Handbook of
North American Indians

Handbook of North American Indians

WILLIAM C. STURTEVANT
General Editor

VOLUME 4

History of Indian-White Relations

WILCOMB E. WASHBURN
Volume Editor

SMITHSONIAN INSTITUTION

WASHINGTON

1988

For sale by the Superintendent of Documents,
U.S. Government Printing Office, Washington, D.C. 20402.

Library of Congress Cataloging in Publication Data

Handbook of North American Indians.

    Bibliography.
    Includes index.
    CONTENTS:

                v. 4. History of Indian-White Relations.

    1.   Indians of North America.
I.   Sturtevant, William C.

E77.H25   970′.004′97   77–17162

History of Indian White Relations Volume Planning Committee

Wilcomb E. Washburn, Volume Editor

William C. Sturtevant, General Editor

Robert F. Berkhofer, Jr.

William T. Hagan

Wilbur R. Jacobs

Francis Paul Prucha

D'Arcy McNickle

Contents

This map is a diagrammatic guide to the 10 culture areas of native North America referred to in this volume and throughout the *Handbook*. These culture areas are used in organizing and referring to information about contiguous groups that are or were similar in culture and history. They do not imply that there are only a few sharply distinct ways of life in the continent. In reality, each group exhibits a unique combination of particular cultural features, while all neighboring peoples are always similar in some ways and dissimilar in others. The lines separating the culture areas represent a compromise among many factors and sometimes reflect arbitrary decisions. For more specific information, see the chapter "Introduction" in volumes 5–15 of the *Handbook* and the discussion in volume 1.

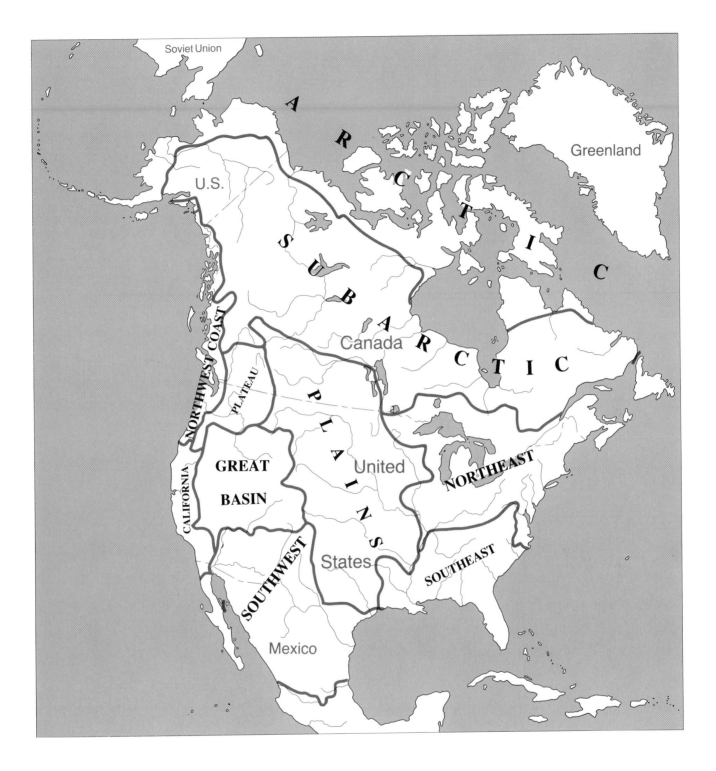

Soviet Union

Greenland

ARCTIC

U.S.

SUBARCTIC

Canada

NORTHWEST COAST

PLATEAU

PLAINS

CALIFORNIA

GREAT

BASIN

United

NORTHEAST

States

SOUTHWEST

SOUTHEAST

Mexico

Conventions for Illustrations

Map Symbol

●	Settlement, fort, or mission
X	Battle
⬭	Body of Water
⌇	River or creek
Sioux	Tribe
Louisbourg	Settlement, fort, or mission
Gila River	Geographical feature

Credits and Captions

Credit lines give the source of the illustrations or the collections where the artifacts shown are located. The numbers that follow are the catalog or inventory numbers of that repository. When the photographer mentioned in the caption is the source of the print reproduced, no credit line appears. "After" means that the *Handbook* illustrators have redrawn, rearranged, or abstracted the illustration from the one in the cited source. All maps and drawings not otherwise credited are by the *Handbook* illustrators. Measurements in captions are to the nearest millimeter if available; "about" indicates an estimate or a measurement converted from inches to centimeters. The following abbreviations are used in credit lines:

Amer.	American	Histl.	Historical
Anthr.	Anthropology, Anthropo-	Ind.	Indian
	logical	Inst.	Institute
Arch.	Archives	Instn.	Institution
Arch(a)eol	Arch(a)eology,	Lib.	Library
	Arch(a)eological	Mus.	Museum
Assoc.	Association	NAA	National Anthropological
Co.	County		Archives
Coll.	Collection(s)	Nat.	Natural
Dept.	Department	Natl.	National
Div.	Division	opp.	opposite
Ethnol.	Ethnology, Ethnological	pl(s).	plate(s)
fol.	folio	Prov.	Provincial
Ft.	Fort	Soc.	Society
Hist.	History	U.	University

Metric Equivalents

10 mm = 1cm	10 cm = 3.937 in.	1 km = .62 mi.	1 in. = 2.54 cm	25 ft. = 7.62 m
100 cm = 1 m	1 m = 39.37 in.	5 km = 3.1 mi.	1 ft. = 30.48 cm	1 mi. = 1.60 km
1,000 m = 1 km	10 m = 32.81 ft.	10 km = 6.2 mi.	1 yd. = 91.44 cm	5 mi. = 8.02 km

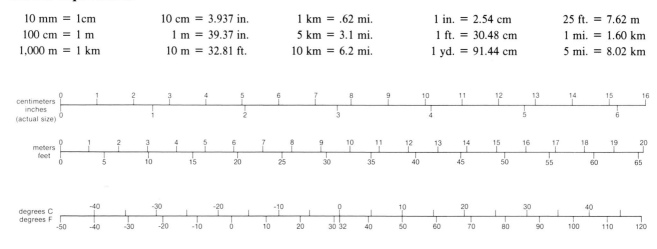

Preface

This is the eighth volume to be published of a 20-volume set planned to give an encyclopedic summary of what is known about prehistory, history, and cultures of the aboriginal peoples of North America who lived north of the urban civilizations of central Mexico.

The aim of this volume is to provide a basic reference work on the history of the interactions in North America between the aboriginal peoples and those, primarily from Europe and Africa, who arrived following 1492. This history is treated according to regional, topical, and temporal categories suitable for the whole continent. Short biographies of non-Indians important in Indian history are included. Volumes 5–15 of the *Handbook*, listed on page *i*, cover aboriginal cultures and their histories in each of the culture areas of North America (see the map on *viii*); each one contains much material on the history of Indian-White relations specific to that area. Other volumes in the *Handbook* are also, like this one, continental in scope. Volume 2 contains detailed accounts of the different kinds of Indian and Eskimo communities in the twentieth century, especially during its second half, and describes their relations with one another and with the surrounding non-Indian societies and nations. A good deal of the recent history of Indian-White relations is covered in that volume. Volume 3 gives the environmental and biological backgrounds within which Native American societies developed; summarizes the early and late human biology or physical anthropology and demography of Indians, Eskimos, and Aleuts; and surveys the earliest prehistoric cultures. It treats many results of Indian-White relations. Volume 16 is a continent-wide survey of technology and the visual arts—of material cultures broadly defined—from prehistoric times up to the present. Volume 17 surveys the Native languages of North America, their characteristics and historical relationships. Volumes 18 and 19 are a biographical dictionary of Indians, Eskimos, and Aleuts. Volume 20 contains an index to the whole, which will serve to locate materials on the history of Indian-White relations in other volumes as well as in this one; it also includes a list of errata found in all preceding volumes.

Preliminary discussions on the feasibility of the *Handbook* and alternatives for producing it began in 1965 in what was then the Smithsonian's Office of Anthropology. (A history of the early development of the whole *Handbook* will be found in volume 1.) Following a planning meeting for the organization of the entire *Handbook* that was held in Chicago in November 1970, a meeting to plan the detailed contents of the *History* volume took place in Cambridge, Massachusetts, on December 31, 1970. This was attended by the General Editor, the Volume Editor, and a specially selected Volume Planning Committee (named on page *v*). This meeting drew up a tentative table of contents for the volume, with lists of qualified specialists on each topic as potential authors. As published, the volume contains 42 chapters essentially as first planned and 16 chapters on new or substantially revised topics and drops 10 chapters proposed in 1970. Of the 60 authors, about one third are those first selected, while the rest are authors on new topics or replacements for people who were unable to accept invitations or later found that they could not meet their commitments to write. (These figures do not include the 294 biographies by 116 authors.)

When authors were invited to contribute a chapter, the Volume Editor indicated what topics should be covered. Authors were also sent a "Guide for Contributors" prepared by the General Editor describing the general aims and methods of the *Handbook* and the editorial conventions. As they were received, the manuscripts were reviewed by the Volume Editor, the General Editor, and sometimes one or more referees. Suggestions for changes and additions often resulted. The published versions frequently reflect more editorial intervention than is customary for academic writings, since the encyclopedic aims and format of the *Handbook* made it necessary to eliminate duplication, avoid gaps in coverage, prevent contradictions, impose some standardization of organization and terminology, and keep within strict constraints on length.

The first draft manuscript submitted was received in the General Editor's office on January 6, 1972, and others followed over the next couple of years. The publication schedule for the whole *Handbook* was then revised, and editorial attention turned to other volumes, which have since been published (see page *i*). In January 1985, intensive work to complete the *History of Indian-White Relations* volume began. At that time, all authors of manuscripts then on hand were asked to revise and bring them up to date, and several new assignments were made. Major changes resulted. Thus the contents of this volume generally reflect the state of knowledge in the mid-1980s rather than in the early 1970s. The first editorial acceptance of an author's manuscript was on August 9, 1983, and the last on July 8, 1987. Edited manuscripts were sent from the Washington office to authors for their final approval between February 6, 1986, and October 5, 1987. These dates for all chapters are given in the list of Contributors. Late dates may reflect late invitations as well as late submissions.

Bibliography

All references cited by contributors have been unified in a single list at the end of the volume. Citations within the text, by author, date, and often page, identify the works in this unified list. Wherever possible the *Handbook* Bibliographer, Lorraine H. Jacoby, has resolved conflicts between citations of different editions, corrected inaccuracies and omissions, and checked direct quotations against the originals. The bibliographic information has been verified by examination of the original work or from standard reliable library catalogs (especially the National Union Catalog and the published catalog of the Harvard Peabody Museum Library). The unified bibliography lists all and only the sources cited in the text of the volume, except personal communications. In the text, "personal communications" to an author are distinguished from personal "communications to editors."

Illustrations

Most of the illustrations—early photographs, drawings, prints, depictions of artifacts, and maps—were located and prepared by the editorial staff, from research in many museums and other repositories, in the published literature, in the editorial files of illustrations collected (but not used) for other *Handbook* volumes, and from correspondence and telephone interviews. Some authors suggested illustrations for their chapters. Locating suitable photographs and drawings, paintings, and engravings was the responsibility of the Illustrations Researcher, Donna Longo DiMichele, with contributions and advice from Joanna Cohan Scherer and using some materials collected by Laura J. Greenberg. Artifacts in museum collections suitable for photographing or drawing were selected by the Artifact Researcher, Ernest S. Lohse. Victor Krantz of the Smithsonian Photographic Laboratory photographed the artifacts illustrated from the Smithsonian collections. The uncredited drawing is by the Scientific Illustrator, Karen B. Ackoff.

All maps were drawn by the *Handbook* Cartographer, Daniel G. Cole, who redrew some submitted by authors and compiled many new ones using information from the chapter manuscripts, from their authors, and from other sources. The base maps for all are authoritative standard ones, especially sheet maps produced by the U.S. Geological Survey and the Department of Energy, Mines and Resources, Canada. Modern political boundaries on maps of past eras are for reference only.

Layout and design of the illustrations have been the responsibility of Lohse, DiMichele, and the Scientific Illustrators, Jo Ann Moore and Karen B. Ackoff. Captions for illustrations were usually composed by DiMichele and Lohse, and for maps by Cole. However, all illustrations, including maps and drawings, and all captions have been approved and sometimes revised by the General Editor or Managing Editor, the Volume Editor, and the authors of the chapters in which they appear.

Acknowledgements

During the first few years of this project, the *Handbook* editorial staff in Washington worked on materials for all volumes of the series. Since intensive preparation of this volume began in 1985, especially important contributions were provided by: the Editorial Assistant, Paula Cardwell; the Production Manager and Manuscript Editor, Diane Della-Loggia; the Bibliographer, Lorraine H. Jacoby; the Bibliographic Assistant, Estella Bryans-Munson; the Researcher, Cesare Marino; the Scientific Illustrators, Jo Ann Moore (through 1986) and Karen B. Ackoff (1987–); the Cartographer, Daniel G. Cole; the Cartographic Technician, Kimberly Rydel; the Illustrations Researchers, Donna Longo DiMichele and Joanna Cohan Scherer; the Assistant Illustrations Researcher, Frances Galindo; the Artifact Researcher, Ernest S. Lohse; the Administrative Specialist, Melvina Jackson; and the Secretaries Tujuanna Evans and Lorretta Williams. Lottie Katz and Eleanor Peterson served as the volunteer assistants for the Bibliographer.

Beginning in January 1985, Ives Goddard served as Managing Editor in addition to his other *Handbook* responsibilities as Linguistic Editor and advisor to the General Editor. He effectively replaced the General Editor during the latter's absence abroad for the year beginning in September 1986.

The Volume Editor would like particularly to acknowledge the exceptional role played by Diane Della-Loggia, Production Manager and Manuscript Editor, in the editorial process. He also thanks Andrea Ludwig who served as a research assistant during the early years of the preparation of volume 4, particularly for the biographies, of which she wrote 26. Estella Bryans-Munson provided research and editorial assistance to the Volume Editor in the later years of the project. Secretarial assistance was provided to him by Susan Daumit Sunkin and Ruby L. Hamblen. Student interns assisted for short periods of time in carrying the project to completion. Among these individuals the Volume Editor would like particularly to cite the contribution of Heather Dodson, who wrote several biographies as well as assisting the Volume Editor in dealing with individual contributors, and D. Sammons-Lohse, who prepared several captions for artifact illustrations.

Acknowledgement is due to the Department of Anthropology, Smithsonian Institution (and to its other curatorial staff), for releasing Sturtevant and Goddard from part of their curatorial and research responsibilities so that they could devote time to editing the *Handbook*. Washburn's participation was supported by the Office of American Studies, Smithsonian Institution, of which he is Director.

Preparation and publication of this volume have been supported by federal appropriations made to the Smithsonian Institution, in part through its Bicentennial Programs.

February 3, 1988   William C. Sturtevant
                                     Wilcomb E. Washburn

Introduction

WILCOMB E. WASHBURN

This volume treats the history of Indian-White relations in North America primarily from the perspective of the institutions and policies of the intruding societies, in response to which the Native cultures changed. The organization of the volume also provides a comparative perspective by considering how each European and Europe-derived nation differed from others in extending its authority and culture over North America.

Other volumes of the *Handbook* treat the specifics of particular events or relationships significant mainly in one region. Volume 4 gives general accounts of the basic themes under which the specifics of Indian-White history are subsumed. The first theme is that of "National Policies," under which the policies of all the state systems that dealt with the American Indians are treated. The second theme is that of "Military Relations," which are covered chronologically from the colonial period to the end of Indian hostilities in the late nineteenth century. Third, the "Political Relations" section concerns the way national policies were implemented through treaties, land transfers, governmental agencies, schools, and the like. Fourth, the section "Economic Relations" is organized according to regions and subjects such as trade goods and Indian servitude. "Religious Relations" is the fifth topic, while "Conceptual Relations" and "Effects of Indians on Non-Indian Cultures" pull together topics such as the Indian hobbyist movement in North America and Europe and the Indian in literature and folk culture. A final section incorporates brief biographies of over 200 non-Indians important in Indian-White relations.

It is apparent that the culture area concept used in the ethnographic volumes does not fit this volume. In part this is because the emphasis is not so much on Indian cultures or Indian tribes as on the impact of Europeans on the social, political, and economic life of Indians. The volume deals also with the impact of the Indian on non-Indian culture. Volume 4 is, as a result, less tribally specific than the other volumes, and more oriented to "the Indian" seen in generic terms by Whites.

In dealing with the interaction of the first comers and later intruders into the Western hemisphere, terms like Indian, White, and Black, Native American and European are inadequate to represent the diverse reality. The term Indian of course, is a misnomer caused by Colum-bus's mistaken belief that he had arrived in the Indies. When it was supposed that Amerigo Vespucci had shown that the Indies were in fact a new continent, a form of his personal name was adopted to parallel Europe, Asia, and Africa. The new misnomer, American, in the initial stages of conquest and settlement referred to the native population but soon was applied to the descendants of the European immigrants. "Euro-American" has been recommended by some to indicate the origin of those who are now designated Americans, but this term is awkward and does not take account of the descendants of those who came by later migrations from Africa, Asia, and the Pacific Islands, to say nothing of those who migrated from within the Americas. The term Native American as a substitute for "Indian" is no longer in favor as it was briefly in the 1960s. Most of those designated by the term continue to call themselves Indians. When the term has been used exclusively for such people it has failed to comprehend its more common use in applying to anyone born in the Americas, whether White, Black, Asian, or Indian. The term Amerindian has a long pedigree but is not commonly used in North America. Even the term Indian, used throughout this volume, is ambiguous not only because of occasional confusion with the inhabitants of India but also because it sometimes does not cover Eskimos (including Inuits and Greenlanders) and Aleuts.

The intermarriage and interbreeding that began with contact have altered the original meaning of all terms that have attempted to freeze so-called racial identities. Most brittle and insubstantial have been the elaborate designations, which grew up in the early Spanish, French, and Portuguese colonies, that attempted to classify mixed ancestry by terms like quadroon and octaroon. All such attempts to categorize the varieties of ancestry are virtually useless, particularly when culture as well as biology is inextricably involved. Even Métis and half-breed have become largely cultural or social labels, rather than biological ones. Hence it is not strange that terms such as White Indian and Apple (Red outside, White inside) arise.

Discussion of the history of "the Indian" is made difficult by the rapid progress of transculturalization (the mutual interchange between Indian and White cultures; Hallowell 1963), acculturation (usually understood as the change of Indian cultures toward Euro-American norms and practices), and assimilation (the absorption and disappearance of Indian individuals and occasionally whole communities into non-Indian society). Yet a discourse distinguishing between Indian and White continues to be valid, despite the difficulty of disengaging the intertwined relationship between the two, as long as Indians occupy a distinct legal status within the United States and Canada both as citizens and as members of tribes having a distinct autonomy and sovereignty within the two republics, and as long as Indians form a distinct ethnic group in North America.

The authors and editors of this volume, mostly historians but some of them anthropologists, write in a tradition of objective or pseudo-objective detachment from the subjects of their inquiry. As John Quincy Adams stated the ideal in 1847, "a Historian . . . must have neither Religion or Country" (J.Q. Adams 1965:36). But no one who looks closely can fail to be moved by the sad record of events by which independent Indian people were destroyed, pushed aside, or assimilated into the culture of European and European-derived White intruders. That emotional commitment, while in a strict sense inconsistent with the methodological and theoretical assumptions of the discipline of history, cannot be excluded from the mind-set of those who practice history. In its extreme form, it can result in a virtual legal indictment. Friar Bartolomé de las Casas asserted that he wrote one of his many historical works about the Spanish conquest so that if God destroyed the Spanish nation for their crimes against the Indians, future generations would know why (Friede and Keen 1971:204). Heizer (1974:v–xi), editor of the California volume of the *Handbook*, expressed this feeling in his preface to a historical study of California Indians.

While acknowledging the destructiveness of the initial clash between Indian and White in North America, students should note that the history of the contact is also a history of rebirth as well as death, of re-creation as well as destruction, both in regard to the Indian population and in regard to Indian tribal organization. The low point in Indian population in the United States following the introduction of European diseases, wars, and relocation was reached about 1900. Since then the Indian population growth has been up. Insofar as Indian tribal autonomy is concerned, the low point was reached about the same time. Since 1934, with the passage of the Indian Reorganization Act, tribal autonomy has been rapidly restored. Judging against an ideal standard, the historian can find many crimes in the Indian-White relationship; judging against a comparative standard (that is, against the history of aboriginal versus intruder populations in other areas of the world), or against a historical standard (the past actions of a society versus its present actions), the history of Indian-White relations in the United States and Canada *is* one that the historian can write about with both rational detachment and emotional commitment.

Volume 4 begins with "National Policies." A summary is provided of the national policies of all the European nations whose activities impinged upon the Native inhabitants of North America. This section can be read both to obtain insights into the policies of particular nations and for the purpose of comparing those policies. While many assume that all European nations acted identically in establishing and justifying the dominant relationship that each developed with the Native inhabitants, in fact national policies differed markedly. The English (and later American) policies, which are the focus of this section, evolved in an extraordinary way, arriving at what during the administration of President Ronald Reagan was denominated a "government-to-government" relationship among the federal government, the states, and the Indian tribes. The late twentieth-century U.S. policy is far different from policies enunciated in earlier centuries when the juridical existence of Indian tribes was often denied. The fact that the present relationships were established in large measure through treaty negotiations testifies to the degree to which English and American authorities recognized the distinct legal character of the Indian tribes and nations with whom they came into contact.

Contrast the English and American policy with that of the French and Spanish. Neither of the continental nations relied on the treaty process or recognized the sovereign legal character of the Indian tribes with which they interacted, at least to the degree that English and American authorities did. In the French and Spanish tradition, Indians might be recognized as distinct minorities requiring treatment different from other colonials, but almost invariably their political independence was quickly curbed as soon as the European authorities could effectively establish control over them. Little residual legal independence was retained by Native inhabitants in areas settled by French and Spanish.

This is not to say that the picture is entirely one-sided. Indeed, the United States is often pictured as having been more cruel and less accommodating to the native Indians than were the Spanish, French, and Portuguese who more readily intermarried and who assimilated Indians more directly into the Latin American cultures that emerged following the conquests. The English empire had less of a place for the American Indian in the social and political structures it re-created in the New World than did the empires of France, Spain, and Portugal. In part this outcome derived from the facts that the English came more often as settlers and colonizers than as conquerors or traders and women were usually included among the colonists. Being accustomed to the concept of contractual relations as the basis for civil government, and coming from a tradition of diffused and localized power in contrast to the highly centralized governments of Spain, France, and Portugal, the English colonial authorities more readily entered into pragmatic agreements with Indian nations.

The Indian population in the areas colonized by the English was also smaller than that to the south. Disease, war, and migration caused the small Indian populations in the north to be supplanted by European-derived populations in a way that never occurred in the south where the Indian population was larger and integration more intense. One would hesitate to call the policies of the other European colonizing powers more egalitarian than the English; but certainly they were more assimilationist in character, even when they reduced the Indian population to a state of practical dependency or oppressive servitude. English and American policies dealt diplomatically and militarily with Indian societies but did not incorporate them directly into the body politic as did their European rivals.

The military confrontation between Indian and White in the New World is too often seen by Americans in twentieth-century terms. Seventeenth-century Europeans are seen as establishing a "beachhead" on a hostile continent, driving rapidly ashore against a determined and unified enemy, consolidating the initial beachheads into an extended "front," and proceeding in a coordinated fashion to destroy "the enemy" and occupy his terrain. In fact, the analogy is seriously flawed. The initial arrival of the Europeans was usually exploratory in character, not hostile. Trade rather than war was the common first relationship between Indian and White. The tiny settlements made by the initial colonists hardly constituted beachheads in a modern military sense. The fortified villages that the Europeans built in time became the nuclei of expansion, but they were initially isolated settlements of a primarily defensive character.

Indians were allies as well as enemies of Europeans. Relationships of peace—albeit a cautious, suspicious peace—were more frequent than relationships of war. European colonization did eventually mean the gradual disappearance of powerful and autonomous Indian tribes in the areas of English settlement, but it distorts history to apply a modern military analogy to this long process.

Not only is the analogy of a sudden seaborne European invasion inadequate, but also the assumption of a unity of purpose among Europeans, on the one side, and Indians, on the other, is flawed. The several European colonies had purposes diverging from one another, and the several English colonies differed in their particular interests and their military responses to challenges to those interests. Even less coordinated were the Indian nations with whom the Europeans came into contact. It is notorious that the Indians failed to unify in the face of the invader and were picked off one by one. "Divide and conquer" is an ancient rule. Despite the efforts of an occasional Indian leader—most notably Tecumseh—urging Indian unity in the face of the European threat, tribal self-interest and ancient intertribal antagonisms were too strong for most of the Indian tribes to resist. For such reasons Indians often preferred to ally themselves with Whites against their traditional Indian foes.

Warfare has always been influenced, and often dominated, by technological changes. The extent to which Indians adopted European technology and Europeans adopted Indian modes of warfare is alluded to in several chapters and can be pursued more fully in the references provided. The question of evaluating the prowess of warriors, Indian and White, is a difficult one. A simple accounting of victories and defeats does not fully assess the individual skills of soldiers and commanders on both sides. Even casualty figures conceal as well as reveal the answer, for sickness and disease often took a greater toll than the weapons of war.

The popular image of "the Indian" as a noble warrior, while it is a stereotype when measured against the complex history of widely dissimilar tribes, is also a reality that remains one of the most impressive legacies of the Indian past. Although the Indian tribes were ultimately conquered, the tradition of Indian bravery lived on not only among the descendants of those who contested with the ancestors of non-Indian Americans but also in the symbolic identity of the United States as a nation: in its coinage, its postage stamps, and in other symbolic representations.

The chapters on "Political Relations" between the agencies of government of Great Britain, the United States, and Canada and the Indians with whom they dealt describe the nuts and bolts of administration beginning with the treaties upon which the relationship was founded and continuing with the agencies of government, such as the Bureau of Indian Affairs in the United States, and the school system, by which the Indian policies of each government were carried into effect. There are general chapters on land transfers and the legal status of the Indian, and finally two chapters outlining the emergence of the Indian rights movement and the effect that unofficial "friends of the Indian" had on government policy. An extraordinary evolution and change occurred in the relationship of Whites and Indians not only in theory but also in practice. There was also a growing movement away from more coercive forms of administration to a more compassionate (but sometimes not more understanding) policy.

The chapters in this volume dealing with "Economic Relations" relate to matters that have received considerable attention by anthropologists and historians. The changes in Indian subsistence patterns caused by the introduction of European technology and European economic demand were of enormous consequence. These changes were set in motion by an expanding economy pivoted upon Western Europe (see Wolf 1982). That economy regulated offerings of labor and the prices of commodities through the mechanisms of labor and commodity markets, a means of allocating effort and resources at wide variance with existing Native economic practices, which de-emphasized impersonal market forces and emphasized barter and gift exchange. The full effect of the impact of a European market ecomomy upon Indian societies and cultures continues to be debated among scholars, but clearly it affected all forms of Indian economic activity: hunting, gathering, agriculture, and the ways in which the lands supporting these activities were controlled by the Indians. Conversely, Indian economic practices and especially the availability of Indian products and Indian labor had major consequences for European economies and societies, both in Europe and to a marked extent as they were transplanted to America.

There is no single economic model upon which one can confidently rest assumptions about the Native American economy. Indians often acquired European goods—particularly metal implements—for purposes different from the uses their makers put them to. Often European goods had symbolic rather than utilitarian significance to the Natives. The chapter on European trade goods deals with the objects of the trade. Other chapters deal with the process by which goods and services were exchanged. Included in this section are several chapters on Indian servitude. It is a sad but important aspect of the interaction between Europeans and Indians that Indians, like Black Africans, were enslaved and, like White Europeans, were indentured. The use of Indian slaves was rarely successful and in most instances was soon supplanted by Black slavery. That the Indian became symbolically identified with an unfettered state (hence the appearance of Indian images in representations of "liberty" United States coinage and stamps) stems from factual evidence as much as it does from imagination.

The final chapter in this section deals with the effect of the Indian upon the natural environment.

The sections of this volume dealing with "Religious Relations" cover not only the traditional Roman Catholic and Protestant missions to the Indians but also Mormon and Russian Orthodox missions. Here the complexities and differentiation within and between denominations has sometimes required a regional treatment. Despite the extensive literature no one can speak with absolute assurance about two critical aspects of the religious relationship: the precise motives of the Europeans supporting the missions and the precise motives of the Natives responding to the missions. Many look cynically and skeptically upon the professions of the Europeans who responded to what they perceived as the "Macedonian cry" (illustrated in the seal of the Massachusetts Bay Colony) to "come over and help" the American Indian. That Christianity often served as a mask to conceal baser

motives is too obvious to underline. Priests accompanied Spanish conquerors and witnessed the reading of the Spanish Requirement to the natives (which informed them of the Pope's donation of their land to the Spanish and of the requirement that they submit to the Spanish). On the other hand, men like Bartolomé de las Casas, from the same religious tradition, recognized the ambiguities and spent their lives fighting for justice for the Indians against their own temporal rulers.

Protestant "friends of the Indian" can be accused of blindness in urging policies such as allotment of land in severalty in the United States in the 1880s, but it is well to remember such reformers felt as strong a moral justification as that felt by those making the accusation. There are many practical considerations to weigh. The religious leaders who urged the government to destroy the tribal structure and give individual Indians the legal security of individual White men pointed in justification to the rapid destruction of the Indian population during national expansion. Better half a loaf than none at all, they reasoned.

From the standpoint of the Indians, the chapters also attempt to answer the question of why the Native populations responded to the missionaries as they did. Was their conversion (when achieved) genuine or feigned, expedient or principled? Was Christianity merely more powerful "medicine" that was embraced as the religion of a "winner" in place of a "losing" traditional religious outlook? The debate over the genuineness of the offer, and reception, of Christianity will go on as long as scholars continue to wrestle with the complex evidence of missionization.

The chapters in the last two sections in the book, "Conceptual Relations" and the "Effects of Indians on Non-Indian Cultures" all illustrate the mutual interaction and influence of Whites upon Indians and Indians upon Whites. In the literature of America and Europe, the Indian frequently emerged as a "noble savage" pointing out by implication, if not directly, the sins of Europeans. So strong was the pro-Indian orientation of some Whites that hobbyist groups and the "counterculture" identified in dress and in action with the Indian, while professional anthropologists presented the Indian position in more scholarly and academic ways.

The varying images of the Indian—as drunken savage or noble natural man—not only are discussed in terms of their specific representations in literature and in the arts but also are analyzed conceptually. These chapters uncover fundamental epistemological and methodological problems inherent in the observer/observed relationship. To what extent have Indians been accurately perceived by outsiders? The study of Indian-White relations is as much a study of Whites as it is of Indians. Both are locked in America in an intimate biological, cultural, and intellectual embrace. It is the purpose of this volume to help to define that relationship.

British Indian Policies to 1783

WILBUR R. JACOBS

British policy toward the Indians in the American colonies evolved over a period of 200 years on an ever-expanding colonial frontier. Imperial policy was, in many respects, based upon trial and error with the mother country's or the individual colony's self-interest in mind. Throughout early American history, from the time of first contacts by English explorers, traders, and seventeenth-century colonists, Indian people were regarded as a curiosity and then as a source of potential wealth. Native American people were seen as temporary owners of the North American continent rich in minerals, furs, fish, agricultural produce (maize, squash, and other food plants domesticated by Indians). Anglo-Americans discovered that Indians could be valuable military allies, especially during the long French and Indian War era (about 1680–1763) and later in the fierce borderland fighting during the American Revolution. Indians were also regarded as a source of labor and enslaved whenever conditions or special circumstances made it possible to form Indian people into a labor force. For example, Indians of New England were captured and deported to work as slaves on British sugar plantations in the West Indies. Evidence of this enslavement is in literature on early New England treaties and in inventories of estates in official records of Jamaica (Jacobs 1974:123–132). And Apalachee Indians, christianized by Spaniards in what is now the southeastern United States, were captured and drafted into slavery as plantation field hands by the Carolinians in the early eighteenth century (Reid 1976: 26–28, 45, 53). Children were often kidnapped from their tribal homes on the southern frontier and sold as domestic servants. Some of the borderland tribes such as the Yamasee participated in this traffic along with White wilderness kidnappers.

British policies that developed were often harsh. Whites who enforced the policy were oftentimes colonials, traders, land speculators, and occasionally missionaries. But real authority for implementing far-reaching policy rested on imperial officers in the colonies such as governors or their treaty negotiators, often called Indian commissioners (appointed by colonial governors with the approval of colonial assembly committees). In "Indian affairs," as they were called, the British colonial adminis-tration gave almost unlimited authority to Crown or proprietory officials in the period before the appointment of Indian superintendents in 1755.

Overall policy allowed no special place for the American Indian, who was regarded as a kind of nonperson. There was no body of imperial law to protect the Indians, and colonials on the cutting edge of settlement were often allowed to make their own Indian policy (providing there was no financial loss to the mother country). Individual colonial legislatures applied their own law to native people who came within the orbit of settled communities. So-called distant "wild" Indians were left to their own as long as they remained friendly and cooperative. Native people were thus valuable as friendly neighbors, as fur trading allies, as military allies, and as landholders. This very practical policy of utilizing Indian people for the advantage of Whites can be seen by examination of hundreds of conferences, treaties, exchanges of gifts, promises, and wampum treaty belts. Much of this exploitation was carried on in the name of "civilizing" Indians (Washburn 1971:3–58; Jacobs 1985:1–67; Ray 1974:3–72; Jennings 1975:3–145, 1984:186–289; Kupperman 1980:25–68).

At the same time one must acknowledge that British Indian policy as it guided a system of administration in public affairs was not without instances of altruism and humanitarian concern for Indians. There were many humane men among the colonials and British officials who were concerned about the welfare of native people. Numerous attempts were made to bring youthful male Indians into colonial schools and colleges. There is no question that in the long history of Indian-White relations in the colony of Pennsylvania, Quakers and Indians had contacts based upon "friendship, sympathy, understand-ing, respect, and love" (Tolles 1963). The two first Indian superintendents appointed in 1755 to oversee Indian relations—Sir William Johnson for the northern depart-ment and Edmund Atkin for the southern department—insisted in their public statements on a policy of fair treatment for their Indian wards at treaty meetings, though both agents appear to have profited in the fur trade business and frontier land speculation at the expense of native people (fig. 1). From examination of provincial records it is clear that many of the colonial leaders (including Roger Williams, William Penn, William Bradford, James Logan, Robert Rogers, Benjamin

Franklin, and Thomas Jefferson), the royal governors, the Indian commissioners, as well as certain officers in the colonial administration and in the Board of Trade and Plantations, the agency governing the colonies, were convinced that equitable dealings with Indians, especially in land transactions, were in the best interest of both the colonies and the mother country. The Board of Trade even went so far as to suggest intermarriage among colonials and Indians as a device for promoting better relations between the races (Jacobs 1985:119).

Sixteenth Century

English policy toward aboriginal people as it evolved not only in America but also in other parts of the world was in large part the result of occupation and utilization of the land (Jacobs 1985:126–150). In the sixteenth century English attitudes toward Indians were not basically different from those of other European nations eager to exploit the riches of the New World. There was no particular concern for Indian rights. Indians were part of the new land and could be courted as allies, beaten off as enemies, or tolerated as people whose land would be partly occupied by the English. English kings made huge grants of lands to their favorite subjects and then claimed territory from sea to sea, from the Atlantic coast of old Virginia westward, including as they thought, the "Island" of California. Such territorial grabbing, not unlike the partition of Africa at a later date, was part of a wild race for wealth with little or no regard for the welfare of native people. Letters patent by Henry VII to John Cabot gave him authority to discover "whatsoever isles, countreys, regions or provinces of the heathen and infidels . . . which before this time have been unknownen to all Christians." Cabot could "subdue, occupy and possesse all such townes, cities, castles and isles of them found." Later Elizabeth I gave Sir Walter Raleigh freedom to "discover, search, find out, and view such remote, heathen and barbarous lands, countries and territories, not actually possessed of any Christian Prince, nor inhabited by Christian People," and liberty to "have holde, occupie, and enjoy" what he found (Washburn 1971:30).

The so-called doctrine of discovery, adopted by England as well as other colonial powers, was behind policy-making justifications for occupation of wilderness land. England in the sixteenth century made arguments for her

A North View of Fort Johnson drawn on the spot by Mr. Guy Johnson Sir Wm. Johnson's Son

Lib. of Congress, Rare Book Div.

Fig. 1. View of Ft. Johnson, Montgomery Co., N.Y., from the north, 1759. Sir William Johnson acquired this estate on the Mohawk River (Q) in 1739 and established it as an important site for councils with Indian delegations and for trade with both Indians and Whites. Notable structures are the Indian council house (I), Indian encampment (K), and Johnson's residence (A). Johnson's influence in Indian affairs varied with the political climate in the colonies and in Great Britain (Gwyn 1979:394–398; vol. 15:475). Most of Johnson's manuscripts, including those discussing Indian councils at Ft. Johnson, are published in Johnson's (1921–1965) papers. Original drawing by Guy Johnson, engraving on copper plates by Hulett, printed in *The Royal Magazine* 1759:opp. 167.

claim to North America by reason of John Cabot's "discovery" of Newfoundland and the New England coast. Indian people were, in time, according to imperial policy, relegated to the status of "subjects," although there were many contemporary Europeans who recognized the superficiality of a claim to immense territory and native subjects by reason of sailing along a coastline or into a mouth of a river. (France claimed much of the heartland of North America because of the discovery of the mouths of the Saint Lawrence and Mississippi rivers by French explorers in 1534 and 1685--Deloria 1974: 99–102.)

It was Supreme Court Justice John Marshall, in 1823, who most clearly defined British policy under the doctrine of discovery. Indian people were regarded as "rightful occupants" of the land, "but their rights to complete sovereignty, as independent nations, were necessarily diminished." Furthermore Indian peoples' title to the land was clouded because "discovery gave exclusive title to those who made it." Indian people, then, according to British policy, had only the "right of occupancy" of the land (Deloria 1974:99–100).

Seventeenth Century

English policy toward the Indians and their lands was further refined in the colony of Virginia at the time of the establishment of Jamestown in 1607 (fig. 2). Business finance of the day, based upon experience that directors of the Virginia Company had in contacts with the East India Company in India, Java, and other areas of the Far East, at first suggested that American Indian "Emperors" were similar to those of the Orient. Yet the Company directors had no intention of expending large sums of money to force a conquest of Virginia Indians to convert them to Christianity. The Virginia Company was willing to fight for a beachhead of land, if necessary. The Company stated that it wished to assert good will to bring Indians Christianity and "cover their naked miserie, with civill use of foode and cloathing." Indians would become part of an English community occupying a portion of abundant lands, which the Indians had neglected to use effectively (E.S. Morgan 1975:47, 54–55). Indeed, the directors were pleasantly surprised to learn of a cordial local Indian reception because Indians were pleased to have a trading post with metal tools and kettles close at hand (Macleod 1928:172–176).

In Virginia as well as in other areas where first contacts with Indians were made, copper kettles and tools were exchanged for maize and furs, and a new technology was gradually diffused throughout the Indian world (Martin 1975). Increasing Indian demand for European goods also made it easier for colonists to obtain land that was needed by the Virginians as they eagerly expanded a profitable tobacco-growing plantation system in the early 1600s. A

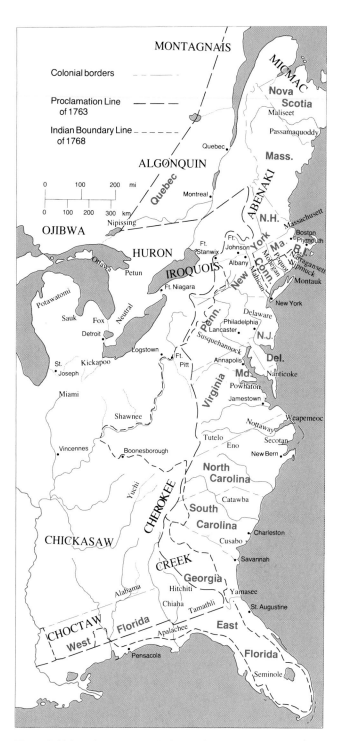

Fig. 2. British settlements and colonies relative to traditional Indian tribal areas in the mid-1700s (J.T. Adams 1943; Cappon 1976; Jacobs 1985).

policy of friendship with the Powhatan confederacy, first initiated by John Smith, was cemented by the marriage of John Rolfe and Pocahontas (Beverley 1705). However, the vigorous White appetite for land inevitably brought Indian hostility resulting in the bloody wars of 1622 and 1644 (Morgan 1975:99, 149). The English colonists then followed a policy of wholesale expansion and extermination of opposing coastal tribes. When the governor of Virginia tried to stem this advance into Indian lands, the result was an uprising of White settlers in 1676, known as Bacon's Rebellion. British troops were sent from England to put down the rebellion, but the governor succeeded in doing so before the arrival of the troops (Washburn 1957).

As in Virginia, Indian people in New England gave the first English colonists a hospitable reception at Plymouth in 1620 and at Massachusetts Bay in 1630. The first policies of settlers, occupying land with the authority of a royal charter, was to establish friendly treaty relations, especially in making land purchases. As Deloria (1974) argues, the early English in Virginia as well as in New England were vitally concerned with land titles, and they wanted very much to avoid occupying Indian lands when there were obvious Indian claimants. Nor did colonists want to give the impression that they were confiscating wilderness lands or swindling the aborigines. Englishmen used a "chain of friendship" legend extant among certain tribes, especially Iroquoians, to justify land ownership of subject Indians (Jacobs 1985; Haan 1976; Jennings 1984: 186–289, 1985:3–65).

Another solution was to create a theory to justify policies that might conflict with Anglo-Saxon traditions, morality, and law. Europeans, it was argued, could justify occupation of the land because they were capable of putting it to a "higher" use, whereas the Indian would, in his "savage" state, put the land to a "lesser" use (Deloria 1974:92). Indians, in other words, had an inadequate yield from the land. The English not only practiced a more intensified form of agriculture but also introduced live-stock and European grasses that made herds of grazing animals profitable. The herds, of course, yielded meat and dairy products (Jennings 1975:62–63). This English method of farming clearly made possible a "higher" use of land by adding the component of herding.

The Indian, regarded as primitive farmer, was increasingly relegated into a racial stereotype, an ignoble savage (Jennings 1975:59). Moreover, Indian men, whose role centered on hunting, fishing, and fighting, appeared "indolent" by comparison with Indian women whose activities more closely approximated White concepts of work. Whites had few pangs of conscience in dispossessing such undeserving savages of their land by what Jennings (1975) has called a "deed game." Indian lands were taken by fraud through fines, through ruination of Indian crops by White livestock, through threats of violence, or through fraudulent deeds signed by drunken chiefs bribed with gifts.

It is true, nevertheless, that many Indian lands were obtained by formal treaty or contract as in Pennsylvania, New York, and in other colonies. The actual purchase of land was agreed upon in what was regarded as fair exchange between legitimate Indian sellers and Anglo-American buyers, but this kind of transaction was not the rule. Indeed, the big acquisitions of Indian land were actually made by wars of conquest, in, for example, the New England wars of 1636–1637 (the Pequot War) and King Philip's War of 1676 (which was, at least in part, a "preventive war" for the conquest of Narragansett Indian land) (Jacobs 1985:121; Leach 1966:66–67; Jennings 1975: 144–145).

There was, then, a policy of confiscation of Indian lands in seventeenth-century Indian wars followed in New England as well as in Virginia. In New England, in particular, the rationale for such a policy is seen through the voluminous writings of Puritan historians. It was Increase Mather who spoke for the Puritan leadership when he wrote, "Lord God of Our Father hath given us for a rightful possession: the lands of Heathen People amongst whom we live" (in Jennings 1975:183).

Seventeenth-century Puritans were probably not such fervent Indian missionaries as their Jesuit counterparts in early New France (Jaenen 1976:41–83) in efforts to convert borderland Indians to Christianity (John Eliot and Thomas Mayhew claimed 2,500 converts). Puritans also attempted, with little success, to enroll individual Indians as Christian students at New England colleges. Roger Williams's policies, usually diverging from his fellow Puritans when it came to Indians, were based upon a respect for Indian rights and culture. Williams's study of Indian societies and languages enabled him to establish a friendly rapport with his Indian wards. Nor did Williams follow a policy of pressing them into becoming Christians. Williams's policy on land transactions, purchasing by agreement from neighboring Rhode Island tribes, was nevertheless ultimately based upon the royal charter given to his colony for the land the settlers of Rhode Island occupied. Earlier, in Massachusetts, Williams had argued that the royal charter in that colony illegally expropriated land of the Indians. Thus Williams, despite his courageous opposition to the royal patent, was eventually obliged to accept a royal charter himself to protect the territory of Rhode Island against encroachments by neighboring English colonies (Washburn 1971:41).

The policy of taking over great areas of wilderness land by royal charter was followed in all of the British continental colonies in the seventeenth century and in the case of Georgia, founded in 1732. Crown or proprietary agents negotiated land purchases from the Indians by treaty, although coastal wars of conquest persisted in the early eighteenth century. The Virginia-Carolina frontier was cleared of Indians by the Tuscarora War of 1711–1712 and the Yamasee War of 1715–1728. Justification for these conquests was usually that there was no alternative to the putting down of Indian "conspiracies." Almost all Indian leaders of the colonial era were cast in the lot of treacherous, sly, underhanded villains who led "conspiracies" against Whites. It is no accident that the Yamasee were practically exterminated as a people in retaliation for having brought about "the great conspiracy of 1715." Thus individual colonies retaliated by a scorched-earth policy in removing coastal tribes, destroying whole villages, towns, and stored food supplies. However, as the remnants of coastal tribes moved into the interior, English colonies faced powerful new confederacies of well armed Indians (Jacobs 1985:12–14).

It was understandable that New England as well as the middle colonies in the late seventeenth century and early eighteenth century were concerned about the maintaining of friendly relations with the greatest of all confederacies, the Six Nations of Iroquois and their Indian allies (R.R. Johnson 1976). Colden (1747) has preserved details of the fierce wilderness fighting of the late seventeenth century in which the Iroquois attempted to protect western beaver hunting territories from Algonquian tribes allied to the French fur trading interests. Since beaver had virtually been exterminated by the mid-seventeenth century in Iroquois home territory (what is now the state of New York) by the Iroquois hunters allied to the Anglo-Dutch fur traders of Albany, the Iroquois became involved in a series of wars with the French and their Indian allies over the possession of western beaver lands of the Great Lakes (Jacobs 1973). English alliance with the Iroquois, called the Covenant Chain, was based upon a series of treaties with the Six Nations (Jacobs 1966; Jennings 1976, 1984).

An overall change in policy toward the Indians in the closing decades of the seventeenth century is depicted in contemporary colonial accounts. There was a shift in White policy because of Indian depopulation. In a letter of 1687, for example, the Reverend John Clayton described native American mortality in Virginia resulting from disease, malnutrition, deprivation, and other factors. The surviving coastal "Indian inhabitants of Virginia are now very inconsiderable as to their members and seem insensibly to decay though they live under English protection and have no violence offered them. They are undoubtedly no great breeders" (in Lurie 1959:56). Indian depopulation was thus a factor in the conquest of coastal and piedmont tribes by the early 1700s.

In the interior, the colonists faced populous confederacies on the frontier from Maine to Georgia. These tribes included northern Algonquians, Six Nations Iroquois, Indians of the Pennsylvania-Virginia frontier (Delawares, Shawnees, Ohio Iroquois), and the tribes of the southern woodlands (Cherokees, Chickasaws, Choctaws, and Creeks).

1700–1763

By the early 1700s Indian relations along the colonial frontier were no longer completely localized. English governors and leaders of colonial assemblies, increasingly concerned over threats from French attacks, were considering measures to bring about a greater degree of colonial unity. Imperial officers at home, as indicated in the long correspondence between the colonial governors and the Board of Trade and Plantations, were vitally conscious of the role interior tribes could play in the European struggle to claim sovereignty over all of the North American continent.

The result of the threat from France or Spain was an accelerated treaty-making process on the part of the various colonies with neighboring powerful Indian confederacies. Several basic considerations lie behind the mass of early Anglo-American treaty literature. Indian affairs were discussed at practically all colonial conferences including the Albany congress of 1754 (Jennings 1976:325–329). The negotiated treaties in the period 1700 to 1763 nearly always concern British attempts to neutralize French influence among the Indians, though there is some mention of Spanish intrigue in certain treaties made with the southern tribes (fig. 4). One more factor that increasingly governed British policy was the expanding inland fur trade. The potential wealth from the exchange of furs for British hardware, textiles, and weapons was partly responsible for the development of a policy of limiting settlement on Indian territories that might destroy the natural habitat of the beaver. Since Indian hunters were also trappers of beaver and skins and furs of other animals, fur trading interests combined with imperial officers in giving the inland tribes a delay in

Royal Ont. Mus., Toronto: HD6313.
Fig. 3. Silver gorget, engraved with the arms of George III, presented to Cherokee chief Outacite by the British for acting as a loyal ally against the French. Historically a symbol of rank in European armies, gorgets were given to Indian leaders in recognition of their allegiance to a particular foreign power. For the British, presentation of a gorget to an Indian chief might also convey the rank of "gorget captain," an official commission in the British army. Width 10.8 cm.

White occupation of the frontier. Nevertheless, British policy was also vitally concerned with established British sovereignty over the land, especially the Ohio Valley, as a gateway to the West. This would protect British fur trading interests as well as the fur trade middlemen among the Iroquois and their allies. Another factor emerged in the negotiations—the actual sale and transfer of big land tracts to Whites through the speculative Anglo-American land companies, such as the Ohio Company of Virginia in the 1750s.

Several of the most important colonial treaties illustrate the foregoing trends in policy. For instance, representatives of the colonies of Pennsylvania and Virginia met with Iroquois at Lancaster, Pennsylvania, in 1744. After accepting valuable gifts from the colonies, the Iroquois declared themselves to be allies by reaffirming the Covenant Chain of friendship. The Indians also acknowledged the right of Virginia settlers to keep lands they had already occupied in the Ohio Valley frontier (Jacobs 1966:112). By concentrating favors at Lancaster on the Onondaga sachem, Canasatago, spokesman for the

Lib. of Congress, Rare Book Div.

Fig. 4. Cover of *The American Magazine and Monthly Chronicle*, 1757–1758. The magazine was founded during the French and Indian War. The illustration depicts the struggle between the English and the French for the favor or loyalty of the Indians. The Englishman (left) holds a Bible in his hand and a bolt of cloth under his arm. The more elaborately attired Frenchman (right) wears a sword and holds a purse of money and a tomahawk. *The American Magazine and Monthly Chronicle* was a British colonial publication, distributed in England and the American colonies. Its purpose was to publish news of both the colonies and Europe (Mott 1938–1968, 1:80–82). Woodcut by an unidentified artist; published by William Bradford, Philadelphia and London.

Ohio Iroquois, who claimed ownership of the Ohio River Valley, White land speculators hoped to tap a rich prize. Indeed Whites hoped to take over the Iroquois claim as their own.

In 1752, at the strategically located trading village of Logstown on the Ohio River, representatives of the newly formed Ohio Company of Virginia negotiated the Treaty of Logstown with Ohio Iroquois claiming the whole Ohio Valley by virtue of the 1744 Lancaster treaty. A Seneca spokesman, Tanaghrisson, protested in 1752, "We never understood, before you told us Yesterday, that the lands then sold were to extend further to the Sun setting than the Hill on the other side of the Alleghany Hill . . . ." (in Jacobs 1966:123). The English, despite Indian protests, at last established, in their eyes, a legal claim to a vast interior hinterland.

1763–1783

Although the British royal government had supported the Ohio Company in its negotiations with Indians, the Crown had second thoughts about permitting speculators to claim the whole interior after the French and Indian War. By the Treaty of Paris in 1763, the English Crown laid claim to all of eastern North America and at a stroke of the pen, without consulting their Indian allies, who had fought French troops and Western Abenaki warriors in several battles, reduced all native people to the status of "subjects." Yet the Indians were not to be ignored, for as a result of the Proclamation of 1763, a boundary along the crest of the Appalachians was established to separate the Indian country from White settlement. The sea to sea claims based on colonial charters were thus nullified at this time. It was also in this year that the uprising and war of Indian independence organized by the Ottawa Pontiac served notice of native American disenchantment with British policy. Unfortunately the Indians were largely ignorant of changes in British policy and had little immediate understanding of the significance of the Proclamation of 1763 (Jacobs 1985:82–103). During the bitter fighting in 1763–1764 Gen. Jeffrey Amherst actually ordered that the Indians around Fort Pitt be infected with gifts of smallpox blankets (Jacobs 1966:185). The Indian uprising failed, and Fort Pitt was easily relieved after a smallpox epidemic broke out among the warriors besieging the fort. In the peace with the Indians that followed, the British were forced to a stalemate settlement allowing only British occupation of western forts. This expensive fortification system requiring a military establishment along the Proclamation line wooed the Indians, but irritated the colonials (Jennings 1976:334–335).

By the "Plan of 1764" an elaborate imperial fur trading system of control at the frontier forts was established, partly to rectify continuing Indian complaints. Such overall regulation might have protected native peoples'

Fig. 5. Engraving of a medal ceremony depicting 2 powerful symbols, the Tree of Peace and the Chain of Friendship, both adopted by the Indians and figuring prominently in treaties and ceremonies. Superintendent William Johnson presented a printed testimonial with this engraving and a medal to Indian chiefs who demonstrated singular loyalty to the British cause. Drawing by Henry Dawkins, 1770. Dimensions 11.5 by 8 cm.

rights in the fur and skin trade as well as their land rights and hunting rights. But the Plan of 1764 as well as the Proclamation of 1763 were difficult to enforce. Pressures from land speculators and fur trading interests in America as well as in England prevailed so that in 1768 at the Treaty of Fort Stanwix, New York, negotiated by Indian Superintendent Sir William Johnson, the Indians were obliged to give a land bonanza to White speculators. Then followed in this year a series of additional treaties setting up an Indian boundary line that established the colonies' western frontiers from Georgia northward through the Carolinas to the Kanawha and Ohio rivers to Fort Pitt and thence northeast to Fort Stanwix, east of Oneida Lake in the Iroquois country. The boundary line in the decade just before the Revolution became an obstacle to White expansionism and did, for a time, bring about a moderated pace in White encroachment upon native lands (Jacobs 1985:94–100; Marshall 1967; Gwyn 1979; Mullin 1986; vol. 15:418–441).

Had the American Revolution not taken place so soon after the establishment of an Indian boundary line, it is possible that there might have been a more deliberate, orderly occupation of the West without the rapid displacement of native American societies. Yet the boundary line concept was not discarded by the Revolutionaries and became a basic concept in U.S. Indian policy to justify "removing" Indians farther west to new boundary lines. It was George Washington who, in a letter of September 7, 1783, to a Congressional committee, attempted to set up policies toward western tribes by suggesting the American boundary line "beyond which we will endeavor to restrain our People from Hunting and Settling" (in Jacobs 1985: 102).

Fig. 6. Joseph Brant, a Mohawk leader (b. 1742/43, d. 1807). An important figure in British-Indian relations, Joseph Brant had a long career as a soldier and statesman. Brant encouraged Indian alliances with the British and commanded Indian forces on Loyalist missions. He first served with the British military during the Seven Years' War. In 1759 Brant fought at Ft. Niagara under Sir William Johnson, beginning a life-long affiliation with the Johnson family. Educated in Indian schools and tutored by missionaries, Brant acted as an interpreter and translator for the Six Nations. He traveled to England in 1775 and 1785 on diplomatic missions on behalf of Indian affairs and claims. A participant in various negotiations with American officials, Brant was wary of the impact of American political activities on Indian affairs (Graymont 1983:803–812). He led Iroquois Loyalists to a settlement on the Grand River, Ont., after the American Revolution (Graymont 1983:806ff.; vol. 15:525–536). Brant believed that it was necessary for Indian people to adopt White customs to survive in the changing conditions of North America (Graymont 1983: 810–811). The peace medal worn by Brant is possibly the George III presentation medal in fig. 7. Watercolor by Wilhelm von Moll Berczy, about 1794.

British policy, meanwhile, toward the Indians during the American Revolution was very much as it had been in the decades before the outbreak of hostilities. After sale of western lands in the 1760s and early 1770s, land jobbers moved into rich areas of Kentucky where colonial frontiersmen committed murders of the family of Logan, an Iroquois. Such outrages brought on a conflict in the Virginia wilderness known as Lord Dunmore's War, in 1774. This was a prelude to Indian fighting on the whole frontier that coincided with the first battles of the American Revolution (Washburn 1975:146–150). William Legge, Earl of Dartmouth, Secretary of State for the Colonies in 1775, took advantage of Indian resentment against colonial land encroachments and urged military commanders such as Gen. Thomas Gage and Indian Superintendents Guy Johnson (northern department) and John Stuart (southern department) to obtain Indian support "when opportunity offers" (Washburn 1975:151; Graymont 1972; O'Donnell 1973). The innocence of the Indians about origins and outbreak of the Revolution is revealed in Superintendent Guy Johnson's simple explanation of the cause of the fighting to the Iroquois: "This dispute was solely occasioned by some people, who notwithstanding a law of the King and his wise Men, would not let some Tea land, but destroyed it, on which he was angry, and sent some Troops with the General, whom you have long known, to see the Laws executed and bring the people to their sences, and as he is proceeding with great wisdom, to shew them their great mistake, I expect it will soon be over" (in Graymont 1972:57).

Warriors from the western Iroquois as well as the Cherokees, Creeks, Shawnees, and other border peoples joined the British cause to inflict blows on the colonial frontier. Yet all the tribes did not attack despite the urging of British officials and the overflow of guns, liquor, and gifts of textiles and hardware into their villages. In time, the larger mass of Indians fought on the side of the King of England, "their ancient protector and friend" (Jennings 1976:341).

When England negotiated treaty terms ending the Revolution in 1783, she broke faith with her Indian allies by ceding their lands to the U.S. without their knowledge (Washburn 1975:157). Gen. Frederick Haldimand, Canadian British commander, made amends to the Iroquois by giving lands to Indians who wished to depart from the United States and make new homes in Canada (fig. 6). The question will always be raised about the price most Indians paid for joining the British cause. Their taking a neutral position might have held off American invasion into Indian territory for a time (Washburn 1975:158), but it is probable that the American frontier expansion of the early nineteenth century would not have respected Indian territory for long. It can be argued that the British concessions to the Americans in 1783 prevented an all-out outburst of revenge attack on Indians by Americans. However, the temporary British occupation of frontier forts after the Revolution (to insure Loyalist claims) was probably responsible for a more aggressive American policy toward Indians in the 1790s, for the Americans regarded interior Indians as allies of the British in control

Smithsonian, Natl. Mus. of Amer. Hist., Natl. Numismatics Coll.: 67.94662.
Fig. 7. George III presentation medal, showing the king's likeness and the British coat of arms. Beginning in the 1760s, medals were struck specifically for presentation to allied Indian leaders; previously their allegiance had been recognized with medals minted for other purposes. Diameter 11.2 cm.

of forts.

British policy from seventeenth-century origins to the time of the Revolution gradually shifts to a concern for welfare of Indians, particularly in the 1760s. As the home government became involved in the Revolutionary conflict, it eventually retreated to a policy of complete self-interest in attempting to win the friendship of the Americans at the Paris peace conference in 1783. The overseas vital interests of England transcended her concern for Indian people, and this accounts for the decision to cede Indian lands to the Americans without permitting Indians to have a role in deciding their own fate (Glenn 1974–1975:81–89; Jennings 1976:341). The history of British Indian policy ends in 1783 where it began in the seventeenth century—on the issue of land.

Dutch and Swedish Indian Policies

FRANCIS JENNINGS

The Dutch became interested in the Americas for the same reason they had earlier ventured to the East Indies: they wanted to trade profitably in the commodities of the country. Trade developed naturally through several stages, each of which implied new relationships with the natives, the colonies of other Europeans, and the European home countries.

In the first stage the Indians were of little or no concern. Dutch merchant ships went to the Newfoundland fisheries early in the sixteenth century, as perhaps also in the late fifteenth, to buy cod from the European fishermen then thronging these waters. Like other Europeans, the Dutch thus became knowledgeable in the geography of the American coast and in the possibilities of a trade in furs. However, French power barred them from intruding upon the fur trade in New France. Turning elsewhere, several venturesome merchants studied the report and map of Henry Hudson, who had explored the Hudson River in 1609 while searching for a passage to the Orient for the Dutch East India Company (Brodhead 1853–1871, 1:25–35; Weslager and Dunlap 1961:25–42). Hudson's voyage had otherwise been of no significance because the East India Company had no interest in America.

From 1611 to 1614 several independent voyages were made by Dutchmen to the Hudson River and along the Atlantic Coast to trade with the natives for peltry and to map the country. In 1614 a Dutch trading company built Fort Nassau on Castle Island (south of Albany) as a year-round trading post (Hart 1959:18–27). An Indian tradition states that a treaty of friendship was made in 1618 between the Indians of the upper Hudson, probably Mahicans, and some Dutch traders who represented themselves as agents of their nation (Jennings 1971a:89).

New Netherland, 1614–1674

The Dutch West India Company

In 1614 four Dutch companies merged into the New Netherland Company, which received a monopoly patent from the States General to make four trading voyages (Hart 1959:33–38). After the patent's expiration on January 1, 1618, competition resumed among the so-

called *voorcompagnieen* until the chartering of a new monopoly, the West India Company, on June 3, 1621. New Netherland was a distinctly secondary concern for this great semisovereign organization that had been conceived partially as a means to prey upon the Spanish and Portuguese empires. The entire western hemisphere, as well as Africa, was its chartered province of action (Van Laer 1908:86–115). Trade with North American Indians promised dependable and regular profit if carefully exploited, but with the disadvantage of being vulnerable to interlopers of other nations. England, especially, was to be feared because England claimed all the territory from Newfoundland to Florida. Anticipating English competition, the West India Company decided upon establishing a permanent agricultural colony to protect its fur trade and to reduce the expense of provisioning its traders (Bachman 1969:54–73).

Being well capitalized and having the benefit of experienced traders' knowledge of American conditions, the company prepared more adequately for its colony than any other colonizing agency had yet done on the Atlantic coast. Its first party landed at Manhattan in May 1624, followed by a larger one the following year, and the colony never experienced the "starving times" suffered by the English colonies. Most of the colonists of the first expedition settled on the upper Hudson, slightly above Castle Island, where they built Fort Orange (fig. 1). Others scattered to the Delaware and Connecticut rivers and some remained at Manhattan, but within two years the dispersed outliers were recalled and concentrated at Manhattan where New Netherland's major community was thereafter located. Fort Amsterdam was built there, and in due course the town acquired the name New Amsterdam (fig. 2) (Bachman 1969:81–89).

England protested to the Dutch States General, but confined its hostility to diplomatic measures. From the Hudson River base, Dutch traders scattered up and down the Atlantic coast, aiming to establish in the New World the same predominance in the carrying trade that they enjoyed in Europe. Among other ventures, in 1627 they taught the colonists of New Plymouth to use wampum in the Indian trade. Since the best sources of wampum were then under Dutch control, the Dutch hoped to make Plymouth a steady wholesale customer for the Indian "money." The two colonies continued to trade for several years to their mutual advantage although Plymouth's Gov. William Bradford asserted that England held sovereignty over the territory claimed by the Dutch (Brodhead 1853–1871, 1:179–181). As a general rule the Dutch would trade anywhere that profit could be made, regardless of friendship or enmity, nationality, or state of diplomatic relations. It was the simple principle by which they had risen to commercial supremacy.

Beyond this principle, the West India Company vacillated in its colonizing policies, and New Netherland grew slowly. In 1629, in order to accelerate population growth without cost to itself, the company issued a Charter of Freedoms and Exemptions for "patroons" who would recruit and finance new settlers. For this service the patroons were granted large tracts of territory and feudal powers of lordship. Interested individuals quickly established patroonships on the Connecticut and Delaware rivers as well as on the Hudson. By 1631 the company changed policy again, made no more grants, and withheld cooperation from the existing patroons. Indian troubles, the difficulties and expense of management from abroad, and the obstructions of an opposed faction in the company wore the patroons down; all failed eventually except Kiliaen van Rensselaer, whose Rensselaerswyck was on the upper Hudson (Van Laer 1908:49–85, 137–153; Bachman 1969:95–139).

The conditions and purposes of colonization determined the colonists' relations with the natives. In this respect one must distinguish carefully between the intentions of the West India Company's European directors and the intentions of its colonial agents and settlers. The directors wished to cultivate Indian good will in order to create an extensive trading network and to establish support for their territorial claims. However, their people on the scene aimed at exploiting the Indians for personal advantage, frequently without care about arousing the hostility of the despised "wild men."

Land Purchases

On the positive side, the company ordered that all lands used by the colony should be purchased from the rightful Indian owners. This practice has often been cited as a singularly benevolent feature of New Netherland. Although it was consistently maintained and undoubtedly did tend to improve Dutch-Indian relations, even this policy was adopted for reasons other than altruism, and it was somewhat vitiated in its effects by trickery in local administration. The policy had originated in a struggle with England for supremacy in the East Indies. As a compromise settlement there, the Dutch and English agreed not to disturb each other in "possessions" already held. On the strength of this precedent the Dutch West India Company determined to create legal possession for

14

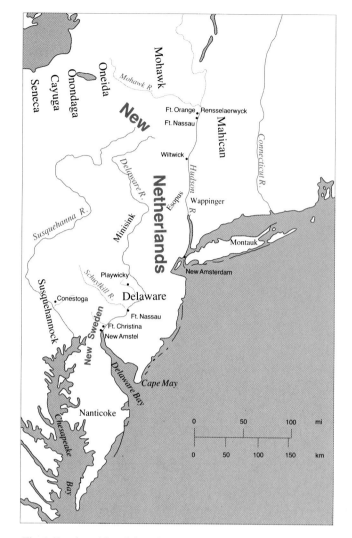

Fig. 1. Dutch and Swedish settlements and colonies relative to adjacent Indian tribal areas in the mid-1600s.

itself of its New Netherland territories by creating written deeds of conveyance of native title (Jennings 1975:132). The company's charter made the contrivance necessary because the charter contained no grant of territory, although it authorized business and military activities that could lead to acquisition of territory. Maximizing its chartered authority, the company formally recognized Indian rights in land so that the recognized right could be formally acquired, "a contract being made thereof and signed by them [the Indians] in their manner, since such contracts upon other occasions may be very useful to the Company" (Van Laer 1924:51–52).

The first use of such a deed upon one of those other occasions was made in a dispute with New Plymouth in 1633 regarding rights to trading posts on the Connecticut River (near Hartford). Englishmen had no precedents for recognition of Indian rights in land. "Purchases" previously made in Virginia had been merely expedients to keep the natives quiet; no legal rights ("civil" rights) were then formally recognized and no deeds were written. As late as

1632 the English Crown had emphatically denied that Indians could have any legal rights to land claimed by Christian princes. However, the Dutch deed tactic impressed Plymouth men with its serviceability, more especially because Plymouth lacked an authentic charter of its own. To counter the Dutch tactic, Plymouth's traders got a deed of their own from another Indian whose right to the land they recognized in order to make it their right. The practice spread thereafter, acquiring a rationale under "natural rights" doctrines that evolved gradually into the "Indian title" of modern United States law (Jennings 1971:529–531).

The Fur Trade

Some Indians were employed by the Hudson Valley Dutch as farm laborers, but the fur trade was the chief vehicle for intersocietal cooperation. In fact, the seal of the province of New Netherland was a beaver surrounded by wampum. The Dutch made little effort to follow the Indians far into the woods although individuals frequently attempted to intercept returning hunters before their arrival in the markets of Fort Orange/Rensselaerswyck, New Amsterdam, or Fort Nassau on the Delaware. Some Dutchmen, such as Arent van Corlaer or Curler, became adept at dealing with Indians in their own villages, but the Dutch never developed a corps of wide-ranging traders to parallel the French coureurs de bois. The market at Fort Orange/Rensselaerswyck acquired predominance in the trade partly because of its favorable location, partly through the expertise and single-mindedness of its residents, and partly through their adroit diplomacy among the Indians. The central position of New Netherland enabled its people to gain strategic advantage in the trade, but it also raised up a host of French, Swedish, and English competitors whose struggles for dominance over the trading Indians quickly expanded competition to antagonism and hostility. If the fur trade promoted

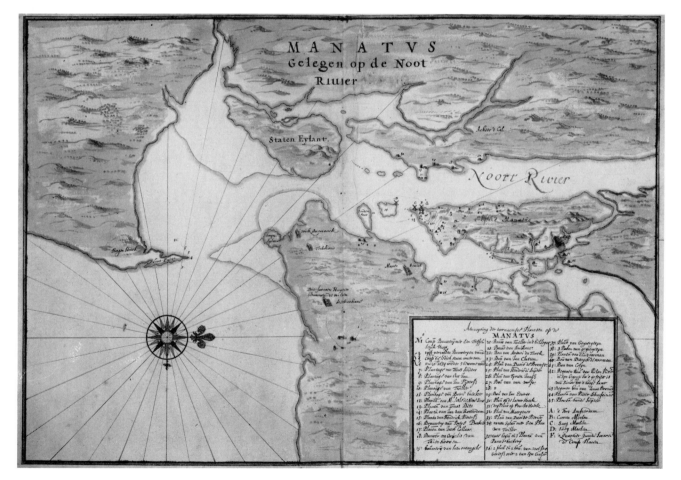

Lib. of Congress, Geography and Maps Div.: NY-NY-1639-Vingboon.
Fig. 2. Copy made about 1660 of a 1639 map "Manatus, Gelegen op de Noo<r>t Rivier" ('Manhattan, situated on the Hudson River'). Oriented with north to the right, this early survey map shows the Hudson River, Manhattan Island, Governor's Island, Staten Island, and New York Bay. Marked out are Dutch plantations and small farms, accompanied by a numbered key referring to their occupants, with Ft. Amsterdam and several mills at the southern tip of Manhattan. In what is now Brooklyn are 4 longhouses, one with the note "This is the type of houses the Indians live in," indicating the villages Wichquawanck, Techkonis, Mareckewich (vol. 15:237), and Keskachaue. The map may have been drawn to encourage settlement in the Dutch colony (Stephenson 1981). Pen and ink and watercolor wash after an original probably by Johannes Vingboons for the West India Company of Holland.

intersocietal cooperation, it also generated intrasocietal conflict (Trelease 1960:45–54, 112–137).

Indian War

Dutch Indian diplomacy developed slowly. In New Netherland's early years it was a simple matter of trade goods as carrots and firearms as clubs. Each community dealt separately with its Indian neighbors and for its own particular interests. Violence occurred sporadically, but it remained small in scale until Gov. Willem Kieft attempted in 1640 to reduce the tribes near New Amsterdam to subjection. Emulating New England, he demanded payment of wampum tribute from Long Island and Hudson Valley tribes, and when this was refused he ordered his mercenary troops to attack. When they proved insufficient for the job, he also hired Indian allies and trainband troops from new towns of ethnic Englishmen who had settled within New Netherland. At least two massacres were committed, comparable in scale and ruthlessness to those of the Pequot War, but the similarity stopped there because the Dutch terror did not succeed. Out of its failure was born a wasting war with tribes on the lower Hudson and Long Island. Being unable to gain decisive victory, the Dutch hired the Mohawk tribe to "arbitrate"; by what means is not explicit, but probably some judicious use or threat of Mohawk force was involved (Jennings 1984:55–57). Although a peace was concluded in 1643, and another in 1645, war broke out again, bringing widespread devastation to both colonists and Indians. In loss of life and destruction of property these Indian wars were without doubt New Netherland's greatest calamity. Kieft claimed to be merely obeying orders from the company, but he produced no documents, the company's directors denied his assertion, and he was lost at sea on his way to an inquiry. Whatever the truth may have been, the States General's committee on the affairs of New Netherland wondered why the instigators of this "unnecessary, bloody and ruinous war" had not been "duly inquired after, or punished." For the future, this sovereign body directed, no war should be waged "against the Aborigines of the country or neighbors of New Netherland, without their High Mightinesses' knowledge" (NYCD 1:388). There was no way, however, for their High Mightinesses to prevent the Indians from rising in rebellion against encroachment and cruelty as they did repeatedly in 1655, 1659, and 1663; and the defensive measures of Gov. Peter Stuyvesant were, naturally and indisputably, warfare (Trelease 1960:60–84; Brodhead 1853–1871, 1:607, 658, 711).

New England

New Netherland's numbers failed to increase rapidly enough to maintain strength relative to New England. Throughout the 1630s and 1640s, offshoots of New England towns established new communities in territories claimed by the Dutch in the Connecticut Valley, on Long Island, and on the mainland coast of Long Island Sound. Some of these new towns accepted Dutch jurisdiction; others refused it, thus advancing English colonial authority ever closer to New Amsterdam. The English within New Netherland constituted an element of doubtful fidelity where, even including the ethnic Englishmen, the population in 1650 amounted only to a total of about 4,000 persons of European stock as compared to about 22,000 in New England; but, lacking the strength to expel the aliens, the Dutch could only request their allegiance and hope for the best.

New Netherland's officials petitioned their company to treat with the English Crown to halt New England's encroachments on territory and trade, but in 1649 the company thrust responsibility back upon Governor Stuyvesant "to live with his neighbors on the best terms possible" (Brodhead 1853–1871, 1:499). There could be no fruitful negotiations with England at a time when civil war made it difficult even to find a viable government to treat with. Besides, relations between the two countries were strained to the point of rupture; when England's internal strife calmed, the new government would turn to war against the Dutch.

Thrown onto his own resources, Governor Stuyvesant opened prolonged negotiations with the United Colonies of New England that culminated in the Treaty of Hartford in 1650. By playing upon conflicts of interest among the English colonies, Stuyvesant gained the support of Massachusetts Bay and New Plymouth for a recognized boundary that protected New Netherland from further advances by the expanding colonies of Connecticut and New Haven. Stuyvesant had the treaty ratified by his West India Company and the States General, but the United Colonies of New England never submitted the treaty for ratification by the English government, choosing instead to assume authority to make treaties by their own right (R. Cohen 1969). It is doubtful that an English government would have confirmed any treaty recognizing the legitimacy of New Netherland's territory.

The Iroquois Alliance

In the Indian diplomacy of the Dutch the alliance with the Mohawks was a change in direction prophetic of the future. In 1626 the Fort Orange Dutch had sided with the Mahicans in a losing war against the Mohawks (Trigger 1971a), but by 1640 most of New Netherland's peltry was coming from far inland through trade or brigandage operated by the Mohawks and affiliated tribes in the League of the Iroquois. Although Governor Stuyvesant distrusted the Mohawks and feared their rise to dominance among the tribes, he had to reckon with their importance to the trade. The prosperity of New Nether-land depended directly upon the capacity of the Iroquois to transmit or grant passage to furs gathered from distant tribes and places. In 1642 the French of Canada founded a mission at Montreal that blocked Iroquois access to Canadian tribes and obstructed Iroquois hijacking of cargoes destined for French markets. Montreal's protection was effective enough to make both the Iroquois and the Dutch resort to desperate measures. In 1645 the Iroquois declared war upon the French-protected Hurons who collected furs from a wide network of interior tribes for trading at Montreal and Quebec. To insure Iroquois success the Dutch sold them firearms, and in 1648 Governor Stuyvesant provided them with the unprece-dented quantity of 400 arms. With these the Iroquois launched shattering blows against the Hurons and their allies from 1649 to 1656. These wars established Iroquois ascendancy along the south shore of Lake Erie and in the upper Ohio Valley, but the Susquehannock tribe, armed by Swedish patrons, remained unconquered (Trigger 1976:751–840; Jennings 1984:85–112). In 1655 Dutch conquest of New Sweden compelled the Susquehannocks to come to terms. For the remainder of New Netherland's existence, Dutch markets on the Hudson and Delaware rivers monopolized the trade of nearly all the Indians in the area covered by the present-day states of New York, New Jersey, Delaware, and Pennsylvania. Dutch policy was to pressure these Indians to stay at peace with one another so as not to interfere with trade, but whether efforts were also made to prevent plundering forays on Indians bound for non-Dutch markets is more difficult to say (Jennings 1968:23–25). Dutch policy made no provi-sion for developing a political confederation or system of tribal organizations. Each tribe was dealt with separately (Ruttenber 1872:54–55, 64).

New Sweden, 1638–1655

New Sweden originated from a commercial union of Swedish aspiration and Dutch experience. In the early seventeenth century Sweden had become a military power capable of swaying the balance of power in Europe, but its industrial and commercial base was relatively tiny and its participation in the Thirty Years' War made the discrep-ancy critical. To improve this situation, King Gustavus Adolphus and the influential Oxenstierna family extended state encouragement to a series of commercial companies, without much success. In the process they became patrons of Willem Usselinx, a disgruntled founder of the Dutch West India Company who had quarreled with his associates. Usselinx was joined by two other stockholders in the company, Samuel Blommaert and Peter Minuit, to provide the management capacity for a new company of mixed Dutch and Swedish capital under a Swedish charter. This New Sweden Company was founded early in

1637 with great ambitions to trade and colonize along the entire coast of North America from Newfoundland to Florida, but in practice it concentrated its activities in the Delaware River and Bay. Its first expedition, under Minuit, sailed up the Delaware in March 1638, built Fort Christina at the mouth of Brandywine Creek, and promptly began trading with the natives (A. Johnson 1911, 1:3–119).

The Swedes were met with protest by traders of the Dutch West India Company in Fort Nassau, whom they countered with policies that had been invented by the Dutch themselves. Since Minuit had formerly been a governor of New Netherland, the adoption of such policies is not surprising. Although the Swedish compa-ny's charter has vanished, it appears from surviving records to have resembled the Dutch company's charter in not providing specifically for a grant of territory. There-fore, imitating the Dutch, the Swedes immediately legiti-mized their presence on the Delaware by purchasing the cession of land from native chiefs. Also like the Dutch, they made the deeds convey more land than the natives intended; and, continuing to follow Dutch example, the Swedes used their deeds to argue that they had acquired rights of jurisdiction as well as property (Jennings 1968: 50–53).

The New Sweden Company's enthusiasm for coloniza-tion was not matched among the common folk at home, and the company had to resort to compulsion to get more settlers. Early returns to stockholders were disappointing-ly low, and the alarmed Dutch West India Company applied pressure to the Dutchmen who held stock in both companies.

In 1641, therefore, the Dutch members of the Swedish company sold their interest, and its ownership became and remained wholly Swedish (A. Johnson 1911, 1:120–134).

The colony made alliances of different sorts with the Delaware and Susquehannock Indians and "bought" lands from both, but the so-called purchases had different kinds of significance. In a familiar application of such terminology Delaware lands were bought for occupation by Swedish villages and trading posts. However, as applied to Susquehannock lands, the "purchase" was "for the sake of trade," which seems to mean that only a monopoly of the peltry produce of the Susquehannocks had been purchased; though Swedish traders traveled into Susquehannock territory, Swedish settlements were not made there.

Close proximity to the Delawares created strain. In 1644 Gov. Johan Printz requested a force of mercenary troops with which to conquer the Delawares outright. As incentive he pointed out that the "rights of conquest" thus acquired would be more substantial in international law than rights of purchase (Myers 1912:103) but the Swedish government failed to provide the requested soldiers. Between New Sweden and the Susquehannocks, trade relations were close but residence was more distant. Friendship was cemented by alliance. In 1643 Swedish provision of arms and advice for the Susquehannocks was instrumental in preventing that tribe's conquest by Maryland (Jennings 1982:220–221). Linderholm (1976: 66–67) states that this is the only time in the Indian wars when the Indians used artillery.

As the Susquehannocks were an important tribe in trade, and as access to them through Chesapeake Bay was controlled by Virginia and Maryland, the alternative access route of the Delaware River became an object of strong competition among the Swedes, the Dutch, and some English adventurers from New Haven. The colonists played traders' leapfrog, each attempting to plant his post closer than the others to the Susquehannock source of supply. The Swedes proved especially adroit in this game by building a strategic post at the Schuylkill River and by dispatching emissaries directly to the Susquehannock homeland (vol. 15:362–367).

In 1642–1643 the Swedes cooperated clandestinely with the Dutch to expel the New Haven English from the Delaware Bay and River, but immediately afterward the Dutch and Swedish colonists resumed struggle with each other (Weslager 1967:89–132). Their tensions in the New World were heightened by conflict in the Old when, after the close of the Thirty Years' War, the Netherlands strove with Sweden for domination of trade in the Baltic Sea.

New Sweden's life was always precarious. Its colonists never numbered as many as 400 and, of these, freemen were in the minority. Only 12 expeditions sailed to it during its 17-year existence. When Gov. Johan Rising took command in 1654, his predecessor had not received even a letter from Swedish authorities for more than six years (A. Johnson 1930:190). Founded in the great era of Swedish imperialism, the colony died as that era entered its twilight under the government of statesmen whose delusions of grandeur led them to overextend their kingdom in every direction. In 1654, taking advantage of the Netherlands' preoccupations in the first Anglo-Dutch War, a Swedish expedition under Rising's command forced capitulation of the Dutch colonists on the Delaware. The act seems to have been performed on Rising's own initiative rather than by instruction from his government. Its effects were highly temporary. The Dutch ended their war with England, and in 1655 they sent a fleet under Governor Stuyvesant to conquer New Sweden. The colony surrendered on September 1, 1655, whereupon its residents came under the jurisdiction of the Dutch West India Company (Hazard 1850:148–151, 178–203).

English Conquest

The cost of conquering New Sweden added more debt to the already overburdened Dutch West India Company that, in 1656, liquidated the amount owed to the city of Amsterdam by ceding to it part of the colony on the Delaware. Although new resources of money and persons were then poured into the city's colony, renamed New Amstel, it continued to be plagued by expensive troubles.

As toward the north, a great problem was encroachment by the English. Maryland claimed by charter the west coast of Delaware Bay and River up to 40° north latitude, about where Philadelphia now stands. The Maryland government intrigued among the motley settlers on the Delaware and formally presented demands to Dutch officials for surrender. These pressures were enhanced by implicit threats of force, which the Dutch accepted as genuine. Numbers of people abandoned the colony to live under Maryland's protection. In a futile effort to bolster its defenses, the city of Amsterdam took over the entire Delaware colony from the West India Company (Hazard 1850:220–351).

At the other end of New Netherland, New Englanders once again moved menacingly along the Atlantic coast and on Long Island and even attempted to get a foothold on a tributary of the Hudson above Fort Orange. Governor Stuyvesant alternately blustered and bargained to maintain his claimed territory against overwhelming numbers. All sides believed that the others were intriguing with the Indians for hostile purposes, and the available evidence suggests that this practice was indeed widespread. In 1664 a fleet commissioned by the Duke of York made New Netherland into New York (Brodhead 1853–1871, 1:670–745).

This conquest did not eliminate intercolonial boundary disputes. New York picked up New Netherland's territorial claims and Indian alliances and acquired New Netherland's quarrels as well. In 1673 the Dutch navy briefly reconquered the former colony, but the peace of 1674 gave it finally to England. The new English governor, Edmund Andros, had resources at his disposal that were largely Dutch and Swedish in ethnic origins, for the English did not immediately flock in to populate the colony. Using Dutch traders, merchants, and interpreters as his agents, Andros built upon the Indian alliances formerly made by the Dutch government. He intensified New York's ties with the Mohawks and the League of the Iroquois. In one respect, he deviated from Dutch policy; under pressure from New England he permitted the Iroquois to enter treaty relationships with the Puritan colonies that developed into a network of alliances involving Iroquois tributaries and a number of English colonies, comprehensively called the Covenant Chain. In Iroquois metaphor this was a "silver" chain as distinguished from the merely "iron" chains that had bound each tribe separately to the Dutch (Jennings 1975: 322–324, 1984:171, 223–375).

The primacy of the community at Fort Orange/ Rensselaerswyck was maintained in the fur trade and Indian diplomacy. Though the place was renamed Albany, little more than the name was changed. It remained essentially a Dutch town until well into the eighteenth century (Kenney 1969:xxi–xxii).

In summary, New Netherland and New Sweden were alike in many particulars. Both were founded by chartered companies and thus were governed indirectly rather than by their national sovereigns. Both aimed at profit through trade with the Indians, and both tried to legitimize themselves through purchase of Indian territories. Strikingly, though both were aware of danger from native resentment, they rated this as something manageable; their greater apprehensions were of conquest by other Europeans. Conquest, when it came, was relatively bloodless and painless for both colonies. Personal liberty and property were confirmed by the conquerors. In contrast to the destruction and bloodshed of New Netherland's Indian wars, conquest entailed little more than the loss of claims to sovereignty.

Sources

The Dutch manuscript sources have been seriously affected by two major losses—the disposition of many of the West India Company's records as waste paper and the 1911 great fire in the Albany capitol. The company's records seem to be irretrievably lost. Since many of the Albany records had been printed in whole or part before the fire, a variety of printed sources published before 1911 supplements the mutilated surviving manuscripts. Of these the most important are Documents Relative to the Colonial History of New York (NYCD), volumes 1, 2, 12–14, and The Documentary History of the State of New York (NYDH). The basic manuscript collection—the New York Colonial Manuscripts—was calendared (O'Callaghan 1865–1866) before the fire. Some of its Dutch language volumes have been translated into English by A.J.F. Van Laer (1908, 1920–1923, 1922, 1924, 1926–1932, 1932, 1935) in typescripts filed with the originals at the New York State Public Library in Albany. Gehring's (1977, 1980, 1981) translations of New York manuscripts correct many errors. Microfilms are available.

The histories and published sources of Brodhead (1853–1871) and O'Callaghan (1846–1848, 1865–1866, NYCD, NYDH), both of whom had had access to the destroyed materials, retain exceptional importance in spite of obsolete interpretations and faulty translations, but O'Callaghan's (1846–1848) History of New Netherland especially has been superseded. Both writers were strongly pro-Dutch. Hart (1959) fills a gap with translations of notarial records in the Amsterdam archives.

Jameson (1909) is a useful miscellany of sources. The best Dutch source on Indian culture is Van der Donck (1841).

No one historian of New Netherland can be called standard. Brodhead's first volume (1853–1871) provides a substantial chronological structure to which Hazard (1850) should be added for the Delaware region. Fernow's (1884) exhaustive discussion of sources must be valued with the knowledge that he also had worked with the manuscripts before the Albany fire. Bachman (1969) and Condon (1968) give alternative modern interpretations of Dutch commerce, Bachman's appearing to have been researched more intensively. Bachman's bibliography may be used as a guide to sources in the Old Dutch language. Kenney (1969) discusses the Dutch social structure.

On Dutch relations with the Indians, Heckewelder (1876) gives the traditions of Mahicans and Delawares, somewhat mixed up together as were his informants when interviewed in the late eighteenth century. Sources on treaties are in Jennings, Fenton, and Druke (1985). Ruttenber's (1872) explanations can neither be overlooked nor accepted without qualification. Hunt (1940) has become a classic on the Indian trade and its wars, but Trelease (1960) gives much needed correctives and a more rounded understanding. Weslager's (1967, 1972; Weslager and Dunlap 1961) volumes are indispensable for the Delaware region; besides his thorough descriptions, he provides translations of source documents not printed elsewhere. Jennings (1966, 1968, 1971, 1971a, 1975, 1981, 1982, 1984) is concerned with problems of accommodation between different cultural systems of politics and property. R. Cohen (1969) is useful for Dutch relations with New England.

A. Johnson (1911, 1930) is standard for New Sweden, both as source translator and as historian, but the reader should carefully distinguish his translated records from his statements about them; the two do not always coincide. Johnson's work is tainted by strong ethnocentric bias displaying itself in chauvinism toward the Swedes as well as racism against the Indians, but his translations are almost all there is in English. Keen (1884) provides a useful corrective in some matters and an extensive discussion of Swedish sources. Lindeström (1925) is the most reliable early Swedish commentator on Indian culture, Campanius Holm (1834) much less so. The eighteenth-century writers Kalm (1937) and Acrelius (1874) are often cited, but their information is derivative as regards New Sweden, and Acrelius especially is wildly wrong on Indian matters. Linderholm (1976) has not been published in translation.

Myers (1912) has collected a volume of Dutch, Swedish, and English sources for the Delaware region that provide the basis for useful comparisons.

French Indian Policies

MASON WADE

France's policy toward the North American Indian evolved rather rapidly over the two centuries of the French empire in North America. It began with the high-minded missionary spirit of the Counter Reformation, but by 1700 it had degenerated into political manipulation to provide the Indian allies that a chronically undermanned empire needed, in order to preserve its claims to a large part of both Canada and the United States against the expansionism of the much more populous British colonies. Parkman's (1897, 1:131) verdict that while "Spanish civilization crushed the Indian; English civilization scorned and neglected him; French civilization embraced and cherished him" remains essentially true. The French, with their lack of racial prejudice, were able to achieve a much closer relationship with the Indian than any other European colonists in North America.

The Northeast

The record of French contacts with the Indians begins with Jacques Cartier's kidnapping of two Iroquoians who were fishing in Chaleur Bay off the Gaspé Peninsula in the summer of 1534. The glowing accounts provided by these Indians of the mythical kingdoms of Hochelaga, Stadacona, and Saguenay aroused French interest in the New World, for they suggested that North America might offer riches comparable to those of Mexico and Peru. François I was induced to back Cartier's voyages in 1535–1536, when he made his way up the Saint Lawrence to the Iroquoian settlements of Stadacona and Hochelaga (vol. 15: 357–360), and in 1541–1542, when he established a base near Quebec for the discovery of the riches of Saguenay and for the search for the Northwest Passage.

The missionary impulse of the Counter Reformation is evident in the dedication of Cartier's account of his second voyage, in which he holds forth to the king "the certain hope of the future augmentation of our said Holy Faith and of your seigneuries and Most Christian name." Cartier (1863:5–6, 31a) observes of the Indians: "By what we have seen and been able to understand of these people it seems to me that they should be easy to tame. May God in His Holy compassion see to it." To achieve his evangelical ends Cartier did not hesitate to kidnap Chief Donnacona, and nine of his band, taking them back to

France in spring 1536. All these Indians died in France, after being duly baptized, before Cartier returned to the Saint Lawrence in 1541.

There can be little doubt that Jacques Cartier was a pious man with strong missionary instincts, but there is much reason to doubt the sincerity of the alleged motives of François I, who in 1540 announced his intention to plant a permanent French colony in the New World, "in order to attain better our announced intention and to do something pleasing to God our creator and redeemer and which may lead to the augmentation of His Holy and sacred name and of our mother Holy Catholic Church of whom we are called and named the first son" (1854–1856,1:3, 5–6). François I had been told by Donnacona of "many mines of gold and silver in great abundance" (Biggar 1930:77), and he had hopes that France might reap as rich a harvest in the north of the New World as Spain had in the South. While the announced purpose of Cartier's 1541 expedition was "to establish the Christian Religion in a country of savages separated from France by all the extent of the earth, and where he [the king] knew that there were no mines of gold and silver, nor other gain to be hoped for than the conquest of infinite souls for God, and their deliverance from the domination and tyranny of the infernal Demon," the long list of men required concluded with six churchmen, while "two goldsmiths and lapidaries" enjoyed much higher priority (Biggar 1930:70–72, 77). There is no mention of missionary work in Cartier's account of this voyage, but much attention was devoted to the discovery of what were thought to be precious stones and metals. The fact that these turned out to be worthless effectively dampened French interest in the New World for a half-century.

Cartier took one step on this voyage that was to pave the way for the rapid expansion of New France. He left two French boys with the Indians to learn their language, just as he had taken two Indian boys back to France with him in 1534. This exchange plan, continued by Samuel de Champlain, was to serve the French well. They had the good fortune, unlike other European newcomers to North America, to find themselves among speakers of Algonquian and Iroquoian languages, which were widely spoken. The expertise their interpreters soon acquired in languages of these families spoken in the Saint Lawrence–Great Lakes area stood them in good stead in the incredibly rapid expansion of the French fur trade to the foothills of the Rockies (the western limit of the Algonquian linguistic family) and in their later vital dealings with the Iroquois. The French first sought to acquire mastery of the Indian languages for purposes of exploration, and later for missionary motives and, as the fur trade became the mainstay of the colony, for commercial purposes.

In the closing years of the sixteenth century François Gravé Du Pont and Pierre Chauvin obtained a 10-year monopoly of the Canadian fur trade and set up a trading post at Tadoussac at the mouth of the Saguenay River, long a rendezvous of the Indians, French fishermen, and Basque whalers (fig. 1). When this enterprise failed to flourish, the monopoly was annulled in 1602 and given to the Company of New France, a joint stock company on the same model as the English and Dutch companies trading with the East Indies. In exchange for a complete monopoly of the fur trade forever, it was to settle 4,000 colonists within 15 years and to see to the conversion of the Indians. But this trading company and subsequent ones failed miserably as colonization agents and only tolerated the missionary activity that they were supposed to support.

When the new company sent out its first expedition in 1603, it included the geographer Samuel de Champlain, who was to become the true founder of New France and to play a major role in the establishment of French relations with the Indians. Soon after Gravé Du Pont and Champlain landed at Tadoussac they made an alliance with the Montagnais that lasted as long as New France did. The French, unlike the Spaniards and the English, did not try to exterminate the relatively sparse Indian population in their region of exploration and settlement, because they needed their aid in the fur trade and in war against European rivals. Circumstances forced them into an alliance with the Algonquian tribes of northeastern North America (Montagnais, Maliseet, Passamaquoddy, and Algonquin, who became the middlemen in the trading of furs for French goods), against the Iroquois Confederacy whose members traded first with the Dutch and then with the English from their homeland in northern New York. At Tadoussac in 1603 the sides were being chosen unconsciously in the Anglo-French struggle for North America, for the Iroquois, the enemies of the Algonquians, after nearly discouraging French colonization through their own efforts, were to become the allies of the English in the struggle for military dominance and control of the fur trade of the interior. The Iroquois were to be the most dreaded enemies of the French, but the hands of all other Indians of the Northeast were raised against the Iroquois because of their ferocity in war, and so the French won the alliance of the greater part of the Indians in the region they were to penetrate. Without these Indian

allies, undermanned New France could not have survived so long as it did.

One French trait that gave them a great advantage in dealing with the Indians was their willingness to learn and adopt Indian ways. Champlain quickly recognized the superiority of the birchbark canoe to the clumsy French skiff. He became convinced that "by directing one's course with the help of the savages and their canoes, a man may see all that is to be seen, good and bad, within the space of a year or two" (Champlain 1922–1936,1:152). With the aid of the canoe the French were able to explore the waterways of the continent during the next century and trace out the routes that were later used by Frenchmen who had mastered the use of the canoe for exploration, trade, and warfare. The willingness of the French to adapt themselves to native ways gave them a great advantage in trade and war over the insular English, who thought the English way was the only way. The Hudson's Bay Company did not adopt the canoe for nearly a century after it began operations. It waited for the Indians to bring furs to its posts, while the French coureurs de bois were tapping its supply lines far to the west.

Champlain established contact with most of the Indian tribes who were to remain allies of the French until the end of New France. Having acquired some idea of the Saint Lawrence–Great Lakes system in summer 1603, during the next three years Champlain explored and mapped the Atlantic coast from Nova Scotia to the juncture of Martha's Vineyard and Nantucket sounds. Encounters with hostile Indians along the densely populated Massachusetts coast (vol. 15:165) led his party to return to Port Royal and its friendly Micmacs, although Champlain wished to explore farther south. Unfriendly Indians thus forced the French to concentrate their colonization efforts in the colder and less fertile regions to the north.

At Port Royal the French and Micmacs helped each other out with provisions, and Membertou and other Indian chiefs were welcomed to the Frenchmen's table. Charles Biencourt de Saint-Just and Robert Gravé Du Pont adapted themselves to Indian ways and learned the Micmac language, and Champlain determined to settle other young Frenchmen among the Indians to become agents and interpreters. The French supplied their Indian friends with muskets and steel-tipped arrows, which enabled Membertou to undertake a successful war against the fierce Massachusett Indians. Fishhooks, iron kettles, other metalware, ornaments, and European clothing also were adopted by the Indians, who in return taught the Europeans the use of tobacco, forest craft, and canoeing. Though the French planted gardens at the short-lived settlement of Saint-Croix and at Port Royal, the Micmac were not agricultural Indians and could not be induced to farm. When moose meat, their staple food, ran out, they

Fig. 1. Indian and French settlements, forts, and trading posts of New France and Louisiana relative to adjacent Indian tribal areas in the 1600s to the mid-1700s (Voorhis 1930; J.T. Adams 1943; Tanner 1986). 1, Rigolet; 2, Esquimaux Baie; 3, Ft. Phelipeaux; 4, Baye de Philipeau; 5, Ft. Bourbon; 6, Moisie; 7, Mingan; 8, Ft. Dauphin; 9, Maison des Dorvals; 10, Îslets de Jeremie; 11, Ft. Maurepas; 12, Saguenay and Tadoussac; 13, Nipisiquit; 14, Ft. Ste-Anne; 15, Lac Nepigon; 16, Lac St.-Jean; 17, Ft. La Reine; 18, Ft. Rouge; 19, La Have; 20, Ft. St. Charles; 21, Abitibi; 22, Ft. St. Pierre; 23, Lorette and Sillery; 24, Quebec and Stadacona; 25, Île d'Orleans; 26, Ft. St. Jean and Ft. La Tour; 27, St. Croix; 28, Camenestiguouia; 29, Michipicoten; 30, Trois-Rivières; 31, Port Royal; 32, Ft. La Pointe; 33, Hochelaga, Lachine, and Montreal; 34, Caughnawaga; 35, Ft. Castine and St.-Sauveur; 36, Sault Ste.-Marie; 37, St. Ignace; 38, Ft. Michilimackinac; 39, Caciaque; 40, Ft. Frontenac; 41, Ft. de la Presentation; 42, Ft. Carillon; 43, Ft. Pepin; 44, Ft. de la baye des Puants and St.-Francois Xavier; 45, l'Huillier; 46, Otinawatawa; 47, Prairie du Chien; 48, Detroit; 49, Ft. St. Joseph; 50, Ft. des Miamis; 51, Ft. Duquesne; 52, Ft. St. Louis; 53, Ouiatanon; 54, Ft. Orleans; 55, Cahokia; 56, Ft. Vincennes; 57, Ft. Ste. Genevieve; 58, Kaskaskia; 59, Juchereau Tannery; 60, Ft. Prudhomme; 61, Pacaha; 62, Arkansas Post; 63, Chicaca; 64, Ft. Rosalie; 65, Biloxi; 66, Mobile; 67, New Orleans; 68, Ft. St. Louis.

had to be saved from starving by French provisions. They acquired a taste for brandy as well as wine and soon priests complained that "since the French mingled with and carry on trade with them, they are dying fast and the population is thinning out" (JR 3:105). Indians thought the French poisoned them, but the missionary Pierre Biard justly blamed their own gluttony and drunkenness.

Revocation of the company's trading monopoly and the destruction of Port Royal and the Jesuit settlement of Saint-Sauveur on the Maine coast by Capt. Samuel Argall of Virginia virtually ended the French effort at colonization in Acadia. It shifted to Quebec, which Champlain founded in 1608. While he laid the basis for good relations with the Indians in his explorations and his efforts to restrain the rival traders who debauched them, it was first the Recollect (Franciscan) and later the Jesuit missionaries (fig. 2) whom he enlisted for the mission of New France who developed these relations into a close and lasting alliance. One of the reasons for choosing Quebec as a base was that it would be "easier to plant the Christian faith and establish such order as is necessary for the preservation of a country" (Champlain 1922–1936, 1:232) among the sedentary Indians of the interior. The new settlement would discourage raids by the Iroquois in the fur traffic from the Great Lakes to the Saint Lawrence and enable the French to meet the Indian traders at the Lachine Rapids (Montreal), a natural entrepot at the intersection of three great waterways. Champlain's persistent desire to explore farther into the interior met opposition from the Montagnais, who did not wish to lose the profitable role of middlemen in the exchange of northern furs for French goods. The French were to encounter similar opposition from other tribes as they pressed westward. But their Indian neighbors were only too glad to have French aid in their war parties against the Iroquois, and Champlain's participation in that of 1609 by the Montagnais, Algonquin, and Huron had momentous consequences for the French in North America (vol. 15:348).

The Iroquois were encountered on Lake Champlain near the future site of Fort Ticonderoga, and Champlain's double-loaded arquebus, which killed two of their chiefs at the first shot, was sufficient to put the much stronger Iroquois party to panic-stricken flight. This brief encounter sealed the alliance of the French with the Algonquians and the Hurons and made the Iroquois their deadliest enemies (vol. 15:350). Thanks to this war party, it was a long time before the French found their way up the Saint Lawrence beyond the Lachine Rapids, for this route was barred by the Iroquois. Like the Hurons, they were forced instead to follow the arduous Ottawa River route to the upper Great Lakes. Actually they had little choice in the matter, for the upper Saint Lawrence would still have been barred to them unless they had allied themselves with the Iroquois. And this alliance was impossible since the French fur trade and the future of the French establishments on the lower Saint Lawrence hinged upon the friendship of the Algonquians and the Hurons.

Continuing the policy that Cartier had started, in June 1610 Champlain persuaded the Algonquins to take home with them a young Frenchmen, Étienne Brûlé, who was to become the first of the coureurs de bois, while the French in turn agreed to take a young Huron, Savignon, to France. Both were to be returned a year later. In 1611 Champlain arranged to have another Frenchman winter with the Hurons to learn their language, as Brûlé already had that of the Algonquins, while Savignon returned

Fig. 2. Cartouche, from *Carte du Canada ou de la Nouvelle France* . . . by Claude Delisle with collaboration from Guillaume Delisle, 1703 (Delanglez 1985:275–298). The cartouche illustrates features of life in New France. The priests, top, left and right, represent two orders active in the colony, the Jesuits and the Franciscan Recollects, and are depicted baptizing and preaching to Indians. The beaver, lower left, was a key trade item, and the fish and the duck, lower right, probably represent provisioning, another aspect of Indian-White trade relations. Engraved by N. Guerard, 1703.

home to spread the prestige of the French among the Hurons (Trigger 1968:115–123). Another young Frenchman, Nicolas de Vignau, was to winter with Chief Tessouat of the Algonquins. These three were intended to serve Champlain in the future as guides and interpreters. By proposing to found a French establishment at Montreal, Champlain further tightened his ties with the Hurons and Algonquins, since they would be saved the long and dangerous journey to Quebec or Tadoussac.

Champlain had higher motives than most of the French fur traders, as his persistent efforts in France to secure missionaries indicate. He may have felt some resentment against the Jesuits for their decision in 1610 to go to Acadia instead of to Quebec as he had asked. In any case the order was not popular with either Henri de Bourbon, Prince de Condé, the absentee governor of New France, or the Huguenot merchants of the northern ports who were interested in developing the colony's trade. So Champlain sought instead "some good friars, with zeal and affection for the glory of God, whom I might persuade to send or come themselves with me to this country to try to plant there the faith" (Champlain 1922–1936, 3:16). He found them among the Recollects of Brouage. Since they were a poor order, vowed to proverty, they had no funds to maintain missionaries. Finally the French bishops agreed to support four missionaries.

Despite these recruits neither missionary work nor colonization flourished in the next few years. The Recollects maintained that to convert the Indians it was necessary to increase the colony, "the greatest obstacle to which was on the part of the gentlemen of the Company, who, to monopolize trade, did not wish the country to be settled, and did not even wish us to make the Indian sedentary, without which nothing can be done for the salvation of these heathen" (Le Clercq in Bishop 1948: 264). The Recollect historian Le Clercq also observed of the Company of New France that they were "very zealous for their trade," but "they care little to deserve God's blessing by contributing to the interest of his glory" (ibid.). Colonization and missionary work were both expensive and incompatible with the fur trade, and the Company would do no more than provide free passage for two missionaries. It was not interested in promoting agricultural settlement, since it wanted its employees to take to the woods, or in helping to domesticate the nomadic Indians who supplied its furs.

Since the fur trade was the economic lifeblood of the colony, its interests dominated all aspects of the life of New France. When in 1622 the Iroquois sent ambassadors proposing a general peace, a peace treaty was only negotiated after considerable opposition from the traders, who felt that if peace were made, the Iroquois would induce the Hurons to trade with the Dutch. But Champlain took good care to keep his commercial fences in repair, and in 1623 sent Gabriel Sagard-Théodat and 13 other Frenchmen to winter with the Hurons, while Étienne Brûlé and two others wintered with the Algonquins. In 1624 the Iroquois themselves came with 35 canoes of furs to trade at the Lachine Rapids. But the peace was broken by the Iroquois in 1627, after provocation from the Montagnais, just as the French became unable to maintain agents and missionaries among the tribes. An Anglo-French War commenced in 1627, and a blockade by British merchants of the Saint Lawrence in 1628 and 1629 cut off supplies from France. Finding no trade goods at Quebec, the Indians took their furs back home or to Albany. The Dutch fur trade nearly doubled between 1626 and 1628, and it quadrupled before the peace treaty in 1632.

However, when the French returned to trading in 1632, they had stronger backing than ever before. The Jesuits had obtained the exclusive right to the mission of New France, since the Recollects were financially unable to continue. The Jesuits launched a vigorous missionary effort, which continued to expand until 1690. Until 1663, when royal government was instituted, the jesuits dominated the life of New France, both religious and secular. Thanks to their excellent connections in high places at

court, they received the support in manpower and funds that both the early trading companies and the Recollects had lacked. Like the Recollects the Jesuits felt that the nomadic tribes, such as the Montagnais and Algonquin, would have to become sedentary and Frenchified, so that "mingled with French traders and settlers, softened by French manners, guided by French priests, ruled by French officers, their now divided bands would become the constituents of a vast wilderness empire, which in time might span the continent" (Parkman 1897,1:131). Their original goal, then, was to found a Christian theocracy, where European and savage would live together in peace.

As for intermarriage, Champlain had already welcomed it. When he told the Indians of the proposed settlement at the Lachine Rapids, he said: "then our young men will marry your daughters, and we shall be one people" (JR 5:211). Indeed intermarriage had already begun. Of four recorded marriages at Quebec between 1604 and 1627, two were those of Frenchmen who espoused Indian "women who were educated in our language and manners, and who had persevered in great understanding, peace, and union with their husbands" (Le Clercq 1691, 1:223). Lescarbot (1907–1914, 3:167) was the only French writer of the period to censure such unions. Though the Jesuits did their best to maintain strict morality in the settlements, the scarcity of French women and the tendency of the coureurs de bois to follow the sexual ways of their Indian hosts doubtless produced many interracial relationships.

French expansionism was marked from the early days of this second beginning of New France. In 1634 Champlain sent the interpreter Jean Nicollet, who had lived among the Algonquins, Nipissings, and Hurons, to visit the Winnebago, who were reputed to live by a western sea. Nicollet carried with him a richly embroidered Chinese robe, in case he should reach the Orient by that sea, which turned out to be Lake Michigan. Nicollet got no farther west than Green Bay, later to become an important fur trading center, where he concluded a treaty with the Indians.

Under the zealous Jesuits the work of the missions prospered, both along the Saint Lawrence and in the interior. The 22 baptisms of 1635 were eclipsed by more than 100 the following year. The numbers increased each year, so that by 1640 more than 1,000 baptisms had taken place in Huronia (vol. 15:383). The missionaries found it easier to minister to the sedentary Hurons than to the nomadic Montagnais and Algonquins, but they encountered resistance from the Huron medicine men. This increased as healthy adult Indians demanded baptism, which at first had been administered chiefly to infants and the dying, though perhaps more as a matter of magical health insurance than of faith. In 1635 the Jesuits started teaching both French and Montagnais children at Quebec; two years later they were teaching Hurons and Algonquins as well. Funds were made available by wealthy philanthropists in France for the establishment of a hospital, a school for Indian girls, and a seminary for Montagnais, Algonquins, and Hurons to train native helpers for the French missionaries. Now that Jesuits had made some progress in the Indian languages, of which they produced the first dictionaries, they found that the harvest of souls went much faster.

By 1638 Father Paul LeJeune, the superior of the mission of New France, could report that superstition, error, barbarism, and sin were being attacked by four means: war was being made upon the enemy on his ground with his own weapons, the Montagnais, Algonquin, and Huron tongues; a hospital was being built in Quebec to care for sick Indians; the Indian seminary was launched; and the effort to make the Indians sedentary was begun with the establishment of two Indian families on the land near Quebec (fig. 3). The Jesuits proposed to gather their converts into separate villages where they could be instructed in agriculture and various trades, as well as in religion. At Sillery and Trois-Rivières, and later at Lorette and Caughnawaga (vol. 15:470), their purpose was to guard their Indian flock against corruption by the lawless coureurs de bois or unruly French soldiers. The Company furthered their plans by giving converted Indians the same rights at its stores as Frenchmen and by providing cleared lands as dowries for Indian girls. But among both students and apprentice farmers there were many backsliders, for aboriginal culture remained strong among the Indians, who did not flourish on a French diet or a French way of life.

The Jesuits made a major contribution both to the development of New France and to modern knowledge of the Indians at this period through the publication of the *Jesuit Relations* (JR), annual reports of the mission of New France, written by the superior but incorporating the observations of all the missionaries. Published each year from 1632 to 1674, they were intended for general readers and designed to obtain support for the missions. They were truthful propaganda, feeding French curiosity about the Indians and the New World, and spurring pious zeal for the conversion of the Indians. They constitute a uniquely valuable source for Indian and French colonial life in the seventeenth century.

The *Jesuit Relations* were directly responsible for the foundation of Montreal in 1642 by a group of pious laymen, who proposed to established a hospital there for the Indians and to work for their conversion. The leader, Paul Chomedey de Maisonneuve, persisted in this purpose despite warnings of danger from the Iroquois from the governor of New France and the Jesuits (Dollier de Casson 1928:91). The new establishment persisted, even though Iroquois attacks grew more savage and frequent, so that for three years the Jesuits were unable to get supplies through to their establishments in Huronia. Then

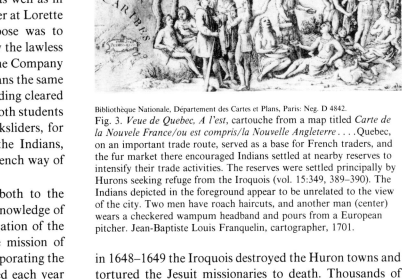

Bibliothèque Nationale, Département des Cartes et Plans, Paris: Neg. D 4842.

Fig. 3. *Veue de Quebec, A l'est*, cartouche from a map titled *Carte de la Nouvele France/ou est compris/la Nouvelle Angleterre . . . .* Quebec, on an important trade route, served as a base for French traders, and the fur market there encouraged Indians settled at nearby reserves to intensify their trade activities. The reserves were settled principally by Hurons seeking refuge from the Iroquois (vol. 15:349, 389–390). The Indians depicted in the foreground appear to be unrelated to the view of the city. Two men have roach haircuts, and another man (center) wears a checkered wampum headband and pours from a European pitcher. Jean-Baptiste Louis Franquelin, cartographer, 1701.

in 1648–1649 the Iroquois destroyed the Huron towns and tortured the Jesuit missionaries to death. Thousands of Hurons were killed and more died of starvation after the devastation of their country. A few survivors reached Quebec in 1650, and the French established a mission village for them, first on the Île d'Orleans and later at Lorette. Other fugitive Hurons joined this colony until it numbered about 600. Another 500 fugitives settled near Lake Superior.

The Jesuits sent missionaries to the Onondagas in 1656. In 1658 they escaped when the Indians planned to kill them. For the first time the French began to talk about eliminating the Indians, since they had become convinced that the Iroquois must be destroyed if the colony were to survive. But the necessary troops for an expedition into the heart of the Iroquois country did not arrive until 1665. Three forts were built that summer to block the Iroquois warpath on the Richelieu River, and the following year Alexandre de Prouville de Tracy led an army into the Iroquois country that achieved little but awed the Iroquois into a peace that lasted for nearly 20 years (vol. 15:356). Then as the French pressed westward into the Iroquois trading territory, with Henri Tonti pioneering in the Illinois country, Antoine Laumet de Lamothe Cadillac at Detroit and Michilimackinac, Daniel Greysolon Dulhut on the Upper Great Lakes, Father Louis Hennepin on the upper Mississippi, and Nicolas Perrot roaming about the whole Great Lakes area, the Iroquois once more attacked New France, massacring the inhabitants of Lachine in 1689. After Louis de Buade de Frontenac's devastation of the Oneida and Onondaga country in 1696 (vol. 15:494), the Iroquois finally made peace with the French and their Indian allies in 1701. They had succeeded in threatening the very existence of New France for over a half-century.

For their part the French placed increasing reliance on their Indian allies as they were more and more outnumbered by the militia of the British colonies and regulars sent from Britain in time of war. During the final Iroquois war they became dependent in the west upon the support of the Illinois, Ottawas, Hurons, and Christian Iroquois to repel the threat to the Great Lakes fur trade. Similarly, in Acadia, after the surrender of the Nova Scotia peninsula to the British in 1713, French missionaries and Indian agents kept the Abenaki, Maliseet, and Micmac active in resisting the advance of the English settlement frontier in northern New England. This policy stimulated the antipapist sentiments of the New England pioneers. Mixed forces of Micmacs and Acadians, led by French regular officers and militant missionaries, kept the Nova Scotia frontier in tumult until the expulsion of the Acadians in 1755.

In the west the French pursued the devious ways of Indian agents, succeeding in keeping a loose coalition of a majority of the tribes in their interest. The only tribe against which the French waged a war of near extermination was the Fox, hereditary enemies of most of the Great Lakes tribes, who were only finally subdued in 1731, after several efforts. The relationships among the western tribes remained turbulent. Though in the east in the final days of New France little reliance was placed upon the western Indians, they did make up the majority of the garrison of Fort Duquesne and were chiefly responsible for Gen. Edward Braddock's defeat in 1755. French regular officers shared the British regulars' contempt for Indian allies, to their cost in wilderness warfare. The British had no useful Indian allies except the Iroquois, while the French had considerable numbers of officers trained in Indian warfare in the western posts, who subsequently served on the Alleghany and Acadian frontiers (fig. 4).

The South and the West

At the beginning of the eighteenth century France occupied the mouth of the Mississippi and asserted her claim, based upon René-Robert Cavelier, Sieur de La Salle's explorations, to its vast watershed. French establishments at Biloxi and New Orleans attempted to use Indian slaves to work the tobacco plantations, but these ran away and it was decided to import Blacks from the French West Indies. The Canadians, who made up the most energetic element of the colony, started a trade in furs that brought them into contact with the Indians. Then the Natchez massacred the French colony at Fort Rosalie, which led to a series of Indian wars. The Chickasaw supported the Natchez, while the Choctaw allied themselves with the French. The French sent their Natchez prisoners as slaves to Santo Domingo. The Chickasaw were aided by traders in the British colonies of North and South Carolina, and this powerful tribe became the chief threat to Louisiana. The French mustered an expedition against them in 1739 that was a complete failure. The Louisiana officials then put their faith in the success of the missionaries' efforts to win over the Indians to Roman Catholicism and the French interest, in order to resist the advance of the British traders over the Appalachian Mountains.

The French occupation of the lower Mississippi led to wide-ranging exploration of the west in the hope of finding gold mines and an overland way to the Pacific. As early as 1682 Pierre Le Sueur had visited the Sioux country, and in 1695 he brought the first Sioux to Montreal. He claimed that he had established a trading post at Lake Pepin on the upper Mississippi and asked and obtained a monopoly of the region's fur trade and mines for 10 years. His monopoly was eventually revoked, after it had been limited to copper and iron mines, on the grounds that he really was only interested in furs. In 1700 he turned up in Louisiana and set out for the Sioux country by boat. Encountering Canadian fur traders after passing the mouth of the Ohio, Le Sueur's party established themselves at Fort l'Huillier on the Blue Earth River. They were soon joined by seven Canadian traders who had been plundered and stripped to the skin by Sioux. The buffalo hunting proved excellent, and soon they were visited by bands of Sioux from whom they bought beaver. They returned to Louisiana with a good supply of beaver and 4,000 pounds of blue earth, which proved worthless. Thus the French established contact with Sioux who ranged westward to the Black Hills and perhaps the Rockies.

In the south Louis Juchereau de Saint-Denis journeyed cross-country to the Rio Grande in 1715. In 1719 Claude-Charles Dutisné went up the Missouri to a village of the Missouri Indians, above Grand River. They would not let him go farther, so he returned to the Illinois and then journeyed on horseback until he reached a village of Osages. They, too, refused to let him go on to a town of the Wichita, their enemies, some distance beyond. But he overroad their opposition and reached the Wichita town, where he was threatened with death as a presumed enemy. The Wichitas would not permit him to continue to the

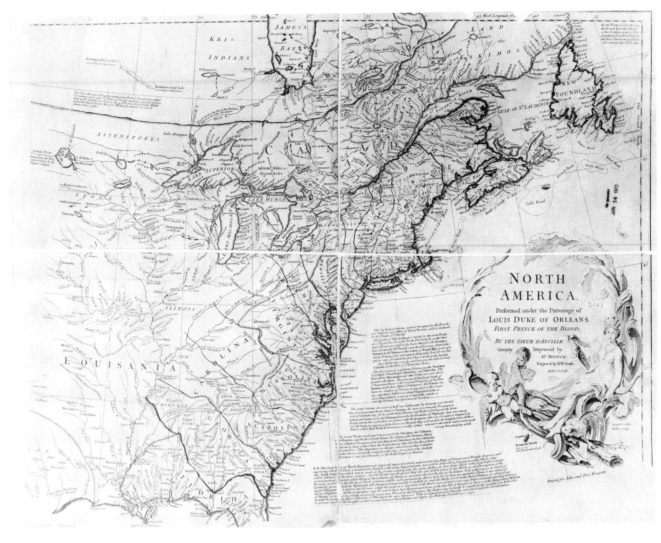

Fig. 4. Detail of *North America*, a 1752 engraving that is a British version of a map originally drawn in France. The inscription adjacent to the cartouche provides detailed information of what can be called the "cartographer's war" between British and French mapmakers. The English commentator points out the absurdity (from the English point of view) of the French claims to certain areas of North America, asserting the authority for the English claim to vast areas by virtue of various treaties, agreements, and purchases negotiated with the Indians. Jean-Baptiste d'Anville, cartographer, with improvements by Solomon Bolton; engraved by Richard W. Seale.

Plains Apaches, a 15-day journey, so he returned home to Illinois (Wedel 1972–1973).

After a Spanish party, supported by Plains Apache warriors, had been routed by the Missouri tribes before it could launch an attack on the French at the Illinois, the French sought to make peace, in the interest of trade, between the Missouri tribes and the Plains Apaches. In 1723 Étienne Venyard, Sieur de Bourgamont, a trader, well known among these tribes, built a post on the Missouri, near the mouth of the Grand River, and in 1724 succeeded in making peace among the Plains Apache and the Missouri, Osage, Kansa, Omaha, and Pawnee. The way was then open for the French to trade with the Spaniards in New Mexico.

The French had the notion that the upper course of the Missouri bent southward and formed a waterway to Mexico. In 1739 Pierre-Antoine and Paul Mallet went up the Platte to the South Fork, followed it for some distance and then turned southward, crossing the Colorado plains. They reached Picuris, Santa Fe, and Pecos and returned by the Arkansas to the Mississippi. The Great Plains had ceased to be terra incognita to the French.

Proposals for renewing the search for the western sea, which had been one of Jacques Cartier's objectives, were raised again in France in 1716, and in 1723 the Jesuit traveler and historian Pierre Charlevoix was ordered to collect all possible information about it in America. After talking to missionaries, officers, voyageurs, and Indians, he came to the conclusion that it formed the western boundary of the Sioux country. Therefore, he planned to establish a mission among the Sioux, from whom the desired information might be obtained. Since the king would not supply the necessary funds, the traditional expedient was adopted of granting a trading monopoly to a company charged with building a fort, chapel, and mission house, and maintaining a garrison. None but pious and virtuous persons were to join the company. Once again there was an incongruous mixture of spiritual and material motives, since the purpose was to attach the Sioux to the French by religious and commercial ties, and to use their knowledge to reach the Pacific, in order to gain entrance to the China trade. The enterprise, begun in 1727, had failed by 1737, largely because of the hostility of the Sioux, incited by the Fox.

Meanwhile a 33-year-old Canadian officer, Pierre Gaultier de Varennes de la Vérendrye, had become interested in the search for the western sea while commanding the post at Lake Nipigon, where he had heard Indian tales of a great salt lake that rose and fell. La Vérendrye decided that the way to the western sea lay to the north of the Sioux country. He sought help from the king but was merely authorized to find the way to the Pacific at his own expense, in return for a monopoly of the fur trade of the region north and west of Lake Superior. In 1731 he began his great effort, building a post at Rainy Lake and later five others (fig. 1). He also built two temporary posts, Fort Rouge on the site of Winnipeg, and another at the mouth of the Saskatchewan. He failed to get any information about the western sea from the Assiniboins, whose westward way was barred by their enemies the Sioux, while the Cree were equally ignorant but more inventive, both with tall tales and imaginary maps. Both assured La Vérendrye that the Mandan knew the way to the western sea and could provide him with guides.

So in 1738 he set out on the month and one-half journey to the Mandan villages. Thanks to the theft of his presents and the disappearance of his interpreter, his visit was relatively fruitless, though he heard tales of mounted men wearing armor, presumably Spaniards, and he was able to leave two men to winter with the Mandan. Upon their return the following fall they told of visiting Indians who seemed to have been in contact with the Spaniards in California. The elder La Vérendrye sent out two of his sons in 1741 and 1742 to seek the assistance of the Mandan in making their way to the western sea, but it became increasingly evident that the Mandan themselves did not know the way. In summer 1742 the two Frenchmen pushed westward with two Mandan guides, encountering Crows and "Snakes" (probably Shoshone), among other Indians, until they saw the Bighorn Range of the Rockies on New Year's Day 1743.

The La Vérendryes had achieved the farthest western penetration of the French. They had done it largely at their own cost, with few followers; and they had survived because of skill in dealing with the Indians. La Vérendrye's sons were disappointed in their hopes of finding a route to the Pacific by way of the Saskatchewan by the revocation of their monopoly, which was given to a favorite of the governor of New France, who abandoned the effort to press westward when he decided that the Hudson's Bay Company had incited the western tribes to oppose it.

The success of French policies toward the Indians is indicated by the great assistance they received from them in exploration and in the fur trade in time of peace, and by the military support they provided in time of war, which alone enabled the French empire in North America to hold out as long as it did against overwhelming odds. The French missionaries continued their work among the Indians after the fall of New France, and from their lexicographic labors are derived much basic knowledge of the Indian languages.

Sources

By far the most important source for French policies toward the Indians is Thwaites's edition in 73 volumes of *The Jesuit Relations and Allied Documents* (JR 1896–1901). This contains the annual reports of the North American missions and much related correspondence. Another major documentary source, though less reliable since it is anti-Jesuit, is Margry's (1876–1886) collection of documents relating to discovery and settlement. *Documents Relative to the Colonial History of the State of New York* (NYCD 1856–1887) contains much material relevant to the long Anglo-French struggle to achieve dominance over the Iroquois.

Valuable material on early French contacts with the Indians is found in works on Cartier (Biggar 1930), Champlain (1922–1936), and other explorers and missionaries (Sagard-Théodat 1866, 1939). Marie de l'Incarnation (1876) provides a penetrating account of the difficulties encountered by the French in trying to educate the Indians and to make them adopt French ways. Le Clercq's (1910) 1691 work is a valuable account of the Micmac. Lahontan (1905, 1931) provides a contrast to the clerical accounts: he helped to launch the cult of the noble savage in France. French-Indian relations in the Mississippi Valley and the Northwest are abundantly documented by Margry's (1876–1886), Shea's (1852), and Kellogg's (1917, 1925) narratives. Perrot (1911), Lafiteau (1724), and Bacqueville de la Potherie (1722) offer detailed accounts of the Indians by Frenchmen who knew them well.

Bailey (1937) has given an admirable anthropological account of early French contact with the Indians. Lanctot's (1963–1965) history of Canada is a critical account of the whole French regime, as is Kennedy's (1950) study. Hunt (1940) stresses the role played by trade in intertribal relations. Trudel (1960) deals with the neglected topic of the *panis*, the Western Indian captives who were used as slaves in New France. Douville and Casanova (1967) have summarized the daily life of Indians during French colonization.

United States Indian Policies, 1776–1815

REGINALD HORSMAN

In the early years of the American Revolution both sides attempted to maintain the friendship of the Indians on the edges of colonial settlement. Many of the officials of the prewar Indian Department remained loyal to the crown, thereby helping to enlist Indian support for the British, and many of the Indians themselves realized that the revolutionaries were the representatives of those advancing farmers who were destroying the Indian way of life. To these Indians the Revolution provided an opportunity to continue the fight against the encroaching frontiersmen. The Indians, often in cooperation with the British, made extensive attacks on large areas of the frontier, particularly in Kentucky, western Pennsylvania, and New York, while military expeditions destroyed Indian villages in western New York as well as in modern Ohio and Tennessee. The hatred engendered by the wartime fighting markedly influenced the shaping of United States policy in the postwar years.

During the Revolution the first steps were taken in the creation of a national Indian policy for the United States. In July 1775 the Continental Congress established Indian departments to supervise three regions: the northern, middle, and southern. Commissioners in these regions were to act on behalf of the Continental Congress and were to attempt to persuade the Indians to remain neutral (JCC 2:174–177). In spite of this effort by the Continental Congress, individual states also continued to conduct their own relations with the Indians.

In the Articles of Confederation, which was drafted in 1777 but did not take effect until 1781, the central government was given a somewhat ambiguous general control over Indian affairs. As part of Article IX it was stated that the United States would have "the sole and exclusive right and power of . . . regulating the trade and managing all affairs with the indians, not members of any of the states, provided, that the legislative right of any state within its own limits be not infringed or violated" (JCC 9:919). This provision was to contribute to the confusion in relations between the United States and the Indians in the 1780s as a number of states by their colonial charters claimed that they owned lands far to the west of their colonial boundaries.

The Confederation, 1783–1789

The Treaty of Paris (September 3, 1783), which ended the Revolution, gave to the United States her independence and a western boundary on the Mississippi River. The treaty ignored the Indians. When European powers transferred territory in the New World it was assumed that each sovereign nation would make its own arrangements with the tribes within its limits.

In establishing an Indian policy the young United States at first chose to ignore colonial precedents. Before the Revolution both the British government and the individual colonies had acknowledged that the Indian tribes possessed a "right of soil" that should be purchased in formal treaty. Although such a policy of formal purchase had not avoided war or injustice, it had brought more order to the frontier advance than would have emerged from a policy of naked conquest. The Continental Congress pursued a different policy in the immediate postwar years.

Congressional committee reports of the fall of 1783 and the spring of 1784 dealt, respectively, with the Indians north and south of the Ohio River. The assumption behind each report was the same: the Indian tribes by joining the British in the Revolution had forfeited their right to the possession of land within the limits of the United States; the new country would be justified in compelling the Indians to retire to Canada or to the unknown areas beyond the Mississippi River; but, it was argued, the United States was prepared to be generous. Some cessions would be demanded as reparation for Indian hostility in the war, but boundary lines would be established that would leave the Indian tribes in possession of land within the United States. It was emphasized that the "right of soil" as well as territorial sovereignty now belonged to the United States, and that the Indians could remain only on her sufferance (JCC 25:681–693, 27: 453–465; Berkhofer 1972).

This postwar policy stemmed from a wartime-inspired hatred of the Indians and from an unwarranted national confidence based on the defeat of England and the establishment of the independence of the United States. It presumed that Indians shocked by the British defeat would willingly acquiesce in uncompensated cessions even

29

though they themselves were undefeated militarily. Even purchase had not prevented war, but at least purchase had provided periods of comparative tranquillity while cession by demand could only produce repeated hostilities. After 1783 the United States was practically bankrupt and had almost no military power, yet she began a policy that would depend on the use of overwhelming force.

The primary aim of postwar Indian policy was to acquire land; a subsidiary aim was to establish peace with the Indians. That this policy was implemented differently north and south of the Ohio River resulted both from the attitude of the individual states, particularly in regard to the problem of western lands, and from the financial needs of the government. Seven of the original 13 states had claims to the eastern half of the Mississippi Valley. These claims stemmed from their original charters, except in the case of New York who claimed by the supposed right of cession by the Iroquois. Before the Articles of Confederation had gone into effect in 1781, it had been agreed that these claims would be ceded for the common good, and that land beyond the colonial boundaries would form a public domain.

By 1786 most of the land between the Ohio and the Mississippi rivers had been ceded to the federal government, but south of the Ohio there was more confusion: Virginia maintained her control over Kentucky; North Carolina did not cede Tennessee until 1789; and Georgia maintained her claim to what is now Alabama and Mississippi until 1802. Thus, the right of the United States to conduct Indian affairs south of the Ohio was challenged by the individual states, and throughout the 1780s the central government had no land to sell in that region. As the Continental Congress desperately wanted to sell land to ease its financial crisis, its main efforts in Indian policy were concentrated north of the Ohio River. In the south the federal government hoped to restrain the states and frontiersmen and avoid Indian war.

The Policy in Practice

Between 1784 and 1786, acting on the principles enunciated in the fall 1783 report of the congressional committee on Indian affairs, the United States dictated treaties to a number of northern tribes with the object of obtaining land in what is now eastern and southern Ohio: Fort Stanwix in 1784 with the Six Nations; Fort McIntosh in 1785 with the Delaware, Wyandot, Chippewa, and Ottawa; and Fort Finney in 1786 with the Shawnee (7 U.S. Stat. 26). At these treaties the representatives of the tribes were told that they had to cede land north of the Ohio as compensation for hostility in the Revolution. Although the land was officially ceded, the treaties were a failure. Encouraged by British agents from Canada, the Indians of the northwest fought in an attempt to block American expansion, and an impoverished Confederation govern-

ment could not raise an army to enforce what it had dictated at the treaty councils.

In the south the central government had little authority in the Confederation period. Settlers from North Carolina advanced onto the lands of the Cherokee in what is now Tennessee, while the state of Georgia ruthlessly appropriated the lands of the Creeks in treaties that in no way represented the desires of the majority of that nation. As both North Carolina and Georgia had not ceded their land claims in the Mississippi Valley, they asserted that the central government had no right to interfere in their internal concerns. In spite of this attitude the central government attempted to bring peace to the southwest, for it wanted to use what troops it could raise to obtain the land north of the Ohio.

In November 1785 the United States signed the Treaty of Hopewell with the Cherokee. The boundary line that was negotiated was a comparatively moderate one, so much so that some of the Whites were left on the Indian side of the line, and the southern states were angered (7 U.S. Stat. 182). Other United States treaties with the southern tribes at this time also attempted to block the extreme demands of the southern states and frontiersmen, but in reality the United States had little or no power in the region. The states did not enforce the Confederation boundary lines, settlers often ignored them, and the Cherokees and Creeks resorted to war in an effort to preserve their lands.

By 1786 it was obvious that the post-Revolutionary Indian policy was a failure. In theory lands in what is now eastern and southern Ohio had been ceded to the United States, but such was Indian hostility to the dictated treaties that most settlers dared not cross the Ohio River. In the south the United States had attempted to restrain the states and the frontiersmen, but the authority of the Confederation was being flouted. In both regions Indian warfare threatened increased costs, a necessity for a larger army, and a continuation of frontier protest against an inefficient central government.

A Shift in Confederation Policy

Against this background of failure the Confederation government gradually reverted to the pre-Revolutionary methods of negotiating with the Indian tribes and obtaining land. For three years the Indian tribes had been treated as nations conquered in war; from 1786 there was an attempt to create a system that would bring greater tranquillity to the frontier. The first step, a comparatively minor one, was the passing of An Ordinance for the Regulation of Indian Affairs on August 7, 1786. By this measure Congress created Indian departments north and south of the Ohio River, each of them under a superintendent who was given the power to grant trade licenses. The main concern of this new ordinance was trade with the

Indians, but the superintendents were to receive instructions from and to report to the secretary of war (JCC 31: 490–493).

In 1787, beset by the problems of increasing Indian hostility and expense, the Confederation began to change the assumptions upon which it based its Indian policy. Secretary of War Henry Knox reported in July 1787 that the United States would need to treble (500 to 1,500) the number of soldiers in the West in order to secure the frontier against Indian attack, but he admitted that Congress did not have the money to provide for this increase. He also admitted that it was difficult to judge whether the advancing settlers or the Indians were in the wrong (Carter 1934–1962, 2:31–35). Increasingly, there was an acknowledgment by the central government that the arrogant policies of the immediate postwar years were consistent neither with justice nor with good sense, and in the summer of 1787 Congress made it clear that while it intended to provide for the continued westward expansion of the United States over Indian lands, it intended if possible to avoid the use of force. This desire was dictated primarily by a wish to avoid the excessive costs stemming from continuous war, but there was also an increasing realization that a question of justice was also involved.

In the Northwest Ordinance of July 13, 1787, Congress outlined its plans for expansion westward across the Old Northwest. The ordinance provided for the creation of three to five states between the Ohio and the Mississippi rivers. Most of that area was in 1787 occupied by a variety of Indian tribes. Yet, in Article III of the ordinance, it was stated: "The utmost good faith shall always be observed towards the Indians; their lands and property shall never be taken from them without their consent; and in their property, rights and liberty, they shall never be invaded or disturbed, unless in just and lawful wars authorised by Congress; but laws founded in justice and humanity shall from time to time be made, for preventing wrongs being done to them, and for preserving peace and friendship with them" (Carter 1934–1962, 2:47). This statement showed in Congress a desire to escape from the assumptions of the postwar period, and a hope that the central government could check the worst excesses being perpetrated by the states and the frontiersmen, but there was no explanation of how expansion over the entire northwest could be made compatible with "justice and humanity" toward the Indians. The central government wanted to obtain land, but increasingly it became clear that it wanted to obtain it by purchase, with a good conscience, and when possible without warfare.

On July 21, 1787, Knox argued in a report to Congress that as the Indians of the northwest had banded together in a confederacy, and had asked for a treaty, the United States should negotiate; the alternative was war. What is more the United States should be ready to pay for the land: "A recurrence to the custom of Britain on this point

will evince," wrote Knox, "that they thought a treaty and purchase money for land, was the most prudent measure and in no degree dishonorable to the nation" (JCC 33: 389). In August a committee of Congress accepted and endorsed Knox's viewpoint. The committee recommended abandoning the postwar policy of dictating treaties to the Indians. The Indians should be treated "more on a footing of equality," and should be convinced of the "Justice and humanity as well as the power of the United States." The United States, argued the committee, should seek peace and trade, and should be prepared to buy land: this would be much cheaper than waging war and dictating treaties (JCC 33:477–481).

Under this reshaped policy the United States signed two treaties with the northwest Indians at Fort Harmar in January 1789. The first treaty confirmed the cessions northwest of the Ohio made at the Treaty of Fort McIntosh in 1785 (7 U.S. Stat. 28); it was signed by the Wyandot, Delaware, Potawatomi, Ottawa, and Sauk tribes, and the United States agreed to pay a small sum for the ceded land. A similar treaty with the Six Nations confirmed the Fort Stanwix treaty of 1784, with the United States paying for the ceded area (7 U.S. Stat. 33). The United States had returned to the principle of purchase.

Confederation Indian policy had been a disastrous failure. The central government had infuriated the Indian tribes by its assumption that the United States had an absolute right to all the land to the Mississippi River by reason of its victory over the British in the Revolution, and its belated return to a policy of purchase only served to convince the Indians of United States weakness. In 1789 Indians along the whole frontier were ready to fight

Fig. 1. Pipe-tomahawk said to have been presented to Seneca leader Red Jacket. The United States government continued the practice, started by the European colonial governments, of giving gifts to prominent chiefs in recognition of their allegiance. This silver-mounted specimen has a silver mouthpiece, silver inlay upon the handle, and a silver insert in the blade engraved with the American eagle. Length 42.7 cm.

to resist the White advance, and the government under the Constitution, which took effect in spring 1789, had first to undo the mistakes of the Confederation before it could carry out its own Indian policies.

The Administration of George Washington, 1789–1797

Under the leadership of Secretary of War Henry Knox the administration of George Washington began to develop a concept of Indian relations that was to dominate the thinking of the government until the debate over the removal policy in the 1820s and early 1830s. In essence Knox wanted to develop a policy that would gradually obtain Indian land, would be as cheap as possible, would avoid war, would redound to the honor of the United States, and would benefit the Indians as well as the advancing frontiersmen. In reporting to the new Senate in May 1789 regarding the treaties of Fort Harmar, Knox told that body of the mistakes made in the immediate postwar period and pointed out that the Indians expected to be paid for the land they ceded (Knox 1834:40–41). In June and July he amplified these views and argued for a policy of morality in the conduct of Indian relations (Knox 1832–1834, 1:12–14, 52–54).

The interest of many early national leaders in a "moral" Indian policy stemmed both from an eighteenth-century view of the natural rights of man and from their concept of the revolutionary nation as an example to the world. After pointing out that considerable force (and thus money) would be needed to wage war on the Indians for their land, Knox argued on June 15, 1789, that even if the United States had the force available it was doubtful whether she should use it in this way: "The Indians being the prior occupants, possess the right of soil. It cannot be taken from them unless by their free consent, or by the right of conquest in case of a just war. To dispossess them on any other principle, would be a gross violation of the fundamental laws of nature, and of that distributive justice which is the glory of a nation" (Knox 1832–1834, 1:13). A policy of peace and purchase was moral and cheap; a policy of war and conquest was immoral and dear. The choice was plain. What was ignored was that a policy of peace and purchase was probably incompatible. Knox's suggestion for fair purchase and for negotiating with the Indians more on a basis of equality did not mean that he considered it possible that the Indians could retain lands desired by the United States. Even when "firm" boundaries were established by treaties, and the Indians given the right to retain the land on their side of the line as long as they wished, it was assumed that future cessions were inevitable. As White settlement crowded up to the boundary lines game would diminish, the Indians would be reduced in number, and those surviving would be willing to sell their land for small sums (Knox 1832–1834, 1:12–14). This analysis had elements of truth in it, but it failed to acknowledge that the Indians would fight when they saw their land and game disappearing, and the tribes dwindling.

Knox and Washington in the early 1790s also sketched the outline of the plan by which they thought expansion over Indian land would benefit the Indians as well as the United States, and by which the reputation of the United States would be enhanced. Their solution was the bringing of civilization and the assimilation of the Indians. Knox, like Thomas Jefferson, assumed that the Indians were men on a lower stage of development, but men capable of improvement. The leaders of the American government assumed that their way of life was the "highest" yet attained and that true generosity was to teach the Indians to live in the American manner. Indeed, this view of the Indian, though ethnocentric, was more generous than that which became quite common by the 1840s and 1850s: the view that the Indian was probably incapable of improvement. Knox realized that the United States could and would be criticized for destroying the Indians. He wrote in July 1789: "How different would be the sensation of a philosophic mind to reflect, that, instead of exterminating a part of the human race by our modes of population, we had persevered, through all difficulties, and at last had imparted our knowledge of cultivation and the arts to the aboriginals of the country, by which the source of future life and happiness had been preserved and extended" (Knox 1832–1834, 1:53).

Both expediency and justice helped convince the United States government in the 1790s that the arrogance of the 1780s, the ruthlessness of the states, and the recklessness of the actual pioneers would have to be curbed. The frontier would still advance, but it would advance with order and not in pell-mell fashion; the Indians would cede their land and would be paid in formal negotiation; the boundaries thus established would be respected by the United States government; the arts of civilization would be imparted to the Indian tribes; and further cessions would be accomplished peacefully. The system was to fail, but in the following decades the United States government attempted to implement it; the government underestimated the difficulties of the task, the resources needed, the hostility of the states, and the opposition of its own frontier population. Perhaps most important of all, it became obvious in the following years that the rapid acquisition of land was far more important to the federal government than the accomplishment of a civilization policy. In the years before 1815 the federal government was more moderate in its attitude toward the Indians than was desired by its own frontiersmen and many of the states, but not surprisingly it responded most promptly to the desires of its own citizens, not to the needs of the Indians.

Ironically, the new government, which very much hoped that it was devising a policy that would avoid war, engaged in extensive military operations in the early 1790s. The Indians of the Old Northwest were embittered by the pressures of the Revolution and of the 1780s. They still hoped to stop the Americans from expanding beyond the Ohio River, and in this ambition they were encouraged by the British in Canada. In order to occupy the lands in what is now eastern and southern Ohio, which had been obtained from the Indians in the 1780s, the United States had to fight.

The military operations of the United States government in the Old Northwest began in 1790 and were concluded temporarily in 1794. At first the efforts were futile; in 1790 military defeats were suffered near what is now Fort Wayne, Indiana, and in November 1791 an American expedition under Arthur St. Clair was overwhelmed by the Indians near the same area. Over 600 of the expedition were killed. Not until Anthony Wayne organized and trained an army from 1792 to 1794 did military victory become possible; this was achieved at the Battle of Fallen Timbers in August 1794. In the south, where Indian war continued in the early 1790s, the states depended upon their own resources, for the federal government used all its available force to make possible the settlement of the land northwest of the Ohio.

The military disasters in the Old Northwest in 1790 and 1791 did not alter the determination of the federal government to inaugurate a new era in relations with the American Indians. In January 1793 Henry Knox wrote to his military commander Anthony Wayne that "if our modes of population and War destroy the tribes the disinterested part of mankind and posterity will be apt to class the effects of our Conduct and that of the Spaniards in Mexico and Peru together" (Knopf 1960:165).

In the 1790s Congress passed a series of measures designed to accomplish its aims of peace and order in its relations with the Indians. The basic laws were the trade and intercourse acts, which were passed on July 22, 1790, on March 1, 1793, and on May 19, 1796. These measures forbade settlement on the Indian side of boundary lines, licensed trade, and provided for the punishment of crimes committed in the Indian country. They also made the tentative beginnings of a civilization policy. By the 1793 act the president was given the power to distribute useful articles to the Indians and the power to appoint temporary agents to help them achieve civilization. To these ends he was allowed to spend $20,000 a year, and in 1796 this sum was cut to $15,000 (Prucha 1962:45–50, 62, 145, 215–217).

The civilization policy was not restricted to the powers granted under the trade and intercourse acts. Various treaties in the 1790s also made provision for the beginning of the civilization policy. In the Treaty of New York, signed with the Creeks on August 7, 1790, it was agreed that the Creeks would be given domestic animals and agricultural tools (7 U.S. Stat. 35). In a similar manner, in the Treaty of Holston with the Cherokee, signed in July 1791, the United States said it would help the Cherokee become "Herdsmen and cultivators" (Carter 1934–1962, 4:60–67). In both these treaties it was also agreed that the United States would send individuals to act as interpreters and to help in the civilization process. Similar provisions were incorporated in many of the Indian treaties of the following years, so that even while the fighting was continuing the Indian treaties incorporated articles designed to facilitate the civilization policy.

Treaty of Greenville

The interrelationship of the new policies with frontier expansion became fully apparent in the circumstances surrounding the Treaty of Greenville, which was signed on August 3, 1795. This treaty set the seal on Wayne's military victory in August 1794 and well demonstrated the bitter experience of the 1780s and early 1790s. Wayne was told to obtain a firm cession of what had been forced from the Indians in the 1780s, but for this he was allowed to spend more money. For yielding eastern and southern Ohio the signatory tribes were given $20,000 in goods and promised an annuity of $9,500. By Article V of the treaty the tribes were guaranteed that they could keep the land west of the Greenville line as long as they desired (7 U.S. Stat. 49–54).

In theory, it would appear that the wording of Article V (and such wording occurred in many of the treaties of these years) was a block to the expansion of the United States, but the instructions to Wayne before the treaty made it clear that this was never envisioned as a problem. Secretary of War Timothy Pickering had written to Wayne on April 15, 1795, indicating why Wayne should not press for additional cessions: "When a peace shall once be established, and we also take possession of the posts now held by the British, we can obtain every thing we shall want with a tenth part of the trouble and difficulty which you would now have to encounter" (Knopf 1960:405). As far back as 1785 Pickering had accepted the argument that moderation and a policy of firm boundaries was the soundest policy; Indians always diminished in numbers in the vicinity of the advancing frontiersmen, the game disappeared, and future cessions were always available for less money (R. King 1894–1900, 1:104–105).

At Greenville in 1795 many Indians believed that they had been given, for as long as they wished to stay, much of the Old Northwest. For the United States government, however, the Greenville line was merely a stage in the acquisition of all the land to the Mississippi River. Governmental leaders considered that they had bought an interlude of peace. Now pioneers would advance toward the boundary lines, and when needed other cessions would be readily available. In the meantime there was hope that

A Proclamation.

By his Excellency ANTHONY WAYNE, Efquire, Major General and Commander in Chief of the Legion of the United States of America.

WHEREAS the Prefident of the the United States of America did nominate and by and with the advice and confent of the Senate, has appointed three commiffioners to hold a treaty with the hoftile Indians at the *Lower Sandufky* on or about the firft day of June next, enfuing, to endeavour to effect a permanent peace with thofe Indians : And whereas it would be highly improper, that any hoftile attempts fhould be made againft any of the Indian towns or fettlements, whilft the aforefaid treaty is pending.

I am therefore ordered by the Prefident, and I do, hereby, in his name, moft folemnly forbid and reftrain any attempts being made againft any of the Indian towns or fettlements until the refult of the treaty is known.

GIVEN under my hand and feal at Head-Quarters, Legionville, this 22d day of April, in the year of our Lord one thoufand feven hundred and ninety three, and in the feventeenth year of the Independence of the United States.

ANTHONY WAYNE.
By order of the Commander
in Chief.
H. DE BUTTS, A. D. C.   tf.

Mass. Histl. Soc., Boston: Timothy Pickering Papers, Vol. 59:165.

Fig. 2. Proclamation issued by Maj. Gen. Anthony Wayne, April 22, 1793. The proclamation refers to one of a series of treaty conferences held with Indians north of the Ohio River following the American Revolution. Eager to ensure successful negotiations and the safety of the treaty commissioners, several White officials issued proclamations like this one prior to the conference. The proclamation was enclosed in a letter from Secretary of War Henry Knox to Commissioners Col. Timothy Pickering, Gen. Benjamin Lincoln, and Beverley Randolph, June 6, 1793. An account of this particular conference, held at Lower Sandusky and attended by Mohawk leader Joseph Brant, is found in Downes (1940:321–325; see also Stone 1838, 2:338–356).

the civilization policy would make the Indians content with their lot, persuade them that their loss of lands had brought progress, and salve the conscience of the United States.

By the mid-1790s the Washington administration had at last been able to inaugurate the policy it had outlined on coming into office. In the north the wars of 1789–1794 had been looked upon as the aftermath of Confederation policy, a complication that had to be resolved before the new policies could take effect. In the south the United States had expended less effort, but by the mid-1790s there was peace in that region; North Carolina had ceded her land claims to the federal government, and an attempt had been made to establish firm boundaries with the Cherokees. These efforts had not been completely successful, and settlers still refused to obey the federal policy of firm boundary lines and an ordered rather than an unrestricted advance. Georgia presented a major complication to federal policy makers as she still claimed land beyond her western borders all the way to the Mississippi River and was pressing hard on the Creeks within the actual state of Georgia. Yet, along the whole length of the frontier the chaos of the 1780s had been replaced by boundary lines that the federal government intended to enforce, the trade and intercourse acts had established rules governing White entry into and conduct in the Indian country, and by the same acts and by the various treaties a civilization policy had been begun. To round out its policies the Washington administration in 1796 also established its own general system of trade with the Indian tribes.

The Factory System

Washington in the mid-1790s asked Congress to establish a system of trade that would win the allegiance of the Indians, avoid the extortions of private traders, and defeat the machinations of the British. On April 18, 1796, Congress responded by establishing the factory system (1 U.S. Stat. 443). The law provided for the setting up of government trading factories (posts) to trade fairly with the Indians; friendship not profit would be their aim. In trading at the government posts the Indians would receive fair value for their pelts; moreover, they would also by obtaining trade goods develop new wants that only the ending of their way of life and the adoption of a full civilization policy could satisfy. After 1806 a superintendent of Indian trade governed the operation of such posts.

The factory system, which lasted until 1822, had difficulties for most of its period of operation, for it had to compete not only with the British traders from Canada but also with private trading interests within the United States. This meant that each renewal of the system brought controversy, and opposition from private interests. When the system finally came to an end, its failure stemmed as much from the bitter opposition of the American Fur Company as from its own weaknesses.

The Advance of Settlement

In the late 1790s the frontier was more peaceful than it had been for a quarter century. The Indians had been told that the government was concerned for their interests, that they had a "right of soil," and that from this time on they would be treated with justice and friendship. They had not been told that the government had every intention of expanding its settlements to the Mississippi River or that some were dreaming of an expansion of United States citizens throughout the continent. They did not need to be told that the generous assertions of federal officials were not echoed by the frontiersmen themselves. Although the federal government, the states with frontier interests, and the actual settlers all assumed that United States settlement would continue to advance, the policies advocated by the federal government were too slow and too moderate to appeal to the actual frontiersmen. To some of the leaders of the United States government the frontier advance over the Indians conjured up reflections on the possibilities for natural man's improvability; but to many of those who actually cut new paths through the West, chopped down trees, and built cabins the Indians were merely another savage obstacle, as the wolf or the wildcat was an obstacle. Henry Knox might talk of the different stages in the progress of man, and a national responsibility to help the Indians to a higher state of civilization, but the pioneer who had defended the Kentucky forts in the Revolution dreamed of a land tamed by the ax and the plough, a land in which natural obstacles, including the wild animals and the Indians, had been eliminated.

In the late 1790s frontiersmen poured in ever increasing numbers across the Appalachians into the Mississippi Valley. In the north numerous settlers entered the rich area east and south of the Greenville line, and by 1800 pioneers were ready and eager to cross onto lands guaranteed to the Indians in 1795. In the south, where the federal government had been far less successful in imposing its point of view, the boundaries were respected far less than in the north. The federal government had never been able effectively to enforce the boundary guaranteed to the Cherokee at the Treaty of Holston in 1791, and in 1798 at Tellico the Cherokee were obliged to cede more land to accommodate settlers who had refused to abide by the earlier boundaries (7 U.S. Stat. 62).

In Georgia there were increasing signs of the clash between federal and state Indian policies that was to bedevil American Indian policy for the next 40 years. Since 1783 the state of Georgia had appropriated Indian land within the state in spite of Indian protests and warfare, and in spite of federal efforts to moderate state demands. The Georgians argued that the federal government was willing to fight to obtain the lands northwest of the Ohio, which could be sold as part of the public domain, but was unwilling to fight to allow the Georgians to settle the land the state owned. In June 1796 the Georgians were infuriated when federal commissioners at the Treaty of Colerain confirmed the Creek boundaries established at the Treaty of New York in 1790 (7 U.S. Stat. 56–60). The Georgia commissioners who had attended the treaty issued a protest arguing that more land should have been obtained. It was clear that Georgia would continue to exert pressure on the Creeks and Cherokees who still occupied much of the state, and the federal government faced the additional problem that Georgia had still not ceded her claims to what is now Mississippi and Alabama.

The federal hope for a general solution of the Indian problem still lay in the ill-financed and weak civilization program. Through this program it was hoped to convince the Indians that the cession of their lands was in their own interest. No thought was given at this time to the additional problem of what would happen if the states and their citizens were unwilling to accept acculturated Indian farmers living on individual plots of land.

The Administration of Thomas Jefferson, 1801–1809

In the administration of President Thomas Jefferson, the Indian policy devised in the 1790s obtained its most lucid and eloquent defender while at the same time revealing in practice its inherent and fatal weaknesses. Jefferson himself well reveals the high hopes and disappointments of American Indian policy in the early nineteenth century. He viewed the Indian in the abstract as the natural man of the eighteenth-century philosophers. His opinion in June 1785 was that "the proofs of genius given by the Indians of N. America, place them on a level with Whites in the same uncultivated state" (Jefferson 1950, 8:185). He believed that the Indians should and could, as rapidly as possible, acquire all the characteristics of the Whites.

Therefore, Jefferson throughout his presidency wrote and spoke of the necessity of bringing civilization to the Indians: "humanity enjoins us to teach them agriculture and the domestic arts; to encourage them to that industry which alone can enable them to maintain their place in existence and to prepare them in time for that state of society which to bodily comforts adds the improvement of the mind and morals" (Richardson 1896–1899, 1:380). To accomplish this end, Jefferson urged the instruction of the Indian men in agriculture and the Indian women in spinning and weaving. At times he went even further and advocated not only cultural change but also intermarriage as the solution to the Indian problem. He told a visiting Indian delegation in December 1808: "You will unite yourselves with us, and join in our great councils and form one people with us and we shall all be Americans. You will mix with us by marriage. Your blood will run in our veins and will spread with us over this great island" (Jefferson 1808:396).

There were two basic weaknesses in Jefferson's ideal hopes for future United States–Indian relations. The first weakness stemmed from a general misunderstanding of the difficulties of acculturation; Jefferson simply did not understand that there was no easy, rapid, or sure way to transform the Indian way of life into a European way of life. This misunderstanding was not peculiar to Jefferson or to the United States; it was common to the age.

A second fundamental weakness of Jefferson's Indian policy was that Jefferson and the American government considered the rapid acquisition of land more important than the bringing of civilization to the Indians. United States frontiersmen were advancing relentlessly across the Mississippi Valley. They wanted protection, and they wanted the government to acquire the rich lands they saw before them. Jefferson himself envisioned the North American continent peopled by emigrants from the United States, and believed that this would be for the good of mankind. Jefferson firmly believed that the United States was the world's best hope against the monarchies and despotisms of Europe. What was good for the United States, thought Jefferson, was good for the world.

When in 1802 and 1803 Jefferson had reason to believe that there was a great danger of Napoleonic France regaining control of the Mississippi River and the lands beyond it, he had no hesitation in urging Gov. William Henry Harrison of Indiana Territory to press for Indian land cessions as rapidly as possible. Jefferson even went so far as to suggest that influential Indian chiefs should be encouraged to go into debt at the government trading houses; they could later pay off their debts by ceding lands (Esarey 1922, 1:69–73). After the Louisiana Purchase was accomplished Jefferson suggested that the removal of the Indians to the land west of the Mississippi River might provide the best solution to problems farther east, but with the exception of discussions with the Cherokee Jefferson abandoned that notion in favor of his general civilization plan. Throughout his administrations he wrote with eloquence of the transformation of the Indian way of life, and in his public messages he exaggerated the extent to which the Indians were in fact abandoning their traditional ways in favor of American ideas. He never acknowledged that by 1809 the policies he had so ardently advocated were a failure; that the United States was

Smithsonian, Dept. of Anthr.: 362061.

Fig. 3. Engraved silver pipe given "to the Delaware tribe of Indians" in 1814 by Gen. William H. Harrison (top). The four sides of the bowl are engraved with: the inscription, the American eagle, clasped hands with the words "Peace and Friendship," and an Indian and an American officer shaking hands (bottom). The officer holds both a traditional straight pipe and the presentation pipe (Klapthor 1965: 88–89). As the custom of presentations continued through the 18th century, the types of silver, pewter, and steel gifts became more varied, from gorgets and arm bands to medals, pipes, and pipe-tomahawks. Length 61 cm.

obtaining land, but the Indians were ready for war; that only a small minority were being transformed by the civilization policy; and that the advance of the frontier was bringing to the Indians not progress but demoralization and disease.

Gov. William Henry Harrison and Tecumseh

From 1802 to 1809 the reality rather than the rhetoric of federal Indian policy was clearly revealed in the Old Northwest. By this time the cessions made at Greenville were not enough to satisfy the demands of the settlers who were crossing the Ohio in ever increasing numbers. If the theories of the 1790s had proved correct two factors would have made further cessions easy and peaceful: first, the Indians would be fewer in number, the game would have diminished, and there would have been little resistance to future cessions; second, civilization policies should have been taking effect, and Indians living on their separate plots of land should have been happy to yield their large, unwanted hunting grounds. Little of this happened as prophesied. There were fewer Indians and less game, but the Indians who had survived were determined to fight to preserve their lands and their way of life. Very few had happily become American farmers, and there was no chance at all that the majority of the Indians would be acculturated before their land was desired. In 1795 most of the land between the Ohio and the Mississippi rivers still belonged to the Indians; only a few thousand United States settlers had crossed the Ohio. Ten years later, determined pressure was being exerted to obtain the whole of what is now Ohio and Indiana for American settlers; no constructive policy was possible when American frontiersmen advanced westward at this speed.

Between 1802 and 1809 Harrison signed a series of treaties with the Indians of the Old Northwest. By 1809 the United States had obtained most of southern Indiana, large parts of present Illinois, and even parts of present Wisconsin. Other commissioners farther east had obtained large cessions in Ohio and Michigan. For the most part these were forced cessions, though with none of the overt coercion of the 1780s. The treaties read as though both sides were in complete accord, but in reality pressure was exerted by the United States until the desired land was obtained. When the Indian negotiators were not cowed by the presence of troops and the insistent pressure of the American negotiators, often individual chiefs were bribed by having personal separate payments written into the treaty agreements.

In the face of these pressures Indian resistance grew to the point of open warfare. From 1805 Tenskwatawa, first at Greenville, Ohio, and then at the village of Prophetstown on the Tippecanoe River in northern Indiana, preached an Indian religious revival—a throwing off of White ways and a return to a distinctly Indian way of life.

His brother Tecumseh argued for political unity among the Indians and maintained that as Indian lands were for the common use of the Indians any treaty by which an individual tribe ceded land to the United States was invalid. By 1810 sporadic fighting broke out in the Old Northwest. In the following year Governor Harrison attacked and destroyed Prophetstown, and many of the Indians of the region were now ready to fight in a hopeless attempt to preserve their lands and their way of life.

The South

The nature and results of American Indian policy in the south in the first decade of the nineteenth century are obscured by the overemphasis on the success of the civilization policy among the Cherokee and to a lesser extent among the Creeks. The civilization policy did have its greatest success among the Cherokee, and a portion of that tribe farmed in the American manner, apparently accepted an "American way of life," and became the victims of the greatest tragedy of the removal policy in the 1830s. Yet, for much of the South, the failure of the civilization policy was as clear as in the Old Northwest. The various tribes attempted to maintain their lands and their own way of life, the government put on great pressure to obtain cessions, and eventually the Indians resorted to warfare in an effort to resist the oncoming American frontiersmen.

Beginning in 1801 a series of treaties weakened the hold of the southern tribes on their lands. When they could not be persuaded to make further territorial cessions, they were urged to yield rights of way for roads and small tracts of land for posts. The process of breaking down resistance was almost continuous between 1801 and 1806, and by 1806 both Creeks and Cherokee were in a precarious position, and the Chickasaw and Choctaw were beginning to feel the American pressure.

The state of Georgia continued to exert particularly strong pressure on the federal government; she felt she had been neglected in that much of the state was still occupied by the Indians. When on April 24, 1802, the state finally agreed to cede its western land claims to the federal government, the United States agreed to act immediately to try to obtain specific lands in the state "as early as the same can be peaceably obtained on reasonable terms." Moreover, the United States pledged in the same manner, to "extinguish the Indian Title to all other Lands within the State of Georgia"(Carter 1934–1962, 5:142–146). The promise to clear the Indian title to Georgia was to become a crucial problem in the creation of federal Indian policy. In the years to come Georgia interpreted it as meaning that, with reasonable speed, all the Indians would be expelled from the state. This interpretation was incompatible with the federal Indian policy of these years, which asked the Indian to give up tribal lands, assume individual

A SCENE ON THE FRONTIERS AS PRACTICED BY THE HUMANE BRITISH AND THEIR WORTHY ALLIES!

Bring me the Scalps
and the King our Master
will reward you!

Reward for
16 Scalps.

Arise Columbia's Sons and forward press,
Your Country's wrongs call loudly for redress,
The savage Indian with his scalping knife
Or tomahawk, may seek to take your life,

By bravery aw'd, they'll in a dreadfull fright
Shrink back for refuge to the woods in flight,
Their British leaders then will quickly shake,
And for those wrongs shall restitution make,

The Bostonian Soc., Boston: 1154.
Fig. 4. Anti-British cartoon, 1812, depicting Indians taking American soldiers' scalps to exchange for rewards from the British. The knife and ax of one Indian (center) are marked with the monogram of King George III. A slip on the British officer's coattail reads "Secret service Money." Drawing probably by William Muldaux, possibly published in a Pennsylvania newspaper.

ownership, and become an American farmer. Between 1802 and 1805 the Creeks reluctantly and unhappily ceded some of their land in Georgia to the federal government, but these cessions were neither extensive enough nor fast enough to suit the Georgians.

The pressure on the Cherokee was reasonably moderate from 1801 to 1803, but from 1803 until 1806 the tribe was pressured into yielding large areas of land. By 1806 East and West Tennessee, which since their settlement by the Whites had been separated by Indian land, were united, and as more settlers came into the state the pressure on the lands retained by the Cherokee became more intense.

After 1806 the southern tribes benefited temporarily from the rise of Indian opposition in the Old Northwest, and from the growing crisis in American foreign relations. The federal government was keen to avoid war in the south if at all possible. The frontiersmen of the region had fewer qualms. Settlers pressed up to and beyond federally guaranteed boundary lines, compelling the government to

choose between expelling the squatters by force (which from time to time throughout this period it did), or eventually arranging for further cessions to acknowledge the fact that the frontiersmen had decided that the time had come to readjust the boundaries. Considering its constituency, it is not surprising that throughout the nineteenth century the federal government was to respond to frontier residents and obtain new cessions.

The War of 1812

James Madison, who became president in 1809, had little real chance to shape an Indian policy; his administration was dominated by the crisis with England. He inherited an Indian policy that had been created in the late 1780s and 1790s, had received its fullest explanation from President Jefferson, but was clearly failing by 1809. The object of obtaining land was being achieved, but most of the Indians were not being "civilized," and outright Indian war seemed likely. From 1809 to 1812, as the United States

38

slowly moved into war against England, warfare broke out between the United States and the Indians in the northwest, and an uneasy peace was maintained in the southwest.

In the war itself many Indians took the opportunity to fight against the United States (fig. 4), even though a large number remained neutral and some even fought on the American side. In the northwest Tecumseh joined the British and helped lead a variety of tribes into battle. His death and the British and Indian defeat at the Battle of the Thames in October 1813 marked the end of effective Indian resistance between the Ohio and the Mississippi rivers. In the southwest many of the Creeks took the opportunity of the war to launch an all-out attack in what is now Mississippi and Alabama. In retaliation Andrew Jackson of Tennessee invaded the Creek country in the winter of 1813–1814, killed numerous Creek warriors, and at the Battle of Horseshoe Bend in March 1814 destroyed their resistance. In August 1814 the Creeks lost over half their lands at the Treaty of Fort Jackson; those who had remained neutral suffered along with those who had engaged in war (7 U.S. Stat. 120–122). As in the Old Northwest the Indians lost any chance of resisting the stream of settlers who were to pour across the Appalachians after the War of 1812.

By 1815 the policy of Henry Knox, Washington, and Jefferson was clearly failing. Formal treaties, strict boundaries, the trade and intercourse acts, the factory system, and expenditures to persuade the Indians to adopt a different way of life had not prevented war, and had not made the Indians happier, or, for the most part, any more like Europeans. Given the problems of acculturation, even if the frontier had advanced slowly the likelihood of the success of any such policy appears extremely doubtful. In reality the pioneers advanced with relentless speed, and frontier state governments were impatient with a federal government that at times appeared to value Indian goodwill almost as much as the concerns of the frontiersmen. Confronted with frontier opposition, the federal government used a variety of means to speed up the acquisition of land. After 1815 the policy makers only slowly and reluctantly acknowledged that the high hopes of the turn of the century had evaporated, and that the efforts to give a moral basis to expansion had failed.

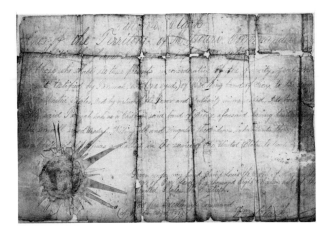

Minn. Histl. Soc., St. Paul.

Fig. 5. Certificate presented to Tamaha, a Mdewakanton Sioux chief, by Gov. William Clark of the Missouri Terr., in 1816. Tamaha was one of only 2 prominent Sioux leaders who did not turn against the United States in the War of 1812 but instead entered its service as a scout and messenger, carrying dispatches from St. Louis to Wis. Imprisoned and threatened by the British, Tamaha refused to divulge any information. For his extraordinary conduct, Tamaha was given a small medal, a captain's uniform, this certificate of commendation, and commissioned chief of the Sioux nation by Clark (Robinson and Thomas 1910:680). Tamaha carried both the medal and certificate on his person until his death in 1863. This is an 1861 copy of the certificate; however, the seal may be the 1816 original. Dimensions 35 by 22.8 cm.

Sources

There is a general analysis of the theory and practice of American Indian policy from 1783 to 1812 by Horsman (1967); a useful study of federal Indian policy in the Revolutionary and Confederation periods is by Mohr (1933). Jones (1982) perceptively discusses the treaty system. The trade and intercourse acts and the creation of an Indian country are dealt with in detail by Prucha (1962). Relations with the southern Indians are treated effectively by Cotterill (1954), Caughey (1938), and Pound (1951); and relations in the Old Northwest to 1795 are covered by Downes (1940). Berkhofer (1965) analyzes the interrelationship of missionary efforts and Indian response; and the concept of the Indian in the United States in the early nineteenth century is discussed by Pearce (1953), Sheehan (1973), and Berkhofer (1978).

United States Indian Policies, 1815–1860

FRANCIS PAUL PRUCHA

The United States government in the years between the War of 1812 and the Civil War built its Indian policy upon the foundation established in the first quarter-century of national existence. It continued to deal with the Indian tribes as separate nations with whom formal treaties were negotiated, but the treaties themselves and the Indian trade and intercourse laws that supplemented the treaty provisions limited Indian sovereignty in many ways.

Underlying United States policy was an overriding concern for the advance of White settlement, for it was an axiom that the expansion of White civilization should not be obstructed or prevented by hunter or agricultural societies, thinly spread over the land and not fully using the resources according to White standards. Military force was used to prevent conflicts between the two races, to enforce the laws and treaties, and to ward off possible interference in American Indian relations by foreign nations.

The United States managed Indian affairs in its own interests without disregarding what it thought were essential elements of Indian welfare. The federal program contained the following points:

(1) protecting Indian rights to lands reserved for them by setting definite boundaries for the Indian country, restricting the Whites from entering the area except under certain controls, and removing illegal intruders;

(2) controlling the disposition of Indian lands by denying the right of private individuals or local governments to acquire land from the Indians by purchase or by other means;

(3) regulating the Indian trade by determining the conditions under which individuals might engage in the trade, prohibiting certain classes of traders, and actually entering into the trade itself;

(4) controlling the liquor traffic by regulating the flow of intoxicating liquor into the Indian country and then prohibiting it altogether;

(5) providing for punishment of crimes committed by members of one race against the other and compensation for damages suffered by one group at the hands of the other;

(6) promoting White standards of civilization and education, in the hope that the Indians would be absorbed into the general stream of White society.

The emphasis on the different elements in federal policy changed as the decades passed and the expansion of the White population pressed more heavily upon the Indian lands. Beginning with a concern to impress American authority on the West and its Indian inhabitants after the War of 1812, the United States by 1860 had extended its jurisdiction across the entire continent and had forced out the Indian tribes in most of the region, confining the native peoples into smaller and smaller areas (Prucha 1984; Washburn 1975).

Asserting American Dominion

The War of 1812 brought defeat to the Indians both in the north (Battle of the Thames, October 5, 1813) and in the south (Battle of Horseshoe Bend, March 27, 1814), but the Treaty of Ghent between the United States and Great Britain, signed on December 24, 1814, did not include Indian participants. The United States government was left the task, therefore, of negotiating treaties with the tribes that had been hostile during the war and of substituting American trade and influence with the tribes of the Northwest for that of the British. At Portage des Sioux at the confluence of the Missouri and Mississippi rivers in the summer of 1815 treaties of peace and friendship were signed with the tribes of the Missouri and upper Mississippi, who had been summoned to the treaty grounds. In subsequent years additional treaties were made with tribes not represented at Portage des Sioux and with the southern tribes (Kappler 1904–1941, 2:110–159). The treaties, however, did not of themselves eliminate the traditional ties that the northwest Indians had had with the British, and for many years the Indian agents on the frontier worked diligently to convince the tribes that they should give up their attachment to the British and come fully into the American orbit.

The federal government was conscious of the need for a positive assertion of United States dominion in the area along the northern border that had been overspread by British traders, as it received warnings from officials on the frontier. Lewis Cass, governor of Michigan Territory, fearing a renewal of British agitation of the Indians against American interests, proposed to the War Department in 1815 that military posts be built to block off the channels

40

of communication by which British traders and their goods infiltrated the American West. President James Madison responded vigorously with directives to expand American military presence in the Northwest to protect the American fur trade and to put a halt to British incursions into American territory and thus to bring the Indians under United States control. In 1815 Fort Mackinac at the straits between Lake Huron and Lake Michigan was regarrisoned, and in 1816 regular army troops established a military post (Fort Howard) at Green Bay at the mouth of the Fox waterway and re-established Fort Dearborn at the site of Chicago. Simultaneously a military expedition up the Mississippi from Saint Louis built Fort Armstrong on Rock Island and Fort Crawford at Prairie du Chien.

These installations provided a defensive cordon of posts, but the exuberant nationalism that blossomed after the War of 1812 demanded a more aggressive display of American authority. Therefore, Secretary of War John C. Calhoun set on foot a two-pronged movement into the Northwest. One expedition, moving from Detroit through the Great Lakes and the Fox-Wisconsin passageway, ascended the Mississippi to the mouth of the Minnesota River where Fort Snelling (at first called Fort St. Anthony) was built in fall 1819 (fig. 1). A second expedition was directed to ascend the Missouri to establish a military post at the mouth of the Yellowstone River or at least as far up the Missouri as the Mandan Villages, near present-day Bismarck, North Dakota. Calhoun believed that trade and presents accompanied by talks were among the most powerful means to control the Indians, and when

these tools were wielded by a foreign power, American frontiers would be constantly exposed to Indian warfare. When the posts were all established and occupied, Calhoun asserted that the fur trade would be thrown into American hands. Although the so-called Yellowstone Expedition failed to attain its goal and Fort Atkinson, built a little above present-day Omaha, marked the farthest point of its advance, American control of the Missouri River and its fur trade was assured. In 1822 another important passageway was controlled by the building of Fort Brady at Sault Sainte Marie.

In the shadow of these military posts, competent Indian agents like Nicholas Boilvin and Joseph M. Street at Prairie du Chien, Lawrence Taliaferro at St. Peter's, Henry R. Schoolcraft at Sault Sainte Marie, and William Clark, superintendent at Saint Louis, were largely successful in convincing the Indians to turn in their British flags and medals and to accept in their place the symbols of American jurisdiction.

Regulation of Trade and Intercourse with the Indians

The fur trade remained a vital concern in United States relations with the Indians, and action was taken in 1816 to cut out of the trade any persons who were not United States citizens (3 U.S. Stat. 332–333). The government factory system of trading houses among the Indians, which had been promoted before the War of 1812 as a means of developing friendship with the Indians by providing necessary trade goods at fair prices, continued after the war. (There were factories after the War of 1812

Fig. 1. Fort Snelling, Minn. Watercolor by Seth Eastman, 1848.

at Fort Confederation, Spandra Bluffs, Sulphur Fork, Fort Osage, Green Bay, Prairie du Chien, Chicago, and Fort Edwards.) But the factory system was opposed by the growing private fur trading interests, of which the American Fur Company (founded in 1808) was the most important, and in 1822 the factories were abolished by Congress (4 U.S. Stat. 35–36).

The trade and intercourse laws sought to prevent intrusion onto the lands guaranteed to the Indians, and the right of the Indians to occupy their lands was repeatedly affirmed. In 1823 Chief Justice John Marshall, in the case of *Johnson and Graham's Lessee* v. *McIntosh* (8 Wheaton 543), reviewed the long history of White and Indian claims to the land, and although holding to the traditional doctrine that the "absolute ultimate ownership" of the land rested in the United States, he declared: "It has never been contended that the Indian title amounted to nothing. Their right of possession has never been questioned." Yet, despite explicit laws and decisions and repeated cases of action to forcibly eject settlers who had illegally invaded the Indian country, the Indians in the long run lost out. The government did not have effective forces to carry out the legislative measures and executive decisions, and it acquiesced in settlements when they had gone so far as to be irremediable. United States policy intended that White settlement should advance and that the Indians should withdraw or be assimilated. Its interest was to make this process as free of disorder and injustice as possible.

To prevent warfare that might result from murders or robberies committed by Indians against Whites or Whites against Indians, the United States provided legal procedures intended to punish such crimes of individuals. Loopholes in the early intercourse acts were plugged by a law of 1817 (3 U.S. Stat. 383), which also clarified the jurisdiction of the courts over various cases. In practice, crimes committed by Indians against Whites were more vigorously prosecuted than crimes by Whites against the Indians.

Special concern was given to the problem of liquor in the Indian trade and its introduction into the Indian country. Although the intercourse law of 1802 had authorized the president to prevent or restrain the distribution of liquor among the Indians, the directives to agents and other measures to control the traders were largely ineffective, and conditions got worse instead of better. The amendment to the 1802 law passed in 1822 provided that the president could direct Indian agents, superintendents, and military officers to search stores of goods going into the Indian country. If liquor was found, the goods were to be forfeited, the trader's license canceled, and his bond put in suit (3 U.S. Stat. 682–683). But there were ambiguities and loopholes in the law, and the powerful trading companies were able to thwart the agents and army officers in the execution of the law.

Discretionary power to admit liquor, which the laws permitted, was removed in 1827, only to be restored in 1831 at the instigation of the fur traders. Finally in 1832 Congress declared: "No ardent spirits shall be hereafter introduced, under any pretence, into the Indian country" (4 U.S. Stat. 564). It was a total prohibition that applied to traders and nontraders alike and allowed no exceptions. The law was clear, but enforcement still was imperfect.

The piecemeal nature of much of the legislation governing relations with the Indians created a need for a codification of the regulations. Moreover, the intercourse act of 1802 had not been completely effective in meeting the problems that arose from contacts between the two races. Regulation of traders was still inadequate and encroachments on Indian lands continued. Secretary of War Peter B. Porter, sensing the lack of a system of principles and rules for the administration of Indian concerns, wrote in 1828 to the two men he considered best qualified to deal with Indian affairs, Governor Cass and Superintendent Clark. Cass and Clark responded enthusiastically and drew up a long report, which outlined a comprehensive system for regulating affairs and establishing a well-organized Indian department. Much of the report repeated previous laws, but additions and modifications indicated the reforms needed (Prucha 1967). The report was submitted to the Senate by Porter (1829). A supplementary statement appeared in the first annual report of Cass, who became secretary of war in 1831. In view of the removal of the Indians from the East, Cass proposed seven principles to govern relations with the Indians: a solemn declaration that the land assigned to the Indians in the West would be theirs forever and that White settlement would never encroach upon it; a determination to exclude all liquor from the Indians' territories; the employment of adequate military force in the vicinity of the Indians to prevent hostility between tribes; encouragement of the Indians to adopt severalty of property; assistance to all who needed it for opening farms and acquiring domestic animals and agricultural implements; leaving untouched as much as possible the institutions and customs of the Indians; and employment of persons to instruct the Indians.

These documents, together with a report of commissioners sent west in 1832 to examine lands for Indian settlement, formed the basis for a new trade and intercourse act of June 30, 1834 (4 U.S. Stat. 729–735). This act defined the Indian country as "all that part of the United States west of the Mississippi, and not within the states of Missouri and Louisiana, or the territory of Arkansas, and, also, that part of the United States east of the Mississippi river, and not within any state to which the Indian title has not been extinguished." The licensing system for trading with the Indians was continued. Superintendents and agents could issue licenses, which ran for two years east of the Mississippi and for three years in the West, and they

42

were given discretionary power to refuse licenses to persons of bad character.

The integrity of the Indian country was guaranteed by a repetition or amplification of previous laws. No Whites were permitted to hunt or trap game in the Indian country, and grazing of cattle on Indian lands without the consent of the Indians was to be punished by fines. Settlement on Indian lands was prohibited. Illegal settlers or other intruders were to be removed by the agents, and the president could authorize the use of military force to effect the removal. The provisions of the 1802 law for indemnification for thefts or damage done to property of either race by members of the other were retained. Stern punishments were provided for anyone introducing liquor into the Indian country or setting up distilleries therein. Although previously the United States had been careful not to interfere in conflicts between Indian groups, the new law authorized the use of military force to prevent or terminate hostilities among the Indian tribes.

A companion bill provided for the organization of the agents and superintendents of the Indian service. One section of it dealt with the issuing of annuities, an increasingly important matter as new treaties of cession were negotiated. Henceforth no payments were to be made on an individual basis, but the whole sum was to be paid to the tribe, that is, to its chiefs or other designated persons. If the Indians so requested, the annuities might be paid in goods (4 U.S. Stat. 737).

Civilization Program

There had been sporadic attempts from colonial days onward to provide schools for the Indians to give them special aid toward adopting White patterns of civilization. Aside from limited government aid for constructing school buildings and some provision of agricultural implements, livestock, and instruments for spinning and weaving, the activities aimed at civilizing the Indians had been the work of voluntary philanthropic groups, among which various missionary societies were prominent. After the War of 1812 the United States government began to play a more active role. In 1819 Congress authorized an annual sum of $10,000 for a "civilization fund." It was to be used at the president's discretion to promote the civilization of the Indians by employing "capable persons of good moral character, to instruct them in the mode of agriculture suited to their situation; and for teaching their children in reading, writing, and arithmetic" (3 U.S. Stat. 516–517). Secretary of War Calhoun determined to use the limited funds to stimulate and aid private organizations. He wrote a circular to missionary societies inviting their participation, and the churches responded enthusiastically. The government aid was joined by sizable private contributions, and the number of schools increased.

Early statesmen had looked for a rapid assimilation of

the Indians into White society. Thomas Jefferson had hoped that the Indians would give up their hunter's existence and adopt the agricultural life of the yeoman farmer. There was, in fact, much change cited by friends of the Indians. Some Indians, educated in White schools, became accomplished in the English language and in American ways. The invention of a syllabary by the Cherokee Sequoya, which permitted the Indians to learn quickly how to read, and the establishment of the *Cherokee Phœnix*, a newspaper printed in English and Cherokee (fig. 2), seemed to many to prove the possibility of the transformation of the Indian nations. However, the great majority of the Indians did not change so rapidly as the optimists predicted and made the complete assimilation of the eastern Indians unlikely. A large proportion of the Indians, in fact, did not desire to give up their customs and traditional ways of life for those of Whites.

Indian Removal

By the 1820s a crisis approached in Indian affairs. The Indians were not being absorbed into the dominant White society, and as White population increased and pressed westward in search of new lands for diversified agriculture in the north and for cotton culture in the south, there was increasing demand by the Whites for the removal of the Indians from their path. There had been a gradual but steady attrition on Indian land holdings in the north, as the separate tribes were consolidated in small areas or were moved westward (Foreman 1946; Prucha 1984). To the treaties before the War of 1812, which had cleared much of Ohio, Indiana, and Illinois of Indian title, were now added new treaties with Wyandot, Wea, Delaware, Miami, Winnebago, Potawatomi, Chippewa, Ottawa, Menominee, Sauk and Fox, Sioux, and other tribes, which opened up large sections of Indiana, Illinois, Michigan, Wisconsin, Iowa, and Minnesota to White exploitation by 1840.

These tribes, for the most part politically weak and disunited, offered little obstacle to the crushing White advance. A threat of an uprising in 1827 by the Winnebagos in what is now Wisconsin was quickly quelled, and increased military occupation of the region made serious Indian resistance impossible. The Black Hawk War of 1832, occasioned by the return of the British band of Sauk and Fox Indians under Black Hawk to their ancestral homes east of the Mississippi from which they had earlier been removed, was a disaster for the Indians and showed their weakness before aggressive White frontiersmen supported by federal troops.

The status of the Indians in the southeastern United States was considerably different and more complex. The so-called Five Civilized Tribes (Cherokee, Creek, Choctaw, Chickasaw, and Seminole) held large areas in Georgia, Alabama, Mississippi, Florida, and parts of

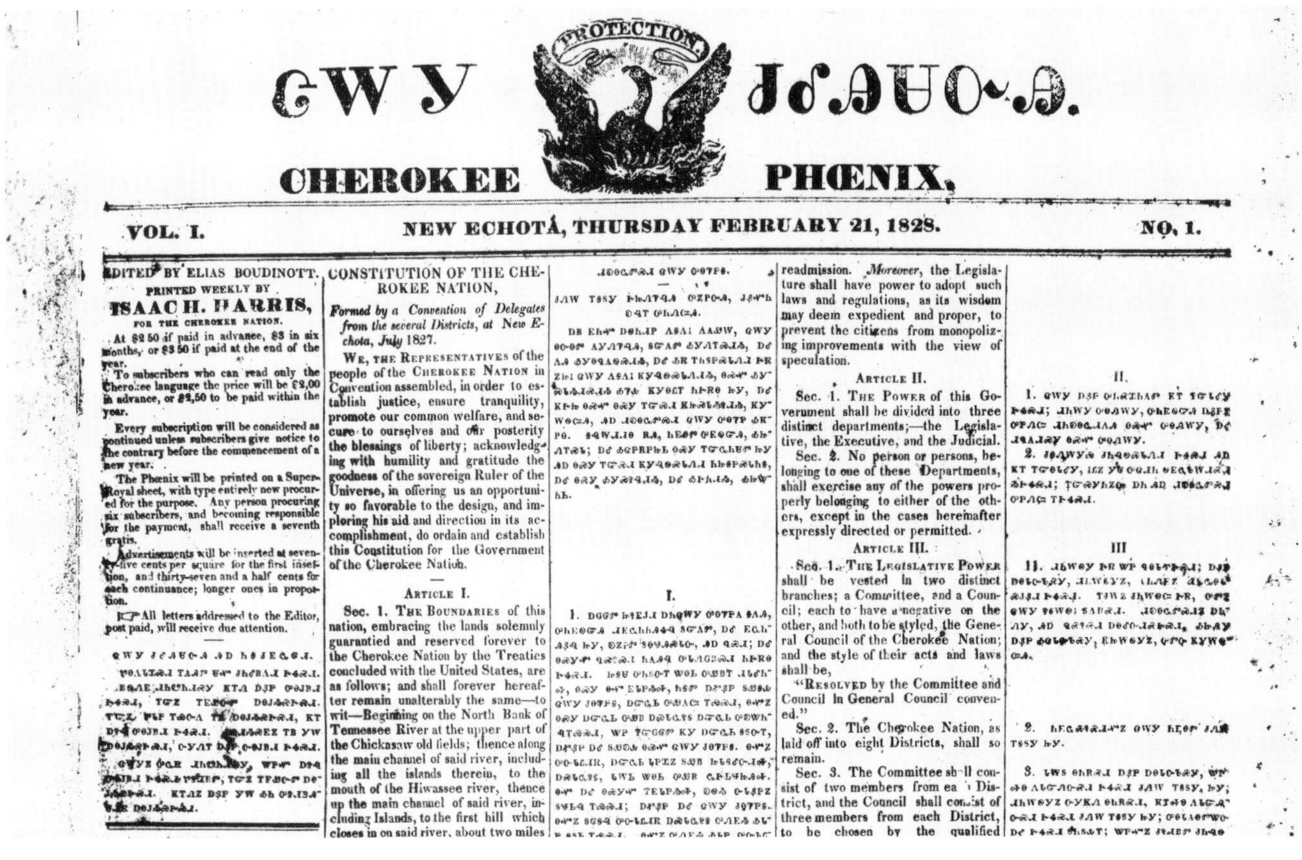
CHEROKEE PHŒNIX.

PROTECTION

VOL. I. NEW ECHOTA, THURSDAY FEBRUARY 21, 1828. NO. 1.

EDITED BY ELIAS BOUDINOTT.
PRINTED WEEKLY BY
ISAAC H. HARRIS,
FOR THE CHEROKEE NATION.

At $2 50 if paid in advance, $3 in six months, or $3 50 if paid at the end of the year.

To subscribers who can read only the Cherokee language the price will be $2,00 in advance, or $2,50 to be paid within the year.

Every subscription will be considered as continued unless subscribers give notice to the contrary before the commencement of a new year.

The Phœnix will be printed on a Super-Royal sheet, with type entirely new procured for the purpose. Any person procuring six subscribers, and becoming responsible for the payment, shall receive a seventh gratis.

Advertisements will be inserted at seventy-five cents per square for the first insertion, and thirty-seven and a half cents for each continuance; longer ones in proportion.

☞All letters addressed to the Editor, post paid, will receive due attention.

CONSTITUTION OF THE CHEROKEE NATION,

Formed by a Convention of Delegates from the several Districts, at New Echota, July 1827.

WE, THE REPRESENTATIVES of the people of the CHEROKEE NATION in Convention assembled, in order to establish justice, ensure tranquility, promote our common welfare, and secure to ourselves and our posterity the blessings of liberty; acknowledging with humility and gratitude the goodness of the sovereign Ruler of the Universe, in offering us an opportunity so favorable to the design, and imploring his aid and direction in its accomplishment, do ordain and establish this Constitution for the Government of the Cherokee Nation.

ARTICLE I.

Sec. 1. THE BOUNDARIES of this nation, embracing the lands solemnly guarantied and reserved forever to the Cherokee Nation by the Treaties concluded with the United States, are as follows; and shall forever hereafter remain unalterably the same—to wit—Beginning on the North Bank of Tennessee River at the upper part of the Chickasaw old fields; thence along the main channel of said river, including all the islands therein, to the mouth of the Hiwassee river, thence up the main channel of said river, including Islands, to the first hill which closes in on said river, about two miles

readmission. *Moreover*, the Legislature shall have power to adopt such laws and regulations, as its wisdom may deem expedient and proper, to prevent the citizens from monopolizing improvements with the view of speculation.

ARTICLE II.

Sec. 1. THE POWER of this Government shall be divided into three distinct departments;—the Legislative, the Executive, and the Judicial.

Sec. 2. No person or persons, belonging to one of these Departments, shall exercise any of the powers properly belonging to either of the others, except in the cases hereinafter expressly directed or permitted.

ARTICLE III.

Sec. 1. THE LEGISLATIVE POWER shall be vested in two distinct branches; a Committee, and a Council; each to have a negative on the other, and both to be styled, the General Council of the Cherokee Nation; and the style of their acts and laws shall be,

"RESOLVED by the Committee and Council in General Council convened."

Sec. 2. The Cherokee Nation, as laid off into eight Districts, shall so remain.

Sec. 3. The Committee shall consist of two members from each District, and the Council shall consist of three members from each District, to be chosen by the qualified

Amer. Antiquarian Soc., Worcester, Mass.

Fig. 2. Portion of the front page of the first edition of the *Cherokee Phœnix*, printed in New Echota, Ga. Elias Boudinot, editor of the newspaper, was assisted by Rev. Samuel Austin Worcester. Boudinot resigned in 1835 when he could no longer support tribal leaders on the removal issue (Perdue 1983). The publication was suspended after 6 years because of the hostility of Georgia authorities, who at one point imprisoned Worcester (Mooney 1975:103–104).

Tennessee and the Carolinas—areas increasingly coveted by land-hungry frontiersmen. Unlike the tribes in the north, they were relatively advanced in a settled agricultural economy, and some of the Indians, indeed, managed large plantations by the use of Black slaves. Moreover, the tribes generally were well-organized politically and had astute leaders, some of them mixed-bloods who spoke English well and were wise in the ways of the Whites. Although the Five Civilized Tribes had all given up large portions of their land, they finally refused to dispose voluntarily of any more. They intended to stay where they were and expected the federal government to fulfill the guarantees it had made in the treaties to protect the tribes' possession of the lands that remained (Van Every 1966; Prucha 1962:213–249).

The relations between the Cherokees and the state of Georgia were critical. On April 24, 1802, the federal government had made an agreement with Georgia whereby the state ceded its western lands to the United States. In return the federal government promised to extinguish the Indian title to lands within Georgia as soon as it could be done peaceably and on reasonable terms. In the 1820s the state began to demand vociferously that the federal government live up to its part of the bargain. President James Monroe refused to be panicked into precipitant action, but he ultimately decided that the only solution to the pressing problem was the exchange of the Indian lands in the East for comparable lands west of the Mississippi, where there would be no federal-state jurisdictional disputes. This was a policy proposed by Thomas Jefferson in 1803, when the Louisiana Purchase made such an exchange of lands feasible, and Jefferson had urged the Indians to move voluntarily. After the War of 1812 the idea had been revived, and some groups of eastern Indians accepted lands west of the Mississippi and moved to new homes (Abel 1908).

Monroe in his annual message to Congress in December 1824 declared that there was only one solution to the Indian problem: the Indians must be induced to move west. On January 27, 1825, he sent a special message to Congress on Indian removal. In it he urged adoption of a liberal policy that would satisfy both the Indians and the Georgians. He asked for a plan that would shield the Indians from impending ruin and promote their welfare and happiness. He thought that such a plan could be made so attractive to the Indians that even those most opposed to emigration would accede to it. Part of his proposal was to set up a government for the Indians in the West that would preserve order, prevent White encroachment, and stimulate civilization. In order to convince the Indians of the government's sincere interest in their welfare, Monroe asked Congress to pledge the solemn faith of the United States to fulfill the arrangements he had suggested. Congress failed to act on Monroe's proposal. Monroe's successor, John Quincy Adams, although hesitant about the policy, could think of no alternative, and he and his cabinet endorsed it.

Meanwhile the situation in Georgia worsened, as the discovery of gold in the Cherokee nation bolstered the demands of the Whites for the Indian lands. Then in 1827 the Cherokee nation adopted a constitution, closely modeled upon that of the United States, and declared its sovereign jurisdiction over its own territory. This action brought a hostile response from Georgia, which complained about having an independent political enclave within its state boundaries. In 1829 the Georgia legislature enacted a law by which the state's jurisdiction would be extended over the Cherokee lands on June 1, 1830.

Georgia had been encouraged in her stand against what she considered Cherokee pretensions by the election of Andrew Jackson as president (for Jackson's policy, see Prucha 1969a; Satz 1975). Jackson was an advocate of Indian removal, and in his first message to Congress in December 1829 he forthrightly told the Cherokees that they could not be supported in their constitutional position and had better move to free areas in the West out of the way of White pressures that were sure to crush and destroy them as a nation. He and his supporters urged the passage of legislation that would enable the president to negotiate with the eastern tribes for their removal.

The Indian removal policy was bitterly debated in Congress and in the public press. Advocates of the policy declared that it was the only means of preserving the Indians, for close contact with the Whites led to the destruction of the weaker race, and that removal would separate the races, enable the government to protect the Indians from encroachment, and permit the Indians to move toward civilization at their own rate. It would ease the threatening conflicts between the southern states and the federal government. Opponents of removal—among whom Secretary of the American Board of Commissioners for Foreign Missions Jeremiah Evarts, and Sen. Theodore Frelinghuysen of New Jersey were outstanding spokesman—argued that justice demanded the protection of the Indians' rights solemnly guaranteed by treaty. Most of the opposition was couched in moralistic terms, but there was also a strong political base for the fight on removal, as pro- and anti-Jackson forces seized upon the issue.

The removal party won in Congress by a narrow margin, and on May 28, 1830, the removal bill became law (4 U.S. Stat. 411–412). The legislation authorized the president to set up districts west of the Mississippi, to which Indian title had been removed, and to exchange such districts for Indian-held lands in the East. It provided payments for improvements on the lands to be given up, for costs of removal, and a year's subsistence in the West for Indians who migrated. Five hundred thousand dollars was appropriated to carry out the act.

Opponents of removal did not slacken their efforts when the bill was passed but continued to fight for the Indians' right to stay on their eastern lands, and an appeal was made to the Supreme Court. The Cherokee nation brought suit against Georgia for violation of Cherokee sovereignty by the extention of its laws over Cherokee territory. Chief Justice John Marshall declared in *Cherokee Nation* v. *Georgia* (5 Peters 1) that the Cherokees, not being a foreign nation in the meaning of the Constitution, could not bring suit in the federal courts, but he reviewed the history of Indian-White relations in the United States and described the Indian tribes as "domestic dependent nations." In *Worcester* v. *Georgia* (6 Peters 515), based on the arrest by Georgia of missionaries in the Cherokee nation, Marshall decided in favor of the Indians, but it was an empty victory, for no action was taken to enforce the decision against Georgia.

The Jackson administration moved forward aggressively to negotiate removal treaties with the Five Civilized Tribes. In 1830 the Treaty of Dancing Rabbit Creek (Kappler 1904–1941, 2:310–319) was signed with the Choctaws, by which the nation agreed to give up the lands in Mississippi in exchange for lands west of Arkansas (DeRosier 1970). In 1832 the Chickasaws signed away their lands and agreed to move to the Choctaw district in the West (Kappler 1904–1941, 2:356–362). Led by astute chiefs, the Chickasaws sold their eastern lands for substantial sums and moved without serious trouble. In the same year the Creeks signed a removal treaty (Kappler 1904–1941, 2:341–343), but delays in actual emigration brought repeated conflicts with the Whites, who moved rapidly into the Creek cession. In 1836 an outbreak of hostilities known as the Creek War was put down by federal troops and state volunteers under Gen. Winfield Scott. The Seminoles, although certain chiefs had signed removal treaties in 1832 at Payne's Landing (Kappler 1904–1941, 2:344–345) and in 1833 at Fort Gibson (Kappler 1904–1941, 2:394–395), resisted attempts to carry out the treaties since many of the Seminoles did not accept them as properly made. From the end of 1835 to 1842 a war raged in Florida between federal forces and the Indians, until all but a handful of Seminoles had been killed or removed to the West.

The Cherokees, led by John Ross (fig. 3), were adamant in refusing to move. Finally in 1835 a small group led by Major Ridge, his son John Ridge (fig.4), and his nephew Elias Boudinot, believing that there was no further hope of survival as a nation in the East, signed the Treaty of New Echota (Kappler 1904–1941, 2:439–449) and migrated to the lands allotted them west of Arkansas (Wilkins 1970). *45*

The Ross party, however, refused to go voluntarily, and in 1837 and 1838 they were forcibly rounded up by the United States army and sent on their way to join the western Cherokees. The Ridges and Boudinot were assassinated by members of the Ross faction in retaliation for having signed away Cherokee land, and the split in the Cherokee nation occasioned by removal persisted until after the Civil War.

The removal treaties with the Choctaw, Creek, and Chickasaw Indians provided for allotments of land to the Indians. The Choctaws received donations of land to heads of families who intended to emigrate, as a substitute for cash payments for abandoned improvements. Allotments in fee simple were granted to heads of families who did not plan to remove, proportionate in size to the number in the family. Such allotments were to enable those who chose to remain to gain freeholds in the ceded lands. The Creek treaty authorized allotments of 320 acres for heads of families and for orphans, as well as 640 acres for each of 90 chiefs. By these arrangements the tribesmen were offered the hope that they might remain on their ancestral lands; on the other hand, the White negotiators, believing that opposition to removal came principally from the chiefs, thought that the arrangements would enable the mass of the Indians to decide for themselves to sell their land and depart.

It was a compromise that did not work. Speculators moved in to acquire Choctaw lands, and spectacular frauds marked the disposition of the Creek lands (Young 1961). The Chickasaw allotments were more generous in size (each single person was allowed 640 acres and families up to 2,680 acres), and they were more fairly administered. These allotments were intended to be temporary homes from which the Indians were committed to remove as soon as possible. The Chickasaw lands were sold for reasonable prices, and the nation moved to the West with considerable wealth (A.M. Gibson 1971). However, the frauds committed among the Choctaws and Creeks and the administrative difficulties gave the allotment policy a bad name, and the Cherokee removal treaty did not contain allotment provisions.

The uprooting of the Indians from the East and the transporting of them to new homes in the West was a traumatic ordeal. The hardships of the journey were enormous, and many Indians died on the way. The Cherokees, whose major movement in 1838 was delayed by bad summer weather, were caught by the winter at the end of the journey, and their "Trail of Tears" became a symbol of the harshness of the removal policy. By 1840 the bulk of the Indians from both north and south were in the

Smithsonian, Natl. Portrait Gallery: NPG. 72.74.
Fig. 3. John Ross (b. 1790, d. 1866) Prior to his political career, Ross served in a Cherokee regiment under Gen. Andrew Jackson and saw action at the Battle of Horseshoe Bend. He was principal chief of the Cherokee 1828–1866 and headed numerous delegations to Washington on behalf of Cherokee land claims and treaties (Moulton 1978). The portrait is signed by Ross and his name appears in Cherokee syllabary (lower left), in transliteration <gu wi s gu wi>. Watercolor and ink on paper from life by John Rubens Smith, 1841.

Buffalo Bill Histl. Center, Cody, Wyo.
Fig. 4. John Ridge (b. 1803, d. 1839). Seeking sympathy for Cherokee rights in the Southeast, in the 1820s Ridge and Elias Boudinot went on a speaking tour in the North. Ridge's other political activities included participation in delegations to Washington and collaboration with U.S. commissioners in the adjustment of land claims of Cherokees forced to emigrate (Dockstader 1977:238–240; Dictionary of Indians of North America 1978, 3:19–21). Painting by Henry Inman, about 1836, after Charles Bird King, Washington, D.C., 1825.

trans-Mississippi regions (Foreman 1932).

The government sought to provide for the welfare of the Indians in the West. It had promised to protect the Indians who had removed from their eastern homes, and to that end a cordon of military posts was established on the "permanent Indian frontier" along the western border of Arkansas and Missouri and then northeasterly across Iowa and southern Minnesota to the Mississippi. Forts Towson and Washita near the Red River marked the southern end. Fort Smith and Fort Gibson on or near the Arkansas border, and Fort Scott, Fort Leavenworth, and Fort Snelling were other major posts in the chain. The forts sought not only to prevent intertribal warfare but also to prevent White encroachment on the Indian lands.

Traders, who profited from the annuity moneys of the Indians, were sharply criticized, and attempts were made to limit their activity (Trennert 1981). An act of March 3, 1847 (9 U.S. Stat. 203–204), gave discretionary authority to the president or the secretary of war to pay annuities to individuals rather than to the chiefs, and with the consent of the Indians, to apply the funds for promoting the happiness and prosperity of the tribes. In some cases annuities were paid semiannually, in order that they might not be quickly squandered by improvident Indians. The law of 1847 struck at the liquor trade by prohibiting the payment of annuities to Indians who were intoxicated or while liquor was within convenient reach and by providing imprisonment for anyone introducing or selling liquor in the Indian country. Indians were made competent witnesses in such cases. A proposal of the Indian Office for a partial return to the factory system, in order to eliminate abuses connected with the system of private traders, came to nothing.

Meanwhile, efforts were continued to provide education and other Europeanizing forces for the Indians (Prucha 1971). Missionary schools, especially manual labor schools such as that established by the Methodists at the Shawnee agency, were encouraged by the government. The Indians were urged to apply annuity and other treaty moneys toward building up schools in the tribes, and some, like the Choctaws and Cherokees, made considerable progress. Any indications of progress were seized upon by reformers and government officials as indications of success, and the more optimistic spokesmen at the end of the 1840s saw the approach of the millennium. Commissioner of Indian Affairs Orlando Brown spoke in 1849 of a great moral and social revolution among the tribes and predicted that they would soon be able to maintain themselves in prosperity and happiness in contact with the White population (ARCIA 1850:22).

Relations between the United States and the tribes were peaceful, and in 1849 Indian affairs, which had been a responsibility of the War Department, was transferred to the newly established Department of the Interior.

Proposals for an Indian State

Serious proposals were made that the Indians who had been removed to the West should form a unified or confederated government there, which might be given territorial status and eventually be admitted to the Union as a state (Abel 1908a). There had been indications of such a move early in the nation's dealings with the Indians. A treaty with the Delawares in 1778 spoke of the possibility of an Indian state in the Confederation, and the Treaty of Hopewell with the Cherokees in 1785 permitted the Indians to send a deputy to Congress, an option never fulfilled. When the removal policy was formulated, ideas of an Indian governmental unit reappeared, and eventual statehood, if not specifically proposed, was hinted at. Jedidiah Morse (1822) proposed such a state in his report to the secretary of war. President Monroe, in his special message to Congress on removal in 1825, stressed the importance of instituting an Indian government in the West as an incentive to emigration, and Secretary of War Cass in 1831 suggested a territorial government for the Indians. The Baptist missionary Isaac McCoy was an ardent and persistent advocate of an Indian state.

Several proposals, in fact, were introduced in Congress, but all failed to pass. One of the most significant of these was the bill of 1834, proposed by the House Committee on Indian Affairs as part of a total legislative package together with the new trade and intercourse law and the law organizing the Indian department. The bill established boundaries for an Indian territory west of Arkansas and Missouri, in which the tribes were to organize a confederated government for their internal affairs. The confederation was to send a delegate to Congress, and the committee hoped for eventual admission of the territory as a state. The bill was opposed by Whites, who questioned the right of the United States to organize such a territorial government for Indians, and by the Indians themselves, who were not inclined to accept a confederated government. In the 1840s and 1850s the project was revived from time to time, but no conclusive action was taken.

New Policy for the West

The dream that removal had solved the Indian problem was soon shattered. The addition of vast new territories in the West that came with the annexation of Texas in 1845, the settlement of the Oregon question in 1846, and the Mexican Cession at the end of the Mexican War in 1848 necessitated an extension of Indian policy to cover the new regions, and the movement of large numbers of persons from the settled regions of the Mississippi valley to Oregon and California brought pressure for opening a corridor to the west through the lands so recently guaranteed to the Indians (Malin 1921).

The new circumstances called for concentration of   *47*

Indians of the plains into southern and northern "colonies," thus beginning a move that developed into the reservation system. Treaties established enclaves of land, on which the Indians were located in order to keep them out of contact with Whites and to provide them with education and new agricultural techniques that would make their restricted existence feasible. In 1858 the commissioner of Indian affairs (ARCIA 1858:9) declared that the "policy of concentrating the Indians on small reservations of land, and of sustaining them there for a limited period, until they can be induced to make the necessary exertions to support themselves" was the only alternative to their extinction (Trennert 1975). The reservation system was adapted to the various regions of the newly acquired West and became an enduring policy of the United States.

Texas

As an independent republic from 1836 to 1845, Texas had developed its own Indian policy (Muckleroy 1922–1923). During his first administration, President Sam Houston inaugurated a policy of peace, friendship, and commerce, with provisions as needed for protection of the frontier against Indians who remained hostile. But depredations did not decrease, as settlers pressed upon the Indian lands, and Houston's successor, Mirabeau B. Lamar, declared the policy of pacification a total failure and began an aggressive program that sought the expulsion or extermination of the Indians. The result was almost continual warfare in which the Indians were removed or pushed back before the advancing Whites. When Houston returned to the presidency at the end of 1841, he reinstituted his pacific policy. Peace treaties were signed with the Indians and new trade relations established; his successor, Anson Jones, followed the same plan. Protective measures were still necessary against hostile tribes, but disturbances on the frontier were lessened and the cost of Indian defense greatly reduced.

With the annexation of Texas, the Indian problems of Texas became the responsibility of the federal government (Harmon 1930; Koch 1925). In a treaty with the important tribes at Council Springs signed on May 15, 1846 (Kappler 1904–1941, 2:411–413), the Indians placed themselves under the protection of the United States and recognized the sole right of the United States to regulate trade and intercourse with them. An act of March 3, 1847, provided funds to carry out the treaty and for the appointment of a special Indian agent, a position filled with distinction by Robert S. Neighbors. Depredations of hostile Indians led to the establishment of a line of military posts in 1848 and 1849, stretching from Fort Worth on the Trinity River in the north and running south to the Rio Grande. When pressure was brought against this line by the Indians, a supplementary line of defense farther to the

west was built during the 1850s. The defense problem was aggravated by Indian raids from Mexico across the Rio Grande.

The federal government's position was complicated by the fact that, although it had responsibility for regulating Indian affairs in Texas, the public lands in Texas remained under control of the state and did not become part of the national public domain. Thus the federal government was limited in making arrangements to provide space and protection for the Indians. However, a Texas law of February 6, 1854, authorized the United States to select and survey areas for the Indians, and two reservations, one on the main fork of the Brazos River and another on the Clear Fork of the Brazos, were set aside for colonization by the Texas tribes. The tribes that settled the former reserve began cultivation with some success; the latter reserve, settled chiefly by the Comanches, was less successful. Ultimately the reservation system broke down because of antagonism of the Whites and continual depredations by the Indians. In summer 1859 the reservation Indians of Texas were moved north across the Red River into Indian Territory. The unsettled nature of Indian affairs in Texas remained an irritant until well after the Civil War.

Pacific Northwest

Large numbers of White settlers arrived in Oregon during the 1840s, especially in the rich agricultural valley of the Willamette River and in the Puget Sound region, and as their numbers increased, conflicts arose with the many small tribes of Indians who inhabited the Pacific Northwest. Missionaries had set up stations in the 1830s, but they were unable to quell antagonisms, and when Marcus Whitman, his wife, and other Whites were killed by Indians in 1847, the federal government realized at last the need for official administration of the territory. The first territorial governor, Joseph Lane, arrived in March 1849 and assumed the ex officio duties of superintendent of Indian affairs for Oregon; however, not until an act of June 5, 1850, did Congress extend the provisions of the trade and intercourse act to Oregon and otherwise provide for Indian affairs in the region. Commissioners were appointed to negotiate treaties with the Indians, with instructions to extinguish Indian title to all lands west of the Cascades and to concentrate the Indians on reservations. They met resistance to their plans from the Indians, and the six treaties they negotiated were rejected by the Senate. Subsequent treaties, too, failed to be ratified (Coan 1921, 1922; Hoopes 1932).

In 1854–1856 new treaties with the tribes in Oregon and Washington were negotiated by Joel Palmer, appointed superintendent of Indian affairs for Oregon in 1853, and Isaac I. Stevens, who was appointed governor of the new Washington Territory in the same year and served ex officio as superintendent of Indian affairs. Stevens also treated with Flathead, Blackfeet, and other tribes in what is now western Montana. The treaties extinguished Indian title to most of the la̲ ⁺ʰᵉ Pacific Northwest, assigned the Indians to rese̲ ̲ ̲vided annuities and other assistance. ̲ ̲stal tribes recognized their f

Meanwhile, t'
Oregon and Wa
the Indians th
River War an
in 1858.

California

The Inc
match
follow
destr
on
eve
ther̲   ̲n
country. Onl̲y ̲   ̲ve
into the new state. In ̲ ̲, ̲ho-
rized three Indian agents for Camorn̲. ̲ame
time it authorized commissioners to nego̲ ̲ eaties
with the California tribes. The first agents, acting as the commissioner before they took up their duties as agents, negotiated 18 treaties in which the Indians acknowledged the sovereignty of the United States and placed themselves under its protection. Reservations were marked out for the Indians, and subsistence, annuities, and other aids were promised. But the Senate, on July 8, 1852, refused to ratify the treaties—in part because of California objections that the reservations comprised some of the most valuable agricultural and mineral land in the state—and the dispossession of the Indians by the Whites continued.

An independent Indian superintendency was created in California in 1852, a post first held by Edward F. Beale, who worked zealously to establish reservations for the California tribes, where they could be protected by military troops and instructed in agriculture and other pursuits. Beale himself established only one reservation, but his successors extended the system, and there developed a pattern of limited reservations under control of agents in the midst of the White population. Military posts were built to protect the reservations and to maintain peace between the Indians and the Whites. The reservations by 1860 were in generally poor condition, and on June 19, 1860, Congress abolished the single superintendency of California and divided the state into northern and southern districts (Ellison 1922; Hoopes 1932).

New Mexico and Utah

Indian affairs in New Mexico were in a critical condition when James S. Calhoun was appointed Indian agent at Santa Fe in 1849. He outlined an able plan to formalize relations with the Pueblo Indians and to mark off boundaries for the lands of the Indians. Although Calhoun was appointed governor of New Mexico Territo- ̲n it was organized in 1850 and held the position of ̲ntendent of Indian affairs ex officio, he was able to ̲nplish little in putting his plans into effect because ̲gress failed to act, and later superintendents were no ̲re successful. Although treaties were signed with the ̲paches and other tribes, warfare was widespread ̲hroughout the 1850s. Only one reservation was estab- ̲ished in New Mexico up to 1860 (Hoopes 1932).

Indian affairs in Utah Territory were provided for by the appointment of the Mormon leader Brigham Young as governor of the territory in 1850, with ex officio duties as superintendent of Indian affairs. Young had deep concern for the Indians, but he aimed to reconcile their interests with the expansion of Mormon settlement. He hoped to persuade the Indians to settle down to an agricultural existence in imitation of the Mormons, and he believed that the Indians would benefit in the long run from the Mormon occupation of their lands. Young's career as Indian superintendent was a stormy one, for he was often at odds with the Indian agents sent to Utah by the Indian Office, who objected to his extensive control. One of the agents, Garland Hurt (appointed 1854), advocated and began a notable experiment in developing Indian farms. Then the whole matter of Indian relations was complicated by the conflict between the Mormons and the federal government that resulted in the Mormon War of 1857–1858. A tragic episode was the Mountain Meadows Massacre of September 1857, in which a band of White emigrants was murdered by Indians and Mormons. In 1857 a separate superintendency for Utah was established, and in 1858 Young was replaced as governor and as superintendent of Indian affairs (Morgan 1948; Hoopes 1932).

Great Plains

In the meantime a policy was formulated and implemented for the Great Plains region, through which the emigrants to the new western territories passed. Heavy use of the Oregon and California Trails in the north-central district and the Santa Fe Trail in the south increased Indian-White contacts, and as the emigrants killed off great quantities of game, the Indians experienced food shortages. In a treaty at Fort Laramie in 1851 (Kappler 1904–1941, 2:594–596), the northern Plains tribes granted to the United States the right to establish roads and military posts in their country and agreed to stop 49 depredations against Whites passing through their lands. Boundaries of the territory occupied by each tribe were defined. The government distributed presents to the Indians and agreed to specified annuity payments. Other treaties with Sioux (fig. 5) and the Treaty of Fort Atkinson in 1853 with Comanche, Kiowa, and Apache had similar provisions (Kappler 1904–1941, 2:600–602).

In a series of treaties negotiated in 1854 and 1855 by Commissioner of Indian Affairs George Manypenny, the central tribes ceded to the government most of their lands in eastern Kansas and Nebraska, leaving behind only a few small reservations (Kappler 1904–1941, 2:451–478). These treaties, while continuing the policies of removal and concentration, also contained provisions for allotments in severalty to Indians who chose to remain on homesteads under fee simple tenure.

The Kansas-Nebraska Act of 1854 provided territorial organization for the region and opened the way for settlement and for transcontinental railroad construction. The rapid push of the Whites into new areas in the West led to open conflict with the Indians, who resisted encroachment upon their lands, and the decade before the Civil War witnessed wars in Texas, on the central plains, and in the Pacific Northwest. The warfare led responsible officials to question whether military control of the Indian service might not be a wise arrangement, and both the secretary of war and the secretary of the interior in 1860 supported a resolution to move the Bureau of Indian Affairs back to the War Department, but Congress did not act. When the Civil War broke out in 1861, it drew attention away from Indian affairs, but serious problems remained.

Newberry Lib., Edward E. Ayer Coll., Chicago.

Fig. 5. Treaty conference with Santee Sioux, Traverse des Sioux, Territory of Minn., July 16, 1851. The federal government signed treaties that summer with 4 bands of eastern Sioux. In return for ceding and leaving certain lands, treaty provisions included the payment of 3 million dollars, some of which was designated for agricultural improvements and for the establishment of manual-labor schools, and other programs intended to help the Sioux become integrated into the national economy and White culture (Kappler 1904–1941, 2:588–593). Sketch by Frank Blackwell Mayer.

United States Indian Policies, 1860–1900

WILLIAM T. HAGAN

1860–1864

By the early 1860s the principal features of the Indian policy the United States would pursue throughout the late nineteenth century had been established. As the Whites began to press upon their lands the Indians were to be persuaded, through negotiations, to cede most of their holdings and locate on reservations. These reservations would be closed to all Whites except those on official business in order to protect the Indians from the corruption and demoralization usually attendant upon the casual contact of frontier Indian and White populations. Initially the reservations would be large enough so that the Indians might depend partially upon hunting, but as they converted to farming and stock raising their holdings would be gradually reduced, making more land available to White settlers (Harlan 1865a). The proceeds from the sale of these surplus lands would help buy cattle and farm implements for the Indians and in other ways relieve the taxpayer of some of the burden of the civilization programs. Meanwhile, the Indian children would be attending schools of the manual labor type developed in the pre–Civil war era. Approximately a generation later the Indians would have progressed to the point that they could receive title to individual farms and blend with the general population.

The outbreak of the Civil War had not brought any significant changes in the general Indian policy. Except in Indian Territory (now Oklahoma) the war had little impact on the Indian population. The United States did raise a few units from among the pro-Union refugees from the Five Civilized Tribes and employed individual Southern Plains Indians as scouts, but there was no effort to make maximum use of Indian manpower. The Confederate leaders, with only limited success, did try to make greater use of Indians in their military forces. Except for the Five Civilized Tribes, which were badly split by the war and suffered tragically, the payment of their annuities in depreciated greenbacks, or the reduced quantity of goods greenbacks could purchase, was the most direct effect the war had on most Indians.

The support that members of the Five Civilized Tribes provided the Confederacy was recognized as early as 1862 as offering the United States an excuse for reducing their

Minn. Histl. Soc., St. Paul: E91.7u/rl.

Fig 1. Sioux Indian farmer, near Yellow Medicine Agency, Minn. Among those groups who supported and enabled federal goals of establishing an agrarian economy among the Indians were the Protestant missionaries in Minn. This Mdewakanton Sioux farmer, Chaska, lived near the mission of Dr. Thomas S. Williamson at Pézutazi. Williamson had brought a farmer to his first post at Lac Qui Parle to teach farming to the Indians (Gates 1935:134–138). While some of the Sioux embraced farming, it was a source of divisiveness among tribal members at the outbreak of the Sioux war in 1862 ("Indian-U.S. Military Situation, 1848–1891," fig. 3, this vol.). While Sioux farmers received goods from agents, nonfarmers were without resources because of delays in government shipments of annuity goods. "Blanket" Sioux who continued to hunt referred to those who farmed as the "pantaloon band" and even "Dutchmen," associating them with nearby German settlers. Whites called the farmers "Improvement Sioux" (Carley 1962:132–133; Anderson 1986:107–116). Photograph by Whitney's Gallery, St. Paul, Minn., 1862.

landholdings in Indian Territory (ARCIA 1862:179). With a population density of less than one person per square mile the territory seemed to Washington officials to be capable of accommodating more Indians. Kansans had been demanding the removal of the tribes placed there in the drive to clear eastern states of their Indian populations, and room in Indian Territory might be found also for some of the tribes in Nebraska.

The continued, indeed accelerated, movement of Whites into the West during the Civil War was accompanied by their demands for more Indian land. The United States made little effort to curtail the influx of Whites and, at least in the case of Nevada, the creation of a new state may have been expedited for political reasons associated with the 1864 elections. Dakota, Colorado, Idaho, and Arizona territories also came into being and by 1865 there was no area in the West, except Indian territory, that was not to some degree open to White settlement.

The influx of miners and settlers forced the Indians to strike back. In the early months of the Civil War the U.S. Army's frontier installations had been virtually denuded of troops. Nevertheless, by the summer of 1863 the United States had more soldiers available for service against the Indians than it had in 1860 (Utley 1967:216). Most of the new units were volunteer regiments raised in the western states and territories. These soldiers had the animus toward Indians common to White frontiersmen, and the conduct of the Colorado troops under Col. John M. Chivington at Sand Creek in 1864 reflected the zeal with which they killed Indians.

Most of the military action on the plains stemmed from the Army's assignment to keep open emigrant and stagecoach routes. In 1862 (12 U.S. Stat. 491) Congress committed the government to much greater efforts to open the West by chartering the transcontinental railroad and pledging to "extinguish as rapidly as may be the Indian title" to the land involved.

An experiment, which if it had developed differently might have brought about a major change in responsibility for Indian affairs, got underway on the Pecos River in eastern New Mexico in 1862. There Brig. Gen. James H. Carleton located 400 Mescalero Apaches and then brought in more than 8,000 Navajos. Although Indian Service personnel were assigned to Bosque Redondo, the War Department controlled the experiment and the Interior Department acquiesced in it. Had Carleton's hopes of a model pueblo on the Pecos been realized, advocates of a transfer of Indian affairs back to the War Department would have been in a much stronger position as that debate developed after the Civil War.

It was apparent by late 1864 that major decisions would have to be made regarding the policy to be pursued toward the Plains Indians. In the wake of Indian raids inspired by the Sand Creek Massacre and White intrusions, Secretary of the Interior John P. Usher (1865:9) went so far as to propose that the hostile Indians had violated their treaties and no further negotiations with them should be attempted. The military posts in the region should be strengthened and the Indians punished. Those that chose peace would be turned over to the Interior Department, which would locate them on reservations and control them without the interference of treaties. In March 1865 (13 U.S. Stat. 572) Congress was sufficiently concerned with the increasing violence on the plains to create a joint committee to investigate.

1865–1867

The Civil War had been over only a few weeks when Secretary of the Interior James Harlan proposed negotiations with the Indians of Kansas, Indian Territory, and the plains (Harlan 1865). In August 1865 two groups of commissioners were dispatched to the West for this purpose. Their instructions reflected current government Indian policy. The commissioners were to persuade as many as possible of the tribes in Kansas to take up residence in Indian Territory. The Five Civilized Tribes there were to be required to sell sufficient land to the United States to permit the location of the additional tribes in Indian Territory. The Five Civilized Tribes also would have to consent to the emancipation of their slaves and their incorporation into the tribe on a basis of equality with other members. The Plains Indians were to be told that the government could not and would not interfere with the westward movement of its peoples, and that the Indians would have to consent to accepting reservations far removed from emigrant trails and railroad routes. As had already been decided, these reservations would be closed to the general White population and would be at first sufficiently large so that the Indians would partially support themselves by hunting. Provisions in the treaties were to be made for schools, and benevolent societies were to be encouraged to assist in this work, although no coercion of the Indian in religious matters or religious monopolies would be permitted on any reservation. Indicative of the degree to which these were to be true negotiations was the instruction to the commissioners to tell the Indians that these treaties might be amended by the Senate and such amendments would not require the concurrence of the Indians.

The commissioners did not secure treaties with the Five Civilized Tribes in 1865, these having to wait for negotiations in Washington the following year. Then the United States purchased approximately half of the holdings of these tribes in Indian Territory. During the next decade and a half a number of other tribes were moved to Indian Territory, including the Sauk and Fox, Potawatami, Osage, Iowa, and several other smaller groups from Kansas, the Pawnee from Nebraska, and the Ponca from South Dakota. The Washington treaties also committed the Five Civilized Tribes to the creation of an all-territorial council in which each tribe would be represented. Its architects hoped it would develop into a full-fledged territorial government, and ultimately into a state.

The 1865 negotiations with the Plains tribes produced treaties with the Kiowa, Comanche, Kiowa-Apache, Cheyenne, Arapahoe, and nine bands of Sioux. But the treaties either did not prescribe reservations for the tribes concerned, due to their opposition to such provisions, or were so unrealistic in size as to be meaningless. The reservation for the Kiowa and Comanche, for example, included a substantial slice of western Texas that that state was not likely to surrender. Meanwhile continued Indian resistence to White intruders stimulated a debate on the Indian policy the United States should pursue.

Few Whites advocated exterminating the Indian population, and those who did were usually Westerners. This was not surprising as those Whites bore the brunt of the Indian violence. The stories of the 1862 Sioux uprising in Minnesota that resulted in the deaths of perhaps 600 or 700 Whites and the steady stream of reports of Indian raids on the Texas frontier helped generate considerable anti-Indian sentiment throughout the West. In contrast, Indian Service personnel generally defended their charges, playing down the raids that did occur and blaming the Whites for keeping the Indians hostile by their invasions of tribal territories.

In Congress all segments of opinion on the Indian question were represented; however, most senators and representatives agreed with the argument of the Indian Service that it was cheaper, and more humane, to feed the Indians than to fight them. The Indians would have to give way before the White settlers, but diplomats rather than soldiers would be employed to achieve the objective. The estimate of the joint congressional committee appointed in 1865 was that it would cost $30,000,000 and require an army of 10,000 men two or three years to subdue the Plains Indians (U.S. Congress. Senate 1867). Senators and congressmen might rail at the idea of taxpayers supporting Indians in idleness, but the argument that it was more economical than fighting them finally won the day for the Peace Policy.

The question of returning to the War Department responsibility for administering the Indians also frequently arose in the post-Civil War years. Proponents of the Army cited evidence of incompetence and corruption among civilian Indian agents and argued that army officers as agents would be more responsible and cheaper and command more respect from Indians who were warriors themselves. The opponents of the Army questioned the competence of military men to instruct the Indians in peaceful pursuits. The latent American hostility to a standing army also undoubtedly worked to the advantage of the Interior Department. Nevertheless, a bill to return the Indian Office to the War Department did pass the House early in 1867 only to fail in the Senate. This was high tide for the Army's supporters, although the issue would not die for another 10 years, and as late as the 1890s there was a period of a few years when nearly half

the agencies were headed by army officers on detached duty.

In spring and summer 1867 members of Congress engaged in a repetition of the debate on the relative merits of feeding or fighting the Indians. Indian resistance to Army efforts to keep the Bozeman Trail open, highlighted by the Indians' spectacular victory over Capt. William J. Fetterman near Fort Philip Kearny in December 1866 fueled the debate. Commissioner of Indian Affairs L.V. Bogy had insisted that the troops were the aggressors and the Sioux, Cheyennes, and Arapahoes had gone to Fort Philip Kearny to negotiate. He proposed sending commissioners to persuade the Indians to return to their reservations (Bogy 1867). Secretary of the Interior Daniel M. Browning asked for an appropriation to finance the mission (Browning 1867). The following month Congress made clear that its role in negotiations was to be decisive, by banning any treaty making until Congress had first appropriated funds for it (15 U.S. Stat. 9). However, not until July, and only over strenuous protests by some Western members of Congress, was a Peace Commission established (15 U.S. Stat. 17). It included a new commissioner of Indian affairs, members of Congress, army officers, and civilians. Its charge was to convince the Indians to locate on reservations; if they failed, provision was made to raise detachments of volunteers to force the Indians into compliance.

The Peace Commission represented an approach to Indian affairs that would become known as the Peace Policy. The Commission produced a new round of treaties in 1867 and 1868, treaties that followed the pattern achieved in less complete form in the 1865 series (fig. 2). The new ones provided distinct reservations and contained provisions for education, isolation from casual contact with Whites, annuities of clothing and useful articles, and allotment of land to individual Indians who sought it. Some of the treaties promised rations for four years; others did not, although the government took it for granted that the Indians would be fed until they could become completely self-supporting by farming and cattle raising.

That the Indians had no desire to give up their nomadic way of life, probably did not understand much of what transpired at the conference with the Peace Commission, and had no political machinery for enforcing compliance of those who had opposed the treaties or had not even been present did not augur well. In some respects the United States had little more than scraps of paper that could provide a legal—by the standards of Whites—basis for forcing Indians onto the reservations.

The government's attitude was that the Indians were bound by these treaties from the instant their leaders signed them; however, the United States was not committed until the Senate ratified the treaties, which might be many months later, and then to appropriate the funds to

Smithsonian, NAA: 3686.
Fig. 2. Members of the Peace Commission meeting with Cheyenne and Arapahoe Indian leaders at Ft. Laramie, Wyo. Terr. Commissioners facing the camera include, center, left to right, Samuel F. Tappan, Bvt. Maj. Gen. William S. Harney, Lt. Gen. William T. Sherman, Gen. John B. Sanborn, Bvt. Maj. Gen. Christopher C. Augur, and Bvt. Maj. Gen. Alfred H. Terry. Also present at the meeting were Nathaniel G. Taylor, president of the Peace Commission and commissioner of Indian affairs and Sen. J.B. Henderson from Mo., chairman of the Senate Committee on Indian Affairs. Photograph by Alexander Gardner, probably May 10, 1868.

implement them required action of both houses. Treaties negotiated with the Southern Plains tribes were not ratified by the Senate for nearly a year and it was several years more before the government began to even approach meeting its financial obligations to these tribes. Typical official reaction was the Peace Commission's condemnation, in October 1868, of the Indians for violating the treaties made a year earlier, and its suggestion that certain privileges accorded tribesmen by the treaties be canceled (ARCIA 1868:371). Nevertheless, the United States had yet to make more than a gesture toward providing the goods and services promised by the same treaties.

1868–1876

In spring 1868 the commissioner of Indian affairs was pleading for Congress to appropriate funds to enable the government to meet its treaty commitments to the Indians and thus to avoid warfare on the Plains. The sum provided when the Peace Commission had been created was nearly exhausted, and the commissioner asked for $1,000,000 to feed 20,000 Indians at an estimated cost of 17½ cents per day (N.G. Taylor 1868). In July (15 U.S. Stat. 222) Congress appropriated only $500,000. It was to cover not only subsistence but also the purchase of tools and other equipment for outfitting the new reservations, as well as

the expense of any additional negotiations with the tribes. To the further disgruntlement of the commissioner and his superior the secretary of the interior, Congress placed the $500,000 at the disposal of, not the commissioner, but Lt. Gen. William T. Sherman, the ranking Army representative on the Peace Commission. For about a year the conduct of government relations with the critical Plains tribes was in the hands of General Sherman and his subordinates. The civilian agents assigned to these tribes were little more than observers.

This was the situation when Sherman's superior, Gen. Ulysses S. Grant, was elected president. As general of the army, Grant had urged the transfer of the Indian Service back to the War Department. As president he clearly hoped to employ as Indian agents some of the officers who were no longer needed on active duty as the military establishment was reduced to peacetime proportions. Accordingly, in the first year of his administration, Grant appointed army officers to fill most of the available agent positions. Surprisingly, he invited the pacifist Society of Friends, which had expressed concern about the quality of Indian Service personnel, to nominate the agents for the two superintendencies that included Nebraska, Kansas, and Indian Territory. Liberal Friends nominated agents for the Northern Superintendency and Orthodox Friends for the Southern, launching the Peace Policy, also called

54

Quaker Policy, of President Grant. Then in January 1870 (16 U.S. Stat. 62) Congress banned the use of retired officers in positions such as Indian agent and followed it in July 1870 (16 U.S. Stat. 319) by forbidding such employment to officers on active duty. To fill the agencies the officers were required to vacate, President Grant directed the secretary of the interior to seek nominations from religious groups that had been doing missionary work among the tribes. In addition to the Friends, 11 different religious groups participated in the selection of agents for 63 of the 75 agencies (Fritz 1963:76–78). Unfortunately, there was much squabbling among them as to which church groups which agencies should be assigned. The Roman Catholics, who felt that their missionary activity on 38 reservations should have qualified them for more than seven agencies, were particularly aggrieved.

The long-run effects of Grant's Peace Policy were minimal. While it may have improved overall efficiency of administration by reducing the incidence of corruption, the Peace Policy did not represent a shift in general objectives of United States Indian policy, nor did it bring to the work the outpouring of church funds that had been hoped for. By placing men who eschewed the use of force in charge of reservations housing warriors for whom raiding was a way of life, the Peace Policy probably protracted the warfare on the southern plains. With Grant's departure from the presidency in 1877 the Peace Policy was permitted by his successor to quietly expire, although here and there a church-sponsored agent secured reappointment at the end of his four-year term.

The Board of Indian Commissioners, another innovation, had a longer life. For several years individuals had been expressing a desire for some type of supervisory body to oversee the Indian Service. In 1869 (16 U.S. Stat. 40) Congress, with the endorsement of the administration, created a board of at least 10 members to be appointed by the President. The Board was charged to "exercise joint control with the Secretary of the Interior over the disbursement" of the funds appropriated for the Indian Department. President Grant issued an executive order June 3, 1869, defining the responsibilities of the Board, and Congress in 1870 (16 U.S. Stat. 360) further delineated its duties. The unpaid members of the Board, whose expenses while on official business were paid by the government, audited purchases for the Indian Service and could inspect agencies. They did not enjoy the degree of power over the Bureau of Indian Affairs some members of the Board had anticipated, leading to some resignations of frustrated commissioners. However, their ability to audit and investigate, and their capacity to mobilize public opinion, did improve the quality of the administration of Indian affairs.

Agencies such as the Board of Indian Commissioners had little direct impact on those tribes the Peace Policy had been conceived to handle. As long as the buffalo roamed the plains it would be difficult to confine the Indians whose way of life had been to follow the great herds. But Indians off the reservation usually came into collision with the growing White population. Some warriors drove off horses and cattle of settlers, and some took scalps and captives. On the other hand, there were many instances of Whites attacking peaceful Indian hunting parties. The Indians fought to hold their land; the Whites called on their government, which had invited them to settle the land, to defend them. Every year Army columns scoured the plains for "hostiles." If the activity intensified sufficiently it would be known as an Indian war. As the Indians whom the Army was called upon to chastise were nominally reservation residents, it inspired considerable bitterness in the relations between the War and Interior Departments. In 1869 the Army had been given jurisdiction over Indians who were off their reservation without permission (ARCIA 1869:452). But the Army found it very difficult to cope with warriors who could slip away from a reservation and then return to its sanctuary with their plunder before troops could even be alerted to move. Nevertheless, increased troop activity on the plains, coupled with better surveillance by the agents and the drastic inroads on the buffalo herds made by the White hide hunters, had virtually ended Indian absences from the southern reservations by 1876, and from the northern reservations by a year later. Some Apaches would continue to resist into the mid-1880s.

Meanwhile, congressmen, who had been led to believe that the treaties negotiated 1865–1868 would enable White occupation of the West at minimum expense to the government, were rebelling against the mounting cost of supporting Indians on reservations. By 1872, 31,000 Indians were being entirely subsisted by the government, and another 84,000 partially (ARCIA 1872:15). There were nearly 1,000 employees at 77 agencies and this did not even approach the number that would be required to provide the services promised the Indians in their treaties.

Commissioner of Indian Affairs Ely S. Parker (the first Indian to hold the position) and Senators Benjamin F. Butler and John Sherman called for an end to the treaty system. Also the representatives, expected to vote appropriations to implement treaties whose ratification process excluded them, were particularly anxious to change the system. Early in 1871 Congress ended the practice of negotiating treaties with tribes as though they were independent powers (16 U.S. Stat. 566) The representatives now had the voice they wished as the agreements that replaced the treaties required the approval of both houses. It was also a more realistic way of dealing with a people whose capacity for independent action had virtually ceased to exist, although it did not make any real difference for several years. Commissioners continued to visit tribes to negotiate for the acquisition of land, and the action of Congress in 1871 did not invalidate existing treaties.

The government was under continuous pressure to further reduce Indian land holdings, and officials did not resist it strenuously. A typical reaction involved the Black Hills, which Indian Commissioner Edward P. Smith advocated persuading the Sioux to sell "for the sake of promoting the mining and agricultural interests of white men" (ARCIA 1875:8–9). By concentrating the tribesmen on a few large reservations, more land would be made available for White settlement, and the cost of administering and supplying the reservation reduced. A particularly appealing solution to the problem was the location of more tribes in Indian Territory. At one time or another between 1868 and 1877 officials proposed moving there all the Indians east of the Rockies, or just the Sioux and Ponca, and perhaps certain Apache tribes.

These plans were generally unsuccessful due to Indian resistance to such propositions and a growing opposition of states neighboring on Indian Territory. These states were happy to push their own Indian populations into Indian Territory, although they objected to states farther removed doing so.

Nor did the planners' hopes for a central government for Indian Territory materialize. Beginning in 1870 Congress underwrote several territorial conferences at Okmulgee, but the council created by the post-Civil War treaties with the Five Civilized Tribes failed as a law-making body, foundering on tribal particularism.

Although the hope was to consolidate Indian agencies, thus reducing the number of salaried employees in the Indian Service, during the period under consideration there actually was a slight increase in the number of agencies. More success was enjoyed in eliminating the superintendencies, of which there had been 14 in 1868. By 1878 there were none. As their function had been to serve as middlemen between the Commissioner of Indian Affairs and the agent, eliminating the superintendents reduced some of the paperwork and increased efficiency. Particularly desirable was the cessation by 1871 of the practice of having territorial governors serve as ex officio superintendents of Indian affairs. Their performance suffered from a conflict of interest in which the settler demanding more land usually benefited at the expense of the Indian.

Two judicial decisions further weakened the position of the Indians. In 1870 the *Cherokee Tobacco* case (11 Wall. 616) helped clear the way for the abolition of the treaty system by affirming the power of Congress to enact legislation in conflict with treaty provisions. A decision in 1873 severely limited Indian rights in reservations to which they did not have a title in fee simple, and this was virtually all except the holdings of the Five Civilized Tribes. In *United States* v. *Cook* (19 Wall. 591) the court had ruled that Indians could not sell the timber of the

reservations they occupied and the decision was interpreted to apply to grass as well. Subsequent legislation permitted reservation Indians to lease grazing rights and to sell down and dead timber, but the *Cook* decision clearly restricted tribal rights in reservations.

The same year as the *Cook* decision, Congress in response to a request of the secretary of the interior provided him five inspectors (17 U.S. Stat. 463). These officials operated independently of the Bureau of Indian Affairs and served the secretary personally. They could be dispatched to any agency at any time and had power to take testimony, audit records, and suspend employees whose performance was in question.

Four actions of Congress in 1874 and 1875 illustrated trends in Indian policy. In 1874 (18 U.S. Stat. Pt 3, 176) and again in 1875 (18 U.S. Stat. 449) laws required male Indians, 18 to 45 years of age, to perform labor if they drew rations from the government. Although they were impossible to enforce, the laws did represent manifestations of congressional discontent with the rising costs of the Indian Service. The same concern was responsible for the limitation on total salaries of agency employees, agents excepted, to $6,000, with the possibility of expansion to an absolute maximum of $10,000 (18 U.S. Stat. Pt 3, 176). Section 7 of the same act struck a blow at tribal organization by requiring that agents issue rations to heads of families rather than to band chiefs. In 1875 Congress extended (18 U.S. Stat. 420) the homestead laws to Indians willing to abandon their tribal relations. Such legislation was consistent with the generally agreed-upon policy of reducing the differences between the Indian and the rest of the population of the United States as rapidly as possible. Although Congress enacted the laws, it was customary for House and Senate Committees to seek the views of the Interior Department on proposed legislation. And, of course, both the president and the secretary of the interior proposed legislation themselves through the appropriate channels.

1877–1887

During this period the overall objectives of United States Indian policy remained unchanged. The government still was committed to reducing the land base of the tribes to make more acreage available to the White population and to converting the Indian into a farmer and stock raiser capable of blending with the general population. The haste with which the first objective was pursued impeded policies designed to achieve the second.

Once all the Indians were gathered on the reservations the magnitude of the problem of feeding them became apparent (fig.3). When the treaties had been written in the post-Civil War years the assumption had been that the Indians would be self-supporting agriculturalists by the time the buffalo had disappeared. However, the Southern

56

Plains tribes conducted their last successful buffalo hunts in 1878 and the herds had disappeared from the northern plains by 1884. In neither section had the Indians made significant progress toward becoming farmers and stock raisers. Unable to feed themselves and denied full rations by a parsimonious Congress, these Indians suffered terribly. Every year during this period, and extending into the 1890s, starving conditions existed on some reservations.

The strain of the unexpected expense of maintaining, even inadequately, the reservation populations continued to inspire support in Congress for concentration of the Indians at fewer locations and further reduction of their land holdings. By concentrating the Indians at fewer locations the cost of administration could be substantially reduced. One plan discussed in 1878 would have eliminated 25 reservations and 11 agencies, and reduced Indian land holdings by 17,000,000 acres (Hyatt 1878). Among other things, under this plan the Utes would have moved to Indian Territory, and for several years this area continued to be considered as a potential home for Indians as widely separated as the Papagos and the Sioux. Other movements, and rumors of movements, kept tribes unsettled and interfered with efforts to get Indians to cultivate individual homesteads.

By persuading the Indians to sell their rights to hunting grounds that as farmers they no longer needed, it was hoped to satisfy the land demands of White settlers and to provide the tribes funds so that they might at least partially assume the burden of the civilization programs. If the land were valuable for timber or minerals, the government's policy was for the Indians to surrender it for White exploitation; however, the sum received by the Indians in exchange for giving up their rights in the land was estimated in terms of its use as agricultural land, a markedly lower figure than if it had been estimated in terms of its timber and mineral resources.

Friction between the War and Interior Departments continued. Army officers warned that starving Indians threatened outbreaks; the Interior Department charged the military with exaggeration and blamed Congress for insufficient appropriations. However, in case of disturbances on their reservations agents had to ask for troops. To enable agents to cope with situations short of crises, Congress responded to the request of the Interior Department and in 1878 (20 U.S. Stat. 86) authorized the payment of Indian police. One of the most successful innovations of the reservation era, the police were the agent's handymen. They guarded the reservations against intruders, returned truant pupils, arrested the drunk and disorderly, and performed numerous other chores for the harried agent (fig. 4).

Fig. 3. Issuing annuity goods to Sioux prisoners at Ft. Randall, Dak. Terr., April 17, 1882. Annuity goods included articles of clothing, bolts of cloth, sewing tools, and cooking utensils. The Hunkpapa Sioux leader Sitting Bull and approximately 137 of his followers, including women and children, were being held at Ft. Randall during this time. They had returned in July 1880 from Canada where they had fled to escape the intensified U.S. military campaign after the Battle of the Little Big Horn in 1876. Photograph probably by Baily, Dix, and Mead.

In 1883 Secretary of the Interior Henry M. Teller assigned the Indian police the additional duty of serving as judges of newly established Courts of Indian Offenses. Obvious problems resulted from the same individuals acting as both policemen and judges, and subsequently Congress was persuaded to provide funds to employ Indians who would serve only in the judicial capacity. Secretary Teller had hoped the courts would discourage the persistence of certain religious and social practices such as the Sun Dance and polygamy. They were more effective in providing local tribunals where the reservation's petty offenders might be brought to trial. Nevertheless, the police and courts combined to help make reservations relatively law-abiding enclaves in the West.

The Courts of Indian Offenses were still in process of formation when the Supreme Court ruled in *ex parte Crow Dog* (109 U.S. 556, 1883) that the United States had no jurisdiction over an Indian accused of murdering another on a reservation. Congress responded to this in 1885 with legislation (23 U.S. Stat. 385) that prohibited seven (later extended to 10) major crimes by Indians on reservations. The *ex parte Crow Dog* decision, despite the legislation it inspired, had strengthened the concept of tribal sovereignty. But three years later, in *United States* v. *Kagama* (118 U.S. 375, 1886), the Supreme Court reversed itself, affirming the jurisdiction of Congress over Indian reservations, while denying such powers to the states.

Another case, *Elk* v. *Wilkins* (112 U.S. 94, 1884), which originated in the attempt of an Indian to vote in an Omaha, Nebraska, election, also touched on the subject of tribal sovereignty. It had even greater significance for Indian citizenship. In this case a federal circuit court ruled that the Fourteenth Amendment did not apply to Indians and that a tribal member could not simply separate himself from the tribe and thus become a citizen of the United States. It was ironic that the decision came at a time when the whole aim of the government's reservation policy was to prepare Indians for citizenship.

Education was recognized as the most important instrument for the transformation of the Indians. In the post-Civil War era Indian Service personnel seldom doubted the capacity of the Indian to be equal to that of the White. There was comparable unanimity on the type of school best adapted to the work, the manual labor school. There the Indian child would be taught the rudiments of reading, writing, and arithmetic, but the main emphasis would be vocational. For the boys there would be agricultural instruction with some training with tools commonly found on farms and reservations. For girls, cooking, sewing, and other household skills, as well as dairying, would be stressed.

That instruction in Indian schools should be in English had been the government's clearly stated policy since 1880; however, it became a greater issue as the mission schools expanded their operations. Some church groups had hoped to minimize resistance to their missionary message by presenting it in the native tongues, and they carried the technique into their educational work. In mid-1887 Commissioner J.D.C. Atkins directed that instruction in all mission schools should be in English and followed a few months later with a threat to expel from reservations any mission schools failing to comply (Atkins

Smithsonian, NAA:86-5320.
Fig. 4. Indian police force, Pine Ridge Agency, Dak. Terr., with Chief of Police George Sword at left. A 50-member police force was first organized at Pine Ridge in 1879 by Agent Y.T. McGillycuddy (Hagan 1966:90). Photograph by C.G. Morledge, about 1890.

1887). Despite a furor, which included charges that the Commissioner had tried to prevent preaching the Gospel in the native tongues, Secretary of the Interior L.Q.C. Lamar and President Grover Cleveland upheld Atkins.

Another issue was the relative merits of boarding and day schools. Until the 1890s the boarding school advocates were far more numerous. Their argument was simple: if the education was to be effective the child must be separated from his family and tribal culture not six, but 24 hours a day. Carried to its logical conclusion this justified the off-reservation training schools of which the Carlisle School, in Pennsylvania, was the best example. The school term at Carlisle was first three years, and then extended to five, and the children did not return home even during vacation periods. Richard H. Pratt, the founder of Carlisle, developed the outing system by which the Indian child was placed with White families during summer vacation periods.

But the advocates of the day school, who argued that a system in which the child went from the schoolroom to his home every day would have an impact on the whole reservation, had economy on their side. The approximate costs of the two types of education were $150 per year per child for the boarding school versus $30 for a day school (ARCIA 1882: xli). For the off-reservation boarding schools there was the additional expense of transportation. Given the reluctance of Congress to meet even the educational provisions of treaties, the more expensive boarding schools met stiff opposition.

With the exception of $100,000 appropriated in the fiscal year 1870–1871, the only government money that had gone to Indian schools between 1860 and 1876 was that obligated by treaties. Fifty thousand Indians, exclusive of the Five Civilized Tribes for whom the government assumed no responsibility for education in this period, had no treaty provisions requiring government support of education. A number of tribes had income from funds created by land sales and assigned some of this money to the maintenance of their own school. Church and charity groups also helped. Nevertheless, probably less than 15 percent of the Indian children were in school in 1875.

During the next two years the last of the plains wars were fought, and the situation on the reservations stabilized. The government now turned its attention to its civilization programs. In 1876 Congress made the first of what would become annual appropriations for Indian education apart from support promised in treaties. The first appropriation was for only $20,000, but the amount grew steadily. It was $75,000 in 1880 and in 1886 had reached $1,000,000 (ARCIA 1900:44).

In 1878 the first Indian students had been enrolled at Hampton in Virginia. In 1879 Carlisle and in 1880 Forest Grove in Oregon opened as boarding schools (fig. 5). Establishment of the schools was financed largely by $500,000 derived from the sale of Osage lands in Kansas.

The success of Carlisle especially led to similar off-reservation institutions at Chilocco in Indian Territory, Genoa in Nebraska, and Haskell in Kansas, the last three all opening in 1884. Congress inhibited further moves in this direction by a rider on the 1886 appropriation bill (24 U.S. Stat. 44) limiting the amount that could be expended in building a boarding school to $10,000, about half of what had been required to build Chilocco, the smallest boarding school. Opponents of off-reservation boarding schools also were responsible for including in the same bill a provision (24 U.S. Stat. 45) that none of the funds the bill appropriated could be used in transporting Indian children to school off-reservation without the permission of their parents.

Government officials had hoped that churches would take an active role in educating the Indian. Even during the era of the Peace Policy there had not been the outpouring of private funds anticipated. Nevertheless, as Congress proved unwilling to meet even the treaty commitments on education, there would be greater dependence on parochial education than Indian Service personnel would have preferred. Generally the churches provided the buildings and selected the teachers and subsidized the entire operation to varying degrees. The government paid tuition for the students attending the boarding, or contract schools as they were called, and if the school were located among Indians drawing rations the school might receive these for its pupils, plus any clothing issued on an annuity basis. As a rule, day schools received only the rations and clothing. For both boarding and day schools sufficient acreage might be assigned them on the reservations for gardens, and sometimes for pastures if they kept herds of cattle.

By 1887 the government was making a real effort to put together an educational system for the Indians. Unfortunately, the effort was being made 20 years after the post-Civil War treaties had created the reservation system. The time period originally allotted to prepare the Indian for integration had nearly elapsed and very little had been accomplished in preparing the Indian for his new status. However, the reduction of his land holdings had proceeded on schedule.

The huge reservations created by the post-Civil War treaties with the Plains Indians had been conceived only as a temporary expedient. The assumption all along had been that these would be reduced in size as their Indian populations ceased to depend on hunting, finally to disappear completely as the individual Indian family settled on its own farm. However, the experience of the Potawatomi in Kansas and some Chippewas in Michigan with their individual allotments was discouraging. Most of these Indians sold their farms, usually at a fraction of their value, as soon as they secured a clear title to them. Leaving large areas to be held in common was not an acceptable solution as the government was under continuous pressure 59

top, Smithsonian, NAA:54, 543; bottom, Oreg. Histl. Soc., Portland:Orh 4456, 571.

Fig. 5. Off-reservation boarding schools. top, Indian students outside the Hampton Normal and Agricultural School, Hampton, Va. The students are posed with a variety of agricultural implements. The school at Hampton was a private institution, founded to serve Black students. The federal government paid a fee for each Indian student enrolled at the school. The students were further subsidized by private support. Arapahoe, Cheyenne, and Kiowa Indians who had been imprisoned in St. Augustine, Fla., were enrolled in Hampton by Lt. R.H. Pratt in May 1878. Photograph by Allen and Rowell, 1879. bottom, Blacksmithing class at the Training School for Indian Youth, Forest Grove, Oreg. Featuring industrial training, in 1882 Forest Grove enrolled 91 pupils from Oreg., Wash. Terr., and Alaska; the blacksmith shop, located in the town, had 7 apprentices and made a profit. The instructor, W.S. Hudson, furnished the buildings and a set of tools (ARCIA 1881:198, 1882:188, 190). Photographed in 1882.

HAGAN

from its White constituents to reduce Indian land holdings. The only politically practical solution was to continue with the reduction of Indian land holdings, but devise some way of ensuring that the Indians held on to the tract that would be allotted them as the reservation was dissolved. The Interior Department's answer was a bill introduced into Congress in 1879 to provide 160-acre allotments to Indian heads of families, and 80 acre allotments to unmarried adults, all allotments to carry patents inalienable for 25 years.

Bills with these basic provisions were before Congress for the next eight years, finally becoming law in 1887. The General Allotment Act (24 U.S. Stat. 338), or Dawes Severalty Act as it is frequently called after Massachusetts Sen. Henry L. Dawes, was important as a statement of general policy (Otis 1973). However, before 1887 Congress by legislation applicable to individual tribes was accomplishing the same end. The General Allotment Act made no provision for purchase of the surplus land after the allotment of a reservation, and after 1887 Congress continued to legislate to provide funds to make the surplus land available for White settlement.

The leasing of Indian land was another issue that the government had to resolve. The rise of the range cattle industry coincided with the creation of the reservations, and cattlemen were anxious to have access to their millions of acres of grasslands. Beginning in the late 1870s the first applications were made for grazing rights. Interior Department officials pled lack of authority to authorize such negotiations, but informal arrangements were made that tended to corrupt both tribal leadership and agency personnel.

The leasing of individual allotments, once these had been made to Indians, was opposed on the grounds that it encouraged idleness among them. Supposedly, exceptions were made only for children and those who for physical reasons were unable to work their allotments. In actual fact, the practice of able-bodied adults leasing their allotments to Whites was widespread.

1888–1900

In 1889 Commissioner Thomas J. Morgan reiterated what had been the policy of the United States since the Civil War: "The Indians must conform to 'the white man's ways,' peaceably if they will, forcibly if they must" (ARCIA 1889:3). The necessity for force arose only during the Ghost Dance revival of 1890–1891, but throughout the last 12 years of the nineteenth century the emphasis was on integration of the Indian into the rest of American society.

The principal reliance to achieve integration continued to be on education. The number of students enrolled in school gradually increased, although by 1900 the system still lacked accommodations for nearly one-quarter of the

Idaho State Histl. Soc., Boise.
Fig. 6. Surveying plats for allotment of land in severalty on the Nez Perce Reservation, Idaho. Anthropologist Alice C. Fletcher, left, who had lobbied for the passage of the Dawes Severalty Act, was special allotting agent on the reservation. She had served as allotting agent in Nebr. among the Omaha Indians 1883–1884 and among the Winnebago Indians 1887–1889 ("Alice Fletcher," this vol.). Photograph by E. Jane Gay, 1890–1893.

potential enrollment. This situation existed despite nearly $3,000,000 of a total appropriation of about $7,700,000 for the Indian Service being allotted to education (ARCIA 1900:44).

Reflecting the importance attributed to education was the action of Congress in 1891 (26 U.S. Stat. 1014) authorizing the commissioner of Indian affairs to enforce school attendance of Indian children. However, the policy first instituted in 1886 of requiring parental consent before children could be sent to schools in other states or territories remained in force.

Significant innovations in Indian education in 1890 were a uniform course of study and standardized textbooks. The following year President Benjamin Harrison placed school superintendents, assistant superintendents, teachers, and matrons under Civil Service.

Commissioner Morgan, who had led in these reforms, also opened an attack on sectarian education. Due to the reluctance of Congress to sufficiently expand the government's Indian school system, increasing reliance had been placed on the contract schools sponsored by church groups. By the early 1890s about one-fourth of the total appropriation for education was going to contract schools, and about two-thirds of this to schools operated by the Roman Catholic church. Amid rumors of a Catholic conspiracy to dominate Indian education, Congress in 1895 began a phased reduction of aid to contract schools.

By 1901 the contract system with church-related groups had come to an end. Mission schools continued to operate on reservations, but without direct federal aid.

Congressional opponents of appropriations for government Indian schools responded to pleas to expand the government's system by reminding Interior Department officials that their oft-stated objective was to blend the Indian with the general population. As early as 1890 the first contracts were made with local school districts to admit Indian students for whom the government would pay tuition. Despite relatively generous tuition payments, local prejudice against Indians led school districts to respond very slowly. A decade later only a few hundred Indian students were attending public schools at federal government expense.

While education programs for Indians lagged, the reduction of their land base continued as planned. For the small reservations where there was only enough land to allot a small farm to each of the reservation's inhabitants, the General Allotment Act of 1887 was generally relied upon. For the larger reservations, which after allotment produced a surplus of land to be purchased from the Indians and made available for settlement by Whites, additional legislation was required as the Interior Department had no funds for this purpose. The General Allotment Act specified that the reservation should be surveyed and allotted before any negotiations for the purchase of surplus land; therefore, special legislation had the additional advantage of speed. Large sections of reservation land could be acquired immediately for White exploitation, with survey and allotment of the remainder to the Indians to occur at a more leisurely pace.

As the Indians took their allotments they frequently—generally for some tribes—revealed no interest in cultivating them. As Whites clamored to have access to this land, Congress in 1891, as part of a law (26 U.S. Stat. 794) that amended the General Allotment Act of 1887, authorized leasing of the allotments for up to three years for farming and grazing, and up to 10 years for mining. The same law approved leasing of land the tribe continued to hold in common for no more than five years for grazing, and again for 10 years for mining. This law removed some of the ambiguity that had plagued the leasing of grasslands.

The Five Civilized Tribes had been specifically exempted from the General Allotment Act, but their day was coming. Since the 1860s government officials had been commenting on their holding land greatly in excess of their needs, as the officials had defined them. Several plans had been proposed that would have placed additional tribes among them, and it was clear that their unique status was to be of a temporary nature, despite all treaty pledges to the contrary.

In 1889 (25 U.S. Stat. 783) a federal court with limited jurisidiction was established in Indian Territory, the opening wedge. Congress also created the Cherokee Commission in 1889 (25 U.S. Stat. 1005) with the mission of negotiating with that tribe for their land west of 96° west longitude and with other tribes of the western part of Indian Territory. The next step was the organization in 1890 of the Territory of Oklahoma to include the area west of the Five Civilized Tribes. As Whites flooded into the new Territory, many others managed to swell the non-Indian population among the Five Civilized Tribes. The newcomers increased the agitation for the breakup of tribal governments and the allotment of Indian lands. To achieve these by negotiation, Congress in 1893 (27 U.S. Stat. 645) established the Dawes Commission, named for ex-Senator Dawes who served as its chairman for 10 years.

The Dawes Commission's proposals met considerable opposition, and its members countered by publicizing the inadequacies of the tribal governments. Despite the obvious resistance of most of the members of the Five Civilized Tribes to any change in their way of life, the government persisted in its efforts. By authorizing a survey of their land in 1895 (28 U.S. Stat. 900) and directing the next year that rolls of the tribal members be compiled (29 U.S. Stat. 339), both steps preliminary to allotment, Congress increased the pressure on the Indians. Four of the tribes submitted to negotiating agreements by which their lands would be allotted. The Cherokees were still holding out in 1898 when Congress passed the Curtis Act (30 U.S. Stat. 495), entitled, ironically, "An Act for the protection of the people of the Indian Territory, and for other purposes." This law provided for the dissolution of the tribal governments and authorized the allotment of their lands. It effectively ended any organized opposition to the Dawes Commission, although passive resistance by some Indians in the form of refusal to accept certificates of allotment continued for many years.

Despite its shabby record regarding Indian land, the government did improve the administration of Indian affairs in the last 12 years of the nineteenth century. President Benjamin Harrison's executive order in 1891 brought under Civil Service not only the positions in the Indian school service but also physicians. In 1894 President Grover Cleveland included assistant teachers and in 1896 extended Civil Service to encompass agency clerks and storekeepers. At the same time Indians were exempted from Civil Service examination for some of the less responsible positions, as part of the general policy of trying to fill more positions in the Indian Service with Indians.

Agents had not been placed under Civil Service, and in 1892 Congress (27 U.S. Stat. 120) directed that the president should fill vacancies as they occurred with army officers unless he believed a civilian were preferable. Under President Cleveland almost half of the nearly 60 agents were army officers. The number declined under President William McKinley and of 15 serving as agents when the Spanish-American War began, 11 were recalled to active duty.

Despite the many statements by officials of the desirability of reducing the number of agents, thus reducing administrative costs, it proved difficult to do so. In 1888 there were 62 agents and for the period 1893–1900 it did not drop below 56. As reservations were dissolved by allotment, Interior Department officials now argued that agents were needed to advise and counsel Indians in this critical period of their careers. And if the Interior Department considered it safe to dispense with an agent, the member of Congress controlling the patronage, or the community that saw a threatened loss of income if an agency were dismantled could be counted on to oppose the move.

An 1893 law (27 U.S. Stat. 614) that permitted an agent's duties to be transferred to the reservation's school superintendent only resulted in a change of nomenclature rather than a reduction of personnel. The administrative head of the agency would be entitled superintendent rather than agent, even though the agency's school might have been closed.

The economy-minded enjoyed more success in reducing the level of subsistence support of the Indians. However, as late as 1900 the government was spending over a million dollars on their rations, about half of it for the Sioux (fig. 7) (ARCIA 1900:5–8). As even for the Sioux this did not provide a full ration, there were charges that the government was permitting Indians to starve. Government officials responded by claiming that the treaties of the post-Civil War period promised rations only

until the Indians could support themselves and that it was unreasonable to expect that over a quarter-century later this aid should be continued.

Although increasingly reluctant to feed Indians in the 1890s, while moving with indecent haste to deprive them of most of their land, the government in some respects did take seriously its role as guardian of the Indians. While it was impossible to withstand pressures for a general reduction in Indian land holdings, Interior Department officials in individual instances did help block legislation that would have worsened the Indian's plight even more, or they protected particular reservations from invasion by Whites (fig. 8). Had it not been for the Interior Department, for example, bills might have become law that would have opened all reservations to prospectors, and would have permitted the state of Washington to terminate at will the nonalienable feature of allotments in that state (Noble 1892). Potentially the most damaging to the Indian tribes, if the Interior Department had collaborated with them, were the thousands of claimants for damages resulting from Indian depredations.

By 1875 claims totaling nearly $10,000,000 had been filed (E.P. Smith 1875), and by 1892 the amount had reached $25,000,000 (Noble 1892a). Of these, some were disallowed for lack of evidence to substantiate them, others were held to be highly inflated. Nor would the government investigators condone claims for consequential or indirect damages.

Congress in 1872 (17 U.S. Stat. 190) had provided that no claims could be paid unless money were specifically

Denver Pub. Lib., Western Hist. Dept., Colo.:F8945

Fig. 7. Ration day. Sioux women wait in line to collect rations at the commissary on the Pine Ridge Reservation, S. Dak. Photograph by C.C. Morledge, probably July 1891.

appropriated for that purpose. The procedure was for the secretary of the interior to report to Congress for payment the ones it judged valid. Up to 1891 Congress had paid $434,570 to claimants with some of the money being deducted from funds payable to the tribes involved. In 1891 (26 U.S. Stat. 851) the jurisdiction over the depredations cases was transferred to the Court of Claims. Fortunately, the statute provided that Indian funds needed for "current and necessary support, subsistence, and education" could not be drawn upon. The Court of Claims also narrowly defined the grounds on which it would recognize claims as valid, thus heading off what could have been judgments that could have completely absorbed the $24,000,000 in trust funds held for the Indians by the government.

As the nineteenth century drew to a close the government was pursuing an Indian policy that had been remarkably consistent since the Civil War. Originally conceived as a peaceful way of facilitating American expansion into the areas controlled in the 1860s by the nomadic tribes, it had stressed negotiation for rights-of-way and gradual reduction of Indian land holdings. In parallel developments the Indian was to be led to abandon hunting for farming and grazing while his children were educated in preparation for citizenship and integration into American society. Negotiation had to be supplemented by force, and Congress had been unwilling to adequately ration the Indians in the critical transition period or support at the level necessary the Indian school system. The Indians themselves tenaciously resisted efforts to absorb them into the larger society. In only one respect, the acquisition of Indian land, had the government's policy achieved its goals.

Sources

For the study of United States national policies, 1860–1900, the best primary sources are the published reports of the Commissioners of Indian Affairs (ARCIA), the collections in the National Archives, and the *Congressional Record*.

The published reports of the Commissioner of Indian Affairs are most readily available in the Congressional Serial Set. Each report contains the commissioner's

Fig. 8. Northern Cheyenne Indians meeting with Brig. Gen. Nelson A. Miles (seated at desk, face in shadow) at Tongue River Agency, Lame Deer, Mont. Two Moon is seated under the shelter, and Lt. Edward W. Casey is standing behind him. The Indians were concerned about local Whites, who coveted their land and hoped for Indian removal. The agent, R.H. Upshaw, appealed to General Miles for assistance in evaluating whether it was in the Cheyenne's best interest to remain on the reservation (ARCIA 1889:236–237). In Oct. 1890 General Miles headed a commission investigating Cheyenne grievances (Weist 1977:141). Photograph by Christian Barthelmess, 1889.

assessment of the current Indian situation as well as any suggested changes in policy and the legislation that would be required to carry them into effect. Although the material is frequently repetitious, and designed to put the best possible face on Indian conditions, the reports are excellent summaries of government policy.

Of the files in the National Archives the two most important for an overview of Indian policy are the Report Books of the Commissioner of Indian Affairs, Record Group 75, and the Letters Sent volumes of the Indian Division of the Office of the Secretary of the Interior, Record Group 48. These contain the correspondence between the Commissioner and the Secretary, and as the former had to seek the approval of the latter for any action of consequence their value is obvious.

As the ultimate voice in establishing policy, due to its control of funds, Congress's role must be followed carefully. Much of the crucial work was done in committee and is not always available to the researcher, but the debates and the votes on the annual appropriation bills are to be found in the *Congressional Record.*

Essential reference works are those by Cohen (1982) and Kappler (1904–1941). Cohen traces the development of a body of Indian law. Kappler's five volumes include the text of laws enacted by Congress and of the treaties with the tribes. Otis (1973) discusses the intentions and results of the Dawes Severalty Act.

For secondary works for the period 1865–1890, consult the bibliographies by Prucha (1977, 1982). The pertinent chapters in Prucha's (1984) two-volume survey of United States Indian policy also provide a good general account of the period. Priest (1942) outlines reform in Indian policy 1865–1887.

The military operations against the Indians are best summarized by Utley (1973). Dunlay (1982) discusses the vital role played by Indian auxiliaries of the United States Army.

The formation of the policies that produced these wars has received the attention it merits. Prucha (1976) traces the role of reformers in shaping these policies 1865–1890. Hagan (1985) covers the first two decades of the most influential of the reform organizations, the Indian Rights Association. The role for church groups provided in the administration of President Grant is dealt with by Keller (1983). An account of Commissioner Ely S. Parker has been provided by William H. Armstrong (1978). Kvasnic-ka and Viola (1979) edited a collection of biographical sketches of all the commissioners of Indian affairs.

For developments in policy late in the nineteenth century, a good source is Hoxie (1984). Prucha (1979) has addressed the controversial subject of the disputes between Protestants and Catholics over the subject of Indian

education. For a general treatment of Indian boarding schools, see David Wallace Adams (1975). Gilcreast (1967) has the best account of Carlisle Indian School and its founder.

Miner and Unrau (1978), Milner (1982), White (1983), and Debo (1940) address the impact of Indian policy on groups of tribes. Miner and Unrau recount the ordeal of the Indians of Kansas under pressure from the United States to reduce their land holdings in that state, or leave it entirely. Milner examines the stewardship of Quaker agents appointed to preside over the Pawnees, Otos, and Omahas. The Pawnees, together with the Choctaws and Navajos, also are the subjects of White who traces the decline of their aboriginal subsistence systems. Debo portrays the tragic history of the Five Civilized Tribes as they struggled to recover from the devastation of the Civil War only to find their tribal governments under assault from the federal government.

The success or failure of policies conceived in Washington depended to a considerable extent on the abilities of the Indian agents charged with execution of these policies. Seymour (1941) provides sketches of several of the best known agents. Tatum (1899) and E.E. White (1965) are accounts by individuals who were members of the Indian Service. Practically all agents testified to the help they received from the police and court systems instituted in the 1870s and 1880s, which have been studied by Hagan (1966). The influential Meriam (1928) report on the economic and social condition of Indians submitted to the secretary of the interior is essential reading.

The best way to reach a judgment about the efficacy of United States policy is to follow its impact on a particular tribe in one of the detailed studies. Virtually all the major tribes have been the subject of histories. Berthrong's (1963, 1976) two volumes on the Southern Cheyennes are models of conventional scholarship. P.J. Powell (1979) has made a commendable effort to employ the usual sources, but to present the history of the Northern Cheyennes from their perspective. Ewers (1958) traces the Blackfoot. Meyer (1967) is the historian of the Santee Sioux, the Indians best known for their clash with Whites in Minnesota in 1862. Olson (1965) approached the story of the Oglala Sioux through the life of one of their chiefs, Red Cloud, who played a prominent role on the Plains in the late nineteenth century. Utley (1963) follows the Sioux from the late nineteenth century. The Chickasaws, one of the Five Civilized Tribes, are fortunate in their historian, Arrell M. Gibson (1971). And Baird (1980) deftly sketches the story of the Quapaws, one of the smaller groups that shared Indian Territory with the Five Civilized Tribes. These are just a sampling of the wealth of tribal studies available.

United States Indian Policies, 1900–1980

LAWRENCE C. KELLY

The evolution of federal Indian policy in the twentieth century may be divided into three distinct time periods. The period from 1900 to 1921 is characterized by the continuation and culmination of the forced assimilation philosophy embodied in the Dawes Severalty Act of 1887. Beginning in 1921 this philosophy came under increasing attack as studies began to reveal the widespread poverty and demoralization that were the true legacy of the land allotment program. Between 1921 and 1947 the individualization of tribal lands and the philosophy of forced assimilation were both gradually modified and then overturned by legislation passed during the New Deal era. Cultural pluralism, with its emphasis upon the preservation and intensification of the Indian heritage, replaced assimilation as the goal of federal policy. In 1947 the argument that Indians would have to be forced to accept the benefits of American civilization was again asserted, and since that time the rival philosophies of forced assimilation and cultural pluralism have alternately controlled the federal decision-making bodies. Beginning in the late 1960s the forces of cultural pluralism once again became dominant in government circles.

1900–1921

Land Allotment and Land Alienation

Although the published records of the Bureau of Indian Affairs are not always reliable and there are frequently contradictions in the statistics published from year to year, it appears that in the years between 1887 and 1900 approximately 32,800 allotments of Indian land, covering 3,285,000 acres, were made. During this same period the federal government forced the cession or sale of approximately 28,500,000 acres of "surplus land" from tribes that were in the process of being allotted. The cession of these lands was, of course, the primary purpose behind the allotment program, for once the Indians were settled on their allotments the remainder of their former reservations could be opened to White settlement. Most of the land cessions in this period occurred in the areas of greatest White interest: the Chippewa areas of Wisconsin and Minnesota, the Sioux country of North and South Dakota, and the Indian lands in central and western Oklahoma

Territory. Most of the allotments also occurred in these areas although sizable numbers of Indians in Oregon, Washington, Nebraska, Montana, and Idaho were also allotted prior to 1900 (ARCIA 1890:38, 1891:43–44, 1912:131–134, 1916:93–99).

From the turn of the century to 1921 an additional 85,860 allotments were made in areas other than Oklahoma. These allotments covered approximately 14,300,000 acres and in addition, outright cessions totaling more than 20,000,000 acres were negotiated. Ninety percent of the land cessions and slightly more than 60 percent of the allotments made during this period occurred during the years from 1900 to 1910 when the movement to break up the reservations reached its peak. During this same 10-year period an additional 101,239 allotments were issued to the enrolled members of the Five Civilized Tribes in eastern Oklahoma who had originally been exempted from the provisions of the Dawes Severalty Act. However, not all these allotments were issued to persons of Indian blood. In addition to 75,340 Indians, allotments were given to 25,888 "intermarried Whites" and "freedmen" (former Black slaves owned by members of the Five Civilized Tribes). The allotment of Indian Territory individualized approximately 15,800,000 acres and released another 3,500,000 acres for later sale. The allotments made in the period 1900–1921 were principally in Oklahoma, the Dakotas, Minnesota, Montana, Wyoming, Idaho, Washington, Oregon, and northern California (ARCIA 1912:131–134, 1915:35–36, 1916:93–99, 1920: 168).

At the same time that the federal government was implementing the allotment policy among reservation Indians, efforts were being made to supply nonreservation Indians with land allotments on the public domain. By 1920 some 8,776 allotments totaling 1,261,586 acres had been awarded to Indians with no legal claim to reservation lands. While Indians in all the western states benefitted from this action, most of the public domain allotments went to Mission Indians in California, the Turtle Mountain group of Chippewa in North Dakota, and the Navajos in New Mexico and Arizona (ARCIA 1915:90–93, 1920: 82).

Major Legislation

The trend of legislation in the period 1900–1921 was in the direction of liberalizing the original provisions of the Dawes Act in order to speed up land transfers from Indian to White hands. The process was most evident in the cases of the Five Civilized Tribes where, as a result of their fee simple title to the lands of the former Indian Territory, there was relatively little surplus land to be sold after allotment.

In 1901, as preparation for allotment and for the admission of Oklahoma Territory to statehood, the enrolled members of the Five Civilized Tribes were declared citizens of the United States (31 U.S. Stat. 1447). In 1904, when many of the allotments in this area had been confirmed and delivered, restrictions on the sale of allotted lands of the Five Civilized Tribes were lifted for the intermarried Whites and the freedmen who were presumed to be competent to handle their own affairs. Two years later, the former Indian Territory tribal governments that had been ordered to dissolve in 1906 were extended, but they were effectively deprived of any real power by a declaration that all their actions were invalid unless approved by the president of the United States. This act of 1906 (34 U.S. Stat. 137–43) also authorized the president to remove the executive officers of the tribes at will and to appoint replacements without the consent of the tribe, authorized the BIA to take control of all schools formerly operated by the tribes, forbade the alienation of full-blood allotments for 25 years, and instructed the secretary of the interior to provide for the speedy disposition of all affairs of the Five Civilized Tribes. Dissatisfied at the slowness with which Indian lands were being alienated and sympathetic to the demands of the new state of Oklahoma that Indian lands be removed from their tax-exempt status, Congress in 1908 passed a sweeping revision of previous legislation relating to alienation of Indian land titles in the former Indian Territory.

By the act of May 7, 1908 (35 U.S. Stat. 312), Congress removed the restrictions on all lands of Indians of less than one-half Indian blood who were members of the Five Civilized Tribes and it also removed the restrictions on all lands except the 40-acre homesteads of Indians of one-half or more but less than three-fourths Indian blood. As a result of the acts of 1904 and 1908 more than 8,000,000 acres of land became subject to Oklahoma taxes, and federal restraints on the alienation of these lands were removed. After 1908 only the lands of approximately 36,000 members of the Five Civilized Tribes remained under restrictions. The protection afforded by these restrictions was more often imaginary than real because the 1908 law placed both the person and the property of minor allottees under the control of the probate courts of Oklahoma rather than the control of the federal government.

Legislation passed in this period for the Five Civilized Tribes was representative of the trend of legislation passed for other Indians. In one way or another most of the acts passed by Congress between 1900 and 1921 provided for the transfer of Indian lands to White ownership. In 1902 Congress approved a bill dealing with the disposition of lands, the allotted owner of which had died before his trust period expired and before a patent-in-fee had been granted him. Under the terms of this act (32 U.S. Stat. 245), the land could be sold with the permission of the secretary of the interior and the proceeds distributed among the allottees' heirs. The justification given for selling the land was that from the proceeds of the sale the heirs would be enabled to amass enough capital to improve their own allotments. The necessity for raising capital for land improvements, so freely acknowledged by this act, highlighted one of the major criticisms of the Dawes Act that would be made in the years after 1921: the failure of the federal government to make available to allotted Indians the financial resources necessary for their economic survival. Like the Radical Republicans of the 1860s who failed to provide newly freed slaves with the means to better themselves materially, so the reformers of the 1880s would be charged with failing to provide for the economic betterment of the Indians whom they had "freed" from what they considered to be the nonprogressive controls of tribal life. By 1920 another 1,373,000 acres of land passed from Indian to White hands under the provisions of this act and although several commissioners of Indian affairs fought to slow the pace of land sales, their efforts were largely unsuccessful (ARCIA 1920:169).

In 1906, as a result of 19 years of experience with the Dawes Act and in recognition of the fact that its original provisions had not always worked to the advantage of the Indians, major modifications were proposed. The resulting Burke Act (34 U.S. Stat. 182) contained several important clauses. First, it proposed to make all Indian lands allotted after May 8, 1906, subject to federal rather than state controls during the 25-year trust period. (Two purposes lay behind this provision: to protect Indians from harmful state laws of descent and partition during the trust period and to make possible better enforcement of federal liquor prohibition laws on Indian lands.) Second, the president of the United States was authorized to extend the trust period beyond 25 years for those Indians not deemed capable of administering their own affairs. Third, citizenship, which had originally been granted with allotment, was to be postponed until the expiration of the trust period and the grant of a patent-in-fee. Fourth, the secretary of the interior was empowered to remove restrictions on allotted lands prior to the expiration of the trust period in those instances where an allottee petitioned for removal and the secretary determined that he was "competent" to handle his own affairs (fig. 1). In recognition of the increased federal responsibility for

Indians during the trust period that the Burke Act conveyed, legislation was passed in 1910 (36 U.S. Stat. 855) giving the secretary of the interior sole authority over the lands of allottees who died prior to receiving a patent-in-fee. This law also made the secretary responsible for determining the heirs of such Indians who died without wills, thus greatly increasing the legal work of the department.

Although the Burke Act was designed both to protect the noncompetent Indian and to speed up the removal of restrictions on those who were competent, the definition of competence was left largely to the discretion of the commissioner of Indian affairs. Commissioner Francis Leupp, who wrote in 1906 that "the legislation of recent years shows conclusively that the country is demanding an end of the Indian question, and it is right," welcomed the act as a means for releasing Indians from federal controls (ARCIA 1906:30). During his administration, 1905–1909, almost all petitions for the removal of restrictions were granted. His successor, Robert G. Valentine, discovered that many of the petitioners during Leupp's administration had been duped by land speculators who subsequently obtained control of the Indian lands for a pittance. Under Valentine, more stringent regulations were adopted and the number of patents-in-fee that were issued declined. But in 1917, Commissioner Cato Sells, who believed that the assimilation of the Indians had been delayed overly long, again applied a more liberal interpretation to competency and thereby opened the floodgates to the removal of restrictions on Indian lands. In the period 1907–1920, 32,150 patents-in-fee were issued under the Burke Act, and restrictions on the sale of 4,213,000 acres were removed (ARCIA 1920:172). No figures exist to determine how many of these acres passed from Indian control, but in 1921 Commissioner Charles Burke, who had authored by law 15 years earlier, applied the brakes to its use and wrote that "experience shows that more than two-thirds of the Indians who have received patents-in-fee have been unable or unwilling to cope with the business acumen coupled with the selfishness and greed of the more competent whites, and in many instances have lost every acre they had" (ARCIA 1921:25).

In 1907 the last major piece of legislation dealing with the alienation of Indian lands was passed (34 U.S. Stat. 1015). By the provisions of this act, Indians who were too old, sick, disabled, or "incompetent" to develop their allotted lands were permitted to sell them and to use the money obtained to better provide for their needs. From 1908 to 1920 another 720,000 acres of land passed from Indian to White control under the provisions of this act (ARCIA 1920:169).

Administration of Federal Policy

Following the passage of the Burke Act in 1906 there was

Fig. 1. Allotment officer Charles A. Bates (center) taking information from Chief American Horse, Oglala Sioux (right), at Pine Ridge Reservation, S. Dak. Billy Garnett, half-Sioux and an official interpreter, U.S. Indian Service, is at left. Pine Ridge Reservation, established in 1868, consisted of 2,721,597 acres. Allotment, which took place 1904–1916, divided the reservation into 8,275 individual tracts that accounted for 2,380,195 acres. Another 182,653 acres were classified as surplus and sold to the government, and 146,633 acres remained tribal land (Fey and McNickle 1959:75–76). Photograph probably by Edward Truman, 1907.

a marked trend away from solving the "Indian problem" by means of legislation. Instead, Congress sought to increase the discretionary powers of the secretary of the interior and the commissioner of Indian affairs. Although each of the commissioners during this period demonstrated sympathy for his Indian wards, each was also firmly wedded to the philosophy of forced assimilation and the allotment of Indian lands. As a result, no efforts were made to halt the gradual disintegration of Indian culture that resulted from the dissolution of Indian tribal lands and governments.

Instead, the emphasis of administrative officers during these early years of the twentieth century was upon what they called "industrial assistance" to the Indians: better methods of leasing Indian lands; improved methods of farming, stock raising, and irrigation; the development of off-reservation job opportunities; and controlled cutting of Indian timber lands. In short, the emphasis was upon the Indian's property rather than his person. Increasingly greater emphasis was also placed upon improving Indian health and sanitation, education, and enforcement of the liquor prohibition laws. In all of these areas, significant improvements were made.

Since the passage of the first act permitting the leasing of Indian allotted lands in 1891, every subsequent commissioner of Indian affairs protested against the leasing principle on the ground that it prevented the Indians from developing their own land. However, so widespread had the principle become by the beginning of the twentieth century that each administration found itself administering a vast estate in behalf of Indians who were attempting to live off their rentals. It was Commissioner Valentine who made the first effective move to cope with this problem, when in 1910 he inaugurated the system of sealed bids administered directly by the commissioner's office instead of by the local superintendent. Not only did he dramatically increase the Indians' revenue from leasing, but also the increased cost of leasing reduced the desire of Whites to use the Indians' land. Commissioner Sells, a Texas banker, further reduced the evils of the leasing system through his successful efforts to encourage Indians to develop their own herds. Recognizing that the Indians' basic problem was a lack of capital with which to purchase blooded stock and to develop their pastures, Sells succeeded in persuading Congress to appropriate large amounts of "reimbursable loans," which enabled Indians to effectively utilize their own lands. As a result, the leasing of Indian lands in stock raising country decreased considerably during this period. Although Sells also attempted to encourage Indian farming through the use of land improvement and implement loans, his efforts in this area were less successful.

Irrigation on Indian lands also received increasing attention after 1900. This was principally occasioned by two factors. First, there was the necessity of providing water on the allotments in the Pacific Northwest and the Rocky Mountain areas (the regions in which the allotment work was concentrated after 1910) if the Indians were to become self-sufficient through farming. Second, after 1910 there was a very real necessity to utilize water rights if the Indians were not to lose them to Whites who, since the passage of the Reclamation Act in 1902, had begun to develop large-scale irrigation projects that drew heavily on waters previously used only by Indians. Millions of dollars, many of them from Indian tribal funds and others from reimbursable appropriations, were poured into these irrigation projects; however, except on the Yakima Reservation the results were disappointing. Most of the allottees refused to farm their irrigated allotments with the result that they were leased to Whites. Others found themselves saddled with discouraging obligations to repay the reimbursable debts on which Congress decreed in 1921 payment must soon begin. However, despite the failure of most of these irrigation projects, the efforts of the federal government to protect Indian title to water flowing through their reservations did result in the important *Winters* v. *United States* decision in 1908. The Supreme Court ruled that Whites adjacent to the Fort Belknap Reservation in Montana could not reduce the quantity of water flowing into the reservation through the construction of dams and reservoirs upstream. Little noticed at the time, this case was cited as the chief defense of Indian water rights in the West (202 U.S. Stat. 564).

Education and health services also became areas of major concern during this period. Although the great growth in Indian schools occurred prior to 1900, important changes in educational method took place after the turn of the century. Medical and health services, almost totally ignored in the nineteenth century, received increasing attention after 1909.

It was Commissioner W.A. Jones who first launched the attack on the boarding school system of Indian education in 1901, when he wrote "the present system, taken as a whole, is not calculated to produce the results so earnestly claimed for it and so hopefully anticipated when it was begun" (ARCIA 1901:1). The boarding schools, Jones went on, were not only expensive to maintain, but also their curriculum was elitist and totally unsuited to the realities of everyday Indian life. Moreover, by supplying Indians with all the necessities of life while they attended school, the boarding schools were actually increasing Indian dependence upon the federal government, rather than making them self-sufficient. Jones called for a shift of emphasis from the nonreservation boarding schools to small reservation boarding schools and day schools, a reform that his successor Francis Leupp enthusiastically enforced. Branding the government boarding schools "simply educational almshouses," Leupp began to close them down at the same time that he launched a spirited campaign to construct day schools throughout the Indian country in an effort "to carry civilization to the Indian [rather than] carry the Indian to civilization" (ARCIA 1907:21–22). Beginning in 1910, Commissioner Valentine shifted the educational emphasis away from federally controlled schools altogether. Through contracts with local school districts he sought to have Indian children in relatively populous areas attend school with their White neighbors. Valentine also ordered the government schools to adopt the curriculum of the public schools in their area. By 1912 there were more Indian pupils in public schools than in government schools, and after 1915 the number of government schools and the number of children enrolled in government schools began slowly to decline (ARCIA 1920:156).

It was not until 1907 that the federal government became concerned about the need for health care and medical facilities among the Indians. In that year the first comprehensive survey of Indian health was conducted; tuberculosis and trachoma were identified as the major diseases among Indians. In 1909 Congress voted a special appropriation to combat these diseases and at the same time it began gradually to increase the total health budget, which in 1905 had stood at only $122,000. By 1921 the annual health appropriation had increased to $375,000, a significant percentage increase, but a figure obviously far below the actual medical needs of Indians.

In 1917 Commissioner Sells announced a far-reaching policy decision that was designed to reduce the number of Indians under federal guardianship. Under this "New Policy," all adult Indians of one-half or less Indian blood were to be declared competent under the provisions of the Burke Act and given complete control of their property, including the right to sell it. All students who received diplomas from government schools, upon reaching age 21, would also be declared competent. The act of 1902, providing for the disposition of inherited land and the act of 1907 that governed the alienation of land belonging to sick, old, and disabled Indians, were henceforth to be interpreted more "liberally"; that is, restrictions on the sale of such lands to Whites would be removed. The time had come, Sells believed, to force many Indians to fend for themselves. During the years 1917–1920 over 21,000 Indians were released from federal protection, their lands patented and made subject to local taxes (ARCIA 1917: 3–4, 1920:40).

As a result of the New Policy and the decision to force patents upon Indians who had not requested them, a lively debate over the future of federal Indian policy commenced. Commissioner Burke, who succeeded Sells in 1921, quickly decided that the New Policy was generally harmful to the Indians and suspended its application. His decision was criticized by many western congressmen who wished to go beyond Sells's criteria for competency and to "emancipate" all allottees of any degree of Indian blood who had received an education comparable to that of White children who had completed the seventh grade. Although Burke successfully resisted congressional pressures to remove restrictions on additional numbers of Indians, the desire to end federal controls over the Indians remained strong throughout his administration.

1921–1947

Albert B. Fall and the Genesis of Reform

The appointment of Albert B. Fall as secretary of the interior in 1921 marked the beginning of a new era in federal Indian policy. Except for his willingness to permit Commissioner Burke to halt the forced application of the New Policy, Fall was in every other way an advocate of terminating federal responsibility over the Indians. During his eight years as senator from New Mexico (1913–1921), Fall frequently advocated the application of the Dawes Act to the Indians of the Southwest whose large nontaxable reservations, he believed, were retarding the economic development of that region. Each time he was defeated by Commissioner Sells who argued that the semiarid lands of the Southwest were not susceptible of supporting the Indians if allotted and that the Indians had not been sufficiently educated to protect themselves.

In the years 1922–1923 Fall introduced or supported four bills that would have greatly impaired Indian property rights, particularly in the Southwest. One of these dealt with a property dispute between Pueblo Indians and White settlers along the Rio Grande that, if passed, would have virtually assured the loss of Indian lands and water rights without compensation, thus possibly threatening the survival of the Pueblo culture. A second bill provided for the allotment in severalty of the Mescalero Apache reservation and the creation of a new national park from a portion of the reservation. The third bill, which applied to all Indians except the Osage and the Five Civilized Tribes, would have given the secretary of the interior power to appraise the value of all remaining tribal properties, to distribute among competent Indians a pro rata share of the tribal wealth, and then to sever these Indians from further federal responsibility. The fourth bill would have opened all Indian reservations created by executive order (as opposed to treaty) to oil development under a complicated plan that would permit the state and the Department of the Interior Bureau of Reclamation to share equally with the Indians in any oil royalties. Since these bills applied mainly to the nonallotted, reservation Indians of Arizona and New Mexico whose cultures had recently become the subject of considerable interest to anthropologists, artists, and conservationists, opposition quickly developed to Fall's plans. The bills were finally defeated in 1924 after a long and bitter conflict between Fall and the pro-Indian groups. The Indian defense groups that had opposed the bills soon launched a vigorous attack on the assimilationist philosophy and the land-allotment system.

Of the various Indian rights societies active in the 1920s, the most vigorous and the most trenchant in its criticisms of federal policy was the American Indian Defense Association. Composed essentially of a very small group of wealthy, liberally oriented individuals from California, the Association received its motive power from its executive secretary, John Collier. A former community organization worker in New York City, Collier concluded in the aftermath of World War I that western civilization was destroying itself and threatening the survival of the rest of the world because of its emphasis on individualism and materialism. Searching for an alternative value system, Collier had discovered in Pueblo society a culture that he believed superior to that of western civilization (Collier 1963:93, 123). Thus, when Fall threatened the economic survival of the Pueblos, Collier quickly joined the opposition. In October 1922 he enunciated the basic goals of the reform program that he and the American Indian Defense Association were to pursue throughout the remainder of the decade: recognition of the Indian right to basic civil liberties; conservation of the remaining Indian reservations through communal and corporate enterprise; the preservation of Indian cultures and societies; and the extension of federal assistance to Indian communities in the form of Farm Loan Bank credits, Department of Agriculture advice and assistance programs, and public health services (Collier 1922:15–20, 63, 66). After the defeat of the Pueblo bill and adoption of a compromise plan basically formulated by Collier, the American Indian Defense Association was formed in 1923 and Collier was charged with the responsibility of securing further reforms of federal Indian policy.

Broadening of the Reform Movement

During the 1920s the only significant Indian legislation was the Indian Citizenship Act of 1924 (43 U.S. Stat. 253). It was during this decade that the first effective challenges to basic Indian legislation since the passage of the Dawes Act were made.

In organizing the resistance to the bill for the settlement of the Pueblo-White land problem, Collier created the All-Pueblo Council to demonstrate the ability of Indians to defend their rights and to organize effectively as a political entity. Throughout the 1920s, despite repeated attempts by the BIA to dissolve the Council, it stubbornly maintained its independence from government controls and served as a symbol of the potential for Indian self-government (fig.2). In time, citing the All-Pueblo Council as an example of Indian capability, Collier and

other reformers began to denounce federal prohibitions against tribal governments and to demand the reinstatement of limited powers of self-government for the tribes.

In 1922–1924 Collier raised the issue of Indian religious freedom when he clashed repeatedly with Commissioner Burke on the issue of enrolling Pueblo Indian children in distant boarding schools and on the right of Indians to hold certain religious ceremonials. Burke, who was misled on the content of the dances by zealous Protestant church groups opposed to any continuation of Indian customs and who was keenly interested in enrolling all Indian children in government schools because of criticism that the government had not kept its promises to the Indians in the area of education, blundered repeatedly in his handling of the religious issue. As a result, although Collier greatly exaggerated the charges of religious persecution, he was able to arouse considerable sympathy for removing administrative restraints on the practice of native religions.

By 1925, mainly as a result of Collier's work, the reform movement launched an attack on the government's handling of Indian property and tribal funds. In several instances, most notably in the case of a bridge built across the Colorado River in Arizona, they were able to demonstrate that Congress had been levying debts against Indian tribal funds, without Indian consent, through the use of the reimbursable debts inaugurated during the Sells administration. Many of the administrative expenses of

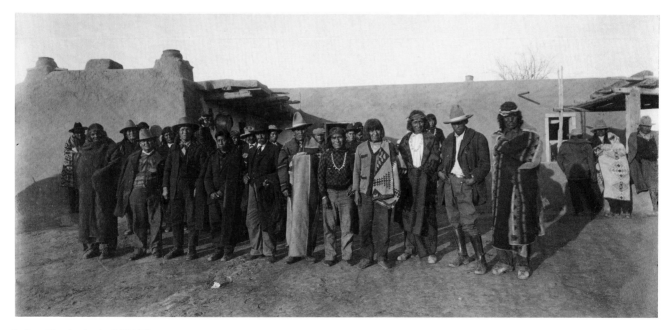

Southwest Mus., Los Angeles, Calif: 24912.
Fig. 2. Governors of the All-Pueblo Council, Santo Domingo, N. Mex., Dec. 10, 1926. A lobbying organization without formal powers, the All-Pueblo Council provided an opportunity for inter-Pueblo communication on issues pertaining to Pueblo-White relations (Spicer 1962:173, 180). When this photograph was made the All-Pueblo Council was meeting on pending federal legislation that seriously threatened Indian religious freedom and the right to self-government. The bill, introduced by Representative Scott Leavitt on behalf of Commissioner of Indian Affairs Charles H. Burke, would have made Indians subject to all federal and civil criminal laws and abolish marriages or divorces formed by Indian custom. Indian courts, with judges selected by superintendents, would have jurisdiction over other offenses. Collier, who organized the meeting, also encouraged the All-Pueblo Council to refrain from joining the BIA-formed U.S. Pueblo Indian Council (Philp 1977:65–69). A constitution for the All-Pueblo Council was signed by 19 Pueblo governors at Santo Domingo on Oct. 19, 1965. Photograph by Charles F. Lummis.

UNITED STATES INDIAN POLICIES, 1900–1980

the BIA were also shown to have come from Indian tribal funds. As a result of these exposures, Congress in 1932 (47 U.S. Stat. 564) authorized the secretary of the interior to adjust or to abolish most of the debts outstanding against Indian tribal funds.

Following the defeat of the bill to open executive order reservations to oil development under terms favorable to the states and harmful to the Indians on whose lands oil might be discovered, Secretary Fall issued an order to this same effect and then resigned from office. In 1927, after a prolonged struggle, the Indian right to all royalties and Indian title to all executive order reservations were upheld (44 U.S. Stat. 1347).

Meriam Report and the Senate Investigation

As a result of the controversy aroused by Secretary Fall's actions, his successor Hubert Work assembled in Washington in 1923 a blue ribbon committee of advisors to assist the government in its execution of federal policy. In general, this "Committee of 100" gave its support to the assimilationist philosophy although it did counsel increased respect for Indian customs and traditions and urged the government to take steps to better protect Indian property. However, the mounting crescendo of reform against federal Indian policy led by Collier forced the administration again to seek outside counsel in 1926. In that year the BIA requested the highly respected and nonpolitical Brookings Institution to undertake a thorough review of federal policy and to make recommendations for its improvement. In early 1928 *The Problem of Indian Administration* (Meriam 1928), popularly known as the Meriam report, was submitted to the secretary of the interior. Much to the surprise of the administration and to reformers like Collier who feared that it would whitewash the BIA, the Meriam report was highly critical of federal policy.

The Dawes Act was severely condemned as a means of separating the Indians from their property. It was labled an obvious failure from the standpoint of Indian welfare, and an immediate halt to the allotment of Indian lands was urged. The BIA was criticized for its misplaced emphasis on Indian property rather than on the person of the Indian. To protect both Indian property and Indian people from further ravages, the Meriam report urged the incorporation of the tribes and the granting of limited powers of decision to Indian tribal councils or business organizations. It urged a large increase in appropriations for Indian health and educational programs, and it urged especially "a change in the point of view" of the government's educational program. Specifically, it called for an end to the enrollment of preadolescent children in the boarding schools and a great increase in the number of day schools. Most important, the report urged the federal government to adopt a policy of cultural pluralism toward the Indians in place of the traditional assimilationist philosophy. While giving "all practicable aid and advice" to those Indians who wished to "merge into the social and economic life of the prevailing civilization," the report urged the government to permit the Indian "who wants to remain an Indian and live according to his old culture" to do so (Meriam 1928:88).

The Hoover Administration

The publication of the Meriam report and the election of Herbert Hoover in 1928 led to many changes in Indian administration and an improvement in Indian welfare during the next four years. Hoover's humanitarian instincts led him to concur in the growing consensus that Commissioner Burke, whose sympathies lay with the traditional approach to Indian affairs, would have to go. In 1929 Hoover appointed two fellow Quakers, Charles Rhoads and Henry Scattergood, to the posts of Indian commissioner and assistant Indian commissioner with the explicit promise that he would back them in the implementation of the Meriam report recommendations. Rhoads and Scattergood and the new secretary of the interior, Ray Lyman Wilbur, were sincere in their efforts to implement the Meriam report; and in the fields of health care, education, administrative reorganization and decentralization of the BIA and the recruitment of better qualified personnel, they were largely successful. On the central issue of land ownership and the formation of tribal councils to administer tribal properties, the Rhoads-Wilbur-Hoover team wavered. All three men were deeply committed to the ideal of individualism and were reluctant to take any steps that might either strengthen tribal cohesion or prolong federal guardianship. Thus, although the Hoover years witnessed the removal of force from the Bureau's dealings with the Indians and a substantial increase in medical and educational services, they did little to halt the allotment of Indian lands or to strengthen tribal decision-making powers.

As a result of the vacillation of the Hoover administration, John Collier persuaded the Senate Indian Affairs Committee to nudge along the reform cause through its own investigation of Indian affairs. Under Collier's leadership, the senators visited most of the major reservations between 1928 and 1932 and came away persuaded that further reforms were necessary. Although most of their time was spent in criticizing the failures of the Rhoads administration, the senators did appear to be in sympathy with the idea of protecting Indian civil rights, curbing the administrative powers of the Indian Bureau, and putting an end to the land-allotment system.

John Collier as Commissioner, 1933–1945

The shift in national leadership occasioned by the 1932

elections resulted in the appointment of Collier as commissioner of Indian affairs. Despite considerable opposition to Collier on the ground that his temperament was too "critical and uncompromising" for a sensitive administrative position, new Secretary of the Interior Harold Ickes, a charter member of the American Indian Defense Association, turned instinctively to Collier as the most knowledgeable man in the field.

During his first year in office, while he was drafting legislation to repeal the Dawes Act, Collier gave impressive evidence of his determination to institute a new order in Indian affairs. He proclaimed the principle of religious freedom for native religions and abolished the forced attendance of boarding school pupils at Christian religious services. Through Secretary Ickes he halted the sale of allotted land, and he cancelled nearly all the reimbursable debts charged against Indian tribal funds. In addition, he ended the 10-year controversy over the Pueblo claims along the Rio Grande in the Indians' favor; pushed through Congress a bill to contract with the states for education, medical care, and relief services; and secured the repeal of 12 statutes passed in the nineteenth century that limited the rights of both Indians and Whites on the reservations in the exercise of their civil liberties. Then, in 1934, he introduced into Congress the Indian Reorganization Act, which represented the culmination of his 12-year effort to end the assimilationist tradition.

The Indian Reorganization Act, as originally submitted, was 52 pages long. As justification for this extreme length, Collier pointed out that it was designed to be the "successor to the greater part of several thousand pages of Indian law," including the Dawes Act. It contained four major provisions, each of which was designed to pave the way for the restoration of Indian autonomy: (1) Indians were to be permitted to organize for local self-government and economic enterprise to the end that "civil liberty, political responsibility, and economic independence shall be achieved;" (2) the policy of Congress would henceforth be to promote "the study of Indian civilization, including Indian arts, crafts, skills, and traditions;" (3) the allotment system was to be abolished and allotments previously made were to be transferred back to tribal control, all former Indian lands that had not been sold were to revert to tribal ownership, additional land was to be purchased for landless Indians, and the federal government was to assist Indians in restoring the fertility of depleted soils; and (4) a special court of Indian affairs, observing procedures and rules consonant with Indian customs and traditions, was to be created to hear all cases involving the new self-governing Indian communities. In order to facilitate the attainment of these goals Congress was asked to appropriate $2,000,000 annually for the purchase of new land; to create a revolving credit fund of $5,000,000 to stimulate economic development on Indian reservations; and to make available educational loans for Indians who wished to attend nongovernmental vocational, trade, and high schools, as well as colleges and universities. In essence, Congress was asked to grant Indians the right to control their own affairs, free from administrative supervision by the federal government and dependent upon it only for financial support (fig. 3).

The original Indian Reorganization bill immediately ran into opposition, both from Indians who opposed the return of individual allotments to tribal control and from the Congress. As a result of Indian opposition, the mandatory provisions calling for the transfer of allotted land back to tribal control were eliminated, and each tribe was permitted to reject the act by referendum. In the Congress, the statement promoting the preservation of Indian culture and civilization was deleted, the Court of Indian Affairs rejected, and the powers of tribal governments and business councils severely curtailed. The final bill signed into law on June 18, 1934 (48 U.S. Stat. 984–986), thus represented a compromise between Collier's dream of a new policy encouraging the growth of Indian society and culture and the traditional forces of assimilation. A dramatic break with the past was achieved through the abolishment of the allotment system and through the authorizations for new land purchases and a credit fund, whose lending capacities were increased to $10,000,000 by Congress. Indian tribes whose lands and tribal cohesion remained essentially intact were given a new lease on life, but those that had been demoralized and stripped of their lands were to find it difficult to rebuild.

Despite the limitations placed on his administration by the compromise nature of the Indian Reorganization Act, Collier found ways to work toward his original goals through the aid of the numerous New Deal agencies. In 1935 he persuaded Congress to create the Indian Arts and Crafts Board (49 U.S. Stat. 891) to promote the economic welfare of Indians through the development of their arts and crafts. Through contracts with the Public Works Administration, the Resettlement Administration and its successor, the Farm Security Administration, he obtained funds to purchase and rehabilitate Indian lands, particularly in the Southwest. From the various relief agencies, especially the Works Progress Administration, he obtained jobs for Indians on soil conservation, irrigation, and road-building projects that further enhanced their landed resources (fig. 4). During Collier's administration, at least until 1942 when the Depression-inspired emergency agencies were phased out, BIA appropriations from all sources averaged about $45,000,000 annually or almost four times annual appropriations for the years 1900–1928. As a result of these greatly increased appropriations, the physical and material aspects of Indian life were greatly improved. However, Collier's attempts to encourage the development of tribal governments, the revival of Indian culture, and the growth of tribal economic enterprise were met by congressional hostility and steadily reduced

Natl. Arch.: RG75N-CHIP-40.
Fig. 3. Delegation from the Minnesota Chippewa Tribe meeting with federal officials in Washington, D.C. left to right, John Hougen, tribal attorney; Charles Roy, Nett Lake Reservation; Frank Broker, chairman of the tribal executive committee, Leech Lake Reservation; Shirley McKenzie, credit agent; Ben Petite, Fond du Lac Reservation; John Herrick, assistant commissioner of Indian affairs; Thomas Artell, White Earth Reservation; Sam Zimmerman, Grand Portage Reservation; M.L. Burns, acting superintendent of the Consolidated Chippewa Agency; and William Nickabaine, Mille Lac Reservation. The Minn. Chippewa Tribe was formed in the 1930s in accordance with the federal Indian Reorganization Act goals for greater tribal self-government and economic autonomy. Chippewas residing on 6 Minn. reservations elected representatives to serve on the tribal executive committee, which had governing powers over interband concerns. Individual reservations retained control over local matters (Danziger 1978:134–135). Photographer unknown, Jan. 1940.

appropriations for implementing the Indian Reorganization Act.

In 1939 the Senate Indian Affairs Committee recommended the repeal of the Indian Reorganization Act, and in 1943 it followed with another bill that would have stripped the BIA of all its essential functions. Although both these attempts to restrict the Bureau failed to become law, Collier resolved in 1944 to defend his administration by an appeal to the House Indian Affairs Committee for a new investigation of Indian affairs. While the House committee report was sympathetic to many of Collier's reforms, it was critical of the extensive bureaucracy that had been created to administer the Indian Reorganization Act, opposed to the continued purchase of nontaxable lands for Indians, and adamant in its insistence that federal policy be redirected toward bringing individual Indians into full and equal participation in American life rather than prolonging their special status as Indians (U.S. Congress. House. Committee on Indian Affairs 1944: 335–349). Following this final rebuff by Congress, Collier resigned from office in January 1945.

Collier's successor, William Brophy, was absent on sick leave during most of his three-year term; and Brophy's successor, John R. Nichols, served only one year before he too resigned. In early 1946 Interior Secretary Ickes also resigned. During the years 1945–1950, as a result, control over Indian affairs passed by default to the Congress.

In 1946 Congress created the Indian Claims Commission (60 U.S. Stat. 1049) in order to settle disputes between the Indians and the federal government dating back to the nineteenth century. From 1950 to 1969 the Claims Commission heard 304 cases and ruled in the Indians' favor in 154 instances; awards totaling $333,000,000 were made (Sorkin 1971:137). Although hailed at the time of its passage as a major victory for the Indians, the Claims Commission awards were actually the entering wedge of the termination policy that developed during the 1950s. As a result of the new wealth created by the awards, congressional committees that favored ending federal supervision over the Indians were given additional support for their position.

The first overt attempt to remove federal protection over the Indians came in 1947 when Acting Commissioner William Zimmerman was subpoened to appear before the Senate Committee on Civil Service and ordered to present a plan for reducing Bureau expenditures. In his testimony, Zimmerman agreed that certain Indian tribes were far enough along the path to acculturation that federal protective services could be removed without serious damage to the Indians involved. He referred particularly to the Menominee and Klamath tribes, which were relatively wealthy as a result of their ownership of rich timber lands. Zimmerman also listed several tribes that could probably be removed from federal jurisdiction within a few years. In submitting his recommendations he counseled caution and attempted to specify criteria that should be applied before the controls were removed. In the years that followed, the criteria that Zimmerman specified were frequently overlooked or ignored in the drive to "emancipate" Indians from federal controls (Zimmerman 1957:36).

1947–1980

Holding the Line

Despite the continued hostility of congressional committees to the Indian Reorganization Act in the postwar period, there was no concerted attack upon the philosophy embodied in that legislation until the early 1950s. Indeed, in the years immediately following the end of World War II there were signs that certain rights previously denied to Indians would be recognized. In 1947 at the instigation of the chief counsel of the Association on American Indian Affairs, Felix Cohen, suits were brought against the states of New Mexico and Arizona for their failure to extend welfare benefits to Indians under the Social Security Act. Both suits were dropped when the states grudgingly complied with the law. In the following year, after the federal Committee on Civil Rights drew attention to the

74

Natl. Arch: RG75N-CARS-153; RG75N-Red-39.
Fig. 4. Works Progress Administration projects on Indian reservations. left, Lena Phoenix, an Indian instructor, teaches beadwork to Northern Paiute girls at the Walker River Day School, Schurz, Nev. The work coupled federal goals of promoting native arts and crafts with economic goals for tribes. Photograph by Arthur Rothstein, 1940. right, Chippewa crew constructing a community center at Ponemah on the Red Lake Indian Reservation, Minn. Photograph by Gordon Sommers, 1940.

disfranchisement of Indians in New Mexico and Arizona, Cohen again brought suits against the two states on behalf of a group of Indian war veterans. Both these cases went to trial and resulted in victories for the Indians (McNickle 1971:152).

On the Navajo reservation in Arizona and New Mexico there were also encouraging signs during these years. The return of thousands of war veterans and defense-plant workers whose absence had eased the economic problems of the reservation during the war years, coupled with severe drought during the summers of 1946 and 1947, brought national attention to the plight of these Indians. In 1947 Congress appropriated $2,000,000 in emergency relief funds for the Navajos and authorized a long-range study for their economic rehabilitation. Two years later a 10-year federal program calling for expenditures of over $88,000,000 was approved by Congress only to be vetoed by President Harry Truman because of an amendment sponsored by Congressman Antonio Fernandez of New Mexico that would have brought the Navajos under state laws and the state courts. In 1950 the Navajo-Hopi Rehabilitation Act was passed following a compromise agreement between the state of New Mexico and the federal government. In return for dropping the Fernandez amendment, permitting the Navajos to draw up a constitution, and providing that the Indians would be consulted on all projects undertaken by the act, the state of New Mexico (and other western states by inference) was promised that the Social Security Administration would accept responsibility for 80 percent of the cost of

welfare aid to elderly or disabled Indians and dependent Indian children. Similar rehabilitation programs for other Indian tribes were subsequently prepared but all failed to gain congressional support.

A report on the reorganization of the executive branch of government brought to an end any optimism that had been aroused by the voting rights and social security decisions. While recommending many welfare and health care proposals favorable to the Indians, the report proposed that the federal government relinquish its responsibilities over the Indians to the states and that Indian tax-exempt status be terminated. Because these recommendations coincided so closely with the congressional sentiment made evident in 1947, federal administrators found it increasingly necessary after 1950 to make concessions to their critics (U.S. Commission on Organization of the Executive Branch of Government 1949: 65–66).

The Withdrawal Policy of Commissioner Myer

In early 1950 the problem of administrative leadership in the Interior Department was solved by the appointment of Oscar Chapman as secretary of the interior and Dillon S. Myer as commissioner of Indian affairs. Myer's experience as director of the Japanese War Relocation Authority from 1942–1946 and his sensitivity to congressional criticism of the Indian Reorganization Act played important roles in his administration of Indian affairs.

Shortly after taking office, Myer announced an important change in administrative policy. Noting that the subsistence farming ideal of the New Deal years was increasingly less viable in the postwar period, and that severe unemployment problems on the reservations were in large part the product of the return of some 113,000 Indians who had left the reservations during the war, Myer resolved to concentrate on relocating young Indians in urban, industrial areas rather than on developing reservation resources. Between 1950 and 1967 some 61,600 Indians were encouraged to relocate in urban areas (Sorkin 1971:121).

In an effort to meet congressional criticism of superfluous personnel and lax administration, Myer also centralized the bureaucracy by greatly enlarging the powers of area administrators. The powers of reservation superintendents were correspondingly reduced and the decision-making powers removed to the more distant regional headquarters. In an attempt to educate Indians in the methods of the White business community, Myer curtailed Indian access to the already limited credit funds administered by the BIA and encouraged Indians instead to rely upon private banks and other lending agencies. To facilitate the willingness of these institutions to make loans to Indians, Myer permitted individual Indians to mortgage their trust and restricted allotments under a previously little-used law passed in 1948 (62 U.S. Stat. 236). Despite these efforts to pacify congressional critics, the House of Representatives in 1952 raised the question of terminating federal responsibility. Shortly before he left office, Myer indicated that in 1952 the Bureau had begun withdrawing its trusteeship over the Indians and had greatly increased its emphasis on the ultimate transfer of Indian Bureau functions either to the Indians themselves or to appropriate state agencies.

Termination and Relocation

Dissatisfaction with the Indian Reorganization Act, constantly growing since the early 1940s, erupted in the Republican-dominated Congress of 1953. Two bills and one resolution, all designed to remove federal controls from Indians, passed through Congress and were signed into law.

House Concurrent Resolution 108 (83d Cong., 1st sess.) called for the termination of federal controls over all Indians in California, Florida, Iowa, New York, and Texas and, in addition, over the following specific tribes: Klamath, Menominee, Flathead, Osage, Potawatomi of Kansas and Nebraska, and the Turtle Mountain band of Chippewa. Later that same month federal liquor prohibition laws on Indian reservations were removed (67 U.S. Stat. 586) (fig. 5); and the Indians of California, Minnesota, Nebraska, Oregon, and Wisconsin (who had requested such a transfer) were placed under the criminal and civil jurisdiction of the states in which they resided (67 U.S.

Stat. 588). Although there was justification for each of these measures, many Indian groups were alarmed by the requirement in the termination resolution that the secretary of the interior submit plans for terminating federal responsibility over other tribes in the near future. Indians were also alarmed by the discretionary power given to other states to extend their laws over Indians living within their boundaries. In signing the bill extending state jurisdiction over the Indians, President Dwight Eisenhower expressed misgiving that the bill did not provide for consultation with the Indians and urged Congress to amend the bill to provide for such consultation at the next session. This was never done. Instead, in 1954 termination bills were introduced not only for the Indians mentioned in the House resolution but also for the mixed Southern Paiute–Utes of Utah, several bands of Indians in western Oregon, and the Indians of Nevada (Watkins 1957:50–51). By 1961 federal supervision had been terminated over the Klamath, Menominee, Alabama and Koasati, Wyandot, Peoria, Ottawa, and several small bands of Southern Paiute–Ute Indians. Bills to terminate federal controls over other Indian tribes were defeated or blocked in Congress, and in 1958 Interior Secretary Fred A. Seaton announced that no further action would be taken toward termination without Indian consent.

In 1953 Commissioner Myer was succeeded by Glenn Emmons, a Gallup, New Mexico, banker and rancher who shared with Myer the belief that the solution to the Indian unemployment problem lay in persuading large numbers of Indians to relocate away from the reservations (fig. 6). Under Emmons the relocation program was continued, but after 1958 when it became apparent that almost half of the Indians enrolled in the program eventually returned to

Lib. of Congress:LC-USF33-1661-M3.
Fig. 5. Sign in tavern window, Sisseton, Sisseton Indian Reservation, S. Dak. Controlling Indian access to alcohol was an issue in Indian-White relations from colonial times into the twentieth century. As in the 1851 treaty between the U.S. and the Sisseton and Wahpeton bands of Sioux, treaties often specified that the sale of liquor on Indian lands was prohibited. Federal legislation enacted in 1953 allowed alcohol on reservations where permitted by state and tribal laws. Photograph by John Vachon, Sept. 1939.

COME TO DENVER

THE CHANCE OF YOUR LIFETIME!

Good Jobs
Retail Trade
Manufacturing
Government-Federal, State, Local
Wholesale Trade
Construction of Buildings, Etc.

Happy Homes
Beautiful Houses
Many Churches
Exciting Community Life
Over Half of Homes Owned by Residents
Convenient Stores-Shopping Centers

Training
Vocational Training
AutoMech., Beauty Shop, Drafting,
Nursing, Office Work, Watchmaking
Adult Education
Evening High School, Arts and Crafts
Job Improvement, Home-making

Beautiful Colorado
"Tallest" State, 48 Mt. Peaks Over 14,000 Ft.
350 Days Sunshine, Mild Winters
Zoos, Museums, Mountain Parks, Drives
Picnic Areas, Lakes, Amusement Parks
Big Game Hunting, Trout Fishing, Camping

Natl. Arch.:RG75N-Reloc-G;RG75N-Reloc-36B.

Fig. 6. BIA relocation program. left, Promotional literature distributed in areas where Indian people usually convened or by BIA relocation officers. Photographer unidentified. right, Cheyenne family from Okla. in their apartment in Denver, where the husband was employed as an airplane cleaner in 1955. Photographic dossiers were made about families, noting their tribal affiliation, former reservation address, the date of relocation, and where the household head worked, including his starting and current wages. The dossiers usually also included a description of the home with a comment about how well the family had adjusted. Photographer unidentified.

the reservation, interest slackened. Although part of the reason for the high return rate was attributable to the culture shock that many Indians experienced in the urban environment, a second factor was the development of rival economic programs. In 1956 Emmons obtained congressional support for the Indian Vocational Training Act (70 U.S. Stat. 986), which provided both advanced vocational training off the reservations and on-the-job training in privately owned industries located on or near Indian reservations. To bring industry to the reservations Emmons encouraged the investment of tribal funds in factories and buildings that were then leased to manufacturing firms. The Indian Vocational Training Act also provided federal wage subsidies to employers who would employ and train Indians. By 1967 the number of Indians who had received advanced vocational training off the reservations stood at 31,556. The on-the-job training program was much less successful. Only 6,223 Indians, more than half of them women, had participated in this program by 1967, and the dropout rate was approximately that of the relocation program, 50 percent. Nevertheless, a Brookings Institution study (Sorkin 1971:115) concluded that the relocation and vocational training programs were

as successful in reducing Indian unemployment as other similar programs for non-Indian poverty groups, such as Job Corps and Neighborhood Youth Corps.

In addition to relocation and vocational training, the Emmons administration placed great emphasis on Indian education. Following the trend begun after World War II, stress was placed upon academic subjects that would prepare young Indians to better compete with their White counterparts in entering college and the professions. Special attention was devoted to the Indians of the Southwest, particularly the Navajos. In the period 1954–1957 over 10,000 new students were enrolled either in public schools or new reservation boarding schools. The educational program was warmly approved by the Congress, which responded with increasingly large appropriations; by 1969 the education budget of the BIA was approaching $100,000,000 annually (Sorkin 1971:39). However, despite the increased emphasis on education, the Indian dropout rate in high school remained high (around 50%); and the number of Indians who successfully completed college, while substantially higher than in the prewar years, continued low.

In 1955 Indian health services were transferred from

U.S. Dept. of the Interior, Bureau of Reclamation, Farmington, N. Mex.: P809-529-1881A.

Fig. 7. Site of the N. Mex. State U. San Juan Branch Agricultural Experiment Station, part of the Navajo Indian Irrigation Project (NIIP). Navajos E.R. Raymond, left, and Frank Sandoval of the Land Investigation Office of the Navajo Tribe examine a map showing the location of the station. The NIIP, a BIA project designed to increase the amount of agrarian land for Navajo subsistence, required cooperation among tribal, federal, and state agencies. The NIIP encountered administrative problems including delays in implementation during the 1960s created by both the BIA and the tribe and the incomplete verification of the amount of available water, which threatened to lead to overcommitment (vol. 10:645–646). Navajo Agricultural Products Industries, an agrarian development project begun in 1970 and based on the resources of the NIIP, posted its first profit in 1986. Photograph by T.R. Broderick, Aug. 15, 1967.

the BIA to the Public Health Service. Dramatic improvements in health care followed almost immediately. Appropriations for Indian health services that were $5,000,000 in 1940 rose to $24,555,000 in 1955 and to $71,775,000 in 1965. A potentially important by-product of this increase in medical and health care has been the interest of the Public Health Service in employing and training Indians in a variety of health skills.

In 1970 almost 60 percent of the Public Health Service personnel working with and among Indians were themselves Indians (Sorkin 1971:51–56).

Self-Determination

The two most important trends in federal policy after 1961--the huge increases in federal expenditures for Indian needs and the growth of pan-Indian organizations that demanded control over programs affecting the Indian community—were both products of the increased recognition of minority groups that characterized domestic affairs in the United States during the 1960s.

In fiscal year 1971 federal appropriations for Indians stood at $626,000,000. While most of this money was earmarked for traditional items such as health, education,

and welfare, significant amounts were allocated to nontraditional areas: home construction and improvement, business and industrial loans, and a multitude of community-action programs begun under the auspices of the Office of Economic Opportunity in 1965. As a result of both the increase in Indian life expectancy (from 51 years in 1940 to 63.5 years in 1964) and the recognition of Indians previously ignored, the number of Indians under the jurisdiction of the BIA grew from 367,000 in 1962 to 452,000 in 1968 (Sorkin 1971:4, 64).

During the 1960s government programs to aid chronically depressed areas and poverty groups were made applicable to Indians. The most important of these were the Area Redevelopment Act of 1961 and the Economic Opportunity Act of 1964. Although the long-range economic effectiveness of the programs initiated by these pieces of legislation was questioned (Steiner 1968: 193–214), there was little doubt that the injections of federal money at least temporarily improved the economic conditions of thousands of individual Indians on the reservations. More important, the experience Indians gained in planning and administering these programs led to the demand that Indians be permitted to plan and administer programs previously controlled by the BIA. A cautious but potentially revolutionary step in the direction of tribal rather than BIA administration of federal funds was made in 1970 when Commissioner Louis R. Bruce signed contracts with both the Zuni and Salt River Pima and Maricopa Indians, permitting them to administer all programs formerly run by the BIA. Similar experiments in education were launched in Arizona and New Mexico where all-Indian school boards were authorized and given full authority over curriculum, the hiring of teachers, and the expenditure of school funds.

In July 1970 President Richard Nixon submitted to Congress a message in which he requested action on the following items in addition to increased funds for health, education, and economic development: (1) repudiation of the termination resolution; (2) legislative authority to empower any tribe to accept responsibility for the operation of federally funded programs in the Department of the Interior and the Department of Health, Education, and Welfare; (3) the restoration to the Taos Indians of 48,000 acres of land surrounding Blue Lake (fig. 8), accomplished December 1970 (84 U.S. Stat. 1437); (4) authority to channel federal education funds to Indians in public schools through tribal governments rather than through local public-school districts; and (5) authority for Indians to enter into long-term leases of their lands (Josephy 1971:223–242). Most of the initiatives sought by Nixon emerged into law or practice. Although sentiment to require termination continued in some quarters, particularly in the Northwest, the impetus was blunted and indeed, reversed, as the Menominee Restoration Act of 1973 (87 U.S. Stat. 770) demonstrated. Recognition of the destructive effects of termination on those tribes (such as the Klamath and Menominee) to which it had been applied reenforced the attitude of most Americans that the special legal status of the Indian tribes should be preserved and strengthened rather than destroyed.

The Indian Self-Determination and Education Assistance Act of 1975 (88 U.S. Stat. 2203) provided statutory authority to allow tribes to assume responsibilities formerly reserved to officials of the BIA and other departments of government. Education funds through this and other education legislation became more available and more subject to control by the Indian tribes. Under the Tribally Controlled Community College Assistance Act of 1978 (P.L. 95-471) other tribes followed the lead of the Navajo, who established a community college in 1969 in which native languages and history were taught.

The American Indian Religious Freedom Act of 1978 (92 U.S. Stat. 469) protected the traditional religious practices and rights of native Americans.

The movement toward self-determination was accelerated by a series of Supreme Court decisions reenforcing and emphasizing "Indian sovereignty" and the power of Indian tribes to assert their economic, political, and cultural authority in appropriate spheres (*Merrion* v. *Jicarilla Apache Tribe*, 455 U.S. 130 in 1982; *Montana* v. *Blackfeet Tribe of Indians*, 105 S.Ct. 2399 in 1985). While

not going so far as some Indian groups wished in, for example, authorizing tribal courts to try and punish non-Indians (*Oliphant* v. *Suquamish Tribe*, 435 U.S. 191 in 1978), these decisions made it unmistakably clear that American Indians, in their tribal capacity, possessed powers of self-government that could not be abridged by states, municipalities, companies, or by the federal government. The Court's decision in *Santa Clara Pueblo* v. *Martinez* (436 U.S. 49) in 1978 went so far as explicitly to uphold the right of a tribe to be governed by its traditional laws and to determine its membership even if it conflicts with civil rights guaranteed individual tribal members and other Americans under the U.S. Constitution. *Martinez* and subsequent decisions placed new responsibilities on Indian courts, the challenge of which was being grappled with in the 1980s.

The Court also, in water cases (*Nevada* v. *U.S.*, 459 U.S. 904 and *Arizona* v. *California*, 460 U.S. 605) in 1983, attempted to solve the complex problem of the division of water resources in the Western states among the states and Indian tribes.

It is not surprising, in the light of the many Supreme Court decisions in the 1960s, 1970s, and 1980s affirming the sovereign powers of the Indian tribes, that the administration of Ronald Reagan enunciated a federal Indian policy based on the concept of a "government-to-

Bureau of Ind. Affairs, SMC, Cartographic Section, Concho, Okla.:303-68-568.
Fig. 8. Taos Pueblo Indians, N. Mex., honor James A. Haley, chairman of the subcommittee on Indian affairs, who introduced a resolution (H.R. 3306) on their behalf to the House of Representatives in 1967. The award to the Taos Indians of trust title to the Blue Lake area and environs was the result of 64 years of petitioning the U.S. government. While the award is significant because of its basis in American Indian religious freedom (Bodine 1978:42), U.S. Senate Report No. 91-1345 clearly states that the decision should not be considered a "precedent for future cases or an expression of national policy in the handling of religious, sacred or ceremonial land claims." Congress wanted to avoid setting a precedent for substituting land for cash awards. Photographed at Taos Pueblo, N. Mex., 1967.

government relationship" among the states, the federal government, and the Indian tribes.

Thus, in the late 1980s the national policy of the United States had changed completely from that of the 1880s, moving from a virtual denial of tribal sovereignty to almost full recognition. Such a major policy shift contained qualifications and apparent contradictions, but the main thrust of the change was clear, and the flourishing state of Indian tribal governments in the 1980s was evidence of this development.

Canadian Indian Policies

ROBERT J. SURTEES

Three nations have exercised sovereignty over portions of Canadian territory: France, England, and the Dominion of Canada. In each case the nation had to accommodate its claims to the presence of native peoples who not only have had legitimate claims of their own but were often essential to the operations of the newcomers seeking to exploit the resources of the northern part of the continent. This required the incoming powers to develop policies—stated and implied, idealistic and pragmatic—that would permit their plans to prosper and yet conform to the reality that another race had preceded them. The incoming powers had varying purposes and methods as they pursued their North American enterprises. Thus, although each regime had to accept portions of the policies developed by its predecessor, each also adopted its own refinements and its own peculiar approaches. The result has been a curious blend of self-interest, paternalism, and declared principles of philanthropy and friendship. Had the native peoples been fully open to accept the newcomers on the newcomers' terms, the task would have been easy. But they were not and they are not. Indians reacted to the European incursions according to self-interest and according to their own heritage. Therefore, Indian policies had to be modified according to the natives' response.

The French Regime

The French were not the first to visit Canadian territory, but they were the first to support their claim to sovereignty by conducting fairly extensive commerce and by attempting to establish permanent trading factories and settlements. Finally one of these took roots when Samuel de Champlain settled his small party at Stadacona (Quebec City) to prepare for the winter of 1608–1609. It was obvious immediately that the survival of this small colony would require the approval and cooperation of the native peoples in the vicinity. The Indians greatly outnumbered the French, the Indians had the requisite knowledge to survive in the Canadian forests, and the Indians had access to the supply of furs that formed the single most important form of wealth to be found there.

The newcomers had assets of their own. They controlled the supply of European trade goods, especially iron products such as kettles and hatchets, which were coveted by people who had hitherto had access only to bone, stone, or wooden weapons and tools. The French also had liquor and firearms, and the further asset of being firmly convinced of the superiority of their civilization, including religion and language. This superiority carried with it the obligation to effect progress among the Indians. There was sufficient mutual dependence to permit the French, from the earliest days, to design and follow Indian policies that allowed their early settlement to grow into an extensive North American empire, and to retain control over it for a century. Even within that successful enterprise, the French were invariably outnumbered in most sectors of their claimed territory, a factor that increased in importance as their ambitions began to clash with other European enterprises in North America. Consequently they had to be circumspect when dealing with their Indian neighbors, for they could not afford to permit their sense of superiority to become overbearing; nor could they appear obsequious, for any sign of weakness could be exploited by their Indian friends as well as by their European rivals in the New World. It was a tenuous road, but one that the French were able to travel effectively for over a century. The policies adopted by the French toward the Indians in that period were successful, it would seem, because they managed to integrate self-interest, strength, and material advantage with the features of friendship and diplomacy found in their missions and trade relations.

Champlain's Policy

In seeking to strengthen the small colony, Champlain initiated several trends that shaped future Indian policy. He began the system of dispatching young Frenchmen into the interior to explore, to learn the Indian languages, and to acquire the means of survival in the North American forests. In agreeing to assist the Hurons and Algonquins on raids against the Iroquois Confederacy in 1609, 1610, and 1615 Champlain sought to cement the commercial relationships between those tribes and the French. It also marked the beginning of the practice that would continue and would reap considerable benefits for the French (Trigger 1971:88). Champlain (1922–1936) himself, in his first years in Canada, undertook extensive exploration that brought the French into contact with numerous tribes in distant regions of the interior. To a large extent the history of New France is the story of this constantly expanding frontier. It was inspired by the Canadian terrain and by the pursuit of the beaver and therefore forms part of France's commercial—not Indian—policy in North America, but it is appropriate to note it in connection with Indian policy since this expansion required that Indian policy be extended into new and distant regions of the continent. This, in turn, had an effect on the manner in which Indian policy was formulated.

Although the prime motive for the French activity on the Saint Lawrence was commerce, the fur trade in particular, a highly important secondary consideration was the goal of converting the Indians to Christianity. Conversion had been adopted as an official goal as early as 1540 (Dickason 1976:19), and it had trickled down sufficiently that the apothecary, Louis Hébert, brought to Canada by Champlain in 1609, would declare that he had come to the New World "pour venir secourir les sauvage plutôt que pour tout autre intérêt particulier" (Jaenen 1973:132). Champlain declared that conversion was not enough; it was necessary also to civilize the Indians, and to him this meant that the Indians should adopt French habits and customs and, eventually, the French manner of thinking. This would not be difficult, thought Champlain, who reported a Huron chief as saying, "we shall easily abandon our life and adopt yours, as our life is wretched in comparison with yours" (Champlain 1922–1936, 3:145). It is more likely that the Huron chief was either attempting to please Champlain or that the chief was misinterpreted, for French efforts and those of all Europeans to promote a civilization program met with meager success, an indication that the Indians possessed a religion and a developed society that they were by no means prepared to abandon. But the goal had been stated, and the end declared to be possible; it would have remarkable longevity, for the policy of civilization and assimilation would remain an integral part of official policy throughout the French regime and long beyond.

There was a strain of self-interest in the goal of civilization. If Indians could be convinced to adopt a sedentary life and to cultivate the soil it would serve the additional ends of providing a more stable supply of food for the young colony and of rendering the Indians easier to control and the French colony more secure.

During the seventeenth century the several principles enunciated during Champlain's long tenure developed according to changing circumstances; variations occurred also according to the manner in which interested individuals or institutions interpreted their assigned or assumed roles within the framework of Indian affairs and declared Indian policy. An indication of the importance of Indian affairs in the society of New France can be seen in the fact that ultimate responsibility for this portfolio rested with the governor. And throughout the French regime there were paradoxes or contradictions in the theories connected to Indian policy. Despite these the French maintained a remarkably successful connection with the Indians they encountered.

French-Iroquois Relations

The first of these concerned the Iroquois Confederacy, known as the League of the Iroquois. Champlain cannot be blamed for this longstanding conflict. He simply engaged in a few skirmishes on the side of the Saint Lawrence Algonquians and Hurons. Rather the geographic position of the Confederacy drew them into a fairly natural alliance with the Dutch at Fort Orange and, after 1664, with the English at Albany, while the French on the Saint Lawrence were drawn, equally naturally, into a commercial alliance with the Huron, Montagnais, and Nipissing. The traditional rivalry between those tribes and the Iroquois, therefore, created a conflict between the French and the Iroquois, a conflict that was exacerbated by the commercial factor. Inasmuch as the confederacy posed a very serious threat to the security, even the existence, of the Saint Lawrence colony, Champlain's belief after 1627 that the Iroquois must be destroyed made sense. But the destruction of the League could also have led to hardship, perhaps even the demise of New France, for without the Iroquois barrier the northern tribes might well have decided to bypass the French and carry their furs to the Hudson River trading posts of the Dutch or the English.

On their southern flank, therefore, the French had a very dangerous situation, but one which they handled rather well. They cooperated with the Hurons throughout the 1630s and 1640s in developing the northern market, they expanded also to Trois Rivières in 1634 and to Montreal in 1642, and in the process they resisted Iroquois attacks until the early 1640s. A truce negotiated in 1645 indicated that the French were willing to treat with the Iroquois, but that treaty was broken and the Iroquois attacks against New France grew more dangerous. When the confederacy succeeded in destroying Huronia in 1649, the French either moved into the interior themselves or permitted other tribes, such as the Ottawas, to assume the middleman role vacated by the Hurons. This policy insured the continued animosity of the Iroquois, which, although dangerous, was preferable to permitting the confederacy to replace the Hurons. The barrier between the Dutch and the northern tribes had to be maintained. The French-Iroquois rivalry continued for another half-century, until hostilities were forsworn at Montreal at the Grand Peace of 1701, during which time the French colony on several occasions rested on the verge of annihilation. The most serious occurred in the 1660s when the colony was so close to collapse that King Louis XIV intervened and sent 1,000 officers and men to defend New France against the Iroquois Confederacy. Again, during King William's War, 1689–1697, the Iroquois threat loomed ominously, and again the French were able to withstand Iroquois strength and even to carry the war into enemy country, especially against the Onondaga (Eccles 1969:103–131).

Frenchification

But these military responses formed only one aspect of French policy regarding the Iroquois. An equally important activity grew from the French conviction that the Indians of their regions should be converted and civilized. Two methods were used to accomplish this end. Priests and brothers, beginning with Champlain's friends, the Recollects, traveled into the Indian country, to live and to preach. The best-known of these efforts were the Jesuit missions in Huronia and, after the dispersal of 1649, in more distant locations such as those on Lake Nipigon. This remained a constant practice throughout the French regime and beyond. A second method was to induce Indians to settle on reserves close to French settlements. This was advocated by the first Recollect priests, by the Jesuits a little later, and by various civil authorities. It was assumed that "the hunting and gathering way of life was incompatible with the discipline required to be good Christians" (Trigger 1971:100). If the natives would settle among or near French settlers and adopt an agricultural way of life it would be easier to teach them French ways and the French religion. It was attempted with temporary success at Sillery between 1637 and 1649 (Stanley 1950: 178–185) and with somewhat greater success at Lorette beginning in 1650. A related experiment was the effort, begun in 1635, to collect Indian children in residential schools where they could be supervised closely and civilized more completely. The Jesuits tried this with Indian boys and the Ursuline nuns tried with Indian girls. By the most optimistic evaluation both must be considered failures, and both were abandoned (Stanley 1949).

The religious orders also observed that placing Indians among French settlers could have negative results because the French did not set the proper example, especially with respect to liquor. They observed further that natives were slow to accept the plough for extended periods when the forests were very near, and the old ways much too easy and too tempting to resist. By 1660 they were prepared to be content with promoting Christianity among the Indians without demanding or expecting full acceptance of the French mores, values, and way of life. Civil authorities perservered somewhat longer in their conviction that a full program of Frenchification was possible, but they too were ready to abandon it by the end of the century (Stanley 1949) and accept the more limited objective of conversion. However, it had became common

for Indians to visit or to live either within or in close proximity to French settlements. This resulted in part at least from necessity in that the vulnerable position of the French on the Saint Lawrence required that they adopt a friendly stance toward their Indian neighbors; but the policies of conversion and Frenchification promoted the practice rather more than might have occurred otherwise. In addition, several Indian villages were promoted by the French. This policy had three consequences.

First, with one exception, the lands upon which these villages were located were formally granted to a religious order for the purpose of ministering to the Indians who were located there (Francis 1983:25–32). This indicated that the Crown had delegated the task of conversion to the orders; it also indicated that the Crown did not recognize Indian title. This did not create difficulties, for the French had occupied a region and had established a sphere of influence, much as the several Indian tribes had done before them (Surtees 1985). The significance of this would come later, after the British conquest. The exception was the village of Sillery. There the land was granted directly to the Indians, but even it was placed "sous la conduite et la direction des PP. de la compagnie de Jésus qui les ont convertys à la foy de Jésus-Christ . . . " (Stanley 1950: 184).

Second, three of these villages were, surprisingly, formed by Iroquois immigrants. The long war between the French and the League of the Iroquois was punctuated by three periods of truce: 1645, 1653–1658, 1666–1687. French Jesuits took advantage of these to establish missions in the Iroquois country and met with moderate success; but the Iroquois converts often found it difficult to maintain their new faith for they were often treated with suspicion, hostility, and even persecution from their unconverted neighbors. To help their charges keep loyal to Roman Catholicism the Jesuits encouraged them to migrate to the French community on the Saint Lawrence. It was a step that had military as well as religious benefits for it would remove the migrants from Dutch (and English) influence and provide Canada with a source of potential warriors. A tract had been granted to the Jesuits for this purpose at Sault Saint Louis in 1647 but it was not until 1667 that the first converts traveled to Canada. They settled first near the French community of La Prairie and for a decade the two races lived side by side, both growing in numbers. The experiment did not last, largely because the brandy traffic created severe problems in the Indian village (Stanley 1950, 1953; Hunt 1940:66–86, 176–181; Jaenen 1984:158–168).

The Jesuit leaders determined that their flock could not flourish because of this debilitating influence. They obtained a tract on the south shore of the Saint Lawrence River near the Lachine rapids, and in 1676 they moved most of the Iroquois converts to the new location. Known as Caughnawaga at Sault Saint Louis, this Indian community grew to include representatives from numerous tribes, but as the years passed it gradually took on a predominantly Mohawk temperament (vol. 15:470). Other Iroquois converts settled near Montreal in 1671, and a mission was soon started on the mountain by the Sulpician Order. But the Mount Royal settlement was also affected by the debilitating brandy trade and the priests determined to move it. They did so, twice: to the Sault-aux-Récollets on the Laprairie River in 1696 and then to the Lake of the Two Mountains in 1721 (Stanley 1950: 205–207) (vol. 15:472). By then there were about 900 Indians, predominantly Mohawk. The evolution of these villages constitutes one of the extreme ironies of the French regime. Their Indian policy, as dictated by commerce, drew the French into an alliance with the Huron and Algonquians north of the Saint Lawrence and required them also to adopt an extremely hostile stance toward the League of the Iroquois. Yet the policy of conversion actually pulled several hundred potential warriors into the very heart of the French colony by 1700. This number would increase dramatically by 1750.

The brandy traffic marks the third consequence of the French policy of establishing Indian villages. And like the French policy toward the Iroquois, this is also something of a paradox. The intent of creating permanent villages was to promote civilization among the Indians. The villages, in close proximity to French communities, were to be the vehicles leading to Frenchification. But several aspects of French society mitigated against this. One was the tendency of French settlers to adopt Indian ways, for example, dress, travel, and warfare. But the most serious was the use of liquor. Virtually all observers of New France wrote of the evil effects of liquor on Indian society. If these were valid it was logical that the advice of the Jesuits and other religious be adopted and the brandy trade be abolished. But it was not, although it was a source of constant dispute among the religious who opposed it, settlers and traders who usually either condoned or practiced it, and the civil authorities who generally felt it was necessary or who sometimes actively promoted it.

Brandy was a source of profit. It was desired by the Indians and therefore was a valuable consumer product. In or near settled areas the trade could not be stopped completely because of Indian demand and because of the French civilians' determination to sell it. In the interior it was even more difficult to stop or even control because of the distance from authorities and because it was much sought, and if the French traders did not supply it, an important trade advantage would be gained by the English who were quite eager to sell rum. Once again commercial considerations dictated one approach and civilization factors directed another. The result was a vacillating policy that took shape according to the dominant personalities in the colony and according to the intensity of trading competition in the interior.

Perhaps the greatest contradiction in French Indian policy concerned the perceived and the actual attitude of the French toward the Indians. Although the French have been characterized as without racial bias, this is not precisely true. Often, Indians were considered inferior by the French, they were segregated where possible, and miscegenation was considered immoral and uncivilized by many. Even the missionaries and parish priests discriminated by dispensing more severe penance to Indian confessants than to French sinners (Jaenen 1969, 1973, 1976, 1984).

French Expansion

During the seventeenth century the French in Canada were reasonably unmolested. The "first British conquest" of 1629–1632 was short-lived, and other attacks were mainly inspired by commercial motives. These the French handled easily as they spread their commercial empire to the north, the west, and the southwest. With the War of Spanish Succession, however, Louis XIV set New France on an imperialistic course that called for control of the Mississippi River and the Ohio River valleys as well the Saint Lawrence–Great Lakes valley and the west. It was a policy that conflicted directly with an expanding Anglo-American frontier that had equally strong designs on the interior. And it was a policy that depended very heavily on securing the support or at least the acquiescence of the Indians. In adopting this stance the French could call on the fruits of the policy they had been following for almost a century.

The expanding French frontier had from the beginning carried two notable groups with it: the trader and the missionary. Both had special reasons for ingratiating themselves with the Indians, and both, in addition to pursuing the goals of either commerce or religion, were avid Frenchmen who were prepared to promote the cause of French culture and the French nation. The governor at Quebec had at his disposal several hundred Frenchmen who were experienced in forest living, Indian diplomacy, and Indian relations and who were willing, even eager, to use that experience in directing the Indians of the interior against the English traders, settlers, and soldiers. The intent was to strengthen the French empire in North America as a means of contributing to the French imperial designs in Europe. The method was that of securing a paramount position in the North American heartland— the Ohio valley and the trans-Appalachian frontier in particular—in order to prevent or retard English expansion from the Atlantic seaboard and also to retain control of the two points of entry against New France, the Hudson River and the Saint Lawrence River.

Specific tactics were integrated into an official Indian policy, beginning with the War of Spanish Succession, to win the Indian's allegiance to the French standard. The coureurs de bois, hitherto considered renegades because they had subverted the normal operation of the government-controlled fur trade, were transformed into instruments of imperial policy. Their experience in the Indian country made them natural diplomats who could promote French interests through the proper distribution of gifts and special honors and medals that were created specially for Indian policy. Another feature of the new policy was the decision to subsidize the fur trade in sensitive areas. English traders had a trade advantage in that they could offer the much coveted trade goods at lower prices than could the French. To offset this the French Crown directed that in strategic areas, such as the Ohio country where English traders were sufficiently close to offer a trading alternative, the posts would be subsidized from the royal treasury. Diplomacy became as important as profit at these posts. By establishing a French presence and by offering both presents and a commercial incentive, these posts were expected to keep the English at bay and to pull the Indians more solidly into the French alliance (Eccles 1969:132–156). It was a policy that, when applied vigorously, served the French well for half a century.

French Indian policy also assisted them in securing their other frontiers during the same period. The Grand Peace of 1701 more or less neutralized the Iroquois Confederacy and the practice of encouraging Iroquois to convert and settle within New France as had those who had moved to La Prairie, Caughnawaga, and Oka in the seventeenth century actually drew many warriors into the French sphere. Two specific actions contributed further to this. One was the move made by a portion of the Caughnawaga settlement, under the direction of the Jesuits, to a new site at Saint Regis. The move was inspired partly by some discontent among the villagers and by a gradual soil depletion there; but it was approved by military and civil authorities who saw strategic advantages in the new location (vol. 15:473; Stanley 1950: 203–205). Likewise, a proposal in 1749 to build a mission at La Présentation at the mouth of the Oswegatchie River on the Saint Lawrence River met with official approval. Indeed the French built a fort at that site, and to this fort-mission the French were able to lure a substantial number of Onondagas and some Cayugas and Oneidas. In addition to religious purposes, the fort-mission was designed to help regulate the fur trade and to ward off the English in that quarter. It must be considered successful in that by the middle of the 1750s the Indian settlement that grew up around it numbered 500 families and one observer noted that migrations to this community had almost denuded the Onondaga country of its population (vol. 15:494–496).

By the Treaty of Utrecht ending the War of Spanish Succession the French were forced to cede to the English the region of Acadia "with its ancient boundaries," but they were not prepared to surrender all control of this seaway approach to their North American empire. They built the Louisbourg fortress on Cape Breton Island, Fort Beauséjour on the isthmus of Chebucto, and marshaled what support they could from the French Acadians and from their Indian allies in the region. The policy regarding the Micmacs, Maliseets, and Abenakis was generally the same as in the Ohio country, but two characteristics were unique to the Acadia frontier. First, the Micmacs, while committing themselves rather more completely than tribes elsewhere to friendship with the French and enmity toward the British, also maintained, more generally than other Indian groups, a loyalty to their own culture and religion. The French, therefore, could depend on Micmac friendship throughout, but they also had to be prepared to accept among the Indians a retention of Indian values, such as an amalgam of the Indian and the Catholic religion. This they were prepared to do. Second, personalities helped to share conditions on the east coast. In particular, active and aggressive priests such as Father LeLoutre were prepared not only to preach Christianity and to promote French interests but also to accompany and to lead war parties against the English settlements and forces in Acadia and New England. It was effective for the French. For the Indians, however, the fierce loyalty they had for the French would prove damaging in the long term. As long as French power remained in Canada the Micmacs and their neighbors were able to sustain a position of relative independence, for their balance of power position, although invariably weighted in favor of France, required a certain degree of circumspection by both European powers. But France was forced to withdraw from Canada when the Seven Years' War ended in 1763 in a British victory. Despite this, the Micmacs' hatred of the English continued. With the French presence removed, the British treatment of the maritime bands would reflect their resentment of that continued animosity.

The British Regime

Although English colonies had had relations with Indians in North America since the first settlements took root at Jamestown and Plymouth, the English government had always remained at least once removed from the actual formulation of Indian policy. The several colonies had handled this aspect of their affairs; and because colonial ambitions often conflicted, especially with respect to expansion and territorial jurisdiction, unity among them was rare, and especially rare when Indian relations were concerned. Indeed this disunity, combined with the unified and centralized nature of French Indian policy, can be cited as a significant factor in explaining the French military abilities during the colonial wars of the seventeenth and eighteenth centuries. It was to offset this problem that England created the Indian Department in 1755, and assigned responsibility for the northern superintendency to Sir William Johnson, an experienced Indian diplomat from New York.

The Military Era

This department was a branch of the military establishment; agents carried military rank and were expected to perform military functions. That is, they were to promote the British cause among the tribes of the interior, using their personal influence, their knowledge of forest diplomacy, and a judicious distribution of gifts in order to woo as many warriors as possible away from the French and attach them to the British. They were also expected to lead, or to direct, Indian war parties against the French, either in solo efforts, or as auxiliaries to a larger force. If it was impossible to secure the active cooperation of the warrior bands, the agents were to try to convince them to remain neutral. Regular officers might complain about the ill-discipline and inconstancy of Indian allies, but the nature of forest warfare and the unquestioned ability of Indians in it meant that such allies had to be sought, and sought assiduously. The defeat of Gen. Edward Braddock's expedition in 1755 provided a vivid and terrifying illustration in support of this policy.

It would be inaccurate to suggest that the new branch contributed overwhelmingly to the defeat of the French in North America, but it did play a role such as in Sir William Johnson's Iroquois attacks along the Hudson River and the Richelieu River. And when the war ended it was this branch of His Majesty's service that was charged with responsibility for Indian affairs in the newly acquired territories as well (Allen 1975). The Department did not have full control, however, for it was directed ultimately by the Commander of the Forces, Jeffrey Amherst, who possessed both a fear and a loathing of Indians. Many of his officers shared these feelings, and were quite pleased to follow Amherst's instructions to restrict the flow of presents, to deny Indians access to the forts recently captured from the French, and in general to reverse the attitude of circumspection that had prevailed while the French were in control of the interior (Hagan 1961: 23–24).

In doing so Amherst and his officers rejected the advice of Superintendent General of Indian Affairs Sir William Johnson. This was a mistake. For almost three years from 1760 to 1763 resentment built up among the tribes of the Ohio country. They resented the British attitude, secretly hoped for the return of the French, and quietly hoarded ammunition and supplies. An Ottawa chief, Pontiac, used this circumstance to organize a bitter and surprisingly strong campaign to drive the British from the Ohio valley. The war ultimately failed, but only after the entire western frontier had been terrorized, eight British forts were either captured or evacuated, and two (Fort Pitt and Detroit) had been subjected to lengthy seiges. The affair was sufficiently frightening to convince the British to return to a policy of gift giving, friendship, and diplomacy in order to retain a peaceful coexistence with the natives. It was a policy that would pertain for seven decades.

Thus when England managed to eject France from Canada in 1759–1760 and then decided to retain Canada in 1763 by the Treaty of Paris, the Indian Department had had formal and official experience in the field for less than a decade, and in that time had concentrated exclusively on the military aspect of Indian affairs. The importance of that feature had been confirmed by Pontiac's uprising and was formally enunciated in the Royal Proclamation of October 7, 1763. In addition to setting forth both Indian and colonial policy for North America, this momentous document reflected the British inexperience and their acceptance of goodly portions of the French Indian program.

By creating, via that document, a vast Indian territory west of the Appalachian highlands, Britain recognized the aboriginal rights to occupancy, a recognition that had been in place de facto since 1754 (Cumming and Mickenberg 1972:26). Those lands were reserved for Indian use: non-Indians were forbidden to enter them except to trade and even then only with a special license to do so from the Indian Department. This trade, furthermore, was to be conducted only at specified posts and under the supervision of the post commander and Indian Department agents. The intent clearly was to keep the colonies from expanding too quickly and to maintain peaceful relations with the Indians. It was vital that there be no repetition of Pontiac's uprising. Over time certain practices developed, always with a view to maintaining harmonious relations between the British and the Indians, and in times of crisis to securing Indian warriors for the British standard. Skilled practitioners of forest diplomacy like Sir William Johnson, Sir John Johnson, Alexander McKee, or Matthew Elliott performed the proper ceremonies intuitively, based on long experience. But newcomers, especially post commanders who rotated frequently, could not draw on such experience. Accordingly these practices were formalized. Special instructions were designed to insure that agents and post commanders would provide rations for visiting Indians, disperse the proper type of gift, use the proper greeting and generally conduct themselves in a manner appropriate to their station and their location (fig. 1). The precise details included in these instructions reveal the importance accorded to Indian affairs. Instructions issued by Gov. Frederick Haldimand in 1783, for example, advised that if an Indian or a group of Indians presented the post commander with a gift upon their arrival, he must respond with a gift of equal or preferably greater value (Public Record Office [London] 42. Vol. 44:189–194).

Until 1830 the general policy remained constant, but

there were ebbs and flows. Obviously times of outright hostility saw the greatest attention paid to the Indian Department. During the American Revolution, bands from Canada, especially the Caughnawaga and St. Regis Iroquois, but also other groups such as the Mississaugas of southern Ontario, were courted assiduously. The same was true during the crisis in the Old Northwest between 1783 and 1796 and during the years leading to and including the War of 1812. At such times the application of British Indian policy extended beyond its normal bounds. The Indian factor figures prominently in Governor Haldimand's decision to retain the western posts in spite of the 1783 Treaty of Paris (Burt 1931). On two occasions Indians from the United States were offered asylum in Canada—the Six Nations of Iroquois in 1783–1784 and Potawatomi and Ottawa of the Detroit River in 1796 (Johnston 1964; Surtees 1982: 152–154). For two years after the Indian victories over the British in 1790 and 1791, the lieutenant governor of Upper Canada (present southern Ontario) seriously proposed the cre-

ation of an Indian barrier state between the United States and British North America (Wise 1953). And even after the British finally evacuated the western posts in 1796, British Indian agents continued to exercise what influence they could among the Indians of the Old Northwest, a practice that has been generally considered as one of the factors leading to the War of 1812.

The years immediately following that conflict witnessed two developments that greatly altered the status of Indians in Canada. First, through a combination of treaties with the borderland tribes and diplomatic demands upon the British government, the United States effectively pulled the Indians under its charge away from the border and away from connections with the British Indian Department and the Six Nations, Chippewa, and Wyandot of Upper Canada. The Canadian Indians had always owed a considerable portion of their stature to this American Indian connection. When that weakened, their importance in Canadian society declined. It declined

Rev. Peter and Mary Dally, Vashon Island, Wash.

Fig. 1. Fort Douglas, Red River Colony, Canada. Gov. Andrew Bulger greets a group of Chippewa Indians from the Red Lake district (now Minn.). Fort Douglas, about 35 miles from the mouth of the Red River, was the seat of the colony's government (Josephy 1970). Pen and ink over pencil by Peter Rindisbacher, about 1823.

further as the non-Indian population of the upper province grew from 80,000 in 1812 to 220,000 by 1830. (Lower 1958:193). By 1827 the Lords of the Treasury in England, having observed this changed circumstance as well as more than a decade of peace with the United States, observed that the Indian Department was no longer necessary and suggested its abolition. It is quite possible that this money saving suggestion would have been adopted had not other developments taken place in the 1820s in Canada and in England.

The Era of Civilization

In Canada, English-speaking missionaries finally began to take an interest in Indian conditions. The most aggressive were the Methodists, whose programs included the convictions that the Indians must be enticed into settling into an agricultural environment in order that they be both christianized and civilized. But the Methodists were directed from the United States, a consideration that concerned Lt. Gov. Peregrine Maitland who feared the missionaries might, in addition to their efforts at promoting civilization and Christianity, promote republican values among their Indian disciples. Thus, although Indian affairs lay beyond his jurisdiction (they were a military matter 1755–1796 and 1816–1830 in Upper Canada) he sponsored a village among the Mississaugas of the Credit River and further suggested that government might be well advised to encourage other such projects in order to avoid the American influence and to promote the Church of England (Quealey 1968:300–333). In England, concurrently, the evangelical movement had begun to promote the idea of better treatment for native peoples generally throughout the empire and, equally important, had succeeded in placing men of this temperament in positions of power. The old policy was summarized by George Murray, Colonial Secretary 1828–1830, as concerned with "the advantage which might be derived from [Indian] friendship in times of war, rather than to any settled purpose of gradually reclaiming them from a state of barbarism and of introducing amongst them the industrious and peaceful habits of civilized life" (PAC 1830). Efforts at "reclaiming them" from a state of barbarism were to involve the congregating of Indians in villages, providing sufficient land for their support, arranging for instruction in agriculture and husbandry, furnishing assistance in building houses, supplying rations, seed and agricultural implements, and, of course, seeing to their instruction in the Christian faith. Some of this land had already been done by private groups such as the Methodists, the Moravians and, of course, by Governor Maitland. In 1830 it became official policy, sanctioned by the colonial secretary and approved, somewhat reluctantly, by the British Treasury (Surtees 1969).

88   For Upper Canada it was a new and to many a very

exciting new program; for Lower Canada it was merely an extension westward of ideas that dated to the *Jesuit Relation* of 1635 (Mealing 1963:39–47) and that had been followed in villages such as Bécancour, Lorette, and Caughnawaga for almost two centuries.

Administratively the Indian Department was split in 1830. Control for Indian Affairs remained with the military secretary in Lower Canada, but it was transferred to the lieutenant governor in Upper Canada. The military connection was completely broken a decade later when the two officers were amalgamated and placed under the authority of the governor general of the United Province of Canada. A further change occurred in 1860 when the imperial government transferred control of Indian affairs to the Province of Canada, which then delegated that charge to the Crown Lands Department. Two years later the position of deputy superintendent general was created. The superintendent general's position continued to be held by a member of the government, a practice begun in 1844 (Leighton 1975:148).

With the formal adoption of a civilization policy, the Indians of Canada became wards of the government. It was paternalistic, of course, but the goal was that of convincing and enabling Indians to become full members of society, and the reserves—with their instructors, agents, teachers and missionaries—were to be the instruments by which that step could be taken. Some of the early land cession treaties had, on the insistence of the Indians involved, tracts of land set apart for the exclusive use of Indians at the Huron Reserve, the Credit River Reserve, the Nutfield Tract, and the Sarnia Reserve. At the time these were merely plots of ground upon which Indians had traditionally conducted a particular enterprise (such as fishing at the mouth of the Credit River) and wished to continue to do so. The new policy of 1830 required that these reserves be developed to pursue the goal of civilization. If such reserves had not been created by the original treaties, government instituted them, as at Coldwater-Narrows, Rice Lake, Mud Lake, or Alnwick; and future land cessions always included provision for reserves for the Indians of the ceded area. In the lower province, east of the Ottawa River, Indian reserves and villages had evolved during the French regime; during the British regime 11 new reserves were created in 1851 when the government authorized a grant of 93,150 hectares of land to native peoples there (Francis 1983:33–35).

As agents of the Indian Department set about the task of implementing the new policy, they encountered resistence from the Indians. They also encountered indifference, hostility, and obstruction from Whites. It was considered necessary, therefore, to buttress the policy through colonial legislation. Accordingly, by 1850 the colonial government had passed laws that protected Indian lands in Upper Canada against trespass by non-Indians, against seizure for nonpayment of debts, and even against taxation since the land was considered as being held in trust by the Crown. Other statutes also forbade the sale of liquor to Indians. In Lower Canada, Indian lands were also protected, but the unique feature of this legislation was the effort to define the designation of "Indian." It was a broad definition that included anyone of native ancestry (by blood or marriage) who belonged to or lived with a recognized Indian band (Francis 1983: 32–33).

Legislation also dealt with and even expanded the goal of civilization. Observers noted that progress in this area since 1830 was at best limited and suggested that it might be facilitated by concentrating the Indian villages in areas where they were surrounded by White communities. Such circumstances could provide opportunities for Indians not only to progress toward a civilized life but also to integrate themselves in the long term into the European environment. Therefore, protection could lead to civilization, which could lead in turn to assimilation (Tobias 1976:16). It was not a new idea. Indeed, the Jesuits had rejected it in the seventeenth century because proximity to Whites was considered detrimental to progress. But mid-nineteenth-century observers felt that the principle was working in Michigan and should be applied in Canada. It was a theory accepted by many missionaries and serves to explain the Methodist support of the government decision to open the Saugeen tract for settlement in 1854 because it would bring the Indians of that remote region into regular contact with Europeans. It was with hopes for the increasing integration of Indians that the legislature of Canada in 1857 passed the "Act to encourage the gradual Civilization of the Indian Tribes in this Province, and to amend the Laws respecting Indians" (20 Vic. cap. 26). The 1857 legislation was a significant legal and theoretical landmark. It confirmed the goal of civilization by announcing the noble intention to "remove all legal distinctions between Indians and other Canadians, and integrate them fully into Canadian Society" (Tobias 1976: 16). Its significance lies in the establishment of the criteria by which progress in that direction could be measured. This was the process known as enfranchisement, which would become a cornerstone of future Indian administration.

If a commission of three—the local Indian agent, the local missionary and a person appointed by the governor—reported that a male Indian was literate, over 21 years of age, of good moral character, and free from debt, then that Indian would be enfranchised, and "all . . . enactments making any distinction between the legal rights and abilities of Indians and those of Her Majesty's other subjects, shall cease to apply to any Indian so declared to be enfranchised, who shall no longer be deemed an Indian within the meaning thereof." The commission could also inquire regarding an Indian male, aged 21–45, and if they found him, though not literate,

"able to speak readily either the English or the French language, of sober and industrious habits, free from debt, and sufficiently intelligent to be capable of managing his own affairs," they could report favorably on his application for enfranchisement (Leslie and Maguire 1978:28). If that man then conducted himself to their satisfaction during a three-year probationary period, he would be enfranchised. In the minds of the legislators and administrators, enfranchisement was a goal that Indians would seek, and to discourage Indians from claiming the distinction falsely the act imposed a penalty of up to six months imprisonment for such action (Leslie and Maguire 1978:27).

In 1859–1861 legislation consolidated the previous statutes of the province and solidified the jurisdiction over Indian affairs by the provincial government in the areas of liquor control, land alienation from reserves, and the control of reserve resources (Leslie and Maguire 1978: 33–34). The goals of Indian policy were, therefore, integrated as was control over them. It had been a lengthy process, for Upper Canada and Lower Canada had developed policies and methods of administration from two distinct origins, but by 1860 these had been united. Official control of Indian affairs had been an imperial responsibility since 1755, but this had been eroded over the years by the declining importance of Indians, and by the growth of representative and then responsible government in the Canadas. The imperial link was finally severed in 1862 when the British government formally transferred authority in this field to the colony.

The Dominion of Canada

After the Dominion of Canada was established in 1867 the federal government, having been charged in the constitution with responsibility for "Indians and lands reserved for Indians," indicated its faith in the policy that it had inherited by taking fairly immediate steps to extend it. In eastern Canada the policy was reinforced consistently through legislation beginning in 1868, revolving around the principle of enfranchisement and its corollary, the institution of elected band councils. In western Canada, it was felt that the bands were not sufficiently advanced for government to impose the eastern model immediately. There government began by concluding a series of land cession treaties, including the now normal schedule of reserves, and then concentrated on assaulting tribal customs and traditions. The ultimate goal throughout was the achievement of enfranchisement. In pursuing this elusive goal from one apparently logical step to the next, the Department of Indian Affairs, through its agents, found itself becoming intimately involved in the local and even the private affairs of Indian bands. As this circumstance developed, the Department became increasingly autocratic and paternalistic in its methods and in its attitude.

The process began first in eastern Canada. The Indian Act of 1868 (31 Vic. cap. 42) confirmed the principle of protection by providing a definition—largely racial—for an Indian and by emphasizing penalties for non-Indians who trespassed on Indian lands. The principle of civilization, leading to assimilation, was also confirmed by the 1869 Enfranchisement Act (Tobias 1976:16–17; 32–33 Vic. cap. 42), which reaffirmed several features of Indian policy and introduced some new ones for the Canadian period.

The Enfranchisement Act gave an Indian the same rights, politically and socially, as non-Indians, including the right to vote. In effect the enfranchised Indian ceased to be an Indian and became a member of Canadian society at large. Although enfranchisement offered a means of measuring the success of the program, only one Indian had relinquished his Indian status since the 1857 law was passed (Leslie 1985:157). This was disconcerting to Indian Affairs officials who viewed enfranchisement as pivotal to Indian policy. Consequently the principle of elected band councils was also introduced in the 1869 legislation, a move designed to promote enfranchisement in two ways.

By "establishing a responsible, for an irresponsible system," wrote Willage Spragge, the deputy superintendent of Indian affairs in 1871, "this provision, by law, was designed to pave the way to the establishment of simple municipal institutions . . . " (Canada 1871:4). This meant that Indians on reserves would grow accustomed to the political institutions that existed off the reserve, and in this fashion would progress in yet another way toward civilization and assimilation. A system of elected band councils would also attack the traditional or hereditary Indian methods of choosing leaders, one of the last vestiges of tribal society that the government wished to remove. The 1869 Act allowed the minister responsible for Indian affairs (who also held the post of superintendent general) to impose such elected councils, but to make it somewhat more palatable the councils' powers were increased beyond minor police and health matters to include things such as the construction and care of public buildings, the maintenance of roads and the repression of intemperance. And chiefs also received the right, upon sanction by the superintendent general, to indicate which of his band members could be enfranchised. The superintendent general in 1869 was Hector Langevin, who declared that large numbers of Indians could be expected to enfranchise through this legislation (Daugherty and Madill 1980, 2:2,3).

From this point onward, the implementation of policy became a series of thrusts and counterthrusts by government through legislation and by Indians through resistence. The comprehensive "Act to amend and consolidate the laws respecting Indians," the Indian Act of 1876 (39

Vic. cap. 18), tinkered slightly with enfranchisement and elected councils. Elected councils became voluntary and could no longer be imposed, and their powers were increased somewhat. Although this consolidated legislation would form the basis of all future Indian acts, it contained only one significant innovation: the location ticket (Tobias 1976:17–18). This was a method designed to promote the acquisition of private property by Indians and still provide protection for them. Reserves were to be divided, under the authority of the superintendent general, into lots that could be assigned to individual band members who had previously shown extensive progress toward a civilized state. The location ticket would be his deed to that plot of land. If, after a three-year period, he demonstrated an ability to use his land effectively—as a White farmer might—he was to be enfranchised and given full title to his property. A ticket of location and immediate enfranchisement could, under this legislation, be granted to any Indian who had demonstrated acceptance of European values and an ability to function in Canadian society by earning professional status as a teacher, minister, lawyer, or doctor. Enfranchisement would serve a double purpose. First, it demonstrated a successful government program. Second, an Indian enfranchised with a location on the reserve would take his land with him, and if enfranchisement were sufficiently widespread it would mean the end of any need for reserves or for an Indian Affairs department.

It was assumed that in the eastern regions of Canada the longstanding contact between Whites and Indians, combined with the longstanding missionary and governmental efforts, had altered Indian society enough to prepare Indians for enfranchisement. Legislation after 1876, therefore, was designed to promote the connected goals of enfranchisement and elected councils, and to counter any Indian opposition to them. Thus in 1880 (43 Vic. cap. 28) the government, because of Indian reticence, re-established the right of the superintendent general to impose the elective system where he judged a band was ready for it; and if traditional leaders were still recognized after the elective process had been imposed the superintendent general could deny them official recognition by declaring that only duly elected councilors would receive the ear of the government. When some bands countered this by simply electing leaders already chosen via traditional means, the government obtained the power through the Indian Advancement Act of 1884 (47 Vic. cap. 27–28) to depose them for intemperance, immorality, or incompetence. This power was reinforced to prohibit persons thus deposed from standing for re-election. The Indian Advancement Act also enhanced the band council's authority in local matters in general and in particular by granting them power to levy taxes on real property; but the powers of the superintendent general, and therefore the powers of the agents in the field, were also increased to include regulations regarding elections as well as the right to call, preside over, advise, participate in, and adjourn band council meetings. As one observer notes, "the agent directed the political affairs of the band" (Tobias 1976: 20).

Political interference was accompanied by financial involvement. Enfranchisement, in large measure, rested on the location ticket so bands could negate the system by neglecting or refusing to allocate lands to band members. After the power to allot lands was removed from the council and vested in the superintendent general, the bands could still resist by refusing to approve the surrender of allocated lands to permit those who held tickets of location to lease or sell their holdings. Accordingly 1884 and 1894 legislation empowered the superintendent general to approve such leases without prior land surrender. In 1898 another statute (61 Vic. cap. 34) permitted the superintendent general to impose regulations regarding health and policing on the reserves when band councils refused to do this themselves and to use band funds for their enforcement (Tobias 1976:20; Daugherty and Madill 1980, 2:18–20, 27-37).

The West

The principal subjects of these measures were the Indians east of Lake Superior. The ultimate goal for the western regions was "the gradual introduction of those agencies which in Canada (i.e. Upper and Lower Canada) have operated so beneficially in promoting settlement and civilization among the Indians" (Surtees 1971:64). Joseph Howe, secretary of state for the provinces and therefore also chief superintendent of Indian affairs, wrote these words in 1871. He obviously adhered to the view that conditions in the recently acquired Canadian West were not yet conducive for that goal. There policy had to concern itself with the acquisition of Indian lands to prepare the way for the transcontinental railway that had just been promised to British Columbia, and with the task of somehow domesticating large numbers of Indians who had not been subjected to any longstanding or consistent contact with a settled White community, who still possessed ample means of continuing to pursue their traditional means of making a living through the chase and through the weir, and who were therefore able to cling tenaciously to their ancient cultures, mores and values.

Changes in the western Indian position took place with frightening alacrity. Between 1871 and 1877, commissioners sent by the federal government concluded seven major land cession treaties with the western tribes, thereby securing the bulk of the lands between Lake Superior and the Rocky Mountains. The Canadian Pacific Railway was completed in 1885; settlement had begun over a decade earlier. By 1880 the mainstay of western Indian life—the buffalo—had almost completely disappeared, and almost all segments of the Cree, Assiniboin, Piegan, Sioux, Blood, and Blackfoot bands had been forced through circumstance to take up residence on the lands provided in the treaties.

They did so without enthusiasm, and some leaders, notably the Plains Cree chiefs Poundmaker and Big Bear, attempted, by organizing large Indian councils in central Saskatchewan in 1883 and 1884, to bring native grievances, forcefully but peacefully, to the government's attention. These efforts came to naught. When the Métis of the region, who had their own grievances against the Canadian government, rose in rebellion in 1885, the more warlike elements among the Western Woods Cree and Plains Cree of Treaty No. 6 region also took up arms. This Northwest Rebellion was quickly crushed by Canadian troops (figs. 2–3).

On the Pacific slope no treaties were concluded, these being deemed unnecessary because colonial policies seemed to preclude them. Also the Pacific coast tribes tended to confine themselves to fairly restricted areas because of the terrain and because of their established patterns of deriving a living from the ocean. However, reserves did exist, and others were created as the interior of British Columbia was opened.

Because the goals of civilization leading to enfranchisement were intended to apply among the tribes in western Canada, government continued to pass legislation to this end. The Department and its agents were drawn even

Public Arch. of Canada, Ottawa: C 1879.
Fig. 2. Louis Riel, a Red River Métis and a leader of the Northwest Rebellion of 1885, addressing the jury. Riel's political activities began in 1869 when Métis unrest grew in response to events associated with government land surveys and political appointments that were believed to threaten Métis rights. Much of the rebellion focused on bicultural issues and aspects of territorial annexation. In a highly politicized trial, Riel was sentenced to death for treason (Thomas 1982: 736–753). Photographer unknown, Regina, Sask., 1885.

more sharply into the practice of regulating Indian life on the reserves.

Government Regulation

Traditional practices were attacked because they promoted pagan beliefs and in doing so helped to resist the absorption of Christian and European values. Thus the Sun Dance popular among the Plains tribes was declared illegal in 1884 (47 Vic. cap. 28). Later even the practice of performing tribal ceremonies in traditional dress at public events like rodeos was also prohibited, to the point that such ceremonies were banned even if ceremonial dress was not worn. The potlatch of the Pacific Coast tribes was considered especially dangerous because its very basis denied the important principle of private property. It too was attacked in 1895 by federal statute (58–59 Vic. cap. 35). A double purpose lay behind efforts to discourage the Plains Cree, Blackfoot, and other tribes of western Canada from the pursuits of hunting and fishing. Such activities were not so productive as in the days of the buffalo hunt, but they could still be practiced, especially if the reserve

served as a base; Indians who did so were resisting the process of civilization in two ways: they were rejecting, or at least retarding, the development of a farming base that was considered essential to progress, and they also were retarding the education of their children who usually accompanied their parents on the hunt. Thus in 1890 the governor of Canada received the authority to have the Manitoba and Territories game laws apply to Indians (53 Vic. cap. 29). Residential and industrial schools were considered to be a means of removing Indian children from the hunt and from other parental influences that slowed their progress toward civilization. But these were also the reasons why Indian parents refused to send their children to the distant White schools. The government reacted by legislating itself the power to require attendance at these schools (57 Vic. cap. 32).

Continued Indian resistance to the policy of civilization caused the government to become even more dogmatic and more involved in local band affairs. In 1917, for example, the superintendent general received authority to dispense band money to assist individual Indians in the purchase of farming equipment, and in 1922 he was

Public Arch. of Canada, Ottawa:C 1872.

Fig. 3. Indians and Whites involved in aspects of the Northwest Rebellion of 1885. left to right, back row: Constable Black, N.W.M.P., Rev. Louis Cochin, Captain Deone, Rev. Alexis Andre, Beverley Robertson; front row: Horse Child, son of Big Bear, Big Bear, A.D. Stewart, and Poundmaker, probably during judicial proceedings. Although Poundmaker and Big Bear met with Louis Riel in June 1884, Indian grievances with the Canadian government differed from those of the Métis. A cut in government rations and starving conditions of the winter of 1883–1884 led to Indian discontent, but Indian violence was perceived by Whites as linked to Riel's activities. After the final battle of the rebellion, Father Cochin was sent by Poundmaker to authorities with a request for peace negotiations, but the request was denied. Although sentenced to 3 years imprisonment for treason, Poundmaker was later recognized as one who worked toward peace. Father Andre, a defense witness at Riel's trial, had earlier disagreed with Riel's activities. Photograph by O.B. Buell, probably Regina, Sask., 1885.

92

empowered to declare general provincial laws applicable to reserves (Tobias 1976:23–24). The former was an effort to promote farming; by having the general laws regarding such matters as motor vehicles and recreational facilities apply on the reserve, the latter was designed to reduce the distinction between reserve and White communities.

During the Canadian regime, therefore, Indian policy was applied rather than formulated. The principles and goals and even the general instruments—the reserves—had been developed during the French and British periods. The application of policy, however, resulted in a series of new tactics by Indian agents and officials—supported by federal legislation. In addition to the thrusts and counterthrusts regarding major issues such as enfranchisement and elected band councils, there were other developments that increased the authority of Indian agents in the areas of policing powers, reserve management, reserve monies, school attendance, and traditional native practices. One example will illustrate. In 1895 legislation granted Indian agents the powers of two justices of the peace with respect to the sections of the Criminal Code concerning liquor (58–59 Vic. cap. 35). In spite of this authority, however, the policy, by the most generous assessment, could not be termed successful. If the enfranchisement yardstick were imposed, it fell very short for fewer than 300 had obtained enfranchisement by 1920 (Tobias 1976:22). Since 1920 the numbers have also been discouraging to administrators.

Two major factors can be cited to account for this. First, the circumstances surrounding Indian affairs mitigated against success. The Indian Department was not considered a very significant part of the public service. In 1900 Minister of the Interior Clifford Sifton felt that the goal of gradual civilization was good, but he was far more concerned with developing Canada's interior, especially in the west, than with promoting the Indian branch (Daugherty and Madill 1980, 2:26). This was a general sentiment among politicians and the public. At times Indian agents were even seen to encourage traditional Indian pursuits like trapping or hunting since these alleviated the pressures for monies from government (Taylor 1984:203). Moreover, the Department had only 1,000 employees in 1939 (Taylor 1984:4), no doubt a reflection of its relative importance, and the range of peoples under its charge was very diverse. It is not surprising that in the twentieth century the aggressive practices of the 1870s and 1880s were softened. The branch, while continuing to pay some homage to the goal of gradual civilization and assimilation, became almost an entrenched social service for maintaining the status quo. "There is no intention," said Deputy Superintendent General Duncan Campbell Scott in 1927, "of changing the well-established policy of dealing with Indians and Indian Affairs in this country" (Taylor 1984:5).

More serious was the second factor, the stubborn

Depart. of Ind. and Northern Affairs, Quebec.
Fig. 4. Members of the Nishga Tribal Council (left to right): Guy Williams, Maurice Nice, Rod Robinson, and Frank Calder, president, in Montreal, Nov. 1971. The Nishga initiated their land claims case in 1967 in the B.C. provincial courts; the case was lost before the Supreme Court of Canada in 1973 (Canada. Indian Claims Commission 1975). The substantive issue of aboriginal title remained unresolved, and the public attention focused on this case forced Canadian politicians to examine native claims. Frank Calder, in 1949, was the first Indian elected to a Canadian legislature, the B.C. Legislative Assembly (Raunet 1984:143–166). Photographer unknown.

determination of Indians to resist government policy. At first this tended to be simply a reflex action opposed to new circumstances and new laws in favor of traditions. It has often been observed that native peoples possessed a different understanding of the treaties than did the British or Canadian officials who negotiated with them. This is also true of other features of Indian policy. Resentment of government interference in practices such as the Sun Dance and potlatch was common, as was the tampering with traditional systems of government and attempts at forced enfranchisement. However, the Indians began gradually to accommodate themselves to the new conditions and to use them differently from the agents' expectation. During the years between World Wars, there was a gradual change in the attitudes of both Indians and government administrators.

The degree of understanding achieved by some Indian people about themselves and their situation . . . . [was] evident in their approach to issues such as the British Columbia land question, enfranchisement, and Indian political associations. The British Columbia Indians wanted to negotiate with governments as equals. Political associations were intended to be channels of communication and vehicles for the determination of matters affecting Indian people and their future.

There began to develop during this period, concepts, of 'being Indian' that differed from mere enfranchisement and were not necessarily incompatible with full Canadian citizenship (Taylor 1984:7).

This concept was difficult for Indian agents to understand; it also grew very slowly for it was difficult to articulate and it was also difficult to circulate among an Indian population that was spread across several hundred reserves. But it did grow, and its growth was increased by the publicity surrounding an exceptional Indian participation in Canada's forces during World War II. This, in turn, led to an unprecedented round of discussions regarding Indian affairs in public circles, followed by the appointment of a parliamentary joint committee, to investigate Indian conditions in Canada. The legislation that resulted—the Indian Act of 1951--did not implement many changes. Rather it brought under the aegis of one statute the full range of legislation regarding Indian affairs; the goals and the policy remained unchanged (15 George VI, cap. 29).

A special commission's report had more dramatic results. This was *The Survey of the Contemporary Indians of Canada* (Hawthorn 1966–1967), a comprehensive report that described the situation of Indians as being generally very greatly depressed, materially (fig. 6), when compared to Canadians in general. It also observed that to correct this circumstance it should not require that an Indian "acquire those values of the major society he does not hold or wish to acquire." The report also made a case for granting a "Citizen Plus" status to Indians, and noted

"possible conflict between the status of citizens plus and the egalitarian attitudes both whites and Indians hold. On the other hand, the reverse status Indians have held, as Citizens minus, which is equally repugnant to a strongly egalitarian society, has been tolerated for a long time, perhaps because it was out of sight and so out of mind of most people" (Hawthorn 1966–1967, 1:6).

The issue of Indian Affairs has seldom been out of the public mind since. Despite the influence that the Hawthorn report had on many persons in the Department of Indian Affairs, it was largely repudiated within the central agencies of the government (Weaver 1981:83–87). The official response, a document entitled "Statement of the Government of Canada on Indian Policy, 1969," generally known as the "White Paper" (Canada. Department of Indian Affairs and Northern Development 1969), rejected the "Citizen Plus" concept in favor of an egalitarian ideology. While disappointed, Indians and other observers could find little fault with the White Paper's declaration that "the legislative and constitutional basis of discrimination be removed" or that "there be a positive recognition

Dept. of Ind. and Northern Affairs, Quebec: 01-03-09-03.
Fig. 5. Sen. James Gladstone (second from left) (b. 1887, d. 1971), first Indian appointed to the Senate of Canada, 1958. Beginning in 1947, Gladstone, a Treaty Indian of the Blood Reserve, Standoff, near Ft. McCloud, Alta., served for many years as president of the Indian Association of Alberta. He was appointed to the Senate by Prime Minister John G. Diefenbaker in fufillment of a campaign promise made by the Conservative party in 1957 to appoint an Indian to this office. Gladstone was cochairman of a parlimentary committee on Indian policy, 1959–1961 (Hugh Dempsy, personal communication 1986). Gladstone is talking with a group of Western Woods Cree men on the Fisher River Agency, Man. Photograph by Hugh Allan, 1958.

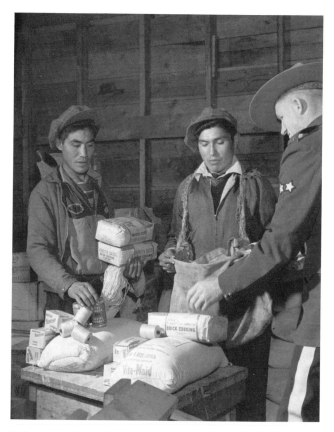

Public Arch. of Canada, Ottawa: PA 114830.
Fig. 6. R.C.M.P. Constable W.H. Christianson assembling supplies for distribution to Hare Indians, Ft. Good Hope, N.W.T. After World War II, when fur prices dropped and natives were settled near towns rather than in the bush, the Canadian government began to provide increased services to the Hare, including welfare and rations. In the late 1950s, regional administrators began to work toward partial decentralization of the Hare bands in order to restore their self-sufficiency (vol. 6:322–324). Photograph by George Hunter, 1953.

by everyone of the unique contribution of Indian culture to Canadian life"; but the proposals to repeal the Indian Act, to assign extensive responsibility for Indian affairs to the provincial governments, and to abolish the Department of Indian Affairs (Surtees 1971:97–98) were considered dangerous, sudden, and an abdication of responsibility. Opposition to the plan was considerable, including articulate criticisms from native people such as Harold Cardinal (1969).

The White Paper was not implemented, but the controversy surrounding it continued. Indian organizations became much more articulate and skillful; and considerable research of historical and sociological nature by academics, by government officials, and by Indians provided in ensuing years a much more substantial information base. Moreover, the resources, particularly oil, in areas where land cessions had not extinguished Indian title, as well as land claims in the treaty areas of Canada kept Indian affairs very much in public view (fig. 7). The effect was more practical than philosophical. The emphasis on enfranchisement was replaced by efforts to strengthen the economic and social conditions on reserves. There remained a desire to "ameliorate" the circumstances of native people, but unlike the theories begun in the nineteenth centuries this effort no longer required Indian acceptance of Christianity and European morals and mores. Nor were the reserves expected to serve as the instruments to promote those twin goals. Rather they were to be homelands, or bases, from which Indian conditions could be improved, and Indians themselves took a much more active role in managing the reserves, as administrators, teachers, or entrepreneurs. This has not been effective everywhere, but it has been sufficiently successful at Walpole Island, Manitoulin Island, and the Grand River reserves, Ontario, to encourage some Indian leaders to seek greater autonomy. It is this that surrounds the debate regarding the concept of "Indian self-government." In essence this concept calls for the granting of

NDP NDP NDP NDP NDP NDP NDP NDP NDP NDP NDP NDP

Native People

The people who were here first should feel it's still their home.

For many generations native people have suffered from discrimination or from paternalistic treatment by insensitive governments.

The New Democratic Party would:
Recognize the rights of native citizens – settle land claims in the North before any change in the form of government in the Territories. The Clark and Trudeau governments all ignored the rights of native people guaranteed by treaty or legislation. New Democrats would include native people's representatives in discussions about changes in the constitution.

We would restore specific rights such as hunting, fishing and trapping, with the agreement of the native peoples themselves, and compensate them when necessary for any loss of those rights. We can have different ways of living in a country as big as Canada, or else we can't claim to have a truly free country.

An NDP government would work in partnership with native people in developing natural resources in the North; we must respect historic sites and burial grounds before developments go ahead.

We would fulfil treaty promises made by the government. Where treaties are obviously unfair, we will negotiate new agreements with the native people affected by them. Where no treaties exist, we will acknowledge legitimate, hereditary titles and negotiate with the bands or tribes concerned.

We would restore full medical and dental services to reserves that were recently cut back by the federal government.

Canada's New Democrats believe that Indians, Inuit and Métis deserve the same right to a good and healthy life as all Canadians. Because that's fair.

New Democratic Party of Canada, Ont.

Fig. 7. Page from campaign literature of the New Democratic Party, 1980. Native land claims and aboriginal rights are campaign issues in Canadian federal elections.

fuller powers—including the right of land alienation, the issuing of bonds, the control over social services—to band councils. As yet it is still a matter of debate (Canada. Parliament. House of Commons 1983). It may experience the same fate as the White Paper. In the meantime the Indian Act of 1951 remains in place. But while there has been no official or formal renunciation of enfranchisement, it is unlikely that there will be a return to applying policy and practice as was done in the nineteenth century or the first half of the twentieth.

Spanish Indian Policies

CHARLES GIBSON

There is no simple or obvious way to apply the concept of national policy to the action of Spain in America, for the historian of this subject is confronted with a multiplicity of policies related more or less closely to the succession of changing circumstances over 300 years. Even by confining attention to policies toward Indians the range is still very great. The situation is compounded in the particular instances, quite numerous, where royal policy competed with and lost out to the policies of political subordinates and private interests. Discrepancies between the professed aims and the local realities of Spanish imperialism require much further study.

Early Spanish-Indian Relations

Christopher Columbus and his followers in the West Indies were concerned with Indians both as curiosities and as slaves, the latter far more than the former. Much of the Spanish movement from one island to another and subsequently from the islands to selected points on the mainland is attributable to the search for new peoples to enslave. Indian slaves were in some instances returned to Spain. But most were worked in agriculture, mining, and other tasks in the island colonies themselves. Enslavement of American Indians followed in general the precedents of Hispanic and other European enslavement of Blacks from the African coast (Sauer 1966; Konetzke 1963).

While enslavement expanded in the early period, an effort to modify the severity of Spanish conduct toward Indians emerged in the legal institution of encomienda, which had its beginnings in Hispaniola under Gov. Nicolás de Ovando after 1501 (Lamb 1956). Encomienda depended on the assignment of groups of Indians to selected Spanish recipients, called encomenderos. Indians were to work for their encomenderos and pay them tribute. The encomenderos in turn were to pay wages to their Indians, to protect and christianize them, and to treat them as free persons. In the official phrase of the sixteenth century Indians were "free vassals of the crown," and it was as free royal vassals that they might be temporarily assigned in encomienda to private colonists. The crown always insisted upon the distinction between encomienda and enslavement; nevertheless, in the first half-century or so of Spanish rule in America, the effective difference remained slight, and as many observers noted, encomenderos bought and sold their Indians, exploited them in labor, abused them, and treated them as if they were slaves (Simpson 1950; Zavala 1935).

In preparation for the first formal legal code governing Spanish-Indian relations in 1512, the monarchy invited new expressions of legal and ecclesiastical opinion. Of the texts submitted the best known are "Concerning the Rule of the Spanish King over the Indies" by the Dominican Matías de Paz, and "Of the Ocean Islands" by the jurist Juan López de Palacios Rubios. Both writers insisted that the king of Spain possessed legitimate title to the lands of America and exercised legitimate dominion over its native peoples. Both emphasized the obligation of the monarch to convert Indians to Christianity, an obligation founded on the papal demarcation decree of 1493 and one that imposed the responsibilities of Christian warfare and humane treatment. Paz argued that Indians could legitimately defend themselves in secular warfare against Spaniards—that is, when no effort was made by Spaniards to convert them to Christianity—since only a war designed to propagate the faith constituted a just Christian war. All such opinions—and the two authors developed their subject in much greater detail—incorporated Christian and juridical views abundantly precedented in the intellectual legacy of antiquity and the Middle Ages. There followed a large corpus of writings, continuous to the nineteenth and twentieth centuries, on the themes of Spanish title to America and Christian treatment of Indians (Parry 1940; Hanke 1949; Carro 1944).

The first formal code appeared as the Laws of Burgos of 1512 with amendments issued from Valladolid in 1513. It is a potpourri of principles and minutiae, focused mainly upon the institution of encomienda. The monarch acknowledged that small progress had been made toward christianization in the two decades following the discovery of America, and the Laws of Burgos identified encomienda as the institution through which effective change might henceforth be realized. Indians were to be congregated and made to live near their encomenderos, who were to instruct them in the faith according to detailed provisions carefully laid down. Indians at the mines were to work for five months and then to rest for 40 days. Encomenderos were to provide cooked meat and other food. Indians were to learn the sacraments, abandon polygamy, sleep on hammocks, and in a number of additional stipulated ways conduct themselves after the manner of Christians. In sum the Laws of Burgos, the fullest expression of royal policy in the first generation of Spanish colonization, emphasized the Christian obligation of both Spaniards and Indians, assumed the practical superiority of Spaniards, and proposed a harmonious relationship that was, in the actual conditions of the sixteenth-century colony, unrealistic and unenforceable (Altamira y Crevea 1938).

Conquest

Conquest, the most celebrated single "policy" of Spanish imperialism, had its remote origins in medieval Christian wars against Moors in Spain. More immediate antecedents of conquest in America appear in the Spanish domination of the Canary Islands in the late fifteenth century and in the slave-raiding expeditions of early West Indian history. The Spanish military expeditions in Cuba under Diego Velázquez in 1511 may be understood as transitional between earlier slave raiding and the great conquests of the mainland. During the age of conquest, 1519 to about 1550, Indians occasionally won individual battles, but the long-term result was Spanish domination over masses of Indians and the establishment of settled regimes within which the Indian population occupied the status of wards and laborers.

A number of particular features of conquest are relevant to a discussion of Spanish policy. A Christian purpose, naively implemented, appeared in the famous Requerimiento, a document read to hostile Indians prior to battle, ordinarily at a distance that rendered it inaudible and in a language that the supposed audience could not be expected to understand. The Requerimiento asserted that if Indians refused to accept a Christian life Spaniards would wage justifiable war against them, and that the resultant damages would be "your fault and not ours" (Hanke 1938). Conquistadors characteristically sought Indian allies against other Indians, the foremost examples being the Tlaxcalans in Mexico and the divided Atahualpa-Huascar factions in Peru (fig. 1). The march into the interior and the subjugation of the capital city were standard conquest practices. While secondary expeditions from newly captured capitals were generally successful, it remains true that subsequent conquering efforts failed in certain more remote regions. Northern Mexico and south-central Chile exemplify areas that fell outside the limits of the great native "'empires'" and that came to be controlled by Spaniards only over a long period and via an advancing Spanish frontier.

The policy of conquest was increasingly criticized after the subjugation of the native "empires," and the principal critic of the age of conquest was Bartolomé de Las Casas, a former encomendero and a Dominican friar and bishop.

Biblioteca Nacional, Madrid: MS 315, f. 470/8.

Fig. 1. An Aztec drawing done in 1565, a sort of bill presented for services on a Spanish expedition to Florida, probably that of De Luna and Villafañe in 1559–1561. The drawing is in a largely Spanish style, although the leader has a speech scroll of the native sort and carries a standard bearing the Aztec glyph representing Tenochtitlán, their capital. The text beneath, written in both Nahuatl and Spanish, reports that 100 Aztec nobles, who provided their own weapons, went to Florida with other Indians, that some died and some returned, and that they were paid nothing although their families were released from laboring for the Spaniards. From the Codex Osuna (Chávez Orozco 1947).

Las Casas expressed an extreme Christian pacifism and humanitarianism, asserting that conquests were illegitimate, that all Spanish relations with Indians should be peaceful, and that Spaniards were obligated to restore to Indian ownership the lands and goods they had taken (Giménez Fernández 1953–1960; Bataillon 1951). Such arguments troubled the conscience of the king, who summoned a formal hearing at Valladolid in 1550 to consider conquest and related questions of legitimacy and morality in Spanish imperialism. Las Casas's opponent in the discussions at Valladolid was Juan Ginés de Sepúlveda, whose position was that conquests were justified as Christian wars because of the superiority of Spanish over Indian civilization and for the propagation of the Christian faith. The writings of Ginés de Sepúlveda are striking examples of the justificatory, rationalized, and apologetic literature concerning Spanish imperialism in the sixteenth century (Hanke 1949:111–132; Sepúlveda 1951). Some subsequent royal enactments tended to uphold the Las Casas position. But for the most part the conquests themselves had been completed by the time of the

97

Valladolid discussion, and the termination of the age of conquest is attributable less to a formal adoption of Las Casas's views (they were in fact never formally adopted) than to the circumstance that no wealthy Indian civilizations remained to be subdued. It should be noted that an unanticipated long-term consequence of Las Casas's criticisms was that they were picked up and reprinted in England, the Low Countries, France, and other countries unfriendly to Spain and that they contributed to the popular, largely Protestant, reputation of Spaniards as bloodthirsty and cruel conquistadors (Juderías y Loyot 1943).

Encomienda

After conquest, encomienda became the most significant, and most controversial, of the institutions governing Spanish-Indian relations. Encomiendas were assigned everywhere that Spaniards went. At first the recipients of encomienda grants tended to be conquistadors. By degrees nonconquistadors, wealthy and influential civilian colonists, and political officials were included within the encomendero ranks. Through the mid-sixteenth century encomienda was the principal institution by means of which Indians performed the labor of the colony and enriched an elite class of colonists. It continued to be an institution of exploitation, with coercion, unremunerated labor exaction, extortion of tribute, and a variety of unauthorized practices.

The monarchy meanwhile vacillated in its position respecting encomienda. On one hand the rising encomendero class assumed the status of a local nobility and threatened royal sovereignty. The monarch was repeatedly enjoined by Las Casas and others to abolish encomienda on Christian humanitarian grounds. On the other hand the king was informed that encomienda was a necessary institution in the colonies and that to terminate it would be to destroy an essential ingredient in the fabric of American life. Several royal attempts to legislate against encomienda proved to be failures. The most important such legislation, embodied in the New Laws of the Indies in 1542, was openly disobeyed or, where efforts were made to enforce it, provoked armed encomendero dissension.

After 1542 royal policy abandoned the goal of outright abolition of encomienda, seeking rather to control it, to surround it with legal limitations, and gradually to incorporate encomienda Indians under direct crown rule. Indian enslavement was then generally confined to individual punishment authorized in court sentences. Encomienda inheritance, for the most part primogenital, was curtailed. Royal officers, especially *visitadores* appointed for this purpose, enforced uniform tribute schedules in encomienda and prohibited the extreme exactions characteristic of the earlier years. The judicial machinery of Spanish imperialism—*audiencias* in the New World

and the Council of the Indies in Madrid—condemned encomienda excesses and increasingly saw to the enforcement of the restrictive legislation. In central Mexico, encomienda progressively lost its hold over Indians during the second half of the sixteenth century. By the end of the century only a small fraction of the Indian population remained under the control of the encomenderos. The change reflected the victory of royal over private authority and the emergence of the expanded bureaucracy characteristic of the reign of Philip II. In effect the monarchy of the first years of the century had confronted a new problem and relinquished control over Indian labor and tribute, whereas the more experienced monarchy of the period after 1550 sought to regain this control and was—as it proved temporarily—successful in doing so (Simpson 1950; Góngora 1951).

Christianization

The Christian purpose loomed large in the justification arguments of the early imperial thinkers, but it was only in the 1520s, when Spaniards confronted great mainland civilizations with millions of inhabitants, that an extensive missionary program for American Indians was initiated. The most important missionaries were Franciscans, Dominicans, Augustinians, and later, Jesuits. The great age of the missionary activity of the first three orders lasted to about 1570, after which royal policy emphasized the secular church and withdrew power from the friars as it was withdrawing power from the encomenderos (Ricard 1933; Tibesar 1953; Armas Medina 1953).

Missionaries understood their task to be not simply the conversion of Indians to Christianity but more fully the education and hispanicization of Indian society. An important aspect of this was *congregación*, whereby scattered Indian families were brought together in new or enlarged nucleated settlements for more effective instruction and a controlled social life (Cline 1949). Increasingly as time passed, missionaries abandoned the more ambitious goals and contented themselves with sacramental instruction and teaching the rudiments of a Christian life. Complete christianization and hispanicization were rarely achieved in Spanish America. The missionaries successfully eliminated human sacrifice and some other non-Christian practices from Indian society, but despite its conspicuous Christian externals the characteristic Indian religion of the seventeenth century preserved many pagan elements. The missionary has commonly received praise from students, for the best missionaries were sincere, dedicated persons of Christian principles, and many were skilled in Indian languages and knowledge of Indian life. The contrast, often made, between the missionary and the conquistador as antithetical (and antagonistic) representatives of the culture of the parent country has some validity. But it should be pointed out also that missionaries shared the pervasive assumptions of Spanish superiority, that their purpose was really to tell Indians how to think and behave, that whipping and imprisonment were standard features of missionary procedure, and that among the missionaries were bigoted, domineering, and exploitative individuals.

The Late Sixteenth Century and After

In the last quarter of the sixteenth century, with the conquests completed, encomienda in decline, and missionary enthusiasm waning, official Spanish attitudes toward Indians assumed forms that would be little changed for the remainder of the colonial period. The imperial regime was characterized by an impoverished monarchy, a powerful and self-centered bureaucracy, administrative torpor and caution, and a widespread disinterest in the welfare of the Indian. A few exceptional persons were dedicated students of Indian civilization in the late sixteenth and seventeenth centuries, but for most Spaniards, both in the parent country and in the colony, Indian "culture" had become a barren subject.

The royal effort to suppress encomienda carried with it some new responses to the problems of crown control over Indians in the late sixteenth century. The state took over and further developed the policies of *congregación*. When encomenderos were eliminated as labor bosses over Indians the state stepped in and for a time regulated Indian labor on a large scale. The regulatory institutions—repartimiento and mita—were effective in distributing Indian laborers to White employers for specified jobs, principally in agriculture and mining, in a rotational labor system. But with a sharp decline in Indian numbers—principally the consequence of European diseases inadvertently carried by the Spaniards—and with the increased demand for labor by a larger White population, rotational and state-controlled labor broke down (Borah 1951; Cook and Borah 1960). While the crown retained control of Indian tribute payment, the successor labor system was one of private hire with a low monetary wage. A further extension of this was peonage, or debt labor. Peonage had become a widespread labor device by the end of the colonial period, but it can hardly be called a "national policy" of Spain, for it developed unofficially without governmental sanction, and though the government came to condone it, its effective history lies in the sector of private enterprise rather than of public administration.

Much the same may be said concerning the progressive alienation of Indian land. Spanish officials to the mid-sixteenth century were fairly careful—though far from wholly scrupulous—in preserving community land in Indian possession. But again with the decline in Indian numbers and with the emergence of a large landholding class of White colonists (hacendados), Indian land became extremely liable to unofficial preemption. In a sense the government's policy was to protect Indian possession of land. But the laws contained many loopholes, the haciendas were ordinarily far stronger than the adjacent Indian communities, and the result was a cumulative land usurpation that left individuals and entire communities landless or with their holdings much reduced. A common condition in many rural areas by the late colonial period was that of the Indian community surrounded by hacienda lands. The economic subordination of the community to the hacienda encouraged a further disintegration of Indian social life and a reconstitution in new, often individual, terms. The standard Indian community of the mid-sixteenth century had combined its traditional organization with the conciliar government common to Spanish towns, all offices being held by Indians. But in towns dominated by haciendas such hispanicized political government frequently collapsed. The crucial relationship became that of the individual Indian worker to the hacienda overseer or *patrón* (Chevalier 1952; Gibson 1964).

The hacienda and the city were focal points of Indian-White (and also Indian-Black) contact in the developed colony, and it was there especially that the ethnically mixed (mestizo) population appeared. The official interest in mestizos, as well as in Blacks, mulattoes, and others was always much less than the official interest in Indians (Mörner 1970).

de Saisset Art Gallery and Mus., Santa Clara, Calif.
Fig. 2. Don Luis Peralta's sword. Peralta (b.1754,d.1851) was the first governor of the Santa Clara Valley and grantee of the Rancho San Antonio, which includes modern-day Alameda and Oakland, Calif. This cavalry sword is typical of arms carried by wealthy Spanish settlers in the late colonial period. The blade carries the inscription "NO ME SACIVES SIN RAZON/NO ME EVAINES SIN HONOR" (Do not draw me without reason/Do not sheathe me without honor). Length 94 cm.

Fig. 3. Mexican lance blade or spontoon, about 1775–1800, stamped with the coat of arms of Castille and Leon on the obverse and the Mexican eagle on a cactus with a snake in its mouth on the reverse. A popular arm of Spanish forces in the New World, the horseman's lance figured prominently in the armament of the expeditions of Hernando de Soto, Cabeza de Vaca, and Francisco de Coronado. Typically 10–14 feet long, the shaft was tipped by an elongated blade. This richly ornamented specimen probably saw service as an insigne. Length 36.3 cm.

Northern Mexico and the Borderlands

Some "borderlands" features relate northern Mexico and the relevant portions of the present United States to the centers of Spanish colonization; other features relate them to other frontier areas of North and South America. In certain respects the borderlands resembled colonial Chile and Paraguay more than Mexico City or Lima, where power, wealth, and elitism were concentrated. Royal authority did not penetrate to the periphery so easily, and enforcement of the law tended to be more relaxed. The frontiers were the locations of the fluctuating societies of the mining camps.

100   Spaniards made contact quite early with the border-

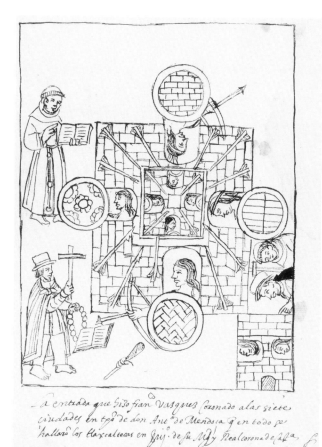

Fig. 4. Pueblo Indians defending a town against Coronado and his Tlaxcalan Indian allies in 1540–1541, as imagined by a 16th-century Tlaxcalan artist. This ink drawing accompanied a description of Tlaxcala written by Diego Muñoz Camargo, a Spanish-educated Tlaxcalan mestizo, which was presented in 1585 to King Phillip II of Spain, by a Tlaxcalan embassy (Acuña 1984). At the top of the page appear the names of provinces reported by Coronado—Señora (Sonora), Quivira, Tiguex, and Çipolla (Cíbola). The legend in Spanish beneath reads: 'The entry which Francisco Vásquez [de] Coronado made into the seven cities [of Cíbola] in the time of [the Viceroy] don Antonio de Mendoza, in all of which the Tlaxcalans were in the service of Your Majesty and the royal crown of Castille'. The drawing is in the early colonial style of New Spain, with features originating in both Spanish and pre-conquest central Mexican Indian artistic traditions.

lands—Juan Ponce de León in Florida in 1512–1513; Francisco Vásquez de Coronado in northern Mexico and the Southwest in 1540–1542--but colonial development and the implementation of imperial policies came relatively slowly (Bourne 1904:157ff.; Bolton 1921; Bannon 1970). An obvious cause is that no Indian civilization north of the Meso-American border appeared sufficiently wealthy or sufficiently impressive to attract concentrated Spanish attention. Spaniards were more than ready to be attracted, as is demonstrated by the belief that cities built of gold existed somewhere in the northern region. But Coronado disproved this myth, and although Coronado's expedition and other northern campaigns of the sixteenth century had some of the characteristics of conquest, no

Museo Naval, Madrid.

Fig. 5. Santa Cruz de Nuca, Spanish base at Friendly Cove, Nootka Sound, Vancouver I. The garrison was established in 1789; the troops' barracks (right rear) were built of large planks. The Spanish corvette *Atrevida* (center) was one of two vessels in the expedition headed by Alejandro Malaspina, commissioned by the Spanish government in 1788 to search for a Northwest Passage, gather scientific data, and create a pictorial record of little known territories. While Malaspina was anchored at Friendly Cove, Nootkan chiefs vied for favorable positions with the Spanish. Chiefs had preferences for different European goods and used their knowledge of competition between European powers to gain advantages (W.L. Cook 1973: 307–313; Cutter 1963:150–155). Ink wash by José Cadero, Aug. 12-28, 1791.

great lands were won and no whole societies subdued and controlled in the classic conquest manner (fig. 4). Additionally, within the borderlands, Florida always had a special and separate character, oriented as it was to the maritime and fortified complex of Havana and the Caribbean and never closely linked with Mexico or the Southwest.

In San Luis Potosí, Zacatecas, and related regions of northern Mexico, the original lure for Spaniards was silver rather than Indian wealth or Indian manpower. Mining became the principal industry after the mid-sixteenth century, and the chief problems were labor recruitment for the extraction and handling of the ores, and supply and protection for the mining areas (Powell 1952). Indian labor was obtained in standard ways: punitive enslavement, encomienda, repartimiento, wage employment, and peonage. But by the standards of central Mexico and Peru the sparse Indian populations never sufficed to support the White population or to meet its needs. In the mines the labor force was made up of Whites, Blacks, mestizos, and mulattoes in addition to Indians, and the conditions of employment were more free than in the coercive Indian labor systems farther south. Organized Indian labor controls broke down in the mines, which came to depend more upon Black slave labor and voluntary hire, for a wage or for a share in the yield (West 1949:228; Howe

1949; Brading 1971). Ranching, one of the important industries of the north, utilized Indian labor only sparingly. The haciendas of northern Mexico were larger and could expand more freely than their counterparts in the south, for the surrounding Indian populations were less sedentary and compact.

The northward movement in New Spain began when encomienda was still in the ascendant and continued until long after encomienda declined. But in general, in the Chichimeca area, the Indian population could not be incorporated in encomienda, for the Indians were of a different type from those of central Mexico and they lacked the precedents of tribute payment and labor service. Encomiendas of a kind were established in Nuevo León in the late sixteenth century (Bolton 1915:288), and in New Mexico a combined encomienda and land-grant system both rewarded the soldiers of the Juan de Oñate conquest of 1598 and served as an incentive for new colonization in the seventeenth century (Bloom 1939; Spicer 1962: 159, 302; Simmons 1969:11). Florida, the only other early Spanish settlement within the boundaries of the present United States, lacked a native population capable of being organized in encomienda terms, and though some of the Florida conquistadors were encomenderos, their possessions were in central Mexico rather than Florida itself. In the later seventeenth century, when

Sonora and Chihuahua were settled, and in the eighteenth century, when Spaniards occupied Texas and California, encomienda was long out of date. Hence only in New Mexico, among borderlands areas of the present United States, were the conditions appropriate for encomienda to be found.

Indian resistance to Spanish civilization in the borderlands was marked by retreat, armed forays, tactics of harassment, and, in the settled regions where Indians were incorporated into the society, open rebellion. One of the most successful of all Indian uprisings in Spanish American history was the Pueblo Revolt of 1680 in New Mexico. The character of Indian society induced some further shifts in emphasis among the institutions of Spanish imperialism. Lay Spanish colonists were not so interested in these Indians. But the frontier conditions provided one of the few remaining grounds, in the late sixteenth century and after, for the continuation of mission labor, and the presence of hostile Indians obligated the state to assume some measures of defense. The mission and the presidio were accordingly characteristic institutions of Spanish occupation in northern Mexico and the Southwest (Bolton 1917). Spanish policy, increasingly reflecting the limited possibilities of a weak European nation, was to provide minimal support for these and to give principal attention to other areas. Selected elements of Spanish Indian policy—Franciscan and (to 1767) Jesuit missions, *congregación*, study of Indian languages—remained locally strong in portions of the borderlands. But even under the threat of British and French expansion in the eighteenth century, Spanish soldiers and missionaries were poorly supported. The eighteenth-century imperial competition in North America—by British and French, by the new government of the United States, and even to some extent by Russia on the Northwest Coast—largely explains Spain's late colonial "defensive expansion" (fig. 5), including the extension of the mission field into California after 1769. But beyond the areas already controlled Spain was a weak and reluctant competitor. Her internal territories, so impressive on a map, were burdens rather than sources of strength. Spanish policy as a whole was never able to take advantage of the formal bestowal of the huge Louisiana Territory following the Seven Years' War. And the principal military emphasis, as well as the principal financial appropriations for defense, continued to be applied not to hostile Indian frontiers but to the traditional areas of international dispute: the Gulf Coast, Saint Augustine, Havana, and the other fortified cities of the Caribbean.

Mexican Indian Policies

EDWARD H. SPICER

Mexico from its beginning as an independent nation regarded the legal status of Indians as an important matter. The first constitution drawn up by the guerrilla leader José María Morelos at Apatzingán in 1814 made the complete equality of Indians, Spaniards, and mestizos the foundation of the political structure. The Plan of Iguala, which in 1821 became the basis for the first period of peace after the outbreak of the War for Independence, also explicitly asserted equality of citizenship for all. This was a departure from the Indian policy of the Spanish empire and had profound effects on the Indians of Mexico.

Spanish Policy: The Background

The Laws of Burgos of 1512 promulgated the social framework for Indian-White relations in New Spain. The structure of encomienda and rules for Indian labor and religion were outlined. In 1542 the legislators of the Spanish empire succeeded in getting Charles V to promulgate the New Laws of the Indies. These were the product of many years of discussion of the Spanish experience of empire, including the destruction of the Indian population of the Antilles. The best of Spanish ethical, philosophical, religious, and practical thought had been brought to bear on the problems of the relationship of Christian Spaniards to American aborigines (Zavala 1964; Hanke 1965). The New Laws became the basis for Indian legislation during the whole remaining period of the existence of the empire. The fundamental principle on which they were reared was that Indians, having souls, were to be treated as any other human beings and were to be brought into the empire as full citizens.

However, this general principle in practice required modification. Indians could not be immediately incorporated as citizens because they first had to be instructed in the ways of Christianity and of Spanish civilization. This called for the establishment of transition communities, the missions, where Indians were to be exempt from the usual citizens' duties such as paying tribute so long as they were under the tutelage of missionaries of the religious orders. Moreover it was recognized that Indians were at a disadvantage when faced with rapacious representatives of European civilization. Experience had shown that special protection was needed if existing Indian communities were to retain their land and control of their governmental institutions (Gibson 1964). Laws prohibited the settling of Spaniards, Negroes, mulattos, and mestizos within prescribed distances of recognized Indian communities and also from grazing cattle or other livestock in their vicinity (Zavala and Miranda 1954:38; Whetten 1948:80–81; Moerner 1970). The regulations grew complex, but from 1591 there was a General Indian Court where Indian grievances were heard and settled. Thus there grew up a kind of special Indian law, built on Spanish recognition of Indian customary law and judicial decisions handed down by the Court (Borah 1983). This law applied only in the milieu of Indian life, not to the population of New Spain generally. The need for transition communities and for the Indian Court was conceived as purely temporary; the ultimate condition of all was to be that of full citizens of the Spanish empire, with all the traditional legal distinctions based on rank, but not on racial or ethnic considerations.

Mexican Policy: Indian Equality

The Plan of Iguala in 1821 did away with all legal distinctions regarding Indians. Article 12 of the Plan stated: "All the inhabitants of New Spain, without any distinction of Europeans, Africans or Indians are citizens of this monarchy with choice of all employment according to merit and disposition" (Gonzalez Navarro 1954:115). When the Plan of Iguala was replaced with a republican constitution in 1824, the same principle of equality of citizenship was maintained. The state constitutions that were enacted during the following decades adhered to the principle, although some introduced certain restrictions. The usual ones had to do with the condition of being a servant or illiteracy and in the state of Sonora persons who went about "shamelessly naked" were excluded from citizenship. Thus the longstanding distinctions that had developed in the Laws of the Indies between Spaniards on the one hand and Indians and *castas* (racially defined groups) on the other were abolished at one stroke (Moerner 1967). There began to be even a sort of taboo on the word Indio 'Indian' in the legal and other literature of Mexico.

However, the legal leveling of all peoples was not consistent with the realities of ethnic life in Mexico and led to nearly 100 years of incessant conflict. Equal citizenship status carried with it several obligations that many Indians up to this time had not been required to fulfill. One was the paying of taxes, another was individual proprietorship of land, and a third was participation with non-Indians in the administration of local government. Nearly every state developed a plan during the years immediately following the War for Independence for surveying and distributing to individuals all lands that had not been so dealt with. These efforts were concerned at first primarily with the land held corporately by Indian communities, that is, land that Indians used as individuals but that was owned and assigned by the Indian town governments. The distribution of the land required surveys by government-appointed commissions. Most of the early state legislation was concerned with safeguards for Indians and included Indian members in the organization set up to do the work (Ezell 1955:205–206). Nevertheless, there were also, as there had always been, non-Indians ready to gain what land they could by whatever means as the new laws were carried out. The result throughout the new republic was armed conflict, as Indians interpreted what was happening as invasion of their territory (Gonzalez Navarro 1954:147–164). The new laws also called for participation of non-Indians in Indian local government, where this had not taken place before. To Indians this appeared as infiltration of their community governments, and resistance was prompt and continuous.

In 1825 in Sonora, Yaquis resisted with armed force and initiated a movement for the foundation of a separate Indian state in the north. Armed conflict went on until 1832 when the Sonorans were finally able, with superior arms, to win decisive battles. From 1831 until 1843 Indians of the state of Guerrero resisted efforts to survey and distribute land. Also in 1831 resistance among Nahuatl-speaking Indians in the state of Mexico led to an anti-White movement that broke out again in the 1840s. From 1847 to 1851, centered at Juchitán in the Isthmus of Tehuantepec, Zapotec Indians were in arms until put down ruthlessly by Benito Juárez, governor of the state of Oaxaca. In 1847 in Yucatán, in 1848 in San Luis Potosí and the surrounding region; in the 1850s in Jalisco, Puebla, Michoacán, and other states; in 1868 in Chiapas; in the 1870s in Querétaro and Hidalgo; in the 1880s in Sonora, Vera Cruz, and Yucatán—in short, everywhere in Mexico Indians rose in armed resistance, and most of these clashes were the recurrent symptoms of continuing rejection of the Mexican government's land policies.

The policy of breaking up corporate holdings intensified through the century rather than abated and hence the Indian conflicts also intensified. The Laws of the Reform began with a law aimed at breaking up primarily the vast church landed estates in 1856, continued with the law of the *baldíos* calling for survey and distribution of all unused land in 1883, and ended with the law eliminating all restrictions on the growth of large individual holdings in 1894. This legislation, building the legal base for breakup of all corporate holdings and placing land tenure on a completely individual basis, lay at the heart of the Indian armed resistance that heightened during the nineteenth century.

Force, Colonization, and Deportation

Indian resistance, smouldering and breaking out sporadically, affected non-Indian attitudes and led to the development of what was essentially undeclared national Indian policy. The constitutions and the laws still did not recognize any aspects of status peculiar to Indians, but there were action programs directed exclusively at Indians. The initial response of the mestizos in governmental positions to Indian reactions against the new land and local government programs was simple application of armed force. Force was met with force, passive resistance was met with force, protest was met with force all over the republic. There was no modification of land policy, except to make it more and more definitely individualistic and hence to fan the flames of conflict. The calling out of soldiers stopped resistance, or else stifled it temporarily, but armed conflict in several regions recurred throughout the nineteenth century and continued to the last year of the Porfirio Díaz regime in 1909. It was most notable in the extreme south among the Mayas of Yucatán and in the north among the Mayos and Yaquis.

Where possible, another approach to Indian resistance by the Mexican government was utilized. This was called "colonization." A Law of Colonization was enacted early in the nineteenth century and subsequently modified (Whetten 1948:154–155). The approach was based on a concept of Indians as not wholly civilized. Mexican policy makers periodically realized that military force was not working to bring Indians to accept the land policies and often then attempted to subsidize non-Indians to take up residence in Indian country and begin to work the land. It was believed that such colonists would demonstrate to the Indians the virtues of "civilized" life and that Indians would follow their ways. A special variety of this program consisted in military colonies, that is, companies of soldiers with their families who took up residence in Indian country and proceeded to farm. This was regarded as the most effective mode of colonization because soldiers were equipped to protect their colonies against Indians who opposed their presence.

Colonization was tried from one end of the republic to the other, sometimes on a grand scale within a specially designated federal district, as in the Sierra Gorda region of central Mexico, with forts and an army of occupation for protection. Generally, it came to be regarded as ineffective in the most recalcitrant instances. Some colonization programs included the placing of resident priests or Roman Catholic sisters in a hostile area in the expectation that, pursuing persuasive methods, they could ease the civilizing process.

In the most persistent conflicts, as in the Sierra Gorda (where the Indians were mostly Huastec) and in Yucatán and Sonora, a third kind of program was developed. The Spanish government had sometimes employed deportation of Indians who resisted Spanish incorporation, for example, Seris in the eighteenth century. The Mexican government did the same. In the Sierra Gorda, Indians who had been captured were shipped to neighboring parts of Mexico, which seemed to result in the spread of resistance, at least at first. In Yucatán beginning in the 1840s the state government began to deport Mayas to Cuba. The federal government protested and decreed that the practice be stopped, but it was not heeded and the traffic in humans continued into the late nineteenth century. About 1900, all other efforts having failed to end Yaqui resistance, the federal government itself under Díaz instituted a large-scale deportation program. Paradoxically Yaquis (and other Indians caught in the net) were shipped to Yucatán.

Armed force, colonization, and deportation did not bring about acceptance of the land policies by Indians. Yet national policy recognized no Indian problems or special governmental obligations. Nor did national policy recognize as a problem the integration of the many different Indian societies into the whole of the republic. It was as though the heritage of Indian problems from the colonial period was regarded as having disappeared with the declaration of equality of citizenship. As Indian problems did develop, there was no corresponding growth of an Indian governmental policy, other than force, for coping with them. In a sense pre-1910 governmental Indian policy could be characterized as laissez-faire.

The Hacienda as Assimilation Mechanism

Quite apart from government policy the integration of Indians into the economic and political whole of the republic was continuous during the nineteenth century. A mechanism for economic incorporation—the hacienda—had developed before the War for Independence. This land and social unit was strengthened progressively by all the legislation of the nineteenth century. Through the operation of the hacienda a private policy regarding Indian integration developed in lieu of any public Indian policy. It ruthlessly ignored the existence of Indian social and cultural units. Its ascendancy in Mexico brought about cultural assimilation on a large scale.

The hacienda was a land-holding unit of very different character from the encomienda of the colonial period (Whetten 1948:90–107). The encomienda, with which most of the higher-rank conquistadores were endowed, included a set of legal relations establishing specific obligations of the encomendero to the people on the land granted (Zavala 1935). Their spiritual and economic welfare was legally in his hands. Inspectors were empowered by the crown to check on conditions, so that the encomendero could be held responsible for inhumane conditions. The haciendas, on the other hand, were outright grants of land with no strings attached. If the land were occupied by Indians, the landlord could evict them or put them to work for himself as he pleased. If they were not good workmen he could evict them and try to attract others. If they were good workmen and he wished them to stay, there were means for holding them.

The most effective of these developed during the nineteenth century was the so-called labor contract method. This enabled a hacendado to force any laborer to remain on the hacienda until any debts that he contracted were paid off. Nearly all haciendas maintained local stores where laborers bought clothing, food, and other items from the landlord. Accounts were managed by the landlord's staff and most laborers were illiterate; the result was a system of debt peonage. By 1900 the great majority of all hacienda workers were attached to haciendas by this means, and nearly the whole of Mexico was covered by haciendas. They were the basic production unit of the republic, and Mexico became a landlord-controlled state.

Thus during the nineteenth century most of the Indians of Mexico became agricultural laborers on the great haciendas. The land between Indian communities was turned into haciendas. Whole villages were incorporated into haciendas. Free Indian communities slowly became, against their will, dependent for subsistence on the big haciendas that intruded as their neighbors. Under the absolutist regime of the landlords the hacienda became an instrument for detribalization and cultural assimilation of Indians throughout Mexico (Spicer 1969).

Work and residence on an hacienda required the acceptance of certain living conditions. A peon renounced, as it were, any political life of his own. He participated in no institution that had any policy-making functions; he held no political office. As haciendas swallowed up villages and individuals, local government almost ceased to exist below the level of the hacendado. The hacendado was the absolute ruler of the hacienda community; he was sometimes totally lacking in humanity and sometimes highly benevolent. Whether or not a hacienda community had a school depended on the landlord. If there was a school the schoolteacher was an employee of the landlord. The Roman Catholic curate had to be acceptable to the landlord. Working conditions were set by the hacendado; protest about conditions was a breach of discipline and subject to whipping or whatever the landlord maintained as punishment. As haciendas grew in number, the peon way of life became the way of the majority of Mexicans. It was built on an extremely low standard of living, a system of economic dependency, illiteracy, and an absence of hope for anything different.

The results were apparent in population figures (Cline 1962:89–90, 93). The Indian population of Mexico in 1810 was approximately 3,700,000, 60 percent of the whole. In 1910 it was less than 2,000,000. The mestizo population on the other hand in 1810 was about 2,500,000 and in 1910 nearly 12,000,000. Indian population had decreased by nearly one-half while mestizo population had nearly quintupled. This seems to mean that most natural increase of Indians resulted in the augmentation of the mestizo population, as children grew up in the peon way of life, under conditions of mestizo cultural dominance. More than 50 percent of the total Mexican population was resident on haciendas (Tannenbaum 1950:141). Indians lived as Indians chiefly only in "regions of refuge" (Aguirre Beltrán 1967), rugged mountain areas such as Highland Chiapas, Nayarit, the Sierra Gorda in San Luis Potosí, the Sierra de Puebla, and similar areas; the Yaqui and the Maya lowland areas were exceptional. It was apparent that rural Mexico through the mechanism of the hacienda had become steadily mestizo, not Indian; this land unit, fostered by the land laws, became an instrument of forced cultural assimilation that had in 100 years brought about the dominance of a new culture—the mestizo—and the near eclipse of the 50 or more Indian cultures of Mexico.

The political revolution of 1910 became, as it progressed, a profound social upheaval. Eleven years were required to resolve the conflicts that had given rise to the overturning of the landlord regime. The Revolution began with the peaceful replacement of one set of big landholders by another. It did not end until the interests of small landholders, industrial workers, and agricultural laborers had been fought for and brought into some relation with one another beginning in 1920 in the administration of Álvaro Obregón. During this period of military conflict, "plans," and constitutional conventions, the interests of Indians as such hardly came to the political surface. The overwhelming issue, besides political dictatorship, was the big landlord and the social structure of the hacienda (Romero Espinosa 1963:28–33). This was phrased as the agrarian problem and focused around forms of land tenure. It was the issue of the landless proletariat in an agricultural country, barely emerging into industrialism. Yet during the Revolution the intense pressures for assimilation under which Indian communities had been living were somewhat lifted; life did not move into the old channels, but there was suddenly more choice.

Rise of Indigenismo

As the major issues of the revolution were brought to an at

least temporary settlement so that they could be resolved further through political process, some Mexican intellectuals reacted against the thinking of earlier counterparts who had, like Lucas Alemán and Justo Sierra, been spokesmen for the landlord regime and the laissez-faire government policy. A justice of the supreme court, Francisco Belmar, in 1910, as the state was crumbling about him, was sufficiently concerned about the "Indian question" to form an association called La Sociedad Indianista Mexicana (the Indianist Society of Mexico) for the purpose of learning about Indians and what might be done about their problems (Comas 1953:70–83). This was a discussion group and met a few times before its dissolution while the Revolution was still in process. It proposed actual study of Indians, representing a strongly felt need for information by the few intellectuals who were at all aware of contemporary Indians.

In a similar tradition but geared for action was the effort of Manuel Gamio, an anthropologist, who set to work studying Nahuatl speakers in the vicinity of San Juan Teotihuacán near Mexico City (Gamio 1922). Gamio continued throughout a long life to pursue this research interest, holding that it was the necessary basis for any sort of government Indian policy. He became an increasingly vital influence on Indian affairs in Mexico. Around him for a time Moisés Sáenz, Luis Villoro, and a few others developed a circle called the Indigenistas or "nativists." The essential features of this viewpoint consisted in: recognition of need for real information, respect for contemporary as well as prehistoric institutions of Indians, the need for government policy to solve special problems of Indians, and the importance of potential and actual contribution of Indian cultures to the general Mexican culture.

Opposing the Indigenistas were others who were concerned about Indian problems, but whose viewpoint was entirely different. One of the most articulate was the man of letters, José Vasconcelos. He held that whatever Indians had to contribute to the developing Mexican culture had already been made, that Indians had nothing of any further value to offer, and that the need was simply for the "incorporation" of Indians into the mestizo culture of Mexico—the great civilization resting on mixed Old and New World origins—the Raza Cósmica, as he called it (Vasconcelos 1948; Vasconcelos and Gamio 1926: 95–102). The policy he advocated was the quickest possible incorporation of the Indians; this would end their problems of poverty and ignorance. It would also strengthen the Mexican people. Vasconcelos, in other words, was convinced that efforts to understand the nature of Indians were futile and that the goal should be their immediate absorption.

There were other viewpoints. There had been for 50 years interest on the part of intellectuals in Indian languages and some, but much less, interest in contemporary Indian cultures. There was a Society for the Study of Nahuatl and various small regional organizations set up to preserve aspects of what were regarded as dying Indian cultures (Comas 1953:83–89). The governor of Chihuahua had proposed in 1906 a law for the protection of the Tarahumara Indians of his state (Comas 1953:66–70). It was fundamentally a protective arrangement, but nevertheless a legal recognition of special Indian problems. The law was never enacted. It is notable that no Indians are known to have gained during this phase of new formulations any kind of national hearing with respect to Indian viewpoints. Only a small number of middle-class intellectuals raised the issues and tried to resolve them. The opposing views of Vasconcelos and Gamio moved into the political arena in the new Department of Public Education during the 1920s, with first Gamio and then Vasconcelos and later other Indigenistas attacking Indian problems through the schools.

The 1917 constitution, like Mexican constitutions before it, made no special provisions for Indians. It was framed by persons who thought in terms of the needs of the poor as against the rich, of the landless as against the landlords, in short in purely economic terms. Thus the legal basis of Indian life in Mexico was not altered by the 1910–1921 Revolution. The policy makers continued to keep ethnic differences separate from political organization. The existing problems connected with integrating the culturally different mestizos and Indians were dealt with at lower levels of policy, as in the Department of Public Education.

Educational Policy, 1920–1934

The first programs consciously directed toward Indian problems were the "direct incorporation" schools of Vasconcelos, the rural schools generally. Vasconcelos opposed any sort of separate institutions for Indians; he spoke against them on the grounds that the United States had compounded problems and hurt the progress of Indians by just such means. He therefore built rural schools for everyone alike and tried to bring the Indians into them. Funds, as the country was recovering from the Revolution, were scarce and there was hardly any trained personnel. Indian problems were lost sight of, to be considered again with the arrival of Sáenz in the Department of Public Education. He tried to institute "community schools" in which local communities would solve their particular problems, as Indians where they were Indian (Saenz 1939:113–170). At the same time during the 1920s small teams of technically trained individuals, "cultural missions," took up residence for short periods in isolated Indian communities and gave varied instruction to all ages. They sought to promote literacy, house improvement, dramatic arts, better sanitation, and much else (Ruiz 1963:91–101).

Administration of President Lázaro Cárdenas: 1934–1940

Meanwhile various ideas were current, such as Lombardo Toledano's idea of separate Indian republics, modeled on the plan of the Soviet Union. Toledano worked out such a plan for his native country, the highlands of Puebla. Some worked on similar schemes for Yucatán and other parts of the republic, but all remained on paper.

It was not until Lázaro Cárdenas became president that a decisive turn in Indian policy took place. He, for the first time, consulted Indians regarding their needs and their views on their place in Mexico as a whole. This led to the formation of a department of Indian affairs, Departamento de Asuntos Indígenas, separate in organization from any of the major departments of government and with a separate budget (Ruiz 1963:142–145). It concerned itself with studies and recommendations, producing monographs and memoranda on Indian conditions and needs. These tended toward plans for structure that would give Indians separate voice from surrounding mestizos in community policy and programs, but they remained nebulous. Another activity consisted in setting up here and there agricultural training schools, such as for the Yaqui. Cárdenas himself, besides instituting serious conferences with Indians in which he tried to understand their needs, set a precedent by establishing a separate "indigenous community" for the Yaquis (Fabila 1940:306–310) and for small groups in Lower California. The indigenous community was given definite boundaries and exclusive Indian ownership of land within those boundaries. This was the first move away from the constitution of 1857, which had eliminated corporate land holding.

In his dealings with Indians growing out of his many visits to their communities throughout Mexico, Cárdenas uniformly in his correspondence and official papers dealt with Indians as "Tribes," giving recognition to their corporate existence. His Departmento de Asuntos Indígenas encouraged the sponsorship by local government agencies of improvement programs for Indians; one such begun as an experiment became a permanent program among the Otomís, the Patrimonio Indígena de Valle del Mesquitál. In 1939 a large-scale effort was launched to prepare alphabets for all the Indian languages of Mexico, to produce bodies of written material in the languages, and to use the written languages in the teaching of literacy as a preliminary to learning Spanish. The Tarascan area in Michoacan was chosen for a pilot project (Ruiz 1963: 162–165).

By the end of Cárdenas's administration, it was clear that a definite Indian policy had taken form for the first time in Mexico, but no subsequent president followed his lead. His immediate successors were not interested or were actively opposed to singling Indians out for special attention. Nevertheless Cárdenas's general approach did

© U. of Ariz. Press, Tucson.
Fig. 1. A national rural school in the Yaqui town of Potam, Sonora, 1939. The school building was replaced with a larger structure in the late 1970s. Attendance, low in the 1930s, increased in the 1960s as other changes in Yaqui-federal relations occurred. Photograph by Rosamond B. Spicer.

develop steadily during the following 30 years, first outside of the Mexican government and then from 1948 on within.

The National Indian Institute

The first Interamerican Indian Congress was held at Pátzcuaro, Michoacan, in 1940 (Comas 1964:48–50). This conference, sponsored by the Pan-American Union and the Organization of American States, marked a turning point in Indian affairs in the Americas and particularly in Mexico. It established an Interamerican Indian Institute to be participated in by all American states and to be a clearing house of information, a study center, and field investigation research unit concerning American Indians. In each American state affiliate organizations, national Indian institutes, with similar functions were planned. Seventeen American states proceeded to set up such national institutes.

The impetus from the conference affected all of Latin America and gave a new turn to events in Indian affairs. Manuel Gamio as director of the Interamerican Indian

Institute from Mexico City gave strong stimulation to the gathering of information. A new era of communication throughout the Americas with respect to Indian problems and programs steadily developed, as the clearing house began to operate. Ideas and influences diffused widely from Canada to Chile.

In 1948, Mexico, after careful planning, established its affiliate with the Interamerican Indian Institute—the National Indian Institute (*Insituto Nacional Indigenista* or INI). Dr. Alfonso Caso, an anthropologist, was chosen as its first director. INI was established as a separate bureau, apart from the traditional major departments of the government, not under the direction of any one, but building its budget for Indian affairs on the recommendations of all departments. For some 15 years it was well financed and developed trained personnel and active programs in a dozen Indian areas of Mexico.

As in every country of the Americas, INI wrestled with the problem of who is an Indian, rejected a definition in terms of race, and settled on a definition in terms of cultural ways, such as language, social institutions, and (less explicitly) sense of identity (Caso 1958). The primary working definition came to be what a community considers itself to be and what it is considered to be by other communities. The object of government-financed Indian programs was declared to be the community, never the individual; individual assistance was a matter for other government departments. Individuals who chose to depart from Indian communities and take up life in mestizo communities were regarded as outside the INI efforts. The integration of Indian communities as wholes into their regions then became the object of INI programs. It was taken as given that there were special problems peculiar to Indians that required special means to be developed for solving them, hence the need for a special government department. The ultimate goal of all action was unforced integration with the nation-state.

INI did not have much money to spend; it was necessary to define its sphere of action accordingly. Thus it undertook to work with only a small portion of those people who might be defined as Indians, namely, those who spoke an Indian language and moreover those among whom there was a high proportion of monolinguals. Highland Chiapas was chosen as a place to begin, where the proportion of monolinguals was in many cases as high as 98 percent. Expansion of the programs took place in other areas where there were high proportions of monolinguals, such as the Mixtec, Tarahumara, lowland Maya, Huichol, and Nahuatl-speaking regions. In these areas the basis of operation was equal respect for the Indian and for the national languages, so that instruction was offered in the native language, and materials for instruction were prepared where they did not exist before, which led to the printing of myths, legends, historical accounts, vocabularies, and primers in several Indian languages.

SPICER

Two other features of INI policy made it exceptional in the Americas. In contrast with the United States, which from the first began the operations of its special agency from within Indian country, whether invited or not, INI set up headquarters outside the Indian territories where it proposed to wait for invitations to enter with its technical and other assistance. The headquarters were called coordinating centers, such as the one at San Cristóbal de las Casas, Chiapas, which was located in a mestizo city surrounded by Indian country with a high density of monolingual Indian speakers. Once established in such a coordinating center, staff members let it be known that they were there to help when asked; they then joined with an Indian community to carry out a desired improvement, such as a health clinic. Policy required that every community seeking help contribute whatever it could, in the form, for example, of labor and materials. INI then contributed the rest from its budget.

The second notable feature of INI policy was the cultural promoters. The central effort was to train natives of Indian communities to serve as bridges between their communities and the mestizo communities of Mexico. This required that individuals not be oriented away from their home communities and that there be positions in which they could work in their communities after training. Promoters in training remained in the INI center within visiting distance of their homes, where they were taught to read and write in their own language as well as Spanish.

INI policy resulted in a wide variety of activities, from the building of schools and roads to the provision of medical aid and schoolroom teaching. However, no offices composed only of government administrators were placed within Indian communities, and hence the local group was not overwhelmed or threatened by the INI staff. The general theory underlying policy was that local decisions should be made by local people, but that some local people should become trained in the ways of the non-Indian world and bring to local decision making some understanding of technological and social advantages of the wider world. In short, the municipal form of government of rural Mexico was not to be modified or bypassed by the federal agency. Increasing participation of Indians in existing local government would bring about a national integration helpful and satisfactory to Indians.

INI thus represented a decisive departure in Indian policy in Mexico. Its efforts emphasized a trend apparent since the 1920s with Gamio's first attempts to build Indian policy related to Indian needs; however, fewer than one-sixth of all Indians, defined on a basis of language, were reached by 1970. Other government agencies, Public Health, Water Resources, Agriculture and Development, as well as Education embodied some elements of the INI approach. The strongest tendency in government during the late 1960s was contrary to the INI approach. Government policy-makers in general tended to stress economic factors to the exclusion of others and to ignore ethnic factors thus making no special provisions for Indians. Political leadership from within the Indian communities will be the most important factor in determining Indian policy in Mexico in the future.

Danish Greenland Policies

FINN GAD

Danish policies toward Greenland are the result of the development of constitutional relations with the island as a territory and with the local population. The constitutional development, as well as the territory's position in international law, must therefore be considered when the various facets of Denmark's policies are examined.

A.D. 985–1721

Until A.D. 985 one cannot speak of political development in relation to Greenland or of a deliberate policy toward the population. After 985 the Norse established a medieval Scandinavian society, having the loosest possible structure and, therefore, great equality and freedom for individuals. Two political-cultural manifestations were of long-range importance: the affiliation of Greenland to Norway in 1261 and the association with the Roman Catholic Church (Greenland was a bishopric under the archbishop of Trondheim from 1126 to 1536) (vol. 5:550). Both manifestations form the basis for the Danish-Norwegian policy that developed during the federation between Norway and Denmark from 1380 to 1814; thereafter it was Danish only (Bobé 1928–1929). The affiliation of 1261 resulted in the obligation of the royal power to maintain peace among the inhabitants of Greenland. The ecclesiastical links created the motivation to support the inhabitants' religious life in a Christian spirit. The disturbed European political and economic situation of the fourteenth and fifteenth centuries made it difficult to carry through these commitments; and it is possible that there was intercultural conflict (vol. 5: 552–553).

During this period the Norse population of Greenland disappeared, and Eskimos immigrated to the coasts around the whole island. Europeans of that time did not have a clear perception of the Eskimos as a particular people; that was not verified until after 1721. To the Danish-Norwegian government the Eskimos (or Greenlanders, as they were in time called), were considered subjects of the king.

From this viewpoint, the Danish-Norwegian government sought with poor economic and technical means to establish a connection between Denmark-Norway and Greenland in the sixteenth and seventeenth centuries (vol.

5:556–557). The Reformation inspired Lutheran Christianity to reach out evangelically to the Norse population who were still believed to live in Greenland. Although this motive became weaker during the centuries, it was still the reason for Hans Egede's missionary enterprise in 1721 (Ostermann 1928–1929). Not until Wilhelm A. Graah's expedition of 1829–1830 was the extinction of the Norse population proved.

A parallel motive for the renewed Danish interest in Greenland was the general European search for the Northwest Passage. Both motives merged in the Danish-Norwegian participation in the competition for mastery of the whaling in the North Atlantic. The Basques, the English, and the Dutch were the most active participants. Having fewer economic resources, the Danish-Norwegian government could only participate to a smaller extent, yet it constantly asserted its sovereignty over the North Atlantic islands (J. Davis 1589; Frobisher 1578).

Chance communication between Europeans and the Eskimos of Greenland resulted in the transfer of elements of European material culture to the natives, an influence that increased when the Dutch trade mission in the Davis Strait developed after 1650, especially after 1713. Unfortunate consequences of contact with Europeans were contagious European diseases such as tuberculosis and, to some extent, kidnapping. From the kidnapping, European knowledge of the Greenlandic Eskimos was increased (Olearius 1656).

A few Danish expeditions maintained communication with Greenland. Toward 1700 there was a growing dissatisfaction, especially from the Icelandic side, regarding the obligations of the Danish-Norwegian king. Even though Hans Egede had in 1709 already made plans for colonization, he had to wait to carry them out because of the Great Nordic War, 1700–1731.

1721–1862

To Hans Egede there was no doubt about the fact that Greenland was one of the Danish-Norwegian king's countries and that the king, as a Christian, had obligations toward the inhabitants, whether they were Norse descendants or "savages," as the inhabitants were often called (Egede 1745). The principles behind his idea were first and foremost to bring the Lutheran conception of faith to the inhabitants, then to support this mission with trading and whaling on the west coast of Greenland (vol. 5:558–564; Ostermann 1928–1929). This plan could only be carried through in close connection with the Danish-Norwegian government, partly because the king was the formal head of the national church (and the mission had to be established in connection with the national church), and partly because the king, as sovereign over Greenland, was the only one who could bestow the privileges necessary to the successful accomplishment of trade in competition with the Netherlands, whose trading activities in Greenland were well known.

The competition from the Netherlands influenced the policy of the government toward the Greenland natives in the first half of the eighteenth century. The government did not want any clash with the Netherlands. Therefore, throughout the eighteenth century, the government's policy was a game between the obligations toward the Greenland population and the consideration of often opposite international interests. After 1777 the Dutch virtually pulled out of the whaling enterprise, but difficulties with the English began. Step by step the Danish-Norwegian government became involved in Greenland policy, until it actually took over the island's trade and administration in 1776 following the foundation of the Royal Greenland Trade Department (Den kongelige grønlandske Handel or KGH). The monopoly and the country's closing to foreigners was established by a royal decree on March 18, 1776 (Gad 1967–1976, 1971–1982).

From 1721, trade activities had grown concurrently with the establishment of more trade centers along the west coast. Bartering the Greenlanders' surplus production of blubber, skin, and whalebones, the trade institutions in Greenland turned to "raw material producing" activities, too, with the employees of the trade organizing the catch themselves. This was especially the case after the establishment of whaling stations in the north (from Holsteinsborg up to and including Disko Bay after 1774).

Meanwhile the mission carried out its concern. Just as the trade, in competition with the Netherlands, wanted expansion of the number of trade centers and thereby expansion of the monopoly, so the mission wanted mission stations, which necessarily had to follow expansion of the trade. The government of Denmark-Norway was organized as an absolute monarchy whose economic policy was characterized by mercantilism and whose main concern of commercial policy was the allocation of monopolies. The national church, including the mission work in Greenland, offered a parallel to this economic monopoly. With some competition from the south Greenland mission of the German Moravian congregation (vol. 5:562), the Danish mission succeeded surprisingly quickly in undermining Eskimo religious concepts and to some extent in substituting Christian ones (fig. 1). The Eskimos'

social institutions, which were bound to their religious concepts, were beaten down but continued to exist as concealed beliefs. The missionaries—the Christian minister and his deputies, the catechists (later Greenlanders)—became spiritual authorities (Ostermann 1928–1929).

In accordance with the Lutheran doctrine, the service was conducted in the mother tongue, which was a dialect of west Greenlandic Eskimo. The missionaries had to learn this language, which required intensive study. A writing system was soon created for Greenlandic, and books were printed using it. Since in Lutheran belief each individual made his own decisions about the fundamental doctrine of the faith, a more general education had to be provided him. Greenlanders, therefore, learned early to read and write.

The services became everyday festivities. The faith was a safeguard for the individual and a help out of spiritual darkness. Since the time of Hans Egede, the missionaries were inspired by a deep Christian pity not only for the Greenlanders' spiritual situation, but also for their material one. The Greenlanders had to be protected and helped materially. The Eskimo society's apparent lawlessness and traditional merciless treatment of widows, old people, and destitute ones called for social care. The distressed Greenlanders took refuge among the missionaries and traders. Help and protection were in keeping with, and supplied by, royal obligation.

In the same way, the trade monopoly gradually took on a protecting character. Presumably it first originated in the interest of the trade in protecting itself against foreign

Arktisk Institut, Charlottenlund, Denmark: 709.
Fig. 1. Greenlander children participating in a Danish-style Christmas celebration with a "tree" that appears to have been constructed from moss and heath. Photograph by Regnar Bentzen, Jakobshavn, West Greenland, 1889.

competitors. When bartering, it was necessary to offer goods for which there was a demand in the Greenlandic daily life. These demands were quickly met, but they required a continuing supply. It soon became a principle that the Royal Greenland Trade Department should intervene as little as possible in Greenlandic household and production traditions in order not to destroy the basis for the existence of the trade. One hesitated, for example, to import firearms but was forced to do so about 1740 by the Dutch competition. The increasing Greenlandic use of firearms does not seem to have interfered destructively in the Greenlandic economy, but neither did the productive capacity increase. On the other hand, it made the whalers and hunters dependent upon repairs and supplies such as gunpowder, lead, and replacement of broken weapons. By sending out quality articles, the trade monopoly sought to protect the Greenlanders against the poorer trade goods of foreigners. Toward 1776, it became another, ever stronger principle to see to it that the Greenlanders did not exhaust the need for their own products. The monopoly thus became to some extent socially responsible.

The trade could not indefinitely refrain from creating a demand for an increasingly wide variety of trade goods. As a result, the Greenlandic dependence upon supplies from abroad increased. In 1770 the Danish trade monopoly was practically absolute. Traditional Eskimo-Greenlandic tools and hunting techniques were preserved. The demand was expanded for articles such as textiles, domestic utensils, tools, and firearms.

An active population policy is a typical mercantile feature. In Greenland it was reflected in the fact that the Greenlanders were kept in their traditional trades, partly by preventing as far as possible their settling at the trade stations, and partly by not tempting the population with a standard of living that their occupations could not support, such as too many imported food luxuries or stimulants. The trade succeeded implicitly in neither. A certain amount of influx to the stations was inevitable because the people who sought the aid of the mission (and of the trade) in emergencies moved to the trade stations (fig. 2).

At this point the trade came into conflict with the mission. In order to provide a steady education, the mission wanted the population gathered for a longer period of time at the trade stations in a particular district (Ostermann 1928–1929).

The expansion of the trade in stimulants such as tobacco, coffee, and tea had various causes. From the 1750s tobacco proved to be extremely useful as a medium of exchange in petty trading; therefore a demand for it slowly sprang up. Nor could one deprive the Danes stationed in Greenland of these stimulants. Through the ever growing number of marriages between the Danes stationed there and the female Greenlanders, the tobacco habit was passed on to the Greenlandic families. Attempts were made to keep alcoholic stimulants away from the Greenlanders, and in the beginning the natives showed little addiction to these stimulants. The communication with the Dutch and English whalers, the influence from the Danes stationed in Greenland, and finally the association between Greenlandic and Danish whalers at the whaling stations that were established in Disko Bay after 1774 accustomed the Greenlanders to alcohol in the form of distilled spirits. Drunk Greenlanders of both sexes became a problem, because at that time alcohol was considered part of a laborer's daily necessities. The brewing of light beer also became common during the eighteenth century among the Greenlanders as well as among Europeans.

The intermittent development of colonial establishments during the years up to 1780, the erosion of native institutions and traditions, the continuous presence of the trade and mission in Greenland, and the activity of the Danes stationed in Greenland resulted in a certain chaotic state inimical to the security of the individual native. Therefore the government intervened, partly through the foundation of the Trade Department in 1774–1776 and partly by the establishment in 1782 of two control posts, consisting of an inspector in the northern part of the west coast and one in the southern part. This division of the country was made for practical reasons. Instructions were issued setting forth regulations for trade with the Greenlanders, in particular prescribing the way in which employees of the trade monopoly must conduct themselves. Thus the government sought to remedy unfortunate tendencies in the development of the trade by official standard measures. The instructions also acted as a political program regulating the stationed Danes' communication with the Greenlanders, the development of the trade, rules for preservation of game, the relationship to foreign ships' crews, the licensing of marriage, and the rules for the upbringing of children of mixed marriages (vol. 5:564–569).

At the same time, a general rate maintained uniform prices both for the Greenlandic products and for those goods that were given in exchange. This pricing policy prevailed in the trade until 1950 and was still carried on to a certain extent in the 1980s. Goods necessary for local consumption were often sold at cost price or at a very low profit. For "useful goods" a price with a reasonable profit was maintained, which covered somewhat more than the costs of production and transportation. The prices of "luxurious goods" were fixed at a considerably higher rate than in Denmark. Certain goods could only be ordered by Europeans stationed in the country. In this way the government could manipulate the prices so that price fluctuations could be prevented. The principle was also dictated by the fact that prices of Greenlandic products had to be kept fairly constant and outside the fluctuations that might prevail in the European and world markets.

Arktisk Institut, Charlottenlund, Denmark: 30.415.
Fig. 2. Danish station at Niaqornat, West Greenland, surrounded by native houses. The wood for the post had to be brought from a location outside of Greenland. Photograph by Arnold Heim, 1909.

The constantly returning periods of hunger and the aid that was necessary in such cases, as well as the needs of the poor, sick, orphans, and others without means, made Johan Friedrich Schwabe, the inspector in the northern part of the country, establish a relief fund for the whaling districts. Its income depended partly on a certain percentage of the Greenlanders' share in the whaling. It was extended to cover this whole part of the country, and later an equivalent system was established in the southern part of the country. The principle was the common twentieth-century Danish one that the population collectively paid from its income to help the indigent. In addition, the northern relief fund paid part of the salary to the first doctor in Greenland. Further action in the fight against disease, such as the vaccination against smallpox after 1804, had to engage the people stationed in the trade and the mission (Gad 1971–1982).

Instruction as well as price policy was introduced for the protection of the Greenlanders, and became one of the goals of the trade. The number of natives employed by the trade in Greenland increased. Greenlanders, particularly children of mixed marriages, entered increasingly into this service. This trend and the palpably beneficial function of the trade caused the trade to stand stronger in the consciousness of the Greenlanders. At the same time the mission became administratively restricted. From 1782 the administration of the trade increasingly recognized, locally in Greenland as well as centrally in Copenhagen,

the social pedagogical obligations of the trade. Administrators tried to adjust their policy accordingly.

In 1784 a fundamental change of government took place in Denmark-Norway that implied a limited liberalization of the absolute monarchy policy, highly marked by physiocratic ideas. The trade monopolies for some of the crown lands were abolished. In the case of Greenland, a commission was created to examine the possibility of abolishing the monopoly. The commission of 1788 consisted partly of leading reform-minded civil servants. However, the commission retreated from a policy of liberalization of Greenland's trade relations because it feared the permanently damaging effect of exploitation of the Greenlanders. The protective obligation was maintained. The commission became relatively permanent (until 1816), and in 1798 it resumed consideration of the matter of liberalization.

The result of a closer examination of the possibilities of liberalization was that the commission did not find the economic, legal, and administrative institutions in the existing west Greenlandic society that were considered necessary in a well-regulated society and that could have a protecting effect for the individual. The Greenlandic population was considered free in the sense that it was not, like the other inhabitants of the kingdom, subjected to any kind of prescribed or mandatory laws. The commission therefore considered whether a civil order, or set of prescribed laws, could be introduced in Greenland accord-

113

ing to Danish pattern. Statements obtained from civil servants in Greenland argued against the proposal. Among other things, they warned against pressing a European order of society upon the Greenlanders: there was no demand for it, and its particular rules would not be understood. A considerable obstacle for change was the Greenlanders' lack of European conceptions of ownership and knowledge of money and its value. The development of Greenlandic society in the desired direction, the commission determined, had to happen through education. The commission sought to establish considerable improvements in the Greenlandic educational system; however, all plans were interrupted by the war of 1807–1814, when the connection between Denmark-Norway and Greenland was broken. The credit notes, which in 1804 had been introduced as a means of exchange in trade, became valueless. Not until the 1820s were they reintroduced. They continued in use until 1950 (Gad 1967–1976).

It was impossible for a reform policy toward Greenland to be carried out until 1825–1830 because of Greenland's isolation during the war of 1807–1814, the Danish national bankruptcy of 1813, the surrender of Norway to Sweden at the peace of Kiel in 1814 (and the subsequent development of Greenland), and the general European economic instability. Meanwhile the west Greenlandic population had gradually increased, yet the basis for existence was still the traditional one. The foreign interest in Greenland and in the surrounding waters dropped considerably, and the monopoly gradually yielded a moderate profit. Economic and political liberalism became increasingly more popular in Denmark. This political climate caused once again proposals for the emancipation of the trade in Greenland and access for private tradesmen. An attempt was made but failed. Therefore, a commission concluded in 1835 that the Greenland policy followed up to that time should be continued in order to protect the Greenlanders from exploitation. It also maintained that future profit from the Royal Greenland Trade Department should be allotted to the Greenlandic society and that Greenland should be self-supporting economically. Consequently, the Trade Department policy had to be designed for constant balance. This made necessary an extremely careful administration of trade because the accumulation of capital would be small and the operating means scarce.

This scarcity of capital left its mark on cultural policy—particularly with regard to education—to 1950. Nevertheless, in 1845 two teachers' colleges for Greenlanders were founded; of these one still exists. Professional education of the Greenlanders was provided for in Greenland and Denmark. Greenlanders were taught to be coopers, carpenters, smiths, and assistants to merchants, and, for girls, midwives. The west Greenlandic language continued to be used, and instruction in the school was given in Greenlandic. The mission's former language policy was maintained.

The international economic interest in Greenland was declining at this time, and consequently the monopoly could operate in relative peace. In Denmark the liberal movement was increasing in strength, and in 1849 the kingdom got a free constitution. The road to this coincided with, among other things, the establishment of local self-government for rural districts and municipalities (Gad 1984). The Danish change of form of government influenced only indirectly the Greenlandic situation. For the sake of the Greenlanders' prosperity, the government still did not dare abolish the monopoly.

1862–1950

In 1862–1863, on the initiative of Hinrich J. Rink and the linguist Samuel Kleinschmidt, a limited local self-government, the system of *forstanderskaber* (vol. 5:569), was established in the west Greenland districts. It had a certain resemblance to the parochial government of 1841 in Denmark. The *forstanderskaber* handled the most common local tasks, which the Greenlanders were able to manage and with which they were personally in touch. This included aid to widows and destitute persons, commercial help and loans, and aid and loans for the building of houses. The economic means that the *forstanderskaber* used to administer these programs resulted from a tax estimated at the value of each district's trade of Greenlandic products, paid by the Trade Department. This was actually a purchase tax, for direct taxation could not be introduced.

At the same time the language policy was carried on by the establishment of printing offices, publication of more books, and a monthly magazine in the Greenlandic language (fig. 3). Kleinschmidt's (1851) spelling reform, grammar, and dictionary were valuable aids. The Royal Greenland Trade Department and the mission met the expenses (apart from the grammar). The language policy was evidently influenced by the corresponding language policy in Schleswig, Denmark (free use of Danish beside German), to a high degree inspired by the ideas of the Danish pastor, poet, and founder of the folk high schools Nikolai F.S. Grundtvig. By publication of Eskimo legends and the study of the Greenlanders' past and present, administrators wanted to deliberately build up a specific Greenlandic cultural development, including political training. By the relatively improved education received by some and by the growing number of Greenlanders employed in the mission's and trade's service, a certain class difference in west Greenland society was created.

The principle that Greenland was to be economically self-supporting was also to have its effect as a security for Greenland's integrity. The same was true of the utilization of possible mineral deposits. The scarcity of capital had

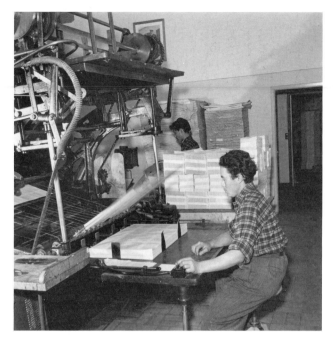

Fig. 3. Printing shop, Godthåb, capital of Greenland. Staffed almost entirely by Greenlanders, the town printing shop publishes materials in the Greenlandic language including translations of English and other European classics. Photograph by Andrew H. Brown, summer 1954.

Fig. 4. Commercial fish processing, Frederikshåb, West Greenland. The women are cleaning cod preparatory to salting. Photograph by James Penfield, 1941 or 1942.

reduced the explorations to local exploitation of surface coal deposits. As a result it early became common for the Greenlanders to participate actively in the mining of coal. When actual mining of coal in the 1920s was carried out it was Greenlandic miners who were employed. This continued until 1971–1972, when the coal mine was shut down as unprofitable. At no time was the coal suitable for export.

Other forms of mining were tried in the nineteenth century (copper, graphite) on a more or less private basis, but they had to be dropped as unprofitable. Because no available Greenlandic manpower could be found and Greenlanders did not feel they should depart from their traditional occupations, they were kept from the hard mining. This concerned the only very profitable mining, the cryolite mine at Ivigtut. The Royal Greenland Trade Department did not have the capital for its operation, so a Danish company was granted the concession of the operation. As a matter of principle the actual ownership of the mine was retained by the Danish state. In Greenland there was no private ownership of territory, only a traditionally decided right to the hunting and fishing areas and the building of houses. All right to soil must fall back to the state according to the old Nordic principle of law: what nobody owns belongs to the king. Therefore, Danish policy was, and still is, to negotiate the concession arrangements, which as far as possible assure that the society, in this case the Greenlandic one, benefits from the profit to a reasonable extent.

Scientific explorations in Greenland and of Greenlandic conditions began with Hans Egede (Bobé 1952; Egede 1745; Rink 1857). They have continued to grow steadily within all branches of science. It has been Danish policy to make it possible for serious scientific examinations and expeditions to be advanced in Greenland, insofar as reasonable economic, scientific, and safety considerations are met. As long as it existed, the monopoly worked as a regulating agent, which was very liberal in regard to entry permits. After 1950 only economy and safety were demanded as conditions of scientific involvement.

Since about 1860 the demand for Greenlandic products has declined. At the same time the population in western Greenland has grown gradually, inhabitants of the Ammassalik and Cape York districts arriving in those districts before 1910. In western Greenland the home consumption of domestic products grew simultaneously with an apparent decline in the seal and whale population. All this, along with the increased import of provisions to Greenland, caused working deficits for the Trade Department. New trades had to be established, but it took time to develop them. But the administration had to be prepared to support them when they appeared. The scarcity of capital called for a careful and hesitant investment policy. The slow pace was also due to the slowly changing climate. Not until 1906 could sheep breeding in southernmost western Greenland get started. The administration did not attempt to organize and support cod fishing until after 1923. Both new trades demanded a fundamental change of the Greenlanders' attitude toward animals and catching in large quantities. Fishing for cod and other fish demanded a private economic change. The Danish policy in Greenland had to concentrate on these "rehabilitation aspects," and at the same time a "pedagogic" management was required. The Trade Department as a production factor became still more central, and the existence of the Greenlanders became increasingly more dependent upon cooperation with the Trade Department. The importation of provisions had to grow continually with the increase of population. Fishing furthered the transition from a primitive economy to a money economy, because the fish did not yield the useful products that sealing had yielded earlier. Consumer goods like clothes and lighting and heating supplies had to be purchased in the stores of the trade, which further increased the importation of outside goods.

The stagnation during the period from 1880 past the turn of the century was coincidental with a trend to increasing rigidity and formality on the part of the *forstanderskaber*. The local government in Greenland was therefore changed by the Administration Law of 1908, so that two provincial councils (Danish *landsråd*) were established, one for the northern part of the west coast, and one for the southern part. Knud Rasmussen, who managed the Cape York district, had earlier established a council of male providers for decisions on local matters. Something equivalent was established in Ammassalik. The west Greenland system was an approximation of the Danish municipal and county systems (Gad 1984).

After World War I the law of 1908 and its effects were examined by a commission set up in 1920 with, among others, three prominent Greenlanders as members. This commission insisted upon the temporary continuance of the monopoly but proposed to work toward its abolition. The Administration Law of 1925 laid down the principles, but it made some changes in the local government that gave greater rights to the *landsråd*. The economic aid that *kommuneråd* and *sysselråd* (municipal and district councils) were going to administer would still result from taxes from the Royal Greenland Trade Department. Church and school were organized by law in 1905 so that the Greenlandic church became a part of the Danish national church under the bishop of Copenhagen. For the first time, instruction in the Danish language was introduced in the elementary schools as a compulsory subject. The change was in response to Greenlandic desires to learn the language as a prerequisite for training in the new trades. The Danish government's reluctance to impose instruction in Danish in Greenland was thus removed on Greenlandic initiative.

Greenlandic society in the twentieth century slowly

modernized, hampered by the scarcity of capital and limited possibilities of investment. The protection policy continued to be maintained. This policy manifested itself internationally by conflicts over the sovereignty of Greenland, brought to an end in 1933 by a judgment of the International Court of Justice in the Hague, the Netherlands. All treaties that have been made with other powers contain a recognition of this protection factor. Within the kingdom, compromises had to be entered into with the Faeroe Islands regarding their fishing at Greenland. By 1939 the monopoly was felt to be a restraint on development due to the scanty investment in Greenland.

The separation between Denmark and Greenland from 1940 to 1945 resulted in Greenlandic society having to stand on its own feet. The local Greenlandic administrative authorities (Danish *landsfogeder*), decided in concert with the united *landsråd* to continue the current policy, lead the development on the same course, and modernize within the limits of the economically possible, but not, at the end of the war, to confront the Danish government with changes of fundamental character.

1950–1983

The developments of the Second World War showed that Greenland could not remain a military vacuum. In 1941 a treaty was entered into with the United States concerning Greenland's defense. After the formation of the North Atlantic Treaty Organization, this treaty was modified in 1951 in consideration of Greenland's strategically central position. In both cases it was the Danish policy to require protective measures for the Greenlanders both socially and militarily. Only in Thule and at Narsarsuaq (Julianehåb district) did military installations have direct influence on the native population; otherwise only indirect influences were felt.

Since Greenland also could not remain as an economic vacuum, the question of the monopoly needed review. This caused a debate to arise, running both in Greenland and Denmark. An investigation of Greenland affairs by a commission was the result, and with consent of the united *landsråd* the new program was initiated in 1950 (Sørensen 1983; vol. 5:574).

The principal lines of the policy determined at that time could be characterized with the words liberalization and privatization as well as modernization. Politically and administratively, this meant a sudden change in practically all respects. The economy was to continue to rest on fishing (fig. 4), which would be developed with both modern vessels and industrial improvement systems on land, which resulted in a concentration of the population (fig. 5).

All institutions, including church, school, local administrative organs, health service, judicial system and enforcement of law and order, and trade and transporta-

Danish Information Office, New York, N.Y.
Fig. 5. Harbor at Jakobshavn, West Greenland, with numerous Danish flags displayed. Photograph by Jorgen Ross.

tion departments had to be changed. This was accomplished partly by new legislation at the time as the transitional decisions and temporary institutions necessary to arrange the changes were established. All this caused technical activity in various forms of building and in the installation of urban facilities.

The improvement of the health service, particularly the successful prevention of tuberculosis, resulted in a population explosion. In the years from 1950 to 1962, the Greenlandic-born population increased by 45 percent, while the number of Greenlanders in the productive age groups remained relatively small. The result was that none of the existing social institutions or activities could keep step with the demands of the developing population. Technical activity had to be accelerated, which brought about an enormous growth in the number of stationed workers and technicians. At the same time, the increase in administrative activities caused an immense expansion of the administrative staff. The balance between the Danish-born and Greenlandic-born living in Greenland was disturbed. The educational institutions could not keep up with this pace, and the Greenlandic population gradually felt left behind. The privatization of the local economic life also resulted in the ousting of Greenlandic small tradespeople, who had established themselves in the early 1950s, by financially stronger and more business-skilled Danes. The salary system also created a cleavage between Danish people, who were paid in European wages and given advantages in the form of free lodging and exemption from taxation, and the Greenlandic born, who were on a lower wage level. This system seemed discriminating even

though that was not its purpose, and a certain frustration grew up in the Greenlandic population.

Critical voices asserted that the postwar developments did not follow the intended policy. The 1955 Committee for the Investigation of Greenland Society was given too few opportunities for real examination. Therefore other political and administrative commissions and councils, including the Greenlandic council consisting of both Danish and Greenlandic politicians, kept in 1964 a firm hand on the development of Greenland. Between 1950 and 1970 two billion Danish kroner were invested in Greenland.

Integration of Greenland with Denmark, which had actually started with the Greenland Church and School Act of 1905, was realized by the Danish Constitution of 1953. With this, the Greenlandic population got two representatives in the legislative assembly, as did the Faeroe Islands, in both cases an overrepresentation in proportion to the population. As for local government, the earlier laws, except that dealing with the change of the constitution, continued; in the case of Greenland, the laws of 1950 continued in effect. The *landsråd* in Greenland therefore had greater competence in certain respects than an equivalent county council in Denmark. Direct taxes still had not been introduced in Greenland. County and town councils got their working capital through excise taxes, especially on beer, wine, liquor, and tobacco.

The feeling of frustration and of being administered from afar without having real influence on the course of the development of their country resulted in a radicalization of the Greenlandic politicians, especially the ones who were recruited from the young people educated in Denmark. Being under the impression that the cod fishing was failing and the prospects of Greenland's economy were doubtful, the Greenlandic politicians searched for a traditional Greenlandic position. They wanted a policy that to a greater extent than that since 1950 relied on Greenlandic premises, both regarding the exploitation of Greenland's natural resources and the consideration of Greenlandic possibilities. They wanted the remote administration remedied by having as many decisions as possible placed under Greenland's local institutions with block grants from the Danish budget (Gad 1984). It is the same principle toward which the Danish domestic policy seems to tend.

Action taken in 1972 by members of the Provincial Council and the Danish Parliament led to the creation of a committee, composed entirely of Greenlanders, which in 1975 suggested the development of a home rule system for Greenland. This resulted in the establishment, also in 1975, of the Commission on Home Rule in Greenland. In 1978, the commission presented formal proposals for a Home Rule Act. Key issues in the negotiation of home rule included aboriginal rights, ownership of resources, and mineral rights. After many hard-fought battles, principally with the Danish prime minister, the Danish Home Rule Act became law on 29 November 1978. Under the act, which became effective on 1 May 1979, a schedule was implemented whereby specific areas of control were gradually transferred to Greenlandic control between 1979 and 1984. Areas of control not specifically mentioned in the act may be transferred to Greenland in the future upon request by Greenland to Danish authorities. Under the Home Rule Act, the Provincial Council was replaced by an elected Provincial Assembly, the first election of which occurred in 1979, followed by a second election in 1983 (vol. 5:714–717).

Russian and Soviet Eskimo and Indian Policies

RICHARD A. PIERCE

Siberia and the northern parts of North America are closely akin in terrain, climate, plant and animal life, and in the economies, cultures, and racial stock of their aboriginal peoples (Levin and Potov 1956; Okladnikov 1968–1969). Conquered by Europeans at the same time and in similar fashion, these peoples were placed under colonial regimes that reflected the historic development of the respective mother countries. The Russian pattern of rule, carried across the Bering Sea in the second half of the eighteenth century, was applied in North America until 1867, when Russia sold Alaska to the United States. The Soviet pattern, based on radically new policies, was imposed on Siberian Eskimos after 1917 (vol. 5: 257–259).

Russian Policies in Siberia

Although frequently invaded, and from 1240 to 1480 under Mongol (Tatar) rule, the population of early Russia nevertheless remained primarily Slavic until the conquest of the Tatar Khanate of Kazan by Ivan the Terrible in 1552. With the subjection of the Tatars and their various subject peoples, Russia became multinational.

Crossing the Ural Mountains in the 1580s, the Russians began a rapid advance eastward, subjugating, one after another, the Voguls, Ostiaks, Yakuts, Buriats, Yukagirs, Kamchadals, and other Siberian peoples. Unfamiliar with firearms, and politically disunited, the natives were no match for the invaders' superior equipment and organization. In 1641 the Russians reached the Pacific coast. By the 1750s they had subdued the last resisting group, the Chukchi, in the far northeast.

In their advance, the Russians overcame their initial handicap of numerical inferiority and the vast extent of the region by building forts, called ostrogs. Placed along important waterways, the ostrogs controlled the chief means of communication and transportation and prevented hostile action by natives (Lantzeff 1943:87).

Once an ostrog was established the local commandants, or vaivodes (Russian voyevoda, sg.), could subdue the natives and impose upon them delivery of yasak (fur tribute). In this they were aided by divisions between tribes. The yasak-paying natives helped to impose the obligation upon their neighbors, while unsubdued groups were hostile to those who accepted the domination. It seems to have been a deliberate policy of the Russians to isolate the tribes by building ostrogs and fomenting intertribal hostility, but as soon as the natives in a newly acquired territory became more or less reconciled to foreign domination the administration tried to introduce peace and order, thus ensuring regular and uninterrupted delivery of yasak.

The government sought especially to make allies of the native upper class. To win this class over, special methods were used. Captive members of the native nobility were treated well and sometimes released in the hope that they would bring their relatives and supporters to the Russian side. Native chiefs who submitted could receive exemption from yasak payment, be granted districts from which they could collect yasak for themselves, or be granted titles. The descendants of even the hostile chiefs were usually allowed to retain their rank and authority.

Flattery and gifts were used to good effect. A new vaivode would receive the local chiefs and their men at the ostrogs. There they heard speeches by the new administrator emphasizing the power and benevolence of the government, and promising new favors and the elimination of evil practices. The natives were then given a feast, where they were encouraged to gorge themselves with food and drink. When the chiefs arrived in town with the yasak from their districts they were given similar feasts and rewarded with gifts of cloth, metal tools, or colored beads. As a result of such tactics, many former native petty principalities or other tribal units became Russian administrative units for the collection of yasak. The native chiefs and "best men" were transformed into Russian government officials who sent their former subjects out to gather furs (Lantzeff 1943:93; Armstrong 1965:117).

Native chiefs who did not respond to such inducements and continued to resist could expect prompt measures. The government did not hesitate to send punitive expeditions, and could use ruthless and unscrupulous methods, including treachery and murder. The Russians generally tried to avoid harsh treatment, since the loss of a native's life meant the loss of the furs that could be delivered, and cruelty toward one was likely to drive away others. The commanders of punitive expeditions were urged to employ persuasion before opening hostilities.

Whenever such measures had succeeded in their

purpose, the natives had to take a solemn oath of loyalty to the tsar and pledge fulfillment of their duties. Appeal was made to the local superstitions, and supernatural agencies were invoked to bring destruction upon those who broke the oath.

Another method of assuring obedience was the practice of taking hostages. The natives of the newly conquered territories were forced to hand over their chiefs and other influential "best men" as guarantees that they would keep the peace. These were supposed to be well treated and fed at the government's expense, but officials often took poor care of their charges. The keeping of hostages was in any case expensive, and guarding them took needed manpower away from productive labor. When sure of its authority the administration usually dispensed with hostages. By the 1770s the practice fell into disuse in Siberia but was employed by fur traders in the Aleutian Islands (Lantzeff 1943:96–97).

Once confident of the loyalty of the natives the government ordered its local officials to treat them kindly. The natives were generally regarded as special wards of the state who needed supervision and protection. It was considered necessary to keep arms from reaching them and to prevent, as far as possible, their demoralization by imported vices because it would affect their economic welfare and their ability to deliver the all-important yasak. Therefore, Russian merchants were forbidden to sell the natives firearms, axes, knives or other objects that could be converted into arms, as well as liquor, tobacco, and gambling devices.

While taking such precautions, the government nevertheless tried to keep the natives satisfied with Russian rule. It listened attentively to their complaints and often gave favorable replies. The local authorities were told repeatedly to protect the natives from any injustice or violence at the hands of Russians and to punish offenders. The vaivodes were told not to require the delivery of yasak from poor, old, sick, or crippled natives. If, for good reason the furs could not be delivered on time, the vaivodes were to extend the date of delivery. Unfortunately, these benign instructions from Moscow were often disregarded.

Interested primarily in the safety of its men and the regular delivery of yasak, the government felt no need to change native customs or tribal organization. Native leaders were allowed to handle their fellow tribesmen in their own fashion. In particular, the administration of justice, unless it involved Russians, was left in the hands of the native chiefs.

Similarly the government did not interfere with native religious practice. However, the conversion of the natives to Christianity had the advantage that baptized men, alienated from their kinsmen and former associates, could enter the Russian service and thus strengthen the garrisons. The baptized women helped to solve the woman shortage in Siberia because they might marry Russian men and baptized natives. To encourage the spread of Christianity the government made gifts to those who embraced the new faith. As the Russians looked upon religion as the main barrier separating them from the natives, the newly baptized were treated on equal terms with Russians.

On the other hand, the government was careful not to encourage the baptism of large numbers of natives. The advantages gained by their conversion were overbalanced by the financial loss as the baptized natives in effect received Russian citizenship and ceased to pay yasak. Consequently the clergy and the local officials were forbidden to use any coercion in converting the natives. Permission from the administration was required for each baptism.

The same considerations affected the government's attitude toward the enslavement of natives by the Russians, but here the government had eventually to yield to the actualities of Siberian conditions. Desiring to preserve as many of the yasak-paying natives as possible, the government at first tried to suppress the acquisition of natives as slaves in Siberia, their sale, or their transportation to Russia. It was recommended that baptized natives be left in Russian settlements, the men be enlisted in the military forces, and the women be married to Russians.

The exceptions made for the baptized natives made it possible for the Russians in Siberia to evade the prohibition of slavery. There were cases of forcible baptism, the enslavement of captives taken during military expeditions, or seized from well-to-do natives, or purchased. Slaves were easy to get because among Siberian people other than Eskimo slavery was an established and widely spread institution, and the Russians were eager to obtain cheap labor and concubines. As a result, the trade continued in spite of government prohibition. From the middle of the seventeenth century the spread of serfdom in European Russia and the legal recognition of it gradually led the government to accept the existence of slavery in Siberia.

In addition to the delivery of yasak, the natives were extensively used in military service, as guides and interpreters, for building and repairing fortifications and roads, as oarsmen and drivers of carts, and for performing personal services to the vaivodes. At first, attempts were also made to use them as farmers, until the gradual arrival of Russian colonists made this unnecessary.

The yasak delivery and other forms of service constituted a heavy burden for the natives, who because of the severe climate already led a precarious existence. In addition to this some of the vaivodes raised the established quota of furs required from the natives, keeping the extra furs for themselves. Others, more cautious, might pretend to buy the extra furs, but at prices far below actual value. Some took from the natives not only their furs, but even their dogs, reindeer, or food supplies. Some natives had to abandon their hunting grounds and fishing places to make way for colonists. Disregarding government instructions, many local administrators mistreated the natives to the point of outright atrocities.

The burdens laid upon them and the plundering and cruelty of the invaders sometimes became intolerable for the natives. One recourse they had was to petition Moscow, but Moscow was far away and two years might elapse before the answer to a petition was known. The local officials often tried to prevent written protests from reaching higher authorities, or intimidated the natives so that they were afraid to complain to investigators. If Moscow ordered correction of the evils the local administrators tended to shield each other or to display lack of vigor in carrying out the orders.

On other occasions the natives resorted to desperate action. Some refused to pay yasak, but this invited punitive action. Others tried to flee, but could be pursued and brought back. There were cases of mass suicides. Others tried rebellion, but they lacked cohesive political and social organization and were usually too divided by mutual hostility to agree on any common action. In western Siberia, where intertribal ties were the strongest, there were several serious attempts, involving several tribes, to shake off the Russian yoke, but all were crushed. Sometimes there were attempts on individual ostrogs, but these were usually secure against attack. Frequently individual tribes or groups within a single tribe would murder the yasak collectors or individual travelers or rob fur and grain shipments. Tortures sometimes inflicted on Russian prisoners reflected the bitterness of the natives toward their masters (Lantzeff 1943:109–114).

In 1822 the Statute for the Administration of Alien Peoples formalized government policy of leaving local administration in the hands of the native leaders, while linking it with higher regional organs of Russian administration. "Settled" natives, in the wording of the statute, were to be treated on a par with Russian peasants, except that they were not required to give military service. The "nomadic" and "wandering" natives were given special forms of social and political organization under their own aristocracy. Yasak continued to be collected in various forms until 1917.

By the nineteenth century the fur resources of Siberia were depleted and no longer played the important part in the revenues of the country they once had. Siberia was becoming important as a place for colonization, at first mainly by exiles, and later by free colonists, and in the second half of the century industry began to develop.

The native people played an increasingly minor role in the development of their homeland. The tribes of the north, especially, tended to be exploited by traders, to whom they were usually heavily in debt. Impoverished, frequently swept by famine or epidemics, most of these groups were declining in population. In the second half of the nineteenth century some of the Yakuts and Buriats profited from selling cattle to the Russian colonists and gold seekers, but heavy Russian colonization at the end of the century led the government to declare some of the best lands "surplus" and available for settlement. Use of the lands for agriculture curtailed traditional nomadic cycles and reduced some of the native herdsmen to poverty.

The degree of acculturation among the natives of Siberia remained low. Illiteracy was almost universal (Armstrong 1965:106).

Russian Policies in Alaska and California

In 1741, sea otter furs brought back to Siberia by survivors of the second Vitus Bering expedition started a rush of traders and hunters from Siberia to the Aleutian Islands (Golder 1922–1925; Fisher 1977). Backed by private companies organized in Irkutsk and Okhotsk, parties moved from island to island along the Aleutian chain and by 1762 had reached the Alaska Peninsula. As they went, they subjugated the natives, often brutally. The natives were essential to the newcomers because of their skill at hunting fur bearing animals in their baidarkas (skin boats) (Pallas 1948).

The Aleuts had only primitive weapons and were unaccustomed to acting in large groups, so they could give the Russians little serious opposition. As in Siberia the Russians declared a rough sovereignty by imposing yasak and by taking hostages as guarantees of good behavior.

The evil practices of the traders went unchecked until 1766, when the government declared the natives of the Aleutian Islands to be Russian subjects and tried to protect them against maltreatment. Yasak payment by Aleuts and other North American natives was abolished in 1788.

Of the numerous companies engaged in the fur trade, one headed by Grigoriĭ Shelekhov proved most successful. Citing the need to check the ruinous competition, to conserve fur resources, to protect the natives, and to explore and conquer new lands for the tsar, Shelekhov agitated for a monopoly. It was granted by imperial decree to his heirs in 1799, in a charter forming the Russian-American Company, to have the sole right to trade in and administer the newly discovered region for the next 20 years (Tikhmenev 1978–1979:41–61). This and charters granted in 1821 and 1844 with accompanying regulations became the instruments by which the region was governed until 1867.

The colonial system created by the charter of 1799 resembled that of the Hudson's Bay Company and the British East India Company. The Russian-American Company became the representative of the crown within the area designated, exercising quasi-governmental authority (Pierce 1976).

The 1799 charter contained no definitive regulation of the status of the natives, except for some general *121* statements. For want of more specific instructions, Aleksandr Baranov, the first chief manager (governor) of Russian America, established virtually at his own discretion a strict order under which Aleuts and Eskimos had to live and work for the Company (Chevigny 1942). As in Siberia, the economy of Russian America was based on furs. Sea otter pelts and seal skins were taken every year by ship to Okhotsk, from there overland to Irkutsk, and thence to Moscow or to Kiakhta, a trading center on the Chinese border, where they were exchanged for Chinese goods. The Aleuts were sent in large parties along the coast each year for sea otters. Some of the early voyages were excessively long, and some natives were killed during storms or Tlingit Indian attacks (J.R. Gibson 1976).

The Company complained frequently to the government about contraband trade by foreign vessels, chiefly from New England, which diverted furs that the Company might have had, and provided the Tlingit in the southern archipelago with better trade goods than the Company had to offer, as well as forbidden items such as liquor and firearms (Khlebnikov 1976). Tlingits used firearms when they attacked and destroyed the Russian settlements of New Archangel (Sitka) in 1802 and Yakutat in 1805. Nevertheless, perennially short of supplies, the Company was forced to make deals with some of the foreign skippers, providing parties of Aleuts to hunt sea otters on the California coast in exchange for trade goods and a share of the peltry.

The order established in practice by Baranov under the charter of 1799 was refined and elaborated by the charters of 1821 and 1844.

In addition to the Russians, the charter of 1821 distinguished the so-called Creoles (the offspring of Russian hunters and native women) from full-blooded natives. The Creoles were Russian subjects forming a separate social group equal to the rank of commoners, that is, to a free station of the Russian people. They had no duties or liabilities toward the Company unless they had been educated at Company expense, and they were free from all taxes. In practice, however, they were mixed in with all social classes of the colonial population, and there was a certain prejudice against them. Since there were few Russian women in the colonies, the Creole class increased. The Company forbade Russians taking their offspring or native wives away from the colonies (Fedorova 1973).

Among the full-blood natives the charter of 1821 distinguished: tribes "inhabiting places administered by the Company" or "Islanders," and tribes "inhabiting the coast of America where the Company has its Colonies." The charter of 1844 distinguished instead: dependent or settled tribes, independent tribes, and "not wholly" dependent tribes. Both charters declared all Russians, Creoles, and the dependent (settled) tribes to be recognized as "Russian subjects" enjoying full protection of the law. Both refrained from stating whether or not the other natives were Russian subjects.

The settled natives lived under a kind of benevolent guardianship intended to favor the interests of the Company and of the natives themselves. The settled tribes—Aleuts and Eskimos—were considered a good-natured and peaceful folk indispensable for the Company's business, and, because of their lightmindedness and irresponsibility, doomed if left alone. They were free from taxes as well as from military or any other duties toward the government and the Company. However, they were not allowed to sell furs to anybody except the Company, and were subject to compulsory service (hunting) for the Company, for which they were paid. To this end the Company was entitled to assign annually half of the male population between 18 and 50 years of age to the hunt and had to pay them at the established rates. Those who rendered this service for three years were replaced by others. The company had to provide the hunters with all necessary equipment and clothes. The charter of 1821 required the pay of natives to be not less than one-fifth that of the Russians, while the 1844 charter provided for pay according to a scale approved by the government. In practice, confirmed by the charter of 1844, native chiefs (toions) had to be confirmed by the chief manager of the Russian-American Company.

The native right to personal property was fully recognized, but the right to landholdings in any form remained unregulated; however, the actual holdings of the natives were to be respected. The Company settled communities of Aleuts on the Pribilof Islands (fig. 1), on Bering Island, and elsewhere in the interest of the fur trade, and in the 1850s consolidated a number of small settlements on Kodiak Island for the intended benefit of the inhabitants.

The Russians converted all the Aleuts to Orthodox Christianity, and as a result of the change in religion, labor service, intermarriage with the Russians, and resettlement, many elements of their original culture were lost. The "not wholly dependent" tribes, chiefly the Tlingit Indians, more numerous and warlike than the Aleuts and with a more complex form of social organization, remained apart. Few adopted Christianity, and few worked for the Russians, although they provided furs in exchange for trade goods, and foodstuffs for the Russian settlement at Sitka (figs. 2–3) (Oswalt 1978).

As for the tribes in the interior of the continent, the Company was required "to make no effort to conquer them," to limit contact with them to trading posts, such as Mikhailovskiy Redoubt (vol. 5:155), if necessary, and to "avoid anything which might lead these people to suspect an intention to violate their independence."

From 1812 to 1841 the Company had a southern extension at Fort Ross, in California. This was at first intended as one of several points that would establish a Russian claim to the entire Pacific coast as far as the

Muzeĭ Antropologii i Étnografii, Akademiā Nauk SSSR, Leningrad: 1142-8.
Fig. 1. The Harbor of St. Paul Island, Pribilof Islands. Seal hides, in various stages of preparation, surround the Aleut semisubterranean dwellings in the foreground. The hides were sent to Novo-Arkangel'sk for use in a variety of ways by the Russian-American Company, including as a packing material. On the hill (left to right) are the administrator's quarters, a store or warehouse, and a chapel built in 1821. Building planks were brought from New Archangel (Blomkvist 1972). (St. Paul Island more than 100 years later is illustrated in vol. 5:175). Pencil drawing by Ilîa Gavrilovich Voznesenskiĭ, Aug. 1843 or 1844.

Spanish possessions, but when this proved impractical the Ross settlement was used as a base of operations for the sea otter trade on the California coast and as a source of food production for the settlements in Alaska. Land was purchased from the natives and three ranchos established. However, the sea otters were soon hunted out, the coastal climate hindered agriculture, and Russia was too preoccupied elsewhere to provide the material support and colonists needed to expand the venture. In 1841 the establishment was sold (Okun´ 1951).

The weakness and vulnerability of the Russian establishment in North America was due partly to the difficulty of conducting a profitable operation in such a northern environment, and partly to failure of the government to take a more positive approach. The effort to simultaneously carry on a profitable commercial enterprise and to exercise governmental functions spread company resources too thinly. The government did not encourage permanent, self-sustaining colonization. Russians who came there did so on a contractual basis to perform specific service for the Company for a specified length of time. Only a few who became too old for Company service and did not wish to return to Russia were accorded "colonial citizenship" (Alekseev 1982).

After the abolition of serfdom in Russia in 1861, measures were taken to improve the administration of Russian America. For some Russian statesmen the duty of natives to work for the Russian-American Company, even with pay, appeared as a kind of bondage or forced labor for the benefit of a private enterprise, and as such incompatible with the new legal order. The exercise of governmental authority by a company seemed obsolete, and the monopolies of the Company out of tune with the spirit of the time.

In 1865 deliberations of the State Council for a new charter led to recommendations that included the release of Aleuts and all dependent natives from obligatory labor for the Russian-American Company and the rights to select their own places of residence and to leave their residences freely. All inhabitants of the colonies settled there permanently were to be divided into natives and colonists; to the colonist class should belong the Creoles. Natives were to be governed by their elected chiefs and colonists by elected elders. The term of obligatory service by Creoles educated at Company expense was to be limited to five years. Russian subjects would be allowed to settle anywhere in the colonial territory not occupied by establishments of the Company or by the present inhabitants, and land for dwellings, farming, and business premises and for cultivation should be allotted to them. No direct taxes were to be levied upon the inhabitants of the colonies. Any inhabitant of the colonies could engage without discrimination or restriction in whatever industry that he might prefer except that of fur hunting (Gsovski 1950:38).

These provisions would have altered fundamentally the order of things in the colonies. However, for considerations of domestic policy, financial difficulties of the Russian government, and reasons of foreign policy, negotiations were meanwhile proceeding for sale of Russian America to the United States, accomplished by treaty on March 18, 1867 (Chevigny 1965; Fedorova 1973).

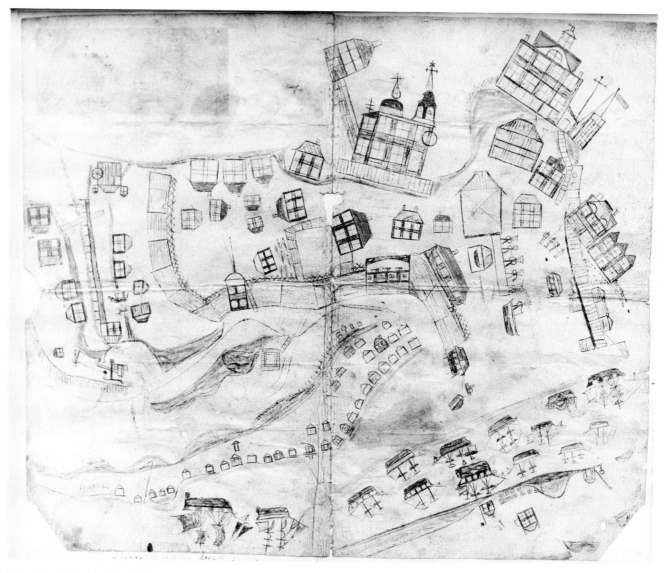

Fig. 2. Native and Russian settlements at Novo-Arkangel'sk, Russian America, drawn by an unknown Indian, probably about 1841. The church and governor's house (upper right) and the stockade with cannons and the railed yard (center) are large in comparison with the Tlingit settlement (lower left). The Tlingit were banned from the site after they attacked and destroyed the original fort in 1802. Fear of native attacks remained in the Russian community and caused a recall of the Tlingit between 1821 and 1826 by Gov. Matvei Muraviev who believed their proximity would allow closer Russian oversight of native activities (Krause 1956:39). In the 1830s native access to the Russian area was restricted to the portcullis that opened into the railed yard used as a market and trade center (Belcher 1843).

Soviet Policy

The Revolution of October 1917 brought a radically new approach to the problem of national minorities in Russia. The Bolsheviks shared the Marxist partiality for large, centralized states, but as a tactical measure they proclaimed the right of all nations to autonomy and self-determination.

Once in power, the Bolsheviks did not want the Russian domain to break up, so wherever possible they overthrew national republics that had split off from Russia during the Revolution, and prevented other groups from achieving independence. A federated Russia proclaimed in 1918, based on the principle of national-territorial autonomy, appeared as a partial solution of minority problems, but it was in practice dominated by the Great Russian majority and merely a step toward restoring central control. The Communist Party, with its highly centralized internal organization and control of state institutions, enabled the Soviet leaders to retain all the important features of a unitary state.

The Union of Soviet Socialist Republics (USSR), organized in 1924, was made up of Union Republics, eventually 15, representing the larger national groups. Less numerous peoples within the union republics were organized in Autonomous Soviet Socialist Republics (ASSR) and still smaller groups into Autonomous Provinces, National Areas, and National Districts, down to

Fig. 3. Views of Sitka, Alaska (formerly Novo-Archangel'sk) drawn from a White artist's perspective, probably about 1867. top, View from the west, showing the stockade separating the Tlingit and White areas and the Indian church (center left) to the rear of the native settlement. bottom, View from the east showing (left to right) the governor's house, the church, and the bishop's residence. Lithographs from Davidson (1869:following pages 118 and 120).

National Village Soviets and National Collective Farms. Politically, each of the Union Republics was supposed to be fully sovereign, but many vital powers were retained by the central government. The ASSRs had even less authority, while the smallest groups, some covering very large areas with but minuscule populations, had little but nominal significance. Although guaranteeing in theory the rights of these minority groups, the Soviet government abolished them at will, altered their boundaries and provinces, and shifted capitals according to economic expediency.

The pragmatic, materialistic nature of communism made the separate political and cultural existence of national minorities dependent on their contributions to the communist cause. If they carried out what were felt to be useful and progressive tasks they might enjoy considerable material benefit. On the other hand, if elements within them presented obstacles to communism they would be summarily dealt with.

Since economic development was of primary importance, colonization and industrialization determined Soviet nationalities policy. The preponderance in the Soviet Union of the Russians and related Slavic peoples meant that local peoples were often swallowed up in a flood of newcomers appearing as a result of timber, oil, mining, manufacturing, or metallurgical development. The influx of colonists destroyed tribal cohesion and unity. Large amounts of money were expended to develop backward regions, but the natives had no say on allocation of finances or on policy.

Besides economic considerations, the minorities were also affected by imposition of alien culture and ideology. The relative neglect of national minorities in pre-1917 Russia was replaced by strenuous efforts to reshape all Soviet citizens. Among the minorities the Communist Party shattered tribal unity by fostering class struggle, campaigned against religion, and suppressed historical and cultural traditions that might aid the survival of national consciousness.

A steady increase in schools for natives was one of the notable achievements of the Soviet regime, but along with education came indoctrination, mistrust of the outside world, and scorn toward native customs. Impressive statistics about volume of publishing in the native languages concealed the fact that much of the material was political or ideological.

In general, the natives had no recourse against these measures. Native leaders who tried to protect the tribal economy or identity were demoted, imprisoned, or executed. The native upper class and intellectual elites were destroyed. Attempts toward cultural and political integration of kindred tribes and nationalities, which might have strengthened their protests, were treated as threats against the state.

Few in number, with less complex cultures, the smaller peoples of the Soviet Union, particularly those of the Far North and Far East, put the intentions of the central government to a special test. Too few to criticize or resist the decisions of the central authorities, these peoples were patronized and given a great deal of publicity, but even they were sometimes the objects of arbitrary decisions and sudden shifts of policy.

After the 1917 Revolution some Russian anthropologists, citing allegedly successful efforts in the United States, Canada, Brazil, and Argentina, wanted to bar Russians from making any use whatever of the territories occupied by these peoples. To carry out this policy a huge bureaucratic apparatus—the Committee of the North—was founded. Five departments dealt with administration and legal matters, economic and financial affairs, scientific research, health, and education. For several years the philanthropic aims of the Committee's founders prevailed. Each tribe had a tribal general assembly, which elected a tribal executive committee. Several related tribes sent delegates to a tribal district congress, which elected a tribal district executive committee. Participation in tribal organizations was not limited by class criteria.

In 1929 the Committee had to apply the principles of class struggle; the well-to-do were pushed from leadership, and from 1930 the tribal administration was abandoned. Regular organs of local government ranging from village soviets to National Areas were created, linked politically and administratively to the rest of the USSR. In 1935 the Committee of the North was abandoned, and its remaining duties placed under the Chief Administration of the Northern Sea Route, a massive body that had among other things to look after the well-being of the Far Northern tribes, direct cultural work among them, organize health services, and help to promote their "sovietization." Then in 1938 all enterprises and institutions that were not directly connected with the development of the Northern Sea Route were handed over to the territorial administrations.

Big state enterprises were another influential factor in the North and Far East. The State Reindeer Trust, the Far Eastern Fishing Trust, and the state organization for fur trading governed vast areas. The employees of these organizations were governed strictly by business, and wanted mainly to fulfill target figures of the state plans. They had no interest in assisting the natives. They seized land and hunting and fishing grounds traditionally belonging to the natives, and even land owned by newly established collective farms of reindeer breeders (Kolarz 1954; Armstrong 1965).

Lack of understanding of the natives was manifested not only by the big state trusts but also in the day to day work of Soviet officials. Administrators were often sent to the Arctic regions to remove them from elsewhere. Some committed abuses against the natives. Even those officials who were idealistic, determined to improve living conditions and promote education among the local peoples, did not necessarily understand the Eskimo or deal with their problems in the best way.

In Moscow, government and Communist Party officials in charge of "native affairs" tended to think in terms of ready made patterns and formulas. They were usually convinced that what was good for urban centers must be equally good for the most remote parts of the Union. This frame of mind made it difficult for them to find the right approach to the special conditions of the Far North. The Soviet authorities for example displayed little understanding of the economic base of the Far Northern peoples—reindeer breeding—and made many blunders concerning it in the 1930s. Failing to understand that the reindeer played a vital part in the life of the Northern tribesmen, and oblivious to tribal customs, they imposed collectivization on the reindeer breeders. The setting up of collective farms and state farms in the native territories of the Arctic regions of the Soviet Far East led to the unleashing of a violent class struggle, which in turn resulted in a drastic drop in the number of reindeer. Only after World War II did the condition improve with more liberal application of the collective farm statute under which collective farm members were encouraged to own small reindeer herds privately.

Education displayed similar shortcomings. The schools tended to be remote from Eskimos' homes and taught the children things that they would be unable to use. Even the vaunted liquidation of illiteracy was complicated. In the 1930s the Far Northern and Far Eastern peoples received an alphabet of their own, the Unified Northern Alphabet. However, this was a Latin alphabet, and after less than six years a decree replaced it with a Cyrillic alphabet. Books in the Latin alphabet had to be destroyed (Kolarz 1954: 72–74).

The benefits achieved under the Soviet regime—the spread of literacy and education, improvement in health, and opportunities in the economy and administration—thus opened the way to a better life for the natives of Siberia. The Siberian Eskimo, along with the culturally similar Chukchi, learned to keep reindeer, and found a good return, through their collectives and state farms, supplying meat to new towns of the region. Their shore collectives hunted whales and seals. By 1969, their district had produced 21 fully qualified Chukchi and Eskimo doctors, enough native teachers to staff its 40 primary and secondary schools (exclusive of schools in the towns), and a number of specialists, scholars, and writers (Mowat 1970:214–215). However, the extensive colonization and development accompanying these advances threatened the destruction of many of the smaller national groups. There was also a high incidence of alcoholism, indicating impaired morale and failure by some to adapt to new conditions.

Colonial Indian Wars

DOUGLAS EDWARD LEACH

Armed conflict has been characteristic of Indian-White relations in eastern North America during most of the period when the two peoples have been in contact. This violence is not made any less grievous by recognizing that long before European colonization began, the Native Americans themselves were engaged in their own rivalries and conflicts. Once the Europeans had arrived and begun their settlements in the sixteenth and seventeenth centuries, the Indians found themselves confronted with antagonists potentially far more dangerous than any previously known among themselves. European culture—technologically advanced in certain critical ways, powerfully self-reinforcing, relentlessly expansive—began challenging a woodlands way of life whose distinctive qualities marked it, for the highly ethnocentric Europeans, as essentially uncivilized, possibly even savage. Worse yet, early Indian-European contacts exposed the Native Americans to deadly epidemic diseases against which they had no immunity and for which they could devise no cures. As a result, the native population was devastated, leaving only relatively small numbers of survivors to resist the European intrusion.

A study of early encounters between groups of Indians and European explorers reveals a variety of attitudes and responses on both sides. According to one of the Norse sagas, when Viking seafarers first sighted a small group of "Skraelings" on an American beach early in the eleventh century, the Europeans attacked without warning, killing all but one who escaped by canoe (Magnusson and Pálsson 1966:60). This apparently unprovoked act of violence provoked a counterattack by natives who, loosing their arrows at the intruding ship, mortally wounded the Viking leader. An inauspicious beginning for Indian-White relations! Five centuries later the Italian explorer Giovanni da Verrazano, coasting from Carolina to Nova Scotia, encountered Indians in at least six, probably more, different places. The majority of these meetings seem to have been friendly, but along the coast of Maine the native inhabitants displayed obvious suspicion and even hostility toward the newcomers (Wroth 1970:133–143). In 1609, when Henry Hudson was exploring New York waterways, he too found that some Indians seemed hospitable while others were openly hostile. The Europeans, on their part, were strongly inclined to distrust even the apparently friendly ones. Groups of Indians who had experienced the widely variant behavior of White explorers and coastal traders reacted in much the same way. On both sides the watchwords became caution and suspicion, if not immediate hostility.

Once the Europeans had advanced from mere probing to actual settlement and colonization, the conditions conducive to armed conflict expanded and intensified. Day-to-day contact between the two peoples became almost commonplace in some areas, as at Jamestown and Plymouth, giving rise to various forms of interpersonal friction. In developing the economies of their new colonies on land acquired from the native inhabitants by default, or some form of bargaining, or intimidation, the Whites soon began revealing the inherently exploitative nature of their endeavors. While the Indians may not have realized the long-range implications of these developments, they had no difficulty recognizing the explicit authority of European firearms. This not only inclined them to avoid confrontation with the newcomers, especially when the Whites came in force, but also sometimes led them into political calculations eventuating in alliances between Indians and Whites. Often the colonists were pleased at the proffer of friendship, for good relations with the local Indians carried obvious advantages. At first the Europeans may not have realized that by accepting such a relationship they were enlarging the possibility of their own involvement in wilderness warfare, as supporters of the local Indians against their enemies. A well-known example occurred in 1609 when the French explorer Samuel de Champlain and two of his men, heavily armed, agreed to accompany an Algonquin and Huron war party on an excursion toward the land of the Mohawks. When the French helped rout a large party of Mohawk warriors, killing several with their firearms, they contributed substantially to the firm establishment of a pattern of alliance and hostility that was to affect French and British America for more than a century (Champlain 1922–1936, 2:95–101; Eccles 1969:24–25). Massasoit's willingness to make a firm treaty of friendship with the colonists of Plymouth in 1621 may be explained, at least in part, by his fear of the Narragansetts to the west. This treaty, in a sense, made the Pilgrims potential enemies of a people they had not even met (Mourt 1963:55–59; Bradford 1952:

80–81). In this fashion groups of colonists and Indians formed relationships and attachments that were to become the warp and woof of an intricate pattern whose central theme was deadly strife.

Even the most ethnocentrically prejudiced early historians had little difficulty recognizing the basic cause of armed conflict—the fact that European colonists were relentlessly engaged in the process of displacing the Native Americans. But there were many, more subtle aspects of the situation that they simply did not perceive or understand. Historians of the late twentieth century have been able to gain a more comprehensive and sophisticated understanding. What has been emerging, as a result, is a fairly clear vision of very diverse groups—of both Whites and Indians—in contact and confrontation, their actions and responses largely determined by human factors such as ambition, fear, greed, land hunger, prejudice, previous experience, religion, tradition, and a desire for vengeance. Seldom is the picture simple.

In general, the conditions working to produce warfare between Indians and Whites in early America may be summarized as: the territorial expansionism of the colonists, depriving the Indians of extensive tracts needed for their subsistence; the practices of White fur and peltry traders who stimulated the Indians to intensive hunting, often abusing and cheating them in the exchange of goods; and the gradual breaking down of Indian culture and independence as a result of disease, the extension of colonial jurisdiction, the activities of Christian missionaries, factionalism within the tribes, and the increasing dependence of the Indians upon trade goods, including firearms and liquor. Permeating all these relationships was a set of assumptions held by most of the colonists— that the Indians were not to be trusted, that the way to keep them docile was to impress them with the terrible might of European colonial government, that European territorial claims and jurisdiction took precedence over the shadowy claims of the tribes, and that European civilization was destined to supplant the "savagery" of native America. Needless to say, the Indian perspective was quite the opposite.

Advantages and Disadvantages at Arms

In warfare between Indians and Europeans, certain advantages and disadvantages were found on each side. Take the matter of weaponry, for example. The Indian traditionally went into combat armed with club or spear, together with bow and arrow. This required fighting at fairly close quarters, often hand-to-hand. The Indian's best weapon, the well-constructed bow, was capable of rapid operation, sending arrow after arrow with considerable velocity and force into a close target, but it was largely ineffective at longer ranges, especially in dense woods, and seldom was able to penetrate European

protective armor. On the other hand, a well-designed European sword was far more deadly than an Indian club or hatchet, while the smoothbore musket, although ponderous and slow in operation, was deadly in execution at close range. During the middle decades of the seventeenth century, as the old matchlock gradually was replaced by the more reliable and easier-to-handle flintlock, the Whites came to have a distinct but temporary advantage in weaponry. The Indians were not slow to recognize this advantage, and they began to acquire muskets for themselves through the channels of trade. Before long, most tribes possessed a fairly good supply of flintlock muskets for use in hunting or war. Not only did the Indians develop a high degree of skill in using the musket and later the rifle, but also some Indians learned how to cast bullets and make minor repairs on their own guns. However, what remained beyond their immediate capability, keeping them dependent on colonial suppliers, was the manufacture of gunpowder.

One advantage possessed by the native inhabitants and never overcome by their White opponents was the intimate knowledge of the land and its resources. Trained from boyhood in the skills of survival in a wilderness environment, the Indian warriors were able to travel great distances in amazingly brief periods of time, living off the land or subsisting on a minimal supply of parched corn. There were occasions, it seems, when they could almost run circles around the heavily encumbered, slow-moving

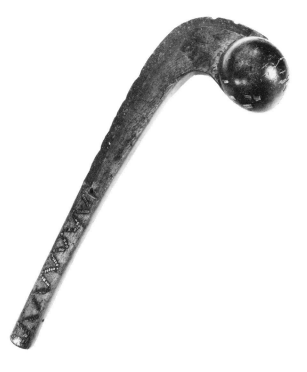

Ashmolean Mus., Oxford: 1685 Cat. B 133-5.
Fig. 1. Ball-headed wooden club from Va. Algonquians. The squared neck and relatively long head ending in a large wooden ball are distinctive of the earliest club forms. Length 54 cm. Collected by John Tradescant before 1662.

companies of colonial militia or regular troops tramping doggedly and noisily through the unfamiliar forest. On more open terrain, the Whites had an advantage in the horse. Cavalry equipped with light carbines or pistols proved quite effective in patrolling extensive areas and riding down fugitive bands of hostile Indians.

One problem that the Whites were very slow to overcome was that of adapting highly developed European military tactics to the actual conditions of wilderness warfare. The Indians, being highly individualistic and often fighting more for personal glory than group advantage, never developed a science of warfare. Two bands seeking combat with each other might scout, and stalk, and skulk, and finally rush into close conflict, with every man for himself. Their most effective tactic was the ambush, with the site very carefully chosen and any telltale evidence skillfully obscured. When fighting against White troops, who were relatively unfamiliar with the terrain and who were employing the close formations and mass evolutions prescribed in European drill manuals, the Indians were able by their own daring and skill as woodsmen to negate, at least to some extent, the White advantage in military technology. So it was that many a time the Europeans discovered, to their cost, that wilderness warfare was a quite different game from the formalized book warfare of the European battlefield. Nevertheless, change came only with painful slowness in the matter of traditional European military formations and tactics. Again and again White troops were marched into the woods by self-assured commanders only to be neatly ambushed and slaughtered by the nimble Indians. The colonists found it agonizingly difficult to fight a foe they could not find but who seemed capable of almost

miraculous movement in the forest. Only in the defense of or attack upon fixed positions such as a village or fort were the Whites generally successful; between such places they were frequent losers.

Quite early, and with some reluctance, the colonists began enlisting friendly Indians to accompany their expeditions as scouts. These Indians often proved invaluable in selecting the best routes, locating the elusive enemy, and preventing ambush. Equally significant was the growing awareness on the part of at least a few colonial commanders that some modification of the prescribed formations and tactics was essential if Indian resistance was to be overcome. Fortunately for the Whites, this was done with moderation. It would have been disastrous for them to abandon all their previous experience and group discipline in order to fight in the loose, individualistic fashion of their enemies. Instead, they retained the discipline and the basic tactical concepts, even while modifying and loosening somewhat the actual practices. For example, although company organization was retained, units learned to spread out when proceeding through wooded country and even developed some skill in enveloping tactics. They likewise came to understand the extreme importance of caution when advancing, alert for any sign of a lurking enemy, and of great care in bivouac to prevent hostile Indians from approaching undetected (Church 1865:102–104, 122–123). In the American wilderness, life was for the alert. What the colonists themselves were beginning to learn about forest warfare toward the end of the seventeenth century, the British regular forces had to learn for themselves in the larger warfare of the eighteenth century, the lesson not being fully absorbed until sometime after Gen. Edward Brad-

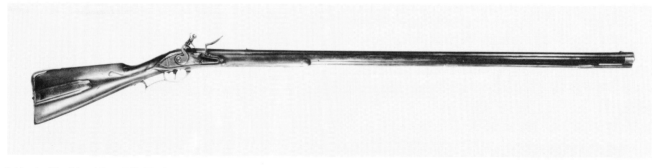

Fig. 2. American long rifle, developed on the colonial Pa. frontier, and acclaimed for its long-range accuracy. Also called the "Kentucky" or "Pennsylvania" rifle, this firearm was the mainstay of colonial militias, where each male citizen had to arm himself and had to seek a compromise between a hunting and military weapon. It saw service in the French and Indian Wars, the Revolutionary War, the War of 1812, and in the sporadic actions against Indians all along the frontier. Its long barrel and exceptional balance were innovations in firearms of the late 17th and 18th centuries. Lacking bayonets and slow to load and fire, these rifles had serious drawbacks in standard military actions but were used effectively by special units that emphasized hit-and-run tactics, such as light infantry, scouts, snipers, and skirmishers. Rifles were particularly effective in conflicts with the Indian where sniping from concealment was the order of the day, where the discipline of close-order charges and volleys was impractical. Certainly, they held a decided advantage over the trade muskets issued to the Indian, which were loaded and fired more quickly but did not approach the accuracy of a long rifle. The rifleman typically carried a powder horn, often elaborately decorated, a powder measure, and shot pouch, all on a single strap slung across the left shoulder. In firing, powder would be measured into the barrel, a round shot extracted, wrapped in a patch of cloth or skin, and rammed down the chamber atop the powder. The cock snapped down, causing the flint to strike off a spark that ignited the powder charge, and with a puff of smoke the ball was propelled through the rifled barrel accurately at distances in excess of 200–300 yards. This rifle, made about 1760, has a birch stalk and is .54 caliber. The maker is unknown. Overall length 151.0 cm.

dock's defeat by French regulars, Canadian militia, and their Indian allies near the Forks of the Ohio in 1755 (fig. 3).

One of the most important advantages possessed by the Whites throughout this period was their strong sense of destiny and their highly developed ability to organize for the achievement of a desired goal. This enabled them to consider every setback as temporary, sure to be redeemed with renewed effort. It was partly this awesome long-range self-confidence, this sense of inevitability, that gave such drive to the westward movement. Also of immense importance, obviously, was the ever-growing advantage of numbers on the side of the Whites. Immigration continued and increased, surpassing decade by decade the complementary effect of a high rate of reproduction. The Indians, in contrast, diminished appreciably as a result of losses in combat and losses to a variety of imported maladies, not the least of which was alcoholism, against which they had little or no resistance. In some epidemics the native inhabitants perished by the hundreds, thereby opening the way for Whites to take over additional territory at little cost.

Further, the colonists generally had continuing access to resources—human, material, financial, technological—enabling them to make up the losses they occasionally sustained. The ships simply kept coming from Europe, laden with people, goods, and knowledge. Material resources, including rum and other trading goods, enabled the colonial governments to bribe Indian leaders and purchase alliances. The tough sinews of the expanding fur trade often bound tribe to colony in a mutual relationship of greed that fostered intertribal hostility and prevented the Indians from achieving any real unity among themselves. Although the various European colonies, even those under the same flag, often failed to cooperate with each other, the Indian tribes were even less cohesive, lacking the sense of a common allegiance and mission that served as a potential unifying influence among the Whites. Even the greatest of the Indian confederations, that of the Iroquois, became weakened by factionalism during the crucial eighteenth century and often could not formulate external policies commanding the wholehearted support of the member tribes. So the Indians faced the growing menace of White expansionism divided and weak (Jennings 1984).

Early Conflicts, 1539–1645

Not every outbreak of violence between Indians and Whites resulted in war. Colonial authorities were inclined to treat Indians as delinquent children, and sometimes were able to damp down explosive hostility among a particular group by seeking out and punishing individual instigators or imposing a repressive penalty on the entire community. Even when spreading violence could not be so easily contained, the early conflicts or wars tended to be sporadic and more or less local in character, although sometimes frightfully bloody. Almost invariably, too, the local Indians were to some degree disunited, thereby providing the colonists with auxiliaries and spies. This sporadic, localized warfare was experienced by nearly every tribe and every European colonizing nation at one time or another. Spaniards were involved long before the English, Dutch, and French began their own permanent settlements.

When the Spanish conquistador Hernando de Soto in 1539–1543 led an armed expedition through what is now the southeastern United States, plundering as he went, he turned the original hospitality of the Timucua, Apalachee, Creek, and other Indians to outrage, and pitched battles ensued. At the same time a comparable adventurer, Francisco Vásquez de Coronado, was exploring the Southwest, also engaging in brief clashes with Indian groups, largely caused by the greed of the intruders and the failure of both peoples to comprehend each other's fears and aspirations. Eventually the Spaniards did manage to plant missions and outpost settlements in the Southeast and Southwest, amidst much grumbling and apprehension on the part of the native inhabitants. In 1680 the Pueblo Indians of New Mexico rose in revolt, temporarily forcing the Whites to withdraw to the south, but the determination and greater resources of the Spaniards eventually prevailed as a reconquest was effected in 1692–1696. The Pueblo Revolt of 1680 "was the end product of culture clash on all levels—material, personal, religious" (Bannon 1970:80).

In the meantime, the English had been experiencing similar trials with some of the Algonquian tribes along the Atlantic coast. Ever since the founding of Jamestown in 1607 the Indians of Virginia had cherished their resentment at being obliged to share the land with the Europeans. Early in 1622, led by the Pamunkey chief Opechancanough, they planned a sudden stroke that, when it fell upon the scattered plantations on March 22, cut down one out of four colonists (Smith 1910:572–583; Sheehan 1980; Vaughan 1978). Before long the surviving colonists were able to rally and defeat the Indians, who again were forced to tolerate the White presence. The principal legacy of the 1622 massacre was a widespread and tenacious impression among English colonists, not only in Virginia but also as far north as New England, that Indians were characterized by treachery and blood-lust. This view was further strengthened in 1644 when a second sudden uprising, again instigated by Opechancanough, took the lives of more than 500 Virginians. The English retaliated, and the conflict lasted two years, destroying Indians along with villages and crops as they drove hard to smash the power they had come to fear. In accordance with what was to become a pattern, the hostile Indians, *131*

Lake Superior

Lake Michigan

Lake Huron

Lake Ontario

Lake Erie

Ottawa R.

Kennebec R.

Connecticut R.

Hudson R.

Delaware R.

Susquehanna R.

Allegheny

Potomac R.

James R.

Kentucky R.

Ohio River

River

Missouri R.

Tennessee River

Arkansas R.

Trombehee R.

Red R.

Roanoke R.

Santee R.

Rio Grande

Little Colorado R.

San José R.

Pecos R.

Ft. Michilimackinac 1763

Ft. Edward Augustus 1763

Ft. Pelee 1763

Ft. Detroit 1763

Ft. St. Joseph 1763

Ft. Miami 1763

Ft. St. Louis 1684

Ft. Ouiatenon 1763

Pickawillany 1752

Chillicothe 1774

Pt. Pleasant 1774

Kerr's Creek 1764

Harrodsburg 1774

Ft. Loudoun 1760

Alabamo 1541

Chickasaw victories v. French 1736

Chicaça 1541

Cabusto 1540

Ft. Rosalie 1729

Mabila 1540

Apalache 1704 San Agustín 1728

Ft. Sandusky 1763

Ft. Presque Isle 1763

Ft. Venango 1763

Penn Creek 1755

Ft. Duquesne (Ft. Pitt) 1753–1763

Braddock's Defeat 1755

Busky Run 1763

Ft. Necessity 1753

Ft. Neally 1756

Paxton 1763

Lancaster 1763

Zwaanendael 1632

Ft. Royal 1644

Machot 1625

Westover 1622

Jamestown 1607–1622

Ft. Nohoroco 1713

Charleston 1715–1717

Pocotaligo 1715

Montreal 1760
Lachine 1689

Ft. St. Frederick (Crown Pt.) 1731–1759

Ft. Carillon (Ft. Ticonderoga) 1755–1759

Ft. Oswego 1756

Saratoga 1745

Schenectady 1690

Ft. Niagara 1759

1696

Tionontoguen 1666

1687 Iroquois villages

Wiltwick 1653-64

Pavonia 1643

New Amsterdam 1655

Norridgewock 1724

Brunswick 1722

Saco 1688

York 1692

Ft. Loyal 1690

Salmon Falls 1690

Peskeompscut 1676

Bloody Br. 1675

Deerfield 1675–1704

Hopewell Swamp 1675

Bridgewater Swamp 1676

Pocasset Swamp 1675

Great Swamp 1675

Block Island 1636

Pequot 1637

Pueblo revolts 1680–1692

Santa Fe 1680-83

Acoma 1598

0   100   200   mi

0   100   200   300   km

Fig. 3. Sites of colonial Indian wars (Paullin 1932; J.T. Adams 1943).

132

LEACH

unable to stand against the greater arms of the Whites (figs. 5-6), were defeated and brought into subordination.

Even more clearly indicative of future developments was the Pequot War of 1637, which occurred in Connecticut almost immediately after the founding of that colony. The Pequots of the area were perceived by the settlers as potentially hostile, although they may have been, in fact, as much victim as villain. Be that as it may, Massachusetts and Connecticut decided that there could be no sure peace in New England until the tribes were taught an unforgettable lesson—the lesson of how disastrous it was for any tribe to bully or resist either the English or other Indians in alliance with the English. Accordingly, an armed force was raised, Mohegan and Narragansett warriors were induced to join the expedition, and soon the unsuspecting Pequots in one principal village found themselves surrounded. The colonial force set fire to the village and then,

Lib. of Congress, Prints and Photographs Div.: LC-USZ62-8962.
Fig. 4. "C[aptain] Smith taketh the King of Pamaunkee prisoner 1608"; detail from an engraved map of Va. by Thomas Vaughn (Smith 1624). This represents an encounter in Jan. 1609 between Smith and Opechancanough in which he seized the leader's scalplock and prodded him with a pistol into a waiting group of armed Indians (Barbour 1964:252–254). The figure of Opechancanough is based on an engraving depicting a North Carolina Indian published by Theodore de Bry in 1590, after an original drawing (vol. 15:277) by John White in 1585. The smaller figures at the left are based on the same de Bry engraving, while the battle scene at the top is heavily influenced by a 1591 de Bry engraving representing a Timucua Indian battle in north Florida, which was based on lost drawings done in 1564 by Jacques le Moyne de Morgues (Feest 1967:22–25; Hulton and Quinn 1964, 2:pl. 123; Le Moyne de Morgues 1977, 2:pl. 105).

with the terrible fervor of crusaders, struck down every Indian—man, woman, or child—who ran out (vol. 15:91). It was mass slaughter (Orr 1897; Vaughan 1979; Salisbury 1982:203–235). Only a remnant of the tribe survived the ensuing campaign of deliberate destruction, and that remnant was parceled out among other tribes in an attempt to extinguish the Pequots as an identifiable people. Between 1643 and 1645 the Dutch on the Hudson River sought to drive home the same lesson to Wiechquaeskeck and Hackensack Indians, at the cost of hundreds of lives. So it was that by mid-seventeenth century in Virginia, New Netherland, and New England a frightful pattern of unrestrained, retributive violence had been fashioned, influencing the conduct of both peoples for decades to come (vol. 15:89–100).

Intensified Warfare, 1675–1689

The expanding Virginia frontier erupted in major violence for the third time in 1675. Indians and Whites charged each other with provocation, but the more significant facts are to be found in the mounting pressure on land and resources caused by White expansionism and Indian migration. When the royal governor of the colony insisted on following a policy that was more defensive than aggressive, outraged frontiersmen found a willing leader in Nathaniel Bacon, formed their own army under Bacon's energetic command, and proceeded to strike at the Indians in the back country. The trouble was that Bacon and his rough-and-ready men were none too particular about which Indians they attacked (Washburn 1957). This activity in 1676 was intertwined with a civil war between Bacon's supporters and those who remained loyal to the governor. Webb (1984) construes the rebellion as a political foreshadowing of the American Revolution rather than a fundamental disagreement over Indian policy. After Bacon's death in October 1676 both the civil war and the conflict with the Indians were concluded, leaving scars that would be visible for many years. The tribes of the Virginia backcountry, many of whom had considered themselves either loyal to the English or neutral in the conflict, were more weak and helpless than ever.

At the same time as Bacon's uprising, New England was undergoing its most terrible ordeal of Indian warfare, terrible for both peoples involved, but especially the Indians. King Philip's War, as this conflict of 1675–1676 is known, began when some of the young men of the Wampanoag tribe, whose sachem was Philip, vandalized a frontier community, and the colonies of New England retaliated with armed force. Soon the warfare spread to other parts of New England, as other tribes joined Philip's resistance movement and began attacking English settlements within their reach. Philip may have been one of the first Indian leaders to catch a vision of a pan-Indian *133*

The Colonial Williamsburg Foundation, Va.: upper left, 7203.C.G.3113F; upper right, C.W.1977–415; 7208.C.G.1821A; center, 7204.C.G.3011H; 7205. C.G.3375C; 7202.C.G.3113F; 7206.C.G.3016C; 7207.C.G.3016A; C.W.1978–9; lower left, C.W.1978-20; 7210.C.G.3016E; lower right, C.W.1978-21; 7211. C.G.3113F.

Fig. 5. Arms and armor found at Wolstenholme Town (present Carter's Grove, near Williamsburg), Va. Settled in 1618, Wolstenholme Town was partly destroyed in the 1622 Indian attacks on the James River settlements. Jamestown itself was warned of the attack and suffered no human losses. These artifacts, the earliest archeological remains uncovered from European attempts to colonize the mid-Atlantic colonies, are shown with items of comparable period and design. upper left, Close helmet, common among English soldiers of the early 17th century but quickly abandoned in Va. as ill-suited to the hot, humid climate of the tidewater. upper right, 17th century broadsword with hilt identical to the recovered pommel and basket guard. center, Musket parts (pan, lock, barrel, and trigger lever) laid out next to complete musket of the period. lower left, 16th century main gauche or left-hand dagger, used as an adjunct to the broadsword in fencing, with comparable blade from Wolstenholme Town. lower right, Complete gunpowder flask with fitted gate and recovered spout. Musket, 150cm in length. Helmet, 28cm in height; rest to scale.

movement designed to halt English expansion and possibly drive the intruders back whence they had come. If so, the vision was only partial and the resistance premature. Although Wampanoags, Nipmucks, and Narragansetts joined forces in response to Philip's cry, Pequots, Mohegans, and others either supported the English colonies or else played an equivocal role, hoping to emerge on the winning side. The English, in contrast, were able to achieve a fair degree of unity through the agency of the New England confederation (United Colonies of New England) and through tenuous appeals for assistance from Sir Edmund Andros, governor of New York (Jennings 1975:298–326; Webb 1984:360–378).

Philip's raiding parties displayed courage, stamina, and skill in their destructive forays against White settlements, so that the colonial authorities had great difficulty contriving any system of defense that would provide reasonable protection for the many small, isolated communities of New England. But again, a greater depth of resources began to make the difference. Gradually learning to make better use of allied Indians as scouts, and adapting tactics to wilderness terrain, the English were able to overcome their earlier handicaps and began to press harder and harder upon the diminishing bands of warriors. One extremely effective tactic was to find and destroy Indian crops and granaries, thereby depriving the enemy of essential supplies. Greatly weakened by hunger, disease, and losses sustained in battle, the Indian cause wavered and, after Philip himself was tracked down and killed in August 1676, collapsed. The Whites dictated the terms of peace (vol. 15:98), which meant that the Indians were reduced to subordination where once they had been free (Leach 1958).

During the second half of the seventeenth century the French, having established themselves at Quebec and Montreal on the Saint Lawrence River, found themselves seriously threatened by the animosity of the Iroquois Confederacy. Here the cause of animosity was not French territorial expansionism, but French support of Algonquian tribes who were enemies of the Iroquois and, most important, French enterprise in the Western fur trade, which threatened to deprive the Iroquois of their distant sources of peltry, thereby excluding them from effective participation in that commerce. Iroquois attacks on groups of Indians who were aiding the French fur trade, on canoemen transporting the furs down the inland waterways toward Montreal, and on outlying French agricultural settlements testified to the depth of anti-French feeling among the Iroquois. In 1687 the French sent a military expedition against the Seneca, westernmost of the five Iroquois tribes, destroying Indian villages and supplies of food without actually breaking the tribe's ability to recuperate and retaliate. Two years later the Iroquois dispatched a major expedition of their own to harass the heartland of New France. Achieving complete surprise, the warriors fell upon the small village of Lachine, located on the same island as Montreal, burning most of the dwellings and killing about 24 French residents. This successful raid roughly coincided with the outbreak of war between England and France, in effect the first blow in a long international struggle that was to end three-quarters of a century later with the expulsion of France from the continent of North America (Jennings 1984:195).

Natl. Park Service, Colonial Natl. Histl. Park, Yorktown, Va.

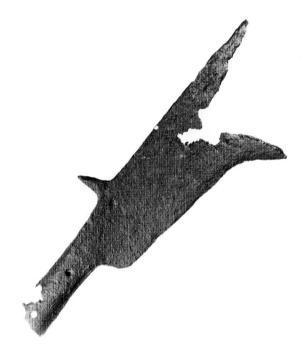

Fig. 6. Brown bill, recovered from excavations at Jamestown, Va. Named for the distinctive brown finish on the blade, this weapon derived from an English agricultural implement of the same name. A favorite among British soldiers, its hooked cutting blade and back spike were used with deadly efficiency. After the Indian massacre of 1622, the Virginia Company petitioned the king for more arms, and 950 brown bills were sent to the settlement in 1623 (Warrant to the Lord Treasurer, Sept. 1622, Kingsbury, *Records* III 676; reprinted in Peterson 1956:322; Plantagenet, *New Albion,* 31, cited in Peterson 1956). Length 49.3 cm.

The Pattern of Warfare

During the period of sporadic hostilities prior to 1690 there evolved a pattern of warfare that was to characterize the struggle throughout the remainder of the colonial period and, in some respects, almost until the disappearance of the frontier. Fundamental was the development of a complex web of relationships in which particular groups of Indians became clients and allies of particular colonies. These relationships grew out of economic ties established in the fur trade and also out of need for support against rivals. Seldom were such relationships absolutely solid and unchanging; on the contrary, the shifting interests of the various groups, both Indian and White, and the changing circumstances in which each was contending called for perpetual revision of allegiances. No tribe or colony ever could feel completely sure of its relationships with other groups across the cultural line.

Doubtless the most prominent element in the evolving pattern of Indian-White warfare was what appears to be cruelty and destruction. Almost from the outset, both peoples acted as though their ultimate objectives could be achieved only by extreme thoroughness in humiliating, hurting, and even obliterating the other. A typical assault on a village, whether Indian or White, included the massacring of human beings, the ravaging of crops and livestock, and the burning of dwellings. The taking of prisoners and plunder also was common practice. Prisoners had value. Indians took White captives for torture, adoption, or to exchange for ransom. Whites took Indian prisoners to be sold into slavery or otherwise held in servitude, or possibly to exchange for White captives. The practice of torturing prisoners to death was well established in some tribes, as was ritual cannibalism. Both practices should be understood not as mere cruelty or barbarism but as traditional, ritualistic, communal rites

The Colonial Williamsburg Foundation, Va., Anthony M. Phillips Coll.: L1985-12.
Fig. 7. Metal passport for "Ye King of Pamunkie," presumably presented to the chieftain of the Pamunkey Indians of eastern Va. by the Virginia General Assembly following passage of an act in March 1661/62 that required all Indian travelers to carry these pieces of identification. Diameter 6.5 cm.

with deep symbolic meanings for the participants (Knowles 1940). Nevertheless, they horrified the Europeans, despite their own penchant for judicial cruelty. Certainly the policy of terrorization and thorough destructiveness in war was deliberate and self-reinforcing. The latest atrocity committed by one side would provoke an even greater retribution by the other, and so the scale of frightfulness was raised. This was warfare at its worst. Inevitably the recollection of such horror became embedded in the folklore of both peoples, where it remained nourishing and renewing old animosities.

One practice requiring special comment is scalping. Anthropologists are unable to say precisely when, where, and why this began. Apparently it had long been practiced among the Native Americans in their own warfare, possibly as a substitute for severing the entire head of a fallen foe (Axtell and Sturtevant 1980). Warriors who had killed in combat brought scalps back to their villages as tangible evidence of their prowess. The Europeans were accustomed to the practice of decapitation as a form of legal execution; in the wilderness of the New World they displayed no reluctance in time of war against hostile Indians to indulge in the same grisly act of retaliation. Then, when colonial governments began offering bounties for enemy scalps, just as was customarily done for identifiable parts of wolves and other predators, the White frontiersmen themselves became scalp hunters. In the famous case of Hannah Dustin, a female captive who paused to slay and then scalp her sleeping captors before making her escape, there can be little doubt that her motive was to collect the bounty (Massachussetts (Colony) 1869–1922, 1:292–293; Mather 1855, 2:634–636).

The wilderness warfare of the seventeenth and eighteenth centuries not only gave vent to the base instincts of greed and cruelty in humanity but also called forth courage and self-sacrifice, enabling a few men of unusual talent and character to stand as distinguished leaders. Such leaders are clearly visible on both sides. One Indian whose dignity and courage won the grudging admiration of his White opponents was Canonchet of the Narragansetts, captured in King Philip's War while on a mission to obtain food for his hungry people. When informed that he was to be executed, this "manly Sachim" replied that "he liked it well, that he should dye before his Heart was soft, or had spoken any thing unworthy of himself" (Hubbard 1865, 2:59–60; Leach 1958:171–172; Harris 1963:46–51). Likewise Annawan of the Wampanoags, one of Philip's righthand men, gained the respect of Capt. Benjamin Church by his gracious and dignified acknowledgment of defeat, but he too was condemned by the authorities (Church 1865:163–175, 179). Other Indians, such as the Mohawk leader Hendrick, who was one of the first to die in the Battle of Lake George in 1755, fought bravely as allies of the British.

Once a tribe had been defeated and rendered incapable

of further resistance, its fate lay in the hands of men whose hearts already were hardened by the cruelties of Indian warfare and perceived the beaten foe only as a dangerous obstacle in the path of civilization. If on some previous occasion the tribe had made formal profession of subordination and loyalty to the colonial government, then its warfare was considered rebellion, and consequently the tribal leaders might be executed as traitors, with other participants sold into slavery, often to the West Indies (Dunn 1972:74). Generally, however, at least a remnant of the defeated tribe would be left more or less intact. For the victors it was unthinkable to let even such a remnant resume the same tribal freedom as before the war, possibly to wax strong again and plot with other Indians for revenge. The solution was to appropriate most of the tribe's former territory by right of conquest, forcing newly elevated Indian leaders to sign a treaty confirming the transfer. Then, for the remnant there would be set aside, supposedly in perpetuity, a strictly limited area of reservation land where the tribe might exist under White supervision. This was the beginning of the ill-fated reservation system, first devised by Virginia in 1646 after the futile uprising of 1644. It worked so favorably for the colonists, while retaining at least a surface appearance of justice and hope for the defeated Indians, that it quickly became an integral part of the evolving pattern of Indian-White relations.

Mass. Histl. Soc., Boston: top 218; center and bottom, 590.
Fig. 8. Helmet, breastplate, and gauntlet from pikeman's armor of the 17th century, Mass. The helmet, known as a pikeman's pot (Peterson 1956), evidently descended from the chapel de fer or chapeau de Montauban of 14th-century France, was popular with European armies as headgear for arquebusiers, musketeers, mounted carabiniers, and pikemen (P. Martin 1967). This breastplate and gauntlet are part of a suit of cuirassier's armor originally owned by Fitz-John Winthrop. Purchased in England between 1658 and 1661, it presumably saw use by Winthrop as commander of Conn. regiments during King Philip's War (1675–1676) and King William's War (1689–1698). Height of helmet, 29.9 cm; others to scale.

International Conflict, 1689–1760

The year 1689 marked a turning point in the history of Indian warfare, for in that year began the first in a series of four great wars among the rival imperialist powers—England, France, and Spain—for predominance in North America, with many of the Indian tribes inevitably caught up on one side or the other as a result of the long-evolving system of alliances. King William's War, the first of these major military conflicts, lasted from 1689 to 1697, when it came to an indecisive conclusion. Spain had remained neutral through that war, leaving the English and French, aided by their respective Indian allies, to test each other's mettle along the extensive northern frontier. But in Queen Anne's War, extending from 1702 to 1713, Spain and France were allied against the British, so that the southern frontier also was a ground of contention, and again the Indians were involved. This second war was concluded with the Peace of Utrecht in 1713, with France ceding Nova Scotia to Britain.

After this there was a long interval of uneasy peace and continuing rivalry short of open hostilities until 1739, when the third war began. At first the War of Jenkins' Ear was primarily a maritime conflict between Britain and Spain, but when France entered the European War of the Austrian Succession in 1744 as an ally of Spain, the war in America became more general, bringing further terror and destruction to Indians and Whites in exposed frontier villages. King George's War, as the British colonists called this latest struggle, was brought to an indecisive end in 1748 with the Peace of Aix-la-Chapelle.

The fourth and last of the great colonial wars began in western Pennsylvania in 1754. Spreading to Europe as Britain and France took up their old rivalry, the conflict exploded into the Seven Years' War. This time Spain remained neutral until near the end. Early in the war the British government made two significant appointments: William Johnson was made superintendent of Indian affairs for the northern frontier, and Edmund Atkin superintendent for the southern frontier. Both men had considerable understanding of Indian ways and Indian needs; Johnson in particular enjoyed a large measure of confidence on the part of important Indian leaders. The two superintendents were largely responsible for recruiting warriors to serve with British expeditions, while attempting to counteract the strong French influence pervading much of the trans-Appalachian West. In these matters no man did more than Johnson to bolster the British cause. The war was concluded in 1763 with the Treaty of Paris, by which terms France was required to withdraw from North America, while Spain had to relinquish her hold on Florida and the southern portions of Alabama and Mississippi.

In general, the contending powers fought for control of the major routes of communication and trade, not only those binding colony to mother country, or colony to colony, but also the great interior routes running deep into the heartland of North America, the routes along which passed the valuable furs on their way to market, and the routes by which traders and pioneers would pursue their interests ever more deeply into the interior of the continent. These were water routes, for the most part, vital portions of the great system of lakes and rivers that extended over such an extensive area from the Atlantic Ocean to the Mississippi River. Along these routes dwelt many of the tribes whose own future would be deeply affected by the outcome. The contending powers built fortified posts at crucial locations along the various routes, and solicited the help of the Indians in defending those forts against the enemy and attacking the opposing forts that the enemy had erected. Under these sometimes bewildering circumstances each tribe sought desperately to perceive and pursue its own best interests, knowing only too well that a faulty decision might mean disaster and perhaps oblivion.

Most influential of all the many groups of Native Americans seeking a path to survival was the Iroquois Confederacy. A coalition of tribes whose geographical location east and south of Lake Ontario gave them extraordinary strategic importance during the long, wearing struggle between the British and the French, the Iroquois assiduously pursued self-interest in both trade and war, managing to develop an impressive hegemony across a vast portion of the interior, with many lesser tribes looking to them for leadership and protection. Through the so-called Covenant Chain, the Iroquois and their client tribes were linked with the province of New York and certain other British colonies, a relationship that proved generally advantageous to most of those involved, and eventually disastrous for the French. In the long run the Covenant Chain served best as an instrument of British imperialism (Aquila 1983; Jennings 1984; Webb 1984:251–406).

One may well ask why the Native Americans were willing to participate in the imperialistic wars of the Europeans, which eventually could work only to their own disadvantage. Often it seemed to them that tangible benefits would accrue if a European power that was less threatening to their immediate interests were victorious over one that appeared menacing and preemptive. So a tribe would cast its lot with one side or the other, hoping for a long-range gain in trade or territorial security. It is also true that Indians frequently joined in colonial military ventures for the promise of pay and plunder. Whenever an enemy village or fort was captured, Indians participating in the victory expected to acquire weapons, clothing, and other goods of value, to drink captured liquor, and to take captives who later might attract ransom. This was predatory warfare, in which Indians and Whites alike displayed a raw kind of greed that was anything but heroic or idealistic.

With some Indians serving actively with the French and others with the British, White troops had frequent opportunity to size up their Indian allies as companions and fellow-soldiers. Many of the commentators were shocked by the way in which Indians gloried in slaughter. Cases of Indian cannibalism after battle, or the deliberate killing of some helpless prisoners and the cruel torture of others, helped strengthen the widespread European belief in the savagery of the American Indian. In addition, White soldiers gained the impression that Indians were strongly motivated by a thirst for revenge against their enemies. A notable case occurred shortly after the Battle of Lake George in 1755. The critically wounded French commander, Jean-Armand de Dieskau, had been captured by the British and was lying helpless in a tent in the British camp. Serving with the British was a contingent of Iroquois warriors who had suffered heavy losses in the battle just ended, their noted leader Hendrick being among those killed by the French. An Iroquois warrior, seeking revenge for these losses, slipped into Dieskau's tent and was barely prevented from murdering the French commander on the spot (NYCD 10:422–423; Johnson 1921–1965, 2:74).

Often, too, the Whites considered their Indian allies capricious and unreliable, mere mercenaries who sometimes sulked when the progress of a campaign or the rewards forthcoming failed to meet their expectations. Commanders found it necessary, on more than one occasion, to wheedle and cajole the Indians into staying through a campaign in which their special abilities were crucially needed. Considering the dubious advantages awaiting the Indians in the colonial wars, and considering also the unreliability of colonial militia in long, wasting campaigns, the behavior of the Indians is not surprising. They also were criticized for their lack of battle discipline, obviously a result of their strong tradition of individualism in warfare. When a raiding party of French and Iroquois, Huron, Nipissing, and Abenaki approached the frontier village of Saratoga, New York, in autumn 1745, for example, their plan was to wait until dawn before launching their attack. As soon as the Indians saw their objective in the darkness, however, they rushed forward impulsively, and the French had no choice but to join in. In the opening phase of the Battle of Lake George, a trap set by the French and Caughnawaga Mohawk and Abenaki allies to destroy an approaching column of British and Iroquois warriors was prematurely sprung when one of the French Indians opened fire. Interestingly enough, this episode was given opposite interpretations by the French and British commanders. Dieskau was convinced that his Indian allies had deliberately betrayed him; William Johnson believed that the premature firing, which saved the British column, was accidental (NYCD 6: 1013, 10:317–318).

138

Despite such annoyances, knowedgeable officers commanding expeditions in wilderness campaigns knew full well the value of loyal Indian scouts, and they were severely handicapped when such auxiliaries proved unavailable. Braddock's disastrous defeat in 1755 was partly attributable to his lack of Indian scouts and the sizable force of Indians operating with the French (fig. 9) (Pargellis 1936:130; Kopperman 1977). Whether the Indians fought well or poorly for one European power or another, the major consideration in all these wars was the imperialistic interest of the contending colonies, not the future well-being and security of the Native Americans.

Wars of Indian Resistance

Interlaced with the great international wars were a number of armed conflicts of a different kind, Indian uprisings in resistance to White expansionism. Usually such wars of resistance against the colonies of one European power were supported if not actually fomented

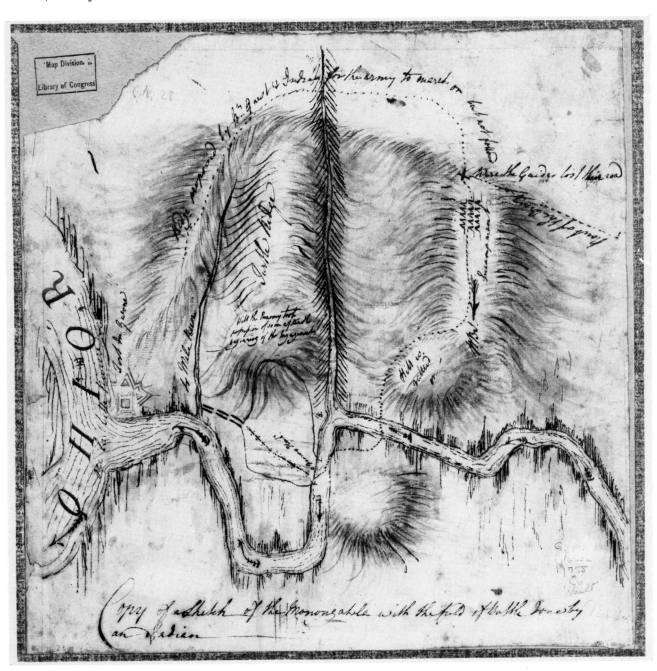

Lib. of Congress, Geography and Map Div.: G3824. P6S26 1755 .C2 vault.
Fig. 9. Manuscript map depicting the battle between Gen. Edward Braddock's forces and the French and Indians, July 9, 1755. An unidentified Indian scout supplied information for the map (Stephenson 1973:190–191). Ft. Duquesne (left, later Ft. Pitt) protected the confluence of the Ohio and Monongahela rivers. Cartographer unidentified.

by one or more rival powers through agents scattered among the tribes. A few of these uprisings, like King Philip's War in 1675, reveal early stirrings of pan-Indianism, but always this potentially powerful force was fatally weakened by Indian rivalry and White intrigue. The Fox War, which began against the French in 1712, is a case in point. Angered by French activity in the West, the Fox Indians, an Algonquian group dwelling in the region between Lake Michigan and the upper Mississippi River in what is now Wisconsin, sought to rally neighboring tribes for a concerted effort to drive off the intruders. For a time they did enjoy some success. By about 1728, however, after years of sporadic warfare, the Indian alliance was disintegrating, and the French still were fighting back. In 1730 a force of French troops aided by other Indians nearly annihilated a large group of Foxes (vol. 15:644), after which the Indian resistance, with some further violence, dwindled away (Alvord 1920:146–148, 160–165; Eccles 1969:148–149).

The Tuscaroras, an Iroquoian tribe in North Carolina, made their bid for independence when they suddenly turned upon the colonists in September 1711, killing dozens of frontier inhabitants at the outset of what was to become known as the Tuscarora War. This struggle, which coincided with the last two years of Queen Anne's War, was precipitated by Indian resentment not only of the usual territorial expansionism of the Whites, but also of the rough, overbearing behavior of British traders and especially their practice of forcing Indians into slavery. South Carolina gave military assistance to North Carolina at this time of crisis. With two forceful expeditions, each consisting of a small nucleus of colonial troops and a large number of allied Indians (Yamasee and others), the government of South Carolina smashed the uprising. After burning the Indians' fort at Nohoroca, 40 miles northwest of New Bern, and slaying hundreds of Tuscaroras, the Carolinians forced the surviving Tuscaroras to accept terms that were greatly to the advantage of the Whites. It was this defeat that started the badly shaken Tuscaroras on their northward trek ultimately to shelter under the wing of the Iroquois Confederacy (Lefler and Newsome 1963:56–61; Sirmans 1966:111; Robinson 1979: 107–110).

Soon after so soundly chastising the Tuscaroras in North Carolina, the government of South Carolina found trouble in its own house. The Yamasee, a group related to the Creek nation, were newcomers in the area between the Savannah River and Beaufort Sound. Their coming had proved profitable to the traders of nearby Charles Town, but as usual the trade created tension and resentment. At dawn on April 15, 1715, the Yamasees, giving no advance warning, massacred a group of Carolina agents and traders in one of their villages. This sudden act of violence inspired other tribes, notably the Creek and Catawba, to join what soon became a spreading frontier war. Battered

by a wave of brutal attacks, the frontier inhabitants abandoned their farms and fled toward Charles Town. The tide of Indian violence swept on, advancing rapidly toward the capital, engulfing desolate plantations as it came. Only when the distraught colony managed to rally its militiamen for decisive counteraction did the tide begin to turn. The Catawbas suffered defeat in the Santee area above Charles Town and soon withdrew from active participation in the war.

Regathering their strength, the Yamasee and Creek renewed the offensive. They drove eastward, crossing the Edisto River, and advanced to within 12 miles of Charles Town before being checked by determined colonial troops. After this, the tide receded for the last time, and Charles Town was safe. The Creek, unsuccessful in their attempt to turn the Cherokee against the Carolinians, withdrew from the struggle in 1717. As for the unhappy Yamasees, whose action had begun the war, they resorted to their former mentors, the Spaniards in Florida, and tried to carry on sporadic raiding activity against the Carolina frontier. Not until 1728, when the Carolinians sent a counterexpedition virtually to Saint Augustine itself and burned the principal Indian village there, did the long Yamasee War come to an end (Crane 1929:162–205; Sirmans 1966:111–117; Corkran 1967:57–60; Robinson 1979:110–120).

New England too had been coming to grips with resentful Indians. Evidence suggests that the Eastern Abenaki were being incited by the French in order to prevent the New Englanders from advancing their line of settlement farther up the Kennebec River, a strategic wilderness route between the Maine coast and Quebec. Serious trouble began in June 1722, when Indian canoemen descended the Kennebec River and attacked the area around Brunswick, Maine, burning houses and making off with a few captives. In response to this raid, the colony of Massachusetts virtually declared war against the Eastern Abenaki, and hostilities spread. This conflict became known as Dummer's War, after the acting governor of the Bay Colony who carried it through to an advantageous conclusion.

The government of Massachusetts believed that the principal *agent provocateur* was a Jesuit missionary named Sébastien Râle, whose headquarters were at the Eastern Abenaki village of Norridgewock on the upper Kennebec. Therefore a military expedition was sent up the river in August 1724 to arrest the missionary and overawe his charges. The troops burst into the village, and of course the Indians immediately began to fight back, Râle himself joining in the resistance. By the time it was over, Râle and a number of the Indians lay dead. The attackers then burned Norridgewock to the ground and returned downriver with scalps as evidence of their victory. Dummer's War was brought to a close in 1727, largely because the Eastern Abenaki found the French unable to provide sufficient military support in the face of a mounting British counteroffensive and equally unable to provide needed trading goods at prices competitive with what the British could offer (Penhallow 1726:107–108; Hutchinson 1936, 2:234–238; Leach 1966:131–133).

In 1729, as the French were about to gain the upper hand over the hostile Fox in the upper Mississippi Valley, 800 miles to the south angry Natchez Indians attacked and destroyed the French Fort Rosalie at the present Natchez, Mississippi. More than 200 French colonists were killed in this sudden eruption that, like so many other similar events in the colonies, was the explosive release of long-accumulating resentment. In response the French called upon the Choctaw for aid and began the ruthless process of subduing the Natchez Indians. The thoroughness with which this was accomplished is reminiscent of New England's vengeance against the Pequots nearly a century before. Hundreds of captured members of the hostile tribe were shipped off to West Indian slavery. Other terrified fugitives, trying to escape French vengeance, took refuge among the Creek, Chickasaw, and even the Cherokees. By 1742 the Natchez tribe had virtually disappeared (Priestley 1939:230–231).

In 1759 a portion of the Cherokee nation became involved in hostilities against the frontiersmen of the Carolinas, in the Cherokee War. At this time the French and Indian War was still in progress, and the British military command sent a powerful expeditionary force to help South Carolina suppress the uprising and pacify the southern frontier. This force, consisting of 1,300 Highlanders and Royal Scots reinforced by colonial rangers and Catawba Indians, advanced into the Cherokee country in 1760. There they plundered and burned several Indian villages and fought a battle with a force of Cherokee warriors trying to block their advance. In the meantime, the hostile Indians were closely besieging Fort Loudoun, an important British outpost deep in the Cherokee country. So effective was this siege that the garrison eventually surrendered upon promise of safe withdrawal. That promise was broken by Indians eager to avenge what they considered an earlier act of treachery by the Whites, the withdrawing garrison being ambushed on the second day after they had left the fort. The British then sent a second military expedition against the Cherokees, again with allied Indians in support, and systematically ravaged villages and crops. In this "scorched earth" campaign 15 Cherokee villages were almost totally destroyed. Finally, late in 1761 a firm peace was arranged, and the chastened Cherokees again aligned themselves with the British (Meriwether 1940:213–240; Corkran 1962:142–272; Leach 1973:487–492; Robinson 1979:217–223).

Pontiac's Uprising, 1763–1766

In every Indian uprising against European expansionism and domination down to the middle of the eighteenth century, the Whites had been able to exploit for their own advantage the intertribal antagonisms that always prevented the Indians from developing a united front. Eventually, however, the concept of pan-Indianism was almost certain to germinate and mature, with the possibility that sometime, in some moment of great crisis, all the Indian peoples would subordinate their differences in a supreme effort to beat back the development of White hegemony. The best opportunity came in 1763 at the end of the Seven Years' War, with the dissolution of French and Spanish control in the vast area east of the Mississippi River. At that time the Indians were rapidly becoming disillusioned with the authoritarian, repressive policy adopted by the victorious British regime, a policy that included rigid economy in the traditional practice of dispensing gifts to the tribes.

Among the Delawares had risen a spiritual leader known as "The Prophet" whose strong, mystical advocacy of the rejection of all aspects of White culture, and the resumption of the traditional virtues of the Indian way, provided a foundation for pan-Indianism. This powerful influence was spreading through the tribes in the Mississippi valley, overcoming old animosities and creating a new sense of cultural identity among the peoples of the forest. Among those who came under the influence of the Delaware Prophet's teaching was Pontiac, a war chief of the Ottawa. This dynamic leader began to see the possibility of transforming the discontentment of the Ottawa, Chippewa, and Potawatomi into action that, with the aid of the French still present in the area, would topple British military power at Detroit and perhaps even drive the British out of the Great Lakes region altogether. It is not clear just how extensive or cohesive Pontiac's "conspiracy" was among the widely scattered tribes of the West prior to the outbreak of actual violence, but the potential of his movement combining the spiritual idealism of the Delaware Prophet with the widespread Indian desire to beat back the British certainly was very great. Once begun, violence spread with amazing rapidity.

Pontiac and his warriors suddenly laid siege to Detroit in May 1763, a siege that was to last for nearly six months. Unlike Detroit, other frontier forts were overwhelmed rapidly, their garrisons usually being taken by surprise and the troops either massacred or held as prisoners. By July the toll included Sandusky, Michilimackinac, and half a dozen other wilderness outposts, as the Delaware, Ohio Iroquois, Miami, Shawnee, and Seneca joined the attack. Fearing the imminent collapse of their whole structure of military power, commerce, and territorial advance in the West, the British gathered their strength to strike back. Their most urgent task was to relieve Detroit and also Fort Pitt at the Forks of the Ohio.

In July Col. Henry Bouquet advanced toward Fort Pitt with fewer than 500 men, mostly regulars, under his command. On August 5, 1763, at Edge Hill 26 miles east of the fort, he encountered a force of Delaware, Shawnee, Wyandot, and Iroquois (fig. 10) returning from harassing the British stronghold. The British column managed to reach a defensible position on high ground as the Indians circled its flanks. Soon the redcoats were completely surrounded. On the following day, the so-called Battle of Bushy Run was resumed. The adroit British commander succeeded in mousetrapping the overeager Indians as they rushed to the attack and routed them with heavy losses (Peckham 1947:212–213; Gipson 1956:111–112).

Staggered by this unexpected setback, the Delaware and Shawnee began to lose their taste for Pontiac's cause, but the Seneca still had an arrow in their quiver. On September 14, they successfully ambushed a convoy of supply wagons along the portage road a few miles south of Niagara. Two companies of troops who hurried to the rescue likewise were badly mauled. This was the worst single defeat inflicted by the Indians during the course of the war, but even a staggering blow such as that could not conceal the fact that Pontiac's uprising had passed its peak. With growing disillusionment and obviously diminishing chances for ultimate victory, the participating tribes already were wavering. The full realization that France actually had been defeated by the British and, as a consequence, had been forced to relinquish her vast territorial interests in North America, contributed significantly to this disillusionment on the part of Indian leaders who had been clinging to the hope of French resurgence. Pontiac tried to keep the movement alive, but after giving up his long, unsuccessful siege of Detroit in autumn 1763, his chances were indeed slim. During 1764 two British military expeditions pacified a large area between the Ohio River and the Great Lakes, receiving from various Indian leaders promises of peaceful behavior and the release of White prisoners. Finally, during 1765–1766, Pontiac himself accepted failure and came to terms with the British authorities.

Conclusion

It is undoubtedly true that when members of the two peoples first began encountering each other along the coast of North America, few if any on either side desired bloodshed and war. Certainly White colonizers had little to lose and everything to gain by establishing peaceful relations with their Indian neighbors, and the Indians themselves often welcomed the newcomers as possible benefactors. Yet increasing contact produced friction, and friction led to violence. Moreover, the rapid increase of the White population and its consequent hunger for more land caused the Indians to become increasingly apprehensive.

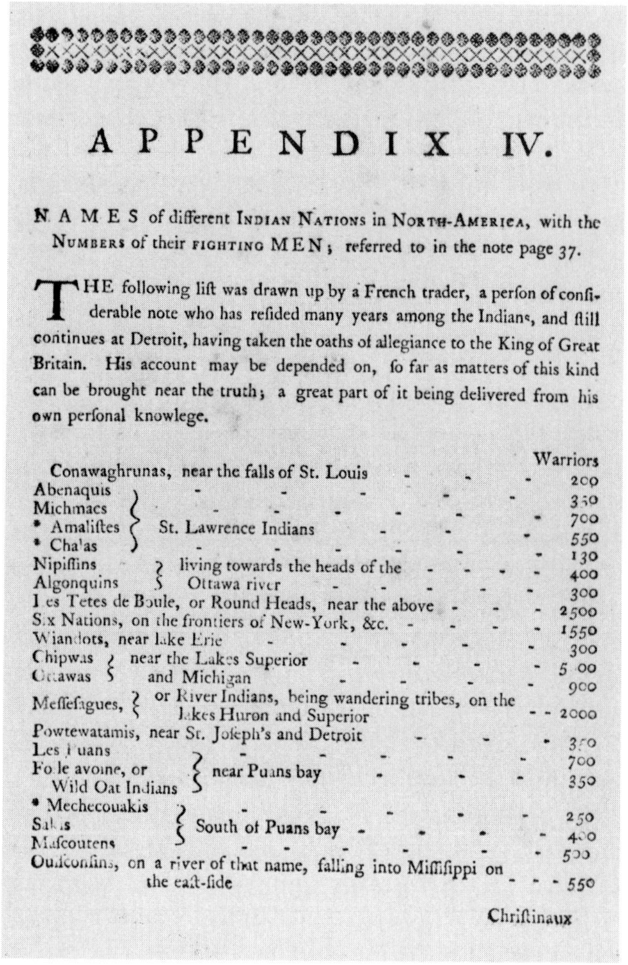

APPENDIX IV.

NAMES of different INDIAN NATIONS in NORTH-AMERICA, with the NUMBERS of their FIGHTING MEN; referred to in the note page 37.

THE following liſt was drawn up by a French trader, a perſon of conſiderable note who has reſided many years among the Indians, and ſtill continues at Detroit, having taken the oaths of allegiance to the King of Great Britain. His account may be depended on, ſo far as matters of this kind can be brought near the truth; a great part of it being delivered from his own perſonal knowlege.

		Warriors
Conawaghrunas, near the falls of St. Louis		200
Abenaquis	St. Lawrence Indians	350
Michmacs		700
* Amaliſtes		550
* Cha'as		130
Nipiſſins	living towards the heads of the Ottawa river	400
Algonquins		300
Les Tetes de Boule, or Round Heads, near the above		2500
Six Nations, on the frontiers of New-York, &c.		1550
Wiandots, near lake Erie		300
Chipwas	near the Lakes Superior and Michigan	5 00
Ottawas		900
Meſſeſagues,	or River Indians, being wandering tribes, on the lakes Huron and Superior	2000
Powtewatamis, near St. Joſeph's and Detroit		350
Les Puans	near Puans bay	700
Fole avoine, or Wild Oat Indians		350
* Mechecouakis	South of Puans bay	250
Sakis		400
Maſcoutens		500
Ouiſconſins, on a river of that name, falling into Miſſiſippi on the eaſt-ſide		550

Chriſtinaux

Brown U., John Carter Brown Lib., Providence, R.I.: 02054, p. 69.

Fig. 10. First page of an appendix listing Indian groups and their fighting men in Canada and La. A published account of Col. Henry Bouquet's campaigns at Ft. Pitt and Bushy Run in 1763 and in the Ohio Territory in 1764 contained information concerning military tactics and equipment, distances between Indian settlements and between White and Indian settlements, and other material believed useful in waging war in North America. Most of the Indian groups listed in this appendix were attached to the French (W. Smith 1765: 70).

Further experience taught them that the exploitative economic drive of the colonists would brook no denial. When isolated acts of violence began exploding into war, bringing terrible suffering to both peoples, a tradition of hostility and hatred was born. After that, neither side had much of an opportunity to perceive the other in undistorted perspective.

Indian warfare against different groups of whites occurred sporadically throughout the period, with the tribes also becoming involved in the great international conflicts from 1689 to 1763. Always there were Indians fighting on both sides of the conflicts. That was one great advantage for the Whites. Another was their more advanced technology, and another their ever-increasing resources, both human and material. With such great advantages belonging to the Whites, the Indians never really had a chance for ultimate success. The way of war, natural and justifiable as it might seem to men such as Opechancanough, Philip, and Pontiac, was not to be the way of redemption for the Indians. Rather, it was to be the way of disaster, leading straight to the reservation or oblivion.

Sources

The bibliography for this topic is diverse and extensive, ranging from captivity narratives and other contemporary accounts to specialized monographs. The best are by Aquila (1983), Axtell (1981), Berkhofer (1978), Ferling (1980), Jacobs (1950, 1985), Jennings (1975, 1984), Kupperman (1980), Nash (1974), Salisbury (1982), Sheehan (1980), Slotkin (1973), Trelease (1960), Vaughan (1965), Wright (1981), and Washburn (1957). Two helpful reference works are DePuy (1917) and Vail (1949); Vail includes an excellent bibliography of North American frontier sources from 1542 to 1800. Sheehan (1969) provides a thoughtful analysis of the basic causes of conflict. The influence of the wilderness experience upon Anglo-American military tactics is discussed in Mahon (1958). For an overview of the colonial wars to 1763, including the major conflicts with Indians, see Leach (1973). That volume, as well as Higham (1975, and Higham and Mrozek 1981, 1986), contain extensive bibliographies. Carp (1986) reviewed several works on early American military history.

Indian–United States Military Situation, 1775–1848

JOHN K. MAHON

The American Revolution

As the American colonies and their mother country began to fight in 1775, both parties had to take the Indians into account, for there were, it was estimated, no less than 35,000 warriors east of the Mississippi River (A.M. Davis 1887:709). But both sides considered the Indians to be savages, especially in their war practices, and were reluctant to use them. Accordingly, American and British agents in America urged them to be neutral (O'Donnell 1963:64; Cotterill 1954:37-56), which suited most of the tribes at the outset. The Oneidas said, "We are unwilling to join on either side of such a contest, for we love you both—old England and new" (Graymont 1972:58).

The British, who had a long established connection with the Indians, were in a better position to make allies of them then the Americans. However, important figures such as Sir Guy Carleton, governor of the province of Quebec, and John Stuart, Indian superintendent for the southern department, were against involving them. On the other hand, Gen. Thomas Gage, commanding general in America, and Guy Johnson, who, after a little interval, succeeded his father, Sir William, as Indian superintendent for the northern department, urged their use. They persuaded William Legge, Earl of Dartmouth, secretary of state for the colonies, to order the use of the Indians, but not until 1777 did England really carry the policy of Indian alliance into effect (O'Donnell 1963:13, 14; Graymont 1972:66, 80; Commager and Morris 1967:999–1002).

On the American side Massachusetts had been the first to involve Indians, enrolling some of the Stockbridge tribe to serve as minutemen in 1775. But throughout 1775 the Continental Congress and George Washington were against enlisting Indians. This sentiment soon changed, and on May 1776 Congress called for at least a partial alliance (Graymont 1972:79, 85, 100; Commager and Morris 1967:1003).

North American Indians had no sense of racial solidarity versus European immigrants. When Whites arrived, they welcomed their assistance in fighting traditional Indian foes. An exception is Cornstalk, a Shawnee chief, who in 1776 appeared at Chota, one of the Overhill Cherokee towns, with 14 headmen from five other tribes to urge the Cherokee to join forces against the Americans. Since this meant war, the older Cherokees objected, but the young warriors, especially Dragging Canoe, sided with Cornstalk (J.P. Brown 1938:141). Notwithstanding the split among them, it was the Cherokee who first went to war, even though John Stuart and the British agent to the Cherokees Alexander Cameron urged them not to do so. American encroachments all around, but particularly in the Watauga area, triggered them. Cameron accompanied the first war party to try to restrain it. By July 1776 almost the entire Cherokee nation, with 2,500 warriors, was at war with the United States (O'Donnell 1963:64, 67).

The Cherokees sought to make mutually supporting attacks on the borders of Georgia, North and South Carolina, and Virginia (fig. 1). Southern Americans assumed that the British were behind this coordination, and the four threatened states entered into a rare sort of joint effort. Georgia put Samuel Jack into the field at the head of 200 militiamen, and in July 1776 his force destroyed Cherokee towns around the head of the Tugaloo River. South Carolina offered 50 pounds per Cherokee scalp and 100 pounds for each live Cherokee prisoner, while sending a substantial force against the middle Cherokee towns, guided by Catawba scouts. As usual, Indian opposed Indian. The South Carolina force merged with one of 2,500 men from North Carolina and proceeded to destroy 30–40 towns. When this Carolina expedition went home in mid-September it turned in 75 scalps for bounty. The Indians left alive in the area where it had operated were soon starving, for their provisions had been effectively destroyed. On October 1, 1776, a Virginia force 1,800 strong marched toward the Overhill towns and demanded that the Cherokees surrender Dragging Canoe and Alexander Cameron. When refused, they overpowered and burned some Cherokee towns. By the end of 1776 most of the Cherokee nation was beaten and unable to continue to fight. In summer 1777 they signed two treaties that ceded wide lands and made heavy concessions to the Americans (J.P. Brown 1938:148, 154–157; O'Donnell 1963:74, 84, 88, 91; Alden 1957:273).

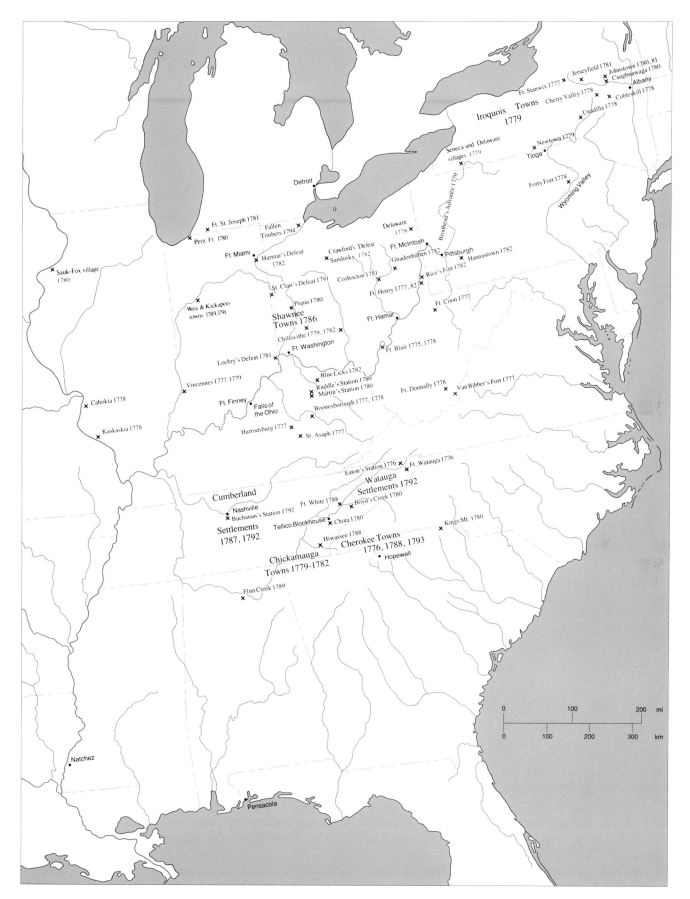

Fig. 1. Sites of Revolutionary and early U.S. battles involving Indians (J.T. Adams 1943; Prucha 1964; Cappon 1976; Tanner 1986).

INDIAN–UNITED STATES MILITARY SITUATION, 1775–1848

Dragging Canoe refused to honor the treaties and withdrew to the Chickamauga Creek area, where other dissidents could rally to him. By the end of 1778 he had 1,000 supporters around him, known as the Chickamauga Cherokees. The British, recognizing that his band had become the dynamic center of Indian power in the south, sent him 2,000 pounds worth of supplies so that he could launch a major campaign in 1779. But before he got started the Americans attacked. Virginia and North Carolina assembled 900 men who embarked on April 10, 1779, to descend by water to the Chickamauga towns. The river approach took Dragging Canoe by surprise, and the American force was able to capture most of the goods supplied by the British and to burn 11 towns (J.P. Brown 1938:161, 171; Alden 1957:273; O'Donnell 1963:199).

The British policy of using Indians as combatants was fully employed in 1777, when two of the British opponents came around. John Stuart tried to get the Creeks, Chickasaws, Choctaws, and Cherokees to act together in alliance with the British, and Guy Carleton at last agreed to permit the Indians to invade the United States. British agents were instructed to try to get the southern Indians to strike the frontiers to aid Gen. William Howe's thrust against Philadelphia and to press the Iroquois to take part in Gen. John Burgoyne's campaign. The pressure to choose sides split the Iroquois Confederacy, for the Seneca, Cayuga, and Mohawk allied strongly with Britain, while the Oneida and Tuscarora remained more favorable to the rebels. The Onondaga wavered in allegiance, first friendly to the Americans, then to the British. Iroquois warriors made up a substantial part of the British forces during 1777 in the Mohawk Valley, centering around Fort Stanwix, and were present with Burgoyne's main column (Graymont 1972:25, 106, 128, 161, 163; O'Donnell 1963: 144; Mohr 1933:50).

Burgoyne's surrender in October 1777 weakened the hold of the British on the northern Indians. But strong supporters of England held most of the Iroquois to the British connection. Principal among those supporters were two Mohawks, Joseph Brant and Mary his sister, the widow of Sir William Johnson, and two rangers, John and Walter Butler, father and son, American Tories who led British soldiers. These urged the Iroquois to make their most destructive efforts during the year 1778. That summer parties directed by John Butler laid waste the Wyoming Valley in northeastern Pennsylvania. On July 4 the militia garrison of Forty Fort, near where the city of Wilkes-Barre now stands, sallied out of its stockade to meet the invaders and fell into an ambush, with heavy loss of life. Butler's Rangers destroyed a great deal of property but killed few civilians (Graymont 1972:158, 174; Commager and Morris 1967:1005–1011).

This was not the case at Cherry Valley the following November. There Walter Butler lost control of the Indians, who did not join in assailing the fort there, but instead spread over the settlement, plundering and killing rebel and Tory alike (Graymont 1972:183).

All the while the White settlements in Kentucky had to fight to fend off extermination. Because of incessant raids by Shawnees and Delawares the settlers finally concentrated in Boonesborough, Harrodsburg, and Saint Asaph's. This left the Indians relatively free to ravage the south bank of the Ohio River from Pittsburgh to the rapids (where what became Louisville stood after 1777). There and elsewhere in the network of rivers in the center of America they were encouraged by Henry Hamilton, lieutenant governor of Upper Canada. From Detroit, Hamilton sent supplies to the Indians of the Ohio and Mississippi River valleys. Americans called him "The Hair Buyer" (Alden 1957:279–280) for his practice of encouraging Indians to bring him scalps of American settlers.

Vincennes, on the Wabash River, was a key point in the Indian trade. Accordingly George Rogers Clark began a gruelling march toward it, and on July 20, 1777, succeeded in capturing it. This caused Henry Hamilton to set out from Detroit. His Indian and White force of 235 men recaptured Vincennes on December 17, 1778. The following month Clark reappeared there and caused four Indian prisoners to be tomahawked where the garrison could see the deed. His object was to influence the British Indians, but the decisive result was Hamilton's decision to surrender on February 5, 1779. Clark's associates expected to be able to gratify their hatred of Hamilton, but Clark would not permit it. Instead, he delivered Hamilton to Gov. Thomas Jefferson of Virginia, who, believing that the name Hair Buyer was merited, let him lie for many months in a dismal dungeon. With Hamilton out of the scene, most of the coordination of the activities of the British Indians in the West disappeared (Commager and Morris 1967:1035–1052; J.P. Brown 1938:172).

Wyoming and Cherry Valley convinced George Washington that he must detach a significant segment from his already overextended Continental Army to break the power of the Iroquois. He ordered Gen. John Sullivan to accomplish "the total destruction and devastation of [the Indian] settlements and capture as many prisoners of every age and sex as possible." It will be essential "that the country may not be merely *overrun* but *destroyed*" (Fitzpatrick 1931–1944, 15:189–190). Sullivan started up the Susquehanna River into the heart of the Iroquois country in July 1779, and Gen. James Clinton marched from Albany to join him. Using surprise-proof formations the two columns merged at Tioga. Commanding 4,400 men Sullivan proceeded to carry out Washington's orders. His men destroyed 40 villages and 160,000 bushels of corn, lost less than 50 men, and were back at their point of departure in September 1779 (fig. 2) (Whittemore 1961: 117–152; Graymont 1972:192–222; Commager and Morris 1967:1011–1021).

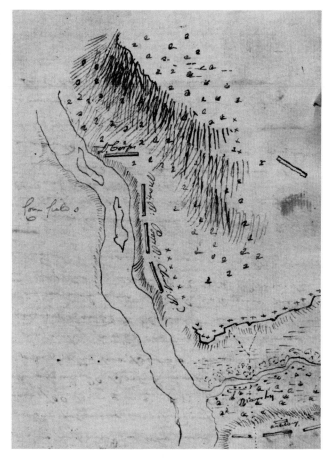

Histl. Soc. of Pa., Philadelphia: Am 643, p. 30, side b.
Fig. 2. Manuscript map, *Sketch of Encampment near Newtown, August 29th*, 1779. The campaign of Gen. John Sullivan is chronicled in the 1779 journal of Lt. Col. Adam Hubley (Jordan 1909). Hubley commanded the main column of the Light Corps, Brig. Gen. Edward Hand's brigade. In addition to daily written accounts of marchs, encampments, battles and other encounters with Indians, Hubley drew a number of maps depicting these. This map depicts the encampment along the Chemung River after the battle at the Seneca village Newtown, where the revolutionaries defeated Tory Rangers and Indian forces led by John Butler and Joseph Brant (vol. 15:508; Waldman 1985:112). The columns of American troops depicted along the right bank of the river are (top to bottom) the Light Corps, Gen. William Maxwell's brigade, Gen. Enoch Poor's brigade, both commanded by Sullivan, and Gen. James Clinton's brigade. One of the many cornfields destroyed during the campaign is shown on the left bank of the river. Prior to destruction, these same fields were often a source of food for the revolutionaries.

Since Wyandots, Ottawas, Chippewas, and Potawatomis had swung for a time to the side of the United States, Col. Daniel Brodhead in command at Pittsburgh proposed leading an army of them against the Iroquois. The Indians were perfectly willing to fight the Iroquois, but Brodhead could not field his Indian army because the frontiersmen refused to supply it in sufficient quantities. So Brodhead marched north with 600 White militiamen, who cut down 600 acres of Indian corn and returned to Pittsburgh with scalps and $3,000 worth of plunder (Downes 1940:249; Commager and Morris 1967: 1021–1028).

Severe as it was, the heavy destruction wreaked by Brodhead and Sullivan did not neutralize the Iroquois and their western neighbors. Complete neutralization would have required a follow-up expedition, but Washington, who was suffering military reverses in the east during 1780 and 1781, had to curtail supplies to the frontier and limit Brodhead to short excursions. What was needed was to capture Detroit, Britain's base for the fur trade and other dealings with Indians, but neither Brodhead nor George Rogers Clark could do it. British officer Henry Bird with 150 Whites and 1,000 Indians was able to descend river valleys as far south as Kentucky, reducing two forts near the Licking River in May 1780; but he quickly withdrew with his plunder (Downes 1940:258).

After Sullivan and Brodhead's campaigns the Iroquois had nothing to lose siding with the British. Even the Oneidas and Tuscororas shifted toward them.

It was the British Indians, under the direction of Joseph Brant, with the help of Butler's Rangers, who took the offensive in the Northeast in spring 1780. Abetted by Guy and John Johnson, they fielded 59 war parties that killed 142 people and captured 160. They devastated the Mohawk and Schoharie valleys. Thereafter Pennsylvania offered a bounty of $1,500 for a ranger's scalp and $1,000 for an Indian's (Graymont 1972:229, 235, 240, 245).

The Delawares had been vacillating between the two White belligerents, but the frontiersmen continued to deny them supplies and the Continental Congress once too often broke its word to them. Therefore, early in 1781 they at last shifted their weight to Britain. Knowing that they were preparing to attack, Daniel Brodhead assailed them first at Coshocton. At the same time Clark, even though Brodhead's operation subtracted from his power, was making one more try to reach Detroit. Behind him came a detachment of Pennsylvania militia under Archibald Lochry, vainly trying to catch up. Joseph Brant, using a ruse, lured it into an ambush on the Ohio River and destroyed it on August 24, 1781 (Downes 1940:263, 270ff.).

The Chickamauga Cherokees, since the heavy blow inflicted on them in 1779, had been quiet, but in 1780, when many of the White men were away, participating in the King's Mountain campaign, Dragging Canoe struck at the frontier settlements. John Sevier, celebrated Indian fighter from the North Carolina frontier, nearly annihilated a party of 80 Chickamauga Cherokees at Boyd's Creek on December 8, 1780. Soon his detachment was absorbed by a column of 400 men form Virginia. The combined force then burned the Cherokee town of Chota and nearby villages on Christmas Day 1780. It moved southward against the Chickamauga Cherokees and effectively destroyed their fighting power (Driver 1932:24–26; J.P. Brown 1938:193–194, 196; O'Donnell 1963:253–254).

During 1781 Spain began to attack the British possessions on the Gulf Coast. Choctaws joined the English to fight off Spaniards, but when in May 1781 the British commander at Pensacola had to surrender to his Spanish foe, not only the Choctaws but all the Indians who adhered to Britain in the Southeast were injured. Now there was no route left open to supply them except overland through Georgia from East Florida. This meant that the tribes farthest west would not be able to get needed goods (O'Donnell 1963:262–267).

Unlike the Cherokees the Creeks took relatively little part in the American Revolution. Although they generally remained loyal to England, they rarely clashed in battle very much with the American rebels. This posture estranged the Cherokees, who resented their unwillingness to aid them (Alden 1957:274–275, 278; O'Donnell 1963: 90).

Indian-White warfare was extensive in 1782. John Sevier thrust once more very bloodily against some Cherokees. At Gnadenhütten, Ohio, militiamen perpetrated a massacre of 90 Delawares who had been converted to the Moravian faith. A more rational and formal campaign was organized under the command of Col. William Crawford of the Pennsylvania militia. No Continentals could be spared to join Crawford, so with about 250 men he engaged an equal number of Indians on June 4 at Sandusky. The next day 140 Shawnees arrived, and some of Butler's Rangers, and by evening the Indians had Crawford completely surrounded. In the end they killed or captured all but a few of his men. Crawford himself, in retaliation for Gnadenhütten, was seized and roasted slowly at the stake. Indian-White relations reached their low point in the Ohio Valley. Emboldened by the destruction of Crawford's army, the Senecas burned Hannastown, Pennsylvania, and unsuccessfully attacked Fort Henry (Wheeling) (J.P. Brown 1938:199; Downes 1940:271; Graymont 1972:253; Commager and Morris 1967:1056, 1058).

The frontiersmen along the Ohio River assembled a force to retaliate. It consisted of Kentucky militia and a company of United States Rangers. Waiting for it in ambush were 30 of Butler's Rangers and 200 Wyandot and other Indians. At the Blue Licks on the Licking River on August 18, 1782, they killed or captured 146 Americans at a cost of 6 Indians killed and 10 wounded (Talbert 1955; Commager and Morris 1967:1060).

The blighted year of 1782 saw a few more scattered operations. George Rogers Clark at the head of 1,000 men followed the Scioto River to Chillicothe, a principal seat of the Shawnee. Early in November he burned five towns and 10,000 bushels of corn. But he could not press on to Detroit. In Georgia there were scattered encounters with pro-British Cherokees (O'Donnell 1963:280; Downes 1940:278–279).

As far back as 1777 Britain had guaranteed territory to some of her Indian allies, but in 1783 she signed the Treaty of Paris, which transferred all the land east of the Mississippi to the new nation without reference to the Indians. The British agents who had drawn the Indians into the conflict protested this, but the government in England took the position that Britain had not ceded the Indians' rights. Said William Petty, the Earl of Shelburne, whose government signed the articles of peace, "The Indian nations were not abandoned to their enemies; they were remitted to the care of neighbors, whose interest it was as much as ours to cultivate friendship with them and who were certainly the best qualified for softening and humanizing their hearts." Specious as this sounds, it held most of the northern Indians to the British connection (Graymont 1972:259–262).

The Articles of Confederation, 1783–1789

In spite of the Treaty of Paris, the Indians continued to seek British aid to hold the land north of the Ohio River. They did not know that England was unwilling to use arms in their cause. Matters reached a crucial stage when in 1783 Pennsylvania and New York began to confiscate Indian lands within their borders. In response, the British were willing to support a grand council of tribes, brought together by Joseph Brant at Sandusky in September 1783. But instead of backing an Indian attempt to regain lost hunting grounds, the British agents sought to curb Indian aggressiveness, for they believed that this was the only way to prevent Indian extermination. The policy of restraint was not successful. Some Indians carried out heavy raids against western Pennsylvania and Virginia settlements in spring 1783 (Downes 1940:279–280).

The Congress of the United States published a significant report dated October 15, 1783. The report was based on the supposition that the Indians had forfeited their lands when they had sided with Britain against the United States. If they were left with any hunting grounds at all it was not because they had rights to them but because of American compassion alone. However, whatever boundaries the United States chose to set between itself and the Indians would be faithfully policed to prevent White encroachment (Downes 1940:284-285; Prucha 1962: 32–33).

In 1784 the Congress brought the First American Regiment into being and in 1785 gave it permanence. The new regiment was to be used on the one hand to influence the Indians to cede land to the United States and on the other to drive trespassers off lands guaranteed to the Indians. The Congress operated on the theories that the tribes were nations and that they understood Euro-American culture. It would use the regiment as a makeweight in the relations between the United States and the Indian nations (Prucha 1969; Mahon 1954; J.R. Jacobs 1947:13–39).

Between 1783 and 1786, various persons, authorized or not, signed a sheaf of treaties with several tribes of

Indians. All the documents were marked by only a few chiefs, none by representatives of any Indian confederation of the sort Joseph Brant was trying to found (Downes 1940:282–283). During those years Georgia ratified three treaties with certain compliant Creeks: Augusta, 1783; Galphinton, 1785; and Shoulderbone, 1786 (Cotterill 1954:65, 66, 72). All three were repudiated by Alexander McGillivray, the central leader of the Creeks in so far as they had one. McGillivray, part Scottish, some French, and part Creek, came as near to being a diplomatist as any Indian leader in any era ever did, and he played the Euro-American powers off against each other with skill. In 1784 he agreed to a treaty that put his people under the jurisdiction and the protection of Spain. The Choctaw and the Chickasaw signed with him (Caughey 1938).

In 1785 the short-lived State of Franklin found some Cherokees who were willing to cede the land lying south of the French Broad River (Driver 1932:89–90). In the same year the United States secured concessions from the Cherokees, Choctaws, and Chickasaws at Hopewell. Several compliant Iroquois marked a treaty at Fort Stanwix in 1784 that transferred Iroquois-claimed land north of the Ohio River to Whites. In January 1785, at Fort McIntosh downriver from Pittsburgh, purported representatives of Wyandot, Delaware, Chippewa, and Ottawa tribes ceded much of the rest of the terrain that later became the state of Ohio (Kappler 1904–1941, 2:3–7).

The Shawnees were the only tribe north of the Ohio River that kept up an active fight between the years 1786 and 1789. Their belligerence brought upon them an American army that in October 1786 destroyed seven towns on the Great Miami River and killed 10 chiefs. Since one of the chiefs was struck down under a flag of truce, the Shawnees became for a time more anti-American than ever.

Joseph Brant steadily attempted to draw the Indians into some sort of confederation. The British abetted him to the extent of allowing major councils to be held at Detroit in 1785 and 1786. In 1786 representatives of almost all the tribes north of the Ohio River agreed to demand abrogation of the land cessions of the 1780s, but they never put together a unit to enforce it. Wyandots, Delawares, and Senecas were shy of Indian union because they knew that they would be first in the path of any United States military action (Downes 1940:296, 299–300).

When all factors had been weighed by the Congress of the United States, the time seemed correct to give political organization to the territory west of Pennsylvania and Virginia. Therefore, in 1787 Congress enacted the Northwest Ordinance, which created a government for the area north of the Ohio River and east of the Mississippi. The new polity, denominated the Northwest Territory, became yet another agency, added to the Congress and the states, to deal with the Indians either by negotiation or by force, or some combination of the two.

Negotiators lost no opportunity to impress the northern tribes with the power of the Whites. Characteristic of the talk were the words of Richard Butler at Fort Finney, Kentucky: "The destruction of your women and children or their future happiness depends on your present choice" (Downes 1940:295). The choice, of course, was to cede land and save the women and children, or refuse to cede and see them wiped out. The Indians recognized that what Butler said was true. Accordingly, when some Senecas came together at Fort Harmar in January 1789, they allowed Arthur Saint Clair, governor of the Northwest Territory, to dictate terms to them. He reaffirmed the boundaries set by the Treaties of Fort Stanwix and Fort McIntosh but gave the Indians permission to hunt in their old lands as long as they were peaceful about it.

Such passivity was not the tone south of the Ohio River. There the Creek council formally declared war on the United States on April 2, 1786. Creek raiding parties killed 82 persons, wounded 29, and captured 140 on the Georgia borders. In 1787 the Chickamauga Cherokees succeeded in virtually isolating the Cumberland settlements. The Cherokees carried out heavy attacks during summer 1788 in the Chickamauga Creek area and around Fort White (later Knoxville). The governor of North Carolina believed that the southern Indians were waging a general war (Alden 1957:357–358).

Finally, the incessant raids brought John Sevier out once more. He summoned the militia of the State of Franklin and conducted a campaign in August 1786 that took from the Cherokee a large new increment of land. In June 1788, he attacked Cherokee towns. But in August Dragging Canoe and his Chickamauga Cherokees met Sevier with a force of only 40 men, whom they stopped at the Hiwassee River and obliged to retreat. In January 1789 Sevier engaged the Indians in the severest action of the Cherokee wars. Known as the Battle of Flint Creek, it cost the Indians no less than 145 dead, and his own army almost no casualities at all. It blunted the aggressiveness of the Cherokees (Alden 1957:357–358; J.P. Brown 1938: 254, 282–289, 297; Driver 1932:30).

The Chickasaws had not at any time been willing to fight against the United States. As for the Creeks, McGillivray learned in January 1788 that Spain was cutting back her aid (Caughey 1938:35–42; Wright 1967), obliging him to seek aid from other White nations.

The Federalist Period, 1789–1800

The United States Constitution, which went into operation in 1789, gave Congress the exclusive power to regulate trade with Indians. They were considered to be outside the Union; the United States would deal with them as foreign nations. Indeed, the survival of the new government depended on how well it did so, diplomatically and militarily. The federal government could handle the diplomatic assignment even if it had to negotiate with many tribes simultaneously, but it had only enough military strength to concentrate in one geographical section at a time. For political reasons the military force was concentrated in the Northwest. The strategy therefore was to try to remain at peace with the tribes south of the Ohio River (Prucha 1969:46).

To keep peace in the south was not simple. Southern frontiersmen mistrusted the federal government and did not expect to receive adequate protection from Indian attack, but they did approve of the continuous federal negotiation with the Indians to allow roads to be built through their lands. More roads were built, and those that already existed, such as that from Natchez to Nashville, became safer than ever before. But they were never perfectly safe. Although 10,000 people passed over the Wilderness Road in 15 years, 100 of them were said to have been killed in the year 1792 alone (J.P. Brown 1938: 225; Nelson 1955:1–14).

The people of Georgia violently disapproved of federal negotiation with the Creeks. The treaty that McGillivray signed in 1790 did not recognize Georgia's claim to the land between the Altamaha and the Saint Mary's rivers but did assert that the federal government had exclusive control of Indian affairs. To both these items the Georgians were in militant opposition (Caughey 1938:45; Pound 1951:58). In 1790 President George Washington issued a proclamation ordering a settlement of White persons to remove from land in the big bend of the Tennessee River that the federal government considered the property of the Cherokees. When the settlers paid no attention to the proclamation, the Cherokees took enforcement into their own hands. Glass, an important chief, surprised the White community so completely that he could have wiped it out, but all he did was tell the people to get off the land (J.P. Brown 1938:318). Under a flag some settlers invited chiefs of the Upper Cherokee towns into a cabin for talks, locked doors, and permitted the son of a man whom the Indians had killed to tomahawk the five. This treachery drove the Upper Cherokee into league with Dragging Canoe (J.P. Brown 1938:277–278).

In October 1790 William Blount became the first governor of the newly created Territory South of the Ohio River (Southwest Territory) and superintendent of Indian affairs for the southern department. Throughout the 1790s he occupied a key position in Indian relations. A heavy speculator in western lands, he was regularly in favor of those policies that would enhance the value of unsettled real estate, the most basic of which was to get the Indians out of the way (Masterson 1954).

The first major military campaign by the United States against Indians took place in 1790. On the north bank of the Ohio River, where Cincinnati now stands, was Fort

Washington. From it, in April, Brig. Gen. Josiah Harmar took out a column that burned some empty Indian towns. Then during the fall he fielded two expeditions aimed at Miami villages. The object of both was to destroy Indian crops, villages, and manpower. The Indians put up detachments from Harmar's command and forced him to countermarch to Fort Washington. The general claimed victory, but the Indians, believing that they had driven him into the fort, became more aggressive (J.R. Jacobs 1947:40–65). Harmar had laid the blame for his having to return to Fort Washington to "the shameful cowardly conduct of the militia" (ASPIA 1:105). Harmar had been forced to rely on militia because the western people had successfully lobbied to be put on the United States payroll at $\frac{2}{3}$ of a dollar a day (Ames 1854, 1:99, 109).

Charles Scott, who had been a general in the Revolution, persuaded the United States to pay for a campaign waged by 750 Kentucky volunteers. His command ravaged the Indians on the Wabash River in May and June 1791. In August, James Wilkinson repeated Scott's performance. To Kentuckians these two expeditions proved that they themselves were a far better instrument to use against Indians than U.S. regulars. They also proved that Harmar had slandered them (J.R. Jacobs 1947:72, 74; McElroy 1909:157–159).

George Washington and his advisors considered Scott's and Wilkinson's excursions as no more than preparation for a heavier thrust to come, not only paid but also directed by the United States government. They knew that to keep the West in the Union they would have to make the next offensive show better results. Washington appointed the governor of the Northwest Territory, Arthur Saint Clair, a Revolutionary officer, to command the new effort.

By autumn 1791 Governor Saint Clair had assembled at Fort Washington (now Cincinnati) 625 regulars, 1,675 of a special type of citizen soldiers denominated "levies," and 470 militiamen. Just before dawn on November 4, 1791, a combined force of Northwest Indians (including Wyandots, Chippewas, Miamis, and Kickapoos) ambushed his camp on the upper Wabash River. Only 1,400 of the American troops even got into position to enter the fight, and 630 of these were killed. Between 250 and 300 others were wounded (fig. 3). The thin bonds that held the frontier in the Union almost broke. If the federal government could not effectively control the Indians, frontiersmen said, what was it good for? Congress called upon the president to provide it with all the papers relative to the campaign, and, when Washington had complied, commenced the first congressional inquiry into the conduct of the executive branch (J.R. Jacobs 1947: 66–123).

Preserving peace with the southern tribes became more difficult in 1791 when the Spanish government replaced Esteban Miró as governor of Louisiana with the Baron

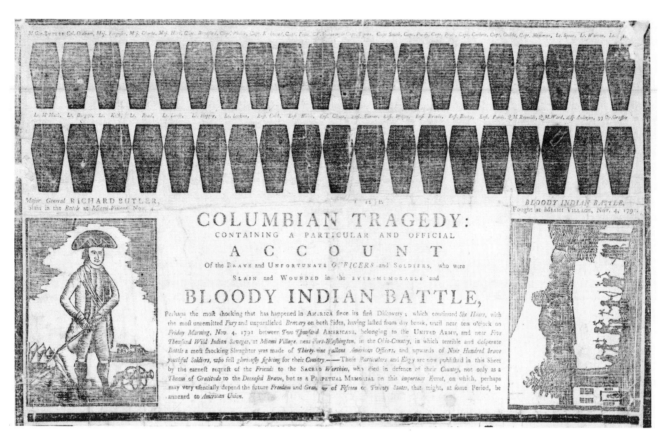

COLUMBIAN TRAGEDY:
CONTAINING A PARTICULAR AND OFFICIAL
A C C O U N T
Of the Brave and Unfortunate Officers and Soldiers, who were
SLAIN and WOUNDED in the ever-memorable and
BLOODY INDIAN BATTLE,

Conn. Histl Soc., Hartford: Bdse/1791/C726t.

Fig. 3. *The Columbian Tragedy*, a broadside describing the defeat of Gov. Saint Clair's forces at Ft. Washington, Nov. 4, 1791, issued as a memorial at the request of "the *Friends* of the Sacred *Worthies*, who died." It included a funeral elegy, a list of officers killed and wounded (not shown), Maj. Gen. Richard Butler (left), and a scene of the battle (right). Broadside printed in Hartford, Conn.

Francisco de Carondelet, who encouraged the southern tribes to draw together into a confederation. He achieved no confederation but did create greater harmony among Creeks, Chickasaws, Choctaws, and Cherokees. Carondelet also set out to nullify the Treaty of New York and to undermine the influence of Alexander McGillivray. He failed in both, but his policy did help to produce attacks on the Cumberland and Watauga settlements in 1792 (Caughey 1938:52; Berry 1917:470; Pratt 1955:66).

Gov. Charles Pinckney, seeing that Creeks and Cherokees were threatening South Carolina, called out 8,000 militiamen and undertook to persuade the federal government to support them. South Carolina also erected blockhouses 10 miles apart along its threatened borders, and Secretary of War Henry Knox agreed to pay rangers to patrol between them. Also, he sent emissaries to the Cherokees, who raised annuities to them by 50 percent (Knox 1792).

In September 1792, a mixed band of Cherokees, Creeks, and Shawnees attacked Buchanan's Station, four miles south of Nashville. The attack was repulsed, but the unusual combination of tribes willing to cooperate in the attack was an omen. White feeling in the territory hardened against the Indians. Gov. William Blount agreed to guarantee, with his own resources, funds borrowed to prepare for attack. Secretary Knox warned Blount not to assault the Indians because the president did not want the war at the north to extend to the south. Blount replied more than once that there was a mounting anger among the frontier people that he might not be able to control (J.P. Brown 1938:359; Masterson 1954:230–240). John Sevier, disregarding the strategy of the federal government, was in the field southwest of Knoxville during October 1792, but the Cherokees were hampered in opposing him by the death of Dragging Canoe, who had been at the center of resistance to Whites (J.P. Brown 1938:329).

The militia of the Southwest Territory threatened the federal policy of peace in the south, during the summer of 1793 attacking a camp of friendly Cherokee even while United States agents were among them. As a result an influential Cherokee chief, John Watts, found himself at the head of a united group, at least for a time. Watts might have permanently injured the White settlements in the Tennessee region if he and his uncle, Doublehead, had not disagreed over methods (J.P. Brown 1938:387ff.). The situation became so desperate that William Blount and others sought to persuade the federal government to wage war on the southern tribes, but Secretary Knox refused (Masterson 1954:24ff.).

151

John Sevier used Blount's absence to strike another blow. In September 1793 with 700 men, he defeated a Cherokee war party, burned towns, and slaughtered cattle. This was his last campaign, and one of the few he ever reported. Not only did he inform the governor but also the secretary of war, whose policy he had flouted. The United States refused to pay his men for many years, but in the end did so, or paid their survivors (Driver 1932: 33ff.; J.P. Brown 1938:393; ASPMA 1:469). James Seagrove, federal agent, was so unpopular among frontiersmen because of the administration's Indian policy that he had to ask the federal troops to escort him through Georgia. He then found it safest to stay in the Creek country until May 1794. There were only 189 regulars stationed in Georgia, but they spent part of their time evicting squatters from Indian land. Georgians cordially hated them for it. Partly to try to ease this antigovernment feeling, Secretary Knox agreed in May 1794 to supply tools for erecting blockhouses every 25 miles along the Georgia border and to pay Georgia militia to garrison them.

As far as the federal government was concerned, the main theater of military operations remained north of the Ohio River. To try to redeem itself with frontiersmen, the administration had in 1792 persuaded Congress to enlarge the military establishment and to reorganize it. The result was the Legion of the United States, composed of 5,120 enlisted men arranged in four sublegions. Each sublegion contained infantry, riflemen, cavalry, and artillery organized so that they could be flexed together. Washington selected Anthony Wayne to command the Legion and to prepare it for a showdown with the Northwestern Indians, a group including Chippewas, Miamis, Delawares, Shawnees, and Potawatomis. But Wayne was not empowered to take the offensive unless specifically ordered by the administration to do so (J.R. Jacobs 1947:124–152).

Wayne had two years to train his men. By 1794 negotiations had broken down, and Knox told him to advance from Fort Washington and settle the score by military means. Wayne moved forward so well guarded that the Indians could not get to his Legion to hurt it. By August he was near Fort Miami, which the British had built in February 1794 in violation of the Treaty of Paris (Burt 1940:136, 137; J.R. Jacobs 1947:153–188).

Every tribe in the Old Northwest was represented in the array of Indians who opposed Wayne's advance, and there were even 100 Cherokees with them. But no central leadership fused them into an army. As a result, when Wayne made his final move toward the British fort on August 20, 1794, only 800 Indian warriors were waiting for him. Those who waited for him had been fasting for days to be pure for battle, and Wayne is said to have slowed his approach in order for them to become weaker from hunger. The strike force was mostly regulars. After a very short skirmish they overran the Indian position.

When the fleeing Indians demanded sanctuary inside the British fort, the British commander was too fearful of American attack to admit them. In the end Wayne made no attempt on the fort and withdrew without precipitating an international incident (ASPIA 1:491; J.R. Jacobs 1947: 153–188).

After the Battle of Fallen Timbers, Wayne and a detachment of troops met with chiefs of Miami, Potawatami, Shawnee, Wea, Piankashaw, Ottawa, Wyandot, and Chippewa bands on August 3, 1795. Recognizing that the Whites were in control of the situation, the Indians ceded a large part of what is now Ohio by the Treaty of Greenville (much of the same land already ceded in Treaty of Ft. McIntosh of 1785). By Jay's Treaty, negotiated during these years, the British yielded to the United States the forts they had promised at the end of the Revolutionary War. Thus in 1796 detachments of the United States Army took over from British garrisons the seven forts through which the Indian trade in the country around the Great Lakes and westward was controlled (fig. 4) (J.R. Jacobs 1947:180).

During 1795 and 1796 an enforced peace of a sort settled over the frontier. Cherokees made peace at Tellico Blockhouse in 1795, and the Creeks ended a 20-year period of warfare when they signed a document at Colerain. White encroachments on guaranteed Indian lands went forward at an unchanged pace, even though in several areas local or regular troops actually evicted a few White families (Cotterill 1954:336).

The National Period, 1800–1832

President Thomas Jefferson sought to cut expenses, particularly in the military services. Appropriations for the army dropped from $2,000,000 in 1801 to $680,000 in 1803; and for the navy from $3,000,000 to $1,000,000 (White 1951:496; Prucha 1969:99).

A trade relationship was to replace a military one, and the government raised the number of its own trading posts to a high of eight. President Jefferson went so far as to suggest that influential chiefs should be encouraged to go into debt at the government trading houses so that they could pay off their debts by ceding land (White 1951:500; Esarey 1922, 1:69–73). Jefferson also urged the Indians to change from hunters and swidden agriculturists to full-time farmers, European-style. Unless this change could be achieved the Indians would never progress toward "civilization." But the attempt created such divisions among some of the Indian societies that it moved them closer to ultimate disaster (Richardson 1896–1899, 1:326, 354–355).

The purchase of Louisiana brought large numbers of new Indians under United States control. It also made possible an alternative to the policy of making European-style farmers out of the natives. For the first time there

Detroit Public Lib., Burton Histl. Coll., Mich.

Fig. 4. View of the southwest corner of Detroit, July 25, 1794. Defense works surround the town. The West Gate, with blockhouse, leads down to the Detroit River. The later site of Windsor, Ont., is across the river. The garrison at Detroit was at various times controlled by the French, British, and Americans. During French occupation, 1701–1760, both Indians and French regarded the fort as a convenient place for trade. The British, 1760–1796, did not welcome Indians into the fort, and trade relations were restricted. The Treaty of Greenville placed the fort in American control. The fort figured prominently in Pontiac's War and was besieged and taken by Tecumseh and British Maj. Gen. Isaac Brock during the War of 1812 (Utley and Washburn 1977:102, passim). Watercolor by "E.H."

was an area into which the Indians might be removed and yet retain their traditional lifeways. Some Cherokees actually migrated as early as 1807 into what became Arkansas, and in a few years about 6,000 of them had gone there (J.P. Brown 1938:471). The French Revolution and its sequels, raging in Europe since 1789, affected Indian-White relations in America. Since it was plain that Upper Canada could not be defended without the aid of the Indians, British officials in Canada, as early as 1807, had commenced to think how to bind the Indians to them if conflict with the United States broke out. Whatever the English did in the wooing of Indians seemed to American frontiersmen to be no less than inviting the Indians to attack them (Pratt 1955:126; Craig 1963:36).

William Henry Harrison, governor of Indiana Territory, saw events as other frontiersmen saw them. His immediate focus was on Prophetstown, a village founded by the Shawnee chief Tecumseh and his brother Tenskwatawa, also called the Shawnee Prophet. Tecumseh was one of the few Indian leaders who had a vision of the need for Indian unity to stop White encroachment. He had the support of many of the small tribes north of the Ohio, so he turned his attention southward. His mother was a Creek. He put together a band of warriors who were trained to perform impressive ceremonies and in the fall of 1811 went south to try to gain allies. He passed from one to the other of the great tribes of the Southeast, urging them to join with the northern Indians, but he could not persuade them (Tucker 1956).

Tecumseh had enjoined his brother to refrain from war until he returned, but Tenskwawata and other leaders became convinced that Harrison, who was marching a

column of about 1,000 men toward them, was determined to wipe out Prophetstown. Rather than leave the initiative to him, the villagers launched a preemptive attack on his camp near the Tippecanoe River, in Indiana Territory on November 7, 1811. After the Battle of Tippecanoe Harrison moved toward Prophetstown, found it abandoned, and destroyed it (fig. 5). Tecumseh upon his return became an ally of the British and helped them in their negotiations for the support of other tribes (Mahon 1972: 20–27).

War of 1812

English policy was in part conditioned by the lucrative fur trade. Accordingly, of highest strategic importance were the settlements around the Great Lakes, from which trade with the Indians had traditionally been carried on. Most important of all were Detroit and Mackinac, for whoever controlled them could also control Lakes Huron and Superior and the Indian trade to the west as far as the Great Plains and to the south as far as New Orleans.

The ministers in London were not happy about using Indians as allies in the War of 1812, but they were persuaded by the commanders in North America that if they did not do so, the Americans would, and the British cause would be lost. They therefore provided substantial sums to feed and maintain their Indian associates. As a result one of their war aims became the conquest of the territory between the border of Upper Canada and the Ohio River. They could settle their Indian allies into this area as a buffer against future American encroachments.

Two days before the surrender of an American army at

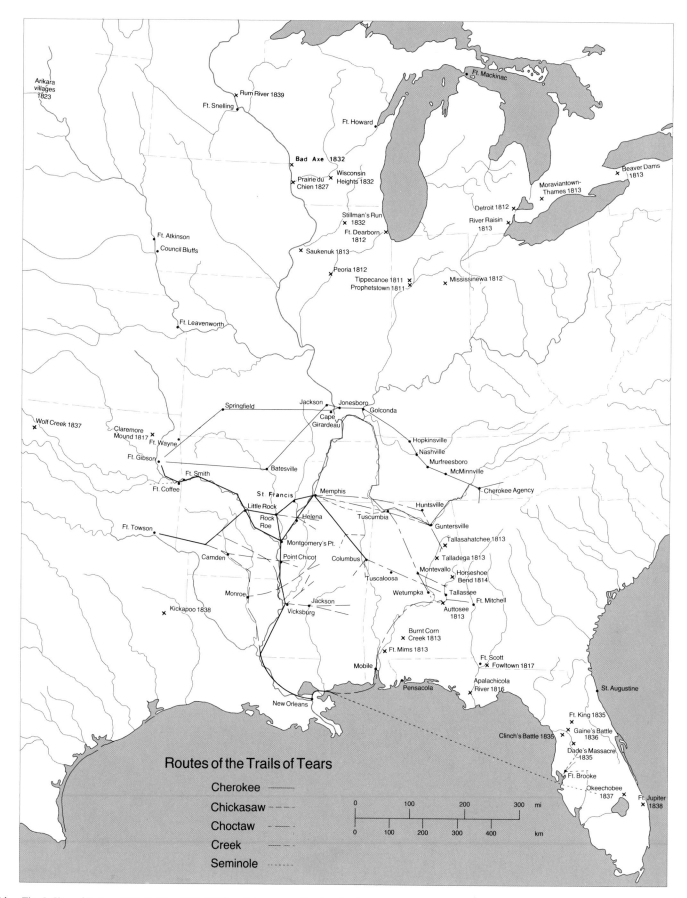

Arikara villages 1823

Rum River 1839
Ft. Snelling
Ft. Mackinac
Ft. Howard

Bad Axe 1832
Prairie du Chien 1827
Wisconsin Heights 1832

Beaver Dams 1813
Moraviantown-Thames 1813
Detroit 1812

Stillman's Run 1832
Ft. Dearborn 1812
River Raisin 1813

Ft. Atkinson
Council Bluffs
Saukenuk 1813
Peoria 1812
Tippecanoe 1811
Prophetstown 1811
Mississinewa 1812

Ft. Leavenworth

Wolf Creek 1837
Springfield
Jackson
Jonesboro
Golconda

Claremore Mound 1817
Ft. Wayne
Cape Girardeau
Hopkinsville
Nashville
Murfreesboro
McMinnville

Ft. Gibson
Batesville
Cherokee Agency

Ft. Smith
St. Francis
Memphis
Huntsville

Ft. Coffee
Little Rock
Rock Roe
Helena
Tuscumbia
Guntersville

Ft. Towson
Montgomery's Pt.
Tallasahatchee 1813
Talladega 1813

Camden
Point Chicot
Columbus
Montevallo
Horseshoe Bend 1814

Tuscaloosa
Wetumpka
Tallassee
Ft. Mitchell

Monroe
Jackson
Vicksburg
Auttosee 1813

Kickapoo 1838
Burnt Corn Creek 1813
Ft. Mims 1813

Ft. Scott
Fowltown 1817

Mobile
Pensacola
Apalachicola River 1816
St. Augustine

New Orleans

Ft. King 1835
Gaine's Battle 1836
Clinch's Battle 1835
Dade's Massacre 1835
Ft. Brooke
Okeechobee 1837
Ft. Jupiter 1838

Routes of the Trails of Tears
Cherokee ——
Chickasaw ----
Choctaw -·-·-
Creek --·--
Seminole ·······

154   Fig. 5. Sites of Indian-White battles, 1811–1848, and the routes of emigrating Indians, 1830–1840 (J.T. Adams 1943; Prucha 1964; Foreman 1953).

MAHON

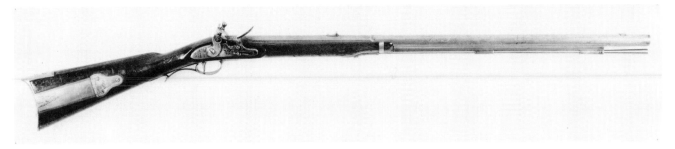

Fig. 6. U.S. rifle Model 1803, the first regulation rifle made for the U.S. Army. Produced at Harper's Ferry Va., this type of flintlock rifle was made to specifications stated by the War Department (Hicks 1940:25–26). The shorter barrel (33 in. or less) and larger caliber (about .54) were changes expressly designed to overcome limitations of the traditional long rifle. Some of its earliest users were members of the 1804–1805 Meriwether Lewis and William Clark expedition (Russell 1960:25), and it was probably also the rifle carried by Zebulon Pike's men into the Southwest in 1805–1806 (Russell 1957:180). The popularity of Model 1803 led to a series of refinements reflected in the issuance of breech-loading and percussion rifles that were standard arms well into the Civil War period. Features of its construction were also copied by private makers in their manufacture of "Plains rifles" and other sporting rifles used by trappers and explorers in the American West throughout the early and mid-1800s. This example was made in 1815. Overall length 126.0 cm.

Detroit, Capt. Nathan Heald had evacuated Fort Dearborn at Chicago. Thus another key point through which the Indians could be controlled fell to the British. The fate of Heald's column illustrated the hazards a European nation ran into when it enlisted Indians in its cause. Although the column had been guaranteed safe conduct by the British, Indians fell upon it and killed nearly 60 people. Only a fragment escaped (Lossing 1869:303–311). Control of the western end of the Great Lakes was now in Britain's hands, and the American defensive perimeter was pushed southward deep into United States territory. Whenever British troops went into action they had Indian help. In most of the actions Tecumseh was involved, directly or indirectly (figs. 7–8).

During January 1813 American forces occupying an exposed position on the River Raisin caved in when attacked by a force of British and Indians. American losses, mostly captured, soared to 800, but what impressed Americans most of all was that the Indians massacred 33 of the wounded prisoners. The number said to have been massacred was inflated by rumor to many times 33, and Americans thereafter went into battle with a new war cry, "Remember the Raisin!" (Mahon 1972:128–131). In the Battle of the Thames on October 5, 1813, Harrison led an army of 5,000, which defeated the remnants of the British and Indian force in western Ontario. More important, they killed Tecumseh, who had personified opposition to American encroachment. His death symbolized the wreck of the fighting power of the Indians of the Northwest (Mahon 1972:182–185).

The tribes south of the Ohio River had done little during the first year of the war of 1812. The Creeks were divided over which, if either, White side they should support and over the cultural change that the United States agents had been pressing upon them. The faction of the Creeks that opposed adopting European-style agriculture and becoming Americanized became known as Red Sticks. In 1812 they fell to fighting the opposite faction,

and early in 1813 came into collision with White Americans. The opening action involving Whites took place at Burnt Corn Creek, Mississippi Territory, on February 9, 1813. A detachment of Mississippi militiamen tried there to intercept a party of Red Sticks who were returning from Pensacola with a pack train of ammunition supplied them by Spain (Halbert and Ball 1895:125–142).

Next, the Red Sticks made a surprise attack on Fort Mims in the same vicinity. Although they killed 400 Whites of all ages and both sexes, they lost 300 of their warriors. What is more, from the White viewpoint they had committed a barbarous massacre and deserved annihilation for it. The immediate result was an invasion into Creek country from three directions. Mississippi Territory, Georgia, and Tennessee each raised a small army and sent it into the Creek heartland in east-central Alabama. Had the three columns been coordinated, the campaign would have been short and final. As it was the

Fig. 7. Compass purportedly given to Tecumseh by the British General Isaac Brock during the summer of 1812. Using Tecumseh's Indian warriors and his own troops, Brock forced the surrender of Detroit on August 16. Diameter 5.5 cm.

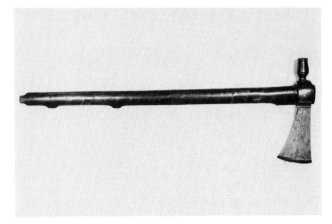

Fig. 8. Presentation pipe tomahawk engraved and given to Tecumseh in 1812 by British Col. Henry Proctor, who led the British land forces after the death of Gen. Brock that year. Ironically, Col. Proctor's caution in attacking American forces led to the British defeat in the Battle of the Thames in 1813 and the death of Tecumseh. The haft is burned in stripes for decoration. Length 66.5 cm.

army from Tennessee, which had the most difficult access route, achieved the decisive results. In their advance they developed a style of attack upon villages that resulted in the capture of all the residents, or the extermination of most of them. The invading White columns were guided and supported by Cherokee warriors, but the Chickasaws, Choctaws, and most of the Cherokee warriors stayed aloof from the conflict (Halbert and Ball 1895:143–76; Mahon 1972:235–242). The Red Sticks prepared to stand off Gen. Andrew Jackson's advance in the Horseshoe Bend of the Tallapoosa River (fig. 9) but were defeated with great loss. Jackson's victory there broke for the next two decades the fighting power of the Creeks and permanently weakened them (Mahon 1972:243–244). After Horseshoe Bend, the Creeks were forced to make an enormous cession of land on August 9, 1814 (Adams 1944:121).

At the very time when the power of the Creeks was being broken, the British formulators of strategy in America were deciding to base their invasion of the Gulf region upon reliance on the Indians. They did not realize that the power of the Creeks had been ruined, that the other major tribes were not committing themselves, and that their only help would have to come from the Florida Indians, who were not numerous (Mahon 1966).

During the War of 1812, including the Creek War, the Indians had shown themselves more willing than usual to attack fortified places and even to besiege them for a time. Generally these attacks were not successful.

The standard American techniques against the Indians were those learned over 200 years: burn Indian villages, destroy standing crops, and kill livestock. Perhaps John Coffee's long enveloping line, adopted by Andrew Jackson, may be considered a new military technique. He trained the units on the tips of his line to turn inward as soon as the center had made contact with the target,

usually a village, and to wrap around it like a net.

The War of 1812 was the last chance for the Indians permanently to alter the history of the United States. Had the tribes listened to Tecumseh, or had they been more skillfully used by the British, they might have affected the outcome of the war and the ultimate fate of the United States. But their chance escaped them, and they never got another.

England, as she had done at the end of the Great War for Empire in 1763 and again after the American Revolution, made at least a gesture toward protecting her Indian allies from future American aggressions. The result was Article IX of the Treaty of Ghent, ending the war, which stipulated that the United States would guarantee to the Indians the same status and territory as they had possessed in 1811. It is hard to see how the American peace commissioners could have acted in good faith when they agreed to this article (Miller 1931–1948, 2:574–575). However, trying to live up to Article IX, from July to October 1815 the United States signed 14 treaties with Indian tribes (Potawatomi, Miami, Sioux, Kickapoo, Wyandot, Osage, Sauk, Fox, Iowa, Kansas, Omaha), guaranteeing them their status as of 1811. But in none of these did it return an acre of land (Prucha 1969:122).

First Seminole War

Since the strongest Indian combinations had been crushed during the War of 1812, in the years that followed the military instrument was used primarily around the perirpheries. Slaves ran away to Spanish Florida and joined the loose aggregation of bands called Seminoles. Since Spain neither would nor could stop this drain, the United States government considered acquiring Florida, if need be by force, and kept a small detachment of regulars in the vicinity of Saint Augustine in 1812. But the idea of conquering Florida was given up lest the United States find herself at war with both England and Spain. So the federal government did not use arms to bring about annexation or to discipline the Indians for harboring runaway slaves.

But Georgia, lacking such inhibitions, sent 117 militiamen into east Florida on September 27, 1812. Also, in February 1813 Tennessee sent a well-appointed body of 250 men for a campaign of destruction that lasted three weeks. Its cost to the Florida Indians was 386 of their cattle driven off or slaughtered, besides a few warriors killed. This campaign wrecked the fighting power of the Florida Indians who dwelt east of the Suwannee River (Patrick 1954:225–236). Turbulence in west Florida centered around a fort on the Apalachicola River that England had built to enable the Indians to defend themselves. The Indians never occupied it, but their Negro allies who did were wiped out on July 27, 1816, by a shot from an American river vessel. The loss of the fort and of

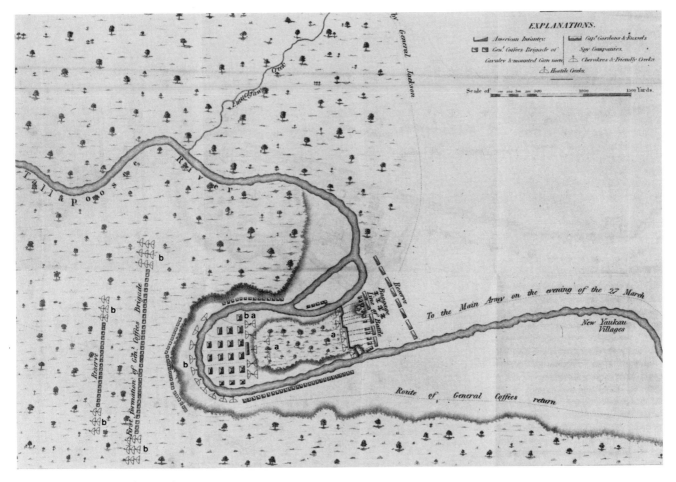

Fig. 9. Detail of map, "The Battle of the Horse Shoe 27th March 1814." Lines of battle are indicated by symbols distinguishing the Red Sticks (a) from the Creeks and Cherokees (b) who supported the Americans. Original engraving in Eaton (1817:opp. 117; a and b added to original map).

its defenders hurt the cause of the Florida Indians, but they continued to be defiant. Their military response is known as the First Seminole War. It began with what was almost a pitched battle near Fowltown, Georgia, on November 21, 1817. Gen. Andrew Jackson reached Fort Scott in March 1818 and hastily penetrated Indian country with 1,500 White soldiers and 2,000 Creeks. In a short time Jackson broke the strength of the Florida Indians west of the Suwannee River (Calhoun 1817).

Spain then saw that it was necessary to transfer Florida to the United States while she could still derive something from it. The treaty of transfer was completed in 1819, and the formal turnover in 1821. As far as the new owner of the land was concerned the Seminoles were an unwelcome appendage to the soil, clearly without any right of permanent ownership in it (Miller 1931–1948, 3:8).

Western Frontier

The administration of Indian affairs was located in the War Department, and as the frontiers pushed westward the Department advanced the fringe of forts. Soon after the War of 1812 army detachments reoccupied Mackinac,

Chicago, and Fort Howard (on Green Bay) and reestablished a line of forts along the Mississippi River. Forts Snelling in Minnesota and Atkinson in Nebraska were begun in 1819, Forts Gibson and Towson in the Oklahoma Country in 1824, and Fort Union in North Dakota in 1828 (Prucha 1969:126–127).

The Arikara, far up the Missouri River, reacting to an influx of traders and trappers, in 1823 attacked a fur gathering party and killed 24 men. This could not go unchallenged if expansion was to continue, so Col. Henry Leavenworth led 340 soldiers out of Fort Atkinson against them. With him as usual were Indian allies, this time 500 Sioux. Together they easily overran the Arikara villages. Some of Leavenworth's subordinates counseled annihilation, but the colonel would not agree to it. This was the first large-scale expedition sent against the Plains Indians (Leavenworth 1823; Prucha 1969:154–155).

Since the Army contained no horse troops, there was only one way to establish regular communications with the tribes beyond the Mississippi, that is, by travel on the rivers. Thus Gen. Henry Atkinson paddled out of Council Bluffs, Iowa, up the Missouri River in May 1825 with 476 men on eight specially designed paddle-wheel keelboats, *157* propelled by the leg power of the soldiers. During the summer Atkinson and his river-borne army covered hundreds of miles and met with many different tribes, some of whom heard of the United States for the first time. The impressive boats, together with the playing of the regimental band and the parading of the troops, left an impression of power on the tribes, even though they often outnumbered their White visitors four to one. The secretary of war reported that during 1825 government agents signed treaties with seven branches of the Sioux nation, and with the Cheyenne, Arikara, Mandan, Hidatsa, Crow, Osage, and Kansa (Nichols 1965:92–102).

By 1828 most of the Creeks were out of Georgia, and the state could concentrate its pressure upon the Cherokees. The Cherokee had in 1827 adopted a constitution, based on that of the United States, in the hope that a legal base would strengthen their position in Georgia. Their hopes rose when the Supreme Court of the United States ruled that the state could not encroach on Cherokee land but fell when President Andrew Jackson refused to enforce the Court's order. Then in 1829 gold was discovered in Cherokee territory, and White miners invaded without giving treaties a thought. At first Jackson sent in the Army to keep order, but he removed it at Georgia's request. The Cherokees were doomed to be moved, but actual removal was yet a decade away.

Reacting to thousands of immigrants arriving to mine lead in the upper Mississippi Valley, Winnebagos murdered three Whites in June 1827, near Prairie du Chien, Wisconsin. The governor of Illinois put a militia detachment in motion, and the governor of Michigan Territory displayed enough power to keep the Sauk, Fox, and Sioux

Fig. 10. Wooden gunstock war club with steel blade, so-called because of its formal resemblance to early musket stocks. These clubs were common Indian weapons in the Old Northwest and among the eastern Plains tribes along the Mississippi and Missouri River drainages. The steel blades were favored trade items and saw use as knives and lance blades, as well as cutting edges on clubs. Length 71 cm. Collected on the upper Missouri River about 1841.

158

from siding with the Winnebago. Although local settlers as usual clamored for Indian blood, General Atkinson sought to avoid spilling it. By show of superior force, he persuaded the Indians to surrender to him Red Bird, the leader who had started the uprising, and other alleged murderers (Nichols 1965:120–134). General Atkinson reopened Fort Crawford at Prairie du Chien, and turned it into the key military position in the Northwest. Using it as a base, he even went so far as to expel a few miners from Indian land. But he could not impose perfect quiet on that frontier, and in 1832 the Black Hawk War occurred there (Nichols 1965:138–139).

Indian Removal, 1832–1848

Out of ever-enlarging relationships with more and more Indian tribes gradually developed the policy of removal of the Indians to some region west of the Mississippi River. Andrew Jackson and other influential men believed that there was no other way to save the Indians from extermination (Prucha 1969a).

A few eastern Indians had gone west in the 1790s, and several thousands of others followed after 1800. These had resettled in Arkansas and southern Missouri, but by the 1820s they were once again in the path of White settlement. As early as 1819 Shawnees, Choctaws, Cherokees, and Delawares had been pushed southward by militiamen from territorial Arkansas. The twice displaced Indians found themselves in what later became Oklahoma, where they were opposed by the Osage. Cherokees and Osages kept up a fight until the United States Army intervened in 1822 (Billington 1949:469; Secretary of War 1828; J.P. Brown 1938:473ff.).

It was the purchase of Louisiana that had provided the empty land essential to a removal policy. The policy had occurred to Jefferson, and President James Monroe, in his final message to Congress, had outlined it. In May 1830 Congress passed the Indian Removal Act and appropriated half a million dollars to carry it out (ASPIA 2:541–542; Foreman 1953:21; Abel 1908:378–380). It was up to the Army to execute the policy. Certain officers, especially Gen. Edmund P. Gaines, undertook to see that removal was effected humanely, but they had little success (Silver 1949:140).

The removal policy brought on severe conflicts. One such "war" began when the Sauk and Fox, led by Black Hawk, returned in 1831 to their former territory in the vicinity of the Rock River in Illinois. The governor of Illinois insisted that Black Hawk had agreed to leave that location forever, and he summoned a militia force to make him go. Black Hawk and his people left but returned the next year and stayed to fight (Stevens 1903:90–99; Nichols 1965:152–175). U.S. army regulars under Gen. Henry Atkinson as well as 3,000 volunteers marched against Black Hawk. At the Battle of Bad Axe on August 2, 1832, they killed 150 Indians, leaving Black Hawk's band too weak to resist further (Nichols 1965:152–175).

One consequence of the Black Hawk War was the reintroduction of horse troops into the regular service for the first time since the War of 1812. A new regiment, called the First United States Dragoons, constituted in 1832, was employed in 1834 and after to show the power of the United States to the Indians west of Arkansas and Missouri. The Kiowa, Comanche, Cheyenne, Wichita, and Osage were fighting the eastern tribes who had moved into what later became Oklahoma (Secretary of War 1834).

In 1834 Congress passed an elaborate Indian Intercourse Act, the object of which was to provide protection for Indians who had been removed from the pathway of White migration. Of course it was up to the Army to provide the necessary sanctions to give the act effect (2 U.S. Stat. 729-738; Prucha 1962:250–273).

The Seminoles in Florida were scheduled to be removed, but late in 1835 they made a stand. Within two weeks they had wrecked the sugar cane industry then flourishing along the Atlantic coast of Saint Augustine (Mahon 1967:87–113: Laumer 1968). Secretary of War Lewis Cass ordered the Army's principal trouble shooter, Gen. Winfield Scott, to proceed to Florida. Scott put into effect a grand converging maneuver designed to trap the Indians between three columns. But by ambush, by nipping supply lines, and by fading when too hard pressed into their difficult terrain, the Seminoles frustrated Scott's design (Mahon 1967:135–167).

Gen. Thomas S. Jesup was in command in Alabama to quell a Creek uprising. His goal was to prevent the Creeks from making a junction with the warring Seminoles. This was achieved; indeed, a Creek regiment went to help the U.S. army subdue the Florida Indians.

At the same time troops as far away as the Great Lakes were rearranged to deter Indian forays. General Gaines was sent to Texas for the same purpose, and Gen. John E. Wool was assigned the task of keeping the Cherokees quiet (ASPMA 7:202, 205, 209, 210, 334, 336, 340, 347–348; Macomb 1836).

The fight in Florida, known as the Second Seminole War, reached its greatest intensity under General Jesup. Jesup became bitter over what he considered Indian faithlessness and abandoned the conventions of so-called civilized war. He determined to do whatever was necessary to get the Indians out of Florida. First, he began to split their Negro allies away from them. Then in October 1837 he captured the most powerful of the Seminole leaders, Osceola, under a flag of truce (fig. 11). Afterward he often violated flags of truce and promises of safe conduct to secure other Indian leaders. Also, he forced captives on pain of death to lead his detachments to Indian hideouts (Mahon 1967:168–189). Against Jesup's wishes, mounted volunteers from all over the Southeast streamed into Florida. At maximum strength he had 9,000 men under his command, far more than he could support or use effectively. Roughly 1,000 of these soldiers, under the direction of Col. Zachary Taylor, encountered close to 500 Indians on Christmas Day 1837 on the northern shore of Lake Okeechobee in the largest pitched battle of the war (Mahon 1967:219–230).

By the time Jesup was relieved in May 1838, his forces had killed 100 Seminoles and captured 2,900. The fighting power of the Florida Indians was reduced, but small bands moved through their native terrain at will, struck where they could inflict injury, and escaped before they could be cornered. This was the posture of things when Zachary Taylor succeeded Jesup. Taylor sought to combat the guerrilla warfare by dividing the terrain into squares 20 miles to a side and placing a blockhouse in the center of each. The garrison of the blockhouse was ordered to patrol its square incessantly. Bloodhounds were tried, but unsuccessfully. More successfully, some chiefs were bribed to move and take their bands with them. Thus, by 1842 only 300 Seminoles were left in Florida Territory, and the war was allowed to run down in the middle of August 1842 (fig. 12) (Mahon 1967:231–320).

As the Second Seminole War had run on year after year, the White method for fighting the Florida Indians had gradually changed. At one extreme was Winfield Scott's European-style scheme of early 1836. At the other was the strategy of 1842: strike the spots vital to Indian survival—villages, crops, and herds; discard the heavy columns that were part Scott's plan, and replace them with small bands operating like rangers; use Negroes, who knew the haunts of the Indians, to guide the troops to hideaways.

Apart from the war in Florida the United States had to deal with about 332,000 other Indians. In 1837 Secretary of War Joel R. Poinsett proposed that there be six or seven posts on the western frontier garrisoned by army regulars, who could instruct local volunteer officers. This system, he believed, would be cheaper than the $458,000 that Indian hostilities were costing each month. General Gaines recommended 11 instead of 7 forts, and in addition a system of roads between the forts, and railroads connecting the line of forts with the center of government. Congress appropriated $100,000 for roads, which was used to build from Fort Leavenworth southward. There was no money left to complete the forts (Homans 1835–1842, 6:68, 289–296). In 1838 Congress established an Indian Territory made up of what became Oklahoma and part of Kansas. Between 1825 and 1842 American troops escorted almost 80,000 Indians there. Most of the movement was carried on without clash of arms, but none of it without the involvement of military personnel. The agent in charge of any given emigration more often than not was a military officer, and the supplies usually came from military stores. Among the bands moved were the

Fig. 11. Osceola (b. about 1804, d. 1838). Oseola's status as a leader during the Second Seminole War was not inherited but stemmed from his efficacy. In 1835 Oseola and other Indian leaders' refusal to confirm the Treaties of Payne's Landing of 1832 and Ft. Gibson of 1833 precipitated war. Oseola died a prisoner at Ft. Moultrie 3 months after his capture. Before burial he was decapitated and his head displayed in a "Medical Museum" (Dockstader 1977:199–200). Oil on canvas from life by Robert J. Curtis at Ft. Moultrie, Jan. 1838.

Creeks in Alabama, who had lost their fight in the mid-1830s. During the same decade the Choctaws were moved. From New York the Senecas, Cayugas, Tuscaroras, and Oneidas departed in the 1830s and 1840s. Out of the Old Northwest came Chippewas, Delawares, Menominees, Miamis, Ottawas, Potawatomis, Shawnees, and Winnebagos (U.S. National Park Service 1963:3).

In 1836 the Senate of the United States and certain Indian headmen ratified the Treaty of New Echota, which gave the Cherokees remaining in the East two years to move. The tribe was split sharply, and most of them, under the leadership of John Ross, denied that the document represented their will. General Wool, on duty in Cherokee country, was so offended by the unfairness witnessed that he asked to be relieved. But the government, stiffened by President Jackson's intransigence, insisted that the Cherokees get out. About 2,000 left voluntarily (Foreman 1953:229–294), but when the deadline date arrived, there were still 15,000 Cherokees in Georgia and North Carolina. Held firm by Ross, they appeared ready to resist displacement. The officer selected

to remove the intransigents was General Scott. His orders for carrying out removal were humane but were ignored in the execution. The Cherokees were rounded up and detained in stockades until the general march could begin. Scott's 3,000 regulars and 4,000 citizen soldiers in the course of the roundup were guilty of rape, robbery, and even murder. But Scott had great respect for John Ross and permitted him to organize the march. Over the objections of some Whites Scott agreed to supply the Indians with sugar, coffee, and soap. Ross started the first party westward in June 1838 but delayed others until fall. The journey then extended into winter, when suffering and mortality ran very high (Foreman 1953:229–294).

Figures on Indian population are not accurate, but the secretary of war stated in 1843 that 89,000 Eastern Indians had been moved west and that 22,846 remained east of the Mississippi River (Secretary of War 1843:278). The Army naturally continued to carry on police duties. After the Second Seminole War, there were two regiments of Dragoons to share such duties. Dragoon detachments traveled along the Oregon and Santa Fe Trails, sometimes as escort and sometimes to warn the Indians not to molest wagon trains. Their officers represented the United States in treaty talks in which the Indians promised to leave alone the migrants dropping off along the way to settle, and agreed to force them to leave the buffalo herds as they were. In the Wisconsin area detachments of soldiers had to repel Winnebagos, Sauks, Foxes, and Potawatamis who sought to return to their old homes (Secretary of War 1843, 1845).

As the 1840s came to an end, the secretary of war reported that the main migration routes had been cleared of Indians. The Army had pushed the Indians aside, either to the headwaters of the Mississippi River or to the territory west of Arkansas and Missouri and north of the Red River. Temporarily, in spite of war with Mexico, the Indian frontier was quieter than it had been since the first decade of the nineteenth century (Secretary of War 1849).

Summary

Citizen soldiers, whether embodied as militia or enrolled as volunteers for specific crises, were central to the military relationship between Indians and Whites. They were more vindictive, more brutal than the regulars, sometimes striving for extermination of the Indians in their locality. But in combat, the Indians gave way more quickly before regulars than before irregulars, as a consequence of the professionals' superior discipline and resultant tighter cohesion.

In most fights against Indians, the White force was a mixture of regulars and militia men. If it was defeated, or made a poor showing, the professionals usually charged it to the misconduct of the citizen soldiers. The latter countered that the Army really did not know how to fight

The Secretary of War presenting a stand of Colours to the 1st Regiment of Republican Bloodhounds

Massacre of the Whites by the Indians and Blacks in Florida.

The above is intended to represent the horrid Massacre of the Whites in Florida, in December 1835, and January, February, March and April 1836, when near Four Hundred (including women and children) fell victims to the barbarity of the Negroes and Indians.

top, New-York Histl. Soc., New York:55121; bottom, Lib. of Congress, Prints and Photographs Div.:LC-USZ62-366.
Fig. 12. Depictions of pro- and anti-Indian sentiments published during the Second Seminole War. top, The use of Cuban bloodhounds to track Indians and their Black allies was only one of several issues that incited public outrage against government treatment of the Seminoles. Francis P. Blair, editor of the Washington *Globe*, points to a map of Florida, while Secretary of War Joel R. Poinsett presents a standard to the "Regiment." Lithograph printed and published by H.R. Robinson, 1837. bottom, Woodcut illustrating in part (top row) the massacre of Maj. Francis L. Dade and his contingent of approximately 100 men by Seminoles and Blacks (Anonymous 1836:frontispiece).

161

INDIAN–UNITED STATES MILITARY SITUATION, 1775–1848

Indians. There was truth on both sides; misconduct among irregulars was not uncommon, since they were green in fighting in groups. With regard to the regulars, the early officers were trained in European methods, and when West Point was founded in 1802, it continued the same sort of training. When confronted by an enemy who refused to line up in the open and fight it out, they had to learn in the field by doing. In general, they were less successful in Indian campaigns than the best of the leaders of citizen soldiers, of whom the conspicuous example was John Sevier.

The United States chose to consider the Indian tribes as nations and negotiate with them after the European manner. It did so primarily because it could wheedle land cessions from the tribes by treaty without having to fight. At all councils seeking treaties, a regular military presence was indispensable. The soldiers were a reminder that violence would be reciprocated.

When tribes were intransigent about ceding land, the government used force, implied if not actual, to get them to yield. In extreme cases, of course, the Army was the coercive agent. Andrew Jackson, who shaped relations between the two races more than any other individual, never thought the Indians worthy of being called nations. To him, when the Indians got in the way, they were insurrectionists, to be subdued and punished. Other leaders thought as Jackson did. The government itself rarely bothered to declare war on Indians: it simply moved militarily against them; nor did it usually take the trouble to conclude a war with a formal peace treaty. Treaties following combat were often instruments of land cession in which peace was only casually referred to.

The Army was often ordered to force the Indians off their lands, but there were cases in which the army's assignment was to expel squatters from ground promised to the Indians. The soldiers carried out this duty, but expulsion of White invaders never lasted. The thrust of migration to the frontiers was so powerful that families, when expelled, returned again and again until the military effort to remove them was halted by political action.

The government sent Army detachments into Indian country to apprehend Indians who had committed crimes against Whites and locked up its captives in the guardhouses of the forts. When the frontier peace was threatened by intertribal wars, army officers tried to persuade the belligerents to turn their dispute over to the United States for settlement. The Indian Intercourse Act of 1834 specifically authorized the use of military force to keep peace among tribes or to halt fighting under way. Attempts to intervene were not usually successful, but the presence of the troops patrolling or garrisoned served to deter large-scale intertribal conflict.

When civilian commissioners were not on hand, Army officers served as Indian agents. In that capacity, and in others, they proved themselves skillful negotiators, because they had more experience with the Indians and were more sympathetic to their cultures than most appointed civilians, whose qualifications were frequently political.

Overall, Indian war parties were not a match for White military forces. One reason was that the numerous bands never united to oppose invasion; quite the contrary, some Indians could always be found fighting on the American side against other Indian bands. Tecumseh, more than any other leader, saw the need for a united effort and did the most to try to draw the tribes together, but even he could not succeed. Another reason was the Indian dependence on White supplies; all the guns and ammunition had to come from White people, as well as any repairs of firearms. Dependence extended to nonmilitary goods too: metal pots, knives, and camp hardware, and even articles of clothing. Only one commodity was always in oversupply: whiskey! It was more powerful in causing Indian downfall than American military power. Officers of the regular army never stopped trying to dry up the whiskey sources but never succeeded. There were at all times civilian suppliers who defied the restrictions and got liquor to the Indians. They also supplied whiskey to the enlisted personnel, where it impaired military efficiency. Alcohol use remained a chronic problem among soldiers but was not so debilitating to the White military effort as it was to the Indian.

In Indian cultures proven success in combat was only one factor in achieving the status of war leader. Cohesion in an Indian army was uncommon. During his brief term as commander, Osceola surely rates as the best of the Indian strategists. Close behind him come Dragging Canoe and Tecumseh, but they excelled more in their unswerving determination not to yield to the American presence than in strategy and tactics.

Indian–United States Military Situation, 1848–1891

ROBERT M. UTLEY

The close of the Mexican War in 1848 suddenly confronted the United States Army with responsibilities of continental proportions. The annexation of Texas in 1845, the resolution of the Oregon boundary dispute in 1846, and the acquisition of New Mexico and California in the peace settlement of 1848 gathered a million square miles under the United States flag. The postwar surge of migration, propelled by the discovery of gold in California in 1848, brought Americans by the thousands to the new territories. Some 200,000 Indians already called these lands home. Moreover, the immigrant trails bisected the Great Plains domain of 75,000 nomads nominally ruled by the Americans since the Louisiana Purchase but until then only lightly touched by their influence. For the next half-century, except for the Civil War, the conflict between White and Indian in the trans-Mississippi West afforded the United States Army its main employment.

The territorial expansion of the 1840s destroyed the hope for a "Permanent Indian Frontier" and thus, rendering a central tenet of U.S. Indian policy obsolete, changed the army's mission. Instead of manning a chain of forts defining the "Permanent Indian Frontier" and separating Whites and Indians, the Army took on the responsibility—theoretically at least—of protecting citizens everywhere in the West. Immigrants, freighters, and stagecoach passengers moving on the great transcontinental trails expected military protection. So did the settlers who made their homes at the end of the trails.

The strongest and proudest of the western tribes resisted the White invasion. Their motives sprang from resentment over the encroachment on their homeland and the destruction of game, timber, grass, and other resources necessary to their way of life; from incidents growing out of racial friction, misunderstandings, and ill treatment by the invaders; and from traditional values that exalted war and awarded high honors to distinguished warriors. They waged a partisan style of warfare that usually confounded opponents using orthodox European military methods. They fought superbly with bow and arrow, lance, tomahawk, and knife, less skillfully with the firearms that fell to them in growing numbers through trade and war.

For the Army, the new West presented military conditions and requirements contrasting with those of the old West of the previous half-century. The soldiers left behind the well-watered woodlands, agriculturally productive and accessible by navigable streams, and moved to plains, mountains, and deserts characterized by great distances, climatic extremes, and scarcity of water, food, and fuel. In this environment mere self-preservation absorbed most of the military effort. The native inhabitants, however, had accommodated to the environment and knew perfectly how to turn it to military advantage. Moreover, most were nomadic, offering an uncertain target. Many, especially on the Great Plains, traveled and fought on horseback. The changed conditions pointed to the need for an expanded logistical apparatus with greater emphasis on land transportation and for a strong mounted arm affording increased mobility (Utley 1967:1–9).

The Frontier Army, 1848–1861

In the 1850s the U.S. Army failed to attain the dimensions dictated by its new western responsibilities. Economy and traditional democratic fears of a standing army kept both staff and line mere shadows of the needed establishment. The authorized strength of the regular Army at the close of the Mexican War was 10,000. Congress lifted this to about 14,000 in 1850 and to about 18,000 in 1855 (Heitman 1903, 2:595–597). Because of the lag of recruitment behind discharge, desertion, and death, actual strength fell below authorized strength by as much as 18 percent. One-fourth of the Army garrisoned eastern stations. Staff, detached service, and furlough made further inroads. In 1857, for example, 11,000 officers and enlisted men spread themselves thinly over the trans-Mississippi West. And this figure shrank with the diversion, at each post, of men for guard and labor details as well as the sick and imprisoned. Little wonder that the obligation to protect every citizen turned out to be so theoretical (Utley 1967:18–58).

The regular Army line consisted of eight infantry regiments, four artillery regiments (mostly infantry except in name), and three mounted regiments. Two of the last were called dragoons and one, mounted riflemen. In 1855

163

Congress allowed two more mounted regiments, these denominated cavalry, and two more infantry regiments. The regiments were led by a professional officer corps of generally creditable competence. It drew both from the United States Military Academy at West Point and, by direct commissioning, from civil life. Most officers were Mexican War veterans. The enlisted complement, recruited largely from city streets in the East, contained a high proportion of criminals, toughs, drunkards, and fugitives from the law and society but also enough adventurous youths and steady foreign immigrants to provide a cadre of reliable soldiers. Year after year desertion, disease, and drunkenness proved costly scourges of the army line.

Beyond the line existed a loose system of command and staff. The general-in-chief in Washington had little real authority. Throughout the 1850s the vain and pompous yet able Winfield Scott held this post and strove unsuccessfully to expand its powers. His momentous feud with Secretary of War Jefferson Davis rocked the War Department for four years, 1853–1857. The most influential authority resided in the commanders of the geographical departments. In 1860 there were six such departments west of the Mississippi: Texas, New Mexico, California, Utah, Oregon, and the West. Seven staff "departments," such as quartermaster, commissary, medical, and ordnance, backed the line from Washington offices and the headquarters of the departments.

Army leaders disagreed over the proper strategy for meeting the new Western responsibilities. Some advocated an extensive network of forts that would permit continuous military occupation of the Indian country. The presence of troops, they argued, would deter hostile action and place the enemy within striking distance in case of trouble. Moreover, the demands of settlers and travelers for visible protection made the proliferation of forts difficult to resist. Opponents of the fixed post contended that the small size of the Army required concentration of units at a few strategic locations from which strong roving columns could operate during the summer months and "show the flag" in the Indian country. During the 1850s a combination of these two. strategies evolved, with not enough forts to cover the Indian country but too many to permit either strong fixed garrisons or strong roving columns.

The fort became the central institution of the frontier army and the building block of frontier defense systems. Lines of forts traced the major transcontinental trails and were welcome way stations to countless overland travelers. Likewise, groups of forts planted in the vicinity of settlements stood, reassuringly if not always effectively, between farmers, stockmen, and miners and the tribesmen whose homeland they threatened. By the eve of the Civil War, 65 such forts dotted the trans-Mississippi West (fig. 1).

Few of these forts were stockaded or otherwise fortified, for Indians rarely threatened a military installation. Rather the typical fort was simply a cluster of buildings—stone, adobe, brick, or wood, depending on local building materials—neatly laid out near a stream or spring. Officers' row faced enlisted men's barracks across a spacious parade ground. Offices, warehouses, shops, stables, and sutler's store stood to the rear and at each end of the parade.

One or two companies, sometimes as many as four or five, held the fort, usually in a combination of mounted and foot troops. Families of some of the officers and sergeants and a handful of civilian employees completed the military community. They led a dismal, uncomfortable existence, characterized by poor food and shelter, isolation, and boredom. The enlisted soldiers' lot also included harsh discipline and nearly continuous fatigue labor that left little time for military pursuits.

Field service now and then varied the dull garrison routine. Usually this meant a scout or patrol in less than company strength. Rarely did such a mission end in combat or even afford a glimpse of the enemy. On the contrary, the principal adversaries were almost always climate and terrain and the results hardship, exhaustion, and frustration. Occasionally commanders mounted elaborate offensives. These were conducted as conventional military operations, in which heavy columns burdened by slow-moving supply trains sought out the enemy and tried to bring him to battle. But the Indians, skilled at guerrilla warfare, usually declined to fight conventional warfare, and such expeditions rarely succeeded. When the Indian could be surprised at home, encumbered by his family and possessions, the troops saw action (Utley 1967:28–58).

Military records count 160 combat actions, varying from harmless exchanges of gunfire to large-scale battles, between 1848 and the outbreak of the Civil War. The Army totaled its own casualties for this period at 13 officers and 197 enlisted men killed and 21 officers and 222 enlisted men wounded. Army estimates of Indian casualties—481 killed, 106 wounded, 194 captured, plus many uncounted—are probably greatly exaggerated (Peters 1966 [5]:9–15).

Major Campaigns, 1848–1861

Great Plains and Texas

On the Great Plains military efforts aimed at protecting travelers on the overland trails who disturbed the Sioux, Cheyennes, Kiowas, and Comanches. In Texas, where Kiowa and Comanche raiding parties from the north ranged the length of the state and deep into Mexico, the Army sought to safeguard the expanding frontier of settlement and the southern transcontinental trails. Reinforcing the diplomatic attempt to neutralize the Plains tribes in the Fort Laramie Treaty of 1851 and the Fort

Fig. 1. Major forts and battles, 1848–1865 (J.T. Adams 1943; Prucha 1964).

Atkinson Treaty of 1853, the Army planted forts at strategic locations: Kearny and Laramie on the Oregon-California Trail; Larned and Union on the Santa Fe Trail; Lancaster, Stockton, Davis, and Bliss on the San Antonio–El Paso Road; and, tracing the Texas frontier from Red River to the Rio Grande, Belknap, Phantom Hill, Cooper, Chadbourne, McKavett, Clark, Duncan, and others.

War came to the Plains in 1854 as a result of the "Grattan Massacre." Near Fort Laramie an inexperienced lieutenant tried to bully a camp of Brulé Sioux into surrendering a man who had killed an emigrant's cow. The Sioux all but annihilated the small military force and then, emboldened by their easy triumph, committed

depredations on the Platte Road. To punish them, in summer 1855 Gen. William S. Harney marched up the Platte with a command of 600 men. On September 3, in the Battle of Blue Water, or Ash Hollow, he fell on Little Thunder's Brulé village and killed or captured half its 250 occupants. Harney then marched through the Sioux homeland to the Missouri River. At Fort Pierre, in March 1856, chiefs of the principal Sioux tribes assembled and made peace with him (McCann 1956; Todd 1962).

The Cheyennes, friends and allies of the Sioux, next tested U.S. military strength. Incidents along the Platte Road in 1856 brought on war. In summer 1857 two columns under Col. Edwin V. Sumner campaigned extensively between the Platte and Arkansas rivers. On

165

July 29, in the Battle of Solomon Fork, Kansas, Sumner's cavalry routed a large force of Cheyenne warriors. Like the Sioux, the Cheyennes broke off hostilities and remained peaceful even as the Pikes Peak gold rush of 1858 rolled over the heart of their domain (Hafen and Hafen 1959).

In Texas, beginning in 1855, Col. Albert Sidney Johnston and the newly organized 2d Cavalry brought fresh energy to defense of frontier settlers against marauding Kiowas and Comanches. Among its officers the regiment counted many future generals of blue and gray, such as Robert E. Lee, George H. Thomas, Earl Van Dorn, and John B. Hood. With Texas Rangers, the cavalrymen struck at the camps north of Red River from which the raiders came. Buffalo Hump's Comanches suffered severely at the Battles of Antelope Hills and Rush Springs, May 11 and October 1, 1858. Another Comanche band was almost wiped out in a bloody action at Crooked Creek, in southern Kansas, on May 13, 1859. In summer 1860 three formidable columns, based on Fort Riley, Kansas, Fort Cobb, Indian Territory, and Fort Union, New Mexico, operated against the Kiowas and Comanches but failed to close in any serious combat. Despite more than a decade of intense military activity, the forays of these tribes along the Texas frontier remained as bloody and destructive in 1861 as they had been in 1848 (Price 1959).

Southwest

In New Mexico, Apaches, Navajos, and Utes preyed on the Rio Grande settlements, and the Army erected a protective system of forts (fig. 1). Tiny garrisons based on these posts contended ineffectually against raiding parties that slipped into the settlements, stole stock and killed citizens, and vanished before pursuit could be organized.

Several offensive movements were mounted against the New Mexico tribes in the 1850s. In the north, following a devastating ambush of a dragoon company at Cieneguilla on March 30, 1854, Lt. Col. Philip St. George Cooke waged a successful campaign against the Jicarilla Apaches that ended hostilities with them for all time. The following year the Army defeated the Capote and Muache Utes and won a temporary peace from the Mescalero Apaches in the Sierra Blanca. In summer 1857 Col. Benjamin L.E. Bonneville conducted aggressive operations against bands of Chiricahua and Western Apache on the upper Gila River. Other Western Apaches interfered with travel and threatened Butterfield stagecoaches on the road to California. Troops from Forts Buchanan and Breckinridge campaigned against them in 1859 and 1860. Early in 1861 an army officer arrested Chief Cochise by deception and incurred the enmity of the Central Chiricahua. Meanwhile, expeditions into Navajo country between the San Juan and Little Colorado rivers reached a climax against this powerful tribe (Utley 1967:142–174).

California

The gold rush was a shattering experience for all the Indians of California. The influx of miners virtually obliterated many of the weak groups that inhabited the mountainous gold districts. A few bands offered a show of resistance but were quickly overrun by military forces or the gold seekers themselves (vol. 8:107–108). The Army laid out a system of forts of which the most important were Tejon, Miller, Reading, Humboldt, and Jones; however, throughout the 1850s, the chief military problem was not Indians but the desertion of soldiers to the gold fields.

Northwest Coast and Plateau

In Oregon and Washington (the latter created a Territory in 1853), the Indian residents proved more formidable than their California neighbors. Major warfare erupted with the Rogue River bands of southern Oregon, the Puget Sound groups, and the Salishan and Sahaptin tribes of the Columbia River basin. Among the Rogue River groups the army maintained Forts Lane and Orford. Fort Steilacoom stood amid the Puget Sound groups. Forts Simcoe and Walla Walla faced the tribes east of the Cascades. Centerpiece of the northwestern defenses was Fort Vancouver, the former Hudson's Bay Company fur post on the lower Columbia.

Almost simultaneously, in 1855, Indian uprisings confronted the northwestern commander, Gen. John E. Wool, with a three-front war. In southern Oregon the Rogue River War marked the climax of several years of friction between settlers and Indians. On the upper Columbia, in the Yakima War, Yakimas, Walla Wallas, Klikitats, Cayuses, Umatillas, Palouses, and Kittitas united loosely behind the dynamic Kamiakin to resist Gov. Isaac I. Stevens's program for opening their homeland to White settlement. Squaxin, Nisqually, and Puyallup (Southern Coast Salish) chose the same moment to oppose Stevens's designs on their Puget Sound domain.

In the Rogue River War Oregon volunteers campaigned throughout the winter against the Rogue and allied bands. Dragoons from Fort Lane occasionally participated, as at the Battle of Hungry Hill on October 31, 1855. In spring 1856 Wool sent a large force against the hostiles. In a series of actions, most notably Big Meadows on May 27–28, regulars and volunteers forced the Indians to surrender and abandon their homeland for small reservations on the coast.

Two expeditions against the Yakimas, in October and November 1855, failed dismally. Some Yakimas crossed the Cascade Mountains and, late in January 1856, helped local warriors lay siege to the village of Seattle. Sailors and marines, backed by a sloop-of-war, put up a successful defense. A "blockhouse war," punctuated by two open battles, brought the conflict on Puget Sound to an end by the spring. East of the mountains, to Wool's disgust, Oregon and Washington volunteers kept the Indians stirred up during the winter. In March 1856 Wool sent a strong command to occupy the Yakima country, especially the vital fishing locations. By August the war had drawn to an inconclusive close.

The uncertain outcome of the Yakima War and the unrest created by the Colville gold rush kept the Columbia basin Indians unsettled. Kamiakin continued to agitate the tribes, concentrating on those east of the Columbia River. In May 1858 a coalition of Spokane, Coeur d'Alene, and Palouse warriors attacked and surrounded a military column under Lt. Col. Edward J. Steptoe. Under cover of night, Steptoe succeeded in extricating his badly mauled command and escaping to Fort Walla Walla. An expedition of 600 men who set out to punish the challengers decisively defeated the Indians in open combat at the Battles of Four Lakes and Spokane Plains, September 1 and 5, 1858. Then the expedition marched up the Spokane River and around Lake Coeur d'Alene, receiving the submission of the hostile groups and hanging their leaders—15 in all. Although Kamiakin escaped, these operations effectively humbled the Columbia basin Indians (Glassley 1953; Burns 1966).

Florida

The last of the Seminole Wars occurred in the Florida swamps, 1856–1858. First under Gen. William S. Harney, then under Col. Gustavus Loomis, troops (primarily state militia) campaigned against these elusive Indians and fought an occasional skirmish until peace talks brought about the removal of 165 to Indian Territory. The rest remained deep in the Florida wilderness, at last, after almost 40 years of warfare, free of a military threat (Prucha 1969:269–306).

Effect of the Civil War

The firing on Fort Sumter, South Carolina, led to the transfer of most regular army units from frontier forts to the eastern theaters of war and the defection of many officers to the South. Legislation in 1861 expanded the regular Army by the addition of nine infantry regiments, one mounted regiment, and one artillery regiment and, eliminating distinctions of dragoons and mounted riflemen, designated all six of the mounted regiments as cavalry. The regular Army remained intact throughout the war; but, despite the augmentation, it wasted away to a mere skeleton as the state volunteer regiments lured its officers with higher rank and competed with bounties for enlisted men. For four years the huge volunteer armies of the Union and Confederacy dominated the American military scene (Utley 1967:211–218).

The war did not slow the westward movement. Migration continued not only from the East but also eastward from the Pacific Slope, as mineral strikes attracted thousands to newly opened areas of the West. Population burgeoned in the Colorado Rockies, on the eastern flank of the Sierra Nevada, along the Clearwater and Snake rivers and the headstreams of the Missouri River, and in the mountains of the Southwest. Territorial organization recorded the population movement—Dakota, Colorado, and Nevada in 1861, Idaho and Arizona in 1863, Montana in 1864, and statehood for Nevada in 1864. Inevitably, all this activity stirred fresh Indian troubles and prompted western insistence on continued military protection despite the demands of the great conflict in the East.

Volunteer forces, raised by the states and territories and mustered into federal service, flowed into the void left by the regulars. By 1862 those stationed in the frontier regions numbered about 15,000 and by 1865, 20,000. In Confederate Texas a specially organized frontier regiment, supplemented by "minuteman" companies, performed Indian duty. Thus, more soldiers served in the West than before the regulars departed. They were better soldiers, too, because the volunteers called forth men of higher physical and mental caliber. Also, as westerners, they viewed the Indian with even less sentiment than the regulars and were less inclined to see merit in any but a violent solution of Indian difficulties.

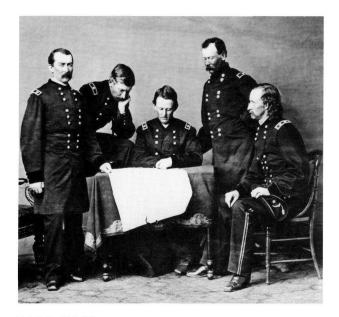

Natl. Arch.: 111-B-4162.
Fig. 2. Union Army generals, some of whom became prominent during the Indian wars. left to right, Maj. Gen. Philip H. Sheridan (b. 1831, d. 1888), Brig. Gen. James W. Forsyth (b. 1834, d. 1906), Maj. Gen. Wesley Merrit (b. 1834, d. 1910), Brig. Gen. Thomas C. Devin (b. 1822, d. 1878), and Maj. Gen. George A. Custer (b. 1839, d. 1876). Photograph by Mathew Brady, Washington, 1864–1865.

167

Major Campaigns, 1861–1865

Great Plains

Surrounded by Whites and driven to violence by agency mismanagement and the rascality of traders, the Santee Sioux in Minnesota revolted in August 1862. Led by Red Middle Voice, Little Shakopee, Little Crow, Inkpaduta, Medicine Bottle, and other chiefs, they destroyed the Redwood Agency, slaughtered some 800 settlers in the Minnesota River valley, made captives of several hundred more, and attempted without success to overwhelm Fort Ridgely. Assembling an army of Minnesota volunteers ultimately numbering more than 1,600, Col. Henry Hastings Sibley marched from Fort Snelling. Following battles at Birch Coulee and Wood Lake in September 1862, rising factionalism among the Sioux leaders led to collapse of the uprising and liberation of the captives. A military commission sentenced 303 Indians to death, but President Abraham Lincoln reduced the number to 38 (fig. 3) (Carley 1961).

Santee refugees from Minnesota and traffic up the Missouri River to the Rocky Mountain gold fields disturbed the Teton Sioux. Gen. John Pope, commanding the Department of the Northwest, decided on a show of force. In summer 1863 he sent two strong columns to Dakota. Under Sibley, now a general, 3,000 men marched west from Minnesota; 1,200 under Gen. Alfred Sully advanced up the Missouri from the south. In late July, northeast of present Bismarck, Sibley fought three engagements with Santee and Teton Sioux, scattering the Santee north to Canada and the Teton west across the Missouri. Sully did not reach the upper Missouri until after Sibley had left, but on September 3, 1863, he trapped and almost annihilated Inkpaduta's Santee village at Whitestone Hill; 300 warriors died in the fight and 250 women and children were taken prisoner.

Sully returned to the upper Missouri in the summer of 1864 with almost 4,000 Iowa, Minnesota, Dakota, and Wisconsin volunteers. Leaving part of them to erect Fort Rice, at the mouth of the Cannonball River, he turned westward with 2,200 men. In an all-day battle at Killdeer Mountain, Sully routed a large coalition of Teton warriors. After skirmishing through the Little Missouri Badlands to the Yellowstone River, he returned to Fort Rice, thwarted in his design to build a fort on the Yellowstone by drought and supply problems.

On the central Plains, the tribes remained relatively quiet until 1864, when efforts of Colorado officials to obtain Indian lands led to costly depredations on travel routes and settlements. The resulting hysteria among the settlers fixed the climate for the infamous Sand Creek Massacre in November, when Colorado volunteers slaughtered some 200 of Black Kettle's Cheyennes, mostly women and children, who thought they had been granted peace and military protection. Sand Creek set the Plains afire and virtually cut off Denver from the East.

General Pope, commanding on the Plains, organized a massive counter-offensive for the summer of 1865. South of the Arkansas River, in a confused sequence of events, Gen. Grenville M. Dodge alternately warred on and negotiated with Kiowas, Comanches, Cheyennes, and Arapahoes. North of the Platte, the Teton Sioux and Cheyenne took the offensive first and carried out a bloody assault on the military garrison of Platte Bridge Station, west of Fort Laramie. A month later Gen. Patrick E. Connor launched almost 3,000 men in three columns into the Powder River country. Connor's troops fought four battles in August and September but, beset by bad weather, logistical breakdown, and desertions, came to the verge of collapse before the campaign ended. On the upper Missouri, where on July 28 a rising Hunkpapa Sioux leader named Sitting Bull openly attacked Fort Rice, General Sully marched uneventfully to Devil's Lake and back. Pope's 1865 offensive, unprecedentedly comprehensive in design and execution, failed to subjugate any Indians. A series of treaties concluded late in 1865 on the upper Missouri and the Little Arkansas proved no more successful in restoring peace to the Great Plains (Ellis 1970; Hoig 1961).

Southwest

Withdrawal of the regulars, followed by the Confederate invasion of New Mexico, stimulated destructive Apache and Navajo aggressions on the Rio Grande settlements and the new Pinos Altos gold mines. Gen. James H. Carleton and a brigade of California volunteers marched eastward in 1862 to help meet the Confederate threat. Arriving too late for this purpose, Carleton and his men, joined by Col. Christopher (Kit) Carson and New Mexico volunteers, fought Indians for the next three years.

Carleton had encountered Apaches on the march from California. Warriors of Cochise and Mangas Coloradas fought his soldiers in Apache Pass of the Chiricahua Mountains on July 15, 1862. Carleton established Fort Bowie to guard the strategic pass. In October and November 1862 Carson swept through the Capitan Mountains of east-central New Mexico and corralled most of the Mescalero Apaches. They were placed on the Pecos River at Bosque Redondo, and Fort Sumner was built to guard them. In January 1863 elements of Carleton's command, under cover of a truce, seized the renowned Eastern Chiracahua Chief Mangas Coloradas and killed him as he supposedly attempted to escape. Carleton also provided military support to the Prescott mining district opened in northern Arizona in 1863. In summer 1864 he organized a "general rising" of both troops and citizens throughout Arizona, but despite several victories they failed to end Apache hostilities.

top left, Smithsonian, NAA:3672-C2; top center, top right, Minn. Histl. Soc., St. Paul: E91.1W/r6, E91.1A/r5; bottom, Lib. of Congress, Prints and Photographs Div.: LC-US262-37940.

Fig. 3. Sioux revolt, 1862. From the beginning of the uprising, the Sioux were divided on the decision to attack Whites. top left, Little Crow (b. about 1820, d. 1863), Mdewakanton band, was a signatory to the Sioux Treaty of Mendota in Aug. 1851 and a leader at the Redwood Agency in 1862. After the battle at Wood Lake, Little Crow fled to Dakota Terr., from which he conducted raids into Minn., and at one time he went to Ft. Garry, Man., for provisions. In the aftermath of hostility toward Indians, Little Crow, who at the time was identified only as an Indian and not by name, was killed by White farmers while gathering food in a field near Hutchinson, Minn. (Carley 1961:19ff.; Anderson 1986). Carte de visite, cropped, by Joel Emmons Whitney, St. Paul, Minn., 1862. top center, Medicine Bottle, Mdewakanton band, who retreated to Canada with Little Shakopee after the battle at Wood Lake. Uneasy about the migration of Sioux refugees to Canada, the British cooperated with Americans in a plot to kidnap Medicine Bottle and Little Shakopee. The 2 were captured in Jan. 1864, imprisoned at Ft. Snelling, and executed at Pilot Knob on Nov. 11, 1865 (Babcock 1962:98; Carley 1961:60–61, 67; Blegen 1963:282). Carte de visite, cropped, by Joel Emmons Whitney, at Ft. Snelling, June 17, 1864. top right, John Other Day (b. 1801, d. 1871), Wahpeton band, a Christian, married to a White woman. An advocate of peace, Other Day warned Whites of an impending attack and escorted a party of 62 settlers from the Wahpeton Agency to Cedar City in Mcleod Co. Other Day was Col. Sibley's scout for the march to Wood Lake. Using the cash reward he received for bravery, Other Day resumed farming after the war (Carley 1961:25–27, 57; Bryant and Murch 1872:116–122). Carte de visite, cropped, by J.E. Martin, St. Paul, Minn., 1862. bottom, Execution by hanging of participants in the Sioux uprising, Mankato, Minn., Dec. 26, 1863. Fear of White violence toward prisoners led authorities to declare martial law in the town (Carley 1961:67). Engraving based on a sketch by Mr. Herman (*Harper's Weekly* 7 (313):37, Jan. 27, 1863).

The most significant achievement of the Carleton-Carson team was the conquest of the Navajos. Throughout the summer and autumn of 1863, Carson's troops ravaged the Navajo country of northeastern Arizona. They killed few Indians but seized their stock, destroyed their crops, and kept them constantly insecure. The climax came with the penetration of the historic Navajo citadel of Canyon de Chelly in January 1864. Throughout 1864 Navajos by the hundreds went to Forts Canby and Wingate, until three-fourths of the tribe had surrendered. In a tragic Long Walk, 8,000 were escorted across New Mexico to the Bosque Redondo Reservation. There they remained until allowed to return to their homeland in 1868. So shattering was the Bosque Redondo experience that the Navajos never again raided the settlements or warred with the Whites (A. Hunt 1958; L.R. Bailey 1964).

Great Basin

General Connor went east at the head of a brigade of Californians. Establishing himself at Salt Lake City, where he built Fort Douglas, Connor patrolled the overland route and campaigned against hostile Utes, Bannocks, and Northern Shoshones. At the Battle of Bear River, Utah, January 27, 1863, he fought and won a bloody engagement with Bear Hunter's band of Northern Shoshone. By the end of 1863 most of the Indians of Utah had been brought to terms (Madsen 1985).

Northern Shoshones interfered with the eastward migration to the Idaho mines. Gen. Benjamin Alvord, commanding in Oregon, established Forts Lapwai and Boise in Idaho and, in concert with Connor, averted this threat. Northern Paiutes, however, proved more troublesome in preying on traffic across Oregon to the mines. Alvord sent Oregon and Nevada volunteers into southeastern Oregon in the summers of 1864 and 1865. They covered the area with military posts, including Forts Klamath and Bidwell, but had to leave the final disposition of these Indians to the postwar regulars (A. Hunt 1950).

California

Provoked by the aggressions of Whites, Shasta, Klamath, and other small groups of northern California, confined to reservations after the Rogue River War of 1855–1856, broke loose in 1862. After two years of bitter warfare conducted by California volunteers, attrition caused the collapse of Indian resistance, and the survivors were returned to their reservations (A. Hunt 1950).

The Frontier Army, 1866–1891

170   The close of the Civil War gave renewed drive to the

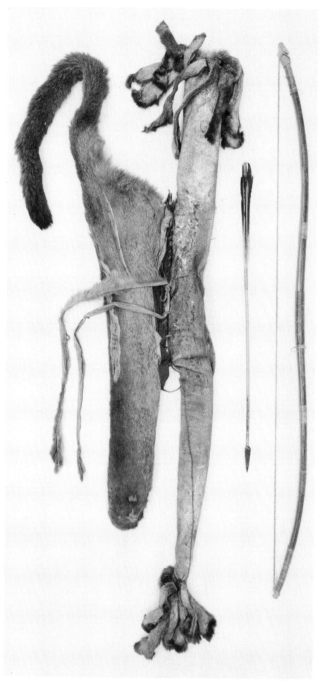

Smithsonian, Dept. of Anthr.: 76684.
Fig. 4. Sinew-backed, double-curved bow, 2-piece hide quiver and bowcase, and metal-tipped arrows fletched with split and trimmed eagle feathers—mainstays of the Indian arsenal even after the availability of muskets and rifles. A rapid rate of fire and easily replaceable parts insured continued reliance on the bow for warfare as well as hunting. Length of bow, 117 cm. Collected from Tall Singer, a Navajo, 1869.

westward movement. Within a quarter-century, 1866–1891, four transcontinental railroads reached the Pacific, new mines were opened and old ones further developed, herds of cattle and sheep overspread the range country, homesteaders broke the prairie sod, and towns and cities took root. Population of the western states and territories swelled from less than two million to eight and one-half million, and seven territories won statehood. In 1890 the Census Bureau could no longer find a distinct frontier of settlement on the map of the West.

One after another during this short span the western Indian tribes met disaster. Their territory shrank under the impact of the White invasion, and there remained, finally, nowhere to retreat. Food resources, especially wild game, dwindled as the habitat contracted and Whites joined Indians in the kill. The buffalo had all but vanished by the early 1880s. Complementing these developments was a federal Indian policy aimed at concentrating the Indians on reservations where they could not interfere with the settlement and development of the West. Here, too, they could be cared for while being "civilized," "educated," and transformed into self-supporting farmers. Loss of land and food inevitably meant loss of freedom and left the Indian little real choice but to go to the reservation.

While continuing to guard travel routes and settlements, the Army increasingly prosecuted large-scale campaigns directed at forcing tribes to settle on reservations or to return to reservations from which they had bolted in rejection of the conditions of reservation life. Most of the wars of 1866–1890 fell into this pattern. In these wars the role of the Army was not so much to conquer the Indians as to seal a fate already ordained by their vanishing base of land and subsistence. Furthermore, as the reservation program gained momentum, the Army increasingly inherited another assignment—to watch over the reservations and make certain the Indians stayed there.

Civil-Military Conflict

The reservation program, involving both the Indian Bureau and the Army, intensified the historic conflict between the two institutions. The Bureau had been a War Department agency before establishment of the Department of the Interior in 1849, and the Army had never reconciled itself to the new order. Military officers regarded the Indian Bureau as corrupt, inefficient, and riddled with partisan and patronage politics; and they ascribed the origins of most Indian hostilities to mismanagement by civilian officials. The Bureau, in turn, scored the Army as meddlesome, arrogant, given too exclusively to purely military solutions, and insensitive to distinctions between friendly and hostile and noncombatant and combatant. Bureau personnel saw the Army as the author of most Indian wars. Both viewpoints contained enough truth to fan the rivalry. For 15 years after the Civil War, friends of the Army in the Congress backed legislation to transfer the Indian Bureau back to the War Department. Several times bills passed the House of Representatives

only to fail narrowly in the Senate.

A major source of discord was the difficulty of distinguishing between hostile and friendly Indians and therefore between military and civil responsibilities. Initially, both the Army and the Indian Bureau welcomed President Ulysses Grant's Peace Policy as providing a rational solution to the vexing problem. All Indians on the reservation would be considered peaceful and the responsibility of the Indian Bureau, all off hostile and the responsibility of the Army. The distinction was artificial and simplistic because there were both kinds of Indians in both places. A trend toward harmony passed quickly, conflict revived, and the Peace Policy reeled under repeated Indian outbreaks.

A fundamental handicap under which both the Indian Bureau and the Army labored was a frame of mind that held groups culpable for the actions of individuals. The Indian police forces the Bureau began to form after 1878 increasingly provided a capability of identifying and moving against individual offenders. But military action continued to be directed against tribes or bands and therefore often fell on "friendlies," or at least neutrals, as well as on "hostiles," and the Army repeatedly exposed itself to charges of making war on peaceful Indians (Utley 1973:187–190).

Strategy

The strategy of Indian warfare remained essentially the same as in previous decades except on a larger scale. One- and two-company forts multiplied throughout the West. By 1880 there were 111, 46 more than in 1860 (fig. 5). Concentration of Indians on reservations permitted a concentration of military garrisons that reduced the number of posts to 62 by 1891. Offensive movements featured heavy columns of infantry and cavalry, burdened by slow-moving supply trains, searching for but only occasionally finding an enemy that could move rapidly, live off the country, and, unless surprised, avoid combat except under favorable circumstances. In short, the Army continued to wage orthodox warfare against a foe skilled in unorthodox methods.

Orthodox methods sometimes worked, as when Indians grew careless or when, burdened by families, they could not travel fast enough. Also, converging columns and winter campaigns improved the chances of success with orthodox methods. Converging columns, even though none made decisive contact, could wear down Indians and harry them into surrendering. Winter campaigns could catch them in a vulnerable season, when less alert to danger, their stock weakened, and food supplies precarious. Finally, the spreading network of railroads and telegraph lines, in addition to furthering western development, gave the Army unprecedented speed of transportation and communication.

171

Fig 5. Major forts and battles, 1866–1891 (J.T. Adams 1943; Prucha 1964).

Few officers advocated or practiced more than token departures from orthodox methods. Gen. George Crook was an exception. He introduced two innovations that, widely applied, might have achieved dramatic results.

One innovation was exclusive reliance on mule pack-trains for supply. Crook refined the science of organizing, equipping, and operating mule trains into a state of high perfection. Able to cut loose from wagon trains, he attained a mobility almost equal to the Indian's. "It was only when General George Crook chased the Indians with a column supplied by mule pack trains," recalled one of Geronimo's followers, "that the Apaches had a hard time staying out of reach" (Betzinez 1959:37).

The other innovation was extensive employment of Indian auxiliaries (fig. 6). Indians had fought allied with Whites against other Indians since colonial times. In the nineteenth century, the U.S. Army had used Indian scouts widely as guides and for reconnaissance. Crook went a step further and employed the scouts as fighters as well. Indian allies matched the special skills of their adversaries and produced a damaging psychological effect on the enemy. "To polish a diamond there is nothing like its own dust," Crook explained. "It is the same with these fellows. Nothing breaks them up like turning their own people against them" (Lummis 1966:17).

This method was not original with Crook. The North

172

Smithsonian, NAA: 56,089.

Fig. 6. Northern Cheyenne scouts. In 1889, Lt. Edward Wanton Casey organized the first group of professionally trained and outfitted Indian scouts as Troop L, 8th Cavalry. The uniformed, equipped scouts were enlisted as regulars and paid $25 a month (Frink 1965:104–106). In this photograph they wear standard-issue clothing including 1880s campaign hats, 5-button shirts and trousers, some with late pattern gauntlets. The man at left holds a saber and wears a buffalo overcoat, an 1884 Mills belt and a muskrat cap. After 1890, special patterns of Indian scout uniforms were authorized. Photograph by Christian Barthelmess, about 1899–1890, Ft. Keogh, Mont.

brothers, Frank and Luther, gained renown with their Pawnee scout battalion on the central Plains in the late 1860s. Nelson A. Miles and George A. Custer also made use of Indian allies. But Crook was the chief advocate. For example, he led Northern Shoshones against Northern Paiutes in Oregon 1866–1868, Pimas and Maricopas against Apaches in Arizona 1872–1873, Eastern Shoshones and Crows against Sioux in Wyoming and Montana in 1876, and White Mountain Western Apaches against Chiricahua Apaches in Arizona 1882–1886.

Despite the example and urgings of Crook and a handful of disciples, however, the army never broke free of conventional methods to fight the style of war in which the Indian excelled (Utley 1973:44–58).

Composition

An act of Congress of July 28, 1866, defined the postwar regular Army. This law increased the cavalry from six to 10 regiments and the infantry from 19 to 45 regiments. Artillery remained at five regiments. Two cavalry and four infantry regiments were composed of Black enlisted men and White officers; and four regiments, offering a haven for wounded veterans, made up the Veteran Reserve Corps. The officer corps drew from both West Pointers and veterans of Civil War volunteer service. Under this law, the regular Army numbered about 54,000. It served both in the Reconstruction South and the frontier West.

Expressing economy drives as well as the progress of Reconstruction programs, Congress in a series of riders to appropriation bills reduced the forces authorized by the act of 1866. An 1869 measure trimmed strength from 54,000 to 37,000 and cut back the infantry to 25 regiments, of which the 24th and 25th (together with the 9th and 10th Cavalry) were Black. An 1870 law lowered the ceiling to 30,000, and beginning in 1874 every army appropriation act carried a proviso limiting enlisted strength to 25,000, or an army with officers of about 27,000. Almost 900 officers made surplus by these cuts were mustered out, while the number of generals permitted the line (as distinct from the staff) fell to 11. Regiments and companies wasted to skeletons, with men scarcely sufficient to mount guard and provide other details, much less perform efficiently in the field. Under the 25,000 limitation, the number of officers and enlisted men actually serving on the Indian frontier averaged less than 20,000 (Heitman 1903, 2:606–613).

After Grant's inauguration as president in 1869, William T. Sherman became commanding general of the army, although, like Winfield Scott before the war, he possessed little real authority and waged a constant power struggle with the secretary of war and the chiefs of the staff bureaus, who reported directly to the secretary. Lt. Gen. Philip H. Sheridan commanded the Division of the Missouri (fig. 5), where most of the severest Indian troubles occurred. West of the Rockies, the Division of the Pacific was commanded by a major general. When Sherman retired in 1883, Sheridan became commanding general, to be succeeded, upon his death in 1888, by John M. Schofield.

In many of its features, the postwar Army resembled its prewar predecessor. Its officer corps and enlisted complement retained about the same composition. Enlisted men came principally from poor urban backgrounds and lacked the mental, physical, and moral qualities of the wartime volunteers. Foreign immigrants, chiefly Irish and German, formed a conspicuous part of the enlisted personnel. Frontier service continued to be marked by boredom, frustration, isolation, hardship, and deprivation. Pay was low, promotion slow, food bad, and shelter minimal. Much of the civilian population scorned soldiers and things military. One authority has called the years between the Civil and Spanish-American wars "the Army's Dark Ages" (Ganoe 1924:298; Utley 1973:10–43).

From 1866 to 1891, the date usually regarded as marking the close of the Indian wars, the Army fought 1,040 combat engagements with Indians. Casualties totaled 69 officers and 879 enlisted men killed and 68 officers and 990 enlisted men wounded. Military estimates, which must be viewed skeptically, record Indian casualties at 4,371 killed, 1,279 wounded, and 10,318 captured (Peters 1966:[4]).

Major Campaigns, 1866–1886

Great Plains

War broke over the northern Plains in 1866 even as peace commissioners tried to quiet Indians still incensed at General Connor's offensive of 1865. Col. Henry B. Carrington established Forts Reno, Phil Kearny, and C.F. Smith to guard the Bozeman Trail, which connected the Platte Road with the Montana gold fields. Prominent in stirring the Sioux and Cheyennes to resist the military penetration was the Oglala Sioux chief Red Cloud. On December 21, 1866, near Fort Phil Kearny, Red Cloud's warriors ambushed and wiped out a force of 80 men under Cap. William J. Fetterman. The disaster alarmed the nation, Carrington was relieved, and reinforcements were sent. The following summer the troops won two resounding victories in the Wagon Box and Hayfield fights. Nevertheless, the Indians effectively prevented use of the Bozeman Trail as an emigrant route (D. Brown 1962).

On the central Plains, scene of railroad construction and heavy travel to Colorado and the Southwest, military authorities believed the Indians to be preparing for war. In spring 1867 Gen. Winfield S. Hancock precipitated a war that neither side may have intended when he attempted, with a show of force, to intimidate a large village of Sioux and Cheyenne near Fort Larned, Kansas. All summer, as warriors raided settlements and travel routes, Lt. Col. George A. Custer and the 7th Cavalry campaigned vigorously throughout western Kansas and southern Nebraska, but a decisive encounter eluded them.

In Washington, peace advocates gained ascendancy, and a peace commission consisting of generals as well as civilian officials went west to negotiate an end to the Plains wars. At Medicine Lodge, Kansas, in October 1867, the southern Plains tribes agreed to withdraw from Kansas and settle on reservations south of the Arkansas River. At Fort Laramie, Wyoming, in spring 1868, the Sioux agreed to accept a "Great Sioux Reservation,"

Smithsonian, Div. of Armed Forces Hist.:14134.
Fig. 7. U.S. Springfield carbine Model 1873. This was the weapon carried by Custer's 7th Cavalry at the Little Big Horn. Breech-loading, single-shot, and .45 caliber, this carbine served the western army 1872–1892. It was slung at the trooper's side by the leather strap and swivel. Convention dictated dismounting before using the carbines, the trooper's six-shot, .45 caliber, Colt revolvers being the handier, more effective weapons when mounted. Carbines used by the frontier army in the post-Civil War period included the highly acclaimed .50 caliber Spencer repeater, and the .50 caliber, single-shot Sharps. Experiments with Henry and later Winchester repeaters gave mixed evaluations, since the side-loading gate and lever action proved overly sensitive to dust and rust, and the army concentrated on breechloaders. However, the lever-action repeaters were the preferred rifle of the settlers and Indians.

essentially present South Dakota west of the Missouri River. But they also won the government's promise to abandon the Bozeman Trail forts and to regard the Powder River country as "unceded Indian territory" in which groups that did not want to live on the Great Sioux Reservation might continue to roam freely. These treaties contained the seeds of future wars.

Conflict came almost at once to the southern Plains. Cheyenne raids on Kansas settlements in August 1868 called forth military retaliation. General Sheridan organized a comprehensive winter campaign featuring formidable columns moving on Indian Territory from Kansas, Colorado, and New Mexico. All Indians not on their newly assigned reservations—Kiowas, Comanches, and Arapahoes as well as Cheyennes—were the target. At the Battle of the Washita on November 27, 1868, Custer's cavalry smashed the Cheyenne village of Black Kettle, a peace chief whose lodges nonetheless harbored warriors fresh from Kansas raids. The chief died in the fighting. On December 25 the New Mexico column, led by Maj. Andrew W. Evans, routed Horse Back's Comanches at the Battle of Soldier Spring. Most of the Kiowas and Comanches escaped Sheridan's troops by assembling at Fort Cobb, which was replaced in January 1869 by Fort Sill on the western flank of the Wichita Mountains. The Cheyennes remained out. In March 1869 Custer pursued them as far west as the Texas Panhandle, where he exacted promises of surrender from key Cheyenne leaders such as Little Robe and Medicine Arrow.

Although most of the Cheyennes eventually fulfilled their promise to Custer, the militant Dog Soldier band struck north to join with the Sioux in the Powder River country. On July 11, 1869, Maj. Eugene A. Carr and elements of the 5th Cavalry shattered a Dog Soldier camp at Summit Springs, Colorado, and killed the famous chief Tall Bull.

The operations of 1868 to 1869, although clearing Kansas of the remnants of the southern Plains tribes, failed to secure lasting peace. The new reservations in Indian Territory festered with discontent as the government failed in some of its treaty promises and as Quaker agents sought to hurry their charges down the road to civilization. The Kiowas and Comanches—those on the Fort Sill Reservation as well as those who clung to freedom on the Staked Plains to the west—never relented in their custom of raiding in Texas and Mexico. Despite some successes in 1871 and 1872, the troops failed to slow the raiding, and the Peace Policy barred them at the reservation boundary. The Cheyennes, too, goaded by White whiskey peddlers and horse thieves, resumed raiding (Leckie 1963; Hoig 1976).

In July 1874, armed with newly won authority to operate on the reservations, General Sheridan organized a comprehensive campaign against the raiding elements of the Cheyenne, Kiowa, and Comanche tribes. Gen. John

Pope and Gen. C.C. Augur provided immediate supervision. Troops took station at the Kiowa-Comanche and Cheyenne-Arapahoe Agencies, and strong columns converged on the Staked Plains from Kansas, New Mexico, Texas, and Indian Territory. On August 30, 1874, Col. Nelson A. Miles and the 5th Infantry routed a force of Cheyennes at the mouth of Palo Duro Canyon, and on September 28 the 4th Cavalry swept through a combined camp of Cheyennes, Kiowas, and Comanches in the canyon itself. All winter, columns probed the Indian haunts, keeping the fugitives constantly on the move. A few more skirmishes occurred, largely bloodless, but the collapse came chiefly because of the sense of insecurity and futility induced by the persistence of the military offensive. Groups surrendered intermittently throughout the winter. By spring 1875, virtually all had given up. This conflict, known as the Red River War, ended hostilities with the tribes of the southern Plains for all time (Haley 1976).

In conformance with the Fort Laramie Treaty of 1868, many Teton Sioux, including Red Cloud himself, settled on the Great Sioux Reservation, Dakota Territory. Others did not, preferring to roam the buffalo country to the north and west as permitted by the treaty. Prominent among leaders of these people were Sitting Bull, Crazy Horse, Black Moon, American Horse, Gall, and Man-Afraid-of-His-Horse.

Both sides broke the treaty. The government failed to provide specified amounts of food and clothing to the reservation Indians. In 1874 a military expedition under Colonel Custer explored the Black Hills, part of the Great Sioux Reservation, and discovered gold (fig. 8). Prospectors rushed to occupy the area. Although less clearly a treaty violation, the Northern Pacific Railroad survey of the Yelowstone River valley in 1873 portended a similar invasion of the unceded territory, and the surveyors and their military escort met armed resistance. For their part, the Sioux continued to commit depredations in Montana, Wyoming, Nebraska, and Dakota. The easy mobility between reservation and hunting groups, moreover, exacerbated the seriousness of this violation, for settlers bitterly condemned policies that permitted Indians to kill and rob Whites in the summer while living on reservation dole in the winter.

The Sioux War of 1876 originated in these conditions. In part to eliminate the raids of the hunting bands and in part to neutralize their opposition to the sale of the Black Hills by making them dependent on the government, the Indian Bureau in November 1875 ordered them to abandon the unceded territory and report to their agencies by January 31, 1876. They failed to comply and, their camps swollen by kinsmen from the reservation, made ready to defend themselves.

General Sheridan organized an offensive of converging columns such as had won the Red River War—Gen.

S. Dak. State Histl. Soc., Pierre:14.
Fig. 8. Custer's expedition in the Black Hills, Dak. Terr., July-Aug. 1874. The official objective of the expedition was military reconnaissance. However, the occurrence of gold in the Black Hills had long been rumored, and 2 miners accompanied the expedition. The party included 1,000 troops of the 7th Cavalry and the 2 companies of infantry, scientists, newspaper correspondents, guides, Arikara Indian scouts, interpreters, a band, and over 100 wagons (Connell 1984:236–249; Utley 1973:244–245). Photograph by W.H. Illingworth.

George Crook from the south, Gen. Alfred H. Terry from the east, and Col. John Gibbon from the west. Winter and a mismanaged attack by part of Crook's command on a Cheyenne camp at the Battle of Powder River delayed the campaign until summer. Strong and confident, the Sioux and Cheyenne coalition traveled in an immense village that could field perhaps 3,000 fighting men. On June 17 a large warrior force turned back Crook at the Battle of the Rosebud. A week later, June 25, the village was attacked by Terry's striking arm, the 7th Cavalry under Custer. In the Battle of the Little Bighorn, renowned in history and folklore, the Indians annihilated Custer and about 225 troopers and inflicted heavy losses on the balance of the regiment in a siege lifted the next day by the approach of Terry and Gibbon (figs. 9–11).

In resounding victory the Sioux and Cheyennes insured their speedy defeat. Heavily reinforced, Terry and Crook campaigned into the autumn, but without success because the Indians had scattered. A fight at Slim Buttes, north of the Black Hills, September 9, 1876, marked the end of the summer operations (fig. 12). The winter campaign of 1876–1877 proved more fruitful. On November 25, 1876, elements of Crook's command smashed Dull Knife's Cheyennes in the Bighorn Mountains of Wyoming. Colonel Miles, planting Fort Keogh on the Yellowstone River, campaigned energetically all winter, first against Sitting Bull, then against Crazy Horse. Combined with peace feelers, military pressure induced one group after another to surrender or simply go back to the reservation. The surrender of Crazy Horse at Camp Robinson, Nebraska, on May 6, 1877, signified the end of the Sioux War.

Pressed by Miles, Sitting Bull had led his people to refuge in Canada in October 1876. There, watched by the North West Mounted Police, he resisted all efforts of the Americans to persuade him to return and accept the reservation. But the scarcity of game made life precarious, and his camps dwindled as people slipped back across the boundary to give up. At last, with only a handful of followers remaining, Sitting Bull surrendered at Fort Buford, Montana, on July 19, 1881 (fig. 13) (J.D. Gray 1976).

Texas

The conquest of the Kiowas and Comanches in the Red River War of 1874–1875 brought to a close the devastating raids on the Texas and Mexican frontiers by Indians from north of Red River; however, from south of the Rio Grande, Indians continued to plague border communities and stockmen as far east as San Antonio. Principal offenders were Kickapoos (refugees from U.S. reservations) and Lipan and Mescalero Apaches. Troops from Forts Clark and Duncan made no headway against the raiders. Diplomatic efforts to induce the Mexican government to restrain the Indians or to permit U.S. troops to cross the border and do so, directed at a nation wracked by revolution and gripped by suspicion of her northern neighbor, proved equally fruitless.

During the 1870s U.S. troops in pursuit or simply in search of Indians repeatedly invaded Mexico. The first major border crossing occurred in May 1873. Backed

176

Fig. 9. Detail from a painting showing the Battle of the Little Bighorn, drawn by White Swan, a Crow scout who was present. The wounded Indian on the horse-drawn travois, upper right, is probably White Swan. The uniformed soldier to the left of White Swan appears to lead the horse bearing him. Sioux and Crow scouts are shown engaging in combat. Crow scouts wear a single feather, their hair in a pompadour with side braids and back hair falling loosely. Sioux warriors wear recumbent feather warbonnets. White Swan's signature mark appears in the lower right corner. Watercolor on muslin.

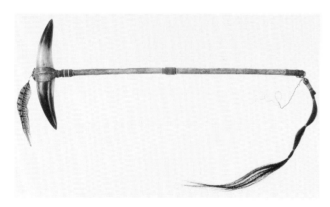

Fig. 10. Sioux tomahawk said to have been collected at the site of the Battle of the Little Bighorn. The 2 buffalo horns are stained red, joined by rawhide. A hawk feather is at the top of the club, a horsehair pendant on the handle. Length of handle, 61 cm.

unofficially by President Grant and General Sheridan, the 4th Cavalry attacked and destroyed three villages—one Kickapoo, one Lipan, and one Mescalero—on the upper San Rodrigo River 40 miles west of Piedras Negras, Coahuila. The Battle of Remolino and the subsequent return of most of the Kickapoos to the United States substantially eliminated the threat from these Indians.

From 1876 through 1878 Gen. Edward O.C. Ord time and again sent troops into Mexico after Lipans and Mescaleros. U.S. cavalry columns hunted the villages of the raiders and in several engagements dealt them severe punishment. On several occasions, too, there were tense confrontations with Mexican troops that came close to armed collision. Ord's policy set off a prolonged diplomatic crisis that brought the two nations close to war. But Mexico, increasingly stable under the regime of Porfirio Díaz and shamed by the violation of her sovereignty, began to send her own troops against the Indians. By 1880, as a result of both U.S. and Mexican operations, the menace had subsided (Utley 1973:344–368).

Fig. 11. Yankton Sioux warbonnet, made in 1872, and said to have been worn at the Battle of the Little Big Horn. The cap is buckskin, covered with split eagle feathers, and surmounted by two split cow horns. A crest of eagle feathers follows along the midline of the cap and down the red stroud trailer edged in ribbon. Length, 164 cm; collected from the owner before 1913.

Fig. 12. Sioux prisoners in front of a lodge taken by Capt. Anson Mills after the fight at Slim Buttes. The Sioux camp consisted of approximately 260 Minneconjou, Brulé, Oglala, and Cheyenne people. Most of the camp's 37 lodges were destroyed during the attack, but soldiers recovered a number of items that the Sioux had supposedly taken from the 7th Calvary at Little Big Horn, including the guidon of Company I displayed in the photograph. Charging Bear (fourth from left), the only Indian identified in the photograph, later became a scout for the army (J.A. Greene 1982:49–50, 71–74, 89). Frank Grouard (far left), who was chief scout for Gen. George Crook in 1876 (Vaughn 1966:187), had been captured in 1869 by a band of Sioux and remained with them for 6 years. Lt. Frederick Schwatka (far right), who led the attack on the village, in later years studied and published about other Native Americans. From a stereograph by Stanley J. Morrow, probably Sept. 13, 1876, near Deadwood, Dak. Terr. (Vaughn 1966:186–187).

Southwest

Warfare with the Apaches continued to wrack New Mexico and Arizona in the postwar years. The Mescalero Apaches broke away from Bosque Redondo in 1865; although they accepted another reservation in the Capitan Mountains near Fort Stanton in 1871, they continued to raid southward across the West Texas travel routes and into Mexico. In central Arizona, Western Apaches and Yavapais disturbed by the Prescott mines fought back. Eight forts sprouted in Apache country (fig. 5), but the garrisons failed to quell the Indians or adapt to their hostile mountain-and-desert environment.

In 1871–1872 Arizona became the scene of expanded efforts, both military and diplomatic. The army sent Gen. George Crook to energize the military effort. The Indian Bureau sent peacemakers. One of these, Gen. Oliver O. Howard, succeeded in persuading Cochise to settle on a reservation. The other, Vincent Colyer, established a

Smithsonian, Dept. of Anthr.: 38811.
Fig. 13. Winchester Model 1866, said to have belonged to Hunkpapa Sioux chief Sitting Bull, and turned in upon his surrender at Fort Buford, N. Dak. Brass tacks decorate the stock, and the initials "St B" have been carved into the stock near the butt. The Winchester repeater was a refinement of the Henry lever action repeater, with side loading gate and .44 caliber, rim-fire cartridge. Indian warriors preferred the Winchester. It was well designed for use while mounted, being lightweight, short, and extremely easy to load and fire. Warriors at the Little Bighorn are known to have used the Winchester against the 7th Cavalry, but it was not the common firearm.

series of reservations for other Apache groups. Finally, freed of civil interference, Crook opened his long-delayed offensive against the remaining hostiles. In the Tonto basin campaign of 1872–1873, directed principally at Yavapais, he demonstrated that, by adopting Indian methods and employing Indian auxiliaries, regular troops could track down and defeat hostile tribesmen. The Battles of Skull Cave and Turret Peak were particularly destructive to the enemy; but more than combat it was Crook's relentless pursuit that wore them down and brought Arizona, for the first time, a genuine respite from Apache aggressions.

The accord began to fall apart in 1875, when General Crook left Arizona. In 1876 the Indian Bureau initiated a program of concentrating all Apaches on the San Carlos Reservation, in the Gila River bottoms. Many Chiricahuas of southeastern Arizona and their Warm Springs kinsmen of southwestern New Mexico opposed concentration. These "renegades," as they came to be labeled by Whites, alternately lived at San Carlos and raided in Arizona and New Mexico from sanctuaries high in the rugged Sierra Madre of Mexico, where still another Chiricahua group already lived. Victorio was the undisputed leader of the Warm Springs "renegades," and increasingly Geronimo gained stature among the Chiricahuas.

From 1877 to 1880 Victorio's warriors terrorized settlements and wore out pursuing soldiers. Whenever troops drew too close or the hostiles needed a rest, they

Smithsonian, Dept. of Anthr.: 8443-B.
Fig. 14. Comanche shield and covers taken from Quahada Comanches in Texas in 1868 by a detachment of the 6th Cavalry out of Fort Griffin. Having attacked a wagon train and stolen all the train's mules, the small band was pursued and taken by surprise at its camp (Rister 1956:74). Rather than burning the band's belongings as had been military practice, some artifacts were shipped to the Army Medical Museum in Washington, D.C., as part of a program to study Indian weapons and military capabilities (G.A. Otis 1868). left, Outer buckskin cover, painted in yellow, red, and blue, with a cluster of red-tailed hawk and cut raven feathers and depictions of 2 muskets. center, Inner buckskin cover, painted in yellow, red, and blue with a red stroud sash hung with red-tailed hawk feathers. Depictions of buffalo or cow's head with horns enclosing a human figure, possibly a priest, are flanked by a spired church with crosses and an Indian figure with breechclout, set above stylized bear paws. Prior to battle, the covers, which displayed symbolic representations that came to the owner through dreams or visions, were removed. right, Buffalo hide shield, thick enough to turn away arrows and musket balls, unadorned except for a strip of horse hair. Diameter of the shield, 50 cm.

INDIAN–UNITED STATES MILITARY SITUATION, 1848–1891

slipped into Mexico. Victorio also stirred up the Mescaleros at Fort Stanton and gave fresh impetus and leadership to their forays. Throughout 1880 Col. Edward Hatch's 9th Cavalry campaigned across the breadth of southern New Mexico. At Hembrillo Canyon on April 7–8 and in the Black Range on May 23 troops and scouts almost snared the quarry. In July, after a Mexican interlude, Victorio tried to reenter the United States through West Texas. In a series of well-conceived and well-executed movements, Col. Benjamin H. Grierson and the 10th Cavalry, out of Forts Davis and Stockton, turned the Indians back. In September, with Mexico's permission, a large expedition under Col. George P. Buell crossed the border in search of Victorio. But on October 15, Mexican troops surrounded and almost annihilated his band at Tres Castillos, Chihuahua. A sharpshooter felled Victorio. His death ended the Mescalero menace, but the survivors of Tres Castillos, under aged Nane, ultimately united with the Chiricahuas in the Sierra Madre to the west.

San Carlos Reservation festered with discontent. Among the White Mountain Western Apaches a shaman named Nakaidoklini preached a religion that the Whites regarded as incendiary. An attempt by Col. Eugene A. Carr to arrest him precipitated a mutiny of Indian scouts and the Battle of Cibicue Creek on August 30, 1881, in which Nakaidoklini was killed and Carr suffered severe losses. On September 1 angry warriors attacked Fort Apache itself.

The excitement created by these events stampeded Chiricahuas at San Carlos who, under Juh, Geronimo, and others, fled the reservation for Mexico. In April 1882 a raiding party from this group, led by Loco, cut a destructive swath across Arizona, gained more adherents at San Carlos, fought off troops under Col. George A. Forsyth at Horseshoe Canyon, and escaped into Mexico only to meet disaster in a battle with Mexican soldiers.

In the wake of the Loco raid trouble broke out again among the White Mountain Apaches. A warrior named Natiotish led 60 followers in a raid on stockmen in the Tonto basin. Converging cavalry units trapped and virtually annihilated the raiders in the Battle of Big Dry Wash, July 17, 1882.

Again the army assigned General Crook to Arizona. Gaining Mexican assent, in May 1883 he personally led an expedition of soldiers and Indian scouts into the heart of the Sierra Madre. In one of the most perilous military ventures of the Indian wars, he succeeded in forcing Geronimo, Naiche, and other Chiricahua leaders into a parley in which, after a week of tense negotiations, they consented to return to San Carlos.

Conditions at San Carlos, including civil-military conflict and government interference with Apache customs, led to still another outbreak in May 1885. Again Crook sent troops and scouts into Mexico. For months they exhausted themselves among the sheer slopes and plunging barrancas of the Sierra Madre. On January 11, 1886, Mexican militia attacked a scout unit and killed Crook's most valuable officer, Capt. Emmet Crawford. Even so, the Chiricahuas, tiring of the chase, agreed to talk with Crook. In a conference at Canyon de los Embudos, March 25–27, 1886, Geronimo and his associates surrendered to Crook. En route to Fort Bowie, however, they obtained mescal from a trader and in a drunken frenzy bolted to the mountains. General Sheridan, now commanding the army, placed conditions on further prosecution of the campaign so offensive to Crook that he asked to be replaced.

Crook's successor, Gen. Nelson A. Miles, made a great show of embracing fresh methods but in fact did not depart importantly from Crook's strategy. Soldiers and scouts scoured the Sierra Madre. In the end, it was Lt. Charles B. Gatewood, an old acquaintance of Geronimo, who won success by going alone into the Indians' Mexican lair and persuading them to give up. Crucial to their decision, moreover, was Miles's action in removing all the reservation Chiricahuas, even Crook's faithful scouts, to military stations in Florida. Geronimo, Naiche, and their handful of followers formally surrendered to Miles at Skeleton Canyon, Arizona, in September 1886. These people, too, were sent to Florida (vol. 10:407–410). The surrender of Geronimo marked the close of Apache hostilities (Thrapp 1967, 1972, 1974).

Alaska

Immediately after the purchase of Alaska from Russia in 1867, U.S. troops under Gen. Jefferson Columbus Davis erected military posts at key coastal locations. The army's chief mission was to oversee a well-established commerce in furs between White traders and Alaska natives—Indians, Eskimos, and Aleuts. Another was to suppress the liquor traffic. But the Army itself engaged in this traffic, and armed collisions provoked by drunken soldiers and Indians caused such scandals that in 1870 all posts save one were abandoned and the garrisons recalled. A token force held Sitka until 1877, when it, too, was withdrawn. Naval and revenue units, better adapted to Alaska's marine character, took over the Army's duties (Utley 1973:181–183).

Great Basin and Plateau

Northern Paiutes continued to plague Oregon as regulars replaced volunteers at the close of the Civil War. The first postwar assignment of General Crook was to command these troops. Against the Paiutes he tested the methods that later, against Apaches and Sioux, gained him fame. Crook's campaign of 1866–1868 featured pack transportation, Northern Shoshone Indian auxiliaries, personal leadership in the field, and aggressive persistence. Operations ranged across the plateau country of Oregon, Idaho, Nevada, and California and involved some 40 combat actions. The dynamic Paiute leader Paulina died in an early engagement. With the surrender of Wewawewa to Crook in July 1868, resistance ended (ARCIA 1868:119).

Trouble was brewing nearby. In 1864 the Modocs had relinquished their homeland on the Oregon-California border, east of the Sierra Nevada, and agreed to live on a reservation with the Northern Paiutes and Klamaths near Fort Klamath, Oregon. The reservation proved uncongenial, and many, acknowledging the leadership of Captain Jack, returned to their California homes. Settlers protested. In November 1872 the Indian Bureau, calling on the Army for help, tried to compel the Modocs to go back to Fort Klamath. They resisted, killed some settlers, and took refuge in the lava beds on the southern shore of Tule Lake, in California.

For five months Captain Jack and his people, with no more than 60 fighting men, defied all efforts to blast and coax them out of their natural fortress. A military force ultimately about 1,000 strong surrounded the lava beds, but an attempt on January 17, 1873, to take them by assault proved a costly failure. Negotiations ended in tragedy on April 11 as Jack and others, in violation of a truce, assassinated Gen. Edward R.S. Canby and fellow peace commissioners (fig. 15). In another assault the troops seized the lava beds, but the Modocs merely withdrew to others farther south. From there on April 26 they fell on a 60-man reconnoitering force and wiped out half of it. Early in May dissension in the Modoc leadership caused the Indians to scatter. Under General Davis, Canby's successor, the troops pursued and by early June 1873 had rounded them all up. Captain Jack and three other leaders were hanged following a military trial of dubious legality, and 155 Modocs were exiled to Indian Territory (Murray 1959; Dillon 1973).

Like the Modoc War, the Nez Perce War of 1877 originated in attempts to force Indians to go to a reservation where they did not want to live. The "nontreaty" Nez Perces had not subscribed to the treaties that established the Nez Perce Reservation on the Clearwater River, Idaho. They preferred to remain in traditional locations on the Salmon River and in the Wallowa valley of eastern Oregon. Threatened with military force if his people did not abandon the Wallowa valley, Chief Joseph acquiesced. En route, however, some of his young men committed depredations. A 100-man cavalry command rushed south from Fort Lapwai, Idaho, and on June 17, 1877, struck the camps of Joseph and White Bird, another nontreaty chief, in White Bird Canyon. The Nez Perces threw back the attackers with heavy casualties, and the war was on.

Gen. Oliver O. Howard took the field with 400 soldiers, both cavalry and infantry. At the Battle of the Clearwater he routed the Indians but failed to follow up his

Smithsonian, NAA:3054-a.
Fig. 15. Modoc women and White men at a camp in the lava beds. left to right, standing: Capt. Oliver C. Applegate, Winema (Tobey) Riddle; seated, center: Laceles and Martha Mainstake; seated, front: Mehunolush and Saukaaduch. Winema and Frank Riddle served as interpreters during the April 1873 peace negotiations at Tule Lake, and Winema saved the life of Alfred B. Meacham, head of a peace commission to the Modocs, during the violence of April 11. The Riddles accompanied Meacham on a speaking tour of the United States in 1875 (Thompson 1971:48, 50, 58–61, 151). Applegate, an agent at the Yainax subagency on the Klamath Reservation, commanded Company B of the Oreg. Volunteer Militia, a unit mostly comprised of Indians (Thompson 1971:28, 34; Riddle 1914:254–256). The seated women were his prisoners. Photograph by Eadweard Muybridge, Tule Lake, Calif., 1873.

advantage. Led by Joseph, Looking Glass, Toohoolhoolzote, and White Bird, about 800 Nez Perces, 500 of them women and children, turned east in a memorable trek across the Bitterroot Mountains to the Montana plains, their objective, at length, safety in Canada. Howard pursued with 700 men. Col. John Gibbon, with infantry units from Montana forts, marched to intercept. Gibbon overtook the Nez Perces on the Big Hole River of southwestern Montana on August 11, but in a tenacious defense they so crippled him that he could not follow. Howard's column, slowed by exhaustion, fell behind (fig. 16).

Crossing Yellowstone National Park, the Indians slipped around a blocking cavalry force under Col. Samuel D. Sturgis, spoiled its pursuit in a fight at Canyon Creek on September 13, and pushed north toward Canada. On the northern edge of the Bear Paw Mountains, 40 miles south of the border, they paused to rest. Here on September 30, 1877, they were attacked by Col. Nelson A. Miles, who had led a command in a forced march from

181

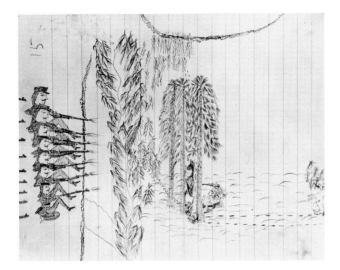

Fig. 16. Indian rendition of a battle, probably the Battle of Clearwater or the Battle of the Big Hole, Nez Perce War of 1877. White soldiers, left, wear dark blue coats, light blue trousers, and forage caps. The 2 Indians, one lying wounded, center, are in a valley under the cover of pines. A horse lies dead at right. The drawing is of the late Plains style of narrative art depicting war scenes (Stern, Schmitt, and Halfmoon 1980:341–376). Pencil drawing on paper linked to the household of Captain Sumkin, Cayuse–Nez Perce, Umatilla Indian Reservation, Pendleton, Oreg.

Fort Keogh to cut off their flight. The battle, after many casualties on both sides, turned into a siege that lasted until October 5, when Chief Joseph surrendered. White Bird and about 300 people succeeded in escaping to Canada. Looking Glass and Toohoolhoolzote had been killed. Like the Modocs, Joseph and his people were sent to Indian Territory (Josephy 1965).

Unsettled by the Nez Perce War and an accumulation of grievances, including the destruction of camas-root grounds by White stockmen, the Bannocks of southern Idaho revolted in spring 1878. They were joined by Northern Paiutes against whom General Crook had warred a decade earlier. General Howard concentrated troops in southeastern Oregon and dogged the hostiles northward all the way to the Columbia River. Defeated at Silver Creek and Birch Creek on June 23 and July 8, they scattered. By the end of the summer, pressed by Howard's columns, most of the Paiutes had returned to their reservations, and Bannock refugees had been apprehended as far east as Yellowstone National Park (Brimlow 1938).

The Utes occupied a large reservation in western Colorado. Mineral strikes in the Colorado Rockies during the 1870s made prospectors covetous of the Ute lands. Part of the reservation was relinquished in 1873, but Coloradoans sought still more. Already apprehensive over the land issue, the Utes had the misfortune in 1878 to be assigned an agent, Nathan C. Meeker, determined to transform them into copies of the White man.

Resistance to the civilization program prompted Meeker, in September 1878, to call for military support. A column marched from Fort Fred Steele, Wyoming, under Maj. T.T. Thornburgh. Ute warriors met it at the reservation boundary and in the Battle of Milk Creek killed Thornburgh and placed the command under siege. At the agency, other Indians killed Meeker and nine employees and carried the agency women into captivity. A relief column under Col. Wesley Merritt rescued the besieged command on October 5 and proceeded to the agency. Thereafter, although the army poured troops into the Ute country from both north and south, the outbreak was suppressed largely by diplomacy. A special agent of Secretary of the Interior Carl Schurz, Charles Adams, joined with the Utes' elder statesman, Chief Ouray, to negotiate the release of the captives and an end to the revolt (Sprague 1957).

End of Hostilities

As one tribe after another gave way to the westward movement of White settlement, the reservation increasingly overshadowed the Army as the dominant instrument of government Indian policy. By 1880 reservations had imprisoned all but the Apaches, and by 1886 they, too, had yielded. Agents, schoolteachers, missionaries, and "practical farmers" strove to make over the Indian in the White image. Indian police and control of rations enforced the agent's will. Confusion, frustration, and despair attended the collapse of traditional values, institutions, and customs. Aggravating this trauma were repeated efforts, often successful, to open "surplus" reservation lands to Whites and repeated failures to provide sufficient rations and other necessities.

Fig. 17. U.S. soldiers collecting Sioux dead into army wagons on the battlefield at Wounded Knee, Pine Ridge, Jan. 1, 1891. A mass grave was dug, no identification of the dead attempted, and no ceremony accompanied the burial (McGregor 1940:80–82). Among the 146 Sioux buried were 84 men and boys, 44 women, and 18 children. Another 20–30 dead or wounded were not found and another 7 Sioux died in a hospital installed on the reservation. Of Whites, 25 died and 39 others were wounded (Prucha 1976:363; Utley 1973:407, 412). A monument was erected on the grave site by Oglala and Cheyenne River Sioux (McGregor 1940:82–83). Photograph by Northwestern Photographic Company, Chadron, Nebr.

Confronted with cultural disaster, Indians all over the West eagerly joined a messianic movement that swept the reservations 1889–1890. Drawing on both Christian and traditional native religious precepts, the Ghost Dance doctrine promised the restoration of the old way of life and the disappearance of all White people. Although the millennium was to be brought about by peaceful means, among the Sioux the Ghost Dance took on violent aspects and precipitated the last important encounter between the Army and Indians (Utley 1984:227–252).

On the Pine Ridge and Rosebud reservations of South Dakota, the Ghost Dancers stirred such defiance and disorder among Oglala and Brulé Sioux that in November 1890 the agents, fearing for the safety of government employees, called for military aid. Gen. Nelson A. Miles sent troops to both agencies. The dancers withdrew to a remote corner of the Pine Ridge Reservation. While the commander at Pine Ridge, Gen. John R. Brooke, tried to coax them back, an attempt to arrest Sitting Bull on the Standing Rock Reservation of North Dakota misfired and the old chief, symbol of Indian resistance for almost 30 years, was shot and killed. Also, a similar effort to apprehend Chief Big Foot ended in the bloodbath of Wounded Knee on December 29, 1890. In this encounter, intended by neither side, the 7th Cavalry and its artillery support, under Col. James W. Forsyth, destroyed a large portion of Big Foot's band, including many women and children (fig. 17). Wounded Knee so infuriated the Sioux that a long and costly war seemed inevitable; however, by

shrewd diplomacy and the concentration of overwhelming force, General Miles obtained the surrender of the rebels on January 15, 1891. Except for a few unimportant incidents, the collapse of the Ghost Dance movement marked the end of armed hostilities between Indians and soldiers in the United States (Utley 1963).

The Army that engaged in these frontier wars saw itself as the vanguard of civilization, sweeping aside the savage and clearing the way for the industrious pioneer. The army in fact participated prominently in the westward movement and contributed significantly to the opening of the West. Forts, patrols, campaigns, and Indian fights gave a sense and sometimes a substance of security to White residents and nudged the Indian farther down the path toward conquest. But contrary to its self-image and the conventional wisdom of later generations, the army did not conquer the Indian. The great westward migration of Americans, depriving him of land and traditional subsistence resources, accomplished that result in the short span of two decades following the Civil War. Thus the Army should be viewed as but one of many instruments of conquest along with miners, stockmen, farmers, traders, freighters, railroad builders, Indian agents, and others.

Sources

Sources for the period 1848–1891 are plentiful. Much

Ariz. Histl. Soc. Lib., Tucson.

Fig. 18. Troop K, 2nd Cavalry, at Zuni Pueblo, N. Mex. Terr., Sept. 14–19, 1897. After the cessation of the wars between Indians and Whites, the U.S. military continued to intervene in Indian-White affairs. Troop K, stationed at Ft. Wingate, N. Mex. Terr., was dispatched to Zuni at the request of civil authorities to assist in the arrest of Indians at that pueblo. The prisoners were brought back to Ft. Wingate (Return of the 2nd Regiment of Cavalry, Army of the U.S., Sept., 1897; Natl. Arch. Microfilm Publication M744, Roll 22). Photographer unknown.

material can be located in various record groups of the National Archives in Washington, D.C., and in local and regional archives. Of specific interest at the National Archives are Record Group 94 (Records of the Adjutant General's Office), Record Group 107 (Records of the Office of the Secretary of War), and Record Group 75 (Records of the Bureau of Indian Affairs).

In addition a variety of published material is available. Bender (1952), Brady (1913), DuBois (1949), J.P. Dunn (1886), Prucha (1964), and Weigley (1967) all offer a broad view of the role of the U.S. Army in the West. The lives and works of specific generals and military personnel are discussed by Athearn (1956), Carpenter (1964), R.G. Carter (1935), E.B. Custer (1885), V.W. Johnson (1962), King (1963), Rister (1944), Rogers (1938), and Wallace (1964). Special attention is drawn to the use of Black soldiers in Indian campaigns by Fowler (1971) and Leckie (1967). A number of memoirs such as R.G. Carter (1935), Cremony (1970), Custer (1874), Lowe (1906), Marcy (1866), and Meyers (1914) offer a more detailed appraisal of the Indian wars and army life in general during the late nineteenth century.

British Colonial Indian Treaties

DOROTHY V. JONES

When the British and the Indians met in treaty negotiations during the colonial period, they brought different diplomatic traditions and expectations to the encounter. Out of the interaction between the two groups, over many years and in many different locations, a new kind of diplomacy took shape. This new diplomacy was neither Indian nor European. It was, rather, a complex mix that changed over time according to changing power relationships. No one planned it that way. It was simply the outcome of prolonged and numerous diplomatic encounters between groups who, for the most part, regarded each other with suspicion and hostility but who found it expedient to enter into negotiations in pursuit of their separate goals.

Compounding the conflicts of interests between them was the fact that the Indians and Europeans were strange to each other. This made relations more difficult because they were relations with strangers whose ways were odd and whose words were suspect. It was here that diplomacy played its key role. Diplomacy is the art of dealing with the stranger and, especially, the stranger group. From that fact comes diplomacy's style and mode of operation. In colonial North America the style was intense because of the proximity of the participating groups and their exclusive unbending pride. Out of the almost-daily interaction among Indians and Europeans came a system of treaties that was complex, flexible, completely satisfactory to none, and yet—on the whole—a remarkable achievement for people whose principles and interests were frequently in opposition.

The colonial treaty system can be seen as a small-scale model of the global system that developed as Europeans spread their technology, their diseases, their ideas, and their quarrels around the world. In the colonial system, as later in the global, groups with different cultural traditions were forced to work out ways to manage their differences. They had to secure collective goals, direct and control conflicts, and facilitate exchanges—while at the same time preserving, to the best of their abilities, their identities and independence. In colonial North America separate diplomatic traditions met and interacted to produce a new kind of diplomacy.

The European Tradition

By the mid-1600s a new state of world affairs was in the process of creation as Europeans spread around the world. There are indications of the new world environment in a 1654 treaty between the Dutch and the English. The treaty established a commission to adjust the many grievances the two powers had against each other for injuries done "in the East Indies, Greenland, Muscovy, Brasil, etc." (C. Parry 1969, 3:251–252). Since North America is included in the treaty article's "etc." this casual listing of European enclaves around the world makes clear the extent of the changes taking place and the strains on European diplomacy.

One of the first acts of the English in colonial Virginia was the "coronation," with cloak and crown, of Powhatan, leader of the Indian confederacy that was the nearest, most necessary, and most threatening to the English (Robinson 1983: 5–6). This coronation was based on the European principle of the hierarchical devolution of authority. Powhatan, who was no stranger to hierarchy within his own group, gave a cloak and some foot coverings in return, on the principle of reciprocity among equals. The issue of principle was thus joined immediately, as was the issue of self-interest. Since each had something the other wanted, they maintained—albeit reluctantly—a dialogue of diplomacy (Watson 1983: 14–21, 33–39).

The European diplomatic tradition (Nicolson 1963: 26–55) out of which the English in colonial Virginia were acting was not well suited to conditions in colonial North America. European diplomacy assumed hierarchy, just as it assumed the centralization of authority and of negotiations.

North American diplomacy was not centralized; it was diffuse. It was not conducted by trained diplomats but by anybody and everybody: by orators, civil leaders, village and provincial councils, missionaries, speculators, traditionalists, dissidents, those with authority and those without. It was a diplomacy that developed its own protocols and ceremonies, and these were rarely European. It was better understood in the centuries when the Indians still had power and the freedom of maneuver than in the centuries when they did not. What happened in the

185

hinterland called colonial North America was the development of a multilateral, multicultural diplomacy unlike the diplomatic tradition of any single participant but partaking of them all. Europeans did not begin with hegemony in the New World. They gained it only gradually, and while they were working toward it, they and their Indian opposites created something new.

American Traditions

In Eastern North America there were at least two different traditions of diplomacy, that of the Mississippi Basin, which centered on the calumet or peace pipe, and that of the Northeast, which centered on the wampum belt or covenant belt. These two traditions can be glimpsed in the work of a remarkable religious, Father Joseph François Lafitau, who from 1712 to 1717 was stationed at Sault Saint Louis, a Jesuit mission on the south bank of the Saint Lawrence River opposite Montreal.

Lafitau's passion to convert the Indians was equaled by his passion to understand them. The result of intensive observation, interviewing, and reading was a two-volume work in 1724 in which Lafitau attempted to understand Indian diplomacy by fitting it within a European frame of reference. In Lafitau's hands the threadbare comparisons to antiquity cast fresh light on the element of the sacred in Indian diplomacy. After comparing the Indians' calumet to the caduceus, Mercury's winged, serpent-entwined staff, Lafitau pointed out that the peace pipe and the caduceus performed similar functions in signaling a diplomatic mission and providing safe conduct, but that the Indians went the ancients one better because they had preserved "the most essential thing in the calumet of peace; it is this pipe, which is I think a veritable altar for the Indians where they offer with all due forms a sacrifice to the sun, a sacrifice which gains for the calumet that respect to which, through a spirit of ancient religion, the sacredness of oaths and the inviolable law of nations are attached, in the same way as these things were formerly attached to Mercury's staff" (1974–1977, 2:181).

By this roundabout route through European antiquity, Lafitau had come to an understanding of one of the essential characteristics of Indian diplomacy. In Indian diplomatic traditions, treaties were not merely temporal agreements. They were sacred collective obligations, to be broken only under peril of divine displeasure. It was a view that had been part of the medieval heritage of European diplomacy. The heritage survived in isolated pockets of the church of which Lafitau was a part, but, in general, European humanists had long since brushed such a view aside.

It was in the New World among the Indians that the sense of sacredness remained strong, informing diplomacy, vivifying it, furnishing the standards of right and wrong, endowing activities with cosmic significance. It is as easy to sentimentalize as to trivialize or ignore this sense of sacredness. It did not, for example, prevent deception, as in Lafitau's (1974–1977, 2:183) story of a Sioux attempt to use peace pipes to deceive an enemy. Nor did sacredness preclude hard bargaining and a careful weighing of policy choices. When the Chickasaws of the lower Mississippi Valley were at war with the French in the early eighteenth century, they sent an embassy to the English on the Atlantic coast, which "entered singing, according to their Custom, and the Great Man of the Chickasaws carrying in his hand a Calamett of Peace . . . " (Robinson 1983:266). Under the protection of the calumet the Chickasaws had come all the way from the Mississippi. They would also have sent a well-armed guard. And when they had done singing, and presenting the pipe, and putting themselves, the English, and the proceedings under divine guidance and protection, they would then bargain like merchant adventurers for powder, shot, guns, horses, and regular access to English supplies while they fought the French.

Ritual Dialogue

What antiquity was to European diplomacy, the Iroquois and the Iroquois Condolence ceremony were to the diplomacy that developed in colonial North America after the coming of the Europeans. Here was the fundamental source for imagery, both visual and verbal. Further, the Condolence ceremony structured the entire form of treaty negotiations from beginning to end (Jones 1984:3–30; Fenton 1985:3–36).

The negotiating was rigid in its demand for a certain order of proceedings couched in particular terms. Indeed, the terminology was so similar from council to council and year to year that the student of diplomacy must read closely to pick out from the ritual dialogue the different subjects that are being introduced and bargained about.

As a purely Iroquois affair, the Condolence ceremony was performed annually at Onondaga, where it served to strengthen the political and social bonds of the League of the Iroquois when performed to install new chiefs (vol. 15: 437–440). This loose confederacy of five, then six separate nations was always in danger of fragmentation, particularly after the strains of European relations were added to the strains of relations within the League and with other Indian nations. The point for diplomacy was the way that the ceremony had defined Iroquois expectations of how separate peoples should meet (M.K. Foster 1985: 106–108). There had to be greeting and response, and mutual cleansing of the spirit so that the negotiation could proceed without obstruction. This meant that past grievances had to be put aside and a new state of affairs created, symbolically as well as actually. How this might work in actual negotiation can be seen in two examples.

In the first, a Delaware speaker at treaty negotiations

with Pennsylvania in 1758 used the formulas from the Iroquois Requickening Address in the Condolence ceremony for the ceremonial cleansing of the spirit that had to precede any substantive talk. "Brother, you desire me to hollow loud, and give notice to all the Indians round about," he said in opening. The Indians had come, but there were still obstructions between the two peoples that had to be removed before real communication could take place. All traces of the everyday world of dirt and discomfort had to be discarded: "I with this string wipe the dust and sweat off your face, and clear your eyes, and pick the briars out of the legs of the Indians that are come here, and anoint one of them with your healing oil, and I will anoint the other." And he gave a string of beads in token of the cleansing (Burke 1760:191).

But cleansing was not all that was needed. What in European terms would be a mutual amnesty for all injuries committed in the past would in Iroquois terms be a burial of the axes that the parties to the negotiations had taken from each other's heads. In the second example, in 1684 a Mohawk speaker said, "We thank the great Sachem of Virginia that the Axe shall be thrown into the Pit." He then gave two beaver skins to confirm the amnesty and said again that he was glad that the Virginians "will bury in the Pit what is past. Let the earth be trod hard over it: or rather, let a strong Stream run under the Pit to wash the Evil away out of our Sight and Remembrance, and that it may never be digged up again." When this was done, literally as well as figuratively, then the new state of peace could take root: "We now plant a Tree, whose top will reach the Sun, and its Branches spread far abroad, so that it shall be seen afar off; and we shall shelter ourselves under it, and live in Peace without molestation" (Robinson 1983:291).

The Iroquois world was not the only one with ceremonial traditions and imagery. There may have been as many as there were groups outside the Iroquois orbit, but scholars have not yet related the bits and pieces of evidence into a coherent whole as they have with the Iroquois. In 1654, for example, some Delawares made a treaty of friendship with settlers in New Sweden, and one of the Delaware negotiators stroked his arm with long, sweeping strokes to show the bonds of amity uniting the two peoples. He then switched to botanical metaphor and likened the joining of the two to the fruit of a gourd that grows without joint or fissure (Kent 1979:26).

A statement by a Creek leader in 1765 suggests another ceremonial diplomatic tradition. "I observe that among the white People Friendship is compared to a chain which links people together," he said. "In our Nation friendship is compared to a Grape Vine, which tho' Slender and Weak when Young, grows Stronger as it grows Older" (Rowland 1911:198).

The rituals of diplomacy are shaped by ceremony, imagery, and symbolism. In their dealings with each other, both Indians and Europeans attached great importance to symbols, although, as one might expect, to different symbols. The members of the governor's council in Virginia in 1680 were alarmed when Charles II sent to the Indians "rich Coronets with Robes, Silver badges, and several other presents." They feared that the Indians, who had not been following the dictates of the council, "may be heightened thereby especially by such Marks of Dignity as Coronets" (Robinson 1983:88). But the Indians, by and large, did not need coronets to "heighten" their standing in their own eyes or those of their fellows. Theirs was a different symbolism with different foundations.

The Concert of the Middle Atlantic

Discussion of diplomacy in colonial North America is limited to the Iroquois and the Middle Atlantic because they have been the subject of the most detailed research. There are hints that equally complex diplomatic systems were functioning in other areas—in New England in the 1600s; in the Southwest, following the Pueblo Revolt of 1680; in the Southeast in the eighteenth century when the Creek Confederacy was forming and the Cherokees were gaining power. Information on these systems is still too meager and scattered for meaningful generalizations to be made.

In October 1758 more than 500 Indians gathered at Easton, Pennsylvania, for negotiations with officials of New Jersey and Pennsylvania. Represented there were all Six Nations of the Iroquois, western Delawares from the Ohio country, eastern Delawares from Pennsylvania, and various smaller groups whose protectorate status vis-à-vis the Iroquois varied from place to place and year to year. During the ceremony that opened negotiations, the Seneca leader Tagheshata stood up to speak for the Indians. Tagheshata "delivered his belts of invitation, which the nations had received to come to the conferences; and desired to see the belts sent by them in return, which the governor said should be given them: and after all ceremonies had passed, the council broke up for this day" (Burke 1760:192).

Here is a view of the Indian diplomatic tradition that centered on the wampum belt or covenant belt. Lafitau (1974–1977, 2:173–175) mentions some of the uses of the wampum belt, and he includes an illustration of a speaker in council, belt in hand (1974–1977, 2:facing p. 185). In this belt-centered negotiation at Easton, the delegates bargained together for 18 days; finally, through a complex balancing of ambitions and interests, they came to an agreement that affected the position of the French in the Ohio Valley, the relationship of the Western Indians to the French and to the Iroquois, and imperial British policy toward colonial expansion (Jennings 1985:54–55). What was happening at Easton was the management of international affairs by conference diplomacy, in which a concert of interested parties works out ways to re-establish a power balance that has been threatened.

In North America a consortium of powers, both great and small, functioned as a restraint on war and as a powerful organizing idea from 1677 to 1775. The participants called their diplomatic arrangements the Covenant Chain (Jennings 1984), but it could be called the Concert of the Middle Atlantic Powers—both Indian and European. (Burke 1760:191–203) makes clear just how this tradition functioned in negotiations. The belts that the Seneca leader Tagheshata displayed and called for were only the first of many that were displayed and exchanged. This was because the belts and the strings of beads or wampum that were also exchanged were an integral part of the negotiations. Without their being proffered and accepted, the agreements had no validity. Each arrangement that was made, each article of the treaty that was being worked out in diplomatic dialogue, had to be validated by such an exchange. This was the outward sign of the principle of reciprocity that underlay Indian diplomacy, and especially Iroquois diplomacy.

Here a distinction must be made between Covenant Chain relationships, which were confirmed and symbolized by wampum belts, and other diplomatic relationships that the Indians of the Northeast might enter into and confirm by a similar exchange of belts. The Covenant Chain was a unique set of diplomatic relationships. It embraced both Europeans and Indians, and it functioned in the specific locale of the Middle Atlantic in a specific time period from the late seventeenth to the late eighteenth century. It cannot be understood in the more general terms of chains and alliances that were used elsewhere, terms that diplomats of the new American nation later appropriated for their own purposes. The generalized use of the specific term Covenant Chain has for years obscured the nature and functioning of the concert of Indian and European powers that centered on the League of the Iroquois and the English in New York. Indeed, one of the many purposes of the 1758 council at Easton was the attempt by Pennsylvanians to make that colony, and not New York, the British center of the Covenant Chain.

What is important to note here is that the crises of the century of the Covenant Chain were dealt with by this unique concert of European and Indian powers functioning through almost continuous negotiations. The powers were held together by proximity and by dozens of formal and informal treaty arrangements, but, of equal importance, they were held together by the grudging realization that the interests of each could best be served by paying some attentions to the interests of all. This concert was destroyed when the American Revolution forced a new set of relationships on all the powers, both American and European. During its existence it was a working demonstration of what can be accomplished through carefully crafted treaty relationships in a contentious, multicultural setting.

Power in Relations

The rough equivalence of power between Indians and Europeans during the colonial period meant that a diplomatic system could be established that tied disparate, self-interested groups into a grid of extended interlocking relationships. The relationships were defined by treaties, and the treaties were a reflection of the leverage of each group during negotiations—a leverage based on power.

The treaties reflected more than power, of course. They can be read as repeated attempts to establish rules of behavior for the contacts of everyday life, as in 1701 when leaders of Pennsylvania and leaders of the Susquehannanock, Shawnee, and Conoy agreed that they would "at all times readily do justice, perform all acts and offices of friendship and goodwill to oblige Each other, to a lasting peace as aforesaid" (Kent 1979:101). The "acts and offices of friendship" were spelled out for situations that might be expected to arise including what each party was to do if it heard rumors of hostile intent. Treaties that dealt with such matters were conscious attempts to create out of the chaos of a warring "state of nature" a universe of intelligible discourse and predictable behavior, of rights and responsibilities. So they reflected values as well as power. It must be noted that power might well determine which group's values predominated in the treaty provisions.

In the second quarter of the eighteenth century the Delawares of Pennsylvania learned about power. No matter how they maneuvered, they could not regain the land they had lost in the Walking Purchase of 1737. They were operating from weakness in the negotiations that led up to their agreement that the Pennsylvanians might make the walk of a day and a half that was to determine the boundaries of the Delaware land cession (Kent 1979: 455–459). And when they protested the manner of the "walk" and tried to secure reparations, they were shut out of meaningful negotiations by the ambition and power of the Iroquois on the one hand and the Pennsylvanians on the other (Kent 1984:45–49). It was a lesson the Delawares never forgot, and it explains much of their later behavior.

Sometimes the power that was expressed in the treaties was not that of the participants but that of a rival for land, or trade, or amity. So in the mid-seventeenth century Swedish negotiations with neighboring Indians for confirmation of a land cession were primarily a reaction to the power of the neighboring Dutch (Kent 1979:27–28). And Spanish willingness in the mid-eighteenth century to depart from their usual practice and negotiate formal treaties with Southeast Indians such as the Choctaw (C. Parry 1969, 49:107-112) was a response to the power

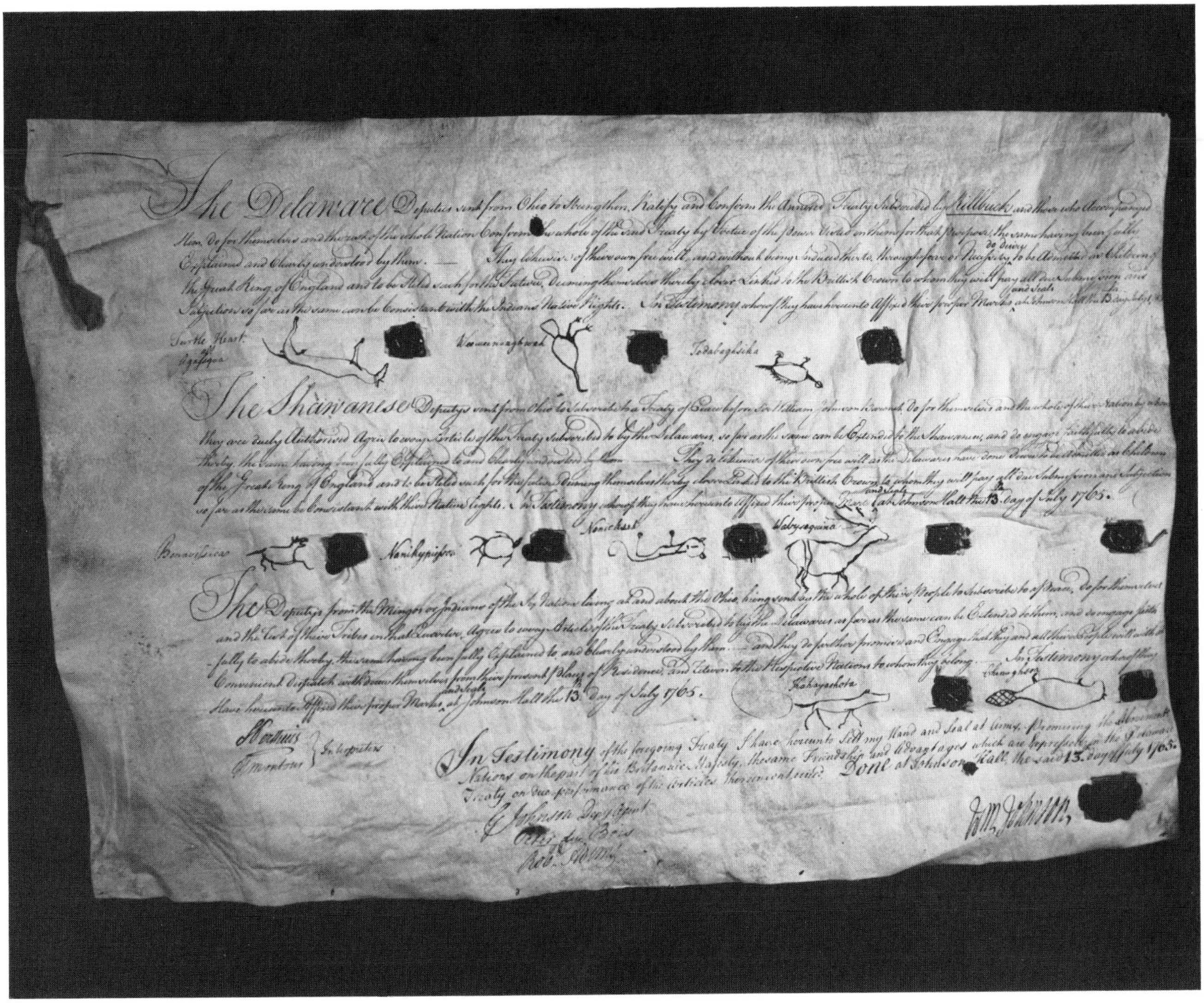

Fig. 1. Treaty between the Delaware, Shawnee, and Mingo (Ohio Valley Iroquois) and Great Britain, July 13, 1765. This treaty was annexed to another one signed by the Delaware on May 8, 1765, under the leadership of Killbuck. The terms of the July 13 treaty were peace, with an additional requirement for the Mingos to remove themselves from their current place of residence. Negotiations took place July 4–14 at Johnson Hall, the home of Superintendent of Indian Affairs William Johnson (Johnson 1921–1965, 4:783). top row of signatures, Delaware chiefs: Agassqua or Turtle Heart, Weeweenoaghwah, Tedabaghsika; second row: Shawnee chiefs Benavissica, Nanikypiessoh, Nanicksah, and Wabysequina; third row: Mingo chiefs Kahayashota and Chenughsoa. British representatives who signed were Deputy Agent Guy Johnson, Peter du Bois, Robert Adams, and William Johnson. Louis Perthuis and H. Montour were interpreters.

conferred on the Indians by the proximity of the new United States. This proximity gave the Creeks, the Cherokees, the Chickasaws, and Choctaws on the Spanish borders an alternative source of arms and alliance. Hence, negotiation became the order of the day.

Finally, power was reflected in another way. Policy makers at the highest level of, for example, the French or British governments, or the Iroquois or Powhatan confederacies, could formulate and proclaim policies. However, to be effective the policies had to be worked out on the ground, through diplomacy, with due regard to power relationships. It was a case of policy proposing, but diplomacy disposing. The Virginians might proclaim, as they did in 1614, that henceforth the Chickahominy

would be "Tassatasses or English men and be King JAMES his subjects" (Robinson 1983:17), but that did not become policy until it became mutual and the Chickahominy behaved as if it were true. The French might take advantage of a lull in their long hostility with the Iroquois to proclaim that the Iroquois were putting themselves under the protection of Louis XIV (Léonard 1693, 5, pt. 14:1-12), but the entire subsequent history of Iroquois-French relations belied the claim.

The crowning example was the British Proclamation of 1763, which forbade British settlement west of the Appalachians. In the transmontane country the various Indian groups held power, and it was to them that the British went to work out a boundary that would make the

Proclamation operative. Five years and 10 treaties later, a continuous boundary from upper New York to the Gulf separated the land and jurisdiction of the Indians from those of the British (Jones 1982:36–92).

What undid the results of this feat of diplomatic negotiation was power. The Iroquois had an inflated notion of their own control over the Shawnees and Delawares of the Ohio and other western Indians, and the British accepted Iroquois assertions. The western tribes decisively rejected the idea that the Iroquois could negotiate on their behalf. Putting negotiation aside, they went to war and brought down the treaty system of 1763–1768 that had excluded them from the exercise of their independent power. They were then caught up in the general return to a warring state that marked the Revolution. For the Indians east of the Mississippi, the warring state did not end until the mid-1790s when a new civil state was put together treaty by treaty. The new civil state was negotiated by Indians and by the Europeans who had become Americans. It reflected, as always, relationships of power, this time to the Indians' great disadvantage.

Conclusion

The focus here has been on the complexity of the process of treaty-making in colonial North America. Once this is understood, then lists of specific treaties and discussions of the significance of particular treaties can be placed against a background that provides theoretical context and a place in a larger conceptual scheme. It is clear that the ideas of European diplomacy that emerged in the late eighteenth century and that formed the conceptual apparatus of nineteenth-century scholars will not serve to illumine the treaties of colonial North America. A diffuse diplomacy, with agreements that were formal and informal, written and unwritten, requires a different analytical approach, yet one that relates the new to the old, the strange to the familiar.

The list of British treaties with North American Indians (compiled by George Chalou) given in table 1 suggests the complexity and extent of the treaty system that developed during the colonial period. The list does not pretend to be complete, because of widely scattered sources and the thick texture of negotiations woven by Europeans and American Indians. When it is also remembered that many treaties were never written down, although they were acted on by both parties, some idea can be gained of the richness and depth of the colonial treaty system and its multilateral, multicultural diplomacy.

Table 1. Indian Treaties with Britain and British Colonies

Date	Parties	Provisions	Sources
Autumn 1607	Powhatan Confederacy–Virginia	peace	Stith 1865:49
Spring 1608	Powhatan Confederacy–Virginia	friendship, peace	Smith 1986:160
Aug. 1608	Rappahannock–Virginia	peace	Stith 1865:72
Aug. 1608	Mannahock–Virginia	friendship	Stith 1865:72
Sept. 1608	Nansemond–Virginia	peace	Stith 1865:74
Apr. 5, 1614	Chickahominy–Virginia	friendship, alliance	Smith 1986:246-247
Apr. 10-15, 1614	Powhatan Confederacy–Virginia	friendship, allegiance	Smith 1986:248-250
Nov. 19, 1619	Powhatan Confederacy–Virginia	alliance	Kingsbury 1906-1935, 3:228
Apr. 2, 1621	Wampanoag–Plymouth	friendship, land cession	Thacher 1832:38
Apr. 1623	Powhatan Confederacy–Virginia	peace	Kingsbury 1906-1935, 4:75, 178, 221-222
Mar. 1634	Indians[a]–Maryland	land cession	Chalmers 1780:207
Nov. 1, 1634	Pequot–Massachusetts	land cession	Bradford 1901, 2:416
Winter 1634	Narragansett–Providence Plantations	land cession	Bartlett 1856-1865, 1:22-24
Spring 1636	Powhatan Confederacy–Virginia	boundary revision	Burke 1804, 3:53
Sept. 1, 1640	Mohegan–Connecticut	land cession	Royce 1899:616
Aug. 27, 1645	Narragansett, Niantic–New England Confederation	peace, captives	Bradford 1952:437-440
Aug. 9, 1646	Wampanoag–Providence Plantations	peace, land cession	Bartlett 1856-1865, 1:31-32
Oct. 1646	Powhatan Confederacy–Virginia	peace, land cession, return of captives	Hening 1969, 1:323-326
May 1650	Indians[a]–Maryland	land cession	Jenkins 1950: Maryland Council Books, 1:41-42

Date	Parties	Provisions	Sources
July 5, 1652	Susquehannock–Maryland	land cession	Bozman 1837, 2:450-451
May 15, 1658	Plymouth Indians–Plymouth Plantation	land cession	Jenkins 1950: Massachusetts Miscellaneous Collection
1664	Jersey Indians[a]–New Jersey	land cession	Craven 1964:38
Apr. 8, 1665	Narragansett–Massachusetts	land cession	Grant and Munro 1908–1910, 1: 791
Apr. 10, 1671	Wampanoag–Plymouth Plantation	allegiance, surrender of arms	MHSC 2d ser., vol. 6:198
Summer 1671	Sakonnet–Plymouth Plantation	allegiance	Hazard 1838-1853, 5:73-74
Sept. 29, 1671	Wampanoag–Plymouth Plantation	allegiance	MHSC 2d ser., vol. 6:193-197
1674	Seneca–Maryland	peace	Craven 1949:373
Mar. 10, 1675	Kiawah–South Carolina	land cession	Royce 1899:636
May 13, 1675	Delaware–New Jersey	peace	NYCD 12:523-524
July 15, 1675	Narragansett–Massachusetts	alliance	Leach 1958:61
Sept. 20, 1675	Susquehannock–Great Britain	land cession	NYCD 12:541
July 3, 1676	Eastern Indians[a]–United Colonies of New England	peace, friendship	Leach 1958:213
May 29, 1677	Pamunkey, Roanoke, Nottaway, Nansemond–Great Britain	peace, allegiance	DePuy 1917:1
July 17, 1677	Eastern Indians[a]– Massachusetts	peace	MHSC 2d ser., vol. 4:378
Aug. 1677	Westo, Cusabo–South Carolina	peace	
July 15, 1682	Delaware–Pennsylvania	land cession	Hazard et al. 1852-1949, 1:47-48
Feb. 28, 1683	Wimbee–South Carolina	land cession	Royce 1899, 2:631
June 23, 1683	Delaware–Pennsylvania	land cession	Hazard et al. 1852-1949, 1:62-65
June 25, 1683	Delaware–Pennsylvania	land cession	Hazard et al. 1852-1949, 1:65
July 14, 1683	Delaware–Pennsylvania	land cession	Hazard et al. 1852-1949, 1:65-66
July 14, 1683	Delaware–Pennsylvania	land cession	Hazard et al. 1852-1935, 1:66-67
Sept. 10, 1683	Delaware–Pennsylvania	land cession	Hazard et al. 1852-1949, 1:67
Oct. 18, 1683	Delaware–Pennsylvania	land cession	Hazard et al. 1852-1949, 1:67-68
Feb. 13, 1684	Cusabo–South Carolina	land cession	Royce 1899:631
June 3, 1684	Delaware–Pennsylvania	land cession	Hazard et al. 1852-1949, 1:88
June 7, 1684	Delaware–Pennsylvania	land cession	Hazard et al. 1852-1949, 1:91-91a
July 31-Aug. 5, 1684	Mohawk, Oneida, Onondaga, Cayuga–New York	land cession, allegiance	Wraxall 1915:10-13
Apr. 10, 1685	Five Nations–Maryland	friendship	Jenkins 1950:Maryland Council Books
July 30, 1685	Delaware–Pennsylvania	land cession	Hazard et al. 1852-1949, 1:92-93
Oct. 2, 1685	Delaware–Pennsylvania	land cession	Hazard et al. 1852-1949, 1:95-96
June 6, 1687	Five Nations–New York	alliance	Jenkins 1950:Penn Manuscripts
Aug. 6, 1687	Five Nations–New York	alliance	Wraxall 1915:13-14
Feb. 25, 1689	Five Nations–New York	alliance, allegiance	NYHSC 1869:165-172
Feb. 3, 1689	Five Nations–New York	alliance, allegiance	Wraxall 1915:14-16
Nov. 29, 1690	Eastern Indians[a]– Massachusetts	peace	Maine Historical Society, 2d ser., Vol. 5:164-166
May 1, 1691	Five Nations–New York	peace, delivery of captives	Maine Historical Society, 2d ser., Vol. 5: 233-235
June 2-4, 1691	Five Nations–New York	alliance	Wraxall 1915:16-17
June 15, 1692	Delaware–Pennsylvania	land cession	Hazard et al. 1852-1949, 1:116-117
July 3-4, 1693	Five Nations–New York	peace	NYCD 4:40-43
Aug. 22, 1694	Five Nations–New York, New Jersey, Connecticut, Massachusetts, Pennsylvania	peace	Jenkins 1950: Penn Manuscripts
Oct. 2, 1696	Five Nations–New York	peace, alliance	NYCD 4:235-241
July 5, 1697	Delaware–Pennsylvania	land cession	Hazard et al. 1852-1949, 1:124-125
July 20-22, 1698	Five Nations–New York	peace	Wraxall 1915:28-30
Nov. 23, 1699	Bear River Indians–North Carolina	land cession	
Aug. 31, 1700	Five Nations–New York	friendship, religion, trade	NYCD 4:727-740
Sept. 13, 1700	Susquehannock–Pennsylvania	land cession	Hazard et al. 1852-1949, 1:133

Date	Parties	Provisions	Sources
Apr. 23, 1701	Susquehannock, Potomac, Shawnee, Onondaga– Pennsylvania	friendship, alliance, trade, land cession	Hazard 1838-1853, 2:14-18
July 19, 1701	Five Nations–Great Britain	land cession, alliance	NYCD 4:908-911
Aug. 1705	Creek–South Carolina	alliance, allegiance	Crane 1928:82-83
June 7, 1706	Conestoga, Potomac, Shawnee–Pennsylvania	trade regulation, friendship	Hazard 1838-1853, 2:253-255
Sept. 29, 1706	Five Nations–New York	alliance	Wraxall 1915:48
July 16, 1709	Five Nations–New York	alliance	Wraxall 1915:69
July 4-10, 1710	Five Nations, Ottawa–New York	alliance	Wraxall 1915:70-74
July 31, 1710	Five Nations, Shawnee, Delaware–Pennsylvania	peace, land	Jenkins 1950: Penn Manuscripts
Aug. 22, 1710	Mohawk–New York	land cession	Wraxall 1915:78-79
May 19, 1712	Delaware–Pennsylvania	friendship	Hazard 1838-1853, 2:571-574
June 8, 1713	Tuscarora–North Carolina	peace	
Jan. 16, 1714	Abenaki–Massachusetts	peace	Winsor 1884-1889, 5:424-425
July 23-28, 1714	Abenaki–Massachusetts	peace	Winsor 1884-1889, 5:424
Sept. 20-27, 1714	Five Nations–New York	peace, friendship	Wraxall 1915:99-100
Feb. 11, 1715	Coree–North Carolina	peace, land cession	Saunders and Clark 1886-1907, 2:168
June 22, 1715	Susquehannock–Pennsylvania	friendship, trade	Hazard 1838-1853, 2:632-633
July 30, 1715	Delaware, Shawnee, Conestoga, Potomac– Pennsylvania	peace	Hazard 1838-1853, 3:12-15
Nov. 15, 1717	Creek–South Carolina	peace	
June 16, 1718	Shawnee, Conestoga, Delaware–Pennsylvania	friendship	Hazard 1838-1853, 3:45-49
Sept. 17, 1718	Delaware–Pennsylvania	land cession	Hazard 1838-1853, 3:318-326
Summer 1721	Cherokee–South Carolina	land cession	Royce 1887:130, 144
Sept. 1721	Five Nations–New York	friendship	Colden 1918:128-134
Aug. 20-Sept. 12, 1722	Five Nations–New York, Virginia, Pennsylvania	peace, boundary settlement	U.S. National Archives 1966: Microcopy 668, roll 1
Sept. 1723	Six Nations–Massachusetts	alliance	Wraxall 1915:148-149
Dec. 15, 1725	Eastern Indians[a]– Massachusetts	peace	Winsor 1884-1889, 5:432
Sept. 14, 1726	Seneca, Cayuga, Onondaga–Great Britain	land cession	NYCD 5:800-801
Apr. 1, 1727	Mattamuskeet–North Carolina	land cession	Saunders and Clark 1886-1907, 3:128-133
July 11, 1727	Eastern Indians[a]– Massachusetts	peace	Winsor 1884-1889, 5:432
Aug. 4, 1727	Eastern Indians[a]– Massachusetts, New York	peace, alliance	Wraxall 1915:171
May 26-27, 1728	Delaware, Shawnee, Conestoga, Potomac– Pennsylvania	peace, friendship	Hazard 1838-1853, 3:310-314
Oct. 1-5, 1728	Six Nations–New York	land cession, alliance	Wraxall 1915:172-175
Sept. 9, 1730	Cherokee–Great Britain	allegiance, return of slaves, peace	Saunders and Clark 1886-1907, 3:128-133
Aug. 31-Sept. 2, 1732	Six Nations–Pennsylvania	friendship	Hazard 1838-1853, 3:447-452
Sept. 7, 1732	Delaware–Pennsylvania	land cession	Hazard et al. 1852-1949, 1:344-347
May 21, 1733	Lower Creek, Yuchi, Yamacraw–Georgia	land cession, amity, trade	C.C. Jones 1883, 1:137-144
June 11, 1735	Creek–Georgia	boundary settlement, alliance	Moore 1840:145-146
Aug. 1, 1735	Caughnawaga Mohawk, Western Abenaki, Housatonic, Scaghticoke, Mohegan–New York	commerce, amity	Wraxall 1915:193
Aug. 27, 1735	Iroquois of Canada– Massachusetts	peace	DePuy 1917:15
Oct. 11, 1736	Seneca, Oneida, Onondaga, Cayuga, Tuscarora– Pennsylvania	friendship, land cession	Hazard et al. 1852-1949, 1:494-498

Date	Parties	Provisions	Sources
Aug. 25, 1737	Delaware–Pennsylvania	land cession confirmation	Jenkins 1950: Pennsylvania, Penn Manuscripts
June 28-July 6, 1738	Penobscot, Norridgewock–Massachusetts	friendship	Winsor 1884-1889, 5:434
Aug. 1, 1739	Shawnee–Pennsylvania	friendship, land cession confirmation	Hazard 1838-1853, 4:345-347
Aug. 21, 1739	Creek–Georgia	land cession, alliance	Candler 1904-1916, 26:485-489
Aug. 1, 6, 1740	Delaware, Mingo–Pennsylvania	peace, friendship, trade regulation	Hazard 1838-1853, 4:432-434, 443-447
Aug. 16-19, 1740	Six Nations–Great Britain	peace, covenant with southern Indians	Wraxall 1915:218-220
May 14, 1741	Seneca–New York	land cession	Wraxall 1915:218-222
June 15-18, 1742	Six Nations–New York	friendship, land cession	Wraxall 1915:226-228
July 2-12, 1742	Six Nations, Shawnee, Delaware, Nanticoke–Maryland, Pennsylvania	land cession, removal of squatters, trade	Van Doren and Boyd 1938:15-34
Aug. 4, 1742	Penobscot, Norridgewock, Pigwacket, Maliseet, St. Francis, Passamaquoddy–Massachusetts	trade problems	DePuy 1917:20
Aug. 1743	Six Nations–Virginia	peace, friendship	Wraxall 1915:231
June 18-20, 1744	Six Nations–New York, Connecticut, Massachusetts	friendship, alliance	Wraxall 1915:233-235
June 22-July 4, 1744	Six Nations–Pennsylvania, Virginia, Maryland	land cession, boundary revision	Van Doren and Boyd 1938:41-79
Oct. 1745	Six Nations–New York, Massachusetts, Connecticut, Pennsylvania	friendship	DePuy 1917:24
Aug. 19-23, 1746	Six Nations, Mississauga–New York, Massachusetts	alliance	Wraxall 1915:247-248
Nov. 13, 16, 1747	Shawnee, Six Nations, Miami–Pennsylvania	alliance	Hazard 1838-1853, 5:145-147, 149-152
July 1748	Six Nations, Miami, Shawnee–Pennsylvania	alliance	DePuy 1917:27
July 23-26, 1748	Six Nations–New York, Massachusetts	friendship	Wraxall 1915:249
Aug. 22, 1749	Six Nations, Delaware, Shomokin–Pennsylvania	land cession	Hazard et al. 1852-1949, 2:33-37
Sept. 1749	Cherokee, Creek–South Carolina	trade regulation	Corkran 1967:151
Sept. 27, 1749	Penobscot, Norridgewock–Massachusetts	peace, return of prisoners	Maine Historical Society 2d ser., Vol. 4:145
July 1, 1751	Six Nations, Catawba–New York, Pennsylvania, Connecticut	peace, union	Wraxall 1915:250-251
Nov. 29, 1751	Cherokee–South Carolina	trade regulation	Corkran 1962:33-34
June 13, 1752	Six Nations–Virginia, Pennsylvania	friendship	Winsor 1884-1889, 5:570
Oct. 13, 1752	Eastern Indians[a]–Massachusetts	peace	Winsor 1884-1889, 5:450
Sept. 21, 1753	Penobscot–Massachusetts	return of captives	Winsor 1884-1889, 5:450
Sept. 29, 1753	Norridgewock–Massachusetts	return of captives	Winsor 1884-1889, 5:450
July 2, 1754	Norridgewock–Massachusetts	peace	Winsor 1884-1889, 5:450
July 5, 1754	Penobscot–Massachusetts	peace	Winsor 1884-1889, 5:450
July 11, 1754	Six Nations–Pennsylvania	land cession	Hazard et al. 1852-1949, 2:147-158
Aug. 29, 1754	Catawba–North Carolina	friendship, land cession	Saunders and Clark 1886-1907, 5:141-144b
Dec. 17, 1754	Six Nations–Great Britain	land cession	
Nov. 24, 1755	Cherokee–Great Britain	land cession	Royce 1887:130, 145
Dec. 1755	Creek–Georgia	friendship	C.C. Jones 1883, 1:502
Jan. 1756	Creek–South Carolina	trade regulation, fort location	Corkran 1967:172
Jan. 8-9, 1756	Delaware groups–New Jersey	trade restrictions	DePuy 1917:35
Feb. 21, 1756	Catawba–Virginia	alliance, fort construction	Stanard 1906:237-244
Mar. 17, 1756	Cherokee–Virginia	alliance, Indian education	Stanard 1906:245-262

193

JONESJONES

Date	Parties	Provisions	Sources
July 1756	Delaware, Shawnee–Great Britain	peace	DePuy 1917:38
Apr. 1-May 22, 1757	Six Nations, Delaware, Nanticoke, Susquehannock–Pennsylvania	alliance	Van Doren and Boyd 1938:167-187
Apr. 1757	Mahican, Shawnee, Nanticoke–Great Britain	friendship	DePuy 1917:41
Aug. 7, 1757	Six Nations, Delaware, Shawnee, Nanticoke, Mahican–Great Britain	peace	DePuy 1917:42
Nov. 3, 1757	Creek–Georgia	land cession, friendship, peace	Candler 1904-1913, 7:665-670
Apr. 22, 1758	Creek–Great Britain	land settlement	Corkran 1967:191
May 1, 1758	Creek–Great Britain	land cession	Corkran 1967:191
Aug. 7-8, 1758	Minisink–New Jersey	peace	DePuy 1917:43
Oct. 1758	Six Nations, Delaware, Mahican, Nanticoke, Minisink–New Jersey, Pennsylvania	peace, land cession	New Jersey State Archives, 1880-1949, 9:139-142
Dec. 21-28, 1759	Cherokee–North Carolina	peace, resumption of trade	
Aug. 12, 1760	Six Nations–Great Britain	friendship	U.S. National Archives 1966: Microcopy 668, roll 1
Aug. 3-12, 1761	Mahican, Tutelo, Nanticoke, Delaware, Conoy, Oneida, Onondaga, Cayuga–Pennsylvania	return of prisoners, land questions	DePuy 1917:46
Dec. 17, 1761	Cherokee–Great Britain	peace, boundary line, return of prisoners	Peckham 1964:204-205
Aug. 11-28, 1762	Delaware, Shawnee, Miami, Conoy, Kickapoo, Six Nations–Pennsylvania	land questions, return of captives	DePuy 1917:47
Nov. 5, 1763	Cherokee, Creek, Choctaw, Chickasaw–Great Britain	boundary definition, peace, land cession	Royce 1899:637
Apr. 3, 1764	Seneca–Great Britain	peace, land cession	NYCD, 7:621-623
July 18, 1764	Huron–Great Britain	peace, alliance	NYCD, 7:650-651
Mar. 26, 1765	Choctaw, Chickasaw–Great Britain	boundary question, land cession	United States 1828-1836, 2:275
May 8, 1765	Delaware–Great Britain	peace	NYCD, 7:738-741
May 28, 1765	Creek–Great Britain	boundary lines	United States 1828-1836, 2:276
July 13, 1765	Shawnee, Mingo–Great Britain	peace	NYCD, 7:754-755
Nov. 18, 1765	Creek–Great Britain	boundary lines	United States 1828-1836, 2:276
July 23-31, 1766	Ottawa, Potawatomi, Ojibwa, Six Nations, Huron–Great Britain	peace	NYCD, 7:854-867
June 2, 1767	Cherokee–Great Britain	boundary lines	Saunders and Clark 1886-1907, 7:462-466
June 5, 1767	Creek–Great Britain	trade regulations	Corkran 1967:259-262
June 22, 1768	Nanticoke–Maryland	land cession	Royce 1899:575
Oct. 14, 1768	Cherokee–Great Britain	land cession	Stanard 1906a:20-23
Nov. 5, 1768	Six Nations–Great Britain	land cession, boundary	U.S. National Archives 1966: Microcopy 668, roll 1
Oct. 18, 1770	Cherokee–Great Britain	land cession	Stanard 1902:360–364
June 3, 1773	Creek, Cherokee–Great Britain	land cession	J. Wright 1873:158
Oct. 2, 1774	Creek–Georgia	peace, friendship, commerce	Force 1837-1853, 1:1138-1139
June 29-July 6, 1775	Six Nations of Ohio, Shawnee, Delaware–Virginia	peace, return of hostages, hunting boundaries	Stanard 1906b:54-78

[a] Band or tribal affiliation not specified in primary or secondary source.

United States Indian Treaties and Agreements

ROBERT M. KVASNICKA

The government of the United States followed the custom established by Great Britain and the colonial governments of negotiating agreements with the Indian tribes (J.H. Martin 1949:1). The term treaty was applied only to formal written documents signed by both parties and not to verbal agreements (Lindquist 1948:421). Some 370 treaties with Indian tribes were formally ratified or perfected and passed into law before the making of treaties with Indians was terminated in 1871. These treaties had the same status, force, and dignity as treaties with sovereign nations (J.H. Martin 1949:1–2).

The treaties were complex instruments that implemented the prevailing Indian policy of the federal government. The most important purpose of many of the treaties came to be the extinguishment of Indian title to land, but secondary considerations were the regulation of commerce with the tribes and the education and acculturation of the Indians to facilitate their assimilation into White society.

Treaties defined the status of tribes as dependent nations and the extent of federal control over tribal affairs and outlined jurisdiction over criminal and civil matters. Some treaty provisions detailed payments for land cessions and improvements by lump sum payments, periodic payments or annuities (fig. 1), or payments in services or commodities; others provided for the allotment of land to individual Indians and the dissolution of tribes. Treaties regulated trade and provided for claims of and against Indians. Some authorized rights-of-way across Indian lands, and others called for the establishment of schools and mills and the employment of teachers and skilled workers such as millers, farmers, and blacksmiths. Many treaties called for the end of hostilities and the maintenance of peace. A few treaties guaranteed tribes hunting and fishing rights in ceded lands (U.S. National Archives 1972:40).

It is estimated that 96 of the ratified treaties dealt in part with the establishment or reaffirmation of peace and the recognition of allegiance to the United States. Two hundred and thirty of the treaties concerned land cessions or related land matters; 76 of these called for Indian removal and settlement in the West. Fifteen treaties established "perpetual annuities," and 19 provided for payment of debts (Lindquist 1948:443–445).

Treaties could be modified by mutual consent of the parties and by subsequent federal statutes. A treaty also could be amended or abrogated by later treaties with the same tribe, a rather common occurrence as some tribes were party to numerous treaties (Lindquist 1948:443; Schmeckebier 1927:59).

The Indians viewed the treaties as a means of preserving themselves as a people (Deloria and Lytle 1984:8) and sought from the federal government a recognition of "their exclusive right to the use and occupancy of a well defined area," and a commitment "to defend and protect their rights within that area from non-Indian encroachment (American Indian Policy Review Commission 1977, 1:145). After the treaty period ended, most tribes came to regard their treaties as sacred pledges on the part of the United States (Deloria and Lytle 1984:8). Succeeding generations of Indians invested the treaties with the moral and symbolic significance accorded other American charters of freedom such as the Declaration of Independence and the Constitution (American Indian Policy Review Commission 1977, 1:111). The federal government's persistence in viewing the treaties strictly as legal documents subject to change and abrogation became a matter of serious contention.

In 1972, when militant Indian leaders organized the Trail of Broken Treaties, nearly 1,000 Indians converged on Washington, D.C., to present to the federal government a 20-point proposal (fig. 2). The first point called for a restoration of the treaty-making authority, and several other points were treaty related. According to the Constitution, Congress has power to regulate commerce with Indians. The federal government rejected the proposals on the grounds that the citizenship conferred on all Indians by the Indian Citizenship Act of 1924 precluded Indians from entering into new treaties with the government (Deloria 1974:xi–xiii).

Historical Survey

The eight treaties concluded during the period of the Confederation, 1778–1789, were recognized by the Constitution (Cohen 1942:33–34) and are included in the official file of ratified Indian treaties. Those that were negotiated during the Revolution emphasized amity and

Fig. 1. Annuity payment to a band of Southwestern Chippewa Indians in Wis., about 1871. The White man at far right is Richard Bardon, acting school teacher and farmer in Superior, Wis. Photograph by Charles A. Zimmerman.

alliance. After the war, treaties extended the protection of the United States to the tribes and ended hostilities with those who had supported Great Britain. Development of a national policy on Indian affairs was hampered by some of the states, who independently negotiated with tribes within their borders (Schmeckebier 1927:16). The Constitution, adopted in 1789, eliminated this division of authority between the central government and the states by vesting the president with the power to make treaties with the advice and consent of the Senate (Article II, Section 2) and by restricting to the Senate the power to regulate commerce with the Indian tribes (Article I, Section 8).

The early postwar treaties were based on the premise that tribal lands belonged to the United States by right of conquest, but in 1788 the decision was made to reimburse the tribes for land cessions. Rapid growth of the White population prompted a series of treaties from 1800 to 1817 extinguishing native title to tribal lands in return for payment of annuities and restricting the Indians to progressively smaller reserves (fig. 3) (Cohen 1942:51). The purchase of Louisiana Territory brought more tribes under United States jurisdiction, but the new territory also offered a solution to the land problem in the states

and in the Old Northwest Territory. In 1804 Congress gave the president authority to grant lands west of the Mississippi River to Eastern tribes in exchange for cessions of their lands east of the river (2 U.S. Stat. 289) (Schmeckebier 1927:26), an option that was not exercised until 1817.

Many Indian tribes defected to the British during the War of 1812, and 20 peace treaties were concluded with the Indians in the two years following its conclusion (Cohen 1942:53). When the Eastern tribes became increasingly reluctant to cede their lands to accommodate the westward surge of Whites after the war, the United States initiated the exchange policy authorized in 1804. The first such treaty, concluded with the Cherokee on July 8, 1817 (7 U.S. Stat. 156), called for the tribe's voluntary removal to a tract of western land proportionate to their cession of eastern land (Cohen 1942:53). Between 1817 and 1843, approximately 170 treaties were negotiated. About 1825 the Plains tribes entered into a series of treaties relating solely to problems of trade and friendship. Other tribes agreed to treaties designed to extinguish tribal land titles (Cohen 1942:61–62). Most treaties made during the years 1817 to 1849 were concerned with the removal of certain tribes to vacant western lands (Cohen 1942:54). As

196

KVASNICKA

UPI/Bettmann Newsphotos, New York City: 1755852.
Fig. 2. Participants in the Trail of Broken Treaties, Nov. 2, 1972, occupying an auditorium at the Bureau of Indian Affairs in Washington, D.C. (See "Indian Rights Movement, 1887–1973," this vol.) The inverted United States flag was the controversial symbol adopted by the American Indian Movement (Matthiessen 1983:36–37). Photograph cropped.

early as 1832, tribes who had removed to Missouri from Illinois and Indiana were agreeing to move still farther west.

The United States acquired Texas by annexation in 1845, the Oregon Country by diplomacy in 1846, and California and most of the Southwest by conquest in 1848. While new treaties continued to be negotiated with tribes in established territories, treaty relations were extended to the tribes in newly acquired areas. In 1846 and 1849 peace treaties were signed with two bands of Ute and in 1849 with the Navajo. Treaties were made with the California tribes in 1851–1852. During the period 1849 to 1853 eight treaties providing for territorial cessions and 10 removal treaties were signed with tribes of the Northeast and the Plains (Cohen 1942:62–63).

The first treaties with Indians in Oregon Territory were negotiated in 1853 although several thousand Whites had settled in the region during the 1840s. Between 1853 and 1857, approximately 60 treaties were concluded, many of which called for the allotment of tribal lands and the opening of surplus lands to White settlement (see Trafzer 1986). The policy of perpetual annuity payments was discarded in favor of fixed sums distributed over a stipulated period of time (Cohen 1942:63).

During the Civil War, 1860–1865, treaties were concluded with several tribes in the West. Treaties also were made with various bands of Chippewa in Minnesota providing for their consolidation on large reservations and the allotment of their land in severalty. Officials of the Confederate States of America negotiated nine treaties of peace and alliance with Plains and Southeast tribes. Following the collapse of the South, the Five Civilized Tribes, who had been semi-autonomous, were penalized for their defection; treaties marking their reconciliation with the United States called for extensive land cessions, the abolition of slavery by the Indians, the extension of civil and property rights to their former slaves or freedmen, and more federal control over the tribes' affairs (Cohen 1942:65).

Warfare with the nomadic Indians of the High Plains resulted in a number of peace treaties signed between 1865 and 1868 that assigned the tribes to reservations. The final ratified treaty concluded with the Nez Perce on August 13, 1868 (15 U.S. Stat. 693), provided for the allotment of their reservation (Cohen 1942:66).

In 1862 Secretary of the Interior Caleb B. Smith questioned the government policy of treating with the Indians as quasi-independent nations and recommended instead that they be treated as wards of the government (Cohen 1942:16). In 1869, Commissioner of Indian Affairs Ely S. Parker, himself a Seneca, urged that the treaty system be abandoned as it fostered unrealistic ideas of nationalism among the tribes. He argued that the tribes could not be considered sovereign nations on an equal basis with the United States as implied by the treaty system because they did not have organizations capable of enforcing compliance with their treaty obligations (Cohen 1942:17–18). This philosophical change, when combined with the House of Representatives' growing dissatisfaction at being excluded from the management of Indian affairs, culminated in the Act of March 3, 1871 (16 U.S. Stat. 544, 566), forbidding further recognition of Indian tribes as nations or independent powers and prohibiting the negotiation of treaties with them. The act did not abrogate existing treaties (Cohen 1942:66).

Negotiations with the Indians did not cease with the termination of the treaty-making power. The reduction of the reservations, largely achieved by negotiations, came after 1871; in the early 1900s negotiations were entered into with some tribes to commute perpetual annuities established by treaties. The documents recording these transactions were commonly called agreements, and they generally became law when ratified by both the Senate and the House of Representatives. Like the treaties, agreements are subject to modification by legislation, but rights created by carrying the agreements into effect may not be impaired (Cohen 1942:67; Schmeckebier 1927:64–65).

One of the chief defects of the treaty system was the federal government's inability, sometimes unwillingness, to enforce the treaties. The government failed to fulfill the terms of many treaties and to protect the treaty rights of the Indians (Cohen 1942:36).

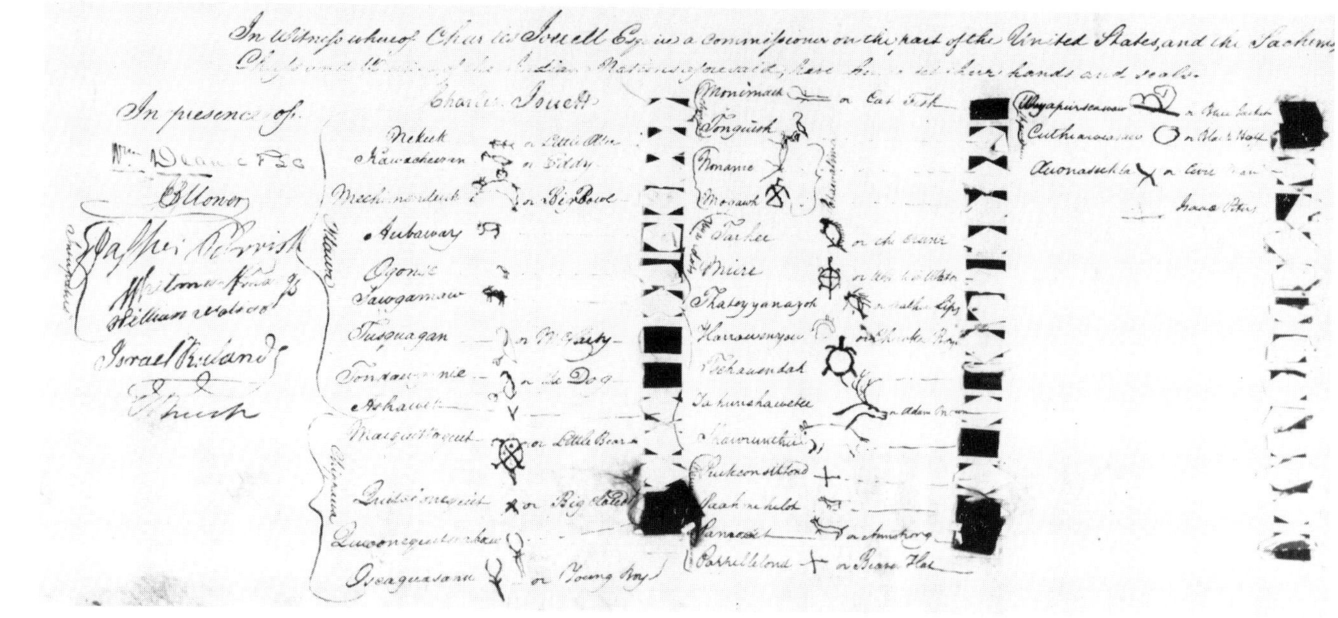
In Witness whereof Charles Jouett Esq. as a commissioner on the part of the United States, and the Sachems

In presence of

Charles Jouett

Natl. Arch.: RG 11, Indian Treaty No. 45.

Fig. 3. Signature page of treaty agreement between the U.S. and the Wyandot, Ottawa, Chippewa, Munsee, Delaware, Shawnee, and Potawatomi Indians at Ft. Industry (Toledo), July 4, 1805. One of 2 documents signed by these tribes on this date, the treaty guaranteed an annuity to be paid in part by the U.S. and in part with money held in trust by the U.S. from the Conn. Land Company and " 'the proprietors of the half million acres of land lying south of lake Erie, called Sufferer's land' " (Kappler 1904–1941, 2:77–78). The treaty, which extended an earlier cession of land claimed at Greenville in 1795 (vol.15:401), became law (7 U.S. Stat. 87). The Indians signed with pictographs placed to the right of their names. first column: witnesses' and interpreters' signatures, William Dean, C.F.L.C.; J.B. Mower; Jasper Parrish; Whitmore Knaggs; William Walker; Israel Ruland; E. Brush. second column: U.S. treaty commissioner, Charles Jouett; Ottawa leaders, Nekick or Little Otter, Kawachewan or Eddy, Mechimenduch or Big Bowl, Aubaway, Ogonse, Sawgamaw, Tusquagan or McCarty, Tondawganie or the Dog, and Ashawet; Chippewa leaders, Macquettoquet or Little Bear, Quitchonequit or Big Cloud, Queoonequetwabaw, Oscaguasanu or Young Boy. third column: Chippewa leaders, Monimack or Cat Fish, Tonguish; Potawatomi leaders, Noname, Mogawh; Wyandot leaders, Tarhee or the Crane, Miere or Walk in Water, Thateyyanayoh or Leather Lips, Harrowenyou or Cherokee Boy, Tschauendah, Tahunehawetee or Adam Brown, Shawrunthie; Munsee and Delaware leaders, Puckconsittond, Paahmehelot, Pamoxet or Armstrong, Pappellelond or Beaver Hat. fourth column: Shawnee leaders, Weyapurscawaw or Blue Jacket, Cutheawcasaw or Black Hoff, Auonaseckla or Civil Man, and Isaac Peters.

The Treaty-Making Process

From 1789 to 1849 responsibility for supervising the negotiation of treaties with the Indians rested with the secretary of war. In 1849 the Office of Indian Affairs was transferred from the War Department to the new Department of the Interior. Actual negotiations were carried out by special commissioners acting for the president, some 200 of whom were appointed during the period 1801–1868 (U.S. National Archives 1972:40; J.H. Martin 1949: 167–174). Upon occasion, the secretary of war or the commissioner of Indian affairs engaged in the negotiations, but usually the commissioners were officials of the Office of Indian Affairs such as superintendents or agents, or other men familiar with the tribes (fig. 4).

Treaty councils held in the field were often festive events marked by much ceremony and considerable oratory on both sides (fig. 5). Sometimes hundreds of Indians gathered and games and feasts were held. The commissioners nearly always distributed food and gifts, and whiskey frequently facilitated negotiations. Often flags and highly prized presidential medals called peace medals were presented to the most important members of the tribe as symbols of their allegiance to the United States ("Presents and Delegations," this vol.).

To impress the tribes with White society's strength the federal government brought many Indian delegations to the District of Columbia for treaty conferences with the commissioner of Indian affairs. The Indians toured the city, attended social functions, and met government officials; some even had interviews with the president. The delegates usually were outfitted with suits of clothes and presented with other gifts. Members of early delegations sat for portraits before they left Washington; later delegations posed for photographers (Viola 1981; J.R. Glenn 1981, 1983; Scherer 1982:148–183; Fleming and Luskey 1986:230–232).

Since few Indians spoke or understood the English language, interpreters were essential to virtually all negotiations. If they were incompetent, misunderstandings and dissatisfaction could result (Schmeckebier 1927: 59). The terms of the treaties were written as simply as possible, and questionable clauses were interpreted as the Indians would have understood them. Technical ambiguities in the treaties also were resolved in the Indians' favor (Cohen 1942:37).

Many of the commissioners were careful not to take

Fig. 4. Canoe bearing treaty commissioner Gov. Lewis Cass, Mich. Terr., and other treaty party members from Fond du Lac, the American Fur Company post at the western end of Lake Superior. While treaty proceedings were held there between the U.S. government and Chippewa Indians, July–Aug. 1826, Cass ordered the canoe made for himself. Chippewa Indians performed all the labor on the 10.97 m by 1.5 m canoe. The red, green, and white paint was probably applied later at Saulte Ste. Marie, Mich. Terr. A bust of an Indian "chief," smoking a pipe, adorned each side of the bow; the rim was striped green, red, and white; and the name *Fond Du Lac* was written on the sides. The awning border was also red, green, and white. A flag was positioned in the stern and a large wooden pipe rested in the bow (McKenney 1827:319–320, 382–383). U.S. superintendent of Indian affairs and a commissioner at the treaty proceedings Thomas McKenney (1827; Viola 1974) gives an informative account of the travels to and preparations for the council and of the proceedings themselves. Watercolor on paper by James Otto Lewis.

advantage of the Indians, but some perpetrated fraud, and others used duress to obtain the Indians' signatures (Schmeckebier 1927:59–61). The lack of tribal organization and unity also created problems for Indians and the government. For purposes of negotiations, commissioners often created "treaty chiefs" whose actions were denounced later by their tribes. Some treaties were negotiated with only a faction of a tribe, one of the most notable being the Treaty of New Echota, signed in 1835 by a group of Cherokees favoring removal (7 U.S. Stat. 478). When the main body of the Cherokee refused to recognize the treaty, they were forcibly transported to the Indian Territory with tragic results.

The government often found that lands ceded by one tribe were claimed by other tribes as well. Consequently, several treaties sometimes were necessary to extinguish Indian claims to a given cession. Misunderstandings also arose over ill-defined land boundaries.

The treaties were signed by the commissioners and the Indian leaders, most of whom made their marks beside their names, and were witnessed by the interpreters and other council participants (fig. 6). When completed the treaties were forwarded through channels to the president, who submitted them to the Senate for approval, an action that in some cases was delayed for years. If major changes were made by the Senate, the amendments were returned to the Indians for their consent. After ratification was completed, the treaties were signed or proclaimed by the president and sent to the State Department for inclusion in the official "Indian Treaty File." The ratified treaties were considered law, and they were published in *U.S. Statutes at Large*.

Although many treaties were rejected by the Senate some of these unratified or rejected treaties took legal effect. The Senate refused to ratify the treaties concluded with the Indians in California; nevertheless, the land cessions authorized by the treaties were recognized. The Court of Claims ruled that the president's signature on a treaty was not essential to its validity by recognizing the legality of the 1851 treaty concluded at Fort Laramie, Dakota Territory, with the Sioux and other tribes, which was ratified but never formally submitted to the president for proclamation (45 C. Cls. 177, 1910).

After 1871, the texts of the agreements were submitted to the Congress in the form of bills, which when approved were enacted into laws (J.H. Martin 1949a:1). Most ratified agreements were published in the annual appropriation acts for the Office of Indian Affairs, but others were printed as separate laws (Schmeckebier 1927:64–65). Some agreements took legal effect without being ratified, since legislation authorizing their negotiation stated they would become effective without further action by Congress. The 1889 agreements with the Chippewas in Minnesota, for example, took effect when approved by the president (25 U.S. Stat. 642).

Sources

The Indian treaties are preserved in the National Archives, Washington, D.C. The State Department filed the original treaties chronologically by the dates they were signed and numbered them in that order. This Indian Treaty File consists of the ratified treaties, 1778–1869, with related papers; copies of seven colonial treaties, 1722–1768; two unnumbered treaties for which the approval and ratification were not completed; and eight unperfected treaties, 1854–1855. The related records usually consist of presidential proclamations, resolutions of approval by the Senate, and printed copies of the treaties. Occasionally there are copies of messages from the president of the Senate, messages or letters of instruction to the treaty commissioners, journals, and related correspondence. A few of the treaties are missing.

The Office of Indian Affairs maintained a separate file of records documenting the negotiation of most ratified treaties, 1801–1868, and unratified treaties, 1821–1869. Included in this file are journals of treaty commissioners, proceedings of councils, reports, and correspondence. The ratified treaty records are arranged numerically by the treaty numbers assigned by the State Department; the unratified treaty files are arranged chronologically by date of signing. Additional documentation on Indian treaties, their negotiation and ratification, is found among the correspondence of the Bureau of Indian Affairs (U.S. National Archives, Record Group 75), and in records of

Fig. 5. Nez Perce Indians in review before the tribe's leaders and U.S. commissioners prior to a treaty conference, May 24, 1855. center, right, Isaac I. Stevens, governor and superintendent of Indian affairs for Wash. Terr., and Joel Palmer, superintendent of Indian affairs for Oreg. Terr., head a group of U.S. representatives. center, left, William Craig, a White interpreter married to a daughter of a Nez Perce headman, stands at the head of a group of Nez Perce leaders including Utsinmalikin, Metat Waptass, Joseph, Lawyer, Old James, and Red Wolf. The parade, followed by equestrian exhibitions and a war dance, was more than a salute; it was a way for the Nez Perce to denote themselves as a powerful people. Palmer and Stevens were each legally responsible only for those Indians who lived within their separate jurisdictions. Stevens was determined to conclude treaties with most of the Indian groups in Wash. Terr. in order to clear the way for a northern route for the Pacific Railroad, for which he supervised a survey, and to free lands for White settlement. This treaty council was arranged to secure treaties with the tribes east of the Cascade Mountains including the Nez Perce, Cayuse, Walla Walla, Umatilla, Yakima, and some groups who lived along the Columbia River. The council was held at Mill Creek in the Walla Walla Valley, Wash. Terr., May–June, 1855 (Josephy 1965:179, 285–332). Pencil drawing and watercolor on prepared color paper base by Gustavus Sohon.

the United States Senate, the War Department, and the Office of the Secretary of the Interior (ARCIA 1872–1906; see also Jones 1982).

There is no segregated series of records relating to Indian agreements similar to those for the Indian treaties. Most of the ratified and unratified agreements and related documents are found in the correspondence files of the Office of Indian Affairs and the Office of the Secretary of the Interior (U.S. National Archives, Record Group 48). Related materials also are among the records of the United States Senate and House of Representatives. Maps of Indian lands ceded by the terms of the treaties and agreements are provided in Royce (1899).

Many of the records pertaining to the negotiation and ratification of Indian treaties and agreements are available in published form. The State Department's Indian Treaty File has been reproduced as National Archives Microfilm Publication M-688, Ratified Indian Treaties, 1722–1869. The treaty file of the Office of Indian Affairs has been published as "National Archives Microfilm Publication T-494 Documents Relating to the Negotiation of Ratified and Unratified Treaties with Various Indian Tribes,

1801–1869" (U.S. National Archives 1960). The texts of the treaties beginning in 1778 are published in Kappler (1904–1941,2), U.S. Congress (1873), and *U.S. Statutes at Large* (see also R. Peters 1848). Some of the earliest treaties and related documents are printed in two volumes of American State Papers (ASPIA 1832–1834; see also U.S. War Department 1826; Commissioner of Indian Affairs 1837). The text of the Indian treaties negotiated by the Confederate States of America are printed in U.S. War Department (1880–1901, series IV, vol. 1:426, 445, 513, 542, 548, 636, 647, 659, 669).

Different ratification and proclamation dates support in general the view that the treaties were ratified by the Senate and proclaimed by the president. However, an examination of the original documents in the State Department's Indian Treaty File shows that during the early years of the republic, particularly under Thomas Jefferson and James Madison, the ratification process was not complete until the president signed the treaty. Many files for these treaties include the Senate Resolution advising ratification, a copy of the treaty signed by the president with the statement that he is ratifying the treaty

Fig. 6. Treaty council meeting at Medicine Lodge Creek, Kans., where negotiations resulted in a treaty with the Cheyenne, Arapaho, Kiowa, Comanche, and Kiowa-Apache tribes of the Plains in Oct. 1867. White participants often had multiple roles in treaty councils. John Howland, a journalist and artist of this somewhat idealized engraving, was also a stenographer for the Peace Commission and a signatory witness for the treaty (D.C. Jones 1966:viii, 36, 103). Engraving in *Harper's Weekly* 11(568):724, Nov. 16, 1867.

with the advice and consent of the Senate, and a second copy of the treaty signed by the president with a statement proclaiming the treaty to be in effect.

The proclamation format apparently was dropped in 1814; the ratification statement was retained, but the date that the president signed the treaty came to be identified as the proclamation date and the date of the Senate Resolution became the ratification date. Before 1815 the ratification and proclamation dates are those of the documents found in the official file. After 1815 ratification dates correspond to those of the Senate Resolutions, and the proclamation dates denote the date that the president signed the treaty. Kappler (1904–1941,2) was inconsistent in the identification of the dates.

Published lists of unratified treaties, ratified agreements, and unratified agreements are not necessarily definitive. Unauthorized treaties and agreements, which occasionally were negotiated by military men or employees of the Office of Indian Affairs, often are buried in correspondence files. Examples are unratified treaties signed with tribes in Oregon (U.S. National Archives 1940) and in 1855 with some bands of Western Shoshone (U.S. National Archives 1957).

The National Archives Trust Fund Board's (1984) select catalog on American Indians lists microfilm publications of records relating to Indian treaties: microfilm M668 reproduces ratified Indian treaties, 1722–1869; microfilm T494 reproduces documents relating to the negotiation of ratified and unratified treaties, 1801–1869. Gasaway, Hoover, and Warden (1980) compiled a Union List of American Indian legal materials that includes several entries under "U.S. Treaties, etc.", all available on microfiche (Law Library Microform Consortium 1981).

There is a considerable body of secondary material on federal Indian treaties and treaty-making. The U.S. Department of the Interior. Office of the Solicitor (1940) compiled a mimeograph compendium of federal Indian laws and treaties. The Institute for the Development of Indian Law (1973-1975) published a chronological list of ratified and unratified treaties and agreements with eight companion volumes of texts. Lists of treaties are in C. Thomas (1910:803–814), and U.S. Congress. House. Committee on Interior and Insular Affairs (1953: 1556–1559). Washburn (1973,4), and Hosen (1985) reprinted the texts of selected Indian treaties. Mills (1924) gives a compilation of laws and treaties relating to the Oklahoma tribes; Fay (1972) presents treaties and land cessions between Sioux bands and the United States. Worcester (1975) edited a collection of papers critical of U.S. treaty-making policy; Viola (1981) presents a discussion of the treaty-making process and how it influenced both Indians and Whites who met in the nation's capital to negotiate treaties. Trafzer (1986) discusses Gov. Isaac Stevens's role in treaty negotiations with northwestern Indians 1850–1855; additional information on treaties may be found in studies of individual Indian tribes. Prucha's (1977, 1982) bibliographies on Indian-White relations in the United States through 1980 list nearly 150 titles under the heading "United States Treaties and Councils."

201

Canadian Indian Treaties

ROBERT J. SURTEES

The Royal Proclamation of 1763

Only about one-half the lands of Canada have been the object of a formal cession agreement, or treaty, between the Indians and the federal government. This somewhat surprising feature of land management can be explained only in historical terms, and the explanation must begin with the Royal Proclamation of October 7, 1763 (Alvord 1908:31–35; Allan 1971:71–20). That document attempted to settle several outstanding issues in British colonial policy in North America, including the boundaries of Quebec and Florida, their respective forms of government, and the nature of the Anglo-American settlement frontier. The Anglo-Americans and the new Canadian subjects of the British Crown were denied access to the lands beyond the Appalachian highlands. Those were declared an enormous Indian Territory, reserved for the use of the tribes who occupied them at the time. Exceptions were made for fur traders who required access to the Indian Territory in order to conduct business, but even they were required to secure formal trading licenses and to restrict their commercial operations to the military posts that Britain maintained at strategic locations such as Ogdensburg, Niagara, Detroit, and Michilimackinac.

While the Territory was thus reserved for Indian occupation, the British clearly did not expect that circumstance to pertain for very long; the document itself provided the means by which portions of the Territory could be alienated from the Indians. The procedure called for the summoning of a formal council, attended by the Indian occupants of the coveted section and by official representatives of the Crown. At this council, called for the express purpose of a land sale, the two sides were to agree on terms and record these in an official deed or treaty. The first such treaty concluded in 1764 concerned a stretch of land on each side of the Niagara River (fig. 1) (Surtees 1982:42), but the first substantial invasion of the Indian Territory via the treaty method came in 1768 with the Treaty of Fort Stanwix (Graymont 1972:3).

The American Revolution removed Britain from her rights of sovereignty over most of the territory between the Appalachian highlands and the Mississippi River, but the rules established by the Proclamation of 1763 contin-ued to apply in those regions that remained part of British North America. Because of the long French regime that preceded the British conquest and retention of Canada in 1763, the Proclamation line that bounded the Indian Territory was drawn somewhat differently in Canada from the way it was drawn in the old British colonies. Over the course of 150 years the French had carved out a sphere of influence, recognized by all parties, along the lower Saint Lawrence River and some of its tributaries. This sphere was recognized by the Proclamation line ("British Indian Policies to 1783," fig. 2, this vol.) (Cumming and Mickenberg 1972:25). Lands lying outside this sphere were to be considered part of the Indian Territory, but two exceptions resulted.

The question of whether or not the regulation of the Proclamation should apply to the Maritime colonies of Canada was raised at the time and has provided the basis for argument ever since. When the Proclamation was issued, Montagu Wilmot, who had recently become governor of Nova Scotia, acknowledged its receipt, but by neglecting to act on it showed that "he obviously did not consider that it related to his province, which had been conquered fifty years earlier" (Upton 1979:62). He ignored it, his successors as governor ignored it; and the future governments of New Brunswick and Nova Scotia also ignored it. While the correctness of that approach is still a matter for debate, the de facto result has been a complete absence of land cession treaties in what have become the three Maritime provinces of Canada. There is a similar absence in the province of Quebec. The Proclamation, it would seem, clearly exempted the lands south of the Lake Nipissing–Lac Saint Jean line. But when it was decreed that Quebec's boundaries in 1867 would lie well north of that line, and then were extended further in 1898 (to the Eastmain River) and in 1912 (to include the Ungava Peninsula) it might have been expected that Proclamation rules would apply and land cession treaties would be required. This did not happen. Rather the rationale applied to the exempted area—that is, that France held that land by right of exploration, conquest, and effective control and had passed this to Britain at the conquest—prevailed after 1867, 1898, and 1912. The signing of the James Bay and Northern Quebec Agreement in 1975 by Native organizations representing East

Main Cree, Montagnais-Naskapi, and Eskimo bands and by the federal and Quebec governments resolved the ambiguity (fig. 2) (Québec 1976).

Indians in the region west of the line from Lake Nipissing to the Saint Lawrence River—largely Ojibwa—felt no pressures from European newcomers for two decades after the conquest. But as the revolt of the American colonies developed into the Revolution, those untroubled times ended; Loyalists began making their way, in small numbers, to the remnants of British North America during the war, and in larger groups when it ended. Their demands for living outside the seigneurial grant region of the lower Saint Lawrence Valley combined with the need to accommodate the Iroquois and other Indian allies of the British with new homelands to convince the governor of Quebec, Sir Frederick Haldimand, to seek settlement lands from the Indians who occupied the regions west of the Lake Nipissing line. That decision, which followed two wartime cessions in 1781, marked the beginning of the treaty era in Canada (Surtees 1982:20, 38–79).

The Early Treaties

The first land cessions were rather simple and uncomplicated arrangements. For a specified amount of money, paid in trade goods, a particular group of Indians agreed to surrender a stated amount of land. Thus, in 1784 the Mississauga bands who occupied the lands at the head of Lake Ontario and north of Lake Erie agreed to sell a tract containing about three million acres in return for £1,180 in goods (Canada 1905–1912, 1: No. 3). It was from this Between the Lakes Purchase area (fig. 1) that the 1843 members of the Six Nations and associated tribes who followed Joseph Brant were provided with the Grand River Valley lands (Johnston 1964). Likewise, in 1790 the "Ottawa, Chippewa, Potowatomie and Huron Nations of Detroit" sold the lands between Lake Erie and the Thames River for £1,200 (Canada 1905–1912, 1: No. 2), and in 1796 the Chippewas gave up London Township for £1,200 and Sombra Township for £800 (Canada 1905–1912, 1: Nos. 6 and 7).

This era of treaty-making activities, which lasted until 1812, was marked by three significant features. First, the early treaties were concluded through a single, one-time payment. Second, several of the early agreements were not recorded properly. The actual deeds of surrender for the Collins Purchase on Lake Simcoe, the Oswegatchie lands on the upper Saint Lawrence River, and the Crawford Purchase of lands on the north shore of Lake Ontario (east of the Trent River) have either been lost or were never fully executed. Also the area on the shore of Lake Ontario from the Etobicoke River to the Trent River as well as a large block south of Lake Simcoe was improperly recorded. In that case, the Mississauga chiefs were enticed

into signing (making marks on) a blank deed (Canada 1905–1912, 1: No. 13). The officials apparently wished to secure accurate landmark descriptions, which they planned to insert in the blank deed later. This irregularity was noted by Lt. Gov. John Graves Simcoe in 1794 and declared invalid by Gov. Guy Carleton, Lord Dorchester, that same year (Cruikshank 1923–1931, 2:138). A modus operandi between the Indians and government officials did permit the settlement of the region, however, and for over 130 years the precise ownership status of this enormous, and valuable, region remained undefined. The Williams Treaty of 1923 claimed to settle this matter (Cumming and Mickenberg 1972:231). Differences of opinion between the Mississaugas and the government of Upper Canada regarding the terms of the Crawford Purchase began to arise in the 1830s and 1840s and were apparently resolved by the conclusion of two new agreements in 1856 (Canada 1905–1912, 1: Nos. 77 and 78). The Onondaga maintained that they never received payments for their territory on the north shore of the Saint Lawrence River. But they moved, on the urging of the British, to the south shore before 1794, and when the Jay Treaty removed the British presence from Ogdensburg this group was dispersed by American Indian agents (vol. 15:495). No claims have been registered regarding the Collins Purchase, and the irregularities there have thus not been faced. Finally, the questionable methods used by several agents of the Indian Department to acquire a block on the Detroit River, known as the Indian Officer's Land, were apparently covered by the McKee Purchase of 1790 (Lajeunesse 1960; Surtees 1982).

A third feature of note was the Indians' wish, in some instances, to retain specific locations for their exclusive use. The Credit River Mississauga, for example, insisted on three such locations: at the mouth of Twelve Mile Creek (Bronte Creek), Sixteen Mile Creek (Oakville Creek), and the Credit River. The first two and much of the third were sold by agreements in 1820 and the remainder of the third in 1846 (Canada 1905–1912, 1: Nos. 14, 22). Likewise, the Ottawas, Hurons, Chippewas, and Potawatomis who agreed to the McKee Purchase in 1790 retained for their exclusive use a substantial tract known as the Huron Reserve and a smaller one, the Huron Church Reserve, both fronting the Detroit River (Canada 1905–1912, 1: No.2). Deputy Superintendent of Indian Affairs Alexander McKee, who negotiated this sale, explained that inclusion of the reserve provisions was the only way he could secure agreement for the treaty (PAC 4: 223). The Huron Church Reserve was sold in 1800, and the Huron Reserve was sold by separate agreements in 1836 and 1914.

It should also be observed that in this era the Indians' position was relatively strong. They outnumbered the newcomers in the early years and even by 1812 the Indian population of the southern regions of the province of

Fig. 1. Major Indian land cessions in southern Ont.: 1, Niagara Purchase; 2, Island of Michilimackinac; 3, Crawford Purchase I; 4, Crawford Purchase II; 5, Indian Officers Lands; 6, Between the Lakes Purchase; 7, St. Regis Purchase; 8, Oswegatchie Purchase; 9, Collins Purchase; 10, Johnson-Butler Purchase; 11, McKee Purchase; 12, Sombra Township; 13, London Township; 14, Grand River; 15, Joseph Brant's Land; 16, Penetanguishe Peninsula; 17, St. Joseph Island; 18, Toronto Purchase; 19, Head of the Lake Purchase; 20, Lake Simcoe Purchase; 21, Rice Lake Purchase; 22, Lake Simcoe-Nottawasaga Purchase; 23, Ajetance Purchase; 24, Rideau Purchase; 25, Tyendinaga; 26, Long Woods Purchase; 27, Huron Tract Purchase; 28, Bond Head–Saugeen Treaty; 29, Bond Head–Manitoulin Treaty and Manitoulin Island Treaty; 30, Robinson-Huron Treaty; 31, Robinson-Superior Treaty; 32, Indian Strip Sale; 33, Saugeen Surrenders; 34, Williams Treaties (Surtees 1982).

Upper Canada constituted better than 10 percent of the total. Moreover, their connections with the Great Lakes area Indians in the United States, the uneasy relations between Britain and the United States, and the traditional military role of Indians were all features that enhanced the importance of Indians in the minds of government and military officials. Yet the land cession treaties were accomplished with remarkable ease. Apart from a few isolated incidents in which surveyors and their crews were harassed or stopped briefly, there was no violence; nor were Indian demands very high, for land was acquired at an average of about 4 pence per acre.

Cessions to 1867

The demands grew stronger as the relative strengths of the two parties—Indian and non Indian—altered in favor of the newcomers. Following the War of 1812, the Indian position weakened. Treaty arrangements in the United States removed most of the Ottawa, Miami, Potawatomi, and Shawnee from the border regions, thereby severing the connection between those tribes and the Indians in Canada. The Upper Canada population also grew rapidly, from about 75,000 in 1812 to 250,000 by 1830 (Lower

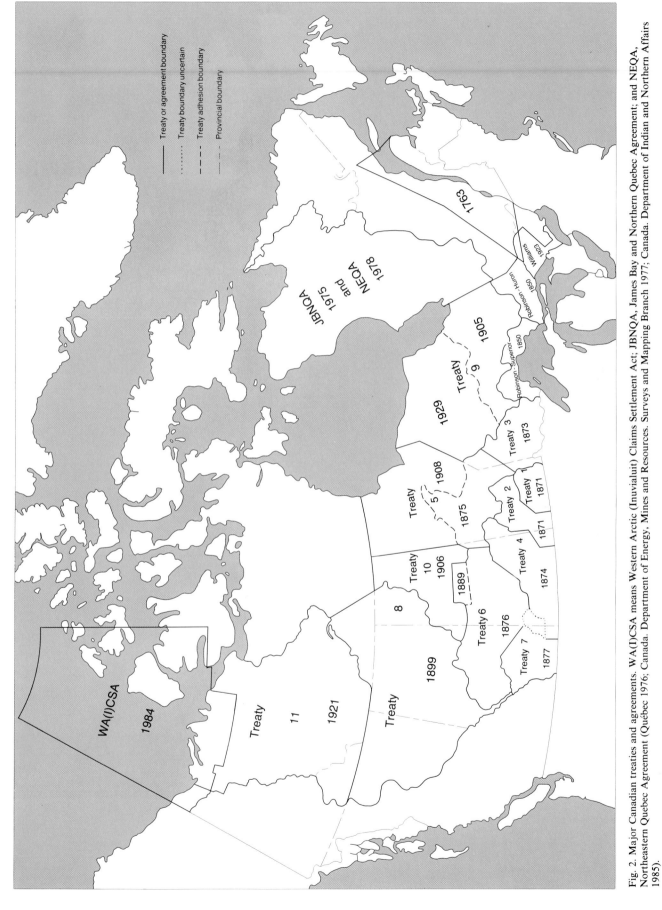

Fig. 2. Major Canadian treaties and agreements. WA(I)CSA means Western Arctic (Inuvialuit) Claims Settlement Act; JBNQA, James Bay and Northern Quebec Agreement; and NEQA, Northeastern Quebec Agreement (Québec 1976; Canada. Department of Energy, Mines and Resources. Surveys and Mapping Branch 1977; Canada. Department of Indian and Northern Affairs 1985).

1958:191). To provide for these newcomers, almost exclusively emigrants from the United Kingdom, the government required more lands from the Indians of Upper Canada. Accordingly six substantial tracts of Indian lands were acquired between 1815 and 1827 (fig. 1). This constituted a second line of settlement, behind the waterfront townships, stretching from the Ottawa River to the eastern shore of Lake Huron, and contained a total of about seven million acres (Surtees 1982:164–207).

Two features of these postwar treaties merit special notice. The first concerns the method of payment. The British government adopted a system of making an annual payment in perpetuity to any band that agreed to sell its land. The intent was to save money (L.F. Gates 1968:159). After the land had been secured from the Indians it could be sold to settlers whose annual interest payment would, it was expected, more than cover the cost of the Indian annuities. The scheme did not function as the British officials had hoped, but the system was continued regardless, and the distribution of "treaty money" became an annual event (fig. 3).

As their relative importance—politically and militarily—declined, the Indians became more wary and began requesting more sophisticated terms. These sometimes included specific reserve areas, as in the Huron Tract Purchase or the Long Woods Purchase (PAC 11:95). But some of the terms also included an agreement that they be permitted to hunt and fish, as had been their custom, throughout the unsettled areas of the surrendered tract. These terms were not actually written into the agreements but were included in the records of the councils that preceded the transactions. A decision in the Supreme Court of Ontario (*The Queen* v. *Taylor and Williams* 1981) held that these terms must be honored, although they do not appear in the actual surrender document.

Two agreements concluded in 1836 by Sir Francis Bond Head, lieutenant governor of Upper Canada, marked something of a watershed in Canadian Indian treaties. On the one hand it can be observed that Bond Head wished to acquire the Saugeen Tract to provide land for settlement and thus defuse a tense political situation in the province. It can be observed also that this was simply the major portion of a general Indian removal scheme to provide settlement territory for the future (Milloy 1978: 165–230). But it should also be noted that Bond Head was restricted in his actions. The British government had in 1830 adopted formally a policy of Indian civilization; and both the policy and the Indians had powerful friends at the colonial office when the following men were Secretary of State for the colonies: George Murray, 1828–1830, Viscount Goderich, 1830–1833, and Lord Glenelg, 1835–1839 (Surtees 1967; Milloy 1978).

Although Bond Head was not himself very sanguine of Indians making much progress toward a civilized state, the well-known sympathies of his superior required that

Pub. Arch. of Canada, Ottawa, Ont.: PA-155156.
Fig. 3. Treaty No. 10 annual $5 per capita payment to Chipewyan Indians at Cold Lake Reserve, Alta. seated, left to right, S.C. Knapp, Indian agent; Pauline Vanier; and Gov. Gen. Georges Vanier, the first vice-regal representatives to participate in the annual distribution. Photograph by Gustav Lunney, June 1961.

he acknowledge and promote the concept. Thus in making his arrangements he promised the Ojibwa of Saugeen and the Chippewas and Ottawas of Manitoulin and surrounding islands that they would have houses built for them and that they would be given proper assistance to enable them "to become civilized and to cultivate land . . ." (Canada 1905–1912, 1: No. 45 ½). The promise to assist treaty-making bands in progressing toward a civilized state was a logical extension of the adoption of that program six years earlier. It would form a significant feature of the substantive treaty arrangements made by Special Commissioner William Benjamin Robinson in 1850 (Canada 1905–1912, 1: Nos. 60 and 61) with the bands of the northern shores of Lake Huron and Lake Superior (figs. 1–2). The reserves set apart in those agreements differed, therefore, from those of the Credit River or those of the Huron Tract Purchase, which had neither stated nor implied that assistance. Such reserves were also included in the Saugeen Surrenders of 1854 (Schmalz 1977; Canada 1905–1912, 1: No. 72) and the Manitoulin Island Treaty of 1862 (Canada 1905–1912, 1: No. 94). Also included in those arrangements, this time in writing, was the guarantee of the right to hunt and fish throughout the ceded tract.

The motives for seeking a land cession treaty varied slightly with each individual surrender, but in general, before 1850, there were two: settlement and military purposes. The acquisition of the waterfront lands in the 1780s and 1790s was clearly in order to provide settlement lands for the Loyalists, although in the case of the Indian allies and in the desire to have an unbroken line of settlement there were military undertones as well. The Niagara Purchase of 1781 (a confirmation of the 1764 deal to which were added the claims of the Mississauga as well as the Seneca) and the acquisition of the Island of Michilimackinac in that same year were motivated mainly by military considerations, as were the purchase of Saint Joseph Island in 1796, the Collins Purchase of 1784, Penetanguishene Peninsula in 1798, and the Lake Simcoe Purchase in 1815. London Township was acquired because Lieutenant Governor Simcoe hoped to establish the provincial capital on the Thames river, and Sombra Township was purchased in 1796 in the expectation that a large number from the groups defeated by American Gen. Anthony Wayne at the Battle of Fallen Timbers might migrate to lands in Canada. The capital was actually built at York, and the migration did not occur, so the two townships were simply made available to White settlement.

The lands acquired through the Robinson treaties had no military value, and almost as little settlement potential. There the desire to exploit the mineral wealth of the Canadian shield provided the purpose. Indeed mining activities, with provincial government approval, had already begun; and the treaties concluded by Robinson were intended to legitimize those operations as well as to provide access for further mining activity. Likewise the acquisition of Manitoulin Island was inspired as much by the desire to exploit the Lake Huron–Georgian Bay fisheries as by a need to provide for settlement.

By 1862, the lands of Upper Canada had been largely alienated from their original inhabitants. There were two exceptions. One was the collective territory of the several reserves. Some of these had been provided by treaties; some had been specially granted as a result of the civilization or reserve policy adopted in 1830; and two—Walpole Island and Wikwemikong on Manitoulin Island—had never been ceded. The other exception was a large pocket lying between the Ottawa River and the line of settlement set between 1818 and 1827. This large block was purchased in 1923 as part of the Williams treaties.

The Numbered Treaties

During the first century of British rule, therefore, a system of land alienation had evolved. Based on the general principles of the Proclamation of 1763, it had taken a form dictated by the changing circumstances that confronted both Indians and the government. While there were some flaws and omissions in its application the system had served government very well. There then occurred, in rapid succession, the Confederation of Canada, the acquisition by Canada of the vast western and northern holdings of the Hudson's Bay Company, the creation of

the Northwest Territories by the Canadian government, and the federal government's decision to link, via settlement and a railway, central Canada with the province of British Columbia, which was admitted to the union in 1871. These developments meant that arrangements had to be made with the Indians who occupied the vast new holdings, for it was decreed by an Imperial Order-in-Council of July 15, 1870, that "any claims of Indians to compensation for lands required for purposes of settlement shall be disposed of by the Canadian government" (Brown and Maguire 1979:36). By including this provision in agreements concerning the Canadian acquisition of the northwest, the imperial government had, in effect, extended the principles of the Proclamation of 1763 into the new regions. It was logical that the new Canadian government should continue to use the system of land alienation that had evolved from those principles and that had served it well to that point. As the treaty system was being applied in the territories it underwent some further refinements and changes in the new circumstances.

The Red River settlement was the first to receive attention. This region had already experienced a lengthy and rocky existence since 1814 when the first Scottish settlers arrived and had to face the hostility of the environment and the animosity of Métis who had preceded them. In the years 1868–1870 it would suffer the further trauma of the Hudson's Bay Company withdrawal and the first Northwest rebellion (Stanley 1960). In the midst of this crisis, which revolved around the lands and the society of the Métis, Indian interests and Indian concerns were pushed somewhat, but not completely, into the background.

It was determined that the 1817 land arrangements of Thomas Douglas, Earl of Selkirk (Brown and Maguire 1979:32), were at best suspect; care was taken to provide the commander of the military expedition sent to suppress the rebellion with an agreement of safe passage for his troops through the Indian country (Stanley 1960:129, 135–136); and there were demands by some Indian bands that proper land cession agreements be made (Tobias 1983:520). The Indians of the disaffected region were dealt with first. Treaty No. 1 (the Stone Fort Treaty) and Treaty No. 2 (the Manitoba Post Treaty) set the pattern for subsequent treaty arrangements in the Canadian West. They also fulfilled, in the minds of the federal government, the condition that in the transfer of lands from the Hudson's Bay Company to the Canadian government proper regard be paid to the Indian inhabitants of the west, and in doing so the federal government extended the treaty making process and, by implication, also extended the region to which the Proclamation of 1763 was to apply (fig. 2).

Negotiations between government representatives and the Cree and Ojibwa of the region took place at Stone Fort (Lower Fort Gary) between July 27 and August 3, 1871

(A. Morris 1880:25–43; Hall 1984). Following the conclusion of Treaty No. 1, the government commissioners moved to Manitoba Post, a Hudson's Bay Company fort at the northern end of Lake Manitoba, and on August 21 concluded Treaty No. 2 with the Chippewa bands there. The Chippewa, West Main Cree, and some others sold 16,700 square miles in southern Manitoba; in return they were promised reserved lands on the ratio of 160 acres for a family of five, the maintenance of a school on each reserve (at the request of the band), the prohibition of the sale of intoxicants on the reserves, a present of three dollars per person, and an annuity of three dollars (raised to five dollars in 1875) for each person (Daugherty 1983). In addition the government promised to provide a bull for each reserve, a cow for each chief, a male and female of all farm animals when the Indians were judged ready to receive them, and a plough and harrow for each Indian settler who actively cultivated the soil. The role of the chiefs was distinguished by the granting of a suit of clothing for signing the treaty and a larger annuity, $25 for chiefs and $15 for headmen. The same terms applied to the area of Treaty No. 2, which involved 35,700 square miles (Daugherty 1983).

Although it can be argued that the young Canadian federal government had not yet set a firm Indian policy

(Tobias 1983), these terms would suggest that it was building on a policy that had been established through the treaty system already consummated in eastern Canada. The principle of using annuities had begun as early as 1818, and the inclusion of reserves had been formalized with the 1850 Robinson treaties. Moreover, the records of treaty negotiations and surrounding documents indicate that while an exact policy may not have been enunciated, there was a determination on the part of the government to secure the lands, and that the Indians of the Canadian west could not have prevented that from taking place (J.L. Taylor 1977). For the Indians' part, it can be observed that they had provided some of the impetus by issuing demands for such land cession agreements and that they learned to bargain somewhat more effectively for better terms in subsequent treaties (Canada 1979). The Northern Ojibwa of Treaty No. 3 (the North-west Angle Treaty) managed to secure a larger initial payment ($12 per person), a larger annuity ($5 per person), larger reserves (a square mile for a family of five), and a guarantee for hunting and fishing rights. The Cree of Treaty No. 6 secured a promise of some health care as well as an additional $1,000 a year for three years for provisions and another $1,500 a year for ammunition and twine. This last provision was raised to $2,000 for the Blackfoot, Blood,

208   Fig. 4. Treaty No. 9 proceedings with Ojibwa and Cree Indians at Flying Post, on the Groundhog River, Ont., 1906.

Piegan, Sarcee, and Assiniboin of Treaty No. 7 (Canada 1979). In general, these slightly altered treaty terms marked refinements in a system that the government intended to apply. The Indians of the west might bargain and resist, but they could not stop it.

By 1877 and the concluding of Treaty No. 7 (the Blackfoot Treaty) the Canadian government had secured control of the western settlement frontier. For about 20 years the treaty system remained in hiatus until settlement and mining enterprises began to exert pressures on Indian bands in the Canadian north. The result of this pressure was another spate of major land cessions in northern Ontario (Treaty No. 9, the James Bay Treaty, 1905 and 1929) (fig. 4), northern Manitoba (an adhesion to Treaty No. 5, in 1908), northern Saskatchewan and a small portion of Alberta (Treaty No. 10, 1906), northern Alberta, the Northwest Territories south of Great Slave Lake, part of northwestern Saskatchewan and northeastern British Columbia (Treaty No. 8, 1899 and 1900) (fig. 5), and the Northwest Territories north of Great Slave Lake and west of the Coppermine River (Treaty No. 11, 1921 and 1922) (Canada 1979). In these several agreements the terms and conditions followed those of the early post-Confederation years.

In Treaty No. 9 the government of Ontario was also a partner because of an 1894 agreement between the federal government and the government of Ontario whereby any future federal treaties with the Indians of Ontario would require the concurrence of the Ontario government (Canada 1931). One condition of the treaty that resulted was that no site suitable for the development of water power exceeding 500 horsepower should be included within the boundaries of any reserve. It was necessary also to include a provincial government in the arrangements surrounding Treaty No. 8, which included land in northeastern British Columbia. An 1876 agreement between the federal government and the government of British Columbia stipulated that "the province would be responsible for negotiating with the Indians for title to their land and setting up reserves" (Madill 1981:44). Reasons for including this portion of British Columbia in Treaty No. 8 were given by Clifford Sifton, the minister responsible for Indian Affairs in 1898:

> As the Indians to the west of the Mountains are quite distinct from those whose habitat is on the eastern side therof, no difficulty ever arose in consequence of the different methods of dealing with the Indians on either side of the Mountains. But there can be no doubt that had the division line between the Indians been artificial instead of natural such difference in treatment would have been fraught with grave danger and have been the fruitful source of much trouble to both the Dominion and the Provincial Governments.

> It will neither be politic nor practicable to exclude from the treaty Indians whose habitat is in the territory lying between the height of land and the eastern boundary of British Columbia, as they know nothing of the artificial boundary,

Royal Canadian Mounted Police Mus., Regina, Sask.
Fig. 5. Chipewyan chief and headmen who accepted Treaty No. 8 at Fond Du Lac, Sask. left to right, Laurent Dziedden, headman; Maurice Piche, chief; and Toussaint, headman. The chief wears a medal that may have been distributed in connection with the treaty. Provisions of the treaty included annual supplies of ammunition, twine, and medical supplies, and a $5 per capita payment (vol.6:273). Photographed in 1899.

and, being allied to the Indians of Athabasca, will look for the same treatment as is given to the Indians whose habitat is in that district (Madill 1981:44–45).

The inclusion of northeastern British Columbia within the boundaries of Treaty No. 8 has been termed "almost accidental" (Madill 1981:i). Such a description has meaning only in terms of the unusual treatment of Indians and Indian lands in that province. Before White settlement of any consequence began on Canada's west coast, the Hudson's Bay Company in 1846 established Fort Victoria as its principal headquarters for the west coast fur trade, and in 1849 the company also assumed responsibility for the colonization of Vancouver Island. Among its obligations in this respect was the protection and welfare of the Indians (Madill 1981:6). Because of the remoteness of the island the British colonial office relied heavily on the Hudson's Bay Company chief factor, James Douglas, to handle Indian affairs according to local conditions. It was with this freedom of movement that Douglas concluded 14 "deeds of conveyance" with some Central Coast Salish Indians of Vancouver Island in the years 1850–1854. These treaties mark the only land cession agreements made by any of the British Columbia Indians before the colony joined Canada in 1871. Because these cessions conveyed lands to the Hudson's Bay Company, and because it was the company and not the Crown that dispensed payments, it has been argued that these agreements do not constitute formal treaties in the same sense as those that apply in other parts of Canada. Certainly this has been the position by governments of British Columbia from the colonial period to the present; and the 1876 Dominion–British Columbia agreement regarding the sale of Indian lands would seem to confirm that view. In that light the description of the British Columbia portion of Treaty No. 8 as "almost accidental" seems logical.

The Status of the Treaties

There is an inconsistency in terms of the legal status of Indian treaties. In rendering a judgment in *R. v. White and Bob* (52 D.L.R. (2d) 481, 1965), the Supreme Court of Canada in 1965 held that an 1854 treaty with the Indians of Vancouver Island took precedence over the British Columbia Game Act. Regardless of the peculiarities of this example, the *White and Bob* decision also demonstrates that a hierarchy has apparently developed in Canadian law as it concerns Indian treaties.

Few would argue that the Indian treaties in Canada constituted solemn agreements between two sovereign states. Levi General, who held the Cayuga title Deskahe, tried to secure international recognition from the League of Nations in Geneva in 1923 but failed. Legal decisions in *Sero* v. *Gault* (20 O.W.N. 16, 50 O.L.R. 27, 1921) and *Logan* v. *Styres* (20 D.L.R. (2d) 416 (1959) O.W.N. 361) have served to reject, formally, full Indian sovereignty. Yet treaties have acquired a status of considerable consequence. The *White and Bob* decision, as well as others such as *R.* v. *Moses* (13 D.L.R. (3d) 50, (1970) 3 O.R. 314), directs that an Indian treaty will supersede provincial legislation. This principle is, furthermore, enunciated in section 87 of the federal Indian Act of 1951 (Canada 1963). But treaties are not supreme. The federal Migratory Birds Convention Act of 1960 appeared to deny hunting and fishing rights enshrined in several of the Indian treaties. It was thus challenged by an Indian from the area of Treaty No. 11 when he was charged with shooting a wild duck out of season. The Supreme Court of Canada upheld the authority of the Canadian Parliament when it ruled in the case of *R.* v. *Sikyea* (S.C.R. 642, 50 D.L.R. (2d) 80, 40 W.W.R. N.S. 306, 44 C.R. 266, 1964) in 1962. This decision, and another in the *R.* v. *Daniels* case S.C.R. 517 (1968), 1 C.C.C. 299 (1969), seems to confirm the principle that federal legislation can be used to override the terms of an Indian treaty. The principle has not been challenged under the Canadian Constitution adopted in 1982.

When first introduced the land cession treaties were designed to provide the British government with a secure and safe method of acquiring lands that were occupied, albeit sparsely, by native people. The reasons for securing land included military considerations, settlement, and mineral and resource exploitation, but the result was always the transfer of actual ownership from Indian to non-Indian hands. In this respect the system worked very well, and governments from 1763 onward were able to acquire the desired lands with remarkable ease. This procedure would be used to acquire lands in the future, whether it be the large tracts in the Canadian north that remain unceded or the smaller tracts—the reserves—portions of which have been purchased, and will likely be purchased, for public purposes such as roadways or wharfs.

As the system evolved, it took on institutional characteristics. The terms of the agreements grew more sophisticated and more elaborate; and the side effects, such as hunting rights, annuity payments, and reserve lands, became established as recognized features of Canadian society. Perhaps most significantly the treaties, because of tests in the courts, obtained entrenched positions in the legal hierarchy.

Indian Land Transfers

ARRELL M. GIBSON

North America on the eve of the European intrusion was populated at a density of less than one person per square mile. Many of the tribes claimed vast territories with fixed village sites and adjacent agricultural lands, the remainder consisting of hunting reserves, all components of what the members of each tribe regarded as their territory. From the Indian viewpoint, this low man-land ratio was ideal and essential for the aboriginal life way. However, Europeans, accustomed to more intensive land occupation and utilization, regarded the Indian method of land use as wasteful and considered much of each tribal estate as vacant territory. The interaction of these conflicting land utilization viewpoints and the concomitant struggle for control of the tribal territories supply the substance for much of the chronicle of American history.

After 1776, a new nation arose in North America to compete with the European claimants for dominion over the land, resources, and native peoples. Quite early in its national life the United States developed an ethos of expansion that committed it to extend American suzerainty to the Pacific shore. Two obstacles intruded momentarily to check the consummation of this national design. One was the presence of several foreign nations in the coveted Western territory. By 1850, through purchase, diplomatic agreement, and war of conquest, the United States had removed alien title to all Western territory and had integrated the land into the national domain. The other obstacle was the occupation of the Western territory by populous and powerful Indian nations, each claiming as tribal estate a substantial portion of what the United States declared to be its national domain. The government of the new nation, pushed by its expanding, agrarian-based population, worked assiduously to extinguish Indian title to the land desired by its citizens. By 1900, the federal government had vested primary title to former tribal territories in itself.

Attitudes Toward the Land

This process of appropriating the Indian estate and transferring land title from the tribes to the public domain for dispensing to American settlers has complex and diverse origins. The intellectual foundation of American rhetoric and policy for tribal land expropriation was derived from political theory, international law, a corpus of supportive writings from Sir Thomas More to Theodore Roosevelt, and nearly 300 years of imperial practice followed by several European nations.

Sir Thomas More in *Utopia* contended that "When any people holdeth a piece of ground void and vacant to no good or profitable use: keeping others from the use and possession of it, which notwithstanding, by the law of nature," "this situation ought thereof to be nourished and relieved" (More 1808:191–192).

Theodore Roosevelt expressed the jingoist view that "the settler and pioneer have at bottom had justice on their side; this great continent could not have been kept as nothing but a game preserve for squalid savages" (Roosevelt 1889–1896, 1:90). All intruder nations assumed dominion, "based on discovery, without regard for the natives." Administrators of European empires in America "insisted on the right of dominion in its acquired territory and that of granting the soil, the rights of the original inhabitants were in but few instances entirely disregarded" (Fletcher 1907:500).

The presumptively imperialist doctrine of Spain, Holland, and France tinctured United States policy for appropriating the Indian estate, but the primary source of American action was derived from British practice. The government of Great Britain and the governments of the British colonies in North America treated the Indian tribes as nations and conducted relations with tribal governments through the treaty process. The United States government in its relations with the Indian tribes under its jurisdiction continued this practice until 1871 when the Indian Appropriations Act (16 U.S. Stat. 544, 566) was adopted. Most land transfers resulting from extinguishment of tribal claim and shift of title to the United States were accomplished through the treaty process.

American Revolution and Confederation

Even before the American Revolution colonial pioneers from the seaboard had migrated into eastern Kentucky and Tennessee, establishing permanent settlements in complete disregard for Indian rights to the land as stated in the Proclamation of 1763, which forbade settlement

Natl. Archives: RG75-M-17.

Fig. 1. Attorneys and witnesses for the Red Pipestone Quarry land claim of the Yankton Sioux, Pipestone, Minn., Sept. 30, 1927. front row, left to right, Richard Jelier, operator of a quarry; James Irving, Yankton Sioux, judge of Probate Court, Pipestone Co., Minn.; Winifred Bartlett, court reporter; others unidentified. fourth row, unidentified, unidentified, F.E. Cron, Yankton Agency farmer; Myron Cohen, Commissioner, U.S. Court of Claims; Moses Standing Bull, Yankton; Jennings C. Wise, attorney for the Sioux; George A. Rice, agriculturalist. fifth row, Rev. Philip Deloria, Yankton, Episcopal missionary; Herber M. Rice, Assistant U.S. Attorney General; R.E. Lee Daniels, Indian agent; unidentified; Giles Pettigreiu, attorney, Flandreau, S. Dak. seventh row, unidentified, James W. Balmer, superintendent of Pipestone Indian School. In the treaty between the U.S. government and the Yankton Sioux, April 19, 1858 (11 U.S. Stat. 743), article 8 secured the right of the Indians to retain access to and use the "red pipestone quarry" in southwestern Minn., and a 1-square mile reserve was platted. In the 1870s a White man, Herbert M. Carpenter, obtained a patent to land within the reserve. Whites began to move into the area and some of them to quarry stone on the reserve. Carpenter would not relinquish title and, based on his plea that the Indians were still permitted to quarry pipestone, the U.S. Circuit Court for Minn. found in Carpenter's favor. The Indians' case was taken by government attorneys to the Supreme Court, which in 1883 found that the reserve was not open to private parties, but the violators remained and increased in number. In 1884 it was discovered that the Cedar Rapids, Iowa Falls and Northwestern Railroad built tracks across the north part of the reserve. In 1887 U.S. troops were sent to the reserve to evict the violators. A plan for settlement, outlined in a bill passed in 1889, stated that evicted settlers could reassert their claims, the land occupied by the railroad would be appraised and the Yankton compensated for it, but only if the Indians approved the act. The Yankton approved the sale of right of way for the railroad but not the settlement plan. In 1892 the federal government built an Indian industrial training school on the Pipestone reserve ("American Indian Education," fig.4, this vol.) over protests of the Yankton. In December 1892 the Yankton and the Department of the Interior agreed to refer the case to the Supreme Court to decide quarry ownership within one year of Congressional ratification of the agreement, failing which the Yankton would simply acquire ownership. The matter was not referred to the Court, and in 1897 the Yankton petitioned the Department of the Interior for legal title to the quarry and compensation for damages. Under the Indian Appropriations Act of 1897 a settlement of $100,000 in cattle and cash was negotiated, with the Yankton retaining sole right to quarry pipestone. But the agreement was rejected by the Senate in 1903 based on the document's premise that the Yankton held title to the quarry. The tribe took their claim to the U.S. Court of Claims in 1911, but that court's decision in 1917 did not decide ownership. When the Yankton refiled a petition in 1924, the court found that they did not own the land and had no rights of occupancy but they did have the right to mine pipestone from the quarry. The case was taken to the Supreme Court, which decided that the Yankton did hold title by virtue of the agreement of 1892 and should be compensated. A settlement of $100,000 plus interest, based on the 1891 value of the land, was awarded in April 1928. The money was distributed to the tribe on a per capita basis, and title of the reserve passed to the U.S. government (Corbett 1978; Nydahl 1950). Photograph by C.E. Sogn Studio, Pipestone, Minn.

west of the mountains. During the 1760s the British government on the one hand ambivalently developed plans to establish a permanent reserve in the trans-Appalachian region for the Indian tribes and, on the other, worked with British and colonial politicians and businessmen to distribute much of the western territory to speculator land companies.

The American Revolution aborted both schemes. Wide Indian support of the British cause including participation in British-led campaigns against American settlements in the West had catastrophic impact, immediate and long-range, on Indians. A pattern evolved. In the War of 1812 and the Civil War, Indians opposed the United States. At the conclusion of each war, their role as vanquished people made it easier for the United States to appropriate their lands.

The American Revolution initiated the conquest process. A case in point was Cherokee support of the British cause. Warriors from this tribe were among the first to do the British bidding in attacking American settlements in the West. On several occasions between 1776 and 1778, Cherokee bands struck hard at the pioneer communities south of the Ohio River. Massed frontier militia forces broke the Cherokee siege on the settlements, forced the Indians to withdraw, then mounted retaliatory campaigns that desolated the Cherokee towns in western North and South Carolina and eastern Tennessee. These operations crushed Cherokee martial power, and thereafter only on isolated occasions were raiding parties from this tribe able to strike the American settlements even on a nuisance raid (Woodward 1963).

During 1777, American frontier leaders extracted from the Cherokees the Treaty of Dewitt's Corner and the Treaty of Long Island whereby the Cherokees ceded claim to all territory in western South Carolina, that part of their range east of the Blue Ridge Mountains divide in North Carolina, and the land occupied by the Watauga and Nolichucky settlements in eastern Tennessee (fig. 2a) (Woodward 1963:97, 98). This marked the beginning of the compression of the vast Cherokee estate in the Southeastern United States, which was completed by the Treaty of New Echota in 1835 (7 U.S. Stat. 330).

British use of Indian armies in campaigns against the Western settlements during the Revolution resulted in drastic reduction in the population of great and powerful tribes filling the territorial interstice between the seaboard and the trans-Appalachian West. The League of the Iroquois was reduced to shambles by American armies, never again able to muster its awesome power of colonial times. After tribal leaders ceded much of their Eastern territory to the United States, several remnants of this confederacy migrated into the Ohio Valley to escape the settlement pressure.

From the American viewpoint, tribes residing on territory claimed by the United States that raided Ameri-can settlements as British mercenaries were constructively tainted with treason. Thus retaliatory campaigns against these Indians by Western militia armies, consistently ending in defeat of the natives, were generally concluded by treaties calling for cession of land to the Americans, righteously extracted as reparations for making war.

British-Tory-Indian armies had carried out brutal, dehumanizing campaigns against American settlements in the trans-Appalachian West. American frontier militias matched their enemy in wanton destruction and general barbarity in their retaliatory strikes. At the close of hostilities, the British and Tories withdrew, but the Indians remained on the land, now the territory of the United States. The memory of Indian atrocities survived for a century, coloring American relations with the tribes. In the surge of the settler tide across the West this image made appropriation of Indian lands easier.

The new United States government, functioning under the Articles of Confederation, began its relations with the Western Indian tribes in the mid-1780s. From the beginning it faced jurisdictional problems. For over a century each of the Atlantic colonies, then states in the American union, had been involved in Indian affairs (fig. 3), including appropriation of Indian lands. After 1763, the British government belatedly had developed a royal policy for managing the Indian tribes and their lands. The Articles of Confederation vested in Congress the exclusive power to regulate the affairs of Indians who were not residents of any state. The states with Western land claims derived from colonial charters and grants had, beginning in 1781, ceded much of the territory between the Appalachians and Mississippi River to the national government, and it was over this territory that Congress was to have full jurisdiction (1 U.S. Stat. 6).

However, this power was limited by reservations of western lands made by several of the states. Connecticut had retained title to a large tract to indemnify its citizens for war damages. Virginia had reserved substantial territory to provide military bounties for troops under the command of George Rogers Clark. North Carolina and Georgia had made conditional grants to the national government. North Carolina regularly ceded, then reclaimed, its western lands, comprising most of Tennessee. And as late as 1802, Georgia retained title to western lands, granting much of the territory embracing the future states of Alabama and Mississippi to a group of speculators under the aegis of the Yazoo Land Company, in complete disregard of Indian title rights or pledges to the national government. To further complicate the jurisdictional issue over Indian tribes and their lands, in 1786 Georgia officials negotiated a treaty with the Creek Nation for cession of all tribal lands east of the Oconee River. In 1794 the Georgia legislature by statute sold these lands—about 35 million acres—to three Yazoo land companies. The land sale to the Yazoo companies led to negotiations between federal agents and

213

214

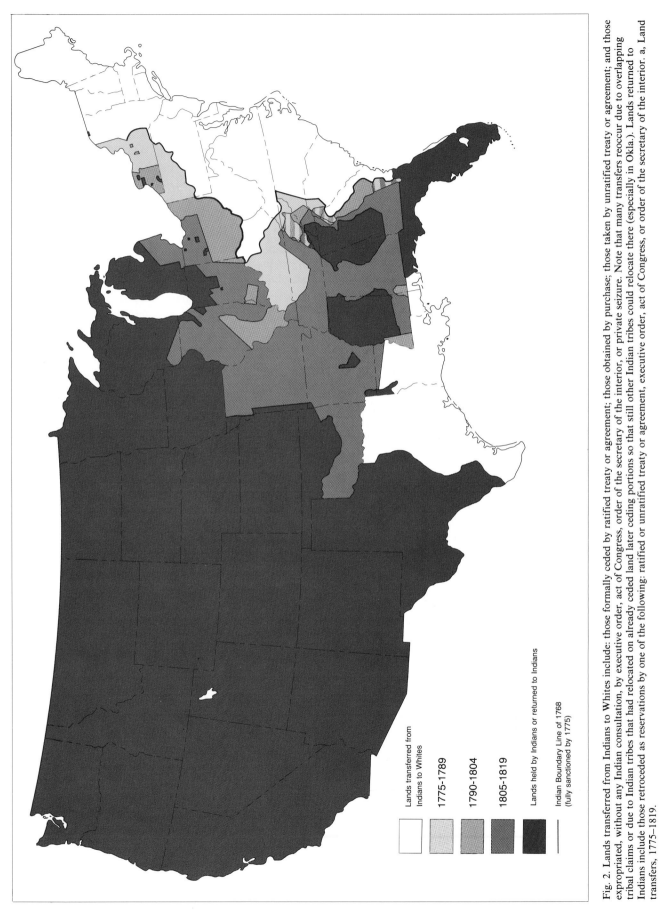

Fig. 2. Lands transferred from Indians to Whites include: those formally ceded by ratified treaty or agreement; those obtained by purchase; those taken by unratified treaty or agreement; and those expropriated, without any Indian consultation, by executive order, act of Congress, order of the secretary of the interior, or private seizure. Note that many transfers reoccur due to overlapping tribal claims or due to Indian tribes that had relocated on already ceded land later ceding portions so that still other Indian tribes could relocate there (especially in Okla.). Lands returned to Indians include those retroceded as reservations by one of the following: ratified or unratified treaty or agreement, executive order, act of Congress, or order of the secretary of the interior. a, Land transfers, 1775–1819.

Lands transferred from
Indians to Whites

1775-1789

1790-1804

1805-1819

Lands held by Indians or returned to Indians

Indian Boundary Line of 1768
(fully sanctioned by 1775)

GIBSON

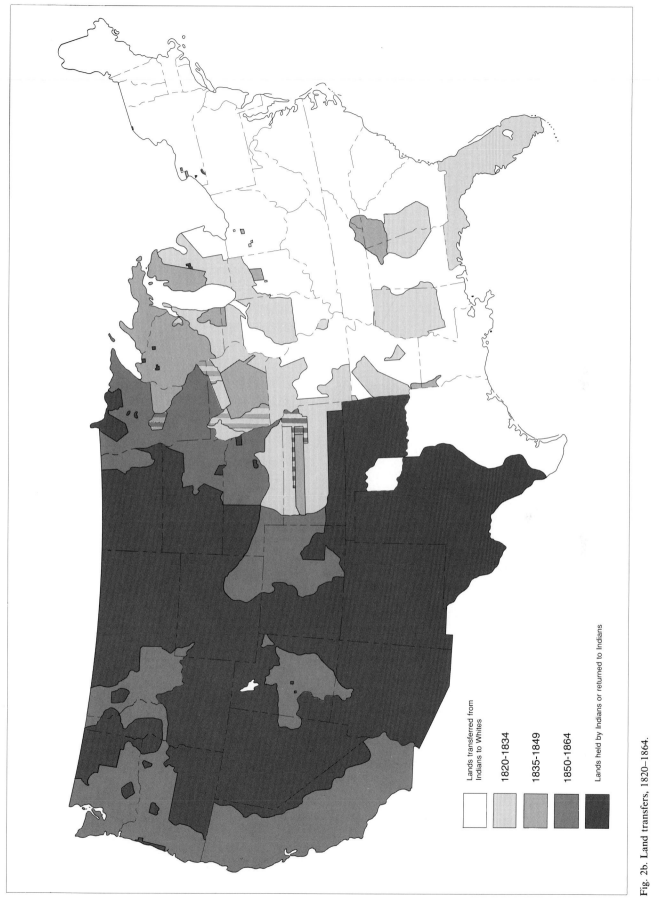

Fig. 2b. Land transfers, 1820–1864.

Lands transferred from
Indians to Whites

1820-1834

1835-1849

1850-1864

Lands held by Indians or returned to Indians

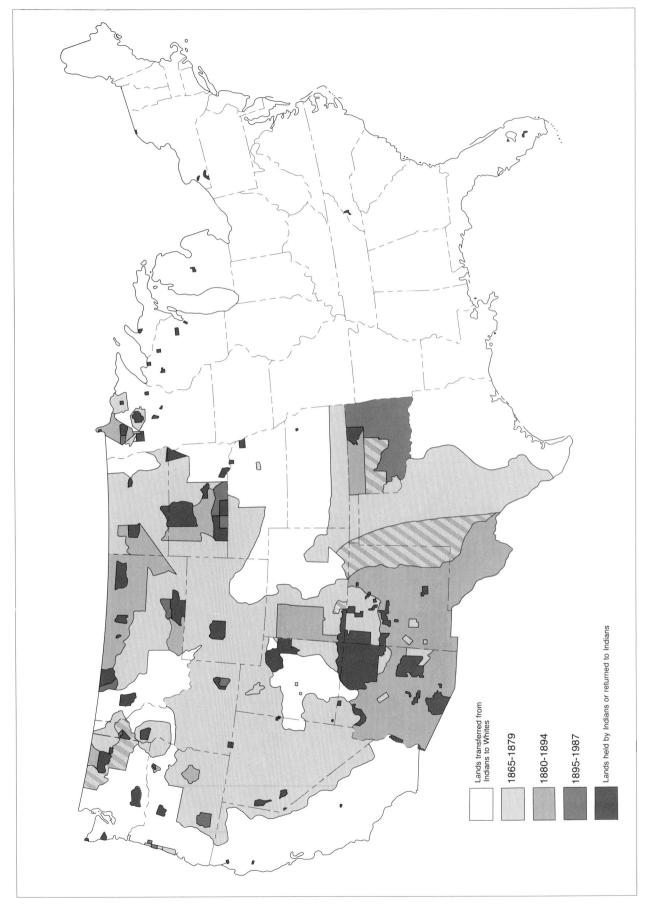

Lands transferred from
Indians to Whites

1865–1879

1880–1894

1895–1987

Lands held by Indians or returned to Indians

Fig. 2c. Land transfers, 1865–1987.

GIBSON

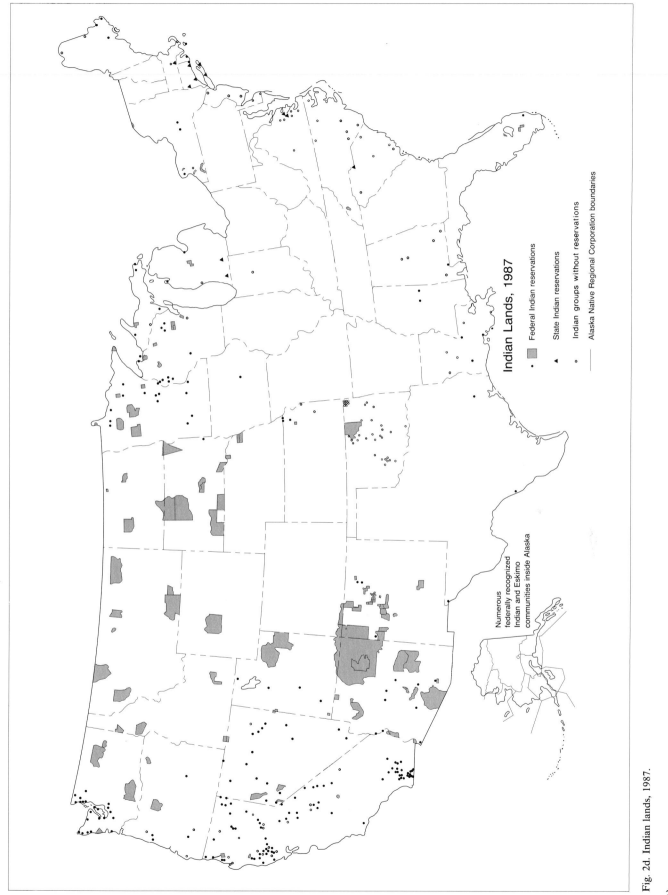

Indian Lands, 1987

Federal Indian reservations

State Indian reservations

Indian groups without reservations

Alaska Native Regional Corporation boundaries

Numerous
federally recognized
Indian and Eskimo
communities inside Alaska

Fig. 2d. Indian lands, 1987.

Georgia officials for a settlement of Georgia's claim to western lands. Georgia ceded its western lands in exchange for $1,500,000 and a pledge that the United States extinguish title to all Indian lands in the state.

In spite of these jurisdictional complications, the national government persevered in its effort to create an Indian policy for the tribes in the western territory. National leaders proceeded on the assumption that while absolute title to the land resided in the national government, the Indian tribes held possessory and occupancy rights to the territory. These rights had to be extinguished by established constitutional process before the land could be considered a part of the public domain, open to settlement.

In 1786 Congress, by statute, asserted its exclusive power to deal with the Indian tribes (R.R. Hill 1904–1937, 32). Further regard for native land rights was stated in the Northwest Ordinance of 1787—"The utmost good faith shall always be observed toward the Indians; their land and property shall never be taken from them without [their] consent, and in their property, rights and liberty, they shall never be invaded or disturbed, unless in just and lawful wars authorized by Congress" (1 U.S. Stat. 50). In addition, Congress created a modest bureaucracy to administer Indian affairs, consisting of two departments or divisions, divided by the Ohio River. Each department was headed by a superintendent or commissioner (R.R. Hill 1904–1937, 32:32, 340–341).

Congress also took steps to extend American dominion over Indian nations through a series of councils presided over by American commissioners. The tribes in the Northern department met with American commissioners at Fort Stanwix in 1784. There the remnants of the League of the Iroquois accepted American suzerainty and surrendered their claims to territory in the Northwest (7 U.S. Stat. 15). A second council with the Northern tribes was held at Fort McIntosh in the Ohio country during 1785. Ottawa, Delaware, Chippewa, and Wyandot leaders acknowledged American dominion and ceded certain tribal lands in the Northwest (7 U.S. Stat. 16). A third council was held at Fort Finney in Kentucky in 1786, where Shawnee leaders acknowledged American dominion and assented to Anglo-American settlement in the Ohio country (7 U.S. Stat. 26). By these treaties the American government agreed to keep settlers off Indian lands. The Muskingum River was set as the boundary for settlement. To thwart American trespass on Indian lands west of the river, Gen. Josiah Harmar constructed Fort Harmar at the mouth of the Muskingum.

The leaders of the Cherokee, Choctaw, and Chickasaw met with American commissioners for the Southern department at Hopewell in South Carolina in 1785–1786 to sign the Treaties of Hopewell whereby they accepted American suzerainty (7 U.S. Stat. 18). The Creek Nation did not accede until 1790 by the Treaty of New York (7

U.S. Stat. 35).

Early National Period

Quite early federal leaders attempted to resolve the jurisdictional dilemma of dealing with the Indian tribes residing in American territory by taking steps to nationalize Indian policy and reduce complications created by actions of the states. In response to President George Washington's request for a policy statement to guide the new government in this regard, Secretary of War Henry Knox and Secretary of State Thomas Jefferson articulated the ideal position from which the United States might proceed. Knox stated that "It would reflect honor on the new government, and be attended with happy effects, were a declarative law to be passed, that the Indian tribes possess the right of the soil of all lands within their limits. . .and that they are not to be divested thereof, but in consequence of fair and bona fide purchases, made under the authority, or with the express approbation, of the United States." Knox added that the different tribes "ought to be considered as foreign nations, not as the subjects of any particular State. Each individual State, indeed, will retain the right of pre-emption of all lands within its limits, which will not be abridged; but the general sovereignty must possess the right of making all treaties, on the execution or violation of which depend peace or war" (ASPIA 1832–1834, 1:53).

Jefferson supported the Knox position and added the concept of the sovereign's "right of pre-emption" in the land that, he declared, the federal government possessed from European imperial precedents and American colonial practice. Jefferson's doctrine of pre-emption acknowledged Indian tenure in the land each tribe occupied and asserted the concomitant power of the sovereign government holding dominion over territory occupied by aboriginal peoples to extinguish their claim through purchase (Lipscomb and Bergh 1904–1905, 17:322, 328–329; Carter 1934–1962, 4:34–35).

During 1793, Congress incorporated the spirit of the Knox and Jefferson statements in a statute that provided that no transfer of Indian-held land to the public domain of the United States would be valid "unless the same be made by a treaty or convention entered into pursuant to the Constitution." Relations with the Indian tribes, including those pertaining to land transfers, trade, and general administration were to be conducted by the president primarily through treaties subject to ratification by the Senate (1 U.S. Stat. 329–330).

In the halls of government well-intentioned leaders drafted an ideal system for conducting relations with the Indian tribes; but in the wilderness harsh, expropriative reality prevailed. The American population more than doubled each decade. Increasing numbers of settlers poured onto the frontier, pressing for more land. Ameri-

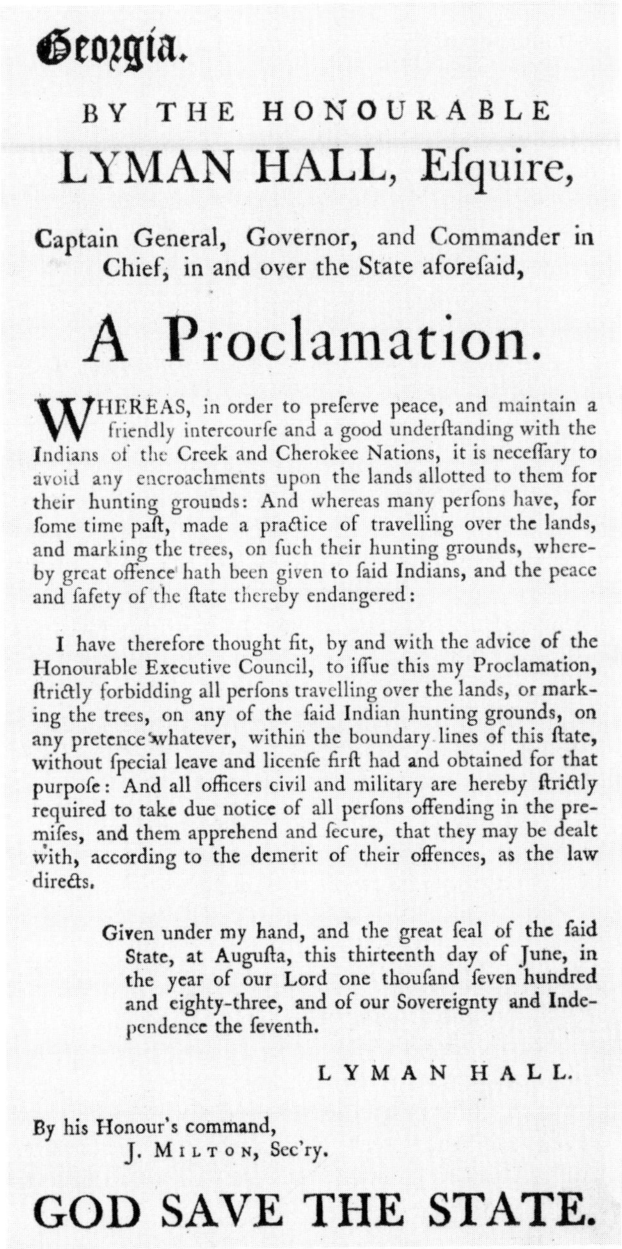

Georgia.

BY THE HONOURABLE

LYMAN HALL, Efquire,

Captain General, Governor, and Commander in Chief, in and over the State aforefaid,

A Proclamation.

WHEREAS, in order to preferve peace, and maintain a friendly intercourfe and a good underftanding with the Indians of the Creek and Cherokee Nations, it is neceffary to avoid any encroachments upon the lands allotted to them for their hunting grounds: And whereas many perfons have, for fome time paft, made a practice of travelling over the lands, and marking the trees, on fuch their hunting grounds, whereby great offence hath been given to faid Indians, and the peace and fafety of the ftate thereby endangered:

I have therefore thought fit, by and with the advice of the Honourable Executive Council, to iffue this my Proclamation, ftrictly forbidding all perfons travelling over the lands, or marking the trees, on any of the faid Indian hunting grounds, on any pretence whatever, within the boundary lines of this ftate, without fpecial leave and licenfe firft had and obtained for that purpofe: And all officers civil and military are hereby ftrictly required to take due notice of all perfons offending in the premifes, and them apprehend and fecure, that they may be dealt with, according to the demerit of their offences, as the law directs.

Given under my hand, and the great feal of the faid State, at Augufta, this thirteenth day of June, in the year of our Lord one thoufand feven hundred and eighty-three, and of our Sovereignty and Independence the feventh.

LYMAN HALL.

By his Honour's command,
J. MILTON, Sec'ry.

GOD SAVE THE STATE.

Amer. Antiquarian Soc., Worcester, Mass.: Evans Coll. 44369.
Fig. 3. Proclamation forbidding the trespass or settlement by citizens of Ga. on Creek and Cherokee Indian lands, 1783. Issued just before the signing of the Peace of Paris, which ended the war between Great Britain and the United States, this document reflects the concern of the state governor for winning the confidence of the Indians, as well as drawing them away from Spanish influence, by appearing protective of Indian land rights (see Caughey 1938:21–25). The proclamation anticipates a Congressional proclamation forbidding unauthorized settlement on or possession of title to Indian lands outside of the states (Tyler 1973:34). Another proclamation addressing similar concerns was issued by the governor of Pa. in 1765; it can be found in the Lib. of Congress, Rare Book Div. (Broadside Portfolio 142, No. 18).

can pioneers settled where they chose, disregarded boundaries set by treaty, antagonized the Indians, and precipitated incidents that often led to frontier wars. The inevitable result of each frontier extension was reluctant tribal assent to new treaties ceding the lands coveted by the settlers. Recurring and accelerating demands for more land forced the federal government to depart from its lofty position of protecting tribal rights to treaty-assigned territory. In simplest terms, political expediency forced this. Pioneer voters sent territorial delegates and congressmen to Washington to frame legislation and develop policy that would provide an ever-expanding reservoir of public land, free of tribal encumbrance, for settlement and development.

Until the War of 1812, settler pressure on the tribes of the trans-Appalachian region produced the periodic reduction or compression of tribal lands. Each settler surge into the West resulted in government officials pressing Indian leaders to surrender a portion of the tribal estate. President Thomas Jefferson discussed with Cherokee leaders and spokesmen for other tribes complete removal west of the Mississippi River to the Louisiana Territory. However, after intense federal diplomatic pressure or military conquest, tribal leaders eschewed removal, generally responding by surrendering those portions of their Eastern domains desired by the settlers, concentrating their people on the steadily reduced tribal lands (Lipscomb and Bergh 1904–1905, 16:432–435).

The federal government had created an administrative apparatus to deal directly with the tribes. Responsibility for Indian affairs resided with the War Department. Several officials assisted the secretary of war including the territorial governor, who also served as the local superintendent of Indian affairs, and the tribal agent. The agent had many duties. He represented the United States in the Indian nation and in the early years was expected to watch for tribal defection from the United States. As the federal government's representative, he had the duty of enforcing federal laws in the Indian country with regard to intruders, traders, contraband traffic, and Indian treaty provisions (Prucha 1962; Seymour 1941).

In President Jefferson's view the Indian agent's function was to promote peace and acquire more land for the settlers by leading the Indians to agriculture as the tribe's primary industry. "When they shall cultivate small spots of earth, and see how useless their extensive forests are, they will sell from time to time, to help out their personal labor in stocking their farms, and procuring clothes and comforts from our trading houses" (Lipscomb and Bergh 1904–1905, 10:357–358). Jefferson expected the federally operated trading houses to serve the purpose of Indian land transfer. He directed agents "to establish among them a factory or factories for furnishing them with all the necessaries and comforts they may wish (Spirituous liquors excepted), encouraging them and especially their leading men, to run in debt for these beyond their individual means of paying; and whenever in that situation, they will always cede lands to rid themselves of debt" (Lipscomb and Bergh 1904–1905, 17:373–374).

During the 1790s the advance of American settlers in

the Northwest was accomplished only after federal armies had waged a series of bloody campaigns to dislodge the determined Indians. The Wyandot, Shawnee, Delaware, Miami, Ottawa, Chippewa, Potawatomi, and Kickapoo were antagonized by intruding survey parties and expanding American settlements. Braced by British agents at Detroit with arms, blankets, provisions and gifts, warriors from these tribes prepared to ravage the expanding American settlements in southern Ohio. During the 1780s Joseph Brant, the Mohawk mixed-blood, had formed a confederacy among the Northwest tribes. The leaders pledged to cede no more land to the United States and repudiated the treaties of Fort Stanwix, Fort McIntosh, and Fort Finney (ASPIA 1832–1834, 1:8–9).

Spokesmen for the confederacy met with American officials at Fort Harmar during January 1789. Arthur St. Clair, governor of the Northwest Territory, would agree to nothing short of the conditions set forth in the three treaties. Settlements in the Ohio country increased, British-armed warriors cut a bloody swath from Chillicothe to the gates of Fort Harmar, and frontier militia companies retaliated in kind with vengeance strikes against the Indian towns on the Maumee (7 U.S. Stat. 28; ASPIA 1832–1834, 1:10).

Beginning in 1790, President Washington ordered troops into the Ohio country to pacify the frontier. In 1793, Gen. Anthony Wayne led an American army into the troubled zone and finally defeated the Indian confederacy forces at the Battle of Fallen Timbers during August 1794. American officials and tribal leaders met at Greenville the following year to sign the Treaty of Greenville whereby the insurgent tribes conceded most of Ohio to the United States. In return federal officials distributed $20,000 worth of goods to the signatory tribes and pledged an annuity of $9,500 (7 U.S. Stat. 49, 51).

War of 1812

The War of 1812 settled the problem of the Indian barrier to American settler advance in the trans-Appalachian region in that this contest destroyed the martial power of the resident tribes. And their weakened postwar state made inevitable their removal to the trans-Mississippi West by the federal government. The western origins of the War of 1812 grew out of the accelerated federal pressure after 1800 on the tribes for additional land cessions. Federal commissioners had achieved spectacular success in reducing the domain of certain tribes in order to keep an ample supply of land available for settlers. A consummate negotiator was Governor William Henry Harrison of Indiana Territory. By 1809 he had completed 15 treaties calling for substantial cessions of territory. In 1809 at Fort Wayne he concluded a treaty with Delaware, Potawatomi, and Miami leaders calling for the cession of over 3,000,000 acres of tribal land in Indiana to the United

States in exchange for trade goods worth about $7,000 and an annuity of $1,750 (7 U.S. Stat. 113, 114).

After Governor Harrison effectuated the Fort Wayne Treaty, Tecumseh, a Shawnee leader of considerable oratorical and organizational talent, confronted him. Tecumseh had formed a confederation of tribes based on nativistic precepts that included rejection of White contact and culture and a moratorium on the cession of Indian lands. Tecumseh repudiated the Fort Wayne Treaty and warned Harrison to keep surveyors and settlers out of the tract ceded by that agreement. There ensued a two-year impasse (Esarey 1922:459–469; Edmunds 1984).

It became apparent to Harrison that if Tecumseh's will prevailed, there would exist a permanent Indian barrier across the northwestern corner of Indiana that would thwart American settler expansion. Therefore, while Tecumseh was south of the Ohio River during late 1811 attempting to ally the Choctaw, Creek, Chickasaw, and Cherokee, Harrison collected a militia army and marched on Prophetstown, the confederated Indian settlement situated near the Wabash River. As a result of the Battle of Tippecanoe, November 7, 1811, Harrison's troops dispersed Tecumseh's followers; this marked the beginning of the War of 1812 in the West.

American armies campaigned widely on the western frontier, but only one operation involving the conquest of an Indian community resulted in land transfer during the period of the war. Most cessions of tribal lands came after the conclusion of hostilities in 1815.

The only Indians south of the Ohio River to take seriously the anti-American teachings of Tecumseh were members of the Red Stick faction of the Creek Nation. These warriors ravaged the frontier settlements of western Georgia and Alabama during 1813–1814. In the Treaty of Fort Jackson the Creek Nation ceded as reparations 22,000,000 acres of land in southern Georgia and central Alabama (7 U.S. Stat. 120).

By 1816 the national government was ready to change drastically its policy of dealing with frontier tribes. First of all, they were in a most unfavorable position from the American viewpoint in that, as members of tribal communities under United States dominion, they had actively supported the British in the War of 1812. As vanquished peoples they could be expected to suffer some penalty, in the form of land reparations, for making war on the United States. In addition, their collective martial power, which peaked under Tecumseh, had been destroyed by American victories.

The awareness of this very important fact by national government officials was articulated by William Clark, superintendent of Indian affairs at Saint Louis. "The relative condition of the United States on the one side, and the Indian tribes on the other" he concluded, had changed substantially. Before the War of 1812, "the tribes nearest our settlements were a formidable and terrible enemy; since then, their power has been broken, their warlike spirit subdued, and themselves sunk into objects of pity and commiseration." Clark recommended that "the tribes now within the limits of the States and Territories should be removed to a country beyond" the Mississippi River "where they could rest in peace" (ASPIA 1832–1834, 2: 653). Thus colonizing the tribes in the path of American expansion in the trans-Mississippi territory became a certain and continuing policy of the national government.

Removing the tribes did not occur in a single year, but was evolutionary, the rate of evacuation determined largely by the press of the settlement line. Tribal remnants were still being relocated in the trans-Mississippi West as late as the 1840s (fig. 4). Also, some Indian communities fell back to lands so unattractive for settlement use that they completely escaped removal to the West, so that late in the twentieth century residual communities of Potawatomi, Menominee, and certain other tribes remained in isolated areas. However, most of the tribes were removed in the period 1815–1825. The treaties that federal commissioners negotiated with tribal leaders provided for cession of lands on the frontier in exchange for new reserves west of the Mississippi and relocation of tribal members at government expense.

Federal officials found removing the tribes residing south of the Ohio River much more difficult. These Indian communities were large: the Cherokee numbered about 20,000 (Woodward 1963), the Choctaw about 20,000 (Debo 1934), the Seminole about 4,000 (McReynolds 1957), the Creek about 22,000 (Foreman 1934), and the Chickasaw about 5,000 (A.M. Gibson 1971). The Cherokee, Choctaw, Creek, and Chickasaw each had a corps of educated bilingual leaders who were worthy adversaries of American commissioners in council. Except for the Red Stick faction in the Creek Nation these tribes had remained loyal to the United States during the War of 1812, supplying troops for Gen. Andrew Jackson's campaigns against the Indian and British enemy. The Southeast tribes did not carry the stigma of making war on the United States as was the case for the Northeast tribes. However, these Indians occupied valuable lands in the states of Georgia, Alabama, Mississippi, Tennessee, and Florida. Each of the Indian nations maintained a tribal government. By treaty with the United States, the tribal governments challenged state sovereignty and comprised, in a sense, a state within a state.

Removal to the West

Both state and federal officials applied intense pressure on the Southeast tribes to move west. Tribal leaders responded by continuing the process of surrendering limited portions of their territory to satisfy settler demands of the moment, and by concentrating their people on the residue.

The Cherokees were the first to succumb to pressure from national officials and to accept a western domain. In 1817, Cherokee leaders negotiated a treaty with General Jackson providing for the surrender of one-third of their eastern lands for a tract of equal size in Arkansas between the White and Arkansas rivers. Emigration was discretionary; by 1835, only about 6,000 Cherokees had moved West (7 U.S. Stat. 156).

The Choctaw were the next tribe to commit themselves to vacating their eastern lands and migrating west. In 1820, General Jackson and Chief Pushmataha concluded the Treaty of Doak's Stand, providing that in return for surrendering to the United States about one-third of their remaining eastern domain the Choctaws were to receive a vast tract of territory west of the Mississippi, extending from southwestern Arkansas to the western boundary of the United States (fig. 2b). The treaty pledged the United States government to supply to each Choctaw warrior who would emigrate a rifle, bullet mold, camp kettle, blanket, and ammunition sufficient for hunting and defense for one year. The treaty also authorized payment for any improvement he left in his ancestral home.

Indian colonists from the Northeast settling in Missouri and from the Southeast settling in Arkansas found their treaty-assigned lands occupied by American settlers. These pioneers had opened farms, established towns, and organized territorial governments. The frontiersmen demanded that the arriving Indians be located elsewhere.

In 1825 Secretary of War John C. Calhoun determined to end for all time the recurring tribal relocations. He reported to President James Monroe the tragedy of periodic uprooting of the tribes to accommodate the American settlers. Calhoun stated that "one of the greatest evils to which they are subject is that incessant pressure of our population, which forces them from seat to seat. . . . To guard against this evil. . .there ought to be the strongest and the most solemn assurance that the country given them should be theirs, as a permanent home for themselves and their posterity . . . ." Calhoun recommended that the region west of Arkansas Territory and Missouri be set aside as a permanent Indian reserve. There, the federal government could colonize the Indian tribes remaining east of the Mississippi River as well as those tribes residing in Arkansas Territory and Missouri (ASPIA 1832–1834, 2:544). President Monroe and his successors, with the support of Congress, implemented Calhoun's recommendation. This colonization zone, situated west of Arkansas Territory and Missouri, was bounded on the north by the Platte River, on the South by the Red River, and extended to the western boundary of the United States. It was by 1830 commonly referred to as the Indian Territory (4 U.S. Stat. 729).

In 1825 the Choctaw surrendered their claim to land in southwestern Arkansas and relocated west of the Arkansas Territory boundary. Three years later the Cherokees

Tippecanoe Co. Histl. Assoc. and Evelyn O. Ball, Lafayette, Ind.

Fig. 4. Potawatomi Indians from the area along the Tippecanoe and Eel rivers with Indian Agent Abel C. Pepper and other government officials in council near Logansport, Ind., July 21, 1837. The removal of the Mich., Wis., Ill., and Ind. Potawatomi bands to lands in the West occurred in stages marked by various treaties, land sales, disagreements about suitable sites in the West, and conflicts over annuity payments (and subsequent disputes with traders) throughout the 1830s. The Indiana or "Wabash" Potawatomi depicted in this drawing first met with Pepper in summer 1834 to discuss plans for removal. An exploration party of chiefs, accompanied by Pepper, approved lands adjacent to the Marais des Cygnes River in Kans. In response to Chief Iowa's request that this land be located away from certain other bands of Potawatomis, the federal government established the Osage River Subagency in Kans. The July 1837 council was to prepare the bands for actual removal; however, only about 52 Potawatomis left for the agency that August. Most of the remaining band members left one year later (Edmunds 1978:255–256, 260, 264, 266). An account of the July 1837 council and the meeting preceding the August 1837 migration can be found in Winter (1948:95–114, 119–147). Drawing in ink and pencil on paper by George Winter.

exchanged their Arkansas domain for a new home in Indian Territory. The Missouri tribes relocated in that portion of the Indian colonization zone that in 1854 became Kansas Territory.

Indian Territory already was occupied by several tribes including the Osage, Quapaw, Kansa, Oto, Missouri, and Ponca. Before federal officials could make land assignments to the eastern Indians, they were required to persuade these local tribes to cede substantial portions of their lands to the United States for reassignment to the emigrating Indians. Through a series of negotiations between 1818 and 1825, the local tribes accepted reduced domains to make room for the emigrating Indians.

The Southeast tribes for the most part were relocated during the 1830s. Georgia, Alabama, and Mississippi legislatures adopted repressive laws that abolished tribal governments and made Indians subject to state law, applying to resident Indians the penalties of the statutes while denying them protection that the law accorded White citizens (Dawson 1831:198–199; Aikin 1833: 224–225; A. Hutchinson 1848:134; Young 1961:14–17). The state of Georgia went so far as to distribute—by means of a lottery—to its citizens the land of the Cherokee

(Woodward 1963:173–177). These actions were designed to pressure the Indians to emigrate to Indian Territory. Tribal leaders appealed to federal officials for protection from oppressive state action as guaranteed by treaties with the United States. President Andrew Jackson refused to intercede on behalf of the Indians, simply advising them to surrender their lands and move West as the only means to escape torment (Prucha 1962:235–238, 247; Foreman 1953:231–232, 247).

Cherokee leaders attempted to obtain respite through action in federal court. In the *Worcester* v. *Georgia* decision (1832), the Supreme Court ruled that the Georgia laws pertaining to the Cherokee were null and void because federal jurisdiction over the Cherokee was exclusive (31 U.S. (6 Peters) 515). Nonenforcement of the decision destroyed the will to resist among many Cherokees, and several tribal leaders prepared for removal.

In 1830, Congress passed the Indian Removal Act, which formalized the colonization process and reiterated federal intent as to Indian land rights in the East (4 U.S. Stat. 411). Between 1830 and 1837, all Southeast tribes signed comprehensive removal treaties ceding their Eastern lands to the United States and accepting new domains

222

in Indian Territory.

In the case of the Creek and Choctaw, government commissioners permitted the removal treaties to contain provisions for allotment. Tribal members who preferred to remain in the East were assigned allotments within the ceded territory, and the allottees thereby became subject to state law. The treaties differed in sums paid to the tribes and government services provided in relocation (7 U.S. Stat. 333, 366).

By the terms of the controversial Treaty of New Echota, the Cherokee Nation surrendered to the United States a domain of about 8,000,000 acres for $5,000,000. The Eastern Cherokees were confirmed in joint ownership with the Western Cherokees in their Indian Territory lands, and this domain was patented to the Cherokee Nation in fee simple. They were obligated to remove within two years after ratification of the treaty; the federal government was to pay the cost of removal and to provide subsistence for the immigrants for one year after arrival in the West (7 U.S. Stat. 478).

The Chickasaw ceded their Eastern lands by the Treaty of Pontotoc in 1832 and the amendatory treaties of 1832–1834. Federal agents were required to survey the Chickasaw land and assign each Indian family a homestead as a temporary residence until the western home was decided upon. Then the Indians were permitted to sell their homesteads to White settlers. The remainder of the Chickasaw territory was to be sold at public auction, the proceeds to go to the Chickasaw general fund. Also the Chickasaws were to pay for the cost of their relocation (7 U.S. Stat. 381, 388, 450).

The Seminoles were the last of the Southeast tribes to experience forced removal to Indian Territory. In 1832 Seminole chiefs signed the Treaty of Payne's Landing. By its terms, the Seminole tribe relinquished all claim to its lands in Florida Territory to the United States and agreed to relocate on Creek lands in Indian Territory within three years. The United States government agreed to pay the cost of removal, to provide subsistence for one year after arrival in the West, and to pay $15,400, plus an annuity of $3,000 for 15 years. In the Treaty of Fort Gibson in 1833 the Seminole agreed to settle on a particular tract of Creek lands west of Fort Gibson (7 U.S. Stat. 368, 423).

Osceola and other patriot leaders refused to be bound by the removal treaties. As a result of their opposition, a faction of the Seminole became embroiled in a costly war with the United States that lasted until 1842. During the protracted struggle, the federal government forcibly removed most of the Seminoles from Florida Territory. In 1842, the United States abandoned its war effort and allowed a small group of Seminoles to remain permanently in Florida (A.M. Gibson 1980:328–329).

In 1855, the land of the Choctaw and Chickasaw in Indian Territory was reduced by a treaty with the federal government whereby the Chickasaw leased the tribal lands situated between the Canadian and Red rivers and designated it the Leased District (11 U.S. Stat. 611). Subsequently federal officials assigned this area as a reservation for some Texas tribes—Wichita groups, Caddo, some Comanche bands, and others—numbering at the time of their removal only about 1,500. For several years these tribes had resided on the Brazos Reserve in northwest Texas. Demands by Texas settlers for reserve lands led federal officials in 1859 to relocate these tribes in the Leased District. Following removal, they were attached to the Wichita Agency, situated in the Leased District (ARCIA 1855:182–186).

Well before the Civil War, the Indian Territory's status as a permanent Indian colonization zone, off-limits to non-Indians, was challenged by the renewed expansion of American settlements into the West. The Kansas-Nebraska Act of 1854 excised land from Indian Territory to create Kansas and Nebraska Territories (10 U.S. Stat. 277).

In 1854 and 1855 Commissioner of Indian Affairs George W. Manypenny concluded agreements with local tribal leaders abrogating treaties that forbade the creation of any organized territory within this Indian colonization zone (7 U.S. Stat. 349, 353). The commissioner reported that the Omaha, Oto, Missouri, Sauk and Fox, Kickapoo, Delaware, Shawnee, Illinois, Miami, and other resident tribes reluctantly signed new treaties and accepted reduced reservations or allotments (Kappler 1904–1941, 2: 608–641, 677–681). The federal government sold the ceded lands to settlers.

The American expansionist surge of the 1840s that carried United States dominion to the Pacific shore produced in the new territory a momentum of expansion, settlement, and development that did not ebb until the close of the century. Discovery of gold in California and the concomitant sweep of the mining frontier across the newly acquired territory into the Pacific Northwest, Great Basin, Rocky Mountain region, and into the Southwest, with recurring gold and silver strikes, rapidly populated portions of the West. This drastically increased activity disturbed the local Indian peoples who then defended their homelands. The inevitable retaliatory military action led to successive Indian defeats and reductions in tribal territory, culminating in assignment of the conquered tribes to drastically reduced reservations out of the Euro-American stream of expansion and development.

Conquest and Compression in the West

The military conquest of the western tribes and compression of tribal territory, which began in 1845, can be divided into three periods. The first period, 1845–1861, conducted largely by regular troops, was particularly successful in California, Oregon, and Washington where,

Fig. 5. Congressman Harry R. Shepard of Calif. with members of the Indian Rights Assoc., Julia Ross Gardner (Northern or Owens Valley Paiute), Celestine Pico von Bulow (Luiseño), and Thomas Largo (Cahuilla), in Washington, D.C., March 3, 1937. The Indian Rights Assoc. helped Calif. Indians to assert claims on land promised in 18 treaties that had been signed by Calif. Indians 1851–1852 but that were never ratified by the U.S. Senate. Eventually the land case was put before the U.S. Court of Claims and an award was made on Dec. 4, 1944, based on claims for the 18 treaty reservations (vol. 8:705–706, 716). Photographer unidentified.

except for scattered pockets of resistance, the Indians after 1861 were no longer a factor to be reckoned with. The Treaty of Fort Laramie in 1851 began the compression process for several tribes of the Plains including the Mandan, Gros Ventre, Assiniboine, Crow, Blackfeet, Cheyenne, and Arapahoe. By this pact the signatory tribes accepted reduced hunting ranges, which ultimately became restricted reservations (Kappler 1904–1941, 2:594). This phase substantially reduced the Indian threat to American expansion and opened vast areas of Indian land to settlement and development.

The second period of the conquest of western lands occurred during the Civil War, 1861–1865. This episode in national history produced the comprehensive militarization of the West. Volunteer infantry and calvary regiments raised in the region's territories and states were kept in combat readiness for service in the East against Confederate armies by campaigning against Indians. Volunteer troops pacified the Northern Shoshone, Bannock, Ute, and other tribes residing near the Oregon-California roads, and their campaigns against the Cheyenne and other tribes of Colorado, Nevada, and Utah territories scattered the Indians and reduced their domains. In New Mexico and Arizona, Gen. Henry H. Carleton's conquest and containment policy at Bosque Redondo emasculated the Mescalero Apache and Navajo will to resist. His troops also campaigned eastward onto the Plains against the Kiowa and Comanche. However, Union regiments were never able to deal decisively with the Western Apache.

224   During the Civil War, the tribes of Indian Territory—

Choctaw, Creek, Chickasaw, Cherokee, and Seminole—signed treaties of alliance with the Confederate States of America. Indian armies fought under the Confederate flag in the contest between Union and Confederate armies for control of Indian Territory. At the close of the war the five tribes through their Reconstruction treaties were required to surrender the western half of Indian Territory to the national government as a penalty for the Confederate alliances and as reparations of war, receiving only minimal compensation for the territory ceded. The Seminole were pressed by federal officials to cede their entire domain to the United States for which they received an average of 15 cents an acre. Subsequently the Seminole purchased a small homeland within the Creeks' reduced territory for which they paid 50 cents an acre. The intent of federal officials in appropriating the western half of Indian Territory was to use the land as a colonization zone for concentrating tribes from other portions of the West (14 U.S. Stat. 155, 156, 755, 769, 785, 799; Abel 1915–1919).

This was compatible with recommendations of a congressional committee that, during the Civil War, had studied extensively the Indian problem in the West and concluded that it was "no longer feasible" to indulge the Western tribes in free, roving existence. To "remove the causes of Indian wars" and to establish peace in the West, the committee concluded that the Indians would have to give up the nomadic life and accept limited reservations and "walk the white man's road" (U.S. Congress. Senate 1867:7).

Fulfillment of this policy in the postwar period provides the substance for the third period of Western conquest. During the period 1866–1886, the federal government assigned tribes to reservations. Those tribes that remained largely unconquered—Sioux, Northern Cheyenne, Kiowa, Comanche, Southern Cheyenne, Arapaho, and Western Apache—did not submit quietly to the new policy. Federal troops campaigned continuously against them until the last tribal holdout, Geronimo's Chiricahua Apache band, capitulated in 1886.

The continuing settlement and development of the West during the postwar period and the concomitant reduction of Indian lands are illustrated in the case of the Kiowa, Comanche, Cheyenne, and Arapaho. In 1865 at the Council of the Little Arkansas, leaders of these tribes signed treaties with American commissioners. They ceded to the United States their claim to all territories south of that stream (fig. 2c). Thereupon federal officials assigned the Cheyenne and Arapaho a domain between the Arkansas and Cimarron rivers in southwestern Kansas and northwestern Indian Territory. The Kiowa and Comanche were assigned a reservation between the Cimarron and Red rivers, extending across western Indian Territory and the Texas panhandle (14 U.S. Stat., 703, 713, 717).

Notwithstanding the Little Arkansas treaties, the soil

of the new Kiowa, Comanche, Cheyenne, and Arapaho domains was soon bloodied by contests between Indians and Euro-American intruders. Settlers pressed onto the eastern margins of the treaty-assigned lands. The flow of traffic along the rivers and the old trails across these tribal ranges increased. American hunters slaughtered the buffalo, essential for the survival of the Plains tribes, for the hides. Because federal officials on the western border refused to protect tribal territorial rights guaranteed by the Little Arkansas treaties, the tribes assumed this function themselves. Settler appeals for protection brought the tribes into bloody contests with the United States army.

Two years later federal commissioners called these tribes into council again at Medicine Lodge Creek. The Treaties of Medicine Lodge in 1867 further reduced the lands of these tribes. The Kiowa and Comanche were assigned a reservation in the Leased District. The Cheyenne and Arapahoe were assigned a reservation in the Cherokee Outlet, bounded by the Cimarron and Arkansas rivers, but they actually settled south of the reservation on the North Canadian River. An executive order in 1869 established a new Cheyenne-Arapahoe reservation in the Leased District (fig. 6) (15 U.S. Stat. 581, 589, 593; see also D.C. Jones 1966).

Extensive military action was required to keep the Indians on their reservations. After considerable combat, all bands had capitulated by late 1875. Military officials at Fort Sill and Fort Reno disarmed the warriors, confiscated the Indians' horses, and arrested their leaders and sent them off to military prison at Fort Marion, Saint Augustine, Florida. Finally leaderless, disarmed, and afoot, the warriors of the Southern Plains tribes were thoroughly pacified. They settled down to the routines of reservation life, most of them demoralized by the drastic changes confronting them (Leckie 1963; A.M. Gibson

U. of Okla. Lib., Western Hist. Coll., Norman: Norman Pub. Lib. Coll. 23.

Fig. 6. Participants in an unofficial council regarding the disbursement of lands and monies belonging to the Cheyenne and Arapaho Indians, Okla. City, Okla. Terr., May 23, 1889. A group of Whites, including former Indian agents and attorneys, wanted to convince the Cheyenne and Arapaho that they had rights to and could sell all lands described in the 1867 Medicine Lodge Treaty, an area known as the Cherokee Outlet, and the 1869 executive order reservation, which had actually superseded the tribes' claims to the Cherokee Outlet. Only a few chiefs and a small number of the educated members of the tribes were invited to this council. The Whites hoped to gain financially from any cession agreements. The Cheyenne and Arapaho were divided on the issues of whether to sell land at all or how to go about such a sale if one was agreed to by a consensus. During this time, federal authorities dismissed as invalid the earlier contract drawn up by the lawyers. An agreement between the federal representatives and the Cheyenne and Arapaho was signed by some chiefs in Oct. 1890; the subsequent garnering of signatures of 70 percent of the adult males, required for submission of the document for Congressional approval, was subject to corruption by the agents and other interested parties (Berthrong 1976: 148–152, 165–167). Congress eventually ratified the agreement wherein the Cheyenne and Arapaho gave up claims to the Cherokee Outlet, and lands in the 1869 executive order reservation were to be allotted at 160 acres for each person. Cheyennes and Arapahoes were each paid 75 silver dollars for their surplus lands. Portions of land were retained for schools, missions, agencies, and military activities. Surplus lands were opened up to White settlement on April 19, 1892 (Ekirch 1974:222–224). Photographer unidentified.

225

1978).

Allotment, Restoration, Termination, and Claims

Federal officials believed that the Indian land system, whereby the Indians held their reservation lands in common with title vested in the tribe, nourished a continuing tribal government. They concluded that the way to break resistive tribal force and communal strength would be to abolish reservations and assign each Indian an allotment of land in fee simple. Private ownership of land, allotment in severalty, would accomplish what 20 years of reservation life had not. What officials failed to acknowledge, but was a compelling force in the movement behind the liquidation of Indian reservations, was that considerable land embraced by Indian reservations held agricul-

U. of Okla. Lib., Western Hist. Coll., Norman: Phillips 1524.

Fig. 7. Choctaw citizens receiving their per capita shares of money derived from the sale of townsites, Smithville, Indian Terr. An 1893 law authorized the Dawes Commission to supervise the allotment of Choctaw, Creek, Cherokee, Chickasaw, and Seminole tribal lands in Indian Territory. In 1898 the Choctaw ratified the Atoka Agreement, which outlined the conditions for the dissolution of lands. In general, under this agreement all land except for public buildings, townsites, and mineral lands would be alloted equally among members of the tribe; citizens would receive equal shares of the proceeds of any town lots that were sold; income from mineral resources would be used for education; and the tribal government would be increasingly limited and ultimately dissolved. Townsite sales began in 1899 under the direction of a 2-member commission, one member an appointee from the Dawes Commission and a second appointed by the Choctaw principal chief. By 1907, the year Okla. became a state, approximately 90 towns were platted. The Choctaw protested the delayed distribution of the sale proceeds, arguing that the money would offset financial problems that were causing some Choctaws to prematurely sell their allotments. Distribution of the townsite money began in 1904 (Debo 1934:246–247, 255–264, 269, 278–280). Photographer unidentified, 1906.

tural promise, and thereby was coveted by homesteaders. By the 1880s settlers had filed upon most of the arable land in the West under the Homestead Act and other federal land-dispensing statutes. Indian reservation lands then, in a sense, comprised the agrarians' last frontier.

Congress passed the Dawes Severalty Act in 1887, which provided for the assignment to each Indian of an allotment of 160 acres of reservation land, to be held in trust by the federal government for 25 years. It applied to virtually all reservation lands with promise for agricultural development. Thus, those reservations in the desert and mountain regions, which at that time were not coveted by Anglo-American settlers for farming and stockraising or by corporate interests for timber and mineral exploitation, escaped the allotment process. In Indian Territory all the reservations were liquidated under the terms of the Dawes Severalty Act as amended or under similar statutes. Each member of each tribe was assigned an allotment (fig. 7). The surplus lands in the West after allotment, amounting to over 60,000,000 acres, were opened to homesteaders. Of the acreage assigned to Indians between 1887 and 1934, 27,000,000 acres, or two-thirds of the land allotted, had passed from Indian to non-Indian ownership (fig. 8) (25 U.S.C. 331–334; 329; 341–342; 348–349; 354; 381; Cohen 1982:138).

In 1934, by the terms of the Indian Reorganization Act, a historic process—compression of the Indian estate—ended. This statute terminated allotment in severalty, restored to tribal ownership surplus Indian lands available for non-Indian purchase, and provided for the acquisition of additional land for the tribes in order to maintain "tribal land bases." During the period 1934–1950, the Indian tribal estate actually increased (48 U.S. Stat. 984; 25 U.S.C. 461–479).

A resurgence of old practices occurred during the 1950s under the rhetoric of "termination," a federally sponsored program to conclude national trusteeship for the American Indian. Termination produced a resumption of transfer of Indian land to non-Indian owners. During the period 1953–1957 about 1.8 million acres of Indian land passed from Indian tenure. Termination slowed during the 1960s and was repudiated by the federal government in 1970. However, threats to Indian land tenure persisted, a primary one being resort to eminent domain by the U.S. Army Corps of Engineers and other federal and state agencies to obtain Indian land for construction of dams and reservoirs (fig. 9) as power and flood control projects, highway right-of-way, and other public purposes (Cahn 1969).

Indian leaders have worked to counter these threats to their surviving tribal estates and have achieved modest success in some instances. They have gained cash awards in settlements of certain claims that alleged unlawful sequestration of tribal lands by state and federal authori-

Fig. 8. Advertisement by the U.S. Dept. of the Interior offering surplus Indian lands for sale, 1910–1911. Once all Indian allotments had been made and certain lands were set aside for schools, missions, and other administrative needs for a particular tribe, the federal government opened up surplus lands to non-Indians. Lands could also be sold under other conditions. Indians age 21 years or older could sell allotments held under a trust patent according to the act of March 1, 1907 (34 U.S. Stat. 1015–1018). Lands for which a patent with restrictions against alienation was issued could be sold according to the act of March 7, 1907 (34 U.S. Stat. 1015–1018), as modified by the act of June 25, 1910 (36 U.S. Stat. 855–856). While the money from the sale was the property of the Indian, the commissioner of Indian affairs assumed the responsibility for the disbursement of the money to the individual (ARCIA 1910:39–40). A provision was also made for the disposal of land by Indians who inherited allotments (so as to insure that individuals would not hold a surplus of land or by individuals deemed as "competent" by the secretary of the interior who then issued a patent in fee. In 1911, 340,000 acres were affected by laws and provisions for disposal, and a total of 150,000 acres were sold for $2,500,000 at an average of $16 per acre (ARCIA 1912: 25–26). The Indian on the poster is Not Afraid of Pawnee, a Yankton Sioux photographed by Delancey Gill in Washington in 1905 (Smithsonian, NAA:3581-b-1).

ties. In other instances the result has been restitution of former tribal land or purchase of other land for tribal use.

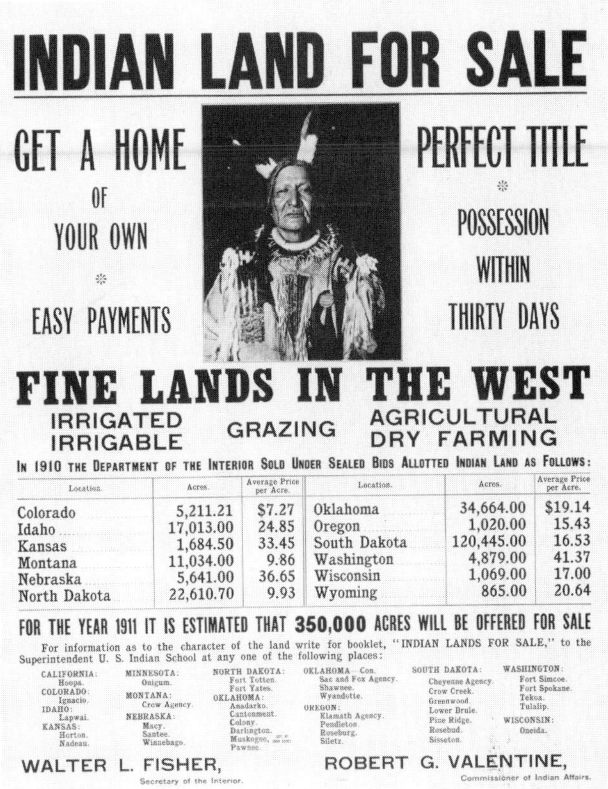

This counter movement in restitution by money or land is the result, largely, of a gradual change in Native American stance from activism to advocacy, from stridency in the streets to persuasive, rational quest for remedy in Congress, state legislatures, and federal courts. The agencies responsible for the change in Native American strategy are reactivated tribal governments supporting leaders capable of fashioning appeals to improve Native

Buffalo and Erie Co. Histl. Soc., Courier-Express Coll., Buffalo, N.Y.

Fig. 9. Tuscarora Indians protesting plans for a reservoir that would flood more than one-fifth of their N.Y. reservation. left to right, William Rickard, John Hewitt, and Wallace Anderson. When the N.Y. State Power Authority (S.P.A. on the sign) made plans in 1957 for the reservoir, the Tuscarora responded through legal channels and physical protest. Although the Federal Power Commission ordered the N.Y. Power Authority to halt its plans, in 1960 the ruling was reversed by the U.S. Supreme Court and the reservoir was built (vol. 15:523–524). Photograph taken 1958.

UPI/Bettman Newsphotos, New York, N.Y.: 1704097.

Fig. 10. Representatives of the St. Regis Reservation hold the treaty of May 31, 1796 (7 U.S. Stat. 55), evidence of their claim of jurisdiction over the town of Hogansburg, N.Y. left to right, Connie Tarbel, Lawrence Lazore, Karoniakesom Thomas, and Standing Arrow at the capitol in Albany, May 10, 1971. The state of N.Y. had erected signs in Hogansburg indicating the entrance to the Mohawk Nation, placing Hogansburg in the township of Bombay and outside the reservation boundaries. At issue was both the Mohawks' claim to Hogansburg and the fact that only the federal government, and not the state, could negotiate with the tribe (Karoniakesom Thomas, communication to editors 1987). St. Regis boundaries have also been disputed on an international scale since Indian land extends into Canada (vol. 15:471, 476–477; Hauptman 1986:146–149). Photographer unidentified.

American life including restitution of the tribal estate. The resort to courts to accomplish these goals has been strengthened by the formation of several Native American legal action groups including the Native American Rights Fund, founded in 1970, which is made up largely of Indians educated as lawyers.

Indian action groups began some restitution work in 1946 when Congress enacted the Indian Claims Commission Act. The Indian Claims Commission considered and settled claims filed by Indian tribes before August 13, 1951, that had accrued prior to the enactment of the act. Surviving Indian communities, if successful in their suits, were awarded monetary compensation for appropriated lands. Damages were based on rates determined by expert witnesses to be the fair value of the land at the time it was appropriated by the federal government. Congress extended the life of the Indian Claims Commission five times to settle the claims before it. The last extension expired on September 30, 1978. On its dissolution, all claims that the Commission had not adjudicated were transferred to the United States Court of Claims, which was also given jurisdiction of Indian claims arising after the establishment of the Indian Claims Commission. The Court of

Claims had a more limited scope; it had jurisdiction only of claims arising "under the Constitution, law or treaties of the United States, or Executive orders of the President, or which otherwise would be cognizable in the Claims Court if the claimant were not an Indian tribe, band or group" (60 U.S. Stat. 1050).

Some tribes have preferred land restitution to monetary compensation. During the 1970s a number of tribes regained possession of former tribal lands (fig. 2d). In 1970 the return of 48,000 acres to the Taos Pueblo culminated a 64-year effort by Taos leaders to regain possession of Blue Lake and its watershed area. In 1975 Congress returned 185,000 acres in the Grand Canyon to the Havasupai tribe in Arizona; Havasupai attempts to regain some of their ancestoral lands had begun in the early twentieth century (90 U.S. Stat. 1990; 84 U.S. Stat. 1437; 88 U.S. Stat. 2089).

Other tribes in the 1970s succeeded in their efforts to restore former lands to their land base. For example, the Confederated Tribes of the Warm Springs Reservation in Oregon received approximately 61,000 acres; the Northern Paiute and Western Shoshone of Fallon Reservation in Nevada regained about 2,700 acres; the Santa Ana and Zia Pueblos in New Mexico recovered 16,000 acres and 4,850 acres, respectively; and the Yakima tribe in Washington secured possession of Mount Adams and 21,000 acres. In

1975 Congress passed legislation authorizing the secretary of the interior to restore surplus lands to tribes (88 U.S. Stat. 1954).

Since the 1970s some tribes have obtained restitution in the form of monetary awards and land. In 1971 Congress enacted the Alaska Native Claims Settlement Act. It represented the largest amount of land ever received by American Indians for the extinguishment of aboriginal title. The Alaska Natives recovered over 40 million acres, 462.5 million dollars, and mineral royalties not to exceed 500 million dollars. Fee simple patents were to be issued to village and regional corporations established by the act. The settlement culminated several decades of efforts by Alaska Native groups to obtain title to their aboriginal lands (85 U.S. Stat. 688).

Tribal remnants, such as Penobscots, Passamaquoddies, and Maliseets in Maine, Wampanoags in Massachusetts, Narragansetts in Rhode Island, Pequots in Connecticut, Mohawks, Oneidas, and Cayugas in New York, and Catawbas in South Carolina—casualties of colonial and early state and national territorial sequestration—also sought restitution in the form of monetary compensation and land. Each tribal claim has been based on the trade and intercourse acts of the 1790s, which required Congress to ratify all land transactions with tribes. Claimant tribes alleged that the requirements of these laws were never met. Most of these tribes have filed lawsuits against state or local governments or private parties owning the claimed lands. In some instances, the tribes have negotiated settlements to their land claims, and Congress had implemented these agreements by enacting Indian claims settlement acts (Campisi 1985).

The Narragansetts were the first to win a settlement of their claims. In 1978 Congress enacted the Rhode Island Indian Claims Settlement Act implementing the negotiated settlement among the Narragansetts, the state of Rhode Island, and other parties to the lawsuits. The Settlement Act provided for the restoration of 1,800 acres of former tribal land, one-half of the land to be donated by the state, the other half to be purchased from private owners with federal funds. Congress authorized the appropriation of 3.5 million dollars to purchase the private lands. The land was to be transferred to a state-chartered and Indian-controlled corporation. In return the Narragansetts agreed to the extinguishment of their land claims and to the extinguishment of their aboriginal title (92 U.S. Stat. 813).

In 1980 Congress enacted a settlement of Penobscot, Passamaquoddy, and Maliseet claims. These tribes claimed aboriginal title to 12,500,000 acres in Maine. Congress authorized the appropriation of $54,500,000 to purchase for these tribes over 300,000 acres of land from private owners, largely lumber and pulp companies. The Maine Indian Claims Settlement Act also created a $27,000,000 trust fund to be invested by the Penobscot and Passamaquoddy tribes. In return the tribes agreed to the extinguishment of their aboriginal title and land claims (94 U.S. Stat. 1785).

Some eastern tribes have not been successful in their efforts to recover former tribal lands or to obtain monetary compensation. In 1978 the Wampanoag claim to 16,000 acres on Cape Cod was denied by the federal district court in Boston on the grounds that the Wampanoags did not constitute a tribe in a federal sense and therefore were not qualified to pursue their claim (444 U.S. 866).

The Indian Claims Limitation Act of 1982 (96 U.S. Stat. 1976) provided for the amendment of the Statute of Limitation for most pre-1966 Indian claims. Permission to file claims not already registered with the secretary of the interior was extremely limited.

229

The Legal Status of American Indians

LAWRENCE BACA

Definition of an Indian

The federal government has considered biological, ethnological, and social factors in the legal history of Indian-White relations. According to the *Handbook of Federal Indian Law*, "if a person is three-fourths Caucasian and one-fourth Indian, it is absurd, from the ethnological standpoint, to assign him to the Indian race. Yet legally such a person may be an Indian. From a legal standpoint, then, the biological question of race is generally pertinent, but not conclusive" (Cohen 1942:2). The 1982 edition of that *Handbook* continues: "Racial composition is not always dispositive in determining who are Indians for the purposes of Indian law. In dealing with Indians, the federal government is dealing with members or descendants of political entities, that is, Indian tribes, not with persons of a particular race. Tribal membership as determined by the Indian tribe or community itself is often an essential element. In fact, a person of complete Indian ancestry who has never had relations with any Indian tribe may be considered a non-Indian for some legal purposes" (Cohen 1982:19). One Circuit Court held in 1912 that persons of one-eighth Indian blood were "of sufficient Indian blood to substantially handicap them in the struggle for existence" and therefore were Indians (Cohen 1942:4). The Supreme Court decided in 1876 that the Pueblo tribes of New Mexico were not to be treated as an Indian group (*United States* v. *Joseph*, 94 U.S. 614, 616) because they were agricultural, Christian, "peaceable, industrious, intelligent, honest and virtuous people. They are Indians only in feature, complexion, and a few of their habits; in all other respects superior to all but a few of the civilized tribes of the country, and the equal of the most civilized thereof." In 1913 (*United States* v. *Sandoval*, 231 U.S. 28) the Supreme Court concluded that federal guardianship and legislative control over the Pueblos *was* appropriate. Citing reports of drunkenness, debauchery, dancing, and communal living, the Court concluded that these *were* Indians and subject to the guardianship of the federal government.

It is generally concluded that the indices of Indianness that may have influenced the courts and federal government in these cases would not be accepted in the 1980s. Who is an Indian may depend on the purpose for which the question is asked. Congressional legislation often contains a definition of who it is meant to affect. The Indian Reorganization Act of 1934 contained this definition:

> The term 'Indian' as used in this Act shall include all persons of Indian descent who are members of any recognized Indian tribe now under Federal jurisdiction, and all persons who are descendants of such members who were, on June 1, 1934, residing within the present boundaries of any Indian reservation, and shall further include all other persons of one-half Indian blood. For the purposes of this Act, Eskimos and other aboriginal people of Alaska shall be considered Indians (48 U.S. Stat. 984).

While there has never been a general definition of the term Indian that could be used by the courts, a good working definition of Indian for general understanding of the legal status of American Indians would be the following: a person, some of whose ancestors lived in America before the arrival of Whites, who is generally considered to be an Indian by the community in which he lives or from which he comes, and who holds himself to be an Indian.

The importance of being able to decide who is and who is not an Indian is readily understandable. The Supreme Court held in 1978 that an Indian tribe cannot exercise criminal jurisdiction over the actions of non-Indians even though those actions occur within the boundaries of the tribe's reservations (*Oliphant* v. *Suquamish Tribe of Indians*, 435 U.S. 191). In 1959 (*Williams* v. *Lee*, 358 U.S. 217), the Supreme Court held that the state courts of Arizona had no authority to hear a debt collection case by a non-Indian against an Indian where the action arose on the Navajo Indian Reservation. The jurisdiction over that matter would lie exclusively with the tribal court. It is likely that a similar action against a non-Indian debtor would, however, be considered outside the tribe's jurisdiction and within the power of the state courts to adjudicate (Cohen 1982). For criminal jurisdiction purposes, crimes by Indians that are committed within the reservation borders are controlled only by tribal or federal laws. In 1974 (*Morton* v. *Mancari*, 417 U.S. 535) the Supreme Court upheld an employment preference for Indians in the Bureau of Indian Affairs, and in 1977 (*United States* v. *Antelope*, 430 U.S. 461) it upheld a criminal statute that applied the federal felony murder rule to Indian country and created a situation where Indians were treated less favorably than they would have been treated under the state law. In both these cases the Court focused on the unique status of Indians as members of political bodies: specifically, as members of recognized tribes (Clinton 1981). In each case the unique status of being Indian affected the outcome. Non-Indians could not and would not receive the special treatment.

Foundations of the Principles of Federal Indian Law

Indian tribes are limited sovereigns that retain their original inherited powers of sovereignty over their peoples and their territories except for those powers specifically removed by treaty, federal law, or by natural implication as a result of their dependent status. An American Indian who is a tribal member has three citizenships. He is a citizen of his tribe, a citizen of the United States, and a citizen of the state in which he resides. A tribal member thus owes allegiance and duty to each of these three sovereigns and receives from each certain benefits and protections.

These basic principles are the foundations of the legal status of American Indians. They are the linchpins of an entire body of federal law that applies only to Indians. Kappler (1904–1941) contains the federal statutes and treaties that govern the lives and affairs of American Indians. Federal regulations, and federal and state court opinions, add to this body of laws that deal only with Indians.

The relationship between the United States government and Indians is unlike that between the government and any other group in America. Indian tribes are political groups as well as part of a larger racial group. This relationship between the United States and American Indians has been called unique. It has been likened to that of a guardian to its ward. It has been called a fiduciary and a trust relationship. The special relationship between Indians and the federal government is established in the Constitution of the United States, which grants to Congress the power "to regulate Commerce with foreign nations, among the states and with the Indian Tribes." (Congressional power to regulate the affairs of Indians has also been found in the war powers and treaty powers of the Constitution.) Second, at the core of all these decisions, laws, and regulations is the fact that Indian tribes are sovereigns and that the relationship between Indian tribes and the United States is a government-to-government relationship. (A list of all Indian tribes in the United States with which the United States maintains a government-to-government relationship is published annually in the *Federal Register*.)

The threads of the fabric that is the legal status of American Indians go back to the formative years of constitutional law and Chief Justice John Marshall, whose guiding hand is still felt as both a restraint and a moving force of the Supreme Court's decisions involving Indian law. Chief Justice Marshall wrote the opinions in *Cherokee Nation* v. *Georgia* (5 Pet. 1 [1831]) and *Worcester* v. *Georgia* (6 Pet. 515 [1832]), the two most influential cases in the early history of the Supreme Court's considerations of the status of American Indians.

The Cherokee Nation requested the Supreme Court of the United States to enjoin the "State of Georgia from the execution of certain laws of that state" over the territory and people of the Cherokee Nation. The case had been brought in the Supreme Court because the constitutional authority of the Court extends to cases between states and foreign states. Therefore, the primary question before the court was whether or not the Cherokee Nation was a foreign state in the constitutional sense and thus capable of bringing the action at all. The Court had no difficulty in finding that the Cherokee Nation was a "state, as a distinct political society, separated from others, capable of managing its own affairs and governing itself" (5 Pet. 10, 11 [1831]). But the Court did not find that the Cherokees were a foreign state.

In 1831, when the case was filed, Indians generally were not citizens of the United States. The fact that they were not citizens was at the core of the Cherokee argument: they were not, as individuals, citizens of the United States, therefore they were foreign to it; a state made up of individuals who are foreigners must be a foreign state. Yet in commercial intercourse with foreign nations and attempts at intercourse between Indian nations and foreign nations, Indians have been considered by the United States and foreign nations to be within the jurisdictional limits of the United States. In treaties, tribes acknowledged themselves to be under the protection of the United States. Thus, the Court could not find them to be foreign states. "They may, more correctly, perhaps be denominated domestic dependent nations. They occupy a territory to which we assert a title independent of their will, which must take effect in point of possession when their right of possession ceases. Meanwhile they are in a state of pupilage. Their relation to the United States resembles that of a ward to his guardian" (5 Pet. 10, 12 [1831]). In the commerce clause of the Constitution, Indian tribes were distinguished from foreign nations and from the states of the union. The Court concluded that the issues might be decided by the Court, but only if the proper parties were before it. "If it be true that the Cherokee nation have rights, this is not the tribunal in which those rights are to be asserted. If it be true that wrongs have been inflicted, and that still greater are to be apprehended, this is not the tribunal which can redress the past or prevent the future. The motion for an injunction is denied" (5 Pet. 10, 20 [1831]).

The proper case to decide the rights of these parties was *Worcester* v. *Georgia* in 1832. Samuel A. Worcester had been convicted, under Georgia law, of living among the Cherokee without a state license. Worcester was a citizen of another state, Vermont, and therefore got his case to the Supreme Court on a writ of error to the Supreme Court of the county of Gwinnett, Georgia. This time the court had before it proper parties and questions that it could consider. It was argued by the Cherokee that the Georgia statutes in question abolished their laws and annihilated their political existence. The Court went to the heart of the issue of what right, if any, the Cherokee had to govern themselves.

> America, separated from Europe by a wide ocean, was inhabited by a distinct people, divided into separate nations, independent of each other and of the rest of the world, having institutions of their own, and governing themselves by their own laws. It is difficult to comprehend the proposition, that the inhabitants of either quarter of the globe could have rightful original claim of dominion over the inhabitants of the other, or over the lands they occupied; or that the discovery of either by the other should give the discoverer rights in the country discovered, which annulled the existing right of its ancient possessors . . . .
> But power, war, conquest, give rights, which, after possession, are conceded by the world; and which can never be controverted by those on whom they descend. We proceed, then, to the actual state of things, having glanced at their origin; because holding it in our recollections might shed some light on existing pretensions (6 Pet. 515, 541–542 [1832]).

The tribes were treated as nations with whom the great powers of Europe could enter into treaties. The United States, as inheritors to the claims of the English Crown, continued that practice. Marshall wrote of the Treaty of Hopewell of 1785 with the Cherokees that there was a mutual exchange of peace between two sovereigns. "This relation was that of a nation claiming and receiving the protection of one more powerful: not that of individuals abandoning their national character, and submitting as subjects to the laws of a master" (6 Pet. 515, 554 [1832]). Marshall reiterated the theme that a nation may ally itself with a stronger nation and still remain an independent nation: "The Cherokee nation, then, is a distinct community, occupying its own territory, with boundaries accurately described, in which the laws of Georgia can have no force, and which the citizens of Georgia have no right to enter, but with the assent of the Cherokees themselves, or in conformity with treaties, and with the acts of congress" (6 Pet. 515, 560 [1832]).

The Court's decision in these two cases, *Cherokee Nation* v. *Georgia* and *Worcester* v. *Georgia*, can be reduced to the simple assertions that the Supreme Court has no original jurisdiction to hear a case brought by an Indian tribe against a state of the union and that the state of Georgia has no jurisdiction to pass laws over the Cherokee Nation of Indians or its territory. Within them are the foundations of the great principles of federal Indian law, of federal-Indian relations, of state-Indian

relations, and of the legal status of the American Indians. In these cases Indian tribes are distinct political communities having the right to make their own laws and be governed by themselves without the interference of state governments. Here also is the root of the trust doctrine that Indian tribes are wards of the national government deserving of its protection, by force or legislation, their property subject to the benefits if its trusteeship. The parallel theme of the federal government having plenary authority over the affairs of Indians finds its seed in this fertile soil as well. As domestic dependent nations, by implication, the tribes lose the sovereign power to deal with nations other than the United States. The doctrine that Indian treaties should be read to mean what they would have meant to the Indians at the time that they were written is also asserted, as is the maxim that where the meaning of a treaty clause is in doubt the doubt shall be resolved in favor of the Indians. All these doctrines are major themes in federal Indian law and are important to the legal status of American Indians.

Indian Citizenship and Civil Rights

On June 2, 1924, all noncitizen Indians born in the United States were made citizens by the Indian Citizenship Act (43 U.S. Stat. 253). The grant of citizenship to Indians did not terminate the duty of the United States to pass laws for the protection of Indians and their property under the principle of wardship or trust responsibility. The Supreme Court had held (*United States* v. *Nice*, 241 U.S. 591) in 1916 that federal citizenship for Indians was not inconsistent with tribal existence.

Prior to the Citizenship Act of 1924, many Indians had acquired citizenship under other federal laws, such as through marriage of Indians to Whites, military service, receipt of allotments, or through treaties (fig. 1). The Supreme Court had held, in 1884, that the Fourteenth Amendment did not automatically make Indians citizens (*Elk* v. *Wilkins*, 112 U.S. 94). In fact, the Senate Judiciary Committee had filed a report by resolution in 1870, concluding that Indians did not become citizens by passage of the Fourteenth Amendment. The universal grant of citizenship by the Act added to the debate about the effects of citizenship on peoples under wardship, peoples over whom the federal government exercised great and extensive powers. The answer, in short, was that Indian citizenship did not alter the power of Congress over Indians. This is an extremely important point for the governance of Indian reservations, as the Supreme Court has held that the states have no jurisdiction over Indians on their reservations so long as they are maintaining tribal relations (*United States* v. *Kagama*, 118 U.S. 375 [1886]). On the other hand, citizenship is not incompatible with the federal guardianship. Citizenship did not extend state jurisdiction into Indian country, although federal citizenship made Indians citizens of the states in which they reside. Nor did the fact of citizenship create any constitutional protection for Indians against the actions of their tribal governments (*Toledo* v. *Pueblo of Jemez*, 119 F. Supp. 429 (1954)).

It has been held that Indians who reside on an Indian reservation and therefore may not be subject to state laws nevertheless have the right to vote for and to run for state and county offices. State laws denying Indians the right to vote because of their status as wards of the federal government or because they maintain tribal membership have been struck down by the courts (Op. Sol. M. 29596; *Harrison* v. *Laveen*, 67 Ariz. 337, 196 P.2d 456 (1948)).

Arguments have periodically been made in the name of Indian equality. Abbot (1888) argued that the goal of the nation should be to equalize the rights and status of American Indians, offering them the same "personal, legal, and political status which is common to all other inhabitants." The argument for equality for Indian citizens re-emerged in the 1980s in the context of jurisdictional issues, hunting and fishing rights, and water rights. Groups such as the Interstate Congress for Racial Equality believe that many of the rights granted to Indians by treaties and other federal laws make Indians more than equal. Some have argued for equality by federal abolition of treaty rights, dissolution of reservations, and termination of trust status of Indian lands. Indians in the nineteenth and twentieth centuries have opposed the "full citizenship" offered (Leupp 1910; U.S. Commission on Civil Rights 1981).

Indians comprise both political and racial groups. As a racial group, Indians are protected by all the civil rights laws and constitutional prohibitions against denials of rights based on race (Cohen 1982). As political groups, Indians are exempt from the application of some state and federal laws within their territories. Because Indians are political groups, Congress may pass laws that favor Indians over non-Indians (*Morton* v. *Mancari*, 417 U.S. 535 [1974]). It is also as political groups, as governments that predate the Constitution, that tribal governments are unrestricted by the Bill of Rights of the Constitution. The Supreme Court early held that the right to a grand jury indictment for a capital offense under the Fifth Amendment did not apply to a tribal prosecution by the Cherokee Nation. The Court's analysis was that the Fifth Amendment was a restriction only on the actions of the federal government and that, while the federal government recognized the powers of the Cherokee Nation and had the power to regulate the manner in which those powers were exercised, it had not created the Cherokee Nation or its government (*Talton* v. *Mayes*, 163 U.S. 376 [1896]).

Federal citizenship did not affect the rights of Indians with respect to tribal government power. Legal commentators lamented the failure of the courts to recognize any constitutional protection enjoyed by Indians against arbitrary actions of tribal governments. In the 1960s, Congress undertook extensive hearings on the rights of Indians under tribal government. These hearings led to

left, State Histl. Soc. of N. Dak., Bismark: Fiske Coll. 372; right, Natl. Arch.: RG48, Central Files 1907–1936, 5–6 General, Competent Indians, Pt. 3.

Fig. 1. Scenes from a ritual of admission to citizenship on 2 reservations. left, Shooting the last arrow on the Standing Rock Reservation, N. Dak., Dec. 18, 1917. James McLaughlin, Indian Service, is standing behind the table. right, Taking hold of a plow at Crow Creek Agency, S. Dak., Nov. 8, 1916. McLaughlin reads from a script as a Sioux takes a plow. Indians deemed "competent" would have their lands allotted in fee simple and were granted citizenship in a ritual developed by the secretary of the interior in 1916 and usually presided over by McLaughlin, a former agent. In this ritual, Indians were told they were to live as White men and women. The ritual used a prepared script. The following activities, each accompanied by a brief speech, were performed for each new citizen: the men used their Indian name for the final time and shot their last arrow; men took a plow and, addressed by their White name, were admonished about the importance of work for a White man; a purse was given as a symbol of thrift; an oath was made while touching the American flag; and, finally, a badge of citizenship, adorned with an eagle, was pinned on their breasts. The ritual for women, somewhat shorter, began with a presentation of a work bag and a purse, accompanied by a speech regarding the nature of the White woman's role in the home and the importance of thrift; an oath was then pledged on the flag; a pin, also adorned by an eagle, awarded. The woman's Indian name was not used in the ritual (Natl. Arch.: RG48, Dept. of Interior, Office of the Secretary, Central Classified File 1907–1936, 5–6, Attorneys and Agents, Competent Indians; Deloria 1971:141–143). left, Photograph by Frank B. Fiske; right, photographer unidentified.

THE LEGAL STATUS OF AMERICAN INDIANS

the enactment of the Indian Civil Rights Act of 1968, passed as Title II of the Civil Rights Act of 1968 (82 U.S. Stat. 73). The Act specifically restricted the actions of tribal governments in ways similar to the restrictions placed on the federal government by the Bill of Rights.

It was the intent of Congress to make a limited intrusion on tribal self-government (Burnett 1972). The Indian Civil Rights Act, moreover, refers to persons, not Indians or tribal members. The protections of the Indian Civil Rights Act apply to non-Indians and Indians, tribal members and nontribal members, when within the jurisdiction of the Indian tribe. Congress thus acknowledged that Indian tribes exercised powers over non-Indians as well as Indians in some instances. While the rights created have the appearance of constitutional rights, they are not. They are statutory rights. In interpreting the act, the federal courts for 10 years after its passage tried to balance the rights of individuals, the intent of Congress that these rights be interpreted in the tribal context, and the cultures of the individual tribes. Congress was clear in restricting the "constitutional" interpretation of some sections by specifically *not* forbidding the establishment of a tribal religion and by requiring those contesting tribal rulings to obtain counsel at their own expense. In other areas courts and some legal commentators simply looked to what the federal courts had said these phrases in the Constitution meant and held them to mean the same thing in the tribal context, in part because constitutional interpretation was a ready reference point and in part because the provisions of the act were called "Constitutional rights" in the statute's title.

The Supreme Court held in the case of *Santa Clara Pueblo* v. *Martinez* (436 U.S. 49) in 1978 that there was no right of action in a federal court created by the passage of the Indian Civil Rights Act, except the right of habeas corpus, specifically created by Section 203. The rights created by the act may be vindicated only in tribal courts. The Court's reasoning was that, because Indian tribes are sovereigns, they are immune from suit, and therefore, actions could not be brought against them in federal courts unless that immunity were waived; but it found that Congress had *not* intended to waive an Indian tribe's immunity from suit in passing the act. Thus, the interpretation of what these rights are and how they apply in a tribal setting are left to the tribes and tribal courts (fig. 2).

The Indian Reorganization Act

Perhaps the most revolutionary piece of federal Indian legislation was the Indian Reorganization Act of 1934 (IRA) (48 U.S. Stat. 984). The Act was meant to encourage Indian economic development, self-determination, and the preservation of tribal organization. The most significant provisions of the act (codified at 25 U.S.C.

Natl. Arch.: RG75-N-Pin-68.

Fig. 2. Indian tribal court, Pine Ridge Reservation, S. Dak. left to right, Rose Ecoffey, clerk and judge; unidentified; Moses Two Bulls, judge. The Indian Reorganization Act of 1934 effected changes in Indian tribunals. Justice was administered either under a code designated by the tribe and approved by the secretary of the interior or under the same judicial regulations that had been used by the Courts of Indian Offenses (Hagan 1966:150–151). Tribal courts, of which 51 were established by 1964, were able to incorporate customs and traditions that were a part of tribal cultures. Although a BIA model was often adopted, tribal courts were better organized to meet the particular needs of the tribe, which, in turn, had more control over the court (Deloria and Lytle 1983:116). Photograph by John Vachon, 1940.

461–479) are: the prohibition of future allotments of Indian lands; the indefinite extension of the trust periods of Indian lands and restrictions against alienation; the restoration of tribal lands previously opened for sale or settlement; giving the secretary of the interior the authority to establish conservation regulations on Indian lands and to declare newly acquired lands Indian reservations; creation of a revolving credit fund for loans to incorporated tribes; creation of preference for the employment of Indians within the Indian Bureau; provision for tribes to organize and adopt constitutional forms of government; provision for the formation of business corporations by the tribes, with charters of corporation issued by the secretary of the interior; and provision for any tribe to avoid the application of the act to its reservation where a majority of the tribal members voted against its application.

In the two years following the act's passage, 181 tribes voted to accept the IRA, and 77 tribes voted against it. Within 12 years, 161 constitutions and 131 corporate charters had been adopted pursuant to the IRA (Anonymous 1972; Cohen 1942:130; Haas 1947; G.D. Taylor

1980).

The powers granted under the act to the tribes are largely powers that the tribes as sovereigns already exercised and are powers that continue to be exercised by many tribes that did not accept the IRA. The Navajo Nation, whose population was some 45,000 at the time of the act's passage, represented half the Indians who rejected the IRA, but in the 1980s the Navajo Nation exercises all the same powers that the IRA tribes do. The basic powers of self-government are inherent powers of sovereign nations. They were neither granted nor restricted by the IRA. The IRA was probably a useful means of achieving an effective and organized tribal government on some reservations where there had previously not been one. Tribal experience under the IRA is as varied as the tribes that accepted it (fig. 3).

Termination

One demonstration of the power of the federal govenment in Indian affairs was the policy of termination of the special status of Indians carried on by the Congress and the executive branch in the 1950s. Since colonial times it was believed by the non-Indian governments that Indian communities would simply disappear over time, as Indian people intermarried with the non-Indian community and as they assimilated Euro-American culture. The federal program of the late 1800s to allot Indian lands to individual Indians and to break up reservations and tribal governments was one governmental effort to assist that assimilation. The allotment program did not succeed. The Indian Reorganization Act halted the allotment program and sought to stabilize tribal governments and to preserve tribal identity. But the desire to assimilate Indians into the American mainstream did not die. Congressional efforts to foster a policy of terminating the special status of American Indians began shortly after passage of the Indian Reorganization Act and may have been a side effect of its enactment.

Various programs such as relocation of individual Indians and their families from their home reservations to urban areas were already in operation when the Congress set forth the policy of termination with the adoption of House Concurrent Resolution 108 in 1953. It stated "the policy of Congress, as rapidly as possible, to make the Indians within the territorial limits of the United States subject to the same laws and entitled to the same privileges and responsibilities as are applicable to other citizens of the United States, to end their status as wards of the United States, and to grant them all of the rights and prerogatives pertaining to American citizenship; and" that "the Indians within the territorial limits of the United States should assume their full responsibilities as American citizens." All tribes and individual Indians in "the states of California, Florida, New York, and Texas" as

UPI/Bettman Newsphotos: 323964 (ACME).
Fig. 3. Chief Victor Vandenberg and Chief Martin Charlo, representatives from the Flathead Reservation, Mont., in Washington, D.C., receive a constitution and by-laws made under the Indian Reorganization Act from Secretary of the Interior Harold Ickes. The confederated Kutenai and Salish tribes of that reservation had the first tribal government established under the Indian Reorganization Act. The reservation was divided into districts, each with representatives to the tribal council, that differed in tribal composition and the proportion of mixed-bloods. Such differences presented difficulties for the new government, and an attempt was made at decentralization in 1936 and 1937. However, continuing problems arose from these differences, and the validity of a "tribal" government was in question on the Flathead Reservation (G.D. Taylor 1980:83–85). Photographed Oct. 29, 1935.

well as five other named tribes "should be freed from federal supervision and control and from all disabilities and limitations specially applicable to Indians" (Washburn 1964:397–398).

House Concurrent Resolution 108 was followed shortly by Public Law 83–280 (67 U.S. Stat. 588), and several termination bills for specific tribes. What is popularly called Public Law 280 is a complex statutory scheme that transferred jurisdiction over Indian lands in several states to those states and provided a mechanism whereby all other states could unilaterally take civil and criminal jurisdiction over Indian lands within their borders. Due to the additional financial burden involved in assuming jurisdiction over Indian lands, few states even attempted to exercise this authority. Public Law 280 was amended in 1968 to provide for tribal consent (82 U.S. Stat. 73), so that no state could take jurisdiction over an Indian reservation without the concurrence of the voting members of the reservation involved. The 1968 amendment also provided authority for states that had previously assumed jurisdiction over any Indian lands to retrocede that jurisdiction to the tribes.

Public Law 280 was one of the major pieces of termination legislation. Its passage greatly diminished the power of Indian tribes during the period 1953–1968 because some tribes were placed within the unilateral power of the states. While the law (para. 1162) specifically reserved to the tribes or the federal government jurisdiction over "the alienation, encumbrance, or taxation of any real or personal property . . . [and] any right, privilege, or immunity afforded under Federal treaty, agreement, or statute with respect to hunting, trapping, or fishing," it removed within the mandatory states—California, Minnesota (except for Red Lake Reservation), Nebraska, Oregon (except for Warm Springs Reservation), and Wisconsin (except for Menominee Reservation, terminated later by specific legislation)—a great measure of sovereign power (Cohen 1982:176; Goldberg 1975; Cree 1974).

The termination process was basically a three-step process. The first was an administrative decision that a tribe was ready for termination. The four tests for termination of federal responsibility were degree of acculturation of the tribe, the economic resources and condition of the tribe, the willingness of the tribe to be relieved of federal control, and the willingness of the state to take over (Tyler 1973:163). The second step was for a congressional termination act for the tribe or tribal groups to be passed. The third step was for the secretary of the interior to develop a plan that included a time when termination would be completed. The time was usually longer for larger tribes with larger land bases. Termination essentially meant the end of the special federal relationship and the end of federal services to the terminated tribes and individuals. Between 1954 and 1962, 109 tribes and bands were terminated. At least 1,362,155 acres of land and 11,466 individuals were affected by the legislation. In summary, the effects of termination were: fundamental changes in land ownership patterns; the end of the trust relationship; the imposition of state judicial and legislative authority; the end of state tax exemptions; discontinuance of special federal programs to tribes and individuals; and the end of tribal sovereignty (Wilkinson and Biggs 1977:152–153).

While the effects of termination were severe, the federal courts have held that tribal existence was not destroyed. Tribal powers remained for maintenance of tribal rolls, regulation of hunting and fishing rights, capacity to contract, capacity to receive grants, and standing to sue in court (Cohen 1982). Thus, all that was terminated was federal recognition. Congress may restore this recognition and special relationship and has done so with several tribes.

As early as 1958, the policy of termination was fading from favor in the government. On July 8, 1970, President Richard M. Nixon announced in a message to Congress that "termination is morally and legally unacceptable, . . . it produces bad practical results, and . . . the mere threat of termination tends to discourage greater self-sufficiency among Indian groups." He asked Congress to "expressly renounce, repudiate and repeal the termination policy as expressed in House Concurrent Resolution 108

of the 83rd Congress" (Deloria and Lytle 1983:20).

Congressional Power Over Indian Affairs

In *Worcester* v. *Georgia* Chief Justice Marshall explained that the Constitution conferred on Congress "all that is required for the regulation of our intercourse with the Indians" (6 Pet. 515 [1832]). The power thus described has been called by the Supreme Court "plenary power" over Indian affairs (Newton 1984). The most far-reaching statement of this seemingly limitless power over the affairs of Indians is found in the case of *United States* v. *Kagama* (118 U.S. 375 [1886]). It followed the case of *Ex Parte Crow Dog* (109 U.S. 556 [1883]), in which the Supreme Court held that the United States District Court for the Territory of Dakota did not have jurisdiction to try an Indian for the murder of another Indian when both maintained tribal relations and where the crime was committed within the boundaries of their home reservation. An attorney general's opinion, issued later that year, stated that the same principle would apply to an Indian from one tribe who went to the reservation of a second tribe and there killed an Indian from a third reservation. Federal law applicable to the Indian country at the time excepted crimes by one Indian against the person or property of another Indian. Public pressure led to congressional reaction and the enactment of the Major Crimes Act in 1885 (23 U.S. Stat. 62), which covered the following offenses (later amended to 16): "murder, manslaughter, rape, incest, assault with intent to kill, assault with a dangerous weapon, arson, burglary, robbery and larceny" when committed by an Indian against the person or property of another within the Indian country, subject to the courts and jurisdiction of the United States (Cohen 1982:163).

An Indian called Kagama was the first man tried under the Major Crimes Act to contest its validity. He was charged with the murder of another Indian on the Hoopa Reservation in California. The essential question before the Court was whether the constitutional power existed to pass such a law over the affairs of Indians maintaining "the usual tribal relations" governing acts occurring within the boundaries of an Indian reservation. The Court's opinion described the tribes as semi-independent and not possessing the full attributes of sovereignty. Congress had enacted in 1871 a statute (16 U.S. Stat. 544) terminating the making of treaties with Indian tribes. Congress had chosen to move to governing Indian relations by acts of Congress rather than by treaty. The court had no trouble in finding the constitutional power to do so. Couched in the language of the government as protector of the Indian tribes, the opinion stated:

> These Indian tribes *are* the wards of the nation. They are communities *dependent* on the United Sates. Dependent largely for their daily food. Dependent for their political rights. They owe no allegience to the States, and receive from

them no protection. Because of the local ill feeling, the people of the States where they are found are often their deadliest enemies. From their very weakness and helplessness so largely due to the course of dealing of the Federal Government with them and the treaties in which it has been promised, there arises the duty of protection, and with it the power. This has always been recognized by the Executive and by Congress, and by this court, whenever the question has arisen (118 U.S. 375, 383–384 [1886]).

Then, in perhaps the single most powerful expression of the authority of the federal government over Indian tribes, the Court's opinion concluded:

"The power of the General Government over these remnants of a race once powerful, now weak and diminished in numbers, is necessary to their protection, as well as to the safety of those among whom they dwell. It must exist in that government, because it never has existed anywhere else, because the theatre of its existence is within the geographical limits of the United States, because it has never been denied, and because it alone can enforce its laws on all the tribes" (118 U.S. 375 [1886]).

To be sure, there are some restraints on the power of the federal government in the regulation of Indian affairs. The notion presented by *Kagama* that the commitment to provide protection for the Indian tribes brings with it the power to do so in any manner it sees fit is tempered by the doctrine that the federal government acts for the benefit of Indian tribes. Thus the notion that treaties are to be read in favor of the Indians is an assumed part of the guardianship theory. The treaties were written by the United States in their language and translated by their interpreters to the Indians. Therefore, the courts have always held the meaning of the language must be taken as what the Indians would have understood it to mean at the time of signing. This concept has been applied to statutes as well, and to regulations written under statutory authority.

The courts have regularly held that Congress has the power to abrogate Indian treaties by statutes passed at a later date that conflict with them. In *Lone Wolf* v. *Hitchcock* (187 U.S. 553 [1903]), the Supreme Court stated: "The power exists to abrogate the provisions of an Indian treaty, though presumably such power will be exercised only when circumstances arise which will not only justify the government in its disregarding the stipulations of the treaty, but may demand, in the interest of the country and the Indians themselves, that it should

do so" (187 U.S. 553, 566 [1903]). The Court in that case also mentioned that the power of Congress over Indian relations was a political one and therefore not subject to the review of the federal courts.

Another case decided in the same term of the Court held that Congress possessed full administrative power over Indian tribal property (*Cherokee Nation* v. *Hitchcock*, 187 U.S. 294 [1902]). In 1914 the Court seemed to narrow that power somewhat when it said that because the Congress's "power is incidental only to the presence of the Indians and their status as wards of the Government, it must be conceded that it does not go beyond what is reasonably essential to their protection, and that, to be effective, its exercise must not be purely arbitrary" (*Perrin* v. *United States*, 232 U.S. 478, 486).

An additional restraint on the seemingly limitless power of the Congress with respect to Indian property is the due process clause of the Fifth Amendment. The federal government must pay just compensation where Indian property is taken for a non-Indian purpose. While this is not a prevention of the exercise of congressional power over Indian property, it is a limitation on its exercise. The Supreme Court in the cases of *Kagama* and *Lone Wolf* had rested the power of Congress to legislate over Indian matters on the dependent status of Indians and the federal responsibility to protect them even from their own improvidence. The Court in later decisions took the notion as a limitation as well, by finding that a congressional exercise of that power must be "tied rationally to the fulfillment of Congress' unique obligation" to Indians. In *Morton* v. *Mancari* (417 U.S. 535 [1974]), where this standard of review was first articulated by the Court, the statutory action that was under scrutiny was the preference for employment of Indians within the Bureau of Indian Affairs. The question was whether or not the Congress could discriminate on the basis of race in favor of Indians. The Court held that, because of the unique nature of the Bureau of Indian Affairs and its relationship to the lives of Indian people, this exercise of power was appropriate; it was tied rationally to the federal obligation to Indians.

The general canons of construction for treaties, statutes, and regulations concerning Indians call for "a broad construction when the issue is whether Indian rights are reserved or established, and for a narrow construction when Indian rights are to be abrogated or limited" (Cohen 1982:225).

Presents and Delegations

FRANCIS PAUL PRUCHA

The United States governed its relations with the American Indians through the web of treaty arrangements negotiated with the tribes, through the legislative enactments of Congress, and through administrative rulings and regulations emanating from the Bureau of Indian Affairs or other executive offices. In these activities the federal government paralleled its activities in other areas of its regular operations.

Because of the peculiar nature of the relations between Indians and Whites, special instruments of policy also came into play. Chief among these were the giving of presents to the Indians, the formal presentation of symbolic gifts to indicate special attachments of friendship and the allegiance of the chiefs to the United States, and the invitation of delegations of influential Indians to the seat of government in the East.

Presents

European nations made extensive use of presents in their diplomacy with the Indians. The British and the French, in their rivalry in the New World, sought to gain the friendship and if possible the alliance of the tribes by a tremendous outlay of presents, and these gifts were often spearheads of White culture among the aborigines (Jacobs 1950). The United States government, in this matter as in others, was obliged to follow the established practices.

George Washington in his annual message to Congress in October 1791 asserted that authority for the president to give presents to the Indians was one of the basic principles for dealing with the Indians, and he sent numerous gifts to the Southeast Indians to hold their friendship while the tribes northwest of the Ohio River were at war with the United States. Early treaties with the Indians after the American Revolution provided for the distribution of presents to the Indians; in some cases they specifically indicated that these gifts should be domestic animals and implements of husbandry.

Such presents provided for by treaty, even those intended to hasten the Indians along the road to the civilization of the Whites, could be considered part of a mutual exchange, as the Indians agreed to submit to American jurisdiction or to cede parcels of land. But the use of presents had considerably wider implications. An example of a thoroughly worked out philosophy of present-giving can be seen in a memorandum on Indian affairs sent by Governor Lewis Cass of Michigan Territory to the secretary of war in 1816. In addition to the moral obligation of the Whites to provide goods for Indians in need, Cass candidly outlined a five-point argument for the distribution of presents to the Indians. First, presents tended to conciliate the Indians and counteract unpleasant circumstances in United States dealings with them; they played upon the hopes of the Indians rather than upon their fears. Second, distribution of presents by the United States was necessary because of the practice of the British in Canada. The United States had to use this means to counteract British influence with the tribes. Third, presents could be used to strengthen and secure the influence of tribal chiefs, whose good will was essential for American policy. Fourth, presents would prevent the Indians from committing depredations upon White citizens. Fifth, the distribution of presents would give influence and importance to United States agents, thus strengthening their position. Cass (1968:45–50) urged the prudent distribution of the presents in such a way as to enhance all these elements of policy.

Presents were an essential element in the negotiating of treaties with the Indians. Not only did the Indians attending the councils expect to be subsisted for the duration of the meeting by the United States, but also other gifts were necessary to gain a conciliatory attitude, without which negotiations were useless. In some cases gifts were used by American commissioners to bribe influential chiefs to agree to the terms of the treaty.

Gifts were carried by American explorers moving into Indian territories as means of showing friendship to the Indians encountered. Thus Meriwether Lewis and William Clark took along light articles for barter and presents, and Zebulon Montgomery Pike was provided with some trifling presents when he ascended the Mississippi in 1805. Indian delegations who went to Washington were provided generously with clothing, entertainment, and refreshments as guests of the government; and presents of food and other goods were on occasion given out by agents on the frontier as rewards to Indians for some good deed or in appreciation for acts of friendship to the United States.

Natl. Arch.: RG75-PU–227.
Fig. 1. A delegation from Jemez Pueblo with the commissioner of Indian affairs. left to right, Emiliano Yepa, interpreter; Juan Pedro; Commissioner John Collier; and Jemez Gov. George Toledo. The governor holds silver-headed canes, symbols of his authority. One cane was presented by Spanish authorities to secular officials appointed to serve at Jemez Pueblo. A Christian cross is engraved on the head of the cane. The other cane was a gift from President Abraham Lincoln, who gave canes to the leaders of the Pueblos in 1863 to affirm the peaceful relations between the 2 governments. Inscribed on the cane is the name of the pueblo, the date 1863, and A. Lincoln. Both canes are kept on display in the governor's home (Sando 1976:203–204). These Jemez Pueblo representatives were discussing land issues probably related to the Ojo del Espíritu Santo land grant (Sando 1982:43–49). Photographed about 1940.

As United States power increased in relation to that of the Indian tribes and the need to conciliate strong groups of Indians who could obstruct American plans and policies weakened, the formal use of presents faded away.

Symbolic Gifts

The presentation of peace medals, flags, and chief's coats differed from the distribution of gifts such as food, clothes, utensils, and tobacco, in that they added a significant new element. They were symbols of the government that presented them, and their acceptance signified special ties of allegiance and friendship. Occasional gifts such as engraved silver pipes or silver-headed canes served the same purpose (fig. 1). And silver gorgets and wrist bands engraved with the arms of the United States given to warriors and lesser chiefs also carried a symbolic message.

Peace Medals

The most important of the special gifts carrying deep political significance were the Indian peace medals. The Spaniards, the French, and the British presented medals to the Indians, and the British especially produced large and magnificent silver medals, each bearing the likeness of the reigning monarch on one side and his coat of arms on the other. The British medals were usually solid medals of silver, impressed in clear relief, and were given to the Indian chiefs as marks of friendship and special recognition (Jamieson 1936; McLachlan 1899). They were highly prized by the Indians, who not only delighted in the decorative aspects of the medals but also esteemed the honor that was signified by possession of a medal bearing the likeness of the king.

The United States found that it was necessary to continue the practice of presenting medals if it hoped to have peaceful relations with the tribes and influence with the chiefs. The federal government began the production of Indian peace medals, which became a settled and extremely important element in American Indian policy (Prucha 1971a; Belden 1927; Morin 1915).

As early as 1787 Henry Knox, the secretary of war under the Articles of Confederation, urged Congress to comply with the request of the Indians for medals, gorgets, and wrist and arm bands bearing the arms of the United States. Congress was pressed for funds, but Knox noted that the Indians would turn in their British medals, which could be melted down to produce new ones. Secretary of State Thomas Jefferson outlined the policy behind the distribution of medals to the Indians; he spoke of it as "an ancient custom from time immemorial. The medals are considered as complimentary things, as marks of friendship to those who come to see us, or who do us good offices, conciliatory of their good will toward us, and not designed to produce a contrary disposition towards others. They confer no power, and seem to have taken their origin in the European practice, of giving medals or other marks of friendship to the negotiators of treaties and other diplomatic characters, or visitors of distinction" (Jefferson 1903–1904, 9:148–161).

The practice took firm hold in the United States. Medals were given to Indian chiefs on important occasions, such as the signing of a treaty, a visit of Indians to the national capital, or a tour of the Indian country by some federal official. Lewis and Clark on their exploratory expedition in 1804–1806 carried a large supply of medals, which they handed out with impressive ceremonies to chiefs along the way. Indian agents on the frontier distributed the medals to their charges, in recognition of friendship and peace with the United States. These Indian agents or treaty negotiators used their own discretion in making the presentations, but they were guided by fixed norms. In 1829, in fact, Governor Cass and Superintendent of Indian Affairs at Saint Louis William Clark, in drawing up a series of regulations for the governance of the Indian department, included the following rules for the presentation of medals and flags.

1. They will be given to influential persons only.
2. The largest medals will be given to the principal village chiefs, those of the second size will be given to the principal war chiefs, and those of the third size to the less distinguished chiefs and warriors.

Fig. 2. Seasons medals, designed by American artist John Trumbull to the specifications of President Washington and Secretary of War James McHenry. Scenes on the reverse were to inspire the Indian to adopt husbandry (upper left), agriculture (upper right), and domestic crafts (lower left). Each carried on the obverse (lower right) an inscription acknowledging Washington's second term of office. The stock lasted through the presidency of John Adams, and the medals were distributed by Meriwether Lewis and William Clark on their expedition of 1804–1806 (Prucha 1971a:16–17). Diameter, 54 mm.

3. They will be presented with proper formalities, and with an appropriate speech, so as to produce a proper impression upon the Indians.

4. It is not intended that chiefs should be appointed by any officer of the department, but that they should confer these badges of authority upon such as are selected or recognized by the tribe, and as are worthy of them, in the manner heretofore practiced.

5. Whenever a foreign medal is worn, it will be replaced by an American medal, if the Agent should consider the person entitled to a medal (Cass and Clark 1829:77–78).

The Indians expected to receive medals, and it was impossible to conduct Indian affairs without the use of them. Thomas L. McKenney, head of the Office of Indian Affairs, in 1829 wrote to the secretary of war about the policy of distributing medals. "So important is its continuance esteemed to be," he said, "that without medals, any plan of operations among the Indians, be it

what it may, is essentially enfeebled. This comes of the high value which the Indians set upon these tokens of Friendship. They are, besides this indication of the Government Friendship, badges of power to them, and trophies of renown. They will not consent to part from this ancient *right*, as they esteem it; and according to the value they set upon medals is the importance to the Government in having them to bestow" (McKenney 1829). Superintendent Clark wrote in 1831 that "the distributing of Medals to the chiefs of the western & Northwestern Tribes, has had a very good effect" in "Securing the influence of the Chiefs of those distant tribes, for the better security of our Traders exposed amongst them; and with a view to the reconciliation of disputes between themselves . . . .A proper distribution of *Medals*, Flags & Chief Coats will give an influence which no other means within my knowledge can be applied with as little expense" (Clark 1831).

Fig. 3. Thomas Jefferson medal, the first of the standard peace medals: a bust of the president on the obverse and a symbol of peace on the reverse. John Reich, employed by Robert Scott, engraver of the U.S. Mint, cut the dies for the 3 medals (Prucha 1971a:90–91, 95). This is the large size. Diameter 105 mm.

Fig. 4. left to right, The Winnebago Prophet, Black Hawk, and Whirling Thunder, Black Hawk's eldest son, painted from life, while prisoners after the Black Hawk War, shortly after meeting with President Andrew Jackson. After their release from a prison at Ft. Monroe, Va., they were taken on a tour as part of an effort by U.S. officials to impress Indians with the size and wealth of American cities and thus discourage them from further uprisings. The trip included public appearances and was accompanied by considerable publicity (Jackson 1955:1–18). The suit worn by Black Hawk was probably the gift of President Jackson. Oil on canvas by James Westhall Ford, May–June, 1833.

In the years after the Civil War the government continued its policy of presenting peace medals to the Indians, but the changing situation of the Indians accentuated changes in the use of peace medals that had already begun to occur in earlier decades. The tribes were no longer diplomatic forces to be conciliated or drawn under American authority, as were the Southeast tribes immediately after the Revolution. There was no longer a problem of exchanging the American medals for British ones, for the political and economic rivalry of United States and Canadian fur traders had ended. There was a diminishing need to recognize chiefs within the tribes, for the sentiment of the age was increasingly to de-emphasize the importance of the chiefs and thus strike at the roots of tribalism, which many reformers came to consider the great obstacle in the acculturation of the Indians.

Peace medals thus tended to lose the great political significance they had once had and to become simply rewards for good deeds or good behavior or even prizes for minor accomplishments that had nothing at all to do with matters of state. Occasionally, in conflicts over policy, the medals were presented to Indians who advanced the government's program—a faint reflection of the earlier usage. But there was a diminished feeling of the sacredness of the medals, for the Indians themselves often requested medals and they were occasionally asked to pay for those they received.

After the large numbers of medals produced for the presidential administrations from Thomas Jefferson through Ulysses S. Grant (it was common for 300 medals to be struck for a single administration), the number of medals struck markedly decreased. In the Rutherford Hayes administration no medals at all were given to the Indians. Medals were no longer ordered in bulk to be used when needed but were purchased from the U.S. Mint when specific occasions arose. The use of the medals had so far deteriorated toward the end of the nineteenth century that their original purposes were almost completely lost sight of. In 1888, in what was perhaps the nadir in

Smithsonian, NAA: 31,374–B.

Fig 5. Indians, mostly Chiricahua Apache, from the San Carlos Agency, Ariz., visiting Washington, D.C., Sept. 1876. seated: Chiquito, Eskiminzin, Sagully, Casadora. standing: wife of Chiquito, Marijildo Grijalva, interpreter, wife of Eskiminzin, Agent John P. Clum, and wife of Casadora. The entire group included 22 Apaches. Clum promoted the trip as a means of improving White perceptions of Indians as well as impressing the Apache with the cultural and geographical features of the U.S., but the BIA would not pay for the trip, so Clum funded it with donations from his friends and his own contributions. From San Carlos the group traveled by wagon, camping in the open until they reached the railroad at El Moro, Colo.; then they traveled by rail and stayed in hotels to visit Pueblo and Denver, Colo.; Kansas City and St. Louis, Mo.; Cincinnati, Ohio; Washington, D.C.; and Philadelphia, where they attended the Centennial Exposition. Several "wild Apache" shows were given enroute in an unsuccessful attempt to raise money to pay for the trip. While in Washington, Commissioner of Indian Affairs John Q. Smith agreed to pay the group's return expenses. The president was out of the city and so no interview was possible. One member of the group, Tahzay, son of Cochise, died of pneumonia in Washington and is buried in the Congressional Cemetery (Clum 1936:185–196). Photograph by Charles M. Bell.

the use of the official peace medals, one silver and one bronze Cleveland medal were sent to the Hoopa Valley Agency in California, to be used as first and second prizes in an agricultural fair conducted for the Indians to stimulate their interest in farming.

In the medals can be read much of the history of the relations between the United States and the Indian tribes. The medals, once the bearers of diplomatic authority between powerful and independent nations, in the end became rewards passed out to dependents of the United States government for good behavior or some trifling individual accomplishment. The silver symbols of peace and friendship that had once served to swing the Indians into the orbit of American authority, that had created jealousy and tension between great nations, that had provided for the chiefs ornaments to be cherished deeply by them and their descendants became little more than weighty trinkets.

The medals given to the Indians were supposed to bear the likeness of the president currently in office, and

medals were produced for each president from Washington to Benjamin Harrison, with the exception of John Adams and William Henry Harrison.

The government presented a number of medals to Indian chiefs during Washington's term of office, but it did not mass produce the medals. Instead, the medals were hand engraved on oval plates of silver, the largest ones roughly four by six inches. On one side was engraved the figure of Washington with that of an Indian in the peaceful gesture of throwing away his tomahawk. The reverse showed an eagle bearing the crest of the United States on its breast, with an olive branch in its right talon, a sheaf of arrows in its left. The most famous of these Washington Indian medals was the one given to the Seneca chief Red Jacket in 1792 (vol. 15:435).

Medals distributed during John Adams's term of office were the so-called seasons medals, which had been produced in England during Washington's second administration (fig. 2). They showed scenes of a farmer sowing grain, women spinning and weaving, and domestic cattle.

The production of Indian peace medals began to be regularized during the administration of Thomas Jefferson (fig. 3). The pattern for the medals was more or less established, although the methods of manufacture were still not quite set. Medals in three sizes were ordered—large (4 inches in diameter), medium (3 inches), and small (2 inches). One feature of the Jefferson medals distinguished them from later medals. They were shells rather than solid medals; the obverse and reverse of the medals were struck separately, then fastened together with a silver band to form a hollow medal. It was a satisfactory expedient as far as the appearance of the medals was concerned, but the Indians compared them unfavorably with the heavy medals they were accustomed to receive from the British.

Beginning with James Madison's administration solid medals were struck in silver, and the sizes were standardized at 3 inches, 2½ inches, and 2 inches. After the Taylor medals, the smallest size was discontinued, and the Grant medal was made in one size only. The medals from Hayes through Cleveland were oval medals, 3 inches long. The last of the peace medals produced specifically for Indians, those of Benjamin Harrison, returned to the round form and were struck in the 3-inch size.

The symbolic designs for the reverses represented two themes in American Indian policy—the desire to maintain relations of peace and friendship with the Indian tribes and the concern of the government to lead the Indians from their own customs to those of the Whites. The policy of changing Indians, whom the Whites saw as hunters relying upon the chase for subsistence, to settled farmers cultivating the soil for a livelihood is forcefully reflected in the designs used for the medals. The early medals depicted President Washington and an Indian chief against a background of agricultural life. The seasons medals, with

Fig. 6. Delegation of Southern Cheyenne and Arapaho men in Washington, D.C. front row: Lame Man, Yellow Eyes, Henry Roman Nose, Turkey Legs, He Bear, Little Chief or White Spoon, Yellow Bear, and Little Man, all Cheyenne. middle row: Black Coyote, Arapaho; Andrew John, Seneca; Leonard Tyler, Cheyenne; Philip Cook, Cheyenne. back row: Cleaver Warden, Arapaho; Bird Chief, Sr., Arapaho; Grant Left Hand, Arapaho; Jesse Bent, Arapaho; and Robert Burns, Cheyenne. A number of the men, both those in traditional and those in citizen clothing, wear peace medals. While in Washington, members of the delegation stayed in a boarding house owned by the Beveridge family, who regularly furnished accommodations for Indian delegates (Viola 1981:124–125). Photographed at the Arts and Industries Building, Smithsonian Institution, Jan.–Feb., 1899.

their agricultural and domestic scenes, were intended to lead the Indians toward the customs of civilized life. The reverse of the medals of Jefferson through Taylor showed clasped hands of friendship, a crossed tomahawk and peace pipe, and the legend PEACE AND FRIENDSHIP. The Fillmore and Pierce medals pictured an Indian in feathered headdress and blanket conversing with a White man, with attributes of Indian and White life in the background. On the Buchanan and Lincoln medals was a savage scene of an Indian in the act of scalping another, contrasted with a center medallion showing a peaceful scene of an Indian plowing, with children playing ball beyond him, and a landscape of White society. Later medals had similar symbolic presentation of the new life expected for the Indians. The Benjamin Harrison medal showed before and after scenes of the Indian, with a banner inscribed PROGRESS.

The government took pains to produce medals of artistic merit, and the best available artists and engravers were engaged. As McKenney (1825) remarked about the medals, "They are intended, not for the Indians only, but for posterity." The Indian peace medals formed the beginning of a "presidential" series of medals, continued by the inaugural medals, and bronze copies of all of them remain available at the United States Mint. A study of the medalists is Chamberlain (1963).

Delegations

Indian delegations were invited to the national capital for visits of friendship and for the purpose of treaty making early in the nation's history. Alexander McGillivray and a group of Creek chiefs, for example, went to New York to sign a treaty of peace in 1790, and in 1792 a delegation of Iroquois, including Red Jacket, journeyed to Philadelphia to confer with Washington and other officials. Eastern Indians had had long contact with the Whites and were acquainted with their strengths and weaknesses; however, meetings in the capital added a special note of solemnity to conferences and negotiations and enabled the United States government to impress the guests with its friendship and its hospitality.

For Indians from the remoter West the invitation of delegations served another significant purpose—to impress upon the Indians the size, population, strength, and accomplishments of the United States. Lewis and Clark were directed to cultivate the friendship of the Indians and were told by President Jefferson: "If a few of their influential chiefs, within a practicable distance, wish to visit us, arrange such a visit with them, and furnish them with authority to call on our officers, on their entering the U.S., to have them conveyed to this place at the public expense" (Ewers 1966:10). In 1804 a delegation of Osages visited the Eastern cities, and in 1805–1806 a group of chiefs from the tribes on the Missouri and Mississippi traveled to Washington, Philadelphia, New York, Providence, and Boston. They met important officials, including the president; they were shown the arsenals and military fortresses of the nation, supplied with clothes and other gifts, presented with silver peace medals, and lionized by the curious crowds. These early visitors from the West were the first in a long series of Indian delegations—Pawnee, Omaha, Oto, Kansas and Missouri Indians in 1821; Sauk and Fox, Iowa, and Piankashaw, brought to Washington by Superintendent Clark in 1824; Choctaw chiefs for a treaty in 1824; Winnebagos with their chief Naw-Kaw in 1828; the defeated Black Hawk and a group of other Sauk and Fox hostages in 1833 (fig. 4); chief Oshkosh and a delegation of Menominees in 1850; and Chippewas under Hole-in-the-Day in 1855—to mention only some of the groups. As contacts with other tribes increased after the Civil War, the old processes were repeated. Numerous delegations of Sioux arrived in Washington to carry on their tribes' relations with the United States, and other western tribes sent representatives (Viola 1981).

The Indians were feted at considerable expense, exchanged speeches with governmental dignitaries, and saw the sights of the cities. They were much impressed by the power of the Whites and returned to their tribes with stories of the wonders they had seen. But the total effect of the visits upon governmental relations with the Indian tribes is difficult to assess. There were disadvantages as well as benefits, for misunderstandings arose if the wrong chiefs were honored, the death of delegates during the visits and on the journey to and from the capital caused ill will, and sometimes the returning delegates were not believed or not heeded.

The visits of the chiefs to the East made possible a significant artistic record of the Indians. Charles St. Mémin's crayon portraits of the Osages in 1804 (Lockwood 1928), Charles Willson Peale's silhouettes of the Missouri River chiefs in 1806 (Ewers 1966), and the numerous portraits painted for the Office of Indian Affairs in the 1820s by Charles Bird King (Viola 1972, 1976) form an incomparable record of the Indians in the early nineteenth century. And the chiefs of the post-Civil War delegations are preserved in the official photographs taken of the visitors and in the portraits taken by commercial photographers in Washington.

Colonial Governmental Agencies

YASUHIDE KAWASHIMA

During a major part of the colonial period, Indian affairs were largely controlled by the individual colonies. Although they realized the seriousness of the Indian situation, the colonies never fully succeeded in dealing effectively with problems in the face of the difficult circumstances surrounding intercolonial conflicts, quarrels between governors and assemblies, and intrigues incited among the Indians by the French. Indian policies were usually initiated by the colonial governors, and the assemblies appropriated funds and passed laws to regulate Indian trade and land and other matters. However, at times, the legislatures handled Indian affairs directly. The colonial governments, whether in their executive or legislative capacities, usually administered Indian affairs through commissioners and agents appointed for specific purposes.

New England Colonies

No other section in British North America developed a more comprehensive system of governmental agencies dealing with Indians than did New England. In Massachusetts, for example, the Indian praying towns were established as early as the 1650s. The colonial legislature, called the General Court, selected White guardians to serve as trustees for the Indian towns and to give advice on all important matters, both executive and judicial, to the various Indian officials, who did much of the routine governing of their own towns (McFarlane 1933:270–271).

More significant was the establishment of the position of superintendent of Indian affairs to supervise not only the praying Indians but also the non-Christian tribes that acknowledged Massachusetts' authority. The office was the first of its kind in English North America. The General Court appointed Daniel Gookin as the first superintendent in 1656, and he held the office until his death in 1687, except for the years 1658 to 1661, when he was in England. He was succeeded by Thomas Prentice, who served until 1709, at which time the office ceased to exist (McFarlane 1933:271; Kawashima 1969a:49, 1986).

Serving as a medium between the guardians of the Indians and the colonial administration, the superintendent had a wide range of functions, which included sitting as judge at the Indian county court, installing new native

officials, "making of orders, and giving instructions and directions" . . . for promoting and practising morality, civility, industry, and diligence, . . . providing teachers for the Indians, distributing 'encouragement' among the rulers," supervising the collection of tithes, and insuring that the Indians observed the Sabbath and attended religious services (Vaughan 1979:294).

In spite of his extensive service to the Indians, Gookin received small reward. It was only later in his life that the Honourable Corporation at London for Propagating the Gospel among the Indians in New England awarded him annually first 15 pounds and then 20 pounds (F.W. Gookin 1912:130). In Plymouth, a similar office of superintendent was established, but it never attained any prominence.

Although the reservation system survived King Philip's War, the guardianship did not. As a result, the Indian villages came to be under the more strict and direct control of the General Court (Kawashima 1969a:44, 1986). It was not until 1694 that the White commissioners appointed by the governor came to rule the native villages. They were authorized not only to exercise the power of justice of the peace over the Indians but also, as their guardians, to handle all kinds of problems concerning their welfare. This system, which proved to be highly effective in administering the village Indians, continued in force for 52 years. A new law of 1746, which was renewed several times during the rest of the colonial period, provided that 24 guardians be chosen by the General Court, instead of by the governor as before, three for each of the eight districts of Natick (Middlesex); Stoughton (Suffolk); Grafton (Worcester); Yarmouth, Harwich, and Eastham (Barnstable); Mashpee, Barnstable, Sandwich, and Falmouth (Barnstable); Plymouth, Pembroke, and Middleboro (Plymouth); Martha's Vineyard; and Nantucket. In the administration of the reservation during the first half of the eighteenth century, the guardians were the most important officials. They assumed the full responsibilities held by both the superintendent and the guardians in the seventeenth century (Kawashima 1969a:49, 1986). But they received only a token award of £5 to 10 a year for their valuable service (MacFarlane 1933:284).

While Plymouth, before its incorporation into the Bay Colony in 1691, followed the Massachusetts policy, other

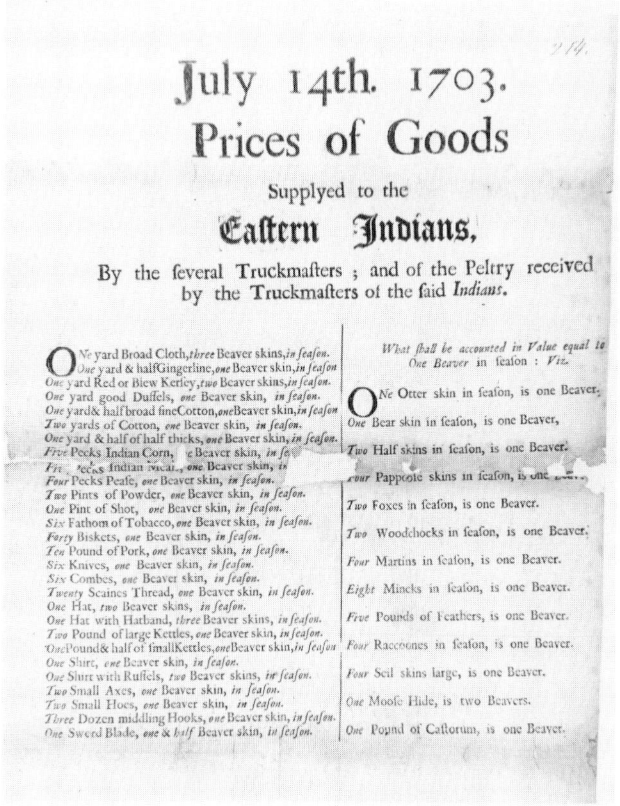

July 14th. 1703.
Prices of Goods
Supplyed to the
Eaſtern Indians,
By the ſeveral Truckmaſters ; and of the Peltry received by the Truckmaſters of the ſaid *Indians.*

ONe yard Broad Cloth, *three* Beaver skins, *in ſeaſon.*
One yard & half Gingerline, *one* Beaver skin, *in ſeaſon*
One yard Red or Blew Kerſey, *two* Beaver skins, *in ſeaſon.*
One yard good Duffels, *one* Beaver skin, *in ſeaſon.*
One yard & half broad fine Cotton, *one* Beaver skin, *in ſeaſon*
Two yards of Cotton, *one* Beaver skin, *in ſeaſon.*
One yard & half of half thicks, *one* Beaver skin, *in ſeaſon.*
Five Pecks Indian Corn, [illegible] Beaver skin, *in ſe*[illegible]
Fi[illegible] Pecks Indian Meal, *one* Beaver skin, *in* [illegible]
Four Pecks Peaſe, *one* Beaver skin, *in ſeaſon.*
Two Pints of Powder, *one* Beaver skin, *in ſeaſon.*
One Pint of Shot, *one* Beaver skin, *in ſeaſon.*
Six Fathom of Tobacco, *one* Beaver skin, *in ſeaſon.*
Forty Biskets, *one* Beaver skin, *in ſeaſon.*
Ten Pound of Pork, *one* Beaver skin, *in ſeaſon.*
Six Knives, *one* Beaver skin, *in ſeaſon.*
Six Combes, *one* Beaver skin, *in ſeaſon.*
Twenty Scaines Thread, *one* Beaver skin, *in ſeaſon.*
One Hat, *two* Beaver skins, *in ſeaſon.*
One Hat with Hatband, *three* Beaver skins, *in ſeaſon.*
Two Pound of large Kettles, *one* Beaver skin, *in ſeaſon.*
One Pound & half of ſmall Kettles, *one* Beaver skin, *in ſeaſon*
One Shirt, *one* Beaver skin, *in ſeaſon.*
One Shirt with Ruffels, *two* Beaver skins, *in ſeaſon.*
Two Small Axes, *one* Beaver skin, *in ſeaſon.*
Two Small Hoes, *one* Beaver skin, *in ſeaſon.*
Three Dozen middling Hooks, *one* Beaver skin, *in ſeaſon.*
One Sword Blade, *one & half* Beaver skin, *in ſeaſon.*

What ſhall be accounted in Value equal to One Beaver in ſeaſon : *Viz.*

ONe Otter skin in ſeaſon, is one Beaver,
One Bear skin in ſeaſon, is one Beaver,
Two Half skins in ſeaſon, is one Beaver.
Four Pappoose skins in ſeaſon, is one [illegible]
Two Foxes in ſeaſon, is one Beaver.
Two Woodchocks in ſeaſon, is one Beaver.
Four Martins in ſeaſon, is one Beaver.
Eight Mincks in ſeaſon, is one Beaver.
Five Pounds of Feathers, is one Beaver.
Four Raccoones in ſeaſon, is one Beaver.
Four Seil skins large, is one Beaver.
One Mooſe Hide, is two Beavers.
One Pound of Caſtorum, is one Beaver.

Mass. State Arch., Boston, Mass.: Mass. Arch., vol. 119:214.

Fig. 1. Broadside from 1703, "Prices of Goods supplyed to the Eastern Indians, . . . " The Mass. General Court probably issued this equivalency list to truckmasters as part of its responsibility as a regulatory agency for trade. The "Eastern" Indians were those tribes who lived in the area now the state of Me., which was formally part of the Mass. colony.

New England colonies did not maintain such close supervision over their Indians as did Massachusetts. In Connecticut prior to 1725 only a small number of the natives had formally submitted to the colony and settled in fixed reservations. The Indian plantations were governed almost exclusively by the sachems. The English guardians did little more than advise the Indian officers. Although their powers were further extended in 1734, the Connecticut guardians did not have nearly so much authority or influence as did the corresponding officials in Massachusetts (MacFarlane 1933:289–292).

In the administration of justice, the Massachusetts General Court in the seventeenth century provided for two special Indian courts—the Indian justice of the peace and the Indian county court—to which one English magistrate was added to appoint the time and place of the court and give consent to the decisions of the Indian judges. Plymouth carried out a similar policy. In the eighteenth century, these special Indian courts were abolished and all the natives came under the jurisdiction of ordinary colonial courts, except those under the White guardians, who were the justices of the peace for the Indians (Kawashima 1969, 1986). In Connecticut and, to a lesser extent, in Rhode Island, the General Court occasionally set up special committees to hear cases involving the natives (MacFarlane 1933:556, 559).

The Indian trade in New England was undertaken by the colonial governments more for political and diplomatic reasons than for a revenue-producing purpose. Throughout the colonial period, commissioners and agents had been appointed to manage the trade, issue licenses, prohibit the sale of certain articles, enforce the provisions of the law, and adjudicate disputes arising from the trade. The year 1694 marked a significant turning point in the Indian trade in Massachusetts, when a law provided for the setting up of public trading establishments, called truck houses, which were designed not only to prevent private settlers from trading with the natives but also to win the friendship of the natives by providing them with cheap and accessible English goods (fig. 1). The managers, called truckmasters, who received salaries ranging from 100 to 120 pounds annually, although they frequently also drew allowances as military officers, played a crucial role in the operation. They were required to keep detailed accounts of all transactions, were prohibited from indulging in private trade with the natives, were allowed to supply the natives with rum only in moderate quantities, and were strictly forbidden to sell goods to the Indians on credit. The key objective of the truckmaster was to undersell the French (MacFarlane 1938:52–53, 56, 59).

The success of the truck houses greatly depended upon the ability and personality of the individual agents. While men like Samuel Moody, Joseph Heath, Joseph Kellogg, Thomas Smith, John Moyes, and Jabez Bradbury proved themselves very capable as the truckmasters, others were not so successful. The truckmasters were responsible for their own conduct, and complaints were often directed to the General Court from both the Indians and the Whites. Although they were occasionally recalled in disgrace, just as were the guardians for the Indians, the truckmasters were usually chosen from among those already esteemed by the Indians (MacFarlane 1938:51–52).

Criticism was often lodged about the management of the Indian trade. In addition to the truckmaster's limited power as to liquor, arms, and ammunition, disagreements between the executive and the legislature over the regulation of the private traders, the expense of maintaining the truck houses, and frequent criticism of the governmental monopoly somewhat hampered the effective operation of the system (MacFarlane 1938:63). Yet the truck house trading system proved to be largely a success and continued with occasional minor changes until the American Revolution.

In eighteenth-century New England, the colonial governments often sent agents on special diplomatic missions among the Indians. They played an important role in establishing friendship with the Indians, in keeping the governments informed of the Indians' attitudes toward the English, and in undermining French influence. The most important figures in this diplomacy with the Indian tribes were the special commissioners, who were selected from among the most influential colonial leaders, sometimes including the governors themselves. These delegates and commissioners as wilderness diplomats attended Indian conferences and concluded many important treaties with the natives. In addition to the formal Indian conferences, commissioners were also appointed to investigate, and often to settle, specific disputes between Indians and Whites (Kawashima 1969:534–537, 1986).

Middle Colonies

Indian affairs in the Middle colonies were handled in a more informal manner. Few permanent governmental agencies dealing with the natives were established, although Indian relations were more vital in this area than in New England. Dealings with the Indians were more personal than institutional. Commissioners and agents were frequently appointed for specific purposes, yet the colonial governments assumed more direct administration of Indian affairs.

In New York, ultimate control of Indian problems during most of the seventeenth century was in the hands of the governor, but the details were necessarily left to the local magistrates. Albany, because of its proximity to the Iroquois, played an important role in New York Indian relations; but until 1696, its management of Indian affairs was held to be one of the duties attached to the local magistracy, and no special commissions or instructions seem to have been issued to define clearly the responsibility. In 1686 Gov. Thomas Dongan granted Albany a city charter, which confirmed Albany's monopoly of the western fur trade and empowered the local authorities to regulate it, thus strengthening their control of Indian affairs as a whole. Robert Livingston was retained as city clerk and ex officio secretary for Indian affairs (Trelease 1960:207–208).

Gov. Benjamin Fletcher broke with tradition in 1696 by taking the management of Indian relations out of the hands of the city magistrates and placing it under a local board of four commissioners for Indian affairs—Peter Schuyler, Mayor Dirck Wessels, Domine Godfrey Dellius, and Evert Banker (Trelease 1960:309). Two years later the Earl of Bellomont, as the governor of New York, renounced Fletcher's commissioners for Indian affairs and returned this function to the city magistrates as a whole, although that body included Schuyler and Wessels, two of the four commissioners involved. Henceforth, quite different from the informal practice prevailing before 1696, the magistrates served in this capacity by virtue of a special commission from the governor. This arrangement lasted well into the next century (Trelease 1960:338–339).

During King George's War, Gov. George Clinton became increasingly dissatisfied with the conduct of the New York Indian commissioners at Albany, who were attempting to keep the Iroquois neutral so that the Indian trade, in which the commissioners themselves were engaged, could go on without interruption. When the commissioners, with the support of the New York assembly, refused to perform their duties, Clinton gave a commission to handle relations with the Iroquois to William Johnson, the most prosperous of all the New York traders and the man who had greatest personal influence with the Iroquois. As "Colonel of the Warriours of the Six Nations" from 1746 to 1751, Johnson was successful in insuring the friendship of the Six Nations of Iroquois, and in persuading them to attack the French. Clinton could not finance his operations without grants from the assembly, with which he was carrying on a bitter struggle over the extent of the royal prerogative. When the assembly did finally act, it met Johnson's bill only in part. In disgust he announced his resignation in 1751. However, Johnson received some satisfaction, when Clinton, in his reports to Thomas Pelham-Holles, Duke of Newcastle, and the Board of Trade, gave him full credit for his achievements. The ineffectiveness of the Albany Indian commissioners increasingly became the target of criticism during the last few years of their existence: the Indians accused the commissioners of a general lack of interest in Indian affairs and made an earnest plea for the appointment of Johnson as agent to the Iroquois (Alden 1940: 199).

In Pennsylvania, Indian affairs were mostly in the hands of the colony's Indian commissioners, who were appointed from time to time to deal with all the Indians. The fact that these commissioners were always leaders of the colony clearly indicates the importance of Indian affairs in Pennsylvania (Jacobs 1966:40–41, 112–113). It was also in this colony that men like Conrad Weiser, George Croghan, Richard Peter, George Thomas, and Andrew Montour, who were thoroughly familiar with the natives' customs, languages, and traditions, provided invaluable services as provincial agents, in delivering presents, preparing and making arrangements for major Indian conferences to be attended by the Indian commissioners, serving as interpreters, and negotiating by themselves on minor problems (Boyd 1938:xx, xxv; Tolles 1957:167).

Despite some regulatory laws and proclamations, Pennsylvania never succeeded in regulating its Indian trade. In 1758, following Massachusetts' example, the Assembly passed a stronger Indian trade act, authorizing special commissioners to supervise the trade, banning the sale of liquor to the Indians, and creating a monopoly for the province of all trade west of the mountains. For the purpose of regulating the trade in the interest of the Indians, this law provided for three trading posts in the

Indian country, operated by provincial officials under the supervision of a committee of the Assembly. By thus placing the Indian trade under the control of the commissioners, it was hoped to put an end to the sharp practices of the conventional commercial traders; however, from the very start the Indian trade commissioners ran into difficulties. Their inability to send enough necessary goods to the Indians doomed their expectation of engrossing the Indian trade (Wainwright 1959:162; A.F.C. Wallace 1949:230–231).

New Jersey and Delaware, which had only a few Indians to deal with within their colonies, developed no special governmental agencies for handling Indian problems. Therefore, Indian affairs were mainly administered within the ordinary governmental structure, provincial and local. On occasion, the assemblies appointed delegates to negotiate treaties with the Indian tribes.

Southern Colonies

In the Southern colonies, Virginia, Maryland, and North Carolina were very similar to the Middle colonies in that they did not establish any permanent government agencies for dealing with the Indians. Because of the absence of any large Indian tribes close to the settled areas of these colonies between the late seventeenth century and the end of the colonial period, the governments of Virginia, Maryland, and North Carolina did not usually take great interest in Indian affairs, either in the enforcement of Indian trade regulations or in the conduct of diplomacy. At times, as in the New England and Middle colonies, these Southern colonies appointed commissioners to negotiate with the Indian tribes as well as to supervise the trade with particular tribes. Special commissioners, both executive-appointed and legislative-appointed, handled not only specific grievances of the Indian tribes but also those of tributary and nontribal Indians regarding land, trade, and administration of justice. The problems concerning the tributary and nontribal Indians were almost exclusively under the control of the executive.

The situation was drastically different in South Carolina, where colonial safety, welfare, and preservation were considered to be largely dependent upon friendly relations with independent tribes such as the Catawbas, Cherokees, Chickasaws, Choctaws, and all the other nations that lived close to the White settlements. South Carolina thus developed quite naturally a better system of governmental Indian agencies than the other Southern colonies. Above all, Indian trade was the most important concern. As early as 1707, the entire trade with the independent tribes was placed under the control of a board of nine commissioners, who were usually members of the assembly and had had experience in Indian affairs. In addition to the regular semiannual meetings, they met frequently: from 1710 to 1715 they averaged two or three meetings each month

from March to December. In their corporate capacity the commissioners were vested with considerable powers: granting annual licenses to traders for an eight-pound fee, prohibiting the sale of liquor and ammunition to Indians, issuing instructions to their agents and traders, and serving as a court of appeal without jury from their agents' decisions in cases involving sums over £10. Each commissioner received a salary of £150 a year. The Indian agent, the central figure in the trade, was required to supervise the trade and to live among the tribe for 10 months each year at an annual salary of £250. He not only had, as a justice of the peace, authority to decide all cases involving sums under £30 between traders themselves and between traders and Indians but also was a political adviser to the tribes as well as the chief adviser of the colonial government on Indian affairs (Crane 1928:149–151; Greene 1963:311–312).

In 1719 the commissioners, whose members were by then reduced to three, received a yearly salary of £300 each and were authorized to participate directly in the trade, while at the same time being permitted to license private traders to trade with Indians residing at least 20 miles from the public trading posts (Crane 1928:193–194, 197–199; Greene 1963:319). Four years later the entire power of the commissioners was placed under a single man with a salary of £600. Seven men served as commissioner between 1724 and 1761. James Moore, the first sole commissioner, who lived for only a month after his appointment, was succeeded by George Chicken. James Herbert became commissioner in 1727, Tobias Fitch in 1733, William Drake in 1734, Childermas Craft in 1739, and, in 1747, William Pinckney, who retained the office until 1761. The commissioner was subject to the directions of the governor and assembly. Chicken and his successors served not only as Indian commissioners but also as their own agents (Crane 1928:201–202). The appointment of a royal superintendent of Indian affairs for the Southern department in 1756 did not diminish Pinckney's authority as the commissioner over the Indian trade. The Commons nominated and controlled the commissioner, and its dominance over this office went unchallenged by either Crown or governor for more than 25 years (Alden 1944:69–70; Greene 1963:313, 315). In 1762, one year after this effective trading law expired, a new law was passed, authorizing five directors to supervise the trade with the Cherokees, which soon proved unprofitable. Between 1764 and 1767 control passed gradually to the royal Indian superintendent and later back to the governor and council (Alden 1944:177, 207–214, 249; Greene 1963:315).

The Indian trade obscured Indian diplomacy in South Carolina until the mid-1730s, but gradually alliances with the Indians or at least assurances of their neutrality became the object of colonial diplomacy. The Commons played an important role, exercising practically unlimited power in the conduct of Indian diplomacy. It decided when to send special agents to the various Indian nations; nominated, instructed, and paid those agents; and determined all matters of expense in regard to Indian affairs, including the giving of presents (Greene 1963:316).

Special agents were regularly employed to negotiate with various Indian tribes during the middle period of the eighteenth century, and the Commons insisted upon nominating them, regarding all such nominations as its right. In 1755, for example, when it voted to send an agent to persuade the Creek chiefs to come to Charleston to regulate the trade, the Common promised to appropriate full expenses of more than 2,000 pounds on condition that Gov. James Glen appoint its nominee, Henry Hyrne, as agent (Greene 1963:318–320). In spite of the repeated objections raised by governors (Glen, William Littleton, and Thomas Boone), which did gradually contribute to the curtailment of its power, the Commons continued to exercise considerable authority until the Crown assumed complete control over Southern Indian affairs in the middle 1760s under royal superintendent John Stuart (Greene 1963:324).

South Carolina handled problems concerning the tributary and nontribal Indians in a manner similar to that of other Southern colonies. Sometimes special commissioners, appointed usually by the proprietors or the Commons, dealt with Indian problems (Crane 1928:138), while on other occasions regular administrative and legislative offices, both colonial and local, handled such problems.

Georgia's Indian policy is a clear reflection of its unique situation as a buffer colony facing strong Southern tribes. From the very beginning the colonial government directed its attention almost entirely toward the independent tribes, whose amicable relations largely determined the Savannah Indian trade and the security of the colony. Until the establishment of the royal government in Georgia in 1754, the trustees regulated the Indian trade. Following the example of South Carolina, Georgia early employed commissioners to carry out its Indian policy. The law of 1734, the first statute ever passed by Georgia, dealt solely with the Indian trade. It not only prohibited trade with the natives without license under penalty of 100 pounds but also empowered the commissioner to manage the entire trade, authorizing him to determine the Indians' complaints based upon their evidence and to award them damages if less than three pounds. The commissioner was not allowed to trade or to receive any gift during his agency and four subsequent years under penalty of 100 pounds.

After 1754, the Indian trade was in the hands of the governor, and the Georgia assembly did not attempt to assume direction of the trade, although in 1758 it did pass an act that required all Indian traders to take out a license and invested the governor with the "sole management and regulation of the Indian Trade" in the colony. The trade remained in the hands of the executive until it passed to the royal superintendent in the mid-1760s. Thus the governor had full authority to appoint commissioners and agents in dealing with Indians. In matters of Indian diplomacy, the governor and council dominated the scene, often directly handling the problem, and as a result the Georgia assembly was excluded from participating in it (Greene 1963:324–325).

British Imperial Administration

Ideas in favor of placing Indian affairs under some centralized authority had often been expressed since the early colonial period, but it was not until 1753 that more definite attention was paid to the problem. In spite of the chaotic and confused situation existing in the colonies, imperial management of Indian affairs was achieved not by cooperative effort or agreement by the colonies themselves but by royal instructions emanating from the ministry in London (Volwiler 1926:116). Finally, in 1756 the British government created two separate Indian departments in North America and appointed a superintendent for each. William Johnson was appointed "colonel" of the Six Nations of Iroquois and their confederates and "sole agent and superintendent" of the Indians with an annual salary of £600 (Alden 1940:208). Edmond Atkin received his appointment as "agent for and Superintendent of" the Indian tribes bordering the Southern colonies, with the word "sole" of Johnson's commission significantly absent. The Earl of Loudoun, commander-in-chief in America, was even given final authority to approve Atkin's appointment as the Southern superintendent (Atkin 1954:xxii). Although the military commanders delivered the commissions, gave instructions, and maintained a close connection with the superintendents, these Indian agents were not directly under the military authority. Until the Revolution, the superintendents considered themselves to be directly, though not primarily, responsible to London (Alden 1944:146).

The superintendents, in theory if not always in practice, conducted the political relations of the English with the Indians, protecting the Indians as well as they could from the traders and speculators, negotiating the boundary lines that were called for after 1763, distributing the presents given to the Indians in the attempt to gain and maintain their good will, and enlisting the Indians in wartime as auxiliary troops (Alden 1944:139–140). From 1765 to 1768, they even attempted to control the trade, until the imperial government finally ordered them to desist, although theoretically, and to a great extent practically, the management of the trade remained in colonial hands (Alden 1944:139–155; Prucha 1962:11).

The Northern department was always considered to be the more important, for which Johnson once recommended twice as many presents as those for the South. Division was indicated by the enumeration of tribes, although roughly speaking the districts were separated by the Potomac and Ohio rivers. Sir William Johnson was superintendent of the Northern department for almost 20 years, until his death in 1774. He was succeeded by his nephew Guy Johnson, who held office until the close of the Revolution. Much of the prestige of the Northern district and of the entire Indian department was due to the ability and influence of William Johnson (Volwiler 1926: 117–118).

In the second year of his superintendency, Johnson selected George Croghan as deputy superintendent in the Northern district. Croghan served in this capacity for 15 years. Until 1760 Johnson had no other deputy, but after the surrender of Canada his staff was increased by the appointments of Daniel Claus, assigned to Canada in 1760, Guy Johnson to New York in 1762, and Maj. Joseph Gorham (who acquired the position through the political influence of his friends in England) to Nova Scotia in 1767. Each drew a salary of £200. Croghan rendered by far the most important services of these four deputy superintendents, because he was assigned specifically to the tribes of Pennsylvania and the Ohio valley, including the distant tribes in the Illinois country, where the friction between Indians and Whites over trade and land was greatest (Volwiler 1926:122; Wainwright 1959: 113).

Croghan's field of operations during the first half of the 1760s expanded so greatly that he could no longer carry on the work by himself. His staff came to include two assistant agents at Fort Pitt, one at Detroit, and one at Michilimackinac, who were all provided with interpreters. Croghan's annual budget for these years called for about £1,000 for salaries. His chief assistant experts were Edward Ward, his half-brother; Thomas McKee, an Indian trader on the Susquehanna; Alexander McKee, son of Thomas and later to be Croghan's successor; and Thomas Hutchins (Volwiler 1926:143–144). In 1771, with totally insufficient financial support for effective dealing with the natives, Croghan, who had until that time been dissuaded by Johnson from leaving the Indian department, decided to retire. Johnson accepted the resignation only on condition that Croghan promise to return to active duty when he had settled his personal affairs. On this understanding, Johnson appointed Alexander McKee deputy agent pro tempore. Croghan remained on call when Indian affairs were critical. Indeed, the native chiefs preferred to deal with him (Wainwright 1959:282).

Atkin, as superintendent of Indian affairs for the Southern department until 1761, was faced with somewhat different problems. His attempt to secure funds for his expenses from the imperial government failed; the Board of Trade merely ordered the governors to cooperate with Atkin, and they referred him to Loudoun for funds and instructions (Alden 1944:70).

Lord Loudoun wished Atkin to assume control of the Indian trade in the South. But when the superintendent asked him for £2,000 in expense money and for permission to draw upon him for further necessary sums, Loudoun referred him to the Southern colonial governments for financial support. Finding himself dependent upon the colonies for financial support, Atkin approached Virginia. At Williamsburg in spring 1757, he succeeded in establishing an organization to deal with Virginia's Indian problems. At the request of George Washington and Gov. Robert Dinwiddie he appointed the well-known frontiersman Christopher Gist as his deputy and placed him in charge of such Southern Indians as should come to Virginia after his own departure; Gist served until his death in 1759. Under authorization from Dinwiddie he also set up a system whereby Cherokee and Catawba parties coming to Virginia would be supervised by "conductors" and guides, consisting of John Watts, Richard Smith, and Thomas Rutherford (Alden 1944: 71–73). While Virginia thus gave the superintendent excellent financial support, Maryland failed, for the most part, in responding to Atkin's call for funds. Pennsylvania, which had some of its tribes under the Southern department, did not fully cooperate with him. As a result, Virginia had to bear most of the financial burden for Indian presents and other costs (Atkin 1954:xxv).

From the time of his appointment in 1756 until his death in 1761, Atkin's importance as a manager of Indian affairs in the French and Indian War steadily declined. He not only had difficulties with many persons entrusted with the management of Indian affairs by Pennsylvania and Maryland, such as Croghan, but also alienated several of the colonial governors by sending them bristling letters (Alden 1944:72; Atkin 1954:xxiv). He did not reach his own colony, South Carolina, until 1758, two years after his appointment, and then spent the following two years traveling among the Creeks and Choctaws and holding conferences with them, returning to Charleston only in 1760. When Lord Loudoun instructed Atkin to obtain 500 Southern Indians to support Gen. John Forbes in an attack on Fort Duquesne in the campaign of 1758, Loudoun, fearing that Atkin might be dilatory, appointed William Byrd as a second agent (Alden 1944:76–77).

Atkin failed to establish a strong Indian department in the South. His appointment was usually regarded by his contemporaries as a mistake. Nor did he have sufficient financial support for the office. The result was that Indian affairs remained largely in the hands of the Southern governors during Atkin's superintendency (Alden 1944: 71, 134; Atkin 1954:xxix). When Governor Boone of South Carolina learned of Atkin's death in 1761, he called upon Jeffrey Amherst, the governor general of British North America in New York, and urged him to recommend John Stuart for the Southern superintendency. As a result, Stuart replaced Atkin as superintendent of the Southern department in 1762 and held the position until 1779. The administration of Stuart was of an entirely different character from that of his predecessor. During the critical years for the British empire, Stuart succeeded in centralizing the Southern department, which had been in a haphazard, decentralized, and often chaotic condition (Shaw 1931:47).

Stuart was assisted by a number of men. Alexander Cameron, who was appointed commissary for the Cherokees in 1764, was soon raised to the rank of deputy superintendent. Stuart also appointed Roderick McIntosh for the upper Creeks and Cowetas and John Struthers for the lower Creeks (Shaw 1931:35, 37). John Stuart's cousin, Charles Stuart, who was first appointed commissary to the small tribes, was promoted to deputy superintendent in 1766. To the Chickasaws John Stuart sent as commissary John McIntosh, who rendered long and faithful service with them. Elias Legardere was stationed at Fort Tombigbee to deal with the Choctaws, and William Struthers was temporarily commissioned as commissary to the Creeks. The Southern superintendent also furnished each of these men with an interpreter and stationed another interpreter, René Roi, at Mobile. Dugald Campbell and John Doigg were appointed commissaries of stores at Mobile and Pensacola respectively (Alden 1944:212–213).

Much of the burden of enforcement in Stuart's department fell on the shoulders of the commissaries and other minor officials, and thus much depended upon the caliber of the commissaries to make Stuart's system effective. In the period 1766–1768, Stuart made several additional appointments. Pierce Acton Sinnott was appointed assistant commissary to live at Fort Appalachie to deal with five lower Creek towns and the Seminoles, Harpain de la Gauterais was chosen as commissary to the six villages of Choctaws and what were referred to as the small tribes, and Lt. James Henderson was employed to replace Legardere. Several interpreters and blacksmiths were also added to the staff during this period. For the West Florida area, the Southern superintendent appointed John McIntosh in 1770 as commissary (without salary), in order to remove the serious trade abuses in the Chickasaw and Choctaw nations, and in the following year gave him back his old post as commissary to Chickasaws. In December 1770 Stuart chose Lt. John Thomas as deputy superintendent for the small tribes (Alden 1944:254–255, 318).

Changing Policies

In the hope of improving the superintendency by making it more efficient and independent, the superintendents presented in 1764 a plan to the Board of Trade. It provided that the Indian trade was to be taken completely out of the hands of the colonies, all colonial laws regulating Indian affairs repealed, and control placed in the hands of the superintendent of each district, who was to be assisted by deputies, commissaries, interpreters, smiths, and missionaries. The superintendents or their deputies were to visit the tribes yearly and were to be empowered to act as justices of the peace. All the trade was to be under the direction and inspection of the superintendents and their deputies. Although the plan was never adopted, Johnson and Stuart proceeded to administer Indian affairs according to this plan (Alden 1944: 242–243; Mohr 1933:7–8; Prucha 1962:22–23). In 1767 Lord Shelburne proposed that the Indian departments be abolished and that Indian affairs revert to the earlier practice of colonial control. His suggestion was rejected but was instrumental in bringing about a compromise between imperial and colonial control (Mohr 1933:8–9). Due largely to the high cost of the imperial establishment, the Indian trade was returned to the control of the colonial governors, but political relations with the Indians remained under the superintendents. Accordingly, Stuart had to issue orders for the discharge of all his commissaries and most of the inferior employees in his department. He was now limited to two deputies and three interpreters including his own. Only Alexander Cameron and Charles Stuart were retained by Stuart as his deputies (Shaw 1931: 42).

The Revolution

British Administration

The coming of the American Revolution necessitated changes in the duties of the superintendents. The Northern department, although it did not disappear as an administrative unit during the Revolution, was gradually confined to Canada and became rather quickly an integral part of the war machine, furnishing Indian auxiliary forces to the British army (Volwiler 1926:117). It is estimated that under Guy Johnson's Northern superintendency there were all together about 50 officers devoting themselves to maintaining the friendship of the Indians for Great Britain (Mohr 1933:62). John Johnson, who had been in England since the fall of 1781, after long negotiating, finally received an appointment in 1782 as superintendent general and inspector general of Indian affairs, thus coordinating Indian affairs in the North under a single head, in contrast to its earlier fragmented state (Graymont 1972:252).

In the Southern department, Stuart retained his interest in the problems of trade and Indian boundaries and made sporadic efforts to regain authority over the trade until the end of his life. He became virtually independent during his last years. In 1777, believing that Guy Johnson had been given a commission as colonel in the army (he was actually made only a colonel of the Indians in his district), Stuart requested that he be given a similar commission. Lord George Germain gave him an empty title of colonel solely for the purpose of enhancing Stuart's prestige among the natives in his department (Alden 1944:152, 155).

Stuart's death early in 1779 caused a division of the department. Cameron and John Graham controlled the western area, from 1779 to 1781 and from 1782 to 1783 respectively; and Col. Thomas Browne controlled the east during the remaining four years of its existence. This division greatly decreased its prestige. Although the two districts were still under the Crown, Cameron and Browne were not imperial administrators. Of necessity the Indian agents were now more directly subject to military rule than they had been during Stuart's lifetime (Shaw 1931: 47–48; Mohr 1933:58; Alden 1944:139–140).

For the imperial superintendents, the role of enlisting the Indian nations on behalf of the Crown against the rebels was difficult indeed. The colonists were quick to regard Indian raids on the frontier as the instigation of the British agents, whether or not this was true (Washburn 1971:50). Nonetheless, the British largely succeeded in retaining the friendship of the major tribes throughout the Revolutionary War. That the British could provide a generous supply of goods to the Indians, while the Americans stood as a symbol of encroachment on the Indian lands, contributed to the success of the British Indian department (Mohr 1933:43; Graymont 1972:90, 164).

One of the largest allotments from the imperial treasury was necessary in order to pay the personnel of the Indian department. Atkin wanted the same salary as that received by Sir William Johnson for the office of superintendent, £600 per year. Deputies such as Croghan received only £200–300 a year, while the salaries of interpreters ranged from £70 to 80. The salaries of gunsmiths, who were much in demand, started at the same rates as those of the interpreters, but they went up as high as £100. In addition, each smith had to be provided with equipment, costing sometimes into the hundreds of pounds. Indians also had to be employed as messengers and translators (Jacobs 1966:73).

The expenditures steadily increased until 1770 when the budgets of the Northern and Southern departments were both fixed at approximately £5,000. From that time the expenses remained relatively stable until the Revolu-

tion. Then they increased very rapidly, reaching in the years 1775 and 1776 about £20,000 annually. They continued to grow during the next three years and reached their maximum about the time of Stuart's death in 1779. But when the expenses began to exceed £20,000 a year, the imperial government was unprepared to maintain such an expensive organization and ordered reduction. From the fall of 1779 until the close of the British administration of Indian affairs, the regular annual allowance was fixed at £3,910 (Shaw 1931:83).

American Administration

With the imperial superintendency turned increasingly into a device for winning friendship for the British, the Americans felt the need of establishing an efficient system of handling Indian affairs. Individual colonies began sending commissioners to the Indians. In June 1775 the Virginia assembly appointed George Washington, Thomas Walker, James Wood, Andrew Lewis, and Adam Stephens commissioners for holding treaties with the Ohio Indians and appropriated £20,000 toward expenses (Mohr 1933:24, 30; Prucha 1962:26–27). On July 12, 1775, the Continental Congress authorized the formation of three departments of Indian affairs: the Northern department including the Six Nations and the Indians to the north of them, the Southern department encompassing the Cherokees and all others to the south of them, and the Middle department covering all tribes between the others. Five commissioners were appointed for the Southern department and three for each of the other two (Schmeckebier 1927:12; Prucha 1962:27–28).

The duties of these Indian commissioners were to deal with the Indians in order to keep their peace and friendship. They were given power to seize the king's Indian superintendents or any of their assistants if they should attempt to turn the natives against the colonies (Graymont 1972:165; O'Donnell 1973:22–24). That Benjamin Franklin, Patrick Henry, and James Wilson were chosen for the Middle department is an indication of the importance attached to the matter (Prucha 1962:28). However, the Americans largely failed in securing the Indians as allies. They even failed to keep the natives neutral. Few American commissioners were experts in Indian affairs, Indians traditionally regarded Americans as encroachers, and, above all, the colonists lacked goods to supply to the Indians.

Interpreters

Throughout the entire colonial period, interpreters played an indispensable role in Indian-White relations, in which they were in reality agents of the governments. The fundamental structural differences between English and the Indian languages, the highly symbolic and allusive character of Indian diplomatic discourse, and the radical disparateness of White and Indian cultures made the translator's job extremely difficult. While a poor interpreter could turn an eloquent speech of the Indian into flat prose, a good one could make a poor speaker very poetic. The job of the Indian interpreters, then, was not simply the literal translation of one language into another. Only those who were thoroughly familiar with the customs and traditions, as well as languages, of both cultures were able to translate accurately and effectively.

The Plymouth stories of Samoset, who spoke some English, and Squanto, who had a better command of English and rendered a valuable service to the infant colony, are well known. Throughout the seventeenth century, in the Middle colonies and Southern colonies as well as in New England, the Indian interpreters were in great demand not only in political relations but also in more ordinary daily functions. At courtroom trials involving the natives, for example, translators were regularly employed.

As the eighteenth century approached and the Anglo-French rivalry in North America began, Indian-White political and diplomatic relations took on an additional significance. In diplomatic negotiations, effective translating was essential, especially in the colonies that dealt with strong Indian tribes. Consequently, the importance of Indian interpreters grew and was gradually institutionalized. Although the office of interpreter was not usually a full-time job and did not command high prestige, the position often involved much more responsibility than its title implied. The interpreters were actually the field representatives of the colonies in their dealings with the Indians, who were required to translate one language to another and simultaneously to serve as messengers and diplomatic agents to the Indian country, sometimes for extended periods of time (Trelease 1960:211–212). Among numerous interpreters (who were usually selected from among those traders, half-bloods, and English-speaking Indians who had good reputations) actively engaged in White-tribal relations, there emerged a small number of highly able persons, who began to assume political roles (Jacobs 1966:41). Essential qualities of these men, who increasingly turned into diplomats in the wilderness, were mastery of languages and full understanding of both the White and Indian cultures. The great success of Sir William Johnson with the Iroquois was due largely to these qualities. Although he usually used interpreters and rarely acted as his own interpreter, he more than once corrected his interpreter's translations. One of Johnson's ablest interpreters, Arent Stevens, was a coworker of Conrad Weiser in his early years and acted as an official interpreter in Albany in the 1740s. During the period 1755–1756, Stevens was Johnson's interpreter in almost every conference Johnson held with the Indians.

A variety of languages spoken by different tribes made it necessary for the English to appoint many different interpreters to deal with specific tribes. In the summer of 1757, for example, when 13 Indian chiefs were invited to the Easton, Pennsylvania, conference, almost all the leading interpreters in the colonies were summoned. Weiser, Croghan, Thomas McKee, John Pumpshire, Moses Tattamy, and others formed a kind of board of interpreters. Weiser, a religious leader, farmer, and head of a large family, had participated in numerous negotiations with the Indians as a provincial interpreter of Pennsylvania and was the senior interpreter at Easton. He was highly respected by both Whites and Indians and was regarded as a faithful, honest, and truly good man, who "spoke their words and our words, and not his" (P.A.W. Wallace 1945:46, 53, 145, 184–186 ff.; Jacobs 1966:41).

Andrew Montour, whom Weiser recommended as interpreter to the Pennsylvania council in 1748 as being "faithful, knowing, and prudent," was the son of an Indian and a French woman and was considered an Iroquoian by the Indians themselves. Montour became actively engaged in the affairs of the Ohio Indians serving both Pennsylvania and Virginia as more than an interpreter (Jacobs 1966:41; Lewin 1966). Croghan, holder of a military commission and an Indian trader, whom Weiser also recommended in 1747 to the Pennsylvania council, often acted as a senior partner of Montour (Jacobs 1966:41). He made many journeys throughout the Ohio valley and negotiated with a number of tribes. From 1756, he was an exceptionally effective deputy superintendent, acting at the same time as his own interpreter (Wainwright 1959:113). Thomas McKee, an Indian trader who married a Shawnee woman and was thoroughly familiar with the Delaware language, had already established himself as a valuable interpreter, messenger, and negotiator by the time he attended the Easton conference as the interpreter for the Crown.

Colorful figures such as Croghan, Montour, Weiser, McKee, Robert Rogers, and Abraham Bosomworth, who regularly served as messengers, arbitrators, and diplomatic agents, were not merely interpreters in the true sense of the term. The word "interpreter" meant more than "translator." It became a title. These men, as forest diplomats, whether they were employed by the colonial governments or by the imperial superintendents, performed the kind of work that not just anyone could handle. Never before and never after in American history did the interpreters play such an essential role in Indian-White politics.

Summary

In the conduct of Indian diplomacy, the colonies did not establish any permanent agencies of government. Special commissioners were the device used to deal with the Indian tribes regarding specific diplomatic problems.

Colonial dealings with the tribes were therefore more personal than institutional. Even after 1756, the colonies that still retained some of the power to handle the problems concerning the Indian tribes continued their former practice. It was not until the start of the American Revolution that the Americans established three superintendents to control Indian affairs. The year 1756 marked an important turning point in the institutional development of governmental agencies concerning the Indians. The imperial government established a full-fledged superintendency of Indian affairs, including two superintendents, deputy superintendents, commissaries, and many other minor offices.

In the matter of trade, the colonies developed formal governmental agencies, such as the truck house system in Massachusetts, the Indian trade commissioners in South Carolina and Georgia, and the special commissioners in Pennsylvania. Problems concerning tributary and nontribal Indians were mostly handled within the existing governmental system, except in New England, where special agencies administered their affairs. In both trade and diplomacy, Indian interpreters played a valuable role in Indian relations throughout the colonial period as agents of government, formal and informal. However, the effective handling of Indian affairs did not necessarily depend upon the effective system of governmental agencies. The individuals who occupied the offices largely determined the effectiveness of the agencies as institutions.

Nineteenth-Century United States Government Agencies

DONALD J. BERTHRONG

The United States Constitution provides the federal government with plenary power over Indian tribes. There is only one specific grant made to Congress in the Constitution dealing with Indians, the power to control commerce with Indians. That authority combined with other general grants such as the ability to make treaties and to appropriate funds for the general welfare has permitted Congress, with the approval of the Supreme Court, to control Indian affairs and to protect the person, property, and welfare of Indian people (*McClanahan* v. *Arizona State Tax Commission*, 411 U.S. 164 [1973]; U.S. Department of the Interior. Office of the Solicitor 1958: 21–22).

Political relations with Indians by central agencies of the national government preceded the adoption of the Constitution. In July 1775 the Continental Congress created northern, middle, and southern departments with commissioners for each department who in turn were authorized to appoint agents to the various Indian tribes. Together, the commissioners and agents were to maintain friendships between the colonies and the Indian tribes and were to prevent British officials from inflaming Indian antagonism against the American colonists (Prucha 1984, 1:35–36). In 1781, the Articles of Confederation recognized that the national government should manage Indian affairs and trade. During the period of the Articles of Confederation, Congress maintained its power to treat exclusively with Indian tribes by approving boundary lines and by prohibiting unauthorized settlement and unlicensed trade in Indian country. Also, Congress in the Northwest Ordinance of 1787 declared that Indians should not lose their lands, property, rights, or liberties except during war approved by Congress (Schmeckebier 1927:12–17).

Soon after the Constitution was ratified, President George Washington and Secretary of War Henry Knox turned their attention to Indian affairs. The first statute under the Constitution of 1789 applicable to Indian affairs, which became law on July 22, 1790 (1 U.S. Stat. 137), was based on earlier precedents, required a license for all Indian traders, provided punishment for those who traded with improper licenses, and invalidated the acquisi-

tion of Indian land other than by an official United States treaty. The 1790 statute also provided that Whites who murdered Indians or committed other crimes against Indians in Indian country would be punished.

The law solved little. President Washington continued to insist in 1791 and 1792 on more permanent means to care for Indians. In 1793, stronger legislation was approved by Congress giving the president a budget for Indian affairs and for gifts to the tribes (1 U.S. Stat. 329). Primarily, the first laws were aimed at lawless frontiersmen and sought to restrain Whites from violating treaties with Indians. The laws did not control the Indian tribes and did little more than regulate Indian trade and the sale of Indian land. In 1796 and 1799, Congress passed laws that specified boundary lines between Indian country and land open for settlement by United States citizens (1 U.S. Stat. 469, 743). Finally, on March 30, 1802 (2 U.S. Stat. 139), a permanent trade and intercourse law, effective until 1834, was enacted, based upon the 1796 and 1799 laws.

Creation of the Bureau of Indian Affairs

President Thomas Jefferson, early in the nineteenth century, continued the Indian system created by his predecessors. The governors of the territories were directed by law to assume the duties of superintendent of Indian affairs. Associated with the territorial governors were temporary agents who were to reside among the Indians and supply them with animals and agricultural implements and also with goods and money. When President Jefferson appointed the temporary agents, he instructed them to "civilize" the Indians by teaching them agriculture and the domestic arts. Through the territorial governor, the agents were required to report to the War Department, to record the events and activities at their agencies, to note the condition of the Indians, to depict the natural history of the region, and to describe the Indians' progress in civilization. The agent and subagents quickly became key factors in White-Indian relations. They made the initial reports on all violations of the Intercourse Acts to the superintendents of Indian affairs, to frontier military commanders, or to the War Department. The agents' success depended upon the balance they could achieve between the needs of the Indians among whom they lived and the demands of the White frontiersmen. If the agent was respected by both Whites and Indians, he could resolve conflicts without resorting to troops or court action.

Not until 1818, when there were 15 agents and 10 subagents among the Indians, were the appointments of these officials regularized by a statute (3 U.S. Stat. 428). Still the agencies themselves, in which the agent worked and lived, existed only by implication even in the 1818 statute, which appropriated funds for the agents' salaries (3 U.S. Stat. 461). Later legislation stressed the authority of the agents to restrict whiskey traffic, to issue trading licenses, and to write the required reports to the War Department (Prucha 1962:52–57).

The haphazard growth of offices managing Indian affairs was also reflected in the statutes establishing and regulating government factories for the Indian trade. For a decade after the factories were instituted in 1796 (1 U.S. Stat. 452), the managers, or factors, were appointed by the president and were responsible to the secretary of the treasury and not to the secretary of war. Finally, an office of the superintendent of Indian trade was established on April 21, 1806, within the War Department. The superintendent of Indian trade and the factors were presidential appointees. The former was charged with the duties of purchasing and distributing Indian goods, acquiring Indian furs and hides, and assuring the Indians a fair market price for the product of their hunts (Peake 1954:6). Gradually, the superintendent of Indian trade became an important advisor to the secretary of war on Indian affairs and the office of the superintendent became an unofficial focus for all matters relating to governmental relations with Indians (fig. 1). Thomas L. McKenney, who was the superintendent during the last six years of the factory system from 1816 to 1822, became a leading advocate of the Indians and sought to promote their welfare (Viola 1974:24). But when Congress abolished the factory system in 1822 (3 U.S. Stat. 678) because of the pressure of the fur traders led by John Jacob Astor, again there was no central agency or office for Indian affairs.

John C. Calhoun, on March 11, 1824, used his authority as secretary of war to create a Bureau of Indian Affairs within the War Department (Viola 1974:93–94). McKenney accepted the appointment to head the new office, and he was given two clerks as assistants although there was no specific congressional authorization for the three new appointees. Secretary Calhoun invested McKenney with the power to supervise the expenditure of appropriations for annuity payments and operational expenses, the disbursal of all federal monies related to Indian affairs, the Indian civilization fund, the settlement of all White and Indian claims arising under the Inter-

Natl. Arch.: RG75, Letters Received by the Superintendent of Indian Trade, 1806–1824.
Fig. 1. Letter from John Johnston, Indian agent to the Shawnee at Piqua Agency, Ohio, to Superintendent of Indian Trade John Mason, March 26, 1812. Johnston requests tobacco, clay pipes, wampum, and Jefferson medals with ribbons for use as presents to the Shawnee. He had been at the newly established post for only 3 weeks and probably intended to use the presents to influence the Shawnee to remain neutral or to align with the Americans in the imminent War of 1812.

course Acts, and the routine War Department correspondence dealing with Indian affairs. Within a few months, McKenney's office became known as the Office of Indian Affairs and quickly a voluminous correspondence from superintendents and Indian agents began to flow over the desks of McKenney and his assistants (Viola 1974:95–96). The informal arrangement disturbed McKenney, who realized that his tenure in office rested only upon the confidence that the secretary of war held in him. For six years, McKenney pressed for legislation that would create an office headed by a commissioner of Indian affairs. A plan, containing McKenney's recommendations, to completely reorganize Indian affairs was written in 1829 by Lewis Cass and William Clark. Three years later, Congress authorized the president to appoint a commissioner of Indian affairs as a subordinate to the secretary of war who would be empowered to direct and manage all Indian affairs and relations with Indian tribes (4 U.S. Stat. 564).

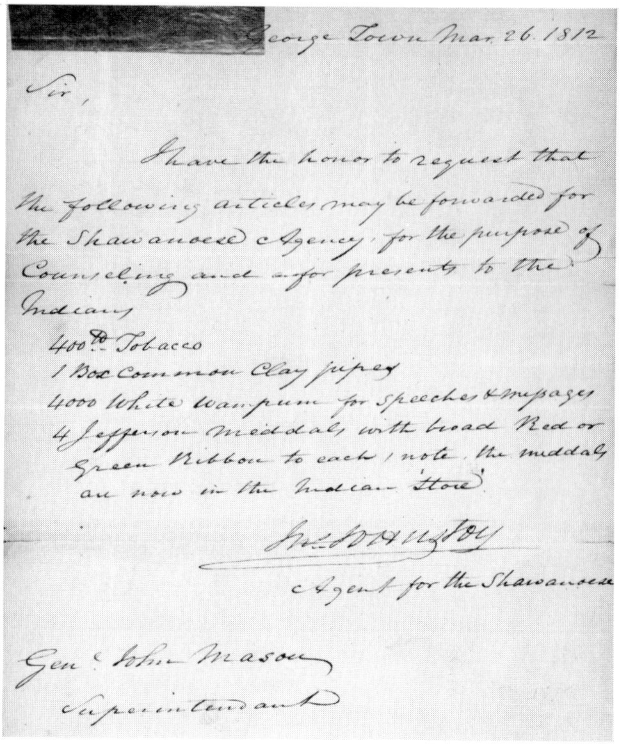

On June 30, 1834, Congress approved a statute that is considered to be the organic law of the Bureau of Indian Affairs (4 U.S. Stat. 735). Earlier, Secretary of War Lewis Cass had noted that legislation on Indian affairs had become "inappropriate and inadequate" because of changing circumstances. The act established new agencies, abolished some old ones, and with certain exceptions continued the territorial governors as ex-officio superintendents of Indian affairs. However, Indian agents in the states were placed directly under the control of the commissioner of Indian affairs. The 1834 act specified the location of the agencies, but the president was given the power to shift the location to meet changing locations of tribes. After 1834, the number of superintendents and agents was increased by special acts, so that the 1834 statute was the last general law for field personnel of the Bureau of Indian Affairs. The transfer of the Bureau of Indian Affairs from the War to the Interior Department in 1849 (9 U.S. Stat. 395) did not materially change the administrative structure of the Bureau, since from the outset the office was predominantly civilian in orientation.

During its evolution and maturation, the Bureau of Indian Affairs became the principal government agency for the management of Indian-White relations. The policies, regulations, and law developed and administered by the Bureau were imposed upon Indians with minimal consideration of their impact upon the Indians or their culture. The Bureau was expected not only to regulate the Indians' fur trade, to control the introduction of liquor into Indian country, to see that justice was served when crimes were committed on Indian land, and to acculturate the Indian but also at proper times to assist in the removal of Indian tribes to reservations.

In the early years of the nineteenth century, military forces of the United States by law also played a role in Indian-White relations. Indian agents were ordered to request assistance from military commanders in the fulfillment of their duties. By 1796, the president was authorized to use troops to remove White settlers who had located illegally upon Indian land and to apprehend any person in Indian country violating Intercourse Acts. Violators by 1800 could only be detained for five days by military authorities before they would be required to deliver the accused to a civil court for the setting of bail except in cases of murder or other capital offenses (Prucha 1962:60–63). When juries of Whites consistently refused to punish their fellow citizens charged with crimes violating the intercourse laws, great consternation was caused among Indian agents as they attempted to assist and protect Indian tribes.

Effective enforcement of the intercourse laws required close cooperation between Indian agents and military commanders on the frontier. Conflicts between the civil and military arms of the War Department were frequent especially when an officer did not respond quickly to an agent's request for assistance. In practice, army officers would cooperate only when they received specific orders emanating from the secretary of war. Effective and able Indian agents, such as Lawrence Taliaferro at Saint Peters, Minnesota, or Benjamin Hawkins among the

Creeks, were frequently powerless because of differences with military commanders (Prucha 1962:64–65). Hawkins, who served the Creeks for nearly two decades before his death in 1816, realized that it was not possible for him, the Indians, or the War Department to check White penetration into Creek country. Despite many provocations, Hawkins, until the War of 1812, persuaded the Creeks to remain peaceful and stimulated them to till their farms, erect permanent homes, and engage in commerce. He also contributed to the decline of Creek power by undermining their communal town life and by destroying the prestige of their traditional tribal leaders (Debo 1941:67–71).

The Removal Period

As American settlers flooded west over the Appalachian mountains, the demand for Indian removal became insistent. In the Ohio country, land cessions led to Tecumseh's heroic efforts to preserve the Indians' way of life. Although blood was spilled north of the Ohio River during the War of 1812 and the Black Hawk War, the key conflict occurred in the Southeast where the Cherokees, Creeks, Choctaws, and Chickasaws lived. Those nations, with substantial populations and considerable human and economic resources, undertook resistance to the advance of the White frontier. Indians of the Ohio country removed more or less voluntarily, but those of the Southeast either refused to sign cession treaties or to emigrate until coerced. Politicians of Georgia, supported by public officials of Alabama and Mississippi, insisted that the United States was obligated to remove the Cherokees because of the 1802 compact by which Georgia ceded her western territory to the United States. President James Monroe on March 30, 1824, categorically denied that the United States government had any such obligation when he stated that "Indian title was in no way affected by the compact with Georgia" (Prucha 1962: 228).

The removal of the Southeast Indians began early. Andrew Jackson in 1814, after subduing the Creek Red Sticks, began to clear the Indians from their domains by forcing the Creeks to cede to the United States about two-thirds of their territory (Debo 1941:82–83). The new states of Mississippi and Alabama added their demands for Indian removal to those earlier voiced by older Southern states. In 1820 the Choctaws were the first of the great Southeast tribes to capitulate (De Rosier 1970:67). Five years later, the Choctaws exchanged their lands east of the Mississippi for a tract of land that comprised approximately the southern one-half of the present state of Oklahoma (De Rosier 1970:80–82). By 1828, the Creeks ceded the remainder of their lands. The prosperous mixed-blood faction of the Creeks moved to Indian Territory while the full-bloods joined their kinsmen in Alabama   *257* where many of them died despite their agent's efforts to assist them with distributions of food and clothing (Debo 1941:94–96).

Where Presidents Monroe and Adams had used a voluntary emigration policy, Andrew Jackson resorted to force. The 1830 Removal Act (4 U.S. Stat. 411) epitomized his Indian policy. That law was first applied to about one-third of the Choctaws who exercised their options to select land in Mississippi rather than move to the West. However, their selections were ignored; when dispossessed, many Mississippi Choctaws joined the bulk of their people in Indian Territory (Debo 1970:102–103). Even Creek submission to state laws in 1829 did not save them. After ceding their lands in Alabama, all but 2,500 Creeks moved to Indian Territory. Those who did not emigrate joined the Cherokees, not realizing that displacement was inevitable. Beginning in 1836, another group of Creeks was transported to Indian Territory without food, clothing, weapons, or cooking utensils. When finally assembled in Indian Territory, the tribal population had declined by 45 percent, the Creek agent discovered (Debo 1941:98–103, 1970:102–103). The very few Creeks who remained were ancestors of the Poarch Creeks of Alabama.

The Cherokees stubbornly refused to part with their lands in northwestern Georgia and smaller areas in three adjacent states. However, one faction of the Cherokees in 1835 signed a cession treaty by which they agreed to remove to Indian Territory within two years. Those who knew the Cherokees said that the faction not signing the treaty and led by John Ross would not consider themselves bound by it (Woodward 1963:180–182, 190). When only 2,000 Cherokees emigrated within the time specified, 7,000 troops, regulars and militia, commanded by Gen. Winfield Scott drove the Cherokees from their homes into stockades. By June 1838, 5,000 people were transported to the West, to be joined later by the remainder of the tribe who moved themselves. Of the 18,000 Cherokees who emigrated after 1835, about 4,000 died in the stockades or enroute to their new lands in Indian Territory (Woodward 1963:195, 205, 218).

Two wars were fought to expel the Seminoles from Florida. Led by Osceola and others, the Seminoles retreated into the Everglades where they were tracked down by bloodhounds and patrols. Small groups were periodically captured and shipped as prisoners to Indian Territory where later lands were reserved for them in 1856 (McReynolds 1957:152 passim). An 1823 census listed 4,883 Seminoles in Florida while in 1836, 3,765 of the tribe had been transferred to Indian Territory (M.H. Wright 1951:228).

Expansion to the Plains and Pacific

258   The annexation of Texas, the Oregon Convention of 1846,

and the Treaty of Guadalupe Hidalgo in 1848 brought additional Indians within the jurisdiction of the United States. For nine years after the annexation of Texas in 1845, Indians in that state had no reservation or agency. The peaceful Caddoes, Tonkawas, and Penateka Comanches were attacked by Texans despite the protests of their agent, Robert S. Neighbors. To save his charges, Neighbors brought the Caddoes and Penatekas to the Washita River in Indian Territory where they received their protection from Fort Cobb and their land and food from the Wichita Agency. When Neighbors returned from his journey, he was murdered by a Texan (Debo 1970: 114–115).

White settlers entered Oregon Country before treaties for land cessions were begun in 1850. Eighteen treaties were arranged with California tribes in 1851 and 1852, but they were never ratified by the United States Senate. Throughout California, the Indians suffered from the influx of gold miners and settlers. The president was authorized to establish five reservations, not exceeding 25,000 acres each, as havens for the California tribes (Schmeckebier 1927:43; Josephy 1968:145, 332–333; Heizer 1974a; Heizer and Almquist 1971).

Emigrants traversing the overland route to the Pacific coast increased the possibilities of conflict with Indians of the Plains. In 1819, Benjamin O'Fallon was appointed Indian agent of the Upper Missouri Agency. Relations between the Indians residing along the Missouri River and fur traders expanded rapidly after the War of 1812 and required substantial supervision. Originally the agent was not assigned responsibility for individual tribes but rather over the region bordering the Missouri River. Subagencies were established in 1824 at the Mandan villages and at the Great Bend of the Missouri, which led to decreased duties for the Upper Missouri Indian agent (E.E. Hill 1967). Until 1834, the Saint Louis Superintendency supervised all the agencies on the Mississippi and Missouri rivers, and after that date the Western Superintendency shared those responsibilities. As national boundaries were expanded, new superintendencies were created for Oregon in 1848, New Mexico and Utah in 1850, California in 1852, and Washington in 1853. When western population growth required further subdivision of older territories, Indian superintendencies were originated that coincided with the new territorial boundaries and the territorial governor became the ex-officio superintendent of Indian affairs. As the field force of the Bureau of Indian Affairs expanded into new geographical regions, new superintendencies were developed to keep supervisory personnel in close contact with their subordinates. Eight years after the Central Superintendency, which replaced the Saint Louis office, was created in 1851, its offices were shifted from Saint Louis to Saint Joseph, Missouri, to Atchison, Kansas, in 1865, and finally to Lawrence, Kansas, in 1869. The Central Superintendency originally was given jurisdiction over all Indian agencies located on the upper reaches of the Missouri, Platte, and Arkansas rivers. In 1861, when Colorado and Dakota territories were organized, the Indian agencies in those areas were shifted from the Central Superintendency to the appropriate territorial superintendency.

The areas of the western Indian agencies when first established were large. Thomas Fitzpatrick, for example, when appointed Indian agent for the Upper Platte and Arkansas Agency, was expected to serve all Indians living and trading along the upper Platte and Arkansas rivers. From his headquarters at Bent's Fort on the Arkansas River, Fitzpatrick was expected to deal with the Cheyenne, Arapahoe, Kiowa, Comanche, Kiowa-Apache, and Oglala and Brulé Sioux and to extend his ministrations to the South and North Platte rivers. As a former fur trader and mountain man with more than 20 years experience among the Indians of the plains and mountains, Fitzpatrick was representative of many Indian agents who distrusted Indians and advocated strong policies for their control. Life among the Indians had taught the traders to be wary of Indians. Although Fitzpatrick wrote in his first report, that "ingratitude, low, mean cunning, cowardice, selfishness and treachery, are the characteristics of the whole race" (ARCIA 1847:243), he believed that the Plains tribes could be controlled by stamping out the illegal liquor traffic, by patrolling the caravan routes with a highly mobile body of troops recruited from old fur trappers, by establishing military posts on the Upper Platte and Arkansas rivers, by ending intertribal hostilities, and by cultivating goodwill among Indians through treaties and presents. Saint Louis Superintendent D.D. Mitchell followed Fitzpatrick's suggestions: a comprehensive peace treaty and demarcation of tribal hunting grounds on the Plains was the result of councils held at Fort Laramie in 1851 when 10,000 Indians from the central and northern plains met with United States commissioners (Berthrong 1963:106–109, 115–116, 118–123; Trennert 1975:181–190).

Peace between Indians and Whites on the Plains quickly succumbed for a variety of reasons. More travelers on the overland roads, more wagon freight trains, more population diffusing into the western mining regions, more aggressive army officers, and constant diminution of buffalo and other game upon which the Indians of the Plains depended for their food supply provided situations that encouraged conflicts. James W. Whitfield, Fitzpatrick's successor for the Upper Platte and Arkansas Agency in 1855, warned that the only way war could be avoided was for the United States government to construct forts on the central plains at strategic points along the principal trails and roads in Indian country. He recommended that Indians be chastised and awed with the power of the government or else they would raid, kill, and prevent the smooth flow of commerce (ARCIA 1856:

116). Until well after the Civil War, Indian agents throughout the West were concerned either with placating their charges with food and goods or trying to mitigate the ravages of war upon the Indian people.

Until 1869, Indian agents and superintendents were political appointees who found ways to use their posts for personal gain. All too frequently, they did not pay the Indians annuity funds due or they delivered inferior goods and spoiled foods furnished by dishonest contractors. In Kansas Territory in the 1850s, Indian agents linked themselves to land speculators and railroad corporations to defraud Indian tribes of land for a fraction of the reservations' value (P.W. Gates 1954:19). Even if an Indian agent were competent and honest, he often found his position untenable. In theory, it was the duty of the Indian agent to make the reservation a place upon which the Indian could be taught agricultural pursuits, be educated, and be protected from disease, hunger, and death. Almost universally, frontier settlers were hostile to their Indian neighbors and constantly encroached upon Indian land, carried off Indian goods and property, and committed acts of violence upon the tribesmen. Local courts and juries were seldom sympathetic to the plight of the Native American. Law infrequently operated for the benefit of Indians even if they were fully supported by their Indian agent and other officials in the Indian Bureau.

The Reservation Era

As the reservation period began after the Civil War and Indian wars became less frequent, the Bureau of Indian Affairs was thoroughly reorganized. A relatively small number of influential people, in and out of Congress, had for some years made known the corruption within and the deficiencies of the Bureau. The powers of the secretary of the interior and the commissioner of Indian affairs remained unchanged, but the Bureau's field personnel and the manner of its selection were modified. At the outset of his administration, President Ulysses Grant tried to substitute surplus army officers in the place of political appointees in the Indian service (Fritz 1963:76). When Congress passed legislation that prohibited military officers from serving in any civil capacity (16 U.S. Stat. 315), President Grant turned to religious bodies for nominations of Indian agents and superintendents. Each denomination that accepted responsibilities within the Indian service appointed an executive committee on Indian affairs to approve all nominations for Indian agents and other agency personnel. The Methodists became accountable for the greatest number of Indians, 54,473, while the Lutherans administered the fewest, 273 (Fritz 1963:76–79). The quality of the Indian agents rose measurably. Still, problems ensued when the churchmen, many of whom never had seen an Indian or who understood little of Indian culture, assumed their posts. The pacifism of the agents representing the Society of Friends was severely strained by the turbulence and intermittent warfare on the Plains, which did not end until after 1876. One Friend, Agent John D. Miles of the Cheyenne-Arapaho Agency, was reprimanded by the church's executive committee on Indian affairs for seeking protection from and for cooperating with troops when his agency was threatened by hostile Cheyenne warriors as the Red River War erupted (Berthrong 1963:387–388).

Hostility between the Senate and House of Representatives over control of Indian affairs accounted for the formation in 1869 of the Board of Indian Commissioners. The Indian Peace Commission of 1867 had succeeded in ending temporarily the widespread Indian wars on the Plains by negotiating treaties that were ratified by the Senate but were unacceptable to the House. During early 1869, the House refused to concur with the Senate's budgetary provisions intended to carry out the Peace Commission's treaties. A compromise was finally agreed to between the two houses of Congress that provided for the usual Indian affairs budget but added a lump sum of two million dollars enabling the president to maintain peace with Indians, to promote civilization among them, to establish reservations as needed, to furnish Indians with necessities of life, and to encourage reservation Indians toward self-support (Fritz 1963:75). The House, however, insisted upon a section within the 1869 appropriation act that provided that the statute did not ratify or approve any Indian treaty proclaimed after July 20, 1867. The section had no legal effect and merely indicated the House's discontent with the conduct of Indian affairs (Prucha 1984, 1:530–531). To supervise further the expenditure of public funds, the Act of April 10, 1869 (16 U.S. Stat. 13), also permitted the president to organize a Board of Indian Commissioners consisting of not more than 10 persons "eminent for their intelligence and philanthropy" to serve without salary. The commissioners, responsible to and under the direction of the president, were to exercise joint control of Indian appropriations with the secretary of the interior. The Board was organized on June 3, 1869, by an executive order.

The Board quickly became involved in the purchasing of annuity goods and agency supplies. The commissioners revised the specifications and the methods of awarding contracts by the Department of the Interior to assure competition and better quality of materials purchased. Congress, in 1870, tried to increase the authority of the Board by directing it to inspect all goods purchased (16 U.S. Stat. 335), and, in the next year, a statute provided that not more than 50 percent of any contract could be paid until all accounts and vouchers had been examined by the Board's executive committee. But the secretary of the interior could override the Board by authorizing payment in full for any contract for Indian goods actually delivered. The Board, throughout its existence, remained in an ambivalent position. It was expected to reform accounting and purchasing systems within the Indian service without having final authority to enforce its recommendations. Through experience, the members of the Board found that they were not expected to oppose too vigorously the policies of the secretary of the interior, the commissioner of Indian affairs, or Congress. Finally, the duties of the Board, in 1882, were limited to visitation of agencies and the inspection of the purchase of Indian supplies, although by law the commissioner was directed to consult with the Board about the purchase of all goods intended for Indians (Schmeckebier 1927:55–57). The Board, nevertheless, composed of members with considerable prestige and status, offered independent advice about major Indian policies. Members were among the most active advocates for the assimilation policy that culminated in the General Allotment Act of 1887 (24 U.S. Stat. 388), more commonly known as the Dawes Severalty Act. The Board of Indian Commissioners was abolished by President Franklin D. Roosevelt by an executive order on May 25, 1933 (U.S. Department of the Interior. Office of the Solicitor 1958:220).

Congressional bickering produced another modification in the relations with Indians and the United States government. During nearly a century before 1871 some 370 treaties had been negotiated by representatives of the central government and tribal authorities (Schmeckebier 1927:59). These treaties, usually unfair to the native Americans, and more than occasionally concluded by fraud, deception, and coercion, were in theory based upon the mutual consent of the parties concerned. Modifications of the terms of the treaties occurred and were justified as necessary and proper for fulfilling the treaties' terms. In such cases, authority for the necessary changes was implicit in the treaty document. Because the House of Representatives disliked being excluded by the Senate in the treaty-making process, the House membership balked when asked to provide funds to carry out the provisions of the treaties in which they had no voice in modifying or ratifying. In the March 3, 1871, Indian Appropriation Act (16 U.S. Stat. 544), the House demanded a section legislating that henceforth Indian groups would not be "acknowledged or recognized as an independent nation, tribe or power with whom the United States may contract by treaty." The act did not invalidate or impair any previously ratified Indian treaty. By this law, Congress in the future could simply legislate without reaching or attempting to achieve a previous understanding with Indians of the United States. Although treaties were no longer needed, the federal government still sought the Indians' consent by seeking prior arrangements when land cessions were being negotiated.

The 1871 act did not alter the position of the Indian within the political system of the United States. Indians were still neither citizens nor aliens since the Fourteenth Amendment of 1868, as interpreted by the Supreme Court, had continued their exclusion from citizenship. The 1871 statute destroyed the concept constructed by Chief Justice of the Supreme Court John Marshall of tribal autonomy and was an initial and important step in weakening intratribal institutions and customs. It was hoped that by reducing the power of tribal institutions, Indians could be more easily absorbed into the political, social, and economic structure of the United States. After 1871, Congress could use the less restrictive legislative process rather than depend upon the traditional and cumbersome treaty-making procedures.

To increase the surveillance over Indian field offices, Congress on February 14, 1873, created the Office of Indian Inspector (17 U.S. Stat. 463). The number of inspectors was initially limited to three and they were appointed by the president with the advice and consent of the Senate for four years unless earlier removed from office by the president. Later Indian appropriation acts changed the number of Indian inspectors. Intended as liaison personnel between Washington and field offices, inspectors were vested with significant powers. Yearly, each superintendency and agency was visited by an inspector who reported directly to the secretary of the interior about all expenditures of money, accounts, and business matters of the jurisdiction, and the number of Indians enrolled at an agency, their physical well-being, their advancement toward civilization, and the uses made of the reservation's resources. If questionable practices or maladministration were apparent, the inspector could assemble information from witnesses under oath; and if it was deemed necessary, he could suspend any superintendent, agent, or employee, designating a temporary replacement subject to the president's approval. When legal proceedings were required to effectuate, to enforce laws, and to prevent violations of law in the administration of Indian affairs, the inspector called upon the proper United States attorney to institute court action (18 U.S. Stat. 422; Stuart 1979:81–84). In 1879 Congress also created special Indian agents whose duties corresponded to those of the inspectors but could also include taking charge of agencies (22 U.S. Stat. 295). Special agents reported directly to the commissioner of Indian affairs on difficult and unusual problems at the various agencies. As the inspection system developed, the superintendencies became superfluous, and they were abolished at various times in the 1870s (Stuart 1979:74). Thereafter, Indian agents were directed to report to and correspond with the commissioner of Indian affairs.

The administrative reforms of the 1870s were slowly incorporated into a rather stable system for the Indian service that continued until the reservation era closed. By the early 1880s, nominations of agents by churches ceased because of disruptive, interdenominational disputes on the reservations and high rejection rates by the Bureau of Indian Affairs of the individuals put forward by church executive committees on Indian affairs. The secretary of the interior then turned once again to political appointees until the civil service reform made its impact after 1891 (Fritz 1963:155–156; Stuart 1979:40–41).

The focal point of all policies and regulations was the Indian agency and its personnel. Indian agents coming to a new reservation faced a bewildering number of tasks. A site for the agency headquarters had to be selected, buildings constructed, Indians fed and clothed, annuity goods, rations (fig. 2), and per capita payments distributed, scanty supplies and agricultural implements doled out, wagon trains for the freighting of supplies from railroads supervised, an educational system begun, diseases among Indians treated, Christian beliefs encouraged, tribal religious ceremonies suppressed, sanitary facilities installed, and Indian hunter-warriors instructed in agricultural and stock-raising techniques. Added to these tasks, the agent was expected to maintain account books balanced to the penny, to conduct a voluminous official correspondence, to placate unruly tribesmen, to council with tribal chiefs, to escort delegations to Washington for visits with the president or lesser functionaries, to protect the reservation from the encroachments of White settlers or cattlemen, to drive out illicit whiskey peddlers and other unauthorized persons, to cooperate with army officers in restraining warriors within the reservation's borders, and to accomplish a multitude of other duties, including keeping themselves fully informed of the frequent changes in administrative procedures flowing from the Washington offices. It was also assumed that the agent would be responsible for all agency employees, which included office clerks, superintendents of schools, teachers, disciplinarians, cooks, blacksmiths, physicians, agency farmers, Indian policemen, Indian judges, herders, and all others employed by the Indian Service. Most agents received an annual salary during the reservation period of $1,500.

The needs of Indians living on reservations varied significantly. Among the Five Civilized Tribes of the Southeast, an Indian agent dealt with educated people who owned large farms, ranches, and business enterprises or who were engaged in profitable professions. Other members of the same tribes were uneducated and needed the full range of agency services. To a lesser degree, other tribes contained some people who except for the fact that they lived on reservations would not have needed much assistance from their agents. Tribes who were able to continue to some degree their traditional subsistence pursuits of fishing, hunting, gathering, and agriculture usually required rations only to supplement their diets. But many Indians became dependent upon the federal government for their livelihood. Congress began appropriating in 1867 small sums to irrigate arid or semi-arid

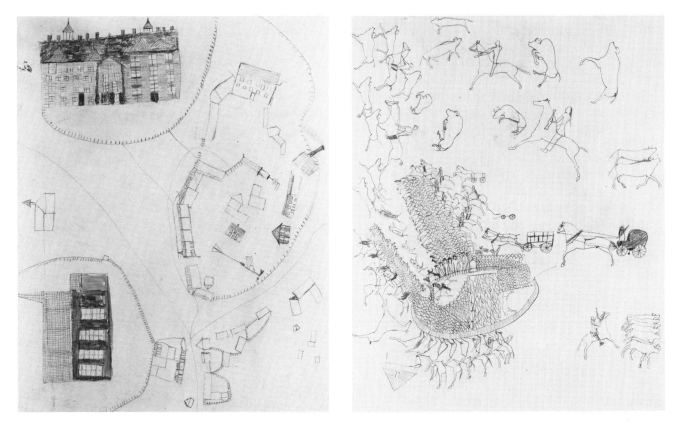

Fig. 2. Indian artists' depictions of Pine Ridge Agency and a cattle issue, about 1890. left, clockwise from lower left, Church; school; agent's compound, enclosed by miscellaneous agency buildings, with a watertank with windmill at one end and a flagpole at the other; traders' quarters. Unidentified artist, pencil and watercolor on paper. right, clockwise from lower left, Corral with a cattle shoot; Indians chasing cattle; the agent in his buggy; and, possibly, an Indian herding cattle. The cattle, especially those farthest from the shoot, are depicted with buffalo-like characteristics, such as humped backs with fur. This may be partially explained by the fact that a beef issue was often organized by the agent as a mock buffalo hunt (Wissler 1938:68–70, 1971:138). Drawing by Sinte, a Sioux, pencil on paper.

reservation lands. Until the twentieth century, however, reservation irrigation projects were developed by agents or superintendents and were of limited benefit to Indian agriculture (Prucha 1984, 2:891–894). The Indians of the Plains suffered the most seriously for the want of food in the decade following the Civil War when they were restricted to their reservations and the White buffalo hunters decimated the vast herds of buffalo. When living freely in their natural environment, Indians stored food for the months when hunting, fishing, or gathering were difficult and unrewarding. As the buffalo and large game became scarce, reserve pemmican supplies could not be stored, and agency rations rarely lasted more than a few days of the ration period, which spanned a week or more. Malnutrition weakened the young and old, making the Indian population susceptible to enervating or fatal diseases, causing the Indian population to decline at all Indian agencies throughout the nineteenth century. Congressional appropriations during the reservation era were rarely sufficient to furnish an adequate diet to the Indians because Congressmen believed that rations destroyed Indian initiative to become self-supporting. Indian agents protested futilely over the late shipments of food stuffs,

often spoiled or wormy when distributed to the Indians, and condemned the use of underweight and diseased cattle that were unfit for human consumption. Pleas from agents that hunger would lead to costly wars were turned aside by Washington officials who frequently warned their subordinates that expenditures above approved budget schedules were in violation of law and were the financial responsibility of the offending Indian agent.

Assimilation Programs

Education, a crucial element in the movement to assimilate Indians, received little emphasis until 1871, when $240,000 was made available. Government day schools, boarding schools on reservations, and nonreservation boarding schools that taught all aspects of White American culture were established during the late nineteenth century ("American Indian Education," this vol.). Legislation in the 1880s and 1890s gave preference to educated Indians in agency employments for which they were qualified. Indians returned from boarding schools became clerks, shop artisans, assistant matrons, disciplinarians, assistant farmers, and interpreters at the agencies. Unfortunately, only a tiny fraction of the graduates could be employed because of the scarcity of jobs at the agencies and because of the prejudice of agents who were more critical of Indian employees than the White employees protected by political influence.

Indian agents struggled unsuccessfully for decades to increase the number of Indians who were self-supporting. Although Indians still retained 138,000,000 acres of land for their own use in 1887 (Hagan 1961:147), very practical difficulties prevented full utilization of that vast domain. Much of the land was located in regions where intensive agricultural techniques were inappropriate. While many tribes grew some cereal crops and cultivated vegetable gardens, systematic attention to large fields of cash crops was antithetical to most Indian ways of life. On the southern Plains, agency personnel for years encouraged Indian people to plant grains only to see the crops wither from droughts and excessive temperatures. Agricultural implements were not furnished to agencies in sufficient quantities. When one agent asked for threshing machines, the commissioner of Indian affairs replied that they were too costly for Indians and that flails should be purchased (Lee 1885). Surplus crops, if ever available, could only be marketed at army posts or at the agencies since railroads were too far distant for practical use. On the Plains and to the west, the potential for ranching was excellent, but that enterprise was not pursued. Since Indians did not use their lands, Whites could see no reason for continuing the reservation system, which only perpetuated indolence and tribal customs. Reformers insisted that by placing Indians on 160-acre allotments, progress would be served. The 1887 Dawes Act (24 U.S. Stat. 388) assumed that by making Indians owners of private property that they would be forced to become farmers, to acquire an education, and to accept Christianity.

The Dawes Act was applied most rapidly to Indian reservations that contained good agricultural land or mineral or timber resources (Debo 1970:256–257). Those Indians to whom the Dawes Act was applied became citizens of the United States and the states or territories in which they resided. Indian relations became more complicated at those agencies where allotments were assigned. Not only did the agent continue with his previous duties dealing with education, farming, health, suppression of Indian ceremonies, and the curtailment of liquor traffic, but also he became the protector of the Indians' private property and civil rights. With some exceptions, Indian allotments were held in trust for a period of 25 years and could not be alienated without the approval of the secretary of the interior. After 1891, the Indian agent was charged with supervision of leasing arrangements for allotments not used by Indians (26 U.S. Stat. 794), an activity that consumed much time of agency personnel. White farmers and ranchers were eager to deal directly with Indians on leasing matters because few Indians understood either their legal rights or the value of their land. Local government officials were also anxious to add Indian property to their tax rolls. Trust property, income derived from it, and funds derived from federal sources were not taxable by local or state governments (U.S. Department of the Interior. Office of the Solicitor 1958: 855–856). Not infrequently, Indian agents resorted to court actions to have trust property stricken from tax rolls. Since allotted Indians were citizens, territorial, state, and local laws were applicable to them. With the approval and cooperation of local law enforcement officials, Indian agents urged that Indians be prosecuted for gambling, the use of liquor and peyote, multiple wives or marriages by Indian customs, vagrancy, or the practice of Indian medicine.

At the end of the nineteenth century, there were 61 Indian agencies maintained by the federal government to distribute goods and provide services for Indian tribes. Two school superintendents had responsibilities similar to those who were in charge of Indian agencies (ARCIA 1899, 1:659–661). The Indian agencies employed 2,562 persons of whom 1,160 were Indians (ARCIA 1899, 1:29). Among Indian employees, 46 percent held appointments for which the salaries were the lowest in the Indian service. Indian reservations contained 81,271,084 acres of land in addition to the acreage held by Indians as allotments (ARCIA 1899, 1:580). Indian tribes had on deposit in trust funds $32,594,188.09 in the United States Treasury and received $1,613,403.93 in interest. Total Indian income from all governmental sources was $6,146,202.91, derived from interest, treaty and agreement money, gratuities, labor, and miscellaneous sources (ARCIA 1899, 1:520, 528). No statistics are available for Indian income from private sources or renumeration for labor and other gainful employment. Congress appropriated $8,237,675.44 for the 1899 fiscal year (ARCIA 1899, 1:1).

Indian population in 1899 was estimated at 267,905, exclusive of the native groups living in Alaska. Reflecting the minimal health care provided Indians, reported deaths during 1899 exceeded births by 1,016. Among the 187,319 Indians for whom vital statistics are available, 23 percent could read, 28 percent could use English for ordinary purposes, 13 percent lived in houses, and 17 percent were communicants in Christian churches (ARCIA 1899, 1: 580–581). In the 275 government day and boarding schools maintained for Indian youths, there were 23,615 pupils enrolled with 1,587 students attending mission, contract, and public schools (ARCIA 1899, 1:21). The United States government spent 32 percent of all appropriated Indian funds for Indian education since it was believed that schools were the most effective means for assimilating the Indian (ARCIA 1899, 1:1).

Twentieth-Century United States Government Agencies

PHILLEO NASH

As the twentieth century opened, American Indian affairs were, in some respects, at the nadir. Indian numbers had been reduced to the point where their continued existence could not be taken for granted. Indians were pushed onto the poorest and least productive lands, and even portions of those were being taken from them as minerals or other unforeseen values appeared. All their affairs were handled by one small government agency, under-funded and ill-equipped to meet the needs of a far-flung, isolated, rural constituency (Schmeckebier 1927).

Much of what was to come was foreshadowed in a landmark case settled by the U.S. Supreme Court in 1908: *Winters* v. *United States* (207 U.S. 564 (1908)), the result of a case filed by the U.S. Department of Justice at the request of the Bureau of Indian Affairs to protect the water rights of Fort Belknap Reservation, Montana, against nearby White settlers. The effect of this decision was to assure Indians of rights to water sufficient to irrigate the lands set aside for them by the creation of the reservation. However, during the 50 years after the *Winters* decision, the United States pursued a policy of assisting family-sized farms on arid Western lands by building dams for irrigation. For example, in the Missouri River basin, the Pick-Sloan Plan, the joint water development program designed by the Army Corps of Engineers and the Bureau of Reclamation in 1944, caused more damage to Indian land than any other public works project in America. The plans ultimately affected 23 different reservations (Lawson 1982). This policy was pursued with little or no regard for Indian water rights and the *Winters* doctrine. This is the story of the American Indian in the twentieth century: rights established in law are not always enjoyed by the Indians because of social, demographic, and economic change.

In the early 1900s Oklahoma was approaching statehood. The Senate Committee on Territories found that some 25,000 U.S. citizens were residing among the Five Civilized Tribes without the full protection of the law. The committee "recommended that the Indian Territory should have a United States court with criminal and civil jurisdiction and that the Indians should become citizens of the United States" (Prucha 1984, 2:740). It was proposed that the state should be created by combining Indian Territory—the home since the early nineteenth century of the Five Civilized Tribes—and Oklahoma Territory—the home since time immemorial of Plains tribes (M.H. Wright 1951). As the plans for statehood matured, it was clear that Indians would have to be included fully in whatever polity should be created but clearly not as "states within a state." Whites began being admitted in 1889, and allotment started in 1891. Only the Osages resisted successfully, and they only with respect to the subsurface rights. The result was the acceptance and incorporation of Indians into the political and economic life of the new jurisdiction. This was accompanied by the rapid decline of the tribal governments and the loss of much valuable land as individual Indian estates were probated in the courts.

Sen. Holm O. Bursum from New Mexico and Secretary of the Interior Albert B. Fall were among those who yearned for the exploration and development of New Mexico's mineral resources. The public domain and Indian lands were in their way. Although the federal Statehood Enabling Act had required New Mexico to concede the Pueblos' rights to their land and water resources, by 1922 non-Indian squatters were making extensive use of Indian water and lands. Senator Bursum introduced and Fall supported a bill that, had it been enacted into law, would have set up procedures that could have only one result: confirmation of title and water rights to the non-Indians with the historic Pueblos short of both land and irrigation water.

Writers and artists, citizens' groups, anthropologists, and the national press voiced their opposition to the Bursum bill. The Indian Bureau, whose own superintendent of the Northern Pueblo agency had criticized the bill, was besieged by public pressure (Prucha 1984, 2:797-800). Commissioner Charles Burke, who had "supported the bill as an administrative measure" (Prucha 1984, 2:799), was accused of failing to protect the rights of the Pueblo Indians (Kelly 1983:213–254).

Many of the best-known defenders of Indian rights in later years first joined in this legislative battle. Among them were William and Leslie Denman and Charles de

Young Elkus of San Francisco; Mable Dodge of Taos, New Mexico; and of course John Collier (Philp 1977: 26–54). The Bursum bill was defeated, but it was significant in two respects: the issues of Indian land and water and the adversaries—friends of the Indians, legislators, and administrators. John Collier and his allies formed a coalition during the New Deal and beyond (Collier 1963; Philp 1977; Kelly 1983; Deloria and Lytle 1984:37–182).

The Meriam Report

By the middle 1920s, the dismal outcome of allotment was becoming known to all Americans (Hoxie 1984). The diminished Indian land base, poverty, ill health, lack of education, lack of development, waste of natural resources, and the need to continue rations were exposed by two major studies of Indian affairs. The earlier of the two originated in Congress. A Select Committee on Indian Affairs conducted widespread investigations into reservation conditions, and its well-publicized report shocked America. Blame for the conditions of poverty and exploitation was laid pretty much at the door of the Bureau of Indian Affairs (BIA). In partial response, the executive branch asked for, and the Brookings Institution conducted, a comprehensive inquiry. Under the authorship of Lewis Meriam of the University of Chicago and actually carried out by a panel of distinguished scholars from many walks of life, the Meriam report is generally regarded as the beginning of the modern era in Indian affairs (Meriam 1928). It covered the entire spectrum of government-Indian relations.

The thrust of the Meriam report went deep. It was sharply critical of the BIA. It was particularly critical of the system of federal education for Indian children, especially of the boarding schools. It generally favored shift of programs to the states again, especially education. Uniting the fields of basic education and community development, it favored community-based schools, not just day schools to replace boarding schools.

Important recommendations were made looking toward the upgrading of personnel in the BIA. The Indian Service had until then operated on a low salary scale and low entrance qualifications to fill its positions. To improve the quality of the Indian Service personnel, the Meriam report recommended that a new classification of positions, "rigid" qualification standards, and higher salaries should be adopted by the Bureau, whose employees were to show "character and personality, and . . . ability to understand Indians and to get along with them" (Meriam 1928:159). In regard to preferential hiring of Indians in the Bureau, the Meriam report noted that "this policy is excellent provided the Indians possess the requisite qualifications, and every effort should be made to give them . . . the training and experience essential. The policy is extremely

unwise when it is given effect by lowering standards" (Meriam 1928:156–157). The policy of preferential hiring of Indians was enforced under the Indian Reorganization Act with notable results. The number of permanent Indian Bureau employees rose from a few hundred in 1933 to over 4,600 in 1940: "Of these, 8 were superintendents, 251 held professional positions, 935 were clerical workers, and approximately 3,475 were in other skilled jobs . . . . Indians in regular and temporary positions represented over half the entire Indian Service personnel" (Prucha 1984, 2:992).

President Herbert Hoover, a Quaker, responded by appointing two Quakers, highly respected officers of the Indian Rights Association of Philadelphia, as commissioner and assistant commissioner of Indian affairs. Charles J. Rhodes and J. Henry Scattergood began promptly to implement the Meriam recommendations (see Tyler 1973:115–124). Unfortunately, the onset of the Depression in 1929 so reduced the funds available that little substantive change took place at the reservation level.

The Indian New Deal

It remained for the New Deal to implement the Meriam report and to extend it with its own policies. President Franklin Roosevelt appointed as Commissioner of Indian Affairs John Collier (table 1) who had been active in Indian affairs since 1922 and a sharp critic of the BIA (Kelly 1983). Taking office in May 1933, Collier immediately put his aides to work drafting the legislation that is known as the Indian Reorganization Act of 1934 (48 U.S. Stat. 984). The act as passed was substantially modified by amendment from what Collier and his staff devised (Deloria and Lytle 1984:140–153, 265–270). The draft legislation offered to the Indian tribes what was, in essence, a cooperative commonwealth within the federal-state relationship. Nevertheless, as enacted and signed into law, the IRA was landmark legislation, set the tribes on the road to self-government, and is the foundation of everything that has been accomplished in Indian affairs in the decades since. The essence of the IRA is that it offered to the American Indian people local self-government and economic development on a tribal, voluntary basis (G.D. Taylor 1980).

A good deal of guidance was offered to the tribes by the BIA, some of it required by the IRA, and some the outcome of the BIA administrators' beliefs about their mission to foster representative government. Thus, a typical constitution provided for a council form of government with officers, usually a chairman, vice-chairman, secretary, and treasurer. Quite often there was an executive or advisory committee. These were very simple governmental forms and procedures designed to follow, as closely as seemed practical at the time, the   *265*

Table 1. Administrators of U.S. Indian Policies, 1789–1986

Secretaries of War, 1789–1832	Year of Appointment
Henry Knox	1789
Thomas Pickering	1795
James McHenry	1796
Samuel Dexter	1800
Henry Dearborn	1801
William Eustis	1809
John Armstrong	1813
James Monroe	1814
William H. Crawford	1815
John C. Calhoun	1817
James Barbour	1825
Peter B. Porter	1828
John H. Eaton	1829
Lewis Cass	1831

Head of Bureau of Indian Affairs within the War Department, 1824–1832	
Thomas L. McKenney	1824
Samuel S. Hamilton	1830
Elbert Herring	1831

Commissioner of Indian Affairs within the War Department, 1832–1849	
Elbert Herring	1832
Carey A. Harris	1836
T. Hartley Crawford	1838
William Medill	1845

Commissioner of Indian Affairs within the Department of the Interior, 1849–1977	
Orlando Brown	1849
Luke Lea	1850
George Manypenny	1853
James W. Denver	1857, 1858
Charles E. Mix	1858
Alfred B. Greenwood	1859
William P. Dole	1861
Dennis Cooley	1865
Lewis V. Bogy	1866
Nathaniel G. Taylor	1867
Ely S. Parker (Seneca)	1869
Francis A. Walker	1871
Edward P. Smith	1873
John Q. Smith	1875
Ezra A. Hayt	1877
Roland E. Trowbridge	1880
Hiram Price	1881
John D.C. Atkins	1885
John H. Oberly	1888
Thomas J. Morgan	1889
Daniel M. Browning	1893
William A. Jones	1897
Francis E. Leupp	1905
Robert G. Valentine	1909
Cato Sells	1913
Charles H. Burke	1921
Charles J. Rhoads	1929
John Collier	1933
William A. Brophy	1945
John R. Nichols	1949
Dillon S. Myer	1950
Glenn L. Emmons	1953
Philleo Nash	1961
Robert L. Bennett (Oneida)	1966
Louis R. Bruce (Mohawk-Sioux)	1969
Morris Thompson (Tanana)	1973
Benjamin Reifel (Sioux)	1976
Raymond Butler (Blackfeet)[a]	1977
Martin Seneca, Jr. (Seneca)[a]	1978
William Hallett (Chippewa)	1979

Assistant Secretary for Indian Affairs within the Department of the Interior, 1977–1986	Year of Appointment
Forrest Gerard (Blackfeet)	1977
Tom Fredericks (Mandan-Hidatsa)[b]	1981
Kenneth Smith (Wasco)	1981
Ross Swimmer (Cherokee)	1985

SOURCES: E.E. Hill 1965, 1:11–12; U.S. Bureau of Indian Affairs 1973:15–17; Kvasnicka and Viola 1979; Prucha 1984, 2:1211–1216; Evelyn Pickett, communication to editors 1986.
[a]Served as acting commissioner.
[b]Served on a temporary appointment.

general councils by which the traditional tribal governments had conducted their deliberations since before White influence.

Once representative governments had been created under these conditions, the authority was automatically extended to the tribes to review agency budgets. The councils provided for were then empowered to represent the tribes in their dealings with state and local governments, as well as the federal government. They were also empowered to choose and retain attorneys to represent them and aid them in their negotiations with public and private agencies.

Extensive provisions were also made for economic development. Of greatest importance, perhaps, was the provision that reversed allotment. The IRA extended indefinitely the 25-year trust period after allotment of Indian lands. By 1934 two-thirds of the landed estate as it existed in 1887, the beginning of allotment, had been lost to Indian ownership. The IRA contemplated the addition of trust lands to make up for the loss, but this provision has never been adequately implemented. Some two million acres of land were purchased under authority of the IRA, but about as much has passed out of tribal ownership through the operation of other unrelated statutes and regulations.

The prohibition on the sale or alienation of tribal trust land is absolute: only Congress can authorize the surrender of tribal trust title. Individual trust land is another matter, and there the secretary of the interior and commissioner of Indian affairs may exercise discretion. It is a heavy responsibility, for the need to protect the Indian land base and the individual's freedom to make decisions to sell are often in conflict.

Close in importance to the protection of the land is the IRA provision with respect to business charters. Once a tribe has voted to accept the IRA and has created the necessary governmental instruments, it may also create a federally chartered corporation with the usual powers necessary to do business, such as borrow money, sue, and enter into contracts. This is a most valuable right, extended only to Indian tribes, because such a corporation has the cloak of federal protection in that it may not be sued without government consent, yet it can initiate similar action against others to protect its assets. And, of course, tribes, being units of government, are not taxed

(Cohen 1982:390).

Of great promise and considerable usefulness in practice is the Revolving Loan Fund authorized by the IRA. Under it, loans may be made to tribal credit committees and through them to individual tribal members. The concept is an important one, related to other New Deal measures such as the Rural Electrification Act. Under this concept, the economically disadvantaged person is able to obtain credit, which would otherwise be unavailable to him, and at interest rates he can afford. The Indian Financing Act of 1974 authorized an additional $50 million and provided for loan guarantees, insurance, and interest to encourage the use of private lenders (Cohen 1982:720).

The New Deal was conservation-oriented, and this interest was reflected in the IRA. The tribes were required, as a condition of receiving the benefits of the Act, to practice sustained yield forestry and to accept the setting aside by the BIA of wilderness areas in the reservations. Agricultural leases of tribal and individual trust lands contained clauses that required soil conservation practices.

For historical reasons, both Oklahoma and Alaska were excluded from the IRA. In these jurisdictions it was felt that the IRA, which was essentially a system of reservation government, was inappropriate. The Five Civilized Tribes had surrendered their autonomy at the time of statehood (Foreman 1934). Accordingly, the benefits of the IRA were extended to Oklahoma in 1936 via a separate statute, the Oklahoma Indian Welfare Act (49 U.S. Stat. 1967). That statute is silent as to tribal government, but it permits the formation of credit unions for economic development. It also makes benefits available to Indians living "on or near" reservations, thus creating eligibility for many thousands of individual trust lands, as well as Indian enclaves in rural and small-town Oklahoma.

Extension of the IRA to Alaska even without settlement of the native claims brought to that part of the United States a completely new relationship to the federal government. Alaska natives were provided with government services by the territorial government of Alaska through the Bureau of Education, which was administered by the secretary of the interior. This Bureau was directed operationally by the commissioner of Indian affairs but was relatively independent of him by virtue of distance, difficulty of communications, and political isolation.

Services to Alaska, in the form of schools and health facilities paid for out of federal funds and designed especially to meet the needs of isolated Arctic villages date from the 1890s for the Aleuts. In the early 1920s the U.S. Revenue Marine Service ship *Bear* began to execute supply missions beyond the range of commercial shipping. The schools thus established and the field medical services

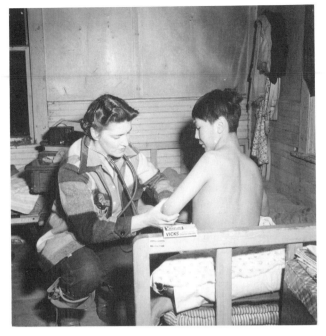

Natl. Geographic Soc.

Fig. 1. A physician from the *North Star* with an Eskimo patient on St. Lawrence I., Alaska. During each of the ship's stops, an orthopedic surgeon from the U. of Chicago, Mary S. Sherman, examined patients. Photograph by Amos Burg, 1950.

thus provided, together with the annual visit of the supply ship, quickly became the foundation of the federal government's Eskimo, Aleut, and Indian program in Alaska.

The Act of May 1, 1936 (49 U.S. Stat. 1250), extending the IRA authority to Alaska, added to this foundation the basic programs of local self-government and economic development. Thus, the fisheries industry of southeast Alaska, so important to the Tsimshian, Tlingit, and Haida communities, quickly came to revolve around cooperative canneries. These were created under the authority of the 1936 Act and funded from the Revolving Loan Fund, which eventually committed 50 percent of its resources to the support of the Alaska canneries.

In Alaska villages, the self-government features of the IRA were generally popular, and soon nearly 100 village governments with associated economic functions had come into being. Although the industrial and productive features of Arctic Alaska were not at that time conducive to economic growth, the creation of cooperative stores to meet the consumer needs of Alaska native communities provided a form of economic development. Nearly all the villages soon had cooperatively owned stores, equipped with credit through the Revolving Loan Fund. These stores maintained a purchasing agent in Seattle and were supplied with merchandise by BIA vessels named *North Star* (fig. 1).

A counterpart to the system of cooperative stores was the Alaska Native Arts Cooperative. In association with the native stores, this cooperative provided a market for   *267* items such as ivory and baleen carving; furs; caribou and reindeer bone, horn, and hoof items. Since credit was advanced to native craftsmen through the stores, there was of necessity a close link between the two cooperatives, which extended the value of the Revolving Loan Fund far beyond advances to the native stores.

The interest in arts and crafts was not limited to the Alaska cooperatives. Independent of the BIA, but intimately associated with it, was the Indian Arts and Crafts Board created by Congress. The legislation made the Board a part of the Interior Department, reporting directly to the secretary of the interior. The Board was granted broad authority to set standards of arts and crafts of Indian manufacture; to aid in the formation of cooperatives and guilds; to label and authenticate items of genuine Indian arts, as against imitations, factory-made products, or foreign imports (fig. 2). The Board was also given authority to establish markets, and through the operation of museums and shops, acquaint the public with the variety and quality of crafts available. Throughout its history, the Indian Arts and Crafts Board has been able to attract to its membership America's most distinguished collectors, artists, and museum directors. Its staff has established a network of cooperatives stretching from Alaska to Florida.

Another significant item of New Deal legislation was the Johnson-O'Malley Act (48 U.S. Stat. 596). Based upon the premise that social services to Indians would ultimately be best supplied by state governments, the act authorized the secretary of the interior to enter into contracts with state and local governments for educational and welfare services.

Under this program, the BIA sought funds from the Congress to make grants to state departments of education and welfare. The objective of such grants was to make the administration of the programs as local as possible (within the federal-state concept), making use of federal rather than local or tribal monies. This program, obviously based on the Meriam report's concept of Indian administration, never achieved more than a bare minimum of its purpose. First the Depression and then war increased the federal government's role in all social services, raised the cost, and diminished the states' ability and desire to perform these functions where Indians were concerned.

A milestone in Indian affairs was reached in 1942 with the completion of *The Handbook of Federal Indian Law* by Felix S. Cohen, an assemblage and summary of the major pieces of legislation, treaties, executive orders, secretarial orders, and opinions of the solicitor that affected Indian affairs. Since there were several hundred treaties and several thousand orders, statutes, and opinions, the codification of them in manual form was a major contribution to the improvement of Indian administration and to Indian participation in the governmental process. A 1958 revision, prepared by the Solicitor of the Interior

Department, was of inferior quality and had limited usefulness. Reworked and published (Cohen 1982) it is a major source of information and interpretation.

The Depression brought many changes to reservations. Unemployment, food distribution, and welfare were no novelty to Indians. But increased and improved social services, with the federal and state governments bringing programs of social betterment to rural areas were new, and they changed reservation life permanently.

The Collier administration moved quickly to turn disaster into an economic development opportunity on the Plains. A loan-in-kind program was initiated whereby drought-stricken cattle were collected from the dustbowl, shipped to reservations in the mountain states with good summer pasture, and subsequently loaned to Indian ranchers in the grazing states on a basis of repayment with calves. Many an Indian cattleman who was established in the mid-twentieth century owed his start to the drought program. And by it, full advantage was taken of the highly successful established whiteface herds in the Southwest reservations—herds established under farm and ranch programs initiated in the pre-World War I period.

Planning and conservation were both very much a part of the New Deal. Both were represented in the Soil Conservation Service of the U.S. Department of Agriculture. Through their common interest in conservation and with similar views on community development, a joint program grew up in the U.S. Department of Agriculture known as Technical Cooperation–Bureau of Indian Affairs (TC-BIA). TC-BIA was eventually to have great significance for American Indians not only in the area of soil conservation but in the form of social and political organization developed by the Navajo.

The prototype was on the Navajo Reservation where TC-BIA made a concerted effort to determine, by social science research, the true social and geographic boundaries of the natural use areas. Eventually these units, called "outfits" by the social scientists in TC-BIA, became the basis for the Chapter House program of the Navajo and were closely linked with the electoral districts by which representation is assured on the Navajo Tribal Council.

The influence of TC-BIA was not restricted to the Navajo. The soil conservation movement was so strongly engrained in the New Deal that its principles and practices—sustained yield forestry, water retention structures, erosion control, contour plowing—were built into the requirements for approved leasing of Indian lands. Soil conservation was something the U.S. Congress could accept more readily than community development.

Another New Deal agency with major significance to American Indians was the Civilian Conservation Corps, a program of training and employment for young men throughout the entire country. These young men, mainly from urban areas, were sent to militarylike camps for a

Natl. Arch.: RG75-N-Five-73.

Fig. 2. Students in arts and crafts class, Wheelock Academy, Okla. The Wheelock School was first established about 1850 by the Choctaw tribe. In 1937 the Indian Arts and Crafts Board developed, in conjunction with the Five Tribes Agency, a project with the Choctaw. While spinning and weaving were not traditional Choctaw crafts, they were promoted in order to develop new skills in an area where traditional crafts were not perceived as marketable. Individual styles were encouraged (Schrader 1983:208–213). Photograph by Andrew T. Kelley, Dec. 14, 1937.

combined program of education and soil conservation work in the national parks. Collier fashioned a separate program, the Emergency Conservation Works, for Indians, and a change was made. Indian men were permitted to live with their families and work at soil conservation, forestry, and resource development on the reservations (fig. 3). The result was a significant, though temporary, increase in income and a strengthening of family ties. Although the program was short in duration, it is remembered on the reservations as a good program.

World War II

World War II put an end to the Civilian Conservation Corps and initiated many other changes in American Indian life. Large numbers, proportionately, of the young men were drafted or volunteered for the armed services. They were readily accepted both by their comrades-in-arms and by the military command. Educationally and experientially, World War II was broadening for many Indians. For women, their role in the extended family was enhanced, while tradition and customary behavior were relatively unchanged (fig. 4). For the young men horizons were broadened, family ties were loosened, and traditional ceremonies were not possible. For some at least, there was a considerable strengthening of the desire to participate in traditional culture—religious, social, and political. At the same time, the postwar return was to reservations underdeveloped and with diminished job opportunities.

Another wartime change came about through the diminishment of the BIA presence. It was not only Indian men who were taken away by war. The middle and upper management of the BIA, at that time still largely non-Indian, went to war in large numbers. The war budget cut heavily into BIA operations, and the commissioner's office was moved from Washington, D.C., to Chicago for the duration. On the reservations, operations were put on hold. Road, school, and hospital construction was halted; and maintenance was cut back. The elaborate economic development planning of the New Deal came to a temporary end.

After the Roosevelt administration, the executive 269

branch leaders who had dominated Indian Affairs—John Collier, Harold Ickes, and Franklin Roosevelt—were gone. Indian affairs in the next decade was directed by Congress. The Senate and House Subcommittees on Indian Affairs and the Indian Affairs Appropriations Subcommittees provided the leadership.

Indian Claims Commission

The Indian Claims Commission Act (60 U.S. Stat. 1049) created a special court in which class actions by and on behalf of American Indians could be brought to correct inadequate compensation for lands taken in the past century. There had to be proof of ownership; contingent fees were permitted, since the clients, Indian tribes, were usually impoverished and the legal research was costly; the valuation had to be at the time of taking; and there were to be offsets for treaty payments, special grants, and forms of compensation other than cash. The Act became law in 1946 and was extended at intervals until 1978 when it was permitted to lapse, and remaining cases were transferred to the U.S. Court of Claims (Cohen 1982:162).

The Indian Claims Commission proved to be a major resource in terms of economic development. Approximately two billion dollars was awarded to the tribes in claims (for example, vol. 11:550–553). Although reimbursement for expenses, including legal fees, reduced the total available, large sums underwrote scholarships, community centers, resource development, and tribal enterprises, among other things.

Termination

During the New Deal, resentment had been developing over what Westerners regarded as government favoritism to Indians, particularly in the area of land use. The Bureau, through the IRA land restoration program, "spent over one and a half million dollars to purchase four hundred thousand acres of cropland to be used by Indians. In addition, tribes regained control of seven million acres of grazing land that had previously been held by white cattlemen under leases made by the Bureau of Indian Affairs" (Deloria and Lytle 1984:184–185). By 1950 "for the first time in 80 years, Indian holdings of land increased—from 48 to 52 million acres" (Fey 1955:396; see also Sutton 1985). Traditional Indians, members and supporters of the Oklahoma-based American Indian Federation, and conservative Democratic and Republican members of Congress voiced their opposition to New Deal reforms and attacked Collier on both political and personal grounds (Tyler 1973:136–143; Philp 1977:187–213; Deloria and Lytle 1984:173–182; see also Washburn 1984). In February 1945 Collier resigned.

For Commissioner of Indian Affairs President Harry S. Truman settled on a strong administrator, Dillon Myer,

Natl. Arch.: RG75-RAFB-30C.
Fig. 3. Jocko family camp of the Indian Emergency Conservation Works, Flathead Indian Agency, Dixon, Mont. The Flathead Agency project focused most of its labor on roads and reservoirs, with some work on timber and trails. This was one of 72 camps on 33 reservations (Philp 1977:121). Photographed 1935.

who had been head of the War Relocation Administration, which had responsibility for secluding 100,000 Japanese Americans during World War II. Under Myer, the Bureau of Indian Affairs pursued a conservative policy and moved toward withdrawal of federal services to tribes. In his address to the convention of the National Congress of American Indians in 1951, Myer stated that "the Bureau [should] not do anything which others can do as well or better and as cheaply. The Bureau should lean over backward to help [Indians] learn to do more things on their own" (cited in Ourada 1979:294–295). He introduced a program to help Indians "relocate" in urban centers with better employment opportunities (Philp 1985). It was also an attempt to relieve the population pressure on the reservations. In 1948, the Bureau had already established placement offices in Denver, Salt Lake City, and Los Angeles to assist members of Southwestern tribes, particularly Navajo and Hopi, to relocate and seek employment in urban areas. By 1958 the Bureau operated 10 relocation offices in major cities. From 1953 to 1960 over 33,000 Indians were involved in the relocation program (Prucha 1984, 2:1082). Critics of the program charged that in some areas as many as 60 percent of relocatees eventually returned to the reservations (Tyler 1973:159). In 1958 the General Accounting Office, after conducting an evaluation of the relocation program, criticized the Bureau, noting that Indians were relocated to areas not offering adequate opportunities, Indians were inadequately prepared for relocation, and minimum standards for selecting relocatees had not been prescribed by the Bureau. Termination began in 1947 when the Congress called on the acting commissioner of Indian affairs for a set of criteria that would mark the readiness of tribes to give up their status as Indians and enter the mainstream, no longer needing the protection of federal trusteeship. With criteria in hand, the Congress then demanded a list of tribes in an advanced state of readiness. The Interior Department was reluctantly forthcoming, and one by one bills terminating the trust and the special status of tribes and individuals as Indian were prepared and several were passed (Tyler 1973:163–173).

The adoption of House Concurrent Resolution 108 (67 U.S. Stat. B132) in 1953 made termination official congressional policy. But Concurrent Resolutions do not become statutes; they are binding on Congress but are not signed by the president and are only advisory to the executive branch. Thus, the position of the federal government remained ambiguous.

House Congressional Resolution 108 has never been revoked, but successive presidents of the United States have declared their opposition to it. In practice, termination was an issue from the end of World War II to about 1960 (Prucha 1984, 2:1013–1084).

Termination was not unique to the 1950s. On the contrary, individual tribes were terminated by special acts of Congress as early as the first half of the nineteenth century. Throughout the history of Indian policy, it seems clear that one of the factors present in all fluctuations was the assumption that eventual assimilation was both inevitable and desirable. What the termination era expressed and provided was an intense experimentation with a small group of tribes.

During the period 1953–1960, 14 termination acts were adopted covering 110 or 111 tribes and bands. The reason for the uncertainty in numbers is that the California Rancheria Act was not specific as to the individual homesteads. Some of the tribes were large (3,270, for

Natl. Arch.: RG75-PU-H-2.

Fig. 4. Honoring a Laguna Pueblo Indian who was a prisoner of war in Germany in 1944. The Air Medal with Oak Leaf clusters, awarded to Frank Paisano, Jr., a lieutenant in the Army Air Force, was presented to his wife Anacita (center, in suit) at Laguna Pueblo. Paisano was imprisoned for 3 years. left to right, Col. Louis W. Proper; Theadore Riley (Old Laguna), U.S. Navy; Frank Siow (Seama Village); Marie L. Paisano, mother of Frank Paisano; Elizabeth Piasano Wacondo, sister of Frank; Gloria Analla Leon; Anacita Lucero Piasano; Frances Ann Piasano Chavez, daughter of Frank; Miguel Lucero; Mary Lucero Jojola; Juanita Lucero (Sandia); Anacita's father, sister, and mother; Paul Thomas (holding flag), U.S. Marines; Francisco Lorenzo (Laguna); and Walter Sarracino (Laguna). Photographed Feb. 4, 1944.

TWENTIETH-CENTURY UNITED STATES GOVERNMENT AGENCIES

example, in the Menominee of Wisconsin); others were bands of a few families. The aggregate number of individuals covered is estimated at 12,450. However, the effect was far greater than the small number of individuals concerned (Cohen 1982:811).

Typically, the language of a termination act required the secretary of the interior to publish in the *Federal Register* a proclamation declaring that the federal trust relationships to former tribal members had been terminated. Thereafter, such individuals were not entitled to any of the services performed for Indians because of their status as Indians. All statutes of the United States that affected Indians because of their status as Indians were declared to be inapplicable to such persons. The laws of the several states then applied to such persons in the same manner as to other citizens within their jurisdiction.

In individual instances, specific provisions were added. Thus, tribal rolls were often closed; tribal land was sometimes sold and the proceeds divided up among former members; land was placed in a private trust; or land was placed in a state corporation. Most exemptions from state taxing authority were ended; tribal sovereignty was effectively though not technically ended (Cohen 1982: 812–813).

Although the executive branch was reluctant to proceed, the states were mostly unwilling to assume the additional expenses of administration and to provide the services, and the tribes were generally opposed; still the process continued.

By 1958, numerous problems had surfaced. The administrative costs increased. Numerous tribes and individuals sued to protect their rights. Shortfalls in the level of health, roads, utilities, and human services appeared. The pace of termination legislation slowed.

In 1958 Secretary of the Interior Fred Seaton made a radio speech in which he effectively retreated from termination except by agreement of the tribes themselves. In 1960 both presidential candidates issued strong statements supporting the sanctity of Indian treaties and Indian rights in general.

In later years, judicial review exposed some of the hidden costs of termination. Termination of some of the California rancherias was invalidated because the Interior Department had never provided the required utilities (water and sewer). The Klamath tribal forest was purchased by the U.S. Forest Service, but the courts later held that the price was inadequate, and Congress had to appropriate additional sums.

The major signal that the termination era had ended was passage of the Menominee Restoration Act in 1973 (87 U.S. Stat. 770). Following passage of the Menominee Termination Act (68 U.S. Stat. 250) in 1954, the Menominee and the state of Wisconsin had struggled unsuccessfully to make the new system work. Arrangements by the Wisconsin legislature to replace the func-

tions formerly provided by federal trusteeship proved inadequate. Tribal leaders concluded that the only way out was to seek legislative retrocession of termination, an event never before attempted successfully.

To the surprise of all concerned, that attempt succeeded in only a few years. The trust was reestablished, and access to federal programs was restored, The act, plus later litigation, established that the tribe had continued its existence and that certain rights, such as hunting and fishing, had never been disturbed. Thus, in the 1980s Menominee County, created by the state of Wisconsin, with its courts and county officers, continues its existence alongside the Menominee tribe with different rights and responsibilities. Later acts of Congress restored tribal status to terminated groups in western Oregon (91 U.S. Stat. 1415), Arizona (92 U.S. Stat. 246, 712), Oklahoma, and Utah (94 U.S. Stat. 317).

The termination era may appear as a unique event, a failed experiment that was soon corrected. But termination was actually an expression of the national will that the ultimate goal of government policy toward Indians was "assimilation."

With an acceptance of cultural pluralism in the United States, termination may be dead. Congress, the judiciary, and the executive branch have all renounced termination, and the tribes have stated firmly that they will not accept it.

The end of the termination era in 1960 brought with it an insistence that federal government control be relaxed at the same time as programs were improved. Dissatisfaction ranged all the way from blaming the BIA for heavy-handed administration to requiring that control be passed to the hands of the Indians. Both of these goals were easier said than done. It was one thing for the Congress to demand better performance. It was another to place administrative responsibility in the hands of the tribes, which varied in their degree of acculturation and fiscal responsibility.

Decentralization of Indian Programs

In the 1960s and 1970s successive administrations distributed functions formerly reserved to the BIA to other federal agencies. As early as the nineteenth century, the BIA, reservation, and tribal council formed a closed political structure into which neither state nor any other federal agency could enter.

But the BIA had a strong desire to improve Indian housing. The money for public housing was appropriated to a wide range of authorities that eventually were consolidated as the Department of Housing and Urban Development. The most appropriate unit to help in Indian housing was the Public Housing Administration. This agency had assisted more than one-half million urban families to have better housing, but, up to the 1960s, had not been able to help even one reservation Indian family. Improved housing requires improved water supply and sanitary waste disposal. Such authority had already been vested in the Indian Health Division of the United States Public Health Service in the Department of Health, Education, and Welfare.

The problem was how to coordinate the activities of three agencies with different missions, in three different cabinet level departments, and with three different appropriation structures. Eventually a formal agreement was worked out among the three departments, and hundreds if not thousands of family housing units have been built on the reservations through tribal housing authorities.

Reaching outside the BIA to find funding for a need the BIA could not meet by itself proved invigorating. The Area Redevelopment Act and the Manpower Development and Training Act of 1962 (76 U.S. Stat. 23) also helped. Greatest help of all was the War on Poverty. The programs of the Office of Economic Opportunity in education, industrial development, credit, and tribal government were designed from the first to be independent of the BIA. At later dates, they were transferred to a number of different departments.

The BIA had developed an expertise over the 175 years of its existence that the newer agencies could not duplicate. Historically, the scattering of programs has resulted in fragmentation and loss of effectiveness. Nevertheless, the diffusion out of BIA had to take place and was significantly advanced by the War on Poverty and its successors.

In matters of health, the BIA was at a particular disadvantage. It was required to provide medical services in frontier areas without the ability to attract first-rate professionals, not being a recognized or established health agency. In 1954 the Indian Health Division was removed from the BIA and put into the Public Health Service, in the Department of Health, Education, and Welfare, which was better able to fund its programs, and it received the benefit of young physicians who could perform their military service as public health officers. By all measurements, the status of Indian health is below that of non-Indians, but there has been significant improvement since the transfer.

The Indian Health Service was also authorized to provide community and individual water and waste disposal systems for Indians. The rationale was one of public health. Originally conceived as an on-reservation program, the Division's water and waste authority was later extended to off-reservation communities. The construction program of the Department of Housing and Urban Development would have been nothing without the water and waste facilities.

The Indian Health Service provides comprehensive health care services to eligible Indians; assists tribes and

Dept. of the Interior, Bureau of Ind. Affairs, Washington: BIA 51, 203LC.
Fig. 5. BIA task force members with Eskimos at Point Hope, Alaska. third from left, Theron Smith, Fish and Wildlife Service pilot; fourth and third from right, task force members, William K. Wheeler (Cherokee), and Secretary of State of Alaska Hugh J. Wade. In order to clarify issues central to Alaska Natives' land claims and other matters, Secretary of the Interior Stewart L. Udall appointed a 3-member Task Force on Alaska Native Affairs to visit the state. Hearings, held in connection with legislation ultimately enacted, are reported in U.S. Congress. Senate. Committee on Interior and Insular Affairs (1968:126–127). Photograph by James E. Officer, third member of the task force, summer 1962.

Native Alaska communities in developing and managing their own health programs; and interacts with federal, state, public, and private organizations in delivering health services to Indian people (U.S. Department of Health and Human Services. Health Resources and Services Administration 1984). The IHS organizational structure includes a national headquarters in Rockville, Maryland; 12 area program offices; and 125 administrative units responsible for delivering health care services to some 960,000 eligible American Indians and Alaska Natives (R.S. Jones 1985:155). In 1985, IHS operated 46 hospitals, 71 health care centers, 66 health centers, and some 200 other treatment locations (U.S. Department of Health and Human Resources. Health Resources and Services Administration 1986:5).

For a comprehensive survey of other federal agencies providing services to American Indians and Alaska Natives see R.S. Jones (1985), T.W. Taylor (1983:65–103), and Americans for Indian Opportunity (1981).

Alaska

By the treaty of purchase of Alaska in 1867 (15 U.S. Stat. 539), the United States promised to treat the indigenous inhabitants of Alaska the same as those in the United States and its territories. But with little information on the distant territory, Congress deferred consideration of issues about Alaska Eskimos, Indians, and Aleuts from decade to decade. Starting in the 1940s, with the advent of defense

273

installations, rapid communication, minerals exploration, and industrial development, firmly based land titles were needed, but there were none.

The Alaska Statehood Act (72 U.S. Stat. 339) brought it to a crisis. By that act, the new state had been promised a large part of the public domain in Alaska, but the Alaska natives claimed all of it.

In the Tee-Hit-Ton decision (348 U.S. Stat. 272 (1955)) the United States Supreme Court held that the United States is not necessarily required to pay compensation for the extinguishment of aboriginal title. This decision, for a time, appeared to be a roadblock to all Alaska development. The discovery of large oil and gas reserves in Alaska made it imperative to find a solution (fig. 5).

The result was the Alaska Native Claims Settlement Act of 1971 (85 U.S. Stat. 688). In effect, the Congress said that while it might extinguish aboriginal title without compensation, it would not do so. The act extinguished all claims based on Alaskan aboriginal title. In return, the United States agreed to provide nearly one billion dollars in direct appropriations and mineral royalties. The act created a system of regional and village corporations, setting aside 40 million acres of land for Alaska natives. The corporations were to receive the land in fee simple, without any restraints on alienation.

Civil Rights

The rapid growth of the civil rights movement and its legislative successes in the 1960s led to the adoption of the Indian Civil Rights Act of 1968 (82 U.S. Stat. 73). A long series of court decisions had held that the tribes, not being states, could act in ways that are constitutionally prohibited to the states. The rights that are protected by the amendments to the Constitution known collectively as the Bill of Rights were not extended to the relations between members of Indian tribes and tribal councils, officers and courts, until and unless Congress provided such protection. Tribes, such as the Pueblos, that have a religious establishment that also functions politically protested that the full provisions of the First Amendment would invade their traditional form of government.

Other provisions were also not included, because they were deemed impractical or as contravening other established rights. Among the omissions are: the guarantee of a republican form of government, the prohibition against an established form of religion, the requirement of free counsel for an indigent accused, the right to a jury trial in civil cases, provisions broadening the right to vote, and prohibition of denial of the privileges and immunities of citizens. The reasons for omitting these provisions appears to be a decision by the Congress to limit its intrusion into

274   Fig. 6. BIA area offices and area boundaries.

tribal independence (Cohen 1982:202–204).

After 1966 congressional enactments iterated the intent to put the tribes into the decision-making process in their own behalf. In education, health, resource development, and many other program areas, Congress has required the presence of Indian representatives at the negotiating table.

This is, in part, due to the findings of the American Indian Policy Review Commission (1977) created by Congress in 1975. The report was a strong statement in support of tribal sovereignty, self-determination, and the federal government's commitment to the trust relationship of federally recognized tribes.

Although the Indians are not solidly united (they have their differences of opinion as much as any other political group) there is a sentiment that the intermediate steps of self-determination and limited self-government contemplated in the Indian Reorganization Act, the cornerstone of government-Indian relations since 1934, are no longer enough. Thus, the position of some tribal leaders is more akin to that of the traditionalists who have never accepted conquest, defeat, or subordination. Lower courts have held that hunting and fishing rights were not invalidated by termination or temporary interpretation. Civil regulation of gambling stakes by a state does not apply where legal gambling is permitted. Tribes may not be required by states to collect excise taxes.

Summary

In the 1980s the Bureau of Indian Affairs continued to be the main government agency responsible for administering the federal trust responsibility to 504 federally recognized tribal entities with a total service population of nearly 800,000 (U.S. Bureau of Indian Affairs 1986:4). Throughout its history (see Jackson and Galli 1977), the Bureau of Indian Affairs underwent several reorganizations but it maintained a basic tri-level organizational structure that included: a central office, or headquarters, located in the nation's capital; 12 area offices throughout the country (fig. 6); and 84 agencies, many located on Indian reservations (Lovett et al. 1984:12–14). In 1983, it was estimated that more than 80 percent of some 15,000 Bureau employees were Indian, reflecting the Indian preference policy enforced by the Bureau and upheld by the Supreme Court in 1974.

Government Indian Agencies in Canada

DOUGLAS SANDERS

Canadian Indian policy focuses around the basic fact of a reserve system. That has been the most constant and the most influential factor since 1637, when the first reserves were established in New France by Roman Catholic religious orders (Jaenen 1976:171–181). The goal of assimilation has also been constant, though specific goals have varied with changing non-Indian values in Canada. Assimilation has meant at different periods different combinations of Christianity, agriculture, education, wage labor, and traditional culture.

The reserve system required two supporting institutions: legislation to give legal form and support to the reserves and a governmental department concerned with the management of the system. Indian legislation began in Nova Scotia in 1762, in Ontario in 1839, and in Quebec in 1850. The four western provinces had no Indian legislation before their incorporation into Canada in 1869–1870. In 1867 the British North America Act—the federal constitution of Canada—assigned legislative jurisdiction over "Indians, and Lands Reserved for the Indians" to the federal Parliament. By 1880 the federal government had consolidated and developed their Indian legislation in much the form it would have until the revisions in 1951 (Leslie and Maguire 1978).

Origins of the Department of Indian Affairs—Upper Canada

By the time of the Royal Proclamation of October 7, 1763, the Indian Department, created in 1755, had little experience in the nonmilitary aspects of Indian affairs such as those presented by the acquisition of the French areas of North America. Lands west of the Allegheny watershed and lands around the great lakes were to be frozen in Indian occupancy—"reserved" to them as their hunting grounds. The acquisition of lands from Indians within established colonies and within the western reserve was formally established as a Crown monopoly (Sanders 1974). The methodology of public assemblies of Indians and treaties was set forth.

In 1763 there were settled patterns of Indian-White relations in Nova Scotia, New Brunswick, and Quebec. The policies of the Royal Proclamation were applied prospectively, not retrospectively. Ontario (Upper Cana-

da) was basically unsettled at the time, and it is in southern Ontario that the policies of the proclamation were applied. Between 1763 and 1867 numerous treaties and surrenders were signed with Indians of the province purporting to cover the land mass of the jurisdiction as it was defined when it entered confederation in 1867. It was also in southern Ontario that the administrative system established by 1763 found its continuity (Scott 1914, 4: 722).

In 1796, by Royal Instructions, Indian affairs in Ontario were transferred from the control of the military to the lieutenant-governor. It was restored to military authority in 1816. "Thereafter the administration was military in character; the officers had military rank, and were entitled to wear a uniform which was established by order in 1823 . . . . Their duties have been described as consisting of 'conveying the presents to the Indians and attending at the different stations where they assembled to receive them with as much military pomp and display as the occasion would admit' " (Scott 1914, 4:723).

In 1830 the conduct of Indian affairs was transferred to civilian jurisdiction under the lieutenant-governor of Upper Canada, who was designated superintendent-general of Indian affairs. This basic change was seen in the orientation of the Indian service, though it was still characterized by military personnel and centralized authority. The Indian service in Ontario, before at least 1862, did not attain adequate authority and organization to function as a competent civil administration concerned with the newly stated goals of government. But, at least, the change in goals was clear. Sir John Colborne, appointed lieutenant-governor in 1828, stated the following goals:

> 1st. To collect the Indians in considerable numbers, and settle them in villages with a due portion of land for their cultivation and support.
> 2nd. To make such provision for their religious improvement, education, and instruction in husbandry as circumstances may from time to time require.
> 3rd. To afford them such assistance in building their houses; rations; and in procuring such seed and agricultural implements as may be necessary, commuting when practicable a portion of their presents for the latter (Scott 1914, 5:333).

This formulation obtained imperial approval, and some money was allotted for the proposed policy. In sharp contrast, Colborne's successor, Sir Francis Bond Head, concluded that removal was the only answer for an Indian population he saw as doomed. He believed "1. that an Attempt to make Farmers of the Red Men has been, generally speaking, a complete Failure; 2. That congregating them for the Purposes of Civilization has implanted many more vices than it has eradicated; and consequently, 3. That the greatest Kindness we can perform towards these intelligent, simple-minded People, is to remove and fortify them as much as possible from all communication with the Whites" (Scott 1914, 5:337). In 1836 Bond Head initiated the "elaborately planned and very expensive" experiment of relocating Indians to Manitoulin Island (Surtees 1967). The program was an immense failure, and relocation attempts were abandoned.

The civilizing policy was buttressed very strongly in 1837 by the Imperial Report of the Select Committee on Aborigines (British Settlements), which advocated the retention of imperial responsibility for natives, to protect them from adverse local interests. In theory Indian affairs in Upper Canada remained an imperial responsibility until 1860, but, in fact, both imperial interest and imperial responsibility steadily declined in the nineteenth century before 1867.

A labyrinthian system developed, an evolution resulting from the military origins of the Indian Department. While a progressive philosophy pervaded Indian policy, the practical economics of the department lagged behind. The men who developed the new policy were philanthropists, not economists or accountants; while they extolled the virtues of reclaiming the savage, they failed to give expression to the equally important questions of everyday finance (Surtees 1967:58–59).

The period was the subject of three special investigative commissions, each of which portrayed an ineffective administration. The first, in 1839–1840, said of the Indian department that "it was not so much a reforming as an organization of this office *ab initio* that is wanting" (Canada. Legislative Assembly 1839–1840,2), it recommended the centralizing of the various governmental functions relating to Indians into the one department (table 1). The chief superintendent testified that "the Indian Office, strange as it may appear, has until lately possessed little or no information respecting the Indians' property, or the funds derived from sales or portions of it" (Canada. Legislative Assembly 1847:411). Indian lands were handled by the Crown Lands Department.

The 1844 report commented that the distribution of presents "has been the chief object for which a separate department for the Indian service has been maintained . . ." (Canada. Legislative Assembly 1847:363). The second report, in 1844, was concerned that the centralization of functions (and, therefore the organization of an Indian department on a clientele basis) "will tend to prolong their state of tutelage and of isolation from the rest of the community" (Canada. Legislative Assembly 1847:380).

While the 1857 report favored centralization of the functions in one department (Canada. Legislative Assembly 1858), and the colonial authorities assumed full control over the Indians in 1860, it was 1862 before "a single agency was created to administer Indian affairs and a permanent head, with the status of a deputy minister, was appointed to that agency . . . .All the major concerns of the Indians—land, timber, fish, and business records— were now under one political head, the Commissioner of Crown Lands" (Hodgetts 1955:223). By 1867 the Indian agency was a civilian department of government, organized as a clientele department (though within Crown lands). The presents had been terminated. The major change that occurred with confederation in 1867 was that this department was separated from Crown Lands by becoming a federal responsibility, while general responsibility for lands remained with the individual provinces of the Dominion of Canada.

Indian Affairs in the Other Uniting Colonies

While it was clearly the Upper Canada Indian legislation and administrative structure that was extended by the federal government after 1867, it should be recognized that separate Indian policies had been pursued in Newfoundland, Nova Scotia (out of which New Brunswick was created), Quebec, Rupert's Land, and British Columbia. The Beothuk Indian population of Newfoundland had been slaughtered by British settlers in the eighteenth and nineteenth centuries. Moravian missionaries had worked with native peoples in Labrador, but no Indian department or Indian legislation was developed.

The formal establishment of a government agency in Nova Scotia originated in the concern to regulate trade with the Indians (Upton 1975a, 1975c; Hutton 1961). The concept of a government monopoly on purchases from the Indians was adopted in 1760, drawing on models in New England. Truck houses were established in which the government assembled goods for trade to the Indians in exchange for furs. The scheme did not pay for itself and was opposed by the Board of Trade in England, which favored private trading. Formal legislation to bar private trading was disallowed by England in 1761, though the following year legislation was permitted that regulated private trading. In 1764 the imperial government adopted a Board of Trade plan to repeal all existing Indian commerce laws in British North America and to establish controlled free trade with the Indians. Commercial trade, in the areas north of Maryland, was to be conducted at designated locations where posts would be established. The agent or commissionary for Indian affairs was replaced by a superintendent with broader responsibility than just the newer trading system.

Table 1. Administration of Indian Affairs in Canada, 1755–1986

Year	Administrative Unit
1755	Sir William Johnson is appointed superintendent of Indian affairs, Northern Department.
1782	The title superintendent-general of Indian affairs and inspector general of the Indian Department replaces that of superintendent of Indian affairs.
1794	The Office of Deputy Superintendent-General is created.
1796	The lieutenant-governor assumes responsibility for Indian affairs in Upper Canada.
1800	The governor-general assumes responsibility for Indian affairs in Lower Canada.
1816	Jurisdiction over Indian affairs in Upper and Lower Canada is transferred to the commander of the forces.
1828	The position of superintendent-general of Indian affairs and inspector general of the Indian Department is abolished and the Office of Chief Superintendent of Indian Affairs created.
1830	The Indian Department is divided into two offices: the lieutenant-governor is responsible for Upper Canada, and the military secretary is responsible for Lower Canada.
	The reserve system is established in Upper Canada.
1841	Union of 1841: the two offices of the Indian Department are amalgamated and placed under the governor-general.
1844	The civil secretary is designated as superintendent-general for Indian affairs and the Office of Chief Superintendent abolished.
1860	Responsibility for Indian affairs is transferred from imperial control to the Province of Canada.
	The Crown Lands Department assumes control of Indian affairs, and the commissioner is appointed chief superintendent.
1867	Confederation: the federal government assumes control of Indian affairs; responsibility is delegated to the Department of the Secretary of State for the Provinces; the secretary of state becomes superintendent general of Indian affairs.
1873	The Department of the Interior is created with an Indian Lands Branch in it; a Board of Commissioners is established to administer Indian affairs in Manitoba, British Columbia, and the North West Territory.
1875	The Indian Boards are abolished; a system of superintendents and agents is established.
1880	An independent Department of Indian Affairs is established; the minister of the interior continues to serve as superintendent-general of Indian affairs and presides over the new department.
1897	General reorganization of the Department of Indian Affairs.
1909	Several distinct branches are established within the Department of Indian Affairs.
1924	Eskimos are placed under the responsibility of the superintendent-general of Indian affairs.
1936	The Department of Indian Affairs becomes a branch of the Department of Mines and Resources as Indian Affairs Branch.
1949	Indian Affairs Branch is transferred to the Department of Citizenship and Immigration.
1962	Reorganization of the Indian Affairs Branch.
1965	Indian Affairs Branch is transferred to the Department of Northern Affairs and National Resources.
1966	Department of Indian Affairs and Northern Development (also known as Department of Indian and Northern Affairs) is established, comprised of: Finance and Management, Personnel, Corporate Policy, Indian and Inuit Affairs, and Northern Affairs.
1973	Office of Native Claims becomes the sixth section in Department of Indian Affairs and Northern Development.

SOURCES: Leslie and Maguire 1978:v–xi; Frideres 1983:26–29; McCardle 1982, 1:22.

The idea of protected lands for the Indians in Nova Scotia developed in the years after 1813. In 1820 Surveyor-General Charles Morris made a report with a plan for the establishment of reserves. By 1834 "the broad outlines of the scheme of Indian reserves" was operative in the province (Hutton 1961:220). In 1841 proposals were accepted for proper surveys of reserves, and Joseph Howe was requested to make recommendations on Indian policy. Howe's recommendations led to the Act of 1842, the first significant reserve-oriented Indian legislation in Nova Scotia. Howe was appointed Indian commissioner under the new legislation. Indian commissioners after

Howe turned more and more to relief; and concern for reserves, as such, passed to the commissioner of Crown lands. In 1867 the positions of commissioner of Crown lands and Indian commissioner were both held by one man, Samuel Fairbanks. Fairbanks became Indian commissioner for the federal government after confederation and in 1868 was appointed dominion agent in Nova Scotia. In Nova Scotia, specific tribes were not assigned to specific reserves; all Indians were equally entitled to all reserves. This practice, at variance with policy in the rest of Canada, remained in effect until the 1950s. When Fairbanks resigned in 1871, Nova Scotia was reorganized by the federal government with local Indian agents reporting directly to Ottawa.

In New Brunswick (Upton 1973), following the pattern in Nova Scotia, reserves were established by grants. The first listing of reserve lands, published in 1838, identified 15 reserves ranging in area from 10 to 16,000 acres. As in Nova Scotia there were many disputes with squatters on reserve lands, and the local government was not prepared to ignore the demands of all the Whites who were claiming Indian reserve lands. In 1844 New Brunswick passed legislation permitting the sale of reserve lands without Indian consent, the resulting funds to be used for the exclusive benefit of the Indians (Cumming and Mickenberg 1972:104). Fifty acres per head of family were to be assigned to the Indians and the balance sold. The Indians would receive a location ticket immediately to their lands and, after 10 years' continuous occupancy, would be eligible for a free grant of title. The Indian would then be able to sell the land without restriction. Between 1844 and 1867, 10,679.5 acres of reserve land had been sold to 109 Whites. That amounted to 16 percent of the reserve land in the province. The native peoples of New Brunswick "had none of the safeguards provided the Indians of Canada, no corps of permanent paid officials to speak for them, no missionaries capable of lobbying for their interests in London, no subventions from the Imperial government" (Upton 1973:43).

British Columbia was an exceptional case. During its short colonial history a reserve system was begun, but no Indian legislation or Indian department was established.

It is with Quebec (Lower Canada) that the most interesting contrasts are to be made. The French policy of direct integration failed. Then there was a policy of integration through the education of Indian children. That failed. A third policy of integration through reserves failed. After that, the practice of segregating Indians on reserves was continued in order to isolate and protect them (Jaenen 1976:183–184).

The Inheritance of Confederation

The main institution inherited by the dominion government from the colonial administrations in Nova Scotia,

New Brunswick, Quebec, and British Columbia was the reserve system. The reserve system was seen as serving conflicting goals: protection and change. Apparently, in the views of the administrators of the period, it served neither goal well.

A decision was made in 1867 to place "Indians, and Lands Reserve for the Indians" under the legislative jurisdiction of the federal government. There are clear reasons why the opposite decision might have been taken. By 1867 significantly different legal and administrative patterns had developed in the colonies that federated. Barring any strong reason for centralized authority, it would clearly have been easier to have left jurisdiction with the provinces. In addition, the provinces were given jurisdiction over land, education, municipal level government, and social welfare matters. Indian-White relations were in a calm period in North America in 1867. The politicians would not have been anticipating immediate military problems. Section 146 of the British North America Act gave the federal government ample powers over the western areas that would later come into confederation. The power over Indians was not a necessary adjunct of western expansion.

It seems most likely that the tradition of imperial control over Indian policy, a tradition that had been ended in Upper Canada in 1860, lay behind the decision. Indian affairs administration in Upper Canada had been with the local representatives of the imperial government, not with the local administration. The logic of centralized and distant control, to override local settler interests that would be in conflict with Indian interests, seems the most likely explanation for federal jurisdiction over Indians and Indian lands in the British North America Act of 1867. The reserve system and the clientele Department become more distinct, more separate from normal national life when they were translated into the federal structure created in 1867.

The Completion of Pacification

In 1869–1870 the imperial government transferred Rupert's Land (the territories covered by the charter of the Hudson's Bay Company) and the North Western Territory (the balance of the west and north, excluding British Columbia) to Canada. In the protracted negotiations with the Hudson's Bay Company and the imperial government, the national government in Ottawa seemed barely aware of a distinct Métis population in the Red River colony, who saw the termination of the Hudson's Bay Company charter as a likely threat to their land and way of life. The Red River rebellion of 1869 led by Louis Riel led to a government policy of making land grants to mixed bloods. This involved land scrip and later scrip redeemable for money. The system was first set forth in the Manitoba Act of 1870 and was later extended throughout the present area of Manitoba, Saskatchewan, Alberta, and the Northwest Territories in response to the second Métis rebellion, the Northwest Rebellion of 1885 (Stanley 1960).

The mixed-blood grants were a parallel policy to the federal treaty policy. Federal treaties, Nos. 1–11, were negotiated from 1871 to 1921 ("Canadian Indian Treaties," fig. 2, this vol.). Clearly the treaty process in Canada changed dramatically from the model followed in southern Ontario. That probably simply reflected the increasingly confident and centralized legal and governmental structure created in Canada by the colonial process and weaker political positions of the tribes. Some of the prairie treaties, for example, No. 7, were negotiated in periods of near desperation for the Indian tribes. With the traditional economic order obviously disintegrating from forces beyond Indian control, the Indian leadership had little choice but to accept the offers of the government commissioners. Their political bargaining position had largely been destroyed. In the negotiations they asked, among other things, for relief in times of famine. That was what was facing them (Stanley 1960; J.L. Taylor 1976).

By 1900 the prairies were pacified, but there were distinct fears of Indian uprisings in British Columbia. The provincial government rejected the notion of Indian title to tribal territories and refused to cooperate with the federal government on the question of treaties. Since British Columbia had entered confederation with control over its land and natural resources, the federal government did not feel it had jurisdiction to establish reserves or

Fig. 2. Prime Minister John G. Diefenbaker with Plains Cree Indians at Maple Creek Reserve, Sask., during his re-election campaign. Photograph by Bill Cadzow, Oct. 1965.

otherwise deal with Indian land questions without the assistance of the provincial government. The Terms of Union in 1871 assumed good will and envisaged reserves being established on the same basis that they had been by the British Columbia government prior to 1871, but in fact there had been no clear or consistent policy in British Columbia before 1871 and the province showed no good will. After two joint federal-provincial royal commissions and lengthy negotiations, the two governments resolved their differences by 1938. Indian protests, asserting aboriginal title, were rejected by a joint committee of the federal Senate and House of Commons in Ottawa in 1929. To make it clear that one hearing was thought to be enough, the Indian Act was amended to prohibit Indians from raising money to put forward claims (LaViolette 1961; R. Fisher 1977; Shankel 1945).

In the 1920s the last treaties were signed in the Northwest Territories, and the treaty process was extended to the new northern limits of Ontario. The Department of Indian Affairs, following on the treaties and other dealings, now had its administrative structure in place nationally.

Indian Affairs, 1945–1985

It is perhaps telling that when Newfoundland and Labrador joined Confederation in 1949, no mention was made of Indians or Inuit though both groups lived in Labrador. No politician of the period would have

Fig. 1. An Eskimo woman signs for a family allowance at Royal Canadian Mounted Police headquarters, Coppermine, N.W.T. Government education, welfare, and health care programs and services were one incentive for Eskimo people to centralize in Eskimo–White communities such as Coppermine in the 1950s (vol.5:409). The family allowance program was intended to provide food, clothing, and miscellaneous items for children. The poster on the wall describes the the program in Inuit and English. Photograph by Richard Harrington, about 1950.

welcomed the extension of Canadian Indian policy to any new area. Other than instituting the disastrous Métis grants policy on the prairies, the federal government had done little with what it had inherited upon confederation. The Indian legislation, the reserve system, the clientele department had simply been extended to the new areas of Canada. In the period after the Second World War the federal government started to come to grips with a population who were unquestionably "second class citizens," who did not have the vote, who had been denied access to liquor since the 1859 Enfranchisement Act (Frideres 1983:23), who were discriminated against by the provinces in their programs, who were even discriminated against in federal programs, and who needed social services (fig. 1). Yet the Indians had a strong claim to national attention in the immediate postwar period for they had had the highest enlistment rate of any group in Canada in the Second World War. The initial Indian demands were for equal treatment in the face of officially structured discrimination.

The federal government established a Joint Senate and House of Commons Committee on the Indian Act, which held hearings from 1946 to 1948. In 1951 the government introduced a new Indian Act. For the first major legislative reform of Indian policy in the life of the country, it was a modest document. Archaic sections prohibiting the potlatch and Sun Dance and the ban on collecting money to advance claims were dropped. The membership system, which had been rather loose, became a set of practically unreadable sections, to be tightly administered by a registrar in Ottawa.

In 1960 under the John Diefenbaker administration,

the federal government extended the federal franchise to Indians with the assurance that it would not affect their status or special rights (fig. 2).

The emergence of Indian political activity can perhaps be dated from the Indian pavilion at Expo 67 in Montreal. The Indian pavilion was financed by the federal government but under Indian control. The pavilion displayed in pictures, print, and sound an Indian view of Canadian history. It represented one of the first Indian political assertions funded by the federal government.

A review of federal Indian policy, conducted within the Department of Indian Affairs, led to a policy proposal by personnel in the Privy Council Office. It was done in a reform atmosphere by people with no background on Indian questions.

The Indian policy proposal of June 1969 was based on the concept of equality (Canada. Department of Indian Affairs and Northern Development 1969). The elements of Indian policy that had been inherited at confederation were to be dismantled. Reserves would go to Indian ownership and be subject to provincial law. The Indian Act would be repealed. The clientele department would be phased out over five years. The Indian would be rewarded with equality and with some transitional money for economic development. The movement to recognize Indian claims, which had progressed, though slowly, in the postwar period, was blunted. "Lawful obligations" would be recognized, but the government indicated that it thought that the only lawful obligations that were outstanding were some treaty promises to supply ammunition for hunting and twine for nets. Prime Minister Pierre Trudeau, explaining the policy, on the question of

left, *The Globe and Mail*, Toronto, Ont.: 69185-01; right, Dept. of Ind. and Northern Affairs, Hull, Que.: 20-02-06-00.
Fig. 3. Responses to the White Paper. left, Dept. of Indian Affairs Minister Jean Chrétien, left, with Harold Sault, Ojibwa, a member of the Union of Ontario Indians. Chrétien had been invited to address the Union about the White Paper he introduced to Parliament in June 1969 (Anonymous 1969). Photograph by Franz Maier, July 4, 1969. right, Response of The Indian Chiefs of Alberta to the White Paper, a formal statement to the federal government entitled *Citizen Plus*, and often called the Red Paper. Some problems for which the Indians proposed solutions were: the lack of an Indian claims commission, reevaluation of treaties, the legal status of Indians, reorganization of the Dept. of Indian Affairs, and representation of Indian history and culture in the schools and in Canadian culture (Patterson 1972:180–181). from left, Chrétien, Pierre Trudeau, and Sen. Paul Martin; second from right Sen. James Gladstone, Blood, and right, Harold Cardinal, Cree. Photographed June 1970.

GOVERNMENT INDIAN AGENCIES IN CANADA

aboriginal rights, said bluntly, "our answer is 'no'!" (in Cumming and Mickenberg 1972:332).

The controversy over the policy proposal, called the White Paper, was a significant stimulus to Indian political activity. Almost all Indian spokespeople in the country opposed it, and the fight against the White Paper became a major issue around which to organize (fig. 3). The federal government began the funding of native political organizations, initially, to hold discussions on the White Paper proposals. By 1971 the government was funding those organizations as continuing political bodies, intermediaries between their Indian constituency and the federal government.

Indian-government relations appear to have been significantly changed by the controversy over the White Paper and the development of the Indian organizations. What is perhaps most telling about the Department of

Indian Affairs in the period is that it appeared to play no initiating role. Even though it was a period in which concern with Indian issues increased dramatically in Canada, no one was making clear proposals for policy. The dominant Canadian assessment was to see the reserve system as part of the problem, not part of the solution. That assessment took concrete form in the White Paper, the final form of which was not the work of the Department of Indian Affairs. The political retreat from the White Paper involved a commitment on the part of the government of Pierre Trudeau to retain the Indian Act and the reserve system until proposals for modification or reform came from the Indian community. Secondly, it involved some recognition by the federal government of Indian claims and the assignment of responsibility to the Department of Indian Affairs to negotiate settlement of those claims.

Dept. of Ind. and Northern Affairs, Ottawa, Ont.: 25-01-06-00.
Fig. 4. Demonstration on Parliament Hill, Ottawa, Ont., against the Quebec Court of Appeals decision on the James Bay hydroelectric project, Nov. 1973. The Quebec provincial government announced the James Bay project in 1971, initiating 3 years of negotiations with the Dept. of Indian Affairs and Northern Development and with Inuit and Indian organizations. During this time the Northern Quebec Inuit Association and the Grand Council of the Cree used the provincial courts to attempt to halt the project until the issue of aboriginal title had been treated. This was unsuccessful, and the Supreme Court of Canada denied the Indian and Inuit appeal for a hearing. The negotiations of the province, the federal government, and the Native organizations eventually resulted in an agreement, reached on Nov. 11, 1975, that had important effects on the administration of Native affairs in Quebec and gave Native people a high level of local control. Some aspects of the agreement were: $225 million (Canadian) in compensation, support for Native management of game conservation, support of hunting subsistence, use of Native languages along with French and English in administration, Native control of schools, and Cree and Inuit regional and local administration of lands (Frideres 1983: 111–112; J.A. Price 1978:259–261, 1979:96–97). Photographer unidentified.

282

The most positive development in the postwar period, in terms of the Department as an institution, was a fairly dramatic increase in budgetary allotments. The traditional underfunding of Indian affairs (Hawthorn 1966–1967) ended. The Department was able to increase its administrative competence, for example, in establishing a well organized Indian lands registry, beginning in 1968. It also expanded its staff in the area of economic development, conscious that it had no in-house competence in this area as late as the middle-1960s. It had great difficulty coping with staffing and policy in new policy areas, such as economic development and land claims. In contrast it became quite efficient on administrative tasks, such as membership and the Indian lands registry.

The new claims policy, announced in 1973, was a response to litigation in British Columbia, Quebec (Jenness 1985), and the Northwest Territories and a general politicization of the issue. The minority Liberal government in Ottawa was facing vocal support of Indian claims by both opposition parties. At issue were major frontier energy projects, primarily the James Bay hydroelectric project in northern Quebec and the proposed Mackenzie valley natural gas pipeline in the Northwest Territories. The 1973 policy sought negotiated settlements of aboriginal title claims. The strongest, immediate pressure was in Quebec, where construction of the James Bay hydroelectric installations was underway (fig. 4). For constitutional reasons distinctive to northern Quebec, the lead in negotiations was taken by the provincial government, not the federal government. Two agreements resulted, one with the Cree and one with the Inuit. Both were approved by referenda and implemented by federal and provincial legislation (Québec 1976). The James Bay and Northern Quebec Agreements were supplemented by an agreement with the Naskapi. A settlement was also negotiated with the Inuit in the Mackenzie delta. But no settlements were achieved for the major claims in British Columbia, the Yukon, and most of the Northwest Territories.

Some progress was made on "specific claims," smaller-scale claims not based on aboriginal title, but none on major claims, although the minister of Indian affairs gained cabinet approval for a formal restatement of claims policy in 1981 and 1982.

By the mid-1970s Indians had become politically assertive. The Dene Declaration of 1975 sought recognition of the Subarctic Athapaskans as a nation within Canada (M. Watkins 1977). The phrase "Indian government" came into common use. The political reformulation of Indian claims was in place in 1978 when Prime Minister Trudeau undertook to amend the Canadian constitution (to end remaining powers in the British Parliament to amend the constitution, to entrench minority language rights, and to add a bill of rights). The National Indian Brotherhood defined constitutional amendment as an Indian issue and demanded constitutional recognition of

George Mully Audio Visual Ltd., Ottawa, Ont.

Fig. 5. Indian women demonstrating against the Indian Act in front of Parliament buildings in Ottawa, July 1979. Minister of Indian and Northern Affairs Jake Epp addresses the group. Under the Indian Act, Indian women who marry non-Indian men lose their status and privileges, and their children are legally non-Indian. However, non-Indian women who marry registered Indian men obtain Indian status and subsequent benefits (Surtees 1971:74). Photograph by George Mully.

treaty and aboriginal rights, and an Indian role in the amendment process (a process always limited to the federal and provincial governments). Indians succeeded in gaining a role in the process, and provisions were added to the Canadian constitution in 1982 recognizing and affirming "existing aboriginal and treaty rights" and promising Indian, Métis, and Inuit involvement in meetings of the prime minister and the provincial premiers (Sanders 1983). The first meeting in 1983 was successful, but after two more the process appeared ineffective owing to opposition from provincial governments and no common front on the part of the aboriginal organizations (Sanders 1986).

The Department of Indian Affairs was in the background as constitutional issues dominated from 1978 to 1985, for the "lead department" on aboriginal constitutional questions was the Department of Justice. On self-government the policy initiatives came not from the Department of Indian Affairs but from the Indian organizations and from the Report of the Special Committee of the House of Commons on Indian Self-Government (Canada. Parliament. House of Commons 1983). In 1985 the federal government enacted self-government legislation for the Sechelt band of Coastal Salish, a small, well-organized band in British Columbia that had been seeking such legislation for a decade.

Indian issues emerged as significant in Canadian political life in the years after the Second World War. Their importance was at least in part because of the success of Indian initiatives in the government's constitutional revision project.

American Indian Education

MARGARET CONNELL SZASZ AND CARMELITA RYAN

Colonial Experiences

New Spain

In the initial stages of New World colonization, the Spanish monarchy had valued the concept of American Indian education as an important agent of acculturation. In the sixteenth century, in central Mexico, where Indian schooling achieved impressive levels, colleges such as Santa Cruz de Tlatelolco educated many fine Indian Latinists. By the mid-seventeenth century goals had changed, and much of the initial enthusiasm espousing higher education for Indians had waned.

In the borderlands Indian education varied considerably. Nevertheless, through the auspices of the ubiquitous mission, the entire area shared a common institution that engendered all formal efforts to educate the Indian.

The Spanish mission system provided the Indian with instruction in prayers and catechism—usually in Spanish—in vocal and instrumental music, and in other activities that might aid in religious services. Thus, mission-educated Indians became bilingual, and, on occasion, literate as well. In addition, missions instructed Indian neophytes in agricultural and mechanical arts, such as woodworking and blacksmithing. Some mission Indians, such as the woodworkers of Pecos Pueblo in northern New Mexico, gained local reputations for the quality of their craftsmanship.

In the late eighteenth century, Spain renewed its efforts to promote Indian education. New legislation called for the establishment of schools within every Indian town of Spain's empire in the Americas. Unfortunately, these education laws had virtually no impact in the borderlands.

After gaining independence in 1821 Mexico undertook a program of secularization of the mission system. Thus, Mexico dismantled the single institution that had housed Indian education under Spanish rule.

New France

The French also relied on Roman Catholic missionaries to christianize the Indians of New France. But attempts to provide religious education for the Algonquian and Iroquoian Indians of the Subarctic and Northeast proved a severe challenge. In addition to the usual language barrier, French missionaries struggled to overcome the difficulties of reaching mobile people who possessed well-developed religions.

The Recollects were the first order to be summoned to New France. They made the initial forays into Huron country, where they taught the youth (Trigger 1976, 1: 430). They also founded a seminary near Quebec where they attempted to educate native children. The Ursulines also opened a monastery in Quebec, where they educated Indian girls.

The powerful and wealthy Society of Jesus soon replaced the Recollects. They also contacted the Hurons, where they established a mission in the late 1630s. The Jesuits' progress among the Hurons in the 1640s was cut short by the virtual destruction and dispersal of this people by their enemy, the Iroquois, by 1650.

Undaunted, the Jesuits searched for new fields. They pushed west in the Great Lakes region to work among the Ottawas; they followed the fur trade as the French voyageurs moved into Illinois country, where the Jesuits established missions among the Illinois. They even approached the lodges of the Iroquois, and despite difficulties, they attracted Iroquois converts who moved to the French settlements. They also continued to maintain their earlier missions among the Abenakis and other Eastern Algonquians.

British Colonies

The education given the Indians took many forms. At the least complicated level individual Indians were taken into colonial homes; sometimes willingly, sometimes as hostages. The colonists taught the Indian boys how to farm and the girls how to keep house, weave, and sew. Both boys and girls were given Euro-American clothing, introduced to colonists' food, and, in general, shown the ways of Euro-American civilization. Ministers instructed the Indians in Christianity, in reading, and in writing. At the most sophisticated level small schools were established for the Indians and provisions made for more advanced education for the more promising Indian youths (fig. 1). Where Indians remained after White settlement, Indian children attended school with White children (Szasz 1988:

chapter 5).

● VIRGINIA The earliest attempt to provide formal schooling for the Indians in the English colonies occurred in Virginia in 1619 when Sir Edwin Sandys, president of the Virginia Company, ordered the sale of 10,000 acres of land in Virginia, the proceeds of which were to be spent to erect an Indian college at Henrico, near the present site of the city of Richmond (Land 1938). At the same time King James ordered the archbishops of Canterbury and York to take up four collections in their dioceses to obtain money to build churches and schools for the Virginia Indians. The monies from the collections, which amounted to £1,500, were to be invested until the construction of the churches and schools began. Meanwhile, the East India School, to prepare the Indians for college, was erected across the James River from Charles City. These endeavors had scarcely begun when they were put to an end by the Virginia Indian uprising of 1622.

Although the settlers extended their former offer to educate Algonquian children in colonial families, it is unlikely that many Indian parents voluntarily complied. Contemporary legislation suggests that those children who did live with Virginia families served essentially as indentured servants (Bell 1930:25–26). Where Indians were educated in English homes, their schooling was similar to that of other Virginia children. With the exception of the wealthy, few children in early Virginia, whether White, Red, or Black, had access to formal schooling.

In 1691 the executors of the estate of Sir Robert Boyle invested £2,400 to provide education for the Indians of Virginia. The College of William and Mary, in Williamsburg, chartered in 1693, was dedicated in part to christianization of the Indians. Through the aid of the Robert Boyle fund, it opened its Indian school in 1700 (Ganter 1935:14, 16). From then until the Revolution, this school educated 75 to 100 Indians. By 1723, sufficient money had accumulated to build a brick building, Brafferton College, to provide living accommodations for the Indians. This Indian school was the longest continually operated school for Indians in the British colonies (Robinson 1952). Nonetheless, it differed significantly from other colonial colleges that enrolled Indians. At Harvard, the College of New Jersey, and Dartmouth, Indian students studied at the college level; at William and Mary, their schooling was at the elementary level.

Under Lieutenant-Governor Alexander Spotswood, Virginia also furnished schooling for western Indians. A Virginia trading company induced some of the Saponi and affiliated tribes to settle apart from the White settlements on a tract of land at Fort Christanna on the Meherrin River near the present Virginia–North Carolina state line. There the trading company built a school for the children (Spotswood 1882–1885, 2:90; Byrd 1966:220). The school, which had 70 students by 1715, closed three years later;

The Newberry Lib., Edward E. Ayer Coll., Chicago, Ill.

Fig. 1. Frontispiece in *A primer, for the use of Mohawk children, to acquire the spelling and reading of their own, as well as to get acquainted with the English, tongue; which for that purpose is put on the opposite page* (Claus 1786). Written by an Indian agent in Montreal, Que., the 98-page primer has sections on the alphabet; words of 1 to 5 syllables in Mohawk and English; words of 6 to 11 syllables in Mohawk only; "a short scripture catechism for children which will serve to explain to them the many principal persons contained in the scriptures," a church catechism in Mohawk and English; other sections, which incorporated English and Mohawk in several ways, containing various Christian prayers, the names of books of the *Old* and *New Testaments*, and a series of questions and answers to be used by missionaries among the Mohawks; and the Mohawk words for numbers. Engraved mezzotint by James Peachy, 1786.

and the settlement was abandoned when the trading company lost its exclusive rights to trade in that area.

● THE CAROLINAS AND GEORGIA In general, Indian education in the southern colonies before the American Revolution closely resembled that of the education provided for the White settlers. The available schooling was designed to provide a good preparation for the few well-to-do youths who were expected to attend college in the colonies or abroad: education for the poor was almost nonexistent. Similarly, the Indian education reached only a small number of the youth.

In 1715 schooling for Indians in the Carolinas could not boast an extensive history. Most of it remained in the hands of the Church of England missionaries in the Society for the Propagation of the Gospel in Foreign Parts

(SPG), and they had not arrived until 1702. Foremost among the missionaries to express concern for Indian education in this period was the Reverend Francis Le Jau. Le Jau's accounts of his years in South Carolina (1706–1717) portray the frustration and despair of one whose efforts to christianize and educate the Indians were constantly undermined by the demands of the deerskin trade (Le Jau 1956:41). In the Carolinas, as elsewhere, the SPG missionaries preferred to work with the settlers, whose living conditions more closely approximated their own. Thus the educational efforts of Carolina SPG missionaries, as well as the occasional schoolmaster funded by the SPG, were limited to Indian youth who were either enslaved or who lived nearby with their families.

Only one Southeastern Indian of this period, a Yamasee youth who was educated for two years in England, demonstrated the promise of civilization idealized by the English. Known as the Yamasee Prince, this young man acquired the material trappings of English civilization and also learned to read and write. But that promise died when his return to Carolina coincided with the Yamasee War, the imprisonment of his father, and the drowning of his Carolinian benefactor.

Georgia's colonial Indian schooling was also restricted by warfare and imperial rivalry. Moreover, if few Indians remained in proximity to the South Carolina settlements after the Yamasee War, even fewer remained near Georgia's settlers when the colony was founded in 1732.

The single endeavor to educate Indians in Georgia involved three groups: a small Creek-Yamasee community known as Yamacraw, located a short distance from Savannah, and two bands of missionaries—John and Samuel Wesley and Benjamin Ingham, of the Church of England—and several Moravians from Saxony (Tyerman 1873; Dallimore 1970–1979, 1:61–78; Fries 1905:71). In 1734, Tomochichi, the mico of Yamacraw, had requested a Christian educator for the Yamacraw children (C.C. Jones 1868:54–72). Two years later his request was answered, but the dream of the old mico was never to be realized in full. Due to a combination of circumstances, the schooling of the Yamacraw children continued intermittently for only about two years. The school itself was initiated by Benjamin Ingham (Wesley 1938, 1: 237). For several months the little structure at Irene, a site adjacent to the Yamacraw village, continued under the co-direction of Ingham and Peter and Catherine Rose, two Moravians (Coulter 1927:2–3; Loskiel 1794:34; Fries 1905:144). With Ingham's departure for England, various Moravians maintained the school until the rumor of war with Spain led to their removal to Pennsylvania. Thus Georgia's single Indian school came to a close.

● NEW ENGLAND AND THE MIDDLE COLONIES In the northern colonies the education provided the Indians was broader in scope: some schooling being considered a necessity for all the White population, the education of the Indians was necessarily given greater consideration there. Although no more successful in the long run than their southern counterparts, several of the New England educational experiments became prototypes of later schooling furnished the Indians. In the first days of the New England colonies, Indian youths, usually hostages, were instructed in English homes. Later, self-governing Indian communities, complete with schools, were established and flourished for a time. Eventually an Indian college was established in association with several colleges, notably at Harvard and Dartmouth.

The Massachusetts Bay Colony witnessed major efforts in Indian education during the seventeenth century. In 1643 the first Protestant Indian mission complete with school in the United States was established on Martha's Vineyard by Rev. Thomas Mayhew, Jr., whose family carried on the mission school for several generations (Banks 1911–1925; Hare 1932; Ronda 1981).

In 1646 Reverend John Eliot, minister of the church in Roxbury, Massachusetts, began his work among the Indians. As he made converts of the Indians, Eliot gathered them into villages (14 were eventually established) where they were trained to live like their White neighbors. Each of the "praying towns" had a school where the Indians were taught to read and write. The first town, Nonantum, near the present site of Newton, was established almost immediately as a community for converts. In 1650 Eliot founded Natick, which became the leading village of the "praying Indians" and soon numbered 150 Indians.

Eliot and Mayhew relied heavily on the cooperation and skills of a number of Indians as translators; and a Nipmuck, James Printer, helped set the type for the Indian Bible of 1663 and other religious works published in Massachusett and English. These publications provided the Indians of southeastern New England with access to western culture through a means unavailable to any other Indian group in colonial America (fig. 2) (Salisbury 1974: 42, 62; Speck 1943:51).

Most New England Indians who attended school during these decades were taught at the school on the Vineyard, its counterpart among the Mashpee on Cape Cod, or in the "praying towns," where some schoolmasters were Indian (Tannis 1970). A small number advanced to the grammar schools in Roxbury or Cambridge. Between the mid-1650s and 1670s perhaps as many as 40 Indian students were enrolled in these two grammar schools. Four of them went on to the Indian college at Harvard, and two (Joel Hiacoomes and Caleb Cheeshahteaumuck) completed their education there. Of the other two, one remained for only a year, and the second died.

From the mid-seventeenth century the Society for the Propagation of the Gospel in New England preached and taught Indians. In the early 1700s the missionaries

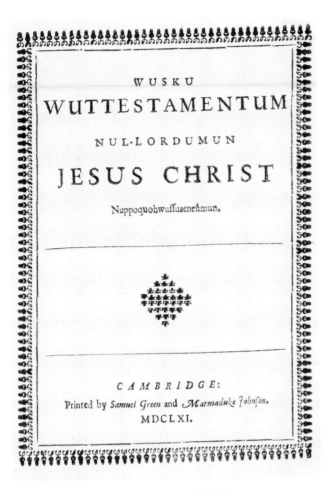

Brown U., John Carter Brown Lib., Providence, R.I.: 0A685/B582m.

Fig. 2. Massachusett title page of the *New Testament*, translated by John Eliot (1661). The title is literally 'the new testament of our Lord Jesus Christ, our savior'. It was printed at Harvard College under the auspices of the Corporation in England for the Propagation of the Gospel Amongst the Indians in New England (Pilling 1891:132–138). When the whole Massachusett bible was issued in 1663, it was the first bible in any language printed anywhere in the Western Hemisphere.

expanded their focus by reaching out to the Indians of southern New England and western Massachusetts. By the mid-1720s they supported several schools in this area, including one at Mohegan, Connecticut, attended by Mohegan, Pequot, and Niantic children. Although it was founded by a White, the Mohegan school eventually came under the supervision of the Mohegan Ben Uncas, III, who served as schoolmaster for over a decade.

Shortly thereafter the commissioners began to fund the work of John Sergeant, who arrived in western Massachusetts in 1734 to begin a 15-year ministry to the Mahican, Housatonic, and Naugatuck. Sergeant opened a day school at Stockbridge for the Indian children; later he introduced a boarding school, as well (Sedgwick and Marquand 1974).

David Brainerd, a Presbyterian missionary to the Mahican near Albany, soon moved to the forks of the Delaware River, where the support of the Society in Scotland for Propagating Christian Knowledge enabled him to work with the Delawares. His brother, John Brainerd, served the Delawares in New Jersey (Brainerd 1865).

The educational work of the Brainerds was paralleled by that of the Moravians, who had moved to Pennsylvania about 1740. Between this decade and the end of the century the Brethren taught Delawares and other Indians in mission sites in Gnadenhütten and Shamokin, Pennsylvania, and later in Ohio and Canada. Despite warfare and prejudice, their persistence was a remarkable commitment to Christian education.

In 1754 Rev. Eleazer Wheelock founded Moor's Indian Charity School in Lebanon, Connecticut, with two Delawares sent by John Brainerd. This school, which was supported by the Society in Scotland for Propagating Christian Knowledge and by grants in land and money from other sources, educated perhaps 60 Indians in its Connecticut location, one-fourth of them girls (McCallum 1932; Szasz 1980; Axtell 1981a). By the 1760s, Wheelock had developed a plan for moving his school to Iroquoian territory where he would employ his own graduates to teach Iroquois youth. This plan failed to materialize, but Sir William Johnson, Indian superintendent for the northern colonies, permitted Wheelock to send individual students to teach Oneida, Tuscarora, and Mohawk youth (Szasz 1988). In 1766 Wheelock sent Samson Occom, a Mohegan who was a Presbyterian missionary among the Indians of southern New England, and a White minister to England. There they raised over £13,000, which was used when Moor's Indian Charity School moved from Connecticut to Hanover, New Hampshire, where it became part of Dartmouth College (L.B. Richardson 1933; Chase 1928).

Wheelock's school, like John Sergeant's boarding school, educated Indians in an environment removed from their own culture. From this perspective, they differed from John Eliot's praying village schools. However, both Eliot and eighteenth-century missionaries trained Indian students in the values and material culture of Whites. At Moor's School boys received a classical education in Latin and Greek, and sometimes even Hebrew. When girls were included in the program in 1761, they were boarded in nearby homes, where they learned to keep house and to sew and went to the school one day a week to learn to read and write. Wheelock educated the girls in order that they might assist the boys "in the Business of their mission" (Szasz 1980).

1776–1860

During the American Revolution Indian education received some thought from the new government as a consequence of their campaign to win support from the Indians in the fight against Great Britain. Funds were made available to ministers and teachers willing to live among the Indians and to serve as diplomatic agents. For example, in 1776 the Continental Congress authorized the Indian commissioners to find a minister and a blacksmith for the Delawares and to determine the terms under which two teachers would live among the Indians in New York. Again, Congress appropriated money to support Indian students at Dartmouth and the College of New Jersey (later Princeton University). Significantly, that same body was not moved to make funds available for southern Indians, who were in open sympathy with the English. Dr. Samuel Kirkland, who had been working as a missionary among the Oneida since 1766, received a charter in 1793 for a school for Indians that he called the Hamilton-Oneida Academy. The next year it closed and was not reopened until 1799. Kirkland's attempt to enroll Indian students failed, and in 1812 the Indian academy was granted a new charter as Hamilton College.

The Society of Friends sent a few missionaries to Indians in the colonial period, Carolina and the Shawnee in Pennsylvania in the early eighteenth century, and by the 1790s they had established themselves among the Oneida, Tuscarora, Delaware, and Shawnee in New York. In 1804 they established a school for boys and in 1825 one for girls on the Alleghany reservation. In 1822 the Society opened a manual training school for the Shawnee Indians on the Au Glaize River in western Ohio. This school, which remained with the Shawnee Indians during their successive removals, was finally located at Shawnee, Kansas, where some of the buildings remain. The Shawnee Manual Labor School, which had the children working part time on the farm or in the house and part time at academic studies, became the prototype for many later schools. It combined academic studies with useful labor and taught the Indians the Protestant work ethic.

During the three decades following the establishment of the federal government in 1789, Indian education received little attention from the new nation. However, the presence of powerful Indian tribes within its boundaries and along its borders prevented the United States from ignoring the matter completely. Consequently, federal funds for the practical training of the Indians were made available through the provisions of Indian treaties, by executive order, and the trade and intercourse laws enacted between 1790 and 1802, under which Congress appropriated $15,000–20,000 annually to purchase farm animals and domestic tools and equipment (Prucha 1984, 1:140). The educational provisions written into treaties negotiated during this period varied widely. Some promised that artisans who could instruct would reside among the tribes. The 1794 treaty negotiated with the Oneida, Tuscarora, and Stockbridge Indians promised that the United States would employ one or two artisans to instruct their young men to be millers and sawyers as well as to keep their mills in repair (7 U.S. Stat. 47). Other

288

U. of Okla. Lib., Western Hist. Coll., Norman: T.L. Ballenger Coll. 7.
Fig. 3. Students at the Cherokee Female Seminary, a secondary school maintained by the Cherokee Nation, Indian Terr. Only Cherokee students were admitted to the academy. There was a companion seminary for young men (ARCIA 1888:205). Photographed about 1900.

treaties authorized the expenditure of tribal money to provide aid for missionaries working with the Indians. Thus in 1803 the Presbyterian missionary among the Cherokee, Gideon Blackburn, was promised aid in the construction of a schoolhouse (McLoughlin 1984:74–75, 284). Finally, some treaties simply stated that a certain portion of the monies received from the sale of Indian lands would be set aside for the education of the Indians.

In the early national period missionaries were active in the Southeast. In 1817 the American Board of Commissioners for Foreign Missions established a mission among the Cherokee at Brainerd, Tennessee. The federal government aided in building the schoolhouse and workshops where boys and girls were taught practical arts (McLoughlin 1984:105–106). By 1820 there were nearly 100 pupils, and others were being turned away for lack of facilities; 100 more pupils were studying in other Cherokee missions (Mooney 1975:95–96, 98).

The mission to the Choctaw at Eliot, Mississippi, was founded in 1818 by Cyrus Kingsbury, a Presbyterian missionary. Soon after, eight Choctaw children were brought to be enrolled, even though the schoolhouse was not yet built. A few months later Kingsbury was invited to a tribal council, at which he proposed that the Choctaws who desired a school would support it financially. Immediately $1,300 in cash and 95 cows were pledged (Cushman 1962:73, 99). Another mission to the Choctaw was founded at Mayhew, Mississippi, in 1821.

In 1819 Congress passed an "act making provision for the civilization of the Indian tribes ajoining the frontier settlements" (3 U.S. Stat. 516) and subsequently authorized setting aside treaty annuities specifically for education in order to provide a constant and fixed sum of money for Indian education. The 1819 act called for an annual appropriation of $10,000 to teach adult Indians agriculture and trades and to teach Indian children reading, writing, and arithmetic (Beaver 1966:68–69). President James Monroe and Secretary of War John C. Calhoun decided to use the money to support the efforts of missionaries and the benevolent societies who had or who would establish schools to educate Indian children. Although this sum was relatively small considering the numbers of Indians to be educated, the "civilization fund," in use until 1873, encouraged the work of missionaries and stimulated public contributions for the support of the missions. Many missionaries who continued to operate schools on the reservations after 1873 received financial support from the federal government over the following two decades in the form of payments of a specified sum of money for each child received into the mission school.

In order to apportion the civilization fund fairly, the government required the heads of all established schools wishing to share in the fund to submit periodic reports including the courses taught, the number of teachers, and sometimes the names of the pupils; a description of the school buildings; and often a brief history of the accomplishments of the year. The local Indian agent, under whose general supervision the school was placed, frequently added remarks or appended a report of his own concerning the educational status of the tribe. An 1824 report of the Bureau of Indian Affairs (which had been created in the War Department early in 1824 to supervise the federal government's relations with the Indians) showed that in that year there were 32 schools with 916 students (McKenney 1824:App. B).

Schools for Indians continued to endorse mainstream concepts of education. Hence, when public schools encouraged the teaching of good behavior, so, too, did the Indian schools. The Presbyterian missionaries had faith in the "character transforming power of education" (Coleman 1985:2). They were not alone in this belief. In 1822 an American Board missionary suggested that Indian students be taught "those habits of sobriety, cleanliness, economy, and industry, so essential to civilized life" (Berkhofer 1965:35). Indeed, missionary reports suggest that much of their energy went into enforcing matters such as regular attendance, respectable progress, and proper behavior (Coleman 1985:12–17; Berkhofer 1965: 16–21, 35–37). If students were to adopt all aspects of American cultural behavior, they needed to learn English, but this posed a problem in virtually every school (McLoughlin 1984:63–68).

Hundreds of Indian schools opened in the early nineteenth century, ranging from those among the Oneida, Tuscarora, and Seneca to the Shawnee mission school established by the Methodists in Indian Territory. The most widespread schooling developed among the tribes of the Southeast, and especially among the Cherokee and Choctaw. Two off-reservation schools for Indians trained a number of these Southern Indians: the American Board of Commissioners for Foreign Missions school at Cornwall, Connecticut (1817–1827), and the Choctaw Academy, located in Kentucky (1825–1842) (Walker 1931: 155–158; C.T. Foreman 1928–1932).

A wide variety of conditions existed in the Indian schools. Some were boarding schools both on- and off-reservation; others were academies. Many operated as manual labor schools, which combined academic and practical training (Berkhofer 1965:36–37; E.C. Adams 1946:35–37). Others remained as day schools, either missionary or tribal. Thus, there was no representative type of Indian school, nor was there a predictable Indian response to these schools.

Several tribes, particularly those living in the Southeast, began to establish common schools, funded and managed by the tribes themselves. The Cherokee, Choctaw, and Chickasaw had begun to do so before they were forced to remove to the west in the 1830s and 1840s.

The Choctaws established their tribal school system in 1833, building 12 log schoolhouses. Four years later, they had 10 tribal schools attended by 217 boys and 46 girls in addition to 12 mission schools attended by 96 boys and 82 girls. Schools of higher education were planned, constructed, and began to offer advanced instruction and manual training. The 1850 Choctaw school report listed Chuahla, Wheelock, Igunobi, and Koosha Female Seminaries; New Hope Academy for girls; Armstrong, Spencer, and Fort Coffee Male Academies, and the Norwalk School for boys. These schools were supported by tribal, missionary, and federal funds. In addition, the Choctaws taught reading, writing, and arithmetic to adults as well as to youths in seven community schools (G. Foreman 1934: 18–77).

The Cherokee Nation was as progressive as the Choctaw tribe in providing schooling for their children. While residing in their eastern lands, the Cherokee had operated a flourishing network of schools. They reopened these and established others shortly after their arrival in Indian Territory. On December 16, 1841, the Cherokee National Council, the tribal governing body, set up a system of 11 schools in the eight Cherokee Districts. The curricula consisted of reading, writing, arithmetic, bookkeeping, English grammar, geography, and history. By 1843 there were 500 students in the schools, and by 1852, 1,100 students in 21 schools and two academies. To administer this system, the Cherokee National Council appointed a general superintendent of the schools in 1853. At this time the Cherokee Nation had a better school system in terms of numbers of schools, teachers, and students than the states of Arkansas and Missouri (G. Foreman 1934:354–410).

Educational efforts among the Chickasaw before their removal to Indian Territory were sporadic and unsuccessful; it was not until long after their removal to Indian Territory that the Chickasaw began to establish tribal schools. Although the Chickasaw had petitioned the federal government in 1842 for funds to establish a large manual labor boarding school, as late as 1847 the Chickasaw agent reported that there was not a single school in operation among that people. Two years later the Chickasaw legislature appropriated funds for six schools. By 1851 they had succeeded in opening the Chickasaw Academy and the next year the Wapauneka Female Manual Labor School under the auspices of the Presbyterians. In 1855, the Chickasaws provided county superintendents to regulate their schools and to supervise their teachers (G. Foreman 1934:99–125).

The Creek Indians, who had been reluctant to establish schools while they were living in the East, were equally slow to establish them after their removal. By 1842 the Creeks had permitted a mission school within their lands with the understanding that the missionaries would not interfere with tribal matters. By 1853 the Creeks had 12 neighborhood schools and two manual training schools (G. Foreman 1934:169–207).

These tribal schools had to close with the passage of the Curtis Act of 1898 (30 U.S. Stat. 495–503), which mandated the end of tribal governments in Indian Territory (G. Foreman 1934; Baird 1967; Debo 1934: 60–64; Welsh 1983).

1860–1928

The Civil War dealt a shattering blow to the school system in Indian Territory. In the decades following many groups of people combined to restore, improve, and expand a system of education for the Indians. Officials of the Bureau of Indian Affairs, missionaries, philanthropists, army officers, church societies, and Indian tribes participated in educational work. The treaties negotiated with the Indians immediately after the war anticipated the establishment of schools and provided for the erection of schoolhouses as soon as "sufficient number of children can be induced to attend school." This clause appears in treaties made in 1868 with the Ute, Sioux, Crow, Northern Cheyenne, Northern Arapahoe, Navajo, Eastern Shoshone, and Bannock (see Kappler 1904–1941).

The Southeast Indian tribes also began to resume their own educational work. By the winter of 1869–1870, for example, the Choctaw school superintendent reported 84 neighborhood schools with an enrollment of 1,746 pupils. The general council of the Choctaw Nation also appropriated the interest accruing from the money provided by the Treaty of Dancing Rabbit Creek of 1830 for education. This money furnished education for 40 Choctaw young men to attend the academies and colleges of the United States—Dartmouth, Yale, and Union, among others.

The federal government then began to build schools, staff them with teachers whose salaries they paid, and maintain them exclusively by means of government appropriations. Although a few schools that would fit this definition had been established earlier (for example, the school at Leech Lake, Minnesota, opened in 1860), it was not until the 1870s that true government schools were established.

To provide the money for a system of Indian education, Congress in 1870 authorized an annual appropriation of $100,000 to be spent exclusively for schooling for the Indians. In 1883 the appropriation jumped dramatically and in 1893 reached about 2.3 million dollars (Priest 1942: 149). Yet in 1880, only one out of every 12 Indian children was receiving an education (ARCIA 1881:36).

More than half the appropriated money went to maintain the day schools on the reservations, which were expected to provide elementary or primary Indian education and to prepare the Indians to attend more advanced schools.

To lower the costs of educating the young Indians while at the same time to increase the efficacy of that education by removing the student from the tribal environment, the concept of the off-reservation boarding school, or industrial school, was propounded by Richard Henry Pratt, who established the most famous of the industrial schools at Carlisle, Pennsylvania, in 1879. The Carlisle Indian Industrial School was the first nonreservation government boarding school for Indians. The industrial school offered instruction in academic subjects and in various trades and vocations. The children were also expected to work part of the time to help defray the cost of the administration of the school itself.

A Civil War veteran and experienced frontier officer, Pratt was placed in charge of 72 Kiowa, Comanche, and Cheyenne prisoners from the Red River War who were exiled to Fort Marion, Florida, in 1875. His success in educating these men encouraged him to transfer 17 of them to Hampton Institute, Virginia, a school for Blacks ("United States Indian Policies, 1860–1900," fig. 5, this vol.) (Peabody 1918; D.W. Adams 1977; Tingey 1978). After a single year there, Pratt persuaded the federal government to donate army cavalry barracks at Carlisle, Pennsylvania, to found an Indian school (Brunhouse 1939; C.S. Ryan 1962; Walker-McNeil 1979). He opened the school with a few Indians from Fort Marion and about 150 others, mainly Sioux.

Carlisle Indian School opened at a time when the federal government had already shown increasing interest in Indian schooling. In 1873 the Indian Bureau had established a Medical and Education Division. Although the Bureau did not form a separate Education Division for another decade, the bureaucratic process for government direction of Indian education had, indeed, begun.

Between 1880 and 1900 the Indian Bureau opened 24 additional off-reservation manual labor boarding schools.

290

Some of them became well known: Forest Grove, Oregon, 1880; Chilocco, Newkirk, Indian Territory, 1884; Haskell, in Lawrence, Kansas, 1884; Albuquerque, 1886 and Santa Fe, 1890, New Mexico; and Phoenix, Arizona, 1890 (fig. 4). But none of them achieved the reputation established by Carlisle. Pratt stamped his personality and his approach to Indian education on this singular institution. During his 24-year superintendency, Carlisle enrolled a total of 4,903 Indians. For Pratt native cultures held no significance; the future of his students lay in their role as mainstream Americans. "The end to be gained," Pratt concluded in a letter to Sen. Henry L. Dawes, "is the complete civilization of the Indian . . . [and] the sooner all tribal relations are broken up; the sooner the Indian loses all his Indian ways, even his language, the better it will be" (R.H. Pratt 1964:266). Pratt counseled all Carlisle students to forget their early years and tribal connections and to become individualized Americans. Hence, a Carlisle education attempted to transform not only material culture—hair styles, dress, ornamentation—but also cultural attitudes and values. The students spent half their day learning reading, writing, and arithmetic and the other half learning farming and trades—harness making, tinsmithing, building barns, houses, and other buildings, tailoring, printing, laying concrete, masonry, and tending machinery. The girls learned cooking, washing, sewing, ironing, dressmaking, and some elementary nursing. All the students worked at the school or on the farms, putting to practical use the lessons learned in the schoolroom. The students who mastered these prerequisites were eligible to participate in Carlisle's pragmatic cultural experience, the "outing system." Carlisle took advantage of its proximity to farms by arranging for students to live with farm families for extended periods. Under contract with the school during this experience, the Indian youth absorbed White American culture through immersion, a method that remained impossible in the isolated boarding-school environment of most contemporary off-reservation schools (Trennert 1979).

Through an ingenious promotion scheme relying on lectures, pamphlets, and "before" and "after" photographs of the students, which illustrated their dramatic change in appearance (vol. 10:662). Pratt convinced the public that Indians could become educated and americanized (Malmsheimer 1985). By 1887 the number of Indian pupils enrolled in school had increased to 10,000 (Prucha 1976:288). Between 1881 and 1897 the number of employees in the educational field service expanded from 238 to 1,936, or from about 11 percent to almost 50 percent of all field service employees (Prucha 1984, 2: 717). Even though the total number of Indians enrolled in school remained a small percentage of the Indian population, it was, nonetheless, a significant dent. By 1900 Indians were enrolled in three types of federal education programs: 81 reservation boarding schools (fig. 5), 25 off-reservation boarding schools, and 147 reservation day schools.

Contract Schools

Although the influence of mission schools declined rapidly after the 1870s, the federal government employed the assistance of schools run by the religious denominations to supplement its growing network of day and boarding schools. Through this system, the Indian Bureau funded the construction of a schoolhouse, provided 160 acres of land, and paid the religious organization an annual fee of 75 dollars per pupil (Fritz 1963:58). The first contract school opened in 1869 on the Tulalip Reservation, Washington. Within a little over a decade, 22 boarding and 16 day schools were operating as contract schools (Prucha 1984, 2:709).

The contract school program appealed primarily to the Roman Catholics (fig. 6). Late entrants into the field of missionary schooling, the Catholics saw in the government offer a tremendous opportunity to compete with Protestant denominations on an equal basis. Their enthusiasm led to rapid expansion: by 1886 two-thirds of the 58 contract schools were under Roman Catholic direction. The Protestant denominations that had sponsored contract schools were unhappy with this, and in 1892 they withdrew. In 1897 Congress phased out the contract school. By 1900, contract schools had ceased to exist, although the Catholics succeeded in winning permission to use tribal funds for mission school support where tribes agreed (Beaver 1966:77–78, 136–138, 156–168; Prucha 1979; Fritz 1963:87–108; Keller 1983:208–209).

The Peace Policy

An even more novel experiment in direct Christian influence over governmental Indian policy emerged with Ulysses S. Grant's Peace Policy, 1869–1881. Although the Peace Policy was many-faceted, one of its most publicized aspects was the revolutionary concept that the Indian Bureau divide all the agencies among the various Christian denominations. Initially this plan was limited to Quaker-appointed agents, but Grant soon extended it to include other denominations. In the 1870s, therefore, every Indian agency fell under the guidance of at least one of about a dozen denominations and missionary organizations. Problems appeared immediately. The apportionment itself was erratic and illogical; the denominational response was less enthusiastic than expected; and the churches encountered tremendous difficulties in obtaining competent men and women willing to work at low salaries in isolated locations. Finally, the new agents were inexperienced and often had little control over the other staff, who were usually political appointees (Fritz 1963: 72–80, 88–93; Prucha 1976:46–63; Beaver 1966:134–168;

292

Natl. Arch.: top left, RG75-GS-6; top right, RG75-EXPM-1; bottom left, RG75-EXP-1D; center left, Mus. of Modern Art:Lincoln Kirstein, New York; Smithsonian, NAA: center right, 76-13460; bottom right, 75-13462.

Fig. 4. Off-reservation boarding schools. top left, Classroom at the Genoa Industrial School for Indian Youth, Genoa, Nebr. The students were predominately Sioux from Rosebud and Yankton agencies. Photograph by Louis R. Bostwick, 1910. top right, Students and superintendent James W. Balmer (standing) in front of the Pipestone Indian School, Pipestone, Minn. Photograph by C.E. Sogn Studio, about 1930. center left, History class at Hampton Institute, Hampton, Va. The federal government used the contract system to enroll Indians in this nonsectarian contract industrial training school in which most students were Black. Among other industrial crafts, students were taught to make harnesses. Around 1900, the students at Hampton filled an order for harnesses totaling more than $2,000 for the New York and Philadelphia department stores of John Wanamaker (ARCIA 1900, 1:14). Photograph by Frances B. Johnston, 1899–1900. center right, Male and female students in the steam laundry at Sherman Institute, Riverside, Calif. Photograph by H.T. Cory, 1914. bottom left, Art class at Phoenix Indian School, Ariz. Photograph by Messinger, June 1900. bottom right, Hopi students in sewing class, Phoenix Indian School. Photograph by H.T. Cory, 1914.

Keller 1983:46–71; Milner 1982). In spite of these obstacles, many of the agents performed their tasks well. Moreover, some of the denominations, such as the Episcopalians, Quakers, and Roman Catholics, were directly involved in schooling of the Indian youth in their assigned agencies (Beaver 1966:152–156). Certain individuals, including the Methodist James H. Wilbur at the Yakima Agency, established strong schooling programs (Keller 1983:159–160).

The educational and civilizing goals of the Peace Policy did not differ from those of the early nineteenth century. They were "to demolish the Indians' communal life, to wreck tribal identity and values, and to implant a different individualist ideology" (Keller 1983:152). Indian children enrolled in schools at this time—whether contract, government, or missionary supported—were taught the virtues held dear by nineteenth-century America.

Administration

In order to manage this burgeoning educational empire, which by 1888 included 126 boarding and 107 day schools with an enrollment of over 10,000 Indian children, the Bureau of Indian Affairs took a number of important steps in the final two decades of the century. First, in 1883, the Bureau appointed J.H. Hayworth as inspector of Indian schools. Within a decade, the Bureau's administrative hierarchy boasted a field superintendent of Indian schools assisted by six field superintendents who did in fact visit and inspect the schools. Hayworth's successor, John H. Oberly, organized the Education Division to direct the Bureau's activities in Indian education. Oberly (in ARCIA 1885) presented the first comprehensive discussion of federal Indian education. He advocated uniform school buildings, textbooks, and teaching methods for all the Indian tribes. He favored the use of boarding schools because they accommodated a greater number of Indian children, took them away from their homes, and provided them with training and discipline (fig. 4).

During the next decade the Bureau of Indian Affairs moved in several ways in the direction Oberly had advocated. In 1892 the Bureau adopted the merit system of appointment of teachers. Until that year the majority of school officials had been appointed for political or personal reasons. By 1896 all employees of Indian agencies except agents and day laborers were included in the civil service. In 1890 the first codification of rules for Indian schools appeared with a suggested course of study and a list of textbooks. These rules were designed for the boarding schools both on and off the reservation. The unpopular day schools were ignored.

Superintendent of Indian Schools Dr. William N. Hailmann in the mid-1890s suggested gradually replacing Indian schools with public schools. The Indian Service began to contract for this kind of education in 1891, offering a per capita payment directly to the individual school for each Indian pupil enrolled. This was to offset the loss of property tax income, since most Indian land was exempt from tax. Public school enrollment for Indians did not expand significantly in the early years, due in part to local anti-Indian sentiment, but by the 1920s it was accelerating rapidly. In 1930 public schools accounted for over half the Indian children enrolled in school (Schmeckebier 1927:225).

By 1900, therefore, the direction of Indian schooling had shifted dramatically. In about three decades it had moved from a limited partnership between the federal government and the churches to an expanding network of federally supported schools. These were supplemented by denominational schools and public schools that enrolled Indians.

Curriculum

The revival of interest in the day school came when Francis E. Leupp became commissioner of Indian affairs in 1904. The educational policy of the Bureau veered away from assimilationist goals, turning to the philosophy supported by Hampton Institute superintendent Samuel C. Armstrong, who had urged practical training for Indians who would remain on reservations. The shift in focus was ostensibly a pragmatic one. Critics argued that industrial schools were simply too expensive for the government to operate, and, contrary to Pratt's assertions, most students from off-reservation institutions failed to become assimilated Americans.

Under the guidance to Estelle Reel, superintendent of Indian education 1898–1910, a uniform curriculum was introduced. Under this program all students in Bureau schools would be taught the basic academic courses taught in White schools as well as sufficient vocational training

293

Fig. 5. Cleaning the grounds of the Seger Colony School, a reservation boarding school under the Cheyenne-Arapaho Agency in Okla. John H. Seger began a settlement at Colony with Cheyenne and Arapaho Indians in 1886 (Berthrong 1976:121). He began the school, his second among these tribes, in 1893. Crops grown on the school farm included wheat, oats, rye, corn, and garden vegetables. Herds of cattle, sheep, horses, and pigs were kept. The farm supplied the school with food; and some pigs and wool brought in a cash income. More than half of the school's staff members were Indians (ARCIA 1900, 1:498–501, 736). Photographed in 1900.

to prepare them for reservation life. Girls were taught domestic science by cooking, washing, sewing, and cleaning the schools. Boys were "given instruction in manual training" while they worked on the school farms raising food for the school or constructing buildings or making repairs on them or providing janitorial services on the school buildings. Institutional labor was thereby transformed into vocational training (fig. 4). In 1922 the Uniform Course of Study was revised to approximate more closely that given in the public schools. Day schools were expanded so that all of them included six grades, and reservation boarding schools were made uniform with eight grades. Nonreservation boarding schools began to offer high school work as a matter of course. In 1921 only Haskell Institute offered high school courses, but by 1929 six schools did. In 1928 almost 90 percent of all Indian children were enrolled in some school. About half of these were attending public schools, and about 10 percent, private and mission schools. Of those attending schools operated by the BIA, 27 percent were enrolled in reservation and off-reservation boarding schools and a much smaller percentage in day schools (Schmeckebier 1927:2, 18). Behind these statistics, education was limited. A large proportion of the children dropped out of school early. For those who remained, the education they received was poor. The educational level of the day schools was low, but it was better at the boarding schools where more advanced course work was offered. This course work was usually unrelated to the environment and culture from whence the students came.

1928–1945

By the 1920s it had become apparent that the misguided reforms of the late-nineteenth century had resulted in a disaster for the Indian people. The policies of Indian land allotment and federal Indian education had inflicted immeasurable damage. The 1920s movement for reform, spearheaded by John Collier, led to the investigation of conditions of Indian life. The publication of these findings, called the Meriam report (1928), was largely devoted to Indian education.

One of the chief objects of criticism was the BIA boarding school, which was viewed as a "grossly inadequate" institution (Meriam 1928:11). All the bleak conditions at the boarding schools came under attack: inadequate food, overcrowding, poor medical service, underpaid and ill-suited teachers, and harsh discipline. Many of these conditions resulted from a stringent budget. Others reflected the assimilationist goals. Still others were common to American education elsewhere. Hence, Estelle Reel's concept of a uniform curriculum was seen as unrealistic: it ignored local conditions and deliberately avoided Indian cultures. The vocational training program had evolved into mere student labor necessary for the schools to operate. Where schools did teach vocational training, the trades were either disappearing from the market or were taught at levels inadequate to secure a job. Thus the concept of training for reservation life had never fulfilled the goals anticipated in 1900. The problem of the runaway became the symbol of the failure of the boarding

294

Fig. 6. St. George's Boarding School, Puyallup Reservation, Wash. Terr. A Roman Catholic school under contract with the federal government, St. George's had an enrollment of 27, an average attendance of 17, and cost the government $1,398.98 in 1889 (ARCIA 1889:388–389). Photograph by Thomas H. Rutter, 1889.

school. The tragic stories of children who had died attempting to return home prompted the conclusion that pre-adolescent children should attend day schools near their homes.

The man largely responsible for composing the education section of the Meriam report, Will Carson Ryan, was named director of Indian education for the BIA in 1930. In his five years in office Ryan attempted to improve educational conditions by developing community schools on the reservations, alleviating poor conditions in the boarding schools themselves, and closing others. Equally important, in the public school realm he was responsible for the legislation that simplified the process by which schools were paid by the federal government for their Indian students. The Johnson O'Malley Act of 1934 (48 U.S. Stat. 596) enabled the states, rather than the individual school districts, to sign contracts with the Education Division of the BIA. Although this improved the funding procedure, the state school systems often used the money for general programs (Szasz 1974: 92–105). As a result, from the 1940s through the early 1970s public schools failed to develop special programs for Indian students.

Both Ryan and his successor, Willard Walcott Beatty, were influenced by the progressive education ideas of John Dewey, and both saw the need for close ties between school and community (Cremin 1961).

During the mid-1930s, the bureau offered to Indian youth the first outside effort in American history to provide schooling that acknowledged the diversity and significance of native cultures. Ryan gradually removed subjects such as algebra, geometry, and ancient history from the regular course of study and added rug weaving,

silver making, pottery making, and tribal history (Szasz 1974:32, 68–88). Beatty developed bilingual texts for Sioux, Navajo, and Pueblo children and began one of the earliest programs in the country for training teachers in the techniques of bilingual instruction. Like some of his predecessors, he understood the need to teach children in their own language (W.W. Beatty 1953).

Between 1933 and 1941 the enrollment at the community day schools almost tripled as nearly 100 new schools were opened. By 1941 the number of Indian children attending the community day schools surpassed the enrollment of 14,000 at the 49 boarding schools (fig. 7) (see Fischbacher 1974: 175–176).

The stringent discipline at some of the boarding schools were eased and the military routine removed. On the other hand, financial exigencies forced a continuation of the practice of student labor to support the schools.

Ryan and Beatty proved more successful in developing vocational training programs at the boarding schools. Except at Haskell Institute, which retained its secretarial training program, and Sherman Institute, Riverside, California, which taught shop courses, the boarding schools shifted emphasis from inadequate industrial training to more rural job-training geared to the needs of the area in which the school was situated (Szasz 1974: 65–66). The boarding schools in the Dakotas, Montana, and Wyoming, for example, concentrated on raising herds of cattle. The Oglala Community High School, Pine Ridge, South Dakota, became famous for the beef cattle and the fine horses that its students raised. The Chilocco School in Oklahoma controlled more than 8,000 acres of land providing instruction in its diversified program of farming. Land irrigation, dry farming, control of erosion, animal husbandry, and plant life were taught in the school. At the Phoenix School, students learned how to operate heavy farm machinery.

The introduction of Indian art into the course of study was successful, especially at the Santa Fe Boarding School, which benefited from a revival of interest in Pueblo and Navajo art (Brody 1971).

1945–1986

World War II touched and changed the lives of all Indians. In addition to those 24,000 who served in the U.S. armed forces, over 40,000 others left their homes to participate in war work. For many, this meant a significant increase in income, but equally important, it introduced new concepts and a greater appreciation for the value of schooling. These changes led Beatty, who remained director of education until 1952, to remold BIA education (W.W. Beatty 1953:11). The most dramatic illustration of this pragmatic shift came in the success of the Navajo Special Education Program, which provided basic schooling for 4,300 overage Navajo students, largely

295

top, Smithsonian, NAA: 45,216–E; Natl. Arch.: bottom, RG75-N-CAR-268, center, RG75-N-PU-480.

Fig. 7. Day schools on reservations. top, Seminole children on Big Cypress Reservation, Fla. Teacher Paul Birney instructs a class of 7 students in a traditional palmetto-thatch building. Photographed Dec. 6, 1940. center, Taos Indian Day School first-grade students, Taos Pueblo, N. Mex. Photograph by Peter Sekaer, 1940. bottom, Classroom chores at the Indian Service Day School on the Fallon Indian Reservation, Nev. Northern Paiute and Western Shoshone students contribute to school maintenance by cleaning their classroom. Photograph by Arthur Rothstein, 1940.

at Intermountain Inter-tribal School in Brigham City, Utah (fig. 8) (Coombs 1962). The goal of the program was to provide in five years the same education the child would have received in 10 or 12 years had he started school at the usual age. The students received vocational training to enable them to find jobs (Szasz 1974: 118–121).

Hildegard Thompson, director of Indian education in the BIA 1952–1965, continued the postwar policies begun by Beatty. Perhaps her greatest contribution lay in the accelerated effort to enroll thousands of Indian children not yet in school. This included a program to provide schooling for 13,000 Navajos unaffected by the Navajo Special Education Program (H. Thompson 1975) and about 1,000 Native Alaskans, many of whom were sent to Chilocco Indian School in Oklahoma.

To combat the rising dropout rate, the BIA began to sponsor summer-school programs in 1960. It was hoped that by raising the educational achievement level of the Indian children, more of them would remain in school. The summer sessions developed four kinds of program: academic schooling, work projects, field trips, and recreation. Academic work was given at all levels from preschool to college preparatory work.

The Branch of Education stressed post high school education to equip Indian youth to compete in the job market. To give the student the option of choosing college, BIA policy emphasized academic rather than vocational training, which was restricted in the last two years of high school. As a result of this policy the number of Indian college graduates tripled between 1961 and 1968: 66 to 181. Another important factor in this growth was the increase in financial support available to Indian students desiring to attend college. Federal assistance had been minimal until the Second World War. The Indian Reorganization Act of 1934 provided a $250,000 loan fund for higher education. By 1969 the BIA allocated $3 million for scholarship aid.

The mission of vocational studies became the responsibility of a few boarding schools. Haskell Institute, which became Haskell Indian Junior College in 1965, added to its course in business and secretarial training courses in electronics, the building trades, and service occupations. Chilocco School, which closed in 1980, offered vocational courses in dry cleaning, auto mechanics, welding, and printing. The Institute of American Indian Arts, which

Natl. Arch.: RG75-N-Intermountain School-10.
Fig. 8. Parade float built by students at the Intermountain Inter-tribal School, Brigham City, Utah. The float theme was "Leaders of Tomorrow." At the rear of the float are 3 students dressed in traditional Navajo clothing in front of a painting of a hogan. In front of the float were 5 students dressed in work clothes and a carpenter's apron; a school graduation robe and cap; a business suit; a soldier's uniform; and a nurse's uniform and cap. The float was part of the Brigham City Peach Day Parade. Photographed Sept. 7–8, 1951.

replaced the Santa Fe Boarding School in 1962, offered post high school work in painting, sculpture, jewelry, ceramics, design, and printing of textiles and creative writing (Aurbach, Fuchs, and Macgregor 1970).

Alaska

Federal government schooling for the Alaska Natives differed from that offered the rest of the Indian children. The administration of native schools in Alaska was assigned to the U.S. Office of Education in 1887 and was transferred to the BIA in 1931, although full control over the activities of the Alaska Natives was not assumed by the BIA until the Indian Reorganization Act was extended in 1936 to include Alaska.

In Alaska, the day school was the center of village organization. The laundries, baths, and workshops located in the school building were available for community use. Boarding schools offered high school level work giving technical training in handicrafts, mechanics, carpentry, sewing, and tanning. Commercial courses trained students to work in the cooperative stores. The course of study was geared to the local industries: fishing, reindeer raising, arts and crafts, and canning. All school personnel are on duty year round either in the villages or in the camps. The school follows the industrial migrants.

In 1942 there were 6,450 children of Alaska Natives

enrolled in government schools, 360 in public schools, and 136 in mission, private, and state schools. By 1972 the number of school-aged children in Alaska was estimated as 21,439. Of this number 6,080 were in government schools (two boarding schools and 53 day schools), 14,459 attending public schools, and 443 in other schools. The number of children aged 5 to 8 who were not attending any school was 454. The number of students over 18 attending various schools was 1,834.

Indian Self-Determination

In the mid-1960s over 90 percent of all Indian children were enrolled in school. By the early 1980s those in BIA schools accounted for only 15 percent of this number; most of the remaining 85 percent were in public schools; only a small percent were in mission schools (Szasz 1983: xi). Indian schooling had, therefore, witnessed another major shift—from BIA domination to that of the public school.

By the mid-1960s the BIA had established Indian advisory boards for almost all its schools and begun contracting with Indian groups to operate their own schools. A new form of "contract school" had come into being. Among the early experiments, two of the Navajo ventures—Rough Rock Demonstration School, Arizona, and Navajo Community College, Tsaile, Arizona—achieved success (vol. 10:665–671) (Coombs 1972; Erickson and Schwartz 1969; Szasz 1974:169–180). Other schools followed their lead and managed to achieve Indian control despite the difficulties of acquiring financial support (Clifford 1973). These included Borrego Pass Day School, New Mexico; Wyoming Indian High School, Wyoming; and tribally controlled community colleges such as Sinte Gleska, South Dakota; Standing Rock, North Dakota; and Fort Berthold, North Dakota (Szasz 1983:xii).

During this era when Indian leaders were advocating self-determination, Indian education was the subject of several studies. The Senate report known as the Kennedy report (U.S. Congress. Senate. Special Subcommittee on Indian Education 1969) led to a national debate on Indian schooling. The National Association for the Advancement of Colored People Legal Defense and Educational Fund (1971) critique of Indian education added to the controversy. At the same time, the U.S. Office of Education was conducting its own investigation of the subject (Fuchs and Havighurst 1972). For a survey of the literature see B. Berry (1969).

The years between 1965 and 1978 witnessed the passage of the most significant legislation on Indian education in American history. The thrust of this legislation was to provide a greater Indian voice in Indian schooling. Since the majority of Indian children were in public school, the new laws focused on developing the

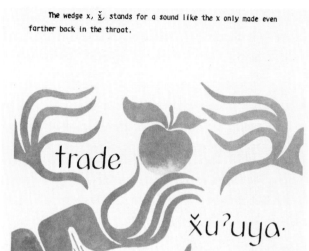

The wedge x, x̌ stands for a sound like the x only made even farther back in the throat.

Practice words :

xaʔałapix̌ (steamer clam)   x̌a·ya (far)
x̌ax̌apx̌t (lecturing)   x̌aša·bis (bone)

Makah Cultural and Research Center, Neah Bay, Wash.

Fig. 9. Page from the *Makah Alphabet Book* (Makah Cultural and Research Center 1979). The book is a text for all Makah language classes taught by the Makah Cultural and Research Center on Neah Bay Reservation, Wash. The classes are for children in kindergarten through high school in the public school, as well as the tribally managed Headstart and adult education programs. The language program has been funded by a National Endowment for the Humanities grant and the Office of Indian Education in the Department of Education. Illustration by Scott Tyler and Chris Walsh.

Indian voice in public school programs funded by the federal government for Indian children. Under Title I of the Elementary and Secondary Education Act of 1965 (79 U.S. Stat. 27) Indian children in public school qualified for special benefits as "children of low-income families." This legislation increased the amount of money available to schools already reimbursed for Indian children through the "federally impacted area" legislation (P.L. 81–874 and P.L. 81–815) of the 1950s and the Johnson-O'Malley Act (Szasz 1974:181–183). Of all the public school programs affecting Indian children only Title I of the Elementary and Secondary Education Act had provided an opportunity, albeit a limited one, for parental involvement and local control. As a result, these special funds, which totaled about $630 million in 1969 and which Congress intended for Indian pupils, generally were spent for all the pupils in a school district (Szasz 1974: 185).

The Indian Education Act of 1972 (86 U.S. Stat. 235, 334–345) mandated parental and community participation in the programs engendered by the impact aid laws. It also encouraged programs that stressed culturally relevant and bilingual curriculum materials (fig. 9). Finally, it established the Office of Indian Education in the Department of Education, directed by a deputy commissioner of education; and it created a National Advisory Council on Indian Education to review applications for grants under the new act. The Indian Self-Determination and Education Assistance Act of 1975 (88 U.S. Stat. 2203) introduced a revolutionary tactic: it incorporated regulations, drafted by Indian leaders, that shifted the traditional control of Johnson-O'Malley programs from public school districts to Indians by direct contracting with Indian groups. For an Indian critique of American Indian education past and present see T. Thompson (1978).

In 1979 there were 43,571 Indian students enrolled in 68 boarding schools, 106 day schools, and 15 dormitories, all BIA-operated; 6,412 Indian students in 33 contract schools; and 171,290 pupils in Johnson-O'Malley funded public schools, for a total of 221,271 (U.S. Bureau of Indian Affairs. Office of Indian Education Programs 1981:1).

By 1985, BIA education programs and operations totaled $273 million, which constituted the largest item in the BIA budget. In 1984 the BIA funded 206 educational facilities, including 72 day schools, 49 on-reservation boarding schools, 8 off-reservation boarding schools, 62 tribally contracted schools, and 15 dormitories (Lovett et al. 1984:14). The BIA also provided grants to 19 tribally controlled community colleges under the Tribally Controlled Community College Assistance Act of 1978 (92 U.S. Stat. 1325). In 1984 over 3,300 Indian students were enrolled in these colleges (Lovett et al. 1984:14–16). In 1983 Sinte Gleska became "the first Indian college in the country to receive accreditation on the 4-year baccalaureate level." A few months later, the Oglala Lakota College, Kyle, South Dakota, also received accreditation (fig. 10) (U.S. Department of the Interior and U.S. Department of Health and Human Services 1984:12).

In 1986 the BIA operated three postsecondary schools: the Haskell Indian Junior College, Lawrence, Kansas, with some 1,000 enrolled Indian students; the Institute of American Indian Arts in Santa Fe, New Mexico, with about 200 students; and the Southwestern Indian Polytechnic Institute in Albuquerque, New Mexico, with some 700 students (U.S. Bureau of Indian Affairs 1986:7). Noting that "the need for off-reservation boarding schools has declined with the development of schools on the reservations" (Lovett et al. 1984:16), in the late 1970s-early 1980s the BIA closed some of its off-reservation boarding schools such as Concho, Fort Sill, and Chilocco in Oklahoma, Stewart in Nevada, and Mount Edgecumbe in Alaska. Despite the protest of Indian students and faculty, Intermountain Inter-tribal School in Utah was closed in 1984. The history of Indian boarding schools is the subject of a video by David Kendall (1985). The

298

Fig. 10. Graduation ceremony at Oglala Lakota College, Kyle, S. Dak. A medicine wheel and an eagle feather or an eagle plume are presented to male and female students, respectively, with their degrees. Carol Shangreaux Martin is being congratulated by Frank Fools Crow. Chartered in 1971, the college offers bachelor's degrees in education, human services, business administration with an emphasis on small business development and tribal management; associate degrees include Lakota studies, nursing, business administration, general studies, human services, education, criminal justice, and applied sciences; vocational education certificates in meat cutting, construction trades, and wildlife and resource management; and high school equivalency diplomas. A BIA police academy operates at the college. Degree students are required to complete a minimum of 15 hours in Lakota subjects. To meet effectively the needs of the Oglala Sioux, the college is decentralized into 9 district centers and is controlled by a board of 12 tribal members. Photograph by Tom Casey, 1982.

boarding school experience of west-central Oklahoma Indians is discussed by McBeth (1983).

An important development in Indian education was the passage in 1968 of Title VII-Bilingual Education Act (81 U.S. Stat. 816), amended in 1974 and 1978, providing financial assistance to state and local educational agencies to meet the educational needs of children of limited English-speaking abilities. Section 706 of the 1968 act and Section 722 of the 1974 and 1978 amendments dealt specifically with bilingual education for Indian children (see Andersson and Boyer 1978:227, 234–235). The 1978 Bilingual Education Act (92 U.S. Stat. 2143) expanded the eligibility for Title VII funding to Indian students from "home environments where a language other than English has had 'significant impact' on their English proficiency" (Leap 1981:228; see also Leap 1978). As a result of sensitive legislation and tribal interest in language maintenance (Leap 1981), the number of American Indian bilingual education programs funded by the Title VII Office of Bilingual Education, Department of Health and Human Services, has grown steadily since 1968. In 1976, the Title VII Office funded 27 Indian language programs

in 32 schools in 13 states; in 1979, 30 Indian language programs in 55 schools in 16 states. By 1986, the number of projects had grown to 89 in 18 states, covering 55 Indian languages and 14,384 enrolled Indian students (D'Alan Huff, communication to editors 1987).

Although bilingual-bicultural education constituted a minor component of BIA education programs, the BIA Office of Indian education has administered a number of bilingual programs under Title I (supplementary programs) and Title VII proper. One of the most successful bilingual programs has been the Primary Eskimo Program, at Bethel Agency, Alaska, serving Yupik-speaking children. The program has been in operation since 1970, providing bilingual-bicultural instruction for Eskimo children and promoting community involvement in the classroom and school meetings; the Yupik Primary Eskimo Program is a maintenance-oriented bilingual program.

The issues and policies of bilingual education were studied by scholars and educators (see Andersson and Boyer 1978). Battiste, Bond, and Fagan (1975) discuss bilingual-bicultural projects. Evans and Abbey (1979)   *299* compiled a bibliography of language arts materials for Native Americans. D. Bradford (1974) and Leap (1978, 1981) analyzed American Indian bilingual education and language maintenance. Spolsky (1978) reviewed several Title VII Indian bilingual education programs. Earlier literature on Indian bilingual education is cited in a bibliography on American Indian education compiled by Nafziger (1970). Two comprehensive bibliographies on Indian education are listed in Prucha (1977:240–273, 1982:71–87).

Indian Rights Movement Until 1887

ROBERT W. MARDOCK

The Colonial Period

Spain was the first colonial power to come into extensive contact with the American Indians. The military conquest was followed by a cultural subjugation through the encomienda system and the Franciscan, Dominican, and Jesuit missions. The subsequent harsh exploitation and violation of basic human rights by the encomenderos aroused the first Indian rights movement in North America. In 1511 Antonio de Montesinos, a Dominican friar, publicly protested the mistreatment of the Indians and demanded that their right to freedom from forced labor and tribute be respected. Three years later a Dominican bishop, Bartolomé de Las Casas, began a lifelong career on behalf of the God-given "natural rights" of the Indians. Las Casas's (1552) critical analysis of Spanish Indian policy helped to bring about the enactment of Spain's New Laws of the Indies of 1542. The laws provided for both a gradual abolition of the encomiendas and for the protection of Indian rights and marked the beginnings of a more humane Spanish-Indian policy (Hanke 1965:17–21, 174). Henceforth the Indian rights proponents in all the North American colonies would be essentially Indian policy reformers attempting to bring the legalization of what they believed to be the natural rights of the aboriginals: life, liberty, and property, and finally, the right to progress from primitive savagery to the European form of civilization.

In California during the eighteenth century the Indians were reduced to virtual serfdom under the mission system. That condition, together with loss of land rights throughout New Spain, came under increasing criticism from humanitarians. But a major Indian rights movement did not get underway until after 1800 when Father Miguel Hidalgo, pastor of Dolores, Texas, and Spanish liberals demanded that all the rights of man be granted to the Indians. In 1810, a series of reform laws accorded equal rights, including citizenship and land ownership, to the Indians of New Spain. However, the application of the reforms was delayed by the inability of many Indians to adjust to the new life, and by mission opposition, so that the majority of Indians failed to achieve equality under Spanish rule or under the liberal policy of the Mexican Republic (Bannon 1970; C.A. Hutchinson 1969).

The French had far-flung economic and religious contacts with the Indian tribes of the Saint Lawrence and Mississippi river regions, but unlike the Spanish and English, acculturation was limited. Property rights were generally recognized, but the conditions to inspire an Indian rights movement did not develop. On a smaller scale the same can be said for the Dutch in New Netherlands and the neighboring Swedish colonists.

In contrast, the expansion of the more densely populated English colonies during the seventeenth and eighteenth centuries brought a broadening confrontation with the Indians and a concurrent concern with Indian rights. In Virginia in 1609 the Anglican Rev. Robert Gray defended Indian land ownership, a position that culminated in a general policy of recognition of their land rights. In 1619 an act forbidding oppression of the Indians was passed by the Virginia assembly, and in 1646, a treaty with the Powhatan Confederacy provided for the lawful redress of Indian grievances and secured their land rights by means of an Indian reservation (Craven 1949: 76–81, 143, 363).

The Puritans of Massachusetts Bay Colony supported missionary activities with the goal of complete conversion to the New England way of life, and under Rev. John Eliot's leadership notable progress was made. But the rights involved were limited to property ownership, education, and church membership (Vaughan 1965:261, 307, 308). The Massachusetts Bay Company charter recognized Indian land ownership, although in 1629, Gov. John Winthrop and the General Court maintained that all untilled land in America was legally vacant until a deed was obtained based upon a grant by the company. This doctrine aroused a controversy with Puritan minister Roger Williams, who questioned the Crown authority to award Indian lands to the colonies without prior agreement by the possessors (P. Miller 1962:2–5). But even though Massachusetts prevailed in the dispute with Roger Williams, the colonists, including Governor Winthrop, abandoned the official position after 1633 and purchased lands directly from recognized Indian owners (Jennings 1971a:521, 522, 536).

Later in the century, Samuel Sewall, a prominent Massachusetts judge and landholder and an official in the Society for the Propagation of the Gospel in New England, helped to foster a more enlightened Indian

301

policy in Massachusetts. He opposed legislation harmful to the Indians, contributed land and funds to facilitate their education and conversion, and insisted that land reserves be set aside for them that were protected from encroachment (Strandness 1967:106–108).

William Penn's three letters to the Indians of Pennsylvania in 1681 and 1682 embodied the colonial period's most advanced concepts of Indian rights. All land transactions and trade relations were to be conducted in a spirit of brotherly love, friendship, and fundamental justice. The Indians were to be protected by equitable laws and a court system utilizing mixed juries of both races (Janney 1970:164–170, 185–186). Penn's principles, applied in a series of treaties between 1682 and 1701, helped to preserve peace in Pennsylvania in subsequent years. Penn came to be held in high esteem by the Indians and by the Indian rights workers of the nineteenth century (Beatty 1939:266–273). A half-century later, Quaker John Woolman engaged in a spirited defense of Indian land rights, to him the key to the Indian problem. A solution would come, he believed, when they were civilized and christianized, by which he meant adopting the ways of their Euro-American neighbors (Woolman 1961:244).

The National Period

Woolman's hopes were dashed during the horrors of the French and Indian war, which, along with Pontiac's Rebellion and the American Revolution, would cost much of the remaining enlightened sympathy for the natives. The negative reaction was more universal than that to the seventeenth-century conflicts, and both missionary and Indian rights work suffered for a time. Despite the trend, humanitarian views prevailed at governmental levels as evidenced by the intent of the Northwest Ordinance of 1787 (1 U.S. Stat. 51–53) to protect the Indians in "their property, rights and liberty" and by the new federal policy, a mixture of humanitarian ideals and pragmatic methods that was strongly influenced by Thomas Jefferson (Sheehan 1973; Prucha 1962).

During the decades following the War of 1812, the principal means by which Euro-American civilization was advanced among the western tribes was through missionary efforts. Indian rights were largely a by-product of the labors of missionary workers who usually supported the Indians, especially when land rights were at stake. These rights were being threatened on a large scale in face of the massive westward movement.

Jedidiah Morse, Congregational clergyman and geographer, visited many of the western tribes for President James Monroe in 1820 and 1821 and reported that the Indians should have the right to an education and ultimately to the "enjoyment of all the rights and privileges of freemen, and citizens of the United States" (1822:80). Upon his recommendation the American

Society for Promoting the Civilization and General Improvement of the Indian Tribes Within the United States was formed in Washington, D.C. With control vested in representatives of federal, state, and territorial governments and leading church denominations, it was to serve as a national body under which Indian rights would be preserved. The society failed to become an effective body but, significantly, Morse's report gave a qualified recommendation for the removal of the eastern tribes to areas farther west. The government's adoption of a removal policy in 1825 divided Indian sympathizers. Some were convinced that survival was dependent on removal, while others insisted that removal was a violation of Indian land and treaty rights. The controversy captured national attention during the 1830s, even to briefly divert William Lloyd Garrison from his antislavery crusade to oppose removal. Tennessee Congressman David Crockett voted against removal, and composer John Howard Payne and Jeremiah Evarts, secretary of the American Board of Commissioners for Foreign Missions labored at length in defense of Cherokee land rights. But it would be the Cherokee Indian missionaries, led by Samuel Worcester and Elizur Butler, who aroused popular sympathy for the Indians and encouraged the Cherokees to battle for their land rights before the Supreme Court (Dippie 1982; McNickle 1949).

Following the failure of the Court fight, Rev. Worcester moved to Indian Territory with the Cherokees where he was joined by Samuel Houston, ex-governor of Tennessee and, in 1830, ambassador from the Cherokee Nation to the United States. Later, as president of the Texas Republic and as U.S. senator, Houston consistently spoke for Indian rights, opposed encroachment on Indian lands, and in 1854 objected to the Kansas-Nebraska bill because it made no provisions for the Indian inhabitants (James 1929:384).

By the 1850s the Indian rights question was nearly submerged by the antislavery movement, although a few Indian sympathizers were agitating for a reform of Indian policy. Among them were Henry Benjamin Whipple, Episcopalian bishop for Minnesota (fig. 1), and John Beeson, an Illinois farmer and abolitionist who became interested in the plight of the western tribes when he migrated to Oregon in 1853. Both men became life-long champions of Indian rights in careers that spanned three decades. During the war years, Whipple and Beeson were able to enlist President Abraham Lincoln's support for reforms and to inspire Congress to initiate an experimental reform program in California.

The population movement into the frontier West, during and following the Civil War, and the resulting widespread Indian warfare aroused government officials and humanitarians to take a new look at Indian policy. Government peace commissioners who negotiated with the hostile Plains tribes in 1867 criticized congressmen,

Fig. 1. Rev. Henry B. Whipple, members of the Northwest Indian Commission, and associates. second from right, Paul Beaulieu, interpreter; fourth from right, probably John G. Morrison, chief of Indian police at White Earth Reservation, Minn.; center, Whipple; far right, John Beaulieu, farmer. Others in the photograph but not specifically identified are: Commissioners John V. Wright of Tenn. and Charles Larrabee of the BIA, White Earth Agent T.J. Sheehan, reporter J.W. Wing, and missionary Isaac Houlgate. The commission was formed to negotiate with the Chippewa Indians of the White Earth Reservation for changes in their reservation through the modification of treaties and the consolidation at White Earth and Red Lake agencies of all Minn. Chippewa and to negotiate with the Indians of Mont.; of Ft. Berthold, N. Dak.; and certain bands of Spokane, Pend d'Oreilles, and Coeur d'Alene Indians in Wash. and Idaho Terr. for the sale or cession of portions of their reservations, and their removal to and consolidation on other reservations (ARCIA 1886:xxxv, 170, 1887:xxvii–xxxii, 129). Photograph by Robinson and Hopper, probably at White Earth Reservation, Aug.–Oct., 1886.

church leaders, and humanitarians for overlooking the mistreatment of the Indians. The commissioners concluded that the civilization of the Indians and the protection of tribal land rights would end frontier warfare (Indian Peace Commission in ARCIA 1868:47).

The Post-Civil War Era

Challenged by the peace commission's report and inspired by the success of the anti-slavery movement, many experienced reformers turned their talents to the cause of Indian policy reform. One declared that the time had come when, "without intermitting our vigilant watch over the rights of black men, it is our duty to arouse the nation to a sense of its guilt concerning the red men" (Child 1868: 15). A few months later Peter Cooper and other prominent New Yorkers, among them Henry Ward Beecher, formed the United States Indian Commission to bring public pressure upon Congress for reform legislation. In Philadelphia the Universal Peace Union, under the leadership of Alfred H. Love, turned its attention to the Indians. Several well-known antislavery veterans, among them Lucretia Mott, Gerrit Smith, and Aaron Powell, worked with Love to memorialize Congress and write letters advocating reforms to President-elect Ulysses Grant. Wendell Phillips vigorously denounced the "extermination policy" advocated by the Army and the frontier settlers. A fierce opponent of racism, and a militant champion of human rights, Phillips stirred up the Indian question, first in Boston, then throughout the nation (W.

Phillips 1870, 1892).

Following the election of 1868, two Quaker committees met with President-elect Grant and gained his support for reform. By March 1869, when Grant took office, the foundation had been laid for a new federal Indian program (Priest 1942; Fritz 1963). Under the label of Peace Policy or Quaker Policy, it incorporated the current ideas on the rights of the Indians, which were to be guarded by church-selected agents and a nonpolitical Board of Indian Commissioners. The primary objective was the civilization of the tribes through education and religious instruction, with full citizenship and cultural assimilation as a final goal. The Indians were to be placed on reservations and cared for by the national government until they had become economically self-supporting and had gained equal political rights (Prucha 1976; Tatum 1899).

A majority of the Indian rights workers believed in the validity of education and religious instruction on the premise that human nature was essentially the same in all races and that the only significant difference between the Indian and White people was in the stage of cultural development. The progressive cultural evolutionary theory held that the Red race would advance in time, and the reformers believed that the process could be accelerated through proper instruction (Mardock 1971).

Many western tribes, among them the Sioux, Ute, Cheyenne, and Apache, strongly opposed the radical cultural changes inherent in the civilization program, and government attempts at enforcement led to periodic warfare. The Canadian government experienced similar

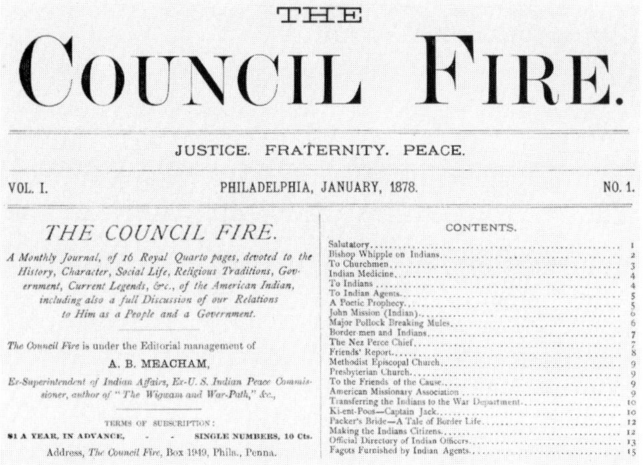

THE

COUNCIL FIRE.

JUSTICE. FRATERNITY. PEACE.

VOL. I. PHILADELPHIA, JANUARY, 1878. NO. 1.

THE COUNCIL FIRE.

A Monthly Journal, of 16 Royal Quarto pages, devoted to the History, Character, Social Life, Religious Traditions, Government, Current Legends, &c., of the American Indian, including also a full Discussion of our Relations to Him as a People and a Government.

The Council Fire is under the Editorial management of

A. B. MEACHAM,

Ex-Superintendent of Indian Affairs, Ex-U. S. Indian Peace Commissioner, author of "The Wigwam and War-Path," &c.,

TERMS OF SUBSCRIPTION:

$1 A YEAR, IN ADVANCE, - - SINGLE NUMBERS, 10 Cts.

Address, *The Council Fire*, Box 1949, Phila., Penna.

CONTENTS.

Smithsonian, John Wesley Powell Lib.

Fig. 2. Section of the front page of the first edition of *The Council Fire,* a journal edited by Alfred B. Meacham and dedicated to Indian rights.

opposition to its reservation-civilization policy. In 1885, a rebellion involving the Canadian Plains tribes led by Louis Riel was repressed by troops ending that nation's most serious outbreak in which Indian treaty rights were involved (McInnis 1969:398–400). The Alaska natives, peripheral to the center of Indian-White contact, merited only occasional Indian rights concern prior to 1887.

The Indian rights groups supported the Peace Policy in the face of political and sectional opposition throughout the 1870s, although many objected to the use of the Army as a policing agency, blaming it for the continued warfare, but they particularly abhorred the enforced removal of tribes to distant reservations. Opposition to removal did not coalesce until 1879 when the Ponca Indians, who were ordered to move from Nebraska to Indian Territory, attempted to return to their homeland. The ensuing controversy brought author Helen Hunt Jackson into the Indian rights movement. Her public criticism of Secretary of the Interior Carl Schurz, whom she blamed for the government's refusal to compromise, and her indictment of past Indian policy (H.H. Jackson 1881) helped to publicize the Indian rights cause and bring a satisfactory solution of the Ponca question.

The Ponca case, together with the Nez Perce War in 1877 and the Meeker Massacre among the Ute in 1878 (vol. 11:534) stimulated renewed public interest in the Indian problem and spawned a second major Indian rights movement. A new group of reformers came into the Indian rights ranks, guided by the social gospel and differing from their predecessors in that they put less emphasis on the spiritual and more on the material and mental progress of the Indians. The doors to civilization, they were convinced, were the schools, individual ownership of land, and the rights of citizenship.

Among the new Indian rights groups was the Women's National Indian Association of Philadelphia founded in 1879, the Indian Rights Association founded in 1882, and the National Indian Defense Association. To coordinate the Indian rights organizations, Albert K. Smiley held a meeting of workers at Lake Mohonk, New York, in 1883, the first of a series of annual conferences that brought a combined weight to bear on the government for legislation of reform proposals (Partington 1911:27–29; Burgess 1971). A general agreement on methods and goals, more bipartisan and national responsibility, and an emphasis on cooperation created a spirit of unity during the 1880s that further distinguished the new phase from the earlier one. Nevertheless, differences over goals and tactics persisted, most forcefully expressed by Alfred B. Meacham and Thomas A. Bland, founders of the National Indian Defense Association, who opposed assimilation and the destruction of tribal organization (fig. 2) (Washburn 1975).

Citizenship had long been a goal of the Indian rights advocates. Alfred H. Love and his Universal Peace Union believed that citizenship was the best hope for Indian progress. Indian congressmen could then present their side of the legislative issues, the right to vote would give Indians political power, and in turn they would resort to the ballot rather than violence to obtain justice. Wendell Phillips insisted that the only valid guarantee for individual Indian rights was citizenship, and Aaron Powell maintained that citizenship was concomitant with the "pure gospel of human rights." Government policy saw citizenship as the capstone in the civilization program, and the majority of Indian rights workers accepted this viewpoint. In 1884 the case of *Elk* v. *Wilkins* (112 U.S. 94), submitted to the courts by the Ponca Indian Committee to determine the citizenship status of the Indians under the Fourteenth Amendment to the Constitution, was decided by the Supreme Court. The decision that the Indians were not within the jurisdiction of the Amendment was a setback to the reformers, but the Court did uphold the power of Congress to confer citizenship on the Indians (Mardock 1971:217, 218).

In 1880 the Board of Indian Commissioners declared that the only solution to the Indian rights problem was the distribution of reservation lands to individual Indians with inalienable title. Several bills incorporating these provisions failed to pass Congress, but by 1885 the belief that individual ownership of land was the best path to self-support and civil rights for the Indians had acquired sufficient backing for the passage of Sen. Henry Dawes's severalty bill in 1887 (24 U.S. Stat. 388). The Dawes bill included provisions for Indian citizenship, together with the allocation of reservation lands to individual tribal members and the sale of the surplus lands to settlers. Most Indian rights workers accepted the Dawes Act as a practical solution to a longstanding problem, convinced that the Indians were on the road to assimilation into the nation's economic and political systems (Washburn 1975).

Indian Rights Movement, 1887–1973

HAZEL WHITMAN HERTZBERG

The Indian rights movement, which won its first great legislative victory in the Dawes Severalty Act of 1887 (24 U.S. Stat. 388), established a pattern that has since appeared before each major change in governmental Indian policy: the formation of new organizations representing new forces that reflect more general reform concerns; the forging of a consensus on the causes of Indian rights violations and the remedies to be applied; and the mobilization of public support through astute use of the media including a symbolic case epitomizing the beliefs of the reformers. The roots of the movement stemmed from the work of earlier rights advocates and the anti-slavery, peace, temperance, and civil service reform movements and the reform Christianity that helped to nourish them all.

In the 1880s the symbolic case was the forced removal of the Poncas to Indian Territory and their tragic attempts to return to their homeland. The Poncas, a peaceable farming tribe friendly to Christianity and willing to adopt the White man's ways, were ideally suited to represent the concerns of the emerging movement. Ponca Chief Standing Bear and Bright Eyes (Susette LaFlesche), an educated Omaha woman, addressed thousands of Americans in meetings held in great halls and small parlors throughout the country. An extensive reform literature and a campaign in the secular and religious press publicized a series of Indian rights violations that went far beyond the Ponca case to the heart of fundamental governmental policy.

By 1887 when the Dawes Act was passed, the reformers had arrived at a consensus. The chief obstacles to Indian progress, they believed, were avaricious Whites, an often corrupt and paternalistic government that did not hesitate to ignore treaty rights, and "the tribal relation" that kept Indians in a backward condition unable either to defend themselves or to advance. A new policy was needed.

The eventual goal of the new policy was the complete assimilation of Indians as individuals into American society and their full participation in the life of a democratic nation. The reformers believed that this transformation required Indian acquisition of Christianity, secure Indian ownership of private property through division of tribal lands, dissolution of the tribes, citizenship, extension to Indians of equal protection of the laws, honest and competent administration, and an education that would equip Indians to become self-reliant, productive members of the society into which they would be absorbed. But while united as to goals, the reformers differed as to the rapidity with which change could take place, the measures to which Indian consent was essential, and the need for honoring existing treaties and agreements.

The standard bearers of the Indian rights movement were three new national organizations buttressed by a number of local groups. The earliest was an interdenominational women's group founded in 1879 in protest against treaty violations. The Women's National Indian Association, led by Mary L. Bonney and Amelia S. Quinton, was dedicated to treaty-keeping, education, and eventually to missionary and social welfare activities. Their campaign to arouse public opinion and to influence the president and the Congress helped to lay the basis for major reforms (Women's National Indian Association 1883–1901).

The Indian Rights Association, founded in 1882 by Herbert S. Welsh and Henry Pancoast, quickly became the most important of the rights organizations. Advocating education, legal protection, and the division of Indian lands in severalty, the Association early established organizational patterns that helped to ensure its continuing leadership and public credibility. These included regular investigation of conditions in "Indian country," a wide correspondence network, a Washington office to monitor legislation and the administration of Indian affairs, a committee of lawyers to aid in drawing up legislation and handling legal cases, and an effective program of public information (Indian Rights Association 1884–1935).

The third organization, the Lake Mohonk Conference of the Friends of the Indian, was first convened in 1883 by Albert K. Smiley, a Quaker member of the federal Board of Indian Commissioners, and thereafter met annually until 1917. The Lake Mohonk Conferences provided a forum for the diverse forces in the movement and a mechanism for arriving at consensus through debate and the adoption of an annual platform. To the meetings came the older humanitarian reformers, the new rights organization members, academics, government officials, and influential persons only tangentially concerned with

Indian rights.

The fight for the passage of the Dawes Act demonstrated the ambiguous character of the reform consensus. Lyman Abbott, the editor of the *Christian Outlook,* an influential leader in general social reform and a man with little experience in Indian affairs, and Gen. Samuel C. Armstrong, the head of Hampton Institute, Norfolk, Virginia, were the chief advocates of compulsory allotment. The Indian Rights Association, the Women's National Indian Association, and a number of individuals favored a voluntary, graduated approach. These differences were submerged in the fight for the Dawes bill, but they often resurfaced in the years that followed (Washburn 1975a).

The only national White organization that opposed the Dawes Act was the National Indian Defense Association. The association sympathized with tribal cultures and favored gradual acculturation through education (Bain 1885; Bland 1906). It did not long survive the passage of the Dawes Act.

Both the dominant and the minor wings of the Indian rights movement were White. It is difficult to ascertain Indian opinion of the allotment policy, although there are indications that some Indians favored it in practice if not in principle. The Five Civilized Tribes, which had developed an acculturated tribal system of communal land holding and education and political institutions, were sufficiently powerful to exempt themselves—temporarily—from its operations (Priest 1942). Most tribes were in no position to act in concert for their own defense, although some attempted in vain to secure the help of the Five Civilized Tribes (Hertzberg 1971).

The Dawes Act provided for the division of tribal lands in severalty at presidential discretion, allotment to individual Indians with a 25-year trust period, and citizenship as soon as the allotment was made. The Indian Rights Association warned in 1887 that its passage opened "a transition of indefinite duration." Although the legal outcome—full citizenship—was reasonably certain, the social outcome was not.

The principle of allotment as embodied in the Dawes Act remained for almost four decades an article of faith for most Indian rights advocates. The severe problems that developed almost immediately were not inherent in the act, they believed, but rather due to faulty administration. Therefore, the organization defended allottee rights and upheld the sacredness of treaties and agreements, attacked the taking of Indian land without Indian consent, opposed incursions on Indian water and mineral rights, fought for civil service reform, the removal of corrupt or incompetent personnel, and the retention of excellent men and women regardless of party.

To most reformers, education to equip Indians for their new life was the cornerstone of an enlightened social outcome. They preferred that Indian children attend public rather than Indian schools. Gradually they came to favor day schools over boarding schools. The Indian Rights Association fought with only partial success to end contracting with religious bodies for the education of Indian children, basing their opposition on the separation of church and state.

Indian citizenship remained an area of controversy. The Association strenuously but unsuccessfully opposed the Burke Act of 1906 (34 U.S. Stat. 182–183), whose effect was to postpone Indian acquisition of citizenship.

The Association also handled numerous rights issues not so directly involved with the Dawes Act. Following the massacre at Wounded Knee in 1891 the Association published a stinging analysis by its field investigator that laid the major, although not sole, responsibility on government ineptitude and broken promises and called for remedial measures. The organization successfully opposed the forced removal of several tribes. It was unsuccessful in its attempt to secure the admission of the Indian Territory occupied by the Five Civilized Tribes as a separate Indian state, to be called Sequoyah, which the Indians maintained had been guaranteed them. Other causes included the protection of water and mineral rights.

Thus the Association frequently upheld legal rights of the tribes to whose dissolution they were also committed. It was the chief friend in court of the Indian and the chief guide to Whites who wished to help them. Over the years the Association became in practice somewhat more sympathetic to reservation life. But their sympathies had severe limitations. In tribal fights between conservatives and progressives, they unhesitatingly supported the progressives. Their hostility to the tribal relation continued: the tribes—although not individual Indians—must finally and irrevocably vanish.

Not until the progressive period was well underway did an Indian wing of the rights movement emerge. It was the result of a small but growing English-speaking Indian middle class; a general, if gradual, acculturation of the tribes; the interminable confusion over the legal status of tribes and individuals; the popularity of the idea of an Indian race transcending tribal boundaries; and the rising tide of progressive reform. These factors made a secular, national pan-Indian movement possible for the first time.

The impetus for the Society of American Indians came from the work of a White sociologist, Fayette A. McKenzie of Ohio State University, who believed that a "race leadership" could build a "race consciousness" on behalf of "all lines of progress and reform, for the welfare of the Indian race in particular, and humanity in general" (Hertzberg 1971:36). The organization was founded in Columbus, Ohio, in 1911 by Dr. Charles A. Eastman (Sioux), Rev. Sherman Coolidge (Arapahoe), Charles E. Daganett (Peoria), Laura Cornelius (Oneida), and Thomas L. Sloan (Omaha). Another leading Indian involved in the preliminary negotiations, Dr. Carlos

Montezuma (Yavapai) initially stayed away, fearful that the Indian Bureau covertly controlled the organization. Among the younger founders were two men strongly influenced by social science: Henry Roe Cloud (Winnebago), a Yale graduate and minister, and Arthur C. Parker (Seneca), an archeologist and ethnologist. All the leaders had spent their childhoods in their tribes and had extensive familial and other connections with the White world. Most had attended White colleges. None was a "typical" representative of his tribe, but most had considerable tribal loyalty and at the same time a vision of Indian unity.

The conference participants had similar backgrounds. Most of them had attended those "nationalizing" institutions, Carlisle Indian School, Pennsylvania, and Hampton Institute. Most were Protestants or Catholics, with some Christian adherents of the Peyote religion (fig. 1). Farmers, small businessmen, Bureau of Indian Affairs employees, teachers, and nurses, these men and women came from the "progressive" wing of their tribes.

The founding conference had a strongly academic and reform flavor. Indians presented papers on educational problems (including Indian art), industrial problems (including farming, mechanical arts, and homemaking), and legal and political problems. The discussions revealed a consensus. Self-help, initiative, and self-reliance, and education, they believed, were essential to progress. The Society organized itself along typical reform lines, with the usual panoply of officers. Membership provisions included "actives" (Indians only) and "associates" (non-voting non-Indians), a pattern that characterized pan-Indian reform and fraternal organization for decades thereafter. Representatives of the Indian Rights Association, Carlisle, and Hampton attended the founding conference.

The Society moved quickly to establish itself (Hertzberg 1971; Society of American Indians 1914). A Washington headquarters was opened. A periodical (*Quarterly Journal* 1913–1915, later *American Indian Magazine* 1915–1920) was established under the editorship of Arthur C. Parker. A legal division with investigative powers was established, together with divisions on membership and education. The committees were comprised of "successful" Indian men and women, including J.N.B. Hewitt (Tuscarora), an anthropologist from the Bureau of American Ethnology, Smithsonian. The Society conducted an annual essay contest for Indian students, promoted American Indian Day, and opened its pages to a diversity of Indian opinion. The organization supported a bill introduced by Society member Congressman Charles D. Carter (Chickasaw) of Oklahoma, which would set up a commission to codify Indian law and determine the exact legal status of Indian tribes and individuals. The Society also called for opening the U.S. Court of Claims to the tribes as well as typical progressive measures such as

Natl. Arch.: RG75-M-3.
Fig. 1. Society of American Indians banquet, Hotel Walton, Philadelphia, Pa., Feb. 14, 1914. The people seated along the rear wall addressed the group: left to right, Charles E. Dagenett (Peoria) and W.J. Kershaw, vice-presidents of the Society; Cato Sells, commissioner of Indian affairs; Rev. Sherman Coolidge (Arapahoe), president of the Society; Arthur C. Parker (Seneca), editor of the Society's journal; Dr. Carlos Montezuma (Yavapai); Richard H. Pratt; and Gabe E. Parker (Choctaw), registrar of the treasury. The dinner meeting, attended by Whites and Indians, followed an afternoon conference at the Philadelphia Academy of Science during which papers were read and a report was given on the annual conference in Denver, Colo. (Parker 1914:56–59). Photograph by William Rau.

educational reform and improved health facilities. At its 1913 conference, the organization favored allotment but did not mention the Dawes Act.

The consensus that supported the Society began to show serious strains by the 1915 conference as factions developed (Hertzberg 1971:135–154). The most important difference was over attitudes toward the Indian Bureau. The "radicals" or "abolitionists," led by Dr. Carlos Montezuma and encouraged by Gen. Richard H. Pratt (who founded Carlisle School), advocated immediate abolition of the Bureau and Indian assimilation on the immigrant model. Another conflict arose over the issue of peyote. In 1918, the organization's secretary, Gertrude L. Bonnin (Sioux) and Dr. Eastman testified at congressional hearings in favor of a bill to outlaw peyote, while a number of members and former members opposed it. At the 1918 conference, the radicals succeeded in carrying a resolution calling for the immediate abolition of the Bureau.

Factionalism could flourish more easily because the Society had neither the resources nor the public support to deliver on its promises. It was unable to secure the legislation it favored or to give sufficient legal help to the many Indians who sought its aid. A meeting of Society leaders with President Woodrow Wilson in 1914 failed to win his backing for its major legislative goals: the Code Commission and Indian access to the Court of Claims.

After World War I new themes began to appear as the Society's leaders called for self-determination for the tribes while continuing to favor a melting pot approach to pan-Indianism. A Society campaign for Indian citizenship came to an abrupt halt in 1919 when members were divided on the matter. Despite efforts to revivify the organization by Sloan, Montezuma, and Father Philip B. Gordon, a Roman Catholic priest, the Society declined rapidly.

Just as the Indian wing of the rights movement was fading into obscurity, a new group of Whites, incensed by a series of depredations against Indians and their lands, entered the movement. Like the advocates of the Dawes Act in the 1880s, the new reformers came to believe that a fundamental change in governmental policy was needed, and they created effective organizations and strategies for the achievement of their purposes (Hertzberg 1971). The new forces coalesced around a symbolic case that dramatized their deep concerns. The case involved the Pueblos, who had retained both cultural cohesiveness and considerable self-governance for centuries and whose art, architecture, ceremonials, and settled modes of community life were immensely appealing to non-Indians. For reformers determined to preserve the tribes they were ideal, although they were no more representative of all tribes than were the Poncas in the 1880s. To John Collier (Philp 1977; Kelly 1983) and to many of the new reformers, the Pueblos became the symbol of what all Indians could be, and indeed were often believed to be. The bill introduced in Congress in 1921 by Sen. Holm O. Bursum threatened to divest the Pueblos of New Mexico of a large portion of their lands in favor of non-Indian trespassers.

Another threat arose in 1922 when Secretary of the Interior Albert B. Fall ruled "executive order reservations," that is, reservations set aside by executive order rather than by treaty, were subject to legislation on the leasing of oil and gas deposits. The tribal titles to some 22,000,000 acres, or almost two-thirds of the remaining tribal estate, were thus placed in jeopardy (Indian Rights Association 1884–1935, 40:28–32).

The first important new voice on behalf of Indian rights came, as in the late 1870s, from an organization of women. In 1921, Stella Atwood was appointed head of an Indian welfare committee of the powerful General Federation of Women's Clubs and, with the advice of John Collier, began to establish state committees (Philp 1977; Indian Rights Association 1921:38,39).

In 1922 two organizations were formed to fight the Bursum bill—the Eastern Association on Indian Affairs, headed by the anthropologist Herbert J. Spinden, and its affiliate, the New Mexico Association on Indian Affairs. The former was able to enlist the support of anthropolo-

gists and businessmen, and the latter engaged the enthusiasm of a group of writers and artists (Anonymous 1923).

In 1923 John Collier organized the American Indian Defense Association. Collier proved a masterful strategist and publicist in defense of Indian rights. He worked closely with progressives in both houses of Congress and with a generation of reformers outside. Collier enlisted the support also of important businessmen and philanthropists (Collier 1963; Kelly 1983).

The new reformers considered the Dawes Act bankrupt, in conception as well as implementation. They placed a high value on the preservation and development of tribal institutions and a relatively low value on individual Indian assimilation. Both the Eastern and New Mexico Associations took a less acerbic view of the Indian Bureau and all its works than did Collier and were less hostile toward Indian assimilation or even acculturation. The evolving cultural pluralist consensus was supported by a public opinion that the new groups helped to create and that tended to favor the preservation of Indian cultures rather than their absorption (Hertzberg 1971).

However different their perspective, the old and new wings of the movement were united in their opposition to the invasions of Indian rights represented by the Bursum bill and the threat to executive order reservations. But on a third they were bitterly divided. This was the "dance order," a prohibition by the BIA issued largely at the instigation of the older reform groups, which sought to stop Indian "giveways" and dances or practices deemed dangerous or immoral. The battle pitted the new reformers, who sought to preserve the rights of Indians to practice traditional tribal customs, against the Indian Rights Association and old reformers, who sought to discredit or forbid them but who were also concerned with the rights of dissidents within the tribes. Eventually, the victory went largely to the new reformers (Philp 1977; Collier 1963).

Faced with powerful criticism from the Indian rights movement on these issues Secretary of the Interior Hubert Work called together in 1923 a Committee of One Hundred to advise him on Indian policy (H. Work 1924). The Committee elected Arthur C. Parker chairman and Fayette A. McKenzie as chairman of the resolutions committee. Membership included most of the leaders of both wings of the White-led Indian rights movement, almost all the former leaders of the Society of American Indians, a number of anthropologists, and a group of distinguished Americans not so directly concerned with Indian affairs.

The most difficult controversy in the Committee revolved around the Pueblo lands case, on which the new reformers were acrimoniously divided. The Committee recommended speedy decisions on Pueblo land cases then in the courts, adequate compensation to the Indians for Pueblo titles annulled with their consent or through government negligence, and compensation to settlers who might be evicted. The significance of the Committee of One Hundred lay in the stimulus it provided to the forging of a new consensus that started from a position closer to the one advocated by the Society of American Indians in its heyday than to that of either the older or newer reformers (Work 1924; Hertzberg 1971; Philp 1977).

In 1924 the Indian Citizenship Act (43 U.S. Stat. 253) passed with the support of both wings of the rights movement. It declared all Indians citizens without affecting any rights to tribal or other property.

While White Indian rights organizations continued throughout the 1920s to fight for Indian rights, as well as to skirmish with one another, rights organizations controlled by Indians were much weaker than in the previous decade. This seemed to be due to the general waning of the reform impulse, the weakening of unifying ideas based on concepts of the melting pot and Indian "race consciousness," the disillusionment of many middle-class Indians with pan-Indian reform, and the demise of Carlisle Indian School.

The National Council of American Indians, founded about 1926, was headed by Gertrude Bonnin, a leader in the Society of American Indians and Peyotist crusader. Apparently formed to induce Indians to participate in politics after the passage of the Indian Citizenship Act in 1924, the Council attempted to be a national intertribal council under the slogan "Help the Indians Help Themselves in Protecting Their Rights And Properties." In practice the National Council was kept alive largely by Bonnin and her husband. The Council itself was little more than a holding operation (Hertzberg 1971).

The American Indian Association, organized in 1922, was also strongly influenced by the society of American Indians and in time came to regard itself as a continuation of that organization. The association stood for standard reform programs such as the establishment of a Court of Claims for Indians. In practice it was largely fraternal and did little to attain its reform goals (Hertzberg 1971).

Three other Indian rights organizations were more localized and have continued in existence since then with varying degrees of vigor and effectiveness. The Indian Defense League of America, primarily based in the Six Nations of New York and Canada, was founded by Chief Clinton Rickard (Tuscarora) in 1926 to ensure that Indians could freely cross the U.S.-Canadian border without going through immigration, a right the organization established in 1928 and thereafter commemorated annually in a Border Crossing Celebration in July (fig. 2). It took until 1969 before the Canadian government recognized the Indians to receive goods across the border duty-free (Hauptman 1986:148–149). After 1928 the League devoted itself largely to immigration cases, educating the public about Indian culture, and mutual aid (Rickard 1973).

Another group with primarily fraternal and social but also reform interests was the Grand Council Fire of Chicago (later the Indian Council Fire), organized in 1923 and composed largely of Indians. Its membership also included Whites, most prominently the secretary, Marion Gridley, who continued to be active in Indian affairs for the next four decades (Hertzberg 1971).

The Alaska Native Brotherhood was founded in 1912 to fight for the rights of the Native peoples in Alaska. This remarkably stable organization for many years maintained relationships with Indian and White groups concerned with Indian rights (fig. 3) (Drucker 1958).

As an outgrowth of the Committee of One Hundred, Secretary of the Interior Work in 1926 asked the Brookings Institution to make a study of the economic and social conditions of American Indians. The group of independent experts headed by Lewis Meriam included Fayette McKenzie and Henry Roe Cloud, who was the only Indian member.

The Meriam (1928) report contained detailed recommendations for change in the administration of Indian affairs buttressed by evidence. The object of work with or for Indians, it pointed out, was to fit them either to merge into the social and economic life of the nation or to live in its presence according to a minimum level of health and decency. Whichever choice Indians made should be respected. The work of the Indian Bureau was conceived of as fundamentally educational. In its conception of the relationships of Indians to the dominant society the Meriam report staked out a middle ground between the two wings of the Indian rights movement.

In response to the Meriam report the Indian Rights Association called a conference, which heartily endorsed the report. The conference agreed on the excellence of three key appointments by President Herbert Hoover: as Secretary of the Interior, Ray Lyman Wilbur, a member of the Committee of One Hundred; as Indian commissioner Charles J. Rhoads, who was president of the Indian Rights Association; and as assistant commissioner, J. Henry Scattergood (Tyler 1973:115–124).

The reform of governmental policies began in earnest. Rhoads and Wilbur were both committed to implementing the recommendations of the Meriam report. Rhoads reorganized the Indian Office, strengthened health and medical services, and, most important, appointed a progressive educator, Dr. Will Carson Ryan, Jr., as Director of Education in the Indian Service (Philp 1977).

Ryan, who had been on the Meriam report staff and was a member of the board of the Indian Rights Association, was enthusiastically backed by both wings of the Indian reform movement. He set about the reorganization of Indian education by strengthening day schools as opposed to boarding schools. Ryan had a conception of the Indian right to education that meant adapting education to varying conditions of tribal life, encouraging 309

Buffalo and Erie Co. Histl. Soc., Courier-Express Coll., Buffalo, N.Y.
Fig. 2. Members of the Indian Defense League during annual march across the bridge joining the U.S. and Canada, July 19, 1969. The Jay Treaty of 1794 and the Treaty of Ghent, 1814, were cited as giving the Indians unconditional rights to trade and passage across the border (Hauptman 1986: 148–149). Photograph by Frank J. Schifferle.

pride in the Indian heritage, helping Indian children attend public school where appropriate, and building on the environmental experiences of children (Szasz 1974).

In October 1929 the Lake Mohonk Conference of Friends of the Indian, which had not met since 1917, was briefly revived to discuss the Meriam report. All the major groups in Indian reform were represented. The unanimous report of the platform committee placed primary emphasis on the improvement of Indian education, health and family life, employment, law and order, and the setting up of an Indian claims commission. The delicate issue of Indian land titles was handled by advocating inalienable Indian home sites to be either guaranteed or restored, thus achieving a compromise between those who favored a modified form of allotment and those who favored a program of consolidation and enlargement of tribally owned lands (Lake Mohonk Conference on the Indian 1930). Despite considerable agreement between old and new reformers, controversies erupted. In 1930–1931 the American Indian Defense Association attacked the Rhoads administration of the Indian Bureau. It complained of the failure of reform in Indian law and of the handling of Indian property (Anonymous 1931). The Indian Rights Association, which had been a severe, if usually polite, critic of the Bureau, stoutly defended the new commissioner and his administration.

After the election of President Franklin D. Roosevelt in 1932, the Indian reform organizations put forward their candidates for the commissionership. The Indian Rights Association urged the continuation of the Rhoads administration. The All-Pueblo Council advocated John Collier, Lewis Meriam, or Nathan R. Margold, the Pueblos' lawyer. An intertribal conference held in Oklahoma suggested Gabe Parker (Choctaw). John Collier, the leader of the newer reformers and the executive secretary of their most influential organization, the American Indian Defense Association, in April 1933 became Roosevelt's commissioner of Indian affairs (Philp 1977; Kelly 1983; Deloria and Lytle 1984:55–182).

The legislative program of the Indian New Deal was evolved in part through consultation with Indian rights organizations. In the development of the program, Commissioner Collier and members of his staff met with representatives of the older and newer reformers, including two Indian organizations, the National Council of American Indians and the Ojisto Council of New York, a women's organizational offshoot of the American Indian Association (Conference on Indian Legislation 1934).

The Indian Reorganization bill, which was the legisla-

Smithsonian, NAA:72,535.
Fig. 3. Members of the Alaska Native Brotherhood and the Alaska Native Sisterhood in parade formation during an annual convention at Ketchikan, 1930. The men wear bandoliers of buckskin backed by red felt with the letters ANB usually appliquéd in felt across the front. The group also used a label pin with a stylized arrow transversing the letters ANB. That design was incorporated in the bandoliers. The Brotherhood's colors are red and yellow, which represent the salmon and the gold of Alaska. The women wear blue and white bandoliers of similar design, with the letters in either white appliqué or beadwork. The blue and white represent the White American concepts of fidelity and purity respectively (Drucker 1958:31–32). Photograph by Fisher Studio, Ketchikan, Alaska.

tive heart of the Indian New Deal, included many of the recommendations proposed by this conference. Most of the reform organizations supported the bill, or major portions of it. The Indian Rights Association, while approving much of the proposed legislation, took serious issue on a number of grounds, also charging that insufficient time had been allowed to secure Indian reactions (Steere 1934).

The most vocal Indian opposition to the bill came from California, Oklahoma, and the Southwest. In Oklahoma the Indian National Confederacy's "principal chief," Joseph B. Bruner (Creek), vigorously denounced Collier. The heart of the Confederacy opposition was the fear that the bill would be destructive of the Oklahoma Indians'

accomplishments of the last 200 years, resulting in less rather than more freedom for Indians, in effect forcing acculturated Indians "back to the blanket" (Hertzberg 1971:289).

Closely allied with the Oklahoma forces was a group of California Indians, the Mission Indian Federation, whose president was Adam Castillo (Cahuilla). Like the Oklahoma group, the Californians believed that the bill's passage would "result in further suffocation of the Indians." They were particularly concerned about the bill's failure to provide a direct Indian voice in the removal of agency superintendents and other BIA employees. At a meeting presided over by Rupert Costo (Cahuilla) the Mission Indian Federation opposed the creation of tribal courts as removing their rights as American citizens and expressed a desire to break away from Indian Bureau control.

But the weight of opinion influential in Indian affairs favored the drastically revised compromise version of the Indian Reorganization Act (48 U.S. Stat. 984–986), which became law in June 1934. Its passage represented both the triumph of the viewpoint of the newer reformers and the culmination of many hopes of the older ones. What Collier had failed to get through legislation, he sought as best he could to achieve through administration (Kelly 1974; Deloria and Lytle 1984:171–182; Washburn 1984).

During the remainder of the 1930s the energies of the Indian rights movement were devoted primarily to the operations of the Indian Reorganization Act. The Indian Rights Association continued its public role of friendly critic, and the American Indian Defense Association continued its vigorous backing of Collier and the Indian New Deal. In 1936, the American Indian Defense Association and the National Association on Indian Affairs, which in 1933 had changed its name from the Eastern Association on Indian Affairs, voted to consolidate as the Association on American Indian Affairs. Oliver LaFarge, president of the new organization, while generally supporting the Indian New Deal, was also somewhat critical of its administration.

In April 1938 the major White religious and lay groups concerned with Indian rights met in Atlantic City. Although differences among the organizations persisted, they were able to unite on a platform opposing repeal of the Indian Reorganization Act, which had been periodically attempted almost since its passage (Federal Council of the Churches of Christ in America 1938).

A new organization, the American Indian Federation, was formed in Gallup, New Mexico, in August 1934 with Joseph B. Bruner from the Indian National Confederacy in Oklahoma as president, and officers from eastern, midwestern, and southwestern tribes. The Federation carried on a bitter campaign against the Indian Reorganization Act (Philp 1977:200–204). By the end of the decade, the Federation was engaged in attempting to secure legislation to award $3,000 to some 4,664 Indians

311

described as voluntary members of the American Indian Federation, and similar payments to each enrolled, recognized, or allotted individual Indian, and his or her heirs, who agreed to accept the full responsibility of American citizenship. The older reformers took a dim view of these activities. This scheme, the Indian Rights Association states, was "as brazen an attempt to stimulate racketeering as we have known to be offered in Congress" (Sniffen 1939:1).

During the 1930s there were few Indian rights organizations, and these were largely regional rather than national in scope. Many Indian reformers were working for the BIA. By the early 1940s many domestic reforms, including Indian reforms, languished.

The immediate occasion for the founding of a new national Indian organization was a meeting of Indian Office employees called in late 1942 in Chicago, then the headquarters of the Indian Bureau, by Commissioner Collier. Collier's purpose was to ask them to sponsor an Indian researcher in Central America as a way of strengthening ties between North and South American Indians. The Indian employees turned down the Commissioner's request on the grounds that they did not truly represent the Indians of North America. Instead they agreed on the need for a represenative national organization of Indians to speak and act for themselves. With the help of Indians in the Chicago area, and Indian Service field agents proceeding with Collier's blessing, plans were formulated for a nationwide organization that would be composed of reservation Indians delegated by the tribes.

D'Arcy McNickle (Flathead), an employee of the BIA and an anthropologist, was one of the leaders in organizing the movement and continued throughout the next three decades to be one of the most influential men in Indian affairs. McNickle stressed that while the prospective organization was starting in the Chicago office of the BIA, it should be a federation of tribes rather than a matter of individual membership (McNickle 1944). A temporary group led by Mark L. Burns (Chippewa) called together the first convention of what was to become the National Congress of American Indians (NCAI) in Denver, Colorado, in November 1944 (fig. 4). Since then it has been the most important pan-Indian rights movement in the country.

The men and women who founded the National Congress of American Indians represented tribes from 27 states. They were Indians prominent in the professions and business, anthropologists, and BIA employees. Many had attended Carlisle or Haskell Institute, Lawrence, Kansas, a number were college graduates, and some were active in non-Indian fraternal organizations. The first president of the NCAI, Judge Napoleon B. Johnson (Cherokee) and its first secretary, Dan M. Madrano (Caddo) reflected the strong Oklahoma influence in the new organization.

NCAI resembled its predecessor, the Society of American Indians, but it was more tribally oriented and broader based.

Natl. Congress of Amer. Indians, Washington, D.C.

Fig. 4. Charter members of the National Congress of American Indians at the Constitutional Convention, Cosmopolitan Hotel, Denver, Colo., Nov. 15–18, 1944. left to right, front row: Edward Cata, San Juan Pueblo; Stephen C. De Mers, Flathead; George Kenote, Menominee; William Fire Thunder, Sioux; Basil Two Bear, Sioux; Martin T. Cross, Gros Ventre; William W. Short, Chickasaw; George La Motte, Chippewa; Roy E. Gourd, Cherokee; Judge N.B. Johnson, Cherokee; Ben Dwight, Choctaw; Irma Hicks, Cherokee; Albert Attocknie, Comanche; George LaVatta, Shoshone-Bannock; Jesse Rowlodge, Cheyenne-Arapaho; Ed Davenport, Fox; John Dick, Chippewa; Luke Gilbert, Sioux; Henry Throssel, Papago; Fred Mahone, Walapai; Grant Iron Lightning, Sioux; Roly Canard, Creek. middle row: Perry Kennerly, Blackfeet; Paul Pitts, Osage; Harry Red Eagle, Osage; John Whitehorn, Osage; Steve Vencenti, Jicarilla Apache; Laell Vencenti, Jicarilla Apache; Sam Burch, Southern Ute; Paul LeGarde, Chippewa; Conner Chappoose, Ute; George Eastman, Sioux; Raymond Graham, Western Shoshone; J.P. James, Creek; David Dozier, Santa Clara Pueblo; Charles E.J. Heacock, Sioux; Archie Phinney, Nez Perce; Joshua Spottedhorse, Sioux; Leona Locust, Cherokee; Clara Spottedhorse, Sioux; Margaret Onefield Richard, Sioux; Beulah M. Abbott, Choctaw; Hazel Christian; Lawrence Appah, Ute; Howard Soontay, Kiowa-Comanche. back row: Andrew Dunlap, Caddo; Henry Standing Bear, Sioux, Walter S. Kimmel, Sioux; Ben Chosa, Chippewa; D'Arcy McNickle, Flathead; Peru W. Farver, Choctaw; John B. Milam, Cherokee; John Max, Sioux; Simon J. Kirk, Sioux; Frank Beaver, Winnebago; Edward L. Rogers, Chippewa; Cornelius S. Aaron, Mohegan; Albert A. Exendine, Delaware; James Dougomah, Kiowa; Dan Madrano, Caddo; Don Whistler, Sauk; Eugene Fisher, Cheyenne; Richard J. Cryer, Potawatomi; Arvid E. Miller, Stockbridge-Munsee; Francis Issues, Northern Cheyenne; James Hawkins, Sioux; Lois Harlan, Cherokee.

Membership in the organization was restricted to persons "of Indian ancestry" and was open to both individuals and groups, with suitable safeguards. Any "Indian tribe, band or community of Indians" could become a member organization. Later non-Indians and organizations could join as associate members. The NCAI was established, according to its constitution: "to enlighten the public toward a better understanding of the Indian race; to preserve Indian cultural values; to seek an equitable adjustment of tribal affairs, to secure and to preserve Indian rights under Indian treaties with the United States; and otherwise to promote the common welfare of the American Indians . . . " (National Congress of American Indians 1946). The delegates called for the establishment of a Claims Commission, which was established by act of Congress in 1946. A Legal Aid and Service Bureau was set up in Washington with Ruth Muskrat Bronson (Cherokee) as director. Bronson, who had retired from the BIA, was on good terms with White reformers and shortly became executive director.

The NCAI immediately cooperated with the Alaska Native Brotherhood in disputes with the Department of the Interior and private firms on fishing, trapping, and timber rights of Alaska Natives.

Another important focus in the fight for Indian rights was aid for the Navajos, the largest tribe in the United States, whose conditions of near starvation, poor health, and lack of educational facilities became matters of widespread public concern. A special Navajo Institute dealing with Navajo relief, irrigation, health, equal rights, and literacy was sponsored in 1947 by the Coordinating Committee on Indian Affairs, a body consisting of the American Civil Liberties Union, Association on American Indian Affairs, General Federation of Women's Clubs, Home Missions Council, Indian Rights Association, and the New Mexico Association on Indian Affairs. Under several names, with varying degrees of cooperation, and with an occasional shift in membership, the committee continued to operate for the next two decades. Indian organizations like NCAI became members in the 1950s, and the Committee's name was eventually changed to the Council on Indian Affairs.

By the end of the 1940s, the Indian rights movement was clearly on the defensive. There was a postwar turning away from national to local concerns. For Indians, as for others, such a trend represented both an opportunity and a danger. The opportunity lay in how much influence people were actually able to acquire in their communities and how real this influence could be made in an increasingly interdependent society. The danger lay in who would actually exert power locally. In Indian affairs, Indians struggled to build a type of local control that would give the tribes a greater voice in their destiny. But other forces, determined also to divest the federal government of some of its powers, hoped to hand over Indian affairs, not to the tribal communities, but to local interests either uninterested in or hostile to Indian welfare.

The war and its aftermath also had another profound effect on Indian affairs. During the war many Indians had left the reservation for the first time to serve in the armed services and to work in war industries (U.S. Bureau of Indian Affairs 1946; Haynie 1984). This extensive experience with the non-Indian world in the U.S. and abroad affected both tribal life and the Indian rights movement. It produced a generation of national and tribal leaders who had developed considerable skill in dealing with the dominant society.

Both groups combined in the fight over termination of federal control over Indian lands. Those who favored termination (or "emancipation") saw it as a way to "get the government out of the Indian business" and to turn back the tribal lands to local control. The opponents of termination saw it as a threat to the continued existence of the tribes. Despite continuing Indian resentment and ambivalence toward the BIA, most Indians did not want to be removed from federal protection. They feared both uncontrolled local interests and also the greed of some fellow Indians who in the past had shown themselves willing to accept immediate individual advantage, financial or otherwise, in the place of long-term communal ownership of tribal lands.

The 1948 NCAI convention in Denver, Colorado, attempted to meet the threat of termination in several ways. One series of proposals was designed to strengthen and support tribal control over tribal affairs. A committee urged that the BIA be reorganized so as to provide for the planning of the affairs of each reservation by reservation people and representatives from the state and federal governments. At the same time, the convention strongly opposed termination of federal trusteeship, whose effect would have been to phase out federal protection of Indian tribes (National Congress of American Indians 1948).

Under Commissioner of Indian Affairs Dillon S. Myer, the drive for termination became more concerted and more serious. The BIA encouraged "relocation" of Indians in the cities on the grounds that the reservation economies could not support their growing populations. The BIA also became more lenient in allowing land sales and issuing fee patents. In addition, regulations gave the BIA power over the selection of tribal attorneys. This power was rescinded in 1952.

The late 1940s and early 1950s saw the growth of a number of state and regional intertribal organizations. Of these, some, like the All-Pueblo Council, had been in existence for several decades. Others, like the newly formed Arizona Inter-Tribal Council organized by Clarence Wesley (San Carlos Western Apache), were probably a response to pressing local issues such as irrigation and water rights. One of the most effective was the Affiliated Tribes of Northwest Indians. NCAI welcomed the organization of these regional Indian organizations. From them came national Indian leadership. When termination legislation came before Congress in the 1950s the arguments were similar to those leading up to the Dawes Act of 1887, but the differences were more significant. This time, the White friends of the Indian were the opponents rather than the advocates of termination, and this time the Indians had their own knowledgeable national and regional organizations to fight the policy. However, despite their opposition, in 1953 Congress adopted House Concurrent Resolution 108, which stated that congressional policy was to make Indians "subject to the same laws and entitled to the same privileges and responsibilities as . . . other citizens . . . and to end their status as wards of the United States, and to grant them all of the rights and privileges pertaining to American citizenship" (see Prucha 1984, 2:1044). Public Law 280 (67 U.S. Stat. 588) gave the states power to extend their civil and criminal laws over Indian reservations in any state without Indian consent (Tyler 1973:161–185).

Probably the crisis over termination was an important factor in a shift of influence within the NCAI away from Oklahoma and toward the northwest and the northern plains. In 1953 the Oklahoma influence in the NCAI was challenged at the moment when the full extent of the crisis over termination was becoming starkly evident to the Indian leadership, although its impact had not yet been fully felt by Indians on the reservation. A new executive director, Helen L. Peterson (Oglala Sioux) (fig. 5), took over in the midst of this crisis. Her professional experience, working with Hispanics and other minorities in community organization, was particularly important because the major thrust of the civil rights movement during this period was for equality and integration, a position that many supporters of Indian rights found in conflict with the Indian assertion of special rights and the Indian desire to retain separate tribal identities. To interpret the Indian position to believers in equal rights and integration was a major task of the NCAI.

At the 1953 NCAI convention, Joseph R. Garry (Coeur d'Alene) from Idaho was elected the new president. Garry had a strong commitment to the tribal land base and tribal integrity. He believed that tribes were "nations within a nation," with a status different from other minorities. "As other groups may be pleading for equality, the American Indian is fighting to retain his superior rights as guaranteed to him by treaties and agreements as the original inhabitants and the giver in good faith of this rich land," Garry (1956) wrote.

The NCAI moved quickly to take the offensive against the plethora of piecemeal termination bills and to ensure that no tribe would be terminated or otherwise seriously

Fig. 5. Participants in a legal workshop to prepare Indian delegates for congressional testimony on termination-related issues. center, wearing headdress, Joseph R. Garry (Coeur d'Alene), president of NCAI. seated, second from right, Helen L. Peterson (Oglala Sioux), executive director of NCAI. NCAI and the Association on American Indian Affairs (1957) organized the workshop to prepare tribal and intertribal council representatives who would be giving testimony regarding health and education, law and order, and water and irrigation at Senate hearings on S. 331, an amendment to the 1953 termination act; Senate Concurrent Resolution 3; and S. 809, all of which would affect federal termination programs. Senate Concurrent Resolution 3 proposed a program of economic development called the Point 4 program; S. 809 called for $200 million in grants and loans for Indian enterprises and non-Indian business near reservations. Neither proposal was supported sufficiently for passage in Congress or the Department of the Interior, which both favored the continuance of existing termination policies (Prucha 1984, 2:1078–1079). Photograph by Swann Studio, Washington, D.C., May 12, 1957.

affected without its consent. In February 1954 NCAI held an emergency conference in Washington to which 43 tribes from 21 states and the territory of Alaska sent delegates representing more than one-third of the nation's Indian population. The conference adopted a "Declaration of Indian Rights" calling for the continuation of the "federal protection and the promise of certain benefits which our ancestors gave forever to the people of the United States [in return for] title to the very soul of our beloved country." Reservations, the delegates declared, "do not imprison us. They are ancestral homelands, retained by us for our perpetual use and enjoyment. We feel we must assert our right to maintain ownership in our own way, and to terminate it only by our consent" (National Congress of American Indians 1954).

The efforts of NCAI and the White Indian reform organizations helped to slow the pace of termination and narrow its scope (fig. 5). Nevertheless, Congress in the 1950s terminated six tribes, of which the most spectacular cases were two timber-rich groups, the Klamath of Oregon (68 U.S. Stat. 718) and the Menominee of Wisconsin (66 U.S. Stat. 250), with results disastrous to the Indians (Stern 1965; Peroff 1982).

The fear of termination and the battle against it brought an unusual degree of unity of purpose among the tribes and support for the NCAI. One consequence was a decisive change in the organizational structure of the NCAI to make it more representative of the tribes. In the early days of NCAI as the organization was seeking to build its strength, a number of Indian groups located in cities or off reservations, as well as voluntary organizations within tribes, had become affiliated as chapters. During the 1950s the constitution was changed and voting group membership was limited to "bonafide Indian tribes" and groups belonging to the Alaska Native Brotherhood and Sisterhood tribes, and the executive council membership was changed to include all member tribes with their representatives selected by the tribal councils. Other Indians were encouraged to join as individuals. Thus the autonomy and integrity of the tribes was asserted within the organization while the NCAI became a more clearly intertribal body.

Yet another result of the threat of termination was increased participation of Indians in voting in general elections. In several close contests in states with large Indian populations the number of Indian votes cast could have contributed the needed margin of victory for a pro-Indian candidate. A survey of congressmen and senators from states in Indian country attested to the effectiveness of Indian political activity on legislation directly affecting them. This growing political awareness was due largely to the work of tribal and intertribal organizations and the NCAI, which interpreted issues, offered information about candidates, and explained the mechanics of voting (H.L. Peterson 1957).

A significant development in the 1950s, which was to have an important impact on Indian rights movements in the 1960s, was the sponsorship by the largely White Indian rights organizations of educational and organizational activities for Indian young people. Beginning in 1955, the New Mexico Association on Indian Affairs, which shortly became the Southwestern Association on Indian Affairs, supported the organization of an Indian Youth Council. Starting in Santa Fe with the Kiva Club at the University of New Mexico as host, the Council expanded rapidly to include other Indian young people in southwestern and western states and Canada meeting in annual conferences. The focus of the group was a wide range of educational, religious, political, and legislative programs.

Paralleling this development was a series of summer workshops for Indian youth, also beginning in 1955. The workshops were a spin-off from the efforts of the Council on Indian Affairs. They were conducted by the Anthropology Department of the University of Chicago and strongly oriented toward "action anthropology." In 1959 the program by mutual agreement was taken over by American Indian Development, Inc., an Indian service organization directed by D'Arcy McNickle. The set of friendships, shared ideas, and common experiences developed in the youth councils and the workshops laid the ground work for the emergence of an Indian youth movement in the 1960s (fig. 6).

After John F. Kennedy's election as president, unofficial groups positioned themselves to influence the policy of the new administration. Prominent among these were the Chicago "action anthropologists" who were preparing to bring together representatives of both reservation and urban Indian groups from all over the country. With Dr. Sol Tax, chairman of the University of Chicago Anthropology Department, as coordinator, preliminary meetings to develop a basic philosophy and program for Indian affairs were held at a number of universities. Position papers and drafts for discussion were circulated. NCAI was deeply involved in this preliminary work.

The American Indian Chicago Conference convened in Chicago on June 13, 1961, attended by several hundred Indians (Lurie 1961). The meeting adopted a Declaration of Indian Purpose, which included a program for Indian affairs. The conference reflected a cultural pluralist approach, emphasizing the responsibility of Indians to preserve Indian cultures before American society absorbed them. A program opposing termination and dealing with resource and economic development, health, welfare, housing, education, law, and relations with federal agencies was adopted. One of the most interesting sections advocated the development of urban Indian centers "in the hands of Indian people" and urged an adequate subsidy for them from the federal government. By this time urban Indian centers already existed in cities having significant Indian populations, such as San Francisco and Chicago. The NCAI "endorsed" but did not "sponsor" the conference, no doubt because of the dissension in its own ranks (Washburn 1985).

The 1950s had been a time of trial for the American Indian rights movement. Paradoxically, the threat of termination had in some ways been a blessing. The danger of termination had brought Indians together in the face of what they believed to be danger to continued tribal existence. The White Indian reform organizations were also united against termination, an important consideration in Indian unity, since factionalism among Indian-interest organizations almost always fosters factionalism among Indians.

The first significant new organization to appear was a youth movement whose leadership had been largely trained in the youth councils and the summer workshops of the 1950s. Some were disenchanted with the views and the activities of many tribal leaders, whom they thought were too conservative, too given to politicking, and not representative of Indian opinion. In August 1961 the National Indian Youth Council (NIYC) was formed in Gallup, New Mexico, with Melvin D. Thom (Northern Paiute) as president and Herb Blatchford (Navajo) as executive director.

Closely allied with the NIYC was the United Scholarship Service, which had been started in 1960 by Elizabeth Clark Rosenthal, an anthropologist who was the daughter and granddaughter of missionaries to Indians, and Tillie Walker (Mandan-Hidatsa), a staff member of the American Friends Service Committee. Both were board members of the Indian Rights Association. The United Scholarship Service, whose original purpose was to assist Indian and Spanish-American students in college, was sponsored by the Board for Home Missions of the United Church of Christ, the National Council of the Episcopal Church, and the Association on American Indian Affairs, organizations that had long been interested in the education of Indian young people. Vine Deloria, Jr. (Standing Rock Sioux), the son and grandson of Episcopal missionaries, became staff associate in charge of this work.

The concerns and strategies of Indian youth, while having a specific Indian cast and context, were much like those of other youth movements. They were especially troubled about problems of identity, alienation, and culture, which they cast in the anthropological terms largely acquired in the summer workshops. From the larger youth movement they also drew a vocabulary that they adapted to Indians: they frequently attacked the "Indian power structure," "Indian Bureau Indians," "middle-class Indians," and "Uncle Tomahawks." Nevertheless, it was much more difficult for them than it was for non-Indian youth to stand firmly on one side of the generation gap. Defining themselves as Indians inevitably involved respect for their Indian cultural heritage, which

Fig. 6. Some participants in the workshops on American Indian Affairs sponsored by American Indian Development, Inc. kneeling, left to right, Gordon Keahbone, Taos Pueblo–Kiowa; unidentified, Pacific Eskimo; Gerald Ignace, Coeur d'Alene; Gerald Brown, Flathead. standing, Dorothy W. Davids, Stockbridge-Munsee; Fran Poafpybitty, Comanche; Michael N. Taylor, Oglala Sioux; Jeri Cross; Clyde Warrior, Ponca; Louise Tansy; Bruce A. Wilkie, Makah; Lenore LeMere, Winnibago. Participants had to be enrolled in a post-secondary program to join the workshops. Taylor later served as director of American Indian Development, Inc., education program officer for the Association on American Indian Affairs, and a member of the American Indian Advisory Council of the Denver Museum of Natural History. Clyde Warrior was a founder of the National Indian Youth Council. Bruce Wilkie was tribal chairman at Neah Bay Reservation and served as executive director of NCAI. Gerald Ignace served as president of the Association of American Indian Physicians. Photographed in Boulder, Colo., 1962.

meant the tribes and their elders. Although many of the NIYC members had close connections with their reservations and tribes, others had been brought up in urban areas or had long lived in the cities with only remote and sporadic relationships with reservation life. It was often unclear whether the "Indian nationalism" that they espoused was tribal, directed to Indian people as a whole, or both. Perhaps their frequent impatience with the NCAI was in part a deflection of youthful rebellion from the tribes to an organization that did not seem to them so traditionally Indian. But even here they were torn between their frequently expressed desire for Indian unity and their frequent criticism of the NCAI as insufficiently militant.

A further conflict was between the early 1960s civil rights movement allegiance to equality and integration and their own commitment to a separate Indian destiny and a special and nonintegrated place for Indians in American society. But there can be little question that the civil rights movement, and especially its youth contingent, exerted a strong influence on Indian young people (Lurie 1965; R.K. Thomas 1965; Witt 1965).

While the National Indian Youth Council was organizing somewhat rebellious college students, the National Congress of American Indians worked closely with the Kennedy administration on its new Indian program, which placed heavy emphasis on increasing the economic viability of the tribes through attracting industry and tourists to reservations while also helping Indians to "relocate" in cities. But the new administration of NCAI was more factional and less efficient than the one it had replaced. It was unable to generate a new program for Indians in the 1960s and less able to hold the confidence of the tribes.

Meanwhile, the National Indian Youth Council moved toward a position of greater militancy. Its Indian equivalent of the "sit-in" was the "fish-in." The first fish-ins took place as a result of controversy in the state of Washington over the off-reservation fishing of several small tribes. The tribes claimed the fishing rights were theirs by treaty, and the state claimed the Indians were fishing illegally (Ryan 1979). Largely on the initiative of the Makah tribal chairman and the NIYC, whose secretary, Bruce Wilkie, was the business manager of the Makah tribe, a meeting of the Washington tribes together with representatives of the NCAI, Northwest Affiliated Tribes, and other intertribal groups, was held to present a proclamation on fishing rights to Gov. Albert Rossellini. The governor agreed to set up an Indian Advisory Board and to protect the sovereignty of the tribes but did not meet the other demands, which included a moratorium on the arrests of Indians who were fishing in "their usual and accustomed fishing grounds" (*Americans Before Columbus*, July 1964).

The response of the NIYC was a fish-in. Like their young non-Indian counterparts, the NIYC had an astute understanding of the uses of the media and symbolic action. Many Indians believed the fish-in undignified and un-Indian. Nevertheless, the Washington state fish-in was the first of a series of confrontations staged by the NIYC and other militant groups, demonstrating how closely Indian rights movements reflected similar movements in the dominant society (Isley et al. 1970).

In order to influence the direction and character of the administration of President Lyndon Johnson, in 1964 the Council on Indian Affairs held a meeting, in the form of an American Indian Capital Conference on Poverty, with a major focus on the role of education within the broader context of health, housing, employment, and "community mobilization." Over 300 Indians and non-Indians attended the sessions in Washington, D.C., in May 1964. The participants came from tribal councils, intertribal groups, the NCAI, the NIYC, the BIA, and Indian rights organizations with a heavy added complement of persons from religious groups. Vice President Hubert H. Humphrey, who had long taken a serious interest in Indian affairs, Commissioner Philleo Nash, and Jack Conway from the President's Task force on Poverty participated. Significantly, the urban Indian centers were poorly represented. None of the future leaders of the extreme Indian militants attended.

A major vehicle for the achievement of reform purposes in the 1960s was the grant—in the form of federal subsidy or foundation aid. In the 1950s the NCAI had made do with modest budgets and modest grants from private foundations, in addition to tribal and other Indian contributions. But in the expansive 1960s all the Indian organizations from moderate to militant increasingly sought grant money from the foundations, from government, and from the churches.

Funding from the federal government created opportunities for Indian people. Many new local Indian organizations were set up for the specific purpose of qualifying for grants. On the one hand this provided important and varied experience and opportunities for Indians, but on the other it divided Indian energies, loyalties, and personnel. Furthermore, tribes had to deal with a multitude of funding groups, often ill-coordinated and frequently at odds with one another. As in the past, White factionalism encouraged Indian factionalism. The net effect was to weaken Indian national organization.

In 1964 the NCAI convention meeting in Denver selected a new executive director in the person of Vine Deloria, Jr. Deloria took office at a time when the NCAI was in serious financial and organizational difficulty. Moreover, the center of gravity in the general reform movement, and especially in the civil rights and student movements, was shifting to more militant elements. White reformers concerned with minorities, almost entirely focused on the Black civil rights struggle, cast their views about Indians in terms of developments in that movement. An ill-defined ideology of cultural pluralism, ranging from simple toleration of differences to the growing support for separate "cultures," encouraged tribal or regional rather than national intertribal efforts. The largely rural constituency of the NCAI was more conservative in approach than the more activist urban-based forces that turned to confrontation politics. At the same time the organization was unable to produce results sufficiently satisfactory to hold the loyalty of a large group of tribes or to exploit the media in the manner of the more militant groups. Despite—or perhaps because of—NCAI's heavy involvement in federal social and economic programs and efforts to attract industry to reservations, its leadership was increasingly challenged by other Indian groups. From this experience, Deloria (1969) concluded that a fundamental need of Indian people was for competent legal services manned by Indians.

As federal programs expanded, state and local organizations emerged to tap Office of Economic Opportunity funds. One of the most important of these was Oklahomans for Indian Opportunity, Inc. headed by LaDonna Harris (Comanche), whose husband was U.S. Senator Fred R. Harris from Oklahoma. The Oklahoma organization soon broadened into a national organization with an Indian-White board and a focus on community organization, economic development, education, and legal defense for both reservation and urban Indians (Harris and Marino 1984).

In 1966 President Lyndon B. Johnson appointed Robert L. Bennett (Oneida), a career employee of the BIA, as commissioner of Indian affairs. (The first and only previous Indian-born commissioner was Ely S. Parker, a Seneca, appointed in 1869.) Bennett had for many years served in various offices in NCAI and was one of its most experienced and devoted supporters. Despite this political victory, the Indian reform movement continued to splinter.

By 1967 the conflict of interests of reservation and urban Indians had assumed serious proportions. In an attempt to bring together urban Indian groups whose major organization vehicles were the urban Indian centers, the Council on Indian Affairs asked Vine Deloria, Jr., to head a committee for an Urban Indian Consultation Conference financed largely by church groups. At the conference held in Seattle, Washington, in January 1968, the participants were more interested in social services for urban Indians than in political action. A few urged affiliation with the NCAI, but this suggestion received little support. The delegates from the Indian centers thereupon met separately, and elected an ad hoc committee whose chairman was Jesse Sixkiller (Cherokee) to form a federation of urban Indian groups. In October 1968 American Indians–United was founded in Chicago with Sixkiller as chairman in a convention attended by representatives from Indian centers in 14 states. The role of the group was declared to be to support and serve Indian centers, providing technical assistance in programming and fundraising, economic development, and cultural expression. One of the first tasks the organization set forth was the development of good relations with the NCAI. However, this attempt to unite off-reservation Indians in a national body and to form an alliance between urban and reservation Indians, despite its brave beginnings, did not come to fruition.

When Indian militancy began in earnest, its development was strengthened by a growing disillusionment among Whites with the Black militant movement, especially with its anti-White rhetoric and appeals to violence. Indian militants shared most of the characteristics of their non-Indian counterparts and developed their own Indian versions of these in their general viewpoint toward society, their attitudes toward those who differed from them, their confrontation politics and use of the media, and their style of life.

In 1968 the question of Indian participation in the Poor People's March on Washington helped to widen the breach between Indian moderates and Indian militants. Some members of the United Scholarship Service and the National Indian Youth Council joined in the demonstrations led by the Rev. Ralph Abernathy of the Southern Christian Leadership Conference. Nevertheless, the NIYC's chairman, Clyde Warrior (Ponca), a charismatic figure with considerable appeal to young Indians, refused to participate although he was often considered a militant. Indians like Vine Deloria, Jr., called Warrior a nationalist rather than a militant, a distinction increasingly used in the more activist wing of the Indian rights movement (Deloria 1969).

The National Congress of American Indians refused to endorse the Poor Peoples' March. In a statement that expressed sympathy with the organizers' ultimate goals and aims, the NCAI asserted that the Poor People had no clear legislative goals and that in the absence of these, with the potentialities for violence inherent in the situation, and with considerable division on the matter within its own membership, the NCAI could not offer its endorsement.

City and campus formed the base of the Indian militant movement. But the Indian tribal population lived in the rural areas least touched by militancy. Both the Indian urban and campus populations were growing, the first due in part to the BIA's relocation program and the second to increased efforts to get Indians to stay in school and to go to college. In 1968 two new Indian organizations came into being in the cities, both led by urban Indians who had extensive contact with other militant groups. In Minneapolis, the American Indian Movement (AIM) was founded, based in the more militant of the Indian centers there. AIM originally focused on a broad array of services for urban Indians, following the pattern of many urban centers. In San Francisco, the United Native Americans, Inc., led by Lehman Brightman (Cheyenne River Sioux) was formed to further "Indian power" and "self-determination." AIM expanded into a national organization while United Native Americans remained essentially California-based. Both played major roles in Indian confrontation politics (U.S. Congress. Senate. Committe on the Judiciary 1976; Weyler 1982; Durham 1983; Matthiessen 1983).

The first dramatic instance of Indian symbolic politics of the late 1960s took place in California. In November 1969 a group of Indians under the name Indians of All Tribes moved onto Alcatraz Island "reclaiming" the island "in the name of all American Indians by right of discovery." The occupiers, many of whom were students, claimed support from other minorities. They announced that Alcatraz would be used as a center for Native American studies, spiritual growth, ecology, and Indian arts and crafts, a training school, and American Indian museum (Blue Cloud 1972a).

The Alcatraz occupation lasted for 19 months. The occupiers formed a population of varying size, some of whom stayed only briefly, others for some time. When they were finally removed by federal marshals, fewer than 30 were left. Meanwhile, their organization initiated or participated in a number of other occupations, for example, the "invasion" of Fort Lawton in Seattle,

Washington (fig. 7), "to press for their right to occupy lands to be declared surplus." A number of participants were arrested (Indians of All Tribes *Newsletter* 1(3) 1970).

Most of the symbolic actions were mounted in or near cities. But in 1970, the militants moved closer to the reservations. At Mount Rushmore in South Dakota, the Black Hills National Monument Movement occupied a part of the famous mountain. The protest was against "many, many broken treaties and promises" and was proclaimed an effort to create "a stronger feeling of unity" among Indians. Among the organizations participating were AIM, the United Native Americans, United Indians of All Tribes, and the National Welfare Rights Organization. South Dakota Indian leaders, including the Oglala Sioux tribal chairman, Gerald One Feather, and the Democratic candidate for state attorney general, Ramon Roubideaux (Sioux) denounced the action, which they asserted was carried out by "out of state Indians" and as offensive to the majority of South Dakota Indians. The protestors pointed out that three of their leaders originally came from the area. Two years later, One Feather and Roubideaux were leaders in the AIM occupation of Wounded Knee. Similar protests were mounted by AIM in a Thanksgiving demonstration that included an action at Plymouth Rock and a boarding of the *Mayflower*, causing some misgivings on the part of local Indians who had planned a more sedate day-of-mourning.

Another type of militant activity concerned the rights of Indian students. A concerted campaign against the BIA Inter-Mountain School for Navajos in Brigham City, Utah, was mounted in 1970 by the National Indian Youth Council, which charged the school with racism, discrimination against members of the Native American Church, Navajo culture, Indian employees, as well as brutality against students. The campaign was later joined by Lehman Brightman of the United Native Americans.

Indian student protests flared at colleges, such as Dartmouth and the University of Oklahoma, over the use of Indian symbols (Washburn 1981). The "Little Red" controversy at the University of Oklahoma over the Indian student dancer who traditionally performed at football games was significant because of Oklahoma's large Indian population. The NIYC demanded abolition of "Little Red," while Indians in Oklahoma were divided on the issue. Supporters of "Little Red" contended that the custom honored the Indians of the state while opponents called it degrading to Indian culture. The controversy was resolved in favor of the continuance of "Little Red" after a legal battle that was ended at the request of NIYC and the university's American Indian Student Office, both prime movers in the dispute (Allen and Dolan 1970; Washburn 1981). Other students' rights battles at colleges and high schools concerned Indian student hairstyles and were much like those in other schools over the same issue. AIM and the Native

Fig. 7. Members of the United Indians of All Tribes during the occupation of Ft. Lawton, Seattle, March 15, 1969. This group was outside the main gates. Photograph by Greg Gilbert.

American Rights Fund were involved in some of the protests and litigation.

Another series of symbolic actions had as their targets museum exhibits, the use and display of Indian artifacts, and archeological digs of Indian burial grounds. These were clearly connected both with resentment against anthropologists and with the desire to identify with the Indian cultural past and reclaim its artifacts from non-Indians. A number of museums and digs were invaded by Indian militant groups often led by AIM, who charged that their exhibits or activities were disrespectful of Indian culture. Occupations and protests were staged at the Field Museum in Chicago and the Southwest Museum in Los Angeles. See Blair (1979), Floyd (1985), and Baker (1985) on the repatriation of Indian artifacts; see Norick (1982), Tymchuk (1984), and Grimes (1986) on the desecration and reburial controversy.

Most of the confrontation politics did not have to do with matters such as jobs. However, in March 1970, the National Indian Youth Council supported by AIM and a Denver Indian organization occupied the BIA office in Littleton, Colorado, charging discrimination in hiring and advancement for Indian employees contrary to the stated BIA policy for Indian preference (fig. 8). Commissioner Louis Bruce (Mohawk-Sioux) flew to Denver to meet with the occupiers and signed several agreements acceding to some of their demands. After Bruce's departure several Indians were arrested, followed by another occupation and a few more arrests. Charging betrayal, AIM thereupon staged demonstrations at other BIA offices in different parts of the country.

In some instances symbolic politics were carried on by the tribes. One highly effective nonmilitant protest

Fig. 8. Indian protestors against Bureau of Indian Affairs policy infractions, Denver, Colo., March 1970.

occurred in New York when the Onondagas demanded that the New York State Museum, Albany, give them wampum belts some of which had been given to the museum by Iroquois leaders to hold in trust. The Onondaga chiefs contended that the belts belonged to them as the Keepers of the Central Fire of the League of the Iroquois and were essential for religious ceremonies; the State Museum's position was that the belts had been acquired in good faith, were not religious in character, and were part of the heritage of all the people of the state. The Onondagas, who had influential backing from non-Indians as well as from Indian leaders like Vine Deloria, won a compromise by action of the state legislature. Some of the belts were to be given to the Onondagas when they had built a museum on the reservation to house them safely (Fenton 1971).

In the northwest, the fishing rights controversy dramatized by the fish-ins continued using both symbolic action and more old-fashioned political pressure. A new organization, the Survival of American Indians Association, was directed by Hank Adams (Assiniboine-Sioux), a veteran of the youth movement and a leader in the fishing struggle. This group was dedicated largely to the effort to secure the treaty rights of Indian fishermen in Washington and Oregon. Much more closely connected with the tribes than many other activists, Adams was also involved in the antiwar movement and in state politics (Waldman et al. 1978, 1:16–17).

Thus, with some exceptions, Indian militancy between 1968 and 1972 did not arise from the reservations or

express their most pressing concerns. Rather the movement engaged in symbolic actions of an urban or campus character. Of all the groups engaging in militant action, the National Indian Youth Council and Survival of American Indians Association were most concerned with tribal affairs. Although occasional alliances were formed with other militant groups, the Indian militants tended to parallel rather than work with their non-Indian counterparts.

It is difficult to estimate to what extent urban and campus Indians supported the militants, whose organization was loose and whose actual membership was small. Available evidence indicates that urban and campus Indians were divided on the issue of militancy and that organized clubs or urban centers tended to concentrate more on local problems of immediate practical concern: discrimination, housing, jobs, education, and fraternal and social activities.

The National Congress of American Indians and the various regional intertribal organizations had a perspective quite different from that of the militants. Their reactions were similar to those of other moderate groups, and their energies were directed to more traditional issues. Although the direct threat of termination had receded, it remained an issue shadowing spokesmen for the tribes in the state houses and in Washington. Resolutions at the 1968 NCAI convention urged self-determination, protection of Indian lands, the participation of Indians in programs affecting reservations and Indian communities, improved health services, anti-pollution measures, and higher education for Indians.

During the convention, a disruption by a group of militants shocked many of the tribal people and probably made it more difficult for the organization to cooperate with and assist urban Indians. Street demonstrations, the delegates concluded, were not the Indian way, urging that Indians work through "regular organizations and governmental channels to effect improvements" (*NCAI Sentinel* Fall 1968).

At the request of President-elect Richard M. Nixon, Alvin M. Josephy, Jr., a Republican who had written on Indian affairs and served in the 1960s as commissioner of the Indian Arts and Crafts Board, made a series of recommendations that included a strong emphasis on "self-determination" and a removal of the BIA to the Executive Office of the President. Other less desirable options, the report stated, included keeping the BIA in the Department of the Interior but placing it under an assistant secretary for Indian and territorial affairs, transferring it to the Department of Health, Education, and Welfare, or setting it up as an independent agency (Josephy 1971:105–139). To the demands of the militants was thus added a powerful voice from a more conservative quarter.

"Abolish the Bureau" had been for decades the

320

persistent cry of some Indian groups. The controversy it engendered had been a major cause of the disintegration of NCAI's predecessor, the Society of American Indians. Now some urban militants and activists used the report to undergird their demand for abolition of the BIA and transfer of its powers to the Indians. But to the tribes, the proposal sounded perilously like a form of termination.

The proposal to move the BIA to the Executive Office, or anywhere else, was firmly rejected by the NCAI at its 1969 convention on the grounds that past failures of the BIA were mainly due to interference in its operation by higher officials in Interior, congressional statements of policy, and inadequate appropriations; although the NCAI was frequently critical of the BIA the suggested alternatives seemed worse. The convention also passed resolutions designed to give the tribes more effective control over their own affairs. At the convention another disruption occurred, further hardening many tribal hearts against the militants.

In late 1970 and 1971, new Indian organizations arose of great moment to the existing Indian rights organizations. They dealt with legal aid for the tribes, analysis of pending legislation, and the formulation of a new philosophy of Indian law to enable the tribes to function both within the American legal system and Indian tribal traditions that often conflicted with it. The latter was the primary emphasis of the Institute for the Development of Indian Law, located in Washington, D.C., founded by Vine Deloria, Jr. The Institute issued a periodical, *I-Lids Legislative Review*, which eventually merged with the *American Indian Journal*, analyzing Indian legislation and carrying articles placing legal problems in broader context. Another organization, the Native American Rights Fund (NARF), growing out of the Office of Economic Opportunity California Legal Services, was established in 1970 largely through the efforts of David Getches, a White lawyer, to provide Indians with legal services. With a staff of lawyers both Indian and White and an Indian steering committee representing a broad spectrum of Indian groups, NARF quickly moved into a number of cases involving Indian rights both on and off the reservation. By 1972, NARF had an Indian director, John E. Echohawk (Pawnee). Another group designed to train lawyers and to disseminate information about Indian legislation through the *American Indian Law Newsletter* was the Indian Law Center at the University of New Mexico, headed by an Indian legal expert, Philip Sam Deloria (Standing Rock Sioux).

The Indian press was another rapidly developing area. The formation of the American Indian Press Service with Charles Z. Trimble (Oglala Sioux) as its president grew out of the need for a national press service focusing on Indian news. During the 1960s there was a proliferation of local publications by Indian groups in addition to the newspapers that many tribes had long published (see

Danky and Hady 1984). General newspapers in areas with significant Indian populations had no ready access to Indian news. Treatment of Indian news in the general press was sporadic and often showed little sophistication or background in Indian affairs. The Indian Press Service provided wide coverage and helped to disseminate news of Indians and the Indian rights movement. Two new pan-Indian newspapers with national circulation among Indians and non-Indians were especially important because of the declining influence of the older rights organizations and their publications. *Wassaja* was one of a number of publications of the American Indian Historical Society in San Francisco. *Akwesasne Notes*, put out by a group on the Saint Regis Reservation at Akwesasne, New York, reprinted Indian news from numerous publications, had a strongly pro-militant stance, and was frequently embroiled in disputes with the tribal council. Both papers, in addition to U.S. Indian news, carried reports of aboriginal movements elsewhere.

All these organizations were staffed entirely or largely by Indians, but none was controlled by the tribes. All performed functions hitherto carried out to some degree by the National Congress of American Indians. While each offered particular services in the Indian world, they held also the possibility of conflict with the NCAI, which remained the only national intertribal body.

The formation of the National Tribal Chairmen's Association in 1971 signaled a further breach between urban and reservation Indians. In part, the chairmen's group grew in response to tribal fears that off-reservation Indians would be favored at the expense of the reservations and also in reaction to the activities of Indian militants.

The Indian programs of the Nixon administration, already floundering in 1971, were in deep trouble with the Indian rights organizations by 1972. There were some welcome exceptions, such as the return of Blue Lake to Taos Pueblo ("United States Indian Policies, 1900–1980," fig. 8, this vol.), some sacred lands to the Yakima, and gains in education. But budget cuts in Indian programs brought forth protests from both the NCAI and the National Tribal Chairmen's Association. The Alaska claims settlement gave Natives some land and money but seriously jeopardized their future rights and their economy.

In fall 1972 Indian affairs took a new turn. Eight Indian organizations, including the National Indian Brotherhood of Canada, NARF, AIM, NIYC, and the National Indian Lutheran Board, met in Denver to plan a "Trail of Broken Treaties–Pan American Native Quest for Justice," a caravan of Indians that would converge on Washington before the election. A 20-point program was drawn up, of which the final draft was composed by Hank Adams (Anonymous 1973). The program envisioned a return to the pre-1871 status of Indian tribes, before most treaties. A new treaty commission to renegotiate treaties would be set up that could contract with tribes; all Indians would be considered in treaty relationship with the government; the question of legal tribal membership renegotiated; a 110-million land base restored; and land, water, natural and economic resources consolidated. The BIA would be abolished to be replaced by an Office of Federal Indian Relations and Community Reconstruction to be housed in the Executive Office of the President, governed by a tripartite board responsible to the president, the Congress and an elected council, and staffed by persons exempt from civil service regulations. National Indian referendum procedures and a national Indian grand jury would be established; and trade, commerce, and transportation of Indians would remain "wholly outside the authority, control, and regulation of the several states." Other less controversial matters, such as the repeal of Klamath, Menominee, and other termination acts were also advocated. In effect the program proposed a quasi-independent Indian nation of nations operating from the White House and including both reservation and urban Indians (*I-Lids Legislative Review* November 1972). The NCAI convention, meeting in October, declined to participate, but the Caravan received considerable support from church groups.

The Caravan, which had gathered at various points throughout the country, arrived in Washington November 1 and 2 shortly before the presidential election of 1972. John O. Crow (Cherokee), Bruce, and other officials met with the group. With police massed outside, the Indians occupied the BIA building, which was renamed the Native American Embassy ("United States Indian Treaties and Agreements," fig. 2, this vol.). A complex series of negotiations and court orders ensued. The occupation ended November 8 after the White House had agreed to set up an interagency task force to meet with representatives of the Trail of Broken Treaties and other Indian groups to discuss grievances and proposals, to recommend that there be no prosecution for the BIA occupation, and to finance the return of some Caravan members with government funds with NCAI serving as the conduit.

The occupiers took with them a considerable number of BIA files and left the building seriously damaged. Reaction was immediate. Robert Burnette (Rosebud Sioux), Caravan co-chairman, denounced its leadership. The National Tribal Chairmen's Association, which had earlier condemned the occupation, called on the president to accept the resignations of Interior and BIA officials who failed to protect the BIA and demanded prosecution of those responsible for the damage. The NCAI director, Charles Trimble, also deplored the destruction in the building and the purloining of records, but stated that the NCAI trod "common path" with many of the Caravan in the 20-point program. Meanwhile many tribal leaders denounced the occupation (*I-Lids Legislative Review*

November 1972; Anonymous 1973).

Commissioner Bruce, Crow, and others involved in the controversy in the BIA were fired, and the administration of Indian affairs delegated to Melvin L. Franklin (Iowa) in the newly created post of assistant to the secretary of the interior for Indian affairs. The BIA was in a shambles, its future was uncertain, and the Indian rights movement deeply divided. The dismantling of the Office of Economic Opportunity and its Indian programs, strongly protested by NCAI, further exacerbated conflicts and fears among American Indians.

It was in this vexed situation that the occupation of Wounded Knee on the Oglala Sioux reservation at Pine Ridge, South Dakota, began. From the viewpoint of AIM, Wounded Knee was an ideal setting for confrontation politics. Dee Brown's (1971) best-selling book, *Bury My Heart at Wounded Knee*, had made Wounded Knee a symbol to many non-Indian Americans, while to Indians, of course, the massacre at Wounded Knee was one of the terrible tragedies of their history. It took place among the Oglala Sioux, whose internal politics were intensely factional.

The drama at Wounded Knee began on February 7, 1973, when 200 armed members of AIM together with Oglalas opposed to the tribal council seized the hamlet, charging Richard Wilson, the elected council head, with corruption, a charge made frequently by those opposed to whatever council was in power at the time. The national leaders of AIM, Russell Means (Oglala Sioux), Clyde Bellecourt (Chippewa), and Dennis Banks (Chippewa), played major roles in the occupation, buttressed by Leonard Crow Dog, Frank Foolscrow, and other traditionalists, and Gerald One Feather and his group (Matthiessen 1983). The Oglala Sioux tribe itself was bitterly divided (Burnette and Koster 1974).

The siege at Wounded Knee lasted for 70 days. It resulted in two deaths of Indians occupying Wounded Knee, one U.S. marshall paralyzed, and the village of Wounded Knee in ruins. When a pact was finally signed between AIM leaders and government negotiators, the tribal government was bypassed.

Behind the drama there were issues not so evident at the time. While Wounded Knee engaged the support of many urban and some reservation Indians, the two national organizations that spoke for tribal Indians, the NCAI and the National Tribal Chairmen's Association, opposed the occupation. For them, the principle of upholding the right of elected tribal governments to run their own internal affairs was at stake, a right that Indian organizations had fought long and staunchly to win and had defended for decades in the courts, in Congress, and in many battles with the BIA itself. If tribal governments could be seriously threatened or overturned by an urban-based Indian movement from outside the reservations combining with dissident factions within them—factions that existed on almost every reservation—then tribal government itself would be endangered. However critical the tribal Indian rights organizations were of the BIA, they feared that its abolition would result in fewer rights and less self-government for the tribes. The White Indian reform organizations sided with the occupation, or tried to play a mediating role, or remained outside the conflict. The Indian Rights Association cautiously supported the militants, while the Association on American Indian Affairs remained largely aloof. Many church groups long involved in Indian affairs aided the occupiers at Wounded Knee. The occupation's immediate effect on Indians was to divide them, further embittering relations between moderates and militants, and between urban-based and reservation organizations. Many Indian moderates also resented the fact that the Wounded Knee occupation largely ignored the kinds of problems with which reservation Indians are necessarily concerned, such as water rights, mineral rights, and other basic issues involving the viability of reservation economies. Such issues are difficult to dramatize or to encapsulate in the news media, but they are essential to tribal survival.

In 1973 when Wounded Knee ended, most of the basic elements that have historically signaled a major change in governmental Indian policy were already in place. Wounded Knee was the climactic symbolic case in a series of cases made more vivid and dramatic as well as romanticized and simplified by television exposure. Major new forces had entered the Indian rights movement, partially displacing those created in the interest of earlier reforms and taking over some of their functions. The associations of the White reformers whose efforts created the Dawes Severalty Act and the Indian Reorganization Act were seriously weakened. There was no longer any organization to which non-Indians automatically turned for information on Indian affairs. A new public opinion had been created in which sympathy for "the movement" was expanded to include almost automatic support for the Indian causes that seemed allied to it. But this opinion was not necessarily well informed on the complexities of governmental Indian policies or the realities of tribal life.

The Indian rights movement has historically been concerned with defending, modifying, or changing governmental policy in Indian affairs. The unique relationship between American Indians and the United States government makes such a focus central and inevitable, although Indian rights movements have been concerned with many other issues as well. With the end of the occupation of Wounded Knee, the necessary consensus on which a new governmental policy could be based had not yet fully emerged but its outlines were already visible. If the Dawes Severalty Act stood for Indian assimilation and the Indian Reorganization Act for tribal self-government, the new policy would stand for "self-determination."

The Fur Trade in the Colonial Northeast

WILLIAM J. ECCLES

Early in the sixteenth century fishermen from western Europe—Basques, Portuguese, Bretons, Normands, English, and Irish—were landing on the North American coast near the Grand Banks fishing grounds and had established trade relations with the Indians. In the beginning, for the Europeans, the trade in furs was merely an adjunct to fishing, but for the Indians it meant a technological revolution within their way of life. Although their flint and other stone cutting tools and weapons were almost as effective as, and in some instances more so, than those made of iron, and the bow and arrow superior to the noisy musket for hunting, yet iron tools and weapons were easily resharpened and the musket was a more deadly weapon. Ironwares, woolen and linen clothing, and trinkets were to be had in exchange for the pelts of a few animals. Yet the old skills were never completely lost; European goods merely made life easier by sparing time and labor. The Indians did not become dependent on them so quickly as has been claimed (Judd and Ray 1980: 40–48).

Manufactured goods were not the only things that the Europeans brought to the Indians. Disease—smallpox, measles, influenza—to which the Indians had little or no resistance, spread among the coastal tribes then far inland (Martin 1978:40–55; Larocque 1982). This resulted in lands that the Indians had cleared and cultivated being abandoned, left vacant for waves of Europeans who came, not to trade, but to settle (Jennings 1975:30; Salisbury 1982). Alcohol, which these Indians had never encountered, was more insidious but it too wreaked havoc (Axtell 1981:257–259). It helped to destroy the fabric of Indian culture by undermining religious beliefs, in which dreams played a prominent part (Vachon 1960; Martin 1978: 75–76). Christian missionaries did their best to eradicate the Indians' religious beliefs. Those who were persuaded to accept Christianity found themselves ostracized by their traditional brethren. Tribes became divided into hostile factions. In the case of the Huron confederacy this contributed greatly to their destruction by the Iroquois. Had it not been that the French authorities insisted that Jesuit missionaries be tolerated among the tribes as a condition of continued trade, they would have been early expelled, if not killed. Eventually the missionaries learned to compromise, to accept and incorporate some Indian

beliefs that allowed the Indians to be at peace with themselves, but for decades they were in turmoil (Trigger 1976; Jaenen 1976a).

It was not until the early years of the seventeenth century that the trade in furs ceased to be merely an adjunct to fishing and become a staple in its own right. It was one particular fur, beaver, that brought this about. In Europe the broad-brimmed Swedish felt hat came into fashion. The best material available for the manufacture of the felt was the soft, barbed, underfur of the beaver. The barbs caused the individual strands to lock tightly together (Crean 1962; Rich 1967:7–8). The European beaver was by this time almost extinct, but fishermen were bringing beaver pelts of far better quality from America. Owing to the colder climate Canadian animals had thicker fur. The demand for beaver and for luxury furs such as marten, otter, ermine, fox, raccoon, and lynx was great. In addition there was an insatiable demand for moose, caribou, and wapiti hides. Since the late Middle Ages, as Europe's population began to increase, more than doubling in the sixteenth century (Rich and Wilson 1967:21), the people had been forced to switch from a predominantly meat to a cereal diet (Mousnier 1954:146–148; Braudel 1973:67; R. Davis 1973:111–119). The resulting relative decline in livestock meant fewer hides for the tanners.

The market for furs and hides thus established, French and Dutch merchants decided to establish permanent posts on the North American mainland. The French had earlier established commercial relations with the Montagnais and Abenaki tribes at Tadoussac, where the Saguenay River flows into the Saint Lawrence ("The Hudson's Bay Company and Native People," fig. 1, this vol). Every summer Indians in the hundreds came to this safe anchorage to meet the ships from Europe (Champlain 1922–1936, 1:105). They quickly learned not to trade with the first ship to arrive but to wait until several had dropped anchor. The ensuing competition made for better terms. Some of these Indians transported their surplus goods to other tribes far in the interior. Two factors enabled them to garner furs from these remote tribes, the birchbark canoe and corn (maize). The canoe was the only means of transport in the northern wilderness. It could carry sizable loads, was light enough to be carried around rapids by one man, was manufactured from materials readily available in the forest; the only tools needed were a knife, an awl, and a hand ax. Corn, which grew in abundance in the upper Saint Lawrence valley, was, when mixed with water and bear grease, a highly nutritious food. The normal ration for voyageurs in the eighteenth century fur brigades was a bushel of corn and seven and one-half pounds of bear grease a man a month (RAPQ 1927–1928:340–341).

With the competition so keen at Tadoussac, some French traders sought to circumvent it by establishing a permanent post, but the cruel winters and scurvy defeated them. Other traders, among them Samuel de Champlain, turned south and established a base in the Bay of Fundy. The Indians did not object to these establishments on their lands; indeed, they welcomed them since the trading posts made goods and services more readily available. The maintenance of permanent posts increased costs greatly, requiring the investment of much more capital. The Indians could not be made to absorb these higher costs. The only way a reasonable return on investment could be obtained was to remove the competition of the summer traders. To this end monopoly privileges were sought from the Crown. These privileges were readily granted to favored individuals since they provided a means for the French Crown to claim sovereignty over vast unknown territories at no cost to the royal treasury (Trudel 1979).

It proved impossible to exclude interlopers along the Atlantic coast. The French monopoly holders therefore moved back to the Saint Lawrence, but this time a thousand miles inland, to the point where the river narrowed almost to cannon range. The Iroquois tribes that had occupied the region when Jacques Cartier had last visited it in 1541 had long since disappeared, and there was no conflict over occupancy or title. At this base, named Québec, Champlain was able to forestall other traders and have first pick of the furs brought by the Huron and Algonquin. For the first quarter-century the French at Québec did not exceed 100. They survived only on the sufferance of the Indians (Trudel 1973:118-160).

In 1609 a disturbing element was introduced into the fur trade in the Northeast. Henry Hudson, seeking a water route to the Pacific, sailed up the the river later named after him, as far as the junction of the Mohawk. Other Dutch ships followed and drove a brisk trade in furs with the Mohawk. In 1614 the Amsterdam merchants, learning from the same experience as the French, obtained trading privileges from the States General and established trading posts on Manhattan island and near the present site of Albany. Like the French at Québec, the only interest these Dutch had was the trade in furs. Costs had to be kept low and settlement was not envisaged. Of the two trading regions, that of the French on the Saint Lawrence and that of the Dutch on the Hudson, the former was decidedly the better. The French post, being more northerly, produced better quality furs, and being vastly greater in extent it produced a far greater volume of furs. In the Saint Lawrence valley and Great Lakes basin the white birch that provided the bark for canoes grew in abundance, whereas to the south it was scarce (Glover 1948). Moreover, the Iroquois nations holding the territory west of the Hudson River prevented the Dutch, and their English successors, from establishing bases on the Saint Lawrence or the Great Lakes. Within some 30 years the lands they occupied were stripped bare of furs, and they too were eager to have a steady supply of European goods. They had therefore either to obtain furs in trade from the northern tribes with whom they had been at war from time immemorial, seize them by force, or acquire new furbearing territory by conquest (Trigger 1976, 2:617–647). The struggle between the rival commercial bases on the Saint Lawrence and the Hudson was to dominate the history of northeastern America for the ensuing 150 years.

On the Atlantic coast, a similar struggle developed between the French in Acadia and the English who had seized and begun to settle the territory both north and south of New Amsterdam. As early as 1602 English seamen, seeking sassafras roots along the New England coast, obtained furs from the Indians, but the price obtained for them in London was then too low to encourage active pursuit of the trade (P.C. Phillips 1961, 1:65). In 1607 an unsuccessful attempt was made to establish a trading establishment on the Kennebec River, but interest in the trade was maintained, and English traders soon came into conflict with the French of Acadia who had extended their trade and missionary activities down the coast. In 1611 Samuel Argall of the Virginia settlement destroyed the recently established French mission and trading base at Mont-Désert bay. The following year, in a similar piratical attack, he destroyed the French post of Port Royal in the Bay of Fundy (Trudel 1973:115–118). Yet the French managed to hang on in the face of growing numbers of English settlers along the New England coast.

One advantage the New England traders did have was a good supply of wampum, obtained from the Narraganset and neighboring tribes (vol. 15:166), a commodity that was highly prized by all the Indian nations. The Puritans were also able, on occasion, to trade their surplus grain for furs with the Indians (P.C. Phillips 1961, 1:114–115). Merchants in England, anticipating rich profits from this trade, were willing to invest in the settlement at Plymouth in return for a monopoly on the marketing of all the furs exported. When, in 1626, the Council of New England superseded the Plymouth Company, it too obtained monopoly privileges from the Crown, but it proved just as difficult for English monopoly holders to exclude inter-lopers as it was for the French.

During the early years of English settlement the fur trade was a mainstay of their as yet feeble economy. In Virginia tobacco quickly came to dominate, but attempts were made by the Assembly to diversify production. The Navigation Act of 1651, which restricted the carrying of tobacco to English ships, caused freight rates to soar, and the restriction of sales to the English market caused the price of the product to drop. This led some of the planters to turn to the fur trade, which quickly expanded south and west into the interior. Otter, opossum, raccoon, muskrat, and beaver were all taken in abundance, but they were of poor quality. Deer hides remained the mainstay of the trade. As the demand for tobacco grew, the need for ever more plantation land pressed hard on the heels of the fur traders (P.C. Phillips 1961, 1:161–185).

It was the fur trade that had enabled both the English and the French to maintain and expand their settlements in the early years. The French were much slower to send out settlers. They were satisfied to maintain mere commercial counters with a handful of men and no women, making no attempt to cultivate the soil, but as the population grew in the English colonies they were forced to change that policy for fear that they would eventually be overwhelmed by force of numbers. The capture of their bases in Acadia and at Quebec by Anglo-Scots adventurers in 1628 and 1629 drove that lesson home. Not until 1632 were the French able to reoccupy their posts (Trudel 1973:172–180).

At this point French policy in North America underwent a radical change. Title to all existing and future possessions of France on the continent was vested in the Company of One Hundred Associates, whose aim was the conversion of the Indians to Christianity. All furs had to be sold to the Company's agents and the profits from their sale were to be used to sustain the missionary drive, given over exclusively to the Society of Jesus. The Company also had to send 200–300 settlers a year to Canada and have 4,000 settled there by 1643 (Trudel 1973:169–172; Campeau 1974).

For the Indians the change from mere trading posts to settlement colonies posed a serious, long-term threat, but, eager as they were for European goods—which included firearms for those of them who embraced Christianity—they had to maintain good relations with the suppliers of those goods.

Where the number of English and Dutch settlers was increasing, Indians found themselves being forced off their land, reduced by military force, and driven farther into the interior. The exception to this development for some 174 years was the League of the Iroquois, who used their combined military might to keep both their Indian foes and the French at bay. They also adroitly used the French as a foil to keep the English of New York in their place (Richter 1983). Although dependent on agriculture rather than hunting for their main source of food, they too had to obtain furs to exchange for European goods, particularly firearms. When their population suffered heavy loss from disease and warfare, Iroquoians raided

neighboring tribes for prisoners, who were then assimilated. Their political strategy was to make peace with some of these tribes in order to concentrate their strength against the others. Thus in 1640 they sought peace with the Hurons while attacking the Algonquians. For the same reason they sought to make peace with the French who at first refused the offer unless their Huron and Algonquian trading allies were included. Subsequently a compromise was reached and a peace arranged, but it did not last long (Trigger 1976, 2:621–664; Dickinson 1982). The Iroquois continued to press their attacks on the Indian allies of the French. The Hurons, their numbers reduced by half when an epidemic of European origin scythed through their villages, and divided among themselves by the Jesuits' proselytizing, were no match for the better armed Iroquois. They were virtually destroyed as a nation (Trigger 1976, 2:725–788). Yet =he Iroquois failed to achieve their end. The Ottawa and other Algonquian tribes, all expert canoemen, then transported their furs directly to the French who, in 1642, had established a mission and trade base on Montreal island (Dollier de Casson 1928:107–115).

At the same time Iroquois raiding parties invaded the territory of the Algonquian tribes to quell them, end their attacks, and take prisoners. Other war parties attacked the French settlements in retaliation for the loss of some of their warriors at the hands of the French (Dickinson 1981) and blockaded the Ottawa River route to Montreal. The western Iroquois invaded the Ohio valley and drove the resident tribes out, only to come into conflict with an advance guard of the French who had outflanked them by way of the Great Lakes and the Mississippi.

By this time the French had more at stake than the fur trade. Neither the French church nor the Crown could permit New France to be destroyed. Settlers and soldiers were hastily recruited (Auger 1955). Although French casualties were not so great as has been maintained (Dickinson 1982), the swiftness and surprise of the Iroquois attacks and the torture ceremony to which many of their prisoners were subjected spread terror throughout the colony (Dollier de Casson 1928: 155ff.). A regiment of regular troops was sent out and the Iroquois forced to come to terms. A few thousand settlers were also sent, raising the population from 2,500 to 10,000 in a decade (Eccles 1964:251). Far more men than women were recruited, and many of them had no experience working on the land. For these men the fur trade offered a far more rewarding way of life than working for wages on another's farm.

In order to stabilize the fur trade and bring some sort of order to the market the Crown fixed the prices of beaver pelts and moose hides. The Compagnie de l'Occident, a Crown corporation (Mims 1912), in return for its monopoly on the marketing of those pelts, had to accept all that the Canadians had to offer. The colonists thus had a

Fig. 1. Projectile points cut from trade kettles. Kettle scrap became knives, tinklers, and ornaments of various kinds for the hair and clothing. left, Bilaterally barbed point dated 1770–1820, excavated from Grand Portage, Minn. right, Stemmed point dated 1732–1750s, recovered at the French Ft. St. Charles, Minn. Left 7.7 cm long; right same scale.

guaranteed market, regardless of its true condition. The law of supply and demand for those commodities had been suspended, hence the profits to be made were guaranteed, the labor less arduous than obtained in the clearing of virgin forest for subsistence farming. Within a decade, some hundreds of young men were off in the west, living among the Indians, pushing into the interior in the search for ever more beaver (Eccles 1964:106-113).

When it proved impossible to stop this exodus of coureurs de bois the Crown tried to curb it by a licensing system that permitted 25 canoes with three men each to voyage to the west each year. The Crown also decreed that an annual fur fair should be established at Montreal and the western Indians encouraged to bring their furs to it so that all the settlers could engage in the trade without quitting their farms for more than a few days. None of these regulations proved effective. The French continued to flood into the west, and by 1675 they had again come into conflict with the Iroquois who were driving all before them in the Ohio valley (Eccles 1959:108-110).

In their quest for a secure source of furs the Iroquois were spurred on by the Albany merchants and the governor of New York, Thomas Dongan, who was determined to challenge both the French hold on the western fur trade and their claim to sovereignty over half the continent. He sent Albany men, escorted by Iroquois and guided by renegade Canadians, to trade with the Ottawa at Michilimackinac, the main French base in the west. The high prices these Albany traders offered in an attempt to break the French hold proved very tempting to the Ottawa (Eccles 1959:177-185).

At the same time the Iroquois harassment of the Canadian traders and their attacks on the Indian allies of the French threatened the French hold on the west. Regular troops were again sent from France. After one ineffectual campaign that ended disastrously, in a second campaign the villages of the Senecas, most powerful and westerly of the Iroquois, were destroyed and a party of Albany traders captured en route to Michilimackinac. That ended Albany's direct challenge to French dominance of the fur trade. It also unleashed fierce attacks by the entire Iroquois confederacy on the French throughout the west. When, in 1689, France and England went to war, the Iroquois, incited and supplied by New York, began ravaging the French settlements around Montreal. For the ensuing eight years New France had to fight desperately to stem the Iroquois assaults and to hold the allegiance of its wavering Indian allies (Eccles 1959:186-272, 328-333).

Ironically this war saw a tremendous expansion of the fur trade. The governor-general of New France, Louis de Buade, comte de Frontenac, established more posts in the west, pleading military necessity. More traders were sent out in the guise of military garrisons for these posts and vast quantities of trade goods were shipped out, labeled as supplies for the Indian allies to press the war against the Iroquois. The result was an astronomical increase in the amount of beaver, most of it of poor quality, flooding back to Montreal. At the same time the amount of fur that the Albany merchants garnered had been reduced to a trickle. The French Crown tried to take drastic measures to stem the flood of beaver, but in vain. To make matters worse the French hat makers had discovered ways to use cheaper materials, reducing the demand for beaver (Eccles 1959: 273-294).

The problem for the French was that for sound economic reasons the trade in beaver should have been suspended until the glut had been consumed, but for political and military reasons this could not be done. The French claimed title to the vast interior of North America, still not knowing its true extent, yet their numbers were pathetically few compared to the burgeoning populations of the English colonies. They were therefore dependent on their alliances with the Indian nations, who would admit the sovereignty or authority of no Europeans over them (Eccles 1984). If the French were to have ceased to provide them with trade goods and the services of blacksmiths and gunsmiths, the French feared that the Indians would have gone over to the English who, ironically, had never proved able to provide these services for more than brief periods. Although this would have meant the removal of a temporary economic liability—the beaver glut—for political reasons France could not allow the English colonies to expand into the west. It was for these reasons that Louisiana and Detroit were established at the turn of the century. From that time on French imperial policy required that the Indian nations, from Hudson Bay to the Gulf of Mexico, be kept in the French alliance. This meant that the French had to supply them with goods and services at competitive prices, and the only thing apart from military support that the Indians had to offer was furs. Thus the French fur trade staggered on, with the Indian nations in an excellent bargaining position (Eccles 1983).

In this imperial rivalry each of the contenders enjoyed certain advantages over the other. The English traders paid higher prices for beaver than did the French, but not for other furs. English woolen cloth (duffles and strouds) was usually cheaper than that manufactured in France, if not always of superior quality, and these cloths had become the mainstays of the trade (Eccles 1979). The English also had fewer scruples over supplying the Indians with unlimited quantities of rum, regardless of the dire consequences. The French had the great advantage of controlling the river routes into the interior. They saved the Indians the trouble of long voyages by taking goods to their villages. They were well provided with birchbark canoes and expert canoe men, two essentials that the English lacked.

The French officials, unlike those of the English colonies, strove to keep their traders and voyageurs under strict control. Officers of the Canadian regular troops were in command at the principal posts. They were held responsible for the maintenance of order and for keeping the tribes in their respective districts at peace, one with another, by no means an easy task. Over and above that, their main duty was to prevent, as far as possible, the Indian nations having any dealings with the English colonists. As a result of their constant contacts with the Indians in their own country, their mastery of the Indians' languages, the need always to court them, the subordination of commercial aims to political ends, and the domination of the aristocratic and military ethos in Canadian society, values much closer to those held by the Indians than those of the English traders who thought only of buying cheap and selling dear. French relations with the Indians were far better than were those of the English (Eccles 1983).

The greatest advantage of all enjoyed by the French was that they did not covet the Indians' land. With their much smaller population concentrated in the Saint Lawrence valley, and with only settlements at Detroit and in the Illinois country, they posed no threat to the Indians' use of the forest as hunting grounds. In fact, French policy required that the Indians be preserved as hunters and warriors. The English, on the other hand, with their much larger population, doubling every generation, were constantly pushing outward, depriving the Indians of their territory (Jennings 1975; Salisbury 1982:190–202). It was thus easy for the French to make much of this English menace and to point out that the best hope of survival for the threatened Indian nations was a military alliance with the French.

The royal officials in Canada had more success preventing the Indian allies trading with the English colonists than they did with the Canadians who, after peace was restored in 1713, developed a thriving and profitable trade with Albany. Within a few years it was estimated that as much as half the beaver brought to Montreal took this route (Lunn 1939; Norton 1974: 121–151). This was, of course, contrary to the strict mercantilist principles of both the French and British governments. From Albany the Canadian traders obtained ample supplies of English duffles and strouds at prices lower than were charged by the Compagnie de l'Occident for the same cloths imported from England, and via the Netherlands when England and France were at war. The royal officials in New York deplored this smuggling and strove to have it stopped since it aided the French to maintain their influence over the Indian nations, but the Albany merchants refused to pay heed. The steady flow of beaver from Montreal to Albany also removed any incentive the Albany merchants might have had to challenge the French by sending their own traders into the northwest. When the royal officials in New York did succeed in persuading the Assembly to prohibit the trade with Canada, the London merchants who supplied the Albany men succeeded in having Parliament suspend the law (Norton 1974:137–147). From their point of view the fur trade was important less for the furs than for the market it provided for English manufacturers.

The principal agents of this trade were the Christian Iroquois at the Jesuit mission at Sault Saint Louis, who had removed from the Five Nations in the mid-seventeenth century for religious reasons and established themselves, under Jesuit auspices, near Montreal. It was they who transported the goods and furs back and forth by way of the Richelieu River, Lake Champlain, and the Hudson River. The Canadian officials could do little to stop them, for no Indian nation would submit to French decrees (Eccles 1984).

During the second quarter of the eighteenth century the Canadian fur trade was called on to aid the advance of European scientific knowledge. In New France this interest was reflected in the field of botany, biology, geology, hydrography, astronomy, and geography. The

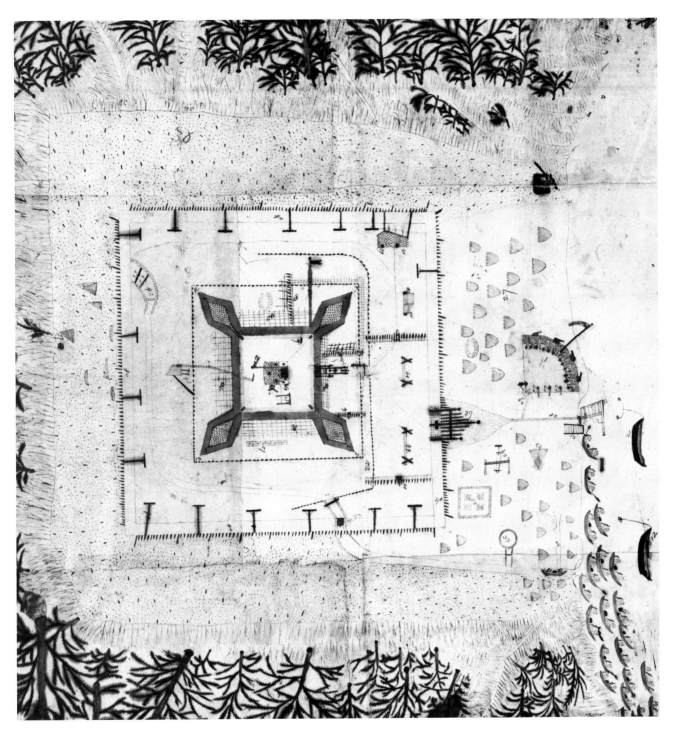

Fig. 2. Plan of York Factory, a Hudson's Bay Company post on the Hayes River at Hudson Bay, Man. Several structures at different locations were named York Factory. The fort illustrated here, completed in 1715, was built of logs and plaster. It had 4 bastions, breastworks, and a double row of palisades and was defended throughout by mounted armaments. The approach to the Hayes River, right, was protected by a battery of cannon. A flotilla of Indian canoes, lower right, is approaching the fort (Cummings et al. 1974:195). Drawing in pen and ink and watercolor by James Isham, about 1743.

government, close to bankruptcy after the 1702–1713 war, declared that the costs of this endeavor would be borne by the fur trade. The officers in the colonial regular troops who were appointed to command at the western posts, and who received monopolies of the trade in their respective areas of command to defray the heavy costs that they were required to sustain in return, were required to send some of their men on probing expeditions to the western ocean (Eccles 1984a:3–5).

It was under such conditions that Pierre Gaultier de

Fig. 3. Jesuit brass rings, popular trade items. The inscriptions may represent the customer's initials (Noel Hume 1969:266) or abstract decorative motifs traceable to 3 prototype designs: L-Heart series, Double-M series, IHS series (Cleland 1972). The rings themselves evidently did not carry any religious significance. At least at Ft. Michilimackinac during the French occupation about 1720–1750, they were not distributed by the resident Jesuit priest (L.M. Stone 1974: 131). These rings were excavated from the French Ft. St. Charles, a settlement at Lake of the Woods, Minn., dating 1732–1750s. Center 2.2 cm diameter; others to same scale.

Varennes, sieur de La Vérendrye and his sons journeyed across the Plains to the Big Horn Mountains and subsequently established bases for an advance westward along the Red, Assiniboine, and Saskatchewan rivers. La Vérendrye's successor in command of the entire region west of Lake Superior and the commandant at Green Bay were likewise enjoined to send their men westward along the Saskatchewan and Missouri rivers. The former was by far the better route. It was more navigable, and one language, Cree, sufficed along its length. Moreover, the tribes on the prairies had little need for European goods. Since they were well supplied with horses, even with bows and lances the great buffalo herds were at their mercy and provided both food aplenty and hides for shelter. There were few furbearing animals on the prairies of any value whereas north of the Saskatchewan lay the forest belt, providing vast quantities of high quality furs (Brebner 1933).

The French traders appear to have paid little heed to the order to seek a route to the western ocean. Their time was too taken up with the fur trade, striving to keep peace among the belligerent tribes, and in preventing them having dealings with the English at Hudson Bay or with the English colonial traders who had begun to cross the Appalachian mountain barrier. It seems likely that a handful of the French did reach the Rocky Mountains.

The French drive into the northwest did serve one economic and political purpose. The rivers on which the western posts were located drained into Hudson Bay. The French were thus able to impede the access of the western tribes to their English rivals at the bayside posts. They dared not block the routes completely; the Indians would never have allowed that. By taking some of their furs to the bay from time to time Indians reasserted their independence and the right to go where they pleased in their land; it also forced the French to be ever solicitous toward them. Yet the voyage to Hudson Bay was long and dangerous through lands where game was scarce. Moreover, there was barely enough time to make the voyage there and back between the spring break-up and the freeze-up in the fall (Ray 1974). Thus it was that the French skimmed off the cream of the trade, and the volume of furs traded at the Hudson's Bay Company posts declined steadily in the first half of the eighteenth century (Ray and Freeman 1978).

To the south the English were striving to break through the ring that the French had forged in the rear of the 13 colonies, for it not only blocked their westward expansion but also constituted a grave threat in the event of war. When Gov. William Burnett of New York proposed seizing control of the Niagara River he received no support from the Assembly. They were satisfied with the existing arrangements whereby furs from Montreal were delivered to their doorsteps. Governor-General of New France Philip de Rigaud de Vaudreuil, on the other hand, acted swiftly. He had a fort built and garrisoned at Niagara (Zoltvany 1974:168–170).

This move upset not only the English but also the Iroquois. Their policy had been one of neutrality since 1701, of preventing both the French and the English from gaining a dominant position. To balance this French move at Niagara they granted the English what they had hitherto adamantly refused, permission to establish a fortified post at Oswego on Lake Ontario in 1725. The New York officials hoped to break through the chain of French posts into the rich fur country of the northwest and seduce the tribes out of their alliance with the French. To block this the French Crown was obliged to subsidize the trade at Forts Frontenac and Niagara from time to time and relax the regulations on the trading of liquor to the Indians. Every means was used—presents, flattery, lavish entertainment at Québec and Montreal, trips to France for the more influential chiefs—to keep the allies away from Oswego and Albany. The French fur trade more than ever was subordinate to political ends. In this contest, the English colonists were their own worst enemies; their trading methods and contemptuous attitude toward the Indians outraged and alienated them (Leach 1966:153–154).

Traders from Pennsylvania and Virginia began to make their way in increasing numbers over the Appalachian range into the Ohio valley. Although the Canadian fur traders had little interest in the low-grade furs and deerskins of the region and would have been content to leave them to the English, a new element had been added—land speculation. In both Virginia and Pennsylva-

330

nia land companies were formed and huge grants of Indian lands obtained from the Crown. Some of the English traders were advance agents of these companies. They wooed the Indians with cheap goods, established posts, flooded the region with rum, and soon dominated the headwaters of the Ohio. The Indians, although warned by the French, could not see that this development posed any serious threat to them (Stanley 1968:33–40). The French, on the other hand, saw their hold on the west seriously threatened.

The French could have countered the Anglo-American fur trade threat by economic means, but against this new menace mere Crown subsidies would not suffice. They felt compelled to resort to military force. Canadian regulars and militia drove the American traders out of the Ohio valley, back over the mountains, destroyed their posts, built Fort Duquesne at the forks of the river, overawed the Indians, and provided them with the goods they desired at heavy cost to the Crown. The Anglo-American response was predictable, a feeble military riposte that the French swiftly and ignominiously crushed. But those brief clashes of arms in the spring and summer of 1754 proved to be the first shots fired in the Seven Years' War.

That the French fur trade and Indian policy had been politically sound was made abundantly plain during the course of the war. The Anglo-Americans found themselves with no Indian allies while their frontier settlements were devastated by Canadian and Indian war parties. Oswego was destroyed in 1756, and the Iroquois, who persisted in remaining ostensibly neutral while many of their young warriors fought with the French, pointedly thanked the governor-general at Montreal for removing that intrusion on their land, thereby serving notice that the French were not to think of occupying the site themselves. The destruction of that fort eliminated the Albany merchants from the fur trade, gave the French control of the Great Lakes, and removed the threat to French communications in the west. Throughout the war the fur brigades left Montreal, but with thousands of warriors assembling there every summer to engage in the war against the British and Americans the supplies of fur diminished. The Indians had little need to hunt beaver and marten; they were kept well supplied with arms and food for their families in return for hunting down American settlers and British soldiers. Scalps and prisoners became the medium of exchange rather than furs. For warriors this was a much more gratifying arrangement (Leach 1973:378–379, 403).

In 1758 the tide of war turned. The Royal Navy and a large army of British regulars, combined with wretched and divided leadership in the French command, finally mastered the French and Canadians. Louisbourg fell, the following year Quebec, and in 1760 the outnumbered French were forced to capitulate at Montreal.

In 1760, prior to the surrender, only five canoes had left for the west. The following year, under British military rule, the trade revived, and over 200 voyageurs were hired. Significantly seven of the 35 merchants who hired them bore English or Scots names. Some of them, like Alexander Henry, were old Albany traders who had moved to Montreal. By the end of the century Anglo-Scots merchants dominated the trade (Ouellet 1966:101–109; Eccles 1969:186–187).

The French Canadians were not the only ones to suffer from the conquest of New France. The plight of the Indians was far worse. Whereas before, the French and the English had had to compete for their support, with French power removed the Indians had no bargaining position. On the orders of British commander in chief Jeffery Amherst, the distribution of "presents" to the Indians ceased. He could see no need to "bribe" the "savages" who had sided with the enemy (Peckham 1947: 71–72). They, on the other hand, had always regarded these "presents" as payments for the right to maintain trading posts and to travel through their lands. At the western posts American and British garrisons took over from the French and treated the Indians with their customary contempt. At the same time, in defiance of laws and treaties, American settlers poured over the mountains onto the Indians' lands in the thousands, the British authorities seemingly unable to stop them. The Indian nations quickly grasped what was in store for them and determined to drive the encroaching settlers off their territory. In 1763 they struck at the British-held posts and supply convoys, then at the settlers. The survivors fled back over the mountains. Although the Indians scored some early successes, inflicting heavy casualties, they could not sustain a lengthy war. When their supplies were exhausted their resistance collapsed.

Meanwhile the Canadian fur trade began rapidly to expand. The trade at Tadoussac was continued as a Crown monopoly and leased to a group of British merchants for £400 a year. To the northeast of these posts, from Anticosti island to the Straits of Belle-Isle, the seal hunt was resumed but the profits were small compared to those of the western fur trade. English, Scots, and some few American merchant traders, based at Montreal and amply supplied with goods and credit by London merchants, obtained licenses from James Murray, the governor of the British province of Quebec, and took over the trade at the old French posts. In an attempt to maintain some semblance of order and curb reprisals by the much abused Indians they were confined to these posts where the commandants could keep an eye on them. The traders complained bitterly at this constraint, and by 1767 the regulations had been eased to enable them to meet the competition of Canadian traders operating out of Saint Louis on the Mississippi, part of Spanish Louisiana (P.C. Phillips 1961, 1:597–603; Sosin 1961:112–113). The trade south of the Ohio was given over to the southern colonies,

Fig. 4. Silver trade cross. Cruciform images, which probably lacked any element of Christian devotion for the Indian, served most often as additions to necklaces and other items of traditional Indian apparel. This cross was fashioned by Robert Cruickshank, Montreal silversmith and supplier to Montreal traders about 1767–1809 (Langdon 1960). It was found at an Ojibwa ricing camp on Big Sandy Lake, Minn., near the site of Sandy House, a North West Company post established in 1794 (I.H. Hart 1926:311; E.A. Hart 1963:2–3). Length 12.7 cm.

Virginia, Maryland, Georgia, and the Carolinas; that to the north of the Ohio went to New York and Pennsylvania. The Montreal traders, like their Canadian predecessors, had little interest in that region. The only serious rival they had was the Hudson's Bay Company, which claimed title to all the land whose rivers flowed into the Bay and a monopoly on the trade throughout this region that stretched to the Rocky Mountains.

The main problem facing the Montreal traders was not competition from either Louisiana or Hudson Bay but that among themselves. This cutthroat competition, which did not stop short of murder, drove the traders to seek out tribes far to the north and west (W.S. Wallace 1954:19–26). By 1770 the "Pedlars," as the Hudson's Bay Company disparagingly referred to the Montreal traders, were on the Saskatchewan River, cutting the flow of furs to the bay. It was the Canadian voyageurs—their skill as

canoemen, their knowledge of the country and of Indian ways, their ability to survive in that harsh environment— that allowed the fur trade to expand as it did. As the trade moved across the northern half of the continent the capital investment required mounted steadily. Goods had to be ordered in England a year previous to their being sent west from Montreal, and the furs to pay for them could not return until the following year. The profits could be great, and the losses ruinous (Innis 1962:166–262).

In 1775–1776, with the outbreak of the American Revolution and the occupation of Montreal by a rebel army, the western fur trade was briefly interrupted, but during the course of the war the Montreal traders eliminated Albany from the trade. In the terms of the treaty ending the war, Britain ceded the territory south of the Great Lakes to the new republic. The Indians whose land it was and the Montreal merchants protested vigorously (Creighton 1937:87–110; Eccles 1984). Partly to assuage them, but mainly to prevent another Indian war, Britain retained possession of several posts in the region, and the concerned fur traders rapidly stripped it of its furs, leaving barely a chipmunk. With the signing of Jay's Treaty in 1794, after granting to the Americans what was not theirs to grant, the British withdrew, abandoning the Indians to their fate.

The Hudson's Bay Company had, in 1774, established its first major western inland post, Cumberland House, on the Saskatchewan, to try to meet the competition of the "Pedlars" who too often pillaged the traders sent inland from the bay. This invasion of the west by the old company, with its solid financial backing, along with the difficulties caused by the American Revolution and the need for more capital to meet increased costs, forced the major Montreal traders to amalgamate. In 1779 the North West Company, a loose partnership comprising 16 shares, was formed for one year. A similar partnership was formed the following year and in 1783 another North West Company was formed, again with 16 shares, for a minimum of five years. These partnerships were friable arrangements; merchant traders joined, quarreled, split off. In 1797 a rival, the XY Company, was formed (Innis 1962:196–201; Rich 1967:172–176, 190–195; Morton 1939:510–518).

The struggle of these companies against each other, and of the two of them against the Hudson's Bay Company, had a devastating effect on the Indians. Liquor, in a form that was euphemistically referred to as "high wine" (a potent mixture of rum, brandy, port, sherry, and water in equal proportions) was used in increasing quantities to lure the Indians with their furs to one company's post over another's. Worse still, in 1781 smallpox swept across the prairies. The few survivors fled, spreading the disease farther (Rich 1967:158–159). Among the tribes hardest hit were the Chipewyan and the Slavey who usually traded at Hudson Bay. This enabled the North West Company to gain the upper hand temporarily. Their fur shipments varied from £165,000 to £242,000 a year; those of the Hudson's Bay Company were only some £30,000 (Rich 1967:158–159, 174).

The Bay Company was also severely handicapped by its lack of canoes and skilled canoe men, and with the renewal of the war with France it had a hard time recruiting men in Britain for service at its posts. The British army and navy scoured the kingdom for men; all who could see lightning, hear thunder, and were not on crutches were deemed fit for His Majesty's service. The Hudson's Bay Company therefore had to take the physical rejects, and they were no match for the tough North West Company voyageurs (Glover 1948). Moreover, these Bay Company servants were just that. They saw no gain to themselves in the unequal struggle where they got the blows for starvation wages and the shareholders in England got the profits. By contrast, the wintering partners of the North West Company knew the ways of the Indian country; they had endured the privations that

their Canadian employees suffered in the hinterland winters and had earned their grudging respect. As fast as the Hudson's Bay Company established posts in the interior the North West Company constructed their posts nearby and beyond, driving the Indians away from their rivals by fair means and foul, denying them food supplies, constantly forestalling them (Rich 1967:187–189).

In 1811 a new threat to the North West Company appeared: land settlement athwart their main supply line. When Thomas Douglas, Earl of Selkirk, gained control of the Hudson's Bay Company in 1809, his aim was to establish a farming colony south of Lake Winnipeg. This area was the main source of the food supply for the western fur trade—pemmican, a concentrated and nutritious food made from dried buffalo meat, pounded fine, mixed with melted buffalo fat and prairie berries, then sewn into buffalo hide sacks. The providers of this essential food were the Métis buffalo hunters who occupied the region at the junction of the Red and Assiniboine rivers. When Selkirk's settlers arrived there in

Fig. 5. Cartouche from *A Map of the Inhabited Part of Canada*, by Claude Joseph Sauthier, 1777, depicting a trading transaction. The map shows a section of the Northeast, including parts of Upper and Lower Canada, northern New York, and northern New England, and the English army's winter quarters for 1776 (Haase and Jantz 1976:133). Engraved by William Faden.

THE FUR TRADE IN THE COLONIAL NORTHEAST

1812 and began to put the plow to the prairie sod it spelled the doom of the buffalo hunt, the Métis nation, the Indians, and Montreal's dominance of the fur trade.

Despite the opposition of the North West Company men, who made life as difficult as possible for the settlers, Selkirk persisted with his scheme, and more colonists were recruited in the Scottish highland. Spurred on by the North West Company men, the Métis in 1814 drove the settlers out, only to see them return the following year. At Seven Oaks in 1816 the governor of the colony and 21 settlers were killed. The survivors were driven out, some to the Hudson Bay posts, the rest to Canada (Gray 1963: 167–173).

But Selkirk succeeded in restoring his colony, and the Hudson's Bay Company finally got the upper hand in the long struggle for control of the fur trade. By this time it was established in the Oregon territory. It was far cheaper to supply the posts there by ship around Cape Horn than by ship to Quebec, then across the continent by canoe. Moreover, the Hudson's Bay Company acquired better manpower, and an answer had been found to the Montrealers' canoes, the York boat. This was a sturdy flat-bottomed, pine-planked boat, with high, wide, slanted sides, sharply pointed at both ends, powered by sail and oars. These boats were maneuverable in fast water, more durable than the birchbark canoe, and capable of carrying as large a load as the fur trade canoe with a smaller crew, thereby effecting a saving of one-third in wages and maintenance costs (E.W. Morse 1969:24). The French Canadian voyageurs had finally met their match (Glover 1948; Morton 1939:454). So too had the Montreal wintering partners. Their loose organization, with the shares held only by active partners, operating on a financial hand to mouth basis, with no capital reserves, and living extravagantly ensured that they could not prevail. In 1821 they were forced to amalgamate as best they could with the Hudson's Bay Company. They were, in fact, absorbed by their old foe (Innis 1962:261–280).

This marked the end of Montreal as the entrepôt of the northern fur trade. The canoe brigades no longer left Lachine for Fort William each spring. Under the new regime trade goods moved by ship to York Factory at the mouth of the Nelson and Hayes rivers, then up river by York boat; or else they went around the Horn to Oregon by ship. Before long they also went by railroad from New York to Saint Paul, then north on Red River by paddle steamer to Lake Winnipeg (Morton 1939; W.L. Morton 1957:167, 173, 175).

In the northwest the amalgamation of the rival companies brought a semblance of peace to a devastated land. Many trading posts were closed to reduce costs, and with the removal of cutthroat competition there was no longer the need to ply the Indians with high wine. At the same time they were at the mercy of the Company, dependent on it for the goods they could no longer do without.

Sources

The primary source material concerning the northeastern fur trade is extensive and scattered. For the trade in the regions within the borders of the United States the documents are in various state archives, public and university libraries, historical societies, and private collections. Many are cited in the preface of P.C. Phillips (1961).

For the Canadian trade under the French regime the mass of documents is staggering. They are to be found in Paris, principally at the Archives Nationales and the Bibliothèque Nationale. The Public Archives of Canada, Ottawa, and the Library of Congress have microfilm of most of these documents.

In Canada the sheer quantity of fur trade documents in the notarial *greffes* at the Archives Nationales du Québec, Montréal, is daunting, and there is a goodly number at the Archives Nationales du Québec in Québec. Another treasure trove, consisting of eighteenth-century Montreal merchants' ledgers, the property of the Château de Ramezay, Montreal, is on deposit at the Public Archives of Canada. The McCord Museum at Montreal possesses documents pertaining to the North West Company.

Some primary source material has been printed, but it must be used with caution. For the seventeenth century the Thwaites edition of the *Jesuit Relations* (JR 1896–1901) is still of great value, but it is being superseded by Campeau (1967, 1979). Also for the early seventeenth century the works of Samuel de Champlain (1922–1936) are invaluable. The papers of Sir William Johnson (1921–1965) contain many insights and nuggets of solid evidence bearing on the roles of the Indians, French, and English in the fur trade. The archives of the Hudson's Bay Company are located in Winnipeg. For the American trade Cuthbertson and Ewers (1939) and Donnelly (1947) are points of departure. Norton (1974) contains a useful bibliography for the New York trade, but the text is vitiated by assumptions and the failure to consult Canadian primary sources. Innis (1962), which is dated, is marred by conclusions not supported and even contradicted by the evidence. P.C. Phillips (1961) is useful for the trade in the English colonies but riddled with errors on the Canadian fur trade.

Works on the Canadian trade by Ray (1974), Ray and Freeman (1978), Allaire (1980), Van Kirk (1980a), Brown (1980), Morantz (1980), Francis and Morantz (1983), and Eccles (1983) have put the fur trade in context by describing the role of the Indians in the trade.

The Hudson's Bay Company and Native People

ARTHUR J. RAY

The Hudson's Bay Company is unique; it is the only business that has maintained a relationship with native peoples living along the shores of Hudson and James Bays for over 300 years and with those living in the lower Mackenzie River valley and British Columbia, for over 150 years.

The growth of the trade routes can be generally traced along the following progression. Prior to 1670, the French developed routes from the Saint Lawrence basin to southern James Bay via the Saguenay and Nottaway rivers, and into the Great Lakes. From 1670 until 1763, the French and the Hudson's Bay Company expanded to the southern Hudson's Bay periphery, to the eastern and southern James Bay interior, to the Great Lakes interior, and west to the Saskatchewan River via Rainy Lake, Lake of the Woods, and Lake Winnipeg. Between 1764 and 1821, the Hudson's Bay Company, North West Company, XY Company, and independent operators competitively spread into the Ontario, Manitoba, Saskatchewan, Alberta, and British Columbia interiors, and north via the Great Slave Lake on the Mackenzie River to the Arctic Circle. From 1822 until 1885, the Hudson's Bay Company and independent operators expanded into northern British Columbia, Yukon Territory, north to the Mackenzie Delta, east into the Mackenzie District interior, and into northern Labrador and northeastern Quebec. After 1885, the Hudson's Bay Company and independent operators extended their routes into the northern Northwest Territories and northwestern Quebec (Ray 1987).

Era of Native Entrepreneurship, 1670–1763

In 1670 Charles II of England chartered the Hudson's Bay Company, giving the company monopoly trading privileges and title to the lands lying within the territory drained by waters flowing into Hudson Bay. This vast region, named Rupert's Land, included the Hudson Bay lowlands, a large section of the Canadian Shield uplands, and portions of the northern Great Plains (fig. 1). As a joint-stock trading company, the Hudson's Bay Company was one of the earliest organizations of this type (Ray and Freeman 1978:10–13). Its development became the primary responsibility of a small group of men known as the Governor and Committee who were elected annually from among the shareholders. Through the company's charter, the Governor and Committee were given the option of building the fur trade along three very different lines. The first involved conducting trade from aboard ships, as had been done between 1668 and 1670. A coasting trade such as this offered the advantage of keeping fixed overhead costs to a minimum. A second option involved developing a "cape and merchant system" in which the Hudson's Bay Company would monopolize the transportation of goods to and from Hudson Bay while independent merchants would build trading establishments and would deal directly with the native peoples. Instead of pursuing either of these options the Governor and Committee decided to establish permanent trading facilities, called factories (Rich 1958–1959, 1:55). Mindful of the overhead costs of building and operating factories, the Governor and Committee adopted a conservative construction program and erected posts only at key locations along the shores of Hudson and James bays. For the first century of the Company's operations, the Governor and Committee remained committed to this policy, refusing to move inland to challenge French trading operations. Parliamentary critics of the Hudson's Bay Company who favored aggressive action for the sake of British imperial interests dubbed this approach the policy of "sleeping by the frozen sea" (Rich 1958–1959, 1:533–555). The decision to "sleep by the frozen sea" had major consequences for Indian–Euro-Canadian relations. It placed the Hudson's Bay Company in direct and sustained contact with its Indian trading partners. At the same time, this policy enabled the Indian entrepreneurs to organize and dominate the inland portion of the company's business for over 100 years.

The original idea of developing a company to trade into Hudson Bay was promoted by Pierre Esprit Radisson and Médard Chouart, sieur des Groseilliers, two men who had been involved in extending the French fur trade to the upper Great Lakes area. They realized that transportation expenses could be lowered substantially by developing a transoceanic link into the heart of the continent. Being unable to obtain French backing for their plan, they sought and obtained English support. Committed to the idea, but knowing little about the native people or the manner in which the North American fur trade was

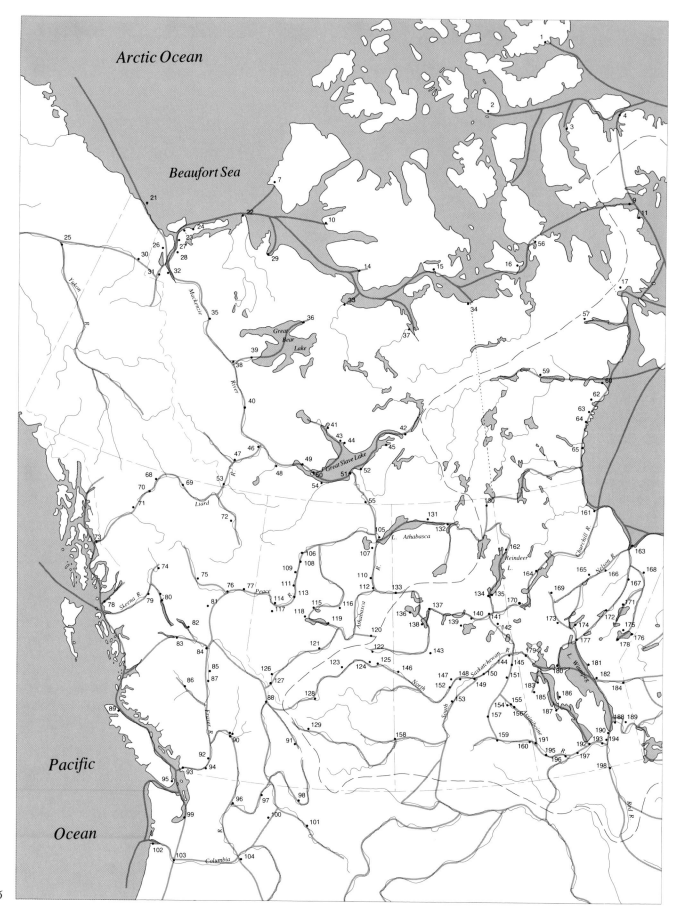

Arctic Ocean

Beaufort Sea

Pacific

Ocean

336

Fig. 1. Historic trade routes and posts of the French (Fr), Hudson's Bay Company (HBC), North West Company (NWC), XY Company (XYC), and independent (Ind) operators with dates of establishment. All posts cited were in use at least 15 years; those indicated with an asterisk were in use during 1987. Since many short-term posts existed, this map is not comprehensive, nor were all these posts in existence at the same time. When more than one operator is named for a post, that post had simultaneous, overlapping, sequential, or interrupted operation. In many cases, nearby place-names differ slightly from the post names. In 1987, the Hudson's Bay Company sold all its trading posts (Voorhis 1930; E.W. Morse 1969; Usher 1971; Canada. Department of Energy, Mines and Resources 1973; Harris and Matthews 1987, 1; Hudson's Bay Company Archives—Provincial Archives of Manitoba 1987). Northwest Terr.—Franklin District: 1, Grise Fiord, Ind, 1961*; 2, Resolute Bay, HBC—Ind, 1961*; 3, Arctic Bay—Tukik, HBC, 1926*; 4, Mitimatalik—Pond Inlet, HBC, 1921*; 5, Clyde River, HBC, 1923*; 6, Broughton I., HBC, 1960*; 7, Sachs Harbour, Ind, 1958*; 8, Netchelik—Pangnirtung, HBC, 1921*; 9, Igloolik, HBC—Ind, 1939*; 10, Holman, HBC, 1939*; 11, Hall Beach, Ind—HBC, 1965*; 12, Frobisher Bay—Iqaluit, HBC, 1949*; 13, Ward Inlet, HBC, 1921; 14, Read I., HBC, 1931; 15, Cambridge Bay, HBC, 1920*; 16, Gjoa Haven, HBC, 1927*; 17, Ft. Hope—Repulse Bay, HBC—Ind, 1850*; 18, Cape Dorset, HBC—Ind, 1913*; 19, Lake Harbour, HBC, 1911*; 20, Port Burwell—Killiniq, HBC—Ind, 1916.* Northwest Terr.—Mackenzie District, Yukon Terr., and Alaska: 21, Herschel I., HBC, 1915; 22, Baillie I.—Cape Bathurst, HBC, 1916; 23, Kittigazuit, HBC, 1912; 24, Port Brabant—Tuktoyaktuk, HBC, 1934*; 25, Ft. Yukon, HBC, 1847; 26, Aklavik, HBC—Ind, 1912*; 27, Reindeer Station, HBC, 1949; 28, Inuvik, HBC—Ind, 1956*; 29, Paulatuk, Ind, 1942*; 30, La Pierre's House, HBC, 1847; 31, Peel's River Post—Ft. McPherson, HBC—Ind, 1840*; 32, Arctic Red River, HBC—Ind, 1901*; 33, Coppermine, HBC, 1928*; 34, Perry River, Ind—HBC, 1926; 35, Ft. Good Hope, NWC—HBC, 1804; Ft. Confidence, Ind, 1837; 37, Burnside River, HBC, 1930; 38, Ft. Norman, NWC—HBC—Ind, 1810*; 39, Ft. Franklin, NWC—HBC, 1812*; 40, Ft. Wrigley, HBC, 1877*; 41, Ft. Rae—Ind, 1852*; 42, Ft. Reliance, Ind—HBC, 1833*; 43, Yellowknife, Ind—HBC, 1937*; 44, Ft. Providence, HBC, 1790; 45, Snowdrift, HBC—Ind, 1926; 46, The Forks—Ft. Simpson, NWC—HBC—Ind, 1804*; 47, Nahanni Butte, Ind, 1915*; 48, Trout River, Ind, 1934; 49, Ft. Providence, HBC—Ind, 1869*; 50, Big Island House, HBC, 1830; 51, Slave Ft.—Ft. Resolution, NWC—HBC, 1786*; 52, Rocher River, HBC—Ind, 1926*; 53, Ft. Liard, NWC—HBC—Ind, 1800*; 54, Hay River, HBC—Ind, 1868*; 55, Ft. Smith, HBC—Ind, 1874.* Northwest Terr.—Keewatin District: 56, Spence Bay, HBC, 1949*; 57, Wager Bay, HBC, 1925; 58, Southampton I.—Coral Harbour, HBC, 1924*; 59, Baker Lake, Ind—HBC, 1916*; 60, Chesterfield Inlet, HBC, 1911*; 61, Cape Smith—Smith I., HBC, 1927; 62, Rankin Inlet, HBC, 1957*; 63, Whale Cove, Ind, 1963*; 64, Tavani, HBC, 1929; 65, Eskimo Point, HBC, 1921*; 66, Tukarak—Sanikiluaq, HBC, 1937*; 67, Charlton I., HBC, 1680. B.C., southeast Alaska, and northwest U.S.: 68, Liard Post—Lower Post, HBC, 1873; 69, Ft. Halkett, HBC, 1829; 70, McDame's Creek Post, HBC, 1873; 71, Dease Lake, HBC, 1837; 72, Ft. Nelson, NWC—HBC, 1805*; 73, Ft. Wrangell—Ft. Stikine—Ft. Highfield, Russian—HBC, 1834; 74, Connolly Post, HBC, 1827; 75, Bear's Lake—Ft. Grahame, HBC, 1870; 76, Hudson's Hope—Rocky Mountain Portage House, NWC—HBC, 1805; 77, Ft. St. John, NWC—HBC, 1806; 78, Ft. Simpson—Port Simpson, HBC, 1831; 79, Hagwilget—Hazelton, HBC, 1866*; 80, Babine Lake—Ft. Babine, HBC, 1822; 81, McLeod's Lake, NWC—HBC, 1805; 82, Ft. St. James, NWC—HBC, 1806*; 83, Fraser Lake, NWC—HBC, 1806; 84, Ft. George, NWC—HBC, 1807; 85, Quesnel, HBC, 1866; 86, Ft. Chilcotin, HBC, 1829; 87, Ft. Alexandria, NWC—HBC, 1805; 88, Boat Encampment, NWC—HBC, 1810; 89, Ft. Rupert, HBC, 1849; 90, Ft. Thompson—Ft. Kamloops, Ind—NWC—HBC, 1812; 91, Kootenay House, NWC—HBC, 1807; 92, Ft. Yale, HBC, 1848; 93, Ft. Langley, HBC, 1827; 94, Ft. Hope, HBC, 1848; 95, Ft. Victoria, HBC, 1843; 96, Ft. Okanagan, NWC—HBC, 1811; 97, Ft. Colville, HBC, 1825; 98, Kootenay Ft., NWC—HBC, 1809; 99, Ft. Nisqually, HBC, 1833; 100, Spokane House, NWC—HBC, 1810; 101, Flathead House—Ft. Connah, NWC—HBC, 1809; 102, Ft. Astoria—Ft. George, NWC—HBC, 1811; 103, Ft. Vancouver, HBC, 1824; 104, Ft. Walla Walla—Ft. Nez Perces, NWC—HBC, 1818. Alta.: 105, Ft. Chipewyan, NWC—HBC, 1798*; 106, Ft. Vermilion, XYC—NWC—HBC, 1800*; 107, Pond's Ft., NWC, 1778; 108, Ft. du Tremble—Keg River, NWC—HBC, 1800; 109, Horse Shoe House—Battle River Post, NWC—HBC, 1803; 110, Ft. McMurray—Ft. McKay, HBC, 1874; 111, McLeod's Ft., NWC—HBC, 1791; 112, Ft. of the Forks—Ft. McMurray, NWC—HBC, 1788; 113, Ft. of the Forks—Peace River, NWC—HBC, 1792*; 114, Ft. Dunvegan, NWC—HBC, 1805; 115, Whitefish Lake, HBC, 1878; 116, Wabasca—Desmarais, HBC, 1889*; 117, Spirit River, HBC, 1888; 118, Lesser Slave Lake, NWC—HBC, 1802; 119, Lesser Slave Lake, NWC, 1799; 120, Lac-la-Biche, NWC—HBC, 1798*; 121, Ft. Assiniboine, HBC, 1823; 122, Ft. Lac d'Orignal—Moose Lake, NWC, 1789; 123, Ft. Augustus—Ft. Edmonton, NWC—HBC, 1795; 124, St. Paul House, HBC, 1866; 125, Buckingham House, HBC, 1792; 126, Jasper House, HBC, 1801; 127, Henry's House, HBC, 1812; 128, Acton House—Rocky Mountain House, NWC—HBC, 1799; 129, Bow River Ft., NWC, 1802. Sask.: 130, Caribou, HBC, 1930; 131, Fond du Lac, HBC, 1845*; 132, Black Lake, HBC, 1959*; 133, Portage la Loche, HBC, 1801*; 134, Clapham House—Southend, HBC, 1795*; 135, Deers River, HBC, 1792; 136, Lac-des-Boeufs—Buffalo Narrows, NWC—HBC, 1790*; 137, Pine River—Patuanak, HBC, 1921*; 138, Île-à-la-Crosse, NWC—HBC, 1776*; 139, Lac la Ronge, NWC—HBC, 1778*; 140, Rapid River House—Stanley House, Ind—HBC, 1778*; 141, Portage du Traite, Ind—NWC—HBC, 1774; 142, Pelican Narrows, NWC—HBC, 1779*; 143, Green Lake House, NWC—HBC, 1781; 144, Cumberland House, NWC—HBC, 1774*; 145, Pas Mountain House, HBC, 1885; 146, Manchester House—Ft. Pitt, HBC, 1786; 147, Hudson's House, HBC, 1776; 148, Prince Albert, HBC, 1868; 149, Ft. St. Louis—Ft. à la Corne, Fr—NWC—HBC, 1753; 150, Ft. Lower Nipawi, Fr, 1748; 151, Egg Lake—Nut Lake, HBC, 1852; 152, Ft. Carlton, 1795; 153, South Branch House, NWC—HBC, 1786; 154, Ft. Alexandria, NWC—HBC, 1780; 155, Ft. Hibernia—Ft. Pelly, HBC, 1795; 156, Carlton House, HBC, 1795; 157, Touchwood Hills, HBC, 1849; 158, Chesterfield House, XYC—NWC—HBC, 1791; 159, Ft. Qu'Appelle, HBC, 1853; 160, Ft. Esperance, NWC, 1787. Man.: 161, Churchill Factory, HBC, 1717*; 162, Lac du Brochet, HBC, 1796*; 163, York Factory—Ft. Nelson, Ind—Fr—HBC, 1682; 164, South Indian Lake, HBC—NWC, 1797; 165, Split Lake House, HBC, 1790*; 166, Gillam, HBC, 1927*; 167, Gordon House—Rock Depot, HBC, 1794; 168, Shamattawa, HBC, 1913*; 169, Nelson House, HBC, 1800*; 170, Pukatawagan, Ind—NWC—HBC, 1793*; 171, God's Lake, HBC, 1825; 172, Oxford House, HBC, 1798*; 173, Wabowden, HBC, 1922; 174, Cross Lake, NWC—HBC, 1794*; 175, Island Lake, HBC, 1818*; 176, Island Lake, NWC, 1803; 177, Jack River House—Norway House, NWC—HBC, 1796*; 178, Maria Portage—St. Theresa Point, HBC, 1947*; 179, Ft. Pasquia—The Pas, Fr—HBC, 1749*; 180, Grand Rapids, HBC, 1864; 181, Poplar River, NWC—HBC, 1806*; 182, Berens River, HBC, 1814*; 183, Shoal River, HBC, 1828; 184, Little Grand Rapids, HBC, 1801*; 185, Swan River, NWC—HBC, 1790; 186, Waterhen Lake House, HBC, 1886; 187, Ft. Dauphin, Fr—NWC—HBC, 1741; 188, Ft. Maurepas—Ft. Bas-de-la-Rivière, Fr—NWC—HBC, 1734*; 189, Lac-du-Bonnet House—Indian Cap Ft., NWC—HBC, 1804*; 190, Rivière aux Morts—Lower Ft. Garry, NWC—HBC, 1803; 191, Ft. Ellice, HBC, 1794; 192, Ft. La Reine—Portage la Prairie, Fr—NWC—HBC, 1738; 193, White Horse Plains House, HBC, 1810; 194, Ft. Gibraltar—Ft. Douglas—Upper Ft. Garry, NWC—HBC, 1807; 195, Ft. Montagne-à-la-Bosse, NWC, 1790; 196, Ft. Souris—Brandon House—Grand Ripple, XYC-NWC-HBC, 1793; 197, Pine Ft., Ind—NWC—HBC, 1768; 198, Pembina, NWC—HBC, 1797. Ont. and Great Lakes-United States: 199, Severn House, HBC, 1680; 200, Attawapiskat House, HBC, 1901*; 201, Kapiskau River, HBC, 1750; 202, Chickney Creek, HBC, 1750; 203, Ft. Albany, HBC, 1679*; 204, Severn Lake—Bearskin Lake, HBC, 1793*; 205, Trout Lake Ft., NWC—HBC, 1793*; 206, Moose Factory, HBC, 1673*; 207, Webequie, HBC, 1942*; 208, Ghost River, Ind—HBC, 1905; 209, Sandy Lake, NWC—HBC, 1798*; 210, Attawapiskat Lake—Lansdowne House, HBC, 1814*; 211, Martin's Falls, HBC, 1784; 212, Ogoki, HBC, 1924; 213, Henley House, HBC, 1743; 214, Gloucester House, HBC, 1777; 215, New Post, HBC, 1880; 216, Pickle Lake, HBC, 1932*; 217, Ft. Mamattawa—English River House, HBC, 1832; 218, Wapiscogamy House—Brunswick House, HBC, 1777; 219, Pikangikum, HBC, 1946*; 220, Cat Lake, HBC, 1788*; 221, Osnaburgh House, HBC, 1786; 222, Cockinagamy Lake, NWC, 1804; 223, Mattice, HBC, 1917; 224, Waupissatiga Lake, HBC, 1800; 225, Devil's Island—Frederick

House, NWC—HBC, 1785; 226, Nakina, Ind—HBC, 1944*; 227, Micabanish House—New Brunswick House, NWC—HBC, 1778; 228, Keenogumisee Lake, HBC, 1794; 229, Langue-de-Terre, Ind, 1785; 230, Red Lake House—Balmertown, NWC—HBC, 1790*; 231, Nipigon House—Ft. Duncan—Wabinosh House, NWC—HBC, 1786; 232, Ft. Outoulibis, Fr, 1684; 233, Ft. La Maune, Fr, 1684; 234, Longlac, NWC—HBC, 1813*; 235, Capoonacagami, NWC—HBC, 1815; 236, Flying Post, NWC—HBC, 1800; 237, Mattagami, Ind–HBC, 1794; 238, Lac Suel, NWC—HBC, 1803*; 239, Missinaibi House, HBC, 1777; 240, Portage de l'Isle, Fr—NWC, 1789; 241, Wepineban—Escabitchewan, NWC—HBC, 1796; 242, Eagle Lake—Dryden, HBC, 1809; 243, Sturgeon Lake Ft., HBC, 1779; 244, Ft. Camanistigoyan—Red Rock—Nipigon, Fr—NWC—HBC, 1678*; 245, Pic, NWC—HBC, 1779; 246, Montizambert—Mobert, HBC, 1888; 247, Michipicoten—Wawa, Fr—Ind—HBC, 1714*; 248, Sturgeon River House, NWC—HBC, 1800; 249, La Ronde Post—Nipissing, NWC—HBC, 1800; 250, Mattawa House, HBC, 1828; 251, Shoal Lake House, HBC, 1831; 252, Camenestiguouia—Mountain Portage—Ft. William, Fr—NWC—HBC, 1679; 253, Batchewana Bay—Mamainse, NWC—HBC, 1814; 254, La Cloche, NWC—HBC, 1808; 255, Whitefish Lake, HBC, 1827; 256, Ft. Frontenac, Fr, 1673; 257; Ft. St. Charles, Fr, 1732; 258, Ft. St. Pierre—Lac la Pluie—Ft. Frances, Fr—XYC—NWC—HBC, 1731; 259, Grand Portage—Ft. Charlotte, Ind—NWC—XYC, 1765; 260, Sault Ste. Marie, Ind—HBC, 1768; 261, Sault Ste. Marie, Fr, 1670; 262, Ft. St. Joseph, NWC, 1765; 263, Mississagi, NWC—HBC, 1800; 264, Ft. St. Ignace, Fr, 1627; 265, Ft. Michilimackinac, Fr, 1712; 266, Ft. Rouille, Fr, 1749; 267, Ft. la Pointe, Fr, 1718; 268, Chagouamigon, Fr, 1663; 269, Ft. Niagara, Fr, 1679; 270, Ft. Baie-des-Puants, Fr, 1717; 271, Ft. Detroit, Fr, 1701; 272, Ft. St. Joseph, Fr, 1691; 273, Ft. Sanduskey, Fr, 1751. Que.: 274, Ft. Wolstenholme—Invujivik, HBC, 1909; 275, Sugluk—Salluit, HBC, 1929*; 276, Wakeham Bay—Kangiqsujuaq, HBC—Ind, 1910*; 277, Payne Bay—Bellin—Kangirsuk, HBC—Ind, 1927*; 278, Ft. Silveright—George River, HBC, 1838; 279, Whale River, HBC, 1869; 280, Leaf River, Ind—HBC, 1905; 281, Ft. Chimo—Kuujjuaq, HBC, 1830*; 282, Baie Philipeau, Fr, 1705; 283, St. Paul, Fr—Ind, 1701; 284, Povungnituk, Ind—HBC, 1921*; 285, South River House—Ft. McKenzie, HBC, 1832; 286, St. Augustin(e), Fr—HBC, 1720*; 287, Gros Mecatina, Fr, 1739; 288, Montagamiou, Fr, 1733; 289, Port Harrison—Inukjuak, HBC, 1920*; 290, Itamamiou, Fr—Ind—HBC, 1733; 291, Ft. Musquarro—Romaine, Fr—NWC—HBC, 1710*; 292, Natashkwan, Fr—NWC—HBC, 1710; 293, Ft. Caniapiscau, HBC, 1834; 294, Nepiochibou, Fr—NWC—HBC, 1710; 295, Richmond Gulf, HBC, 1923; 296, Mingan, Fr, 1661; 297, Little Whale River, HBC, 1749; 298, Ft. Nitchequon—Nichikun, Fr—HBC, 1725; 299, Cormoran, Fr—NWC—HBC, 1661; 300, Great Whale River—Poste-de-la-Baleine—Kuujjuaraapik/Whapmagoostui, HBC, 1756*; 301, Ft. Manicouagan, Fr, 1730; 302, Ft. Moisie, Fr, 1722; 303, Sept-Îles, Fr—Ind—NWC—HBC, 1679; 304, Kanaaupscow, HBC, 1921; 305, Godbout, Ind, 1828; 306, Ft. George—Big River—Chisasibi, HBC, 1805*; 307, Neoskweskau, HBC, 1793; 308, Ft. Temiskamay, HBC, 1825; 309, Papinachois, Fr, 1694; 310, Nouveau Comptoir—Wemindji, HBC, 1959*; 311, Ft. Mistassini, HBC, 1812; 312, Îles-de-Jérémie—Bersimis, Fr—HBC, 1730*; 313, Mille Vaches—Portneuf, Fr—HBC, 1665; 314, East Main Factory, HBC, 1698*; 315, Nemiscau, Fr—HBC, 1685; 316, Ft. Mistassini, Fr, 1674; 317, Ft. Bon Desir, Fr, 1732; 318, Tadoussac, Fr—NWC—HBC, 1599; 319, Ft. Charles—Rupert's House—Waskasanish, Fr—HBC, 1667*; 320, Ft. Nikabau, FR, 1661; 321, Ft. Chicoutimi, Fr—Ind—NWC—HBC, 1676; 322, Pike Lake, HBC, 1826; 323, Ashuapmuchuan, Fr—HBC, 1690; 324, Pointe Bleue, Fr—Ind—NWC—HBC, 1720; 325, Lac St. Jean, Fr—NWC—HBC, 1665; 326, Waswanipi House, NWC—HBC, 1815; 327, Obijuan, HBC, 1827; 328, Kikendatch, Fr—HBC, 1700; 329, Weymontachingue, HBC, 1821; 330, Quebec, Fr, 1608; 331, Ft. Migiskan, HBC, 1828; 332, Manouane, HBC, 1847*; 333, Trois Rivières, Fr—NWC—HBC, 1634; 334, Abitibi, Fr—Ind—NWC—HBC, 1686; 335, Grand Lac, Ind—NWC—HBC, 1785; 336, Kakabonga, HBC, 1851; 337, Rivière Deserte—Desert Post, HBC, 1832; 338, Lac des Sables, NWC—HBC, 1820; 339, Lac des Deux Montagnes, Fr—NWC—HBC, 1663; 340, Ft. Maisonneuve—Montreal, Fr, 1642; 341, Ft. Temiscaming, Fr—Ind—NWC—HBC, 1679; 342, Lac des Allumettes—Ft. William, HBC, 1823; 343, Ft. Coulonge, FR—NWC—HBC, 1680. Newf.: 344, Nachvak, HBC, 1868; 345, Davis Inlet, Ind—HBC, 1869; 346, Aillik, HBC, 1840; 347, Sandwich Bay—Cartwright, Ind—HBC, 1775*; 348, Kaipokok, Ind—HBC, 1837; 349, Rigolet, Fr—Ind—HBC, 1734; 350, Ft. Cap Charles, Fr, 1735; 351, Anse au Loup, Fr, 1710; 352, Baie des Esquimaux—Northwest River, Fr—Ind—HBC, 1743*; 353, Kenemich River, Ind—HBC, 1799; 354, Ft. St. Modet, Fr, 1735; 355, Mud Lake, HBC, 1906; 356, Sandy Banks House, HBC, 1836; 357, Ft. Nascopie, HBC, 1838; 358, Winokapau, HBC, 1830; 359, Ft. Naskapis, Fr, 1730.

conducted, the Governor and Committee depended heavily on the advice of these two Frenchmen. It is not surprising that many of the earliest trading goods of the Hudson's Bay Company were of French manufacture. Building from their initial inventory, the Governor and Committee quickly commissioned English copies of French merchandise. By the early eighteenth century most of the Hudson's Bay Company's trading goods were made in England (Ray 1980).

Trade Goods

Indian people played an important role in the expansion and improvement of the Hudson's Bay Company's line of English-made goods. This was possible because the Governor and Committee realized that they needed to pay close attention to the kinds of goods that were in demand, the features Indians liked and disliked about the company's goods, and the merchandise the French supplied. Chief factors were ordered to solicit this information from their Indian trading partners and relay what they learned in annual reports sent from the posts to London. Furthermore, chief factors were instructed to purchase from the Indians any French trading goods that they considered superior to their own. Indian complaints about Hudson's Bay Company goods forwarded to the Governor and Committee were brought to the attention of suppliers, who were expected to address the problems raised. Whenever French goods were sent from Hudson Bay the Governor and Committee examined them carefully to determine whether copies should be made or whether new and improved lines of merchandise introduced. In this way, the Hudson's Bay Company's operation was very sensitive to Indian needs and desires. This was especially so whenever French competition for Indian furs was strong.

Indians exhibited a strong preference for firearms and metal tools that were lightweight and durable (fig. 2). High-quality textiles were also popular (Ray 1980: 266–267, 1987). English manufacturers had difficulty meeting Indian expectations. In particular, the manufacture of metal goods that were lightweight and able to withstand harsh usage under subarctic winter conditions was a major problem (Ray 1980). It is also clear that the Indians were quick to respond to the opportunity to make comparisons between English and French merchandise. Frequently they claimed that the French goods were superior (Eccles 1979:430–431; Innis 1962). Clearly it was in the Indian's interest, as a bargaining ploy, to highlight

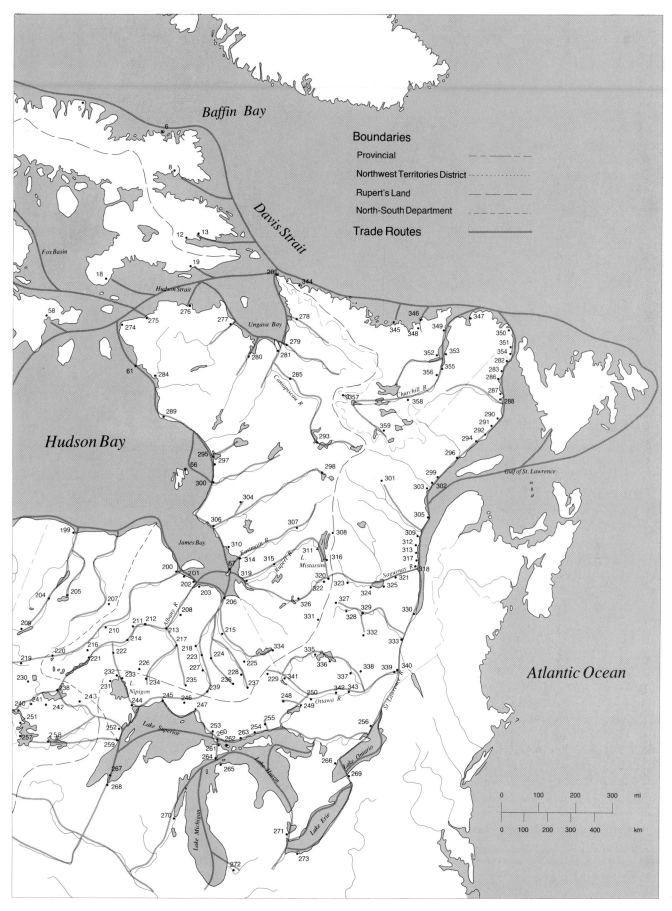

Baffin Bay

Boundaries

Provincial ‑ ‑ ‑ ‑ ‑ ‑

Northwest Territories District ·············

Rupert's Land ‑ ‑ ‑ ‑ ‑

North-South Department ‑ ‑ ‑ ‑ ‑

Trade Routes ▬▬▬▬▬▬

Davis Strait

Fox Basin

Hudson Strait

Ungava Bay

Caniapiscau R.

Churchill R.

Hudson Bay

Gulf of St. Lawrence

James Bay

Eastmain R.

Rupert R.

L. Mistassini

Saguenay R.

Atlantic Ocean

Albany R.

L. Nipigon

Lake Superior

Lake Michigan

Lake Huron

Ottawa R.

St. Lawrence R.

Lake Ontario

Lake Erie

| 0 | 100 | 200 | 300 | mi |

| 0 | 100 | 200 | 300 | 400 | km |

THE HUDSON'S BAY COMPANY AND NATIVE PEOPLE

all the real and imagined shortcomings of English goods. In this way the Indians were able to manipulate the English and the French and to upgrade their merchandise (fig. 3).

Exchange Rates

One major difference between trade dominated by the Hudson's Bay Company and aboriginal trade was that the aboriginal trade was not based upon a standard medium of exchange. Hence, the Governor and Committee decided to establish an accounting and trading standard for their posts that recognized beaver pelts as the staple of the business. Beaver values were assigned to all goods, furs, and provisions that the Indians exchanged. There were two types of beaver pelts: coat beaver, pelts worn by Indians for a winter or more prior to trading; and parchment beaver, the skins taken and processed exclusively for exchange purposes. Both types were rated equal, and the unit of account came to be known as the Made Beaver. The initial trading standard of the Hudson's Bay Company was set by Radisson and Groseilliers, presumably with reference to current French standards. The Governor and Commitee set the official rates of exchange annually. The Made Beaver accounting system was used officially until 1810.

The Made Beaver exchange rates were changed very infrequently (Rich 1960:49). In fact, in the short-term these standards appeared to be virtually inelastic. Given the ebb and flow of competition with the French for the Indians' furs and the fluctuations of the commodity and trade goods markets in Europe, this price rigidity seems remarkable. Rich speculated that it may have been the result of the unwillingness of Indians to respond to market forces because Indians operated in a context in which sociopolitical considerations, rather than impersonal supply and demand forces, played a paramount role in establishing price schedules. Rotstein (1967, 1970) agreed that prices were set through political negotiations and treaties. However, Ray and Freeman (Ray 1975–1976; Ray and Freeman 1978) demonstrated that official exchange rates were not the actual exchange rates. Rather, these standards served only as reference points. This would have been necessary because the official rates expressed equivalents only in terms of prime furs. The value of other furs, such as summer, small, and damaged pelts, had to be determined by dickering. And, in the case of trade goods measured out at the time of sale (such as powder, shot, cloth, tobacco, brandy, and beads), Indians and traders usually haggled about the fullness of the measures but not about the measures themselves (fig. 4) (Ray and Freeman 1978:95). Analysis of the post accounts reveals that during the eighteenth century Hudson's Bay Company traders always obtained more for their goods than the official rates specified, but the amount of the excess was influenced by the intensity of French competi-

Fig. 2. Trade kettle of hammered brass, trimmed in iron with a hand-forged iron bail, stamped "HBC" within the upper rim. Made in England about 1830, this is typical of kettles traded through the Hudson's Bay Company. Various manufacturers turned these out over the years to meet the constant Indian demand for metal utensils. After the kettles became scrap, Indians used the metal to fashion projectile points ("The Fur Trade in the Colonial Northeast," fig. 1, this vol.). Diameter 52 cm.

tion (Ray and Freeman 1978:93–94, 125–197). This seems to indicate that Indians did respond to local market forces.

Records reveal that Indians repeatedly pressured the company for better prices for their marten (valued at one-third Made Beaver). The Hudson's Bay Company's traders favored meeting the Indian demand part way, but the Governor and Committee steadfastly refused (Ray and Freeman 1978:178; Ray 1985a). They were unwilling to sacrifice any of the profit margin that they made on this key commodity. In contrast, the French were often forced to trade goods at unprofitable rates after 1700 in order to compete with Anglo-American traders (Eccles 1969: 132–156) and because they wished to retain the Indians as military allies. In other words, the French motive for trading with the Indians was more political than economic after 1700 (Eccles 1983).

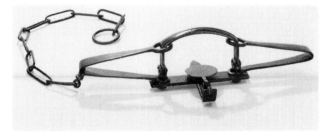

Fig. 3. Hand-forged beaver trap made by Sewell Newhouse, considered among the best makers in the mid-1800s. Similar traps were sold to many trading outfits in the United States and Canada. Length 34.5 cm.

Trading Customs

The initial structure that developed to facilitate Indian–Hudson's Bay Company interaction incorporated trading customs from both cultures. Barter trade was preceded by an elaborate gift-giving ceremony of native origin. This practice (Rich 1958–1959; Rotstein 1967; Ray 1974; Ray and Freeman 1978; Francis and Morantz 1983) was a form of balanced reciprocity that served to cement and renew bonds of friendship between the Hudson's Bay Company and its Indian partners. Indian bands rallied behind a leader, called a trading captain, who was a good orator, knew the trading routes, and was a skilled bargainer (Ray 1974; Ray and Freeman 1978; Francis and Morantz 1983). The Hudson's Bay Company men gave the trading captain a suit of clothing. Other band elders were also dressed in suits that denoted their lower status. After food, alcohol, and tobacco were consumed, the band assembled in the fort and the trading captain made a gift to the chief factor of one or two furs he had collected from his followers. Once these formalities were concluded, barter trade commenced.

For most of the eighteenth century barter took place through the "hole-in-the-wall" (Rich 1958–1959; Ray and Freeman 1978). This consisted of a wicket that opened from the warehouse onto a trading room where the Indians assembled. The trading captain was allowed into the warehouse to oversee the Hudson's Bay Company clerks as they dealt with his followers. This was done to reassure the Indians that the general terms of trade agreed to were being followed.

The extension of credit to Indians became an essential feature of the Hudson's Bay Company's trade before the end of the seventeenth century. Customarily an Indian was given an advance that was equivalent to a portion of his average return. He was expected to repay it in the following year unless extraordinary circumstances made this impossible. In this way provision was made to enable Indians to obtain the items they wanted even if their returns were insufficient in the short-term. Credit trade would have been compatible with Indian concepts of balanced reciprocity and in accord with aboriginal trading

Fig. 4. Shot measures. Sold by the pound, lead shot was measured into standard-sized metal cups. These were used at the Hudson's Bay Company post on Albany Island, Ont., possibly as late as 1900. Height of cup 7.3 cm.

practices since the period of time in which transactions had to be completed (balanced) was set by mutual agreement. Significantly, in keeping with their own traditions, Indians regarded their debts as personal obligations to their traders who advanced the credit rather than as something they owed to the company. This caused problems for the company whenever personnel changes were made at a post.

Beside helping Indians cope with periodic shortfalls credit was used by traders to generate and reinforce customer loyalty whenever competition with other traders and companies was strong. Company traders hoped Indians would feel obligated to return and clear their debts despite the presence of other traders who might offer more attractive terms. Credit was also used to increase the per capita consumption of goods by Indians. The fur trade commissioner in 1929 claimed this was possible because Indians considered that the amount of credit an individual obtained was a measure of the status a hunter had in the eyes of the local post manager. To retain that status, the hunter had to pay his debts regularly (Hudson's Bay Company 1929). Credit and barter trade may also have been used to create a sense of dependency in native hunters, who were given a line of credit by the fur trader. Thus credit and barter trade put the company's agents in a very strong position to create psychological and economic dependency.

Company Organization

The Hudson's Bay Company developed a centralized and hierarchical labor management system. North American operations were placed under the control of a governor. Management of the various posts was the responsibility of a senior officer, who held the rank of chief factor, and a council of fellow officers. The senior officers held commissions. Generally officers were sufficiently educated so that they could serve as traders, bookkeepers, and writers. During the first century of operations there was some upward mobility, and skilled tradesmen who served several years in the company were sometimes able to attain officer rank. The remaining men at the factories were servants (laborers) who were hired on three- to five-year contracts. This arrangement produced ranked social pyramids at all trading posts (Foster 1973:33–35). A sharp division existed between officers and servants, and within each of these two classes an employee's position was ranked by occupation. Each position from that of laborer to that of the commanding officer entitled a man to certain privileges and charged him with a particular set of responsibilities. The commanding officer was responsible for successful trade and the welfare of all the men under his authority. This hierarchical pattern mirrored English social traditions. The head of the household served as father and as employer to the other members who were both his children and his servants (Foster 1975:57).

Initially, the Governor and Committee prohibited fraternization between company men and native women. They feared liaisons might cause friction with Indian men, might lead to debauchery of the officers and men, and might lead to an unacceptable increase in the consumption of provisions at the posts. In spite of this prohibition Hudson's Bay Company men did fraternize with Indian women, and a population of European-Indian ancestry began to develop around the posts. Identified in later company records as "mixed-bloods," "half-breeds," "country born," and "citizens of Hudson's Bay" (Brown 1980, 1980a, 1985; Foster 1973, 1986; Judd 1980; Van Kirk 1980, 1980a), these people came to constitute a significant component of the native population that began to settle around the bayside posts, a population of East Main Cree that came to be known as the Home Guard Cree.

The Indian groups who went to the bayside posts to trade were band-organized hunters and foragers. Key features of their societies included equal access to land; no accumulation of surplus; insignificant investment in material goods; flexible social arrangements; strongly egalitarian social and political arrangements; and generalized reciprocity as the predominant mode of exchange. This socioeconomic tradition was entirely different from the strict hierarchy of the British immigrants and the Hudson's Bay Company itself.

By the early eighteenth century, the development of the Home Guard Cree population and the growing number of illegal liaisons between company men and native women had a strong impact on the Hudson's Bay Company's

trading operations. Long-distance trade with interior groups who visited the posts once a year or less often were conducted in the usual manner, and these groups brought in the bulk of the company's fur returns. But relations with the Home Guard Cree developed along different lines. These Indians were not treated to elaborate gift exchange ceremonies every time they visited the posts, because contact was continuous for all practical purposes, and of greater importance, kinship bonds had been forged between the Home Guard and the men at the posts. Although these links bound the Home Guard to the company, they also caused problems. By taking advantage of their kinship affiliations, Company officers and men gained access to the fur returns of a segment of the Home Guard Cree, and an illegal "private trade" sprang up (Graham 1969:281–286; Ray and Freeman 1978:117–119, 184–185). In this trade the Company men smuggled in trading goods and secretly took out the furs exchanged for them. Success in the venture usually involved the clandestine cooperation of senior officers at the posts and ship captains. The value was probably small by comparison to the Hudson's Bay Company's official trade.

North West Company Competition, 1764–1821

While the Hudson's Bay Company remained at the coastal posts, the French built a small chain of posts extending from Lake Superior to the forks of the Saskatchewan River (fig. 1) in order to intercept Indians traveling to Hudson Bay and gain most of their furs. Apparently the French did secure a major share of the fur production of southern Rupert's Land, but they did not exert enough pressure to force the company to move inland. The losses in the volume of Hudson's Bay Company trade were more than offset by rising fur prices on the London market. Thus, the period of strongest English-French rivalry was a time when the Company was able to pay some of the highest dividends in its history (McKay 1936:339–340; Ray 1985a). This situation changed sharply beginning in the late 1760s when the North West Company took over and expanded the overland network of the French. Between 1774 and 1787 they pushed beyond the middle Saskatchewan River to Great Slave Lake in the northwest and westward to the North Saskatchewan. Between 1788 and 1800 they explored and began to develop the Mackenzie River valley as well as the Peace River and North Saskatchewan routes across the Rocky Mountains (fig. 1). As early as 1774 the North West Company had drawn off enough of the Hudson's Bay Company trade to force it to begin building an inland network of posts. For the next 47 years the two groups of traders were locked in an intensive struggle that centered on the area between Lake Superior and the Peace River valley.

This rivalry had a profound impact on Native–Euro–Canadian economic and social relations. Indian middlemen were largely eliminated from the territory south and east of Lake Athabasca. Simultaneously, a large market for provisions developed in the prairie–mixed forest region and in the boreal and mixed forests (Ray 1984). Prairie provisions became the mainstay of the diets of the men who manned the growing number of canoe and boat brigades operated by the fur trade companies, while woodland foodstuffs fed the men stationed at posts in the boreal forests. In the mixed forest–prairie–steppe area, the provision market became more important than the fur market.

The escalating intensity of competition had a very negative effect on the fur and game resources of the boreal and mixed forests. Before 1763 most Indian groups had to travel substantial distances to reach trading posts, and the capacity of their canoes was limited to the equivalent of about 300 prime winter beaver pelts, or 150 per man (Ray and Freeman 1978:161). This placed an upward limit on the per capita consumption of trade goods by Indians and moderated the negative impact the fur trade had on the environment (Ray 1978). The situation changed substantially between 1763 and 1821. By 1821 relatively few Indians lived very far (over 200 miles) from a trading post in the vast territory lying between the Churchill River and James Bay. Indeed, in a hotly contested area Indians did not have to leave their winter hunting and trapping camps since the traders began building in the native encampments small temporary structures called "flying posts" or "log tents." Alternatively, traders made periodic visits to Indian camps over the course of the winter. These practices were intended to reduce a trader's risk of losing the entire winter hunt of a native group to a rival in the spring. By proliferating the number of supply points in these ways, traders encouraged Indians to exert greater hunting pressures on furbearing species.

By 1821 beaver populations were in sharp decline south and east of the Churchill River. The pattern and rate of this decline has been carefully documented for the area between Lake Winnipeg and James Bay, known to the fur traders as the "Petite Nord" (Lytwyn 1981). In addition to furbearers, game animal populations, especially moose, were adversely affected by the hunting pressures that developed in response to the local provision markets generated by woodland trading posts (C.A. Bishop 1974: 245–249; Ray 1974:117–124). As a result, Indians found themselves vulnerable to periodic food shortages. With increasing frequency they were forced to turn to the local trading post for assistance. The traders were able to respond to the Indians' growing need by importing foods from the mixed forest–prairie–steppe, from Europe, and from eastern North America (C.A. Bishop 1974:189–197; Ray 1974:111–124, 137–165). In some areas, such as the Rainy River region, deer and moose were so scarce by the 1820s that the Hudson's Bay Company had to import buffalo hides for the local Ojibwa to make moccasins and

clothing (Ray 1974:147). Thus, for many Subarctic Indians, economic dependence was becoming a fact of life by the early nineteenth century (Ray 1984a).

The expansion of the trading networks of the North West Company and the Hudson's Bay Company affected Native–Euro-Canadian socioeconomic relations in a variety of other ways. Burgeoning manpower requirements meant that significant seasonal employment opportunities developed for native peoples for the first time. The companies faced the very difficult task of moving the bulk of their furs and supplies during a relatively short open-water season. Neither company was able to obtain enough European or French Canadian labor to accomplish this. Facing an acute manpower shortage, the Governor and Committee ruled that mixed-bloods could be hired as permanent employees. However, the prohibition against hiring Indians on a permanent basis remained in place in order that Indians not be diverted from traditional hunting and gathering activities.

The North West Company recruited French Canadians in Quebec. These men had to be supplemented with Indians, many of Iroquois descent, and Métis (French speakers of French and Indian background). The Indians and Métis who worked for the North West Company generally served as laborers at the posts or as paddlers on the canoe brigades. French Canadians, on the other hand, served as bowmen and sternmen on brigades, and as clerks and skilled tradesmen at posts. Management of local operations was the responsibility of the wintering partners, largely of English and Scottish descent (Brown 1980a:35–42). By 1820 the labor forces employed by the two competing merchant groups were ethnically diverse and included three native groups: Métis, English-speaking mixed-bloods, and Indians. Jobs were strongly linked to ethnic background, and native peoples occupied the lowest levels in evolving labor hierarchies.

Proliferation of trading posts during the period also profoundly altered the social order by facilitating Indian-White social interaction. Initially this led to an increase in the number of liaisons between White men and Indian women, bringing about a rapid growth of the Métis population. Also, interaction with Plains Indian groups was more extensive than during the French occupation. Thus, a sizable Plains Métis population developed that was distinctly different in terms of its economic orientation from that of the Subarctic mixed-bloods. By 1821 the Métis populations were sufficiently large that most White men chose wives from these groups rather than from Indian bands (Brown 1980a:70–80; Van Kirk 1980a: 95–122). Thus, by 1821 both merchant groups had established strong kinship bonds with their Indian trading partners.

Reflecting these various economic and demographic factors, a sharply stratified social order developed around trading posts. Occupying the upper echelons were the 343

Fig. 5. Cree women and Red River cart in northern Alta. The Red River carts were constructed entirely of local wood and rawhide. Photograph by H.G. Cochrane, 1882.

Euro-Canadian officers. Laborers holding permanent contracts, who included Whites, Métis, and mixed-bloods, constituted the middle class. In contrast to the North West Company, in the Hudson's Bay Company system upward mobility was possible at this time, and a few mixed-blood men were able to move into the officer class (Judd 1980a:310; Brown 1980a:45–50). Beneath the class of permanent laborers were the seasonal workers. In both companies this class was composed mostly of Métis and Indians.

Era of Monopoly, 1821–1862

In 1821 the Hudson's Bay Company and North West Company joined forces, bringing the era of ruinous competition to a close. The British Parliament gave the newly amalgamated concern a 20-year monopoly on the trade in Rupert's Land and extended these privileges to the Mackenzie drainage basin and the Pacific region. The Governor and Committee divided the territory into the Northern and Southern departments, which were subdivided into districts (fig. 1). Affairs in each department were regulated by a governing council, whose decisions had to be ratified by the Governor and Committee. Council members consisted of chief factors and chief traders who were in charge of departmental districts. A governor presided over each council. George Simpson was appointed governor of the Northern Department in 1822 and of the Southern Department in 1826. In 1839 he was named Governor in Chief of Rupert's Land, a position he held until his death in 1860 (Galbraith 1976; Morton 1944). In 1822, Simpson was concerned with transforming the fur trade into a profitable enterprise. He eliminated superfluous posts and manpower resulting from the company's merger (Judd 1980:130).

Native people were affected in two ways by Simpson's

economy moves: those mixed-bloods who remained in the company's service found that the reduction in size of the labor force combined with the adoption of some North West Company traditions served to diminish opportunities for upward mobility, and those who merely supplied the company also had reduced opportunities. In 1821 the number of commissioned officers was set at 53 (25 chief factors and 28 chief traders). These were the elite who collectively shared 40 percent of the trading profits of the company. After 1821, postmasters and clerks were all recruited outside the northwest; mixed-blood men were effectively excluded from these ranks. When commissioned officers with mixed-blood sons protested this practice, the Governor and Committee responded by creating the position of apprentice postmaster. This action merely served to highlight discriminatory hiring policies. European officer recruits, who knew nothing of the country and often had no better education than the officers' sons, did not have to apprentice. Few mixed-bloods who signed on as apprentice postmasters were ever promoted.

A large percentage of the men who retired or were terminated by the Company in and after 1821 were mixed-bloods. Many took up residence in Red River Colony (in present-day Manitoba), where the economic livelihood was based on an economy that combined farming with commercial and subsistence buffalo hunting. The produce of the buffalo hunt was sold to other colonists and to the Hudson's Bay Company. As time passed, the Métis became heavily involved in transportation activities, using their two-wheeled Red River carts to haul cargoes for the company and the colony. In addition, they found summer employment working on the company's York boat brigades between the colony, York Factory, Norway House, and the Saskatchewan district (vol. 6:361–371).

Within the French Métis and English mixed-blood communities, particularly the former, there was a strong entrepreneurial tradition. Simpson decided that it made good sense to let these people trade with Indians in the southern areas of Rupert's Land so long as they obtained their goods from, and sold their furs to, the Hudson's Bay Company. The system worked well enough initially, but a serious problem soon developed. The Red River traders quickly learned that they could increase their profit margins by buying goods and selling furs south of the U.S. border. As a result, a clandestine trade sprang up that by the 1840s seriously undermined the Hudson's Bay Company's monopoly position in the prairie–mixed forest region. In an effort to stop this illegal trade, the company arrested a free trader named Pierre Guillaume Sayer and tried him at Red River in 1849 for violating the Hudson's Bay Company monopoly trade privileges. While Sayer was found guilty of the charge, community pressure forced the company to accept a suspended sentence. The Métis considered this a major victory and proclaimed the trade to be free. Indeed, thereafter the Hudson's Bay Company made no effort to enforce its monopoly by legal challenges. The Red River free traders remained a potent force in southwestern Rupert's Land into the late nineteenth century (Brown 1980a; Foster 1986; Pannekoek 1976; Spry 1983; Van Kirk 1980).

Simpson's economic measures also affected the livelihoods of Indians not employed by the company. His beaver conservation program was an example of such a policy. By 1821 the only areas where the Hudson's Bay Company could expand its operations were the lower Mackenzie valley, the Yukon, and New Caledonia (the interior of present British Columbia). All except New Caledonia were remote and costly to develop. Simpson decided that beaver trapping had to be placed on a sustained yield basis in older areas where the company held sway. To accomplish this conservation goal, he introduced district fur quotas, established open and closed seasons for beaver, and prohibited the trade of summer and cub beaver (Ray 1975). In addition, beaver preserves were established on islands in southern James Bay where a rudimentary kind of fur farming was attempted. Simpson's conservation policy was applied primarily to the woodlands between James Bay and the Churchill River. As a result of depletion of beaver stocks and company regulations regarding beaver, Cree and Ojibwa Indians in this region became increasingly dependent upon the muskrat, a species of lesser value and greater temporal variability than the beaver. The scarcity of resources in this region also set in motion a migration of natives, some of whom joined their Plains Indian relatives (Ray 1974: 94–116), while others moved toward Red River Colony.

Simpson recommended altering native land tenure systems by assigning bands to specific tracts of land in order to restrict their trapping activities and not run the risk of having adjacent Indian groups trespass on their lands and take beaver left behind for propagation purposes. However, for such a radical plan to be successful, he realized that Indians had to be distant from "frontier areas" (zones of competition) such as the American border and the prairie–mixed forest region. Also, the native subsistence economy had to become more oriented to localized resources like hare and fish rather than to mobile game animals like moose and woodland caribou. For Simpson's scheme to work Indians already had to be highly dependent on the company. Initially the Hudson's Bay Company's efforts to alter native land tenure systems were most successful in northern Ontario and the northern portions of the prairie provinces.

In sharp contrast to the measures designed to increase beaver populations in districts protected from competition were Simpson's efforts to eliminate beaver altogether in frontier districts exposed to American traders. Elsewhere, the company hoped to offset diminished returns from older areas by expanding the trade in newer regions.

In addition to trying to change native economies, Simpson attempted to alter the Hudson's Bay Company's trading practices, but he met with only limited success. Simpson believed that the pre-trade gift exchange ceremony was an "extravagence born of competition" and he wanted to eliminate it (Ray 1974:194–198). Of course this was an impossibility in areas where American and Red River free traders operated, but even where the company was unopposed, native resistance was strong enough that curtailment of gift-giving, rather than its total elimination, was the best that could be achieved. Also, the practice of giving ammunition and food to the sick and infirm as a kind of welfare assistance was continued. The idea was that the destitute could attach themselves to a good hunter by giving him the ammunition in exchange for a share in his return. Simpson appreciated that this practice served to discourage Indians from settling in the vicinity of posts to obtain aid.

To improve profit margins Simpson proposed downgrading the quality of trading goods, particularly cloth and high-priced Brazilian tobacco. These were key items in the trade of the western interior of Canada. The Governor and Committee balked at the idea of importing cheaper quality goods, particularly the suggestion to sell lighter weight cloth, pointing out that the company did have an obligation to consider the Indians' well-being. Poor quality clothing and cloth would jeopardize the health of groups living in an arctic or subarctic environment, but the Governor and Committee were willing to experiment with luxury items. For example, tobaccos were imported from the United States; however, Indians found the new tobaccos to be unacceptable, and this experiment was terminated.

By the early 1860s distinctive socioeconomic subregions had emerged in the central and western interior areas of Canada. In the Hudson Bay–James Bay lowlands most West Main Cree had developed very strong social and economic links with the trading posts. A sizable component of their income was derived by provisioning the posts, particularly through hunting geese and fishing. Trapping was still important, but depletion of furbearers along the coast was a serious problem (Ray 1982, 1984a). Summer employment in the company was very important for Indians and mixed-bloods, as hunting and trapping incomes were often not sufficient to meet the per capita demands of Indians for goods. As these summer jobs became more crucial, the Hudson's Bay Company traders adopted the practice of awarding jobs to the most reliable hunters and trappers. In this way seasonal employment opportunities were used to reinforce more traditional economic activities (Ray 1984a:10). York Factory and Moose Factory (fig. 6) provided the greatest number of jobs; a sizable mixed-blood labor force was employed on a permanent basis to assist with warehousing, shipping, trade good manufacturing and repair, as well as ship building and repair activities.

The important role that the mixed-blood labor force played in the life of the communities of Moose Factory and York Factory may have served to lesson the negative social impact that exclusion from the officer ranks had in other settlements. For example, at Moose Factory the shipbuilding and repair facility was the lifeblood of the community, and its last manager was a mixed-blood. Thus, in this instance a mixed-blood was in a high-status position even though he was not a commissioned officer. The case suggests that the socioeconomic structure of the bayside settlements may have differed from that of Red River partly because of their different economic orientation. Also, the less diverse ethnic composition of the bayside communities as compared to Red River may have favored a somewhat different pattern of social development.

The economic position of Indians living in the woodlands north and northwest of the Churchill River was very different. Most of this area, except the Peace River district, escaped the negative effects of Hudson's Bay Company–North West Company rivalry (cf. vol. 6:273). And, reflecting the later arrival of the traders, Indians were much less dependent on the trading posts. Indeed, Asch (1975, 1977) suggests they remained largely independent of the trading posts. Krech (1984:99–146), on the other hand, indicates that the Slavey and Dogrib were drawn into the orbit of the trading posts but were not in any way economically dependent upon them. Yerbury (1980) suggests that trading post bands began to emerge and patterns of interdependency were being established between 1821 and 1870 along the Mackenzie River.

In the mixed forest–prairie-steppe area, the Indian and Métis economies reached their zeniths between 1821 and 1870. During this period the commercial buffalo hunts grew rapidly. Initially the hunt was oriented to securing provisions for the Hudson's Bay Company and the Red River Colony. However, by the 1840s a strong market developed for robes; after 1865 the demand shifted to hides (Ray 1974:195–216, 1984; Roe 1970), the bulk of which were exported to the United States. High transportation costs prevented the Hudson's Bay Company from playing a major role in this trade. The presence of American and Red River free traders provided Indians with competitive markets for their products, enabling them to be independent of their suppliers. Simpson complained that the Plains Indians were "insolent" and "independent," rarely visiting the company's forts more frequently than once every three years (Ray 1974:207).

Considered in the context of the hierarchical paternalistic trading system that the Hudson's Bay Company had established, Simpson's observation offers a clue about the degree of economic and psychological dependency that existed between native groups and the Hudson's Bay Company. For instance, while Plains Indians were always

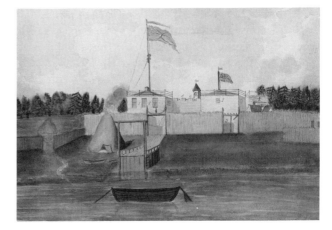

Glenbow Museum, Calgary, Alta.
Fig. 6. East view of Moose Factory, on the Moose River, Ont. The section of the fort topped by the larger flag is the dwelling flanker; to its right, topped by the smaller flag, is the warehouse and the north flanker; the right aperture is the principal gateway; the dock leads to the boatyard door. Outbuildings include the shipwrights' workshop, smith, forge, kitchen, brewhouse, and cattle sheds. The post is in the area inhabited by the West Main Cree, where in the early 19th century many of the Cree bands were referred to by the name of the post at which they traded (vol. 6:230) or as Home Guard Cree. The artist, who was of Welsh and local Indian descent, was born in Rupert's Land and employed at Moose Factory as a laborer, canoeman, and cooper (A.M. Johnson 1967). Watercolor by William Richards, about 1804–1811.

described as being "insolent," Subarctic groups were said to include many "good Indians" who were defined as being "steady," "always paid their debts," and so forth. Indians described in this fashion usually were strongly dependent on the company.

The economic relationships that developed between the Métis and the Plains Indians during the period were complex. It is clear that some activities were symbiotic, such as trade, and others, such as buffalo hunting, often caused conflicts. The conflicts were exacerbated by the retreat of the buffalo herds to the southwest. This trend increased tensions not only between the Métis and Blackfoot, but also with other groups as all buffalo hunters were drawn into a shrinking range (Cowie 1913: 305–306). Thus, well before the collapse of the buffalo hunting economy in the 1880s, signs of the end were manifest.

Twilight of the Old Order, 1863–1885

Other developments in the 1860s foreshadowed the end of the fur trade economy built in the mercantilistic era. In 1863 the controlling interest in the Hudson's Bay Company was sold to the International Financial Society, men concerned with real estate speculation and promotion, agricultural development, and railway construction. Attention was focused upon efforts to obtain a quick return on their investment in the Hudson's Bay Company through the sale to the British or Canadian government of the real estate the company claimed by virtue of the 1670 charter. Many shareholders favored having the Hudson's Bay Company divest itself of its fur trading operations altogether. However, they were opposed on this point of view by the company's officers, who still shared in the profits of the fur trade, and by other investors whose interests in the company predated the 1863 sale (Ray 1985a).

The Governor and Committee's attempt to arrange a quick sale of Rupert's Land was unsuccessful. An agreement was not reached with the Canadian government (formed in 1867) until 1869. The Canadian government permitted the Hudson's Bay Company to retain title to one-twentieth of the land in the prairie-mixed forest region and title to developed lands around its trading posts. The accord had several important consequences. By failing to sell all of its real estate interests in one large transaction, the Hudson's Bay Company had to make a long-term commitment to economic development in the prairie-mixed-forest region. Therefore, the Hudson's Bay Company backed any government or private schemes that favored that goal, such as construction of the transcontinental railway. Meanwhile, the Governor and Committee took the view that the fur trade would have to continue to provide the company with its major source of income. The Governor and Committee proposed to increase capital investment in the fur trade, develop retail sales, and promote land sales as settlement warranted (Ray 1985).

The Governor and Committee noted that in the boreal forest region aggregate fur volumes had not declined in the 1860s and as long as markets for furs were strong, reasonable profits could be expected. They planned to improve the company's competitive position by economizing its own operations and by modernizing its transportation network—introducing steamboats to the Red River, Lake Winnipeg, the Saskatchewan River, and the Mackenzie Basin. One advantage of introducing steamboats was that they would reduce the Hudson's Bay Company's heavy dependence on native laborers in the summer. It was anticipated that native laborers would be attracted to new economic development in the region, which would pay higher wage rates than the company would pay.

The sale of Rupert's Land to the Canadian government affected economic relations between native peoples and the Hudson's Bay Compnay in a variety of ways, many of which were not anticipated by the Governor and Committee. When transferring title and civil authority to the Canadian government, the Hudson's Bay Company passed along the obligation to look after the welfare of the native peoples. Although native welfare became the legal responsibility of the Canadian government after 1870, too often the government lacked the financial and manpower resources, and perhaps the will to fulfill this obligation. Frequently the Hudson's Bay Company had to provide

assistance when hunts or crops failed. As long as fur trade profit margins were sufficient, the company continued to shoulder this burden. The Canadian government also wished to extinguish aboriginal title in the tracts of land that lay along the proposed railway and where agricultural colonization was planned. Between 1871 and 1877 this task was accomplished with the signing of Treaties 1 through 7. Indians ceded land in exchange for: the establishment of reserves, one-time cash payments to band members, a supply of farm tools and livestock, annuities, small annual allowances for certain supplies, and the obligation to provide schooling (Brown and Maguire 1979). By virtue of the Manitoba Act of 1870, Métis land claims were also recognized. One and one-quarter million acres were set aside in Manitoba for people of Indian-White ancestry.

Although the cash settlements to Indians were small by comparison to the settlement that the Hudson's Bay Company received for its claim, they had an important impact on the continuing fur trade economy in the boreal and mixed forest areas. The treaties served to inject cash into the northern economy for the first time, and the native peoples were the conduit. Of the utmost importance, Indians received this income regardless of whether they hunted or trapped. The presence of cash encouraged independent merchants to move into areas under treaty and compete with the Hudson's Bay Company in the merchandising business. This established a trend whereby merchandising and fur buying were separated. Indians were able to seek the best prices for goods and for furs. Company records indicate that itinerant merchants trailed the government treaty parties every year in the hope of profiting from the immediate business these payments generated. The Hudson's Bay Company actively participated as well.

The other major economic development that took place during this period was the building of the Canadian Pacific Railway. Railroad construction and related interests gave the native people their first opportunity to work for employers other than the trading companies. These new employment opportunities served to establish local wage rates. For example, in 1900 Indians at Moose Factory went on strike to be paid the same wages that railway construction crews were receiving farther south.

Competition and a Changing Order, 1885–1914

The completion of the Canadian Pacific Railway in 1885 marked a very important turning point in the economic history of Canadian native peoples. The railway opened the prairie to settlers, and the Hudson's Bay Company's land sales rose sharply. Also, retail sales greatly expanded. By 1914 the company's net incomes from these two lines of activity exceeded that derived from the fur trade. This meant that the company's relations with the native people

Pub. Arch. of Canada, Ottawa, Ont.: PA-118768.

Fig. 7. Plains Cree Indians and Hudson's Bay Company personnel at Fort Pitt, Sask. front, left to right, Four Sky Thunder; Sky Bird; Matoose; Napasis; Big Bear; William McKay or William McClean, head of the post; Otto Dufresne, cook; Louis Goulet, Métis; Stanley Simpson, accountant; Alen McDonald, constable, N.W.M.P.; H. Rowley, constable (seated); Corporal R.B. Sleigh; H.L. Edmund; and Henry Dufresne, half-Indian son of Otto Dufresne. rear, left to right, Patsy Carrol; Leduc or Leonais; Billy Anderson; unidentified; and Fred C. Roby and Larry O'Keefe, constables. The Cree men wear European-style hats adorned with plumes and blankets. Rowley holds a tobacco carrot and sits by a bucket (see vol. 6:151) in front of what is probably a Red River cart. The Hudson's Bay Company began operations at Fort Pitt in 1829 to serve the trade with the Blackfoot. Three years later a smallpox epidemic caused the deaths of two-thirds of the Blackfoot, and the fort became a trade center for the Crees who moved onto the Plains into the depopulated area. The fort, located on the Saskatchewan River, was an important provisioning center with a good supply of buffalo and pasture for horses (Dempsey 1984:16–17; Innis 1962:296–297, 302). Big Bear regularly traded at Fort Pitt and his affinity and respect for the traders played a part in his role as leader, both when his leadership was strong and during the 1885 uprising (see "Canadian Indian Policies," fig. 3, this vol.), when his political influence waned (Dempsey 1984:26, 168–171). Photograph probably by Ernest G. May and Boone, about 1885.

occupied less of the attention of the Governor and Committee than had been the case previously. Instead, these affairs were left largely in the hands of the company's fur trade commissioner.

By the time of the outbreak of World War I, the Hudson's Bay Company faced a variety of competitors throughout the boreal forest region. Cash fur buyers were particularly active along the railway lines and in the immediate hinterlands of cities such as Montreal, Sudbury, Winnipeg, Prince Albert, and Edmonton. Some operated as far to the northwest as the lower Mackenzie River valley. By keeping their overhead costs to a minimum and maintaining very close contact with current fur market conditions via telegraph, cash buyers were able to operate on a very narrow profit margin. Thus, generally they were in the position to offer Indians the best prices for their furs.

In addition to cash fur buyers, the Hudson's Bay Company had to contend with more traditional traders, most of whom were small-scale operators who would arrange to obtain goods on credit from merchants or

wholesalers in cities. These small operators were particularly active in the hinterlands of Winnipeg and northern Ontario, and some of these traders may have had longstanding associations with the fur trade. Between 1899 and 1920 larger trading firms had made their appearance also. These included Paris-based Revillon Frères, Boston-based Lamson & Hubbard, and Edmonton-based Northern Trading Company. All these firms operated networks of posts spread over relatively large areas. Competition was especially vigorous in the Mackenzie River valley, the woodlands between the Saskatchewan and Churchill rivers, the James Bay area, and along the railway lines of northern Ontario and Quebec. With the federal government making treaties with more Indian groups, Indian agents became important economic agents. They promoted various schemes, such as part-time farming in the southern boreal forest area, and by dispensing economic aid they eventually challenged the dominant economic position that traders had held for so long.

Although these processes were undermining the older

348

Fig. 8. A Hudson's Bay Company 250th anniversary celebration, Lower Fort Garry, Winnipeg, Man. Chief Kinnewakan presents a decorated pipe to Sir Robert Kindersley, who smoked it, as did a number of other participants in the ceremony. This event was part of the Red River Pageant in Winnipeg, which also included a York boat and canoe flotilla down the Red River and a powwow at Lower Fort Garry (Hudson's Bay Company 1920). Hudson's Bay Company anniversary celebrations occurred across Canada, opening in Winnipeg on May 3, 1920, and closing in Victoria on May 24. Photographed May 3, 1920.

paternalistic order of the fur trade, it was not swept away entirely. Part of the reason for the slow rate of change related to the unwillingness of the Canadian government to assume the social overhead costs associated with the fur trade economy. Also, the government feared that any liberal provision of economic assistance might serve to discourage the Indians from pursuing their hunting and trapping activities. The Hudson's Bay Company shared this concern to a considerable extent. However, the Company was forced to temper this concern in light of the fact that its economic future was dependent upon the existence of the native labor force.

The Hudson's Bay Company continued to provide relief to sick and destitute Indians and write off a portion of its credit trade as uncollectable. The Governor and Committee regarded these losses as a welfare payment that was a necessary expense of the business. When giving relief to the sick and destitute the company billed the government for the expenses. Usually, the government paid them. Also, when the government authorized relief for Indians, the Hudson's Bay Company was frequently called upon to distribute it. In this way between 1885 and 1914 the paternalistic fur trade economy was beginning to give way in the boreal forest of central Canada, and a new fur trade was emerging that operated within the context of the national state.

Transformation of the Old Order, 1915–1945

The outbreak of World War I marked an important turning point in the Hudson's Bay Company fur trade. In 1914 the London market was temporarily closed by the war, depriving the company of its traditional market. Accordingly, the Governor and Committee ordered their men in Canada not to buy any furs from Indians during the winter and spring of 1914. During and after the war fur auction houses were active in the United States and developed in Canada. Auction houses facilitated the expansion of the activities of the cash fur buyers by providing quick turnover of inventories. Also, buyers who used an auction house's services regularly were able to obtain credit. The Hudson's Bay Company responded to the appearance of cash fur buyers by establishing cash fur purchasing agencies in towns along the southern peripheries of the boreal forest, in the prairie provinces, and along the railways of northern Ontario and Quebec. These agencies bought furs from small-scale traders and cash buyers. In addition, where necessary the Hudson's Bay Company introduced lower prices for customers purchasing with cash (rather than barter) at its trading posts. After World War I the Hudson's Bay Company also began to buy controlling interests in key fur auction houses, most notably those in Montreal and Winnipeg.

Despite these adjustments to the changing structure of the industry, the Hudson's Bay Company never fully recovered from the effects of its slow response to wartime market conditions, and it was unable to bridle its competitors to the extent it had in earlier periods. As a result, the company lost a major portion of its share of the raw fur production of Canada, and by 1940 the Hudson's Bay Company was obtaining less than 50 percent of the output of most regions.

The construction of the second transcontinental railway between 1903 and 1912 shifted the southern frontier of the fur trade farther north, opening a larger territory to small operators. In 1920 the directors of the Hudson's Bay Company shifted the focus of the corporation's fur trading activities to the High Arctic, where competition would be less severe. The northward shift meant that the Eskimo assumed a much more important role than had been the case.

A more traditional trading pattern was continued in the High Arctic. In the southern boreal forest the credit and barter trade continued with cash becoming increasingly important. Also, large retail concerns, such as the T. Eaton Company, introduced catalogue sales (Hudson's Bay Company 1929).

Although the fur trade remained highly competitive into the 1930s, thereby increasing the purchasing power of native peoples, their economic welfare was a growing concern. Intensive hunting and trapping created problems of severe resource depletion. Beginning in the 1890s provincial governments began to play active roles in resource management. However, in some areas, such as the James Bay and Hudson Bay lowlands, depletion occurred, and Indians led a precarious existence.

The Hudson's Bay Company did not believe that the Canadian government was living up to its responsibilities in the area of native welfare (Indian and Eskimo) and shared the opinion that the future of these peoples was at risk. The Hudson's Bay Company's directors held the view that White Canadians would never be willing to work in the bush trapping for the relatively low rates of return that native peoples found acceptable. In an effort to assure the survival of their native labor force, in 1920 the Hudson's Bay Company established a Development Department. Its primary responsibility was improving native health and economic welfare. This involved undertaking research into the health conditions of native people, developing vitamin and other nutritional supplements, and exploring economic activities that native people could pursue in addition to the fur trade. Handicrafts were among the activities that were promoted. The Canadian government generally supported the company in these ventures.

In 1939 the fur trade economy collapsed temporarily with the outbreak of World War II. The postwar period was markedly different from the preceding era in that the government, through various kinds of social programs, became the dominant agent in the economic life of the native peoples. The fur trade continued in the 1980s, but the industry contributed a much smaller share of the total native income than it did in the past. Company paternalism was replaced by social programs of the government.

Indian Trade in the Trans-Mississippi West to 1870

The history of Indian-White relations in the trans-Mississippi West has been entwined with the history of Euro-American efforts to find and extract resources from lands formerly or, in some cases still, occupied by Indian tribes. Among the more important extractive industries was the fur trade (Chittenden 1902; Innis 1962; P.C. Phillips 1961).

The significance of the fur trade was felt in other than economic terms, for instance, in the ecological impact of commercial fur hunting on previously stable ecosystems (Wishart 1979; Kay 1979) and in the importance furbearing animals assumed in the mythology, religious observances, diets, and material cultures of various Native American societies. The trade may well have been the most important meeting ground between Indians and Whites from first encounter to the beginnings of the reservation era (Peterson and Anfinson 1984).

In the trans-Mississippi West, as in the Northeast and Canada, the exchange of material commodities became the economic vehicle for Indian-White cooperation, cultural accommodation, and the fusion of the two biologically (Giraud 1945; Gilman 1982; Peterson and Brown 1985). The trade had a profound impact in attracting Native Americans to Euro-American ideas, material culture, and lifeways as well as in alienating many individuals and ethnic groups from these same acculturative influences (O. Lewis 1942; Jablow 1950; Ewers 1958). Ultimately, the trade encouraged the transculturation of numerous Euro-Americans who contributed to the growth of a bicultural, biethnic population in the West (Lamar 1977; Swagerty 1980; R.M. Craven 1982).

Several summary statements about the nature of Indian involvement in the trade can be made. First, the fur trade of the Far West extended and was built upon long established Indian trade networks that involved the exchange of numerous commodities in addition to peltries and hides. Second, there was no single contact experience or pattern of response in the trans-Mississippi West, even within culture areas or among close linguistic relatives. Neither Indian nor White societies exerted dominance over the other, and ethnic and social boundaries were maintained despite the influences of long-term processes of assimilation and acculturation (Spicer 1961).

Third, in sharp contrast to the experiences of many native societies in eastern North America and parts of the Canadian West (Ray 1974; Ray and Freeman 1978; Jacobs 1966; White 1983), even those tribes most deeply involved in the trade of the trans-Mississippi West during the peak decades in the eighteenth and early nineteenth centuries did not trade their autonomy for dependence until tribal lands were alienated and reservations established. Although the exchange disproportionately benefited the invader cultures for most of the historic period (Wishart 1979:214–215; Hickerson 1973; Klein 1983), Euro-American hegemony over the native peoples was not established until the trade gave way to other forms of White exploitation in the mid-nineteenth century (Lamar 1977).

The trade wrought important changes in the material culture, art, subsistence patterns, gender roles, and social and political structures of the tribes in the trans-Mississippi West (O. Lewis 1942; Ewers 1972; Vaughan and Holm 1982; Klein 1983; Brasser 1985). Less clear are changes in environmental ethics, spiritual beliefs, and ceremonial behavior, brought on by commercial hunting, of the sort suggested for the Ojibwa, Cree, and Micmac (Martin 1978; A. Tanner 1979).

Native American Trade Before White Contact

Centuries before Euro-American penetration of the Far West, Native Americans had established networks of trails and trade relationships (fig. 1). Prized trade commodities, such as marine shells, obsidian, and turquoise traveled hundreds, and in some cases, thousands of miles from their origins. Among closely related peoples, intraregional exchange of commodities bearing common social and ceremonial value was well organized throughout the continent. In addition, certain places served as important "trade centers" (Ewers 1968), with routes to elaborate "trade nets" (W.R. Wood 1972, 1980).

All major trade centers were located among sedentary native populations with surplus-abundant economies able to selectively harvest and trade food and other commodi-

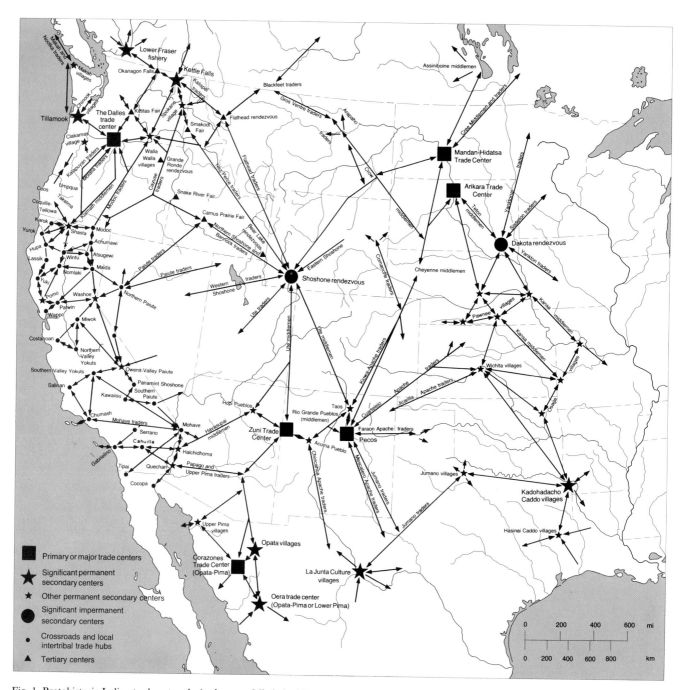

Fig. 1. Protohistoric Indian trade networks in the trans-Mississippi West. Primary trade centers had permanent resident populations and surplus subsistence economies in the form of garden crops for the Southwest and Plains (Wood 1980; Ewers 1954), fish for the Plateau and Northwest Coast. Permanent secondary trade centers with resident populations are differentiated by the relative volume of trade and density of the host trading population into 2 levels of significance. Significant impermanent secondary trade centers were at shifting locations. Tertiary trade centers, which usually lacked permanent resident populations, follow "minor trading points" (Wood 1980:101). Many correspond to trade fairs or subsistence sites (Griswold 1970; Chance and Chance 1985). Crossroads or local trade hubs served as points of intertribal trade (Davis 1961; vol. 8: 690–693).

ties to nonhorticultural and fellow farming or fishing neighbors. In the Southwest, some of the earliest of these centers such as Casas Grandes, Snaketown, and Chaco Canyon may have been linked to Mesoamerica through resident and itinerant middlemen (Di Peso 1974). By the sixteenth century, none of these well-known population clusters still functioned as a major redistribution point (Di Peso 1974:3; vol. 9:75–90, 131–161), but other centers,

especially Pecos Pueblo, Zuni, and the Hopi mesas bustled with multiethnic trade activity when Spaniards entered the region (Riley 1976, 1978, 1982). Trading webs emanating from the Puebloan heartland connected the province to the Plains, Great Basin, Sonora, and California (vol. 10:711–722).

Other sixteenth-century secondary centers included the Quechan (vol. 10:86–98), the Halchidhoma (Dobyns

1981a), Upper Pima and Papago (Dobyns 1976; Riley 1982:63–65), and the La Junta culture villages at the junction of the Rio Grande and Rio Conchos of Texas and Chihuahua (Kelley 1952; Applegate and Hanselka 1974). Far more than the sites of seasonal trade fairs, these centers collectively formed an efficient chain recognized as the Greater Southwest (Kelley and Kelley 1975; Pailes and Whitecotton 1979; Riley 1986).

On the northern Plains, well before horses and European trade goods intensified the frequency and diversity of interethnic exchanges, a self-sufficient and surplus-abundant trading system as elaborate as that of the Southwest had been established. The primary focuses of this system were the earth lodge villages of the Arikaras near the mouth of Grand River and those of the Mandan-Hidatsa near the mouth of the Knife River in present-day South Dakota and North Dakota respectively. A favorable geographic location as well as resource and craft specialization enabled these tribes to assume the position of middlemen linking riverine horticulturalists with upland hunters (Ewers 1954, 1968:14–33). This east-west network is labeled the Middle Missouri system (W.R. Wood 1972, 1980).

It is still unclear how many and from what distance separate ethnic groups traveled to the village bazaars of the Missouri River (Bowers 1950:14–18; W.R. Wedel 1961:181–193). However, by 1805 Crow, Assiniboin, Plains Cree, Cheyenne, Arapaho, Kiowa, Kiowa-Apache, and Comanche of the Plains traded dried meat, deer hides, bison robes, mountain sheep bows, and other leather goods for garden produce and Knife River flint at the Mandan-Hidatsa center and were joined by bands of Teton Sioux at the Arikara center on a regular basis (Ewers 1968:17–18; Wood and Thiessen 1985:4–5).

A second type of indirect trade, later borrowed by White traders, was the "rendezvous." Trading parties from different bands met at a prearranged time and place in order to exchange goods, many of which had been acquired through direct trade with other tribes. The rendezvous was also an occasion for ceremonial and social activities at the interband and intertribal levels. At least two major rendezvous were active at the time of white contact. The Dakota Rendezvous, held on the James River in present-day South Dakota, was a pan-Siouan gathering of Tetons, Yanktons, and Sissetons. Goods acquired at the rendezvous were transported to various midwestern tribes, including some groups east of the Mississippi River. The Shoshone Rendezvous, held regularly in southwestern Wyoming, linked Plateau and Great Basin tribes with the Middle Missouri system via Crow middlemen. The Shoshone Rendezvous also became the major exhange point for horses during protohistoric and early historic times, enabling numerous tribes to acquire Spanish, French, and English trade goods a generation or more before they actually glimpsed a White trader (Ewers

1968:17–18; Haines 1938, 1976:92–94).

A third major trade system stimulated direct and indirect exhange throughout the Plateau and Northwest Coast culture areas. The vortex of the Pacific-Plateau system was The Dalles of present-day Oregon (W.R. Wood 1980:101–102; French 1961). The Wasco-Wishram living at The Dalles and the Wayam subgroup of Tenino at Celilo Falls were both the middlemen for Pacific Coast and Plateau products and the primary processors of dried and smoked fish, which were sold to Yakima, Kittitas, Klikitat, Umatilla, and Nez Perce traders (Anastasio 1972:161). The Lower Columbia Chinookans served as middlemen for shells, whale bone, oil, and other Northwest Coast items, all the while procuring shellfish and producing baskets for trade at The Dalles (Griswold 1970: 150–154: Ruby and Brown 1976:3–23).

The variety of trade goods, the intensity and volume of trade, and the plethora of cultures that manufactured and processed these goods is unparalleled elsewhere in North America. For example, whale and seal bone, cooking and cosmetic oils, and ornamental shells went from the Pacific Coast directly to the West and Southwest; obsidian and other stone tools were brought from the Great Basin; pipestone (catlinite), parfleches, buffalo bone beads, feather headdresses, and buffalo robes arrived from the Plains across the Plateau. Baskets, canoes, minerals and plant materials for paint, peltries, and hides were offered by traders from other parts of the Plateau; food plants such as wapatoo, camas, acorns, and bitterroot arrived from the Plateau, California, and Great Basin.

Items traded at The Dalles have been found in archeological sites from Alaska to California and over 1,000 miles east in the Missouri River trade centers (W.R. Wood 1980:103). The extensive distribution network associated with the Pacific-Plateau trade system, like those of the Greater Southwest and Middle Missouri systems, confirms that the tribes of the trans-Mississippi West were linked by a web of commercial relationships on the eve of European contact. Indian-White trade relations must therefore be viewed as an elaboration of native patterns rather than as a European innovation (Ewers 1968).

Euro-American Trade, 1530–1805

Spanish Sphere

The first Europeans to follow the highways of trade were Spaniards, in the sixteenth century (fig. 2) (Riley 1976; Quinn 1977; Sauer 1971). The Spaniards carried saddlebags filled with beads, mirrors, hawkbells, blades, and other trifles to exchange for items of native production as well as for human services. They did not find precious metals in any abundance, having to settle instead for foodstuffs, pottery, baskets, pearls, turquoises, and, when

353

in need of bedding and new coats, furs and hides. At times the conquistadors bartered for such commodities; more often they demanded and forcibly seized them. Although a handful of Spaniards returned to Mexico with favorable reports, the traffic in Indian commodities was given low priority well into the seventeenth century. Of the hundreds of items that Indian traders circulated throughout the Greater Southwest, few ranked high on the Spanish gauge (Riley 1971, 1976).

Although the western Spanish borderlands would become a major arena of fur and robe production only after Mexican independence, Spaniards were fully cogni-

zant of the varieties and locations of hides and furs—both on the hoof and in Indian lodges. But robe and hide production was not stimulated initially due to unrealistic Spanish expectations regarding the true wealth of the region, the small scale of colonization efforts in the northern borderlands, and the logistics of transporting large quantities of any commodity from remote northern colonies to major Spanish ports (Weber 1971:12–31; Moorhead 1958).

Certainly, by the middle of the seventeenth century under direct Spanish colonial rule, exploitative labor systems such as the encomienda, missionization, hispani-

354   Fig. 2. Major historic trade routes and posts to 1824 (Meinig 1968; Hart 1980; Wishart 1979; Garrett 1982, 1984, 1984a, 1985, 1986, 1986a, 1986b).

cization, and intermarriage had redirected some aspects of Pueblo trade and production away from traditional networks and into Spanish hands. This pattern was to characterize all Spanish mission settlements from Texas to California by the end of the eighteenth century.

In the Southwest, the Spaniards built a series of royal highways, ostensibly to connect their towns and missions, which carried a growing interregional trade prompted by native surpluses. Much of the traffic was in hides, furs, and deerskins obtained through Puebloan trade with Plains tribes and collected as tribute by Spanish governors (Weber 1971:17–22).

The volume and proceeds of this first "fur trade" in the West have never been quantified, but cargo inventories and reports from trade fairs officially sanctioned by Spanish authorities at Taos, Pecos, and Picuris hint at its importance in the regional economy. For example, in one caravan that left Santa Fe in 1639, 122 painted buffalo hides and 198 chamois skins were sent south along with 68 leather jackets, shirts, and trousers produced in workshops by Indians (Bloom 1935). Two decades later, upon leaving office, Gov. Lopez de Mendizabal shipped 1,350 deerskins, 1,200 antelope skins, four bundles of at least 100 elk skins as well as a quantity of buffalo hides (Weber 1971:20–21).

Spanish demand increased the quantities of hides and furs brought to traditional trade centers such as Pecos where, in 1786, the Comanches alone supplied over 600 hides (A.B. Thomas 1932:306). At Taos, which attracted Utes, Navajos, Pawnees, and other tribes, an official truce was proclaimed each summer after 1723 for the purpose of trade (Hallenbeck 1950:214). In 1760, one priest reported that the Utes brought to this "great fair," "captives to sell, pieces of chamois, many buffalo skins, and, out of the plunder they obtained elsewhere, horses, muskets, shotguns, munitions, knives, meat, and various other things" (E.B. Adams 1954:57).

Additional hides and furs were obtained by both legal and illegal traders and hunters operating directly among the plains cultures in the eighteenth and nineteenth centuries. In theory, all traders were to be licensed, a practice Mexico perpetuated well after 1821; in reality many traders never secured the governor's permission (Weber 1971:21–29). In the multiethnic milieu of colonial New Mexico and Texas, three groups deserve mention in the context of trade. Genízaros were descendants of Spaniards and Plains Indians who had been captured, bought, or ransomed by Spaniards (vol. 9:198–200). A direct result of Pueblo and Spanish trade with Plains tribes (Swadesh 1974), they lived in a dozen villages in northern New Mexico after 1800. Comancheros functioned as middlemen in the lucrative and vigorous commerce with Comanches, other Plains groups, and eventually with Mexicans and Anglos between 1786 and 1860 (J.E. Haley 1935; Kenner 1969:78–97). A third group of Hispanos and

mestizos—the ciboleros—teamed up with Pueblo hunters and seasonally combed the Plains for bison. The ciboleros alienated some of the Plains tribes because they bypassed Indian middlemen and competed directly for the Spanish trade in hides and meat. These hunters relied upon Pueblo military auxiliaries for most of the Spanish era, traveling in well-armed groups often numbering over 100 men (O.L. Jones 1966). They suffered heavy losses, but as late as the 1870s, ciboleros continued to harvest diminishing herds of American bison on the southern Plains (Kenner 1969: 98–114).

Small scale entrepreneurs like the ciboleros and the Comancheros ranged from the Pacific to the Gulf during the Spanish regime. However, control and direction of most of the trade in the Greater Southwest, the Great Basin, and California, as well as on the Plains, remained in Indian hands. Pre- and protohistoric patterns of Indian trade persisted at traditional primary and secondary centers, although often modified by European ideas and commodities. Nowhere is this better demonstrated that at Pecos Pueblo, the most important crossroads linking the Southwest and Plains culture areas. Pecos middlemen monopolized the westward diffusion of Plains-processed items (Kidder 1932:42–44, 1958:313–314; Gunnerson 1974; Riley 1978; Kessell 1979). Inter-Indian trade among the Southwest, Plains, and Great Basin in historic times was significant (vol. 9:201–205, vol. 11:238–255).

Several conclusions can be drawn about Spanish-Indian trade in the West. Despite radical demographic decline and population shifts due to disease (Simmons 1966; Schroeder 1972:54, 62; Ewers 1973; Dobyns 1976), environmental stress (Zubrow 1974; Upham 1982), increased intertribal warfare between Plains and Southwestern tribes (O.L. Jones 1966; Kenner 1969), and Spanish-directed acculturation (Spicer 1954, 1962), the Greater Southwest trade network remained intact during the entire Spanish era (Riley 1982).

On the other hand, the new goods and livestock accompanying the European presence both increased the variety and altered the value of trade commodities. The most important Spanish importations were horses, which spread throughout the Plains in the seventeenth century and became deeply integrated into all of Plains culture by 1800, bearing ceremonial and social as well as utilitarian value (Haines 1938, 1976; Roe 1955; Ewers 1955). Other Spanish innovations that the trade in horses carried as far away as the Middle Missouri trade centers included mules, saddles, bridles, wool and cotton blankets of Navajo or Pueblo weave, and Spanish trade beads (Ewers 1968:25–26).

Spanish material culture was also introduced into the Pacific-Plateau systems from three sources, only one of which actually involved Spaniards. Trade items from the village fairs of the Middle Missouri system flowed westward on horseback with Crow and Nez Perce traders along former foot trails. English and French copper kettles, blades, axes, metal arrowheads, and a few North West Company guns reached the Plateau on these horses before any of the mountain tribes had any direct contact with White traders (Ewers 1955:7–11).

Most horses and what Spanish material culture they bore diffused north from the Shoshone Rendezvous in parfleches of Plateau riders (Anastasio 1972:127–130). This revolution in transportation enabled more frequent interregional trade and communication between culturally diverse strangers, all the while increasing hostilities among horse-hungry tribes (Haines 1976:58–98). Horse raiding and individual feats of thievery gained high status in most Plains and Plateau societies once these animals were culturally important (Wissler 1914; Ewers 1955: 240ff.; Roe 1955).

Horse culture altered social and political organization, and that in turn had an important effect on the values native societies placed on ownership, inheritance, and the exchange of commodities. Euro-American traders consistently had difficulty grasping native definitions of wealth and poverty and in understanding the prestige and shame ascribed to giveaways and hoarding by Plains, Plateau, and Northwest Coast societies (Kehoe 1981:290–298, 421–422; K.M. Weist 1973; Codere 1950, 1961:441–446). The greater availability and variety of prestige items compounded this misunderstanding because many Euro-American traders could not (or would not) engage in the prescribed rituals of reciprocal gift-giving. During the Spanish regime, such prolonged face to face contacts with noncolonized peoples were minimal.

The exception to this pattern occurred on the Northwest Coast. As a response to the Russian presence there, Spanish vessels widened their arc of navigation to include the Pacific Northwest in the 1770s, using the Californias as harbors and resupply points. The Spanish entered the pelagic mammal trade of the Northwest with great zeal (W.L. Cook 1973:41–58). Indian-processed pelts of the sea otter were first introduced into the Orient by the Spaniards in the 1730s. Spain enlisted as trading partners several Northwest Coast groups, including the Haida and Nootkans, who in turn traded with other coastal and inland groups within the Pacific-Plateau system (R. Fisher 1977:1–23).

The European innovation of trafficking directly off the coast or at prearranged villages along the seaboard was not exclusively a Spanish idea; the Russians had been mining the coastal trade with great success since the 1740s in northwestern North America (J.R. Gibson 1978a: 56–57). However, the appearance of Juan Pérez's ship, *Santiago*, in 1774 sparked international competition for pelagic furs. By 1780 the waters of the Pacific Northwest were crowded with Russian, Spanish, English, and American ships whose decks served as trading fairs for coastal tribes.

What developed along the Pacific coast from Oregon to Alaska and most intensely at Nootka Sound was a brief period of easy trading and high profits for a few Europeans followed by a dramatic inflationary spiral ("The Maritime Trade of the North Pacific Coast," this vol.). In the preindustrial, precapitalist environment, natives rather than Europeans dictated the terms of trade. It was quite common for native traders to demand 100 percent more in goods per fur, only a year after first contact. At Nootka, for example, one piece of copper yielded 10 skins in 1786. By 1792, when 21 ships anchored to trade along the Northwest Coast, the rate of exchange was one piece of copper for each pelt, leaving one Englishman to conclude "we found to our cost, that these people, . . . possessed all the cunning necessary to the gains of mercantile life" (Meares 1790:141–142). Furthermore, the coastal groups knew high-quality iron and premium quality textiles and would not settle for less. Although this pattern lasted only until the 1820s when the Hudson's Bay Company gained control of the land-based coastal traffic, no other trade relations in the annals of the West were ever so balanced as those of the Northwest Coast (R. Fisher 1977:1–23).

By the time Spain withdrew its claim to Nootka Sound in 1795, many trade items of Spanish origin or transport had passed into native hands, and items of greater long-term value than furs had been collected as scientific curiosities. These masks, baskets, carved objects, and other cultural artifacts gave the Western world its first glimpses of natives of the Far West and preconditioned attitudes that would affect later contact and trade (Cutter 1963a; Gunther 1972).

The wide diffusion of trade goods and the general pattern of Spanish-Indian relations did not lead to radical culture change anywhere in the West during the Spanish era except where forced missionization divorced natives from their cultural heritage as in Alta California (Cook 1943,1). Spaniards tended to accept native compartmentalization of European and native lifeways so as to coexist and to win souls for Catholicism. In fact, once Spaniards capitalized upon preexisting Indian trade networks in the West, commodity exchange among native groups and with the resident Spanish minority became an important economic as well as diplomatic, political, and social avenue for communication and coexistence.

French Sphere

Frenchmen penetrated the Plains and Southwest culture areas by way of the lower Mississippi River (McDermott 1965). Traders under the French flag also entered the trans-Mississippi West from the northeast via Lake Superior and the Canadian prairies, using the Middle Missouri system trade centers as collection depots and wintering posts (fig. 2) (Wood and Thiessen 1985:3–8).

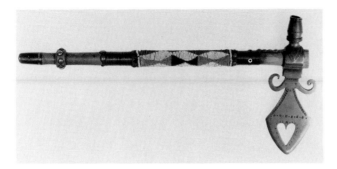

Oreg. Histl. Soc., Portland: 1116–1.
Fig. 3. Tomahawk of the spontoon type, probably made and distributed principally by the French in the 18th century. With the closing of the French trade after the Louisiana Purchase of 1803, these distinctive tomahawks were presumably made by American, British, and Canadian manufacturers (Peterson 1965:25). This tomahawk carries many of the hallmarks of the Indian trade: brass tacks, thick wraps of copper wire, and hide grips covered in seed beads. Collected from Cayuse after 1847. Length 56 cm.

In comparison with French colonial efforts in eastern North America, activities beyond the Mississippi pale in overall significance. And, for the region as a whole, the French physical presence, the length of French occupancy, and the spatial extent of the French trading network were minimal when compared with Spanish, English, and Anglo-American spheres (Bolton and Marshall 1920: 280–288). Yet, in several geographic regions the French influenced Native American cultures profoundly. Furthermore, the strategies for economic and social interaction with Indian trade partners that the French developed in the Northeast and transferred to the West directly affected Spanish, British, and American trade behavior after 1763 (fig. 3) (Trigger 1976; Heidenreich and Ray 1976).

French reconnaissance of the Mississippi watershed revealed that the Pawnee, Osage, and Wichita were engaged in direct commerce with tribes to their south and west and indirectly with the Spaniards. Evidence of this trade was visible in the presence of horses and Spanish riding equipment among the Caddoans on the Red River of Texas, who acquired them from Jumano (Sauer 1980: 240–243; Kelley 1955) and Wichita traders (Schroeder 1962; Wedel 1979). At 1700, when first contacted by French traders, the Wichita were the most important link between the Southwest and Southeast culture areas.

The French employed a strategy of favored nation diplomacy and sought to form the most advantageous partnerships with the cultures west of the Mississippi. However, intercolonial wars and the lack of Crown support ensured stagnation of trade until 1712 when the French government granted a 15-year monopoly to Antoine Crozat, a wealthy French businessman. Crozat faced problems from the outset despite his wide-ranging authorities, which entitled him to a monopoly of all the mining, agricultural, and Indian commerce of Louisiana except for the trade in beaver pelts. Beaver were not to be trapped, traded, or purchased in order to dispose of the surplus furs generated by the trade of New France (P.C. Phillips 1961, 1:370–372).

Crozat's trading empire was superimposed on a preexisting French, Spanish, and Indian trade oriented toward French Biloxi and Mobile and Spanish Pensacola where Indian slaves, deerskins, peltries, and bison robes were exchanged for sugar, tobacco, cocoa, molasses, and brandy. In order to increase the volume and flow of trade, Crozat's first move was to encourage the expansion of French trading posts throughout Louisiana. The major focus of this expansion remained in the Southeast culture area, but some efforts were made to open trade with the numerous river and prairie-oriented cultures due west of the Illinois country (Surrey 1922; Nasatir 1952, 1:1–12; P.C. Phillips 1961, 1:373–374).

Bénard de la Harpe was instrumental in establishing direct French contact with tribes of the southern Plains after 1719 when a French post was built among the Nasoni Caddo on the Red River, upriver from the Caddo post at Natchitoches opened in 1713 (Margry 1876–1886, 6:241–306). La Harpe contacted nine Wichita bands and sealed military and trade agreements that were to endure to 1763 (John 1975:212–218). The Wichita (Wedel 1971) had become horse-herders as well as expert hoe-gardeners by the time of La Harpe's visit (Holder 1970: 28–33, 79, 111).

The French success on the Plains hinged on several factors. First, reliable trading partnerships had to be established. In the posthorse, pregun stage, gifts of a limited number of firearms to men of chiefly authority served this purpose (Secoy 1953). Second, lacking strength in numbers, the French were forced to rely upon middlemen tribes for trade and military protection of French trade routes and posts. Although some Plains tribes could trace their middlemen status to pre-European contact, intertribal competition for middleman trade intensified during the eighteenth and early nineteenth centuries especially among Caddoan and Siouan-speaking riverine horticulturalists. The French were the first to manipulate, with varying degrees of success, both traditional and newly created animosities and alliances on the northern and central Plains (Holder 1970:79–85). Third, the trade was dependent upon peaceful relations. Because conflicts among tribes increased dramatically after the introduction of horses and guns, the French and all Euro-Americans were forced to bend their diplomatic skills to peacemaking.

Charles Claude du Tisné made two sorties from the Illinois country in 1718–1719 to explore the Missouri River and to conclude alliances with the most powerful inland middlemen—the Pawnees and the Apaches. In rapid succession, trade alliances were made with the Osages and the Wichitas, but attempts to reach the Plains Apache were temporarily blocked by their Wichita rivals

357

(Wedel 1972–1973).

In a bold move that opened up the Missouri River to French traders, du Tisné contacted the Pawnees directly in 1719, promising guns and presents in exchange for a trading alliance and favored-nation status in the French sphere (Margry 1876–1886, 3:311–312; Hyde 1951:38). The agreement required periodic renewal in the 1720s as intertribal rivalries intensified in the quest for guns, but the method, when backed with presents, proved as successful on the Plains as in the Northeast during the European wars for empire (John 1975:217–225; Haines 1976:79–80).

The French were aided in their expansion of the Mississippi-based trade by the contraction of Spanish trade in east Texas between 1662 and the founding of San Antonio in 1718 and by increased Indian dependency on the new tools of warfare. French design also benefited from the defeat of Pedro de Villasur and his army of 42 Spanish soldiers and 70 Pueblo auxiliaries who had been sent in 1720 to reconnoiter French activities on the southern Plains. Armed with French guns, the Pawnees and their Kansa allies (Unrau 1971:56–58) killed 45 of the Spanish-Pueblo party and forced the rest to retreat to Santa Fe (O.L. Jones 1966:100–102).

The victory opened the door for Étienne Veniard de Bourgmont, who arrived from France in 1723, to secure trading alliances with all Plains tribes not in the French fold, especially the Cuartelejo Apaches (Gunnerson 1974: 121, 223). After building Fort Orléans on the banks of the Missouri River, Bourgmont pressed his mission among the lower Missouri River tribes, securing by the end of 1724 initial pacts of friendship and commerce with the Missouri, Osage, Kansa, Oto, Pawnee, Iowa, and Illinois. An alliance was also struck between these tribes and representatives of one or more divisions of Plains Apaches (Margry 1876–1886, 6:312, 398–449; Haines 1976:80–81), who were then residing in semipermanent villages in present-day Nebraska, Kansas, and Colorado (Gunnerson and Gunnerson 1971:11–12; vol. 10:389).

Peace was short-lived. Once Bourgmont left, his efforts were undermined by New Orleans–based slavers willing to pay higher prices for human cargoes than for furs. While the French counted 50,000 skins in the Louisiana trade during 1725 (John 1975:220–221), unspecified lots of Apache men, women, and children, supplied primarily by the Pawnee and Osage (R. White 1983:152–154; Din and Nasatir 1983) and secondarily by the Kansa middlemen (Haines 1976:82–83; Unrau 1971:60), found ready buyers in French markets.

Direct French contact with the Mandan-Hidatsa-Arikara dates to 1738 when Pierre Gaultier de Varennes, sieur de La Vérendrye, accompanied a party of Assiniboin traders bound for the easternmost Mandan villages on the Heart River. The French strategy involved building an extensive chain of posts from Lake Superior to the Pacific to serve the triple purpose of tapping the wealth of the interior, claiming those lands for France, and outbidding England and Spain in the process (G.H. Smith 1980).

The La Vérendrye family figured prominently in this grand scheme, as did the Indians of the Middle Missouri network. In 1742 and again in 1743, two sons of La Vérendrye continued the quest for a waterway to the Pacific. The identity of the various tribes contacted by the French explorers is not clear, but there is considerable evidence that in addition to the Mandan, they parleyed with the Arikara (Meyer 1977:24–26). Many other tribes farther south and west were also contacted. It is difficult to determine what impact, if any, the La Vérendryes had on intertribal relations. Certainly little trade flowed into French hands as a result of these treks, in part because of French preoccupation with intertribal and international struggles east of the Mississippi.

The western sphere was not totally neglected before relinquishment of French claims to North America in 1763. In 1739, Peter and Paul Mallet crossed the Plains to Santa Fe and opened the doors of commerce between Louisiana and New Mexico (Folmer 1939). Governor Jean-Baptiste Le Moyne, Sieur de Bienville, of Louisiana soon dispatched other licensed traders to take advantage of the opportunity to bring in desperately needed Mexican silver specie in exchange for French textiles, metal goods, and exotic spices (Loomis and Nasatir 1967:54–61). However, after the 1724 Bourgmont alliances, French control of the Indian trade and rapport with tribal allies in the Lower Missouri district began to deteriorate. In the late 1720s and early 1730s, several French voyageurs and military personnel were killed in the aftermath of the Fox Wars by Osage and Missouri as well as Fox warriors. Symptomatic of growing diplomatic and commercial ailments, in 1741, a French expedition bound for New Mexico was blocked in its ascent of the Canadian River by a war party of Osage whose kindred had recently killed several French traders in the Arkansas district.

As French control of both the Indian trade and her own citizens in Indian country waned (Nasatir 1952, 1: 23–30), continued dependence upon middleman tribes, especially the Osage, became critical. Exports flowing toward New Orleans from the Illinois country could, in theory, bypass the Osage, but traffic up the Missouri could not. The French were forced to rely upon the Osage for transshipment of commodities, primarily slaves, deer and bear skins, and secondarily beaver, river otter, and other small mammal furs (G.A. Bailey 1973:33–35). Around 1750 the Osage and their allies, the Missouri, were supplying the French with an annual average of 80 packs of skins (Nasatir 1952, 1:50). As dependency on European technology increased and as the Osage became irreversibly caught in the market economy of the fur trade, they would tax their environment heavily, supplying 950 packs of skins annually by 1800 (Mayhall 1962:26–27).

On the eve of the French and Indian War, French traders cast a wide net, carrying on sporadic legal and illegal traffic with Spaniards in New Mexico and Texas as well as supplying Comanches with guns for their wars against Utes, Apaches, Spaniards, and Pueblos (A.B. Thomas 1940:17–34). Voyageurs licensed in Louisiana were operating in Indian villages on or within easy range of the Missouri and Mississippi watersheds. However, after 1744, they faced competition throughout the Missouri River country from unlicensed French coureurs de bois from Canada, many of whom were accused of defrauding the natives, abducting Indian women, and supplying brandy, especially among the Oto and the Skiri Pawnee, who complained loudly to agents of Governor Bienville. Theft of traders' pelts and goods became more common as the Osage, Iowa, and other tribes used the competition among the French as an opportunity to enlarge their middleman positions (Din and Nasatir 1983:44–45).

In an effort to stamp out the illegal competition and restore order, the Company of the Indies leased the entire Missouri Indian trade to the Canadian entrepreneur Joseph Deruisseau who was required to sell the peltry of the district exclusively to the Company. By this agreement, the Indian trade of Canada and Louisiana was officially divided for the first time by the French Company (Nasatir 1952, 1:35–41).

Deruisseau fulfilled his obligations by building Fort Cavagnolle in the domain of the Kansa during the mid-1740s. From this outpost, the Company temporarily improved its control of the Indian trade, policed the Missouri country for deserters and illegal traders, and assembled expeditions bound for Spanish New Mexico. Until the opening shots were fired in the Seven Years' War, this first "Santa Fe Trade" enjoyed a limited prosperity largely because Jumano middlemen and Comanche bands were willing to allow French traders to cross their territories (Bolton 1917a).

The trade about the fort was disappointing, however, and the French troops failed to keep the Canadian voyageurs from operating independently in the Indian villages. The voyageurs slashed prices of trade goods, regaled Indians with brandy, and guaranteed purchase of all furs. In 1752 a trader named Avion even lured the Kansa away from their main village at Cavagnolle to a new location on the Kansas River, resulting in French financial failure. Fort Cavagnolle was soon abandoned, an invitation to illegal French traders and English agents who took advantage by inciting unrest among the Missouri River tribes (Unrau 1971:65–70).

Between 1756 and 1763, the French focused their energies on the Seven Years' War. Policy in the West aimed primarily at protecting the Plains tribes from English influence and in keeping intertribal warfare to a minimum. In this the French succeeded, but the changing of flags in towns and posts along the Mississippi and Missouri as a result of the treaty of 1763 did not signal an equivalent transfer of control over the Indian trade of the interior. For the next 38 years, Spain claimed the Illinois, Missouri, and Louisiana districts as her own, but in reality these remained tribal districts where a small number of Spaniards and Frenchmen operated within altered, but still sovereign native communities (Bannon 1974).

Under Spanish rule, the Indian trade of the West increased in volume. However, the plan of Spanish authorities in 1763 to build a string of posts to collect furs and dispense trade goods at 50-mile intervals along the Missouri River failed to materialize (Nasatir 1952, 1:59). In addition to the Arkansas Post, only Fort Carondelet on the Osage River (completed in 1795) and a handful of wintering posts in Upper Louisiana operated as major European transsshipment points in addition to Saint Louis. Wars on the continent, preoccupation with the lucrative trade on the lower Missouri, lack of European personnel, and energies and monies spent to retain middleman suppliers (especially the Osage) discouraged Spanish advance much beyond her immediate native trading partners (Din and Nasatir 1983:385ff.). The continued domination of the daily operations of the trade by French personnel and their reluctance to conform to the Spanish monopoly-licensing system also restricted geographic expansion. Nevertheless, the local districts were profitable for the oligopolies operating out of Saint Louis and New Orleans (Foley and Rice 1983).

The most important residential and commercial enclave of the Franco-Spanish trade sphere was Saint Louis, founded in 1764, which soon replaced the French centers at Cahokia (founded 1699), Kaskaskia (1703), and Sainte Geneviéve (1732) as the emporium of the Missouri River (Nasatir 1952, 1:58–74). In Saint Louis and its environs, a Creole society emerged as a result of intermarriage between the leading French and Spanish families, and between those same families and the most powerful Indian middlemen tribes. The pattern of creating Indian-White political and economic alliances through marriage was well established elsewhere in the French sphere (Dickason 1985). In Upper Louisiana, the Osage were particularly important in this regard and were courted and wed by the leading merchant-capitalist families in Saint Louis, especially the Chouteaus (Foley and Rice 1983; Thorne 1984). As French, Spanish, Métis, and later Anglo-American traders moved up the Missouri into the Middle Missouri trade system and beyond into the Rockies, similar kinship alliances were forged (H.H. Anderson 1973; Swagerty 1980).

In the region beyond the lower Missouri, the greatest threat to the Spanish trade sphere was the English presence to the north and east. As in the Southeast, national rivalries and intrigues between Spain and England affected diplomatic and commercial relations with Indians between 1763 and 1803. After 1783, Anglo-

American encroachments also disrupted Spanish-Indian relations on the Plains as traders from the United States called "fillibusters" illegally entered Texas in search of horses. Some, like Philip Nolan, were eventually stopped by Spanish bullets, but others carried on a contraband trade with the Comanches and other tribes eager to acquire American trade goods (Loomis and Nasatir 1967: 74–80; Glass 1985).

During the final years before American takeover of Louisiana, French and Métis personnel continued to extend the Franco-Spanish sphere onto the Plains by way of overland and waterborne trade. English competition by the newly created North West Company and expansion of Hudson's Bay Company operations forced more aggressive tactics on the Missouri. In 1790, Jacques D'Église became the first Spanish-licensed trader to enter the Mandan-Hidatsa main villages. There he found a French-Canadian named Ménard who had been in residence as a free trader since some time between 1778 and 1783 (Wood and Thiessen 1985:27, 43; Nasatir 1952, 1:82–83).

Ménard's life is illustrative of a pattern of accommodation coined by the French and duplicated by the English and Americans. Ménard lived among the Mandan for a quarter of a century with a native wife and was supplied on credit from Brandon House, a Hudson's Bay Company post on the Assiniboine River. At 1795, these "residenters" or "tenant traders" were responsible for one-fourteenth of the total business in furs in all of Canada (Rich 1967:188). At least 14 such residenters, including Toussaint Charbonneau, are known to have resided at the Mandan-Hidatsa center from the late 1770s to the early 1800s. As free traders, they often accompanied native merchants on their journeys, crossing ethnic and network boundaries. Ménard traveled with the Hidatsas to Crow camps in eastern Montana. Many others like Ménard resided in native villages and camps throughout the Canadian and American Wests (Wood and Thiessen 1985: 42–47).

Men like Ménard of French Canadian and Métis background established small-scale commercial hegemonies in Indian trade zones and served as cultural brokers and interpreters in the growing direct trade between Whites and Indians during the American and British periods. They provided a cultural buffer for tribes on the threshold of stiff competition with entire brigades of White trappers and traders during the nineteenth century. Their descendants and cousins comprised at least one-fourth of the rank and file of the Anglo-dominated trade of the mountain West (Swagerty 1980:161).

Alarmed by D'Eglise's reports of British-backed trade, Spanish authorities launched a more vigorous program of encouraging direct commerce between remote parts of Spanish North America by enticing Saint Louis merchant-traders to risk capital on the Upper Missouri. In 1794, the Company of Explorers of the Upper Missouri was chartered to expel residenters and to exploit the fur resources of the Middle and Upper Missouri. Several expeditions cordelled their way up the Missouri in the 1790s but were ineffective in channeling much of the Mandan-Hidatsa-Arikara trade down the Missouri into Spanish warehouses. By 1803, the trade of the northern Plains still had not been won by any European power (Nasatir 1952, 1:82–115; Hafen 1965–1972, 1:35–37; Alwin 1979).

The Western Interior, 1805–1824

The period of greatest intensity in the Indian trade of the Far West began around 1805 and ended about 1870. Concurrently, the Indian tribes of the West suffered demographic decline, intensifying warfare, and a diminishing subsistence base. The Euro-American-induced trade was a prime agent in the process of biological and cultural change, but it was only one of a series of overlapping, complex phenomena at work in the nineteenth-century West. The transformative effects of the trade were more subtle, less immediately erosive than the mining, farming, and ranching frontiers (Swagerty 1980). Still, the result was near-catastrophic.

As in most contact frontiers, the process began and was accelerated by waves of epidemic disease brought by Euro-American carriers. In the 1780s as many as one-third of all native residents in the Northern Plains, Southwest, and Northwest died as smallpox swept the West, supplemented by cholera or bubonic plague in Texas (Mooney 1928; L.M. Scott 1928; Ewers 1973; Thornton 1986). Streptococcal infections attacked the Sioux in 1798 and were reported among the Assiniboin and Cree by 1801. Five years later, Mandans and Blackfeet suffered strep as well as influenza. Measles and whooping cough carried away thousands on the Northern Plains in 1819 and 1820, and an estimated 4,000 Comanches died that same decade from smallpox (J.F. Taylor 1977: 79–80). Measles struck in 1806 and again in 1827 killing thousands in the missions of California (Cook 1943, 1:19–20).

On the High Plains the scourge was smallpox, affecting the Arikara, Arapaho, Gros Ventre, Crow, and Pawnee in 1831–1832. By 1833, whooping cough and cholera were noted among the Mandan and Hidatsa (J.F. Taylor 1977: 80). In the Pacific Northwest, much of the Columbia River valley was depopulated by influenza, 1831–1838 (L.M. Scott 1928; Taylor and Hoaglin 1962; Ruby and Brown 1976:185–200).

The great smallpox outbreak of 1837 on the Northern Plains cut in half the Indian population of the Plains. By year's end, the greatest trading cultures of the Middle Missouri system had been all but wiped out; seven-eighths of the Mandan and over one-half of the Arikara were gone (Dollar 1977).

During the same decade, in California, New Mexico,

and Texas—all under Mexican rule—diseases took heavy tolls among Indian populations (Cook 1943, 1:17–22; Ewers 1973; Weber 1982:237). Many other epidemics followed in the 1840s and beyond. Cumulatively, the biological impact of these pathogenic destroyers did much to alter both the level and the nature of Indian trade activity.

Stimulation of the trade after the epidemics of the 1780s came from both private and government sources. Acquisition of Louisiana Territory in 1803 gave the United States formal diplomatic cause for investigating French, Spanish, Russian, and English activities among tribes of the West and for assessing the region's trade potential. United States government–sponsored expeditions under Meriwether Lewis and William Clark, 1804–1806; Zebulon Pike, 1805–1806, 1806–1807; and Thomas Freeman, 1806; as well as published accounts by North West Company explorers (especially Alexander MacKenzie) encouraged entrepreneurial capital formation in the East (J.L. Allen 1975; Jackson 1981; Flores 1984).

These early American probes into the West provided valuable scientific, geographic, and ethnographic information and contributed to increased interest in a land-based fur trade (Cutright 1969; Ronda 1984). Lewis and Clark reported extensively on the fur resources of the upper Missouri and the Columbia Basin and urged Americans to enter the competition in order to prevent North West Company and Hudson's Bay Company traders from further expansion into Louisiana Territory. They also advocated establishing American trading posts in or around native primary and secondary trade centers and on the Yellowstone and Marias rivers in order to control the Missouri and its tributaries. Posts on the Milk River and the Little Missouri would, in the judgment of Clark, secure the fur trade to the mouth of the Columbia, enabling Americans to reach Canton directly from Pacific bases on the Northwest Coast (P.C. Phillips 1961, 1: 257–258).

As Lewis and Clark descended the Missouri in 1806 to report their findings, they met 11 separate parties of American traders headed upriver to tribes in the Arikara, Sioux, and Pawnee sectors of the Middle Missouri system (Thwaites 1904–1905, 5:242, 335, 341). Apparently, the raising of the American flag over Louisiana had done little to disrupt the customary relations between Saint Louis merchants and the Mandan villages. However, after 1806 relations changed dramatically as the geographic focus of the trade shifted to the upper Missouri. Accompanying the shift were large numbers of foreign fur and hide hunters—Whites, Hawaiians, Blacks, and Iroquois, Shawnee, and Delaware Indians—who competed with one another as well as with resident hunters (Clark 1934; Duncan 1972; Porter 1934; Ewers 1963; Nicks 1980; Karamanski 1982).

The age of the American beaver men and buffalo robe traders arrived as the Pueblos and the Mandan-Hidatsa-Arikara were struggling to rebound from the 1780s epidemics. It was a propitious time for outsiders to take advantage of the weakness of traditional trade centers. In some cases, tribes less adversely affected by epidemics took over the middleman role of other groups, such as Sioux inroads on the Arikaras' status. When visited by Lewis and Clark, the Arikara had not yet lost their position as mediators between east-west, and to a lesser extent, the north-south tribes (Orser 1984a, 1984).

In the Southwest, once-powerful Pecos continued to serve as the major trade center between the Pueblos and the Plains, but the Comanches—also struck heavily by smallpox—were persuaded to sign a treaty of peace in 1786. Even with combined Pueblo, Spanish, and Comanche military and commercial alliances, continued demographic decline and Apache raiding sapped the strength of Pecos. By 1815, the days of the trade fairs were over (Kessell 1979:401ff.).

A different pattern applied to tribes such as the Blackfoot, Assiniboin, and Plains Cree. At a disadvantage when compared with horse-wealthy Crow, Northern and Eastern Shoshone, and Nez Perce, by 1806 bands of Blackfoot, Piegan, and related tribes had begun to consolidate into larger ethnic units in order to strengthen their military and trading powers and to aggressively stake out their territory in the wars for furs, horses, and guns (O. Lewis 1942; Ewers 1955; Haines 1976:120–134).

Still another pattern distinguished the Sioux, who continued to host the annual Dakota Rendezvous. They expanded onto the Plains, pushing other tribes south and west. By 1805, the Sioux were recognized by Lewis and Clark as the dominant power on the Missouri River (J.A. Hanson 1975; R. White 1978; Ronda 1984).

In 1806, despite redistribution of power among the Plains tribes, access to the abundant furbearers of the trans-Mississippi West was firmly controlled by the Indian majority. Euro-American success hinged on the willingness of outsiders to follow customary trade protocol and to give good measure for commodities and privileges received. Interested parties who understood and respected these guidelines were usually accommodated; those who violated or ignored them were often treated with hostility (Ewers 1976).

The Spanish and French systems of licensing a limited number of traders for the exclusive or near-exclusive trade with individual tribes had won Indian cooperation and approval in part because posts were not built in large numbers within Indian domains. And, the few posts that had been constructed served primarily as collection and redistribution depots and only secondarily as defensive works and residential quarters for White personnel. The difference between primary and secondary motives was critical from the Indian point of view. During the French and Spanish regimes, Indian middlemen had been pitted against one another in the spiraling quest for trade goods, but their status had not been challenged, and the most powerful tribes, such as the Osage and the Pawnee, were never intentionally avoided or bypassed.

Under American auspices, the Saint Louis-based traders experimented with various strategies of expansion on the upper Missouri from 1807 to 1826 (Wishart 1979: 41–53). Spanish and French mercantile families of Saint Louis such as the Chouteaus, Prattes, Gratiots, and Cabannes provided seed capital and business acumen and were joined by Americans such as John Jacob Astor and William H. Ashley in the early nineteenth century (Foley and Rice 1983; Porter 1931; Clokey 1980). Field partners and leaders—the diplomatic corps of the trade—hailed from a wide variety of backgrounds, but most were old hands in the Indian trade of Louisiana or were veterans of major reconnaissance expeditions (Clarke 1970). By the 1820s inexperienced Anglo-Americans emerged from Missouri, Virginia, Kentucky, and Tennessee to supersede French-Americans, French-Canadians, and Spanish-Americans in field leadership roles. Men in the rank and file represented the ethnic and linguistic diversity generations of trade had already produced in the colonial fur trade societies of New France and Louisiana, but French-Canadians and Americans of French extraction, many of whom were Métis, were relegated to the lower tiers of the occupational ladder (Fehrman 1972; Swagerty 1980).

A new American approach, evident by the 1820s, rested on several ill-founded assumptions. First, entrepreneurs Manuel Lisa and William H. Ashley naively believed that the Arikara middlemen and their Teton Sioux neighbors could be courted into submission or ignored as Whites and Métis passed through their lands to more lucrative fur-bearing zones upriver. Denying Indians their middleman prerogatives incurred resentment and invited violence. In 1823, 14 Ashley men were killed and nine wounded as their keelboats passed through Arikara country. In retribution, the Arikara villages were assaulted, and the trade center physically destroyed. Most of the residents fled in advance of the attack, but in leaving their villages, they abandoned forever their role as the connective link in the southern sector of the Middle Missouri system. After 1823, the Arikara periodically harassed White traders, but their numbers and influence clearly had waned (Morgan 1964; Orser 1984).

Another costly assumption concerned the system of labor. Under American rule, Lisa and Ashley challenged the division of labor accepted by French, British, Spaniards, Russians, and Americans in most previous and contemporary trade spheres, wherein Indian hunters controlled the production aspects of the trade. Organized originally as "parties," later as "companies," and finally into military-like "brigades," American-based personnel out of Saint Louis did not merely trade; they also trapped

Smithsonian, Dept. of Anthr.: 729.
Fig. 4. Steel dagger of the type referred to as hand dag or stabber. Common trade items on the Northern Plains, these were large and heavy enough for routine camp chores, yet functional fighting knives. This hilt consists of two bone pieces riveted to the steel shank. The sheath is buckskin ornamented with seed beads. Collected by George Gibbs from the Blackfoot before 1862. Approximate length of knife, 33 cm.

and hunted, avoiding Indian middlemen and their native suppliers altogether (Chittenden 1902, 1:1–4). Direct competition insured the enmity of the Blackfoot and Gros Ventre in part because White, Métis, and Eastern Indian trappers violated the spiritual as well as the physical realm of the Blackfoot. Beaver was regarded as sacred and was not hunted at all by some bands (Ewers 1958:49–50).

A xenophobic response to American trappers generally and to select British personnel in particular characterized Blackfoot, and to a lesser degree Crow, Gros Ventre, Sarcee, and Assiniboin attitudes from 1809 to approximately 1831. During those years, dozens of White trappers and traders were slain in the region beyond the Yellowstone; and thousands of dollars in trade goods, packs of furs, and horses fell into Indian hands (Chittenden 1902, 2:850–854). Various explanations have been offered about the "Blackfoot threat" to life and the "Crow threat" to property that plagued a generation of American fur trade personnel. The stabbing to death of He-that-looks-at-the-Calf, a would-be gun and horse thief, by a member of the Lewis and Clark expedition has traditionally been cited as the root of the feud (Coues 1893, 3: 1102–1105).

An alternative explanation focuses on the American government's open door policy giving all tribes in the intermountain West an equal opportunity to trade for American manufactures under the Intercourse Act of 1802 and the Trading House Act of 1806. Arming Crows and Flatheads was not perceived as egalitarian by Piegan, Blood, or Blackfoot tribesmen who had long struggled to control the flow of guns and other goods (Chittenden 1902, 2:721; Ronda 1984:243–244). Lewis and Clark failed not so much by counting coup on a noisy thief, but by spreading ideas of democracy in the Indian trade and by directly challenging Blackfoot superiority over tribes

362

on their perimeters.

In 1807 the Blackfoot were in no mood to relinquish their position. Their dependency on Assiniboin and Cree middlemen had been broken only in the 1780s and 1790s by the opening of North West and Hudson's Bay Company posts on the South Saskatchewan River, which provided direct access to guns, rum, and manufactured goods (Giannettino 1977). Blackfoot hegemony from the Saskatchewan to the Musselshell was subsequently achieved by providing the British traders food rather than furs. Provisions of fresh buffalo meat, pemmican, and horseflesh enabled English traders to replenish post larders and to mount brigades in the field for the more abundant, taboo-free trade in prime beaver north of the Saskatchewan (Ewers 1958:31ff.).

The British gave the Blackfoot cause for alarm even before the arrival of American explorers and trappers. In 1805, Chesterfield House, built at the confluence of the Red Deer and South Saskatchewan rivers as a convenience for Blackfoot and Gros Ventre traders, was abandoned by the Hudson's Bay Company as a revenue-saving measure (Rich 1958–1959, 2:219–220). Fearing exposure to Gros Ventre attack as well, by 1805 the Company had retreated to the North Saskatchewan River to conduct Plains trade from Rocky Mountain House and Edmonton House, forcing the Blackfoot to resume the longer treks of the 1790s (Smyth 1984).

Inconveniences were tolerable; encirclement by Whites and traditional Indian rivals equipped with firearms, traps, and tools supplied by English and American traders or Indian middlemen was not acceptable to the Blackfoot. In the same year that Chesterfield was closed, the Nez Perce joined the Crow during their annual caravan across the Plains to the Mandan trade center and returned to the Rockies with six guns. On their part, the Crow traded 250 horses acquired that year at the Shoshone Rendezvous to the Hidatsas, who in turn provided 200 guns. Most of the major Plateau and Rocky Mountain tribes contacted by Lewis and Clark had few, if any guns, but that was soon to end. Although Zebulon Pike reported that only five percent of the Teton Sioux possessed firearms in 1806, and Lewis and Clark noted very few guns among the otherwise wealthy Northern Shoshone, the Hidatsa offered the Cheyenne 200 fusils for an equal number of horses that critical year.

Between 1807 and 1809, North West Company traders built posts among the Kutenai and Flathead, sewing tighter the circle around the Blackfoot. It did not take the Flatheads long to learn how to use their new trade guns. With 20 marksmen they boldly crossed the divide in 1810 to hunt buffalo in the Blackfoot country. A battle ensued at the base of the Rocky Mountains in which 16 Blackfoots died. Decades of intertribal violence followed (Jablow 1950; Ewers 1958:52, 1968:27–28, 49ff.).

Hostility toward Whites bivouacked in Blackfoot, Flathead, Gros Ventre, and Crow country in the first quarter of the nineteenth century is understandable in light of the fact that Americans were entering tribal lands not primarily to trade with Indian hunters and consumers, but to trap their fur-bearing resources and to live off the game of their hunting territories. Not surprisingly, until 1831, when the Blackfoot agreed to allow the American Fur Company to build Fort McKenzie in the heart of their lands, no company—British or American—safely wintered their trappers in the Piegan-patrolled districts. American strategists followed the British and French pattern of building "posts," "factories," or "houses" at commercial crossroads; however, after the demise of the United States factory system in 1822, standardization and regulation of trading practices in the Far West were virtually nonexistent (Peake 1954; Prucha 1962).

In fact, with the exception of the factory at Fort Osage, the U.S. government did not officially supervise any activities of fur trade personnel in the West until the 1830s and then only in an advisory capacity. The open door to the West led to unrestricted competition, destabilizing relations between resident tribes and assorted traders, trappers, and travelers who made their own policy when given the opportunity. Field leaders and company owners who respected Indian trade protocol and sought a diplomatic agreement from resident tribes usually were permitted to build their posts and safely winter their personnel. However, most of the American companies in the period from 1807 to 1850 attempted to circumvent formal diplomacy with Indian leadership, leaving the establishment of peaceful relations to individual field captains and brigade leaders. When such relations failed, trappers were attacked on streams and traders ambushed on trails.

The first major American expedition to test the upper Missouri diplomatic waters left Saint Louis in 1807 under the leadership of Manuel Lisa. Although the party of 50–60 Franco-, Spanish-, and Anglo-Americans was threatened by angry Arikara middlemen as they cordelled their way upriver, the men succeeded in reaching Absaroka intact. Once in Crow country, they established friendly relations and built a small post on the Yellowstone River at the mouth of the Bighorn. From this base, called Fort Raymond, traders fanned out with packhorses full of trade goods. Other employees worked streambeds and ponds, trapping and processing furs (Oglesby 1963).

A successful season encouraged backers in Saint Louis to finance Lisa's trading association, which, after 1812, was known as the Missouri Fur Company. Its strategy was to funnel furs out of the Middle Missouri trade network via a string of trading posts from the Mandan down to the Omaha middleman villages near Council Bluffs. Such posts would not infringe on Indian trappers and hunters but would protect company trapping parties heading into the upper Missouri country from harassment. The company's main party of trappers and traders then consisted of 160 men, including some Delaware Indians, who were to work in large groups establishing collecting points and defensive redoubts in friendly tribes' domains.

Implementation of this strategy resulted in an expanded Fort Manuel Lisa on the site of the old Fort Raymond in 1809 and construction of smaller posts to serve the Arikara-Mandan-Hidatsa (Lisa's Post, built 1809), Teton and Yankton Sioux (Cedar Island Post, 1809), and Omaha, Oto, Iowa, and Pawnee (Fort Lisa, 1812) trade. Feeling safety in numbers, groups of trappers also expanded into Blackfoot country in 1809, building Fort Henry and the Three Forks Post. However, by 1812, Piegan and Gros Ventre reprisals and the loss of more than 20 men to the Blackfoot forced Lisa to retreat to the Middle Missouri system (Dunwiddie 1974; Schilz 1984).

The Missouri Fur Company continued to send expeditions to the Northern Plains until 1824, although after Lisa's withdrawal from the company in 1819 and his death the following year, the new management faced stiff competition from four other companies operating northwest of the Mandan villages. A renewed effort to build posts on the upper Missouri led to construction of Fort Benton in 1821. But in 1823, Blackfoot warriors killed two field leaders and five employees and sold the Americans' cache of over 1,000 furs to the Hudson's Bay Company at Edmonton House for $15,000. These and other losses proved to be the end for the company, which closed its ledgers in 1824. Clearly the Lisa and Ashley strategies had worked against rather than with the grain of the Middle Missouri and Northern Plains trade networks. Even so, many American officials and financiers blamed the British rather than their own fur men for the losses of 1823 (Nasatir 1939; Oglesby 1963; Dunwiddie 1974; Wishart 1979:41–47).

Mistrust and suspicion recalled another experiment in the Far West that ended in American withdrawal. In 1810, John Jacob Astor organized the Pacific Fur Company as a subsidiary of a pan-continental American Fur Company (founded 1808). Astor proposed to capitalize on both the Indian trade and the China trade by using the Columbia River delta as a transshipment point between New York and Canton. For three years the Pacific Fur Company struggled at the mouth of the Columbia suffering heavy loss of men and material. When news of impending British invasion arrived at Fort Astoria in 1813, the management sold its assets to the North West Company (Irving 1964; Porter 1931).

During the Pacific Fur Company's short tenure in the Northwest, efforts to compete with the North West Company for the trade of the Plateau tribes led to the building of She-Whaps Post in interior British Columbia and Fort Spokane in Washington state adjacent to North West Company posts and Fort Okanogan near the Columbia River. Had the company remained in business, its nascent Clearwater Post, built at the junction of the Snake and Clearwater rivers among the Nez Perce, might have profited from proximity to the finest horse breeding trade nexus in the Northwest, which drew native traders from throughout the region. However, the Astorians and their successors discovered to their chagrin that the Nez Perce "spurned the idea of crawling about in search of furs, viewing trapping as a lifestyle only fit for women and slaves" (Josephy 1965:45–48; Meinig 1968:48–53; Wishart 1979:116–120; Ross 1849:219).

Despite stiff competition, an estimated $100,000 in furs was warehoused from the 1812–1813 season alone. These included 17,705 pounds of beaver, 16 grizzly bear hides, 71 black bear skins, and 68 sea otter. In addition, the Pacific Fur Company had purchased 80,000 seal skins in trade with the Russians at Sitka, and plans had been laid for expansion into the Pacific-Plateau trade system (Meinig 1968:39–53).

British Activities in the Inland Northwest to 1824

Astor's plan for the Northwest had involved resupply from Boston, transshipment to China with an essential communication link overland between St. Louis and Astoria. The merits of this plan did not escape North West Company officers, who rehired several Astorians including the veteran trader, Alexander Ross (Davidson 1918: 135–138).

Ross undertook the unenviable task of convincing the Plateau tribes to hunt beaver and to allow the company's spring "express" to ferry and pack furs out of the Columbia District. Several of these tribes, including the Nez Perce and the Palouse, had been alienated by Pacific Fur Company personnel whom they considered stingy and arrogant. One employee had erected a gallows and hanged a Nez Perce in response to a robbery (Josephy 1965:48–51). From the other point of view, Indian thievery and occasional ambush justified English justice and economics. Seven trappers were slain in 1813 by Bannocks along the Boise River. They had been trapping streams without the permission of the resident tribes. This event was not to be forgotten in British camps (Ross 1956: 13, 170–171).

From 1814 to 1816, as the North West Company attempted to circumvent native prerogatives by expressing goods and pelts through the Plateau area, their brigades were halted by Indian opposition. Yakima, Cayuse, Palouse, Walla Walla, and Nez Perce warriors harassed North West Company boats and exchanged shots with Whites. Plateau warriors captured Alexander Ross and his party claiming "[t]hese are the men who kill our relations, the people who have caused us to mourn" (Ross 1956:11–13, 23). The Ross party eventually was freed, but relations throughout the district remained at an impasse until 1816 when the Montreal-based company acquiesced to native middleman traders and transportation systems by entrusting to Indian leaders all freighting and inland transshipment, with the exception of the annual general express to Montreal.

The move placated some tribes; however, a counterproductive policy was attached to the new company orders. To increase profits and to obviate the necessity of maintaining trading posts among so many "warlike and refractory natives," who could not be persuaded to trap beaver for the British, formidable squadrons of nonresident Indian and non-Indian trappers were organized to "range" and strip the interior of fur resources. Furs were to be inventoried at Fort George for the annual cargo bound for China (Ross 1956:56–58). The strategy was successful enough to warrant continuation after the North West Company and the Hudson's Bay Company merged in 1821 (Williams 1983:48–53).

After 1816, the British companies assembled a highly stratified and specialized work force that employed numerous workers from outside the region. Iroquois, Cree, Nipissing, and Abenaki male trappers, hunters, and camptenders joined Orkney Islanders, French-Canadian, and Métis personnel under the direction of Scottish and English officers on the brigades. Many Indian and Métis wives, as well as some children, accompanied husbands and fathers on these extended treks into the interior (Ross 1956; P.S. Ogden 1950, 1961, 1971; W.T. Atkin 1934).

Eastern Indians, especially christianized Caughnawaga Mohawks, lent complexity to the inland Northwest trade. Although their numbers are difficult to assess because so many were "free trappers" or former company employees known as "freemen" (Nicks 1980), by 1821 the Iroquois made up nearly one-third of the hired hands in the Columbia District (Karamanski 1982:9; Ross 1956:194). Highly valued by Euro-American officers for their skills at setting and filling traps with castorum (Ewers 1963:6) and as canoe-men (Cox 1957:364), the Iroquois were also known for their strong sense of independence, even while engaged to the Company, and their proclivity to desert when better opportunities arose. Alexander Ross (1956: 194) considered them "sullen, fickle, cowardly and treacherous," while Ross Cox (1957:364) labeled them "quarrelsome, revengeful, and sometimes insubordinate." Even so, few North West Company or Bay Company operations in the Far West after 1818 lacked Iroquoian personnel (vol. 15:544–546).

Their presence posed a special dilemma for resident tribes. Native reaction to Northeast Indians and to Hawaiians (who were called Kanakas) was mixed. Some tribes on whose lands posts and depots had been erected extended to Hawaiian and Iroquoian men the courtesy of a marriage partner from the women in their villages (R.C. Clark 1934; Nicks 1980:94). Others, especially the Gros Ventre, and to a lesser extent the Carrier, Cree, Beaver, and Blackfoot, greatly resented Iroquois willingness to

trap out entire regions without regard to season or the furbearers' age or sex. Many Iroquois were killed for their lack of respect; others survived by forming freemen family bands and by receiving preferential treatment from Euro-American companies who employed and supplied them (Nicks 1980; Karamanski 1982). Still others settled among Indian groups, demonstrably influencing tribes such as the Flathead by attracting converts to Roman Catholicism and by teaching, in tandem with missionaries, Plateau and Plains tribes the art of farming (Ewers 1948, 1963; Fahey 1974:64ff.).

Unlike the independent Iroquois, the Hawaiians had by 1830 proven themselves the least expensive and the most reliable wage laborers available to the English in the Columbia District. In the 1790s, Hawaiian males constituted the vast majority of deckhands and navigators on British ships bound for the Northwest, and by 1825, 300 Hawaiians were active in the pelagic and terrestrial trade. Hawaiians were highly regarded for their aquatic skills, as sailors, paddlers, and divers. Dozens of Hawaiians also lived in villages attached to Hudson's Bay Company forts where they worked in pastoral and artisan-mechanic capacities as well as in freighting. Others could be found among American mission and fur trade settlements deep in the interior (Ross 1956:194; Blue 1924; Chance and Chance 1976; Duncan 1972; Lamar 1985:307–310).

The intrusion of sizable numbers of foreigners in tandem with Euro-American disregard of Indian trade protocol complicated traditional intertribal animosities and intensified intertribal conflict. As the British built well-fortified blockhouses, barracks, and warehouses within tribal hunting territories and sent out well-armed brigades of nonresident trappers to harvest the river valleys, frustrations mounted among resident tribes from the coast to the Rockies. In 1818, for example, the molesting of several Cowlitz women by Iroquois men led to a skirmish in which a dozen Cowlitz and one Iroquois died and to a cessation of all traffic on the lower stretches of the Columbia (Ross 1956:129–134). Not until 1825 with the shift of headquarters from Fort George in Chinook country to Fort Vancouver in the domain of the Clatsop and Cowlitz would wounds heal enough to resume productive trade (Ross 1956:129–134; Ruby and Brown 1976:165–166, 1981:30–31, 42, 50–51).

The Western Interior, 1824–1850

From 1824 to 1850, intense competition among Euro-Americans for control of the trade of the trans-Missouri West pulled Indians and Whites into sharper conflict and closer cooperation than at any previous point in the historic period. During these critical years, American economic activities expanded into Mexican as well as British trade and settlement spheres (fig. 5). By 1850, with the annexation of Texas, California, and the Oregon

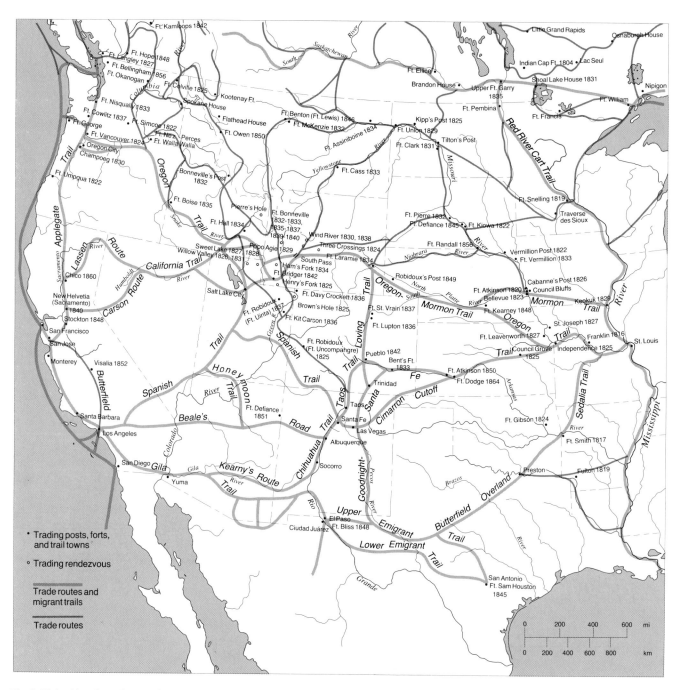

Fig. 5. Major historic trade and migrant routes and posts after 1824 (Meinig 1968; Wishart 1979; Garrett 1982, 1984, 1984a, 1985, 1986, 1986a, 1986b).

Country, the atmosphere of Indian-White relations in the trade clouded, giving way to the stormy decades of "Indian wars," treaty-making, and the establishment of reservations (Trennert 1975; Utley 1984).

In 1825, the wholesale price of beaver stood at a premium of between three and six dollars per pound; by 1850, the price had fallen to an unprofitable two dollars per pound. Beaver would be trapped after mid-century, but attention had already shifted to South American nutria and North American muskrat and raccoon pelts, as well as buffalo robes and provisioning of the trade (G.

Simpson 1931:177; Hafen 1965:83; Clayton 1967:64–67; Wishart 1979:141ff.). Individual trappers and fur trade companies who had not diversified by 1850 experienced unemployment and economic stagnation. Beaver alone was not enough.

Ironically, the land-based fur trade of the West never constituted more than one percent of the United States gross national product, even in the peak decades of the 1820s and 1830s (Dodds 1977:426). Only in 1833 did U.S. fur exports exceed $800,000. Internationally, as well, the fur trade of the United States was of minor significance

366

(Clayton 1967:70). Yet, if the fur trade did not affect the living standard of the vast majority of Whites living east of the Mississippi from 1790 to 1870, it was the most significant activity affecting the domestic and international economies of dozens of Indian societies from the Missouri to the Pacific for at least half a century. Out of Saint Louis alone, in the years from 1807 to 1840, an annual average of between $200,000 and $300,000 in trade goods flowed westward, yielding an equal number of dollars in furs (Chittenden 1902, 1:8).

Some tribes benefited from the Euro-American trade wars, acquiring wealth and prestige through access to and redistribution of White manufactured goods. Profits from the trade accrued to Indians as well as Whites, although the meaning of accumulated wealth varied considerably among participant tribes (Ewers 1976:17). Where wealth demanded the fulfillment of economic, social, and often ceremonial obligations, "giving" assumed greater importance than "selling" or "buying" (Suttles 1968; K.M. Weist 1973).

The long-term effects of sustained trade with Whites also varied by tribe and depended upon influences beyond the scope of Indian-White trade relationships. By 1850, as treaty-making, mining rushes, and White settlement ushered in new problems, many western Indians who had participated directly in the White trade began to refer to the earliest days of the White trade, when horses, guns, and furs made them powerful and wealthy, as a "golden age" (Holder 1967:138).

The relative importance Indians assigned the trade with Euro-Americans may be seen in Sioux pictographic and oral expressions called winter counts. Painted on hides, these images served as annual calendars and, when interpreted by a "keeper" of the count, as a history of the group in that year (Howard 1976). The presence and presents of Whites occupy considerable space in the winter counts of some Plains tribes in the period 1790–1880. However, among the Western Dakota, the deeds and importance of Whites, so pervasive from 1790 to 1819, dim in significance after 1820. Procurement of buffalo, unusual forces in nature, and the internal history of the band commanded more attention in the counts than the White trader or his goods up to 1850 (Henning 1982).

Elaboration of culture in this period characterized every major trading group. The expanded trade gave more tribal members access to time- and labor-saving devices. In the process, it increased the number of native people actively participating in the Indian-White trade and accelerated the rate of Indian economic dependency.

The White-directed trade in this period challenged or changed the subsistence rounds of many tribes and diverted some tribes from their former role in the intertribal and interregional trade (Mishkin 1940; O. Lewis 1942; Holder 1970; R. White 1983). There had always been specialization of labor and commodities in the

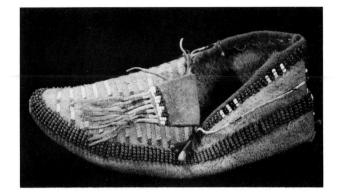

Smithsonian, Dept. of Anthr.: 1899.
Fig. 6. Soft-soled Sioux moccasin of smoke-tanned hide using pony beads, an important trade commodity. The beads, predominantly blue interspersed with red, white, and yellow, line the outsole, flap, ankle, and heel. Quilled bands of red, purple, and yellow decorate the toe. All stitching is done in sinew thread. Tin tinklers holding tufts of yellow-dyed horsehair are tied to the quilled ankle thong. Small glass beads rapidly replaced quillwork, though initially design patterns remained simple. This moccasin uses both kinds of ornament. Collected by Lt. G.K. Warren on the upper Missouri River, presumably in the 1850s. Length 28 cm.

Indian-centered trade. However, the White-directed exchanges forced alterations in the division of labor, in gender roles, and, in some cases, in social organization as men, women, and children killed, skinned, cured, and marketed animal products (K.M. Weist 1983; Klein 1983). Women in horse-rich societies such as the Blackfoot and the Crow may have increased their political and economic status during the nineteenth century (Ewers 1955:315; Lowie 1935:60–61, 1982:78–83). Other analysis suggests that the trade benefited Indian males at the expense of Indian females. Within once egalitarian buffalo cultures, the power, wealth, and prestige associated with the trade flowed only to males, eroding the position of women (Klein 1980:134). Case studies of the Cheyenne (J.H. Moore 1974) and the Devil's Lake Sioux (Albers 1982) as well as work on Northern Plains cultures (Klein 1977, 1983) complement rather than substantially revise previous emphasis on the impact of Euro-American material culture and staple production of animal products, especially for the Plains (O. Lewis 1942; Jablow 1950).

The reasons for these changes are rooted in the larger economic scale of the trade and the change in mode of production from a subsistence economy to a market economy among hunting tribes. By the 1840s, over 90,000 buffalo robes poured into Saint Louis annually, and this increased to an average of 100,000 robes per year for the 1850s (Sunder 1965:17). The demand for hides far outstripped Indian ability to produce them using conventional means. Thus, Plains women, like the Subarctic Montagnais, no longer participated in the hunt, but remained in camp spending far more time fleshing and tanning hides than formerly. Even so, the average Plains woman could produce no more than 20–30 robes per season, whereas her husband could provide four to eight skins per hunt (Ewers 1955:150; Flannery 1953:61, 73), and his band of 15–20 men could kill about 1,000 bison on the fall hunt (Hornaday 1889:465).

The immediate effect on Plains society, in addition to increased labor for women, was an increase in polygyny. As long as buffalo were plentiful, even extra wives could not cure and tan robes as fast as their husband brought them into camp. The increased demand for female processors intensified intertribal warfare and interband raiding for wives, whose victims in turn left more widows available for remarriage (O. Lewis 1942:38ff.; Ewers 1958: 134ff.). The demand also increased the cost of bride purchase and, concomitantly, heightened the necessity for a family to accumulate bridewealth (Flannery 1953: 171–194). On the Northern Plains, the new dynamics of trade resulted in an increase in the numbers of women and children who fell victim to captivity. Numbers are impossible to assess, but every tribe owned captives.

Two regions—the upper Missouri and the Rocky Mountains—became focuses of the fur and robe trade after 1824. The Southwest and the Northwest continued to attract attention and to yield quantities of furs, hides, and by-products; however, the trade of those two areas was more diverse and has been less intensively studied than the Northern Plains and intermountain West. The differing annual cycles of operations and seasonal rounds associated with these two systems have been analyzed by Wishart (1979: figs. 8, 10, 19, 21).

The Rocky Mountain system developed as a result of Saint Louis–based trappers' failure to respect Middle Missouri and Northern Plains Indian trade protocol. After White losses among the Blackfoot and the Arikara in 1823, William H. Ashley, with field partner Andrew Henry, turned their attention away from the upper Missouri and toward the central Rockies where, in 1824, a party under Jedediah S. Smith charted a route through the mountains in present-day South Pass, Wyoming (Morgan 1964:93–98). Wagons and pack animals would no longer be restricted to the eastern slope of the continental divide. American fur men envisioned expansion over the mountains on to the Columbia Plain (Lamar 1977:1132).

In 1825 Ashley's men managed to penetrate the Hudson's Bay Company sphere, competing directly with Hudson's Bay Company brigades in the Snake River country and Flathead Post region (Ashley in Morgan 1964:100ff.). In July, all 120 Ashley men converged on Henry's Fork of the Green River, duplicating with their White "rendezvous" a system familiar to the Eastern Shoshone and their neighbors.

The American rendezvous system endured for 14 years. Its major purpose was to reassemble trapping parties once a year for the transshipment of furs eastward and the reorganization and resupply of widely dispersed mountain-based employees, most of whom were non-Indian. An additional benefit was the opportunity to purchase furs from independent freemen and free trappers. The Indian trade of the intermountain West was not a major consideration in the selection of rendezvous sites from 1825 to 1840; however, a successful trapping season and summer's gathering both depended upon peaceful Indian relations. Ashley and his successors chose south-central sites for their convocations not only because of the convenient access to South Pass and the Platte River overland route but also because the Green River country was far from the Blackfoot and close to secondary resupply and market centers on the Columbia Plain and in the Southwest. The region provided easy access to all major furbearing zones, yet it was fairly isolated from the major centers of intertribal and Indian-White confrontation (Dale 1941; Ashley in Morgan 1964; Gowans 1975).

Trapping parties financed out of Saint Louis, Montreal, Fort Vancouver, and Taos all experienced difficulties in their Indian relations, largely because the system avoided Indian producers. A few trading alliances developed with Crows, Northern and Eastern Shoshones, Nez Perce, Flatheads, and other tribes, but the firmest and most secure relationships were formed not at the company or brigade level, but by individuals who intermarried into Indian society (Swagerty 1980).

Anglo-, Spanish-, and French-Americans had the option under Ashley's system of working as *engagés* for an annual salary, as "skin trappers" who were outfitted at the rendezvous by the company on a credit system, or, as "free trappers" who were at liberty to sell furs to the highest bidder (Chittenden 1902, 1:3, 3:938–942; Wishart 1979: 125). None of these men enjoyed the comforts of company-built residences or the safety of the stockades, benefits available only to traders with capital (Lamar 1977).

The Rocky Mountain trapping system produced windfall profits for a few entrepreneurs like Ashley, who abandoned fur collecting for freighting and state politics in 1826 (Clokey 1980). Most White participants in the system were fortunate to leave the trade with their lives and their equipment after an average of 15 years' service (Oglesby 1967; Swagerty 1980:161, 163). Of the approximately 3,000 White and Métis trappers and traders active in the West from 1810 to 1845, over one-half worked the northern and southern Rockies. This region was the scene of fierce competition for furs between 1824 and 1850, a rivalry that fostered the individualism, for which American "mountain men" gained a reputation (Carter and Spencer 1975).

Many original Ashley men continued in the trade, reorganizing themselves into small companies such as Smith, Jackson, and Sublette, which made modest profits from 1826 to 1830. During the company's short history, Smith crossed and mapped the Great Basin and revived a trading nexus between Mexican California and Americans in the rendezvous country. For three years, Smith's southwestern expeditions mined the Sierra Nevadas, but the party paid for other trappers' atrocities both in 1826 when Mohaves (previously attacked by American and Mexican trappers based in Taos) cut down eight of his men and in 1828 when Umpqua Indians (alienated first in 1818 by Iroquois trappers) slew 14 Smith employees near the Willamette Valley (Morgan 1953:193, 256, 329–330; Ross 1956:132–134; Brooks 1977).

The prospect of greater profits in the Southwest prompted Smith, Jackson, and Sublette to sell out in 1830 to new partners organized as the Rocky Mountain Fur Company. This company lasted only four years before it too suffered dissolution and reorganization. Small partnerships would continue to wrestle for the intermountain trade from 1834 to 1840, forming, disbanding, and reforming themselves. From a business point of view, no other fur trade frontier was so unstable as the Rocky Mountain system from 1830 to 1840 (Hafen 1965:103ff.; Wishart 1979:141–174).

The Rocky Mountain system depended upon steady supply from Saint Louis and Taos, plentiful beaver harvests, high prices for furs in the mountains and at market, precision in coordinating the rendezvous and the overland express, and, most important, the tolerance of resident tribes. For the first five years, all these conditions were met. After 1830 the system fell into disequilibrium. As beaver prices plummeted in the 1830s, employees of the Rocky Mountain Fur Company foolishly invaded Blackfoot hunting territory (D. Berry 1961; Wishart 1979). In retaliation, the Blackfoot killed 40–50 White and Métis trappers each season in the 1830s (M.C. Ross 1951:148; Dunwiddie 1974).

The Rocky Mountain system also declined due to competition from other systems of trade involving fewer risks and higher return on investment. The lucrative traffic that commenced in 1821 between citizens of the United States and citizens of the Republic of Mexico along the Santa Fe Trail amounted to $190,000 in gross receipts by 1824 (Simmons 1977). The trade indirectly benefited Indians as manufactured goods formerly unavailable from Mexican sources then flowed into the region from the East. Freight wagons outbound from Missouri also carried Franco- and Anglo-Americans eager to trap furs as independents or to join their Mexican counterparts as suppliers in the Indian trade. Many of these men made Taos and Santa Fe their permanent base, marrying Hispanic or Indian women and challenging other White (as well as Indian) traders and trappers in the southern Rockies (Duffus 1930; Cleland 1950; Weber 1971, 1982: 122ff.; J.J. Hill 1930).

Several independent business concerns such as Bent, St. Vrain, and Company of St. Louis and Gantt and Blackwell did manage to secure a respectable share of the fur and Indian trade. Bent's Fort, built in 1833 on the upper Arkansas, was the largest American citizen-owned and operated business concern in the Southwest prior to 1848. Its location near the United States–Mexico boundary was a magnet for southern Plains tribes, especially the Arapaho and the Cheyenne, with whom the Bents were linked by marriage, as well as for parties of American and Mexican trappers, hunters, and traders (Lavender 1954).

In the northern Rockies, direct competition from the American Fur Company and the Hudson's Bay Company sealed the demise of the Rocky Mountain system. In 1823 a Western Department of the American Fur Company was organized in Saint Louis to conduct business on the upper Missouri and in the Platte River country. The Company eased its way into the upper stretches of the Missouri, and by 1830 American Fur Company men had become permanent fixtures, there to stay until the Indians and the animals played out (Porter 1931).

American Fur Company officials gave no quarter to opponents—Red or White. They undercut White competition by inflating prices for furs, absorbing short-term losses in the interest of long-term stability and monopoly. On the Missouri, the American Fur Company absorbed Columbia Fur Company assets and posts in 1827, creating a subsidiary, the Upper Missouri Outfit, of the Western Department. Until the mid-1830s, American Fur Company management pursued mergers, price wars, and buyouts with other competitors such as the Rocky Mountain Fur Company and Sublette and Campbell. The efforts to establish hegemony on the Missouri coalesced in 1834 with Astor's retirement from the trade and purchase of the Western Department by Pratte, Chouteau, and Company of Saint Louis. Within two years, the leading families of Saint Louis had reestablished complete control of the Missouri River Indian trade, but in the mountains small associations and modest partnerships continued to reap respectable harvests throughout the 1830s (Hafen 1965: 104–165; Clayton 1967).

The American Fur Company also installed new modes of efficiency such as an elaborate credit system and more reliable order and delivery systems for furs and trade goods. Transportation innovations included the use of steamboats up the Missouri as far as Fort Union (fig. 7) by 1832. The age of steam enabled rapid delivery to post sutlers and Indian traders (Chittenden 1903; Wishart 1979:79–114). The system forced standardization of trade goods and trade values and in the process stripped the trade of much of its symbolic, aesthetic, and human meaning. Still, furs and robes arriving at wintering posts and large forts alike had to be negotiated out of the hands of native male traders with the same skills of personal communication and barter of precorporate days.

The success of the American Fur Company was built on the mistakes of Lisa and his successors. The Company focused intently on accommodating resident tribes' subsistence, consumption, and trade patterns so as to draw every possible marketable commodity produced by Plains

Indians into one of the many depots, regional posts, and wintering posts that were erected throughout the upper Missouri and Platte country from 1826 to 1840. The most important of these was Fort Union (built 1829), which served as the head for steamboat navigation for the entire system. Other major depots followed: Fort Clark in 1831, Fort Pierre (formerly Ft. Tecumseh) rebuilt in 1832 (fig. 8), and Fort McKenzie in 1832 (fig. 5). By 1835, every major Plains tribe had access to at least one American Fur Company post within a reasonable distance of its hunting and camping territories (Chittenden 1902, 1:321ff.; Wishart 1979:53–65).

Trading posts on the Missouri, the Columbia, and elsewhere came to symbolize and to function as microcosms of Western civilization. In addition to commercial emporia and Indian general stores, posts served as interethnic recreation and community centers where "post" or "Home Guard" Indians could be visited by tribal kin and friends. Trading posts also provided medical, dietary, and spiritual support to increasingly large numbers of Indian clients from the 1830s on (Ewers 1972:6–7; Athearn 1967:19–34; Hussey 1957; Chance 1973). With the end of the rendezvous system in 1840, trading posts became essential for companies operating in the central and southern Rockies. In all, 140 fur posts, large and small, were erected in the West during the American fur trade years (Chittenden 1902, 3:947).

In 1831, the American Fur Company succeeded where its predecessors had failed, negotiating a truce with the Blackfoot that led to the building of Fort McKenzie among the Piegan in 1832. Then, in 1835, the American Fur Company purchased Fort William (renamed Fort Laramie) from Sublette and Campbell, thereby gaining control of both the robe and fur traffic (figs. 9–10). Fort McKenzie alone warehoused almost 1,000 packs of robes and a wealth of furs, skins, and by-products each year from 1834 to 1840. By 1841, the post was returning 21,000 buffalo robes annually, making it by far the most

The Thomas Gilcrease Inst. of Amer. Hist. and Art, Tulsa, Okla.: 1326.1093.
Fig. 7. Cree Indians and Whites in the chief trader's office, Ft. Union. Ft. Union was built around 1829 by Kenneth McKenzie, a partner in the Upper Missouri Outfit unit of the American Fur Company, to establish a place where free traders from both the mountain and riverine areas could converge. It was a well-equipped fort and supported a large number of *engagés*, artisans, and clerks (Chittenden 1902, 1:326, 3:958–960). In this scene, a pipe decorated by a White man and presented to the Cree chief Le Tout Piqué (standing at center) is being smoked for the first time. The chief addresses the group after placing a buffalo robe around the shoulders of Edwin T. Denig, the chief trader (seated in the arm chair). The interpreter, Battiste (probably seated on the floor, second from left), translated from Cree into French. Two of the Cree men on the bench were named Rassade au Cou and Bras Cassé. The artist, a guest at the ceremony, may have portrayed himself next to Denig. At the end of the ceremony the Cree were served cooked meat and sweetened coffee (Kurz 1937:203–205). Ink and pencil on paper by Rudolph F. Kurz, Oct. 19, 1851.

Smithsonian, NAA:2856-82.
Fig. 8. Ft. Pierre, Minn. Terr., as seen from the Missouri River. An American Fur Company post established on the west bank of the river in 1832, Ft. Pierre was a central post in the Sioux-White trade. Blockhouses were in the southeast and northwest corners, and the main gate was in the east wall of the stockade (Wilson 1902:270–273). The artist of this drawing wrote that 12 Teton Sioux men guarded goods delivered by the *St. Ange*, a ship on which he was a passenger. Sioux men saluted them when the ship departed the following day (Kurz 1937:71). The post became a military fort in 1855. Pencil drawing by Rudolph F. Kurz, July 4, 1851.

productive fort in the interior West. By 1840, Fort Laramie produced an average of 1,000 packs of robes annually as well as lesser amounts of small furs. Both depots were beneficiaries of the transition from beaver to buffalo products (Chittenden 1902, 1:309ff.; P.C. Phillips 1961, 2:415–429; Hafen and Young 1938; Wishart 1979: 61–65).

Trade 1850–1870

The American Fur Company remained in business on the upper Missouri through 1865, withdrawing before the great slaughter of buffalo by White hide-hunters commenced in earnest in the 1870s (Sunder 1965). Because of its economic size, its reliance upon an Indian clientele, its longevity, and its geographical extent, the American Fur Company affected Plains Indian lives to a greater degree than any other American business concern in the nineteenth-century trade. Widespread availability of glass, metal, ceramic, and cloth goods at sutlers' counters prompted both a revolution in everyday technology and a florescence of artistic creativity on the Plains. As metal pots replaced buffalo paunches on native hearths, Indian artisans experimented with new materials, colors, designs, and motifs, integrating them into the social and ceremonial spheres. The elaboration of mid-nineteenth century Plains Indian material culture can best be seen in stylized robe and tepee-cover painting; pad saddles and tailored hide coats ornamented with beaded and quilled rosettes; colorful woven sashes; the decorative use of mirrors, military buttons and belt buckles, brass tacks and commemorative "peace medals;" and the spread of floral

beadwork (Ewers 1972; R.P. Koch 1977).

American Fur Company traders were also instrumental in native political life. Company interpreters served as cultural brokers at treaty councils in the 1850s and 1860s, often providing essential diplomatic skill in negotiating concessions and compromises (H.H. Anderson 1973: 245–252; Hanson 1966; DeMallie 1980). American Fur Company personnel were indirectly responsible from 1820s through the mid-1860s for the relative success or failure of certain governmental Indian policies, especially after the demise of the factory system.

For example, in 1832, the United States Congress prohibited the use of alcohol in the Indian trade and soon met fierce opposition from small and large companies alike. Liquor continued to flow illegally into Indian country, with significant negative effects (De Smet 1905, 1:158–59, 4:1214–1215; Maximilian 1904–1907, 2:254; Stein 1974; Sage 1956:245–259, 1982:49–50). By the 1830s, liquor had become an important, if not essential item in the trade.

Not all Indians, Métis, or Whites drank. Despite intensive contact and cajoling from 1807 to the 1860s, the Crow of the Yellowstone rarely touched "white man's crazy water" (Ewers 1972:18). But other Indian tribes as well as occupational groups like the voyageur class considered alcohol an important privilege, and, at times, a necessity. Thus, distillers, bootleggers, and rum smugglers continued to do a brisk business in the Far West (Saum 1965:150–151; G. Simpson 1931:320–321; Miller 1976: 37).

Congress no more than the clergy or military was effectively able to change the predilections or preferences of entire Indian tribes or their White suppliers. During the final years of the Indian-based trade, Indians and Whites traded, smoked, imbibed, and slept together (Peterson and Brown 1985). Wherever there were fur trade posts, there was intermarriage between members of a diverse array of tribes and Euro-American nationalities (Brown 1980a). The children of such unions played an important role as interethnic brokers and paved the way for a bicultural society unique in the annals of Indian-White relations (Ewers 1968:57–67; Peterson and Brown 1985).

On the northern Plains, even before the fur trade ended, mixed-bloods far outnumbered White fur trade personnel and were more numerous than the full-blood members of any single Indian tribe. Some of these mixed-bloods settled among their mothers' relatives and identified themselves as tribal members after reservation agencies replaced fur trading posts throughout Indian country (H.H. Anderson 1973; Swagerty 1980). Others joined the growing ranks of the Métis, whose camps were sprinkled along both sides of the Canadian border from the Red River to the Rockies after 1860. Plains Métis remained active in the hide and robe trade until 1884 (Hornaday 1889:500–505), long after their full-blood

Fig. 9. Exterior view of Ft. Laramie, Nebr. Terr. Constructed in 1834 by William Sublette and Robert Campbell at the junction of the Laramie and North Platte rivers, the post was purchased by the American Fur Company in 1836. As the nexus between the Rocky Mountain and upper Missouri fur trade systems, the fort was an important depot for Whites on the Oregon Trail (R. Tyler 1982:between pages 76 and 201). The defensive architecture of the high walls and bastions was typical of American Fur Company posts, as was the presence of Indian lodges and intensive trading activity in its environs. This painting and fig. 10 are based on the artist's field sketches made while he accompanied an American Fur Company caravan in 1837 (McCracken 1978:154). Watercolor on paper by Alfred Jacob Miller, 1858–1860.

cousins had been forced to give up the hunt for life on the reservation. Thereafter, they constituted a landless minority on the Plains of Canada and the United States (J.K. Howard 1952; Dusenberry 1958; Peterson and Brown 1985).

The late trade produced casualties throughout the West. Although American Fur Company and Hudson's Bay Company personnel in the Rocky Mountain trade had been befriended by and had married into a number of tribes, many Indians resented denial of their former, or what they considered their rightful, place in the trade. Unlike the trade-induced feud that erupted at the 1832 rendezvous at Pierre's Hole in southern Idaho, which pitted Plateau tribes and their White and eastern Indian allies against the Blackfoot, most confrontations were limited to scuffles between bands and individual White or Indian trappers, or between company servants and their employers (Hafen 1965:123–126; W.C. Hayden 1972;

Gowans 1975:74–95).

In the Hudson's Bay Company sector economic reforms after 1821 resulted in spectacular expansion, rapidly reducing many of the small tribes of the Northwest and Plateau to dependency (G. Simpson 1931; J. McLoughlin 1941–1944). Although tribes in the Northwest had no cause to fear immediate dispossession from English settlers, increasing subservience to the company credit system caused resentment. But during the British period, few Indians took up arms against the Hudson's Bay Company, which worked with rather than against its Indian clientele ("The Hudson's Bay Company and Native People," this vol.).

Under the direction of Hudson's Bay Company Governor George Simpson and Chief Factor Dr. John McLoughlin, Fort Vancouver, built 1824–1825, served as the distribution center, craft-specialization workhouse, and interethnic residential compound of the Company's

Fig. 10. Interior view of Ft. Laramie, Nebr. Terr. Watercolor on paper by Alfred Jacob Miller, 1858–1860.

northwestern interests (Hussey 1957). Other posts built after 1825 included Fort Colvile near the Columbia River fishery at Kettle Falls (Oliphant 1925), Fort Langley at the mouth of the Fraser River, Fort Nisqually on Puget Sound, and Fort Boise on the Snake River, built to oppose American Nathaniel Jarvis Wyeth's Fort Hall at the junction of the Snake and Portneuf rivers (Swinney and Wells 1962). In 1836 the Hudson's Bay Company bought out Wyeth, becoming the sole fur trade post proprietor on the Pacific slope until American takeover of the Oregon Country after 1846 (Beidleman 1957; Rich 1967).

In the Northwest, many Indian trader families settled at Oregon City, French Prairie, and Champoeg in the Willamette valley and were joined by free trader families after the demise of the Rocky Mountain system (Victor 1870; Hussey 1967). Others joined full-blood in-laws on reservations as they had on the Northern Plains (H.H. Anderson 1973). Still others set down permanent roots

with their Mexican and Indian families at Taos, New Mexico, and in communities in southern Colorado not far from Bent's Fort (LeCompte 1978; R.M. Craven 1982). Napa Valley, California, also attracted a small group of diverse trade personnel (Bancroft 1886–1890; 23:17–21; Camp 1972) as did fur trade forts that were converted into freighting hubs or military compounds such as Fort Bridger and Fort Laramie in Wyoming (R.S. Ellison 1931; Hafen and Young 1938; Swagerty 1980).

After 1850, Euro-American companies interested in the Indian trade expanded their operations so as to cash in on a diversified traffic in Indian annuities, the provisionment of reservations and U.S. military posts, and the supply of White towns and farming communities. Indian and Métis producers themselves increasingly lost purchasing power, experiencing stiff competition from White hunters over the only major resources remaining—robes and hides on the Plains, fish and furs in the Northwest. On the Plains, at 1869, an estimated four million bison still grazed south of the Platte River with some one-half million remaining in the north. That year the Union and Central Pacific railroads joined tracks, initiating the great slaughter for robes, hides, and tongues. Between 1872 and 1874, over three million buffalo fell to White hide hunters while another one-half million were killed by Indians and settlers. By 1876, the southern herd was gone (Hornaday 1889:490–501; Garretson 1938:108–129).

The northern herd faced a similar fate after the Battle of Little Big Horn. On the upper Missouri, I. G. Baker and Company of Fort Benton, Montana replaced its parent, the American Fur Company, after 1863, having shipped 70,000 robes in that year. By 1883, volume had declined to 5,000 robes, and in 1890, only about 1,000 animals remained (Hornaday 1889:504–525; Sunder 1965: 260–265).

As the century drew to a close, the Indian trade in furs and hides ceased to provide a viable livelihood for most western Indians. Members of some tribes adjusted to the reservation-based economy, by supplying utilitarian and ceremonial objects such as beaded bags and apparel, baskets, carved masks, textiles, pipes, and medicine bags to private collectors and salvage anthropologists in the employ of museums. This adaptive strategy continued into the twentieth century, augmented by the growing tourist trade (McNitt 1962). Where it was possible to imitate the old way of life, some western tribes continued to process and supply natural products such as hides and furs to White wholesalers. Indian profits from this trade were modest.

The interethnic trade in raw and finished commodities in the trans-Mississippi West, which long antedated White contact, did not die entirely with Indian loss of land and resources. But the volume, variety, and control of exchanges among individuals, tribes, and cultural areas would never again duplicate the elaborate networks of late prehistoric and early historic times.

The Maritime Trade of the North Pacific Coast

JAMES R. GIBSON

On the North Pacific coast the maritime fur trade began in the 1780s. Although American and English involvement in the coast trade is best known (W.K. Lamb 1944; Wike 1951; R. Fisher 1977, 1977a), the Russian participation lasted longer than that of any other nationality (J.R. Gibson 1980). The early or boom period of the trade was before 1812. By 1829 land furs outnumbered sea furs, and by 1842 American traders had withdrawn, leaving the overworked field to the Russians and the English. During this late period the trade changed considerably, and these changes can be traced in several unpublished American logs and journals from the 1810s and 1820s and in the manuscript records of the Russian-American and Hudson's Bay Companies for the 1820s and 1830s, as well as in the business correspondence of the leading Boston shipowners. By the 1840s the furbearers had been so depleted by overhunting and the fur markets had been so depressed by changing fashion that the coast trade was negligible.

Not all Northwest Coast Indians had access to sea otters, which were the mainstay of the maritime fur trade. These marine mammals were endowed with a dark, thick, lustrous coat that became by far the most valuable fur on the world market. "Other furs bear no proportion, in value, to those of the sea-otter," declared the owners of one of the earliest English trading voyages (Meares 1790: App. A). In 1829 it took more than 10 beaver pelts—the pillar of the continental fur trade—to equal the value of one sea otter skin (Green 1915:85–86), although by then the latter was admittedly scarcer than the former. A prime pelt of "this beautiful and elegant Fur" would be as large as five and one-half feet by three feet and glossy black (A. Walker 1982:127, 146). Sea otters frequented the protective kelp beds of the North Pacific littoral from Japan to Mexico, feeding on sea urchins, mollusks, and starfish. But there were gaps in this range, particularly between Cape Flattery and Trinidad Bay. Around the mouth of the Columbia River sea otters, although not plentiful, were large in size and high in quality, so that the natives set a "great value on them" (M. Roe 1967:128). Consequently, the maritime fur trade was negligible on the southern half of the Northwest Coast; besides, that stretch was not well sheltered for vessels, and its natives were neither very numerous nor very friendly. The Northern Northwest coast tribes—the Tlingit, Haida, Tsimshian—as well as the Bella Coola, Kwakiutl, Nootka, Coast Salish, and Chinookans were most important in the trade and the northwestern California tribes the least. In fact, after about 1800 the maritime fur trade was largely confined to the Northern group alone.

Precontact Indian Trade

Although not all coastal natives had an opportunity to hunt the sea otter, all of them prized its resplendent coat. Robes of sea otter fur, like those of mountain goat "wool" (hair) and whistling marmot fur, were esteemed as objects of beauty, wealth, and prestige, as well as warmth. Traders found that "the cloaths wore universally on the coast are made of skins sewed together in various forms" (Beresford 1789:189; see also Meares 1790:321–324, 328–329). Each of these robes or cloaks, termed "cotsacks" or "cutsarks" by the White traders, consisted of usually three sea otter skins. For one captain the Tlingits of Yakutat Bay "stripped themselves almost naked, to spin out their trade as far as possible" (Beresford 1789:169).

The creature's flesh was eaten, too. So with the coming of Euro-American traders the Indians did not have to initiate an untried activity in order to meet White demands; rather, they had simply to intensify a traditional occupation. Hunting singly with harpoon and bow and arrow was replaced by hunting severally by the sweep-and-surround method. And the gun was adopted as a hunting weapon.

Furthermore, the Indians already had a strong tradition of barter among themselves and with interior groups. Intracoastal trade was voluminous and extensive, thanks to the fact that "the environment of the Northwest Coast cultures is neither uniformly rich and dependable within any tribal area nor precisely the same from area to area" (Suttles 1962:536). "Southern" were exchanged for "northern" articles, and coastal for interior products. This traffic was increased by Euro-American traders, who were not slow to see the profit in buying items from one tribe and selling them to another for skins (fig. 1).

Both scarce and specialized commodities were traded up and down the coast for decorative and practical purposes alike: mountain goat hair "blankets" (ceremoni-

375

Smithsonian, Dept. of Anthr.: 2662.
Fig. 1. Carved mask inset with bits of abalone, an item traded aboriginally up and down the western coast of North America. Early Spanish traders routinely stopped at Monterey Bay, Calif., to take on the abalone to transport north. Later American traders, at the request of the natives, also carried the coveted abalone. Its decorative uses were many, ranging from simple personal ornaments to incorporation into elaborate sculptural representations. Holes drilled in 6 of the bits of abalone indicate they were probably recycled from another ornament. Probably Tsimshian. Collected by the U.S. Exploring Expedition of 1838–1842; height 28.4 cm.

al robes), ermine skins, native copper plates, and spruce-root baskets from the Tlingit; dugout cedar canoes from the Haida; mountain goat horn spoons, Raven rattles, dance headdresses, and eulachon oil from the Tsimshian; mountain goat hair and horn from the Bella Coola, the best hunters on the coast of that animal; yellow cedarbark robes and wooden utensils from the Kwakiutl; dugout cedar canoes, sharks' teeth, and dentalia from the Nootkans; dogs' hair blankets from the Coast Salish; elk hides and slaves from the Chinookans; and tobacco and abalone shells from the Yurok (Heizer 1940). Dentalium shells were one of the most popular and widespread commodities; they were especially prized by the Yurok, who used them as money. Even more valuable were elk hides, most of which probably came from the Willamette Valley. They were "always in great demand on the Northern Coast" (Jackman 1978:34) as "leather war dresses" for use in the frequent intertribal clashes.

Although the Northwest Coast was rather isolated from the rest of aboriginal North America by mountain ranges, there was intercourse through the mountain wall wherever major rivers afforded routeways. The Chinookans exemplified transmountain contact at the busy marketplace and prolific fishery of The Dalles, where dried salmon and dentalium shells and eventually Euro-American wares were swapped for land furs, mountain sheep horn, buffalo robes, rabbitskin robes, jade celts, obsidian blades, native tobacco, baskets, horses, and slaves from the Nez Perce and Cayuse. The Coast Salish trafficked with the Chilcotin and Lower Carrier, the Tsimshian with the Upper Carrier and Sekani, and the Tlingit with the Tahltan and other Athapaskans. Land furs, moose and caribou hides, ermine skins, jade celts, and porcupine quill embroidery went from the interior Indians to the coast via the Fraser, Nass, Stikine, and Chilkat river valleys. Control of two of these routeways—the Stikine and the Chilkat—helped to make the Tlingit the strongest and the richest of the coastal groups. And their interior clients were among the last to be tapped by Hudson's Bay Company posts. Also, the Tlingit virtually monopolized several of the most valuable native goods: placer copper, ermine skins, and superior baskets and robes. In addition, they were the closest middlemen to precious Asiatic iron. Finally, their principal villages, which were sited toward the heads of the long inlets, were less accessible to attack by other natives or Euro-Americans.

The Russian Period

The first Euro-Americans to make contact with the Northwest Coast Indians were the Russians. In 1742 the Vitus Bering–Alexsei Chirikov expedition returned to Kamchatka from the Gulf of Alaska with hundreds of sea otter skins, which were found to bring handsome prices in North China, where the upper class valued sea otter fur as both decorative trim and snug garb in winter. From 1743 to 1800 100 ventures of Russian promyshlenniki (fur traders) obtained more than 8,000,000 silver rubles worth of skins (Makarova 1975:209–217). In 1799, alarmed by the vicious competition among the several Russian companies and by the prospect of international entanglement, the tsarist government chartered a joint-stock monopoly—the Russian-American Company—to exploit and administer Russian America (see Okun 1951; Tikhmenev 1978–1979; "Russian and Soviet Eskimo and Indian Policies," this vol.).

Thus, the Russians enjoyed a lead in the maritime fur trade of nearly a half-century, and this advantage was compounded by their control of the habitats of the most valuable sorts of *Enhydra lutris*, Kurilian-Kamchatkan and Aleutian, whose fur was blacker, denser, and glossier than that of the Northwest Coast and New Albionian-Californian "sea beavers." It was not until the superior

376

varieties were depleted that the Russians advanced to the Northwest Coast proper in 1788, whereupon they engaged other Euro-American traders in a competition that was eventually to exterminate the local strain. By 1800 three-quarters of the Russian-American Company's sea otter skins were coming from Sitka Sound (Khlebnikov 1973: 34).

Also, the company benefited from the financial and political backing of the czarist government, the establishment of permanent bases on the coast (fig. 2), particularly the colonial capital of Novo-Arkhangel'sk (New Archangel) on Baranof Island (founded 1799 and again in 1804 after it was destroyed by Tlingits), and the use of the Aleut and the Koniag Eskimo, the world's best hunters of sea otters (J.R. Gibson 1980:224–225). In fact, Russian participation in the Northwest trade amounted more to hunting than trading, with their vessels serving to transport and protect hunting parties of kayaks. Consequently, the low quantity and quality and the high price of Russian trade goods (stemming from the backwardness of Russian manufacturing and entrepreneuring) were not crucial, the company being able to get pelts in return for paltry Aleut and Eskimo wages in kind.

The Russians were not accustomed to marine hunting, or to seafaring in general for that matter, so they became dependent upon the coastal natives of Alaska (see J.R. Gibson 1978). The hunting of elusive sea otters in the open sea from flimsy kayaks with short harpoons was a daunting task that the Aleutian and Kodiak islanders practiced from childhood and took years to master. With such highly skilled and largely defenseless hunters cheaply available, the Russians declined to learn how to hunt otters themselves. In late spring and early summer hunting parties of at least 15 one-hatched kayaks under a Russian foreman put to sea at dawn and paddled in formation, close enough beside each other to spot any sea otters; a paddle was raised upon sighting an otter and all or some of the kayaks surrounded the animal and gradually tightened the circle as it tired, harpooning it when it surfaced close to them. The Aleut, who were better kayakers than the Eskimo were particularly proficient; their craft—light, fast, and maneuverable, with a shallow draft—were well suited to the pursuit of otters in the kelp and shellfish beds of the rocky coastal waters. They also did the hunting of fur seals on the Pribilof Islands for the Russians. All Aleut males between the ages of 15 and 50 were required to labor for the Russian-American Company (Veniaminov 1840, 2:172); in 1832 they constituted nearly one-third of company employees in Russian America (Wrangell 1980:22). The Aleut and Eskimo became so essential that as late as 1861 two government inspectors concluded that "in speaking with the Aleuts or with all of the natives in general we involuntarily became convinced that they are not slaves of the company, rather it has become their slave" (Rimskiĭ-

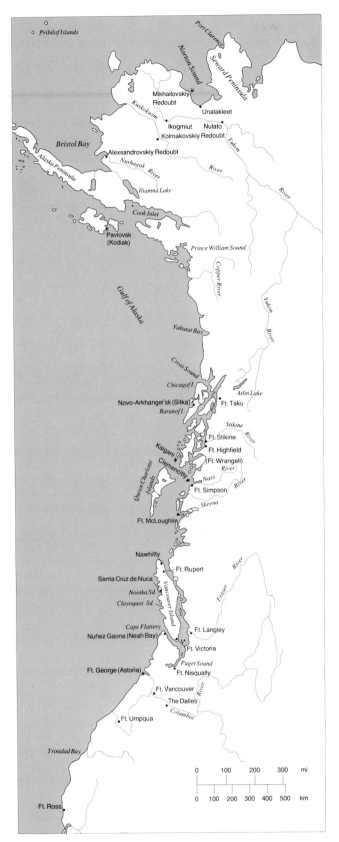

Fig. 2. Spanish, Russian, British, and American fur trade posts along the North Pacific coast during the late 18th and early 19th centuries (Dmytryshyn and Crownhart-Vaughan 1979; Tikhmenev 1978–1979; Vaughan and Holm 1982).

THE MARITIME TRADE OF THE NORTH PACIFIC COAST

Korsakov 1863:315).

Russian trading voyages per se remained infrequent, thanks, too, to the difficulty of navigation of the narrow, shallow channels among the islands of the Alexander Archipelago and the hostility of the Tlingit. The negligible profit was another deterrent. Russian prices for Indian furs were set by the Russian-American Company's head office in Saint Petersburg and hence could not be quickly changed to meet competition, whereas English and American prices could be adjusted on the spot (Litke 1835–1836, 1:134–135). The Russian-American Company was unable to match the quality and the price of the trade goods of the more efficient Hudson's Bay Company and American shipmasters, who could offer the Indians from two to three times as much as the Russians for sea otter skins (J.R. Gibson 1980a:131). In 1839 Gov. Ivan Kupreyanov reported from Sitka that "year by year I see the Tlingit drawn more and more from our territory to the English frontier" (U.S. National Archives 1802–1867, roll 42:403v., 446).

More important was the long haul for Russian furs from the coast across the North Pacific and Eastern Siberia to the Mongolian frontier at Kyakhta, one of only two border crossings where Russia was permitted to traffic with China. Equally disadvantageous was the inability of the usually undermanned and often undersupplied Russian-American Company to subdue the Tlingit (Lisiānskiĭ 1814:242). The Tlingit were militarily formidable, employing orderly battle formations, donning hide and slat cuirasses (which together could stop musket shot), gorgets, and bone helmets, and eventually wielding firearms. American traders supplied the Tlingit with powder, shot, muskets, and even falconets, instructed them in their use, and incited them against the Russians. The Sitka Tlingit had muskets and falconets, as well as iron breastplates, by 1805. Chief Kotlean owned 20 of the "best" muskets and was an "excellent" marksman (Lisiānskiĭ 1814:231, 238–239; Langsdorff 1813–1814, 2). They destroyed Sitka itself in 1802 and threatened it as late as 1855, and periodically they killed the Russian-American Company's native hunters (Khlebnikov 1976:145). The Tlingit were never completely pacified by the Russians, whose warships could seldom reach the main Indian villages far up the tortuous inlets and "canals." Thus, Russian participation in the maritime fur trade of the Northwest Coast did not extend south of the Alexander Archipelago, and it remained marginal figuratively as well as literally. That marginality was deepened in 1839, when the Hudson's Bay Company leased the mainland panhandle of Alaska from the Russian-American Company, whose Northwest activity thereafter was restricted to the offshore islands.

The intensive hunting of sea otters, coupled with the animal's low fertility, hastened the Russians' advance across the far northern Pacific and along its northeastern shore, as well as the abatement of their maritime fur trade. The Russian take of sea otter skins in Cook Inlet, for example, fell from 3,000 in the first year (1789) to 2,000 in the second, 800 in the third, 600 in the fourth, and 100 in 1812 (Tikhmenev 1978–1979, 1:151). The rapid depletion of sea otters prompted a number of conservation measures (temporary bans on hunting in certain places or certain times or of certain animals) and attempts to find alternative sources of fur, particularly in the interior of Alaska. In the early 1790s a Russian party probably reached as far as the lower Yukon River by way of Iliamna Lake and discovered its fur resources, but it was not until the late 1810s that better trained and better equipped ventures began to reconnoiter the northern interior systematically. Starting with Pëtr Korsakovskiy's probe of Bristol Bay and the lower Kuskokwim River in 1818–1819 and ending with Lavrentii Zagoskin's exploration of the upper Yukon and Kuskokwim in 1843–1844, 15 land and sea expeditions (vol. 5:150) uncovered plentiful land furbearers, friendly Eskimos and Indians who were willing to trade, a network of navigable rivers for transport, and a readymade native trading system (Tikhmenev 1978–1979, 1:176–185, 348–351). Several new trading posts arose: Aleksandrovskiy Redoubt (1820) on the Nushagak River, Kolmakovskiy Redoubt (1832) on the Kuskokwim (Oswalt 1980), Mikhailovskiy Redoubt (1833) on Stuart Island in Norton Sound, Ikogmiut (1836) and Nulato (1839) on the lower Yukon, and Unalakleet (1837) on Norton Sound (fig. 2). Principally beaver, fox, and river otter pelts were acquired by the inland posts, and the composition of the Russian-American Company's fur catch changed accordingly. The firm's exports of sea otters and fur seals, respectively, from North America decreased from 73,000 and 1,232,400 during its first charter (1797–1821) to 25,400 and 458,500 during its second (1822–1842) and 25,900 and 372,900 during its third (1843–1862). By contrast, its exports of beavers increased from 34,500 to 162,000 to 157,000 and of foxes from 107,138 to 159,674 to 131,981, while its exports of river otters doubled between each of the three charter periods (Tikhmenev 1978–1979, 1:153, 207, 360). Sea furs (sea otters, fur seals, sea lions) as a percentage of the company's North American fur exports dropped from 84 to 56 to 52 percent.

These figures are somewhat misleading, however. Many of the land furs came not from the interior posts but from the streams and ponds of the coast itself and its archipelagos, as well as from the Hudson's Bay Company, which provided 50,000 river otters in the decade of the 1840s (and probably all the 1842–1863 river otter exports) in return for exclusive trading rights to the mainland Alaska panhandle. The Russian-American Company with its blue glass beads, copperware, and ironware failed to divert completely (or even mostly) the longstanding native trade between northeastern Siberia and central Alaska via

378

Bering Strait, whereby on dogsled in winter and in umiak in summer Athapaskan furs and Eskimo walrus tusks from Alaska were exchanged for Russian tobacco, iron and copper utensils, beads, and knives and Chukchi reindeer hides (up to 1,000 annually) from Chukotka via Eskimo middlemen on the islands of the northern Bering Sea, the latter adding the fats, oils, and skins of sea mammals to the traffic (VanStone 1979:63–69; Wrangell 1980:30–32). In 1842–1843 Nulato, for instance, collected 3,125 beaver pelts for the Russian-American Company but 5,500 furs still remained in native hands for the trans-Bering trade. Zagoskin's expedition was designed to intercept this trade, but it failed to do so. One reason was the fact that Indian furs from the Yukon River Valley brought from four to six times as much at the private Russian trading posts on the Kolyma and Anadyr rivers as at Mikhailovskiy Redoubt (Zagoskin 1967:183). And from 1850 American whaling ships began visiting Port Clarence on the Seward Peninsula to barter hardware, firearms, and liquor for furs and walrus ivory (VanStone 1979:90). The Russian-American Company lacked sufficient capital, personnel, and supplies, as well as detailed, accurate intelligence, to dominate the interior trade. So the natives of the uppermost reaches of the Yukon remained virtually untouched, the Russians managing only infrequent and indirect contact through Indians on the middle Yukon and Copper rivers, plus the Tlingit.

The Spanish Period

The Spaniards sent three expeditions to the Northwest Coast, in 1774, when Capt. Juan Pérez in the *Santiago* reconnoitered as far north as the Alexander Archipelago and obtained some sea otter skins from the Haida. Spain outfitted a series of expeditions from San Blas, Mexico, to the Northwest Coast in the last quarter of the eighteenth century to assess and forestall Russian and English encroachment. Naval outposts were established to protect New Spain's northwestern frontier: Santa Cruz de Nuca (1789–1795) on Vancouver Island (see "Spanish Indian Policies," fig. 5, this vol.) and Nuñez Gaona (1792) on the Olympic Peninsula (fig. 2).

Spanish interest in the Northwest Coast remained military. They wanted simply to keep the coast unexplored and undeveloped as a desolate buffer against foreign penetration of the Californias and Mexico. Only one of the Spanish voyages was a trading venture. Alta California's missions and ranchos produced abundant grain and beef, but foreign trade was prohibited by the Laws of the Indies. Also, the northern frontier of New Spain was chronically undermanned (Shaler 1808:161). The Spanish source of sea otter skins remained the California coast (Ogden 1941), and the California Indians were neither willing nor skilled hunters of sea otters. After 1800 most of the traffic was conducted by American and Russian poachers.

top, The British Lib., London; bottom, Natl. Lib. of Australia, Canberra: Rex Nan Kevell Coll. NK53/J.

Fig. 3. Scenes from James Cook's third voyage. top, Unidentified Northwest Coast Indians in canoes approaching the ship *Resolution*, probably for trade. Watercolor by James Webber, 1778. bottom, The *Discovery* (left) and the *Resolution* anchored in Nootka Sound. Watercolor and ink by William Ellis, 1778.

The British Period

It was Capt. James Cook's third voyage that brought his country into the Northwest trade (fig. 3). In 1778 his two ships refitted for a month in Nootka Sound, where his crewmen bought sea otter skins (literally off the Indians' backs) for scraps of iron; more were subsequently purchased in Cook Inlet for glass beads. At the end of 1779 the prime skins were sold in Canton for a return of £90 on an investment of one shilling (Cook and King 1784, 3:437; Lloyd and Anderson 1959:21–22). Little wonder that the crew's eagerness to return to the Northwest Coast approached mutiny. Others became just as eager, alerted by the publication in the first half of the 1780s of both the official and unofficial accounts of Cook's last voyage. The first Englishman to exploit his findings was Capt. James Hanna and 30 crewmen in 1785 in a brig fittingly named *Sea Otter*. He anchored in Nootka Sound for five weeks and procured 560 skins, which fetched from $20,600 to $24,000 at Canton in 1786 to defray an outlay of $17,000 (Beresford 1789: 315–316; A. Walker 1982:199). By that year there were seven English trading vessels on the coast; however, by 1803 the English had disappeared from the coast trade (fig. 4). From the beginning they had been obliged to hurdle the monopolistic privileges of the British East India and South Sea companies. The latter, although moribund, had been granted the exclusive right to English trade in the Pacific and the former to English trade in China, so sea otter skins were procurable only in the preserve of one monopoly and disposable only in that of the other. Some English "coasters" obtained licenses from both companies, some from either, and some from neither and risked becoming "fair and lawful prizes" of licensed vessels; still other ships masqueraded under foreign flags (Austrian, Portuguese, Swedish) to circumvent the restrictions. The "Honorable John Company" usually permitted English trading vessels to export furs to Canton but for a percentage of the proceeds. Moreover, the East India Company did not allow English maritime traders to export Chinese goods to England; instead, they were given specie for their furs in the form of bills payable on London. Thus, the last and most profitable leg of the England–Northwest

Coast–China circuit—the sale of Chinese teas, silks, porcelains, and curios in Western Europe—was denied English coasters, who consequently received 20 percent less for their skins than their American counterparts (O'Neil 1930:265). The monopolistic impediments were finally removed in 1834, but by then there were few sea otters left to buy or sell.

The American Period

Probably the first shipmaster to ply the New England–Northwest Coast–South China circuit was Capt. Robert Gray, who sailed in 1788. Gray set the pattern for American trading voyages, most of which originated in Boston. Just as Salem dominated American trade in the Indian Ocean, so Boston commanded its country's traffic in the North Pacific. Nearly all the owners, captains, and crews of American coasters were from Boston. Their vessels were small for navigating the winding and narrow channels and inlets of the fiorded coast, well-manned and heavily armed for repelling Indian attacks, and copper-bottomed for stemming seaweed, barnacles, and worms. The ships cleared Boston in the fall, doubled Cape Horn in

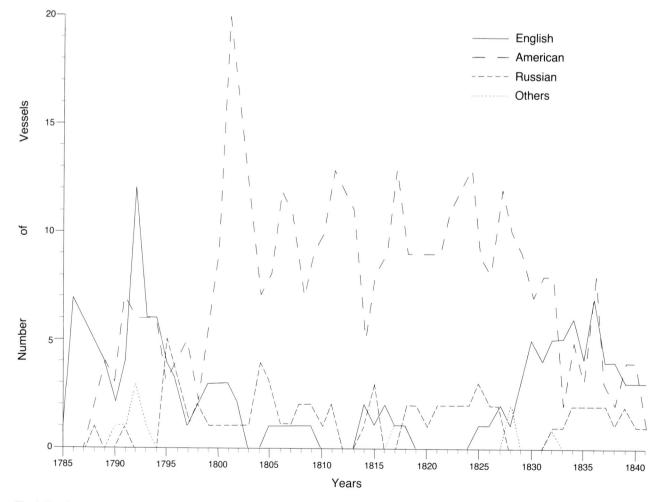

380   Fig. 4. Trading and hunting vessels to the Northwest Coast, 1785–1841.

the Antarctic summer, and hailed the coast in the spring, when the Indians were returning to the outer coast from their inland winter villages. The shipmasters spent spring and summer on the coast in search of sea otter skins.

By late summer the Indians were shifting to the inner coast for forest hunting, the fall salmon run, and wooded winter shelter, and trade was ending. Before quitting the coast American captains made sure that their furs had been cleaned and packed in casks or chests to prevent contamination by vermin. In addition, water, wood, and food (fish, venison, fowl, and berries) were replenished, holds were smoked to kill rats and mice, and ships repaired for the long voyage to China. After three weeks they made port in the Hawaiian Islands (Meares 1790: lxxiii) and continued to the Portuguese colony of Macao, where a licensed pilot was hired and an official permit was secured that allowed the ships to proceed to Whampoa Roads, the anchorage for all foreign merchantmen. From Whampoa the cargoes were lightered in chop boats a dozen miles upriver to Canton itself and stored in the large warehouses that were rented from the security merchants. Americans virtually monopolized the sea otter traffic in Canton.

It was often late winter before the Yankees sold their furs for cash and bought a load of teas, silks, nankeens, and porcelains, plus pharmaceuticals, spices, and sundry bric-a-brac, for the large European and burgeoning American markets. Particularly tea was taken, for the Chinese merchants were usually so overstocked that they would not only sell it at a reasonable price but also accept goods in return at a high rate, as well as do so with dispatch. Moreover, the American public savored tea as much as the English (Cleveland 1842, 1:100; Krusenstern 1813, 2:331–332).

After replenishing their provisions, the American merchantmen sailed across the Indian Ocean to the Cape of Good Hope, which was rounded in spring, and made for Cape Cod (Morison 1961:77). Altogether American ships made at least 127 voyages between the United States and China via the Northwest Coast from 1788 through 1826 (Latourette 1927:255–261).

American domination of the Northwest trade continued until the first half of the 1830s, when first the Hudson's Bay Company and then the Russian-American Company began concerted trading on the coast. By then, American traders were abandoning the coast trade anyway, for it had peaked long before. The prospect of a quick and easy fortune had resulted in overtrading and overhunting. By diversifying their business some American traders were able to continue, but their take of skins remained negligible. In 1827 Capt. William Martain of the *Louisa*, the most experienced and successful of all of the American shipmasters on the coast, spent nearly the entire year trading and managed to get a mere 160 sea otter skins (U.S. National Archives 1802–1867, roll 31:76), as many

as one could have gotten in a single good day in the 1790s. Even the old Sitka market, with its inveterate demand for provisions and manufactures, finally became overstocked. By the end of 1827 the Russians had procured enough supplies from the Bostonians to last two years (Hudson's Bay Company 1821–1835:22). The veteran Capt. Andrew Blanchard spent two summer months at Sitka in 1827 but was able to get only $1.75 for each of his fur seal skins—from one-half to three-quarters the former rate (U.S. National Archives 1802–1867, roll 31:2v.–3).

The resurgence of English participation in the coast trade was engineered by George Simpson, who became governor of the Hudson's Bay Company's territory in North America after the absorption of the rival North West Company in 1821. Governor Simpson overhauled Company operations, reducing costs and eliminating competitors, including American mountain men west of the Continental Divide and American coasters north of the Columbia. A new "naval department" was designed to pursue the coastal trade by means of both posts and vessels. By 1832 the Company had a post, Fort Simpson (fig. 5), at the mouth of the Nass and several vessels on the coast, including the American brig *Lama*, which was bought with its captain and crew. Fort McLoughlin followed in 1833 near Dean Channel and Forts Stikine and Taku in 1840 near the mouth of the Stikine (fig. 2). The success of the American trade began to flag as soon as the company, with its enormous financial resources and experienced employees, began to shadow and outbid American ships in 1829, although at first it lacked suitable vessels, capable seamen, and sufficient goods. In 1833 the English *Lama* collected one-third of all the furs that were traded on the coast that year, the rest going to the two new posts and to Sitka (Hudson's Bay Company 1821–1835: 48v.). Again in 1837 the Hudson's Bay Company resolved "to get the furs at any price or at least raise them so high that any which may fall into the hands of our Opponents will yield a loss or at least no profit," this being "considered the only means by which the Coast can be kept clear of Opponents" (Hudson's Bay Company 1831–1866:10). The outcome of this policy is shown in table 1, which demonstrates the extent of the company's domination of the coast trade in the late 1830s.

In 1839, when the Hudson's Bay Company leased the Alaska panhandle from the Russian-American Company, American trading vessels were unable to ensure profitable voyages through sales at Sitka, and the last arrived in 1841. The Hudson's Bay Company was able to reduce by as much as 40 percent the "extravagant" prices that the Indians had been receiving from Yankee traders (10 blankets for 1 sea otter skin, compared with from 6 to 8 blankets from the English) (Hudson's Bay Company 1831–1866:139–139v., 146v.).

The Process of Trade

Some shipmasters preferred to cruise, others to sojourn. Sojourning was better because more skins were obtained, since few Indians were willing to chase a ship several miles offshore and to trade hurriedly, whereas a sojourner would meet more than 2,000 Nootkans in Nootka Sound in 1786, at least 3,000 Nootkans in Clayoquot Sound in 1791, up to 2,000 Haidas at Kaigani in 1799, and as many as 2,000 Tlingits in Sitka Sound in 1805 (Howay 1941:382; Jackman 1978:99; Lisiánskiĭ 1814:237; A. Walker 1982: 122).

Having sighted an Indian village, shipmasters fired their cannon to alert the inhabitants. The approach of the natives presented a curious and fearsome spectacle to the Euro-Americans. The carved and painted dugout canoes could be as long as the trading ships and carry as many men, who were cloaked with furs, disfigured by scars, daubed with red ocher, coiffed in braids sprinkled with fish oil and eagle down, and adorned with shell nose and ear rings and copper collars or bone necklaces, as well as—in the case of the northern Indians—tattooed and the women labreted. They greeted the ships with an "agreeable" song, keeping time to a drum beat with their paddle strokes. As a sign of friendship they threw white feathers onto the sea, and as an even stronger sign a chief and a captain might eventually exchange surnames. The canoes crowded around the ships (fig. 3, top) and trading was done over the side or on the deck; in the latter case few natives, often only the chief, were allowed on board at one time for security reasons.

The Indians were just as eager to trade as the Euro-Americans. Apparently the Haida exceeded other northern Indians in "keenness in trade," perhaps partly because more of their furs were the more valuable sea otter and perhaps, too, partly because they had less opportunity for transmountain trade with interior natives on the mainland. As traders the Indians proved not only as keen as Euro-Americans but also as shrewd, as sensitive to supply and demand, and as vulnerable to fashion (R. Fisher 1977a). Often a chief handled all the trade of his tribe. In doing so he was disposing of communal resources (not only furs but provisions, too), for which he was responsible. If he were bested in trading, he lost not only wealth but also prestige and perhaps even rank and subjects as well; therefore, it was important to him to strike a bargain.

The captain directed his ship's trade, and he and the chief began in the traditional Indian manner by exchanging gifts—"always with an expectation of a return . . . of equal value" (Ingraham 1971:130). Shipmasters soon discovered, however, that skins received in this way always cost more than those purchased in trade (perhaps because they were less likely to shortchange the natives at the outset in order to stimulate traffic), so they tried to avoid gift exchanges, although this could not always be done for fear of insulting the Indians and losing their business.

Before trading began it was likewise customary to fix a price for prime skins as a standard of value. This entailed a great deal of haggling, and only after a couple of days of such bantering was a skipper able to "break trade," much to his and his crew's exasperation. The Indians were skillful traders who viewed barter as more than simply a commercial transaction; to them it was also a political and

Fig. 5. Ft. Simpson with Tsimshian houses, B.C. An important Hudson's Bay Company post, Ft. Simpson was established in 1831 near the Nishga at the mouth of the Nass River. However, the location was changed to the Tsimshian Peninsula when, among other reasons, the trader John Kennedy married the daughter of the Tsimshian leader Legaik. A large Tsimshian settlement was built at the walls of the fort. This "home guard" exerted considerable control over the trade by acting as middlemen and keeping prices high (R. Fisher 1977:26, 28–31, 41). Pen and ink drawing by James Swan, about 1875.

social event that should not be hurried.

Small articles were added to the primary Euro-American goods as presents but were in fact part of the price. Different individuals wanted different assortments, so that equivalents had to be established: an iron pot equaled an ax, a knife a file, a pocket mirror a pair of scissors. The Indians would try hard to get more than the equivalent, and these attempts were resisted to avoid antagonizing those natives who had already traded at the equivalent. At the same time the Indians kept the price of their skins from falling by monopolizing the traffic of a moored vessel, excluding other Indian sellers and not allowing them to participate until their own stock of furs had been exhausted, and even then only under certain restrictions (Cook and King 1784, 2:278). Whenever other Indians managed to break the monopoly, they charged less for their skins (A. Walker 1982:110–111).

Table 1. American and English Returns from the Coast Trade, 1835-1838

	Sea Furs		Land Furs	
	American	English	American	English
1835	89	254	4,850	12,051
1836	43	130	2,197	12,930
1837	0	108	0	13,907
1838	0	136	0	14,011

Source: Hudson's Bay Company 1826-1860.

The Euro-American traders were struck by the honesty of the Indians in trade, at least at first (Howay 1941:195, 208; Portlock 1789:113, 118, 264; Vancouver 1798, 1:204, 240, 326, 348, 2:269, 278, 385, 394, 409), although they were not above blackening sea otter pelts with charcoal, glossy black being the most desirable color (A. Walker 1982:62–63), or diluting animal oil with water (Cook and King 1784, 2:279). But the maritime fur traders were even more impressed by the Indians' commercial aptitude. What a member of a French trading venture said of the Tlingits of Sitka Sound in 1791 applied equally to the other Indian groups of the coast: "They examined with the most scrupulous attention, turned about in every way, all that was presented to them, and they knew very well how to discover defects and point them out: on the other hand, they employed art and cunning in setting off their merchandise . . . ." (Fleurieu 1801, 1:192). In the middle 1830s the Kaigani Haidas were considered "the most difficult Indians on the coast to deal with" (Work 1945: 21–22), probably because they were in the best location for upping the bidding among competing Russian, American, and English traders.

The natives were quick to take advantage of the presence of competitors to drive the best bargain. One shipmaster commonly tailed another in the expectation that he could outcompete the other, just as in the continental fur trade rival companies often sited their posts near each other (Freeman and Dungey 1981). The Indians then went back and forth between the competing ships in order to raise the price of their skins. "Nothing pleases them better than to have two vessels thus opposing each other," commented Chief Trader John Work (1945: 36) of the Hudson's Bay Company. To counter this tactic American traders assigned each of their vessels to a certain stretch of the coast and divided the returns equally (at least until 1827, when ostensibly there were no longer enough sea otters to justify this practice) (Hudson's Bay Company 1821–1835:21v., 27v.). But even when trading vessels were scattered the Indians "are soon acquainted with what vessels are at different parts . . . and set a value on their furs accordingly" (Ingraham 1971:203). At Fort Simpson the Tsimshian would "very often" even falsely report that they had sighted an American ship "in hopes of receiving a better price for their Skins" from the Hudson's Bay Company post (Hudson's Bay Company 1831–1866:88). In order to get a higher price some chiefs "held back" their furs until the trading vessels were about to leave in September and were therefore anxious to dump their goods and complete their cargoes (Hudson's Bay Company 1821–1835:22).

The higher Indian demand and the lower Euro-American offer inevitably produced a compromise. Thus, in Sitka Sound in early 1799 the Tlingit offered one sea otter skin for one musket and the *Eliza*'s captain demanded four or five skins, and after three days of haggling the two sides settled on three skins (Jackman 1978:34–35). Some skippers feared that "should they [the Indians] raise their price from what they at present [1792] require, the trade will be no longer worthy of anyone's attention, for ruin must certainly follow" (Ingraham 1971: 203). But the Indian's response to supply and demand never reached that inelastic point. The Indians, of course, tried to keep fur prices as high as possible. And it was not long before the natives put prices on other articles that were in demand by shipmasters. By 1829 Tongass was the only place on the northern coast where trading vessels could wood and water free of charge; elsewhere they had to pay in goods (Green 1915:76–77).

The Euro-American traders devised their own stratagems to counter the commercial wiles of the Indians. Skippers tried to win the favor of fur-laden chiefs by giving them presents, allowing them access to the ship's cabin and its larder, offering them passage to another village, teaching them the proper use of trade goods, and taking them to Macao, Boston, or Hawaii. Less successful were attempts to establish permanent factories on the coast (for year-round trading) and to leave temporary agents with the natives (to monopolize their furs).

Meanwhile, the tendency for competing vessels to bid up fur prices continued. To defeat this inflation shipmasters resorted to price fixing. In spring 1835, for example, the American vessels *Bolivar Liberator* and *Europa* and the English *Lama* "acted in concert" in order to keep the price of beaver no higher than three blankets for two pelts, dividing the returns equally (Tolmie 1963:312). Often, however, price fixing did not last because one confederate could not resist the temptation to exceed the fixed price and thereby reap a windfall of skins. There was also the danger that the Indians might retaliate by withholding their skins until the free market had been restored.

Another Euro-American tactic was to locate "newer" Indians, that is, those who had had little contact with trading vessels, for "not having been visited By Ships often they are not so knowing and Clammorous and of Course the skins purchased proportionally cheap" (M. Roe 1967: 71–72). Inevitably, however, "newer" Indians became "older" Indians. A similar step was the bypassing of Indian traders in order to deal directly (and more cheaply) with the suppliers. Many, if not most, of the skins that were traded by the natives of the outer coast were not bagged by them but acquired from inland Indians by barter and even plunder. That is what happened when, after exhausting his stock of furs, a chief would ask a shipmaster to wait a few days until he had procured more. Not one-fiftieth of the skins that were for sale at Kaigani, for instance, were caught by the Haida; they obtained them from inland natives for one-half the price that they received from shipmasters (Jackman 1978:67–68). Increasingly trading vessels sailed farther up the channels and inlets in order to circumvent the Indian middlemen. The middlemen tried (in vain) to keep their sources of supply a secret and to deceive the shipmasters by declaring that the waterways were impassable or the interior natives murderous, while the captains tried to discover the whereabouts of the sources by plying the Indians with liquor.

After 1792 Nootkan-Kwakiutl trade was intercepted, and by the end of the decade Nootka Sound had been largely abandoned by trading vessels. Nootkan resentment, aggravated by periodic insults to Chief Maquinna, culminated in the capture of the *Boston* in 1803 and the killing of nearly all its crew. Then the Queen Charlottes became dominant, but by 1799 they had not half the skins that they formerly had, again because the trading vessels intercepted the trading expeditions that brought most of the archipelago's supply from the mainland. Then Sitka Sound became preeminent until its fur supply was preempted by merchantmen sailing up Menzies Strait between Baranof (Sitka) and Chichagof Islands (Jackman 1978:88–89). Similarly, by the middle 1810s Chief Concomly's Lower Chinookans had been bypassed. They had long kept their interior suppliers at bay by telling them that White shipmasters were evil and would enslave them, but now the inlanders canoed downriver every summer to the Columbia River mouth to truck directly with the Euro-Americans (Corney 1965:153–154).

Hudson's Bay Company posts also eliminated some middlemen. Chief Trader John Work reported from Fort McLoughlin in 1835 that the local Indians were "disturbed" over the Company's monopoly "and also the loss of the Interior trade or a considerable part of it, as the Interior Indians dispose of their furs themselves at the fort, and they do not pass through the hands of the others as formerly" (Work 1945:77).

Obstacles to Trade

The obstacles to trade included those common to all long ocean voyages of the time: weather, environmental conditions, disease, and Spanish, English, and French privateers and warships. The Northwest Coast itself had its own perils: persistent rain, contrary winds, thick fogs (particularly around the Queen Charlottes), strong tides, and unknown shallows.

More serious was the gradual decline of fur prices. As supply rose from the middle 1780s, demand and hence prices fell, reaching their nadir in the middle 1790s. Between 1785 and 1792 the price of skins fell threefold at Canton (and rose fourfold on the Northwest Coast) (Meany 1915:40). Conversely, with the depletion of sea otters on the coast supply decreased and demand and hence prices increased. The higher prices for the fewer skins permitted at least some fur traders to stay in business.

The two most formidable problems for Northwest maritime traders arose on the coast itself, and they were not unrelated: the rapid depletion of sea otters and the even more rapid worsening of Euro-American–Indian relations. Initially the Indians were curious, polite, and friendly, and the Euro-Americans were similarly impressed with their honesty and fairness in trade. Perhaps because many of the Euro-Americans were "transient traders" (albeit not infrequently returning ones) they were wont to treat the Indians more callously and brutally than if, like the land fur traders, they had to live among them permanently. White violations of native customs undoubtedly gave offense, too. The initial hospitality and friendliness of the Indians soon changed to antipathy and hostility. Once the Euro-Americans, too, were no longer novel, they were regarded as members of distant tribes, as potential enemies, for they were obviously not relatives, and as such they were fair game for theft or even murder (Duff 1964:56).

Euro-Americans were responsible for various abuses: the selling of defective goods, the forcible taking of skins, and the kidnapping of chiefs to force trade or to ransom for skins (Vancouver 1798, 2:364). Several times the Haida chief, Altatsee, was enticed aboard ship, clapped in irons, and ransomed for skins. Eventually the Indians would ask the identity of the captain (and sometimes the flag) of a vessel before agreeing to trade because some skippers became known for their dishonesty (Jackman 1978:36, 53).

The Indians, of course, responded in kind (Howay 1925), "continually remembering their injuries, and never forgiving till they have obtained sufficient revenge," according to one captain (Jackman 1978:47). The Indians' sense of revenge was not only strong but also applicable to any other Whites, as they saw all White men as belonging to one tribe and therefore sharing the guilt of any of its members. Thus, after being victimized by one vessel, they would seek revenge on the next, despite its "innocence." This was the basis of the so-called "unprovoked" and "treacherous & unexpected" attacks of the Indians (S. Hill 1815–1822:8).

Occasionally the Indians succeeded in capturing trading vessels and killing their crews. By 1805, American shipmasters told the Russians at Sitka, they had lost six ships to the natives (Tikhmenev 1978–1979, 2:157). One of the bloodiest losses occurred in 1811, when John Jacob Astor's ship *Tonquin* was captured at Clayoquot Sound; all hands and some 100 Nootkans were killed. Ironically, "very often" the trading vessels were attacked with the very arms that they themselves had sold, and on the very day of the sale (Choris 1822:9). Although a flotilla of 50-foot war canoes bristling with two dozen armed and whooping Indians in warpaint must have been a daunting sight, most traders' ships were well-manned and well-armed, and attacks were usually easily repulsed (those vessels that were overpowered were victims of surprise rather than frontal assaults). In the middle 1820s American coasters generally exceeded 200 tons, mounted several cannon and swivel guns, and carried a couple of dozen men with muskets, pistols, sabers, and daggers (G. Simpson 1947:79). Precautions were taken: they seldom put into port singly, and otherwise they stood offshore; no trading was done at night, and during the day only a few canoes were allowed alongside at one time; no Indians were permitted to come aboard; and they had to be unarmed, while every crewman stood on guard and all cannon were loaded with double grapeshot, with a match burning at each of them. Any hostilities normally ended in a standoff, although the Indians suffered more casualties because of greater Euro-American firepower. By 1825 Kaigani was the only anchorage on the entire coast where American vessels did not have to take precautions (Scouler 1905:192). The Tlingit became particularly hostile, perhaps partly because they were more numerous and better armed than other coastal tribes.

More serious than the souring of relations was the diminution of sea otters. In 1792–1793 there was an "Astonishing Quantity" of sea otters along the northern coast in particular (Puget 1793:66, 71v.). In the late 1780s a trading vessel could obtain up to 2,500 skins in one season with little difficulty. On the Queen Charlottes, for example, one captain got 300 skins in half an hour in 1787 (Beresford 1789).

The great profits accruing to both Indians and White traders eventually led to overhunting of the sea otter resource and overstocking of the Indian market. The animal itself was particularly vulnerable. Its reproductivity was low, generally one offspring per dam per year. Perhaps because of this, the mother was exceptionally regardful, so much so that she refused to abandon her pup under any circumstances, with the fatal result that both were bagged. Also, her pelt was more valuable than her mate's, so that dams bore the brunt of hunting. Finally, the creature's pelt remained prime all year as insulation against cool ocean waters; this fact invited year-round hunting and hastened depletion. Whereas Capt. Charles Bishop had found in 1795 that the waters around the Queen Charlottes "abound with Sea otters" (M. Roe 1967: 62), John Work noted in 1835 that "now scarcely any is to be found" (Work 1945:40). Of the several sorts of *Enhydra lutris*, only that of the Northwest Coast, where competition was most intense, was hunted to extinction. This was reflected in the declining number of skins taken by American vessels on the coast, from an unknown but probable peak in 1795 or 1796 (when prices at Canton reached their nadir), to 18,000 in 1800 to 15,000 in 1802 to annual averages of 14,837 in 1804–1807, 9,592 in 1808–1812, and 3,100 in 1813–1814 to 4,300 in 1815, 3,650 in 1816, 4,177 in 1817, and 4,500–4,800 in 1818 (Cowdin 1846:536; Roquefeuil 1823, 2:307–308; Phelps 1850:6). In the early 1820s the yearly American take was only 3,000–4,000 skins (U.S. National Archives 1802–1867, roll 28:245; see also Howay 1973:161), and by the middle 1840s no more than 200 skins of "very ordinary" quality were taken by trading vessels annually (Cowdin 1846:536).

Changes in Trade

Like the price of skins, the coast trade was anything but static. From its inception until its demise traffic changed constantly and rapidly, especially during the period of greatest competition—from 1791 through 1802—when overpricing and overhunting necessitated frequent adjustments. At first, trading vessels sailed in pairs to Nootka Sound (fig. 3), Cook Inlet, and Prince William Sound. These were the places where Cook had procured furs (Beresford 1789:xvii). After 1788, English and American traders avoided Cook Inlet because by then the Russians "had got entire possession of the river," and within five years they had "almost hunted out" the water body (Meares 1790:312; Tikhmenev 1978–1979, 2:32). Thereafter Euro-American traders concentrated on the coast between Cross and Puget sounds, with occasional forays southward to the Columbia River and northward into the straits, where the Russians became dominant. During the 1790s Nootka Sound was the foremost "mart for peltry" (Portlock 1789:3). Within the sound Friendly Cove was just that (at least until around 1800, when Chief

Maquinna's forbearance broke). There was plenty of timber and water, as well as numerous Indian customers. The sound was visited by 30 ships in 1792, including 21 trading vessels (Vancouver 1798, 3:124–125, 127, 498). By then, however, sea otters were already becoming scarce there and the locus of the coast trade was shifting from Vancouver Island to the Queen Charlotte Islands and the Alexander Archipelago; Kaigani Harbor at the southern tip of the archipelago became the favorite English and American rendezvous. Close behind were Clemencitty at the entrance to Portland Canal and Nawhitty at the northern extremity of Vancouver Island (fig. 2). Sitka Sound was also frequented.

Before the turn of the century, too, trading vessels were no longer sailing in tandem. At first they had sailed "in company" for safety and security against accidents, enemy vessels, and hostile natives, but this soon changed. Many skins were missed because "one would [could] have been collecting the Skins to the Northward, while the other was doing the same to the Southward" (A. Walker 1982:191). Now, too, there were fewer skins to share, and accumulated knowledge of the coast had made solo voyaging safer. Furthermore, no longer did vessels range up and down the coast in quest of skins; greater competition induced them to remain longer in fewer anchorages. Keener competition also brought vessels closer to shore and prompted less trading over the side (with chiefs only on board) and more trading on the deck with more tribesmen as the shipmasters tried to ingratiate themselves. Eventually, as the Indians received more abuse and acquired more ordnance, trading "at arm's length" was restored.

As the number of competitors increased and the number of sea otters decreased, by about 1800 vessels needed two seasons to complete a cargo, so they took to wintering at Hawaii or on the coast itself. Some captains spent the winter hunting sea otters on the southern coasts, employing Tlingit and Haida marksmen. Consequently, the duration of a Boston–Northwest Coast–Canton–Boston venture lengthened to as many as five years from two years or less initially.

By the 1810s there were already so few otters left that American shipmasters were commonly "dividing the skins," that is, cooperating by trading on halves, with a crewman from each vessel aboard the other to monitor the returns (Howay 1973:135). The growing Indian military threat triggered cooperation in defense, too; vessels plied the coast "in company." In addition, the higher risks necessitated larger crews, which from about 1820 were augmented by skilled Hawaiian hands.

Trade goods, particularly those demanded by the Indians but also those accepted by the Euro-Americans, were among the first things to change. The natives wanted goods for both practical and aesthetic purposes. Generally they preferred articles that could be readily counted and compared and were therefore suitable for potlatches; thus,

The St. Louis Art Mus., Mo.: 268:1982.

Fig. 6. Potlatch copper, one of the most impressive additions to the material inventory of Northwest Coast tribes. Ship captains traded copper plates carried for hull sheathing and other copper items to the Indians, who fashioned these into elaborate shields, symbols of authority. No coppers made from native ore are known. If these were made, they must have been smaller given the limited availability of native copper. Collected from the Tsimshian, Prince Rupert, B.C.; probably 1800–1850. Height 110.7 cm.

portable, storable, and uniform goods were desired (Wike 1951:90). In the last half of the 1780s the Indians demanded principally iron, copper, and colored glass beads, although beads, like all trinkets, were accepted mainly as introductory and conciliatory gifts (their use as trade goods seems to have been limited to Cook Inlet and Prince William Sound, where they were popularized by the Russians).

The first Spanish visitors found iron and copper already present among the Haida and Nootkans in 1774. They had probably obtained the iron through long-distance trade via Bering Strait from Russian posts in Siberia, and some may have come across the mountains from Hudson's Bay Company posts (some may even have drifted in flotsam across the North Pacific from the Far East) (T.A. Rickard 1939). Some native copper was procured from the basin of the Copper River. These traditional sources of supply could not satisfy Indian demand, so the natives pressed the trading vessels, particularly for iron (probably because it was more suitable than copper for use in weapons and tools and because it was rarer than copper on the coast). The iron was used for fishhooks, arrowheads, and lancetips in place of stone, shell, and bone, as well as for blades for chisels, adzes, and daggers, but not for axes or hatchets.

Copper was demanded almost as much as iron. It was used for bracelets, ear and hair ornaments, and robe bangles. And from sheet copper the Northern Northwest coast tribes made the famous copper shields that loomed so large in the potlatches of the nineteenth century (fig. 6) (Gunther 1972:131).

After Whites satisfied Indian demand for metal, blue cotton cloth became the commanding inducement. Before the end of the decade it was joined by readymade clothing (especially great coats), blankets, and duffels, and all of them remained in demand until the end of the coast trade.

Firearms were introduced shortly after textiles. Certainly the Nootkans were using firearms by 1788 (Howay 1941:62). It was not long before intertribal trade had diffused guns up and down the coast. By 1792 the Coast Salish were not yet supplied with firearms (probably

because their native neighbors were wont to war on them rather than trade with them), but the Kwakiutl of the Strait of Georgia had been "amply provided" with muskets by the Nootkans (Vancouver 1798, 1:343; Moziño 1970:80–81, 88). By the end of the 1792 trading season the Tlingit had "plenty" of guns, and among them ammunition was "always the first demand" (fig. 7) (Barkley 1836). Already by 1794 the market was glutted (Wike 1951:41), but guns remained a staple trade good, thanks to their utility as a weapon and their symbolization of wealth. Every trading vessel carried an armorer to repair Indian as well as its own firearms (and to forge made-to-measure articles). In the early 1820s American traders got one-third of their sea otter skins for guns (and the rest for blankets and woolen cloth) (U.S. National Archives 1802–1867, roll 28:245). The muskets and pistols were used by the Indians mainly for warfare, not only among themselves but also against Whites. The Nootkans, at least, preferred guns to bows and arrows for hunting land animals and shore birds (Moziño 1970:48). Indeed, the natives mastered firearms quickly.

Apparently the only restraint shown by traders was

Muzeĭ Antropologii i Ėtnografii; Akademiia Nauk SSSR, Leningrad.
Fig. 7. The *Nikolai I*, a Russian-American Company steam-driven paddle-wheel boat used for the fur trade with the Tlingit in the Kolosh Straits. The ship carried tobacco, lead, powder, and woolen clothing to exchange for furs and potatoes. Armed with 14 guns, the *Nikolai I* was the first craft built in the company's Novo-Archangel'sk shipyard. The boat is shown near the magnetic observatory (right) on the southeast side of Japanese I., across from Novo-Archangel'sk (Blomkvist 1972:145–147). Native Alaskans were employed as sailors and mates by the Russian-American Company. Drawing by Ilia G. Voznesenskii, about 1844.

THE MARITIME TRADE OF THE NORTH PACIFIC COAST

their reluctance to trade blunderbusses, which fired several balls at one time (whereas muskets, with a smaller bore and a longer range, fired one ball at a time). Thus, armed with the best guns (besides lances, bows and arrows, sabers, and daggers) and adept in their use, the Indians were a potent force (R. Fisher 1976 to the contrary).

Alcohol and tobacco were almost as pernicious as firearms. Both were introduced around 1800. Before the arrival of White traders the Haida and Tlingit cultivated a variety of tobacco, which they mixed with lime and chewed, and the Yurok grew and smoked tobacco, but intoxicants were unknown. The initial Indian distaste for alcohol was overcome by persistent offerings by explorers in a spirit of friendship and by traders bent on ingratiation and intoxication. By 1800 it was used in large amounts as a trade good (Howay 1942). Thereafter "Indian rum"—from one-quarter to one-half rum and the rest water—was commonly given to open trade. By 1829 rum and guns were "the articles upon which the Indians place the greatest value" and they yielded shipmasters the "greatest profit" (Hudson's Bay Company 1826–1860:16v.–17). The Russian-American Company preferred to trade rum, for it was sold at 180 percent above cost, so that a large beaver skin could be bought for one and one-half gallons of rum (U.S. National Archives 1802–1867, roll 36: 175v.–176). At this time the rival Hudson's Bay Company also gave one and one-half gallons of watered rum for a large beaver skin. After the Americans had withdrawn from the coast trade, the two companies agreed in 1842 to ban the trading of alcohol, but within a few years this pact was broken.

About the same time molasses, rice, bread, and "Indian sugar" (half sugar, half bran) were introduced. Initially the Nootkans, at least, abhorred salt and liquor but relished rice and biscuit (A. Walker 1982:187). Before long the Haida even preferred molasses to rum and would trade a prime sea otter skin for four bottles. Molasses with rice or bread was the best seller on the coast in 1802 (Jackman 1978:57, 120), and either concoction remained in demand until the close of the coast trade. Like rum and tobacco, molasses with bread was eventually given as a present rather than traded for skins (D'Wolf 1968:19–20).

Other Euro-American wares like wire and paint were traded but never so heavily as guns and blankets. Trinkets probably had the longest life of all trade goods. Most of them were ornamental personal effects, such as beads, which were worn as necklaces, bracelets, and anklets. "Small" trade in beads, buttons, "China cash" (holed Chinese coins), spoons, nails, fishhooks, scissors, mirrors, combs, handkerchiefs, and the like served two functions: as gifts to broach trade and as barter for provisions. These items could be traded for fish, venison, wildfowl, berries, wapatoos, greens, water, and whale oil for ships' lamps.

Besides bringing Euro-American goods to the coast,

White traders also bought and sold coastal goods that had long supported intertribal trade: abalone and dentalium shells, ermine skins, elk hides, eulachon oil, and slaves—anything that could be exchanged for furs. Elk hides, mostly from the lower Columbia, were "always in great demand on the Northern Coast," thanks to the virtually incessant intertribal warfare (Cowdin 1846:534). The hides were bleached white in the sun and folded double or treble into armor that covered a warrior from his neck to his heels.

Slaves were traded up and down the coast and across the mountains to the interior. The chief victims, apart from the California Indians, seem to have been the Coast Salish, who were periodically terrorized by flotillas of Kwakiutl and even Haida war canoes. To the Tlingit in the early 1830s a slave was worth two sea otter or 25 beaver skins (Wrangell 1980:32). Shipmasters were not long in taking advantage of this additional medium of exchange for furs (by 1800 at least), buying slaves at the mouth of the Columbia and in the Strait of Juan de Fuca and selling them on the northern coast. Occasionally they also traded Hawaiian women as slaves.

Slaves were often employed as concubines and prostitutes and offered to the Euro-American traders (Jackman 1978:60). In 1817 an English trader found that Trinidad Bay, California, was the "only place on the coast where we could not induce the females to visit the ship" (Corney 1965:165). During the middle 1820s at Sitka Tlingit concubines (mostly slaves) even tended to impoverish their Russian keepers (whose gifts went to the native owners of the concubines) (Khlebnikov 1976:71).

Such sexual intercourse had two results: the diffusion of venereal disease and the appearance of mixed-blood offspring. This group of mixed bloods would have been more numerous and might have persisted had it not been for infanticide. A missionary reported in 1829 that the offspring of White traders and unmarried native girls were often killed at birth (Green 1915:45, 51). The Haida chief Cow told the missionary that "all the young women of the tribe visit ships for the purpose of gain by prostitution, and in most cases destroy their children, the fruit of this infamous intercourse" (Green 1915:68). By contrast, Alaska Creoles—the mostly illegitimate offspring of Russian fathers and Aleut and Koniag Eskimo mothers—multiplied rapidly. By 1843 Creoles outnumbered Russians in the colony by two to one (Golovnin 1965:table A; Rossiĭsko-Amerikanskaia Kompaniia 1843:30). They helped to offset the shortage of Russian manpower.

As sea otters diminished, the Indians offered other products for Euro-American goods: provisions, timber, concubines, and even curios (fig. 8). In 1829 "more or less boards" were sawn on the coast and sold in Hawaii by trading vessels (Green 1915:76). Tongass Harbor on Revillagigedo Channel (the most popular wintering place) was reputed in the middle 1830s "to be the best on this

Fig. 8. Carved figure of a ship's officer in argillite with an ivory face. Haida carvers often took aspects of European culture as their subject matter. Frequent visits by fur traders supported a considerable curio market, and by at least the 1840s, figures, platters, and pipes were plentiful. No date of collection has been preserved, but it is datable by stylistic features to the 1840s; height 40 cm.

part of the coast whence to obtain spars, and other wood, for shipping" (J. Dunn 1844:286). The Tlingit sold halibut, potatoes, and venison in large amounts to the Russians and even took jobs at Sitka (fig. 7) (J.R. Gibson 1978). But it was the Haida who seem to have adjusted the most. In 1829 they were "fierce for trade" and offering potatoes (an introduced crop), reed hats, argillite pipes, fish, fowl, eggs, and berries, besides furs (Green 1915:86). Such provisionment undoubtedly increased the food-procuring activities of the natives.

Impact of Trade

Northwest Coast voyages, which enjoyed more popularity and more prestige among New England seamen than any other, undoubtedly because they were more profitable, created many well-to-do Boston families (Morison 1961: 76–77). Certainly the multiplier effect on New England's economy must have been appreciable.

It is easier to assess the impact of the maritime fur trade on the Indians. For the natives the coast trade was neither just destructive nor just constructive but both. It was positive in that the new materials and the new ideas were adapted by the Indians to suit their own needs, and they stimulated the development of their culture. Generally Euro-American goods supplemented, not supplanted, Indian products, and they served to further, not initiate, changes. Thus, trinkets did not replace dentalia as

valuables or ornaments; blankets did not replace cedar bark or even fur robes; muskets and pistols did not replace lances, bows and arrows, and knives; sails and rudders did not replace paddles in canoes; fishing line did not replace harpoons, nets, or weirs; farming did not replace fishing or hunting; bread, rice, and potatoes did not replace smoked salmon, dried herring roe, pounded hemlock cambium, venison, and berries; Chinook Jargon or English did not replace native languages; metal tools did not replace stone or bone implements; and so on. Yet all these innovations were accepted and put to good use. And customs that repelled Euro-American traders—labret wearing, head flattening, corpse carrying, lice picking, hair greasing, body tattooing, funeral sacrificing—were not discontinued, although they became somewhat less common. In other words, the maritime fur trade did not revolutionize coastal Indian society. After all, the Northwest Coast Indians were decidedly mercantile and commercial before White contact, and the maritime fur trade came to them, not vice versa, and they accepted it readily on their own terms (Wike 1951:92–107).

If the coast trade did not bring revolution, it certainly brought material prosperity. The sale of furs brought more income, and Euro-American technological innovations increased Indian output. Woodworking was enhanced, for example (Wike 1951:75–79). More wealth meant more ceremonies, which required more artistic products like totem poles, masks, rattles, and robes, which were also in demand by White traders as curios (Duff 1964:57, 59).

The increased demand for furs meant more hunting and trading between the coastal and interior tribes, with attendant cultural influences. For example, the Sekani began to discard their bilateral descent system in favor of exogamous matrilineal phratries accompanied by crests and potlatches; the Babine Lake Carrier adopted phratry and crest systems, as well as the potlatch and labret; and the Athapaskans around Atlin and Teslin Lakes were so acculturated that they came to be considered Tlingits (Duff 1964:58; Harris and Ingram 1972:184–185). The increased traffic may have promoted more alliances, too, as between the Nootkans and the Kwakiutl, as one group sought to benefit commercially from another (Wike 1951: 99–100). It undoubtedly generated more potlatching, for the greater wealth made possible more frequent and more lavish giveaways. In 1803, for instance, Chief Maquinna dispensed 100 muskets, 400 yards of cloth, 100 looking glasses, and 20 kegs of gunpowder at a single potlatch (Jewitt 1815:39–40).

At first the increased potlatching strengthened the position of chiefs like the Nootkans Maquinna of Nootka Sound and Wickaninnish of Clayoquot Sound, Tatoosh of the Makah, Concomly of the Lower Columbia Chinookans, Kotlean of the Sitka Tlingits, and Cow of the Kaigani Haidas. Because they controlled hunting and trading, they grew richer and stronger. Eventually, however, their position was debased by a proliferation of chiefs, since wealth could be acquired not only by hereditary clan chiefs but also by skillful individual hunters. The higher death rate resulting from gunfire, disease, and alcoholism likewise meant that more positions of rank became available.

There was unquestionably a negative impact as well. The health of the Indians, Koniag Eskimo, and Aleut was impaired by alcohol and tobacco, and their numbers were reduced by epidemics and firearms. Because their hunting skill was so necessary to the Russian prosecution of the maritime fur trade, the Aleut were severely exploited. At first sea otter skins were exacted from them as tribute, and hostages were taken to ensure payment. After 1794 this practice was replaced by compulsory labor, with the Aleuts becoming, in effect, serfs who were paid in food, clothing, and tobacco. They were separated from their families, moved to new hunting grounds, forced to work hard, and exposed to cold, hunger, accidents, diseases, and Indian enemies. By 1790, after a half-century of Russian contact, the Aleut population may have decreased by as much as two-thirds (Sarychev 1952:211). This toll prompted the Russians to use more Eskimos, whose ability with kayak and harpoon was second only to that of the Aleut (Davydov 1977:194–195). Such exploitation led to a decline in Kodiak Island's native population from 5,700 in 1792 to 1,500 in 1834 (Khlebnikov 1979:24; Veniaminov 1840, 1:vi).

The Indian population of the Northwest Coast fell drastically from about 125,000 in 1780 to less than 100,000 in 1825 (vol. 7). Natives learned to consume brandy, wine, and beer, coffee and tea, sweets, and bread, which were detrimental to their diet. Alcohol promoted sexual promiscuity, which in turn spread syphilis. Guns made Indian warfare more deadly. Mainly for these reasons the Indian population of Nootka Sound fell from perhaps as many as 3,000 to 4,000 in 1788 to 1,500 in 1804 (Jewitt 1815:115, 142; Meares 1790:229). When the natives began to cluster around trading posts for commercial favors or protection or out of curiosity, they exposed themselves to epidemics. The most virulent of several diseases was smallpox, which arrived with the first Euro-Americans on either the *Santiago* in 1774 or the *Favorita* and *Princesa* in 1779. A Kaigani chief said in 1795 that two-thirds of the local Haidas had succumbed to the disease (M. Roe 1967:83; Green 1915:39). There is evidence of smallpox having struck Chinookans in 1776 or 1778 and in 1801 or 1802 (Thwaites 1904–1905, 4:50–51, 241). In the late 1830s smallpox killed one-third of the Indians north of Fort Simpson (J. McLoughlin 1941–1944, 1:271). This demographic disaster broke the back of northern Indian resistance to Euro-American encroachment, both territorial and cultural (R. Fisher 1977:21–23, 44–45 to the contrary; J.R. Gibson 1982–1983).

The coast trade also promoted slavery, increasing the number, distribution, and exploitation of slaves (Averkieva 1971:331). The increased slave raiding in turn helped to depopulate peripheral areas such as the lower Fraser Valley and the Puget Sound lowland (Wike 1951:99).

The impact of the Northwest Coast trade would have been worse if there had been more posts. As it was, the White maritime fur traders were mostly seasonal visitors, not permanent residents, and the cultures of the Indian and Eskimo tribes continued to develop during its operation.

Economic Relations in the Southeast Until 1783

DANIEL H. USNER, JR.

Economic relations with European colonies affected Southeast Indians in many ways. Inside the hundreds of Indian villages that dotted the region from the Chesapeake Bay to the Texas Big Thicket, important continuities as well as changes occurred in the way people produced and distributed food, clothing, and other material goods. During the formative years of colonization, coastal Indian communities contributed much-needed food and information in Florida, Virginia, Carolina, and Louisiana. Less familiar than this early contribution is the fact that many Indians who survived colonial wars in the seventeenth and early eighteenth centuries—remnants of defeated tribes—continued to provide goods, services, and labor to colonial settlements. Many Indian villages participated to varying degrees in even wider networks of long-distance exchange. European commerce perhaps had its most profound influence through this nexus of economic life, well known to historians as the fur trade, since it transmitted deadly microbes, drew native products, and introduced foreign manufactures across aboriginal and newly formed trade systems.

Although frequently used, words like "dependency" or "decline" seem inadequate for characterizing the nature of economic change wrought among Indians by relations with the colonial populations. Economic relations with European colonies certainly imposed hardships and problems upon Indian livelihood and deeply altered society and politics throughout Indian communities. But countervailing forces inherent in American Indian cultures, as well as those devised by them on the spot, helped preserve some fundamental values and basic patterns that proved essential for their survival over the colonial era. Village economies rested upon an age-old mixture of hunting-gathering, farming, and trading activities. And while exposure to peoples and products from Europe and Africa affected the relative importance of these activities, the cyclical pattern of procuring seasonally diverse resources was maintained by most Indian communities in the Southeast. The principle of reciprocity, by which the exchange of material goods was subsumed within social and political relations, guided Indian nations in their formal trade with the colonies. Insistence by tribal leaders that prices be fixed, commerce regulated, and gifts granted often coincided with the needs of colonial governments and thereby buffered Indian societies from the commercial revolution being spearheaded in the Southeast by the fur trade. And while in many ways those communities living nearest colonial settlements appeared to be the most debilitated Indian groups, their unique set of economic activities—petty marketing, working for wages, and even begging—allowed them to adjust without completely losing their social autonomy.

By the middle of the eighteenth century, economic relations between Southeast Indians and colonists centered around an extensive trade in deerskins. Charleston and New Orleans each exported more than 100,000 pounds of skins annually during the late 1750s, in the midst of the global war raging between France and England, while Savannah, Saint Augustine, and Pensacola were shipping additional volumes (Crane 1981:330; Surrey 1916:204–211). From localized exchange around colonial outposts, the fur trade had evolved into competing networks of commerce that penetrated far into the interior of the Southeast (fig. 1). While Great Britain, Spain, and France vied for essential alliances with Indian nations on the grand scale of diplomacy, colonial governments tried to regulate what Indian Superintendent for the Southern Colonies Edmond Atkin called "a very considerable Branch of Commerce" inside the respective trade zones (Jacobs 1967:6). The Indian nations, meanwhile, exerted their own customs and exigencies upon the deerskin trade.

Forms of participation in the deerskin trade networks changed through time and varied among both the Indian and colonial populaces. Some tribes struggled to maintain middlemen positions between European traders and Indian producers, often at the risk of going to war. Others expanded their own hunting activities in order to produce more deerskins for the commercial trade. They relied upon very formal channels of diplomacy in order to contain economic exchange within a political alliance. Still other Indian groups chose to market additional or alternative kinds of products, such as foodstuffs and livestock, on a less formal basis. Inside colonial society import-export merchants accumulated wealth from the deerskin trade and clashed frequently with other interest groups, like planters or backcountry settlers. Traders dealt most personally with Indian villagers, extending a line of credit that originated in European cities and reached Indian hunting camps in the Southeast.

Formation of Trade Networks

The deerskin trade first penetrated the southeastern interior during the 1640s, when Virginians established Fort Henry at the Appamattox River falls. John Lederer, William Byrd, and others subsequently expanded commerce down the piedmont, and by the 1670s Tutelos, Saponis, and Monacans were bringing their furs to the rendezvous at Occaneechee Island. While these tribes tried to secure a middleman position between the traders from James River and other Indians to the south and west, Englishmen like James Needham and Gabriel Arthur

sought direct contact with the populous Cherokees in the Appalachian mountains (Robinson 1979:55–60). In large part, the conflict known as Bacon's Rebellion that erupted in Virginia in 1675 was a revolt by frontier colonists against Gov. William Berkeley's efforts to regulate this expansion of Indian trade (Washburn 1957:27–28, 161–162).

From their foothold in Florida, meanwhile, the Spaniards extended their own trade with Southeast Indians into the interior. Deerskins had probably accompanied other items, such as sassafras, ambergris, and goods salvaged from wrecked ships, traded by coastal Florida Indians with Europeans since the sixteenth century. But beginning in the 1640s Florida governors encouraged a large-scale deerskin commerce with the Lower Creeks. The mission Indians of San Marcos de Apalache, who

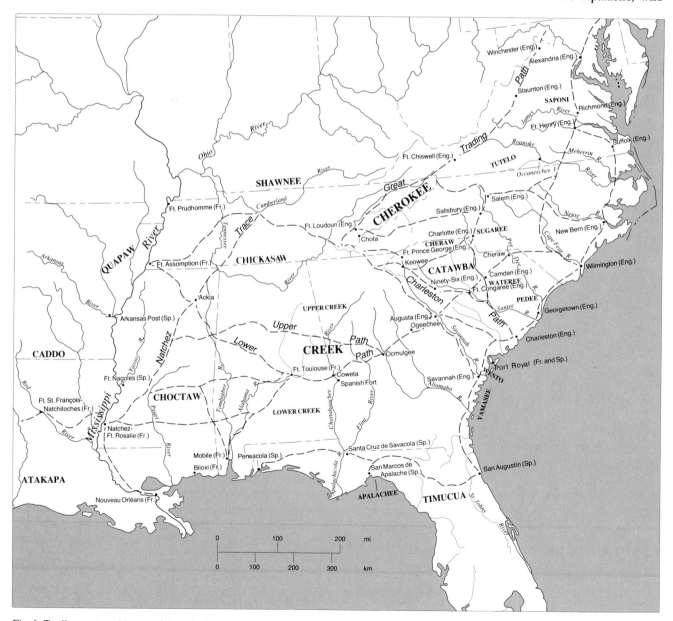

392   Fig. 1. Trading posts and routes of the colonial Southeast (J.T. Adams 1943; P.C. Phillips 1961; Cappon 1976; Garrett 1983).

already supplied corn, beans, wheat, and beef to Saint Augustine and coastal traders, were employed as packhorsemen and interpreters for Spanish officers seeking deerskins up the Apalachicola valley (Bushnell 1986).

By the end of the seventeenth century, South Carolina surpassed both Virginia and Florida in the expansion of the peltry trade across the Southeast. Founded in 1670, Charleston rapidly became the major entrepôt for the exportation of both deerskins and Indian slaves from the region. In 1674 the English formed an alliance with the powerful Westos, who had already acquired some firearms from the Virginia deerskin trade and now raided neighboring Indian groups for captives to sell to Charleston merchants. When the Westos begrudged the efforts of English traders to bypass them and deal directly with other Indians, Carolina waged a war against them in 1680. Those Westos who escaped death and slavery dispersed, while the Shawnees who aided the British became the new masters of trade on the Savannah River. Disgruntled refugees from the missions in Spanish Florida, who became known as the Yamasees, settled behind Port Royal and joined the Shawnees in gathering deerskins and capturing slaves for commerce with the English. The Sugarees, Cheraws, and other Indian groups in the Wateree and Pedee valleys, meanwhile, were also being drawn into the Carolina trade sphere (Crane 1981:3–28).

The Charleston-based trade reached the Lower Creek towns in 1685 when Henry Woodward led a packtrain to Coweta on the Chatahoochee River. English traders successfully diverted a growing volume of deerskins from the Spaniards' Apalachee-based trade and used the alliance with the Creeks to expand trading and raiding to the Mississippi River. The Spaniards responded with military forays up the Apalachicola valley and with trade restrictions on arms and horses that might reach English allies. An important turning point was reached in 1701, when failure to acquire horses from the Apalachees led the Creeks to attack. The subsequent series of English and Indian raids against the Florida Indian missions, during Queen Anne's War, guaranteed British dominance of the deerskin trade for a long time to come (Crane 1981: 71–88).

Trade conditions inside the expanding Carolina system, nevertheless, fomented deep resentment among Indian trading partners. Mounting indebtedness and encroachment on hunting territory drove the Yamasees to a violent revolt in 1715 (Haan 1981). Indians from other tribes joined the Yamasees in ousting English traders and attacking English settlements, sending a wave of terror along the Carolina seaboard. With assistance from Catawba and Cherokee allies especially, the British reversed the rebels' advances, dispersed the Yamasees, and enslaved many survivors of the rebellious groups. This war sparked important reforms in Carolina trade policy and produced a stronger defense system on the colonial frontier (Crane 1981:162–186).

Beginning in 1699 the French developed a separate deerskin trade network in Louisiana under the direction of men like Jean-Baptiste Le Moyne, Sieur de Bienville, and Henri de Tonti. As in the other southern colonies, small-scale exchange with Indians around the military posts and nascent settlements grew into a specialized commerce in peltry that reached many Indian villages in the interior. Caddos on the Red River, Quapaws on the Arkansas, and smaller tribes in the lower Mississippi Valley all produced deerskins for exportation through New Orleans, but the Choctaws living in the piney hill country up the Tombigbee and Pearl rivers were the most prized trade partner in this French-Indian alliance system (Usner 1985). After the Yamasee War English traders managed to strengthen their ties with the Chickasaws, who lived in the midst of French-allied Indians and posed a constant threat to Louisiana's security in the Mississippi valley. Many Choctaws and Upper Creeks also took advantage of English trade opportunities. A split within the Choctaw nation between pro-French and pro-English factions broke into a bloody civil war in 1746, but Louisiana managed to hold onto its access to deerskins and even food supplies produced by the populous Choctaw Indians (Galloway 1982; R. White 1983:54–68).

Economic Change at the Village Level

Choctaw economic life at the village level illustrates how the seasonal cycle of economic activities characteristic of Southeast Indians was affected by trade with Europeans. By the second quarter of the eighteenth century, the Choctaw population was reduced to approximately 13,000 people, half its precolonial size. Each of the 50 or so villages averaged just over 250 inhabitants. The Choctaws continued to plant their crops on select bottomlands along the streams or bayous that bordered their villages. Whereas the hills and bluffs of Choctaw country were covered by a mixed pine and oak forest, the lowlands supported a cypress and oak forest with thick patches of cane. The villagers cleared the cane-breaks by cutting and burning, preparing productive fields without much labor and without animal fertilizers. Seeds of corn were sown directly into the nutritive ashes of burnt wood and cane. This system of agriculture required that lowland fields be left fallow after several harvest seasons for new vegetation to grow (Usner 1981:163–166; R. White 1983:19–26).

Groups of entire families planted and harvested these large fields, but in smaller household gardens Choctaw women grew beans, small corn, tobacco, and an array of vegetables introduced by Europeans and Africans. After these gardens were sown and as soon as bayou waters receded, usually by the beginning of May, the Choctaws planted their staple corn, pumpkins, and melons on the village bottomlands. From then until the harvest in 393

August, the women generally weeded and tended to all the crops, misleading some passing observers to believe that Indian men did not till the soil. Men and women in most Southeast tribes actually worked the fields together at planting and harvest time much as Europeans, the essential difference being that the fields in Choctaw, Chickasaw, and other Indian villages belonged to female lineages. When in May 1732 a French officer requested military assistance from the Choctaw town of Boucfouca, on the Pearl River, the men "begged me please to ask for people from the neighboring villages, since they could not furnish me all I needed on account of their planting" (Rowland and Sanders 1927–1984, 1:146). At every spring planting the men "help their wives in the labour of the fields" (Romans 1775:58).

As among the other large interior tribes of the Southeast—the Cherokees, Creeks, and Chickasaws—hunting, gathering, and fishing occurred around Choctaw villages with minimal impediment from the colonial populace. However, the peltry trade did alter economic life by encouraging the Choctaws to spend more time during the winter months hunting for game away from their villages. Small camps of 10 or so families traveled along rivers and bayous to hunt deer and bear in large quantities. In January 1772 a British cartographer spotted along the Tombigbee River "a hunting camp of Choctaws . . . who invited us on shore, treated us very kindly, and spared us some venison, bear's meat and oil." He observed that whenever members of the camp killed a deer or bear, they divided the liver up and sent a piece to each fire in the camp, whereupon the men of the family burned it. This is one indication that the commercial market had not extinguished all traditional hunting rituals. Excluded from this ceremony but certainly active in these camps, the women stayed near the palmetto huts in order to prepare the meat, skins, and oil for their own use and for sale to colonists (Romans 1775:56, 215).

From their villages and winter camps, Choctaw hunters employed various methods of procuring meat and skins. On hunting expeditions they burned away the undergrowth in small patches of forest. These controlled fires both enhanced the nutritional quality of the plants that deer browsed on and eased passage for the animals through the woods. Southeast Indians generally also set fires to prairies to drive deer and smaller mammals into hunting range. In another popular method of hunting, the men carried deer heads to decoy the animals and then shot them at close range. Black bears hibernating along thickly vegetated waterways in mid-winter were smoked out of hollow trees and shot as they emerged. Choctaws still used traps and blow-guns to catch raccoons, opossums, and other small game, while fish were taken with wooden and bone hooks, spears and weirs, and poisonous herbs. But the musket became their principal means of shooting the white-tailed deer for commercial trade (Le Page du Pratz

1774:134, 256; Romans 1775:44).

The material culture of the Choctaws was undoubtedly affected by the trade goods acquired through their exchange of deerskins. By 1750 merchandise needed annually for the Choctaw trade included approximately 5,000 meters of woolen cloth (called Limbourg), 1,700 blankets, 2,500 trade shirts, 150 muskets, 4,000 pounds of gunpowder, 300 pieces of scarlet ribbon, and 30 gross of woodcutter knives (Usner 1981:134). Metalware and textiles were adopted into the household economy, but Indians changed their cooking methods and clothing styles very selectively during the eighteenth century. The most disruptive product received through the deerskin trade was alcohol: brandy from the French and rum from the English. Liquor adversely affected the health and well-being of many Choctaw families. It greased the wheels of commerce by inducing Indian hunters to expand their accumulation of peltry for the European trade (R. White 1983:84–86).

The Choctaws produced things other than deerskins for trade with the colonial populace. Men sold their labor as guides, packhorsemen, and rowers to officials and traders. New and old food plants, poultry, and hogs were all brought by Choctaw peddlers to settlers and soldiers and even to townspeople in Mobile. The production of Old World foods altered the landscape of village life, changing the mixture of garden crops and requiring vigilance over livestock, but the most dramatic innovation came from Choctaws who raised horses. Many Southeast Indians participated in the movement of horses from west to east during the eighteenth century, and some groups became skillful breeders and traders of horses. The Choctaw pony was a highly prized commodity among colonists and other Indians (Adair 1775:340, 457–458).

Changes After 1763

During the second quarter of the eighteenth century, these and other changes were introduced to a growing number of Indian villages as the deerskin trade expanded more widely across the Southeast. Following the Yamasee War, the Cherokees steadily became South Carolina's single most important trade partner. Eleazer Wiggan was the first trader to set up a trading post in Cherokee country, and by the 1720s Fort Congaree was a way-station for packtrains moving seasonally between Charleston and the Cherokee towns. While the Cherokees contributed more and more deerskins to Carolina's commerce, perhaps as many as 25,000 pelts by mid-century, traders from the new colony of Georgia assumed a dominant position in the Creek villages to the south (Goodwin 1977:88–99; Spalding 1977:90–95; Corkran 1967:82–102).

Competition among the English colonies for Indian trade fueled the development of the deerskin commerce across much of the Southeast. Rivalry between the British and French empires was responsible for chronic tension in a zone of overlap between colonial regions, which Choctaws and Upper Creeks effectively used to their advantage by trading with both sides and bargaining for better exchange rates. The Seven Years' War intensified conflict between European trade spheres in the Southeast but involved much less military confrontation there than in the Northeast. Cherokee grievances against the English made them receptive to French overtures and drove them into very costly warfare in 1759 (Alden 1944; Corkran 1962).

The most significant changes in Indian-European economic relations occurred over the decades after the Treaty of Paris was signed in 1763. Great Britain took possession of Florida, while Spain acquired Louisiana from France. This new geopolitical arrangement gave the English greater control over the flow of deerskins from Indian villages in the southeastern interior. The Creeks and Choctaws found themselves encircled by British colonists for the first time. English traders could reach their villages from the Gulf Coast towns of Pensacola and Mobile in West Florida. At treaty councils held in the spring of 1765, Indian leaders like Tomatly Mingo of the Choctaw expressed hope that the English would pick up where the French left off, "Supplying my Wants by proper Presents and also by furnishing a plentyfull Trade." However, many spokesmen voiced complaints against new abuses already being committed by English traders: trading excessive amounts of alcohol, cheating and robbing, and committing physical violence (Rowland 1911, 1:211–255; Corkran 1967:229–272).

Great Britain's efforts to regulate Indian trade and prevent these kinds of troubles were largely futile during the 1760s and 1770s, and the American Revolution suddenly upset any order that might have been achieved. The Cherokees' trade suffered most during the war, especially when Continental soldiers and militiamen invaded their villages in 1776. The other large tribes in the Southeast—Creeks, Choctaws, and Chickasaws—fared better by avoiding any firm allegiance with Great Britain or the rebellious colonies. They demanded that trade avenues remain open, playing a shrewd diplomatic game between the two sides (O'Donnell 1973).

Overall the southeastern deerskin trade continued to flourish into the 1780s, Charleston, Savannah, Pensacola, and New Orleans exporting large volumes of peltry to Europe. Tanneries there processed the better quality skins into gloves and other soft leather goods. Other skins were dehaired and limed, then stretched at ordinary temperatures until they became sheets of parchment, from which bookbindings were made.

As their political leverage weakened during this period, especially after the United States became a sovereign power, Indians became increasingly vulnerable to aggressive trade practices and unfair exchange conditions. Liquor flowed into their villages in larger quantities. Traders moved through Indian country more freely, many even hunting and farming for themselves. Spain retrieved the Floridas after the American Revolution and allowed British merchants to operate the Indian trade. One firm in particular, Panton, Leslie & Company, began to expand monopoly power over the large interior tribes. The deerskin trade became highly commercialized, and Indian hunters fell into deeper indebtedness as time went on. Beginning in the 1790s, the United States government entered this commerce with its own trade factories and used the increasing dependency of Southeast Indians to acquire their land (Coker and Watson 1986).

Trade Goods

E.S. LOHSE

The distribution of goods, as political gifts or as items of exchange, was one of the most important carriers of European civilization to the Indian tribes of North America. Trade goods, in finished or raw form, milled and machined or made by hand, served to quickly and irrevocably unite the Indian to the European. From earliest contact, America's aboriginal inhabitants were hungry for all kinds of exotic manufactures and materials. Once channels for trade were opened, Indians obtained all sorts of useful and fascinating metal tools, clothing, and decorative items that earned prestige. The drive for these goods prompted acceptance of the foreigners, albeit grudging in many instances, and created ties of association traces of which remained in the 1980s.

The Allure of Industrial Age Technology

All across North America, Indian groups wanted articles of European manufacture or raw materials transported by White traders to meet native demands. The acquisition of these articles intensified purely aboriginal economic systems as on the Northwest Coast, or greatly elaborated costume and personal adornment as on the Plains, or were used pragmatically by colonial powers and their Indian allies to direct favorable economic relationships and political alliances as in the Great Lakes area.

Trade goods were powerful incentives to the closer bonding of Indian and White political, economic, and social systems. White and Indian alike used European products to direct actions to political ends, to establish favorable trading relationships, and to cement social intercourse. Guns traded to the Algonquians by the French or to Iroquoians by the Dutch and British were to foster military advantages for the protection and expansion of territories and markets of both White and Indian. The motives for both cultures were parallel; trade goods maintained effective partnerships based on mutual advantage. The ultimate supremacy of one side over the other hinged on control of supplies wanted by the other. Acceptance of European goods by the Indian had a practical economic basis in many instances, since metal tools of European design often outperformed traditional tools produced by the nonindustrial Indian societies. Sharp-edged steel axes and knives were more efficient than stone axes and knives, and metal kettles and pots and pans were far more durable and transportable than native creations in clay and vegetal materials. Scissors and files were marvelous innovations that speedily showed advantage in processing hides, making clothes, creating tools in soft stone, or in the manufacture and repair of the new metal tools. These kinds of trade items simply had no effective counterparts in traditional Indian material culture and were quickly adopted by aboriginal populations as vast improvements over traditional tools. Other trade goods, as a class, usually decorative, allowed greater artistic elaboration of traditional Indian designs. Beads, tin cones, bells, ribbons, and other gewgaws of the Indian trade were used to enhance aboriginal fashion and to establish prestige through already accepted channels of display and ostentatious consumption of exotic or expensive items.

Goods Adopted by Indians

Firearms were desired by Indians from the first contact with Europeans. With its machined steel barrel, brass and iron finishes, and heavily varnished, carved wood stock, the gun was physically attractive and was first prized for notions of magical attributes. Only later was it held to be a superior weapon. At first, only powerful individuals could obtain a gun. Later, although guns could be had by anyone for a price, they still demonstrated the wealth of the owner. Of course, the gun held no real initial advantage over the bow and arrow. The bow and arrow was more efficient than the matchlocks and smoothbore muskets that the Indian first acquired, was at least as accurate, if not more so, at long distances, and most important, materials for its manufacture were always close at hand. It was not until the advent of the lever action repeaters of the late nineteenth century that any claim could reasonably be made for the technical superiority of the gun. Bernardo De Gálvez, governor of New Spain, stated in 1786 that since it was impossible to defeat the Indians as long as they continued to use the bow, every effort should be made to arm the Indians with guns and thereby reduce the conflict to more manageable terms (Gálvez 1951:47–49).

Complete descriptions of the various kinds of trade goods and their impact or lack of impact on traditional

Indian lifeways would fill volumes. Good surveys detailing the range of materials traded to the American Indian include Russell (1957, 1967), A. Woodward (1970), Wheeler et al. (1975), and Gilman (1982). An exceptional publication series on many aspects of the fur trade is the *Museum of the Fur Trade Quarterly*, published in Chadron, Nebraska. This essay attempts only to characterize broadly the role that trade goods played in the Indian's life. Discussion will focus on specific, illustrated items of Indian material culture.

Traditional skin clothing underwent profound modifications with the adoption of articles of White manufacture. Whole articles of clothing were, of course, obtained by the American Indian as replacements for his hide and woven garments. Cloth shirts, pants, and jackets were prestige items at first contact, obtainable only for the wealthy and powerful. They were also more comfortable and adaptable than the stiff hide garments of native manufacture. Most commonly, the Indian consumer had access to smaller, less expensive items of personal adornment. Beads, paints, dyes, tin bangles, and other odds and ends of the trader's stock allowed great elaboration of traditional native patterns of design and decoration. In the earliest periods, large glass beads were strung only in necklaces or as earrings since they were costly and their size and irregular shape did not allow for replication of traditional appliqué and overlay work found in aboriginal quillwork and hair embroidery. Later, with the introduction of small, regularly shaped glass beads, which could be sewn down in tight, uniform decorative surfaces, work in quills and embroidery diminished. The modification of aboriginal dress pattern did not consist entirely of enhanced ornamentation, as European cloth garment designs were quickly copied by Indian clothiers. Hide was adapted to cloth designs, particularly the great coat or officer's uniform coat with its tapered waist, flared skirt, and exaggerated cuffs and collar.

The hide coat shown in figure 1 is characteristic of those modeled on European cloth garments. These were particular favorites of the Ojibwa, Cree, Red River Métis, and others in the Great Lakes region but were found all over the North American continent as Indian-White contacts expanded. This coat has woven quillwork epaulets, quillwork medallions, quilled embroidery in floral patterns, and quill-wrapped and beaded fringes. The design and layout of these quilled decorations, as well as the fringed sleeves and simple straight cut of the shoulder, have obvious parallels in the traditional Plains man's hide shirt (fig. 1). Placement of the beaded decoration on the chest, shoulders, and arms of the shirt is comparable to that on the coat. And the taper of the traditional hide shirt, following the natural shape of the skins, is echoed in the flared skirt of the coat.

Indian clothiers created garments that looked like European clothes, but they did not necessarily change their traditional methods of manufacture. Proportions changed, and distinctive nonfunctional design elements like cuffs and collars were added, but sinew was used for sewing the skins and the native seamstress used tailoring that had its origin in the manufacture of hide clothes. Indians were not producing crude copies of European clothes; rather, aboriginal clothiers brought expertise in the working of hides to the application of European style.

Women's clothing, like the men's, shows selective incorporation of European articles in both design and decoration. Finished dresses, like shirts and pants for the men, might be available at the larger trading posts, but costs were prohibitive. Usually, only the wives and daughters of traders had ready-made dresses, and even for them, it was far more common that they or their servants made them from cloth bought at the post. Indian women away from the trading post got stroud and other cloth in trade and fashioned these into dresses based on native patterns.

Figure 2 shows two dresses made in traditional style. On the hide dress, with beaded yoke, pendants of tubular glass beads hung with Chinese coins take the place of deer hooves or elk teeth. These coins were popular trade items particularly on the Northwest Coast, where natives used them on clothing and elkhide armor. These coins may have been traded inland from the coast through native contacts, or they may have been carried in trading post stock. Quite often, particularly in the late nineteenth century, traders carried a wide range of exotic items ranging from those that were long a focus of aboriginal trade like dentalia, abalone, and cowrie shells, to surplus U.S. Army buttons, sleigh bells, satin ribbons, civilian buttons, old uniforms and clothing, bits and pieces of chain, or rolls of copper wire.

The blue and red stroud dress (fig. 2) was cut and sewn on the traditional hide pattern. The pendant flaps at the sides of the hem are imitations of the legs of the animal skin. The yoke is laced with elk teeth perforated for suspension from hide thongs. In this example, non-Indian manufactured material is used in a traditional Indian design, just the reverse of the hide coat in figure 1, where European tailoring was applied to native materials.

The key point is that the Indian, although intemperate in his borrowing and application of European trade goods, was actually quite conservative in retaining traditional designs and modes of decoration. Cloth for dresses was cut and sewn in traditional fashions that derived from the use of animal skins. Foreign materials like the Chinese coins were simply inserted into traditional design patterns. White material culture was adopted, but it did not necessarily convey any basic cultural-societal changes on the part of the Indian consumer, only an appreciation of the different, the exotic, the useful.

Cradles, a major form of artistic expression, also represent as well as any artifact the admixture of Indian

left, Minn. Histl. Soc., St. Paul: 8303.2; Smithsonian, Dept. of Anthr. 175754.

Fig. 1. Men's clothing. left, Front and back views of an Indian-made hide coat of the mid-1800s that was modeled on European cloth coats sold by traders. This example, probably Red River Métis, was owned by Alexander Ramsey. right, Front and back views of a scalp shirt of the Minneconjou Sioux chief and 1890 Ghost Dance organizer Kicking Bear. Collected by James Mooney at the Cheyenne River Agency, Dak. Terr., 1869. Length of left 112 cm, right to same scale.

and White cultures. The Cheyenne cradle in figure 3 is lined with trade cloth and completely covered with glass seed beads in geometric patterns. Attached to the thongs at the head end are large blue glass trade beads, dentalium shells, cowrie shells, and brass bells. The bells sounded at each movement of the horse when the cradle was slung at the mother's side and attracted the attention of the child when the cradle was propped against a tepee or tree. Cradles of aboriginal design used stone, bone, wood, or seed beads instead of the glass trade beads, dentalium and cowrie shells supplied through aboriginal trade, and deer hooves or bird bills as jinglers. The back boards of the cradle are machined lumber that was cut, shaped, and

assembled by the maker of the cradle.

Figure 4 depicts a trade gun, gun accessories, and items whose native manufacture depended on adaptation of the gun complex. Adoption of the gun forced a number of unforeseen changes in aboriginal lifeways. First, ownership of the gun brought a heavier dependence upon White-controlled lines of supply, because a gun required gunpowder and balls of lead as well as a wide range of materials, tools, and skills difficult to find in the wilderness that was still the Indian's home. Over the course of time, Indian groups did develop their own blacksmiths and gunsmiths. Still, repairs were often distinctly Indian, perhaps a broken gunstock wrapped in

Smithsonian, Dept. of Anthr.: left, T-14884; right, 76240.
Fig. 2. Trade goods in women's clothing. left, Traditional skin dress with heavily beaded yoke fringed by Chinese coins on beaded hide pendants (top center shows detail). Style indicates a Northern Plains origin, while use of large glass seed beads suggests a pre-1870 date for manufacture (collection data unavailable). right, Stroud dress cut on traditional lines, with elk teeth laced on the yoke (bottom center shows detail). Bought from Rosa White Thunder, Brulé Sioux, by Capt. R.H. Pratt, superintendent of the Carlisle Indian Industrial School, Pa., which she attended, 1884. Length of left 129 cm; other to same scale.

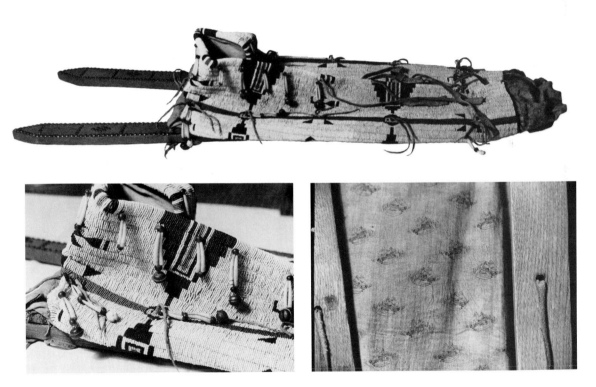

Smithsonian, Dept. of Anthr.: 394635.
Fig. 3. Cheyenne cradle. The leather case is completely beaded and sports brass bells, cowries, dentalia, and large trade beads strung on hide pendants (bottom left). The back is lined with trade cloth printed with horse heads (bottom right). Collected in Mont., about 1900; length 100.3 cm.

rawhide or bullet molds carved in soft stone and set in carved wooden grips. Indians of the Carolinas in 1709 commonly straightened musket barrels by bending them in a notch cut in a tree (J. Lawson 1966:27, 172). The essential element that could not be substituted for—and which tied the native consumer to the White trader—was powder. A more insidious factor that accelerated Indian dependence on the gun, at the expense of the bow and arrow, was the havoc that guns and their noisy discharges wreaked on wildlife. Hunting patterns changed as noisier weapons made the game more difficult to approach. Where once the bow and arrow was remarkably efficient in the close stalking employed by Indian hunters, the later necessity for accurate long-distance shooting gave the edge to the gun.

The musket shown in figure 4e, with flintlock and characteristic dragon sideplate, is typical of the kind of arm traded to the Indian by the North West and Hudson's Bay companies in the late eighteenth and most of the nineteenth centuries. Short, lightweight, of moderately large caliber, and functionally designed for rough use and standardized for easy repair, the smoothbore trade musket was admirably suited for use in a wide range of environments and climates. So successful was this design, often called the Northwest trade gun, that the Indian consumer refused to accept guns without certain trademarks. For instance, Indians dealing with John Long near Lake Abitibi, Ontario, in 1778, carefully scrutinized a case of guns before consenting to trade (Thwaites 1904, 2:145). This strong preference on the part of the Indian led American trading companies and the federal Office of Indian Trade to order muskets from American, English, and Belgian makers that copied in every detail the English trade musket. Some manufacturers copied marks so closely that the maker's name was used with a letter left

out or substituted (Hanson 1955:27). Ramsey Crooks, president of the American Fur Company, wrote James Henry of the Boulton Gunworks in Nazareth, Pennsylvania, explaining that he had to order English Northwest guns as his people could not successfully trade any other kind to the Indians (Nute 1945, 2:453, No. 4310).

Typical accessories for the gun-using Indian hunter were in the main indistinguishable from those carried by non-Indian backwoodsmen. A bag carried shot, flints, gun worms, files, and other appliances judged necessary for use and repair of the gun in the field (fig. 4d). Different sizes of shot could be carried: balls for single shot charges and pellets for multiple-shot loads where the smoothbore musket effectively performed as a shotgun. A powder horn, made by the owner or supplied by the trader, and often personalized with engravings, held the powder and kept it dry. Optional equipment included a horn powder measure, which was used to accurately dispense the proper load down the barrel. Flints could be purchased in bulk lots from the trader or, more conveniently, made by the gun user.

Signs of the retention of traditional Indian material culture, even within the gun complex adopted from the Whites, are frequent. For instance, discarded gun barrels found reuse as tent stakes, picket pins, pry bars, flutes (fig.

Smithsonian, Dept. of Anthr.: a, 130786; b, 152974; c, 96617; d, Minn. Histl. Soc., St. Paul: Mus. Coll.: 69.51, Archaeol. Coll.: 63.65.1; 64.179.3; 68.49.2; Natl. Park Service Coll.: 21CK6 173–5; 21CK6 1963 94–8; 21CK6 1963 564–5; e, Smithsonian, Div. of Armed Forces Hist: 387266.

Fig. 4. Gun, gun accessories, and tools made by Indians from gun parts. a, Catlinite pipe with lead inlay. Collected from Boy, an Ojibwa chief, on Crow Wing River, Minn., 1845. b, Gun barrel–flesher. The muzzle serves as handle, the barrel cut, and the end flattened and serrated. Collected by James A. Mooney from the Kiowa, Indian Terr., 1891. c, Four-hole flute made from the muzzle half of a gun barrel, with shallow, square gains cut above the holes as finger guides. Collected by J.W. Fewkes from the Mescalero Apache, Ariz., 1896. d, Pouch, powder horn, powder measure, different gauge lead balls, wormers, flints, and assorted files, all necessities for use of the smoothbore musket. Pouch and powder horn are without collection data but must date 1800–1860. Other specimens were recovered from archeological sites in Minn. and Canada. e, British Northwest gun, showing characteristic brass serpent sideplate and big iron trigger guard designed for use with mittens. No provenience information available. This type, distributed across North America, was used into the late 19th century. Length of a 18 cm; rest to same scale.

4c), and hide scrapers (fig. 4b). Lead balls and the bars from which they were made would be melted down and used to inlay catlinite pipes (fig. 4a) and other objects of native manufacture like wooden pipestems and the handles of tomahawks.

It is then not a simple matter of the Indian being dependent upon the White trader for all his wants; and the acceptance of articles of White manufacture did not indicate a complete scrapping of the native lifeway and material culture. Examples of Indian ingenuity in applying materials and objects of non-Indian manufacture to the making of traditionally designed artifacts are common. Not only was the Indian not a passive consumer of "superior" White goods, but also he was not constrained by the limited choices of objects and designs presented to him by the trader. Wherever and whenever possible, the Indian freely adapted non-Indian artifacts to uses that had direct analogues in traditional material culture. This propensity to innovation tied to maintenance of traditional lifeways and continued use of artifacts designed through literally thousands of years of trial and error shows that Indian culture was surviving European contact. Adoption of many items simply reflected appreciation of aspects of superior industrial-age technology. Metal proved a better performer and far more durable than stone or bone. Gunpowder allowed more success in hunting and warfare with a lower level of requisite skill and investment of labor than traditional weapons. The appearance and lifeway of the Indian was changing, but the changes were in large part controlled by the aboriginal consumers of trade goods.

One class of trade goods that is particularly good in demonstrating the wide range of uses to which the American Indian put European tools is the file. In this instance, Indian adaptation or reuse was most likely not immediate. Files were valued items, essential for resharpening and repairing the various metal tools available through trade with Whites. Once dulled or broken, the tempered steel of the file offered a marvelously broad range of potential reuses.

Figure 5 shows only a few of the possible uses of a file. It could be made into a chisel, knife, hide scraper, or a strike-a-light (Russell 1967:fig. 97d, 349–354; Hanson 1955:68; Gilman 1982: fig. 194).

The Indian as Market Director and Consumer

The Indian in his role as active consumer directed the trade market, his demands voiced or assessed prompting the manufacture of tools that had no direct parallel in non-Indian economies. The metal quill flattener shown in figure 6 is one such example. Interestingly, this tool had no direct ancestor in Indian practice either, since quills were flattened during aboriginal quillwork by the quill-worker between her teeth, with her fingernail, or with a flattened piece of antler or bone. Here then, is a metal tool in a new form, one that was designed to tap a perceived market. Tooled steel implements like this one proved popular and were part of trader's stocks on the northern Plains and in the Great Lakes region in the late nineteenth century.

Another trade item that was produced only for the Indian market, which is often assumed to be solely a product of Indian manufacture because it is so strongly a

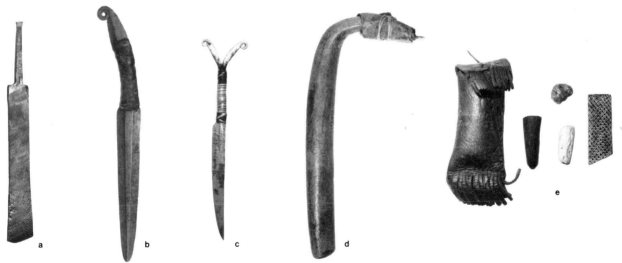

a, Minn. Histl. Soc., Archaeol. Coll., St. Paul: 4718; Smithsonian, Dept. of Anthr.: b, 49116; c, 1635; d, 152970; e, 6972.
Fig. 5. Indian use of steel files. a, File made into a chisel by flattening and sharpening the distal end into a blade. The tang has been flattened by hammering. Collected about 1900 at Mille Lacs Lake, Minn. b-c, knives of Athapaskan type made from files. The characteristic sweeping ears were made from the tangs. b, Collected by E.W. Nelson, Alaska, before 1882; c, collected on the Anderson River, Alaska, before 1866. d, Plains-style hafted hide scraper, a section of sharpened file lashed to a wooden handle. Collected by James A. Mooney from the Kiowa, Indian Terr., 1891. e, Fire-making kit of flint, file strike-a-light, pouch, punk, and tinder horn. Collected by E. Palmer from the Comanche, Texas, 1868. Length of a 27.5 cm; rest to same scale.

Fig. 6. left, Traditionally styled quill bag of beaded intestine holding red-dyed and undyed quills. Collected from the Sioux, 1866. right, Machined steel porcupine quill flattener. Date of collection and locale unknown. Length of left 23 cm; right to same scale.

part of the popular Indian image, is the catlinite pipe. Actually, White manufacturers were supplying machine-turned catlinite pipes to Indian traders. The Northwest Fur Company made nearly 2,000 pipes between 1865 and 1868 and traded these to the Indians on the upper Missouri River (Hayden 1869:274). These pipes seem to have been simple, of generally large size, with a high bowl, sharply right-angle bowl-stem juncture, and marked prow. They were not, presumably, elaborately carved as in figure 4a. White manufacture of pipes, beginning with the creation of the distinctive pipe tomahawk and carrying on to manufacture of catlinite and cast metal pipes of the calumet type, shows vividly how White traders and mercantilists studied the needs of the Indian in order to produce objects that he would desire (Washburn 1966).

Traders also carried items of Indian manufacture for sale to other Indians. This, of course, had its origin in the long-established trade patterns of the American Indian, but it is worthy of note that traders contributed to cultural exchange between Indian tribes as well as between the Indian and the White. For instance, Sioux moccasins were popular trade items, considered the finest by many Great Basin, Plateau, and Plains tribes in the late nineteenth century. It would not be remarkable if a trader's stock contained a broad range of items from many Indian tribes. An Ojibwa bandolier bag, a Navajo blanket, a Crow-made hide shirt, or Blackfoot leggings would sell very well among other tribes.

Traders also brought raw materials of all kinds to their Indian customers, many of which had a long history of trade through purely aboriginal channels. Feathers, claws, tanned hides, hair, robes—anything of value—found its way into the trade. Traders were, in effect, joining extant aboriginal trading systems rather than imposing European systems. The trading of raw materials or items of Indian manufacture in a real sense simply underpinned the successful trade of non-Indian manufactured goods.

Adoption of some trade items, like the gun, did in fact

Fig. 7. Comanche bone hairpipe breastplate with German silver pendant. Collected by E. Palmer from the Comanche, Indian Terr., 1867. Length 30 cm.

have very deep ramifications that forever changed some aspects of traditional Indian life and brought the Indian closer to White society. Changes were made constantly; developments that can now be traced to the adoption of one item or sets of items could not have been predicted by the Indian or the non-Indians involved in the trade. The Indian was borrowing those items that seemed technologically superior or that seemed to have the potential to enhance his life in some other way, as in the expansion in design and color supplied by commercial dyes, paints, pigments, glass beads, satin ribbons, and dyed fabrics. Indian society changed markedly in the course of a very few years, measured in decades rather than in the thousands of years of the prehistoric record, but it was still Indian society, not White or some pale reflection of White society.

Traditional, in a very simple sense, can be taken to mean what was general at some time prior to a specified change. For instance, the hairpipe breastplate shown in figure 7 is distinctively Indian and yet is made up almost entirely of European manufactures. This is the oldest known example of an item that is very strongly identified with the apparel of the Plains warrior (Ewers 1965:58). However, the bone hairpipes that make up the breastplate were made from cow bones by White manufacturers. The brass beads at the ends of each hairpipe were popular trade items. The leather spacers on which the hairpipes and beads were strung were cut from commercial harness leather. The German silver pendant, of the type carried on Spanish headstalls, may or may not have been made by an Indian smith. The use of hairpipes in a breastplate is a comparatively late innovation. The earliest portrayers of Indian life on the Plains show that the original hairpipes, of shell, were used principally as necklaces, pendants suspended from the ears, or as pendants hung from apparel. Made by White artisans on the East coast, they were expensive and, for the Indian, hard to get in any numbers. In the mid-1800s, use of cow bones and enhanced technology greatly increased the supply of hairpipes. With more hairpipes came their use on long straps, bandoliers, and in the distinctive breastplates. Nothing about the items is traditionally Indian, yet they are Indian, because the design and assembly is certainly Indian. It was the Indian who took the various trade items and combined them in a distinctive way.

Trade goods, then, are not just diagnostic items indicative of a certain period or time. They are also not just something that "primitive" Indians adopted and that are reflective of advanced White civilization and its machine age technology. Artifacts are documents in themselves, reasonable reflections of historical events, cultures, values, and social and economic changes. American Indians made choices that led to profound changes in their cultures. But Indian societies did not wane or cease to exist when artifacts of White technology were adopted. To the contrary, these adoptions and the concomitant changes in aboriginal material culture and social, ideological, and economic organization reflect the evolution of Indian culture.

Indian Servitude in the Northeast

YASUHIDE KAWASHIMA

Faced with a constant problem of scarcity of labor, English colonists in the Northeast made attempts from the very beginning to obtain Indian labor. The natives were exploited in four ways: as slaves, indentured servants, apprentices, and free laborers.

The Whites tried to enslave Indians whenever they could. Principle was not so much at issue as convenience. The Puritans justified the enslavement of the prisoners taken in a just war. Following the Pequot War in 1637, for example, Massachusetts not only enslaved 48 captive women and children within the colony but also sold some fierce Pequot warriors to the West Indies in exchange for more docile Blacks, who became the first Negro slaves in New England (Kawashima 1986:214–215). Similar measures were taken in King Philip's War (Lauber 1913: 108–111). On September 16, 1676, Maj. Richard Waldron at Dover, New Hampshire, captured 400 peaceful Abenakis and sent one-half of them to Boston to be sold into slavery (Hubbard 1865, 2:28). On rare occasions, the settlers also purchased enslaved war prisoners from the Indian tribes (Northrup 1900:304, 306; Trelease 1960: 202). In addition, New England had many "Spanish Indians," the slaves who had been brought from the Spanish Indies with Negroes (Lauber 1913:162–164). Although there was general distribution of Indian slaves throughout the colonial period, their number was not large. In Massachusetts, which had the largest Indian slave population in the North, there were in 1790, according to the census report (Anonymous 1847:214; Lauber 1913:109–110), only 200 half-breed Indians among the entire slave population of 6,000.

Unlike Massachusetts and Plymouth, which sold Indian captives freely into slavery, both inside and outside their borders, Rhode Island passed anti-slavery legislation by 1676. However, the law was not effective, and the perpetual bondage of Indians became established and legally acceptable in Rhode Island during the eighteenth century (Sainsbury 1975:382–387).

In the Middle colonies, the number of native slaves was much smaller than that in New England. New York had the largest Indian slave population in the region. Although the colonial authorities discouraged it and on several occasions prohibited it by law (NYCD 13: 537–538), Indian slavery continued throughout the colo-

nial period. New Netherlands did sell during the 1640s Indian war captives to the West Indies, but few such natives were kept as slaves within its jurisdiction. Nor did the distribution of New England Indian captives greatly affect New York, under Dutch or English rule. The limited number of native slaves held in the colony were mostly Spanish Indians, but the Indian slave trade never became a general custom (Lauber 1913:112–113; New York State Historical Association 1961, 1:317–319, 342, 2:300–301). Even in Pennsylvania, "a free colony for all mankind," where there was some protest against slavery (Commager 1963:37–38), the Indian slave existed along with the Black slave. However, the number of native slaves, almost all of whom were brought from other colonies or the Spanish Indies, never reached even 1 percent of the entire slave population (Herrick 1926:96). In New Jersey and Delaware slavery did exist, but the number was very small (Pomfret 1973:92–93, 211; N.J. Arch. 20:111, 21:190, 210).

Enslavement of the natives through kidnapping was practiced by the colonists, especially by New Englanders. All the Indians in the Northeast were fully aware of this custom, although strong tribes like the Five Nations of Iroquois had never fallen victim. As a matter of diplomacy rather than for humanitarian reasons, most of the Northern colonies made kidnapping of Indians a capital crime (Lauber 1913:160–162, 165–167), yet the laws were only casually enforced. The practice thus continued but did not develop into a full-scale means of recruiting slave labor.

The word "slave" was not clearly defined but was used in an imprecise way, often interchangeably with "servant," in the Northern colonies. The Puritans considered their Indian and Black workers, even when they were actually slaves, as part of their families and so usually referred to them as servants, rarely as "slaves" (L.J. Greene 1942:168–169). Nor did the slavery in the North fit well into the concept of the uniquely American slavery in the South. Perhaps the only exception was the practice in the middle of the eighteenth century of the so-called Narragansett Planters in the southern corner of Rhode Island, where a large number of Indians and Blacks were employed for stock-farming on an extensive scale. There, slavery reached a development unusual in the Northern

404

colonies. South Kingstown, for example, contained 223 Indians and 333 Blacks in 1730 and 193 Indians and 380 Blacks in 1748, nearly one-half of whom were slaves in the true sense of the term (Channing 1886:5–23; Sainsbury 1975:390). In general the Northern slaves, who were used as house servants and for other menial work, were treated more like White servants and given the same privileges and rights enjoyed by them. The main difference between servant and slave was the length of service.

By far the greatest amount of Indian labor was used in the form of indentured servitude, in which the natives contracted to work for certain periods of time for specified compensation. Indians were in fact among the earliest of such servants in North America. The New Englanders recognized the effectiveness of this kind of servitude for utilizing native labor, but in the early decades of settlement few Indians found their way into English homes as servants because the colonists regarded the keeping of Indians in their families as more or less dangerous. Therefore, native servants did not reach important numbers until the first half of the eighteenth century (Towner 1955:135, 140, 150). The Indian indentured servants, like the White, were entitled to fair and just treatment by their masters, and the courts saw to it that they received it. Many of the Indian criminals were also sold as indentured servants. The labor of the Indian male was usually valued three times as much as that of the female (Kawashima 1986:137–139, 174–176).

Although the colonial authorities endeavored, through legislation and court order, to guarantee justice to the Indian servants, the natives were more often the object of abuses than the Whites (Towner 1955:267–268). While protection of the indentured natives was their constant concern, the colonial governments took the growing number of Indians in the White communities to be a serious threat for maintaining order and security, although the actual number had never been great (Lauber 1913:144–145, 290–292). Repeated legislation restricting the importation of Indians as servants reveals the fact that the settlers regarded Indian labor, for the most part, as unimportant.

In New York, which had the largest number of Negro slaves in the North in the eighteenth century, indentured servants did not become so important as in New England. The number of Indian servants was very small, though larger than that of Indian slaves. The colony had no large group of natives from which such servants could be drawn, nor did indentureship as a form of labor ever become popular (New York State Historical Association 1961, 2:305–307). In Pennsylvania, the increasing number of indentured servants from Europe not only substituted for slaves but also made Indian labor totally unattractive (Herrick 1926:97). Nor did the colony have a large amount of nontribal Indians readily available for labor in any form. In other Middle colonies, too, the number of native indentured servants remained inconspicuous (Pomfret 1973:92, 211; N.J. Arch. 11:41, 58–59, 186, 24:269).

A numerically less important form of voluntary servitude was apprenticeship, the central part of which involved the learning of a particular skill in exchange for service for a specific term. The majority in this servitude were children. Due to the loose use of the word "apprenticeship," which included all kinds of contractual agreements involving labor (McKee 1935:82), there are numerous Indian apprentices recorded. True Indian apprentices were very few.

Indians who were apprenticed in New England and New York were treated basically the same as the White apprentices, but occasionally some degree of discrimination existed. Indian minors, like Blacks, were often in the same category at law as orphans and pauper children; thus, they were not infrequently bound out to longer terms, sometimes until 24 or 31 years of age, without reference to the parents' ability to support them (Morris 1946:388). Most Indian apprentices were employed for general work, not for trade (Lauber 1913:293; McKee 1935:85). Pennsylvania, where apprenticeship was recognized as an important form of labor next to the indentureship, had few available Indians, nor did the Whites show preference for natives. In New Jersey and Delaware, few cases of Indian apprenticeship are recorded.

Since the early years of settlement in the Northeast, Indians had also been employed for wages. The colonial authorities required settlers to get permission before employing Indians. As a free laborer the Indian was considered to be no more reliable or trustworthy than a slave, but many leading colonists, especially in New England in the seventeenth century, customarily hired such natives, either individually or in a group. Although most of these Indians were unskilled workers, doing chores such as cutting timber, some possessed a trade or handicraft (Lauber 1913:292–294; Pomfret 1973:60).

Hired servants generally enjoyed more advantages than the slaves, but there was not much demand for the natives except as general labor. These free Indians, whom the records refer to as "late servants" or "labourers," were decidedly small in number, though they were consistently used throughout the colonial period, especially in New England (Kawashima 1986:108–109). Indeed, many of the Indian indentured servants who completed their terms of servitude were more likely to make new contracts than to become free laborers. Furthermore, Indians were excluded from some particular jobs in the White communities, while they were required to get special licenses to work in other capacities, such as porters and chimney sweepers. Occasionally efforts were made to enlist idle free Indians and Blacks living in the White communities for public work (Kawashima 1986:136, 213–214).

From the points of view of both Indian and White, Indian servitude was neither successful nor attractive. The native population was too small to make any substantial contribution to the colonists' labor shortage. Nor did the Whites see any desirable quality in the Indian labor. It was not regarded as a substitute, but only a poor supplement. For the natives, the colonial system of labor provided no opportunities for advancement.

In New England, Indian labor, though used regularly throughout the colonial period, contributed only in a limited way because of the small numbers involved. In New York and Pennsylvania, where Black slavery and White indentured servitude, respectively, dominated the labor scene, the native labor was negligible. But in all sections of the Northeast, the trend is clear. By the end of the eighteenth century, changing circumstances such as abolition of slavery, constant inflow of European immigrants, industrialization, and decline of indentureship and apprenticeship gradually brought about a large population growth of non-Indian common workers. Consequently, an insignificant number of Indian laborers among them became simply unnoticeable as a group.

Indian Servitude in the Southeast

PETER H. WOOD

Patterns of involuntary servitude were traditional and commonplace among the early Southeast Indians, as elsewhere on the continent. Enemies captured in intertribal wars were commonly enslaved, and occasionally Indians would barter away the freedom of fellow tribesmen, family members, or even themselves in order to preserve peace, obtain food, or repay a debt. War captives were sometimes mutilated, usually by cutting away part of one foot, in order to reduce the possibility of rebellion or escape (Swanton 1946:816). But generally slaves dressed, ate, and labored in a manner very similar to their masters, and the most common form of manumission was through adoption into the tribe. Such servitude was non-hereditary and local in nature (Hudson 1976:253–255). Nevertheless, Indians from the Carolina region were carried north across the Appalachians to serve among the Iroquois. And in 1565 Spaniards establishing an outpost at Saint Augustine reported that Indians who had come from Cuba were living as slaves among tribes in Florida (Lauber 1913:30). This is a reference to Cuban refugees absorbed by the Calusa of southwest Florida (Dobyns 1983:255).

The introduction of coastal tribes to European conceptions of slavery had begun earlier in the sixteenth century. White explorers who could not obtain Native Americans by gift or purchase resorted to kidnapping local inhabitants. Ayllón (1521), Gómez (1525), and Narváez (1528) all took captives in the name of Spain. Hernando de Soto carried two Florida natives to Cuba in 1538 to train them as interpreters for his expedition the next year in which he explicitly intended to procure Indian slaves. Spaniards carried several thousand Southeast Indians to the West Indies during the sixteenth century, but their devastating new diseases and brutal military tactics reduced the numbers they could transport. By the 1540s the Spanish government was seeking to end the practice of enslaving Indians and was encouraging the use of African labor in its American colonies (J.L. Wright 1981:129–131).

Indian servitude among the French began somewhat later. Giovanni da Verrazano in 1524, Jacques Cartier in 1534 and 1535, and Jean Ribault in 1562 had each sought to carry off Indians for the crown of France, but the regular use of Indian slaves by Frenchmen did not develop until they started to colonize the Gulf Coast around 1700. Even then the practice was limited; several hundred French at Fort Louis de Louisiane had fewer than a dozen Indian slaves in 1704. When Nicolas de La Salle visited Fort Louis three years later he reported that Frenchmen from Canada were encouraging wars between Indian tribes farther north to obtain slaves to sell in Louisiana. By 1708 there were at least 80 Indian slaves in the province, most of them young women, and a similar number had died soon after enslavement. But the French settlers had already made known their dissatisfactions with such labor, stated their willingness to pay cash for Negro slaves, and requested permission to sell Indian slaves for Blacks in the West Indies. In 1710 the French minister of marine vetoed this prospect (Usner 1981:6). Although dozens of Natchez, Fox, and Chickasaw war captives were exported from Mobile and New Orleans, such trade proved intermittent. While 1,400 Africans were imported in the first five years after the Western Company was chartered in 1717, the number of Indian slaves retained by Whites in Louisiana never exceeded several hundred, and by the 1740s most of these had disappeared, their descendants augmenting the free White or enslaved Black populations.

The enslavement of Native Americans developed most among the English. Before 1640 colonists in Massachusetts and Virginia had bartered captive Indians for Blacks in the West Indies. By 1676 Indians taken in Bacon's Rebellion in Virginia and King Philip's War in New England were being sold as slaves (C.T. Foreman 1943:31). But the Carolina region rapidly became "preeminent in the use and exportation of Indian slaves" over the next half-century (fig. 1) (Winston 1934:431). White settlers arrived in 1670 via the Caribbean where they had been exposed to Black and Indian slavery, and in wars during the first 10 years with the Coosa, Stono, and Westo tribes local leaders profited from enslaving Indian captives. The London proprietors realized that such activities endangered the security of the colony, so in 1682 they instructed the new governor not "to suffer any Indians to be sent away from Carolina." But prominent colonists argued that purchasing war captives from Indian allies such as the Shawnee saved them from possible death and that offering a settler the right to take slaves made him more willing to enlist in Indian wars. Gradually the proprietors gave way, attempting only to impose certain licensing controls on the human traffic (Crane 1928:18–21).

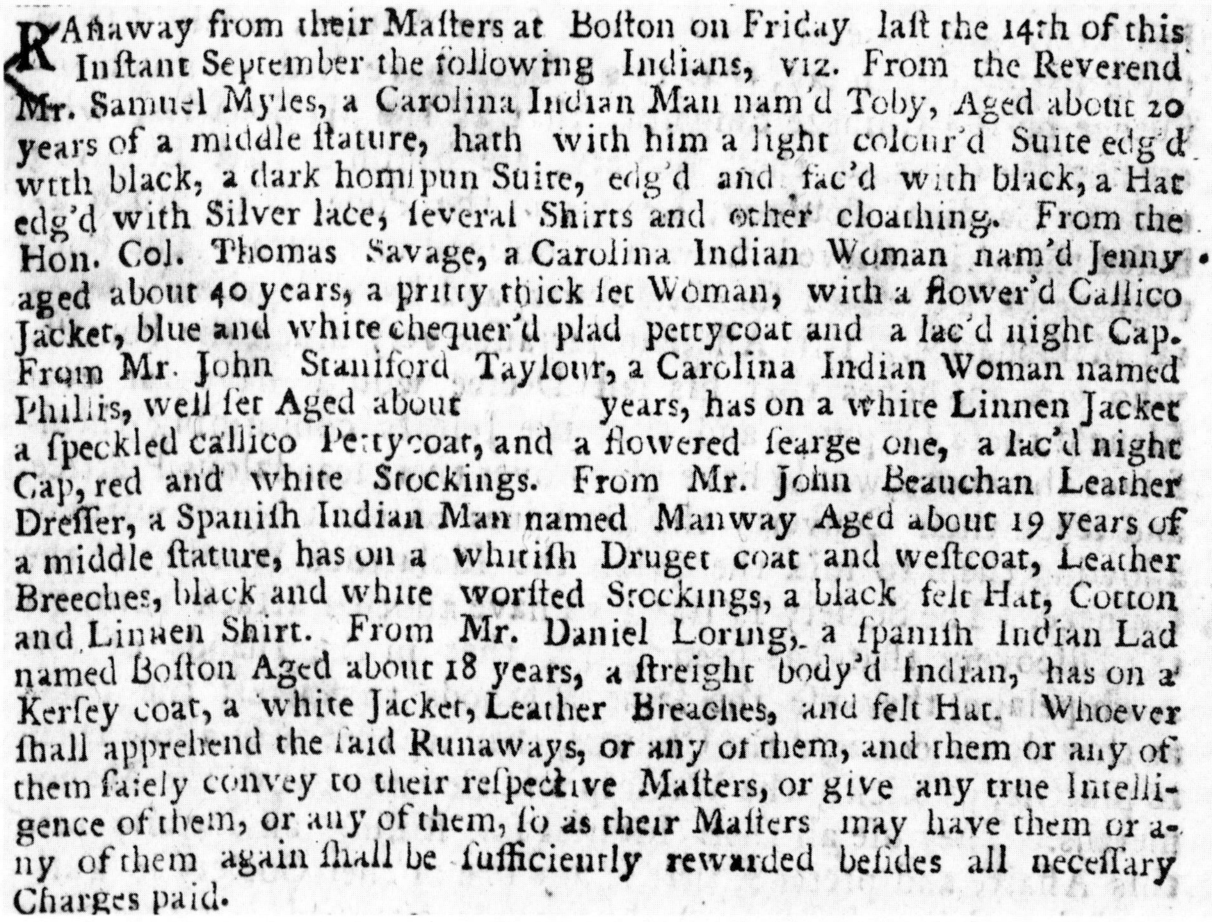

RAñaway from their Masters at Boston on Friday last the 14th of this Instant September the following Indians, viz. From the Reverend Mr. Samuel Myles, a Carolina Indian Man nam'd Toby, Aged about 20 years of a middle stature, hath with him a light colour'd Suite edg'd with black, a dark homspun Suite, edg'd and fac'd with black, a Hat edg'd with Silver lace, several Shirts and other cloathing. From the Hon. Col. Thomas Savage, a Carolina Indian Woman nam'd Jenny, aged about 40 years, a pritty thick set Woman, with a flower'd Callico Jacket, blue and white chequer'd plad pettycoat and a lac'd night Cap. From Mr. John Staniford Taylour, a Carolina Indian Woman named Phillis, well set Aged about   years, has on a white Linnen Jacket a speckled callico Pettycoat, and a flowered searge one, a lac'd night Cap, red and white Stockings. From Mr. John Beauchan Leather Dresser, a Spanish Indian Man named Manway Aged about 19 years of a middle stature, has on a whitish Druget coat and westcoat, Leather Breeches, black and white worsted Stockings, a black felt Hat, Cotton and Linnen Shirt. From Mr. Daniel Loring, a spanish Indian Lad named Boston Aged about 18 years, a streight body'd Indian, has on a Kersey coat, a white Jacket, Leather Breeches, and felt Hat. Whoever shall apprehend the said Runaways, or any of them, and them or any of them safely convey to their respective Masters, or give any true Intelligence of them, or any of them, so as their Masters may have them or any of them again shall be sufficiently rewarded besides all necessary Charges paid.

Mass. Histl. Soc., Boston.
Fig. 1. Advertisement calling for the return of 5 runaway Indian slaves, 3 from Carolina and 2 probably from Spanish Florida, to their Boston masters, published in the *The Boston News-Letter*, Sept. 17, 1711.

In Carolina, as in Louisiana, the fluctuating White commerce in Indian slaves reached its peak in the early eighteenth century (D.I. Bushnell 1908). In 1703 there were only 350 Indian slaves in South Carolina and almost 10 times as many Blacks. Five years later, as a result of raids against the Yamasee, Apalachee, and Timucua of northern Florida, 1,400 Indians made up nearly one-fourth of the colony's slave population, which had come to exceed the free White population (5,500 to 4,080). Of 1,100 Indian adults the majority were women, since hundreds of male captives were transported to other colonies as far off as New England and the West Indies. Among Carolina's Black slaves, in contrast, men outnumbered women by more than three to two early in the eighteenth century, with the result that numerous slave children were born of Black-Indian unions (P.H. Wood 1974:143–144).

The Tuscarora War between 1711 and 1713 led to the sale of more than 400 Indian slaves by the North Carolina government, and captives taken in the Yamasee War that followed made South Carolina the leading source of Indian slaves. But while Indians were still being exported from Charleston annually by the score, Blacks were beginning to be imported from Africa by the hundreds, and after 1720 the relative and absolute numbers of Indian slaves held by Whites in the Southern colonies declined steadily (Grinde 1977:39–41). An Anglican minister reported that the comparative figures for Black and Indian slaves in Saint Thomas Parish, South Carolina, in 1720, 1724, and 1728 respectively were 800 and 90, 950 and 62, and 1,000 and 50 (Klingberg 1941:32, 34). The value of Indian slaves in the White economy continued to decrease, and those recorded in colonial inventories during the remainder of the eighteenth century were generally bound to Whites who held little property.

If several thousand Southeast Indians endured slavery among European colonists during the seventeenth and eighteenth centuries, why did not this condition spread farther and last longer? The answer lies in several factors beyond the simple "love of freedom" occasionally cited.

408

Although Southeast tribes were more populous than those farther north, there were too few Indians to satisfy the incessant labor demands of a steadily increasing European population oriented toward plantation agriculture. High susceptibility to imported diseases further reduced the availability and attractiveness of Indians for servitude among Whites. Indians were less experienced than many Africans in aspects of large-scale semitropical agriculture, and they were more able to escape and return to their traditional homes. Rather than risk the diplomatic and military uncertainty created by enslaving Indians, Whites established incentives to reward Native Americans for catching and returning runaway Black slaves (Willis 1963: 157–176).

By the nineteenth century, as Southeast Indians ceased to be seen as slaves among the Whites, several tribes gave added sanction to the longstanding pattern of retaining Black slaves. Most notably the Cherokees, in their efforts to conform to a White definition of "civilized" behavior that would prevent removal, enacted formal codes governing the enslavement of Blacks (Perdue 1979:57; see also Halliburton 1977).

The number of Black slaves among the Cherokees rose from 583 in 1809 to 1,592 in 1835, and it had reached 4,000 by the time the Cherokee chiefs in Oklahoma declared emancipation in February 1863 (Roethler 1964). Although Black freedmen were admitted by treaty to full citizenship in the Cherokee Nation, some settled in separate communities and a few even sought to return to Africa (McLoughlin 1974).

Indians, therefore, not only were enslaved by other Indians and later by White invaders, but some eventually became the owners of Black slaves. Like so much in the history of the Southeast, the topic of Native American servitude involves the interdependence of all three racial groups.

INDIAN SERVITUDE IN THE SOUTHEAST

Indian Servitude in the Southwest

ALBERT H. SCHROEDER AND OMER C. STEWART

Sixteenth Century

Slavery in the true sense, wherein an Indian became the absolute subject of a Spaniard, without freedom or personal rights, was forbidden by Spanish law in the opening years of the sixteenth century (Haring 1963:39; Bourke 1894:195, 197). However, the encomienda system introduced into the Southwest (Scholes 1935:78–79), first authorized in the Americas in 1503 (Haring 1963:40) and born of the semifeudal and earlier heritage of Spain, was a labor grant to Spanish landowners to exact labor and tribute from Indians up to 1549, after which labor was forbidden (Simpson 1950:37). This practice often led to substituting personal service without pay for tribute, also prohibited by Spanish law but resorted to on the frontiers of New Spain (Gibson 1966:52, 60; Haring 1963:53, 57).

Though captives taken in war at various periods in the sixteenth century could be sentenced to personal servitude or slavery for a designated number of years (Haring 1963: 49–50), they could not be sold, bartered, or transferred as of 1618 (Bourke 1894:197). However, in the Southwest, captives often were treated as chattel in trade with an assigned value and used in the payment of debts. They also could be purchased by Indian servants living in Spanish households, and even after baptism, the captives were traded or sold. In some cases, servants inherited material property and land from their owners (Twitchell 1914, 1: 29, 50, 73, 83–84, 90).

Captives among Southwestern tribes, whether Indian or Spanish, faced a variety of treatment, ranging through cannibalism, ritual cannibalism, slavery, chattel, adoption in the tribe, and marriage.

The beginning of Indian servitude of one type or another in the Southwest might extend from prehistoric times as a result of influences from Mexico. Whether marriage by capture existed prior to Spanish entry has not been demonstrated. The first record of Indian capture of Spaniards in the northern Southwest is that of Álvar Nuñez Cabeza de Vaca and his shipwrecked companions in Texas in 1528 (Bancroft 1884–1889, 1:61). The earliest occurrences of Spanish slaving expeditions into the Southwest are those of Nuño de Guzman in the 1530s, working northward out of southern Sinaloa, Mexico (Hodge 1937:4; Bancroft 1884-1889, 1:59). Perhaps by

way of retaliation, the Ópatas of Sonora in 1540 attempted to capture members of Francisco Vázquez de Coronado's army (Hammond and Rey 1940:269).

Instances of Indian captives, slaves, or refugees among Plains and Pueblo tribes are mentioned in reports of this same expedition of 1540–1541--a Jumano woman among the Teyas in the Texas Panhandle (Schroeder 1962:13), a male adult and a young man from the Wichita among the Pecos, and a captive at one of the Tiwa Pueblos (Hammond and Rey 1940:219, 235, 256). One of the Mexican Indians who took flight after their Spanish masters were killed on the Plains in 1595 was held captive by Apaches before he escaped to Pecos and later San Juan Pueblo, New Mexico (Hammond and Rey 1953, 1:418). The roles of these individuals in other than their own societies are not known.

The Indians referred to as slaves or captives when Spaniards entered the northern Southwest were adults. Whether all represent slaves or were exiles from their country, like the Zuni male Fray Marcos de Niza found among Indians of southern Arizona in 1540 (Hammond and Rey 1940:72), remains a question. Some may have voluntarily taken refuge among the Pueblos as did some of Coronado's Mexican Indians at Zuni (Hammond and Rey 1940:271) and two of Gaspar Castaño de Sosa's in 1591 (Hammond and Rey 1953, 1:319).

In the middle 1500s, along the southern borders of the Southwest, some 2,000 households of Spanish Black slaves lived in the Zacatecas area, including a few in two padres' households (Mecham 1927:52–53). Similar slaves are recorded in Nueva Vizcaya in the 1580s (Hackett 1923–1937, 1:111). At that time, tribes neighboring on these Spanish settlements normally killed their enemies but did capture Indian women and children strong enough to travel with them (Powell 1952:52), using children to later fight in their ranks (Bancroft 1874–1876, 1:629). In the Durango region, into the early 1600s, captives were eaten, a practice noted as far north as the Jovas (Bancroft 1884–1889, 1:317; Mecham 1927:64–65, 171). Partial or ritual cannibalism in the 1540s occurred farther north among the warring Yuman-speaking tribes living along the lower Colorado River who cut out and ate the hearts of some of their captives, sometimes keeping women captive (Hammond and Rey 1940:133, 135, 138, 146).

Ritual cannibalism also apparently occurred among Texas Gulf tribes when first met by Spaniards (Newcomb 1961: 78).

Though compulsory Indian labor in mines was abolished in the middle 1500s, the law was generally disregarded. This led to more explicit regulation of Indian labor in 1589 (Mecham 1927:220; Haring 1963:48ff.), but again other irregular practices were resorted to as the frontier moved north, away from the Black slave market.

In the late 1500s, Spaniards raided out of north-central Mexico into Chihuahua to obtain Indian labor for mining ventures (Gallegos Lamero 1927:3, 14–16; Hammond and Rey 1928:270; Pérez de Luxán 1929:52–55, 60–61; Bolton 1952:137–138, 144, 171), as they did against royal orders to the northwest of Durango in the Acaxee country, which led to an Indian rebellion in 1601–1602. Captive Spaniards and servants also were held by Tepehuans. Tobosos, Conchos, and Tarahumaras in the middle 1640s also revolted against treatment almost as slaves in the mines or elsewhere (Bancroft 1884–1889, 1:313–314, 326, 352, 356).

Expeditions into New Mexico in the late 1500s contained Indian servants in their muster rolls (Bolton 1952:144, 170), as well as slaves with monetary values assigned (Hackett 1923–1937, 1:423). Antonio de Espejo's entrada of 1582–1583 into New Mexico for some reason obtained an Apache woman held by the Hopis and took a girl from Apaches near Acoma. He also captured two men at Pecos, one of whom he took to Mexico so his language could be learned (Pérez de Luxán 1929:112, 120; Hammond and Rey 1953, 1:321; Bolton 1952:192). Castaño de Sosa in 1591 did the same with an Indian woman from a Galisteo Basin Pueblo (Hammond and Rey 1953, 1:321), an act for which he was arrested (Hackett 1923–1937, 1:219). There is little doubt that at the time of Spanish entry the Indians of the Southwest, from the Zacatecas area north to the Yumans, Hopis, and Pecos, as well as in the Plains and Texas, held captives either for cannibalism in the south or for other purposes there and elsewhere. The Spanish explorers into New Mexico up to the 1590s only took a few captives already held by the Indians, one Apache, and a few others from whom they planned to learn their language.

The first governor of New Mexico in 1599, following a battle and on the theory that it was a just war, sentenced Acoma adult captives to 20 years of personal servitude (the first occurrence in the northern Southwest), the children to the church, and the elderly to the care of the neighboring Apaches (Hammond and Rey 1953, 1:478). Enslavement of Pueblo Indians by the Spaniards was rare (Scholes 1935:83). Though Spanish law otherwise prohibited enslavement of Indians as early as 1526, governors of the early 1600s in New Mexico, whose powers permitted them to govern honestly or as a tyrant (Scholes 1935:75), organized raids against Indians on the Plains, seized orphans for use as servants, and used forced labor for building projects, both church and state (Scholes 1936:22, 25, 32, 149, 154–155, 160; Hackett 1923–1937, 1:130). Juan de Eulate, governor 1618–1625, went so far as to transport Indians to New Spain to be sold as slaves, for which he was fined and had to pay for their return to New Mexico (Scholes 1936:164; Benavides 1916:56–57). Luis de Rosas, governor 1637–1641, not only conducted slave raids against Apaches and Utes and engaged in illegal trade with tribes on the Plains but also established a workshop in Santa Fe in which his captives labored (Benavides 1916:300–301), a practice prohibited by law in 1632 (Gibson 1966:146). In the mid-1600s, captives still were being transported to Parral, Chihuahua, to work in the mines. Unconverted Plains Indians also brought in captives to exchange for food (Hackett 1923–1937, 1: 186–187, 191–192). Apaches and Navajos of this period took Spanish and Pueblo captives of their own (Scholes 1937–1940:150).

Seventeenth Century

Tribes bordering the northern fringe of Spanish settlement in southern Chihuahua and Coahuila in the late 1600s practiced cannibalism and used captive Indian or Spanish women for menial tasks or for trade, children often being adopted in the tribe (Griffen 1969:11–12, 119, 122). By 1675, Spaniards in Coahuila, exploring into west Texas, found considerable discord among tribes, each capturing one another's children, as well as Spanish youngsters, for use as servants or for trade (Bolton 1952:301–302, 308).

The missions of the seventeenth century used unpaid Indian laborers as helpers in the church and for other purposes, and they often suffered physical punishment (Scholes 1936:165, 1937–1940:144–145). Civil government in New Mexico also enlisted cheap labor using Pueblo Indians for piñon, salt, and similar expeditions and transport to Chihuahua (Scholes 1935:81–82, 1937–1940: 394–395, 1938:67–68).

Continued mistreatment of the Indians and the attempted suppression of their ceremonies so intricately woven into their everyday life (Scholes 1935:80–81) led to the Pueblo Revolt of 1680 and the retreat of the Spaniards to El Paso de Norte where the roster of the survivors included several Indians listed as servants (Chavez 1954). By way of retaliation against the Pueblos, one governor suggested all-out warfare, including enslavement for 10 years of all captives from age 16 up (Hackett 1942, 1:45, 134, 221).

Spaniards expanding into Sonora in the late 1600s, using flimsy excuses, attacked a converted Pima ranchería in 1688 to obtain labor for mines in spite of the fact that the king, in an attempt to abolish such practices, had issued an order two years before, stating that all new converts for the first 20 years would not be required to give tribute, serve on estates, or work in mines (Kino 1948, 1:109, 142). This, however, did not legally stop the Spaniards in Sonora from capturing unconverted Janos and Jocomes who were distributed as slaves among the soldiers (Kino 1948, 1:162). The Sobaipuri Pimas also took Jocome children prisoners as well as those of Apaches expanding south into Sonora (Kino 1948, 1: 176–177, 199, 2:34). In a Spanish-Pima campaign of 1701 against Apaches, the Pimas captured 16, four of whom they sold to the Spaniards (Kino 1948, 1:295).

During the absence of the Spaniards in New Mexico, between 1680 and 1692, those Piros who remained in New Mexico were practically exterminated by other Pueblos. Survivors, including male adults, were held captive in various Pueblos because many of their kindred joined the Spaniards in their exodus (Twitchell 1914, 2:184; Espinosa 1942:23, 234, 252; Hackett 1942, 2:329). Similar treatment was suffered by Awatovi in 1701, when the other Hopis sacked the Pueblo, killing the men and distributing the women and children among the Hopi villages (Bandelier 1890–1892, 2:371–372; Wilson 1972), much as the Spaniards and various tribes distributed captives among their troops and warriors in their campaigns against one another. Continued dissatisfaction with treatment by the Spaniards after their return caused the Picuris in 1696 to take refuge on the Plains where at least some reportedly became slaves of Apaches who also sold Pawnee captives in New Mexico (A.B. Thomas 1935: 60–61, 69, 74).

Eighteenth Century

After the Pueblo Revolt the encomienda system was not reinstituted (Espinosa 1942:363), and the Spaniards began to rely more heavily on the capture of unconverted Indians for local labor and export. The depredations of the newly arrived Comanches with Ute allies in northern New Mexico in the first decade of the 1700s drew Spanish retaliation, and in one successful campaign in 1716, the governor and his brother divided the captives between them, whom they sold in Nueva Vizcaya (Twitchell 1911–1917, 1:430). Comanches eight years later carried off half of the Jicarilla Apache women and children from a rancheria friendly to the Spaniards (A.B. Thomas 1932: 58). The Comanches from the north thus became a new source for captives, most of whom in the past, up to the early 1700s, came from Plains tribes. Nearby southern Utes and eastern Apaches were among the unfortunates. Comanches and Apaches made up the greatest number of captives during the 1700s (D.H. Snow 1970:42). The Comanches in turn, pressing Lipan Apaches south on the Plains in the 1740s, captured Apache women and children in their drive (Bancroft 1884–1889, 1:622). Apparently the Comanches held some of their captives as slaves (A.B. Thomas 1940:171).

Navajos and Utes were at war with one another from about 1715 to the 1750s. During this period Navajos were driven west (A.B. Thomas 1940:138) and had little contact with the Spaniards, aside from an occasional missionary effort, until the 1770s (Reeve 1959). As a result, most of the Navajo captives of this period probably reached New Mexico as chattel traded by the Utes to the Spaniards. Navajos in the 1770s, in close contact with the Gila Apaches, became involved in the Apache war with the Spaniards (A.B. Thomas 1931:37). This resulted in Spanish campaigns against Navajos in 1774 and the capture of men, women, and children.

By 1785 Navajos joined the Spaniards against Apaches and remained on relatively friendly relations with New Mexico (Reeve 1960) until 1804 when Navajos attacked Cebolleta. In the following year, the Spaniards marched into Canyon de Chelly, and again Navajo captives appeared in the Rio Grande valley (Reeve 1971:111–113). Animosities continued into the American period, each side taking captive children and women from the other until the Navajos were interned at Fort Sumner, New Mexico, in the 1860s.

In the middle and late 1700s, Yuman speakers along the lower Colorado traded captive children to Sonorans for horses, and Halchidhomas disposed of captives to Pimas and Papagos, a practice that continued into the 1840s (Dobyns et al. 1957:48). Apaches and Seris carried off Spanish and converted Indians of Sonora, the Apaches and Spaniards sometimes exchanging prisoners, the extra captives among the Apaches also being traded for horses and knives. In some cases, Indian and Spanish captives of Apaches preferred to remain with them, or, if ransomed, made their way back to them (Pfefferkorn 1949:43, 144, 146, 149–150), indicating their treatment was not necessarily that of a slave. In a general campaign against the southern Apaches in the 1770s and later, a number of women and children were taken (A.B. Thomas 1932).

Tribes coming into Taos to trade in the 1700s brought a variety of material including Indian captives (Twitchell 1911–1917, 1:454; Hackett 1923–1937, 3:487; A.B. Thomas 1940:111–112, 134–135), as did the Utes in their trade in and after the 1740s at Abiquiu (Domínguez 1956: 253), a practice continued into the American period, mostly at the expense of Southern Paiutes (Snow 1929:69; Hill 1930:18–20, 22–23; Malouf and Arline 1945: 380–381). By the 1780s, Pawnees raided Comanche rancherias east of the Pecos, capturing women and children (A.B. Thomas 1932:322). Navajos of this period attacked a party of Hopis, killing the men and capturing the women and children (ibid.:232), but more often raided the Utes and Southern Paiutes in the 1800s, preferably for women for household use or sale to Mexicans. These women could marry into the tribe, but not adult male captives who suffered many indignities. The Mormons in the 1850s brought an end to slave trade between Utah and

New Mexico (Malouf and Arline 1945:382, 386ff.) While most Spanish captives prior to the late 1700s came from tribes east of New Mexico, most after that date were obtained from the northwest, west, and southwest.

Conclusion

Though some reports exist of Apache captives being treated well (Cremony 1970:265), others in the mid-1800s indicate treatment similar to that of the Navajos (ibid.: 54–55, 266). The Pimas, on the other hand, in their hostilities with Yavapais, used their captives primarily for trade with Sonorans (Ives 1939:110; Ezell 1961:29) as the Utes and Plains tribes did with their captives traded to New Mexicans. One of the Pima captives in 1871 was a Yavapai, who was purchased from them and educated to become Dr. Carlos Montezuma, a Chicago physician (fig. 1) (F. Russell 1908:55; Spicer 1962:530).

Because of the variety of treatment in the Southwest given by the Spaniards or Indians to their captives, the term slave cannot be broadly applied except in those instances of personal servitude without pay or rights. The unfortunates acquired by capture obviously changed status if retained by their captors, sometimes coming to own property or marrying into the capturing group. In other instances, as chattel, their treatment or rights could change, particularly if purchased, traded, or ransomed to become servants, laborers, or *genízaros* (non-Pueblo Indians, ransomed captives or mixed-bloods living in Spanish fashion, sometimes in villages of their own) (Hackett 1923–1937,3:401–402). Spanish servants and captured children and women often were baptized (A.B. Thomas 1940:111–112, 173), and some captives of the Navajos and Apaches either formed the basis for a new clan or were adopted in a clan. It has been suggested that these devices of the Spaniards and Indians served to formally integrate the captives they retained into their respective societies (Brugge 1968:128).

Captives were a part of Indian custom and society at the time the Spaniards entered the Southwest. Spanish law permitted enslavement of captives of rebellious tribes for a specified length of time, but this was often disregarded on the frontier. The major practice introduced by the Spaniards appears to have been treatment of captives as chattel, assuming that captives among Indians at the time of Spanish entry in the Southwest were not used in the same fashion.

In any case, after the settlement of Spaniards in the northern Southwest, trade in Indian captives by Indians

Smithsonian, NAA: 55,530.

Fig. 1. Carlos Montezuma, about 7 years old. He and his 2 sisters, captured by Pimas, were sold separately. The boy was purchased for $30 at a village near Florence, Ariz., by an Italian photographer and artist, Carlo Gentile. He was baptized as Carlos Montezuma under Gentile's patronage (Iverson 1982:5–6). Photograph by Napoleon Sarony, 1871–1872.

mushroomed among surrounding tribes in exchange for Spanish trade items. The Spaniards in turn used traded captives as well as their own captives as servants, laborers for work in mines in Chihuahua, or allowed them to live as free men, many of whom resided in towns, Indian pueblos, or settlements of *genízaros* (Twitchell 1914, 2:219, 238, 248, 250, 330).

In the southern part of the Southwest, tribes early lost their identity through decimation or missionization and intermarriage. Most of those who survived took refuge or lived in mountain retreats away from Spanish settlements. The lack of demand for labor for mining ventures in the northern Southwest, where mining was practically nonexistent, probably played a major role in the survival of Indian groups in this region and helped to generate large numbers of mixed-bloods in the Spanish population.

Indian Servitude in California

ROBERT F. HEIZER

Servitude is here defined as the forced detention of persons whose labor or person is used to the advantage of others. Servitude may take the form of slavery per se, or slavery de facto. Indian servitude in California took two main forms. The first was a purely native institution where Indians were held as slaves by other Indians; the second was a form of bondage or peonage of Indians that came into being after European discovery and settlement and that was either officially condoned by the successive Spanish or Mexican or American governments or was legalized by statute.

Aboriginal Times

In northwestern California a group of five tribes (Tolowa, Yurok, Wiyot, Hupa, Karok) all exhibited the same kind of wealth-oriented culture. Of these five nations the Yurok was the most numerous and well-off and exhibited the regional type of civilization most incisively. According to Yurok law a family upon whom was levied a justifiable claim for compensation for some injury—homicide, insult, property destruction—must pay up in actual goods that had fixed values (for example, canoes, dentalium beads, valuable ceremonial regalia) or, lacking these, provide a male or female person who became the "debt slave" and whose labor was devoted to his owner's advantage. Such debtor slaves could be passed on to a second party in substitute satisfaction of a claim for damages, though this was rare. Such debtor slavery was humiliating, and persons so held might be freed after many years upon payment of a pro-rated portion of the original amount of the claim if his family's fortunes improved.

What might be termed "voluntary slavery" also was known. Individuals whose families were starving in times of drought or when the salmon runs failed might offer themselves as slaves to rich persons who owned productive fishing spots or acorn lands since such men were more likely to have plenty of food. In addition, a man who had run up big expenses for curing or a funeral and could not pay might voluntarily become the slave to a third party who, in exchange, would pay his debts (L. Thompson 1916:183–184).

A benevolent owner might buy his slave a wife; the children then belonged to the master. When a master wished to marry his female slave he paid a token bride price to her parents, this act proving that it was to the services and not to the person that the owner had rights. Slaves did not run away since giving them refuge would lead to financial liability, and if they sought asylum in a neighboring tribe they would be killed as unknown and dangerous outsiders. Debtor slaves seem to have accepted their inferior social position without objection. Prisoners taken in battle with neighboring tribes were held until a settlement was agreed upon and then restored. Such captives were not ransomed, but merely held as levers to bring pressure on the other side to agree to a settlement. Kroeber (1925:32; Elmendorf and Kroeber 1960:344) variably estimates the number of slaves in aboriginal Yurok society as "probably not over one-twentieth, certainly not over a tenth" and "probably not over one percent." Exact figures on numbers of slaves are not recorded. Yurok slavery was not very efficient in economic terms judging from the fact that such a person was valued at from one to two strings of dentalium shells.

The Tolowa (Gould 1966:83) practiced the Yurok form of debtor slavery but to a notably less degree. The Hupa did likewise but ordinarily demanded a life in return for a killing if the guilty party refused to pay compensation in wealth items. The Wiyot and Karok knew the custom of debtor slavery, but it was rarely practiced.

Prisoners taken in war were kept as slaves by the Shasta (Kroeber 1925:296). The Juaneño held as slaves captured women and children only (ibid.:647). In general it seems that female slaves were not sexually exploited, overworked, or ill-treated, though occasionally a captive was sacrificed in a spirit of revenge by a man whose relative had been killed in battle (Forde 1931:168). The apparent reason for keeping them was to serve as a public reminder of the tribe's prowess in war.

The Modoc raided the Achuwami, Atsugewi, and Northern Paiute for captives. Such prisoners were either held by the Modoc as slaves or, more commonly, were sold to the Klamath who took them to the market at The Dalles on the Columbia River where they were again sold (V.F. Ray 1963:144–145). Kroeber (1925:308) suggests that the commercial aspect of slave raiding is a historic development that occurred after the horse became available, but Ray (1963) was told that slave-keeping was an aboriginal Modoc institution.

Historic Times

Interpretations vary on how to classify the social position of the approximately 54,000 Indian converts that were drawn into the 21 Franciscan missions of California between 1769, when the first mission was established at San Diego, and 1834, when the missions were secularized by order of the Mexican government. Some critics of the mission system have considered the mission neophytes to have been in a condition of simple servitude (for example, Hittell 1885–1897, 1:519). Other scholars have analyzed in detail and with objectivity the operation of the mission system and the Indian response to missionization, concluding that "there can be no serious denial that the mission system, in its economics, was built upon forced labor" since the evidence for physical restraint and compulsion is clear and abundant (Cook 1943, 1:95). Military expeditions to seize natives for conversion were common in the 1769–1834 period (Cook 1943, 1:77–79).

The theory of missionization was that the Indian was to be instructed in such a way that he would become "civilized" and made a useful member of society (C.A. Hutchinson 1969:70–81, 109, 222), but in 1834 when about 15,000 converted natives were released when the missions were disestablished, it is clear that the program had been a miserable failure. Many Indians after 1834 moved into the interior of California to take up residence with their unconverted brethren who still followed the aboriginal way of life. Others voluntarily attached themselves, or were forced to do so, to ranches where they were subject to the conditions of peonage (Cook 1943, 2:5, 27–28). Mariano Guadalupe and Salvador Vallejo, Mexicans with large landholdings near Sonoma, raided Wappo, Lake Miwok, Pomo, and Patwin groups to obtain laborers for their agricultural and construction projects (Cook 1943, 3:9, 51; G. Simpson 1847:177–178). This kind of serfdom for the purpose of providing labor on the large ranches prevailed through the Mexican period after 1834 until 1850.

Americans who had been awarded land grants by the Mexican government before 1846 also applied the prevailing peonage system of labor. Among these may be mentioned J.A. Sutter, J. Bidwell, T. Cordua, R. Livermore, G. Yount, and B. Redding (Cook 1943, 3:46–52). At Sutter's Fort (now Sacramento) in 1846 Sutter was described as keeping "600 or 800 Indians in a complete state of slavery" (Clyman 1928:129; see also Heizer and Almquist 1971:18–20).

California was admitted to the Union in 1850 with the understanding that it was to be a nonslaveholding state. The California constitutional convention held in September and October 1849 at Monterey effectively blocked Indians and Blacks from voting, and the first session of the state legislature in 1850 passed the Act For the Government and Protection of Indians, which was amended slightly in 1860 (Heizer and Almquist 1971:212–217). The act permitted any White person "obtaining a minor Indian, male or female, from the parents or relations of such Indian minor, and wishing to keep it" to go before a justice of the peace and secure a certificate "authorizing him or her to have the care, custody, control and earnings of such minor, until he or she obtain the age of majority," the age of majority being defined for males as 18 and females as 15. The penalty for failure to adequately feed and clothe or to inhumanely treat such indentured Indian minors was a fine of not less than 10 dollars. The act further provided that in event of complaints "in no case shall a white man be convicted of any offense upon the testimony of an Indian." The act as amended in 1860 extended the period of indenture by defining the age of majority of male indenturees under 14 at 25 years, of females under 14 at 21. Males over 14 could be indentured until they were 35 and females until they were 25. From 1850 until April 1863 (when the act was repealed four months after the Emancipation Proclamation) the kidnapping and sale or indenture of California Indians was common. The indenture documents have for the most part disappeared, but one lot of 114 Humboldt County indentures dating from 1860 to 1863 has been preserved. In 70 of these 110 persons aged from 2 to 50 were bound over. Forty-nine of these 110 individuals were between the ages of 7 and 12. Seven of these are listed as "taken in war" or "prisoner of war," referring to children aged 5, 7, 9, 10, and 12. Four children are listed as "bought" or "given." One indenture concerns a child of 3, another two children of 4 years of age. Ten married couples, some of them with children, were indentured (Heizer and Almquist 1971: 51–57). Without documentary evidence for the number of indentures of Indians in California for the period 1850–1863, it can only be estimated that as many as 10,000 persons were involved. Illegal sale of Indian minors was perhaps as common, judging from what documents (newspaper articles, letters from army officers, and Indian agents) have been preserved, so an estimate of the number of native Californians sold or placed in legal bondage for this period is about 20,000. Women and children were secured either by outright capture or after a native village was attacked by regular army troops or volunteer military companies. Those who were captured by regular troops were usually placed on reservations, and those persons seized by groups who can only be called slave-hunters were sold (Heizer and Almquist 1971:40–46).

In addition to the (illegal) outright sale of Indians to Whites, and about which there is abundant evidence (ARCIA 1861:149, 1862:315, 1867:117), Section 20 of the 1850 Act for the Government and Protection of Indians authorized "any Justice of the Peace Mayor or Recorder of any incorporated town or city" to hire out to the highest bidder any Indian classed as a vagrant, for a period of not more than four months. This practice was common, but since it was rarely made a matter of permanent record it can only be estimated in frequency from newspaper accounts and records. For example, a letter written by Charles Brinley, overseer of Abel Stearns's Rancho Alamitos at Los Angeles, asks Stearns "to deputize someone to attend the auction that usually takes place at the [Los Angeles] prison on Monday's and buy me five or six Indians" (Heizer and Almquist 1971:48–49).

It is clear that until the end of the Civil War California citizens and courts acted as though Indian slavery or servitude was legal, or at least permissible (cf. Pitt 1966: 57–58, 204–205; Eaves 1910:82–104).

Ecological Change and Indian-White Relations

RICHARD WHITE AND WILLIAM CRONON

Several themes should be kept in mind when surveying the environmental history of Indian-white relations in North America. The first is that a great many myths obscure the understanding of this subject. There has long been a tendency in the United States, encouraged by the environmental movement of the 1960s and 1970s, to view Indians as "original conservationists," people so intimately bound to the land that they have left no mark upon it (MacLeod 1936; Speck 1938; Deloria 1970:181–197; Jacobs 1972: 19–30). Depictions of Indians as savages wandering in the wilderness or as innocent children living gratefully off nature's bounty are cultural artifacts of Europe; they have little to do with the actual lives of Native Americans (H.N. Smith 1950; Pearce 1953; Sheehan 1973; Slotkin 1973). Indeed, the very word wilderness in the sense of a natural landscape unaffected by human use has little meaning for most of aboriginal North America. To assert that Indians lived on pristine "virgin land" not only ignores the human influences that had long reshaped pre-Columbian North America but also "naturalizes" Indians in a way denies both their histories and their cultures. Just as important, to portray Indians as "conservationists" or "ecologists" is fundamentally anachronistic (Martin 1978: 157–188).

A second theme of Indian environmental history has to do with broad similarities in Indians' actual uses of the natural world. Given their diversity, it is dangerous to generalize about Indian land-use practices; nonetheless, certain common features emerge when they are contrasted with those of Europeans. Agriculture on the two continents differed dramatically. In Indian North America, in places where crops were raised, they were almost always integrated into hunting, fishing, and gathering economies that required more physical mobility than was typical of European communities. However intimate the relation of certain Plains peoples to the bison herds, no North American ungulate species had been fully domesticated, so that dairy products, woven textiles, and animal power sources were generally lacking. In many parts of the continent—the Arctic, Subarctic, much of the Great Basin, and the Northwest Coast—agriculture was not practiced at all, though nonagricultural subsistence practices differed radically in different regional environments. Throughout the continent, seasonal cycles, ecologically

and culturally defined, governed the physical movement of Indian communities among different environmental sources of subsistence. Indian economies typically protected themselves from environmental fluctuations by incorporating a wide variety of different resources into these seasonal cycles. When one such resource failed to appear during a given season of the year, others were almost always available to support a community. These in turn were usually articulated in terms of a clear sexual division of labor in which (to overgeneralize) men concentrated on hunting and fishing, and women on horticulture and gathering (H. Driver 1969; Jorgensen 1980).

The ways Indians used the environment profoundly influenced the historical landscapes of North America. Indian activities brought changes to the continent's forests, grasslands, and deserts, whether by modifying vegetational assemblages, by encouraging or discouraging the spread of animal populations, or by creating habitats best suited to human settlements. The tools and methods Indian peoples used to gain food, shelter, and clothing before White contact varied widely. Some techniques, such as irrigation, were localized; other techniques, such as burning, were in use across the continent.

The notion that Indians passively "adapted" to their regional environments must be avoided. Natural systems clearly limited human uses of land, and in the trivial sense that Indians did not do the impossible, they adapted. But if regional environments were diverse, Indian uses of them were even more diverse. Nature offered not one, but many ways for human beings to live in a given region. More important, it gave no clues as to what might be an "optimum" way to live, for only culture could provide the values that defined what an optimum use of land might be. Indians were no more passive or "adaptive" in choosing such environmental values than Europeans were, and out of their choices and spiritual beliefs flowed the material changes they imposed upon the landscapes of North America.

The third theme of Indian environmental history is simply that anthropogenic change of North American landscapes accelerated with the arrival of the Europeans. The story of Indian-White relations cannot be framed solely in political or diplomatic or even cultural terms, for the very ground over which Indians and Euro-Americans

417

were struggling shifted as they did so. Part of the process of environmental change involved incompatible uses of different habitats, as when Europeans imposed fences or fixed property boundaries on landscapes that had lacked them. Part of it derived from the reduction or elimination of indigenous species—species that had been fundamental to earlier Indian economies—as they experienced new and heavier human use; at the same time, the introduction of alien species shifted ecosystems and economies alike. And part of the process involved fundamental differences in Indian and European conceptions of spiritual nature.

Indian Conceptions of Nature

North American Indian conceptions of nature and culture generally intersect in two ways. On the one hand, human beings are part of nature by virtue of being biological beings living within a material world. On the other, natural beings such as plants and animals are also part of a human cultural world. Perhaps the clearest example of this can be found among the Algonquian peoples of the northern United States and Canada. Among both the Ojibwa and the East Cree, for instance, natural and cultural worlds overlap. In the Cree world game animals exist as persons who "participate simultaneously in two levels of reality, one 'natural' and one 'cultural' " (A. Tanner 1979:137). The interaction of hunters and game animals becomes a social relationship, often expressed in terms of friendship or love. In a properly conducted hunt the animals offer themselves voluntarily to be killed (A. Tanner 1979:138, 146, 148).

In consequence, the boundaries between human and nonhuman communities become difficult to define. Just as nature and culture shade into one another, so do natural and supernatural phenomena. One class of spirits exists as personified natural forces, while another class of spirits "own" or are "masters" of particular animal species (A. Tanner 1979:114–116, 139). Human beings thus act properly and successfully in nature not merely through practical environmental knowledge but also through spiritual relations with the masters of the game and with the animals themselves (A. Tanner 1979:122; Hallowell 1976:357–386; Black 1977, 1977a; Charlevoix 1744, 2:144; JR 50:289).

For Indian communities that view the world through these lenses, few distinctions are made between what outsiders might regard as common-sense environmental knowledge and those magical activities that induce an animal to surrender to a hunter. A hunting technique of the Winnebago, for example, involved shooting an arrow down the trail of the quarry deer the day before an actual hunt. The hunter did not regard the arrow falling on the trail as a preliminary to the hunt or as a substitute for hunting skills; the arrow and the subsequent hunt were an "indissoluble whole" and were employed only under well-defined conditions (Radin 1924:15–16). Similar ceremonies were used by the Navajo to request hunting success both from the Talking Gods who controlled game animals and from the animals themselves (W.W. Hill 1938:98). Among the Winnebago, the Navajo, and the Cree, then, the "practical" and the "spiritual" paralleled each other (A. Tanner 1979:134). Neither alone could make the hunt successful.

In the Southeast, this conception of the complex community relationships among animals, plants, and human beings became even more elaborate when applied to disease. Like many Indians, the Cherokee constructed their medical theories on the premise that animals caused illnesses as a way of retaliating against hunters whose activities were wanton, careless, or disrespectful of animal remains. Despite this dangerous power that animals could wield, human beings were not entirely defenseless against it, for a number of plant allies had agreed to furnish them with specific remedies against animal-induced disease. Much of Cherokee medicine involved selecting plants appropriate to the animal causing a particular illness. To treat sickness being sent by deer, for instance, doctors made a compound of four plants known in Cherokee as "Deer Ear," "Deer Shin," "Deer Eye," and "Deer Tongue" (Mooney 1890:47). The Cherokee thus established cultural congruences among the plants they saw as connected to certain animals and then used those plants to treat the diseases they thought those animals caused.

By using these techniques Native American groups sought to manipulate nature to serve their own purposes. This was particularly true among horticultural peoples, who established intricate symbolic schemes representing natural systems and their seasonal cycles that could be ritually manipulated. Such cultural systems differed (and continue to differ) profoundly in detail, but they were often based on perceived natural oppositions between earth and sky, winter and summer, male and female; these in turn were elaborated into cultural categories that could be applied to the entire natural world. The Creek, Cherokee, and other Southeast Indians, for example, conceived of the world in terms of an opposition between "upper" and "lower" worlds, with "this world" suspended between. It was the duty of Indian peoples to maintain the balance between the upper and lower worlds, by keeping separate those things that belonged to each. This task gave them what has been called an "almost obsessive concern with purity and pollution" (Hudson 1976: 121) in their efforts to prevent the mixing of things from opposing categories.

As another example of such horticultural belief systems, the people of the Tewa Pueblos developed a quite different set of cultural classifications, but these too were inspired by natural oppositions. The Tewas elaborated their social organization and ritual cycle from natural dualities marked by the solar equinoxes and by the opposition between hot and cold temperatures. From those two sets of poles, ritual divisions could be applied to phenomena ranging from disease, to plants and animals, to society itself. The Tewa system of summer and winter chiefs reflects this duality (Ortiz 1969:118–119).

Whether Indians understood their place in the natural environment in terms of a series of social relationships among spirits, human beings, and nonhuman organisms, or in terms of ritual classificatory systems, they showed little reluctance about trying to control that environment. For the East Cree, "much of the religious thought of the hunters is concerned with the state of the natural environment, with how the environment may be controlled, and with the reason for failure when hunters are unable to exercise that control" (A. Tanner 1979:211). The same is even more true of agricultural peoples. The ritual cycle of the Tewas is designed to "harmonize man's relations with the spirits, and to insure that the desired cyclical changes will continue to come about in nature" (Ortiz 1969:98). Above all, their agricultural rituals are designed to procure rain (Ortiz 1969:106). Similarly, the Pawnee quite literally believed that their ceremonial cycle perennially insured that corn would grow and buffalo would prosper (Weltfish 1965). In all these ways, Indian religions and ritual practices confirmed the crucial role human beings played in facilitating the movement of natural cycles.

Indian Transformations of Landscape

One key determinant of Indian environmental influence was simple population density. In the Arctic and Subarctic, environmental conditions and social organization both contributed to the lowest population densities in North America, on the order of 1.7 persons per 100 square kilometers; this was lower than was typical of more temperate regions (vol. 6:141, 173, 275, 372, 534; vol. 5: 164, 206, 479–480, 486; Hallowell 1949; Krech 1978; Dobyns 1983:34–45). Because northern biological cycles moved between dramatic annual extremes in the relative abundance of subsistence resources, human numbers and impacts there remained small relative to places elsewhere on the continent. No agriculture was possible, so localized shifts in game animal populations probably remained the most significant human effects on natural landscapes. Anthropogenic forest fires may occasionally have affected wide areas of the Subarctic landscape, but there is little evidence that the use of fire for hunting was widespread in the region (Flannery 1939:14, 167; Day 1953:338–339; vol. 6:86).

South of the Subarctic, population densities were generally higher, ranging from perhaps a little over one person per 100 square kilometers in the deserts of Nevada to over 300 persons per 100 square kilometers in the more fertile areas of the East (Dobyns 1983:34–45). In the deciduous woodlands of the Northeast, Algonquian and Iroquoian peoples living in more temperate climates attained higher population densities in part by combining annual cycles of hunting and gathering with a horticultural cycle derived from the Meso-American corn-squash-bean cultigen complex. Crops were planted chiefly by Indian women during April and May, and a mixture of gathering, fishing, and small-game hunting sustained communities until the fall harvest. Villages would then break into smaller bands to participate in the fall and winter deer hunts, living off harvested corn when meat supplies fell short (Wallace 1970:49–75; Salisbury 1982: 30–39; Cronon 1983:34–53).

Agricultural fields in the vicinity of permanent villages could become quite extensive, and these, combined with the effects of gathering wood for fuel, resulted in localized deforestation. After the soil fertility of such fields had begun to decline, they were abandoned and new lands cleared to replace them. The result was to maintain early successional stages in the vicinity of Indian villages, creating a patchy landscape of grasslands, shrublands, and young woods. In addition, many communities followed the practice of setting fire to portions of the forest around them, opening up the landscape still further. The promotion of mixed grasslands and young woods simultaneously provided forage for animals such as deer, hare, beaver, turkey, grouse, and quail. Although these species were not "domesticated" in any conventional sense of the word, Indians played a significant role in managing their numbers and use.

In the Southeast, similar alterations of the landscape reflected the agricultural and hunting demands of Indian peoples. The prehistoric peoples had concentrated their settlements and cleared fields along the terrace lands bordering major rivers; moving out from those bases, they hunted the surrounding forest and prairie lands. After epidemics had largely depopulated prehistoric centers, the nations who inhabited the region following European contact tended to live along smaller streams. There they still farmed terrace lands, but the old fields of the prehistoric people became prime hunting grounds. In the region as a whole, the distribution of fields and villages changed over time, but the overall pattern remained the same: ribbons of fields ran along the terraces and were surrounded by hunting areas of forest, prairie, and abandoned fields.

Within this landscape, Southeast Indians acted to increase the abundance of those plants and animals they needed for food and clothing. To produce the corn, beans, and squash that formed the staples of their diets, they practiced swidden agriculture, cutting and burning existing vegetation to establish their fields. Within fields that contained beans as well as corn, nitrogen-fixing bacteria on the roots of the legumes replaced some of the nitrogen that corn extracted from the soil, but the beans never put

419

back all that the corn took out. As fields declined in fertility, Indians abandoned them and cleared new ones. They were selective in their clearing, paying attention to soil quality and also, in some areas, sparing wild fruit and nut trees (Sauer 1971:181, 282–284). Under ideal conditions, this agriculture was remarkably productive and, when supplemented by hunting, fishing, and gathering, it provided the tribes of the Southeast with a secure subsistence.

The game that hunters took in upland forests and prairies had fewer direct connections than crops did with human alterations of the environment, but it too was influenced by the ways people modified habitats. Indians burned both to clear lands and to hunt game, but the influence of anthropogenic fire in creating deer habitats varied from region to region within the Southeast. In the upland pine-hardwood forests, burning appears to have encouraged herbaceous growth, particularly of those plants most palatable to deer (R. White 1983:10–11). On the prairies, old fields, and openings, the fires retarded normal successional patterns and maintained the edge habitats in which deer thrive. However, along the Gulf Plain fire degraded rather than improved deer habitat. In this region, longleaf pine, a fire-resistant species, dominated a region that otherwise would have been oak-hickory forests with a higher average carrying capacity for deer. The combination of poor agricultural soils and scarce game made this perhaps the least inhabited section of the region (Chapman 1932; R. White 1983:11; Pyne 1982: 112).

The Plains provide one of the most intriguing examples of Indian uses of the environment. This is a land of abundant grass and often catastrophic drought. Before the horse the southern and central Plains were inhabited by Caddoan peoples who farmed the river valleys along its margins and who seasonally ventured out onto the plains to hunt buffalo. Permanent residents of the plains were confined to small groups of nomadic peoples, and even they apparently engaged in a more limited horticulture. The women—the horticulturalists of the tribes of the Plains margin—had by the late nineteenth century evolved a series of crop varieties that had been adjusted to local conditions over long periods of time (Will and Hyde 1964). These villagers too exerted pressure on the environment. Their activities gradually exhausted local timber supplies and diminished the fertility of cornfields, so they were forced to move their settlements. Later, their widespread burning of the grasslands, together with the fires set by surrounding nomads, reduced the quantity of timber along stream and river margins where it would otherwise have existed. Because such environmental changes gradually undermined the subsistence base of the community itself, the life of such a village, barring attack from the outside, would appear to have been about 30 years (Wells 1970; R. White 1983:183–185).

In the Southwest and Great Basin, aridity set limits on human land use, but there too the environment hardly dictated a specific or optimal use. The Hopi, Apache, and Southern Paiute, for example, all shared desert environments, but their systems of land use differed significantly. Each modified the land to suit their needs. For instance, the desert around Black Mesa, where the Hopis built their villages, is hardly ideal for agriculture. The lands are high and dry, with the critical rainfall of July and August usually amounting to only three or four inches; that the Hopis even attempted agriculture under such conditions is remarkable. Once they did so, climate and the scarcity of water severely restricted when and where they could plant (Bradfield 1971:2).

Despite such conditions, environment by no means determined the cultural accommodations the Hopis made in responding to them. To compensate for aridity, the Hopis planted special varieties of corn with a greatly elongated mesocotyl and a single deeply thrusting radicle instead of seminal roots. The unusual mesocotyl and radicle allowed corn to germinate even when planted as much as 10 inches deep and to make maximum use of moisture preserved deep beneath the ground's sandy surface (Bradfield 1971:5–6). But such corn could not be planted everywhere. The Hopis had to select fields that successfully preserved the moisture from melting winter snows and also captured runoff from rain and snow elsewhere on the mesa. These fields were located on clay soils overlain by sand, and they dotted the valleys that were carved into the mesa's sides. The Hopis located their fields in these valleys by noting the size of key indicator plants, particularly the rabbit brush and its associated species. Such fields, barring catastrophic arroyo cutting, were the sites of an agriculture that was permanent rather than shifting, since floodwaters and the silt they carried fertilized as well as watered the fields. In the desert the Hopis constructed an agricultural economy that included not only corn, beans, and squash, but also cotton and, after contact with the Spanish, orchards (Bradfield 1971: 12–19).

Farming clearly involves modifying the landscape, but Indians shaped the Southwest much more widely, if less dramatically, with fire. Fire drives by Apaches and Papagos of the Gila River system in the Sonoran Desert were apparently important in keeping grasslands from becoming chaparral. Apaches set fires as a hunting technique, and these fires in turn encouraged plant successions that helped increase game populations (Dobyns 1981:34–43). In the Great Basin, Indians also set fires to encourage the germination of wild plant seeds and the growth of wild tobacco (Steward 1933:281). Fires set by hunters in the Plateau culture area were major ecological factors in shaping foothill grasslands and mountain woodlands (Gruell 1985; Flores 1983:329; Arno 1985:82).

The barren high desert environment of the Great Basin demanded much of the people who lived there, and they of necessity forged a subsistence system that was at once alert to all possible food sources and flexible enough never entirely to depend on one or two. The Northern and Southern Paiute and Western Shoshone depended on mobility and flexibility to survive. They used a variety of fish, plants, and animals that were abundant and easily harvested only for brief periods. The Southern Paiute and Western Shoshone used their intricate knowledge of desert environments to gather what they could, storing one food whenever possible to guard against the failure of another element in their elaborate seasonal cycle. No family or band could depend entirely on their own resources; boundaries were flexible and the population readjusted itself to seasonal scarcity or abundance. A poor yield of ricegrass in the territory of one Northern Paiute band, for example, required that band to move into the territory of another where food was more abundant. Such shifts were only temporary, since a poor yield of ricegrass rarely meant that other seasonal plant foods—say, the piñon crop in the fall—would fail to be plentiful in the migrant band's own territory. Although the various Paiute groups might seem to have been the people most forced to take the land as found, a closer look shows environmental manipulation even here. Many Northern Paiute groups burned vegetation to encourage wild plants, with some sowing seeds after the fires (Steward 1941:281; Downs 1966). The Owens Valley Paiutes burned to encourage the growth of certain desirable plants, and they increased the yield of several plants by practicing limited irrigation (Steward 1933, 1930:150).

In California, many of the techniques found among the Great Basin peoples occurred again. The Diegueño and Luiseño irrigated and cultivated wild plants (Bean and Lawton 1973:xv, xxvii). Far more than in the Great Basin, California Indians used fire to shape the environment. Indian fires in the Sacramento Valley and neighboring foothills reduced "brush cover to favor a parkland of grasses, trees, and intermittent stands of brush" (Lewis 1973:17). By maintaining early successional stages, Indians provided a favorable environment for deer. Burning the chaparral was particularly important. After the fire had reduced woody species, a variety of grasses, forbs, and sprouts on regenerating chaparral provided an abundance of game food. In higher mountain regions, frequent ground fires set by Indians left the larger trees undamaged, destroyed needles and debris, encouraged shrubs and herbaceous plants, and maintained the forest as a parkland with open spaces between the trees. Such a forest provided more abundant animals and easier hunting. Regular burning, by eliminating debris, reduced the likelihood that catastrophic crown fires, which were capable of entirely destroying the forest, would occur (Lewis 1973:25–35, 1985).

In the coastal regions of the Pacific Northwest and along the major rivers that reached into the interior, the seasonal cycles of Indian peoples clearly centered on the annual spawning runs of salmon and steelhead, but subsistence extended beyond fishing. Around the fishing runs, many coastal peoples created an elaborate cycle of gathering and hunting. This cycle meant much more than simple variety in their diet; it was a hedge against those years in which salmon runs failed. This was true not only of the Coast Salish but also of the Kwakiutl, Haida, and other tribes farther north (Drucker and Heizer 1967). To increase the yields of this hunting and gathering system, Southern Coast Salish groups such as the Skagit, Snohomish, and Kikiallus significantly modified local environments. They burned the scattered prairies to increase yields of bracken (whose roots were ground to flour) and camas (whose bulbs were dried and stored). There is a little evidence that the Salish regularly burned forests, but prairie fires did occasionally spread into surrounding woods and could, under proper conditions, cause immense conflagrations. Burned-over sections of forest were common at White settlement. These fires helped to maintain the dominance of Douglas fir, the seedlings of which, unlike those of hemlock and cedar, could not grow unless the mature trees of the overstory were eliminated (R. White 1980).

If, then, one were to summarize the ways in which Indians modified North American landscapes prior to the start of European settlement, several subsistence practices would clearly be counted among the most important and widespread. Hunting and, where available, fishing were significant sources of food and clothing virtually everywhere on the continent, but their effects on local animal populations were determined by human population densities, the abundance of game species apart from Indian influence, and the extent to which hunter-gatherer economies were supplemented by horticulture. The agricultural activities of North, Southeast, and Southwest Indians yielded substantial landscape change not only on croplands themselves but also on old fields where different successional stages coexisted in a complex system of altered habitats. Everywhere on the continent, burning wood to cook food and warm lodges produced local deforestation. Much more dramatic was the use of fire to burn wild grasslands and forests. No single Indian practice contributed to more dramatic changes in North American environments.

Postcontact Environmental Change

Disease

The most immediate environmental change in Indian lives brought by European landings on American shores was also the most invisible and insidious: the introduction of pathogenic microorganisms against which Indians had virtually no immunity. Indian susceptibility to diseases like smallpox, chicken pox, measles, influenza, and malaria was a function of several phenomena. Most immediately, it was caused by their failure to maintain the historical transmission of antibodies from mother to child that is one of the species' most effective biological defenses against disease. That in turn resulted from their ancestors' passage through arctic environments where low winter temperatures and low population densities made it impossible for pathogens to survive, and from their lack of the domesticated animals with which Old World populations share several key disease organisms (Crosby 1972, 1976; McNeill 1976).

Wherever Indians encountered Europeans for any extended period of time, disease and depopulation were the eventual results. In the four decades following Columbus's arrival, massive epidemics killed millions of Indians in the Caribbean basin and in Central and South America. Although early epidemics are very poorly documented in North America, they were probably already beginning to occur to a limited degree in coastal areas during the sixteenth century and had brought significant depopulation by the early seventeenth century (Dobyns 1983). They recurred well into the nineteenth century among peoples with no previous experience of a particular disease. Mortality rates varied with the specific disease organism, population density, the season of the year, a community's historical immunity, and so on, but at their worst they could range as high as 80 or 90 percent. Some communities appear to have survived their encounters with disease more easily than others, and that tendency increased as historical exposure, mergers with other groups, and biological immunity rose. Nonetheless, as late as 1837, the Mandan of the Missouri River were virtually wiped out by smallpox (Crosby 1976:299).

The indirect effects of disease may have been at least as important as direct ones in bringing environmental change to North American habitats. The strain placed on economic subsistence practices, hierarchies of political power, and ritual belief systems in societies drastically reduced must have been quite extraordinary. Areas that had supported large populations, such as the major terraces of Southeastern rivers, or the coastal bays and salt marshes of the Northeast, suddenly became depopulated. Villagers were forced to move into new alliances with each other, shuffling the decks of kin networks and political alliances to accommodate their altered circumstances. These changes, like depopulation itself, were bound to have significant effects on the ways Indians used the plants and animals around them.

The Fur Trade and Resource Exhaustion

422   The epidemics occurred at precisely the same time that Indian economies were being drawn into new trading relations with European merchants. Indian reasons for participating in the fur trade were diverse and numerous. They included the symbolic and ritual power attributed to certain European goods and the simple material attractions of European trade goods, whether those had to do with the sharpness of metal tools, the warmth and colorfulness of woolen fabrics, or the effectiveness of firearms in certain types of hunting and warfare. Alcohol rapidly came to have an extraordinary and destructive attraction to Indians, the reasons for which are not entirely clear (Vachon 1960; Stanley 1953; Miller and Hamell 1986). Precontact trading networks facilitated the movement of furs and European goods along known transport corridors; these in a sense simply expanded their repertoire to include new bundles of goods. Disruption of status systems in the wake of epidemic depopulation may well have contributed to the willingness of Indians to participate in the trade (Cronon 1983; Ceci 1977; Salisbury 1982).

Whatever the reasons, the net effect of the fur trade was to begin a process whereby the animals of the hunt gradually became trading commodities, although the older spiritual relations of the traditional hunt could persist long after animal furs had begun to be sold in European markets (A. Tanner 1979). The fur trade entailed the integration of European goods and traders into Indian gift relations and kin networks as much as it did the linkage of Indian economies to merchant capitalism and the North Atlantic economy ("The Hudson's Bay Company and Native People," this vol.). Complex hybrid economies and cultural exchanges resulted, and all had environmental consequences.

In association with European contact, but often far ahead of actual European settlement, major changes occurred in the distribution of North American fauna. Native species dwindled or disappeared and exotic species appeared in sizable numbers. Alterations in flora were even more far-reaching, but these changes tended to come after actual Euro-American settlement. The destruction of big game species did not begin immediately; there is evidence that some of these species were actually increasing in number and range during the period following contact. Bison appear to have been expanding east of the Mississippi, and white-tailed deer, taking advantage of the new habitats opened after riverine lands had been abandoned by peoples following epidemics, may also have increased their populations in the Southeast (Rostlund 1960; R. White 1983:10–11).

Although there is little doubt that local overhunting did occur in aboriginal North America, such overhunting never seriously threatened regional populations of game animals before the advent of the fur trade. The population of those animals whose pelts provided the basis for various fur trades—beaver all over the continent, white-tailed deer in the Southeast, buffalo on the Plains, and sea otter in the Northwest Coast and California—plummeted toward regional or total extinction (Matthiessen 1959). Not all this destruction was the work of Indian hunters, but they played a critical role.

Despite suggestions that Northern Algonquians engaged in a war of revenge against the beaver because they believed that the animal had wantonly caused epidemics, the bulk of available evidence suggests that Indians overhunted game animals in order to obtain the goods offered by Europeans (Martin 1978; Krech 1981). Indian demand for European goods, while quite real, was not automatically large enough to threaten game populations. Nor were native cultural and political barriers against overhunting rapidly and easily overcome. The stimulation of demand and the breakdown of safeguards against overhunting were the result not only of the fur trade but also of social and political developments that were altering the native landscapes of North America. Generalizations upon the environmental consequences of the trade are thus hazardous. Not only did the animals that traders sought differ from place to place and period to period, but the trade itself ranged from a relatively straightforward economic exchange in some areas to a single element in much larger political relationships elsewhere. Moreover, the trade itself cannot be taken in isolation; it was but a component of a larger Indian subsistence economy and had to exist in balance with it.

Overhunting as a response to the fur trade did not occur everywhere. Certain tribes—the Pawnees and Crows being perhaps the most notable—managed to control alcohol consumption and frustrated traders by keeping their trade within well-defined limits (Wishart 1979:6). Groups that were central to the imperial balance of power in North America, such as the Iroquois, received needed goods as gifts and thus were less dependent on the hunt.

For overhunting to occur several conditions had to be met. Indians needed the technological capability to take game in numbers sufficient to threaten the survival of a species. They had to desire or require European goods in sufficient quantities to invest the labor necessary to hunt out game animals. During the hunt, they had to have access to the resources necessary to maintain hunters and their families if the fur-bearing animals themselves did not yield enough meat and garments for subsistence. They had to be able to hunt in a region without threat of disruptive attacks by other peoples. Finally, they had to be able to justify, within their own system of values, the elimination of entire species.

The first factor, technology, seems to be the least important. Northern Indians possessed a native technology and hunting techniques perfectly capable of eliminating the beaver before Whites came. Among buffalo hunters the bow and arrow remained the preferred weapon even after the introduction of the gun. The horse more than the gun increased the efficiency of the hunt, but mounted hunters harvested the herds for years without seriously depleting them. Firearms did make overhunting of white-tailed deer easier, but hardly insured their destruction (Martin 1978).

The second factor, demand for trade goods, could lead to depletion even when limited if exchange rates were high and furbearers few. Classic cases include the destruction of beaver in many tribal territories in the Northeast and the elimination of sea otters on the Northwest Coast. When Indian demand was inelastically low, as it often was, and game was abundant, trade might persist for years with only gradual or limited depletion. In the Great Lakes, where beaver and other game animals were abundant over much of the area, depletion of furbearers occurred gradually (Alcoze 1981; Kay 1977:158; Beauharnois and Hocquart 1737). Hunters quickly eliminated beaver and large game in the lands around the overcrowded refuge centers of people who had fled the Iroquois attacks, but game remained abundant elsewhere, both because Indian demand remained limited and because part of that demand could be met by gifts from rival European empires. Even after overhunting of the beaver had clearly occurred, Indians around Green Bay still quit hunting as soon as they had obtained their basic necessities, and if the requisite European goods were available from other sources, they often refused to hunt for furs at all (Kay 1979:402–403; Ray 1980).

When Indian demand for trade goods, for whatever reason, led to overhunting, Indian hunters had several alternatives. If depletion affected only some fur-bearing species, native hunters could simply turn their attention to other animals. With the decline of beaver, for example, first the Menominee and Winnebago and later the Sioux began hunting less valuable species, such as the muskrat, that remained abundant (Kay 1979:413; Anderson 1984:109). If alternative species were not able to support the trade, a group might take measures, either on their own or at the instigation of traders, to conserve or replace depleted species. Another response to the depletion of species was the organization of hunting territories of the Algonquian peoples of eastern Canada. The specific arrangements varied, and the details have been a matter of controversy (vol. 6:25–26).

The third factor, access to resources, is evinced in the tendency of Indian hunters operating in depleted environments to become dependent on traders for food. Where animals such as the white-tailed deer or the buffalo were a source of both food and skins, overhunting eliminated a community's principal source of food supplies and clothing. Beyond this, traders often bought or harvested Indian foodstuffs themselves in order to pay advances to Indians short of supplies during the winter or spring. After gift exchanges gave way to credit transactions, Indians in debt could be induced to hunt more intensively. On the other hand, without food Indians would be diverted from fur hunting to subsistence hunting or fishing (Bishop 1974:24, 183–186). Such dependence, of course, only increased as traders encouraged tribes such as the Ojibwa to move into regions of the Canadian Shield that, despite their respectable yield of furs, offered few of the other resources on which Ojibwa life depended. Hunters in this situation quickly came to depend on traders not just for access to European goods but also for food and clothing (Ray 1974: 147, 225; Bishop 1974:196).

The fourth factor, freedom from warfare, is important because moving onto new hunting grounds often meant infringing on lands already hunted by others. If the hunters already in possession of hunting lands resisted the incursions of new hunters, game depletion might be halted simply because borderland rivalry rendered the region too dangerous for fur hunting and thus protected animal populations. In such disputed zones game populations could recover. This phenomenon appears to have taken place in the borderlands between the Sioux and Chippewa in the eighteenth and nineteenth centuries, in the southern borderlands of the Choctaw, Creek, and Chickasaw in the seventeenth and eighteenth centuries, and in portions of the Great Lakes region that were initially emptied of their inhabitants during the Iroquois wars of the seventeenth century (Hickerson 1965; R. White 1983).

These political constraints on overhunting vanished when Europeans moved in to establish peace. When the French secured an uneasy peace in Ontario and southern Michigan among the Ottawa, Mississagua (Ojibwa), Huron-Petun, and the Iroquois, for example, the result was overhunting. French traders complained that for the first time Indians were slaughtering all beavers in the area regardless of age. There was little sense in conserving shared lands or game if rivals would reap the benefits of so doing. Similarly, the Iroquois had complained during an earlier peace that Illinois hunters, contrary to accepted custom, were killing all beavers and sparing no breeding stock (Bacqueville de la Potherie 1722, 3:176–177; NYCD 9:162–163; Lahontan 1905, 1:82). Peace in the Southeast brought similar results among the Choctaw and Chickasaw in the eighteenth and early nineteenth centuries, where the victims were white-tailed deer (R. White 1983; Hatley 1977).

Once begun, the search for fresh hunting lands could instigate a cycle of overhunting, expansion, conflict, and eventually renewed overhunting, but none of these was inevitable. In emerging onto the Plains, groups such as the Teton Sioux, the Assiniboin, and Plains Cree in effect broke this cycle as they transformed their own economies and used the buffalo to become less dependent on European goods. Their connection to the fur trade before the last brief period of the robe trade was as provisioners of the northern fur trapping brigades, producing pemmi-

can for their consumption. These tribes and others contributed to the demise of the buffalo, but their role was relatively minor. White Americans, more than Indians, were principally responsible for the destruction of the bison herds (Ray 1974:131–133, 147).

But the question still remains: even if the job of persuading Indians to overhunt was a long and complicated one, why didn't Indians do more to conserve the depleted animal species upon which their well-being increasingly depended? How did they justify the slaughter of entire species of animals? This is again a question that can only be answered for particular groups involved in particular aspects of the fur trade, but a look at the logic of two groups—Northern Algonquians in the beaver trade and Sioux in the buffalo trade—can perhaps clarify the general patterns.

For Northern Algonquians, beavers, like other animals, were under the control of masters of the game. Their abundance depended on human relations with these masters of the game and on the respect accorded individual animals. The decline of a species meant that Indians had either not observed proper ritual forms or else relations with the game master for that species had deteriorated. Two solutions suggested themselves. Conservation, one such response, appears to have been adopted among contemporary East Crees. Among the Crees, native beliefs about depletion have led to a hunting system that insures the maintenance of desired species. Respect for the animals involves killing only those that are needed. Although a given territory may be hunted out almost completely, it is then allowed to go unhunted until game animals are once more abundant.

But there is no necessary correlation between such beliefs and modern conservation. Great Lakes Algonquians, for example, could just as consistently consider their increased hunting to be right and "necessary," since they still treated animal remains with respect and still only killed the number of animals needed to acquire goods that were "necessary" (Kay 1985:124–125). The critical element seems to be whether hunters believed their increased killing for trade to constitute disrespect for animals. Sporadically, religious leaders among the Algonquians would assert a connection between declining game populations and irresponsible fur hunting. The Shawnee Tenskwatawa made such arguments in the early nineteenth century. His followers appear to have reduced their hunting for trade, but such religiously inspired conservation appears to have been both unusual and temporary. In most areas it could not overcome dependence on the trade (Public Archives of Canada 1807).

A second example of Indian responses to overhunting can be found in Sioux actions during the late nineteenth century. These show that Indian beliefs about animals could actually make conservation in the twentieth century sense more difficult in situations where animal populations were declining. Like the Algonquians, the Sioux believed that the abundance of animals was a function of the way they were treated and of ritual relations with them. For them, the disappearance of the buffalo was a sign that buffalo were not being treated with the proper respect; in response, the animals were withdrawing underground. But the Sioux could also see that it was not they but the Americans who were mistreating buffalo. When the Ghost Dance religion promised to restock the plains with buffalo, it was thus being perfectly consistent with Sioux ecology and environmental beliefs (DeMallie 1982:390–391).

Domesticated Animals

Association with Euro-American settlers led to a rise in domesticated animals—cattle, sheep, horses, and pigs. The northward dispersal of the horse enabled numerous tribes on the margins of the Plains to move out into the grasslands to exploit the bison herds. Tribes such as the Comanches are better understood as horse pastoralists who happened to exploit the buffalo, as opposed to buffalo hunters who happened to use horses. For the Comanches, horses were sources of food as well as vehicles for hunting, transportation, and war (Downs 1964). In the Great Lakes region, the movement of the Potawatomi, Sauk, and Fox onto prairie lands was accompanied by adoption of the horse at about the same time that Choctaws were beginning to raise small ponies for transportation and food (Clifton 1984). In the central valley of California, horses stolen from Spanish and Mexican rancheros became a basic food item in Indian diets (G. Phillips 1983). And on the Northwest Coast even tribes living in the western foothills of the Cascades became herders, receiving horses from the much larger herds of the Plateau and northern Great Basin. Everywhere in North America south of the Subarctic, the horse gradually became an essential part of Indian subsistence practices.

Cattle too became regionally important. The Nez Perce and their neighbors built up large cattle herds, as did the Papagos of the Southwest (Josephy 1965; Manuel, Ramon, and Fontana 1978:522–525). So too did many Southeast Indians, such as the Choctaw and Chickasaw (fig. 1). Virtually everywhere in the East, cattle eventually ranged throughout prairies and open woodlands where deer had once thrived. In the Southeast, Indians also kept pigs in the frontier manner, allowing them to range freely in the woods. Finally, in the Southwest, the Navajo and to a lesser degree the Pueblos became accomplished shepherds. Sheep and horses initially complemented agriculture among the Navajo and gave them increased security in facing the irregular subsistence cycles of a harsh and arid land.

As an example of the divergent ways that peoples living in similar environments might choose to utilize the horse,

Natl. Arch.: RG75-AO-21-2.
Fig. 1. Chickasaw cattleman Darius Cravatt, Ada, Okla., Oct. 24, 1973.

both the Pawnee and the Teton Sioux benefited from the northward spread of horses. Both groups at the time they acquired the horse lived on lands bordering the Plains. For the Teton Sioux, the acquisition of horses meant more effective buffalo hunting, greater security of subsistence, and a general movement away from dependence on the fur trade.

For tribes like the Sioux, maintaining horse herds through the rigors of the Plains winter became one of their most important environmental challenges. Because the short bunch grasses of the High Plains remain nutritious even after their topgrowth has dried and withered, horses could graze until snow covered the ground. After that, horses often depended on the young growth of cotton-woods and on cottonwood bark harvested by their Indian owners. Even with the widespread cutting of these trees, which grew only on narrow stream margins and hence could easily become depleted across wide areas, many horses still died in bad winters. Replacing them meant raiding, usually directed against tribes living in more southern areas where milder winter weather meant greater survival of the horse herds. This pattern of horse starvation and Indian raiding appears to have been among the most important reasons for the longstanding tendency of many Plains nomads to migrate gradually south and west, but this is a matter of controversy. They sought to move not only toward the original source of horses but toward the milder southern lands where the animals could better survive the winter (R. White 1978, 1983; Osborn 1983; Albers and James 1985).

In contrast the Pawnee were horticulturalists, and although horses certainly increased the efficiency of their seasonal buffalo hunting on the plains, the animals, unless carefully watched, also threatened the unfenced crops Pawnee women planted along the tributary streams of the Platte and Loup rivers. There were also problems in trying to feed them during the late fall before departure on the winter hunt, during the hunt itself, and in the early spring when the Pawnee returned to their villages to plant. Paradoxically, in a land of abundant grass the horses could nonetheless starve because the tall grasses of the eastern plains store their nutrients in their rhizomes and their dried stalks thus have little food value. In the fall, Pawnees fed the horses corn nubbins or grazed them in sheltered areas such as Grand Island, where fresh grass was available. During the winter, the Pawnees, like the nomads, cut and fed them the bark and small branches of cottonwood trees.

The real danger came in the early spring, when the horses, already weakened by a harsh winter, had to carry the Pawnees and their dried meat and equipment back to the earth lodge villages at a time when new grass had not yet normally appeared. The Pawnee could not wait for the grass to appear, or they would arrive home too late to plant; however, if they left too early they would lose their horses, along with the stores of dried meat they carried. The Pawnees' eventual solution was to manipulate the environment to produce earlier growth of grasses. They methodically burned the lands around their villages and along the routes to their Plains hunting grounds. By removing dead top growth and debris, the Pawnees made sure that the soil warmed more quickly and the grass sprouted sooner. They thus managed to fit the horse into an existing subsistence cycle at the same time that the Teton Sioux used the animal to create a subsistence cycle that was largely new (R. White 1983:180–186).

Outside of the horse on the Plains, probably no animal was integrated more fully into an Indian way of life than sheep were among the Navajos. The Navajos were horticulturalists, hunters, and raiders before they obtained the herds and remained so afterwards; but the addition of herds of sheep did give them a prosperity and environmental security they had lacked. Rather than depending on a single food or activity to produce a surplus that hedged against famine, the Navajo relied on a mixed subsistence base. A group that hunted, farmed, and grazed sheep was more secure than a group that relied on only one such activity. The herds thus became a critical link in Navajo subsistence. Particularly after the Navajo return from the Bosque Redondo in the 1860s, during a period when they came close to hunting out their newly constricted lands,

sheep alone often stood between them and famine (R. White 1983).

Among the different Indian peoples who adopted them, domesticated animals undoubtedly had some of the same environmental effects among Indian communities as they did among European ones, though in general Indian pastoralism probably had less concentrated effects because of the lower population densities involved. Weed species were undoubtedly encouraged in places where animals were kept in large numbers. New concepts of animal ownership encouraged patterns of raiding and theft that, if not entirely new, took on new meaning for Indian cultures, especially among peoples in the trans-Mississippi West where the horse herds were so regularly threatened with starvation. Among horticulturalists, greater attention had to be paid to protecting crops in places where animals were kept. The problem of feeding animals during scarce seasons of the year could encourage deforestation and erosion alike. Despite these potential problems, the adoption of domesticated animals appears to have been a very viable response for Indian peoples who found themselves confronted with declining populations of the native species on which they had formerly depended for food.

Just as Indians were quick to incorporate European tools into their earlier patterns of subsistence, so too were they willing to become pastoralists relying on the introduced animals for a substantial portion of their social and economic life.

The Reservation Era

With the beginning of the reservation era in the United States, fundamental changes occurred in relationships among Indian peoples and the land. During the nineteenth century, the logic by which Indian peoples were permitted to maintain a partial land base meant that they could retain only those lands not immediately suitable to agricultural use by Whites. Under the allotment policy of the Dawes Severalty Act of 1887, even Indian lands that were agriculturally marginal were opened to White settlement. The process left in shambles native subsistence systems that were already suffering from widespread decline of game and loss of critical agricultural lands. Even in areas such as the Northwest Coast and the Southwest where fishing, grazing, or agricultural economies remained largely intact, environmental crises were postponed rather than prevented.

Nineteenth-century policies and treaties shaped Indian reservation boundaries in ways that deprived them of agricultural land, severely constrained their hunting practices, and generally truncated the environmental foundations of their economies. Ironically, those same

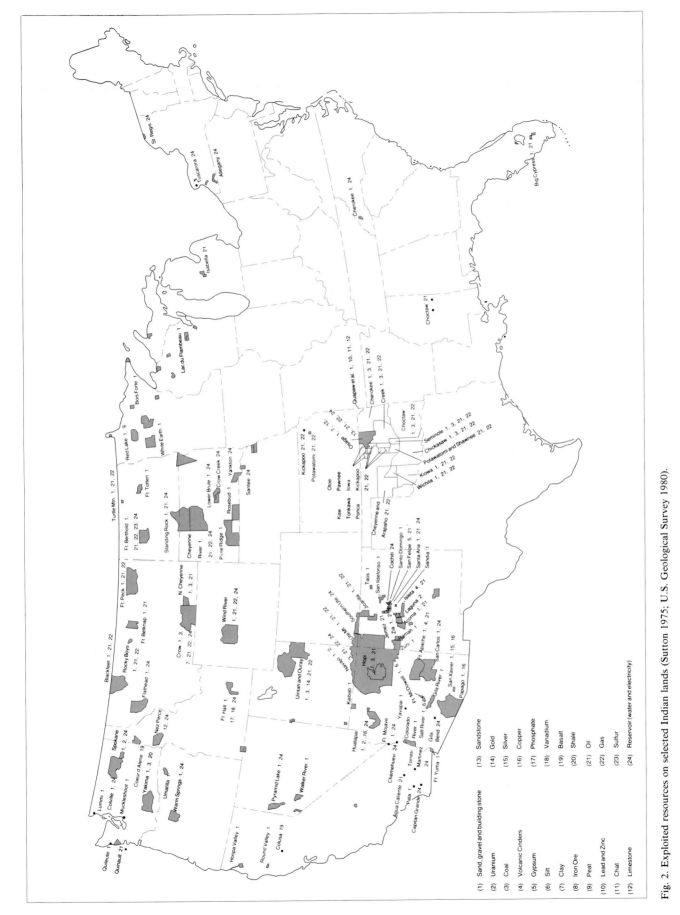

Fig. 2. Exploited resources on selected Indian lands (Sutton 1975; U.S. Geological Survey 1980).

(1) Sand, gravel and building stone
(2) Uranium
(3) Coal
(4) Volcanic Cinders
(5) Gypsum
(6) Silt
(7) Clay
(8) Iron Ore
(9) Peat
(10) Lead and Zinc
(11) Chat
(12) Limestone
(13) Sandstone
(14) Gold
(15) Silver
(16) Copper
(17) Phosphate
(18) Vanadium
(19) Basalt
(20) Shale
(21) Oil
(22) Gas
(23) Sulfur
(24) Reservoir (water and electricity)

427

policies unknowingly left Indians with nonsubsistence resources—coal, gas, oil, and uranium—that would become valuable in the twentieth century (fig. 2). The treaties also left western Indians with water rights that were even more valuable (Hundley 1978, 1982). Many of the most important issues in Indian environmental politics during the twentieth century would revolve around the ways such resources would be exploited on reservation lands (see Americans for Indian Opportunity 1981, 1982).

In addition, nineteenth-century treaties, even when they were ignored by Whites for years, guaranteed that Indians would be free from state regulation in their traditional hunting and fishing. Particularly after the 1974 decision in the case of *United States* v. *State of Washington*, the willingness of the courts to uphold these rights has restored an important degree of Indian control over the environment. In particular, Indian fishing rights in the wake of that case appeared to take priority over most non-Indian access to resources protected by treaty (Josephy 1982:177–211). In addition, legislation such as the National Environmental Policy Act of 1969 and the American Indian Religious Freedom Act of 1978 forced public agencies to take the cultural heritage of Indians into consideration in land planning decisions (Clemmer 1985: 147). Protecting Indian cultural and religious practices in this way has had unforeseen environmental implications by enabling Indians to demand that landscapes of religious significance be preserved. The courts, for example, in the early 1980s prevented the U.S. Forest Service from logging timber in the Blue Creek area of northern California, in part because it was sacred land for the Yurok, Karok, and Tolowa Indians (*Northwest Indian Cemetery Protective Association et al.* v. *Max Peterson et al.*, C-82-4049 SHW, 1983).

The result of these post-1960 developments is that while the vast majority of Indian peoples have lost access to the resources necessary to feed, shelter, and clothe themselves through their own efforts, some groups have nonetheless regained some access to fish and game, and some control over sacred sites. Furthermore, some tribes control valuable nonrenewable resources that they cannot develop without outside capital and technical skills. Their attempts to rescue themselves from poverty through the sale of such resources has at best retarded their long slide into dependency, and such gains have sometimes been purchased at the cost of disastrous consequences for their land and health. As a single instance, the opening of the Navajo reservation to uranium mining has been a source of income but has also left the tribe with occupational injuries, high cancer rates, and the long-term legacy of radioactive tailings (Samet et al. 1984). Continuing pressure to develop Indian resources forces Indian communities to make choices about how to reconcile their own environmental values with their need for income.

During the twentieth century tribal peoples have had to

UPI/Bettman Newsphotos, New York: 870684(ACME).
Fig. 3. Cession of lands on the Fort Berthold Reservation, N. Dak., for Garrison Dam. front row, left to right, George Gillette, chairman of the reservation business council, and Secretary of the Interior Julius A. Krug. Krug signs the document while representatives of the Three Affiliated Tribes of Mandan, Arikara, and Hidatsa look on. The dam flooded 152,000 acres of reservation land (Lawson 1985:172). Photographed May 20, 1948.

struggle against the values, power, and economic goals of the dominant society in order to assert their control over reservation lands. The damming of the Missouri River in the late 1940s and early 1950s under the Pick-Sloan plan, a project whose benefits, such as they were, went to Whites, resulted in Indians losing most of their arable and wooded land on the Standing Rock, Cheyenne River, Crow Creek, and Fort Berthold reservations in North and South Dakota (figs. 2, 3). On one edge of this massive project, the Oahe Dam flooded 160,889 acres formerly owned by the Standing Rock and Cheyenne River Sioux, including their best rangeland, most of their gardens and farms, and nearly all their timber, wild fruit, and wildlife resources (Lawson 1982:29, 49–50).

Far more common than too much water has been too little, and in the West irrigation projects themselves have threatened Indian agriculture. Attempts by White settlers to monopolize the water of the Milk River and thus deny the Indians of the Fort Belknap Reservation, Montana, the means of irrigating their lands precipitated the legal struggle that yielded the *Winters* doctrine of 1908, in which the courts tried to guarantee Indians adequate water for their own needs. Interpretation of the doctrine has only yielded more litigation (Hundley 1978, 1982).

Such developmental issues have also impinged on areas where at first glance they might appear to be irrelevant. Stock reduction among the Navajos during the New Deal, for example, was the result of severe overgrazing of the Navajo reservation. By the 1930s, such overgrazing had been taking a serious toll on Navajo lands for at least 20 years. The overgrazing itself had been promoted by encouragement on the part of the government for the

WHITE AND CRONON

Navajos to increase their herds, even as their population rose and they lost access to traditional off-reservation grazing lands. The Bureau of Indian Affairs acted to drastically reduce the number of sheep, goats, and horses that the Navajos grazed. While the reduction was necessary to halt the deterioration of the Navajo herd economy, it also preserved Boulder Dam, whose reservoir, officials believed, would be destroyed by silt eroding from the Navajo reservation. Unfortunately, the consequence of the policy was to remove an important support from an economy that had come to rely on sheep for a key aspect of subsistence (R. White 1983).

Alaska

Perhaps the single most dramatic example of their ecological quandary has been the fate of the Alaska Natives under the terms of the Alaska Native Claims Settlement Act of 1971. In return for extinguishing native title to the whole of Alaska, which had never been acquired by treaty, Alaska Natives were given $962.5 million and 44 million acres, approximately 10 percent of state land. These enormous resources were to be distributed under a scheme that divided native communities into regional and village corporations; individual natives became shareholders in these entities.

Corporations were not allowed to distribute their shares to non-natives for 20 years, which meant that in 1991 control over the land from which Alaska Natives derived their livelihoods could pass entirely out of native hands. Leaving aside potential environmental changes relating to petroleum or mineral development that might diminish the caribou herds or the salmon runs, the bankruptcy of village or regional corporations could easily yield circumstances under which Natives would lose access to the hunting and fishing around which their entire way of life revolved (Berger 1985). The ultimate success of this attempt to control ecological impact remained unclear.

Protestant Churches and the Indians

R. PIERCE BEAVER

Protestants of a number of denominations have supported missions to the Indians in British America and in the United States. Especially during the early colonial period and at times in the nineteenth century, mission policy has had links to the general civil and political policies of the secular authorities.

The Colonial Period

Evangelization of the native inhabitants of North America was often alleged to be the dominant motive for British exploration and colonization (Williamson 1931; L.B. Wright 1943; Lucas 1930; Beaver 1966:7ff.). The Virginia charters of 1606 and 1609 declared the conversion of the inhabitants to be the principal goal of colonization; and the parsons who preached the annual sermons for the Virginia Company rang the changes on that theme (A. Brown 1897, 1:53, 67–68, 74, 236, 337, 463, see also 283–291 for sermons; L.B. Wright 1943:92–94, 99–102). Many have been puzzled by the slowness with which the settlers acted on the avowed missionary profession of the charter and company. It has been suggested that the colonists were militarily too weak and the Powhatan Confederacy too strong for the situation to be favorable to missionizing, and that the English needed the friendship and help of the Indians too much to allow evangelization, which ultimately had a political end of subjugation in view. Acculturation and christianization consequently began to be effective only after the defeat of the Powhatan tribes following the 1622 massacre (Nash 1975).

The charters of Plymouth, Massachusetts, and Connecticut likewise claimed that the king was bent on "reducing and conversion of such savages as remain wandering in desolation and distress to civil society and the Christian religion" (New Plymouth Company 1836; Massachusetts (Colony) 1853–1854, 1:17; Connecticut (Colony) 1850–1890, 2:8, 1900, 2:8). It was to be the New England missions in which such professions of missionary zeal would be brought to fruition. The final voicing of such a motive to colonization was in the case of Pennsylvania. Friends preached to Indians as a matter of personal concern, but no corporate mission was undertaken during the colonial period (Kelsey 1917). The evangelistic motive was not officially expressed in the instance of Georgia, but the governor, his trustees, and at least one preacher made the last profession that colonization was for the sake of evangelization. Gov. James Oglethorpe induced Bishop Thomas Wilson to write a manual that would enable settlers to instruct Indians in the Christian faith. A parcel of land was granted to Moravian missionaries as their base of a mission to the Creek, but that venture speedily ended when the missionaries refused to bear arms at a time when an invasion of Spaniards from Florida was expected (Lucas 1930:69; Rundle 1734; T. Wilson 1759; Schwarze 1923:6–14).

The settlers of Plymouth and Massachusetts saw their invasion of New England as an action of Divine Providence bringing the western lands into the kingdom of Christ. At first they seemed to think, despite the charter and the seal of the colony (fig. 1), that this goal was to be accomplished by the displacement of the Indians. After a generation many decided that the intention of God was the conversion of the Indians, and, once launched, the mission came to be regarded as "one of New England's peculiar glories." Evangelization was simple in motivation: first, giving glory to God, and second, compassion for the ruined spiritual and physical state of the Indians (Mather 1820, 1:7). Except for Eleazer Wheelock in the eighteenth century, there was little thought given to the conversion being cheaper than war or to the expediency of creating a bulwark of Protestant Indians against the French in Canada. The mission was not a form of moral restitution for the plundering of the lands of the Indians, because the Puritans held that they had bought "empty" land from the Indians at their own price and had turned it into productive farms (Stoddard 1722; Washburn 1964: 101–110, 162–208, 1959). On motivation generally see Beaver (1962, 1968).

The mission might be undertaken to realize the glory of God, but the gardening of the wilderness required the conversion of the Indians in order to justify the Puritan's understanding of himself as the highest model of the Christian civilized man. The Indian had to be transformed into this model in order to justify the claim (Pearce 1952, 1953; Vaughan 1965; Carroll 1969:11–13, 123–125; Nash 1975). This motive to mission effort was to have a tremendous impact on methods.

The General Court of Massachusetts began to address

Amer. Antiquarian Soc., Worcester, Mass.

Fig. 1 Seal of the governor and Company of Mass. Bay, depicting an Indian with a scroll reading "Come over and help us." This woodcut, while the earliest New England depiction of an Indian in print, is derived from several earlier versions of the seal made in London. The Indian wears a girdle of leaves and holds a straight-backed bow. The iconographic representation is conventional and derived from 16th–century European stereotypes of South American Indians. No descriptions of New England Indians discuss leaf, or feather, girdles (Simmons 1982), and the Indian's garment is probably based on Brazilian Indian feather skirts. Woodcut and print by John Foster, on a broadside issued by the General Court, Boston, 1681.

itself to the evangelization of the Indians in 1644 and in 1646 instructed the ministers each year to select two of their number as preachers to the Indians (Massachusetts (Colony) 1853–1854, 2:6–7, 84, 134, 176–179). However, by that date two missions were already in preparatory stages. Why the delay in launching the mission? There was little chance for evangelization until the Massachusett Indians recognized Puritan authority and ceded land in 1644 (Nash 1975; Jennings 1971b; Salisbury 1974; Axtell 1972; Ortega y Medina 1958; for a good survey of the course of the seventeenth-century missions see Vaughan 1965:235–308).

Thomas Mayhew in 1641 purchased a group of 16 islands including Nantucket, Martha's Vineyard, and the Elizabeths. His son, Thomas, Jr., directed the first settlement at Edgartown on Martha's Vineyard in 1642; and the father set up as proprietor. Indian land claims were honored, title purchased, and then the lands were resold to English settlers. The son had studied theology, and he was elected minister when the church was gathered. Thomas, Jr., already knew the Massachusett language, and he soon began evangelizing the Indians. This inaugurated a unique family mission by the Mayhews lasting through five generations (Hare 1932). The young pastor employed a quiet, individual approach. He spent every Sunday night in conversation with a young man named Hiacoomes, who was baptized in 1643, served Mayhew as assistant, and was the first ordinand in 1670. Public services began in 1646, and after two years conversions multiplied. A covenant for a Christian community was drawn up in 1652, and the first Indian church, with Indian officers, was organized in 1670, by which time there were some 3,000 Christians in the islands living in towns under their own sachems. The delay was due to a desire to prove to Whites that the Christian profession of the Indians was equal to their own. The other islands and some of the mainland were evangelized from the Vineyard.

Meanwhile John Eliot, pastor at Roxbury, had launched the mission on the mainland (Mather 1820; see also Winslow 1968; Beals 1957; Vaughan 1965:245–252, 286–287). After he had spent some time in language study, Eliot began public preaching in autumn 1646 and soon was regularly holding services at a dozen different locations. His church called an assistant in order to give him freedom for the Indian work. He enlisted friends, who usually had to preach and teach through interpreters: for example, Daniel Gookin in Massachusetts and John Cotton and Richard Bourne in Plymouth Colony. The first town was gathered at Nonantum but soon moved to Natick in 1651, the land being set aside by the General Court. Other towns were also established by the legislature, and by 1674 there were 14 towns of "praying Indians" with a reported population of 2,200 on the mainland and 1,800 to 2,600 on the island. Indians were admitted into membership in English churches also, but the extent of the practice is not clear.

King Philip's War of 1675–1676 seriously disrupted the towns and destroyed most of them. The mission never fully recovered, for the Christian Indians had been victims of the wrath of both White settlers and non-Christian Indians. The number of Indians was henceforth diminished in eastern Massachusetts, and only slight remnants were extant in the late twentieth century, with small churches at Mashpee on Cape Cod and at West Tisbury on the Vineyard (Kellaway 1962; Beaver 1966:125–152; Lindquist 1923).

While the mission was in decline in eastern Massachusetts during the eighteenth century, a second enterprise was initiated in the 1730s. Solomon Stoddard, at Northampton, called for a new obedience to the purposes of God and the founding fathers of the colony in 1722 (Stoddard 1722). The new interest was sparked into action when the Society in Scotland for Propagating Christian Knowledge had to find missionaries to support in order to claim a legacy, and in 1731 wrote to Gov. Jonathan Belcher and others. This led in 1733 to the ordination of three Harvard College graduates for service at northern points: Stephen Parker for Fort Richmond, Ebenezer Hinsdell to Fort Dummer, and Joseph Seccombe to Fort George (Beaver 1966:33–73). The mission soon failed, supposedly because of the prior influence of the French Roman Catholic missionaries.

However, a more promising mission was already beginning in the Housatonic Valley of western Massachusetts, considered to be beyond the reach of adverse White influences. Ministers brought the Housatonic Mahicans to the attention of the governor and commissioners in Boston, and the Rev. Nehemiah Bull of Westfield and Rev. Stephen Williams of Springfield were sent to those Indians to confer with them about a mission. Williams carried a favorable report to Boston, and the mission was authorized in the summer of 1734. A missionary was found in the person of a Yale College tutor, John Sergeant. The governor made Sergeant's ordination at Deerfield on August 31, 1735, the climax of a great regional council with the Indians (Beaver 1966:75–103).

Once again the Massachusetts legislature bought land and established a township for the converts and inquirers, naming it Stockbridge. Its establishment contained a fatal flaw: allotments were made to four English families who were expected to provide the Indians with examples of Christian piety and English civilization. Eventually the Whites would displace the Indians (Axtell 1985:196–204). Sergeant was preaching in Mahican within three years. A day school and a boarding school were flourishing institutions. When the missionary died in July 1749, he had baptized 182 persons, of whom 129 were living then in the village, and of whom 42 were full communicants. The town counted 20 houses in English style and 218 inhabitants. The Christian Indians had become recognized as a separate tribe, the Stockbridge nation.

Sergeant was succeeded by Jonathan Edwards, who left in 1758 to become president of the College of New Jersey (Princeton). Under the next pastor, Stephen West, the church was divided into Indian and English congregations, and the Indians entrusted to John Sergeant, Jr. The pressure by Whites was so great that after the Revolution the Indians sold their lands and migrated to a tract ceded to them by the Oneidas in central New York, called New Stockbridge (Belknap and Morse 1816), having followed

Samson Occom and his Mohegans. White pressure again induced them to move in 1820 to Ohio, and then by stages into the Green Bay region of Wisconsin, where the Stockbridge Reservation remained in 1987. The tribe was granted citizenship in 1843. The church was reorganized under the American Board of Commissioners for Foreign Missions in 1827, but the affiliation later became Presbyterian (Lindquist 1923:126–131).

Also touching the Housatonic Valley, but in Connecticut and across the border in New York, were important missions of the Moravian Church undertaken by missionaries from the center at Herrnhut, Saxony. Christian Heinrich Rauch began the mission at Shekomeko in Dutchess County in 1740 and built the main station at Wechquadnach (present Indian Pond), which is bisected by the state line. A branch station was established at Schaghticoke on the Housatonic River. Prosperous towns of farmers and craftsmen following the Moravian liturgical pattern of community life rapidly developed. But White settlers wanted them eliminated. After imprisonment on charges of being French agents, the missionaries were ejected from Connecticut, while in New York the missionaries were harassed by official persecution because the pacifists refused militia duty. A sheriff terminated the services and instruction on December 15, 1744. After Parliament recognized the Moravian church as an ancient episcopal church, settlers at Wechquadnach asked the authorities at Bethlehem to send missionaries, who served as pastors to the Whites and worked with the Indians at Schaghticoke (Moravian Historical Society 1860; D.C. Smith 1948; Hamilton 1900).

The Moravians had removed from Georgia to Nazareth, Pennsylvania, in 1740, and to Bethlehem in 1743. Bethlehem became headquarters and the base for the Indian missions (fig. 2). Missionaries were supposed to be

left, Brown U., John Carter Brown Lib., Providence, R.I.: 30650; right, Natl. Arch.: RG22-FFA-314.
Fig. 2. The Moravian Church and Native people. left, Baptizing Indians (Cranz 1757), presumably Delawares and Mahicans at Bethlehem, Pa. Indicated by letters are: the minister performing the baptisms (A), the Indians being baptized (B), Indian lay assistants (C), and the Indian congregation, with the men depicted wearing cloth matchcoats, on the left, and the women in clothing of European style, on the right (D). Engraved plate. right, Carmel Mission, on Nushagak Bay, Alaska. The mission and its school were established next to the Yupik Eskimo village of Kanulik in 1885. An industrial school and a hospital were later built. The site was abandoned about 1910 (Orth 1967:187), but the church remained active in the area. Photograph by N.B. Miller, 1890.

self-supporting, but that was impossible among the Indians in the forests, and the missions were supported by the 42 industries of Bethlehem (Danker 1971; Gollin 1967; Hamilton and Hamilton 1967). A mission to the Delawares was begun at Meniolagomeka near the Wind Gap in the Blue Mountain, and Mahicans from Wechquadnach and Shekomeko joined that community. Settlers forced abandonment in 1755, and the converts moved to a new site called Gnadenhütten, where 11 were killed by allies of the French. After several years of disruption and removals when the French Indians began attacks in 1763, the Christian Indians were interned on an island in the Delaware River at Philadelphia while a mob sought to massacre and scalp them. They were shipped to New York, but the authorities there returned them to Philadelphia, where another mob threatened.

The same story was repeated for the Delaware missions, and even for a new mission to the Munsees on the Allegheny River, as they moved westward by stages, until David Zeisberger and John Heckwelder led them to Schönbrunn in eastern Ohio, supposedly far from White penetration. The peaceful, pious, industrious villages of Gnadenhütten, Lichtenau, Schönbrunn, and Salem were founded. But the Revolution brought chaos, and the mission was destroyed when a party of American militiamen murdered 90 unresisting men, women, and children at Gnadenhütten on March 8, 1782. The sorrowful story of unending migration ended in Canada with the founding of Fairfield, Ontario, in 1792, and the successor mission at New Fairfield, on the Moravian town reserve, was in 1902 turned over to the Methodist Church of Canada (E.E. Gray 1956).

Another mission of the Society in Scotland for Propagating Christian Knowledge related to the New England work was that of David Brainerd (D. Brainerd 1822; Beaver 1966:105–124), who was commissioned on November 22, 1742, a year after Azariah Horton was sent to work with the Montauks of Long Island. Brainerd went to Kaunaumeek, southeast of Albany, and commuted to Stockbridge for language study. Next he located at the Forks of the Delaware (Easton, Pennsylvania), itinerated on the Susquehanna, and finally in the spring of 1745 settled among Indians in the neighborhood of Crosswicks, New Jersey. The Indians were swept into a revival marked by "spiritual" manifestations just like those that characterized revivals in White communities at the time. A mass movement of conversion developed. A Christian town based on farming and crafts arose. After Brainerd's death in 1747, his brother John succeeded him. A few decades later the state appropriated the land to White uses and packed the Indians off to Brothertown near New Stockbridge, New York.

The Iroquois tribes of New York constantly attracted the attention of the New Englanders, and in 1747 the Boston representatives of the Society in Scotland sent Elihu Spencer to Oquaga on the Susquehanna River, where Gideon Hawley (former schoolmaster at Stockbridge) also served from 1753 to 1756 (Beaver 1966:186; Dexter 1885, 2:89–92, 205–208; Barnes 1932:418). Eleazer Wheelock's mission made the most persistent effort to move out of New England to the Iroquois. Wheelock was the most creative strategist among New England missionaries, but he always lacked sufficient means to support his men. Due to his temperament and inability to cooperate with others he was usually at odds with his missionaries and his constituents (McClure and Parish 1811; W.B. Sprague 1857–1869, 1:493–499; Wheelock 1763; McCallum 1932; Beaver 1966:211ff.).

The inspiration for his mission came to Eleazer Wheelock through his tutoring of the Mohegan lad, Samson Occom; and later he always attempted to exploit this Indian for the sake of public relations. Like many another Connecticut parson, Wheelock took boys into his home at Lebanon Crank and taught them. Occom spent four years studying under the pastor. Thwarted in going on a mission to the Cherokees, Occom served as missionary and pastor to the Montauks of Long Island and the Mohegans and Niantics of eastern Connecticut (fig. 3), except for a brief effort with the Oneidas, from 1749 throughout the remainder of his life. He received a little financial help from the New England and Scottish societies and from individuals. He was ordained by the Presbytery of Long Island on August 30, 1759. Occom went to England and Scotland with the Rev. Nathanael Whitaker from 1765 to 1768 to raise funds for Wheelock. He along with his son-in-law, Joseph Johnson, and brother-in-law, David Fowler, held consultations with the Oneidas between 1773 and 1775, receiving from that tribe a tract of land to which the Mohegans and Montauks might remove. The Revolution interrupted removal, but in 1784 Occom led most of his people to Brothertown. He died at New Stockbridge in 1792 (Blodgett 1935; L.B. Richardson 1933; Beaver 1966:153–183).

Wheelock's experience with the young Occom inspired him with the idea that he could recruit and train Indian and English youths together and support them as missionaries. The Indian youths would have their faith and piety confirmed by the White students' example, and the Whites would provide an example of the civilization to which they should acculturate. The White students would gain from their classmates a knowledge of Indian vernaculars and customs. Both types of students would then be commissioned as missionaries. More Indians than Whites were desired, because they could be more effective in their own society and be supported much more cheaply. However, Wheelock in the end came to doubt their reliability and effectiveness because the results did not measure up to his expectations. The root cause of that seems to have been, not the inferiority of the Indian agents, but Wheelock's own sense of superiority and his

Mr. Occom's Addreſs

TO INDIAN HIS BRETHREN.

On the Day that MOSES PAUL, an Indian, was executed at NEW-HAVEN, on the 2d of SEPTEMBER, 1772, for the Murder of MOSES COOK.

I.

MY kindred Indians, pray attend and hear,
With great attention and with godly fear;
This day I warn you of that curſed ſin,
That poor, deſpiſed Indians wallow in.

II.

'Tis drunkenneſs, this is the ſin you know,
Has been and is poor Indians overthrow;
'Twas drunkenneſs that was the leading cauſe,
That made poor Moſes break God's righteous Laws.

III.

When drunk he other evil courſes took,
Thus hurried on, he murdered Moſes Cook;
Poor Moſes Paul muſt now be hang'd this day,
For wilful murder in a drunken fray.

IV.

A dreadful wo pronounc'd by God on high,
To all that in this ſin do lie;
O deviliſh beaſtly luſt, accurſed ſin,
Has almoſt ſtript us all of every thing.

V.

We've nothing valuable or to our praiſe,
And well may other nations on us gaze;
We have no money, credit or a name,
But what this ſin does turn to our great ſhame.

VI.

Mean are our houſes, and we are kept low,
And almoſt naked, ſhivering we go;
Pinch'd for food and almoſt ſtarv'd we are,
And many times put up with ſtinking fare.

VII.

Our little children hovering round us weep,
Moſt ſtarv'd to death we've nought for them to eat;
All this diſtreſs is juſtly on us come,
For the accurſed uſe we make of rum.

VIII.

A ſhocking, dreadful ſight we often ſee,
Our children young and tender, drunkards be;
More ſhocking yet and awful to behold,
Our women will get drunk both young and old.

IX.

Behold a drunkard in a drunken fit,
Incapable to go, ſtand, ſpeak, or ſit,
Deform'd in ſoul and every other part,
Affecting ſight! enough to melt one's heart.

X.

Sometimes he laughs, and then a hideous yell,
That almoſt equals the poor damn'd in hell;
When drown'd in drink we know not what we do,
We are deſpiſed and ſcorn'd and cheated too.

XI.

On level with the beaſts and far below
Are we when with ſtrong drink we reeling go;
Below the devils when in this ſin we run,
A drunken devil I never heard of one.

XII.

My kindred Indians, I intreat you all,
In this vile ſin never again to fall;
Fly to the blood of CHRIST, for that alone
Can for this ſin and all your ſins atone.

XIII.

Though Moſes Paul is here alive and well,
This night his ſoul muſt be in heaven or hell;
O! do take warning by this awful ſight,
And to a JESUS make a ſpeedy flight!

XIV.

You have no leaſe of your ſhort time you know,
To hell this night you may be forc'd to go;
Oh! do embrace an offer'd CHRIST to-day,
And get a ſealed pardon while you may.

XV.

Behold a loving JESUS, ſee him cry,
With earneſtneſs of ſoul, "Why will ye die?"
My kindred Indians, come juſt as you be,
Then Chriſt and his ſalvation you ſhall ſee.

XVI.

If you go on and ſtill reject Chriſt's call,
'Twill be too late, his curſe will on you fall;
The Judge will doom you to that dreadful place,
In hell, where you ſhall never ſee his face.

Fig. 3 *Mr. Occom's Address to His Indian Brethren* (Occom 1772), written in metered verse. In this moral injunction, the Mohegan missionary Samson Occom admonishes his "kindred Indians" to abstain from drunkenness, which he claims to have brought them to a deplorable state. The minister further counsels Indians to become Christians and so save themselves from a fate similar to that of Moses Paul, a Christian Wampanoag, who committed a murder while drunk. Paul had been a member of the Provincial Regiment under Col. Israel Putnam during the French and Indian War and later served on a naval warship. At Paul's request Occom delivered a sermon to him in public, prior to his execution. The last part of the sermon was addressed specifically to Indians and dealt with drunkenness in particular (Blodgett 1935:138–144). The sermon was later printed in numerous editions. The broadside verse, of uncertain authorship, is a summary of the sermon. Other versions of the broadside were also published.

inability to trust an Indian and treat him as an equal (Axtell 1985:204–215).

All missions to the Iroquois out of Boston between 1761 and 1766 failed. They were supported by the Society in Scotland for Propagating Christian Knowledge and a short-lived Massachusetts society (Beaver 1966:185ff; Kellaway 1962:194–196, 205–208). But in that last year Samuel Kirkland began a permanent mission to the Oneidas. He had studied at the College of New Jersey after leaving Wheelock's school. He had a considerable measure of success with the Oneidas, and when the Revolution erupted he was able to keep them friendly to the Americans (Lennox 1932).

There was one mass movement, the conversion of the Mohawk nation to adherence to the Church of England. It was undertaken with a small amount of missionary assistance, but it was actually a spontaneous movement inspired by Superintendent of Indian Affairs for the Northern Department William Johnson and the Mohawk Joseph Brant.

This Anglican mission to the Mohawks had been started with the approval and support of Queen Anne and the archbishop of Canterbury by the new Society for the Propagation of the Gospel in Foreign Parts. The first missionary, Thoroughgood Moore, took up residence in Albany in 1704, but the mission was in a very anemic state until Henry Barclay's appointment in 1737. Barclay reported in 1743 that only a few hundred Mohawks remained unbaptized.

Johnson and Brant were convinced that the Indians could become Christians and still be Indians. They disturbed the Mohawk culture very little, adding Anglican liturgical practices to traditional customs. Loyal to England, the Mohawks moved to Ontario after the Revolution (Lydekker 1938; Klingberg 1940; Buell 1903; Flexner 1959; Pond 1893; H. Chalmers 1955; L.A. Wood 1922).

Strategy and Methods

Only two New Englanders concerned with christianizing the Indians questioned the general aims and goal of the mission. Roger Williams, the Baptist leader, made no effort at evangelization. He was opposed to "Christianizing" the natives into the state church (Vaughan 1965: 118–120, 239–240, 302–303). Dr. Charles Chauncy was much more deeply committed to mission than Williams, and he thought Indian civilization would be compatible

with Christianity. The gospel by its own inherent power could naturally effect any necessary change (Chauncy in Beaver 1966:190–209). The aim of all the missions was so to preach the gospel that sinful souls might be saved through faith in Jesus Christ and the converts gathered into churches. But most of them had the further aim that the Indian must conform to English civilization (Beaver 1969).

Preaching was the primary means of evangelization, and teaching the second. Some Protestant missionaries preached and taught in the vernacular, especially the Congregationalists and Moravians, but most were limited by having to speak through an interpreter. Preaching was heavily theological and intended to move the hearers to a conviction of sin and repentance. The Moravians told principally of the love of Christ, and David Brainerd also stressed God's love and grace.

The Indians were baptized as soon as converted and manifesting evidence of repentance and faith. In the first generation testing was protracted over many years until churches were eventually organized. The first was Natick in 1660 (Mather 1820, 1:499ff.). However, in the following century the Stockbridge church was organized simultaneously with John Sergeant's arrival in 1734.

Indians were admitted into membership in New England White churches, but the standard practice was to establish Christian Indian towns on land granted by the legislature, and on which the state also built the church and the schoolhouse. Segregated in this fashion, the converts and inquirers could be protected from the influence of bad Whites and bad Indians, the pastors could maintain discipline, and the teachers could nourish the people in religion and conformity to English civilization. But the towns were never a bulwark against White encroachment.

Catechizing was the first step in evangelization and Christian nurture. John Eliot's catechism, published in Massachusett in 1653, was the first book by Protestants ever printed in an Indian language (Eliot 1880:xvii). The Shorter Westminster and other catechisms were also used, and Brainerd improvised catechization. Instruction was in both the vernacular and English by White and Indian teachers. Eliot's grammar, *Indian Primer*, *Indian Dialogues*, and *Logick Primer* were basic texts (Pilling 1891: 127–130; Eliot 1904). Farming, carpentry, and blacksmithing were taught to men and boys, while women learned the domestic arts and crafts. During the early period a few promising youths were sent to the Boston

Latin Grammar School and to Harvard College, where a special residence was erected. The experiment was abandoned soon after 1700. John Sergeant at Stockbridge contributed to Protestant missions a new institution of prime importance, namely, the boarding school. It was a farm school where children were removed from parental and tribal influence and educated in Christian faith and piety and in the ways of English civilization (Sergeant 1743:3–4). Day schools were everywhere, but only Eleazer Wheelock took up the idea of the boarding school and adapted it to his peculiar scheme of missions.

Worship, devotions, evangelism, general education, and Christian education in the vernacular demanded literature, and John Eliot pioneered in providing it. In addition to the books in Massachusett previously named, Eliot and other Congregationalist missionaries produced a few other new compositions and a number of translations, the great achievement being Eliot's translation and printing of the whole Bible, completed in 1663. Sergeant put material into Mahican, and the *Book of Common Prayer* was printed in Mohawk, and the Moravians printed some small works in Delaware (Kellaway 1962: 125–126; Winship 1945; Vaughan 1965:253, 276–279; Hopkins 1753:13, 69; Lydekker 1938:156, 182–183; Pilling 1891).

The capstone of the mission system was the recruiting and training of a native ministry. Native teachers were employed in even greater numbers. The New England missionaries believed that the Indians were men with intellect and the power of reason, and they could be made to fulfill their potential by the transforming power of the gospel. White missionaries would always suffer limitations, from which the Indians working among their own people would be free. The Indians would complete the evangelization begun by the Whites. About 1700 there were 37 Indian ministers in Massachusetts. With the decline of the Indians in eastern Massachusetts the native pastors also declined and disappeared. The next company of them chronologically were associated with Wheelock and Samson Occom, and they were active through the period of the Revolution.

The activities of the agents of Massachusetts in London and the publication of the early Eliot tracts initiated a movement of concern in Parliament, which resulted in an act establishing the Society for the Propagation of the Gospel in New England in 1649. This is the very first Protestant missionary society, and it set the precedent for missions to be conducted and supported by voluntary societies incorporated by the authority of the state. After 1660 this society was rechartered as the Company for the Propagation of the Gospel in New England and Parts Adjacent in North America, and was popularly known as the New England Company. The Commissioners of the United Colonies of New England served until their dissolution in 1684 as the local agents who dealt directly with the missionaries. Thereafter the board of commissioners was made up of eminent clergymen and laymen in the vicinity of Boston (Kellaway 1962:199ff.).

The Society in Scotland for Propagating Christian Knowledge (called the Scottish Society), founded 1701, chartered in 1709, appointed a Boston board of commissioners in 1733 and began to support Indian missions, notably Stockbridge. There was overlapping between the two boards, and often it is difficult to distinguish between them.

Dr. Thomas Bray was led by his experiences in America to found three Anglican societies: the Society for Promoting Christian Knowledge in 1699, the Society for the Propagation of the Gospel in Foreign Parts in 1701, and Dr. Bray's Associates. The first was intended to provide libraries and other assistance to Anglican clergy in the colonies, the second to convert heathen and bring dissenters into the Church of England, and the third to provide schools and catechists for the Black slaves (Klingberg 1940).

It is impossible to learn to what extent individuals and local churches supported the missionaries. The earliest known local society was formed in Boston for support of the mission to Oquaga in 1747, and a regional Society for Propagating Christian Knowledge was chartered by the legislature of Massachusetts in 1762 (Kellaway 1962: 194–196). The king did not approve, and further organization had to await independence. Harvard College and the College of New Jersey had Indian mission funds, which supplemented grants from Great Britain.

Missions in a New Nation

The Indian missions were orphans during the Revolution. The New England Company turned permanently to Canada, while the Society in Scotland found it impossible to transmit funds. Samuel Kirkland was paid by Congress as a combined missionary, chaplain, and political agent among the Oneidas and other Iroquois (Lennox 1932: 92ff.; Beaver 1966a:54–56). Mahican and some White ministers were similarly employed or subsidized (Beaver 1966a:56–58).

It was difficult after the war to take up the old programs again. The frontier was rapidly moving west, and the settlements there appeared to the churchmen of the seaboard as being veritable dens of heathenism. The new country might be populated only by White and Red pagans if missionaries were not sent there. So it happened that missions to frontiersmen swallowed up the men and money raised for all evangelization, even in those societies that named the Indians as the first of their objects. New societies abounded. The Boston-centered Society for the Propagation of the Gospel among the Indians and Others in North America was founded in 1787, and the Moravian Society for Propagating the Gospel among the Heathen in the same year (Eckley 1806:App. 25–36; Elsbree 1928: 49–51; K.G. Hamilton 1940: 114–124). The Philadelphia Society of Friends set up an Aborigines Committee in 1795 (Kelsey 1917:92), which sent an educational mission to the Seneca (A.F.C. Wallace 1970). The Connecticut Missionary Society and the Massachusetts Missionary Society were established in 1789 and 1799 respectively, but despite some efforts they were unable to launch permanent Indian missions (Missionary Society of Connecticut 1800:14; Elsbree 1928:55–56). The New York Missionary Society of 1795 was a response to the example of the London Missionary Society, as was the Northern Missionary Society in the State of New York, founded the next year (Anonymous 1800:5–15; Elsbree 1928:51–56). They sent missionaries to the Tuscarora and other Iroquois peoples. The New York Society planned a very ambitious mission to the Chickasaw in 1799 that might have spearheaded a whole new era of mission activity, but it failed (Beaver 1966:235–248). Soon there were 20 to 30 societies, nearly all professing to be equally concerned about Indians, frontiersmen, and overseas heathens, but only a few made good on any objective save the frontiersmen (Elsbree 1928). The best account of the societies is by Chaney (1976).

Overseas missions were eventually established through a student movement in 1810, which resulted in the organization of the American Board of Commissioners for Foreign Missions (Strong 1910:3–16). It was responsible for missions to nonbelievers in general, and missions to American Indians were undertaken as well as those to India and elsewhere, beginning with the Cherokee. Half the personnel and funds were devoted to Indian missions in 1820. In 1827 the missions of the United Foreign Mission Society were taken over through merger. Among the tribes served were the Cherokee, Choctaw, Chickasaw, Osage, Stockbridge, Ojibwa, Creek, Pawnee, Nez Perce, Flathead, Sioux, Abenaki, and groups in Ohio and Michigan. Until the Civil War period the American Board of Commissioners maintained the most extensive enterprise of evangelization of Indians (Strong 1910:35–55). By 1860 the Board had sent 182 men and 290 women to the various tribes (American Board of Commissioners for Foreign Missions 1861). This was a joint venture of Congregationalists, Presbyterians, and Dutch Reformed churchmen. The Triennial Convention of Baptists for Foreign Missions, formed in 1814, within three years was giving national oversight to work among the Cherokee and in the Midwest that had originally been under local societies (Torbet 1955:26–30). This board in 1839 had sent 100 missionaries compared to 320 under the American Board of Commissioners. The Presbyterian Western Missionary Society in 1802 was active in the Midwest. When the Presbyterian Church in the U.S.A. divided in 1838, the New School churches remained with the American Board while the Old School General Assembly took over the Board of Foreign Missions established in 1836 and sent missionaries to Indians as well as to peoples overseas (A.J. Brown 1936). There were 20 persons in Indian work in 1839. Methodists working with Indians were largely under control of local annual conferences, and reporting to the denominational Missionary Society was sporadic and haphazard (Barclay 1949–1957, 1: 200–212, 2:112–285). The story began with the licensing of John Stewart in 1818 and the approval of his mission to the Wyandots at Upper Sandusky, Ohio, in 1819 (Barclay 1949–1957, 1:203–205). The Moravian attempt to reestablish the mission in eastern Ohio failed, and the continuing community in Canada went through a long period of decline (E.E. Gray 1956). A new motive to mission was heard, namely, atonement for the terrible wrongs inflicted on the Indians (Anonymous 1816:118–122; Beaver 1966 a: 62, 63), but it was the federal government's desire to use the missions in civilizing the Indians that was much more powerful than any ideological or theological motive in stimulating new mission projects.

Civilization and Evangelization

The missions of the colonial period had laid great stress on educating the Indians generally in agriculture and crafts and those persons destined for ministry in the liberal arts and theology. The aim was to civilize them according to the British pattern. The same emphasis continuing in the new missionary endeavors after independence was achieved with even greater stress on agricultural and craft education. This began with the New York Missionary Society's mission to the Chickasaw in 1799 (Beaver 1966: 235–248). There was never any argument over whether the aim of missions was "evangelization" or "civilization," since the two were regarded as twin objectives. The debate was about sequence: did one begin with evangelizing and move on to civilizing, or was the order to be reversed? Some persons believed that the gospel could be understood and accepted only when a sufficient degree of civilization had been achieved; others held the position that conversion had to come first, because only acceptance of the gospel could awaken a desire for civilization. Whatever the theory about sequence, actually both activities were stressed and the school was regarded as the chief means of evangelism. The exception was the Society of Friends mission to the Seneca on the Allegheny, a purely educational project.

The American Board missions usually pioneered in both theory and practice overseas and among the Indians, and other boards and societies accepted their models. What developed in Cyrus Kingsbury's Brainerd Mission to the Cherokees was more or less duplicated by other agencies. A school was built before a church, and education was the major activity, although conversion and church planting were inextricably interwoven with it.

The Lancasterian system of instruction used by the British dissenters (Anglicans generally used the "British National" system) was generally employed. The use of the more advanced pupils as tutors to the less advanced multiplied the teaching force. Day schools were satellites of the central station boarding schools, and they afforded places for worship and preaching. There were Sunday schools for Blacks, presumably the slaves of the Indians. When Kingsbury moved on to the Choctaws he soon established a system of four boarding schools and 32 day schools. There was itinerant preaching from all central stations.

The stated policy of the United Foreign Missionary Society in their third annual report, in 1820, adopted when it launched the mission to the Osage, well reveals the strategy of the missions:

> The Board have declared it to be their object to promote amongst the Indians not only the knowledge of Christianity, but also of the arts of civilized life. Besides the branches of learning taught in common schools, the boys will be instructed in agriculture, and the mechanic arts, —and the girls in spinning, weaving, sewing, knitting, and household business. They have also resolved that in every establishment there shall be a superintendent and an assistant, who shall be Ministers of the Gospel, a schoolmaster, a farmer, a blacksmith, a carpenter, and other such mechanics as shall be found necessary, all of whom come under the general denomination of *Missionary*. This number may be increased as occasion shall require, and at every station there shall be a Physician, by profession; or a person acquainted with the practice of physic.

The ordained men were the administrators, but all—teachers, farmers, millers, carpenters, and the wives—were simultaneously teachers and evangelists.

English was the language of instruction at Brainerd and other Cherokee stations in the beginning, but when it was discovered how little was understood through the alien tongue, there was a switch to instruction in Cherokee. George Guess (Sequoya) devised a writing system for the language, and thenceforth progress was rapid among the Cherokees. This experience induced the American Board missionaries to use the vernacular languages generally, and the later Sioux Mission is a good example of what was achieved (fig. 4). However, too few of the other denominations were willing to have their missionaries devote the time and energy necessary to mastery of the vernacular, and they had to use interpreters much of the time. Learning in the English language schools was superficial.

Such a program of education and christianization worked out very well among the Cherokees and Choctaws in their original homelands and in the Dwight Mission among the Cherokees who moved west of the Mississippi in 1821. It enabled the transplanted peoples of the Five Civilized Tribes to recover and move forward after removal. However, those peoples were settled and acculturated to the White culture to a great degree. The program failed utterly when addressed to the Osage and other Plains Indians (Graves 1949). Large investments in

Lib. of Congress, Rare Book Div.: Broadside Portfolio 174, No. 43.
Fig. 4. Poster with Indian names in Sioux and English, probably those of students in the Touch-the-Cloud School, operated by the Congregational Church under Rev. T.L. Riggs, missionary. Nos. 1–17 are male names and 18–40 are female names; the English translations are not accurate. The poster was printed at the Santee Normal Training School at the Santee Agency, Nebr., also operated by the Congregational church (American Missionary Association). The use of Indian languages for instruction, often by Native teachers, was considered by the Congregational church to be highly effective, but the practice was ultimately rejected by the federal authorities who subsidized the schools (Meyer 1967:187–190; ARCIA 1886:52–53, 1887:161–162). Printed 1886–1913.

land, buildings, equipment, a big mission family, and the like were futile and wasteful. Indians accustomed to shifting their residence moved far away from such centers after a year or two. A few missionaries traveled with the people and some children were brought into the boarding school. The essential features of the system were tenaciously held, but very little could be achieved by a central station until the Indians were restricted in their movements. This induced many missionaries early to favor reservations.

Without government aid there would have been far less mission effort in the first half of the nineteenth century. Administration of Indian affairs fell originally to the War Department. Secretary of War Henry Knox, believing that practical education in agriculture and arts was the only possible alternative to extermination for Indians, looked to the churches to carry out his scheme. However, Knox was reluctant to allow teaching of Christianity to Indians not yet converted, so little was done (Beaver 1966a:63–66; ASPIA 1832–1834, 4:235). The seemingly bright future of the American Board mission to the Cherokees undertaken by Cyrus Kingsbury with aid from the War Department in 1816 provided the needed special stimulus (Walker 1931; ASPIA 1832–1834, 4:477–478). President James Madison's message to Congress in January 1818 emphasized the urgency of an educational program. The bill to establish a permanent "civilization fund" passed Congress in March 1819 (3 U.S. Stat. 516–517).

The War Department rule after 1820 was to provide

two-thirds the cost of buildings (ASPIA 1832–1834, 4: 273). Thirty-one grants in 1820, totaling $16,605, were given to the Baptist Cherokee schools at Great Crossings and Valley Towns, to the Moravians at Springplace, the Osage schools of the United Foreign Missionary Society, the Cherokee Brainerd and Eliot schools of the American Board of Commissioners, the Foreign Mission School at Cornwall, Connecticut, the Baptist mission at Fort Wayne, a Presbyterian Choctaw school, and to the Oneida School of the Hamilton Baptist Missionary Society in New York (ASPIA 1832–1834, 4:271–273). The school at Cornwall prepared Hawaiians, American Indians, and Africans for the evangelization of their own peoples. By 1826 subsidized schools numbered 38, including one Roman Catholic and one Episcopal school.

Tribes such as the Cherokee and Choctaw readily invested part of their government annuities in the schools, almost as much as the government grants. The missions themselves spent 15 to 18 times the amount of the federal grant (ASPIA 1832–1834, 4:669). Nevertheless, probably very little would have been given by church people without the stimulus of the civilization fund.

The successful acculturation of the Cherokees and others of the Five Civilized Tribes confirmed the opinions of the mission leaders and many philanthropists that Indians could be brought to accept the White American cultural and spiritual values and social and economic way of life. There was little to sustain that hope with respect to most of the tribes as they were uprooted and forced into poverty. For every instance of success in acculturation there were 10 of failure. The missions were usually a force for disintegration of the Indian society, and they joined the settlers, the Army, and government policy in the process of disruption. Their persistent attack on the religion of the Red man and their relegating of all his beliefs and ritual practices to the realm of superstition deprived the missionaries of use of the Indian spiritual values and ideas as bridges to the gospel and to acceptance of the Christian faith in terms meaningful to Indians (see Bowden 1981). The cultural product was usually something different from both the traditional society and the White pattern (Berkhofer 1965).

Where the missions were least dogmatic and coercive and sought to show Christian principles in practical, friendly relations, the Indians had the best opportunity to fashion a synthesis of traditional and White American religious and social values and customs. The outstanding example is Handsome Lake's religion, which emerged among the Allegany Senecas (A.F.C. Wallace 1970: 239–337). Even the concept of sin and the practice of confession, along with the requirement of temperance, were combined with traditional Iroquois beliefs and practices.

Lib. of Congress, Print and Photograph Div.: LC-US262-38006.
Fig. 5. Church of St. Columba's, on Gull Lake, Minn. Terr., established among the Chippewa by the Protestant Episcopal Church in 1852 at the request of Rev. John Johnson (Enmegahbowh, d. 1902), an Ottawa raised among the Chippewa. In Canada he became a Methodist and later attended a Methodist school in Jacksonville, Ill. Ordained as a Methodist preacher, Johnson served the Chippewa of the upper Mississippi beginning in 1839. When St. Columba's was built, Johnson acted as assistant and interpreter in the Episcopal church. He was ordained as an Episcopal priest in 1859 and was given charge of the Gull Lake mission. During the tumultuous period of the Sioux revolt of 1862, Johnson was the only missionary to remain in the area. In 1869 St. Columba's was moved to the White Earth Reservation, Minn., where Johnson, who brought followers from Gull Lake with him, was again in charge. When he was joined by another missionary in 1873, the 2 men began a school for training Indian clergy. Johnson also often traveled as Bishop Henry B. Whipple's assistant and interpreter. The church at Gull Lake was the first Episcopal church for Indians west of the Mississippi (Hodge 1907–1910, 1:425; W.H. Hare 1926). Wood engraving from *Frank Leslie's Illustrated Newspaper*, Jan. 26, 1856:109.

Removal and Disruption

The church and state partnership in missions to the Indians continued smoothly until the federal government adopted a policy of removal through both persuasion and coercion. That policy was incompatible with the earlier one of "civilizing," although many a missionary deluded himself that he could both evangelize and civilize if he could accompany some tribe to a place remote from all other White interference. Nearly every school that had been established under the "civilization fund" was destroyed by the removal program. While many portions of tribes were voluntarily moving west under White aggression, official pressure was first exerted on the tribes along the eastern Great Lakes. James B. Finley at the Methodist mission to the Wyandots at Upper Sandusky, Ohio, opposed removal because it would destroy the hope of christianization and civilization (Finley 1840, 1853, 1857) while the Baptist Carey Mission at Niles, Michigan, was the seat of the most rabid advocate of removal, Isaac McCoy (McCoy 1840; Schultz 1972). McCoy lobbied Congress, the administration, and the Baptist Triennial Convention on behalf of removal, beginning in 1824; and in 1828 he induced the Convention to present a memorial to Congress. That body also printed and distributed a pamphlet on the subject by the missionary (McCoy 1840: 321–323).

McCoy and his Baptist neighbors had the same views as the rest of the frontier population about the desirability of removing the Indians from the lands east of the Mississippi, but he was actually convinced that it was the only way to save the Indians. Pressure by settlers had forced relocation of his mission twice, and he had no sooner become established at Carey Mission than he found White interference made that site untenable. It was with genuine conviction and a passion for the welfare of the people that he contended for removal and strove for the establishment of Indian Territory (Schultz 1972; Beaver 1966a:95–102).

Other and more dispassionate ideas than those held by frontier Baptists—philanthropic ideas—ruled the hearts and minds of many Congregationalists and Presbyterians of the long-settled East where an Indian had become a rarity. When the possibility of general removal was first raised, the American Board favored it largely because of the persuasive advocacy of an influential member, Dr. Jedidiah Morse, in 1820 (Morse 1822) and because of the sad experience with the Indians by the three early New York societies that it had absorbed. However, the aggression of the state of Georgia against the Cherokees transformed this Board into a stalwart champion of Indian rights. It was largely through the ministry of the American Board's stations at Brainerd (Chickamauga), Carmel, Creekpath, Hightower, Willstown, Haweiss, Candy's Creek, and New Echota that the Cherokees had come to be recognized as a Christian nation by the War Department (Stokes 1950, 1:709). The stimulus provided by the missions had resulted in swift and effective acculturation of the tribe to White American culture and politics without loss of native genius and identity (Walker 1931; Starkey 1946; Bass 1936). When the Cherokees' suit against Georgia in the Supreme Court was dismissed because of lack of jurisdiction, since the tribe was not a foreign nation but a "domestic dependent nation," the Board through its secretary, Jeremiah Evarts, and members who were senators and representatives lobbied Congress and the administration, while the missionaries directly defied Georgia. Evarts also wielded a mighty pen in his essays published in the *National Intelligencer* and his pamphlets.

Locally nine missionaries—six of the American Board personnel, two Moravians, one Baptist—issued a formal defense of the Cherokees and defiance of Georgia at New Echota on December 29, 1830, soon seconded by some Methodists (Anonymous 1830:363–364). The Georgia legislature retaliated by enacting a law that punished by four years of imprisonment at hard labor any person residing in Cherokee territory who had not sworn an oath of allegiance to the state of Georgia. Soon missionaries were in jail, and after a series of legal actions two American Board men were sentenced to four years at hard labor. The Baptists and Methodists disowned the stand taken by their missionaries, but the American Board championed their imprisoned agents (Beaver 1966a: 111–114). When the Supreme Court in February 1832 pronounced judgment in favor of the missionaries and the tribe, President Andrew Jackson refused to enforce it. The federal government then set the army to the task of removing the Cherokees to a new home west of the Mississippi River (Foreman 1932). The enforced removal of the other Southeast tribes followed, all at the cost of tremendous human suffering. It was the Congregationalists, the Dutch Reformed, and the party of Presbyterians affiliated with the American Board of Commissioners for Foreign Missions who opposed removal and championed Indian rights. Other churchmen acquiesced or were silent.

The Society of Friends also emerged as foes of removal and champions of the rights of the Indians in defending the Senecas in the legal theft of their lands by the Ogden Land Company in New York in 1838–1842 (Society of Friends 1840; N.T. Strong 1841; Kelsey 1917).

Missionaries of the American Board fostered the growth of solid, substantial congregations among the Cherokees and Choctaws. But the majority of the peoples of the Southeast tribes were more attracted to the less exacting and more emotionally expressive models of the Baptist and Methodist churches. These predominated both before and after removal. The American Board fell into disfavor with a large part of its northern constituency because it refused to reject contributions from slaveholders and to expel slave-owning Cherokees and Choctaws from the churches related to it. Many persons withdrew support and organized the American Missionary Association. The missionaries among the Cherokees and Choctaws themselves denounced the Board and severed relations. The Board of Foreign Missions of the Presbyterian Church in the U.S.A. was pressed to take on support of those missionaries and did so just before the outbreak of the Civil War, but there had been enough early Presbyterian mission action to found the Presbytery of Indian Territory in 1840 and the Creek Presbytery in 1848 (Coleman 1985:52–63). Both the White settlers and the Indian church members were favorable to secession, and at the opening of the war in 1861 the Synod of Arkansas including the Indian churches of the Territory entered the Presbyterian Church of the Confederacy (Drury 1952: 388–389). The majority of people of the Five Civilized Tribes became Southern Baptists by assimilation (R. Hamilton 1930).

The American Board of Commissioners for Foreign Missions along with the Old School Presbyterians attempted the same high standard, exacting methods of evangelism and Christian nurture to the tribes of Michigan and Wisconsin and the diverse remnants among them transplanted from farther east, but enduring results were meager. The Baptists and Methodists worked the same area (Barclay 1949–1957, 2:113–170).

Missions meanwhile jumped across the continent to the Oregon Country. In 1835 the Methodists sent a party of four men, headed by Jason Lee, to the Willamette Valley (Brosnan 1932; Hines 1899; Barclay 1949–1957, 2: 200–262; Josephy 1965:120–126). That year Dr. Marcus Whitman and Samuel Parker scouted for the American Board of Commissioners for Foreign Missions. The following year Dr. Whitman founded a mission among the Cayuse near Walla Walla, and Henry S. Spaulding another among the Nez Perce at Lapwai, Idaho (Drury 1936, 1937, 1958, 1963–1966; Eells 1882, 1886; Josephy 1965:129–284). There was rivalry between the Protestant and Jesuit missionaries in the region, although there were instances of mutual helpfulness (Hinman 1933:65–66, 69–70; Burns 1966:30–36, 174–177; Josephy 1965: 206–207, 216, 247–252, 253–259).

The murder by Indians of the Whitman family among a total of 14 Whites at Whitman's station in 1847 left only a small Christian remnant among the Cayuse. The Nez Perce mission had appeared flourishing, but Spaulding was expelled by the government Indian agent. Some Christians remained faithful (Josephy 1965:281, 289–290). Spaulding was able to return in 1871, when he came back as a Presbyterian missionary and government instructor (Josephy 1965:432–433; Drury 1936). His return coincided with a revival stimulated by a party of Yakimas, and there was then rapid growth of the church (K.C. McBeth 1908:75–83; Hinman 1933:70–71). The first minister was ordained in 1879, and at the close of the century there were seven ministers and six churches (K.C. McBeth 1908:252–253).

The Sioux were the other main target of mission action before the Civil War. Dr. Thomas S. Williamson and the Pond brothers, Samuel and Gideon, were the pioneers in 1834, attempting to reach the Sioux from stations at Lake Harriet near Saint Anthony Falls and at Lac Qui Parle (S.C. Bartlett 1876; Riggs 1869, 1887; Pond 1893). Stephen Riggs soon joined them. The agent of the American Fur Company, the half-Sioux Joseph Renville, aided them as interpreter and advisor. Despite the wandering life of the tribe, two churches were gathered before 1850. Episcopal Oneidas had moved from New York to Minnesota, and Bishop Henry B. Whipple provided ministry to them. Then he extended his interest to other tribes, and in 1860 he began a mission to the Sioux (Whipple 1899).

Injustices and stupidities involved in locating the Sioux on thoroughly unsuitable reservations, failure to keep treaty provisions, and the issuance of wretched rations combined to stimulate a massive uprising of the Sioux in 1862. Hundreds of White settlers were killed, and a few hundred were captured. The christianized Indians, many of whom had helped White persons escape, suffered along with the settlers. The demand for punishment, even for extermination, of the Sioux was louder and more universal than usual after an Indian "war." The Sioux who had been most responsible for the action largely fled to Canada, while the remainder were interned under horrible conditions. Hundreds were condemned by military courts to be hanged, but after President Abraham Lincoln had reviewed the case only 38 were executed ("Indian–United States Military Situation, 1848–1891," fig. 3, this vol.) (Riggs 1869; Hinman 1933:77ff.).

The missionaries ministered to the Sioux, and Stephen Riggs of the American Board was appointed chaplain and interpreter. J.S. Williamson toiled along with his father, Dr. Thomas S. Williamson. The condemned men were moved to Mankato, Minnesota, and the women, children, and other men were put in a camp near Fort Snelling. A "revival movement" led by a Christian elder, Robert Hopkins, brought large numbers to church services and even to conversion. Dr. Williamson and Gideon Pond baptized 274 persons in a single ceremony and eventually a total of 306, while an Episcopal missionary baptized nine others. Progress was made in literacy and religious instruction. There was a similar movement in the camp. The missionaries continued their ministry after the condemned men were moved to Davenport, Iowa, for three years of imprisonment and the others transported to Crow Creek. Large portions of the Bible were translated and a new edition of the Sioux hymnal prepared. When all the prisoners were released in 1866 and located on the Santee Sioux reservation in Nebraska, the churches of the prison and of the camp were united. This became a center for the evangelization of the Sioux elsewhere, largely through the work of Indian pastors and evangelists (Hinman 1933:91–92). When the two Presbyterian denominations merged, the American Board handed over the larger part of the Sioux churches to the Presbyterian Church in the U.S.A., and gave over the others to the American Missionary Association. The Board of Foreign Missions of the Presbyterian Church in the U.S.A. turned all the Indian work over to the Board of Home Missions.

President Grant's Peace Policy

Once the Civil War had ended and slavery had been abolished, efforts on behalf of the freedman did not absorb all the energies of the philanthropists and reformers, and they turned their attention to the sad plight of the Indians and demanded justice for them (Mardock 1971). The Bureau of Indian Affairs and the agency service were generally regarded as hopelessly corrupt. The idea of involving the churches in the Indian service began with a bill that failed to pass Congress in 1867, but the idea quickly gained advocacy, and the question was asked

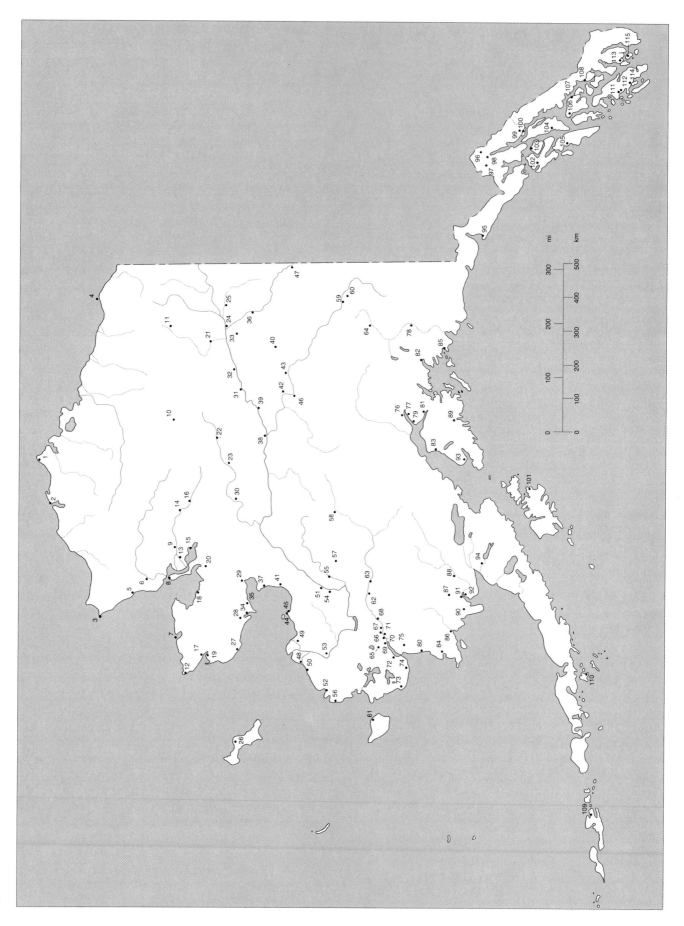

442

Fig. 6. Historic Protestant-Indian missions with dates of earliest denominational establishment, if known. When the first mission of any denomination is known for a site, that denomination and its date of founding are noted followed by other appropriate denominations listed in alphabetical order. For sites where the earliest mission is unknown, all appropriate denominations are merely listed in alphabetical order. Since many short-term ministries existed, this map is not comprehensive, nor were all of these missions in existence at the same time. Where more than one mission is noted for a town, that town had simultaneous, overlapping, sequential, or interrupted missions (Barclay 1949–1957; Beaver 1979; Bowden 1981; Lane, Markoe, and Schulte 1926; Copplestone 1973; Department of Town and Country Church and Indian Work 1962; Garritt 1886; Gaustad 1962; Mooney 1907b; Sweet 1964, 1964a, 1964b, 1964c; A.C. Thompson 1890). The denominations are abbreviated: A, Assemblies of God; B, American and Conservative Baptist; Br, Church of the Brethren; C, Church of God; Co, Congregationalist or United Church of Christ; D, Disciples of Christ; E, Episcopal or Anglican; Ev, Evangelical; F, Society of Friends or Quakers; L, Lutheran; M, Methodist; Me, Mennonite; Mo, Moravian; N, Nazarene; P, Presbyterian; Pe, Pentecostal; Pr, Protestant Board; R, Reformed; SA, Salvation Army; SB, Southern Baptist; SDA, Seventh Day Adventist.

Fig. 6a. Alaska: 1, Barrow, 1878, P, A, E; 2, Wainwright, A, P; 3, Point Hope, 1890, E, A; 4, Kaktovik, A, P; 5, Kivalina, E, F; 6, Noatak, F; 7, Shishmaref, L; 8, Kotzbue, 1897, F, A, B, E; 9, Kiana, F; 10, Anaktuvuk Pass, P; 11, Arctic Village, E; 12, Wales, 1890, Co, M; 13, Noorvik, F; 14, Ambler, F; 15, Selawik, B, F; 16, Shuangnak, F; 17, Teller Mission, L; 18, Deering, F; 19, Teller, 1894, L; 20, Buckland, F; 21, Venetie, B, E; 22, Allakaket, 1902, E; 23, Hughes, E; 24, Fort Yukon, 1898, E, A, B, SB; 25, Chalkyitsik, A, B, E; 26, Savoonga, 1878, P; 27, Nome, 1900, E, A, Ev, L, M, P; 28, White Mountain, Ev; 29, Koyuk, Ev; 30, Huslia, E; 31, Stevens Village, A, E; 32, Beaver, A, E; 33, Birch Creek, A; 34, Golovin, Ev; 35, Elim, Ev; 36, Circle, 1898, E; 37, Shaktoolik, A, Ev; 38, Tanana, 1892, E; 39, Rampart, 1900, E; 40, Chena, 1908, E; 41, Unalakleet, A, Ev; 42, Minto, A, E; 43, Fairbanks, 1905, E, A, Ev, F, M, SA, SB; 44, Stebbins, A; 45, St. Michael, 1886, E, A; 46, Nenana, 1911, E, A; 47, Eagle, E; 48, Alakanuk, A; 49, Kotlik, A; 50, Sheldon Point, A; 51, Grayling, E; 52, Scammon Bay, Ev; 53, Mountain Village, Ev; 54, Anvik, 1886, E; 55, Shageluk, E; 56, Hooper Bay, Ev; 57, Iditarod, 1911, E; 58, McGrath, A; 59, Tanacross, E; 60, Tok, SB; 61, Mekoryuk, Ev; 62, Aniak, A; 63, Kolmakof, 1885, Mo; 64, Chistochina, Pe; 65, Kasigluk, Mo; 66, Akiachak, Mo; 67, Akiak, Mo; 68, Tuluksak, Mo; 69, Napakiak, Mo; 70, Bethel, Ev, Mo; 71, Kwethluk, Mo; 72, Tuntutuliak, Mo; 73, Kipnuk, Mo; 74, Kwigillingok, Mo; 75, Eek, Mo; 76, Wasilla, Pe; 77, Chugiak, M; 78, Chitina, SB; 79, Anchorage, A, B, C, Ev, F, L, M, P, SA, SB; 80, Quinhagak, Mo; 81, Girdwood, M; 82, Valdez, 1906, E; 83, Kenai, M; 84, Goodnews, Mo; 85, Cordova, 1908, E, A; 86, Togiak, Mo; 87, Aleknagik, Mo; 88, Ekwok, B; 89, Seward, M; 90, Manokotak, Mo; 91, Dillingham, A, Mo; 92, Nushagak, 1885, Mo; 93, Homer, M; 94, King Salmon, B; 95, Yakutat, A, P; 96, Skagway, 1898, E; 97, Klukwan, A, P; 98, Haines, A, SA; 99, Juneau, 1886, P, A, E, M, SA; 100, Douglas, 1887, F, E, M; 101, Kodiak, 1893, B; 102, Pelican, A; 103, Hoonah, A, P, SA; 104, Angoon, A, P; 105, Sitka, 1878, P, E, M; 106, Kake, 1892, F, A, P, SA; 107, Petersburg, P, SA; 108, Wrangell, 1877, P, A, E, SA; 109, Unalaska, 1890, M; 110, Unga, 1886, M; 111, Klawock, P, SA; 112, Craig, P; 113, Ketchikan, 1898, E, M, P, Pe, SA; 114, Hydaberg, A, P; 115, Metlakatla, 1915, P, A.

why the churches did so much for the heathen overseas and so little for the Indians at home (ARCIA 1871: 26–50). The Washington, D.C., *Weekly Chronicle* in an editorial on September 14, 1867, suggested that the Society of Friends, known to be trusted by the Indians, be asked to rescue the service from corrupt politics (Kelsey 1917:165; Janney 1867:514). The Hicksite Friends held a conference on Indian affairs in Baltimore and informed

the administration of their willingness to be of service without compensation. At the instigation of the Orthodox Friends Iowa Yearly Meeting, a joint conference of all Friends meetings was conducted in Baltimore in 1869, and a delegation from it went to Washington and presented a memorial to President-elect Ulysses Grant, while the very next day a group of representatives of the Liberal Friends made a similar representation (Kelsey 1917:165–167). All were impressed by Grant's profound sympathy with the Indians. About the same time Major General W.B. Hazen, at Fort Cobb, Indian Territory, proposed using on the agencies and reservations the practical type of missionary who had made up the "mission family" of a station in the earlier period (ARCIA 1869:97).

Meanwhile, the Rt. Rev. Henry B. Whipple, Episcopal Bishop of Minnesota, had been trying to rally his church to genuine concern for the Indians and had been lobbying with Congress and the president on behalf of Indian rights. He finally got positive action from the Board of Missions of his church in 1868 (Whipple 1899:521–548) and simultaneously reported to the United States Peace Commission. That body memorialized Congress asking the government to enlist in supervision of the Indian service capable, reliable, politically independent men who would not be reimbursed from the public treasury (ARCIA 1869:95–96). Grant in his inaugural address declared that he favored "any course towards the Indians which tends to their civilization and ultimate citizenship" (Richardson 1896–1899, 7:8).

Grant's initial reform took the shape of making a Seneca Indian, Ely S. Parker, commissioner of Indian affairs, and discharging all but two of the old superintendents and replacing them with Army officers. The Liberal and the Orthodox Friends respectively were asked to nominate superintendents and agents for those two districts (Kelsey 1917:168, 170–172, 187; Milner 1982: 1–26). Grant, in his next annual message, declared himself satisfied with the results (Richardson 1896–1899, 7:38).

Congress in 1869 established a fund of $2,000,000 "to enable the President to maintain peace" among the Indians (16 U.S. Stat. 40). This is the origin of the term Peace Policy (Keller 1983; Fritz 1963; Rahill 1953; Beaver 1966a:123–176). A board of men "eminent for their intelligence and philanthropy" was to be appointed by the president to exercise joint control with the secretary of the interior over the Bureau of Indian Affairs. Secretary Jacob D. Cox managed to have the board's role limited in the bill as passed to inspection and advice. There was no integral relation to the Bureau, and the board was powerless except to the extent that it could marshall public opinion and political support. This Board of Indian Commissioners was in its early stage popularly called a "church board," because its members were active laymen in the Presbyterian, Methodist, Congregational, Episcopal, Baptist, and Friends churches. The chairman was the *443*

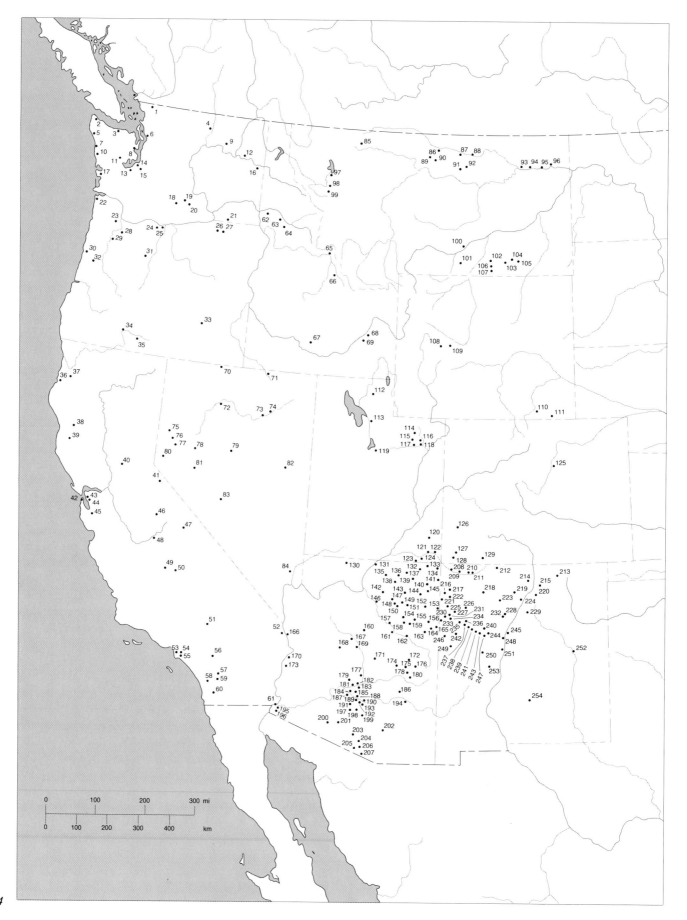

Fig. 6b. Washington: 1, Nooksak, 1880, M; 2, Neah Bay, 1896, P, L; 3, Port Angeles, 1944, A; 4, Omak, Pe; 5, La Push, L; 6, Marysville, C; 7, Queets, SB; 8, Tracyton, M; 9, Nespelem, M; 10, Quinalt, M; 11, Skokomish, Pr; 12, Wellpinit, 1882, P; 13, Nisqualli, 1839, M; 14, Tacoma, P; 15, Puyallup, 1860, P; 16, Tshimakain, 1838, Pr, Co, P; 17, Shoalwater, 1883, E; 18, White Swan, D, M; 19, Wapato, A, D; 20, Toppenish, C, D; 21, Waiilatpu, 1836, Pr, P. Oregon: 22, Clatsop, 1840, M; 23, Beaverton, SB; 24, Wasco, 1836, M; 25, Celilo, C; 26, Pendleton, 1882, P; 27, Cayuse, 1838, Pr, P, A; 28, Willamette Falls, 1834, M; 29, Willamette, 1835, M; 30, Siletz, M; 31, Warm Springs, 1875, P, SB; 32, Alsea, M; 33, Malheur, Pr; 34, Chiloquin, 1876, M; 35, Beatty, 1898, M. California: 36, Humboldt, 1908, E; 37, Hoopa, A, M, Me, P, SB; 38, Covelo, M, Pe; 39, Willits, 1875, M; 40, Auburn, A; 41, Markleeville, A; 42, San Francisco, R, SB; 43, Berkeley, L; 44, Oakland, SB; 45, San Jose, M; 46, El Portal, A; 47, Bishop, 1912, P; 48, Friant, A; 49, Porterville, A; 50, Tule River, M; 51, Daggett, A; 52, Needles, 1903, P, N; 53, Los Angeles, B, E, M; 54, Bell Gardens, A, SB; 55, Norwalk, M; 56, Banning, Mo; 57, Palomar Mountain, N; 58, Valley Center, 1904, E, A; 59, La Jolla, 1905, E; 60, El Cajon, SB; 61, Winterhaven, 1945, N, A. Idaho: 62, Lapwai, 1836, Pr, C, M, P; 63, Kamiah, 1838, Pr, P; 64, Clearwater, 1840, Pr; 65, North Fork, P; 66, Lemhi, 1871, M; 67, Shoshone, 1898, E; 68, Blackfoot, SB; 69, Ft. Hall, A, E, M. Nevada: 70, McDermitt, 1955, A, SB; 71, Owyhee, 1914, P, A; 72, Winnemucca, SB; 73, Carlin, SB; 74, Elko, Pe; 75, Pyramid, B, E; 76, Nixon, 1894, E, A; 77, Wadsworth, 1900, E; 78, Fallon, Pe; 79, Austin, SB; 80, Carson City, B; 81, Schurz, 1875, M, B, E, Pe, SB; 82, Ely, SB; 83, Tonopah, SB; 84, Overton, SB. Montana: 85, Browning, 1876, M, Me, SB; 86, Havre, Pr; 87, Ft. Belknap, A; 88, Dodson, R; 89, Box Elder, 1918, L; 90, Rocky Boy, A, L; 91, Hays, A, Pr; 92, Lodgepole, A; 93, Frazer, Pe; 94, Wolf Point, 1870, M, P, SB; 95, Poplar, 1880, P, A, Pe, SB; 96, Brockton, P; 97, Flathead, 1838, Pr; 98, St. Ignatius, A; 99, Arlee, Pr; 100, Billings, 1958, B, SB; 101, Pryor, 1914, B, A; 102, Crow Agency, 1870, M, B, C, SB; 103, Busby, 1904, Me, Pe; 104, Lame Deer, Me, Pe, SB; 105, Ashland, Me, Pe; 106, Lodge Grass, 1905, Pe, A, B; 107, Wyola, B. Wyoming: 108, Ft. Washakie, 1870, E; 109, Ethete, 1875, M, A, E; 110, Laramie, 1890, E; 111, Cheyenne, 1861, L, E. Utah: 112, Brigham City, SB; 113, Salt Lake City, R, SB; 114, Whiterocks, 1904, E; 115, Roosevelt, A, SB; 116, Ft. Duchesne, 1896, E, Pe; 117, Uintah Valley, 1875, P; 118, Randlett, 1898, E; 119, Leland, 1904, E; 120, Blanding, A, SB; 121, Bluff, E; 122, Montezuma Creek, E; 123, Oljato, 1950, P, E; 124, Monument Valley, 1961, SDA. Colorado: 125, Denver, A, L, R; 126, Naturita, Pe; 127, Cortez, B, SB; 128, Towaoc, 1891, P; 129, Ignacio, A, SB. Arizona: 130, Fredonia, Pe; 131, Page, B, N; 132, Dinnehotso, A; 133, Mexican Water, B, Ev; 134, Teec Nos Pos, R, SB; 135, Kaibito, B, N; 136, Shonto, A, B; 137, Kayenta, 1910, P, A, N, Pe; 138, Tonalea, A, B, N, Pr; 139, Chilchinbito, 1955, N; 140, Many Farms, L, SB; 141, Red Rock, R; 142, Tuba City, 1910, P, A, B, Me, SB; 143, Piñon, SB; 144, Salina, N; 145, Chinle, 1926, L, F, Me, N, P, SB; 146, Cameron, 1961, A, N, SB; 147, Hotevilla, Me; 148, Oraibi, 1893, Me; 149, Polacca, A, B; 150, Second Mesa, B; 151, Keams Canyon, 1894, B, Me, N; 152, Ganado, 1901, P, A, Me, SB; 153, Ft. Defiance, Window Rock, St. Michaels, 1899, E, A, Ev, M, N, Pr, SB; 154, Tees To, A, N; 155, Greasewood, Pe; 156, Klagetoh, C, Me; 157, Leupp, 1910, P, N, SB; 158, Dilkon, 1956, N, Pe; 159, Indian Wells, 1910, P, A, SB; 160, Flagstaff, A, N, SB; 161, Winslow, 1951, N, A, Pe, SB; 162, Holbrook, 1945, SDA, A, Pe, SB; 163, Navajo, 1957, N; 164, Chambers, Ev; 165, Houck, A; 166, Mohave, A; 167, Clarkdale, 1907, P; 168, Prescott, 1907, P, A; 169, Camp Verde, A; 170, Parker, 1914, P, A, N, Pe; 171, Payson, SB; 172, Show Low, 1959, A; 173, Poston, B, N; 174, Cibique, A, L; 175, Carrizo, A; 176, McNary, A; 177, Ft. McDowell, 1907, P; 178, Cedar Creek, A; 179, Glendale, Me; 180, White River, 1895, L, A, SB; 181, Phoenix, 1914, P, A, L, M, Me, N, P, Pe, SB; 182, Scottsdale, 1870, M, A, P; 183, Mesa, P, SB; 184, Laveen, 1930, SDA, A, P, SB; 185, Guadalupe, Pe; 186, San Carlos, 1872, R, A, L, SB; 187, Gila Crossing, Pe; 188, Santan, A, SB; 189, Bapchule, 1870, M, A, P; 190, Blackwater, P; 191, Maricopa, 1872, R, A; 192, Sacaton, 1870, P, A, SB; 193, Coolidge, P, SB; 194, Bylas, A; 195, Yuma, 1900, M, A; 196, Sommerton, 1944, N, A; 197, Stanfield, 1950, A; 198, Casa Grande, A, SB; 199, Eloy, A; 200, Ajo, A; 201, Hickiwan, A; 202, Tucson, 1888, P, A, N; 203, Quijotoa, Pe; 204, San Luis, N; 205, Sells, A, N, P, Pe, SB; 206, Vamori, 1919, P; 207, San Miguel, P. New Mexico: 208, Shiprock, A, E, M, R, SB; 209, Fruitland, A, E, Ev, SB; 210, Farmington; A, C, E, M, N, R, SB, SDA; 211, Bloomfield, Me; 212, Dulce, 1958, A, R, SB;

213, Cimarron, P; 214, Carson, A, E; 215, Taos, Pe, SB; 216, Toadlena, R; 217, Newcomb, A, R; 218, Counselor, SB; 219, Abiquiu, P; 220, Chamisal, Pe; 221, Navajo, 1868, P, A, L, R; 222, Naschitti, R; 223, Cuba, 1950, Br, A, SB; 224, Espanola, A, SB; 225, Tohatchi, R, SB; 226, Crownpoint, A, R, SB; 227, Pinedale, A; 228, Jemez, 1851, P, SB; 229, Santa Fe, A, SB; 230, Gallup, Mentmore, 1948, N, A, Pe, R, SB; 231, Church Rock, Rehoboth, 1903, R, SB; 232, San Ysidro, 1955, A; 233, Manuelito, A; 234, Ft. Wingate, Perea, Pe, R, SB; 235, Thoreau, F, Pe; 236, Prewitt, A, Ev, Pe; 237, Bluewater Lake, Pe; 238, Milan, SB; 239, Grants, A, SB; 240, Paguate, N; 241, San Fidel, Pe; 242, Ramah, 1949, N; 243, Cubero, SB; 244, Canoncito, A, N, SB; 245, Albuquerque, A, N, SB; 246, Zuni, 1876, P, R, SB; 247, Laguna, 1851, P, B, N; 248, Isleta, SB; 249, Fence Lake, SB; 250, Alamo, Pe; 251, Bosque, SB; 252, Santa Rosa, N, P; 253, Magdelena, SB; 254, Mescalero, A, P, Pe, R, SB.

Episcopalian, William Welsh, who resigned when he discovered that the Board was powerless. He was replaced by Felix R. Brunot (Slattery 1901). Vincent Colyer was the secretary. After prodigious efforts seemed to have been in vain, all but one of the Board resigned in 1874, and the vacancies were filled with men who for half a dozen more years were said to be representatives of churches. The Board lingered on until 1933.

President Grant on the recommendation of the Board of Indian Commissioners turned to the churches' mission boards and asked them both to nominate superintendents and agents and to supervise them (Board of Indian Commissioners 1881:6). Grant declared that this would be missionary work, and the boards were expected both to supply agents and to carry on missionary action (Richardson 1896–1899, 7:109–110; ARCIA 1870:10). The theory seemed to be that a reservation should be assigned to the church already having a mission there or one nearest to it, but there was no clear principle of assignment. Vincent Colyer made the original selection (ARCIA 1870:5, 96, 98). Secretary Cox sent invitations to the American Missionary Society, the Board of Foreign Missions of the Presbyterian Church in the U.S.A., the Missionary Society, of the Methodist Episcopal Church, the Board of Foreign Missions of the Reformed Church in America, the American Unitarian Association, the Board of Missions of the Domestic and Foreign Missionary Society of the Episcopal Church, and to the American Church Missionary Society. The two bodies with the longest experience in Indian missions were ignored, namely, the American Board of Commissioners for Foreign Missions and the Moravian Church; but eventually the American Board was given one agency. Later a few small agencies were assigned to the Evangelical Lutheran Church, the United Presbyterian Church, and the Christian Church (Disciples of Christ). The three churches with the largest number of Indian members—the Southern Baptists, Southern Methodists, and Southern Presbyterians—were ignored for political reasons. Two of the Boards chosen had no Indian missions and one had no missions anywhere, and it withdrew. All others accepted the invitation, and missions were established on many reservations (fig. 6). Roman Catholic participation was invited in   *445*

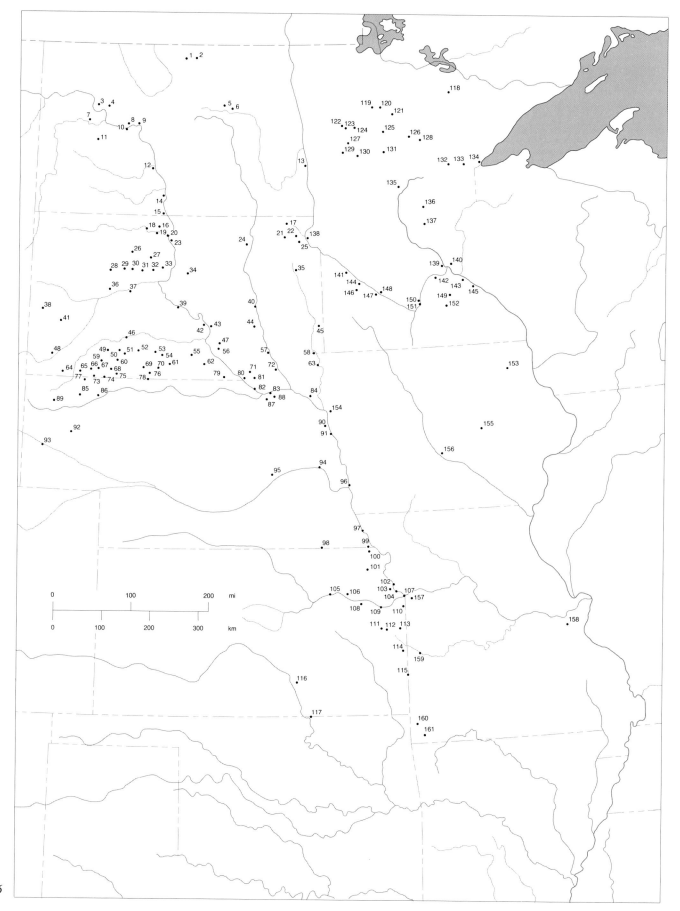

Fig. 6c. North Dakota: 1, Dunseith, 1899, E, Pr; 2, Belcourt, 1954, A, L; 3, New Town, 1922, Co, E; 4, Parshall, 1899, Co; 5, Ft. Totten, 1876, P, E, SB; 6, Tokio, 1957, L, A, P; 7, Mandaree, 1916, Co; 8, Emmet, E; 9, Garrison, 1885, Co; 10, Ft. Berthold, 1873, Pr; 11, Halliday, 1922, Co; 12, Mandan, SB; 13, Fargo, L; 14, Cannon Ball, 1905, E, Co, SB; 15, Ft. Yates, A, E, SB. South Dakota: 16, McLaughlin, E, Pr; 17, Veblen, E, P; 18, Bullhead, E; 19, Little Eagle, 1891, Co, E; 20, Wakpala, A, E; 21, Eden, P; 22, Sisseton, 1870, P, A, E, Pr, SB; 23, Mobridge, 1963, A, E; 24, Aberdeen, M; 25, Peever, E, P; 26, Isabel, E, Pe; 27, White Horse, E; 28, Faith, E; 29, Dupree, E; 30, Lantry, 1925, Co, E; 31, Eagle Butte, 1895, Co, E, SB; 32, Ridgeview, E; 33, La Plant, 1894, Co; 34, Gettysburg, E; 35, Watertown, 1884, E; 36, Howes, 1910, Co; 37, Cherry Creek, 1890, Co, E; 38, Lead, 1888, E; 39, Pierre, 1840, P, E; 40, Huron, 1836, E; 41, Rapid City, 1888, E, A, M, SB; 42, Lower Brule, 1872, E, P; 43, Ft. Thompson, Crow Creek, 1864, Pr, E, P; 44, Woonsocket, 1884, E; 45, Flandreau, 1869, P; 46, Kadoka, E; 47, Pukwana, E, P; 48, Hot Springs, 1946, M; 49, Potato Creek, E; 50, Wanblee, E; 51, Longvalley, P; 52, Norris, A, E; 53, White River, E; 54, Wood, A; 55, Ideal, E; 56, Red Lake, 1890, E; 57, Mitchell, 1884, E; 58, Sioux Falls, 1888, E; 59, Kyle, E; 60, Hisle, E; 61, Okreek, E; 62, Dixon, P; 63, Canton, 1884, E; 64, Oelrichs, P; 65, Oglala, E, P; 66, Manderson, E; 67, Porcupine, E, Me, P; 68, Allen, C, E; 69, Parmalee, 1908, Co, E; 70, Mission, A, B, E; 71, Ravinia, E; 72, Olivet, 1884, E; 73, Wounded Knee, C, E, P; 74, Batesland, E; 75, Martin, E, P; 76, Rosebud, 1884, E; 77, Pine Ridge, 1880, E, M, Me, P, SB, SDA; 78, St. Francis, E; 79, St. Charles, 1891, Co; 80, Pickstown, E; 81, Wagner, A, P; 82, Greenwood, P; 83, Springfield, 1880, E; 84, Vermillion, 1884, E. Nebraska: 85, Spotted Tail, E; 86, Gordon, C; 87, Niobrara, 1866, Co, E, P; 88, Santee, 1856, E, Co, F; 89, Red Cloud, 1871, E; 90, Winnebago, 1869, F, P, R; 91, Blackbird Hill, 1846, P, F, M, R; 92, Alliance, E; 93, Scottsbluff, C; 94, Otoe-Omaha, 1833, B; 95, Pawnee, 1834, P, F, Pr; 96, Otoe-Ottawa-Omaha, 1846, P; 97, Nemaha, F; 98, Otoe, F; 99, Iowa-Sac, 1834, P. Kansas: 100, Iowa-Sac-Fox, 1833, M, B, P; 101, Horton, M; 102, Ft. Leavenworth, 1833, M, F; 103, Delaware, 1832, M; 104, Munsee, Mo; 105, Kansa, 1830, M; 106, Potawatomi, 1837, B, F, M; 107, Delaware-Wyandot, 1832, B, M; 108, Topeka, 1835, M; 109, Lawrence, 1848, M, SB; 110, Shawnee, 1829, M, B, F; 111, Ottawa, 1837, B; 112, Peoria-Potawatomi, 1833, M; 113, Wea, 1834, P, B; 114, Miami, 1847, B; 115, Osage, 1824, Pr; 116, Wichita, M, SB; 117, Arkansas City, M. Minnesota: 118, Orr, M; 119, Red Lake, 1842, Pr, E, P, Pe; 120, Redby, 1878, E; 121, Squaw Lake, 1878, E; 122, Fosston, M; 123, Lengby, M; 124, Bagley, 1876, E, L; 125, Cass Lake, 1881, E, Pr; 126, Ball Club, A; 127, Naytahwaush, 1893, E; 128, Pokegama, 1840, Pr; 129, White Earth, 1852, E, A, Pr; 130, Ponsford, E; 131, Leech Lake, Walker, 1833, Pr, B, E; 132, Sandy Lake, 1831, Pr, P; 133, Fond du Lac, 1833, Pr, M, P; 134, Duluth, L, M; 135, Gull Lake, 1852, E; 136, Mille Lacs, Onamia, 1840, M, Pe; 137, Milaca, Pr; 138, Browns Valley, 1834, P, E; 139, Minneapolis, 1854, Pr, A, E, Ev, M, N; 140, St. Paul, 1834, Co, E, M; 141, Lac Qui Parle, 1834, Pr, Co, P; 142, Shakopee, E; 143, Welch, 1906, E; 144, Yellow Medicine, Granite Falls, 1852, Pr, Co, P; 145, Red Wing, 1848, Co; 146, Cottonwood, P; 147, Redwood Falls, 1860, E; 148, Morton, 1886, E; 149, Hazelwood, 1854, Co; 150, Traverse des Sioux, 1843, Pr; 151, St. Peter, 1844, Pr; 152, Faribault, 1858, E. Iowa: 153, Winnebago, 1833, Pr; 154, Sioux City, 1883, E; 155, Sac and Fox, Tama, 1872, L, P; 156, Des Moines, E. Missouri: 157, Kansas City, SB; 158, Union, 1820, Pr; 159, Rich Hill, 1821, P; 160, Seneca, 1839, M; 161, Anderson, SB.

a different manner, and although Catholics claimed 38 agencies on the grounds of priority of action and proximity, they were assigned eight agencies. A central agency was created in 1874, the Bureau of Catholic Indian Missions, and it vigorously developed the missions on all possible sites (Rahill 1953).

The action of the Grant administration powerfully stimulated mission expansion. The Episcopal Indian work had just been taken over by the central mission board of that church, a special Indian committee or commission was established, and the missionary jurisdiction of Niobrara was created with William Hobart Hare as bishop (M.A.D. Howe 1911; Robbins 1913:134, 299–304, 322–323). The Presbyterian Church in the U.S.A., already probably as active in Indian work as the American Board, received 10 agencies, and it greatly augmented its ministry. The Reformed, Unitarian, and Baptist boards did little or nothing to establish new missions, but in general the others expanded markedly. The missions of the Society of Friends were notable for the high quality of their unified administrative and mission work, each agency being virtually a mission station. Agents were carefully selected for missionary motivation as well as personal integrity, business ability, and concern for the Indians (Kelsey 1917:176, 179, 184; ARCIA 1879:71). The wide expansion is evident in the statistics of 1873 compared with those of 1869. Whereas in the earlier year there were 15 Protestant missionaries, 10 schools, and 17 teachers with 594 pupils, in 1873 there were 74 missionaries, 90 church buildings, 69 schools, 86 teachers, 2,690 primary and 7,419 secondary students (ARCIA 1873: 332–347). The objective of the missions was still evangelization and civilization, and there was very little appreciation and use of the Indian cultural heritage, except that the Episcopal and Congregational missionaries used the Sioux language rather than English (fig. 4). The Protestant agencies, having been accustomed to practice comity in mission work abroad (Beaver 1962a), generally accepted their exclusive assignments and those made to others. There was relatively little rivalry other than the hostility and competition between Protestants and Roman Catholics. Protestant unity was encouraged by an annual meeting. The Board of Indian Commissioners regularly called a meeting with representatives of the mission boards, and at a certain point it ceased being under the auspices of the Commissioners and became an informal discussion of mission problems and issues by the persons sent by the boards. Eventually the annual meeting with the Commissioners became the Lake Mohonk Conference of the Friends of the Indian.

The boards in general exercised much care in selecting agents, stressing genuine Christian and missionary commitment, integrity, ability to get along well with people, and compassion for the Indians (Beaver 1966a:141–146; Rushmore 1914:34–35). The Baptists and Methodists, who had the largest percentage of membership in frontier areas, were dependent largely on local ecclesiastical bodies, pastors, and influential laymen for recommendations, which were not always objective and disinterested. They also tended to appoint ordained ministers (Barclay 1949–1957, 3:324–328). A better job of screening was done by national mission boards not so intimately involved with frontiersmen. When graft was eliminated, the salary of an agent was far too small to sustain even a self-sacrificing man with missionary motivation and his

Fig. 6d. Oklahoma: 1, Quapaw, 1843, M, F; 2, Miami, SB; 3, Dewey, M; 4, Wyandotte, 1871, F; 5, Ponca City, 1939, N, M; 6, Pawhuska, F, SB; 7, Bartlesville, 1820, Pr; 8, Enid, SB; 9, Grove, 1958, SB; 10, Hominy, 1908, F; 11, Collinsville, Pe; 12, Spavinaw, 1960, SB; 13, Jay, 1832, B, E, M, SB; 14, Morrison; 15, Pawnee, 1908, SB, M; 16, Claremore, M, SB; 17, Salina, 1860, SB, M; 18, Eucha, 1926, SB; 19, Seiling, A, Me; 20, Longdale, A; 21, Kenwood, Me; 22, Colcord, 1952, SB; 23, Tulsa, 1950, SB, M; 24, Locust Grove, 1926, SB, M; 25, Rose, 1915, SB; 26, Kansas, 1912, SB; 27, Canton, 1883, Me, SB; 28, Oakhurst, 1848, P, SB; 29, Broken Arrow, M; 30, New Springplace, Oaks, 1838, Mo, L; 31, Watts, 1950, SB; 32, Fay, 1909, E; 33, Watonga, 1898, B, E, M; 34, Kingfisher, M; 35, Sapulpa, M, SB; 36, Glenpool, SB; 37, Bixby, M, SB; 38, Coweta, M, SB; 39, Mounds, M; 40, Hulbert, 1850, SB, M; 41, Tahlequah, 1913, SB, M; 42, Proctor, 1914, SB; 43, Park Hill, 1829, Pr, C, M, P; 44, Stilwell, 1845, SB, M, P, Pe; 45, Hammon, 1950, SB, A, Me; 46, Arapaho, SB; 47, Geary, 1898, B; 48, Darlington, 1880, Me; 49, Stroud, SB; 50, Preston, M; 51, Muskogee, B, M, SB; 52, Weatherford, M; 53, Cheyenne and Arapaho Agency, F; 54, Sac and Fox Agency, F; 55, Okmulgee, A, M, SB; 56, Braggs, SB; 57, Bunch, 1915, SB, A, P; 58, Clinton, 1953, SB, M, Me, Pe; 59, El Reno, M, SB; 60, Oklahoma City, M, Pe, SB; 61, Prague, SB; 62, Schulter, M; 63, Hitchita, SB; 64, Oktaha, SB; 65, Marble City, M; 66, Union City, 1821, P, B; 67, McLoud, 1883, F, SB; 68, Shawnee, B, M, SB; 69, Castle, M; 70, Okemah, M, N, SB; 71, Henryetta, M, SB; 72, Checotah, SB; 73, Vian, M, SB; 74, Cheyarha, P; 75, Weleetka, SB; 76, Muldrow, SB; 77, Gracemont, SB; 78, Eufaula, 1832, Pr, B, M, P, SB; 79, Arkoma, 1832, B, M; 80, Seminole, 1848, P, M, SB; 81, Wetumka, M, SB; 82, Dustin, 1870, SB; 83, Hanna, SB; 84, Stigler, P; 85, Keota, SB; 86, Hobart, B, M, Pe; 87, Mountain View, B, M; 88, Carnegie, M, Pe, SB; 89, Ft. Cobb, B, M; 90, Anadarko, 1887, P, B, E, F, M, Pe, SB; 91, Maud, P, SB; 92, Bowlegs, 1884, P, SB; 93, Wewoka, 1848, P, M, SB; 94, Yeager, M; 95, Holdenville, M, SB; 96, Quinton, M; 97, McCurtain; 98, Apache, M, R; 99, Konawa, SB; 100, Sasakwa, 1888, SB; 101, Calvin, SB; 102, Fletcher, M; 103, Byars, P; 104, Allen, M; 105, McAlester, M, SB; 106, Krebs, SB; 107, Wilburton, 1894, P, SB; 108, Red Oak, SB; 109, Elgin M; 110, Ada, M, SB; 111, Indiahoma, 1936, N, A, Me; 112, Cache, A, M, N; 113, Lawton, B, F, M, Me, Pe, R, SB; 114, Duncan, SB; 115, Roff, P, SB; 116, Stonewall; 117, Centrahoma, 1929, P, M; 118, Wardville, P; 119, Talihina, M, P, SB; 120, Whitesboro, M; 121, Walters, 1937, SB, B, M, N; 122, Ft. Arbuckle, 1852, P; 123, Sulphur, SB; 124, Coalgate, P; 125, Honobia, 1914, P; 126, Connerville, M; 127, Lehigh, 1888, P, N; 128, Smithville, P; 129, Watson, P; 130, Wapanucka, P; 131, Atoka, 1887, P, M, SB; 132, Snow, M; 133, Pickens, P; 134, Battiest, P; 135, Bethel, M, P; 136, Lane, 1925, P, M; 137, Finley, M; 138, Tishomingo, M, SB; 139, Fillmore, P; 140, Antlers, M; 141, Ardmore, SB; 142, Bently, M; 143, Oleta, M; 144, Sobol, M; 145, Ft. Washita, 1843, M; 146, Spencerville, 1846, P; 147, Rufe, M, P; 148, Wright City, 1951, P, A, M; 149, Marietta, Pe; 150, Calera, SB; 151, Bennington, M, P; 152, Boswell, 1882, P, M; 153, Soper, SB; 154, Hugo, 1850, P, M, SB; 155, Wheelock, Millerton, 1832, Pr, P; 156, Broken Bow, 1906, P, M, Pe; 157, Eagletown, 1887, P; 158, Garvin, P; 159, Achille, SB; 160, Idabel, M, P; 161, Tom, 1890, P. Texas: 162, Ft. Worth, A, SB; 163, Grand Prairie, SB; 164, Dallas, A, M, SB; 165, Livingston, 1949, A, P. Arkansas: 166, Lee's Creek, 1848, Pr; 167, Harmony, 1821, Pr; 168, Dwight, 1820, Pr, P; 169, Fairfield, 1830, Pr; 170, Mt. Zion, 1840, Pr. Louisiana: 171, Elton, A; 172, Baldwin, SB; 173, Duloc, M.

family. The extreme isolation of some posts was another major obstacle. Some boards supplemented the governmental salary with a grant from their own funds. But the most potent factor in hampering and finally destroying the system was political interference. On the one hand, the Indian Bureau could easily circumvent the mission boards and the Board of Indian Commissioners, while, on the other hand, politicians could exercise a variety of powers to delay fatally or control outright the actual appointment of an agent to almost any reservation. Good and effective agents were often harassed unmercifully. Corrupt agents

that the mission boards had accepted only reluctantly or refused to nominate brought undeserved criticism on the boards. More and more the boards were bypassed in the appointments.

The state of affairs became so intolerable under Commissioner of Indian Affairs Ezra A. Hayt in 1880 that the Orthodox Friends and the Reformed Church withdrew from the system. The boards were not asked for a single nomination during the James Garfield administration. President Chester Arthur's Secretary of the Interior, H.M. Teller, declared that there was no such thing as a Peace Policy and terminated the relationship with the mission boards (Board of Indian Commissioners 1881:53; Beaver 1966a:151). Secretary Carl Schurz in 1881 opened the reservations to all denominations for mission work provided that rivalry did not jeopardize peace (Anonymous 1881:129).

All cooperation between government and the churches in Indian education did not end with the rejection of the Peace Policy. Missions contracted with the Bureau to carry on schools on many reservations, and these were subsidized. A conflict between Roman Catholics and Protestants over these contract schools was the chief factor in the abolition of the practice in 1897 (Prucha 1979). It was largely inspired and directed by a Baptist clergyman, educator, and former Civil War general, Thomas J. Morgan, whom President Benjamin Harrison appointed commissioner of Indian affairs. He and the Bureau of Catholic Indian Missions contended in a struggle with no holds barred (Beaver 1966a:162–167). Morgan proposed taking away education of Indian children and youths from all the churches and substituting government direction under the local laws of each state. Morgan left office to become corresponding secretary of the American Baptist Home Mission Society and became the chief spokesman for the nativist, anti-Catholic American Protective Association. Convinced by Morgan that Catholic operation of Indian schools with federal money was but the first step in the capture of the public schools by the church hierarchy, the American Protective Association made a major issue of government support of any Indian mission schools (Desmond 1912). Morgan practically blackmailed Protestant denominations and their mission boards into repudiating subsidy for schools. Congress in making the appropriations in 1895 limited support of contract schools and on June 7, 1897, decreed that "it is to be the settled policy of the government to hereafter make no appropriation whatever for education in any sectarian school" (Stokes 1950, 2:289–290). The Indian Appropriation Act of 1899 stated that it was making the "final appropriation for sectarian schools" (Stokes 1950, 2:290). Thereafter a few Protestant schools and many Roman Catholic ones were conducted on the basis of contracts with particular tribes, and funds administered by the commissioner of Indian affairs under

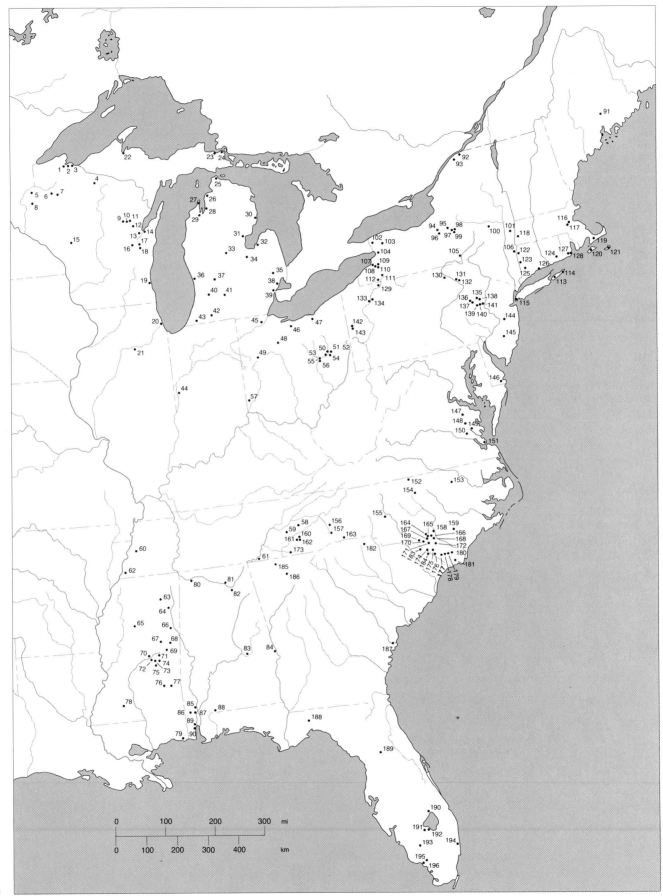

Fig. 6e. Wisconsin: 1, La Pointe, 1830, Pr; 2, Ashland, 1878, P; 3, Odanah, 1845, Pr, M, P; 4, Lac du Flambeau, 1885, P; 5, Yellow Lake, 1833, Pr; 6, Stone Lake, P; 7, Courderay, A; 8, Luck, A, M, Pr; 9, Bowler, 1935, L; 10, Gresham, 1898, L, A, P; 11, Keshena, A; 12, Shawano, 1968, M; 13, Oneida, 1826, P, A, E, M; 14, Green Bay, 1825, E, P, Pr; 15, Black River Falls, 1878, Co; 16, Winnebago, Co; 17, Stockbridge, 1828, Pr; 18, Brothertown, 1842, M; 19, Milwaukee, A. Illinois: 20, Chicago, A, E, SB; 21, Potawatomi, 1824, M. Michigan: 22, L'Anse, 1832, M; 23, Bay Mills, A; 24, Sault Ste. Marie, 1826, B, E, M; 25, Mackinaw, 1823, Pr, Co; 26, Charlevoix, 1833, M; 27, Northport, M; 28, Kewadin, M; 29, Traverse City, 1838, P, M; 30, Oscoda, M; 31, Standish, M; 32, Chippewa, 1845, L; 33, Mt. Pleasant, 1926, N, M, Pe; 34, Saginaw, M; 35, Lakeville, 1841, M; 36, Ottawa, 1839, Pr; 37, Grand Rapids, 1825, B, A, M; 38, New Gnadenhütten, 1782, Mo; 39, Detroit, B; 40, Allegan, M; 41, Ottawa, 1840, E; 42, Nottawa, 1847, M; 43, Carey, Niles, 1822, B. Indiana: 44, Wea, 1818, B. Ohio: 45, Maumee, 1822, Pr, P; 46, New Salem, 1787, Mo; 47, Pilgerrah, 1786, MO; 48, Upper Sandusky, 1806, P, M; 49, Wapakoneta, 1816, F; 50, New Schönbrunn, 1779, Mo; 51, Schönbrunn, 1772, Mo; 52, Goshen, 1798, Mo; 53, Salem, 1780, Mo; 54, Gnadenhütten, 1772, Mo; 55, Coshocton, 1774, Mo; 56, Lichtenau, 1776, Mo; 57, Gekelemukpechünk, 1771, Mo. Tennessee: 58, Sevierville, SB; 59, Cherokee, 1803, P, B; 60, Ripley, SB; 61, Brainerd, 1817, Pr; 62, Memphis, SB. Mississippi, 63, Chickasaw, 1821, Pr; 64, Chickasaw, 1820, P; 65, Eliot, 1818, Pr, M; 66, Mayhew, 1820, Pr; 67, Louisville, Me; 68, Mashulaville, Me; 69, Preston, Me; 70, Carthage, SB; 71, Philadelphia, 1799, M, A, Me, SB; 72, Walnut Grove, SB; 73, Sebastopol, SB; 74, Union, SB; 75, Conehatta, SB; 76, Heidelberg, SB; 77, Six Towns, 1825, Pr; 78, Bogue Chitto, Pe; 79, Pascagoula, SB. Alabama: 80, Chickasaw, 1826, Pr; 81, Chickasaw, 1799, Pr; 82, Cherokee, 1820, Pr, M; 83, Creek, 1822, B; 84, Creek, 1822, M; 85, McIntosh, F, SB; 86, Citronelle, SB; 87, Mt. Vernon, M; 88, Atmore, 1953, SB; 89, Chickasaw, SB; 90, Mobile, SB. Maine: 91, Indian Island, B. New York: 92, St. Regis, Hogansburg, A, E, M; 93, Massena, M; 94, Syracuse, E, M; 95, Oneida, 1766, Co, B, E, F, M; 96, Onondaga, 1830, M, E; 97, New Stockbridge, 1785, Co; 98, Brotherton, 1786, Co; 99, Pine Woods; P; 100, Ft. Hunter, 1712, E; 101, Kaunaumeek, 1743, Co, Mo; 102, Tuscarora, 1796, F, P; 103, Tonawanda, 1820, B, P; 104, Buffalo Creek, 1811, Pr; 105, Oquaga, 1747, Co; 106, Shekomeko, 1740, Mo; 107, Lower Cattaraugus, 1808, F, P, Pr; 108, Upper Cattaraugus, 1797, F, P, Pr; 109, Lawtons, A; 100, Gowanda, M; 111, Salamanca, 1798, F, P; 112, Tunesassah, 1804, F, P, Pr; 113, Shinnecock, 1741, P; 114, Montauk, 1741, E, P; 115, Brooklyn, P. Massachusetts: 116, Nonantum, 1646, Co; 117, Natick, 1651, Co; 118, Stockbridge, 1734, Co, Mo; 119, Mashpee, 1660, Co, B; 120, Martha's Vineyard, 1643, Co; 121, Nantucket, 1646, Co. Connecticut: 122, Wechquadnach, 1749, Mo; 123, Schagticoke, Pachgatgoch, 1742, Mo; 124, Mohegan, 1673, Co; 125, Poodatook, 1743, Mo; 126, Branford, 1651, Co. Rhode Island: 127, Wakefield, 1929, N; 128, Narragansett, 1721, Co. E. Pennsylvania: 129, Cornplanter, 1795, F, P; 130, Sheshequin, 1769, Mo; 131, Wyalusing, 1763, Mo; 132, New Friedenshütten, 1765, Mo; 133, Goschgoschunk, 1766, Mo; 134, Lawunkhannek, 1769, Mo; 135, Wechquetank, 1760, Mo; 136, Gnadenhütten, 1746, Mo; 137, New Gnadenhütten, 1754, Mo; 138, Meniolagomeka, 1742, Mo; 139, Nain, 1757, Mo; 140, Friedenshütten, 1746, Mo; 141, Forks of the Delaware, 1744, E; 142, Kuskuski, 1769, Mo; 143, Friedensstadt, 1770, Mo. New Jersey: 144, Crosswicks, 1745, E, P; 145, Brotherton, 1745, P. Delaware: 146, Millsboro, M. Virginia: 147, Tappahannock, SB; 148, King William, SB; 149, West Point, SB; 150, Providence Forge, 1922, SB; 151, Hampton, 1886, E. North Carolina: 152, Hamer, M; 153, Hollister, 1958, SB; 154, Fairview, 1914, M; 155, Salisbury, SB; 156, Pleasant Grove, 1900, M; 157, Asheville, SB; 158, Fayetteville, 1922, SB, A; 159, Clinton, 1910, SB, M; 160, Cherokee, E, M, SB; 161, Bryson City, SB; 162, Whittier, SB; 163, Sandy Plains, 1908, M; 164, Raeford, 1954, SB; 165, Lumber Bridge, Shannon, 1919, SB, M; 166, Parkton, SB; 167, Red Springs, 1924, SB, M; 168, St. Pauls, SB; 169, Laurinburg, 1896, SB; 170, Maxton, 1874, M, SB; 171, Pembroke, 1882, SB, M; 172, Lumberton, 1879, SB, M, Pr; 173, Valleytown, 1820, B, M; 174, Rowland, 1906, M, SB; 175, Fairmont, 1880, SB; 176, Ashpole Center, 1880, M; 177, Chadbourn, 1949, SB; 178, Hallsboro, 1902, SB; 179, Lake Waccamaw, SB; 180, Bolton, 1945, SB; 181, Prospect, 1886, M. South Carolina: 182, Hickory Grove, 1926, M; 183, Clio, 1891, SB, M; 184, Hamer, 1912, M. Georgia: 185, Springplace, 1801, Mo, M; 186,

Cherokee, 1819, Pr, B; 187, Irene I., 1735, Mo. Florida: 188, Tallahassee, P; 189, Ocala, 1911, E; 190, Okeechobee, SB; 191, Moore Haven, M; 192, Clewiston, SB; 193, Immokalee, 1899, E; 194, Ft. Lauderdale, SB; 195, Ochopee, SB; 196, Everglades, 1905, E.

treaties were transmitted to the missions. These contract schools also generally received the rations that would be due the children were they on the reservation with parents and not in the boarding school. The mission stations had normally been built on reservation land, and in 1922 Congress authorized the gift of land up to 160 acres to missions that were at that date using the land for school purposes.

An example of the new missions stimulated by the Peace Policy is the case of the Blackfeet. Abortive efforts by Presbyterians and Jesuits had been made in the 1840s (Harrod 1971:19–38). The government agent invited a Jesuit mission in 1859 to effect the "civilizing" of the tribe, but it was in the implementation of the Peace Policy in 1874 that a permanent Jesuit presence was effected. The missionaries aimed at making the Indians practicing Catholics and settled farmers. They attacked the traditional culture and religion in almost every particular. Then the reservation was assigned to the Methodist Episcopal Church by the government, and the Jesuits resented this. The Methodists assigned an ordained minister as agent in 1876, and he and the Catholic missionaries came into sharp conflict when he took his missionary mandate seriously. The Methodists also tried to turn the Blackfeet into farmers on their individual plots, and they had no regard for Blackfeet culture. Both missions used the coercive power of government to bend the Indians to their will. Neither of the missions completely destroyed the old culture, nor did they achieve a copy of White society; and the ultimate result was something between the two, with the missions being able to point to the existence of a few organized churches (Harrod 1971; L.B. Palladino 1922:185–229; Barclay 1949–1957, 3: 350–351).

Church and mission board advocacy of Indian rights reached an alltime high during the period of the Peace Policy (Beaver 1966a:177–206). The enlistment of many additional agencies under the Peace Policy, their initial association with the Board of Indian Commissioners, and especially the annual meeting had as an important by-product the fostering of a broad front on behalf of justice and rights among the mission agencies. They were both vocal apologists for, and critics of, the policy, and cultivated public opinion. They sought to convert the frontiersmen who demanded extermination of the Indians and those who wanted them left alone to die off speedily. At the end of the nineteenth century, as at its beginning, the claim was being made that the wild Indian is deteriorating and dying out, while the christianized Indian is improving and increasing. It was said to be far cheaper to christianize and civilize than to exterminate. Two missionaries could be maintained at the cost of one soldier

(Anonymous 1878:38). The churches should voice the conscience of the people "until it shall be impossible to return to the old ways of Indian fraud and corruption."

The advocacy of Indian rights took many forms. There was an annual crop of resolutions by ecclesiastical bodies. Much effort went into organization of Indian rights associations of an interdenominational character, while Episcopalians and Friends created numerous denominational societies that provided goods and services as well as fostered public concern (Beaver 1966a:183–184; "Indian Rights Movement, 1887–1973," this vol.). The Commission of Indian Missions of the Episcopal Church was the most active of denominational agencies in lobbying and in practical ministry (Beaver 1966a:184–185). Transfer of Indian affairs from the Department of the Interior to the War Department was vigorously and continuously fought (Beaver 1966a:189–190), and an independent Indian Department was proposed (Whipple 1899:545, 560). Individual personal rights, the termination of wardship of tribes, the application of civil law in all matters relating to Indians, the granting of land in severalty, and the bestowal of citizenship upon Indians were perennial goals sought by the Protestant agencies (Beaver 1966a:193–197). Education, stimulated by conversion and Christian faith, was as in the past to be the chief means to those desired goals, and the federal government should provide the Indians with the equivalent of the common public school system (Beaver 1966a:197–200).

Indian Territory and Oklahoma

The government's policy of removal concentrated more Christian Indians in Indian Territory than anywhere else in the country, in fact more than in the entire remainder of the United States and its territories. Isaac McCoy made surveys for the government, lobbied, and labored for exclusive possession of the land by the Indians, holding fast to his dream (Schultz 1972:161–203). Mission boards and national church bodies passed innumerable resolutions in vain. Settlers entered in even greater numbers. The churches followed both Indians and Whites. The great majority of these Christians were the peoples of the Five Civilized Tribes. The rigors of the Civil War, especially invasion by federal troops and postwar raids by bands of armed men, left the churches and missions in utter confusion. Between 1863 and 1867 the Northern Presbyterians lost all contact with the tribes among whom their main activity was concentrated and remained in touch only with the Chippewa, Ottawa, Omaha, and the Iowa Indian Orphan Institute (Faust 1943:357). The older churches of the Cherokee and Choctaw had entered the Southern Presbyterian Church in 1861, and the northerners declared that this denomination did absolutely nothing for them (ARCIA 1882:48). The Board of Home Missions as well as the Board of Foreign Missions sent in missionaries. Eventually all the Indian work was merged under the former in 1893 (Faust 1943:403–421). The Synod of Indian Territory was organized at Vinita on September 7, 1887, with Presbyteries of the Cherokee Nation, Choctaw, and Muskogee. Action by the Cumberland Presbyterian missionaries brought sufficient results to organize the Synod of Indianola in 1898, and when it merged with the (Northern) Synod in Indian Territory in 1906 it had six presbyteries, largely consisting of Indian churches (Drury 1952:217–389). The united body was called the Synod of Oklahoma. Ethnic Indian presbyteries were gradually absorbed into the predominantly White bodies, but Choctaw Presbytery continued into the 1950s.

The Baptist churches were evidently self-sufficient and received little attention from the mission board of the Southern Convention, which reported chiefly on the Creek, among whom there were 88 churches with a membership of 4,289 in 1886 (Board of Indian Commissioners 1886:21). The board ventured into educational work with the establishment of Levering Mission School for Creeks (Board of Indian Commissioners 1881:45). In 1906 they appointed Rev. A.J. Washburn superintendent of all the Five Civilized Tribes (R. Hamilton 1930:92). The American or Northern Baptists concentrated on the Territory, and despite their losses to the Southern Convention they reported in 1881 that one-tenth the population was Baptist. Cherokee churches numbered 61, Creek 46, Choctaw 34, Chickasaw 6, and Seminole 7 (R. Hamilton 1930:57). They made their "Indian university," Bacone College, their major resource for ministerial and lay leadership training. It was founded at Tahlequah in 1879 and moved to Muskogee in 1886. The Cherokee leader, William P. Ross, told the Board of Indian Commissioners in 1871 that his people were largely Baptists and Methodists (Board of Indian Commissioners 1871:170).

Many Cherokee and other churches had adhered to the Methodist Episcopal Church, South, and were organized in an Indian Mission Conference, which came to include White and Black members as well as Indians. There were 90 churches in the Conference in 1889, which were served by 53 preachers on "the effective list," plus 147 local preachers. Indian members numbered 4,954 compared to 3,616 others, but settlers were pouring into the country so fast that by the following year the White members outnumbered the Indians 4,173 to 3,909 (Board of Indian Commissioners 1889:42, 43, 1890:51; Barclay 1949–1957, 3:347–349). The work among the Cherokee, Choctaw, Creek, Chickasaw, and Osage was by then so blended with the White ministry and activity that reporting was difficult (Board of Indian Commissioners 1892:118). Intermarriage, especially by Cherokees and Choctaws, speeded assimilation in the churches.

Although there was increasing overlapping and competition, until the 1930s or 1940s there were few churches other than Baptist, Methodist, and Presbyterian among the people of the Five Civilized Tribes. The Moravians had followed their people from the original Springplace in Georgia and had established New Springplace in Indian Territory, but their community was always small. The United Evangelical Lutheran Church (Danish) maintained a mission, churches, and a school among the Cherokees in the Oaks district from 1892.

The Southern Baptists in 1922 were reported to have 26 Cherokee churches with 41 ministers and an active membership of 1,750; 12 Chickasaw churches with 10 ministers and only 189 active members; 27 Choctaw churches with 32 ministers and 341 active members; 20 Muskogee and Wichita churches with 35 ministers and 470 active members. There were also 17 churches in the region unaffiliated with the Baptist Associations, having 16 ministers and 170 active members (Lindquist 1923: 430–432; see also R. Hamilton 1930). This picture scarcely accords with the claims of Baptist predominance a half-century earlier.

The Methodist Episcopal Church, South, reported about 100 churches with a membership of 2,800 (R. Hamilton 1930:168–170). The Southern Presbyterians had 20 churches with 11 ministers, two licentiates, 10 candidates, and 536 communicants. The Presbyterian Church in the U.S.A. had four Cherokee churches with 250 members and one pastor; 27 Choctaw and Chickasaw churches with 450 members and 12 native pastors; and five Seminole and Creek churches with 150 members and three native pastors.

The mission boards related to the above churches had operated schools with government assistance during the era of the Peace Policy, there being then more than 20 day and boarding schools. After the termination of subsidies a dozen of those schools continued as government institutions. In 1922, only four distinctly Protestant schools existed, namely, the Goodland School and Oklahoma Presbyterian College at Durant under the Presbyterian Church in the U.S., the Lutheran School of nine grades at Oaks, and Bacone College at Muskogee run by the Baptists (North). However, at that time the Southern Methodists were establishing the Willis Folsom Training School at Smithville and the Women's Board of the Presbyterian Church, U.S.A., was reopening the Dwight School (Lindquist 1923:158–160).

No other tribal communities in the region were so large as the churches of the Five Civilized Tribes. Remnants of the peoples of the eastern Great Lakes were settled in the northeast corner of Oklahoma, all of them having previously been associated with missions—Senecas, Cayugas, Ottawas, Eastern Shawnees, Wyandots, Peorias, and Miamis—plus Quapaws and Modocs from the west. Except for the Catholic Modocs, these tribes had come under the care of the Society of Friends through their administrative service under the Peace Policy. There was

discontinuity between the early United Foreign Mission Society–American Board–Presbyterian mission to the Osages and the early twentieth-century work of the Southern Baptists and Friends (Lindquist 1923:173–176; R. Hamilton 1930:114–176; Kelsey 1917).

Another grouping of displaced eastern Indians was in what was known as the Shawnee Superintendency: Absentee Shawnees, Sauk and Foxes, Kickapoos, and Potawatomis, plus the Iowa tribe. The Baptists among the Sauk and Foxes changed their affiliation from the Northern to Southern Conventions (R. Hamilton 1930: 138–149). The Friends worked with the Shawnee, and the Southern Baptists took over the former Friends' mission to the Ponca. They also established a mission to the Pawnee, founding the first church in 1906. The National Indian Association began missions among the Ponca, Pawnee, and Oto in 1883, but soon turned them over to the Methodists (R. Hamilton 1930:115–135; Lindquist 1923:176–180).

The remaining concentration of missions was in the Kiowa Superintendency, where the Northern Baptists and five other churches launched often overlapping evangelistic efforts between 1886 and 1907. The Baptists ministered to the Kiowa, Comanche, Wichita, and Caddo. The Methodist Church, South, went to those same tribes along with the Reformed Presbyterian Church. The Mennonite Brethren established a mission to the Comanche, and the Reformed Church in America instituted one among the Apache and Comanche. About one-third of these peoples were said to be Protestant in 1922. The earlier Episcopal and Congregational missions to the Cheyenne and Arapahoe tribes were replaced by a vigorous Mennonite mission at Cantonment, Fonda, Hammon, Clinton, and Canton, as well as by a Reformed Church effort at Colony, and Northern Baptist efforts at Calumet, Kingfisher, Watuga, and Greenfield. The Peyote religion provided competition in the first quarter of the twentieth century (Lindquist 1923:184–195; Page 1915).

The course of political development in Indian territory with its consequent effect on Indian society was bitter medicine for the Baptists and Methodists, who had clung to Isaac McCoy's certainty that the area would always be a sanctuary where the indigenous population could develop unhampered by White intrusion and aggression. The other missions desired such protection but never expected it to prevail. The influx of White settlers was constantly protested, and this was a recurrent subject of discussion at the meeting of mission agencies following the annual session of the Board of Indian Commissioners. "Observe the sacred treaties! Preserve the national honor!" was the watchword. Then quickly, in hope of protecting both Indians and legitimate White settlers from exploiters and ruffians, the new watchword became "one good government for the whole territory" with laws, enforcement officers, and courts displacing the fictitious and ineffective national tribal governments (Board of Indian Commissioners 1882:8–9, 1894, 1895:6–7). The churches generally hailed the working out of the provisions of the Dawes Severalty Act and the merger of Indian and Oklahoma territories and admission of the state of Oklahoma into the union on November 16, 1907. Nevertheless, the developments that had brought about statehood had rather thoroughly thwarted the aims, goals, and projects of the missions, although the assimilation of the Cherokees and other tribes to White American culture through intermarriage and accommodation was what the missionaries and their supporters had been advocating for two centuries.

The Twentieth Century

The churches were not stirred to new concern by a significant change in government policy or by a keener awareness of the Indians' plight, and consequently few additional churches embarked on mission programs. The older missions augmented their activities. The Presbyterian Church in the U.S.A. in 1904 conducted missions in California to the Hupa, Shasta, and others; in Oregon to the Umatilla; in Washington to the Makah, Puyallup, and Spokane; in Idaho to the Nez Perce, Bannock and Northern Shoshone; in Utah to the Shivwits Southern Paiute; in Arizona to the Mohave, Navajo, Pima, and Papago; in New Mexico to Laguna Pueblo; in Colorado to the Ute; in Indian Territory to the Cherokee, Choctaw, Creek, Seminole, and Kiowa; in Kansas to Iowas and Sauks; in Nebraska to Omaha and Winnebago; in the Dakotas and Montana to Sioux; and in New York to Iroquois (B.M. Brain 1904). Some smaller agencies that had begun work before the turn of the century, such as the General Conference Mennonite Church among the Arapahoe and Cheyenne and the Christian Reformed Church among the Navajo and Zuni, gradually expanded (Hinman 1933:138–155; Lindquist 1923:59; Christian Reformed Church, Board of Foreign Missions 1914; Dolfin 1921; Beets 1940; DeKorne 1947). A comprehensive survey begun by the Interchurch World Movement in 1919 and completed by the Committee on Social and Religious Surveys in 1921 listed 23 churches engaged in Indian missions (Lindquist 1923:428–429). But in three instances two churches are combined under one name, and the actual number of churches is 26.

In addition, there were small programs by the Reformed Church in the United States among the Winnebagos in Wisconsin (Casselman 1932) and single missions by the Gospel Union, Wesleyan Methodists, and Seventh Day Adventists. The Reformed Church in America had launched missions to seven tribes, and two bodies of Lutherans were ministering to four tribes. One interdenominational society of women was at work, namely, the National Indian Association, which pioneered in new missions and, when they had developed, turned them over to denominational boards (Lindquist 1923:433–434, also xiii).

The large mission programs were still those of the older agencies. The Presbyterian Church in the U.S.A. had 125 churches among 43 tribes; the Methodist Episcopal Church, 43 churches among 25 tribes; the Episcopal Church, 93 churches in 13 tribes (fig. 7); the Northern Baptists, 32 churches in 20 tribes; the Southern Baptists, 114 churches in 14 tribes; the Methodist Episcopal Church South, 78 churches among 8 tribes; and the Southern Presbyterians, 20 churches in 4 tribes. The total number of Indian churches by 1921 was 597 among 175 tribes. Personnel included 268 ordained Indian ministers and 550 other Indian church workers, compared to 160 ordained White ministers. The churches had a total of 32,164 communicants with another 80,000 counted as Protestant adherents. There were 38 schools with 2,262 pupils. The usual organizations in White churches were duplicated in the Indian churches: 332 Sunday schools, 137 young people's societies, and 251 women's societies (fig. 8).

The survey revealed that there were 40 reservations with 46,000 inhabitants untouched by either Protestant or Roman Catholic missions (Lindquist 1923:xiv).

Most notable geographic expansion had been in the Southwest. Few of the missions undertaken before 1900 had endured (Spicer 1962:516–526). The mission to the Pima begun independently by Charles H. Cook in 1870 and taken over by the Presbyterian Church in the U.S.A. in 1878 is an exception, as is the Presbyterian mission to the Pueblo Indians at Laguna and Jemez dating from 1851. Cook represents the best in missionary ministry. He founded and fostered churches, and about half the Pimas had been baptized by him by the year 1899. He chose as elders former village headmen who could maintain morality and social order. There was positive acculturation, and Christian faith provided a new force for community integration. Indigenous ministers were recruited and trained. Cook served until 1911. The Lutherans at Fort Apache, Arizona, also maintained their mission.

When the Indians of the area began to attract the attention of tourists, the mission boards took notice of them. The Reformed Church in America opened a mission to the Mescalero Apache in 1907 and took over another to the Jicarilla Apache in 1914. They began the Papago mission in 1903, that at Fort Mohave in the same year, and the Camp Verde mission in 1907. This was their only mission that used the vernacular languages (Spicer 1962:518). The Methodist Episcopal, Presbyterian U.S.A., Episcopal, Christian Reformed, Gospel Union, Plymouth Brethren, and the Seventh Day Adventist churches were all drawn to the Navajo, while Mennonites and Northern Baptists went to the Hopi. The Plymouth

Arch. of the Episcopal Church, Austin, Tex.: top, PHO 2.103; center, RG106-18-6; bottom, RG106-18-5.

Fig. 7. The Episcopal Church in Alaska and the Great Basin in the early 20th century. top, Alaska Natives, probably Kutchins, and Whites in front of a hospital operated by the Episcopal Church in Circle, Alaska. The mission and hospital were established by the first bishop for Alaska, Rev. Peter T. Rowe, in the 1890s, when what was then Circle City was a mining boom town. The Indians had already been baptized, and many were familiar with their Native prayer books, hymns, and Bibles (Stuck 1920:54–57), which would have been those produced by Archdeacon Robert McDonald (vol. 6:78). In the 1970s the station was known as Trinity Mission and was served by diocesan staff. Photograph by Hudson Stuck, 1904. center, Junior Auxiliary of the Church of St. Mary the Virgin, Nixon, Nev. The mission, serving a Northern Paiute community from Pyramid Lake Reservation, was established around 1894. Children were taught English and crafts; women were taught to sew (W.H. Hare 1926:19–21). Photograph by Ruth D. Harmon, 1925. bottom, Church of the Good Shepherd, Ft. Hall Reservation, Idaho. The girls probably attended the girls' school run by the Episcopal church. The photograph was taken when a brick from a church in Jamestown, Va., was incorporated into the wall of the school under construction. In the 1970s the church served Northern Shoshone and Bannock Indians and local Whites. Photographed in 1921.

home missions from 1870 to 1882, vigorously fostered Indian and White missions (Drury 1952; Lazell 1960). In 1882 he went to Alaska as both territorial superintendent of education and Presbyterian superintendent of missions. He introduced the reindeer as livestock and fostered White and Native missions, sometimes in conflict with the existing Russian Orthodox missions.

The transfer of the administration of the Indian missions from foreign mission boards to home mission boards probably brought some loss for a few years. The issues of the use of Indian languages, the recruiting and training of a native ministry, self-support, and cultural accommodation or indigenization might have been faced earlier. The foreign mission boards had a common organ to deal with such matters from 1893 onward, namely, the Conference of Foreign Mission Boards of the United States and Canada, renamed the Foreign Missions Conference of North America, and later the Division of Overseas Ministries of the National Council of Churches of Christ in the U.S.A. After the termination of the annual meetings of board secretaries during the period of the Peace Policy the home mission people lacked opportunity for regular discussion and consultation. Many of them participated in the Indian Rights Association and the Lake Mohonk Conference, but these were not mission organs. Not until 1908 did the home mission boards organize the Home Missions Council. The next year that new body established its committee on Indian affairs, bringing together 14 denominations, the American Bible Society, the Young Men's and Young Women's Christian Associations, and the Indian Rights Association (Handy 1956:54–55). The Presbyterian member, Dr. Thomas C. Moffatt, was the leading spirit in its organization and served as the first chairman. The committee's purpose was to promote comity, persuade boards to take over unoccupied fields, strive for cooperation in mission work, and lobby with government on behalf of Indian rights and welfare. The

Brethren began their ministry to the Walapai in 1917. The Protestant mission impact on the Southwest tribes included "the regeneration of community life disorganized by the reservation system" as well as "the stimulation of political factionalism and community disorganization" (Spicer 1962:518). Another response to missionary impact was the rise of the syncretistic religion founded by Silas John Edwards among the Apaches before 1920 (vol. 10: 486–487).

Sheldon Jackson, the Presbyterian superintendent of

PROTESTANT CHURCHES AND THE INDIANS

Fig. 8. Christian Endeavor Society under the auspices of the Presbyterian Church at New Kasaan, Alaska, a Haida village. left front, Pat Skulka. front row, center, Walter Frank; to his right, Lydia Isaacs and her daughter Bessie. second row, center, Julia Johns Davis, in large hat. third row, second, third, and fourth from left, Mason Frank, John Baronovich, Mrs. John Baronovich. Photograph by H.B. Herrick, 1890–1896.

Council of Women for Home Missions joined the committee in 1919, and the name was changed to Joint Central Committee on Indian Affairs.

The purpose of this augmented committee was stated to be the coordination of all Protestant forces as far as possible in Indian work; to improve the level of religious instruction in the federal, public, and mission schools; and to call a representative conference on a united program for the Indians. The Conference of Christian Workers among the Indians was held at Wichita, Kansas, in September 1919 (Handy 1956:74; Lindquist 1923:xi). It dealt with religious instruction in government schools, the development of a well trained Indian ministry, and surveys. The most important result of the conference was that Dr. G.E.E. Lindquist began serving as director of religious work at Haskell Institute at Lawrence, Kansas, in 1922, and soon there were such directors in eight schools in eight states (Handy 1956:89).

Lobbying in Congress was directed in the beginning largely toward prevention of federal aid to sectarian schools. Examples are opposition to the proposed grant of 300,000 acres of land to a Roman Catholic school and a monetary grant of $20,000 to the (Protestant) California Indian Rights Association (Handy 1956:56). In the 1920s the committee combated the Peyote religion and its legalization. It was the agent for 23 Protestant denominations in 1923 in an effort to protect Pueblo lands. It constantly sought larger appropriations for medical and social programs. A careful watch over the Indian service was kept, and protests made when some action was deemed unjust or ill-advised.

The Joint Central Committee on Indian Affairs contin-

ued to represent and coordinate the Indian ministry of the mainstream Protestant churches. (When numerous ecumenical or cooperative agencies merged in 1950 to form the National Council of Churches of Christ in the U.S.A., the committee was carried over into the new structure as a unit of the new Division of Home Missions.) Two major projects of the Committee were the seminars or sectional conferences on the Indian ministry in the North American Home Missions Congress at Washington, D.C., in December 1930, and the National Congress on Home Missions at Columbus, Ohio, in January 1950 (North American Home Missions Congress 1930, 1; Lindquist and Carter 1951). One result of the former was the formation of the National Fellowship of Indian Workers, which provided those ministering to the Indians with a professional organ for study, consultation, planning, and improvement. Regional divisions of the Fellowship allowed for more local fellowship and consultation.

The Indian office of the Council during this period continued to maintain liaison between missions and government and to administer programs of religious work in seven government schools (Handy 1956:149). There was an occasional joint seminar with government officers to discuss common problems. Cooperation with other concerned agencies was fostered, such as a Conference on Indian Affairs held at Atlantic City in 1938 by the Home Missions Council, the Council of Women for Home Missions, the Indian Rights Association, and the American Association on Indian Affairs. The old objectives of acculturating the Indian to the national White culture, securing the end of wardship, the granting of land in severalty, and full citizenship were pursued.

Then the general harmony between the missions and the government was disrupted when Commissioner of Indian Affairs John Collier introduced a policy that the churches considered to be diametrically opposed to what they had sought as goals for the Indians throughout 300 years. The Indian Reorganization Act of 1934 was regarded as stopping the trend toward individual ownership of land. The Joint Central Committee on Indian Affairs in 1938 declared that the national administration allowed by its policy little opportunity for cooperation with the evangelistic, educational, and health programs of the church mission boards (Handy 1956:167–168). Religious work directors were provided in the government boarding schools, and by 1947 there were 12 full-time and four part-time workers (Handy 1956:199).

There was a genuine effort made to upgrade education in the boarding high schools, and the Baptist Bacone College at Muskogee, Oklahoma, added collegiate level courses. Belatedly attention was given to recruiting and training a native ministry. Cook Christian Training School at Phoenix was taken over from the Presbyterian mission by the Home Missions Council to be a union institution for the preparation of ministers and other

Fig. 9. Students from the Carlisle Indian Industrial School who were participants in the Sunday school of a local Methodist Episcopal Church. Indian students were often in segregated classes at churches (Lonna M. Malmsheimer, communication to editors 1987). front row, left to right: William Stelle (standing), Nelson Smith, Edward Snake, Simon Smith, Thomas Metoxen, Carl Lieder, Edmund, Charlie Wheelock, Peter Cornelius, Chester Cornelius, Jesse Cornelius, Harry Martin. second row: Richard Somers, Arlonzo Schondoah, Isaac Williams, Dennison Wheelock. third row, standing: James Cornelius, Adam Metoxen, Wilkie Sharpe, S.A. Bender, Robert Matthews, Luther Kuhns. Photograph by John N. Choate, 1888 to 1890.

church workers.

An investigation of the Indian ministry in 1948 located 232 Indian ministers, 71 percent of whom were in Oklahoma (Belvin 1949). Half of all ordained ministers served the Five Civilized Tribes, and 36 percent were Southern Baptist ministers. The average membership per church was reported as 65 in the churches they served.

The survey made for the 1950 National Congress on Home Missions revealed that 36 denominations were then engaged in Indian missions, of which 15 were constituent members of the Home Missions Council (Lindquist and Carter 1951:31ff.). Thirteen agencies had begun work within the previous 20 years. The Assemblies of God, the major Pentecostal body, was working with 19 tribes in 10 states, the Christian and Missionary Alliance with 16 tribes in five states, and the Church of the Nazarene with 14 tribes in six states. Religious ministry was being carried on in 375 communities, at 437 stations, by 833 workers, working with a church membership of 39,200 and a Protestant constituency of about 140,000. Some 333 workers were involved in 215 projects, including 213 native workers. Lindquist and Carter (1951) reported on many aspects of church life and work, noting the apparent lack of concern about conserving and using the Indian

culture and its values as well as the social concern of the major White churches, reflected in the ministry to urban Indians.

1950s–1970s

Ministry to the city-dwelling Indians, who after the end of World War II began to move from reservations into urban areas, was the most urgent and creative new form of service in mission work in the 1950s and 1960s (fig. 10). Rapid City, South Dakota, was chosen by the Committee on Indian Work for a special study because, although small, it was typical (Lindquist and Carter 1951:54–67). This resulted in the establishment of a program of ministry by the Division of Home Missions of the National Council of Churches, the Rapid City Council of Churches, and the local County Council. An Indian Service Center at Phoenix served local residents and transients, and reported an attendance of 8,254 for the year 1948 (Lindquist and Carter 1951:68–69). A notable program was that taken in Minnesota under the United Church Committee on Indian Work organized 1952–1953, in which were united the Minnesota Council of Churches, the local Councils of the Twin Cities, the

457

Fig. 10. Mohawk worshipers in Cuyler Presbyterian church in Brooklyn, N.Y. Mohawks, most of whom were originally from Caughnawaga, Que., began to attend the church in small numbers in the 1930s. By the 1950s about 25 Mohawks had joined the church with a slightly larger number attending the monthly service in Mohawk conducted by Pastor David M. Cory (right). Cory uses a Mohawk hymnal that he and 2 Mohawk parishioners, Josephine Skye and Margaret Lahache, translated. The hymnal is also used on the Caughnawaga Reserve. Cory also translated a version of the New Testament gospels into Mohawk. Periodically the Mohawks produced an Indian pageant for the other members of the congregation. Most of the Mohawk men worked in high steel construction in New York City (Conly 1952; J. Mitchell 1960). Photograph by E. Anthony Stewart, about 1952.

National Council of Churches, and local churches and organizations (United Church Committee on Indian Work 1957). Rather than maintaining a center it supplied services, including housing, public relations, social service in many forms, a volunteer corps of workers with men, and a hospitality program. This program became a model for others. By 1958 14 percent of Protestant workers were in urban situations (Lively 1958:7).

The body of missionaries and church workers seems to have remained much the same since the 1960s. But integration of the Indian congregations and programs into the national and local church life and work makes it extremely difficult to obtain a clear overview of the Indian mission. For example, in the complete reorganization of all the mission and service activities of the United Presbyterian Church in the U.S.A. under a new program agency in 1973, a central office for American Indian work disappeared and responsibility scattered through a number of departments, such as Race Relations and Church Development. The same thing happened a few years earlier to eliminate the Indian office of the National Council of Churches. The extensive Episcopal Church Indian ministry in contrast remained unified and coordinated (Episcopal Church. National Committee on Indian Work 1973, 1970; Meredith 1973), and the United Methodist Church has a central office.

Forms of ministry aimed at social and economic problems and situations have come to match the educational ministry, and they predominate over the former evangelistic emphasis, which has given way to more of a pastoral concern.

There has been a marked change in attitude toward Indian culture, and the missionaries no longer present a solid front on the desirability of complete assimilation. In 1958 44 percent of Roman Catholic workers and 35 percent of Protestant workers were still strong advocates of assimilation, but 11 percent of Roman Catholics and 9 percent of Protestants evaluated Indian culture highly and wanted it conserved, and 57 percent of Protestants and 37 percent of Roman Catholics took a middle ground requiring the retention of certain positive values in assimilation (Lively 1958). More astounding is the revelation that 74 percent of the Roman Catholics, 81 percent of Episcopalians, 75 percent of Congregational Christians, and 53 percent of Methodists believed that the Indian religions are almost entirely or for the most part reconcilable with Christianity. The Congregational Christian Church (now United Church of Christ) took the view that the Indian American needed to be encouraged in the rediscovery of the basic values of his own culture, and in the assimilation of those cultural patterns of White society best suited to the upholding of persons as whole and free people. The United Presbyterian statement was similar.

However, the missions have been slow in implementing their newer insights, and the missionaries have been even slower in handing over authority and control to the Indian Christians. In the 1970s Indian political protest expressed resentment, claims for redress of wrongs, and aspirations for Indian people through sometimes violent confrontation. The impatience of Christian Indians with White missionary leadership, frustration over continuing dependence, and a positive approach to their cultural and religious heritage brought about a revolt within the churches parallel to the expression of Indian resentment and claims in society generally. The 1970s were a time of conflict, confusion, and radical change in the Indian Christian community. There were protests in 1971 over the Presbyterian Ganado mission project in Arizona (G.P. Noble 1971); and in 1970 the dormitories of Augustana College in Sioux Falls, South Dakota, were occupied by the American Indian Movement as a protest against the inaction of Lutheran and other churches (Deloria 1973: 21, 58).

The evidence seems to indicate that within the Indian Christian community the Indian churches will be controlled by the Indians themselves and will make their own cultural adaptation as well as theological reinterpretation.

For a directory of Indian, Aleut, and Eskimo churches see Beaver (1979).

Mormon Missions to the Indians

JOHN A. PRICE

The Church of Jesus Christ of Latter-day Saints was formally organized on April 6, 1830, in Feyette, New York, following about 10 years during which Joseph Smith, Jr., claimed to have received revelations from Heaven, visions from God the Father and his son Jesus Christ, and visitations from spiritual beings. Although one might say that the church, known as the Mormon church, came out of the general religious revitalization movement in the northeastern United States from the 1820s to the 1840s, Mormons claim Joseph Smith was a prophet called by God and directed by the Holy Spirit to restore the Christian church and direct its development. The new religion could be thought of as a Christian protest against both the Catholic and Protestant churches. It claimed continuing divine revelation to answer certain questions that were important in the early nineteenth century: the utopian design of society, and priesthood positions for all adult men; God's cosmic plan, including temple rituals that could provide some assurance of a successful afterlife; and the origin and history of the American Indians, by migration out of Israel but with wars and degradations until they were like the local Iroquois.

The revelation that caused the greatest difficulty for the Mormon church concerned the endorsement of polygyny, which was announced publicly in 1844 and accepted by the membership in 1852. Another teaching prohibits use of alcohol, tobacco, tea, and coffee.

The church received its first unique scripture in 1830 with the publication of the Book of Mormon (J. Smith 1830), which is held to be sacred history of the New World, comparable to the Bible. Mormons believe that Joseph Smith was the divinely selected translator of a set of gold plates that were revealed to him in New York and that were inscribed in "reformed Egyptian hieroglyphics." The Book of Mormon is accepted by Mormons as a history primarily concerned with a migrant group led by a Jewish prophet by the name of Lehi who would have arrived in the New World about 589 B.C. Nephi, one of the sons of Lehi, kept the records of his people and was progenitor of one of the main branches of New World peoples, referred to as the civilized Nephites. Laman, the oldest but rebellious son of Lehi, was ancestor of a competing society, the Lamanites, who survived the wars between the two societies to become the American Indians, but for their sins "God did cause a skin of blackness to come upon them" (2 Nephi 5:21), like the Blacks before them in the Old World.

According to the Book of Mormon, the Lord said to Nephites, "Go forth among the Lamanites, thy brethren, and establish my word . . . they had undertaken to preach the word of God to a wild and hardened and a ferocious people; a people who delight in murdering the Nephites, and robbing and plundering them" (J. Smith 1830:238). According to Mormons these are the first missionaries to the Indians, from about 91 to 77 B.C. in North America.

In the early years of the "restored" church the Mormons believed that once the Indians were told of their history and their place in the church they would convert to Mormonism by the thousands. In fact, one of the prophecies in the Book of Mormon states that "in the last days" of the world before the millennium the Indians will be converted to the true church by Whites, and within a few generations they shall become a "white and delightsome people" (2 Nephi 30:5-6). Based on this scripture, and backed by pronouncements from Mormon authorities, the practice developed to refuse full membership, such as male priesthood and receiving temple ordinances, to Blacks yet to accord membership to American Indians.

Early Missions

In 1830–1831 Oliver Cowdery led a mission to the Indians. They preached to a group of Senecas at Cattaraugus near Buffalo, New York; to a camp of Wyandots in Sandusky, Ohio; to a small Shawnee camp in Independence, Missouri; and to Delawares along the Kansas River (fig. 1). Through a translator Cowdery told the Indians that they had once been affluent and powerful peoples, but had become wicked, and God was punishing them. But "if the red man would receive this Book [of Mormon] and learn the things written in it, and do according thereunto, they should be restored to all their rights and privileges; should cease to fight and kill one another; should become one people . . . Then should the red men become great, and have plenty to eat and good clothes to wear, and should be in favor with the Great Spirit" (P.P. Pratt 1938:54–55).

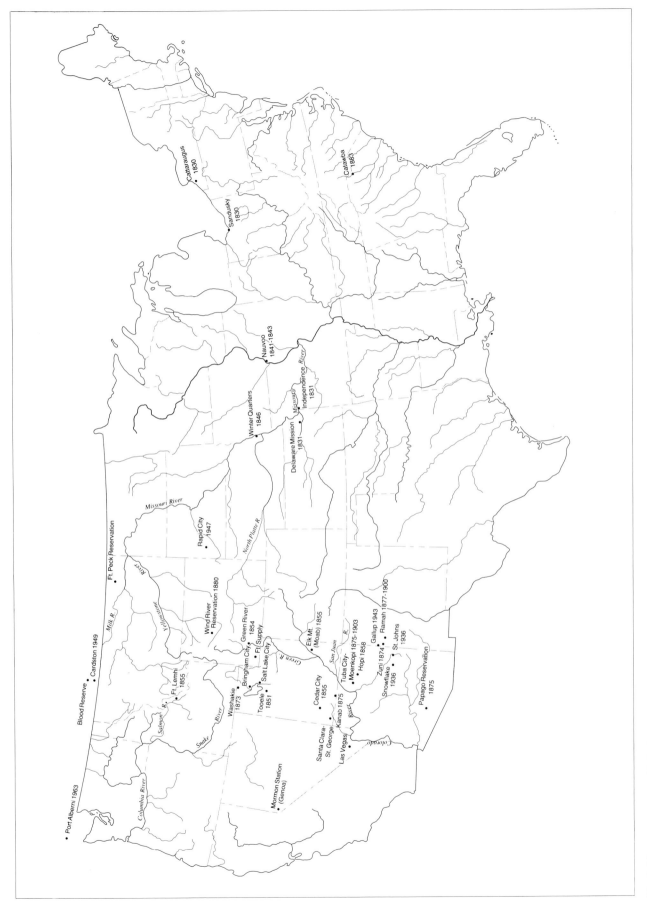

Fig. 1. Mormon contacts with Indians since the mid-19th century.

PRICE

The missionaries reported enthusiastic Indian acceptance of this message. In fact, Mormonism is the only faith in which North American Indians are featured in the holy scripture, and this may hold some appeal to Indian converts.

A group of Sauk and Fox led by Keokuk went to the Mormon community in Nauvoo, Illinois, in 1841. Joseph Smith told them they would become a prosperous people. He advised them to be peaceful. The Mormons provided a feast and a band concert as the Indians entertained with their dances. In 1843 three Potawatomi chiefs visited Nauvoo to see if the famous prophet could help prevent the theft of their land, horses, and cows by Whites.

Settlement in Utah

The next Indian missions were not sent out until 1854, in Utah. In the meantime the Mormons had been forced to move westward several times; Brigham Young, the president of the church, led the resettlement centered in Salt Lake City, Utah. When the Mormons arrived in the Salt Lake Valley in 1847 they were the first permanent White settlers in the Great Basin. However, non-Mormon settlers immediately began coming into the territory. Thus, the church felt an immediate need to establish control over as much land as possible, to establish a secure state, free from the harassment the church had received in New York, Ohio, Illinois, and Missouri. They began to create a separate state, to be called Deseret. The Indian "missions," where Indians were encouraged to farm, were seen as part of this regional organization. To some extent

Mormons and Indians became allies against advancing White settlement (vol. 11:508–510).

In 1853 Brigham Young assigned Orson Hyde the task of leading missionaries to settle in the area of the Green River, Wyoming, to work with the Shoshone. His instructions were not to use military force if possible, but to "preach civilization to them, try and teach them how to cultivate the soil, to instruct them in the arts and sciences if possible, and by that means prevent trouble for our frontier settlements and emigrant companies" (Coates 1972:4). In 1854, 39 missionaries went to the Green River where they built a two-story structure they called Fort Supply as an outpost in Eastern Shoshone country (R.S. James 1967). Young encouraged Mormon men to marry "the Indian maidens" and to instruct the Indian leaders.

In 1854 and 1855 other missionaries were sent to Indian missions: 41 to Elk Mountain, near Moab, Utah (Law 1959), to Ute, Southern Paiute, and Navajo; 27 to Salmon River, Idaho (J.D. Nash 1967), to Bannock, Northern Shoshone, Flathead, Nez Perce, and Blackfeet; and 23 to Cedar City and Santa Clara, Utah (fig. 2) (Corbett 1952), to Southern Paiute, Hopi, and Yuman-speaking tribes. It was soon apparent that only two or three men in each mission group were at all effective at proselytizing the Indians; these several men served repeatedly to solve Indian-White conflicts: James S. Brown, George W. Hill, Jacob Hamblin, Ira Hatch, among others. Hamblin settled disputes with Gosiutes west of Tooele, Utah, in 1851; and in 1858 Hamblin, Hatch, Dudley Leavitt, Thales Haskell, and Samuel Knight revolved conflicts with Mohaves.

left, Utah State Histl. Soc., Salt Lake City:970.52P.1; right, Southern Utah State College, Special Collections and Zion Photo Company, Cedar City, Utah.
Fig. 2. Southern Paiutes and Mormons. left, Baptism of Southern Paiutes by David H. Cannon of the Church of Jesus Christ of Latter Day Saints near St. George and Santa Clara, Utah. About 200 Southern Paiute men, women, and children were baptized and then received gifts of food from the Mormons (Alter 1944:67). Photograph by Charles R. Savage, March 20, 1875. right, Southern Paiute and White participants in a gardening project sponsored by the Mormon church in Cedar City, Utah. Church members in this area organized a number of projects for Indians, including after-school tutoring, voter education and registration, construction of a chapel, and handicraft promotion. Photograph by Homer C. Jones, July 16, 1962.

MORMON MISSIONS TO THE INDIANS

Several of these men married Indian women, in addition to their White wives. The missions of the 1800s combined functions of exploration, military defense, and agricultural settlement with religious proselytizing. In the 1850s they helped reduce the widespread Indian raiding of caravans and stopped the Ute raids for Southern Paiute children to be sold south as slaves (Malouf 1966:14). They tried to induce the Indians to become settled farmers.

In 1858 Brigham Young called all outlying missions and settlements in to help defend the central Great Basin settlements, when the U.S. government sent troops from Fort Leavenworth to stamp out the supposed rebellion by the Mormons. Young also established martial law, had the mountain passes into the Great Basin guarded, and attempted to create alliances with the Indians against the U.S. Army.

Mormons colonized a large area of Indian territory with relatively little bloodshed. They received predictably more organized and more military reactions from the horse-riding societies, such as the Eastern Shoshone and Eastern Ute in the Great Basin and the Navajo and Apache in the Southwest. They had predictably more passive reactions from the Western Ute, Western Shoshone, Northern Paiute, Southern Paiute, and Washoe in the Great Basin. The agricultural Hopi, Zuni, and Pima-Papago the Mormons considered more peaceful, more civilized, and better prospects for conversion to Mormonism than any other Indians they met in the West.

The passivity of the Western Shoshone, Northern Paiute, and Washoe is apparently the main reason why a Mormon Indian mission was never sent into the western area of the Basin: these Indians were no military threat. There were Mormon settlers there, in places such as Genoa in western Nevada, but they experienced no significant Indian resistance. Missions were sent to the north, northeast, southeast, and south in the 1850s. Then in the 1870s Mormon settlements were purposely built near more peaceful, agricultural Indians in the southwest: near the Hopi at Moenkopi in 1875 (C.S. Peterson 1973) and near the Zuni at Ramah, New Mexico, in 1877. Hundreds of Navajos were baptized at Kanab, Utah, in 1875. In 1876 when Brigham Young appointed Ammon Tenney as president of the Arizona–New Mexico Indian Mission he asked him to locate favorable sites for Mormon settlements (Smiley 1972).

In 1873 George Hill led a group of missionaries into southern Idaho to the Bannock and Northern Shoshone and baptized about 100 Indians (R.O. Brown 1956). Coates (1972:8) claims that Hill's success with the Shoshone was due to his use of pictures, their belief in the validity of experiences such as the visions of Joseph Smith, and their wish to escape the government reservation system. After the initial proselytizing, the Indians were settled on farmland 35 miles north of Brigham City, Utah, which they called Washakie after an Eastern Shoshone

chief who was usually receptive to the Mormons. Teams of Mormon farmers, craftsmen, and teachers helped these Shoshones create an agricultural community that was fully operating in the 1880s. These Indians were mormonized and integrated into all local church positions. In 1885 L.W. Warner, a full-blood Shoshone, was sent on a mission from this community to proselytize other Indians.

The first missions to the Hopi, 1858–1860, did not succeed (vol. 9:525–526). In 1874 the first mission was sent to Zuni. In 1878 missionary Llewellyn Harris was at Zuni when a reported smallpox epidemic was raging. He is given credit for curing people by laying his hands on them and praying for them.

In 1883 a Mormon mission to the Catawba in South Carolina was begun, and it became a permanent mission in 1897. It resulted in the conversion of nearly the entire tribe. By 1934, 95 percent of the 300 Catawbas were Mormon believers (Hudson 1970:77–80; D.S. Brown 1966:340–347).

In 1885 an Indian mission farm was established outside the Eastern Shoshone reservation by Amos Wright and James Brown. But during 1887–1936, there was very little organized Indian missionary work. The federal government was trying to stop the Mormon practice of polygyny, Indian agents were uncooperative, and many Indian conversions did not last. In 1900 the Ramah, New Mexico, mission closed. In 1903 the Tuba City–Moenkopi mission closed when Indian agents ordered the Mormon settlement removed from Indian land.

The church's attitude toward Indians has been that they must be both civilized and proselytized, ultimately to be assimilated into Mormon society. Neither nineteenth nor twentieth-century relationships, however, have reached that ideal. For example, in the 1855 mission to the Indians in Idaho (R.O. Brown 1956), George Hill briefly preached to a group of Northern Shoshones who came into the missionary camp and then baptized the entire group in the church. He said he knew only a few words of their language. Then the missionaries simply moved on. In northern Idaho they baptized 56 Indians in a single session, although the meaning of such baptism to the Indians was obviously very different from its meaning to the Mormons. Amos Wright baptized 422 Eastern Shoshones during his four-week mission in fall 1880, and during a seven-week mission to the Zuni in 1876 111 Indians were baptized.

Competition among different Christian sects led to an early Bureau of Indian Affairs ruling that only one denomination would be allowed on a reservation or a section of the large ones. Since Mormons had little standing with the U.S. government until 1900, other denominations were officially approved for reservations even in Utah. Until the order of Commissioner of Indian Affairs John Collier in 1934 declaring religious freedom on Indian reservations, Mormons worked only on the fringe.

The Twentieth Century

In explaining the paucity of permanent Indian conversions prior to 1936, Flake (1965:85–86) wrote that "the Mormon religion was rigidly based upon European culture and would not yield to lowering itself until a common ground with the Indians was reached . . . The Church was quite willing to wait for as many generations as necessary for the Indians to learn modern civilization . . . .then the Mormons hoped to step in and find the Indians more able to live and accept their religion."

In 1936 missionaries were again active among Indians in Arizona and New Mexico. The Navajo-Zuni Mission, started in Gallup in 1943, became in 1947 a model for Indian programs. A mission at Rapid City, South Dakota, was founded soon after that.

A Mormon mission to Canadian Indians was centered in Cardston, Alberta, in 1949. In 1963 Nootkans on Port Alberni Reserve, British Columbia, were proselytized.

Dozens of Mormon families in the nineteenth century adopted Indian children, at first after buying them from slave raiders who had threatened to kill them. In later years adoption was in order to "civilize" and convert the children. After 1949 this kind of intimate missionary work through assimilation was organized in the Indian Student Placement Program (C.R. Bishop 1967). Reservation children from the families of both Mormons and non-Mormons are taken into White families to live during the school year and are then returned to their reservation homes during the summer. By 1976 over 20,000 Indian children had participated in this "foster parent" program, with each child usually returning to the same White family each year (Beaver 1979:77). This has led to extensive direct contacts between White Mormons and Indian Mormons because the White foster families often visit their foster child's Indian family in the summer. Intermarriage between Indians and Whites is avoided whenever possible.

Golden Buchanan (1960:5,12), as the director of Mormon missions, outlined a program for missionaries to the Indians. "The program should be one of assimilation and integration as rapidly as possible . . . .First, make friends. Then get into the home as soon as you can . . . .it will be helpful if you have in your hands some pictures of Indian people, of the ruins of Central and South America . . . .They like pictures . . . ." The missionary was given a model method of introducing Mormon religion to an Indian—pictures, prayer, songs, and stories. In 1963 *Indian Liahona*, an illustrated magazine for Mormon Indians, was started, published in Salt Lake City.

The place of the Indian in the religious history of the Book of Mormon and the Mormon belief in the extreme importance of genealogical lineage has meant that Indians (and Polynesians) have been heavily missionized, while Blacks were not missionized at all. However, in 1978 Blacks' exclusion from the priesthood was ended, and in 1981 a new edition of the Book of Mormon altered the desired state of "White and delightsome" to "pure and delightsome."

With an increasingly large and self-sufficient membership of Indians, there has been a transition of the position of Indian communities in the Mormon church from missions to the ordinary Mormon organization of religious "stakes" and local "wards" aided by mission "branches." Brigham Young University, which has the largest enrollment of Indians in any American university, has a ward, a Lamanite Club, and other organizations that tend to keep Indians segregated. In 1975 there were about 300 Mormon missionaries working with Indians in the U.S. and Canada, about 40 of whom were full-blood Indians. The Church had about 150 wards or mission branches that were predominantly of U.S. or Canadian Indians. The largest number, about 60, was in the Southwest, but other areas with Mormon Indians were the Catawba Reservation, South Carolina; Sully Lake in North Dakota; Papago in Arizona; Fort Peck in Montana; Blood Reserve in Alberta; and Port Alberni Reserve in British Columbia. The presence of a Mormon Indian ward on or near a reservation usually means than there are at least 20 Indian families actively involved in the church. About 100 Indians were sent on missions to other Indians in 1987.

Sources

Additional sources on the Mormon missions to the Indians include the work of Mormon missionaries Jacob Hamblin (P.D. Bailey 1948; C.S. Peterson 1971), Zadock K. Judd (D.W. Judd 1968), James S. Brown (J.S. Brown 1900), Thomas D. Brown (T.D. Brown 1972), and Hubert Case (Stowell 1963). W.A. Jennings (1971) discusses Mormon presence among the Delaware in Kansas in the 1830s; Flake (1965) traced the history of Mormon missionary work among the Hopi, Navajo, and Zuni; the response of the Rimrock Navajo to the Mormons is addressed by Rapoport (1954); K.W. Parry (1972) looked at a Mormon mission as an agent of social change among the Blood Indians of Canada. Barney (1986) addressed the relationship between Mormonism and the Ghost Dance religion of 1890. Mormon-Indian relations were analyzed by J. Brooks (1944).

Roman Catholic Missions in New France

LUCIEN CAMPEAU, S.J.

The territory explored and occupied by France in North America during the seventeenth and eighteenth centuries contained an immense population of Indian tribes, mostly Algonquian-speaking, but also Iroquoian and Siouan. This essay will review the work of French Catholic missions to the Indians throughout this area, including the border regions that were disputed by the English.

Early Missions, 1611–1629

The first missionary to the Indians in New France was a secular priest named Jessé Fléché who in 1610 baptized more than 100 Micmacs, including a chief, Membertou, and his family. Fléché was overzealous; he neglected church rules by baptizing persons who had no understanding of the catechism.

The first Jesuits, Pierre Biard and Enemond Massé, did not arrive at Port Royal until May 22, 1611, although their order had been invited to New France as early as 1604. Anxious to avoid Fléché's mistakes, the Jesuits determined to learn the local languages and to refrain from any administration of the baptism while doing so. This was a source of violent disputes with the colonial leaders, the Biencourts. Evangelization became impossible. The Jesuits made an attempt at Saint Sauveur, but they were routed by the Englishman, Sir Samuel Argall, in 1613 and returned to France.

At Samuel de Champlain's request in 1615, the Recollects of Paris sent four missionaries: Denis Jamet, Superior; Joseph Le Caron; Jean Dolbeau; and Brother Pacifique Duplessis. The French worked among two categories of Indians: nomadic hunting and fishing groups and sedentary groups who cultivated the fields. The nomads, of Algonquian linguistic stock, included the Montagnais, who congregated each summer at Tadoussac, and the Algonquin, natives of the Saint-Maurice and Ottawa rivers, who traded at Trois-Rivières. The sedentary villagers, the Hurons, lived farther away. They were the western merchants who came to sell furs to the French by way of the Ottawa River, crossing Algonquin country. To the French, the nomads were pure savages whose roaming ways were hard to reconcile with Christianity; while not abandoning them, the Recollects placed their main hope in the Hurons, whose agricultural habits seemed to predispose them to the faith (fig. 1).

The Recollects were soon discouraged; they were too dependent on the French merchants. Following the nomads on the hunt was a strenuous task; and life among the Hurons, isolated, was hardly easier. They hoped to make more progress by giving the children a French education in a seminary in Quebec, and in 1620 they built a convent on the Saint Charles River. It was not a success. Finally, in 1629, the war between the French and the English ruined the French establishment. A 1619 effort made in Acadia by the Recollects of Aquitaine met even less success and was abandoned in 1624.

In 1625 the Jesuits arrived at Quebec. There were five: Charles Lalemant, Enemond Massé, Jean de Brébeuf, Anne de Noüe, and Brother François Charton. At first they stayed at the Recollect convent; later they took up residence on the opposite bank of the Saint Charles River. They began methodically learning the local languages. Having adopted the Recollect point of view concerning ability of adult Indians to become Christians, the Jesuits' main concern was to create seminaries for the boys.

When the domination of the Huguenot merchants became unbearable, Father Philibert Noyrot tried to obtain a change in administration, and Armand Jean du Plessis, Duc de Richelieu, founded the New France Company, dedicated to the creation of a French Catholic colony on the Saint Lawrence. But Quebec fell to the English and all the missionaries were sent home in 1629.

Capuchin Missions in Acadia, 1632–1654

In 1629 two Jesuits were serving in the post of Sainte Anne du Grand-Cibou on Cape Breton Island, and in 1630 the Recollects of Aquitaine, resuming their mission of 1619–1624, sent two members of their order to Fort Loméron on Cape Sable (fig. 2). But the most important missionaries in Acadia at this time were the French Capuchins. Theirs was the first mission established on Canadian soil by authority of the Roman Congregation "De Propaganda Fide." Six of them made the crossing with Isaac de Razilly and 300 colonists. They began evangelizing the Indians: in Nova Scotia, Micmacs; on the Saint John River, Maliseets; on the Saint Croix River, Passamaquoddys; and on the Penobscot River, Eastern

Lib. of Congress, Rare Book Div.
Fig. 1. Title page of *Le Grand Voyage du Pays des Hurons* (1632) by Gabriel Sagard-Théodat, a lay brother in the Recollect order who lived from 1623 to 1624 at Carhagouha, where the mission was called Saint Gabriel (Shea 1855:167). The mission was founded by Joseph Le Caron. The Huron figures at the top may be copied from Champlain's descriptions (Tooker 1964:6–7). Engraved copperplate, printed by Denys Moreau.

Abenakis.

Richelieu wanted the Capuchins to have a monopoly in this region, but they were hindered by the presence of Recollects. Their mission was interrupted in 1654 when Robert Sedgewick came from Boston with a fleet, seized Port Royal, and imposed English authority along the whole East coast. The Capuchins reluctantly went back to France, and they never returned to Acadia.

Jesuit Missions, 1632–1659

The Jesuits' return to Quebec in 1632 was improvised. Three of them embarked from France with Emery de Caën: Paul LeJeune, Anne de Noüe, and Brother Gilbert Burel. Two more, Ambroise Davost and Antoine Daniel,

went with Champlain to Sainte Anne du Grand-Cibou where they spent the first year rebuilding the ruins of their former missions. In 1633 all were reunited in Quebec, where de Brébeuf and Massé joined them. As in the time of the Recollects, their primary concerns were to learn the native languages and to establish seminaries for the Indian boys.

LeJeune spent the winter of 1633–1634 with a Montagnais family on the south bank of the Saint Lawrence. In 1634 the Huron mission was reestablished with de Brébeuf as head, assisted by Davost and Daniel. They brought servants with them also.

The plan to create seminaries for young Montagnais was unsuccessful; the children could not endure the confinement of a European house and a fixed routine. From the earliest years, however, a few adult family heads had displayed some interest in Christian doctrine. Father LeJeune developed a plan to take in families in permanent mission settlements, on the model of Jesuit work in Paraguay. To accustom the Indians to sedentary life and to free them from dependence on the hunt, it was thought necessary to build cottages, a church, a missionary residence, and a fort against the Iroquois and to clear and cultivate the land. In 1634 the Jesuits joined the French in the foundation of a post at Trois-Rivières where they hoped to attract the Algonquian tribes of the upper Saint Lawrence and of the Saint Maurice and to settle them in such an establishment. Once this plan was conceived the Jesuits proceeded to reserve land near the French posts, based on the principle that the Indians were the original landowners. This effort was the origin of the principal Jesuit seigneuries: Sillery, near Quebec; Cap-de-la-Madeleine, near Trois-Rivières; and La Prairie, near Montreal (fig. 2).

From 1637 Noël Brulart de Sillery, in France, assumed the cost of clearing and construction at Sillery. On February 22, 1639, he set up a fund of 20,000 livres, producing an income of 1,500 livres a year for maintenance. The Sillery establishment, dedicated to Saint Joseph, was begun with two Montagnais families; the registers show 118 baptisms between 1638 and 1640. In 1639 three hospital nuns or Augustinian sisters from Dieppe came to found a hospital. Father Barthélemy Vimont judged Sillery to be an appropriate location, and the hospital was built there in 1640.

Despite its success, the mission had problems. To begin with there was disease: smallpox ran riot, attacking the two original heads of families, one of whom died in 1639. Once the epidemic passed, the population began to grow again. Jean-Baptiste Etinechkaouat and Noël Negabamat were elected chiefs, and a captain was appointed to direct catechism and prayers. Work in the fields was shared by all, under the direction of the Jesuit brothers and a few Frenchmen. Part of their subsistence came from eel fishing, for which Sillery had always been the center.

ROMAN CATHOLIC MISSIONS IN NEW FRANCE

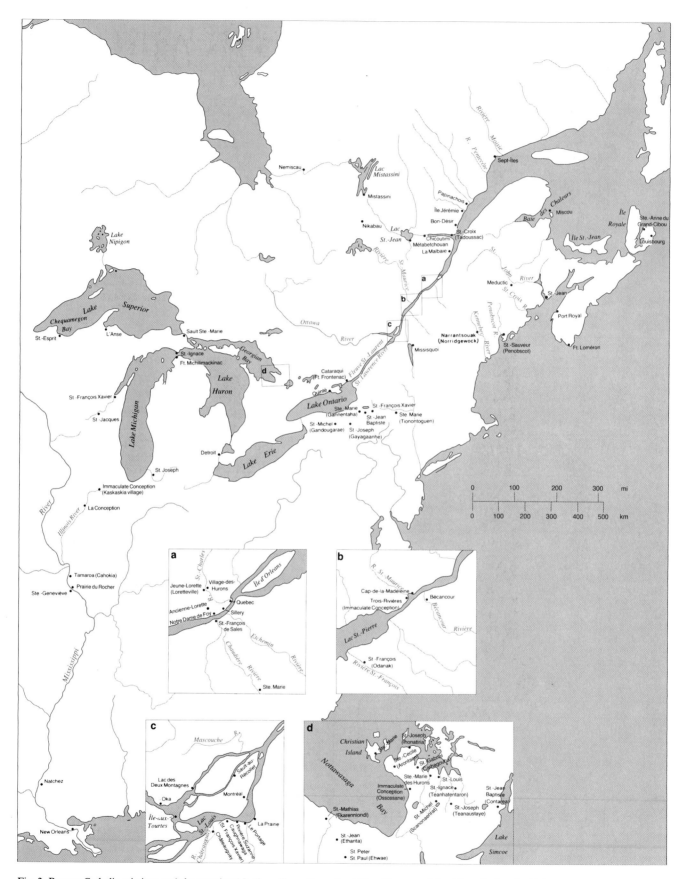

Fig. 2. Roman Catholic missions and the associated Indian villages throughout New France and Louisiana during the 17th and early 18th centuries (JR 10, 34, 51, 63; Tanner 1986; vol. 15:123–136, 137–159, 368–388, 394–397, 418–441, 594–601).

CAMPEAU

During the winter the neophytes and their families left the mission for the hunt; but they continued to observe Sundays, and on important feast days they returned to make their devotions at the church. Some lived in the French manner inside the mission, while others pitched their tents alongside. They provided a colorful spectacle in their skin garments overlaid with fabrics bought from the French and adapted to their tastes. Their Christian fervor was great. Polygamy disappeared, as did the nocturnal trysts of young men and women; and young Christians began to ask the missionaries to sanction their marriages.

Sillery's influence was not limited to the Montagnais. The Attikamègues of the Saint Maurice, the Algonquins of the Ottawa, and the Hurons of Georgian Bay acquired their first notions of Christianity there; many were baptized. In 1642 a liberated Western Abenaki prisoner was treated at the Sillery hospital, and through him the fame of the settlement spread. Father Gabriel Druillettes visited the Western Abenaki in 1646.

The number of Christians increased until in 1646 there were 120. Sillery became a headquarters whence the missionaries fanned out along the Montagnais hunting trails. The Iroquois posed a constant threat to the mission, and local Indians were afraid to settle there. Construction of a stockade around the church began in 1649 and was finished in 1651. While some Christian Indians lived at the mission, a far greater number merely passed through each year to reaffirm their faith or to receive their first catechism.

Each summer the Indians of the Saguenay flocked to Tadoussac to trade furs. They had learned of the Jesuits from the Sillery neophytes, and in 1640 they invited Father LeJeune to meet them at Tadoussac, where he went the following year. Visiting the Tadoussac mission, named Sainte Croix, became an annual event. New Christians returning home up the Saguenay became proselytizers and invited missionaries to their remote homelands. Fathers Druillettes and Jean de Quen were the principal figures of these journeys into the wilderness. In 1652 de Quen opened two centers of assembly, at the mouth of the Métabetchouane on Lac Saint-Jean and on the Pentecôte River among the Montagnais. The missionaries, notably Father Charles Albanel, began regularly wintering with the Indians. This kind of mission proved more fruitful and better adapted than the settlement system. Father Jacques Buteux adopted it among the Attikamègues as well in 1650.

The Trois-Rivières mission settlement was founded in 1634, in the name of the Immaculate Conception. The affluence of non-Christian traders was thought to provide a poor example for the Christians, so the mission was moved a few years later to a property belonging to Jean de LaFerté, abbot of La Madeleine. When the French encroached on surrounding lands, the Jesuits were granted two leagues of the riverbank, from Saint Maurice downstream, and inland to the depth of the seigneury. The Cap de la Madeleine mission flourished several years, then dwindled away as profit-seeking and traffic in brandy became uncontrollable passions among the French.

It was among the Hurons that the Jesuits made their most important effort. Three priests (with six servants) founded the mission in 1634, and others joined them in succeeding years. They numbered 14 priests in 1640, 19 in 1648. Father de Brébeuf, the first superior, devised a system whereby his colleagues were to settle in the principal villages, where they would be lodged and fed in the Huron manner with the help of French servants. The first residence, called Saint Joseph, was created at Ihonatiria. From there, the missionaries dispersed to other villages and even to other tribes, the Petuns and the Neutrals. They were attacked by disease in 1636, but by 1637 there were enough Jesuits to open a new residence, Immaculate Conception, at Ossossane. The following year the Hurons deserted Ihonatiria, and the Saint Joseph residence was moved to Teanaustaye. Little progress was made in evangelization. Disease ravaged the Indians, who blamed it on the sorcery of the missionaries, but tempers cooled as the epidemic subsided. In 1638 the Jesuits baptized their first healthy adult, Tsiouendaentaha (JR 14:77–95).

In summer 1638 Father Jérôme Lalemant came from France to replace de Brébeuf as superior. Lalemant conceived a new plan, to reunite the missionaries in a French-style central residence situated away from the Huron villages. There they would receive students for catechism and other instruction, and from there the priests would be sent out, by twos, to preach in the villages. Sainte-Marie-des-Hurons was finished in the spring of 1640, and the Ossossane and Teanaustaye residences were abandoned. From this time on, a growing movement toward conversion became evident. Christian communities took shape in the principal villages, chapels were built, and the missionaries took up permanent residence, returning to Sainte-Marie only to renew their spirits among their brothers. The fortified post at Sainte-Marie, augmented by a hospital, served as a refuge for natives harassed by the Iroquois. Father Paul Ragueneau succeeded Jérôme Lalemant as superior in 1644. The Jesuits attended to the Neutrals as well as the Hurons, while the Nipissings, who camped in Huron territory during the winter, formed a separate mission. In 1646 a mission to the Petuns was opened. The other missions prospered, and the fathers met only sporadically at Sainte-Marie. Father Antoine Daniel was the first to perish at the hands of the Iroquois, at Teanaustaye on July 4, 1648. The following spring de Brébeuf and Gabriel Lalemant met the same fate on March 16 and 17, 1649, at Saint Ignace and Saint Louis; two others died later that year. The Hurons evacuated their villages and the missionaries followed them, setting fire to Sainte-Marie on May 15, 1649. The devastated nation took refuge on Christian Island where a new mission of Sainte-Marie was established. The following year a party of survivors left for Quebec, under the leadership of Father Ragueneau and the remaining missionaries.

Permanent Establishments on the Saint Lawrence, 1660–1760

The year 1660 marked a new departure for the Catholic missions. Although they expanded toward the west, their greatest success was in the mission settlements on the Saint Lawrence.

First there was the Huron establishment. The small group of refugees who had gone to Quebec in 1650 settled on the Île d'Orléans. There the Iroquois continued to harass them until they were forced to return to Quebec proper, where a fort was constructed for them. In 1668 the Jesuits built them a village, Notre-Dame-de-Foy, in the Sillery seigneury. Father Pierre-Joseph-Marie Chaumonot lived in the Sillery mission and ministered to them. In 1674, because of poor location, the village was moved to the neighboring seigneury, Saint Gabriel. There new cabins were erected around a brick church situated on an elevation; this was Notre-Dame-de-Lorette (Ancienne-Lorette). The faith of the Christian Hurons drew the admiration of the French and their little church became a place of pilgrimage where the governor and the bishop went to pray. Some Iroquois joined the Hurons there to practice Christianity. In 1697 the village was again relocated, to a place called Jeune-Lorette, while the old mission became a French parish (vol. 15:389–393). After Chaumonot, the most important missionary there was Father Pierre-Daniel Richer who directed the mission from 1716 to 1761.

In 1668, on his way to make the first clearing for the La Prairie seigneury, Father Pierre Raffeix encountered in Montreal a group of seven Oneidas who wanted to become Christians, and he invited them to spend the winter with him and his workers. In 1669 he sent them to complete their instruction at Notre-Dame-de-Foy, and they were baptized. This was the nucleus of the La Prairie establishment. Iroquois of the Five Nations, especially Mohawks, soon flocked there, and Christianity flourished. In 1676 Father Jacques Frémin obtained permission for the Indians to clear a new territory bordering the seigneury on the south side of the Saint Lawrence. The mission was moved there, and a new church built between Rivière La Tortue and Le Portage. By 1679 there were 400 believers there. In 1680 Frémin obtained from the French king a grant of the Sault-Saint-Louis property between the La Prairie and Châteauguay seigneuries. In 1689 the village was again moved, upstream, opposite the rapids. Father Jacques Bruyas was in charge. There was another transfer in 1696, to the Suzanne River, and a final move, to the

Fig. 3. Scene during the ceremony of the beatification of Kateri Tekakwitha (b. 1656, d. 1680), a Mohawk Indian, in Rome, Italy. Pope John Paul II is listening to a presentation by members of a delegation of about 500 Indians from 35 tribes in the United States and Canada who attended the ceremony and brought gifts to the pontiff. Tekakwitha, who was declared venerable in 1934, was the first American Indian to be beatified (Anonymous 1980). Tekakwitha was baptized by Rev. Jacques de Lamberville in 1676 at the Mohawk Valley village of Caughnawaga and died at the St. Lawrence River village of the same name (vol. 15:470; Donohoe 1895:222–229). A shrine to Blessed Kateri is in Fonda, N.Y. Photograph by Vittoriano Rastelli, June 22, 1980.

present site of Caughnawaga, in 1714. The mission was always in need of self-defense, first against the hostility of Louis de Buade de Frontenac and then against the greed of the brandy merchants who coveted the Iroquois trade. During the eighteenth century the French merchants of Montreal waged a fierce battle against the Desaulnier sisters, who had the commercial franchise in the mission. In the end French policy had the effect of transforming missions everywhere into military posts. Contact with the garrisons was disastrous for the native Christians; nevertheless, it was imposed at Caughnawaga and contributed in no small way to cooling Iroquois affection for the French.

In 1673 the Christian Hurons of La Prairie quarreled with the Christian Iroquois and emigrated to Montreal. The Sulpicians took them in but hesitated to form them into a mission for fear of offending the Jesuits. However, in 1676, they were established at Montagne, on the present site of the Grand Séminaire of Montreal. The original group expanded from year to year, and it had the advantage of a perfect organizer in François Vachon de Belmont. From 1680 to 1700 he devoted himself to the task of instilling French culture in his flock, a task he reproached the Jesuits for neglecting. He built houses, a chapel, and a fort. He founded a Sisters of the Congregation school for girls, while he taught the boys himself. Drunkenness, caused by the proximity of Montreal, was a problem; the mission was accidentally burned down by drunkards in 1694. De Belmont rebuilt it, but in 1696 he removed those most inclined to drink to a site at Sault-au-Récollet, where a small church and a fort were built. In

1700 the whole Montagne mission was moved there, followed by the Sisters' school in 1701. But Sault-au-Récollet was still thought to be too close to the French settlements, so in 1721 the mission was moved to Oka where Algonquin and Nipissing groups, originally combined at the Île-aux-Tourtes, were also brought in.

In May 1675 some 30 non-Christian Western Abenakis took refuge at Sillery where they were received by Father Jacques Vaultier who instructed and baptized them. More Abenakis joined them from year to year, and in 1683 Father Jacques Bigot settled them at Sainte-Marie, on the Chaudière River; they were transferred later to the mouth of the same river. The new village, called Saint-François-de-Sales, numbered 600 in 1689. This settlement attracted the Abenakis as Caughnawaga had the Iroquois. People went to settle there or merely to receive instruction and to return, converted, to New England—so many that the missionaries were forced to follow the neophytes back to their homes. Fathers Jacques and Vincent Bigot and Joseph Aubery were the most famous of these ministers. Saint-François-de-Sales prospered, but around 1706 its inhabitants emigrated to Bécancour and the Saint-François River, which were to become the sites of the two main Abenaki villages on the Saint Lawrence. A mission on the Missisquoi River was added in 1743 (fig. 2). The Abenakis were staunch allies of the French and wrought havoc in the English colonies.

Distant Jesuit Missions, 1660–1760

On Lake Superior in 1660 were the remains of the Petun and Nipissing missions in addition to a large number of tribes, mostly Algonquian, who were known to the Jesuits by name alone. After two vain attempts to penetrate the region, Father René Ménard, along with donné Jean Guérin, succeeded in 1660. After a halt at Sault Sainte Marie, Ménard lost his way and died in August 1661, en route to Chequamegon Bay where early Christian Petuns had taken refuge. Guérin strove to take his place among the Indians but died accidentally in 1662. Father Claude Allouez came to replace him in 1665. Allouez founded the mission of Saint-Esprit at Chequamegon Point and evangelized the tribes who met there, including the Sioux, and the Nipissings at Lake Nipigon. In 1667 he went to Quebec for help and on his return in 1669 he founded the mission of Saint-François Xavier and there he preached to the tribes on Green Bay. In 1669 Father Claude Dablon founded Sault Saint Marie. The following year under Father Jacques Marguette the Saint-Esprit mission emigrated to Michilimakinac. This was to become the mission of Saint Ignatius, increasingly the center for the Ottawa missions, which spanned Lakes Superior, Huron, and Michigan. In 1673 Marquette and Louis Jolliet journeyed down the Mississippi to the Arkansas River. In 1674 Marquette founded the mission of the Immaculate Con-

ception to the Kaskaskias, which Allouez later served from his mission of Saint-François-Xavier. Among the tribes touched by this apostolate were the Petun, Ottawa, Ojibwa, Miami, Fox, Sauk, Sioux, Cree, and the several tribes of the Illinois. Jesuit expansion to the south was hindered after 1678 by René-Robert Cavelier, sieur de La Salle, who reserved this region for the Recollects, while on the Great Lakes they were opposed by Frontenac, who would have liked to expel them. The coureurs de bois, whom Frontenac favored, trafficked in brandy, which was disastrous for the missions. This plague had been checked under Joseph-Antoine LeFebvre de La Barre and Jacques-René de Brisé de Denonville. It reappeared during the second government of Frontenac, thanks largely to the French commanders in the Western posts, of whom most damaging was Antoine Laumet de Lamothe Cadillac who attempted to annex the missionaries when he founded Detroit. The Great Lakes missions declined, to the point that the Jesuits burned the mission at Michilimakinac in 1705 and abandoned it. Reestablished by order of the French king, its vigor was lost. Soon only one Jesuit remained at Detroit to serve the Christian Petuns and Ottawas.

The Iroquois tribes fascinated the Jesuits from the outset. Father Isaac Jogues died in 1646 in an early effort to evangelize the Mohawks. In 1654 Father Simon LeMoyne visited Christian Hurons held captive at Onondaga. As a result, a Jesuit mission, Sainte Marie, was founded at the Onondaga village of Gannentaha in 1655; but it was evacuated in 1658 because of hostility from neighboring tribes (JR 44:185–187, 213–217). After the pacification of the Iroquois in 1666, the Jesuits opened missions to each of the Five Nations. Brandy, which the Albany Dutch sold to the Mohawks (and through them to their neighbors) was the missions' worst problem. Fathers Jean Pierron, Jacques Frémin, Etienne de Carheil, and Jacques Bruyas distinguished themselves in this apostolate. La Salle's explorations angered the Indians, especially the Seneca, who in 1682 were on the point of conflict with the French and threatening to involve the other nations. Governors La Barre and Denonville tried unsuccessfully to subdue them. This led to the interruption of the Iroquois missions in 1684; they were not resumed until 1702 with the sending of Father Jacques de Lamberville to the Onondaga and Fathers Julien Garnier and François Vaillant to the Seneca. Other missionaries settled among the Oneidas and the Cayugas in succeeding years. But the Iroquois, jealous of their autonomy, were torn between their interest in English commerce and their fascination with the French "Prayer" (as they called Catholicism). English diplomacy won out and in 1709 the Jesuits had to leave for Montreal.

From the Great Lakes the focus of the missions shifted southward to the Illinois tribes. In 1689, Father Jacques Gravier founded the Mission-du-Rocher (Ste. Genevieve), *469* on the Mississippi River, reuniting the Kaskaskia, Peoria, and Moingwena groups of the Illinois Indians. In 1700 Father Gabriel Marest moved it to the Mississippi River where he cultivated a fervent Christian following. In 1696, Father Pierre Pinet founded the mission to the Tamaroa at Cahokia on the Mississippi, but he had to abandon it some years later when the Bishop of Quebec gave it to the Missions-Etrangères. In 1699 Pierre Le Moyne d'Iberville founded Louisiana at the mouth of the river. Jesuits went there in the early years, but withdrew when Bishop de St.-Vallier made conditions unacceptable for them. The colony was left without priests. In 1723 Bishop de Mornay brought in the Capuchins who lived in New Orleans and held authority along the river up to Natchez, that is, roughly, over the territory south of the Arkansas. The rest of the Mississippi and the length of the Ohio were reserved for the Jesuits. This territory formed the Jesuit mission of Louisiana, which was separate from the Ottawa mission and had its own superior. The Jesuit superior lived in New Orleans, as did the Capuchin superior, a situation that occasioned conflicts of jurisdiction, as both were vicars-general of the Bishop of Quebec. The Jesuits ministered to the French and the Indians both and created missions to the Choctaw, Alabama, Arkansas, and Illinois. Only the Illinois were evangelized with success; the other tribes sympathized with the French but were little influenced by Catholicism, largely because of the bad examples set by the French soldiers and the passion for brandy. The Jesuit missions ended in 1762, with the suppression of their order in France.

The Montagnais mission was very active after 1660. Father François de Crespieul, the principal organizer, spent his entire missionary life there. He built churches at Métabetchouan, Chicoutimi, Papinachois Bay, and Nikabau and established missions at Mistassini Lake, Némiscau, and the Moisie River, thereby covering the known (Crown) domain with Christian outposts. A permanent missionary residence was built at Metabetchouan and Father François Malherbe started a farm. By the end of the seventeenth century the nomadic Indians of the domain were all nominally Christian.

When Crespieul died in 1703 the flourishing mission was largely abandoned because the Jesuits had no one to send there, and commerce was reduced almost to nothing. Father Pierre Laure rebuilt the mission after 1720. He established mission posts and built chapels at Bon-Désir, Chicoutimi, Îles-de-Jérémie, and La Malbaie; and he composed a dictionary, a grammar, and religious books in Montagnais. Father Claude Coquart took over the mission in 1746 and built a chapel at Sept-Îles, while each year he traveled around to the various mission outposts. He died in 1765. The last Jesuit missionary to the Montagnais was Father Jean-Baptiste de LaBrosse. He taught the Indians reading and singing and had pious books printed for them. His intelligent activity assured the Indians' Christian perseverance despite the scarcity of priests.

The arrival of a group of Abenakis at Sillery prompted the creation of Jesuit missions in the Eastern Abenakis' own territory. At the request of Governor Denonville, Father Jacques Bigot went to Penobscot in 1667. His brother Vincent replaced him shortly after and evangelized the Penobscots and Kennebecs. In 1694 Bigot established a permanent mission at Penobscot, and Father Sébastien Râle founded the Norridgewock mission on the Kennebec River. Father Joseph Aubery established the Maliseet mission at Meductic in 1701. These three missions, which served as centers for diffusion into surrounding areas, were very successful and contributed strongly to tying the Acadian and New England tribes into the French alliance. After the Treaty of Utrecht in 1713, the missionaries became objects of general hostility in New England because, in the interest of conserving their flocks, they defended the French thesis that limited the Acadian treaty cessions to the Nova Scotia peninsula, leaving New Brunswick and northern Maine to the French. Fathers Jean-Baptiste Loyard (Meductic) and Pierre de La Chasse (Penobscot) were not excessively harassed; but Râle was in territory claimed by Great Britain. During Dummer's War the Penobscot mission was destroyed, and Râle was killed in 1724 during the destruction of Norridgewock.

The Norridgewock and Penobscot missions were reestablished a few years later. Father Jacques de Siresme rebuilt Norridgewock in 1728. The Meductic mission, under Fathers Guillaume Loyard and Charles Germain, was more sheltered from English attack. Germain remained there until the fall of Canada, serving the Saint-Jean mission as well, and taking in Acadian refugees in 1755.

Other Missions, 1667–1760

From the time of their arrival, the Sulpicians wanted to take part in the missions to the Indians. Montreal was founded to promote the missions, and the ministry had been promised to the associates of Jean-Jacques Olier, founder of the Sulpician order. Two young Sulpicians, François de Salignac-Fénelon and Claude Trouvé, arrived in June 1667. They volunteered to open an Iroquois mission at Quinté Bay, north of Lake Ontario, and received permission in 1668. Trouvé was named superior. The two priests lived among the Iroquois, following the Indians' way of life. Three more Sulpicians joined them in 1669. That same year René de Bréhant de Galinée and François Dollier de Casson journeyed west as far as Sault Sainte Marie, exploring for new mission territory. The Quinté mission was affected by the foundation of Fort Frontenac and its associated mission of Cataraqui in 1672, the governor allocating this region to the Recollects. However, the mission was maintained until 1680 when

Trouvé abandoned it to return to France. A few Sulpicians, notably Charles de Breslay, also worked in the Acadian missions from 1720 to 1755. Their most successful work was in the mission at Oka, which was still being served by Sulpicians in the 1980s. However, for the most part, the Sulpicians ministered to the French.

The priests of the Séminaire des Missions-Etrangères of Quebec and Paris were more involved in Indian missions. Acadia was their first mission-ground. They ministered to the French and evangelized the Indians at once. Their first missionary to the Indians was Father Louis-Pierre Thury who was sent in 1684 to help the curé of Port Royal, Louis Petit. He had care of the Micmacs, Maliseets, and Penobscots along the coast from the Baie des Chaleurs to the Penobscot River. Antoine Gaulin succeeded Thury in 1698; he was a great missionary who, most often alone, attended to the spiritual needs of the Micmacs and the Maliseets until 1730. He had much to put up with, the poverty he was left to, as much as the opposition of certain French officers. When he returned to Quebec, worn out by work and age, Pierre Maillard, a young priest from the Missions-Etrangères, succeeded him. Maillard learned Micmac remarkably well and exerted a great influence on the Indians. He remained among his neophytes after the conquest of Canada until his death in 1762.

The Missions-Etrangères also had a mission to the Illinois. Eager to participate in evangelizing the Indians of the Mississippi, in 1698 they requested the whole territory south of the Missouri River. They asked to establish their first mission among the Tamaroa tribe, whom they viewed as the gateway to this vast country. The Jesuits had already begun to evangelize this tribe but were forced to give way to the Missions-Etrangères who sent three priests the first year. Led by zealous priests the Tamaroas became a flourishing Christian congregation; but the mission declined during the last years of the French regime, for lack of missionaries. The Indians abandoned the mission, and it became a French parish. In 1760 the last curé sold off the seminary properties and left the post.

Frontenac would have liked to substitute the Recollects for the Jesuits in the native missions. From the moment of their return to Quebec he urged the Recollects to occupy the posts that were open. Thus he sent them to Miscou and Acadia, in defiance of Bishop de Laval; he entrusted to them the parochial duties of Fort Frontenac on Lake Ontario and assigned them to accompany La Salle on his travels and explorations. But the Recollects were successful evangelists only in Acadia.

When Île Royale (Cape Breton Island) was established after 1713 the Recollects of Quebec were entrusted with the administration of the French parishes and the Indian missions outside Louisbourg, while Louisbourg proper was left to the Recollects of Bretagne who were brought in from Plaisance. They worked in Acadia until 1729 when the governor of Port Royal expelled them from the English possessions. Subsequently they lost interest in the Acadian missions and returned to Quebec.

Sources

The fundamental source for the history of the French Jesuit missions in North America is the *Jesuit Relations* (JR 1896–1901). The most important general work on this topic is that by Rochemonteix, the first part (1895–1896) covering the seventeenth century and the second part (1906) the eighteenth century. A good deal of data was collected by Shea (1886–1892). Special studies on the missionary activities of the various religious communities during the French period are restricted to the works by Candide de Nant (1927) on the Capuchin missions in Acadia, Campeau (1967) on the first Jesuit mission in Acadia, and Jouve (1915) on the first Recollect mission in Quebec.

Useful early histories are those of Sagard-Théodat (1866), DuCreux (1664), Le Clercq (1691), Le Tac (1888), and Charlevoix (1744). Faillon (1865–1866) is a general history of New France up to 1675. Gosselin (1890, 1911–1914) has described the Canadian church from the time of Bishop de Laval to the English conquest.

Published collections of documents include the *Relations inédites* (Mission du Canada 1861), the *Collection de manuscripts* (Quebec. Provincial Archives 1883–1885), the Jesuit journal edited by Laverdière and Casgrain (1871), and the materials gathered by Margry (1876–1886).

The most important collections of manuscripts are those in the Archivum Romanum Societatis Iesu, Rome; the Archives de Saint-Sulpice, Montreal; the Archives du Séminaire de Québec, Quebec; the Archives de l'Archevêche de Québec, Quebec; the Public Archives of Canada, Ottawa; the Archives de la Province de Québec, Quebec; and the Archives de la Société de Jésus de la Province du Canada Français, Saint-Jérôme, Quebec.

Roman Catholic Missions in California and the Southwest

SHERBURNE F. COOK AND CESARE MARINO*

California

The Roman Catholic Church entered California in 1769, when the Gaspar de Portolá–Junipero Serra expedition crossed the border of Baja California, and, on its way north, founded the first mission at San Diego (Crespí 1927). In its composition and operation, it followed the pattern laid down by the viceroys of New Spain in their occupation of Baja California and the American Southwest. The immediate objective was two-fold: to establish military bases, or points of resistance to aggression by other European powers, and to convert the natives to Christianity. In order to carry out these purposes the party consisted of a company of soldiers under Gaspar de Portolá, and a small group of missionaries of the Franciscan order, chief among whom was Junipero Serra. All contact with the natives was to be in the hands of the friars (Shea 1855).

On this first entrance, which reached as far north as San Francisco Bay, two missions were organized, San Diego de Alcalá in 1769 and San Carlos Borromeo de Carmelo (Carmel) in 1770. Others were established at intervals until the last, San Francisco Solano (Sonoma), was formed in 1823 (fig. 1) (Bowman 1965). Some essential data concerning all of these is given in table 1.

The important process of conversion to the Christian faith involved more than baptism and instruction in doctrine, for the Indian entered upon an entirely new life, one to which he was completely unaccustomed. In the beginning of each mission the inhabitants of the immediate vicinity were converted and organized as the embryo establishment. Very rapidly, however, the friars extended their efforts so as to bring into the fold the villages more or less distant until a limit was imposed by some natural obstacle, or by the time and energy necessary for travel (fig. 2). Thus, in general, the radius of conversion reached a day's journey from the mission as a center. Where the density of population warranted, and the width of intermission gaps required, new missions were founded. This process continued until the coastal strip was thor-

oughly saturated, about the year 1800.

The missionized area extended inland from the coast, in the south approximately to the San Gabriel, San Bernardino, San Jacinto, and Santa Rosa mountains, to below the present Mexican border. In the center the line crossed the Tehachapi range and followed the summits of the Diablo Range as far north as the Carquinez Strait. Beyond San Francisco Bay the mission influence was felt only as far as Santa Rosa and the Napa Valley.

After 1805, in order to obtain new converts, it was necessary to penetrate the semidesert region of southern California, to reach beyond the coast ranges into the San Joaquin Valley, and to cross San Francisco Bay. In these efforts the clergy were strongly assisted by the military, who organized repeated expeditions to the interior in the decades following the year 1800. A new wave of converts entered the missions, and the interior Indian groups were brought face to face with the advancing forces of Christianity.

Population

Careful records were kept at the missions of baptisms, marriages, and deaths, but some of the pertinent books have been destroyed or lost. A good many of the annual reports sent to Mexico by the chief administrative officers of the missions are still in existence. Some are in the Bancroft Library, University of California at Berkeley, and the Huntington Library, San Marino, California, together with numerous other documents relating to mission affairs. Most of the available records were examined by Bancroft (1886–1890) and by Engelhardt (1908–1915) for their historical works, which jointly form the indispensable core of knowledge concerning the California missions.

Engelhardt (1908–1915, 3:653) computed the totals for each mission up to the end of 1832. Bancroft consolidated all the annual reports he could find and made estimates of the values for missing years. In view of the many gaps and mistakes in the records, the two presentations of the mission population are not identical. The approximations must contain an error of at least 5 percent.

---

*The section on California was written by Cook; that on the Southwest, by Marino.

Fig. 1. Roman Catholic missions and mission sites in California and the Southwest in the 17th and 18th centuries. Numerous other small missions or *visitas*, having a chapel but no resident priest, also existed throughout this region (Bannon 1970; Bolton 1960; Adams and Chavez 1956; Griffen 1979; Kessell 1976; F.C. Lockwood 1934; Spicer 1962; vol. 8:99–127; vol. 10:137–148, 250–263, 276–289). California: 1, San Francisco Solano; 2, San Rafael Arcángel; 3, San Francisco de Asís; 4, San José de Guadalupe; 5, Santa Clara de Asís; 6, Santa Cruz; 7, San Juan Bautista; 8, San Carlos Borromeo de Carmelo; 9, Nuestra Señora de la Soledad; 10, San Antonio de Padua; 11, San Miguel Arcángel; 12, San Luis Obispo de Tolosa; 13, La Purísima Concepción; 14, Santa Inés; 15, Santa Bárbara; 16, San Buenaventura; 17, San Fernando Rey de España; 18, San Gabriel Arcángel; 19, San Juan Capistrano; 20, San Luis Rey de Francia; 21, San Diego de Acalá; 22, San Pedro y San Pablo; 23, Imaculata Concepción. Arizona: 24, San Francisco de Oraibi; 25, San Bartolomé de Xongopavi; 26, San Bernardo de Aguátubi; 27, San Xavier del Bac; 28, Tumacácori; 29, Guevavi. New Mexico: 30, San Gerónimo de Taos; 31, San Lorenzo de Picurís; 32, Abiquíu; 33, Las Trampas; 34, San Juan; 35, Español; 36, Santa Cruz; 37, Santa Clara; 38, San Ildefonso; 39, Nuestra Señora de Guadalupe de Pojoaque; 40, San Francisco de Nambe; 41, San Lorenzo de Tesuque; 42, Santa Fe; 43, San Diego de los Jémez; 44, San Buenaventura de Cochití; 45, Nuestra Señora de los Angeles de Pecos; 46, Santo Domingo; 47, Nuestra Señora de la Asunción de Zia; 48, Santa Ana; 49, San Felipe; 50, Galisteo; 51, Bernalillo (Sandia); 52, Halona (Zuni); 53, San José de la Laguna; 54, Albuquerque; 55, Hawikuh; 56, San Esteban de Ácoma; 57, San Antonio de Isleta; 58, Tomé; 59, Alamillo; 60, Socorro. Baja California Norte: 61, El Descanso; 62, San Miguel Arcángel; 63, Guadalupe del Norte; 64, Santo Tomás de Aquino; 65, Santa Catarina Mártir. Sonora: 66, San Marcelo de Sonóita; 67, San Estanislao del Ootcam; 68, San Valentín; 69, Caborca; 70, Pitiquito; 71, San Luis Bacoancos; 72, Santa María; 73, Busanic; 74, San Bernardo; 75, San Lázaro; 76, Saric; 77, San Simón y San Judas del Síboda; 78, Cocospera; 79, Santa Teresa; 80, Tubutama; 81, Cuquiárachi; 82, Oquitoa; 83, Imuris; 84, Remedios; 85, Cuchuta; 86, Batepito; 87, San Miguel; 88, San Ignacio; 89, Bacoachi; 90, Turicachi; 91, Magdalena; 92, Dolores; 93, Chinapa; 94, Bavispe; 95, Cucurpe; 96, Arizpe; 97, Bacerac; 98, Tuape; 99, Sinoquipe; 100, Oputo; 101, Huachinera; 102, Banamichi; 103, Cumpas; 104, Opodepe; 105, Huépac; 106, Huásabas; 107, Aconchi; 108, San Pedro de la Conquista (Pitic); 114, Mátape; 115, Bacanora; 116, Bacanora; 117, San José de Pimas; 118, Tecoripa; 119, Ónavas; 120, Cumuripa; 121, Belem; 122, Huirivis; 123, Rahum; 124, Potam; 125, Vicam; 126, Torim; 127, Bacum; 128, Cocorit. Chihuahua and Texas: 129, San Lorenzo; 130, Ysleta del Sur; 131, Senecu del Sur; 132, Socorro del Sur; 133, San Antonio de Casas Grandes; 134, Santa Ana de Torreón; 135, San Francisco; 136, San Pedro de Namiquipa; 137, Yepómera; 138, Santo Tomás; 139, San Gerónimo; 140, Tutuaca; 141, San Andres; 142, Nombre de Dios; 143, Santa Ana de Chinarras; 144, Tomóchic; 145, San Antonio de Julimes; 146, Santa Isabel; 147, Santiago de Babonoyaba; 148, San Pedro de Conchos; 149, Cárichic; 150, Satevó; 151, Sisoguichic; 152, San Francisco de Borja; 153, San Francisco de Conchos; 154, San Felipe.

473

ROMAN CATHOLIC MISSIONS IN CALIFORNIA AND THE SOUTHWEST

The total neophyte population increased from zero in 1769 to 20,000 in 1805. It then rose slowly to a maximum of approximately 21,000 in 1824. It declined to 17,000 by 1832, and subsequently dropped sharply.

Further information comes from the baptism and death records contained in the annual reports and also in the surviving mission books themselves. As of 1832 Engelhardt (see table 1) shows a cumulative total of 87,787 baptisms, of whom perhaps 3,000 were of non-Indians. The Bancroft compilation yields a somewhat lower value, approximately 83,000, but does not include non-Indians. On the other hand both totals include baptisms from two sources, the converted heathen and those born in the mission. At the beginning the former group predominated heavily, but toward the end of the period the balance shifted. According to the Bancroft compilation, which is based on these reports, out of 83,000 baptisms, a little more than 53,000 were converts, leaving 30,000 who were mission born.

Aggregation and Labor

In order to understand the interaction between clerical California on the one hand and the native peoples on the other, it is necessary to appreciate the underlying theory and method of the mission system. The primary objective was to convert the heathen to Christianity and to induct them into full membership in the Roman Catholic Church. The cultural and social background of the Indians was given careful consideration, and the process of religious instruction was modified as might be desirable. At the same time the lot of the Indian was to be improved in the material as well as in the religious sense. He was to be lifted from savagery and taught the arts of civilization in order that he might assume a respected position in society.

If this double purpose was to be fulfilled it was necessary that the as yet unreduced natives should be placed under a paternalistic but firm administration that would proceed with the task of civilization in an orderly, effective manner. This administration would be provided by competent missionaries in an establishment that was equipped to supply all material necessities as well as to furnish proper spiritual guidance. In practical terms this meant a substantial amount of regimentation and discipline.

Fig. 2. Native dance at the Mission of San Francisco de Asís (Mission Dolores). Although the mission is in the aboriginal territory of the Costanoan, neophytes were also brought to it from the Patwin, Miwok, Esselen, and Yokuts tribes (vol. 8:351, 400, 486). The sixth California mission to be established, San Francisco de Asís was founded by Franciscan priests Francisco Palóu and Peter Cambón. Watercolor painting by Louis Choris, Oct. 1816.

474

Table 1. California Mission Statistics

Missions, south to north	Year founded	Neophytes in 1832	Baptisms to 1832	Deaths to 1832	In territory of Indian tribe
San Diego de Alcalá	1769	1,455	6,522	4,322	Diegueño
San Luis Ray de Francia	1798	2,788	5,399	2,718	Luiseño
San Juan Capistrano	1776	900	4,340	3,126	Juaneño
San Gabriel Arcángel	1771	1,320	7,825	5,670	Gabrieleño
San Fernando Rey de España	1797	782	2,784	1,983	Fernandeño
San Buenaventura	1782	668	3,875	3,150	Chumash
Santa Bárbara	1786	628	5,556	3,936	Chumash
Santa Inéz	1804	360	1,348	1,227	Chumash
La Purísima Concepción	1787	372	3,255	2,609	Chumash
San Luis Obispo de Tolosa	1772	231	2,644	2,268	Chumash
San Miguel Arcángel	1797	658	2,471	1,868	Salinan
San Antonio de Padua	1771	640	4,419	3,617	Salinan
Nuestra Señora de la Soledad	1791	339	2,131	1,705	Costanoan
San Carlos Borromeo de Carmelo	1770	185	3,827	2,837	Costanoan
San Juan Bautista	1797	916	4,016	2,854	Costanoan
Santa Cruz	1791	284	2,439	1,972	Costanoan
Santa Clara de Asís	1777	1,125	8,536	6,809	Costanoan
San José de Guadalupe	1797	1,800	6,673	4,800	Costanoan
San Francisco de Asís	1776	204	6,898	5,166	Costanoan
San Rafael Arcángel	1817	300	1,821	652	Coast Miwok
San Francisco Solano	1823	996	1,008	500	Coast Miwok
Total		16,951	87,787	63,789	

SOURCE: Engelhardt (1908-1915, 3: App. J., 653).

Probably the basic difficulty with the implementation of the program lay in the sudden and drastic change of environment to which the Indian converts were thus subjected. The California tribes were organized in small, sedentary groups, each with its own territory and each with its individual body of tradition and culture. The missionaries, following accepted practice, removed these groups either as a whole, or by single persons, and assembled them at a common focus, the mission. The Indian neophyte, consequently, was forced to depart from his ancestral mode of behavior and adopt a new culture.

It is significant that the four southernmost missions departed to some extent from the principle of complete centralization. Whether for cultural, climatic, or geographical reasons, the missions from San Gabriel Arcángel (vol. 8:543) to San Diego de Alcalá permitted a much looser organization than did those of the center and north. Indeed, they went so far as to establish satellite settlements such as San Bernardino and Pala where the converts might live under conditions closely simulating those obtaining in their natural habitat. The friars among the Chumash and Costanoans, on the contrary, insisted rigorously that their neophytes live together in a common set of buildings.

The effect of overaggregation was magnified by the mission custom of confining all unmarried males and females to separate quarters and permitting no freedom in sexual relationships. This course of action was justified by the White lay population as well as by the clergy on moral grounds, and in fact it is difficult to see how a system grounded upon the ethics of the Roman Catholic Church could operate otherwise. Yet the physical confinement and the restriction of social as well as sexual intercourse was completely contrary to native custom and acted as a powerful source of irritation.

A factor related to aggregation and confinement, and one concerning which there has always been bitter controversy, is forced conversion. It was the firm policy of the missionary fathers, and was an integral part of the church doctrine, that natives should not be accepted for conversion on any but a voluntary basis. This principle was adhered to faithfully during the first years of occupation, and indeed at all times when the local population was being brought into the mission. When the

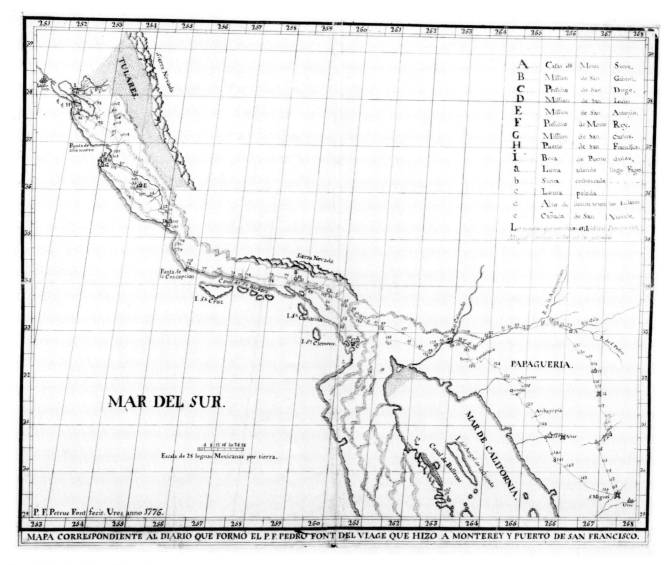

MAPA CORRESPONDIENTE AL DIARIO QUE FORMÓ EL P. F. PEDRO FONT DEL VIAGE QUE HIZO A MONTEREY Y PUERTO DE SAN FRANCISCO.

Brown U., John Carter Brown Lib., Providence.
Fig. 3. Manuscript map detailing the route of the second expedition of Juan Bautista de Anza, Sept. 1775 to June 1776, which extended from Horcasitas, Mexico, to San Francisco Bay, where the missions of San Francisco de Asís and Santa Clara de Asís were established. The map was made by Father Pedro Font to accompany the first of his diaries, which describe the entire journey including Indians encountered in its course. The dotted lines show the expedition route. Each day's journey is referred to by number, and the letters in the key (upper right) indicate significant sites (Font 1930). Drawn in ink on paper, June 1776.

radius of activity was extended, however, beyond easy access to the native villages, the friars were not able to go personally to areas far from their home and persuade the Indians to make the long remove to the mission establishment. Thus grew up the system whereby parties of civilians or soldiers went out and literally captured large numbers of Indians who were then taken to the missions and made Christians by threat or exercise of force.

This device for obtaining converts was employed principally in the north. From the southern missions a few expeditions went out, but many members of the more distant tribes were christianized in situ, and many of them never lived permanently at the mission itself. The establishments among the Chumash and Salinan as far north as San Antonio de Padua Mission (fig. 4) drew their converts

primarily from populations within a short distance. The northern missions, in particular San Francisco de Asís, San José de Guadalupe, Santa Clara de Asís, Santa Cruz, and San Juan Bautista, within 20–30 years after their foundation had gathered in the Costanoans to the last person (Cook 1943). Thereafter, they depended upon expeditions that rounded up masses of Yokuts and Miwok (vol. 8:400). In the later years of the period, the missions San Rafael Arcángel and San Francisco Solano built up their congregations by the exercise of some degree of compulsion exerted upon the remnants of the local villages and drew heavily upon distant tribes such as the Pomo, southern Patwin, and Lake Miwok.

Another factor that has been the occasion for much comment is that of forced labor. The critics of the system

476

have maintained that the Indians were subjected to a modified peonage, almost slavery, under which they were obliged to contribute excessive physical exertion. The friends of the missions answer that maximal labor on the part of the neophytes was essential. The mission was a self-supporting unit. Not only subsistence but also almost all other commodities had to be produced at home. Moreover, foreign manufactured articles, such as tools, cloth, and church furniture had to be imported from Mexico and Spain, and had to be paid for with surplus raw materials, predominantly hides and tallow. It was unavoidable that the neophytes be called upon for not only unskilled but also in many cases for rather highly skilled labor. In supplying this, the Indians were obliged to put forth a consistent effort that required them to work for several hours nearly every day. It was not the physical strain that was so distasteful, for the tasks were not onerous, but rather the unremitting demand. The California Indian could not readily adapt to this regimen, for his practice had been to work only at intervals as need directed.

It is undoubtedly true that the numerous attempts of the mission Indians to avoid their assigned tasks were met by disciplinary measures of significant severity. Furthermore, occasional misdemeanors and a few major offenses were punished harshly, although the code of the missionaries forbade any but the most temperate corrective procedures. The contemporary documents are filled with complaints and accusations against the friars on the part of not only the Indians themselves but also the White civilians and soldiers, many of whom were hostile to the missions (vol. 8:102).

Smithsonian, MAH: Anthr. Arch. No. M-1082.

Fig. 4. Prayer board, a form of hornbook primer, giving prayers and songs in the Salinan, Latin, and Spanish languages. Prepared at San Antonio de Padua Mission in 1817 by a Franciscan, Rev. Pedro Cabot, the board was to teach Indians the liturgy. The board is made from Monterey cypress, a local wood, covered by a colonial laid paper, and printed in red and black ink. left (obverse), Prayers and songs in Salinan, Spanish, and Latin, with musical notations; right (reverse), Catholic prayers referred to as the Acts of Faith, Hope, and Charity in Salinan and Spanish. Size 31.5 cm by 21.6 cm.

Disease and Fugitivism

Primarily responsible for the reduction in population was the introduction of epidemic and contagious disease. The effect may be seen particularly in the birth and death rates among the neophytes. An aboriginal, premission equilibrium may be assumed with birth and death rates of approximately 50 per 1,000 persons a year. Among the converts who were living at the missions the crude birth rate in the decade 1770–1780 was very close to this value. Thereafter it underwent a consistent decrease until by 1830 it had fallen to about 30 per 1,000. Various causes have been assigned as contributing to the decline. such as the widespread incidence of venereal disease and the common practice of induced abortion. It is also probable that a rising male-female sex ratio, which had reached 1.35 by 1834, and which correspondingly reduced the relative number of childbearing women, was reflected in an apparent reduction in crude birth rate. This view is supported by the fact that the ratio of children to reproductive females remained nearly constant throughout the mission period.

The crude death rate for the total population was close

to 70 per 1,000 in the decade 1770–1780. The increase above the presumed aboriginal rate is probably referable to the trauma of removal to a strange environment plus exposure to diseases introduced by the Spaniards. It then rose to the level of 85 per 1,000 by the year 1800, after which date it declined to its initial value. Especially striking were the changes in the child death rate, which in the first decade was close to 140 per 1,000 children, a value much higher than in the aboriginal condition. Then it increased to an average of 170 per 1,000 annually in the decade 1790–1800. The child deaths were also subject to great fluctuations, the peaks of which denoted severe epidemics. The worst of these was in 1806 when measles carried off fully one-third of the small children (Cook 1943:13–22). After 1800, the average mortality among children decreased notably until at the close of the missions it had fallen to 110 per 1,000 children, a value significantly below that found at the beginning. It is quite likely that the mission-born population was undergoing rapid readjustment with respect to health and vitality, and that if the missions had not been destroyed the trend of declining population would soon have reached equilibrium and might well have reversed itself.

Another important factor was fugitivism. Many of the new converts together with not a few mission-born neophytes resented existence under the mission system. When antagonism to their current surroundings built up to a critical level of intensity, there were, for the disaffected neophytes, only two possible courses of action. They could revolt by force of arms or they could abscond. The first course was difficult to achieve in the face of a strong military establishment, but it did occur in 1824 at Missions La Purísima Concepción and Santa Barbara (vol. 8:103). The second course was easy and satisfied with little effort the desire for the old way of living.

By the year 1800, fugitivism had become the most difficult problem confronting the friars, and indeed threatened to break down the entire mission structure. It is not strange, therefore, that every method was used to check the constant movement toward absenteeism and outright apostasy. Persuasion was employed where possible. Otherwise punishment was inflicted upon confirmed runaways and military expeditions were sent out to capture fugitives and return them to their missions. However, even these measures proved relatively ineffectual. A study of the mission records (Cook 1940:27–28, 1943:58–61) indicates that the cumulative desertions up to 1834 amounted to over 5,000, and that in the last two or three decades of mission existence the number of current runaways averaged somewhere near 10 percent of the population. After secularization the proportion increased phenomenally.

Secularization

Prior to the first expedition in 1769 the Franciscans were given complete authority in Alta California, and they exercised this authority until 1834. The successful war of independence waged by Mexico against Spain insured the ultimate displacement of the Catholic church from its position of temporal control of the California missions. Agitation to this end began in 1826, but the process was not completed until 1834. The crucial change was the removal of the missionary friars and their replacement by the secular clergy. In other words, the Indians ceased to be neophytes and hence protected socially and economically by the church. Instead, they assumed the position of parishioners who were ordinary citizens, and who were members of the civil community, subject to all the pressures and requirements of that status (Bowman 1958). Those in the missionary arm of the church opposed the plan strongly. Bancroft (1886–1890, 3:309) stated the argument of the friars succinctly: "that the Indians were absolute masters of the soil and all the mission property, but that they were still children requiring parental control, and that the friars alone were qualified to exercise that control."

When the church was overruled and the missions placed in civilian hands, the results were disastrous from the standpoint of the material welfare of the missions and the social as well as the material welfare of the neophytes. Within a decade the administrators who were placed in charge of the establishments had sold or looted all available physical resources. In the meantime the Indians followed their own devices.

Most of those who had been born and raised in the missions, and who knew no other form of existence, tended to remain there. Others spread out into the local communities and ranches, where they maintained a tenuous spiritual association with the mission but depended for food and shelter upon charity and upon casual employment by land owners and ranchers. In the south a series of small pueblos had been founded, populated by ex-neophytes who managed, with at least partial success, to operate independent communities. The remainder, released of all restraint, fled to their unconverted kinsmen in the interior.

The ultimate fate of the mission population can be ascertained approximately from the figures scattered through Bancroft (1886–1890, 3 and 4). In 1834, after four years of demoralization, there were 15,000 neophytes in the missions themselves (Bowman 1958). In 1840 there were about 5,000 living at the missions, with another 3,000–4,000 scattered over the local countryside but still carried on the mission rolls. The loss, 8,000–9,000, was referable almost entirely to flight to the interior tribes. By 1845 those who remained at the missions or were attached to local communities had been reduced to not much more than 3,000, with perhaps another 3,000 who were dispersed but whose whereabouts was known. Thereafter, the ex-mission population sank still lower, but there has never been an adequate estimate made of their number or distribution.

For nearly 30 years the missions remained in private hands. However, in 1862, by an act of the United States government, most of them were returned to the ownership of the Roman Catholic church. The church then reinstated the Franciscan order as the controlling agency. Santa Barbara was never sold and is the only mission to be in constant occupation since the day of its foundation. La Purísima Concepción and San Francisco Solano have become public property.

In most of the missions, at least since 1862, there has been maintained a parish church and many of the former neophytes retained their old religious connection, although in the status of parishioners. No California Indians entered orders or became priests. As parishioners they fused with the Spanish-speaking population of the state and have been regarded in the same light as all members of the congregations of the church.

The Indians from the Central Valley returned to their native homes but conserved their religion and the Spanish tongue. Many of them became persons of consequence in their community. The former mission Indians, together with many Mexicans, formed settlements where they were served by clergymen from the coast and later from the valley towns. Numerous other Indians were converted. The result was the formation of strongly Catholic rancherias in the Sierra Nevada foothills. In general no more attention has been devoted to Indians than to other Catholics, except that, as a rule, the priests have gone to them rather than they to the priests.

The south has seen much the same process of maintaining intercourse with former mission Indians, although the work has been made easier by the existence of many already established centers and rancherias. Some of these have enjoyed an uninterrupted relationship with the Catholic clergy since before secularization; others among the older centers have been converted into small reservations under the Bureau of Indian Affairs, with their religious affiliation entirely Roman Catholic. Throughout the years since 1850 the church has retained the loyalty and affection of its Indian parishioners.

The Southwest

Fray Marcos de Niza's 1539 exploration of Zuni Country (Bandelier 1887, 1929) and Francisco Vásquez de Coronado's entrada of 1540 marked the opening of Spanish Catholic missionary efforts in the Southwest. When Coronado withdrew from the region in 1542, the three Franciscan fathers who had volunteered to remain behind were killed by the Indians. In 1580, three other Franciscan missionaries attempted to set up a permanent mission among the Pueblos, but they too were eventually killed by the natives (Shea 1855:77–78). Formal colonization of Pueblo country was begun by Juan de Oñate in 1598 (Hammond and Rey 1953, 1966; Thoma 1896:50–65) whose motivation appears to have been primarily a missionary one (vol. 9:179). Within a few months after taking up residence at the Tewa Pueblo of San Juan, Oñate had succeeded in gaining the formal submission of both Eastern and Western Pueblos (Mooney 1910:892). He divided the region of Nuevo México, which had been declared a missionary province of the Franciscan Order, into seven mission districts each under a Franciscan friar (Thoma 1896:60).

By the early 1600s two main missionary frontiers had been established in northwestern New Spain, "one in the south [Sonora], where the missionary side of the Spanish advance was under the direction of the Jesuits, and one in the north [Nuevo México] where the Franciscans commanded the missions" (Spicer 1962:24). The Pueblo missions flourished under the energetic fathers Gerónimo de Zárate Salmerón and Alonso de Benavides, whose writings provide important information on this early period of Indian-White relations in the Southwest (Benavides 1916, 1945; Zárate Salmerón 1966). By the Franciscan fathers' own estimates, which might have been exaggerated, in 1630 the Pueblo missions counted some

Lib. of Congress, Prints and Photographs Div.: LCUSZ62-29347.
Fig. 5. Feast day at San Esteban del Rey Mission, Acoma Pueblo, N. Mex. The 2 men and 2 women lead a procession during which a statue of a saint is carried from the church to the site of the feast day dances. Photograph by Charles F. Lummis, 1890.

60,000 christianized Indians in 90 Pueblos served by 50 priests, from the Rio Grande valley to the Hopi mesas (Mooney 1910:893; vol. 9:519–520). Nevertheless, the Indians' nominal acceptance of Catholicism and their forced submission to Spanish authority did not result in true conversion to Christianity. The suppression of native ceremonies and dances, destruction of ritual paraphernalia, and public punishment of native priests and medicine men did not weaken the traditional Pueblo religion and world view. In an effort to crush native religious resistance, in 1661 the Franciscan leadership decreed the "absolute prohibition of all kachina dances, and missionaries were instructed to seek out all materials of 'idolatry' . . . . Kivas, the Pueblo ceremonial rooms, were raided and in a short time sixteen hundred kachina masks were captured and destroyed, as well as prayer feathers and images of various kinds" (Spicer 1962:160–161). The growing discontent of the Indians eventually matured into a full-scale revolt that struck Pueblo country in the summer of 1680. Twenty-one missionaries out of the 33 in residence at the Pueblo missions and some 400 of the Spanish colonists were killed by the Indians. "The fact that the majority of the Spaniards were allowed to escape indicated that the major objectives of the revolt were, first to eliminate the mission system and, second, to drive all Spaniards out of Pueblo country" (Spicer 1962:163). Until the reconquest by Diego de Vargas in 1692–1694, the Pueblo Indians lived free from Franciscan missionary presence and Spanish rule. Resentment against the Spaniards, particularly the friars, continued after the reconquest, and in 1696 the Pueblos of Picuris, Taos, and Jemez, plus some Tewas, Tanos, and Keresans rose again killing five missionaries and a number of White settlers and soldiers (vol. 9:186).

The eighteenth century brought a less oppressive Spanish domination and a reduced missionary activity among the Pueblo Indians, who had suffered great population losses due to war, migrations, dispossession, and enslavement. The fewer Franciscan missionaries were unable to win the true conversion of the Indians, who adopted a strategy of religious accommodation referred to by some anthropologists as compartmentalization:"keeping their own organization and viewpoint quite separate from that of the Catholic Church, [the Pueblos] nevertheless accepted and sharply defined functions of the latter in their lives. They integrated fragments of Catholicism, but not the system, and hence it is no cause for wonder that the Catholic Church regarded no Pueblo village as a Catholic community" (Spicer 1962: 508; see also Dozier 1961). The Franciscans were even less successful in their efforts to establish permanent missions among the Jicarilla Apache 1733, among the Navajo in 1746 and 1749, and at Hopi in 1776. Eventually, during the following decades, the Franciscans also reduced to a minimum their activities among the Rio Grande Pueblos, while closing their mission at Zuni in 1820.

During the Mexican period, 1821-1846, the state of the Pueblo missions worsened due to lack of missionaries and funds (see vol. 9:206–208). Ironically, when the Pueblos came under American rule in the mid-1800s, the Catholic Church assumed a more open and tolerant attitude toward the Indians in the attempt to contain the new presence of Protestant missionaries (Spicer 1962).

In addition to the works already cited, other sources on the Catholic Indian missions of New Mexico include the writings of Fray Francisco Atanasio Domínguez (Adams and Chavez 1956), Kessell (1979, 1980), and H. W. Kelly (1941). The early missionary efforts of the Franciscans are discussed by Scholes (1937) and McCarty (1981, 1983); Franciscan methods of indoctrination are presented by Matson and Fontana (1977), while Van Well (1942) dealt with the educational aspects of the Southwest missions. The problem of cultural conflict in the context of the Spanish missionary program to the Pueblos has been addressed by Bowden (1975, 1981), while Dozier (1958) focused on the influence of Spanish Catholicism on Rio Grande Pueblo religion.

The history of the Franciscan presence in Arizona has been traced by Engelhardt (1899); information on the Catholic missions among the Navajo and Apache is found in volume 10. Brugge (1968) reviewed the material pertaining to the Navajo in the Catholic Church records of New Mexico. There are biographies of Anselm Weber, O.F.M., a missionary to the Navajo 1898–1921 (Wilken 1955) and Albert Braun, O.F.M., missionary to the Mescalero Apache (Emerson 1973).

The Jesuit missions among the Tarahumara, Mayo, Yaqui, Seri, Lower Pima, Ópata, Papago, and Upper Pima are discussed by Spicer (1962:25–151, 502–516). Bannon (1955) traced a history of the mission frontier in Sonora, 1620–1687. Dunne (1948) presents the early Jesuit missions among the Tarahumara. The Jesuit missionaries themselves left important accounts of their experiences among the Indians. Andrés Pérez de Ribas (1645) was the first missionary among the Yaqui; Adam Gilg's (1692) letter deals with the early stages of the Seri mission, and Joseph Neumann's (1682, 1725, 1969) writings with the Upper Tarahumara and their revolts between 1629 and 1724. Ignaz Pfefferkorn's (1949), Joseph Och's (1965), and Juan Nentvig's (1863, 1980) descriptions of Sonora and Arizona in the 1750s and 1760s contain valuable material on their experience as missionaries. See also Spicer (1962:308–333) and Plozer's (1976) compilation of documents on the organization and methods of the Jesuit missions in New Spain. The pioneering work of Italian Jesuit Eusebio F. Kino (1948) in California, Sonora, and Arizona is recorded in his historical memoir of Pimería Alta. The vast literature on Kino includes a biography (Bolton 1960) and a survey of the missions he founded (Lockwood 1934); see also Burrus (1961). The period in northwestern New Spain from 1711 until the expulsion of the Jesuits in 1767 is covered by Donohue (1969). McCarty (1981) and Kessell (1976) discuss the work of the Franciscans on the Arizona-Sonora mission frontier after 1767. See also individual tribal chapters in volume 10 for each tribe's response to the Catholic missionary program in the Greater Southwest.

Roman Catholic Missions in the Southeast and the Northeast

CLIFFORD M. LEWIS

The Southeast

The Spanish missions are an integral and important part of the history of Spain in America. Once the new continents were discovered, their inhabitants' conversion to Christianity took precedence, at least in theory, over economic exploitation and political dominance. The mission process was the main device for the acculturation of the American Indian.

To make for skilled and smooth administration of the apostolate to the Indians, very few religious orders were entrusted with mission activity. Early in the sixteenth century, Spanish missions were conducted principally by the Franciscans, Dominicans, and Augustinians. In 1566, the Jesuit order was enabled by the king of Spain to open missions in Florida and when opportunity presented in Mexico and Central and South America. At a later date the Carmelite and Capuchin fathers and several groups of sisters became engaged in mission work in North America. The Franciscans (chiefly the Order of Friars Minor), had the greatest number of Spanish Indian missions, their activities reaching from coast to coast. Members of religious orders were preferred to diocesan clergy, because by reason of their own vow of poverty and varied sources of support, it was easier to provide for their necessities. They were also somewhat easier to supervise, since protests or requests by the Crown could be made to one central head instead of to bishops of many dioceses. In spite of this, the church in America has never been without its "secular" missionaries.

Spanish mission philosophy was forged early, accelerated by the experience on Hispaniola, where the population was reduced to a very few thousand through disease and hard labor in gold and silver mines, coupled with radical changes in a life previously supported easily by natural sources of food. As the supply of workers dwindled, the Spanish began to import Indian slaves captured on surrounding islands and along the Florida coast. A few Dominican priests assigned to Hispaniola in 1510 protested, on the island and to the king in Spain. The result was the Laws of Burgos of 1512 and 1513, which gave some protection to the Indians.

Lucas Vasquez Ayllon, a wealthy auditor of the Hispaniola courts, was sympathetic with those espousing the cause of Indian freedom (Shea 1886–1892). When Ayllon attempted to establish a Spanish settlement in 1526, possibly on Winyah Bay within the present boundaries of South Carolina, he took as chaplains three Dominicans. Ayllon died and the mission failed.

Florida witnessed both directly and indirectly the effects of the philosophy of Bartolomé de Las Casas, an advocate of the Indians (Hanke 1949; Friede and Keen 1971). The Dominican Luis Cancer de Barbastro obtained royal permission for an ill-fated attempt to return Indians captured in Florida and at the same time establish a mission without accompaniment of soldiers—a policy that had succeeded for him in Guatemala.

Florida

For the purposes of this section, Florida includes not only the present state of Florida but also the southeastern coastal region as far north as Virginia and west as far as Mississippi.

There were several attempts to carry the Gospel to the natives before the founding of Saint Augustine in 1565. Both regular and secular clergy accompanied all properly authorized explorations of Florida, at least from 1521. Missions to the Indians played a key role in the plans of Pedro Menéndez de Avilés after his appointment as adelantado of Florida (Lyon 1976). Menéndez brought in diocesan priests to care for his settlements and their nearby Indians and sent Father Sabastian Montero with Juan Pardo to start mission work, with the help of soldiers, along the string of forts the Spaniards for a short time maintained in a northwesterly direction. Montero himself stayed for six years teaching Christian doctrine, reading, and writing at Guatari in present Anderson County, South Carolina. Reflecting a general policy of Menéndez, he worked principally with chiefs and presumably with their children. At the same time Menéndez distributed Spanish children as catechists along the line of populated islands on the Atlantic Coast. Thus was established in Florida the policy of relying on young boys to learn the Indian languages quickly, later acting as interpreters and teachers of the missionaries.

Menéndez's next move was to send two Dominicans with soldiers to Chesapeake Bay to start a mission but also to seek for a reputed passage to China. They were guided by a native of that section of the coast, who had been baptized in Mexico as Don Luis de Velasco. Bad weather and poor guidance by Don Luis combined to thwart this settlement, and on a majority vote the party elected to go to Spain, thus escaping the wrath of the adelantado.

● JESUITS   Menéndez now redoubled his efforts, begun in 1565, to obtain Jesuit missionaries, giving them to understand he wanted none other. In 1566 the forerunners of a contingent of Jesuits arrived in Florida. Their leader, Father Pedro Martínez, was killed near the Saint Johns River while seeking directions from the Indians, and the ship bearing Father Juan Rogel and Brother Francisco Villarreal was blown out to sea and ended up in Havana. While there the new missionaries became more familiar with Menéndez's master plan for Florida. Missions would be wrapped all around the Florida peninsula, starting from Tocobaga in Tampa Bay and would reach all the way to Virginia. Evidently Menéndez was dropping the western penetration by Pardo in favor of the Chesapeake Bay as a possible link with China. These missions should pacify the Indians on the route pursued by the treasure fleets around the Gulf Coast to Havana, and from Havana following the Gulf Stream along the coast to the Carolinas and thence across to Spain. The importance of this plan was amply confirmed by the growing attempts of the English and Dutch as well as the French to exploit the resources of the Atlantic Coast, and to attack the treasure fleets, attempts that did not cease with the establishment of Saint Augustine.

Jesuits participated in the plan by taking children of the Florida chiefs to Havana. There they founded, in 1568, a school teaching Spanish and the fundamentals of Christianity, fitting the Indian boys to assist the mission priests. Wives, too, might participate in this scheme. Some of the older Indian youths were even taken to Spain, so that returning they might relay to their tribes an impression of the scale of Spanish achievement, power, and population.

When the Jesuits came to Cuba they learned that Menéndez already had discovered the Calusa just south of the Caloosahatchee River, and in 1567 Father Rogel was established at the tribal chief's village probably on Mound Key in Estero Bay, where a fort was built enclosing houses and a small chapel. Similar detachments were settled at Tocobaga, Tequesta (Miami), started as a mission by Brother Villarreal, Santa Lucia (Jensen Beach), San Agustín, San Mateo on the Saint Johns River, Santa Catalina (St. Catherines Island, Georgia), Tupiqui on the mainland opposite, at Santa Elena (Parris Island) with its adjunct Orista 12 miles away (fig. 1). At the cost of their lives Jesuits refused army support at Ajacán in Virginia.

The missions at Tocobaga and Santa Lucia lacked permanently stationed priests, and both garrisons were conquered by the natives. Troops arrived at Villarreal's mission just in time to prevent the same thing there.

Father Rogel started the mission among the Calusa. He also visited many of the other settlements, though his call at Ajacán was only to seek his eight companions. He brought back to Havana the lone survivor of the Virginia mission, Alonso de Almos. The rest had been slain by Indians led by the convert Don Luis in 1571. All the Jesuit priests and one brother at one time or another were stationed, at least temporarily, at the San Antonio fort mission among the Calusa.

A most complicated problem faced the Jesuits, as well as other missionary groups. Their background as well as their faith compelled them to get rid of native religion as quickly as possible. Menéndez was inclined to temporize, but he finally took the responsibility of forcing the Calusa chief Don Felipe to destroy the ceremonial equipment of the tribe, which he is reputed to have done "in fear and trembling." Don Felipe had come into power after the Spaniards, sensing a threatened rebellion by his predecessor, Carlos, had taken Carlos's life.

In fairness to the Jesuit effort, its apparent lack of success cannot be evaluated purely on the basis of counting converts. The Jesuits wanted the early converts in particular to be thoroughly grounded in the faith and in some cases they preferred a year of more of instruction. Several of the young natives taken to Havana for tutelage died there. The Jesuits wisely chose to baptize the chiefs first, although they made some exceptions. The overall policy took care of two difficulties: danger of undermining the chief's influence and the reluctance of his subjects to set themselves up in opposition to their rulers. The Jesuits who survived the difficulties of the Florida experience gained a more realistic outlook on the patience required by the conversion process.

In the eighteenth century the Jesuits attempted to reestablish the Florida missions. The Indians of Los Martires on their trips to Cuba requested missionaries. The Italian-born Jesuits Joseph J. Alaña and José Monaco responded. They mapped the entire keys and set up headquarters on the southern coast of Florida. Their success was modest at best.

● FRANCISCANS   After the Jesuits left Florida in 1572, the Franciscans in the following year began mission activity that lasted nearly two centuries and ended only with the first evacuation of Spaniards in 1763. For 20 years the British ruled Florida, only to return it in 1783 to Spain, but mission work thereafter under Spanish auspices was negligible and limited to West Florida.

The Franciscans worked under almost the same difficulties as the Jesuits, but they had the experience of an established order, a much larger group of volunteers to cover a vast mission territory, and decision-making

482

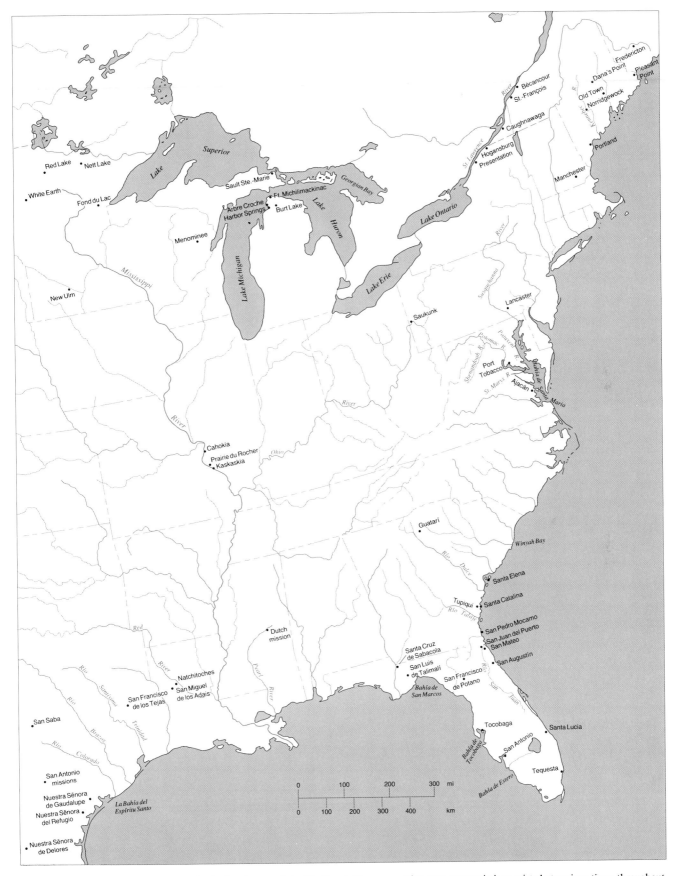

Fig. 1. Selected missions and other sites in the Southeast and the Northeast. Numerous other temporary missions existed at various times throughout Florida and Texas. See "Roman Catholic Missions in New France," fig. 2, this vol., for other missions in New France and Louisiana.

ROMAN CATHOLIC MISSIONS IN THE SOUTHEAST AND THE NORTHEAST

superiors relatively close at hand. Finally, they had a more established system of civil government to back them up, though the relationship between cleric and governor was never ideal, and most later governors did not support the conversion efforts with the energy displayed by Menéndez.

At least by 1602, the Franciscan friary in the pueblo of Saint Augustine had expanded into a custodio—a unit midway between a friary and a province—subject to the Holy Gospel province centering in Mexico City. This Florida custodio soon became the Province of Santa Elena de la Florida, with territory reaching from Cuba to South Carolina.

Although the Franciscans were what is called an "exempt order," their missions were subject to surveillance by the bishop of the diocese, with headquarters in Cuba. It is a matter of no little wonder that only two episcopal visitations, those of 1606 and 1674–1675, were made during the entire mission history of Florida. The Franciscan Luís Gerónimo de Oré visited in 1614 under orders of the commissary general, and again in 1616–1617, when he acted in the capacity of delegate of the bishop of Cuba as well. Records of these visitations provide the most complete information on the growth of the missions. A few maps of the mission, reports of censuses, and letters to Spanish officials are also available. Much confusion results from the changing of mission names, sometimes occasioned by the removal of missions to new tribal locations.

An understanding of the recruitment and education of the missionaries is necessary in evaluating their accomplishments. Before 1622, this process could be visualized as chiefly a matter of internal Franciscan policy, but in that year Pope Gregory XV instituted the Papal Congregation for the Propagation of the Faith, and that organization's interest extended to the individual missionary's original selection and even to his performance in the field. Within the Franciscan order, uniform approaches to educational philosophy and activity were achieved by meetings of Franciscans from various provinces. Schools for missionaries were set up in various places, chiefly in Europe, with stress on the study of native languages and educational method. The Indians in Florida freely expressed their preference for American-born rather than European-born instructors.

From the very beginning in Florida, missionaries strove to learn the native languages. The Jesuits had been motivated in this study when they found teaching through interpreters ineffective. The Franciscan Francisco Pareja translated Spanish works into Timucua (fig. 2) and composed a grammar in that language. Father Gregorio de Movilla likewise translated two religious works into Timucua. At the increasing insistence of the Crown, however, Indian children later formally as well as naturally learned Spanish.

Institucion del SS. Sacramento
hiti, tuque nocomi puquamota napatirota aboma, mihabety, anecolofiromanta eatamala Anoreqema,nihihabeleta hibuantema hiti puqua

inibiti, vquafiromãta eatema enetela Diofi maniniqe, mine, yfomima, yaha,nihihabeletantema, enenotichule, anoeyocarema, enetamale.

Smithsonian, NAA.
Fig. 2. Illustration from *Cathecismo, y Examen para los que Comulgan, En lengua Castellana, y Timuquana* (1627) by Francisco Pareja. This catechism, printed in Timucua and Spanish, served primarily as instruction in the Catholic religion, especially regarding the sacrament of communion. The text reproduced here is Timucua, and the illustration depicts devils carrying off a soul. Woodcut reproduced from a microfilm of the original in the British Lib., Dept. of Printed Books.

The Franciscans had the good fortune to be able to supply hundreds of missionaries to Florida, but since they were spread over several generations, there were never more than about 70 for all the northern part of Florida (including Georgia). Only occasionally could they afford more than one man per *doctrina*, or teaching center. In addition to this responsibility, the missionary usually had to care for one or more outlying *visitas* where he would say Mass on Sundays or holy days.

Florida was a difficult mission for the Franciscans, inasmuch as the friars did not and could not successfully beg enough money from the sparse Spanish population. The Crown itself assumed the responsibility of the Franciscans' support, but as this support trickled through several distributors, it became scanty indeed.

Because of Indian uprisings and unrest possibly generated by French traders and refugees, the accomplishments of the Franciscans during the first 10 years were modest. Their first efforts, except for southern Florida, were made in virtually the same places where the Jesuit missions had been located, and the focal point was the same, Santa Catalina. In addition, they began the successful San Pedro Mocamo mission on Cumberland Island, which by 1588 numbered many converts.

Improved recruitment and mission management by 1616 at the time of Fray de Oré's second visitation had produced 6,000 converts. By 1618 there were 4,000 more and 1,000 under instruction, reflecting a sudden influx of missionaries in 1615. When the second episcopal visitation was made in 1673–1674, there were more than 13,000 confirmations (an accurate enumeration from the bishop's visitation) (Wenhold 1936). The census taken then seems to indicate a total of 26,000 Christian Indians, which may reflect the difficulty of communicating with all the converts in Florida and Georgia, for by 1673 there would be few Indians still living from the time of the first confirmation in 1606.

The missions of the early years were helped no little by sympathetic Florida governors, but the Franciscans were sensitive to encroachment of government officials into their sphere of responsibility. Even more so they resented quartering of troops in areas not absolutely requiring it.

During the late sixteenth and early seventeenth centuries, the Franciscans consolidated their gains along the East coast and pushed west in a reasonably straight line as far as Tallahassee. It was during this period that they came as close as American missionaries ever did to the creation for the Indian of the ideal social order visualized by Bartolomé de Las Casas. Except for attacks by seamen, there was little military danger from enemies from without. The Spanish Indians were discouraged from the possession and use of firearms (which later was greatly to their disadvantage). Their native corn production increased. Grazing of cattle was popular with the Indians and probably more so in the few areas where they were assigned horses for supervision. Herds of up to 2,000 cattle were reported.

The western mission of the Franciscans proved helpful to settlers in the eastern seacoast region where food was scarce. Their agriculture improved by the friars, the Apalachee were able to send 3,000–4,000 bushels of maize and beans yearly to Saint Augustine. They also shipped deer skins and salted turkey to Saint Augustine, Havana, and Spain, and there were deliveries of the same items, including live pigs and chickens, to the east coast.

Because of the trade and the presence of soldiers, the

mission of San Luís de Talimali was the principal one, with 1,400 Indian residents, in 1674. In spite of the obvious danger from rival colonies, the friars continued to oppose stationing of troops as injurious to mission work.

The natives displayed good cooperation in the building of churches and houses, again a type of labor they must have identified with their tradition. Nevertheless, the tendency to fix their residence and attend schools resulted in important though not profound changes in their culture, perhaps more from the standpoint of communication than from labor. They could read and write Timucua as well as Spanish—an accomplishment eventually common to the tribes in the older missions.

There was little social distinction between Spaniard and Indian, at least in the missions. The Franciscans even encouraged marriage of soldiers or other Spaniards to Indian women. A conspicuous example was the marriage to a Spaniard of the Indian woman Dona Maria, who ruled at San Juan del Puerto.

The policy of keeping the Indians in a domestic rather than a military pose was commendable. However, this vulnerability led to the conquest of the missions by the English and their Creek Indian allies, under the leadership of Gov. James Moore of Carolina. He was responsible for campaigns in 1702, 1704, and 1706–1707, as a result of which three Franciscans were killed. Many of the missionized Indians, inadequately armed at the last minute, were killed and large numbers carried off to slavery or its equivalent on the eastern coast. The missions survived but a few decades more and were thereafter able to serve but a fraction of the population.

The Florida experience had been a trying one for the Franciscans. They had lost 10 men in all, slain by the Indians or the English. In Georgia in 1597, a widespread Indian revolt took five Franciscan lives. This revolt was occasioned in part by Franciscan attempts to keep the office of mico from a non-Christian Indian with two wives. More missionaries were killed by a western revolt in 1643 and by English attacks in the early 1670s.

Lower Mississippi Area

The missions of the lower Mississippi region started under the French, passed to the Spanish, to Great Britain, and finally to the Americans, with notable gaps in service at the stages of transition. When the United States through purchase in 1803 and war in 1812 had acquired all the South except Texas, the Catholic Church was too poorly organized and small in numbers to undertake decisive missionary work in Louisiana territory. The Jesuit Order, which had conducted mission work there from 1726 to 1763, maintained a small mission at Fort Toulouse, Arkansas, among the Choctaw (Delanglez 1935; O'Neill 1966). The Capuchins were responsible for the longest-lasting and largest Indian mission in the lower Mississippi

Valley, that of the Apalachee outside Mobile (Vogel 1928). In the nineteenth century Father Roquette was a missionary among the Louisiana Choctaw (Le Breton 1947).

To complicate the mission situation, the new American nation was pushing westward and demanding the relocation of the Indians (fig. 3), a policy enacted into federal law in 1830. Meanwhile, English and American land acquisition had resulted in the migration of several tribes into the Mississippi Valley. From there and from the East, beginning in 1830, they began the arduous trek to Indian Territory.

The Choctaw mission of the Dutch Carmelites in Mississippi is an example of the promise and the difficulties of missions in south-central United States. Beginning in 1831, the majority of the Choctaw withdrew to the Indian Territory under great hardship, but about 3,000 remained behind, only to be cheated out of promised land by Whites and Indian agents. The bishop of the Natchez diocese, embracing the entire state of Mississippi, in 1883 recruited from the Netherlands the Reverend Bartholomew J. Bekkers, who went to the town of Tucker in Neshoba County (where a Choctaw reservation was later established). In the 15 years after his arrival, Father Bekkers was able to build a few little churches, baptize 725 Indians, and perform 80 marriages. In 1899 a contract was signed with five Dutch religious under Father Augustine Breek. The Reverend Cyrus Byington's Choctaw grammar was used for instruction conducted under the Carmelites with teaching sisters and nurses. When the Indian chief Tom Billy died in 1900, the missions virtually collapsed from lack of financial aid and ineffective leadership. Three of the Carmelites went to the Indian territory along with many Choctaws (Lickteig 1969).

Texas

As was true in Florida and California, the Spanish missions in Texas were in part a response to challenges by a foreign power. In California the opponent was Russia, in Florida it was France, and in Texas it was again the French, who provided a reason for the more easterly Spanish missions. The financial drain of Spain's worldwide responsibilities dictated that the equipping and supporting of mission stations and presidios be undertaken preferably where a dual benefit existed: the security of the Spanish borderlands and the salvation of the natives.

The Spanish had been seeking the gulf coast fort established and abandoned by René-Robert Cavelier, sieur de La Salle in 1687 but did not find it until 1689, under the leadership of Capt. Andrés de León and Father Damien Massanet, who at this time founded the mission of San Francisco de los Téjas for the Indians somewhat east of the Trinity River. After a few years, when danger from the French seemed past, this mission was abandoned.

Sporadic attempts were made to establish missions in the El Paso area beginning in 1630, but the first serious attempt, among the Manso and Suma Indians, came in 1659 when Father San Francisco founded the mission of Nuestra Señora de Guadalupe. With the aid of another father and 10 families of Christian Indians, he built a church of mud and branches and a monastery thatched with straw. The priests furnished the mission, providing ploughs, laborers, carpenters, and implements of various kinds. In addition, they supplied livestock, thousands of head of cattle, sheep, and goats, and 200 horses (Castañ-

left, Tippecanoe Co. Histl. Assoc. and Evelyn O. Ball, Layfayette, Ind.; right, Smithsonian, NAA:763–b.

Fig. 3. Potawatomi Indians and the Catholic Church. left, Bishop Simon Bruté preaching to the Potawatomi at the beginning of their emigration from Ind. to Kans. (see "Indian Land Transfers," fig. 4, this vol.). Many of the Potawatomi present were from the Yellow River area where the Catholic mission was administered by Rev. Benjamin Marie Petit and others (Winter 1948:48–49). Drawing in ink and pencil on paper by George Winter, Sept. 1838. right, Contract boarding school for Potawatomi children at Saint Mary's Mission on the Kansas River, Kans. In 1846 the Potawatomis from the Osage River and Council Bluffs subagencies together moved to a reservation on the Kansas River. Saint Mary's Mission was established there in 1848 by Jesuit missionaries, the Revs. Christian Hoecken, Maurice Gaillard, Felix L. Verreydt, and Brother Andrew Mazella (Garraghan 1938, 2:605–615, 619–625). Photograph by Alexander Gardner, 1867.

eda 1936–1958, 1:249).

Several other missions were also begun late in the seventeenth century along the Río Grande, three of these being near El Paso (O'Rourke 1927). The growth of some of these missions was due to Indian revolts in New Mexico and consequent flight of many Spaniards and their Indian converts. The growth of the line of missions farther down the river was doubtless also due in part to the desirability of being close to water and the intention to facilitate the movement of Spanish civilization toward its objectives in New Mexico, but they were due in part to the requests of the Jumanos as early as 1683. From the beginning, the great mobility of many of the Texas tribes caused the missions no end of difficulty. This mobility was increased by the acquisition of horses, which many of the natives learned to tend and ride while working in the presidio.

The Spanish were always conservative in the gift or sale of firearms to Indians. The natives therefore welcomed the firearms supplied by the French traders. The traditional advantage the Spanish always thought they had in combat was diminished. Then there was the temptation of neophytes to take vacations among their pagan brethren on the occasion of certain hunts or during attractive rituals when restraints might be discarded. One of the greatest difficulties throughout Spanish America was the Indian's susceptibility to certain diseases, particularly smallpox, from which the natives usually fled, leaving the padres to take care of the sick.

Almost as difficult as the missionaries' life with the Indians were the drawbacks of their Spanish environment, where captains frequently cheated their own soldiers by charging high prices for goods and forcing the soldiers for mere subsistence to work in the mines and on ranches, even at the expense of leaving vital forts inadequately staffed.

After 25 years of passivity following the La Salle episode, the French again became aggressive on the eastern frontier. They built a fort at Natchitoches on the Red River in Louisiana and began trading with the Indians. The Spanish demonstrated their boldness by building the mission of San Miguel de los Adais inside Louisiana territory and very close to the French fort at Robaline. That the Spanish did not take their frontier posts too seriously is demonstrated by the fact that when the French, in 1719, attacked their positions from Natchitoches, the Spanish pulled back to San Antonio, where in 1720, near Valero, they founded the mission of San Jose y San Miguel de Aguayo. The most famous of the Texas missions, of course, was the Alamo, founded in 1718 under the name of San Antonio de Valero. Associated with it were a presidio and a pueblo also under the name of San Antonio (fig. 4). With new resolve and larger forces, in 1721 the Spanish restored their forts in eastern Texas. After nine years of quiet, the Spanish built three missions on the San Antonio River south of the Alamo. Of all the mission churches in Texas, only a half dozen in San Antonio have been fully restored.

Long hours of travel, insufficiency of food and clothing, and lack of cooperation from the secular arm made the missionaries' life an ordeal. At least a dozen died violent deaths, mostly at the hands of the Indians, but some as victims of Whites. They pleaded largely in vain to make the fierce Apaches and Comanches mission subjects rather than enemies to be hunted and exterminated. At San Sabá they almost achieved this objective of friendship with the Apaches, only to see the opportunity vanish during an assault by the Comanches in which two of the missionaries lost their lives. Perhaps the best-known missionary in Texas was the Venerable Anthony Margil (d. 1726), veteran of arduous missions in Mexico and Guatemala, who labored chiefly in the east and central parts of Texas.

The last mission in Texas was established in 1793 on Goff Bayou in Calhoun County. It was given the name of Nuestra Señora del Refugio. Its purpose was to provide a gathering place for Christian Indians who had lost contact with their former missions on the Gulf coast. But this establishment was the beginning of the end of the missions in Texas. In the judgment of Bolton (1917), the missions failed because the priests were unable to persuade the Indians to locate permanently near the missions for education and protection. This was certainly a chief contributing cause of their decline, but it was a decline hastened by the Mexican order secularizing the missions in 1794. The mission as an institution in a few years came to an end.

The number of Indian converts in Texas has been estimated as roughly equivalent to those of California and of Florida.

The Northeast

Maryland

The English missions to the Indians of Maryland and adjacent areas are chiefly identified with Father Andrew White, both because of his work and his accounts of mission activity in the early years.

A. White (1910) described the object of the plantation as "first and chiefly, to convey into the said land and neighbouring parts the light of the Gospel and of the truth, where it is certain no knowledge of the true God has ever shed its beams . . . ."

The story of the Maryland-Pennsylvania missions is one of success and failure, of lasting conversions and of death and dispersion. Contributing most to the success was the receptivity of the Algonquian tribes nearest the early English settlement. The Yaocomaco residing around Saint Mary's River, Maryland, were in the act of removing to land more inaccessible to Susquehannock attacks when

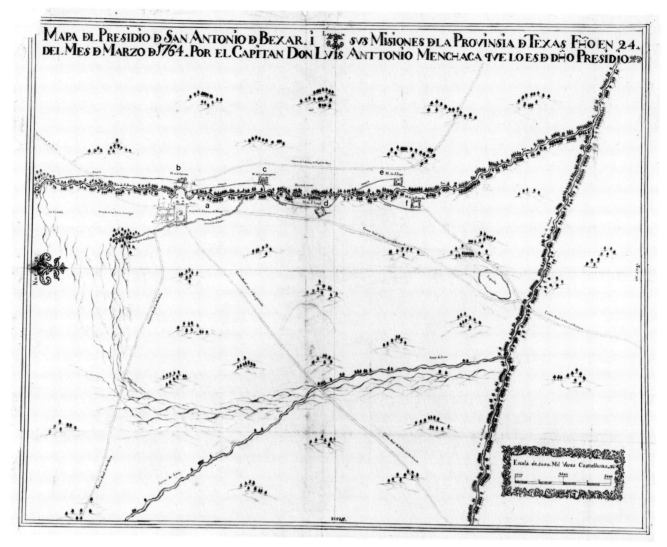

Fig. 4. Manuscript map and plan of the Presidio de San Antonio de Bexar (a) and the nearby missions: San Antonio (b), La Concepción (c), San José (d), San Juan (e), and la Espada (f) on the San Antonio River. North is to the left. Drawn by Luis Antonio Menchaca, March 24, 1764.

Fathers White and John Altham arrived on the scene. The chief gave them a house a few miles from the Potomac, which they immediately converted into a chapel. Tribes with which the Jesuits enjoyed some success included the Patuxent, Potapaco, Potomac, Piscataway, and the Anacostank.

Gov. Leonard Calvert, with Father Altham and some retainers, soon after their arrival cruised up the Potomac in a pinnace making friends with the Potomac Indians on their way but having as their principal objective the cultivation of the chief of the Piscataway, the most powerful of the Maryland leaders. Chitomachen, as he was called, later made Father White welcome in his home, willingly dismissed his concubines, and together with his wife, family, and some retainers, was received into the church in a solemn ceremony after lengthy instructions. Before long, well over 100 converts were made in his villages. The chief's daughter was tutored at Saint Mary's,

becoming first the charge of Margaret Brent, and then the wife of her brother Giles Brent.

Throughout the mission years the religious personnel in Maryland were mainly Jesuit. In 1673, Franciscans came to Maryland and enjoyed friendly relations with the Jesuits.

The Jesuits, particularly Father Rigby on the Patuxent River and Father White among the Piscataway, quickly set about trying to master the Algonquian dialects. Father Rigby composed a brief Indian language cathechism. Despite difficulties the Jesuits were able to form Indian congregations, particularly Piscataway and Patuxent, who remained loyal whether staying at home or scattered abroad. Part of the missionaries' success was doubtless due to their willingness to partake of Indian lodging, food, and hospitality. The Indians, on the other hand, were quick to adopt the clothing and utensils distributed by the missionaries.

As means of supporting their missionary efforts, the Jesuits were permitted to participate in the original land distribution, made on the basis of 100 acres for each person brought to the colony. Additional land was given the Jesuits by Indian chiefs, with the understanding that the Jesuits would use the land for the building of chapels and as a support for their religious services. Governor Calvert challenged the right of anyone to accept property from Indians without his permission. He expropriated the gift-lands and redistributed them to suit his purpose.

Defense of Jesuit ownership of land, if such a defense is required, lay in the missionaries' desire to expend the greater share of their time on the Indian missions. The concept of support of pastoral work from a broad section of church membership had not yet taken root; tenant farms seemed to supply the Jesuits' only reliable income.

In the few years after 1644, missionary work was seriously handicapped by the war in England between Royalists and Parliamentarians, which had its counterpart in Maryland. Father White and Father Copley (alias Philip Fisher) were seized and taken to England, where Copley was eventually released but Father White was detained for three years. Father White was 68; his superiors did not wish him to return to the missions. Copley returned to put the Jesuit mission again in order. Three new Jesuit missionaries fled from the civil strife or were carried off, supposedly to Virginia, in 1645 or 1646, and were never heard from again.

During the Puritan uprising of 1655, which denied religious existence to Catholics and Anglicans, Jesuit buildings in Maryland were destroyed. Two priests fled, probably to the mouth of the Shenandoah. A law was passed forbidding the Jesuits to "meddle" with the Indians.

When conditions became more propitious, the Jesuit superior took up residence on Port Tobacco Creek, in Charles County, in a house called Saint Thomas, where most of his parishoners were Piscataway.

Pennsylvania

The first religious aid to the Pennsylvania tribes probably came from the north rather than from Maryland. During the month of July 1643, the Jesuit Isaac Jogues, a prisoner among the Mohawks, was taken on a journey of some 200 miles, seemingly down into Susquehannock territory. As he went from village to village, he managed to baptize the sick, including the man who had cut his bonds at the third village where he had been taken after his captivity in New York.

The Jesuits from Maryland had long been caring for the Piscataway and Susquehannock, that dimly defined amalgam forged out of the long conflicts among the Iroquoian and Algonquian groups in southern Pennsylvania and Maryland. So many Piscataway women had been carried off captive to the Susquehanna Valley that the missionaries who spoke the Algonquian language probably experienced little difficulty in making themselves known.

Father Henry Harrison, S.J., served the Pennsylvania mission at a critical period of its existence. He had been brought to New York from Europe by the Catholic governor, Thomas Dongan, in the hope that he and other English missionaries might take over the Five Nations missions from the French. This plan naturally was resisted by the Canadian governor. The entire idea collapsed when Governor Dongan was succeeded by a governor inimical to Catholicism. Dongan sold the acquisition rights to the Susquehanna land, acquired by New York from the Susquehannocks, to his erstwhile rival, William Penn, for a pittance. Thus Father Harrison ended up in the Pennsylvania missions in 1687. He labored there until his death in 1700.

Not only Father Harrison but also Fathers Joseph Greaton and Richard Molyneux each in his turn shared in the Pennsylvania mission out of Maryland. According to early Cumberland historians, Father Greaton went to Conewago, in southern Pennsylvania west of the Susquehanna, in the early 1720s, as a missionary to the Indians. Father Molyneux went up from Maryland at the request of the Proprietary of Pennsylvania to attend the Indian council at Lancaster in 1744. As a result of this and other councils, arrangements were made to recompense the Iroquois for ownership they had acquired by conquest of the Susquehanna lands.

Maine

The Revolutionary War in America wrought several changes affecting the progress of Catholic missions among the Indians. Freedom of worship guaranteed by some state constitutions and later made nationwide by an amendment of the United States Constitution enabled Roman Catholic missionaries to move and act more and more freely. The Revolution also produced a growing independence from European custom and thought.

Aware of the close linguistic relationship of the Eastern and Western Abenaki and the Delaware, the Jesuit Father Claude Virot in 1757 had transported possibly as many as 20 Abenakis from the Saint François and Bécancour missions on the Saint Lawrence to Saukunk, a Delaware village on the Ohio several miles below Fort Duquesne. The object was not only to remove the Abenaki from the dangers of alcohol but also to use them in the conversion of the Delaware and possibly other tribes. Only a few conversions were made before the leading Delaware chief forcibly brought an end to Virot's plan. The Abenaki missions remained in the 1980s at Saint François and Bécancour.

To appreciate fully the remarkably firm attachment of the Maine Algonquian tribes to Christianity through three

N.B. Prov. Arch., Fredericton: MBE/T-170.
Fig. 5. Maliseet Indians and Roman Catholic priest on Corpus Christi Day, Kingsclear, N.B. Photograph by George T. Taylor, 1887.

and one-half centuries, it will be well to recall briefly the mission accomplishments during the period of French responsibility. The first serious attempt at systematic missionary work was an outgrowth of the papal organization known as the Congregatio de Propaganda Fide, founded in part in the Church's desire for missions independent of national interests. For the first time in the history of what was to become United States territory, the Propagation, as it was familiarly known, undertook a mission enterprise. The new order of Capuchins founded seven permanent missions from Nova Scotia to the Kennebec River in Maine. The 20 years of labor by some 40 Capuchin missionaries was one of the factors in the long attachment of these Algonquian tribes to the Catholic faith. The Jesuits gradually supplanted the Capuchins in these missions and were responsible for transplanting a majority of the Abenaki to reductions on the Saint Lawrence. From there some of their members returned to Norridgewock, Maine, as forerunners of the missionaries.

The English victory in the French and Indian War, formalized in the Treaty of Paris in 1763, created problems for the missions. Canada had become a British possession, and to make matters more difficult the Jesuit Order was suppressed in France by King Louis XV, leading indirectly to the abandonment of the New England missions by the Jesuits, since their means of support was largely denied them. To complicate the problem, potential missionaries from the Vicar Apostolic of London were in short supply.

Help for New England's Catholic Indians came from an unexpected source—from the concerned Col. John Allan, whom the Massachusetts government appointed in 1777 as superintendent of the eastern tribes. Appeals broadcast by the Penobscot with the help of Colonel Allan brought temporary ministration by an exiled French priest in Boston, who baptized 65 and married 12 couples.

From 1791, John Carroll, the first Roman Catholic bishop of the United States, became sympathetic with the

Maine Indians' pleas for a missionary. These requests were repeatedly relayed to the bishop by Indian agent Allan, a Protestant. Allan likewise aided the Passamaquoddy Indians, who were fortunate in obtaining the ministrations of two French Sulpician exiles in succession, the second of whom, Jean de Cheverus, became the first bishop of Boston. He was succeeded by another French refugee, Jacques-René Romagne, who served the Passamaquoddy nearly a score of years until his return to France in 1818.

To care for the religious and educational needs of the Indians at the Old Town mission, in the 1870s the bishop of Portland obtained four Sisters of Mercy from Manchester, New Hampshire. The Sisters proved themselves adaptable by occupying the four room wigwam that had been given up to them by the tribal chief, Stockvesin Swassin. The Sisters' work provides a good study of adaptation and acculturation guided by a group of intelligent women (Leger 1929). The Sisters on the Penobscot immediately set about learning the tribal language and translating the catechism into the Indian tongue. In 1879 additional Sisters from Manchester set up a mission with schools on the reservation at Pleasant Point opposite Deer Island on Passamaquoddy Bay. They also gave four months' yearly service to a separated group of Passamaquoddy Indians at Dana's Point on the Schoodic Lakes.

The first conversions to Catholicism among the Maliseet and Passamaquoddy occurred in the seventeenth century, and these people have been nominally Catholic since the eighteenth century (fig. 5). Since the 1920s their religious needs have been supplied by the Franciscan Fathers (O.F.M.). Sisters of Charity teach the early grades in a government-sponsored school.

A renaissance of native culture, encouraged by Catholic Church leadership and by the Union of New Brunswick Indians at Frederickton, included conducting the liturgy in the Indian language in a setting of Indian art and music. Religious instruction, too, was given in the Indian tongue. In Maine, likewise, the Division of Indian Services, with headquarters in Bangor, in which the Catholic clergy have played an important role, provided community development and technical assistance, particularly through a privately funded Indian Resource Center.

New York

Virtually the only remaining Catholic mission of any consequence in the 1970s in the state of New York was that of the Saint Regis Mohawks, on the border of the United States and Canada, in a community that originated from a migration of Catholic Iroquois from Caughnawaga, near Montreal.

Religious supervision of the Catholic members is divided among three dioceses, those of Ogdensburg, New

Fig. 6. Saint Regis Reservation, N.Y., 1838. Engraving by William Henry Bartlett, originally published 1840.

York; Alexandria, Ontario; and Valleyfield, Quebec. A grade school for boys and girls was administered by Sisters of Saint Ann. Stationed at the mission for many years was Father Michael Jacobs, S.J., himself a bilingual native.

Midway in the eighteenth century a mission was established with a log house as temporary chapel. The village became a seat of the Jesuit mission named for Saint Francis Regis (fig. 6). The mission grew by addition in 1806 of a group originally settled at Oswegatchie, where a small band of Iroquois was all that remained of the Presentation mission established by the Sulpician Father François Piquet, in 1748, on the site of Ogdensburg (Shea 1886–1892, 1:614–618). This mission once numbered about 3,000 drawn chiefly from the Onondaga and Cayuga through the visits of Piquet.

Of the approximately 5,000 Indians on the Saint Regis Reservation in the 1970s, approximately 80 percent were Catholics, who worshiped in a church built in 1791. For a number of years, the liturgy, in part, was carried out in the Mohawk language.

Great Lakes Area

After the Revolutionary War the new American nation was not long in pushing to the West. England's command of Indian allies disappeared after the War of 1812. The American advance of the frontier was least successful in the area that became Minnesota, Wisconsin, and Michigan, where some of the original occupants held fast. To their ranks were added portions of eastern tribes fleeing before the Whites migrating to farmlands in the Great Lakes region and western territory.

The northern missions embraced many tribes and sites. The flourishing missions that the French had in Michigan were virtually abandoned by reason of American independence and the conquest of Canada by the English. Indian participation in the French and Indian War, Pontiac's rebellion, the American Revolution, and the War of 1812 made missionary work virtually impossible west of the Alleghenies.

Early in the nineteenth century missions in the northern territory had to rely almost exclusively on Europeans. One of these was Gabriel Richard, a Sulpician priest of many accomplishments who in the 1820s was a delegate to the U.S. House of Representatives from the Michigan Territory. Arriving from France in 1792, he ministered to Indians and Whites at Prairie du Rocher, Kaskaskia, and Cahokia in the Illinois country, and to the

Indians of Sault Sainte Marie, Fort Michilimackinac, Arbre Croche, and Georgian Bay in and around Michigan. With the first printing press in Michigan he published a Bible for Indians, and as a member of the House he watched over their interests in Washington.

For some years, missions have been conducted by Jesuits at Sault Sainte Marie in northern Michigan and by Franciscans at Burt Lake, Cross Village, and at Harbor Springs, where a school for Indians was conducted by Sisters of Notre Dame.

In Wisconsin the early French missionaries made many converts among the Menominee. After the passage of many years following the French departure, the Menominee lost their Christian affiliation, but the tribe welcomed Catholic missionaries in 1854. In Menominee County in the 1980s 95 percent were Catholic. Several missions are served by Franciscan priests, and schools are directed by Sisters of Saint Joseph of Carondolet and Franciscan Sisters of Christian Charity. Diocesan priests also had some mission responsibility.

In Minnesota there are several missions, chiefly to the Chippewa, served by Benedictine Fathers all originating at the Collegeville, Minnesota, abbey. Benedictine sisters assist the priests and brothers. The only other order of priests connected with mission work are the Oblates of Mary Immaculate, at Nett Lake. In northwestern Minnesota, there were missions at Red Lake and White Earth reservations and at Fond du Lac and New Ulm. At Red Lake, one of the most populous missions, over half the residents were Catholic.

Sources

The principal source for the Jesuit period in Florida is Zubillaga (1946), which, with a lengthy introduction and bibliography, contains more than 500 pages of letters and contemporary short histories pertaining to the brief Jesuit experience. Zubillaga also wrote a narrative of the mission (1941).

There is no comparable compilation for the Franciscan missions in Florida. However, a good deal of correspondence related to mission matters has been extracted from the archives in Seville and Simancas and is in the Stetson Collection in the P.K. Yonge Library of the University of Florida, Tallahassee. Material dealing with the coastal missions has been calendared by the St. Augustine Foundation. The Mission of Nombre de Dios had received the entire collection on microfilm as part of its aim to become a research center for early Florida history, especially of the church and the missions.

Two contemporaries of Menéndez have written very similar works on the history of his accomplishments in Florida, including the Jesuit missions (Solís de Merás 1923; Barrientos 1902). Connor (1925–1930) translated and annotated two volumes dealing with Spanish activities in Florida from 1526 to 1580.

Documents pertaining to the Virginia venture of the Jesuits are presented in original and translation by Lewis and Loomie (1953).

Original documents and translations of the first visitation of Florida, by Bishop Altamirano, O.P., are given by Father V.F. O'Daniel, O.P. (1917), while a description of this visitation is supplied by Mary Ross (1926).

Fray Luis Gerónimo de Oré (1936) wrote an account based on his two official visits to Florida, translated under the title *The Martyrs of Florida*. The work deals principally with the five deaths of Franciscans in Georgia in 1597 but also describes a Spanish exploration of the Chesapeake in 1588 with references to the earlier Jesuit mission in southern Virginia. Geiger (1937, 1940) assists in understanding the work of the missionaries and includes lists of missions for various periods. Biographies of Franciscan missionaries killed in the United States are contained in Habig (1947). Boyd, Smith, and Griffin (1951) describe the destruction of Apalachee missions. Gannon (1965) describes Catholic missions in Florida, while Keegan and Tormo Sanz (1957) and Borges (1961) treat mission methods. A concise history is by Pohlkamp (1936). Barth (1945) includes much valuable information on Florida missions in a work of wider scope on the Franciscan philosophy of missions. Lanning (1935) thoroughly describes the Spanish missions of Georgia, although the remains he suggested were of mission buildings are actually structures left from the much later rum industry.

Castañeda translated and edited the history of Texas missions by Fray Juan Augustín Morfi (1935). He drew on other extensive documentary discoveries in Mexico for a seven-volume work with an important bibliography (Castañeda 1936–1958). J.T. Ellis (1965) published a capable modern account of the Texas missions, while Eckhart (1967) maps their locations, and Weddle (1964) is a thorough study of a single site.

The most important primary source for the Maryland mission is Andrew White's (1874) story of the journey to America, 1633–1634, coupled with the annual letters and triennial catalogues during succeeding years. The letters through the year 1642 were probably the work of Andrew White. For many years thereafter the letters are brief and infrequent, for correspondence was difficult and reports of missionary work among the Indians were suppressed for the safety of the enterprise. In addition to Father White's Latin version, Gov. Leonard Calvert sent an English version, slightly different, to his business partner. This and many other documents pertaining to early Maryland were edited by C.C. Hall (1910). The chief source on the Jesuit missions in Maryland is the four-volume work by Hughes (1907–1917). Complete lists of Jesuit missionaries and their activities were issued by Beitzell (1959); see also Beitzell (1968).

The colonial missions in Maine are treated in J.T. Ellis

(1965), while Guilday (1922) gives details on the efforts of American Catholic missionaries. Good summaries are in Rahill (1953) and Leger (1929). Information on the status of the missions in 1973 was obtained directly from the mission personnel.

For missions in New York see Shea (1886–1892, 1), Mooney (1910a), and Hewitt (1910).

The Franciscan missions among the Chippewa and Menominee of Wisconsin and the Ottawa of Michigan are treated by Habig (1958:497–561). Among the missions conducted by the Sacred Heart order of sisters was one to the Potawatomi (Callan 1957:632–659).

Roman Catholic Missions in the Northwest

ROBERT I. BURNS, S.J.

A half-century of Roman Catholic intimations prepared the coming of the missionaries in the Pacific Northwest. A few Spanish friars from coastal ships left crucifixes and hymns (W.L. Cook 1973; Blanchet et al. 1956), but the ubiquitous Catholic Iroquois and French Canadians serving the fur companies constituted the main influence, as they mingled, married, or settled with most tribes from the southern Northwest Coast to the Plateau. Ross (1956: 194–195) described, before 1825, how one-third of the Hudson's Bay employees in the Northwest were devout Catholic Iroquois. Blanchet et al. (1956:217–218, 184–185, 228) found that the French free trappers (but not the corrupting *engagés*) had "prepared for a long time" the priests' arrival among the Colville, Lakes, Nez Perces, Sanpoils, Spokanes, Okanagons, Wenatchis, and "most of the Indians." The trader Berland catechized the Kutenais; Pierre Pambrun, the Cayuses, Nez Perces, and neighbors; and Gabriel Prudhomme, the Flatheads. Premissionary travelers noted fragments such as Sunday observance and the Catholic sign of the cross (Wyeth 1899; J. Dunn 1844: 210, 235–236). In 1825 delegates from both north and south among the Plateau tribes asked the Hudson's Bay Company's Gov. George Simpson for the French "Master of Life." Around 1816 a band of 24 Caughnawaga mission Iroquois under Ignace Lamoose settled among the Flatheads (Ewers 1963) insistently preaching Catholicism and the need for priests, both to Flatheads and to Nez Perces and other bands who joined their annual hunt on the Plains. Before 1834 some Catholic "Iroquois-Flatheads" moved from the Rockies to settle near Kansas City. As early as 1821 the French-Canadian community in the Northwest petitioned Saint Louis for priests (Burns 1966; Palladino 1894; Rothensteiner 1928).

Like so many of their Plains neighbors, the Plateau Indians sent a delegation, probably two Flatheads and two Nez Perces, though without interpreters, to Saint Louis in 1831 on a religious quest, receiving baptism and Catholic symbols "with eagerness" at the cathedral. Responding to a published fraud (Garraghan 1938, 2:236–244; Burns 1966:17–18) that these unintelligible seekers had asked for the "Book of Heaven," a Methodist mission went to the Northwest Coast in 1834 and a Presbyterian mission to the Nez Perces and Cayuses in 1836. Receiving no priests, the Flatheads in 1835 sent the French-speaking Iroquois Young Ignace and his two sons to Saint Louis as representing Flathead, Nez Perce, Cayuse, Colville, Kutenai, and Pend d'Oreille. In 1837 Ignace Lamoose led a Nez Perce–Flathead party, destroyed by the Sioux. In 1839 Young Ignace and another Iroquois made the final, successful quest (Garraghan 1938, 2:248–249).

The Jesuits

The Jesuits, to whom the American hierarchy in 1833 had committed the evangelization of the trans-Mississippi tribes, dispatched the Belgian Pierre De Smet from the Potawatomi mission to the Rockies. Following his 1840 reconnaissance, the order in 1841 opened as base missions Saint Mary's (Flathead) and Sacred Heart (Coeur d'Alene) (fig. 1); in 1844 Saint Ignatius (Kalispel) and Saint Francis Xavier as a coastal center; and in 1845 the outriding stations Assumption (lower Kutenai), Holy Heart of Mary (Kutenai), Saint Francis Borgia (Pend d'Oreille or upper Kalispel), Saint Francis Regis (Crees), Saint Peter's (Lakes), and Saint Paul's (Colville, with neighbors like Sanpoils) (fig. 2). Saint Joseph's (Okanagons) and four stations served British Columbia tribes. The network waxed and waned as missions moved, closed temporarily, collapsed, or multiplied, consolidating during the critical 1850s in the northeast interior and Rockies. Scanty resources limited the dream of recreating in the Northwest those Indian "republics" for which the order has been famous in Latin America—educational-agricultural Reductions, with their Indian-culture methodology (Burns 1966:48–55; De Smet 1905).

Each mission, with its sometimes imposing church, village, farms, and mills, held a portion of the extraordinarily scattered and nomadic units comprising its quasi-tribe, hosting the rest on transient visits or feasts; each also served a roving circuit of hundreds of miles, touching most tribes from the Columbias over to the Blackfeet but at first leaving the southern interior rather to Oblates and diocesan missions. Recovering from a series of external crises attendant upon growing American presence, from the Cayuse War of 1847 to the Northern Indians' War of 1858–1859, the network reopened the Colville (1863) and Flathead (1866) missions, a Spokane mission (1867, Saint Michael's), and incorporated the Nez Perce Saint Joseph's

Lib. of Congress, Prints and Photographs Div.: LC-USZ62-4422.
Fig. 1. Sacred Heart Mission, Wash. Terr. Established by Jesuits among the Coeur d'Alene, Sacred Heart and its priests played a role in Indian-White relations during the treaty period and wars of the mid-19th century. Geographically isolated from White settlement, it was an important center for Coeur d'Alene life. The building was constructed by Indian labor on the north bank of the Coeur d'Alene River. A barn, stables, storeroom, mill, smithy, bakery, and priests' residence were built adjacent to the church. About 40 Coeur d'Alenes settled there, with many other families in residence for brief periods (Burns 1966:119, 192, passim). Pencil drawing by Gustavus Sohon, 1858.

and the Yakima Saint Joseph's (early 1870s). In the 1880s the network absorbed or opened missions to the Umatilla (Saint Andrew's, 1888) and Okanagon-Columbia (Saint Mary's, 1887) (Bischoff 1945).

By 1890 Palladino (1894) reported for Montana alone 9 missions and stations, holding 7,000 of the census total of 10,000 Indians, with 500 boys and 500 girls in 9 Indian schools; 18 priests, 20 other Jesuits, 14 Sisters of Providence and 60 Ursuline nuns served these. Saint Ignatius mission then ran 10,000 cattle, 5,000 horses, 1,200 swine, and 6,000 fowl; marketed a surplus from their irrigated farms; and deployed a showplace set of public buildings. The Flathead and Coeur d'Alene mission presses from 1876 to 1899 poured out Indian imprints, of which 89 are extant (Schoenberg 1957). The missionaries, from 1854 directed from Turin in Italy, came from the Jesuit educational establishment in many countries; three Belgians, a German, an Italian, and a Frenchman founded the network, soon joined by a Dutchman, a Swiss, a Maltese, an Irishman, a Frenchman, two Belgians, and three Italians, with a wave of Italians arriving subsequently due to unrest in Italy. Eminent were Joseph Cataldo, Jerome D'Aste, Pierre De Smet, Joseph Giorda, Adrian Hoecken, Joseph Joset, Joseph Menetrey, Gregory Mengarini, Lawrence Palladino, Nicholas Point, Anthony Ravalli, and Stephen de Rougé. The Jesuits' linguistic, historical, and artistic contributions (especially Point 1967); their educational, medical, and pioneering roles; and their championing of Indian rights were impressive. Their mission network comprised part of the order's California province from 1907 and of its Oregon province from 1932, their institutional promise blighted but their obscure, continuing service to the tribes invaluable (see

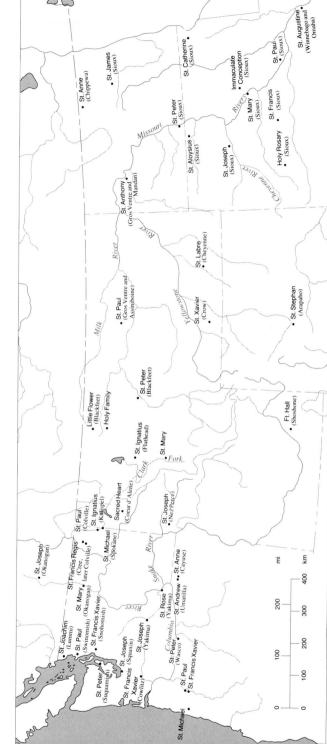

Fig. 2. Roman Catholic missions and the tribes that they served in the Northwest and northern Plains from the mid-19th through the 20th centuries. Throughout these areas were mission stations as well, where crosses were erected and traveling missionaries met local tribes for field services and other religious activities (Beaver 1979; Schoenberg 1987).

495

Schoenberg 1982).

*The Plains**

In the early 1820s, Louis Valentine Du Bourg, bishop of Louisiana, whose diocese included part of the trans-Mississippi West, was authorized by Secretary of War John C. Calhoun to proceed with his plans for Catholic missionary activity among the Indian tribes on the Upper Mississippi and Missouri rivers. Answering Bishop Du Bourg's appeal, the first Maryland Jesuits led by Charles Van Quickenborne arrived in Saint Louis, Missouri, in 1823. The following year the Jesuits opened a boarding school for Indian children at Florissant, near Saint Louis, and soon began their missionary work among the Osage, who had already been visited by father Charles De La Croix in 1822. Van Quickenborne's visit to the Osage villages on the Neosho River in 1827 marked "the formal opening of the missionary activity of the Missouri Jesuits among the Indian tribes of the West" (Garraghan 1938, 1: 184).

A permanent mission among the Osage was established in 1847 by Father John Schoenmakers, and a year later the first church was erected at Osage Mission in southeastern Kansas. In 1851, Paul Mary Ponziglione, an Italian Jesuit, joined Schoenmakers at the mission. Together they labored for several decades primarily among the Osage and neighboring Quapaw, extending their missionary zeal also to tribes in Indian Territory such as the Ottawa, Chippewa, Sauk and Fox, Kansa, and Ponca. Ponziglione eventually visited the Cheyenne and Arapaho at North Fork Agency, Indian Territory, but these tribes' efforts to secure Catholic missionaries in the 1870s were frustrated by the government's Peace Policy, which assigned them to another denomination (Rahill 1953). It was not until 1884 that Saint Stephen's Mission was established among the Northern Arapahoe on the Wind River Reservation, Wyoming, by John Jutz of the Buffalo Mission of the Society of Jesus (Reilly 1980:11). Ponziglione was later assigned briefly to Saint Stephen's Mission after leaving Osage Mission in 1887. The history of the Osage Mission is discussed by Garraghan (1938, 2:493–593) and Fitzgerald (1937, 1939). Graves (1916) compiled the life and letters of Schoenmakers, Ponziglione, and other Jesuits at Osage Mission. Curtis (1977) analyzed the relations between the Quapaw and the Roman Catholic Church. M.U. Thomas (1938) discussed the Catholic presence on the Oklahoma frontier, 1824–1907.

Following an unsuccessful mission among the Kickapoo in northern Kansas, in the late 1830s the Jesuits established Saint Mary's mission among the Potawatomi, active until the late 1870s (Garraghan 1938, 2:175–235, 594–699, 3:1–65). From the Potawatomi mission, the Jesuit fathers Felix Verreydt, Christian Hoecken, De

St. Gregory's Abbey, Shawnee, Okla.
Fig. 3. Chief Enoch Hoag (Caddo) addressing Bishop Francis C. Kelly, St. Patrick's Indian School, Anadarko, Okla. After celebrating mass for more than 200 Kiowa, Comanche, Apache, and Caddo Indians, the bishop confirmed 40 individuals. Following these ceremonies, speeches were given on the mission school's lawn by Enoch Hoag, Frank Bossin (Kiowa), and the bishop (Hitta 1925). Photographed on March 30, 1925.

Smet, and others carried their missionary activity to several Plains tribes and to Northeast Indians who had relocated west of the Mississippi. In 1838, De Smet visited the Oto on the Platte River (Laveille 1915:81–82) and the Omaha on the Missouri in northeastern Nebraska. In 1855, the Omaha unsuccessfully petitioned Bishop John B. Miége, Vicar-apostolic of the Indian Territory east of the Rocky Mountains, for missionaries (Garraghan 1938, 2:465). The Ponca Indians camped on the Niobrara river in Nebraska were also visited by De Smet on his way to Sioux country in 1848 (Laveille 1915:208; Garraghan 1938, 2:463–464).

From the Potawatomi Mission at Council Bluffs, in 1839 and 1840 respectively, De Smet and Hoecken made missionary excursions among the Yankton Sioux on the Vermillion River in present-day South Dakota, opening the Upper Missouri region to Catholic missionary work (Duratschek 1947:39–59). During the 1840s and 1850s De Smet made repeated visits to the Sioux, gaining their respect and admiration. Such was De Smet's popularity among many Plains tribes that he was officially invited by the U.S. government to participate in several treaty negotiations with the Indians between 1851 and 1868 (De Smet 1905, 2: 675–681; Duratschek 1947:47). Between 1851 and his last visit to the Sioux and Upper Missouri tribes in 1870, De Smet ministered among the Yankton, Yanktonai, and Teton bands (see excerpts of De Smet's record of baptisms in Garraghan 1938, 2:472–487), visiting also Sitting Bull's camp in 1868 (Laveille 1915: 347–358; Garraghan 1930). Despite De Smet's efforts, a permanent mission among the Sioux was not established until 1876, when Abbot Martin Marty took residence at Fort Yates, on the Standing Rock reservation, which had been assigned to the Catholic Church under the Peace

* This section on the Plains missions was written by Cesare Marino.

Fig. 4. Members of the Little Shield family, on First Communion Day, Standing Rock Reservation–Ft. Yates, N. Dak. The new communicant wears a white communion dress and veil, and the man and woman wear the emblems of the St. Joseph's and St. Mary's Societies respectively. These societies were organized at Ft. Yates in 1888 at the invitation of the Benedictine Fathers at Standing Rock Reservation. When first organized the societies were oriented to enhance and reinforce the missionaries' teachings through oratory; later there were more religious discussion groups and some social activities. Before becoming members of the societies, individuals had to receive the sacraments of baptism, Holy Communion, and, if necessary, marriage. Men had badges and women had blue veils and medals. Within the societies there were many offices to be filled, such as singer, standard bearer, visitor of the sick, church servant or marshall, waiter, and horse trader (Duratschek 1947:98–99). Photograph by Frank B. Fiske, about 1910.

Policy (fig. 4). The missionary work of Abbot Martin and the Benedictines among the Sioux is discussed by Duratschek (1947:60–120) and Fitzgerald (1940). When in the early 1880s the reservations were opened to all religious denominations, the Jesuit missionaries returned among the Sioux: in 1884 they established Saint Francis Mission at Rosebud, and in 1887 Holy Rosary Mission at Pine Ridge (Duratschek 1947:121–222). In the early 1890s, the Benedictines established a Catholic mission among the Sioux on Cheyenne River reservation. For a history of Catholic Indian missions in South Dakota see Duratschek (1947).

The mission of Saint Labre among the Northern Cheyenne in Montana was opened by the Ursuline Sisters in 1884, who were joined a year later by the Jesuit fathers A. van der Velden and Peter P. Prando. In 1886, Prando

established Saint Xavier's Mission among the neighboring Crow (Palladino 1894:203–234). Together with other Italian Jesuits, he also labored among the Blackfeet, whose St. Peter's Mission, opened in 1857, was relocated several times (see Harrod 1971). In the 1880s the Jesuits also returned among the Gros Ventre and the Assiniboine on Fort Belknap Reservation, Montana, where in 1885 Frederick Eberschweiler established Saint Paul's mission (Palladino 1894:197–203). For additional sources on Roman Catholic Indian missions see Ronda and Axtell (1978). Bantin and Thiel (1984) compiled a guide to Catholic Indian mission records in Midwest repositories.

Diocesan Missions

While the Jesuits and their nun auxiliaries monopolized most of what pioneers called the interior—the "wild tribes" from the Cascades into the Rockies—diocesan and Oblate priests worked especially along the coast and the lower interior (fig. 5). There French Canadians established the main or diocesan church, which enclaved the Jesuit network. For the French subjects at its 28 posts and for Indian stability, the Hudson's Bay Company in 1838 permitted Quebec's bishop to send, through his Red River vicariate, F.N. Blanchet and Modeste Demers (Ruby and Brown 1981:81–83; Lyons 1940). By 1845 they had established the church among the 1,000 French Canadians (nearly all "married to native women of different tribes") and had preached to scores of tribes along the coast and the Columbia and Fraser rivers. Helped by their graphic invention, the Catholic Ladder, they claimed 3,000 adult converts and had baptized many hundred Indian infants and dying (Blanchet et al. 1956). Their early Vancouver and Chinook registers alone name individual Indians married, buried, or baptized from almost 50 tribes, plus some 400 names designated merely "Indian"; larger groups include 60 Cascades, 16 Chehalis, 119 Chinookans, 104 Cowlitzes, 18 Crees, 31 Iroquois, 130 Klikitats, 26 Lakes, 19 Nisquallys, 39 Okanagons, 10 Pend d'Oreilles, 14 of Chief Seattle's Suquamish, 20 Tumwaters, and 25 Walla Wallas, with lesser numbers from tribes or subdivisions like the Cayuse, Clatsop, Clackamas, Clallam, Klamath, Molala, Nez Perce, Sanpoil, Shuswap, Snohomish, Spokane, Tillamook, Lower Umpqua, and Wasco (Warner and Munnick 1972).

In the wake of confusing civil and ecclesiastical claims, Catholic authorities in Rome in 1843 combined all the American (still under Saint Louis) and some Canadian Northwest areas into a vicariate answering (through Red River) to Quebec; but in 1846 it was elevated to a separate metropolitan province of the United States (the only one besides all-embracing Baltimore). Its main division, coast versus interior, gave way in the 1850s and 1860s to a lateral split, Archbishop F.N. Blanchet holding the southern half from ocean to Rockies, his brother Augus-

Fig. 5. Service during the dedication of the Catholic church at Seshelt Indian Reserve, B.C., a Salish community. Because the size of the crowd exceeded the church's capacity the service was conducted in a tent. In the 1860s Oblate missionaries established communities designed to promote culture change among the Sechelt Indians. Missionaries often appointed a couple of village "chiefs," while other Indians were appointed to inform on fellow villagers' behavior. Those Indians who joined the community had to stop many native practices, such as potlatches and dances, abstain from alcohol, and build European-style houses (R. Fisher 1977:138–139). Photograph by Charles S. Bailey and Hamilton G. Neelands, June 1890.

tine Magloire Blanchet the northern, suffragan diocese. These shrank in 1868 respectively to the areas of modern Oregon and Washington states to allow a vast Idaho (with western Montana) vicariate. These and further remappings have relevance for the Indians, partly because dioceses or vicariates also sent missionaries (and also served Indians in the more parochial establishments), and partly because Jesuit and other missionaries later worked simultaneously in White and Indian apostolates, becoming a bridge between Indian and White worlds and a point of mutual interpretation (Bradley and Kelly 1953; Schoenberg 1962). A.M. Blanchet, at first holding an abortive Walla Walla diocese, obtained from Provence in 1847 the new Oblates of Mary Immaculate for a Cayuse (Saint Ann's) and three Yakima missions (Saint Rose's, Immaculate Conception, Saint Joseph's), where Casimir Chirouse, Charles Pandosy, and Pascal Richard labored during a war-troubled decade, eventually abandoning their turmoil for the Tulalip and allied coastal missions among tribes like the Lummi, Snohomish, Suquamish, and Swinomish (W.L. Davis 1943; Waggett 1947; Leflon 1961–1970, 3:159–177).

Diocesan missionaries besides Demers and the Blan-

chets included J.B. Bolduc (Puget Sound tribes), J.B. Brouillet (Cayuse, Umatilla, later a founder of the national Bureau of Catholic Indian Missions), Adrian Croquet (40 years among the mixed tribes of Grande Ronde Reservation, Oregon), Toussaint Mesplié (Chinookans, Wasco, Northern Paiute), Louis Rousseau (mixed tribes at The Dalles), and L.M. St. Onge (Yakima). The coastal tribes, swept by disease and progressively demoralized by White concentration there, proved a disappointing mission field. There and in the interior the diocesan role increased in the twentieth century.

Indian Catholicism

In 1845 Blanchet et al. (1956:232) estimated that 6,000 Northwest Indians were Catholic, half of them under Jesuits. By 1875 the Jesuits alone had 7,000 faithful (Burns 1966:363–364)—including 2,000 Flathead Confederates (Flatheads, Kalispels, Kutenais, Pend d'Oreilles), 2,000 on the northwestern Plateau, 500 Yakimas, 300 Spokanes, and 200 Nez Perces. Diocesan missions counted 800 Umatillas and Walla Wallas, and 400 Northern Paiutes, with 2,000 of mixed groups under Oblates at

Puget Sound (Warner and Munnick 1972).

The Cayuse War in 1847 symptomized a vast unrest affecting even remote mission Indians, contributing to a 15-year closing of Flathead missions. The Yakima War in 1855 similarly represented general antipathy to American as against French missionary control and agitated all the mission tribes. The great Northern Indians' War of 1858 was a general coalition of interior Indians centering on the mission tribes. The Nez Perce War of 1877, in appearance a romantic episode, again threatened general outbreak. In these and numerous lesser troubles, the missioners worked to restrain the tribes, protect their Indians, and secure fair treaties. They were prominent too in the 1855 treaty tour of Gov. Isaac I. Stevens of Washington Territory and contributed heavily to Stevens's scientific materials in his congressional railroad surveys. Outstanding peace makers included Cataldo, De Smet, Joset, and Ravalli, all officially acknowledged by civil authorities; more than any man, Joset ended the 1858 war, with the army sending De Smet on a subsequent peace tour (Burns 1947, 1961, 1966).

The whiskey trade, Stevens's reservation treaties, gold rushes, and the Americanizing Peace Policy of President Ulysses Grant in 1870 were blows to the Indian missions. Additional converging factors caused a precipitate decline by the turn of the century: overwhelming White settlement facilitated by the railroad, destruction of the buffalo, acculturative and land policies of the government, and the settlers' indifference and hostility contributed. Indian missions became a footnote to the White church, institutionally a failure but in terms of individual Indians a continuing success.

Ecclesiastical framework and personnel, however vital, convey little about Northwest Indian Catholicism itself, as yet unexplored despite abundant documentation. The mutually assimilative impact of Indian society and its European-American Catholicism has especially gone unstudied. Since Catholicism is a way of life, teaching implicitly as much as by dogma, any social structure such as a tribe absorbs, expresses, and transforms it differently; only ruthless abstraction allows discussion of Northwest tribal Catholicism in common terms. Moreover, since the tribes experienced progressive acculturation from 1830 to 1910 and American Catholicism experienced its own radical changes, the relational structure must be plotted in terms of evolutionary dynamics.

So international a missionary body spared these Indian societies a single nationalist formation, thus conferring more cultural freedom. Since missionaries were scarce and villages frequently moved, priests tended to plant the religious seed, minimize demands, and trust to spiritual growth—a liberating methodology. The more structured Reduction system of the Jesuits for the minority settling at a mission was minimally acculturative, though it did reject institutions like polygamy, slavery, warfare at will,

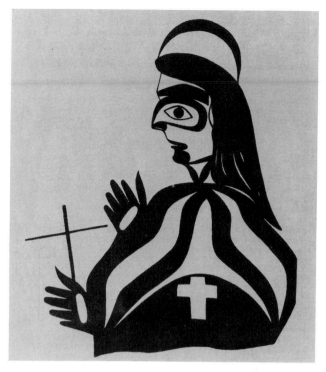

Oblate Missions, 1979 (139), Ottawa, Ont.
Fig. 6. Depiction of Christ by a Nootka artist. Incorporating Native and Christian symbols, the design originally appeared on the cover of a program for the ordination of a White priest, Rev. Terrance J. McNamara, O.M.I. The ceremony, which included parts spoken in the Salish language Cowichan and incorporated Indian motifs and traditions, took place at Quamichan Longhouse, Duncan, B.C., on July 15, 1979. Rev. McNamara worked in Indian schools and taught in a Native studies program at Camosun College, Victoria, B.C., prior to his ordination (Nyland 1979). Design by Tim Paul, Hesquiat band.

and native religious elements not susceptible of "accommodation" to Catholicism. The increasing American ambiance, threatening Indian survival, later demanded that the missions more deliberately assimilate.

A priority need for understanding the Northwest Coast and Plateau Indians—aggregating between 30 and 100 "tribes," speaking dozens of languages, dispersed over one-tenth of the continental United States, and undergoing a century-long, kaleidoscopic change (especially from converging Plains, French-Canadian, and American influences)—is a history of Christian life in each tribal entity, yielding disparate models. Tribe differed from tribe, not only in its locally determined structure and in the balance of religious elements it favored, but also in its basic psychological profile; and segment sometimes differed from segment. One unit might reject Christianity, conceive a grossly material interest, split bitterly between Protestant and Catholic, embrace one passionately but then cool, slowly swing over, or respond only to a single charismatic missionary. External forces could combine with religious to divide and redefine a tribe. Thus the buffalo-hunting or blanket Nez Perces drifted rather into the Hudson's Bay or "French" orbit, as either pagan or Catholic; the relatively sedentary faction became open to

Fig. 7. Joseph F. Brown, S.J., a Blackfeet Indian, at St. Ignatius Mission, Flathead Reservation, Mont., on the day of his ordination. The ordination was attended by Blackfeet, Flathead, and Kalispel people, many of whom wore traditional clothing. Rev. Brown is offering his first blessing as a priest. Prior to his ordination Rev. Brown was a teacher at Sacred Heart Mission, Caldwell, Idaho (Balfe 1948). During his ministry Rev. Brown served in many Indian Catholic communities. Photographed June 16, 1948.

American and Protestant influences and more readily accepted trousers and short hair.

An historical, religious sociology should analyze: the stratum of Indian catechists and lay leaders, emotional patterns in favored devotions and transformed festivities, reexpression of ascetical and mystical-prophetic tendencies, restructuring of the warrior-hunter ethos (prayer before battle, no war on Sundays, no scalping, courage and killing as charity in defending community), and novel artistic expression. Among the "difficult" Coeur d'Alenes in 27 locations for example, the mission decisively altered previous political decentralization, discredited Stellam as prototribal leader, created true headship under Vincent, and displaced him by Seltis in the 1858–1859 troubles; the mission-based economic and affiliate strength eventually

conferred on Seltis also regional hegemony. Joset discerned three separate Coeur d'Alene psychologies. Chief Vincent characterized their corresponding Catholicisms: "In the mountains there is faith, at the lake it is half and half, on the prairie it is superstition" (Burns 1966:189). The new religion had given the mountain villages an ascendancy that had helped convert the previously dominant lake and prairie people.

By 1858 the bulk of the Coeur d'Alene tribe rode annually to the Plains buffalo, had evolved a Christian war ethic, and were suffering the worst of their several spiritual crises, in fury against Whites. In the 1870s while abandoning the buffalo, shifting largely to an agricultural economy, and even loaning Whites money at interest, they remained Indian in dress, language, organization, and political independence, with a well-armed 40-man Militia of the Sacred Heart. Their annual Corpus Christi festivities attracted 1,000 Plateau Indians even from pagan tribes, with horse racing, gambling, and growing violence. As befit a tribe in which women some times performed a public role, they produced the most formidable Christian visionary-ascetic of the Plateau, Louise Sighouin (fl. 1840s). Ritual, medals, banners, beads, rousing hymns, rigorous Sunday observance, and community prayer exercised strong attraction; their precontact voluntary whippings as punishment carried over into their penitential life. The handsome Renaissance church they built without nails in the wilderness near Cataldo, Idaho, from 1848 to 1855, 40 by 90 feet and 25 feet high, became a tourist sight (fig. 1).

A more complex religious profile in expanded detail could be devised for each tribe from the missionaries' prolific writings (see archival and published sources in Burns 1966; E. Carriker et al. 1976; Schoenberg 1957). The warrior Flathead Confederates, whose mission and patriarchal leaders attracted national and European fame, particularly invite attention. The many mission and diocesan reports over four states offer data for comparative religious statistics.

Roman Catholic Missions in the Arctic

LOUIS-JACQUES DORAIS AND BERNARD SALADIN D'ANGLURE

Greenland

The very first attempts by Roman Catholic missionaries to enter into contact with the Eskimo took place in Greenland. In 1266 priests from the diocese of Garðar (in southern Greenland, created to provide for the spiritual needs of Scandinavian colonists) sailed northward along the east coast, trying to contact the Eskimos who were then living in the northern part of the country. Their expedition was unsuccessful; unable to meet any of the natives, they turned back (Seumois 1954:290). Catholics did not try to establish themselves in Greenland again until seven centuries later, by which time the majority of the population had been Lutherans for two hundred years.

In 1960 the Oblate fathers opened a house at Godthåb (Nuuk), the capital. In 1967 there were about 10 Catholic Greenlanders (Wolfe 1967).

First Missionaries

In Canada and Alaska, after difficult beginnings the Catholic missionaries won over a fairly large number of Eskimos. In 1658 an Eskimo woman, a prisoner of the Micmac Indians, was "instructed and baptized" by Jesuits and lived "in the French manner like a good Christian" (JR 45:69). Systematic work was begun by the Oblates of Mary Immaculate fathers who, shortly after their arrival in Canada in 1844, developed their apostolate in Indian territory.

Eager to expand more into the north, they made several incursions into Eskimo territory but were unable to establish themselves. As early as 1860 Roman Catholic missionaries visited Fort McPherson, on the Peel River, Northwest Territories, where they preached to Kutchin Indians and perhaps Mackenzie Delta Eskimos at the post. During the next 60 years the Oblates made a dozen missionary visits to the Eskimo, in Canada as well as Alaska (table 1).

The obstacles encountered by these first missionaries were largely political. Alaska belonged to Russia, and the Canadian Arctic, to the Hudson's Bay Company. Russia traditionally gave preference to Orthodox missionaries, while the Hudson's Bay Company, after several centuries of fierce struggles with the French Catholics, was more inclined to favor the representatives of the Church of England. For these reasons, any attempt on the part of the Catholics to build a permanent establishment prior to the cession of Alaska to the United States in 1867 and of Rupert's Land to the Dominion of Canada in 1870 was bound to fail.

Psychological and cultural barriers—insecurity, mutual suspicion—faced missionaries to the Eskimos in this early period. Fathers Jean-Baptiste Rouvière and Guillaume LeRoux were murdered near Coppermine, Northwest Territories, by two Copper Eskimos in 1913 (Whalley 1960).

The period of first contact was followed by an era of proselytism, frequently competitive. In many areas Catholics were preceded by representatives of other Christian faiths: Russian Orthodox, Presbyterian, and Moravian in Alaska; Anglican in Canada; Moravian in Labrador. Thus the second period in the history of the Catholic church in the Arctic was based on a "struggle for souls."

Alaska

The development of the Alaska missions began in 1887 with the installation of the Jesuits in the area. It was they who spread Catholicism among the Eskimo and were the moving forces in the majority of parishes in northern Alaska.

From the beginning they came in force: their numbers rose from three priests and one lay brother in 1887, to six priests and four brothers in 1890, and 15 priests and nine brothers in 1905. The number of mission residences increased from two in 1887 (the missions of Holy Cross—half Ingalik Indian and half Eskimo—and Nulato, a Koyukon Indian village where Norton Sound Eskimos traded) to six in 1905 (table 2). Nuns went to assist the fathers. They belonged to the following orders: Sisters of Saint Ann (arrived 1888), Sisters of Providence (1901), Sisters of Our Lady of the Snows (1933), and Ursuline Sisters.

When the Jesuits arrived in Alaska, Orthodox and Protestant missionaries had long been established there and the great majority of Eskimos already professed to be Christian. Thus there was competition among the religious groups, although it was not so strong as it might

501

Table 1. Oblate Missionaries Before the Establishment of Permanent Missions in the Arctic

Year	Missionary	Place Visited	Group
1860	Henri Grollier	Ft. McPherson, N.W.T.	Mackenzie Delta Eskimo
1865	Émile Petitot	Ft. Anderson, N.W.T.	Mackenzie Delta Eskimo
1868	Gasté	Keewatin, N.W.T.	Caribou Eskimo
1872	Charles Arnaud	Kuujjuaq, Que.	Inuit of Quebec
1873-1874	Isidore Clut and Lecorre	Kotlik, Alaska	Southwest Alaska Eskimo
1880	Zacharie Lacasse	Kuujjuaq, Que.	Inuit of Quebec
1881	François-Xavier Fafard	Kuujjuaq, Que.	Inuit of Quebec
1887	Lacasse	Kuujjuaq, Que.	Inuit of Quebec
1890-1896	Lefebvre	Ft. McPherson, N.W.T.	Mackenzie Delta Eskimo
1901	Arsène Turquetil	Keewatin, N.W.T.	Caribou Eskimo
1906	Turquetil	Keewatin, N.W.T.	Caribou Eskimo
1913	Jean-Baptiste Rouvière and Guillaume LeRoux	Coppermine, N.W.T.	Copper Eskimo
1920	Fallaize	Coppermine, N.W.T.	Copper Eskimo

SOURCES: Seumois 1954; Carriere 1964.

Table 2. Catholic Missions among the Alaska Eskimo

Year	Eskimo Catholics	Permanent Missions	Priests	Nuns
1887	?	2	3	0
1890	?	3	6	3
1905	3,000	6	15	33
1916	3,500	6	21	?
1925	4,000	7	21	?
1937	4,500	12	22	?
1950	5,300	14	?	?
1970	6,700	13[a]	18	17
1975	6,750	13[a]	16	27
1985	7,000			

SOURCES: Santos 1943; Seumois 1954; Catholic Church Directories 1973, 1975.
[a]Not counting Nulato (included in previous years), which is not in Eskimo territory.

have been. Orthodox, Protestant, and Catholic clergy seem to have agreed quickly on a division into zones of influence. It is even said that Orthodox and Protestant missionaries encouraged their flocks to convert to Catholicism where they could not themselves provide adequate religious services (Santos 1943).

Competition was also mitigated by the fact that the various Christian groups soon had to define themselves with respect to the United States government. As early as 1895, for example, the federal government created its own school system and abruptly discontinued subsidies for the mission institutions. This did not prevent the mission schools from continuing to function, on a private basis, but their importance was diminished.

Catholic proselytism in Alaska seems to have been much less aggressive than in Canada.

Canada

The history of the development of missions among the

Canadian Eskimo was marked by competition between Catholics and Anglicans. While the Oblates were the first to establish themselves on the west shore of Hudson's Bay (where Father Arsène Turquetil founded the Chesterfield Inlet mission among Caribou Eskimo in 1912), they were long preceded by the Church of England in the North West Territories (where Aklavik was founded by the Catholics in 1924) and in the Ungava and northern Quebec (where the first Catholic mission was opened in 1936 among Labrador Eskimos at Wakeham Bay). The belated establishment of the Catholics in northern Quebec is mainly due to the fact that from 1911 to about 1935 the evangelization of this region was entrusted to the Eudists who, in contrast to the Oblates, were not interested in opening missions in Eskimo country. There was no entente between Catholics and Protestants, as in Alaska. Each was there with the object of "saving" the greatest possible number of souls; and the most effective means for doing so was to multiply the number of mission posts, in order not to leave the field open to the opposition. This

Fig. 1. Mission work of Rev. Bellarmine Lafortune, S.J., among Bering Strait Eskimo. left, Sleds made in a workshop attached to the Holy Angels mission in Nome, established in 1905 by Rev. Lafortune, who is standing at left. The workshop supported a cottage industry and also served as a recreation center. These sleds were ordered by Vilhjálmur Stefánsson for his second exploration (vol.5:11). Photograph by Lomen Brothers, July 17, 1913. right, Teaching catechism to King I. children. Rev. Lafortune began to build a church on King I. in 1929 and spent most of his time there until his death in 1947 (Renner 1979). Photograph by Rev. Bernard Hubbard, S.J., 1938.

explains the proliferation of Catholic missions between 1930 and 1950 (table 3).

The more or less complete absence of Canadian government influence in the region before the 1950s gave the two rival forces the opportunity to develop social activities in conjunction with their religious work. Perhaps the most concrete effects of mission work in Canada were in this field: from 1925 to 1955 almost all the schools and hospitals in Eskimo territory were under the mission aegis. Here too there was competition, facilitated by government subsidies to mission schools and hospitals (Jenness 1964:45). The Catholics and the Anglicans each directed their own school and hospital systems, with no effort to coordinate their respective social services. For example, at Aklavik in 1931 there were two missions, two

schools, and two hospitals, for a population of 411 (Jenness 1964:46).

In this struggle, for which they were the stakes, the Eskimo had nothing to say. Many missionaries thought of them as "big children," subject only to instinct, whom it was necessary to "civilize" at any cost (for example, Duchaussois 1921; Buliard 1949).

It is not surprising that the Eskimo, caught between two opposing groups of missionaries, were confused. Some of them followed the Catholics at one moment, the Anglicans at another, trying to profit from the advantage, both material (implements, food, clothing) and spiritual, offered by the representatives of each church. Others syncretized, trying to interpret Christianity in light of traditional beliefs (vol. 5:503–504).

Table 3. Catholic Missions among the Canadian Eskimo

Year	Eskimo Catholics by Diocese				Permanent Missions	Priests	Nuns
	Mackenzie–Ft. Smith Diocese	Hudson Bay Diocese	Labrador-Schefferville Diocese	Total Communicants			
1925	20	80	0	100	3	6	0
1950	252	1,113	25	1,390	25	51	17
1970	600	1,850	50	2,500	29	40	7
1983	650	3,120	80	3,850	26	26	11

SOURCES: Seumois 1954; Choque 1969, 1969a; Canada 1973, 1983.

503

SSC - Photocentre, Ottawa, Ont.: 62-3233.
Fig. 2. Christmas celebration at Pelly Bay, N.W.T. Father Frans Van de Velde distributes presents to Eskimos in a large igloo constructed for the holiday festivities. Photograph by Doug Wilkinson, Dec. 1961.

Eskimo Catholicism Since 1950

It was not until after 1950, with the beginning of massive acculturation, that religious activities became less proselytizing and aggressive.

The late 1950s and early 1960s were a turning point in the history of Catholic missions in both Canada and Alaska. The missionaries must have felt the influence of the Vatican II Council and the spirit of ecumenism pervading the Christian community of the time. Competitive proselytism gave way to transformation of existing missions into organized parishes.

The complete nationalization of social services, education (in 1975 the Catholics of Alaska had only one school, Saint Mary's, in Eskimo territory, while in Canada all learning institutions were under state direction), and health favored the new importance given to the internal organization of the Catholic communities, especially in Canada. The era of conversions and competition (in every domain) was replaced by one of religious consolidation. Several missions were closed, especially in areas where the Roman Catholic church had few adherents. By contrast, the growing number of Euro-Americans working in Eskimo country required the founding of new establishments to serve this population: Barrow, Alaska (1954); Inuvik, Northwest Territories (1957); Happy Valley,

504

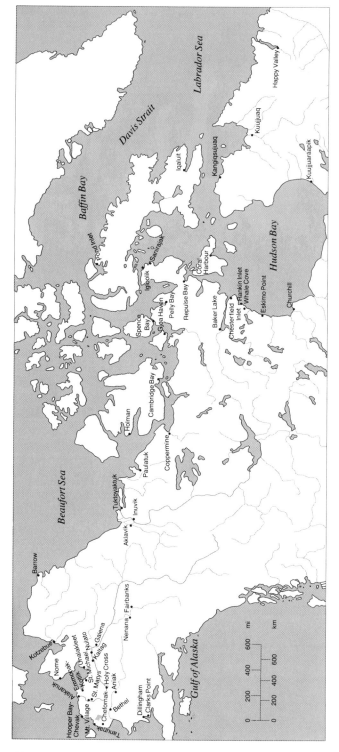

Fig. 3. Catholic missions in the Arctic region since the late 19th century.

Newfoundland (1958); and Frobisher Bay, Baffin Island, Northwest Territories (1959).

The movement toward consolidation was accompanied by a concern for Eskimoizing the church. Thus among the Canadian Eskimo the direction of several missions without resident pastors was entrusted to native catechists. In

1984 there were three such missions: Gjoa Haven, Spence Bay, and Cambridge Bay, all Northwest Territories. In Alaska, where there have been native catechists since the beginning of the century, they were given increased responsibilities. To train these catechists, special schools were founded at Pelly Bay, Northwest Territories, in 1969 and Bethel, Alaska, in 1970 (Choque 1969:12; Didier 1973:15).

The effort to bring the native population into the church organization has not yet extended to ordination of Eskimo priests. Unlike the Anglican, Protestant, and Orthodox churches, the Roman Catholic Church in Alaska and Canada has not developed an indigenous clergy. The only Eskimo to have achieved the priesthood is a Greenlander, from a country where Catholicism has only a handful of adherents.

Nevertheless, there are a few Eskimo coadjutor brothers and nuns. As early as 1929 an Alaska catechist entered the Jesuit novitiate, but he died three years later, before taking his vows. In 1933, again in Alaska, the bishop of Fairbanks founded the native community Sisters of Our Lady of the Snows (seven nuns in 1947). Similar vocations have been formed since then among the Canadian Eskimos. In 1951 the first Canadian Eskimo nun took her vows (vol. 5:388–389).

The contemporary Catholic church in the Arctic seems to have renounced proselytism and excessive competition and to have devoted itself increasingly to the task of consolidation, the formation of parishes directed by native leaders, and the preparation of a liturgy in the Eskimo language. Nor have these efforts prevented the Catholic missionaries from working, when they can, in the socio-economic domain; for example, the Canadian Oblates have contributed to the foundation of at least six Eskimo cooperatives (Haramburu 1971:130).

The impact of the Catholic missions on Eskimo society is hard to measure. The number of conversions has been largest where the Catholics were the first missionaries in the area, such as the west shore of Hudson's Bay and the Pelly Bay region, Northwest Territories. Elsewhere, in areas already under Christian influence, they have had difficulty being accepted by the population.

Unlike the representatives of other churches, the Jesuits and Oblates seem to have been little concerned with the systematic transformation of the socioeconomic conditions of the traditional or semitraditional Arctic populations. They did not force the Eskimos to settle around the missions or even directly encourage them to do so. More often, the missionaries went to the hunting camps of their followers, whose customs and conditions of life they tried, at least in part, to adapt to. It is probably this attitude of respect for traditional life that explains why the Catholic Eskimos have a much less negative attitude toward their past than have most others. This viewpoint also encouraged the missionaries to produce numerous linguistic and anthropological works; for example, the work of Petitot (1887), Métayer (1973), Mary-Rousselière (1964, 1976), and Schneider (1970). Together with other denominations, the Catholic Church gives its full support to the Eskimos' struggles for the respect of their native rights. These struggles constitute one of the main themes discussed on the occasion of Pope John Paul II's meetings with the Indians and Eskimos during his visit to Canada in September 1984.

The meticulous observation of Catholic rituals by the Eskimo does not mean that traditional beliefs and attitudes have completely disappeared. One may cite by example the case of a Canadian Eskimo who, while a fervent and informed Catholic, refused to take communion during her menstrual periods, thus perpetrating, in a Christian context, a traditional food taboo.

In 1984 the 11,000 or so Roman Catholic Eskimos were served by some 40 permanent missions (missions having at least one priest or catechist in residence), belonging to six dioceses (fig. 3).

505

The Russian Orthodox Church in Alaska

SERGEI KAN

From the beginning of its development, the Russian Church entered into close alliance with the Russian state. While the church endeavored to uphold in society the proper respect and obedience toward the government, the imperial power preserved the sanctity of Orthodoxy, the doctrines and customs of the church, and took measures for the material support of the church and the clergy. From the fourteenth century on, missionary efforts of the Russian Church were closely linked to the colonization of the native peoples of Siberia by the Russians (Lantzeff 1943). At times the christianization even outdistanced the expansion of the state. The Russian missionary activity in North America was an extension of the Orthodox Church's Siberian venture (see Bolshakoff 1943; Glazik 1954).

The first native Alaska group encountered by the Russian *promyshlenniki* (fur trappers, hunters, fur traders) were the Aleut. Between the 1740s and the 1780s, Aleut relations with the Russians ranged from military conflicts to trade and diplomacy. By the end of the eighteenth century, after a series of military defeats and accompanying depopulation, the Aleut resistance to the intruders had been crushed and their labor began to be used by the *promyshlenniki* to obtain furs of marine animals. Gradually, the Aleuts established trading partnerships and affinal relationships with individual *promyshlenniki* and began accepting aspects of Russian material and spiritual culture. The first baptisms of the Aleuts occurred in the initial stages of contact. Thus Andrei Tolstykh was perhaps the first to begin baptizing the natives in the 1740s. Steven Glotov, who discovered the Fox Islands in 1759, stayed on for three years, baptizing many Aleuts and instructing them in the rudiments of Christianity (Veniaminov 1984:233–234). Various goals were pursued by the Russian seafarers in their efforts to bring the natives into the Orthodox Church. On the one hand, they were sincere in their faith, believing in the superiority of Orthodoxy and the spiritual and social benefits it could bring. On the other hand, by baptizing the Aleuts, they brought them further under the Russian control, establishing patron-client relationships with individuals who often served their godfathers loyally. Thus the newly baptized natives represented a reliable labor force during the time when competition between fur trading companies intensified, creating a labor shortage.

Grigorii Shelekhov, whose fur trading company began to play the leading role in Alaska, was particularly devoted to spreading Christianity among the natives. After establishing Russian rule on the island of Kodiak in 1748, he began baptizing the Koniag Eskimo, beginning with the children given to him as hostages by their parents. Shelekhov established a school on Kodiak where the natives were taught reading, writing, arithmetic, as well as the basic precepts of Christianity. By the time he departed from Kodiak 40 Koniags had been baptized, and more had expressed a desire to become Orthodox.

In 1790–1791 Evstrat Delarov, the head of Shelekhov's company's establishment on Kodiak, assisted Father Vasilii Sivtsov, chaplain of the Joseph Billings expedition, in persuading the natives to be baptized, particularly students of the Kodiak school. Sivtsov baptized 93 males and 33 females, Aleut and Koniag, some of whom had already been baptized by the *promyshlenniki*, and performed what some sources believe to be the first marriage ceremony involving a Russian man and a native woman (Afonsky 1977:18).

In his petitions to the Russian government, which contained requests for the imperial patronage of his undertaking and the granting of a monopoly to his company, Shelekhov emphasized the willingness of native Alaskans to be baptized. He asked that a clerical mission or at least a priest be assigned to the Aleutian Islands and Kodiak and agreed to bear all the expenses involved in maintaining a church there. He also asked that several natives from among his best students be permitted to study for the priesthood in the Irkutsk seminary, Russia.

1793–1824

Shelekhov's requests were favorably received by the Holy Synod and the empress Catherine II. In 1793 Metropolitan Gabriel appointed a group of clergymen under the leadership of Archimandrite Iosaf Bolotov to go to Alaska. The Kodiak mission consisted of eight monks and two novices from the Valaam Monastery in northern Russia noted for the strictness of its discipline and the simplicity of its life. On the way to Kodiak, the missionaries baptized 100 Aleuts in Unalaska. On September 24, 1794, they arrived in Kodiak (Afonsky 1977:16). In 1796 the first Orthodox church in America, Holy Resurrection of Our Lord, at Saint Paul's Harbor on Kodiak, was consecrated (fig. 1).

The natives of Kodiak, particularly the young, were eager to learn the ways of their conquerors and expressed a desire to be baptized. In 1795 Iosaf reported that on Kodiak, the nearby islands, and on the Alaska Peninsula 6,740 natives (mostly Aleut and Koniag Eskimo) had been baptized and 1,573 weddings had been performed. In the same year Hieromonk Iuvenaliĭ baptized 700 Chugach Eskimos of the Prince William Sound area, and from there went to the Kenai Peninsula, where a large number of Tanaina Indians were baptized. In the meantime, Father Makariĭ labored with success in the Aleutian Islands, where he baptized 2,442 persons and married 536, including 36 mixed couples.

In 1794 Ivan Golikov, Shelekhov's partner, petitioned Metropolitan Gabriel for the establishment of a separate see in America and promised his company's support for the bishop and the clergy. In 1796 the Holy Synod and the government responded favorably. The new prelate was to bear the title Bishop of Kodiak, functioning as a vicar of the Irkutsk Diocese. The government awarded 4,030 rubles annually for the upkeep of the bishop and his residence; The rest of the money was supposed to be provided by the Shelekhov-Golikov Company. Archimandrite Iosaf was to become the first American bishop. In 1799 he was consecrated in Irkutsk, but on the return voyage to Alaska, he and most other members of the Kodiak mission perished in a shipwreck.

The activity of the Alaska missionaries was severely hampered by these losses as well as the illness of several of the remaining monks, who concentrated their efforts on the natives of the Kodiak area, holding church services, teaching children, and instructing adults in gardening and various Russian trades. Until the 1820s the relationship between the missionaries and the Russian-American Company, established in 1799, was rather strained (Afonsky 1977:32–41; Kovach 1957:63–69, 81–114). The missionaries objected to the "immoral" behavior of the *promyshlenniki*, especially their "free use" of native women and various forms of exploitation and mistreatment of the natives. Prior to 1799, the monks were also embroiled in the quarrels between rival commercial companies (Afonsky 1977:32–38). In 1799 the Russian-American Company not only received monopoly powers for the commercial use of Alaska resources but also became the official representative of the Russian state in Alaska. Thus the chief manager of the company, Aleksandr Baranov, embodied both civil authority and economic control. The church, as in Russia, had to be subservient to the interests of the secular authorities, which in turn were obliged to care for it. A collective memorandum against the company's abuses of the natives

and the missionaries was sent by the monks in 1804. In response to it, the Holy Synod sent Hieromonk Gedeon to investigate the situation and to revive the activity of the mission.

Gedeon stayed in Kodiak from 1804 to 1807 and was able to improve the relationship between the missionaries and the company to a certain extent. He also organized a two-grade school for the natives where not only reading and writing but also catechism, grammar, geography, and history were taught. By 1807 it enrolled 100 students and was maintained by the company. One of its best students, a Creole, Prokopiĭ Lavrov, accompanied Gedeon to Saint Petersburg, where he studied at a seminary. He returned to Kodiak in 1810 to serve as a priest, but could not get along with the *promyshlenniki*, and left for Siberia a year later. Gedeon recorded ethnographic data on the Koniag and translated the Lord's Prayer into their language (L.T. Black 1977a; Valaam Monastery 1978; Lîâpunova 1979).

By 1823 the only remaining missionary in Alaska was Father Herman, who spent 14 years as a hermit on Spruce Island where he died in 1837. He won the admiration of the local natives with his kindness and dedication to defending them from the Company's mistreatment. Father Herman's school and orphanage on Spruce Island contributed to the strengthening of Orthodoxy among the Koniag. A person of extraordinary spiritual strength and charisma, he began to be seen as a holy man capable of performing miracles and was canonized as the first Alaska saint by the Orthodox Church in America in 1971 (Valaam Monastery 1978; Golder 1972).

Although the Holy Synod decided in 1811 to close the episcopal see in Kodiak, Tsar Alexander I disagreed and ordered the Synod to look for a candidate to fill the see. During the period between 1794 and 1821, the financial situation of the Alaska mission was rather poor. The 1799 charter given to the Russian-American Company did not specifically mention its responsibility for the mission. Only in 1821, when the charter was renewed, did the company become obliged to support the mission and insure an adequate number of priests. The company provided 7,142 rubles annually to support the mission, plus another 6,300 rubles accumulated from offerings to the church in the colonies. The Russian government provided 5,450 rubles annually (Tikhmenev 1978–1979, 1: 196–197). In 1816 a priest was assigned to Novo-Arkhangel'sk (the new capital of Russian America, present-day Sitka), but only in the 1820s were the systematic missionary activities resumed.

1824–1840

When he arrived in Unalaska in 1824, Father Ivan Veniaminov found every Aleut baptized, including children who had been baptized by their parents. Veniaminov (1984) described the Aleuts as people who knew little

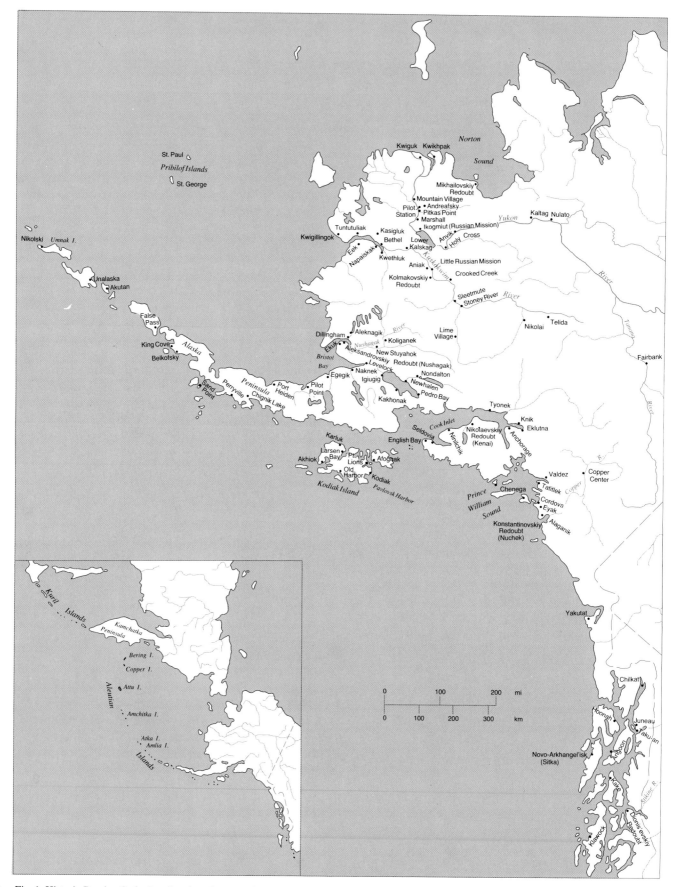

508   Fig. 1. Historic Russian Orthodox church and community sites in Alaska (Beaver 1979; B.S. Smith 1980).

about Christianity, but whose devotion to the new religion was strong and sincere. They had already abandoned shamanism and destroyed their shamanistic paraphernalia. Most of the "heathen superstitions" had either been abandoned or were losing their force. They listened carefully to Veniaminov's sermons and were exemplary in their performance of religious duties, including confession, communion, and fasting. They even prayed in private in their homes. In addition many Aleuts were eager to learn to read and write Russian and Aleut.

Veniaminov built the first church in the Aleutian Islands in 1825, the Church of the Holy Ascension in Unalaska. He also built a chapel on Umnak Island. He learned the local language and, with the help of an Aleut chief, Ivan Pan'kov, designed an alphabet and translated the Scriptures into Aleut (L.T. Black 1977). By 1840 he had already translated and published a short catechism, the Gospel of Saint Matthew, and other religious texts. A man of many talents, Veniaminov wrote textbooks, taught school, and conducted meteorological, zoological, and ethnographic research (Veniaminov 1984; Stepanova 1947; P.D. Garrett 1979; Kan 1984).

Veniaminov labored in close cooperation with the first Creole priest in Alaska, Father Iakov Netsvietov , a native of Atka, who studied at the Irkutsk Seminary and was appointed the first Atka priest in 1828 (Netsvietov 1980, 1984). In 1830 he built a church in Atka. He helped to translate and corrected the translation of the Gospel of Saint Matthew into Aleut made by Veniaminov. He also translated into Atka Aleut the first chapter of the Gospel of Saint Luke and other religious texts. The Atka parish included Amlia, Amchitka, Attu, Copper (Mednyĭ), and Bering islands and Kurils, all of which Netsvietov visited regularly.

Veniaminov resided in Unalaska till 1834. During that period he became the first priest to visit the Bristol Bay region, where on the Nushagak River the Aleksandrovskiy Redoubt was built by the Russian-American Company in 1818. There he preached to and baptized 13 Aglurmiut Eskimos and gave permission to the redoubt manager to baptize natives when they themselves requested it. When Veniaminov returned in 1832, he found that the parish had grown to include 70 natives. A chapel was built in Nushagak upon the order of the company chief manager.

In 1834 Veniaminov was transferred to Novo-Arkhangel'sk (New Archangel), where he remained until 1838. The Russian-American Company established a permanent foothold there in 1804, but its relationship with the Tlingits remained strained. The Russians rarely ventured outside the fort, and the Tlingit traders were allowed to enter it only in small numbers ("Russian and Soviet Eskimo and Indian Policies," fig. 2, this vol.). This made Veniaminov's missionary work very difficult. He was able to begin his proselytizing only in 1837–1838, after a

smallpox epidemic killed many Tlingit shamans and elders, upholders of traditional religion. It undermined the natives' trust of their own healers and demonstrated to them the power of the Russians, invincible to the new disease. Gradually some of the Tlingit began accepting the vaccine administered by the company. Veniaminov obtained permission of the local "chiefs" (heads of matrilineages) to visit their homes. He also conducted outdoor services at the Dionis'evskiy Redoubt established by the Russians at the mouth of the Stikine River, in the territory of the Southern Tlingit. The services attracted the attention of a large number of natives (Barsukov 1887–1901, 3:641–647; Veniaminov 1984; Kan 1984).

By 1840 20 Sitka Tlingits had been baptized, some of them women living with the Russians and Creole employees of the company, others Tlingit chiefs and aristocrats courted by the company and attracted by the splendor of the Orthodox ritual and the possibility of establishing special ties with high-ranking company officials who acted as their godfathers. One of the obstacles to the Tlingit conversion was their perception of the Sitka Aleut as Russian slaves who had lost their freedom after accepting the Russian religion (Tikhmenev 1978–1979, 1: 191). It appears that the Tlingit reaction to missionization had a lot to do with their indigenous notions about rank and prestige (Kan 1983, 1985:198).

Veniaminov played the key role in strengthening and expanding the Alaska mission. His approach to missionization represented a Russian Orthodox tradition of considerable tolerance of native customs, emphasis on using native languages, and reliance on persuasion rather than force or bribery in gaining converts. Veniaminov was inspired by his predecessors in Alaska, who in 1799 received an instruction similar to the one given to Siberian missionaries in 1769 (Afonsky 1977:22–23). On the basis of this and other documents as well as his own experience in Alaska, Veniaminov (1899) composed his famous *Instruction*.

According to Veniaminov, the missionary had to rely on the power of his sermons and not on force, threats, presents, or the backing of local authorities. He had to be sensitive to the local ecological, economic, and cultural circumstances and traditions, and not to demand that his native parishioners carry out all the duties that the Christians in Russia did. For example, the rules of fasting could be relaxed in areas where meat was the major staple, or fewer restrictions were to be imposed upon the marriages among the natives than among the Russians. An Orthodox missionary was never to deride native customs but instead had to observe them carefully and record detailed information on local culture. While he had to discourage the "bad" customs contrary to Christianity, such as shamanism, he also had to give the natives credit for the "good" ones, such as helping the needy. He was also strongly encouraged to learn the local language, to be able to preach without interpreters, and to translate religious texts and prayers. Veniaminov's ultimate goal was the creation of alphabets for all the Alaska native languages and the spread of literacy among them. In accordance with the views of his predecessors in Siberia and Alaska, Veniaminov insisted on training natives to become clergymen. Thus, similar to the Russian-American Company, which relied heavily on Creoles and natives in its operations, the Orthodox Church in Alaska relied on the Creole and native clergy.

It must be pointed out that there existed another missionary tradition in Russia that emphasized coercion and the Russification of native peoples as its ultimate goal. Its proponents looked with suspicion at the translations of Christian literature into native languages and preferred to rely on Russian priests rather than native ones (Vdovin 1979). This approach gained more support in the end of the nineteenth century, when the Russian government was dominated by nationalists and Russificators (Popov 1874; Kharlampovich 1904). In Alaska itself, Veniaminov's enlightened approach to missionization was not put into practice by all missionaries, many of whom lacked his education and patience. The tolerance of all Orthodox missionaries, including Veniaminov, had its limits, and their journals and reports refer to admonitions of native Orthodox for continuing practices such as shamanism, polygamy, memorial feasts, and dances (Netsvietov 1984: 54–58; Salamatov 1862–1863; Kamenskii 1985; Kan 1984, 1985, 1987).

Despite this, Veniaminov's ideas exerted a strong influence on the Alaska mission, especially after 1840, when he was consecrated in Saint Petersburg as Bishop Innocent, "Bishop of Kamchatka, the Kuril and Aleutian Islands." Russian America finally had its own bishop and was no longer administered from Irkutsk. In 1841 Bishop Innocent returned to Sitka with several new clergymen to begin his energetic work in Alaska. His main efforts were directed toward establishing an administrative diocesan center in Sitka, traveling throughout the enormous diocese, establishing a seminary in Sitka to train native clergy, and creating new missionary districts in Nushagak, Kenai, and Kuikhpak (Yukon) (Afonsky 1977:57; Barsukov 1897–1901).

In his report on the conditions of the Orthodox Church in America published in Russia in 1840, Veniaminov (1972) summed up the results of the first period of Russian missionization. As of 1840, the Alaska diocese included the Sitka parish consisting of 1,035 Russians and Creoles, 78 Aleuts, and 20 Tlingits. The Unalaska church had 42 Russians, 212 Creoles, and 1,497 Aleuts. The Atka parish numbered 50 Russians, 145 Creoles, and 587 Aleuts. It included Bering Island with its 147 Aleuts brought from Atka, and the Kuril Islands inhabited by 99 Ainu, 104 Eskimos brought from Kodiak, and 9 Russians. The Kodiak parish included 73 Russians, 482 Creoles, 794

Tanainas, 448 Chugach Eskimos, and 1,831 Koniag Eskimos. The Nushagak River area had over 200 baptized Eskimos. In addition a small number of Bering Strait Eskimos were baptized in 1838 at Mikhailovskiy Redoubt in Norton Sound. Twenty-five Russian and 15 Creole members of the Church resided in Mikhailovskiy and Novo-Aleksandrovskiy redoubts. Finally the Russian Church in North America included 39 Pomo Indians of California baptized at Fort Ross.

The Aleut were singled out by Bishop Innocent as exemplary Christians (fig. 2). Although some secular Russian observers (for example, Golovin 1979:21) claimed that the reason for the Aleut dedication to Orthodoxy was their total submission to Russian authority, most scholars agree that by the middle of the nineteenth century their spiritual and social culture had already undergone significant changes due to the incorporation of Russian customs and beliefs, that Christianity had become the core of the Aleut world view replacing aboriginal religion to a large extent, and that the church served as the focus of community integration. Some scholars (L.T. Black 1977: 100) also suggest that a similarity between the indigenous Aleut religion and Orthodoxy contributed to the success of Christianity among them. Many Aleut churches and chapels (including two chapels on the Pribilof Islands) were supported by donations from Aleut hunters and built by them under Russian overseers ("Russian and Soviet Eskimo and Indian Policies," fig. 1, this vol.). Some of the carving inside these churches was done by native craftsmen trained by the Russians (D.J. Ray 1981:58–59; L.T. Black 1982:127). Village parishes elected their own wardens, who were usually local chiefs or other high-ranking persons. Despite the general success of Orthodoxy, the Aleut did retain some of their pre-Christian beliefs, glimpses of which appeared in some of the missionary reports as late as the 1860s. For example, a priest on Atka reported that in 1862 some Aleut hunters consulted as an oracle a mummy of a famous ancestor hidden in a cave. The purpose of their visit was to obtain information on the outcome of their hunting expedition (Salamatov 1862–1863).

The only other native Alaska people classified by the company as "truly dependent" were the Koniag. While their status and relationship with the Russians resembled that of the Aleut, their Christianity, according to Bishop Innocent, was much weaker, despite a continuous presence of missionaries on Kodiak. Many of the Koniag remained unbaptized, and many of the baptized ones did not consecrate their marriages in the church. "Adultery" (wife exchange?) was prevalent, confessions frequently avoided, and church services rarely attended, except on holidays. Worst of all, shamanism persisted, and most Koniags refused inoculation during the 1838 epidemic of smallpox, while the Aleut accepted it gladly. The bishop concluded that the Kodiak church needed better organiza-

right, Presbyterian Histl. Soc., Philadelphia.
Fig. 2. Russian Orthodox Church on the Aleutian Is. left, Very Reverend Archpriest Ismael Gromoff, an Aleut from the Priboloff Is., holding a Russian icon. Rev. Gromoff serves in the Holy Ascension of Our Lord Cathedral in Unalaska. The icon, along with others, was hidden by Aleuts during the World War II evacuation of the islands (Hess 1981). Photograph by Bill Hess, 1981. right, Sod covered church with free-standing belfry on Attu. Photographed about 1900.

tion and the Koniag had to be protected from a bad influence of the Russian *promyshlenniki* whose own Orthodoxy was far from perfect. In fact, in 1841–1842 a turn for the better occurred under the leadership of a new manager of the Kodiak department of the company and a new priest. Many shamans accepted baptism and allegedly abandoned their practices; many Christian natives repented and improved their church attendance and behavior. Religious texts and prayers were being translated into their language by the missionaries.

The natives of the Kenai Peninsula, Prince William Sound, and the Alaska Peninsula were classified by the Company as "semi-dependent." In reality their dependence on the Russians was very limited and their contacts with company employees were generally limited to trade, and some participation in local hunting parties sent out by the Russians. Only a few of the natives were hired to work for the local company posts and trading centers on a long-term basis. Their Christianity was characterized by Bishop Innocent as weak, due primarily to rare visits by the missionaries and occasional conflicts with the Russians. Shamanism and other traditional religious practices were particularly strong among the Tanaina, both Christian and non-Christian.

The Nushagak natives, also considered "semi-dependent," were described as resembling the Aleut in their peaceful character and voluntary acceptance of baptism. At the same time, they were only rarely visited by priests, who could not cover the large territory they inhabited. In 1842 a special Nushagak mission was created under the leadership of Father Il'ia Petelin. The people listened to

him gladly and became diligent in the fulfillment of their religious duties. By 1842 from 200 to 250 Eskimos had joined the Nushagak church, and some even burned the masks used in aboriginal ceremonies to prove the sincerity of their conversion (Van Stone 1967:24–25).

1840s–1867

The 1840s–1850s period was the time of territorial expansion, opening of schools, and increasing the number of clergy. Bishop Innocent was behind all these activities. In 1842 he undertook his first missionary journey throughout the diocese, visiting Kodiak, Unalaska, Atka, Kamchatka, and Siberia. The journey took about one year of traveling by company vessels, native bidarkas, and dog sleds. He made three more such trips before 1850. In 1843, a two-story building was constructed in Sitka by the Russian-American Company to house the bishop, the Chapel of Annunciation, the seminary established in 1845, the library, and the orphanage ("Russian and Soviet Eskimo and Indian Policies," fig. 3, this vol.). The goal of the seminary was to train clergymen, primarily Creole and native, to serve the Alaska diocese. Among its subjects were several native languages, as well as medicine, and even physics, which was supposed to help the missionaries understand nature and fight native superstitions. The seminary numbered over 40 students. In 1858 the archbishop's cathedra was transferred to a Siberian town, Blagoveshchensk, along with the seminary. The Holy Synod approved a plan to create two vicar bishops for the large diocese. Archimandrite Pëtr Sysakov, the dean of

511

the Sitka seminary, was consecrated as the Bishop of Novo-Arkhangel'sk.

During the last 25 years of the Russian-American Company, the educational system improved considerably. The Orthodox Church was responsible, as in Russia itself, for the elementary education of the children in each parish. Church schools existed in most of the major settlements and trading centers. While most of the Russian, Creole, Aleut, and Koniag Eskimo children received elementary education, only a small number of the total population of other Orthodox native groups received instruction (Starr 1972:5–12). In 1841 there were six religious schools in Russian America, with 10 teachers, 146 students, and 260 dropouts. In 1851 7 schools had 12 teachers, 316 students, and 16 dropouts (Starr 1972:32). The instructional materials used in the Alaska schools were similar to those of the Russian parish schools.

According to its new charter of 1844, the Russian-American Company continued supporting the Church, including supporting the clergy and construction of the major churches, including the Sitka Cathedral of Saint Michael in 1848. In some places, such as Unalaska, the sale of candles and voluntary offerings (including gifts of furs from parishioners sold by the missionaries to the company) maintained the churches and chapels. Native Church workers received the same compensation from the company as its other employees. According to Black (Netsvietov 1980:xx), the clerical salaries in Alaska were far in excess of salaries of the Russian clergy elsewhere. On the other hand, their living conditions were often more difficult than in Russia, especially in the more isolated settlements. The parish priests and other clergymen supervised native morality, defended natives from abuses by company employees (which declined somewhat), distributed medications, and even administered vaccination during epidemics. Between 1840 and 1867, when Alaska was sold to the United States, the Orthodox Church grew from four churches and four priests to one cathedral, nine churches, 35 chapels, nine priests, and two deacons. Its membership was 11,562 in 1860 (table 1) and, according to Afonsky (1977:64), reached the figure of approximately 15,000 in 1867.

Creole clergymen continued to play an important role in missionary work, especially in the Aleutians and in the Kuikhpak mission. Netsvietov, when transferred to the Yukon in 1845, brought several Creoles to assist him. The Kuikhpak and other missions located in the more remote areas depended heavily on the assistance of Creoles and natives (see Netsvietov 1984:ix-xx, 469–482).

Among the main difficulties faced by the missionaries were the small number of church workers and the great distances they had to travel to visit their parishioners. For that reason most of the missions were located either on the coast or along the rivers, which could be navigated during the summer. In the winter some of the missionaries traveled by dog team. Not all the missionaries possessed the spiritual strength, tact, courage, and the knowledge of the local cultures and languages, qualities demanded by Bishop Innocent and demonstrated by people such as Netsvietov. Some clergymen were discouraged by the difficulties, including their parishioners' persistent aboriginal beliefs and lack of devotion to the church. In the last decades of the Russian presence in North America, more missionaries arrived from Russia. Some were sent to this remote diocese by their superiors trying to get rid of undesirables. They lacked understanding of the local conditions and especially resented the missions' reliance on Creoles and natives. They also criticized what they perceived as lenience in Creole and native marriages, and the involvement of some of the clergy in trading relationships with the natives as a means of survival (Netsvietov 1984:xviii-xx).

The degree of devotion to Orthodoxy among various native groups continued to differ. The Aleut continued to be seen as the best Christians. Many of the men and some of the women were literate in Russian and Aleut and knew many of the church hymns and prayers. By 1867 the Russian Church was perceived by them as part of the Aleut way of life. The Koniag Eskimo's Orthodoxy was strengthened, particularly during the period of Father Pëtr F. Kashevarov's service, 1850–1879. He was the first priest born and raised on Kodiak and was very popular among the Koniag. According to his records, in 1867 the Kodiak parish included 65 Russians, 703 Creoles, 19 Tlingits, and 1,605 "Aleuts" (mostly Koniag and some Aleut).

In the 1840s the Kenai mission was established, with the construction of a chapel at Nikolaevskiy Redoubt in 1841 and the arrival of a special missionary, Hieromonk Nikolai, in 1845. Nikolai reported in 1848 that the natives listened to him attentively, carried out their Christian duties diligently, and gave up their traditional songs and dances, replacing them with religious songs (some of them in their own language), which they became very fond of. Among the converts were shamans who allegedly became good Christians. In 1859 the Kenai mission included 80 Tanainas. In his later reports (Townsend 1974), Hieromonk Nikolai mentioned the persistence of shamanism and his punishment of shamans with genuflections. It appears that the Tanaina behavior in this respect resembled that of many other native Alaskans, who promised to abandon "paganism" at the time of baptism but subsequently returned to it. Some of them did not see any contradiction between Christian and indigenous beliefs, which led to the development of religious syncretism in many areas. By 1867 all the Tanaina (close to 1,000) were at least nominally Christian (Townsend 1974).

The Kenai mission included other native groups, such as the Chugach Eskimo, who numbered 450 in 1859 and resembled the Koniag in their attitude to Orthodoxy. The

Table 1. Orthodox Christians in Russian America in 1860

Nationality	Males	Females	Total
Russians	576	208	784
Creoles	853	823	1,676
Aleut and Koniag	2,206	2,185	4,392
Tanaina	430	507	937
Chugach	226	230	456
Eyak	73	75	148
Ahtna	17	1	18
Maarmiut	18	1	19
Aglurmiut	19	20	39
Aziagmiut (?)	105	101	206
Kusquqvagmiut	755	640	1,395
Kuigpagmiut	226	153	379
Ingalik	262	213	476
Kolchan	97	93	190
Tlingit	221	226	447
Total			11,562

SOURCE: Tikhmenev 1978-1979, 1:384.

Eyak Indians had also been baptized and numbered 148 in 1859. Finally a few Ahtna Indians from the Copper River who visited Konstantinovskiy Redoubt in Prince William Sound were baptized there. In 1859 they numbered 18, and in 1862 Golovin (1979:26) reported that "their nomadic life and the distance from the Konstantin redoubt, as well as their casual attitude toward their new religion, means that they very rarely participate in religious ceremonies, and many have forgotten that they are Christians."

The size of the Nushagak mission increased dramatically during this period. Under Father Il'ia Petelin, the Church of the Apostles Peter and Paul was built in 1844. In 1848 the Church numbered 1,080 natives. While some of the older people refused baptism, the younger ones were in favor of it and brought their children to be baptized. In the early 1850s Hieromonk Nikolai visited all the villages in the region and was well received. Some of the Eskimos were afraid to be baptized, believing that it would lead to contamination with epidemic diseases whose origin was in the poison allegedly put by the priest into the communion cup. While the inhabitants of the communities located closer to the mission were more dedicated to the church, those occupying the upriver area refused communion and behaved improperly during services (DRHA 2:136–137; see also Van Stone 1967). The Kuskokwim River Eskimo were baptized by missionaries from Nushagak as well as Ikogmiut on the Yukon.

The spreading of Orthodoxy among the Eskimos and Athapaskan Indians of the Yukon River area was largely the result of Father Iakov Netšvietov's labor, from 1845 when the mission center was established at Ikogmiut till 1863 when he left for Sitka (Netšvietov 1984). Netsvetov traveled extensively throughout his enormous parish, baptizing Kuigpagmiut, Maarmiut, Kayaligmiut, as well as some Kotzebue Sound Eskimo. He also reached and baptized some of the Ingalik, Kolchan, and Lower Yukon Koyukon. Under his leadership a chapel was built at Mikhailovskiy Redoubt in 1845 and the Church of the Elevation of the Holy Cross in Ikogmiut (Russian Mission) in 1859.

The missionary influence was stronger in areas located closer to Mikhailovskiy Redoubt, Ikogmiut, and the Kolmakovskiy Redoubt on the Kuskokwim River (Oswalt 1980). Farther from these centers of Russian activity, native converts continued pre-Christian practices. Thus unable (or unwilling) to forbid a potlatch at Ikogmiut, Netsvetov asked the natives to postpone it until after Christmas. The Eskimo followed his request. In another community he allowed the natives to complete their ceremonies and then began hearing their confessions and administering communion. He found shamans in more remote villages to be his major adversaries, instigating other natives to refuse baptism or communion (Netšvietov 1984). In the coastal village of Pastolik the native dwellings were decorated with paper icons, and certificates of baptism were carefully preserved in wooden boxes, but many of the Christians could not remember their own baptismal names (Zagoskin 1967:281).

The state of the Tlingit missionization was also rather weak. Although the number of converts steadily increased, especially in the early 1840s, and reached 447 in 1860, more than half the Sitka Tlingit and the great majority of the inhabitants of the rest of the Tlingit communities remained unbaptized. The majority of the converted natives had only a vague understanding of Orthodoxy, attended the services infrequently, and often failed to confess and receive communion. The construction of Trinity Church for the Sitka Tlingit on the border between the Russian fort and the native village in 1849 and the translation of some prayers and parts of the Gospel in the Tlingit language contributed to the increase of the church membership but did not produce dramatic changes. The hostile relations between the Russians and the Indians and the limited interaction between them were serious obstacles in Tlingit christianization. In 1855 the local Tlingit attacked the Russians and desecrated the Trinity Church. Many of them, particularly the aristocracy, preferred to attend the services at Saint Michael Cathedral where the Russians prayed, but the Russian-American Company could not allow large numbers of Indians to enter the town. In the middle of the 1860s, the Tlingit still demanded gifts in return for accepting baptism and insisted that high-ranking company officials serve as their godfathers (Militov 1865). Few church marriages or burials were reported for this period, with most Tlingits continuing to cremate their dead. Some agreed to have their relatives buried by the church but later exhumed the bodies and cremated them. While some Tlingit converts, particularly those working for or married to the Russians, were probably more dedicated, the majority of them seemed to perceive baptism as a means to achieve various political and commercial ends. Toward the end of the Russian presence, the Tlingit from other communities began to show interest in the church, but the missionaries lacked the means and were afraid to travel through the bays and inlets of southeastern Alaska (Kan 1983, 1985, 1987).

1867–1917

The sale of Alaska to the United States in 1867 radically changed the status of the Orthodox Church. It became a Russian mission in a foreign country. The church retained the right to serve the needs of its members—natives, Creoles, and a small number of Russians who chose to remain in Alaska—but it lost its economic base, the financial support of the Russian-American Company. Many of the clergy returned to Russia, so that in 1870 there were only four priests left in Alaska, two of them in Sitka.

In the late 1870s, various non-Orthodox missions began proselytizing among the Alaska natives, including those who identified themselves as Orthodox. Many of these new missionaries had a negative view of the Orthodox mission and frequently attacked it as backward, corrupt, and even anti-American. Secular authorities often sympathized with and supported American missionaries in their struggle with Orthodoxy over the souls of native Alaskans. After 1885, when Sheldon Jackson, a Presbyterian minister, became the federal superintendent of education for Alaska, Alaska was divided among the non-Orthodox missions. Many of the public schools in 1880s–1900s were staffed with missionaries who combined secular and religious subjects. In 1903 there were 82 missions and missionary churches in Alaska, only 16 of them being Orthodox.

During the Americanization of Alaska, the Orthodox Church managed to survive and even strengthen its position in some parts of Alaska. In 1870 the Holy Synod established a new independent episcopal see in San Francisco, where the first Orthodox Church was created in 1868. Archimandrite Ioann Mitropol'skii was appointed the Bishop of this new Aleutian and Alaskan Diocese. In 1872 the bishop's cathedra and the Ecclesiastical Consistory, as well as the pastoral school, were transferred to San Francisco. (The same cathedra, located in New York, governed the entire Orthodox Church in America in 1987.) By the decree of the Russian government of August 4, 1870, the State Council had to provide financial support for the Alaska churches. Additional support was provided by the Missionary Society established in 1870 in Russia. However, the Alaska mission remained poor, especially compared to its Protestant and

Fig. 3. Parish schools. top, Father Ivan Soboleff, right, with Tlingit students at the St. Andrew parish school, Killisnoo. Photograph by Vincent I. Soboleff, 1896–1908. bottom, Classroom in the bishop's residence in Sitka. After 1867, Indian and White children attended classes here. Seminary students were also taught here from 1906 to 1910. Paintings of Tsar Nikolai II, left, and Father Ivan Veniaminov, second from left, hang on one wall. Photograph by Elbridge W. Merrill, 1899–1917.

Catholic rivals. Some local psalm-readers and teachers had to resign or combine their duties with various other occupations in order to survive.

In 1876 Bishop Ioann was recalled to Russia, and the Diocese had no bishop till 1879; the pastoral school closed during that time. Among Alaska's subsequent bishops, Bishop Vladimir Sokolovskii, Bishop Nikolai Ziorov, and Bishop Tikhon Belavin were the most active. Bishop Vladimir brought 22 clergymen with him to America and began using English in the church services. He also reestablished the pastoral school that trained clergymen for Alaska (some of the students were brought from Alaska as children). Bishop Nikolai established missionary schools in Sitka and Unalaska and promoted the organization of native temperance societies and brotherhoods. Bishop Tikhon became the Archbishop of the Archdiocese of the Aleutians and North America and transferred the ecclesiastical administration to New York in 1905. During the same period a special vicariate for Alaska was created. A survey of the Alaska vicariate for the year 1905 indicates that it was comprised of 17 churches and 72 chapels; it was served by 17 priests and 21 other church workers. Its membership was 10,376, including 64 Russians, 501 Serbs and other Slavs, 2,166 Creoles, 3,618 Eskimos, 1,906 Aleuts, 2,026 Indians, and 95 others (Innokentiĭ 1906:295).

The Alaska clergy in that era consisted of two major types. On the one hand, many of the parishes, especially in the Aleutians and on the Yukon, were served by the Alaskan-born Creole and native priests and subordinate clergymen. They were more tolerant of their parishioners' transgressions and often spoke the local native languages (B.S. Smith 1982). They were also poorly educated in some cases. On the other hand there were missionaries from Russia, some of whom were well educated and urbane and longed to return to their motherland (Kan 1984; Kamenskiĭ 1985). They were Russian patriots and nationalists, but in the Alaska context they could not engage in Russificatory activities similar to those carried out by some Orthodox missionaries in Russia (Vdovin 1979). A few of them followed Veniaminov's tradition of recording information on native cultures (Kamenskiĭ 1985).

The Russian Alaska mission continued its educational efforts, increasing the number of schools and students (fig. 3). The largest schools were located in parishes where natives were numerous and strongly dedicated to Orthodoxy, as in Unalaska and Kodiak. In some communities, where native congregations were large, the Russian school competed with non-Orthodox and public schools and consequently had fewer students. In some areas, the Orthodox parish schools played the role of public schools. Contrary to Protestant accusations, Orthodox schools taught English and by and large did not instill anti-American attitudes in students. Besides the subjects taught in parish school in Russia, missionary schools in Alaska instructed native children in hygiene, "moral rules," and gardening. Some schools also taught reading and writing in the native languages using Cyrillic alphabets.

In 1906 a seminary was reopened in Sitka to train clergymen for Alaska. Many of the students were natives who later played an important role in the survival of Orthodoxy in Alaska after 1917. Native Alaskan languages were included in the curriculum. Thus the Orthodox Church continued its tradition of presenting Christianity in the native languages. In the post-1867 era, a number of translations of religious texts and prayers into Tlingit, Aleut, Yupik, and other Alaska languages were printed and used in church services and instruction (Oleksa 1979). Despite these efforts many of the schools in smaller and more remote parishes had only a small

Alaska Histl. Lib., Juneau: top, PCA 1; bottom, PCA 57–43.

Fig. 4. Russian Orthodox brotherhoods among the Tlingit. top, Saint John the Baptist Society, Killisnoo. The first brotherhood was established in Sitka, and other communities soon followed. front row, second from left, Father Ioann Soboleff, the local priest; fifth from left, Bishop Innocent. Photograph by Vincent I. Soboleff, 1905–1906. bottom, Society of Temperance and Mutual Aid of St. Michael the Archangel and the Brotherhood of St. Gabriel, Sitka. Members of the St. Michael Brotherhood wear diagonal sashes and those of St. Gabriel wear crossed sashes. St. Michael Brotherhood was established in 1896. A split occurred in 1904 and a number of members established the St. Gabriel Brotherhood. The split followed the lines of two feuding clans (Kan 1985). Photograph by Elbridge W. Merrill, 1915–1920.

number of students, and the rate of absenteeism remained high. The school year continued to be short, because the children were removed from the schools by their parents during their annual subsistence-related migrations.

A new phenomenon in the religious life of native Alaskans were the church brotherhoods and the societies of temperance and mutual aid (fig. 4). These sodalities were modeled upon the organizations established by the Orthodox Church among the Slavic immigrants in the United States and Canada. In Alaska their major goals were to fight intemperance, strengthen ties among church members, create funds to help the poor, and to increase the role of native parishioners in maintaining church property. In some parishes the brotherhood statutes were more specific and included prohibitions against gambling, quarreling, shamanism, memorial feasts for the dead, and other vices, old and new (Kamenskiĭ 1985; Kan 1985). Brotherhoods had their own insignia and elected their own officers. The clergy supervised brotherhood activities and used weekly brotherhood meetings to instruct the members in religious and moral subjects. In some communities, such as Sitka, brotherhoods became semi-independent native sodalities, whose leadership tended to be the traditional aristocracy. While undoubtedly strengthening native Orthodoxy and community solidarity these organizations (at least among the Tlingit) did little to fight "heathen customs" and inadvertently strengthened the indigenous social system (Kan 1985). At the same time, temperance societies in many communities helped bring down the level of drinking.

The Orthodox Church was one of the few voices that spoke out against the mistreatment suffered by native Alaskans after 1867. Orthodox priests helped draft petitions from natives to local officials and occasionally to the president of the United States, in which the true story of the Americanization of Alaska was told. For example, a petition sent to the president by the Sitka Tlingit leaders in 1897 stated several grievances against local businessmen and the White population in general (Khliantych 1897; Kamenskiĭ 1985:134–136). The best known among such documents was a letter sent to President William McKinley by Bishop Nikolai of Alaska in 1897. The bishop attacked as adversaries of his church and of the native people of Alaska the Alaska Commercial Company and Sheldon Jackson (Afonsky 1977:85; Anonymous 1897). One of the most common complaints voiced by the

Orthodox priests in their reports to church superiors and American officials was the forcing of Orthodox children to attend non-Orthodox schools and to live in non-Orthodox orphanages, such as the Methodist orphanage in Unalaska.

Although Orthodox missionaries were in favor of "native progress," they did not equate christianization with Westernization, as the Protestants did. Following Veniaminov's tradition, they were ambivalent about technological and economic progress of the natives, and argued that traditional subsistence activities and even some indigenous social institutions had to be preserved. This position, the use of native languages, greater tolerance of indigenous customs, or at least the absence of power to fight them, made Orthodoxy generally more attractive to the conservative segment of native communities, where the split between the "conservatives" and the "progressives," that is, the more acculturated, began to occur (see Kan 1983, 1985; B.S. Smith 1980).

Individual Parishes

Aleuts remained among the most loyal members of the Orthodox Church. In the second half of the nineteenth century they identified so strongly with the Russian culture and Orthodoxy that many of them did not recognize or understand the meaning of the sale of Alaska and continued to consider themselves Russian subjects.

left, Alaska Histl. Lib., Juneau: PCA 57-35; right, Glenbow-Alberta Inst., Calgary, Alta.: ND-1-162.
Fig. 5. Funereal and mortuary observances incorporating Native and Orthodox features. left, body of the chief of the Tlingit *łukʷnaxʔádi* clan laid out in his lineage house where weekly meetings of the St. Michael Brotherhood were also held. The chief's wife sits by the Euro-American coffin flanked by an Orthodox candlestick. An arch decorated with the name of the brotherhood and other Christian symbols decorates the wall, right. The Native items are all decorated with crests. A ceremonial hat with potlatch rings, out of which hangs an ermine panache, rests on the coffin. Such hats are valuable heirlooms of a clan or house lineage. On the wall, left, hangs a mantle that appears to be painted hide with fur trim along the top edge. Leaning against the mantle are probably a dance baton, left, and chief's staff, right. Photograph by Elbridge W. Merrill, 1900–1910. right, Eskimo cemetery in Andreafsky (St. Mary's). Lomen Brothers photograph, 1905–1915.

Some parents were reluctant to send their children to public schools out of fear that they would forget how to speak Russian. Aleut resistance to Methodist missionary propaganda was so strong that the new mission failed to attract any natives. Native chiefs continued to be elected as church wardens, local people served as lay readers, and the church itself remained the focus of community integration.

The situation on Kodiak was similar, with the exception of the behavior of some Creoles influenced by Americans. They began to despise the Koniag Eskimo and decreased their financial support of the church. Nevertheless they remained in the same church with the natives, since Orthodoxy does not allow schism in parishes. Unlike the Aleut, most of the Koniag could not read, write, or even speak Russian, and in smaller villages rarely visited by a priest, people no longer understood the meaning of prayers in Church Slavonic. Nevertheless most of the Koniag remained Orthodox, and the Protestants had little success on Kodiak (Shalamov 1904).

The Chugach Eskimo were also predominantly Orthodox. Christianity was stronger in Nuchek (Hinchinbrook Island), where the priest resided, but was weaker in outlying villages. Missionary work was revitalized by a Kodiak-born Creole priest, Father Andrew Kashevarov, who served in Nuchek from 1894 to 1897.

The Kenai mission experienced difficult times between 1867 and 1881, when there was no resident priest and a Creole, Vasiliĭ Orlov, remained in charge. In the 1880s–1890s missionary work was revived, with the center of the mission located in Nikolaevskiy Redoubt. Ninilchik, Seldovia, and several other villages had literate lay readers and maintained their chapels and churches in good condition. Smaller villages did not see the priest so often, and Christianity there was weaker. According to Townsend (1965:293), most of the Tanaina considered themselves Orthodox, accepted Christian sacraments, celebrated Orthodox holidays, and attended services when the priest came through. However, the aboriginal beliefs and practices remained strong, including shamanism, polygamy, wife exchange, and memorial feasts for the dead. Although burial had already replaced cremation, grave houses were still constructed on top of the graves, with food, water, and personal possessions of the deceased placed inside (fig. 5). Some Christian beliefs were syncretized with indigenous ones and became part of the people's daily life. Local chiefs (Russian *toions*) and their assistants remained in charge of parish affairs, as they had been since the time of the Russian-American Company. In the 1900s, in the Lake Iliamna area, non-Orthodox missionaries converted some Tanainas from the Orthodox faith, but many of the Kenai people remained Orthodox.

The Eyak remained Orthodox too, but until the 1890s they were rarely visited by the priest and had a vague idea of Christianity. In the 1890s–1900s the Chugach area missionary began to visit Eyak villages, reviving Orthodoxy among this small group. The number of Orthodox among the Ahtna increased during this period, because natives visiting Knik and other coastal communities for trade were baptized there in the 1880s–1890s. In the 1910s a priest from Tatitlek visited the Ahtna at Copper Center. By the end of the nineteenth century, over 100 Ahtnas were listed as members of the Russian Church, but their communities did not have a resident priest.

After 1867 the number of Orthodox Eskimo in the Nushagak area continued to grow. By the end of the 1870s, it was one of the largest Orthodox parishes in Alaska, with its membership reaching 2,400. The strength of Orthodoxy was proved when the Moravians attempted to establish a stronghold on the Nushagak in the 1880s (VanStone 1967). Despite the Moravian efforts to force Orthodox children into their schools and the gifts distributed among the adults, very few natives converted. The Moravian mission closed in 1906. Conversion to Orthodoxy did not mean the disappearance of traditional beliefs and ceremonies. Wife-exchange, shamanism, offerings to carved "idols," pre-Christian mortuary practices, and memorial feasts were particularly strong among the Kiatagmiut and the Tuyuryarmiut.

Similar difficulties confronted the Orthodox mission on the lower Yukon. Orthodoxy was stronger among the Kuigpagmiut residing closer to the center of the mission in Ikogmiut (fig. 6) (vol. 5:238). The more distant groups, especially the Kusquqvagmiut of the Kuskokwim River area, were nominally Christian but engaged actively in shamanism, believed in sorcery, and preferred to dispose of their dead in wooden boxes placed on the surface with logs piled up on top. The influence of Christianity on the aboriginal religion was minimal, even around Saint Michael and Ikogmiut (E.W. Nelson 1899:421). Many of the Yukon and some of the Kuskokwim area Eskimo remained unbaptized around the turn of the century. Some of them continued to believe that baptism brought illness and death. The situation improved somewhat during the service of a dedicated missionary, Father Amphilokhiĭ Vakul'skiĭ. As the head of the Yukon mission between 1900 and 1912, he traveled widely throughout the area by dog sled and boat. The Moravian mission at Bethel established in 1885 was more successful than the Nushagak one, but many of the Kuskokwim River natives remained Orthodox (Oswalt 1963a).

In the Athapaskan region, Orthodoxy was the strongest among the Kolchan. Although there was no resident priest on the upper Kuskokwim River, by 1900 all the Kolchan had become Orthodox and were characterized by the missionaries as more devout than the Kusquqvagmiut Eskimos (Hosley 1966:147). The first churches were built at Nikolai and Telida villages in 1914–1915, with the two communities becoming the focal points for the remaining Kolchan. The aboriginal potlatch merged with the Ortho-

top, Alaska Histl. Lib., J.E. Thwaites Coll., Juneau: PCA 18-8; bottom, W.A. Durham Coll.: PCA 85-17.
Fig. 6. Russian Orthodox churches near Eskimo dwellings in southwest Alaska. top, Transfiguration of Our Lord Church and semisubterranean, sod-covered Eskimo dwellings, Nushagak. Photograph by John E. Thwaites, 1906–1932. bottom, Elevation of the Holy Cross Church and a chapel in the community of Ikogmiut (Russian Mission). The Kuigpagmiut structures in the foreground are summer dwellings. Photograph by William A. Durham, 1890–1910.

dox Christmas in 1915 (vol. 6:621). Orthodoxy among the Ingalik declined by the end of the nineteenth century, due to irregular visits by the Ikogmiut missionary and competition from Roman Catholics, who in 1888 established a mission at Holy Cross, and Episcopalians, who in 1887 established a mission at Anvik. In 1895 the Russian Church still claimed over 100 Ingalik members, but in the 1930s Osgood found only a feeling of nostalgia for the Orthodox Church among the Ingalik (Van Stone 1979). Orthodoxy remained strong among the Lower Yukon Koyukon Indians in the 1870s–1880s, when Catholic missionaries arrived there. However, the rare visits by the Russian priests and the establishment of a Catholic Mission at Nulato in 1887 led to the disappearance of Orthodoxy among this group (Loyens 1966).

518   The Orthodox Church was much more successful

among the Tlingit. In the initial period after the sale of Alaska, its influence on the Sitka Tlingit remained weak, with clergymen complaining about native indifference to church services, pagan burial practices, and so forth. In 1876 Bishop Ioann reported to the Holy Synod that the Tlingit demanded payment for embracing Christianity and sending their children to school (DRHA1:162). Besides these difficulties, the Orthodox mission had to compete with the Presbyterians who began proselytizing in southeastern Alaska in the late 1870s. This well-financed mission established schools and churches in several Tlingit communities, including Sitka, and made some converts. However, by forcing native children into the school and attacking important traditional practices such as the potlatch, the Presbyterians lost their appeal among the more conservative segment of the Tlingit population. In the mid-1880s this group began voluntary conversion to Orthodoxy, and by the early 1890s, a large part of the Sitka Indians were Orthodox. This movement coincided with the increase of the Russian missionary activities in southeastern Alaska (see Kamenskiĭ 1985; Kan 1983, 1985). During that period Orthodoxy spread to most Tlingit communities, including Juneau, Hoonah, Killisnoo/Angoon (fig. 4), Taku-an, Chilkat, Yakutat, Kake, and Klawock. In the 1900s the Inland Tlingit traveled from Atlin, British Columbia, to Juneau to be baptized and to celebrate Christmas. The lack of funds and manpower, as well as the competition from Presbyterian and Salvation Army missionaries, prevented Orthodoxy from establishing permanent parishes in many Tlingit villages. By 1917 only Sitka, Juneau, Hoonah, and Killisnoo had Russian churches, and only in Sitka were Orthodox Indians the majority of the population. Nevertheless, Orthodoxy had strong influence on the native world view, particularly in the sphere of mortuary rituals (fig. 5) (Kan 1987), beliefs about power, and so forth. Orthodox holidays became part of the Tlingit annual cycle and the native fishermen began the spring fishing season after their boats had been blessed by the Russian priest (Kan 1985).

1917–1985

The Russian revolution of 1917 brought new difficulties to the Orthodox mission in Alaska. The financial support from the government ended, and very few clergymen continued to arrive from Russia. Many priests served for years without receiving a salary and had to find additional jobs to support their families. Many communities left without a resident priest had to rely on local native readers. To a large extent, it was due to their efforts that Orthodoxy survived its most difficult years in Alaska. The condition of the Alaska natives was just as poor as in the previous period, especially prior to World War II.

In the twentieth century the non-native population of

Fig. 7. Weddings. left, Wedding party in the Bering Strait Eskimo community of St. Michael. Photograph by Lomen Brothers, July 1, 1906. right, Marriage of Peter and Christine Kosbruk in St. John the Theologian Church, Perryville, a Pacific Eskimo community on the Alaska Penninsula. Photographed 1937–1941.

Alaska increased dramatically and so did the non-Orthodox missionization. Although the Orthodox Church did lose some members in this period, it was also able to gain new ones. The Aleut and Koniag and other Eskimos of the Alaska Peninsula remained loyal to the Church (vol. 5:178) (fig. 7), by and large rejecting the proselytizing of fundamentalist churches (D.M. Jones 1976; N.Y. Davis 1971; Berreman 1955). Many Aleuts remained literate and used the Russian alphabet to write religious and secular texts in Aleut (Ransom 1945). Orthodox brotherhoods continued to be active throughout the 1940s–1950s. The Chugach also remained devout, with new parishes established in Cordova and Valdez.

By the 1930s all the Ahtna had become Orthodox, many baptized in the mid-1920s by the Cordova priest, Father Tikhon Lavrishchev. However, by the 1950s Orthodoxy was replaced by fundamentalist Christianity and other non-Orthodox denominations (Frederica de Laguna, personal communication 1985). The Tanaina have been influenced by Pentecostal and other Protestant denominations since the 1950s, and some of them converted. Nevertheless, strong Orthodox communities remained in the Cook Inlet and the Lake Iliamna area (Townsend 1965). The Nushagak and the Kuskokwim regions remained Orthodox strongholds. Although other denominations continued their work in this part of Alaska, many natives remained Orthodox, and new churches were built in several communities (fig. 8). Orthodoxy became firmly established in Eskimo social and religious life, with church holidays structuring the annual cycle and church brotherhoods taking on many of the functions of village councils (Oswalt 1963; Van Stone 1967). Orthodoxy also continued to be the major denomination among the Eskimo of the lower Yukon, between Ikogmiut and Saint Michael, as well as among the Kuskowim River Kolchan (Hosley 1966). Many of the Sitka and, to a lesser extent, Juneau, Hoonah, and Angoon Tlingit remained Orthodox. In Sitka and Juneau, Orthodoxy tends to be the religion of the traditionalists and their families (Kan 1979–1984, 1983, 1985, 1987).

While the Christian beliefs and rituals have gradually replaced many of the indigenous ones, some of the key traditional religious notions and ceremonies have been syncretized with Orthodoxy and thus survived. For example, the Tlingit cycle of mortuary and memorial rituals has incorporated the Orthodox custom of having a memorial feast following a memorial church service on the fortieth day after a person's death (Kan 1987). The Orthodox Church itself has adopted more tolerant attitudes toward native customs since the 1960s (Tarasar 1975:291–293).

The 1960s and 1970s were the beginning of a new era in the life of Orthodoxy in Alaska (Tarasar 1975:289–300). Ten native priests were ordained by Bishop Amvrossy Merejko, 1956–1966. Under Bishop Theodosius Lazor, 1967–1972, the number of priests increased to 22. A number of middle-aged native men, who had served as church wardens and readers, were ordained to serve their villages as priests, after studying with Orthodox priests in Sitka. In 1967 a new parish consisting of representatives of all native Alaska peoples was established in Anchorage. In 1986 the parish of Fairbanks (with a similar membership) was working on building a church. Since 1968 periodic all-Alaska diocesan assemblies have taken place, bringing together clergy and lay leadership. In 1970 the Orthodox Church of Russia formally granted total self-government to the Orthodox Church in America, though the Alaska Diocese retained the name "Russian Orthodox" for

Fig. 8. Communion service during the consecreation ceremony of a new Russian Orthodox church in Kasigluk, an Eskimo community in the Yukon–Kuskowim delta. The man near the table is a deacon. Photograph by James H. Barker, 1977.

historical reasons (Tarasar 1975).

In 1973 under Bishop Gregory Afonsky the Saint Herman Pastoral School was established. In 1977 it became a seminary training native priests and other church workers, including women (who can serve as readers, choir directors, and teachers). The number of priests in Alaska tripled after 1941; in 1985 there were 33 priests serving 80 parishes, more than half of them natives (Joseph P. Kreta, personal communication 1985). In addition native people served as deacons and readers and carried out other church duties. The revival of Orthodoxy in Alaska coincided with (and was stimulated by) the increase of the native political activism and cultural renaissance, as well as the improvement of native education, medical services, and economic conditions, particularly since the passage of the Alaska Native Claims Settlement Act in 1971. The Orthodox Church continued to use native languages in its services, especially in areas where they were still widely used, for example, Central Yupik. At the same time it has largely replaced Church Slavonic with English to meet the needs of the younger people for whom English is the main language. Although, by and large, the Orthodox Church does not extend its influence beyond the communities that have been Ortho-

dox for many years, several churches were built in native villages that never had them, for example, Mountain Village on the Yukon. Nine new churches were consecrated in 1985. The number of Orthodox people in Alaska in 1985 was approximately 15,000–18,000 (Tarasar 1975).

The Alaska identity of the Orthodox Church has been strengthened by the canonization of two Alaska saints, Saint Herman the Wonderworker in 1970 and Saint Innocent, the Apostle of America in 1977, and two martyrs, Saint Juvenalii and Saint Peter the Aleut in 1980.

Sources

Most of the primary sources on the history of the Orthodox Church in Alaska are in Russian (B.S. Smith 1980). Important documents on the subject are in the Frank A. Golder Archives (Library of Congress, Manuscript Division, and the Suzzalo Library of the University of Washington, Seattle) and the Yudin Collection (Library of Congress, Manuscript Division). The largest collection in the United States is the Alaska Church Collection, Manuscript Division, Library of Congress (Basanoff 1933; Dorosh 1961), which has been microfilmed. It contains documents on most of the Alaska parishes, primarily for

Fig. 9. Interior of Sts. Peter and Paul Chapel, Pitkas Point, an Eskimo community in southwest Alaska. The chapel is decorated for Christmas. The star, lower left, is used for the Orthodox Christmas ritual of starring during which carols are sung. Photograph by Myron Wright, 1978.

the period 1794–1867, with some parishes covered to the early twentieth century. Excerpts from this collection were translated into English in the 1930s by scholars from the University of Alaska, Fairbanks (DRHA 1936–1938). A valuable source of demographic and historical data is the *Index to Baptisms, Marriages and Deaths in the Archives of the Russian Orthodox Greek Catholic Church in Alaska* (i.e., Alaska Church Collection, 1816–1866; 1890–1899; 1900–1936). It is available on microfilm (20 rolls) from the manuscript Division of the Library of Congress. In addition English translations of some documents from the Alaska Church Collection appeared

in Oswalt (1960), Shalkop (1977), Townsend (1974), Kamenskiĭ (1985), and, most important, Netsvietov (1980, 1984). Besides the Alaska Church Collection, parish records and other documents could be found in the Archives of the Alaska Diocese in Kodiak, Alaska, and the Archives of the Orthodox Church in America in Syosset, New York. The Archives of the Alaska Diocese contain the valuable Veniaminov Papers (1821–1840), which are letters, reports, and travel journals of Bishop Innocent (see also Sturdza 1857). Several parishes are also represented there, with many of the documents pertaining to the Yukon Mission. Most of the documents cover the 1846–1915 period (see B.S. Smith 1980). The Archives in Syosset contains miscellaneous parish records and the correspondence of local clergy with the church headquarters; most materials represent the period between the 1880s and the 1970s. Some of the Alaska parishes, including Sitka, the center of the Alaska Diocese, have kept a few documents from the nineteenth and the first half of the twentieth centuries (Kan 1979–1984). The Alaska Historical Library in Juneau contains some primary sources on the history of the Orthodox mission in Alaska in the nineteenth and the twentieth centuries, including the M.Z. Vinokouroff Collection. References to the activities of the Russian Church could also be found in the Records of the Russian-American Company, 1802, 1817–1867, located in the National Archives. Several Orthodox periodicals contain references to the church in Alaska. The most important among them is the *Russian Orthodox American Messenger*, published in Russian (and English during some periods), between 1896 and 1973. *Tserkoynye Vedomosti* [Church Register], published in Russia, 1888–1917, featured articles and short reports on Alaska. Barbara S. Smith (1980) has completed an annotated index of Alaska references in the *Russian Orthodox American Messenger*.

One of the major collections of primary sources on this subject in the Soviet Union is the *Tsentral'nyi Gosudarstvennyi istoricheskii arkhiv* (especially *fond Synoda*) [The Central State Historical Archive, the Synod Collection] in Moscow.

White Conceptions of Indians

ROBERT F. BERKHOFER, JR.

From the very beginning of White penetration of the western hemisphere, Europeans realized that it was inhabited by peoples divided among themselves. Even Christopher Columbus on his first voyage distinguished between peaceful and hostile Indians on the basis of cannibalism and military ardor. Subsequent Spanish explorers, conquerors, and writers noted the differences among the many Indian societies of the New World, especially between the Aztec and Inca civilizations and other peoples. Both French and English explorers remarked the contrasts between the Eskimos and other peoples to the south of them. Early English adventurers into Virginia spoke of "Indians," "savages," and "infidels" in one breath at the same time as they carefully studied the various alliances and specific characteristics of the tribes around Jamestown. The ability to differentiate one tribe from another only increased as White knowledge accumulated over time, but the general term *Indian* or a synonym continued to coexist with and in spite of such information. If past Whites understood the many differences among Native American peoples, why did they persist in using the general designations, which, semantically speaking, required the lumping together of all Native Americans as a collective entity in spite of their diversity?

The "Indian" is the Native—or original—American conceived and imagined as an "other." In the paradigm of human understanding of other human beings according to race or ethnicity, it is the rule for the members of the self-designated in-group to divide themselves from those they categorize as an outgroup. The idea of the Indian was the classification of the original, native inhabitants of the western hemisphere as alien and other by fifteenth- and sixteenth-century Europeans and their descendants. In this paradigm, the others are understood as without, or at least deficient, in the virtues, traits, values, and habits self-consciously ascribed to the in-group by its members. Such withoutness or deficiency can be evaluated as good or bad, noble or ignoble, in the others' behavior, outlook, and institutions, but always in contrast to the in-group's artifacts, government, religion, and economy. Such a conceptual paradigm lay at the base of the whole conception and understanding of the "Indian" from the time of Columbus to the present.

The definition and characterization of *Indian* as a general term for Native Americans as collective other in the White mind is the subject of this chapter as opposed to the history of the images and conceptions of specific tribes by Whites or of Native Americans' imagery of themselves collectively or individually. General surveys of imagery are Hoover (1976), Berkhofer (1978), R. Sanders (1978), Takaki (1979), Turner (1980), Drinnon (1980), Stedman (1982), Dippie (1982), Lemaire (1986).

Foundations: Early European Nomenclature and Imagery

What Europeans termed the discovery of the New World and its inhabitants was, of course, a product of the changing economic and intellectual world of Western Europe at the time. The rising spirit of nationalism and the emergence of nation-states in that area spurred exploration of the non-European world and divided it into national spheres of colonization. The printing press disseminated information in words and pictures about the new-found lands and expanded European knowledge of other peoples and their ways of life (Chiappelli 1976; Honour 1975a, 1975:1–117; Bucher 1981; Dickason 1984: 3–84). But if Europeans added a fourth part, America, to the traditional tripartite division of the inhabited world, they comprehended that new world in terms of their familiar conceptual categories and values (Elliott 1970, 1972; Todorov 1984; R. Sanders 1978). That New World peoples were perceived and comprehended according to old ways of thinking during the first century and one-half after Columbus's voyages can be seen in the terminology, the methods of description, and the overall images of them contained in the White explorers' accounts and the travel literature of the period.

The specific term Indian as a general designation for the inhabitants of North and South America derives from Columbus. Under the impression that he had landed among islands off Asia, he called the peoples he met *los Indios*. So natural did the term seem to him that in the letter announcing his discovery its first appearance occurs as an aside (Jane 1930:3, 5, 17). Regardless of whether Columbus thought that he had landed among the East Indies or near Japan, he probably would have used the same term for the natives, because India stood as a synonym for all Asia east of the Indus River at the time, and Indies was the broadest term available for all the area he claimed according to royal grant (Lach 1965, 1:4; Morison 1974:26, 30). Even after Columbus' error was corrected by subsequent explorations, the Spanish continued to employ *Indios* for all peoples of the New World. From the Spanish term came eventually the French *Indien*, the German *Indianer*, and the English *Indian* as the general name for original North and South Americans.

Not only was the general term a bequest of the Spaniards to Europe but so was the basic imagery of the Indian. In the mid-sixteenth century what educated Europeans knew of the geography and inhabitants of the Americas came mainly from Spanish sources. Collections of travel accounts and chronicles of Spanish discoveries appeared as early as the first decade of the 1500s, but the first comprehensive collection of travel literature was compiled by Ramusio (1970) in three volumes during the 1550s. In the third volume devoted to the New World, all the extracts and journals are of Spanish origin except for Giovanni da Verrazzano and Jacques Cartier for the French. Likewise, the first translated materials on the Americas published for the English in the same decade drew largely upon Spanish accounts except for some reports of Italians (Arber 1885). The only important exceptions are the reports of the cannibalistic Tupinamba of South America (Hemming 1978:1–23).

The basic themes that would pervade so much of White thinking on Native Americans for the next few centuries were well developed in the literature on the Spanish conquest and settlement of the Americas. Using the twin criteria of Christianity and civilization of the Spanish variety, Indians were found wanting in a long list of attributes: letters, laws, government, clothing, arts, trade, agriculture, marriage, morals, metal goods, and above all religion. Judgments upon these lacks might be kind and sympathic or harsh and hostile, but no one argued that the Indian was as good as a European in this early period.

Neither discovery that the new lands were indeed a New World nor the conquest of the Aztec and Inca civilizations changed the essential understanding of the Indian as a generic conception for the inhabitants of the Americas. Knowledge of Aztec and Inca achievements in art, agriculture, or social and political organization added to the concrete information about the diversity of peoples but did not alter the overall stereotype of the Indian (see B. Keen 1971:172; cf. Pagden 1982:75–79; Elliott 1972). If the Aztecs, for example, possessed sophisticated governmental, agricultural, and social systems, they also practiced a religion that appeared to European eyes as the very worship of the Devil with its emphasis on human sacrifice. Indians might therefore have the wrong kinds as well as too little religion or government in addition to the other negative qualities attributed to the stereotype, but they

were always in Christian error and deficient in civilization according to European standards of measurement.

Under this impression, no wonder Spaniards debated what means were necessary to bring the Indian in line with their ideals of Christian civilization. Was the very nature of the Indian so bestial, so far removed from civility, as to demand force and ultimately enslavement to accomplish his conversion to Christ and Spanish ways? Or was the Indian sufficiently rational and potentially "human," therefore able to achieve these goals through peaceful means or example alone? The Dominican friar Bartolomé de Las Casas, appalled by the depopulation caused by Spanish exploitation of the natives, was the most vigorous publicist and lobbyist for the side favoring peaceful means and Indian freedom. He therefore portrayed the Indians as essentially virtuous:

> God created these simple people without evil and without guile. They are most obedient and faithful to their natural lords and to the Christians whom they serve. They are most submissive, patient, peaceful and virtuous. Nor are they quarrelsome, rancorous, querelous, or vengeful. Moreover they are more delicate than princes and die easily from work or illness. They neither possess nor desire to possess worldly wealth. Surely these people would be the most blessed in the world if only they worshipped the true God (Las Casas in Hanke 1935:20).

His opponents argued for the conquest and the enslavement of the Indians on the basis of their natural inferiority, their sinfulness, and their barbarous institutions. In short, they resorted to an image of the bad Indian (Hanke 1935, 1949, 1959, 1974; Friede and Keen 1971; Pagden 1982; Todorov 1984:146–182).

To what extent these conceptions of the Spaniards became the preconceptions of the French and the English in their subsequent contact with Native Americans is difficult to tell, for the basic values and orientations of the Spaniards lie at the foundation of French and English thinking also. Thus, whether influenced by Spanish reports or not, French and English explorers saw Native Americans in the light of Christianity and civilization and made the same comparisons as had the Spaniards. That such judgments had to be the outcome of contact of French and Englishmen with Indians was reinforced by the type of native societies and cultures that they encountered. Rather than peoples with sophisticated social and governmental organizations like the Aztec, the explorers of these two nations met "wilder" Indians, and so perhaps the denomination of these peoples as savages seemed more appropriate to early explorers from those two countries (Chinard 1911; Atkinson 1935; Jaenen 1976; Gagnon 1984; Dickason 1984). For early English imagery, there are many good books (Cawley 1938: 344–395; Blanke 1962:186–282; R. Nash 1982:55–86; R.B. Davis 1978; Pennington 1979:175–194; H.C. Porter 1979; Sheehan 1980; Kupperman 1977, 1980; Quinn 1985: 157–237; Fishman 1979). 523

Fig. 1. Illustrations from *Mémoires de l'Amérique septentrionale* (1703), a narrative by Lahontan. left, *Sauvages* of Canada. The males are labeled: left to right, a *sauvage* going to the hunt; a married or elderly *sauvage* promenades through the village; a young *sauvage* promenades through the village. The woman is labeled: a female *sauvage* carries her infant in her arms. All the clothing and the cradleboard have little semblance to native costume. The tunic worn by the hunter is similar to a coat worn by a French explorer. The other 2 males carry double-curved bows unlike any bow used by Northeast tribes. These 2 figures have a distinctly Classical appearance in costume and stance. While Northeast tribes did live in palisaded villages, this village has been rendered in a simplified form. right, Proselytizing to Indians. Two White men use an image of a Christian God to convert natives. One Indian wears a South American Indian feather headdress and skirt. Lahontan never went to areas where such trees grow. The shelters are merely rudimentary drawings of longhouses. Lahontan was in Canada from 1683 to 1693, where he served as an officer in the French army. During this period he became familiar with Senecas, Cayugas, and other Iroquois, Ojibwas, Ottawas, and possibly Arikaras whom he hunted with, was allied with, or fought against. He was selected, because of his ability to speak Algonquian, in 1687 by Gov. Brisay de Denonville, to head a detachment at Ft. St.-Joseph on the Sainte-Claire River and in 1690 by Gov. Louis de Buade de Frontenac to negotiate peace with the Iroquois. Lahontan discussed philosophical questions regarding the Noble Savage, his origins, and spirituality in his widely read travel narratives (1703) on North America (Hayne 1969). Engravings.

Sixteenth-century Frenchmen, Italians, and Englishmen generally employed a variant of the Latin *silvaticus* 'forest inhabitant, man of the woods', for the Indian. Although English usage switched to Indian as the general term for Native Americans in the seventeenth century, the French continued to use *sauvage* (fig. 1) as the preferred term until the nineteenth century. The image behind this term is probably the ancient one associated with the "wild man." According to medieval legend and art, the wild man was a hairy, naked, club-wielding child of nature who existed half-way between humanity and animality. Isolated from mankind in woods, caves, or clefts, he hunted animals or gathered plants for his food. French and English explorers were therefore both surprised and not surprised by the cultures they encountered when compared to what they expected of "wild" strangers. According to Morison (1971:428), French in the early period always called Indians *sauvages*, later *peaux-rouges*, and sometimes *indigènes* (see also Dickason 1984:63–80). On the English use of savage, consult Kupperman (1980: 111–112).

Less used than *Indian* and *savage* but still prevalent among early English synonyms for Native Americans were the terms *infidel, heathen,* and *barbarian.* Both *infidel* and *heathen* were based on religious criteria and derive from ancient Jewish and early Christian distinctions between themselves and other peoples. In fact, at the time of the initial English colonization of the New World, the word "nation" still retained its older meaning of a people or race usually heathen as well as the modern meaning of country or kingdom. In brief, the term designated a foreign people of another religion or culture as well as the territory they occupied. Given such ambiguous meaning for the word and the nationalistic outlook emerging then, small surprise that Englishmen applied "nation" to what later was called a "tribe." The latter term did not really replace the former until well into the nineteenth century. *Barbarian* contrasted, of course, with one who was civilized and stemmed from the ancient Greeks' prejudice against peoples whose languages sounded like babble to them and therefore seemed without reason (Pagden 1982:15–26, 119–145). By the sixteenth century, *barbarian* and *heathen* had come to be almost interchangable in English usage (Rowe 1964:5–7).

In comparing their own societies and cultures with those of the Native Americans, Europeans created images both favorable and unfavorable to the Indian. Chinard (1911) concluded that the French descriptions of Indians in the sixteenth century could be classified as favorable or unfavorable in their estimate of Indian characteristics and virtues (see also Kennedy 1950; Jaenen 1976:12–40; Dickason 1984:61–84). The same may be said of sixteenth- and seventeenth-century English accounts (Cawley 1938: 344–395; Blanke 1962:186–282; H.M. Jones 1964:1–70; Nash in Dudley and Novak 1972:55–86; Berkhofer 1978: 3–31; Sheehan 1980:9–64; cf. Kupperman 1980). By the middle of the seventeenth century, then, the practice of using a general name for all Native Americans regardless of social organization or of cultural complexity was well established, and with the general name went a set of stereotyped characteristics evaluated favorably or unfavorably according to the commentator.

Increased knowledge of the fundamental differences among peoples of the world also seemed to promote Europeans' recognition of the similarities among themselves. The transition in thinking can perhaps be seen best in the increasing use of "Europe" for self-reference during the fifteenth and sixteenth centuries in preference to the older "Christendom." Another indication would be the new word *continent* to characterize the new geographical notions (Washburn 1962:2–4). The basic attributes ascribed to continents showed most vividly in the symbolic pictures applied to title pages and to maps or in the representation of various peoples in the pageants of the period, but the same meaning lay behind the more prosaic written descriptions and discourses on the peoples of the world. Europeans portrayed their own continent in terms of intellectual, cultural, military, and political superiority, for Europa was usually pictured wearing a crown, armed

with guns, holding orb and scepter, and handling or surrounded by scientific instruments, palette, books, and Christian symbols. While Asia was richly dressed, rarely did she possess superior signs of power, learning, or religion. America and Africa appeared naked, and America usually wore a feathered headdress and carried a bow and arrow. In short, Europe represented civilization, Christianity, and learning confronting nature in America (Hay 1957; Honour 1975a, 1975:84–117; Dickason 1984: 202–229; Boorsch 1976:503–515).

The general terms *heathen, barbarian, pagan, savage,* and even *Indian* revealed these criteria of judgment at the same time that they validated the use of a collective term for all peoples of other continents. The European takeover of the New World first by Spanish conquest and later by French and English invasion proved to Europeans, at least, the superiority of themselves. Common concepts plus successful conquest reinforced the stereotype of the deficiency of "savages" everywhere and validated the continued use and the glossing over of the growing knowledge of specific social and cultural differences

Lib. of Congress, Rare Book Div.
Fig. 2. Figure from the title page of *The American Magazine and Historical Chronicle,* Volume 2, April 1745. The city is probably Boston; however, the Indians do not resemble those of New England tribes. The man, child, and woman at left wear upright feather headdresses and feather or leaf skirts. The man carries a straight back bow and a calumet, which would have been used in the Northeast. However, the palm trees, kegs (for rum?), and woman, right, with the basket of fruit on her head, together with the costumes, suggest that the image is modeled after South American or Carib Indians. Woodcut by J. Turner, printed by Rogers and Fowle, Boston, 1745.

among New World peoples. Even among themselves and the peoples they had long known well, Europeans correlated whole nationalities with uniform moral and intellectual attributes, so no wonder they should stereotype the new peoples they met elsewhere.

Part of this stereotyping of national as well as continental characteristics must be ascribed to the confusion among the realms of culture and biology, nation and race long prevalent (Stocking 1968). Thus general terms embracing stereotyped characteristics made sense to Whites and could exist alongside knowledge of specific societies with individual characteristics. One important consequence of this stereotyping was the continuance of the general term Indian to blend character and culture into one stereotype.

In spite of fusing race and culture under nationality and character, Europeans during the initial centuries of contact with Native Americans did not see color as a significant way of describing or understanding the Indian. Unlike the European deprecation of Africans as black, Indians were considered basically White and their coloration, if noticed, was attributed to the sun's rays, peculiar cosmetics, or some other such influence. Not until the eighteenth century did "red skin" enter descriptions as prelude to the more racist thought patterns of the nineteenth century (Vaughan 1982; Gagnon 1976; Jaenen 1976:22–23; Kupperman 1980:35–37).

Persisting White Presuppositions about the Indian

The centuries-long confusion and melding of biology and culture, nation and race, as the way of understanding human societies probably account for several persistent practices found throughout the history of White images and comprehension of Native Americans as Indians: generalizing from one tribe's society and culture to all Indians, conceiving of Indians in terms of their deficiencies according to White ideals rather than in terms of their own various cultural values, and combining moral evaluation with descriptions in the image of Indians.

That almost all accounts in the sixteenth century do not portray systematically or completely the customs and beliefs of any one tribe probably results from the newness of the encounter and the feeling that all Indians were characterized by the same basic qualities (cf. Rowe 1964; Hulton and Quinn 1964). Although eyewitness accounts and discourses by those who had lived among Native Americans in the seventeenth and eighteenth centuries often describe in detail the lives of a specific tribe or tribes, they also in the end generalize from this knowledge to all Indians. The famous sources on Native American cultures during the colonial period of the United States, for example, invariably treat their tribes as generally similar enough to all Indians in culture and beliefs, if not in specifics, to serve as illustrations of that race in thought

and deed (for example, Adair 1775). Even in the century that saw the rise of professional anthropology, most social scientists as well as their White countrymen continued to speak and write as if a specific tribe and all Indians were interchangeable for the purposes of description and understanding of fundamental cultural dynamics and social organization (cf. Stewart and Newman 1951). In the late twentieth century few Whites seem to realize that the word Indian is an abstraction as opposed to various tribal peoples and individual Native Americans as Deloria (1969) tried to remind them. (For Canada, see Churchill, Hill, and Hill 1978:47.)

Another persistent theme in White imagery is the tendency to describe Indian life in terms of its deficiency in relation to White standards and ways rather than a positive description in line with the framework of the specific culture under consideration. Just as early European explorers of new found lands could not convey what they had seen and experienced but by words familiar to their listeners and readers, so later Whites throughout the centuries appear forced to perceive and conceive of the Indian in general, or even specifically as individuals and tribes, according to the customs, values, and classifications familiar to their own contemporaries. Therefore, Native Americans were usually described not for what they were in their own eyes but from the viewpoint of the invaders into their lands. Images of the Indian, accordingly, were and are usually what they were not or had not in White terms and ideals, rather than in terms of individual tribal cultures and social systems.

Description by deficiency all too readily led to characterization, and so most of the White studies of Indian cultures were (and are) also examinations of Indian character. Later White understanding of the Indian, like that of earlier explorers and settlers, expressed moral judgments upon lifeways as well as presented their description, or mixed ideology with ethnography, to use modern terms. Ethnographic description according to modern standards could not truly be separated from ideology and moral judgment until the complete acceptance of *both* the ideals of cultural pluralism and moral relativism in the twentieth century, and even then only a few Whites truly practiced the two ideals in their outlook on Native Americans. Thus description combined moral evaluation with ethnographic detail, and moral judgments frequently passed for science. No matter how many ethnographic details a modern scholar can derive about specific tribes from a past White source, the image as a whole contained in that source usually embodies from a modern point of view material of an ideological cast in addition to and combined with the scientific information. If ideology is fused with ethnography in eyewitness sources, then images created by Whites who never had firsthand experience with Native Americans usually contained little more than stereotype and moral judgment (fig. 3).

Whether describing physical appearance or character, manners or morality, economy or dress, housing or sexual habits, government or religion, Whites overwhelmingly measured the Indian as a general category against those beliefs, values, or institutions they ascribed to themselves at the time. For this reason, many commentators on the history of White Indian imagery see Europeans and Americans as using anti-images of themselves to describe Indians and the anti-images of Indians to describe themselves (Pearce 1965). Such a negative reference group could be used to define White identity (Sheehan 1973) or to prove White superiority over the worst fears of their own depravity. If the Puritans could project their own sins upon people they called savages, then the extermination of the Indian became a cleansing of those sins from their own midst as well as the destruction of a feared enemy (Meade 1971; Salisbury 1972; Slotkin 1973).

Since White views of Indians are inextricably bound up with the evaluation of their own society and culture, then ambivalence of Europeans and Americans over the worth of their own customs and civilization would show up in their appraisal of Indian life. Even with the image of the Indian as a reverse or negative prototype of White life (the most common and the most persistent image in the history of White conceptions), Whites drew two different conclusions about the nature or quality of Indian existence. That Indians lacked parts or all of White civilization could be viewed as bad or good depending upon the observer's feelings about his own society or the use to which he wanted to put the image. In line with this possibility, commentators upon the history of White imagery of the Indian have found two fundamental but contradictory conceptions of Indian culture, which reflect the two basic positions of Whites about the values of their own time and the institutional manifestations of those over time. These

Fig. 3. *William Penn's Treaty with the Indians, when he founded the province of Pennsylvania in North America.* The painting, often used as a metaphor for peace, is a romanticized version of the English treating with the Delaware in 1683. While the painting is notable for its departure from the use of Classical attire to illustrate historical characters, it is not an accurate rendition of a 17th-century treaty. For example, no wampum is being used nor is there a council fire; however, the trade goods would have been present (Francis Jennings, communication to editors 1986). The cradleboard and the way in which the infant is bound is mostly fictional, but the embroidery on the woman's garment is correct. The male Indian, second to the right of Penn, wears a horned bonnet of a type worn by Plains Indians. The garment and leggings of the kneeling Indian are similar to Delaware styles as are the feather roaches. A detailed discussion of the original painting and subsequent versions is in E.S. Brinton (1941). Oil painting on canvas by Benjamin West, 1771.

527

WHITE CONCEPTIONS OF INDIANS

basic positions are generally designated the good and bad, or favorable and unfavorable, images for short (Berkhofer 1978; Billington 1981; Monkman 1981; Stedman 1982).

In general and at the risk of oversimplifying some four centuries of imagery, the good Indian appears friendly, courteous, and hospitable to the initial invaders of his lands and to all Whites as long as Whites honored treaties mutually entered into with the tribe. Along with handsomeness of physique and physiognomy went great stamina and endurance. Modest in attitude if not always in dress, the good Indian exhibited great calm and dignity in bearing, conversation, and even under torture. Brave in combat, he was tender in love for family and children. Pride in himself and independence of other persons combined with simplicity of life and wholesome enjoyment of nature's gifts. In short, according to this version, the Indian lived a life of liberty, simplicity, and innocence.

On the other side, a list of almost contradictory traits emerged of the bad Indian in White eyes. Nakedness and lechery, passion and vanity led to lives of polygamy and sexual promiscuity among themselves and constant warfare and fiendish revenge against their enemies. When habits and customs were not brutal they appeared loathsome to Whites. Cannibalism and human sacrifice were the worst sins, but cruelty to captives and incessant warfare ranked not far behind in the estimation of Whites. Filthy surroundings, inadequate cooking, and certain items of diet repulsive to White taste tended to confirm a low opinion of Indian life. Indolence rather than industry, improvidence in the face of scarcity, thievery, and treachery added to the list of traits on this side. Concluding the bad version of the Indian were the power of superstition represented by the "conjurers" and "medicine men," the hard slavery of women (Smits 1982) and the laziness of men, and even timidity or defeat in the face of White advances and weaponry. Thus this list substituted license for liberty, a harsh lot for simplicity, and dissimulation and deceit for innocence. In short, this image contrasted the ignoble savage with the noble one.

Along with the persistence of the dual image of good and bad and general deficiency went a curious timelessness in the defining of the Indian as other. The history of White imagery reveals at its core that the quintessential Indian was and is thought outside the dictates of time and history in Western thought. Fundamentally the Indian is conceived of in a static temporal context, as neither having history nor being affected by history until White contact. In spite of centuries of contact and the changed conditions of Native American lives, Whites picture the "real" Indian as the one before contact or during the early period of that contact. That Whites of earlier centuries should picture the Indian as historyless makes sense given their lack of knowledge about the past of Native American peoples and the shortness of their encounter. That later Whites should harbor the same assumption seems surpris-

Lib. of Congress, Prints and Photographs Div.

Fig. 4. Cartoon with caption "Lo the Poor Indian, Oh why does the white man follow my path!" An appearance of the phrase "Lo, the poor Indian" is Alexander Pope's *An Essay on Man*:

"Lo, the poor Indian whose untutor'd mind
Sees God in clouds, or hears him in the wind;
His soul proud Science never taught to stray
Far as the solar walk or milky way;" (1773–1774:Epistle I).

The Indian is shown drunk, in tattered garments of White and Native derivation and his exaggeratedly featured face has a comic, foolish countenance. The cartoon and its caption's intent can be interpreted at several levels. "Lo the poor Indian" is always in reference to Indians who are taken advantage of or pitiable in some way. "Why does the white man follow . . ." could be mocking Whites, perhaps those who live in the East, who call the Indian and his way of life noble and exemplary. The cartoon could also be criticizing those Whites, who moving West, bring alcohol and other disruptive influences to Indian cultures. Engraving by Parsloe and Vance, New York, 1875.

ing given the discoveries of archeology and the changed condition of the tribes as the result of White contact and policy (Trigger 1980).

If Whites of the early period of contact invented the Indian as a conception and provided its fundamental meaning through imagery, why did later generations perpetuate that conception and imagery without basic alteration although Native Americans had changed? The answer to this question must be sought partially in the very contrast between Red and White society that gave rise to the White idea of the Indian as an other in the first place. Since Whites primarily understood the Indian as an antithesis to themselves, then civilization and Indianness

BERKHOFER

as they defined them would forever be opposites. Only civilization had history and dynamics in this view, so therefore Indianness must be conceived of as historyless and static. If the Indian changed through the adoption of civilization as defined by Whites, then he was no longer truly Indian according to the image. Because the Indian was judged by what Whites were not, change toward what Whites were made him ipso facto less Indian. The history of White-Indian contact increasingly proved to Whites, particularly in the late eighteenth and nineteenth centuries, that civilization and Indianness were inherently incompatible and verified the initial conception that gave rise to the imagery. Death through disease and warfare decimated the aboriginal population in the face of White advance and gave rise by the time of the American Revolution to the idea of the vanishing race and "lo! the poor Indian" imagery (fig. 4). If Whites feared the Indian as a threat to life and morals when alive, they regarded him with nostalgia upon his demise—or when that threat was safely past. Indians who remained alive and who resisted adoption of civilization appeared to accept White vices instead of virtues and so became those imperfect Indians: the degraded or reservation images. Complete assimilation would have meant the total disappearance of Indianness. If one adds to these images the conceptions of progress and evolution, then one arrives at the fundamental premises behind much of White American understanding of the Indian from about the middle of the eighteenth century to the twentieth century. Under these conceptions civilization was destined to triumph over savagery, and so the Indian was to disappear either through death or through assimilation into the larger, more progressive White society (Dippie 1982; cf. Sheehan 1973; Pearce 1965). Nineteenth-century frontiersmen acted upon this belief; missionaries and philanthropists tried to cope with the fact. In the twentieth century anthropologists rushed to salvage ethnography from the last living members of some tribes, and historians treated Indians as dead after early contact with Whites. In these ways modern Native Americans and their contemporary cultures have largely disappeared from the White imagination, except where Indian activism reversed this historic trend.

The Noble Savage: the Good Indian in Literature and Art

What is called the good or favorable image of the Indian resulted from or was strongly influenced by the primitivistic tradition of Western civilization. By the time of the Renaissance, the Judeo-Christian and Greco-Roman myths of Eden and Arcadia, or Paradise on Earth and the Golden Age, had merged to people lands far away to the westward or long ago in the past with citizens who dwelt in an ideal(ized) landscape and gentle climate and lived in harmony with nature and reason. Such peoples existed free of history's burdens and modern society's complexities. Such myths influenced Spanish perceptions of natives in the New World and their hunt for fabled cities and fountains of youth. Some French and English explorers and settlers believed the Indians they encountered still lived in the Golden Age.

The primitivistic tradition did not create the favorable version of the Indian from whole cloth; rather it shaped the vocabulary and the imagery the explorers and other White travelers used to describe their actual experience in the New World. The accounts of explorers, missionaries, and other early travelers and settlers seemed therefore to provide the factual basis, hence the validation, for the primitivistic faith of the political and social theorists and artists. (Washburn 1957a and 1976: 335–350 argues that Indian tribes did indeed display the virtues attributed to them by the Noble Savage convention.) What written accounts prompted in the European imagination was reinforced by the noble Indians portrayed by the artist in André Thevet's *Cosmographie* in 1575 and the engravings in Theodor De Bry's 1590 edition of Thomas Hariot's *Briefe and True Report of the New Found Land of Virginia* (1972) and his 1591 edition of Jacque Le Moyne de Morgue's *Brevis Narratio eorum quae in Florida Americae provincia Gallis acciderunt* (Hulton et al. 1977). Likened to classical statues in poses and garb, these images of the Indian became standard illustrations for texts about Native Americans for two centuries. (On the role of the artist in sixteenth-century discovery voyages, see Hulton and Quinn 1964:29–36. On other early artistic representations of the Indian, see Weitenkampf 1949a; Feest 1967; P.D. Thomas 1971; Honour 1975a, 1975:3–83; Sturtevant 1976.)

In this way the American Indian became part of the "good savage" tradition so long a correlate of the Golden Age or paradisical mythology of Western civilization. Indians were used, as were other discovered peoples, as convention for specifying the hopes and desires of European authors for a simpler world, for criticizing obliquely or directly the institutions and customs of their own societies, or for providing new imagery for the intellectual, literary, and artistic styles of the day (Baudet 1965; Fairchild 1928). Whether the Indians north of Mexico were ever as influential in this tradition as those of the Antilles, Brazil, and the Inca and Aztec empires (B. Keen 1971:138–248) is difficult to say, because most European authors used the Indian generically for their purposes.

That the Indians north of Mexico came to loom large in the French image of the Noble Savage must be ascribed mainly to the voluminous *Relations* (JR 1896–1901) of the Jesuits in New France. Published annually from 1632 to 1674 and sporadically before and after those years, the *Relations* from the Canadian missions often provided flattering descriptions of some Native Americans and

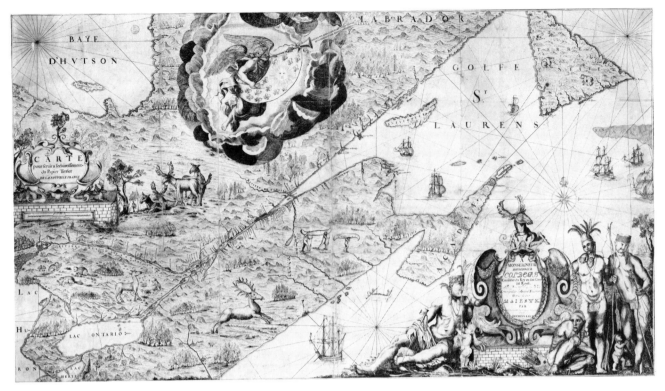

Fig. 5. Map titled *Carte pour servir a l'éclaircissement du Papier Terrier de la Nouvelle France*. The cartouche exemplifies the association between the Noble Savage and North America. While the Indians display realistic elements of material culture, their forms are classical in nature. The left figure wears a checkered wampum headband (as does the figure to the far right) and holds a T-shaped pipe decorated with beads. He, and the figure second from the right, wear shell gorgets. The arrow quiver by the crouching figure seems to be made from a bear's head. On the map appear Indians with birchbark canoes, and groups of longhouses indicate several Iroquois villages. Other map details include fauna such as moose, other elk or deerlike animals, beaver, fox, and bear. French territory is depicted quite accurately on the map, but British North America is only presented schematically. Map by Jean-Baptiste Louis Franquelin, 1678.

their ways of life in order to gain contributions from the faithful and to refute their Jansenist and atheist opponents. Although the Jesuits generally found their Canadian charges more savage than noble, their allusions otherwise—usually to converts, however—provided the basis for eighteenth-century deists and philosophers to prove that a beneficient state of nature existed among the Hurons of New France (Chinard 1934:122–187; Kennedy 1950; Healey 1958; Altherr 1983; Walsh 1982; Dickason 1984). Another tactic that ennobled the Indians of North America was the trend, especially among the French, to compare the Indians of the New World with the ancient peoples of the Old. From Marc Lescarbot's sixth book in his *Histoire de la Nouvelle France*, published in 1609, to Joseph Lafitau's (1724) work, the natives of New France were steadily elevated in wisdom and status if not in actual culture and custom by comparison with the highly regarded ancients. English travelers and settlers, on the other hand, provided little material (Frantz 1967:72–158; Randolph 1973) to glorify the Indian with the exception of John Lawson (Diket 1966), Cadwallader Colden (F.A. Crane 1952:31–37), and John Adair (Washburn 1973a), nor did the Noble Savage ever become so fashionable in English letters as he did on the French literary scene

(Bissell 1925; but see Daiutolo 1983 on Quaker attitudes).

The transition from the description of the American Indian as a Noble Savage to the use of the noble American Indian as a critic of European society and culture is difficult to date, but scholars generally concede that most of the milestones occurred in France from the late sixteenth century to the late seventeenth century. Scholars usually credit Michel Montaigne's synthetic combination of French and Spanish accounts of Mexican and South American Indians with French skepticism and humanism as being the first full-length portrait of the Noble Savage as critic of contemporary European civilization and a model of what men ought to be and could be (Chinard 1911:193–218; Fairchild 1928:15–21; Chiappelli 1976: 63–89, 107–164; R. Sanders 1978:199–210, 256–262; H.C. Porter 1979:137–152). The transition had been completed by the time of publication of Fénelon's (1845) *Aventures de Télémaque* in 1699 and Lahontan's (1931) dialogues in 1703 (fig. 1). Both men praised the Hurons' sensible ways of life compared to the corruption and complexity of European civilization. Jean-Jacques Rousseau, Voltaire, Denis Diderot, and other famed philosophers of the eighteenth century had but to continue a tradition well established by their day of using the Noble Savage in

530

general and the American Indian in particular for their critical, moral, and political purposes (Chinard 1934: 341–398; Honigsheim 1945, 1952; Duchet 1963, 1971; David 1948; Atkinson 1935; Hubert 1923; Symcox in Dudley and Novak 1972:223–248; R.L. Emerson 1979).

The cult of the Noble Savage, especially as rational critic, was far less developed outside France, and what polemical and satirical use there was of the noble American Indian in England generally stemmed from French influence. Although John Locke offered the Indian as example for his benevolent state of nature, the political and satirical use of the Native American mainly stems from the visit of four chiefs, three Mohawks and one Mahican, to England in 1710 (Bond 1952). In that country the rational savage soon fused with or was succeeded by the sentimental savage as a precursor of romanticism (Fairchild 1928; Bissell 1925; Whitney 1934:7–136), but neither the rational nor the sentimental Indian ever achieved the popularity in England that he did in France, perhaps because that country had already had its revolution. In the English colonies the literary and ideological use of the Noble Savage appeared on the scene only during the Revolutionary era (Aldridge 1950; Pearce 1965: 136–146; Sheehan 1973:89–116).

By the end of the eighteenth century certain trends had become clear in the history of the Noble Savage convention. To the extent that the Noble Savage was used to criticize European institutions of the period, to that extent the supporters of orthodox religion (Reed 1964), old regimes, the contemporary social order, or just the civilized amenities (Fairchild 1928:327–338), all felt compelled in their defense of the status quo to point out the presumably brutish existence lived by contemporary primitives. In one way the whole dispute over the advantages and disadvantages resulting from the discovery of the New World and the degeneracy of the American Indian must be viewed as an attack upon the idea of the Noble Savage and therefore as part of the larger struggle in the realm of ideas over the possibilities of political and social reform in the second half of the eighteenth century (Gerbi 1973:3–324). The American and French Revolutions marked the turning point in this phase of the Noble Savage convention, for both sides to the dispute could point to the dramatic real world to support their contentions rather than the hypothetical world of the Noble Savage. For the Noble Savage convention in art, see E. Parry (1974:14–34) and Honour (1975a, 1975:84–137).

Equally clear in the history of the Noble Savage convention by the end of the eighteenth century was the transformation of the literary primitive from a man of reason and good sense into a man of emotion and sensibility: the romantic savage as opposed to the enlightened savage. Although the trend to the romantic savage culminated in the early nineteenth century, its beginnings must be traced far back into the Enlightenment. The

opposition of nature to the artificiality of civilization, the stress on the long ago and the far away, and even the concern over the superiority of impulse and instinct over reason had long been an important part of primitivistic thinking. The European use of the American Indian according to romantic conventions culminated in Thomas Cooper in England and François-René de Chateaubriand in France. What had been in England a good adventure story of sentimental love amidst exotic scenery and American Indians reached its height under romantic premises in the long poem by Campbell (1809), *Gertrude of Wyoming*, relating how the love of two White youths on the Pennsylvania frontier ended tragically in the Wyoming Massacre of 1778 (Fairchild 1928:258–267). Chateaubriand's (1801) *Atala* depicted the ill-fated love of two Indians from warring tribes but embodied the French fashion, first popularized by Rousseau, to internalize the relation between man and nature by fusing the wildness of men in other places with the wildness within all men (Thorslev in Dudley and Novak 1972:290–292; Slotkin 1973:370–382; for the art inspired by *Atala* see Honour 1975a:286–302, 1975:220–225).

Just as European intellectuals dropped the Noble Savage as a subject for formal literature, American authors and artists took up the convention as part of their quest for a (high) cultural identity to match their country's newly acquired political independence. The only time the Indian figured prominently in the so-called higher forms of American literature and art occurred between the War of 1812 and the Civil War, as authors and artists sought American themes and materials to replace those inherited from abroad. If cultural nationalism caused United States authors and artists to turn to the Indian and the forest for subject matter, the importation of romanticism from Europe enabled the elevation of such subject matter to literary and artistic respectability. As long as the neo-classical perspective and subject matter of eighteenth-century rationalism dominated American letters, then the Indian was not really appropriate material for the American author seeking literary reputation at home or abroad. Romanticism came late to the United States, but its emphasis on indigenous traditions, folk customs, and the glorification of the national past fit in well with the drive toward cultural nationalism (P.R. Cox 1970:49–97).

Given romantic premises, the Indian, whether a good or a bad image, made an ideal subject for American high culture. Whether American litterateurs looked to the past, to nature, or to exotic peoples in their country, they found the Indian each time. Certainly the American forest possessed a grandeur, an expanse, and a wildness unknown to European nature, sublimer by far than the meek pastoral scenes across the Atlantic. Part of the wildness of the American forest came from the nature of its inhabitants and the horrors of native warfare in White eyes. The tortures, vengeance, escapes, and ambushes of Indian warfare aroused a variety of emotions of the most romantic sort. Compared to the future Americans envisaged for themselves, their past looked meager indeed for the artist looking for ruins and ancient monuments. But the mysterious Indian burial mounds gained much attention at this time as the American equivalent of European ruins and castles. Even when an American author looked to the short history of his country, he found the Indian a prominent participant in the colonial struggles and even in the Revolution. The Indians, moreover, were an exotic folk with quaint customs, heroic acts, and alive to the impression of nature around them. Their language was filled with picturesque allusion and metaphor, and their legends equaled the tales of Old World folk. Indian rhetoric had long existed as kind of literature in the form of treaty proceedings (Buntin 1961: 521–599; Wroth 1928; Drummond and Moody 1953; cf. Sorber 1972). The Cayuga Logan's famed speech in 1774 was compared by Thomas Jefferson to that of the Greek orators, and it was memorized from McGuffey readers by school children in the nineteenth century (Sandefur 1960; Washburn 1966a). Perhaps the best known publication of Indian legends was the compilation of Ojibwa and other tribes' tales published by Schoolcraft (1839), which later served Henry Wadsworth Longfellow as the source for *Hiawatha* (1855; cf. Mitchell 1981:151–187 for the larger "preservation" context of Indian culture in the nineteenth century).

Perhaps most romantic of all was the impression of the Indian as rapidly passing away before the onslaught of civilization (fig. 6). The nostalgia and pity aroused by the dying race produced the best kind of romantic sentiment and gave that sense of fleeting time beloved of romantic sensibilities (Dippie 1982:1–44). The tragedy of the dying Indian, especially as represented by the last living member of a tribe, became a staple of American literature and art beginning with Philip Freneau's (1786) poems and made its mark upon world literature through James Fenimore Cooper's *The Last of the Mohicans* (1826). To truly pity the dying Indian, American authors had to transform him from a bloodthirsty demon into a Noble Savage. That transformation occurred late in the United States compared to Europe. Just as it has been said that the Europeans could easily ennoble the Indian because of their remoteness from savage warfare, so commentators have pointed out that authors and artists of the eastern United States conceived of the Indian as noble only after that region was no longer subject to Indian conflict. Even then the number of truly Noble Savages in books or paintings was relatively few and relegated to the far away and the long ago.

For the artist of the time the noble Indian was to be found only in the wild West beyond the corruption of advancing civilization. Fears of the imminent passing of

The N.-Y. Histl. Soc., New York.

Fig. 6. *The Indian: The Dying Chief Contemplating the Progress of Civilization.* The figure is rendered in a Classical pose. Its moccasins are woodland style, but the imaginative feather headdress resembles a South American form. Sculpted in white marble by Thomas Crawford, Rome, 1856.

the Red race prompted painters to rush westward to capture the likenesses of these noble beings before it was too late. The portraits of Charles Bird King, which became color lithographs in McKenny and Hall's (1842–1844) history; the Indian gallery painted by George Catlin that toured the United States and Europe in the 1830s and 1840s; and the paintings of Seth Eastman, which were reproduced as illustrations by Schoolcraft (1851–1857) all helped to popularize the image of the noble Indian before the settlement of the West. By reliance upon classic analogy and romantic conventions in art, these artists and others ennobled the Indian on canvas (H. McCracken 1959; Haberly 1948; Ewers 1956; McDermott 1961; Bushnell 1932; Flexner 1962:77–102; Kinietz 1942; Coen 1969:64–120; Gerdts 1974; Honour 1975a, 1975: 227–247). Just how much of these works is ethnography and how much ideology and whether they are more realistic portrayals of Indians than art of previous centuries is the subject of Weitenkampf (1949a, 1949), Ewers (1949, 1967), and Viola (1977).

Similarly, the authors of poems, plays, and novels conceived of the Indian as noble only before White contact or during the early stages of the encounter between White and Red cultures. Thus many famous Indians such as Pocahantas (Hubbell 1965; P. Young 1962; cf. R.D. Green 1975) and King Philip (F.A. Crane 1952:182–231) were revived as noble figures in the literature influenced by cultural nationalism during the first half of the nineteenth century. Perhaps the culmination of the

Fig. 7. Broadside announcing a massacre of Whites by Indians. This broadside copies another broadside advertising captivity narratives of 2 White women from a frontier settlement and of a man from Kentucky (Lib. of Congress, Rare Book, Div.: Broadside "War and Pestilence"). The women were captured after a massacre in their settlement. Printed about 1832.

tendency to romanticize the dead Indian at the expense of living ones was Longfellow's (1855) epic poem, *Hiawatha*. Confusing the Iroquois hero with an Ojibwa myth figure (vol. 15:422), Longfellow placed Hiawatha's noble deeds and love in the picturesque forests before the coming of White people. Even the Iroquois of Lewis Henry Morgan's (1851) ethnography can be seen as part of this trend to romanticize a golden age of Indian life prior to White contact, for his description of primitive democracy and utopian harmony in the League of the Iroquois takes place outside the story of actual White-Iroquois relations and history (F.A. Crane 1952; Keiser 1933:22–97; Pearce 1965:169–236; P.R. Cox 1970).

Of all American authors, James Fenimore Cooper probably did the most to make the American Indian a literary type in world literature, but his Indians were delineated according to the premises and conventions of his time in the United States. Eleven of his novels featured Indians, of which the best known now and the best sellers then were the five depicting the adventures of Leatherstocking or Natty Bumppo. Like so many authors of his era, Cooper knew little or nothing of Native Americans directly, and so his works reveal the typical confusion of one tribe with another in customs, names, and languages (Ten Kate 1922:509–515). He showed Indians as both noble and savage according to the traditional favorable and unfavorable images, for their character and personality excited romantic emotions. Following the judgments of his chief source, the Moravian missionary John Heckwelder, Cooper's good Indians resemble Christian Delawares and his ignoble Indians behave like Heckeweilder's descriptions of their enemies, the Iroquois (P.A.W. Wallace 1954; Parker 1954). Moreover, his good Indians, although not necessarily Christian converts, act like the Christian and natural aristocrats he admired, live apart from their tribe, or are often the last surviving members of their tribe, and play their roles in locales historically situated between savagery and civilization. Not only did Cooper subscribe to the contemporary White Americans' tension between progress and simple nature, savagery and civilization, but also he obeyed the conventions of the novel of the time in not allowing an Indian, no matter how noble, to marry a White. Even Leatherstocking himself was too Indianized and lower class to breach these conventions of the traditional romantic novel. Although Cooper's bad Indians far outnumbered his few noble ones, Lewis Cass and others at the time and later Francis Parkman criticized his superficial and unrealistic portrayal of Indian thought and emotions as too sentimental (F.A. Crane 1952:114–181; Keiser 1933:101–143; Folsom 1966:36–59; H.N. Smith 1970; T. Martin 1976; Sequeira 1978; Milder 1980). Frederick (1956) defends Cooper's Indian imagery; compare P.A.W. Wallace (1954). On White ambivalence toward "half bloods," see Scheick (1979).

By the 1850s the Indian in general and the Noble Savage in particular began to bore the sophisticated reading public and to reveal their literary limitations to men of letters. Although Longfellow's *Hiawatha* achieved great success during this decade, it was quickly ridiculed in one satirical imitation after another as were other standard Indian themes of the period (F.A. Crane 1952: 223–225, 326–329, 387). The use of the Indian to produce an American literature in the quest for cultural identity and nationalism had run its course along with the romanticism that sustained the image. The Indian mainly became a literary staple of popular culture while serious men of letters searched elsewhere for inspiration and subjects except for a few authors of the local color school in the late nineteenth century. If the chief writer of this school, Mark Twain, displayed White prejudices against the Indian in *Roughing It* (cf. Denton 1971–1972 with H.L. Harris 1975), lesser writers of the same genre romanticized the Indian as noble (Joaquin Miller) or sentimentalized over his fate (Helen Hunt Jackson) (Odell 1939:153–211, 224–226; Byers 1975-1976). In general, see Keiser (1933:233–292), G.E. Jones (1958), and Shames (1969) for this later period.

Artists of the late nineteenth century perpetuated the usual stereotypes of the Indian under the guise of greater realism. Coen (1969:121–131) and E. Parry (1974: 115–163) provide brief overviews. Even the photographers attempting to capture the "authentic" Indian before he passed off the stage of history sought the romantic, primitive Indian in costume and habitat more than actual native lives in transition (Taft 1938:248–310; A. Thomas 1981–1982; Mitchell 1981:134–150; Lyman 1982).

Commentators disagree just when Native Americans first began receiving realistic portrayals by Whites in literature and journalism.

If the criteria of realistic presentation of the Indian in literature becomes the treatment of Native Americans as individuals rather than as Indians, as human beings and not assemblages of tribal traits, all placed in an everyday situation, then the Indian novel cannot said to have begun long before the publication of Oliver La Farge's Pulitzer Prize-wining *Laughing Boy* in 1929 (McNickle 1971; T.M. Pearce 1972; Gillis 1967; Schulz 1964; cf. on Edwin Corle's *Fig Tree John*, Beidler 1977). In the wake of *Laughing Boy's* popularity came the novels of the first generation of White-educated Native American writers: *Flaming Arrow's People* by James Paytiamo (1932), Acoma; *Sundown* by John Joseph Mathews (1934), Osage; *Brothers Three* by John Oskinson (1935), Cherokee; and *The Surrounded* by D'Arcy McNickle (1936), Flathead. White recognition of the Native American writing the Indian novel arrived with N. Scott Momaday, Kiowa, winning the Pulitzer Prize for *House Made of Dawn* (1968).

By 1980 courses in American Indian literature had appeared on college campuses, and a scholarly specialty had developed its own canon of Indian authors and the beginnings of a literary criticism (for example, Lincoln 1983; Monkman 1981). In spite of such developments, White American authors, like movie-makers, still exploited the supposedly "real Indian" as foil or allegorical figure to expose the selfishness, provincialism, and crassness of their own culture (Gage 1974; Olivia 1973; Cleary 1980; cf. Hoover 1976:273–279, 341–353), just as D.H. Lawrence had decades earlier (L.D. Clark 1976; cf. Frost 1980). Most horrifying to Native American scholars and leaders was the continuing popularity of what

appeared to them to be blatant White misrepresentations of native cultures, all the while purporting to be more authentic reconstructions than previous ones (for example, Medicine 1979; Albers and James 1981).

The Bad Indian in White Imagination and Ideology

The ideological conventions that undergird the Bad or Ignoble Savage image of the Indian are as old and as embedded in Western civilization as those of the Noble Savage. As a consequence of such ancient prejudices, Indian deficiences all too quickly became savagism in the eyes of Europeans. Thus Indian culture was likened to that of beasts in the field, Indian religion became the Devil's own, and Indian warfare was bloody, incessant, and cruel (Sheehan 1980:37–88).

Lurking at the base of this image was European fascination with Indian cannibalism and human sacrifice. As a result of Columbus's descriptions of the practice of anthropophagy among the Caribs, whom he called *caníbales*, the term *cannibalism* came into use for the practice of man-eating. In 1503 and 1505 Amerigo Vespucci provided sensational accounts of killing, storing, cooking, and consuming human flesh by the Brazilian Tupinamba, and other books on these same peoples as well as Spanish reports of Aztec religious rituals culminating in massive human sacrifice fixed Indian savagism in European minds (Hemming 1978:24–68; Pagden 1982:80–90). These accounts were republished with vivid illustrations by Theodor De Bry in the 1590s (Bucher 1981).

Although the negative evaluation of the North American Indian as ignoble savage originated in European observations, it never prevailed or persisted in that continent's literature and art in the way that it did in North America's. Belles lettres and formal art can hardly be said to have existed in the English colonies before the American Revolution. The opening pages of literary histories of the United States discuss chiefly the journals, chronicles, promotional tracts, sermons, and histories penned in the colonies rather than the poetry, plays, and novels upon which such history is usually grounded. New England far excelled other regions in the production of these so-called subliterary genres, and it is primarily there that the imaginative transformation of the Native American from the Indian of contact into the Indian of symbol and myth took place during the colonial period of American cultural history. Both the reason for the outpouring of published works and the mythologizing of the Indian must be ascribed to the Puritan beliefs of the region's writers.

For the Puritan the Indian as well as himself were part of the cosmic drama willed by God to reveal His sovereignty and grace. In this drama the Puritans saw themselves as chosen of the Lord for the special purposes of bringing forth a New Zion, and those who fled England to the shores of North America believed they had founded just the holy commonwealth God decreed. The history of New Englanders, when conceived of as that of a chosen people, naturally reminded the pious of the trials of the Israelites of old. Like the Old Testament Jews, the Puritans had fled a corrupt Egypt, in their case England, for the promised land, and like the ancient Israelites they too landed in the desert or wilderness, often spoken of as "howling" or "savage" and inhabited by Satan's agents (Heimert 1953; Carroll 1969; R. Nash 1982:23–43). The journey into the wilderness became as much a controlling metaphor for the story of the Puritans collectively as the spiritual pilgrimage formed the basis of the personal narrative of conversion, and the struggle between Puritans and Indians, who were one of the forces of evil, represented externally what the conflict between conscience and sin did internally (Pearce 1952; Meade 1971; Salisbury 1972; Slotkin 1973:57–179; W.S. Simmons 1981).

To Puritan divines and laymen alike, the interaction of Native Americans with the New England saints represented something larger in significance than mere contact. Hospitality and kindness represented not native friendliness and goodness but the Lord's mercy to his chosen people. Gov. William Bradford of Plymouth Plantation wrote of Squanto, whose crucial assistance to the Pilgrims enabled them to survive in the new environment, as "a Spetiall instrument sent of God for their good beyond their expectation" (quoted in Gay 1966–1969, 1:35–36). On the other hand, Indian character and culture in general showed Native Americans to be in the clutches of Satan. They therefore expected the horrors of native warfare both because of the unregenerate state of the Indians and because God must send periodically a scourge to chastise His chosen people in their pride and in their departure from his Word. Thus the good and the bad images of the Indian served the same didactic purposes for the Puritan imagination. By the late seventeenth century, devout Puritans eulogized the faith of the founding fathers of New England and lamented the lack of zeal in their descendants, and King Philip's War in 1675 seemed to confirm the warnings of the godly about the imminent threat of a humbling experience sent by the Lord. The war gave vivid meaning to the jeremiads about the decline of Puritan piety, and its coming and hard-won victory were used in sermons, histories, and tracts to point out the lessons for New England (J.M. Morse 1952:105–129; Slotkin 1973:57–93; Buntin 1961:176–344).

Among the spate of literature preaching this theme were the first captivity narratives published in New England. The lessons drawn from Indian capture by the minister's wife who published the first of the genre in 1682 are revealed in its title: *The Soveraignty and Goodness of God, Together with the Faithfulness of His Promises Displayed: Being a Narrative of the Captivity and Restau-* *ration of Mrs. Mary Rowlandson; Commended by Her, to All that Desire to Know the Lord's Doing to, and Dealings with Her.* What made this genre so effective was the bringing of the larger forces of God and Satan, Puritan and Savage into the microcosm of personal experience through embodiment of the image of the bad Indian. She summarized in her preface the basic nature of her captors as "Atheistical, proud, wild, cruel, barbarous, brutish, (in one word) diabolical creatures . . . , the worse of heathen." Ministers soon picked up this method of impressing the power of the Lord and the sinfulness of His people upon their audience both for its drama and its message. In the end, the bad image of the Indian triumphed over the good one in the Puritan imagination (Slotkin 1973:94–115; Meade 1971:32–57). Southern colonists produced few captivity narratives (R.B. Davis 1978, 1:215–219, 427–428).

The evolution of the captivity narrative from Puritan jeremiad into gothic novel and commercial anthology by the last decade of the eighteenth century points to the future uses of negative Indian imagery in the American imagination. The best-seller status of the captivity narrative (Mott 1947:20–22) led to the retention of its basic premise of the horrors Whites suffered under Indian "enslavement" but with a variation of style and intellectual thrust as the climate of opinion and literary fashions changed. The twin trends of commercialism and literary self-consciousness culminated after the American Revolution in the first collection of accounts inspired by commercial reasons, published in 1793, and in Charles Brockden Brown's (1799) gothic novel. Compilations of captivity accounts continued to be published throughout the nineteenth century (Drake 1851; Buntin 1961:43–174; Meade 1971:58–117; M.J. Thorne 1982; Vail 1949:22–61). Van Der Beets (1973), Vaughan and Clark (1981), and Levernier and Cohen (1977) are histories of the genre.

The blood-and-gore sensationalism of the commercially inspired and highly successful captivity narratives became part of the Western formula in popular literature during the second half of the nineteenth century. Although the Western did not invariably depend upon the bad image of the Indian, it often used the conflict between Red and White to provide drama and suspense. Adventure stories of the Western type with Indians appeared in cheap periodicals, based upon the captivity narrative, the growing legends of Daniel Boone and Davy Crockett, the popularity of Cooper's Leatherstocking Tales, and the ignoble savages presented in the romantic novels of the period (Keiser 1933:38–174; Pearce 1965; Slotkin 1973; Zanger 1967; Barnett 1975; Drinnon 1980, 3).

As distribution improved and the potential market enlarged in the 1850s, the dime novel appeared. Although the publishing house of Beadle and Adams did not invent the genre, it standardized the length, uniformly packaged the product, innovated in advertising, and issued regularly

Fig. 8. Illustrations from 2 of the dime novel series published by Beadle and Adams. Although the illustrations were drawn by a small group of artists, one man was responsible for the majority of them. Most covers were probably executed after the artist read the first 1 or 2 chapters of the book. top left, Cover from reprint of *Malaeska; The Indian Wife of the White Hunter*, by Ann S. Stephens, about 1860. The story takes place during the colonial period in New York City and the Catskill Mountains. top center, Frontispiece from *The Seminole Chief; (Billy Bowlegs) or, The Captives of the Kissimmee* by Lt.-Col. Hazelton, Aug. 29, 1865. top right, Cover from *The White Brave; or The Flower of the Lenape Lodge* by Capt. Murray, June 18, 1872. The story centers on a Delaware chief in 1799. bottom left, Cover from *The Fighting Trapper; or, Kit Carson to the Rescue* by Capt. James F.C. Cooper (Edward S. Ellis), May 21, 1879. bottom center, *Red Renard the Indian Detective; or, The Gold Buzzards of Colorado*, by William F. Cody, Sept. 29, 1886. Whether Cody wrote all his novels himself is disputed. bottom right, *Captain Ready the Red Ransomer; or, Nick Peddie's Wild West Inheritance* by Leon Lewis, Feb. 1, 1888 (Johannsen 1950, 1:8–9, 31, 81, 86, 95, 2:6, 59–60). Drawings probably all by George G. White. Engravings for Dime Novels by Nathaniel Norr and Company, New York, and for Dime Library by John Karst, New York.

for 10¢ what had cost 10 to 15 times as much in hard covers. Their first number in mid-1860 reprinted *Malaeska; The Indian Wife of the White Hunter*, a love story that became a best-seller (fig. 8) (Mott 1947:149–150). Another best-seller published in the same year was *Seth Jones: or, The Captives of the Frontier*, in which Edward S. Ellis had his hero captured by Indians, tortured in vivid detail, chased melodramatically, and revealed finally as someone of sufficiently high status to marry a good White woman. Ellis's paperback hit upon the right formula. What had been creative tension between civilization and savagery in Cooper's and others' novels in the earlier period became production by formula in cheap literature after 1860. In the many series issued by Beadle and Adams and their competitors, frontier adventure provided more titles than any other subject, and the last battles with the Plains Indians probably did not hurt sales or improve the image of the Indian in these novels. (The Indian is not particularly stressed by the authorities on cheap literature, but see the text and especially the pictures in Pearson 1929 and Johannsen 1950–1962.)

By the mid-1880s, the cowboy gained prominence over the former Western heroes: the Boones and Crocketts, the copies of Leatherstocking, and the mountain men and trappers of the far West. Whether based upon the supposed exploits of real men like Buffalo Bill (William F.) Cody, Wild Bill Hickock, and others of the Plains West or upon the imagined adventures of the fictional heroes with the alliterative names of the Deadwood Dick variety, these new Western protagonists displayed ever

greater feats of horsemanship, riding, and escape from ever bloodthirstier savages and outlaws. Perhaps all this action and gore signified that the dime novel and the nickel library had become juvenile literature as well as a formula with little new to offer the adult reader.

The Western formula and cheap literature had its impact upon the stage at home and abroad, on foreign literature, and in the popular arts (fig. 9). The Wild West shows and circuses were dime novels come alive, and they thrilled audiences in Europe and the United States. Fittingly the prototype show in 1884 featured a hero made famous by the cheap literature of the period, Buffalo Bill. Among the standard performers in the show were "wild" Indians acting their savage images, and one year Sitting Bull even toured with the show (C.T. Foreman 1943: 190–209; Barry 1975; Billington 1981:48–50).

The images of the Indian according to the Western formula were impressed upon the American imagination by the popular artists of the day as well. By this period the modern image of the "classic" Indian as a horse-mounted, befeathered Plains tribesman had superseded the older representations of De Bry and successors (Ewers 1965a, 1971) (fig. 10). Besides the vivid illustrations drawn to capture the cheap literature reader's attention, Currier and Ives produced many chromolithographs depicting standard Indian themes according to good as well as bad images. Perhaps the most famous artist of the Old West in the late nineteenth century was Frederick Remington, whose sculptures, engravings, and paintings, like his stories, portrayed a hostile Red race deserving of extinc-

Lib. of Congress, Prints and Photographs Div.: left, LC-USZ62–46512; right, LC-USZ62–19801.
Fig. 9. Nostalgia for the Indian as a "dying race" in early 20th-century art. left, *Memories*. An aged Indian regards a buffalo skull, while in the sky ghostlike figures of buffalo are pursued by mounted hunters. The image can be interpreted as representing both the memories of an aged Indian no longer able to hunt and the loss of a way of life for an entire people. Oil painting by John Innes, 1922. right, *Victim of Fate*. The demise of the buffalo herds in the 1880s was concurrent with dramatic changes in Plains Indian culture. While in this painting only the Indian lies dead, the buffalo is also wounded. The Indian and the buffalo are portrayed as victims of the westward advance of White American development. Oil painting by Henry H. Cross, 1898.

537

WHITE CONCEPTIONS OF INDIANS

tion (H. McCracken 1959; G.E. White 1968:94–121; Hassrick 1973).

Visual representation of White Indian imagery immeasurably increased in the twentieth century. The nickelodeons and penny arcades showed cowboys and Indians on their brief reels, and one of the first, if not the first, motion picture in the modern sense of sustaining a single narrative line depicted *The Great Train Robbery* in 1903 according to Western conventions. Whether derived from popular or elite literature or the director's imagination, the elements of chase, action, violence, suspense, and dramatic scenery of the Western all lent themselves well to film presentation and became a staple of the developing motion picture industry in the early decades of the twentieth century (see "The Indian in the Movies," this vol.).

Radio and television adopted the conventions of the motion picture industry. One of the few Westerns on radio featured the famous Lone Ranger and his stereotyped Indian ally, Tonto. The rapid acceptance of commercial television by the American public in the early 1950s challenged the cinema industry, but the same old themes of Indians, vicious or noble, for or against settlers or miners or soldiers or helpless White women were trotted out on the new medium (Brauer and Brauer 1975). Savages, Indian princesses, squaw men, and wise chiefs were joined by Indian football heroes and soldiers after Jim Thorpe captured public attention (Reising 1974) and Native Americans served in the United States Armies during the two World Wars. In spite of these heroes, the Indian was generally portrayed as a person of little culture and less language. Speaking "How!" and "ugh!" dialogue and wearing combination, if not phony, tribal dress, Native Americans were usually shown with little concern for tribal differences in languages (Stedman 1982:58–73), customs, and beliefs.

Historians have generally adopted the prejudices of their countrymen in favor of national White progress and policies and hence a view of the Indian as deserving of his fate before the onslaught of civilization. The nineteenth-century historians George Bancroft and Francis Parkman employed the romantic conventions of scenery and character delineation to depict the deceitfulness of Indian diplomacy and the horrors of savage warfare (Levin 1959: 133–142; Pearce 1965:162–168; Callcott 1970:168–169; Vitzhum 1974). Parkman in his magisterial history of the conflict between France and England for dominion over North America pictured the Indian as inferior and celebrated the demise of the Red race in the face of White advance (Nye 1967; Wade 1942; Gale 1973; Jennings 1963; Jacobs 1972:83–93; Shulman 1971). Hubert Howe Bancroft (1874–1876) likewise subscribed to the ideas of savagism and civilization in picturing the aboriginal people occupying the Pacific coast of North America as mere prelude to the more interesting White societies to follow (Caughey 1946:118–139; Dippie 1982:98–102).

Similarly, Edward S. Ellis, the dime novel author, and Edward Eggleston, a writer of popular literature, promulgated the same basic views in their popular histories written around 1900 (Benson 1973). American schoolbooks perpetuated these same themes of White supremacy, Indian inferiority, progress, and manifest destiny (Hauptman 1977). Canadian historians uniformly utilized the image of the savage Indian in the nineteenth century and well into the twentieth to enhance French exploits and achievements during the so-called Heroic Period before 1763 (D.B. Smith 1974; cf. Walker 1971).

This view received full academic respectability when it became the dominant interpretation of American history as a result of Frederick Jackson Turner's frontier thesis. As originally presented in 1893, the thesis rested upon the premises of social progress and evolution fashionable in the late nineteenth century, and so, naturally, pictured the Indian as an obstacle to White settlement and the coming of civilization (D.A. Nichols 1972). Although scholars questioned details of Turner's thesis beginning in the 1920s, its basic premises and interpretation of the Indian were not really challenged until after World War II (cf. Walker 1971). H.N. Smith (1950) demonstrated that much of what Turner and other historians had accepted as fact about White westward expansion constituted nineteenth-century American mythology about the frontier. Applying this idea specifically to Native Americans, Pearce (1953) argued that White Americans from 1750 to 1850 had created the image of the Indian from their ideology of the opposition of savagism and civilization in order to justify their policies of extinction and assimilation. Books on White Indian imagery in the late 1970s developed the themes of racist stereotyping by Whites in thought and action (Hoover 1976; Berkhofer 1978; R. Sanders 1978; Takaki 1979; Drinnon 1980; Sheehan 1980; F.W. Turner 1980; Dippie 1982; Stedman 1982). Almost all the books offered implicit, if not blatant, critiques of White American racism, economic imperialism, and cultural hegemony. Some even seemed to reinvent stereotypes of their own in their ardent quest for the origins of American racism, Indian wholeness with the earth, and native spiritual wisdom (Fiedler 1969; Zolla 1973; Takaki 1979).

To correct the views disseminated by White historians, Native Americans founded the American Indian Historical Society in 1964 (Henry and Costo 1967). Through critiques of traditional history texts (J. Henry 1970) and the publication of monographs and a journal, *The Indian Historian* (1964–1980), the members of this organization hoped to correct the usual stereotypes of Native Americans and their past and to produce what they considered a more accurate view of Indian history. White scholars dedicated to the same goal of accuracy had already banded together in the American Society for Ethnohistory. Combining both anthropological insight and historical

538

Circus World Mus., Baraboo, Wis.
Fig. 10. The Plains Indian as representative of all Indians. Iron Tail (Oglala Sioux) was one of 3 models used for the design of the Indian head nickel (Dockstader 1977:122–123). The Wild West show, 101 Ranch, engaged Iron Tail from 1913 to 1916 and promoted him as the nickel's model. He was previously with Buffalo Bill's Wild West Show. Lithograph by The Strobridge Lithograph Company, 1913–1916.

investigation, these ethnohistorians hoped to correct traditional historians' omissions of Indians' perspectives as well as to eliminate anthropologists' assumptions of the timeless Indian (Voegelin 1954:1–3). The success of these goals can be seen in the rise of American Indian history courses, the publication of many ethnohistories, and the efforts to redefine the nature of the American frontier.

Explanations of Indian Otherness

Anthropology as an academic specialty and a professional subcommunity became established in the 1890s, but its concerns in regard to the Indian can be traced back hundreds of years in the questions that have dominated White discussions of the relation between Native Americans and the rest of the human species. How can one account for the origins of the Indians and their location in the Western Hemisphere? How can one explain the differences in complexion, customs, institutions, and languages from other peoples in general and Whites in particular? Were the observed differences inherent and immutable or relative and changeable? How should the Indian be ranked in relation to other societies known to White Europeans and Americans? The history of the answers to these questions reveals that the Indian, like other non-Whites, more often than not proved to White thinkers what they already assumed to be true rather than creating new theories or upsetting old prejudices.

Religion

The initial formulation of these questions and their answers occurred within a Christian framework. For traditional Catholics and Protestants during the first centuries of contact, the Christian cosmogony that explained the origin and history of all human-kind also had to explain the Indians' presence in the New World and the state of their society according to the traditional story given in Genesis of Adam and Eve first peopling the Earth and the descendants of Noah repeopling the planet after the Flood. If the New World and its inhabitants went unmentioned in the Bible or in classical authorities, then the Indians had to be traced through known peoples back to their biblical origins to preserve the monogenetic account of God's creation of all humans in a single act at one time in the past. Speculations upon cultural affinities led thinkers to propose connections between the Indians and almost all the peoples of the ancient world. First proposed in print by José de Acosta (1589) the idea of

539

migration across a land bridge from Asia to America became the preferred means of connection. To account for the amazing diversity of custom and language in the New World from any known in the Old, speculators resorted to the theories of degeneration from the original stock over time or the influences of environment. Whether or not they saw the Indian as degenerate, Christians had to believe in his humanness and in his possession of a soul, for according to Genesis all people possessed but one inheritance and therefore were of one blood in the beginning (Huddleston 1967; Hodgen 1964; D.C. Allen 1949:113–137; Wasserman 1954:456–468; Meek 1976: 37–67).

Naturally, the Christian world view and its explanation of Indian diversity and origins continued long beyond the 1680s, the decade conventionally said to begin the Enlightenment, but about that time thinkers critical of traditional religious and political beliefs gave a new twist to old thoughts sufficient for many scholars to claim that the modern social sciences began then. For the majority of Whites who remained Christians, these new thoughts and those of succeeding centuries had to be grafted on or reconciled with traditional scriptural history or be rejected. During subsequent periods of religious revival, the theory of Indian degeneration regained its appeal (for example, Henry R. Schoolcraft in the 19th century; see Freeman 1965). The question of Indian origins remains an intriguing problem for scholars and lay persons alike (Buntin 1961:354–361; Boorstin 1948:68–80; Sheehan 1973:45–65; Haven 1856; Winsor 1889; Haller 1971: 69–94; Wauchope 1962).

Environmentalism

The effect of physical environment as an explanation of human social and cultural diversity goes back at least to the ancient Greeks, but as a way of analyzing the place of the American Indians among the races of man it was particularly characteristic of Enlightenment thought. (Glacken 1967 provides a general history of environmental thought.) Environmental explanations of Indian life originated in Europe, but this approach especially appealed to thinkers in the United States (Sheehan 1973: 1–44; Pearce 1965:76–104; Bieder 1986:16–54). Grounded upon the basic biological and psychological theories of the time, it seemed to account for racial diversity in terms of the liberal social ideals of the era as well as its scientific knowledge. As part of the secularization of thought during the seventeenth and eighteenth centuries, philosophers came to believe that revelation would discover the laws governing human actions and history to be as stable and unchanging as those put forth by the great Newton for the cosmos. If laws for the human realm were to display the same uniformity and universality as governed in the larger universe, then the science of

man must be grounded upon a fundamental human nature common to all people. The diversity of complexions, customs, and institutions must be explained by principles applicable to all human beings.

By accepting also the short time span of the biblical account of creation, Enlightenment thinkers were still faced with explaining the varieties of the human species about which they received increasing information from European exploration, settlement, and conquest in all parts of the world. Generally men of the period assumed in accordance with their fundamental cosmology that species were fixed for all time with little or no possibility of transforming from one into another, for they really knew of no mechanism by which such mutation could occur (Glass, Temkin, and Straus 1959; J.C. Greene 1959: 129–174). Varieties on the other hand could and did change from their initial creation, and so natural causes had to be found for these alterations in line with the basic outlook of the era.

Environmentalism became the preferred explanation. To the extent that the psychology of the time presumed mental processes a function of environment, particularly according to Lockean sensationalism, then this approach to human diversity was reinforced. This definition of species and explanation of varieties of mankind preserved the monogenetic interpretation presumed by Christian and nonbeliever alike while it also accounted for the obvious racial differences so engraved upon the White mind. Under this theory, all men were created equal by their Creator and the variations were due to purely natural causes. As the Philadelphia scientist, Benjamin Rush, succinctly summarized the theory (quoted in Bieder 1986: 10): "Human nature is the same in all Ages and Countries; and all differences we perceive in its characters in respect to Virtue and Vice, Knowledge and Ignorance, may be accounted for from Climate, Country, Degrees of Civilization, from Government and other accidental causes." Indians therefore became products both of the social and physical environment in the confused mixture of character and circumstance that constituted environmental theory at that time. The best example of environmental theory applied to the Indian was S.S. Smith's (1965) 1787 essay.

The assumptions of environmentalism could lead to arguments supporting the degeneration of the Indian as well as his equality with all men as the eighteenth-century debate over the advantages and disadvantages of the discovery of America demonstrated. The great eighteenth-century French naturalist Georges Louis Leclerc, comte de Buffon included Native Americans in his generalizations about the degeneration and deficiency of New World animals and plants (Duchet 1971:229–280). Other thinkers inimical to the idea of the Noble Savage picked up and amplified his ideas and soon reached the inevitable conclusion that if European animals introduced into the Western Hemisphere degenerated then so too would

European peoples (Gerbi 1973; but see Chinard 1947; Sheehan 1973:66–88). Thus Americans defended their own enlightenment and the possibility of progress of their country by denying the facts claimed by the degenerationists (Hoover 1976:60–79). In doing so, they naturally proved the Indian at least equal in potential to the White man if not in present accomplishments. Such a defense of the American Indian appeared in 1785 as part of Thomas Jefferson's contribution to the larger debate (Jefferson 1954:43–65, 199–202).

The Enlightenment idea of progress and of conjectural history also bolstered assumptions of Indian inferiority. In so far as Native Americans like other alien peoples figured in the history of European expansion around the world, their conquest justified in White minds their understanding of their own history as progress. Stressing the commonness of all human nature and the uniformity of the laws of human behavior over all time, the intellectuals of the era presumed that present conditions of primitive peoples could be taken to represent the previous history of civilized society. Although the American Indian played but a slight role in overall Enlightenment thought (Honigsheim 1952), most writers presumed that Indian beliefs and customs exemplified the earlier stages of existence in the natural history of mankind, for as Adam Ferguson wrote in 1767 (quoted in Burrow 1966:12): "It is in their [the Indians'] present condition that we are to behold, as in a mirror, the features of our progenitors." In English political philosophy the image of the bad Indian was used by Thomas Hobbes to demonstrate that the life of man in the original state of nature was "solitary, poore, nasty, brutish, and short," while John Locke employed the image of the good Indian to prove, on the contrary, that the state of nature was indeed benevolent because "in the beginning all the world was America." Thus had the systematic explication of correspondence between Indian and ancient cultures in regard to origins, religions, and other institutions culminated in the theoretical or conjectured history of all mankind (Hodgen 1964:295–430; Meek 1976).

The comparison of societies became a theory of progression that led easily to the ranking of peoples. By analogy between the life cycle of a human being and the history of the species, philosophers, especially in France and Scotland, produced a history of the sequence of stages of society that the race had passed through to reach the height presumably exemplified by eighteenth-century Europe. This idea was not new at the time, for it can be found in the ancient writers and in Spaniards Bartolomé de Las Casas and José de Acosta, for example (Pagden 1982:146–200), but the intellectual context that gave real meaning to such a sequence did not develop until the late eighteenth century. Whether such stages were grounded in the ability of the human intelligence, as French philosophers wrote, or on the modes of subsistence and the division of labor, as Scottish writers maintained, the Indian ranked low or at the bottom of the scale (Meek 1976; R.L. Emerson 1979; Stocking 1975). This theory of progress as applied to the American Indian received extensive treatment in William Robertson's *History of America* (1811–1812), a book particularly influential in shaping American leaders' comprehension of the Indian (Hoebel 1960). Although citizens of the new nation debated the accuracy of Robertson's picture of the Indian, they accepted the Scottish philosophers' version of progress just as they had its environmentalism in explaining the Indian (Bieder 1986). This thinking illustrated that Whites of the time could both hold to the equality of the human species and yet rank Indians as inferior in achievement and act accordingly in attitude and policy as did Benjamin Rush and Thomas Jefferson (Kunitz 1970; Binder 1968:82–119; Drinnon 1980:78–98; Takaki 1979: 55–65; Sheehan 1973). European and American thinkers alike saw cultural diversity, but they did not approve of it as an ideal (cf. Duchet 1971; Popkin 1973).

Social Evolution

What had been conjecture in the eighteenth century became science in the succeeding century under evolutionism. The theories and findings of the many evolutionarily grounded sciences provided a new context for the theoretical history of mankind. The history of human institutions and customs came to be seen in terms of development like all other things in the universe. Both in social science and history, scientific status was given genealogy through the genetic method of explanation according to evolution. Societies and cultures were portrayed as slow accumulations obeying laws natural and evolutionary. The findings of archeology demonstrated that the origins of human society and culture did not form fully developed at one time but grew rather from slow beginnings just as had other elements in the universe. The destruction of the biblical chronology gave the life sciences longer scope to achieve the transformations needed to explain present-day forms, and the increased antiquity of man offered a longer time span for the conjectural historian. If human beings were the end-product of a long process of evolution, could not the institutions and customs of civilization be developed from savagery in the same manner according to the same basic laws (J.C. Greene 1959)?

Evolutionism became the framework for anthropology by the late nineteenth century, especially for the division called ethnography or ethnology, through the application of the comparative method and conjectural history. The method remained fundamentally the same as developed by eighteenth-century thinkers, but in the hands of Edward Tylor and John Lubbock in England and Lewis Henry Morgan in the United States it gained authority and comprehensiveness for the treatment of human culture and societies. If the trend to utilize more and better authenticated data was new, the basic assumptions continued to be the same as earlier: uniformity of human mental characteristics and abilities over space and time so as to allow the comparison of peoples regardless of geography or history, similarity of stages in the course of cultural evolution of all peoples, and the use of European standards and the idea of progress to measure the direction and amount of development. In brief, these and other leading anthropologists of the era took over the eighteenth-century conceptual or logical relationships of a classificatory scheme embracing all coexisting and previous peoples and made it into a sequential relationship in a time series through analogy to the transformism of organic growth (Murphree 1961; Burrow 1966; cf. Voget 1967; M. Harris 1968:108–249).

The implications of evolutionary anthropology for the scientific image of the Indian and the use of Native American ethnography in the new discipline can be seen most vividly in the writings of Lewis Henry Morgan (B.J. Stern 1931; Resek 1960; Bieder 1986:194–251). Although L.H. Morgan (1851) spoke of the Iroquois as representative of all Indians and presumed the ideas of progress and stages of development in what is often hailed as the first modern ethnography in the United States, he employed comparison only incidentally in his exposition of familial and governmental relationships. The insight into kinship relations afforded by the Iroquois L.H. Morgan (1870) extended to all. Using kinship systems as clues to previous social organization, he reconstructed the conjectural history of the family and marriage (Trautmann 1987). L.H. Morgan (1877) espoused a full-fledged theory of evolution. In addition to the family, he traced the institutions of government, property, and technological innovation and economic development. As he measured the "ratio of progress," the American Indians had advanced beyond the "zero" of lower savagery but had fallen far behind the superior Aryan and Semitic races. Such evolutionary presuppositions and the example of Morgan justified the research and findings of the departments of anthropology being established in the museums and universities during the late nineteenth century. John Wesley Powell, the first head of the Bureau of American Ethnology founded in Washington in 1879, hoped to shape the work of his colleagues along these lines (Darrah 1957:255–269, 355–360; Darnell 1969:1–139; Hinsley 1981:125–189; Moses 1984; cf. Mark 1980; for Canadian developments, see Cole 1973).

Scientific Racism

The great evolutionary anthropologists of the nineteenth century used the term "culture," in the singular and not the plural sense. Given their belief in progress, they ranked all lifeways, including those of Native Americans, in hierarchical order. In their attempts to explain the failure of some societies to reach the same top stage of civilization ascribed to themselves, they resorted to the racist modes of thinking common to their times. Though they thought of culture as extra-somatic, they were unclear on the mechanism of transmission. So long as they confused culture and biology, they frequently had to adopt racial characterizations of peoples to explain the diversity of human cultures in spite of their uniformitarian, and therefore theoretically egalitarian, assumption of the psychic unity of all mankind.

Scientific racism accomplished the "biologization of history," to use M. Harris's (1968:107) telling expression, by equating the cultural hierarchy assumed under the idea of progress with the physical and mental differences popularly believed to exist among human groups. Certain counter-assumptions about the common origin of the human species and the significance of the environment prevented most eighteenth-century thinkers from carrying racist thinking to its logical extreme as a science, but the fusion of several trends in the nineteenth century convinced most social scientists in the second half of that and the early decades of the twentieth centuries of the scientific truth of racism. Polygenetic as opposed to monogenetic explanation of human origins moved from a Christian heresy confined to a few brave thinkers in the seventeenth and eighteenth centuries to a widely debated issue in the nineteenth. Although still a minority opinion, the increasing number of polygenists pointed to a changing religious atmosphere and the coming divorce between religion and the scientific study of human origins. As evolution in all forms became increasingly acceptable to thinkers, most assumed that cultural evolution was parallel to biological evolution and maybe even part of it. Last, the use of comparative anatomy to study racial differences was supposed to offer firm scientific basis for what so many thinkers had long assumed about the differences among various people.

Before a science of race could start, the ad hoc groupings of common knowledge had to be given scientific status through a classification system. The division of all mankind into a few races instead of many nations or peoples began in the last quarter of the seventeenth century with François Bernier and William Petty, but neither man singled out Native Americans as a separate race (J.S. Slotkin 1944:459–460; Hodgen 1964:418–425). Although eighteenth-century classifiers differed upon the number of races, they usually listed the American Indian as a separate race (J.S. Slotkin 1944:461–466; J.C. Greene 1954:31–41). The stereotype of the Indian entered the mainstream of scientific thought through Linné's (1758–1759) classification of all living creatures into a single system. Following eighteenth-century practice, he included all known specimens of the human race as one species, *Homo sapiens*, and then divided it into several varieties. *Homo americanus* was essentially the traditional White image of the Indian, for he described him as reddish, choleric, beardless, content, free, painted with red lines, and governed by custom. His confused mixture of geography, color, physique, customs, personality, and even the theory of the four humors as well as his Europocentric bias reveals the state of scientific classification of the human species at the time.

Such gross comparisons of physical appearance, culture, and geography continued well into the next century, but some scholars as early as the late eighteenth century sought to place the subject of race upon more scientific grounds through the detailed and quantified study of anatomy. Beginning at that time, scientists commenced measuring facial angles and cranium sizes in order to differentiate the races. Craniometry or craniology, the study of the size of the brain, shape of the skull, and nature of the suture, reached its height with the invention of the cranial or cephalic index in Sweden in 1842 and the treatises of the 1840s and 1850s. In the United States the concern with crania was part of the pro-slavery argument for the Black's inherent inferiority, but incidental to the measurement of Black and White skulls was the study of Red ones (Bieder 1986:55–103). From these beginnings came the discipline of physical anthropology.

By the 1860s the cultural hierarchy of social progress had been fused with the racial hierarchy of physical anthropology, and evolutionary biology only seemed to confirm the conventional wisdom. Ascent up the ladder of social evolution was closely linked to mental capacity and mental capacity was presumed a function of brain or cranial size. Whether such differences were due to environmental adaptation or to polygenetic inheritance, the conclusion was the same: the lower races not only possessed darker skins and crude manners but also inferior organic equipment. What eighteenth-century scholars ascribed to the progress of reason or social stages in the history of nations, nineteenth- and early twentieth-century scientists attributed to innate mental capacity and biological superiority in the history of races.

Regardless of whether the Indian was measured against cultural history or biological destiny, Whites in this period pictured his race as redder in color and more "other" in conception (Vaughan 1982). Evolutionary and racist assumptions in the new discipline of psychology proved among other things that Indians, like other savages, depended more on instinct than reason in their affairs. D.G. Brinton (1890) applied such ethnic psychology to Native Americans. That instinct governed Indians may also be found in the early issues of the *American Anthropologist*, founded in 1889, and in some of the articles in Hodge (1907–1910, 1:53–56, 964–972, 2: 238–240, 311-313). These presuppositions shaped the Indian displays in museums and the exhibits of man in the world's fairs after the Centennial Exhibition of 1876 in Philadelphia. Museums and fairs alike used the Indian to exemplify the earlier state of human beings prior to mankind's ascendancy to its nineteenth-century apex, especially in the progress of technology (Hinsley 1981; Lester 1972; Trennert 1974; Rydell 1984).

Anthropology

Scientific racism continued into the early decades of the twentieth century as part of the social scientific mainstream in the United States (Cravens 1978; Hoover 1976: 279–301), but a new school of anthropology arose to challenge its basic assumptions during the same period. Although the concept of culture in a modern anthropological sense did not prevail in the social sciences in the United States until the 1930s at the earliest (Kroeber and Kluckhohn 1952), the basic assumptions of relativism, pluralism, and functionalism that underlay it were abundantly foreshadowed, by 1915, in the work of Franz Boas and his students, who sought to replace the conjectural approach of evolutionary history with a more scientific method based upon empirical research. These scholars stressed detailed fieldwork among specific tribes over theoretical speculation and condemned the comparative method for ripping cultural elements out of their context to fit a preconceived scheme. In their own research they emphasized the wholeness of cultures over comparisons across cultures, examined the distribution of traits rather than their origins, and preferred the mapping of cultures in the New World to the elaboration of a cross-societal taxonomy based upon evolution. The method of Boasian anthropology therefore became the intensive study of localized culture traits shared by social groups or the lifeway and beliefs of a single group. The concept of culture provided a rallying point for the professionalization of anthropology as a distinct, formal discipline as its practitioners formed new university departments (Darnell 1969; Stocking 1968:133–233; M. Harris 1968:250–372; Matthews 1970; Cravens 1978:89–120; Dippie 1982: 231–236, 281–284).

As applied to Native Americans, the Boasian approach meant intensive fieldwork among one or a few tribes and the classification of cultures according to areas of trait distribution. Boas himself concentrated upon the Northwest Coast tribes, while Clark Wissler and Robert Lowie studied intensively the Plains Indians, Alfred Kroeber the California Indians, and Paul Radin the Winnebago. In other words, they studied Native Americans as tribes and as cultures not as the Indian, but they did strive to understand them as they had once existed in the past and not as they lived when the anthropologist visited the tribe. Although tribal ethnography can be traced back in American anthropology to Henry Rowe Schoolcraft or Lewis Henry Morgan, never before this period had tribes been studied so completely or so intensively for their own sake by so many anthropologists in light of the modern assumptions of cultural relativity and pluralism. The product of this work was at first the mapping of various modes of subsistence, social organization, languages, customs, and beliefs according to their distribution in aboriginal America. These maps of distribution led to the designation of culture areas by the ways of life considered most characteristic before the coming of White peoples, especially for the museum display of native artifacts. To the extent that New World anthropology was presumed unable at that time to depend upon dated records of culture change and diffusion, anthropologists chose to infer the history of culture change from geographical distribution (Kroeber 1931). The first general works on Native Americans incorporating the views of the Boas School were Wissler's (1917) survey and Parsons's (1922) anthology.

The history of anthropological theory in the United States and knowledge of Indian cultures has increased greatly since the 1920s, but the basic presuppositions of cultural pluralism and relativism as established by Boas and his followers remain as fundamental to the new developments as they were earlier. American anthropologists came to understand culture as a holistic configuration as well as patterned, as a mental blueprint as well as behavior manifestation, as historicist as well as historical. Benedict (1934) presented these presuppositions to the general reader through her description of three cultures, two of which were Native American (Pueblo and Kwakiutl). She hoped to persuade her readers that the integrative holism of individual cultures was as important as their diversity (Modell 1983). Since the mid-1930s English social anthropology, the structuralism of Claude Lévi-Srauss, and even a new evolutionism arose to challenge the long-dominant school of Franz Boas (Erasmus 1953: 74–146; M. Harris 1968:393–687; Voget 1960; Hoover 1976:272–301, 341–381), but these new intellectual styles did not repudiate the cultural pluralism and relativism fundamental to the profession.

Imagery as Justification for White Policy

The imagery outlined here possessed real implications both for the White policymakers who used the conceptions of the Indian to justify their actions toward Indians and for those Native Americans treated as Indians under those policies. Regardless of the real motives prompting White governmental leaders, Indian agents, philanthropists, or military officers in their dealings with Native Americans, the idea of the Indian stood at the very heart of the rationales for the policies they followed. Without repeating what is covered elsewhere in this volume on the same topics, this chapter concludes with an examination of the relationship between White Indian imagery and: the

justification for White expansion and settlement upon Native Americans' lands; White military activities and the conquest of the population; the dependency and wardship status of the Indian under White law; and White religious and educational work among the tribes (Berkhofer 1978: 113-195; Dippie 1982).

The most obvious use of the "Indian" image pertained to the conflict over land title. European nations claimed title to New World lands through peaceful or military conquest and subsequent settlement. Royal charters to explorers and settlement agencies treated the new found lands as either uninhabited or peopled by persons with imperfect or no legal title to the lands upon which they lived. Native Americans were denied title to their lands according to European theory because they lacked Christianity or because they lacked adequate habits of civilization. A heathen religion demanded conversion to Christ's kingdom and, if the natives resisted, justified conquest to promulgate White religion. Failure to cultivate the land in accord with the dictates of the Bible as interpreted by Whites of the time also justified joint occupation of the land with the Native American possessors, if not outright dispossession of the Indian. If White interpretation of God's words and international custom justified the original opinions on native title, then the ideas of civilization and progress, after their invention in the eighteenth century, plus the secularized conception of natural rights came to justify imperfect title and expropriation in that century.

The founding of the United States infused new meaning into White Americans' conception of progress and civilization, but the effect was the same as the old thinking on the new nation's policies toward native title and land acquisition. Thus, for example, policymakers in the United States made the traditional division between occupational and sovereign title the basis for their approach to Native American lands under their jurisdiction. They continued to employ the deficiency image of the Indian to justify continued removal of tribes westward (fig. 11) and ultimately allotment of tribal lands in the last decades of the nineteenth century. For the religious White, God continued to demand the spread of Christian civilization over the pagan's sparsely settled lands. The secular-minded could see destiny manifest in the technological progress of the United States and the social evolutionary theories applied to races and societies at the time as sufficient justification and explanation for what they presumed had to happen to Indian occupation of lands. For some or even many Whites, the Indians received a bargain in the exchange of their lands for Christianity and civilization (Kimmey 1960), but Native American acceptance of these gifts was no guarantee that acculturation would promote firmer Indian title to lands as the Cherokees discovered in the 1830s. The deficiency and the savage warrior images tainted even this tribe under the demand for removal, so powerful a rationale were they for White land policy. (Works especially important for Indian imagery in relation to White land policy are Juricek 1970; Washburn 1959; Eisinger 1948; Jennings 1971b; Weinberg 1935:72-92; Dippie 1982; Sheehan 1973:243-275.)

More than mere deficiency was needed to justify war and conquest, and the ignoble Indian provided that rationale. Whites consistently called native resistance to White incursion "treacherous," native methods of warfare "savage," and native victories "massacres." From the earliest Spanish, French, and English battles with various tribal peoples to the last wars on the Plains, White soldiers, government officials, writers and reporters at the time and historians later often pictured the conflict as a struggle between civility and savagery, between innocence and duplicity. Some scholars, in fact, claim to discern a cycle of imagery dependent upon the course of White-Indian relations in an area. The peaceful relations of initial contact and native hospitality to the early White comers fostered an image of the good Indian in the minds of the Whites. The wars that followed from land acquisition and dispossession due to the expansion of White settlement generated the image of the bad Indian. Finally, the elimination of the Indian "menace" and White hegemony over the remaining natives in the area brought a return of the good image and even nostalgia for a dying race. The cycle has been developed most explicitly for early Virginia history (for example, Nash in Dudley and Novak 1972:55-86), but the cycle seems the basis of the longstanding practice among scholars to consider distance in space or time as lending enchantment to Indian life in the minds of Whites while proximity breeds bitterness if not contempt.

Americans thought too many Europeans romanticized the Indian they did not have to confront directly in the forests and plains of America. French and English writers adopted the noble and romantic savage conventions in literature and art in the eighteenth century, but American writers waited until the following century and the defeat of the Indians in the eastern part of the United States before using the same themes. It was only then basically that Easterners wanted to save the poor Indian through extensive missionary work at the same time as the Westerners saw those efforts as mere obstacles to doing unto the Indian what the Easterners had done years earlier (fig. 4) (Nichols 1971; Evans 1967:9–68; cf. Riley 1984). Under these impressions, those Whites favoring military conquest of the Indians for land and for subordination needed only to promulgate and act upon the "realistic" views of frontierspeople rather than the sentimental opinions of Whites removed from actual contact with Native Americans (cf. Leonard 1974; Skelton 1976).

The deficient image alone was sufficient to justify the peculiar position Native Americans have occupied in relation to White law and government, but the concep-

U. of Mich., William L. Clements Lib., Print Div., Ann Arbor.

Fig. 11. Andrew Jackson depicted as the "Great Father." Jackson was a key figure in U.S. policy decisions to remove American Indians from the eastern areas of the nation to the West. Although the Indians' clothing is not uncharacteristic for some groups, the Indians appear diminutive and doll-like in this picture. They are portrayed as at once dependent upon and manipulated by Jackson who represents the paternal relationship of the federal government of Indians. Engraving, probably around 1830.

tions of the Indian as savage or as inferior in mind or ability offered additional arguments to those proposing subordinate status legally for the Native American. If Native Americans as independent tribes before White conquest posed anomalies for European and American conceptions of national sovereignty, they continued to present problems to lawmakers deciding their fate after defeat. If after conquest Indians were alloted special reservations upon which to reside, so too were they given special laws under which to live. White laws generally circumscribed the personal liberties, the economic relations, and the political power and privileges of the Native American when designated an *Indian*. In the name of protecting Indians from their own incompetency in handling civilized institutions and the vices of White civilization, Whites proclaimed laws to restrict trade, land transactions, and alcohol among Indians. In general the Indian was not considered a person under White law and therefore incapable of entering into many kinds of legal transactions and political relationships. In the United States, for example, federal law generally treated the Native American as a ward, placing his own land and money in trust for him at times. Symbolic of the peculiar and inferior status of the Indian in the United States was the long-time denial of citizenship to the Native American. Although other persons born on American soil were considered citizens under law, Indians who were native to the United States had to wait for special laws or the Indian Citizenship Act of 1924 to achieve full citizenship, and even then states continued to curtail their privileges. Discussions of United States presidents' images of Indians and their resultant policies may be gleaned from Binder (1968), Prucha (1971b), L.H. Parsons (1973), Sinkler (1971), Sheehan (1973), Satz (1975), and D.A. Nichols (1978).

Again the Indian as deficient in White values and institutions seemed to be the prevailing image behind White philanthropic effort over the centuries. Although the content of civilization and what it meant to Whites changed over the centuries, Indian lack of it and its metaphysical correlate in White minds, Christianity, justified White missionary, educational, philanthropic, and welfare programs from the beginning of European settlement. White succession to title and occupancy had

been justified upon the basis of the benefits the natives would receive from Christian missionization. Thus, lack of the proper religion both provided Whites with their rationale and defined the object of their philanthropic activity (for example, Kennedy 1950; Berkhofer 1965; N. Lewis 1968; Beaver 1966, 1969; Mardock 1971; Prucha 1976, 1979; Bowden 1981). Whether or not missionaries were racists is raised by Coleman (1980; cf. Cocks 1975). White-maintained, White-directed, and White-taught educational systems among Indian tribes, whether financed by private White charities or by government funds, sought nothing less than the conversion of the Indian to the White culture of their time (Ahern 1976; Bannan 1978). Thus, philanthropists, like other Whites, pictured Indians according to their own rather than their charges' needs.

Conclusion

Even the briefest historical survey of White conceptions, images, and attitudes about the Indian leads one to several evident but perplexing conclusions. Although scholars agree that Europeans and White Americans alike generally inspected the Indian as an other by means of a mirror held up to their own lives at the time, they disagree upon what of White society and culture was reflected at the

ABORIGINAL SUSCEPTIBILITY.

MAN-WITH-FRAYED-EAR. — What for you cry?
MAN-AFRAID-OF-RED-HEADED-HORSE. — Injun
think what dam shame he 's Injun!

THE REASON OF THE INDIAN OUTBREAK.
General Miles declares that the Indians are starved into rebellion.

Lib. of Congress: left, LC-USZ62-55997; right, LC-USZ62-56003.
Fig. 12. Political cartoons. Political cartoons were a vehicle by which conceptions of Indians were promoted. left, The reservation-bound Indian as self-deprecating. This cartoon appeared in an issue of *Puck's Library* devoted to the theme "Out West." In it, Indians were presented as fools, savages, or at their best when dead. Cartoon by Kembil in *Puck's Library*, No. 18:22, December 1888. right, Cartoon suggesting that Indian agents are profiting from graft stemming from reservation supplies while Indians starve. The cartoon appeared about one month after Gen. Nelson A. Miles sent troops to the Pine Ridge and Rosebud reservations where the Ghost Dance was active and about a week before the massacre at Wounded Knee. While this particular cartoon appears to be sympathetic toward Indians, the publisher was generally critical of them and was probably more concerned with criticizing the political system surrounding Indian-related policies. The publisher also used Indians as characters and sarcastic references to them in political commentary and cartoons about non-Indian-related issues. Lithograph in *Judge* 19(479):214, Dec. 20, 1890, based on
546   drawing by Hamilton.

time. Some scholars accept White professions of ideals and ideas as the true White image of the Indian, but others believe that actions toward Native Americans spoke louder than words in ascertaining the real White images and conceptions of Indians in any situation. To oversimplify somewhat, the first group of scholars sees the imagery as an integral part of White cultures and as an independent variable in explaining White behavior toward Native Americans; the second group understands the imagery to be a variable dependent upon the political and economic relationships prevailing in White societies at various times. Usually the former concentrates on ideas and imagery, while the latter emphasizes policy and actual behavior toward Native Americans.

Still less do scholars concur upon just how much Whites could see beyond the reflected mirror image of their society to the realities of Native American existence. Just as the motives of the producer of the historical sources influenced the nature of the image, so the goal of the modern-day investigator affects what is looked for and found in the history of White Indian imagery. Some investigators seek to illustrate changing intellectual and cultural trends through the use of Indian materials, while others try to ascertain how those trends determined White understanding of the Indian. Still others wish to condemn past White ideals, policies, and actions as demonstrated in the treatment of Native Americans. In the present as in the past, to understand the Indian is to understand an "other" according to one's own culture.

Ultimately, then, it is to the history of White values and ideas that one must turn for the conceptual categories, classificatory schema, explanatory frameworks, the moral criteria by which past and present Whites perceived, observed, evaluated, and interpreted Indians as others. In this sense, the scholarly understanding of past White images becomes the latest phase of a centuries-old White effort to understand the Indian. Thus any history of that scholarship must explore how present-day opinions, including so-called scientific conceptions of the Indian, evolved from past imagery as well as how current interpreters look at past imagery through the prism of present-day concerns.

Relations Between Indians and Anthropologists

NANCY OESTREICH LURIE

Both Indians, as a particular kind of minority population, and anthropology, as a particular kind of scholarly discipline, operate within a larger sociopolitical environment that for a long time was conducive to mutually satisfactory and functionally adaptive relations. Some time after World War II, this largely if not entirely unplanned symbiosis began to deteriorate. The reciprocal basis of the relationship had been undercut; and whatever warm feelings still existed between particular Indian people and particular anthropologists, anthropology as a discipline no longer offered much to the Indian population. Yet, anthropologists still turned to the Indian population to forward the interests of the discipline.

In probing into the methods and personalities of anthropology's founding fathers and mothers it is clear that many of the early, self-trained scholars must have struck the particular Indians they worked with as decidedly unlovable (for example, Lurie 1966). Nevertheless, they managed to do as much creditable research as their contemporaries who exhibited greater sensitivity. By the turn of the twentieth century when the first university-trained and more theoretically sophisticated scholars began entering the field, they still obtained their data by whatever rough and ready methods would accomplish the task; however, by that time the professionalization of the discipline increased opportunities to compare experiences. Anthropologists became aware of field techniques as embodying more than thoroughness and dogged persistence. Terms such as empathy, rapport, and participant observation became part of the anthropologists' working vocabulary. Eventually, anthropologists began to take it for granted that they should make a sincere effort to maintain cordial relations and conform as much as possible to the local value system. By the 1950s anthropologists began teaching courses and publishing texts on field techniques in order to properly sensitize their students. Yet, it was only then that Indians expressed their resentment! Although anthropologists had recognized the need to change for the better in their personal relationships in the field, anthropology as a discipline and a profession had undergone changes that tended to militate against good working relationships with Indians as a people.

548   Four significant periods can be discerned in the development and deterioration of symbiosis between Indian people and anthropology. From the 1830s to about 1870, the Indian population contributed much to anthropology without being aware of doing so. Between the 1870s and 1920s, despite conscious interaction between anthropologists and Indians, anthropologists were not fully aware of the extent of their usefulness to the Indian interest. During the 1930s and 1940s, the nature of the symbiosis was manifest, at least in large part, to both sides. By the early 1950s, new factors affecting Indians as a minority and other new factors affecting anthropology as a discipline began to erode the basic structural relations underlying symbiosis.

The Initiation of Symbiosis 1830-1870

American anthropology is indebted to the Native American for far more than a vast store of rich and varied data. Given the complex of intertwined questions posed by the simple presence of the Indians, it was probably inevitable that in North America anthropology should develop as a multifaceted discipline, subsuming to a large extent what are usually considered separate disciplines in Europe (cf. Hallowell 1960). In North America, "the study of man" was holistic, comparative, and bicultural almost from its inception as the scientific approach to long-standing philosophical speculation about the origin of the American Indian. American scholars saw the presence of a distinctive race, impressive earthworks and simple stone tools, a multiplicity of tongues, and a great range of customs as interrelated parts of a single question peculiar to the New World. Thus, while anthropology in North America was broad in concept from the start, it tended to focus almost entirely on one population, the American Indians.

Henry Rowe Schoolcraft (1839) was typical of the general naturalists of the nineteenth century who studied rocks, minerals, flora and fauna, and the Indian at first hand. Most of his ethnographic data were collected in the course of his career as an agent and superintendent for the Bureau of Indian Affairs from 1822 to 1841 in the Great Lakes region. He says of his own work, "respecting these legends and myths . . . .they are versions of oral relations from the lips of the Indians, and are transcripts of the thought and inventions of the aboriginal mind . . . .They place the man altogether in a new phasis. They reflect him as he is" (1856: vii).

Similarly, Lewis Henry Morgan's life work was stimulated by the interest in Indians of the same White elite that delighted in Henry Wadsworth Longfellow's *The Song of Hiawatha*. Seeking a pattern for the organization and ritual of a men's social club, L. H. Morgan, a lawyer, soon abandoned his interest in make-believe upon discovering the real Indian world and went on to produce his monumental tome, *The League of the Ho-dé-no-sau-nee, or Iroquois* (1851). This work was to set the theoretical tone of American anthropology for generations to come and act as a model of ethnological research and reporting.

Although it was Bronislaw Malinowski who made explicit, systematic, and respectable the field technique known as participant observation, the publication of Malinowski's journals proved disillusioning to many anthropologists because, apparently, Malinowski never rid himself of lingering racism and patronizing colonialism (Malinowski 1967; M.L. Wax 1972). Personal data comparable to Malinowski's diaries from Schoolcraft (1851), Morgan (L.A. White 1959), and their successors well into the twentieth century such as Franz Boas (Rohner 1966) reveal energetic collectors of information who operated out of what might be called field offices. They saw little need to mingle cozily within the tribal communities as an essential feature of fieldwork; however, they knew the value of trying to comprehend things from the Indians' point of view. Even Boas donned blanket and headband while attending feasts among the Kwakiutl at Alert Bay in 1896, and frequently he went barefoot around the village (Rohner 1966:190). The trouble was that these anthropologists considered what they were interested in as somehow more truly Indian than the rest of Indian life going on around them. Committed to the then contemporary common-sense view as to the Indians' future, they did not delve into the adaptive nature of changes taking place before their very eyes.

For the most part, individual Indians with whom the early scholars worked, such as Morgan's Iroquois associate, Ely Parker, seemed to agree with White opinion that the Indians would lose their distinctive identity; but they were motivated to record their native heritage for posterity. As expressed by Schoolcraft, "the man, it may be, shall pass away from the earth, but these tributes to the best feelings of the heart will remain" (1856:xxiii).

Mutual Exploitation, 1870-1930

Although we tend to associate the tradition of painstaking fieldwork as beginning with Franz Boas, earlier research of a high order was inspired by Morgan's example. The professionalization and increasing sophistication of anthropology as a university-taught discipline in which Boas played a key role built upon the data and experience of self-trained forerunners who had gone into the field with private means or under museum or government sponsorship. Nevertheless, it was the Indians' steadily worsening condition that operated to the benefit of anthropology from about 1870 to 1930 as much as the theoretical and methodological refinement that developed within the discipline itself.

Most Whites who went among the Indians did so to hasten the Indians' sociocultural demise in the name of God and country or to improve their own fortunes at the Indians' expense. Anthropologists, interested in neither of these ends, brought a rare quality, simply the desire to know and understand. Furthermore, albeit for reasons of their own, anthropologists were as distressed as the Indians that the Indians' traditions were being systematically repressed and destroyed. A mutual bond was thus easily established. The anthropologist, by his or her very presence and dedicated labors, acknowledged as worthy of the greatest intellectual respect those very things that Indian agents forbade as "savage" and missionaries denounced as "pagan."

Indians themselves entered the ranks of professional anthropology at a time when there were few anthropologists. John Napoleon Brinton Hewitt, a Tuscarora, and Francis La Flesche, an Omaha, began their careers as interpreters and field assistants about 1880 and soon became anthropologists in their own right on the staff of the Smithsonian Institution's newly formed Bureau of Ethnology. In succeeding years, considering the small number of Indians who entered college, a surprisingly large number have taken degrees in anthropology. If anthropologists relied on Indians to supply data, Indians discovered anthropology as a new profession uniquely adapted to their interests and talents.

By chance, anthropologists fanned out into many reservation communities at a time when White officialdom was losing patience with the Indians' curious unwillingness to understand they were supposed to vanish. This circumstance played a large part in ushering in and sustaining the so-called golden age of American anthropology from about 1880 to 1920 (Mead and Bunzel 1960).

Anthropologists, taking little heed of the political changes that were taking place around them, generally thought more highly of the Indians than they did of the Whites on the reservations. And the Indians knew it. There were, of course, individual anthropologists who actively championed the Indians and fought abrogation of their communal rights; for example, James Mooney (Hertzberg 1971:262–266) and Frank Hamilton Cushing (Gronewold 1972:46); however, in general, anthropologists appear to have accepted the Indians' misfortunes as the workings of providence rather than the result of calculated policy they could question and oppose as scientists and citizens. Alice Fletcher was a notable exception who recognized something could be done on behalf of the Indians by lobbying at the federal level. Unfortunately, she put her considerable influence behind the Omaha Allotment Act of 1882 and the Dawes Severalty Act of 1887 (Lurie 1966a), mistaking popular opinion regarding the Indians' inevitable assimilation for scientific truth as revealed in the evolutionary theory of her day.

It was probably just as well for the Indians that the first university-trained scholars who came upon the scene about the same time that the disastrous effects of allotment began to occur simply stuck to their work as anthropologists. Although the criticism is overdrawn that Boas was not interested in theory, at least his cautiousness made his students leery of trying to apply untested theory to practical problems on a major scale as Fletcher had done. Avoiding humanitarian sins of commission, yet they were not without sins of omission as scientists. Concentrating entirely on the Indian side (and on only certain of the Indians), they overlooked the development and effects of cultural pluralism in the reservation areas. Young Indians who had never gone on a vision quest or counted coup were exploring mechanisms for tribal survival as their ancestors had adapted to the fur trade and the horse, albeit against much tougher odds. Anthropologists, meanwhile, went on about their business of trying to reconstruct what they conceived of as static, "aboriginal" lifeways of the Indian tribes. It was thought that although all living evidence of the Indians might eventually disappear, the anthropologists' records could meet all scientific needs, analyzed synchronically and comparatively in the "ethnographic present," a conceptualization that McNickle (1971a:30) criticizes aptly as "a kind of cookie-cutter device that clipped away and discarded that which was antecedent or subsequent."

Whatever their theoretical myopia, anthropologists' interest in traditional Indian customs afforded psychic support and cultural vindication to desperately aggrieved people. The conservative Indian people anthropologists tended to work with most closely were beset, on the one hand, by culturally arrogant Whites and, on the other, by members of their own tribes who, estranged by White education and socioeconomic pressures, seemed to be going over to the side of the enemy in fulfillment of the goals of governmental assimilation policy regarding Indians. Anthropologists on reservations usually developed warm friendships among the people with whom they worked. Overtly or by implication, they played on the theme that they were performing a service of preserving the memory of a vanishing race. But perhaps the Indians were not all that fatalistic and paid closer attention to the changing actuarial facts of Indian life than did the anthropologists whose primary concerns were with people of reproductive age.

Certainly there were Indians who resisted blandishments and bribes to part with still viable, sacred knowledge. It is also worth pondering whether Indian people sometimes put up with anthropologists not because they really appreciated having them around but because they were such a thorn in the side of other Whites they liked even less. It must have been obvious to Indian people that a natural antipathy existed between anthropology and bureaucracy—whether federal or clerical. Anthropologists made no secret of what they thought of White ethnocentrism. Even Fletcher evoked criticism from the missionary element who agreed with her on allotment. Her study of Indian music, dance, and ritual appeared to give importance to the work of the devil that the missionaries wanted to expunge from human memory forever (Lurie 1966a:83).

There is the strong possibility that anthropologists sometimes unwittingly served Indian purposes by presenting innovations and ideas not available from other White sources. Indians may have regarded anthropology as placing their knowledge in a state of suspended animation for their own future use rather than embalming it permanently for the anthropologists' purposes. Consider, as an example, the highly conservative Wisconsin Winnebago (Lurie 1969–1972). Never confined to a reservation, these people had been under little pressure from the government or missionaries. They resented Paul Radin for having published information about the tribal religion. Most of Radin's research had been done between 1908 and 1913 with the enclave of the tribe that had been removed to a reservation in Nebraska in the 1860s. In contrast to the Wisconsin people, the Nebraska Winnebago had experienced the difficulties attendant on allotment and problems with the Indian Bureau that were fairly typical of the general Indian scene by the turn of the twentieth century.

In 1950, among the Nebraska Winnebago, Radin was recalled with genuine fondness by the knowledgeable elders. By his own admission, Radin had exploited the zeal of converts to the Peyote religion to divulge the rite of the Medicine Lodge and won a good deal of animosity thereby (Radin 1945:35–49). Radin had been downright devious in obtaining other sacred data. He explained candidly that there were old men in Nebraska who would not speak with him. Since it was vital to anthropology that their knowledge of myth and legend not die with them, he got their young kinsmen into his debt by gifts and favors. The payoff he wanted and got was the old men's stories. It is possible that Radin was being used by the old men as much as he was using the young men. In the first place, he paid twice for the stories since he also supplied the young men with the appropriate gifts to approach the elderly people for their wisdom. Second, it is possible that the old men really *wanted* to convey their knowledge to their own people but recognized that the feckless young were not inclined to go to the trouble and expense to obtain it without Radin's prodding. The young who had turned old by 1950 apparently also appreciated the effect of Radin's work on their lives.

This thought casts new light on Radin's (1923:47) observation that "owing to the fact that the Winnebago have for some time been accustomed to the use of a syllabic alphabet borrowed from the Sauk and Fox, it was a comparatively easy task to induce them to write down their mythology and, at times, their ceremonies, and then have an interpreter translate them." Was it an "easy task" because Radin's request suggested they could preserve and pass on their knowledge in this way among themselves as well? By Radin's time, compulsory school attendance and economic exigencies prevented children and young adults from spending the long hours among their elders that were required to gain knowledge in a traditional fashion. In this same context, there is no question that anthropologists were responsible for introducing mechanical recording devices (beginning with cylinder recorders around 1900) among the Indians, who quickly acquired and adapted them to their own uses.

Radin belonged to the generation of Boas's early students whose approach reflected the master in his more imperious days of fieldwork. Later students, influenced by a more mellow Boas and the winds of functionalism blowing from England, began to take an active interest in contemporary Indian society, empathizing with its concerns. By 1930 Boas himself presented a different image from the very young man of 1886 who would photograph a totem pole no matter how the owner felt about it (Rohner 1966:164).

Boas endeavored to explain the economic functions of the potlatch to Canadian authorities who sought to stamp it out as a wickedly wasteful, pagan rite, and he also tried to get them to return some coppers that had been taken from the Indians without compensation and sent to a museum. He even went so far as to intervene on behalf of the Indian community at Fort Rupert, British Columbia (fig. 1), to improve sanitary facilities, taking his arguments all the way to the provincial capitol when he could get no action on the matter at the local level of Indian administration (Rohner 1966:201ff.).

Activities of this kind became increasingly characteristic of the reciprocal relations between anthropologists and Indian people and were gradually taken for granted, like participant observation, as inherent in the nature of any fieldwork.

Mutual Benefit, 1930–1950

Although anthropologists in general clung to the notion of the vanishing Indian, as early as 1898 WJ McGee (1960) recognized what he termed "piratical acculturation" whereby one society acquires items from another to enrich

Amer. Philosophical Soc., Philadelphia.
Fig. 1. Franz Boas (back row, far right) with George Hunt, his Kwakiutl informant and assistant, and Hunt's family at Ft. Rupert, B.C. Hunt worked closely with Boas in the field and contributed substantially to Boas's publications (Codere 1966:xviii–xxxi). Photographed about 1900.

and sustain itself without losing its sense of "autochthonous" identity. The tremendous interest in acculturational studies that began in the 1930s can be traced in large part to the strictures of Malinowski regarding the futility of trying to reconstruct a culture from old recollections and still observable "survivals." A signal work was Margaret Mead's *The Changing Culture of An Indian Tribe* (1932), a contemporary description of the Omaha who had been the subject of Fletcher's work (Fletcher and La Flesche 1911). Tracing the deleterious effects of the allotment policy, Mead showed how differently it had been perceived and adapted to by the Indians compared to the expectations of Fletcher and her White associates.

Meanwhile, several significant developments on the Indian scene were to have a profound effect on American anthropology and its relations with Indian people. Although most Indians under federal jurisdiction were not subject to conscription in World War I, many volunteered. Like the old Wild West show performers who traveled widely, they saw a larger world of adaptable socioeconomic models than the narrow alternatives thrust upon them by the government and missionaries. They began to rediscover the old idea of confederacy for united action that segregation on reservations had discouraged. Rather than militant campaigns, the new confederacies appealed to the White public and brought pressure on Congress. In 1922, for example, the All-Pueblo Council was formed to combat proposed federal legislation that *551* would have alienated vast areas of Pueblo lands (Fey and McNickle 1959:83). A valuable ally in these endeavors was John Collier, who responded to Indians on their terms. He enlisted women's clubs, anthropologists, and other civic-minded people as a national pressure group supporting the Pueblo's efforts that succeeded in defeating in 1922 the bill introduced by Sen. Holm O. Bursum.

In 1933 Collier was appointed commissioner of Indian affairs by Franklin Roosevelt and brought a whole new philosophy to Indian administration. Profoundly impressed by the beauty and worth of Indian culture, particularly the Pueblos, with which he was most familiar, Collier also considered the relativistic approach of anthropology highly congenial to the Indian point of view. Collier focused his attention on upgrading material standards and encouraging self-determination of Indian communities. His enabling legislation was the Indian Reorganization Act of 1934, based on Indian opinion and advice. In 1935 Collier established an applied-anthropology unit to help implement the new policy.

Several facets of the Collier regime served to reinforce a good opinion of anthropology so far as Indian people were concerned. Many of the things that Indians agreed with in Collier's administration derived from anthropological sources. First, there was respect for Indian traditions. Second, the kind of reciprocal relations that had become the norm at the level of the individual anthropologist's fieldwork were given broad expression at the level of national policy. Finally, although the new tribal constitutions were often inadequate to the tasks of self-government within the Indian communities, they served an extremely important function in allowing the communities to enter into contracts to deal with the federal government and the larger society. The Indian Reorganization Act, in effect, reasserted rights of Indians to operate as tribal entities—rights that had been systematically undercut since treaty making had been discontinued in 1871. Although anthropologists were not aware of it at the time, their most important contribution was in forwarding the legal and political education of Indian communities. Indian people themselves had been struggling to gain leverage in the larger system and Collier's program expedited fulfillment of a felt need. But the Indians soon outdistanced their mentors in political sophistication. By 1944, for example, the National Congress of American Indians was formed with two objectives in mind: to lobby in regard to legislation concerning the Indian interest; and to act as a clearing house of information and expertise in putting the Indian Reorganization Act to work.

During World War II Congress disregarded entreaties to support the policy Collier had initiated in 1934. The most obvious problems of Indian poverty were temporarily alleviated by income from men in the armed services and the fact that many Indian people left home to work in defense factories. Collier and Indian leaders knew the Indians would return to the reservations when the war ended, but Congress remained complacent in the old expectation that the Indians were on their way to vanishing into the larger society. Meanwhile, most of the anthropologists also left the reservations to become involved in the war effort in various ways. With the end of the war, changes set in for Indians as a minority and for anthropology as a discipline that worked against the continuation of symbiotic relationships between them.

Symbiosis Deteriorates, 1950–

The quiet buildup of Indian bitterness with anthropology over a period of some two decades exploded publicly with the appearance of an article by Vine Deloria, Jr. (1969a), excerpted from his forthcoming book, *Custer Died For Your Sins* (1969), which took to task not only anthropologists but also missionaries, Congress, and the BIA. Many anthropologists were offended by Deloria's biting wit and also appalled to discover that they were as subject to criticism as those other sinners whom they had traditionally scorned out of a sense of empathy with Indian people. But, according to Deloria, anthropology's association with Indian people was as insensitive and self-serving as that of other White-dominated institutions.

Controversy soon arose over Deloria's contention that "not a single . . . anthropologist . . . came forward to support the tribes against the detrimental policy" of termination (1969:98). As a mater of record, individual anthropologists had opposed termination strenuously in regard to particular tribes with which they were familiar and in support of Indian-rights organizations that led the fight against termination in general (for example, Ostrom and Stern 1959; Stewart 1948). The views of at least two anthropologists were brought to the attention of Congress (Sturtevant 1954; Tax 1957). But Deloria contended that the termination sentiment in Congress that began to take form even before the close of World War II called for the anthropological profession to take an organized stand (Vine Deloria, Jr., personal communication 1971).

In historical perspective, it is difficult to imagine how the American Anthropological Association could have taken a public stand on an issue such as termination in the 1950s. It was not until the late 1960s that the discipline and the Association had achieved the kind of activist outlook respecting national and even international policy issues that would have suggested such a course. As evidence of this assessment, one might mention the fact that the early 1950s also saw the rise of McCarthyism, which was a direct threat to many scholars, including some anthropologists, and a general cause of scholarly concern for the future of academic freedom. Anthropologists discussed the problem unofficially among themselves but no one proposed a public resolution to put the

Association on record regarding the issue of McCarthyism, which had important and immediate bearing for many more anthropologists than the termination issue.

It is perhaps remarkable that any anthropologists had the acumen to take a firm stand against termination at the outset insofar as House Concurrent Resolution 108 of 1953 merely enunciated the philosophy of Congress. Implementation that made the disastrous nature of termination evident to many more people was developed over a period of years in special acts for each terminated tribe. At least in the early stages of discussion of termination, even Indian opinion was divided as to its seriousness. The Menominee, who were terminated in 1954, as the first tribe to be subjected to the policy, considered the issue a local matter they could handle themselves and turned down an offer of help from the Association of American Indian Affairs, whose active membership included anthropologists (Alexander Lesser, personal communications 1971; Lurie 1969–1972). The Klamath, also terminated in 1954, included a faction that actually lobbied in favor of their termination (Stern 1965).

The alleged failure of anthropology to rally in behalf of the Indians against termination was not a grievance that was widely shared by Indian people until it was expressed by Deloria. Yet, Deloria's scathing rebuke of anthropologists struck a respondent chord among Indian people. There is no question that the termination issue figured in the growth of Indian dissatisfaction with anthropologists; however, this attitude developed after termination had become established as policy. While Indian communities were struggling to cope with the continuing threat of termination and the general nature of Indian policy and programs after 1953, anthropology became caught up in concerns of its own; and fieldwork studies tended to disregard what was really troubling Indian communities (Lurie 1962).

In retrospect, it is possible to trace why relations deteriorated between anthropologists and Indian people. Anthropology suddenly had been faced with a variety of challenges since the late 1940s in regard to a dramatic increase of university students and a veritable explosion of new theoretical and methodological interests in the discipline. Meanwhile, because of World War II, the postwar Indian policy, and a rapidly changing national climate of opinion regarding minorities, Indians faced new crises, were exposed to new ideas, and were developing new survival strategies. The concerns of anthropology and the concerns of the Indian population ceased to mesh by accident or design in their mutual interest as had been the case prior to the war.

Until the early 1950s there were not many Indian communities under anthropological study at any one time. The fieldworker was usually a lone investigator dependent on the local Indians' goodwill to conduct research that was vital to his career. Few professors had more than one or two field students to supervise at a time and could keep close track of their activities to offer ready guidance and advice. The enormous postwar bulge in college enrollments that began to be felt in graduate programs a few years later produced significant alterations in anthropology as an academic discipline. It is worth noting that while all disciplines felt the impact of the postwar developments, anthropology as the youngest of the social sciences experienced particularly profound and rapid changes. Departments expanded to meet not only the increase in student enrollments in general but also the interest in anthropology that had been awakened in the world's peoples by the war. New departments sprang up. Texts, courses, and field schools were developed to train the great numbers of new students. American anthropology had begun with a concentration on the American Indian, and it was apparently an automatic response to continue to turn to the Indian communities as handy places for students to learn their trade. Despite efforts of academic advisers to guide students and imbue them with the essential ethics of fieldwork, there were just too many anthropologists and would-be anthropologists. Better-known tribes in the Plains and Southwest particularly were overrun. Researchers simply set up shop or organized field schools with little concern about coordinating plans with other anthropologists to avoid oversaturating Indian communities and replicating studies that began to strike Indian people as not very useful to their interests.

It was particularly unfortunate that at this time the relatively new field of applied anthropology, which had drawn much inspiration and valuable experience from the Collier administration of the BIA, had shifted much of its emphasis to areas outside North America. The very people who were best informed and qualified to sense the growing crisis in Indian life and perhaps offer significant assistance were in demand to work in the Trust Territory of the Pacific Islands, other United States and United Nations programs, and foundation-funded projects in Latin America, Asia, and elsewhere.

In addition, despite the volume of study on Indian reservations from about 1950 onward, there was a tendency in the discipline to view American Indian research as passé. Advanced and better-qualified students were encouraged to undertake their serious, doctoral field study overseas. Many established anthropologists who had begun careers as North Americanists took advantage of postwar research opportunities to begin new research interests in more exotic, untouched areas. Thus, circumstances conspired to deflect intensive social and intellectual interest from the American Indians during a period when they could ill afford this kind of neglect.

A final problem that was no less unfortunate for being understandable was that studies conducted in American Indian communities remained entrenched in a methodological tradition that viewed the local reservations as

553

natural, bounded, and isolated social universes. This tended to delay awareness of what was happening on the larger Indian scene. The postwar years saw a sharing of knowledge and the generation of commonality of sentiment among tribes across the country. Well before 1960 an astonishing number of tribal, regional, and intertribal newssheets had sprung into being (Ortiz 1971). Powwows, traditional occasions for members of different tribes to get together, also proliferated. By the 1960s there were many intertribal organizations besides the National Congress of American Indians. Because of the BIA relocation program that had been coupled with the objective of termination to disperse and assimilate the Indian population, there was an unprecedented mingling in urban areas of members of widely separated tribes. Sharing news and views widely, Indian people found that common experiences and grievances transcended tribal differences and even old antipathies. Pan-Indian opinion began to crystallize in regard to Indians' problems and the White world. These shared conclusions inevitably included ideas about anthropology.

In the early 1950s a joke came out of the Southwest (long a swarming ground of anthropologists) that the average Navajo family consisted of a mother, father, three children, and an anthropologist. By the early 1960s Indians across the country were telling the joke as applying to the average Indian family, sometimes with the bitterly sophisticated twist of "3.5 children." Younger Indians' perceptions of anthropology as practiced after the war did not concur with the friendly view older Indian people had of "their" anthropologists whose ethnographies were used as reference works, though often surreptitiously, even by very traditional people. More recent publications, reflecting changing theoretical and methodological interests in anthropology, began to come through to Indian people as irrelevant at best and often downright insulting. Although anthropology did not intend to be pejorative, it did not take into full account the increased literacy among American Indians, their searches for help in a critical period among the writings of a profession they had considered friendly to their interests, and their unfamiliarity with scientific jargon. Personality and culture studies relying on the terminology of psychopathology to describe modal personality types for cross-cultural comparisons made whole communities appear mildly neurotic or seriously disturbed. Revival of the functionalist-evolutionist controversy in the postwar years and rehabilitation of evolutionary theory employed terminology that also had unintentionally offensive connotations for the living representatives of cultures discussed in the ethnographic present as "primitive" (cf. Hsu 1964). Finally, anthropology became increasingly enamored of quantitative approaches borrowed from sociology and with the awesome hardware that could be employed in connection with them. Doleful statistics appeared on delinquency, drinking, and dropouts with little ethnographic attention paid to the underlying sense of desperation as Indian communities watched their hopes that had been raised in the 1930s go aglimmering under the threat of termination, pressures to relocate, and a general policy orientation that was diametrically opposed to Indian aspirations. The eventual "discovery" of urban Indians soon led to studies that often ignored the growing sense of community among intertribal city populations but bristled with statistics on gradients of individual "adjustment" to city life. Total assimilation was often tacitly accepted as the criterion of successful adjustment while despairing reaction to injustice and a desire to return home to the reservation were treated as a kind of personal failure.

When the large-scale anthropological invasion of Indian life began, the discipline seemed to have a lot of money that Indian people soon concluded could be better applied directly to community improvement or research that Indians could use to argue their case in the halls of Congress and before the courts. Indians knew the extent of their problems and did not need them delineated in tables, Gutman scales, and chi-squares comprehensible only to social scientists. They needed financial and, above all, political and legal help to get at the root cause of their difficulties. Thus, since about 1960, the legal profession seems to have usurped anthropology's role as champion and ally of the Indian (Dobyns 1968).

Anthropologists were not entirely oblivious to Indians' problems and some shared the Indians' sense of frustration in trying to change congressional sentiment during the 1950s. Furthermore, in many quarters, anthropologists were still looked upon as friends and allies. In 1960 Professor Sol Tax was invited to address the annual convention of the National Congress of American Indians (fig. 2), at which time he proposed a plan whereby Indians could mobilize as a highly visible pressure group, publicizing their problems and making the nature of their aspirations known before the government and general public. The result was the American Indian Chicago Conference of 1961 (Lurie 1961). In some ways, it succeeded too well in fulfilling the tenets of action anthropology Tax was in the process of developing. Determined that he and his staff would merely supply the wherewithal and mechanics of coordination, Tax, the role of anthropology, and even the fact of the conference itself were soon forgotten as Indian people in succeeding years built, expanded, innovated, and improved upon the theme of unity and mutual assistance and optimism generated at the conference. The National Indian Youth Council, for example, was a direct outgrowth of the Chicago gathering. These young people in turn organized the first "fish-in" demonstration on the Northwest Coast, an approach that older, more prominent Indian participants at Chicago did not understand or approve of. Other demonstrations and conferences followed solely from Indian initiative. No doubt there would have been similar developments without the Chicago Conference, but Tax's effort was a timely catalyst to instruct and inspire, and, most important, allow for an immediate exchange of a tremendous variety of Indian ideas (Lurie 1961; Washburn 1985).

Unfortunately, increasing communication among Indian people worked to the disadvantage of anthropology in several ways. First, there was the diffusion of growing antipathy to the volume and nature of postwar research on Indians. Because anthroplogists had always been closely associated with Indians and Indians seemed to have more problems than ever, somehow anthropology must be to blame. At least anthropologists were always there as handy targets to work off generalized hostility toward the White world and its institutions. Second, the publicity accorded Indian efforts in the 1960s and 1970s to attract attention to their problems made Indians a popular issue. Just at the time that anthropologists were trying to restore better working relationships, the reservations swarmed with sociologists, psychologists, journalists, folklorists, philosophers, political scientists, educationalists, and scholars of every ilk. Many came with grants, credentials, accouterments and questions that Indian people had long associated solely with anthropologists. Such new discoverers of the Indian often accepted the designation of anthropologist as a role Indian people understood but often were totally unaware of the discipline's basic ethics. Even Deloria (1969:83) realized that the more recent scholarly visitors to the reservations were not all anthropologists when he wrote his chapter entitled "Anthropologists and Other Friends," but he lumped them together anyway.

In addition, Indians in the 1960s were visited by hordes of counterculture adherents, Indian buffs, Volunteers In Service To America (VISTAs), and a host of church-supported young people bent on doing good and seeking their own identity or salvation but often simply getting underfoot in a kind of pathetic parody of the anthropologist's role as participant observer. How were Indians to know the *real* anthropologists?

Indian people began striking out at all aspects of the discipline that developed along its distinctive holistic and biocultural lines in North America because of the presence of the Indian. Indian groups have disrupted archeological work, decrying it as "grave robbing" and "desecration of our ancestors' bones." Museums have been targets for angry demonstrations and demands have been made for the return of artifacts once gratefully consigned to the safety of museums by concerned Indian custodians who feared destruction of tribal heirlooms at the hands of missionaries or neglect by unconcerned heirs. Linguistic research has been criticized as "stealing our languages too" for scholarly purposes of no benefit to the Indians. Young Indian people who may never have met an anthropologist were conditioned to react negatively to the

Fig. 2. Sol Tax (left) and D'Arcy McNickle, Flathead, at the 17th annual convention of the National Congress of American Indians. Tax was the presiding officer of a meeting of college and university representatives. The session's presentations addressed tribal goals for programs and services offered by colleges and universities. McNickle, who was director of American Indian Development, Inc., an Indian service organization, addressed the first topic (National Congress of American Indians 1960). Photograph by Mile High, Denver, Colo., Nov. 15, 1960.

very word "anthro," which was popularized but not invented by Deloria as a term of opprobrium covering all aspects of cultural anthropology. Even the Society for Applied Anthropology attracted a cadre of outraged Indians at its annual meeting of 1970.

In the 1980s there were archeological sites under excavation in cooperation with local Indian communities, for example, Ozette Village on the Makah Reservation, Washington, and projects undertaken by the Schoharie Museum of the Iroquois, New York. Anthropologists were closely involved at Indian request in the development of Indian museums, of which there are many, and in making museum resources available to Indian groups. Indian language courses, utilizing personnel and methods from anthropology, were developed for Indian studies programs on many college campuses and even in some primary and secondary schools serving Indian communities ("American Indian Education," fig. 9, this vol.). Language classes were held on nearly every reservation with an active group of native speakers and in urban areas with substantial Indian communities. Anthropologists also were involved in a host of studies from survey research to very traditional research in cooperation with Indian groups, and young Indian people were still taking degrees in anthropology.

The building of new symbioses was triggered by Indian discontent with the discipline. Moreover, there were good interpersonal relations between individual anthropologists and given Indian groups all along, but these were not sufficient to maintain a shining image of the discipline as a whole. Between the 1950s and 1970s, the cordial relationships were localized, perhaps considered exceptional by the Indian people concerned, while Indian hostility toward anthropology became a generalized, ideological rallying point in the cause of Indian unity.

The turmoil may have had the salutary effect of carrying anthropology beyond its long-standing concern with the role of the individual in the field to deeper consideration of the role of the discipline as a whole in regard to the peoples with which it works. It is probably significant and indicative of American anthropology's continuing debt to the American Indian that at the very time Indian unrest stirred deeper social awareness on the part of North Americanists, the discipline as a whole was faced with similar challenges and new questions of ethical and social responsibility around the world. If the American Anthropological Association was incapable of seeing any role for itself in the termination policy in the early 1950s, since the 1970s the Association and other anthropological organizations have joined forces in opposing American and other nations' policies that threaten the survival and rights of native peoples.

The Indian Hobbyist Movement in North America

WILLIAM K. POWERS

A generalized, romantic interest in American Indians by non-Indians has given rise to a movement primarily centered in the United States known by its constituents as "the hobby."

A hobbyist may be defined as a non-Indian who has a wide range of interests in American Indian subjects, but mainly in arts and crafts, Indian dancing, and singing. Although here regarded as a movement, hobbyism has no national organization but rather comprises independent groups organized at the local, state, and regional levels. No statistical studies have been made of hobbyism and no population figures are available, but based on the distribution of various hobbyist publications it can be determined that: one or more hobbyist groups are located in every major city; the greatest clustering of groups is in the Midwest, especially Wisconsin, Illinois, Indiana, Ohio, and Michigan; and the average group is composed of approximately 20 members.

The primary activity of hobbyist groups is the sponsorship of powwows, indoor and outdoor activities in which hobbyists dress in Indian costumes and participate in Indian dances modeled after what anthropologists call pan-Indian celebrations (Howard 1955). Indian singing is usually provided by American Indians, and dancing is accompanied by trading, feasting, and other kinds of social activities. Outdoor powwows are usually conducted over a weekend, and participants camp out in tents, campers, and tepees.

Both hobbyist groups and powwows are often temporary as a result of merger and factionization. Since the Bureau of Indian Affairs Indian relocation program of 1954, increasing numbers of American Indians have been near urban areas and been able to participate in these powwows. Similarly, Indian hobbyists have attended powwows sponsored by American Indians both on and off reservation.

Origins

American Indian hobbyism has flourished as a self-conscious movement since the end of World War II; however, its genesis may be traced to a number of youth organizations established around 1900. Largest of these organizations is the Boy Scouts of America, which was incorporated by Congress in 1910. Many outdoor activities were modeled after real or putative American Indian themes. Particular focus was placed on Indian lore by two of three men who are recognized as co-founders of Scouting in America—Daniel Carter Beard, outdoorsman and author of children's books from New York, and Ernest Thompson Seton, a naturalist and author from Canada (the third man was James E. West, a Washington, D.C., attorney who became the first Chief Scout Executive).

Although other organizations such as Girl Scouts, U.S.A., Camp Fire Girls, Young Men's Christian Association, Young Men's Hebrew Association, and Boys' Clubs have contributed to the dissemination of Indian lore, the Boy Scouts remain the most influential. As part of its program, young people are encouraged to learn Indian costume making, dancing, sign language, and other customs and crafts. In 1911, the Indian Lore Merit Badge, which gave formal recognition of achievement in Indian lore activities, was initiated.

In 1915, Indian lore became even more popular when the Order of the Arrow, a national Scout camping fraternity, was founded by E. Urner Goodman and Carroll A. Edson at Treasure Island Scout Camp near Philadelphia. Ceremonies of initiation into the "Arrow" were based on Indian themes, and local lodges and chapters were given Indian names. The Order of the Arrow primarily focused on service-oriented projects, and only a small percent were active in Indian programs.

Much of the direction in Indian lore programs was provided in the writings of Beard (1909), Buttree (1930), R. Hubbard (1927, 1935), W.B. Hunt (1942), Mason (1944, 1946), Parker (1927), Salomon (1928), E. S. Seton (1902), and authors writing in *Boys' Life*, the national Scout magazine. More serious students extracted information from publications of the Smithsonian Institution, Bureau of American Ethnology; American Museum of Natural History, New York; and other institutions.

The growth of membership in Scouting, and its age grouping into Boy Scout troops and, later, Cub Scout dens

Powwow Trails, Somerset, N.J.
Fig. 1. Hobbyists from Indianapolis, Ind. The women's names are followed by the tribe from which their clothing design originates. left to right, Margaret Seider, Potawatomi; Carol Puckett, Miami-Delaware; Jane Webb, Potawatomi; Karen Kemp, Mascouten; unidentified; and Pam Barrett, Mascouten. Photographed 1965.

for younger boys, and Explorer posts, a coeducational program for high school youths, helped to transform individually oriented Indian lore projects into group activities. Foremost of these activities was the performance of Indian pageants and local Scout shows. Enthusiasts such as Ralph Hubbard traveled the United States and Europe producing Indian pageants. The particular interpretive repertory of dances soon became the stock in trade of Indian lore. Putative dances such as the "Great Plains War Dance," "Sioux Buffalo Dance," "Ghost Dance," and "Eagle Dance" were learned by thousands of boys.

By the 1930s and 1940s, some Scout groups seemingly devoted more time to the Indian lore program than was officially recommended by the national Scout office. In some localities, Scout officials gave an ultimatum to local Scout groups to de-emphasize Indian lore or leave Scouting. The majority of groups compromised, but other continued Indian lore independently, primarily focusing their attention on providing public performances in order to "perpetuate the arts and crafts of the American Indian." The independent groups became the nucleus of hobbyist groups, although many Scout-affiliated groups still considered themselves hobbyists as well as Scouts.

The American Indian Hobbyist

The publication of *The American Indian Hobbyist* in

September 1954 serves as a convenient historical marker in the development of hobbyism. Recognizing that the term "hobbyist" was in use before the publication and that hobbyist-like activities had preceded the magazine by at least 45 years, the publication of a magazine confirmed that there was some concerted effort to share information among people with similar interests in the American Indian.

The American Indian Hobbyist was founded by Norman Feder, a former Boy Scout from New York City who had moved to Los Angeles.

The first issue clearly indicated a merger between independent groups and Boy Scouts. *The American Indian Hobbyist* contained a calendar of Indian events, profile of an Explorer post specializing in Indian lore, directions for learning a new dance, an article on beadwork, where to obtain Indian movies, and a report on the 39th anniversary conference of the Order of the Arrow. A column called "Horse Trader Joe" featured classified advertisements in *The American Indian Hobbyist* such as: "Will trade or sell pair of loom beaded Chippewa leg wraps, also a fine old knife sheath spot-stitch floral design, very small, small beads, 12" long with old knife."

The very language of *The American Indian Hobbyist* indicated that a certain amount of sophistication regarding Indian material culture was present. Under the direction of Feder, this sophistication progressed rapidly, witnessed by articles on esoteric subjects such as split-horn bonnets, yarn leg wraps, and blanket capotes.

Feder became interested in museology and later served as an assistant curator of the Museum of the American Indian, Heye Foundation, New York City; curator of American Indian Art at the Denver Art Museum; and guest curator at New York's Whitney Museum for its "Two Hundred Years of North American Art," which was opened concurrent with his major publication, *American Indian Art* (Feder 1971).

Authenticity versus Interpretation

Up to and through the publication of *The American Indian Hobbyist*, hobbyism had been primarily craft-oriented. Many hobbyists became proficient in various techniques of beadwork, quillwork, feather work, and costume making. Costumes were then worn at public performances. "Artifakery" (the attempt to duplicate museum specimens, but not on a commercial or fraudulent basis) became the target for the more serious hobbyists. Second in importance was learning a repertory of Indian dances that could be performed for the public. Most dances were learned initially from books, especially Mason (1944). Others were learned at rehearsals for Scout pageants.

During the publication of *The American Indian Hobbyist*, individual hobbyists and groups achieved various levels of competence in craftwork, dancing, and singing, which was considered the most difficult of hobbyist activities. Based on a person's proficiency, hobbyists began differentiating between those individuals who had more intimate knowledge of Indians gained through field trips to reservations and who were master craftsmen and outstanding dancers, and novices, namely the "lipstick and towel school," which received its appellation from the fact that beginners (especially boys in the Cub Scouts) painted their faces with lipstick and wore bathroom towel breechclouts. Those who had achieved relative acuity in craftwork and who had become, for the most part, leaders of the various independent hobbyist groups became known as "superhobbyists." The term was partly complimentary and partly derogatory inasmuch as "superhobbyists" were usually regarded the most knowledgeable but also the most aloof from the mainstream of hobbyist activities.

A great deal of attention was focused on whether an individual or group was "authentic" or "interpretative." The former term was assigned to those hobbyists who preferred to duplicate actual Indian artifacts and learn dances from the Indians. The latter term referred to the policy of some groups whose members fabricated their own interpretations of American Indian dances. Some of the long-time leaders in the movement feared that even the word "hobbyist" was somehow derogatory to the American Indians upon whose cultures the hobby was founded and that the study of American Indians could not be relegated to a kind of human stamp-collecting.

Pan-Indianism and Powwows

In January 1960 Feder abdicated editorship of *The American Indian Hobbyist*, turning it over to a group of young men from Alton, Illinois, calling themselves the Society for American Indian Tradition. Under the editorship of Richard R. McAllister, a graduate student at Saint Louis University, *The American Indian Hobbyist* was published under its original title for one year, after which the name was changed to *American Indian Tradition* with hopes of promoting a wider readership among universities, libraries, and American Indians themselves.

The new title also reflected a change in values of American Indian hobbyists. In the 1950s and 1960s, increasing numbers of hobbyists were making field trips to American Indian communities to learn things firsthand. Similarly, more Indians were migrating to the cities. Some American Indians on relocation learned about local hobbyist groups and were invited to become members. To craftsmanship and excellence in Indian dancing were added two important esteem factors: "Real" Indians were now members of hobbyist groups and, most important, some hobbyists had been adopted into Indian families. Additionally, the hobby was changing from the male-centered program held over from Scouting to family-oriented activities with great interest in hobbyism being demonstrated by young women (fig. 1). Firsthand experience in American Indian celebrations led to a gradual change from public performances to Indian activities for their own sake. Interest in current Indian affairs also waxed, and the pan-Indian complex that had been reportedly emerging in many Indian communities became the hobbyist model for indoor and outdoor activities. The term "powwow," which was becoming commonly used by American Indians to signify music and dance events, designated hobbyist events as well. The term "powwow circuit" was introduced in *American Indian Tradition* suggesting that hobbyists should try to learn music and dance from Indians by attending numerous clusters of Indian powwows held during the summer. Further emphasis was placed on hobbyists sponsoring their own powwows. Independent hobbyist groups and ad hoc committees began sponsoring annual events such as the Monroe Powwow (New York) (fig. 2), the Oglewanagi Powwow (Cleveland), the "Detroit" Powwow, the Red Shield Powwow (Baltimore), and the Witayapi Powwow (Los Angeles).

These powwows were modeled after northern and southern Plains celebrations and included War Dances, Round Dances, Two-steps, and Forty-nines as well as specialty dances such as the Hoop Dance. Dances were usually held outdoors in an arbor or in indoor gymnasiums. Indian singers were employed by the committees, and contests were held in Junior and Senior War Dances and "old-time" dancing as well as cloth and buckskin dress contests for women and tiny tot contests for the third generation of hobbyists' children. In addition to dancing and singing, traders, many of whom were from nearby reservations, were invited to sell their wares, and campers were encouraged to set up tepees for which prizes were awarded.

Although the direction of hobbyism became imitative of pan-Indianism, hobbyists could clearly differentiate between those factions known as "old-timers" who were identified by interests and costumes representing historic periods; "Boy Scouts," a term of derogation that implied amateurism (although in all fairness, Scout groups such as the Order of the Arrow had increased their sophistication about Indians comparable to non-Scout hobbyists); and the mainstream of which a relative few were considered "superhobbyists." The mainstream was mainly differentiated by its members' costumes, which tended to be modern (post-1930), and their interests, which were mainly pan-Indian oriented. Proficiency in dancing attained through participation in powwows plus ownership of one or more costumes sometimes valued at as high as $1,000 became the main criteria of the hobbyist.

The ability to "sing Indian" also gave status to individuals and groups. Songs were learned from commercial recordings beginning in the 1940s, but by the 1950s hobbyists were recording Indian songs in native communities using their own wire and tape recorders. Trading songs directly and through the mail became another hobbyist pastime. Similarly, recording fees became part of the payment to visiting Indian singers at hobbyist powwows. Some hobbyist groups, such as the Medicine Drum Society of Staten Island, New York, and the Tecumseh Lodge (an Order of the Arrow Lodge), became proficient enough to sing at Indian celebrations.

At either end of a wide spectrum, hobbyism boasted that some members had entered teaching, social work, art, and academics (all related to American Indians) on one side, while others had "gone native," moving to Indian reservations where they took up permanent residence. Hobbyism also boasted that its membership was comprised of all people, ranging from professionals to blue-collar workers. Powwows had become a focal point of much of their social life, a subculture in which marriage partners found each other and produced a generation of children who grew up in an atmosphere in which it was difficult to separate non-Indian from Indian culture. Although hobbyists came from a wide range of economic backgrounds, until the late 1950s there was little racial integration save for a handful of Hispanics, Orientals, and Blacks, mostly integrated into urban hobbyist groups. A tacit philosophy decreed that it was appropriate for Whites to dress and paint up but that "others" looked "strange" posing as Indians. Even as late as the 1940s "real" Indians were somewhat regarded as curiosities by some hobbyists.

The social issues prevalent in the United States in the 1950s also affected hobbyism. Especially in the east,

Fig. 2. Annual Monroe Powwow, N.Y. The man at left and the woman in the center foreground wear clothing with an emphasis on Northeast Indian design. Photograph by William K. Powers, 1964.

Blacks and Puerto Ricans began participating in hobbyist powwows. Some hobbyists attempted to block powwow integration by requiring dancers to participate by special invitation only. Ironically, after only a few special invitation dances, Indians themselves helped to open the powwows to non-Whites by claiming that all people were invited to dance at Indian celebrations and they saw no reason to prohibit people because of racial or ethnic background. Some discrimination persisted, and it was not until the mid–1960s that Blacks and Puerto Ricans were winning dancing and singing contests.

American Indian Tradition continued to provide an ideological base to hobbyism, one which promoted "authenticity" and "Indianness" as goals to be sought. Then in 1962, after three years of intensive publishing and proselytizing, the magazine ran into financial problems and was forced to discontinue publication.

A newsletter called *Powwow Trails* was established by William K. Powers and Marla N. Powers in April 1964. The title was selected to appeal to American Indians and hobbyists who were primarily interested in attending or sponsoring powwows. It contained a monthly calendar of Indian and hobbyist events, as well as articles on material culture, powwow organization, music, and dance. Editorials stressed organization of powwows and involvement of American Indians as singers, dancers, and judges at hobbyist powwows. Emphasis was also placed on unification of groups into state or regional associations based on an apparently successful model in Texas. In the mid–1960s, in addition to the Texas Indian Hobbyist Association, there arose similar associations in Florida, Louisiana, Pennsylvania, New England, Greater New York, and California. Powers (1966) provided instruction in a number of pan-Indian dances. The emphasis on secular dances was partly due to the growing philosophy among hobbyists that Indian religious dances, once a mainstay of Indian shows, should not be performed for the public. *Powwow Trails* was published until 1970.

The organization of state and regional associations led hobbyists to consider the feasibility of a national organization. Although none was ever formed, national events were held, mainly due to the efforts of Tyrone H. Stewart, a former member of the California Indian Hobbyist Association who, in 1967, founded the publication, *American Indian Crafts and Culture*, with headquarters in Tulsa, Oklahoma. In 1969, Stewart was able to organize the first National Indian Hobbyist Powwow, which took place in Denver, Colorado. At the Second National Powwow, held in Sedalia, Missouri, in 1972, over 1,000 campers—of whom 600 were dancers—participated. Two drums (song groups), one "northern" (Sioux) and one "southern" (Ponca), provided the singing.

Stewart continued editing *American Indian Crafts and Culture*, which grew from a newsletter to magazine format until 1974, when he founded a full-color journal called *Indian America*. This publication lasted only four issues because of the exorbitant costs of its production.

Continuing, however, was a modest publication called *Whispering Wind*, which was founded in 1967 by editor Jack B. Heriard under the auspices of the Louisiana Indian Hobbyist Association. In 1987, it was the only publication devoted to the same interests addressed by Feder in the original *American Indian Hobbyist*, and it was then the longest-lived hobbyist publication in North America.

Throughout the history of hobbyism, especially during the 1960s, there was a continuing debate over a proper name to adequately describe its aims and interests. "Indian lore" was rejected mainly because of its early association with Scouting. The term "hobbyist" itself was being rejected by many for philosophical reasons. In 1972, the New England Hobbyist Association, under the direction of Ron Head, voted to change its name to the American Indianist Society. This group in particular had as a subsidiary interest the objective of providing educational resources to elementary and secondary schools in New England and, in some school systems, curricula to be used in teaching units on the American Indian, as well as bibliographies to schools and public libraries. Elsewhere, such as in Ohio, hobbyists formed American Indian Cultural Associations with similar academic interests.

Beginning in the 1970s, some groups were criticized by American Indians, mainly non-Indian performance groups rather than powwow-oriented hobbyists, for indiscreet use of religious dances. This led to a further evaluation of Indian awareness. Hobbyism in general has tended both to reinforce the stereotype of the American Indian and to dispel some of the myths. In the 1980s hobbyists were attempting to dispel the myths.

The Indian Hobbyist Movement in Europe

COLIN F. TAYLOR

The term "Indian hobbyism" describes a wide range of nonprofessional interests in North American Indians displayed in European countries. Although the term "hobbyist" is useful, it is generally disliked by most of the individuals to whom it is applied; and just as in North America, it is rejected by many who feel that the interest cannot be equated to other leisure activities, since it usually involves a very deep commitment. The description "American Indianist" has gained some acceptance.

The interest of a committed hobbyist generally begins at an early age, manifesting itself in activities such as costume making and powwows. The powwows form an important activity of a typical hobbyist group and involve dressing up and dancing and singing, frequently in public. Such involvement and exposure clearly demands considerable knowledge of the subject and many hobbyists, often after much study, display unusual expertise in these fields. As the interest develops, individuals often choose to emphasize one or more activities, such as craftwork, collecting, camping (generally in tepees), joining political support groups in aid of American Indians, lecturing, researching, or writing.

Most individuals have a somewhat romanticized view of Indian life, and an interest in Plains Indian culture is often dominant. Although hobbyists are from many occupations, they are primarily blue-collar workers. Hobbyism is male dominated, but it is not uncommon to find wives and children participating.

Few hobbyists have had the formal training in American anthropology enjoyed by their professional colleagues, but their acquisition of knowledge and methodology has often followed very similar paths. Their interest generally leads to a life-long commitment and a life-style that frequently determines friendships and social activities.

United Kingdom

There has long been a fascination for American Indians in Europe (fig. 1), which began soon after the discovery of America, and "the allegorical symbol of the Americas in European art was the figure of an 'Indian' female wearing a feathered crown and skirt" (Howard 1978:33).

A major influence in the United Kingdom was the

Liverpool Mus., Natl. Mus. and Galleries on Merseyside, England.

Fig. 1. Sir John Caldwell, an Irish baronet, in clothing collected from Eastern Great Lakes area Indians. Caldwell obtained these items while he served in an English regiment in North America from 1774 to 1780 during which time he was stationed at Ft. Detroit and Ft. Niagara. In this period he spent a great deal of time among Ojibwa Indians (Brasser 1976:2, 180). Artist unidentified, oil on canvas, about 1780.

writings of George Catlin (1841). His exhibitions of ethnographical material from the Plains Indians, particularly in Egyptian Hall, Piccadilly, London, in the mid-nineteenth century, were given wide and sympathetic press coverage. Later editions of his books were published in large quantities, many being aimed at the young reader (Catlin 1861, 1868), so that Catlin's popular interpretation early awakened a broad and general interest in the American Indian, and his work became a standard source of information for several generations of readers in the United Kingdom until the mid-twentieth century.

Although no other books received such wide public

acclaim in Great Britain as Catlin's, there were a number of nineteenth-century British writers who maintained and stimulated the interest in North American Indians, for example, Ballantyne (1893), W.A. Bell (1869), and Butler (1875; Hannabuss 1987). The writings of Ernest Thompson Seton, particularly *Two Little Savages* (1903), became readily available. In his *Book of Woodcraft and Indian Lore*, Seton (1912:vii) wrote: "when I was a boy, I hungered beyond expression for just such information as I have tried herein to impart." Such sentiments were subsequently to be recognized by several English hobbyists.

Archibald Belaney (b.1889, d.1938), better known as Grey Owl, apparently inspired by the visits of Buffalo Bill (William F. Cody) to England at the turn of the twentieth century, wrote a number of widely read books on the great outdoors, wild animals, and Indians. His name became a household word, and he personally pleaded the cause of the American Indian to King George VI in 1937 (Dickson 1939). A Grey Owl Society was formed in Hastings, Sussex, in spring 1982 (Feest 1983:6).

One of the earliest British amateurs to pursue the study of American Indians in a really systematic way was the London businessman, William Blackmore (b.1827, d.1878). In December 1868 he exhibited and discussed his collection of Indian photographs at the invitation of the American Ethnological Society in New York and in April 1872 spent "a pleasant evening discussing Indians and the West" with President and Mrs. Ulysses Grant at the White House (Brayer 1949, 1). In September 1867, Blackmore founded a museum in Salisbury, Wiltshire, where he housed a collection of books (about 1,000 on the American Indian), photographs (at least 2,000), ethnological material, and data on the bison (C.F. Taylor 1980:15). He became a recognized authority on the Plains Indian. He donated many hundreds of negatives of Indian subjects to the Smithsonian Institution in 1872. W. Blackmore's (1868–1869) amateur but scholarly contribution to American Indian ethnology was important in both its direct and indirect influence on subsequent generations of Englishmen, and others, who also took up the study of the American Indian as a hobby (C.F. Taylor 1980).

Unrelated to William Blackmore, Edward H. Blackmore (d. 1983) of Eastbourne, Sussex (fig. 2), gained recognition as an authority and lecturer on the North American Indian. Once described "as more Sioux than the Sioux themselves" (T. Clarke 1939), Blackmore commenced lecturing in the 1930s to a wide audience of natural history and archeological societies, schools, and youth organizations. A true romantic, he nevertheless combined as sound scientific knowledge with a schoolboy's enthusiasm and presented his subject in a popular and highly interesting way. Friends of Blackmore influenced him considerably. Philip Godsell (1938), who emigrated to Canada in 1903 to work for the Hudson's

Eastbourne Herald, Eastbourne, England.
Fig. 2. Edward H. Blackmore dressed in northern Plains Indian style garments. The double trailer headdress was constructed by Blackmore with eagle feathers obtained from his friend Oskenonton. Blackmore's wife, Clare, made the beaded leggings. Blackmore carries a beaded Sioux pipe bag, a catlinite pipe, and foxskin bag containing materials used to light the pipe. Photograph by Doug Barnes, Eastbourne, Sussex, April 1972.

Bay Company, was a friend of many Blackfoot, Assiniboine, and Cree Indians, photographs of whom he sent to Blackmore, 1940–1961. Another friend was the Mohawk singer, Oskenonton, who took the role of Hiawatha, performing at the Royal Albert Hall, London, 1930–1945. It was Oskenonton who obtained for Blackmore raw materials for craftwork, such as tanned buckskin, eagle feathers, and beads. Clare Sheridan, an enthusiast for American Indian studies but better known as a sculptor and writer, had visited the Blackfoot Indians in Canada and the United States where she modeled six heads from life. She recalled Edward Blackmore as "the most convincing instance of reincarnation that I have ever met . . . .who can transform himself at will into the most perfect and finest type of Redskin Indian . . . .who has a Redskin soul and a Redskin heart, Redskin wisdom and knowledge, and all the finer Redskin traits" (in E.H. Blackmore 1950:2). Ernest Thompson Seton invited Blackmore to visit his College of Indian Wisdom at Santa

Fe, New Mexico, to help teach the making of war bonnets. Blackmore's unselfish support to the romantic, artist, hobbyist, and amateur scholar alike stabilized and fostered the American Indian interest in Great Britain, particularly after 1938.

Blackmore's collection of North American Indian material, including Blackfoot regalia collected by Clare Sheridan (B. Taylor 1984), was transferred to the Hastings Museum, Sussex. In the 1980s the Hastings Museum sponsored a Junior Indian Club and held annual powwows in Blackmore's honor as well as for Albert Burdett (b. 1916, d. 1983).

Burdett was a skilled craftworker and an early museum researcher. In common with several other British hobbyists, he was greatly influenced by the collections that he studied. He made a number of replicas, one outstanding example being a shirt decorated with quill-wrapped horsehair, which is in the Leather Museum, Northampton.

The American Library, opened at the United States Information Service in London in 1942, soon recognized the interest in American Indians in the United Kingdom (books on the subject came next in popularity to books on the Civil War). At the time of its closing in 1965, it had about 100 books pertaining to Indians.

There were brief contacts by the Boy Scouts and other youth movements with Indians and Indian lore in the first half of the twentieth century. Unlike their American cousins, British Boy Scouts and Girl Guides never developed Indian lore in their activities to any great extent. There is nothing, for example, comparable to the American Scout's Order of the Arrow. Although Sir Robert Baden-Powell frequently referred to the North American Indian in his Scout handbook (Baden-Powell 1909) and also expressed the hope that the Indian sign language might be adopted by Scouts throughout the world (Tomkins 1926), his firsthand experience with native groups in British colonies in Africa and India tended to direct attention away from North America. However, the Indians of America were represented at the Boy Scouts' Jamboree at Olympia, London, in 1920 (Salomon 1928), and again at Birkenhead, England, in 1929. During World War II, at least one scout studied with J.F. Burshears of the La Junta, Colorado, Boy Scout troop who called themselves Koshare Indians.

Although such contacts created some activity in Indian lore it was not until the formation of the English Westerners' Society in 1954 with its affiliated *Brand Book* and *Tally Sheet* that organized groups of hobbyists emerged. *The American Indian Hobbyist* magazine was founded in America in 1954, but it appears that the Westerners' publications were more influential in the United Kingdom for at least a decade. North American Indians were interpreted by the ethnological group of the Westerners' Society not only through their research papers published in the *Brand Book* but also by exhibi-

Colin Taylor, Hastings, East Sussex.

Fig. 3. Founding, and other, members of the North American Indian group of the English Westerners' Society at one of the group's early exhibitions. left to right, Charles Clayton, John Datlen, Ian West, Edward H. Blackmore, Ann Robinson, Fiona Robinson, and Colin Taylor. All the members wear central or northern Plains style garments. Photograph by Russell Robinson, Woldingham, England, 1960s.

tions, the first of which was held at Orpington, Kent, in May 1960 (I.M. West 1961:12). Founder members of this group, such as E.H. Blackmore, Ian M. West, and Colin F. Taylor, together with Russell Robinson from the Tower of London (fig. 3) combined their collections of artifacts. For more than a decade, exhibitions were regularly organized for Scout groups (both British and American), youth clubs, historical societies, and museums, in particular the American Museum in Britain at Claverton Manor, Bath, which was for a number of years host to the Westerners' Society (Dallett 1965). By invitation small teenage groups gave displays of Indian dancing. A particularly active group in this respect was that run by S.H. Walker, who had in 1960 organized a Scout group in Birmingham with interests oriented toward American Indian dancing. The American Indian exhibitions were held annually at Bath.

C.F. Taylor's (1971–1984) surveys indicated that there were initially four hobbyist groups in Great Britain consisting of 10–35 members, all in southern England. While dancing was a prominent activity, collecting, an interest in art, research, and craftwork were all considered important facets of the hobby.

In 1965, the Sioux Indian Dancers' Club was formed by Maurice Oakeshott, a former scoutmaster, with Edward H. Blackmore as president. This group of about 15 members was initially strongly influenced by the older members of the Westerners' Society and combined ethnology with Indian dancing. Because of their association with a stable organization where they had the opportunity of meeting visiting U.S. Americanists such as the ethnologist J.C. Ewers and the "superhobbyist" Sam Cahoon, and because of Blackmore's reputation, they grew rapidly.

The Westerners' Society continues and ethnological interests are still significant, primarily in the so-called

American Indian Study series, which was initiated in 1981 to meet a growing need for comparatively rapid distribution of research carried out by Society members contributing to knowledge in the field of North American Indian studies. Topics covered in extended essays have been as diverse and specialized as an analysis of the political history of the Oglala Sioux to a reconsideration of the so-called Wanata costume in the Royal Scottish Museum, Edinburgh. However, former members more oriented toward American Indian song and dance, craftwork, and artwork have largely reorganized independently.

A myriad of groups often cater to specialized interests. For example, the Native American and Pre-Columbian Arts Movement put emphasis on producing copies of American Indian arts and crafts; a support group of the North West Indian Women's circle, which seeks to draw attention to the problems and issues affecting all Indian women, formed in London. Other groups identified in 1985 included the Sheffield American Indian Circle; the White Eagle Dance Team, and the North American Historical Society, both in Birmingham; the Mother Earth Lodge in Leighton Buzzard, Bedford; the East Anglian American Indian Eagle Dance Team from Ipswich, Suffolk; Four Directions, run by David Meanwell of Heathfield; and the American Indian Movement in Yorkshire.

Some groups have been disbanded. For example, the Sioux Indian Dancers' Club ceased in 1975, several of its founder members forming The Black Crow Dancers in 1979. Together with the Earth Lodge Singers (fig. 4) and generally accompanied by others, they form a mainstay at any powwow. Members of the Earth Lodge Singers have made tepees and a full-sized earth lodge, and many are outstanding craftworkers. One enthusiast made a fully beaded Crow-style cradle for her baby son.

Fig. 4. Hobbyist groups in England. left, Black Crow Dancers and White Shield Dancers. left to right, Charles Clayton, Keith Lord, John Powell, and John Kirkby at Soca Cheta Hall, Norwood, South London. Photograph by Colin Taylor, 1983. right, Members of the Earth Lodge Singers at a wedding powwow. The Cockerton family—Paul, Jennifer, Samuel Joseph, and Penny—are dressed in garments of traditional Blackfoot and Sioux design, all made by themselves or another English hobbyist. Photograph by Michael Hopkinson, Uckfield, Sussex, April 1984.

THE INDIAN HOBBYIST MOVEMENT IN EUROPE

Despite these activities, several expressed a wish to be independent of club or group type organization. They preferred a looser knit expression of mutual interest with other individuals and families by correspondence and ad hoc meetings and generally avoided publicity or close involvement with the mainstream. Several supported the protests of the Canadian Indians who lobbied Parliament regarding treaty obligations (C.F. Taylor 1979). In common with a number of their American counterparts, some individuals (such as Fraser Pakes, who joined the Nakoda Institute, Morley, Alberta) turned professional in the field of American ethnology, while others, although still amateurs in the field, have been acknowledged as making genuine contributions to Native American studies (Howard 1978:42; Wood and Liberty 1980:120; Pakes 1983).

Hobbyists often emphasize the spirituality of their identification with Indians. They hold what others may consider an idealized image of the North American Indian, encompassing a concern for the despoliation of the environment (a sentiment expressed by Grey Owl in the 1930s), cultural survival of minority groups, and a quest for spiritual awareness.

Sentiments of this type were apparent in the middle 1970s with the foundation of the Onaway Trust of Leeds, Yorkshire. A registered charity, its trustees believe that Europeans and White Americans have lost the ability to live in harmony with the natural world. Along with traditional Indians, through its projects and magazines, the Trust seeks to help Western man "to rediscover this vital balance and harmony and oneness with nature" (James Bradley, personal communication 1984). The Trust predominantly funds projects conceived and staffed by Native Americans themselves, American journalists acting as observers initially when funding is requested. Donations to the Yellow Thunder Camp, the Dakota Indian Movement in the Black Hills, South Dakota; Akwesasne Freedom School on the Mohawk reservation, New York; the Buffalo Robe project in Alberta, and a lecture tour in England for Russell Means have been made. By 1984 over $600,000 for Indian-related projects had been raised. Important to the success of Onaway is the support of the various English hobbyist groups and

De Kiva, Bennebroek, The Netherlands.
Fig 5. Hobbyist movement in The Netherlands. left, Cover of the periodical *De Kiva*, Jan.-Feb. 1985; design by Koos Van Oostrom. right, H. Loers, member of De Kiva. Photographed in The Netherlands, about 1963.

individuals, many of whom donate proceeds of powwows, exhibitions, and the like to the Onaway fund.

The Continent

Parallel interests have developed in a number of other European countries, particularly where historical, early contacts were made with North America.

In Sweden, for example, awareness of the colony of New Sweden on the Delaware River influenced the founding of Indianklubben, which was formed in 1959 by Olof Norbeck, a retired banker, whose main interests centered on the Delaware, Mohegan, and Mahican and their descendants. The club consisted of 30–35 members who met several times a year to discuss Indians and books, to show films, and to exhibit photographs. It published a yearbook containing articles on North American Indians written by members of the club and translated three books on Indians into Swedish, including Catlin (1841). Erik Englund, a longstanding member of the club, who popularized the North American Indian in Sweden, wrote a book in Danish for schools (1971), while the poet Einar Malm published scholarly works on Indian chiefs, such as Sitting Bull (1970). Another Indian club in Stockholm, called Svensk-indianska forbundet (The Swedish Indian League), printed an occasional periodical called *Indian-Bulletinen*, which was concerned with voicing the wrongs committed against the contemporary Indian. They have also been active in collecting money and clothes for Indians. In contrast to American, British, and other European hobbyists, powwow activities and craftwork seem to have found little expression in Sweden. Swedish contributions to North American Indian studies have been described by Hultkrantz (1984).

In Germany there is a long tradition of interest in North American Indians. In the closing years of the nineteenth century, the writer Karl May (b. 1842, d. 1912), composed a series of magazine articles on Amercian Indians, later expanded (1893). The May publications continued in the twentieth century to be a significant influence on the continent. It also seems probable that early Western traveling shows, such as Buffalo Bill's, exerted considerable influence on the development of some German hobbyism (Conrad 1987).

At Radebeul, near Dresden, German Democratic Republic, is the Indianer Museum that was founded by the publishers of the May books. They developed a smaller one after 1945 in Bamberg, Upper Franconia, Federal Republic of Germany. May himself did not collect American Indian material, and the majority of specimens in the Radebeul Museum, renamed Karl May Museum, were assembled partly by exchange and loans from German museum collections by Patty Frank (b.1876, d.1959), who was active in Buffalo Bill's show around 1900. In 1985 there were 21 hobbyist groups in the German Democratic Republic, including traditional hobbyist groups such as the Interessengemeinschaft Mandan-Indianer of Taucha, who have their annual tepee camp near Triptis (with participation from other Eastern European countries) and more political groups such as the AG Völkerkunde/Indianistik am Jugendklub haus Walter Barth in Leipzig.

The earliest documented regular instance where Germans dressed as Indians was at the annual Taucha market in a suburb of Leipzig in the late nineteenth century, which remained popular until it was officially discouraged in the 1940s. Hobbyist groups in Germany, some apparently as early as the 1910s, were founded in Dresden, Frankfurt, and Munich (Conrad 1987). These early activities led to the first "Indian Council" in Germany, which was held in Karlsruhe, Baden-Württemberg, in 1951. Traditionally, the Council met each year with 50-60 tepees pitched and some 300 participants. Some 60-70 Indian clubs existed in Germany in 1972 although the interest of many club members was often both fleeting and superficial; nevertheless, as in the United Kingdom, there were a number of individuals whose interests put them in the category of amateur scholars with the major emphasis on research and collecting. The activities of these clubs varied, and in most cases there was considerable emphasis on social events with a carnival-like atmosphere. The competitions of roping, whip-handling, and square dancing among the cowboy factions of such clubs are paralleled by archery and knife and tomahawk throwing of the "Indians." A gathering in Nidda, about 60 kilometers from Frankfurt am Main, Hesse, in June 1981 may be taken as typical of the annual events of group hobbyism in Germany. It was attended by some 3,000 Western fans who represented wide-ranging interests, cowboys, mountain men, North West Mounted Police, and soldiers of the Union and Confederate armies. However, the Indian village dominated, having almost 200 tepees with participants "dressed in their finest elaborately beaded or quilled buckskins, 1840 to 1870 style." In their efforts to obtain authentic costumes, these enthusiasts imported entire North American porcupine hides in order to get the quills. The council was officially opened "with the re-enactment of a Wyoming treaty signing" (Hoeldtke 1981:10).

Such three-day functions are attended by groups from all over Germany, Belgium, France, and England. Contacts have been made with Indians in North America, a number of whom have attended the event.

The activities of the German Indianist groups have been addressed over the years by a variety of publications; among the earliest was *Der Dakota Scout*, which gave rise to *Kalumet*, which began publication in 1969. Since then other publications such as *Amedian* and *Deutsch Indianischer Kreis* have been concerned with contemporary Indian affairs, while *Magazin für Amerikanistik*, published in Braunschweig, focuses mainly on romantic and

Western literature. The society, Arbeitskreis für Nordamerikanische Indianer launched its journal *Indianer Heute* in the late 1960s and attempted to direct traditional German interest in Indians toward contemporary Indian problems and politics. Its function was then taken over by *DANAI-Notes* (Deutsche Arbeitsgemeinschaft für Nordamerikanische Indianer), which was succeeded in 1984 by *Informationsdienst-Indianer Heute* published in Berlin with the main aim being "to inform the public of the real situation of the Native Americans and to support them through petition and letter campaigns, donation-drives etc." (R.S. Kelly 1984:14).

In Holland, "Jack" Heyink founded *De Kiva* in May 1964 and published it six times a year. This group brought together a number of individuals who had pursued the study of American Indians as a hobby for many years (fig. 5). In 1972 there were 600 members of the club with about two powwows held each year; while a few individuals were concerned with craftwork and Indian dancing, the orientation of interest was broadly scientific and the powwows often took on the aspect of a scientific congress. An important activity of the group was the financial and moral help its members gave to the contemporary Indian. For example, in 1971 the cause of the Nisqually Indians concerning their fishing rights was taken up by some *De Kiva* subscribers who were lawyers in an attempt to get the Indian cause before the International Court of Justice at The Hague. In 1985, with the new name of Werkgroep Nord Amerikaanse Indianen in Nederland en België, Dutch members annually joined members in Belgium in the popular tepee camps with supporting powwows. Activities in support of the American Indian have been extended, including an annual scholarship and also donation to Indian-initiated projects.

Another particularly active support group in Holland is NANAI (Nederland Actiegroep Nord Amerikaanse Indianen), which was founded in 1973. Its objectives have been to support Indian tribes in their political struggles, by giving information to the Dutch people about the contemporary situation in North America through lectures to schools and other organizations. Members have also mounted a photographic exhibition and written protest letters to North American governments (Bolhuis 1983: 22). NANAI published a monthly newspaper, *NANAI Notes*, which was mailed to 1,600 supporters, and in addition produced brochures on Canadian and U.S. Indians as well as more specialized subjects such as Indian camping and the prophesies and problems of the Hopi Indians.

In Belgium, WAIA (Werk Actiegroep Indiaans Amerika) was founded in response to the killing of numbers of Indians in the Brazilian rain forests and to the confrontations at Alcatraz and Wounded Knee. A major aim of WAIA was to keep Dutch-speaking Belgians informed about the political situation of Native Americans, which is done through the production of brochures, posters, and exhibitions of past and present American Indian culture (Bruggerman 1985).

In France, the interest in American Indians was mainly centered in the magazine *Western Gazette*, which was founded in 1964, and which was strongly biased toward other facets of the American West (D. DuBois 1970; Gunhold 1966). Although no coherent Indian dance groups existed in France, exhibitions of American Indian life and customs were organized by one of France's best-known hobbyists and collectors, Maurice Dérumaux. French enthusiasts traveled to Germany to participate in the annual Indian councils (Hoeldtke 1981).

Soconas Incomindios, the Italian hobbyist group with explicit political goals, published a magazine, *Tepee*. A number of Italian hobbyists have firm contacts with similarly oriented friends in Czechoslovakia (Milos Ekstein, personal communication 1983). An Italian who pioneered in American Indian research was Giacomo Costantino Beltrami (b. 1779, d. 1855) who explored the Upper Mississippi region in 1823; his collection of Indian objects is in the Museo Civico "E. Caffi," Bergamo, Italy (Marino 1986).

Several individuals in Switzerland with hobbyist interests have achieved wide recognition as deeply involved in American Indian studies. Among the earliest of these was Rudolph F. Kurz (b. 1818, d. 1871), who collected Indian weapons, decorations, and apparel. His collections and those of the businessman and enthusiast Lorenz Alfonse Schoch are in the Berne Historical Museum (J. Thompson 1977). Gottfried Hotz, a Zurich schoolteacher, formed a large collection of Indian artifacts (Hotz 1974), which is maintained by Hans Läng (1983). Joseph Balmer (fig. 6) "taught himself to read and write in the Dakota (Sioux) language, and formerly conducted an extensive correspondence with old-timers on reservations in North and South Dakota" (Howard 1978:41).

In Czechoslovakia there were several committed hobbyists who made their own costumes and camped in tepees (Zelva 1983:11). Some also wrote for the magazine *Winaminge,* which contains articles by both professional and amateur scholars of the North American Indian and has further references to the development of Czech hobbyism (Kandert 1982).

In Finland, Finncomindos produces a magazine concerned with American Indian cultural history.

In Poland, the Polski Ruch Przyjaciot Indian (Polish Movement of Friends of the American Indian) was formalized in 1981, with hobbyism and scholarly research as goals. The Polish movement is discussed in detail by Nowicka (1987).

In the Soviet Union, the largest and best organized group is in Leningrad, which acts through the Inter-Union House of Creative Activities. Called the Leningrad Indian Club, it was formed in the late 1970s; it influenced most

Fig. 6. Joseph Balmer in garments of Sioux Indian design, obtained from the Red Cloud family at Pine Ridge, S. Dak. Photograph by René Groebli, Switzerland, 1962.

other groups, organizing annual powwows generally held near Leningrad. The total number of participants at such powwows is generally about 60, and in 1984 there were 20 tepees pitched. The major activities and goals of the Soviet groups were "to study and promote true knowledge of North American Indian cultures, to practice scouting and forestry and woodsmanship; to imitate Indian art, compose songs on the American Indian theme and in solidarity with their ideals and rights" (Alexandr Vashchenko, personal communication 1985). Connections with European hobbyists seemed mainly limited to similar organizations in the German Democratic Republic with whom there were exchange visits.

There were at least three different hobbyist groups in Hungary, one of the earliest being founded in the 1930s by the anthropologist Ervin Baktay (Richman 1967). One of the largest groups was developed in Budapest in 1963, when four boys about the age of 16 started to play at being Indian. These were joined by others with more ethnologically based interests who shared the founders' views about "Indianness" as a habit of life, and the "game" gradually changed into a more faithful imitation of the life of the Northern Plains Indians (George Gereby, personal communication 1985). The group had no common name but consisted of six "tribes" in four camps, every member identifying himself by the tribal name. The major and unique activity of the group, which took place during a two-week summer camp generally in the forests of the Bakony Hills, was the "warpath" or "hunt." The Hungarian hobbyists' war game was complex and highly symbolic where participants counted coup, symbolically captured horses, and sought to accomplish the four major coups to become a recognized (Crow) pipe-holder. Although the war game activity gave coherence to the whole group, craftwork, singing, dancing, sweat-bathing, feasting, and making ceremonies were also listed as important activities (Tibor Balazs, personal communication 1985). For the majority of the group, their inspiration was spiritual; those that participated felt that they shared an inborn, natural quest for the hardships, freedom, and glory of the idealized warrior life of the North American Plains Indian.

569

Indians and the Counterculture, 1960s–1970s

STEWART BRAND

In the mid-twentieth century events led to the emergence of a youthful counterculture in America that sought and found much to share with American Indians, particularly traditional and politically active Indians. The counterculture was an equalizing current set in motion by American urban-industrial success—all the new wealth, power, leisure, and guilt. Some of the sources of the phenomenon were: the baby boom of World War II, which presented the 1960s with an unusually large youth population; increased affluence and leisure, which supplied the youth with the means and confidence to pursue their own projects; channels of immediate access to news of political and culture change; psycho-active drugs termed "psychedelic"—LSD, mescaline, psilocybin, marijuana, etc.; American Blacks' campaign for equal rights; the American government's long war in Vietnam, inspiring alienation; fear of world-wide political crisis, leading to a ferment of spiritual revival, search, and invention; and recognition of world-wide ecological crisis, reinforcing departure from faith in high technology and disembodied intellectuality.

In the 1960s the children of excess startled their elders with a pervasive headlong romantic movement. Membership traits (one consciously joined) included colorful or ragged garments, long hair on males, sexual promiscuity, use of drugs for pleasure and insight, esoteric and eclectic religious activity, high mobility, scant identification with job or family, rebellious politics, earnest commitment to group process and honesty, and language that evolved rapidly to stay ahead of usurpation by the movement's vast and fascinated audience.

Rediscovery of Indians

American Indians, ever the object of romantic interest, were a particular study of this new group. From a distance Indians looked perfect: ecologically aware, spiritual, tribal, anarchistic, drug-using, exotic, native, and wronged, the lone genuine holdouts against American conformity and success.

The new counterculture loved the old. There was a big increase in sales of books about Indians, particularly where specific spiritual or practical lore was presented, even if not always authentic (Neihardt 1972; Waters 1969;

Castañeda 1968; Laubin and Laubin 1957). Canvas tepees appeared at every counterculture enclave. The most common headgear on young men and women was a headband. The San Francisco Human Be-In, a pivotal event in 1967, was subtitled "A Gathering of the Tribes" (fig. 1). They called themselves "hippies," "freaks," and also "longhairs"—the same term used for Traditionals of an Indian tribe. Many gave themselves new personal names, Indian-style (in contrast to hobbyist practice, which was to seek adoption and naming by a tribe).

Some of the reservations were soon embarrassed by an influx of young White voluntary primitivists ready to join the tribe uninvited. Many Indians who were busy fighting their way out of poverty were not charmed by these bizarre children telling them how to be Indian. But some perceived the frequent sincerity and intelligence of the newcomers and met it with their own. Most of the interaction was temporary and shallow, but there were two major areas of real sharing: peyote and politics.

Peyote

There is support for Slotkin's (1956) thesis that the swift spread of peyote use among Indians was a response to massive culture change. Another population, young Americans generally, became subject to overwhelming acceleration of events and also responded with a proliferation of drug use. The major difference was that the Indians had a shared effective ritual in the Peyote religion meeting and the Whites did not.

In February 1962 several young Whites from the counterculture in the San Francisco area held an informal Peyote meeting on Mount Tamalpais to celebrate a solar eclipse. By summer 1962 they and other White friends were traveling to Woodfords, California, in the Sierras to attend Peyote meetings with Paiutes, Washoes, and San Francisco area Navajos. Several of the Whites moved to the Carson Valley in Nevada and established steady relations with the Indians and Peyote. This pioneer group in time numbered 25–30. As they gradually became skilled, several emerged as competent leaders and meeting officers, notably Rick Mallory, Jack Loeffler, David Melville, Jimmy Hopper, and John Kimmey.

In 1965 most of the group migrated to the Santa Fe

Fig. 1. Poster advertising the Human Be-In, Jan. 14, 1967.

area to be closer to Texas sources of peyote and the stricter meetings of the Southwest. In 1968 the group was incorporated in New Mexico as The American Church of God and had a steady membership of some 200. Four-fifths of the group were Whites mostly in their early 20s and semitransient. The rest were Indians, mostly 50–70 years old, from tribes all over the Southwest. There were a few Black participants and in 1972 a few Chicanos. The non-Indians knew 40–50 Indian Peyote songs and had introduced some 40 songs of their own. They had learned the power of ritual and of personally experienced religion from teachers such as Little Joe Gomez, Henry Gomez, John Gomez, and Tellus Good Morning (all Taos), John Pedro (Arapaho), Wilbur Doss (Navajo), Emerson Decora (Winnebago), and Paul Manarko (Jicarilla Apache). Leonard Crow Dog (Sioux), who ran mixed meetings in Rosebud, South Dakota, summarized the liberal Peyotists' attitude to White participation: "If they can take it, they can take it."

Mostly the young Whites were looking for elder voices they could completely respect. Among the Traditionals (or those presenting themselves so) willing to talk to them were Thomas Banyacya, David Monongye, John and Mina Lanza (all Hopi), Eddie Box (Southern Ute), Harvey Goodbear (Cheyenne-Arapaho), Oren Lyons

(Onondaga), Mad Bear Anderson (Tuscarora), Essie Parrish (Pomo), Rolling Thunder (Cherokee–Western Shoshone), Samu (Chumash), Stella Leach (Oglala Sioux), and traditional-leaning young Indians such as Larry Bird (Santo Domingo–Laguna) and Fred Coyote (Wailaki). It is impossible to summarize what was taught by the Indians. The poet Gary Snyder suggested the general subject was "commitment to the continent," or "radical traditionalism."

Politics

With the founding in the 1960s of pan-Indian national organizations such as the National Indian Youth Council and the American Indian Movement something new entered Indian affairs, the energy of youthful pride. It came in part from the college educations that more young Indians were receiving. It came in part from the "Black pride" development in the civil rights movement. And it came in part from Indian elders who had never let it go.

By 1964 and the beginning of the long fight over Indian fishing rights in the Pacific Northwest, there was also the beginning of participation by young White radicals who had registered Black voters with the Student Nonviolent Coordinating Committee in Mississippi and shut down the University of California, Berkeley, with the Free Speech Movement and then heard about Indian causes and wanted to help. They had learned a little humility from exclusivist Black Power and were to learn still more from conservative Red Power. More than other White do-gooders the counterculture young people were able to listen and try things the Indians' way.

As time and confrontations progressed the Indians could increasingly count on logistical as well as moral support from young Whites. The "Indians of All Tribes" who took possession of Alcatraz in 1969 relied largely on San Francisco Bay area artists and students for food, water, and transportation to the island. Money was raised for Alcatraz, for an Indian well-baby clinic in Berkeley, and for a Traditional Indian Cultural Foundation through benefits performed by rock bands such as The Grateful Dead and Big Brother and the Holding Company. When in 1970 a group of northern California Indians occupied land owned by Pacific Gas & Electric and were arrested, the Indian children were cared for by a traveling commune called the Hog Farm. At the same time in New Mexico White longhairs gave significant financial help to the Taos Indians in their successful fight for ownership of Blue Lake. In 1969 some of the early White Peyotists (Jack Loeffler, Jimmy Hopper) responded to requests from Hopi and Navajo Traditionals for aid in stopping the strip mines on reservation land. They organized the very effective Black Mesa Defense Fund, which carried on national publicity, aided technical research, and in 1972 took the Indians before the United Nations Conference on

571

the Human Environment in Stockholm.

Mutual Reinforcement

There was cultural mixing. Elderly traditional Indians could be seen engaged in uncharacteristic friendly hugs and direct eye contact with strangers. The Institute of American Indian Arts, founded in Santa Fe in 1962 by the Bureau of Indian Affairs, gave young Indians and White artists influential access to each other, yielding hybrid-vigorous art. In 1971 Gary Snyder was invited to read his poetry at Indian high schools in the Southwest and found the students at schools such as Fort Wingate (Navajo) near Gallup, New Mexico, divided into two groups called by the students the "stomps" (cowboy image, country and western music, 60%) and the "cats" (hippie image, rock and roll, 40%). The "cats" dug Gary's poetry and wanted to hear all he knew about Chinese and Japanese culture.

American Indians provided the counterculture with a living identity base. In turn the popular counterculture encouraged respect and support for traditional Indian ways among young Indians. The counterculture grew from the excess of the cities and left to ground again in rural values, infusing them with city energy. The longhair convergence was mutual reinforcement, a mutual loosening of dominant White strenuousness.

The Indian in Literature in English

LESLIE A. FIEDLER

There are a number of literary works written in English by White American authors that attempt to describe Indian life from an Indian point of view. The earliest of these to survive is *The Delight Makers*, which was written by the pioneering anthropologist, Adolf F. Bandelier (1890), with actual photographs of life in a Pueblo as illustrations. Other writers, including Mary Austin, Oliver LaFarge, Frank Waters, and William Eastlake, have followed his example; but such works seem always to fall somewhere between a tour de force and a hoax, because no White writer is fully convincing as having seen life through Indian eyes. And, in any case, what has chiefly intrigued writers in English is the encounter of the White man and the Indian as experienced by the White man.

In the United States that encounter has from the first been felt as central to American literature and life, since it represents the "making of Americans": the transformation of the consciousness of transplanted Europeans into something new in the presence of an alien people at home in the wilderness. In this sense, Indians play a secondary role in American literature (and all the more so in British), being finally more symbolic than real. Nonetheless, it would be impossible to write a significant study of American literature without mentioning any book dealing with White portrayals of Red men.

British Images

Indeed, if there is any mythology native to White America, it is based on its earliest encounters with Indians. Long before the end of the eighteenth century, when the United States and its literature were simultaneously invented, travelers had already written accounts of meetings with the aboriginal Americans in the wilderness (Hakluyt 1892; Purchas 1905). Meanwhile, missionaries had begun to record their vicissitudes, and White captives carried off by Red men had described their hardships and escapes. Later, fur trappers and traders told their hair-raising tales or persuaded writers as distinguished as Washington Irving to write them.

It is hard to tell history from myth in such accounts, though these earliest attempts to create an image of the Indian for the American imagination usually presented themselves as "true relations" of fact. Capt. John Smith may seem to have fabricated rather than recorded the story of his encounter with Pocahontas; but his early readers took as literal truth the fanciful tale of his rescue from death by a beautiful Indian princess, which he did not actually include in any version of his "history" of the Virginia plantation (1616, 1624) until after all the other major participants were dead. At this point, it scarcely matters whether it was fact or not, since the story of Pocahontas has assumed in the intervening centuries another kind of truth: the truth of dreams and legends. And in this guise, it has continued to haunt the imaginations of speakers of English on both sides of the Atlantic.

The pictures that have survived of Captain Smith's young Indian rescuer may be all different from one another, and none of them may look at all like a native of Virginia, but they have been transformed by dreams into the icons of a popular and sentimental myth of reconciliation between Red and White, which for centuries has moved poets and novelists and, in the beginning, particularly playwrights. In their works, the stone ax of Powhatan hangs threateningly forever over the bared head of the English captain, and the tawny body of Pocahontas in eternally interposed to save him (fig. 1). Yet the early verse laureates of Pocahontas, like Seba Smith (1841) or George Pope Morris (1857) are forgotten; and even the writers of once immensely popular dramas, like James Nelson Barker (1808) and George Washington Parke Custis (1830) are recalled only by scholars. As for the early novels and half-fictional "biographies," they blur into each other and the featureless mass of defunct popular literature.

Nevertheless, the Pocahontas legend has not died. It persists not only in primers, popularizing histories, juvenile literature, and B-movies but also distinguished twentieth-century poems like Vachel Lindsay's "Our Mother Pocahontas" (1923) and Hart Crane's *The Bridge* (1930), quite respectable modern dramas like Virgil Geddes's *Pocahontas and the Elders* (1933), and in contemporary novels of first rank, like John Barth's *The Sot-Weed Factor* (1960).

Moreover, the Indian princess survives, even less expectedly, in British literature, reappearing, for instance, in the nineteenth century, when that eminent Victorian, William Makepiece Thackeray, wrote *The Virginians*

573

Fig. 1. Pocahontas and Capt. John Smith, illustrations from British and American narratives. top, "King Powhatan commands C[aptain] Smith to be slayne, his daughter Pokahontas beggs his life"; detail from an engraved map of Va. by Thomas Vaughan (Smith 1624). Printed by James Reeve. bottom, "Pocahantas ran with mournful destraction to the block," frontispiece from *Captain Smith and Princess Pocahontas*, by John Davis (1817). Engraving by H.A., printed by William Green.

narrator as having written a Pocahontas play but also includes a Pocahontas poem, presumably written by that narrator's brother. Moreover, David Garnett, a member of the circle that surrounded Virginia Woolf, improbably returned to the theme in *Pocahontas, or the Non-Pareil of Virginia* (1933), perhaps the most successful, subtle, and deeply moving of all the fiction produced on the subject, with the possible exception of Barth's.

It seems odd that the English should be so concerned with Pocahontas in light of their failure to exploit in depth any other major Indian myth developed on this side of the Atlantic. But, after all, Pocahontas did marry an Englishman, and actually died in England, after having been introduced under her baptismal name of Rebecca at the Court of King James I. Except in this form, however, the Indian is strangely absent from literature of Great Britain throughout the nineteenth and twentieth centuries, though William Shakespeare's hybrid savage, Caliban, suggested to him in part by early chronicles of encounters with the natives of the West Indies, already possessed the imagination of the seventeenth century. There is even a story that Pocahontas saw *The Tempest* during her English sojourn; and, in any case, she, along with other imported American aborigines, had made the Indian visible to Englishmen while the Jamestown Colony was still fighting for life.

Moreover, the tradition of the stage Indian continued to flourish on into the eighteenth century; though, after Shakespeare, it was the Spanish-American encounter with the Incas and Aztecs that captured the fancy of playwrights such as Sir William Davenant, John Dryden, and Richard Brinsley Sheridan, whose *Pizzaro* (1800) was one of the major stage successes of its time. The poetry written by those as eminent as Robert Southey tends to deal with the Spanish conquest, North American Indians being left pretty much to American poets, some of whom were read in England as well, like Timothy Dwight, Joel Barlow, and Sarah Wentworth Morton.

The novel is the last major genre in England to make the Indian its subject; and there is only one distinguished English fictionist who deals with the theme: Tobias Smollett, who introduced a brief Indian captivity episode into *The Expedition of Humphry Clinker* (1794). Indians did not fare very well in English fiction during the nineteenth century and after, not even in those thrillers and boys' adventure books that attracted so large an audience during the reign of Victoria. In Robert Louis Stevenson's (1889) novel, Indians remain peripheral and shadowy

(1859), a historical novel set in the early eighteenth century. In it, he not only portrays his Anglo-American

figures. The only truly popular book published in England between the accession of Victoria and World War I in which Indians play a major role is James Barrie's *Peter Pan* (1910). In it, Indians pursue pirates, even as pirates pursue children, and Tiger Lily, the Princess of the Pickaninny Tribe, is a kind of minor heroine. But James Barrie's attitude toward her and her tribesmen is jocular and condescending.

Perhaps the first English literary man (and the last?) to take Indians quite seriously was D.H. Lawrence, whose life-long concern with native Americans ("kindled by Fenimore Cooper") eventually took him to live in New Mexico, where he wrote essays on Indian life (1927) and produced at least two important Indian fictions, *The Plumed Serpent* (1926) and "The Woman Who Rode Away" (1928). To these works a rival novelist, Wyndham Lewis in *Paleface* (1929), responded with a scorn much more typically English, branding them the products of White self-hatred and an unworthy sentimentalization of savagery.

American Fiction

Eighteenth and Early Nineteenth Centuries

In the United States, the situation is quite different; for there is scarcely a major figure in American literature, especially in the realm of the novel, who has not been concerned with the White-Red encounter. The very earliest American novelists, from Ann Eliza Bleecker (1793) in her *History of Maria Kittle*, deal with the theme of Indian abduction, which also inspired the first American fictionist of real talent, Charles Brockden Brown. Brown made Red-White warfare a part of the nightmare horror of his dreamlike *Edgar Huntly* (1799) and argued in its preface that "the incidents of Indian hostility" constitute the central American subject, which must replace the antiquarian trappings of English Gothic.

But it is, of course, James Fenimore Cooper who creates for the entire Western world the image of the Redskin as "vanishing American," noble and ignoble, but in any case doomed. Much of his fiction is based on pre-existent models: the Indian captivity stories, in particular, and the work of missionaries and proto-anthropologists such as Heckewelder (1820), who had first satisfied the hunger of "civilized" White Americans to know what Indian life on the frontier was like.

Moreover, from sources like Alexander Henry (1809), a fur trapper who in the early nineteenth century wrote an account of his adventures in the wilderness, he derived the mythic story of a love between White man and Red that transcends the hostility of their peoples. It is a myth of extraordinary potency, later translated to the relations of Whites and non-Whites in general, including Polynesians and Blacks; but in Cooper it appears only in the *Leather-Stocking Saga* (1954), the five volumes written in the

Fig. 2. Book plate showing a helmeted Minerva, the Roman goddess of wisdom and the arts, handing a book to a kneeling Indian, who offers his tomahawk in exchange. The Latin motto on the bookcase is *Emollit mores* 'It makes one's behavior gentler' (Ovid, *Ex Ponto* 2: 9.47), and the scene is intended as an emblematic illustration of the civilization of savages through literacy and learning. Engraving by Peter Maverick for the N.Y. Soc. Lib., 1789.

1840s in which he recounted backward the life-long companionship of the White woodsman Natty Bumppo and his Indian comrade, Chingachgook.

Cooper wrote other Indian books, including the pious *The Oak Openings* (1848) and *The Wept of Wish-ton-Wish* (1829), not primarily concerned with the interethnic love between lonely males. And in these, he continued to depict nostalgically and sentimentally the expropriation and destruction of the first Americans, defending the same in the name of Christianity and civilization.

This vision of the Indian bitterly resisting the end of his world that history demands persists in vulgarized form in the dime novels of the nineteenth century, in which the undercurrent of White nostalgia and guilt, everywhere present in Cooper, is replaced by a celebration of violence and a simple-minded joy in the victory of White civilization. And it was acted out in Wild West shows, even as it was being frozen into classic form in the standard Western of the early twentieth century, best represented perhaps by Zane Grey's *The Vanishing American* (1925).

But it has survived also in pulp stories, cheap hard cover novels, and paperback originals, as well as in the movies that helped make the childhood of most living Americans, and in the child's game of Cowboys and Indians, in which kids took into the streets what had moved them in the darkened theater. Its most popular manifestation was perhaps "The Lone Ranger," which began as a radio show based on a Zane Grey novel, was translated to television, comic strips, and comic books, making the name of the Indian, Tonto, better known than that of Chingachgook (fig. 3).

Even in his own time, Cooper was already being imitated by writers of smaller talent like N.M. Hentz, author of *Tadeuskind, the Last King of the Lenapes* (1825). And in the years immediately after his heyday, his view of the Indian was adapted to the more romantic "Southern" imagination by William Gilmore Simms in *The Yemassee* (1835), even as it was being violently reacted against in Robert Montgomery Bird's *Nick of the Woods* (1837), which pictures the Red-White encounter as almost unmitigatedly brutal. But the only work of the nineteenth-century imitators that compares to Cooper in uniqueness and power (though not in coherence or popularity), is John Neal's *Logan* (1822), which uses the Indian tale as an occasion for translating the Gothic Satanism of George Gordon, Lord Byron, to the American woods, and should therefore be considered, perhaps, more in the school of Charles Brockden Brown than that of Cooper.

Late Nineteenth Century

Those whom Cooper moved most deeply and profitably were those writers of the American Renaissance: Emerson and Henry David Thoreau, Herman Melville and Nathaniel Hawthorne, Walt Whitman and (just a little earlier than the rest) Edgar Allen Poe. Poe attempted only two full-scale novels, in which he turned, as he typically did not in his short stories, to American themes, specifically to Indians. The setting of *The Narrative of A. Gordon Pym* (1838), the one novel he actually finished, is the sea rather than the wilderness, but the constant companion of his stowaway hero is a half-breed Indian called Dirk Peters, a figure at once horrific and sympathetic.

And in the abortive *Journal of Julius Rodman* (1840), Poe moves into the Western woods, drawing heavily on published accounts of the Meriwether Lewis and William Clark expedition into Indian territory—in an attempt perhaps to capture the large audience already devoted to reading Westerns. It is in *Gordon Pym*, however, that he tries to adapt the Cooper theme of the woodland companions to shipboard life; and what he failed to do was accomplished by Melville in *Moby Dick* (1851).

Melville turned the Noble Savage into a Polynesian in the course of his attempt. Nonetheless, Indians are not absent from his imagination even in that novel, for the last figure described before the *Pequod* sinks forever is Tashtego, a Gay Head Indian, who is nailing the flag to the mast. And in *The Confidence-Man* (1857), Melville offers a cameo portrait of the Indian hater, the professional killer of Redskins, who in seeking revenge against the "savages" becomes himself the most abominable savage of all.

It is the anti-myth not only to that of the "good companion" but also to Pocahontas, in which love binds together Redskin and Paleface as warfare ends in a marriage and reconciliation. Nor was Melville alone in evoking it. It was already present in Bird (1837) and in Hentz (1825), though not until 1851 did it pass into the public domain with the appearance of the most widely read of such gospels of hate, James Quinlan's *Tom Quick, the Indian Slayer* (1851).

The sole major American writer who was himself possessed by the spirit of Indian-hating does not appear until after the Civil War (Melville was only "trying on" attitudes he had encountered in the works of Western history writer James Hall), when in Mark Twain's *Innocents Abroad* (1869) certain virulent anti-Indian passages are introduced without apparent motivation, passages echoed in *Roughing It* (1872). From Cooper, whom he pretended to despise, Twain had adapted the theme of the "male good companions," but the only Noble Savage he could imagine loving is a Black one; and the only Indians in *Huckleberry Finn* (1884) are therefore "literary" ones, as imaginary as his pirates and "A-rabs." Twain's sole published portrait of an Indian character is the Injun Joe of *Tom Sawyer* (1876), a sadistic destroyer, and an especial nightmare threat to women and children. Injun Joe is, to be sure, a "half-breed," mythological projection of the White man's fear of miscegenation, the hybridization of the two American cultures.

This same fear of "mongrelization" is otherwise projected in the figure of the renegade, the turncoat White man. Best known of such nightmare figures is Simon Girty, which the otherwise unknown Emerson Bennett gave classic form in a novel called *The Renegade* (1848), though the nineteenth-century California poet Joaquin Miller (1871, 1874) thrilled literary circles in America and England during his own lifetime with tales of having actually played such a role.

Most American writers of first rank, however, have eschewed the anti-myth, choosing to re-dream the loving encounter of the White refugee from civilization and the Noble Savage, like Henry David Thoreau in *A Week on the Concord and Merrimack Rivers* (1849). Of all American writers, Thoreau was, perhaps, the one most persistently concerned with the Indian (R.F. Sayre 1977). A collector of Indian relics and lore, he died with the word "Indians" on his lips and left behind some 1,500 pages of notes for an encyclopedic work on the subject. He also

Fig. 3. Detail of the title page from *The Lone Ranger* (Vol. 1, No. 108, 1957) comic book. In this episode, the Lone Ranger takes the lead in not only protecting Whites but also protecting an Indian, Tonto, from another group of Indians.

dealt with Indians at length in *The Maine Woods* (1864).

Thoreau (1849) not only retells Alexander Henry's woodland idyll but also recounts, as a kind of control or counterbalance, the tale of Hannah Dustan: an Indian captive who killed and scalped 10 Indians, including seven children, in revenge for the death of her own baby. The notion of the avenging mother, with its suggestions of an endless enmity between Indian braves and White women, is quite as important a myth of Red-White relations as that of Love in the Woods and the Indian Hater, and seems, indeed, the female equivalent of the latter. The story of Hannah Dustan possessed the imaginations of many influential writers: essayists like Thoreau, theologians like Cotton Mather, and fictionists like Nathaniel Hawthorne, who retold it as a story for children.

Mather clearly approves of Hannah, whom he thinks of as a heroic representative of the Church, resisting diabolic savagery, quite like some Hebrew heroine of old; Hawthorne clearly reads her as a shrewish harridan warring against whatever it is that male Americans secretly dream. Only Thoreau, by juxtaposing the stories of Henry's love for his Indian friend with Dustan's feud with her Indian captor, suggests the interconnectedness of the two stories. And a century later, that connection is made explicit in Ken Kesey's *One Flew Over the Cuckoo's Nest* (1962).

The protagonist of that twentieth-century novel, a rebellious White male fleeing society like Henry or Natty Bumppo before him, learns that, quite like his predecessors, he, too, must find an Indian comrade. And with that comrade, a six-foot eight-inch psychotic half-breed called mockingly Chief Broom, he engages in a monumental struggle with Big Nurse, super-female representative of *577* what Huck Finn referred to contemptuously as "sivilization," that is, a repressive social order. That a dramatized version of Kesey's book was acted out by Indians when they temporarily took over the abandoned jail on Alcatraz in 1969 seems absolutely just; for in it, at long last, the Indian does not vanish, but survives his White companion and returns at the end of the story to his fellow tribesmen.

Oddly enough, Walt Whitman, though obsessed by the notion of love between comrades, nowhere projects the image of the "male good companions" that are White and Red. His ideal companions are apparently White on both sides; and the Indian enters his earlier poetry in a female form more closely related to Capt. John Smith's fantasies than Fenimore Cooper's: as the bride of the White trapper in "Song of Myself," for instance, and the Red Women come to repair his mother's chairs in "The Sleepers." When he returned to Indian themes in later life, it was the popular sentimental tradition that moved him—leading him to produce an elegy for Gen. George Custer in "From Far Dakota's Cañons" and for the "vanishing American" in "Red Jacket (From Aloft)," "Yonnindio," and "Osceola."

All in all, Whitman in his treatment of Indians is less close to other writers of the American Renaissance, who appealed to an elite, largely male audience, than he is to the spokesmen for a counter-tradition that addressed a larger readership including females. But the Red Man is central in that tradition, too. Philip Freneau, for instance, earliest of the genteel poets, survives in school anthologies in a handful of poems dealing with Indians, dying and dead, the best known of them being *The Indian Burying Ground* (1786).

So, too, his successors, who included a host of female versifiers, continued to exploit this most authentic of American subject matters. William Cullen Bryant develops with characteristic melancholy the pathos of a vanished race in "An Indian at the Burial Place of His Fathers" (1875). And John Greenleaf Whittier pursues the same sentimental subject in prose as well as verse, giving fullest expression to the theme first explored in certain juvenile poems in his fictional *Leaves from Margaret Smith's Journal* (1849).

But, of course, the culmination of this tradition is that American epic, Henry Wadsworth Longfellow's *Hiawatha* (1855), a poem whose language and tone made it from the start available to all readers, children and adults, male and female, educated and uneducated. Even now, it must be the most widely read and best remembered, if not the most respected and honored, attempt to assimilate Indian legend to White mythology in the New World. Its marked and monotonous metric—imitated from the Finnish epic, *The Kalevala* (Crawford 1891)—sticks stubbornly in the mind. Though the sources of its form are disconcertingly European, those of its subject matter are authentically native; for Henry Schoolcraft (1845, 1851–1857), however unreliable, was a diligent scholar of the folklore of the first

Americans, and he played for Longfellow the same role that Heckewelder had played for Cooper.

Indians did not fare so well in the hands of the prose writers of the genteel tradition as they did in the hands of the poets. Harriet Beecher Stowe, for example, was so obsessed by the plight of the Black slave that she seemed scarcely aware of the problems besetting Red men in the United States. Yet in one of her novels, considerably less well-known than *Uncle Tom's Cabin*, the nostalgic *Old Town Folks* (1869), she included acute and moving portraits of Indians attempting to live in White civilization after their conversion to Christianity. Her sketches are more realistic than mythic or sentimental, and perhaps for that very reason they have refused to stay in the American imagination. The popular novel *Ramona* was by Helen Hunt Jackson (1885), an extraordinary woman who took on Theodore Roosevelt himself in a polemical discussion about the place of Indians in American life. The novel embodies a defense of Indian values against their White defamers.

Twentieth Century

Women writers have expressed sympathy for Indians in fiction, often of the most popular variety. Edna Ferber's *Cimmaron* (1930) is an example on the level of the best-seller. And perhaps the most distinguished book of the kind is Willa Cather's *Death Comes for the Archbishop* (1927). It is a species of fiction rather rare in American literature, immortalizing the encounter between Roman Catholicism and the Indian culture of the old Southwest.

Most American books dealing with Indians, when they have any religious dimension at all, tend to be Protestant. However, a notable novel was based on the *Jesuit Relations* (JR 1896–1901), Leonard Cohen's complex and fascinating *Beautiful Losers* (1966). Cohen's book deals with Catherine Tekakwitha, a Canadian Indian who pledged herself in the seventeenth century to a life of perpetual chastity for the sake of Jesus Christ and whom the Roman Catholic Church has declared venerable.

There is one Indian woman who has moved the imaginations of American popular writers, both male and female. She is derived from the rather shadowy figure of Sacajawea, the Northern Shoshone woman who helped guide the Lewis and Clark expedition. During the first wave of feminism in the early twentieth century, she took on a symbolic importance in excess of her historic role and was recreated for the American imagination in Eva Emory Dye's *The Conquest* (1902) and the semifictional biography of Grace Raymond Hebard (1932). Such books, though they may glorify women (and sometimes love), still subscribe to the notion of the vanishing American and attempt to justify the destruction of Indian culture.

But what of the popular literature of anti-feminism, those widely read expressions of "masculine protest," which begin, perhaps, with Owen Wister's *The Virginian* (1902)? There are Indians in such books, of course, but they are, except the works of John G. Neihardt (1932, 1951) relegated to a secondary role—and seem, as tests of manhood, interchangeable with bad White men. In the struggle between Christian values and the code of the West, between a "male" ethic of individually enforced law and order and a "female" ethic of forgiveness and nonviolence, the problems of expropriation and genocide are pushed into the background. In the popular Western of the age of Theodore Roosevelt, the essential mythical struggle is felt to be not that between Red savages and White females, as it was in the age of Andrew Jackson. It is rather between White men who have learned to be Noble Savages and White women who cling still to the European tradition: the cowboy and the schoolmarm.

In the 1960s certain heroes of the age of Jackson and after had become villains or clowns, including Jackson himself and General Custer and Buffalo Bill—as anyone can discover by reading a play such as Arthur Kopit's *Indians* (1969), or poems like Gary Snyder's "A Curse on the Men in Washington, Pentagon" (1967) or novels like Kesey's *One Flew Over the Cuckoo's Nest* (1962) and Thomas Berger's *Little Big Man* (1964).

It is with such books as these and John Barth's *The Sot-Weed Factor* (1960) that the encounter between White Men and Red returns once more to the center of major American fiction after a long absence. To be sure, two of the major novelists of the 1920s, Ernest Hemingway and William Faulkner, who continued to dominate the literary scene until their deaths after World War II, wrote about Indians. But Hemingway stories such as "Ten Little Indians" (1938) and his burlesque novel *Torrents of Spring* (1926) are not among his most highly prized or most frequently reprinted works. And even Faulkner's "The Bear" (1942), that much esteemed account of a boy's initiation under the tutelage of a wilderness guide half-Black and half-Red, is overshadowed by his more ambitious long fictions. In the 1930s, 1940s, and 1950s, the two most important schools of fiction, the Southern and the urban Jewish, tended to scant the Indian theme almost entirely.

It is minor writers or provincial ones, like Oliver La Farge (1929, 1937, 1942), and Frank Waters (1942, 1963, 1966), or popular entertainers without "literary" ambitions, like Max Brand, or oddly intermediate figures like A.B. Guthrie (1947, 1949) and Vardis Fisher (1958, 1965) who keep the tradition alive in what the reigning critics of the time tended to consider a semirespectable underground. But with the 1960s the situation changed, even as American society was changing, and the vanishing American unexpectedly re-appeared. But the neo- or meta-Western, in which he is revived, is quite different from anything written in the past, whether anti-Indian or pro-Indian.

Still in some sense nostalgic and sentimental, such fiction is also irreverent and farcical; but even more unprecedented than its new tone is a new uncertainty, most clearly expressed in *Little Big Man*, but also to be found in stories such as Dorothy Johnson's *Man Called Horse* (1965), about exactly what it means to "be an Indian." The protagonist in *Little Big Man* shuttles back and forth between two mutually incomprehensible cultures and ends by leaving himself unsure not only about whether he is "really" Red or White but also about the larger question of whether "Red" and "White" are not finally questions of attitudes and values rather than blood and race.

Moreover, the revival of the Indian in the neo-Western led to the rediscovery of earlier books on Indians read in their own time chiefly by "professional Westerners" and scholars, such as Bandelier's *The Delight Makers* (1890). Yet the Indian tales of Jack London remain uncollected and unread. Even so fascinating a figure as Joaquin Miller (1874), who apparently helped lead an Indian revolt in 1855 (facts are hard to tell from fancy in his own account) is not rediscovered. And Hamlin Garland's *The Book of the American Indian* (1923) does not even live the life of academic book-lists like his *Son of the Middle Border* (1917). Mary Austin, though she has been the subject of more doctoral dissertations than any other writer about Indians except Cooper and Longfellow, remains still a classroom assignment.

Yet the books that achieved popularity in the 1970s resembled those of Miller and Garland in theme and quality: they presented themselves as fact rather than fiction but operated in the minds of their readers as works of imagination or even mythology. They are not notably better books, not even in the case of the two best examples, *Black Elk Speaks* (Neihardt 1932) and *Ishi in Two Worlds* (T. Kroeber 1961). *Ishi* recounts the difficult and beautiful friendship that developed between Alfred L. Kroeber and the sole surviving Yahi Indian, whom Kroeber brought to San Francisco in 1911. Theodora Kroeber's book, written after the death of the two principals, is reminiscent and nostalgic, a footnote to the theme of the vanishing American. *Black Elk Speaks*, on the other hand, presents itself as the product not of memory but transcription: the undoctored record of a surviving Indian describing a life still living for him, though history for others. Yet the book, like all such books, is in part the creation of its White author, who had spent his career, from 1906 on, composing prose fiction and narrative poems about the Indian wars (Neihardt 1925, 1935). And that suspicion is compounded by reading *When the Tree Flowered* (1951), a candidly fictional work by Neihardt, which also purports to record the conversations of an aged Indian and a young White man. Records of Neihardt's interviews with Black Elk were transcribed and annotated by DeMallie (1984).

A literature by Indians about Indians began to appear 579

in the 1960s, written in English, of course, and therefore available to the American mass audience. Vine Deloria's *Custer Died For Your Sins* (1969) is one example, along with *We Talk, You Listen* (1970). N. Scott Momaday, less bitter and ironic, wrote books that include nostalgic essays such as *The Journey of Tai-me* (1967) and *The Way to Rainy Mountain* (1969), along with a novel, *House Made of Dawn* (1968), which won the Pulitzer Prize for fiction in 1969. A professor of English literature, Momaday shares in both cultures, and makes, therefore, an admirable interpreter and intermediary between Red and White.

There have been many translations of older Indian poetry into English by poets both Red and White, the most successful perhaps being those collected in *Shaking the Pumpkin* (Rothenberg 1972; see also Cronyn 1972).

An Indian who most possessed the contemporary imagination, particularly among the young, in the 1970s was a Yaqui sorcerer and wise man who entered literature in a trilogy written in English by Carlos Castañeda (1968, 1971, 1972). Its first volume, *The Teachings of Don Juan* (1968), became an immediate underground best seller in colleges and high schools, largely because "Don Juan" was the spokesman for a mythical view of the world totally opposed to rationalism, and for a magical way of manipulating reality totally opposed to science. Presented as traditionally "Indian," his views correspond a little too aptly, perhaps, with those of certain exponents of cults associated with the use of hallucenogenic drugs (Baldwin 1977); and one cannot help suspecting that Castañeda's book may be only allegorically or fictionally "true" (Spicer 1969a; De Mille 1976, 1980).

It matters very little, however, whether the Don Juan trilogy is the actual account of a dialogue between an anthropologist and an Indian shaman or instead another effort, so essential in White American fiction, to find and release the true voice of the Indian. Such uncertainty is characteristic of White American literature from the start, for the Red man has always been confused by his White expropriators with certain repressed elements in their own psyches, leading Thoreau to remark that some day Americans would no longer be sure whether their forests had contained actual Indians or only their own "shadows cast upon the trees."

The Indian militancy of the 1970s reminded White America and the world that the American Indian was indeed alive, if not always well.* And it was the Sioux, who had made headlines at Wounded Knee in 1973, who captured once again the imagination of thousands of uninformed readers with the best-selling novel *Hanta Yo* (1979), by White author Ruth Beebe Hill. Based ostensibly on a Sioux winter count and years of research, *Hanta Yo* is the saga of a Lakota band around 1800. Praised by critics and the press for its epic language and unique narrative style, *Hanta Yo* was apparently conceived by its author as a literary tribute to the traditional world of the Plains Indians, epitomized by the fictional Mahto band. Ironically, the reaction of the Sioux Indians to the book was overwhelmingly negative (JoAllyn Archambault, communication to editors 1987). The Sioux denounced Hill's misrepresentations of traditional Lakota religion and sexuality, noting also that *Hanta Yo* created "new and defamatory stereotypes . . . of American Indians" (Sinte Gleska College Staff Senate 1980; see also Sinte Gleska College, Lakota Studies Department 1980; Medicine 1979). Anthropologists joined the Indians in condemning the book (DeMallie 1979; Powers 1979).

This controversy had a less publicized precedent in Hyemeyohsts Storm's *Seven Arrows* (1972), an allegorical and episodic fictional narrative centered around traditional Cheyenne religion and beliefs. *Seven Arrows* presented itself, quite presumptuously, as the first book about the traditional ways of the Plains Indians written entirely by an American Indian. The Northern Cheyenne condemned the book both for its content and its color plates of spurious "Indian" symbols, which they felt made "a blasphemous travesty of the Cheyenne Way" (Costo 1972: 41; see also J.H. Moore 1973). However, Larson (1978: 112–126) gave *Seven Arrows* a positive review. Storm's *Song of Heyoehkah* (1981) followed the visual format of *Seven Arrows*; the narrative itself is a fictional account of the indoctrination of a White man into the traditional world view of the Indian and is clearly reminiscent of Castañeda.

The *Seven Arrows* and *Hanta Yo* controversies were indicative of the role American Indians were taking in scrutinizing not only works by anthropologists (see Deloria 1969:83–104), but also by fiction writers. Indians did not limit themselves to criticism; from the early 1970s they made important original contributions to American literature (K. Lincoln 1983). In this literary expression of what had long been an oral tradition, modern Indian writers often chose to reflect the conflicts and contradictions of contemporary American Indian life: the reservation and the urban experience, the war veterans, the police, and the problem of alcohol, insidious enemy of the Indian body and soul. Some of these key elements characterize the early writings of Indian authors such as Leslie Marmon Silko (Laguna), Simon J. Ortiz (Acoma), and Joseph Little (Mescalero Apache), who were among the contributors to *The Man to Send Rain Clouds* (Rosen 1974), a collection of short stories by Native Americans. These and many other American Indian writers found a congenial forum for their work in *Sun Tracks*, a literary magazine featuring prose, poetry, and photography by Native Americans. The magazine began publication in 1971, sponsored by the American Indian Student Club and the Department of English at the University of Arizona in Tucson.

A number of outstanding Indian novelists emerged

*The remainder of the chapter was written by Cesare Marino.

from a growing body of Native American writers. James Welch (Blackfeet/Gros Ventre) captured a personal story of reservation and nearby rural town life in *Winter in the Blood* (1974), praised as "an almost flawless novel, certainly one of the most significant pieces of fiction written by an American Indian" (Larson 1978:140). In the end, it is right on the reservation that the nameless narrator finds refuge from the White man's world and memories of death. More acute is the sense of despair and alienation that transpires from Welch's second novel, *The Death of Jim Loney* (1979), the story of a Gros Ventre half-blood who can find a solution to his problematic life only by putting an end to it (actually, he sets himself up to be killed by the police). With *Fools Crow* (1986), Welch reaches back to the late nineteenth century to share with a member of a small Piegan band an evocative story of life, death, and survival.

Similar historical realism pervades *Wolf and the Winds* (1986), a posthumous novel by White author Frank B. Linderman. Like *Fools Crow, Wolf and the Winds* is a eulogy of traditional Indian life on the Northern Plains, here experienced in the mid-nineteenth century by a Gros Ventre protagonist named Wolf. Toward the end, the encroachment of the White "wasters" raises Wolf's pan-Indian consciousness. To the Gros Ventre elders who hoped the Black Hills war would bring death to their enemies the Sioux, Wolf warned: "No, it is not good . . . .I hate the Sioux and the Cheyennes as you do, as we all do, but they are red men, as we are. If the white men wipe [them] out . . . we shall be next" (Linderman 1986:185). The appeal for Indian unity echoes more explicitly in *Winter Count* (1967), by Sioux author Dallas Chief Eagle, as the legendary Hunkpapa leader Sitting Bull declared: "We must unite to survive, to defeat the white man who is our enemy" (Chief Eagle 1967:95). This theme reaches a climax in *Indians' Summer* (1975), by Shawnee author Nasnaga (Roger Russell). While America celebrates her two-hundredth birthday, several Indian nations declare their independence and unite to wage guerrilla warfare against the United States. The Indians gain world-wide political and military support and in the end the intertribal coalition, the Anishinabe-waki Democracy, is recognized by Washington as an independent nation.

A shift from the overtly political and confrontational tone of Nasnaga's novel toward an analysis of the cultural and psychological implications of modern Indian-White interaction characterized much of American Indian literature in the late 1970s and early 1980s. The mixed-blood, already a protagonist in *The Surrounded* and *House Made of Dawn*, became a recurring theme in *Darkness in Saint Louis Bearheart* (1978) and *Earthdivers: Tribal Narratives of Mixed Descent* (1981) by Chippewa author Gerald R. Vizenor. Similarly, unlike Welch's portrayal of Jim Loney as a loser, Tayo, the protagonist of Leslie Silko's *Ceremony* (1977), emerges from his cathartic experience as a redeemed mixed-blood who is able to overcome evil and restore harmony to his Pueblo by acting as a sort of modern-day trickster. Mixed-bloods are many of the characters in *Love Medicine* (1984) by Louise Erdrich (Turtle Mountain Chippewa), as well as the protagonist in *The Jailing of Cecelia Capture* (1985) by Janet Campbell Hale (Sioux). This is undoubtedly a reflection of the important roles mixed-bloods play in contemporary American Indian life and literature (Schöler 1986:93–94, 1984:137–144).

An example of a successful novelist of mixed Indian-White descent is Martin Cruz Smith, who gained international fame with *Gorky Park* (1981). In his *Nightwing* (1977) the setting is Hopi country, where the death of an old Indian sets the stage for a prophetic mystery that will end with the destruction of the infected bats threatening the Southwest. With *Stallion Gate* (1986) Smith combined history and fiction in a novel where duty, love and betrayal, and cultural conflict unfold around Sergeant Joe Peña, a Pueblo Indian, caught in the midst of the development of the atomic bomb at Los Alamos, in the heart of Rio Grande Pueblo land. The Indian Southwest is also the theater of Tony Hillerman's detective mysteries centered around the fictional protagonist Jim Chee of the Navajo Tribal Police in *People of Darkness* (1980), *The Dark Wind* (1982), *The Ghostway* (1984), and *Skywalkers* (1986).

American Indian authors such as Simon Ortiz (1977, 1983, 1983a), Anna Lee Walters (Pawnee-Otoe; 1985), Joy Harjo (Creek, 1983), Linda Hogan (Chickasaw, 1981, 1985), Paula Gunn Allen (Laguna, 1983), and Michael A. Dorris (Modoc, 1987) have also made unique contributions to American literature. In the 1980s, a number of anthologies featuring prose and poetry by Native American writers were published (see Hobson 1981; R. Green 1984; Dodge and McCullough 1985): they reflected the vitality of what K. Lincoln (1983) called a literary renaissance among American Indians. Earlier discussions of American Indian literature include A. Chapman (1975), Larson (1978), and Velie (1981), who focused on Momaday, Welch, Silko, and Vizenor.

The place of the Indian, both mythical and real, in American literature is discussed by Fiedler (1969) and Keiser (1933). Louise K. Barnett (1975) analyzed American racism in literature, 1790–1890, with regard to the Indian. Elémire Zolla (1973) offered a comprehensive treatment of the Indian image in Anglo-American literature. Beidler and Egge (1979) compiled an annotated bibliography of the American Indian in short fiction; Colonnese and Owens (1985) published a critical bibliography of American Indian novelists. Krupat and Swann (1987) edited a collection of essays on Native American literature. Monkman (1981) discussed the images of the Indian in English-Canadian literature. Prucha (1977: 363–367) has a bibliography on the Indian in literature.

The Indian in Non-English Literature

CHRISTIAN F. FEEST

North American Indians and Eskimos have played a small but at times influential role in European literature.

Literature in French

Both substantial information and speculative theories on the native inhabitants were published in France following French discoveries in the Americas beginning in the sixteenth century. From the very beginning opinion was divided on the question whether the Indians were unspoiled children of the forest or senseless brutes (Chinard 1911).

The first French novel on Canada, possibly based on personal experience (Du Périer 1601), was soon dramatized by Du Hamel (1603) at the expense of the little local color contained in the original. More ethnographic is a poem by Lescarbot (1612) written on his way home from Canada. In America, seventeenth-century Jesuits also made use of local events for their stage plays (Roy 1890).

The Indian as a "naked philosopher," important in eighteenth-century literature, was introduced by Lahontan (1703a). His and other French explorers' data on the Indians were relied on by the writers of exotic literature until 1800.

Arlequin sauvage (Delisle 1722), the most influential early play on Indians, portrays the disenchantment of a young Huron man with European civilization. The Indian remained a favorite on stage in *La Sauvagesse* and *Les Mariages de Canada* (Le Sage and d'Orneval 1735, 1735a), Chamfort's (1764) variant of the English Inkle and Yarico motif, and *Hirza, ou Les Illinois* (Billardon de Sauvigny 1767), all of which feature the obligatory Indian-White love story in a romantically tragic form. The Indian novel developed more slowly. Some of the stories in Le Sage (1732) relate to adventures among Canadian Indians. The fictional Abaquis of Florida figure in Prévost (1728–1738), who later compiled a collection of voyages (1747–1780). Whereas data on different tribes (even including Mexican) are strangely mixed in these works, Le Beau (1738) is so well put together that his novel has occasionally been used as a source on Indians of eastern Canada. Other romantic French prose includes an Iroquois triangle story (Anonymous 1776) and a German-influenced *Inkle et Iarico* (Anonymous 1778), a tale of an Indian woman ultimately sold into slavery by her lover, a shipwrecked Englishman whose life she had saved. There is little important poetry on Indians.

Critical views of the idealistic picture of the Indians were expressed in prose by Maubert de Gouvest (1752, 1769), on stage by Voltaire (1767), and in philosophical writings by the encyclopedists and by de Pauw (1768–1771). Chateaubriand's (1801, 1802, 1827) Indian novels have little to do with their author's visit to America; rather, they center around traditional French concepts of Indians to which the beneficial influence of Christianity on the natives is added. His works had a considerable impact on later writers on Indians (Chinard 1918, 1919). For more details on the seventeenth and eighteenth centuries see Chinard (1935).

Louisiana French authors contributed substantially to this genre of literature. Le Blanc de Villeneufve (1814) wrote a tragedy in which he pleaded for the "hommes de la nature." His more realistic picture derives from the fact that he had lived for seven years among the Choctaws. Adrien E. Rouquette (1841, 1879) and Dominique Rouquette (1839), two lyrical poets, included the Indian in their praise of nature. Adrien even dressed like an Indian to achieve his ideal of becoming part of nature. Deléry (1878) pitied the vanishing Indian, implying parallels with the fate of the Louisiana French. Bouis (1847) romanticized the Indian in James Fenimore Cooper fashion, while Eyma (1854) would not pity the "brigands about whom Chateaubriand has deceived the public." French Canadian writers include Fréchette (1877), Marmette (1877), and Girard (1910).

For political reasons, French interests shifted from the former colonies to Mexico and the Southwestern border region. Gabriel Ferry, Gustave Aimard, and Paul Duplessis had been in Mexico themselves and capitalized on this interest in their novels. Their plots usually feature a White hero, preferably of French origin, his equally heroic Indian friend, and the antagonism between friendly and hostile tribes (chiefly Comanche versus Apache). Ferry (especially 1850, 1855), became the most influential of the three. Duplessis (1856, 1859, 1864) produced 60 volumes in 10 years, some of them also on North Africa; Aimard (for example, 1858, 1858a, 1865, 1866, 1872) produced 50 volumes (some co-authored by d'Auriac 1866, 1867, 1878) mainly on the Americas and not limited to the Southwestern borderlands. In their wake, other writers exploited this favorite subject. Révoil (1876, 1878, 1884), traveler, hunter, and translator of Reid and Friedrich Gerstäcker, and Noir (1899, 1899a) are examples.

Twentieth-century French fiction partly continued in the style of Ferry and Aimard and partly followed modern trends by dealing with descriptions of Indians on reservations or by concentrating on Indian and Eskimo life to the exclusion of White heroes. Most of these books were written for juvenile readers. Authors include Cerbelaud-Salagnac (1937, 1953); Swiss writers Villoz (1956) and De Cesco (1957, 1961); the Swiss anthropologist Gabus (1941, 1951), who had field experience among the Eskimo; the Belgian Droit (1943); and the French Canadian Thériault (1960, 1961, 1963, 1964), who is best known for his *Agaguk* (1958). Camus (1978; Camus and Grenier 1984), who claims to have an Iroquois father and who grew up in Yukon Territory, has published Indian fiction and science fiction. On America in French literature see also Lebel (1952) and Viatte (1954).

Literature in German

Although German interest in America became intense around 1500 and publications on America were numerous thereafter (Sixel 1966), the North American Indian did not become a topic of German writers until Bodmer (1756) and Gessner (1756) introduced the Inkle and Yarico motif on the German stage (L.M. Price 1937). The John Smith–Pocahontas story was used in Scheibler's (1781) novel and Rose's play, which had been written in 1771 but was published in 1784 "due to the current interest in such things." This interest partly reflects foreign influence (translations from French and English sources) but more important, actual and journalistic German involvement in American matters during the Revolution (Hatfield and Hochbaum 1899). *Der Hessische Officier* (Weppen 1783), for example, deals with German mercenaries and also features Indians. Seume's poem "Der Wilde" (1801) is likewise influenced by the author's past as an impressed mercenary soldier (cf. Friedrichs 1984).

Poetry largely portrays heroic death among the Indians (Schubart 1787; Krauseneck 1778; Schiller 1797). Herder (1778) published translations of Indian poetry in his *Volkslieder*. Other works of that period include Kotzebue's play *Die Indianer in England* (1790), La Roche (1798), and Grosse (1793). French and English ideas about the savage were of guiding importance for German writers throughout the eighteenth century. Zschokke (1804, 1820) briefly mentions Indians and praises them as independent, honest, virtuous men of nature, free of religious intolerance. Both Chamisso (1831) and Lenau (1838) had visited America before writing their poems

lamenting the fate of the Indians in view of the advancing frontier. Freiligrath (1838), inspired by Lenau's experiences, wrote a cycle of poems describing the adventures of an emigrated poet who, disappointed with American life, finally settled among the Indians. This romantic concept of Native Americans, which was reinforced by the emphatic acceptance of Chateaubriand and particularly Cooper in Germany (Barba 1914; Rossbacher 1972), was attacked in the novels of Biernatzki (1840) and Lewald (1847). However, this criticism could not stop the rapid increase of Indian fiction. German promotional literature for emigrants and travel narratives (more than 50 titles between 1815 and 1850) kept the public informed about North America. Sealsfield (1843–1846) and Gerstäcker (for example, 1844, 1847, 1862) were the first German writers specializing in American subjects. Both had firsthand experience and consequently pictured the Indian more realistically than previous authors, romantic patterns permeating their work notwithstanding. On the period before 1850 see also P.C. Weber (1926) and H. Meyer (1929).

Armand (Friedrich Strubberg) also combines realistic detail with romantic idealization (fig. 1). Since he had been involved in the German colonization of Texas, the Comanche are frequently described from observation. Others of the 57 volumes published late in his life (for example, 1858, 1858a, 1859, 1859a, 1860, 1867, 1868) reflect impressions of an earlier visit to America (Barba 1913). The German element in the United States is prominent in his and in Ruppius's (1861, 1862) writings where exotic subject matter is combined with German nationalism. Möllhausen (for example, 1861, 1865, 1878, 1880) wanted his Indian novels to be regarded as illustrative counterparts to his serious books of travel (Barba 1916). German-American author Straubenmüller (1858) revisited Pocahontas.

Of those who never saw America, Scherr (1853) was influenced by Cooper beyond his selection of King Philip's War as his topic, while Spielhagen (1871) describes German colonization of the Mohawk valley around 1750. During the same period, translations of books on America, mainly fiction, flooded the market. The works of Robert Montgomery Bird, William Gilmore Simms, Mayne Reid, Charles Murray, Ferry, Aimard, and others had a wide distribution. Ferry (1850) went through around 40 different German editions by 1980. Translations of 378 volumes were published in the *Amerikanische Bibliothek* between 1852 and 1871. Periodicals like *Das Ausland*, *Die Gartenlaube*, *Das Sonntagsblatt* (founded by Ruppius), and *Uber Land und Meer* carried factual and fictional information about the New World.

Another important agent contributing to the surge of Indian fiction was the rise of juvenile literature. Nieritz (1846) introduced the Eskimo to the young ones. Hoffmann (1845) started with an abridgement of Cooper and

Fig. 1. left, Title page and, right, illustration from *Na Zapadīe Ameriki* 'In the American West' (1896), a Russian translation of a novel by Armand. The illustrations show some Indians as noble savages who protect White, female innocents from other Indians, portrayed as hostile and barbaric. Such novels, in which Indians fight other Indians, gave authors the opportunity to present the two opposing views of Indians held by Whites. Illustrations by W. Zweigle.

for 40 years continued to lean on the writings of others. During the last quarter of the century more than 100 authors published approximately 1,000 titles of Indian fiction, chiefly in Kleine Volkserzählungen, Neue Volksbücher, Volks- und Jugenderzählungen, Kleine Jugendbibliothek, Indianer- und Volksbibliothek, Collection Wild-West and a dozen similar series consisting of from two to eight printed sheets. The authors (among the most prolific were Ludwig Foehse, A.H. Fogowitz, W. Frey, J. and P. Grundmann, Franz Pistorius) freely stole from more successful writers and from one another; and while frequently focusing on Indians, they also wrote on adventures in other fields of colonial enterprise. The themes of these writings range from the lives of chiefs through descriptions of border warfare to loving Indian maidens and superstitious medicine men; but very often they refer to contemporary news like the outbreaks from reservations or the deeds of Sitting Bull and Buffalo Bill (William F. Cody). The Sioux lead in frequency of description, followed by the Apache, Comanche, Seminole, and Blackfoot.

The Indian craze slowed down around 1900 when the wars in Asia and stories relating to German colonies in Africa become more popular. A special variety of this type of literature was Roman Catholic missionary stories for pious readers (Anton Huonder, Joseph Spillmann). Only a few writers of this period deserve particular mention. Karl May (1913–1969) ranks first in view of his later success (fig. 2). Influenced by Ferry and based on data from Albert Gatschet, Robert von Schlagintweit, Ross Browne, and others, May's descriptions are better than the average but still far removed from reality. The few "good" Indians in his novels are mainly those who have been "improved" by Germans or by Christianity. They are contrasted with those originally innocent pagans who have been corrupted by "Yankee civilization."

Wörishöffer (1880) relied in her extended ethnographic descriptions chiefly on Wied-Neuwied (1839–1841); Felde (1900, 1903) is among the better authors writing in the

Fig. 2. Illustration titled "Ein Wiedersehen" 'A Reunion' from *Der Ölprinz* 'The Oil Prince' (1891), a novel by Karl May. Shatterhand, left, and Winnetou embrace. The theme of White-Indian friendship, especially Germans and Indians, is prominent in May's novels. Illustration by O.H.

Fig 3. Title page of *Der Arrapahu* 'The Arapaho' (1900), a novel by Max Felde. Illustration by J.V.C.

vein of May (fig. 3); while Pajeken (1891, 1895) unsuccessfully tried to counteract the allegedly harmful effects of romantic Indian fiction by writing moralizing stories said to be based on his own experiences. Bessels (1891) is one of the few German authors of Eskimo fiction. On the period to 1900 see also S. Schroeder (1934) and Barba (1913a). Augustin (1982) is an anthology of German Indian poems, 1700–1900.

Franz Kafka's (1983) short prose piece on dreaming to be an Indian may serve as an indication that the subject matter was not exclusively relegated to trivial literature. Other early twentieth century authors include Droonberg (1921, 1925), who prominently included Indians in his vivid descriptions of life in the wilds of Alaska and Canada where he had lived for some time. Gagern (1925, 1927a) described the Indian as seen and detested by the Virginia and Kentucky frontiersmen but also (1927) pitied his doom caused by the contact with the White man in one of the first novels without White heroes.

Although some Nazi ideologists deplored the enthusiasm for other races in literature, the 1930s brought a new high for the German Indian novel. Steuben (1930, 1931,

1932, 1933, 1934, 1936, 1938, 1953), an author of edifying nationalistic literature, wrote a series of successful and well-researched novels relating to the life of Tecumseh. The moral of his story was that even the most heroic acts of resistance are bound to fail in the absence of national and racial unity. The Tecumseh story was instantly taken up by other authors (Hoffmann-Harnisch 1935; Schauwecker 1942). Historical topics became the rule. Stimulating accounts of bravery and Germanic references abound in dozens of Indian novels published between 1933 and 1945. Gymir (1940), for example, claimed Norse descent for the Narragansett Canochet and other coastal Indian leaders.

After World War II, the Indian craze increased in the Federal Republic of Germany with reissues of classics (35 million copies of May's works were sold between 1954 and 1971) and many new titles, few of them with original ideas. A series of biographies of Indian chiefs was published by Swiss writer Ernst Herzig (1951, 1954, 1956, amongst others). Woodland Indians are the subject of novels by Austrian writers Weiser (1933, 1936, 1969,

1970) and Recheis (for example, 1967, 1967a). The best German book on Indian life, written by anthropologist Lips (1947), was first published in English. Osceola as a leader of the Indian resistance is placed in a contemporary context for young readers by H. Martin (1972). The "Four Indian Kings" and their 1710 visit to London (vol. 15:474) is presented as a case study of English colonialism for adults by Kühn (1974).

Because Karl May was regarded as petit bourgeois and reactionary until 1983 in the German Democratic Republic, local appetite for Indian fiction had to be satisfied otherwise. Novels of superior quality were produced by Welskopf-Henrich both in a six-volume account of the fate of a small Lakota band emigrating to Canada after the Battle of Little Big Horn (1951-1955), as well as in novels with a contemporary setting (for example, 1969, 1972). Pro-Indian and antiimperialist attitudes characterize her works as also those of Daumann (1957, 1957a, 1958) and Jürgen (1950, 1951). For a discussion of the Indian in German history text books see Everwien (1972); for Indians in German children's books compare Lutz (1980).

Other Literatures

Translations of classics such as Cooper, Chateaubriand, Ferry, Aimard, and May have appeared in most European and in a few Asian languages (for example Cooper in Japanese, May in Malay). Besides, many modern works have been translated from some European languages into others, often without regard to quality.

Written literature has been produced by Greenland Eskimos (vol. 5:640-645). As one would expect, there are some very good Eskimo novels in Danish. Both Mikkelsen (1920, 1921) and Freuchen (1927, 1928, 1930, 1934) belong to the category of ethnographer-novelists. Gredsted (1918, 1922, 1932) wrote successful Indian stories in Danish, and Voss (1960) is a modern example of the same genre. For Swedish, the writings of Ericson (1963, 1963a, 1964, 1965, among others) may be mentioned. In Linderholm (1975), Little Beaver, a descendant of Swedish colonists, united two warring tribes to beat the Whites and free the Black slaves.

In Dutch, there are numerous series, such as *Arendsoog-serie* or *Texas Rangers serie.* Modern novelists include Eggermont (1960), Van Hichtum (1960), Frank (1954, 1959), and Wilkeshuis (1968), who do not limit themselves to Indian topics. Contemporary poetry inspired by Indian themes is offered by Schierbeek (1982). Dutch and Belgian comic strips on Indians are discussed by Malcorps (1982).

Salgari's books of adventure, which have been compared to those of May, include several on Indians (for example, 1896, 1905, 1908). Among later Italian authors of juvenile literature are Fabietti (1950) and Gelardini De Barbo (1959). *Grandi romanzieri* is an example of a series with Indian titles. For original and translated literature see also Solimano (1983:127-132); for Italian comic strips see Bertieri and Musso in Solimano (1983) and Pompa (1983).

In many countries of Eastern Europe, a substantial body of popular nonfiction on Indians was published to counterbalance the distortions of fiction (for example, Šolc 1968; Stingl 1966, 1969). Polish books include the writings of Sat-Okh (Stanislaw Suplatovich) who claims to be half-Polish and half-Shawnee, Arkady Fiedler, Nora Szeponska, and Wieslaw Wernic. In Alfred Szklarski's *Tomek na wojenne sciezce* (1978), a Polish youth who sees the parallels between tsarist domination of Poles and American oppression of Indians gives sometimes paternalistic advice to his Indian friends. In Russian fiction, Pushkin's extensive 1836 review of Tanner's captivity (Vashchenko 1987:307) was not followed by a surge of Indian fiction. Mikhail M. Prishvin's work on Grey Owl, *Seraia sova* (1938), is actually one of the few such books. In Hungarian, juvenile literature both on Indians (for example, M. Ronaszegi) and on Eskimos (B. Lengyel) has been added to the classic Belányi (1865). There are several Western series in Turkish, besides Indian-related books for the young (Anonymous 1963, 1965; Uğurkan 1956).

On the whole subject of the Indian in non-English literature compare Ten Kate (1922), Plischke (1951), and Billington (1981).

The Indian in Popular American Culture

RAYNA GREEN

From the time when Europeans first came to the Americas, the Indian was a central figure in the New World iconography. Nowhere was he more central than in the expressive forms of American popular culture. These oral, visual, and dramatic expressions are vital forms in American culture. They describe, codify, and present the image of the Indian while defining the set of operative values by which Anglo-Americans have approached the Native American. By oral forms are meant ballads, tales, legends, anecdotes, sayings, and ethnic slurs. Visual forms consist of advertisements, items of decorative art and craft, or any other plastic and graphic form. Dramatic-ideational forms include games and gestures, popular entertainments and pastimes, sports, and social organizations. For a more detailed discussion, see R.D. Green (1971, 1973).

As these expressions acted together with events and ideas, they projected, extended, reinforced, and maintained the images of the Indian that suited the uses of the culture in any given region, time, or situation. Each mode of expression acted with, informed, and supported every other, even when they may have been in conflict thematically. In the interchange can be seen the evocative power, the salience, and the aesthetic appeal of certain themes and behaviors—the fixation, for example, on the Indian princess; the attraction to the drunken, eloquent, vanishing Indian; the Indian as Nature's Nobleman (Deloria 1969; Dorson 1946; Dippie 1970) or the common allure of "playing Indian." Such themes were transmitted widely by artistic and social forms to a popular audience.

Predisposition toward the Indian as savage, defined in terms of his cultural differences, his inability or unwillingness to give up his culture and become White, and the manifestations of those cultural differences in his hostile actions toward Whites appears throughout the body of material. Yet predispositions toward an understanding of the Indian as admirable, noble, and exotic are also repeated. These statements, defined again in terms of the Indian's cultural differences, in terms of the virtues that stemmed from his "natural, primitive" state and manifested in his native skills as well as in his noble acts toward Whites, are part of the body of ideas that describe and prescribe for the White experience of the Indian.

The diverse regional and situational circumstances in which Whites encountered the Indian do not account entirely for the ambivalence and contradiction with which the image of the Indian is weighted. The uses of that ambivalence are visible, for example, in the positive attitude toward what are overtly defined as negative characteristics of the Indian. The only good Indian, these vernacular expressions tell us, is one who is alive as well as dead, noble as well as ignoble, exotic as well as dirty and common, violent and savage as well as gentle.

Though these items are products of the vernacular tradition, they do have their roots in many other traditions, and the diverse sources for these expressions account, in part, for the contradictory components and uses of the Indian image in American culture. Given different sources of content, form, and style, and the xenophobic sociocultural framework into which they were channeled, and given the gap between the stated public doctrine and actual behavior with respect to the Indian (and other non-White groups in America), it is little wonder that stereotyping took place.

What follows is a description of the kinds of vernacular expression and their sources, the manner of expression peculiar to each kind of medium, and the manner of expression peculiar to vernacular expression as a whole. Classification is based on surface distinctions between types of material, though much overlap occurs in the actual use of these materials in the culture. Since the materials that form the substance of this analysis are numerous, the samples and references are inclusive for type only, rather than for the complete body of material.

Oral Expression

Oral expression and those expressions passed on by customary example that include oral components (games and songs) are highly mobile and may exist in variants. They are formulaic, dramatic, descriptive, and symbolic forms. Though most of the oral expressions included here would come under the heading "folklore," many come from both popular culture and elite culture and are often spread through print and through the institutional forms of the national culture (such as schools) as well as by word of mouth.

One source of American oral expression is those

European conventions from high culture that predispose Whites toward a view of the Indian as Noble Savage, exotic and admirable creature, and the "natural" man. Second, there are those elements, motifs, and tale types (S. Thompson 1932–1936; Aarne 1961) from Indo-European narrative tradition and folk belief that were imported into the repertoire of New World expression. The Indian replaced or acted with the conventional personae (tricksters, clever fellows, fools, and stupid fellows) and inherited conventional actions (tricks, wise retorts, fabulous hunts) and elements of folk belief (magic acts, ghostly revenge, the existence of devils) from European tradition (Coffin 1971:202). Thus, the tendency of oral tradition to become attached to new situations, events, and people forced the Indian into roles not necessarily his by achievement.

Third, historical and regional encounter, whether friendly or unfriendly, with real Indians of all kinds of behavior fed oral tradition. But because the popular mind is disposed to seek formulas (stereotypes and the like) with which to interpret experience, and because too many different kinds of Indians and Whites interacted on too many different levels to provide a single interpretive framework, the tales based on historical experience are more likely to express the formulas of folklore than the details of fact.

Regional and temporal factors enter into the historical experience as well. Expressions were most abundant in times of greatest contact between Whites and Indians, and negative expressions were most abundant in areas and times when interaction between Indians and Whites was hostile (H.W. Thompson 1962:48–69; Coffin 1971: 187–206; E. Speck 1949). Thus, after about 1830, when fear of conflict in the East was greatly reduced, folk and popular expression in the East took on its nostalgic, sentimental, positive quality with respect to the Indian. But actual conflict, fear of conflict, and persistent geographic and live reminders of conflict kept the mythos negative in the West.

Other expressive forms of popular and elite culture feed into and are fed by folk expression. The popular stage (Rourke 1942:60–75), material culture and the plastic and graphic arts, literature, music (J.C. Hickerson 1970, 1970a; Hallowell 1957), popular entertainments and pastimes—all synthesize and reinterpret folk forms. They often bring expressions with opposing themes into geographic and ideological areas where other themes once dominated. The popular stage, for example, brought the positive song, "Little Mohea," to areas where most expression was negative.

Legends

Legends were elaborated largely from the late seventeenth through the late nineteenth century. They are distinguished in part by analogues in European tradition. H.W. Thompson (1962:48) and Coffin (1971:202) repeat a European story (Tale Type 38, Aarne 1961), that became the Indian Hater legend of Tom Quick, who was accosted by two Indians who meant to kill him. He was splitting logs and asked them to help before he would go with them. He had them put their hands in the split, and then knocked out the wedge, trapping them so he could escape. The legends—the Lovers' Leap tales, for example—are also distinguished by their repetition in the body of Indian-White lore (Baughman 1966: A968.2, K666, K547.2, K625.26, K656, K657a, K657c, X333, X690, X691), by their formulaic structure and content, by their specific placement in time and place, and by sincere belief in them. Both national and local legends abound, with the national ones, like Pocahontas Saving Capt. John Smith and Squanto Helping the Pilgrims, spread primarily through print in educational institutions and reinforced by visualization. Others were spread through oral tradition at the folk level. They are often attached to historical personages, local characters, events, and physical points of geography, thus forming a folk history of Indian-White relations. A number are said to have been told by Indians themselves, but few are verifiable in Indian tradition. For some tales that can be documented in Indian tradition, see L.J. Davidson (1948). The large body of fantastic (Dorson 1946), explanatory, local place-name (Huden 1962; H.W. Thompson 1962:455–456), and place-lore tales indicates the importance of the Indian on the psychological, historical, and geographic landscape in folk tradition.

A significant number of tales that treat of White folk belief with regard to Indians (monsters, ghostly revenge, curses) reveal some of the fear and guilt with which the Indian was and is approached by Whites. The Squaw Ghost—a common tale of an Indian ghost dressed in black haunting a particular spot every night—is told as a moral lesson. "The significance of the legend is that it is a means for getting even for the inhuman treatment of the Indians by the whites. The ghost was to scare the white people" (Kiebler 1955). These tales plus the romantic ones of Tragedy and Treasure, and Lovers' Leaps (J.W. Allen 1963; L. Pound 1949; Hurley 1951; Skinner 1896) validate the image of the Indian as an exotic. How many areas do not have a bluff or high place still unhaunted by the moans and cries of an Indian princess, torn by her own people from her brave—a warrior from an enemy tribe—a princess who chose to die by leaping over a precipice rather than face life without her lover or with one she did not love at all?

The romantic tales tend to be more literary than the historical ones, which affirm the view of the Indian as a savage by repeating tales of massacres, murders, captivities, and atrocities. Many are the stories of murders where Indians dashed out the brains of innocent babies against trees or made pouches from the skins of White babies

(H.W. Thompson 1962:65). Some few humorous aspects appear, often in the place-name tales, such as the story of how Passadaumkeag, Maine, got its name. "Drunk Injun says, 'Passa-de-rum-keg,' and so the town was named" (E.D. Ives 1971). Aspects of the Indian's nobility appear in the national legends, which always stress aid and friendship to Whites. Attitudes generally followed contact patterns; mixed attitudes can be found in all regions.

● ANECDOTES Anecdotes—Short first or third person narratives—were established and circulated from the beginning of English contact to the closing of the frontier. They recount personal experiences with or recollections of Indians. They were so popular in the nineteenth century that several collections perpetuated anecdotes common both to oral tradition and to print (G. Turner 1836; Newcomb 1835; Blake 1850; P. Thompson 1857; Merrill 1837). Their personalization appeals to the listener's sense of truth, though many are formulaic and have the components of legends, folktales, and jokes. Anecdotal structure does not depend on the formulas, and thus overt feelings and attitudes are more clearly stated than in the other oral genres. Many are humorous and deal with complex, multi-level relationships, ones less abstract or dramatic than those described in legend or song. Indians often appear more as named individuals than as anonymous abstract types: as humorous, for example, but also as possessing a sense of humor (Dorson 1946:113). Anecdotes speak of the daily commonplaces in contact relationships—recreation, trade, local characters, and minor incidents.

They speak of Indians and their savage acts, of unfriendly encounters, of Indian vices and failings (laziness, stupidity, drunkenness, gluttony, theft, violence, untrustworthiness, and trickery); but often the accounts of vice are cause for humor as well as dismay. One account tells of a party of Indians in the service of the American government who, during the Black Hawk wars of 1832, came upon a party of hostile Indians killed by White soldiers. They "commenced a most inhuman butchery of the dead bodies," cutting out the hearts and devouring them "raw and bleeding." Such, the narrator sadly concludes, "is the natural man!" (G. Turner 1836, 2:93). But in a more common sort of anecdote, the Indian propensity for theft is treated humorously. "At one time, Indian Sam picked up an axe which someone had left carelessly in the front yard. The Indian took it to Johnny Anderson who had a store at the time and tried to sell it. 'No,' said Anderson, 'I don't want to buy it; it's not good, it's not steel.' 'Yes, yes,' the Indian protested eagerly, 'all steal, all steal!' " (Kyes 1953). Often, the anecdote details some aspect of Indian custom or behavior that, though not regarded as a vice, stresses the incompatibilities of White and Indian culture. Many are the tales of Indians who would simply walk into a White's house and take whatever food was there. And in others, like the tale of

Trucky's Specialty, the Whites express revulsion at Indian food habits. Trucky was an Ottawa, a local character in the Muskegon, Michigan, area. A White man, a friend of Trucky's, was on his way homeward when he became hungry and decided to stop at Trucky's to eat. When he arrived, "he found Trucky preparing some soup which smelled delicious. Just then he [Trucky] stirred the stew, and Hubbard saw coming to the top a head of a muskrat, fur and all. For some reason or other, he lost his appetite, and went on his way to Muskegon" (Kyes 1953).

An important body of tales, connected to these, deals with Indian encounters with White technology and customs, the often disastrous attempts (regarded as humorous by Whites) by Indians to imitate White behavior and culture. In the anecdote, Big Storm on Lake, an old Indian was sitting in a hotel lobby pretending to read the newspaper. Some White men, knowing he could not read, decided to ask him what the news was. "Big storm on lake," he replied, "many ships sink." They knew that was impossible since they'd not heard of it. But he pointed to the account. "See," said the Indian, "ship upside down lake." He was holding the newspaper upside down (Kyes 1953).

A large number of anecdotes treat of Indian virtues as well (cleverness, bravery, generosity, stoicism, eloquence, kindness); however, these, like the legends, are usually connected to Indian virtue only insofar as those virtues benefit Whites. Many tell of generous repayments of gifts to Whites who had done the Indians some small (usually not equal) favor, or of Indian knowledge that became indispensable to Whites.

Another body of material deals with the Indian as he was mistreated and misunderstood by Whites, and these tales often stress the dignity, perceptivity, and eloquence of the Indian as he rebukes or replies to the White man. In one that epitomizes Indian-White relations, an Indian and a White man are sitting on a log. The Indian asks the White man to move over a little and the White man does so. He repeats his request several times until the White man says that if he moves over again, he will fall off the log. And the Indian replies: "That is what the white man expects the Indian to do. Keep moving until we are in the other waters" (Opie and Opie 1959:328). In another, an Indian attends the trial of a friend, and when his friend is sentenced, he approaches the judge. He points to the figure of Liberty in the courtroom and says "What that?" "Liberty," replied the judge. "Who him?" asked the Indian of another figure. "Justice," replied the judge. "Where him live now?" asked the Indian (Kyes 1953).

An important group of anecdotes deals with the Indian and his response to Christianity, its missionaries and followers. These are less apologetic than the songs on similar subjects, and they tell of humorous retorts to missionaries and responses to attempts to christianize Indians as well as revealing Indian interpretations of doctrine. In the tale Dogmas of Religion, or, Indian Politeness, a Swedish missionary tells a group of Indians about Adam and Eve and the Messiah, and the Indian leader offers to tell him some tales. The missionary, disgusted by native revelations, says: "What I deliver to you are sacred truths—but what you deliver to me is fable—fiction." And the chief, not knowing how to respond to such rudeness, retorted: "My brother, it seems to me that the tutors of your youth neglected your education. I blame them for not having instructed you in the rules of common civility. Did you not see that we Red men—who understand and practice those rules—readily believed all your stories? Why then, do you refuse to believe ours?" (Turner 1836, 1:20–21).

Many anecdotes, as with other genres, combine references to Indian vices and virtues in the same tale, expressing the very conflict that exists in the White understanding of the Indian. Many a tale admiringly acknowledges the Indian's cleverness and acumen in obtaining liquor from the gullible White man while, at the same time, deploring the Indian's weakness for liquor.

● JOKES Jokes did not appear until the late nineteenth century and were repeated sporadically until the third quarter of the twentieth. They are separated from anecdotes in terms of their primary purpose (entertainment), style (short narrative characterized by a punch-line ending), appearance in time, and analogues in tradition to other folktale and joke types (Little Moron, shaggy dog, ethnic, pun). There are riddles (When is an Indian not an Indian? When he's a wooden Indian—C.G. Shaw 1939: 131), shaggy dog stories with puns (the son of the squaw of the two hides is equal to the sons of the squaw of the hippopotamus), and ribald jokes (A White tells a squaw with 11 children that her husband ought to be hung, and she replies, "Ugh, Pretty Well Hung!"). The Indian as aggressively sexual is expressed uniquely in the joke genre. Ethnic jokes often ridicule Indians together with other minority groups (Clements 1969:M3.0). There are numerous Lone Ranger–Tonto jokes (the Lone Ranger killed Tonto because he finally found out what Kemo Sabe meant).

Stupidity and filthiness are characteristics commonly attributed to outgroups in ethnic jokes. In one, a rich White man befriends and is befriended by an old Indian. He learns Indian ways and lives among Indians for several months. In gratitude for the experience, he takes the old Indian back to his well-appointed house to live for a while. The Indian was particularly impressed with the plumbing facilities, and expressed admiration for everything. One day, however, the neighbors heard a scream, and rushing in, they found the White man dead, murdered beside the toilet. The Indian admitted killing the White man, and when they asked why, he said, pointing to the White man and the toilet, "Mess 'em up stream!" Other jokes do not stress specific characteristics, merely using Indian charac-

ters (chiefs, squaws, Tonto, Hiawatha) as frames for puns and jokes. Most jokes use some form of pidgin English.

Songs

Songs are products primarily of the eighteenth and nineteenth centuries, but some few were written in the twentieth century. Different types (parodies of music and text, ballads, lyrics, humorous, obscene) stem from different sources (print, oral tradition, recorded popular music, the popular stage, political movements) (Fife and Redden 1954; Laws 1964:B11, 12, H8, 10, 11, 15). Some songs commemorate specific events; others treat of general feelings and impressions. They display variation in terms of the Indian image conveyed through space, time, and group, but both "bad" and "good" Indian songs were heard by people in different social levels in different regions due to their widespread transmission in popular forms on the stage and in the popular press (Fife and Redden 1954:392–394). There is an enormous body compared to the number for other racial and ethnic outgroups, due to the unique vision of the Indian as a romantic figure. Moreover, the songs are more explicit and descriptive about Indians (as Whites saw them) than are the minstrel songs about Blacks. Since songs have a stronger tendency than other genres toward emotional expression and abstraction and must present "information" in a compact form, the Indians therein are rarely complex human types. They appear as extreme types with little dimension.

Indians are complete savages. "I is for Indian, He is going to slay," says an alphabet song of the early nineteenth century (Randolph 1946–1950, 4:405). The murderous Indians slay a mother and her children in "The Haunted Falls."

> There they danced and sang about her, heeding not
>   the words she cried;
> Cast her on the rocks beneath them, and in agony
>   she died.
> It was revenge they were after and revenge
>   that they had found,
> And they burned those sleeping babies and the
>   dwelling to the ground (O.W. Burt 1958:144–146).

Other songs, obviously from the folk level, inspired by hostile contact, define the Indian by his savage acts toward Whites. Many songs that have their origin in experiences of pioneer members of the Church of Jesus Christ of Latter-Day Saints are on this level (Hallowell 1957:242–243). And yet, like Young Alban who saved Amandy, a White girl, from an "unmerciful throng" of his own people and returned her to her parents, asking food and their friendship, they are admirable, noble beings (Carlisle 1952:115). Few comic Indians are found in song (Fife and Redden 1954:391).

As is the case with other genres, the source of the song

seems to dictate the image conveyed. When comedy is found, the song usually came from popular music, such as the country and western "Kawli-jah" of the 1950s, or the popular stage, as did "On An Indian Reservation."

> Whiteman went to fish one summer, met an
>   Indian maid—a hummer,
> Daughter of Big-Chief-Spare-the-Rod.
> Whiteman threw some loving glances, took this
>   maid to Indian dances,
> Smoked his pipe of peace, took chances living
>   in a tepee of fur.
> Rode with her on Indian ponies, gave her diamond rings,
>   all phonies . . .
> His dream of love soon faded. Napanne looked old
>   and jaded;
> Just about like any other squaw.
> Soon there came papoose in numbers; redskin
>   yells disturbed his slumbers
> Whiteman wonders at his blunders; soon the
>   feathers droop upon his head . . . (Anonymous 1955).

Comedy also comes from political movement songs (Charters 1955:80–81; Haylemon 1938) or from the parody impulse. Some bawdy humor exists, usually drawn from children's or organizational lore. The source of humor in many songs is drawn from pidgin English, which is present even when the content is serious, or from an ironic description of Indian activities or character.

Songs of the Pity and Admiration cycle (Fife and Redden 1954:379–394) had their origins in the East and Midwest and on the popular stage. These, like the fragments of "The Indian Lament" quoted below, mourn the Indian's loss of land and freedom, the doom of the Red man, the beauty and exotic quality of his natural state, and the shame of the White man's depredations on the Indian.

> At first they began to intrude on our soil,
> As their numbers increased they drove
>   weaker to spoil;
> They've driven us away from our own happy shore,
> Where the smoke of our council fires
>   rises no more . . .
> Oh, the time when the Redmen were lords
>   of the soil,
> We lived out our ease free from sorrow and toil . . .
> So farewell to our parents and children so brave,
> We must now go Westward and find there
>   a grave (Gordon 1939).

The Shakers romanticized the Indian, even in contact situations. A large number of Shaker songs, always in dialect and usually written as tableaux in which the Shakers would take the parts of Indians and make "Indian" gestures, praised Shaker love and the Christian message brought to Indians (E.D. Andrews 1962:69–75). Other religious songs also defend Christianity and, again in dialect like "The Indian Convert" (W. Walker 1939:133; Barry 1960, 6:18) sentimentalize the "primitive" Indian.

> In de dark woods, no Indian nigh,
> Den me look heb'n and send up cry
> Upon my knee so low,
> But God send angel, take 'em care . . .
> If Indian heart do pray . . .
> God hear poor Indian in de wood,
> So me lub him and dat be good . . .
> De joy I felt, I cannot tell,
> To tink dat I was saved from hell.
> Through Jesus' streaming blood.
> Dat I am saved by grace divine,
> Who am de worst of mankind,
> O glory be to God (Sullivan 1846).

Another important kind of song, stemming from direct contact, treats of sexual, marital, and love relationships between White men and Indian women or tragic half-bloods ("Cherokee Woman"). No doubt mirroring what were real and common relationships, the songs nevertheless reiterate a romanticized view of the Indian as exotic and reify the Indian Princess complex of ideas. In "Little Mohea" (Barry 1960, 6:15–18), the "fair Indian lass" lives in a coconut grove. She takes in a White stranger, feeding and clothing him and promising him undying love. He returns home to find that "none would equal compare with the lass of Mohea," and he returns to her and her paradise to live forever. More realistic in tone, but little expressed or enacted, is the song about a relationship between a White woman and an Indian man and the severe disapproval of such relationships by Whites (Barry 1960, 4:9–10). A small number of highly romanticized songs, such as "Hiawatha" (Charters 1955:78) and "The Indian Bride's Farewell" (Sullivan 1846) treat of romance between Indians, but they talk less of Indians than of the beautiful natural environment.

The large body of imaginative children's songs includes lullabies and camp songs (Cushing 1936), which sentimentalize and glamorize the Indian by glorifying the natural environment or using the Indian as incidental interest with "Indian" words, rhythms, and artifacts. School songs and cheers stress more aggressive characteristics. Only one really negative expression was found among children's songs, in a jump-rope rhyme:

> Indian, Indian, lived in a tent.
> Indian, Indian, never paid rent.
> She borrowed one, she borrowed two,
> And passed the rope over to Y-O-U (Abrahams 1969:245).

Common use of pidgin English in the children's songs perpetuates the stereotype in children's minds even when the content is not specifically negative. As in the children's songs, the Indian does appear as incidental interest in a large number of other songs, most of them Western (Fife and Redden 1954:390–392).

Proverbs and Epithets

Ethnic slurs, sayings, and traditional phrases appeared from the late eighteenth through the early twentieth century. The Indian and Indian practices had considerable influence on descriptive language in America. Many phrases such as "burying the hatchet" and "Indian file" enriched American English (Hallowell 1957:237). But another set of negative (though occasionally neutral or ambiguous) sayings and names in references to Indians and Indian characteristics exist in response to the White encounter with Indians.

There are relatively few names compared with the number Whites use for Blacks and Jews, and even with the number Blacks use for Whites (Tarpley and Moseley 1971: 25–46). As with Jews, most names refer to attributes of personality, character, and behavior rather than to physical characteristics. The one that refers to a physical aspect—Redskin—is not the most negative though the most commonly used.

Sayings, names, and phrases represent "folk cliches . . . the simplest ones of which convey stereotypes" (Jansen 1957:185–186; many of the following examples appear in R.F. Adams 1968). Some are temporally restricted, like "savage," or regionally restricted, like "siwash." With few exceptions (Redskin; the only good Indian is a dead Indian), most were never in wide circulation. The most widely used were and still are general names for the Indian (Injun; Redskin; Redman) with semicomic names applied to individuals (Tonto; Chief) next, and names that refer to supposed propensities of the Indian (gut-eater; hair-lifter) last in frequency of use. Only one positive term, Mansito, can be found, but this applied only to Christian Indians. Most sayings are negative (wild as an Indian; off the reservation), though some convey ambivalence (sly or cunning as an Indian; vanishing Indian). Phrases, words, and sayings most frequently refer to those events (Indian powwow), situations or conditions (Indian ring), persons (Indian giver, siwash), objects or things (Indian coffee for 'whiskey'; where the Indian shot him for 'navel'), or actions (working harder than an Indian, H. Pearce 1946) regarded negatively by Whites. Use of these in the twentieth century is usually restricted to children's conversation, expressive forms in popular culture, such as cinema and television, and some geographic areas where the Indian still has high visibility.

Visual Representations

From the engravings of Theodor De Bry in the sixteenth century the Indian was a visually significant figure in American expressive culture. Those visual symbols were at the same time abstract and representative, concrete and symbolic, descriptive and suggestive.

Many types of graphic and plastic expressions featured the Indian, and the sources for those representations are as complex as those for oral tradition. In addition to general European conventions, there were the artistic European conventions, which ordinarily stressed the positive, virtu-

Peabody Mus. of Salem, Mass.: M9487.

Fig. 1. Drawing of a ship figurehead *King Philip*. The figurehead demonstrates a combination of Classical form, including the oratorical stance, and elements of Northeast Indian costume with what appear to be a feather roach or hair ornament, leggings, moccasins, and a tomahawk. Pencil and watercolor sketch by John W. Mason, about 1854.

ous side of the Indian, and which were extrapolated from the philosophical and literary conventions already discussed. They manifested themselves in the many artistic forms and art historical modes of American material culture. The first of these, the Classic, is indicated by the rounded, graceful lines of the body, the oratorical stance (fig. 1), and the dress: the toga or kiltlike drapes, the martial trappings of the Roman warrior god or goddess (Diana of the Hunt) and the sandals and diadems of classical antiquity. Thus the Indian is seen as classical virtue translated into the natural statesman-warrior, the antique hero in the New World complete with all the ideological and political significance classical references had for the new democracy (fig. 2). When the artist Benjamin West saw the Apollo Belvedere, he exclaimed, "My God, how like it is to a young Mohawk warrior!" (Coen 1969:40). The Romantic or Primitivist mode combines with the classic to reinforce the Noble Savage complex of ideas. This amalgamation is accomplished by alternating the exotic dress of the primitive (the furs and skins, half-naked bodies, leaves, jewelry, and feathers of the South American, Plains, and Northeast Indians) with dress appropriate to the Victorian ladies of the day in their flounced overskirts and capped sleeves. This mode includes heavy visual emphasis on the natural, "native" setting. In the idea of the picturesque as articulated by the romanticists, the Indian is understood as the beautiful and tragic representative of a primitive, dying world, which

592

GREEN

Joslyn Art Mus., Omaha, Nebr.:1965.424. 1–2.
Fig. 2. Cast candelabras. Figures of Indians are used to represent the Northern (left) and Southern hemispheres. They were made for the 1904 St. Louis Exposition. Originally cast in bronze, the figures were silver-plated by their first owner. Height approximately 60 cm.

must give way to "civilization" and to progress (Pearce 1965; Washburn 1964:pl. 9; Liebers 1965:185). The Indian is to America what ruins were to Europe (Coen 1969: 16–20). Finally, there is some movement toward artistic Realism, though this appears less frequently than any of the other modes. This mode accentuates ethnographically correct dress and paraphernalia and realistic facial features. Realism came into its own, if too dramatically, after photographers, Western travelers, artists, and Wild West shows had provided an abundance of Plains figures on which to model visual representation (Ewers 1965a).

Few of these modes appeared in their pure forms, and Classic dress is as likely to appear on a figure with South American Indian jewelry as a designated Mohawk is to appear with a tepee in the background. In one vernacular painting, used widely as a calendar cover, Pocahontas and her fellow Virginia Indians are dressed as Plains figures. The various modes and attitudes with which they were freighted demanded unrealistic portrayals. The Neoclassic mode demanded light-skinned, Caucasian Greco-Roman faces. A set of implicit, covert sexual standards in

Anglo-American society demanded that Indian women be lighter-skinned and more Caucasian than Indian men, even when they appeared in the same picture. Moreover, the society permitted portrayals to include sexual references (bare or prominent bosoms) for females even when tribal dress and ethnography denied the reality of the reference.

Historical encounter, the third source of concepts, added to and complicated artistic conventions. Historical referents—battles, massacres, meetings, personages (fig. 3)—and semihistorical referents—legends, apocrypha, half-truths—are widespread. Whether abstract or literal, these references are usually to Indian-White relations though they can occasionally appear for the Indian alone. Indians are seen winning or losing battles, fleeing from the White man's advance, saving a White man or massacring his wife and children.

Included in the historical input are certain iconographic and symbolic elements that define the Indian's symbolic roles in America's history. The Indian is often seen as symbol of America, embodying her qualities, standing for her virtues and flaws. The first significant set of figures connected with America was that of the Indian Queen and the Indian Princess (Fleming 1968, 1965). These figures created conventions that were maintained in later symbolic uses and were reinforced by the Four Continents theme in which De Bry–like South American Indians represented America (LeCorbeiller 1961; Fleming 1968). Later the Indian continued to appear not so much *as* but *with* various symbols of America like the flag and the eagle. Yet he also appears as a figure of the past, a symbol for the Old World as well as for the New. He is both ruins and representative of the dying order; the White man's boats sit in his harbor, suggesting what is to come.

Oral traditional sources feed into visual representation just as visual representation feeds into them. Beyond the correspondence of characters and events appearing in both forms, which points up the influence of historical event (real or legendary) on expressive culture, many visual items inspired pieces of oral tradition (R.D. Green 1971). Yet the comic Indian, so much a part of oral tradition, is slighted in the visual mode. While Blacks are almost always treated in a comic vein visually, Indians are rarely dealt with in that manner. When the Indian is comic, however (more in twentieth-century advertising materials and cartoons than in any other medium), the visual expressions take on the components of standard jokes about outsiders. Thus, the Indian appears as a grotesque, undersized, big-nosed, buck-toothed savage; or he appears as a straightforward representation made humorous by the addition of comic elements from oral tradition such as pidgin English and indications of stupidity, humorlessness, and drunkenness.

593

Brown U. Lib., Anne S.K. Brown Military Coll., Providence, R.I.: UB1811sf-1.
Fig. 3. Advertisement for a patent medicine with historical reference to the 1811 battle between Whites and the followers of the Shawnee Prophet. The name Tippecanoe is after the Indiana Terr. battle site. Chromolith, about 1890.

Cigar-Store Indians

The classic cigar-store sculpture appeared from the late sixteenth through the early twentieth centuries; its most popular period of representation was 1850–1880 (Christensen 1952:40, 43). The cigar-store Indians had both commercial and decorative functions. These figures were the best-known visual representation of the Indian, and they were so popular they inspired jokes, elements of popular speech (wooden Indian), plays (Sanborn 1911: 73), cartoons, which inevitably pictured drunken encounters or fights with and amorous advances toward figures (see the *Police Gazette* of 1884 and *Harper's Weekly* of 1908), and popular anecdotes (Sanborn 1911:41). A large industry produced the figures, which stood in front of and on counters in tobacco shops (fig. 4). The earliest traceable figure in America appeared in Pennsylvania in 1770, though a figure of Pocahontas was rumored to have been in Boston in 1730 (Christensen 1952:42). There were many kinds of shop figures, but most were Indians, having their origin in England as early as 1617 (Fried 1970:112). Small figures called Black Boys or Virginie Men were first used to represent the tobacco trade or one of its companies, and they wore the skirt, crown, and medallion associated with the De Bry South American type of

Indians. Later Indians were life-sized or larger and exhibited other forms of dress, but the Black Boy persisted as an Indian on tobacco graphics throughout the nineteenth century. The fact that many later figures were done by professional artists and shipcarvers could account for the stylized fanciful aspects as well as for the classical influences, but not for popular acceptance of the figures as Indian or for the maintenance of such conventions by nonprofessional artists. Carvers rarely used models for figures, and realism was not especially valued by them (Christensen 1952:48; Pendergast and Ware 1953:22; Fried 1970:81).

Carvers gave the different types names based on their stance, dress, and sex. Most were called Chief, Pocahontas, or Squaw. Chiefs were divided into Warriors, Hunters, Scouts, Trappers, Bucks, Braves, and Captain Jacks (named either after an Indian hater of oral tradition who dressed as an Indian to pursue the murderers of his family or for a Modoc leader, Kientapoos, who was called Captain Jack after a White miner of that name whom he was thought to resemble—Fried 1970:50, 148). Though some differences in dress, stance, and paraphernalia existed, the types were often indistinguishable from one another and their characteristics were mixed. With few exceptions, all were large, aggressive, armed Indians.

594

Many exhibited classical features, stance, and clothing or South American/Northeast mixed dress. Some few were realistic, and some few were grotesque and comic. A number were given specific names of real or fictional figures like Keokuk, Sitting Bull, Black Hawk, or Hiawatha. Some had abstracted names like "Lo" for "Lo, the Poor Indian," a sentimentalized nineteenth-century embodiment of the vanishing Indian, while others had comic names like Big-Chief-Me Smoke-Em. Most, however, were unnamed, ideal types. Females were called Pocahontas, Squaw, or Maiden. Pocahontases and Maidens, embodying the Indian Princess theme, were usually smaller than Squaws, and had more Caucasian or infantile features and wore classical or romantic dress. Squaws were more likely to have exposed or prominent bosoms and have a papoose on their backs. Some were armed, but unless they embodied the classical Diana-of-the-Hunt idea, most were less aggressive than the males and held out a bundle of cigars or tobacco leaves as well as an outstretched, welcoming hand.

Other Carved and Cast Figures

Indian motifs in nautical carving were common 1773 to 1875. They were three-dimensional or bas-relief wood figures of males and females. They stood both as single figures and as figures in scenes and had both decorative and symbolic functions. Often they were given the name of a well-known fictional or real Indian like King Philip (fig. 1) or Minnehaha. They appear to represent the symbolic virtues of a ship, its sailors, America ("Rattlesnake"), or simply Indians in general (Brewington 1962:46, 50–53, fig. 14). The figure of the Indian Princess was much admired, and it often replaced the conventional female figurehead (Lipman 1948:28). Indian chiefs and warriors were also popular, most often taking the stance and features of a Classical orator (fig. 1). The paraphernalia he carried or the name of the ship marked the figure as Indian. Stern carvings had bas-relief figures that varied from South American, abstract designs like Shanunga to symbolic, fanciful designs like *The American Indian* (fig. 5).

Weathervanes were manufactured and used widely throughout the late eighteenth and early nineteenth centuries. They were made of wood and cast or cut metal and were ordinarily low-relief silhouettes. Some few were two-dimensional. They were both homemade and commercially manufactured, and all had primarily pragmatic and secondarily decorative and symbolic functions. They were common in New England and the mid-Atlantic states and are thought to have been used by farmers as signs that the land was gained legitimately from Indians and that the owner was friendly (K. Fitzgerald 1967:76). The same figures on locomotives, 1875–1900, were also thought to tell Indians of White friendship when trains traveled in hostile territory (Lipman 1948:53). The majority were depicted as armed with a bow and arrow, tomahawk, knife, or gun, and stood in a ready-to-fire position, pointing the direction of the wind. All were male. They often appeared in nature scenes with animals or greenery. Their features are rarely distinguishable, but were often grotesque when detailed with the exaggerated large nose. They usually wear an upright feather headdress and the feather cloth or skirt of the Black Boy. A few represent specific Indians like Tammany, a figure used as a political party symbol (Lipman 1948:30), or Massasoit, once used as a symbol for the Commonwealth of Massachusetts (K. Fitzgerald 1967:71). Other well-known vanes include: the "Shem Drowne" vane (fig. 6), which stood on Province House in Boston, inspired the Nathaniel Hawthorne tale "Drowne's Wooden Vane," and provoked a local children's belief that the Indian would fire his arrow at noon (Lipman (1948:50); and the symbol for the Improved Order of Red Men.

A number of figures were produced in connection with popular entertainments like circuses and were purely decorative and noncommercial in function. Circus wagons featured semihistorical scenes out of national legendry and other abstract scenes like "The Coming of the White Man" (Fried 1970:fig. 84). Others, much like cigar-store figures, appeared as carrousel (Fried 1964: fig. 166) and pilot-house figures. A number of cast metal andirons and cast metal stove plates showing South American Indians were common in the mid-Atlantic states in the late eighteenth and early nineteenth centuries (Lipman 1948: 143; Dependahl 1971). Some few folk figures, like a crudely carved Pennsylvania farm gatepost were used like weathervanes. There were few toys. Only two have been found in tradition: a jointed, cut metal doll (Lipman 1948: 109) and a crude whirligig in the Shelburne Museum, Shelburne, Vermont. Later, the twentieth-century tourist trade demanded souvenir dolls, and these, almost all Plains types, are found widely throughout the Southwest and West in tourist shops (St. George 1953:12–13).

Medals, Coins, and Stamps

Numismatic items were issued from the late eighteenth through the twentieth century. They had a pragmatic purpose as a medium of exchange along with important secondary functions of decoration and commemoration. The specially issued medals had a limited circulation while the coins were more widespread. Presidential Peace Medals or Red Jacket medals (Washburn 1964:pl. 23, 342; Belden 1927; Prucha 1971a) were issued by early presidents to heads of visiting tribal delegations and were meant to be symbolic of treaty agreements and friendliness between a tribe and the White government. Later (Prucha 1971a:xiv), they came to be given simply as a reward for cooperation, and many unofficial medals were struck and top left, top center, top right, Natl. Gallery of Art, Index of Amer. Design, Washington: Mich-Ca-59, Mich-Ca-30, and Mass-Ca-101; bottom, Lib. of Congress, Prints and Photographs Div.: LC-USZ162-38019.

Fig. 4. Cigar-store Indian figures. top left, Figure with mixed South American and Northeast North American Indian elements in its costume. The original polychrome painted wooden figure was displayed in the streets of Cleveland, Ohio. The figure dates from about 1865; height approximately 1.93 m. Watercolor, gouache, colored pencil, and graphite on paperboard by Eugene Croe, 1935–1942. top center, Female figure, carved of wood, 1812–1860; height approximately 1.54 m. Gouache and graphite on paperboard by Walter Hochstrasser, 1935–1942. top right, Wood figure displaying grotesque, comic features and dating from the 19th century; height approximately 1.5 m. Watercolor, colored pencil, and graphite on paper by Victor Muollo, 1935–1942. bottom, "Indians Trading at a Frontier Town," depicting Ute Indians engrossed in a cigar-store figure. The carved figure is described in an accompanying paragraph as the "ideal Indian . . . very unlike the real creature." The women, referred to as "squaws," are said to do all the work because the "warriors . . . consider every kind of labor degrading to a man" (*Harper's Weekly* 19(966):537, July 3, 1875). Engraving by Tavernier-Frenzy.

given away by traders. The medals were so significant and widespread that artists added them to representations of Indians as a matter of course, confusing them with the trade medals worn by Black Boys and the jewelry worn by South American Indians. Common representation on the medallions were crossed peace pipes, busts of the issuing president, two hands shaking, or an Indian sharing a pipe with a White man, both men usually military, leaderlike figures. Some few had allegorical scenes, such as the Andrew Johnson medals showing one Indian scalping another, with a central scene of an Indian in full headdress plowing a field. These were to illustrate the superiority of the White way over the savage mode (Prucha 1971a:120). Other commemorative medals were struck for various purposes, such as the one for the Society for the Veterans of Indian Wars showing an Indian defeat and another for the Missouri Centennial showing an Indian pointing to a White man coming in the distance (Liebers 1965:184).

Coins in circulation varied from the Indian-head penny, 1859–1909, to the famous buffalo nickel with the pictures of two endangered species—the Plains Indian on one side and the buffalo on the other ("White Conceptions of Indians," fig. 10, this vol.). On the penny, the Indian was the symbol of America, and the features were of the Miss Liberty face later to appear on the twentieth-century dime. Other coins were the Half and Quarter Eagles, 1908–1929, with a Plains Indian head on one side and the eagle on the other. The same coins were issued from 1796 to 1908 with a Liberty head. Another was the Eagle, 1908–1933, showing a Plains type with Caucasian features (Liebers 1965:140, 169, 174).

A few commemorative postal stamps have been issued. They were standard artistic renderings of individuals, such as Crazy Horse and Jim Thorpe. More common were objects, such as Navajo rugs.

Etchings

Carvings were done throughout the late eighteenth and nineteenth centuries by amateurs who recorded their own or historical experiences on objects of everyday use and on decorative objects. There were representative, often symbolic scenes of experience and conflict with Indians. On gunstocks and powderhorns (Washburn 1964:pl. 8; Grancsay 1965), the conflict of westward movement was a common scene. Ivory scrimshaw carvings tended more toward abstract, less personalized scenes, much like the stern carvings and figureheads. These were also more classical than those in the West.

Ceramics, Glassware, and Textiles

Items of decorative art were not characteristically produced in a particular period, though most available examples fall into the nineteenth century. The predominant influence, considering the decorative functions and the elite origin, was from classical, neoclassical, and romantic art. All the objects have commemorative and pragmatic functions as well. On such objects is visible the reinforcement of the image of the Indian as an exotic creature. He is seen here, as elsewhere, as colorful, interesting, attractive, and evocative. Many items, like Delft china jars, were made in Holland and England for the tobacco trade but distributed widely throughout the United States. These showed South American Indians. Others, not involved with trade, commemorated American historical scenes, events, and movements (fig. 7). The use of the Indian as a symbol of America or of the New World was common. Indians were used infrequently, however, on the important pieces of Liverpool china, whose transfer designs dealt with American scenes (McCauley 1942; Dependahl 1971).

Textiles portraying Indians were produced in the eighteenth and nineteenth centuries. These objects were primarily decorative though also pragmatic and commemorative in function. Some single-figure representations exist, but scenes were more prevalent. Bedspreads, curtains, handkerchiefs, pieces of upholstery fabric (Washburn 1964:pl. 21), and needlepoint detail battle scenes and symbolic and iconographic scenes like the Four Continents. William Penn's Treaty With the Indians, copied from either Benjamin West or Edward Hicks, is the most common scene on textiles (Brinton 1941). Some few folk pieces exist, but these are not widespread.

Painting

Beyond the paintings of Indians rendered by professional artists and meant for a smaller, usually elite, audience, a large number of important vernacular (naive, folk, nonacademic, primitive) paintings have included the Indian as a subject fit for portrayal. Some of the best-known and most

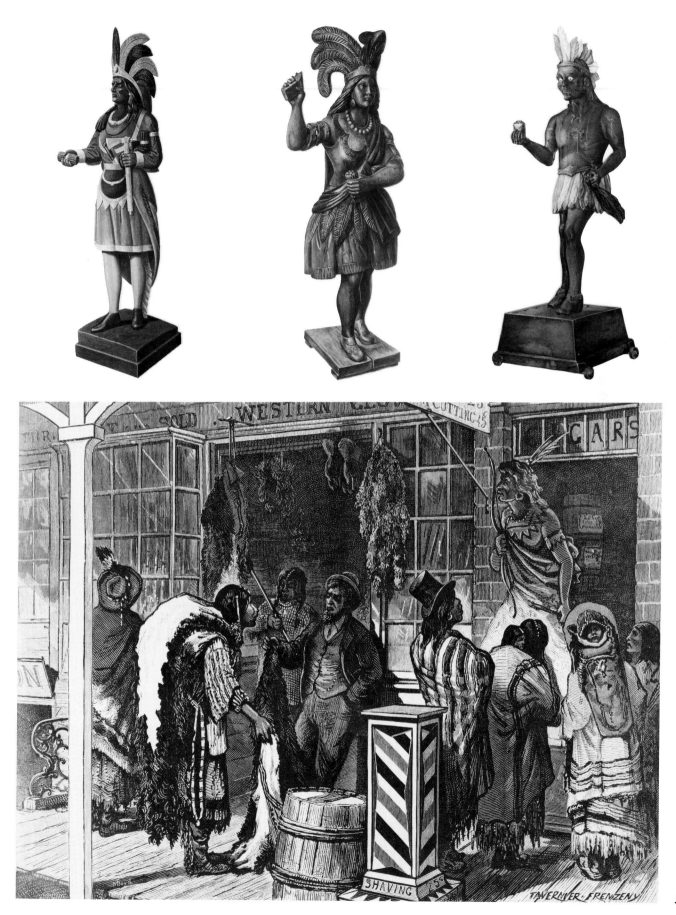

597

THE INDIAN IN POPULAR AMERICAN CULTURE

Fig. 5. Nautical carving. Stern carving from the Plymouth, Mass., ship *The American Indian*, with the Indian figure in fanciful dress, in a Classical reclining pose. The positioning of the figure among animals reinforces the notion of the Indian as a creature of nature. However, the use of an African lion intensifies the fancifulness of the scene. Polychrome painted wood, 1785; length approximately 3 m.

influential visualizations of the Indian are found in such paintings, done by untrained artists who were often deficient in the skills of perspective. These paintings circulated in small regional areas among friends and neighbors, were carried through larger areas and sold by the artists themselves, or were consigned, like many of the large murals in the mid-nineteenth century, to traveling shows and circuses. The many versions of Pocahontas Saving Capt. John Smith, William Penn's Treaty With the Indians ("White Conceptions of Indians," fig. 3, this vol.), and Custer's Last Stand include versions by these untrained, often unknown artists, which made their way onto calendars and cheap prints for decoration. Because they were also reproduced on artifacts, these painted versions of the primal scenes of American history, mythic and real, were spread widely to a popular audience. Such visualizations, like the Anheuser-Busch rendering of Custer's Last Stand, which hung over nearly every bar in the country during the period 1875–1920 (D. Russell 1968), were largely responsible for the public's great familiarity with and attachments to those scenes and to the images of the Indian conveyed in them.

Other paintings repeat the themes peculiar both to oral tradition and to other forms of visualization. The sentimentalized Christian Indian appears in paintings like *Indian Lament*, which shows a Red child of nature mourning beside a white cross (his White friend? a converted Indian friend? his culture?). The friendly relationships between Whites and Indians, modeled on the Pocahontas/William Penn/Medicine theme are repeated in these kinds of paintings, and numbers of Indians and White men shake hands over treaties and understandings that will eventually be broken. However, the theme is what is important. Related to this theme are the numbers of paintings of individual Indians—chiefs and leaders—that focus on them as representatives of Indian virtues, particularly those that involve native skills and the

attachment to the land (examples are in Garbisch 1966).

Of course, the savagery of the Indian is also widely memorialized in the many renderings of Custer's Last Stand (D. Russell 1968), and Indian attacks on forts, settlements, settlers, and wagon trains.

The several versions of the infamous murder of Jane MaCrae show two dark, half-naked, and sinister savages as they are about to murder the very fair-skinned Jane, her bosom bared to their knives. In these paintings as in the ballads are revealed the scenes that epitomize the popular history of Indian-White relations, the popular sense of the Indian and his multitextured character.

Tobacco and Other Advertisements

Tobacco advertisements were a by-product of the industry, which began in the late sixteenth century, and were important commercial products in their own right. The Indian image was widely used by the industry due to the association of the Indian with the "gift" of tobacco (fig. 8). These graphics exhibit the widest range of representation in all the visual media because of the long persistence of the industry. Early connections to Europe through trade assured the domination of European artistic conventions. Black Boys, South American, Northeast, Plains, romantic, realistic, and neoclassical types appear. Many appear in a natural setting with the usual confusions of artifacts, dress, and facial features; others are pictured with the paraphernalia of the tobacco industry. Still others appear with symbols of America or with a classical muse type who seems to be representative of "civilization." Associated with tobacco, the muse seems to indicate a symbolic alliance in the tobacco trade of native knowledge and White civilization. The muse may also be seen to suggest doubt about the native origins of the knowledge.

Famous Indians (Uncas, Red Cloud, Black Hawk, Pocahontas, Wenonah) appear as brand-name designa-

598

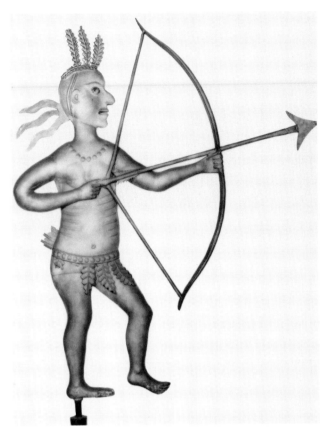

Mass. Histl. Soc., Boston.
Fig. 6. Hammered copper-molded weathervane with eyepieces of glass. Made by Shem Drowne, Boston, about 1716. Height approximately 132 cm.

tions and representations. Almost always, they are strong, aggressive, leader types as are the tribal names used for brands. General names for Indians, usually for social roles as Whites perceived them, are widely used (Great Chief, Indian Princess, Grand Sachem). Often, the title is general, indicating aggressiveness (Warpath, Heroine, Frontier, Huntress). The accompanying scenes are of hunting and making war. The implied associations are of strength, power, and aggressiveness, which are carried over into the twentieth century in the advertising industry's insistence on the connections between manliness, individualism, and tobacco products. Nearly all figures, even females, are armed. Many are Classic, martial types, though there is some minor Romantic strain in the tobacco graphics.

As commercial graphics developed in the nineteenth and twentieth centuries, industry used the Indian as a brand-name designation, visual motif, and advertising symbol and as an illustration for books (almanac, recipe, and dream books) and objects (little wool and silk pieces with Indian designs) given out with the products. Graphics and objects became collectors' items during and after their prime period of circulation (Burdick 1953:42–45).

Some brands (Duryea's Refined Maizena Indian Corn,

Joslyn Art Mus., Omaha, Nebr.:1959.429.A-B.
Fig. 7. Covered compote in a pattern originally named "Pioneer" and later "Westward Ho." The Indian figure is dressed in feathers and skins and portrayed in a woodland setting, emphasizing the Indians' connection with the natural world. The dish was probably made by the Phila. company, James Gillinder and Sons, 1876–1877. Clear, pressed glass, height about 30cm.

Hudson's Bay Company) stressed the historical or regional connections with the Indian, but others (Piel's Beer, Wilson's Corned Beef) used the Indian as a comic logotype while having no connection to the Indian. Some food, medicine, and cosmetic promotions (Pocahontas and Indian Princess Perfumes, Land O'Lakes Butter) traded on folk wisdom about Indian beauty and featured Noble Savage, Classic types with Caucasian features as logotypes. Others (Missouri Pacific Railway, Sky Chief Line) traded on the Indian reputation for speed, strength, and agility and used Plains types. Still others, with an eye

599

Fig. 8. Tobacco advertisements. left, The Frontier. Lithograph by Major and Knapp, New York, 1865. right, Indian Girl Chewing Tobacco. The paddle steamer on the river symbolizes the encroachment of civilization. Lithograph by C. Hamilton and Company, St. Louis, Mo., 1874.

for tourist appeal (Heskill's Hotel, "At the Sign of the Indian Queen"; Squaw Mountain Inn; Niagara Falls's Maid of the Mist) used exotic Classic or South American types while stressing place legends, real and invented, to attract trade. Other products and companies used names of Indian social roles (Chief, Princess, Queen, Squaw), the general names for the group (Savage, Indian) (fig. 9), some few tribal names (Shawmut, Mohawk), Indian words common to or indicative of the region (Oswego, Patchogue, Kinniquinique), or personal names of famous Indians (Chief Joseph, Black Hawk, Wessacumcan, Massasoit) or literary Indians (Ramona, Hiawatha). Many companies, especially in the mid-Atlantic states, used Penn's Treaty With the Indians on advertising literature. Others used grotesque, comic Indians and pidgin English poems and sayings to attract customers. Some few used negative characteristics to sell the product but most did not. Over 100 companies and brands used an Indian designation during the nineteenth century (Landauer 1940).

Picture Cards

Picture card graphics were circulated widely from about 1850 through the first half of the twentieth century. A commercial industry produced items with commercial, decorative, and commemorative functions. Advertising and trading cards were used by salesmen as calling cards, advertising supplements, and promotional gifts, but they were also popular as collectors' items. They followed the visual patterns of other commercial products. Souvenir, greeting, playing, and picture post cards were popular and widely circulated between 1880 and 1892 and were well illustrated with Indians and scenes of Indian life (Burdick 1953). Since they were popular along with foreign scenes, flags, actors, animals, pirates, and historical scenes, Indians obviously conformed to the image of an exotic.

Portraits of chiefs and medicine men were the most popular, followed by scenes of daily life, hunting buffalo, and dancing. Almost all figures were Plains males. Stereoscopic cards were available before 1844 but became popular after 1876 when Mathew Brady's improved photography methods made more realistic scenes possible. Travel scenes of the Old West were the most requested (Burdick 1953). Some show Indians on the warpath, while others picture local tourist legends or the familiar chiefs and scenes of daily life.

Dramatic Expressions

Dramatic expression works on a number of levels—oral, visual, and behavioral. The impact manifests itself primarily in dramatic behavior, although ideas, attitudes, and feelings are as much a part of the expressions as the actions. In these expressions, ideas about the Indian are conveyed by Whites who insist on certain aspects of Indian personality, culture, and behavior and on certain aspects of Indian-White relationships. For the most part, Whites and Blacks "play Indian," taking over "Indian roles." They begin by claiming that the person speaking is part-Indian through the bloodline of a putatively Indian grandmother (usually Cherokee). White and Blacks then "become" Indian, thus being granted authority to express how Indians behave.

The Indian makes his impact in drama in both negative and positive ways, though as in other forms of expression, even the negative aspects of Indian behavior as perceived by Whites are ultimately viewed as necessary and positive.

Entertainments and Pastimes

● WILD WEST SHOWS AND CIRCUSES Buffalo Bill's Wild West Show and Congress of Rough Riders, 1884–1938, was the first show and the prototype for at

600

Fig. 9. Indian model for Savage Arms rifles. The model was the central feature for an advertisement that appeared in a popular magazine in the early 1970s. The company's trademark, located on the rifle stock, is a profile of an Indian male with high cheek bones, slightly hooked nose, and feathered Plains-style warbonnet. Photographed about 1970.

least 10 major shows that were on the road in the late nineteenth and early twentieth centuries (Schwartz 1970: 657). Cowboys, soldiers, Indians, and the conflicts between them, as well as the showier aspects of their separate lives and daily activities were the inevitable focus of these spectacles. Later shows presented the Indian with exotic warriors from foreign countries, animals, circus clowns, and freaks. The Indian's prominence in such shows as well as in the Western myths is clear. The Indian was indispensable as a foil for Buffalo Bill (William F. Cody) and for other Western heroes in the nineteenth century (Sell and Weybright 1955:45). The shows reconfirmed James Fenimore Cooper's Natty Bumppo conventions for Western Whites who became half-Indian in dress and manner. The Wild West show, circus Indians, and dime novels set the conventions for cowboy and Indian portrayal in twentieth-century cinema. Conflicts, though faked, had psychological reality for Whites and often for Indians who, like Sitting Bull, performed in the show. Arthur Kopit's play *Indians* (1969) provides a striking analysis of this aspect.

Not to be overlooked are the graphics associated with

these entertainments (fig. 10). Thousands of posters, couriers, advance heralds, and programs revealed the activities that took place in the shows and the image of the Indian they conveyed. Indians were presented as aggressors—attacking the Deadwood Stage, forts, settlements, troops, and wagon trains—while Buffalo Bill's men, dressed as cavalry or cowboys, rescued those attacked and won the battle. Custer's Last Stand was enacted after Sitting Bull joined the show, and Indians were presented as victorious villains. They also performed dances and riding tricks, thus combining the savage with the Noble Savage, exotic mode. Later shows, particularly circuses, presented Indians as comic/exotic figures, but this portrayal was short-lived and not so common as the warrior-villain presentation. Posters displayed, in the order of their frequency: Indians mounted; hunting buffalo; attacking stages, forts, and wagon trains; and dancing and playing games.

● MEDICINE SHOWS The medicine show began in the late eighteenth century and reached its prime with traveling shows numbering in the hundreds between 1865 and 1900 (A.M. Gibson 1967:35). Over 80 Indian brands were on the market, 1840–1920, and the White "Indian" or herb doctor was a familiar figure to most Americans in that period (Landauer 1940) (fig. 11). An Indian or someone dressed as an Indian played the drum, danced, appeared in colorful costume, and performed feats to illustrate his health and strength. At first based on Indian performance alone, the shows later added other popular entertainments.

The industry was based on folk wisdom about natural Indian medical knowledge (Hallowell 1957:241; V.J. Vogel 1970:138). The Indian was represented as a healer, knowledgeable in nature's ways, superior in health and physical endurance to Whites. This representation exists in conflict with the picture of the Indians as a diseased and dying race. The Indian was used as a visual motif, brand-name designation, advertising logotype, and illustration for objects and literature given out with the product. The commercial function here as well as the kind of product sold dictated the use of a positive image. Pictures are primarily of peaceful, Northeast or Southeast Indians. The Indian is pictured as giving help and medicine to the ailing White man, but rarely to other Indians. Many females, often bare breasted, help the males in giving medicine to or making medicine for ailing Whites. In some pictures a classical muse gives the knowledge of medicine to the Indian; and in others the Indian gives the medicine to a classical, Aesculapian figure. Several brands named after Indians have pictures of medicine men, who represent Indian strength, health, and natural knowledge. On other labels famous leaders are featured (Joseph Brant, Osceola, Red Jacket, Pocahontas), ones admired for their friendship to Whites or for their leadership qualities even though they were often in conflict with Whites. The

left, Amon Carter Mus., Ft. Worth, Tex.:56.70; right, Lib. of Congress, Prints and Photographs Div.: LC-S6-338.
Fig. 10. Wild West shows. left, Tiger Bills Wild West. Lithograph stockposter by Riverside Printing Company, Milwaukee, Wis., 1909–1934. right, Cowboys, Indians, and other performers in Pawnee Bill's Wild West Show with tepee, post office, and painted backdrop. Photograph by Erwin E. Smith, 1908–1910.

names of tribes are generally of "peaceful," nonaggressive ones like the Cherokee or Kickapoo, except when the medicine was supposed to be "strong"; in that case, names that implied aggression (Modoc, Nez Perce) were used. Women in the medicine scenes are generally more Caucasian and classical in appearance than the men, but since the advertisements stress "natural" qualities of the Indian, both are more realistic in features and dress than those in other visual modes.

● GAMES AND GESTURES Most formal games are products of the twentieth century, though the gestures that form an essential part of the games predate the games themselves. Included are informal games with understood but loosely structured sets of rules, more formal games with rigid rules, and standard gestural systems, all of which require the player to assume the role of and a set of attitudes toward the Indian. The common children's game, Cowboys and Indians, requires the Indian to speak pidgin English (How! Ugh! Me no go); to whoop like an Indian by placing the hand over the mouth and emitting a series of staccato yells (Woo-woo-woo!); to assume a set of gestures, "Indian" signs and elements of pseudo–sign language (arm upraised at elbow in greeting, two fingers behind head to indicate feathers); and to dress in rudimentary elements of "Indian" costume and armament, many improvised and some manufactured for the popular game and role.

The "Indian" can assume an antisocial, aggressor role and even "play dirty" in contrast to the "cowboy" who enacts the standard "good guy" role. There are no known games in which the player takes the role of "Jew" or "Negro," and the Indian role, though explicitly negative, is implicitly a desirable one.

The gestures of the "Indian," adapted from the conventions of real sign language and the stereotyped Wild West show Indian as maintained in Western movies, were carried over into American sign language for the deaf (2-fingered gesture representing war paint on the cheeks to mean 'Indian'), the popular barroom game of "Indian," in which players are required to assume an "Indian sign," and to make it in order while beating an Indian rhythm with the foot. One who misses his sign in turn must swallow his drink at one gulp. Note also the use of verses or utterances that accompany games, such as the jump-rope rhyme already discussed and "Indian file" and "Indian wrestling," which convey no particular message with regard to image though the influence of the Indian is observable.

● SPORTS In sports is found one of the most significant areas of impact of the Indian on American vernacular culture. The use goes beyond adoption of Indian games like lacrosse into the White sports repertoire and the possible influences of Indian athletes on the nature of a game (Jim Thorpe on football). The use here varies from such nonloaded influences to the very loaded use of Indian names and visual images for sports teams, and to the ideas

Lib. of Congress, Prints and Photographs Div.: top left, LC-USZ62-55635; top right, LC-USZ62-55633; bottom left, LC-USZ62-4636; top right, LC-USF34-80943.
Fig. 11. Details from patent medicine labels and a traveling medicine show. top left, Red Jacket Stomach Bitters. Buyers were told that the recipe came from "the great Indian chief Red Jacket" to a Dr. Chapin who perfected it. The roach, ear ornaments, blanket robe, and stylized cloth leggings of the figure would be appropriate for the historical Red Jacket, a Seneca leader. Lithograph by Edward Mendel, Chicago, 1864. top right, Cherokee Liniment. Engraving by C.J. Hollis, Philadelphia, 1856. bottom left, Old Sachem Bitters, Wigwam Tonic. The figure wears moccasins, stylized cloth leggings with exaggerated fringe, a bear claw necklace, and sashes similar to styles worn by Northeast tribes. His headdress is a South American Indian style. However, his skirt, shirt, cape, and coin necklace, in combination with his stance, are reminiscent of a Classical warrior. The Indian is depicted as noble and contemplative while a battle scene occurs behind him. Lithograph by Sarony, Major, and Knapp, New York, 1859. bottom right, Medicine show booth at a fair sponsored by a local Indian association. The men are unidentified. The title "paw maw" on the sign miscopies a spelling of *powwow* in its historical sense of 'shaman' or 'medicine man'. Photograph by John Collier, Jr., Windsor Lock, Conn., Oct. 1941.

THE INDIAN IN POPULAR AMERICAN CULTURE

about the Indian inherent in the use of such names. While the use of such names does not generally appear to carry the weight of the beliefs and practices associated with totemism among primitive peoples, such a use does appear to be the same sort of pseudototemic complex found in the uses of insignia and name-group designations in the American armed forces (Linton 1920:296–300). The power of the names and their representative embodiments to attract semireverential attitudes, belief in the power of the name when invoked (chanted) to bring good luck and guardianship, the exclusive use of such names by groups and the identification of the members of that group with their totemic embodiment ("He's a Redskin"), and the use of the totemic figure as a decoration or means of personal

adornment all match the characteristics of pseudototemic complexes.

The most visible area of impact lies in the choice of an Indian tribal name for a team or school mascot. Again, the choice is often made on a regional basis ("Seminoles" for a Florida team, "Chippewas" for a Michigan team), but as with other usages, tribal names may be chosen without regard for a connection to a region ("Seminoles" for an Arkansas team). The general term for Indians ("Indians," "Redskins") is used more often than tribal names, however, and names indicative of Indian social status ("Chiefs," "Braves," "Warriors") are also widespread. Whatever the type of name used, the choice seems to indicate a connection of the Indian, and thus the team,

THE DEATH OF OLD TAMMANY AND HIS WIFE LOCO FOCO.

Fig. 12. The Indian figure Tammany, an example of the use of an Indian persona to represent a group whose agenda is not at all related to Indian life and that acts outside of conventional boundaries. The late 17th-century Delaware chief Tamanend became the subject of legendary tales about his benevolence that were circulated by Whites, who began various societies under the patronage of Tammany. The societies conducted "Indian" activities, such as dances and calumet smoking, and had an "Indian" official structure. Similar societies were established as early as the French and Indian War. The groups were primarily political in nature but also had social and charitable functions (Mooney 1910b). Lithograph copyrighted by H.R. Robinson, N.Y., 1837.

with aggressive behavior (Scalpers), stoic bearing, militance, and, ironically, an ability to win. Warlike male roles are stressed and implied in the choice of such names. In 1971, seven professional teams and more than 30 colleges had Indian names, symbols, or mascots. In 1987 there were only two college teams with such mascots.

The choice of an Indian mascot, logotype, or symbol, even if the team name is not loaded, introduces new elements into the image. Mascots are often brought in for the entertainment of the crowd, and many are comic. Ordinarily, an Indian or a White costumed as an Indian performs, and he is always dressed as a Plains tribesman in full war regalia no matter what the team association. He does "war dances" when the team has scored or needs to score, or performs in a dance with the band at half time. Another form of live mascot is an animal (a buffalo or pinto horse) that stands for Indian characteristics. As common is the use of a graphic Indian as a logotype connected with the team's publicity. This logo can be a stern, stoic, buffalo-nickel type but most often is a comic caricature. These join with pidgin English advertisements or cheers ("Hail to the Redskins/Hail Victory/Braves on the Warpath/Fight for old D.C./Scalp 'em, Swamp 'em, We will take 'em big score/ Read 'em, Weep 'em, Touchdown we want heap more"—Coffey 1972). After complaints were made, the scalping reference was removed from the song.

Since 1968 various Indian groups have agitated to change the use of Indian names, logotypes, and mascots in sports teams. A number have changed their comic logotype for a more serious, dignified one or have dropped the association altogether (Stanford University, Dartmouth College). Indian groups brought suit during 1971-1972 against the Cleveland Indians regarding Chief Wahoo, a comic logotype (Anonymous 1972a); the Atlanta Braves for Chief-Noc-a-Homa, a dancing mascot; and the Washington Redskins for their very name (Coffey 1972).

Social Organizations and Events

The image of the Indian inspired and instructed ritual, behavior, and ideologies controlling a number of organizations, one of which has had great influence in American vernacular culture. Two organizations, the Boy Scouts of America and the Improved Order of Red Men, stressed positive, if stereotypic virtues and skills of the Indian. The Boy Scouts, with their emphasis on manliness, the outdoors, and survival skills, insisted on Indian craft and technology for Scouts. The Scouts's Order of the Arrow carried the Indian emphasis into the expressive arts, and taught Indian dancing and costume—always Plains—carried to elegant, decorative extremes (Boy Scouts of America 1967). The Improved Order of Red Men, much like other fraternal organizations, stressed Christian and

La. State Mus., New Orleans: LSM 1971.37.
Fig. 13. Member of a New Orleans Mardi Gras Indian group called Wild Magnolia Tribe. Theodore Emile Dollis, a "chief," wears a costume composed of red and white ostrich-feather plumes and beaded panels with stylized figures of Indians on them. The lower panel shows a man wearing a feather bustle and breechcloth.Photographed July 1971, at the La. State Mus.

patriotic virtues framed in "Indian" language in terms of "Indian" virtues. The Order gave officers names of Indian leadership roles; members wore "Indian" costume and used pidgin English and sign language in rites. In the 1980s the Young Men's Christian Association developed the Indian Guides program in which fathers (braves) share activities with their daughters (princesses) that are similar to the Boy Scouts'.

The Society for Veterans of Indian Wars was constructed on a negative understanding of the Indian. Meetings were celebrations of victories or commiserations with the defeats endured, accompanied by accounts of Indian savagery, trickery, and cowardliness, as well as White bravery and heroism while serving in the Indian wars. The Indian was a rallying symbol for veterans, much like the "carpetbagger" or "Yankee" for Southern veterans after the Civil War. A minor association of the Indian chief Tamanend with the Tammany Society (or Columbian Order) of New York City was well known (fig. 12). Formed about 1786 for social, ceremonial, and patriotic reasons, the society soon became a dominant political force, ruling New York City politics in the nineteenth century. Its symbol was an Indian, but the association with the image was slight.

Another organization is the Mardi Gras Indian Association of New Orleans. Made up almost entirely of Blacks, the "Indians" dress up and act according to a stereotypic folk ideal of real American Indians, as an attraction at New Orleans' annual Mardi Gras parade (fig. 13). Started in the late nineteenth century under circumstances now unknown, the tradition does not seem to be based on any real ties with American Indian people or culture, but on an Afro-Caribbean performance tradition and on an image projected to this Black community by way of comic books, posters, photographs, even children's coloring books. Each year the "Indians" put together elaborate costumes made of ostrich feathers, fringe-like ribbons, and large beaded and sequined patches depicting supposed scenes of Indian life. They may paint their faces with streaks of color, and the "chiefs" carry tall staves with shields decorated with the individual insignia derived from their "tribal" names: Black Eagles, Wild Magnolias, Yellow Pocahontas, Cherokee Hunters, and others. As each "tribe" marches an unannounced route through the city, the members sing songs and dance as wildly as their costumes permit. Accompaniment for the singing is percussive only; rhythms reminiscent of West African or Caribbean syncopated music are beat out on tambourines. The songs are in a call and response form, often improvised, and often in non-English vocables (Wilhelmsen 1971, 1972, 1972a, 1972b; Lomax 1950:14).

Many texts, objects, and photographs of objects discussed in this chapter are in the author's possession. For locations of specific pieces, see R.D. Green (1973).

Sources

The Fife Mormon Collection at Utah State University, Logan, contains many examples of song, legend, and anecdote. The Archive of Folk Song in the Music Division of the Library of Congress is a rich source for song. Examples of forms of oral expression are available in the Folklore Archives and the Archives of Traditional Music of Indiana University, Bloomington; the Randall V. Mills Archive of Northwest Folklore at the University of Oregon, Eugene; and the Folklore Collections in the Department of Folklore and Folklife at the University of Pennsylvania. See J.C. Hickerson (1972) for a listing of other folklore archives.

Among depositories for visual materials, the Maryland Historical Society, Baltimore, has a good collection of cigar-store sculptures. Ship carvings and scrimshaw objects are in the Mystic Seaport Marine Historical Association, Mystic, Connecticut. Cigar-store figures, nautical carvings, weathervanes, locomotive ornaments, and miscellaneous items are in the collections of: the New York State Historical Association, Cooperstown; the Museum of Early American Folk Arts, New York; the Abby Aldrich Rockefeller Folk Art Collection, Williamsburg, Virginia (Little 1957); the National Museum of American History, Washington, D.C.; and the Shelburne Museum, Shelburne, Vermont, which also exhibits ceramics, glassware, and textiles. All kinds of decorative art and craft are found in the H.F. du Pont Winterthur Museum, Winterthur, Delaware, and in the Joslyn Art Museum, Omaha, which also contains paintings of Indians. Watercolor renderings of all the types of vernacular objects may be found in the Index of American Design, National Gallery of Art, Washington, D.C. Tobacco and medicine advertising materials are housed in the Library of Congress, Prints and Photographs Division; the National Museum of American History, Smithsonian; and the New York Public Library, Landauer Collection of the Indian in Advertising Materials. From the U.S. Patent Office in Washington, D.C., can be obtained dates and distribution data for commercial products and advertising.

Graphics and other ephemera associated with the most popular form of dramatic expression—the Wild West show—are collected at the Buffalo Bill Historical Center, Cody, Wyoming; the Buffalo Bill Museum, Golden, Colorado; Circus World Museum, Baraboo, Wisconsin; the Amon Carter Museum of Western Art, Fort Worth, Texas; and the Smithsonian Museum of American History.

The Indian in the Movies

MICHAEL T. MARSDEN AND JACK NACHBAR

Realism has never been an important tradition in American movies. Hollywood-produced films, like most other forms of commercial popular entertainment, have relied on familiar story patterns, stereotyped characterizations, and well-known personalities in order to appeal to as broad a public as possible. As a consequence, the accurate presentation of North American Indian cultural patterns and the immense cultural differences between the hundreds of Native societies have been mostly ignored in American movies. The feathered headresses, skillful horsemanship, reliance on hunting, and tailored hide clothing that typify Native life in most pictures were in reality characteristic of only about two dozen Plains tribes in the 1800s, and not of the hundreds of other Indian societies, who included fishermen or farmers and who wore a variety of clothing taken from their various local resources (Price 1973:153–154).

Another conspicuous distortion of Native American culture has been the corruption of Native languages. It is understandable, given the overall tendency of the movies to avoid unnecessary complexities, that most Indians in films speak English. But the inept, rudimentary English spoken by most Indian characters in the low-budget Westerns of the 1930s and 1940s, instead of capturing the figurative language characteristic of Native speech patterns, only seemed to heighten the sense of Indian barbarism. The use of Native languages became more common after 1950, but it was still enough of a novelty to hear Blackfoot spoken in *Across the Wide Missouri* in 1951 and Navajo as late as 1955 in the remake of *The Vanishing American* that several critics felt it necessary to point out these uses of Native languages in their reviews.

What many point to as yet another misrepresentation of Native life, White performers taking roles as Indians, is also the result of Hollywood commercial necessities. After 1910 highly publicized movie stars became the financial backbone of the film industry. The star's presence in a movie has been traditionally both a central attraction to the paying audience and a lure to encourage financial backers to invest in specific films. As a result, whenever Indian characters are central in a film, they have nearly always been played by well-known White performers. Capable Native performers such as the Cherokees Iron Eyes Cody and Chief Thundercloud, the Seneca Chief John Big Tree, the Chickasaw Rodd Redwing, the Yakima Chief Yowlachie and the Mohawk Jay Silverheels all worked in films for several decades but invariably in minor roles or as sidekicks to the White Western heroes. Helen Hunt Jackson's (1884) popular novel *Ramona* has been filmed four times, and each film has featured White stars as the tragically fated Indian lovers, Ramona and Alesandro: Mary Pickford and Henry B. Walthall in 1910, Adda Gleason and Monroe Salisbury in 1916, Dolores del Rio and Warner Baxter in 1928 (a silent film but featuring the famous song), and Loretta Young and Don Ameche in 1936. A possible high point for the inappropriate casting of Whites in major Indian roles may have been reached in 1964 when John Ford's *Cheyenne Autumn* presented the epic story of the brave attempt of 286 Cheyennes to flee an Oklahoma reservation and return to their Yellowstone River country homeland by featuring as the Indian heroic characters the White performers Ricardo Montalban, Gilbert Roland, Victor Jory, Dolores del Rio, and Sal Mineo.

Films of the 1970s ostensibly began paying more meticulous attention to authentic Native cultural patterns; however, Georgakas (1972:26) has found that these pictures, despite possibly good intentions, are full of important cultural errors and as a result "tell us very little about the Native Americans." The most notorious example of such cultural muddling is *A Man Called Horse* in 1970, which by employing mostly Native performers, using authentic Sioux dwellings and other artifacts, and speaking the Sioux language throughout the film created the surface of Sioux life in the early 1800s with unusual accuracy. However, on a deeper level, Sioux life is completely misrepresented. Sioux motives for fighting in the film are incorrect as are depictions of Sioux attitudes toward their elderly. Worst of all, the Sun Dance ceremony is shown not to be a sacred religious rite but a rather barbaric test of courage. The rites themselves are mistakenly a recreation of rites of the Mandan, traditional enemies of the Sioux (Georgakas 1972). A possible reason for such misrepresentations is offered by P. French (1973: 76–93), who argues that many of the films about Indians made after 1950 are about White rather than Native concerns. *Flap*, 1970, for example, while on one hand being a comedy-drama about contemporary reservation

Indians who demonstrate for their rights is, on the other hand, an allegory about all the American protest movements of the late 1960s. When the Indian leader Flapping Eagle (Anthony Quinn) is assassinated during a demonstration, references to protest heroes Robert Kennedy and Martin Luther King, Jr., are purposely apparent. Ralph Nelson (1970:26), director of *Soldier Blue*, 1970, has admitted that while his film was loosely based on the Sand Creek Massacre, Colorado, of 1864, he also intended the picture to demonstrate the horrors of the American presence in Vietnam.

During the 1960s and 1970s film scholars, citing the inaccuracies about Native life on film, waved accusing fingers at Hollywood with increasing frequency as American society came to realize its social sins in regard to minorities and unassimilated cultures. Such censure may have satisfied the national soul's yearning for a catharsis of self-accusation, but unfortunately the criticism that results from such social assaults is often little more than Hollywood scapegoating. In essence, these arguments charged that because a social problem exists and Hollywood reflects it on film, Hollywood must have created the problem in order to exploit it for box-office value (for example, Friar and Friar 1972:2). There are two major unwarranted assumptions in that argument. The first is that Hollywood was responsible for stereotyping the American Indian (Spears 1971:361), and the second is that Hollywood never does more than reflect the single-minded values of a majority society. There is as much danger of obscuring the truth about American Indians through these critical rantings about how Hollywood has warped the American imagination on the topic of Native Americans as there is in relying on movies for total knowledge about the world.

The Dramatic Inheritance

Interest in the "noble savages" of the wilderness is certainly as old as rumors about a continent covered with gold. Hollywood, rather than inventing White attitudes toward Indians, in fact merely continued popular conceptions about Native Americans that were already over 200 years old (Bataille and Silet 1980). As numerous scholars have pointed out, the first truly popular literature in America was the Indian captivity narrative, a literary genre with hundreds of titles in print by 1800. Interest in and imaginings about America's native inhabitants became a national leisure-time activity. White relationships with the Indians were quickly and permanently woven into the fabric of American popular arts; a meeting of cultures as epical as this one was bound to have permanent ramifications, either conscious or unconscious. It has even been suggested that Indian treaties were in reality dramas. "These treaties were essentially plays—chronicle plays—recording what was said in the parleys, including bits of

action, the exchanges of gifts, of wampum, the smoking of pipes, the many ceremonials with dances, cries and choral songs. Even the printed form of the treaties was dramatic: the participants were listed like a cast of characters, and precise notations were made as to the ceremonial action. Symbolic phrases were used to seal promises, even to raise questions" (Rourke 1942:61–62).

A very successful play entitled *Ponteach, or The Savages of America*, published in England in 1766, was the first American Indian play (Sears 1982). It was written by Robert Rogers, an Indian trader and ranger in the French and Indian War. By the dawn of the nineteenth century, the Indian had become the central character on American stages throughout the country (Nye 1970:148). By 1808 a play entitled *The Indian Princess, or La Belle Sauvage* was enthralling audiences with its story of the courageous Pocahontas. The doomed hero and the forest maiden of that famous story became featured players in more than 50 plays between 1810 and 1840. As the Indian was depicted in an increasingly romantic manner, the audience came in large numbers. Some theorized that America in its search for a past turned to the ready-made and accessible past in the American Indian—not the Indian of the present or future, for that was realistic and problematic, but the Indian of the past, the dying Indian who was believed to be romantically passing from the scene (Rourke 1942:73; Pearce 1965). Vardac (1949) argues that the nineteenth-century theater audience became interested in "pictorial sensations." The emphasis on pictorial effects, and thus realistic stage techniques, joined hands with an emphasis on romantic themes to produce a very popular American theater in the mid- and late nineteenth century.

By the late nineteenth century the Indian ceased to be the center of theatrical attention; however, the West continued to fascinate audiences and Indians became part of the emerging Western spectacles. Perhaps one of the most famous of these Western plays was *The Scouts of the Prairie*, which was performed in Chicago in 1872 for the first time. It starred Buffalo Bill (William F. Cody) and his friend, Texas Jack. The play's dramatic effects, including "a temperance lecture, a lasso exhibition, a prairie fire, a lovely Indian princess (played by an Italian girl from Chicago), and a knife fight with ten Indians" insured a fantastic popularity. "After increasing the number of Indians to twenty-five, adding horses, and inserting a ballet by ten Indian maidens, Cody took the show on the road for one of the most successful tours in American theatrical history" (Nye 1970:149). Thus, the romanticized West married the realistic stage presentation and gave birth to highly successful popular entertainment.

While Cody toured cities of America and Europe with his Wild West show, the theater's next step was to use still photographs projected as backdrops for the action, an innovation that was widely in use by the late 1800s and early 1900s. The omega point of this trend was reached when a stage production of *Ramona* in 1916 was presented as "a novelty in moving-picture shows rather than as a stage play," with each act and the prologue beginning with people who sing and dance, and each blending into moving pictures telling the story (Vardac 1949:83).

Only motion pictures could provide the realism American audiences were beginning to expect in their entertainment. And motion pictures could easily capitalize on existing popular story forms, especially those dealing with Indians and the West. So began America's cinematic love affair with the Indian, which was to change character and direction many times. During that time, the filmic treatments of the American Indian, although culturally inaccurate and stereotyped, would be as varied as the popular imagination would allow. There has never been a strict "Hollywood version" of the American Indian; there have been many Hollywood versions of America's first citizens, some more respectful than others, and some racist. Although movies were a new medium, they were limited by the conventions in characterization and narration that govern all the mass-produced popular arts. In the search for subject matter, producers encountered an extremely popular tradition about the frontier and the Noble Savages who lived there.

The first movies in which American Indians were the primary subject matter were made during the first days of the American film industry for Thomas Edison's Kinetoscope machines in the 1890s. Films such as *Sioux Ghost Dance*, 1894; *Eagle Dance*, 1898; and *Serving Rations to the Indians*, 1898 followed the normal formats of the Kinetoscope parlor "peep shows" of the day. They were documentaries less than a minute long and were filmed in a single camera setup that recorded an event, ceremony, or curiosity. However, the tremendous success of Edwin S. Porter's *The Great Train Robbery* in 1903 was a sure indication that the future of popular films, including those about Native Americans, was to be the narrative form.

As numerous film historians have shown, the audiences that attended the movies in the decade after 1903 were composed largely of the young and the poor—those who could not afford expensive entertainments and those who lacked the sophistication to appreciate subtle stories and drama. The images of the Indian in the one- and two-reel films of this period, therefore, conformed to the images that had developed in the popular art forms of the nineteenth century that had appealed to such an audience: stage melodramas, Wild West shows, and dime novels. All these forms had presented three primary Indian stereotypes that, with some variation, were continued in the movies. Dating back to her original appearance in the drama *The Indian Princess* in 1808, Pocahontas became popular culture's predominant image of the Indian woman. Deeply affectionate, yet maidenly, the Pocahontas figure always provides a sentimental tear or two by aiding her White brethren, often at the sacrifice of her own

life. The second image, equally sentimental, was first established in the popular frontier novels of James Fenimore Cooper and was later present in dime novels and in Wild West shows. He may be termed the Noble Anachronism and is characterized by a high degree of natural virtue made more poignant by the audience's knowledge that his race and probably he himself are doomed by an oncoming White culture not compatible with his admirable but primitive mode of living. The third popular Indian stereotype, immortalized in hundreds of dime novels and action melodramas and in the famous attack on the Deadwood Stage in Buffalo Bill's Wild West show, is the Savage Reactionary. The Indian fitting this image is a killer because he detests the proper and manifest advancement of a White culture clearly superior to his own and often because of his own primal impulses. He must be annihilated for the good of civilization.

1903–1913

Since the cinema lent itself so well to the presentation of exciting outdoor action, it is not surprising that the dramatic possibilities inherent in the Savage Reactionary stereotype made it from the beginning the most common image of the Indian in films. In 1903 in American Mutuscope and Biograph's production *Kit Carson*, Carson and a group of trappers are without provocation set upon by a band of treacherous Indians and all are murdered but Kit. In 1904 Carson returned in Biograph's *The Pioneers* and with his band of intrepid scouts gains sweet and deadly revenge on another group of Indians who had attacked and massacred a pioneer family. The biggest of all the early Savage Reactionary pictures was a five-reel extravaganza filmed in 1913 appropriately entitled *The Indian Wars*. The film recreated five famous Indian–U.S. Army battles, used 1,000 Indian extras, and featured the actual appearance of two of the most famous of all Indian fighters, Buffalo Bill and Gen. Nelson A. Miles.

Indians were often expected to be vicious; a press release for a 1911 film, *Ogallalah*, read: "It is savage and cruel as Indians are by nature." However, very often the Savage Reactionary was treated with a degree of understanding and sympathy by first being provoked to go on the war path. *The Invaders*, for example, a 1912 two-reeler produced by Thomas A. Ince, features a Sioux attack on a fort but not until a treaty between the Sioux and the government has been broken by the Whites. One of D.W. Griffith's last two-reelers, *The Battle at Elderbush Gulch*, 1913, pictures Indians brutally slaughtering women and children but only after the chief's son has been shot to death by a White settler.

The Pocahontas image of the Indian woman also first appeared in the 1903 *Kit Carson* when an Indian maiden helps Kit escape and is killed by the chief for her good deed. For the next 10 years this romantic figure, young, 609 beautiful, and self-sacrificing, would come to the aid of Whites almost as often as the Savage Reactionary would murder or capture them. Pocahontas herself appeared as the title character in films made in 1908 and 1910 while merely the titles of other pictures of the period reveal the sentimentalized nature of the central women characters: *The Squaw's Sacrifice*, 1909; *Red Wing's Loyalty*, 1910; *The Heart of a Sioux*, 1910; *The Indian Maid's Sacrifice*, 1911. In one of the more complex Pocahontas films of the era, Ince's *The Heart of an Indian*, 1913, a young Indian mother grieves over the death of her baby but receives some comfort when she accepts the care of a White infant captured in a raid by her tribe on a White settlement. Later, as Whites and Indians bloodily fight each other, the Indian woman takes pity on the now grieving White mother and returns her child to her even though it means the renewal of the Indian mother's own sorrow. Thus, in the midst of an atmosphere of violent racial hatred, the emotions of suffering and love induced by the shared experience of motherhood created a touching incident of interracial compassion.

A popular variation of the Pocahontas image was the Indian maiden or wife doomed to a tragic love for a White man. In *The Kentuckian*, 1908, for example, an Indian maiden rescues a young man, marries him, gives birth to his son, and finally kills herself so her husband can return to White society without embarrassment. An even more pathetic story is Griffith's *Comata the Sioux*, 1909, in which an Indian woman and her baby die of starvation and exhaustion trying to get away from her White husband whom she has discovered is unfaithful to her.

The Noble Anachronism manifested itself during the early period of film production in two quite different ways. The first was the Indian playing the part of hero and relying on his native customs and skills to win the day. The Sioux hero in Griffith's *The Redman and the Child*, 1908, rescues a child and chases down two White kidnappers in conventional heroic fashion. Yet, it is the Indian characteristics of the hero that make him especially interesting. The opening shot of the film reveals him carefully constructing a bow, and just before the climactic chase he throws an Indian blanket over his shoulders and prays to the Sioux deities. Another example of extraordinary virtue on the part of the Native American occurs in a 1912 French-made film, *The Red Man's Honor*, in which Red Hawk achieves a good reputation at a fort for his scouting skills but voluntarily returns to his native village to face an undeserved execution because he had promised to do so.

The second common portrayal of the Noble Anachronism, perhaps in part due to the notoriety in the early years of the century of the career of Indian athlete Jim Thorpe, was the Indian who went away to college but whose native instincts make it impossible to fully enter civilized White society. A trade advertisement for Grif-

fith's 1908 *Call of the Wild* stated the case bluntly: "So it is with the Redman. Civilization and education cannot bleach his tawny epidermis, and that will always prove an insurmountable barrier to social distinction." The ad goes on to describe the story of an Indian honor student and football star from the Carlisle school (Thorpe's alma mater) whose declaration of love for a White woman is indignantly repulsed, whereupon he reverts to his Native clothes and feathers, carries off the woman, and is prevented from raping her only by "the call of a Higher Voice" (Niver 1971:397). Education as portrayed in early movies could also lead Indians to alienation from their own culture. In the 1911 *Curse of The Red Man*, a stint at an Eastern college only leads the protagonist to a mania for whiskey, which in turn leads to his being rejected by his own tribe.

Thousands of one- and two-reel films were produced by the American movie industry between 1903 and 1913. Of these, several hundred dealt with Indian subject matter. Although a great majority of these hundreds may loosely be termed Westerns, and although the Indians in most of these fit the three stereotypes, the necessarily experimental nature of an industry in its initial growing stages and the sheer quantity of film product made it possible for Native Americans to receive a greater variety of treatments in film than in any other period of movie history. Almost every familiar situation had its exceptions. Even intermarriage sometimes was successful. In *The Indian Land Grab*, 1910, a sophisticated White woman tries to lure a young brave away from doing his tribal duty of demanding Indian land rights in Washington. In the end, however, the woman falls in love with the Indian, helps him regain the Indian lands, and follows him into the woods to live with him among his people. Many films went beyond White-Red stories and dealt exclusively, if not altogether accurately, with Native American life. *Hiawatha* was filmed in 1909 and made again in 1913 using Indian performers in one of the first feature-length films. *The Legend of Scar Face*, 1910, and *In The Long Ago*, 1913, both based their stories on supposedly ancient Indian legends. Love in Indian village life was depicted in Griffith's *The Mended Lute*, 1909, and in his *The Squaw's Love*, 1911, with both films presenting happy endings.

1913–1950

When the feature-length film began to replace the one- and two-reeler in American theaters in 1913, the total number of films produced quite obviously decreased. Consequently, less experimentation with the image of the Native American was attempted. There were, of course, still some exceptions to the three stereotypes. *Massacre*, 1934, featured Richard Barthelmess as the son of a Sioux chief who is educated and a star Wild West show performer, but who returns to his reservation to heroically rescue his tribal lands from White exploiters and who eventually is appointed federal representative to the reservation. Even more of an exception was a late silent film, *The Silent Enemy*, 1930, which featured an all-Indian cast reenacting the Ojibwa struggle to avoid starvation in northern Canada in the era before White contact. The entire picture was filmed outdoors and climaxed not with the usual battle but with the discovery and hunting of a giant herd of caribou. Unfortunately, *The Silent Enemy* proved to be financially unsuccessful and its attempt to dramatically but accurately depict Native life was quickly abandoned by commercial filmmakers.

Of the three Indian stereotypes that continued into this period from the early history of the movies, the Pocahontas image became the least used, although two screen stories featured the sentimentalized, doomed Indian girl and were continually popular during the period. Cecil B. DeMille's 1913 *The Squaw Man* was the first Western feature-length film. In the film a loving Indian wife commits suicide to prevent fighting between a White posse and her Indian tribe and so her husband can send their son East to be educated without the husband's feeling guilty. The story was so successful that DeMille remade it twice, in 1918 and 1931. But as Western stars of the 1920s such as Tom Mix and Ken Maynard placed greater and greater emphasis on daring stunting, the emphasis of the Western became more on fast action than on sentimentality. Furthermore, low-budget Westerns of the 1930s and 1940s mainly appealed to youth who disliked Western tenderness. And so the Pocahontas figure was no longer seen in Westerns with any regularity until the 1950s when a new Indian consciousness on the part of filmmakers brought about her return.

The low-grade Westerns featured the same star in several films per year. Emphasis was put on the star's exceptional physical skills on one hand and on cheap production methods on the other. Shooting two films at once became common as did running the same action footage in several movies. As a result the Savage Reactionary remained the predominant Indian screen stereotype. Not only were bands of marauding savages good adversaries for the heroics of the star, but also long shots of feathered riders made for exciting action sequences and were eminently reusable.

Savage Reactionaries were also a central image in the "big" feature movies of the period, the Western epics chronicling the triumph of civilization over the untamed frontier. In these epics, Indians became convenient symbols of the untamed element of the wilderness. Great masses of aggressive savages became protagonists in the first Western epics, *The Covered Wagon*, 1923, and *The Iron Horse*, 1924. In the late 1930s and early 1940s Indians violently opposed civilized advances such as the railroad in *Union Pacific*, 1939; the stage line in *Stagecoach*, 1939, the settlement of a state in *Arizona*, 1940; and the

telegraph in *Western Union*, 1941. Gen. George Custer's "last stand" was a popular historical incident throughout the period as at least eight films were made about it, the most lavish being *The Flaming Frontier*, 1926, and *They Died With Their Boots On*, 1941. All the Custer films of this period glorified the general as a martyr to the cause of White manifest destiny.

Most of the epic films ignored historical accuracy in favor of American patriotism, but most also ascribed some validity, even nobility, to the violent actions of the Indians. In a 1927 film about the infamous defeat of the British Gen. Edward Braddock, *Winners of the Wilderness*, the Indians are graphically shown killing and torturing British-American troops. But later Chief Pontiac allows the film's star, Tim McCoy, to go free because McCoy had earlier defeated Pontiac in a hand-to-hand fight but had allowed Pontiac to live. The most viciously anti-Indian of all the filmed epics of the conquest of the frontier is undoubtedly King Vidor's *Northwest Passage*, 1940. In that film Spencer Tracy as Maj. Robert Rogers leads his gallant Rangers in 1759 to the Indian village of Saint Francis in Canada where he delivers a hysterical speech about the horrors of Indian atrocities and orders his men to kill every Indian man, woman, and child, which his Rangers subsequently do. *Northwest Passage* ends with Tracy impressively silhouetted against the skyline, his slaughter of the Indians having obviously made him into a kind of frontier saint.

During the years after 1913 the Noble Anachronism largely ceased being a hero and also quit going to college. Instead, perhaps owing to the predominance of the Western "star" in films, he took on the function of either being protected by the superior White hero or acting as the hero's loyal helpmate, much as a squire would aid a knight, or as a son would serve his father. In both cases "nobility" became synonymous with being an object of White paternalism.

The formula for the protected-by-the-White-hero stories usually involved crooked Whites stirring up normally virtuous Redskins to the brink of violent rebellion whereupon the hero would dispose of the White villains and the Indians would return to their reservation and docility. So rigid was this formula that Tim McCoy, who had served as Indian adviser on *The Covered Wagon* (fig. 1) and several other Western epics before becoming a star in his own right, and who had a sincere concern for the injustices suffered by Native Americans, tried to include his own screen death in the 1932 film, *End of the Trail*, in order to illustrate the tragic futility of Indian-White hostilities. Instead, Columbia Pictures changed the ending and McCoy, at film's end, had only an arm wound and had been appointed Indian agent (Tuska 1970–1971, 2(3):26–29). The formula probably reached its most absurd proportions in Tom Mix's last picture, the 1935 serial, *The Miracle Rider*. Even though the story takes

Smithsonian, NAA: left, 1659-C; right, 55,752.
Fig. 1. On location for *The Covered Wagon*, near Walker Lake, Nev. left, White technical advisor Tim McCoy poses with Wovoka, a Northern Paiute, a leader of the 1890 Ghost Dance. right, Northern Arapahoe men from Ft. Washakie, Wyo.; Wovoka, seated; and a White actor at far left. The Arapahoe men acted in the film along with 750 Indians from various Western tribes who were included in the attack sequence (Hilger 1986:39). Both photographed in 1923.

place in 1935 and the Indians are buying modern tractors for their reservation, the Indians nevertheless wear nineteenth-century native costumes and are about to be frightened off their land by Whites using a radio-controlled glider the Indians superstitiously believe to be a malevolent deity. At the end, when Mix saves the day, he is appointed director of Indian affairs for "having done more for the Indian than any man in history."

The Noble Anachronism as loyal helpmate is, of course, best illustrated by that "faithful Indian companion," Tonto, the pal of the Lone Ranger. Fran Striker first created the Masked Rider of the Plains for radio in 1932. The Ranger came to the movies in a 1938 serial, *The Lone Ranger*, and Tonto appeared on the screen in several more films, steadfastly aiding the forces of civilized law and justice and often acting as translator for the monolingual Lone Ranger. However, his role remained decidedly secondary to that of the Ranger, and the Masked Man invariably had most of the ideas. In Spanish, *tonto* means 'fool' or 'numbskull', but Striker did not intend the name to be interpreted in Spanish.

The father-son relationship hinted at in the Lone Ranger stories was even more obvious in the long-running Red Ryder film series (28 films from 1940 through 1949) in which Ryder had to constantly put up with the antics of his youthful Indian pal, Little Beaver. A small exception to the father-son relationship occurred in 1944 when Chief Thundercloud appeared with Hoot Gibson and Bob Steele in *Outlaw Trail* and *Sonora Stagecoach* as a fully contributing member of the Trail Blazers.

A film that until the early 1970s was believed lost,

George B. Seitz's 1925 *The Vanishing American*, has proved to be not only the most ambitious of the Noble Anachronism pictures but also quite possibly one of the most interesting commercial films ever produced by the Hollywood film industry. Beginning with a title card quoting Herbert Spencer on evolutionary survival of the fittest, continuing with a long prologue to the story about the races of people who have from the beginning of time inhabited an area of the American Southwest, and ending with the death of the Indian protagonist as an illustration of the biblical quote, "He that loseth his life for my sake will find it," *The Vanishing American* attempts on an epic scale to reconcile the forces of history and evolution within a pattern of Christian love. Nophaie, the film's hero, played with enormous authority and dignity by Richard Dix, sees Navajo horses stolen and sold to the U.S. Army. Nevertheless, he fights valiantly in World War I only to return with his Navajo friends to discover a crooked Indian agent has stolen their land. Yet, despite these affronts, his love of the White schoolmarm and hers for him convinces him of the validity of her religion, and he dies trying to keep an uprising of his people against the Whites from killing members of either race. It may be argued that because Nophaie's heroism was induced by White Christianity it therefore is somewhat condescending toward Native American culture and religion. However, the lavish production, Dix's performance, the obvious approval for the romance between the Red man and the White woman, and most important, Nophaie's assumption, at the end, of the qualities of a savior obviously meant to be associated with Christ made the presentation of the

612

Indian hero in *The Vanishing American* during the racially sensitive 1920s an act of both great skill and bravery.

1950–1975

The third quarter-century of American film production witnessed the end of the low-grade Western. Nevertheless, the depiction of the American Indian maintained the traditional Indian stereotypes. However, these films have a greater self-consciousness about how White history had distorted Red-White relations. An early manifestation of the development occurred in David O. Selznick's lavish 1946 *Duel in the Sun* in which the half-Indian Pearl Chavez (Jennifer Jones) is psychologically destroyed by White racial prejudices against her. Two John Ford–directed Westerns in the late 1940s also helped prepare the way. *Fort Apache*, 1948, featured Henry Fonda as an arrogant fort commander who sneers, "Your word to a breechclothed, savage, illiterate, uncivilized murderer and treaty breaker? There is no question of honor between an American officer and Cochise," and who in arrogance later precipitates a cavalry-Indian battle in which Fonda's troops are slaughtered. When a similar plot occurred in *Two Flags West* in 1950, it was definitely established that the Savage Reactionary may have acted as he did because of White tyranny. A second Ford film, *She Wore A Yellow Ribbon*, 1949, featured a memorable scene between John Wayne as an aging cavalry officer and Chief John Big Tree as an old chief no longer completely in control of his young, headstrong warriors. As the two men talk over old times, the problems both are having with their young charges, and the pleasures of retiring to go hunting, a rare moment on the screen occurs—a conversation between two people from widely differing cultures brought together by a mutual respect that never for a second allows the slightest hint of condescension.

The major influence on the new image of the Indian in post-1950 films (as virtually all film critics agree) was Delmer Daves's lovingly made and financially successful 1950 Western, *Broken Arrow* (fig. 2). In the film Tom Jeffords (James Stewart) studies the culture of the Apaches so he can speak with the famous Apache leader, Cochise (Jeff Chandler), about stopping a long and bloody White and Indian war. He (and by implication the film audience) is surprised to learn that the feared and detested Cochise is in reality a man of honor and integrity. It is, in fact, finally Cochise who becomes the film's hero by passionately refusing to break the peace treaty once it is made.

Walk the Proud Land, 1956, featured Audie Murphy as a religious Indian agent paternalistically removing chains from the legs of Apache chiefs and telling them they must learn to live like Whites. As late as 1971 in *Big Jake* and 1973 in *Cahill, U.S. Marshal*, John Wayne accomplished

Fig. 2. Scenes from the 1950 version of *Broken Arrow*. top, Cochise (Jeff Chandler) talks with Tom Jeffords (James Stewart). bottom, Jeffords marries Sonseeahray (Debra Paget), an Apache character.

his heroics with a faithful Indian companion. But such films after 1950 became increasingly rare. These relationships are on the basis of the respect for skills rather than on the father-son basis of the relationships in films of the Lone Ranger–Red Ryder era. *Broken Arrow* in its portrayal of Cochise had effectively destroyed the passivity of the Noble Anachronism stereotype and in its place substituted an equally romantic image—the heroic, but very probably doomed, hero. Soon after the release of *Broken Arrow*, in *The Devil's Doorway*, 1950, Robert Taylor played an educated Eastern Shoshone, a Civil War veteran, who dies fighting for land rightfully his. *Hiawatha*, 1952, ignored the H.W. Longfellow story completely and instead had the title character bring peace between traditional enemy Ojibwas and Sioux in what in reality looked like a hidden Hollywood attack on the Cold War. *Apache*, 1954, portrayed as a hero a follower of Geronimo who refused to surrender to Whites, and the actions of Geronimo himself were dramatized as admirable in *Geronimo*, 1962. Crazy Horse and Sitting Bull, the former

613

THE INDIAN IN THE MOVIES

villains of innumerable film treatments of Custer's Last Stand, received sympathetic treatments in *Crazy Horse*, 1953, and *Sitting Bull*, 1954. And in *Tell Them Willie Boy is Here*, 1969, Willie is killed by Whites because he honorably insists on maintaining Indian customs in a White world where they are unlawful. Two non-Western biographical films of the period also created portraits of the admirable yet doomed Indian. Burt Lancaster played the famous Indian sports hero in *Jim Thorpe, All American*, 1951, whose story related how Thorpe became the greatest athlete in American history only to lose his honors and his status because he did not understand White-formulated rules separating amateur from professional athletes. In *The Outsider*, 1961, Tony Curtis portrays Ira Hayes, the Indian hero of Iwo Jima who is physically destroyed by a publicity campaign he is talked into participating in, and who finally dies alone and drunk.

Half-bloods had rarely been treated as heroes before 1950, but after *Broken Arrow*, they too joined the pantheon of admirable Noble Anachronisms in films such as *The Half-Breed*, 1952; *Broken Lance*, 1954; *Reprisal*, 1956; *Flaming Star*, 1960; and *Nevada Smith*, 1966. In *Billy Jack*, 1971, and *The Trial of Billy Jack*, 1974, the hero goes through Indian religious ceremonies (and is himself a half-blood) for no other reason it would appear than the assumption that the association with Indians would make the character more attractive to the film's youthful audience.

The lovely, sacrificial Pocahontas maiden also returned to romantic popularity in the post-1950 era and, like her early movie ancestors, was very often ready to die in the arms of her White husband or lover. *Broken Arrow*; *Across the Wide Missouri*, 1951; *Hondo*, 1953; *A Man Called Horse*, 1970; *Little Big Man*, 1971; *Jeremiah Johnson*, 1972; and *The Man Who Loved Cat Dancing*, 1973--all have Indian women married to Whites who die either during the film or in the background of the film's story.

If the continuation of the image of the sacrificial Indian woman hints at a corresponding continuation of an American fear of miscegenation, other films of the period indicated such a fear was breaking down. One of the mountainmen in *The Big Sky*, 1952, is convinced by his companions that his desertion of an Indian woman was wrong and he subsequently returns to her. Rod Steiger in *Run of the Arrow*, 1956, lives for a period of time with the Sioux, but when he decides at the film's conclusion to return to White society, he takes his Sioux wife and adopted child with him. Even when death occurs in an interracial marriage after 1950 it is often to illustrate the beauty of the relationship. In John Farrow's admirable *Hondo*, the title character (John Wayne) falls in love with a White widow (Geraldine Page) only after he discovers in her personality many of the same qualities he had found earlier in his Apache wife, now dead.

Indians continued to be Savage Reactionaries during the 1950s and later, especially in low-budget films; but some filmmakers used the stereotype for serious purposes. John Ford's *The Searchers*, 1956, Sam Peckinpah's *Major Dundee*, 1964, and Robert Aldrich's *Ulzana's Raid*, 1972 all present horrendously destructive Indian killers, but all three films use the image to illustrate a parallel destructive impulse in the Indian's White pursuers. *Soldier Blue* and *Little Big Man* recreate the Sand Creek and Washita River, Texas, massacres of the Indians in an attempt to reverse the Savage Reactionary stereotype by making the White soldiers the true bestial savages.

The plot of *When the Legends Die*, 1972, traced the life of a teenaged Ute who is forced to forsake the "old ways" he had learned from his parents and who grows up to be a success in the White world as a rodeo star, but who in the end returns to the Ute reservation and his cultural roots. While the picture was free of the traditional Indian stereotypes, it was also not a commercial success. Violating audience expectations in commercial films, as had been shown as early as 1930 in *The Silent Enemy*, has always been financially dangerous. Experimental films in the 1970s played an unusually large role in breaking the screen Indian free from the confinements of stereotypes. Kent MacKenzie's *The Exiles*, 1961, documents the lifestyle of a group of poor Native Americans living in San Francisco. Susan Dyal's *Navajo Rain Chant* uses animation to show in less than three minutes the organic relationship between Navajo culture and the designs on Navajo blankets. Phillip Greene's documentary, *The Long Walk*, traces the history of the Navajo nation from the 1860s to the 1960s and the Navajo-run Rough Rock School. Robert Primes's *Legend Days Are Over*, 1973, presents a series of natural scenes to accompany the narration of a 91-year-old Indian woman remembering her cultural past. Some other non-Hollywood films praised for a sensitive depiction of Native American life include *Ballad of Crowfoot, End of the Trial, Mass for the Dakota Sioux, Now That The Buffalo Are Gone, Ishi in Two Worlds, Tahtonka*, and *Circle of the Sun* (Clark and Vickery 1969–1970:27, 46–47).

During the late 1960s and 1970s Native Americans themselves began to get more directly involved in determining their roles on the screen. In 1966 Jay Silverheels led the formation of two Los Angeles groups, the Indian Actors Guild and the Indian Actors Workshop, to teach acting skills to Indian performers and to promote the use of Native people in Native roles. In 1972 Kiowa author N. Scott Momaday's (1968) Pulitzer-Prize-winning novel, *House Made of Dawn*, was produced with a script by Momaday and with Native American performers and financing. The direct involvement of Native Americans in film production and the sensitive films about Native life made by noncommercial, experimental filmmakers hint at the limitations that have always been present in Hollywood films about Indian life and also at possible corrections of these limitations. The history of the depiction of Native peoples during the first three-quarters of a century of commercial movie production reveals a wide degree of variety on the scale of general human conduct by both Indian and White characters but, at the same time, reflects a general ignoring of the subtle cultural differences between groups of Native peoples. Therefore, it would appear that careful depictions of North American Indian history and various cultural patterns might be eventually best shown on film by those whose primary interests are centered on Indian life itself rather than on entertainment, which must necessarily appeal to a mass audience.

1976–1987

After 1976 traditional movie Westerns no longer had box-office appeal (Tuska 1985). As a result, by 1980 the production of Westerns had become all but nonexistent. One consequence of this decline in the production of Westerns was a corresponding lessening of movies with Native American characters. During the five year period, 1980–1984, for example, only 15 films with speaking parts for Indian characters were released. This is less than half the number of films with Indian characters released in 1970–1974 or 1960–1964 (Hilger 1986:105–162). Of these 15 films, only three are traditional Westerns. Within this smaller number of films the three basic types of Indian stereotypes persist. However, these stereotypes are presented within a context of a modern sensibility about Indian subject matter first seen in *Broken Arrow* in 1950. Such a sensibility recognizes Native Americans as more than mere impediments to the establishment of a superior White culture but fails to insist on a meticulous presentation of Native American life and culture.

Indian characters continued to appear as villains during the decade, but no longer as savage reactionaries slowing White manifest destiny. In *Greyeagle*, 1977, the title character, like many earlier movie Indian bad guys, kidnaps a young White woman. However, in this film, the kidnapping is motivated: the woman is in reality the daughter of a Cheyenne chief. Some Indian villains plot their nefarious schemes in the contemporary world, where White-Indian conflict symbolizing civilization versus savagery is no longer an issue. Billy Bear in *48 Hours*, 1983, is a violent killer, but his murderous impulses are not tied to his race, and he is paired with an even nastier White partner. In *Firestarter*, 1984, the heavy is identified as a Navajo, but his villainy is tied to his being a corrupt government agent.

The Pocahontas stereotype also continued into the 1980s. In *Sacred Ground*, 1982, the Indian wife of a White trapper dies soon after giving birth to a healthy infant. The trapper, desperate for someone to nurse the baby, kidnaps

the wife of a Paiute chief. Later, after stopping an armed battle between the Paiutes and the trapper, the kidnapped woman chooses to leave her Paiute husband and her village to live with the White trapper because she has grown attached to the child she nurses. Two made-for-television films show Indian women as less self-sacrificial than in *Sacred Ground*, but they are still closely related to the Pocahontas type. The storylines in *Centennial*, 1978, and *The Legend of Walks Far Woman*, 1982, both feature strong Indian women through several decades of their lives. Yet they are pictured as so perfect and their sufferings are so continual and unjust that the same overstated sentimentality is aroused in the viewer as was aroused by the earlier, more simplistic Pocahontas stereotypes.

Since 1975 Noble Anachronisms have been the most frequently used Indian stereotype on movie screens. Like the other two stereotypes, Noble Anachronisms have undergone changes to make them more palatable to contemporary moviegoers. This change is clearly seen, for example, in the 1981 remake of the original story of the Lone Ranger, *The Legend of the Lone Ranger*. In this film Tonto is once again a trusty sidekick in the service of the Masked Man, but here Tonto shows a raised consciousness. In one scene he articulates for members of his tribe his reasons for riding with the Ranger, and in another he lectures President Ulysses Grant about Grant's obligation to honor government treaties with the Indians.

The most common use of the Noble Anachronism was to suggest how the close-to-nature lifeways of these admirable characters are desirable alternatives to decadent White ways of living. In *Buffalo Bill and the Indians, or Sitting Bull's History Lesson*, 1976, Buffalo Bill is portrayed as a bragging, drunken incompetent, while Sitting Bull is presented as the true man of the West, both spiritually and physically at home on the frontier. *Eagle's Wing*, 1979, a British production, dramatizes the struggle between a city-bred trapper and a Comanche chief to possess a wild horse. The film makes the chief a symbol of the elemental freedom in nature, a freedom that the trapper comes to envy and desire.

A notable variation on the Noble Anachronism stereotype is the image of the Indian as a possessor of exotic, occult secrets. *Nightwing*, 1979, shows vampire bats released through tribal magic. The main character in *Altered States*, 1980, engages in hallucinogenic rites of ancient Indian origin to obtain a new level of consciousness. In *The Manitou*, 1978, a Sioux medicine man living in the contemporary world exorcises a demon from a White woman. Even in *Windwalker*, 1980, a film much praised for its portrayal of Crow and Cheyenne life in the eighteenth century and for its dialogue that is spoken in the appropriate Native languages, the title character magically returns from the dead to unify his family. This emphasis on the spiritual exoticism of Native Americans brings the screen Indian full circle. Just as Edison's one-minute movies in the 1890s were sold to audiences eager to view the strange otherness of Native peoples, so too do audiences in the 1980s go to the movies for the pleasure of seeing Indians whose mystical lore makes them fascinatingly different.

A few films after 1975 have broken with Indian stereotypes and have dealt with Native Americans living in twentieth-century America with sensitivity and honesty. *Three Warriors*, 1977, and a Canadian film, *Dreamspeaker*, 1979, for example, both relate the struggles of young Native Americans to sort out the conflicts between the heritage of their Native past and the realities of living in an urban environment in the present. Two other films present sympathetic biographies of noted Native American athletes. *Spirit of the Wind*, 1982, tells the story of Alaska dogsled racer George Attla, Jr., and *Running Brave*, 1983, shows how the Sioux Billy Mills became an Olympic long-distance gold medalist. Unfortunately, all four of these films, like earlier films that tried to break through long-established Indian stereotypes, proved to be commercially unsuccessful.

Native Americans have appeared on movie screens in a great number of guises from heroic to villainous, from comic to pathetic (Bataille and Silet 1985). Yet, after thousands of movies featuring Indian characters, only a handful of films have shown Native American life with cultural accuracy (Bagley 1980). Hollywood Indians entered the movies already weighed down by more than a century of stereotyping in popular drama and fiction. The movies have modified these stereotypes but have never eliminated them (O'Connor 1980).

Non-Indian Biographies

In this section are brief biographical sketches of 294 individuals who were not Indians but had a significant impact on the history of Indian-White relations in North America. Inclusion is restricted to those who were deceased at the time this volume was prepared. All U.S. commissioners of Indian affairs meeting these criteria are included. These sketches often omit significant aspects of the subjects' lives outside the field of Indian affairs. Further information on some may be located by consulting the index in this and other volumes of the Handbook. Volumes 18 and 19 of the Handbook are reserved for a biographical dictionary of Indians.

Abbott, Lyman 1835–1922

Indian affairs were among the many reform interests of Lyman Abbott, Congregational clergyman and editor of the *Christian Union*, after 1893 the *New Outlook*, an influential journal of liberal Christianity and progressivism published in New York. Abbott took an extreme position in favor of assimilation of Indians into society (as opposed to gradualists like Herbert Welsh and Senator Henry Dawes). He called for immediate "annihilation" of reservations, division of Indian lands, abrogation of treaties if necessary to achieve these objectives, and immediate citizenship and voting rights. He early advocated separation of church and state in Indian education and federally maintained compulsory public schools for Indians. A leader in the Mohonk Conferences, he was also a member of the Indian Rights Association and an associate member of the Society of American Indians (I.V. Brown 1953; L. Abbott 1901, 1915, 1921). The Abbott papers are at Bowdoin College, Brunswick, Maine. HAZEL WHITMAN HERTZBERG

Abel, Annie Heloise 1873–1947

A leading historian of the American Indian, Abel was born in Fernhurst, Sussex, England, and raised in Kansas. She received her B.A. in 1898 and her M.A. in 1900, writing her master's thesis on Indian reservations in Kansas (Abel 1904). After graduate study at Cornell University, 1900–1901, she returned to Kansas to teach high school and do research on American Indian history.

In 1903 Abel entered Yale University and received the Bulkley fellowship in history. Her Ph.D. dessertation on Indian removal (Abel 1908) established her as a major historian of federal Indian policy. This was the beginning of a long career in publication of Indian histories, diaries, and documents relating to the West. She felt her greatest contribution to scholarship was *The Slaveholding Indians* (Abel 1915–1925), covering the problems of the Southern Indians during the Civil War and Reconstruction. Although sympathetic to the Indians she wrote about and critical of government Indian policy, she maintained a high level of scholarly objectivity and accuracy in all her works.

Abel had a distinguished college teaching career (Prucha 1971c; Kelsey 1973) and also served as historian in the United States Office of Indian Affairs in 1913 (see also Anonymous 1947). BARBARA GRAYMONT

Abraham about 1787–after 1870

Abraham, a runaway slave from Pensacola, was about 1825–1845 the principal Seminole interpreter, a counsellor to head chief Micanopy, and the principal chief of the Seminole Maroons (the Blacks associated with the Seminole). His busk name was Sohanac or Souanakke Tustenukke. He accompanied his master on a mission to Washington, 1825–1826, and received his freedom for his services. Although he witnessed the "removal" treaties of Payne's Landing, Florida (May 9, 1832), and Fort Gibson, Indian Territory (March 28, 1832), he was active both in preparing resistance to removal and as a commander in the war that erupted on December 28, 1835. However, he was always ready to treat with Whites and so negotiated a truce with Gen. Edmund Gaines in March 1836. Abraham was also largely responsible for negotiating the Treaty of Camp Dade (March 6, 1837) by which the Indians undertook to go west provided their Blacks were permitted to accompany them. When that provision was violated and the war resumed, Abraham remained a prisoner and, as guide and interpreter, strove to bring about the surrender of the hostiles. Early in 1839 he was shipped to Indian Territory where he served as interpreter. He was employed by the Seminole subagency, 1843–1845, until discharged for habitual intoxication. In 1852 he was interpreter for the delegation that unsuccessfully tried to persuade Billy Bowlegs, chief of the Florida Seminole, to move west. After accompanying the chief to Washington and New York and back to Florida, Abraham returned to Indian Territory, where, late in 1870, he was reported as still living on Little River. For additional information see Porter (1946, 1971). KENNETH WIGGINS PORTER

Adair, James about 1709–about 1783

Best known for his *History of the American Indians* (1775), Adair, a Scotch-Irish immigrant to the southern colonies, established himself by 1735 as a trader among the Southeast Indians. Although he dealt with all the major tribes of the Southeast he found his true home among the Chickasaw where he lived in the 1740s and 1750s with his Chickasaw wife. Adair performed diplomatic duties as well as acting as a trader. He played an important role in encouraging the Choctaw to throw off their allegiance to the French in 1746. However, the opportunity to win over this important tribe to the

617

English side was lost by what Adair regarded as the inexperience and incompetence of Gov. James Glen of South Carolina. Adair's claims for losses incurred in the enterprise were treated harshly by the colonial authorities and led him to publish caustic attacks on those involved. Although alienated from the formal society of the coast, Adair periodically helped the colony, once by leading a body of Chickasaws during the 1760 Cherokee War. In his *History*, Adair expressed his ire against the incompetence of royal administrators and his admiration for the noble quality of his Indian friends. Although his book is often ridiculed for his speculation on the Jewish origin of the Indians, it is a rich mine of useful anthropological information on the Indians of the Southeast by an acute observer. The circumstances of his death are unknown, but he seems to have died shortly after the Revolution probably while among the Indians of the Southeast. For further information see Sirmans (1966) and Washburn (1973a). WILCOMB, E. WASHBURN

Amherst, Jeffrey 1717-1797

A British major general and experienced commander of Hessian troops, Amherst was sent to America in 1758 as commander-in-chief of the army fighting the French. Forces under his command captured the French fortress of Louisburg in 1758. His later military accomplishments included the capture of Ticonderoga and Crown Point and the occupation of Montreal in 1760, completing the conquest of Canada. In the last days of his Canadian campaign, Amherst had the aid of thousands of Indian warriors, subsidized by generous gifts of food, clothing, tools, and weapons. After 1760, Amherst instituted a policy of strict economy, discontinuing Indian gifts. At this time, Indians were in need of basic supplies; crops had not been cared for; women demanded the finery given to them by the French; and, worst of all, British officers at the forts declined to give the Indians ammunition for hunting. Outraged Indians would take bold measures to get these prizes. Although Superintendent William Johnson and other Indian agents protested against Amherst's policy of economy, the general refused to alter his view.

Partly as a result of the desperate situation created by Amherst, the Indians, in an explosion of violence, joined Pontiac in the Indian war of 1763. Amherst, who looked down upon the Indians as savages, spread smallpox at Fort Pitt by giving Indians blankets from soldiers who had the disease. He had no real understanding of the significance of the Indian war he had a hand in making. For details on Amherst and his Indian policy, see Jacobs (1985), Parkman (1898), and Peckham (1947). WILBUR R. JACOBS

Anza, Juan Bautista de 1736-1788

Anza, son of a Spanish army officer, was born at the presidio of Fronteras near present-day Douglas, Arizona. His career as a military officer on the frontier was a brilliant one, and he rose steadily in rank from lieutenant (1754) to captain (1760) to lieutenant colonel (1774) and colonel (1782). From 1778 to 1787 he was governor of New Mexico (Ivancovich 1960). He was nicknamed "the hard-riding captain," and it is estimated that in his life he traveled 20,000 miles on horseback. In 1775 he was placed in command of 240 colonists, who successfully traveled from Tubac (presidio of Tucson) across the Colorado River and the Mohave Desert to Monterey on the central California coast. This group founded the presidio and mission at San Francisco in 1776 (Bowman and Heizer 1967).

Thirteen diaries were written on the expedition, and they contain a wealth of ethnographic information, especially on the Quechan tribe (Bolton 1930, 1931). Of especial interest is the detailed autobiography of the Quechan leader Salvador Palma (probably dictated by him to Anza), which is the earliest such document on record referring to Indians of the western United States (Bolton 1930, 5; Bowman and Heizer 1967:148-155). ROBERT F. HEIZER

Armstrong, Samuel Chapman 1839-1893

Armstrong was born in the Hawaiian Islands, the son of missionary parents who specialized in educational work. He attended Oahu College in the islands, then graduated from Williams College. He compiled a distinguished record of personal bravery and leadership in the U.S. Army during the Civil War, attaining the rank of brevet brigadier general and the command of a Black regiment. At the end of the war, Gen. O.O. Howard persuaded him to take charge of the Freedmen's Bureau at Hampton, Virginia, and the administration of some 10,000 Blacks. Armstrong suggested a school for young Blacks, and with the help of the American Missionary Association and the Freedmen's Bureau he opened Hampton Institute in 1868. Armstrong's interest in Indians was the result of his answering the appeal of another army officer, Richard Henry Pratt, to accept 17 former Indian prisoners at Hampton in 1878, while Pratt organized a separate Indian school in Pennsylvania. Thereafter, Armstrong continued to accept Indians at Hampton Institute, though in small numbers. By 1892, 25 Indians had graduated from Hampton of the 345 who had attended. Unlike Pratt, who disagreed with him on this point, Armstrong saw the objective of Indian education to be to prepare students for useful lives on the reservations. Hampton's so-called Education For Life envisioned the education of "head, heart, and hand" through the teaching of a skilled trade. Indian and Black alike were to be trained in life as they would most probably live it (S.C. Armstrong 1883, 1904, 1913). For biographical details see Talbot (1904), L. Abbott (1921), Peabody (1918), and Start (1892). Armstrong's papers are in the Williams College Library, Williamstown, Massachusetts, and in the Hampton Institute Archives. E. ARTHUR GILCREAST

Ashley, William Henry 1778–1838

Ashley was a Virginian by birth, a Missourian by choice. He experimented in a variety of occupations before finding a lucrative and satisfying niche in the Indian and fur trades of the Far West. Early ventures in lead mining, freighting, and trading produced little success; but Ashley's determination was eventually rewarded with the purchase of a gunpowder manufacturing company on the eve of the War of 1812.

During the war, Ashley served as captain, colonel, and eventually general in the militia. By 1819 he had moved to Saint Louis where success continued in real estate transactions. The Indian trade of the trans-Missouri West attracted Ashley's resources and his personal attention for the next six years. From 1822 to 1826 Ashley, in partnership with Andrew Henry, organized and directed new strategies for extracting furs from the West. Ashley personally led three expeditions and instituted fundamental changes in the trade. Instead of relying on Indian procurers and processors of furs, Ashley hired his own trappers and thus avoided Indian middlemen as well as native processors. These brigades scoured streams and ponds of the Rocky Mountain West and did not return to fixed fur trade posts for re-outfitting and deposition of their cache. Instead, annual rendezvous were held in parklands long used by Northern and Eastern Shoshone and other Indian traders.

The Ashley formula was a short-term bonanza for its architect, who sold out to Smith, Jackson, and Sublette in 1826. Thereafter, Ashley continued to profit from the trade by selling furs on commission and by selectively supplying small companies active in the West. His main focus turned toward politics, and he was elected to the U.S. House of Representatives, serving 1831–1838. During his last years, Ashley was a strong advocate of aggressive military and diplomatic policy toward Indians and other Euro-Americans active in the West. His legacy is that of the success of free enterprise at the expense of natural resources (especially beaver) and diplomatic relations with resident native trader-cultures, most of which were alienated by Whites circumventing well-established protocol and respect for trade spheres.

Ashley's papers are located primarily in the Missouri Historical Society, Saint Louis, and in the New-York Historical Society, New York. Ashley's biography (Clokey 1980) may be supplemented with his writings (Morgan 1964) and information on Ashley, his partners, employees, and associates (Hafen 1965–1972). WILLIAM R. SWAGERTY

Astor, John Jacob 1763–1848

Born in Walldorf, Germany, Astor came to New York City in 1784 and soon entered the fur trade. His connections with American Indians were almost entirely through his employees in various fur companies (notably the American Fur Company, 1808–1834), for Astor himself probably never went farther west than the vicinity of Canandaigua, New York.

Astor played a key role in bringing Indians into a dependence on trade goods and in enlarging White knowledge of the Indian country and its inhabitants. He eventually controlled the trade of the Great Lakes, Upper Mississippi, and Upper Missouri regions. His agents even distributed medals bearing Astor's likeness. His unsuccessful attempt to gain control of the fur trade of the Pacific Northwest inspired Washington Irving's classic *Astoria* (1964).

Astor had two important influences on Indians. First, in 1822 he achieved the abolition of the government-owned trading posts, or factories, which sought to lure the Indians away from alcohol-dispensing private traders by supplying them goods at cost. Second, the American Fur Company's agents were notably successful in introducing alcohol into the Indian country in spite of government legislation.

In 1834 Astor withdrew entirely from the fur trade. For a more detailed biography see Porter (1931). KENNETH WIGGINS PORTER

Atkin, Edmond 1708–1761

Born in England, Atkin spent his boyhood in South Carolina. During the 1730s he and one John Atkin, probably a close relative, established an Indian trading business in Charleston. The venture was so successful that Atkin, as a leading provincial Indian trade merchant, won an appointment to the governor's council of South Carolina. Atkin moved to England in 1750 where he remained for six years composing two lengthy documents on Indian-white relations that established his reputation as an authority. The first of these works was a history of the revolt of the Choctaw Indians against the French, a 30,000-word narrative detailing the exploits of Red Shoes, a Choctaw chief who allied his people with the English. The second was a comprehensive report on Indian relations throughout the British colonies and a plan for setting up an imperial superintendency system. Atkin's report and plan, written in 1755, were largely responsible for his appointment as superintendent of Indian affairs for the Southern Department in 1756. These documents provide a historical portrait of the Southeast Indians unequaled in his time. Atkin himself was largely unsuccessful in treaty-making with the

Southeast tribes after his appointment; however, he did help to create a scheme for the administrative control of Indian-white relations that would have provided a measure of justice for both Indians and Whites had the American Revolution not destroyed it. For details on Atkin's career and writings see Jacobs (1967, 1985), Parish (1943), and Alden (1944). WILBUR R. JACOBS

Atkins, John DeWitt Clinton 1825–1908

Born in Henry County, Tennessee, Atkins graduated from East Tennessee University (University of Tennessee) in 1846. He studied law and passed the bar but never practiced. Instead he spent the next four decades engaged in political affairs. Atkins served in the Tennessee House of Representatives, 1849–1851, the State Senate of Tennessee, 1855–1857, and the United States Congress, 1857–1859. The Civil War saw him a lieutenant colonel in the 5th Tennessee Regiment in the Confederate Army, but ill health cut short his military career. Atkins then directed his energies toward political activity on behalf of the Confederacy until the war ended. After again serving in Congress, 1873–1883, Atkins served as commissioner of Indian affairs, 1885–1888, during which time the Dawes Severalty Act of 1887 became law. Atkins was in favor of this legislation, for he saw allotment as the best solution to the Indian "problem." For additional biographical information see Moore (1923). For statements of Atkins's policy see ARCIA (1885, 1886, 1887). ANDREA LUDWIG

Atkinson, Henry 1782–1842

Atkinson entered the Army in 1808 as a captain. After service in Louisiana and later in New England during the War of 1812, he moved west as commander of the Missouri Expedition in 1819. For the rest of his life he remained in the West, where he worked closely with William Clark in dealing with the Indians. In 1825 he and Benjamin O'Fallon served as joint commissioners to sign treaties of peace and friendship with the tribes of the upper Missouri Valley (Nichols 1963). Two years later Atkinson led troops into central Wisconsin to awe the Winnebago into an uneasy peace. In 1832 he commanded the forces engaged in the Black Hawk War against the Sauk and Fox tribes. He directed the removal of the Potawatomi from Missouri in 1837 and three years later moved the Winnebago from Wisconsin into Iowa. Atkinson considered himself a policeman of the frontier, not an Indian fighter, as he strove to prevent conflict between Whites and Indians and also between contending groups of Indians. Details of his relations with the Indians are in Nichols (1965). Official correspondence about his dealings with the Indians may be found in the Records of the Office of Indian Affairs and the War Records Branch of the National Archives, Washington, and in the Black

Hawk War Papers at the Illinois State Historical Library, Springfield. ROGER L. NICHOLS

Bacon, Nathaniel 1647–1676

Bacon was the leader of an unsuccessful rebellion of frontier residents against the royal governor of Virginia, Sir William Berkeley, in 1676–1677, in the course of which he died. Bacon's Rebellion was interpreted in different ways by historians in the three centuries following its occurrence, the most common interpretation being that it was an attempt at political reform in the colony. That interpretation, presented by Wertenbaker (1940) and Webb (1984), was challenged by Washburn (1957, 1987), who insisted that the conflict grew out of policy differences toward Indians held by the governor and by Bacon and his followers. Bacon insisted that the Indians—even those allied and under the protection of the English—had no rights that an Englishman need respect. Berkeley attempted to restrain unauthorized and treacherous attacks on the Indians by Bacon and his frontiersmen, but the attempt led to civil war in the colony, the burning of the capital Jamestown, and the exile of Governor Berkeley to the Eastern Shore of Virginia, from whence he was able to mount a counterattack and put down the rebellion before the arrival of English troops and commissioners sent from England by Charles II. WILCOMB E. WASHBURN

Baldwin, Frank D. 1842–1922

Born in Manchester, Michigan, Baldwin began a military career at the age of 19, serving as an officer in the Michigan volunteers during the Civil War. After the war he joined the regular army and served as an officer in the Indian wars of the Southwest frontier and on the northern Plains. In the late 1870s Baldwin served in Montana and skirmished with Sitting Bull at Red Water River in 1876.

During the 1880s Baldwin was Judge Advocate of the Military District of the Columbia, Washington Territory. In this capacity he adjudicated disturbances on the Moses and Colville reservations. He served actively in quelling the Sioux activities related to the Ghost Dance of 1891 around the Pine Ridge Agency, South Dakota.

In 1894, Baldwin was appointed agent of the Kiowa Agency at Anadarko, Oklahoma Territory, with responsibility for the Kiowa, Comanche, Kiowa-Apache, Wichita, Caddo, and Western Delaware tribes. During his tenure, he encouraged agriculture and stock raising, but with limited success in the difficult environment. He also worked against ratification of the Jerome allotment agreement of 1892, claiming that the Indian signatures were obtained by fraud. Originally Baldwin asked for a five-year postponement of the terms of the agreement; in 1897 he asked for an indefinite postponement, believing that frontier Whites would be able to gain control of the

Indians' land very quickly. Congress debated the Jerome agreement but authorized it in 1901, and the reservation allotment was carried out.

In 1898 Baldwin returned to military duty to serve in the Philippines during the Spanish-American War. For further information see A.B. Baldwin (1929), Miles (1911), Rister (1928), and Wellman (1947). HENRY E. FRITZ

Barton, Benjamin Smith 1766–1815
Born and educated in Pennsylvania and Europe, Barton was a teacher at the College of Philadelphia (W.P.C. Barton 1816; Jeffries 1969) and a member of the American Philosophical Society, Philadelphia, which houses his papers. Of his articles on various aspects of Indian culture (Barton 1788–1789, 1799; Bieder 1972:37–119), he is best known for his book *New Views of the Origins of the Tribes and Nations of America* (1797), which brought together Indian vocabularies gathered by correspondence and his own fieldwork in an attempt to discover Indian origins. ROBERT E. BIEDER

Bartram, William 1739–1823
William Bartram, son of the botanist John Bartram, spent his childhood at his father's internationally renowned botanical garden in Philadelphia, where he attended college. A brief and not very successful career as a merchant ended when William joined his father as his assistant and companion on an extended plant-gathering exploration through the Carolinas, Georgia, and East Florida, 1765–1766 (J. Bartram 1942). His own career as a naturalist was assured when a London physician agreed to support him in another collecting tour through the South (Bartram 1943), which became one of the most famous journeys into the Southern wilderness ever chronicled. In the course of his peregrinations, 1773–1777, William Bartram met and observed the Creek, Cherokee, and Choctaw (Bartram 1853, 1791). The 1791 work ranks among the half-dozen most important contemporaneous sources for the study of the Southeast Indians and their habitat during the late eighteenth century. The most authoritative edition is F. Harper (1958), which lists Bartram manuscript collections. LOUIS DE VORSEY, JR.

Beale, Edward Fitzgerald 1822–1893
Beale was attached to the U.S. Navy, participated in the conquest of California, and was the bearer of official dispatches to Washington announcing the discovery of gold in California. He resigned from naval service in March 1851 and was appointed in November 1852 by President Millard Fillmore as general superintendent of Indian affairs for California. In 1853, on the basis of his report on conditions of the California Indians, Congress authorized the president to establish five military reser-

vations on unoccupied lands, not to exceed 25,000 acres each, and appropriated $250,000 for removal of Indians to these reservations and for their support. Beale operated with difficulty partly because of problems caused by the issuance in 1851–1852 of unauthorized expenditures by three Indian treaty commissioners. The first reservation Beale founded was Tejon, sometimes called San Sebastian, between the San Joaquin Valley and Los Angeles. Beale's aim was to gather the California Indians on the reservations, clothe and house them, make them economically self-sufficient through farming, and protect them with a military detachment stationed on each reserve. Problems arose over Beale's accounts, and he was removed from office in June 1854. Beale's successor, T.J. Henley, approved of and continued Beale's general policies. Beale in 1857 purchased title to the Tejon Ranch, which included the Tejon Indian reservation after it was abandoned and the Indians were moved to Tule River. Beale served the federal government in several capacities after 1854 including a term as surveyor-general of California and envoy to Austria-Hungary, 1876–1877 (Beale 1954; Bonsal 1912; Crouter and Rolle 1960). ROBERT F. HEIZER

Beckwourth (Beckwith), James P. about 1800–1866
Beckwourth, son of Sir Jennings Beckwith and a mulatto, was born in Frederick County, Virginia, the family moving to Missouri about 1809. Except for employment, 1837–1838, by the U.S. Army in the Seminole Wars in Florida, Beckwourth's entire life was spent in close association with western Indians. Beckwourth went to the Rocky Mountains with William H. Ashley's 1824 expedition and again in 1825. He remained in the mountains until 1836, during which time he was employed by the Rocky Mountain Fur Company and the American Fur Company. He became a chief of the Crow Indians and with them engaged in numerous battles with other tribes. He trapped in the Southwest and made two journeys to California, remaining there from 1848 to 1856. In 1850 he discovered Beckwourth Pass. Returning to Colorado, he worked as a storekeeper for a while and was involved in the Sand Creek Massacre, 1864. He turned to scouting for the Army and died while on one of these assignments to the Crow Indians. For further information see Bonner (1856) and Wilson (1972). ELINOR WILSON

Beede, Cyrus 1828–1908
In a career in the Indian Service that stretched, intermittently, over a period of 30 years, Beede held positions as agent, chief clerk to the central superintendent, special agent, and inspector. His original appointment by President Ulysses Grant stemmed from his membership in the Society of Friends. Subsequent appointments were due in part to the influence of Sen. W.B. Allison of Iowa. A

fervent supporter of the Peace Policy, Beede also brought sound business training to his administration of Indian affairs (Anonymous 1908). WILLIAM T. HAGAN

Beeson, John 1803–1889

Beeson was born in Stoke, Lincolnshire, England, where he attended grammar school and at age 14 underwent a religious conversion to Methodism, an experience that later directed him into humanitarian reform work. He and his wife emigrated to New York State in 1830 and to Illinois in 1834. There he practiced farming, worked for the temperance cause, and aided slaves along the Underground Railroad. In spring 1853, he moved his family to Oregon, where the Rogue River Indian War, 1853–1856, convinced him that the Indians had been wronged, and he vowed to work for Indian rights "until justice was done." His efforts angered his Oregon neighbors, and in 1856 he was forced to return to the East Coast where he published and lectured on Indian rights, a crusade that occupied him for 30 years. In 1860, he published the only issue of *The Calumet* (Beeson 1860), a journal advocating the reform of Indian policy. The slavery issue and the Civil War distracted attention from the Indian question, but Beeson continued his work, meeting with President Abraham Lincoln and with congressional leaders. He organized public meetings and helped to initiate a movement for the reform of Indian policy. Beeson supported the federal government's Peace Policy in the 1870s and worked closely with several Indian rights groups. He advocated Indian citizenship and education and strongly opposed the suggested transfer of Indian affairs to the War Department. For more on his career see Fritz (1963) and Mardock (1971). Much of Beeson's correspondence on Indian policy is in the National Archives. ROBERT W. MARDOCK

Bent, Charles 1799–1847

Born in Virginia, Bent early moved to Saint Louis with his family. After several jobs he was attracted to the fur trade and eventually became a partner in the Missouri Fur Company. All this time he gained experience in dealing with Indians, and he even served briefly as subagent for the Iowa tribe. In 1828 Bent turned his attention toward the Santa Fe trade, joining with Ceran St. Vrain in a partnership that dominated the entire Southwest. In 1833 the partners built Bent's Fort on the Arkansas River and began trading with the tribes in the vicinity. From this position, Bent came to rule the trade with the Cheyenne, Arapaho, Kiowa, and Comanche. His influence and good reputation with the Indians enabled him to play a prime role in maintaining what peace existed along the Santa Fe Trail. When American troops occupied New Mexico in 1846, Gen. Stephen W. Kearny named Bent civil governor of the province. Indian affairs were chaotic in New Mexico at the time.

Bent's great experience with Indians led him to make one of the first realistic assessments of the problems facing the United States. His recommendations to the commissioner of Indian affairs for securing peace suggested that agents immediately be sent to the tribes and that the military establish forts in the Indian country (Bent 1846; Dunham 1952). Due to the uncertainty over the legal status of New Mexico, his proposals were not enacted until 1851, by which time considerable blood had been spilled. In early 1847, dissident Mexicans enlisted the aid of the Pueblo Indians in attempting a revolt in New Mexico. They succeeded in killing Governor Bent and several others before being crushed. Details on Bent's life are in Lavender (1954) and Dunham (1965). ROBERT A. TRENNERT

Beverley, Robert about 1673–1722

Born in Virginia and schooled in England, Beverley became a prosperous landowner and representative in the House of Burgesses. He is the author of *The History and Present State of Virginia*, published in London in 1705 and revised for a second edition of 1722, which remains one of the best sources on the coastal tribes of Virginia. Beverley's portrayal of the Indians is partly based upon the writings of John Smith, Father Louis Hennepin, Baron de Louis Armand Lahontan, and John Bannister and partly on personal observation. For example, he gives a long discussion on Indian religion derived from an Indian informant whom he plied with copious amounts of cider. What distinguishes Beverley's writing is his portrayal of the Indians as people with a culture that had much to offer Whites. He discusses the wampum, agriculture, weapons, tools, houses, recreation, and medicines of the Virginia Algonquians and the impact of European civilization on their own. Beverley's *History* was influential in bringing immigrants to Virginia. For biographical data and appraisals of Beverley's *History*, see L.B. Wright (1940, 1953), Beverley (1947), and Jacobs (1977). WILBUR R. JACOBS

Bland, Thomas Augustus 1830–?

Bland was born in Bloomfield, Indiana, was educated in the public schools, and studied medicine at the Eclectic Medical College in Cincinnati. He served as a surgeon in the Union Army during the Civil War. In 1864, he became editor of the *Home Visitor* (Indianapolis), founded the *Northwestern Farmer* in 1865, but moved to Chicago in 1871 to edit the *Scientific Farmer*. In 1877, he assisted Alfred B. Meacham on a lecture tour of the Midwest in support of a reformed Indian Peace Policy. Bland moved to Washington, D.C., in 1878 and became an editor (with Meacham and his wife, Mary C. Bland) of the *Council Fire*, a periodical dedicated to the promotion of the reservation system with eventual citizenship and assimilation of the Indians. During the next 30 years he served as president of the Eclectic Medical Society and published books on current public issues, farming, medicine, spiritualism, and Indian rights. In 1885 Bland and Meacham founded the National Indian Defense Association in Washington, D.C. By this time Bland had reversed his earlier position and insisted that the government should withdraw completely from its wardship over the Indians in order that they might have full cultural freedom. He and the Association worked to prevent the passage of the Dawes Severalty Act on the grounds that it was a menace to Indian tribal organization. After the passage of the act in 1887 Bland contended that the Indians should not be forced to take up land allotments although he admitted that severalty was probably the ultimate solution. Bland represented a minority view often standing well outside the mainstream of the Indian policy reform movement. For further biographical information, see Banta (1949–1981, 1). ROBERT W. MARDOCK

Bloomfield, Leonard 1887–1949

A Germanist and for decades one of the world's leading linguists, Bloomfield began about 1919 a systematic study of the Central Algonquian languages. He worked with Cree, Ojibwa, and especially with the Menominee Indians of Wisconsin, for whose language and way of life he had enormous respect and among whom he developed close friendships. His reconstruction of Proto-Algonquian, using the standard methods of comparative linguistics, is paradigmatic, and his description of Menominee, published posthumously in 1962, is one of the finest accounts of any language in the world. For biographical details and complete bibliography, see Hockett (1970). CHARLES F. HOCKETT

Boas, Franz 1858–1942

Trained as a physicist and geographer in his native Germany, Boas's interests shifted to ethnology after a geographical expedition to Baffinland in 1883. He settled in the United States in 1886, after the first of many field trips to the Indians of the Canadian Northwest. In the next few years he served as editor of *Science*, taught anthropology at Clark University, Worcester, Massachusetts, and supervised physical anthropological work for the Chicago World's Columbian Exposition of 1893. In 1895 he settled permanently in New York, where he was associated with the American Museum of Natural History until 1905, and with Columbia University until his retirement as professor of anthropology in 1936. By 1896, Boas had established himself as one of the country's leading anthropologists and had developed a systematic critique of the prevailing cultural evolutionary point of view. In a series of articles (culminating in Boas 1911a), he established the basis for modern anthropological thought on problems of race and cultural determinism. He published major contributions to two subdisciplines

Smithsonian, NAA: MNH 8302.

Fig 1. Franz Boas, wearing a yellow cedar-bark blanket and posing as a singer in a Kwakiutl hamatsa dance. This and other poses imitating various participants in the dance were the basis of life-size mannequins in a diorama in the U.S. Natl. Mus. (Smithsonian) (Hinsley and Holm 1976). Photographed Jan.-Feb. 1895.

of anthropology: the charter of modern descriptive linguistics (Boas 1911), and an attack on the static assumptions of classical physical anthropology (Boas 1910). These works, and his own ethnographic researches on the tribes of the Northwest Coast (especially the Kwakiutl), which continued until 1931, helped to define the pattern of North American Indian research (fig. 1). Boas played a crucial role in establishing anthropology as an academic discipline, and the several generations of his students included most of the leading figures in American anthropology down to 1950. Boas also had great impact on the race assumptions of American intellectuals generally, especially through the activities of his last decade, which were largely devoted to attacking Nazi racial theories. For biographical details and intellectual interpretation, see Kroeber et al. (1943), which contains a full Boas bibliography, Goldschmidt (1959), Herskovits

(1953), and Stocking (1974). For a somewhat critical assessment, see White (1963). For collections of Boas's shorter writings, see Boas (1940) and Stocking (1974). The Boas papers are in the American Philosophical Society, Philadelphia. GEORGE W. STOCKING, JR.

Bogy, Lewis Vital 1813–1877

Born in Missouri Territory, Bogy served in the Black Hawk War of 1832, graduated from Transylvania University in Lexington, Kentucky, with a law degree in 1835, and practiced law and politics in Missouri for many decades. He served in the Missouri legislature twice, in 1840, and in 1854, where he led the anti-Benton faction. Secretary of the Interior O.H. Browning appointed Bogy commissioner of Indian affairs in November 1866, and he served until 1867, when the Senate would not confirm his appointment. Bogy was in favor of negotiating an end to Indian land claims so that the frontier regions could be open to White settlement and development. Bogy's business and family connections with firms from which he had directed the Indian Office to procure supplies led to a congressional investigation (A.C. Davis 1867). In addition, Bogy's term as commissioner was entangled in partisan Reconstruction politics. His public career may be traced in the *Missouri Republican*, Saint Louis, and the *Missouri Statesman*, Columbia. Biographies may be found in Bay (1878), Reavis (1875:223–238) and Unrau (1979). ANDREA LUDWIG

Boone, Daniel 1734–1820

Boone was one of the truly important American frontiersmen. Born in Berks County, Pennsylvania, he moved with his family to the North Carolina frontier in 1750. At the outbreak of the French and Indian wars, Boone went as a wagoner and got his first taste of Indian fighting when Gen. Edward Braddock's army met defeat in July 1755. He began his serious penetration of Kentucky in the spring of 1769. In the following two years Boone established himself as an expert on frontier land location and was often consulted in litigation over conflicting claims. Following Lord Dunmore's War in 1774 Boone became associated with the Transylvania Land Company as a land scout and pathfinder. In 1774–1775 the Company was engaged in negotiating a land-cession agreement with the Cherokee. Anticipating the signing, Boone and a party of men blazed a trail through the Cumberland Gap and established the first site of Boonesborough on the Kentucky River. In January 1778 Boone was briefly held captive by the Shawnee. In the summer of 1778, he led the successful defense of Boonesborough against Indian attack. Once Indian raids against the Kentucky settlements had ceased, immigrants crowded in and Boone worked as an expert land locator and a competent surveyor. Until 1790 he also engaged in merchandising, tavern keeping, and farming. From 1788

to 1791 he served in the Virginia General Assembly, first from the Kentucky area, then from Kanawha County in western Virginia. In 1799 he and his family migrated to Missouri. He frequently was in armed conflict with the Indians, but at other times he came into friendly association with them. For additional information see Bakeless (1939), Boone (1823), Bruce (1934), Flint (1833), and Thwaites (1902). THOMAS D. CLARK

Bowles, William Augustus 1763–1805

Bowles began his association with the Creeks in 1779 when he ran away to them from his Maryland Loyalist regiment in Pensacola, rejoining it after a few months in the company of some Creek warriors. After the Revolution he went to the Bahamas, where British interests backed his return to the Creeks with arms and ammunition in 1788. He married Mary Perryman, a daughter of the Lower Creek leader Tom Perryman, by whom he had a son, Little Billy, and perhaps a daughter. In 1789–1791 he led a group of five young Creeks and and Cherokees to London with petitions addressed to George III, but failed to gain support for invading Mexico as "generalissimo" of the fictitious "United Nation of Creeks and Cherokees," for attacking the U.S., and for trading privileges in conflict with the Creek trade monopoly held by the British firm of Panton, Leslie and Co. based in Spanish Florida. On his return, the Upper Creek leader Alexander McGillivray placed a price on his head. In 1792 Bowles and a force of about 100 Lower Creeks took the Panton, Leslie store at Saint Marks, but Bowles was soon captured by the Spaniards and sent to New Orleans, then Spain, then Manila. On his way back to Spain in 1797, he escaped off the coast of Sierra Leone and went to England, where he adopted the title "Director-General of the Muscogee Nation" and took the supposed Creek name Eastajoca (perhaps a nickname, *ísti čó·ka* 'writings person'). Returning to the Lower Creeks he issued a proclamation on October 31, 1799, expelling all U.S. and Spanish agents from the largely imaginary "state of Muskogee." In 1800 with a force of Lower Creeks and Seminoles he briefly held the Spanish fort at Saint Marks. In 1803 the Upper Creeks turned Bowles over to the Spaniards in Mobile, whence he was sent to Havana where he died in captivity. Much of the evidence on Bowles's career is from his own self-promoting, almost megalomanic propaganda. A thorough, well-documented biography (Wright 1967) is severely biased in his favor; Sturtevant (1979) argued a different view. WILLIAM C. STURTEVANT

Braddock, Edward 1695–1755

Experienced in European military campaigns and with a reputation as a severe disciplinarian, Major General Braddock was sent to America as commander-in-chief of military forces at the beginning of the French and Indian

War in February 1755. After meeting with five colonial governors at Alexandria, Virginia, he led an army of 1,400 regulars, 700 colonials, and 8 Indian guides westward on a road cut through the wilderness toward Fort Duquesne, the French bastion at the forks of the Ohio River. Braddock's Indian guides, led by Indian agent George Croghan, met the first of 224 French soldiers and Canadians and 600 Indian warriors. On July 9 Braddock himself and over half of his army and officers were killed as Indian and French forces, using the natural protection of undergrowth, trees, and rocks, easily slaughtered the British troops, who maintained close formation. Unfortunately for the British, political rivalry between governors Robert Dinwiddie of Virginia and James Glen of South Carolina had prevented a force of 600 Cherokee warriors from joining Braddock's army. These Indians might have changed the course of the battle. For details, see Jacobs (1966), Gipson (1958–1960), McCardell (1958), Sargent (1855), and M.W. Hamilton (1976). WILBUR R. JACOBS

Brainerd, David 1718–1747

Born into the New England aristocracy, Brainerd was expelled from Yale for his advocacy of the Great Awakening religious movement. Denied a degree, he studied theology privately and in 1742 received both a license to preach in Connecticut and appointment as a missionary to the Indians by the Society in Scotland for the Propagation of Christian Knowledge. Beginning in April 1743, he ministered for a year to the natives of Kaunaumeek, between Albany, New York, and Stockbridge, Massachusetts, before persuading them to move to Stockbridge to be under the Rev. John Sergeant. In June 1744, having been ordained by the New York Presbytery, he began a brief peripatetic career among the Delawares, near present Easton, Pennsylvania, and Freehold and Cranberry, New Jersey. Although his own intense piety was exemplary, his tubercular condition and ignorance of the Indian tongue attenuated his religious impact on the Delawares. He served only four years in the field before his death. For further information see D. Brainerd (1793, 1749) and Edwards (1881). JAMES AXTELL

Bridger, James 1804–1881

Bridger was born in Virginia but moved to Saint Louis in 1812. At eighteen, he answered William H. Ashley's advertisement for "enterprising young men" and, from 1822 to 1839, was a trapper in the Rocky Mountains. He found the Great Salt Lake in 1824 and, from 1830 to 1834, owned the Rocky Mountain Fur Company with four partners. From 1840 to 1853, he operated Fort Bridger, on the Oregon Trail, in partnership with Louis Vasquez. From 1854 to 1868, he acted as guide and scout for many army explorations, railroad surveys, and hunting expeditions. From 1868 to his death, he lived on land he had bought near Kansas City.

Bridger married three Indian women: Cora, a Flathead, by whom he had three children; a Ute, who died giving birth to Virginia; and Mary, a Shoshone, by whom he had two more children.

Bridger was famous for his geographical knowledge and his tall tales. His Indian fighting was largely defensive. Although his knowledge of Indian customs was remarkable, he retained his identity as a White and his daughter, Virginia, who looked after him in his old age, married a White. For further information see Dodge (1905), Alter (1962), and Ismert (1968). HARVEY LEWIS CARTER

Brinton, Daniel Garrison 1837–1899

Brinton was born in Chester County, Pennsylvania, graduated from Yale University in 1858, and Jefferson Medical School in 1860. After the Civil War, he returned to Philadelphia to practice medicine, devoting his spare time to the study of American Indian mythology, language, and religion, particularly in Middle America. His over 200 publications include eight volumes on aboriginal American literature (1882–1890), a collection of essays (1890a), and several books on mythology (1868, 1882, 1897) in North America.

Brinton's primary scientific affiliation was with the American Philosophical Society in Philadelphia. He held the first North American university position in anthropology, beginning at the University of Pennsylvania in 1886. He proposed the first comprehensive classification of the Indians of North and South America, based on linguistic comparison (1891). He was the foremost American proponent of evolutionism, believing that the American Indian constituted a single race, culture, and linguistic family (Darnell 1967).

Brinton's personal papers are in the Rare Book Collection of the Van Pelt Library, University of Pennsylvania. REGNA DARNELL

Brown, Orlando 1801–1867

Brown, son of Kentucky's first representative to Congress, was born in Frankfort, Kentucky. He studied at Princeton and at Transylvania University, Lexington, Kentucky, where he received a law degree in 1823. Most of his life's work was spent as editor of the Frankfort *Commonwealth*. In 1840 he became interested in Whig politics, and this led him to an association with John G. Crittenden. With the election of Zachary Taylor in 1848, Crittenden managed to get Brown appointed commissioner of Indian affairs in 1849. Brown entered the office with reluctance and without any knowledge of Indian affairs. He soon discovered that Secretary of the Interior Thomas Ewing intended to run the Indian Office himself.

625

Two significant events occurred during Brown's administration. First, because White travelers had to pass through Indian territory to reach the lands acquired in the Mexican War, the Indian Office decided that a major treaty with the Plains tribes had become necessary, and the Treaty of Fort Laramie was signed in 1851. The second event revolved around Secretary Ewing's ordering payment of claims held by traders against several tribes. Since these claims had been declared fraudulent by the preceding administration, the Democratic party publicly charged Brown with fraud, and he resigned in June 1850 (Clift 1951). Manuscript materials concerning Brown's year as Indian commissioner are in the National Archives, the Kentucky Historical Society, Frankfort, and The Filson Club, Louisville, Kentucky (O. Brown 1849–1850, 1849–1850a, 1849–1850b). ROBERT A. TRENNERT

Browning, Daniel M. 1846–1903

Born in Benton, Illinois, Browning graduated from the State University of Indiana in 1866 with a law degree. He was active as a judge and in Illinois Democratic politics until 1893, when he was able to secure the appointment of commissioner of Indian affairs. With the recent conversion of many government jobs to the civil service, Browning found few opportunities to place his political associates in patronage jobs. During his term of office, 1893–1897, Browning relied on the bureaucracy for the routine administration of the department; and Congress and Secretary of the Interior Hoke Smith took the lead on policy. Browning was noted for encouraging Indian agents to enroll Indian children in government day schools rather than the contract schools run by religious groups, regardless of the parents' wishes, but his administration left little impact on the Indian Office (Hagan 1979). ANDREA LUDWIG

Brunot, Felix Reville 1820–1898

Brunot was born in Newport, Kentucky, but spent his childhood in Pittsburgh, Pennsylvania. He was educated at Jefferson College, Cannonsburg, Pennsylvania, and practiced civil engineering until 1842, when he entered the milling business in Rock Island, Illinois. In 1847 he returned to Pittsburgh, invested in the steel manufacturing industry, and began the philanthropic work that would occupy much of the remainder of his life.

In 1869 President Ulysses Grant appointed him to the Board of Indian Commissioners, whose duties were to oversee the expenditures of the Indian Bureau and the overall operation of the Indian Peace Policy. He served as the Board chairman, visiting western Indian tribes and working for the advancement of the civilization program. The board had no official authority over the interior Department or the Indian Bureau, and by 1873 its recommendations were often ignored. For this reason,

Fig. 2. Commissioner of Indian Affairs Charles H. Burke (seated) and Mrs. Redbird Smith (seated) after a meeting of the Cherokee Kituhwa Society founded by Red Bird Smith. Photographed in Cherokee Hills, near Gore, Okla., May 15, 1927.

and Congressional refusal to establish a separate department of Indian affairs, Brunot and the five remaining original Board members resigned in 1874. Brunot contended that the powerlessness of the Board made it ineffective in correcting the abuses in the Indian service and believed that a department of Indian affairs, with cabinet status, was the best instrument for the achievement of Indian rights and civilization.

Brunot continued to serve the cause of Indian rights through active support of the Peace Policy. He also served as president of the National Reform Association, 1873–1898; founded the Pittsburgh branch of the Evangelical Alliance; and served as a trustee of the YMCA, 1881–1898 (Slattery 1901). ROBERT W. MARDOCK

Burke, Charles H. 1861–1944

Burke was born in Batavia, New York, moved to Dakota Territory in 1882, and was shortly thereafter admitted to the bar. In 1898 he was elected as a Republican to the U.S. House of Representatives where he served from 1899 to 1907 and again from 1909 to 1915. As a member of the House Indian Affairs Committee, Burke actively supported the implementation of the Dawes Severalty Act of 1887, but in 1906, recognizing that certain of its provisions were harmful to the Indians, he authored a major amendment to it. The "Burke Act" (34 U.S. Stat. 182) freed Indians from the imposition of state laws during the 25-year trust period that accompanied allotment, postponed the award of citizenship until the expiration of the trust period, authorized the extension of the trust period beyond 25 years in the case of Indians who were judged incompetent to handle their own affairs, and empowered the secretary of the interior to lift restrictions on allotted lands prior to the expiration of the trust period for those Indians who were competent. Following his defeat for the U.S. Senate in 1914, Burke retired to Pierre, South Dakota, where he entered the real estate investment business.

In 1921 President Warren Harding appointed Burke commissioner of Indian Affairs. Throughout most of his eight years as commissioner, Burke was under severe attack by reformers, both those who believed assimilation should be accelerated and those who wished to abandon it. His attempts to expand the education and health programs were ineffectual because Congress did not appropriate enough funds, and Burke did not vigorously pursue greater appropriations. His controversial handling of issues of religious freedom in the Pueblos and the condition of Oklahoma Indians caused both President Herbert Hoover and the Senate Indian Affairs Committee to press for his resignation (fig. 2). For further information see Kelly (1979b) and Corey (1923). LAWRENCE C. KELLY

Butrick, Daniel Sabin 1789–1851

Butrick was a Presbyterian missionary affiliated with the American Board of Commissionerss for Foreign Missions, who labored among the Cherokees before and after their removal west. Born in Windsor, Massachusetts, he was ordained in Boston in 1817 and soon thereafter reached the Cherokee Nation, where he dedicated the rest of his life to the care of Cherokee souls. He was assigned to Brainerd, Carmel (Talonagy), Creek Path, Hightower, Haweis, Candy's Creek, and other mission stations in the East; in the West he was associated with Fairfield, Mount Zion, and Dwight Mission. However, Butrick preferred itinerant preaching to sedentary mission service. In 1823–1824 he traveled over 3,400 miles to 171 meetings, but for all these efforts he baptized only 18 adults and 25 children.

Butrick confronted chronic moral contradictions and personal crises. Enthusiasm for the missionary calling was interrupted by bouts of self-doubt and despair. Pragmatic neutrality in Cherokee political struggles vied with outspoken activism and outrage over the injustices of the local situation. His scholarly interests in certain aspects of traditional native culture clashed with acute dismay over polygamy, conjuring, ball games, stomp dancing, and drinking.

Butrick emigrated west with Richard Taylor's detachment of Cherokees in November 1838 and faithfully served the Cherokees from his arrival in Indian Territory in 1839 until his death.

Butrick's correspondence with mission officials in Boston and his diaries survive in the Houghton Library,

Harvard University. The material he collected to write a history of the Cherokees with John Howard Payne is on file at the Newberry Library, Chicago. RAYMOND D. FOGELSON

Calhoun, James S. about 1802–1852

Born in South Carolina, Calhoun moved in 1830 to Columbus, Georgia, where he prospered in the shipping business. During the Mexican War, he led two Georgia battalions and rose to the rank of lieutenant-colonel. In 1849 Calhoun was appointed U.S. Indian agent in Santa Fe. Though without any particular qualifications for the job, he proved to be an honest and capable administrator (Abel 1915). Unusually energetic, he made numerous recommendations and some of his proposals were implemented long after his death. The problems he faced were extremely difficult but not atypical: hostile Indians of various tribes and factions, unscrupulous Indian traders, an empty treasury, and corrupt local politicians. Receiving little money or support from Washington, he took matters into his own hands, issuing orders without authority, for example, to control trade with the Indians (L. Crane 1928). He complained frequently to the Indian Bureau and constantly requested additional military troops to stabilize the countryside. In this he was unsuccessful and his relations with the military mission in the area were often strained by personality clashes and disagreement on proposed actions. In 1849 Calhoun succeeded in negotiating a treaty with the Navajo. When the treaty failed to allay the belligerence of some tribal members, Calhoun authorized voluntary retaliatory expeditions and encouraged friendly Indians to make war against the tribe (Reeve 1939). In 1850 New Mexico was established as a territory, and Calhoun was appointed its first governor and superintendent of Indian affairs (Trennert 1975). Calhoun's correspondence and a biography are found in Abel (1915). HENRY E. FRITZ

Calhoun, John Caldwell 1782–1850

Born in South Carolina, Calhoun died in Washington, D.C., after 40 years of almost continuous national service. As secretary of war 1817–1825, Calhoun supervised Indian affairs. He promoted Indian removal to the west. He supported vigorously the factory system of Indian trade but saw it abolished in 1822 by Congress. By administrative action in 1824 he created the first Bureau of Indian Affairs, as part of the War Department. He initiated the long-term program for the civilization of the Indians, under an annual appropriation of $10,000, and arranged generous grants for buildings and tuition to mission schools. For details see Meriwether, Hemphill, and Wilson (1959–1984) and references given therein. W. EDWIN HEMPHILL

Carondolet, Francisco Luis Hector, Baron de
1748–1807

A nobleman of French origin who pursued a military career in Spain, Carondolet participated in the Algerian expeditions and in the capture of Pensacola in 1781. As *Intendente* and governor of the province of Guatemala, 1788–1792, he demonstrated abilities as an administrator and governor of Spaniards and Indians, founding towns, colonizing lands, and "civilizing" Indians. As governor of Louisiana, 1792–1797, he tried to maintain peace and security among the Indians, signing in 1793 the Treaty of Nogales with the Creeks, Cherokees, Choctaws, Chickasaws, and Alabamas, which ratified the agreements they had made with Spain since 1784. In 1795, with the Georgians selling Indian lands, he advised some 30,000 Indians to emigrate to the other side of the Mississippi. He tried to end the traditional warfare between Creeks and Chickasaws, succeeding in founding the fort of San Fernando de las Barrancas de Margot and seeking Choctaw mediation. He attempted to defend the Caddo, in the west, against the attacks of Choctaw invaders. He received embassies from all these tribes and supported them with gifts from Mobile, Pensacola, and Natchez. In 1798 he was transferred to Quito, Ecuador, as president and governor, where he served until his death. Documents on his career are in Spain in the Papeles de Cuba section of the Archivo General de Indias, Seville, and in the Estado section of the Archivo Histórico Nacional, Madrid. See also the biography by Larrea (1968). VICENTA CORTES ALONSO

Carson, Christopher 1809–1868

Born in Kentucky and brought up in Missouri, Christopher (Kit) Carson ran off to Santa Fe at 16. His career as a trapper began in 1829 and continued until 1842, when he visited Missouri. From 1842 to 1848, he won fame as a guide for John C. Frémont's first three explorations and as scout and courier in the Mexican War. From 1854 to 1861, he was Ute Indian agent at Taos. As Colonel (brevetted Brigadier General, 1865) of New Mexico Volunteers he campaigned against both Confederates and Indians, 1861–1865. In 1863 he led a military campaign against Mescalero Apaches. In 1864 he was in charge of pursuing Navajos and confining them at Fort Sumner, New Mexico. This plan was in response to the Navajo raiding of Pueblo livestock and the Navajo attack on Fort Defiance in 1860. His battle with Kiowas and Comanches at Adobe Walls in 1804 led to the first treaty with them in 1865. Settling in Colorado after the Civil War, he died after a trip to Washington on behalf of the Utes.

Carson's first wife was an Arapaho, by whom he had two children; his second, a Cheyenne; and his third, Josefa Jaramillo, a Mexican, by whom he had eight children.

Carson was no Indian hater, as often depicted. As a trapper he fought when attacked or robbed. He was a better than average Indian agent. The fictional Carson has often obscured the historical Carson. For further information see H.L. Carter (1968) and Guild and Carter (1984). HARVEY LEWIS CARTER

Cass, Lewis 1782–1866

Cass was born in New Hampshire, but as a young man he moved to Ohio, where he practiced law and served in the state legislature. During the War of 1812 he distinguished himself as an officer on the northwest frontier. In 1813 Cass began his long career in Indian affairs with his appointment as governor of Michigan Territory, a position he held until 1831. Dealings with the Indians were a major part of his official duties, and he promoted an orderly administration of the Indian service that would treat the Indians justly (Cass 1968). He was direct and fearless in his relations with them and traveled extensively in the Indian country. His interest in the Indians was scientific as well as administrative (E.S. Brown 1953), and he soon became one of the best-informed officials of the government on Indian matters, writing articles on Indian subjects (Cass 1826, 1827, 1830) and strongly influencing the development of American Indian policy in the period. Although deeply sympathetic to the Indians, Cass saw no future for them unless they accepted the civilization of the Whites, and he was active in negotiating treaties by which Indian land holdings were reduced. Having accepted Jackson's position on Indian removal, Cass was appointed secretary of war in 1831, and he became deeply involved in the removal of the Indians from the southeastern states. At the end of 1836 he was appointed minister to France, and his subsequent career as senator from Michigan, candidate for the presidency in 1848, and secretary of state in Buchanan's administration had little bearing on Indian matters. Details on his handling of Indian affairs are in Prucha (1967) and McLaughlin (1889). FRANCIS PAUL PRUCHA

Catlin, George 1796–1872

Born in Pennsylvania, Catlin attended the academy at Wilkes-Barre and in 1817 the law school of Reeves and Gould in Litchfield, Connecticut. He began practicing law in Susquehanna County, Pennsylvania, but his artistic interests soon prevailed. He was elected a member of the Pennsylvania Academy and exhibited 12 paintings at the American Academy of Fine Arts in New York in 1828.

Catlin said his decision to portray Indian life was prompted by seeing a delegation from a western tribe passing through Philadelphia. With William Clark's help in Saint Louis in the summer of 1830, Catlin began his lifelong task of recording and interpreting the tribes of the Great Plains. Between 1830 and 1836 he traveled from North Dakota to Oklahoma (Catlin 1841), painting some 500 portraits, landscapes, and scenes of Indian life in a rapid, direct, and accurate style (Ewers 1956). In 1837 he began exhibiting his paintings and Indian artifacts in the East, with the hope that Congress would purchase the collection. In 1839 he took his "Indian Gallery" to England, where it was received with enthusiasm.

Catlin displayed his collection in the Louvre, Paris, in 1845. He returned to England in 1848, lost his collection to creditors in 1852, and over the next six years made two long trips to South America. The first trip was extended up the West Coast of North America to Alaska. Paintings made during these trips and sketches of his early subjects were combined, during the next decade in Brussels, into a cartoon collection, which Catlin brought to New York in 1871 in a final, unsuccessful attempt to interest Congress in his life's work. Most of these cartoons now belong to the National Gallery of Art in Washington (fig.3). The original collection, redeemed by

Joseph Harrison of Philadelphia, was presented to the Smithsonian Institution by his widow in 1879 (Halpin 1965).

For further information see Donaldson (1887), Haberly (1948), and H. McCracken (1959). WILLIAM TRUETTNER

Chandler, Zachariah 1813–1879

Born in New Hampshire, Chandler moved to Detroit in the 1830s and became a successful businessman. He entered politics in 1848, was mayor of Detroit in 1851, and was elected to the United States Senate in 1857, where he remained until defeated in 1874. Grant then appointed Chandler, who had been a staunch Unionist, secretary of the interior. Chandler tried to reform the department, especially the Indian Office. Chandler left at the end of the Grant administration, returning to the Senate. Chandler's papers are in the Manuscript Division of the Library of Congress and in the Burton Historical Collection in the Detroit Public Library, Michigan. See the *Annual Reports of the Secretary of the Interior* and the

Natl. Gallery of Art, Washington: Paul Mellon Coll. 1965. 16.80.
Fig. 3. *Catlin Feasted by the Mandan Chief.* George Catlin met with Four Bears in July or Aug. 1832. Oil on card mounted on paperboard by George Catlin, 1865–1870.

records of the Interior Department in the National Archives for details of his term. For further biographical information see Trani (1975), Detroit Post and Tribune (1880), Harris (1917), and George (1969). ANDREA LUDWIG

Chouteau, Jean Pierre 1758–1849

Born in New Orleans, in 1764 Chouteau moved to Saint Louis, then a fledgling settlement founded by his father, Pierre de Laclède Liguest, and stepbrother Auguste. Together these three men turned the settlement into one of the most important trade centers for Indian and White wares. The family traded extensively among the Osage and recognized the importance of learning their language and customs. The Indians regarded the family highly, welcomed their trade, and allowed them to live among them when the need arose. Relations with other Whites proved complex for the Chouteaus since the territory was alternately claimed by the French, Spaniards, and English. Skilled in diplomacy, the Chouteaus managed to protect their business interests and strengthen their ties with the Indians without jeopardizing their relations with the regime in power. When the United States acquired the territory in 1804, President Thomas Jefferson sought an Indian agent who could resolve the continuing conflict in the regions, and Chouteau was commissioned as U.S. Indian agent for the Upper Louisiana region. Chouteau succeeded in his tasks as mediator; nevertheless, he fell under a great deal of criticism. It was the government's policy to provide the Indians with trade goods in hopes of establishing peace, and many suspected Chouteau of using this practice to his own commercial advantage. If this was in fact the case, the outcome was favorable to the United States, for during the War of 1812, Chouteau secured the Osages' loyalty to the United States. As a result, Saint Louis, an important trade center, remained free from attack. Despite Chouteau's success in pacifying Indian-Indian and Indian-White conflicts, he was relieved of his government duties in 1818. He thereupon returned to his family's trading interests, although he also willingly advised government agents working in the region as well as those working in Washington on Indian affairs. For further details see Foley and Rice (1983). HEATHER C. DODSON

Church, Benjamin 1639–1717/8

Born at Plymouth, Church began his career as a carpenter. Commissioned a captain in the Plymouth forces during King Philip's War, 1675–1676, Church distinguished himself against the Wampanoags in the later stages of the war, after recruiting his own volunteer force of Whites and Indians. He was the first commander in Plymouth or Massachusetts Bay to employ Indian troops and the first to make use of the natives' tactics of forest warfare. By his example, English fears and preju-dices against using Indians were broken down, enabling the colonies to achieve victory. As a result of his achievements during the war, Church's land holdings and political influence increased greatly. During King William's War, 1689–1697, and Queen Anne's War, 1702–1713, Major Church was called upon five times to lead expeditions against the Abenakis in Maine. Using the same tactics and many of the same men as in 1676, he again rounded up many prisoners with few casualties to his own troops. However, because of the larger scale of these wars and the lack of an effective English strategy, Church's tactics failed to produce the same spectacular results. Instead of being hailed as a hero, he met with severe criticism. While full of self-praise, Church's own account, recorded by his son, is the best history of his activities (Church 1865, 1867). For background, see S.A. Drake (1897). NEAL SALISBURY

Clark, William 1770–1838

Clark was born in Virginia, but as a boy he moved with his family to Kentucky. In the late 1780s and early 1790s he participated in several campaigns against the Indians living north of the Ohio River. After managing the family plantation for six years, in 1803 Clark became co-leader of the Lewis and Clark expedition, and on that historic journey he gained much knowledge of and experience in dealing with the Indians living along the route. In 1807 Clark became principal Indian agent for Louisiana Territory and brigadier general of its militia. In 1813 he became governor of Missouri Territory (the northern part of Louisiana Territory, after the admission of the state of Louisiana). Following the admission of Missouri to the Union as a state, in 1822 Clark was appointed superintendent of Indian affairs at Saint Louis. Both as governor and as superintendent of Indian affairs, Clark had jurisdiction over most of the tribes of the trans-Mississippi West and, except for a short time, those of Illinois. Known to them as the "Red-Headed Chief," Clark had a real sympathy for the Indians and sought to promote their best interests as he understood them. He supported the policy of removing Southeast Indians west of the Mississippi and played a large role in its execution.

Adequate through the expedition, but sketchy for the last 25 years of Clark's life, is Bakeless (1947). A detailed biography covering the period to 1813 is Loos (1953), and a brief general treatment is Steffen (1977). For further information see Osgood (1964) and Thwaites (1906). JOHN L. LOOS

Clum, John P. 1851–1932

Clum was born in New York the son of a poor farmer. After attending Rutgers College for a year, he obtained a job with the U.S. Signal Corps and was assigned to Santa Fe, New Mexico. In 1873, he was appointed Indian agent in charge of 4,500 Apaches at the San Carlos Reservation, Arizona. Sympathetic toward the Indians and honest in his dealings with them, Clum earned their respect and affection. Declaring self-government and self-enforcement as goals, he set up a tribal court and organized a force of Apache police who proved loyal, efficient, and reliable. However, his efforts led to occasional conflicts with the military and the Indian Bureau. In 1876 Clum became involved briefly in the entertainment business, traveling throughout the East with a "Wild Apache" show that he founded. The enterprise proved a financial failure and the entourage returned to Arizona after visiting Washington, D.C. ("Presents and Delegations," fig. 5, this vol.). In 1877 Clum and his Indian police gained fame by trapping Geronimo and his renegades at Ojo Caliente and arresting them—the only time the Apache leader was ever forcibly captured. Soon afterward, he resigned as agent because of disgust at Indian Bureau intrigues (Seymour 1941). Clum spent the rest of his life in the West. Initially he lived in Tuscon where he bought a newspaper. In 1880 he moved to Tombstone, Arizona, serving as its first mayor and as publisher of the *Epitaph*. His last years were spent in Los Angeles. The best account of Clum's life as Apache agent is found in Clum (1936). For further information see Hagan (1966). HENRY E. FRITZ

Cody, William, Frederick 1846–1917

One of the most mythologized figures of the American frontier, "Buffalo Bill" Cody was born in Iowa and grew up in the vicinity of Fort Leavenworth, Kansas. As a young man he participated in the Colorado gold rush, rode for a time with the Pony Express, and served as a scout for the Union army in Tennessee operations during the Civil War and in Kansas campaigns against the Kiowa and Comanche. In 1867–1868 Cody was employed to furnish meat for the Kansas Pacific railway construction crews, and by his proficiency in the slaughter of buffalo earned his famous nickname. Some of his exploits were glorified and popularized by publicist Ned Buntline, and Cody in 1872 took to the theater, playing himself in a series of action melodramas produced in Chicago and eastern cities. During the next decade he alternated between acting on the stage and scouting for the cavalry against the northern Plains Indians. In 1883 he organized his Wild West Show, which capitalized on his reputation as an Indian fighter and casually exploited Indian heroes, like Sitting Bull, with whom Cody maintained a friendship. The rest of his life was spent promoting the show on its national and European tours (fig. 4) and developing a ranch near present Cody, Wyoming.

Denver Public Lib., Western Hist. Dept.: F.9623.

Fig. 4. William F. Cody. left to right, Brave Chief, Eagle Chief, Knife Chief, Young Chief, all Pawnee; Cody; American Horse, Rocky Bear, Flys Above, and Long Wolf, all Sioux. Photograph by Anderson, New York, 1886.

Cody (1879) wrote an autobiography. R.J. Walsh (1928) analyzes the creation of the Cody legend, and Croft-Cooke (1952) and D.B. Russell (1960) examine his life. Photographs of Cody and his shows are in the Wanamaker Collection, Department of Anthropology, Indiana University, Bloomington. P. RICHARD METCALF

Cohen, Felix S. 1907–1953

Born in New York City, Cohen graduated from City College, studied philosophy at Harvard and law at Columbia, and engaged briefly in private practice. Cohen joined the staff of Solicitor Nathan Margold at the Department of the Interior in 1933. His 14 years at the Department involved a myriad of legal problems, many of which concerned the Indian—self-government, land titles, and treaty rights. He served in the Interior Department as legislative draftsman (Indian Reorganization Act of 1934), Assistant and Associate Solicitor, and as Chairman of the Department's Board of Appeals. Cohen gained a reputation as a skilled and tireless advocate, legislative draftsman, and administrator who directed a 250-lawyer litigation force. His most memorable accomplishment was the completion of the *Handbook of Federal Indian Law* (Cohen 1942). Not to be confused with the 1958 work of the same name, Cohen's book was based on his compilation, along with Theodore H. Haas of 46 volumes of federal laws and treaties. After leaving the Department in January 1948, he continued, while in the midst of a career that included law practice, teaching, and scholarly writing, as an advocate of Indian rights through Indian identity. Among other accomplishments, his argument won the right to vote for Indians in the two states where it was still denied them. There is a collection of some of Cohen's writings (L.K. Cohen 1960), and a complete bibliography in the 1969 printing of his *Handbook*. DONALD ROPER

Colden, Cadwallader 1688–1776

Born in Ireland, Colden obtained an A.B. at the University of Edinburgh and came to America in 1710. In Philadelphia, where he began a medical practice, Colden interested himself in science, which became a lifelong pursuit. In 1718, Colden moved to New York with the office of Master of the Weigh House. He held a series of offices, including that of surveyor general of New York, which enabled him to become a wealthy man by profiting from Indian land transactions and fees. As governor of New York, Colden also negotiated Indian treaties.

In 1727, in New York, he published the first edition of *The History of the Five Indian Nations Depending Upon the Province of New York in America*; the book was revised and enlarged in a 1747 London edition published in two volumes. The first volume narrates the history of Indian affairs and the history of the Iroquois tribes from the time of first contacts with Europeans through the

Natl. Archives: RG75-PU-WA-56.

Fig. 5. Commissioner of Indian Affairs John Collier with Hopi Indians. The men are Tawaguaptewa, right, village chief (vol. 9:529), and his adopted son Myron. Photographed at Oraibi, Ariz., Sept. 16, 1943.

Treaty of Ryswick in 1697. The second volume consists of a series of fur trade manuscripts that form a documentary history of the Iroquois and other tribes in the early eighteenth century. Colden's *History* is surprisingly modern in its emphasis upon the Indian form of government, the ecological impact of the fur trade on the beaver population, and the Iroquois culture in peace and war.

For details on Colden's life and historical work, see Jacobs (1973) and Nammack (1969). WILBUR R. JACOBS

Collier, John 1884–1968

Although Collier is best known for his attempts to reform federal Indian policy in the years 1923–1945, his entire life was devoted to a series of reform causes. The central theme running throughout his various activities was his denunciation of individualism and materialism and his championing of community enterprise and esthetic values.

From 1907 to 1919 Collier worked in the immigrant wards of New York City where he sought to create community organizations that would assume responsibility for political, economic, and cultural decisions affecting the neighborhood. In 1919 he left New York for California to work among immigrants and migrant workers there. In 1920 he lost his position with the state of California in the midst of the "Red scare." It was at this time that Collier discovered the Pueblo Indians of New Mexico. In 1921 he resolved to preserve the Indian way of life as the last example of community life in a world whose emphasis upon individualism, he believed, was tearing it apart.

From 1923, when he organized the American Indian Defense Association, to 1933 Collier provided the leadership for an assault upon the land allotment provisions and the assimilationist philosophy of the Dawes Severalty Act of 1887. He successfully defended Indian title to the remaining reservations, forced the removal of restrictions on the practice of Indian religious ceremonials, and prepared public opinion for further reforms enacted into law in 1934 in the Indian Reorganization Act. During his years as Indian commissioner, 1933–1945, Collier fought for the revival of Indian tribal governments, the rehabilitation and enlargement of Indian reservations, and the encouragement of Indian culture. However, he never succeeded in convincing Congress that the assimilation of Indians into White society should be abandoned as national policy. The Collier years witnessed a lessening of assimilationist pressure upon the Indians of the Southwest (fig. 5), but in other parts of the country, particularly the Dakotas and Oklahoma, the attempt to revive tribal societies met with only slight success. See Collier (1947, 1963), Philp (1977, 1979), and Kelly (1983). LAWRENCE C. KELLY

Collins, Henry Bascom 1899–1987

Collins graduated from Millsaps College, Jackson, Mississippi. After working for three summers for the Smithsonian at Pueblo Bonito, New Mexico, and receiving a master's degree from George Washington University, he was hired as an assistant curator in the division of ethnology of the Smithsonian's U.S. National Museum. From 1925 to 1929, Collins was mainly interested in the archeology of the Southeastern United States.

Collins was best known for discoveries at Saint Lawrence Island, Alaska, 1927–1937, proving for the first time that Eskimo cultures had ancient roots in the Bering Strait and were not recent arrivals from Canada as had been previously thought (fig. 6). On Saint Lawrence Island, Collins excavated a series of sites where he found evidence of an unbroken sequence of changes in Eskimo art styles going back 2,000 years. This research resolved nearly a century of scholarly squabbles and the concerns of Arctic peoples about their history.

In 1948, Collins began research on Canadian prehistory at the invitation of Diamond Jenness of the National Museum of Canada. Through excavations of Frobisher Bay, Resolute, Southampton Island, and other locations, 1948–1955, Collins provided important new data and interpretations on Dorset and Thule Eskimo cultures. He trained the first generation of Canadian nationals who specialized in Arctic prehistory. The Canadian work led Collins to a synthesis of Alaskan, Canadian, and Greenlandic prehistory.

Collins was president of the Washington Anthropological Society, 1938–1939, and was vice president of the Society of American Archeology in 1942 and 1952. During World War II, he directed the Ethnogeographic Board. In 1945 he helped found the Arctic Institute of North America, serving as director of its Board of Governors in 1948, as chairman of its Arctic Bibliography Committee, 1947–1967, and several times as a member of its Board of Governors. Collins was acting director of the Smithsonian's Bureau of American Ethnology during the last two years of its existence, 1963–1965. For a partial bibliography of his writings see volume 5:744–745. WILLIAM W. FITZHUGH

Colyer, Vincent 1824–1888

Colyer was born in New York City of English immigrant parents. One of seven children, and fatherless at an early age, Colyer worked in a store until age 19 when he became an art student under John R. Smith. He later studied at the National Academy of Design, was elected a member in 1849, and opened a New York studio. His canvasses reflected a strong sympathy for the anti-slavery movement, and upon the outbreak of the Civil War he raised a Black regiment and served as its commanding officer. An active member of the YMCA, he advocated organization of the U.S. Christian Commission to provide for the spiritual and physical welfare of the troops. After the war, he turned his attention to Indian rights, and in 1868 he became the secretary of the newly founded United States Indian Commission, a private organization devoted to the reform of Indian policy. In 1869, President Ulysses Grant appointed him to the Board of Indian Commissioners whose function was to oversee the expenditures of the Indian Bureau under the Peace Policy program. Serving as secretary of the Board, he traveled to Alaska, Arizona, and other western territories, 1869–1872, to help implement the reservation policy among the Indians of those regions. Colyer was convinced that all the tribes could be civilized and warfare ended if the humanitarian principles of the Peace Policy were fully applied. For further information on his Indian rights work, see his correspondence in the National Archives and Mardock (1971). ROBERT W. MARDOCK

Smithsonian, NAA: 4905.
Fig. 6. Henry B. Collins with Nunivak Eskimo children at Nash Harbor, Nunivak I., Alaska. Photograph probably by T. Dale Stewart or C.G. Harold, summer 1927.

Cook, Charles Henry 1838–1917

Born in Germany, Cook emigrated to the United States when 17. He served in the United States cavalry, 1857–1865, fighting in the Indian wars and in Civil War battles in New Mexico. After his discharge, he joined the Methodist church. From 1871 to 1877, Cook taught the first government day school for the Pima Indians. He worked as a trader and clerk 1878–1880 while conducting religious services for the Pima. He joined the Presbyterian church, was ordained in 1881, and thereafter worked as a full-time missionary. Under his guidance, seven churches were constructed among the Pima. In 1890, Cook founded what grew into the Cook Christian Training School. He baptized over 1,800 individuals. Much of his religious work was carried out in the Pima language. Cook was an outspoken defender of the Pima in their water rights problems. After 43 years among the Pima, he retired in 1913. The most complete references to Cook include Ladies' Union Mission School Association (1893) and J.M. Hamilton (1948). SUSAN BLOOM LOBO

Cooley, Dennis N. 1825–1892

Born in New Hampshire, Cooley went into business and then studied law. He moved to Dubuque, Iowa, in 1854 and began the practice of law. Politically active in the Republican Party, he served in the District Supreme Court of Iowa and in 1864 was appointed by President Abraham Lincoln as commissioner to South Carolina to decide title to property. Most important, he was secretary of the National Republican Congressional Campaign Committee in 1864, a post which appears to have led to his appointment as commissioner of Indian affairs in 1865 by his friend Secretary of the Interior James Harlan. Believing that administrative reorganization, higher salaries, and penal punishments might alleviate some of the graft in the Bureau, Cooley promoted these ideas. He also attempted to clarify the overlapping jurisdictions of the Army and the Bureau in the handling of Indian affairs. In other respects, he carried out Harlan's plans, which included assignment of Indians to reservations so that large tracts of land could be opened to settlement, and the assimilation of Indians into American culture. In 1865 Cooley chaired a commission that negotiated land cession treaties with tribes in Indian Territory. When his political support eroded, he resigned as commissioner in 1866 (Roberts 1979). ANDREA LUDWIG

Cooper, James Fenimore 1789–1851

Cooper was born in Burlington, New Jersey, but moved while very young to what is now Cooperstown, New York. He had no firsthand experience of a frontier life, and the only Indians he seems to have known were a few Christian Indians. What he knew about aboriginal Indian life he learned from John Heckewelder's writings. More important to him were certain notions of the primitive and heroic derived from the novels of Sir Walter Scott.

Cooper wrote nearly 50 novels, but he is remembered by most readers only for the five Leatherstocking Tales, especially *The Last of the Mohicans* (1826). He also dealt with Indian themes in other novels (Cooper 1829, 1843, 1848) and in three novels that dealt with the relations between a Black man and a Red man (Cooper 1845, 1845a, 1846). LESLIE A. FIEDLER

Cox, Jacob Dolson 1828–1900

Lawyer, amateur scientist, major general in the Union Army, and governor of Ohio, Cox was appointed secretary of the interior by President Ulysses Grant in 1869. As a reformer, he was instrumental in establishing the Board of Indian Commissioners and championed Grant's Peace Policy. Cox took a firm stand against political patronage, which led to his resignation in 1870. His papers may be found in the Oberlin College Library, Ohio, and in the Historical Society of Ohio, Columbus. There is a biography of Cox by Schmiel (1969) and a brief one in Trani (1975). See also Ewing (1902) and W. C. Cochran (1901). ANDREA LUDWIG

Crawford, Thomas Hartley 1786–1863

Crawford was born in Chambersburg, Pennsylvania, and after graduating from Princeton College in 1804 he studied and practiced law in Pennsylvania. He was elected to Congress in 1829 as a Jacksonian Democrat and served until 1833 when he became a member of the Pennsylvania state legislature. He first became involved in Indian affairs in 1836 when President Andrew Jackson appointed him to a commission to investigate alleged frauds in the purchasing of Creek allotments. Crawford's report was a condemnation of the fraud and speculation committed against the Creeks (Crawford and Balch 1836–1838). In 1838 President Martin Van Buren appointed Crawford commissioner of Indian affairs. As commissioner until 1845, Crawford proved to be an especially able and energetic administrator. He attempted to improve the administrative machinery of Indian policy, to expedite the removal of the Seminoles and other Eastern tribes to the West, and to promote tranquil Indian-White relations in the trans-Mississippi West. He also sought ways to speed up the acculturation process. In 1845 President James K. Polk nominated Crawford to a judgeship in Washington, which he held until his death (Lanman 1876). Details of his attitude toward the Indians and his handling of Indian affairs are in Prucha (1971) and Satz (1975, 1979, 1986). The largest collections of Crawford manuscripts are in the National Archives (Record Groups 75 and 107) and the Historical Society of Pennsylvania, Philadelphia (Joel R. Poinsett Papers). RONALD N. SATZ

Cresap, Thomas 1694–1790

Born in Skepton in Yorkshire, England, Cresap came to Baltimore at the age of 21 but almost immediately was the center of conflict between Maryland and Pennsylvania in what was known as the Conojacular War, a boundary dispute in an area on the Susquehanna River opposite present-day Columbia, Pennsylvania. Cresap lost. After next failing in a fur trading venture, he moved in 1741 to Old Town, a former Shawnee village located on the north bank of the Potomac River, about 15 miles above the later location of Fort Cumberland. Indians, particularly Iroquois, frequented Cresap's settlement.

In 1748 Cresap became a leader in developing the western land schemes of the Ohio Company of Virginia. During the early phases of the French and Indian War, Gen. Edward Braddock's forces spent much time at Old Town. Following the French and Indian War the Proclamation of 1763 forbade settlements in the lands west of the Alleghenies, but Cresap was a leader in ignoring the Proclamation, establishing settlements at Redstone Creek on both sides of the Monongahela River. Cresap participated in the Revolutionary War, although handicapped by old age. For his broader career see K.P. Bailey (1944). KENNETH P. BAILEY

Crespi, Juan 1721–1782

Father Crespi, a Spanish Franciscan missionary, arrived in the Americas in 1749 and went to Baja California in 1767 to supervise Mission La Purísima Concepción. He went to Alta California in 1769 as part of the settlement expedition headed by Gov. Gaspar de Portolá of Baja California, with Father Junípero Serra as its religious leader. Marching in two contingents from San Fernando Vellicatá in Baja California, the Portolá expedition established a mission and a presidio at San Diego, the first Spanish settlement in what is today the state of California. There the priests initiated their proselytizing of Alta California Indians. The expedition continued north to San Francisco Bay and returned to San Diego, continually making contact with Indians along the route (Priestley 1946:22–33). As the only priest to travel the entire 1,500 miles, Father Crespi was commissioned to assemble a composite diary of the journey, including a description of the Indians whom the expedition encountered.

In 1770, Father Crespi again marched north with Portolá. Arriving at Monterey Bay, he met Father Serra, who had come from San Diego by sea, and helped him found Mission San Carlos Borromeo at Carmel. Father Crespi later participated in and wrote about two other expeditions: Pedro Fages's 1772 land exploration of the San Francisco Bay area and Juan Pérez's 1774 voyage that landed in what is today Canada. Following his return to Carmel in 1774 with Pérez, Father Crespi devoted himself to mission activities until his death. Most of his efforts involved the proselytizing and converting of California Indians to Roman Catholicism.

Father Crespi's special contribution came in the form of his diaries, correspondence, and mission records. His diaries, in particular, have become one of the basic records and most widely used sources on eighteenth-century Spanish California. These included perceptions of California Indian life, Indian-Spanish relations, and the impact of the Catholic Church on California Indians. Crespi also wrote about Canadian Indians observed during the 1774 Pérez voyage. The basic published source is Crespi (1927), which contains the diaries. See also Priestly (1946). CARLOS E. CORTÉS

Crocket, David 1786–1836

Crockett began life in Greene County, North Carolina. Often called a champion of Indian rights, he first rose to prominence serving in the military under Andrew Jackson in the Creek Indian War of 1813–1815, where he participated in several battles. About 1818 Crockett began a career in Tennessee politics and eventually served in the state legislature between 1821 and 1824. He was elected to Congress in 1827. As a congressman he became involved in the fight to defeat the Indian removal bill of 1830. He is reported to have delivered a speech in the House of Representatives on May 19, 1830 (later published under his name) attacking Jackson and the removal bill. His opposition to the bill was widely used by northern humanitarians in their crusade to protect the homelands of the Southeast Indians, but to no avail. Crockett's support for the Indians may have been politically motivated (Shackford 1956). After the passage of the removal bill Crockett became aligned with the Whig party. He lost his congressional seat in 1835 and moved to Texas where he died at the Alamo.

Biographies are numerous and not always reliable. Various approaches are Crockett's autobiography (1834), Rourke (1934), and Shackford (1956). ROBERT A. TRENNERT

Croghan, George ?–1782

Croghan, an Anglican, came to Pennsylvania from Ireland in 1741 and engaged in the Indian trade, becoming within a few years the colony's largest trader, with a home base in what is now Cumberland County. His operations were mainly in the Ohio Country. Ruined by the French invasion of the Ohio Valley in the early 1750s, Croghan was with Col. George Washington on the Fort Necessity campaign in 1754, and the next year he led Gen. Edward Braddock's Indian scouts. Continuing active in the French and Indian War, he was with the army when it captured Fort Duquesne.

For the next 15 years he supported Sir William Johnson as his principal deputy to the western Indians. A heavy and unsuccessful land speculator, he made his home at Pittsburgh. Croghan's tremendous influence over the natives was generally acknowledged. Opposed to Gen. Jeffrey Amherst's Indian policy, he went to London in an unsuccessful effort to reorganize the Indian department. Huge purchases of land in New York led to his building a large establishment at Lake Otsego, but by the early 1770s he was again bankrupt and in exile at Pittsburgh.

Forced to come East by the Revolutionary authorities at Pittsburgh, who did not trust him, he died at Philadelphia in obscurity and poverty. For further information see Volwiler (1926) and Wainwright (1947, 1959). Croghan's personal papers are at the Historical Society of Pennsylvania, Philadelphia. NICHOLAS B. WAINWRIGHT

Croix, Teodoro de 1730–1791

Born near Lille, France, Croix entered the Spanish Army at the age of 17, serving in Italy and Flanders, and receiving the cross of the Teutonic Order in 1756. In 1766 he accompanied his uncle, Viceroy Carlos Francisco de Croix, Marqués de Croix, to Mexico, where he rose to the rank of brigadier and was castellan of Acapulco and inspector general of New Spain troops. He returned to Spain in 1771–1772, where he served with his former Flemish company until 1776, when he was appointed commandant general, directly responsible to the Crown, of the new military government of the vast interior provinces—New Vizcaya, Sonora, Sinaloa, the Californias, Texas, New Mexico, Coahuila—founded chiefly for the purpose of solving the increasing problems of the long, thin line of defense of the northern frontier of New Spain against the depredations of hostile Indians, especially the Apache and Comanche. He administered the interior provinces until 1783, when he was appointed Viceroy of Peru, where he served until 1790. The task he faced in creating a new system of civil and military government for the interior of New Spain to subdue the hostile tribes and guard against encroachments by the English on the east and the Russians on the northwest was enormous, and scholars differ about the efficiency and success of his measures (A.B. Thomas 1941; Bobb 1962). For further information see Alessio Robles (1938) and de Palo (1973). ELEANOR B. ADAMS

Crook, George 1829–1890

Native of Ohio and graduate of West Point in 1852, Crook became the Army's foremost Indian fighter in the final quarter-century of hostilities. Quiet and unpretentious, he developed both military and diplomatic skills sharpened by insight into Indian mentality and culture. Better than any other general he understood the military conditions and requirements of Indian warfare. He also deeply sympathized with the Indians and lamented their treatment by the government and frontier settlers. Highlighting Crook's career were the Paiute operations of

1866–1868, the Tonto Basin campaign in Arizona in 1872–1873, the Sioux War of 1876, and Apache operations in 1882-1886. Crook papers are in the Rutherford B. Hayes Memorial Library at Fremont, Ohio, and the U.S. Army Military History Research Center at Carlisle Barracks, Pennsylvania. See also Bourke (1891), Crook (1946), and Vaughn (1956). ROBERT M. UTLEY

Curtis, Edward S. 1868–1952

Curtis was born in Wisconsin but reached manhood on the shores of Puget Sound. He became a photographer, largely self-trained, and in 1895, after much landscape work, began to focus on Indians, funding his extensive fieldwork from the profits of his successful Seattle portrait studio. In 1906 the immensely wealthy J. Pierpont Morgan agreed to finance Curtis's project to produce *The North American Indian* (Curtis 1907–1930). Curtis established The North American Indian, Inc., and while untrained himself, employed able Indian and White researchers, including A.B. Upshaw, George Hunt, W.E. Myers, and Frederick W. Hodge, to amass and edit ethnographic material covering over 80 different peoples throughout western North America. Curtis considered Indians a "vanishing race," and many of the thousands of images he produced for both his scholarly text and popular publications (for example, Curtis 1914) are elegiac in mood or reconstructions of bygone customs (Lyman 1982). He made movie footage of Hopi ceremonies as early as 1904 and used it, together with music and slides, in an elaborate "picture-opera" in 1911 (Gidley 1987). In 1914, working with the Kwakiutl, Curtis completed the first feature-length narrative documentary film, *In the Land of the Head-Hunters,* and later worked intermittently in Hollywood (Holm and Quimby 1980; Gidley 1982). As his major text appeared only in a limited edition, it fell into oblivion until a revival in the 1970s. Biographical data may be found in Graybill and Boesen (1976). MICK GIDLEY

Cushing, Frank Hamilton 1857–1900

A member of the first Bureau of American Ethnology expedition to the Southwest in 1879, Cushing is generally credited with having laid the foundations for scientific study of the ethnology and archeology of the area. The first anthropologist to study a culture as participant observer, he remained at Zuni Pueblo from 1879 to 1884, living with the family of the Zuni governor. He learned the Zuni language, adopted Zuni dress, and was accepted into the tribe, eventually winning admission to the Bow Priesthood and appointment as First War Chief.

Largely self-trained in his profession, Cushing built on skills developed during his boyhood in central New York, when he spent much time in the collection and experimental reproduction of Indian artifacts. After one term at Cornell University, he was appointed to the Smithsoni-

Smithsonian, NAA: MNH S.I. 8254.

Fig. 7. Frank Hamilton Cushing posed for mannequin of Sioux warrior figure that became part of the exhibits of the U.S. Natl. Mus. (Smithsonian). Photographed about 1894.

an Institution; he maintained that connection the rest of his life (fig. 7).

In 1887–1888 Cushing directed the Hemenway Southwestern Archaeological Expedition, discovering and excavating, near Tempe, what was probably the largest pre-Spanish community in southern Arizona. The resulting collection went to the Peabody Museum of Harvard University. Later, in the Florida Keys, Cushing discovered the ruins of an Indian civilization, until then entirely unknown, whose elaborate settlements had been constructed over the water on mounds artificially built up out of sea shells. The large collection derived from his excavations there was divided between the Smithsonian and the University of Pennsylvania Museum.

His major writings are about Zuni (1883, 1896, 1901, 1920, 1941). Probably his most influential contribution, apart from pioneering the participant observation approach and the practice of experimental reproduction of

Indian craftwork, was his exposition of Zuni "mytho-sociologic" organization (F.H. Cushing 1896).

Cushing's papers are mainly divided between the Smithsonian National Anthropological Archives and the Hodge-Cushing Collection of the Southwest Museum, Los Angeles. Biographical information and comment on his professional career may be found in McGee et al. (1900) and in articles by Fontana (1963), Pandey (1972), and J.D. Green (1975). Other important sources are Haury (1945) and Brandes (1965). For a bibliography of works by and about Cushing, see especially Brandes, Green, and Pandey. JESSE D. GREEN

Custer, George Armstrong 1839–1876

Flamboyant, unorthodox, contradictory, intensely controversial in his own time and later, Custer has come down in history and legend as the best known of the U. S. Army's Indian-fighting generals. "Custer's Last Stand" is firmly planted in the national memory. Graduated from the U.S. Military Academy in 1861, Custer achieved fame and high rank as a hard-hitting Civil War cavalryman. Ending the war a major general at the age of 25, he became lieutenant colonel of the regular Seventh Cavalry in the shrunken peacetime army. In 1867 he commanded a column in Gen. W.S. Hancock's campaign against the southern Plains Indians in Kansas. Court-martialed and suspended for a year because of certain alleged offenses in this campaign, Custer returned to duty to win the Battle of the Washita, November 27, 1868, against Black Kettle's Southern Cheyennes and to participate prominently in Gen. P.H. Sheridan's subsequent operations in Indian Territory and Texas. From 1873 to 1876 Custer and his regiment garrisoned Fort Abraham Lincoln, Dakota Territory. In 1873 he commanded the cavalry arm of Gen. D.S. Stanley's escort for the Northern Pacific Railroad survey and fought two actions with Sitting Bull's Sioux on the Yellowstone. In 1874 he led an expedition that explored and discovered gold in the Black Hills, part of the Sioux Reservation. In the Sioux War of 1876, which sprang in part from the violation of the Black Hills, Custer was a subordinate commander in one of the three columns that converged on the Sioux country of the Powder and Yellowstone River valleys. On June 25, 1876, Custer attacked a huge Sioux and Cheyenne village on the Little Bighorn River in south-central Montana. Part of the regiment succeeded in holding out until help came, but Custer and five companies, about 225 officers and soldiers, fell before the onslaught of overwhelming numbers of warriors. Of Custer's immediate command, none survived.

Custer's career is voluminously documented, but see especially E.B. Custer (1885), W.A. Graham (1926, 1953), E.I. Stewart (1955), Monaghan (1959), and Connell (1984). ROBERT M. UTLEY

Dale, Thomas ?–1619

After two decades of service with English forces in the Netherlands, Dale in 1611 was hired by the Virginia Company of London to discipline its disorderly colony. During five years as marshall and sometimes acting governor, Dale ended the strife between settlers and Indians that had existed since 1607. When he failed to draw Chief Powhatan into open combat and could not crush the Indians in scattered raids, Dale kidnapped and held hostage the chief's daughter, Pocahontas, until Powhatan met English demands. In the interval, Dale had Pocahontas instructed in Christianity. She soon converted to Anglicanism, married John Rolfe (after Dale consented to Rolfe's famous request for permission to marry "one whose education hath bin rude, her manners barbarous, her generation accursed"), and bore a son Thomas, named for Dale. In 1616 Dale and the Rolfes visited England to promote the colonial venture. After his wife's death in 1617 Rolfe returned to Virginia while Dale turned his attention to the East Indies where he died of disease. For further information see A. Brown (1890, 2: 869–874), P.A. Bruce (1929, 1: 43–56), and Hamor (1615). ALDEN VAUGHAN

Dart, Anson 1797–1879

Born in Brattleboro, Vermont, Dart became a druggist in New York City, then moved to Wisconsin in the 1830s to speculate in real estate. Because of his strong support of the Whig Party, Dart was appointed first superintendent of Indian affairs under Oregon's territorial government in 1850. Shortly after his arrival in the Pacific Northwest in October 1850, he began to suppress the liquor trade, enforce the Intercourse Act as amended in 1847, and settle increasingly difficult Indian-White relations. The Oregon Donation Land Act, operative 1850–1854, brought thousands of land-hungry Americans into the region. Dart had to secure land cessions from Indians who, in many cases, had already experienced flagrant seizure of their homes, hunting grounds, and fishing sites. In 1851 he visited tribes east of the Cascades and selected the site of the Umatilla Reservation. He promised that the government would not interfere in the Indian religions and that tribes should decide on which missionaries and teachers were to settle in their lands. On the coast Dart secured treaties with the Chinookans and Tillamooks, setting aside specific reservations. He treated with the Clackamas and a dozen bands of Athapaskan speakers on the southwest Oregon coast. Dart's 13 treaties ceded six million acres, but, though he went to Washington, D.C., with his agreements, none was ratified by the Senate. Dart held other government posts, including one in Europe. The only biography of Dart is Anonymous (1941). STEPHEN DOW BECKHAM

Dawes, Henry Laurens 1816–1903

Born in Cummington, Massachusetts, Dawes was educated at Yale College. He joined the bar in 1842, and, having moved to Pittsfield, began a successful career in state politics, holding a number of elective offices. He entered Congress in 1857 and served there continuously until his election to the Senate in 1875. He retired from the Senate in 1892. Dawes engaged in a wide range of legislative activities in both houses of Congress but was best known for his work as chairman of the Committee on Indian Affairs in the Senate, a post he held for 16 years. His greatest contribution to Indian affairs was the Dawes Severalty Act of 1887, which enrolled individual Indians as citizens of the United States and awarded them land as their private property. He was a leader of the assimilation movement, which was designed to incorporate the Indian fully into American life.

Despite the frequent failings of the Dawes Act to transform Indian customs and the increased criticism of assimilation in the 1890s, Dawes argued adamantly that the only long-range solution to the Indian problem was the absorption of the Indian into American life. In this cause, he actively supported educational efforts and the work of humanitarian groups. In his retirement he served as head of the commission sent to the Five Civilized Tribes to persuade them to abandon voluntarily their tribal governments. Despite the logic of his absorption policy and the letter of the law, which permitted Indians to select land anywhere in the public domain, Dawes continued to support the idea that educated Indians should return to their former reservation areas and serve as missionaries of civilization among other Indians. The apparent failure of the assimilation policy led to sharp criticism of the Dawes Act by 1900.

Dawes's papers are in the Library of Congress, and the papers of the Dawes Commission are at the Oklahoma Historical Society, Oklahoma City. For further information see Dawes (1880, 1899), Hoar (1903), and Gilcreast (1967). E. ARTHUR GILCREAST

Denver, James William 1817–1892

Denver's two temporary appointments as commissioner of Indian affairs were minor phases of his colorful public career. He is best known for lending his name to the capital of Colorado. A graduate of Cincinnati Law School, Ohio, in 1844, he served in the Mexican-American and Civil Wars, resigning with the rank of brigadier-general. Between these conflicts, he traveled to California, was elected to that state's Senate in 1851, was appointed secretary of state of California in 1853, and represented California in the United States Congress, 1855–1857, where he chaired the Select Committee on Pacific Railroads (Smiley 1901). President James Buchanan appointed him commissioner of Indian affairs (April 1857), governor of Kansas Territory in December

1857, and again commissioner in October 1858. Denver continued the policy of concentrating and confining Indians via treaty and land title extinguishment. He practiced law from the end of the Civil War until his death.

A thorough, well-documented, but uncritical biography is Barns (1949); see also Chaput (1979). Many of Denver's papers are located in the Manuscript Division of the Library of Congress and the Division of Manuscripts in the University of Oklahoma Library at Norman. ANDREA LUDWIG

De Smet, Pierre Jean 1801–1873

Fascinated with Indians, De Smet left Belgium to join the American Jesuits in 1821 and was ordained in 1827. When the Roman Catholic hierarchy entrusted to Jesuits the evangelization of the trans-Mississippi tribes, De Smet worked among the Potawatomi, within the ancient tradition of Reductions and cultural accommodation, 1837–1839. Responding to the Flathead appeals, he founded a Northwest Jesuit mission network from the Rockies to the Pacific, 1840–1846. Not a systematic missionary thereafter, he worked irregularly with over 100 tribes, notably the Blackfeet, Coeur d'Alene, Crow, Flathead, and Sioux, baptizing thousands. He served as publicist for the Indian to Europe by prolific writings in six languages and by 16 trips to Europe, and he channeled men and money to the missions. Of impressive physique and charm, his appeal to Indians had no parallel in the nineteenth century, a phenomenon amply attested by military, political, frontier, and Indian notables. Outstanding as a peacemaker, both officially for the government seven times and also between tribes, he penetrated Sitting Bull's camp to stop a war in 1864. His voluminous writings on the Indians can be sampled in De Smet (1843, 1847, 1863, 1863a, and 1905); see also Laveille (1915). ROBERT I. BURNS, S.J.

Dewdney, Edgar 1835–1916

An elected Member of the Canadian Parliament, 1872–1879, Dewdney was appointed Indian Commissioner for the North-West Territories in 1879 at a time when the buffalo were being destroyed and Indians were moving to their reserves. Although Métis unrest resulted in the Northwest Rebellion of 1885, most Indians refrained from joining because of Dewdney's handling of the situation. He was appointed lieutenant-governor of the territories in 1881, concurrent with his post of Indian Commissioner, and had his term extended to 1888 partly as the result of petitions from Indians. He was superintendent-general of Indian affairs for Canada, 1888–1892, and lieutenant-governor of British Columbia, 1892–1897. For further details, see Baptie (1968) and H.J. Morgan (1898). HUGH A. DEMPSEY

Dickson, Robert about 1765–1823

Dickson was born in Scotland, migrated to Canada about the close of the American Revolution, and entered the fur trade. He was employed in 1787 as interpreter and storekeeper of government goods at the great Indian council held at Michilimackinac. As a result of that activity he began trade with the Sioux. He and his associates established trading posts in the interior of the Upper Mississippi Valley within the area bounded by the Mississippi, the James, and the DesMoines rivers. His chief post was at Lake Traverse, where in 1797 he married the sister of Red Thunder, a Sioux chief. Dickson raised his family in the midst of her people.

At first friendly and helpful to the United States, Dickson later became antagonistic, because of the Indian policy of the United States and restrictions imposed on his trade west of the Mississippi after the acquisition of Louisiana. When the War of 1812 broke out, Isaac Brock of Upper Canada chose Dickson as agent to keep the Indians of the Northwest friendly, and to lead them to Canada to join the British forces. Dickson led a party of Sioux, Winnebago, and Menominee in the British capture of Michilimackinac, July 17, 1812, and indirectly aided in the capture of Detroit.

Dickson's power and influence awakened jealousy in the military men in the Northwest and led to his arrest at the end of the war and dismissal from service in 1815. A hearing in London cleared his name. At the behest of Thomas Douglas, earl of Selkirk, Dickson undertook to create an agricultural and industrial settlement of Indians and traders on the site of Grand Forks, North Dakota. However, Selkirk and Dickson died before it could be developed.

Dickson's papers in the United States are in the State Historical Society of Madison, Wisconsin, and the South Dakota Historical Society, Pierre. In the Canadian Public Archives, Ottawa, see Series C (Military Affairs), Series S (Secretary of State Papers: Indian Affairs Upper Canada), and the Selkirk Papers. For further information see Coues (1895), Cruikshank (1892), Kellogg (1935), and Tohill (1928–1929). A.P. NASATIR

Dole, William Palmer 1811–1889

Born in Vermont, Dole moved with his parents to Ohio and later to Indiana, where he became a successful merchant and politician. He served for eight years in the Indiana legislature, then moved to Paris, Illinois, in 1860, where he began to take a prominent role in Republican politics. He was a delegate to the Republican National Convention in Chicago in 1861, and he was one of the political leaders who helped to convince Indiana delegates to vote for Lincoln. He was appointed commissioner of Indian affairs in 1861, and served until July 1865, longer than any other commissioner until William Jones took the office in 1897.

Dole sought to develop a reservation system that would guarantee the Indians peaceful tenure of their land and help them to become assimilated. He looked upon the treaty system as the best method for securing Indian rights in the face of a hostile Congress. Pursuing this goal, Dole and his agents negotiated about 40 Indian treaties and managed to get about half of them approved, including several treaties with Indians of the far Southwest. Contrary to Dole's recommendation, Congress consistently refused to recognize aboriginal land titles for the Southwest tribes, but Dole's treaties helped to provide the basis for successful claims by these Indians a century later. He was forced out of office by the scandal of the Sand Creek Massacre, Colorado Territory, in 1864, although he was not directly involved in the affair. He lived in Washington, D.C., for the rest of his life, working as a claims agent. See H. Kelsey (1979) and Carmony (1971). HARRY KELSEY

Dorsey, James Owen 1848–1895

Dorsey entered the Theological Seminary of Virginia in 1867 and in 1871 was ordained a deacon of the Episcopal Church. From 1871 until 1873 he worked as a missionary among the Ponca. He was then forced by ill health to return to parish work in Maryland, where he began to compile a grammar and dictionary of the Ponca language. In 1877 Joseph Henry, Secretary of the Smithsonian Institution, referred Dorsey to Major John Wesley Powell who had just been given charge of the Smithsonian's collection of American Indian vocabularies. In 1878 Powell hired Dorsey to undertake ethnological study among the Omaha. Returning to the newly founded Bureau of Ethnology in 1880, Dorsey prepared an important work on Omaha sociology (Dorsey 1884) and continued his studies of the Omaha-Ponca language. His was the first definitive classification of the Siouan linguistic family (Dorsey 1885). He made numerous field trips to other Siouan groups—Winnebago, Iowa, Oto, Quapaw, Kansa, Osage, Dakota, Biloxi, Tutelo—as well as an extensive linguistic survey of the tribes of the Oregon coast (Dorsey 1889). Dorsey prepared major works on Siouan religion (Dorsey 1894), Omaha and Ponca mythological and historical texts (Dorsey 1890, 1891a), Siouan sociology (Dorsey 1891, 1897), the Biloxi language (Dorsey and Swanton 1912), and edited a Dakota dictionary, grammar, texts, and ethnography (Riggs 1890, 1893). Most of Dorsey's material, including extensive Siouan vocabularies and texts, is unpublished and in the Smithsonian National Anthropological Archives. For biographical details see Hewitt (1895). RAYMOND J. DEMALLIE

Dougherty, John 1791–1860

As a Kentucky recruit of the Missouri Fur Company, Dougherty joined Manuel Lisa's upriver expedition of

1809. In 1810 hostile Blackfeet ruined an effort to establish a post at Three Forks, and Dougherty joined Andrew Henry's party in crossing the Continental Divide, the first American party to do so since Meriwether Lewis and William Clark. Exploration of the Teton-Yellowstone region followed. Extensive knowledge gained in trade with various tribes of the Nebraska-Dakota region secured for Dougherty, in 1819, the job of interpreter and deputy under Benjamin O'Fallon, Indian agent at Fort Atkinson (above Omaha). At this outpost he became a key figure in events related to the Stephen Long expedition and explorations of the Rocky Mountain Fur Company. In 1827 Dougherty succeeded O'Fallon as Indian agent for the Upper Missouri tribes, a post he held until 1839. During this period his agency was at Belle Vue (below Omaha), but he traveled frequently among Saint Louis, Fort Leavenworth, and the villages of the Iowa, Kansa, Pawnee, Omaha, Oto, Sioux, and other tribes. His diplomatic skills and forceful personality gained him wide praise, but his campaign against the use of alcohol among the tribes created political enemies who forced his dismissal.

Subsequently, Dougherty entered Missouri politics. The fourth phase of his remarkable career, 1849–1855, saw him in the role of freighter and post trader at Forts Kearny and Laramie, military posts on the Platte Route during the California gold rush. His agency letters and reports in the National Archives and his business papers in the Missouri Historical Society, Saint Louis, comprise his legacy. The only documented biography is Mattes (1971). See Maximilian (1906:234–260) and Wilson (1953) for further information. MERRILL J. MATTES

Drake, Samuel Gardner 1798–1875

Born in Pittsfield, New Hampshire, Drake briefly served as a school teacher before embarking upon his life's work as the proprietor of a rare book shop in Boston. He soon developed an abiding interest in history and helped form the New England Historic and Genealogical Society in 1845. Most of his interest centered about the Indians, particularly in New England. He eventually became one of the foremost Indian historians of his day, doing research among many vanishing sources and publishing some of the first serious accounts of the subject (1832, 1841, 1851; Church 1851). Although occasionally expressing sympathy for the Indian, he wrote largely to document for future White generations the hardships their ancestors faced in settling America. ROBERT A. TRENNERT

Duncan, William 1832–1918

A British lay missionary of the Church Missionary Society (Anglican), Duncan's proselytism among the Coast Tsimshian Indians of British Columbia led to the founding of the Christian villages of Metlakatla, B.C.,

and New Metlakatla, Alaska. Duncan inaugurated radical cultural change among the Tsimshian with conversion and resettlement strategies that were emulated by other nineteenth-century missionaries to these people. He arrived at Fort Simpson in 1857 at the height of postcontact cultural and economic florescence among the Lower Skeena River Tsimshian, who had moved their villages to the area surrounding the fort. In May 1862 Duncan led a group of about 50 converts to found the village of Metlakatla at the site of the deserted winter villages on Metlakatla Passage. Soon after they left, a disastrous smallpox epidemic struck at Fort Simpson and other Indians followed them. The next year Legaik, the highest-ranking chief of the Lower Skeena River tribes, joined the converts at the new village. Duncan commanded that his followers give up their traditional way of life and established Metlakatla as a model, self-sustaining Victorian community, which had a population of 1,100 by 1879. In 1887, after several years of conflict with officials of the Anglican church, Duncan left British Columbia with some 800 followers to found Port Chester, later New Metlakatla, on land given them by the United States government on Annette Island in Alaska (Arctander 1909; Church Missionary Society 1869; J. Usher 1974; Wellcome 1887). MARJORIE M. HALPIN

Duponceau, Peter Stephen 1760–1844

Born in France, Duponceau emigrated to America in 1777. A lawyer and philologist, he was corresponding secretary and later president of the American Philosophical Society, Philadelphia. Deeply interested in American Indian languages, he exchanged views about them with other scholars, particularly John Heckewelder and John Pickering. He was honored for an essay on the grammatical typology of American Indian languages, based on Algonquian (Duponceau 1838). His papers are among the manuscript collections of the American Philosophical Society (Duponceau 1820–1844, 1815–1834). For a biography see Knott (1930). MARY HAAS

Eells, Myron 1843–1907

Eells was born near Spokane, Washington, the son of missionaries. He was educated at Pacific University (Forest Grove, Oregon) and at Hartford Theological Seminary. He was Congregational missionary on the Skokomish Reservation, western Washington, from 1874, and published an account of his first 10 years of missionary work (Eells 1886), also valuable as an ethnographic source. Eells was a prolific writer on ethnology and on the history of Pacific Northwest Indian missions. His ethnological contributions include some of the earliest detailed accounts of western Washington Indian customs and beliefs (Eells 1877); for a partial listing of Eells's articles, books and manuscripts see Ruby and Brown (1976a:121–122). Notable as anthropological sources are a description of acculturative change on the Skokomish Reservation in the late 1870s (Eells 1877) and a summary ethnographic account of the tribes with whom he was primarily involved as missionary, the Twana, Chemakum, and Clallam (1889). His historical works are sources for Indian and White contacts in a wide area of the Northwest (Eells 1881, 1882, 1883, 1894). Unpublished manuscripts of Eells are in the library of Whitman College (Walla Walla, Washington). Eells (1985) contains biography as well as a detailed bibliography. WILLIAM W. ELMENDORF

Egede, Hans P. 1686–1758

Born in Harstad, Norway, Egede initiated the Danish-Norwegian colonization of Greenland. As a Lutheran priest in northern Norway he became interested in the fate of the Christian Norse population in Greenland and gained support to settle in West Greenland in 1721 with his family. He did not find the Norsemen but did missionary work among the Greenlanders until 1736, when he went to Denmark. His sons, Poul and Niels, continued his work. Egede published valuable information concerning the geography of Greenland and the language and culture of the West Greenlanders (Egede 1738, 1741; Bergsland and Rischel 1986). See Bobé (1952), Myklebust (1958:279–291), and *Norsk Tidsskrift for Misjon* (1986), a 300-year anniversary issue, for further information. INGE KLEIVAN

Eliot, John 1604–1690

Commonly referred to as the "Apostle to the Indians," Eliot was born in Essex County, England, and educated at Cambridge, arriving in Boston in November 1631. While serving as pastor at Roxbury after 1632 he also maintained a career as missionary to the Indians of Massachusetts. His decision may have reflected, in addition to altruistic motives, an effort by the leaders of Massachusetts to avert criticism in England of the dismal efforts to christianize the colony's Indians up to the 1640s.

After mastering the Massachusett language, Eliot gave his first sermon on October 28, 1646. Spurred on by what Eliot claimed to be an enthusiastic reception from the Indians and with economic assistance after 1649 from the Society for the Propagation of the Gospel in New England, he established the first of the "praying towns" at Natick in 1651. Intent upon civilizing as well as christianizing the Indian, Eliot created 14 of these towns with a total population of about 2,500 Indians by 1675. Two of the towns achieved full Congregational Church status—Natick and Hassawesitt. Since Eliot believed adherents to Puritanism required a knowledge of the Bible, he translated the Old and New Testaments into Massachusett and had them published in one volume in 1663--the first complete Bible printed anywhere in the New World. As further aids to converting the Indian, he also translated a primer, a grammar, a logic manual, and some sermons.

Eliot's attempts to protect the "praying Indians" from Puritan attacks during King Philip's War, 1675–1676, and his opposition to the enslavement of Indian captives earned him the hatred of those colonists who sought a policy of harsh retaliation. Despite the setbacks of the war and the decline in the population of the "praying towns" after 1676, Eliot continued his missionary endeavors until his death. The fullest treatments of Eliot are in Mather (1691), Vaughan (1965), Winslow (1968), Salisbury (1974), and Jennings (1971). RICHARD L. HAAN

Elliott, Matthew about 1739–1814

Born in Ireland, Elliott came to America in 1761. Before the American Revolution he traded out of western Pennsylvania into the region northwest of the Ohio River, forming attachments with the Shawnee that lasted throughout his life. After some indecision he decided to join the British in the Revolution, and in 1778 he fled to Detroit with Alexander McKee and Simon Girty. For the remainder of the Revolution he served in the British Indian Department. After 1783 he traded out of Detroit, and in the early 1790s he worked for the British Indian Department in advising and supplying the Indians of the Old Northwest. In 1796 he was appointed superintendent of Indian affairs at Amhertsburg, upper Canada, but he was dismissed in the following year. At a time of crisis between England and the United States in 1808 Elliott was reappointed as superintendent, and in the years before the War of 1812 he was an influential advisor of Indians from United States territory who visited Amherstburg. During the war itself Elliott served in the field with the Indian allies of the British. There is a biography of Elliott by Horsman (1964). REGINALD HORSMAN

Evans, James 1801–1846

A Methodist missionary, Evans invented a syllabic writing system for Cree in 1840, variants of which were later used for several other languages. In 1987 it continued to be widely used in native magazines, books, and newspapers. He also published an Ojibwa primer in 1837 and a Cree hymnal in 1841 (J. Evans 1837, 1954). For further details see McLean (1890), Landon (1930), and Peel (1958, 1974). HUGH A. DEMPSEY

Evarts, Jeremiah 1781–1831

Born in Vermont, Evarts graduated from Yale College in 1802. With the founding of the American Board of Commissioners for Foreign Missions in 1810, Evarts began an active association with that body that lasted until his death. He was elected a corporate member in 1812, served as treasurer from 1811 to 1822, and became corresponding secretary, 1822–1831. From the last position he handled all the Congregational missions to the American Indians. Under his supervision nearly all the missions to the Cherokees, both East and West, were founded (Tracey 1840). Evarts developed a special concern for the success of these missions. He knew them well both from correspondence with the missionaries and through visits in 1822 and 1826 (Walker 1931; Evarts 1956). With the movement to move the Cherokee west of the Mississippi River in the late 1820s, Evarts became involved in defending Indian interests (Evarts 1981). He published 24 essays entitled "Essays on the Present Crisis in the Condition of the American Indians" in the *National Intelligencer* (Evarts 1829), which protested against the removal effort. These essays, along with his publication of speeches opposed to removal (Evarts 1830), were widely reprinted and did much to focus attention on the protest movement. Georgia politicians, who favored removal, used Evarts as an example of the type of humanitarian who would prefer civil war to removal. Papers regarding Evarts's activities are in the records of the American Board of Commissioners, the Houghton Library, Harvard University. For additional information see E. Tracey (1845). ROBERT A. TRENNERT

Filson, John 1747–!788

Filson was born in East Fallowfield Township, Chester County, Pennsylvania, and raised on a farm. He became a schoolteacher. In his mid-thirties Filson, lured by accounts of land speculation in the West, left Pennsylvania for Lexington, Kentucky. Once there he continued teaching and began surveying land. As a surveyor Filson met and interviewed many of the hunters and pioneers who settled the area. In 1782 he wrote an account of Daniel Boone's Chillicothe expedition. In 1784 he published *The Discovery, Settlement and Present State of Kentucke*, which included an ethnographic essay on the various Indian tribes found in the area. It stands as the first history of Kentucky. The detail and accuracy of Filson's map of Kentucky made it a valuable reference tool.

In 1785 he set off to document the Illinois country. By 1786 he had completed his investigations, but no published work resulted. In 1788 he joined Mattias Denman, Col. Robert Patterson, and Judge John Cleves Symms in their plan to settle what later became Cincinnati. While surveying lands for this purpose, Filson separated from his party and was killed by Indians. For further information see J.W. Coleman (1954) and Durrett (1884). HEATHER C. DODSON

Fitzpatrick, Thomas 1799–1854

One of the original pioneers of the Rocky Mountain fur trade, Fitzpatrick went west in the early 1820s. After the fur trade declined he remained on the frontier leading emigrant parties westward. He probably knew more about the Plains Indians than any other White man then living. In 1846, at the insistence of Sen. Thomas H. Benton, he was named Indian agent for the newly created Upper Platte and Arkansas Agency, serving in that position until 1854. Under his jurisdiction were the Arapaho, Cheyenne, Kiowa, Comanche, and some bands of the Sioux. Although sympathetic to the Indians and maintaining a good reputation among the tribes, Fitzpatrick strongly believed the Indians must make way for White expansion and that they should adopt agriculture. If the Indians resisted, he advocated a military solution, believing the only thing they respected was armed might. He was one of the first and continuing advocates of placing garrisons on the Oregon Trail. Fitzpatrick was also instrumental in fostering the treaty of Fort Laramie in 1851, the first major treaty with most of the Plains tribes. His biographies (Hafen and Ghent 1931; Hafen and Hafen 1969) describe his entire career. Most primary sources concerning his activities as Indian agent are in the National Archives (T. Fitzpatrick 1846–1854). ROBERT A. TRENNERT

Fletcher, Alice Cunningham 1838–1923

Active in various Indian rights organizations, Fletcher turned to professional anthropology after studying archeology at the Peabody Museum of Harvard University. In 1881 she visited the Omaha reservation with the dual purpose of studying traditional culture and offering her services to help the Omaha people. In fear of removal to Indian Territory, the Omaha told Fletcher that they wanted a "strong paper" to make their lands secure. Accordingly, Fletcher drafted a petition, signed by 55 Omaha men, requesting the allotment of reservation lands and the granting of full titles to Indian landowners (Fletcher and La Flesche 1911:636–638). Fletcher gave public lectures in Washington, D.C., to publicize the Omaha cause, and on August 2, 1882, the Omaha Act was passed by Congress—a prototype for the Dawes Severalty Act of 1887. Fletcher was appointed special agent to carry out the Omaha land allotment (fig. 8). In this she was assisted by Francis La Flesche, an Omaha whom Fletcher adoped as a son and who continued in a career in anthropology. The Omaha, in gratitude for her services, gave Fletcher permission to study their religion and culture. She later carried out allotments for the Winnebago and Nez Perce ("United States Indian Policies, 1860–1900," fig. 6, this vol.). She published a survey volume on the progress of education and civilization among U.S. Indians (Fletcher 1888). Fletcher officially joined the Peabody Museum in 1886 and in 1891 received a fellowship that provided for her Indian studies. She was the first anthropologist to undertake the serious study of American Indian music (1893, 1894). Her major contributions were studies of Dakota, Omaha, and Pawnee rituals (Fletcher 1883, 1884, 1904), and the ethnography of the Omaha (Fletcher and La Flesche 1911). She was also a frequent lecturer and a popularizer of the American Indian. Fletcher was president of the Anthropological Society of Washington in 1903, and president of the American Folk-lore Society in 1905. For biographical details and bibliography see La Flesche (1923), Lurie (1966), Mark (1980), and R.H. Welch (1980). Fletcher's unpublished manuscripts are in the Smithsonian Institution, National Anthropological Archives. RAYMOND J. DEMALLIE

Forsyth, James William 1836–1906

Born in Maumee, Ohio, Forsyth attended the U.S. Military Academy, graduating in 1856. After the Civil War, he served as a cavalry officer with Sheridan in the West and was in the campaign against the Bannocks in 1878. Colonel Forsyth was in command of the 7th Cavalry at Wounded Knee Creek on December 29, 1890, when his soldiers and Big Foot's Minneconjou Sioux exchanged fire. Forsyth reported the deaths of 25 soldiers and more than 200 Indians. In the official inquiry Forsyth was criticized for the way he had deposed his troops, but he did not lose his regimental command. In 1894 he became a brigadier general; he retired from the Army in 1897 with the rank of major general. For details of Forsyth's life and career, see Chandler (1960), Heitman (1903), and Utley (1963). DEE BROWN

Forsyth, Thomas 1771–1833

Born in Detroit of an Irish father and Canadian mother who ran an inn, Forsyth entered the fur trade in 1790. He traded among the Ottawa at Saginaw until 1796, when he formed a fur-trade partnership with a Mr. Richardson at Quincy, Illinois. In 1804 he formed another such partnership, with his half-brother John Kinzie, and settled at Peoria with his wife Keziah Malotte, with whom he eventually had four children.

Prior to the War of 1812, Forsyth was appointed Indian subagent, moving to Saint Louis at the outbreak of hostilities. He managed to keep the powerful Potawatomi neutral during the war, thus irritating the British who consequently put a price on his head. He managed the Peoria agency until 1819, when he was instructed to ascend the Mississippi River to reconnoiter and treat with the Indian tribes along the way (Forsyth 1872). Later in 1819 he was appointed to full Indian agent and stationed at Fort Armstrong, near Rock Island, where he supervised the Sauk and Fox tribes. He gained the respect of these Indians and helped conclude a treaty with them in 1822 (Forsyth 1911–1912, 2:183–245). His relatively enlightened views regarding United States–Indian relations are revealed in an 1815 letter to Gov. William Clark (Forsyth 1834).

Forsyth retired in 1830 and removed to Saint Louis, where he died. His papers are in the Missouri Historical

Smithsonian, NAA:4473.

Fig. 8. Alice Fletcher, second from the left, seated, with Indian and White women at a Presbyterian mission on the Omaha Reservation, Walthill, Neb. Photographed 1883–1884.

Society, Saint Louis, and the State Historical Society of Wisconsin, Madison. Some are published (Forsyth 1888). WILLIAM W. QUINN, JR.

Franklin, Benjamin 1706–1790

A native of Boston, Franklin moved at age 17 to Philadelphia. A philosopher, inventor, scientist, and statesman, his political and diplomatic career during the era of the American Revolution and his experiments on the nature of electricity made him one of the most widely known and internationally influential Americans of all time.

Franklin's active involvement with Indian affairs occurred primarily during his service in Pennsylvania's colonial assembly, 1736–1757. He regarded Indians with humane respect, sympathy, and curiosity, and often took their side in disputes with Whites such as the infamous "Walking Purchase" episode of 1737 and the murder of 20 Conestoga Indians by the "Paxton Boys" in 1763. He used the Iroquois confederacy as an example when arguing for his plan of intercolonial union in 1754, and in 1784, while serving as United States ambassador to France, he published *Remarks Concerning the Savages of North America*, which was widely read in Europe and which demonstrated a firsthand knowledge of Indian culture. Franklin always found it ironic that Indians should be termed "savages" for no reason except that "their manners differ from ours, which we think the perfection of civility; they think the same of theirs" (Franklin 1784:19). The most useful biography is Van Doren (1938), and Ford (1890) is the most complete Franklin bibliography. A complete edition of Franklin papers is being edited by Labaree and Willcox (1959–1986). The largest collections of manuscript materials pertaining to Franklin are in the American Philosophical Society in Philadelphia, the Library of Congress, and the Franklin Collection of the Yale University Library. P. RICHARD METCALF

Fraser, Simon 1776–1862

Fraser was a fur trader and explorer who joined the North West Company in 1792 and became a partner in 1801. In 1805 he went to northern British Columbia, building the first forts west of the Rocky Mountains—Fort McLeod in 1805, Fort St. James and Fort Fraser in 1806, and Fort George in 1807. He also was the first White man to meet the Carrier Indians. In 1808 he made an exploratory trip down the Fraser River, which was named in his honor. During this voyage, he was the first European to meet many Indian bands along the river, some of whom greeted him with hostility. In 1809 Fraser moved to Athabasca district and later to Red River, retiring in about 1819. Sources on his career include Hutchinson (1950), W.K. Lamb (1960), and V.L. Denton (1929). HUGH A. DEMPSEY

Frelinghuysen, Theodore 1787–1862

Born in New Jersey, Frelinghuysen graduated from Princeton in 1804 and was admitted to the bar in 1808. He served in many public offices: attorney-general of New Jersey, 1817–1829; United States senator, 1829–1835; mayor of Newark, 1836–1839; and in many private ones: president of the American Board of Commissioners of Foreign Missions for 16 years and president of the American Bible Society from 1846 until his death. His significance in Indian affairs stems from his ardent opposition to the removal of the Cherokees west of the Mississippi. He foresaw that removal would be a continual demand and pleaded for the Indian the right "of a free exercise of his own will" (Evarts 1830:24). This position and his stance on the abolition of slavery (Frelinghuysen 1824) undoubtably won him the title "Christian statesman." In 1839 Frelinghuysen retired from the law and became chancellor of the University of the City of New York. In 1850 he became president of Rutgers, a position he held until his death (see Erdman 1931). Frelinghuysen's papers are in the Library of Congress. ANDREA LUDWIG

Gaines, Edmund Pendleton 1777–1849

A leading figure of the Indian-fighting Army between the War of 1812 and the Mexican War, Gaines was also an outspoken officer who waged constant war with his superiors and colleagues, especially Winfield Scott, as well as with the Indians. Gaines served as a commissioner to the Creek Indians in 1817, then joined Andrew Jackson in operations against these Indians and the Seminoles of the Georgia-Florida frontier. Gaines held an important field command in the Black Hawk War of 1832 and led an expedition in 1835 against the Seminoles during which he was wounded in action. He authored detailed plans for western frontier defense in 1838 and 1840. For a biography see Silver (1949). ROBERT M. UTLEY

Gallatin, Albert 1761–1849

Gallatin was secretary of the treasury under Presidents Jefferson and Madison and later was minister to France and, briefly, to England. Retiring from public life he became president of the National (later Gallatin) Bank in New York City. He published the first reasonably comprehensive classification of the American Indian languages of the United States and the British and Russian possessions of North America (Gallatin 1836). This, together with his work on vocabularies (Gallatin 1848), formed the base on which J.W. Powell (1891) built his definitive linguistic classification. Gallatin founded the American Ethnological Society in 1842. For further biographical information see Adams (1879) and Walters (1957). The largest collection of Gallatin's papers is on microfilm at New York University. There are state papers in the Library of Congress and the New-York Historical Society. MARY HAAS

Gates, Merrill Edward 1848–1922

Gates earned a Ph.D. from the University of the State of New York in 1880. He was president of Rutgers College, 1882–1890, and president of Amherst College, 1890–1899. From 1892 to 1898 he was president of the American Missionary Association and became a licensed preacher of the Congregational Church in 1899. His religious interest was expressed by membership in the American Bible and American Tract Societies. Yet his major activity for years was his service as an adviser on Indian affairs.

Gates joined the Board of Indian Commissioners in 1884, served as its chairman 1890–1899, and as its secretary from 1899 to 1912. During these years the Board was less influential than it had been, but Gates was close to the center of its activity. He also served as president of the Lake Mohonk Conference of the Friends of the American Indian for eight years (M.E. Gates 1907). In those capacities Gates opposed the reservation system (M.E. Gates 1885). Additional information about Gates is incorporated in the General Correspondence of the Board of Indian Commissioners in the National Archives, Record Group 75. LORING B. PRIEST

Gatschet, Albert Samuel 1832–1907

Born in Switzerland, Gatschet emigrated to the United States in 1868. He applied his linguistic training and experience in European languages to the study of North American Indian languages, first by publishing a series of vocabularies from the Southwest and Plains collected by travelers (Gatschet 1876). Hired by John Wesley Powell as philologist for the Geographical and Geological Survey of the Rocky Mountain Region in 1877, Gatschet's first major fieldwork was among the Klamath. He was a staff member of the Bureau of (American) Ethnology from the time of its organization in 1879 until his retirement for reasons of health in 1905. His work is particularly valuable for his field studies of poorly known, genetically isolated, and remnant languages. Among the larger language families he concentrated on Muskogean and Algonquian. His major fieldwork was among the Catawba, 1881; Louisiana Choctaw and Chitimacha, 1882; Tonkawa, Lipan Apache, Kiowa, Kiowa-Apache, Atakapa, Natchez, Yuchi, and Modoc, 1884–1885; Biloxi, Tunica, Comecrudo, Cotoname and Hitchiti, 1886–1887; Peoria, Shawnee, Arapaho, and Cheyenne, 1892–1893; Miami, 1895; Passamaquoddy, 1896, 1898; and Micmac, 1899. He also worked extensively with members of Indian delegations visiting Washington and with boarding school students and in all made studies of nearly 100 languages. His papers are in the National Anthropological Archives, Smithsonian Institution; his publications, on a wide array of topics but principally linguistic, are listed in his obituary (Mooney 1907a). IVES GODDARD

Gibbs, George 1815–1873

Rejecting a law career and duties as librarian of the New-York Historical Society, George Gibbs rushed west in 1849. This Harvard-educated scholar explored the Pacific Slope from 1849 to 1860. He served as surveyor and secretary for the Oregon Indian Commission of 1851; interpreter and cartographer to the northern California commission of 1851–1852; geologist and naturalist for the Pacific Railroad surveys in Washington Territory, 1853; secretary to Gov. Isaac Stevens's Indian Commission on Puget Sound, 1854–1855; and geologist-naturalist on the Northwest Boundary survey, 1857–1860. These travels afforded him excellent opportunity for linguistic and ethnographic studies. He annually shipped artifacts to the Smithsonian. In treaty negotiations on Puget Sound he insisted on guarantees of fishing rights. In 1861 Gibbs moved to Washington, D.C., and published linguistic studies on Yakima, Chinook Jargon, Chinook, Clallam, Lummi, and Nisqually (Gibbs 1862, 1863, 1863a, 1863b, 1877). His accounts of Indians in the West appeared in the Schoolcraft series (Gibbs 1853) and in the *Pacific Railroad Reports* (Gibbs 1855). He also studied Northwest coast mythology (E.E. Clark

1955–1956). Gibbs edited manuscripts and wrote guides for fieldwork for the Smithsonian, penned accounts on geology and cartography, and was a founder of the Anthropological Institute of New York and the American Philological Society. His papers include over 100 manuscripts in the Smithsonian Institution National Anthropological Archives. For his biography see Beckham (1969). STEPHEN DOW BECKHAM

Girty, Simon about 1745–1818

Born on the Pennsylvania frontier, Simon Girty was a captive among the Seneca from 1756 to 1759. He became fluent in their language and at various times between 1766 and 1774 was employed as Iroquoian interpreter at Pittsburgh by the Indian Department. In 1775 he declared for the colonies, serving as interpreter, ambassador to the Six Nations of Iroquois, and lieutenant of Virginia troops; however, he came to resent the treatment he had received from American authorities, and in 1778 deserted to the British at Detroit. There he rejoined the Indian Department, on whose pay and pension rolls he remained until his death. Girty was a skilled linguist, an expert diplomat, and a fearless fighter. Together with Alexander McKee and Matthew Elliott, Girty coordinated and directed Indian hostilities against the Americans from 1778 until 1783, and after the Revolution he was instrumental in cementing Indian loyalty to Great Britain. Girty participated in most of the major frontier battles between 1778 and 1794. He died on his farm near Amherstburg, Ontario. American accounts of Girty stress his brutality and savagery, but some evidence suggests these are exaggerations. For a guide to the principal documentary sources on Girty see Thwaites (1906a) and Beers (1964); Horsman (1964) presents valuable sketches. Butterfield's (1890) and T.W. Boyd's (1928) biographies are inadequately researched and frequently inaccurate. RICK TOOTHMAN

Gist, Christopher 1705–1759

Gist spent his early years in Baltimore as a plantation owner, hunter, surveyor, road builder, merchant, and fur trader. In 1745, having gone broke, he moved to the North Carolina frontier on the Yadkin River. From 1750 to 1752 Gist made two explorations for the Ohio Company in Ohio, Kentucky, and present-day West Virginia. He kept an excellent journal for each expedition (Darlington 1893). In 1752 Gist established a settlement in western Pennsylvania between the Monongahela and Youghiogheny rivers. For the next few years "Gist's Plantation" became the headquarters of English western activities. In 1753 George Washington and Gist journeyed into the Ohio country to order the French out of the Ohio Valley. In 1754 Gist was with Washington on his expedition to establish a fort at the forks of the Ohio. Following Gen. Edward Braddock's defeat in 1755 Gist, through the sponsorship of Washington, became a captain of the Scouts, and then deputy Indian agent under Edmond Atkin. His biggest responsibility was to supply Southern Indians to scout for British troops, particularly for Gen. John Forbes for his expedition of 1758. It was while engaged in this work that Gist contracted smallpox and died near Winchester, Virginia. Gist's career has been fictionalized by a historical forgery (Horn 1945), which claims Gist lived on for another decade and had an Indian family (for correction see Middleton and Adair 1947). K.P. Bailey (1976) is a full biography. See also Dorsey and Dorsey (1969) and K.P. Bailey (1939). KENNETH P. BAILEY

Gookin, Daniel 1612–1687

Gookin was born in Kent, England. Although he visited in Virginia at his father's plantation as early as 1630, it was not until 1641 that he migrated to Virginia. Just after the Indian massacre of 1644, Gookin, an ardent Puritan, moved to Massachusetts as a result of Gov. William Berkeley's policy of strict conformity to the Anglican church. He eventually settled at Cambridge and became an influential man, serving in many public capacities. Nothing stands forth more saliently than his work among the American Indians. Gookin's interest in the natives, which developed during his experiences in Virginia, intensified when he came to know John Eliot, his Roxbury neighbor. In 1656, Gookin was appointed superintendent of the Indians, a post he held until his death, except for the years 1658 to 1661, while he was in England. He administered the affairs of the Massachusetts Indians, while Eliot taught them. Gookin wrote three books: on the Indians in New England (1792), on the Christian Indians during King Philip's War (1836), and on the history of New England (never printed and now lost). F.W. Gookin (1912), W.F. Gookin (1913), and Vaughan (1979) provide further information on the man and his contributions. YASUHIDE KAWASHIMA

Greenwood, Alfred Burton 1811–1889

Born in Georgia, Greenwood graduated from the University of Georgia, studied law, and was admitted to the bar in Georgia in 1832. He was a member of the Arkansas House of Representatives, 1842–1845; was state prosecuting attorney, 1845-1851; a circuit judge, 1851–1853; and United States Congressman, 1853–1859. He was commissioner of Indian affairs in May 1859. As commissioner, he believed that the administration of Indian affairs would be improved if the military played a more prominent role, if the Intercourse Law were revised, and if the Indian could be transformed into an agricultural capitalist. In spring 1861, with the secession of Arkansas and because of his strong belief in nonintervention in the slavery question, he resigned. Greenwood served the Confederacy, by recruiting Cherokees and Choctaws for the war effort (Wilkinson 1961). Thereafter he practiced law until his death.

See Hallum (1887:273–274) and Roberts (1979a) for additional information. ANDREA LUDWIG

Gregg, Josiah 1806–1850

Born in Overton County, Tennessee, Gregg spent three years in Illinois, moved to Missouri in 1812, and in 1825 to Independence. Given a fairly liberal education, he acquired a knowledge of medicine and surgery, and was dubbed a doctor. (In 1845–1846 he attended medical school in Louisville, and was granted an honorary degree.) He never practiced, except for a short period late in his life in Mexico. He tried his hand at almost everything: school teaching, studying law, overland trading, surveying, writing, and even gold mining.

In 1831 Gregg set out with a caravan from Independence to Santa Fe. He learned Spanish and became a trader making trips to Santa Fe and Chihuahua. Between 1831 and 1840, he crossed the Plains four times, and in the last year toured the prairies. He went to Texas in 1841. In 1844 he published *Commerce of the Prairies*, a popular account of the Southwest trade (Gregg 1954).

In 1846, when war broke out with Mexico, Gregg volunteered, joining Gen. John Wool unofficially as a war correspondent and also as a guide and interpreter for the army. He joined in the California gold rush.

For further information see Connelley (1921), Coy (1932), Fulton (1941–1944), and Twitchell (1924). A.P. NASATIR

Grey Owl 1889–1938

Born in Hastings, England, as Archibald Stansfeld Belaney, Grey Owl (Wa-sha-quon-asin) arrived in Canada in 1906. He spent nearly 20 years among the Ojibwa of northeastern Ontario. In his books (1931, 1934, 1935, 1936) and his British and North American lecture tours, 1935–1938, he described the northern wilderness. He claimed to have been raised by an Apache mother on the banks of the Rio Grande. Several accounts provide biographical information (Anahareo 1972; Dickson 1939; D.B. Smith 1971; and G. Hutchinson 1985). DONALD B. SMITH

Haile, Berard 1874–1961

Born in Canton, Ohio, Haile entered the Franciscan Order in 1891 and was ordained in 1898. In 1900 he went to the newly established mission to the Navajo Indians at Saint Michaels, Arizona. He spent over 50 years of his life as a missionary, 10 years in charge of the mission at Lukachukai, Arizona, but most of the time at the mission at Saint Michaels. Convinced that it was fruitless to try to convert the Navajos to Christianity without first becoming able to communicate with them fluently in their own language and learning as much as possible about their native religion, Father Berard devoted much of his time to linguistic and ethnographic studies. His numerous publications in these fields, many of which were produced by the press that he established at the mission, earned him the title of "Scholar to the Navajo" among his Franciscan colleagues. The Navajos themselves said of him that he was one of the very few White men who spoke their language "like a Navajo."

All his papers and unpublished manuscripts are at the Special Collections Division of the Library of the University of Arizona, Tucson. A preliminary bibliography of his published works (D.M. Powell 1961) contains over 40 items of which 20 concern Navajo ceremonialism and mythology. Father Berard began his most intensive linguistic work in 1928, and in 1930 he was made a research associate in the Department of Anthropology of the University of Chicago. His most important linguistic works are *Learning Navaho* (1941–1948) and *A Stem Vocabulary of the Navaho Language* (1950–1951). LELAND C. WYMAN

Hale, Horatio Emmons 1817–1896
Born at Newport, New Hampshire, to a literary family, Hale entered Harvard in 1833. He interviewed Indians camped nearby and personally set into type 50 copies of his first publication, on the Penobscot language (Hale 1834). Hale was appointed philologist with the U.S. Exploring Expedition to the Pacific, under Capt. Charles Wilkes, 1838–1842, during which he confirmed the affinity of Malay and Polynesian languages, worked on languages of Australia, and treated the difficult languages of the Northwest Coast of America (Hale 1846). He guided the work of Franz Boas for the British Association for the Advancement of Science.

Settling in Clinton, Ontario, Hale soon tired of the practice of law and undertook the study of Iroquoian languages. At the Six Nations Reserve he made the important discovery that Tutelo was a Siouan language (Hale 1883a). His second discovery was the existence of two manuscripts written in Mohawk and Onondaga in the orthography of the Anglican missionaries and dating from the mid-eighteenth century (Hale 1833). In editing these two manuscripts Hale combined textual reconstruction with informant interviews in a productive way. In dating Iroquoian language splits he anticipated glottochronology. He was a member of the American Philosophical Society, the Royal Society of Canada, and was active in both the British and American Associations for the Advancement of Science. He was president of the American Folk-lore Society. Gruber (1967) discusses his place in anthropology. Hale's papers went up in smoke when his study at Clinton, Ontario, burned. WILLIAM N.

Hare, William Hobart 1838–1909
Born in Princeton, New Jersey, Hare moved to Philadelphia in 1843 where he attended the Episcopal Academy and the University of Pennsylvania. Choosing to enter the ministry, he became a student at the Episcopal Divinity School and was admitted to the diaconate in 1859. In 1862 he asked for a transfer to the Minnesota diocese. There he saw the aftermath of the Sioux uprising of 1862 and the Indian wars that followed, an experience that eventually led him to be the Indians' advocate. Hare returned to pastoral work in Philadelphia in 1864. His work for the Indians began when he was elected as the Bishop of the Missionary Jurisdiction of Niobrara in 1872 in present South Dakota, where he ministered to the Sioux and Cheyenne. Convinced that the education of Indian children would break down the wall between the races and facilitate total assimilation, Bishop Hare founded five boarding schools. He opposed the reservation as a permanent system and favored the Dawes Severalty Act of 1887 as a way to bring the intermingling of Indians and Whites. In 1883 he was elected Bishop of South Dakota. He moved from the Yankton Agency to Sioux Falls, where he founded the All Saints School, and ministered to both Whites and Indians until his death. In 1891–1892 he served as a missionary bishop in Japan and China. For further biographical information see M.A.D. Howe (1911). ROBERT W. MARDOCK

Harlan, James 1820–1899
Harlan graduated from Asbury University (now DePauw University) in 1845, and pursued careers as educator, merchant, lawyer, and politician. Elected to the United States Senate in 1855, he chaired the Committee on Public Lands that drafted the Homestead Act. President Abraham Lincoln appointed Harlan secretary of the interior in 1865. Harlan made a valiant effort to rid the department of thieves and incompetents, but with the assumption of the presidency by Andrew Johnson, with whom he clashed, Harlan resigned in 1866. After his resignation, he was accused of petty graft and corruption in the sale of Cherokee land. These charges were not proved, though the stigma affected his future political career. Miscellaneous Harlan papers may be found in the Iowa State Department of History and Archives, Des Moines. For further biographical information see Trani (1975) and Brigham (1913). ANDREA LUDWIG

Harney, William Selby 1800–1889
Born in Tennessee and educated at Nashville's Cumberland College, Harney entered the United States Army as a lieutenant in 1818. During 45 years of active duty, he rose to the rank of brevet major general and at various times commanded the Second Dragoons and military departments in Texas, Florida, Oregon, and the Missouri

Valley. Proud, boisterous, and tempermental, Harney earned distinction as a relentless Indian fighter during the Black Hawk and Second Seminole Wars and subsequent campaigns in Texas and the upper Great Plains (O. Griswold 1949). He was best known for crushing Chakaika's Seminoles in the Florida Everglades in 1840 and mercilessly drubbing Little Thunder's Brulé Sioux in Nebraska in 1855 (G.R. Adams 1970). Despite his reputation, Harney generally advocated negotiation and strong frontier defenses as the best means of implementing American Indian policy and keeping peace between White men and Red, and he blamed unscrupulous White traders and agents for many of the problems between the two races (H.S. Anderson 1963). Regarding Indians as an inferior people, he believed that to survive they must adopt White civilization, and he supported this view while serving on the Peace Commission of 1867–1868. The Missouri Historical Society, Saint Louis, holds his few remaining papers. Details of his role in Indian affairs are in Reavis (1878) and G.R. Adams (1983). GEORGE R. ADAMS

Harris, Carey Allen 1806–1842

Harris was born in Williamson County, Tennessee. As a young man he became active in politics as a Nashville newspaper publisher and then as a lawyer. In the early 1830s Harris moved to Washington and served as a War Department clerk in the confidence of Secretary of War Lewis Cass and President Andrew Jackson. In 1836 he received the appointment of commissioner of Indian affairs. As commissioner between 1836 and 1838, Harris played an important role in expediting the removal of many Eastern tribes and strengthening the government's control over the trans-Mississippi Indian country. He was active in ejecting the Cherokees from their lands in the Southeast, the Seminole from Florida, the Creeks from Alabama, and the Chickasaw from Mississippi. In the case of the Seminole, Harris's directives assisted White planters in acquiring the Black slaves of the departing Indians. In the case of the Chickasaw, Harris used his authority—threatening military force and withdrawal of rations—to force Indians to comply with removal orders. Harris promoted the removal of tribes from the Old Northwest at the same time he attempted to resettle New York Indians in the vacated areas.

For the relocated Indians, Harris promoted the establishment of local schools in the West to make Indian youth more amenable to government policies. He also advocated the granting of territorial status to the Indian country in order to permit close government supervision of the emigrant tribes by a governor.

In autumn 1838 President Martin Van Buren ordered Harris to resign from office when he refused to answer charges that he had speculated in Indian allotments. Harris then took up residence in Arkansas where he

served as an official of the Real Estate Bank in Little Rock. Details of his attitude toward the Indians and his handling of Indian affairs are in Satz (1975, 1979b). The major source of Harris correspondence is the National Archives (Record Groups 75 and 107). RONALD N. SATZ

Harrison, William Henry 1773–1841

Harrison was born at Berkeley Plantation, Virginia. He served as a military officer in the Northwest Indian Wars, 1791–1794; as Indiana territorial governor, 1800–1813; and as Indian treaty negotiator, 1814–1815. Three factors affected Harrison's Indian policy: his desire to please President Thomas Jefferson, settler influence, and his compassion (Goebel 1926:89–127). His Indian dealings carried out presidential land accession programs; he first controlled, then reflected, settlers' desires; and he showed a sometimes paternal concern for Indians, in that he sought to protect them from whiskey and unregulated trade and, through treaty, to safeguard them from extermination. Balancing this was his political proclivity, which sacrificed the Indian concept of land use and culture. After gaining experience at the Treaty of Greenville, 1795, Harrison concluded numerous general and tribal treaties, 1802–1815, that added 30 million acres to the United States.

Harrison also controlled the Indian by force. Tenskwatawa and Tecumseh, whose influences contradicted Harrison's, were defeated at the Battles of Tippecanoe, 1811, and the Thames, 1813. Harrison's influence upon American Indian affairs must rest with his treaty negotiations and the precedence they held in the formative years of United States Indian policy. The best assessment of Harrison is Goebel (1926), which contains an extensive bibliography of Harrison's original papers. See also Pirtle (1900), J.A. Green (1941), and Cleaves (1939). JOHN J. NEWMAN

Hawkins, Benjamin 1754–1816

Born in North Carolina and educated at Princeton, Hawkins served for a time as a French interpreter on George Washington's staff during the Revolution. In 1781 he was elected to the Continental Congress, where he became heavily involved in Indian issues. In 1785 he was appointed one of the commissioners who negotiated the first federal treaty with the Cherokee, and the following year he signed similar agreements with the Choctaw and the Chickasaw. In 1790 he took a seat in the U.S. Senate. During his term, Hawkins advised President Washington on Indian affairs and was called upon to aid in negotiations with the Creek of Georgia. In 1796 the President appointed him superintendent for all Indians south of the Ohio River, a post he held until his death. Hawkins proved to be an honest and able administrator and won the respect of most Whites as well as numerous Indians. His sympathy for the Indians incurred the wrath of many frontiersmen, especially from Georgia (A.H. Hall 1934). He was able to keep the Indians at peace for 16 years and was instrumental in negotiating the end of the Creek War of 1813–1814. Hawkins traveled extensively throughout Indian country. A keen observer, he kept a detailed journal that provided accounts of Indian agriculture and customs as well as descriptions of the land (Hawkins 1848). For his correspondence see Hawkins (1916).

The best biography is Pound (1951); see also Pound (1942) and Harmon (1932). HENRY E. FRITZ

Haworth, James M. 1832?–1885

Although raised a Quaker, Haworth left the sect during the Civil War, serving as an officer in an Ohio regiment (Hagan 1976:92). Returning to the Society of Friends after the war, he was appointed agent to the Kiowa, Comanche, and Apache reservation in 1873 (Hiatt 1958). He followed the dictates of the Quakers, dispensing with the military guard from Fort Sill at the agency and generally favoring peaceful persuasion rather than coercion (R.N. Richardson 1933). He presided over the agency during the troubles of the 1874–1875 Red River War. He later urged that the agency be moved from Fort Sill to Anadarko to escape the influence of the Army. Due to malaria, he resigned in 1877, effective in 1878. In 1878 he served on the commission that carved the Rosebud and Pine Ridge reservations from the larger Sioux reservation (G.W. Kingsbury 1915). In 1879 Haworth moved to Olathe, Kansas, where he was employed as an Indian inspector. Two years later, he was appointed inspector of Indian schools. When the office of Indian school superintendent was created by Congress in 1882, Haworth became its first incumbent. He proved a competent and faithful officer. HENRY E. FRITZ

Hayt, Ezra A. 1823–1902

A wealthy New York businessman, Hayt was a member of the Board of Indian Commissioners with the responsibility for the quality of food and supplies provided to the Indians, 1874–1877. During his term as commissioner of Indian affairs, 1877–1880, there were controversies surrounding hostilities with the Nez Perce, Bannock, Northern Cheyenne, and Ute. Hayt advocated an Indian police force, allotment, compulsory education for the Indian, and consolidation of many tribes on fewer reservations. He replaced an unprecedented number of agents in order to obtain competent and honest officials, ignoring the Peace Policy practice of appointing religiously affiliated agents. Hayt was accused of negligent management after Agent Nathan C. Meeker and others were killed by some Utes in 1879. Along with other charges of mismanagement, this led to his removal from office. For more detail, see Priest (1942), Waltmann (1962), and Meyer (1979). ANDREA LUDWIG

Hearne, Samuel 1745–1792

Hearne was born in London and, when aged about 12, was placed in the Royal Navy. He joined the Hudson's Bay Company as a seaman in 1766. In 1769, the Company sent him to search for the source of free copper known to exist somewhere northwest of Hudson Bay and to establish the latitude of the coast of North America in that region. His first two attempts, in 1769 and 1770, were unsuccessful. On his third attempt, December 1770–June 1772, his Chipewyan guide Matonabbee took him to the mouth of Coppermine River, where the Indians with whom they were traveling massacred a band of Eskimos. Hearne considered the copper deposits unexploitable, and his reckoning of the Arctic coast, in error by about 200 miles to the north, was corrected by John Franklin in 1826. No White man traveled again through much of the territory he had explored until the 1890s. In 1782, Hearne was obliged to surrender Fort Prince of Wales to the French.

On his retirement, Hearne settled in London. Hearne's (1958) journal described the search for a Northwest Passage and the geography, natural history, and people of a hitherto little-known region of the Subarctic (see also Hearne 1958a). For more information see G. Speck (1963) and J.T. Wilson (1949). ALAN COOKE

Heckewelder, John 1743–1823

Heckewelder was born in England, his father having left Saxony in order to participate in the evangelical efforts of the United Brethren. The family moved to the Moravian settlement at Bethlehem, Pennsylvania, in 1754. Heckewelder was a Moravian missionary to the Delaware Indians in Pennsylvania and Ohio between 1771 and 1810. In 1773 he became the resident missionary and de facto administrator of six flourishing communities of christianized Delaware Indians in the valley of the Muskingum and at other locations in the Ohio country. He returned to Bethlehem in 1786, but in 1801 he returned to the Ohio country to superintend a reservation of Moravian Indians. In 1810 he went back to Bethlehem and soon after began to write his valuable ethnological treatises on the Delaware Indians (Heckewelder 1819, 1820; P. Wallace 1958). ANTHONY F.C. WALLACE

Hennepin, Louis Antoine 1626–1705

Born at Ath, Belgium, Hennepin completed classical studies before joining the Recollect order in 1643. He then studied at Bethune and at Montargis in France. In 1675 he was one of five Recollect missionaries sent to New France in the company of Réné-Robert Cavelier, sieur de La Salle. The following spring, he and a companion built a mission house at Cataracoui (Fort Frontenac, now Kingston) and ministered to the Iroquois of the environs. In autumn 1678, Hennepin set out with La Salle's party for the Mississippi region. The following

April, Hennepin was captured by a Sioux war party that took him to a Sioux village in present-day Minnesota. There he was adopted by Chief Aquipoguetin and his six wives. Hennepin took advantage of this privileged position to study the language, customs, and beliefs of the Sioux. In July, Hennepin accompanied a hunting party led by Chief Ouasicoudé to the Wisconsin River. Then in September, Hennepin was given permission to leave the Sioux country; he returned to France where he wrote a description of the region (1683) that soon went through several French editions and was translated into Italian, Dutch, and German.

In 1687, Hennepin ran afoul of both civil and ecclesiastical authorities in France and Belgium; he, therefore, retired to Holland where he published two more descriptions of his alleged trip down the Mississippi (1697, 1698). Hennepin tried to resume his missionary work in the colony in 1699 but Louis XIV forbade him to set foot on North American soil. For additional information see Delanglez (1941) and Stengers (1945). CORNELIUS J. JAENEN

Herring, Elbert 1777–1876
Herring was born in Connecticut, but he became identified with political and social life in New York after graduating from Princeton College in 1795. He served with distinction as a member of the New York bar and also held several appointive positions before being named head clerk of the Indian Bureau by President Andrew Jackson in August 1831 (McAdam 1897–1899, 1:357). When Congress created the position of commissioner of Indian affairs in 1832, Jackson followed the advice of Secretary of War Lewis Cass and appointed Herring to that office. As commissioner between 1832 and 1836, Herring became deeply involved in efforts to promulgate Jackson's removal policy. He was a thorough advocate of that policy and seriously doubted whether the Indians could continue to survive unless they emigrated West and drastically altered their ways of life. The aspects of Indian life that Herring found wanting included their civil laws, their alleged distaste for farming, their communal landholding patterns, and their religious beliefs. Herring steadfastly maintained that only when the Indians adopted Christianity and private property and learned to farm and work at mechanical trades could they save themselves from extinction. To reach these goals, he emphasized education.

Details on his attitude toward the Indians and his handling of Indian affairs are in Satz (1975, 1979a). Herring's writings on Indian affairs are in the National Archives (Record Groups 75 and 107). RONALD N. SATZ

Holmes, William Henry 1846–1933
An archeologist and artist, Holmes began his career by sketching natural history specimens for the Smithsonian

Institution. He soon became a leading artist for the U.S. Geological Survey, 1872–1889, winning renown for illustrations accompanying the reports of Ferdinand V. Hayden's 1872 Yellowstone expedition and Clarence Dutton's explorations of the Grand Canyon in 1880 (Hayden 1873; Dutton 1882). His experiences on Hayden's 1874–1876 survey in southwestern Colorado led him into archeology, and he became a recognized authority on Indian antiquities. As a consequence, Holmes was appointed to important positions in the anthropological and museum professions, including terms as head curator of anthropology at Chicago's Field Museum, 1894-1897; head curator of anthropology at the U.S. National Museum 1897–1902 and 1909–1920; chief of the Bureau of American Ethnology, 1902–1909; and director of the original National Gallery of Art, 1920–1932. Holmes's anthropological interests included areas as diverse as the Virginia tidewater and the Yucatan. The obituaries by Hough (1933) and Swanton (1936) include bibliographies. P. RICHARD METCALF

Horn, Tom 1860–1903
Horn was an adventurer of enigmatic character. Born in Missouri, he ran away to Santa Fe when 14. There he drove mules, learned Spanish, and came under the tutelage of Al Sieber, an army scout. In 1876, he went with Sieber to the San Carlos Agency where he met Geronimo and learned to speak Apache. Horn, as a scout and interpreter, was involved in the negotiations and forays that led to the surrender of Geronimo in 1886. In 1890, Horn became a Pinkerton agent and, later, a stock detective in Wyoming. He also served in the Spanish-American war. Horn was accused of the murder of a 14-year-old boy in 1901, and for this he was hanged. The question of his innocence and of his character is explored in several biographies (Paine 1962; Monaghan 1946; Raine 1944; Coe 1927; and T. Horn 1904). ANDREA LUDWIG

Horse, John about 1812–1882
John Horse—known in Mexico as Juan Caballo and Juan de Dios Vidaurri—was perhaps better known in the United States by his nickname, Gopher John, from his boyhood prank of selling a brace of "gopher" terrapins over and over again to an army officer. Born a slave in Florida to a Seminole Indian father and a Black mother, the Seminole War gave him the opportunity to distinguish himself, both as a hostile in association with Chiefs Osceola, Wild Cat, and Alligator, and, after his surrender in April 1838 on a promise of freedom for Seminole Maroons who would "come in," in inducing other hostiles to surrender.

In the Indian Territory, to which he was removed in 1842, he allied himself with Wild Cat in striving for Seminole independence and protection for the Seminole

Maroons. He traveled to Washington in 1844 as interpreter to a delegation headed by Wild Cat and in 1845–1846 as representative of the Seminole Maroons. After the United States attorney general on June 28, 1848, declared illegal the war-time promise of freedom to Seminole Maroons who surrender, Horse, in 1849, founded Wewoka, later the Seminole capital, as a city of refuge. Later that year, with Wild Cat, he led an exodus of Seminole Indians and Blacks to Mexico, where they were settled in Coahuila as military colonists.

There Horse distinguished himself both by leading his people in battle against marauding Indians and Texas slave-hunters and by his obdurate refusal to permit their use in Mexican civil wars (Porter 1951). After the United States Civil War most of the Blacks returned to the United States, where some served effectively as army scouts, 1870–1914. John Horse himself, after being badly wounded in an assassination attempt at Fort Clark, Texas, on May 19, 1876, returned to the Seminole Maroon village of Nacimiento, Coahuila, and is said to have taken a leading part in destroying a band of outlaw Indians near San Carlos, Chihuahua (Porter 1952).

When in 1882 claimants to the Seminole Maroons' land at Nacimiento ordered their removal, John Horse went to Mexico City and obtained an order recognizing the Seminole claim, but he never returned. He was almost certainly the "Juan Caballo" who died of pneumonia in a Mexico City hospital on August 9, 1882. Descendants of his band maintain ownership of the Nacimiento land grant. A biography is in Porter (1970). KENNETH WIGGINS PORTER

Houston, Samuel 1793–1863
Born in Rockbridge County, Virginia, Houston was closely associated with Indians most of his life. As a youth in Tennessee, he ran away and lived with the Cherokee for nearly three years. There he developed a strong sympathy for the Indian and his way of life, although he fought against the Creek tribe during the War of 1812. After the war, serving as an agent for the government, he helped convince some of the Cherokee to remove west of the Mississippi, a move that he saw as being in the Indian interest. Houston then went into politics, following the political creed of Andrew Jackson and serving in the House of Representatives, 1823–1827, and as governor of Tennessee 1827–1829. In 1829 he suddenly resigned and joined his Cherokee friends in Arkansas. He was adopted into the tribe and became a champion of Indian rights, trying to force the government to end its neglect of the Indians and honor past pledges (Gregory and Strickland 1967). He went to Texas in 1833, participating in the Revolution of the Republic. During the period of the Texas Republic, 1836–1845, Houston worked hard, but ineffectually, to provide justice for the Comanche and other Texas tribes. In 1846,

when Texas entered the Union, Houston assumed a seat in the U.S. Senate. He held this post for the next 14 years, during which time he often defended Indian interests.

Reliable biographies include Friend (1954), James (1929), and Wisehart (1962). Of his own writings there are Williams and Barker (1938) and the autobiography (Day and Ullom 1954). Manuscript material is spread throughout the country, although a great deal has been collected at the Texas State Library and the University of Texas Library, Austin. ROBERT A. TRENNERT

Howard, Edgar 1858–1951
Born in Osceola, Iowa, Howard entered the Iowa College of Law, but failed to graduate. Elected to the House of Representatives in 1923 as a liberal Democrat from Nebraska, he became a member of the Committee of Indian Affairs and established a reform record. Howard introduced a series of Indian claims bills, worked to protect Indian allotments, and helped prevent the confiscation of Indian oil reserves on executive-order reservations. Chairman of the Committee on Indian Affairs at the beginning of the New Deal, he sponsored and defended the Indian Reorganization Act of 1934, but his bid for reelection in 1934 proved unsuccessful. Howard's private papers are in the Nebraska State Historical Society, Lincoln. For an analysis of his political performance consult W.E. Christensen (1955). KENNETH PHILP

Howard, Oliver Otis 1830–1909
A native of Maine, the one-armed "praying general" of Civil War fame brought profound religious convictions and a keen social consciousness to his military career. In 1872 he negotiated an end to 10 years of hostility with Cochise's Chiricahua Apaches in Arizona. In 1877, while commander of the Department of the Columbia, he pursued the Nez Perce in their unsuccessful effort to reach a haven in Canada, and in 1878 he directed the campaign that suppressed the Bannock–Northern Paiute uprising. He wrote extensively of his Indian experiences (O.O. Howard 1881, 1907, 1908). His papers at Bowdoin College, Brunswick, Maine, have supported a competent biography (Carpenter 1964). ROBERT M. UTLEY

Hrdlička, Aleš 1869–1943
Of Czech origin, Hrdlička came to America in 1882 at the age of 14. After graduating from medical school in 1894, he studied anthropology in Paris. His introduction to Indians was in 1898, when he accompanied the explorer Carl Lumholtz to Mexico. From 1903 to 1942 he served as the first curator of physical anthropology in the U.S. National Museum, Washington (fig.9). During this period he traveled widely, made a huge collection of Indian skeletons, and published voluminously. He played an important role in the development of physical anthropology as a discipline. He founded and edited the

American Journal of Physical Anthropology, 1918–1942. In 1930 he founded the American Association of Physical Anthropologists. For a biography see A.H. Schultz (1945). T. DALE STEWART

Hunt, Philemon Burgess 1837–1915

Born in Kentucky, Hunt served in the 4th Kentucky Mounted Infantry during the Civil War. In 1878, he was appointed agent of the Kiowa-Comanche-Apache Reservation, a position he held until 1885. In 1878, the Kiowa Agency was consolidated with the Wichita Agency north of the Washita River, and the Agency moved to Anadarko.

Hunt issued rations and annuity goods directly to the heads of families, rather than to chiefs, which undercut traditional political authority. He encouraged individual families to settle on homesteads rather than in band camps and to send their children to the Carlisle Indian Industrial School in Pennsylvania.

The biggest changes on the reservation under Hunt came with the end of the buffalo and the start of a new relationship with Texas cattlemen. Annual buffalo hunting parties, which were escorted by troops, supplemented the rations appropriated by Congress. In the winter of 1878–1879, the parties failed completely to find any animals. Supplies had to be bought from ranchers on credit, and emergency supplies sent from Fort Sill.

Congress refused to increase the appropriation for rations, thus precipitating a five-year-long food crisis. Hunt solved the problem by taking advantage of the Texas cattlemen who were allowing their stock to cross the unfenced Red River. In return for supplying cattle to Indians, Hunt allowed the cattlemen to use the reservation lands. The action was unauthorized but eased the immediate problem. After considerable debate, both in Washington and within the tribes, in 1885 the arrangement was formalized in leases with the cattlemen. The proceeds were distributed in semiannual "grass money" payments. Although they were modest payments, the money allowed the purchase of luxury items not available before.

There is no published biography of Hunt. See Hagan (1971, 1976) for details of his tenure and of the "grass money" controversy. THOMAS W. KAVANAGH

Ickes, Harold L. 1874–1952

Born in Pennsylvania, Ickes graduated from the University of Chicago in 1897 and obtained his law degree in 1907. He became active in municipal and state reform. In the 1920s when Secretary of the Interior Albert B. Fall pursued policies that would break up Indian landholdings and water rights so that these could be easily acquired by grazing, mining, and timber enterprises, Ickes became involved in efforts to improve the

Smithsonian, NAA: Aleš Hrdlička Papers, Series 15, Box 8.
Fig. 9. Aleš Hrdlička on Kodiak I., Alaska. He is standing at the Uyak Bay archeological site in an "outdoor museum" that he organized for the interest of visitors to the site. Photographed in 1934.

NON-INDIAN BIOGRAPHIES

economic and cultural status of the tribes and to safeguard them from aggressive White interests and the indifference of the government. In 1933, Ickes was appointed secretary of the interior and enlisted John Collier as commissioner of Indian affairs. Ickes and Collier were able to bring about the termination of the 50-year-old allotment policy, which had already stripped the Indians of almost half their tribal land holdings, and to push through Congress the Indian Reorganization Act of 1934, designed to engender an equitable relationship between the federal government and Indian tribes.

Ickes believed not only that the economic rehabilitation of the Indian tribes was a matter of first importance but also that the government should assist them in managing their own affairs within a framework of civil and cultural freedom and opportunity rather than continue the policy of coercion, forced anglicization, and social fragmentation that had been followed for so many years.

Equally close to Ickes's heart was the issue of the conservation of the country's natural resources. He battled before, during, and after his tenure as secretary to protect this national heritage from shortsighted exploitation by powerful private interests. Nor were these two major goals unrelated, since attainment of his objectives for the Indians was closely tied to keeping their lands and water out of the hands of the same forces that were grasping for other parts of the public domain.

Ickes resigned in 1946. He then wrote newspaper columns that championed the causes of minority rights and conservation. For further information see Ickes (1943, 1953). RAYMOND W. ICKES

Jackson, Andrew 1767–1845

Born in South Carolina, Jackson as a young man moved to Tennessee, where as lawyer, landowner, and politician, he became identified with the new West. In 1813–1814, as major general of the Tennessee militia, he mounted a decisive campaign against the hostile Creeks in Alabama; his defeat of them at the Battle of Horseshoe Bend and the Treaty of Fort Jackson that followed meant the extinguishment of Indian title to large parts of Alabama and Georgia. Jackson's military success at New Orleans, subsequent to the Creek War, made him a national hero. His pursuit of Indians into Spanish-owned Florida in 1818 brought official criticism, but it did nothing to weaken his popular image as an Indian fighter and advocate of frontier interests. His political career developed rapidly, and as president he eagerly accepted the policy of Indian removal inaugurated by his predecessors, supporting Georgia in its drive to rid the state of the Indians. The Indian Removal Act of 1830, which he advocated, led to the negotiation of removal treaties with the Five Civilized Tribes and the forceful removal of those who would not depart voluntarily. Faced with a serious jurisdictional problem between the federal gov-

ernment and the southern states, Jackson believed that the best interests of the Indians as well as of the United States lay in their migration to the West, but his action won him great opposition from the Indians and their friends at the time and severe criticism from later historians. For divergent views of Jackson's Indian policies, see Binder (1968), Prucha (1969a), Remini (1977–1984), and Satz (1975). FRANCIS PAUL PRUCHA

Jackson, Helen Hunt 1831–1885

Jackson's importance rests primarily upon writings completed near the end of her life on the condition of the Indians. Already noted for her literary output, Jackson wished to stir up national indignation on behalf of Indian rights. In *A Century of Dishonor* (1881) she exposed the story of government mistreatment of the Indian. While preparing her books, Jackson circulated tracts and petitions, wrote letters to newspapers, and toured the country taking jibes at officials then dealing with the Indians.

Following the furor created by *A Century of Dishonor*, she received a commission from the Department of Interior to investigate the condition of the Indians in California. Her experiences there with the natives formed part of her romantic novel *Ramona* (1884). Her saccharine style reconstructed the Indian as a synthetic type that never was. Yet the book occupies an important place in reformist literature, ranked along with *Uncle Tom's Cabin*.

For further information see Nevins (1941) and Odell (1939). ANDREW ROLLE

Jackson, Sheldon 1834–1909

Jackson, a Presbyterian clergyman born in upstate New York, was educated at Union College and Princeton Theological Seminary. After 1877, he devoted his energies to education and missionary work in Alaska and, with representatives of other denominations, worked out a division of mission fields in the territory. In the 1880s he established a mission school and anthropological museum at Sitka.

In 1885 Jackson was appointed the first general agent for education in Alaska and, in 1892, he sponsored the importation of domestic reindeer from Siberia for the benefit of Eskimo subsistence. In the years that followed, he made annual inspection trips to schools and reindeer herds throughout Alaska, resigning as general agent in 1906.

Jackson's annual reports concerning his educational duties appeared in Reports of the Commissioner of Education for 20 years beginning in 1886. S. Jackson (1880) wrote on Alaska and its missions and on the reindeer program (1891–1908). For additional information concerning Jackson's involvement in the program see D.J. Ray (1965). Biographies have been written by R.L. Stewart (1908) and Lazell (1960). Jackson's manuscripts are in the National Archives; the Sheldon Jackson Museum, Sitka; and the Presbyterian Historical Society, Philadelphia. JAMES W. VANSTONE

Jefferson, Thomas 1743–1826

Jefferson presented his interpretation of American Indian society in the 1780s in *Notes on the State of Virginia* (1954). Jefferson expressed broad sympathy for the Indian's capacity for improvement, but he granted little legitimacy to the existing native culture. He pursued his lifelong interest in the Indian by assembling native vocabularies, excavating a burial mound on the Rivanna River, searching for Indian origins, and collecting native artifacts.

His vocabularies were stolen in 1809, though a remnant survives in the American Philosophical Society, Philadelphia. As an archeologist, Jefferson's work was close to professional. His collections of artifacts come largely from the gifts of Indian delegations that visited the capital and from western travelers whom Jefferson encouraged to send him trophies of their expeditions. Such activity was characteristic of an eighteenth-century natural historian.

When Jefferson assumed national office, first as secretary of state and then as president, he attempted to apply the benevolent attitude he had developed from observation of the Indians. His high opinion of the natives coupled with his optimistic view of the future of the new nation led him to believe that the Indians would quickly adopt European civilization. This hope he saw partly confirmed by the changes that took place in the early nineteenth century in the social economy of the southern tribes. Jefferson's benevolence sometimes justified force and manipulation when the Indians did not adopt civilization and retire from their lands as quickly as the frontier advanced. In the later years of his presidency, Jefferson began to doubt that the Indians would reach the stage of incorporation before they were destroyed by the advance of American settlement. Consult D. Malone (1948–1974, 1 and 2), Prucha (1962), McLoughlin (1988), and Sheehan (1973). BERNARD W. SHEEHAN

Johnson, William 1715–1774

Born in Ireland, Johnson immigrated to America about 1738 and settled in the Mohawk River area in charge of an estate belonging to an uncle. In the late 1730s and early 1740s he began a career of real estate speculation and fur trading that brought him a fortune. In all his business activities Johnson allied himself with the Six Nations of Iroquois, particularly the Mohawks. Called Warraghiyageh by the Indians, he acquired their confidence, especially through Hendrick, a Mohawk chief. During King George's War, beginning in 1744, Johnson was appointed Indian agent by the colony of New York and enlisted Mohawk warriors on the British side. In

1745–1746 he was instrumental in checking French influence among the Iroquois by diplomacy and by giving presents. He also provisioned the post of Oswego, and he cooperated with Anglican ministers of the Society for the Propagation of the Gospel in Foreign Parts in their preaching and teaching among the Iroquois. At his home called Johnson Hall (close to the modern city of Johnstown, New York), built in 1763, this Irish immigrant established a headquarters for Indian diplomacy and business, flanked by blockhouses and quarters for visiting Indian embassies. Appointed superintendent for the northern Indian department during the French and Indian War in 1755, Johnson was also a major general who led troops against the French in a victory of that year. Aided by the Mohawks, Johnson aquired support from other Iroquois tribes that eventually helped Gen. Jeffrey Amherst in the conquest of Canada in 1760. At the Treaty of Fort Stanwix in 1768, Johnson took the lead in setting up an Indian boundary line that gave a measure of protection to the Indians as well as huge profits to his land-speculating associates.

After the death of his White wife, Catherine, Johnson lived with a Mohawk, Caroline, who bore him three children. Another Mohawk woman, Molly Brant, sister of the chief Joseph Brant, seems to have been the mother of eight more of his children, for whom he made provision in his will.

Johnson's sympathy was with the imperial government as the Revolution approached. His real significance appears to have been as a speculator in opening up the Mohawk valley area for peaceful settlement and assisting in mobilizing Indian allies to bring about the French defeat in North America.

For more detail see Johnson (1921–1965), Flexner (1959), Jacobs (1985), M.W. Hamilton (1976), and Marshall (1967). WILBUR R. JACOBS

Jones, Evan fl. 1805–1840s

Evan Jones was a missionary to the Cherokee whose life remains relatively obscure. As an independent Baptist minister he first passed through the Cherokee Nation in 1805 where he became interested in the tribe. In 1817 the Baptist Board of Foreign Missions appointed the Rev. Humphrey Posey to found a mission among the Cherokee, a task completed in 1820 with the establishment of the Valley Towns Mission in eastern Tennessee. Jones came to this mission as a teacher. In 1824 Posey retired and Jones was ordained pastor of the mission in 1825, retaining this position until 1838. Jones spent much of his time riding circuit, preaching, and trying to provide the tribe with education. He was extremely interested in developing methods for converting the Cherokee language into print. The Valley Towns Mission was relatively successful in obtaining Indian converts. As the movement to remove the Cherokee west of the Mississippi gained strength, Jones worked closely with missionaries of other denominations in defending tribal homelands. After the Cherokee removal treaty was signed in 1835, Jones was arrested by federal troops and forced out of Indian country, the government considering him an obstacle to enforcing the treaty. Jones went west with the tribe when they were ejected from Tennessee in 1838 and suffered along with his friends on the Trail of Tears. Jones continued his missionary activities among the Cherokee in their new homes in Indian Territory. Material on Jones's missionary activities is in Peck (1840) and D. Malone (1956). ROBERT A. TRENNERT

Jones, William A. 1844–1912

Born in Wales, Jones was a railroad manager, served as county superintendent of schools, as mayor of Mineral Point, Wisconsin, and in the Wisconsin House of Representatives before his appointment as commissioner of Indian affairs in 1897. He viewed the reservation system, rations and annuities, and lingering Indian cultural traditions as obstacles to the assimilation of the Indian. He was enthusiastic about industrial education to enable Indians to learn skills marketable off the reservation. Jones used allotment and the withholding of rations and annuities to force the Indians to work. For further information about Jones's term see W. David Baird (1979). ANDREA LUDWIG

Kane, Paul 1810–1871

Kane studied painting in Canada, the United States and Europe and was determined to paint Indian views after meeting George Catlin in London. Kane spent the season of 1845 painting the Ojibwa and other tribes near the Great Lakes and from 1846 to 1848 he traveled to Fort Garry, Fort Edmonton, and over the mountains to Fort Vancouver, becoming one of the first professional artists to paint portraits and scenes of the Cree, Blackfoot, Kutenai, Spokan, Chinookans, and coastal tribes. Kane's (1925) book is a valuable source of ethnographic data. For further information see Harper (1971). HUGH A. DEMPSEY

Kent, James 1763–1847

Born in New York state, Kent graduated from Yale College in 1781 and immediately began his lifelong connection with the law. An ardent Federalist, Kent was temperamentally unsuited for the rough-and-tumble of politics, and was much happier on the bench where he was able to make policy relatively free from rancor. Appointed to the New York Supreme Court in 1798, he was promoted to chief justice in 1804 and became chancellor of the state in 1814. After retirement in 1823 Kent revised his highly influential *Commentaries on American Law* (Kent 1826).

Kent developed the concept that though the Indian tribes were in an inferior position they still maintained their sovereignty. Kent's opinion in *Goodell* v. *Jackson* (20 Johnson's Reports 716, N.Y., 1823) was followed by the United States Supreme Court in *Worcester* v. *Georgia* (6 Peters 515, 1823). A general biographical work is Horton (1939). The bulk of Kent's papers are at the Library of Congress. DONALD ROPER

Kenton, Simon 1755–1836

Born in Virginia to a farming family, Kenton showed no interest in tilling soil. Although he learned to sign his own name, he never learned to read and write. At the age of 16 Kenton knocked a man unconscious and mistakenly thought him dead. He fled Virginia. Changing his name to Simon Butler he lived off the land with two other companions in northern Kentucky. By the age of 18 he had established himself as a skilled hunter and guide whose services were sought by those settling the territory. He was employed as a military spy during Lord Dunmore's War and kept the governor of Virginia abreast of Indian activity along the borderlands. After the war Kenton resumed his services as scout and hunter for groups of White settlers under the direction of George Rogers Clark, military commander of the Kentucky frontier. The remainder of his family moved to Kentucky in the early 1780s. On learning that the man he had fought in his youth had not died, Kenton resumed use of his family name.

In 1793 Gen. Anthony Wayne appointed Kenton major, and Kenton organized 100 Kentucky volunteers in a campaign against the Indians. In 1802 he moved to Ohio and took up lands near Urbana. Noted for his courageous campaigns against various Indian tribes, Kenton was not a wanton Indian killer. When troops stationed at Urbana plotted to kill a group of Indians who had sought refuge within the White settlement, Kenton alone voiced opposition, declaring that the troops would have to kill him first. Sensing his deep conviction the soldiers relented. For further information see Kenton (1930), Cochran (1932), and McDonald (1838). HEATHER C. DODSON

Kingsbury, Cyrus 1786–1870

After graduating from Brown University in 1812 and three years later from Andover Theological Seminary, Kingsbury was ordained a Congregationalist minister in 1815 and appointed a missionary the next year to the Cherokee by the American Board of Commissioners for Foreign Missions. In beginning the first Indian missions of that society in 1816, he founded, near present-day Chattanooga, Tennessee, Brainerd station, modeled upon the large manual-labor boarding school plan (Walker 1931). Although Kingsbury did not invent the principles of this model community method of Indian acculturation, his practical application of the method was instrumental in getting the United States government to fund such institutions among various Indian tribes after 1819 (Berkhofer 1963). In response to Choctaw requests, the American Board sent Kingsbury in 1818 to establish similar missions in that tribe, among whom he remained for the rest of his life (Cushman 1962; De Rosier 1972). When the Choctaw were forced to remove westward in the early 1830s (Lankford 1984), Kingsbury founded a new station in Indian territory. In opposition to the American Board's stand against slave-holding by the Southeast tribes in the two decades before the Civil War, Kingsbury was one of the many missionaries attempting a neutral stand on the issue in order to continue his work among the Choctaws (Lewit 1963). After the American Board withdrew from the Southeast tribes in 1859, his work was supported by the Old School Presbyterians until 1861, and later by the Southern Presbyterian missionary agency. A.S. Spalding (1975) is a full-length biography, and Kingsbury's life can be traced through manuscript sources, the largest number being among the American Board papers deposited at Harvard University. ROBERT F. BERKHOFER, JR.

Kino, Eusebio Francisco 1645–1711

Born of Italian parents at Segno in the Tyrol, Kino was educated by German Jesuits at Trent, Hall, Innsbruck, and Ingolstadt. He entered the Society of Jesus as a member of the Upper German Province in 1665 and later set aside a promising career as a mathematician-scientist to accept a missionary assignment to the New World. Appointed cartographer for a royal expedition to California in 1683, Kino explored the "island" and established a mission at La Paz (Kino 1952). The California venture failed and Kino was reassigned to the mission to the Pima Indians in Sonora and Arizona. He founded the mission of Dolores at the Upper Pima village of Cosari in 1687. For the next 24 years he explored the mountainous deserts, selected 27 mission sites, and directed the construction of 14 mission complexes. Through his knowledge of Piman language and culture he introduced Western thought and method to Piman and Yuman settlements scattered over 50,000 square miles. His missionary skills benefited Piman economy by the introduction of cattle raising and more varied agriculture. His explorations proved the peninsularity of California (Burrus 1971) and the feasibility of overland supply. Although Kino is remembered by Western society for his achievements as a missionary, cartographer, historian, and rancher, he was himself primarily dedicated to the welfare of the indigenous peoples of northwestern New Spain (Kino 1948). His approach to acculturation can be reviewed in his life of Saeta (Polzer 1971). The bibliography on Kino is extensive (Smith, Kessel, and Fox 1966);

Bolton (1960) remains the standard biography. CHARLES POLZER, S.J.

Kirkland, Samuel 1741–1808

Son of a minister at Norwich, Connecticut, Kirkland enrolled in the school of Eleazar Wheelock at Lebanon in 1761, to be educated along with Indians, including some Mohawks whose language he decided to learn. The next fall Kirkland entered what is now Princeton, graduating in absentia with the class of 1765, having already departed for the Seneca country. His journal of 1764–1765 of his trip to Kanadasegea (modern Geneva, New York), though written from notes later in life, is typical of the man at his best, affording vignettes of travel in winter, reception of strangers, the Onondaga council, his adoption, and beliefs concerning dreams and death. Kirkland was ordained at Lebanon in July 1766 and returned to Iroquoia for the Society in Scotland for the Propagation of Christian Knowledge, this time settling at Oneida where, save brief absences, he passed the rest of his days.

The societies that supported his work expected him to send journals regularly. The first journals contain the sharpest observations of Indian life, although his letters of negotiations between 1774 and 1794 are richer, more meaningful documents.

Kirkland strongly defended the integrity of the Oneida and Tuscarora communities that he served. He broke with Wheelock, frustrating his agents at the 1768 Fort Stanwix treaty from obtaining lands near Oneida for the Indian charity school and advocating education of Indians at home in the useful arts. In 1770 Kirkland put himself under the Boston Board of Commissioners for the London Company for the Propagation of the Gospel in New England and Parts Adjacent in America. The Harvard Corporation also contributed. Although William Johnson had welcomed Kirkland, and the Oneida chiefs would protest that their minister did not interfere in state matters, Johnson became concerned over the growing independence of the Oneidas and Tuscaroras and their gradual alienation from the Crown. Kirkland deserves partial credit for keeping the Six Nations quiet and out of the Shawnee war with the Virginians, and only he brought the Oneida and Tuscarora to the patriots' cause during the Revolution. After the war, he assisted Timothy Pickering of Salem in concluding a series of treaties that kept the Six Nations from involvement in warfare in the Ohio country, and he collaborated in plans for their gradual civilization. On the occasion of his election to the American Academy of Arts and Sciences in 1791, Kirkland contributed a census of the Six Nations (Fenton 1953:585). His 1791 "Plan of Education for the Indians . . . " is quite free of racism and shows remarkable insight into how culture is acquired; the plan bore fruit in the chartering of Hamilton Oneida Academy in

1793, afterward Hamilton College (Ibbotson and North 1922).

Kirkland's (1980) papers in the Hamilton College Library, Clinton, New York, are an indispensible record of Indian and White affairs during the period. See also Graymont (1972). WILLIAM N. FENTON

Kroeber, Alfred L. 1876–1960

Kroeber was a foremost student of American Indians, his active fieldwork extending from 1899, when he studied the Arapaho, Ute, Northern Shoshone, and Bannock, to 1954, when he recorded Mohave myths. His voluminous writings on American Indian ethnography concentrate on California Indians, among whom he worked from 1901 on, after he established the Department of Anthropology at the University of California, Berkeley. His broad interests led him into anthropological theory, folklore, linguistics, and Peruvian archeology—all fields in which he displayed special competence. He founded the Museum of Anthropology at Berkeley and served as its director until his retirement in 1946, and his efforts helped establish the University of California Publications in American Archaeology and Ethnology, 1903–1960, which went through 50 volumes. The biography written by his wife (T. Kroeber 1970) describes the man, and obituaries by his colleagues (Steward 1961; Hymes 1961) assess his professional contributions; for a bibliography see Gibson and Rowe (1961). ROBERT F. HEIZER

Lacombe, Albert 1827–1916

Father Lacombe was an Oblate priest in the Canadian west who published a Cree grammar and dictionary as well as other books in Cree and Blackfoot. In 1861 he founded Saint Albert mission for Cree-Métis; in 1865, Saint Paul des Cris; and in 1895, Saint Paul des Métis, all for Cree and Métis farmers (Breton 1955; Mac Gregor 1975). HUGH A. DEMPSEY

La Farge, Oliver Hazard Perry 1901–1963

La Farge, from an artistically and intellectually prominent Rhode Island family, went on archeological expeditions to Arizona in 1921, 1922, and 1924 while studying anthropology at Harvard (A.M. 1929) and undertook archeological and ethnological investigations of Mayans in Mexico and Guatemala in 1925, 1927, and 1932 under the auspices of Tulane and Columbia universities. His experiences with Arizona Indians inspired the writing of his novel *Laughing Boy* (1929), a Navajo love story that communicated a feeling of realism by its wealth of ethnographic detail and concomitant impression of psychological authenticity; it won the Pulitzer Prize in 1930. In Guatemala La Farge obtained data on the Mayan calendar that was still in use among the Jacaltec and the Chuj and its correlation with the European calendar, research that led to basic contributions to Mayan studies.

As he continued his career as a writer of fiction and popular works on Indians, he was active in Indian welfare and support organizations. After serving as a director of the Eastern Association on Indian Affairs, 1930–1932, he was elected its president in 1933, a post he held, through its successive renamings as the National Association on Indian Affairs and the American Association on Indian Affairs (when it merged with the Indian Defense Association in 1937), until he stepped down to enter military service in 1942. He was re-elected president in 1948 (the name Association on American Indian Affairs having been adopted in 1946) and served until his retirement in declining health in 1962. While working for Commissioner of Indian Affairs John Collier, La Farge was one of the team that developed the practical Navajo orthography (vol. 10:667). Besides the Navajo, his closest associations were with the Jicarilla Apache and Santa Clara Pueblo. His papers are in the University of Texas, Austin; the biography by McNickle (1971) includes further references. IVES GODDARD

Lafitau, Joseph-Françeois 1681–1746

Son of a merchant family of Bordeaux, France, Lafitau entered the Jesuit order, receiving the rigorous classical education of that society. In 1711 he was ordained a priest and granted permission to go to the missions of New France. He arrived in Canada toward the close of a period of intense French hostilities with the Five Nations of Iroquois. Reporting at Quebec, he was ordered to Sault-Saint-Louis (Caughnawaga) opposite Montreal. He remained 1712 to 1717 among the "praying Iroquois." This settlement, already 30 years old, had a winter population of 600, which doubled in summer; but intensive horticulture had depleted the soil, firewood was scarce, and the brandy traders were a menace. Lafitau manifested some ability in the language, and his genuine interest in Iroquois culture paid dividends. He left detailed descriptions of housing, the composition of households, and the classificatory kinship system; his chapters on the activities of men and women, local government, and warfare are classics (Lafitau 1724; Fenton and Moore 1974–1977).

In 1717 Lafitau was sent to France, where he shared the duties of the procuratorship until 1732, after which until 1741 he was solely in charge. He was near libraries and he found time to write. He returned to Canada 1727–1729 as superior of the mission.

Lafitau was not just another comparatist; he developed a method of reciprocal illumination in which he used his own field observations to throw light on the customs of antiquity, which afforded him clues to discoveries. In his view the savages of the New World were men, the Iroquois were people in their own right, and their customary ways were worthy of study and respect. For

more information see Fenton (1969).
WILLIAM N. FENTON

La Follette, Robert M., Sr. 1855–1925
Congressman (1885–1890), governor of Wisconsin (1901–1905), United States Senator (1906–1925), and independent candidate for the presidency (1924), La Follette was one of the strongest legislative supporters of Indian rights during the Progressive era. Although his vision of Indian reform was limited by the Progressives' cultural biases and constituted only a fraction of his total reform interests, La Follette was generally recognized by Indians as an important ally. In 1906, appointment to the Senate Indian Affairs Committee provided La Follette with an unexpected outlet for his Progressive interests. By attracting public attention, he was able to prevent sale of the Five Civilized Tribes' mineral rights to railroad companies under an amendment to the Curtis Act. In 1908, he secured passage of a bill, frequently referred to as the La Follette Act, to end wasteful use of Chippewa and Menominee reservation timber by lumber companies in Wisconsin. Although his defense of Indian rights was largely determined by their close relation to Progressive issues, La Follette providently advocated allowing Indians greater control of their resources. La Follette continued to serve on the Indian affairs committee until his death.

La Follette (1960) wrote an autobiography; see also La Follette and La Follette (1953). La Follette papers may be found in the State Historical Society of Wisconsin, Madison, and the Library of Congress. CAROLYN J. MATTERN

Lane, Joseph 1801–1881
Born in North Carolina Lane lived in Kentucky and Indiana before gaining national prominence for service in the war against Mexico. Shortly after his return to his farm in Indiana in 1848, he was named first territorial governor of Oregon, a region that included, at the time of his assuming duties in 1849, the entire Pacific Northwest. Operating initially also as superintendent of Indian affairs, Lane attempted to pacify the region's natives, disturbed by increasing White encroachment. He made small payments to aggrieved tribes but was firm in threatening military action. In June 1850 he concluded a provisional treaty with the Takelma of the Rogue River Valley in southern Oregon. A year later he led a company of volunteer soldiers into the region and joined Major Philip Kearny in a 10-day war with these Indians. In August 1853 Lane again fought the Takelma as commander of the volunteer and government forces. His operations forced the Treaty of Table Rock, which ceded most of the Rogue River Valley to the government. In 1860 Lane was nominated on a states-rights ticket for

vice-president of the United States. His pro-Southern sympathies brought political ruin.

Lane's papers include collections in the Bancroft Library, University of California, Berkeley; University of Oregon, Eugene; Oregon Historical Society, Portland; and Indiana University, Bloomington. For biographical details see Lane (1878), Hendrickson (1967), and Beckham (1971). STEPHEN DOW BECKHAM

Laurie, John Lee 1899–1959
A schoolteacher from Calgary, Canada, Laurie was secretary of the Indian Association of Alberta, 1944–1956, and treasurer, 1956–1959. As its only non-Indian member for several years, he helped transform the Association into a strong political force and was directly responsible for Canadian Indians receiving benefits such as old-age assistance and improved health services in the 1940s. He was named honorary chief Red Crow of the Blood, White Cloud of the Assiniboine, and Sitting Eagle of the Sarcee (Anonymous 1959). Laurie's papers are in the Glenbow-Alberta Institute, Calgary. HUGH A. DEMPSEY

Lea, Luke 1810–1898
Born in Tennessee, Lea was the nephew of the Luke Lea who served in Congress 1833–1837 and eventually became Indian agent at Fort Leavenworth, Kansas, 1849–1851. The younger Lea held various minor political offices in Tennessee before moving to Mississippi. In 1849 he ran as the Whig candidate for governor of the state and was soundly defeated. As a reward for supporting Zachary Taylor, Lea was appointed commissioner of Indian affairs in 1850. Lea was committed to the idea of "civilizing" the Indians and felt that this could best be done by assigning all tribes to permanent homes within well-defined boundaries, where they could farm. To accomplish this task it was necessary to expand the Indian Bureau into areas of the Far West where the government had never before taken any responsibility.

The reorganization of the Indian department became a reality in February 1851, when a new system of superintendencies and agencies received congressional sanction. The significant feature of this act was the creation of three full superintendencies for all the tribes east of the Rockies. As part of the same plan and also to clear all tribes away from the Oregon Trail, Lea helped engineer the treaty of Fort Laramie in 1851, which assigned lands to the Cheyenne, Arapaho, Mandan, Gros Ventre, Crow, Blackfeet, and Sioux. This was the first time most of these tribes had entered into serious agreement with the federal government. Lea intended to use the assignment of specific lands to encourage the tribes to end their nomadic ways. Lea also negotiated the removal of the small border tribes from Nebraska and Kansas. In 1853 he was replaced as commissioner (Trennert 1979b). ROBERT A. TRENNERT

Lee, Jason 1803–1845

Lee was born near Stanstead, Quebec, Canada. He was converted to Methodism during a frontier revival in 1826 and three years later enrolled in a religious academy at Wilbraham, Massachusetts, where he embarked on a career of preaching and teaching. In 1833 Lee responded to the concern for an Oregon mission; with his nephew, Rev. Daniel Lee, he set out overland for the Pacific Northwest in 1834. The Lees located their station in the center of the Willamette Valley among the Kalapuya Indians. Lee found the people badly ravaged by the epidemics of 1829–1832 and in 1835 opened a school with a dozen orphans as students. The Methodist program was one of "civilization" and "salvation"; all instruction was in English and emphasized manual labor, agriculture, and Christian values. Reinforced by 30 adult laborers in 1840, Lee embarked on an expansion program for stations at Fort Nisqually, The Dalles, Clatsop Plains, and Oregon City. His success among the Indians was negligible. His contribution toward bringing American settlers to Oregon was immense. Lee was dismissed by his supporting Mission Society in 1844; his stations were closed in 1845. His papers and reports are held by the Bancroft Library, University of California, Berkeley, and the Oregon Historical Society, Portland. Biographies include Brosnan (1932). STEPHEN DOW BECKHAM

Leupp, Francis Ellington 1849–1918

Born in New York City, a graduate of Williams College in 1870 and Columbia law school in 1872, Leupp was a renowned journalist who maintained a lifelong interest in the Indian. He was assistant editor of the New York *Evening Post*, 1874–1878; part-owner and editor of the Syracuse *Herald*, 1878–1885; and bureau chief for the Washington *Evening Post*, 1885–1904.

Leupp's interest in the Indian made him a frequent visitor to the Indian reservations of New York when a young man, and later he made several extended Western journeys. In 1895 he became agent for the Indian Rights Association. He was sent by Secretary of the Interior Hoke Smith as his confidential representative to Ute negotiations concerned with opening their land to settlement in 1895 (Leupp 1895). In 1896–1897, Leupp served on the Board of Indian Commissioners. President Theodore Roosevelt sent him to investigate accusations against the officials responsible for the welfare of the Kiowa, Comanche, and Apache in 1902. From 1905 to 1909, Leupp served as commissioner of Indian affairs (Parman 1979).

Leupp saw the Indian as an individual—not to be transformed but to be improved—and believed in the efficacy of a manual education in order that the Indian could become independent not only of the tribe but of the government. Leupp emphasized day schools and off-reservation employment for Indians. For detail of his views see Leupp (1905, 1910, 1914). ANDREA LUDWIG

Lewis, Meriwether 1774–1809

President Thomas Jefferson chose U.S. Army captain Lewis to lead the Corps of Discovery in its exploration of the Louisiana Purchase, from Saint Louis to the Pacific, 1804–1806. An excellent Indian diplomat, he won friends from the Oto to the Tillamook. Only two tribes received him with hostility, the Arikara and the Piegan. After the expedition, William Clark continued his friend's work with the Indian nations of the West. For further information see Bakeless (1947), Dillon (1965), and Thwaites (1904–1905). RICHARD H. DILLON

Lisa, Manuel 1772–1820

First to exploit the Fur trade of the Rockies in 1807, Lisa built and maintained trading posts with all the Missouri River tribes. He married the daughter of an Omaha chief. A master of Indian diplomacy, he was appointed subagent by William Clark and was instrumental in keeping the Sioux neutral during the War of 1812. For further information see Chittenden (1902, 1:125–136), Douglas (1911, 1964), and Oglesby (1963). RICHARD E. OGLESBY

Livingston, Philip 1686–1749

The second son of Robert Livingston, Philip succeeded to the family manor upon his father's death in 1728. He had studied for the law and was admitted to the New York bar in 1719. In the next year he followed his father as a commissioner for Indian affairs and as secretary for Indian affairs for the colony of New York under a direct Crown commission. In 1724, Gov. William Burnet nominated him to the Governor's Council to which he received appointment in 1725.

Livingston served Governor Burnet as emissary to the acting governor of Canada in a vain effort to halt the building of a French fort at Niagara. In his last years, Livingston became embroiled in quarrels with Gov. George Clinton over handling Indian relations. The governor charged Livingston with selling arms to the French-allied tribes and also with stealing some Mohawk lands. Clinton urged Livingston's removal from the secretaryship for Indian affairs and all other public offices, but the London authorities ignored the governor's demands. Philip Livingston retained his offices until his death. For further information see Livingston (1910). LAWRENCE H. LEDER

Livingston, Robert 1654–1728

Livingston arrived in Albany, New York, in 1674 as the final transfer of New Netherland to the English took place. Although born in Scotland, he had spent his youth in Rotterdam and consequently had a good command of both Dutch and English. His father had been a prominent Calvinist clergyman, and this gave Robert contacts in the Boston mercantile community. He quickly utilized both advantages, beginning as an Albany merchant, and moved into several minor governmental offices where his bilingualism proved advantageous. He married Alida Schuyler Van Rensselaer in 1679, gaining connections with prominent political and mercantile families in the colony and, in 1686, possession of a 160,000-acre manor. In 1675 Livingston became secretary to the Board of Commissioners for Indian Affairs, beginning a long association until 1721 with the colony's dealings with the Iroquois Indians. He became most influential in Indian affairs during the administrations of Governors Robert Hunter and William Burnet, helping to design the ill-fated efforts of those governors to destroy French influence in the fur trade. He also collaborated with Cadwallader Colden in the preparation of his *History of the Five Indian Nations* by making available the records in his possession. Those records have been published (R. Livingston 1956) as has a definitive biography of Livingston (Leder 1961). LAWRENCE H. LEDER

Longfellow, Henry Wadsworth 1807–1882

Longfellow's attitudes and sensibility were deeply influenced by his university education in Germany. He devoted much of his life to a study of comparative literature, which he taught at Harvard. Perhaps his chief contribution to American culture resides in his opening it to European influences. But by the popular audience he is less well remembered for his criticism, translation, and adaptation of European poetry, including his notable rendition of Dante, than for his poems on American subjects, *Evangeline, The Courtship of Miles Standish*, and especially *Hiawatha*. Though its form is based on a Finnish model, *Hiawatha* represents Longfellow's most notable attempt at making an epic poem on native themes. Longfellow's view of the Red man is based on inadequate scholarship and distorted by a sentimental Christian belief that Indian culture was and should be doomed. (See J.A. Russell 1928). LESLIE A. FIEDLER

Lorimier, Pierre Louis 1748–1812

Lorimier was born of French descent near Montreal. At the age of 21, he traveled to the Miami River and traded with various Indian tribes from his post called "Lorimie's." During the Revolutionary War, he aided British efforts and incited numerous Indian raids on American settlements. In 1778 he gained notoriety by capturing Daniel Boone. In 1782, Lorimier was forced to flee after his trading post was destroyed by an army led by George Rogers Clark. In 1787 Lorimier moved to Spanish territory west of the Mississippi and quickly built up a lucrative trade with the Indians. His good relations with

the tribesmen proved valuable in protecting towns and settlements. The Spanish showed their gratitude by granting him large concessions of land and by appointing him commandant of a district. Lorimier continued to have much influence in the area after the Louisiana Purchase and was appointed one of the judges on the court of common pleas. Respected by Indians for his sense of justice, he served both the Spanish and the Americans as interpreter and conciliator. Often on critical occasions he made dangerous trips to persuade tribes to keep the peace. Uneducated formally, Lorimier spoke French, English, and several Indian tongues fluently. He was a brave commander, an able leader, and a successful businessman. In 1808 Lorimier laid out the town of Cape Girardeau from his land grants. Lorimier successively married two half-blood Shawnee women and had several children, including a son who attended West Point. A short biographical sketch of Lorimier is found in Quaife (1965). HENRY E. FRITZ

Lowie, Robert H. 1883–1957

Born in Vienna, Lowie was educated in New York, received his Ph.D. in anthropology at Columbia under Franz Boas in 1908, and was attached to the American Museum of Natural History, New York, until 1921, when he became professor at the University of California, Berkeley. His fieldwork was carried out among the Chipewyan, Shoshone, Ute, Northern Paiute, Hidatsa, Mandan, Arikara, Assiniboine, Blackfoot, Akwa'ala, Hopi, Washoe, and especially the Crow.

He published over 500 titles (including reviews) on a wide range of subjects—anthropological theory, ethnography, folklore, kinship, philosophy, biography, and linguistics (Kroeber 1957, 1958). A number of his books had an important influence (Lowie 1917, 1920, 1924, 1937, 1948).

For an obituary and a bibliography of Lowie's published writings see Radin (1958) and Lowie, Lowie, and Richardson (1958); for an edited collection of his shorter papers see Lowie (1960). ROBERT F. HEIZER

McBeth, Susan L. 1833–1893

Born near Sterling, Scotland, Susan McBeth emigrated as an infant with her parents to Wellsville, Ohio. Educated at Steubenville, she taught at the University of Fairfield, Iowa. From 1859 to 1861 she taught and carried on missionary activity among the Choctaw in Oklahoma but was obliged to leave on the outbreak of the Civil War, during which she worked in a hospital at Jefferson Barracks, Missouri. Later she undertook mission work in Saint Louis and about 1872 suffered a stroke. In 1873 she went to the Nez Perces Indian Reservation, Idaho, first as a government teacher, and from 1874 for most of the next 20 years as missionary and trainer of young Nez Perces for the Presbyterian ministry. Her sister Kate C. McBeth joined her in 1879 (K.C. McBeth 1908). For other notices of the work of the McBeth sisters see M.M. Crawford (1936:11–13) and E. Eells (1914:296–298). According to D.E. Walker (1968:40–41, 55–59) the religious and social effects of earlier Presbyterian missionaries among the Nez Perce were strongly reinforced under the McBeth sisters. A grammar and a vocabulary of the Nez Perce language compiled by Susan McBeth are deposited in manuscript in the Smithsonian Institution, National Anthropological Archives. Papers and letters of both McBeth sisters are in the Idaho State Historical Society, Boise. WILLIAM W. ELMENDORF

McCoy, Isaac 1784–1846

Born in western Pennsylvania, as a young man McCoy felt the call to preach and became a self-educated Baptist minister in the Indiana Territory near Vincennes. There he became aware of the condition of the Indians in the region and decided to direct his missionary efforts to them rather than White settlers. He began with the Wea but soon turned to the Miami. Subsequently he established Potawatomi and Ottawa missions in the Michigan Territory.

As the White frontier moved toward his missions, McCoy became imbued with the idea of a permanent Indian country in the west. There, removed from the deleterious influence of White settlers, the Indians might gradually adapt to Christian civilization. McCoy supported Andrew Jackson's removal policy, although he criticized its emphasis on removal rather than colonization (McCoy 1827). He conducted explorations for the War Department in what is now Kansas and Oklahoma. During the course of removal he located and surveyed the western lands for most of the emigrant tribes.

McCoy established new Indian missions in the west, but he devoted most of his time to the formal organization of the Indian Territory. He worked closely with Sen. John Tipton on an organization bill, which passed the Senate in 1838 but did not come before the House. Thereafter, his chief concern was to foster peaceful relations between emigrant and indigenous tribes. McCoy's correspondence and journals are in the archives of the Kansas State Historical Society, Topeka. He wrote a history of Baptist Indian missions (McCoy 1840). For biographical details and an analysis of McCoy's effort to establish an Indian state see Schultz (1972) and E.J. Lyons (1945). GEORGE A. SCHULTZ

McGillycuddy, Valentine Trant O'Connell 1849–1939

In 1869 McGillycuddy obtained a medical degree from the Marine Hospital in Detroit, Michigan. When his health suffered as an intern in 1871, he took a leave of absence from the hospital and joined a survey group as assistant engineer. For three years he helped survey Lake Michigan and eventually became surgeon for the expedition. He joined W.J. Twining of the United States Engineering Corps in his survey of the boundary line between the United States and British America as both topographer and surgeon. In 1875 he served in the same capacities for John Wesley Powell in his exploration of the Black Hills. Under Gen. George Crook, as surgeon in the field, McGillycuddy saw military action against Sitting Bull. While stationed at Fort Robinson as assistant post-surgeon, McGillycuddy treated Indian patients. He became dissatisfied with government treatment of the Cheyenne and traveled to Washington, D.C., to discuss the matter with Commissioner of Indian Affairs E.A. Hayt. While there McGillycuddy obtained the position of Indian agent at Pine Ridge, South Dakota, where he served seven years. His policy reflected a belief that White usurption of Indian lands was inevitable. His responsibility lay in making the Red Cloud Sioux self-sufficient farmers and ranchers. Although some of the younger Sioux shared McGillycuddy's views, Red Cloud and other leaders did not. Red Cloud repeatedly filed complaints against the agent. Although all complaints were found groundless, suspicions against McGillycuddy mounted and in 1886 he resigned. After leaving Pine Ridge he worked for the Public Health Service and, in the 1920s, served as a hotel physician in Berkeley, California. For further details see McGillycuddy (1941). HEATHER C. DODSON

McKee, Alexander about 1738–1799

The son of a Pennsylvania fur trader, McKee joined the British Indian department in 1760. In 1771 he became deputy Indian agent at Pittsburgh. He adhered to the British cause at the outbreak of the Revolution and in 1778 made his escape from Pittsburgh to British headquarters at Detroit. McKee served in the field from 1778 until 1783, coordinating, supplying, and occasionally participating in the Indian war effort against the American frontier. Aided by his considerable prestige among the Indians, McKee served to the end of his life as Britain's chief diplomat and ambassador to the Ohio Valley Indians. In 1794 his long service was rewarded by his appointment as deputy superintendant general and deputy inspector general for Indian affairs. His biography is by Hoberg (1934, 1935). RICK TOOTHMAN

McKee, Redick fl. 1850–1876

Redick McKee, a Virginian, was the chairman and purchasing and disbursing agent among the three Indian commissioners appointed by President Millard Fillmore in 1850 to go to the new state of California. The commission was to report on the number, character, and condition of the Indian tribes in California and to negotiate treaties for securing peace between the gold miners and native peoples. McKee and his colleagues

(O.M. Wozencraft from Louisiana and George W. Barbour from Kentucky) in 1851–1852 entered into treaty-making arrangements with Indian groups, mainly those in the area where gold mining was being carried out and where Indian-White altercations were most common (C.L. Hoopes 1970; Heizer 1972). McKee's main treaty work is described by Gibbs (1853) and J. McKee (1853). The entire mission came to nothing, because the Senate, which on September 28, 1850, had authorized the treaties, refused to ratify them on July 8, 1852.

By 1851 the commission had run out of funds and McKee prevailed upon the collector of the Customs House in San Francisco to advance $5,000 to carry on its work. When this amount did not arrive from Washington to reimburse the customs collector, McKee borrowed money to repay the advance by mortgaging his own property. Unable to repay the bank, his house and other property were foreclosed and sold in 1863. After numerous appeals the Bureau of Indian Affairs paid McKee $2,234 in 1865, and Congress in 1870 granted further reimbursement in the amount of $7,424. In 1876 McKee was still petitioning for reimbursement in the amount of $50,910 for losses incurred in his ill-advised move to finance the federal government's treaty-making fiasco. No record has been located to show that McKee ever received further satisfaction. ROBERT F. HEIZER

McKenney, Thomas Loraine 1785–1859

Born into a Quaker family on Maryland's Eastern Shore, McKenney spent his early years as a merchant, first in Maryland and then in the District of Columbia. After brief service in the War of 1812, he returned to private business where he remained until April 1816, when President James Madison appointed him superintendent of Indian trade. McKenney administered the factory system, as the network of government-owned trading houses for the Indians was known, until Congress abolished it in 1822. He became editor of the *Washington Republican and Congressional Examiner*, a semiweekly newspaper founded solely to support Secretary of War John C. Calhoun's bid for the 1824 presidential nomination. Calhoun's candidacy was short-lived, but he rewarded McKenney by naming him superintendent of Indian affairs, a position the secretary of war established without legislative sanction in the War Department in March 1824. McKenney served capably as the first head of the Bureau of Indian Affairs until August 1830, when President Andrew Jackson removed him from office. McKenney spent the remainder of his life lecturing and writing about Indian affairs (McKenney 1846). McKenney pioneered the study of North American ethnology (McKenney and Hall 1842–1844), establishing in his War Department office a remarkable collection of books, manuscripts, artifacts, and paintings, which he called his "archives of the American Indian," and he was the

architect of two government programs that had tremendous impact on Native Americans in this period. He drafted the Indian Civilization Act in 1819, which provided $10,000 annually for the support of schools in the Indian country, and he sponsored the Indian Removal Act of 1830, which provided for the relocation of eastern tribes west of the Mississippi River. For a comprehensive study of McKenney and his role in Indian affairs, see Viola (1974). HERMAN J. VIOLA

Mackenzie, Ranald Slidell 1840–1889

A graduate of the military academy at West Point in 1862, Mackenzie took command of the 4th Cavalry in 1871. During the next decade he led it in campaigns against Kickapoo and Apache in Mexico, both northern and southern Plains Indians, and Western Apache in Arizona. He also was called in at the time of the Ute uprising in 1878 and supervised their removal the following year. He demonstrated in 1872 that troops could operate on the Staked Plains of Texas and eastern New Mexico and ended that Indian sanctuary. At Palo Duro Canyon, Texas, in 1874 and again in the attack on Dull Knife's Cheyenne in 1876, Mackenzie inflicted severe property losses on Indians and helped force them to reservations. In an attack on the Comanche on McClellan Creek in 1872, he captured over 100 women and children and held them for several months as hostages for the good behavior of their relatives.

Although implacable in his pursuit of bands termed hostile, Mackenzie earned the respect of the Quaker Indian Agent James M. Haworth. In April 1875 Mackenzie arranged the surrender of the last Comanche band and treated the Indians leniently. He used army rations to help the Kiowa agency through food crises and appealed through military channels for better rations for the Indians. He also was responsible for an unsuccessful effort to launch the Kiowa and Comanche on careers as cattle and sheep raisers.

In December 1883 Mackenzie was disabled by mental illness and was retired from the army the following March. For his career in the West see Nohl (1962) and Pate (1987); for his campaigns on the Texas frontier see Wallace (1964, 1967–1968). WILLIAM T. HAGAN

McLaughlin, James 1842–1923

Born and reared in Ontario, McLaughlin received an eighth-grade education before serving a three-year apprenticeship in a blacksmith shop. As as apprentice he learned how to operate and maintain sawmills and gristmills. In 1863 he moved to Saint Paul, Minnesota, where he married Marie Louise Buisson, who had a full knowledge of Sioux language and custom from her grandmother, a Mdewakanton Sioux. In 1865 McLaughlin obtained United States citizenship, and for the next several years worked as both a blacksmith and a traveling

Smithsonian, NAA: 56,650.
Fig. 10. James McLaughlin at the dedication of the Standing Rock, Standing Rock Agency. left to right, foreground, Sitting Bull, Hunkpapa Sioux; McLaughlin; and Joe Primeau, interpreter. Photograph by David F. Barry, No. Dak., 1886.

salesman. In 1871 McLaughlin was hired as a blacksmith at Fort Totten, northern Dakota Territory, a Sioux reservation, but the agent there trained him as an Indian agent. In July 1876 McLaughlin obtained the appointment as official agent at Fort Totten. In 1881 he was transferred to the Sioux reservation at Standing Rock (fig. 10). White malcontents filed complains against him, questioning his integrity and job performance; none was substantiated. In 1895 McLaughlin declined the position of assistant commissioner of Indian affairs but accepted a position as a United States Indian inspector. Throughout his government service, McLaughlin adhered to the Indian policy of the day and strove to make Indians self-sufficient by encouraging them to give up their own traditions and adopt those of the Whites (J. McLaughlin 1910, 1936). McLaughlin was greatly respected by both Indians and Whites for his thoroughness and dedication (Pfaller 1978). HEATHER C. DODSON

Macleod, James Farquharson 1836–1894
Macleod was appointed assistant commissioner of the North-West Mounted Police in Canada, 1874–1877, and commissioner, 1877–1880. He was the first Canadian official to contact the Blackfoot tribes in 1874 and established a bond of trust that resulted in the signing of Treaty No. 7 with the tribes in 1877. For further information see J.P. Turner (1950). HUGH A. DEMPSEY

McLoughlin, John 1784–1857
Born in the parish of Rivière-du-Loup, Quebec, McLoughlin trained in medicine in Montreal. He early entered the fur trade and served the North West Company for two decades. By 1821 McLoughlin was in charge of Fort William on Lake Superior. In 1825 he

assumed command in Oregon and relocated the company's headquarters to Fort Vancouver. He governed the Pacific Northwest from 1825 to 1846 as chief factor of the Hudson's Bay Company. McLoughlin fixed policies and practices that shaped economic and political relations with the Indians of the region. He saw his firm as distinct in its powers and engaged in one pursuit—seeking wealth through the fur trade. To achieve this end, McLoughlin pursued peace with the Indians but did not hesitate to send out armed parties to punish or overawe the natives if troubles had occurred or threatened. McLoughlin's marriage to an Indian woman and the intermarriage of other company employees and Indians cemented relationships that preserved peace in the Columbia District throughout most of his tenure. He scrupulously followed his company's policy of not using alcohol in the trade with the native inhabitants. McLoughlin retired to Oregon City at the falls of the Willamette in 1846. The official correspondence of McLoughlin (1941–1944, 1948) and his superiors is filled with comments on the Indians of western North America. Biographies include R.C. Johnson (1935) and Montgomery (1934). STEPHEN DOW BECKHAM

Mallet, Pierre-Antoine 1704?–? and Paul Mallet
Pierre Mallet, trader, explorer, and first White man to travel from Illinois to Santa Fe, was a native of Montreal. He and his younger brother, Paul, drifted to Michilimackinac and to the Illinois country about 1734. In 1739, the Mallet brothers, together with six others, ascended the Platte River, and guided by an Indian slave, reached Santa Fe. They returned to Missouri in 1740.

Possibilities of opening trade and finding a route to the Western Sea based on the Mallets' information were now in the minds of the French officials of Louisiana. The Mallets served as guides to the unsuccessful Fabry de La Bruyère expedition of 1741. They then settled in the Arkansas country and engaged in trade. On a journey to establish trade relations between merchants of New Orleans and Santa Fe in 1750, Pierre was arrested and taken to Santa Fé. Considered as a harbinger of illegal French contraband traders, he was sent to Chihuahua and Mexico City and eventually to Spain where he was imprisoned. Frontier officials were ordered to stop all illicit commerce immediately. Thus ended the ambitious plan of the French governor to send goods to New Mexico in exchange for silver. Nevertheless, the Mallet brothers played a pioneering role in developing trade and commerce from the Illinois country to Santa Fe. Of their later life and activities little is known. Principal manuscripts are to be found in the Archives Nationales, Paris; Archivo Histórico Nacional, Madrid; and Archivo General de la Nación, Mexico. For further information see Bolton (1917), Folmer (1939), and Nasatir (1952). A.P. NASATIR

Manypenny, George Washington 1808–1892

Born in Pennsylvania, Manypenny moved to Ohio in 1830, was in the newspaper business, was admitted to the bar, and served as a clerk of common pleas for Muskingum County. He was rewarded for his political activities by being appointed commissioner of Indian affairs in 1853.

Manypenny advocated a change in the status of the Indian from that of a member of a semiautonomous state to that of ward, a guarantee of protection for the Indian's annuity from dishonest agents and his land from rapacious settlers, and an end to the policy of removal. His views encompassed the concept of allotment, agricultural "colonies," and, most important, the complete exclusion of the military from Indian affairs. During his term, 52 treaties were negotiated, mainly within the newly created territory of Kansas-Nebraska, by which 174 million acres of land were ceded by Indian tribes and thus opened to White settlement.

After leaving office in 1857, Manypenny remained active in Indian affairs, supporting reformers (Manypenny 1867). In 1876 he served as chairman of the Sioux Commission that secured cession of the Black Hills, Dakota, and in 1880 on the Ute Commission, which selected reservations for the Ute and supervised their removal. Manypenny wrote *Our Indian Wards* (1880), a history of Indian affairs sympathetic to the Indians. For more information see Fritz (1972) and Kvasnicka (1979). ANDREA LUDWIG

Marshall, John 1755–1835

A lifelong Virginian, Marshall was a soldier in the Revolution, a lawyer, politician, diplomat, and chief justice of the United States Supreme Court, 1801–1835. His opinion for the Court in *Worcester* v. *Georgia* (6 Peters 515, 1832) maintained that while the Cherokee Nation might be dependent it was still sovereign, and in the absence of treaty stipulations to the contrary was exempt from Georgia's jurisdiction. He had declined applying this rule the previous year in *Cherokee Nation* v. *Georgia* (5 Peters 1, 1831) and his *Worcester* opinion marked acceptance of the principle of Indian sovereignty contained in Justice Smith Thompson's *Cherokee Nation* dissent. There are a number of interesting and important questions about the Marshall court's actions in the Cherokee cases (J.C. Burke 1969). There is a complete annotated bibliography on Marshall (Servies 1956). For his papers see H. Johnson et al. (1974–1984). His thought and work is discussed by R.K. Faulkner (1968), and Haskins and Johnson (1981). DONALD ROPER

Mason, John 1600–1672

Born in England, Mason served as an officer in the Netherlands before sailing for Massachusetts Bay in 1632. In 1635 he joined the migration from Dorchester to Windsor, Connecticut. The new settlement constituted a major challenge to the Pequot Indians who had hitherto dominated Indian-European trade in the lower Connecticut Valley and eastern Long Island Sound. The issue was decided in 1637 when Mason led a joint Connecticut-Massachusetts force, supported by Mohegans and Narragansetts, up the Mystic River for a predawn attack on one of the Pequots' two villages. After the remaining Pequots were hunted down, the English enslaved some survivors, and their Indian allies assumed jurisdiction over the rest. Connecticut was then open for settlement, and the English were the dominant force in southern New England. For Mason, as for most Puritans, God had engineered the victory (J. Mason 1736). For the next 35 years Mason was in charge of Connecticut's Indian and military affairs. His policy was to ally with and to protect the Mohegan and to harass the Narragansett and Eastern Niantic. As deputy governor and New England Confederation commissioner, Mason was a leading voice in expressing the repeated fears of a Narragansett "conspiracy" against the English. His role as both war leader and protector of the Mohegan enabled him to profit immensely as a landowner. The biography by G.E. Ellis (1848) is more reliable though less comprehensive than that of L.B. Mason (1935). For historical treatment, see Salisbury (1982). NEAL SALISBURY

May, Karl 1842–1912

Born near Dresden, Saxony, May was blind until the age of five, became a teacher, and served almost eight years in prison for theft and fraud before taking up writing in 1875. By 1971 46 million copies of the German edition of his collected works had been published plus translations in more than 25 languages. As a result, May's novels and tales of adventure take a prominent place in German popular and juvenile fiction. Although less than one-third of his writings (May 1913–1969) deal with North American Indians, his fame rests largely on them (24 million copies). His Mescalero Apache hero Winnetou became the symbol for the noble but vanishing North American Indian for many central Europeans.

Contrary to his claim that his stories were based on his actual experiences, he did not visit America until 1908. In writing on American subjects he leaned heavily on published primary accounts, the works of other novelists, and his own imagination (Cracroft 1963).

While most critics agree on his low literary merits, May in his time was attacked principally as a Catholic or Social Democrat although he was neither. Officials of the Third Reich (some of their leaders avid May readers) found his strong nationalist sentiments agreeable but deplored his religious overtones. After World War II May was considered a clerical and chauvinist writer of the petty bourgeoisie in the German Democratic Republic, but in the 1980s he was rehabilitated as an antiracist defender of the oppressed.

May's autobiography (supplemented by other data in 1913–1969, 34) and Wollschläger (1965) add biographical data and introduce the extensive literature on May. CHRISTIAN F. FEEST

Mayhew, Thomas 1593–1682

The son of an English yeoman, Mayhew began as a textile merchant. In 1631 he migrated to New England to oversee the plantation and enterprises of Matthew Craddock. When the operations failed to profit sufficiently, Mayhew was dismissed under a cloud of suspicion. He continued to engage in various enterprises on his own until 1641 when he purchased patents to Martha's Vineyard, Nantucket, and the Elizabeth Islands off Cape Cod. Here Mayhew established a feudal domain with himself as governor, chief justice, and "Lord of the Manor of Tisbury." His son, Thomas Jr., an ordained minister, began preaching to the Massachusett-speaking Indians on the islands, achieving far greater success than the mainland Puritan missionary, John Eliot. In 1657 his son was lost at sea, and Mayhew, unable to procure a replacement, began preaching to the Indians himself. Unlike Eliot, the Mayhews countenanced a certain amount of pantheism during the transition period, rather than requiring that converts dispense completely with the native religion before worshiping the Christian God. Mayhew likewise converted the Indians *before* insisting that they adopt the secular institutions of "civilization." As a result, conversions on the islands tended to be more gradual, less disruptive of native life, and more lasting than Eliot's. Mayhew also protected the Indians against abuses by the islands' White settlers—one of the griev-

ances repeatedly expressed in the 1660s and 1670s by settlers opposed to Mayhew's feudalism. While the family ultimately lost its hereditary claims to the islands, it continued to dominate the Indians in a missionary capacity into the nineteenth century. See Banks (1911–1925, 1:117–130, 213–247), Hare (1932), and Salisbury (1972) for details of Mayhew's life. NEAL SALISBURY

Meacham, Alfred 1826–1882

Born in Indiana, Meacham was lured by gold to California in 1850 and to eastern Oregon in 1863 where he operated a hotel and toll road near the Umatilla Indian Reservation. A confirmed free-soil advocate, temperance campaigner, and supporter of Ulysses S. Grant, Meacham was appointed Oregon's Superintendent of Indian Affairs in 1869. He firmly espoused reform. He advocated "civilization" programs, moral agents, and Indian participation in governance. In 1869 Meacham inaugurated the policy of allowing Oregon Indians to decide how to spend annuity funds and wrote in his annual report: "If they are men, treat them as such, and not as children" (ARCIA 1870:156). He pushed for manual labor schools and allotment in severalty. He was equally adamant about protecting treaty rights. Meacham's policies and views brought strong pressure for his dismissal. He was relieved in December 1871 as he was arguing for laws to recognize Indian citizenship. In January 1873 he was named to the Commission of Peace to the Modocs. On April 11 he was attacked by some Modocs, shot four times, and left for dead. This critical event confirmed in him a desire to head a national effort for Indian rights. Through the Meacham Lecture Company in 1873–1874, in association with Dr. T.A. Bland in the journal *Council Fire*, 1878–1880, and through literature (Meacham 1875, 1876), Meacham fought for the cause. For his biography see Phinney (1963). STEPHEN DOW BECKHAM

Medill, William about 1802–1865

Born in New Castle County, Delaware, Medill studied law before moving in 1830 to Lancaster, Ohio, where he entered Democratic politics, serving several terms in the state legislature before being elected to Congress in 1838. Defeated for re-election in 1842, Medill eagerly accepted the position of second assistant postmaster general in the Polk administration in 1845. Near the end of 1845, Polk appointed Medill to the position of commissioner of Indian affairs (D.L. Smith 1954). As commissioner between 1845 and 1849, Medill used his office as a means of funneling patronage jobs to Democrats in Ohio and other areas of the Old Northwest. In addition to his political ambitions, he was interested in promoting better Indian-White relations. He supported the establishment and maintenance of manual labor schools in the trans-Mississippi Indian country, fought to uphold the federal laws regulating Indian trade and prohibiting the sale of whiskey to Indians, and defended the Omaha Indians against Mormon intruders. Despite such attempts to promote Indian welfare, Medill's overriding concern was the establishment of safe corridors across the Indian country created by the Indian Removal Act of 1830, which after the Mexican War stood as a barrier to the newly acquired possessions on the Pacific coast. Medill's subsequent career as governor of Ohio, comptroller of the treasury, and Peace Democrat in 1863 had little bearing on Indian affairs.

For information on Medill's attitude toward the Indians and his handling of Indian affairs see R.H. Faust (1975), Prucha (1971), Satz (1975), and Trennert (1972, 1973, 1975, 1979a). The most important source of manuscripts relating to his term as Indian commissioner is Record Group 75 of the National Archives and Record Service. The Medill papers in the Library of Congress document his use of the prerogatives of his office as commissioner to enhance his own political standing. RONALD N. SATZ

Meigs, Return J. 1740–1823

Born in Connecticut the son of a hatter, Meigs joined a state regiment in 1772 and participated in numerous Revolutionary War battles. Promoted to lieutenant-colonel, he achieved hero status by leading his troops to victory on the Sag Harbor expedition. After the war, Meigs took an active interest in the Ohio Company. In 1788, he led a group of settlers to the Ohio territory and drew up a set of laws for the new settlement.

In 1801 Meigs accepted the dual appointment of Indian agent to the Cherokee and agent of the War Department in Tennessee. During his 22 years at this post, he proved an able administrator and a skillful diplomat. He played an important role in negotiating land cession treaties, settling boundary disputes, and implementing the removal policy. Though he served the interests of the government, Meigs retained the confidence of his Indian wards. Genuinely sympathetic with the Indians, he worked hard to improve their welfare. A strong believer in the value of education and instruction in the ways of civilization, he not only distributed household and farming implements but also assisted and advised individual Indians. He dispensed justice fairly, punishing both the White trespasser and the Indian lawbreaker. He also encouraged self-government and worked closely with the Cherokee Council. In 1820 Meigs advanced the opinion that the Cherokee were so advanced that they needed no further government aid. Despite initial agreement by President James Monroe, the proposal was never realized because of opposition from nonprogressive Cherokee and state officials fearful of independent Indian farms (W.R.L. Smith 1928). The

best study of Meigs's career as Indian agent is H.T. Malone (1956). HENRY E. FRITZ

Meriam, Lewis M. 1883–1972

A statistician by profession, Meriam was a lifelong student of public administration. A graduate of Harvard and the George Washington University Law School, he was employed by the Office of the Census, 1905–1912, the federal Children's Bureau, 1912–1915, and the newly organized Institute for Government Research in 1915. In 1920 when the Institute became a part of the Brookings Institution, Meriam was made senior research associate, and by his retirement in 1951 he had risen to the post of vice-president of Brookings.

Meriam's contribution to the field of Indian affairs resulted from his appointment in 1926 as technical director of the survey of Indian affairs, a study commissioned by the Rockefeller Foundation and conducted by the Institute for Government Research. Meriam (1928) edited the survey report, *The Problem of Indian Administration*, which condemned the land allotment provisions of the Dawes Severalty Act and urged the federal government to adopt a policy of cultural pluralism in place of the traditional goal of Indian assimilation. Meriam was a candidate for the office of commissioner of Indian affairs in 1932 but he withdrew to support the candidacy of John Collier, who was subsequently appointed. LAWRENCE C. KELLY

Merriam, C. Hart 1855–1942

Merriam was by training and chief interest a zoologist, although he earned an M.D. and practiced medicine from 1879 to 1885. From 1885 to 1910 he was attached to the U.S. Biological Survey. He is given primary credit for developing the idea of life zones. Early natural history fieldwork in the West led him to an interest in Indians, and from 1910 until his death, with support of a fund established by E.H. Harriman, he visited Indian groups, mainly in California, and recorded their language, ethnoscience and ethnogeography. His writings are voluminous and concern mainly zoology and to a lesser extent, anthropology (W.H. Osgood 1945). The mass of ethnographic data and photographs accumulated by him was deposited at the University of California in 1950 (Heizer 1969a) and since that time certain portions have been published (Merriam 1962, 1966–1967). His interest in zoological species distributions (Merriam 1974) was paralleled in his interest in identifying and determining the tribal distributions of California Indians. His independent researches into these matters led to conclusions quite similar to those reached by Kroeber and his students. A considerable body of linguistic data (vocabularies, word lists for plants and animals) remains in manuscript form.

Smithsonian, NAA.
Fig. 11. C. Hart Merriam in his office. Photograph by Virum Bailey, Washington, Feb. 23, 1930.

Merriam was keenly aware of and sympathetic to the plight of Indians, and his testimony in Senate hearings was often helpful in securing favorable government action on their behalf (fig. 11). ROBERT F. HEIZER

Miles, Nelson A. 1839–1925

A Boston crockery salesman who made good in the Civil War Volunteers, Miles served with distinction on the postwar frontier. To military ability he added ambition and vanity, which made him controversial and widely disliked. As colonel of the 5th Infantry, he commanded a column in the Red River War of 1874–1875, which ended hostilities with the southern Plains tribes; played a significant part in destroying the power of the Sioux and Cheyenne during 1876–1880; and headed off the flight of the Nez Perce in 1877, thus preventing their escape to Canada (J.M. Carroll 1978). In 1886 he succeeded Gen. George Crook as commander in Arizona and directed the final phase of operations against Geronimo's Chiricahua Apaches. In 1890–1891 he commanded the army concentrated on the Sioux reservations to counter the Ghost Dance troubles. His career is documented in both autobiographical (Miles 1896, 1911) and biographical writings (V.W. Johnson 1962). ROBERT M. UTLEY

Miró, Esteban Rodríguez 1744–1795

Miró entered the Spanish army at the age of 16 and reached the rank of colonel after serving with Bernardo de Gálvez in the West Florida campaigns of the American Revolution. He was appointed acting governor of Louisiana in 1782 and made permanent governor in 1785 when his patron Gálvez was commissioned viceroy of New Spain. While governor at New Orleans, Miró endeavored to use the Southeast Indians as a barrier against American expansion (Burson 1940), and he intrigued with the American malcontent James Wilkinson for the purpose of pulling Kentucky and Ohio valley settlements away from the United States. He was closely directed by orders from Spain in these and all important aspects of his administration. With the population of Louisiana he was mildly popular and remembered as benevolent and constructive. In 1791 Miró was dismissed from the governorship and charged with malfeasance in office. Returning to Madrid, he succeeded in clearing himself. Miró's dealings with the Indians are detailed in Serrano y Sanz (1916), Berry (1917), and Caughey (1938). P. RICHARD METCALF

Mitchell, David Dawson 1806–1861

Born in Virginia, Mitchell became one of the famous men of the fur trade on the Upper Missouri. Working for the American Fur Company between 1828 and 1838, he developed a reputation for ability to deal with the Blackfeet and Assiniboine. While in charge of Fort McKenzie, Mitchell entertained artist Carl Bodmer and Maximilian, Prince of Wied, giving them great assistance in recording Indian life on the Upper Missouri (De Voto 1947; Mattison 1965). In September 1841 Mitchell was appointed superintendent of Indian affairs at Saint Louis, giving him responsibility for all tribes west of the Rockies. We was an able administrator and very vigilant in protecting the Indian. His attempts to enforce the liquor laws led to opposition by the traders and resulted in his replacement in October 1843. However, his successor, Thomas H. Harvey, proved even more obnoxious to the traders and in 1849, Mitchell was again appointed Indian superintendent (Trennert 1973). During the next four years Mitchell played his greatest role in Indian affairs. His main concern was to clear all tribes from the main routes of westward travel. These efforts reached a climax in 1851 when Mitchell headed the government negotiating team at the treaty of Fort Laramie and secured the desired terms. Mitchell was replaced as superintendent in 1853. Most of his correspondence while superintendent is in the National Archives. ROBERT A. TRENNERT

Mix, Charles E. 1810–1878

Born in Connecticut, Mix moved to Washington, D.C., when he was about 18 years old. After his business apparently failed in the economic panic of 1837, Mix found a job in the Office of Indian Affairs, where he established a reputation for integrity and efficiency and soon became the highest-paid clerk in the office. In the 1850 reorganization of government offices Mix was named chief clerk of the Indian Bureau, an extremely important job, second only to that of commissioner of Indian affairs. Mix was acting head of the bureau during the frequent absences of the commissioners from Washington. In addition, he supervised the clerical staff, prepared routine correspondence with agents and superintendents in the field, and handled daily communications between the bureau and the office of the Secretary of Interior, as well as relations with the Treasury Department, the War Department, and the Congress. Probably his most important contribution was an 85-page pamphlet entitled *Office Copy of the Laws, Regulations, Etc., of the Indian Bureau, 1850*, which Mix (1850) compiled for the use of Indian Bureau employees during the first year he was chief clerk. It remained the only such book of rules for the Indian Bureau during the next two decades. Mix seems to have begun writing most of the annual reports for the Bureau, or at least to have compiled basic reports for the commissioner to revise slightly and sign. Mix served under a dozen commissioners during his 30-year career with the Bureau and was himself appointed commissioner for a few months in 1858 (H. Kelsey 1979a). Mix was able to provide a basic policy continuity during a long period of change for the Indians and official neglect of their needs. He retired from the Indian Bureau in 1869 and worked for several years as an agent specializing in Indian claims.

There is no biography of Mix, and there are no known collections of Mix papers, except the voluminous official records of the Office of Indian Affairs in the National Archives. Some aspects of his work are covered in H. Kelsey (1971, 1973a). HARRY KELSEY

Montour, Andrew ?–1772

Montour was the son of Madame Montour and an Iroquois, and his mixed racial and cultural heritage permitted him to serve as a cultural broker between the English colonists and the Indians in his career as interpreter and trusted intermediary. He was employed by the governments of Pennsylvania and Virginia; he also served under Indian Superintendent Sir William Johnson. His public career extended from 1742 through 1768 and included participation in the making of the treaties of Lancaster in 1748, Logstown in 1752, and Fort Stanwix in 1768. At Logstown his aid was essential in gaining the transfer of Indian land to the Ohio Company. He was with Washington at Fort Necessity. He led the Indian allies of the English against French Indian allies during the French and Indian War and Pontiac's Rebellion. Although accused of making extravagant demands for

Smithsonian, NAA: 2458-F.

Fig. 12. James Mooney with a Navajo man at a trading post in Keams Canyon, Ariz. Photographed winter, 1892–1893.

his services, Montour proved to be a good friend to the English, who needed his aid in negotiating treaties and in providing much needed intelligence about Indian attitudes and activities. George Washington, Pennsylvania interpreter Conrad Weiser, and Gov. Robert Dinwiddie of Virginia had high regard for the ability of this illiterate who had extensive knowledge of Algonquian and Iroquoian languages, English, and French and knew the customs of the Indians. At the same time, he was generally respected by the Indians as an honest agent who could be trusted accurately to convey their views to the English as well as fairly to present the English position to them. The chiefs of the Six Nations regarded him as an Indian and affirmed that he was a chief on the Council of the Six Nations. For biographical details see Lewin (1966) and Darlington (1893). ROBERT BRUNKOW

Mooney, James 1861–1921

After a brief career with his home-town newspaper in Richmond, Indiana, Mooney joined the staff of the Bureau of American Ethnology, Smithsonian Institution, in 1885, remaining a Bureau employee until his death. Although his interests in North American Indians were catholic (fig. 12), his field trips and published research centered on Eastern Cherokees and Southern Plains tribes including Arapaho, Cheyenne, Kiowa, and Kiowa-Apache. Mooney contributed over 500 signed articles to the *Handbook of American Indians North of Mexico* (Hodge 1907–1910) and amassed large amounts of data on Indian population history. His major publications were on Eastern Siouan tribes (1894), history of Ghost Dance and Sioux outbreak (1896), Cherokee myths and sacred formulas (1891, 1900), Kiowa calendar history (1898), Cheyenne history (1907), and Indian population statistics (1928). Almost all his work is free of ethnocentric attitudes and unilinear cultural theories prevalent during this period, especially among early Bureau scholars. Mooney interceded with government and religious authorities, as far as his position would allow, for Indian economic and cultural needs, objecting to certain restrictions and conditions, and testifying in favor of Peyote ceremonies. The National Anthropological Archives holds Mooney's letters, field notes, grammars, and bibliographies, as well as extensive unpublished material on peyote, Kiowa and Cheyenne heraldry, Cherokee medical formulas, and population notes. A small collection of Mooney letters is in the Oklahoma Historical Society, Oklahoma City. For additional biographical details see Anonymous (1922), Bass (1954), and Moses (1984). WILLIAM COLBY

Moorehead, Warren K. 1866–1939

Born in Siena, Italy, Moorehead (fig. 13) was the son of American missionaries who returned to their native Xenia, Ohio, soon after his birth. By the time of his entrance into Denison University in 1882, he was widely known as a dealer in Indian antiquities. Following his college years, Moorehead served on the staff of the Smithsonian Institution. Between 1891 and 1893 he was employed as a field assistant to Frederick Ward Putnam, gathering archeological materials for exhibit at the World's Columbian Exposition. From 1901 until his retirement in 1938, he was curator and later director of the department of archeology at Phillips Academy, Andover, Massachusetts. Moorehead's attention was drawn to the problems of living Indians while employed as a correspondent for the *Illustrated American* at the Pine Ridge agency, South Dakota, in 1890. He served on the Board of Indian Commissioners from 1908 until the dissolution of the board in 1933. Throughout this period he sought to protect traditional cultures, fought for Indian land rights, and attempted to remove political influences from the administration of Indian affairs. He opposed the principles of the Dawes Severalty Act and the policy of easy alienation of Indian lands. His own account of the conduct of the Bureau of Indian Affairs between 1890 and 1914 emphasizes land frauds and the malfeasance of Bureau personnel (Moorehead 1914, 1925). For biographical details see Weatherford (1956) and D.S. Byers (1939). The Moorehead manuscript collection is held by the Ohio Historical Center, Columbus. TOM D. CROUCH

Smithsonian,NAA: S.I. 11,756.
Fig. 13. Warren K. Moorehead, right, at an archeological excavation of a grave, Ft. Ancient, Warren Co., Ohio. Photograph by C.J. Strong, about 1886.

Morgan, Lewis Henry 1818–1881

Born in Aurora, New York, Morgan was educated at Aurora Academy, then Union College, and on graduation read for the law before taking up a lucrative practice for the burgeoning corporations of Rochester. But his real interests were natural history and Indians, and as a young man he founded a secret society, the Gordian Knot, which became the Grand Order of the Iroquois, with chapters in the territories of the Five Nations. In this effort he knew Henry Rowe Schoolcraft, and he soon met the Seneca Ely S. Parker. Their collaboration in collecting the ceremonies of the Senecas, delineating social organization, describing and collecting their arts and industries, and mapping place names soon led, through a series of papers, to the *League of the . . . Iroquois* (L.H. Morgan 1851), the first scientific account of an Indian tribe. In Minnesota in 1858 Morgan discovered that the Ojibwa have the same classificatory kinship system as the Seneca, and this started him on a massive search for similar and variant systems in the New and Old World, which caused him to give up his law practice and devote himself wholly to science. He thought he might so demonstrate the Asiatic origin of the American Indians. L.H. Morgan's (1871) *Systems of Consanguinity and Affinity of the Human Family* began as a historical inquiry but culminated in a theory of social evolution. His great theoretical work *Ancient Society* (1877) has had a wide readership. His late literary work, *Houses and House-Life of the American Aborigines* (1881), may be his best theoretical statement. Morgan served a term in the New York Assembly, but failed to gain the office of commissioner of Indian affairs, was denied an ambassadorship, and declined a professorship at Cornell. He was elected to the National Academy of Sciences in 1875 and four years later was president of the American Association for the Advancement of Science. Morgan's papers are in the Rush Rhees Library, University of Rochester; his ethnological collections are shared by the New York State Museum, Albany, and the Rochester Museum of Science. For further information see B.J. Stern (1931), Resek (1960), and Trautmann (1987). WILLIAM N. FENTON

Morgan, Thomas Jefferson 1839–1902

Born in Franklin, Indiana, Morgan was educated at Franklin College. After service in the Civil War, where he won fame as a commander of Black troops, he entered Rochester Theological Seminary. Although ordained a Baptist minister in 1869, he was prominent chiefly for his work in public education. Appointed commissioner of Indian affairs in 1889, he was a strong advocate of assimilation of the Indians, and he cooperated fully with the humanitarian reformers of the Lake Mohonk Conference of the Friends of the American Indian. His most important work was his his detailed plan for universal government education for the Indians, which he set forth in his first annual report and disseminated in published speeches and articles (T.J. Morgan 1890, 1891). He worked hard to carry out allotments on reservations. His goal was to turn all the Indians into patriotic American citizens and enable them to compete successfully in the White society. His strong support of public schools for the Indians won him the enmity of Roman Catholics, who unsuccessfully sought to prevent his confirmation by the Senate and who opposed him during his entire term (Sievers 1952). After leaving office in 1893 he became corresponding secretary of the Baptist Home Mission Society and editor of its magazine, in which he continued to urge Indian education programs. There is a biography of Morgan by Prucha (1979a). FRANCIS PAUL PRUCHA

Morice, Adrien-Gabriel 1859–1938

Born in Saint-Mars-sur-Colmont, France, Morice joined the Oblates of Mary Immaculate in 1877. He then spent nearly 30 years in British Columbia working with the Indians before moving to Manitoba, where he continued his scientific career writing on linguistics, anthropology, and history. He made basic contributions to the study of the Athapaskan languages of Canada. For a short biography and bibliography, see Carrière (1972). GASTON CARRIÈRE

Morse, Jedidiah (1761–1826)

Born in Woodstock, Connecticut, Morse attended Yale College and, after his graduation in 1783, opened a school for young women at New Haven. He studied for the ministry, was ordained in 1786, and began a 30-year pastorate at the First Congregational Church in Charlestown, Massachusetts. Because of his deep interest in the work of civilizing the Indians he was appointed by the secretary of war in 1820 to visit the border tribes and devise the most suitable plan to "advance their civilization and happiness" (Morse 1822). Throughout his life, Morse was involved with religious controversy, consistently defending the traditional Calvinist orthodoxy of the New England church. He edited the *Panoplist* (1805–1810), forerunner of the *Missionary Herald*, and was one of the founders of Andover Theological Seminary in 1808, the New England Tract Society in 1814, and the American Bible Society in 1816. He also served as secretary of the Society for the Propagation of the Gospel among the Indians. A political as well as a religious conservative, he helped found *The Mercury and New England Palladium* to defend and publicize Federalist party views. Morse published several popular books on geography, 1784–1802, which had wide circulation. For biographical details see W.B. Sprague (1874). ROBERT W. MARDOCK

Morton, Samuel G. (1799–1851)

Born in Philadelphia, Morton earned degrees in medicine from 1820 to 1823. Thereafter he practiced medicine, did research at the Academy of Natural Sciences, and taught anatomy at the Philadelphia Medical College. Owing to his large collection of Indian skulls and his book *Crania Americana* (1839), he has been called the father of American physical anthropology. For a biography see Meigs (1851). T. DALE STEWART

Morton, Thomas (about 1579–1646)

Born into minor English gentry, Morton was trained in the law. In 1624 he migrated to New England to establish a trading post at the site of Quincy, Massachusetts. In the following year, with his senior partners and most of their indentured servants gone, Morton led the other servants in a revolt against the remaining partner, granting them freedom and equal partnerships. He renamed the post Merrymount, erected a maypole, and invited the local Massachusett Indians to join the festivities there. Such

Natl. Congress of Amer. Ind., Washington.
Fig. 14. Commissioner of Indian Affairs Philleo Nash at the 18th annual convention of the National Congress of American Indians. left to right, front row, Osley B. Saunooke, Eastern Cherokee; Miss Indian America VIII Brenda Bearchum, Northern Cheyenne and Shoshone-Bannock; Nash; Angus Wilson, Nez Perce; Loretta Green, Nez Perce; Nancy Halfmoon, probably Nez Perce. Photograph by Helen Gehrke, Lewiston, Idaho, Nov. 18–22, 1961.

interracial conviviality was sufficient to arouse the deepest anxieties among the nearby Plymouth colonists, but even more serious was Morton's growing success as a fur trader. Merrymount not only represented the antithesis of the Puritans' fundamental concepts of morality and community but also endangered their profits. In 1628 Morton was arrested by the Plymouth authorities and banished to England. When he returned a year later, the Massachusetts Bay Company had established an outpost at Salem. Morton was quickly arrested for failing to acknowledge the religious and political jurisdiction, and the economic monopoly, of the company. Back in England Morton cooperated with efforts to discredit the Bay Company and have its charter revoked. In 1643 he returned to New England a final time and was again arrested, this time going to Maine. Morton's account of the Indians (T. Morton 1883) is a mixture of noble-savage idealization and accurate ethnology. He repeatedly stresses the Indians' humanity and urges their conversion to Anglicanism as a means of realizing their full potential for virtue. For more details, see Connors (1969) and Salisbury (1982). NEAL SALISBURY

Nash, Philleo 1910–1987
Born in Wisconsin, Nash graduated in anthropology from the University of Wisconsin and earned his doctorate from the University of Chicago. As his dissertation project, he studied religious revivalism among the Klamath Indians.

For several years following graduation, Nash taught anthropology at the University of Toronto and the University of Wisconsin. In the 1940s he entered federal employment, becoming a minority affairs specialist on President Harry Truman's staff. In 1958 he was elected lieutenant governor of Wisconsin. He served as a member of a Task Force on Indian Affairs early in 1961, and in September 1961 the Senate confirmed his nomination as commissioner of Indian Affairs.

From the beginning of his term as commissioner, Nash concentrated his efforts on obtaining enlarged appropriations for education and resource development and on involving other federal agencies in raising the living standards of Indian communities. He persuaded the Department of Labor to extend the Manpower Development and Training Act to reservation communities and, shortly afterward, secured the participation of the Department of Commerce in Indian programs. A drive to improve reservation housing gained support and assistance from agencies of the Department of Housing and Urban Development.

To coordinate Bureau of Indian Affairs activities and keep track of what other agencies were doing on the reservations, Nash set up a division of economic development. He also greatly strengthened the office of tribal operations, thereby improving the BIA's ability to assist tribal council members with programming funds from claims cases and carrying out other new economic ventures.

Nash established close relations with many Indian leaders. He attended their regional and national meetings (fig. 14), often staying up all night singing with them. He was also a frequent visitor to the reservations and to the native villages of Alaska. Nash resigned as commissioner in 1966. He was the last non-Indian and the only anthropologist to hold the office.

P. Nash's publications include reflections on his federal service (1979, 1986); see also Szasz (1979). JAMES E. OFFICER

Neighbors, Robert S. (1815–1859)
Neighbors was born in Virginia, orphaned while an infant, and received little formal education; in 1836 he moved to Texas. He served in the Army of the Republic and in 1845 became agent for the Lipan Apache and Tonkawa tribes, breaking with custom by spending considerable time in Indian camps. After annexation he became a special, federal Indian agent and played a prominent role in councils held with Comanches and other tribes. In 1854, with Capt. R.B. Marcy, he selected two sites for Indian reservations. As supervising agent for Texas Indians he attempted to safeguard reservation Indians, but hostile Whites forced abandonment of the reservations. Neighbors moved his charges to Indian Territory successfully. On his return he was murdered by a White settler. For further information see A.A. Neighbors (1936), Neighbours (1956), and R.N. Richardson (1952). W.W. NEWCOMB

Oberly, John H. 1837–1899

A journalist and politician from Ohio, Oberly, filled the role of commissioner of Indian affairs, 1888–1889. Oberly had been the superintendent of Indian schools since May 1885 and had also been appointed by President Grover Cleveland to serve on the Civil Service Commission. Thus, he strongly endorsed civil service reform in the Indian Bureau. A member of the executive committee of the National Indian Defense Association, he believed that education should precede citizenship and severalty. Education, in this case, did not mean intellectual enlightenment, but inculcation of the work ethic. Oberly also believed that if the Indian would not accept "civilization," then he must be compelled by the government to do so. When the Republicans regained control of the federal bureaucracy in 1889, Oberly returned to journalism.

For more see F.A. O'Neil (1979a). ANDREA LUDWIG

O'Fallon, Benjamin 1793–1842

Born near Lexington, Kentucky, O'Fallon became the ward of his uncle, the explorer William Clark, in Saint Louis following the death of his father around 1794. After leaving school, he opened a milling establishment, which he sold in 1816, turning his attention toward the Indian trade. With assistance from his influential uncle, he became an Indian agent at the agency-factory in Prairie du Chien, Wisconsin. In 1817 he helped conclude a treaty with the Oto and Ponca tribes.

In 1819 O'Fallon was appointed "Agent for Indian Affairs on the Missouri," also acquiring the title of major. He established headquarters at Council Bluffs, and supervised the Omaha, Oto, Missouri, and Pawnee tribes, among others. In 1821 he accompanied a Pawnee tribal delegation touring the Eastern states. In 1825 O'Fallon accompanied Gen. Henry Atkinson to the headwaters of the Missouri River, making treaties of trade and friendship with 12 different tribes. During his service with the Indian Office, he earned a reputation both for integrity and expertise in Indian culture. He was a critic of corruption in the Indian trade system (O'Fallon 1834:328).

O'Fallon retired from the Indian Office in 1827, returned to Saint Louis where he worked for Andrew Jackson's campaign, and later became a principal in the Missouri Fur Company. He retired to Jefferson County. His papers and manuscripts are in the Missouri Historical Society, Saint Louis. See also Reid and Gannon (1929). WILLIAM W. QUINN, JR.

O'Reilly, Alexander 1722–1794

O'Reilly was a native of Ireland who served all his life in the Spanish army. After participating in numerous European campaigns and earning the rank of lieutenant general, he was made governor of Louisiana in the aftermath of the 1768 Creole rebellion against the first Spanish governor, Antonio de Ulloa. O'Reilly arrived at New Orleans in July 1769 with a force of 2,000 men and quickly crushed the uprising, executing several of its leaders and imprisoning others. These forceful measures earned him the sobriquet "Bloody O'Reilly" among the French Louisianans and gave rise to a continuing debate among historians as to his character and the justifications for his actions.

In Indian affairs O'Reilly attempted to stabilize relations with tribes bordering the province by abolishing traffic in Indian slaves. He ordered stern action against French or British traders caught in Spanish territory and changed the previous pattern of open Indian trade by restricting it to friendly tribes—a policy that remained in force throughout the period of Spanish rule. By February 1770 O'Reilly had completed his mission of pacification. He returned to Spain in honor, where he served the rest of his life in the highest ranks of the Spanish military. Texada (1970) details O'Reilly's brief governorship and discusses the positions of other historians. O'Reilly's approach to Indian relations is detailed in Bolton (1914) and Kinnard (1949). P. RICHARD METCALF

Owen, Robert Latham 1856–1947

Owen was born in Lynchburg, Virginia, to Robert Latham Owen, a prosperous civil engineer and Narcissa Chisholm Owen, a well-educated woman of Cherokee descent. In 1874 Owen secured a scholarship to Washington and Lee University and graduated three years later with both bachelor's and master's degrees. On the advice of his mother, Owen moved to Indian Territory and accepted a teaching position among the Cherokee, thus beginning a long and varied career of Indian service. In 1880 he joined the bar and in 1885 was appointed Indian agent to the Cherokees. As such he focused his attention on land disputes. In 1890 he became attorney for the Choctaws and succeeded in winning claims against the United States government for them as well as the Eastern and Western Cherokees. When Oklahoma was admitted into the Union in 1907, Owen was elected to the United States Senate and served three terms. Although his senatorial interests were not restricted to Indian issues he spent a good deal of his time on them. In 1925 Owen retired from the Senate and opened a law practice in Washington, D.C. For further information see Keso (1937). HEATHER C. DODSON

Painter, Charles C.C. ?–1895

Painter began his work for the cause of Indian rights in 1883 as the Washington, D.C., agent for the Indian Rights Association. He did much of the fieldwork for the new organization by guiding the congressional legislation favored by the Association and by investigating all legislation affecting the Indians. The Association maintained that practical and businesslike methods were necessary for the solution of the Indian problem, and Painter concurred. He believed that Indian policy should have definite goals in order to achieve real progress. Among the goals were education, citizenship, and individual ownership of land. His insistence that the Dawes Severalty Act must appeal to White interests to enable its passage led to the elimination of a provision that would have prohibited the sale of surplus reservation lands to White settlers. He effectively lobbied for the Dawes bill (Painter 1887) and his efforts gained the Indian Rights Association a share of credit for securing its passage in 1887. Painter wrote numerous books and pamphlets on Indian policy that were published by the Indian Rights Association from 1883 to 1893 (for example, 1885, 1886, 1889). In January 1894 he was appointed to the Board of Indian Commissioners and served until his death. Much of his correspondence on Indian rights is deposited in the National Archives. ROBERT W. MARDOCK

Palmer, Edward 1831–1911

Although lacking formal education, Palmer qualified himself as a medical man and served as a contract surgeon at Army posts in Colorado, Kansas, and Arizona, 1862–1867, and as medical officer at the Kiowa-Comanche agency in what is now Oklahoma in 1868. After this he gave up medicine and devoted himself to collecting biological and other material in Mexico and the western United States. His notes and observations, and his collections of ancient and modern artifacts, are important sources of information on Indian ethnology and archeology. His longest original paper was *Food Products of the North American Indians* (E. Palmer 1871). A biographical account of Palmer, with details of his itineraries and collections, remarks on archival sources, and a full bibliography, is available (McVaugh 1956). ROGERS MCVAUGH

Palmer, Joel 1810–1881

A pivotal figure in Indian policy in Oregon, Palmer was born to Quaker parents in Ontario, Canada. In 1845 he journeyed overland from Indiana to Oregon to examine conditions for settlement. His classic emigrant's guide *A Journal of Travels Over the Rocky Mountains* (1847), containing Chinook Jargon and Nez Perce vocabularies, was published as he set out with his family again for the Far West. Palmer served as commissary-general and commissioner of peace in Oregon Territory during the Cayuse War of 1847–1848. From 1853 to 1856 he was the territorial superintendent of Indian affairs and extinguished title to two-thirds of the Indian land in Oregon; of his 11 treaties, three were rejected by the Senate. Palmer opposed plans to remove all Indians of western Oregon to arid reservations east of the Cascades. He instituted humane policies for beleaguered Indians during

the wars of 1855–1856. He advocated, located, and established the Siletz and Grand Ronde reservations. A miller, corporate director, miner, farmer, state legislator, candidate for governor, and agent at Siletz from 1871–1873, he died at Dayton, Oregon. Palmer's papers are at the University of Oregon, Eugene. See Spaid (1950) for an assessment of his Indian policy. STEPHEN DOW BECKHAM

Parkman, Francis 1823–1893

Born in Boston, Parkman graduated from Harvard in 1844. During the summer of 1846 he traveled westward on the Great Plains, to Fort Laramie on the Oregon Trail. He then moved southward to the basin of the Medicine Bow, where he lived for a short time with a band of Oglala Sioux. The record of this experience, first published by installments in the *Knickerbocker Magazine*, appeared in book form (Parkman 1849). Parkman's experience with the Sioux gave him, as a pioneer in comparative ethnology, background to recreate the narrative of Indian life in his history of Pontiac's rebellion (Parkman 1851). Although Indian people parade through his later books, it is Parkman's book on the Ottawa chief Pontiac that remains his best work on the American Indian. Parkman portrayed Pontiac as a major figure in American frontier history; however, Parkman's view of the Indian war of 1763 as a conspiracy obscured the fact that the Indians were fighting for self-determination. The ferocity of the Indians portrayed in Parkman's books reflected his concern with the dramatic fabric of his narrative. He needed heroes and villains, and the Indian was a convenient negative figure to put in the path of his major actors such as René-Robert Cavelier, Sieur de La Salle and Father Isaac Jogues.

For biographical additions and commentary on Parkman's writings, see Levin (1983), Parkman (1898), and Jennings (1985a). WILBUR R. JACOBS

Payne, John H. 1791–1852

Born in New York City, Payne attended Union College and quite early attained international fame as an actor and dramatist. He is best remembered as the author of the lyrics to "Home Sweet Home." In 1833 he visited the Creeks and Cherokees and planned to write a history of the Cherokees in collaboration with Daniel S. Butrick, a resident Congregational missionary. Payne's arrival among the Cherokees coincided with the period when political pressure for Cherokee removal had reached a climax. Payne became a confidant of Chief John Ross, a friendship that was deepened when both were illegally arrested and jailed by the Georgia militia. Payne wrote several influential newspaper articles espousing the Cherokee cause, and his pen was apparently responsible for many of the eloquent Cherokee pleas sent before Congress and elsewhere. He was employed by the Cherokees as a lobbyist in Washington in 1838 to try to secure the most favorable terms possible for the inevitable removal. In 1840, Payne revisited his relocated Cherokee friends in Indian Territory, where he made observations on the reorganization of the Cherokee Nation and conducted a rare interview with Sequoya. In 1841 he was employed by the War Department to research Indian treaties. Payne served as American consul to Tunis from 1843 to 1844 and from 1851 until his death.

Payne's first volume on Cherokee history was apparently completed and ready for publication, but it has not survived. However, 14 volumes of his and Butrick's notes, containing invaluable material on Cherokee social and religious customs, are preserved in the Newberry Library, Chicago (Payne and Butrick 1835–1838). The most complete of several biographies of Payne is by Overmyer (1957); this work contains a comprehensive bibliography of works by and about Payne. RAYMOND D. FOGELSON

Penn, William 1644–1718
The son of one of the wealthiest and most influential families in England, Penn became one of the most famous and respected spokesmen for the Quaker faith. He developed an interest in American settlements during the 1670s, and after Penn's father died, King Charles II quieted his debts to the Penn family by granting William proprietorship and right of governance over the lands that became Pennsylvania. Penn hoped his province could become a "holy experiment" governed according to principles of brotherhood, rule of law, and personal liberty for colonists and native inhabitants alike; however, his goals were not widely shared, and he spent the rest of his life struggling with challenges to his faith and position from enemies in England and trying to achieve governmental harmony among the assertive factions of his colonists. Though Pennsylvania quickly became rich, Penn gained almost nothing from it, was confined for a time in a debtor's prison, and died disillusioned. In his dealings with the Indians Penn strove to be scrupulously fair; but he shared the European belief in an idealized noble savage, had minimal contact with Indians, and was naive as to the possibility of cooperation between colonists and Indians. His philosophy of benevolence and justice did give rise to an enduring myth of Quaker success in Indian relations, which influenced government Indian policies into the twentieth century. For Penn's writings and broad career see Spence (1932) and the biography by Peare (1956); for his dealings with the Indians see Kelsey (1917). P. RICHARD METCALF

Petitot, Emile 1838–1917
Born in Grancy-le-Château, France, Petitot joined the Oblates of Mary Immaculate in 1860. In 1862, he was sent to the missions of the Canadian North. He lived at Fort Good Hope, Northwest Territories, and traveled extensively. He worked among many Indian tribes but mostly among the Kutchin and Hare.

Bad health forced him to go to France in 1874 where he published his important French-Eskimo dictionary (1876a) and his comparative vocabularies of Canadian Athapaskan languages (1876).

He returned to Fort Good Hope in 1876, but only for a short time. Sickness obliged him to leave the North, and after working at Cold Lake, Alberta, 1879–1881, he returned to France where he served as a parish priest in Mareuil-les-Meaux, 1886–1917.

During his stay in the North Petitot became an authority on Indian languages. He also gathered much information on geography, geology, paleontology, and ethnography, which forms the basis of his numerous books and papers in many French scientific periodicals. GASTON CARRIERE

Pickering, Timothy 1745–1829
Pickering was born and reared in Salem, Massachusetts, graduated from Harvard, supported the Revolution, and served as adjutant general, quartermaster general, and on the Board of War, helping to supply Gen. John Sullivan's campaign against the Iroquois in 1779. Indian commissioner in 1790, he conducted a council with the Seneca at Tioga Point, Pennsylvania. The next year he held a council with the Six Nations at Newtown (Elmira), New York. In 1792, while postmaster-general, he was host to 60 Iroquois in Philadelphia and arranged for agricultural education in their tribes. With Gen. Benjamin Lincoln and Beverly Randolph he journeyed to the Detroit River in 1793 and held a nerve-wracking council with the Western tribes. In 1794 he concluded a major treaty with the Six Nations at Canandaigua and another treaty with the Oneida, Tuscarora, and Stockbridge at Oneida. While secretary of war 1795–1796 and secretary of state 1795–1800, he supervised some Indian relations, directing Gen. Anthony Wayne on the Treaty of Greenville and advising various agents. A Massachusetts senator and representative, 1803–1817, he championed justice for Indians. His role in Indian affairs is covered in E.H. Phillips (1966) and Clarfield (1980) and his entire career in Pickering and Upham (1867). Pickering's papers are in the Massachusetts Historical Society, Boston (Smith et al. 1896). EDWARD HAKE PHILLIPS

Pinart, Alphonse 1852–1911
Although Pinart was born and died in France, he was an Americanist of notable experience and attainments. Interested in linguistics at an early age, Pinart recorded ethnographic details and vocabularies and made museum collections among the Aleut, Koniag Eskimo, and Tlingit Indians of Alaska in 1871–1872. In 1875–1876 he spent several months in Arizona and British Columbia. In

1877–1878 he and L. de Cessac on a joint expedition sponsored by the French government conducted archeological explorations in the Santa Barbara region, California (Reichlen and Heizer 1963), and recorded linguistic data from surviving mission Indians south of San Francisco (Heizer 1952). From 1882 to 1885 he made expeditions to Panama and Central America. His writings were abundant (Parmenter 1966), and many of these are important because of their early date and high quality. Pinart had an ambition to publish a comprehensive study of American Indian languages. One volume (concerning Chiapanec) did appear in print in 1875 (Parmenter 1966:15), but the publication of the great mass of materials collected or copied by him was never realized. His material culture collections are deposited in the Musée de l'Homme, Paris, in the Musée des Antiquités Naturales de Saint-Germain-en-Laye, and in the museum of Boulogne-sur-Mer, France. The signed original copies of his California vocabularies are in the Bancroft Library, University of California, Berkeley. The original version (Harrington 1934) of Boscana's 1822 *Chinigchinich* secured by him or de Cessac at Santa Barbara in 1880–1881 is in the Bibliothèque Nationale, Paris (Kroeber 1959). Pinart must be given equal rank in importance with Stephen Powers as one of California's early and important ethnographers. ROBERT F. HEIZER

Point, Nicolas 1799–1868

Point was born at Rocroy in northern France. He was ordained to the priesthood in 1831. In 1835 he was sent with several other Jesuit priests to conduct a college at Lebanon, Kentucky. In 1837 he was directed to open a college at Grand Coteau, Louisiana. He left there in 1840 for Saint Louis, Missouri, where he joined the party of Father Pierre Jean De Smet bound for the Flathead country. The group reached the Flathead nation in August 1841. From that date until the spring of 1847 Point labored at evangelizing the Flathead, the Coeur d'Alene, and other neighboring nations. He spent the winter of 1846–1847 with the Blackfeet at the American Fur Company's Fort Lewis. Though a devoted missionary, Father Point is chiefly remembered for the six richly illustrated volumes of the manuscript journals he kept while among the Indians (Point 1850). He had early manifested some artistic talent, which he put to excellent use in painting numerous scenes of Indian life. The four volumes pertaining to the Plateau Indians of Oregon and Idaho were published (Point 1967; McDermott 1952). Returning from the Oregon country, Point went to Canada where he spent most of his remaining life as a missionary to the Ottawa Indians of Manitoulin Island, Ontario. JOSEPH P. DONNELLY, S.J.

Pope, John 1822–1892

From 1862 to 1886 Pope, a Civil War veteran, held major commands in the West, directing campaigns against the Sioux, 1862–1865; Kiowa, Comanche, and Southern Cheyenne, 1874–1875; Ute 1879–1880; and Apache. He also attempted to keep illegal White settlers out of Indian Territory. Repeatedly criticizing federal Indian policy and its administration, he believed military control of Indian affairs would benefit both Indians and government while favoring assimilation of Indians into White society. He was sincerely concerned with the welfare of Indians for military and humanitarian reasons. For further information see Ellis (1970). RICHARD N. ELLIS

Powell, John Wesley 1834–1902

Born in Mount Morris, New York, Powell grew up on the frontier in Ohio, Wisconsin, and Illinois. He attended various colleges but did not graduate. He served in the Union Army in the Civil War, attained the rank of major, and lost his lower right arm at the battle of Shiloh. After the war he led natural history expeditions to the West, culminating in his explorations of the Colorado River system between 1869 and 1872. During the 1870s he directed the United States Geological and Geographical Survey of the Rocky Mountain region.

From 1868 through 1880 Powell conducted intermittent studies of the Numic-speaking peoples of the Great Basin and of tribes in northern California. In 1874 Powell and G.W. Ingalls (1874) produced a report on Great Basin Indian affairs. Under Powell's direction, John K. Hillers photographed American Indians (D.D. Fowler 1972). In 1880 Powell directed the first census of "untaxed" Indians for the United States Census.

In 1879 Powell founded the Bureau of Ethnology (after 1894 the Bureau of American Ethnology) of the Smithsonian Institution, serving as its first director until his death. Between 1881 and 1894 he served concurrently as director of the United States Geological Survey. Under Powell's direction, the Bureau of Ethnology staff and its numerous collaborators conducted extensive archeological, linguistic, and ethnographic studies of North American Indians and made collections of ethnographic and archeological artifacts for the United States National Museum. Powell directed the compilation of bibliographies on American Indians that were used in Hodge's (1907–1910) *Handbook* and the completion of a linguistic classification of American Indian languages (Powell 1891). The results of these studies are in three publication series that Powell initiated, the *Contributions to North American Ethnology* and the Bureau of Ethnology *Annual Reports* and *Bulletins*. Powell was a founder and president of the Anthropological Society of Washington.

Biographical and bibliographical data on Powell and the Bureau are contained in Fowler and Fowler (1969)

and Terrell (1969). His ethnographic studies and collections are reported in Fowler and Fowler (1971), Fowler and Matley (1979), and Fowler, Euler, and Fowler (1969). Powell's ethnographic manuscripts and correspondence are in the Smithsonian Institution, National Anthropological Archives, and Record Group 57 in the National Archives, Washington, D.C. See also Warman (1903). DON P. FOWLER

Powers, Stephen 1840–1904

In 1875 Powers, who was a newspaper journalist and author, was commissioned to make a collection of Indian material culture on the eastern slope of the Sierras and in California for the Centennial Exhibition of 1876. He carried out this assignment and wrote a series of reports that were published under the editorship of John Wesley Powell as *Tribes of California* (S. Powers 1877; Fowler and Fowler 1970). Powers was not a professional anthropologist, and he made no further contributions in this field.

Tribes of California is a basic work on California Indian ethnography. It was the first effort to treat the native cultures of the area systematically. Archeology, though little known and understood, is treated in a special chapter, as is ethnobotany. The map was the first one published that attempted to define the territorial extent of language families. Kroeber (1925:ix) paid Powers's volume high praise while at the same time recognizing that it must be used with caution, saying that the author "possessed an astoundingly quick and vivid sympathy, a power of observation as keen as it was untrained, and an invariably spirited gift of portrayal." Powers can be truly called the father of California Indian ethnography. ROBERT F. HEIZER

Pratt, Richard Henry 1840–1924

A career Army officer, Pratt founded the Carlisle Indian School in 1879 with 82 children from the Sioux tribes in Dakota Territory. Despite the opposition of the Army, he served as superintendent of Carlisle until his dismissal in 1904 for insubordination, the result of his opposition to Indian Bureau policy. Pratt made an original contribution to educational policy with his concept of the Eastern boarding school, providing both academic and manual training. He held inflexibly to the idea that the only way to get the Indian into the mainstream of American life was to isolate him from the tribal environment and put him into contact with White civilization. See Eastman (1935), Gilcreast (1967), and Utley (1964) for further information. Pratt's papers are in the Beinecke Library, Yale University. E. ARTHUR GILCREAST

Priber, Johann Gottlieb fl. 1734–1744

Priber, known as Christian Priber, a German immigrant to South Carolina in 1734, an army officer of some

education, settled in the Cherokee town of Great Tellicoe in 1736. He preached the formation of a Christian, communal republic consisting of all the tribes of the Southeast to the Mississippi. Priber's objectives included the preservation of Indian independence from European encroachment and the creation of a society worthy of European emulation.

Adopting Indian language and dress, Priber's influence grew and with it the suspicions of English furtraders who believed him to be a French spy. An attempt by the South Carolina authorities to arrest him as a troublemaker was thwarted by the Cherokee in 1739, but he was captured in 1743 on route to Mobile and died in prison at Fort Frederica, Georgia, several years later. The best discussions of Priber are Crane (1919), Gipson (1936–1970, 4:61–62), and Sirmans (1966). RICHARD L. HAAN

Price, Hiram 1814–1901

Price, a banker from Iowa, former congressman, and advocate of temperance, was commissioner of Indian affairs, 1881–1885. In order to transform Indians into copies of White Americans, Price forbade many Indian customs, such as certain dances, plural marriages, the destruction of property by mourners, and shamans' practices. He also planned to withhold rations so that Indians would take up farming and other work. A devout Methodist, he sought religious men as Indian Service personnel. Like many of his predecessors, Price viewed allotment as the primary answer to the Indian "problem" (Waltmann 1962). For more information see Gue (1895) and F.A. O'Neil (1979). ANDREA LUDWIG

Putnam, Frederic Ward 1839–1915

Putnam's first interest and his formal training were in the field of zoology, which he studied under Louis Agassiz. After a brief career as a curator and director of the Museum of the Peabody Academy of Science at Salem, Massachusetts, he turned his attention to anthropology. In 1875 he was appointed curator of the Peabody Museum of American Archeology and Ethnology at Harvard University. From a very modest beginning he developed this museum into one of the finest research institutions for American archeology. In 1886 he became the first Peabody Professor of American Archeology and Ethnology at Harvard, and he trained most of the professional workers in his specialty during his career. He organized the Department of Ethnology and Archeology for the World's Columbian Exposition held in Chicago in 1894, where he planned and directed the first public Museum for Anthropology in the United States. Following this he became part-time curator of anthropology at the American Museum of Natural History, to which he brought his chief assistant at the Columbian Exposition, Franz Boas, and he subsequently got Boas established at Columbia College. In 1903 Putnam became part-time professor of anthropology and director of the Anthropological Museum at the University of California. With Alfred L. Kroeber he established another museum, a teaching department, and a series of publications in anthropology. Besides organizing and directing five museums and their publications he served for 25 years as permanent secretary of the American Association for the Advancement of Science and in 1898 was elected its president. For further biographical information see Boas (1915), R.W. Dexter (1966, 1966a, 1976, 1980), Kroeber (1915), and Tozzer (1935). There is a bibliography of Putnam by F.H. Mead (1909). RALPH W. DEXTER

Quinton, Amelia Stone (Swanson) 1833–1926

Born in New York and educated in an academy there, Quinton had been a teacher and temperance organizer before her friend and fellow Baptist Mary Lucinda Bonney awakened her concern for Indian rights. In Philadelphia in 1879 the two women committed themselves to winning for the Indians popular and congressional support. Quinton would organize, while Bonney would supply funds. Out of this partnership grew the first significant organization of friends of the Indian, later known as the (Women's) National Indian Association (see Wanken 1981).

By early 1882 the Association mustered 100,000 supporters for a congressional petition written by Quinton that called for a program to assimilate the Indians: education, citizenship, and allotment of tribal lands to individual Indians. Quinton traveled, organized, wrote, and spoke extensively to gain popular support for the Dawes Severalty Act providing for allotment and Indian citizenship, which passed in 1887.

From 1887 through 1905 (except one year) Quinton served as president of the Association. She organized new chapters, inspected Indian reservations, lobbied in Washington, and set up many missions among the Indians, which were eventually transferred to various denominations. She worked for reform in Indian administration and for the total destruction of all aspects of Indian culture. She was not a cultural relativist. Active in Indian work through 1909, Quinton was moved by humanitarianism, the missionary zeal of nineteenth-century Protestantism, and a conviction that all races were endowed with equal potential.

Details of Quinton's activities and statements of her philosophy are in published records of the Women's National Indian Association, 1883–1926; the Lake Mohonk Conference of the Friends of the Indian, 1885–1906; and Board of Indian Commissioners, 1884–1896. For her biography and an account of the Association, see Westing (1971). IRENE J. WESTING

Randlett, James F. 1832–1915

Randlett served in the Union Army during the Civil War and reentered the Army in 1867. In 1893 he was detailed as agent for the Uintah and Ouray Reservation Utes. Although retired from the Army in 1896, he continued as Indian agent until 1897. In 1899 Randlett was appointed to the difficult Kiowa, Comanche, and Wichita Agency and served as agent there until 1905. A man of great integrity and administrative ability, he succeeded admirably in a position few handled well. The best single source for information on Randlett is his Army Commissioned Personnel File in the National Archives. For his career at the Kiowa, Comanche, and Wichita Agency, see Hagan (1976:219ff.). WILLIAM T. HAGAN

Râle, Sébastien 1657–1724

Born in Pontarlier, France, Râle joined the Society of Jesus when he was 18. He was ordained at Lyons and sailed for Canada in 1689. His first two years were spent at the refugee Eastern Abenaki mission near Quebec, where he began his French–Eastern Abenaki dictionary (Râle 1833). A second tour of two years at Kaskaskia and Michilimackinac gave him the opportunity to learn Ottawa, Huron, and Illinois. In 1694 he founded the Eastern Abenaki mission at Norridgewock on the Kennebec River in Maine, which he guided for the next 30 years.

Râle's mission lay in the disputed area of Acadia that France ceded to England by the Treaty of Utrecht in 1713. The priest supported the pro-French factions that opposed the English claims to Abenaki territory and checked the tentative advances of Protestant ministers sent to woo his flock. His steady opposition led the English to put a price on his head. Twice his mission church was destroyed and the village sacked by English troops before he was finally killed, scalped, and mutilated. Among the booty seized was his dictionary, which reflects more than 30 years of observation and is the principal source on the Caniba dialect of Eastern Abenaki. A few of his letters survive in the Harvard and Cornell University libraries.

Râle has evoked strong and contrasting reactions from both contemporaries and historians, usually along national and religious lines. Morrison (1970, 1975, 1984) and Axtell (1985) restore historical balance to the accounts of Francis (1845) and Baxter (1894). Leger (1929), and Lord, Sexton, and Harrington (1944), describe the religious context of his work from both sides of the frontier. JAMES AXTELL

Remington, Frederic 1861–1909

Born at Canton, New York, Remington attended Yale University Art School 1878–1880. His highly successful career as illustrator, painter, sculptor, and writer was launched shortly after sensational news stories concerning Apache raids in Arizona enlivened popular interest in Indians and the West in 1885. From that time until his death, Remington played an important role in shaping American impressions of Indian life.

Remington was an outspoken critic of U.S. Indian policy, which he regarded as bungling, bureaucratic, and heartless. In his journalistic essays, he argued that since Indians made excellent soldiers, they should be trained, armed, and incorporated into the structure of the regular army. In his fiction, literary essays, oils, and bronzes, he depicted the Indian as a tragic figure of American history. His most arresting treatments of Indian subjects concerned the complex relations between Indians and Whites. Among such treatments, *John Ermine of the Yellowstone* (Remington 1902), a novel, best demonstrates the extent of Remington's personal involvement.

G.E. White (1968) links Remington with Theodore Roosevelt and Owen Wister as an Easterner who discovered affirmative values in the West. McCracken (1947) considers him primarily as a chronicler of colorful Western history. Vorpahl (1972, 1978) gives the fullest analysis of his writing and a critical biography. Significant collections of Remington art are at the Whitney Gallery in Cody, Wyoming; the Gilcrease Institute in Fort Worth, Texas; and the Frederic Remington Art Memorial in Ogdensburg, New York. The bulk of Remington's diaries and manuscripts are housed at the Remington Art Memorial. BEN MERCHANT VORPAHL

Rhoads, Charles J. 1872–1954

Born in Germantown, Pennsylvania, Rhoads was from a devout Quaker family and graduated from Haverford College. His career was centered about the city of Philadelphia where he was active in banking, education, and philanthropy. In 1899 Rhoads was elected a director of the Indian Rights Association and in 1927, its president. As a result of close work with Herbert Hoover in YMCA and American Red Cross activities in 1918–1919, he was chosen by Hoover to serve as commissioner of Indian affairs in 1929. Rhoads was reluctant to accept the post of commissioner but did so after receiving President Hoover's promise that he would support Rhoads in his efforts to implement the reforms outlined in the Meriam report. He appointed another Quaker, Joseph Henry Scattergood, as his assistant. For two years he worked closely with John Collier, executive secretary of the American Indian Defense Association, on reforms, before Collier became a critic. They disagreed on the advisability of further allotments and on the taxation of Indians; Rhoads favored both.

During Rhoads's four years in office appropriations for Indian health and education swelled greatly and significant reforms were implemented in both areas. Rhoads was also responsible for an administrative reor-

ganization of the Indian Bureau, which resulted in a sweeping change in personnel. Rhoads resigned in 1933 with the change in presidential administration. He and Scattergood continued their campaign for assimilation of Indians through the Indian Rights Association. A cautious reformer, both by training and by instinct, Rhoads was a transitional figure between the nineteenth-century goal of racial assimilation and the New Deal goal of cultural pluralism. For further information see Kelly (1968, 1979a). LAWRENCE C. KELLY

Riggs, Alfred Longley 1837-1916

Born at Lac-qui-parle mission in Minnesota, A.L. Riggs was the eldest of the nine children of Stephen Return Riggs, missionary to the Santee Sioux. He graduated from Knox College, Galesburg, Illinois, and attended the Theological Seminary of Chicago from 1860 to 1862. In 1870 he joined the Congregationalist mission to the Sioux (Riggs 1880), establishing himself at Santee Agency, Nebraska. He began the Santee Normal Training School, which became one of the foremost Indian boarding schools, renowned for its emphasis on the use of the Sioux language for instruction. After 1877 Riggs was involved in editing the Dakota newspaper *Iapi Oaye* and its English counterpart, *The Word Carrier*, which were printed on the school press. He continued his work at Santee until his death. RAYMOND J. DEMALLIE

Riggs, Stephen Return 1812-1883

Born in Ohio, Riggs was educated at Jefferson College and the Western Theological Seminary at Alleghany. Riggs and his wife Mary Ann joined the Congregationalist mission to the Sioux Indians of Minnesota, sponsored by the American Board of Commissioners for Foreign Missions. In 1837 they established themselves at Lac-qui-parle mission among the Wahpeton Sioux. There, together with other members of the mission, and relying principally on the assistance of Joseph Renville, a mixed-blood Sioux trader, they began studying the Sioux language and preparing translations of the scriptures. The first of these was published in 1839, and the entire Sioux Bible was printed in 1879. Combining his own efforts with those of other missionaries, particularly Jedidiah D. Stevens, Samuel W. Pond, Gideon H. Pond, and Thomas S. Williamson, Riggs edited a Sioux grammar and dictionary (Riggs 1852). In 1842 Riggs began a new mission at Traverse des Sioux, but in 1846 he returned to Lac-qui-parle. In 1854 Riggs and Williamson consolidated their missionary efforts at Hazelwood near the Santee Agency. In the aftermath of the Santee uprising, Riggs served in 1862 as chaplain for the military expedition led by Henry H. Sibley against them, and in 1863 he acted as interpreter. In 1865 Riggs moved to Beloit, Wisconsin, and organized a mission and school among the Santee Sioux prisoners at Davenport. In 1870 he organized a mission at the Sisseton agency. In 1872 he moved back to Beloit, where he remained, devoting the remainder of his life to overseeing the Sioux missions and preparing Sioux translations. For bibliography see Pilling (1887:60–66). From 1873 until his death he edited *Iapi Oaye*, the Sioux language newspaper. Riggs (1869) is a description of Santee culture and a history of the Sioux missions. Riggs (1887) is an account of his own work with the Sioux. RAYMOND J. DEMALLIE

Rousseau, Jean-Jacques 1712-1778

Born in Switzerland, Rousseau moved to Paris where he became a novelist, essayist, and political theorist. His works, including *Du Contract Social* (1762) and the *Discours sur l'Origine . . . de l'Inégalité* (1755) are immensely influential but also ambiguous and confused. Some scholars have argued that even the notion of the Noble Savage generally attributed to him results from a mistaken reading of his text. But that scarcely matters; since, mistaken or not, it has possessed the minds of many important Europeans and Americans, including the most notable writers on Indian themes, beginning with James Fenimore Cooper. LESLIE A. FIEDLER

Rowlandson, Mary White about 1635–about 1678

The wife of a minister in Lancaster, Massachusetts, Mary Rowlandson, with her three surviving children, was taken captive during an attack on the village on February 10, 1676, during King Philip's War. For 11 weeks she moved with her Indian captors throughout Massachusetts and New Hampshire until she was ransomed on May 2 with her two surviving children. She described her experiences in her account of her captivity (Slotkin and Folsom 1978), which was frequently reprinted and became a model for Indian captivity narratives and a standard against which to measure popular "best sellers" (Slotkin 1973, 1985; Washburn 1977–1983). WILCOMB E. WASHBURN

Sapir, Edward 1884–1939

Sapir did extensive linguistic fieldwork among the North American Indians and encouraged students to do so. Among numerous articles and monographs (Mandelbaum 1949) influential contributions are *Language* (Sapir 1921), his essay on time perspective (Sapir 1949), and his proposed reduction of Powell's (1891) 55 families of Indian languages to six superstocks (Sapir 1949a). For biographical information and evaluations of Sapir's work from a number of perspectives, see Cowan, Foster, and Koerner (1986). Sapir's papers form part of the Boas collection of the American Philosophical Society, Philadelphia, and some materials on Nootka are in the National Museum of Canada, Ottawa. MARY HAAS

Scattergood, Joseph Henry 1877–1953

Born in Philadelphia, Scattergood was a Quaker and a graduate of Haverford and Harvard. A close personal friend of fellow Quaker Charles J. Rhoads, Scattergood joined the reform administration when Rhoads became commissioner of Indian affairs in 1929. Scattergood and Rhoads worked as a team with Scattergood specializing on financial matters and filling in when the commissioner was away. Under their direction appropriations for Indian affairs increased, and work on implementing reform recommendations in the Meriam report was successfully undertaken, especially in the area of education.

Achievements were modest in the last two years of the Rhoads-Scattergood administration, because they were forced to spend much of their time defending subordinates from a variety of critics, including John Collier. For further information see Downes (1945), Anonymous (1953), and Prucha (1984, 2:926–939). LORING B. PRIEST

Schermerhorn, John Freeman 1786–1851

Reared in Schenectady, New York, Schermerhorn graduated from Union College and Andover Seminary. From 1816 to 1832 he served the Dutch Reformed Church in New York state. During that time he also was active in New York and national politics. Schermerhorn's Indian work extends from 1832 to 1837. From 1832 to 1834 he served as one of three commissioners to the western territory. In 1835 he negotiated the treaty of removal with the Cherokees. And in 1836 he worked to remove the Six Nations of Iroquois from New York. He was dismissed from office in 1837. Schermerhorn was President Andrew Jackson's most knowledgeable, active, and notorious Indian commissioner, from 1832 to 1837. The best source for Schermerhorn's career is Van Hoeven (1972) and Schermerhorn (1914). Schermerhorn's correspondence is in the National Archives, Record Groups 46, 75, 94, 107. JAMES VAN HOEVEN

Schoolcraft, Henry Rowe 1793–1864

Born in northern New York, Schoolcraft moved to the west in 1818. His book on the Missouri lead mines (Schoolcraft 1819) impressed Secretary of War John C. Calhoun, and together with his friendship with Gov. Lewis Cass of Michigan Territory obtained for him first a position as Indian agent in 1822 and later the acting superintendency of Indian affairs for Michigan. While Indian agent he married Jane Johnston, a half-blood Ojibwa. Schoolcraft valued his contact with the Johnston family, for through them he learned about Ojibwa culture. In 1832 his interest in Indian culture and devotion to missionization led him to found the Algic Society for promoting the civilization and christianization of the Indian (Schoolcraft 1851). Dismissed from his post as agent for political and financial reasons in 1841,

Schoolcraft moved to New York City (Bieder 1972), where he wrote popular books about Indians as a livelihood (Schoolcraft 1843, 1845). Membership in the New-York Historical Society and the American Ethnological Society helped Schoolcraft receive a commission in 1845 to take a census of New York Indians, which resulted in *Notes on the Iroquois* (Schoolcraft 1846). From 1849 to 1857 the federal government sponsored his compilation of a six-volume work on the Indian tribes of the United States (Schoolcraft 1851–1857) that, even more than his other works, underscored his paternalistic attitude toward the Indians (Freeman 1960) and his belief that they would become extinct unless they accepted Christianity. The Library of Congress and the Burton Historical Collection, Detroit Public Library, house the largest collections of Schoolcraft's personal papers; the National Archives contains his official reports. ROBERT E. BIEDER

Schurz, Carl 1829–1906
Born in Cologne, Germany, Schurz attended the University of Bonn intent on becoming a professor, but his plans were interrupted by civil unrest. He became a political activist, joining the movement for a united Germany. His political activities forced him out of Germany in 1849, and after brief stays in France and England, Schurz emigrated to the United States. In 1852 Schurz bought farmland, speculated in real estate, and dabbled in small business, but he soon found that his real talents lay in public speaking. At first he lectured only in German, but as he gained more command over English he began addressing English-speaking audiences. As a renowned speaker, Republican, and antislavery activist, Schurz proved a highly dedicated and effective campaigner for Abraham Lincoln in 1860, and Lincoln awarded him the ministry to Spain in 1860 in recognition of his work. In 1861 Schurz entered the Army, serving as general throughout the Civil War. In 1869 he was elected senator from Missouri.

In 1877 President Rutherford B. Hayes appointed Schurz secretary of the interior. Schurz resolved to reform the department and free it of graft. Although his efforts proved somewhat successful, his dealings with the Indians did not. Schurz continued the accepted practice of removing tribes to Indian territory. The effects proved devastating and forced Schurz to reconsider his Indian policy. In so doing he promoted allotment and encouraged the Indian to support himself as the White man did. To this end Schurz also encouraged the establishment of Indian schools such as Carlisle Industrial School, which was founded in 1879. Schurz's term as secretary of the interior ended in 1881. He spent the remainder of his years as a writer and public speaker. For details see Trefousse (1982). HEATHER C. DODSON

Schuyler, Peter 1657–1724
Born in Albany into a prominent Dutch family with extensive landholdings and commercial interests, Schuyler served in the local militia and became involved in border warfare. In 1686, when Albany received its charter, Schuyler became its first mayor and head of the Board of Indian Commissioners. During the Leisler Rebellion, Schuyler took a leading role in keeping Jacob Leisler's influence out of Albany and out of Albany's relations with the Iroquois. He continued to maintain a significant influence with the Iroquois and worked to reduce French influences among the tribes. Schuyler played a prominent role in the Canada expeditions of 1709 and 1711, and in 1710 he visited England with three Mohawks and one Mahican, known as the Four Kings of Canada. He had a tempestuous political career in the colony and was removed from his public offices by Gov. William Burnet in 1720. For additional information see Schuyler (1885). LAWRENCE H. LEDER

Scott, Hugh Lenox 1853–1934
An 1876 West Point graduate, Scott served 20 years on the Plains frontier and gained a reputation as a friend of the Indian. He commanded an Indian scout company, 1892–1897; superintended the Chiricahua Apaches, 1894–1897; and resolved troubles with the Navajos, 1908 and 1913, Kickapoos in 1908, Hopis in 1911, Apaches in 1912, and Paiutes in 1915. He published widely on Plains Indian history and culture, especially the sign language, on which he was a leading authority. After retiring as Army chief of staff in 1917, he continued his studies. He served 1919–1929 on the Board of Indian Commissioners (fig. 15). His autobiography is Scott (1928). ROBERT M. UTLEY

Scott, Winfield 1786–1866
Virginian, military hero of the War of 1812 and Mexican War, and presidential candidate, Winfield Scott endured as a controversial public figure for half a century. He exercised field command in the Black Hawk War of 1832 and for a time in 1835 in the perennial Seminole War. In 1838 he superintended removal of the Cherokees to a new homeland west of the Mississippi. As commanding general of the U.S. Army, 1841–1861, he gave overall direction to operations against the Seminoles and the tribes of the western territory acquired from Mexico and England in the 1840s. There are Scott papers in the Library of Congress and the New-York Historical Society. A competent biography is C.W. Elliott (1937). See also Prucha (1969) and Utley (1967). ROBERT M. UTLEY

Sells, Cato 1859–1948
A rancher-banker from Cleburne, Texas, Sells's appointment as commissioner of Indian affairs in 1913 resulted primarily from his loyal support of the Democratic

Lib. of Congress, Prints and Photographs Div.
Fig. 15. Hugh Scott at the 60th-anniversary celebration commemorating the signing of the treaty between tribes of the Southern Plains and the United States at Medicine Lodge. left to right, George Hibbard; his wife; Mrs. George Hunt, Kiowa; Scott; George Hunt, Kiowa; W.H. Sears. Photographed at Medicine Lodge, Kans., Oct. 1927.

nominee, Woodrow Wilson, in the 1912 elections. Sells served throughout the Wilson administration, 1913–1921 (fig. 16).

Although Sells was responsible for increasing Indian usage of grazing land, as opposed to leasing it to White cattlemen and for improving the property rights of Indian minors among the Five Civilized Tribes in Oklahoma, he is best remembered for his policy of forced patenting of Indian trust lands. In 1906 an amendment to the Dawes Severalty Act empowered the secretary of the interior to remove restrictions on allotted Indian lands prior to the expiration of the 25-year trust period if he determined that the allottee was competent to handle his own affairs. This power was used sparingly until Sells's administration.

In 1917, in an attempt to hasten the assimilation of Indians and to end their special status as wards of the federal government, Sells launched what he called the New Policy. Henceforth, all adult Indians of one-half or less Indian blood were to be recognized as competent in terms of the 1906 act. In addition, all Indian students who received diplomas from government schools would also be declared competent to handle their own affairs

upon reaching the age of 21. Between the years 1917 and 1920 over 21,000 Indians were released from federal protection, their lands fee-patented and made subject to local taxes. Many of them subsequently lost their land and in 1921 Sells's successor, Charles Burke, put a halt to the policy. Sells's interpretation of the 1906 act was ruled illegal by a federal court in 1924, and legislation was enacted during the 1920s to restore the lost lands or their equivalent to the original Indian owners; for more detail on his term as commissioner see Kelly (1979).
LAWRENCE C. KELLY

Sergeant, John 1710–1749

Sergeant graduated from Yale in 1729. After two years of theological study and four as a college tutor, he was appointed in July 1735 by the Society for Propagating the Gospel among the Indians in New England to minister to the Housatonic Indians in Berkshire County, Massachusetts. With the assistance of a schoolmaster, and a school, church, and land grant from the Massachusetts General Court, he turned Stockbridge into "the most impressive Indian settlement in New England" (Kellaway 1962: 276).

Fig. 16. Commissioner of Indian Affairs Cato Sells (front row, second from left) with a delegation of Osage Indians. The Osages came to Washington to discuss issues connected with federal administration of their mineral resources. Photograph by Natl. Photo Company, Washington, about 1920.

In 14 years, despite alcoholism, native resistance, and unsavory Dutch influences, Sergeant had baptized 182 of the 218 inhabitants, received 42 into church membership, and won the respect of most with his "catholic temper" and command of their language (Dexter 1885: 396–397). He translated prayers, biblical passages, and the shorter catechism into Mahican. Shortly before his death, Sergeant was granted funds to establish a boarding school for Indian boys and girls that would unite academic study with work training, a plan he had publicized six years earlier (Sergeant 1743). For further information see Hopkins (1753), E.F. Jones (1854), and Axtell (1986).

JAMES AXTELL

Serra, Junipero 1713–1784

Born in Petra, Majorca, Spain, Serra entered the Franciscan Order at Palma in 1730 and was ordained a priest in 1738. At Palma he was librarian at the Convento de San Francisco, taught philosophy, and upon obtaining his doctorate in theology taught at the Lullian University. Desiring to become a missionary among the Indians of America, he sailed for the New World in 1749 and in 1750 entered the College of San Fernando, Mexico City, whence he was sent to the Sierra Gorda missions in northeastern Querétaro among the Pame Indians. Between 1752 and 1758 he was instrumental in building five beautiful and sturdy missions still in use in the 1980s. He learned the native language and introduced agriculture, animal husbandry, commerce, and the useful arts.

Recalled to Mexico City in 1758, he was assigned to administrative duties and occasional preaching tours through central and southern Mexico. When the Jesuits were removed from Spanish America Serra was chosen as president of their missions in Lower California, 1768–1769. In 1769, when Spain occupied Upper California, Serra accompanied the first overland expeditions to

San Diego and founded nine missions between San Diego and San Francisco, 1769–1784 ("Roman Catholic Missions in California and the Southwest," this vol.).

Serra letters and reports reveal his genuine love for the Indians (Tibesar 1955–1966). For further information see Geiger (1959). Principal depositories of original Serra materials are the Santa Barbara Mission Archive, California; Archivo General de la Nación and Biblioteca Nacional, Mexico City; Archivo de Indias, Seville, Spain; and University of Texas, Austin. MAYNARD GEIGER

Seymour, Flora Warren 1888–1948

Born in Cleveland, Flora Warren Smith graduated from George Washington University, law school, and received a doctorate in law in 1916. While she continued to practice law, she became best known for her prolific writing on Indian subjects.

From 1906 to 1912 she served in the United States Indian Service. Her interest in the American Indian was thus already established in 1915 when she married George Steele Seymour. Her knowledge of Indian affairs was recognized when she was appointed to the Board of Indian Commissioners in 1922. In 1924 appeared the first of her many books about Indians written for children. Biographical books for youth and for adults about frontier Americans soon followed.

Seymour's particular fame rests upon her studies of Indian history, which revealed her feeling that "Indians should be treated as human beings, not as museum pieces or as perpetual dependents." The process of assimilation, she believed, was inexorable in spite of efforts to hold it back, and she opposed the policies of John Collier. Her views on assimilation dominate her books (for example, Seymour 1926, 1929). She also made contributions to Indian scholarship (Seymour 1930, 1941). Her papers are in the Eleanor de Smith Memorial Library, Niles, Michigan. LORING B. PRIEST

Sheridan, Philip Henry 1831–1888

An Ohioan and West Point graduate of 1853, Sheridan served in the Pacific Northwest before winning high rank in the Civil War. He led the campaign of 1868–1869 against the southern Plains tribes, then headed the Military Division of the Missouri from 1869 to 1883. The large-scale operations of the 1870s gainst the tribes of this vast command—the Great Plains, Texas, New Mexico, and part of the Rocky Mountains—fell under his overall direction. As commanding general of the Army from 1883 to 1888, he figured prominently in the conduct of the last Apache warfare in Arizona. His service is documented in personal papers in the Library of Congress, his autobiography (P.H. Sheridan 1888), and a study of his frontier years (Hutton 1985). ROBERT M. UTLEY

Sherman, William Tecumseh 1821–1891

Blunt, articulate, and dogmatic, Sherman emerged from the Civil War the nation's second-ranking soldier. He commanded the Military Division of the Missouri until 1869, when he was elevated to commanding general of the Army, a post he held until retirement in 1883. This position afforded little formal authority over military operations, but his powerful personality and towering prestige gave him pervasive influence. Sherman viewed the opening of the West as a great national enterprise, and against Indians who resisted government authority he advocated total war such as he had practiced in the South in the Civil War. His role in Indian affairs is richly documented in his personal papers in the Library of Congress and is the subject of an excellent monograph (Athearn 1956). ROBERT M. UTLEY

Sieber, Al 1844–1907

Born in Germany, as a young man Sieber emigrated with his family to the United States, eventually settling in Minneapolis, Minnesota. He had no formal education and began his fighting career as a Civil War soldier. The period for which Sieber is probably remembered most is when he served as chief of scouts under Gen. George Crook in Arizona. His primary duty was to lead Indian scouts in the campaign to conquer "hostile" Indians and confine them, along with cooperative Indians, to reservations. His Indian subordinates served him well throughout this campaign basically because he was honest with them and treated them fairly and respectfully. Toward the end of his career, Sieber was accidentally shot in the leg while attempting to arrest the notorious Apache Kid. As a consequence, he became permanently disabled but continued serving the government until 1890, when he was fired because of differences between him and the new agent at San Carlos Reservation, Arizona. For Sieber's career see F.C. Lockwood (1942), Williamson (1931), and Thrapp (1964). NED ANDERSON

Slocum, Frances 1773–1847

In 1778 Slocum was captured by Delaware Indians at her home near Wyoming, Pennsylvania. She was adopted by a Delaware family and given the name Weletawash. She married a Delaware man who disappeared after a battle at Fort Wayne in 1814. Her second marriage was to a Miami, Shepancanah, with whom she had four children; her Miami name was Maconaquash. She remained at his village on the Wabash through government largesse although the Miami people were removed to the West in 1840. She preferred to retain her Indian identity even after being rediscovered by her White family in 1835. For further biographical information see Winger (1936), Meginness (1891), Slocum (1908), and M.B. Phelps (1905). ANDREA LUDWIG

Smiley, Albert K. 1828–1912

Born in Vassalboro, Maine, and educated at Haverford College, Smiley founded and headed several academies in a number of Eastern states. In 1869, with his brother Alfred he purchased property at Lake Mohonk outside Poughkeepsie, New York, and constructed a resort hotel that was noted for its austere Quaker rules for guests. Smiley's religious interests brought him into contact with humanitarian circles that dealt with the Indian, and his reputation as a fair and impartial arbiter earned him an appointment in 1879 to the Board of Indian Commissioners. In 1889 he was named chairman of a commission of three to select reservations for the Mission Indians of Southern California and in 1895 chairman of a committee of investigation on the proposed uniting of the tribes in western Nevada.

His role in Indian work was chiefly as a catalyst for other groups and individuals interested in the Indian. Beginning in 1883, Smiley annually invited the leaders in Indian work, as his guests, to confer on the Indian problem at the Lake Mohonk retreat. As many as 200 people attended these three-day conferences, known as the Lake Mohonk Conference of the Friends of the Indian, Smiley established the procedures of the conferences and served as peacemaker among the often argumentative groups. He insisted that any recommendations for Indian policy that were to be designated as a Mohonk platform should have the endorsement of all participants. A select committee presented the annual platform to the Indian Bureau and the administration. President Grover Cleveland credited the Mohonk group in his first administration with persuading him to abandon a scheme to gather all Indians on a single reservation. The Conference published a detailed annual report and continued to meet beyond Smiley's death. For further information see Trueblood (1897) and L. Abbott (1921). E. ARTHUR GILCREAST

Smith, Edward Parmelee 1827–1876

Born in Connecticut, Smith graduated from Yale and Andover Theological Seminary. Ordained in 1856, he became a Congregational minister. Smith's work with the American Missionary Association led to his appointment in 1871 as agent for the Minnesota Chippewa where he was involved in a plan to sell their pine to provide income for them. In 1873 he accompanied Gen. O.O. Howard on a peace mission to the Apaches of the Southwest.

Smith held the position of commissioner of Indian affairs 1873–1875, and he defended the Peace Policy. He supported the demand that Indians work in return for government-furnished supplies. He advocated severalty and the creation of a formal code of law for the Indian. He believed that treaties could be broken in the higher interest of the United States and Indian nations and that military intervention in Indian affairs was permissible

when required. He did not, however, advocate the transfer of the Bureau to the War Department. For further information see A.F. Beard (1909:205) and R.C. Crawford (1979). ANDREA LUDWIG

Smith, Jedediah 1799-1831

A native of New York state, Smith's career was launched in 1822 at Saint Louis when he joined William Ashley's keelboat expedition to trade among the Upper Missouri tribes. In 1823, after a hostile encounter with Arikaras, he led a trail-blazing band overland from Fort Kiowa to South Pass and the beaver-rich Green River. At the Cache Valley rendezvous of 1826 he became a partner of David Jackson and William Sublette in the Indian trade and then pioneered the first known traverse of the Great Basin, from Great Salt Lake to San Diego. In 1827, from a beaver camp in the Sierras, he made a central crossing of the Great Basin to Great Salt Lake and the Bear Lake rendezvous with his partners. Again he crossed the desert to California, losing most of his party to hostile Mohaves. From Los Angeles he trapped and explored northward to the Umpqua River in Oregon. There he narrowly escaped the fate of most of the members of his party when they were attacked at night, asleep and defenseless, and methodically slain by Lower Umpqua Indians. Smith remained at Fort Vancouver on the Columbia until 1829 when he rejoined his partners after a trek through Nez Perce and Flathead country. In 1830 his partnership was sold to a combine headed by Jim Bridger and Thomas Fitzpatrick. In 1831 he went on a trading expedition from Saint Louis to Santa Fe. On the dreaded Cimarron Cut-off he was making a side trip to search for water when he was ambushed and speared to death by Comanches. He left only a fragmentary journal; his definitive biographer is Morgan (1953). Also see H.L. Carter (1971), Morgan and Wheat (1954), and M.S. Sullivan (1936). MERRILL J. MATTES

Smith, John 1580?-1631

Smith came to America in 1607 with the expedition that founded Virginia; for the next two and one-half years he dominated the colony's relations with the Indians. His principal goals were to persuade the Indians to permit English settlement and exploration and to coerce them into providing food whenever the colony was in need. Smith explored and mapped much of Chesapeake Bay during his first six months, but when he probed beyond the falls of the James River he was captured by the Powhatan tribe. Chief Powhatan released Smith after Pocahontas, "his favorite daughter," pleaded for the captive's life, according to Smith's later recollections. While he remained in the colony (of which he was president 1608–1609), the English had willing help from Pocahontas who apparently idolized Smith, grudging cooperation from Powhatan who recognized the long-range implications of English colonization, and sporadic opposition from local tribes that resented Smith's bullying tactics.

In keeping with his earlier military exploits, Smith used cajolery or threats to get what he wanted. After Smith left Virginia he made a brief exploration of New England where he had occasional contact with the natives. More important were his subsequent writings, which kept his contemporaries informed about English colonization and which fostered their incipient contempt for Indian rights and culture.

For further information see Barbour (1964), K. Glenn (1944), B. Smith (1953), and Smith (1910). ALDEN VAUGHAN

Smith, John Quincy 1824–1901

Born near Waynesville, Ohio, Smith attended Miami University at Oxford, Ohio, for a short period. A farmer and politician, he served in the Ohio Senate and House of Representatives. In 1872 he was elected to the United States House of Representatives. When defeated for reelection, Ulysses Grant appointed Smith commissioner of Indian affairs in 1875, a post he held until asked to resign by Secretary of the Interior Carl Schurz in 1877.

According to Smith's letters, he had a low opinion of Indians and their culture. He favored allotment, sale of "surplus" land to Whites, and consolidation of all Indians on a few reservations. He was in favor of the Peace Policy use of religious workers as Indian agents. When Indians did not follow directives for removal, he ordered the Army into action. During Smith's term, many charges of corruption and incompetence were leveled against Smith and other high officials in the Indian Bureau. For more detail see Waltmann (1962) and E.E. Hill (1979). ANDREA LUDWIG

Spalding, Henry H. 1803–1874

Born in Steuben County, New York, Spalding graduated from Western Reserve College, Hudson, Ohio. He prepared for the ministry in Lane Theological Seminary. In 1836 the American Board of Commissioners for Foreign Missions assigned him and his wife, Eliza, to the Oregon Territory. The Spaldings traveled overland to the Pacific that year with Marcus and Narcissa Whitman and established mission stations in the region's interior. The Spaldings located at Lapwai, Idaho, among the Nez Perce. Spalding insisted on basing his mission program on agriculture and commenced farming in 1837. In 1840 he printed a pamphlet in the Nez Perce language to instruct his pupils, the first item to be printed in the Pacific Northwest. With the murder of the Whitmans in 1847 by Cayuse Indians the labors of the American Board in the Oregon interior came to an end, and the Spaldings settled in the Willamette Valley. On June 24, 1850, Henry Spalding was named Indian agent for the

territory. He assisted Superintendent Anson Dart in treaty work on the Oregon seaboard in 1850–1851 but was dismissed less than a year later because of his disagreements with his superior and absences caused by his wife's illness. In 1859 Spalding returned to Idaho and in 1862 to Lapwai, then site of the area's Indian agency. He resumed preaching among the Nez Perce and continued, with some interruptions, until his death. Spalding papers include collections at the Oregon Historical Society, Portland, and Whitman College, Walla Walla, Washington. For biographical assessment see Drury (1936). STEPHEN DOW BECKHAM

Speck, Frank G. 1881–1950

Of Hudson River Dutch and Mahican descent, Speck spent part of his childhood at Mohegan, Connecticut, in the care of Fidelia A. Fielding, the last speaker of the Mohegan language. He received bachelor's and master's degrees from Columbia University, the M.A. as a student of Franz Boas, who strongly influenced his research interests and methods and supervised his PhD dissertation on Yuchi ethnography. His final degree was awarded in 1908 by the University of Pennsylvania, where he taught anthropology for his entire career.

Speck was the leading ethnographer of the Indians of eastern North America, visiting their communities nearly every year from about 1900 until his death. Emphasizing the recovery of moribund cultural detail, he recorded masses of information that would otherwise have been completely lost. He published almost 250 papers and some 30 monographs and books on at least 35 different Indian groups ranging from Labrador and Maine to Oklahoma and Louisiana; he was also an important collector of artifacts for many different U.S. museums. His salvage ethnography and linguistics (for example, among the Catawba and the Indians of Virginia and southern New England) was of extreme importance, and he also studied contemporary culture (for example, among the Creek, Cherokee, Naskapi, Montagnais, and Iroquois). His work on family hunting territories and the religious aspects of hunting among northern Algonquians is especially significant. His interests included ritual, mythology, social organization, folk biology, and material culture.

His scholarly work had long-lasting social consequences, especially for the recognition of the many groups of whose distinct cultural and historical traditions he was the first (and sometimes the only) serious student. For some of these and other Indian communities he provided direct but quiet encouragement and assistance on political reorganization.

Speck's surviving fieldnotes are in the American Philosophical Society, Philadelphia (Freeman 1966). For biographical information and appreciation by some of the many students and other anthropologists he influenced, see Hallowell (1951), A.F.C. Wallace (1951), and Blankenship (1988). WILLIAM C. STURTEVANT AND JOHN WITTHOFT

Squier, Ephraim George 1821–1888
Born in New York, Squier began his archeological explorations with the Ohio Valley mounds, later excavated New York mounds, and, while in diplomatic service, sites in Central and South America (Squier and Davis 1848; Squier 1851; Stanton 1960:82–89; Bieder 1872:305–366). A member of the American Ethnological Society and an Indian sympathizer, Squier also wrote on Indian religion (Squier 1848, 1851a). ROBERT E. BIEDER

Stevens, Isaac Ingalls 1818–1862
Simultaneously Washington Territory's first governor, Indian superintendent, and transcontinental-railroad explorer in 1853, the controversial Stevens gathered Indian data and labored to open the Pacific Northwest by removing its tribes onto reservations (Trafzer 1986). His stormy tour in 1855 to sign treaties, especially with the Nez Perce and neighbors, with the Flathead Confederacy, and with the Blackfeet, precipitated the Yakima and other Indian wars, 1855–1858. See J.T. Hazard (1952) and Hazard Stevens (1901) for biographies. ROBERT I. BURNS, S.J.

Stewart, John 1787–1823
Born in Powhatan County, Virginia, of free Black parents, Stewart moved to Marietta, Ohio, at the age of 21, where he did odd jobs. In 1815, he felt he received a divine message ordering him to preach the gospel to the Indians. In spring 1816 he left for the frontier, visiting the Munsee Delaware at Pipetown on the Sandusky River. The Delaware were pleased with Stewart's singing of hymns and invited him to remain among them, but he soon moved farther northwest to Upper Sandusky, where about 700 Wyandots lived. Stewart began preaching the Methodist faith to the Wyandots although he was not an ordained minister and though some believed that he was a runaway slave. Stewart's religious zeal and melodious voice in singing hymns soon won him many converts among the Wyandots. Jonathan Pointer, a Black man who had been a captive since childhood and spoke Wyandot, served as the interpreter of Stewart's sermons. The Indian subagent and interpreter, William Walker, defended Stewart against the efforts of the White traders to persuade the Wyandots to drive him from their country. Several Wyandot leaders resisted Stewart, but others were converted.

After the Wyandot ceded most of northwestern Ohio to the United States in August 1817, Stewart was adopted into the Wyandot tribe, given a share of their annuities, and presented with a section of land for his mission in the center of their reservation. In 1819, the Reverend Moses

M. Henkle visited Stewart's mission and thereafter licensed Stewart to preach and incorporated his mission under Methodist jurisdiction. In 1821, the Methodists sent the Reverend James B. Finley to Upper Sandusky to take charge of the mission, erect a school, and assist Stewart. Stewart had combatted the influence of the White traders and native shamans as well as the use of liquor. In 1842 the Wyandots sold the last of their lands in Ohio, and the Upper Sandusky mission came to an end. Most of what is known about Stewart is found in Mitchell (1827), Badger (1851), and Finley (1840). FRANK T. SIEBERT, JR.

Street, Joseph Montfort 1782–1840
Born in Lunenburg County, Virginia, Street read law in the office of Henry Clay and eventually practiced law in Tennessee and Kentucky. In 1806 Street began publishing a controversial Federalist journal, *The Western World*, in Frankfort, Kentucky. During six years there he fought several duels, was shot while unarmed, and lost a costly libel suit. Then he removed to Shawneetown in southern Illinois.

From 1812 to 1827 Street served as court clerk, postmaster, recorder of deeds, and brigadier-general of the militia at Shawneetown. In 1827 he was appointed Indian agent for the Winnebago at Prairie du Chien, Wisconsin. Street was a staunch defender of the Indians against unscrupulous Whites and even government officials who sought to deny or cheat them, yet he was also a strong advocate of allotment in severalty, christianization, citizenship, and in general "civilization" for Indians. The Winnebago and Menominee tribes remained neutral during the Black Hawk War of 1832 as a result of his efforts and these tribes' respect for him. Street was transferred to Rock Island in 1835 to supervise the Sauk and Fox and remained there until 1837. After a brief return to Prairie du Chien a year later, in addition to a tour of the eastern states with several chiefs, he went to Iowa and selected the site for the new Sauk and Fox agency on the Des Moines River. Having lived and worked there for two years, he died at Agency City, Iowa.

Street's papers are found in the Historical Society of Iowa, Des Moines, and the Historical Society of Wisconsin, Madison. For detailed accounts of his life and fur-trade relations, see Street (1895) and I.M. Street (1929). WILLIAM W. QUINN, JR.

Stuart, John 1718–1779
Born in Inverness, Scotland, Stuart was in youth engaged in commerce in Spain. He traveled around the world on an expedition, 1740–1744, and settled as a merchant in Charleston, South Carolina, in 1748. Becoming bankrupt, he enlisted as an officer in the South Carolina militia and served in the Cherokee War, 1760–1761. 687

Captured by the Cherokee at Fort Loudoun, he was befriended and enabled to escape by his friend, Chief Attakullakulla (Little Carpenter). Recommended by Gen. Jeffery Amherst, he was appointed British superintendent for Indian affairs in the southern department of North America in 1762 and held that office until his death. Before 1775 he strove to maintain peace on the frontiers of the Southern colonies, to regulate the trade with the Indians, and to prevent rapid expansion of White settlements. At the outbreak of the War of Independence he fled from Charleston to Saint Augustine and thence to Pensacola. Stuart was beloved by the Cherokee. He did not instigate the first Indian attacks upon the revolutionaries but later enlisted Indians to serve with contingents of British regulars and Loyalists against the colonists. Extensive official correspondence of Stuart is preserved in the Thomas Gage Papers, William L. Clements Library, University of Michigan, Ann Arbor, and in the Colonial Office Papers of the British Public Record Office, London. His career is chronicled by Alden (1944). JOHN R. ALDEN

Sublette, William Lewis 1799–1845

Born near Stanford, Kentucky, Sublette received little, if any, formal education. He was active in the Western fur trade, 1823–1840, as trapper, trader, and outfitter. A Jacksonian Democrat influential in Indian affairs, he narrowly missed appointment to an Indian superintendency in 1845. The Missouri Historical Society, Saint Louis, holds the Sublette family manuscripts. For further information see Nunis (1959) and Sunder (1959, 1968). JOHN E. SUNDER

Swan, James G. 1818–1900

Born in Medford, Massachusetts, Swan was apprenticed in Boston to a ship chandler, studied admiralty law, became a ship-fitter, and read voraciously about the Pacific Coast, a region visited by his uncle 1806–1810. Swan journeyed to California in 1850 and in 1852 settled on Willapa Bay, Washington, as an oysterman. He compiled voluminous field notes and sketches of the Indians. In 1854 he became a collector of customs and served the territory's Indian Commission in treaty negotiations with the Chehalis, Chinookans, Cowlitz, and Quinault. Swan (1857) published a compendium of his Indian studies and travel experiences, including Chehalis and Chinookan vocabularies. Swan became secretary to Gov. Isaac I. Stevens of Washington Territory. From 1862 to 1866 Swan was Indian agent to the Makah at Neah Bay. On seven major expeditions in the 1870s and 1880s, he traveled to southeast Alaska to collect artifacts and sketch the Indians (Swan 1870, 1876). Between 1880 and 1892 he authored a dozen articles on subjects such as fur seals, fish, and tattooing among the Haida. Swan's papers include 73 volumes of diaries, journals, and letters

in the University of Washington library, Seattle, and 125 sketches and watercolors in private hands. For a biography see McDonald (1972). STEPHEN DOW BECKHAM

Swanton, John Reed 1873–1958

Swanton was educated at Harvard and Columbia, and after receiving his PhD in 1900 he went to work for the Bureau of American Ethnology, Washington, from which he retired in 1944. His first fieldwork was on the Lakhota (Teton Sioux) language, 1899. Upon joining the BAE he initially investigated the Northwest Coast tribes and completed major ethnographic and linguistic publications on the basis of his fieldwork among the Haida, 1900–1901, and Tlingit, 1904. He then turned his attention to the tribes of the lower Mississippi Valley and the Southeast, which were the major focus of his research for the remainder of his career. On numerous field trips (nearly every year 1907–1919 and 1929–1931) and by studying historical and archival sources he made important studies of the ethnography or languages, or both, of the Alabama, Atakapa, Biloxi, Caddo, Catawba, Chickasaw, Chitimacha, Choctaw, Creek, Hitchiti, Houma, Kitsai, Koasati, Natchez, Ofo, Timucua, Tunica, and Wichita. His descriptive monographs and collections of source materials provide the basic ethnohistorical and ethnographic documentation for these groups as well as important linguistic materials. He served as chairman of the U.S. De Soto Commission, 1936–1939 and wrote its final report, a determination of the route across the Southeast taken by Hernando de Soto in 1540. His general papers on social organization, based on ethnographic data from North America, were considered significant refutations of social evolutionary theories and formed the basis for subsequent typologies. Swanton's papers are in the National Anthropological Archives, Smithsonian Institution. A comprehensive bibliography of his scholarly writings is in the biographical memoir by Steward (1960); see also Fenton (1959). IVES GODDARD

Taliaferro, Lawrence 1794–1871

Born in King George County, Virginia, Taliaferro enlisted in the infantry during the War of 1812. In 1818 he resigned from the Army to assume charge of the Indian agency at Fort Saint Anthony, later renamed Fort Snelling, Minnesota. For the following 20 years Taliaferro served continuously as Indian agent. His position was a difficult one. On the one hand, he was confronted with the longstanding enmity between the two main tribes under his jurisdiction, the Eastern Sioux and the Southwestern Chippewa, aggravated by the territorial pressures of the advancing White frontier. On the other hand, the activities of trappers, traders, and the American Fur Company often interfered with and complicated the agent's role as peace-keeper among tribes and between them and the United States. While an honest and zealous agent and a strong supporter of American westward expansion, Taliaferro also manifested uncommon empathy and concern for the rights of the Indians, taking an uncompromising stand against unscrupulous Whites and their illegal trade of liquor to the Indians.

In 1824 Taliaferro led a delegation of Sioux and Chippewa to Washington to arrange for a convocation of all the tribes of the middle and upper Mississippi region. The grand council, held the following summer, resulted in the Treaty of Prairie du Chien between the U.S. and the Sioux, Chippewa, Sauk and Fox, Menominee, Iowa, Winnebago, and a portion of the Ottawa and Potawatomi tribes. Peace among the tribes and boundary lines of their respective territories were established.

Enmity between the Sioux and the Chippewa was not resolved by the 1825 treaty, and it remained a continuous vexation for Taliaferro until 1827 when jurisdiction over the Chippewa was transferred to another agency. Taliaferro then focused his attention on the Minnesota Sioux, whom he unsuccessfully attempted, with missionary help, to transform into Christian farmers. He was more successful in securing several territorial cessions from the Sioux, whose large delegation Taliaferro accompanied to Washington in 1837.

Toward the White traders, Taliaferro always voiced contempt and dislike, as he was convinced they wanted "to enslave the poor Indian body and mind to their dictatorial will" (Satz 1975:110–111). He believed the traders of the American Fur Company to be scoundrels, and for their part American Fur Company officials attempted repeatedly to have Taliaferro removed from office.

In 1839, Taliaferro resigned his post as Indian agent at Fort Snelling, leaving behind a strong legacy of fair dealing with the Indians. Taliaferro reentered military service from 1857 to 1863, when he finally retired.

Taliaferro left a voluminous and detailed record of his military life and long term as Indian agent; manuscript materials are available on microfilm from the Minnesota Historical Society, Saint Paul (H. White 1966). His portrait is attributed to Catlin (Coen 1971). For further information see Babcock (1924), Satz (1975), Taliaferro (1891), and G.C. Anderson (1986). CESARE MARINO

Tanner, John 1780?–1847?

The son of a Kentucky pioneer family, Tanner was captured in 1789 by a raiding party led by a man who kept him at the Ojibwa-Ottawa village of Saginaw for two years and then traded him to an Ottawa woman, who accepted him as a son. For nearly 30 years he lived as an Indian in the Ojibwa country between Lake Superior and Lake Winnepeg, marrying, and raising a family. Around 1820 he began to make efforts to regain his identity as a White man, and for several years moved back and forth between Indian and White society, finally settling as a

government interpreter at Sault Sainte Marie. Unable to adjust psychologically to his divided heritage or overcome the social barriers thrown up against him, Tanner was in constant conflict with both his White and Indian associates, none of whom could trust him to be one of them. In 1846 he was suspected of murdering Henry R. Schoolcraft's brother James and fled Sault Sainte Marie just ahead of bloodhounds and a lynch mob, never to be seen again. Someone else later confessed to the murder. J. Tanner's *Narrative* (1830) is one of the most significant Indian captivity accounts, recounting in a frank and intensely personal way the situation of those trapped on the border between two cultures but belonging to neither world; it is also an important ethnographic source (see also Désy 1983). Tanner's last years are discussed in O'Meara (1962), which includes a bibliography of source materials on Tanner's life. P. RICHARD METCALF

Tatum, Laurie 1822–1900

On July 1, 1869, Laurie Tatum, a member of the Society of Friends, became the Indian agent at Fort Sill on the Wichita Reservation. The Kiowa were warriors and raiders who showed the utmost arrogance to Tatum and took every kindness as a concession or act of cowardice. However, Tatum was a Quaker of heroic proportions and the Indians discovered that intimidation was useless against him.

The greatest problem facing Tatum was keeping the Kiowa and Comanche on the reservation and halting their raids into Texas. The raids continued through 1870 and 1871, during which time many fresh scalps and White captives were brought back to the reservation. Tatum recommended to Acting Commissioner William F. Cady that if rations or annuity goods were issued or ransoms paid the Indians would be encouraged to continue committing depredations and taking captives.

Tatum first tested this policy in 1872, demanding the release of three White captives without ransom from the Kiowa Chief Lone Wolf. No annuity goods would be issued until the chief complied. The captives were given up and eight others were surrendered shortly thereafter. Although Tatum did not condone the use of military force it is not unlikely that an expedition in the summer of 1872 against the Comanche influenced Tatum's method.

The arrest and conviction of several leading Kiowa chiefs—Satank, Satanta, and Big Tree—for raids in Texas were due to Tatum's efforts. It was his testimony that convicted Satanta and Big Tree and also his intervention that caused their death sentences to be reduced to life imprisonment. He was concerned that their deaths might bring reprisals.

Tatum's position became difficult as the other Kiowa chiefs began to clamor for the release of Satanta and Big Tree. This was further complicated by well-meaning but uninformed people in the settled areas who considered the imprisonment an injustice. Tatum was opposed to the release of Satanta, and when he was overruled, he resigned his position on March 31, 1873. For additional information see Tatum (1899), Rister (1940), Seymour (1941), and Cutler (1971). HENRY E. FRITZ

Taylor, Alexander S. 1817–1876

Born and educated in South Carolina, Taylor left home in 1837, traveled widely in India and Southeast Asia, and went to California in 1848 during the gold rush. He served as clerk of the U.S. District Court in Monterey until 1860 when he moved to Santa Barbara. He developed an interest in California history and bibliography of the Spanish-Mexican period, 1542–1846, and wrote extensively for California newspapers (Cowan 1933). He drew up in 1864, but never published, the first map showing locations of California Indian tribes (Heizer 1941). His chief publication of anthropological interest is *Indianology of California* (A.S. Taylor 1860–1863). This miscellany, which appeared in a newspaper, contains a great deal of original and copied information from archives, much of which has otherwise disappeared. ROBERT F. HEIZER

Taylor, Nathaniel G. 1819–1887

Born in Tennessee, Taylor graduated from Princeton. He became a Methodist minister and served in Congress. He was appointed commissioner of Indian affairs in 1867, when partisan politics and corruption were rampant in the Bureau. The army was using force against Indians throughout the West, at great cost. Taylor recommended negotiating peace with all tribes, consolidating them on three huge reservations, and providing education and training for them. Taylor was a member of the Peace Commission of 1868, which reported on the poor conduct of many Indian agents and tried to make peace with the western tribes. When Ulysses Grant was elected, Taylor resigned. In his retirement he farmed and preached. For more information see Unrau (1979). ANDREA LUDWIG

Teit, James Alexander 1864–1922

Born in the Shetland Islands, Teit emigrated to Canada as a young man and settled at Spence's Bridge, British Columbia, near a village of Thompson Indians. He developed an interest in these people, learned their language, and became intimately acquainted with their customs. In 1895 he met Franz Boas, whom he aided as a field collaborator during the next 25 years, contributing a large body of data on the ethnology and mythology of Plateau tribes, much of it published under Boas's editorship (Teit 1898, 1900, 1906, 1909, 1909a, 1912, 1912a, 1928, 1930). He also collected ethnographic articles and natural history specimens for the Geological Survey of

Canada, materials now in the National Museum, Ottawa; the Field Museum, Chicago; and the American Museum of Natural History, New York. Teit's materials are basic to any study of Plateau Indian cultures, but he was more than a scientific recorder of customs. His warm personal empathy with Indian peoples and sympathy with their social problems led him to initiate the organization of an association of British Columbia tribes for protection of their interests, in which he served as secretary for some years. As an ethnographer, Teit had unusual and perhaps unique qualifications, although lacking any conventional academic training. An evaluation of his work was presented in an obituary by Boas (1922). See also J.J. Banks (1970). WILLIAM W. ELMENDORF

Teller, Henry Moore 1830–1914

Born in Allegany County, New York, to a poor farming family, Teller pursued a higher education and eventually began reading law. In 1858 Teller set out for Illinois to join the law practice of Hiram A. Johnson. In 1861, Teller joined Johnson in Colorado. In 1876 Teller was elected to the United States Senate, where he took an active interest in Indian affairs, and in 1882 Chester A. Arthur appointed Teller secretary of the interior (Trani 1975:138–140).

Teller's Indian policy stood in direct opposition to that of his predecessor Carl Schurz. Whereas Schurz pushed hard for landholding in severalty, Teller advocated tribal allotments and continued tribal organization. He favored the sale of excess Indian lands in hopes of restricting traditional Indian activities such as hunting and encouraging sendentary activities such as farming. Teller also opposed boarding schools. He advocated reservation schools that emphasized vocational training and enrolled both male and female students. Wanting to make education compulsory for all Indian children, Teller acknowledged the futility of educating only a small sector of the Indian population. He recognized the difficulty educated Indians faced when graduating from off-reservation schools and returning to reservation life. He wished to ease their assimilation into White society by assimilating more of their own society. Although Teller's Indian policy was well defined it met with little support. Teller returned to the Senate after serving three years in the Cabinet. For further information see E. Ellis (1941). HEATHER C. DODSON

Thayer, James Bradley 1831–1902

Born in Massachusetts, Thayer was educated at Harvard College and Harvard Law School. In 1874, after practicing law for many years, he became a professor in the law school, a position he held until his death. During his tenure, he was considered a leading scholar of constitutional law and the law of evidence (Thayer 1893).

Thayer became interested in the legal status of the American Indian in the 1880s and was a leading proponent of the Dawes Severalty Act of 1887 (Thayer 1888). However, he believed that the Dawes Act was too slow an instrument to bring all Indians immediately under the United States legal system. Therefore, with the help of the Law Committee of the Indian Rights Association, he drew up the Thayer Bill, which would have secured this goal. Thayer failed to get congressional approval for his proposals, and he wrote articles that severely criticized the Indian policy of the period (Thayer 1891). Being unsuccessful in achieving his goal, Thayer's interest in the issue faded (Prucha 1973). Thayer's papers are located in the Harvard Law School Library in Cambridge, Massachusetts. ANDREA LUDWIG

Thomas, William Holland 1805–1893

Born near Waynesville in western North Carolina, Thomas moved with his widowed mother to a small farm on the Oconaluftee River near Quallatown, a settlement of Mountain (or Eastern) Cherokees. As a young man, Thomas operated a store on Soco Creek where members of Chief Yonaguska's band of Mountain Cherokees traded. Living among the Cherokees, Thomas learned their language and customs and soon earned their friendship and trust. Yonaguska adopted him as his son.

Thomas taught himself law, became a respected attorney and a successful businessman, and was elected to the state legislature in 1848. In 1831 the Quallatown Cherokees named him their agent and attorney. The previous year Congress had passed the Indian Removal Act that set the stage for the (fraudulent) Treaty of New Echota of 1835 by which the Cherokee Nation agreed to remove to Indian Territory (Foreman 1932). Even though the Eastern Cherokees were both geographically and politically separated from the rest of the Cherokee Nation they too were faced with the removal threat. Thomas's position on the removal issue appears to have changed at times (M. Russell 1956:54–99; Finger 1984:20–59); however, in the end Thomas succeeded in gaining for the Quallatown Cherokees the right to remain in the East. He pleaded their case before Congress and the North Carolina legislature and used his own money and funds appropriated by Congress to purchase over 50,000 acres on behalf of the Indians (W.H. Thomas 1853, 1858). These lands, which became known as the Qualla Indian Boundary, constitute the main tract of the Eastern Cherokee Reservation.

During the Civil War, Thomas organized and was commanding officer of two Confederated regiments known as Thomas's Legion of Indians and Highlanders in which some 400 Eastern Cherokees served (Crow 1982).

Between 1873 and 1874 Thomas was involved in two lawsuits the Eastern Cherokees brought against him (and other Whites) to clear their title to the lands Thomas still held in trust for them. The arbitrators eventually ruled that title was vested in the Eastern Cherokees as a tribe.

In 1877 Thomas entered the state insane asylum in Morganton, where he died. Considering the nature and extent of Thomas's close association with the Eastern Cherokees, Finger (1984:171) concluded that, "without him there would have been no Eastern Band of Cherokees. Despite a normal measure of human shortcomings, he was the best friend the Indians ever had."

M. Russell's (1956) biography also lists a bibliography of Thomas's papers. CESARE MARINO

Thompson, Smith 1768–1843

A lifelong New Yorker, Thompson read law with James Kent after graduating from Princeton. As a recipient of political preferment, Thompson served on the New York Supreme Court from 1802 until appointed secretary of the navy in 1818. In 1823, President James Monroe appointed Thompson to the United States Supreme Court, and he served until his death. Perhaps Thompson's greatest opinion, in a career with few distinctions, was the dissent he delivered in *Cherokee Nation* v. *Georgia* (5 Peters 1, 1831), asserting that despite their dependent status, Indian tribes retained their sovereignty. The following year, in *Worcester* v. *Georgia* (6 Peters 515, 1832), this dissenting opinion became the majority position. Thompson often followed the reasoning of his mentor and longtime colleague, James Kent, in his opinions. For a detailed discussion of this aspect of Thompson's judicial career see Roper (1963). Thompson's papers are in the Library of Congress, the New-York Historical Society, and the New York Public Library. DONALD ROPER

Thorpe, George 1575–1622

A former member of Parliament and a pensioner of James I, Thorpe in 1620 went to Virginia to administer lands set aside by the London Company for an Indian college. He had earlier taken an Indian boy into his home and taught him to write; in America his interests continued to focus on the education of the natives, although his immediate responsibility was to supervise farmers assigned to cultivate the college lands. He was also a member of the governor's council. Unlike most of the colonists who, he complained, gave the Indians "nothinge but maledictions and bitter execrations," Thorpe befriended them and sought to reduce racial tensions. His ultimate goal was conversion of the Indians, especially Chief Opechancanough, to Christianity. Thorpe was killed in the Indian rebellion of March 22, 1622. For additional information see A. Brown (1890, 2:1031) and Kingsbury (1906–1935). ALDEN VAUGHAN

Trowbridge, Charles Christopher 1800–1883
Born in Albany, New York, Trowbridge served, after 1819, as private secretary to Gen. Lewis Cass and in various capacities in the Michigan Superintendency of Indian Affairs. On the basis of his own fieldwork he wrote ethnographies of several tribes of the Old Northwest and compiled vocabularies and paradigms to document their languages (Kinietz 1946; Trowbridge 1938, 1939). There is a biographical sketch by J.V. Campbell (1883). ERMINIE WHEELER-VOEGELIN

Trowbridge, Roland Ebenezer 1821–1881
Born in New York, a graduate of Kenyon College, Trowbridge was a farmer and a politician. A Republican, he served in the Michigan Senate and twice in the United States House of Representatives. In March 1880, President Rutherford Hayes appointed Trowbridge, a friend from college, commissioner of Indian affairs, but Trowbridge was very ill and could do little in that position. For more information see Goldman (1979). ANDREA LUDWIG

Underhill, John 1597–1672
Born in England, Underhill was brought up in the Netherlands where his father and later he himself served as officers against the Spaniards. Emigrating to Massachusetts Bay in 1630, he was immediately chosen a militia captain. In the Pequot War of 1637, Underhill participated in the invasion of Block Island and in the predawn massacre led by John Mason of a Pequot village on the Mystic River. The massacre enabled the English to supplant the Pequots as the dominant force in southern New England. Underhill justified the incident by comparing the Puritan cause to that of King David in the Old Testament (J. Underhill 1638). Underhill returned to Boston in time to be banished as both an Antinomian heretic and adulterer. After serving as "governor" of a short-lived plantation at Piscataqua, New Hampshire, he moved to Long Island and joined New Netherlands Gov. Willem Kieft's futile but bloody effort to expel all Indians from the New Amsterdam area. In March 1644 he repeated Mason's strategy of 1637 and led the massacre of an Indian village at Pound Ridge. When war broke out between the English and Dutch in 1652, Underhill helped reinforce New England's fears of a Dutch-Indian conspiracy, issued a one-man declaration of independence from Dutch rule, and led the capture of a small island of Dutch territory inside Connecticut. There is no reliable biography of Underhill; the one by Shelley (1932) should be used in conjunction with historical accounts (for example Vaughan 1965; Salisbury 1982; Trelease 1960). NEAL SALISBURY

Valentine, Robert Grosvenor 1872–1916
Before his appointment as commissioner of Indian affairs in 1909, Valentine, a graduate of Harvard, was an administrator and the originator of the profession of industrial counseling. He had taught English at the Massachusetts Institute of Technology, worked in banking and industry, and served as secretary to Commissioner Francis Leupp and as supervisor of Indian schools and assistant commissioner of Indian affairs.

Valentine had great respect for the Indian as an individual, and his Indian policy was based upon finding a place for the individual Indian in the economic life of the nation. He supported allotment in order to make the Indian economically independent. Improved health services and industrial education were priorities for him, as was the bureaucratic restructuring of the Indian Service and the professionalization of its personnel.

Valentine had to deal with serious problems during his tenure—the Pima Indians of Arizona were without adequate water supplies, and there was massive land fraud on the White Earth Reservation in Minnesota. Valentine's papers are in the J.P. Kinney Collection, Cornell University Library, Ithaca, New York. For more detail on his term as commissioner see Putney (1979). ANDREA LUDWIG

Veniaminov, Ivan Evseevich 1797–1879
Born in Irkutsk province, Siberia, and first named Ioann Evseevich Popov, Father Veniaminov was a Russian Orthodox Church missionary in Alaska, Metropolitan of Moscow, ethnographer, and linguist. At age nine he was sent to Irkutsk Seminary where he was given the surname Veniaminov.

In 1823, two years after graduating from Irkutsk Seminary as an ordained priest, Father Veniaminov was sent to Unalaska Island where he converted the Aleuts to Christianity, taught them building trades, and founded a boys' school to teach them reading, writing, and Christianity. He learned Aleut, wrote the first Aleut-Russian dictionary and Aleut grammar, invented an Aleut alphabet, and translated the liturgy, catechism, and the gospel of Matthew into Aleut.

In 1833, Veniaminov transferred to Novo-Arkhangel'sk and had some success in converting nearby Tlingits to Christianity. In 1838, Veniaminov left America for Saint Petersburg. Two years later he published his classic study of Aleut culture (Veniaminov 1840).

Becoming a monk in 1840, he took the name Innokentii (Innocent) and was appointed bishop of the newly formed Kamchatka, Kuril, and Aleutian diocese based at Novo-Arkhangel'sk. During the next 27 years, he helped spread Christianity to the natives in his diocese and had the Holy Scriptures translated into Aleut, Yakut, and Kuril.

In 1868, Bishop Innocent became the Metropolitan of Moscow and Kolomensk, holding that post until his death. His papers are in the Alaska Historical Library and Museum, Juneau. For further information see C.R. Hale (1888), Veniaminov (1886–1888), Kashevarov (1927), Stepanova (1949), and Shenitz (1967). WINSTON L. SARAFIAN

Vial, Pedro 1746?–1814

Pedro or Pierre Vial, native of Lyons, France, came to North America early in his life, and became an outstanding explorer, guide, and Indian interpreter. Well liked by the Indians, he lived among them as a gunsmith. In the 20 years following 1786, he traveled the wilderness between Santa Fe, San Antonio, Natchitoches, and Saint Louis, establishing and pioneering routes of communication for Spain. He was used by Spain in her attempt to hold her frontier possessions and the loyalty of the Indians against the more aggressive and feared Anglo-Americans. In 1792–1793, he opened the road between Santa Fe and Saint Louis. It was the speed of that trip that made the Spanish authorities realize the nearness of Santa Fe to the United States. Vial must have spoken, or at least understood, several Indian tongues, for he dealt with Wichitas, Comanches, Jicarilla Apaches, Osages, Kansas, and other Indians.

Although all Frenchmen were suspected and ordered arrested in 1795, Vial was released but not permitted to leave New Mexico. In 1797, he deserted to the Comanches and went from there to Missouri where he remained for three years, at times with interests in mining near Mine à Breton. By 1803, Vial was back in service with the Spaniards in Santa Fe. In 1808, he was issued a license to hunt on the Missouri by Gov. Meriwether Lewis; he was back in Santa Fe in November 1809. He died in Santa Fe in 1814 and was buried there. Vial could not write Spanish and wrote badly in his native French.

For more information see Loomis and Nasatir (1967), and Nasatir (1952, 1974). A.P. NASATIR

Walker, Francis Amasa 1840–1897

Born in Massachusetts, Walker graduated from Amherst, studied law, and served in the Civil War. He was appointed commissioner of Indian affairs by President Ulysses Grant in 1871 and served until 1873. Walker deplored the action of Congress in terminating the treaty relationship with Indian tribes in 1871, since he felt that the government was left without an adequate legal basis for negotiating (F. Walker 1874:11–13). A political economist and statistician of international reputation, a newspaper editor (Springfield *Republican*), an educator and administrator, Walker's accomplishments include the rationalization of the method of taking the United States census, the vitalization of the Massachusetts Institute of Technology as its president from 1881 to

1897, and a long list of publications in varied fields. See Munroe (1923) for biographical information and a bibliography of Walker's writings. For details of his official term see Miner (1979). ANDREA LUDWIG

Walker, James Riley 1849–1926

Walker received his M.D. from North West Medical School in 1873. In 1878 he joined the Indian Service as a doctor among the Chippewa at Leech Lake, Minnesota. He tried to check the smallpox epidemic there in 1883. Walker remained with the Chippewa until 1893 when he was transferred after accidentally wounding an Indian during an attempt to confiscate a supply of illegal whiskey. Walker then served at Colville Agency, Washington, and at Carlisle Indian School, Pennsylvania. In 1896 he was transferred to Pine Ridge Reservation, South Dakota, where he remained until his retirement in 1914. There his major medical work was in the prevention and treatment of tuberculosis. He devoted a great amount of effort to studies of Sioux culture, under the guidance of Clark Wissler. Walker gained the confidence of the older Oglala medicine men and was accepted by them as one of their number. His account of Oglala religion (1917) and three volumes of collected papers (1980, 1982, 1983) are basic sources of Sioux ethnography. For biographical details, see J.R. Walker (1980). Walker's unpublished papers are in the State Historical Society of Colorado, Denver, and the Department of Anthropology of the American Museum of Natural History, New York. RAYMOND J. DEMALLIE

Washburn, Cephas 1793–1860

Born in Randolph, Vermont, and educated at the University of Vermont, Washburn became a Congregational missionary to the Western Cherokee. In 1819 the American Board of Commissioners for Foreign Missions sent him to work with the Cherokee at the Brainerd Mission in Tennessee. There Washburn joined his sister, Susanna, and her missionary husband Alfred Finney in taking an interest in that portion of the tribe that had agreed to move to Arkansas in 1817 (Finney and Washburn 1821–1825; R.S. Walker 1931; Malone 1956a). In 1820 Washburn and Finney visited the Western Cherokee in their new homes and made arrangements for a mission. In 1821 the two ministers were officially transferred to Arkansas, where they established the Dwight Mission and Indian school. Operating out of this mission, Washburn became the dominant Christian influence on the Western Cherokee, at times presiding over as many as 16 missionaries and assistants (Tracey 1840). When the Eastern Cherokee were moved to Indian Territory in 1835, the Dwight Mission served to coordinate all missionary efforts. Washburn did have some difficulty after this with the portion of the tribe led by John Ross, who resented the missionary influence among the Cherokee. C. Washburn (1869) left an account of his work among the Cherokee. Papers regarding his activities are in the records of the American Board kept at the Houghton Library, Harvard University. ROBERT A. TRENNERT

Washington, George 1732–1799

Washington, as first president of the United States, was, along with Henry Knox, an architect of the Indian policy of the newly formed nation. The thrust of the Indian policies Washington urged upon Congress was toward peace, protection of Indian land rights, and the regulation of trade. Details of Indian-White relations during the Revolution and the early years of the Republic may be found in Graymont (1972), Prucha (1962), and Washburn (1975).

Washington's papers are in the Library of Congress. An extensive biographical bibliography may be found in Fitzpatrick (1936). ANDREA LUDWIG

Wayne, Anthony 1745–1796

Born in Waynesboro, Pennsylvania, Wayne early became an activist in the independence movement both as a politician and soldier. Following a career as a Revolutionary War officer, he unsuccessfully tried surveying and gentleman farming. Elected as a representative to Congress from Georgia in 1791, he was unseated because of an election fraud. Beset by marital problems which denied him easy access to his family farm a few miles from Philadelphia, he applied for the position of commander-in-chief of the United States Army, then stationed on the northwest frontier. Even though he was not President George Washington's first choice for the position, Wayne accepted the appointment in April 1792. From that time until the mounting of the "active campaign" on July 28, 1794, he raised and trained an effective force that won a decisive victory over the Indian confederacy at Fallen Timbers, August 20, 1794. It was this humbling defeat of the British-inspired Indians that led to the imposed peace, the Treaty of Greenville in 1795, and eventually to the British surrender of their posts in the Old Northwest in 1796. By this peace, nearly three-quarters of the present state of Ohio was opened to White settlement and the groundwork was laid for the eventual settlement of the entire Northwest Territory. In the summer of 1796, Wayne formally accepted the British-held forts of Miami, Detroit, and Michilimackinac on behalf of the United States. He died while returning from this mission. There are biographies by T. Boyd (1929) and Wildes (1941). See also Knopf (1961). RICHARD C. KNOPF

Weiser, Conrad 1696–1760

Weiser was the province of Pennsylvania's Indian agent to the Iroquois confederacy during the years leading to and culminating in the French and Indian War. He was born in Würtemburg and moved with his family in 1710 to New York state along with other German refugees from the Thirty Years' War. As a youth he lived with the Mohawk Indians and learned to speak the language. After the family's removal to Pennsylvania in 1723, he established himself as a substantial frontier farmer and community leader. But he also was repeatedly employed by Pennsylvania officials and other colonial figures as an adviser on Indian affairs. He frequently visited Iroquois, Delaware, and other Indian communities and council sites on errands of diplomacy and regularly served as Pennsylvania's interpreter at important treaties. He was trusted by both Indians and colonists and helped to resolve peacefully many difficult economic, social, and political confrontations between Indians and Whites. His extensive correspondence, journals, and treaty records provide an intimate picture of Indian-White relations in Pennsylvania and New York during the first half of the eighteenth century. See the biography by Paul A.W. Wallace (1945). ANTHONY F.C. WALLACE

Welsh, Herbert 1851–1941

As a member of a Philadelphia merchant family, Welsh enjoyed the luxury of choosing his full-time profession as a humanitarian reformer. After graduating in 1871 from the University of Pennsylvania and spending two years studying art in Paris, Welsh returned to Philadelphia and a life of seemingly inexhaustible energy devoted to his reform interests. Most notably in 1882 he was the instrumental organizer of the Indian Rights Association, in which he then served 35 years as the corresponding secretary and 11 years as president, his most productive years being in the 1880s and 1890s. Welsh focused the lobbying efforts of the Indian Rights Association on civilizing, christianizing, and americanizing the American Indian, all of which he believed mutually inclusive. Caring more for the economic than cultural rights of the American Indian, he specifically emphasized education, private property ownership in land, legal protection, incorruptible agents under a civil service system, and a gradual reduction of government rations. He sought as his goal the demise of the Indianness in American Indians and their emergence as American citizens without a separate sovereignty. See H. Welsh (1892) and Hagan (1985). FRED NICKLASON

Welsh, William 1807–1878

Born into an Episcopalian Philadelphia merchant family, Welsh went to work in his father's office at the age of 16. He subsequently developed a penchant for public service that in his fifties included philanthropic work for American Indians. Welsh organized the 1868 meeting of reformers who sought to eliminate corruption in the Bureau of Indian Affairs, and that resulted in the congressional establishment on April 10, 1869, of the Board of Indian Commissioners. Welsh, first chairman of the board, resigned within one month in protest against its having responsibility for policy without the authority for practical enforcement. His continued interest in Indian affairs eventually led to a congressional investigation of the Bureau of Indian Affairs. Following the resignation of all the remaining original members of the Board of Indian Commissioners in 1874, he despaired of a peaceful, civilian elimination of graft and isolated himself ideologically by supporting military control of Indian affairs (W. Welsh 1874). FRED NICKLASON

Wheeler, Burton K. 1882–1975
Born in Hudson, Massachusetts, Wheeler graduated from the University of Michigan Law School. Elected to the Senate in 1923 as a Democrat from Montana, Wheeler joined a bipartisan coalition of liberals who used Indian affairs as a focal point for their reform efforts. A member of the Senate Indian Affairs Committee, Wheeler helped prevent the confiscation of Indian oil reserves on executive order reservations, exposed the practice of using tribal funds for public improvements needed by Whites, and assisted the Flathead in safeguarding their water power rights. More important, Wheeler was instrumental in starting the Senate investigation of the Indian Bureau that laid the groundwork for future reform. Chairman of the Indian Affairs Committee in 1934, he introduced the Wheeler-Howard bill at the request of Commissioner John Collier. Wheeler had not read this bill, but when he discovered that it created self-governing Indian communities, tribal ownership of land, and a separate Court of Indian Affairs, he became a critic of the Indian New Deal. His opposition caused a series of amendments that resulted in the more conservative Indian Reorganization Act. Fearful that Collier's policies would segregate the Indians from White society, and hostile toward the Franklin Roosevelt administration for a variety of other reasons, he introduced a bill in 1937 to repeal the Indian Reorganization Act. This effort failed, but Wheeler continued his opposition until 1946, when he lost his bid for reelection. His autobiography (Wheeler and Healy 1962) offers a personal account of his career, while Ruetten (1961) describes his activities in the Senate between the wars. KENNETH PHILP

Wheelock, Eleazar 1711–1779
Born in Windham, Connecticut, Wheelock was educated at Yale. In 1735 he became pastor of the second Congregational church in Lebanon, where he gained renown as a powerful preacher during the revivalism of the Great Awakening of the 1740s. Among his other activities he often tutored students preparing for college, and in 1743 he began instructing Samson Occum, a Mohegan. Impressed by Occum's progress, Wheelock

developed a plan for the education and christianization of Indians, involving separation from the tribal environment at a coeducational boarding school, instruction in "husbandry" and "housewifery," and preparation to return to their people as missionaries. The school was begun in 1754 and by 1765 had received 39 students from the Delaware, the Iroquois, and the New England tribes and had graduated 10 missionaries and teachers who were working among the Iroquois. However, Wheelock had become disgusted with the "ineptitude" and residual "savage character" of even his best students and was disillusioned by opposition to his efforts from Indian Superintendent William Johnson and from even his own parishioners. From the beginning his school had enrolled White students as well as Indian, and he had visions of enlarging his domain to include the administration of a college. When Samson Occum returned in 1768 with £12,000 from a fund-raising tour of Britain, Wheelock used the money to establish Dartmouth College at Hanover, New Hampshire, where he removed with his family and students in 1770. The English trustees of the fund were not informed of the move until after the fact, and Occum was so enraged by what he felt to be a violation of the donors' intents that he broke permanently with Wheelock. Wheelock became Dartmouth's first president, and though he continued to direct his Indian education program it received less and less of his attention, and after he died Dartmouth soon became a college of and for Whites. The work of the Indian school is recounted in the series of narratives by Wheelock (1763), and the early years of Dartmouth are described by L.B. Richardson (1932). Full details of Wheelock's life can be found in the biography by McCallum (1939). The Wheelock family papers and correspondence are in the archives of Dartmouth College. P. RICHARD METCALF

Whipple, Henry B. 1822–1901
Whipple was born in Adams, New York, attended Presbyterian schools, and was a student at Oberlin College in 1838 and 1839. During the 1840s he decided upon a ministerial career and was ordained in 1849. Following parish service in Rome, New York; Saint Augustine, Florida; and Chicago, he was elected as the first Episcopalian bishop of the frontier diocese of Minnesota in 1859. The demoralized condition of his native charges, the Chippewa and Eastern Sioux tribes, convinced him that the federal Indian system needed to be reformed and that the only hope for the Indians was in their civilization and christianization. In 1860, he expressed his concern to President James Buchanan and warned of the imminence of a Sioux uprising, which did occur two years later. Following the suppression of the Sioux, Bishop Whipple drew up a six-point plan embodying a complete overhaul of the Indian policy and sent it to President Abraham Lincoln. He later conferred with

Lincoln and helped to convince him that reforms were needed. These efforts marked the start of a lifelong work for Indian rights through letters and memorials to presidents, Indian Bureau officials, and congressmen. He soon won the respect of both Whites and Indians, who called him "Straight Tongue"; and his advice on Indian matters was often solicited by humanitarians and government officials. For an account of his Indian rights work, see his autobiography (1899), Fritz (1963), Mardock (1971), and P.E. Osgood (1958). His papers are in the National Archives and the Minnesota Historical Society, Saint Paul. ROBERT W. MARDOCK

White, Elijah 1806–1879

White was born in New York state and educated in the medical college in Syracuse. In 1836 the Methodist Church appointed him physician for its Oregon missions, and he set out by sea with his family. He arrived in Oregon in 1837 after teaching briefly in Hawaii. White, who had frequent conflicts with others, quarreled with Rev. Jason Lee, head of the Methodist mission, and in 1841 returned to the East, where he secured appointment as Indian subagent for all territory west of the Rockies. In 1842 he outfitted a wagon train of over 100 emigrants and led them to Oregon. As Indian agent White drew up a code of laws for the Nez Perce and secured their approval of the measures. He also worked in 1842–1843 to quell increasing restiveness among the Cayuse and Walla Walla, who were displeased with White incursions and the settlement of missionaries in their homelands. White's attempts to regulate the American residents of Oregon were thwarted, but he participated in the establishment of a provisional government in the Willamette Valley in 1843. He left Oregon in 1845 and returned, without a government appointment, in 1850 to promote a townsite at the mouth of the Columbia River. In 1861 White was again named special Indian agent, but he soon located in California, where he died. He spent his last years as a physician. White's western adventures appeared in A.J. Allen (1850). His official reports were published (White 1846, 1861). White (1879) is his autobiography. STEPHEN DOW BECKHAM

Whitman, Marcus 1802–1847

An experienced physician of New York-Massachusetts background, the Presbyterian Whitman was sent by the American Board of Commissioners for Foreign Missions as a missionary-physician in response to the appeal of the 1831 Flathead-Nez Perce delegation to Saint Louis. After reconnaissance with Samuel Parker at the Green River, Wyoming, rendezvous in 1835, he married Narcissa Prentiss and established the Cayuse mission Waiilatpu in the Walla Walla Valley. His companions founded the Nez Perce mission at Lapwai; reinforcements, increasing personnel to 13, allowed for a station among the

Spokane. Despite a decade of religious, educational, and medical devotion, the Cayuse became cold, then hostile, especially when Waiilatpu became a stop along the Oregon Trail and when the doctor's medicine failed to halt a measles epidemic. In 1847 14 people at the mission were massacred by Cayuses, in 1848 there was the Cayuse War, and the mission network collapsed thereafter. Drury (1958, 1963–1966, 1973) has detailed the story and edited many documents, with their observations on the Indians. ROBERT I. BURNS, S.J.

Williams, Roger 1603?–1683

London born and Cambridge educated, Williams arrived in Boston in February 1631. Williams is best known for his banishment from Massachusetts in 1636 because of his maverick religious views, which led to his founding of Rhode Island, but he also drew the ire of the Puritan magistrates by questioning the colony's claim to the land without compensation to the Indians. More significant, perhaps, were his efforts at diplomacy among the southern New England tribes. He was instrumental in bringing over the Narragansett to the Puritan side in the Pequot War, 1636–1637, and in maintaining their neutrality during much of King Philip's War, 1675–1676.

Williams's expertise in Indian affairs rested in good measure on his knowledge of the culture and language of the southeastern New England Indians, which he displayed in his *Key into the Language of America* (1643). Williams desired the christianization of the Indian; but, unlike many Puritans, he refused to force their conversion, explaining in his *Christenings Make Not Christians* (1645) that no church polity could prove it had the right to impose its religion upon others, even heathens. The standard biographies of Williams are Brockunier (1940), Winslow (1957), and Covey (1966). Williams's religious and political ideas are discussed by P. Miller (1953) and E.S. Morgan (1967). The best edition of Williams's writings is the reprint of the Narragansett Club edition of 1866 by Russell and Russell (1963). RICHARD L. HAAN

Wirt, William 1772–1834

Born and indifferently educated in Maryland, Wirt moved to Virginia in his late teens. Affable and eloquent, Wirt was considered one of the great advocates of his era. He was also a man of letters (Wirt 1803, 1817), but his literary work was ephemeral. In 1817 President James Monroe appointed Wirt Attorney General. He remained in that position 11 years and helped define the modern character of that office. Giving the appearance of eschewing politics, Wirt was an ardent anti-Jacksonian (Cain 1965) and was the Anti-Mason Party's presidential candidate against Andrew Jackson in 1832. Perhaps because of his anti-Jackson animus, Wirt agreed to represent the Cherokee Nation against infringement by the state of Georgia. As Attorney General Wirt's opinions on Indian sovereignty were contradictory (J.C. Burke 1969), but in marshaling the Cherokee legal effort, he formulated the position that Indian tribes retained their sovereignty against the states that was accepted by a minority of the Supreme Court in *Cherokee Nation* v. *Georgia* (5 Peters 1, 1831), and ultimately by a majority of the Court the following year in *Worcester* v. *Georgia* (5 Peters 515, 1832). A definitive work on Wirt is J.C. Burke (1965). Wirt's papers are located at the Maryland Historical Society, Baltimore. DONALD ROPER

Wissler, Clark 1870–1947

A native of Indiana, Wissler studied education and psychology, taking his doctorate at Columbia in 1901. While there he was heavily influenced by Franz Boas, and his interests turned primarily toward anthropology. He joined the staff of the American Museum of Natural History in New York in 1902 and served as curator of its Department of Anthropology from 1907 to 1942. In 1924 he was appointed to the faculty at Yale and was professor of anthropology from 1931 to 1940. Wissler's only extensive fieldwork was done among the Blackfoot and other northern Plains tribes from 1902 to 1905. While his monographs on that region prompted an era of anthropological concentration on the Plains Indians, his most significant professional contributions were the support and direction he gave to the projects of others, and the publication of two general studies (1917, 1923). These books, which helped immeasurably to disseminate the concepts of anthropology to scholars in other disciplines, have served as introductions to anthropology for generations of students. Details on Wissler's life and career and a bibliography of his works can be found in the obituaries by Murdock (1948) and Lowie (1949). P. RICHARD METCALF

Worcester, Samuel Austin 1798–1859

Worcester, who was born in Worcester, Massachusetts and attended the University of Vermont, is often called the most important missionary to the Cherokee. In 1825 he was ordained a minister in the Congregational church and immediately departed to take up his life's work with the Cherokee Indians. He served his first two years at the Brainerd Mission in Tennessee, where he was one of the primary instruments in making the new Cherokee syllabary, invented by Sequoya, suitable for printing. In 1827 he was transferred to New Echota, the capital of the Cherokee Nation. There Worcester, believing that the use of native languages was a significant way of propagating the gospel, continued his work on the Cherokee writing system. In 1828, with the help of Elias Boudinot and other Cherokee leaders, the *Cherokee Phoenix*, a tribal newspaper, came into being (Gabriel 1941). Worcester spent the next several years writing religious tracts and translating the Bible into Cherokee. When pressure for

removing the Cherokee from their homelands in Georgia reached a climax in 1830, Worcester and other missionaries stood in the forefront of resistance. Claiming they were exempt from state law, the missionaries refused to obey Georgia laws forbidding White residence among the Indians. In 1831 Worcester and Elizur Butler were arrested, convicted, and sentenced to four years at hard labor. Attorney William Wirt used this action to bring the Cherokee case before the United States Supreme Court. In 1832 the court ruled, in the case of *Worcester* v. *Georgia*, that the missionary must be released and also that the tribe enjoyed the protection of the federal government. President Andrew Jackson refused to enforce the decision. Worcester was released from prison in 1833, by this time convinced that removal was inevitable. In 1835 he moved west, along with the tribe, to Indian Territory. He spent the rest of his life helping the Cherokee adjust to their new homes. His activities included establishing the Park Hill Mission, printing the Bible and an almanac in Cherokee, and organizing many religious societies. For biographical details see Bass (1936) and Wilkins (1970). Papers regarding his missionary activities are in the records of the American Board of Commissioners for Foreign Missions kept at the Houghton Library, Harvard University. ROBERT A. TRENNERT

Wraxall, Peter ?–1759

Born in England to a family with social and political connections, Wraxall had probably spent some time in the Netherlands before coming to New York as a soldier in 1746. He quickly returned to England and remained there until 1752 when he arrived again in New York. While in England he secured royal appointment in 1750 as secretary for Indian affairs in the colony, a position that had earlier been held by Robert Livingston and then by his son Philip. Wraxall attended councils and kept records of the agreements. In 1754 he became secretary to the Albany Congress where he came to the attention of William Johnson. In the same year he sent to Lord Halifax his "An Abridgment of the Records of Indian Affairs," one of the major sources on Anglo-Indian relations from 1678 to 1751. His purpose was to attack the Albany fur traders and Indian commissioners, who were not aggressively promoting English as opposed to French interests with the Indians. This document probably played a vital role in the reorganization of the control of Indian affairs, including the appointment of William Johnson as superintendent of Indian affairs for the northern department. Wraxall served until his death as Johnson's secretary. For further information see Wraxall (1915). LAWRENCE H. LEDER

Wright, Asher 1803–1875

Born at Hanover, New Hampshire, Wright attended Dartmouth College and graduated from Andover Theological Seminary. After being ordained in 1831, he went directly to the Senecas at Buffalo Creek Reservation as a missionary for the American Board of Commissioners for Foreign Missions.

Wright (1842) devised the first adequate orthography for Seneca, and he persuaded his sponsors to equip him with a press and the special type needed to print it; in 1841 he set up the Mission Press, which produced the first books printed in Buffalo (Pilling 1888:175–177; Howland 1903:158). The journal *The Mental Elevator*, with its numbers denominated by the moons in Seneca, ran for 19 issues until April 15, 1850. The purpose of this journal, as its title says, was to "lift up the minds" of the Senecas with translation of Scripture, notices of worthy men and women, and matters relating to politics and business. It was preceded in 1836 by an elementary reading book in Seneca, prepared by his wife Laura. They also translated a hymnal. Wright in later years answered queries on social organization for Lewis Henry Morgan (Stern 1933). And Wright himself left a general sketch on the Seneca (Fenton 1957).

During the "seven years of trouble," 1837–1845, as the Senecas referred to their unsuccessful struggle to keep their Buffalo lands from the promoters of the Ogden Land Company, Wright is credited with having secured the "Compromise Treaty" of 1842, which saved the Allegany and Cattaraugus reservations. In the revolution that followed the removal, the life chiefs were overthrown and the republic of the Seneca Nation was established. Wright had brought the literacy that enabled the Senecas to write their own laws and constitution. In 1847, the childless Wrights took in the orphans of a typhoid epidemic, and in 1854 Philip E. Thomas, a wealthy Quaker of Baltimore, founded the Thomas Asylum for Orphan and Destitute Indian children, which endured for a century.

The papers of the American Board of Commissioners for Foreign Missions, Houghton Library, Harvard University, contain reports and letters of the Wrights. Other materials are in the Parker Papers in the Library of the American Philosophical Society, Philadelphia. Fenton (1956) gives further details. WILLIAM N. FENTON

Young, Brigham 1801–1877

Born in Whitingham, Vermont, Young was poorly educated but practical and hardworking. He was a carpenter, painter, and glazier and was at 16 years of age already at work as a craftsman. After removing to western New York, he was converted to the Mormon church and was baptized in 1832. He met the prophet, Joseph Smith, Jr., who sent him on a mission to Canada the same year.

Young was made an apostle in 1835, and in 1836 he served as a missionary in the East. As a dedicated loyalist to Joseph Smith, he was instrumental in the removal of

the major portion of the Mormons from Ohio to Missouri in 1838 and later helped to organize the removal to Nauvoo, Illinois. Young was one of the most successful of all the Mormon missionaries in foreign lands. His mission to Great Britain in 1840 and 1841 led to the conversion of literally thousands from the working classes in and around Liverpool and the industrial Midlands. He was on yet another mission when Smith was assassinated in 1844.

Young began his leadership of the Mormons in 1844 on tenuous grounds. He acted as head of the church because of his position as president of the Quorum of the Twelve Apostles, but it was not until December 1847 that he was named president and prophet of the church while the headquarters of that group reposed at the Missouri River near Council Bluffs. During the removal to Utah, Young was able to consolidate his power in the church.

After the territory of Utah was created in 1850, Young was appointed territorial governor and ex officio superintendent of Indian affairs. Under his leadership, Whites took the best lands, the Indians entered a period of decline, war ensued, and the Whites won. Even though Young was replaced as governor in 1858, his influence over Indian affairs remained great. He urged the expulsion of the Utes from central Utah and put pressure on the federal government to accomplish this. Young attempted to create an "outer cordon" of Mormon settlement, a defensive perimeter against other White settlements. The failure of this outer cordon occurred in part in the 1850s when Indian difficulties at both Elk Mountain, Utah, and Fort Lemhi, Idaho, caused the abandonment of those posts.

Instrumental in founding 100 Mormon communities, Young was a major figure in both Indian and White affairs in the West until his death. For further information see Hirshson (1969) and Hunter (1940). FLOYD A. O'NEIL

Zeisberger, David 1721–1808

In his first years of service in the Moravian missions, 1744–1755, Zeisberger studied Iroquoian languages and had duties as an emissary and interpreter. These activities were curtailed by the French and Indian War, and in 1765 he began the task of establishing mission towns for Algonquian speakers, starting with a nucleus of Delaware and Mahican converts. His instructions were, among other things, to learn Delaware, translate scripture and hymns into that language, and teach literacy. The missions won the support of the Delaware chiefs and were brought to Ohio in 1772 from the Allegheny and the Susquehanna. Zeisberger remained with these missions through the disruptions and relocations brought on by the Revolution, and in 1792 founded the town of Fairfield on the Thames near Thamesville, Ontario. He died in Goshen, Ohio.

Zeisberger wrote numerous translations of religious materials into Delaware (see Lieberkuhn 1821), a Delaware primer (1776), grammatical and lexical studies of Onondaga and Delaware (for example, 1827, 1887, 1887–1888), and an ethnographic treatise (1910). De Schweinitz's biography (1871) may be supplemented by the published diaries (1885, 1912). Zeisberger's unpublished papers are principally in the Archives of the Moravian Church, Bethlehem, Pennsylvania, and in the Houghton Library, Harvard University. IVES GODDARD

Contributors

This list gives the academic affiliations of authors at the time this volume went to press. Parenthetical tribal names identify Indian authors. The dates following the entries indicate when each manuscript was (1) first received in the General Editor's office; (2) accepted by the General Editor's office; and (3) sent to the author (or, if deceased, a substitute) for final approval after revisions and editorial work.

BACA, LAWRENCE R. (Pawnee), American Indian Bar Association, Alexandria, Virginia. The Legal Status of American Indians: 9/19/85; 8/4/86; 2/26/87.

BEAVER, R. PIERCE (emeritus), Divinity School, University of Chicago, Chicago, Illinois. Protestant Churches and the Indians: 2/14/74; 3/5/87; 8/27/87.

BERKHOFER, ROBERT F., JR., Department of History, University of Michigan, Ann Arbor. White Conceptions of Indians: 6/18/74; 5/26/87; 10/1/87.

BERTHRONG, DONALD J., Department of History, Purdue University, West Lafayette, Indiana. Nineteenth-Century United States Government Agencies: 4/15/74; 9/19/86; 2/17/87.

BRAND, STEWART, Whole Earth Review, Sausalito, California. Indians and the Counterculture, 1960s–1970s: 5/25/72; 6/23/87; 9/2/87.

BURNS, ROBERT I., S.J., Department of History, University of California, Los Angeles. Roman Catholic Missions in the Northwest: 7/24/73; 2/10/87; 6/23/87.

CAMPEAU, LUCIEN, S.J. (emeritus), Department of History, University of Montreal, Quebec. Roman Catholic Missions in New France: 5/31/72; 3/13/87; 7/17/87.

COOK, SHERBURNE F. (deceased), Pacific Grove, California. Roman Catholic Missions in California and the Southwest: 3/2/72; 4/27/87; 8/6/87.

CRONON, WILLIAM, Department of History, Yale University, New Haven, Connecticut. Ecological Change and Indian-White Relations: 5/8/86; 8/4/86; 3/2/87.

DORAIS, LOUIS-JACQUES, Département d'Anthropologie, Université Laval, Ste-Foy, Québec. Roman Catholic Missions in the Arctic: 4/30/74; 2/18/87; 6/24/87.

ECCLES, WILLIAM J. (emeritus), Department of History, University of Toronto, Ontario. Fur Trade in the Colonial Northeast: 1/3/73; 11/30/84; 4/21/87.

FEEST, CHRISTIAN F., Museum für Völkerkunde, Vienna, Austria. The Indian in Non-English Literature: 11/28/72; 5/14/85; 9/8/87.

FIEDLER, LESLIE A., Department of English, State University of New York, Buffalo. The Indian in Literature in English: 4/6/73; 6/26/87; 9/16/87.

GAD, FINN (deceased), Gentofte, Denmark. Danish Greenland Policies: 11/16/73; 12/17/85; 2/6/86.

GIBSON, ARRELL M. (deceased), Department of History, University of Oklahoma, Norman. Indian Land Transfers: 8/12/74; 5/14/85; 2/18/87.

GIBSON, CHARLES (deceased), Keeseville, New York. Spanish Indian Policies: 1/6/72; 11/18/85; 3/26/86.

GIBSON, JAMES R., Department of Geography, York University, Downsview, Ontario. The Maritime Trade of the North Pacific Coast: 11/30/81; 9/1/83; 5/15/87.

GREEN, RAYNA D. (Cherokee), American Indian Program, National Museum of American History, Smithsonian Institution, Washington, D.C. The Indian in Popular American Culture: 5/4/72; 7/6/87; 9/25/87.

HAGAN, WILLIAM T., Department of History, State University College, Fredonia, New York. United States Indian Policies, 1860–1900: 1/19/74; 12/10/85; 5/30/86.

HEIZER, ROBERT F. (deceased), Department of Anthropology, University of California, Berkeley. Indian Servitude in California: 3/3/72; 8/9/83; 3/17/87.

HERTZBERG, HAZEL WHITMAN, Program in Social Studies, Teachers College, Columbia University, New York. Indian Rights Movement, 1887–1973: 8/22/73; 8/4/86; 3/23/87.

HORSMAN, REGINALD, Department of History, University of Wisconsin, Milwaukee. United States Indian Policies, 1776–1815: 5/5/72; 11/5/85; 3/27/86.

JACOBS, WILBUR R., Department of History, University of California, Santa Barbara. British Indian Policies to 1783: 5/16/77; 1/15/86; 3/28/86.

JENNINGS, FRANCIS (emeritus), Indian History Center, Newberry Library, Chicago, Illinois. Dutch and Swedish Indian Policies: 12/6/72; 2/6/86; 4/11/86.

JONES, DOROTHY V., Newberry Library, Chicago, Illinois. British Colonial Indian Treaties: 1/29/86; 7/17/86; 3/3/87.

KAN, SERGEI, Department of Anthropology, University of Michigan, Ann Arbor. The Russian Orthodox Church in Alaska: 6/26/85; 8/10/85; 7/13/87.

KAWASHIMA, YASUHIDE, Department of History, University of Texas, El Paso. Colonial Government Agencies: 3/5/73; 9/12/86; 2/5/87. Indian Servitude in the Northeast: 12/22/73; 12/1/86; 2/27/87.

KELLY, LAWRENCE C., Department of History, North Texas State University, Denton. United States Indian Policies, 1900–1980: 12/13/72; 11/22/85; 5/21/86.

KVASNICKA, ROBERT M., National Archives and Records Administration, Washington, D.C. United States Indian Treaties and Agreements: 9/10/74; 7/9/85; 1/23/87.

LEACH, DOUGLAS E. (emeritus), Department of History, Vanderbilt University, Nashville, Tennessee. Colonial Indian Wars: 6/21/72; 1/3/86; 4/2/86.

LEWIS, CLIFFORD M., S.J. (deceased), Wheeling College, Wheeling, West Virginia. Roman Catholic Missions in the Southeast and Northeast: 9/25/72; 4/23/87; 7/20/87.

LOHSE, E.S., Handbook of North American Indians, Smithsonian Institution, Washington, D.C. Trade Goods: 10/1/86; 1/5/87; 4/8/87.

LURIE, NANCY O., Anthropology Section, Milwaukee Public Museum, Milwaukee, Wisconsin. Relations Between Indians and Anthropologists: 1/15/73; 6/12/87; 9/2/87.

MAHON, JOHN K. (emeritus), Department of History, University of Florida, Gainesville. Indian–United States Military Situation, 1775–1848: 6/7/72; 1/23/86; 4/10/86.

MARDOCK, ROBERT W. (retired), Department of History, Millikin University, Decatur, Illinois. Indian Rights Movement Until 1887: 5/31/72; 8/19/86; 2/4/87.

MARINO, CESARE R., Handbook of North American Indians, Smithsonian Institution, Washington, D.C. Roman Catholic Missions in California and the Southwest: 3/2/72; 4/27/87; 8/6/87.

MARSDEN, MICHAEL T., Department of Popular Culture, Bowling Green State University, Bowling Green, Ohio. The Indian in the Movies: 8/16/74; 7/8/87; 10/5/87.

NACHBAR, JACK G., Department of Popular Culture, Bowling Green State University, Bowling Green, Ohio. The Indian in the Movies: 8/16/74; 7/8/87; 10/5/87.

NASH, PHILLEO (deceased), Department of Anthropology, American University, Washington, D.C. Twentieth-Century United States Government Agencies: 7/1/85; 7/17/86; 2/26/87.

PIERCE, RICHARD A. (emeritus), Department of History, Queen's University, Kingston, Ontario. Russian and Soviet Eskimo and Indian Policies: 6/16/72; 12/10/85; 2/7/86.

POWERS, WILLIAM K., Department of Anthropology, Rutgers University, New Brunswick, New Jersey. The Indian Hobbyist Movement in North America: 9/22/72; 6/15/87; 8/12/87.

PRICE, JOHN A., Department of Anthropology, York University, Downsview, Ontario. Mormon Missions to the Indians: 1/17/75; 5/14/85; 7/1/87.

PRUCHA, FRANCIS PAUL, S.J., Department of History, Marquette University, Milwaukee, Wisconsin. United States Indian Policies, 1815–1860: 5/2/72; 1/2/85; 2/28/86. Presents and Delegations: 5/15/72; 1/2/85; 1/21/87.

RAY, ARTHUR J., Department of History, University of British Columbia, Vancouver. The Hudson's Bay Company and Native People: 3/29/85; 4/19/85; 5/12/87.

RYAN, CARMELITA S., National Archives and Records Administration, Washington, D.C. American Indian Education: 6/4/86; 8/4/86; 4/20/87.

SALADIN D'ANGLURE, BERNARD, Département d'Anthropologie, Université Laval, Ste-Foy, Québec. Roman Catholic Missions in the Arctic: 4/30/74; 2/18/87; 6/24/87.

SANDERS, DOUGLAS, Faculty of Law, University of British Columbia, Vancouver. Government Indian Agencies in Canada: 7/20/76; 7/17/86; 3/19/87.

SCHROEDER, ALBERT H. (retired), National Park Service, Santa Fe, New Mexico. Indian Servitude in the Southwest: 3/15/73; 12/2/86; 3/5/87.

SPICER, EDWARD H. (deceased), Department of Anthropology, University of Arizona, Tucson. Mexican Indian Policies: 8/24/72; 2/4/86; 3/25/86.

STEWART, OMER C. (emeritus), Department of Anthropology, University of Colorado, Boulder. Indian Servitude in the Southwest: 3/15/73; 12/2/86; 3/5/87.

SURTEES, ROBERT J., Department of History, Nipissing University College, North Bay, Ontario. Canadian Indian Policies: 9/6/85; 12/10/85; 2/14/86. Canadian Indian Treaties: 6/5/85; 7/14/85; 3/31/87.

SWAGERTY, WILLIAM R., Department of History, University of Idaho, Moscow. Indian Trade in the Trans-Mississippi West to 1870: 3/3/86; 8/4/86; 5/12/87.

SZASZ, MARGARET CONNELL, Department of History, University of New Mexico, Albuquerque. American Indian Education: 6/4/86; 8/4/86; 4/20/87.

TAYLOR, COLIN F., Sussex, England. The Indian Hobbyist Movement in Europe: 8/21/72; 5/14/85; 8/21/87.

USNER, DANIEL H., JR., Department of History, Cornell University, Ithaca, New York. Economic Relations in the Southeast Until 1783: 5/7/87; 5/21/87; 5/21/87.

UTLEY, ROBERT M., Santa Fe, New Mexico. Indian–United States Military Situation, 1848–1891: 3/12/73; 1/31/86; 5/9/86.

701

WADE, MASON (deceased), Windsor, Vermont. French Indian Policies: 5/9/72; 10/31/85; 2/18/86.

WASHBURN, WILCOMB E., Office of American Studies, Smithsonian Institution, Washington, D.C. Introduction: 1/21/86; 2/28/86; 6/13/86.

WHITE, RICHARD, Department of History, University of Utah, Salt Lake City. Ecological Change and Indian-White Relations: 5/8/86; 8/4/86; 3/2/87.

WOOD, PETER H., Department of History, Duke University, Durham, North Carolina. Indian Servitude in the Southeast: 8/11/75; 8/4/86; 4/14/87.

702

List of Illustrations

This list identifies the subjects of illustrations, organized by chapter. All artists, photographers, and some individuals depicted (but not collectors) are included. Every identified individual depicted is found in the index, which also covers the captions. Tables are not listed here.

Bibliography

This list includes all references cited in the volume, arranged in alphabetical order according to the names of the authors as they appear in the citations in the text. Multiple works by the same author are arranged chronologically; second and subsequent titles by the same author in the same year are differentiated by letters added to the dates. Where more than one author with the same surname is cited, one has been arbitrarily selected for text citation by surname alone throughout the volume, while the others are always cited with added initials; the combination of surname with date in text citations should avoid confusion. Where a publication date is different from the series date (as in some annual reports and the like), the former is used. Dates, authors, and titles that do not appear on the original works are enclosed by brackets. For manuscripts, dates refer to time of composition. For publications reprinted or first published many years after original composition, a bracketed date after the title refers to the time of composition or the date of original publication.

ARCIA = Commissioner of Indian Affairs
1849- Annual Reports to the Secretary of the Interior. Washington: U.S. Government Printing Office. (Reprinted: AMS Press, New York, 1976–1977.)

ASPIA = American State Papers. Indian Affairs
1832–1834 Documents, Legislative and Executive of the Congress of the United States. Class 2: Indian Affairs. 2 vols. Washington: U.S. Government Printing Office.

ASPMA = American State Papers. Military Affairs
1832–1861 Documents, Legislative and Executive of the Congress of the United States. Class 5: Military Affairs. 7 vols. Washington: U.S. Government Printing Office.

Aarne, Antti A.
1961 The Types of the Folktale. 2d rev. ed. Helsinki: Suomaleinen Tiedeakatemia.

Abbot, Austin
1888 Indians and the Law. *Harvard Law Review* 2(4): 167–179.

Abbot, Lyman
1901 The Rights of Man: A Study in Twentieth Century Problems. Boston: Houghton, Mifflin.

1915 Reminiscences. Boston: Houghton, Mifflin.

1921 The Smiley Brothers, Lovers of Hospitality. Pp. 28–44 in Silhouettes of My Contemporaries, by Lyman Abbott. Garden City, N.Y.: Doubleday.

1921a General Samuel Chapman Armstrong. Pp. 136–154 in Silhouettes of My Contemporaries, by Lyman Abbott. Garden City, N.Y.: Doubleday.

1921b Silhouettes of My Contemporaries. Garden City, N.Y.: Doubleday.

Abel, Annie H.
1904 Indian Reservations in Kansas and the Extinguishment of Their Title. *Transactions of the Kansas State Historical Society for 1903-1904*, Vol. 8:72–109. Topeka.

1908 The History of Events Resulting in Indian Consolidation West of the Mississippi. Pp. 233–450 in *Annual Report of the American Historical Association for the Year 1906.* Washington.

1908a Proposals for an Indian State, 1778–1878. Pp. 87–104 in *Annual Report of the American Historical Association for the Year 1907.* Washington.

————, ed.
1915 The Official Correspondence of James S. Calhoun While Indian Agent at Santa Fe and Superintendent of Indian Affairs in New Mexico, Collected Mainly from the Files of the Indian Office. Washington: U.S. Government Printing Office.

1915–1925 The Slaveholding Indians. 3 vols. Vol. 1: The American Indian as Slaveholder and Secessionist. Vol. 2: The American Indian as Participant in the Civil War. Vol. 3: The American Indian Under Reconstruction. Cleveland, Ohio: A.H. Clark. (Reprinted: Scholarly Press, St. Clair Shores, Mich., 1978.)

Abrahams, Roger D., ed.
1969 Jump-rope Rhymes: A Dictionary. Austin: University of Texas Press.

Acosta, José de
1589 De natura noui orbis Libri duo; et De promulgatione Euangelii, apud barbaros, siue De procuranda Indorvm salute libri sex. Salamanca: Guillelmus Foquel.

Acrelius, Israel
1874 A History of New Sweden; or, The Settlements on the River Delaware [1759]. William M. Reynolds, trans. *Memoirs of the Historical Society of Pennsylvania* 11. Philadelphia.

Acuña, René, ed.
1984 Relaciones geográficas del siglo XVI: Tlaxcala. Vol. 1. (*Instituto de Investigaciones Antropológicas, Serie Antropológica* 53) Mexico City: Universidad Nacional Autónoma de México.

Adair, James
1775 The History of the American Indians, Particularly Those Nations Adjoining the Mississippi, East and West Florida, Georgia, South and North Carolina, and Virginia. London: Printed for Edward and Charles Dilly. (Reprinted: Watanga Press, Johnson City, Tenn., 1930; Argonaut Press, New York, 1966.)

Adams, David W.
1975 The Federal Indian Boarding School: A Study of Environment and Response, 1879–1918. (Unpublished Ph.D. Dissertation in Education, University of Indiana, Bloomington.)

1977 Education in Hues: Red and Black at Hampton Institute, 1878–1893. *South Atlantic Quarterly* 76(2):159–176.

Adams, Eleanor B.
1953–1954 Bishop Tamarón's Visitation of New Mexico, 1760. *Historical Society of New Mexico Publications in History* 15. Albuquerque.

Adams, Eleanor B., and Angelico Chavez, eds.
1956 The Missions of New Mexico, 1776: A Description [by Fray Francisco Atanasio Domínguez] with Other Contemporary Documents. Albuquerque: University of New Mexico Press. (2d ed. in 1976.)

Adams, Evelyn C.
1946 American Indian Education: Government Schools and Economic Progress. Morningside Heights, N.Y.: King's Crown Press.

Adams, George R.
1970 The Caloosahatchee Massacre: Its Significance in the Second Seminole War. *Florida Historical Quarterly* 48(4):368–380.

1983 General William Selby Harney: Frontier Soldier, 1800–1889. (Unpublished Ph.D. Dissertation in History, University of Arizona, Tucson.)

Adams, Henry
1879 The Life of Albert Gallatin. Philadelphia: J.B. Lippincott.

1944 The War of 1812. H.A. DeWeerd, ed. Washington: Infantry Journal Press.

Adams, James T., ed.
1943   Atlas of American History. New York: Charles Scribner's Sons.

Adams, John Quincy
1965   The Great Design: Two Lectures on the Smithson Bequest, by John Quincy Adams. Wilcomb E. Washburn, ed. Washington: The Smithsonian Institution.

Adams, Ramon F.
1968   Western Words: A Dictionary of the American West. Rev. and enl. ed. Norman: University of Oklahoma Press.

Afonsky, Gregory
1977   A History of the Orthodox Church in Alaska, 1794–1917. Kodiak, Alas.: St. Herman's Theological Seminary.

Aguirre Beltrán, Gonzalo
1967   Regiones de refugio, el desarrollo de la comunidad y el proceso dominical en Mestizo América. *Instituto Indígenista Interamericano, Ediciones Especiales* 46. Mexico.

Ahern, Wilbert H.
1976   Assimilationist Racism: The Case of the 'Friends of the Indian.' *Journal of Ethnic Studies* 4(2):23–32.

Aikin, John G., comp.
1833   A Digest of the Laws of the State of Alabama.... Philadelphia: A. Towar.

Aimard, Gustave
1858   Les Pirates de la prairie. Paris: Amyot.

———
1858a   Le Chercheur de pistes. Paris: Amyot.

———
1865   Un Hiver parmi les Indiens Chippewais. In Les Plumes d'or. P.H.C. Féval, ed. Paris: E. Dentu.

———
1866   Les Gambucinos. Paris: Amyot.

———
1872   Les Scalpeurs blancs. Paris: E. Dentu.

Aimard, Gustave, and Jules-Berlioz d'Auriac
1866   Le Scalpeur des Ottawas. Paris: P. Brunet.

———
1867   Jim l'Indien. Paris: P. Brunet.

———
1878   L'Aigle noir des Dacotahs. Paris: A. Degorce-Cadot.

Albers, Patricia C.
1982   Sioux Women in Transition: A Study of Their Changing Status in Domestic and Capitalistic Sectors of Production. Pp. 175–234 in The Hidden Half: Studies of Plains Indian Women. P. Albers and B. Medicine, eds. Washington: University Press of America.

Albers, Patricia C., and William R. James
1981   Historical Fiction as Ideology: The Case of *Hanta Yo. Radical History Review* 25:148–161. New York.

———
1985   Historical Materialism vs. Evolutionary Ecology: A Methodological Note on Horse Distribution and American Plains Indians. *Critique of Anthropology* 6:87–100. London.

Alcoze, Thomas M.
1981   Presettlement Beaver Population Density in the Upper Great Lakes Region. (Unpublished Ph.D. Dissertation in Zoology, Michigan State University, East Lansing.)

Alden, John R.
1940   The Albany Congress and the Creation of the Indian Superintendencies. *Mississippi Valley Historical Review* 27(2):198–210.

———
1944   John Stuart and the Southern Colonial Frontier: A Study of Indian Relations, War, Trade, and Land Problems in the Southern Wilderness, 1754–1775. Ann Arbor: University of Michigan Press. (Reprinted: Gordian Press, New York, 1966.)

———
1957   The South in the Revolution, 1763–1789. Baton Rouge: Louisiana State University Press.

Aldridge, Alfred O.
1950   Franklin's Deistical Indians. *Proceedings of the American Philosophical Society* 94(4):398–410. Philadelphia.

Alekseev, A.I.
1982   Osvoenie russkimi li͡ud'mi Dal'nego Vostoka i Russkoĭ Ameriki [The Colonization of the Far East and of Russian America by the Russian People.] Moscow: Nauka.

Alessio Robles, Vito
1938   Coahuila y Texas en la época colonial. Mexico City: Editorial Cultura.

Allaire, Gratien
1980   Les Engagements pour la traite des fourrures–évaluation de la documentation. *Revue d'Histoire de l'Amérique Française* 34(1):3–26. Montreal.

Allen, A.J., comp.
1850   Ten Years in Oregon. Ithaca, N.Y.: Mack, Andrus.

Allen, Don C.
1949   The Legend of Noah: Renaissance Rationalism in Art, Science, and Letters. *Illinois Studies in Language and Literature* 33(3–4). Urbana.

Allen, John L.
1975   Passage Through the Garden: Lewis and Clark and the Image of the American Northwest. Urbana: University of Illinois Press.

Allen, John W.
1963   Legends and Lore of Southern Illinois. Carbondale: University of Southern Illinois Press.

Allen, Paula Gunn
1983   The Woman Who Owned the Shadows. San Francisco: Spinsters.

Allen, Robert B., and Jim Dolan
1970   New Little Red to Sit This Dance Out. *Daily Oklahoman* 79(257):1–2. Oklahoma City.

Allen, Robert S.
1971   A History of the British Indian Department in North America, 1755–1830 (*National Historic Sites Manuscript Record* 109). Ottawa: Department of Indian Affairs and Northern Development.

———
1975   The British Indian Department and the Frontier in North America, 1755–1830. *Canadian Historic Sites, Occasional Papers in Archaeology and History* 14. Ottawa.

Altamira y Crevea, Rafael
1938   El Texto de las Leyes de Burgos de 1512. *Revista de Historia de América* 4:5–79. Mexico City.

Alter, J. Cecil
1944   The Mormons and the Indians. *Utah Historical Quarterly* 12(1–2):49–98.

———
1962   Jim Bridger [1925]. Norman: University of Oklahoma Press.

Altherr, Thomas L.
1983   "Flesh Is the Paradise of a Man of Flesh": Cultural Conflict Over Indian Hunting Beliefs and Rituals in New France as Recorded in *The Jesuit Relations. Canadian Historical Review* 64(2):267–276.

Alvord, Clarence W.
1908   The Genesis of the Proclamation of 1763. *Michigan Pioneer and Historical Society, Historical Collections* 36:20–52. Lansing.

———
1920   The Illinois Country, 1673–1818. Springfield: Illinois Centennial Commission.

710

Alwin, John A.
1979   Pelts, Provisions and Perceptions: The Hudson's Bay Company Mandan Indian Trade, 1795–1812. *Montana: The Magazine of Western History* 29(3):16–27.

American Board of Commissioners for Foreign Missions
1861   Memorial Volume of the First Fifty Years of the American Board of Commissioners for Foreign Missions. Rufus Anderson, ed. Boston: The Board.

American Indian Policy Review Commission
1977   Final Report: Submitted to Congress May 17, 1977. 2 vols. Washington: U.S. Government Printing Office.

Americans for Indian Opportunity
1981   Handbook of Federal Responsibility to Indian Communities in Areas of Environmental Protection and Individual Health and Safety. Albuquerque: Americans for Indian Opportunity.

[1982]   Messing with Mother Nature Can Be Hazardous to Your Health: A Final Report on the Environmental Health Impacts of Development on Indian Communities.... Albuquerque, N.M.: Modern Press.

Ames, Seth, ed.
1854   Works of Fisher Ames. 2 vols. Boston: Little, Brown.

Anahareo [Gertrude Bernard]
1972   Devil in Deerskins: My Life with Grey Owl. Toronto, Ont.: New Press.

Anastasio, Angelo
1972   The Southern Plateau: An Ecological Analysis of Intergroup Relations. *Northwest Anthropological Research Notes* 6(2):109–229. (Reprinted: University of Idaho, Moscow, 1975.)

Anderson, Gary C.
1984   Kinsmen of Another Kind: Dakota-White Relations in the Upper Mississippi Valley, 1650–1862. Lincoln: University of Nebraska Press.

1986   Little Crow, Spokesman for the Sioux. St. Paul: Minnesota Historical Society Press.

Anderson, Harry H.
1973   Fur Traders as Fathers: The Origins of the Mixed-blooded Community Among the Rosebud Sioux. *South Dakota History* 3(3):233–270.

Anderson, Harry S.
1963   Harney v. Twiss; Nebraska Territory, 1856. *The Westerners Brand Book* 20(1):1–3, 7–8. Chicago.

Andersson, Theodore, and Mildred Boyer
1978   Bilingual Schooling in the United States. 2d ed. Austin, Tex.: National Educational Laboratory Publishers.

Andrews, Charles M.
1912–1914   Guide to Materials for American History, to 1783, in the Public Records Office of Great Britain. 2 vols. Washington: Carnegie Institution of Washington.

Andrews, Edward D.
1962   The Gift to Be Simple: Songs, Dances and Rituals of the American Shakers. New York: Dover.

Annals of Congress see U.S. Congress 1832–1856

Anonymous
1778   Inkle et Iarico: Histoire américaine. *Bibliothèque des Romans* 28. Paris.

1800   An Account of the Institution, Progress and Present State of the New York, Missionary Society. *The New-York Missionary Magazine* 1:5–15.

1816   What Are the Motives Which Should Induce the Churches in the United States to Attempt the Conversion and Civilization of the Indians? *The Panoplist and Missionary Magazine* 12(1):118–122. Boston.

1830   The American Indians. *Missionary Herald* 26(11):363–364. Boston.

1836   An Authentic Narrative of the Seminole War; Its Cause, Rise and Progress, and a Minute Detail of the Horrid Massacres of the Whites, by the Indians and Negroes in Florida, in the Months of December, January and February. Providence, R.I.: D.F. Blanchard.

1847   Population of Massachusetts. *Collections of the American Statistical Association* 1(1):121–214. Boston.

1878   The Indian Question. *Missionary Herald* 74(2):38. Cambridge, Mass.

1881   [Indian Reservations Opened to All Religious Denominations.] *Missionary Herald* 77(4):129. Cambridge, Mass.

1897   Bishop Nicholas' Complaint: He Tells the President That His Church Is Made to Suffer. *The Washington Post* (November 5):6.

[1908]   Cyrus Beede [Obituary]. *Western Work* 12(2). Oskaloosa, Iowa.

1922   James Mooney. *American Anthropologist* 24(2):209–214.

1923   Draft New Policies on Indian Welfare: Tentative Program Adopted Here Aims at Magna Carta of Red Man's Rights. *New York Times* (June 10), sect. 2:4.

1931   The Cruelest of the Ironies of Official Indian Policy. *American Indian Life* 17:41–42. San Francisco.
        [R.F.]
1941   [Biographical Sketch of Anson Dart] (Unpublished typescript, WPA project biography, in Archives Division, State Historical Society of Wisconsin, Madison.)

1947   Recent Deaths: Annie H. Abel Henderson. *American Historical Review* 52(4):833–834.

1953   [Obituary of] Joseph Henry Scattergood. *New York Times*, June 16:4.

[1955]   [Song.] (Manuscript in Randall V. Mills Archive of Northwest Folklore, University of Oregon, Eugene.)

1959   Dr. John L. Laurie Dies at His Home. *The Calgary Herald*, April 7:20. Calgary, Alta.

1963   Miki kizilderililer arasinda. Istanbul: Güniz Basimevi.

1964   The History of the Museum. *Museum of the American Indian, Heye Foundation. Miscellaneous Series* 55. New York.

1965   Amerika vahsileri arasinda bir Türk kizi. Istanbul: no publisher.

1969   NCAI Launches Billboard "Image" Campaign. *The Amerindian: American Indian Review* 17(5):1.

1969a   Indians Denounce Chretien. *The Montreal Star*, July 5.

1972   Comment: Tribal Self Government and the Indian Reorganization Act of 1934. *Michigan Law Review* 70(5):955–986.

1972a   Indian Group Brings Suit Against Cleveland Indians. *Northwest Arkansas Times*, January 19:13. Fayetteville.

1973   BIA: We're Not Your Indians Anymore. Rooseveltown, N.Y.: Akwesasne Notes.

711

———
1980 The Long Road to Sainthood. *Time* 116(1):42–43.

Applegate, Howard G., and C. Wayne Hanselka
1974 La Junta de los Rios del Norte y Conchos. *Southwestern Studies Monograph* 41. El Paso, Tex.

Aquila, Richard
1983 The Iroquois Restoration: Iroquois Diplomacy on the Colonial Frontier, 1701–1754. Detroit, Mich.: Wayne State University Press.

Arber, Edward, ed.
1885 The First Three English Books on America 1511–1555 A.D. Edinburgh: Turnbull and Spears. (Reprinted: Kraus Reprint, New York, 1971.)

Arctander, John W.
1909 The Apostle of Alaska: The Story of William Duncan of Metlakhatla. New York: Fleming H. Revell Company.

Armand *see* Strubberg, Friedrich Armand

Armas Medina, Fernando de
1953 Cristianización del Perú [1530–1600]. *Publicaciones de la Escuela de Estudios Hispano-Americanos de Sevilla* 75. Seville, Spain.

Armstrong, Samuel C.
1883 The Indian Question. Hampton, Va.: Hampton Normal School Steam Press.

———
1904 The Founding of Hampton Institute. *Old South Leaflets, General Series* 6(149).

———
1913 Education for Life. Hampton, Va.: Hampton Normal and Agricultural Institute Press.

Armstrong, Terence
1965 Russian Settlement in the North. Cambridge, England: University Press.

Armstrong, William H.
1978 Warrior in Two Camps: Ely S. Parker, Union General and Seneca Chief. Syracuse, N.Y.: Syracuse University Press.

Arno, Stephen F.
1985 Ecological Effects and Management Implications of Indian Fires. Pp. 81–86 in Proceedings—Symposium and Workshop on Wilderness Fire, Missoula, Mont., November 15-18, 1983. *U.S. Department of Agriculture, Forest Service. Intermountain Forest and Range Experiment Station, Ogden, Utah. General Technical Report* INT-182. Washington: U.S. Government Printing Office.

Arrington, Leonard J.
1970 The Mormons and the Indians: A Review and Evaluation. *The Record - Friends of the Library, Washington State University* 31. Pullman.

Asch, Michael
1975 The Impact of Changing Fur Trade Practices on the Economy of the Slavey Indians. *Canada. National Museum of Man. Mercury Series, Ethnology Service Papers* 28(2):646–657. Ottawa.

———
1977 The Dene Economy. Pp. 47–61 in Dene Nation: The Colony Within. Mel Watkins, ed. Toronto: University of Toronto Press.

Association on American Indian Affairs
1947 Navajo Institute Report. *The American Indian* 4(1):1–4. New York.

Athearn, Robert G.
1956 William Tecumseh Sherman and the Settlement of the West. Norman: University of Oklahoma Press.

———
1967 Forts of the Upper Missouri. Englewood Cliffs, N.J.: Prentice-Hall. (Reprinted: University of Nebraska Press, Lincoln, 1972.)

Atkin, Edmund
1954 Indians of the Southern Colonial Frontier: The Edmund Atkin Report and Plan of 1755. Wilbur R. Jacobs, ed. Columbia: University of South Carolina Press.

Atkin, W.T.
1934 Snake River Fur Trade, 1816–24. *Oregon Historical Quarterly* 35(4):295–312.

Atkins, J.D.C.
1887 [Letter to the President of the United States, Dated December 9, 1887, re Use of English as Language of Instruction in Both Government and Mission Schools.] (Manuscript, Letters Sent by the Indian Division of the Office of the Secretary of the Interior, 1849–1903, Vol. 53:211–215, M606, Record Group 48, Natural Resources Branch, National Archives, Washington.)

Atkinson, Geoffroy
1935 Les Nouveaux horizons de la renaissance française. Paris: E. Droz.

Auger, Roland J.
1955 La Grande recrue de 1653. Montreal: Société Généalogique Canadienne-française.

Augustin, Siegfried, ed.
1982 Nadowessiers Totenlied: Der Indianer im Gedicht. Munich, Germany: Ronacher-Verlag.

Aurbach, Herbert H., Estelle Fuchs, and Gordon Macgregor
1970 The Status of American Indian Education: An Interim Report of the National Study of American Indian Education to the Office of Education-HEW. University Park: The Pennsylvania State University.

Averkieva, Julia
1971 The Tlingit Indians. Pp. 317–342 in North American Indians in Historical Perspective. Eleanor B. Leacock and Nancy O. Lurie, eds. New York: Random House.

Axtell, James
1972 The Scholastic Philosophy of the Wilderness. *William and Mary Quarterly, 3d ser. Vol.* 29(3):335–366. Williamsbury, Va.

———
1981 The European and the Indian: Essays in the Ethnohistory of Colonial North America. New York: Oxford University Press.

———
1981a Dr. Wheelock's Little Red School. Pp. 87–109 in European and the Indian: Essays in the Ethnohistory of Colonial North America. New York: Oxford University Press.

———
1985 The Invasion Within: The Contest of Cultures in Colonial North America. New York: Oxford University Press.

———
1986 The Rise and Fall of the Stockbridge Indian Schools. *The Massachusetts Review* 27(2):367–378. Amherst.

Axtell, James, and William C. Sturtevant
1980 The Unkindest Cut, or Who Invented Scalping? *William and Mary Quarterly 3d ser. Vol.* 37(3):451–472. Williamsburg, Va.

Babcock, Willoughby M., Jr.
1924 Major Lawrence Taliaferro, Indian Agent. *Mississippi Valley Historical Review* 11(3):358–375.

———
1962 Minnesota's Indian War. *Minnesota History* 38(3):93–98.

Bachman, Van Cleaf
1969 Peltries or Plantations: The Economic Policies of the Dutch West India Company in New Netherland, 1623-1639. *The Johns Hopkins University Studies in Historical and Political Science, 87th Ser. No.* 2. Baltimore, Md.

Bacqueville de la Potherie, Claude C. Le Roy
1722 Histoire de l'Amérique septentrionale. 4 vols. Paris: J.L. Nion and F. Didot.

Baden-Powell, Robert S.S.
1909   Scouting for Boys: A Handbook for Instruction in Good Citizenship. Rev. ed. London: C.A. Pearson.

Badger, Joseph
1851   A Memoir of Rev. Joseph Badger. Hudson, Ohio: Sawyer, Ingersoll. (Reprinted in 1900.)

Bagley, Annette Traversie, ed.
1980   The Native American Image on Film: A Programmer's Guide for Organizations and Educators. Washington: The American Film Institute.

Bailey, Alfred G.
1937   The Conflict of European and Eastern Algonkian Cultures, 1504–1700: A Study in Canadian Civilization. *Publications of the New Brunswick Museum, Monograph Series* 2. St. John's.

Bailey, Garrick A.
1973   Changes in Osage Social Organization 1673–1906. *University of Oregon Anthropological Papers* 5. Eugene.

Bailey, Kenneth P.
1939   The Ohio Company of Virginia and the Westward Movement, 1748–1796: A Chapter in the History of the Colonial Frontier. Glendale, Calif.: Arthur H. Clark.

_____
1944   Thomas Cresap: Maryland Frontiersman. Boston: Christopher Publishing Company.

_____
1976   Christopher Gist: Colonial Frontiersman, Explorer and Indian Agent. Hamden, Conn.: Archon Books.

Bailey, Lynn R.
1964   The Long Walk: A History of the Navajo Wars, 1846–68. Los Angeles: Westernlore Press.

Bailey, Paul D.
1948   Jacob Hamblin: Buckskin Apostle. Salt Lake City, Utah: Bookcraft.

Bain, J.W.
1885   Too Much Book. *Council Fire and Arbitrator* 8(3):45. Washington.

Baird, W. David.
1967   Spencer Academy, Choctaw Nation, 1842–1900. *Chronicles of Oklahoma* 45(1):25–43.

_____
1979   William A. Jones, 1897–1904. Pp. 211–219 in The Commissioners of Indian Affairs, 1824–1977. Robert Kvasnicka and Herman J. Viola, eds. Lincoln: University of Nebraska Press.

_____
1980   The Quapaw Indians: A History of the Downstream People. Norman: University of Oklahoma Press.

Bakeless, John L.
1939   Master of the Wilderness: Daniel Boone. New York: W. Morrow.

_____
1947   Lewis and Clark: Partners in Discovery. New York: Morrow.

Baker, Charles
1985   In My Opinion: Indian Artifacts and Museums: A Question of Ownership. *History News* (April):14–16.

Baldwin, Alice Blackwood
1929   Memoirs of the Late Frank D. Baldwin, Major General, U.S.A. Los Angeles: Wetzel Publishing Company.

Baldwin, Neil
1977   [Review of] The Castaneda Series: The Teachings of Don Juan .... *Journal of Psychedelic Drugs* 9(4):347–349.

Balfe, Joseph A.
1948   Blackfeet's Own Priest: First Indian Priest in N.W. *The Indian Sentinel* 28(7):99–100.

Ballantyne, Robert M.
1893   The Young Fur-traders; or, Snowflakes and Sunbeams from the Far North. London: T. Nelson and Sons.

Bancroft, Hubert H.
1874–1876   The Native Races of the Pacific States of North America. 5 vols. San Francisco: The History Company.

_____
1884–1889   History of the North Mexican States and Texas. 2 vols. San Francisco: A.L. Bancroft.

_____
1886–1890   The History of California. 7 vols. San Francisco: The History Company.

Bandelier, Adolph F.A.
1887   Histoire de la colonisation et des missions de Sonora, Chihuahua, Nouveau-Méxique, et Arizona jusqu'à l'année 1700. 7 Pts. (Manuscript Lat. 14111 in Vatican Library, Rome.)

_____
1890   The Delight Makers. New York: Dodd, Mead.

_____
1890–1892   Final Report of Investigations Among the Indians of the Southwestern United States Carried on Mainly in the Years from 1880 to 1885 .... (*Papers of the Archaeological Institute of America, American Series* 3–4). 2 vols. Cambridge, Mass.: J. Wilson and Son.

_____
1929   The Discovery of New Mexico by Fray Marcos of Nizza. *New Mexico Historical Review* 4(1):28–44.

Banks, Charles E.
1911–1925   The History of Martha's Vineyard, Dukes County, Massachusetts. 3 vols. Boston: G.H. Dean. (Reprinted: Dukes County Historical Society, Edgartown, 1966.)

Banks, Judith Judd
1970   Comparative Biographies of Two British Columbia Anthropologists: Charles Hill-Tout and James A. Teit. (Unpublished M.A. Thesis in Anthropology, University of British Columbia, Vancouver.)

Bannan, Helen M.
1978   The Idea of Civilization and American Indian Policy Reformers in the 1880s. *Journal of American Culture* 1(4):787–799. Bowling Green, Ohio.

Bannon, John F.
1955   The Mission Frontier in Sonora, 1620–1687. James A. Reynolds, ed. New York: United States Catholic Historical Society.

_____
1970   The Spanish Borderlands Frontier, 1531–1821. New York: Holt, Rinehart and Winston.

_____
1974   The Spaniards in the Mississippi Valley: An Introduction. Pp. 3–15 in The Spanish in the Mississippi Valley, 1762–1804. John F. McDermott, ed. Urbana: University of Illinois Press.

Banta, R.E., comp.
1949–1981   Indiana Authors and Their Books. 3 vols. [Vols. 2 and 3 compiled by Donald E. Thompson.] Crawfordsville, Ind.: Wabash College Press.

Bantin, Philip C., and Mark G. Thiel
1984   Guide to Catholic Indian Mission and School Records in Midwest Repositories. Milwaukee, Wis.: Marquette University Libraries, Department of Special Collections and University Archives.

Baptie, Sue
1968   Edgar Dewdney. *Alberta Historical Review* 16(4):1–10.

Barba, Preston A.
1913   The Life and Works of Friedrich Armand Strubberg. *Americana Germanica* 16. Philadelphia.

_____
1913a   The North American Indian in German Fiction. *German-American Annals* 15. Philadelphia.

——— 1914 Cooper in Germany. *German-American Annals* 16. Philadelphia.

——— 1916 Balduin Möllhausen: The German Cooper. *Americana Germanica* 17. Philadelphia.

Barbour, Philip L.
1964 The Three Worlds of Captain John Smith. Boston: Houghton, Mifflin.

Barclay, Wade C.
1949–1957 History of Methodist Missions. 3 vols. New York: The Board of Missions of the Methodist Church.

Barker, James N.
1808 The Indian Princess; or La Belle sauvage. Philadelphia: T. and G. Palmer.

Barkley, Frances
[1836] Reminiscences. (Manuscript in Provincial Archives of British Columbia, Vancouver.)

Barnes, Viola F.
1932 Gideon Hawley. P. 418 in Vol. 8 of Dictionary of American Biography. New York: Charles Scribner's Sons.

Barnett, Louise K.
1975 The Ignoble Savage: American Literary Racism, 1790–1890. Westport, Conn.: Greenwood Press.

Barney, Garold D.
1986 Mormons, Indians and the Ghost Dance Religion of 1890. Lanham, Md.: University Press of America.

Barns, George C.
1949 Denver, the Man: The Life, Letters and Public Papers of the Lawyer, Soldier, and Statesman. Wilmington, Ohio: Shenandoah Publishing House.

Barrelet, James
1953 La Verrerie en France de l'époque gallo-romaine à nos jours. Paris: Librairie Larousse.

Barrie, Sir James M.
1910 Peter Pan: Retold in Story from J.M. Barrie's Dramatic Fantasy. G.D. Drennan, ed. New York: Barse and Hopkins.

Barrientos, Bartolomé
1902 Vida y hechos de Pedro Menéndez de Aviles. Pp. 1–152 in Dos antiguas relaciones de la Florida. Genaro García, ed. Mexico: J. Avilar.

Barry, Phillips, ed.
1960 Bulletin of the Folk-song Society of the Northeast, 1930–1937 [Reprint]. Introduction by Samuel P. Bayard. *Publications of the American Folklore Society, Bibliographical and Special Series* 11. Philadelphia.

Barry, Roxana
1975 Rousseau, Buffalo Bill and the European Image of the American Indian. *Art News* 74(December): 58–61.

Barsukov, Ivan P., ed.
1897–1901 Pis'ma Innokentiia, mitropolita moskovskago i kolomenskago, 1828–1878 (Letters of Innocent, Metropolitan of Moscow and Kolomena, 1828–1878). 3 vols. St. Petersburg.

Barth, John
1960 The Sot-weed Factor. Garden City, N.Y.: Doubleday.

Barth, Pius J.
1945 Franciscan Education and the Social Order in Spanish North America (1502–1821). Chicago: University of Chicago Press.

Bartlett, John R., ed.
1856–1865 Records of the Colony of Rhode Island and Providence Plantations, in New England. 10 vols. Providence, R.I.: A. Crawford Greene and Brothers. (Reprinted: AMS Press, New York, 1968.)

Bartlett, Samuel C.
1876 Historical Sketch of the Missions of the American Board Among the North American Indians. Boston: American Board of Commissioners for Foreign Missions.

Barton, Benjamin S.
[1788–1789] Essay Towards a Natural History of the North American Indian. (Manuscript essay in Barton Papers, American Philosophical Society, Philadelphia.)

——— 1797 New Views of the Origins of the Tribes and Nations of America. Philadelphia: John Bioren.

——— 1799 Observations and Conjectures Concerning Certain Articles Which Were Taken Out of an Ancient Tumulus, or Grave, at Cincinnati.... *Transactions of the American Philosophical Society* 4:181–215. Philadelphia.

Barton, William P.C.
1816 A Biographical Sketch ... of ... Professor Barton. Philadelphia: n.p.

Bartram, John
1942 Diary of a Journey Through the Carolinas, Georgia, and Florida: From July 1, 1765, to April 10, 1766. Francis Harper, ed. *Transactions of the American Philosophical Society* 33(1). Philadelphia.

Bartram, William
1791 Travels Through North and South Carolina, Georgia, East and West Florida, the Cherokee Country, the Extensive Territories of the Muscogulges, or Creek Confederacy, and the Country of the Chactaws.... Philadelphia: James and Johnson.

——— 1853 Observations on the Creek and Cherokee Indians. *Transactions of the American Ethnological Society* 3(1). New York.

——— 1943 Travels in Georgia and Florida, 1773–74: A Report to Dr. John Fothergill. Francis Harper, ed. *Transactions of the American Philosophical Society* 33(2):121–242. Philadelphia.

Basanoff, V.
1933 Archives of the Russian Church in Alaska in the Library of Congress. *Pacific Historical Review* 2(1):72–84.

Bass, Althea
1936 Cherokee Messenger. Norman: University of Oklahoma Press.

——— 1954 James Mooney in Oklahoma. *Chronicles of Oklahoma* 32(3):246–262.

Bataille, Gretchen M., and Charles L.P. Silet, eds.
1980 The Pretend Indians: Images of Native Americans in the Movies. Ames: The Iowa State University Press.

——— 1985 Images of American Indians on Film: An Annotated Bibliography. New York: Garland.

Bataillon, Marcel
1951 La Vera Paz, roman et histoire. *Bulletin Hispanique* 53(3):235–300. Bordeaux, France.

Battiste, Marie A., Richard A. Bond, and Barbara M. Fagan
1975 Study of Bilingual-bicultural Projects Involving Native American, Indo-European, Asian and Pacific Language Groups. Palo Alto, Calif.: American Institute for Research.

Baudet, Henri
1965 Paradise on Earth: Some Thoughts on European Images of Non-European Man. Elizabeth Wentholt, trans. New Haven, Conn.: Yale University Press.

Baughman, Ernest W.
1966 Type and Motif-index of the Folktales of England and North America. The Hague, Netherlands: Mouton.

714

Baxter, James P.
1894   The Pioneers of New France in New England, with Contemporary Letters and Documents. Albany, N.Y.: J. Munsell's Sons.

Bay, William Van Ness
1878   Reminiscences of the Bench and Bar of Missouri . . . . St. Louis, Mo.: F.H. Thomas.

Beale, Marie
1954   Decatur House and Its Inhabitants. Washington: National Trust for Historic Preservation.

Beals, Carleton
1957   John Eliot, the Man Who Loved the Indians. New York: Julian Messner.

Bean, Lowell J., and Harry W. Lawton
1973   Some Explanations for the Rise of Cultural Complexity in Native California with Comments on Proto-agriculture and Agriculture. Pp. v–xlvii in Patterns of Indian Burning in California: Ecology and Ethnohistory. Henry T. Lewis, ed. *Ballena Press Anthropological Papers* 1. Ramona, Calif.

Beard, Augustus F.
1909   A Crusade of Brotherhood: A History of the American Missionary Association. Boston: The Pilgrim Press. (Reprinted: AMS Press, New York, 1972.)

Beard, Daniel C.
1909   The Boy Pioneers: Sons of Daniel Boone. New York: Charles Scribners Sons.

Beatty, Edward C.O.
1939   William Penn as Social Philosopher. New York: Columbia University Press.

Beatty, Willard W., ed.
1953   Education for Cultural Change: Selected Articles from Indian Education, 1944–1951. Washington: Bureau of Indian Affairs.

Beauharnois, Claude de la Boische de Beauharnois et de Villechauve, and Gilles Hocquart
1737   Mémoire au Ministre. *Archives Nationales, Colonies IIA,* Vol. 67, folio 100–101. Paris.

Beaver, R. Pierce
1962   American Missionary Motivation Before the Revolution. *Church History* 31(2):216–226.

1962a   Ecumenical Beginnings in Protestant World Mission: A History of Comity. New York: Thomas Nelson and Sons.

1966   Church, State, and the American Indians: Two and a Half Centuries of Partnership in Missions Between Protestant Churches and Government. St. Louis, Mo.: Concordia Publishing House.

1966a   Pioneers in Mission: The Early Missionary Ordination Sermons, Charges, and Instructions: A Sourcebook on the Rise of American Missions to the Heathen. Grand Rapids, Mich.: W.B. Eardmans.

1968   Missionary Motivation Through Three Centuries. Pp. 113–151 in Reinterpretation in American Church History. Jerald C. Brauer, ed. Chicago: University of Chicago Press.

1969   Methods in American Missions to the Indians in the Seventeenth and Eighteenth Centuries: Calvinist Models for Protestant Foreign Missions. *Journal of Presbyterian History* 47(2):124–148. Philadelphia.
——————, ed.
1979   The Native American Christian Community: A Directory of Indian, Aleut, and Eskimo Churches. Monrovia, Calif.: Missions Advanced Research and Communication Center.

Beckham, Stephen D.
1969   George Gibbs: Historian and Ethnologist. (Unpublished Ph.D. Dissertation in History, University of California, Los Angeles.)

1971   Requiem for a People: The Rogue Indians and the Frontiersman. Norman: University of Oklahoma Press.

Beers, Henry P.
1957   The French in North America: A Bibliographic Guide to French Archives, Reproductions, and Research Missions. Baton Rouge: Louisiana State University Press.

1964   The French and British in the Old Northwest: A Bibliographical Guide to Archive and Manuscript Sources. Detroit, Mich.: Wayne State University Press.

Beeson, John
1860   Autobiography. *The Calumet* 1(1):7–9.

Beets, Henry
1940   Toiling and Trusting; Fifty Years of Work of the Christian Reformed Church Among Indians . . . . Grand Rapids, Mich.: Grand Rapids Printing Company.

Beidelman, Richard G.
1957   Nathaniel Wyeth's Fort Hall. *Oregon Historical Quarterly* 58(3):197–250.

Beidler, Peter G.
1977   Fig Tree John: An Indian in Fact and Fiction. Tucson: University of Arizona Press.

Beidler, Peter G., and Marion F. Egge
1979   The American Indian in Short Fiction: An Annotated Bibliography. Metuchen, N.J.: Scarecrow Press.

Beitzell, Edwin W.
1959   The Jesuit Missions of St. Mary's County, Maryland. Abell, Md.: Privately printed. (2d ed. in 1976.)

1968   Life on the Potomac River. Abell, Md.: Published privately. (Reprinted in 1979.)

Belányi, Ferenc
1865   Vadonban: Regények az Eszak Amerikai Allamokból. Pest: no publisher.

Belcher, Sir Edward
1843   Narrative of a Voyage Round the World, Performed in Her Majesty's Ship Sulpher, During the Years 1836–1842, Including Details of Naval Operations in China from December 1840, to November 1841. London: H. Colburn.

Belden, Bauman L.
1927   Indian Peace Medals Issued in the United States. New York: The American Numismatic Society.

Belknap, Jeremy, and Jedidiah Morse
1816   The Report of a Committee of the Board of Correspondents of the Scots Society for Propagating Christian Knowledge, Who Visited the Oneida and Mohekunuh Indians in 1796. *Massachusetts Historical Society Collections for 1798, 1st. ser.* Vol. 5:12–32. Boston.

Bell, Sadie
1930   The Church, the State, and Education in Virginia. Philadelphia: Sadie Bell.

Bell, William A.
1869   New Tracks in North America: A Journal of Travel and Adventure Whilst Engaged in the Survey for a Southern Railroad to the Pacific Ocean During 1867–8. 2 vols. London: Chapman and Hall.

Belvin, Benjamin F.
1949   The Status of the Indian Ministry. Shawnee: Oklahoma Baptist University Press.

Benavides, Alonso de
1916   The Memorial of Fray Alonso de Benavides, 1630. Mrs. Edward E. Ayer, trans. Frederick W. Hodge and Charles F.

Lummis, ann. Chicago: Privately Printed. (Reprinted: Horn and Wallace, University of New Mexico Press, Albuquerque, 1965.)

1945   Fray Alonso de Benavides' Revised Memorial of 1634. Frederick W. Hodge, George P. Hammond, and Agapito Rey, eds. Albuquerque: University of New Mexico Press.

Bender, Averam B.
1952   The March of Empire: Frontier Defense in the Southwest, 1848–1860. Lawrence: University of Kansas Press.

Benedict, Ruth
1934   Patterns of Culture. New York: Houghton, Mifflin.

Bennett, Emerson
1848   The Renegade: A Historical Romance of Border Life. Cincinnati, Ohio: Robinson and Jones.

Benson, Ronald M.
1973   Ignoble Savage: Edward Eggleston and the American Indian. *Illinois Quarterly* 35 (February): 41–51.

Bent, Charles
1846   [Letter to William Medill, Commissioner of Indian Affairs, Dated Santa Fe, N.M., November 10, 1846] (Manuscript, Document HM 13230 in Henry E. Huntington Library, San Marino, Calif.)

Beresford, William
1789   A Voyage Round the World; But More Particularly to the North-West Coast of America; Performed in 1785, 1786, 1787 and 1788, in the King George and Queen Charlotte, by Captains Portlock and Dixon. George Dixon, ed. London: G. Goulding.

Berger, Thomas
1964   Little Big Man. New York: Dial Press.

Berger, Thomas R.
1985   Village Journey: The Report of the Alaska Native Review Commission. New York: Hill and Wang.

Bergsland, Knut, and Jørgen Rischel, eds.
1986   Pioneers of Eskimo Grammar. *Travaux du Cercle Linguistique de Copenhagen* 21. Copenhagen.

Berkhofer, Robert F., Jr.
1963   Model Zions for the American Indians. *American Quarterly* 15(2):176–190.

1965   Salvation and the Savage: An Analysis of Protestant Missions and American Indian Responses, 1787–1862. Lexington: University of Kentucky Press. (Reprinted: Greenwood Press, Westport, Conn., 1977.)

1972   Jefferson, the Ordinance of 1784, and the Origins of the American Territorial System. *William and Mary Quarterly 3d ser., Vol.* 29(2):231–262. Williamsburg, Va.

1978   The White Man's Indian: Images of the American Indian from Columbus to the Present. New York: Alfred A. Knopf.

Berreman, Gerald D.
1955   Inquiry into Community Integration in an Aleutian Village. *American Anthropologist* 57(1):49–59.

Berry, Brewton
1969   The Education of the American Indians: A Survey of the Literature. Washington: U.S. Government Printing Office.

Berry, Don
1961   A Majority of Scoundrels: An Informal History of the Rocky Mountain Fur Company. New York: Harper.

Berry, Jane M.
1917   The Indian Policy of Spain in the Southwest, 1783–1795. *Mississippi Valley Historical Review* 3(4):462–477.

Berthrong, Donald J.
1963   The Southern Cheyennes. Norman: University of Oklahoma Press.

1976   The Cheyenne and Arapaho Ordeal: Reservation and Agency Life in the Indian Territory, 1875–1907. Norman: University of Oklahoma Press.

Bessels, Emil
1891   Aniligka: Eine poetische Erzählung aus dem hohen Norden. Stuttgart, Germany: Otto Baisch.

Best, George
1938   The Three Voyages of Martin Frobisher in Search of a Passage to Cathay and India by the North-west, A.D. 1576–8. Vilhjálmur Stefánsson, ed. London: Argonaut Press.

Betzinez, Jason
1959   I Fought with Geronimo. Wilbur S. Nye, ed. Harrisburg, Pa.: Stackpole.

Beverley, Robert
1705   The History and Present State of Virginia, in Four Parts. London: Printed for R. Parker.

1722   The History of Virginia, in Four Parts. 2d ed. London: Printed for B. and S. Tooke.

1947   The History and Present State of Virginia. Louis B. Wright, ed. Chapel Hill: University of North Carolina Press.

Bieder, Robert E.
1972   The American Indian and the Development of Anthropological Thought in the United States, 1780–1851. (Unpublished Ph.D. Dissertation in History, University of Minnesota, Minneapolis.)

1986   Science Encounters the Indian, 1820–1880: The Early Years of American Ethnology. Norman: University of Oklahoma Press.

Biernatzki, Johann C.
1840   Der braune Knabe, oder die Gemeinde in der Zerstreuung. Altona, Germany: Hammerel.

Biggar, Henry P., ed.
1930   A Collection of Documents Relating to Jacques Cartier and the Sieur de Roberval. Ottawa: Public Archives of Canada.

Billardon de Sauvigny, Edme Louis
1767   Hirza, ou Les Illinois. Tragédie. Paris: Vve Duchesne.

Billington, Ray A.
1949   Westward Expansion: A History of the American Frontier. New York: Macmillan.

1981   Land of Savagery, Land of Promise: The European Image of the American Frontier in the Nineteenth Century. New York: W.W. Norton.

Binder, Frederick M.
1968   The Color Problem in Early National America as Viewed by John Adams, Jefferson, and Jackson. The Hague: Mouton.

Bird, Robert M.
1837   Nick of the Woods; or, The Jibbenainosay: A Tale of Kentucky. 2 vols. Philadelphia: Carey, Lea and Blanchard.

Bischoff, William N.
1945   The Jesuits in Old Oregon, a Sketch of Jesuit Activities in the Pacific Northwest, 1840–1940. Caldwell, Idaho: Caxton Printers.

Bishop, Charles A.
1974   The Northern Ojibwa and the Fur Trade: An Historical and Ecological Study. Toronto: Holt, Rinehart and Winston of Canada.

Bishop, Clarence R.
1967   A History of the Indian Student Placement Program of the Church of Jesus Christ of Latter Day Saints. (Unpublished

M.A. Thesis in Social Work, University of Utah, Salt Lake City.)

Bishop, Morris
1948   Champlain: The Life of Fortitude. New York: Octagon Books.

Bissell, Benjamin H.
1925   The American Indian in English Literature of the Eighteenth Century. *Yale Studies in English* 68. New Haven, Conn. (Reprinted: Archon Books, Hamden, Conn., 1986.)

Black, Lydia T.
1977   Ivan Pan'kov: An Architect of Aleut Literacy. *Arctic Anthropology* 14(1):94–107.

————, ed. and trans.
1977a   The Konyag (The Inhabitants of the Island of Kodiak) by Iosaf [Bolotov] (1794–1799) and by Gideon (1804-1807). *Arctic Anthropology* 14(2):79–108.

Black, Mary B.
1977   Ojibwa Power Belief System. Pp. 141–151 in The Anthropology of Power: Ethnographic Studies from Asia, Oceania, and the New World. Raymond D. Fogelson and Richard Adams, eds. New York: Academic Press.

1977a   Ojibwa Taxonomy and Percept Ambiguity. *Ethos* 5(1):90–118.

Blackmore, Edward H.
1950   Leaflet "All About Red Indians." Eastbourne, England: Published by the author.

Blackmore, William
1868–1869 The North American Indians: A Sketch of Some of the Hostile Tribes, Together with a Brief Account of Gen. Sheridan's Campaign of 1869 Against the Sioux, Cheyenne, Arapaho, Kiowa, and Comanche Indians. *Journal of the Ethnological Society of London*, n.s. 1(3):287–320.

Blair, Bowen
1979   American Indians vs. American Museums: A Matter of Religious Freedom. *American Indian Journal* 5(5):13–21, (6):2–6.

Blake, John L.
1850   Anecdotes of the American Indians, Illustrating Their Eccentricities. Hartford, Conn.: C.M. Welles.

Blanchet, Francis N.
1878   Historical Sketches of the Catholic Church in Oregon, During the Past Forty Years. Portland, Oreg.: Catholic Sentinel Press.

Blanchet, Francis N., J.B. Bolduc, Modeste Demers, and Antoine Langlois
1956   Notices and Voyages of the Famed Quebec Mission to the Pacific Northwest. Being the Correspondence, Notices, etc., of Fathers Blanchet and Demers, Together with Those of Fathers Bolduc and Langlois. Carl Landerholm, trans. Portland: Oregon Historical Society.

Bland, Thomas A.
1906   Pioneers of Progress. Chicago: T.A. Bland.

Blanke, Gustav H.
1962   Amerika im englishen Schrifttum des 16. und 17. Jahrhunderts (*Beiträge zur Englischen Philologie* 46). Bochum-Langendreer, Germany: Heinrich Poppinghaus.

Blankenship, Roy, ed.
1988   The Life and Times of Frank G. Speck (1881–1950), American Ethnologist. *University of Pennsylvania Publications in Anthropology* 4. Philadelphia. In press.

Bleecker, Ann Eliza
1793   The Posthumous Works in Prose and Verse; To Which Is Added a Collection of Essays, Prose and Poetical, by Margaretta V. Faugeres. New York: T. and J. Swords.

Blegen, Theodore C.
1963   Minnesota: A History of the State. Minneapolis: University of Minnesota Press.

Blodgett, Harold W.
1935   Samson Occum. Hanover, N.H.: Dartmouth College Publications.

Blomkvist, E.E.
1972   A Russian Scientific Expedition to California and Alaska, 1839–1849. Basil Dmytryshyn and E.A.P. Crownhart-Vaughan, trans. *Oregon Historical Quarterly* 73(2):101–170.

Bloom, Lansing B.
1935   A Trade Invoice of 1638. *New Mexico Historical Review* 10(3):242–248.

1939   The Vargas Encomienda. *New Mexico Historical Review* 14(4):366–417.

Blue, George V.
1924   A Hudson's Bay Company Contract for Hawaiian Labor. *Oregon Historical Quarterly* 25(1):72–75.

Blue Cloud, Peter or Aroniawenrate
1972   Not In Anger. *Clear Creek* 2(1):52.

1972a   Alcatraz Is Not an Island. Berkeley, Calif.: Wingbow Press.

Board of Indian Commissioners
1869–1933 Annual Reports. Washington: U.S. Government Printing Office.

Boas, Franz
1910   Changes in Bodily Form of the Descendants of Immigrants, *61st Congress, 2d sess. Senate Document* 208. Washington.

1911   Handbook of American Indian Languages. Pt. 1 *Bureau of American Ethnology Bulletin* 40. Washington.

1911a   The Mind of Primitive Man. New York: Macmillan. (Reprinted: Free Press, New York, 1965.)

1915   Frederic Ward Putnam. *Science* n.s. 42 (1080):330–332.

1922   James A. Teit. *American Anthropologist* 24(4):490–492.

1940   Race, Language, and Culture. New York: Macmillan. (Reprinted: University of Chicago Press, Chicago, 1982.)

Boas, George
1948   Essays on Primitivism and Related Ideas in the Middle Ages. Baltimore, Md.: Johns Hopkins Press.

Bobb, Bernard E.
1962   The Viceregency of Antonio María Bucareli in New Spain, 1771–1779. Austin: University of Texas Press.

Bobé, Louis
1928–1929 [A Short Survey of Greenland History.] In Vol. 3 of Greenland. M. Vahl, G.C. Amdrup, L. Bobé, Ad. S. Jensen, eds. Copenhagen: C.A. Reitzel.

1952   Hans Egede: Colonizer and Missionary of Greenland. Copenhagen: Rosenkilde and Bagger.

Bodine, John J.
1978   Taos Blue Lake Controversy. *Journal of Ethnic Studies* 6(1):42–48.

Bodmer, Johann J.
1756   Inkel und Yariko. [Lindau, Germany]: no publisher.

Bogy, L.V.
1867   [Letter to Orville H. Browning, Secretary of the Interior, Dated February 11, 1867, re Solving the Indian Problem.] (Manuscript, Report Books of the Bureau of Indian Affairs, Vol. 16:152–153, M348, Natural Resources Branch, Record Group 75, National Archives, Washington.)

Bolhuis, Gerda
1983   The Netherlands Actiongroup for North American Indians. *American Indian Workshop Newsletter* 14(October): 22–23. Vienna.

Bolton, Herbert E.
1914   Athanase de Mézières and the Louisiana-Texas Frontier, 1768–1780. 2 vols. Cleveland, Ohio: Arthur H. Clark.

———
1915   Texas in the Middle Eighteenth Century: Studies in Spanish Colonial History and Administration. *University of California Publications in History* 3. Berkeley.

———
1917   The Mission as a Frontier Institution in the Spanish-American Colonies. *American Historical Review* 23(1):42–61.

———
1917a   French Intrusions into New Mexico, 1749–1752. Pp. 389–407 in The Pacific Ocean in History: Papers and Addresses Presented at the Panama-Pacific Historical Congress . . . July 19–23, 1915. H. Morse Stephens and Herbert E. Bolton, eds. New York: Macmillan. (Reprinted: Pp. 150–171 in Bolton and the Spanish Border Lands. John F. Bannon, ed., University of Oklahoma Press, 1964.)

———
1921   The Spanish Borderlands: A Chronicle of Old Florida and the Southwest. New Haven, Conn.: Yale University Press.

———
1930   Anza's California Expeditions. 5 vols. Berkeley: University of California Press.

———
1931   Font's Complete Diary: A Chronicle of the Founding of San Francisco. Berkeley: University of California Press.

———
1952   Spanish Explorations in the Southwest, 1542–1706 [1916], New York: Barnes and Noble.

———
1960   Rim of Christendom, a Biography of Eusebio Francisco Kino, Pacific Coast Pioneer. New York: Macmillan. (Reprinted: University of Arizona Press, Tucson, 1984.)

Bolton, Herbert E., and Thomas M. Marshall
1920   The Colonization of North America, 1492–1783. New York: Macmillan.

Bond, Richmond P.
1952   Queen Anne's American Kings. Oxford, England: Clarendon Press.

Bonner, T.D.
1856   The Life and Adventures of James P. Beckwourth, Mountaineer, Scout, and Pioneer, and Chief of the Crow Nation of Indians. New York: Harper and Brothers. (Reprinted: University of Nebraska Press, 1972.)

Bonsal, Stephen
1912   Edward Fitzgerald Beale: A Pioneer in the Path of Empire, 1822–1903. New York: G.P. Putnam's Sons.

Boone, Daniel
1823   Life and Adventures of Col. Daniel Boone, the First White Settler of the State of Kentucky. Brooklyn, N.Y.: C. Wilder.

Boorsch, Suzanne
1976   America in Festival Presentations. Pp. 503–515 in Vol. 1 of First Images of America: The Impact of the New World on the Old. Fredi Chiappelli, ed. 2 vols. Berkeley: University of California Press.

Boorstin, Daniel J.
1948   The Lost World of Thomas Jefferson. New York: Henry Holt.

Borah, Woodrow
1951   New Spain's Century of Depression. *Ibero-Americana* 35. Berkeley, Calif.

———
1983   Justice by Insurance: The General Indian Court of Colonial Mexico and the Legal Aides of the Half-real. Berkeley: University of California Press.

Borges, Pedro
1961   Los Conquistadores espirituales de América. *Publicaciones de la Escuela de Estudios Hispano-Américanos de Sevilla* 132. Seville, Spain.

Bouis, Amédée
1847   Le Whip-poor-will, ou Les Pionniers de l'Orégon. Paris: Comon.

Bourke, John G.
1891   On the Border with Crook. New York: Scribners. (Reprinted: Time-Life Books, Alexandria, Va., 1980.)

———
1894   The Laws of Spain in Their Application to the American Indians. *American Anthropologist* 7(2):193–201.

Bourne, Edward G.
1904   Spain in America, 1450–1580. New York: Harper and Bros.

Bowden, Henry W.
1975   Spanish Missions, Cultural Conflict and the Pueblo Revolt of 1680. *Church History* 44(2):217–228.

———
1981   American Indians and Christian Missions: Studies in Cultural Conflict. Chicago: University of Chicago Press.

Bowers, Alfred W.
1950   Mandan Social and Ceremonial Organization. Chicago: University of Chicago Press.

Bowman, J.N.
1958   The Resident Neophytes of the California Missions, 1769–1834. *Quarterly of the Historical Society of Southern California* 40(2):138–148. Los Angeles.

———
1965   The Names of the California Missions. *The Americas: A Quarterly Review of Inter-American Cultural History* 21(4):363–374.

Bowman, J.N., and Robert F. Heizer
1967   Anza and the Northwest Frontier of New Spain. *Southwest Museum Papers* 20. Los Angeles.

Boyd, Julian P., ed.
1938   Indian Treaties Printed by Benjamin Franklin, 1736–1762. Philadelphia: Historical Society of Pennsylvania.

Boyd, Mark F., Hale G. Smith, and John W. Griffin
1951   Here They Once Stood: The Tragic End of the Apalachee Missions. Gainesville: University of Florida Press.

Boyd, Thomas W.
1928   Simon Girty, the White Savage. New York: Minton, Balch.

———
1929   Mad Anthony Wayne. New York: Charles Scribner's Sons. (Reprinted in 1942.)

Boy Scouts of America
1967   Boy Scout Handbook. New York: Boy Scouts of America.

Bozman, John L.
1837   The History of Maryland, Its First Settlement, in 1633, to the Restoration, in 1660. 2 vols. Baltimore, Md.: James Lucas and E.K. Deaver. (Reprinted; The Reprint Company, Spartanburg, S.C., 1968.)

Bradfield, Maitland
1971   The Changing Pattern of Hopi Agriculture. *Occasional Papers of the Royal Anthropological Institute* 30. London.

Bradford, Deborah
1974   Bilingual Education for Native Americans. Washington: U.S. Office of Indian Education.

Bradford, William
1901   Of Plymouth Plantation. 2 vols. Boston: Wright and Potter.

1952   History of Plymouth Plantation, 1620–1647. Samuel E. Morison, ed. New York: Alfred A. Knopf. (Reprinted: Capricorn Books, New York, 1962.)

Brading, David A.
1971   Miners and Merchants in Bourbon Mexico 1763-1810. *Cambridge Latin American Studies* 10. Cambridge, England.

Bradley, Cyprian, and Edward J. Kelly
1953   History of the Diocese of Boise, 1863–1952. Boise, Idaho: n.p.

Brady, Cyrus T.
1913   Indian Fights and Fighters. New York: Doubleday, Page.

Brain, Jeffrey
1979   Tunica Treasure. Cambridge, Mass.: Harvard University Press.

Brain, Belle M.
1904   The Redemption of the Red Man: An Account of Presbyterian Missions . . . . New York: Presbyterian Church in the U.S.A., Board of Home Missions.

Brainerd, David
1749   An Account of the Life of the Late Reverend Mr. David Brainerd . . . Boston: D. Hinchmen.

————
1793   Mirabilia Dei inter Indicos; or, The Rise and Progress of a Remarkable Work of Grace, Among a Number of the Indians, in the Provinces of New-Jersey, and Pennsylvania; Justly Represented in a Journal Kept . . . .by David Brainerd, ...Worcester, Mass.: Leonard.

Brainerd, Thomas
1865   The Life of John Brainerd, the Brother of David Brainerd, and His Successor as Missionary to the Indians of New Jersey. Philadelphia: Presbyterian Publication Committee.

Brandes, Raymond S.
1965   Frank Hamilton Cushing: Pioneer Americanist. (Unpublished Ph.D. Dissertation in History, University of Arizona, Tucson.)

Brasser, Ted J.
1976   Bo'jou, Neejee: Profiles of Canadian Indian Art (A Travelling Exhibition). Ottawa: National Museum of Man.

————
1985   In Search of Métis Art. Pp. 221–230 in The New Peoples: Being and Becoming Métis in North America. Jacqueline Peterson and Jennifer S.H. Brown, eds. Winnipeg: University of Manitoba Press.

Braudel, Fernand
1973   Capitalism and Material Life, 1400–1800. Miriam Kochan, trans. London: Weidenfeld and Nicolson.

Brauer, Ralph, and Donna Brauer
1975   The Horse, the Gun and the Piece of Property: Changing Images of the TV Western. Bowling Green, Ohio: Bowling Green University Popular Press.

Brayer, Herbert O.
1949   William Blackmore: A Case Study in the Economic Development of the West. Vol. 1: The Spanish Mexican Land Grants of New Mexico and Colorado, 1863–1878. Denver, Colo.: Bradford Robinson.

Brebner, John B.
1933   The Explorers of North America, 1492–1806. New York: Macmillan. (Reprinted: World Publishing, Cleveland, Ohio, 1964.)

Breton, Paul E.
1955   The Big Chief of the Prairies: The Life of Father Lacombe. [Edmonton, Alta.]: Palm Publishers.

Brewington, Marion V.
1962   Shipcarvers of North America. Barre, Mass.: Barre Publishing Company.

Brigham, Johnson
1913   James Harlan. Iowa City: The State Historical Society of Iowa.

Brimlow, George F.
1938   The Bannock Indian War of 1878. Caldwell, Idaho: Caxton Printers.

Brinton, Daniel G.
1868   Myths of the New World. A Treatise on the Symbolism and Mythology of the Red Race of America. New York: Leypoldt and Holt. (Reprinted: St. Clair Shores, Mich., Scholarly Press, 1972.)

————
1882   American Hero-myths: A Study in the Native Religions of the Western Continent. Philadelphia: H.C. Watts.

————
1882–1890 Brinton's Library of Aboriginal American Literature. 8 vols. Philadelphia: Privately printed.

————
1890   Races and Peoples: Lecture on the Science of Ethnography. New York: N.D.C. Hodges.

————
1890a   Essays of an Americanist. Philadelphia: Porter and Coates.

————
1891   The American Race: A Linguistic Classification and Ethnographic Description of the Native Tribes of North and South America. New York: N.D.C. Hodges.

————
1897   Religions of Primitive Peoples (American Lectures on the History of Religion, 2d ser., 1896–1897). New York: G.P. Putnam's Sons.

Brinton, Ellen Starr
1941   Benjamin West's Painting of Penn's Treaty with the Indians. *Bulletin of the Friend's Historical Association* 30(2):99–167.

Brockunier, Samuel H.
1940   The Irrepressible Democrat, Roger Williams. New York: The Ronald Press Company.

Brodhead, John R.
1853–1871 History of the State of New York. 2 vols. New York: Harper and Bros.

Brody, J.J.
1971   Indian Painters and White Patrons. Albuquerque: University of New Mexico Press.

Brooks, George R., ed.
1977   The Southwest Expedition of Jedediah S. Smith: His Personal Account of the Journey to California, 1826–1827. Glendale, Calif.: Arthur H. Clark.

Brooks, Juanita
1944   Indian Relations on the Mormon Frontier. *Utah Historical Quarterly* 12(1-2):1–48.

Brosnan, Cornelius J.
1932   Jason Lee, Prophet of the New Oregon. New York: Macmillan.

Brown, Alexander, ed.
1890   The Genesis of the United States . . . . 2 vols. Boston: Houghton, Mifflin. (Reprinted: Russell and Russell, New York, 1964.)

————, comp. and ed.
1897   The Genesis of the United States . . . ; a Series of Historical Manuscripts . . . . 2 vols. Boston: Houghton, Mifflin.

Brown, Arthur Jr.
1936   One Hundred Years: A History of the Foreign Missionary Work of the Presbyterian Church in the U.S.A. New York: Revell.

Brown, Charles B.
1799   Edgar Huntly; or, Memoirs of a Sleepwalker. 3 vols. Philadelphia: H. Maxwell.

Brown, Dee
1962   Fort Phil Kearny: An American Saga. New York: Putnam.

1971   Bury My Heart at Wounded Knee: An Indian History of the American West. New York: Holt, Rinehart and Winston.

Brown, Douglas S.
1966   The Catawba Indians: The People of the River. Columbia: University of South Carolina Press.

Brown, Elizabeth S.
1953   Lewis Cass and the American Indian. *Michigan History* 37(3):286–298.

Brown, George, and Ron Maguire
1979   Indian Treaties in Historical Perspective. Ottawa: Department of Indian and Northern Affairs, Research Branch.

Brown, Ira Vernon
1953   Lyman Abbott, Christian Evolutionist: A Study in Religious Liberalism. Cambridge, Mass.: Harvard University Press.

Brown, James S.
1900   Life of a Pioneer: Being the Autobiography of James S. Brown. Salt Lake City: Cannon and Sons. (Reprinted as: Giant of the Lord: Life of a Pioneer, Salt Lake City, 1960.)

Brown, Jennifer S.H.
1980   Linguistic Solitudes and Changing Social Categories. Pp. 147–159 in Old Trails and New Directions: Papers of the Third North American Fur Trade Conference. Carol M. Judd and Arthur J. Ray, eds. Toronto: University of Toronto Press.

1980a   Strangers in Blood: Fur Trade Company Families in Indian Country. Vancouver: University of British Columbia Press.

1985   Métis. Pp. 1125–1127 in Vol. 3 of Canadian Encyclopedia. James H. Marsh, gen. ed. Edmonton, Alta.: Hurtig.

Brown, John P.
1938   Old Frontiers: The Story of the Cherokee Indians from Earliest Times to Their Removal to the West, 1838. Kingsport, Tenn.: Southern Publishers.

Brown, Orlando
1849–1850   [Letters Sent and Received by Orlando Brown as Commissioner of Indian Affairs.] (Manuscript, Letters Sent and Letters Received, Office of Indian Affairs, Record Group 75, National Archives, Washington.)

1849–1850a [Letters and Documents Concerning Brown's Term as Commissioner of Indian Affairs.] (Manuscript, Orlando Brown Papers, Kentucky Historical Society, Frankfort.)

1849–1850b [Letters Concerning Brown's Term as Commissioner of Indian Affairs.] (Manuscript, Orlando Brown Papers, Folders 36 and 37, The Filson Club, Louisville, Kentucky.)

Brown, Ralph O.
1956   The Life and Missionary Labors of George Washington Hill. (Unpublished M.A. Thesis in History, Brigham Young University, Provo, Utah.)

Brown, Thomas D.
1972   Journal of the Southern Indian Mission: Diary of Thomas D. Brown. Juanita Brooks, ed. Logan: Utah State University Press.

Browning, Orville H.
1867   [Letter to L.F.S. Pastor, President of the Senate, Dated February 7, 1867, re Appropriations.] (Manuscript, Letters Sent by the Indian Division of the Office of the Secretary of the Interior, 1849–1903, Vol. 7: 153, M606, Record Group 48, Natural Resources Branch, National Archives, Washington.)

Bruce, Henry A.B.
1934   Daniel Boone and the Wilderness Road. New York: Macmillan.

Bruce, Philip A.
1929   The Virginia Plutarch. 2 vols. Chapel Hill: University of North Carolina Press. (Reprinted: Russell and Russell, New York, 1971.)

Brugge, David M.
1968   Navajos in the Catholic Church Records of New Mexico, 1694–1875. *Navajo Tribe Parks and Recreation Department, Research Section Report* 1. Window Rock, Ariz.

Bruggerman, Walther
1985   [W.A.I.A. Brochure on the "Werk Actiegroep Indians Amerika," English Version.] Sint-Niklaas, Belgium.

Brunhouse, Robert L.
1939   The Founding of Carlisle Indian School. *Pennsylvania History* 6(2):72–85.

Bry, Theodor de
1591   Brevis Narratio eorum quae in Florida Americae provincia Gallis acciderunt. Frankfurt am Main, Germany: S. Feirabendius.

Bryant, Charles S., and Abel B. Murch
1872   A History of the Great Massacre by the Sioux Indians in Minnesota, Including the Personal Narratives of Many Who Escaped. Saint Peter, Minn.: E. Wainwright and Sons.

Bryant, Williams C.
1875   Poems. New York: Appleton.

Buchanan, Golden R.
[1960]   Teaching Aids for Lamanite Missionaries. Salt Lake City, Utah: Church of Jesus Christ of Latter Day Saints, Indian Relations Committee.

Bucher, Bernadette
1981   Icon and Conquest: A Structural Analysis of the Illustrations of de Bry's Great Voyages. Basia Miller Gulati, trans. Chicago: University of Chicago Press.

Buell, Augustus C.
1903   Sir William Johnson. New York: Appleton.

Buliard, Roger
1949   Inuk "Au dos de la terre"! Paris: Editions Saint-Germain.

Buntin, Arthur A.
1961   The Indian in American Literature, 1680–1760. (Unpublished Ph.D. Dissertation in History, University of Washington, Seattle.)

Burdick, Jefferson R., ed.
1953   The American Card Catalog. Syracuse, N.Y.: J.R. Burdick and others.

Burgess, Larry E.
1971   "We'll Discuss it at Mohonk." *Quaker History: The Bulletin of the Friends Historical Association* 60(1):14–28.

1972   The Lake Mohonk Conferences on the Indian, 1883–1916. (Unpublished Ph.D. Dissertation in History, Claremont Graduate School, Claremont, Calif.)

[Burke, Edmund]
1760   Treaty with the Indians. *The Annual Register* 2:191–203. London.

1804   Selected Works. E.J. Payne, ed. 3 vols. Oxford, England: Clarendon.

Burke, Joseph C.
1965   William Wirt: Attorney General and Constitutional Lawyer. (Unpublished Ph.D. Dissertation in History, Indiana University, Bloomington.)

1969   The Cherokee Cases: A Study in Law, Politics and Morality. *Stanford Law Review* 21(3):500–531.

Burnett, Donald L., Jr.
1972   An Historical Analysis of the 1968 'Indian Civil Rights' Act. *Harvard Journal on Legislation* 9(4):557–626.

720

Burnette, Robert, and John Koster
1974   The Road to Wounded Knee. New York: Bantam.

Burns, Robert I.
1947   Père Joset's Account of the Indian War of 1858. *Pacific Northwest Quarterly* 38(4):285–307.

_____
1961   Indians and Whites in the Pacific Northwest (*Jesuit Contributions to Peace*, *1850–1880*). San Francisco: University of San Francisco.

_____
1966   The Jesuits and the Indians Wars of the Northwest (*Yale Western Americana Series* 11). New Haven, Conn.: Yale University Press.

Burrow, J.W.
1966   Evolution and Society: A Study in Victorian Social Theory. Cambridge, England: Cambridge University Press.

Burrus, Ernest J. ed. and trans.
1961   Kino's Plan for the Development of Pimería Alta, Arizona and Upper California. Tucson: Arizona Pioneers' Historical Society.

_____
1971   Kino and Manje, Explorers of Sonora and Arizona. (*Sources and Studies for the History of the Americas* 10) Rome: Jesuit Historical Institute.

Burson, Caroline M.
1940   The Stewardship of Don Esteban Miró, 1782–1792 . . . . New Orleans, La.: American Printing Company.

Burt, Alfred L.
1931   A New Approach to the Problem of the Western Posts. Pp. 61–75 in *Report of the Annual Meeting of the Canadian Historical Association*. Toronto

_____
1940   The United States, Great Britain and British North America from the Revolution to the Establishment of Peace After the War of 1812. New Haven, Conn.: Yale University Press.

Burt, Olive Wooley, ed.
1958   American Murder Ballads and Their Stories. New York: Oxford University Press. (Reprinted: Citadel Press, New York, 1964.)

Bushnell, Amy Turner
1986   Background and Beginnings of the Deer Skin Trade: Spanish Documentary Evidence. (Paper read at the American Society for Ethnohistory Meeting, Charleston, S.C., November 1986.)

Bushnell, David I., Jr.
1908   The Account of Lamhatty. *American Anthropologist* n.s. 10(4):568–574.

_____
1932   Seth Eastman: The Master Painter of the North American Indian. *Smithsonian Miscellaneous Collections* 87(3). Washington.

Butler, William F.
1875   The Great Lone Land: A Narrative of Travel and Adventure in the North-west of America. 7th ed. London: S. Low, Marston, Low, and Searle.

Butterfield, Consul Willshire
1890   History of the Girtys. Cincinnati, Ohio: Robert Clarke. (Reprinted: Long's College Book Store, Columbus, Ohio, 1950.)

Buttree, Julia M. *see* Seton, Julia M.

Byers, Douglas S.
1939   Warren King Moorehead. *American Anthropologist* 41(2):286–294.

Byers, John, Jr.
1975–1976 The Indian Matter of Helen Hunt Jackson's *Ramona*: From Fact to Fiction. *American Indian Quarterly* 2(4):331–346.

Byrd, William
1966   The Prose Works of William Byrd of Westover: Narratives of a Colonial Virginian. Louis B. Wright, ed. Cambridge, Mass.: Harvard University Press.

Cahn, Edgar S., ed.
1969   Our Brother's Keeper: The Indian in White America. New York: World Publishing.

Cain, Marvin R.
1965   William Wirt Against Andrew Jackson: Reflection of an Era. *Mid-America* 47(2):113–138.

Calhoun, John C.
1817   [Letter to Andrew Jackson, Dated December 26, 1817, re Orders for Jackson to Assume Command of Fort Scott and Related Issues.] (Manuscript, Records of the Office of the Secretary of War, Letters Sent, Military Affairs, Vol. 9:439–440, M6, Military Reference Branch, Record Group 107, National Archives, Washington.)

Callan, Louise
1957   Philippine Duchesne: Frontier Missionary of the Sacred Heart, 1769–1852. Westminster, Md.: The Newman Press.

Callcott, George H.
1970   History in the United States, 1800–1860; Its Practice and Purpose. Baltimore, Md.: Johns Hopkins Press.

Camp, Charles L.
1972   George C. Yount. Pp. 411–420 in Vol. 9 of The Mountain Men and the Fur Trade of the Far West. LeRoy R. Hafen, ed. 10 vols. Glendale, Calif.: Arthur H. Clark.

Campbell, James V.
1883   Biographical Sketch of Charles Christopher Trowbridge. [Detroit, Mich.: State Pioneer Society of Michigan.] (Reprinted: *Michigan Pioneer Collections* 6:478–491, 1907.)

Campbell, Thomas
1809   Gertrude of Wyoming: A Pennsylvania Tale. London: T. Bensley.

Campeau, Lucien
1967   Monumenta Novae Franciae. Vol. 1: La Première mission d'Acadie, 1602–1616. (*Monumenta Historica Societatis Iesu*, Vol. 96; *Monumenta Missionum Societatis Iesu*, Vol. 23). Quebec: Les Presses de l'Université Laval.

_____
1974   Les Cent-associés et le peuplement de la Nouvelle-France, 1633–1663. Montreal: Éditions Bellarmin.

_____
1979   Monumenta Novae Franciae. Vol. 2: Etablissement à Québec, 1616–1634. (*Monumenta Historica Societatis Iesu*, Vol. 116; *Monumenta Missionum Societatis Iesu*, Vol. 37). Quebec: Les Presses de l'Université Laval.

Campisi, Jack
1985   The Trade and Intercourse Acts: Land Claims on the Eastern Seaboard. Pp. 337–362 in Irredeemable America: The Indians' Estate and Land Claims. Imre Sutton, ed. Albuquerque: University of New Mexico Press.

Camus, William
1978   Les Oiseaux de feu, et autres contes peaux-rouges. Paris: Gallimard.

Camus, William, and Christian Grenier
1984   Cheyennes 6112 (*Collection Folio Junior Science Fiction* 17). Paris: Gallimard.

Canada
1871   Annual Report of the Secretary of State for the Year 1870. Ottawa: Queen's Printer.

_____
1905–1912 Indian Treaties and Surrenders, from 1680 to 1890. 3 vols. Ottawa: B. Chamberlin. (Reprinted: Queen's Printer, Toronto, 1971.)

_____
1931   The James Bay Treaty, Treaty No. 9 and Adhesions Made in 1929 and 1930. Ottawa: King's Printer.

1963   The Indian Act, 1951, with Amendments of 1952–1953, c. 41 and of 1956, c. 40. Ottawa: Queen's Printer.

1973   Le Canada ecclésiastique, 1973–1974. Montreal: Librairie Beauchemin.

1979   Treaty Agreements Between the Indian People and the Sovereign in Right of Canada; Chart Prepared by the Treaties and Historical Research Centre. Ottawa: Indian and Northern Affairs Canada.

1983   Canada Catholic Church Directory. Montreal: Publicité BM.

Canada. Department of Energy, Mines and Resources. Surveys and Mapping Branch
1977   Indian Treaties. Rev. Map. Ottawa: Queen's Printer. (Originally published in 1970.)

Canada. Department of Indian Affairs and Northern Development
1969   Statement of the Government of Canada on Indian Policy. Ottawa: Queen's Printer.

Canada. Department of Indian and Northern Affairs
1985   The Northern Quebec Agreements, Government of Canada Involvement. [Ottawa]: Department of Fisheries and Oceans of Canada, Indian and Northern Affairs, Canada, and Environment Canada.

Canada. Indian Claims Commission
1975   Indian Claims in Canada: An Introductory Essay and Selected List of Holdings. Ottawa: Indian Claims Commission, Research Resource Center.

Canada. Legislative Assembly
1839–1840   Report of Committee No. 4 on the Indian Department. In Report on the Public Departments. Vol. 2. *Journals. Legislative Assembly, Upper Canada.* Ottawa.

1847   Report on the Affairs of the Indians in Canada. Sect. 3. *Journals. Legislative Assembly.* App. T. Ottawa.

1858   Report of the Special Commissioners to Investigate Indian Affairs in Canada. *Sessional Papers.* App. 21, Pt. 1. Ottawa.

Canada. Parliament. House of Commons
1983   Indian Self-government in Canada; Report of the Special Committee on Self-government. Ottawa: Supply and Services Canada.

Canada. Senate
1970   Report of the Special Senate Committee on Poverty. 28 Parliament, 2-3 sess. Ottawa: Queen's Printer.

Candide de Nante
1927   Pages glorieuses de l'épopée canadienne: Une mission capucine en Acadie. Paris: Librairie Saint-François.

Candler, Allen D., comp.
1904–1913   The Colonial Records of the State of Georgia. 26 vols. Atlanta: Georgia State Legislature. (Reprinted: AMS Press, New York, 1970.)

Cappon, L.J., ed.
1976   Atlas of Early American History: The Revolutionary Era, 1760–1790. Princeton, N.J.: Princeton University Press for the Newberry Library.

Cardinal, Harold
1969   The Unjust Society: The Tragedy of Canada's Indians. Edmonton, Alta.: Hurtig.

Carley, Kenneth
1961   The Sioux Uprising of 1862. St. Paul: Minnesota Historical Society.

1962   As Red Men Viewed It: Three Indian Accounts of the Uprising. *Minnesota History* 38(3):126–249.

Carlisle, Irene Jones
1952   Fifty Ballads and Songs from Northwest Arkansas. (Unpublished M.A. Thesis in Languages and Literature, University of Arkansas, Fayetteville.)

Carmony, Donald F., ed.
1971   William P. Dole: Wabash Valley Merchant and Flatboatman. *Indiana Magazine of History* 67(4):335–363.

Carp, Wayne E.
1986   Early American Military History: A Review of Recent Work. *Virginia Magazine of History and Biography* 94(3):259–284.

Carpenter, John A.
1964   Sword and Olive Branch: Oliver Otis Howard. Pittsburgh, Pa.: University of Pittsburgh Press.

Carrière, Gaston
1964   L'Oeuvre des Oblates de Marie-Immaculée dans le Nord canadien oriental. Pp. 395–425 in Le Nouveau-Québec: Contribution à l'étude de l'occupation humaine. J. Malaurie and J. Rousseau, eds. (*Bibliothèque Arctique et Antarctique* 2) Paris: Mouton.

1972   Adrien-Gabriel Morice, o.m.i. (1859–1938): Essai de bibliographie. *Revue de l'Université d'Ottawa* 42:325–341.

Carriken, Eleanor et al.
1976   Guide to the Microfilm Edition of the Oregon Province Archives of the Society of Jesus; Indian Language Collection: The Pacific Northwest Tribes. Spokane, Wash.: Gonzaga University.

Carriker, Robert C.
1985   Joseph Cataldo, S.J.: Courier of Catholicism to the Nez Perces. Pp. 109–139 in Churchmen and the Western Indians, 1820–1920. Clyde A. Milner, II and Floyd A. O'Neil, eds. Norman: University of Oklahoma Press.

Carro, Venancio D.
1944   La Teología y los teólogos-juristas españoles ante la conquista de América. 2 vols. *Publicaciones de la Escuela de Estudios Hispano-americanos de Sevilla* 6. Madrid.

Carroll, John M., ed.
1978   After the Battle: Sturgis - 7th Cavalry, Miles - 5th Infantry [1878–79]. Bryan, Tex.: Published by the Author.

Carroll, Peter N.
1969   Puritanism and the Wilderness: The Intellectual Significance of the New England Frontier, 1629–1700. New York: Columbia University Press.

Carter, Clarence E., comp.
1934–1962   The Territorial Papers of the United States. 26 vols. Washington: U.S. Government Printing Office.

Carter, Harvey L.
1968   Dear Old Kit: The Historical Christopher Carson with a New Edition of the Carson Memoirs. Norman: University of Oklahoma Press.

1971   Jedediah Smith. Pp. 331–348 in Vol. 3 of The Mountain Men and the Fur Trade of the Far West. LeRoy R. Hafen, ed. 10 vols. Glendale, Calif.: Arthur H. Clark.

Carter, Harvey L., and Marcia C. Spencer
1975   Stereotypes of the Mountain Men. *Western Historical Quarterly* 6(1):17–32. Logan, Utah.

Carter, Robert G.
1935   On the Border with Mackenzie; or, Winning West Texas from the Comanches. Washington: Eynon. (Reprinted: Antiquarian Press, New York, 1961.)

Cartier, Jacques
1863   Bref récit et succincte narration de la navigation faite en MDXXXV et MDXXXVI par le capitaine Jacques Cartier aux iles de Canada, Hochelaga, Saguenay et autres [1580]. Paris: Librairie Tross.

1949   Premier voyage de Jacques Cartier (1534). Pp. 79-112 in Vol. 1 of Les Français en Amérique pendant la première moitié du XVIe siècle. Charles A. Julien, Herval Beauchesne, and T. Beauchesne, eds. Paris: Presses Universitaires de France.

Casas, Bartolomé de las
1552   Breuissima relacion de la destruycion de las Indias; colegida por el Obispo do fray Bartolome de las Casas, o Casaus, de la orden de Sãcto Domingo. Seville, Spain: Sebastian Trugillo. (Reprinted as: History of the Indies, Harper and Row, New York, 1971.)

Caso, Alfonso
1958   Indigenismo. Mexico: Instituto Nacional Indigenista.

Cass, Lewis
1826   Indians of North America. *North American Review* 22:53–119.

1827   Service of Indians in Civilized Warfare. *North American Review* 24:365–442. (Reprinted as: Remarks on the Policy and Practice of the United States and Great Britain in Their Treatment of the Indians. Boston: F.T. Gray, 1827.)

1830   Removal of the Indians. *North American Review* 30:62–121.

1968   A Memorandum of Lewis Cass: Concerning a System for the Regulation of Indian Affairs. Francis P. Prucha and Donald F. Carmony, eds. *Wisconsin Magazine of History* 52(1):35-50.

Cass, Lewis, and William Clark
1829   [Report of February 10, 1829.] Pp. 77–78 in *20th Cong., 2d sess. Senate Document* No. 72 (Serial No. 181). Washington.

Casselman, Arthur V.
1932   The Winnebago Finds a Friend. Philadelphia: Heidelberg Press.

Castañeda, Carlos
1968   The Teachings of Don Juan: A Yaqui Way of Knowledge. Berkeley: University of California Press.

1971   A Separate Reality: Further Conversations with Don Juan. New York: Simon and Schuster.

1972   Journey to Ixtlan: The Lessons of Don Juan. New York: Simon and Schuster.

Castañeda, Carlos E.
1936–1958   Our Catholic Heritage in Texas, 1519–1936. Paul J. Folk, ed. 7 vols. Austin: Von Boeckmann-Jones.

Cather, Willa
1927   Death Comes for the Archbishop. New York: Alfred Knopf.

Catholic Church. Directories
1973   Directory for the Diocese of Fairbanks. (Manuscript.)

1975   The Official Catholic Directory. New York: P.J. Kennedy and Sons.

Catlin, George
1841   Letters and Notes on the Manners, Customs, and Condition of the North American Indians. 2 vols. London: Tosswill and Myers. (Reprinted: Dover Publications, New York, 1973.)

1861   Life Amongst the Indians: A Book for Youth. London: S. Low.

1868   Last Rambles Amongst the Indians of the Rocky Mountains and the Andes. London: S. Low and Marston.

Caughey, John W.
1938   McGillivray of the Creeks. Norman: University of Oklahoma Press. (Reprinted in 1959.)

1946   Hubert Howe Bancroft: Historian of the West. Berkeley: University of California Press. (Reprinted: Russell and Russell, New York, 1970.)

Cawley, Robert R.
1938   The Voyagers and Elizabethan Drama. Boston: D.C. Heath. (Reprinted: Kraus Reprint, New York, 1966.)

Ceci, Lynn
1977   The Effect of European Settlement and Trade on the Settlement Pattern of Indians in Coastal New York, 1524–1665: The Archaeological and Documentary Evidence. (Unpublished Ph.D. Dissertation in Anthropology, City University of New York.)

Cerbelaud-Salagnac, Georges
1937   Sous le signe de la tortue. Paris: Edition Alsatio.

1953   Aux Mains des Iroquois. Roman. Paris: Edition Fides.

Chalmers, George
1780   Political Annals of the Present United Colonies from Their Settlement to the Peace of 1763. London: George Chalmers.

Chalmers, Harvey
1955   Joseph Brant: Mohawk. East Lansing: Michigan State University Press.

Chamberlain, George S.
1963   American Medals and Medalists. [Annandale, Va.]: Turnpike Press.

Chamfort, Sebastien R.N.
1764   La Jeune indienne: Comédie en une acte et en vers. Paris: Chez Cailleau.

Chamisso, Adalbert von
1831   Rede des alten Kriegers Bunte Schlange: Das Mordtal. In Gedichte. Leipzig, Germany: Weidman.

Champlain, Samuel de
1922-1936   The Works of Samuel de Champlain [1626]. Henry P. Biggar, ed. 6 vols. Toronto: The Champlain Society. (Reprinted in 1971.)

Chance, David H.
1973   Influences of the Hudson's Bay Company on the Native Cultures of the Colville District. *Northwest Anthropological Research Notes* 7(1), *Memoir* 2. Moscow, Idaho.

Chance, David H., and Jennifer Chance
1976   Kanaka Village, Vancouver Barracks, 1974. *University of Washington, Office of Public Archaeology. Institute for Environmental Studies, Reports in Highway Archaeology* 3. Seattle.

1985   Kettle Falls 1978: Further Excavation in Lake Roosevelt. *University of Idaho Anthropological Reports* 84. Moscow.

Chandler, Melbourne C.
1960   Of Gary Owen in Glory: The History of the Seventh United States Cavalry Regiment. [Annandale, Va.]: The Turnpike Press.

Chaney, Charles L.
1976   The Birth of Missions in America. South Pasadena, Calif.: William Carey Library.

Channing, Edward
1886   The Narragansett Planters: A Study of Causes. *Johns Hopkins University Studies in Historical and Political Science* 4. Baltimore, Md. (Reprinted: Johnson Reprint, New York, 1973.)

Chapman, Abraham, ed.
1975   Literature of the American Indian: Views and Interpretations. A Gathering of Indian Memories, Symbolic Contexts, and Literary Criticism. New York: New American Library.

Chapman, H.H.
1932   Is the Longleaf Type a Climax? *Ecology* 13(4):328–334.

Chaput, Donald
1979   James W. Denver, 1857, 1858–59. Pp. 69-75 in The Commissioners of Indian Affairs, 1824–1977. Robert M. Kvasnicka and Herman J. Viola, eds. Lincoln: University of Nebraska Press.

Charlevoix, Pierre F.X. de
1744   Histoire et description générale de la Nouvelle-France, avec le journal historique d'un voyage fait par ordre du roi dans l'Amérique Septentrionale. 6 vols. Paris: Rollin Fils.

Charters, Ann, comp.
1955   The Ragtime Songbook: Songs of the Ragtime Era, by Scott Joplin . . . .and Others. New York: Oak Publications.

Chase, Frederick
1928   History of Dartmouth College and the Town of Hanover, New Hampshire (to 1815). John K. Lord, ed. 2d ed. Brattleboro, Vt.: Vermont Print.

Chateaubriand, François-René
1801   Atala, ou, Les Amours de deux sauvages dans le désert. 5th ed. Paris: Migneret.

1802   René, ou, Les Effets des passions, pour servir de suite à Atala. Paris: [Migneret.]

1827   Les Natchez. 2 vols. Brussels: P.J. de Mat.

Chauncy, Charles
1966   The Sermon [1762]. Pp. 190–209 in Pioneers in Mission, by R. Pierce Beaver. Grand Rapids, Mich.: Eardmans.

Chavez, Angelico
1954   Origins of New Mexico Families in the Spanish Colonial Period. Santa Fe: Historical Society of New Mexico. (Reprinted: William Gannon, Santa Fe, N.M., 1975.)

Chávez Orozco, Luis
1947   Códice Osuna [1878]. Mexico City: Edicíones del Instituto Indigenista Interamericano.

Chevalier, François
1952   La Formation des grands domaines au Méxique; terre et société aux XVIe-XVIIe siècles. Travaux et Mémoires de l'Institut d'Ethnologie 56. Paris.

Chevigny, Hector
1942   Lord of Alaska: Baranov and the Russian Adventure. New York: Viking.

1965   Russian America: The Great Alaskan Venture, 1741–1867. New York: Viking.

Chiappelli, Fredi, ed.
1976   First Images of America: The Impact of the New World on the Old. 2 vols. Berkeley: University of California Press.

Chief Eagle, Dallas
1967   Winter Count. [Boulder, Colo.: Johnson.]

Child, Lydia M.
1868   An Appeal for the Indians. New York: William P. Tomlinson.

Chinard, Gilbert
1911   L'Exotisme américain dans la littérature française au XVIe siècle. Paris: Librairie Hachette. (Reprinted: Slatkine Reprints, Geneva, Switzerland, 1978.)

1918   L'Exotisme américain dans l'oeuvre de Chateaubriand. Paris: Librairie Hachette.

1919   Contribution à l'étude des sources de Chateaubriand. University of California Publications in Modern Philology 7. Berkeley.

1934   L'Amérique et le rêve exotique dans la littérature française au XVIIe et au XVIIIe siècle. Paris: Librairie E. Droz. (Reprinted: Slatkine Reprints, Geneva, Switzerland, 1970.)

1947   Eighteenth Century Theories on America as Human Habitat. Proceedings of the American Philosophical Society 91(1):27–57. Philadelphia.

Chittenden, Hiram M.
1902   The American Fur Trade of the Far West: A History of the Pioneer Trading Posts and Early Fur Companies of the Missouri Valley and the Rocky Mountains and of the Overland Commerce with Santa Fe. 3 vols. New York: Francis P. Harper.

1903   History of Early Steamboat Navigation on the Missouri River: Life and Adventures of Joseph La Barge. 2 vols. New York: Francis P. Harper.

Choque, C.
1969   Une Ecole de catéchistes esquimaux. Eskimo 79:12–15. Churchill, Man.

1969a   Attachez vos ceintures. Pt. 2. Eskimo 79:3–10. Churchill, Man.

Choris, Louis
1822   Voyage pittoresque autour du monde avec des portraits de sauvages d'Amérique, d'Asie, d'Afrique, et des Iles du Grand Ocean; des paysages des vues maritimes, et plusieurs objets d'histoire naturelle. Paris: Didot.

Christensen, Erwin O.
1952   Early American Wood Carving. Cleveland, Ohio: World.

Christensen, William E.
1955   The Legislative Career of Edgar Howard. (Unpublished M.A. Thesis in History, University of Nebraska, Lincoln.)

[Christian Reformed Church, Board of Foreign Missions]
1914   Navaho and Zuni: Mission Work of the Christian Reformed Church. Grand Rapids, Mich.: Grand Rapids Printing Company.

Church, Benjamin
1851   The History of the Great Indian War of 1675 and 1676, Commonly Called Philip's War. Also, the Old French and Indian Wars, from 1689 to 1704. With Numerous Notes and an Appendix, by Samuel G. Drake. Rev. ed. Hartford, Conn.: S. Andrus.

1865   The History of King Philip's War [1716]. Henry M. Dexter, ed. Boston: J.K. Wiggin.

1867   The History of the Eastern Expeditions of 1689, 1690, 1692, 1696, and 1704 Against the Indians and French. Henry M. Dexter, ed. Boston: J.K. Wiggin and Wm. Parsons Lunt.

Churchill, Ward, Norbert Hill, and Mary Ann Hill
1978   Media Stereotyping and Native Response: An Historical Overview. The Indian Historian 11(4):45–56.

Church Missionary Society
1869   Metlahkatlah: Ten Years' Work Among the Tsimsheean Indians. London: Church Missionary House.

Clarfield, Gerard H.
1980   Timothy Pickering and the American Republic. Pittsburgh, Pa.: University of Pittsburgh Press.

Clark, Ella E., ed.
1955-1956 George Gibbs' Account of Indian Mythology in Oregon and Washington Territories. Oregon Historical Quarterly 56(4):293-325; 57(2):125–167.

Clark, Joan, and William Vickery
1969-1970 Vanishing Americans. Film Library Quarterly 3 (Winter):27, 46–47.

Clark, L.D.
1976   D.H. Lawrence and the American Indian. D.H. Lawrence Review 9(Fall):305–372.

Clark, Robert C.
1934   Hawaiians in Early Oregon. *Oregon Historical Quarterly* 35(1):22–31.

Clark, William
1831   [Letter of January 22, 1831 to John H. Eaton.] (In Letters Received, Record Group 75, M234, Roll 749, National Archives, Washington.)

Clarke, Charles G.
1970   The Men of the Lewis and Clark Expedition: A Biographical Roster of the Fifty-one Members and a Composite Diary of Their Activities from All the Known Sources. Glendale, Calif.: Arthur H. Clark.

Clarke, Tom
1939   Big Chief of Sussex Downs: Eastbourne's Edward Blackmore More Sioux than the Sioux. *Reynolds News*, March 1939. London.

Claus, Daniel
1786   A Primer for the Use of the Mohawk Children, to Acquire the Spelling and Reading of Their Own as Well as to Get Acquainted with the English Tongue . . . .London: Printed by C. Buckton.

Clayton, James L.
1967   The Growth and Economic Significance of the American Fur Trade, 1790-1890. Pp. 62–72 in Aspects of the Fur Trade: Selected Papers of the 1965 North American Fur Trade Conference. Russell W. Fridley, ed. St. Paul: Minnesota Historical Society.

Cleary, Michael
1980   Finding the Center of the Earth: Satire, History, and Myth in *Little Big Man. Western American Literature* 15(3):195–211.

Cleaves, Freeman
1939   Old Tippecanoe: William Henry Harrison and His Time. New York: Scribner's Sons. (Reprinted: Easton Press, Norwalk, Conn., 1986.)

Cleland, Charles E.
1972   From Sacred to Profane: Style Drift in the Decoration of Jesuit Finger Rings. *American Antiquity* 37(2):202–210.

Cleland, Robert G.
1950   This Reckless Breed of Men: The Trappers and Fur Traders of the Southwest. New York: Alfred A. Knopf.

Clemens, Samuel L.
1869   Innocents Abroad . . . .(by Mark Twain). New York: Harper.

————
1872   Roughing It (by Mark Twain). New York: Harper.

————
1876   The Adventures of Tom Sawyer (by Mark Twain). New York: Harper.

————
1884   The Adventures of Huckleberry Finn (by Mark Twain). New York: Harper.

Clements, William
1969   The Types of the Polack Joke. *Publications of the Folklore Forum, Bibliography and Special Series* 3. Bloomington, Ind.

Clemmer, Richard
1985   The Pinon-pine—Old Ally or New Pest? Western Shoshone Indians vs. the Bureau of Land Management in Nevada. *Environmental Review* 9(2):131–149.

Cleveland, Richard J.
1842   A Narrative of Voyages and Commercial Enterprises. 2 vols. Cambridge, England: John Owen.

Clifford, Gerald M.
1973   The Theory of Indian Controlled Schools. Boulder, Colo.: no publisher.

Clift, C. Glenn, ed.
1951   The Governors of Kentucky, 1792–1824, the Old Master, Colonel Orlando Brown, 1801–1867. *The Register of the Kentucky Historical Society* 49:5–27.

Clifton, James
1984   From Bark Canoe to Pony Herds: The Lake Michigan Transportation Revolution, 1750–1755. (Paper presented at the Chicago Maritime Conference, 1984.)

Cline, Howard F.
1949   Civil Congregations of the Indians in New Spain, 1598-1606. *Hispanic American Historical Review* 29(3):349-369. Durham, N.C.

————
1962   Mexico, Revolution to Evolution, 1940–1960. London: Oxford University Press.

Clinton, Robert N.
1981   Isolated in Their Own Country: A Defense of Federal Protection of Indian Autonomy and Self-government. *Stanford Law Review* 33(6):979–1068.

Clokey, Richard M.
1980   William H. Ashley: Enterprise and Politics in the Trans-Mississippi West. Norman: University of Oklahoma Press.

Clum, Woodworth
1936   Apache Agent: The Story of John P. Clum. Boston: Houghton, Mifflin.

Clyman, James
1928   James Clyman, Frontiersman, 1792–1881: The Adventures of a Trapper and Covered-wagon Emigrant as Told in His Own Reminiscences and Diaries. Charles L. Camp, ed. San Francisco: California Historical Society.

Coan, C.F.
1921   The First Stage of the Federal Indian Policy in the Pacific Northwest, 1849-1852. *Quarterly of the Oregon Historical Society* 22(1):46–89. Portland.

————
1922   Adoption of the Reservation Policy in the Pacific Northwest, 1853–1855. *Quarterly of the Oregon Historical Society* 23(1):1–38. Portland.

Coates, Lawrence G.
1972   Mormons and Social Change Among the Shoshoni, 1853-1900. *Idaho Yesterdays* 15(4):3–11.

Cochran, Samuel L.
1932   Simon Kenton. Strasburg, Va.: Shenandoah Publishing House.

Cochran, William Cox
1901   General Jacob Dolson Cox: Early Life and Military Services. Oberlin, Ohio: Bibliotheca Sacra Company.

Cocks, James F., III
1975   The Selfish Savage: Protestant Missionaries and Nez Percé and Cayuse Indians, 1835–1847. (Unpublished Ph.D Dissertation in History, University of Michigan, Ann Arbor.)

Codere, Helen
1950   Fighting with Property: A Study of Kwakiutl Potlatching and Warfare, 1792–1930 (*American Ethnological Society Monograph* 18) New York: J.J. Augustin.

————
1961   Kwakiutl. Pp. 431–516 in Perspectives in American Culture Change. Edward H. Spicer, ed. Chicago: University of Chicago Press.

————, ed.
1966   Kwakiutl Ethnography, by Franz Boas. Chicago: University of Chicago Press.

Cody, William F.
1879   The Life of Hon. William F. Cody: Known as Buffalo Bill, the Famous Hunter, Scout and Guide; An Autobiography. Hartford, Conn.: F.E. Bliss. (Reprinted: University of Nebraska Press, Lincoln, 1978.)

Coe, Charles H.
1927   Juggling a Rope; Lariat Roping and Spinning, Knots and Splices. Also, The Truth About Tom Horn "King of the Cowboys." Pendleton, Oreg.: Hamley.

Coen, Rena Neumann
1969   The Indian as Noble Savage in 19th Century American Art. (Unpublished Ph.D. Dissertation in Fine Arts, University of Minnesota, Minneapolis.)

————
1971   Taliaferro Portrait: Was It Painted by Catlin? *Minnesota History* 42(8):295–300.

Coffey, Shelby
1972   Indians Open War on Redskins. *Washington Post*, March 30, F:1.

Coffin, Tristram P.
1971   Uncertain Glory: Folklore of the American Revolution. Detroit, Mich.: Folklore Associates.

Cohen, Felix S.
1942   Handbook of Federal Indian Law. Washington: U.S. Government Printing Office. (Reprinted: University of New Mexico Press, Albuquerque, 1971.)

————
1982   Felix S. Cohen's Handbook of Federal Indian Law: 1982 Edition. Renard Strickland, ed. Charlottesville, Va.: Michie Bobbs-Merrill.

Cohen, Leonard
1966   Beautiful Losers. New York: Viking Press.

Cohen, Lucy Kramer, ed.
1960   The Legal Conscience: Selected Papers of Felix S. Cohen. New Haven, Conn.: Yale University Press. (Reprinted: Archon Books, Hamden, Conn., 1970.)

Cohen, Ronald
1969   The Hartford Treaty of 1650: Anglo-Dutch Cooperation in the Seventeenth Century. *New-York Historical Society Quarterly* 53(4):311–332. New York.

Coker, William S., and Thomas D. Watson
1986   Indian Traders of the Southeastern Spanish Borderlands: Panton, Leslie and Company and John Forbes and Company, 1783–1847. Pensacola: University of West Florida Press.

Colden, Cadwallader
1727   The History of the Indian Nations Depending on the Province of New-York in America. New York: William Bradford.

————
1747   The History of the Five Nations of Canada, Which Are Dependent on the Province of New-York in America, and Are the Barrier Between the English and French in That Part of the World . . . 2 vols. London: T. Osborne.

————
1918   The Letters and Papers of Cadwallader Colden. *Collections of the New York State Historical Society for the Year 1917.* New York.

Cole, Douglas
1973   The Origins of Canadian Anthropology, 1850–1910. *Journal of Canadian Studies* 8(1):33–45. Peterborough, Ont.

Coleman, J. Winston, Jr.
1954   John Filson, Esq., Kentucky's First Historian and Cartographer. Lexington, Ky.: Winburn Press.

Coleman, Michael C.
1980   Not Race, But Grace: Presbyterian Missionaries and American Indians, 1837–1893. *Journal of American History* 67(1):41–60.

————
1985   Presbyterian Missionary Attitudes Toward American Indians, 1837–1893. Jackson: University Press of Mississippi.

Collier, John
1922   The Red Atlantis. *Survey* 49(October): 15–20, 63, 66.

————
1947   The Indians of the Americas. New York: W.W. Morton.

————
1963   From Every Zenith: A Memoir. Denver, Colo.: Swallow Publishing.

Colonnese, Tom, and Louis Owens
1985   American Indian Novelists: An Annotated Critical Bibliography. New York: Garland.

Comas, Juan
1953   Ensayos sobre Indigenismo. Mexico: Instituto Indigenista Interamericano.

————
1964   La Antropología social aplicada en México (*Series Antropología Social* 1). Mexico: Instituto Indigenista Interamericano.

Commager, Henry S., ed.
1963   Documents of American History. 7th ed. New York: Appleton-Century-Crofts.

Commager, Henry S., and Richard B. Morris, eds.
1967   The Spirit of Seventy-Six: The Story of the American Revolution as Told by Participants. New York: Harper and Row.

Commissioner of Indian Affairs
1837   Treaties Between the United States of America and the Several Indian Tribes, from 1778 to 1837; with a Copious Table of Contents. Washington: Longtree and O'Sullivan.

Condon, Thomas J.
1968   New York Beginnings: The Commercial Origins of New Netherland. New York: New York University Press.

Conference on Indian Legislation
1934   [Minutes of Conference Held at the Cosmos Club, Washington, January 7, 1934.] Mimeo.

Conly, Robert L.
1952   The Mohawks Scrape the Sky. *National Geographic Magazine* 102(1):133–142.

Connecticut (Colony)
1850–1890 The Public Records of the Colony of Connecticut, 1636–1776. 15 vols. Hartford, Conn.: Case, Lockwood, and Brainerd.

————
1900   Charter of the Colony of Connecticut, 1662. Hartford, Conn.: Case, Lockwood, and Brainerd. (Reprinted: Tercentenary Commission–Yale University Press, New Haven, Conn., 1933.)

Connell, Evan S.
1984   Son of the Morning Star. San Francisco: North Point Press.

Connelley, William E.
1921   Dr. Josiah Gregg, Historian of the Old Santa Fé Trail. Pp. 334–348 in *Proceedings of the Mississippi Valley Historical Association for the Year 1919–1920.* Vol. 10(2).

Connor, Jeannette M., ed. and trans.
1925–1930 Colonial Records of Spanish Florida: Letters and Reports of Governors and Secular Persons. 2 vols (*Publications of the Florida State Historical Society* 5). Deland: The Florida State Historical Society.

Connors, Donald F.
1969   Thomas Morton. (*Twayne's United States Authors Series* 146.) New York: Twayne Publishers.

Conrad, Rudolf
1987   Mutual Fascination: Indians in Dresden and Leipzig. Pp. 455–473 in Indians and Europe. Christian Feest, ed. Aachen, Germany: Rader Verlag.

Cook, James, and James King
1784   A Voyage to the Pacific Ocean. 3 vols. London: W. and A. Strachen.

Cook, Sherburne F.
1940   Population Trends Among the California Mission Indians. *Ibero-Americana* 17. Berkeley, Calif.

1943   The Conflict Between the California Indian and White Civilization. 4 vols. *Ibero-Americana* 21–24. Berkeley, Calif. (Reprinted: University of California Press, Berkeley, 1976.)

Cook, Sherburne F., and Woodrow Borah
1960   The Indian Population of Central Mexico, 1531–1610. *Ibero-Americana* 44. Berkeley, Calif.

Cook, Warren L.
1973   Flood Tide of Empire: Spain and the Pacific Northwest, 1543–1819. New Haven, Conn.: Yale University Press.

Coombs, L. Madison
1962   Doorway Toward the Light. Lawrence, Kans.: Haskell Press.

1972   Rough Rock Revisited: The Indian Voice in Education, How Can It Be Best Heard? *The Arizona Teacher* (March-April):11, 22-24.

Cooper, James Fennimore
1826   The Last of the Mohicans, a Narrative of 1757. Philadelphia: H.C. Carey.

1829   The Wept of Wish-ton-wish. Philadelphia: Carey, Lea and Carey.

1843   Wyandotte; or, The Hutted Knoll. Philadelphia: Lea and Blanchard.

1845   The Chainbearer; or, The Littlepage Manuscripts. New York: Burgess, Stringer.

1845a   Satanstoe; or, The Littlepage Manuscripts. New York: Burgess, Stringer.

1846   The Redskins; or, Indian and Injun: Being the Conclusion of the Littlepage Manuscripts. New York: Burgess, Stringer.

1848   The Oak Openings; or, The Bee Hunter. New York: Burgess, Stringer.

1954   The Leatherstocking Saga; Being Those Parts of The Deerslayer, The Last of the Mohicans, The Pathfinder, The Pioneers, and The Prairie Which Specially Pertain to Natty Bumppo . . . Allan Nevins, ed. New York: Pantheon Books.

Corbelt, Pearson H.
1952   Jacob Hamblin, the Peacemaker. Salt Lake City, Utah: Deseret Book Company.

Corbett, William P.
1978   The Red Pipestone Quarry: The Yanktons Defend a Sacred Tradition, 1858–1929. *South Dakota History* 8(2):99–116.

Corey, Herbert
1923   He Carries the White Man's Burden. *Collier's* 71(May 12):13.

Corkran, David H.
1962   The Cherokee Frontier: Conflict and Survival, 1740–62. Norman: University of Oklahoma Press.

1967   The Creek Frontier, 1540–1783. Norman: University of Oklahoma Press.

Corney, Peter
1965   Early Voyages in the North Pacific, 1813–1818 [1896]. Fairfield, Wash.: Ye Galleon Press.

Costo, Rupert
1972   "Seven Arrows" Desecrates Cheyenne. *The Indian Historian* 5(2):41–42.

Cotterill, Robert S.
1954   The Southern Indians: The Story of the Civilized Tribes Before Removal. Norman: University of Oklahoma Press.

Coues, Elliott, ed.
1893   History of the Expedition Under the Command of Lewis and Clark. 4 vols. New York: Francis P. Harper.

————, ed.
1895   The Expeditions of Zebulon Montgomery Pike, to the Headwaters of the Mississippi, Through the Louisiana Territory, and in New Spain, During the Years 1805-6-7. 3 vols. New York: F.P. Harper. (Reprinted: Dover, New York, 1987.)

Coulter, E. Merton
1927   Mary Musgrove, "Queen of the Creeks": A Chapter of Early Georgia Troubles. *Georgia Historical Quarterly* 11(1):1–30.

Covey, Cyclone
1966   The Gentle Radical: A Biography of Roger Williams. New York: MacMillan.

Cowan, Robert E.
1933   Alexander S. Taylor, 1817–1876: First Bibliographer of California. *Quarterly of the California Historical Society* 12(1):18–24. San Francisco.

Cowan, William, Michael K. Foster, and Konrad Koerner, eds.
1986   New Perspectives in Language, Culture, and Personality: Proceedings of the Edward Sapir Centenary Conference, Ottawa, 1–3 October, 1984. (*Studies in the History of the Language Sciences* 41) Amsterdam: John Benjamins.

Cowdin, Elliot C., ed.
1846   The Northwest Fur Trade. *Hunt's Merchant's Magazine* 14(4):532–539.

Cowie, Isaac
1913   The Company of Adventurers: A Narrative of Seven Years in the Service of the Hudson's Bay Company, 1867–1874 . . . .Winnipeg, Man.: William Briggs.

Cox, Paul R.
1970   The Characterization of the American Indian in American Indian Plays, 1800–1860, as a Reflection of the American Romantic Movement. (Unpublished Ph.D. Dissertation in Education, New York University, New York City.)

Cox, Ross
1957   The Columbia River, or Scenes and Adventures During a Residency of Six Years on the Western Side of the Rocky Mountains Among Various Tribes of Indians Hitherto Unknown . . . .Edgar I. Stewart and James R. Stewart, eds. Norman: University of Oklahoma Press.

Coy, Owen C.
1932   Josiah Gregg in California. Pp. 185–213 in Vol. 2 of New Spain and the Anglo-American West; Historical Contributions Presented to Herbert Eugene Bolton. Charles W. Hackett et al., eds. 2 vols. [Lancaster, Pa.: Lancaster Press.]

Cracroft, Richard H.
1963   The American West of Karl May. (Unpublished M.A. Thesis in English, University of Utah, Salt Lake City.)

Craig, Gerald M.
1963   Upper Canada: The Formative Years, 1784–1841. Toronto: McClelland and Stewart.

Crane, Fred A.
1952   The Noble Savage in America, 1815–1860: Concepts of the Indian with Special Reference to the Writers of the Northeast. (Unpublished Ph.D. Dissertation in History, Yale University, New Haven, Conn.)

Crane, Hart
1930   The Bridge; a Poem. New York: H. Liveright. (Reprinted in 1970.)

Crane, Leo
1928   Desert Drums: The Pueblo Indians of New Mexico, 1540–1928. Boston: Little, Brown.

Crane, Verner W.
1919   The Southern Frontier in Queen Anne's War. *American Historical Review* 24(3):379–395.

————
1928   The Southern Frontier, 1670–1732. Durham, N.C.: Duke University Press.

————
1981   The Southern Frontier, 1670–1732. New York: W.W. Norton.

Cranz, David *see* Moravian Church

Craven, Rebecca McDowell
1982   The Impact of Intimacy: Mexican-Anglo Intermarriage in New Mexico, 1821–1846. El Paso: Texas Western Press for the University of Texas at El Paso.

Craven, Wesley F.
1949   The Southern Colonies in the Seventeenth Century, 1607–1689. Baton Rouge: Louisiana State University Press.

————
1964   New Jersey and the English Colonization of North America. Princeton, N.J.: D. Van Nostrand.

Cravens, Hamilton
1978   The Triumph of Evolution: American Scientists and the Heredity-environment Controversy, 1900–1941. Philadelphia: University of Pennsylvania Press.

Crawford, John M.
1891   The Kalevala, the Epic Poem of Finland. n.p.: Columbian Publication Company.

Crawford, Mary M.
1936   The Nez Perces Since Spalding - Experiences of Forty-one Years at Lapuai, Idaho. Berkeley, Calif.: The Professional Press.

Crawford, Richard C.
1979   Edward Parmelee Smith, 1873–75. Pp. 141–147 in The Commissioners of Indian Affairs, 1824–1977. Robert M. Kvasnicka and Herman J. Viola, eds. Lincoln: University of Nebraska Press.

Crawford, Thomas H., and Alfred Balch
1836–1838   [Three Manuscript Report Books Unbound Papers, Creek Removal Records.] (In Records of the Bureau of Indian Affairs, Record Group 75, National Archives, Washington.)

Crean, J.F.
1962   Hats and the Fur Trade. *Canadian Journal of Economic and Political Science* 28(3):373–386. Toronto.

Cree, Linda
1974   The Extension of County Jurisdiction Over Indian Reservations in California: Public Law 280 and the Ninth Circuit. *Hastings Law Journal* 25(6):1451–1506. San Francisco.

Creighton, Donald G.
1937   The Commercial Empire of the St. Lawrence, 1760–1850. Toronto: Ryerson Press. (2d ed.: Macmillan, Toronto, 1956.)

Cremin, Lawrence A.
1961   The Transformation of the School: Progressivism in American Education, 1876–1957. New York: Columbia University Press.

Cremony, John C.
1970   Life Among the Apache. Glorieta, N.M.: Rio Grande Press.

Crespí, Juan
1927   Fray Juan Crespí: Missionary Explorer on the Pacific Coast, 1769–1774. Herbert E. Bolton, ed. and trans. Berkeley: University of California Press. (Reprinted: AMS Press, New York, 1971.)

Crockett, David
1834   A Narrative of the Life of David Crockett, of the State of Tennessee. Philadelphia: E.L. Carey and A. Hart.

Croft-Cooke, Rupert
1952   Buffalo Bill: The Legend, the Man of Action, the Showman. London: Sidgewick and Jackson.

Cronon, William
1983   Changes in the Land: Indians, Colonists, and the Ecology of New England. New York: Hill and Wang.

Cronyn, George W., ed.
1972   American Indian Poetry: An Anthology of Songs and Chants. New York: Ballantine Books.

Crook, George
1946   General George Crook: His Autobiography. Martin F. Schmitt, ed. Norman: University of Oklahoma Press. (Reprinted in 1986.)

Crosby, Alfred W.
1972   The Columbian Exchange: Biological and Cultural Consequences of 1492. Westport, Conn.: Greenwood Press.

————
1976   Virgin Soil Epidemics as a Factor in the Aboriginal Depopulation of America. *William and Mary Quarterly, 3d ser., Vol.* 33(2):289–299. Williamsburg, Va.

Crouter, Richard E., and Andrew F. Rolle
1960   Edward Fitzgerald Beale and the Indian Peace Commissioners in California, 1851–1854. *Quarterly of the Historical Society of Southern California* 42(June):107–132. Los Angeles.

Crow, Vernon H.
1982   Storm in the Mountains: Thomas' Confederate Legion of Cherokee Indians and Mountaineers. Cherokee, N.C.: Press of the Museum of the Cherokee Indian.

Cruikshank, Ernest A.
1892   Robert Dickson, the Indian Trader. *Collections of the State Historical Society of Wisconsin* 12:133–153. Madison.
————, ed.
1923–1931   Correspondence of Lieut. Governor John Graves Simcoe, with Allied Documents Relating to His Administration of the Government of Upper Canada. 5 vols. Toronto: Ontario Historical Society.

Cumming, Peter A., and Neil H. Mickenberg, eds.
1972   Native Rights in Canada. 2d ed. Toronto: Indian-Eskimo Association of Canada and General Publishing Company.

Cumming, W.P., S.E. Hillier, D.B. Quinn, and G. Williams
1974   The Exploration of North America, 1630–1776. New York: G.P. Putnam's Sons.

Curtis, Edward S.
1907–1930   The North American Indian: Being a Series of Volumes Picturing and Describing the Indians of the United States and Alaska. Frederick W. Hodge, ed. 20 vols. Norwood, Mass.: Plimpton Press. (Reprinted: Johnson Reprints, New York, 1970.)

————
1914   Indian Days of the Long Ago. Yonkers-on-Hudson, N.Y.: World Book Company. (Reprinted: Tamarack Press, New York, 1975.)

Curtis, Ralph E., Jr.
1977   Relations Between the Quapaw National Council and the Roman Catholic Church, 1876–1927. *The Chronicles of Oklahoma* 55(2):211–221.

Cushing, Frank H.
1883   Zuni Fetiches. Pp. 3–45 in *2d Annual Report of the Bureau of American Ethnology for the Years 1880–1881.* Washington.

————
1896   Outlines of Zuni Creation Myths. Pp. 321–447 in *13th Annual Report of the Bureau of American Ethnology for the Years 1891–1892.* Washington.

1901   Zuni Folk Tales. New York: G.P. Putnam's Sons. (Reprinted: Alfred A. Knopf, New York, 1931.)

1920   Zuni Breadstuff. *Museum of the American Indian, Heye Foundation. Indian Notes and Monographs* 8. New York.

1941   My Adventures in Zuni [1882]. Santa Fe, N.M.: The Peripatetic Press. (Reprinted: American West Publishing Company, Palo Alto, Calif., 1970.)

Cushing, Helen Grant, comp.
1936   Children's Song Index. New York: H.W. Wilson.

Cushman, Horatio B.
1962   History of the Choctaw, Chickasaw and Natchez Indians. Angie Debo, ed. New York: Russell and Russell.

Custer, Elizabeth B.
1885   Boots and Saddles; or, Life in Dakota with General Custer. New York: Harper and Brothers. (Reprinted: University of Oklahoma Press, Norman, 1976.)

Custer, George
1874   My Life on the Plains; or, Personal Experiences with Indians. New York: Sheldon.

Custis, George W.P.
1830   Pocahontas; or, The Settlers of Virginia. Philadelphia: C. Alexander.

Cuthbertson, Stuart, and John C. Ewers, eds.
1939   A Preliminary Bibliography on the American Fur Trade. St. Louis, Mo.: U.S. Department of the Interior, National Park Service.

Cutler, Lee
1971   Lawrie Tatum and the Kiowa Agency, 1869–1873. *Arizona and the West* 13(3):221–244. Tucson.

Cutright, Paul R.
1969   Lewis and Clark: Pioneering Naturalists. Urbana: University of Illinois Press.

Cutter, Donald C.
1963   Early Spanish Artists on the Northwest Coast. *Pacific Northwest Quarterly* 54(4):150–157.

1963a   Spanish Scientific Exploration Along the Pacific Coast. Pp. 151–160, 243–245 in The American West: An Appraisal. Robert G. Ferris, ed. Santa Fe: Museum of New Mexico Press.

DRHA=Documents Relative to the History of Alaska
1936–1938   Alaska History Research Project, 1936–1938. (Manuscripts in the Library of Congress, Washington.)

Daiutolo, Robert, Jr.
1983   The Early Quaker Perception of the Indian. *Quaker History* 72(2):103–119.

Dale, Harrison C., ed.
1941   The Ashley-Smith Explorations and the Discovery of a Central Route to the Pacific, 1822–1829. Rev. ed. Glendale, Calif.: Arthur H. Clark.

Dallett, Francis J.
1965   The American Museum in Britain, Calverton Manor, Bath. Wilmington, Del.: The Wemyss Foundation.

Dallimore, Arnold
1970–1979   George Whitefield: The Life and Times of the Great Evangelist of the Eighteenth-century Revival. 2 vols. Westchester, Ill.: Cornerstone Books.

Danker, William J.
1971   Profit for the Lord: Economic Activities in Moravian Missions and the Basel Mission Trading Company. Grand Rapids, Mich.: Eardmans.

Danky, James P., and Maureen E. Hady, eds. and comps.
1984   Native American Periodicals and Newspapers, 1828–1982: Bibliography, Publishing Record, and Holdings. Westport, Conn.: Greenwood Press.

Danziger, Edmund J., Jr.
1978   The Chippewas of Lake Superior. Norman: University of Oklahoma Press.

Darlington, William M., ed.
1893   Christopher Gist's Journals with Historical, Geographical and Ethnological Notes and Biographies of His Contemporaries. Pittsburgh, Pa.: J.R. Weldon.

Darnell, Regna D.
1967   Daniel Garrison Brinton: An Intellectual Biography. (Unpublished M.A. Thesis in Anthropology, University of Pennsylvania, Philadelphia.)

1969   The Development of American Anthropology, 1879–1920: From the Bureau of American Ethnology to Franz Boas. (Unpublished Ph.D. Dissertation in Anthropology, University of Pennsylvania, Philadelphia.)

Darrah, William C.
1957   Powell of the Colorado. Princeton, N.J.: Princeton University Press.

Daugherty, Wayne
1983   Treaty Research Report: Treaty One and Treaty Two. Ottawa: Department of Indian and Northern Affairs, Research Branch.

Daugherty, Wayne, and Dennis Madill
1980   Indian Government Under Indian Act Legislation, 1868–1951. Ottawa: Department of Indian and Northern Affairs, Research Branch.

Daumann, Rudolf H.
1957   Sitting Bull; Grosser Häuptling der Sioux. Berlin: Verlag Neues Leben.

1957a   Die vier Pfeile der Cheyenne. Berlin: Verlag Neues Leben.

1958   Der Untergang der Dakota. Berlin: Verlag Neues Leben.

David, Jean
1948   Voltaire et les Indiens d'Amérique. *Modern Language Quarterly* 9(1):90–103.

Davidson, George
1869   Pacific Coast. Coast Pilot of Alaska, (First Part). From Southern Boundary to Cook's Inlet. Washington: U.S. Government Printing Office.

Davidson, Gordon C.
1918   The North West Company. *University of California Publications in History* 7. Berkeley. (Reprinted: Russell and Russell, New York, 1967.)

Davidson, Levette J.
1948   White Versions of Indian Myths and Legends. *California Folklore Quarterly* 7(2):115–128.

Davis, A.C.
1867   Frauds of the Indian Office: Argument of A.C. Davis Before the Committee on Indian Affairs of the House of Representatives, January 12, 1867. Washington.

Davis, Andrew M.
1887   The Employment of Indian Auxiliaries in the American War. *English Historical Review* 2(8):709–728.

Davis, James T.
1961   Trade Routes and Economic Exchange Among the Indians of California. *University of California Archaeological Survey Reports* 54. Berkeley. (Reprinted: Pp. 1–80 in Aboriginal California: Three Studies in Culture History. Robert F. Heizer, ed., University of California Press, Berkeley, 1963.)

Davis, John
1589   The First Voyage of M. John Davis, Undertaken in June 1585 for the Discoverie of the Northwest Passage. Written by M. John Marchant. London: no publisher.

———   Captain Smith and Princess Pocahontas, an Indian Tale. Philadelphia: Benjamin Warner.

Davis, Nancy Yaw
1971   The Effects of the 1964 Alaska Earthquake, Tsunami, and Resettlement on Two Koniag Eskimo Villages. (Unpublished Ph.D. Dissertation in Anthropology, University of Washington, Seattle.)

Davis, Ralph
1973   The Rise of the Atlantic Economies. Ithaca, N.Y.: Cornell University Press.

Davis, Richard B.
1978   Intellectual Life in the Colonial South, 1585–1763. 3 vols. Knoxville: University of Tennessee Press.

Davis, William L.
1943   Mission St. Anne of the Cayuse Indians, 1847–1848. (Unpublished Ph.D. Dissertation in Anthropology, University of California, Berkeley.)

Davydov, Gavriil I.
1977   Two Voyages to Russian America, 1802–1807. Colin Bearne, trans. (Materials for the Study of Alaska History 10.) Kingston, Ont.: The Limestone Press.

Dawes, Henry L.
1880   The Indian Policy: Speech of Hon. Henry L. Dawes of Massachusetts, in the Senate of the United States, April 5, 1880. [Washington: U.S. Government Printing Office.]

———
1899   Have We Failed with the Indian? Atlantic Monthly 84(502):280–285.

Dawson, William C., comp.
1831   Compilation of the Laws of the State of Georgia, 1819–1829 [etc.]. Milledgeville, Ga.: Grantland and Orne.

Day, Donald, and Harry H. Ullom, eds.
1954   The Autobiography of Sam Houston. Norman: University of Oklahoma Press. (Reprinted: Greenwood Press, Westport, Conn., 1980.)

Day, Gordon M.
1953   The Indian as an Ecological Factor in the Northeastern Forest. Ecology 34(2):329–346.

Debo, Angie
1934   The Rise and Fall of the Choctaw Republic. Norman: University of Oklahoma Press. (Reprinted in 1961.)

———
1940   And Still the Waters Run: The Betrayal of the Five Civilized Tribes. Princeton, N.J.: Princeton University Press.

———
1941   The Road to Disappearance. Norman: University of Oklahoma Press.

———
1970   A History of Indians in the United States. Norman: University of Oklahoma Press.

De Bry, Theodor see Bry, Theodor de

De Cesco, Federica
1957   Le Foulard rouge. Verviers, Belgium: Gérard.

1961   Cathy des Navajos. Verviers, Belgium: Gérard.

Deetz, James
1971   Man's Imprint from the Past: Readings in the Methods of Archaeology. Boston: Little, Brown.

Defouri, James H.
1893   The Martyrs of New Mexico: A Brief Account of the Lives and Deaths of the Earliest Missionaries in the Territory. Las Vegas, Nev.: Revista Catolica.

DeKorne, John C.
1947   Navaho and Zuni for Christ: Fifty Years of Indian Missions, Grand Rapids, Mich.: Christian Reformed Board of Missions.

Delanglez, Jean
1935   The French Jesuits in Lower Louisiana (1700–1763). Catholic University of America. Studies in American Church History 21. Washington.

———
1941   Hennepin's Description of Louisiana, a Critical Essay. Chicago: Institute of Jesuit History.

———
1985   A Jean Delanglez, S.J. Anthology: Selections Useful for Mississippi Valley and Trans-Mississippi American Indian Studies. Mildred M. Wedel, ed. New York: Garland.

Deléry, Charles
1878   Chroniques indiennes. Comptes Rendus 1 (January).

Delisle, Louis François
1722   Arlequin sauvage, comédie en trois actes. Paris: Hochereau. (Reprinted: Century Modern Language Series, N.A. Goodyear, ed., New York, 1928.)

Deloria, Vine, Jr.
1969   Custer Died for Your Sins: An Indian Manifesto. New York: Macmillan.

———
1969a   Custer Died for Your Sins. Playboy 16 (August):131.

———
1970   We Talk, You Listen: New Tribes, New Turf. New York: Macmillan.

———
1971   Of Utmost Good Faith. New York: Bantam Books.

———
1973   God is Red. New York: Grossett and Dunlap. (Reprinted: Dell, New York, 1983.)

———
1974   Behind the Trail of Broken Treaties: An Indian Declaration of Independence. New York: Delacorte Press.

Deloria, Vine, Jr., and Clifford M. Lytle
1983   American Indians, American Justice. Austin: University of Texas Press.

———
1984   The Nations within: The Past and Future of American Indian Sovereignty. New York: Pantheon Books.

DeMallie, Raymond J.
1979   Ayn Rand Meets Hiawatha [A Review of Hanta Yo.] The Nation 228(16):469–470.

———
1980   Touching the Pen: Plains Indian Treaty Councils in Ethnohistorical Perspective. Pp. 38–53 in Ethnicity on the Great Plains. Frederick C. Luebke, ed. Lincoln: University of Nebraska Press.

———
1982   The Lakota Ghost Dance: An Ethnohistorical Account. Pacific Historical Review 51(4):385–405.

———, ed.
1984   The Sixth Grandfather: Black Elk's Teachings Given to John G. Neihardt. Lincoln: University of Nebraska Press.

DeMille, Richard
1976   Castañeda's Journey: The Power and the Allegory. Santa Barbara, Calif.: Capra Press.

———, ed.
1980   The Don Juan Papers: Further Castañeda Controversies. Santa Barbara, Calif.: Ross-Erikson.

Dempsey, Hugh A.
1984   Big Bear: The End of Freedom. Lincoln: University of Nebraska Press.

Denton, Lynn W.
1971–1972   Mark Twain and the American Indian. Mark Twain Journal 16(1):1–3. New York.

Denton, Vernon L.
1929   Simon Fraser. Toronto: Ryerson Press.

dePalo, William A., Jr.
1973   The Establishment of the Nueva Vizcaya Militia During the Administration of Teodoro de Croix 1776–1783. *New Mexico Historical Review* 48(3):223–249.

Dependahl, Deborah L.
[1971] Indians in the Winterthur (Henry Francis Dupont Winterthur Museum) Collection. (Typed list of numbers and descriptions of artifacts representing Indians; in Rayna Green's possession.)

DePuy, Henry F., comp.
1917   A Bibliography of the English Colonial Treaties with the American Indians, Including a Synopsis of Each Treaty. New York: The Lenox Club. (Reprinted: AMS Press, New York, 1971.)

De Rosier, Arthur H., Jr.
1970   The Removal of the Choctaw Indians. Knoxville: University of Tennessee Press.

――――   Cyrus Kingsbury—Missionary to the Choctaws. *Journal of Presbyterian History* 50(4):267–287.
1972

De Schweinitz, Edmund A.
1871   The Life and Times of David Zeisberger, the Western Pioneer and Apostle of the Indians. Philadelphia: J.B. Lippincott.

De Smet, Pierre Jean *see* Smet, Pierre Jean de

Desmond, Humphrey J.
1912   The A.P.A. Movement: A Sketch. Washington: The New Century Press. (Reprinted: Arno Press, New York, 1969.)

Désy, Pierrette
1983   Trente ans de captivité chez les indiens Ojibwa. As told by John Tanner. Paris: Payot.

Detroit Post and Tribune
1880   Zachariah Chandler: An Outline Sketch of His Life and Public Services. Detroit, Mich.: The Post and Tribune Company.

De Voto, Bernard
1947   Across the Wide Missouri. Boston: Houghton, Mifflin.

Dexter, Franklin B.
1885   Biographical Sketches of the Graduates of Yale College, with Annals of the College History. New York: Henry Holt.

Dexter, Ralph W.
1966   Contributions of Frederic Ward Putnam to the Development of Anthropology in California. *Science Education* 50(4):314–318.

――――   Frederic Ward Putnam and the Development of Museums of Natural History and Anthropology in the United States. *Curator* 9(2):151–155.
1966a

――――   The Role of F.W. Putnam in Developing Anthropology at the American Museum of Natural History. *Curator* 19(4):303–310.
1976

――――   F.W. Putnam's Role in Developing the Peabody Museum of American Archaeology and Ethnology. *Curator* 23(3):183–194.
1980

Dickason, Olive P.
1976   Louisbourg and the Indians: A Study in Imperial Race Relations, 1713–1760. Ottawa: Parks Canada.

――――   The Myth of the Savage and the Beginnings of French Colonialism in the Americas. Edmonton: University of Alberta Press.
1984

――――   From "One Nation" in the Northeast to "New Nation" in the Northwest: A Look at the Emergence of the Métis. Pp.
1985

19–36 in The New Peoples: Being and Becoming Métis in North America. Jacqueline Peterson and Jennifer S.H. Brown, eds. Winnipeg: University of Manitoba Press.

Dickinson, John A.
1981   Annaotaha et Dollard vus de l'autre côté de la palissade. *Revue d'Histoire de l'Amérique Française* 35(2):163–178. Montreal.

――――   La Guerre iroquoise et la mortalité en Nouvelle-France, 1608–1666. *Revue d'Histoire de l'Amérique Française* 36(1):31–54. Montreal.
1982

Dickson, Lovat
1939   Half-Breed: The Story of Grey Owl (Wa-Sha-Quon-Asin). London: Peter Davis.

Dictionary of Indians of North America
1978   John Ridge. Pp. 19–21 in Vol. 3 of Dictionary of Indians of North America. Harry Waldman et al., eds. St. Clair Shores, Mich.: Scholarly Press.

Didier, Théophile
1973   Hudson Bay-Alaska 1972. *Eskimo* n.s. 5:10–21. Churchill, Man.

Diket, A.L.
1966   The Noble Savage Convention as Epitomized in John Lawson's "A New Voyage to Carolina." *North Carolina Historical Review* 43(4):413–429.

Dillon, Richard H.
1965   Meriwether Lewis: A Biography. New York: Coward McCann.

――――   Burnt-out Fires: California's Modoc Indian War. Englewood Cliffs, N.J.: Prentice-Hall.
1973

Din, Gilbert C., and Albert P. Nasatir
1983   The Imperial Osages: Spanish-Indian Diplomacy in the Mississippi Valley. Norman: University of Oklahoma Press.

Di Peso, Charles C.
1974   Casas Grandes: A Fallen Trade Center of the Gran Chichimeca. 3 vols. *Amerind Foundation Series* 9. Dragoon, Ariz.

Dippie, Brian W.
1970   The Vanishing American: Popular Attitudes and American Indian Policy in the 19th Century. (Unpublished Ph.D. Dissertation in American Studies/History, University of Texas, Austin.)

――――   The Vanishing American: White Attitudes and United States Indian Policy. Middletown, Conn.: Wesleyan University Press.
1982

Dmytryshyn, Basil, and E.A.P. Crownhart-Vaughan, eds. and trans.
1979   The End of Russian America: Captain P.N. Golovin's Last Report, 1862. Portland: Oregon Historical Society.

Dobyns, Henry F.
1968   Therapeutic Experience of Responsible Democracy. Pp. 268–291 in The American Indian Today. Stuart Levine and Nancy O. Lurie, eds. Baltimore, Md.: Penguin Books.

――――   Spanish Colonial Tucson: A Demographic History. Tucson: University of Arizona Press.
1976

――――   From Fire to Flood: Historic Human Destruction of Sonoran Desert Riverine Oases. *Ballena Press Anthropological Papers* 20. Socorro, N.M..
1981

――――   Trade Centers: The Concept and a Rancherian Culture Area Example. (Unpublished paper presented to the American Society for Ethnohistory Conference, Colorado Springs.)
1981a

_____
1983   Their Number Become Thinned: Native American Population Dynamics in Eastern North America. Knoxville: University of Tennessee Press.

Dobyns, Henry F., et al.

1957   Thematic Changes in Yuman Warfare. Pp. 46–71 in Cultural Stability and Cultural Change. *Proceedings of the 1957 Annual Spring Meeting of the American Ethnological Society.* Verne F. Ray, ed. Seattle. (Reprinted: AMS Press, New York, 1985.)

Dockstader, Frederick J.
1977   Great North American Indians: Profiles in Life and Leadership. New York: Van Nostrand Reinhold.

Dodds, Gordon B.
1977   Fur Trade in the United States. Pp. 422–426 in The Reader's Encyclopedia of the American West. Howard R. Lamar, ed. New York: Thomas Y. Crowell.

Dodge, Grenville M.
1905   Biographical Sketch of James Bridger, Mountaineer, Trapper and Guide. New York: Unz and Company.

Dodge, Robert K., and Joseph B. McCullough, eds.
1985   New and Old Voices of Wah'Kon-Tah. New York: International Publishers.

Dolfin, John
1921   Bringing the Gospel in Hogan and Pueblo, 1896–1921. Grand Rapids, Mich.: Van Noord.

Dollar, Clyde
1977   The High Plains Smallpox Epidemic of 1837–38. *Western Historical Quarterly* 8(1):15–38.

Dollier de Casson, François
1928   A History of Montreal, 1640–1672, from the French of Dollier de Casson. Ralph Flenley, ed. New York: E.P. Dutton.

Domínguez, Francisco A.
1956   The Missions of New Mexico, 1776: A Description, by Fray Francisco Atanasio Domínguez, with Other Contemporary Documents. Eleanor B. Adams and Fray Angelico Chavez, eds. Albuquerque: University of New Mexico Press.

Donaldson, Thomas
1887   The George Catlin Indian Gallery in the U.S. National Museum (Smithsonian Institution), with Memoir and Statistics. Washington: U.S. Government Printing Office.

Donck, Adriaen van der
1841   A Description of the New Netherlands [1656]. Jeremiah Johnson, trans. *Collections of the New-York Historical Society* 2d ser., Vol. 1:125–242. New York.

Donnelly, Joseph P.
1947   A Tentative Bibliography for the Colonial Fur Trade in the American Colonies: 1608–1800. *St. Louis University Studies, Monograph Series, Social Sciences* 2. St. Louis.

Donohoe, Thomas
1895   The Iroquois and the Jesuits: The Story of the Labors of Catholic Missionaries Among the Indians. Buffalo, N.Y.: Buffalo Catholic Publications.

Donohue, John A.
1969   After Kino: Jesuit Missions of Northwestern New Spain, 1711–1767. Rome: Jesuit Historical Institute.

Dorosh, John T.
1961   The Alaska Russian Church Collections. *Quarterly Journal of the Library of Congress* 18(4):193–203.

Dorris, Michael A.
1987   A Yellow Raft in Blue Water. New York: H. Holt.

Dorsey, James O.
1884   Omaha Sociology. Pp. 205–370 in *Third Annual Report of the Bureau of American Ethnology for the Years 1881–1882.* Washington.

_____
1885   On the Comparative Phonology of Four Siouan Languages. Pp. 919–929 in *Annual Report of the Smithsonian Institution for 1883.* Washington.

_____
1889   Indians of the Siletz Reservation. *American Anthropologist* o.s. 2(1):55–61.

_____
1890   The Cegiha Language. *Contributions to North American Ethnology* 6. Washington.

_____
1891   The Social Organization of the Siouan Tribes. *Journal of American Folk-Lore* 4(15):257–266, 331–342.

_____
1891a   Omaha and Ponka Letters. *Bureau of American Ethnology Bulletin* 11. Washington.

_____
1894   A Study of Siouan Cults. Pp. 351-544 in *11th Annual Report of the Bureau of American Ethnology for the Years 1889–1890.* Washington.

_____
1897   Siouan Sociology: A Posthumous Paper. Pp. 205–244 in *15th Annual Report of the Bureau of American Ethnology for the Years 1893–1894.* Washington.

Dorsey, James O., and John R. Swanton
1912   A Dictionary of the Biloxi and Ofo Languages . . . *Bureau of American Ethnology Bulletin* 47. Washington.

Dorsey, Jean M., and Maxwell J. Dorsey
1969   Christopher Gist of Maryland and Some of His Descendants, 1679–1957. Chicago: John S. Swift.

Dorson, Richard M.
1946   Comic Indian Anecdotes. *Southern Folklore Quarterly* 10(2):113–128.

Douglas, Walter B.
1911   Manuel Lisa. *Missouri Historical Society Collections* 3(3):232–268, 4(4):367–406. St. Louis.

_____
1964   Manuel Lisa. A.P. Nasatir, ed. New York: Argosy-Antiquarian.

Douville, Raymond, and J.D. Casanova
1967   La Vie quotidienne des Indiens au Canada à l'époque de la colonie française. Paris: Hachette.

Downes, Randolph C.
1940   Council Fires on the Upper Ohio: A Narrative of Indian Affairs in the Upper Ohio Valley Until 1795. Pittsburgh, Pa.: University of Pittsburgh Press.

_____
1945   A Crusade for Indian Reform, 1922–1934. *Mississippi Valley Historical Review* 32(3):331–354.

Downs, James F.
1964   Comments on Plains Indian Cultural Development. *American Anthropologist* 66(2):421–422.

_____
1966   The Two Worlds of the Washo: An Indian Tribe of California and Nevada. New York: Holt, Rinehart and Winston.

Dozier, Edward P.
1958   Spanish-Catholic Influences on Rio Grande Pueblo Religion. *American Anthropologist* 60(3):441–448.

_____
1961   Rio Grande Pueblos. Pp. 94–186 in Perspectives in American Indian Culture Change. Edward H. Spicer, ed. Chicago: University of Chicago Press.

Drake, Samuel A.
1897   The Border Wars of New England, Commonly Called King William's and Queen Anne's Wars. New York: Charles

Scribner's Sons. (Reprinted: Corner House Publishers, Williamstown, Mass., 1973.)

Drake, Samuel G.
1832   Indian Biography, Containing the Lives of More Than Two Hundred Indian Chiefs . . . .Boston: Josiah Drake.

1841   The Book of the Indians; or, Biography and History of the Indians of North America, from Its First Discovery to the Year 1841. Boston: O.L. Perkins etc. (Reprinted: AMS Press, New York, 1976.)

1851   Indian Captivities, or Life in the Wigwam; Being the True Narratives of Captives Who Have Been Carried Away by the Indians, from the Frontier Settlements of the U.S., from the Earliest Period to the Present Time. Auburn, N.Y.: Derby and Miller.

Drinnon, Richard
1980   Facing West: The Metaphysics of Indian-hating and Empire Building. Minneapolis: University of Minnesota Press.

Driver, Carl S.
1932   John Sevier, Pioneer of the Old Southwest. Chapel Hill: University of North Carolina Press.

Driver, Harold
1969   Indians of North America. 2d ed. Chicago: University of Chicago Press.

Droit, Jean
1943   Etoile solitaire, guerrier Dakota. Tournai, France: Casterman.

Droonberg, Emil
1921   Minnehaha. Stuttgart, Germany: Dieck.

1925   Das Siwash-Mädchen. Leipzig, Germany: W. Goldmann.

Drucker, Philip
1958   The Native Brotherhoods: Modern Intertribal Organizations on the Northwest Coast. Bureau of American Ethnology Bulletin 168. Washington. (Reprinted: Scholarly Press, St. Clair Shores, Mich., 1977.)

Drucker, Philip, and Robert F. Heizer
1967   To Make My Name Good: A Reexamination of the Southern Kwakiutl Potlatch. Berkeley: University of California Press.

Drummond, A.M., and Richard Moody
1953   Indian Treaties: The First American Dramas. Quarterly Journal of Speech 39(1):15–24.

Drury, Clifford M.
1936   Henry Harmon Spalding, Pioneer of Old Oregon. Caldwell, Idaho: Caxton Printers.

1937   Marcus Whitman, M.D., Pioneer and Martyr. Caldwell, Idaho: Caxton Printers.

1952   Presbyterian Panorama: One Hundred and Fifty Years of National Missions History. Philadelphia: Westminster Press.

1958   The Diaries and Letters of Henry H. Spalding and Asa Bowen Smith Relating to the Nez Perce Mission, 1838–1842. Glendale, Calif.: Arthur H. Clark.

1963–1966   First White Women Over the Rockies: Diaries, Letters, and Biographical Sketches of the Six Women of the Oregon Mission Who Made the Overland Journey in 1836 and 1838. Glendale, Calif.: Arthur H. Clark.

1973   Marcus and Narcissa Whitman, and the Opening of Old Oregon. 2 vols. Glendale, Calif.: Arthur H. Clark.

DuBois, Daniel
1970   Mode indienne. Western Gazette, March:7–10. Paris.

DuBois, John V.D.
1949   Campaigns in the West, 1856–1861: The Journal and Letters of Colonel John Van Deusen DuBois. George P. Hammond, ed. Tucson: Arizona Pioneers Historical Society.

Duchaussois, Pierre J.B.
1921   Aux Glaces polaires: Indiens et Esquimaux. Paris: Oeuvre des Missions.

Duchet, Michèle
1963   Bougainville, Raynal, Diderot et les sauvages du Canada. Revue d'Histoire Littéraire de la France 63(2):228–236. Paris.

1971   Anthropologie et histoire au siècle des lumières: Buffon, Voltaire, Rousseau, Helvétius, Diderot. Paris: François Maspero.

Ducreux, François
1664   Historiae canadensis, seu Novae-Franciae, libri decem, ad annum usque Christi MDCLVI. Paris: S. Cramoisy et S. Mabre-Cramoisy.

Dudley, Edward, and Maximilian E. Novak, eds.
1972   The Wild Man within: An Image in Western Thought from the Renaissance to Romanticism. Pittsburgh, Pa.: University of Pittsburgh Press.

Duff, Wilson
1964   The Impact of the White Man. Anthropology in British Columbia Memoir 5. Victoria.

Duffus, Robert L.
1930   The Santa Fe Trail. London: Longmans, Green.

Du Hamel, Jacques
1603   Acoubar, ou La Loyauté trahie. Tragédie. Rouen, France: Raphaël du Petit.

Duncan, Janice K.
1972   Minority without a Champion: Kanakas on the Pacific Coast, 1788–1850. Portland: Oregon Historical Society.

Dunham, Harold H.
1952   Governor Charles Bent: Pioneer and Martyr. Pp. 219–267 in Original Contributions to Western History. Noley Mumey, ed. The Westerners Brand Book 7, 1951. Denver, Colo.

1965   Charles Bent. Pp. 27–48 in Vol. 2 of The Mountain Men and the Fur Trade of the Far West. LeRoy R. Hafen, ed. 10 vols. Glendale, Calif.: Arthur H. Clark.

Dunlay, Thomas W.
1982   Wolves for the Blue Soldiers: Indian Scouts and Auxiliaries with the United States Army, 1860–90. Lincoln: University of Nebraska Press.

Dunn, Jacob P.
1886   Massacres of the Mountains: A History of the Indian Wars of the Far West. New York: Harper and Bros.

Dunn, John
1844   History of the Oregon Territory and British North-American Fur Trade; with an Account of the Habits and Customs of the Principal Native Tribes on the Northern Continent. Philadelphia: G.B. Zieber.

Dunn, Richard S.
1972   Sugar and Slaves: The Rise of the Planter Class in the English West Indies, 1624–1713. Chapel Hill: University of North Carolina Press.

Dunn, Stephen P., and Ethel Dunn
1962   The Transformation of Economy and Culture in the Soviet North. Arctic Anthropology 1(1):1–28.

Dunne, Peter M.
1948   Early Jesuit Missions in Tarahumara. Berkeley: University of California Press.

Dunwiddie, Peter W.
1974   The Nature of the Relationship Between the Blackfeet Indians and the Men of the Fur Trade. *Annals of Wyoming* 46(1):123–134. Cheyenne.

Du Périer, Antoine
1601   Les Amours de Pistion. Paris: Thomas de la Ruelle. (Reprinted: Editions de l'Université d'Ottawa, 1943.)

Duplessis, Paul
1856   Le Batteur d'estrade. 5 vols. Paris: A. Cadot.

———
1859   Les Mormons. 5 vols. Paris: A. Cadot.

———
1864   Les Peaux-rouges. Paris: A. Cadot.

Duponceau, Peter S.
[1815–1834] Philological Note-book. (9 Notebooks. Manuscript 61 in American Philosophical Society Manuscript Collection, Philadelphia.)

———
[1820–1844] Indian Vocabularies. (Manuscript 60 in American Philosophical Society, Manuscript Collection, Philadelphia.)

———
1838   Mémoire sur le système grammatical des langues de quelques nations indiennes de l'Amérique du Nord. Paris: A. Pihan de La Forest.

Duratschek, Mary C.
1947   Crusading Along Sioux Trails: A History of the Catholic Indian Missions of South Dakota. Yankton, S.D.: Benedictine Convent of the Sacred Heart.

Durham, Jimmy
1983   Columbus Day. Minneapolis: West End Press.

Durrett, Reuben T.
1884   John Filson, the First Historian of Kentucky: An Account of the Life and Writings, Principally from Original Sources. Louisville, Ky.: J.P. Morton. (Reprinted in 1890.)

Dusenberry, Verne
1958   Waiting for a Day That Never Comes: The Dispossessed Métis of Montana. *Montana: The Magazine of Western History* 8(2):26–39. (Reprinted: Pp. 119–136 in The New Peoples: Being and Becoming Métis in North America. Jacqueline Peterson and Jennifer S.H. Brown, eds. Winnipeg: University of Manitoba Press, 1985.)

Dutton, Clarence E.
1882   Tertiary History of the Grand Cañon District, with Atlas. *United States Geological Survey Monographs* 2. Washington.

D'Wolf, John
1968   A Voyage to the North Pacific and a Journey Through Siberia More Than Half a Century Ago [1861]. Fairfield, Wash: Ye Galleon Press. (Reprinted: Rulon-Miller, Bristol, R.I., 1983.)

Dye, Eva Emory
1902   The Conquest: The True Story of Lewis and Clark. Chicago: A.C. McClurg.

Eaton, John H.
1817   The Life of Andrew Jackson, Major General in the Service of the United States: Comprising a History of the War in the South, from the Commencement of the Creek Campaign, to the Termination of Hostilities Before New Orleans. Commenced by John Reid and Completed by John Henry Eaton. Philadelphia: M. Carey.

Eaves, Lucile
1910   A History of California Labor Legislation. *University of California Publications in Economics* 2. Berkeley.

Eccles, William J.
1959   Frontenac: The Courtier Governor. Toronto: McClelland and Stewart.

———
1964   Canada Under Louis XIV, 1663–1701. Toronto: McClelland and Stewart.

———
1969   The Canadian Frontier, 1534–1760. New York: Holt, Rinehart and Winston. (Reprinted: University of New Mexico Press, Albuquerque, 1974, 1983.)

———
1979   A Belated Review of Harold Innis' "The Fur Trade in Canada." *Canadian Historical Review* 60(4):419–441. Toronto.

———
1983   The Fur Trade and Eighteenth Century Imperialism. *William and Mary Quarterly* 3d ser. Vol. 40(3):341–362. Williamsburg, Va.

———
1984   Sovereignty Association, 1500–1783. *Canadian Historical Review* 65(4):475–510. Toronto.

———
1984a   La Mer de l'Ouest: Outpost of Empire. Pp. 1–14 in *Rendezvous: Selected Papers of the Fourth North American Fur Trade Conference, 1981.* Thomas C. Buckley, ed. St. Paul, Minn.: The Conference.

Eckhart, George B.
1967   Spanish Missions of Texas, 1680–1800. *The Kiva* 32(3):73–95.

Eckley, Joseph
1806   A Discourse Before the Society for Propagating the Gospel Among the Indians and Others in North America: Delivered Nov. 7, 1805. Boston: E. Lincoln.

Edmunds, R. David
1978   The Potawatomis, Keepers of the Fire. Norman: University of Oklahoma Press.

———
1984   Tecumseh and the Quest for Indian Leadership. Boston: Little, Brown.

Eells, Edwin
1914   Eliza and the Nez Perce Indians. *Washington Historical Quarterly* 5(4):288–299.

Eells, Myron
1877   The Twana Indians of the Skokomish Reservation in Washington Territory. *Bulletin of the United States Geological and Geographical Survey of the Territories* 3(1):57–114.

———
1881   History of the Congregational Association of Oregon, and Washington Territory; the Home Missionary Society of Oregon and Adjoining Territories; and the Northwestern Association of Congregational Ministers. Portland, Oreg.: House of Himes.

———
1882   History of Indian Missions on the Pacific Coast: Oregon, Washington and Idaho. Philadelphia: The American Sunday-School Union.

———
1883   Marcus Whitman, M.D., Proofs of His Work in Saving Oregon to the United States, and in Promoting the Immigration of 1843. Portland, Oreg.: House of Himes.

———
1886   Ten Years of Missionary Work Among the Indians at Skokomish, Washington Territory, 1874–1884. Boston: Congregational Sunday-School and Publishing Society. (Reprinted: Shorey Book Store, Seattle, Wash., 1972.)

———
1889   The Twana, Chemakum, and Klallam Indians of Washington Territory. Pp. 605–681 in *Annual Report of the Smithsonian Institution for 1887.* Washington. (Reprinted: Shorey Book Store, Seattle, Wash., 1971.)

———
1894   Father Eells; or, The Results of Fifty-Five Years of Missionary Labors in Washington and Oregon: A Biography of Rev. Cushing Eells, D.D. Boston: Congregational Sunday-School and Publishing Society.

1985   The Indians of Puget Sound: The Notebooks of Myron Eells. George P. Castile, ed. Seattle: University of Washington Press.

Egede, Hans P.
1738   Omstaendelig og udførlig relation, angaaende den grønlandske missions begyndelse of forsaettelse, samt hvad ellers mere der ved landets recognoscering, dets beskaffenhed, og indbyggernes vaesen of leve-maade vedkommende, er befunden [Circumstantial and Detailed Relation Concerning the Beginning and Continuation of the Greenland Mission, and whatever else was Found at the Country's Reconnaissance Relating to its Condition and the Inhabitants' Nature and Way of Life.] Copenhagen: Trykt hos J.C. Groth.

1741   Det gamle Grønlands nye perlustration eller natural historie, og beskrivelse over det gamle Grønlands situation, luft, temperament og beskaffenhed [The New Perlustration or Natural History of Old Greenland, and Description of the Situation, Air, Temperament, and Character of Old Greenland]. Copenhagen: J.C. Groth.

1745   A Description of Greenland Shewing the Natural History, Situation, Boundaries, and Face of the Country . . . London: C. Hitch. (Reprinted: T. and J. Allman, London, 1818.)

Eggermont, J.L.
1960   Kleine Bever, de Owaga-indiaan. Harlem, The Netherlands: De Spaarneilad.

Eisinger, Chester E.
1948   The Puritans' Justification for Taking the Land. *Essex Institute Historical Collections* 84(2):131–143. Salem, Mass.

Ekirch, Arthur H., Jr.
1974   Cheyenne and Arapaho Indians *vs.* the United States: Historical Background. Pp. 175–226 in Arapaho-Cheyenne Indians. New York: Garland.

Eliot, John
1661   The New Testament of Our Lord and Saviour Jesus Christ; Translated into the Indian Language and Ordered to Be Printed by the Commissioners of the United Colonies in New-England. Cambridge, Mass.: Samuel Green and Marmaduke Johnson.

1880   The Indian Primer; or, The Way of Training Up of Our Indian Youth in the Good Knowledge of God, 1669. Edinburgh, Scotland: Andrew Elliot.

1904   The Logic Primer [1672]. Cleveland, Ohio: Burrows Brothers.

Elliott, Charles W.
1937   Winfield Scott, the Soldier and the Man. New York: Macmillan.

Elliott, John H.
1970   The Old World and the New, 1492–1650. Cambridge, England: Cambridge University Press.

1972   The Discovery of America and the Discovery of Man. *Proceedings of the British Academy* 58:101–125. London.

Ellis, Edward S.
1860   Seth Jones; or, The Captives of the Frontier. New York: I.P. Beadle.

Ellis, Elmer
1941   Henry Moore Teller, Defender of the West. Caldwell, Idaho: Caxton Printers.

Ellis, George E.
1848   Life of John Mason of Connecticut. Pp. 307–438 in Vol. 13 of The Library of American Biography. 25 vols. Jared Sparks, ed. Boston: Little, Brown.

Ellis, John T.
1965   Catholics in Colonial America. (*Benedictine Studies* 8) Baltimore, Md.: Helicon Press.

Ellis, Richard N.
1970   General Pope and U.S. Indian Policy. Albuquerque: University of New Mexico Press.

1979   Robert L. Bennett, 1966–69. Pp. 325–331 in The Commissioners of Indian Affairs, 1824–1977. Robert M. Kvasnicka and Herman J. Viola, eds. Lincoln: University of Nebraska Press.

Ellison, Robert S.
1931   Fort Bridger: A Brief History. Caspar: The Historical Landmark Commission of Wyoming. (Reprinted: The Wyoming State Archives, Museums and Historical Department, Cheyenne, 1981.)

Ellison, William H.
1922   The Federal Indian Policy in California, 1846–1860. *Mississippi Valley Historical Review* 9(1):37–67.

Elmendorf, W.W., and Alfred L. Kroeber
1960   The Structure of Twana Culture With Comparative Notes on the Structure of Yurok Culture. *Washington State University Research Studies, Monographic Supplement* 2. Pullman.

Elsbree, Oliver W.
1928   The Rise of the Missionary Spirit in America, 1790–1815. Williamsport, Pa.: Williamsport Printing and Binding Company.

Emerson, Dorothy
1973   Among the Mescalero Apaches: The Story of Father Albert Braun, O.F.M. Tucson: University of Arizona Press.

Emerson, Roger L.
1979   American Indians, Frenchman, and Scots Philosophers. *Studies in Eighteenth Century Culture* 9: 211–236. Madison, Wis.

Engelhardt, Zephyrin
1899   The Franciscans in Arizona. Harbor Springs, Mich.: Holy Childhood Indian School.

1908–1915   The Missions and Missionaries of California. 4 vols. San Francisco: James H. Barry.

Englund, Erik
1971   Indianernas när, vär, hur. Stockholm: Forum.

Episcopal Church. National Committee on Indian Work
1970   This Land is Our Land; The American Indian in American Society, 1970. [New York: The Executive Council of the Episcopal Church.]

1973-   Newsletter. [New York: The Executive Council of the Episcopal Church.]

Erasmus, Charles J.
1953   Las Dimensiones de la cultura: historia de la etnología en los Estados Unidos entre 1900 y 1950. Bogota, Columbia: Editorial Iqueima.

Erdman, Charles R., Jr.
1931   Theodore Frelinghuysen. Pp. 16–17 in Vol. 7 of Dictionary of American Biography. Allen Johnson, et al. eds. New York: Scribner's.

Erdrich, Louise
1984   Love Medicine. New York: Holt, Rinehart, and Winston.

Erickson, Donald A., and Henrietta Schwartz
1969   Community School at Rough Rock. (U.S. Department of Commerce Doc. PB 184571.) Springfield, Va.: National Technical Information Service.

Ericson, Stig
1963   Präriens pionjärer. Stockholm: Albert Bonnier.

735

1963a   Indianupproret. Stockholm: Albert Bonnier.

1964   Diligensöverfallet. Stockholm: Albert Bonnier.

1965   Vilda Västernshjältar. Stockholm: Albert Bonnier.

Esarey, Logan, ed.
1922   Messages and Letters of Governor William Henry Harrison. 2 vols. Indianapolis: Indiana Historical Commission.

Espinosa, J. Manuel
1942   Crusaders of the Rio Grande: The Story of Don Diego de Vargas and the Reconquest and Refounding of New Mexico. Chicago: Institute of Jesuit History.

Estergreen, M. Morgan
1962   Kit Carson: A Portrait in Courage. Norman: University of Oklahoma Press.

Evans, G. Edward, and Karin Abbey
1979   Bibliography of Language Arts Materials for Native North Americans. Los Angeles: University of California, American Indian Studies Center.

Evans, James
1837   The Speller and Interpreter in Indian and English for the Use of the Mission Schools, and Such as May Desire to Obtain a Knowledge of the Ojibway Tongues. New York: D. Farnshaw.

1954   Cree Syllabic Hymn Book [1841]. Margaret V. Ray, introd.; Raymond B. Horsefield, trans. *Bibliographical Society of Canada Facsimile Series* 4. Toronto.

Evans, James L.
1967   The Indian Savage, the Mexican Bandit, the Chinese Heathen — Three Popular Stereotypes. (Unpublished Ph.D. Dissertation in Literature, University of Texas, Austin.)

Evarts, Jeremiah
1829   Essays on the Present Crisis in the Condition of the American Indians; First Published in the National Intelligencer, Under the Signature of William Penn. Boston: Perkins and Marvin.

————, ed.
1830   Speeches on the Passage of the Bill for the Removal of the Indians Delivered in the Congress of the United States, April and May, 1830. Boston: Perkins and Marvin.

1956   Through the South and the West with Jeremiah Evarts in 1826. J. Orin Oliphant, ed. Lewisburg, Pa.: Bucknell University Press.

Everwien, Folkert
1972   Dort, wo die Massachusets hausten. Norden, Germany: Arbeitsgruppe für nordamerikanische Indianer.

Ewers, John C.
1948   Gustavus Schon's Portraits of Flathead and Pend d'Oreille Indians, 1854. *Smithsonian Miscellaneous Collections* 110(7). Washington.

1949   An Anthropologist Looks at Early Pictures of North American Indians. *New York Historical Society Quarterly* 33(4):223–234.

1954   The Indian Trade of the Upper Missouri Before Lewis and Clark: An Interpretation. *Bulletin of the Missouri Historical Society* 10(4):429–446. St. Louis.

1955   The Horse in Blackfoot Indian Culture; with Comparative Material from Other Western Tribes. *Bureau of American Ethnology Bulletin* 159. Washington. (Reprinted: Smithsonian Institution Press, Washington, 1980.)

1956   George Catlin, Painter of Indians and the West. Pp. 483–506 in *Annual Report of the Smithsonian Institution for 1955*. Washington.

1958   The Blackfeet: Raiders on the Northwestern Plains. Norman: University of Oklahoma Press.

1962   Mothers of the Mixed Bloods. *El Palacio* 69(1):20–29.

1963   Iroquois Indians in the Far West. *Montana: The Magazine of Western History* 13(2):2–10.

1965   Hair Pipes in Plains Indian Adornment: A Study in Indian and White Ingenuity. *Anthropological Papers* 50, *Bureau of American Ethnology Bulletin* 164. Washington.

1965a   The Emergence of the Plains Indian as the Symbol of the North American Indian. Pp. 531–545 in *Annual Report of the Smithsonian Institution for 1964*. Washington.

1966   "Chiefs From the Missouri and Mississippi" and Peale's Silhouettes of 1806. *Smithsonian Journal of History* 1(1):1–26.

1967   Fact and Fiction in the Documentary Art of the American West. Pp. 79–95 in the Frontier Reexamined. John F. McDermott, ed. Urbana: University of Illinois Press.

1968   Indian Life of the Upper Missouri. Norman: University of Oklahoma Press.

1971   Not Quite Redmen: The Plains Indian Illustrations of Felix O.C. Darley. *American Art Journal* 3(2):88–98.

1972   The Influence of the Fur Trade Upon the Indians of the Northern Plains. Pp. 1–26 in People and Pelts: Selected Papers of the Second North American Fur Trade Conference. Mavina Bolus, ed. Winnipeg, Man.: Peguis Publishers.

1973   The Influence of Epidemics on the Indian Populations and Cultures of Texas. *Plains Anthropologist* 18(60):104–115.

1976   Indian Views of the White Man Prior to 1850: An Interpretation. Pp. 7–23 in Red Men and Hat Wearers: Viewpoints in Indian History. Daniel Tyler, ed. Fort Collins: Colorado State University.

Ewing, James R.
1902   Public Services of Jacob Dolson Cox, Governor of Ohio and Secretary of the Interior. Washington: The Neale Publishing Company.

Eyma, Louis X.
1854   Les Peaux-rouges. Paris: D. Giraud.

Ezell, Paul H.
1955   Indians Under the Law: Mexico, 1821–1847. *América Indígena* 15(3):199–214.

1961   The Hispanic Acculturation of the Gila River Pimas. *Memoirs of the American Anthropological Association* 90. Menasha, Wis.

Fabietti, Alfredo
1950   I lupi di montagna. Como, Italy: A. Noseda.

Fabila, Alfonso
1940   Las Tribus Yaquis de Sonora: su cultura y Anhelada autodeterminación. Mexico City: Departmento de Asuntos Indígenas.

Fahey, John
1974   The Flathead Indians. Norman: University of Oklahoma Press.

736

[Faillon, Etienne-Michel]
1865–1866   Histoire de la colonie française en Canada. 3 vols. [Montreal]: Bibliothèque paroissiale.

Fairbanks, Charles H.
1973   The Florida Seminole People. Phoenix, Ariz.: Indian Tribal Series.

Fairchild, Hoxie N.
1982   The Noble Savage: A Study in Romantic Naturalism. New York: Columbia University Press. (Reprinted: Russell and Russell, New York, 1961.)

Faulkner, Robert K.
1968   The Jurisprudence of John Marshall. Princeton, N.J.: Princeton University Press. (Reprinted: Greenwood Press, Westport, Conn., 1980.)

Faulkner, William
1942   Three Famous Short Novels: Spotted Horses; Old Man; The Bear. New York: Random House.

Faust, Harold S.
1943   The Presbyterian Mission to the American Indians During the Period of Indian Removal, 1838–1893. (Unpublished Ph.D. Dissertation in Anthropology, Temple University, Philadelphia.)

Faust, Richard H.
1975   William Medill: Commissioner of Indian Affairs, 1845–1849. *Old Northwest* 1(June):129–140.

Fay, George E., ed.
1972   Treaties, and Land Cessions, Between the Bands of the Sioux and the United States of America, 1805–1906. *University of Northern Colorado, Museum of Anthropology, Occasional Publications in Anthropology, Ethnology Series* 24. Greeley.

Feder, Norman
[1971]   American Indian Art. New York: Harry N. Abrams.

Federal Council of the Churches of Christ in America
1938   American Indians and the Indian Service. *Bureau of Research and Survey Information Service* 17(24). New York.

Fedorova, Svetlana Grigor'evna
1973   The Russian Population in Alaska and California: Late 18th Century-1867 (*Materials for the Study of Alaska History* 4). Richard A. Pierce and Alton S. Donnelly, eds. and trans. Kingston, Ont.: Limestone Press.

Feest, Christian F.
1967   The Virginia Indians in Pictures, 1612–1624. *Smithsonian Journal of History* 2(1):1–30.

1983   The Grey Owl Society. *American Indian Workshop Newsletter* 15 (December):6. Vienna.

Fehrman, Richard J.
1972   The Mountain Men: A Statistical View. Pp. 9–15 in Vol. 10 of The Mountain Men and the Fur Trade of the Far West. LeRoy Hafen, ed. Glendale, Calif.: Arthur H. Clark.

Felde, Max *see* Kaltenboeck, Johann

Fénelon, François de Salignac de la Mothe
[1845]   Aventures de Télémaque, fils d'Ulysse [1699]. New ed. Philadelphia: E. Barrington and G.D. Haswell.

Fenin, George N., and William K. Everson
1962   The Western, from Silents to Cinerama. New York: Orion Press.

Fenton, William N.
1953   A Calendar of Manuscript Materials Relating to the History of the Six Nations or Iroquois Indians in Depositories Outside of Philadelphia, 1750–1850. *Proceedings of the American Philosophical Society* 97(5):578–595. Philadelphia.

1956   Toward the Gradual Civilization of the Indian Natives: The Missionary and Linguistic Work of Asher Wright (1803–1875) Among the Senecas of Western New York. *Proceedings of the American Philosophical Society* 100(6):567–581. Philadelphia.

————, ed.
1957   Seneca Indians by Asher Wright [1859]. *Ethnohistory* 4(3):302–321.

————
1959   John Reed Swanton, 1873–1958. *American Anthropologist* 61(4):663–668.

————
1969   Joseph–François Lafitau (1681–1748), Precursor of Scientific Anthropology. *Southwestern Journal of Anthropology* 25(2):173–187.

————
1971   The New York State Wampum Collection: The Case for Integrity of Cultural Treasures. *Proceedings of the American Philosophical Society* 115(6):437–461. Philadelphia.

————
1985   Structure, Continuity, and Change in the Process of Iroquois Treaty Making. Pp. 3–36 in The History and Culture of Iroquois Diplomacy. Francis Jennings et al., eds. Syracuse, N.Y.: Syracuse University Press.

Fenton, William N., and Elizabeth L. Moore, eds. and trans.
1974–1977   Customs of the American Indians Compared with the Customs of Primitive Times, by Joseph-François Lafitau. 2 vols. Toronto: The Champlain Society.

Ferber, Edna
1930   Cimmaron. Garden City, N.Y.: Doubleday.

Ferguson, Leland, ed.
1977   Historical Archaeology and the Importance of Material Things. Columbia, S.C.: Society for Historical Archaeology.

Ferling, John E.
1980   A Wilderness of Miseries: War and Warriors in Early America. Westport, Conn.: Greenwood Press.

Fernow, Berthold
1884   New Netherland, or the Dutch in North America. Pp. 395–442 in Vol. 4 of Narrative and Critical History of America. Justin Winsor, ed. 8 vols. Boston: Houghton, Mifflin.

Ferry, Gabriel
1850   Le Courreur des bois. Paris: F. Didot.

1855   Le Dragon de la reine, ou Costal l'Indien. Paris: L. Potter.

Fey, Harold E.
1955   Our National Indian Policy. *The Christian Century* (March 30):395–397.

Fey, Harold E., and D'Arcy McNickle
1959   Indians and Other Americans: Two Ways of Life Meet. New York: Harper and Bros. (Rev. ed. in 1970.)

Fiedler, Leslie A.
1969   The Return of the Vanishing American. New York: Stein and Day.

Fife, Austine E., and Francesca Redden
1954   The Pseudo-Indian Folksongs of the Anglo-American and French Canadian. *Journal of American Folklore* 67(265):239–251, (266):379–394.

Filson, John
1784   The Discovery, Settlement and Present State of Kentucke [etc.]. Wilmington, Del.: James Adams. (Reprinted: Peter Smith, Gloucester, Mass., 1975.)

Finger, John R.
1984   The Eastern Band of Cherokees, 1891–1900. Knoxville: University of Tennessee Press.

Finley, James B.
1840   History of the Wyandott Mission at Upper Sandusky, Ohio, Under the Direction of the Methodist Episcopal Church. Cincinnati, Ohio: J.F. Wright and L. Swormstedt.

1853   Autobiography of Rev. James B. Finley, or Pioneer Life in the West. Cincinnati, Ohio: Methodist Book Concern.

1857   Life Among the Indians; or, Personal Reminiscences and Historical Incidents Illustrative of Indian Life and Character. D.W. Clark, ed. Cincinnati, Ohio: Curts and Jennings.

Finney, Alfred, and Cephas Washburn
1821–1825   Mission Among the Cherokees of Arkansaw. *The Missionary Herald* 17:147–152, 211–214; 18:71–76, 141–144, 287–289, 380–383; 19:81–82, 172–174; 20:46–47, 76–79, 345–348. Boston.

Fischbacher, Theodore
1974   A Study of the Role of the Federal Government in the Education of the American Indian. San Francisco: R and E Research Associates.

Fisher, Raymond H.
1977   Bering's Voyages: Whither and Why. Seattle: University of Washington Press.

Fisher, Robin
1976   Arms and Men on the Northwest Coast, 1774–1825. *BC Studies* 29(Spring):3–18.

1977   Contact and Conflict: Indian-European Relations in British Columbia, 1774–1890. Vancouver: University of British Columbia Press.

Fisher, Vardis
1958   Tale of Valor; A Novel of the Lewis and Clark Expedition. Garden City, N.Y.: Doubleday.

1965   Mountain Man: A Novel of Male and Female in the Early American West. New York: Morrow.

Fishman, Laura Sehroger
1979   How Noble the Savage? The Image of the American Indian in French and English Travel Accounts, ca. 1550–1680. (Unpublished Ph.D. Dissertation in History, University of New York, New York City.)

Fitzgerald, Ken
1967   Weathervanes and Whirligigs. New York: Crown.

Fitzgerald, Mary P.
1937   Osage Mission, a Factor in the Making of Kansas. *Mid-America* 19 (July):182–196.

1939   Beacon on the Plains. Leavenworth, Kansas: Saint Mary College.

1940   Bishop Marty and His Sioux Missions, 1876–1896. *South Dakota Historical Collections* 20:523–558.

Fitzpatrick, John C., ed.
1931–1944   The Writings of George Washington. 39 vols. Washington: U.S. Government Printing Office.

1936   George Washington (Feb. 11/22, 1732–Dec. 16, 1799). Pp. 509–527 in Vol. 19 of Dictionary of American Biography. Allen Johnson et al., eds. 21 vols. New York: Charles Scribner's Sons.

Fitzpatrick, Thomas
1846–1854   [Letters Sent by Thomas Fitzpatrick While Indian Agent.] (Manuscript, Letters Received, Upper Platte and Arkansas Agency, Office of Indian Affairs, Record Group 75, National Archives, Washington.)

Flake, David K.
1965   A History of Mormon Missionary Work with the Hopi, Navaho, and Zuni. (Unpublished M.A. Thesis in History, Brigham Young University, Provo, Utah.)

Flannery, Regina
1939   An Analysis of Coastal Algonquian Culture. *Catholic University of America Anthropological Series* 7. Washington. (Reprinted: AMS Press, New York, 1983.)

1953   The Gros Ventres of Montana. Pt. 1: Social Life. *Catholic University of America Anthropological Series* 15. Washington.

Fleming, E. McClung
1965   The American Image as Indian Princess. *Winterthur Portfolio* 2:65–81. Winterthur, Del.

1968   Symbols of the United States: From Indian Queen to Uncle Sam. Pp. 1–24 in Frontiers of American Culture. Ray Brown et al., eds. West Lafayette, Ind.: Purdue University Studies.

Fleming, Paula R., and Judith Luskey
1986   The North American Indians in Early Photographs. New York: Harper and Row.

Fletcher, Alice C.
1883   The Sun Dance of the Ogalalla Sioux. Pp. 580–584 in Vol. 31 of *Proceedings of the American Association for the Advancement of Science for 1882*. Salem, Mass.

1884   Indian Ceremonies. Pp. 260–333 in *16th Report of the Peabody Museum of American Archaeology and Ethnology for 1883*. Cambridge, Mass.

1888   Indian Education and Civilization: A Report Prepared in Answer to Senate Resolution of February 23, 1885 . . . .*48th Cong, 2d sess. Senate Exec. Doc.* 95 (Serial No. 2264) Washington: U.S. Government Printing Office.

1893   A Study of Omaha Indian Music. *Papers of the Peabody Museum of American Archaeology and Ethnology, Harvard University* 1(5):237–307. Cambridge, Mass. (Reprinted: Kraus Reprint Corporation, New York, 1978.)

1894   Love Songs Among the Omaha Indians. Pp. 153–157 in *Memoirs of the International Congress of Anthropology, Chicago, 1893*. Staniland Wake, ed. Chicago: Schulte.

1904   The Hako: A Pawnee Ceremony. Pp. 5–372 in *22d Annual Report of the Bureau of American Ethnology for 1900–1901*. Washington.

1907   Governmental Policy. Pp. 499–503 in Vol. 1 of Handbook of American Indians North of Mexico. Frederick W. Hodge, ed. 2 vols. *Bureau of American Ethnology Bulletin* 30. Washington.

Fletcher, Alice C., and Francis La Flesche
1911   The Omaha Tribe. Pp. 17–672 in *27th Annual Report of the Bureau of American Ethnology for 1905–1906*. Washington. (Reprinted: Johnson Reprint Corporation, New York, 1970.)

Fleurieu, Charles P.C. de
1801   A Voyage Round the World 1790–1792 Performed by Étienne Marchand. 2 vols. London: T.N. Longman. (Reprinted: Da Capo Press, New York, 1969.)

Flexner, James T.
1959   Mohawk Baronet: Sir William Johnson of New York. New York: Harper.

1962   That Wilder Image: The Painting of America's Native School from Thomas Cole to Winslow Homer. Boston: Little, Brown.

Flint, Timothy
1833   Biographical Memoirs of Daniel Boone, the First Settler of Kentucky. Interspersed with Incidents in the Early Annals of the Country. Cincinnati, Ohio: N. and G. Guilford.

Flores, Dan L.
1983   Zion in Eden: Phases of the Environmental History of Utah. *Environmental Review* 7(4):325–344.

———, ed.
1984   Jefferson and Southwestern Exploration: The Freeman and Custis Accounts of the Red River Expedition of 1806. Norman: University of Oklahoma Press.

Floyd, Candace
1985   The Repatriation Blues: Museum Professionals and Native Americans Wrestle with Questions of Ownership and Disposition of Tribal Materials. *History News* (April):6–12.

Foley, William E., and C. David Rice
1983   The First Chouteaus: River Barons of Early St. Louis. Urbana: University of Illinois Press.

Folmer, Henri
1939   The Mallet Expedition of 1739 Through Nebraska, Kansas and Colorado to Santa Fe. *Colorado Magazine* 16(5):161–173.

Folsom, James K.
1966   The American Western Novel. New Haven, Conn.: Yale University Press.

Font, Pedro
1930   Font's Complete Diary of the Second Anza Expedition. Pp. 97–112 in Vol. 4 of Anza's California Expeditions. Herbert E. Bolton, ed. Berkeley: University of California Press.

Fontana, Bernard L.
1963   Pioneers in Ideas: Three Early Southwestern Ethnologists. *Journal of the Arizona Academy of Science* 2(3):124–129.

1965   On the Meaning of Historic Sites Archaeology. *American Antiquity* 31(1):61–65.

1965a   The Tale of a Nail: On the Ethnological Interpretation of Historic Artifacts. *Florida Anthropologist* 18(3, Pt. 2):85–102.

Force, Peter, comp.
1837–1853   American Archives: Consisting of a Collection of Authentic Records, State Papers, Debates, and Letters and Other Notices of Public Affairs. 9 vols. Washington: M. St. Clair Clarke and Peter Force. (Reprinted: Johnson Reprint Corporation, New York, 1972.)

Ford, Paul L., ed. and comp.
1890   "The Sayings of Poor Richard;" the Prefaces, Proverbs and Poems of Benjamin Franklin [etc.]. Brooklyn, N.Y.: Privately printed [by G.P. Putnam's Sons].

Forde, C. Daryll
1931   Ethnography of the Yuma Indians. *University of California Publications in American Archaeology and Ethnology* 28(4):83–278. Berkeley.

Foreman, Carolyn T.
1928–1932   The Choctaw Academy. *Chronicles of Oklahoma* 6(4):453–480; 9(4):382–411; 10(1):77–114.

1943   Indians Abroad, 1493–1938. Norman: University of Oklahoma Press.

Foreman, Grant
1932   Indian Removal: The Emigration of the Five Civilized Tribes of Indians. Norman: University of Oklahoma Press.

1934   The Five Civilized Tribes. Norman: University of Oklahoma Press. (Reprinted in 1974.)

1946   The Last Trek of the Indians. Chicago: University of Chicago Press.

1953   Indian Removal: The Emigration of the Five Civilized Tribes of Indians. 2d ed. Norman: University of Oklahoma Press.

Forsyth, Thomas
1834   [Letter to Governor William Clark, Dated St. Louis, September 22, 1815.] P. 79 in American State Papers. Vol. 2: Indian Affairs. Washington: Gales and Seaton.

1872   Journal of a Voyage from St. Louis to the Falls of St. Anthony, in 1819. Pp. 188–215 in *Wisconsin State Historical Society, Report and Collections* 6. Madison.

1888   Letter-book of Thomas Forsyth, 1814–1818. Reuben G. Thwaites, ed. Pp. 316–355 in *Wisconsin State Historical Society Collections* 11. Madison.

1911–1912   An Account of the Manners and Customs of the Sauk and Fox Nations of Indian Tradition. Pp. 183–245 in Vol. 2 of Indian Tribes of the Upper Mississippi Valley and Region of the Great Lakes. E.H. Blair, ed. 2 vols. Cleveland, Ohio: Arthur H. Clark.

Foster, John E.
1973   The Country-born in the Red River Settlement. (Unpublished Ph.D. Dissertation in History, University of Alberta, Edmonton.)

1975   The Homeguard Cree and the Hudson's Bay Company: The First Hundred Years. Pp. 49–64 in Approaches to Native History. D. Muise, ed. *Canada. National Museum of Man. Mercury Series. History Division Papers* 25. Ottawa.

1986   The Plains Métis. Pp. 375–405 in Native Peoples: The Canadian Experience. Bruce Morrison and C.R. Wilson, eds. Toronto: McClelland and Stewart.

Foster, Michael K.
1985   Another Look at the Function of Wampum in Iroquois-White Councils. Pp. 99–114 in The History and Culture of Iroquois Diplomacy. Francis Jennings et al., eds. Syracuse, N.Y.: Syracuse University Press.

Fowler, Arlen L.
1971   The Black Infantry in the West, 1869–1891. Westport, Conn.: Greenwood Press.

Fowler, Don D., ed.
1972   "Photographed All the Best Scenery:" Jack Hiller's Diary of the Powell Expedition, 1871–1875. Salt Lake City: University of Utah Press.

Fowler, Don D., and Catherine S. Fowler
1969   John Wesley Powell, Anthropologist. *Utah Historical Quarterly* 37(2):152–172.

1970   Stephen Powers' "The Life and Culture of the Washoe and Paiutes." *Ethnohistory* 17(3–4):117–149.

———, eds.
1971   Anthropology of the Numa: John Wesley Powell's Manuscripts on the Numic Peoples of Western North America, 1868–1880. *Smithsonian Contributions to Anthropology* 14. Washington.

Fowler, Don D., and John F. Matley
1979   Material Culture of the Numa: The John Wesley Powell Collection, 1867–1880. *Smithsonian Contributions to Anthropology* 26. Washington.

Fowler, Don D., Robert C. Euler, and Catherine S. Fowler
1969   John Wesley Powell and the Anthropology of the Canyon Country. *U.S. Geological Survey Professional Paper* 670. Washington.

Francis, Convers
1845   Life of Sebastian Râle. Pp. 159–323 in Vol. 7 of The Library of American Biography. 2d series. Jared Sparks, ed. Boston: Charles C. Little and James Brown.

Francis, Daniel
1983   A History of the Native Peoples of Quebec, 1760–1807. Ottawa: Indian and Northern Affairs Canada.

Francis, Daniel, and Toby Morantz
1983   Partners in Furs: A History of the Fur Trade in Eastern James Bay, 1600–1870. Montreal: McGill-Queen's University Press.

739

François I
1854–1856   Edits, ordonnances royaux, déclarations et arrêts du conseil d'État du roi concernant le Canada. 3 vols. Quebec: E.R. Fréchette.

Frank, Theo
1954   De latste tomahawk. Alkmaar, The Netherlands: Kluitmann.

——— 1959   De Speurtocht van Dakota Bill. Alkmaar, The Netherlands: Kluitmann.

Franklin, Benjamin
1784   Two Tracts: Information to Those Who Would Remove to America. And, Remarks Concerning the Savages of North America. Dublin, Ireland: Printed for L. White.

Frantz, Ray, W.
1967   The English Traveller and the Movement of Ideas, 1660–1732. Lincoln: University of Nebraska Press.

Fréchette, Louis H.
1877   La Dernière Iroquoise. In Pêle-mêle: Fantaisies et souvenirs poétiques. Montreal: Lovell.

Frederick, John T.
1956   Cooper's Eloquent Indians. *Publications of the Modern Language Association of America* 71(5):1004–1017. Menasha, Wis.

Freeman, Donald B., and Frances L. Dungey
1981   A Spatial Duopoly: Competition in the Western Canadian Fur Trade, 1770–1835. *Journal of Historical Geography* 7(3):252–270. London.

Freeman, John F.
1960   Henry Rowe Schoolcraft. (Unpublished Ph.D. Dissertation in History, Harvard University, Cambridge, Mass.)

——— 1965   Religion and Personality in the Anthropology of Henry Schoolcraft. *Journal of the History of the Behavioral Sciences* 1(4):301–313.

——— 1966   A Guide to Manuscripts Relating to the American Indian in the Library of the American Philosophical Society. Philadelphia: American Philosophical Society.

Freiligrath, Ferdinand
1838   Der ausgewanderte Dichter. In Gedichte. Stuttgart, Germany: J.G. Cotta.

Frelinghuysen, Theodore
1824   An Oration: Delivered at Princeton, New Jersey, Nov. 16, 1824. [Princeton, N.J.]: Princeton Press.

French, David
1961   Wasco-Wishram. Pp. 357–430 in Perspectives in American Indian Culture Change. Edward H. Spicer, ed. Chicago: University of Chicago Press.

French, Philip
1973   Westerns: Aspects of a Movie Genre. New York: Viking Press.

Freneau, Philip M.
1786   The Poems of Philip Freneau. Philadelphia: F. Bailey.

Freuchen, Peter
1927   Storfanger: En Roman om Hudsons-Bugtens Eskimoer. Copenhagen: Hasselbalch.

——— 1928   Rømningsmand: En Roman om Eskimoer. Copenhagen: S. Hasselbalch.

——— 1930   Ivalu: En Roman fra Polareskimoernes Land. Copenhagen: S. Hasselbalch.

——— 1934   Eskimo. Copenhagen: Gyldendal.

Friar, Ralph E., and Natasha A. Friar
1972   The Only Good Indian: The Hollywood Gospel. Drama Book. New York: Specialists.

Frideres, James S.
1983   Native People in Canada: Contemporary Conflicts. Scarborough, Ont.: Prentice-Hall of Canada.

Fried, Frederick
1964   A Pictorial History of the Carousel. New York: A.S. Barnes.

——— 1970   Artists in Wood: American Carvers of Cigar-store Indians, Show Figures, and Circus Wagons. New York: C.N. Potter.

Friede, Juan, and Benjamin Keen, eds.
1971   Bartolomé de Las Casas in History: Toward an Understanding of the Man and His Work. DeKalb: Northern Illinois University Press.

Friedrichs, Michael
1984   Meine halbhuronische Personalität: Seumes unfreiwilliger Kanada-Besuch 1782-83 und seine literarischen Folgen. *Zeitschrift der Gesellschaft für Kanadastudien* 41(6):71–82.

Friend, Llerena
1954   Sam Houston, the Great Designer. Austin: University of Texas Press. (Reprinted in 1969.)

Friends, Society of
1840   The Case of the Seneca Indians in the State of New York. Philadelphia: Merrihew and Thompson.

Fries, Adelaide
1905   The Moravians in Georgia, 1735–1740. Raleigh, N.C.: Edwards and Broughton.

Frink, Maurice
1965   Photographer on an Army Mule. With Casey E. Barthelmess. Norman: University of Oklahoma Press.

Fritz, Henry E.
1963   The Movement for Indian Assimilation, 1860–1890. Philadelphia: University of Pennsylvania Press. (Reprinted: Greenwood Press, Westport, Conn., 1981.)

——— 1972   Introduction. Pp. xi–xviii in Our Indian Wards, by G.W. Manypenny. New York: Da Capo Press.

Frobisher, Sir Martin
1578   A True Discourse of the Late Voyages of Discovery for Finding of a Passage to Cathaya and India by the North West. London: no publisher. (Reprinted: The Three Voyages of Martin Frobisher . . . Works Issued by the Hakluyt Society, 1st ser., Vol. 38., London, 1867.)

Frost, Richard H.
1980   The Romantic Inflation of Pueblo Culture. *American West* 17(1):4–9, 56–60.

Fuchs, Estelle, and Robert J. Havighurst
1972   To Live on This Earth: American Indian Education. Garden City, N.Y.: Doubleday. (Reprinted: University of New Mexico Press, Albuquerque, 1983.)

Fulton, Maurice G., ed.
1941–1944   Diary and Letters of Josiah Gregg. 2 vols. Norman: University of Oklahoma Press.

Gabus, Jean
1941   Milouka l'esquimaux. Lausanne, Switzerland: Payot.

——— 1951   Agpa, chasseur esquimau. Groningen, The Netherlands: Walters.

Gad, Finn
1967–1976   Grønlands Historie. 3 vols. Copenhagen: Nyt Nordisk Forlag.

——— 1971–1982   The History of Greenland. 3 vols. Montreal: McGill-Queen's University Press.

——— 1984   Grønland: Politikens Danmarkshistorie. Copenhagen: Politikens Forlag.

Gage, Duane
1974   William Faulkner's Indians. *American Indian Quarterly 1(1):27–33.*

Gagern, Friedrich von
1925   Der Marterpfahl. Leipzig, Germany: P. Reclam.

————   Der tote Mann, Roman der roten Rasse. Berlin: Paul Parey.
1927

1927a   Das Grenzerbuch. Berlin: Paul Parey.

Gagnon, François-Marc
1976   "Ils se peignent le visage . . . " réaction européenne à un usage indien au XVIe et au début de XVIIe siècles. *Revue d'Histoire de l'Amérique Française* 30(3):363–381. Montreal.

1984   Ces hommes dit sauvages: l'histoire fascinante d'un préjugé que remonte aux premiers découvreurs du Canada. Montreal: Libre Expression.

Galbraith, John S.
1976   The Little Emperor: Governor Simpson of the Hudson's Bay Company. Toronto: Macmillan of Canada.

Gale, Robert L.
1973   Francis Parkman. New York: Twayne Publishers.

Gallatin, Albert
1836   A Synopsis of the Indian Tribes within the United States East of the Rocky Mountains, and in the British and Russian Possessions in North America. Pp. 1–422 in *Transactions and Collections of the American Antiquarian Society* 2. Cambridge, Mass. (Reprinted: AMS Press, New York, 1973.)

1848   Hale's Indians of North-west America, and Vocabularies of North America. Pp. 1–130 in *Transactions of the American Ethnological Society* 2. New York.

Gallegos Lamero, Hernán
1927   The Gallegos Relation of the Rodriguez Expedition to New Mexico. George P. Hammond and Agapito Rey, eds. *Historical Society of New Mexico Publications in History* 4. Santa Fe.

Galloway, Patricia
1982   Choctaw Factionalism and Civil War, 1746–1750. *Journal of Mississippi History* 44(4):289–327.

Gálvez, Bernardo de Gálvez
1951   Instructions for Governing the Interior Provinces of New Spain, 1786. Donald E. Worcester, ed. and trans. Berkeley, Calif.: The Quivira Society.

Gamio, Manuel
1922   La Población del Valle de Teotihuacán. 3 vols. Mexico, D.F.: Departamento de Antropología, Instituto Nacional.

Gannon, Michael V.
1965   The Cross in the Sand: The Early Catholic Church in Florida, 1513–1870. Gainesville Fla.: St Augustine Foundation.

Ganoe, William A.
1924   The History of the United States Army. New York: D. Appleton.

Ganter, Herbert L.
1935   Some Notes on the "Charity of the Honorable Robert Boyle, Esq., of the City of London, Deceased." *William and Mary Quarterly 2d ser.,* Vol. 15(1):1–39. Williamsburg, Va.

Garbisch, Edgar W.
1966   101 American Primitive Water Colors and Pastels from the Collection of Edgar William and Bernice Chrysler Garbisch, October 8–November 20. Washington: U.S. National Gallery of Art.

Garland, Hamlin
1917   Son of the Middle Border. New York: Macmillan.

————   The Book of the American Indian. New York: Harper.
1923

Garnett, David
1933   Pocahontas; or, the Nonpareil of Virginia. London: Chatto and Windus.

Garraghan, Gilbert J., ed.
1930   Father De Smet's Sioux Peace Mission of 1868 and the Journal of Charles Galpin. *Mid-America* 13(October):141–163.

1938   The Jesuits of the Middle United States. 3 vols. New York: America Press. (Reprinted: Arno Press, New York, 1978.)

Garrett, Paul D.
1979   St. Innocent, Apostle to America. Crestwood, N.Y.: St. Vladimir's Seminary Press.

Garretson, Martin S.
1938   The American Bison: The Story of Its Extermination as a Wild Species and Its Restoration Under Federal Protection. New York: New York Zoological Society.

Garrett, Wilbur E., ed.
1982   The Making of America: The Southwest. Map. *National Geographic Magazine* 162(5).

————, ed.
1983   The Making of America: Deep South. Map. *National Geographic Magazine* 164(2).

————, ed.
1984   The Making of America: Central Rockies. Map. *National Geographic Magazine* 166(2).

————, ed.
1984a   The Making of America: Far West. Map. *National Geographic Magazine* 165(4).

————, ed.
1985   The Making of America: Central Plains. Map. *National Geographic Magazine* 168(3).

————, ed.
1986   The Making of America: Pacific Northwest. Map. *National Geographic Magazine* 170(2).

————, ed.
1986a   The Making of America: Northern Plains. Map. *National Geographic Magazine* 170(6).

————, ed.
1986b   The Making of America: Texas. Map. *National Geographic Magazine* 169(3).

Garritt, J.B.
1886   The North American Indians. Pp. 5–38 in Historical Sketches of the Missions Under the Care of the Board of Foreign Missions of the Presbyterian Church. Philadelphia: Woman's Foreign Missionary Society of the Presbyterian Church.

Garry, Joseph R.
1956   Subversion Threatens Indian Justice. (Unpublished manuscript in Hazel Hertzberg's possession.)

Gasaway, Laura N., James L. Hoover, and Dorothy M. Warden, comps.
1980   American Indian Legal Materials: A Union List. Stanfordville, N.Y.: E.M. Coleman.

Gates, Charles M.
1935   The Lac Qui Parle Indian Mission. *Minnesota History* 16(2):133–151.

Gates, Lillian F.
1968   Land Policies of Upper Canada. Toronto: University of Toronto Press.

Gates, Merrill E.
1885   Land and Law as Agents in Educating Indians. Washington: U.S. Indian Affairs Bureau.

————   Mohonk Indian Conferences. Pp. 928–929 in Vol. 1 of
1907   Handbook of American Indians North of Mexico. Freder-

ick W. Hodge, ed. 2 vols. *Bureau of American Ethnology Bulletin* 30. Washington.

Gates, Paul W.
1954   Fifty Million Acres: Conflict Over Kansas Land Policy, 1854–1890. Ithaca, N.Y.: Cornell University Press.

Gatschet, Albert S.
1876   Zwölf Sprachen aus dem Südwesten Nordamerikas (Pueblos und Apache-Mundarten; Tonto, Tonkawa, Digger, Utah). Weimar, Germany: Hermann Böhlau.

Gaustad, Edwin S.
1962   Historical Atlas of Religion in America. New York: Harper and Row. (Reprinted in 1976.)

Gay, Peter
1966–1969   The Enlightenment, an Interpretation. 2 vols. New York: Alfred A. Knopf.

Geddes, Virgil
1933   Pocahontas and the Elders: A Folkpiece in Four Acts. Chapel Hill, N.C.: M.A. Abernathy.

Gehring, Charles T., ed.
1977   New York Historical Manuscripts: Dutch, Vols. XX–XXI, Delaware Papers (English Period). Baltimore, Md.: Genealogical Publishing.

———, ed. and trans.
1980   New York Historical Manuscripts: Dutch, Vols. GG, HH, and II: Land Papers. Baltimore, Md.: Genealogical Publishing.

———, ed. and trans.
1981   New York Historical Manuscripts: Dutch, Vols. XVIII–XIX, Delaware Papers (Dutch Period). Baltimore, Md.: Genealogical Publishing.

Geiger, Maynard J.
1937   The Franciscan Conquest of Florida, 1573–1618. Washington: The Catholic University of America.

1940   Biographical Dictionary of the Franciscans in Spanish Florida and Cuba, 1528–1841 (*Franciscan Studies* 21). Paterson, N.J.: St. Anthony Guild Press.

1959   The Life and Times of Fray Junípero Serra, O.F.M. or, The Man Who Never Turned Back, 1713–1784: A Biography. 2 vols. Washington: Academy of American Franciscan History.

Gelardini De Barbo, Renata
1959   Sotto la tenda indiana. Brescia, Italy: Editr. La Scuola.

Georgakas, Dan
1972   They Have Not Spoken: American Indians in Film. *Film Quarterly* 25(3):26–32.

George, Mary Karl
1969   Zachariah Chandler: A Political Biography. East Lansing: Michigan State University Press.

Gerbi, Antonello
1973   The Dispute of the New World: The History of a Polemic, 1750–1900. Rev. ed. Jeremy Moyle, trans. Pittsburgh, Pa.: University of Pittsburgh Press.

Gerdts, William H.
1974   The Marble Savage. *Art in America* 62 (July-August):64–70.

Gerstäcker, Friedrich W.
1844   Streif- und Jagdzüge durch die Vereinigten Staaten Nord-Amerikas. 2 vols. Dresden, Germany: Arnoldische Buchhandlung.

1847   Mississippi-Bilder. 3 vols. Leipzig, Germany: Arnoldische Buchhandlung.

1862   Heimliche und unheimliche Geschichten. 2 vols. Leipzig, Germany: Arnoldische Buchhandlung.

Gessner, Salomon
1756   Inkel und Yarico. Zweyter Theil [A prose continuation of Bodmer's poem of the same name]. Zürich, Switzerland: Orell und Füssli.

Giannettino, Susan
1977   The Middleman Role in the Fur Trade: Its Influence on Interethnic Relations in the Saskatchewan-Missouri Plains. *Western Canadian Journal of Anthropology* 7(4):22–33.

Gibbs, George
1853   Journal of the Expedition of Colonel Redick M'Kee, United States Indian Agent, Through North-Western California. Performed in the Summer and Fall of 1851. Pp. 99–177, 634 in Vol. 3 of Historical and Statistical Information Respecting the History, Condition and Prospects of the Indian Tribes of the United States. Henry R. Schoolcraft, ed. 6 vols. Philadelphia: Lippincott, Grambo. (Reprinted: University of California Archaeological Research Facility, Berkeley, 1972.)

1855   Report of Mr. George Gibbs to Captain McClellan, on the Indian Tribes of the Territory of Washington, 1854. Pp. 419–462 in Vol. 1 of Report of the Secretary of War Communicating the Several Pacific Railroad Explorations. 3 vols. Washington: A.O.P. Nicholson, Printer.

1862   Grammar and Dictionary of the Yakama Language. New York: Cramoisy Press.

1863   A Dictionary of the Chinook Jargon, or Trade Language of Oregon. New York: Cramoisy Press.

1863a   Alphabetical Vocabulary of the Chinook Language. New York: Cramoisy Press.

1863b   Alphabetical Vocabularies of the Clallam and Lummi. New York: Cramoisy Press.

1877   Dictionary of the Niskwalli. *Contributions to North American Ethnology* 1:285–361.

Gibson, Ann J., and John H. Rowe, comps.
1961   A Bibliography of the Publications of Alfred Louis Kroeber. *American Anthropologist* 63(5):1060–1087.

Gibson, Arrell M.
1967   Medicine Show. *American West* 4(1):34–39, 74–79.

1971   The Chickasaws. Norman: University of Oklahoma Press.

1978   The St. Augustine Prisoners. *Red River Valley Historical Review* 3(2):259–270.

1980   The American Indian: Prehistory to the Present. Lexington, Mass.: D.C. Heath.

Gibson, Charles
1964   The Aztecs Under Spanish Rule: A History of the Indians of the Valley of Mexico, 1519–1810. Stanford, Calif.: Stanford University Press.

1966   Spain in America. New York: Harper and Row.

Gibson, James R.
1976   Imperial Russia in Frontier America: The Changing Geography of Supply of Russian America, 1784–1867. New York: Oxford University Press.

1978   European Dependence Upon American Natives: The Case of Russian America. *Ethnohistory* 25(4):359–385.

1978a   Old Russia in the New World: Adversaries and Adversities in Russian America. Pp. 46–65 in European Settlement and Development in North America: Essays on Geographical Change in Honour and Memory of Andrew Hill Clark. James R. Gibson, ed. Toronto: University of Toronto Press.

1980   The Russian Fur Trade. Pp. 217–230 in Old Trails and New Directions: Papers of the Third North American Fur Trade Conference. Carol M. Judd and Arthur J. Ray, eds. Toronto: University of Toronto Press.

1980a   Russian Expansion in Siberia and America. *The Geographical Review* 70(2):127–136. New York.

1982–1983   Smallpox on the Northwest Coast, 1835–1838. *BC Studies* 56(1):61–81.

Gidley, Mick
1982   From the Hopi Snake Dance to the Ten Commandments: Edward S. Curtis as Filmmaker. *Studies in Visual Communication* 8(3):70–79.

1987   The Vanishing Race in Sight and Sound: Edward S. Curtis' Musicale of American Indian Life. In Prospects: An Annual of American Cultural Studies. Jack Salzman, ed. New York: Cambridge University Press.

Gilcreast, Everett A.
1967   Richard Henry Pratt and American Indian Policy: A Study of the Assimilation Movement, 1877–1906. (Unpublished Ph.D. Dissertation in History, Yale University, New Haven, Conn.)

Gilg, Adam
1692   [Letter to the Reverend Father Rector of the College of the Society of Jesus at Brünn in Moravia . . . 1692.] Daniel Matson, trans. (Manuscript cited in Spicer 1962:590.)

Gillis, Everett A.
1967   Oliver La Farge. Austin, Tex.: Steck-Vaughn.

Gilman, Carolyn
1982   Where Two Worlds Meet: The Great Lakes Fur Trade. St. Paul: Minnesota Historical Society.

Giménez Fernández, Manuel
1953–1960   Bartolomé de Las Casas, 1474–1566. 2 vols. *Publicaciones de la Escuela de Estudios Hispano-Americanos de Sevilla* 70–71. Seville, Spain.

Ginsberg, Allen
1956   Howl, and Other Poems. San Francisco: City Lights Pocket Bookshop.

Gipson, Lawrence H.
1936–1970   The British Empire Before the American Revolution. 15 vols. Caldwell, Idaho: Caxton Printers. New York: A.A. Knopf.

1956   The Triumphant Empire: New Responsibilities within the Enlarged Empire, 1763–1766 (*The British Empire Before the American Revolution* 9.) New York: Alfred A. Knopf.

1958–1960   The British Empire Before the American Revolution. 3 vols. [Rev. ed.] New York: A. Knopf.

Girard, Rodolphe
1910   L'Algonquine: Roman des jours héroïques du Canada sous la domination française. Montreal: Compagnie de Publication de "La Patrie".

Giraud, Marcel
1945   Le Métis canadien: son rôle dans l'histoire des provinces de l'Ouest. *Travaux et Mémoires de l'Institut d'Ethnologie* 44. Paris.

Glacken, Clarence J.
1967   Traces on the Rhodian Shore: Nature and Culture in Western Thought from Ancient Times to the End of the Eighteenth Century. Berkeley: University of California Press.

Glass, Anthony
1985   Journal of an Indian Trader: Anthony Glass and the Texas Trading Frontier, 1790–1810. Dan L. Flores, ed. College Station: Texas A & M University Press.

Glass, Bentley, Owsei Temkin, and William L. Straus, Jr., eds.
1959   Forerunners of Darwin, 1745–1859. Baltimore, Md.: Johns Hopkins Press.

Glassley, Ray H.
1953   Pacific Northwest Indian Wars: The Cayuse War of 1848, the Rogue River Wars of the '50s, the Yakima War, 1853–56, the Coeur d'Alene War, 1857, the Modoc War, 1873, the Nez Perce War, 1877, the Bannock War, 1878, the Sheepeaters War of 1879. Portland, Oreg.: Binfords and Mort.

Glazik, Josef P.
1954   Die russisch-orthodoxe Heidenmission seit Peter dem Grossen. Münster, Germany: Aschendorffsche Verlagsbuchhandlung.

Glenn, Elizabeth J.
1974–1975   Some Aspects of Indian Culture Affecting the American Revolution in the West. *Indiana Social Studies Quarterly* 27(3):81–89.

Glenn, James R.
1981   The 'Curious Gallery': The Indian Photographs of the McClees Studio in Washington, 1857–1858. *History of Photography* 5(3):249–262.

1983   De Lancey W. Gill: Photographer for the Bureau of American Ethnology. *History of Photography* 7(1):7–22.

Glenn, Keith
1944   Captain John Smith and the Indians. *Virginia Magazine of History and Biography* 52(4):228–248.

Glover, Richard
1948   The Difficulties of the Hudson's Bay Company's Penetration of the West. *Canadian Historical Review* 29(3):240–254. Toronto.

Godsell, Philip H.
1938   Red Hunters of the Snows: An Account of Thirty Years' Experience with the Primitive Indian and Eskimo Tribes of the Canadian North-west and Arctic Coast . . . London: Robert Hale.

Goebel, Dorothy Burne
1926   William Henry Harrison: A Political Biography. *Indiana Historical Collections* 14, *Biographical Series* 2. Indianapolis. (Reprinted: Porcupine Press, Philadelphia, 1974.)

Goldberg, Carole E.
1975   Public Law 280: The Limits of State Jurisdiction Over Reservation Indians. *U.C.L.A. Law Review* 22(3):535–594.

Golder, Frank A.
1922–1925   Bering's Voyages: An Account of the Efforts of the Russians to Determine the Relation of Asia and America. 2 vols. *American Geographical Society Research Series* 1–2. New York.

1972   Father Herman, Alaska's Saint. *Orthodox Alaska* 4(6):1–10. Kodiak.

Goldman, Michael A.
1979   Roland E. Trowbridge, 1880–81. Pp. 167–172 in The Commissioners of Indian Affairs, 1824–1977. Robert M. Kvasnicka and Herman J. Viola, eds. Lincoln: University of Nebraska Press.

Goldschmidt, Walter, ed.
1959   The Anthropology of Franz Boas: Essays on the Centennial of His Birth. [Menasha, Wis.]: American Anthropological Association.

Gollin, Gillian L.
1967   Moravians in Two Worlds: A Study of Changing Communities. New York: Columbia University Press.

Golovin, P.N.
1979   The End of Russian America: Captain P.N. Golovin's Last Report, 1862. Basil Dmytryshyn and E.A.P. Crownhart-Vaughan, trans. Portland: Oregon Historical Society.

743

Golovnin, Vasilii M.
1965   Puteshestvie vokrug sveta, sovershennoe na voennom shliupe "Kamchatka" v 1817, 1818 i 1819 godakh flota kapitanom Golovninym [Trip Around the World Aboard the Military Sloop "Kamchatka" in 1817, 1818, and 1819 by Fleet Captain Golovnin]. Moscow: Izdatel'stvo "Mysl'." (Reprinted: University of Hawaii Press, Honolulu, 1979.)

Góngora, Mario
1951   El Estado en el derecho indiano: época de fundación, 1492–1570. Santiago de Chile: Universidad de Chile.

González Navarro, Moisés
1954   Instituciones indígenas en Mexico independiente. Pp. 113–170 in Métodos y Resultados de la política indigenista en Mexico, by Alfonso Caso, et al. *Memorias del Instituto Nacional Indigenista* 6. Mexico.

Goodwin, Gary C.
1977   Cherokees in Transition: A Study of Changing Culture and Environment Prior to 1775. *University of Chicago. Department of Geography Research Paper* 181.

Gookin, Daniel
1792   Historical Collections of the Indians in New England . . . .Pp. 141–226 in *Massachusetts Historical Society Collections, 1st ser.,* Vol. 1. (Reprinted: Arno Press, New York 1972.)

————
1836   An Historical Account of the Doings and Sufferings of the Christian Indians in New England, in the Years of 1675, 1676, 1677. *Archaeologia Americana: Transactions and Collections of the American Antiquarian Society* 2:423–534. (Reprinted: Arno Press, New York, 1972.)

Gookin, Frederick W.
1912   Daniel Gookin, 1612–1687: Assistant and Major General of the Massachusetts Bay Colony; His Life and Letters and Some Account of His Ancestry. Chicago: Privately Printed [R.R. Donnelly].

Gookin, Warner F.
1913   Major-General Daniel Gookin. *Cambridge Historical Society Publications* 7:95–103. Cambridge, Mass.

Gordon, Robert
[1939]   Indian Lament. (Manuscript 964 in Archives of Folk Songs, Music Division, Library of Congress, Washington.)

Gosselin, Auguste H.
1890   Vie de Mgr de Laval, premier évêque de Québec et apôtre du Canada, 1622–1708. 2 vols. Quebec: L.J. Demers et Frère.

————
1911–1914   L'Église du Canada depuis Monseigneur de Laval jusqu'à la conquête. 3 vols. Quebec: Laflamme et Proulx.

Gossett, Thomas F.
1963   Race: The History of an Idea in America. Dallas, Tex.: Southern Methodist Press.

Gould, Richard A.
1966   The Wealth Quest Among the Tolowa Indians of Northwestern California. *Proceedings of the American Philosophical Society* 110(1):67–89. Philadelphia.

Gowans, Fred R.
1975   Rocky Mountain Rendezvous: A History of the Fur Trade Rendezvous, 1825–1840. Provo, Utah: Brigham Young University Press.

Graham, Andrew
1969   Andrew Graham's Observations on Hudson's Bay, 1767–91. Glyndwr Williams, ed. London: Hudson's Bay Record Society.

Graham, William A.
1926   The Story of the Little Big Horn: Custer's Last Fight. New York: The Century Company.

————
1953   The Custer Myth: A Source Book of Custeriana. Harrisburg, Pa.: Stackpole.

Grancsay, Steven V.
1965   American Engraved Powder Horns: A Study Based on the J.H. Grenville Gilbert Collection. Philadelphia: Ray Riling Arms Books.

Grant, W.L., and James Munro, eds.
1908–1910   Acts of the Privy Council of England. 3 vols. London: His Majesty's Stationery Office.

Graves, William W.
1916   Life and Letters of Fathers Ponziglione, Schoenmakers, and Other Early Jesuits at Osage Mission. St. Paul, Kansas: W.W. Graves.

————
1949   The First Protestant Osage Missions, 1820–1837. Oswego, Kansas: Carpenter Press.

Gray, Elma E.
1956   Wilderness Christians: The Moravian Mission to the Delaware Indians. Ithaca, N.Y.: Cornell University Press. (Reprinted: Russell and Russell, New York, 1973.)

Gray, John D.
1976   Centennial Campaign: The Sioux War of 1876. Fort Collins, Colo.: Old Army Press.

Gray, John M.
1963   Lord Selkirk of Red River. Toronto: Macmillan.

Graybill, Florence Curtis, and Victor Boesen
1976   Edward Sheriff Curtis: Visions of a Vanishing Race. New York: Thomas Crowell.

Graymont, Barbara
1972   The Iroquois in the American Revolution. Syracuse, N.Y.: Syracuse University Press.

————
1983   Thayendanega. Pp. 803–812 in Vol. 5 of Dictionary of Canadian Biography, 1801–1820. Frances G. Halpenny, gen. ed. Toronto: University of Toronto Press.

Gredsted, Torry
1918   Paw, en Dansk Indianerdrengs Eventye. Copenhagen: Hasselbalch.

————
1922   Praeriens Søn. Copenhagen: Hasselbalch.

————
1932   Paw i Urskoven. Copenhagen: S. Hasselbalch.

Green, James A.
1941   William Henry Harrison, His Life and Times. Richmond, Va.: Garrett and Massie.

Green, Jesse D.
1975   The Man Who Became an Indian. *The New York Review of Books* 22(9):31–33.

Green, Jonathan S.
1915   Journal of a Tour on the North West Coast of America in the Year 1829, Containing a Description of a Part of Oregon, California and the North West Coast and the Numbers, Manners and Customs of the Native Tribes. New York: C.F. Heartman.

Green, Rayna D.
1971   Culture Seen and Not Heard: The Uses of Visual Materials in Folkloristic Analysis. (Unpublished paper presented to the Annual Meeting of the American Folklore Society, Washington.)

————
1973   The Image of the Indian in the Popular Imagination: An Analysis of Oral, Visual, and Ideational Materials. (Unpublished Ph.D. Dissertation in Folklore and American Studies, Indiana University, Bloomington.)

————
1975   Traits of Indian Character: The "Indian" Anecdote in American Vernacular Tradition. *Southern Folklore Quarterly* 39(3):233–262.

744

————, ed.
1984   That's What She Said: Contemporary Poetry and Fiction by
            Native American Women. Bloomington: Indiana Universi-
            ty Press.

Greene, Jack P.
1963   The Quest for Power: The Lower Houses of Assembly in the
            Southern Royal Colonies, 1689–1776. Chapel Hill: Univer-
            sity of North Carolina Press.

Greene, Jerome A.
1982   Slim Buttes, 1876: An Episode of the Great Sioux War.
            Norman: University of Oklahoma Press.

Greene, John C.
1954   Some Early Speculations on the Origin of the Human Races.
            American Anthropologist 56(1):31–41.

1959   The Death of Adam: Evolution and Its Impact on Western
            Thought. Ames: Iowa State University Press.

Greene, Lorenzo J.
1942   The Negro in Colonial New England, 1620–1776. New
            York: Columbia University Press. (Reprinted: Kennikat
            Press, Port Royal, N.Y., 1966.)

Gregg, Josiah
1954   Commerce of the Prairies [1844]. Max L. Moorhead, ed. 2
            vols. Norman: University of Oklahoma Press.

Gregory, Jack, and Rennard Strickland
1967   Sam Houston with the Cherokees, 1829–1833. Austin:
            University of Texas Press. (Reprinted in 1976.)

Grey, Zane
1925   The Vanishing American. New York: Harper and Brothers.

Grey Owl [Archibald Stansfeld Belaney]
1931   Men of the Last Frontier. London: Country Life. (Reprint-
            ed: Macmillan, Toronto, 1976.)

1934   Pilgrims of the Wild. Toronto: Macmillan. (Reprinted in
            1968.)

1935   Sajo and Her Beaver People. Toronto: Macmillan. (Reprint-
            ed: Peter Davies, London, 1974.)

1936   Tales of an Empty Cabin. Toronto: Macmillan. (Reprinted
            in 1975.)

Griffen, William B.
1969   Culture Change and Shifting Population in Central-north-
            ern Mexico. Anthropological Papers of the University of
            Arizona 13. Tucson.

1979   Indian Assimilation in the Franciscan Area of Nueva
            Vizcaya. University of Arizona Anthropological Papers 33.
            Tucson.

Griffin, Grace G.
1946   A Guide to Manuscripts Relating to American History in
            British Depositories Reproduced for the Division of Manu-
            scripts of the Library of Congress. Washington: U.S.
            Library of Congress.

Grimes, Ronald L.
1986   Desecration of the Dead: An Inter-religious Controversy.
            American Indian Quarterly 10(4):305–318.

Grinde, Donald, Jr.
1977   Native American Slavery in the Southern Colonies. The
            Indian Historian 10(2):38–42.

Griswold, Gillett
1970   Aboriginal Patterns of Trade Between the Columbia Basin
            and the Northern Plains. Archaeology in Montana 11(2–3).
            Missoula.

Griswold, Oliver
1949   William Selby Harney: Indian Fighter. Tequesta: The
            Journal of the Historical Association of Southern Florida
            9:73–80.

Gronewold, Sylvia
1972   Did Frank Hamilton Cushing Go Native? Pp. 33–50 in
            Crossing Cultural Boundaries. Solon T. Kimball and James
            B. Watson, eds. San Francisco: Chandler.

Grosse, Karl
1793   Adelhait von Florida. Berlin: Vieweg.

Gruber, Jacob W.
1967   Horatio Hale and the Development of American Anthro-
            pology. Pp. 5–37 in Proceeding of the American Philosophi-
            cal Society 111(1). Philadelphia.

Gruell, George E.
1985   Indian Fires in the Interior West: A Widespread Influence.
            Pp. 68–74 in Proceedings—Symposium and Workshop on
            Wilderness Fire; Missoula, Mont., Nov. 15–18, 1983. U.S.
            Department of Agriculture, Forest Service. Intermountain
            Forest and Range Experiment Station, Ogden, Utah. General
            Technical Report INT–182. Washington: U.S. Government
            Printing Office.

Gsovski, Vladimir
1950   Russian Administration of Alaska and the Status of the
            Alaskan Natives. 81st Cong. 2d sess. Senate Document No.
            152 (Serial No. 11401). Washington: U.S. Government
            Printing Office.

Gue, B.F.
1895   The Public Services of Hiram Price. Annals of Iowa 3d ser.,
            Vol. 1(8):585–602.

Guild, Thelma S., and Harvey L. Carter
1984   Kit Carson: A Pattern for Heroes. Lincoln: University of
            Nebraska Press.

Guilday, Peter
1922   The Life and Times of John Carroll, Archbishop of
            Baltimore, 1735–1815. New York: The Encyclopedia Press.

Gunhold, G., ed.
1966   Western Gazette 27 (Nov.-Dec.). Paris.

Gunnerson, Dolores A.
1974   The Jicarilla Apaches: A Study in Survival. DeKalb:
            Northern Illinois University Press.

Gunnerson, James H., and Dolores A. Gunnerson
1971   Apachean Culture: A Study in Unity and Diversity. Pp.
            7–27 in Apachean Culture History and Ethnology. Keith H.
            Basso and Morris E. Opler, eds. Anthropological Papers of
            the University of Arizona 21. Tucson.

Gunther, Erna
1972   Indian Life on the Northwest Coast of North America as
            Seen by the Early Explorers and Fur Traders During the
            Last Decades of the Eighteenth Century. Chicago: Universi-
            ty of Chicago Press.

Guthrie, Alfred B.
1947   The Big Sky. New York: William Sloane Associates.

1949   The Way West. New York: William Sloane Associates.

Gwyn, Julian
1979   Sir William Johnson. Pp. 394–398 in Vol. 4 of Dictionary of
            Canadian Biography, 1771–1800. Frances G. Halpenny,
            gen. ed. Toronto: University of Toronto Press.

Gymir, Gerda [Gerda Morris]
1940   Der Sontschem: Ein Volk kämpft für Freiheit und Ehre
            gegen Puritaner. Cologne, Germany: Schroeder.

Haan, Richard L.
1976   The Covenant Chain: Iroquois Diplomacy on the Niagara
            Frontier, 1697–1730. (Unpublished Ph.D. Dissertation in
            History, University of California, Santa Barbara.)

1981   The "Trade Do's Not Flourish as Formerly": The Ecologi-
            cal Origins of the Yamassee War of 1715. Ethnohistory
            28(4):341–358.

Haas, Theodore
1947   Ten Years of Tribal Government Under IRA. Washington: U.S. Indian Service.

Haase, Yorck A., and Harold Jantz
1976   The New World in the Treasures of an Old European Library (Exhibition Catalog of the Duke August Library, Wolfenbüttel, Germany). Braunschweig, Germany: Waisenhausdruckerei.

Haberly, Lloyd
1948   Pursuit of the Horizon: A Life of George Catlin, Painter and Recorder of the American Indian. New York: Macmillan.

Habig, Marion A.
1947   Heroes of the Cross: An American Martyrology. 3d ed. Paterson, N.J.: St. Anthony Guild Press.

1958   Heralds of the King: The Franciscans of the St. Louis-Chicago Province, 1858–1958. Chicago: Franciscan Herald Press.

Hackett, Charles W., ed.
1923–1937   Historical Documents Relating to New Mexico, Nueva Vizcaya, and Approaches Thereto, to 1773. Adolph F.A. Bandelier and Fanny R. Bandelier, colls. 3 vols. *Carnegie Institution of Washington Publication* 330.

————, ed.
1942   Revolt of the Pueblo Indians of New Mexico and Otermín's Attempted Reconquest, 1680–1682. Charmion C. Shelby, trans. 2 vols. Albuquerque: University of New Mexico Press. (2d ed. in 1970.)

Hafen, LeRoy R.
1965   A Brief History of the Fur Trade of the Far West. Pp. 17–176 in Vol. 1 of The Mountain Men and the Fur Trade of the Far West. LeRoy R. Hafen, ed. 10 vols. Glendale, Calif.: Arthur H. Clark.

————, ed.
1965–1972   The Mountain Men and the Fur Trade of the Far West. 10 vols. Glendale, Calif.: Arthur H. Clark.

Hafen, LeRoy R., and William J. Ghent
1931   Broken Hand: The Life Story of Thomas Fitzpatrick, Chief of the Mountain Men. Denver, Colo.: Old West Publishing Company. (Reprinted: University of Nebraska Press, Lincoln, 1981.)

Hafen, LeRoy R., and Ann W. Hafen, eds.
1959   Relations with the Indians of the Plains, 1857–1861. Glendale, Calif.: Arthur H. Clark.

1969   Thomas Fitzpatrick. Pp. 87–105 in Vol. 7 of The Mountain Men and the Fur Trade of the Far West. LeRoy R. Hafen, ed. 10 vols. Glendale, Calif.: Arthur H. Clark.

Hafen, LeRoy R., and Francis M. Young
1938   Fort Laramie and the Pageant of the West, 1834–1890. Glendale, Calif.: Arthur H. Clark.

Hagan, William T.
1961   American Indians. Chicago: University of Chicago Press.

1966   Indian Police and Judges: Experiments in Acculturation and Control. New Haven, Conn.: Yale University Press.

1971   Kiowas, Comanches, and Cattlemen, 1867–1906: A Case Study of the Failure of U.S. Reservation Policy. *Pacific Historical Review* 40(3):333–355.

1976   United States - Comanche Relations: The Reservation Years. New Haven, Conn.: Yale University Press.

1979   Daniel M. Browning, 1893–97. Pp. 205–209 in The Commissioners of Indian Affairs, 1824–1977. Robert M. Kvasnicka and Herman J. Viola, eds. Lincoln: University of Nebraska Press.

1985   The Indian Rights Association: The Herbert Welsh Years, 1882–1904. Tucson: University of Arizona Press.

Haile, Berard
1941–1948   Learning Navaho. St. Michaels, Ariz.: St. Michaels Press. (Reprinted in 1971–1972.)

1950–1951   A Stem Vocabulary of the Navaho Language. 2 vols. St. Michaels, Ariz.: St. Michaels Press. (Reprinted: AMS Press, New York, 1975.)

Haines, Francis
1938   The Northward Spread of Horses Among the Plains Indians. *American Anthropologist* 40(3):429–437.

1976   The Plains Indians. New York: Thomas Y. Crowell.

Hakluyt, Richard
1892   Voyages in Search of the North-West Passage. London: Cassell.

1962   Voyages. John Masefield, ed. 8 vols. London: J.M. Dent.

Halbert, Henry S., and Timothy H. Ball
1895   The Creek War of 1813 and 1814. Chicago: Donohue and Henneberry.

Hale, Charles R.
1888   Innocent of Moscow, the Apostle of Kamchatka and Alaska. [New York]: Privately printed. (Reprinted from the *American Church Review* of July 1877.)

Hale, Horatio E.
1834   Remarks on the Language of the St. John's or Wlastukweek Indians, with a Penobscot Vocabulary. Boston: Privately printed.

1846   Ethnography and Philology. United States Exploring Expedition During the Years 1838, 1839, 1840, 1841, 1842. Under the Command of Charles Wilkes, U.S.N. Vol. 6. Philadelphia: Lea and Blanchard. (Reprinted: The Gregg Press, Ridgewood, N.J., 1968.)

1883   The Iroquois Book of Rites. (*Brinton's Library of Aboriginal American Literature* 2) Philadelphia: D.G. Brinton. (Reprinted: University of Toronto Press, Toronto, 1978.)

1883a   The Tutelo Tribe and Language. Pp. 1–49 in *Proceedings of the American Philosophical Society* 21(114). Philadelphia.

Hale, Janet Campbell
1985   The Jailing of Cecelia Capture. New York: Random House.

Haley, J. Evetts
1935   The Comanchero Trade. *Southwestern Historical Quarterly* 38(3):157–176.

Haley, James L.
1976   The Buffalo War: The History of the Red River Indian Uprising of 1874. Garden City, N.Y.: Doubleday.

Hall, Arthur H.
1934   The Red Stick War: Creek Indian Affairs During the War of 1812. *Chronicles of Oklahoma* 12(3):264–293.

Hall, Clayton C., ed.
1910   Narratives of Early Maryland, 1633–1684. New York: Barnes and Noble. (Reprinted in 1967.)

Hall, D.J.
1984   A Serene Atmosphere? Treaty 1 Revisited. *Canadian Journal of Native Studies* 4(2):321–358.

Hallenbeck, Cleve
1950   Land of Conquistadores. Caldwell, Idaho: Caxton Printers.

Haller, John S., Jr.
1971   Outcasts from Evolution: Scientific Attitudes of Racial Inferiority, 1859–1900. Urbana: University of Illinois Press.

Halliburton, R., Jr.
1977   Red Over Black: Black Slavery Among the Cherokee Indians. Westport, Conn.: Greenwood Press.

Hallowell, A. Irving
1949   The Size of Algonkian Hunting Territories: A Function of Ecological Adjustments. *American Anthropologist* 51(1):35–45.

――――
1951   Frank Gouldsmith Speck, 1881–1950. *American Anthropologist* 53(1):67–87.

――――
1957   The Backwash of the Frontier: The Impact of the Indian on American Culture. Pp. 229–258 in The Frontier in Perspective, W.D. Wyman and C.B. Kroeber, eds. Madison: University of Wisconsin Press.

――――
1960   The Beginnings of Anthropology in America. Pp. 1–90 in Selected Papers from the *American Anthropologist*, 1888–1920. Frederica De Laguna, ed. Evanston, Ill.: Row, Peterson.

――――
1963   American Indians, White and Black: The Phenomenon of Transculturalization. *Current Anthropology* 4(4):519–531. (Reprinted: Pp. 498–529 in Contributions to Anthropology: Selected Papers of A. Irving Hallowell, University of Chicago Press, Chicago, 1976.)

――――
1976   Contributions to Anthropology: Selected Papers of A. Irving Hallowell. Chicago: University of Chicago Press.

Hallum, John
1887   Biographical and Pictorial History of Arkansas. Vol. 1. Albany, N.Y.: Weed, Parsons. (Reprinted: Southern Historical Press, Easley, S.C., 1980.)

Halpin, Marjorie
1965   Catlin's Indian Gallery: The George Catlin Paintings in the United States National Museum. Washington: Smithsonian Institution.

Hamilton, John M.
1948   A History of the Presbyterian Church Among the Pima and Papago Indians of Arizona. (Unpublished M.A. Thesis in Anthropology, University of Arizona, Tucson.)

Hamilton, John T.
1900   A History of the Church Known as the Moravian Church or Unitas Fratrum, or The Unity of the Brethren, During the Eighteenth and Nineteenth Centuries. Bethlehem, Pa.: Times Publishing Company.

Hamilton, John T., and Kenneth G. Hamilton
1967   History of the Moravian Church: The Renewed Unitas Fratrum, 1722–1957. [Bethlehem, Pa.: Interprovincial Board of Christian Education, Moravian Church in America.]

Hamilton, Kenneth G.
1940   John Ettwein and the Moravian Church. Bethlehem, Pa.: Times Publishing Company.

Hamilton, Milton W.
1976   Sir William Johnson: Colonial American, 1715–1763. Port Washington, N.Y.: Kennikat Press.

Hamilton, Robert
1930   The Gospel Among the Red Men: The History of Southern Baptist Indian Missions. Nashville, Tenn.: Sunday School Board of the Southern Baptist Convention.

Hammond, George P., and Agapito Rey, eds.
1928   Obregón's History of Sixteenth Century Explorations in Western America, Entitled: Chronicle, Commentary, or Relation of the Ancient and Modern Discoveries in New Spain, and New Mexico, Mexico, 1584. Los Angeles: Wetzel.

――――, eds.
1940   Narratives of the Coronado Expedition, 1540–1542. Albuquerque: University of New Mexico Press. (Reprinted: AMS Press, New York, 1977.)

――――, eds.
1953   Don Juan de Oñate, Colonizer of New Mexico, 1595–1628. 2 vols. Albuquerque: University of New Mexico Press.

――――, eds.
1966   The Rediscovery of New Mexico, 1580–1594. Albuquerque: University of New Mexico Press.

Hamor, Ralph
1615   A True Discourse of the Present Estate of Virginia. London: John Beale for William Welby. (Reprinted: DaCapo Press, New York, 1971.)

Handy, Robert T.
1956   We Witness Together: A History of Cooperative Home Missions. New York: Friendship Press.

Hanke, Lewis
1935   The First Social Experiments in America: A Study in the Development of Spanish Indian Policy in the Sixteenth Century. Cambridge, Mass.: Harvard University Press.

――――
1938   The "Requerimiento" and Its Interpreters. *Revista de Historia de América* 1:25–34. Mexico City.

――――
1949   The Spanish Struggle for Justice in the Conquest of America. Philadelphia: University of Pennsylvania Press.

――――
1959   Aristotle and the American Indians: A Study in Race Prejudice in the Modern World. London: Hollis and Carter.

――――
1965   The Spanish Struggle for Justice in the Conquest of America. Boston: Little Brown.

――――
1974   All Mankind is One: A Study of the Disputation Between Bartolomé de Las Casas and Juan Ginés de Sepúlveda in 1550 on the Intellectual and Religious Capacity of the American Indians. DeKalb: Northern Illinois University Press.

Hannabuss, Stuart
1987   The West: Some Victorian Variants. *Antiquarian Book Monthly Review* 14(2):96–100.

Hanson, Charles E., Jr.
1955   The Northwest Gun. *Nebraska State Historical Society Publications in Anthropology* 2. Lincoln.

――――
1966   James Bordeaux. *Museum of the Fur Trade Quarterly* 2(1):2–12.

Hanson, James A.
1975   Metal Weapons, Tools and Ornaments of the Teton Dakota Indians. Lincoln: University of Nebraska Press.

Haramburu, R.
1971   L'Oeuvre des missionnaires. Pp. 127–135 in Atti del Congresso Internazionale Polare. Silvio Zavatti, ed. Civitanova Marche, Italy: Istituto Geografico Polare.

Hare, Lloyd C.M.
1932   Thomas Mayhew: Patriarch to the Indians (1593–1682). New York: D. Appleton. (Reprinted: AMS Press, New York, 1969.)

Hare, William H.
1926   The Church in Story and Pageant. Indian Tribes and Missions: A Handbook of General History of the North American Indians; Early Missionary Efforts and Missions of the Episcopal Church. Hartford, Conn.: Church Mission Publishing Company.

Haring, Clarence H.
1963   The Spanish Empire in America. Rev. ed. New York: Harcourt, Brace and World.

747

Hariot, Thomas
[1972]   A Briefe and True Report of the New Found Land of
           Virginia [1590]. New York: Dover Publications.

Harjo, Joy
1983   She Had Some Horses. New York: Thunder's Mouth Press.

Harlan, James
1865   [Letter to William P. Dole, Dated June 22, 1865, re Renewal
           of Talks with Indians Following the Civil War.] (Letters
           Sent by the Indian Division of the Office of the Secretary of
           the Interior, 1849–1903, 5:262–263, M606, Record Group
           48, Natural Resources Branch, National Archives, Wash-
           ington.)

————
1865a   [Letter to Major General Pope, Dated July 6, 1865, re
           Removal of Indians from Established Reservations.] (Let-
           ters Sent by the Indian Division of the Office of the
           Secretary of the Interior, 1849–1903, 5:278–281, M606,
           Record Group 48, Natural Resources Branch, National
           Archives, Washington.)

Harmon, George D.
1930   The United States Indian Policy in Texas, 1845–1860.
           Mississippi Valley Historical Review 17(3):377–403.

————
1932   Benjamin Hawkins and the Federal Factory System. North
           Carolina Historical Review 9(2):138–152.

Harper, Francis, ed.
1958   The Travels of William Bartram. Naturalist's Edition, with
           Commentary and an Annotated Index. New Haven, Conn.:
           Yale University Press.

Harper, J. Russell, ed.
1971   Paul Kane's Frontier. Austin: Published for the Amon
           Carter Museum, Fort Worth, and the National Gallery of
           Canada by the University of Texas Press.

Harrington, John P.
1934   A New Original Version of Boscana's Historical Account of
           the Sun Juan Capistrano Indians of Southern California.
           Smithsonian Institution Miscellaneous Collections 92(4).
           Washington.

Harris, Donald A., and George C. Ingram
1972   New Caledonia and the Fur Trade: A Status Report.
           Western Canadian Journal of Anthropology 3(1):179–195.

Harris, Helen L.
1975   Mark Twain's Response to the Native American. American
           Literature 46(4):495–505.

Harris, LaDonna, and Cesare Marino
1984   Indian Tribal Governments: Problems and Challenges on
           the People's Road to Sovereignty. Centerboard: Journal of
           the Center for Human Relations Studies 2(1):19–27. Nor-
           man, Okla.

Harris, Marvin
1968   The Rise of Anthropological Theory: A History of Theories
           of Culture. New York: Thomas Y. Crowell.

Harris, R. Cole, and Geoffrey J. Matthews, eds.
1987   Historical Atlas of Canada. Vol. 1: From the Beginning to
           1800. Toronto: University of Toronto Press.

Harris, William
1963   A Rhode Islander Reports on King Philip's War: The
           Second William Harris Letter of August, 1676. Douglas E.
           Leach, ed. Providence: The Rhode Island Historical Soci-
           ety.

Harris, Wilmer C.
1917   Public Life of Zachariah Chandler, 1851–1875. Lansing:
           Michigan Historical Commission.

Harrod, Howard L.
1971   Mission Among the Blackfeet. Norman: University of
           Oklahoma Press.

Hart, Evan A.
1963   Rare Trade Cross - Lost and Found. Minnesota History
           News (December):2–3.

Hart, Herbert M.
1980   Tour Guide to Old Western Forts. Boulder, Colo.: Pruett
           Publishing Company.

Hart, Irving H.
1926   The Site of the Northwest Company Post on Sandy Lake.
           Minnesota History 7(4):311–325.

Hart, Simon
1959   The Prehistory of the New Netherland Company: Amster-
           dam Notarial Records of the First Dutch Voyages to the
           Hudson; City Archives of Amsterdam. Amsterdam: City of
           Amsterdam Press.

Haskins, George L., and Herbert A. Johnson
1981   Foundations of Power: John Marshall, 1801–15. (History of
           the Supreme Court of the United States 2) New York:
           Macmillan.

Hassrick, Peter H.
1973   Frederic Remington: Paintings, Drawings and Sculpture in
           the Amon Carter Museum and the Sid W. Richardson
           Foundation Collections. New York: Harry N. Abrams.

Hatfield, James T., and Elfrida Hochbaum
1899   The Influence of the American Revolution Upon German
           Literature. Americana Germanica 3(3–4):338–385.
           Philadelphia.

Hatley, Marvin T., III
1977   The Dividing Path: The Direction of Cherokee Life in the
           Eighteenth Century. (Unpublished M.A. Thesis in Anthro-
           pology, University of North Carolina, Chapel Hill.)

Hauptman, Laurence M.
1977   Mythologizing Westward Expansion: Schoolbooks and the
           Image of the American Frontier Before Turner. Western
           Historical Quarterly 8(3):269–282.

————
1986   The Iroquois Struggle for Survival: World War II to Red
           Power. Syracuse, N.Y.: Syracuse University Press.

Haury, Emil W.
1945   The Excavation at Los Muertos and Neighboring Ruins in
           the Salt River Valley, Southern Arizona. Papers of the
           Peabody Museum of American Archaeology and Ethnology,
           Harvard University 24(1). Cambridge, Mass.

Haven, Samuel F.
1856   Archaeology of the United States; or, Sketches, Historical
           and Bibliographical, of the Progress of Information and
           Opinion Respecting Vestiges of Antiquity in the United
           States. Smithsonian Contributions to Knowledge 8. Washing-
           ton.

Hawkins, Benjamin
1848   A Sketch of the Creek Country in the Years 1798 and 1799.
           Georgia Historical Society Collections 3(1). Savannah. (Re-
           printed: The Reprint Company, Spartanburg, S.C., 1982.)

————
1916   Letters of Benjamin Hawkins. Georgia Historical Society
           Collections 9. Savannah. (Reprinted: The Reprint Compa-
           ny, Spartanburg, S.C., 1974.)

Hawthorn, Harry B., ed.
1966–1967 A Survey of the Contemporary Indians of Canada: A
           Report on Economic, Political, Educational Needs and
           Policies. 2 vols. Ottawa: Indian Affairs Branch.

Hay, Denys
1957   Europe: The Emergence of an Idea. Edinburgh: University
           Press.

Hayden, Ferdinand V.
1869   Description of Pipestone Quarry and Specimens of Rock.
           Proceedings of the American Philosophical Society
           10(76):274–275. Philadelphia.

1873   Sixth Annual Report of the United States Geological Survey of the Territories. Washington: U.S. Government Printing Office.

Hayden, Willard C.
1972   The Battle of Pierre's Hole. *Idaho Yesterdays* 16(2):2–11.

Haylemon, Merle, coll.
1938   A Hunting Song. WPA Project, Pittsburgh. (Manuscript in Archives of Folksong, Pennsylvania WPA Files, Library of Congress, Washington.)

Hayne, David M.
1969   Louis Armand de Lom d'Arce de Lahontan. Pp. 439–445 in Vol. 2 of Dictionary of Canadian Biography. 11 vols. Toronto: University of Toronto Press.

Haynie, Nancy A., comp.
1984   Native Americans and the Military, Today and Yesterday. Fort McPherson, Ga.: U.S. Army Forces Command Information Branch.

Hazard, Joseph T.
1952   Companion of Adventure: A Biography of Isaac Ingalls Stevens, First Governor of Washington Territory. Portland, Oreg.: Binfords and Mort.

Hazard, Samuel, ed.
1838–1853 Minutes of the Provincial Council of Pennsylvania from the Organization to the Termination of the Proprietary Government. 16 vols. Harrisburg: Theophilus Fenn.

1850   Annals of Pennsylvania, from the Discovery of the Delaware, 1609–1682. Philadelphia: Hazard and Mitchell.

Hazard, Samuel et al., eds.
1852–1949 Pennsylvania Archives. 138 vols. Harrisburg: Commonwealth of Pennsylvania.

Healey, George R.
1958   The French Jesuits and the Idea of the Noble Savage. *William and Mary Quarterly, 3d ser.*, Vol. 15(2):143–167. Williamsburg, Va.

Hearne, Samuel
1958   A Journey from Prince of Wales's Fort in Hudson's Bay to the Northern Ocean, in the Years 1769, 1770, 1771, and 1772 [1795]. Richard Glover, ed. Toronto: Macmillan.

1958a   Coppermine Journey; An Account of a Great Adventure, Selected from the Journals of Samuel Hearne. Farley Mowat, ed. Boston: Little, Brown.

Hearting, Ernie [Ernst Herzig]
1951   Rote Wolke. Einsiedeln, Switzerland: Waldstatt.

1954   Stumpfes Messer. Einsiedeln, Switzerland: Waldstatt.

1956   Geronimo. Einsiedeln, Switzerland: Waldstatt.

Hebard, Grace Raymond
1932   Sacajawea. Glendale, Calif.: Arthur H. Clark.

Hebard, Grace Raymond, and E.A. Brininstool
1922   The Bozeman Trail: Historical Accounts of the Blazing of the Overland Routes into the Northwest, and the Fights with Red Cloud's Warriors. 2 vols. Cleveland, Ohio: Arthur H. Clark.

Heckewelder, John G.E.
1819   An Account of the History, Manners, and Customs of the Indian Nations, Who Once Inhabited Pennsylvania and the Neighboring States. *Transactions of the Committee of History, Moral Science and General Literature of the American Philosophical Society* 1. Philadelphia.

1820   A Narrative of the Mission of the United Brethren Among the Delaware and Mohegan Indians from Its Commencement in the Year 1740 to the Close of the Year 1880.

Philadelphia: M'Carty and Davis. (Reprinted: Arno Press, New York, 1971.)

1876   History, Manners, and Customs of the Indian Nations Who Once Inhabited Pennsylvania and the Neighbouring States [1819]. Rev. ed. William C. Reichel, ed. *Memoirs of the Historical Society of Pennsylvania* 12. Philadelphia.

Heidenreich, Conrad E., and Arthur J. Ray
1976   The Early Fur Trades: A Study in Cultural Interaction. Toronto: McClelland and Stewart.

Heimert, Alan
1953   Puritanism, the Wilderness, and the Frontier. *New England Quarterly* 26(3):361–382.

Heitman, Francis B., comp.
1903   Historical Register and Dictionary of the United States Army, from Its Organization, September 29, 1789, to March 2, 1903. Washington: U.S. Government Printing Office. (Reprinted: University of Illinois, Urbana, 1965.)

Heizer, Robert F.
1940   The Introduction of Monterey Shells to the Indians of the Northwest Coast. *Pacific Northwest Quarterly* 31(4):399–402. Seattle.

1941   Alexander S. Taylor's Map of California Indian Tribes, 1864. *Quarterly of the California Historical Society* 20(2):171–180. San Francisco.

————, ed.
1952   The Mission Indian Vocabularies of Alphonse Pinart. *University of California Anthropological Records* 15(1):1–84. Berkeley.

————, ed.
1969   Man's Discovery of His Past: A Sourcebook of Original Articles. Palo Alto, Calif.: Peek Publications.

————, comp.
1969a   Catalogue of the C. Hart Merriam Collection of Data Concerning California Tribes and Other American Indians. Berkeley: University of California, Archaeological Research Facility, Department of Anthropology.

1972   The Eighteen Unratified Treaties of 1851–1852 Between the California Indians and the United States Government. Berkeley: University of California Archaeological Research Facility.

1974   They Were Only Diggers: A Collection of Articles from California Newspapers, 1851–1866, on Indian and White Relations. *Ballena Press Publications in Archaeology, Ethnology and History* 1. Ramona, Calif.

————, ed.
1974a   The Destruction of California Indians: A Collection of Documents from the Period 1847 to 1865 in Which Are Described Some of the Things That Happened to Some of the Indians of California. Santa Barbara, Calif.: Peregrine Smith.

Heizer, Robert F., and Alan J. Almquist
1971   The Other Californians: Prejudice and Discrimination Under Spain, Mexico, and the United States to 1920. Berkeley: University of California Press.

Hemingway, Ernest
1926   Torrents of Spring: A Romantic Novel in Honor of the Passing of a Great Race. New York: Scribner.

1938   The Short Stories of Ernest Hemingway: The First Forty-Nine Stories and the Play The Fifth Column. New York: Scribners.

Hemming, John
1978   Red Gold: The Conquest of the Brazilian Indians, 1500–1760. Cambridge, Mass.: Harvard University Press.

749

Hendrickson, James E.
1967   Joe Lane of Oregon: Machine Politics and the Sectional Crisis, 1849–1861. New Haven, Conn.: Yale University Press.

Hening, Walter W., ed.
1969   The Statutes at Large: Being a Collection of All the Laws of Virginia, from the First Session of the Legislature in the Year 1619 [1819–1823]. 13 vols. Charlottesville: University of Virginia Press.

Hennepin, Louis
1683   Description de la Louisiane; nouvellement decouverte au sud'oüest de la Nouvelle France, par ordre du roy. Paris: Sebastien Huré.

——
1697   Nouvelle découverte d'un très grand pays situé dans l'Amérique entre le Nouveau Mexique et la Mer Glaciale. Utrecht, The Netherlands: G. Broedelet. (Reprinted: A New Discovery of a Vast Country in America. 2 vols. Canadiana House, Toronto, 1969.)

——
1698   Nouveau voyage d'un pays plus grand que l'Europe . . . .Utrecht, The Netherlands: A. Schouten.

Henning, Elizabeth R.P.
1982   Western Dakota Winter Counts: An Analysis of the Effects of Western Migration and Culture Change. Plains Anthropologist 27(95):57–65.

Henry, Alexander
1809   Travels and Adventures in Canada and the Indian Territories Between the Years 1760 and 1776. 2 Pts. New York: I. Riley. (Reprinted: Garland, New York, 1976.)

Henry, Jeannette
1970   Textbooks and the American Indian. Rupert Costo, ed. San Francisco: Indian Historian Press.

[Henry, Jeannette, and Rupert Costo]
1967   The American Indian Historical Society. The Indian Historian 1(1).

Hentz, Nicholas M.
1825   Tadeuskind, the Last King of the Lenape: An Historical Tale. Boston: Cummings, Hilliard.

Herder, Johann G.
1778   Volkslieder. Leipzig, Germany: Weygand. (Reprinted: G. Olms, New York, 1981.)

Herrick, Cheesman A.
1926   White Servitude in Pennsylvania: Indentured and Redemption Labor in Colony and Commonwealth. Philadelphia: J.J. McVey. (Reprinted: Negro Universities Press, New York, 1969.)

Herskovits, Melville J.
1953   Franz Boas: The Science of Man in the Making. New York: Charles Scribner's Sons. (Reprinted: A.M. Kelley, Clifton, N.J., 1973.)

Hertzberg, Hazel W.
1971   The Search for an American Indian Identity: Modern Pan-Indian Movements. Syracuse, N.Y.: Syracuse University Press.

——
1975   [Interview with Frank W. Parker, Denver, Colo., June, 1975.] (Tape in Hertzberg's possession.)

Herzig, Ernst see Hearting, Ernie

Hess, Bill
1981   Aleuts Recall Horrors of Relocation. Tundra Times 18(38):1.

Hewitt, J.N.B.
1895   [Obituary of] James Owen Dorsey. American Anthropologist o.s. 8(2):180–183.

——
1910   Oswegatchie. P. 162 in Vol. 2 of Handbook of American Indians North of Mexico. F.W. Hodge, ed. 2 vols. Bureau of American Ethnology Bulletin 30. Washington.

Hiatt, Burritt M.
1958   James M. Haworth, Quaker Indian Agent. Bulletin of the Friends Historical Association 47(2):80–93.

Hickerson, Harold
1965   The Virginia Deer and Intertribal Buffer Zones in the Upper Mississippi Valley. Pp. 43–65 in Man, Culture and Animals: The Role of Animals in Human Ecological Adjustments. Anthony Leeds and Andrew P. Vayda, eds. American Association for the Advancement of Science Publication 78. Washington.

——
1973   Fur Trade Colonialism and the North American Indian. Journal of Ethnic Studies 1(2):15–44.

Hickerson, Joseph C.
[1970]   A Brief List of Works Relating to the Use of American Indian Music in Composition. (Typescript in Archives of Folksong, Library of Congress, Washington.)
——, comp.
[1970a]   A Brief List of Composers Utilizing American Indian Music. (Typescript in Archives of Folksong, Library of Congress, Washington.)
——, comp.
[1972]   A List of Folklore and Folk Music Archives and Related Collections in the U.S. and Canada. (Typescript in Archives of Folksong, Library of Congress, Washington.)

Hicks, James E.
1940   Notes on United States Ordnance. 2 vols. Mount Vernon, N.Y.: Hicks.

Higham, Robin, ed.
1975   A Guide to the Sources of United States Military History. Hamden, Conn.: Archon Books.

Higham, Robin, and Donald J. Mrozek, eds.
1981   A Guide to the Sources of United States Military History: Supplement 1. Hamden, Conn.: Archon Books.
——, eds.
1986   A Guide to the Sources of United States Military History: Supplement 2. Hamden, Conn.: Archon Books.

Hilger, Michael
1986   The American Indian in Film. Metuchen, N.J.: Scarecrow Press.

Hill, Edward E., comp.
1965   Records of the Bureau of Indian Affairs. 2 vols. (U.S. National Archives, Preliminary Inventories 163.) Washington: U.S. National Archives and Record Service.

——
1967   Historical Sketches for Jurisdictional and Subject Headings Used for Letters Received by the Office of Indian Affairs, 1824–1880. Washington: U.S. National Archives and Record Service.

——
1979   John Q. Smith, 1865–77. Pp. 149–153 in The Commissioners of Indian Affairs, 1834–1977. Robert M. Kvasnicka and Herman J. Viola, eds. Lincoln: University of Nebraska Press.

Hill, Joseph J.
1930   Spanish and Mexican Exploration and Trade Northwest from New Mexico into the Great Basin, 1765–1853. Utah Historical Quarterly 3(1):3–23. Salt Lake City.

Hill, Roscoe R., ed.
1904–1937   Journals of the Continental Congress, 1774–1789. 34 vols. Washington: U.S. Government Printing Office.

Hill, Ruth Beebe
1979   Hanta Yo: An American Saga. Garden City, N.Y.: Doubleday.

Hill, Samuel
1815–1822   Journal and Log of Two Voyages: The Ophelia from Boston
to Chile, China, etc. and Return to Boston, January 1815 to
February 28, 1817. The Packet, Boston to China and Three
Voyages Between China and South America and Return to
Boston, April 17, 1817 to July 10, 1822. (Manuscript in the
New York Public Library.)

Hill, W.W.
1938   The Agricultural and Hunting Methods of the Navaho
Indians. *Yale University Publications in Anthropology* 18.
New Haven. (Reprinted: AMS Press, New York, 1978.)

Hillerman, Tony
1980   People of Darkness. New York: Harper and Row.

1982   The Dark Wind. New York: Harper and Row.

1984   The Ghostway. New York: Harper and Row.

1986   Skinwalkers. New York: Harper and Row.

Hilliard, S.B.
1972   Indian Land Cessions. Map, suppl. No. 16. *Annals of the
Association of American Geographers* 62(2). Washington.

Hines, Harvey K.
1899   Missionary History of the Pacific Northwest. Portland,
Oreg.: H.K. Hines.

Hinman, George W.
1933   The American Indian and Christian Missions. New York:
Fleming H. Revell.

Hinsley, Curtis M., Jr.
1981   Savages and Scientists: The Smithsonian Institution and the
Development of American Anthropology, 1846–1910.
Washington: Smithsonian Institution Press.

Hinsley, Curtis M., and Bill Holm
1976   A Cannibal in the National Museum: The Early Career of
Franz Boas in America. *American Anthropologist*
78(2):306–316.

Hirshson, Stanley P.
1969   The Lion of the Lord: A Biography of Brigham Young.
New York: Alfred A. Knopf.

Hitta, Aloysius
1925   Indians Welcome Bishop Kelley. *The Indian Sentinel*
5(3):108.

Hittell, Theodore H.
1885–1897   History of California. 4 vols. San Francisco: Pacific Press
Publishing House.

Hoar, George F.
1903   Autobiography of Seventy Years. 2 vols. New York: C.
Scribner's Sons.

Hoberg, Walter R.
1934   Early History of Colonel Alexander McKee. *Pennsylvania
Magazine of History and Biography* 58(1):26–36.

1935   A Tory in the Northwest. *Pennsylvania Magazine of History
and Biography* 59(1):32–41.

Hobson, Geary, ed.
1981   The Remembered Earth; an Anthology of Contemporary
Native American Literature. Albuquerque: University of
New Mexico Press.

Hockett, Charles F., ed.
1970   A Leonard Bloomfield Anthology. Bloomington: Indiana
University Press. (Abridged ed., University of Chicago
Press, Chicago, 1987.)

Hodge, Frederick W., ed.
1907–1910   Handbook of American Indians North of Mexico. 2 vols.
Bureau of American Ethnology Bulletin 30. Washington.
(Reprinted: Rowman and Littlefield, New York, 1971).

1937   History of Hawikuh, New Mexico, One of the So-called
Cities of Cibola. (*Publications of the Frederick Webb Hodge
Anniversary Publication Fund* 1) Los Angeles: Southwest
Museum.

Hodgen, Margaret T.
1964   Early Anthropology in the Sixteenth and Seventeenth
Centuries. Philadelphia: University of Pennsylvania Press.

Hodgetts, John E.
1955   Indian Affairs: The White Man's Albatross. Pp. 205–225 in
Pioneer Public Service: An Administrative History of the
United Canadas, 1841–1867. Toronto: University of Toronto Press.

Hoebel, E. Adamson
1960   William Robertson: An 18th Century Anthropologist-
Historian. *American Anthropologist* 62(4):648–655.

Hoeldtke, Frank
1981   Welcome to the Wild West in Germany. *The Calgary
Herald*, July 4:10. Calgary, Alta.

Hoffman, Walter J.
1896   The Menomini Indians. Pp. 3–328 in *14th Annual Report of
the Bureau of American Ethnology for the Years 1885–1886.*
Washington.

Hoffmann, Franz
1845   Narramatta und Conanchet. Stuttgart, Germany: Stoppani.

Hoffmann-Harnisch, Wolfgang
1935   Manitus Welt versinkt. Berlin: Drei Masken.

Hogan, Linda
1981   Daughters, I Love You. Denver, Colo.: Loretto Heights
College.

1985   Seeing Through the Sun. Amherst, Mass,: University of
Massachusetts Press.

Hoig, Stan
1961   The Sand Creek Massacre. Norman: University of Oklahoma Press.

1976   The Battle of the Washita: The Sheridan-Custer Indian
Campaign of 1867–69. Garden City, N.Y.: Doubleday.

Holder, Preston
1967   The Fur Trade as Seen from the Indian Point of View. Pp.
129–139 in The Frontier Re-examined. John F. McDermott, ed. Urbana: University of Illinois Press.

1970   The Hoe and the Horse on the Plains: A Study of Cultural
Development Among North American Indians. Lincoln:
University of Nebraska Press.

Holm, Bill, and George I. Quimby
1980   Edward S. Curtis in the Land of the War Canoes: A Pioneer
Cinematographer in the Pacific Northwest. Seattle: University of Washington Press.

Holm, Thomas Campanius
1834   A Short Description of the Province of New Sweden. Now
called, by the English, Pennsylvania in America. Peter S.
Du Ponceau, ed. and trans. *Memoirs of the Historical Society
of Pennsylvania* 3 (Pt. 1). Philadelphia.

Homans, Benjamin, ed.
1835–1842   Army and Navy Chronicle. 13 vols. Washington: Benjamin
Homans.

Honey, William B.
1952   English Pottery and Porcelain. 4th ed. London: Adam and
Charles Black.

Honigsheim, Paul
1945   Voltaire as Anthropologist. *American Anthropologist*
47(1):104–118.

1952   The American Indian in the Philosophy of the Enlightenment. *Osiris* 10:91–108.

Honour, Hugh
1975   The New Golden Land: European Images of America from the Discoveries to the Present Time. New York: Pantheon Books.

1975a   The European Vision of America. Cleveland, Ohio: Cleveland Museum of Art.

Hoopes, Alban W.
1932   Indian Affairs and Their Administration, with Special Reference to the Far West, 1849–1860. Philadelphia: University of Pennsylvania Press.

Hoopes, Chad L.
1970   Redick McKee and the Humboldt Bay Region, 1851–1852. *California Historical Quarterly* 49(3):195–219.

Hoover, Dwight W.
1976   The Red and the Black. Chicago: Rand McNally.

Hopkins, Samuel
1753   Historical Memoirs, Relating to the Housatunnuk Indians or, An Account of the Methods Used and the Pains Taken, for the Propagation of the Gospel . . . [Based largely on John Sergeant's manuscripts, now lost.] Boston: S. Kneeland. (Reprinted: W. Abbatt, New York, 1911.)

Horn, Tom
1904   Life of Tom Horn, Government Scout and Interpreter. John Coble, ed. Denver, Colo.: The Louthan Book Company.

Horn, William F.
1945   The Horn Papers: Early Westward Movement on the Monongahela and Upper Ohio, 1765–1795. Scottsdale, Pa.: Herald Press.

Hornaday, William T.
1889   The Extermination of the American Bison, with a Sketch of Its Discovery and Life History. Pp. 367–548 in *Annual Report of the United States National Museum for 1887*. Pt. 2. Washington. (Reprinted: Shorey Book Store, Seattle, Wash., 1971.)

Horsman, Reginald
1964   Matthew Elliott, British Indian Agent. Detroit, Mich.: Wayne State University Press.

1967   Expansion and American Indian Policy, 1783–1812. East Lansing: Michigan State University Press.

Horton, John T.
1939   James Kent, a Study in Conservatism, 1763–1847. New York: D. Appleton-Century. (Reprinted: Da Capo Press, New York, 1969.)

Hosen, Frederick E.
1985   Rifle, Blanket, and Kettle: Selected Indian Treaties and Laws. Jefferson, N.C.: McFarland.

Hosley, Edward H.
1966   Factionalism and Acculturation in an Alaskan Athapascan Community. (Unpublished Ph.D. Dissertation in Anthropology, University of California, Los Angeles.)

Hotz, Gottfried
1974   Indianer Nordamerikas: Katalog zur Sammlung Hotz der Stadt Zürich. Zurich, Switzerland: Städtisches Schulamt.

Hough, Walter
1933   William Henry Holmes. *American Anthropologist* 35(4):752–764.

Howard, James H.
1955   Pan-Indian Culture of Oklahoma. *Scientific Monthly* 18(5):215–220.

1976   Yanktonai Ethnohistory and the John K. Bear Winter Count. *Plains Anthropologist Memoir* 11. Lincoln, Neb.

1978   The Native American Image in Western Europe. *American Indian Quarterly* 4(1):33–56.

Howard, Joseph K.
1952   Strange Empire: A Narrative of the Northwest. New York: Morrow.

Howard, Oliver O.
1881   Nez Perce Joseph, an Account of His Ancestors . . . . Boston: Lee and Shepherd. (Reprinted: Da Capo Press, New York, 1972.)

1907   My Life and Experiences Among Our Hostile Indians. Hartford, Conn.: A.D. Worthington. (Reprinted: Da Capo Press, New York, 1972.)

1908   Famous Indian Chiefs I Have Known. New York: The Century Company. (Reprinted in 1916.)

Howay, Frederick W.
1925   Indian Attacks Upon Maritime Traders of the North-West Coast, 1785–1805. *Canadian Historical Review* 6(4)287–309.

————, ed.
1941   Voyages of the "Columbia" to the Northwest Coast, 1787–1790 and 1790–1793. Boston: Massachusetts Historical Society.

1942   The Introduction of Intoxicating Liquors Amongst the Indians of the Northwest Coast. *British Columbia Historical Quarterly* 6(3):157–169. Vancouver.

1973   A List of Trading Vessels in the Maritime Fur Trade, 1785–1825 (*Materials for the Study of Alaskan History* 2). Kingston, Ont.: Limestone Press.

Howe, M.A. DeWolfe
1911   The Life and Labors of Bishop Hare: Apostle to the Sioux. New York: Sturgis and Walton.

Howe, Walter
1949   The Mining Guild of New Spain and Its Tribunal General, 1770–1821 (*Harvard Historical Studies* 56). Cambridge, Mass.: Harvard University Press.

Howland, Henry R.
1903   The Seneca Mission at Buffalo Creek. Frank H. Severance, ed. *Publications of the Buffalo Historical Society* 6:125–161.

Hoxie, Frederick E.
1984   A Final Promise: The Campaign to Assimilate the Indians, 1880–1920. Lincoln: University of Nebraska Press.

Hsu, Francis L.K.
1964   Rethinking the Concept "Primitive." *Current Anthropology* 5(3):169–178.

Hubbard, Ralph
1927   Handicraft. Pp. 538–547 in Handbook for Boys. New York: Boy Scouts of America.

1935   American Indian Crafts, Including Suggestive Outlines and Bibliography of Indian Lore. New York: Plume Trading and Sales Company.

Hubbard, William
1865   The History of the Indian Wars in New England from the First Settlement to the Termination of the War with King Philip, in 1677. Samuel G. Drake, ed. 2 vols. Roxbury, Mass.: W. Elliot Woodward. (Reprinted: Lenox Hill, New York, 1971.)

Hubbell, Jay B.
1965   The Smith-Pocahantas Literary Legend. Pp. 175–204 in South and Southwest: Literary Essays and Reminiscences, by J.B. Hubbell. Durham, N.C.: Duke University Press.

Hubert, René
1923   Les Sciences sociales dans l'Encyclopédie: la Philosophie de l'histoire et le problème des origines sociales. Paris: Felix Alcan.

Huddleston, Lee E.
[1967]   Origins of the American Indians: European Concepts, 1492–1729. Austin: University of Texas.

Huden, John C., comp.
1962   Indian Place Names of New England. *Museum of the American Indian. Heye Foundation Contributions* 18. New York.

Hudson, Charles M.
1970   The Catawba Nation. Athens: University of Georgia Press.

_____
1976   The Southeastern Indians. Knoxville: University of Tennessee Press.

Hudson's Bay Company
1821–1835 [George Simpson Correspondence Book, Inward.] (Manuscript D.4/121 in Hudson's Bay Company Archives, Provincial Archives of Manitoba, Winnipeg, Canada.)

_____
1826–1860 [Fort Vancouver Correspondence, Inward.] (Manuscript B.223/c/1 in Hudson's Bay Company Archives, Provincial Archives of Manitoba, Winnipeg, Canada.)

_____
1831–1866 [Fort Simpson (Nass) Post Journal.] (Manuscripts B201/a/3 and B201/a/4 in Hudson's Bay Company Archives, Provincial Archives of Manitoba, Winnipeg, Canada.)

_____
[1920]   [Album 57–58, Documenting Hudson's Bay Company's 250th Anniversary.] (Documents in Unclassified Dead Dossier 7, Provincial Archives of Manitoba, Winnipeg, Canada.)

_____
1929   [Annual Report of the Fur Trade Department.] (Manuscript A 74/43 in Hudson's Bay Company Archives, Provincial Archives of Manitoba, Winnipeg, Canada.)

Hughes, Thomas
1907–1917 History of the Society of Jesus in North America, Colonial and Federal. 4 vols. New York: Longmans, Green.

Hultkrantz, Åke
1984   Swedish Contributions to North American Indian Studies. Pp. 16–35 in *North American Indian Studies* 2. Pieter Hovens, ed. Göttingen, West Germany: Edition Herodot.

Hulton, Paul and David B. Quinn
1964   The American Drawings of John White, 1577–1580, with Drawings of European and Oriental Subjects. 2 vols. Chapel Hill: University of North Carolina Press.

Hulton, Paul, et al.
1977   The Work of Jacques Le Moyne de Morgues: A Huguenot Artist in France, Florida, and England. London: British Museum Publications.

Hundley, Norris, Jr.
1978   The Dark and Bloody Ground of Indian Water Rights: Confusion Elevated to Principle. *Western Historical Quarterly* 9(4):455–482.

_____
1982   The "Winters" Decision and Indian Water Rights: A Mystery Reexamined. *Western Historical Quarterly* 13(1):17–42.

Hunt, Aurora
1950   The Army of the Pacific: Its Operations in California, Texas, Arizona, New Mexico, Utah, Nevada, Oregon, Washington, Plains Region, Mexico, etc., 1860–1866. Glendale, Calif.: Arthur H. Clark.

_____
1958   Major General James Henry Carleton, 1814–1873: Western Frontier Dragoon. Glendale, Calif.: Arthur H. Clark.

Hunt, George T.
1940   The Wars of the Iroquois: A Study in Intertribal Trade Relations. Madison: University of Wisconsin Press. (Reprinted in 1960.)

Hunt, Walter B.
[1942]   Indiancraft. Milwaukee, Wis.: Bruce Publishing Company.

Hunter, Milton R.
1940   Brigham Young, the Colonizer. Salt Lake City, Utah: Deseret News. (Reprinted, 4th rev. ed., Peregrine Smith, Santa Barbara, Calif., 1973.)

Hurley, Gerald T.
1951   Buried Treasure Tales in America. *Western Folklore* 10(3):197–216.

Hussey, John A.
1957   The History of Fort Vancouver and Its Physical Structure. [Takoma, Wash.]: Washington State Historical Society.

_____
1967   Champoeg: Place of Transition, a Disputed History. Portland: Oregon Historical Society.

Hutchinson, Anderson
1848   Code of Mississippi: Being an Analytical Compilation of the Public and General Statutes of the Territory and State with Tabular References to the Local and Private Acts, from 1789 to 1848 . . . .Jackson, Miss.: Price and Fall.

Hutchinson, Cecil A.
1969   Frontier Settlement in Mexican California: The Híjar-Padrés Colony and Its Origins, 1769–1835. New Haven, Conn.: Yale University Press.

Hutchinson, Geoff
1985   Grey Owl: The Incredible Story of Archie Belaney, 1888–1938. [Brede, East Sussex, England: G. Hutchinson.]

Hutchinson, Thomas
1936   The History of the Colony and Province of Massachusetts-Bay [1767]. Lawrence S. Mayo, ed. Cambridge, Mass.: Harvard University Press.

Hutchison, Bruce
1950   The Fraser. Toronto: Clarke, Irwin and Company. (Reprinted in 1982.)

Hutton, Elizabeth A.
1961   The Micmac Indians of Nova Scotia to 1834. (Unpublished M.A. Thesis in History, Dalhousie University, Halifax, N.S.)

Hyatt, Ezra A.
1878   [Letter to Carl Schurz, Secretary of the Interior, Dated May 23, 1878, re Consolidation and Removal of Indians.] (Manuscript, Report Books of the Bureau of Indian Affairs, 30:554, M348, Natural Resources Branch, Record Group 75, National Archives, Washington.)

Hyde, George E.
1951   Pawnee Indians. Denver, Colo.: University of Denver Press.

Hymes, Dell
1961   Alfred Louis Kroeber. *Language* 37(1):1–28.

Ibbotson, Joseph D., and S.N.D. North, eds.
1922   Documentary History of Hamilton College. Clinton, N.Y.: The College.

Ickes, Harold L.
1943   The Autobiography of a Curmudgeon. New York: Reynal and Hitchcock.

_____
1953   The Secret Diary of Harold L. Ickes. New York: Simon and Schuster.

Indian Rights Association
1884–1935 Annual Reports of the Board of Directors of the Indian Rights Association (Incorporated). 52 vols. Philadelphia: Office of the Indian Rights Association.

753

Ingraham, Joseph
1971   Journal of the Brigantine Hope on a Voyage to the Northwest Coast of North America, 1790–92. Mark D. Kaplanoff, ed. Barre, Mass.: Imprint Society.

Innis, Harold A.
1962   The Fur Trade in Canada: An Introduction to Canadian Economic History [1930]. New Haven, Conn.: Yale University Press.

Institute for the Development of Indian Law
1973–1975   The American Indian Treaties Series. 9 vols. Washington: Institute for the Development of Indian Law.

Inter-American Indian Institute
1943   Convention Between the United States of America and Certain Other American Republics Respecting the Inter-American Indian Institute. (Treaty Series 978). Washington: U.S. Government Printing Office.

Irving, Washington
1964   Astoria: or, Anecdotes of an Enterprise Beyond the Rocky Mountains [1836]. Edgeley W. Todd, ed. Norman: University of Oklahoma Press.

[Isley, Mary B., et al., comps.]
1970   Uncommon Controversy: Fishing Rights of the Muckleshoot, Puyallup, and Nisqually Indians: A Report Prepared for the American Friends Service Committee. Seattle: University of Washington Press.

Ismert, Cornelius M.
1968   James Bridger. Pp.85–104 in Vol. 6 of The Mountain Men and the Fur Trade of the Far West. LeRoy R. Hafen, ed. Glendale, Calif.: Arthur H. Clark.

Iverson, Peter
1982   Carlos Montezuma and the Changing World of Indians. Albuquerque: University of New Mexico Press.

Ives, Edward D., coll.
1971   How Passadaum Keag (Maine) Got Its Name. (Letter of April 12, 1971; in Rayna Green's possession.)

Ives, Ronald L., ed. and trans.
1939   Sedelmayr's Relacion of 1746. *Anthropological Papers* 9, *Bureau of American Ethnology Bulletin* 123. Washington.

JCC=U.S. Continental Congress
1904–1937   Journals of the Continental Congress, 1774–1789. Worthington C. Ford et al, eds. 34 vols. Washington: U.S. Government Printing Office.

JR=Thwaites, Reuben G., ed.
1896–1901   The Jesuit Relations and Allied Documents: Travel and Explorations of the Jesuit Missionaries in New France, 1610–1791. The Original French, Latin and Italian Texts, with English Translations and Notes. 73 vols. Cleveland, Ohio: Burrows Brothers. (Reprinted: Pageant, New York, 1959.)

Jablow, Joseph
1950   The Cheyenne in Plains Indian Trade Relations, 1795–1840. *Monographs of the American Ethnological Society* 19. New York.

Jackman, S.W., ed.
1978   The Journal of William Sturgis. Victoria, B.C.: Sono Nis Press.

Jackson, Curtis E., and Marcia J. Galli
1977   A History of the Bureau of Indian Affairs and Its Activities Among Indians. San Francisco: R and E Associates.

Jackson, Donald
1955   Ma-ka-tai-me-she-kia-kiak, Black Hawk: An Autobiography. Urbana: University of Illinois Press.

————
1981   Thomas Jefferson and the Stony Mountains: Exploring the West from Monticello. Urbana: University of Illinois Press.

Jackson, Helen Hunt
1881   A Century of Dishonor: A Sketch of the United States Government's Dealings with Some of the North American Tribes. New York: Harper and Brothers. (Reprinted in 1965.)

————
1884   Ramona: A Story. Boston: Roberts Brothers.

Jackson, Sheldon
[1880]   Alaska and Missions of the North Pacific Coast. New York: Dodd, Mead.

————
1891–1908   Annual Report[s] on Introduction of Domestic Reindeer into Alaska, 1st–16th, 1890–1906. Washington: U.S. Government Printing Office.

Jacobs, James R.
1947   The Beginnings of the U.S. Army, 1783–1812. Princeton, N.J.: Princeton University Press.

Jacobs, Wilbur R.
1950   Diplomacy and Indian Gifts: Anglo-French Rivalry Along the Ohio and Northwest Frontiers, 1748–1763. Stanford, Calif.: Stanford University Press.

————
1966   Wilderness Politics and Indian Gifts: The Northern Colonial Frontier, 1748–1763. Lincoln: University of Nebraska Press.

————, ed.
1967   The Appalachian Indian Frontier: The Edmond Atkin Report and Plan of 1755. Lincoln: University of Nebraska Press.

————
1972   Dispossessing the American Indian: Indians and Whites on the Colonial Frontier. New York: Scribner.

————
1973   Cadwallader Colden's Noble Iroquois Savages. Pp. 34–58 in Vol. 3 of The Colonial Legacy. Lawrence H. Leder, ed. 4 vols. New York: Harper and Row.

————
1974   The Tip of the Iceberg: Pre-Columbian Indian Demography and Some Implications for Revisionism. *William and Mary Quarterly, 3d ser.,* Vol. 31(1)123–132. Williamsburg, Va.

————
1977   Robert Beverley: Colonial Ecologist and Indian Lover. Pp. 91–99 in Essays in Early Virginia Literature Honoring Richard Beale Davis. J.A. Leo Lemay, ed. New York: Burt Franklin Press.

————
1985   Dispossessing the American Indian: Indians and Whites on the Colonial Frontier. 2d rev. ed. Norman: University of Oklahoma Press.

Jaenen, Cornelius J.
1969   The Frenchification and Evangelization of the Amerindians in Seventeenth Century New France. *Canadian Catholic Historical Association Study Sessions* 35:57–71.

————
1973   The Meeting of the French and Amerindians in the Seventeenth Century. *Revue de l'Université d'Ottawa* 43(1):128–144.

————
1976   Friend and Foe: Aspects of French-Amerindian Cultural Contact in the Sixteenth and Seventeenth Centuries. New York: Columbia University Press.

————
1976a   The Role of the Church in New France. Toronto: McGraw-Hill Ryerson.

————
1984   The French Relationship with the Native Peoples of New France and Acadia. Ottawa: Indian and Northern Affairs Canada.

James, Marquis
1929   The Raven: A Biography of Sam Houston. New York: Grosset and Dunlap. (Reprinted: Chelsea House, New York, 1983.)

754

James, Rhett S.
1967   Brigham Young - Chief Washakie Indian Farm Negotia-
            tions, 1854–1857. *Annals of Wyoming* 39(2): 245–256.

Jameson, J. Franklin, ed.
1909   Narratives of New Netherland, 1609–1664. New York:
            Charles Scribner's Sons. (Reprinted: Barnes and Noble,
            New York, 1967.)

Jamieson, Melvill A.
1936   Medals Awarded to North American Indian Chiefs,
            1714–1922, and to Loyal African and Other Chiefs in
            Various Territories within the British Empire. London:
            Spink and Son.

Jane, Lionel C.
1930   Select Documents Illustrating the Four Voyages of Colum-
            bus . . . . London: Printed for the Hakluyt Society.

Janney, Samuel M.
1867   Indian Affairs. *Friends' Intelligencer* 24(33):513–514.
            Philadelphia.

1970   The Life of William Penn [1851]. Freeport, N.Y.: Books for
            Libraries Press.

Jansen, William H.
1957   A Culture's Stereotypes and Their Expression in Folk
            Clichés. *Southwestern Journal of Anthropology*
            13(2):184–200.

Jefferson, Thomas
1808   [Speech to Visiting Indian Delegation, Dated December
            1808.] (Manuscript, Letters Sent by the Secretary of War
            Relating to Indian Affairs. Vol. B:396. Record Group 75,
            National Archives, Washington.)

1903–1904   Letter to Carmichael and Short, Dated Philadelphia, June
            30, 1793. Pp. 148–161 in Vol. 9 of The Writings of Thomas
            Jefferson. Andrew A. Lipscomb and Albert E. Bergh, eds.
            20 vols. Washington: Thomas Jefferson Memorial Associa-
            tion.

1950–   Papers of Thomas Jefferson. Julian P. Boyd, ed. Princeton,
            N.J.: Princeton University Press.

1954   Notes on the State of Virginia [1787]. William Peden, ed.
            Chapel Hill: University of North Carolina Press.

Jeffries, Theodore W.
1969   A Biographical Note on Benjamin Smith Barton
            (1766–1815). *Isis* 60(2):231–232.

Jenkins, William S., comp.
1950   Guide to the Microfilm Collections of Colonial and Early
            State Records. Washington: U.S. Government Printing
            Office.

Jenness, Diamond
1964   Eskimo Administration, II: Canada. *Arctic Institute of
            North America Technical Paper* 14. Montreal. (Reprinted in
            1972.)

1985   Aboriginal Rights: The James Bay Experience. Pp. 265–285
            in The Quest for Justice: Aboriginal Peoples and Aboriginal
            Rights. Menno Boldt and J. Anthony Long with Leroy
            Little Bear, eds. Toronto: University of Toronto Press.

Jennings, Francis
1963   A Vanishing Indian: Francis Parkman versus His Sources.
            Pennsylvania Magazine of History and Biography
            87(3):306–323.

1966   The Indian Trade of the Susquehanna Valley. *Proceedings of
            the American Philosophical Society* 110(6):406–424.
            Philadelphia.

1968   Glory, Death, and Transfiguration: The Susquehannock
            Indians in the Seventeenth Century. *Proceedings of the
            American Philosophical Society* 112(1):15–53. Philadelphia.

1971   The Constitutional Evolution of the Covenant Chain.
            Proceedings of the American Philosophical Society
            115(2):88–96. Philadelphia.

1971a   Virgin Land and Savage People. *American Quarterly*
            23(4):519–541.

1971b   Goals and Functions of Puritan Missions to the Indians.
            Ethnohistory 18(3):197–212.

1975   The Invasion of America: Indians, Colonialism and the
            Cant of Conquest. Chapel Hill: University of North
            Carolina Press.

1976   The Indians' Revolution. Pp. 319–348 in The American
            Revolution/Explorations in American Radicalism. Alfred
            F. Young, ed. DeKalb: Northern Illinois University Press.

1981   Jacob Young: Indian Trader and Interpreter. Pp. 347–361
            in Struggle and Survival in Colonial America. David G.
            Sweet and Gary B. Nash, eds. Berkeley: University of
            California Press.

1982   Indians and Frontiers in Seventeenth Century Maryland.
            Pp. 216–241 in Early Maryland and the World Beyond.
            David B. Quinn, ed. Detroit, Mich.: Wayne State Universi-
            ty.

1984   The Ambiguous Iroquois Empire: The Covenant Chain
            Confederation of Indian Tribes with English Colonies from
            Its Beginning to the Lancaster Treaty of 1744. New York:
            W.W. Norton.

1985   Iroquois Alliances in American History. Pp. 37–65 in The
            History and Culture of Iroquois Diplomacy: An Interdisci-
            plinary Guide to the Treaties of the Six Nations and Their
            League. Francis Jennings et al., eds. Syracuse, N.Y.:
            Syracuse University Press.

1985a   Francis Parkman: A Brahmin Among Untouchables. *Wil-
            liam and Mary Quarterly 3d. ser.,* Vol. 40(3):305–328.
            Williamsburg, Va.

Jennings, Francis, William N. Fenton, and Mary Druke, eds.
1985   Iroquois Indians: A Documentary History of the Six
            Nations and their League; Guide to the Microfilm Collec-
            tion. Woodbridge, Conn.: Research Publications.

Jennings, Francis, et al., eds.
1985   The History and Culture of Iroquois Diplomacy: An
            Interdisciplinary Guide to the Treaties of the Six Nations
            and Their League. Syracuse, N.Y.: Syracuse University
            Press.

Jennings, Warren A.
1971   The First Mormon Mission to the Indians. *Kansas Histori-
            cal Quarterly* 37(3):288–299.

Jewitt, John R.
1815   Narrative of the Adventures and Sufferings of John R.
            Jewitt. Middletown, Conn.: Seth Richards. (Reprinted: Ye
            Galleon Press, Fairfield, Wash., 1967.)

Johannsen, Albert
1950–1962   The House of Beadle and Adams and Its Dime and Nickel
            Novels: The Story of a Vanished Literature. 3 vols. Norman:
            University of Oklahoma Press.

John, Elizabeth A.H.
1975   Storms Brewed in Other Men's Worlds: The Confrontation
            of Indians, Spanish, and French in the Southwest,
            1540–1795. College Station: Texas A and M University
            Press.

Johnson, Alice M.
1967   James Bay Artist William Richards. *The Beaver* (Sum-
            mer):4–10.

755

Johnson, Amandus
1911   The Swedish Settlements on the Delaware, 1638–1664. 2 vols. Philadelphia: University of Pennsylvania Press.
———, trans. and ed.
1930   The Instruction for Johan Printz, Governor of New Sweden. Philadelphia: The Swedish Colonial Society.

Johnson, Dorothy M.
1965   A Man Called Horse. New York: Ballantine Books. (Formerly titled: Indian Country.)

Johnson, Herbert A. et al., eds.
1974–1984   The Papers of John Marshall. 4 vols. Chapel Hill: University of North Carolina Press.

Johnson, Richard R.
1976   The Search for a Usable Indian: An Aspect of the Defense of Colonial New England. *Journal of American History* 64(3):623–651.

Johnson, Robert C.
1935   John McLoughlin: Patriarch of the Northwest. Portland, Oreg.: Metropolitan Press.

Johnson, Virginia W.
1962   The Unregimented General: A Biography of Nelson A. Miles. Boston: Houghton, Mifflin.

Johnson, Sir William
1921–1965   The Papers of Sir William Johnson. James Sullivan et al., eds. 15 vols. Albany: University of the State of New York.

Johnston, Charles M., ed.
1964   The Valley of the Six Nations: A Collection of Documents on the Indian Lands of the Grand River. Toronto: University of Toronto Press.

Jones, Charles C., Jr.
1868   Historical Sketch of Tomo-chi-chi, Mico of the Yamacraws. Albany, N.Y.: Joel Munsell. (Reprinted: Kraus Reprint Company, Millwood, N.Y., 1975.)

———
1883   The History of Georgia. 2 vols. Boston: Houghton, Mifflin. (Reprinted: The Reprint Company, Spartanburg, S.C., 1965.)

Jones, Dorothy M.
1976   Aleuts in Transition: A Comparison of Two Villages. Seattle: University of Washington Press.

Jones, Dorothy V.
1982   License for Empire: Colonialism by Treaty in Early America. Chicago: University of Chicago Press.

———
1984   Splendid Encounters: The Thought and Conduct of Diplomacy. Chicago: University of Chicago Library.

Jones, Douglas C.
1966   The Treaty of Medicine Lodge: The Story of the Great Treaty Council as Told by Eyewitnesses. Norman: University of Oklahoma Press.

Jones, Eldred D.
1965   Othello's Countrymen: The African in English Renaissance Drama. London: Published for the University College of Sierra Leone by Oxford University Press.

Jones, Electa F.
1854   Stockbridge, Past and Present; or, Records of an Old Mission Station. Springfield, Mass.: S. Bowles.

Jones, George E., Jr.
1958   The American Indian in the American Novel (1875–1950). (Unpublished Ph.D. Dissertation in American Literature, New York University, New York City.)

Jones, Howard M.
1964   O Strange New World: American Culture; the Formative Years. New York: Viking Press.

Jones, Oakah L., Jr.
1966   Pueblo Warriors and Spanish Conquest. Norman: University of Oklahoma Press.

Jones, Richard S.
1985   Federal Programs of Assistance to American Indians: A Report Prepared for the Select Committee on Indian Affairs of the United States Senate. Washington: U.S. Government Printing Office.

Jordan, John W.
1909   Adm. Hubley, Jr., Lt. Colo. Comdt. 11th Penna. Regt, His Journal, Commencing at Wyoming, July 30th, 1779. New York: J.B. Lippincott.

Jorgensen, Joseph G.
1980   Western Indians: Comparative Environments, Languages, and Cultures of 172 Western American Indian Tribes. San Francisco: W.H. Freeman.

Josephy, Alvin M., Jr.
1965   The Nez Perce Indians and the Opening of the Northwest. New Haven, Conn.: Yale University Press.

———
1968   The Indian Heritage of America. New York: Alfred A. Knopf.

———
1970   The Artist Was a Young Man: The Life Story of Peter Rindisbacher. Fort Worth, Tex.: Amon Carter Museum.

———
1971   Red Power: The American Indians' Fight for Freedom. New York: American Heritage Press.

———
1982   Now That the Buffalo's Gone: A Study of Today's Indians. New York: Alfred A. Knopf.

Jouve, Odoric
1915   Les Franciscains et le Canada: L'Établissement de la foi, 1615–1629. Quebec: Couvent des Ss. Stigmates.

Judd, Carol M.
1980   "Mixt Bands of Many Nations": 1821–70. Pp. 127–146 in Old Trails and New Directions: Papers of the Third North American Fur Trade Conference. Carol M. Judd and Arthur J. Ray, eds. Toronto: University of Toronto Press.

———
1980a   Native Labour and Social Stratification in the Hudson's Bay Company's Northern Department, 1770–1870. *Canadian Review of Sociology and Anthropology* 17(4):306–314.

Judd, Carol M., and Arthur J. Ray, eds.
1980   Old Trails and New Directions: Papers of the Third North American Fur Trade Conference. Toronto: University of Toronto Press.

Judd, Derrel W.
1968   Zadok Knopp Judd: Soldier, Colonizer, Missionary to the Lamanites. (Unpublished M.A. Thesis in History, Brigham Young University, Provo, Utah.)

Juderías y Loyot, Julián
1943   La Leyenda negra: Estudios acerca del concepto de España en el extranjero. 9th ed. Barcelona: Editorial Araluce.

Jürgen, Anna see Müller-Tannewitz, Anna

Juricek, John T.
1970   English Claims in North America to 1660: A Study in Legal and Constitutional History. (Unpublished Ph.D. Dissertation in History, University of Chicago, Chicago.)

Kalm, Pehr
1937   The America of 1750; Peter Kalm's Travels in North America: The English Version of 1770. Revised from the Original Swedish with Translation of New Material from Kalm's Diary Notes. Adolph B. Benson, ed. and trans. 2 vols. New York: Wilson-Erickson.

Kaltenboeck, Johann [Max Felde]
1900   Der Arrapahu (*Kamerad-Bibliothek* 3). Stuttgart, Germany: Union.

———
1903   Villa Biberheim. Stuttgart, Germany: Union.

Kamenskiĭ, Anatoliĭ
1985   Tlingit Indians of Alaska [1906]. Sergei Kan, trans. (*The Rasmuson Library Historical Translation Series* 2). Fairbanks: University of Alaska Press.

Kan, Sergei
[1979–1984] [Ethnographic Notes from 14 Months' Fieldwork Among the Tlingit of Alaska.] (Manuscripts in Kan's possession.)

———
1983   Russian Orthodox Missionaries and the Tlingit Indians of Alaska, 1880–1900. (Paper presented at the Second Laurier Conference on North American Ethnohistory and Ethnology, Huron College, University of Western Ontario, London.)

———
1984   Nineteenth Century Russian Missionaries in Southeastern Alaska: Ethnographers and Agents of Change. (Unpublished paper presented at the Annual Conference of the American Society for Ethnohistory, New Orleans, La.)

———
1985   Russian Orthodox Brotherhoods Among the Tlingit: Missionary Goals and Native Response. *Ethnohistory* 32(3):196–222.

———
1987   Memory Eternal: Russian Orthodox Christianity and the Tlingit Mortuary Complex. *Arctic Anthropology* 24. (1):32–55.

Kandert, Josef
1982   Jak si lidehorajc. Prague: Naprstek Museum.

Kane, Paul
1925   Wanderings of an Artist Among the Indians of North America....Toronto: Radisson Society of Canada. (Reprinted: C.E. Tuttle, Rutland, Vt., 1967.)

Kappler, Charles J., ed. and comp.
1904–1941   Indian Affairs: Laws and Treaties. 5 vols. Washington: U.S. Government Printing Office. (Reprinted: AMS Press, New York, 1971.)

Karamanski, Theodore J.
1982   The Iroquois and the Fur Trade of the Far West. *The Beaver* 312(4):4–13. Winnipeg, Man.

Kashevaroff, Andrew P.
1927   Ivan Veniaminov, Innocent, Metropolitan of Moscow and Kolomna. *Alaska Magazine* 1(2–4):49–56, 145–150, 217–224.

Kawashima, Yasuhide
1969   Jurisdiction of the Colonial Courts Over the Indians in Massachusetts, 1689–1763. *New England Quarterly* 42(4):532–550.

———
1969a   Legal Origins of the Indian Reservation in Colonial Massachusetts. *American Journal of Legal History* 13(1):42–56.

———
1986   Puritan Justice and the Indian: White Man's Law in Massachusetts, 1630–1763. Middletown, Conn.: Wesleyan University Press.

Kay, Jeanne
1977   The Land of La Baye: The Ecological Impact of the Green Bay Fur Trade, 1634–1836. (Unpublished Ph.D. Dissertation in Geography, University of Wisconsin, Madison.)

———
1979   Wisconsin Indian Hunting Patterns, 1634–1836. *Annals of the Association of American Geographers* 66:402–418. Washington.

———
1985   Native Americans in the Fur Trade and Wildlife Depletion. *Environmental Review* 9(2):118–130.

Keegan, Gregory J., and Leandro Tormo Sanz
1957   Experiencia misionera en la Florida (siglos XVI y XVII). Madrid: Instituto Santo Toribo de Mogrovejo.

Keen, Benjamin
1971   The Aztec Image in Western Thought. New Brunswick, N.J.: Rutgers University Press.

Keen, Gregory B.
1884   New Sweden, or The Swedes on the Delaware. Pp. 443–502 in Vol. 4 of Narrative and Critical History of America. Justin Winsor, ed. 8 vols. Boston: Houghton, Mifflin.

Kehoe, Alice B.
1981   North American Indians: A Comprehensive Account. Englewood Cliffs, N.J.: Prentice Hall.

Keiser, Albert
1933   The Indian in American Literature. New York: Oxford University Press. (Reprinted: Octagon Press, New York, 1975.)

Kellaway, William
1962   The New England Company, 1649–1776: Missionary Society to the American Indians. New York: Barnes and Noble.

Keller, Robert H., Jr.
1983   American Protestantism and United States Indian Policy, 1869–82. Lincoln: University of Nebraska Press.

Kelley, J. Charles
1952   Factors Involved in the Abandonment of Certain Peripheral Southwestern Settlements. *American Anthropologist* 54(3):356–387.

———
1955   Juan Sabeata and Diffusion in Aboriginal Texas. *American Anthropologist* 57(5):981–995.

Kelley, J. Charles, and Ellen A. Kelley
1975   An Alternative Hypothesis for the Explanation of Anasazi Culture History. Pp. 178–223 in Collected Papers in Honor of Florence Hawley Ellis. Theodore R. Frisbie, ed. *Papers of the Archaeological Society of New Mexico* 2. Albuquerque.

Kellogg, Louise Phelps, ed.
1917   Early Narratives of the Northwest, 1634–1699. New York: Charles Scribner's Sons.

———
1925   The French Regime in Wisconsin and the Northwest. Madison: The State Historical Society of Wisconsin. (Reprinted: Cooper Square Publishers, New York, 1968.)

———
1935   The British Regime in Wisconsin and the Northwest. Madison: The State Historical Society of Wisconsin. (Reprinted: Da Capo Press, New York, 1971.)

Kelly, Henry W.
1941   The Franciscan Missions of New Mexico, 1740–1760. *Historical Society of New Mexico, Publications in History* 10. Albuquerque.

Kelly, Lawrence C.
1968   The Navajo Indian and Federal Indian Policy, 1900–1935. Tucson: University of Arizona Press.

———
1974   Choosing the New Deal Indian Commissioner: Ickes vs. Collier. *New Mexico Historical Review* 49(4):269–288.

———
1979   Cato Sells, 1913–21. Pp. 243–250 in The Commissioners of Indian Affairs, 1824–1977. Robert M. Kvasnicka and Herman J. Viola, eds. Lincoln: University of Nebraska Press.

———
1979a   Charles James Rhoads, 1929–33. Pp. 263–271 in The Commissioners of Indian Affairs, 1824–1977. Robert M. Kvasnicka and Herman J. Viola, eds. Lincoln: University of Nebraska Press.

———
1979b   Charles Henry Burke, 1921–29. Pp. 251–261 in the Commissioners of Indian Affairs, 1824–1977. Robert M. Kvasnicka and Herman J. Viola, eds. Lincoln: University of Nebraska Press.

1983   The Assault on Assimilation: John Collier and the Origins of Indian Policy Reform. Albuquerque: University of New Mexico Press.

Kelly, Robert S.
1984   The Native American Information Center. *American Indian Workshop Newsletter* 17 (June):14. Vienna.

Kelsey, Harry
1971   William P. Dole and Mr. Lincoln's Indian Policy. *Journal of the West* 10(3):484–492. Los Angeles.

1973   A Dedication to the Memory of Annie Heloise Abel-Henderson 1873–1947. *Arizona and the West* 15(1):1–4.

1973a   The California Indian Treaty Myth. *Southern California Quarterly* 55(3):225–238. Los Angeles.

1979   William P. Dole, 1861–65. Pp. 89–98 in The Commissioners of Indian Affairs, 1824–1977. Robert M. Kvasnicka and Herman J. Viola, eds. Lincoln: University of Nebraska Press.

1979a   Charles E. Mix, 1858, Pp. 77–79 in The Commissioners of Indian Affairs, 1824–1977. Robert M. Kvasnicka and Herman J. Viola, eds. Lincoln: University of Nebraska Press.

Kelsey, Rayner W.
1917   Friends and the Indians, 1655–1917. Philadelphia: The Associated Executive Committee of Friends on Indian Affairs.

Kendall, David M., dir. and ed.
1985   Another Wind Is Moving: The Off-Reservation Indian Boarding School. Donald D. Stull and Jerry Schults, producers. Video. Berkeley, Calif.: [Distributed by] University of California Extention Media Center.

Kennedy, John H.
1950   Jesuit and Savage in New France. New Haven, Conn.: Yale University Press.

Kenner, Charles L.
1969   A History of the New Mexican-Plains Indian Relations. Norman: University of Oklahoma Press.

Kenney, Alice P.
1969   The Gansevoorts of Albany: Dutch Patricians in the Upper Hudson Valley. Syracuse, N.Y.: Syracuse University Press.

Kent, Donald H., ed.
1979   Pennsylvania and Delaware Treaties, 1629–1737. (Early American Indian Documents: Treaties and Laws, 1607–1789, Vol. 1). Alden T. Vaughan, ed. Frederick, Md.: University Publications of America.

1984   Pennsylvania Treaties, 1737–1756. (Early American Indian Documents: Treaties and Laws, 1607–1789, Vol. 2) Alden T. Vaughan, ed. Frederick, Md.: University Publications of America.

Kent, James
1826   Commentaries on American Law. 2 vols. Philadelphia: Blackstone. (Reprinted: Gryphon, Birmingham, Ala., 1986.)

Kenton, Edna
1930   Simon Kenton: His Life and Period, 1755–1836. Garden City, N.Y.: Doubleday, Doran and Company.

Keppler, Joseph
1929   The Peace Tomahawk Algonkian Wampum. *Museum of the American Indian, Heye Foundation, Indian Notes* 6(2):130–138. New York.

Kesey, Ken
1962   One Flew Over the Cuckoo's Nest. New York: Viking Press.

Keso, Edward E.
1937   The Senatorial Career of Robert Latham Owen. Nashville, Tenn.: George Peabody College for Teachers.

Kessell, John L.
1976   Friars, Soldiers, and Reformers: Hispanic Arizona and the Sonora Mission Frontier, 1767–1856. Tucson: University of Arizona Press.

1979   Kiva, Cross, and Crown: The Pecos Indians and New Mexico, 1540–1840. Washington: U.S. National Park Service.

1980   The Missions of New Mexico Since 1776. Albuquerque: University of New Mexico Press.

Kharlampovich, Konstantin V.
1904   O khristianskom prosveshchenii inorodzev. Iz perepiski arkhiepiskopa Veniamina Irkutskogo s N.I. Il'minskim. [On the Christian Enlightenment of the Natives. From the Correspondence Between Veniamin, Archbishop of Irkutsk and N.I. Il'minskii.] Kazan', U.S.S.R.: no publisher.

Khlebnikov, Kyrill T.
1973   Baranov: Chief Manager of the Russian Colonies in America (*Materials for the Study of Alaska History* 3). Richard Pierce, ed. and Colin Bearne, trans. Kingston, Ont.: The Limestone Press.

1976   Colonial Russian America: Kyril T. Khlebnikov's Reports, 1817–1832. Basil Dmytryshyn and E.A.P. Crownhart-Vaughn, trans. Portland: Oregon Historical Society. (Originally published in Russian in 1861.)

Kidd, Kenneth E.
1961   The Cloth Trade and the Indians of the Northeast During the Seventeenth and Eighteenth Centuries. Pp. 48–56 in *Royal Ontario Museum, Art and Archaeology Division Report for 1961.* Toronto.

Kidder, Alfred V.
1932   The Artifacts of Pecos (*Papers of the Southwestern Expedition* 6). New Haven, Conn.: Published for Phillips Academy by Yale University Press.

1958   Pecos, New Mexico: Archaeological Notes. *Papers of the Robert S. Peabody Foundation for Archaeology* 5. Andover, Mass.

Kiebler, Edwin
1955   [Legend No. 58, Told by Edwin Kiebler to Helen Demarest.] (Indian Folklore Series 7.0.3., Indiana University, Bloomington.)

Kimmey, Fred M.
1960   Christianity and Indian Lands. *Ethnohistory* 7(1):44–60.

King, James T.
1963   War Eagle: A Life of General Eugene A. Carr. Lincoln: University of Nebraska Press.

King, Rufus
1894–1900   The Life and Correspondence of Rufus King. Charles R. King, ed. 6 vols. New York: G.P. Putnam's Sons.

Kingsbury, George W., ed.
1915   History of the Dakota Territory. 5 vols. Chicago: J.S. Clark.

Kingsbury, Susan M., ed.
1906–1935   The Records of the Virginia Company of London. 4 vols. Washington: U.S. Government Printing Office.

Kinietz, W. Vernon
1942   John Mix Stanley and His Indian Paintings. Ann Arbor: University of Michigan Press.

1946   Delaware Culture Chronology. [*Indiana Historical Society*] *Prehistory Research Series* 3(1). Indianapolis.

Kinnard, Lawrence, ed.
1949   Spain in the Mississippi Valley, 1765–1781. 3 vols. Washington: U.S. Government Printing Office.

Kino, Eusebio F.
1948   Historical Memoir of Pimería Alta: A Contemporary Account of the Beginnings of California, Sonora, and Arizona, by Father Eusebio F. Kino, S.J., Pioneer Missionary Explorer, Cartographer, and Ranchman, 1683–1711. Published for the First Time from the Original Manuscript in the Archives of Mexico. Herbert E. Bolton, ed. and trans. 2 vols. in 1. Berkeley: University of California Press. (Reprinted: AMS Press, New York, 1976.)

1952   Father Kino at La Paz, April 1683. Charles N. Rudkin, trans. Los Angeles: Dawson's Bookshop. (Original: Relación Puntual de 1683.)

Kirkland, Samuel
1980   The Journals of Samuel Kirkland; 18th Century Missionary to the Iroquois, Government Agent, Father of Hamilton College. Walter Pilkington, ed. Clinton, N.Y.: Hamilton College.

Klein, Alan M.
1977   Adaptive Strategies and Processes on the Plains: The 19th Century Cultural Sink. (Unpublished Ph.D. Dissertation in Anthropology, State University of New York, Buffalo.)

1980   Plains Economic Analysis: The Marxist Complement. Pp. 129–140 in Anthropology on the Great Plains. W. Raymond Wood and Margot Liberty, eds. Lincoln: University of Nebraska Press.

1983   The Political Economy of Gender: A 19th Century Plains Indian Case Study. Pp. 143–179 in The Hidden Half: Studies of Plains Indian Women. Patricia Albers and Beatrice Medicine, eds. Washington: University Press of America.

Kleinschmidt, Samuel
1851   Grammatik der grönlandischen Sprache; mit teilweisem Einschluss des Labradordialekts. Berlin: Walter de Gruyter.

Klingberg, Frank J.
1940   Anglican Humanitarianism in Colonial New York. Philadelphia: Church Historical Society. (Reprinted: Books for Libraries Press, Freeport, N.Y., 1971.)

1941   An Appraisal of the Negro in Colonial South Carolina: A Study in Americanization. Washington: Associated Publishers.

Knopf, Richard C., ed.
1960   Anthony Wayne, a Name in Arms: Soldier, Diplomat, Defender of Expansion Westward of a Nation; The Wayne-Knox-Pickering-McHenry Correspondence. Pittsburgh, Pa.: University of Pittsburgh Press.

1961   Anthony Wayne and the Founding of the United States Army. Columbus: Ohio State Museum.

Knott, Howard H.W.
1928–1937   Pierre Etienne DuPonceau. Pp. 525–526 in Vol. 5 of Dictionary of American Biography. Allen Johnson et al., eds. 20 vols. New York: Scribner's.

Knowles, Nathaniel
1940   The Torture of Captives by the Indians of Eastern North America. Proceedings of the American Philosophical Society 82(2):151–225. Philadelphia.

Knox, Henry
1792   [Letter to William Blount, Dated 9 October 1792, re Declaration of War by Cherokees.] (Correspondence of the War Department Relating to Indian Affairs, Military Pensions, and Fortifications 1791–1797, 1:99–101, M1062, Military Reference Branch, Record Group 107, National Archives, Washington.)

1832–1834   [Reports to the President of the United States, Dated June 15, 1789 and July 7, 1789.] Pp. 12–14 and 52–54 in American State Papers. Class 2: Indian Affairs. Walter Lowrie and M. St. Clair Clarke, eds. 2 vols. Washington: Gales and Seaton.

1834   Report on the Treaties Made at Fort Harmar on January 9, 1789 with Certain Northern and Northwestern Indians; Submitted to the U.S. Senate by the President of the United States. Pp. 40–41 in Annals of Congress, 1st Cong., 1st sess. 1789. Joseph Gales, comp. Vol. 1. Washington: Gales and Seaton.

Koch, Lena C.
1925   The Federal Indian Policy in Texas, 1845–1860. Southwestern Historical Quarterly 28(3):223–234, (4):259–286; 29(1):19–35, (2):98–127.

Koch, Ronald P.
1977   Dress Clothing of the Plains Indians. Norman: University of Oklahoma Press.

Kolarz, Walter
1954   The Peoples of the Soviet Far East. New York: Frederick A. Praeger.

Konetzke, Richard
1963   Entdecker und Eroberer Amerikas: Von Christoph Kolumbus bis Hernán Cortés. Frankfurt am Main, Germany: Fischer Bücherei.

Kopit, Arthur
1969   Indians: A Play. New York: Hill and Wang.

Kopperman, Paul E.
1977   Braddock at the Monongahela. [Pittsburgh, Pa.]: University of Pittsburgh Press.

Kotzebue, August F.F. von
1790   Die Indianer in England. Leipzig, Germany: Kummer.

Kovach, Michael G.
1957   The Russian Orthodox Church in Russian America. (Unpublished Ph.D. Dissertation in History, University of Pittsburgh, Pittsburgh, Pa.)

Krause, Aurel
1956   The Tlingit Indians: Results of a Trip to the Northwest Coast of America and the Bering Straits. Erna Gunther, trans. (Monographs of the American Ethnological Society 26). Seattle: University of Washington Press.

Krauseneck, Johann C.
1778   Lied eines Wilden. In Gedichte. Bayreuth, Germany: Lübeck.

Krech, Shepard, III
1978   Disease, Starvation, and Northern Athapaskan Social Organization. American Ethnologist 5(4):710–132.

1981   Indians, Animals and the Fur Trade: A Critique of Keepers of the Game. Athens: University of Georgia Press.

1984   The Subarctic Fur Trade. Vancouver: University of British Columbia Press.

Kroeber, Alfred L.
1915   Frederic Ward Putnam. American Anthropologist 17(4):712–718.

1925   Handbook of the Indians of California. Bureau of American Ethnology 78. Washington.

1931   The Culture-area and Age-area Concepts of Clark Wissler. Pp. 248–265 in Methods in Social Science. Stuart A. Rice, ed. Chicago: University of Chicago Press.

1957   Robert H. Lowie (1883–1957). Pp. 141–145 in American Philosophical Society Yearbook for 1957.

1958   Robert H. Lowie. *Sociologus* n.s. 8(1):1–3.

1959   Problems on Boscana. *University of California Publications in American Archaeology and Ethnology* 47(10):282–293. Berkeley.

Kroeber, Alfred L., and Clyde Kluckhohn
1952   Culture: A Critical Review of Concepts and Definitions. *Papers of the Peabody Museum of American Archaeology and Ethnology, Harvard University* 47(1). Cambridge.

Kroeber, A.L., R. Benedict, M.B. Emeneau, M.J. Herskovits, G.A. Reichard, and A. Mason
1943   Franz Boas, 1858–1942. *Memoirs of the American Anthropological Association* 61. Menasha, Wis.

Kroeber, Theodora
1961   Ishi in Two Worlds. Berkeley: University of California Press.

1970   Alfred Kroeber: A Personal Configuration. Berkeley: University of California Press.

Krupat, Arnold, and Brian Swann, eds.
1987   Recovering the Word: Essays on Native American Literature. Berkeley: University of California Press.

Krusenshtern, A.J. von
1813   Voyage Round the World, in the Years 1803, 1804, 1805, and 1806, by Order of His Imperial Majesty Alexander the First, on Board the Ships Nadeshda and Neva, Under the Command of Captain A.J. von Krusenshtern of the Imperial Navy. Richard B. Hoppner, trans. London: John Murray.

Kühn, Dieter
1974   Festspiel für Rothäute. Frankfurt am Main, Germany: Suhrkamp.

Kummings, Donald D.
1981   "Nature's Children": The Image of the Indian in Philip Freneau. *Indian Journal of American Studies* 119(1):25–38. Hyderabad, India.

Kunitz, Stephen J.
1970   Benjamin Rush on Savagism and Progress. *Ethnohistory* 17(1–2):31–42.

Kupperman, Karen Odahl
1977   English Perceptions of Treachery, 1583–1640: The Case of the American "Savages." *The Historical Journal* 20(2):263–287.

1980   Settling with the Indians: The Meeting of English and Indian Cultures in America, 1580–1640. Totowa, N.J.: Rowman and Littlefield.

Kurz, Rudolph F.
1937   Journal of Rudolph Friedrich Kurz. *Bureau of American Ethnology Bulletin* 115. Washington.

Kvasnicka, Robert M.
1979   George W. Manypenny, 1853–57. Pp. 57–67 in The Commissioners of Indian Affairs, 1824–1977. Robert M. Kvasnicka and Herman J. Viola, eds. Lincoln: University of Nebraska Press.

Kvasnicka, Robert M., and Herman J. Viola, eds.
1979   The Commissioners of Indian Affairs, 1824–1977. Lincoln: University of Nebraska Press.

Kyes, Alice
1953   [Anecdote 38, Told by Alice Kyes to Sally Ferrill.] (Manuscript in Folklore Archives and Archives of Traditional Music, 1.0., Indiana University, Bloomington.)

Labaree, Leonard W., and William B. Willcox, eds.
1958–1986   The Papers of Benjamin Franklin. 25 vols. New Haven, Conn.: Yale University Press.

Lach, Donald F.
1965   Asia in the Making of Europe. Vol. 1, Book 1: The Century of Discovery. 2 vols. Chicago: University of Chicago Press.

Ladies' Union Mission School Association
1893   Among the Pimas; or, The Mission to the Pima and Maricopa Indians. Albany, N.Y.: Printed for the Ladies' Union Mission School Association.

La Drevetière, Louis François
1722   Arlequin sauvage. Comédie en trois actes....Paris: Hochereau.

La Farge, Oliver
1929   Laughing Boy. Boston: Houghton Mifflin.

1937   The Enemy Gods. Boston: Houghton Mifflin. (Reprinted: University of New Mexico Press, Albuquerque, 1975.)

1942   The Changing Indian. Norman: University of Oklahoma Press.

Lafitau, Joseph-François
1724   Moeurs des sauvages amériquains, comparées aux moeurs des premiers temps. 2 vols. Paris: Saugrain l'aîné.

1974–1977   Customs of the American Indians Compared with the Customs of Primitive Times [1724]. 2 vols. William N. Fenton and Elizabeth L. Moore, eds. and trans. Toronto: The Champlain Society.

La Flesche, Francis
1923   [Obituary of] Alice C. Fletcher. *Science* n.s. 58 (1494):115.

La Follette, Belle Case, and Fola La Follette
1953   Robert M. La Follette, June 14, 1855 - June 18, 1925. New York: MacMillan.

La Follette, Robert M., Sr.
1960   La Follette's Autobiography: A Personal Narrative of Political Experiences [1913]. Madison: University of Wisconsin Press.

Lahontan, Louis Armand de Lom d'Arce de
1703   Nouveaux voyages de Mr. le baron de Lahontan dans l'Amérique septentrionale. 2 vols in 1. The Hague: Frères l'Honoré.

1703a   Suplément aux Voyages du baron de Lahontan, où l'on trouve des dialogues curieux entre l'auteur et un sauvage de bon sens qui a voyagé. The Hague: Frères l'Honoré.

1905   New Voyages to North America by the Baron de Lahontan [1703]. Reuben G. Thwaites, ed. 2 vols. Chicago: A. C. McClurg.

1931   Dialogues curieux entre l'auteur et un sauvage de bon sens qui a voyagé, et Mémoires de l'Amérique septentrionale, publiées par Gilbert Chinard. Baltimore, Md.: Johns Hopkins Press.

Lajeunesse, Ernest J., ed.
1960   The Windsor Border Region: Canada's Southernmost Frontier; A Collection of Documents. Toronto: The Champlain Society.

Lake Mohonk Conference on the Indian
1930   Report of the Thirty-fifth Lake Mohonk Conference on the Indian, Oct. 16–18, 1929. Poughkeepsie, N.Y.: Lousing-Broas Printing for the Lake Mohonk Conference.

Lamar, Howard R.
1977   The Trader on the American Frontier: Myth's Victim. College Station: Texas A and M University Press.

1985   From Bondage to Contract: Ethnic Labor in the American West, 1600–1890. Pp. 293–326 in The Countryside in the Age of Capitalist Transformation: Essays in the Social History of Rural America. S. Hahn and J. Prude, eds. Chapel Hill: University of North Carolina Press.

Lamb, Ursula
1956   Frey Nicolás de Ovando, gobernador de las Indias, 1501–1509. Madrid: Consejo Superior de Investigaciones Científicas, Instituto Gonzalo Fernández de Oviedo.

Lamb, W. Kaye, comp.
1944   A Bibliography of the Printed Writings of Frederic William Howay. *British Columbia Historical Quarterly* 8(1):27–51. Vancouver.

————
1960   The Letters and Journals of Simon Fraser, 1806–1808. Toronto: Macmillan.

Lanctot, Gustave
1963–1965   History of Canada. 3 vols. Cambridge, Mass.: Harvard University Press.

Land, Robert H.
1938   Henrico and Its College. *William and Mary Quarterly 2d ser.*, Vol. 18:453–498. Williamsburg, Va.

Landauer, Bella C.
1940   The Indian Does Not Vanish in American Advertising. New York: New York Historical Society. (Manuscript copy in collection of the New York Public Library, New York City.)

Landon, Fred, ed.
1930   Selections from the Papers of James Evans, Missionary to the Indians. [Toronto: no publisher.]

Lane, Mrs. A.H., Mrs. John Markoe, and Mrs. Bernard Schulte
1926   Indian Tribes and Missions: A Handbook of General History of the North American Indians; Early Missionary Efforts and Missions of the Episcopal Church. Hartford, Conn.: Church Missions Publishing Company.

Lane, Joseph
1878   [Autobiography.] (Manuscript PA 43 in Bancroft Library, University of California, Berkeley.)

Läng, Hans C.
1983   *Indianer-Almanach*. Zurich, Switzerland: Tanner and Staehlin.

Langdon, John E.
1960   Canadian Silversmiths and Their Marks, 1667–1867. Lunenburg, Vt.: Stinehour Press.

Langsdorff, Georg H. von
1813–1814   Voyages and Travels in Various Parts of the World, During the Years 1803, 1804, 1805, 1806 and 1807. 2 vols. London: Henry Colburn.

Lankford, George E.
1984   Trouble at Dancing Rabbit Creek: Missionaries and Choctaw Removal. *Journal of Presbyterian History* 62(1):51–66.

Lanman, Charles
1876   Biographical Annals of the Civil Government of the United States, During Its First Century. Washington: Anglim. (Reprinted: Gale Research Company, Detroit, Mich., 1976.)

Lanning, John T.
1935   The Spanish Missions of Georgia. Chapel Hill: University of North Carolina Press. (Reprinted: Scholarly Press, St. Clair Shores, Mich., 1971.)

Lantzeff, George V.
1943   Siberia in the Seventeenth Century: A Study of the Colonial Administration. *University of California Publications in History* 30. Berkeley.

La Roche, Sophie von
1798   Erscheinungen am See Oneida. Leipzig, Germany: H. Graff.

Larocque, Robert
1982   L'Introduction de maladies européenes chez les autochtones des XVIIe et XVIIIe siècles. *Recherches Amérindiennes au Québec* 12(1):13–24.

Larrea, Carolos M.
[1968]   Barón Luis Hector de Carondelet; el vigésimonono presidente de la Real Audiencia de Quito. [Quito]: Corporación de Estudios y Publicaciones.

Larson, Charles R.
1978   American Indian Fiction. Albuquerque: University of New Mexico Press.

Las Casas, Bartolomé *see* Casas, Bartolomé de las

Latourette, Kenneth S.
1927   Voyages of American Ships to China, 1784–1844. *Transactions of the Connecticut Academy of Arts and Sciences* 28:237–271. New Haven.

Lauber, Almon W.
1913   Indian Slavery in Colonial Times within the Present Limits of the United States. *Columbia University Studies in History, Economics and Public Law* 134. New York. (Reprinted: Corner House, Williamstown, Mass., 1970.)

Laubin, Reginald, and Gladys Laubin
1957   The Indian Tipi: Its History, Construction and Use. Norman: University of Oklahoma Press.

Laumer, Frank
1968   Massacre! Gainesville: University of Florida Press.

Laveille, Eugène
1915   The Life of Father De Smet, S.J. (1801–1873). Marian Lindsay, trans. New York: P.J. Kenedy and Sons.

Lavender, David S.
1954   Bent's Fort. New York: Doubleday. (Reprinted: University of Nebraska Press, Lincoln, 1972.)

Laverdière, Charles H., and Henry R. Casgrain, eds.
1871   Le Journal des Jésuites, publié d'après le manuscrit original conservé aux Archives du Séminaire de Québec. Quebec: L. Brousseau.

LaViolette, Forrest E.
1961   The Struggle for Survival: Indian Cultures and the Protestant Ethic in British Columbia. Toronto: University of Toronto Press. (Reprinted in 1973.)

Law Library Microform Consortium
[1981]   Native American Legal Materials Collection. Microfiche. Honolulu, Hawaii: Law Library Microform Consortium.

Law, Wesley R.
1959   Mormon Indian Missions - 1855. (Unpublished M.S. Thesis in History, Brigham Young University, Provo, Utah.)

Lawrence, David H.
1923   Studies in Classic American Literature. New York: T. Seltzer.

————
1926   The Plumed Serpent. New York: Alfred A. Knopf.

————
1927   Mornings in Mexico. New York: Alfred A. Knopf.

————
1928   The Woman Who Rode Away; and Other Stories. London: Martin Secker.

Laws, G. Malcolm, Jr.
1964   Native American Balladry. *Publications of the American Folklore Society, Bibliographical and Special Series* 1. Philadelphia.

Lawson John
1966   A New Voyage to Carolina [1709]. Ann Arbor, Mich.: University Microfilms.

Lawson, Michael L.
1982   Dammed Indians: The Pick-Sloan Plan and the Missouri River Sioux, 1944–80. Norman: University of Oklahoma Press.

————
1985   Federal Water Projects and Indian Lands: The Pick-Sloan Plan, a Case Study. Pp. 169–185 in The Plains Indians of the

Twentieth Century. Peter Iverson, ed. Norman: University of Oklahoma Press.

Lazell, J. Arthur
1960   Alaskan Apostle: The Life Story of Sheldon Jackson. New York: Harper.

Leach, Douglas E.
1958   Flintlock and Tomahawk: New England in King Philip's War. New York: Macmillan.

————
1966   The Northern Colonial Frontier, 1607–1763. New York: Holt, Rinehart and Winston.

————
1973   Arms for Empire: A Military History of the British Colonies in North America, 1607–1763. New York: Macmillan.

Leap, William L.
1978   American Indian English and Its Implications for Bilingual Education. Pp. 657–669 in 29th Georgetown Roundtable on Languages and Linguistics, 1978: International Dimensions in Bilingual Education. J. Alatis, ed. Washington: Georgetown University School of Languages and Linguistics.

————
1981   American Indian Language Maintenance. *Annual Review of Anthropology* 10:209–236. Palo Alto, Calif.

Leavenworth, Henry
1823   [Letter to the Adjutant General, Dated Fort Atkinson, August 30, 1823 re Battle with Arikaras.] (Letters Received, Records of the Adjutant General's Office, Vol. 7, M567, War Records Branch, Record Group 94, National Archives, Washington.)

Le Beau, Claude
1738   Avantures du Sr. C. Le Beau, avocat en parlement, ou voyage curieux et nouveau, parmi les sauvages de l'Amérique septentrionale. 2 vols. Amsterdam, The Netherlands: Herman Uytwerf.

Lebel, Roland
1952   Les Etablissements français d'outre-mer et leur reflet dans la littérature. Paris: Larose.

Le Blanc de Villeneufve, Paul Louis
1814   La Fête du Petit blé, ou l'héroisme de Poucha-Houmma. New Orleans: Courrier de la Louisiane.

Le Breton, Dagmar Renshaw
1947   Chahta-Ima: The Life of Adrien Emmanuel Rouquette. Baton Rouge: Louisiana State University Press.

Leckie, William H.
1963   The Military Conquest of the Southern Plains. Norman: University of Oklahoma Press.

————
1967   The Buffalo Soldiers: A Narrative of the Negro Cavalry in the West. Norman: University of Oklahoma Press.

Le Clercq, Chrétien
1691   Premier établissement de la Foy dans la Nouvelle France. 2 vols. Paris: A. Auroy. (Reprinted: [English translation], J.G. Shea, New York, 1881.)

————
1910   New Relation of Gaspesia, with the Customs and Religion of the Gaspesian Indians [1691]. W.F. Ganong, ed. and trans. Toronto: The Champlain Society.

Lecompte, Janet
1978   Pueblo, Hardscrabble, Greenhorn, the Upper Arkansas, 1832–1856. Norman: University of Oklahoma Press.

Le Corbeiller, Clare
1961   Miss America and Her Sisters: Personification of the Four Parts of the World. *The Metropolitan Museum of Art Bulletin* 19(8):209–223. New York.

Leder, Lawrence H.
[1961]   Robert Livingston, 1654–1728, and the Politics of Colonial New York. Chapel Hill: University of North Carolina Press.

Lee, Jesse M.
1885   [Letter to J.D.C. Atkins, Commissioner of Indian Affairs, Dated August 3, 1885.] (Cheyenne and Arapaho Agency Letterbooks, Vol. 9:14–15; Cheyenne and Arapaho Agency Records, Indian Archives, Oklahoma Historical Society, Oklahoma City.)

Lefler, Hugh T., and Albert R. Newsome
1963   North Carolina: The History of a Southern State. Rev. ed. Chapel Hill: University of North Carolina Press.

Leflon, Jean
1961–1970   Eugene de Mazenod, Bishop of Marseilles, Founder of the Oblates of Mary Immaculate, 1782–1861. 4 vols. Francis D. Flanagan, trans. New York: Fordham University Press.

Leger, Mary C.
1929   The Catholic Indian Missions in Maine, 1611–1820. *Catholic University of America Studies in American Church History* 8. Washington. (Reprinted: AMS Press, New York, 1974.)

Leighton, James D.
1975   The Development of Federal Indian Policy in Canada, 1840–1890. (Unpublished Ph.D. Dissertation in History, University of Western Ontario, London.)

Le Jau, Francis
1956   The Carolina Chronicle of Dr. Francis Le Jau, 1707–1717. Frank J. Klingberg, ed. *University of California Publications in History* 53. Berkeley.

Leland, Waldo G., ed.
1932–1943   Guide to Materials for American History in the Libraries and Archives of Paris. 2 vols. Washington: Carnegie Institution of Washington.

Lemaire, Ton
1986   De Indiaan in ons Bewustzijn: de Ontmoeting van de Oude met de Nieuwe Wereld. Baarn, The Netherlands: Ambo.

Le Moyne de Morgues, Jacques
1977   The Work of Jacques le Moyne de Morgues: A Huguenot Artist in France, Florida and England. Paul Hulton et al., eds. 2 vols. London: British Museum Publications.

Lenau, Nikolas
1838   Neuere Gedichte. Stuttgart, Germany: Hallberger.

Lennox, Herbert J.
1932   Samuel Kirkland's Mission to the Iroquois. (Unpublished Ph.D. Dissertation in Anthropology, University of Chicago, Chicago.)

Léonard, Frédéric, comp.
1693   Recueil des traitez de paix, de trêve, de neutralité, de confédération, d'alliance, et de commerce, faits par les rois de France, avec tous les princes et potentats de l'Europe, et autres . . . . 6 vols. Paris: F. Leonard.

Leonard, Thomas C.
1974   Red, White and the Army Blue: Empathy and Anger in the American West. *American Quarterly* 26(2):176–190.

Le Page du Pratz, Antoine
1774   The History of Louisiana. London: T. Becket. (Facs. reproduction: Louisiana State University Press, 1975.)

Le Sage, Alain René
1732   Les Avantures de Monsieur Robert Chevalier, dit de Beauchêne, capitaine de flibustiers dans la Nouvelle France. Paris: E. Ganeau.

Le Sage, Alain-René, and P. d'Orneval
1735   La Sauvagesse. *Théâtre de la Foire ou l'Opéra-comique* 9:222. Paris.

————
1735a   Les Mariages de Canada. *Théâtre de la Foire ou l'Opéra-comique* 9:301. Paris.

Lescarbot, Marc
1609   Histoire de la Nouvelle France... Paris: Jean Milot. (Reprinted as: History of New France, Greenwood Press, New York, 1968.)

1612   La Défaite des sauvages Armouchiquois par le Sagamos Memberton et ses alliés sauvages de la Nouvelle France au mois de juillet 1607. In Les Muses de la Nouvelle France, by Marc Lescarbot. Paris: Jean Millot.

1907–1914   The History of New France, W.L. Grant, trans. 3 vols. Toronto: The Champlain Society.

Leslie, John
1985   Commission of Inquiry into Indian Affairs, in the Canadas, 1828–1858. Ottawa: Department of Indian and Northern Affairs Canada.

Leslie, John, and Ron Maguire, eds.
1978   The Historical Development of the Indian Act. 2d ed. Ottawa: Department of Indian and Northern Affairs, Corporate Policy Research Branch.

Lester, Joan
1972   The American Indian: A Museum's Eye View. The Indian Historian 5(2):25–31

Le Tac, Sixte
1888   Histoire chronologique de la Nouvelle-France ou Canada, depuis sa découverte (mil cinq cents quatre) jusques en l'an mil six cents trente deux. Paris: G. Fischbacher.

Leupp, Francis E.
1895   The Latest Phase of the Southern Ute Question: A Report. Philadelphia: Office of the Indian Rights Association.

1905   Outlines of an Indian Policy. Outlook 79(April 15):946–950.

1910   The Indian and His Problem. New York: Charles Scribner's Sons. (Reprinted: Arno Press, New York, 1971.)

1914   In Red Man's Land: A Study of the American Indian. New York: Fleming H. Revell Company. (Reprinted: Rio Grande Press, Glorieta, N.M., 1976.)

Levernier, James, and Hennig Cohen, eds.
1977   The Indians and Their Captives. Westport, Conn.: Greenwood Press.

Levin, David
1959   History as Romantic Art: Bancroft, Prescott, Motley, and Parkman. Stanford Studies in Language and Literature 20. Stanford, Calif.

1983   Modern Misjudgments on Racial Imperialism in Hawthorn and Parkman. The Yearbook of English Studies 12:145–148.

Levin, Maksim Grigor'evich, and L.P. Potov, eds.
1956   Narody Sibir [The Peoples of Siberia]. Moscow: Izdatel'stvo Akademii Nauk SSR. (English translation by Steven Dunn, University of Chicago Press, Chicago, 1964.)

Lewald, Fanny
1847   Diogena. Leipzig, Germany: Brockhaus.

Lewin, Howard
1966   A Frontier Diplomat: Andrew Montour. Pennsylvania History 33(2):153–186.

Lewis, Clifford M., and Albert J. Loomie
1953   The Spanish Jesuit Mission in Virginia, 1570–1572. Chapel Hill: University of North Carolina Press for the Virginia Historical Society.

Lewis, Henry T., ed.
1973   Patterns of Indian Burning in California: Ecology and Ethnohistory. Ballena Press Anthropological Papers 1. Ramona, Calif.

1985   Why Indians Burned: Specific Versus General Reasons. Pp. 75–80 in Proceedings–Symposium and Workshop on Wil-

derness Fire; Missoula, Mont., Nov. 15–18, 1983. U.S. Department of Agriculture, Forest Service. Intermountain Forest and Range Experiment Station, Ogden, Utah. General Technical Report INT-182. Washington: U.S. Government Printing Office.

Lewis, Norman
1968   English Missionary Interest in the Indians of North America, 1578–1700. (Unpublished Ph.D. Dissertation in History, University of Washington, Seattle.)

Lewis, Oscar
1942   The Effects of White Contact Upon Blackfoot Culture with Special Reference to the Role of the Fur Trade. Monographs of the American Ethnological Society 6. New York.

Lewis, Wyndham
1929   Paleface: The Philosophy of the Melting Pot. London: Chatto and Windus.

Lewit, Robert T.
1963   Indian Missions and Antislavery Sentiment: A Conflict of Evangelical and Humanitarian Ideals. Mississippi Valley Historical Review 50(1):39–55.

Liapunova, Roza G.
1979   Zapiski ieromonakha Gedeona (1803–1807)–odin iz isto-chnikov po istorii i etnografii Russki Ameriki [Notes of Hieromonk Gedeon (1803–1807) – One of the Sources on the History and Ethnography of Russian America]. Pp. 215–229 in Problemy Istorii Etnografii Ameriki [Issues in the History and Ethnography of America]. Moscow:Nauka.

Liapunova, Roza G., and S.G. Fedorova, eds.
1979   Russkaia Amerika v neopublikovannykh zapiskakh K.T. Khlebnikov [Russian America in Unpublished Writings of K.T. Khlebnikov]. Leningrad: Izdatel'stvo "Nauka".

Lickteig, Franz-Bernard
1969   The Choctaw Indian Apostolate. The Sword 19(1):31–39, (2):63–78, (3):41–58.

Lieberkuhn, Samuel
1821   The History of Our Lord and Saviour Jesus Christ... Translated into the Delaware Indian Language by the Rev. David Zeisberger. New York: Daniel Fanshaw.

Liebers, Arthur
1965   U.S. Coins: The Collector's Guide and Handbook of Values. New York: Putnam.

Lincoln, Kenneth
1983   Native American Renaissance. Berkeley: University of California Press.

Linderholm, Helmer
1975   De Röda Kömpar. Stockholm: Tidens Förlag.

1976   Nya Sveriges Historia: Vart Stora Indianäventyr. Stockholm: Tidens Förlag.

Linderman, Frank B.
1986   Wolf and the Winds. Norman: University of Oklahoma Press.

Lindeström, Peter
1925   Geographia Americae, with an Account of the Delaware Indians, Based on Surveys and Notes Made in 1654–1656. Amandus Johnson, trans. Philadelphia: The Swedish Colonial Society.

Lindquist, Gustavus E.E.
1923   The Red Man in the United States: An Intimate Study of the Social, Economic, and Religious Life of the American Indians. New York: Doran.

1948   Indian Treaty Making. Chronicles of Oklahoma 26(4):416–448.

Lindquist, Gustavus E.E., with E. Russell Carter
1951   Indians in Transition: A Study of Protestant Missions to Indians in the United States. New York: National Council

of Churches of Christ in the U.S.A., Division of Home Missions.

Lindsay, Vachel
1923   Collected Poems. New York: Macmillan.

Linné, Carl von
1758–1759 Caroli Linnaei . . . Systema Naturae per Regna Tria Naturae. 10th rev. ed. 2 vols. Holmiae: Laurentii Salvii.

Linton, Ralph
1920   Totemism in the A.E.F. *American Anthropologist* 26(2):296–300.

Lipman, Jean Herzberg
1948   American Folk Art in Wood, Metal and Stone. New York: Pantheon.

Lips, Julius E.
1947   Zelte in der Wildnis . . . .Zurich, Switzerland: Büchergilde Gutenberg.

Lipscomb, Andrew, and Albert Bergh, eds.
1904–1905 The Writings of Thomas Jefferson. 20 vols. Washington: Thomas Jefferson Memorial Association.

Lisianskiĭ, Urey
1814   A Voyage Round the World in the Years 1803, 4, 5 and 6; Performed, by Order of His Imperial Majesty Alexander the First, Emperor of Russia, in the Ship Neva. London: John Booth and Longman et al.

Litke, Fedor Petrovich
1835–1836 Voyage autour du monde, exécuté par order de sa Majesté l'empereur Nicolas Ier, sur la corvette le Séniavin e, dans les années 1826, 1827, 1828 et 1829, par Frédéric Lutké . . . Paris: Didot Frères.

Little, Nina Fletcher, comp.
1957   Abby Aldrich Rockefeller Folk Art Collection. Boston: Little, Brown.

Lively, Anne O.
1958   A Survey of Mission Workers in the Indian Field. New York: National Council of Churches of Christ in the U.S.A.

Livingston, Edwin B.
1910   The Livingstons of Livingston Manor: Being the History of That Branch of the Scottish House of Callendar Which Settled in the English Province of New York During the Reign of Charles II . . . .New York: Knickerbocker Press.

Livingston, Robert, comp.
1956   The Livingston Indian Records, 1666–1723. Lawrence H. Leder, ed. Harrisburg: Pennsylvania Museum and Historical Associations.

Lloyd, Christopher, and R.C. Anderson, eds.
1959   A Memoir of James Trevenen. London: Printed for the Navy Records Society.

Lockwood, Frank C.
1934   Story of the Spanish Missions of the Middle Southwest; Being a Complete Survey of the Missions Founded by Padre Eusebio Francisco Kino . . . .Santa Ana, Calif.: Fine Arts Press.

————
1942   Al Sieber: Man of Blood and Iron. *University of Arizona Bulletin* 13(3), *General Bulletin* 6:17–40. Tucson.

Lockwood, Luke V.
1928   The St. Memin Indian Portraits. *New York Historical Society Quarterly Bulletin* 12(1):3–26.

Lomax, Alan
1950   Mr. Jelly Roll: The Fortunes of Jelly Roll Morton. New York: Grosset and Dunlap.

Longfellow, Henry Wadsworth
1855   The Song of Hiawatha. Boston: Ticknor and Fields.

Loomis, Noel M., and Abraham P. Nasatir
1967   Pedro Vial and the Roads to Santa Fe. Norman: University of Oklahoma Press.

Loos, John L.
1953   A Biography of William Clark, 1770–1838. (Unpublished Ph.D. Dissertation in History, Washington University, St. Louis, Mo.)

Lord, Robert H., John E. Sexton, and Edward T. Harrington
1944   History of the Archdiocese of Boston . . . .1604–1943. 3 vols. New York: Sheed and Ward.

Loskiel, George H.
1794   History of the Mission of the United Brethren Among Indians in North America. London: The Brethren's Society for the Furtherance of the Gospel.

Lossing, Benson J.
1869   The Pictorial Field Book of the War of 1812 . . . .New York: Harper and Bros.

Lovett, Vince, Larry Rummel, Dick Hardwick, Glen Robertson, and Vince Monico
1984   American Indians; U.S. Indian Policy: Tribes and Reservations; BIA: Past and Present; Economic Development. Washington: U.S. Government Printing Office.

Lowe, Percival G.
1906   Five Years a Dragoon ('49 to '54) and Other Adventures on the Great Plains. Kansas City, Mo.: Franklin and Hudson.

Lower, Arthur R.M.
1958   Canadians in the Making: A Social History of Canada. Toronto: Longmans, Green. (Reprinted: Greenwood Press, Westport, Conn., 1981.)

Lowie, Robert H.
1917   Culture and Ethnology. New York: D.C. McMurtrie. (Reprinted: Basic Books, New York, 1966.)

————
1920   Primitive Society. New York: Boni and Liveright.

————
1924   Primitive Religion. New York: Boni and Liveright.

————
1935   The Crow Indians. New York: Farrar and Rinehart.

————
1937   History of Ethnological Theory. New York: Holt, Rinehart and Winston.

————
1948   Social Organization. New York: Rinehart.

————
1949   Supplementary Facts About Clark Wissler. *American Anthropologist* 51(3):527–528.

————
1954   Indians of the Plains. Lincoln: University of Nebraska Press.

————
1960   Selected Papers in Anthropology. C. Du Bois, ed. Berkeley: University of California Press.

Lowie, Robert H., Louella Cole Lowie, and Madge D. Richardson, comps.
1958   Bibliography of Robert H. Lowie. *American Anthropologist* 60(2):362–375.

Loyens, William J.
1966   The Changing Culture of the Nulato Koyukon Indians. (Unpublished Ph.D. Dissertation in Anthropology, University of Wisconsin, Madison.)

Lucas, Charles P.
1930   Religion, Colonising, and Trade, the Driving Forces of the Old Empire. London: Society for Promoting Christian Knowledge.

Lummis, Charles F.
1966   General Crook and the Apache Wars. Turbese L. Fiske, ed. Flagstaff, Ariz.: Northland Press.

Lunn, Jean
1939   The Illegal Fur Trade Out of New France, 1713–60. Pp. 61–76 in *Canadian Historical Association Report for 1939*. Ottawa.

Lurie, Nancy Oestreich
1959 Indian Cultural Adjustment to European Civilization. Pp. 33–60 in Seventeenth Century America: Essays in Colonial History. James G. Smith, ed. Chapel Hill: University of North Carolina Press.

1961 The Voice of the American Indian: Report on the American Indian Chicago Conference. *Current Anthropology* 2(5):478–500.

1962 Comments on Bernard J. James Analysis of Ojibwa Acculturation. *American Anthropologist* 64(4):826–833.

1965 An American Indian Renascence? *Midcontinent American Studies Journal* 6(2):25–50. Lawrence, Kans.

1966 Women in Early Anthropology. Pp. 29–81 in Pioneers of American Anthropology. June Helm, ed. (*American Ethnological Society Monograph* 43) Seattle: University of Washington Press.

1966a The Lady from Boston and the Omaha Indians. *The American West* 4(3):31.

[1969–1972] [Ethnographic Field Research on the Menominee.] (Unpublished fieldnotes in Lurie's possession.)

Lutz, Hartmut
1980 Images of Indians in German Children's Books. Pp. 82–102 in The Slant of the Pen: Racism in Children's Books. Roy Preiswerk, ed. Geneva, Switzerland: World Council of Churches, Program to Combat Racism.

Lydekker, John W.
1938 The Faithful Mohawks. Cambridge, England: The University Press.

Lyman, Christopher M.
1982 The Vanishing Race and Other Illusions: Photographs of Indians by Edward S. Curtis. Washington: Smithsonian Institution Press.

Lyon, Eugene
1976 The Enterprise of Florida: Pedro Menéndez de Avilés and the Spanish Conquest of 1565–1568. Gainesville: University Presses of Florida.

Lyons, Emory J.
1945 Isaac McCoy: His Plans and Work for Indian Colonization. *Fort Hayes Kansas State College, History Series* 1; *General Series* 9. Topeka.

Lyons, Letitia M.
1940 Francis Norbert Blanchet and the Founding of the Oregon Missions (1838–1848). Washington: Catholic University of America Press.

Lytwyn, Victor
1981 The Historical Geography of the Fur Trade of the Little North and Its Expansion into the Winnipeg Country to 1821. (Unpublished M.A. Thesis in History, University of Manitoba, Winnipeg.)

MHSC=Massachusetts Historical Society.
1792–1915 Collections. 70 vols. 10 series. Cambridge and Boston: The Society.

McAdam, David, ed.
1897–1899 History of the Bench and Bar of New York. 2 vols. New York: New York History Company.

McBeth, Kate C.
1908 The Nez Perce Since Lewis and Clark. New York: Fleming H. Revell.

McBeth, Sally J.
1983 Ethnic Identity and the Boarding School Experience of West-central Oklahoma Indians. Washington: University Press of America.

McCallum, James D., ed.
1932 The Letters of Eleazer Whelock's Indians. Hanover, N.H.: Dartmouth College Publications.

1939 Eleazar Wheelock, Founder of Dartmouth College. Hanover, N.H.: Dartmouth College Publications.

McCann, Lloyd
1956 The Grattan Massacre. *Nebraska History* 37(1):1–25.

McCardell, Lee
1958 Ill-starred General: Braddock of the Coldstream Guards. Pittsburgh, Pa.: University of Pittsburgh Press.

McCardle, B. Ellen
1982 Indian History and Claims: A Research Handbook. 2 vols. Ottawa: Department of Indian and Northern Affairs, Corporate Policy Research Branch.

McCarty, Kieran R.
1981 A Spanish Frontier in the Enlightened Age: Franciscan Beginnings in Sonora and Arizona, 1767–1770. Washington: Academy of American Franciscan History.

1983 Franciscans North from Mexico, 1527–1580. Pp. 237–280 in Franciscan Presence in the Americas: Essays on the Activities of the Franciscan Friars in the Americas, 1492–1900. Francisco Morales, ed. Potomac, Md.: Academy of American Franciscan History.

McCauley, Robert H.
1942 Liverpool Transfer Designs on Anglo-American Pottery. Portland, Me.: Southworth-Anthoensen Press.

McClure, David, and Elijah Parish
1811 Memoirs of the Rev. Eleazer Wheelock, D.D., Founder and President of Dartmouth College and Mooa's Charity School ....Newburyport, Mass.: Edward Little.

McCoy, Isaac
1827 Remarks on the Practicability of Indian Reform, Embracing Their Colonization. Boston: Lincoln and Edmands.

1840 History of Baptist Indian Missions: Embracing Remarks on the Former and Present Condition of the Aboriginal Tribes: Their Former Settlement within the Indian Territory, and Their Future Prospects. Washington: W.M. Morrison.

McCracken, Harold
1947 Frederic Remington, Artist of the Old West; with a Bibliographical Check List of Remington Pictures and Books. Philadelphia: J.B. Lippincott.

1959 George Catlin and the Old Frontier. New York: Dial Press. (Reprinted: Bonanza Books, New York, 1984.)

McCracken, I.
1978 The West of Buffalo Bill: Frontier Art, Indian Crafts, Memorabilia from the Buffalo Historical Center. New York: Henry N. Abrams.

McDermott, John F.
1952 De Smet's Illustrator: Father Nicolas Point. *Nebraska History* 33(1):35–40.

[1961] Seth Eastman: Pictorial Historian of the Indian. Norman: University of Oklahoma Press.

———, ed.
1965 The French in the Mississippi Valley. Urbana: University of Illinois Press.

McDonald, John
1838 Biographical Sketches of General Nathaniel Massie, General Duncan McArthur, Captain William Wells, and General Simon Kenton: Who Were Early Setters in the Western Country. Cincinnati, Ohio: E. Morgan and Son.

McDonald, Lucile
1972 Swan Among the Indians: Life of James G. Swan, 1818–1900. Portland, Oreg.: Binfords and Mort.

McElroy, Robert M.
1909   Kentucky in the Nation's History. New York: Moffat, Yard.

MacFarlane, Ronald O.
1933   Indian Relations in New England, 1620–1760: A Study of a Regulated Frontier. (Unpublished Ph.D. Dissertation in History, Harvard University, Cambridge, Mass.)

———
1938   The Massachusetts Bay Truck-houses in Diplomacy with the Indians. *New England Quarterly* 11(1):48–65.

McGee, W J
1960   Piratical Acculturation. Pp. 793–800 in Selected Papers from the *American Anthropologist*, 1888–1920. Frederica de Laguna, ed. Evanston, Ill.: Row, Peterson.

McGee, W J et al.
1900   In Memoriam: Frank Hamilton Cushing. *American Anthropologist* 2(2):354–380.

McGillycuddy, Julia E.B.
1941   McGillycuddy Agent: A Biography of Dr. Valentine T. McGillycuddy. Stanford, Calif.: Stanford University Press.

MacGregor, James G.
1975   Father Lacombe. Edmonton, Alta.: Hurtig.

McGregor, James H.
1940   The Wounded Knee Massacre; From Viewpoint of the Sioux. Baltimore, Md.: Wirth Brothers.

McInnis, Edgar
1969   Canada: A Political and Social History. Toronto: Holt, Rinehart and Winston of Canada.

McKay, Douglas
1936   The Honourable Company: A History of the Hudson's Bay Company. Indianapolis, Ind.: Bobbs-Merrill.

McKee, John
1853   Minutes Kept by John McKee, Secretary, on the Expedition from Sonoma Through Northern California. Pp. 134–187 in *33d Congress. Special Session. Senate Executive Doc.* No. 4 (Serial No. 688). Washington: U.S. Government Printing Office.

McKee, Samuel D., Jr.
1935   Labor in Colonial New York, 1664–1776. *Columbia University Studies in History, Economics, and Public Law* 410. New York. (Reprinted: Ira J. Friedman, Port Washington, N.Y., 1963.)

McKenney, Thomas L.
1824   [Letter to the Secretary of War, 24th Nov. 1824.] (Printed copy in Anthropology Library, Smithsonian Institution, Washington.)

———
1825   [Letters of September 17, and October 13, 1825 to Samuel Moore, Director of the Mint.] (Letters Sent to the Office of Indian Affairs, Record Group 75, National Archives, Washington.)

———
1827   Sketches of a Tour to the Lakes, of the Character and Customs of the Chippeway Indians and of Incidents Connected with the Treaty of Fond du Lac. Baltimore, Md.: Fielding Lucas, Jun'r. (Reprinted: Imprint Society, Barre, Mass., 1972.)

———
1829   [Letter of December 21, 1829 to John H. Eaton.] (P. 199 in Vol. 6 of Letters Sent to the Office of Indian Affairs, Record Group 75, National Archives, Washington.)

———
1846   Memoirs, Official and Personal; with Sketches of Travels Among the Northern and Southern Indians . . . .2 vols. in 1. New York: Paine and Burgess (Reprinted: University of Nebraska Press, Lincoln, 1973.)

McKenney, Thomas L., and James Hall
1842–1844   History of the Indian Tribes of North America, with Biographical Sketches and Anecdotes of the Principal Chiefs. 3 vols. Philadelphia: D. Rice and J.G. Clark.

McLachlan, Robert W.
1899   Medals Awarded to the Canadian Indians. Montreal: no publisher.

McLaughlin, Andrew C.
1889   The Influence of Governor Cass on the Development of the Northwest. *American Historical Association Papers* 3(2):67–83.

McLaughlin, Jack
1988   Jefferson and Monticello: The Biography of a Builder. New York: H. Holt.

McLaughlin, James
1910   My Friend the Indian. Boston: Houghton Mifflin.

———
1936   My Friend the Indian; or, Three Heretofore Unpublished Chapters of the Book . . . .Usher L. Burdick, ed. Baltimore, Md.: The Proof Press.

McLean, John
1890   James Evans, Inventor of the Syllabic System of the Cree Language. Toronto: William Briggs.

MacLeod, William C.
1928   The American Indian Frontier. New York: A.A. Knopf.

———
1936   Conservation Among Primitive Hunting Peoples. *Scientific Monthly* 43(December):562–566.

McLoughlin, John
1941–1944   The Letters of John McLoughlin from Fort Vancouver to the Governor and Committee . . . 3 vols. E.E. Rich, ed. Toronto: The Champlain Society.

———
1948   Letters of Doctor John McLoughlin Written at Fort Vancouver, 1829–1832. Burt B. Barker, ed. Portland: Oregon Historical Society.

McLoughlin, William G.
1974   Red Indians, Black Slavery and White Racism: America's Slaveholding Indians. *American Quarterly* 26(4):367–385.

———
1984   Cherokees and Missionaries, 1789–1839. New Haven, Conn.: Yale University Press.

McNeill, William H.
1976   Plagues and Peoples. Garden City, N.Y.: Anchor Press/Doubleday.

McNickle, D'Arcy
1936   The Surrounded. New York: Dodd, Mead.

———
1944   [Remarks to Indian Groups in Chicago, January 1944.] (In Hazel W. Hertzberg's possession.)

———
1949   They Came Here First. Philadelphia: Lippincott. (Reprinted: Octagon Books, New York, 1975.)

———
1971   Indian Man: A Life of Oliver LaFarge. Bloomington: Indiana University Press.

———
1971a   Americans Called Indians. Pp. 29–63 in The North American Indian in Historical Perspective. Eleanor Leacock and Nancy Oestreich Lurie, eds. New York: Random House.

McNitt, Frank
1962   The Indian Traders. Norman: University of Oklahoma Press.

Macomb, Alexander
1836   [Letter to Lewis Cass, Secretary of War, Dated Washington, June 21, 1836, re Relief of Florida Volunteers Posted on the Withlacoohee.] (Letters Sent by the Headquarters of the Army, 1828–1903, 5/3:109–111, M857, Military Reference

Branch, Record Group 108, National Archives, Washington.)

McReynolds, Edwin C.
1957   The Seminoles. Norman: University of Oklahoma Press.

McVaugh, Rogers
1956   Edward Palmer, Plant Explorer of the American West. Norman: University of Oklahoma Press.

Madill, Dennis
1981   British Columbia Indian Treaties in Historical Perspective. Ottawa: Indian and Northern Affairs Canada, Research Branch.

Madsen, Brigham D.
1985   The Shoshoni Frontier and the Bear River Massacre. Salt Lake City: University of Utah Press.

Magnusson, Magnus, and Hermann Pálsson, trans.
1966   The Vinland Sagas: The Norse Discovery of America. New York: New York University Press.

Mahon, John K.
1954   Pennsylvania and the Beginnings of the Regular Army. *Pennsylvania History* 21(1):33–44.

———
1958   Anglo-American Methods of Indian Warfare, 1676–1794. *Mississippi Valley Historical Review* 45(2):254–275.

———
1966   British Strategy and Southern Indians: War of 1812. *Florida Historical Quarterly* 44(4):285–302.

———
1967   The History of the Second Seminole War, 1835–1842. Gainesville: University of Florida Press.

———
1972   The War of 1812. Gainesville: University of Florida Press.

Maine Historical Society
1869–1916   Documentary History of the State of Maine. 24 vols. Portland: The Society.

Makah Cultural and Research Center
1979   Makah Alphabet Book. Forks, Wash.: Olympic Graphic Arts.

Makarova, Raisa V.
1975   Russians on the Pacific, 1743–1799 (*Materials for the Study of Alaska History* 6). Richard A. Pierce and Alton S. Donnelly, trans. Kingston, Ont.: The Limestone Press.

Malcorps, John
1982   Van Tomahawks en martelpalen: De Indiaan in het stripverhaal. Pp. 53–56 in Vanwege mijn rode huid. J. Van Vaerenbergh and A. Devos, eds. Leuven, Belgium: INFODOK.

Malin, James C.
1921   Indian Policy and Westward Expansion. *Bulletin of the University of Kansas* 22(17), *Humanistic Studies* 2(3). Lawrence.

Malinowski, Bronislaw
1967   A Diary in the Strict Sense of the Term. Norbert Guterman, trans. New York: Harcourt Brace and World.

Malm, Einar
1970   Sitting Bulls Krig. Stockholm: Rabén and Sjögren.

Malmsheimer, Lorna M.
1985   'Imitation White Man': Images of Transformation at the Carlisle Indian School. *Studies in Visual Communication* 11 (Fall):54–75.

Malone, Dumas
1948–1974   Jefferson and His Time. 5 vols. Boston: Little, Brown.

———
1956   Cherokees of the Old South: A People in Transition. Athens: University of Georgia Press.

Malone, Henry T.
1956   Return Jonathan Meigs, Indian Agent Extraordinary. *East Tennessee Historical Society Publications* 28(1):3–22.

———
1956a   Cherokees of the Old South: A People in Transition. Athens: University of Georgia Press.

Malouf, Carling
1966   Ethnohistory in the Great Basin. Pp. 1–38 in The Current Status of Anthropological Research in the Great Basin: 1964. Warren L. d'Azevedo et al., eds. *University of Nevada, Desert Research Institute Social Science and Humanities Publications* 1. Reno.

Malouf, Carling, and A. Arline
1945   The Effects of Spanish Slavery on the Indians of the Intermountain West. *Southwestern Journal of Anthropology* 1(3):378–391.

Mandelbaum, David G., ed.
1949   Selected Writings of Edward Sapir in Language, Culture and Personality. Berkeley: University of California Press.

Manuel, Henry F., Juiliann Ramon, and Bernard L. Fontana
1978   Dressing for the Window: Papago Indians and Economic Development. Pp. 511–577 in American Indian Economic Development. Sam Stanley, ed. The Hague: Mouton.

Manypenny, George W.
1880   Our Indian Wards. Cincinnati, Ohio: R. Clark.

Marcy, Randolph B.
1866   Thirty Years of Army Life on the Border. New York: Harper and Bros.

Mardock, Robert W.
1971   The Reformers and the American Indian. Columbia: University of Missouri Press.

Margry, Pierre, ed.
1876–1886   Découvertes et établissements des français dans l'ouest et dans le sud de l'Amérique septentrionale, 1614–1754: Mémoires et documents originaux. 6 vols. Paris: D. Jouaust. (Reprinted: AMS Press, New York, 1974.)

Marie de l'Incarnation
1876   Lettres de la révérende mère de l'Incarnation, première supérieure de monastère des Ursulines de Québec. New ed. Pierre François Richardeau, ed. Paris: Librairie Internationale-catholique Tournai.

Marino, Cesare
1986   A Preview of the Beltrami Collection with a Note on North American Ethnographic Materials in Italian Museums. *Council for Museum Anthropology Newsletter* 10(2):2–14.

Mark, Joan T.
1980   Four Anthropologists: An American Science in Its Early Years. New York: Science History Publications.

Marmette, Joseph
1877   Le Tomahawk et l'epée. Quebec: L. Brousseau.

Marshall, Peter
1967   Sir William Johnson and the Treaty of Fort Stanwix, 1768. *Journal of American Studies* 1(2):149–179.

Martin, Calvin
1975   The Four Lives of a Micmac Copper Pot. *Ethnohistory* 22(2):111–133.

———
1978   Keepers of the Game: Indian-animal Relationships and the Fur Trade. Berkeley: University of California Press.

Martin, Hansjörg
1972   Überfall am Okeechobee: Vom Freiheitskampf der Seminolen-Indianer (*Rororo Rotfuchs* 4). Reinbeck, Germany: Rowohlt.

Martin, John H., comp.
1949   List of Documents Concerning the Negotiation of Ratified Indian Treaties, 1801–1869. *National Archives Publication* 49–31, *Special List* 6. Washington.

———, comp.
1949a   List of Documents Concerning the Negotiation of Ratified Indian Agreements, 1872–1904. (Manuscript Finding Aid

in Scientific, Economic and Natural Resources Branch, National Archives, Washington.)

Martin, Paul
1967   Arms and Armour from the 9th to the 17th Century. Rutland, Vt.: Charles E. Tuttle.

Martin, Terence
1976   Surviving on the Frontier: The Doubled Consciousness of Natty Bumppo. *South Atlantic Quarterly* 75(4):447–459. Durham, N.C.

Mary-Rousselière, Guy
1964   Paleo-Eskimo Remains in the Pelly Bay Region, N.W.T. *Anthropological Series* 61, *National Museum of Canada Bulletin* 193(1):162–183. Ottawa.

1976   The Paleoeskimo in Northern Baffinland. Pp. 40–57 in Eastern Arctic Prehistory: Paleoeskimo Problems. Moreau S. Maxwell, ed. *Memoirs of the Society for American Archaeology* 31. Salt Lake City.

Mason, Bernard S.
1944   Dances and Stories of the American Indian. New York: Ronald Press.

1946   The Book of Indian Crafts and Costumes. New York: Barnes.

Mason, John
1736   A Brief History of the Pequot War; Especially of the Memorable Taking of Their Fort at Mistick in Connecticut in 1637. Boston: S. Kneeland and T. Green. (Reprinted: Martha Helligso, Omaha, Neb., 1981.)

Mason, Louis B.
1935   The Life and Times of Major John Mason of Connecticut, 1600–1672. New York: G.P. Putnam's Sons.

Massachusetts (Colony)
1853–1854   Records of the Governor and Company of Massachusetts Bay in New England. Nathaniel Shurtleff, ed. 6 vols. Boston: William White.

1869–1922   The Acts and Resolves, Public and Private, of the Province of Massachusetts Bay. 21 vols. Boston: Wright and Potter.

Masterson, William H.
1954   William Blount. Baton Rouge: Louisiana State University Press.

Mather, Cotton
1691   The Life and Death of the Renown'd Mr. John Eliot; Who Was the First Preacher of the Gospel to the Indians in America. London: Printed for John Dunton.

1820   Magnalia Christi Americana, or The Ecclesiastical History of New England . . . .[1702]. 2 vols. Hartford, Conn.: Silas Andrus.

Mathews, John J.
1934   Sundown. New York: Longmans, Green.

Matson, Daniel S., and Bernard L. Fontana, eds. and trans.
1977   Friar Bringas Reports to the King: Methods of Indoctrination on the Frontier of New Spain, 1796–97. Tucson: University of Arizona Press.

Mattes, Merrill J.
1965–1972   John Dougherty. Pp. 113–141 in Vol. 8 of The Mountain Men and the Fur Trade of the Far West. LeRoy R. Hafen, ed. 10 vols. Glendale, Calif.: Arthur H. Clark.

Matthews, Fred H.
1970   The Revolt Against Americanism: Cultural Pluralism and Cultural Relativism as an Ideology of Liberation. *The Canadian Review of American Studies* 1(1):4–31.

Matthiessen, Peter
1959   Wildlife in America. New York: Viking Press.

1983   In the Spirit of Crazy Horse. New York: Viking Press.

Mattison, Ray H.
1965   David Dawson Mitchell. Pp. 241–246 in Vol. 2 of Mountain Men and the Fur Trade of the Far West. LeRoy R. Hafen, ed. 10 vols. Glendale, Calif.: Arthur H. Clark.

Maubert de Gouvest, Jean H.
1752   Lettres iroquoises. 2 vols. À Irocopolis. [Lausanne, Switzerland]: Chez lez Vénérables.

1769   Lettres Chérakéesiennes; mises en françois de la traduction italienne par J.J. Rufus. [Fictitious imprint on t.p.] Rome: l'Imprimerie du Sacré College de la Propagande.

Maximilian, Prince of Wied
1843   Travels in the Interior of North America, 1832–34. H. Evans Lloyd, trans. 2 vols. London: Ackermann.

1904–1907   Travels in the Interior of North America. Pp. 234–260,in Vol. 22 of Early Western Travels, 1748–1846. Reuben G. Thwaites, ed. 32 vols. Cleveland, Ohio: Arthur H. Clark.

May, Karl F.
1891   Der Ölprinz: Eine Erzählung für die reifere Jugend. Stuttgart, Germany: Union Deutsche Verlagsgesellschaft.

1893   Winnetou, der rote gentleman . . . Freiburg, Germany: F.E. Fehsenfeld.

1913–1969   Gesammelte Werke. 74 vols. Radebeul and Bamberg, Germany: Karl May Verlag.

Mayhall, Mildred P.
1962   The Kiowas. Norman: University of Oklahoma Press.

Meacham, Alfred
1875   Wigwam and Warpath, or The Royal Chief in Chains. Boston: J.P. Dale.

1876   Wi-ne-ma (the Woman Chief) and Her People. Hartford, Conn.: American Publishing Company.

Mead, Frances H.
1909   Bibliography of Frederick Ward Putnam. Pp. 601–627 in Putnam Anniversary Volume: Anthropological Essays Presented to Frederick Ward Putnam in Honor of His Seventieth Birthday, April 16, 1909. Franz Boas, ed. New York: G.E. Stechert.

Mead, Margaret
1932   The Changing Culture of an Indian Tribe. New York: Columbia University Press.

Mead, Margaret, and Ruth L. Bunzel, eds.
1960   The Golden Age of American Anthropology. New York: G. Braziller.

Meade, James G.
1971   The "Westerns" of the East: Narratives of Indian Captivity from Jeremiad to the Gothic Novel. (Unpublished Ph.D. Dissertation in American Literature, Northwestern University, Evanston, Ill.)

Mealing, S.R., ed.
1963   The Jesuit Relations and Allied Documents: A Selection. Toronto: McClelland and Stewart.

Meany, Edmond S., ed.
1915   A New Vancouver Journal on the Discovery of Puget Sound, by Members of the Chatham's Crew. Seattle: n.p.

Meares, John
1790   Voyages Made in the Years 1788 and 1789, from China to the North West Coast of America. London: Logographic Press. (Reprinted: Da Capo Press, New York, 1967.)

Mecham, John L.
1927   Francisco de Ibarra and Nueva Vizcaya. Durham, N.C.: Duke University Press.

Medicine, Bea
1979   *Hanta Yo*: A New Phenomenon. *The Indian Historian* 12(2):2–6.

Meek, Ronald
1976   Social Science and the Ignoble Savage. New York: Cambridge University Press.

Meginness, John F.
1891   Biography of Frances Slocum, the Lost Sister of Wyoming. Williamsport, Pa.: Heller Brothers. (Reprinted: Arno Press, New York, 1974.)

Meigs, Charles D.
1851   A Memoir of Samuel Geo. Morton, M.D., Late President of the Academy of Natural Sciences of Philadelphia. Philadelphia: T.K. and P.G. Collins.

Meinig, Donald W.
1968   The Great Columbian Plain: A Historical Geography, 1805–1910. Seattle: University of Washington Press.

Melville, Herman
1851   Moby-Dick; or, The Whale. New York: Harper and Brothers.

1857   The Confidence Man: His Masquerade. New York: Dix, Edwards.

Meredith, Howard L.
1973   The Native American Factor. New York: Seabury Press for the Executive Council of the Episcopal Church.

Meriam, Lewis
1928   The Problem of Indian Administration. Baltimore, Md.: Johns Hopkins Press. (Reprinted: Johnson Reprint, New York, 1971.)

Meriwether, Robert L.
1940   The Expansion of South Carolina, 1729–1765. Kingsport, Tenn.: Southern Publishers.

Meriwether, Robert L., W. Edwin Hemphill, and Clyde N. Wilson, eds.
1959–1984   The Papers of John C. Calhoun. 16 vols. Columbia: University of South Carolina Press.

Merriam, C. Hart
1962   Studies of California Indians. Berkeley: University of California Press.

1966–1967   Ethnographic Notes on California Indian Tribes. 3 Pts. Robert F. Heizer, ed. and comp. *University of California Archaeological Survey Reports* 68. Berkeley.

1974   Selected Works of Clinton Hart Merriam. Keir B. Sterling, comp. New York: Arno Press.

Merrill, Rufus, comp.
1837   A Collection of Indian Anecdotes. Concord, N.H.: W. White.

Métayer, Maurice, comp.
1973   Unipkat, tradition esquimaude de Coppermine, Territoires-du-Nord-Ouest, Canada. 3 Pts. *Centre d'Etudes Nordiques, Collection Nordicana* 40–42. Quebec.

Meyer, Hildegard
1929   Nord-Amerika im Urteil des deutschen Schrifttums bis zur Mitte des 19. Jahrhunderts. (*Übersee-Geschichte* 3) Hamburg, Germany: Friederichsen, de Gruyter.

Meyer, Roy W.
1967   History of the Santee Sioux: United States Indian Policy on Trial. Lincoln: University of Nebraska Press.

1977   The Village Indians of the Upper Missouri: The Mandans, Hidatsas, and Arikaras. Lincoln: University of Nebraska Press.

1979   Ezra A. Hayt, 1877–80. Pp. 155–166 in The Commissioners of Indian Affairs, 1824–1977. Robert M. Kvasnicka and Herman J. Viola, eds. Lincoln: University of Nebraska Press.

Meyers, Augustus
1914   Ten Years in the Ranks, U.S. Army. New York: Stirling Press.

Middleton, Arthur P., and Douglass Adair
1947   The Mystery of the Horn Papers. *William and Mary Quarterly 3d ser.,* Vol. 4(4):409–445. Williamsburg, Va.

Mikkelsen, Ejnar
1920   Norden for Lov og Ret. Copenhagen: Gyldendal.

1921   John Dale. Copenhagen: Gyldendal.

Milder, Robert
1980   *The Last of the Mohicans* and the New World Fall. *American Literature* 52(3):407–429.

Miles, Nelson A.
1896   Personal Recollections and Observations of General Nelson A. Miles. Chicago: Werner. (Reprinted: Da Capo Press, New York, 1969.)

1911   Serving the Republic: Memoirs of the Civil and Military Life of Nelson A. Miles. New York: Harpers. (Reprinted: Books for Libraries, Freeport, N.Y., 1971.)

Militov, Nikolaï
1865   Report on the Condition of the Tlingit Parish in Sitka. [Manuscript 81, box 32, f. 24 in Alaska State Historical Library, M.Z. Vinokouroff Collection, Juneau.]

Miller, Christopher L., and George R. Hamell
1986   A New Perspective on Indian-White Contact: Cultural Symbols and Colonial Trade. *Journal of American History* 73(2):311–328.

Miller, David H., ed.
1931–1948   Treaties and Other International Acts of the United States of America. 8 vols. Washington: U.S. Government Printing Office. (Reprinted: W.S. Hein, Buffalo, N.Y. 1977.)

1976   The Fur Men and Explorers View the Indians. Pp. 25–45 in Red Men and Hat Wearers: Viewpoints in Indian History. Daniel Tyler, ed. Fort Collins: Colorado State University.

Miller, Joaquin
1871   Songs of the Sierras. Boston: Roberts Brothers.

1874   Unwritten History; Life Amongst the Modocs. Hartford, Conn.: American Publishing Company.

Miller, Perry
1953   Roger Williams: His Contribution to the American Tradition. New York: Bobbs-Merrill.

1962   Roger Williams: His Contribution to the American Tradition. New York: Atheneum.

Milloy, John S.
1978   The Era of Civilization: British Policy for the Indians of Canada, 1830–1860. (Unpublished Ph.D. Dissertation in History, Oxford University, Oxford, England.)

Mills, Lawrence
1924   Oklahoma Indian Land Law; a Second Edition of The Lands of the Five Civilized Tribes in Oklahoma . . . .with a Compilation of All Treaties, Acts of Congress, [etc.]. St. Louis, Mo.: Thomas Law Book Company.

Milner, Clyde A., II
1982   With Good Intentions: Quaker Work Among the Pawnees, Otos, and Omahas in the 1870s. Lincoln: University of Nebraska Press.

Mims, Stewart L.
1912   Colbert's West India Policy (*Yale Historical Studies* 1). New Haven, Conn.: Yale University Press. (Reprinted: Octagon Books, New York, 1977.)

Miner, H. Craig
1979   Francis A. Walker, 1871–73. Pp. 135–140 in The Commissioners of Indian Affairs, 1824–1977. Robert M. Kvasnicka

and Herman J. Viola, eds. Lincoln: University of Nebraska Press.

Miner, H. Craig, and William E. Unrau
1978   The End of Indian Kansas: A Study of Cultural Revolution, 1854–1871. Lawrence: Regents Press of Kansas.

Mishkin, Bernard
1940   Rank and Warfare Among the Plains Indians. (*Monographs of the American Ethnological Society* 3). New York: J.J. Augustin.

Mission du Canada
1861   Relations inédites de la Nouvelle-France (1672–1679) pour faire suite aux anciennes relations (1615–1672). 2 vols. Paris: C. Douniol.

Missionary Society of Connecticut
1800   Proceedings of the Trustees of the Missionary Society of Connecticut, Relative to a Mission Among the Indians. *Connecticut Evangelical Magazine* 1(1):14–19. Hartford.

Mitchell, Joseph
1827   The Missionary Pioneer, or A Brief Memoir of the Life, Labours, and Death of John Stewart . . . . New York: J.C. Totten.

————
1960   The Mohawks in High Steel. Pp. 3–36 in Apologies to the Iroquois, by Edmund Wilson. New York: Vintage Books.

Mitchell, Lee Clark
1981   Witnesses to a Vanishing America: The Nineteenth Century Response. Princeton, N.J.: Princeton University Press.

[Mix, Charles E., comp.]
1850   Office Copy of the Laws, Regulations, etc., of the Indian Bureau. Washington: Gideon and Company, Printers.

Modell, Judith S.
1983   Ruth Benedict: Patterns of a Life. Philadelphia: University of Pennsylvania.

Möllhausen, Balduin
1861   Der Halbindianer. Leipzig, Germany: Costenoble.

————
1865   Die Mandanenwaise. Berlin: Janke.

————
1878   Die Reiher. Berlin: Janke.

————
1880   Der Schatz von Quivira. Berlin: Janke.

Moerner, Magnus
1967   Race Mixture in the History of Latin America. Boston: Little, Brown.

————
1970   La Corona española y los foraneos en los pueblos de Indios de América. *Instituto de Estudios Ibero-Americanos, Publicaciones serie A, Monografías* 1. Stockholm.

Mohr, Walter H.
1933   Federal Indian Relations, 1774–1788. Philadelphia: University of Pennsylvania Press.

Momaday, N. Scott
1967   The Journey of Tai-Me. Santa Barbara: University of California Press.

————
1968   House Made of Dawn. New York: Harper, Row.

————
1969   The Way to Rainy Mountain. Albuquerque: University of New Mexico Press.

Monaghan, James [Jay]
1946   The Legend of Tom Horn, Last of the Bad Men. Indianapolis, Ind.: Bobbs-Merrill.

————
1959   Custer: The Life of General George Armstrong Custer. Boston and Toronto: Little, Brown. (Reprinted: University of Nebraska Press, Lincoln, 1971.)

Monkman, Leslie
1981   A Native Heritage: Images of the Indian in English-Canadian Literature. Toronto: University of Toronto Press.

Montgomery, Richard G.
1934   The White Headed Eagle: Builder of an Empire, John McLoughlin. New York: Macmillan.

Mooney, James
1890   Cherokee Theory and Practice of Medicine. *Journal of American Folk-Lore* 3(1):44–50.

————
1891   The Sacred Formulas of the Cherokee. Pp. 301–397 in *7th Annual Report of the Bureau of American Ethnology for the Years 1885–1886*. Washington.

————
1894   The Siouian Tribes of the East. *Bureau of American Ethnology Bulletin* 22. Washington.

————
1896   The Ghost-dance Religion and the Sioux Outbreak of 1890. Pp. 641–1136 in Pt. 2 of *14th Annual Report of the Bureau of American Ethnology for the Years 1892–1893*. Washington.

————
1898   Calendar History of Kiowa Indians. Pp. 129–439 in Pt. 1 of *17th Annual Report of the Bureau of American Ethnology for the Years 1895–1896*. Washington.

————
1900   Myths of the Cherokee. Pp. 3–548 in Pt. 1 of *19th Annual Report of the Bureau of American Ethnology for the Years 1897–1898*. Washington.

————
1907   The Cheyenne Indians. *Memoirs of the American Anthropological Association* 1:357–478. Lancaster, Pa.

————
1907a   [Obituary of] Albert Samuel Gatschet, 1832–1907. *American Anthropologist* 9(3):561–570.

————
1907b   Missions. Pp. 874–909 in Vol. 1 of Handbook of American Indians North of Mexico. Frederick W. Hodge, ed. 2 vols. *Bureau of American Ethnology Bulletin* 30. Washington.

————
1910   Tammany. Pp. 683–684 in Vol. 2 of Handbook of American Indians North of Mexico. Frederick W. Hodge, ed. 2 vols. *Bureau of American Ethnology Bulletin* 30. Washington.

————
1910a   Saint Regis. Pp. 412–413 in Vol. 2 of Handbook of American Indians North of Mexico. Frederick W. Hodge, ed. 2 vols. *Bureau of American Ethnology Bulletin* 30. Washington.

————
1928   The Aboriginal Population of America North of Mexico. *Smithsonian Miscellaneous Collections* 80(7):1–40. Washington.

————
1975   Historical Sketch of the Cherokee. Chicago: Aldine.

Moore, Francis
1840   A Voyage to Georgia [1744]. *Collections of the Georgia Historical Society* 1:80–152. Savannah.

Moore, John, ed.
1923   Tennessee, the Volunteer State, 1769–1923. 4 vols. Chicago: The S.J. Clarke Publishing Company.

Moore, John H.
1974   Cheyenne Political History, 1820–1894. *Ethnohistory* 21(4):329–359.

Moorehead, Warren K.
1914   The American Indian in the United States, Period 1850–1914. Andover, Mass.: The Andover Press. (Reprinted: Books for Libraries Press, Freeport, N.Y., 1969.)

————
1925   Plan of Reorganization of the United States Indian Service. Andover, Mass.: no publisher.

Moorhead, Max L.
1958   New Mexico's Royal Road: Trade and Travel on the Chihuahua Trail. Norman: University of Oklahoma Press.

Morantz, Toby
1980   The Fur Trade and the Cree of James Bay. Pp. 39–58 in Old Trails and New Directions: Papers of the Third North American Fur Trade Conference. Carol M. Judd and Arthur J. Ray, eds. Toronto: University of Toronto Press.

Moravian Church
1757   Kurze, zuverlässige Nachricht von der, unter dem Namen der Böhmisch-Mährischen Brüder bekannten Kirche Unitas Fratum, Herkommen, Lehrbegriff, äussern und innern Kirchen-Verfassung und Gebräuchen . . . .No place: no publisher.

Moravian Historical Society
1860   A Memorial of the Dedication of Monuments. Erected by the Moravian Historical Society, to Mark the Sites of Ancient Missionary Stations in New York and Connecticut. Reichel W. Cornelius, ed. New York: C.B. Richardson.

More, Thomas
1808   Utopia [1516]. T.F. Didbin, ed. Raphe Robinson, trans. 2 vols. London: Bulmer.

Morfi, Juan Agustín
1935   History of Texas, 1673–1779. Carlos E. Castañeda, trans. 2 vols. *Quivira Society Publications* 6. Albuquerque.

Morgan, Dale L.
1948   The Administration of Indian Affairs in Utah, 1851–1858. *Pacific Historical Review* 17(4):383–409.

————
1953   Jedediah Smith and the Opening of the West. New York: Bobbs-Merrill.

————, ed.
1964   The West of William H. Ashley: The International Struggle for the Fur Trade of the Missouri, the Rocky Mountains, and the Columbia, with Explorations Beyond the Continental Divide, Recorded in the Diaries and Letters of William H. Ashley and His Contemporaries. Denver, Colo.: The Old West Publishing Company.

Morgan, Dale L., and Carl I. Wheat
1954   Jedediah Smith and His Maps of the American West. San Francisco: California Historical Society.

Morgan, Edmund S.
1967   Roger Williams: The Church and the State. New York: Harcourt, Brace and World.

————
1975   American Slavery, American Freedom: The Ordeal of Colonial Virginia. New York: W.W. Norton.

Morgan, Henry J.
1898   The Canadian Men and Women of the Time: A Handbook of Canadian Biography. Toronto: William Briggs.

Morgan, Lewis H.
1851   League of the Ho-dé-no-sau-nee or Iroquois. Rochester, N.Y.: Sage Books. (Reprinted as League of the Iroquois, Corinth Books, New York, 1962.)

————
[1871]   Systems of Consanguinity and Affinity of the Human Family. *Smithsonian Contributions to Knowledge* 17. Washington. (Reprinted: Humanities Press, New York, 1966.)

————
1877   Ancient Society, or Researches in the Lines of Human Progress from Savagery Through Barbarism to Civilization. New York: Holt. (Reprinted: World Publishing Company, Cleveland and New York, 1963; Gordon Press, New York, 1976.)

————
1881   Houses and House-life of the American Aborigines (*Contributions to North American Ethnology* 4). Washington: U.S. Geological and Geographical Survey of the Rocky Mountain Region. (Reprinted: University of Chicago Press, Chicago, 1905.)

Morgan, Thomas J.
1890   Indian Education. [Washington: U.S. Government Printing Office.]

————
1891   The Present Phase of the Indian Question. (*Boston Indian Citizenship Committee Publication* 10) Boston: F. Wood.

Morin, Victor
1915   Les Médailles décernées aux Indiens d'Amérique. *Proceedings and Transactions of the Royal Society of Canada 3d ser.*, Vol. 9:277–353. Ottawa.

Morison, Samuel E.
1961   The Maritime History of Massachusetts 1783–1860 [1921]. Boston, Mass.: Houghton Mifflin. (Reprinted: Northeastern University Press, Boston, 1979.)

————
1971   The European Discovery of America: The Northern Voyages, A.D. 500–1600. New York: Oxford University Press.

————
1974   The European Discovery of America: The Southern Voyages, A.D. 1494–1616. New York: Oxford University Press.

Morris, Alexander
1880   The Treaties of Canada with the Indians of Manitoba and the North-west Territories, Including the Negotiations on Which They Are Based, and Other Information Relating Thereto. Toronto: Willing and Williamson. (Reprinted: Coles, Toronto, 1971.)

Morris, George P.
1857   The Prose and Poetry of Europe and America. New York: Leavitt and Allen.

Morris, Richard B.
1946   Government and Labor in Early America. New York: Columbia University Press. (Reprinted: Octagon Books, New York, 1965.)

Morrison, Kenneth M.
1970   Sebastien Rale vs. New England: A Case Study of Frontier Conflict. (Unpublished M.A. Thesis in History, University of Maine, Orono.)

————
1975   The People of the Dawn: The Abnaki and Their Relations with New England and New France, 1602–1727. (Unpublished Ph.D. Dissertation in History, University of Maine, Orono.)

————
1984   The Embattled Northeast: The Elusive Ideal of Alliance in Abenaki-Euroamerican Relations. Berkeley: University of California Press.

Morse, Eric W.
1969   Fur Trade Canoe Routes of Canada/Then and Now. Ottawa: Queen's Printer. (Reprinted: University of Toronto Press, Toronto, 1979.)

Morse, Jarvis M.
1952   American Beginnings: Highlights and Sidelights of the Birth of the New World. Washington: Public Affairs Press.

Morse, Jedidiah
1822   A Report to the Secretary of War of the United States on Indian Affairs. New Haven, Conn.: S. Converse. (Reprinted: Augustus M. Kelly, New York, 1970; Scholarly Press, St. Clair Shores, Mich., 1972.)

Morton, Arthur S.
1939   A History of the Canadian West to 1870–71: Being a History of Rupert's Land (the Hudson's Bay Company's Territory) and of the North-west Territory (Including the Pacific Slope). London: Thomas Nelson and Sons.

————
1944   Sir George Simpson: Overseas Governor of the Hudson's Bay Company; A Pen Picture of a Man of Action. Toronto: J.M. Dent and Sons.

Morton, Samuel G.
1839   Crania Americana; or, A Comparative View of the Skulls of Various Aboriginal Nations of North and South America. Philadelphia: J. Dobson.

Morton, Thomas
1883   New English Canaan [1637]. Charles F. Adams, Jr., ed. Boston: Prince Society. (Reprinted: Arno Press, New York, 1972.)

Morton, W.L.
1957   Manitoba, a History. Toronto: University of Toronto Press.

Moses, Lester G.
1984   The Indian Man: A Biography of James Mooney. Urbana: University of Illinois Press.

Mott, Frank L.
1938–1968 A History of American Magazines. 5 vols. Cambridge, Mass.: Harvard University Press.

————
1947   Golden Multitudes: The Story of Best Sellers in the United States. New York: Macmillan.

Moulton, Gary E.
1978   John Ross, Cherokee Chief. Athens: University of Georgia Press.

Mourt, G.
1963   A Journal of the Pilgrims at Plymouth: Mourt's Relation [1622]. Dwight B. Heath, ed. New York: Corinth Books.

Mousnier, Roland
1954   Les XVIe et XVIIe siècles: Les progrès de la civilisation européenne et le déclin de l'orient (1492–1715) (Histoire Generale des Civilisations 4). Paris: Presses Universitaires de France.

Mowat, Farley
1970   Sibir: My Discovery of Siberia. Toronto: McClelland and Stewart.

Moziño, José M.
1970   Noticias de Nutka: An Account of Nootka Sound in 1792. Iris H. Wilson, trans. Toronto: McClelland and Stewart.

Muckleroy, Anna
1922–1923 The Indian Policy of the Republic of Texas. Southwestern Historical Quarterly 25(4):229–260; 26(1):1–29, (2):128–148, (3):184–206. Austin, Tex.

Müller-Tannewitz, Anna [Anna Jurgen]
1950   Blauvogel, Wahlsohn der Irokesen. Berlin: Verlag Neues Leben.

————
1951   Das Indianerspiel. Reutlingen, Germany: Ensslin and Laiblin.

Mullin, Michael
1986   Sir William Johnson, Cultural Brother. (Research Paper, in preparation for publication; copy in W.R. Jacob's possession.)

Munroe, James P.
1923   A Life of Francis Amasa Walker. New York: Henry Holt.

Murdock, George P.
1948   Clark Wissler, 1870–1947. American Anthropologist 50(2):292–304.

Murphree, Idus L.
1961   The Evolutionary Anthropologists: The Progress of Mankind. The Concepts of Progress and Culture in the Thought of John Lubbock, Edward B. Tylor, and Lewis H. Morgan. Proceedings of the American Philosophical Society 105(3):265–300. Philadelphia.

Murray, Keith A.
1959   The Modocs and Their War. Norman: University of Oklahoma Press.

Myers, Albert C., ed.
1912   Narratives of Early Pennsylvania, West New Jersey, and Delaware, 1630–1707 New York: Charles Scribner's Sons.

Myklebust, Olav, G., ed.
1958   Hans Egede: Studier til 200-årsdagen for hans dod 5, November 1958 [Studies on the Occasion of the 200th Anniversary of His Death]. Studies of the Egede Institute 8. Oslo.

NAACP Legal Defense and Education Fund
1971   An Even Chance: A Report on Federal Funds for Indian Children in Public School Districts. New York.

N.J. Arch.=Whitehead, William A. et al., eds.
1880–1949 Documents Relating to the Colonial, Revolutionary and Post-revolutionary History of the State of New Jersey. 42 vols. Newark, N.J.: Various Publishers.

NYCD=O'Callaghan, Edmund B., ed.
1853–1887 Documents Relative to the Colonial History of the State of New York; Procured in Holland, England and France, by John R. Brodhead. 15 vols. Albany, N.Y.: Weed, Parsons.

NYDH=O'Callaghan, Edmund B., ed.
1849–1851 The Documentary History of the State of New York. 4 vols. Albany, N.Y.: Weed, Parsons.

NYHSC=New York Historical Society
1868   Collections. Albany: The Society.

Nafziger, Alyce J., comp.
1970   American Indian Education: A Selected Bibliography. Supplement 1. Las Cruces: New Mexico State University.

Nammack, Georgianna C.
1969   Fraud, Politics, and the Dispossession of the Indians: The Iroquois Land Frontier in the Colonial Period. Norman: University of Oklahoma Press.

Nasatir, Abraham, ed.
1939   The International Significance of the Jones and Immell Massacre and of the Arikara Outbreak in 1823. Pacific Northwest Quarterly 30(1):77–108.

————, ed.
1952   Before Lewis and Clark: Documents Illustrating the History of the Missouri, 1785–1804. 2 vols. St. Louis, Mo.: St. Louis Historical Documents Foundation.

————
1974   More on Pedro Vial in Upper Louisiana. Pp. 100–119 in The Spanish in the Mississippi Valley, 1762–1804. John F. McDermott, ed. Urbana: University of Illinois Press.

Nash, Gary B.
1972   The Image of the Indian in the Southern Colonial Mind. William and Mary Quarterly 3d ser., Vol. 29(2):197–230. Williamsburg, Va.

————
1974   Red, White, and Black: The Peoples of Early America. Englewood Cliffs, N.J.: Prentice-Hall.

————
1975   The Political Dimension of the Seventeenth Century Missions. (Paper presented at the International Congress on First Images of America, Los Angeles, February 7.)

Nash, John D.
1967   The Salmon River Mission. Idaho Yesterdays 11(1):22–31.

Nash, Philleo
1979   Anthropologist in the White House. Practicing Anthropology 1(3):3, 23–24.

————
1986   Science, Politics, and Human Values: A Memoir. Human Organization 45(3):189–201.

Nash, Roderick
1982   Wilderness and the American Mind. 3d ed. New Haven, Conn.: Yale University Press.

Nasnaga (Roger Russell)
1975   Indian's Summer. New York: Harper and Row.

National Archives Trust Fund Board
1984   American Indians: A Select Catalog of National Archives Microform Publications. Washington: U.S. General Services Administration, National Archives Trust Fund Board.

National Congress of American Indians
1946   Constitution and By-laws. In Proceedings of the 3d Annual Convention of the National Congress of American Indians, November 6–9, 1946, Oklahoma City, Okla.

1948   [Minutes of the Convention, December 13–18, 1948, Denver, Colorado.] Mimeo.

1954   [Emergency Conference of American Indians on Legislation, February 25–28, 1954.] Mimeo.

1960   [17th Annual Convention, Denver, Colorado.] (Records of the NCAI Conventions, Box 13, National Anthropological Archives, Smithsonian Institution, Washington.)

National Congress of American Indians and Association on American Indian Affairs
1957   [Legal Workshop on American Indian Legislative Problems.] (Records of the NCAI in Box 10, National Anthropological Archives, Smithsonian Institution, Washington.)

Neal, John
1822   Logan, the Mingo Chief. London: J. Cunningham.

Neighbors, Alice Atkinson
1936   Life and Public Work of Robert S. Neighbors. (Unpublished M.A. Thesis in History, University of Texas, Austin.)

Neighbours, Kenneth F.
1956   Robert S. Neighbors in Texas, 1836–1856: A Quarter Century of Frontier Problems. (Unpublished Ph.D. Dissertation in History, University of Texas, Austin.)

Neihardt, John G.
1925   The Song of the Indian Wars. New York: Macmillan.

1932   Black Elk Speaks, Being the Life Story of a Holy Man of the Oglala Sioux. New York: William Morrow.

1935   The Song of the Messiah. New York: Macmillan.

1951   When the Tree Flowered; An Authentic Tale of the Old Sioux World. New York: Macmillan.

1972   Black Elk Speaks: Being the Life Story of a Holy Man of the Oglala Sioux. Rev. ed. New York: Pocket Books. (Reprinted: University of Nebraska, Lincoln, 1979.)

Nelson, Edward W.
1899   The Eskimo About Bering Strait. Pp. 3–518 in 18th Annual Report of the Bureau of American Ethnology for the Years 1896–1897. Washington. (Reprinted: Smithsonian Institution Press, Washington, 1983.)

Nelson, Harold L.
1955   Military Roads for War and Peace, 1791–1836. Military Affairs 19:1–14. Washington.

Nelson, Ralph
1970   Massacre at Sand Creek. Films and Filming 16(6):26–27.

Nentvig, Juan
1863   Rudo Ensayo, tentativa de una descripción geográfica de la provincia de Sonora [1762]. San Augustin de la Florida. [Albany: Munsell].

1980   Rudo Ensayo: A Description of Sonora and Arizona in 1764. Albert Francisco Pradeau and Robert R. Rasmussen, eds. and trans. Tucson: University of Arizona Press.

Netsvíetov, Iakov
1980   The Journals of Iakov Netsvetov: The Atkha Years, 1828–1844. Lydia T. Black, trans. Kingston, Ont.: The Limestone Press.

1984   The Journals of Iakov Netsvetov: The Yukon Years, 1845–1863. Lydia T. Black, trans. Richard A. Pierce, ed. Kingston, Ont.: The Limestone Press.

Neumann, Joseph
1682   [Letter of February 20.] (Manuscript, in Bolton Collection, Bancroft Library, University of California, Berkeley.)

1725   Historia seditionum quas adversus Societatis Jesú missionarios eorumque auxiliatoris moverunt nationes indicae ac potissimum Tarahumara in America Septentrionali regnoque Novae Cantabriae, jam toto ad fidem catholicam propemodum redacto. Prefacio 15 April 1724. (Manuscript in Bolton Collection, Bancroft Library, University of California, Berkeley.)

1969   Révoltes des Indiens Tarahumara (1629–1724). Luis Gonzalez, ed. and trans. Paris: Institut des Hautes Etudes de l'Amérique Latine de l'Université de Paris.

Nevins, Allan
1941   Helen Hunt Jackson, Sentimentalist vs. Realist. American Scholar 10(3):269–285.

Newcomb, Harvey
1935   The North American Indian: Being a Series of Conversations Between a Mother and Her Children; Illustrating the Character, Manners, and Customs of the Natives of North America. Vol. 1. Pittsburgh, Pa: Luke Loomis.

Newcomb, William W., Jr.
1961   The Indians of Texas: From Prehistoric to Modern Times. Austin: University of Texas Press.

New Plymouth Colony
1836   The Compact with the Charter and Laws of the Colony of New Plymouth. Boston: Dutton and Wentworth.

Newton, Nell J.
1984   Federal Power Over Indians: Its Sources, Scope, and Limitations. University of Pennsylvania Law Review 132(2):195–288.

New York State Historical Association
1961   History of the State of New York. Alexander C. Flick, ed. 10 vols. Port Washington, N.Y.: Ira J. Friedman.

Nichols, David A.
1972   Civilization Over Savage: Frederick Jackson Turner and the Indian. South Dakota History 2(4):383–405.

1978   Lincoln and the Indians: Civil War Policy and Politics. Columbia: University of Missouri Press.

Nichols, Roger L., ed.
1963   General Henry Atkinson's Report of the Yellowstone Expedition of 1825. Nebraska History 44(2):65–82.

1965   General Henry Atkinson: A Western Military Career. Norman: University of Oklahoma Press.

1971   Printer's Ink and Red Skins: Western Newspapermen and the Indians. Kansas Quarterly 3(4):82–88.

Nicks, Trudy
1980   The Iroquois and the Fur Trade in Western Canada. Pp. 85–101 in Old Trails and New Directions: Papers of the Third North American Fur Trade Conference. Carol M. Judd and Arthur J. Ray, eds. Toronto: University of Toronto Press.

Nicolson, Harold G.
1963   Diplomacy. 3d ed. New York: Oxford University Press.

Nieritz, Gustav
1846   Der kleine Eskimo und die Trompete. Berlin: Simion.

Niver, Kent R., comp.
1971   Biograph Bulletins: 1896–1908. Bebe Bergsten, ed. Los Angeles: Locare Researh Group.

Noble, Gaile P.
1971   The Ganado Project: Any 'Change' for the Navajo Reserva-
            tion? *The Christian Century* 88(3):78–80.

Noble, John W.
1892   [Letter to the Chairman of the Committee on Indian
            Affairs, Dated April 23, 1892, re the Alienation of Indian
            Land in Washington State.] (Letters Sent by the Indian
            Division of the Office of the Secretary of the Interior,
            1849–1903, 75:310–312, M606, Record Group 48, Natural
            Resources Branch, National Archives, Washington.)

———
1892a   [Letter to the President of the Senate, Dated June 24, 1892,
            re Claims Against Indians.] (Letters Sent by the Indian
            Division of the Office of the Secretary of the Interior,
            1849–1903, 76:86–96, M606, Record Group 48, Natural
            Resources Branch, National Archives, Washington.)

Noël Hume, Ivor
1969   Historical Archaeology. New York: Alfred Knopf.

Nohl, Lessing H., Jr.
1962   Bad Hand: The Military Career of Ranald Slidell
            Mackenzie, 1871–1889. (Unpublished Ph.D. Dissertation in
            History, University of New Mexico, Albuquerque.)

Noir, Louis S.
1899   Chez les Apaches: Les Rubis du Colorado. Paris: Fayard.

———
1899a   Chez les Sioux: Une française captive chez les Peaux-rouges.
            Paris: Fayard.

Norick, Frank
1982   The Reburial Controversy in California. *Council for Muse-
            um Anthropology Newsletter* 6(3):2–6.

North American Home Missions Congress
1930   Report of Commissions, Addresses and Findings, Washing-
            ton, D.C., December 1–5, 1930. Washington: Home Mis-
            sions Council of North America.

Northrup, Ansel J.
1900   Slavery in New York: A Historical Sketch. *State Library
            Bulletin. History* 4. Albany, N.Y.

Norton, Thomas E.
1974   The Fur Trade in Colonial New York, 1686–1776. Madi-
            son: University of Wisconsin Press.

Nowicka, Ewa
1987   The "Polish Movement of Friends of the American
            Indians." Pp. 599–608 in Indians and Europe: An Interdis-
            ciplinary Collection of Essays. Christian F. Feest, ed.
            Aachen, Germany: Rader Verlag.

Nunis, Doyce B., Jr.
1959   The Sublettes of Kentucky: Their Early Contribution to the
            Opening of the West. *The Register* 57:20–34.

Nute, Grace Lee, ed.
1945   Calendar of the American Fur Company's Papers. 3 vols.
            *Annual Report of the American Historical Association for the
            Year 1944.* Washington.

Nydahl, Theodore L.
1950   The Pipestone Quarry and the Indians. *Minnesota History*
            31(4):193–208.

Nye, Russel B.
1967   Parkman, Red Fate, and White Civilization. Pp. 152–163 in
            Essays on American Literature in Honor of Jay B. Hubbell.
            Clarence Gohdes, ed. Durham, N.C.: Duke University
            Press.

———
1970   The Unembarrassed Muse: The Popular Arts in America.
            New York: Dial Press.

Nyland, Agnes C.
1979   In God's Good Time. *Oblate Missions* 139(Fall):11–16.

O'Callaghan, Edmund B.
1846–1848   History of New Netherlands; or, New York Under the
            Dutch. 2 vols. New York: D. Appleton.

———
1865–1866   Calendar of Historical Manuscripts in the Office of the
            Secretary of State, Albany, N.Y. 2 vols. Albany, N.Y.:
            Weed, Parsons.

Och, Joseph
1965   Missionary in Sonora: The Travel Reports of Joseph Och,
            S.J., 1755–1767. Theodore E. Treutlein, ed. and trans. San
            Francisco: California Historical Society.

O'Connor, John E.
1980   The Hollywood Indian: Stereotypes of Native Americans in
            Films. Trenton: New Jersey State Museum.

O'Daniel, V.F., trans.
1917   Documents: The First Episcopal Visitation in the United
            States (1606). *Catholic Historical Review* 2(4):442-459.

Odell, Ruth
1939   Helen Hunt Jackson ("H.H."). New York: D. Appleton-
            Century.

O'Donnell, James H.
1963   The Southern Indians in the War of Independence,
            1775–1783. (Unpublished Ph.D. Dissertation in History,
            Duke University, Durham, N.C.)

———
1973   Southern Indians in the American Revolution. Knoxville:
            University of Tennessee Press.

O'Fallon, Benjamin
1834   [Letter of January 21, 1822 to Sen. Thomas Benton.] P. 328
            in American State Papers. Vol. 2: Indian Affairs. Washing-
            ton: Gales and Seaton.

Ogden, Adele
1941   The California Sea Otter Trade, 1784–1848. Berkeley:
            University of California Press. (Reprinted in 1975.)

Ogden, Peter S.
1950   Snake Country Journals, 1824–25 and 1825–26. E.E. Rich
            and A.M. Johnson, eds. (*Publications of the Hudson's Bay
            Record Society* 13). London: Hudson's Bay Record Society.

———
1961   Snake Country Journal, 1826–27. K.G. Davies and A.M.
            Johnson, eds. (*Publications of the Hudson's Bay Record
            Society* 23). London: Hudson's Bay Record Society.

———
1971   Peter Skene Ogden's Snake Country, 1827–28 and 1828–29.
            Glyndwr Williams, ed. (*Publications of the Hudson's Bay
            Record Society* 28). London: Hudon's Bay Record Society.

Oglesby, Richard E.
1963   Manuel Lisa and the Opening of the Missouri Fur Trade.
            Norman: University of Oklahoma Press.

———
1967   The Fur Trade as Business. Pp. 111–127 in the Frontier Re-
            examined. John F. McDermott, ed. Urbana: University of
            Illinois Press.

Okladnikov, A.P., ed.
1968–1969   Istoriia Sibiri [History of Siberia]. 5 vols. Leningrad: Nauka.

Okun', Semen Bentsionovich
1951   The Russian-American Company. Carl Ginsburg, trans.
            (*Russian Translation Project Series of the American Council
            of Learned Societies* 9) Cambridge, Mass.: Harvard Univer-
            sity Press.

Olearius, Adam
1656   Vermehrte newe Beschreibung der muscowitischen und
            persischen Reyse, etc. Schleswig, Germany: no publisher.

Oleksa, Michael
1979   The Orthodox Mission and Native Alaskan Languages: A
            Brief Overview. *Orthodox Alaska* 8(1):1–12. Kodiak.

Oliphant, J. Orin
1925 Old Fort Colville. *Washington Historical Quarterly* 16(1):29–48, 83–101. Seattle.

Olivia, Leo E.
1973 Thomas Berger's *Little Big Man* as History. *Western American Literature* 8(1–2):33-54. Fort Collins, Colo.

Olson, James C.
1965 Red Cloud and the Sioux Problem. Lincoln: University of Nebraska Press.

O'Meara, Walter
1962 The Last Portage. Boston: Houghton Mifflin.

O'Neil, Floyd A.
1979 Hiram Price, 1881–85. Pp. 173–179 in The Commissioners of Indian Affairs, 1824–1977. Robert M. Kvasnicka and Herman J. Viola, eds. Lincoln: University of Nebraska Press.

————
1979a John H. Oberly, 1888–89. Pp. 189–191 in The Commissioners of Indian Affairs, 1824–1977. Robert M. Kvasnicka and Herman J. Viola, eds. Lincoln: University of Nebraska Press.

O'Neil, Marion
1930 The Maritime Activities of the North West Company, 1813–1821. *Washington Historical Quarterly* 21(4):243–267. Seattle.

O'Neill, Charles E.
1966 Church and State in French Colonial Louisiana: Policy and Politics to 1732. New Haven, Conn.: Yale University Press.

Opie, Iona A., and Peter Opie
1959 The Lore and Language of Schoolchildren. Oxford, England: Clarendon Press.

Ore, Luis Jeronimo de
1936 The Martyrs of Florida, 1513–1616. Maynard Geiger, trans. New York: J.F. Wagner.

O'Rourke, Thomas P.
1927 The Franciscan Missions in Texas (1690–1793). Washington: The Catholic University of America. (Reprinted: AMS Press, New York, 1974.)

Orr, Charles, ed.
1897 History of the Pequot War: The Contemporary Accounts of Mason, Underhill, Vincent and Gardener. Cleveland, Ohio: Helman-Taylor.

Orser, Charles E., Jr.
1984 Understanding Arikara Trading Behavior: A Cultural Case Study of the Ashley-Leavenworth Episode of 1823. Pp. 101–107 in Rendezvous: Selected Papers of the Fourth North American Fur Trade Conference, 1981. T.C. Buckley, ed. St. Paul, Minn.: North American Fur Conference.

————
1984a Trade Good Flow in Arikara Villages: Expanding Ray's "Middleman Hypothesis." *Plains Anthropologist* 29(103):1–12.

Ortega y Medina, Juan A.
1958 Ideas de la evangelización anglosajona entre los indígenos de los Estados Unidos de Norte-america. *América Indígena* 18(2):129–144.

Ortiz, Alfonso
1969 The Tewa World: Space, Time, Being, and Becoming in a Pueblo Society. Chicago: University of Chicago Press.

————
1971 An Indian Anthropologist's Perspective on Anthropology. *The Indian Historian* 4(1):11–14.

Ortiz, Simon J.
1977 Song, Poetry and Language-Expression and Perception. Tsaile, Ariz.: Navajo Community College Press.

————
1983 Fightin': New and Collected Stories. New York: Thurder's Mouth Press.

————, ed.
1983a Earth Power Coming; Short Fiction in Native American Literature. Tsaile, Ariz.: Navajo Community College Press.

Orth, Donald J.
1967 Dictionary of Alaska Place Names. *U.S. Geological Survey Professional Paper* 67. Washington.

Osborn, Alan J.
1983 Ecological Aspects of Equestrian Adaptations in Aboriginal North America. *American Anthropologist* 85(3):563–591.

Osgood, Ernest S., ed.
1964 The Field Notes of Captain William Clark, 1803–1805. New Haven, Conn.: Yale University Press.

Osgood, Phillips E.
1958 Straight Tongue: A Story of Henry Benjamin Whipple, First Episcopal Bishop of Minnesota. Minneapolis, Minn.: T.S. Denison.

Osgood, Wilfred H.
1945 Biographical Memoir of Clinton Hart Merriam, 1855–1942. (Bibliography . . . by Hilda W. Grinnell.) *National Academy of Sciences Biographical Memoirs* 24(1):1–57. Washington.

Oskison, John M.
1935 Brothers Three. New York: Macmillan.

Ostermann, Hother B.S., ed.
1928–1929 A History of the Mission. Pp. 269–341 in Vol. 3 of Greenland. M. Vahl, G.C. Amdrup, L. Bobé, Ad. S. Jensen, eds. 3 vols. Copenhagen: C.A. Reitzel.

Ostrom, Vincent, and Theodore Stern
1959 A Case Study of Termination of Federal Responsibilities Over the Klamath Reservation. (Report to the Commission on the Rights, Liberties and Responsibilities of the American Indian.) Mimeo.

Oswalt, Wendell H., ed.
1960 Eskimos and Indians of Western Alaska, 1860–1868: Extracts from the Diary of Father Illarion. *Anthropological Papers of the University of Alaska* 8(2):101–118. College.

————
1963 Napaskiak, an Alaskan Eskimo Community. Tucson: University of Arizona Press.

————
1963a A Mission of Change in Alaska: Eskimos and Moravians on the Kuskokwim. San Marino, Calif.: The Huntington Library.

————
1978 The Kuskowagamiut: Riverine Eskimos. Pp. 103–143 in This Land Was Theirs: A Study of North American Indians. 3d ed. New York: Wiley.

————
1980 Kolmakovskiy Redoubt: The Ethnoarchaeology of a Russian Fort in Alaska. *University of California. Institute of Archaeology. Monumenta Archaeologica* 8. Los Angeles.

Otis, Delos S.
1973 The Dawes Act and the Allotment of Indian Lands. Francis Paul Prucha, ed. Norman: University of Oklahoma Press.

Otis, George A.
1868 [George A. Otis, Curator Army Medical Museum to Warren Webster, Chief Medical Officer, District of Texas, January 15, 1868.] (In Letter Book No. 3, Surgeon General's Office, Medical Museum of the Armed Forces, Institute of Pathology Archives, Washington.)

Ouellet, Fernand
1966 Histoire économique et social du Québec, 1760–1850: Structure et conjuncture. Montreal: Fides.

Ourada, Patricia K.
1979 Dillon Seymour Myer, 1950–53. Pp. 293–299 in The Commissioners of Indian Affairs, 1824–1977. Robert M. Kvasnicka and Herman J. Viola, eds. Lincoln: University of Nebraska Press.

Overmyer, Grace
1957   America's First Hamlet, Washington Square. New York: New York University Press.

PAC=Public Archives of Canada
1755–1886   Claus Papers. 27 vols. (Manuscript Group 19, F1, Public Archives, Ottawa.)

————   1807   Substance of a Talk Delivered at Le Maioutonong, Entrance of Lake Michigan, by the Indian Chief Le Maigours or the Trout, May 4, 1807. (Manuscript in Public Archives of Canada, M.G. 19, F 16. Ottawa.)

————   1830   [Murray to Kempt, January 25, 1830.] (Manuscript, Record Group 10, Records Relating to Indian Affairs. Vol. 116. Ottawa.)

————Manuscript Division
1971–1977   General Inventory: Manuscripts. 8 vols. Ottawa: Public Archives of Canada.

Pagden, Anthony
1982   The Fall of Natural Man: The American Indian and the Origins of Comparative Ethnology. Cambridge, England: Cambridge University Press.

Page, Elizabeth M.
1915   In Camp and Tepee: An Indian Mission Story. New York: Revell.

Pailes, R.A., and Joseph W. Whitecotton
1979   The Greater Southwest and the Mesoamerican 'World' System: An Exploratory Model of Frontier Relationships. Pp. 105–122 in The Frontier: Comparative Studies. W.W. Savage Jr., and S.I. Thompson, eds. Norman: University of Oklahoma Press.

Paine, Lauran
1962   Tom Horn: Man of the West. London: John Long.

Painter, Charles C.C.
1885   Facts Regarding the Recent Opening to White Settlement of Crow Creek Reservation in Dakota. Philadelphia: Indian Rights Association.

————   1886   A Visit to the Mission Indians of Southern California, and Other Western Tribes. Philadelphia: Indian Rights Association.

————   1887   The Dawes Land in Severalty Bill and Indian Emancipation. Philadelphia: Indian Rights Association.

————   1889   The Oklahoma Bill, and Oklahoma. Philadelphia: Indian Rights Association.

Pajeken, Friedrich J.
1891   Im wilden Westen Nordamerikas. Stuttgart, Germany: F. Loewe.

————   1895   Mitasha-sa, das Pulvergesicht. Stuttgart, Germany: F. Loewe.

Pakes, Fraser
1983   The Indian Hobbyist as Ethnohistorian. (Paper presented at the American Society for Ethnohistory, Albuquerque, New Mexico, November 1983.)

Palladino, Lawrence B.
1894   Indian and White in the Northwest; or, A History of Catholicity in Montana. Baltimore, Md.: John Murphy.

————   1922   Indian and White in the Northwest. 2d ed. Lancaster, Pa.: Wickersham.

Pallas, Peter S.
1948   Bering's Successors, 1745–1880: Contributions of Peter Simon Pallas to the History of Russian Exploration Toward Alaska. J.R. Masterson, and Helen Brower, eds. Seattle: University of Washington Press. (Reprinted from Pacific Northwest Quarterly 38(1–2), 1947.)

Palmer, Edward
1871   Food Products of the North American Indians. Pp. 404–428 in Report of the Commissioner of Agriculture for 1870. Washington.

Palmer, Joel
1847   Journal of Travels Over the Rocky Mountains. Cincinnati, Ohio: J.A. and U.P. James.

Pandey, Triloki Nath
1972   Anthropologists at Zuni. Proceedings of the American Philosophical Society 116(4):321–337. Philadelphia.

Pannekoek, Frits
1976   The Rev. Griffiths Owen Corbett and the Red River Civil War of 1869–70. Canadian Historical Review 57(2):133–149. Toronto.

Pargellis, Stanley M., ed.
1936   Military Affairs in North America, 1748–1765: Selected Documents from the Cumberland Papers in Windsor Castle. New York: D. Appleton-Century.

Parish, John C.
1943   Edmond Atkin, British Superintendent of Indian Affairs. Pp. 147–160 in The Persistence of the Westward Movement and Other Essays. Berkeley: University of California Press.

Parker, Arthur C.
1914   The Quaker City Meeting of the Society of American Indians. Quarterly Journal of the Society of American Indians 2(1):56–59.

————   1927   The Indian How Book. New York: George H. Doran.

————   1954   Sources and Range of Cooper's Indian Lore. New York History 35(4):447–456.

Parkman, Francis
1849   The California and Oregon Trail: Being Sketches of Prairie and Rocky Mountain Life. New York: G.P. Putnam.

————   1851   History of the Conspiracy of Pontiac and the War of the North American Tribes Against the English Colonies After the Conquest of Canada. Boston: C.C. Little and J. Brown.

————   1897   The Jesuits in North America in the Seventeenth Century. 2 vols. Boston: Little, Brown.

————   1898   The Conspiracy of Pontiac and the Indian War After the Conquest of Canada. Boston: Little, Brown.

————   1898a   Works. 12 vols. Boston: Little, Brown.

Parman, Donald L.
1979   Francis Ellington Leupp, 1905–1909. Pp. 221–232 in The Commissioners of Indian Affairs, 1824–1977. Robert M. Kvasnicka and Herman J. Viola, eds. Lincoln: University of Nebraska Press.

Parmenter, R.
1966   Explorer, Linguist and Ethnologist: A Descriptive Bibliography of the Published Works of Alphonse Louis Pinart, with Notes on His Life. (F.W. Hodge Anniversary Publication Fund 9). Los Angeles: Southwest Museum.

Parry, Clive, ed.
1969–   The Consolidated Treaty Series. 231 vols. Dobbs Ferry, N.Y.: Oceana Publications.

Parry, Ellwood
1974   The Image of the Indian and the Black Man in American Art, 1590–1900. New York: G. Braziller.

Parry, John H.
1940   The Spanish Theory of Empire in the Sixteenth Century. Cambridge, England: Cambridge University Press.

Parry, Keith W.
1972   To Raise These People Up: An Examination of a Mormon Mission to an Indian Community as an Agent of Social

Change. (Unpublished Ph.D. Dissertation in Anthropology, University of Rochester, Rochester, N.Y.)

Parsons, Elsie C., ed.
1922   American Indian Life by Several of Its Students. New York: B.W. Huebsch.

Parsons, Lynn H.
1973   "A Perpetual Harrow Upon My Feelings": John Quincy Adams and the American Indian. *New England Quarterly* 46(3):339–379.

Partington, Frederick E.
1911   The Story of Mohonk. Fulton, N.Y.: Morrill Press.

Pate, J'Nell L.
1987   Ranald S. Mackenzie. In Soldiers West. Paul A. Hutton, ed. Lincoln: University of Nebraska Press.

Patrick, Rembert W.
1954   Florida Fiasco: Rampant Rebels on the Georgia-Florida Border. Athens: University of Georgia Press.

Patterson, E. Palmer, II
1972   The Canadian Indian: A History Since 1500. Don Mills, Ont.: Collier-Macmillan Canada.

Paullin, Charles O.
1932   Atlas of the Historical Geography of the United States. John K. Wright, ed. Washington and New York: Carnegie Institution and the American Geographical Society of New York.

Pauw, Cornelius de
1768–1771   Recherches philosophiques sur les Américains. 3 vols. Berlin: G.J. Decker.

Payne, John H., and Daniel S. Butrick
1835–1838   Payne-Butrick Papers. (Manuscript notes for a proposed history of the Cherokees. 14 vols. In Ayer Collection, Newberry Library, Chicago).

Paytiamo, James
1932   Flaming Arrow's People, by an Acoma Indian. New York City: Duffield and Green.

Peabody, Francis G.
1918   Education for Life: The Story of Hampton Institute, Told in Connection with the Fiftieth Anniversary of the Foundation of the School. Garden City, N.Y.: Doubleday, Page. (Reprinted: McGrath Publishing Company, College Park, Md., 1969.)

Peake, Ora B.
1954   A History of the United States Factory System, 1795–1822. Denver, Colo.: Sage Books.

Pearce, Helen
1946   Folk Sayings in a Pioneer Family of Western Oregon. *California Folklore Quarterly* 5(3):229–242.

Pearce, Roy H.
1952   The "Ruines of Mankind": The Indian and the Puritan Mind. *Journal of the History of Ideas* 13(2):200–217.

————
1953   The Savages of America: A Study of the Indian and the Idea of Civilization. Baltimore, Md.: Johns Hopkins University Press.

————
1965   Savagism and Civilization: A Study of the Indian and the American Mind. Baltimore, Md.: Johns Hopkins University Press.

Pearce, Thomas M.
1972   Oliver LaFarge. New York: Twayne Publishers.

Peare, Catherine Owens
1956   William Penn: A Biography. Philadelphia: Lippincott.

Pearson, Edmund L.
1929   Dime Novels; or, Following an Old Trail in Popular Literature. Boston: Little, Brown.

Peck, Solomon
1840   History of the Missions of the Baptist General Convention. Pp. 353–528 in History of American Missions to the Heathen. Worcester, Mass.: Spooner and Howland. (Reprinted: Johnson Reprint, New York, 1970.)

Peckham, Howard H.
1947   Pontiac and the Indian Uprising. Princeton, N.J.: Princeton University Press. (Reprinted: University of Chicago Press, Chicago, 1961.)

————
1964   The Colonial Wars, 1689–1762. Chicago: University of Chicago Press.

Peckham, Howard, and Charles Gibson, eds.
1969   Attitudes of the Colonial Powers Toward the American Indian. Salt Lake City: University of Utah Press.

Peel, Bruce B.
1958   How the Bible Came to the Cree. *Alberta Historical Review* 6(2):15–19.

————
1974   Rossville Mission Press: The Invention of the Cree Syllabic Characters, and the First Printing in Rupert's Land. Montreal: Osiris Publications.

Peña y Cámara, José M. de la
1958   Archivo General de Indias de Sevilla: Guia del visitante. Valencia, Spain: Tip. Moderna.

Pendergast, Anthony W., and W. Porter Ware
1953   Cigar-store Figures in American Art. Chicago: Lightner.

Penhallow, Samuel
1726   The History of the Wars of New-England with the Eastern Indians. Boston: T. Fleet for S. Gerrich and D. Henchman.

Pennington, Loren E.
1979   The Amerindian in English Promotional Literature, 1575–1625. Pp. 175–194 in The Westward Enterprise: English Activities in Ireland, the Atlantic, and America, 1480–1650, by K.R. Andrews, N.P. Canny, and P.E.H. Hair. Detroit, Mich.: Wayne State University Press.

Perdue, Theda
1979   Slavery and the Evolution of Cherokee Society, 1540–1866. Knoxville: University of Tennessee Press.

————
1983   Cherokee Editor: The Writings of Elias Boudinot. Knoxville: University of Tennessee Press.

Pérez de Luxán, Diego
1929   Expedition into New Mexico Made by Antonio de Espejo, 1582–1583 as Revealed in the Journal of Diego Pérez de Luxán, a Member of the Party. George P. Hammond and Agapito Rey, eds. (*Quivira Society Publications* 1). Los Angeles.

Pérez de Ribas, Andrés
1645   Historia de los trivmphos de nvuestra Santa Fee entre gentes las más barbaras y fieras del Nuevo Orbe. Madrid: A. de Paredes. (Reprinted: Editoral Layac, Mexico, 1944.)

Peroff, Nicholas C.
1982   Menominee Drums: Tribal Termination and Restoration, 1954–1974. Norman: University of Oklahoma Press.

Perrot, Nicolas
1911   Memoir on the Manners, Customs, and Religion of the Savages of North America. Pp. 23–272 in Vol. 1 of The Indian Tribes of the Upper Mississippi Valley and Region of the Great Lakes. Emma H. Blair, ed. Cleveland, Ohio: Arthur H. Clark.

Peters, Joseph P., comp.
1966   Indian Battles and Skirmishes on the American Frontier, 1790–1898. New York: Argonaut.

Peters, Richard, ed.
1848   United States Statutes at Large. Vol. 7: Treaties Between the United States and the Indian Tribes. Boston: C.C. Little and James Brown.

Peterson, Charles S.
1971   The Hopis and the Mormons, 1858–1873. *Utah Historical Quarterly* 39(2):179–194.

————
1973   Take Up Your Mission: Mormon Colonizing Along the Little Colorado River, 1870–1900. Tucson: University of Arizona Press.

Peterson, Harold L.
1956   Arms and Armour in Colonial America, 1526–1783. Harrisburg, Pa.: Stackpole Books.

————
1965   American Indian Tomahawks. *Museum of the American Indian. Heye Foundation. Contributions* 19. New York.

Peterson, Helen L.
1957   American Indian Political Participation. *Annals of the American Academy of Political and Social Science* 311(May):116–126.

Peterson, Jacqueline, and John Anfinson
1984   The Indian and the Fur Trade: A Review of Recent Literature. Pp. 223–257 in Scholars and the Indian Experience. W.R. Swagerty, ed. Bloomington: Indiana University Press for the Newberry Library.

Peterson, Jacqueline, and Jennifer S.H. Brown, eds.
1985   The New Peoples: Being and Becoming Métis in North America. Winnipeg: University of Manitoba Press.

Petitot, Emile
1876   Dictionnaire de langue Dènè-Dindjié, dialects Montagnais ou Chippéwayan, Peaux de Lièvre et Loucheux, etc. Paris: E. Leroux.

————
1876a   Vocabulaire françois-esquimau: Dialecte des Tchiglit des bouches du Mackenzie et de l'Anderson. (*Bibliothèque de Linguistique et d'Ethnographie Américaines* 3) Paris: E. Leroux.

————
1887   Les Grands esquimaux. Paris: E. Plon, Nourrit.

————
1970   Les Amérindiens du nord-ouest Canadien au 19e siècle selon Emile Petitot. Ottawa: Department of Indian Affairs and Northern Development, Northern Science Research Group.

Pfaller, Louis L.
1978   James McLaughlin: The Man with an Indian Head. New York: Vantage Press.

Pfefferkorn, Ignaz
1949   Sonora: A Description of the Province (1756–1767). Theodore E. Treutlein, ed. and trans. Albuquerque: University of New Mexico Press.

Phelps, Martha B.
1905   Frances Slocum, the Lost Sister of Wyoming. New York: The Knickerbocker Press.

Phelps, William
[1850] Solid Men of Boston in the Northwest. (Manuscript P–C 31, Bancroft Library, University of California, Berkeley)

Phillips, Edward H.
1966   Timothy Pickering at His Best: Indian Commissioner, 1790–1794. *Essex Institute Historical Collections* 102(3):163–202.

Phillips, George
1983   Commerce in the Valley: Indian-White Trade in Mexican California. (Paper presented at the American Historical Association Meeting, Dec. 1983.)

Phillips, Paul C.
1961   The Fur Trade. 2 vols. Norman: University of Oklahoma Press.

Phillips, Wendell
1870   Wendell Phillips to the United States Indian Commission. *The Standard* 1(2):101. Cincinnati, Ohio.

1892   Speeches, Lectures and Letters. 2 vols. Boston: Lee and Shepard.

Philp, Kenneth R.
1977   John Collier's Crusade for Indian Reform, 1920–1954. Tucson: University of Arizona Press.

————
1985   Stride Toward Freedom: The Relocation of Indians to Cities, 1952–1960. *Western Historical Quarterly* 16(1):175–190.

Phinney, Edward S.
1963   Alfred B. Meacham: Promoter of Indian Reform. (Unpublished Ph.D. Dissertation in History, University of Oregon, Salem.)

Pickering, John, *see* Râle, Sébastien

Pickering, Octavius, and Charles W. Upham
1867–1873   The Life of Timothy Pickering. 4 vols. Boston: Little, Brown.

Pierce, Richard A., ed.
1976   Documents on the History of the Russian-American Company (*Materials for the Study of Alaskan History* 7). Marina Ramsey, trans. Kingston, Ont.: Limestone Press.

Pilling, James C.
1887   Bibliography of the Siouan Languages. *Bureau of American Ethnology Bulletin* 5. Washington.

————
1888   Bibliography of the Iroquoian Languages. *Bureau of American Ethnology Bulletin* 6. Washington.

————
1891   Bibliography of the Algonquian Languages. *Bureau of American Ethnology Bulletin* 13. Washington.

Pirtle, Alfred
1900   The Battle of Tippecanoe. *Filson Club Publications* 15. Louisville, Ky.: J.P. Morton.

Pitt, Leonard
1966   The Decline of the Californios: A Social History of the Spanish–speaking Californians, 1846–1890. Berkeley: University of California Press.

Plischke, Hans
1951   Von Cooper bis Karl May. Düsseldorf, Germany: Droste Verlag.

Poe, Edgar Allen
1838   The Narrative of Arthur Gordon Pym of Nantucket. New York: Harper and Brothers.

————
1840   The Journal of Julius Rodman: Being an Account of the First Passage Across the Rocky Mountains of North America Ever Achieved by Civilized Man. Philadelphia: William E. Burton.

Pohlkamp, Diomede
1936   Spanish Franciscans in the Southeast. *Franciscan Education Conference* 18(18).

Point, Nicolas
[1850] Souvenirs des Montagnes Rocheuses. [Manuscript, Archives of the Jesuits of Canada, St. Jerome, Quebec.]

————
1967   Wilderness Kingdom: Indian Life in the Rocky Mountains, 1840–1847: The Journals and Paintings of Nicolas Point. Joseph P. Donnelly trans. and ed. New York: Holt, Rinehart and Winston.

Polzer, Charles W., ed. and trans.
1971   Kino's Biography of Francisco Javier Saeta, S.J. (*Sources and Studies for the History of the Americas* 9.) Rome: Jesuit Historical Institute.

————, ed.
1976   Rules and Precepts of the Jesuit Missions of Northwestern New Spain. Tucson: University of Arizona Press.

778

Pomfret, John E.
1973   Colonial New Jersey: A History. New York: Charles
            Scribner's Sons.

Pompa, Cristina
1983   L'Immagine degli Indiani nel fumetto popolare italiano. Pp.
            65–70 in Cultura Planetaria: Omologazione o diversità?
            Roma: A.R.C.I.

Pond, Samuel W., Jr.
1893   Two Volunteer Missionaries Among the Dakotas; or, The
            Story of the Labors of Samuel W. and Gideon H. Pond.
            Boston: Congregational Sunday-School and Publishing
            Society.

Popkin, Richard H.
1973   The Philosophical Basis of Eighteenth-Century Racism. Pp.
            245–262 in Racism in the Eighteenth Century. Harold E.
            Pagliaro, ed. *Studies in Eighteenth Century Culture* 3.
            Cleveland, Ohio.

Popov, Evgeniĭ
1874   Ob userdiĭ k missionerskomu delu [On Missionary Zeal]. 2d
            ed. Perm, U.S.S.R.: Popova's Publishing Company.

Porter, Harry C.
1979   The Inconstant Savage: England and the North American
            Indian, 1500–1660. London: Duckworth.

Porter, Kenneth W.
1931   John Jacob Astor: Business Man. 2 vols. Cambridge, Mass.:
            Harvard University Press.

1934   Negroes and the Fur Trade. *Minnesota History*
            15(4):421–433.

1946   The Negro Abraham. *Florida Historical Quarterly*
            25(1):1–43.

1951   The Seminole in Mexico, 1850–1861. *Hispanic American
            Historical Review* 31(1):1–36.

1952   The Seminole Negro-Indian Scouts, 1870–1881. *Southwest-
            ern Historical Quarterly* 55(3):358–377.

[1970]   O Freedom Over Me!: The Saga of John Horse (Gopher
            John), ca. 1812–1882, and His People, the Seminole
            Negroes, in Florida, the Indian Territory, Texas, and
            Coahuila. (Unpublished manuscript in Porter's possession.)

1971   The Negro Abraham. Pp. 295–338 in The Negro on the
            American Frontier. Kenneth W. Porter, ed. New York:
            Arno Press.

Porter, Peter B.
1829   Statement of a Revised System of Laws and Regulations . . .
            for the Government of the Indian Department. *20th
            Congress, 2d sess. Senate Document* No. 72 (Serial No. 181).
            Washington.

Portlock, Nathaniel
1789   A Voyage Round the World, But More Particularly to the
            North-West Coast of America; Performed in 1785, 1786,
            1787, and 1788 in the King George and Queen Charlotte,
            Captains Portlock and Dixon. London: John Stockdale and
            George Goulding. (Reprinted: Da Capo Press, New York,
            1968.)

Pound, Louise
1949   Nebraska Legends of Lovers' Leaps. *Western Folklore*
            8(4):304–313.

Pound, Merritt B.
1942   Colonel Benjamin Hawkins—North Carolinian—Benefac-
            tor of the Southern Indians. *North Carolina Historical
            Review* 19(1):1–21, (2):168–186.

1951   Benjamin Hawkins: Indian Agent. Athens: University of
            Georgia Press.

Powell, Donald M.
1961   A Preliminary Bibliography of the Published Writings of
            Berard Haile, O.F.M. *The Kiva* 26(4):44–47.

Powell, John Wesley
1891   Indian Linguistic Families of America North of Mexico. Pp.
            1–142 in *7th Annual Report of the Bureau of American
            Ethnology for the Years 1885–1886.* Washington.

Powell, John Wesley, and G.W. Ingalls
1874   Report of Special Commissioners J.W. Powell and G.W.
            Ingalls on the Condition of the Ute Indians of Utah; the Pai-
            Utes of Utah, Northern Arizona, Southern Nevada, and
            Southeastern California. Washington: U.S. Government
            Printing Office.

Powell, Peter J.
1981   People of the Sacred Mountain: A History of the Northern
            Cheyenne Chiefs and Warrior Societies, 1830–1879. 2 vols.
            San Francisco: Harper and Row.

Powell, Philip W.
1952   Soldier, Indians, and Silver: The Northward Advance of
            New Spain, 1550–1600. Berkeley: University of California
            Press.

Powers, Stephen
1877   Tribes of California. (*Contributions to North American
            Ethnology* 3) Washington: U.S. Geographical and Geologi-
            cal Survey of the Rocky Mountain Region.

Powers, William K.
1966   Here Is Your Hobby: Indian Dancing and Costumes. New
            York: G.P. Putnam's Sons.

1979   The Archaic Illusion. (A review of *Hanta Yo.*) *American
            Indian Art Magazine* 5(1):68–71.

Pratt, Julius W.
1955   History of United States Foreign Policy. New York:
            Prentice-Hall.

Pratt, Parley P.
1938   The Autobiography of Parley Parker Pratt: One of the
            Twelve Apostles of the Church of Jesus Christ of Latter Day
            Saints . . . Salt Lake City, Utah: Deseret Book Company.

Pratt, Richard H.
1964   Battlefield and Classroom: Four Decades with the Ameri-
            can Indian, 1876–1904. Robert M. Utley, ed. New Haven,
            Conn.: Yale University Press.

Prévost d'Exiles, Antoine F.
1728–1738   Le Philosophe anglais, ou, Histoire de Monsieur Cleveland,
            fils naturel de Cromwell, écrite par lui-mesme . . . 8 vols.
            Paris: Jacques Guerin.

Prévost d'Exiles, Antoine F. [et al.]
1747–1780   Histoire générale des voyages. 25 vols. La Haye, France: P.
            de Hondt.

Price, George F.
1959   Across the Continent with the Fifth Cavalry [1883]. New
            York: Antiquarian Press.

Price, John A.
1973   The Stereotyping of North American Indians in Motion
            Pictures. *Ethnohistory* 20(2):153–171.

1978   Native Studies: American and Canadian. Toronto:
            McGraw-Hill Ryerson.

1979   Indians of Canada: Cultural Dynamics. Scarborough, Ont.:
            Prentice-Hall of Canada.

Price, Lawrence M.
1937   Inkle and Yarico in Germany and Switzerland. Pp. 75–134
            in Inkle and Yarico Album. Berkeley: University of
            California Press.

Priest, Loring B.
1942   Uncle Sam's Stepchildren: The Reformation of United States Indian Policy, 1865–1887. New Brunswick, N.J.: Rutgers University Press. (Reprinted: Octagon Books, New York, 1969.)

Priestley, Herbert I.
1939   France Overseas Through the Old Régime: A Study of European Expansion. New York: D. Appleton-Century.

1946   Franciscan Explorations in California. Glendale, Calif.: Arthur H. Clark.

Prishvin, Mikhail M.
1938   Seraía Sova [Grey Owl]. In Molodaía gvardiía 9–12. Moscow. (Reprinted: Pp. 80–240 in Vol. 4 of Sobranie sochineniĭ v vos′mi tomakh, V.V. Kzinov et al., eds., Moscow, 1982–1986.)

Prucha, Francis P.
1962   American Indian Policy in the Formative Years: The Indian Trade and Intercourse Acts, 1790–1834. Cambridge, Mass.: Harvard University Press.

1964   A Guide to the Military Posts of the United States. Madison: State Historical Society of Wisconsin.

1967   Lewis Cass and American Indian Policy. Detroit, Mich.: Wayne State University Press.

1969   The Sword of the Republic: The United States Army on the Frontier, 1783–1846. New York: Macmillan.

1969a   Andrew Jackson's Indian Policy: A Reassessment. Journal of American History 56(3):527–539.

1971   American Indian Policy in the 1840s: Visions of Reform. Pp. 81–110 in The Frontier Challenge: Responses to the Trans-Mississippi West. John G. Clark, ed. Lawrence: University Press of Kansas.

1971a   Indian Peace Medals in American History. Madison: State Historical Society of Wisconsin.

1971b   The Image of the Indian in Pre-Civil War America. Pp. 2–19 in Indiana Historical Society Lectures, 1970–1971: American Indian Policy, by Francis P. Prucha, William T. Hagan, and Alvin M. Josephy, Jr. Indianapolis: Indiana Historical Society.

1971c   Annie Heloise Abel. Pp. 4–6 in Notable American Women 1607–1950. Edward T. James et al., eds. Cambridge, Mass.: Belknap Press of Harvard University Press.

——, ed.
1973   Americanizing the American Indians: Writings by the "Friends of the Indian," 1880–1900. Cambridge, Mass.: Harvard University Press.

1976   American Indian Policy in Crisis: Christian Reformers and the Indian, 1865–1900. Norman: University of Oklahoma Press.

1977   A Bibliographical Guide to the History of Indian-White Relations in the United States. Chicago: University of Chicago Press.

1979   The Churches and the Indian Schools, 1888–1912. Lincoln: University of Nebraska Press.

1979a   Thomas Jefferson Morgan, 1889–93. Pp. 193–203 in The Commissioners of Indian Affairs, 1824–1977. Robert M. Kvasnicka and Herman J. Viola, eds. Lincoln: University of Nebraska Press.

1982   Indian-White Relations in the United States: A Bibliography of Works Published, 1975–1980. Lincoln: University of Nebraska Press.

1984   The Great Father: The United States Government and the American Indians. 2 vols. Lincoln: University of Nebraska Press.

[Puget, Peter]
[1793]   A Log of Proceedings of His Majesty's Armed Tender Chatham . . . (Microfilmed Manuscript in the Library of the University of British Columbia, Vancouver.)

Purchas, Samuel
1905   Hakluytus Posthumus, or Purchas His Pilgrimes. Glasgow, England: J. MacLehose and Sons.

Pushkin, Alexander S.
1949   Sobraniie sochineniĭ v 10 tomakh. Vol. 7. Moscow-Leningrad: Akademía Nauk.

Putney, Diane T.
1979   Robert Grosvenor Valentine, 1909–12. Pp. 233–242 in The Commissioners of Indian Affairs, 1824–1977. Robert M. Kvasnicka and Herman J. Viola, eds. Lincoln: University of Nebraska Press.

Pyne, Stephen J.
1982   Fire in America: A Cultural History of Wildland and Rural Fire. Princeton, N.J.: Princeton University Press.

Quaife, Milo M., ed.
1965   The Journals of Captain Meriwether Lewis and Sergeant John Ordway (1803–1806). Madison: The State Historical Society of Wisconsin.

Quealey, Francis M.
1968   The Administration of Sir Peregrine Maitland, Lieutenant Governor of Upper Canada, 1818–1828. (Unpublished Ph.D. Dissertation in History, York University, Toronto, Ont.)

Québec
1976   The James Bay and Northern Québec Agreement. Quebec City: Editeur officiel du Québec.

Quebec, Provincial Archives
1883–1885   Collections de manuscrits contenant lettres, mémoires, et autres documents historiques relatifs à la Nouvelle-France, recueillis aux archives de la Province de Québec, ou copiés à l'étranger, mis en ordre et édités sous les auspices de la Législature de Québec, avec table, etc . . . .Quebec: A. Coté.

Quinlan, James E.
1851   Tom Quick, the Indian Slayer, and the Pioneers of Minisink and Wawarsink. Monticello, N.Y.: DeVoe and Quinlan.

Quinn, David B.
1977   North America from Earliest Discovery to First Settlements: The Norse Voyages to 1612. New York: Harper and Row.

1985   Set Fair for Roanoke: Voyages and Colonies, 1584–1606. Chapel Hill: University of North Carolina Press.

RAPQ=Rapport de l'Archiviste de la Province de Québec
1927–1928   Mémoire sur les postes du Canada adressé à M. de Surlaville en 1754, par le chevalier de Raymond. Quebec.

Radin, Paul
1923   The Winnebago Tribe. Pp. 35–560 in 37th Annual Report of the Bureau of American Ethnology for the Years 1915–1916. Washington.

1924   Primitive Man as Philosopher. New York: D. Appleton.

1945   The Road of Life and Death: A Ritual Drama of the American Indians. New York: Pantheon Books.

1958   Robert H. Lowie, 1883–1957. *American Anthropologist* 60(2):358–361.

Rahill, Peter J.
1953   The Catholic Indian Missions and Grant's Peace Policy, 1870–1884. Washington: The Catholic University of America.

Raine, William M.
1944   Famous Sheriffs and Western Outlaws. New York: The New Home Library.

[Râle, Sébastien] "Sebastian Rasles"
1833   A Dictionary of the Abnaki Language in North America. John Pickering, ed. Pp. 370–574 in *Memoirs of the American Academy of Arts and Sciences* n.s. 1. Cambridge, Mass.

Ramusio, Giovanni Batista
1970   Navigationi et viaggi . . . [1550–1559]. 3 vols. Amsterdam: Theatrum Orbis Terrarum.

Randolph, J. Ralph
1973   British Travelers Among the Southern Indians, 1660–1763. Norman: University of Oklahoma Press.

Randolph, Vance, ed.
1946–1950   Ozark Folksongs. 4 vols. Columbia: State Historical Society of Missouri.

Ransom, Jay E.
1945   Writing as a Medium of Acculturation Among the Aleut. *Southwestern Journal of Anthropology* 1(3):333–344.

Rapoport, Robert N.
1954   Changing Navaho Religious Values: A Study of Christian Missions to the Rimrock Navaho. *Papers of the Peabody Museum of American Archaeology and Ethnology, Harvard University* 41(2). Cambridge, Mass.

Raunet, Daniel
1984   Without Surrender, Without Consent: A History of the Nishga Land Claims. Vancouver, B.C.: Douglas and McIntyre.

Ray, Arthur J.
1974   Indians in the Fur Trade: Their Role as Trappers, Hunters, and Middlemen in the Lands Southwest of Hudson's Bay 1660–1870. Toronto: University of Toronto Press.

1975   Some Conservation Schemes of the Hudson's Bay Company, 1821–50: An Examination of the Problem of Resource Management in the Fur Trade. *Journal of Historical Geography* 1(1):49–68.

1975–1976   The Early Hudson's Bay Company Account Books as Sources for Historical Research: An Analysis and Assessment. *Archivaria* 1(1):3–38.

1978   Competition and Conservation in the Early Subarctic Fur Trade. *Ethnohistory* 25(4):347–357.

1980   Indians as Consumers in the Eighteenth Century. Pp. 255–271 in Old Trails and New Directions: Papers of the Third North American Fur Trade Conference. Carol M. Judd and Arthur J. Ray, eds. Toronto: University of Toronto Press.

1982   York Factory: The Crisis of Transition, 1870–1880. *The Beaver* 312(Autumn):26–31.

1984   The Northern Great Plains: Pantry of the Northwestern Fur Trade, 1774–1885. *Prairie Forum* 9(2):263–280.

1984a   Periodic Shortages, Native Welfare, and the Hudson's Bay Company, 1670–1930. Pp. 1–20 in The Subarctic Fur Trade. Shepard Krech III, ed. Vancouver: University of British Columbia Press.

1985   Planning for the Future: The Hudson's Bay Company at the Crossroads of Canadian History. (Paper presented at the Fifth North American Fur Trade Conference, June 1985, Montreal.)

1985a   Buying and Selling Furs in the Eighteenth Century. Pp. 95–115 in Explorations in Canadian Economic History: Essays in Honour of Irene M. Spry. Duncan Cameron, ed. Ottawa: University of Ottawa Press.

1987   The Fur Trade in North America: An Overview from a Historical Geographical Perspective. In Wild Furbearer Management and Conservation in North America. Milan Novak, James Baker, and Martyn Obbard, eds. Toronto: Ontario Ministry of Natural Resources, Wildlife Branch.

Ray, Arthur J., and Donald B. Freeman
1978   "Give Us Good Measure": An Economic Analysis of Relations Between the Indians and the Hudson's Bay Company Before 1763. Toronto: University of Toronto Press.

Ray, Dorothy J.
1965   Sheldon Jackson and the Reindeer Industry of Alaska. *Journal of Presbyterian History* 43(2):71–99.

1981   Aleut and Eskimo Art: Tradition and Innovation in South Alaska. Seattle: University of Washington Press.

Ray, Verne F.
1963   Primitive Pragmatists: The Modoc Indians of Northen California (*American Ethnological Society Monographs* 38). Seattle: University of Washington Press.

Reavis, Logan U.
1875   St. Louis, the Future Great City of the World. St. Louis, Mo.: Gray and Baker.

1878   The Life and Military Services of Gen. William Selby Harney. St. Louis, Mo.: Bryan, Brand.

Recheis, Käthe
1967   Kleiner Adler und Silberstern. Vienna: Herder.

1967a   Red Boy. Vienna: Herder.

Reed, Eugene E.
1964   The Ignoble Savage. *Modern Language Review* 59(1):53–64.

Reeve, Frank D.
1939   The Government and the Navaho, 1846–1858. *New Mexico Historical Review* 4(1):82–114.

1959   Navajo-Spanish Peace: 1720–1770s. *New Mexico Historical Review* 34(1):9–40.

1960   Navajo-Spanish Diplomacy, 1770–1790. *New Mexico Historical Review* 32(2):200–235.

1971   Navajo Foreign Affairs, 1795–1846. Eleanor B. Adams and John L. Kessell, eds. *New Mexico Historical Review* 46(2):100–132.

Reichlen, Henry, and Robert F. Heizer
1963   La Mission de Léon de Cessac en Californie, 1877–1879. *Objets et Mondes* 3(1):17–34.

Reid, John P.
1976   A Better Kind of Hatchet: Law, Trade, and Diplomacy in the Cherokee Nation During the Early Years of European Contact. University Park: Pennsylvania State University Press.

Reid Russell, and Clell G. Gannon, eds.
1929   Journal of the Atkinson-O'Fallon Expedition. *North Dakota Historical Quarterly* 4(1):5–56.

Reilly, Bob
1980   Christianity comes to the Plains. *The Wind River Rendez-vous* 10(1):[10–11]. St. Stephens, Wyo.

Reising, Robert
1974   Jim Thorpe: Multi-cultural Hero. *The Indian Historian* 7(4):14–16.

Remington, Frederic
1902   John Ermine of the Yellowstone. New York: Macmillan. (Reprinted: Gregg Press, Ridgewood, N.J., 1968.)

Remini, Robert V.
1977–1984   Andrew Jackson and the Course of American Empire. 3 vols. New York: Harper and Row.

Renner, Louis L.
1979   Pioneer Missionary to the Bering Strait Eskimos: Bellar-mine Lafortune, S.J. Portland, Oreg.: Binford and Mort.

Resek, Carl
1960   Lewis Henry Morgan, American Scholar. Chicago: University of Chicago Press. (Reprinted in 1973.)

Révoil, Bénédict-Henry
1876   A Travers les prairies: Les Peaux-rouges de l'Amérique du Nord, excursions, chasses, etc. Limoges, France: E. Ardant.

1878   Le Panthère-noire. Tours, France: A. Mame.

1884   L'Indienne abandonne. Limoges, France: A. Barbou.

Rhonda, James P.
1984   Lewis and Clark Among the Indians. Lincoln: University of Nebraska Press.

Ricard, Robert
1933   La "Conquête spirituelle" du Mexique: Essai sur l'apostolat et les méthodes missionnaries des Ordres Mendiants en Nouvelle-Espagne de 1523–24 à 1572. *Travaux et Mémoires de l'Institut d'Ethnologie* 20. Paris.

Rich, E.E.
1958–1959   A History of the Hudson's Bay Company, 1670–1870 (*Publications of the Hudson's Bay Record Society* 21, 22). 2 vols. Toronto: McClelland and Stewart.

1960   Trade Habits and Economic Motivation Among the Indians of North America. *Canadian Journal of Economics and Political Science* 26(1):35–53.

1967   The Fur Trade and the Northwest to 1857. Toronto: McClelland and Stewart.

Rich, E.E., and C.H. Wilson, eds.
1967   The Economy of Expanding Europe in the Sixteenth and Seventeenth Centuries (*The Cambridge Economic History of Europe* 4). Cambridge, England: Cambridge University Press.

Richardson, James D., comp.
1896–1899   A Compilation of the Messages and Papers of the Presidents, 1789–1897. 10 vols. Washington: U.S. Government Printing Office.

Richardson, Leon B.
1932   History of Dartmouth College. Hanover, N.H.: Dartmouth College Publications.

————, ed.
1933   An Indian Preacher in England; Being Letters and Diaries Relating to the Mission of the Reverend Samson Occum ....Hanover, N.H.: Dartmouth College.

Richardson, Rupert N.
1933   The Comanche Barrier to South Plains Settlement: A Century and a Half of Savage Resistance to the Advancing White Frontier. Glendale, Calif.: Arthur H. Clark.

1952   Robert Simpson Neighbors. Pp. 267–268 in Vol. 2 of *Handbook of Texas*. 2 vols. Austin: Texas State Historical Association.

Richman Robin
1967   From the Journals of a Dedicated Jesuit: Rediscovery of the Lost World of the American Indian. *Life Magazine* (Dec. 11):52–71. Amsterdam, The Netherlands.

Richter, Daniel K.
1983   War and Culture: The Iroquois Experience. *William and Mary Quarterly 3d ser.,* Vol. 40(4):528–559. Williamsburg, Va.

Rickard, Clinton
1973   Fighting Tuscarora: The Autobiography of Chief Clinton Rickard. Barbara Graymont, ed. Syracuse, N.Y.: Syracuse University Press.

Rickard, T.A.
1939   The Use of Iron and Copper by the Indians of British Columbia. *British Columbia Historical Quarterly* 3(1):25–50. Vancouver.

Riddle, Jeff C.
1914   The Indian History of the Modoc War and the Causes That Led to It, by Jeff C. Riddle, the Son of Winema (the Heroine of the Modoc War). [San Francisco]: no publisher.

Riggs, Stephen R., ed.
1852   Grammar and Dictionary of the Dakota Language. *Smithsonian Contributions to Knowledge* 4. Washington.

1869   Tah´-koo Wah-kan´; or, The Gospel Among the Dakotas. Boston: Congregational Publishing Society. (Reprinted: Arno Press, New York, 1972.)

1887   Mary and I: Forty Years with the Sioux. Boston: Congregational Sunday-School and Publishing, Society. (Reprinted: Corner House Publications, Williamstown, Mass., 1971.)

1890   A Dakota-English Dictionary. James O. Dorsey, ed. (*Contributions to North American Ethnology* 7.) Washington: U.S. Geographical and Geological Survey of the Rocky Mountain Region.

1893   Dakota Grammar, Texts and Ethnography. James O. Dorsey, ed. (*Contributions to North American Ethnology* 9.) Washington: U.S. Geographical and Geological Survey of the Rocky Mountain Region.

Riley, Carroll L.
1971   Early Spanish-Indian Communication in the Greater Southwest. *New Mexico Historical Review* 46(4):285–314.

1976   Sixteenth Century Trade in the Greater Southwest. *Southern Illinois University. University Museum Mesoamerican Studies* 10. Carbondale.

1978   Pecos and Trade. Pp. 53–64 in Across the Chichimec Sea: Papers in Honor of J. Charles Kelley. Carroll L. Riley and Basil C. Hedrick, eds. Carbondale: University of Southern Illinois Press.

1982   The Frontier People: The Greater Southwest in the Protohistoric Period. *Southern Illinois University. Center for Archaeological Investigation Occasional Paper* 1. Carbondale.

1986   An Overview of the Greater Southwest in the Protohistoric Period. Pp. 45–54 in Ripples in the Chichimec Sea: New Considerations of Southwestern - Mesoamerican Interactions. Frances J. Mathieu and Randall H. McGuire, eds. Carbondale: Southern Illinois University Press.

Riley, Glenda
1984   Women and the Indians on the Frontier, 1825–1915. Albuquerque: University of New Mexico Press.

Rimshkiĭ-Korsakov, V., ed.
1863   Iz putevykh pisem P.N. Golovina [From the Travel Notes of P.N. Golovin]. *Morskoi sbornik* 6:275–340. Moscow.

Rink, Hinrich J.
1857   Grønland geographisk og statistisk beskrevet [Greenland Geographically and Statistically Described]. 2 vols. Copenhagen: A.F. Høst.

Rister, Carl C.
1928   The Southwestern Frontier, 1865–1881: A History of the Settlers, Indian Depredations and Massacres, Ranching Activities, Operations of White Desperadoes and Thieves, Government Protection, Building of Railways, and the Disappearance of the Frontier. Cleveland, Ohio: Arthur H. Clark.

_____
1940   Border Captives: The Traffic in Prisoners by Southern Plains Indians, 1835–1875. Norman: University of Oklahoma Press.

_____
1944   Border Command: General Phil Sheridan in the West. Norman: University of Oklahoma Press.

_____
1956   Fort Griffin on the Texas Frontier. Norman: University of Oklahoma Press.

Robbins, H., ed.
1913   A Handbook of the Church's Mission to the Indians, in Memory of William Hobart Hare, an Apostle to the Indians. Hartford, Conn.: Church Missions.

Roberts, Gary L.
1979   Dennis Nelson Cooley, 1865–66. Pp. 99-108 in The Commissioners of Indian Affairs, 1824–1977. Robert M. Kvasnicka and Herman J. Viola, eds. Lincoln: University of Nebraska Press.

_____
1979a   Alfred Burton Greenwood, 1859–61. Pp. 81-87 in The Commisioners of Indian Affairs, 1824–1977. Robert M. Kvasnicka and Herman J. Viola, eds. Lincoln: University of Nebraska Press.

Robertson, William
1811–1812   History of America. Vols. 6–7 of [Works]. Philadelphia: T. Bioren and T.L. Plowman.

Robinson, Doane, and Cyrus Thomas
1910   Tamaha. P. 680 in Handbook of American Indians North of Mexico. Frederick W. Hodge, ed. 2 vols. *Bureau of American Ethnology Bulletin* 30. Washington.

Robinson, W. Stitt, Jr.
1952   Indian Education and Missions in Colonial Virginia. *Journal of Southern History* 18(2):152–168. Lexington, Ky.

_____
1979   The Southern Colonial Frontier, 1607–1763. Albuquerque: University of New Mexico Press.

_____, ed.
1983   Virginia Treaties, 1607–1722. (Early American Indian Documents: Treaties and Laws, 1607–1789, Vol. 4) Alden T. Vaughan, ed. Frederick, Md.: University Publications of America.

Rochemonteix, Camille de
1895–1896   Les Jésuites et la Nouvelle-France au XVIIe siècle d'après beaucoup de documents inédits: Portraits et cartes. 3 vols. Paris: Letouzey et Ané.

_____
1906   Les Jésuites et la Nouvelle-France au XVIIIe siècle, d'après des documents inedits, avec cartes. 2 vols. Paris: Picard et fils.

Roe, Frank G.
1955   The Indians and the Horse. Norman: University of Oklahoma Press.

_____
1970   The North American Buffalo: A Critical Study of the Species in Its Wild State. 2d ed. Toronto: University of Toronto Press.

Roe, Michael, ed.
1967   The Journal and Letters of Captain Charles Bishop on the North-west Coast of America, in the Pacific and in New South Wales, 1794–1799. Cambridge, England: Cambridge University Press.

Roethler, Michael D.
1964   Negro Slavery Among the Cherokee Indians, 1540–1866. (Unpublished Ph.D. Dissertation in History, Fordham University, Bronx, N.Y.)

Rogers, Fred B.
1938   Soldiers of the Overland: Being Some Account of the Services of Gen. Patrick Edward Conner and His Volunteers of the Old West. San Francisco: Grabhorn Press.

Rohner, Ronald P.
1966   Franz Boas: Ethnographer on the Northwest Coast. Pp. 149–222 in Pioneers of American Anthropology. June Helm, ed. (*Monographs of the American Ethnological Society* 43.) Seattle: University of Washington Press.

Romans, Bernard
1775   A Concise Natural History of East and West Florida. New York: Printed for the author. (Reprinted: Pelican Publishing, New Orleans, 1961.)

Romero Espinosa, Emilio
1963   La Reforma agraria en México. Mexico City: Cuadernos Americanos.

Ronda, James P.
1981   Generations of Faith: The Christian Indians of Martha's Vineyard. *William and Mary Quarterly 3d ser.,* Vol. 38(3):369–394. Williamsburg. Va.

Ronda, James P., and James Axtell
1978   Indian Missions: A Critical Bibliography. Bloomington: Indiana University Press.

Roosevelt, Theodore
1889–1896   The Winning of the West. 4 vols. New York: G.P. Putnam's Sons.

Roper, Donald M.
1963   Mr. Justice Thompson and the Constitution. (Unpublished Ph.D. Dissertation in History, Indiana University, Bloomington.) (Published: Garland, New York, 1987.)

Roquefeuil, Camille de
1823   Journal d'un voyage autour du monde, pendant les années 1816, 1817, 1818 et 1819, par M. Camille de Roquefeuil. Paris: Ponthieu.

Roquette, Adrien E.
1841   Les Savanes, poésies américaines. Paris: J. Labitte.

_____
1879   La Nouvelle Atala, ou; La Fille de l'esprit. New Orleans: Imprimeries du Progatetr [!] catholique.

Roquette, Dominique
1839   Meschacébéennes: Poésies. Paris: Sauvaignat.

Rose, Johann W.
1784   Pocahontas. Ansbach, Germany: Haueisen.

Rosen, Kenneth, ed.
1974   The Man to Send Rain Clouds: Contemporary Stories by American Indians. New York: Random House.

Rosenteil, Annette
1983   Red and White: Indian Views of the White Man, 1492–1982. New York: Universe Books.

Ross, Alexander
1849   Adventures of the First Settlers on the Oregon or Columbia River: Being a Narrative of the Expedition Fitted Out by John Jacob Astor, to Establish the "Pacific Fur Company." London: Smith, Elder.

_____
1956   The Fur Hunters of the Far West [1855]. Kenneth A. Spaulding, ed. Norman: University of Oklahoma Press.

Ross, Marvin C., ed.
1951   The West of Alfred Jacob Miller (1837). Norman: University of Oklahoma Press. (Reprinted in 1968.)

Ross, Mary
1926   The Restoration of the Spanish Missions in Georgia. *Georgia Historical Quarterly* 10(3):171–199.

Rossbacher Karlheinz
1972   Lederstrumpf in Deutschland; zur Rezeption James Fenimore Coopers beim Leser der Restaurationszeit. Munich, Germany: Fink.

Rossiĭsko-Amerikanskaĭa Kompaniĭa
1843–1865   Otchet Rossiĭsko-Amerikanskaĭ Kompaniĭ Glavnago Pravleniĭa za odin god . . . [Reports of the Russian-American Company by the Governors for the Year . . .]. St. Petersburg: Shtaba Inspektora.

Rostlund, Erhard
1960   The Geographic Range of the Historic Bison in the Southeast. *Annals of the Association of American Geographers* 50(4):395–407. Washington.

Rothenberg, Jerome, ed.
1972   Shaking the Pumpkin; Traditional Poetry of the Indians North Americas. Garden City, N.Y.: Doubleday.

Rothensteiner, John
1928   History of the Archdiocese of St. Louis in Its Various Stages of Development from A.D. 1673 to A.D. 1928. 2 vols. St. Louis, Mo.: Blackwell Wielandy.

Rotstein, Abraham
1967   Fur Trade and Empire: An Institutional Analysis. (Unpublished Ph.D. Dissertation in Economics, University of Toronto, Toronto.)

————
1970   Karl Polanyi's Concept of Non-market Trade. *Journal of Economic History* 30(1):117–130.

Rourke, Constance M.
1934   Davy Crockett. New York: Harcourt, Brace.

————
1942   The Roots of American Culture, and Other Essays. Van Wyck Brooks, ed. New York: Harcourt, Brace. (Reprinted: Kennikat Press, Port Washington, N.Y., 1965.)

Rousseau, Jean-Jacques
1755   Discours sur l'origine et les fondements de l'inégalité parmi les hommes. Amsterdam: M.M. Rey.

————
1762   Du Contract social; ou, Principes du droit politique. Amsterdam: M.M. Rey.

Rowe, John H.
1964   Ethnography and Ethnology in the Sixteenth Century. *Kroeber Anthropological Society Papers* 30(Spring):1–19. Berkeley, Calif.

Rowland, Dunbar, ed.
1911   Mississippi Provincial Archives: English Dominion, 1763–1781. Nashville, Tenn.: Brandon Printing.

Rowland, Dunbar, and Albert G. Sanders, eds.
1927–1984   Mississippi Provincial Archives: French Dominion. 5 vols. [Vols. 4 and 5 ed. by P.K. Galloway and published by Louisiana State University, Baton Rouge.] Jackson, Miss.: Press of the Mississippi Department of Archives and History.

Rowlandson, Mary W.
1682   The Soveraignty and Goodness of God, Together with the Faithfulness of the Promises Displayed: Being a Narrative of the Captivity and Restoration of Mrs. Mary Rowlandson; Commended by Her, to All That Desire to Know the Lord's Doing to, and Dealings with Her. Cambridge, Mass.: Samuel Green.

Roy, Pierre G., ed.
1890   La Réception de Monseigneur le Vicomte d'Argenson par toutes les nations du pais de Canada à son entrée au gouvernement de la Nouvelle-France [1658]. Quebec: Léger Brousseau.

Royce, Charles C.
1887   The Cherokee Nation of Indians: A Narrative of Their Official Relations with the Colonial and Federal Governments. Pp. 121–378 in *5th Annual Report of the Bureau of American Ethnology for the Years 1883–1884.* Washington.

————, comp.
1899   Indian Land Cessions in the United States. Pp. 521–997 in *18th Annual Report of the Bureau of American Ethnology for the Years 1896–1897.* Washington.

Ruby, Robert H., and John A. Brown
1976   The Chinook Indians: Traders of the Lower Columbia. Norman: University of Oklahoma Press.

————
1976a   Myron Eells and the Puget Sound Indians. Seattle, Wash.: Superior Publishing Company.

————
1981   Indians of the Pacific Northwest: A History. Norman: University of Oklahoma Press.

————
1986   A Guide to the Indian Tribes of the Pacific Northwest. Norman: University of Oklahoma Press.

Ruetten, Richard T.
1961   Burton K. Wheeler of Montana: A Progressive Between the Wars. (Unpublished Ph.D. Dissertation in History, University of Oregon, Eugene.)

Ruiz, Ramón Eduardo
1963   Mexico: The Challenge of Poverty and Illiteracy. San Marino, Calif.: The Huntington Library.

Rundle, Thomas
1734   A Sermon Preached at St. George's Church, Hanover Square, on Sunday, February 17, 1733 [or 4], to Recommend the Charity for Establishing of the New Colony of Georgia. London: T. Woodward and J. Brindley.

Ruppius, Otto
1861   Der Prairie-Teufel. Berlin: Duncker.

————
1862   Im Westen: Erzählungen aus dem amerikanischen Leben. Berlin: F. Duncker.

Rushmore, Elsie M.
1914   The Indian Policy During Grant's Administrations. Jamaica, N.Y.: Marion Press.

Russell, Carl P.
1957   Guns on the Early Frontiers: A History of Firearms from Colonial Times Through the Years of the Western Fur Trade. Lincoln: University of Nebraska Press.

————
1960   The Guns of the Lewis and Clark Expedition. *North Dakota History* 27 (Winter):25–34.

————
1967   Firearms, Traps and Tools of the Mountain Men. New York: Alfred A. Knopf. (Reprinted: University of New Mexico Press, 1977.)

Russell, Don
1968   Custer's Last, or The Battle of the Little Big Horn in Picturesque Perspective . . . Fort Worth, Tex.: Amon Carter Museum of Western Art.

Russell, Donald B.
1960   The Lives and Legends of Buffalo Bill. Norman: University of Oklahoma Press.

Russell, Frank
1908   The Pima Indians. Pp. 3–390 in *26th Annual Report of the Bureau of American Ethnology for the Years* 1904–1905. Washington.

Russell, Jason A.
1928   Longfellow: Interpreter of the Historical and the Romantic Indian. *Journal of American History* 22(4):327–347.

Russell, Mattie
1956   William Holland Thomas: White Chief of the North
            Carolina Cherokees. (Unpublished Ph.D. Dissertation in
            History, Duke University, Durham, N.C.)

Ruttenber, E.M.
1872   History of the Indian Tribes of Hudson's River; Their
            Origin, Manners and Customs, Tribal and Sub-tribal
            Organizations, Wars, Treaties, etc., etc. Albany, N.Y.: J.
            Munsell.

Ryan, Carmelita S.
1962   The Carlisle Indian Industrial School. (Unpublished Ph.D.
            Dissertation in History, Georgetown University, Washing-
            ton.)

Ryan, Joe
1979   Indian Treaties, Indian Fish: The Controversy of Fishing in
            Common. *American Indian Journal* 5(4):2–10.

Rydell, Robert W.
1984   All the World's a Fair: Visions of Empire at American
            International Expositions, 1876–1916. Chicago: University
            of Chicago Press.

Rydén, Stig
1963   Discovery in the Skokloster Collection of a 17th-Century
            Indian Head Dress from Delaware. *Ethnos*
            28(2–4):107–121. Stockholm.

Sabin, Edwin L.G.
1935   Kit Carson Days, 1809–1868: "Adventure in the Path of
            Empire." Rev. ed. 2 vols. New York: The Press of the
            Pioneers.

Saenz, Moisés
1939   México integro. Lima: Torres Aguirre.

Sagard-Théodat, Gabriel
1866   Histoire du Canada et voyages que les Frères Mineurs
            recollects y ont faicts pour la conversion des infidèles depuis
            l'an 1615; avec un dictionnaire de la langue huronne. 4 vols.
            Paris: E. Tross.

————
1939   Father Gabriel Sagard: The Long Journey to the Country of
            the Hurons [1632]. George M. Wrong, ed. Toronto: The
            Champlain Society.

Sage, Rufus B.
1956   His Letters and Papers, 1836–1847, with an Annotated
            Reprint of His Scenes in the Rocky Mountains and in
            Oregon, California, New Mexico, and the Grand Prairies.
            LeRoy R. Hafen and Ann W. Hafen, eds. 2 vols. Glendale,
            Calif.: Arthur H. Clark.

————
1982   Rocky Mountain Life; or, Startling Scenes and Perilous
            Adventures in the Far West, During an Expedition of Three
            Years [1857]. Lincoln: University of Nebraska Press.

Sainsbury, John A.
1975   Indian Labor in Early Rhode Island. *New England Quarter-
            ly* 48(3):378–393.

St. George, Eleanor
1953   The Dolls of Yesterday. New York: Charles Scribner's Sons.

Salamatov, Lavrentiĭ
1862–1863   Journal (Atka). (Unpublished manuscript in Alaska Church
            Collection, D-45.)

Salgari, Emilio
1896   Le Avventure del padre Crespel nel Labrador. Turin, Italy:
            Speirani.

————
[1905]   I minatori dell'Alaska, avventure .... Genoa, Italy:
            Donath.

————
1908   Sulle frontiere del Far-West. Florence, Italy: Bemporad.

Salisbury, Neal E.
1972   Conquest of the "Savage:" Puritans, Puritan Missionaries,
            and Indians, 1620–1680. (Unpublished Ph.D. Dissertation
            in History, University of California, Los Angeles.)

————
1974   Red Puritans: The "Praying Indians" of Massachusetts Bay
            and John Eliot. *William and Mary Quarterly, 3d ser.* Vol.
            31(1):27–54. Williamsburg, Va.

————
1982   Manitou and Providence: Indians, Europeans, and the
            Making of New England, 1500–1643. New York: Oxford
            University Press.

Salomon, Julian H.
1928   The Book of Indian Crafts and Indian Lore. New York:
            Harper and Brothers. (Reprinted in 1973.)

Samet, Jonathan, Daniel Kutvirt, Richard J. Waxweiler, and
Charles Key
1984   Uranium Mining and Lung Cancer in Navajo Men. *New
            England Journal of Medicine* 310(23):1481–1484.

Sanborn, Katherine A.
1911   Hunting Indians in a Taxi-cab. Boston: R.G. Badger.

Sandefur, Ray H.
1960   Logan's Oration—How Authentic? *Quarterly Journal of
            Speech* 46(3):289–296.

Sanders, Douglas E.
1974   Canadian Courts and the Concept of Indian Title. Pp. 4–34
            in Proceedings of the First Congress of the Canadian
            Ethnology Society. Jerome H. Barkov, ed. *Canada. Nation-
            al Museum of Man. Mercury Series. Ethnology Service Paper*
            17. Ottawa.

————
1983   The Indian Lobby. Pp. 301–332 in And No One Cheered:
            Federalism, Democracy, and the Constitution Act. Keith
            Banting and Richard Simeon, eds. Toronto: Methuen.

————
1986   An Uncertain Path: The Aboriginal Constitutional Confer-
            ences. Pp. 63–77 in Litigating the Values of a Nation: The
            Canadian Charter of Rights and Freedoms. Joseph M.
            Weiler and Robin M. Elliot, eds. Toronto: Carswell.

Sanders, Ronald
1978   Lost Tribes and Promised Lands: The Origins of American
            Racism. Boston: Little, Brown.

Sando, Joe S.
1976   The Pueblo Indians. San Francisco: Indian Historian Press.

————
1982   Nee Hemish: A History of Jemez Pueblo. Albuquerque:
            University of New Mexico Press.

Santos, Angel
1943   Jesuitas en el Polo Norte; la misión de Alaska. Madrid:
            Consejo Superior de Investigaciones Científicas, Instituto
            Gonzalo Fernández de Oviedo.

Sapir, Edward
1921   Language: An Introduction to the Study of Speech. New
            York: Harcourt, Brace.

————
1949   Time Perspective in Aboriginal American Culture: A Study
            in Method [1916]. Pp. 389–462 in Selected Writings of
            Edward Sapir. David G. Mandelbaum, ed. Berkeley:
            University of California Press.

————
1949a   Central and North American Languages. Pp. 169–178 in
            Selected Writings of Edward Sapir. David G. Mandelbaum,
            ed. Berkeley: University of California Press.

Sargent, Winthrop, ed.
1855   The History of an Expedition Against Fort Duquesne in
            1755; Under Major-General Edward Braddock.
            Philadelphia: Lippincott, Grambo.

Sarychev, Gavrill A.
1952   Puteshestvie po severo-vostochnoĭ chasti Sibiri, Ledovitomu
        moriū i Vostochnomu okeanu [Expedition to the Northeast-
        ern Part of Siberia, the Arctic Sea and the Eastern Ocean].
        Moscow: Gosudarstvennoe izdatel'stvo geograficheskoi li-
        teratury.

Satz, Ronald N.
1975   American Indian Policy in the Jacksonian Era. Lincoln:
        University of Nebraska Press.

────────
1979   Thomas Hartley Crawford, 1838–45. Pp. 23–27 in The
        Commissioners of Indian Affairs, 1824–1977. Robert M.
        Kvasnicka and Herman J. Viola, eds. Lincoln: University of
        Nebraska Press.

────────
1979a   Elbert Herring, 1831–36. Pp. 13–16 in The Commissioners
        of Indian Affairs, 1824–1977. Robert M. Kvasnicka and
        Herman J. Viola, eds. Lincoln: University of Nebraska
        Press.

────────
1979b   Carey Allen Harris, 1836–38. Pp. 17–22 in The Commis-
        sioners of Indian Affairs, 1824–1977. Robert M. Kvasnicka
        and Herman J. Viola, eds. Lincoln: University of Nebraska
        Press.

────────
1986   The Mississippi Choctaw: From the Removal Treaty to the
        Federal Agency. Pp. 3–32 in After Removal: The Choctaw
        in Mississippi. Samuel J. Wells and Roseanna Tubby, eds.
        Jackson: University Press of Mississippi.

Sauer, Carl O.
1966   The Early Spanish Main. Berkeley: University of California
        Press.

────────
1971   Sixteenth Century North America: The Land and the
        People as Seen by the Europeans. Berkeley: University of
        California Press.

────────
1980   Seventeenth Century North America. Berkeley, Calif.:
        Turtle Island Foundation for the Netzahualcoyotl Histori-
        cal Society.

Saum, Lewis O.
1965   The Fur Trader and the Indian. Seattle: University of
        Washington Press.

Saunders, William, and Walter Clark, eds.
1886–1907   The Colonial Records of North Carolina. 26 vols. Raleigh:
        P.M. Hale.

Sayre, Robert F.
1977   Thoreau and the American Indians. Princeton, N.J.:
        Princeton University Press.

Schauwecker, Franz
1942   Thecumseh: Erhebung der Prärie. Berlin: Safari.

Scheibler, Carl F.
1781   Leben der Pocahuntas, einer amerikanischen Prinzessin.
        Berlin: Calwe.

Scheick, William J.
1979   The Half-Blood: A Cultural Symbol in 19th Century
        American Fiction. Lexington: University Press of Ken-
        tucky.

Scherer, Joanna Cohan
1982   Indians: The Great Photographs That Reveal North Ameri-
        can Indian Life, 1847–1929, from the Unique Collection of
        the Smithsonian Institution. New York: Bonanza.

Schermerhorn, Richard
1914   Schermerhorn Genealogy and Family Chronicles. New
        York: Thomas A. Wright.

Scherr, Johannes
1853   Die Pilger der Wildniss: Historischer Roman. Prague:
        Tabor, Kober.

Schierbeek, Bert
1982   Binnenwerk. Amsterdam, The Netherlands: Atheneum.

Schiller, Friedrich von
1797   Nadowessier Totenlied. Musenalmanach für das Jahr 1797.
        Tübingen, Germany: Cotta.

Schilz, Thomas F.
1984   The Gros Ventres and the Upper Missouri Fur Trade,
        1806–1835. Annals of Wyoming 56(2):21–28.

Schmalz, Peter S.
1977   The History of the Saugeen Indians. Ontario Historical
        Society, Research Publication 5. Ottawa.

Schmeckebier, Laurence F.
1927   The Office of Indian Affairs: Its History, Activities and
        Organization. Baltimore, Md.: Johns Hopkins Press. (Re-
        printed: AMS Press, New York, 1972.)

Schmiel, Eugene D.
1969   The Career of Jacob Dolson Cox, 1828–1900: Soldier,
        Scholar, Statesman. (Unpublished Ph.D. Dissertation in
        History, Ohio State University, Columbus.)

Schneider, Lucien
1970   Dictionnaire français-esquimau du parler de l'Ungava et
        contrées limitrophes. Université Laval. Centre d'Études
        Nordiques. Travaux et Documents 5. Quebec.

Schöler, Bo
1984   Coyote Was Here: Essays on Contemporary Native Ameri-
        can Literary and Political Mobilization. Aarhus, Denmark:
        Seklas.

────────
1986   USA: Literature and Politics Among North American
        Indians. IWGIA Newsletter 48:78–110. Copenhagen.

Schoenberg, Wilfred P.
1957   Jesuit Mission Presses in the Pacific Northwest: A History
        and Bibliography of Imprints, 1876-1899. Portland, Oreg.:
        Champoeg Press.

────────
1962   A Chronicle of the Catholic History of the Pacific
        Northwest, 1743–1960, Arranged After the Manner of
        Certain Medieval Chronicles and Annotated with Copious
        Notes for Further Reference. Portland, Oreg.: Catholic
        Sentinel Press.

────────
1982   Paths to the Northwest: A Jesuit History of the Oregon
        Province. Chicago: Loyola University Press.

────────
1987   A History of the Catholic Church in the Pacific Northwest,
        1743–1983. Washington: Pastoral Press.

Scholes, France V.
1935   Civil Government and Society in New Mexico in the
        Seventeenth Century. New Mexico Historical Review
        10(2):71–111.

────────
1936   Church and State in New Mexico, 1610–1650. New Mexico
        Historical Review 11(1–3):9–76, 145–178, 283–294.

────────
1937   Church and State in New Mexico, 1610–1650. Albuquer-
        que: Historical Society of New Mexico.

────────
1937–1940   Troublous Times in New Mexico. New Mexico Historical
        Review 12(2):134–174, (4):380–452; 15(3):249–268.

────────
1938   Notes on the Jemez Mission in the 17th Century. El Palacio
        44(7–15):61–71, 93–102.

Schoolcraft, Henry R.
1819   A View of the Lead Mines of Missouri, Including Some
        Observations on the Mineralogy, Geology, Geography,
        Antiquities, Soil, Climate, Population and Productions of
        Missouri and Arkansas and Other Sections of the Western
        Country. New York: Charles Wiley.

1821   Narrative Journal of Travels Through the Northwestern Regions of the United States; Extending from Detroit Through the Great Chain of American Lakes, to the Sources of the Mississippi River. Albany, N.Y.: E. and E. Horsford.

1825   Travels in the Central Portions of the Mississippi Valley: Comprising Observations on Its Minerals, Geography, Internal Resources, and Aboriginal Population. New York: Collins and Hannay.

1828   The Chippewa Indians. *North American Review* 27:89–114.

1829   Civilization and Conversion of the Indians. *North American Review* 28:354–368.

1834   Narrative of an Expedition Through the Upper Mississippi to Itasca Lake, the Actual Source of This River. New York: Harper.

1839   Algic Researches, Comprising Inquiries Respecting the Mental Characteristics of the North American Indians. 2 vols. New York: Harper and Brothers.

1843   Alhalla; or, The Lord of Talladega: A Tale of the Creek War. New York: Wiley and Putnam.

1845   Oneóta; or, Characteristics of the Red Race of America; from Original Notes and Manuscripts. New York: Wiley and Putnam.

1846   Notes on the Iroquois; or, Contributions to the Statistics, Aboriginal History, Antiquities and General Ethnology of Western New York. New York: Bartlett and Welford.

1851   Personal Memoirs of a Residence of Thirty Years with the Indian Tribes on the American Frontiers . . . .Philadelphia: Lippincott, Grambo.

1851–1857   Historical and Statistical Information Respecting the History, Condition and Prospects of the Indian Tribes of the United States. 6 vols. Philadelphia: Lippincott, Grambo.

1856   The Myth of Hiawatha and Other Oral Legends, Mythologic and Allegoric of the North American Indians. Philadelphia: J.B. Lippincott.

Schrader, Robert F.
1983   The Indian Arts and Crafts Board: An Aspect of the New Deal Indian Policy. Albuquerque: University of New Mexico Press.

Schroeder, Albert H.
1962   A Re-analysis of the Routes of Coronado and Oñate into the Plains in 1541 and 1601. *Plains Anthropologist* 7(15):2–23.

1972   Rio Grande Ethnohistory. Pp. 41–70 in New Perspectives on the Pueblos. Alfonso Ortiz, ed. Albuquerque: University of New Mexico Press.

Schroeder, Samuel
1934   Amerika in der deutschen Dichtung von 1850 bis 1890. (Unpublished Ph.D. Dissertation in Literature, University of Heidelberg, Heidelberg, Germany.)

Schubart, Christian F.D.
1787   Der sterbende Indianer an seinen Sohn. In Gedichte. Stuttgart, Germany: Herman.

Schultz, Adolph H.
1945   Biographical Memoir of Aleš Hrdlička, 1869–1943. *National Academy of Sciences, Biographical Memoir* 23(12):305–338. Washington.

Schultz, George A.
1972   An Indian Canaan: Isaac McCoy and the Vision of an Indian State. Norman: University of Oklahoma Press.

Schulz, Franz
1964   Der nordamerikanische Indianer und seine Welt in den Werken von Ernest Hemingway und Oliver LaFarge. Munich, Germany: Max Hueber.

Schuyler, George W.
1885   Colonial New York: Philip Schuyler and His Family. 2 vols. New York: C. Scribner's Sons.

Schwartz, Joseph
1970   The Wild West Show: 'Everything Genuine'. *Journal of Popular Culture* 3(4):656–666.

Schwarze, Edmund
1923   History of the Moravian Mission Among the Southern Indian Tribes of the United States. Bethlehem, Pa.: Times Publishing Company.

Scott, Duncan C.
1914   Indian Affairs, 1763–1841. Pp. 695–725 in Vol. 4 and 331–352 in Vol. 5 of Canada and Its Provinces: A History of the Canadian People and Their Institutions by One Hundred Associates. Adam Shortt and Arthur G. Doughty, gen. eds. 23 vols. Toronto: T. and A. Constable at the Edinburgh University Press.

Scott, Hugh L.
1928   Some Memories of a Soldier. New York: Century.

Scott, Leslie M.
1928   Indian Diseases as Aids to Pacific Northwest Settlement. *Oregon Historical Quarterly* 29(2):144–161.

Scouler, John
1905   Dr. John Scouler's Journal of a Voyage to N.W. America. *Oregon Historical Quarterly* 6:54–75, 159–205, 276–287.

Scoville, Warren G.
1950   Capitalism and French Glassmaking, 1640–1789. *University of California Publications in Economics* 15. Berkeley. (Reprinted: Johnson Reprint, New York, 1968.)

Sealsfield, Charles
1843–1846   Gesammelte Werke. 14 vols. in 15. Stuttgart, Germany: Metzler.

Sears, Priscilla F.
1982   A Pillar of Fire to Follow: American Indian Dramas, 1808–1859. Bowling Green, Ohio: Bowling Green University Popular Press.

Secoy, Frank R.
1953   Changing Military Patterns on the Great Plains (17th Century Through Early 19th Century). (*Monographs of the American Ethnological Society* 21) Locust Valley, N.Y.: J.J. Augustin.

Secretary of War
1827–1849   Annual Reports of the Secretary of War. Washington: U.S. Government Printing Office.

Sedgwick, Sarah C., and Christina S. Marquand
1974   Stockbridge, 1739–1974. Stockbridge, Mass.: Berkshire Traveller Press.

Sell, Henry B., and Victor Weybright
1955   Buffalo Bill and the Wild West. New York: Oxford University Press.

Sepúlveda, Juan Ginés de
1951   Democrates segundo: O, de las justas causas de la guerra contras los indios [1540]. Angel Losada, ed. Madrid: Consejo Superior de Investigaciónes Científicas, Instituto Francisco de Vitoria.

Sequeira, Isaac
1978   The Frontier Attack on Cooper, 1850–1900. *Indian Journal of American Studies* 8(1):25–35. Hyderabad, India.

787

Sergeant, John
1743   A Letter from the Revd. Mr. Sergeant of Stockbridge, to Dr. [Benjamin] Colman of Boston; Containing Mr. Sergeant's Proposal of a More Effectual Method for the Education of Indian Children . . . Boston: Rogers and Fowle.

Serrano y Sanz, Manuel
1916   España y los Indios Cherokis y Chactas en la Segunda Mitad del Siglo XVIII. Seville, Spain: Tip. de la "Guia Oficial."

Servies, James A., comp.
1956   A Bibliography of John Marshall. Washington: U.S. Government Printing Office.

Seton, Ernest T.
[1902]   The Birch Bark Roll of Woodcraft. New York: A.S. Barnes.

1903   Two Little Savages: Being the Adventures of Two Boys Who Lived as Indians and What They Learned. New York: Doubleday.

1912   The Book of Woodcraft and Indian Lore. Garden City, N.Y.: Doubleday.

Seton, Julia M.
1930   The Rhythm of the Redman in Song, Dance and Decoration. New York: A.S. Barnes.

Seume, Johann G.
1801   Gedichte. Leipzig, Germany: P. Reclam.

Seumois, A.V.
1954   Etapes historiques de la mission esquimaude. Prêtre et Missions 12(7–8):290–296. Quebec.

Seymour, Flora Warren
1926   The Indians Today. Chicago: B.H. Sanborn.

1929   The Story of the Red Man. New York: Longmans, Green.

1930   Lords of the Valley, Sir William Johnson and His Mohawk Brothers. New York: Longmans, Green.

1941   Indian Agents of the Old Frontier. New York: D. Appleton-Century. (Reprinted: Octagon Books, New York, 1975.)

Shackford, James A.
1956   David Crockett, the Man and the Legend. John B. Shackford, ed. Chapel Hill: University of North Carolina Press.

Shalamov, Tikhon
1904   Po missii: Iz pokhodnogo zhurnala aliaskinskago provoslavnago missionera [Around the Mission: From the Field Journal of an Alaskan Orthodox Missionary]. New York: Tipografiia Amerikanskii Pravoslavnyi Viestnik.

Shaler, William
1808   Journal of a Voyage Between China and the North-western Coast of America, Made in 1804. American Register 3(1):137–175.

Shalkop, Antoinette
1977   The Travel Journal of Vasilii Orlov. Pacific Northwest Quarterly 68(3):131–140.

Shames, Priscilla
1969   The Long Hope: A Study of American Indian Stereotypes in American Popular Fiction, 1890–1950. (Unpublished Ph.D. Dissertation in English, University of California, Los Angeles.)

Shankel, George E.
1945   The Development of Indian Policy in British Columbia. (Unpublished Ph.D. Dissertation in History, University of Washington, Seattle.)

Shaw, Charles G.
1939   Speaking of Wooden Indians. Antiques 36(3):131–133.

Shaw, Helen L.
1931   British Administration of the Southern Indians, 1756–1783. Lancaster, Pa.: Lancaster Press. (Reprinted: AMS Press, New York, 1981.)

Shea, John G., ed.
1852   Discovery and Exploration of the Mississippi Valley: With the Original Narratives of Marquette, Allouez, Membré, Hennepin, and Anastase Douay. New York: Redfield.

1855   History of the Catholic Missions Among the Indian Tribes of the United States, 1529–1854. New York: T.W. Strong.

1866   The History of the Five Indian Nations Depending on the Province of New York by Cadwallader Colden. New York: T.H. Morrell.

1886–1892   A History of the Catholic Church within the Limits of the United States, from the First Attempted Colonization to the Present Time. 4 vols. New York: J.G. Shea.

Sheehan, Bernard W.
1969   Indian-White Relations in Early America: A Review Essay. William and Mary Quarterly 3d ser., Vol. 26(2):267–286. Williamsburg, Va.

1973   Seeds of Extinction: Jeffersonian Philanthropy and the American Indian. Chapel Hill: University of North Carolina Press.

1980   Savagism and Civility: Indians and Englishmen in Colonial Virginia. Cambridge, Mass.: Cambridge University Press.

Shelikhov, Grigorii Ivanovich
1981   A Voyage to America, 1783–1786. Marina Ramsay, trans. Richard A. Pierce, ed. Kingston, Ont.: Limestone Press. (Translated from the 1812 edition with indication of variations from the 1787 and 1793 editions.)

Shelly, Henry C.
1932   John Underhill, Captain of New England and New Netherland. New York: D. Appleton.

Shenitz, Helen A.
1967   Alaska's "Good Father." Pp. 121–130 in Alaska and Its History. Morgan B. Sherwood, ed. Seattle: University of Washington Press.

Sheridan, Philip H.
1888   Personal Memoirs of P.H. Sheridan, General, United States Army. 2 vols. New York: Charles L. Webster.

Sheridan, Richard B.
[1800]   Pizzarro: A Play in Five Acts. Altered from Kotzebue by Richard Brinsley Sheridan. New York: M. Douglas.

Shulman, Robert
1971   Parkman's Indians and American Violence. The Massachusetts Review 12(2):221–239.

Sievers, Harry J.
1952   The Catholic Indian School Issue and the Presidential Election of 1892. Catholic Historical Review 38(2):129–155.

Silko, Leslie Marmon
1977   Ceremony. New York: Viking Press.

Silver, James W.
1949   Edmund Pendleton Gaines, Frontier General. Baton Rouge: Louisiana State University Press.

Simmons, Marc
1966   New Mexico's Smallpox Epidemic, 1780–1781. New Mexico Historical Review 41(4):319–326.

1969   Settlement Patterns and Village Plans in Colonial New Mexico. Journal of the West 8(1):7–21.

1977   Santa Fe and Chihuahua Trail. Pp. 1084–1085 in The Reader's Encyclopedia of the American West. Howard R. Lamar, ed. New York: Thomas Y. Crowell.

Simmons, William S.
1981   Cultural Bias in the New England Puritans' Perception of Indians. *William and Mary Quarterly 3d ser.*, Vol. 38(1):56–72. Williamsburg, Va.

Simms, William G.
1835   The Yemassee: A Romance of Carolina. New York: Harper and Brothers.

Simpson, Sir George
1847   Narrative of a Journey Round the World During the Years 1841 and 1842. London: Henry Colburn.

———
1947   Part of Dispatch from George Simpson, Esqr., Governor of Ruperts Land, to the Governor and Committee of the Hudson's Bay Company, London, March 1, 1829; Continued and Completed March 24 and June 5, 1829. E.E. Rich, ed. Toronto: The Champlain Society.

———
1968   Fur Trade and Empire: George Simpson's Journal Entitled Remarks Connected with the Fur Trade in the Course of a Voyage from York Factory to Fort George and Back to York Factory, 1824–1825. Frederick Merk, ed. Rev. ed. Cambridge, Mass.: Belknap Press.

Simpson, Leslie B.
1950   The encomienda in New Spain: The Beginning of Spanish Mexico. Rev. ed. Berkeley: University of California Press.

Sinkler, George
1971   The Racial Attitudes of American Presidents from Abraham Lincoln to Theodore Roosevelt. Garden City, N.Y.: Doubleday.

Sinte Gleska College, Lakota Studies Department
[1980]   Hanta Yo: Authentic Farce. A Critical Review. Rosebud, S.D.: Sinte Gleska College.

———
1985   Mystic Warrior: A Critique. *Sinte Gleska College News* 7(2):4–5, 18. Rosebud, S.D.

Sinte Gleska College Staff Senate
1980   [Resolution Denouncing *Hanta Yo*; Adopted by Unanimous Vote, February 8, 1980. Sinte Gleska College, Rosebud, S.D.]

Sirmans, M. Eugene
1966   Colonial South Carolina: A Political History, 1663–1763. Chapel Hill: University of North Carolina Press.

Sixel, Friedrich W.
1966   Die deutsche Vorstellung vom Indianer in der ersten Hälfte des 16. Jahrhunderts. *Annali del Pontificio Museo Missionario Etnologico Lateranense* 39:9–230.

Skelton, William B.
1976   Army Officers' Attitudes Toward Indians, 1830–1860. *Pacific Northwest Quarterly* 67(3):113–124.

Skinner, Charles M.
1896   Myths and Legends of Our Land. 2 vols. Philadelphia: J.B. Lippincott.

Slattery, Charles L.
1901   Felix Reville Brunot, 1820–1898. New York: Longmans, Green.

Slotkin, James S.
1944   Racial Classifications of the Seventeenth and Eighteenth Centuries. *Transactions of the Wisconsin Academy of Sciences, Arts and Letters* 36:459–467. Madison.

———
1956   The Peyote Religion: A Study in Indian-White Relations. Glencoe, Ill.: Free Press. (Reprinted: Octagon Books, New York, 1975.)

Slotkin, Richard
1973   Regeneration Through Violence: The Mythology of the American Frontier, 1600–1860. Middletown, Conn.: Wesleyan University Press.

———
1985   The Fatal Environment: The Myth of the Frontier in the Age of Industrialization, 1800–1890. New York: Atheneum.

Slocum, Charles E.
1908   History of Frances Slocum, the Captive. Defiance, Ohio: Published by the author.

Slotkin, Richard, and James K. Folsom, eds.
1978   So Dreadful a Judgment: Puritan Responses to King Philip's War, 1676–1677. Middletown, Conn.: Wesleyan University Press.

Smet, Pierre Jean de
1843   Letters and Sketches, with a Narrative of a Year's Residence Among the Indian Tribes of the Rocky Mountains. Philadelphia: M. Fithian.

———
1847   Oregon Missions and Travels Over the Rocky Mountains in 1845–46. New York: E. Dunigan.

———
1863   Western Missions and Missionaries: A Series of Letters. New York: J.B. Kirker.

———
1905   Life, Letters and Travels of Father Pierre-Jean de Smet, S.J., 1801–1873; Missionary Labors and Adventures Among the Wild Tribes of the North American Indians, Embracing Minute Description of Their Manners, Customs, Games, Modes of Warfare and Torture, Legends, Tradition, etc. Hiram M. Chittenden and Alfred T. Richardson, eds. 4 vols. New York: Francis P. Harper.

Smiley, Jerome C.
1901   History of Denver; with Outlines of the Earlier History of the Rocky Mountain Country. Denver: Denver Times, Times-Sun Publishing Company. (Reprinted: Unigraphic, Evansville, Ind., 1971.)

Smiley, Winn
1972   Ammon M. Tenney: Mormon Missionary to the Indians. *Arizona History* 13(2):82–107.

Smith, Barbara Sweetland
1980   Russian Orthodoxy in Alaska: A History, Inventory, and Analysis of the Church Archives in Alaska with an Annotated Bibliography. [Anchorage]: Alaska Historical Commission.

———
1982   Cathedral on the Yukon. *The Alaska Journal* 2(2):4–6, 50–55.

Smith, Bradford
1953   Captain John Smith, His Life and Legend. Philadelphia: Lippincott.

[Smith, Charles C. et al., eds.]
1896   Historical Index to the Pickering Papers. *Collections of the Massachusetts Historical Society* 58 (6th ser., Vol. 8). Boston.

Smith, De Cost
1948   Martyrs of the Oblong and Little Nine. Caldwell, Idaho: Caxton Printers.

Smith, Donald B.
1971   Grey Owl. *Ontario History* 63(3):161–176.

———
1974   Le Sauvage: The Native People in Quebec Historical Writing on the Heroic Period (1534–1663) of New France. *Canada. National Museum of Man. Mercury Series. History Division Paper* 6. Ottawa.

Smith, Dwight L.
1954   William Medill, 1853–1856. Pp. 68–71 in The Governors of Ohio. Columbus: Ohio Historical Society.

Smith, Edward P.
1875   [Letter to Columbus Delano, Secretary of Interior, Dated June 30, 1875, re Claims Filed Against Indians to January 1875.] (In Report Books of the Bureau of Indian Affairs,

26:315–318, M348, Natural Resources Branch, Record Group 75, National Archives, Washington.)

Smith, Fay J., John L. Kessell, and Francis J. Fox
1966   Father Kino in Arizona. Phoenix: Arizona Historical Foundation.

Smith, Gerald A., and Clifford J. Walker
1965   Indian Slave Trade Along the Mojave Trail. San Bernadino, Calif.: San Bernadino County Museum.

Smith, G. Hubert
1980   The Explorations of the La Vérendryes in the Northern Plains, 1738–43. W. Raymond Wood, ed. Lincoln: University of Nebraska Press.

Smith, Henry N.
1950   Virgin Land: The American West as Symbol and Myth. Cambridge, Mass.: Harvard University Press.

1970   Consciousness and Social Order: The Theme of Transcendence in the Leatherstocking Tales. *Western American Literature* 5(3):177–194. Fort Collins, Colo.

Smith, John
1616   A Description of New England. London: H. Lownes. (Reprinted: W. Veazie, Boston, 1865.)

1624   The Generalle Historie of Virginia, New England and the Summer Isles. London: Printed by I.D. and I.H. for Michael Sparks. (Reprinted: Pp. 273–784 in Captain John Smith, Works, 1608–1681. Edward Arber, ed. Birmingham, England, 1884.)

1910   Travels and Works of Captain John Smith, President of Virginia, and Admiral of New England, 1580–1631. Edward Arbor, ed. 2 vols. Edinburgh: John Grant.

1986   The Complete Works of John Smith. Philip L. Barbour, ed. 3 vols. Chapel Hill: University of North Carolina Press.

Smith, Joseph, Jr.
1830   The Book of Mormon. Palmyra, New York. Printed by E.B. Grandin for the author.

Smith, Martin C.
1977   Nightwing. New York: Norton.

1981   Gorky Park. New York: Random House.

1986   Stallion Gate. New York: Random House.

Smith, Samuel
1765   The History of the Colony of Nova-Caesaria or New Jersey: Containing an Account of Its First Settlement, Progressive Improvements, the Original and Present Constitution, and Other Events, to the Year 1721. With Some Particulars Since; and a Short View of Its Present State. Philadelphia, Pa.: David Hall. (Reprinted as Expedition Against the Ohio Indians, University Microfilms, Ann Arbor, Mich., 1966.)

Smith, Samuel S.
1965   An Essay on the Causes of the Variety of Complexion and Figure in the Human Species [1787]. Winthrop D. Jordan, ed. Cambridge, Mass.: Harvard University Press.

Smith, Seba
1841   Powhatan: A Metrical Romance, in Seven Cantos. New York: Harper and Brothers.

Smith, W.R.L.
1928   The Story of the Cherokees. Cleveland, Tenn.: The Church of God Publishing House.

Smits, David D.
1982   The "Squaw Drudge:" A Prime Index of Savagism. *Ethnohistory* 29(4):281–306.

Smollett, Tobias G.
1794   The Expedition of Humphry Clinker. 2 vols. London: C. Cooke.

Smyth, David
1984   The Struggle for the Piegan Trade: The Saskatchewan Versus the Missouri. *Montana: The Magazine of Western History* 34(2):2–15.

Sniffen, M.K., ed.
1939 $3,000 for $1. *Indian Truth* 16(4):1–2. Philadelphia.

Snow, David H.
1970   [Review of] Navajos in the Catholic Church Records of New Mexico, 1694–1874. *El Palacio* 76(4):41–42.

Snow, William J.
1929   Utah Indians and Spanish Slave Trade. *Utah Historical Quarterly* 2(3):66–73. Salt Lake City.

Snyder, Gary
[1967]   A Curse on the Men in Washington, Pentagon. New York: Communication Company.

Society of American Indians
[1914]   The Society of American Indians, a National Organization of Americans. Washington: The Society.

Society of Friends *see* Friends, Society of

Šolc, Václav
1968   Nejstarši Američane. Prague: Nakladatelstvi dětské knihy.

Solimano, Sandra, ed.
1983   I Cerchi del mondo: Proposte di letture. Genoa, Italy: Comune di Genova.

Solís de Meras, Gonzalo
1923   Pedro Menéndez de Avilés, Adelantado, Governor and Captain-General of Florida. Jeannette M. Connor, trans. *Publications of the Florida State Historical Society* 3. Deland.

Sorber, Edna C.
1972   The Noble Eloquent Savage. *Ethnohistory* 19(3):227–236.

Sorensen, Axel Kjaer
1983   Danmark-Grønland i det 20. århundrede; en historisk oversigt. Copenhagen: Nyt Nordisk Forlag.

Sorkin, Alan L.
1971   American Indians and Federal Aid. Washington: Brookings Institution.

Sosin, Jack M.
1961   Whitehall and the Wilderness: The Middle West in British Colonial Policy, 1760–1775. Lincoln: University of Nebraska Press.

South Dakota Council of Churches, Department of Racial and Cultural Relations
1962   Statements–Philosophy of Indian Work. n.p.: The Council.

Spaid, Stanley S.
1950   Joel Palmer and Indian Affairs in Oregon. (Unpublished Ph.D. Dissertation in History, University of Oregon, Salem.)

Spalding, Arminta Scott
1975   Cyrus Kingsbury: Missionary to the Choctaws. (Unpublished Ph.D. Dissertation in History, University of Oklahoma, Norman.)

Spalding, Phinizy
1977   Oglethorpe in America. Chicago: University of Chicago Press.

Spears, Jack
1971   Hollywood: The Golden Era. New York: A.S. Barnes.

Speck, Ernest
1949   How to Scalp an Indian. Pp. 194–199 in the Sky is My Tipi. Mody C. Boatwright, ed. *Publications of the Texas Folklore Society* 22. Austin.

Speck, Frank G.
1938   Aboriginal Conservators. *Bird-lore* 40(4):258–261. New York

1943　　A Note on the Hassanamisco Band of Nipmuc. *Massachusetts Archaeological Society Bulletin* 4(4):49–56. Attleboro.

Speck, Gordon
1963　　Samuel Hearne and the Northwest Passage. Caldwell, Idaho: Caxton Printers.

Spence, Mary K.
1932　　William Penn: A Bibliography, a Tentative List of Publications About Him and His Work. *Pennsylvania Historical Commission Bulletin* 1. Harrisburg.

Spicer, Edward H.
1954　　Spanish-Indian Acculturation in the Southwest. *American Anthropologist* 56(4):663–678.

1961　　Types of Contact and Processes of Change. Pp. 517–544 in Perspectives in American Indian Culture Change. Edward H. Spicer, ed. Chicago: University of Chicago Press.

1962　　Cycles of Conquest: The Impact of Spain, Mexico and the United States on the Indians of the Southwest, 1533–1960. Tucson: University of Arizona Press.

1969　　Política gubernamental e integración en México y Estados Unidos. *América Indígena, Annuario Indigenista* 29(December):49–64. Mexico City.

1969a　　[Review of] The Teachings of Don Juan: A Yaqui Way of Knowledge [by] Carlos Castañeda. *American Anthropologist* 71(2):320–322.

Spielhagen, Friedrich
1871　　Deutsche Pioniere. Berlin: O. Janke.

Spolsky, Bernard
1978　　American Indian Bilingual Education. Pp. 332–361 in Case Studies in Bilingual Education. Bernard Spolsky and Robert L. Cooper, eds. Rawley, Mass.: Newberry House Publishers.

Spotswood, Alexander
1882–1885　　The Official Letters of Alexander Spotswood, Lieutenant-Governor of the Colony of Virginia, 1710–1722 . . . 2 vols. Richmond: Virginia Historical Society. (Reprinted: AMS Press, New York, 1973.)

Sprague, Marshall
1957　　Massacre: The Tragedy at White River. Boston: Little, Brown.

Sprague, William B.
1857–1869　　Annals of the American Pulpit; or, Commemorative Notices of Distinguished American Clergymen of Various Denominations, from the Early Settlement of the Country to the Close of the Year Eighteen Hundred Fifty-five. With Historical Introductions. 9 vols. New York: Robert Carter and Brothers.

1874　　The Life of Jedidiah Morse. New York: Anson D.F. Randolph.

Spry, Irene M.
1983　　The "Private Adventurers" of Rupert's Land. Pp. 49–70 in The Developing West. John E. Foster, ed. Edmonton: University of Alberta Press.

Squier, Ephraim G.
1848　　New Mexico and California. *American Review* n.s. 2(November):503–528.

1851　　Aboriginal Monuments of the State of New York, Comprising the Results of Original Surveys and Explorations. *Smithsonian Contributions to Knowledge* 2(9). Washington.

1851a　　The Serpent Symbol, and the Worship of the Reciprocal Principles of Nature in America (*American Archeological Researches* 1). New York: George P. Putnam.

Squier, Ephraim G., and E.H. Davis
1848　　Ancient Monuments of the Mississippi Valley, Comprising the Results of Extensive Original Surveys and Explorations. *Smithsonian Contributions to Knowledge* 1. Washington.

[Stanard, William G., ed.]
1902　　Treaty with the Cherokees at Lochabor, S.C., 1770. *Virginia Magazine of History and Biography* 9(2):360–363.

————, ed.
1906　　A Treaty Between Virginia and the Catawbas and Cherokees, 1756. *Virginia Magazine of History and Biography* 13(3):225–264.

————, ed.
1906a　　Virginia and the Cherokees, etc.: The Treaties of 1768 and 1770. *Virginia Magazine of History and Biography* 13(1):20–36.

————, ed.
1906b　　Treaty Between Virginia and the Indians of Fort Dunmore (Pittsburg) June, 1775. *Virginia Magazine of History and Biography* 14(1):54–78.

Stanley, George F.G.
1949　　The Policy of "Francisation" as Applied to the Indians During the Ancien Regime. *Revue d'Histoire de l'Amérique Française* 3(3):333–348. Montreal.

1950　　The First Indian "Reserves" in Canada. *Revue d'Histoire de l'Amérique Française* 4:178–210. Montreal.

1953　　The Indians and the Brandy Trade During the Ancien Régime. *Revue d'Histoire de l'Amérique Française* 6(4):489–505. Montreal.

1960　　The Birth of Western Canada: A History of the Riel Rebellion. Toronto: University of Toronto Press. (Reprinted in 1970.)

1968　　New France: The Last Phase, 1744–1760. Toronto: McClelland and Stewart.

Stanton, William
1960　　The Leopard's Spots: Scientific Attitudes Towards Race in America, 1815–1859. Chicago: University of Chicago Press.

Starkey, Marion L.
1946　　The Cherokee Nation. New York: Knopf.

Starr, Jerome L.
1972　　Education in Russian Alaska. *Alaska State Library Historical Monographs* 2. Juneau.

Start, Edwin A.
1892　　General Armstrong and the Hampton Institute. *New England Magazine* n.s. 6(4):442–460.

Stedman, Raymond W.
1982　　Shadows of the Indian: Stereotypes in American Culture. Norman: University of Oklahoma Press.

Steere, Jonathan M.
1934　　The Collier Bill. *Indian Truth* 11(5):1–8. Philadelphia.

Steffen, Jerome O.
1977　　William Clark: Jeffersonian Man on the Frontier. Norman: University of Oklahoma Press.

Stein, Gary C.
1974　　A Fearful Drunkenness: The Liquor Trade to the Western Indians as Seen by European Travelers in America, 1800–1860. *Red River Valley History Review* 1(1):109–121.

Steiner, Stanley
1968　　The New Indians. New York: Harper and Row.

Stengers, Jean
1945　　Hennepin et la découverte du Mississippi. *Bulletin de la Société Royale Belge de Géographie d'Anvers [for]* 1945:61–82. Brussels.

Stepanova, M.V.
1949   I. Veniaminov kak etnograf [I. Veniaminov as an Ethnographer]. *Akademiſa Nauk SSSR. Trudy Institut Etnografiſ* n.s. 2:294–314. Moscow.

Stephenson, Richard W.
1973   Maps from the Peter Force Collection. *Quarterly Journal of the Library of Congress* 30(3):183–204. Washington.

_____
1981   [Descriptive Guide Accompanying Facsimile Map "Manatus Situated on the North River."] (In Geography and Map Division, Library of Congress, Washington.)

Stern, Bernhard J.
1931   Lewis Henry Morgan, Social Evolutionist. Chicago: University of Chicago Press. (Reprinted: Russell and Russell, New York, 1967.)

Stern, Theodore
1965   The Klamath Tribe: A People and Their Reservation. Seattle: University of Washington Press.

Stern, Theodore, Martin Schmitt, and Alphonse F. Halfmoon
1980   A Cayuse-Nez Percé Sketchbook. *Oregon Historical Quarterly* 81(4):341–376.

Steuben, Fritz *see* Wittek, Erhard

Stevens, Frank E.
1903   The Black Hawk War. Chicago: Frank E. Stevens.

Stevens, Hazard
1901   The Life of Isaac Ingalls Stevens, by His Son. 2 vols. Boston: Houghton, Mifflin.

Stevenson, Robert Louis
1889   The Master of Ballantrae, a Winter's Tale. London: Cassell.

Steward, Julian H.
1930   Irrigation without Agriculture. *Papers of the Michigan Academy of Science, Arts, and Letters* 12:149–156. Ann Arbor.

_____
1933   Ethnography of the Owens Valley Paiute. *University of California Publications in American Archaeology and Ethnology* 33(3):233–350. Berkeley.

_____
1941   Culture Element Distributions, XIII: Nevada Shoshone. *University of California Anthropological Records* 4(2):209–359. Berkeley.

_____
1960   John Reed Swanton, February 19, 1873–May 2, 1958. Pp. 329–349 in *National Academy of Sciences, Biographical Memoirs* 14. Washington.

_____
1961   Alfred Louis Kroeber, 1876–1960. *American Anthropologist* 63(5):1038–1060.

Stewart, Edgar I.
1955   Custer's Luck. Norman: University of Oklahoma Press. (Reprinted in 1971.)

Stewart, Omer C.
1948   Indians Today: History in the Making. Program #438, November 13. Department of Radio Production, University of Colorado, Boulder. Mimeo.

Stewart, Robert L.
1908   Sheldon Jackson, Pathfinder and Prospector of the Missionary Vanguard in the Rocky Mountains and Alaska. New York: F.H. Revell.

Stewart, T.D., and Marshall T. Newman
1951   An Historical Resume of the Concept of Differences in Indian Types. *American Anthropologist* 53(1):19–36.

Stingl, Miloslav
1966   Indiáni bez tomahavků, Prague: Svoboda.

_____
1969   Indiáni na válečné stezce. Prague: NV.

Stith, William
1865   The History of the First Discovery and Settlement of Virginia [1747]. New York: Joseph Sabin.

Stocking, George W., Jr.
1968   Race, Culture, and Evolution: Essays in the History of Anthropology. New York: Free Press.

_____
1974   The Shaping of American Anthropology, 1883–1911: A Franz Boas Reader. New York: Basic Books.

_____
1975   Scotland as the Model of Mankind: Lord Kames' Philosophical View of Civilization. Pp. 65–89 in Toward a Science of Man: Essays in the History of Anthropology. Timothy H.H. Thoresen, ed. The Hague: Mouton.

Stoddard, Solomon
1722   An Answer to Some Cases of Conscience Respecting the Country. Boston: B. Green.

Stokes, Anson P.
1950   Church and State in the United States. 3 vols. New York: Harper.

Stone, Lyle M.
1974   Fort Michilimackinac, 1715–1781. East Lansing: Michigan State University, Publications of the Museum.

Stone, William L.
1838   Life of Joseph Brant-Thayendanega: Including the Border Wars of the American Revolution, Sketches of the Indian Campaigns of Generals Harmar, St. Clair, and Wayne . . . 2 vols. New York: George Dearborn.

Storm, Hyemeyohsts
1972   Seven Arrows. New York: Harper and Row.

_____
1981   Song of Heyoehkah. San Francisco: Harper and Row.

Stowe, Harriet Beecher
1869   Oldtown Folks. Boston: Fields, Osgood.

Stowell, Addie
1963   The Red Man's Hope. Dallas, Tex.: Royal Publishing Company.

Strandness, Theodore B.
1967   Samuel Sewall: A Puritan Portrait. East Lansing: Michigan State University Press.

Straubenmüller, Johann
1858   Pocahontas; oder, Die Gründung von Virginien. Baltimore, Md.: W.R. Schmidt.

Street, Ida M.
1929   Joseph M. Street's Last Fight with the Fur Traders. *Annals of Iowa 3d ser.*, Vol. 17(1):105–148.

Street, W.B.
1895   General Joseph M. Street. *Annals of Iowa 3d ser.*, Vol. 2(2–3):81–105.

Strong, Nathaniel T.
1841   Appeal to the Christian Community; on the Condition and Prospects of the New-York Indians, in Answer to a Book . . . .New York: E.B. Clayton.

Strong, William E.
1910   The Story of the American Board: An Account of the First Hundred Years of the American Board of Commissioners for Foreign Missions. Boston: Pilgrim Press.

Strubberg, Friedrich Armand
1858   Bis in die Wildnis. 4 vols. Breslau, Germany: E. Trewendt.

_____
1858a   Amerikanische Jagd- und Reiseabenteuer aus meinem Leben in den westlichen Indianergebieten. Stuttgart, Germany: J.G. Cotta.

_____
1859   Scenen aus den Kämpfen der Mexicaner und Nordamerikaner. Breslau, Germany: E. Trewendt.

792

1859a   An der Indianer-Grenze. 4 vols. Hannover, Germany: C. Rümpler.

1860   Ralph Norwood. 5 vols. Hannover, Germany: C. Rümpler.

1867   Friedrichsburg, die Colonie des deutschen Fürstenvereins in Texas. 2 vols. Leipzig, Germany: Friedrich Fleischer.

1868   Aus Armand's Frontiersleben. 3 vols. Leipzig, Germany: J. Wurner.

1896   Na zapadĭe Ameriki. [In the American West.] n.p.: F.A. Bitepazha.

Stuart, Paul
1978   The Indian Office: Growth and Development of an American Institution, 1865–1900 (*Studies in American History and Culture* 12). Ann Arbor, Mich.: University Microfilms International Research Press.

Sturdza, Aleksandr S.
1857   Pamĭatnik trudov provoslavnykh blagoviestnikov russkikh s 1793 do 1853 goda [Memorial to the Labors of Russian Orthodox Missionaries from 1783 to 1853]. Moscow: V tip.V. Goté.

Sturtevant, William C.
1954   Statement of William C. Sturtevant Regarding S 2747 and H.R. 7321. Pp. 1136–1137 in Joint Hearing Before the Subcommittee on Interior and Insular Affairs . . . *83rd Congress 2d session on S 2747 and H.R. 7321.* Pt 8, Seminole Indians, Florida, March 1 and 2. Washington.

1976   First Visual Images of Native Americans. Pp. 417–454 in Vol. 1 of Images of America. The Impact of the New World on the Old. Fredi Chiappelli, ed. 2 vols. Berkeley: University of California Press.

1979   The Cherokee Frontiers, the French Revolution, and William Augustus Bowles. Pp. 61–91 in The Cherokee Indian Nation, a Troubled History. Duane H. King, ed. Knoxville: University of Tennessee Press.

Sturtevant, William C., and Richard H. Manville
1966   Early Specimens of the Eastern Wolf. *Chesapeake Science* 7(4):218–220.

Sullivan, Marian Dix
1846   Indian Bride's Farewell. (Manuscript in Archives of Folk Songs, Music Division, Library of Congress, Washington.)

Sullivan, Maurice S.
1936   Jedediah Smith, Trader and Trail Breaker. New York: Press of the Pioneers.

Sunder, John E.
1959   Bill Sublette, Mountain Man. Norman: University of Oklahoma Press.

1965   The Fur Trade on the Upper Missouri, 1840–1865. Norman: University of Oklahoma Press.

1968   William Lewis Sublette. Pp. 347–359 in Vol. 5 of The Mountain Men and the Fur Trade of the Far West. LeRoy R. Hafen, ed. 10 vols. Glendale, Calif.: Arthur H. Clark.

Surrey, Nancy Maria
1916   The Commerce of Louisiana During the French Regime, 1699–1763. New York: Columbia University Press.

1922   The Commerce of Louisiana During the French Regime, 1699–1763. *Louisiana Historical Quarterly* 5(1):19–33.

Surtees, Robert J.
1967   Indian Reserve Policy in Upper Canada, 1830–1845. (Unpublished M.A. Thesis in History, Carleton University, Ottawa.)

1969   The Development of an Indian Reserve Policy in Canada. *Ontario History* 61:87–98.

1971   The Original People. Toronto: Holt, Rinehart and Winston.

1982   Indian Land Cessions in Ontario, 1762–1862: The Evolution of the System. (Unpublished Ph.D. Dissertation in History, Carleton University, Ottawa.)

1985   A Cartographic Analysis of Indian Settlements and Reserves in Southern Ontario and Southern Quebec, 1763–1867. Ottawa: Department of Indian and Northern Affairs, Canada.

Suttles, Wayne
1962   Variation in Habit and Culture on the Northwest Coast. Pp. 527–537 in *Proceedings of the 34th International Congress of Americanists.* Vienna.

1968   Coping with Abundance: Subsistence on the Northwest Coast. Pp. 56–68 in Man the Hunter. Richard B. Lee and Irven De Vore, eds. Chicago: Aldine.

Sutton, Imre
1975   Indian Land Tenure: Bibliographical Essays and a Guide to the Literature. New York: Clearwater.

———, ed.
1985   Irredeemable America: The Indians' Estate and Land Claims. Albuquerque: University of New Mexico Press.

Swadesh, Frances Leen
1974   Los Primeros pobladores: Hispanic Americans of the Ute Frontier. Notre Dame, Ind.: University of Notre Dame Press.

Swagerty, William R., Jr.
1980   Marriage and Settlement Patterns of Rocky Mountain Trappers and Traders. *Western Historical Quarterly* 11(2):159–180.

1981   Beyond Bimini: Indian Responses to European Incursions in the Spanish Borderlands, 1513–1600. 2 vols. (Unpublished Ph.D. Dissertation in History, University of California, Santa Barbara.)

Swan, James G.
1857   The Northwest Coast; or, Three Years' Residence in Washington Territory. New York: Harper and Brothers.

1870   The Indians of Cape Flattery, at the Entrance to the Strait of Fuca, Washington Territory. *Smithsonian Contributions to Knowledge* 16(8). Washington.

1876   The Haida Indians of Queen Charlotte's Island, British Columbia. *Smithsonian Contributions to Knowledge* 21(4). Washington.

Swanton, John R.
1936   Biographical Memoir of William H. Holmes, 1846–1933. (Bibliography compiled by Ella Leary) *National Academy of Sciences, Biographical Memoirs* 27(10):223–252. Washington.

1946   The Indians of the Southeastern United States. *Bureau of American Ethnology Bulletin* 137. Washington. (Reprinted: Smithsonian Institution Press, Washington, 1979.)

Sweet, William W.
1964   Religion on the American Frontier. 4 vols. New York: Cooper Square Publishers.

Swinney, H.J., and Merle W. Wells
1962   Fort Boise: From Imperial Outpost to Historic Site. *Idaho Yesterdays* 6(1):15–39.

Szasz, Margaret Connell
1974　　Education and the American Indian: The Road to Self-determination, 1928–1973. Albuquerque: University of New Mexico Press.

――――　1979　　Philleo Nash, 1961–66. Pp. 311–323 in The Commissioners of Indian Affairs, 1824–1977. Robert M. Kvasnicka and Herman J. Viola, eds. Lincoln: University of Nebraska Press.

――――　1980　　"Poor Richard" Meets the Native American: Schooling for Young Indian Women in Eighteenth-Century Connecticut. *Pacific Historical Review* 49(2):215–235.

――――　1983　　Introduction. Pp. ix–xxiii in To Live on This Earth: American Indian Education, by Estelle Fuchs and Robert J. Havighurst. Albuquerque: University of New Mexico Press.

――――　[1988]　　Indian Education in the American Colonies, 1607–1783. Albuquerque: University of New Mexico Press. In press.

Szklarski, Alfred
1978　　Tomek na wojenne ściezce. [Tomek on the Warpath.] Vol. 8. Katowice, Poland: Śląsk.

Taft, Robert
1938　　Photography and the American Scene: A Social History, 1839–1889. New York: Macmillan. (Reprinted: Dover Publications, New York, 1964.)

Takaki, Ronald T.
1979　　Iron Cages: Race and Culture in Nineteenth Century America. New York: Knopf.

Talbert, Charles G.
1955　　A Roof for Kentucky. *Filson Club Historical Quarterly* 29(2):145–165. Louisville, Ky.

Talbot, Edith A.
1904　　Samuel Chapman Armstrong, a Biographical Study. New York: Doubleday, Page. (Reprinted: Negro Universities Press, New York, 1969.)

Taliaferro, Lawrence
1891　　Auto-biography of Maj. Lawrence Taliaferro [1864]. *Minnesota Historical Society Collections* 6(2):189–255.

Tannenbaum, Frank
1950　　Mexico: The Struggle for Peace and Bread. New York: Alfred A. Knopf.

Tanner, Adrian
1979　　Bringing Home Animals: Religious Ideology and Mode of Production of the Mistassini Cree Hunters. New York: St. Martins Press.

Tanner, H.H., ed.
1986　　Atlas of Great Lakes Indian History. Norman: University of Oklahoma Press for the Newberry Library.

Tanner, John
1830　　A Narrative of the Captivity and Adventures of John Tanner During Thirty Years' Residence Among the Indians of the Interior of North America. Edwin James, ed. New York: G. and C. and H. Carvill. (Reprinted: Ross and Haines, Minneapolis, Minn., 1956.)

Tannis, Norman E.
1970　　Education in John Eliot's Indian Utopias, 1646–1675. *History of Education Quarterly* 10(3):308–323.

Tarasar, Constance J., gen. ed.
1975　　Orthodox America, 1794–1976: Development of the Orthodox Church in America. Syosset, N.Y.: Orthodox Church in America, Department of History and Archives.

Tarpley, Fred, and Ann Moseley, eds.
1971　　Of Edsels and Marauders. Commerce, Tex.: Names Institute Press.

Tatum, Laurie
1899　　Our Red Brothers and the Peace Policy of President Ulysses S. Grant. Philadelphia: J.C. Winston. (Reprinted: University of Nebraska Press, Lincoln, 1970.)

Tax, Sol
1957　　Termination Versus the Needs of Positive Policy for American Indians. *Congressional Record* 103:(July 3:116.) [Paper presented at Central States Anthropological Society Meeting, May 4, 1957, Madison, Wisconsin. Extension of remarks of Hon. Barratt O'Hara of Illinois in the House of Representatives.]

Taylor, Alexander S.
1860–1863　　Indianology of California. *The California Farmer and Journal of Useful Sciences* Vols. 13–20, February 22, 1860–October 30, 1863. San Francisco.

Taylor, Betty
1984　　Clare Sheridan (1885–1970). Hastings, England: Published by the author.

Taylor, Colin F.
1971–1984　　[Survey Questionnaires on European Indian Hobbyists.] (Manuscripts in Taylor's possession.)

――――　1979　　Reading the Smoke Signals. *The Guardian*, May 2:12. London.

――――　1980　　Ho, for the Great West! Indians and Buffalo, Exploration and George Catlin: The West of William Blackmore. Pp. 8–49 in *25th Anniversary Publication of the English Westerners Society*. London.

Taylor, Graham D.
1980　　The New Deal and American Indian Tribalism: The Administration of the Indian Reorganization Act, 1934–45. Lincoln: University of Nebraska Press.

Taylor, Herbert C., and Lester L. Hoaglin, Jr.
1962　　The Intermittent Fever Epidemic of the 1830's on the Lower Columbia River. *Ethnohistory* 9(2):160–178.

Taylor, John F.
1977　　Sociocultural Effects of Epidemics on the Northern Plains, 1734–1850. *Western Canadian Journal of Anthropology* 7(4):55–81.

Taylor, John L.
1984　　Canadian Indian Policy During the Inter-War Years, 1918–1939. Ottawa: Department of Indian and Northern Affairs.

――――　1976　　The Development of an Indian Policy for the Canadian North-west, 1869–79. (Unpublished Ph.D. Dissertation in History, Queen's University, Kingston, Ont.)

――――　1977　　Canada's North-west Indian Policy in the 1870s: Traditional Premises and Necessary Innovations. Pp. 104–110 in Approaches to Native History in Canada. D.A. Muise, ed. Canada. National Museum of Man. Mercury Series. History Division Paper 25. Ottawa.

Taylor, Nathaniel G.
1868　　[Letter to Orville H. Browning, Secretary of the Interior, Dated April 6, 1868, re Need to Appropriate Funds Promised to Indians by the United States Government.] (In Report Books of the Bureau of Indian Affairs, 17:240, M348, Natural Resources Branch, Record Group 75, National Archives, Washington.)

Taylor, Theodore W.
1983　　American Indian Policy. Mt. Airy, Md.: Lomond Publications.

Teit, James A.
1898　　Traditions of the Thompson River Indians of British Columbia. *Memoirs of the American Folk-Lore Society* 6. (Reprinted: Kraus Reprint, New York, 1969.)

794

1900   The Thompson Indians of British Columbia. Franz Boas, ed. *Memoirs of the American Museum of Natural History* 2(4); *Publications of the Jesup North Pacific Expedition* 1(4). New York. (Reprinted: AMS Press, New York, 1975.)

1906   The Lillooet Indians. *Memoirs of the American Museum of Natural History* 4(5); *Publications of the Jesup North Pacific Expedition* 2(5). New York. (Reprinted: AMS Press, New York, 1975.)

1909   Two Tahltan Traditions. *Journal of American Folk-Lore* 22(85):314–318.

1909a   The Shuswap. *Memoirs of the American Museum of Natural History* 4(7); *Publications of the Jesup North Pacific Expedition* 2(7). New York. (Reprinted: AMS Press, New York, 1975.)

1912   Traditions of the Lillooet Indians of British Columbia. *Journal of American Folk-Lore* 25(98):287–371.

1912a   Mythology of the Thompson Indians. *Memoirs of the American Museum of Natural History* 12; *Publications of the Jesup North Pacific Expedition* 8(2). New York. (Reprinted: AMS Press, New York, 1975.)

1928   The Middle Columbia Salish. Franz Boas, ed. *University of Washington Publications in Anthropology* 2(4):89–128. Seattle.

1930   The Salishan Tribes of the Western Plateaus. Pp. 23–396 in *45th Annual Report of the Bureau of American Ethnology for the Years 1927–1928.* Washington. (Reprinted: Shorey Book Store, Seattle, Wash., 1973.)

Ten Kate, Herman F.C.
1922   The Indian in Literature. Pp. 507–528 in *Annual Report of the Smithsonian Institution for 1921.* Washington.

Terrell, John U.
1969   The Man Who Rediscovered America: A Biography of John Wesley Powell. New York: Weybright and Talley.

Texada, David K.
1970   Alejandro O'Reilly and the New Orleans Rebels. Lafayette: University of Southwestern Louisiana.

Thacher, James
1832   History of the Town of Plymouth; From Its First Settlement in 1620, to the Year 1832. Boston: Marsh, Capen and Lyon.

Thackeray, William M.
1859   The Virginians: A Tale of the Last Century. New York: Hurst.

Thayer, James B.
1888   The Dawes Bill and the Indians. *Atlantic Monthly* 61(365):315–322.

1891   A People without Law. 2 Pts. *Atlantic Monthly* 68(408):540–551, (409):676–687.

1893   The Origin and Scope of the American Doctrine of Constitutional Law. Indianapolis, Ind.: Bobbs-Merrill.

Thériault, Yves
1958   Agaguk. Paris: Grasset. (Reprinted: Quinze, Montreal, 1981.)

1960   La Revanche du Nascopie. Montreal: Beauchemin.

1961   La Loi de l'Apache. Montreal: Beauchemin.

1963   Nakika, le petit Algonquin. Montreal: Leméac.

1964   Nanya, le petit Esquimau. Montreal: Beauchemin.

Thevet, André
1575   La Cosmographie vniverselle d'André Thevet, cosmographe dv roy . . . .2 vols. Paris: P.L. L'Hulier.

Thoma, Francisco de
1896   Historia popular de Nuevo México, desde su descubrimiento hasta la actualidad. New York: American Book Company.

Thomas, Alan
1981–1982   Photography of the Indian: Concept and Practice on the Northwest Coast. *BC Studies* 52:61–85.

Thomas, Alfred B., ed.
1931   Governor Mendinueta's Proposals for the Defense of New Mexico, 1772–1778. *New Mexico Historical Review* 6(1):21–39.

————, ed. and trans.
1932   Forgotten Frontiers: A Study of the Spanish Indian Policy of Don Juan Bautista de Anza, Governor of New Mexico, 1777–1787. Norman: University of Oklahoma Press.

1935   After Coronado: Spanish Exploration Northeast of New Mexico, 1696–1727. Norman: University of Oklahoma Press.

1940   The Plains Indians of New Mexico, 1751–1778: A Collection of Documents Illustrative of the History of the Eastern Frontier of New Mexico. Albuquerque: University of New Mexico Press.

————, ed. and trans.
1941   Teodoro de Croix and the Northern Frontier of New Spain, 1776–1783. (From the Original Documents in the Archives of the Indies, Seville, Spain). Norman: University of Oklahoma Press.

Thomas, Cyrus
1910   Treaties. Pp. 803–814 in Vol. 2 of Handbook of American Indians North of Mexico. Frederick W. Hodge, ed. 2 vols. *Bureau of American Ethnology Bulletin* 30. Washington.

Thomas, Lewis H.
1982   Louis Riel. Pp. 736–753 in Vol. 11 of Dictionary of Canadian Biography. Henry Pilon, ed. Toronto: University of Toronto Press.

Thomas, Mary U.
1938   The Catholic Church on the Oklahoma Frontier, 1824–1907. (Unpublished Ph.D. Dissertation in History, St. Louis University, St. Louis, Mo.)

Thomas, Philip D.
1971   Artists Among the Indians, 1493–1850. *Kansas Quarterly* 3(4):3–12.

Thomas, Robert K.
1965   Pan-Indianism. *Midcontinent American Studies Journal* 6(2):75–83. Lawrence, Kans.

Thomas, William H.
1853   A Letter to the Commissioner of Indian Affairs, with the Claims of the Indians Remaining in the States East. Washington: Buell and Blanchard.

1858   Explanation of the Fund Held in Trust by the United States for the North Carolina Cherokees. Washington: L. Towers.

Thompson, Augustus C.
1890   Moravian Missions: Twelve Lectures. New York: Charles Scribner's Sons.

Thompson, Erwin N.
1971   Modoc War, Its Military History and Topography. Sacramento, Calif.: Argus Books.

Thompson, Harold W.
1962   Body, Boots and Britches: Folktales, Ballads, and Speech from Country New York [1939]. New York: Dover.

795

Thompson, Hildegard
1975   The Navajos Long Walk for Education: A History of Navajo Education. Tsaile Lake, Ariz.: Navajo Community College Press.

Thompson, Julie
1977   The North American Indian Collection: A Catalogue. Bern, Switzerland: Bern Historical Museum.

Thompson, Lucy
[1916] To the American Indian. Eureka, Calif.: [Cummis Print Shop.]

Thompson, Pishey
1857   Anecodotes of the North American Indians and Notices of Natural History of the Immediate Neighbourhood of the City of Washington, United States. Boston: John Noble.

Thompson, Stith
1932–1936 Motif-index of Folk Literature. 6 vols. Bloomington: Indiana University Press.

Thompson, Thomas, ed.
1978   The Schooling of Native America. Washington: American Association of Colleges for Teacher Education in Collaboration with the Teacher Corps, U.S. Office of Education.

Thoreau, Henry D.
1849   A Week on the Concord and Merrimack Rivers. Boston: J. Munroe.

———
1864   The Maine Woods. Boston: Ticknor and Fields.

Thorne, Melvin J.
1982   Fainters and Fighters: Images of Women in Indian Captivity Narratives. *The Midwest Quarterly* 23(4):426–436.

Thorne, Tanis C.
1984   The Chouteau Family and the Osage Trade: A Generational Study. Pp. 109–120 in Rendezvous: Selected Papers of the Fourth North American Fur Trade Conference, 1981. T.C. Buckley, ed. St. Paul, Minn.: North American Fur Trade Conference.

Thornton, Russell
[1986] American Indian Holocaust and Survival: A Population History Since 1492. Norman: University of Oklahoma Press.

Thrapp, Dan L.
1964   Al Sieber, Chief of Scouts. Norman: University of Oklahoma Press.

———
1967   The Conquest of Apacheria. Norman: University of Oklahoma Press.

———
1972   General Crook and the Sierra Madre Adventure. Norman: University of Oklahoma Press.

———
1974   Victorio and the Mimbres Apaches. Norman: University of Oklahoma Press.

Thwaites, Reuben G.
1902   Daniel Boone. New York: D. Appleton.
———, ed.
1904   John Long's Journal, 1768–1782. Vol. 2 of Early Western Travels, 1748–1846. Cleveland, Ohio: Arthur H. Clark. (Reprint of Voyages and Travels of an Indian Interpreter and Trader, London, 1791.)
———, ed.
1904–1905 Original Journals of the Lewis and Clark Expedition, 1804–1806. 8 vols. New York: Dodd, Mead. (Reprinted: Antiquarian Press, New York, 1959.)

———
1906   William Clark: Soldier, Explorer, Statesman. *Missouri Historical Society Collections* 2(7):1–24.

———
1906a   Descriptive List of Manuscript Collections of the State Historical Society of Wisconsin. Madison: State Historical Society of Wisconsin.

Tibesar, Antonine
1953   Franciscan Beginnings in Colonial Peru. *Publications of the Academy of American Franciscan History, Monograph Series* 1. Washington.
———, ed.
1955–1966 Writings of Junípero Serra. 4 vols. Washington: Academy of American Franciscan History.

Tikhmenev, Peter A.
1978–1979 A History of the Russian-American Company. 2 vols. Richard A. Pierce and Alton S. Donnelly, trans. and eds. Seattle: University of Washington Press.

Tingey, Joseph W.
1978   Indians and Blacks Together: An Experiment in Biracial Education at Hampton Institute (1878–1923). (Unpublished Ph.D. Dissertation in Education, Columbia University Teachers College, New York.)

Tobias, John L.
1976   Protection, Civilization, Assimilation: An Outline History of Canada's Indian Policy. *Western Canadian Journal of Anthropology* 6(2):13–30.

———
1983   Canada's Subjugation of the Plains Cree, 1879–1885. *Canadian Historical Review* 64(4):519–548.

Todd, John B.S.
1962   The Harney Expedition Against the Sioux: The Journal of Capt. John B.S. Todd. Roy H. Mattison, ed. *Nebraska History* 43(2):89–130.

Todorov, Tzevetan
1984   The Conquest of America: The Question of the Other. Richard Howard, trans. New York: Harper and Row.

Tohill, Louis A.
1928–1929 Robert Dickson, British Fur Trader on the Upper Mississippi. *North Dakota Historical Quarterly* 3(1):5–49, (2):83–128, (3):182–203.

Tolles, Frederick B.
1957   James Logan and the Culture of Provincial America. Boston: Little, Brown. (Reprinted: Greenwood Press, Westport, Conn., 1978.)

———
1963   Nonviolent Contact: The Quakers and Indians. *Proceedings of the American Philosophical Society* 107(2):93–110. Philadelphia.

Tolmie, William F.
1963   The Journals of William Fraser Tolmie, Physician and Fur Trader. Howard T. Mitchell, ed. Vancouver, B.C.: Mitchell Press.

Tomkins, William
1926   Universal Indian Sign Language of the Plains Indians of North America . . . San Diego, Calif.: Published by the author. (Reprinted: Dover Publications, New York, 1969.)

Tooker, Elisabeth
1964   An Ethnography of the Huron Indians. *Bureau of American Ethnology Bulletin* 190. Washington.

Torbet, Robert G.
1955   Venture of Faith: The Story of the American Baptist Foreign Mission Society and the Woman's American Baptist Foreign Mission Society, 1814–1954. Philadelphia: Judson Press.

Towner, Lawrence W.
1955   A Good Master Well Served: A Social History of Servitude in Massachusetts, 1620–1750. (Unpublished Ph.D. Dissertation in History, Northwestern University, Evanston, Ill.)

Townsend, Joan B.
1965   Ethnohistory and Culture Change of the Iliamna Tanaina. (Unpublished Ph.D. Dissertation in Anthropology, University of California, Los Angeles.)

1974 Journals of Nineteenth Century Russian Priests to the Tanaina: Cook Inlet, Alaska. *Arctic Anthropology* 11(1):1–30.

Tozzer, Alfred M.
1935 Biographical Memoir of Frederic Ward Putnam, 1839–1915. *National Academy of Sciences, Biographical Memoirs* 16(4). Washington.

Tracey, Ebenezer
1845 Memoir of the Life of Jeremiah Evarts, Esq. Boston: Crocker and Brewster.

Tracey, Joseph
1840 History of the American Board of Commissioners for Foreign Missions. Pp. 9–346 in History of the American Missions to the Heathen from Their Commencement to the Present Time. Joseph Tracey et al., eds. Worcester, Mass.: Spooner and Howland. (Reprinted: Johnson Reprint, New York, 1970.)

Tracey, Joseph, Solomon Peck, Enoch Mudge, William Cutter, and Enoch Mack
1840 History of American Missions to the Heathen: From Their Commencement to the Present Time. Worcester, Mass.: Spooner and Howland.

Trafzer, Clifford E.
1986 Indians, Superintendents, and Councils: Northwestern Indian Policy, 1850–1855. Lanham, Md.: University Press of America.

Trani, Eugene P.
1975 The Secretaries of the Department of the Interior, 1849–1969. Washington: Smithsonian Institution, National Anthropological Archives.

Trautmann, Thomas R.
1987 Lewis Henry Morgan and the Invention of Kinship. Berkeley: University of California Press.

Trefousse, Hans L.
1982 Carl Schurz: A Biography. Knoxville: University of Tennessee Press.

Trelease, Allen W.
1960 Indian Affairs in Colonial New York: The Seventeenth Century. Ithaca, N.Y.: Cornell University Press.

Trennert, Robert A., Jr.
1972 The Mormons and the Office of Indian Affairs: The Conflict Over Winter Quarter, 1846–1848. *Nebraska History* 53(3):381–400.

1973 William Medill's War with the Indian Traders, 1847. *Ohio History* 82(1–2):43–62.

1974 A Grand Failure: The Continental Indian Exhibition of 1876. *Prologue* 6(2):118–179.

1975 Alternative to Extinction: Federal Indian Policy and the Beginnings of the Reservation System, 1846–1851. Philadelphia: Temple University Press.

1979 Peaceably If They Will, Forceably If They Must: The Phoenix Indian School, 1890–1901. *Journal of Arizona History* 20(3):297–322.

1979a William Medill, 1845–49. Pp. 29–39 in The Commissioners of Indian Affairs, 1824–1977. Robert M. Kvasnicka and Herman J. Viola, eds. Lincoln: University of Nebraska Press.

1979b Luke Lea, 1850–53. Pp. 49–56 in The Commissioners of Indian Affairs, 1824–1977. Robert M. Kvasnicka and Herman J. Viola, eds. Lincoln: University of Nebraska Press.

1981 Indian Traders on the Middle Border: The House of Ewing, 1827–54. Lincoln: University of Nebraska Press.

Trigger, Bruce G.
1968 The French Presence in Huronia: The Structure of Franco-Huron Relations in the First Half of the Seventeenth Century. *Canadian Historical Review* 49(2):107–141.

1971 Champlain Judged by His Indian Policy: A Different View of Early Canadian History. *Anthropologica* n.s. 13(1–2):85–114.

1971a The Mohawk-Mahican War (1624–28): The Establishment of a Pattern. *Canadian Historical Review* 52(3):276–286.

1976 The Children of Aataentsic: A History of the Huron People to 1660. 2 vols. Montreal: McGill-Queen's University Press.

1980 Archaeology and the Image of the American Indian. *American Antiquity* 45(4):662–676.

Trowbridge, Charles C.
1938 Meeārmeear Traditions [1824–25]. Vernon Kinietz, ed. *University of Michigan, Museum of Anthropology, Occasional Contributions* 7. Ann Arbor.

1939 Shawnee Traditions [1824–25]. Vernon Kinietz and Erminie W. Voegelin, eds. *University of Michigan, Museum of Anthropology, Occasional Contributions* 9. Ann Arbor.

Trudeau, Pierre
1972 Remarks on Aboriginal and Treaty Rights; Excerpts from a Speech Given August 8th, 1969, in Vancouver, British Columbia. Pp. 331–332 in Native Rights in Canada. Peter A. Cumming and Neil H. Mickenberg, eds. 2d ed. Toronto: Indian-Eskimo Association with General Publishing Company.

Trudel, Marcel
1960 L'Esclavage au Canada français: Histoire et conditions de l'esclavage. Quebec: Les Presses Universitaires Laval.

1973 The Beginnings of New France, 1524–1663. Toronto: McClelland and Stewart.

1979 Histoire de la Nouvelle-France. 3 vols. Montreal: Fides.

Trueblood, Benjamin F.
1897 Mohonk and Its Conferences. *New England Magazine* n.s. 16(4):447–464.

Tucker, Glenn
1956 Tecumseh, Vision of Glory. Indianapolis, Ind.: Bobbs-Merrill.

Turner, Frederick W.
1980 Beyond Geography: The Western Spirit Against the Wilderness. New York: Viking Press.

Turner, George
1836 Traits of Indian Character: As Generally Applicable to the Aborigines of North America. 2 vols. Philadelphia: Key and Biddle.

Turner, John P.
1950 The North-west Mounted Police, 1875–1893. 2 vols. Ottawa: E. Cloutier, King's Printer.

Turner, Katharine C.
1951 Red Men Calling on the Great White Father. Norman: University of Oklahoma Press.

Tuska, Jon
1970–1971 In Retrospect: Tim McCoy. *Views and Reviews* 2(1):10–27, (2):12–29, (3):22–40, (4):12–41.

1985 The American West in Film: Critical Approaches to the Western. Westport, Conn.: Greenwood Press.

Twain, Mark *see* Clemens, Samuel L.

Twitchell, Ralph E.
1911–1917   The Leading Facts of New Mexico History. 5 vols. Cedar Rapids, Iowa: The Torch Press.

————, comp.
1914   The Spanish Archives of New Mexico. 2 vols. Cedar Rapids, Iowa: The Torch Press.

————
1924   Dr. Josiah Gregg, Historian of the Santa Fe Trail *Publications of the Historical Society of New Mexico* 26. Santa Fe.

Tyerman, Luke
1873   The Oxford Methodists: Memoirs of the Rev. Messrs. Clayton, Ingham, Gambold, Hervey and Broughton, with Biographical Notices of Others. New York: Harper and Brothers.

Tyler, Ron, ed.
1982   Alfred Jacob Miller: Artist on the Oregon Trail. Fort Worth, Tex.: Amon Carter Museum.

Tyler, S. Lyman
1973   A History of Indian Policy. Washington: U.S. Government Printing Office.

Tymchuk, Michael
1984   Skeletal Remains: In Defense of Sensitivity and Compromise. *Council for Museum Anthropology Newsletter* 8(3):2–8.

Uğurkan, Turhan
1956   Eskimo cocuğu. Istanbul: Ozyürek yay.

Underhill, John
1638   Newes from America; or, A New and Experimentall Discoverie of New England. London: J.D. for Peter Cole. (Reprinted: *Massachusetts Historical Society Collections 3d ser.*, Vol. 6:1–28, 1837.)

United Church Committee on Indian Work
[1957]   A Mission to Indian Americans in the City: Summary Report of a Survey by A.Z. Mann. [Minneapolis, St. Paul, Minn.]: no publisher.

United States
1828–1836   Laws Respecting Public Lands. 2 vols. Washington: Gales and Seaton.

U.S. Bureau of Indian Affairs
1946   Indians in the War. Chicago: U.S. Department of the Interior, Bureau of Indian Affairs.

————
1973   Federal Indian Policies . . . from the Colonial Period Through the Early 1970's. Washington: U.S. Government Printing Office.

————
1986   American Indians Today: Answers to Your Questions. Washington: U.S. Government Printing Office.

U.S. Bureau of Indian Affairs. Office of Indian Education Programs
1981   Statistics Concerning Indian Education, Fiscal Year 1979. Washington: U.S. Government Printing Office.

U.S. Commission on Civil Rights
1981   Indian Tribes; A Continuing Quest for Survival: A Report of the United States Commission on Civil Rights. Washington: U.S. Government Printing Office.

U.S. Commission on Organization of the Executive Branch of Government
1949   Social Security and Education, Indian Affairs: A Report to Congress. *81st Cong., 1st sess. House Document* No. 129. Washington: U.S. Government Printing Office.

U.S. Congress
1832–1856   Annals of Congress. 42 vols. Washington: U.S. Government Printing Office.

————
1873   A Compilation of All the Treaties Between the United States and the Indian Tribes Now in Force as Law. Washington: U.S. Government Printing Office.

U.S. Congress. House. Committee on Indian Affairs
1944   An Investigation to Determine Whether the Changed Status of the Indian Requires a Revision of the Laws and Regulations Affecting the American Indian. Report of the Select Committee to Investigate Indian Affairs and Conditions . . . .Pursuant to H. Res. 166. *78 Cong., 2d sess. House Report No. 2091 (Serial No. 10848).* Washington: U.S. Government Printing Office.

U.S. Congress. House. Committee on Interior and Insular Affairs
1953   Report with Respect to the House Resolution Authorizing the Committee on Interior and Insular Affairs to Conduct an Investigation of the Bureau of Indian Affairs; Pursuant to H. Res. 698. *82d Cong., 2d sess. House Report No. 2503 (Serial No. 11582)* Washington: U.S. Government Printing Office.

U.S. Congress. Senate
1867   Condition of the Indian Tribes: Report of the Joint Special Committee, Appointed Under Joint Resolution of March 3, 1865, With an Appendix. *39th Cong., 2d sess., Senate Report No. 156 (Serial No. 1279).* Washington: U.S. Government Printing Office.

U.S. Congress. Senate. Committee on Interior and Insular Affairs
1968   Alaska Native Claims. Hearings on S. 2906, February 8–10. Washington: U.S. Government Printing Office.

U.S. Congress. Senate. Committee on the Judiciary
1976   Revolutionary Activities within the United States: The American Indian Movement; Report of the Subcommittee to Investigate the Administration of the Internal Security Act and Other Internal Security Laws. (Committee Print) *94th Cong. 2d sess.* Washington: U.S. Government Printing Office.

U.S. Congress. Senate. Special Sub-Committee on Indian Education
1969   Indian Education: A National Tragedy, A National Challenge. [Kennedy Report] *91st Cong., 1st sess. Senate Report No. 501 (Serial No. 12836).* Washington.

U.S. Department of Health and Human Services. Health Resources and Services Administration
[1984]   Indian Health Service: A Comprehensive Health Care Program for American Indians and Alaska Natives. Rockville, Md.: U.S. Department of Health and Human Services, Public Health Service.

————
1986   Indian Health Service: Chart Series Book, April 1986. Washington: U.S. Government Printing Office.

U.S. Department of the Interior, and U.S. Department of Health and Human Services
1984   Moving Toward Self-Sufficiency for Indian People: Accomplishments 1983–84. Washington: U.S. Government Printing Office.

U.S. Department of the Interior. Office of the Solicitor
1940   Statutory Compilation of the Indian Law Survey: A Compendium of Federal Laws and Treaties Relating to Indians. 46 vols. Mimeo.

————
1958   Federal Indian Law. Washington: U.S. Government Printing Office.

U.S. Geological Survey
1980   Indian Lands: Oil, Gas, and Minerals on Indian Reservations (in production, 1978). Map. Reston, Va.: U.S. Geological Survey.

U.S. Library of Congress, Law Library. Foreign Law Section *see* Gsovski, Vladimir

U.S. National Archives
1802–1867   Records of the Russian-American Company: Correspondence of Governors General. (Rolls 27–28, 31–33, 36, 39,

41–42, File No. M-11, Loc. 10-37-4 in the National Archives, Washington.)

1940   Records of the Oregon Superintendency of Indian Affairs, 1848–73. (Microfilm Publication M2. 29 rolls. Natural Resources Branch, Record Group 75 in National Archives, Washington.)

1957   Letters Received by the Office of Indian Affairs, 1824–81: Utah Superintendency. (Microfilm Publication M234. 962 rolls. Natural Resources Branch, Record Group 75 in National Archives, Washington.)

1960   Documents Relating to the Negotiation of Ratified and Unratified Treaties with Various Indian Tribes, 1801–1869. (Microfilm Publication T494. 10 rolls. Natural Resources Branch, Record Group 75 in National Archives, Washington.)

1966   Ratified Indian Treaties of the United States, 1722–1869. (Microfilm Publication M668, 16 reels, Natural Resources Branch, Record Group 11 in U.S. National Archives, Washington.)

1972   Select Catalog of National Archives Microfilm Publications: The American Indian. *National Archives Publication 72-27.* Washington.

U.S. National Park Service
1963   Soldier and Brave; Indian and Military Affairs in the Trans-Mississippi West. New York: Harper and Row.

U.S. War Department
1826   Indian Treaties, and Laws and Regulations Relating to Indian Affairs; to Which Is Added an Appendix, Containing the Proceedings of the Old Congress, and Other Important State Papers, in Relation to Indian Affairs. Samuel S. Hamilton, comp. Washington City: Way and Gideon, Printers.

1880–1901   The War of the Rebellion: A Compilation of the Official Records of the Union and Confederate Armies. 70 vols. in 128. Washington: U.S. Government Printing Office.

Unrau, William E.
1971   The Kansa Indians: A History of the Wind People, 1673–1873. Norman: University of Oklahoma Press.

1979   Nathaniel Green Taylor, 1867–69. Pp. 115–122 in The Commissioners of Indian Affairs, 1824–1977. Robert M. Kvasnicka and Herman J. Viola, eds. Lincoln: University of Nebraska Press.

Upham, Steadman
1982   Politics and Power: An Economic and Political History of the Western Pueblo. New York: Academic Press.

Upton, Leslie F.S.
1973   Indian Affairs in Colonial New Brunswick. (Manuscript in Upton's possession.)

1975   Indian Policy in Colonial Nova Scotia, 1783–1871. *Acadiensis* 5(1):3–31.

1975a   Colonists and Micmacs. *Journal of Canadian Studies* 10(3):44–56.

1979   Micmacs and Colonists: Indian-White Relations in the Maritimes, 1713–1867. Vancouver: University of British Columbia Press.

Usher, Jean
1974   William Duncan of Metlakatla: A Victorian Missionary in British Columbia. Ottawa: National Museums of Canada.

Usher, John P.
1865   Report of the Secretary of the Interior for the Year 1864. *38th Cong., 2d sess. House Executive Document* No. 1(5), (Serial No. 1220). Washington: U.S. Government Printing Office.

Usher, Peter J.
1971   Fur Trade Posts of the Northwest Territories, 1870–1970. Ottawa: Department of Indian Affairs and Northern Development.

Usner, Daniel H., Jr.
1981   Frontier Exchange in the Lower Mississippi Valley: Race Relations and Economic Life in Colonial Louisiana, 1699–1783. (Unpublished Ph.D. Dissertation in History, Duke University, Durham, N.C.)

1985   The Deerskin Trade in French Louisiana. Pp. 75–93 in *Proceedings of the 10th Meeting of the French Colonial Historical Society*, April 12–14, 1984. Philip P. Boucher, ed. Lanham, Md.: University Press of America.

Utley, Robert M.
1963   The Last Days of the Sioux Nation. New Haven, Conn.: Yale University Press.

————, ed.
1964   Battlefield and Classroom: Four Decades with the American Indian. New Haven, Conn.: Yale University Press.

1967   Frontiersmen in Blue: The United States Army and the Indian, 1848–1865. New York: Macmillan.

1973   Frontier Regulars: The United States Army and the Indian, 1866–1891. New York: Macmillan.

1984   The Indian Frontier of the American West, 1846–1890. Albuquerque: University of New Mexico Press.

Utley, Robert M., and Wilcomb E. Washburn
1977   History of the Indian Wars. Anne Moffat and Richard F. Snow, eds. New York: American Heritage Books.

Vachon, André
1960   L'Eau-de-vie dans la société indienne. Pp. 23–32 in *Canadian Historical Association Report for 1960*. John P. Heisler and Paul E. Dumas, eds. Ottawa.

Vail, Robert W.G., ed.
1949   The Voice of the Old Frontier. Philadelphia: University of Pennsylvania Press. (Reprinted: Octagon Books, New York, 1970.)

Valaam Monastery
1978   The Russian Orthodox Religious Mission in America, 1794–1837 [1894]. Richard A. Pierce, ed. Colin Bearne, trans. Kingston, Ont.: The Limestone Press.

Vancouver, George
1798   A Voyage of Discovery to the North Pacific Ocean, and Round the World; in Which the Coast of North-west America Has Been Carefully Examined and Accurately Surveyed . . . .3 vols. London: G.G. and J. Robinson and J. Edwards. (Reprinted: Da Capo Press, New York, 1967.)

Van Der Beets, Richard, ed.
[1973]   Held Captive by Indians: Selected Narratives, 1642–1836. Knoxville: University of Tennessee Press.

Van Doren, Carl
1938   Benjamin Franklin. New York: Viking Press.

Van Doren, Carl, and Julian P. Boyd, eds.
1938   Indian Treaties Printed by Benjamin Franklin, 1736–1762. Philadelphia: Historical Society of Pennsylvania.

Van Every, Dale
1966   Disinherited: The Lost Birthright of the American Indian. New York: Morrow.

Van Hichtum, N.
1960   Kell, de jonge Koper-Eskimo. Alkmaar, The Netherlands: Kluitman.

Van Hoeven, James W.
1972   Salvation and Indian Removal: The Career Biography of the Rev. John F. Schermerhorn, Indian Commissioner. (Unpublished Ph.D. Dissertation in Religion, Vanderbilt University, Nashville, Tenn.)

Van Kirk, Sylvia
1980   Fur Trade Social History: Some Recent Trends. Pp. 160–173 in Old Trails and New Directions: Papers of the Third North American Fur Trade Conference. Carol M. Judd and Arthur J. Ray, eds. Toronto: University of Toronto Press.

1980a   Many Tender Ties: Women in Fur Trade Society, 1670–1870. Winnipeg, Man.: Watson and Dwyer.

Van Laer, Arnold J.F., ed. and trans.
1908   Van Rensselaer Bowier Manuscripts, Being the Letters of Kiliaen Van Rensselaer, 1630–1643, and Other Documents Relating to the Colony of Rensselaerswyck. Albany: University of the State of New York.
————, ed. and trans.
1920–1923   Minutes of the Court of Fort Orange and Beverwyck, 1652–1660. 2 vols. Albany: University of the State of New York.
————, ed. and trans.
1922   Minutes of the Court of Rensselaerswyck, 1648–1652. Albany: University of the State of New York.
————, ed. and trans.
1924   Documents Relating to New Netherland, 1624–1626, in the Henry E. Huntington Library. San Marino, Calif: Henry E. Huntington Library and Art Gallery.
————, ed. and trans.
1926–1932   Minutes of the Court of Albany, Rensselaerswyck and Schenectady, 1668–1685. 3 vols. Albany: University of the State of New York.
————, ed. and trans.
1932   Correspondence of Jeremias van Rensselaer, 1651–1674. Albany: University of the State of New York.
————, ed. and trans.
1935   Correspondence of Maria van Rensselaer, 1669–1689. Albany: University of the State of New York.

Van Stone, James W.
1967   Eskimos of the Nushagak River: An Ethnographic History. *University of Washington Publications in Anthropology 15.* Seattle.

1979   Ingalik Contact Ecology: An Ethnohistory of the Lower-Middle Yukon, 1790–1935. *Fieldiana: Anthropology* 71. Chicago.

Van Well, Mary S.
1942   The Educational Aspects of the Missions in the Southwest. Milwaukee, Wis.: Marquette University Press.

Vardac, A. Nicholas
1949   Stage to Screen: Theatrical Method from Garrick to Griffith. Cambridge, Mass.: Harvard University Press. (Reprinted: Da Capo Press, New York, 1987.)

Vaschenko, Alexander
1987   Some Russian Responses to North American Indian Cultures. Pp. 307–320 in Indians and Europe. Christian F. Feest, ed. Aachen, Germany: Rader.

Vasconcelos, José
1948   La Raza cósmica: Mision de la Raza Iberoamericana, Argentina y Brazil. Mexico City: Espasa-Calpe Mexicana.

Vasconcelos, José, and Manuel Gamio
1926   Aspects of Mexican Civilization (Lectures on the Harris Foundation, 1926). Chicago: University of Chicago Press.

Vaughan, Alden T.
1965   New England Frontier: Puritans and Indians, 1620–1675. Boston: Little, Brown.

1978   "Expulsion of the Salvages:" English Policy and the Virginia Massacre of 1622. *William and Mary Quarterly 3d ser.,* Vol. 35(1):57–84. Williamsburg, Va.

1979   New England Frontier: Puritans and Indians, 1620–1675. Rev. ed. New York: W.W. Norton.

1982   From White Man to Redskin: Changing Anglo-American Perceptions of the American Indian. *American Historical Review* 87(4):917–953.

1983   Narratives of North American Indian Captivity: A Selective Bibliography. New York: Garland Publishing.

Vaughan, Alden T., and Edward W. Clark, eds.
1981   Puritans Among the Indians: Accounts of Captivity and Redemption, 1676–1724. Cambridge, Mass.: Belknap Press.

Vaughan, Thomas, and Bill Holm
1982   Soft Gold: The Fur Trade and Cultural Exchange on the Northwest Coast of America. Portland: Oregon State Historical Society.

Vaughn, Jesse W.
1956   With Crook at the Rosebud. Harrisburg, Pa.: Stackpole.

1966   Indian Fights: New Facts on Seven Encounters. Norman: University of Oklahoma Press.

Vdovin, Innokentiĭ S., ed.
1979   Khristianstvo i Lamaizm u korennogo naseleniia Sibiri [Christianity and Lamaism Among the Aboriginal Population of Siberia]. Leningrad: Nauka.

Velie, Alan R.
1981   Four American Indian Literary Masters: N. Scott Momaday, James Welch, Leslie Marmon Silko, and Gerald Vizenor. Norman: University of Oklahoma Press.

Veniaminov, Ivan Evĭeevich Popov, comp.
1840   Zapiski ob ostrovakh Unalashkinskago otdĭela [Notes on the Islands of the Unalaska District]. 3 vols. in 2. St. Petersburg: Russian-American Company.

1886–1888   Tvoreniia Innokentiia, Mitropolita Moskovskago [Works of Innocent, Metropolitan of Moscow]. Ivan P. Barsukov, ed. 3 vols. in 2. Moscow: Sinodal'naia Tip.

1899   Natavlenie Vysokopreosviashchennago Innokentiia, byvshago Arkhiepiskopa Kamchatskago, Kurilskago, i Aleutskago [Teachings of the Most Reverend Innocent, Late Archbishop of Kamchatka and the Kuril and Aleutian Islands]. New York: Amerikanskiĭ Pravoslavnyi Viestnik.

1972   The Condition of the Orthodox Church in Russian America: Innokentiĭ Veniaminov's History of the Russian Church in Alaska. Robert Nichols and Robert Croskey, eds. and trans. *Pacific Northwest Quarterly* 63(2):41–54.

1984   Notes on the Islands of the Unalaska District [1840]. Lydia T. Black and R.H. Geoghegan, trans. Richard A. Pierce, ed. Kingston, Ont.: The Limestone Press.

Vespucci, Amerigo
1916   Mundus novus [1503–1504]. Princeton, N.J.: Princeton University Press.

Viatte, Auguste
1954   Histoire littéraire de l'Amérique française des origines à 1950. Quebec: Laval.

Victor, Francis F.
1870   The River of the West: Life and Adventure in the Rocky Mountains and Oregon Embracing Events in the Life-time of a Mountain Man and Pioneer, with The Early History of the North-western Slope. Hartford, Conn.: The Columbian Book Company.

Villoz, Robert
1956   Terres glacées. Neuchâtel, Switzerland: Delachaux et Niestlé.

Viola, Herman J.
1972   Invitation to Washington: A Bid for Peace. *American West* 9(1):19–31.

1974   Thomas L. McKenney: Architect of America's Early Indian Policy, 1816–1830. Chicago: Swallow Press.

1976   The Indian Legacy of Charles Bird King. Washington: Smithsonian Institution Press.

1977   How *Did* an Indian Chief Really Look? *Smithsonian* 8(3):100–104.

1981   Diplomats in Buckskins: A History of Indian Delegations in Washington City. Washington: Smithsonian Institution Press.

Vitzhum, Richard C.
1974   The American Compromise: Theme and Method in the Histories of Bancroft, Parkman, and Adams. Norman: University of Oklahoma Press.

Vizenor, Gerald R.
1978   Darkness in Saint Louis Bearheart. Saint Paul, Minn.: Truck Press.

1981   Earthdivers: Tribal Narratives of Mixed Descent. Minneapolis: University of Minnesota Press.

Voegelin, Erminie W.
1954   A Note from the Chairman. *Ethnohistory* 1(1):1–3.

Vogel, Claude L.
1928   The Capuchins in French Louisiana (1722–1766). *Catholic University of America Studies in American Church History* 7. Washington.

Vogel, Virgil J.
1970   American Indian Medicine. Norman: University of Oklahoma Press.

Voget, Fred W.
1960   Man and Culture: An Essay in Changing Anthropological Interpretation. *American Anthropologist* 62(6):943–965.

1967   Progress, Science, History and Evolution in Eighteenth and Nineteenth Century Anthropology. *Journal of the History of Behavioral Sciences* 3(2):132–155.

Voltaire, François Marie A.
1767   Le Huron; ou, l'Ingénu. 2d ed. Lausanne, Switzerland: no publisher.

Volwiler, Albert T.
1926   George Croghan and the Westward Movement, 1741–1782. Cleveland, Ohio: Arthur H. Clark. (Reprinted: AMS Press, New York, 1971.)

Voorhis, Ernst
1930   Historic Forts and Trading Posts of the French Regime and of the English Fur Trading Companies. Ottawa: Department of the Interior.

Vorpahl, Ben M.
1972   My Dear Wister: The Frederic Remington - Owen Wister Letters. Palo Alto, Calif.: American West Publishing Company.

1978   Frederic Remington and the West: With the Eye of the Mind. Austin: University of Texas Press.

Voss, Tage
1960   Pawnee's sidste kamp. Copenhagen: Aschehoug.

Wade, Mason
1942   Francis Parkman: Heroic Historian. New York: Viking Press. (Reprinted: Archon Books, Hamden, Conn., 1972.)

Waggett, George M.
1947   The Oblates of Mary Immaculate in the Pacific Northwest of U.S.A., 1847–1878. *Etudes Oblates* 6 (January–March):7–88. Ottawa.

Wainwright, Nicholas B., ed.
1947   George Croghan's Journal, 1759–1763; from the Original in the Cadwallader Collection of the Historical Society of Pennsylvania. *Pennsylvania Magazine of History and Biography* 71(4). Philadelphia.

1959   George Croghan: Wilderness Diplomat. Chapel Hill: University of North Carolina Press.

Waldman, Carl
1985   Atlas of the North American Indian. Molly Brown, illus. New York: Facts on File Publications.

Waldman, Harry, et al., eds.
1978   Dictionary of Indians of North America. 3 vols. St. Clair Shores, Mich.: Scholarly Press.

Walker, Alexander
1982   An Account of a Voyage to the North West Coast of America in 1785 and 1786. Robin Fisher and J.M. Bumsted, eds. Toronto: Douglas and McIntyre.

Walker, Deward E., Jr.
1968   Conflict and Schism in Nez Percé Acculturation: A Study of Religion and Politics. Pullman: Washington State University Press. (Reprinted: University of Idaho Press, Moscow, 1985.)

Walker, Francis A.
1874   The Indian Question. Boston: J.R. Osgood.

Walker, James R.
1917   The Sun Dance and Other Ceremonies of the Oglala Division of the Teton Dakota. *Anthropological Papers of the American Museum of Natural History* 16(2):49–221. New York. (Reprinted: AMS Press, New York, 1979.)

1980   Lakota Belief and Ritual. Raymond J. DeMallie and Elaine A. Jahner, eds. Lincoln: University of Nebraska Press.

1982   Lakota Society. Raymond J. DeMallie, ed. Lincoln: University of Nebraska Press.

1983   Lakota Myth. Elaine A. Jahner, ed. Lincoln: University of Nebraska Press.

Walker, James W.
1971   The Indian in Canadian Historical Writing. *Canadian Historical Association Historical Papers for 1971*:21–51. Ottawa.

Walker, Robert S.
1931   Torchlights to the Cherokees: The Brainerd Mission. New York: Macmillan.

Walker, William
1939   The Southern Harmony Songbook [1835]. New York: Hastings House.

Walker-McNeil, Pearl L.
1979   The Carlisle Indian School: A Study of Acculturation. (Unpublished Ph.D. Dissertation in Anthropology, American University, Washington.)

Wallace, Anthony F.C.
1949   King of the Delawares: Teedyuscung, 1700–1763. Philadelphia: University of Pennsylvania Press. (Reprinted: Books for Libraries Press, Freeport, N.Y., 1970.)

1951   The Frank G. Speck Collection. *Proceedings of the American Philosophical Society* 95(3):286–289. Philadelphia.

1970   Death and Rebirth of the Seneca. New York: Knopf.

801

Wallace, Ernest
1964   Ranald S. Mackenzie on the Texas Frontier. Lubbock: West
            Texas Museum Association.
_____, ed.
1967–1968   Ranald S. Mackenzie's Official Correspondence Relating to
            Texas, 1871–1873; 1873–1979. 2 vols. Lubbock, Tex.: West
            Texas Museum Association.

Wallace, Paul A.W.
1945   Conrad Weiser, 1696–1760, Friend of Colonist and Mo-
            hawk. Philadelphia: University of Pennsylvania Press.
            (Reprinted: Russell and Russell, New York, 1971.)

_____
1954   Cooper's Indians. New York History 35(4):423–446.
_____, ed.
1958   Thirty Thousand Miles with John Heckewelder. Pittsburgh,
            Pa.: University of Pittsburgh Press. (Reprinted as: The
            Travels of John Heckewelder in Frontier America, Univer-
            sity of Pittsburgh Press, Pittsburgh, Pa., 1985.)

Wallace, W. Stewart
1954   The Pedlars from Quebec; And Other Papers on the
            Nor'westers. Toronto: Ryerson Press.

Walsh, Martin
1982   The Condemnation of Carnival in the Jesuit Relations.
            Michigan Academician 15(1):13–26.

Walsh, Richard J.
1928   The Making of Buffalo Bill. Indianapolis, Ind.: Bobbs-
            Merrill.

Waltmann, Henry G.
1962   The Interior Department, War Department and Indian
            Policy, 1865–1887. (Unpublished Ph.D. Dissertation in
            History, University of Nebraska, Lincoln.)

Walters, Anna Lee
1985   The Sun Is Not Merciful: Short Stories. Ithaca, N.Y.:
            Firebrand Books.

Walters, Raymond, Jr.
1957   Albert Gallatin: Jeffersonian Financier and Diplomat. New
            York: Macmillan. (Reprinted: University of Pittsburgh
            Press, Pittsburgh, Pa, 1969.)

Wanken, Helen M.
1981   "Woman's Sphere" and Indian Reform: The Women's
            National Indian Association, 1879–1901. (Unpublished
            Ph.D. Dissertation in History, Marquette University, Mil-
            waukee, Wisc.)

Warman, P.C.
1903   Catalogue of the Published Writings of John Wesley Powell.
            Pp. 131–187 in John Wesley Powell: Proceedings of a
            Meeting Commemorative of His Distinguished Services,
            Held in Columbian University Under the Auspices of the
            Washington Academy of Sciences, February 16, 1903.
            Proceedings of the Washington Academy of Sciences 5 (July
            18):99–187. Washington.

Warner, Mikell D., and Harriet D. Munnick, eds. and trans.
1972   Catholic Church Records of the Pacific Northwest: Van-
            couver, Vols. I and II; and Stellamaris Mission. St. Paul,
            Oreg.: French Prairie Press.

Washburn, Cephas
1869   Reminiscences of the Indians. Richmond, Va.: Presbyterian
            Committee of Publication. (Reprinted: Press-Argus, Van
            Buren, Ark., 1955.)

Washburn, Wilcomb E.
1957   The Governor and the Rebel: A History of Bacon's
            Rebellion in Virginia. Chapel Hill: University of North
            Carolina Press.

_____
1957a   A Moral History of Indian-White Relations. Ethnohistory
            4(1):47–61.

_____
1959   The Moral and Legal Justifications for Dispossessing the
            Indians. Pp. 15–33 in Seventeenth Century America: Essays

in Colonial History. James M. Smith, ed. Chapel Hill:
            University of North Carolina Press.

_____
1962   The Meaning of "Discovery" in the Fifteenth and Sixteenth
            Centuries. American Historical Review 68(1):1–21.

_____
1964   The Indian and the White Man. New York: New York
            University Press.

_____
1966   Symbol, Utility, and Aesthetics in the Indian Fur Trade.
            Minnesota History 40(4):198–202.

_____
1966a   Logan's Speech, 1774. Pp. 60–64 in Vol. 1 of An American
            Primer. Daniel J. Boorstin, ed. 2 vols. Chicago: University
            of Chicago Press.

_____
1971   Red Man's Land/White Man's Law: A Study of the Past
            and Present Status of the American Indian. New York:
            Charles Scribner.

_____
1973   The American Indian and the United States: A Documenta-
            ry History. 4 vols. New York: Random House.

_____
1973a   James Adair's "Noble Savage" in The Colonial Legacy. Vol.
            3–4: Historians of Nature and Man's Nature; Early
            Nationalist Historians. Lawrence Leder, ed. New York:
            Harper and Row.

_____
1975   The Indian in America. New York: Harper and Row.

_____
1975a   The Assault on Indian Tribalism: The General Allotment
            Law (Dawes Act) of 1887. Philadelphia: J.B. Lippincott.
            (Reprinted: R.E. Krieger, Malabar, Fla., 1986.)

_____
1976   The Clash of Morality in the American Forest. Pp. 335–350
            in Vol. 1 of First Images of America: The Impact of the New
            World on the Old. Fredi Chiappelli, ed. 2 vols. Berkeley:
            University of California Press.
_____, ed.
1977–1983   The Garland Library of Narratives of North American
            Indian Captivities. (311 titles in 111 volumes). New York:
            Garland.

_____
1981   The Indian Symbol: A Positive Stereotype. The Dartmouth
            Review, February 9:13.

_____
1984   A Fifty-year Perspective on the Indian Reorganization Act.
            American Anthropologist 86(2):279–289.

_____
1985   Ethical Perspectives in North American Ethnology. Pp.
            50–64 in Social Contexts of American Ethnology,
            1840–1984. Proceedings of the American Ethnological Soci-
            ety, 1984. Washington.

_____
1987   Stephen Saunders Webb's Interpretation of Bacon's Rebel-
            lion. Virginia Magazine of History and Biography
            95(3):339–352.

Wasserman, Maurice M.
1954   The American Indian as Seen by the Seventeenth Century
            Chroniclers. (Unpublished Ph.D. Dissertation in History,
            University of Pennsylvania, Philadelphia.)

Waters, Frank
1942   The Man Who Killed the Deer. New York: Farrar and
            Rinehart.

_____
1963   Book of the Hopi. New York: Viking Press.

_____
1966   The Woman at Otowi Crossing. Denver, Colo.: A. Swallow.
            (Reprinted: Ohio University Press, Athens, 1987.)

_____
1969   Book of the Hopi. New York: Ballantine Books. (Reprinted
            in 1972.)

802

Watkins, Arthur V.
1957   Termination of Federal Supervision: The Removal of
            Restrictions Over Indian Property and Person. *Annals of the
            American Academy of Political and Social Science*
            311(May):47–55. Philadelphia.

Watkins, Mel, ed.
1977   Dene Declaration. Pp. 3–4 in Dene Nation: The Colony
            Within. Toronto: University of Toronto Press.

Watson, Adam
1983   Diplomacy: The Dialogue Between States. New York:
            McGraw-Hill.

Wauchope, Robert
[1962]   Lost Tribes and Sunken Continents: Myth and Method in
            the Study of American Indians. Chicago: University of
            Chicago Press.

Wax, Murray L.
1972   Tenting with Malinowski. *American Sociological Review*
            37(1):1–13.

Weatherford, John W.
1956   Warren King Moorehead and His Papers. *Ohio Historical
            Quarterly* 65(2):179–190.

Weaver, Sally
1981   Making Canadian Indian Policy: The Hidden Agenda
            1968–1970. Toronto: University of Toronto Press.

Webb, Stephen S.
1984   1676: The End of American Independence. New York:
            Alfred A. Knopf.

Weber, David J.
1971   The Taos Trappers: The Fur Trade in the Far Southwest,
            1540–1846. Norman: University of Oklahoma Press.

———
1982   The Mexican Frontier, 1821–1846: The American South-
            west Under Mexico. Albuquerque: University of New
            Mexico Press.

———
1926   America in Imaginative German Literature of the First Half
            of the Nineteenth Century. *Columbia University Germanic
            Studies* 19. New York.

Weddle, Robert S.
1964   The San Sabá Mission, Spanish Pivot in Texas. Austin:
            University of Texas Press.

Wedel, Mildred M.
1971   J.-B. Bénard, Sieur de la Harpe: Visitor to the Wichitas in
            1719. *Great Plains Journal* 10(2):37–70.

———
1972–1973   Claude-Charles Dutisné: A Review of His 1719 Journeys.
            Great Plains Journal 12(1–2):4–25, 147–173.

———
1979   The Ethnohistoric Approach to Plains Caddoan Origins.
            Nebraska History 60(2):183–196.

Wedel, Waldo R.
1961   Prehistoric Man on the Great Plains. Norman: University
            of Oklahoma Press.

Weigley, Russell F.
1967   History of the United States Army. New York: Macmillan.

Weinberg, Albert K.
1935   Manifest Destiny: A Study of Nationalist Expansionism in
            American History. Baltimore, Md.: Johns Hopkins Univer-
            sity Press.

Weiser, Franz X.
1933   Der Sohn des weissen Häuptlings. Vienna: Fahne Mariens.

———
1936   Der Gesandte des grossen Geistes. Vienna: J. Habbel.

———
1969   Orimha der Irokese. Vienna: Kremayr and Scheriau.

———
1970   Orimha, der Waldläufer. Vienna: Kremayr and Scheriau.

Weist, Katherine M.
1973   Giving Away: The Ceremonial Distribution of Goods
            Among the Northern Cheyenne of Southeastern Montana.
            Plains Anthropologist 18(60):97–103.

———
1983   Beasts of Burden and Menial Slaves: Nineteenth Century
            Observations of Northern Plains Indian Women. Pp. 29–52
            in Hidden Half: Studies of Plains Indian Women. P. Albers
            and B. Medicine, eds. Washington: University Press of
            America.

Weist, Tom
1977   A History of the Cheyenne People. Billings: Montana
            Council for Indian Education.

Weitenkampf, Frank
1949   Early Pictures of North American Indians: A Question of
            Ethnology. *Bulletin of the New York Public Library*
            53(12):591–614.

———
1949a   How Indians Were Pictured in Earlier Days. *New-York
            Historical Society Quarterly* 33(4):213–222.

Welch, James
1974   Winter in the Blood. New York: Harper and Row.

———
1986   Fools Crow. New York: Viking.

Welch, Rebecca Hancock
1980   Alice Cunningham Fletcher, Anthropologist and Indian
            Rights Reformer. (Unpublished Ph.D. Dissertation in
            American Civilization, George Washington University,
            Washington.)

Wellcome, Henry S.
1887   The Story of Metlakhatla. New York: Saxon.

Wellman, Paul I.
1947   Death on Horseback: Seventy Years of War for the
            American West. Philadelphia: J.B. Lippincott.

Wells, Philip V.
1970   Historical Factors Controlling Vegetation Patterns and
            Floristic Distributions in the Central Plains Region of
            North America. Pp. 211–221 in Pleistocene and Recent
            Environments of the Central Great Plains. Wakefield Dort
            and J. Knox Jones, Jr., eds. *University of Kansas, Depart-
            ment of Geology, Special Publication* 3. Lawrence.

Welsh, Herbert
1892   How to Bring the Indian to Citizenship, and Citizenship to
            the Indian. Philadelphia: Indian Rights Association.

Welsh, Michael
1983   The Road to Assimilation: The Seminoles in Oklahoma,
            1839–1936. (Unpublished Ph.D. Dissertation in History,
            University of New Mexico, Albuquerque.)

Welsh, William
1874   Indian Office: Wrongs Doing and Reforms Needed, an
            Open Letter to President Grant. Philadelphia: no publisher.

Welskopf-Henrich, Liselotte
1951–1955   Die Söhne der grossen Bärin. Berlin: Altberliner Verlag.

———
1969   Stein mit Hörnern. Halle, Germany: Mitteldeutscher Ver-
            lag.

———
1972   Der siebenstufige Berg. Halle, Germany: Mitteldeutscher
            Verlag.

Weltfish, Gene.
1965   The Lost Universe: The Way of Life of the Pawnee. New
            York: Basic Books.

Wenhold, Lucy L., ed.
1936   A 17th Century Letter of Gabriel Díaz Vara Calderón,
            Bishop of Cuba, Describing the Indians and Indian Mis-
            sions of Florida. *Smithsonian Miscellaneous Collections*
            95(16). Washington.

Weppen, Johann A.
1783   Der Hessische Offizier in Amerika. Göttingen, Germany: Dietrich.

Wertenbaker, Thomas J.
1940   Torchbearer of the Revolution, the Story of Bacon's Rebellion and Its Leader. Princeton, N.J.: Princeton University Press.

Weslager, Clinton A.
1967   The English on the Delaware: 1610–1682. New Brunswick, N.J.: Rutgers University Press.

————
1972   The Delaware Indians: A History. New Brunswick, N.J.: Rutgers University Press.

Weslager, Clinton A., with Arthur R. Dunlap
1961   Dutch Explorers, Traders and Settlers in the Delaware Valley, 1609–1664. Philadelphia: University of Pennsylvania Press.

Wesley, John
1938   The Journal of the Rev. John Wesley, A.M. Nehemiah Curnock, ed. 8 vols. London: Epworth Press.

West, Ian M.
1961   Exhibitions of the Society. *Brand Book, English Westerners Society* 3(2).

West, Robert C.
1949   The Mining Community in Northern New Spain: The Parral Mining District. *Ibero-Americana* 30. Berkeley, Calif.

Westing, Irene J.
1971   Amelia Stone Quinton. Pp. 108–110 in Vol. 3 of Notable American Women, 1607–1950: A Biographical Dictionary. Edward T. James, ed. 3 vols. Cambridge, Mass.: Harvard University Press.

Weyler, Rex
1982   Blood of the Land: The Government and Corporate War Against the American Indian Movement. New York: Everest House.

Whalley, George
1960   Coppermine Martyrdom. *Queen's Quarterly*:591–610. Kingston, Ont.

Wheeler, Burton K., and Paul Healy
1962   Yankee from the West. Garden City, N.Y.: Doubleday. (Reprinted: Octagon Books, New York, 1977.)

Wheeler, Robert C., Walter A. Kenyon, Alan P. Woolworth, and Douglas A. Birk
1975   Voices from the Rapids: An Underwater Search for Fur Trade Artifacts, 1960–73. St. Paul: Minnesota Historical Society.

Wheelock, Eleazer
1763   A Plain and Faithful Narrative of the Original Design, Rise, Progress, and Present State of the Indian Charity School at Lebanon in Connecticut. Boston: Richard and Samuel Draper.

Whetten, Nathan L.
1948   Rural Mexico. Chicago: University of Chicago Press.

Whipple, Henry B.
1899   Lights and Shadows of a Long Episcopate; Being Reminiscences and Recollections of the Right Reverend Henry Benjamin Whipple, D.C., LL.D., Bishop of Minnesota. New York: Macmillan.

White, Andrew
1874   Relatio Itineris in Marylandiam [1635–1638]. William McSherry, comp. Edwin A. Dalrymple, ed. (*Maryland Historical Society Fund Publication* 7). Baltimore, Md.: J. Murphy.

————
1910   An Account of the Colony of the Lord Baron of Baltimore, 1633. Pp. 1–10 in Narratives of Early Maryland, 1633–1684. Clayton Colman Hall, ed. New York: Charles Scribner's Sons.

White, Elijah
1846   Concise View of Oregon Territory: Its Colonial and Indian Relations . . . Washington: T. Barnard.

————
1861   Testimonials and Records Together with Arguments in Favor of Special Action for Our Indian Tribes . . . Washington: R.A. Waters.

————
1879   Emigration to Oregon. (Manuscript in Bancroft Pacific Manuscripts, Bancroft Library, University of California, Berkeley.)

White, Eugene E.
1965   Experiences of a Special Indian Agent [1893]. Norman: University of Oklahoma Press.

White, G. Edward
1968   The Eastern Establishment and the Western Experience: The West of Frederic Remington, Theodore Roosevelt, and Owen Wister. New Haven, Conn.: Yale University Press.

White, Helen McCann
1966   Guide to a Microfilm Edition of the Lawrence Taliaferro Papers. St. Paul: Minnesota Historical Society.

White, Leonard D.
1951   The Jeffersonians: A Study in Administrative History, 1801–1829. New York: Macmillan.

White, Leslie A., ed.
1959   The Indian Journals, 1856–62. Ann Arbor: University of Michigan Press.

————
1963   The Ethnography and Ethnology of Franz Boas. *Texas Memorial Museum Bulletin* 6. Austin.

White, Richard
1978   The Winning of the West: The Expansion of the Western Sioux in the Eighteenth and Nineteenth Centuries. *Journal of American History* 65(2):319–343.

————
1980   Land Use, Environment, and Social Change: The Shaping of Island County, Washington. Seattle: University of Washington Press.

————
1983   The Roots of Dependency: Subsistence, Environment and Social Change Among the Choctaws, Pawnees, and Navajos. Lincoln: University of Nebraska Press.

Whitney, Lois
1934   Primitivism and the Idea of Progress in English Popular Literature. Baltimore, Md.: Johns Hopkins Press.

Whittemore, Charles P.
1961   A General of the Revolution: John Sullivan of New Hampshire. New York: Columbia University Press.

Whittier, John Greenleaf
1849   Leaves from Margaret Smith's Journal in the Province of Massachusetts Bay, 1678–9. Boston: Ticknor, Reed and Fields.

Wied, Maximilian, Prinz von
1839–1841 Reise in das innere Nord-Amerika in den Jahren 1832 bis 1834. 2 vols. Coblenz, Germany: J. Hoelscher.

Wied-Neuwied *see* Wied, Maximilian, Prinz von *see also* Maximilian, Prince of Wied

Wike, Joyce A.
1951   The Effect of the Maritime Fur Trade on Northwest Coast Indian Society. (Unpublished Ph.D. Dissertation in Political Science, Columbia University, New York City.)

Wildes, Harry E.
1941   Anthony Wayne, Trouble Shooter of the American Revolution. New York: Harcourt, Brace. (Reprinted: Greenwood Press, Westport, Conn., 1979.)

Wilhelmsen, Finn
1971   The Mardi Gras Indians. Pp. 50–53 in Portraits of New Orleans Jazz: Its Peoples and Places. Raymond J. Martinez, ed. New Orleans, La.: Hope.

————
1972   Creativity in the Songs of the Mardi Gras Indians of New Orleans, Louisiana. *Louisiana State University Folklore Miscellany* 3(3):56–74.

————
1972a   Verbal, Body and Territoriality Concepts Among the Mardi Gras Indians of New Orleans, Louisiana. (Unpublished report in Wilhemsen's possession.)

————
1972b   The Self Image in Black Culture and Its Bearing Upon the Mardi Gras Indians as a Social Institution. (Paper given at the Louisiana Folklore Society Meeting, April 29, 1972.)

Wilken, Robert L.
1955   Anselm Weber, O.F.M., Missionary to the Navaho, 1898–1921. Milwaukee, Wis.: Bruce

Wilkenshuis, Cornelis
1968   Kleine sneeuwveer. The Hague, The Netherlands: Van Goor Zonen.

Wilkins, Thurman
1970   Cherokee Tragedy: The Story of the Ridge Family and the Decimation of a People. New York: Macmillan.

Wilkinson, Charles F., and Eric R. Biggs
1977   The Evolution of the Termination Policy. *American Indian Law Review* 5(1):139–184.

Wilkinson, Means
1961   Greenwood, Sebastian County, Arkansas. Greenwood, Ark.: Farmer's Bank.

Will, George F., and George E. Hyde
1964   Corn Among the Indians of the Upper Missouri [1917]. Lincoln: University of Nebraska Press.

Willey, Gordon R., and Jeremy A. Sabloff
1980   A History of American Archaeology. 2d ed. San Francisco: W.H. Freeman.

Williams, Amelia W., and Eugene C. Barker, eds.
1938   The Writings of Sam Houston, 1813–1863. 8 vols. Austin: University of Texas Press. (Reprinted: Jenkins Publishing Company, Austin, Tex., 1970.)

Williams, Glyndwr
1983   The Hudson's Bay Company and the Fur Trade, 1670–1870. *The Beaver*, Outfit 314(2):4–86.

Williams, Roger
1643   A Key into the Language of America . . . .London: Gregory Dexter.

————
1645   Christenings Make Not Christians . . . .London: Jane Coe. (Reproduced from original in the British Museum.)

————
1963   The Complete Writings of Roger Williams [1866]. 7 vols. New York: Russell and Russell.

Williamson, Dan R.
1931   Al Sieber, Famous Scout of the Southwest. *Arizona Historical Review* 3(4):60–76.

Williamson, James A.
1931   A Short History of British Expansion. 2d ed. New York: Macmillan.

Willis, William S.
1963   Divide and Rule: Red, White, and Black in the Southeast. *Journal of Negro History* 48(3):157–176.

Wilson, Elinor
1972   Jim Beckwourth: Black Mountain Man and War Chief of the Crows. Norman: University of Oklahoma Press.

Wilson, Elizabeth I.
1953   Calendar of Papers of John Dougherty, 1832–1863. (Unpublished M.A. Thesis in History, St. Louis University, St. Louis, Mo.)

Wilson, J.Tuzo
1949   New Light on Hearne. *The Beaver*, Outfit 280 (June):14–18.

Wilson, John P.
1972   Awatovi—More Light on a Legend. *Plateau* 44(3):125–130.

Wilson, Thomas
1759   The Knowledge and Practice of Christianity Made Easy to the Meanest Capacities; or, An Essay Toward an Instruction for the Indians. 9th ed. London: D. Dod.

Winger, Otho
1936   The Lost Sister Among the Miamis. Elgin, Ill.: The Elgin Press.

Winship, George P.
1945   The Cambridge Press, 1638–1692. Philadelphia: University of Pennsylvania Press.

Winslow, Ola
1957   Master Roger Williams: A Biography. New York: MacMillan.

————
1968   John Eliot, Apostle to the Indians. Boston: Houghton Mifflin.

Winsor, Justin
1884–1889 Narrative and Critical History of America. 8 vols. Boston: Houghton Mifflin.

————
1889   The Progress of Opinion Respecting the Origin and Antiquity of Man in America. Pp. 369–412 in Vol. 1 of Narrative and Critical History of America. Justin Winsor, ed. 8 vols. Boston: Houghton Mifflin.

Winston, Sanford
1934   Indian Slavery in the Carolina Region. *Journal of Negro History* 19(4):431–440.

Winter, George
1948   The Journals and Indian Paintings of George Winter, 1837–1839. Indianapolis: Indiana Historical Society.

Wirt, William
1803   The Letters of the British Spy. Originally Published in the *Virginia Argus* in August and September, 1803 . . . .Richmond, Va.: Samuel Pleasants, Jr.

————
1817   Sketches of the Life and Character of Patrick Henry. Philadelphia: James Webster.

Wise, S.F.
1953   The Indian Diplomacy of John Graves Simcoe. Pp. 36–44 in *Canadian Historical Association Report*. Toronto.

Wisehart, Marion K.
1962   Sam Houston, American Giant. Washington: Robert B. Luce.

Wishart, David J.
1979   The Fur Trade of the American West, 1807–1840: A Geographical Synthesis. Lincoln: University of Nebraska Press.

Wissler, Clark
1914   The Influence of the Horse in the Development of Plains Culture. *American Anthropologist* 16(1):1–25.

————
1917   The American Indian: An Introduction to the Anthropology of the New World. New York: Douglas C. McMurtrie.

————
1923   Man and Culture. New York: T.Y. Crowell.

————
1938   Indian Cavalcade; or, On the Old-Time Indian Reservations. New York: Sheridan House.

————
1971   Red Man Reservations [1938]. New York: Collier Books.

805

Wister, Owen
1902   The Virginian: A Horseman of the Plains. New York: Macmillan.

Witt, Shirley H.
1965   Nationalistic Trends Among American Indians. *Midcontinent American Studies Journal* 6(2):51–74. Lawrence, Kans.

Wittek, Erhard [Fritz Steuben]
1930   Der fliegende Pfeil. Stuttgart, Germany: Franck.

————
1931   Der rote Sturm: Eine Erzählung aus dem ersten Indianerkriege um den Ohio . . . .Stuttgart, Germany: Franckh.

————
1932   Tecumseh und der Lederstrumpf. Stuttgart, Germany: Franckh.

————
1933   Schneller Fuss und Pfeilmädchen. Stuttgart, Germany: Franckh.

————
1934   Der strahlende Stern. Stuttgart, Germany: Franckh.

————
1936   Tecumseh, der Berglöwe. Stuttgart, Germany: Franckh.

————
1938   Der Sohn des Manitu. Stuttgart, Germany: Franckh.

[1953]   Tecumsehs Tod: Eine Erzählung vom Kampfe eines roten Mannes für sein Volk. Stuttgart, Germany: Franckh.

Wörishöffer, Sophie
1880   Auf dem Kriegspfade. Bielefeld, Germany: Velhagen and Klasing.

Wolf, Eric R.
1982   Europe and the People without History. Berkeley: University of California Press.

Wolfe, M.C.
1967   Greenland. Pp. 752–754 in Vol. 6 of New Catholic Encyclopedia. New York: McGraw-Hill.

Wollschläger, Hans
1965   Karl May in Selbstzeugnissen und Bilddokumenten. Hamburg, Germany: Rowohlt.

Women's National Indian Association
1883–1901   Annual Reports of the Women's National Indian Association. 19 vols. Philadelphia: The Association.

Wood, Louis A.
1922   The War Chief of the Six Nations: A Chronicle of Joseph Brant. Toronto: Glasgow, Brook.

Wood, Peter H.
1974   Black Majority: Negroes in Colonial South Carolina from 1670 through the Stono Rebellion. New York: Alfred A. Knopf.

Wood, W. Raymond
1972   Contrastive Features of Native North American Trade Systems. Pp. 153–169 in For the Chief: Essays in Honor of Luther S. Cressman. Fred W. Voget and Robert L. Stephenson, eds. *University of Oregon Anthropological Papers* 4. Eugene.

————
1980   Plains Trade in Prehistoric and Protohistoric Intertribal Relations. Pp. 98–109 in Anthropology on the Great Plains. W. Raymond Wood and Margot Liberty, eds. Lincoln: University of Nebraska Press.

Wood, W. Raymond, and Margot Liberty
1980   Anthropology on the Great Plains. Lincoln: University of Nebraska Press.

Wood, W. Raymond, and Thomas D. Thiessen, eds.
1985   Early Fur Trade on the Northern Plains: Canadian Traders Among the Mandan and Hidatsa Indians, 1738–1818; the Narratives of John Macdonell, David Thompson, François-Antoine Larocque, and Charles McKenzie. Norman: University of Oklahoma Press.

Wood, William
1977   New England's Prospect [1634]. Alden T. Vaughan, ed. Amherst: University of Massachusetts Press.

Woodward, Arthur
1970   The Denominators of the Fur Trade: An Anthology of Writings on the Material Culture of the Fur Trade. Pasadena, Calif.: Westernlore Press.

Woodward, Grace Steele
1963   The Cherokees. Norman: University of Oklahoma Press. (Reprinted in 1982.)

Woolman, John
1961   The Journal of John Woolman, and a Plea for the Poor [1774]. John G. Whittier. New York: Corinth Books.

Worcester, Donald E., ed.
1975   Forked Tongues and Broken Treaties. Caldwell, Idaho: Caxton Printers.

Work, Hubert
1924   Indian Policies: Comments on the Resolutions of the Advisory Council on Indian Affairs. Washington: U.S. Government Printing Office.

Work, John
1945   The Journal of John Work, January to October, 1835. Henry D. Dee, ed. *Archives of British Columbia Memoir* 10. Victoria.

Wrangell, Ferdinand P.
1980   Russian America: Statistical and Ethnographic Information (*Materials for the Study of Alaska History* 15). Mary Sadouski, trans. Richard A. Pierce, ed. Kingston, Ont: The Limestone Press.

Wraxall, Peter
1915   An Abridgement of the Indian Affairs Contained in Four-folio Volumes, Transacted in the Colony of New York from the Year 1678 to the Year 1751. Charles H. McIlwain, ed. Cambridge, Mass.: Harvard University Press.

Wray, Charles F., and Harry L. Schoff
1953   A Preliminary Report on the Seneca Sequence in Western New York, 1550–1687. *Pennsylvania Archaeologist* 23(2):53–63.

Wright, Asher
1842   Go'wăna gwa'ih Sat'hah yon de'yăs dah'gwah . . . .A Spelling Book in the Seneca Language; with English Definitions. Buffalo-Creek Reservation: Mission Press.

Wright, J. Leitch, Jr.
1967   William Augustus Bowles, Director General of the Creek Nation. Athens: University of Georgia Press.

————
1981   The Only Land They Knew: The Tragic Story of the American Indians in the Old South. New York: Free Press.

Wright, James
1873   Report of Sir James Wright on the Condition of the Province of Georgia, on 20th Sept. 1773. *Collections of the Georgia Historical Society* 3:158–179. Savannah.

Wright, Louis B.
1940   The First Gentlemen of Virginia: Intellectual Qualities of the Early Ruling Class. San Marino, Calif.: The Huntington Library.

————
1943   Religion and Empire: The Alliance Between Piety and Commerce in English Expansion, 1558–1625. Chapel Hill: University of North Carolina Press.

————
1953   The Colonial Search for a Southern Eden. [University, Ala.]: University of Alabama Press.

Wright, Muriel H.
1951   A Guide to the Indian Tribes of Oklahoma. Norman: University of Oklahoma Press.

Wroth, Lawrence C.
1928   The Indian Treaty as Literature. *Yale Review* 17(4):749–766.

1970   The Voyages of Giovanni da Verrazzano, 1524–1528. New Haven, Conn.: Yale University Press.

Wyeth, Nathaniel J.
1899   The Correspondence and Journals of Captain Nathaniel J. Wyeth, 1831–1836: A Record of Two Expeditions for the Occupation of the Oregon Country. Eugene: University of Oregon Press.

Yerbury, Colin
1980   The Social Organization of the Subarctic Athapaskan Indians: An Ethnohistorical Reconstruction. (Unpublished Ph.D. Dissertation in Anthropology, Simon Fraser University, Burnaby, B.C.)

Young, Mary E.
1961   Redskins, Ruffleshirts, and Rednecks: Indian Allotments in Alabama and Mississippi, 1830–1860. Norman: University of Oklahoma Press.

Young, Philip
1962   The Mother of Us All: Pocahantas Reconsidered. *Kenyon Review* 24(3):391–415.

Zagoskin, Lavrentiĭ Alekseevich
1967   Lieutenant Zagoskin's Travels in Russian America, 1842–1844: The First Ethnographic and Geographic Investigations on the Yukon and Kuskokwim Valleys of Alaska. Henry N. Michael, ed. (*Anthropology of the North: Translations from Russian Sources* 7) Toronto: Published for the Arctic Institute of North America by the University of Toronto Press.

Zanger, Jules
1967   The Frontiersman in Popular Fiction, 1820–1860. Pp. 141–153 in The Frontier Re-examined. John F. McDermott, ed. Urbana: University of Illinois Press.

Zárate Salmerón, Gerónimo de
1966   Relaciones: An Account of Things Seen and Learned by Father Jerónimo de Zárate Salmerón from the Year 1538 to the Year 1626. Alicia R. Milich, trans. Albuquerque: Horn and Wallace.

Zavala, Silvio
1935   La encomienda indiana. Madrid: Imprenta Helenica.

1964   The Defense of Human Rights in Latin America, Sixteenth to Eighteenth Centuries. Paris: UNESCO.

Zavala, Silvio, and José Miranda
1954   Instituciones indígenas en la colonia. Pp. 29–112 in Métodos y resultados de la política indigenísta en México. Alfonso Caso, et al. *Memorias del Instituto Nacional Indígenista,* 6. Mexico.

Zeisberger, David
1776   Essay of a Delaware-Indian and English Spelling-Book for the Use of the Schools of the Christian Indians on Muskingum River. Philadelphia: Henry Miller.

1827   A Grammar of the Language of the Lenni Lenape or Delaware Indians. Peter Stephen Du Ponceau, trans. Philadelphia: American Philosophical Society.

1885   Diary of David Zeisberger, a Moravian Missionary Among the Indians of Ohio, 1781–1798. Eugene F. Bliss, ed. and trans. 2 vols. Cincinnati: Robert Clarke.

1887   Zeisberger's Indian Dictionary: English, German, Iroquois—The Onondaga and Alonquin—The Delaware. Eben N. Horsford, ed. Cambridge, Mass.: John Wilson.

1887–1888   Essay of an Onondaga Grammar . . . .[1776]. John Ettwein, trans. *Pennsylvania Magazine of History and Biography* 11(4):442–453; 12(5):65–75, 233–239, 325–340.

1910   History of the Northern American Indians. Archer B. Hulbert and William N. Schwarze, eds. *Ohio State Archaeological and Historical Quarterly* 19(1–2):1–189. Columbus.

1912   The Diaries of Zeisberger Relating to the First Missions in the Ohio Basin [1767–1769]. (*The Moravian Records* 2) Archer B. Hulbert and William N. Schwarze, eds. and trans. *Ohio State Archaeological and Historical Quarterly* 21(1):1–125. Columbus.

Zelva, Malá
1983   Jubilejni IV. Setkani na severu. *Winaminge* 4:11. Prague.

Zimmerman, William, Jr.
1957   The Role of the Bureau of Indian Affairs Since 1933. *Annals of the American Academy of Political and Social Science* 311(May):31–40. Philadelphia.

Zolla, Elémire
1973   The Writer and the Shaman: A Morphology of the American Indian. Raymond Rosenthal, trans. New York: Harcourt, Brace, Jovanovich.

Zoltvany, Yves F.
1974   Philippe de Rigaud de Vaudreuil: Governor of New France, 1703–1725. Toronto: McClelland and Stewart.

Zschokke, Heinrich
1804   Die Prinzessin von Wolfenbüttel. Zurich, Switzerland: Orell.

1820   Die Gründung von Maryland. Zurich, Switzerland: Orell.

Zubillaga, Felix
1938   Padre Pedro Martínez, 1533–1566: La primera sangre jesuitica en las misiones norteamericanos. *Archivum Historicum Societatis Iesu* 7:30–53. Rome.

1941   La Florida: la misión jesuitica (1566–1572) y la colonización española. *Bibliotheca Instituti Historici S.I.* 1. Rome.

1946   Monumenta antiquae Floridae. *Monumenta Historica Societatis Iesu* 69. Rome.

Zubrow, Ezra B.W.
1974   Population, Contact and Climate in the New Mexican Pueblos. *Anthropological Papers of the University of Arizona* 24. Tucson.

Index

American Indians-United: 318
American Missionary Association: 440, 441, 618, 645, 685
American Missionary Society: 445
American Philological Society: 646
American Philosophical Society: 621, 625, 641, 648, 655
American Protective Association: 449
American Red Cross: 679
American Society for Ethnohistory: 538
American Society for Promoting the Civilization and General Improvement of the Indian Tribes Within the United States: 302
Amerindian; synonymy: 1
Amherst, Jeffrey: 10, 86, 251, 331, 618, 636, 655, 688
Anacostank; missions to: 488
Anderson, Billy: *348*
Anderson, Mad Bear: 571
Andre, Alexis: *92*
Andros, Edmund: 18, 135
Anglo-Dutch War: 18
Anglo-French War: 24
Anheuser-Busch: 598
Annawan: 136
Anne (Queen of England): 435
Anthropological Society of Washington: 644, 676
anthropology: 106, 108, 126, 136, 539, 541–544, 548–556, 575, 580, 584, 586, 623–624, 625, 633, 643–644, *644*, 671, 672, 690, 697. applied anthropology: 553. archeology: 307, 319, 528, 651, 655, 658, 670, *670*, 674, 676–678, 687. ethnography: 526, 529, 541–544, 549, 623, 637–638, 640, 641–642, 646–647, 658, 661, 663, 667, 670–671, 674, 675–677, 686, 688, 689, 690, 692, 693, 699. Indian anthropologists: 549, 643. Indian criticism of: 319, 548, 552–556. in Indian rights movements: 308, 315, 549–550, 552–556, *555*, 643–644. participant observation: 549, 555, 637–638. physical anthropology: 543, 623, 652–653, *653*, 671. *See also* language, research on; research
Anza, Juan Bautista de: *476*, 618
Apache: 49, 50, 55, 56, 172, 180, 411, 420, 462, 647, 650, 660, 681, 685. hostilities with U.S. troops: 663, 676, 684. language: 651. missions to: 453, 480, 487, *496*. prisoners: 410, 412, 413. raiding: 166, 168, 361, 636, 678–679. religion: 455. reservations: 178–179, 630–631. as slaves: 358, 411, 412. trade alliances: 357. warfare: 178–180, 303, 359, 412, 636–637, 684. White depictions of: 582, 584, 613, *613*, 614
Apache, Chiricahua: 681. Central: 166. delegations: *242*. Eastern: 168. hostilities with U.S. troops: 166, 168, 173, 224, 652, 668. raiding: 179–180. warfare: 180
Apache, Cuartelejo; trade alliances: 358
Apache, Gila: 412
Apache, Jicarilla: *312*, 571, 658, 693. hostilities with U.S. troops: 166. missions to: 454, 480. as slaves: 412
Apache, Lipan: 646, 672. raiding: 176–177.

as slaves: 412
Apache, Mescalero: 52, *400*, 580. allotment: 70. hostilities with U.S. troops: 166, 168, 224, 628. missions to: 454, 480. raiding: 176–177. warfare: 178, 180. White depictions of: 666
Apache, Plains: 27. trading alliances: 357–358
Apache, Western; hostilities with U.S. troops: 166, 224, 663. San Carlos: 313. U.S. alliance: 173. warfare: 178. White Mountain: 173, 180
Apache Kid: 684
Apalachee: 131. agriculture: 485. fur trade: 393. missions to: 485–486, 492. as slaves: 5, 408
Appah, Lawrence: *312*
Applegate, Oliver C.: *181*
Aquipoguetin: 651
Arapaho: *54*, 259, 306, *307*, *312*, 571, 643, 646, 658, 669. disease: 360. education: 60, *294*. hostilities with U.S. troops: 168, 175, 224, 225. intermarriage: 628. land cessions: *225*. missions to: 453, 454, 496. trade: 353, 369, 622. treaties: 53, *201*, 224, 290, 659
Arapahoe, Northern: *612*. education: 290. missions to: 496
Arbeitskreis für Nordamerikanische Indianer: 568
archeology. *See* anthropology
Arctic Institute of North America: 633
Area Redevelopment Act: 78, 273
Argall, Samuel: 22, 325, 464
Arikara: *524*, 660, 661, 685. disease: 360, 361. hostilities with U.S. troops: 157. land cessions: *428*. scouts: *176*. trade: 353, 358, 360, 361, 362, 363, 364, 368. treaties: 158
Arizona Inter-Tribal Council: 313
Arkansas; missions to: 470
Armand: 583, *584*
Armstrong. *See* Pamoxet
Armstrong, John: 266
Armstrong, Samuel Chapman: 293, 306, 618–619
Armstrong Male Academy: 289
Arnaud, Charles: 502
Artell, Thomas: *74*
Arthur, Chester A.: 449, 690
Arthur, Gabriel: 392
arts and crafts: 267–268, 350, 371, 374, *389*, 396–403, *398*, *399*, *402*, 490, *499*, 572, 633, 670. Indian hobbyists: 557, 558, 559, 562, 563, 565, 568, 569. instruction in: 295, 296–297, 307, 435, 437
Ashawet: *198*
Ashley, William Henry: 362, 364, 368, 619, 621, 625, 685
assimilation: 2, 32, 40, 43, 61, 66, 88, 89, 91, 93, 105, 106, 351, 458, 462, 463, 529, 550, 552, 617, 622–623, 627, 634, 639, 640, 648, 656, 679, 684. Indian resistance to: 92, 93. missions to Indians: 435, 440, 452–454, 499–500. policies: 72, 82, 88, 89, 90, 91, 95, 98, 235, 260, 261, 262–264, 271, 272, 279, 291, 293, 294, 301, 303, 304, 305, 307, 538, 554, 671, 676, 678, 682, 690, 694. treaty provisions for: 195. White opposition to: 70, 308, 633,

667. *See also* Canadian period, civilization policy; United States period, termination policy
Assiniboine: 28, 91, 320, 424, 563, 659, 661, 668. disease: 360. missions to: 497. trade: 353, 358, 361, 362, 363. treaties: 209, 224
Association of American Indian Physicians: *316*
Association on American Indian Affairs: 74, 311, 313, *314*, *316*, 316, 323, 553, 658
Astor, John Jacob: 256, 362–364, 369, 385, 619
Atahualpa-Huascar: 97
Atakapa: 646, 688
Athapaskans, Northern; Christianity: 513. relations with Canada: 283. technology: *401*. trade: 376, 379, 389. treaties: 638
Atkin, Edmond: 5, 137, 249, 250, 252, 391, 619–620, 647
Atkin, John: 619
Atkins, John DeWitt Clinton: 58–59, 266, 620
Atkinson, Henry: 157–158, 620, 673
Atlanta Braves: 605
Atoka Agreement: *226*
Atsugewi; as slaves: 414
Attakullakulla: 688
Attikamègues: missions to: 467
Attla, George, Jr.: 616
Attocknie, Albert: *312*
Atwood, Stella: 308
Aubaway: *198*
Aubery, Joseph: 469, 470
Augur, Christopher C.: *54*, 175
Augustana College: 458
Auonaseckla: *198*
Austin, Mary: 579
Avion: 359
Awatovi Pueblo; as slaves: 412
Ayllon, Lucas Vasquez: 407, 481
Aziagmiut. *See* Eskimo, Bering Strait
Aztec: 97, 522, 523, 529, 534, 574

B

Bacon, Nathaniel: 133, 620
Bacone College: 452, 453, 456
Bacon's Rebellion: 8, 133, 392, 407, 620
Baden-Powell, Robert: 564
Baktay, Ervin: 569
Baldwin, Frank D.: 620–621
Balmer, James W.: *212*, *292–293*
Balmer, Joseph: 568, *569*
Bancroft, George: 538
Bancroft, Hubert Howe: 538
Bandelier, Adolf F.: 573, 579
Banker, Evert: 247
Banks, Dennis: 322
Bannister, John: 622
Bannock: *312*, 364, 650, 658, *672*. hostilities with U.S. troops: 170, 182, 224, 644, 652. missions to: 454, *455*, 461, 462. treaties: 290
Banyacya, Thomas: 571
Baptist Triennial Convention. *See* Triennial Convention of Baptists for Foreign Missions
Baranov, Aleksandr: 122, 507
barbarian; synonymy: 524, 525

809

819

833

552, 693. European diplomacy: 185, 190. fraud: 199. Indian diplomacy: 186–187, 538. legal interpretation: 232, 237, 272. peace: 24, 40, 163, 165, 168, 186, 187, 195, 196, 197, 259, 302, 361, *527*, 596, 598, 600, 613, 620, 662–663. presents to Indians: 238–239, 259. provisions: 33, 43, 47, 48–50, *50*, 53, 57, 59, 63, 149, 195, 196, 206, 208, 220, 221, 223, 288, 290, 301, 428. Spanish: 149, 628. violations: 52, 54, 255, 302, 305, 321–322, 685. *See also* specific treaties and agreements

Treaty Indians: *94*

Treaty No. 1: *205*, 207

Treaty No. 2: *205*, 208

Treaty No. 3: *205*, 208

Treaty No. 4: *205*

Treaty No. 5: *205*, 209

Treaty No. 6: 91, *205*, 208

Treaty No. 7: *205*, 209, 280, 664

Treaty No. 8: *205*, 209, *209*

Treaty No. 9: *205*, *208*, 209

Treaty No. 10: *205*, *206*, 209

Treaty No. 11: *205*, 209, 210

Treaty of Camp Dade: 617

Treaty of Colerain: 35

Treaty of Council Springs: 48

Treaty of Dancing Rabbit Creek: 45, 290

Treaty of Dewitt's Corner: 213

Treaty of Doak's Stand: 221

Treaty of Easton: 187, 188

Treaty of Fort Atkinson: 50, 164–165

Treaty of Fort Finney: 30

Treaty of Fort Gibson: 45, 160, 223, 617

Treaty of Fort Industry: *198*

Treaty of Fort Jackson: 39, 220, 654

Treaty of Fort Laramie: 49. 1851: 164, 199, 224, 626, 643, 659, 668. 1868: 174–175

Treaty of Fort McIntosh: 30, 31, 149, 152

Treaty of Fort Stanwix: 149, 202, 655, 657, 669

Treaty of Fort Wayne: 220

Treaty of Ghent: 40, 156, *310*

Treaty of Greenville: 33–34, 35, 37, 152, *153*, *198*, 220, 649, 675, 694

Treaty of Guadalupe Hidalgo: 258

Treaty of Hartford: 16

Treaty of Holston: 33, 35

Treaty of Hopewell: 30, 47, 149, 218, 232

Treaty of Lancaster: 669

Treaty of Logstown: 10, 669

Treaty of Long Island: 213

Treaty of Manitoulin Island: 206

Treaty of Medicine Lodge: 174, *201*, 225, *225*, *682*

Treaty of Mendota: *169*

Treaty of New Echota: 45, 160, 199, 213, 223, 691

Treaty of New York: 33, 35, 151, 218

Treaty of Nogales: 628

Treaty of Paris: 10, 29, 86, 87, 137, 148, 152, 395, 490

Treaty of Payne's Landing: 45, 160, 223, 617

Treaty of Pontotoc: 223

Treaty of Portage des Sioux: 40

Treaty of Prairie du Chien: 689

Treaty of Ryswick: 632

Treaty of Table Rock: 659

Treaty of Utrecht: 85, 470, 678

tribal government: 2, 45, 73, 158, 221, 227–228, 235–236, 261, 265–266, 322–323, 623, 631, 632, 633, 667, 690, 695. band councils: 89, 90, 93. courts: *71*, 79, 103, 230, 234, *234*, 246, 307, 309, 311, 631. dissolution of: 62, 67, 222, *226*, 264, 290, 305, 306, 639. establishment of: 126, 552. funds: 71, 73. legal status: 231, 232, 233–235, 274. *See also* Indian police; Indian Reorganization Act

Tribally Controlled Community College Assistance Act of 1978: 298

Triennial Convention of Baptists for Foreign Missions: 437, 439–440

Trimble, Charles Z.: 321, 322

Trouvé, Claude: 470

Trowbridge, Charles Christopher: 692

Trowbridge, Roland Ebenezer: 266, 692

truck houses. *See* trading posts and stores

Trudeau, Pierre: *281*, 281, 282, 283

Truman, Harry S.: 75, 270, 672

Trumbull, John: *240*

Tschauendah: *198*

Tsimshian peoples; ceremonies: *386*. Coast: 641. economy: 267. missions to: 641. Nishga: *93*. trade: 375, *376*, 376, *382*, 383

Tsiouendaentaha: 467

Tumwater; missions to: 497

Tunica: 646, 688

Tupinamba: 523, 534

Turner, Frederick Jackson: 538

Turner, J.: *525*

Turquetil, Arsène: 502

Turtle Heart. *See* Agassqua

Turtle Mountain band. *See* Ojibwa (Chippewa)

Tuscarora: 8, 140, 307, 309, 549, 571, 657. in American Revolution: 146, 147. education: 287, 288, 289. missions to: 437. removal: 160. treaties: 192, 288, 675. warfare: 8, 140

Tuscarora War: 8, 140

Tusquagan: *198*

Tutelo: 640, 648. fur trade: 392. treaties: 194

Twain, Mark: 534, 576

Twana: 642

Twining, W.J.: 662

Two Bear, Basil: *312*

Two Bulls, Moses: *234*

Two Moon: *64*

Tyler, Scott: *298*

Tylor, Edward: 541

U

Udall, Stewart L.: *273*

Ulloa, Antonio de: 673

Umatilla: 166, 498. missions to: 454, 495, 498. reservation: 638. trade: 353. treaties: *200*

Umpqua, Lower. *See* Siuslawans and Coosans

Unalakleet: 378

Uncas: 598

Uncas, Ben, III: 287

Underhill, John: 692

Union College: 290

Union of New Brunswick Indians: 490

Union of Ontario Indians: *281*

United Church Committee on Indian Work: 457

United Colonies of New England: 16, 135

United Foreign Missionary Society: 437, 438, 439

United Indians of All Tribes: 318–319, *319*

United Native Americans, Inc.: 318–319

United States Army: 52, 53, 55, 158, 159, 160, 162–166, 171, 172, 174, 181–183, 224, 257, 303, 304, 462, 609, 634, 650, 690. appropriations for: 152, 163, 167, 173. cavalry: 159, 166, 173–177, *174*, *176*, *178*, *179*, 180, *183*, 631, 638, 663. Indian troops: *173*, 173. officers as agents: 162, 443. role in trade: 152. U.S. Rangers: 148. *See also* military service by Indians; scouts, Indian; scouts, non-Indian

United States Court of Claims: 64, *224*, 228, 270, 307, 308

United States government; Army Corps of Engineers: 227, 264. Board of Indian Commissioners: 55, 260, 303, 304, 305, 443–453, 626, 633, 635, 645, 650, 660, 670, 674, 681, 684, 685, 695. Bureau of Reclamation: 70, 264. Census Bureau: 171, 676. Civilian Conservation Corps: 268, 269. Civil Service: 62, 293, 673. Department of Agriculture: 71, 268. Department of Commerce: 672. Department of Housing and Urban Development: 272, 273, 672. Department of Justice: 264. Department of Labor: 672. Department of the Interior: 47, 52, 53, 56, 57, 61, 62, 73, 171, 198, 200, 201, 268, 271, 308, 313, *314*, 452, 625–626, 629, 632, 635, 648, 653–654, 669, 681, 690. Department of the Treasury: 669. Emergency Conservation Works: 269, *270*. Farm Security Administration: 73. Forest Service: 272, 428. Freedman's Bureau: 618. Indian Health Service: 273. National Archives: 199. Office of Bilingual Education: 299. Office of Economic Opportunity: 78, 317, 322. Office of Education: 297. Office of Indian Education: *298*, 298. Pick-Sloan Plan: 264, 428. Public Health Service: 78, 273. Public Works Administration: 73. Resettlement Administration: 73. Social Security Administration: 75. Soil Conservation Service: 268. State Department: 199. U.S. Mint: *241*, 241, 243. War Department: 40, 47, 50, 53, 55, 57, *155*, 157, 164, 171, 200, 219, 255, 256, 257, 438, 452, 622, 627, 628, 649, 662, 663, 667, 668, 675, 685. War Relocation Administration: 270. Works Progress Administration: 73, *75*. *See also* Bureau of Indian Affairs; legislation, United States; reservations and reserves; United States Army

United States Indian Commission: 303, 633

United States period: 29–39, 40–50, 51–65, 66–80, 144–162, 189. acculturation: 32, 35–36, 61, 73, 171. Alaska purchase: 514. allotment policy: 46, 59, 61, 66, 67–68, 69, 70, 195, 197, 226–227, 263, 294, 304,

835